WHO WAS WHO

VOLUME XI

2001–2005

WHO'S WHO

An annual biographical dictionary
first published in 1849

WHO WAS WHO

WHO WAS WHO VOLUME XI

WHO WAS WHO

2001–2005

A COMPANION TO

WHO'S WHO

CONTAINING THE BIOGRAPHIES
OF THOSE WHO DIED DURING
THE PERIOD 2001–2005

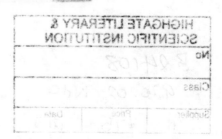
A & C BLACK
LONDON

FIRST PUBLISHED 2006
BY A & C BLACK PUBLISHERS LTD
38 SOHO SQUARE, LONDON W1D 3HB

ISBN-10 0 7136 7601 9
ISBN-13 978 0 7136 7601 3

Printed and bound in Great Britain by William Clowes Ltd, Beccles, Suffolk

PREFACE

This, the eleventh volume of biographies removed from *Who's Who* on account of death, contains the entries of those who died between 2001 and 2005. Those whose deaths occurred before the end of 2000, but were not reported until after the volume of *Who Was Who* covering the years 1996–2000 had been published, are listed as Addenda at the beginning of the biographical section.

The entries are as they last appeared in *Who's Who*, with the date of death added and in some cases further information, such as posthumous publications. It has not always been possible to ascertain the exact date of death, and the editors will welcome such information for inclusion in the next edition of this volume.

CONTENTS

ABBREVIATIONS USED IN THIS BOOK

Some of the designatory letters in this list are used merely for economy of
space and do not necessarily imply any professional or other qualification.

A

AA Anti-aircraft; Automobile Association; Architectural Association; Augustinians of the Assumption; Associate in Arts

AAA Amateur Athletic Association; American Accounting Association

AAAL American Academy of Arts and Letters

AA&QMG Assistant Adjutant and Quartermaster-General

AAArb Member, Association of Arbitrators (South Africa)

AAAS American Association for the Advancement of Science

AABC (Register of) Architects Accredited in Building Conservation

AAC Army Air Corps; Amateur Athletic Club

AACCA Associate, Association of Certified and Corporate Accountants (now see ACCA)

AACE Association for Adult and Continuing Education

AAF Auxiliary Air Force (now see RAuxAF)

AAFCE Allied Air Forces in Central Europe

AAG Assistant Adjutant-General

AAI Associate, Chartered Auctioneers' and Estate Agents' Institute (later, after amalgamation, ARICS)

AAIL American Academy and Institute of Arts and Letters (now see AAAL)

AAM Association of Assistant Mistresses in Secondary Schools

AAMC Australian Army Medical Corps (now see RAAMC)

A&AEE Aeroplane and Armament Experimental Establishment

A&E Accident and Emergency

A and SH Argyll and Sutherland Highlanders

AAPS Aquatic and Atmospheric Physical Sciences

AAS American Astronomical Society

AASA Associate, Australian Society of Accountants (now see FCPA)

AASC Australian Army Service Corps

AATSE Australian Academy of Technological Sciences and Engineering

AAUQ Associate in Accountancy, University of Queensland

AB Bachelor of Arts (US); able-bodied seaman; airborne; Alberta (postal)

ABA Amateur Boxing Association; Antiquarian Booksellers' Association; American Bar Association

ABBSI Associate Member, British Boot and Shoe Institute

ABC Australian Broadcasting Commission; American Broadcasting Companies; Amateur Boxing Club; Associate, Birmingham Conservatoire

ABCC Association of British Chambers of Commerce

ABI Association of British Insurers

ABIA Associate, Bankers' Institute of Australasia

ABINZ Associate, Bankers' Institute of New Zealand

ABIPP Associate, British Institute of Professional Photography

ABIS Association of Burglary Insurance Surveyors

ABM Advisory Board of Ministry

ABNM American Board of Nuclear Medicine

ABP Associated British Ports

Abp Archbishop

ABPI Association of British Pharmaceutical Industry

ABPsS Associate, British Psychological Society (now see AFBPsS)

ABRC Advisory Board for the Research Councils

ABS Associate, Building Societies' Institute (now see ACBSI)

ABSA Association for Business Sponsorship of the Arts

ABSM Associate, Birmingham and Midland Institute School of Music

ABTA Association of British Travel Agents

ABTAPL Association of British Theological and Philosophical Libraries

AC Companion, Order of Australia; Ante Christum (before Christ)

ACA Associate, Institute of Chartered Accountants

Acad. Academy

ACARD Advisory Council for Applied Research and Development

ACAS Advisory, Conciliation and Arbitration Service; Assistant Chief of the Air Staff

ACBSI Associate, Chartered Building Societies Institute

ACC Association of County Councils; Anglican Consultative Council

ACCA Associate, Association of Chartered Certified Accountants (formerly Chartered Association of Certified Accountants)

ACCE Association of County Chief Executives

ACCEL American College of Cardiology Extended Learning

ACCM Advisory Council for the Church's Ministry (now see ABM)

ACCS Associate, Corporation of Secretaries (formerly of Certified Secretaries)

AcDip Academic Diploma in the History of Art

ACDP Australian Committee of Directors and Principals

ACDS Assistant Chief of Defence Staff

ACE Association of Consulting Engineers; Member, Association of Conference Executives; Allied Command Europe

ACENVO Association of Chief Executives of National Voluntary Organisations (now see ACEVO)

ACEO Association of Chief Education Officers

ACertCM Archbishops' Certificate in Church Music

ACEVO Association of Chief Executives of Voluntary Organisations

ACF Army Cadet Force

ACFA Army Cadet Force Association

ACFAS Association Canadienne-Française pour l'avancement des sciences

ACFHE Association of Colleges for Further and Higher Education

ACG Assistant Chaplain-General

ACGI Associate, City and Guilds of London Institute

ACGS Assistant Chief of the General Staff

ACI Airports Council International (Europe)

ACIArb Associate, Chartered Institute of Arbitrators

ACIB Associate, Chartered Institute of Bankers

ACIBS Associate, Chartered Institute of Bankers in Scotland

ACII Associate, Chartered Insurance Institute

ACIM Associate, Chartered Institute of Marketing

ACIS Associate, Institute of Chartered Secretaries and Administrators (formerly Chartered Institute of Secretaries)

ACLS American Council of Learned Societies

ACM Association of Computing Machinery

ACMA Associate, Chartered Institute of Management Accountants (formerly Institute of Cost and Management Accountants)

ACMI Associate, Chartered Management Institute

ACNS Assistant Chief of Naval Staff

ACommA Associate, Society of Commercial Accountants (now see ASCA)

ACORD Advisory Committee on Research and Development

ACOS Assistant Chief of Staff

ACOST Advisory Council on Science and Technology

ACP Association of Clinical Pathologists; Associate, College of Preceptors; African/Caribbean/Pacific

ACPO Association of Chief Police Officers

ACR Accredited Conservator-Restorer

ACRE Action with Rural Communities in England

ACS American Chemical Society; Additional Curates Society

acsc passed Advanced Command and Staff Course

ACSEA Allied Command South East Asia

ACSM Associate, Camborne School of Mines

AcSS Member, Academy of Learned Societies for the Social Sciences

ACT	Australian Capital Territory; Australian College of Theology; Associate, College of Technology; Association of Corporate Treasurers
ACTSS	Association of Clerical, Technical and Supervisory Staff
ACTT	Association of Cinematograph, Television and Allied Technicians
ACTU	Australian Council of Trade Unions
ACU	Association of Commonwealth Universities
ACWA	Associate, Institute of Cost and Works Accountants (now see ACMA)
AD	Dame of the Order of Australia; *Anno Domini* (in the year of the Lord); Air Defence
aD	ausser Dienst
ADAS	Agricultural Development and Advisory Service
ADB	Asian Development Bank; Associate of the Drama Board (Education)
ADB/F	African Development Bank/Fund
ADC	Aide-de-camp; Association of District Councils
ADCM	Archbishop of Canterbury's Diploma in Church Music
AD Corps	Army Dental Corps (now RADC)
ADC(P)	Personal Aide-de-camp to HM The Queen
ADEME	Assistant Director Electrical and Mechanical Engineering
Ad eund	*Ad eundem gradum* ; and *see under* aeg
ADFManc	Art and Design Fellow, Manchester
ADGMS	Assistant Director-General of Medical Services
ADipC	Advanced Postgraduate Diploma in Management Consulting
Adjt	Adjutant
ADJAG	Assistant Deputy Judge Advocate General
ADK	Order of Ahli Darjah Kinabalu
ADM	Advanced Diploma in Midwifery
Adm.	Admiral
ADMS	Assistant Director of Medical Services
ADOS	Assistant Director of Ordnance Services
ADP	Automatic Data Processing
ADPA	Associate Diploma of Public Administration
ADS&T	Assistant Director of Supplies and Transport
Adv.	Advisory; Advocate
AdvDip	Advanced Diploma
ADVS	Assistant Director of Veterinary Services
ADWE&M	Assistant Director of Works, Electrical and Mechanical
AE	Air Efficiency Award
AEA	Atomic Energy Authority; Air Efficiency Award (now see AE); American Economic Association
AEAF	Allied Expeditionary Air Force
AEC	Agriculture Executive Council; Army Educational Corps (now see RAEC); Atomic Energy Commission
AECMA	Association Européenne des Constructeurs de Matériel Aérospatial
AEE	Atomic Energy Establishment
AEEU	Amalgamated Engineering and Electrical Union
AEF	Amalgamated Union of Engineering and Foundry Workers (later AEU, then AEEU); American Expeditionary Forces
aeg	*ad eundem gradum* (to the same degree-of the admission of a graduate of one university to the same degree at another without examination)
AEI	Associated Electrical Industries
AELTC	All England Lawn Tennis Club
AEM	Air Efficiency Medal
AER	Army Emergency Reserve
AERE	Atomic Energy Research Establishment (Harwell)
Æt., Ætat.	*Ætatis* (aged)
AEU	Amalgamated Engineering Union (later AEEU)
AF	Admiral of the Fleet
AFA	Amateur Football Alliance; Associate, Institute of Financial Accountants
AFAIAA	Associate Fellow, American Institute of Aeronautics and Astronautics
AFASIC	Association for All Speech Impaired Children
AFB	Air Force Base
AFBPsS	Associate Fellow, British Psychological Society
AFC	Air Force Cross; Association Football Club
AFCAI	Associate Fellow, Canadian Aeronautical Institute
AFCEA	Armed Forces Communications and Electronics Association
AFCENT	Allied Forces in Central Europe
AFD	Doctor of Fine Arts (US)
AFDS	Air Fighting Development Squadron
AFGE	Associate Fellow, Guild of Glass Engravers

AFHQ	Allied Force Headquarters
AFI	American Film Institute
AFIA	Associate, Federal Institute of Accountants (Australia)
AFIAP	Artiste, Fédération Internationale de l'Art Photographique
AFIAS	Associate Fellow, Institute of Aeronautical Sciences (US) (now see AFAIAA)
AFIMA	Associate Fellow, Institute of Mathematics and its Applications
AFM	Air Force Medal
AFNORTH	Allied Forces in Northern Europe
AFOM	Associate, Faculty of Occupational Medicine
AFRAeS	Associate Fellow, Royal Aeronautical Society (now see MRAeS)
AFRC	Agricultural and Food Research Council (now see BBSRC)
AFRSPSoc	Associate Fellow, Remote Sensing and Photogrammetry Society
AFSOUTH	Allied Forces in Southern Europe
AFV	Armoured Fighting Vehicles
AG	Attorney-General
AGAC	American Guild of Authors and Composers
AGARD	Advisory Group for Aerospace Research and Development
AGAvA	Associate, Guild of Aviation Artists
AGC	Adjutant General's Corps
AGH	Australian General Hospital
AGI	Alliance Graphique Internationale; Associate, Institute of Certificated Grocers
AGR	Advanced Gas-cooled Reactor
AGRA	Army Group Royal Artillery; Association of Genealogists and Record Agents
AGSM	Associate, Guildhall School of Music and Drama; Australian Graduate School of Management
AHA	Area Health Authority; American Hospitals Association; Associate, Institute of Health Service Administrators (later AHSM)
AHA(T)	Area Health Authority (Teaching)
AHQ	Army Headquarters
AHRB	Arts and Humanities Research Board (now see AHRC)
AHRC	Arts and Humanities Research Council
AHSM	Associate, Institute of Health Services Management
AH-WC	Associate, Heriot-Watt College, Edinburgh
ai	*ad interim*
AIA	Associate, Institute of Actuaries; American Institute of Architects; Association of International Artists
AIAA	American Institute of Aeronautics and Astronautics
AIACE	Association Internationale des Anciens des Communautés Européennes
AIAgrE	Associate, Institution of Agricultural Engineers
AIAL	Associate Member, International Institute of Arts and Letters
AIAS	Associate Surveyor Member, Incorporated Association of Architects and Surveyors
AIB	Associate, Institute of Bankers (now see ACIB)
AIBD	Associate, Institute of British Decorators
AIBP	Associate, Institute of British Photographers
AIC	Agricultural Improvement Council; Associate of the Institute of Chemistry (later ARIC, MRIC; now see MRSC)
aic	armour infantry course
AICA	Associate Member, Commonwealth Institute of Accountants; Association Internationale des Critiques d'Art
AICE	Associate, Institution of Civil Engineers
AIChE	American Institute of Chemical Engineers
AICPA	American Institute of Certified Public Accountants
AICS	Associate, Institute of Chartered Shipbrokers
AICTA	Associate, Imperial College of Tropical Agriculture
AID	Artificial Insemination by Donor
AIDB	Accountancy Investigation Discipline Board
AIDS	Acquired Immunity Deficiency Syndrome
AIE	Associate, Institute of Education
AIEE	Associate, Institution of Electrical Engineers
AIF	Australian Imperial Forces
AIFireE	Associate, Institution of Fire Engineers
AIG	Adjutant-Inspector-General
AIH	Associate, Institute of Housing
AIHort	Associate, Institute of Horticulture

AIIA	Associate, Insurance Institute of America; Associate, Indian Institute of Architects
AIIMR	Associate, Institute of Investment Management and Research
AIIRA	Associate, International Industrial Relations Association
AIL	Associate, Institute of Linguists
AILA	Associate, Institute of Landscape Architects (later ALI)
AIM	Associate, Institution of Metallurgists (later MIM); Australian Institute of Management; Alternative Investment Market; Advanced Institute of Management Research
AIMarE	Associate, Institute of Marine Engineers
AIMBE	American Institute for Medical and Biological Engineering
AIMC	Associate, Institute of Management Consultants
AIME	American Institute of Mechanical Engineers
AIMgt	Associate, Institute of Management (now see ACMI)
AIMSW	Associate, Institute of Medical Social Work
AInstM	Associate Member, Institute of Marketing
AInstP	Associate, Institute of Physics
AInstPI	Associate, Institute of Patentees and Inventors
AIP	Association of Independent Producers
AIPR	Associate, Institute of Public Relations
AIProdE	Associate, Institution of Production Engineers
AIQS	Associate Member, Institute of Quantity Surveyors
AIRCENT	Allied Air Forces Central Europe
AIRTE	Associate, Institute of Road Transport Engineers
AIRTO	Association of Independent Research and Technology Organizations
AIS	Associate, Institute of Statisticians (later MIS)
AISA	Associate, Incorporated Secretaries' Association
AIStructE	Associate, Institution of Structural Engineers
AITI	Associate, Institute of Translators and Interpreters
AITP	Associate, Institute of Town Planners, India
AJAG	Assistant Judge Advocate General
AJEX	Association of Jewish Ex-Service Men and Women
AK	Knight, Order of Australia; Alaska (postal)
AKC	Associate, King's College London
AL	Alabama (postal)
ALA	Associate, Library Association (now see MCLIP); Association of London Authorities
Ala	Alabama
ALAA	Associate, Library Association of Australia
ALAI	Associate, Library Association of Ireland
ALAM	Associate, London Academy of Music and Dramatic Art
ALCD	Associate, London College of Divinity
ALCM	Associate, London College of Music
ALCM (TD)	Associate, London College of Music (Teaching Diploma)
ALCS	Authors Lending and Copyright Society
ALFSEA	Allied Land Forces South-East Asia
ALI	Argyll Light Infantry; Associate, Landscape Institute (now see MLI)
ALICE	Autistic and Language Impaired Children's Education
ALLC	Association for Literary and Linguistic Computing
ALP	Australian Labor Party
ALPSP	Association of Learned and Professional Society Publishers
ALS	Associate, Linnean Society; Amyotrophic Lateral Sclerosis
Alta	Alberta
ALVA	Association of Leading Visitor Attractions
AM	Albert Medal; Member, Order of Australia; Master of Arts (US); Alpes Maritimes
AMA	Association of Metropolitan Authorities; Assistant Masters Association (later AMMA, now see ATL); Associate, Museums Association; Australian Medical Association
AMARC	Associated Marine and Related Charities
Amb.	Ambulance; Ambassador
AMBIM	Associate Member, British Institute of Management (later AIMgt)
AMC	Association of Municipal Corporations
AMCST	Associate, Manchester College of Science and Technology
AMCT	Associate, Manchester College of Technology
AMDEA	Association of Manufacturers of Domestic Electrical Appliances
AME	Association of Municipal Engineers

AMEME	Association of Mining Electrical and Mechanical Engineers
AMet	Associate of Metallurgy
AMF	Australian Military Forces
AMFL	Allied Command Europe Mobile Force Land
AMICE	Associate Member, Institution of Civil Engineers (now see MICE)
AMIChemE	Associate Member, Institution of Chemical Engineers
AMIEE	Associate Member, Institution of Electrical Engineers (now see MIEE)
AMIERE	Associate Member, Institution of Electronic and Radio Engineers
AMIMechE	Associate Member, Institution of Mechanical Engineers (now see MIMechE)
AMInstCE	Associate Member, Institution of Civil Engineers (now see MICE)
AmInstEE	American Institute of Electrical Engineers
AMINucE	Associate Member, Institution of Nuclear Engineers
AMIRSE	Associate Member, Institute of Railway Signalling Engineers
AMIStructE	Associate Member, Institution of Structural Engineers
AMMA	Assistant Masters & Mistresses Association (now see ATL)
AMN	Ahli Mangku Negara (Malaysia)
AMP	Advanced Management Program; Air Member for Personnel
AMRC	Association of Medical Research Charities
AMRINA	Associate Member, Royal Institution of Naval Architects
AMRSH	Associate Member, Royal Society of Health
AMS	Assistant Military Secretary; Army Medical Services
AMSI	Associate Member, Securities Institute
AMSO	Air Member for Supply and Organisation
AMTE	Admiralty Marine Technology Establishment
AMTRI	Advanced Manufacturing Technology Research Institute
ANA	Associate National Academician (US)
ANAF	Arab Non-Arab Friendship
Anat.	Anatomy; Anatomical
ANC	African National Congress
ANECInst	Associate, NE Coast Institution of Engineers and Shipbuilders
Anon.	Anonymously
ANU	Australian National University
ANZAAS	Australian and New Zealand Association for the Advancement of Science
Anzac	Australian and New Zealand Army Corps
AO	Officer, Order of Australia; Air Officer
AOA	Air Officer in charge of Administration
AOC	Air Officer Commanding
AOC-in-C	Air Officer Commanding-in-Chief
AOD	Army Ordnance Department
AOER	Army Officers Emergency Reserve
APA	American Psychiatric Association
APACS	Association of Payment and Clearing Systems
APD	Army Pay Department
APEX	Association of Professional, Executive, Clerical and Computer Staff
APHA	American Public Health Association
APIS	Army Photographic Intelligence Service
APM	Assistant Provost Marshal
APMI	Associate, Pensions Management Institute
APNI	Alliance Party of Northern Ireland
APR	Accredited Public Relations Practitioner
APS	Aborigines Protection Society; American Physical Society
APsSI	Associate, Psychological Society of Ireland
APSW	Association of Psychiatric Social Workers
APT&C	Administrative, Professional, Technical and Clerical
APTC	Army Physical Training Corps
AQ	Administration and Quartering
AQMG	Assistant Quartermaster-General
AR	Associated Rediffusion (Television); Arkansas (postal)
ARA	Associate, Royal Academy
ARACI	Associate, Royal Australian Chemical Institute
ARAD	Associate, Royal Academy of Dancing
ARAeS	Associate, Royal Aeronautical Society
ARAgS	Associate, Royal Agricultural Societies (ie of England, Scotland and Wales)
ARAIA	Associate, Royal Australian Institute of Architects
ARAM	Associate, Royal Academy of Music

ARAS   Associate, Royal Astronomical Society
ARBA   Associate, Royal Society of British Artists
ARBS   Associate, Royal Society of British Sculptors
ARC   Architects' Registration Council; Agricultural Research
           Council (later AFRC); Aeronautical Research
           Council; Arthritis and Rheumatism Council
ARCA   Associate, Royal College of Art; Associate, Royal
           Canadian Academy
ARCamA   Associate, Royal Cambrian Academy of Art
ARCIC   Anglican-Roman Catholic International Commission
ARCM   Associate, Royal College of Music
ARCO   Associate, Royal College of Organists
ARCO(CHM) Associate, Royal College of Organists with Diploma
           in Choir Training
ARCP   Affiliate, Royal College of Physicians
ARCPsych   Associate Member, Royal College of Psychiatrists
ARCS   Associate, Royal College of Science; Accreditation
           Review and Consulting Service (now see ISI)
ARCST   Associate, Royal College of Science and Technology
           (Glasgow)
ARCUK   Architects' Registration Council of the United Kingdom
ARCVS   Associate, Royal College of Veterinary Surgeons
ARE   Associate, Royal Society of Painter-Printmakers (formerly
           of Painter-Etchers and Engravers); Arab Republic of
           Egypt; Admiralty Research Establishment
AREINZ   Associate, Real Estate Institute, New Zealand
ARELS   Association of Recognised English Language Schools
ARIAS   Associate, Royal Incorporation of Architects in Scotland
ARIBA   Associate, Royal Institute of British Architects (now see
           RIBA)
ARIC   Associate, Royal Institute of Chemistry (later MRIC;
           now see MRSC)
ARICS   Professional Associate, Royal Institution of Chartered
           Surveyors (now see MRICS)
ARINA   Associate, Royal Institution of Naval Architects
ARLIS   Art Libraries Association
ARLT   Association for the Reform of Latin Teaching
ARMS   Associate, Royal Society of Miniature Painters
ARP   Air Raid Precautions
ARPS   Associate, Royal Photographic Society
ARR   Association of Radiation Research
ARRC   Associate, Royal Red Cross; Allied Command Europe
           Rapid Reaction Corps
ARSA   Associate, Royal Scottish Academy
ARSC   Association of Recorded Sound Collections
ARSCM   Associate, Royal School of Church Music
ARSM   Associate, Royal School of Mines
ARTC   Associate, Royal Technical College (Glasgow) (now see
           ARCST)
ARWA   Associate, Royal West of England Academy
ARWS   Associate, Royal Society of Painters in Water-Colours
AS   Anglo-Saxon
ASA   Associate Member, Society of Actuaries; Associate of
           Society of Actuaries (US); Australian Society of
           Accountants; Army Sailing Association; Advertising
           Standards Authority; Alment Aksjeselskap
ASAA   Associate, Society of Incorporated Accountants and
           Auditors
ASAI   Associate, Society of Architectural Illustrators
AS&TS of SA Associated Scientific and Technical Societies of
           South Africa
ASAQS   Association of South African Quantity Surveyors
ASBAH   Association for Spina Bifida and Hydrocephalus
ASC   Administrative Staff College, Henley
ASCA   Associate, Society of Company and Commercial
           Accountants
ASCAB   Armed Services Consultant Approval Board
ASCAP   American Society of Composers, Authors and Publishers
ASCE   American Society of Civil Engineers
ASCHB   Association for Study of Conservation of Historic
           Buildings
AScW   Association of Scientific Workers (later ASTMS)
ASD   Armament Supply Department
ASE   Amalgamated Society of Engineers (later AUEW, then
           AEU, subsequently AEEU); Association for Science
           Education
ASEAN   Association of South East Asian Nations
ASH   Action on Smoking and Health
ASIAD   Associate, Society of Industrial Artists and Designers
ASLE   American Society of Lubrication Engineers

ASLEF   Associated Society of Locomotive Engineers and
           Firemen
ASLIB or Aslib Association for Information Management (formerly
           Association of Special Libraries and Information
           Bureaux)
ASM   Association of Senior Members; Australian Service
           Medal
ASME   American Society of Mechanical Engineers; Association
           for the Study of Medical Education
ASO   Air Staff Officer
ASSC   Accounting Standards Steering Committee
ASSET   Association of Supervisory Staffs, Executives and
           Technicians (later ASTMS)
AssocEng   Associate of Engineering
AssocISI   Associate, Iron and Steel Institute
AssocMCT   Associateship of Manchester College of Technology
AssocMIAeE Associate Member, Institution of Aeronautical
           Engineers
AssocRINA Associate, Royal Institution of Naval Architects
AssocSc   Associate in Science
Asst   Assistant
ASTA   Association of Short Circuit Testing Authorities
ASTC   Administrative Service Training Course
ASTMS   Association of Scientific, Technical and Managerial Staffs
           (subsequently part of MSF)
ASVU   Army Security Vetting Unit
ASWE   Admiralty Surface Weapons Establishment
ATA   Air Transport Auxiliary
ATAE   Association of Tutors in Adult Education
ATAF   Allied Tactical Air Force
ATC   Air Training Corps; Art Teacher's Certificate
ATCDE   Association of Teachers in Colleges and Departments of
           Education (now see NATFHE)
ATCL   Associate, Trinity College of Music, London
ATD   Art Teacher's Diploma
ATI   Associate, Textile Institute
ATII   Associate Member, Chartered Institute (formerly
           Incorporated Institute, then Institute) of Taxation
ATL   Association of Teachers and Lecturers
ato   Ammunition Technical Officer
ATP   Association of Tennis Players
ATPL (A) or (H) Airline Transport Pilot's Licence (Aeroplanes),
           or (Helicopters)
ATR (BC)   Art Therapist Registered (Board Certified)
ATS   Auxiliary Territorial Service (now see WRAC)
ATTI   Association of Teachers in Technical Institutions (now see
           NATFHE)
ATV   Associated Television (formerly Association TeleVision)
AUA   American Urological Association; Association of
           University Administrators
AUCAS   Association of University Clinical Academic Staff
AUEW   Amalgamated Union of Engineering Workers (later
           AEU, then AEEU)
AUS   Army of the United States
AUT   Association of University Teachers
AVCC   Australian Vice-Chancellors' Committee
AVCM   Associate, Victoria College of Music
AVD   Army Veterinary Department
AVLA   Audio Visual Language Association
AVMA   Association for Victims of Medical Accidents
AVR   Army Volunteer Reserve
AWA   Anglian Water Authority
AWHCT   Associate, West Ham College of Technology
AWO   Association of Water Officers (now see IWO)
AWRE   Atomic Weapons Research Establishment
aws   Graduate of Air Warfare Course
AZ   Arizona (postal)

B

b   born; brother
BA   Bachelor of Arts
BAA   British Airports Authority; British Accounting
           Association
BAAB   British Amateur Athletic Board
BAAL   British Association for Applied Linguistics
BAAS   British Association for the Advancement of Science
BAB   British Airways Board

BAC	British Aircraft Corporation
BAcc	Bachelor of Accountancy
BaccPhil	Baccalaureate in Philosophy
BACM	British Association of Colliery Management
BACSA	British Association for Cemeteries in South Asia
BACUP	British Association of Cancer United Patients
BAe	British Aerospace
BAED	Bachelor of Arts in Environmental Design
B&FBS	British and Foreign Bible Society
BAFO	British Air Forces of Occupation
BAFPA	British Association of Fitness Promotion Agencies
BAFTA	British Academy of Film and Television Arts
BAG	Business Art Galleries
BAgrSc	Bachelor of Agricultural Science
BAI	*Baccalarius in Arte Ingeniaria* (Bachelor of Engineering)
BAIE	British Association of Industrial Editors
BALPA	British Air Line Pilots' Association
BAO	Bachelor of Art of Obstetrics
BAOMS	British Association of Oral and Maxillo-Facial Surgeons
BAOR	British Army of the Rhine (*formerly* on the Rhine)
BAOS	British Association of Oral Surgeons (*now see* BAOMS)
BAppSc(MT)	Bachelor of Applied Science (Medical Technology)
BAPS	British Association of Plastic Surgeons
BARB	Broadcasters' Audience Research Board
BARC	British Automobile Racing Club
BArch	Bachelor of Architecture
Bart	Baronet
BAS	Bachelor in Agricultural Science
BASc	Bachelor of Applied Science
BASCA	British Academy of Songwriters, Composers and Authors
BASEEFA	British Approvals Service for Electrical Equipment in Flammable Atmospheres
BASES	British Association of Sport and Exercise Sciences
BASW	British Association of Social Workers
Batt.	Battery
BBA	British Bankers' Association; Bachelor of Business Administration
BBB of C	British Boxing Board of Control
BBC	British Broadcasting Corporation
BBFC	British Board of Film Classification
BBS	Bachelor of Business Studies
BBSRC	Biotechnology and Biological Sciences Research Council
BC	Before Christ; British Columbia; Borough Council
BCAR	British Civil Airworthiness Requirements
BCC	British Council of Churches (later CCBI)
BCE	Bachelor of Civil Engineering; Before the Christian Era
BCh or BChir	Bachelor of Surgery
BChD	Bachelor of Dental Surgery
BCIA	British Clothing Industries Association
BCL	Bachelor of Civil Law
BCMF	British Ceramic Manufacturers' Federation
BCMS	Bible Churchmen's Missionary Society
BCOF	British Commonwealth Occupation Force
BCom or BComm	Bachelor of Commerce
BComSc	Bachelor of Commercial Science
BCPC	British Crop Protection Council
BCS	Bengal Civil Service; British Computer Society
BCSA	British Constructional Steelwork Association
BCSC	British Council of Shopping Centres
BCTS	Bristol Certificate in Theological Studies
BCURA	British Coal Utilization Research Association
BCYC	British Corinthian Yacht Club
BD	Bachelor of Divinity
Bd	Board
BDA	British Dental Association; British Deaf Association; British Dyslexia Association
Bde	Brigade
BDQ	Bachelor of Divinity Qualifying
BDS	Bachelor of Dental Surgery
BDSc	Bachelor of Dental Science
BE	Bachelor of Engineering; British Element
BEA	British East Africa; British European Airways; British Epilepsy Association
BEAMA	Federation of British Electrotechnical and Allied Manufacturers' Associations (*formerly* British Electrical and Allied Manufacturers' Association)
BE&A	Bachelor of Engineering and Architecture (Malta)
BEARR	British Emergency Aid for Russia and the Republics
BEC	Business Education Council (*now see* BTEC)
BEc	Bachelor of Economics
BECTU	Broadcasting, Entertainment, Cinematograph and Theatre Union
BEd	Bachelor of Education
Beds	Bedfordshire
BEE	Bachelor of Electrical Engineering
BEF	British Expeditionary Force; British Equestrian Federation
BEM	British Empire Medal
BEMAS	British Educational Management and Administration Society
BEME	Brigade Electrical and Mechanical Engineer
BEng	Bachelor of Engineering
BEO	Base Engineer Officer
Berks	Berkshire
BES	Bachelor of Environmental Studies
BESO	British Executive Service Overseas
BEVA	British Equine Veterinary Association
BFI	British Film Institute
BFMIRA	British Food Manufacturing Industries Research Association
BFPO	British Forces Post Office
BFSS	British Field Sports Society
BFUW	British Federation of University Women (*now see* BFWG)
BFWG	British Federation of Women Graduates
BGCStJ	Bailiff Grand Cross, Most Venerable Order of the Hospital of St John of Jerusalem
BGS	Brigadier General Staff
BHA	British Hospitality Association
Bhd	Berhad
BHF	British Heart Foundation
BHL	Bachelor of Hebrew Letters
BHRA	British Hydromechanics Research Association
BHRCA	British Hotels, Restaurants and Caterers' Association (*now see* BHA)
BHS	British Horse Society
BI	British Invisibles
BIBA	British Insurance Brokers' Association
BIBRA	British Industrial Biological Research Association
BICC	British Insulated Callender's Cables
BICERA	British Internal Combustion Engine Research Association (*now see* BICERI)
BICERI	British Internal Combustion Engine Research Institute
BICSc	British Institute of Cleaning Science
BIDA	British Interior Design Association
BIEC	British Invisible Exports Council (*now see* BI)
BIEE	British Institute of Energy Economics
BIFU	Banking Insurance and Finance Union
BIIBA	British Insurance & Investment Brokers' Association (*now see* BIBA)
BIM	British Institute of Management
BIR	British Institute of Radiology
BIS	Bank for International Settlements
BISF	British Iron and Steel Federation
BISFA	British Industrial and Scientific Film Association
BISPA	British Independent Steel Producers Association
BISRA	British Iron and Steel Research Association
BITC	Business in the Community
BJ	Bachelor of Journalism
BJOG	British Journal of Obstetrics and Gynaecology
BJP	Bharatiya Janata Party
BJSM	British Joint Services Mission
BJur	Bachelor of Law
BKSTS	British Kinematograph, Sound and Television Society
BL	Bachelor of Law; British Library
BLA	British Liberation Army
BLDSA	British Long Distance Swimming Association
BLE	Bachelor of Land Economy
BLegS	Bachelor of Legal Studies
BLESMA	British Limbless Ex-Servicemen's Association
BLitt	Bachelor of Letters
BM	British Museum; Bachelor of Medicine; Brigade Major; British Monomark
BMA	British Medical Association
BMedSci	Bachelor of Medical Science
BMEO	British Middle East Office

BMet	Bachelor of Metallurgy
BMEWS	Ballistic Missile Early Warning System
BMG	British Military Government
BMH	British Military Hospital
BMilSc	Bachelor of Military Science
BMJ	British Medical Journal
BMM	British Military Mission
BMR	Bureau of Mineral Resources
BMRA	Brigade Major Royal Artillery
Bn	Battalion
BNA	British Nursing Association
BNAF	British North Africa Force
BNC	Brasenose College
BNEC	British National Export Council
BNF	British National Formulary
BNFL	British Nuclear Fuels Ltd
BNOC	British National Oil Corporation; British National Opera Company
BNP	Banque Nationale de Paris
BNSC	British National Space Centre
BNSc	Bachelor of Nursing Science
BOAC	British Overseas Airways Corporation
BoT	Board of Trade
Bot.	Botany; Botanical
BOTB	British Overseas Trade Board
BOU	British Ornithologists' Union
Bp	Bishop
BPA	British Paediatric Association (later CPCH; *now see* RCPCH)
BPG	Broadcasting Press Guild
BPharm	Bachelor of Pharmacy
BPIF	British Printing Industries Federation
BPMF	British Postgraduate Medical Federation
BProc	Bachelor of Procurationis
BPsS	British Psychological Society
BR	British Rail
Br.	Branch
BRA	Brigadier Royal Artillery; British Rheumatism & Arthritis Association
BRB	British Railways Board
BRCS	British Red Cross Society
BRE	Building Research Establishment
Brig.	Brigadier
BRIT	British Recording Industry Trust
BritIRE	British Institution of Radio Engineers (*now see* IERE)
BRNC	Britannia Royal Naval College
BRS	British Road Services
BRTP	Bachelor of Regional and Town Planning
BRurSc	Bachelor of Rural Science
BS	Bachelor of Surgery; Bachelor of Science; British Standard
BSA	Bachelor of Scientific Agriculture; Birmingham Small Arms; Building Societies' Association
BSAA	British South American Airways
BSAP	British South Africa Police
BSAS	British Society of Animal Science
BSBI	Botanical Society of the British Isles
BSC	British Steel Corporation; Bengal Staff Corps
BSc	Bachelor of Science
BScA, BScAgr	Bachelor of Science in Agriculture
BSc(Dent)	Bachelor of Science in Dentistry
BScEng	Bachelor of Science in Engineering
BSc (Est. Man.)	Bachelor of Science in Estate Management
BScN	Bachelor of Science in Nursing
BScSoc	Bachelor of Social Sciences
BSE	Bachelor of Science in Engineering (US); Bovine Spongiform Encephalopathy
BSES	British Schools Exploring Society
BSF	British Salonica Force
BSFA	British Science Fiction Association
BSFS	Bachelor of Science in Foreign Service
BSI	British Standards Institution
BSIA	British Security Industry Association
BSJA	British Show Jumping Association
BSME	Bachelor of Science in Mechanical Engineering; British Society of Magazine Editors
BSN	Bachelor of Science in Nursing
BSNS	Bachelor of Naval Science

BSocSc	Bachelor of Social Science
BSRA	British Ship Research Association
BSRIA	Building Services Research and Information Association
BSS	Bachelor of Science (Social Science)
BST	Bachelor of Sacred Theology
BSurv	Bachelor of Surveying
BSW	Bachelor of Social Work
BT	Bachelor of Teaching; British Telecommunications
Bt	Baronet; Brevet
BTA	British Tourist Authority (*formerly* British Travel Association)
BTC	British Transport Commission
BTCV	British Trust for Conservation Volunteers
BTDB	British Transport Docks Board (*now see* ABP)
BTEC	Business and Technology (*formerly* Technician) Education Council
BTh	Bachelor of Theology
BTP	Bachelor of Town Planning
BTS	Bachelor of Theological Studies
Btss	Baronetess
BUAS	British Universities Association of Slavists
Bucks	Buckinghamshire
BUGB	Baptist Union of Great Britain
BUNAC	British Universities North America Club
BUPA	British United Provident Association
BURA	British Urban Regeneration Association
BV	Besloten Vennootschap
BVA	British Veterinary Association; British Video Association
BVC	Bar Vocational Course
BVetMed	Bachelor of Veterinary Medicine
BVI	British Virgin Islands
BVM	Blessed Virgin Mary
BVMS	Bachelor of Veterinary Medicine and Surgery
BVSc	Bachelor of Veterinary Science
BWI	British West Indies
BWM	British War Medal

C

C	Conservative: 100
c	child; cousin; *circa* (about)
CA	Central America; County Alderman; Chartered Accountant (Scotland and Canada); California (postal)
CAA	Civil Aviation Authority
CAABU	Council for the Advancement of Arab and British Understanding
CAAV	(Member of) Central Association of Agricultural Valuers
CAB	Citizens' Advice Bureau; Centre for Agricultural and Biosciences (*formerly* Commonwealth Agricultural Bureau)
CABE	Commission for Architecture and the Built Environment
CACTM	Central Advisory Council of Training for the Ministry (later ACCM; *now see* ABM)
CAER	Conservative Action for Electoral Reform
CAF	Charities Aid Foundation
CAFCASS	Child and Family Court Advisory and Support Service
CAFOD	Catholic Agency for Overseas Development
CAJ	Committee on the Administration of Justice
CALE	Canadian Army Liaison Executive
Calif	California
CAM	Communications, Advertising and Marketing
Cambs	Cambridgeshire
CAMC	Canadian Army Medical Corps
CAMRA	Campaign for Real Ale
CAMS	Certificate of Advanced Musical Study
CAMW	Central Association for Mental Welfare
C&G	City and Guilds of London Institute
Cantab	*Cantabrigiensis* (of Cambridge)
Cantuar	*Cantuariensis* (of Canterbury)
CAP	Common Agricultural Policy
Capt.	Captain
CARD	Campaign against Racial Discrimination
CARE	Cottage and Rural Enterprises
CARICOM	Caribbean Community
CARIFTA	Caribbean Free Trade Area (*now see* CARICOM)
Carms	Carmarthenshire

CAS	Chief of the Air Staff
CASE	Council for the Advancement and Suppport of Education
CASI	Canadian Aeronautics and Space Institute
CAT	College of Advanced Technology; Countryside Around Towns
CATE	Council for the Accreditation of Teacher Education
Cav.	Cavalry
CAWU	Clerical and Administrative Workers' Union (later APEX)
CB	Companion, Order of the Bath; County Borough
CBC	County Borough Council
CBCO	Central Board for Conscientious Objectors
CBE	Commander, Order of the British Empire
CBI	Confederation of British Industry
CBII	Companion, British Institute of Innkeeping
CBIM	Companion, British Institute of Management (later CIMgt)
CBiol	Chartered Biologist
CBNS	Commander British Navy Staff
CBS	Columbia Broadcasting System; Confraternity of the Blessed Sacrament
CBSI	Chartered Building Societies Institute (now see CIB)
CBSO	City of Birmingham Symphony Orchestra
CC	Companion, Order of Canada; City Council; County Council; Cricket Club; Cycling Club; County Court
CCAB	Consultative Committee of Accountancy Bodies
CCAHC	Central Council for Agricultural and Horticultural Co-operation
CCBE	Commission Consultative des Barreaux de la Communauté Européenne
CCBI	Council of Churches for Britain and Ireland (now see CTBI)
CCC	Corpus Christi College; Central Criminal Court; County Cricket Club
CCE	Chartered Civil Engineer
CCETSW	Central Council for Education and Training in Social Work
CCF	Combined Cadet Force
CCFM	Combined Cadet Forces Medal
CCG	Control Commission Germany
CCH	Cacique's Crown of Honour, Order of Service of Guyana
CChem	Chartered Chemist
CCHMS	Central Committee for Hospital Medical Services
CCIA	Commission of Churches on International Affairs
CCIPD	Companion, Chartered Institute of Personnel and Development
CCIS	Command Control Information System
CCJ	Council of Christians and Jews
CCLRC	Council for the Central Laboratory of the Research Councils
CCMI	Companion, Chartered Management Institute
CCPR	Central Council of Physical Recreation
CCRA	Commander Corps of Royal Artillery
CCRE	Commander Corps of Royal Engineers
CCREME	Commander Corps of Royal Electrical and Mechanical Engineers
CCRSigs	Commander Corps of Royal Signals
CCS	Casualty Clearing Station; Ceylon Civil Service; Countryside Commission for Scotland
CCSU	Council of Civil Service Unions
CCTA	Commission de Coopération Technique pour l'Afrique; Central Computer and Telecommunications Authority
CCTS	Combat Crew Training Squadron
CD	Canadian Forces Decoration; Commander, Order of Distinction (Jamaica); Civil Defence; Compact Disc
CDA	Co-operative Development Agency
CDC	Centers for Disease Control and Prevention
CDEE	Chemical Defence Experimental Establishment
CDipAF	Certified Diploma in Accounting and Finance
CDir	Chartered Director
Cdo	Commando
CDRA	Committee of Directors of Research Associations
Cdre	Commodore
CDS	Chief of the Defence Staff
CDU	Christlich-Demokratische Union
CE	Civil Engineer
CEA	Central Electricity Authority

CEC	Commission of the European Communities
CECD	Confédération Européenne du Commerce de Détail
CECG	Consumers in European Community Group
CEDEP	Centre Européen d'Education Permanente
CEDR	Centre for Effective Dispute Resolution
CEE	Communauté Economique Européenne
CEED	Centre for Economic and Environmental Development
CEF	Canadian Expeditionary Force
CEFAS	Centre for Environment, Fisheries and Aquaculture Science
CEFIC	Conseil Européen des Fédérations de l'Industrie Chimique
CEGB	Central Electricity Generating Board
CEH	Centre for Ecology & Hydrology
CEI	Council of Engineering Institutions
CEIR	Corporation for Economic and Industrial Research
CEM	Council of European Municipalities (now see CEMR); College of Emergency Medicine
CEMA	Council for the Encouragement of Music and Arts
CeMGA	Centre for the Measurement of Government Activity
CEMR	Council of European Municipalities and Regions
CEMS	Church of England Men's Society
CEN	Comité Européen de Normalisation
CENELEC	European Committee for Electrotechnical Standardization
CEng	Chartered Engineer
Cento	Central Treaty Organisation
CEnv	Chartered Environmentalist
CEO	Chief Executive Officer
CEPES	Comité européen pour le progrès économique et social
CEPS	Center for Economic Policy Studies
CEPT	Conférence Européenne des Postes et des Télécommunications
CERL	Central Electricity Research Laboratories
CERN	Organisation (formerly Centre) Européenne pour la Recherche Nucléaire
CERT	Charities Effectiveness Review Trust
CertCPE	Certificate in Clinical Pastoral Education
CertDS	Certificate in Dramatic Studies
Cert Ed	Certificate of Education
CertITP	Certificate of International Teachers' Program (Harvard)
CertTP	Certificate in Town Planning
CEST	Centre for Exploitation of Science and Technology
CET	Council for Educational Technology
CETSW	Council for Education and Training in Social Work
CF	Chaplain to the Forces; Companion, Order of Fiji
CFA	Canadian Field Artillery
CFE	Central Fighter Establishment
CFM	Cadet Forces Medal
CFPS	Certificate of Further Professional Studies
CFR	Commander, Order of the Federal Republic of Nigeria
CFS	Central Flying School; Chronic Fatigue Syndrome
CGA	Community of the Glorious Ascension; Country Gentlemen's Association
CGeog	Chartered Geographer
CGeol	Chartered Geologist
CGIA	Insignia Award of City and Guilds of London Institute (now see FCGI)
CGLI	City and Guilds of London Institute (now see C&G)
CGM	Conspicuous Gallantry Medal
CGRM	Commandant-General Royal Marines
CGS	Chief of the General Staff
CH	Companion of Honour
Chanc.	Chancellor; Chancery
Chap.	Chaplain
ChapStJ	Chaplain, Order of St John of Jerusalem (now see ChStJ)
CHAR	Campaign for the Homeless and Rootless
CHB	Companion of Honour of Barbados
ChB	Bachelor of Surgery
CHC	Community Health Council
Ch.Ch.	Christ Church
CHE	Campaign for Homosexual Equality
ChLJ	Chaplain, Order of St Lazarus of Jerusalem
(CHM)	see under ARCO(CHM), FRCO(CHM)
ChM	Master of Surgery
Chm.	Chairman or Chairwoman
CHN	Community of the Holy Name
CHSC	Central Health Services Council

ChStJ	Chaplain, Most Venerable Order of the Hospital of St John of Jerusalem
CI	Imperial Order of the Crown of India; Channel Islands
CIA	Chemical Industries Association; Central Intelligence Agency
CIAD	Central Institute of Art and Design
CIAgrE	Companion, Institution of Agricultural Engineers
CIAL	Corresponding Member of the International Institute of Arts and Letters
CIArb	Chartered Institute of Arbitrators
CIB	Chartered Institute of Bankers
CIBS	Chartered Institution of Building Services (now see CIBSE)
CIBSE	Chartered Institution of Building Services Engineers
CIC	Chemical Institute of Canada
CICAP	Criminal Injuries Compensation Appeal Panel
CICB	Criminal Injuries Compensation Board
CICHE	Committee for International Co-operation in Higher Education
CICI	Confederation of Information Communication Industries
CID	Criminal Investigation Department
CIE	Companion, Order of the Indian Empire; Confédération Internationale des Etudiants
CIEx	Companion, Institute of Export
CIFE	Council (formerly Conference) for Independent Further Education
CIGasE	Companion, Institution of Gas Engineers (now see CIGEM)
CIGEM	Companion, Institution of Gas Engineers and Managers
CIGRE	Conférence Internationale des Grands Réseaux Electriques
CIGS	Chief of the Imperial General Staff (now see CGS)
CIHR	Canadian Institutes of Health Research
CIIA	Canadian Institute of International Affairs
CIL	Corpus inscriptionum latinarum
CILT	Chartered Institute of Logistics and Transport
CIM	China Inland Mission; Chartered Institute of Marketing
CIMA	Chartered Institute of Management Accountants
CIMarE	Companion, Institute of Marine Engineers
CIMEMME	Companion, Institution of Mining Electrical and Mining Mechanical Engineers
CIMgt	Companion, Institute of Management (now see CCMI)
CIMGTechE	Companion, Institution of Mechanical and General Technician Engineers
CIMR	Cambridge Institute for Medical Research
C-in-C	Commander-in-Chief
CINCHAN	Allied Commander-in-Chief Channel
CIOB	Chartered Institute of Building
CIPA	Chartered Institute of Patent Agents
CIPD	Companion, Institute of Personnel and Development (now see CCIPD); Chartered Institute of Personnel and Development
CIPFA	Chartered Institute of Public Finance and Accountancy
CIPL	Comité International Permanent des Linguistes
CIPM	Companion, Institute of Personnel Management (later CIPD)
CIPR	Chartered Institute of Public Relations
CIR	Commission on Industrial Relations
CIRES	Co-operative Institute for Research in Environmental Sciences
CIRIA	Construction Industry Research and Information Association
CIRP	Collège Internationale pour Recherche et Production
CIS	Institute of Chartered Secretaries and Administrators (formerly Chartered Institute of Secretaries); Command Control Communications and Information Systems; Commonwealth of Independent States
CISAC	Confédération Internationale des Sociétés d'Auteurs et Compositeurs; Centre for International Security and Arms Control
CIT	Chartered Institute of Transport; California Institute of Technology
CITB	Construction Industry Training Board
CITD	Certificate of Institute of Training and Development
CITP	Chartered Information Technology Professional
CIU	Club and Institute Union
CIV	City Imperial Volunteers
CIWEM	Chartered Institution of Water and Environmental Management
CJ	Chief Justice

CJC	Companions of Jesus Christ
CJM	Congregation of Jesus and Mary (Eudist Fathers)
CL	Commander, Order of Leopold
cl	cum laude
Cl.	Class
CLA	Country Land & Business Association (formerly Country Landowners' Association)
CLIC	Cancer and Leukemia in Childhood
CLIP	Common Law Institute of Intellectual Property; Chartered Institute of Library and Information Professionals
CLit	Companion of Literature (Royal Society of Literature Award)
CLJ	Commander, Order of St Lazarus of Jerusalem
CLP	Constituency Labour Party
CLRAE	Congress (formerly Conference) of Local and Regional Authorities of Europe
CLY	City of London Yeomanry
CM	Member, Order of Canada; Congregation of the Mission (Vincentians); Master in Surgery; Certificated Master; Canadian Militia
CMA	Canadian Medical Association; Cost and Management Accountant (NZ)
CMAC	Catholic Marriage Advisory Council
CMarSci	Chartered Marine Scientist
CMath	Chartered Mathematician
CMB	Central Midwives' Board
CMC	Certified Management Consultant
CME	Continuing Ministerial Education
CMet	Chartered Meteorologist
CMF	Commonwealth Military Forces; Central Mediterranean Force
CMG	Companion, Order of St Michael and St George
CMILT	Chartered Member, Chartered Institute of Logistics and Transport
CMIWSc	Certified Member, Institute of Wood Science
CMJ	Commander, Supreme Military Order of the Temple of Jerusalem
CMLJ	Commander of Merit, Order of St Lazarus of Jerusalem
CMM	Commander, Order of Military Merit (Canada)
CMO	Chief Medical Officer
CMP	Corps of Military Police (now see CRMP)
CMS	Church Mission (formerly Church Missionary) Society; Certificate in Management Studies
CMT	Chaconia Medal of Trinidad
CNAA	Council for National Academic Awards
CND	Campaign for Nuclear Disarmament
CNI	Companion, Nautical Institute
CNO	Chief of Naval Operations
CNOCS	Captain Naval Operational Command Systems
CNR	Canadian National Railways
CNRS	Centre National de la Recherche Scientifique
CNZM	Companion, New Zealand Order of Merit
CO	Commanding Officer; Commonwealth Office (after Aug. 1966) (now see FCO); Colonial Office (before Aug. 1966); Conscientious Objector; Colorado (postal)
Co.	County; Company
Coal.L or Co.L	Coalition Liberal
Coal.U or Co.U	Coalition Unionist
CODEST	Committee for the Development of European Science and Technology
C of E	Church of England
C of I	Church of Ireland
C of S	Chief of Staff; Church of Scotland
COHSE	Confederation of Health Service Employees
COI	Central Office of Information
CoID	Council of Industrial Design (now Design Council)
Col	Colonel
Coll.	College; Collegiate
Colo	Colorado
Col.-Sergt	Colour-Sergeant
Com	Communist
Comd	Command
Comdg	Commanding
Comdr	Commander
Comdt	Commandant
COMEC	Council of the Military Education Committees of the Universities of the UK
COMET	Committee for Middle East Trade

Commn	Commission
Commnd	Commissioned
CompAMEME	Companion, Association of Mining Electrical and Mechanical Engineers
CompICE	Companion, Institution of Civil Engineers
CompIEE	Companion, Institution of Electrical Engineers (now see FIEE)
CompIERE	Companion, Institution of Electronic and Radio Engineers
CompIGasE	Companion, Institution of Gas Engineers
CompILE	Companion, Institution of Lighting Engineers
CompIMechE	Companion, Institution of Mechanical Engineers
CompInstE	Companion, Institute of Energy
CompInstMC	Companion, Institute of Measurement and Control
CompIWES	Companion, Institution of Water Engineers and Scientists
CompOR	Companion, Operational Research Society
CompTI	Companion of the Textile Institute
Comr	Commissioner
Comy-Gen.	Commissary-General
CON	Commander, Order of the Niger
ConfEd	Confederation of Education Service Managers
Conn	Connecticut
Const.	Constitutional
CONUL	Council of National and University Librarians
Co-op.	Co-operative
COPA	Comité des Organisations Professionels Agricoles de la CEE
COPEC	Conference of Politics, Economics and Christianity
COPUS	Committee on the Public Understanding of Science
Corp.	Corporation; Corporal
Corresp. Mem.	Corresponding Member
COS	Chief of Staff; Charity Organization Society
COSA	Colliery Officials and Staffs Association
CoSIRA	Council for Small Industries in Rural Areas
COSLA	Convention of Scottish Local Authorities
COSPAR	Committee on Space Research
COSSAC	Chief of Staff to Supreme Allied Commander
COTC	Canadian Officers' Training Corps
CP	Central Provinces; Cape Province; Congregation of the Passion
CPA	Commonwealth Parliamentary Association; Chartered Patent Agent; Certified Public Accountant (USA)
CPAG	Child Poverty Action Group
CPAS	Church Pastoral Aid Society
CPC	Conservative Political Centre
CPCH	College of Paediatrics and Child Health (now see RCPCH)
CPE	Common Professional Examination
CPEng	Chartered Professional Engineer (of Institution of Engineers of Australia)
CPFA	Member or Associate, Chartered Institute of Public Finance and Accountancy
CPHVA	Community Practitioners & Health Visitors' Association
CPhys	Chartered Physicist
CPL	Chief Personnel and Logistics
CPLS	Certificate of Professional Legal Studies
CPM	Colonial Police Medal
CPR	Canadian Pacific Railway
CPRE	Campaign to Protect Rural England (formerly Council for the Protection of Rural England)
CPRW	Campaign for the Protection of Rural Wales
CPS	Crown Prosecution Service; Certificate in Pastoral Studies
CPSA	Civil and Public Services Association (now see PCS); Church of the Province of South Africa
CPSM	Council for Professions Supplementary to Medicine
CPSU	Communist Party of the Soviet Union
CPsychol	Chartered Psychologist
CPU	Commonwealth Press Union
CQ	Chevalier, National Order of Quebec
CQSW	Certificate of Qualification in Social Work
CR	Community of the Resurrection
cr	created or creation
CRA	Commander, Royal Artillery
CRAC	Careers Research and Advisory Centre
CRAeS	Companion, Royal Aeronautical Society
CRAG	Clinical Resources and Audit Group
CRASC	Commander, Royal Army Service Corps

CRC	Cancer Research Campaign (now see CRUK); Community Relations Council
CRCP(C)	Certificant, Royal College of Physicians of Canada
CRE	Commander, Royal Engineers; Commission for Racial Equality; Commercial Relations and Exports; Conference of Rectors of European Universities (formerly Association of European Universities)
Cres.	Crescent
CRMP	Corps of Royal Military Police
CRNCM	Companion, Royal Northern College of Music
CRO	Commonwealth Relations Office (now see FCO)
CRUK	Cancer Research United Kingdom
CS	Civil Service; Clerk to the Signet
CSA	Confederate States of America; Child Support Agency
CSAB	Civil Service Appeal Board
CSB	Bachelor of Christian Science
CSC	Conspicuous Service Cross; Congregation of the Holy Cross
CSCA	Civil Service Clerical Association (later CPSA)
CSCE	Conference on Security and Co-operation in Europe
CSci	Chartered Scientist
CSD	Civil Service Department; Co-operative Secretaries Diploma; Chartered Society of Designers
CSDE	Central Servicing Development Establishment
CSEU	Confederation of Shipbuilding and Engineering Unions
CSFI	Centre for Study of Financial Innovation
CSG	Companion, Order of the Star of Ghana; Company of the Servants of God
CSI	Companion, Order of the Star of India
CSIR	Commonwealth Council for Scientific and Industrial Research (now see CSIRO)
CSIRO	Commonwealth Scientific and Industrial Research Organization (Australia)
CSM	Civil Service Medal (Fiji)
CSO	Chief Scientific Officer; Chief Signal Officer; Chief Staff Officer; Central Statistical Office (now see ONS)
CSP	Chartered Society of Physiotherapists; Civil Service of Pakistan
CSS	Companion, Star of Sarawak; Council for Science and Society
CSSB	Civil Service Selection Board
CSSD	Czech Social Democratic Party
CSSp	Holy Ghost Father
CSSR	Congregation of the Most Holy Redeemer (Redemptorist Order)
CStat	Chartered Statistician
CSTI	Council of Science and Technology Institutes
CStJ	Commander, Most Venerable Order of the Hospital of St John of Jerusalem
CSU	Christlich-Soziale Union in Bayern
CSV	Community Service Volunteers
CSW	Certificate in Social Work
CT	Connecticut (postal)
CTA	Chaplain Territorial Army; Chartered Tax Adviser
CTB	College of Teachers of the Blind
CTBI	Churches Together in Britain and Ireland
CTC	Cyclists' Touring Club; Commando Training Centre; City Technology College
CText	Chartered Textile Technologist
CTh	Certificate in Theology
CTR(Harwell)	Controlled Thermonuclear Research
CU	Cambridge University
CUAC	Cambridge University Athletic Club; Colleges and Universities of the Anglican Communion
CUAFC	Cambridge University Association Football Club
CUBC	Cambridge University Boat Club
CUCC	Cambridge University Cricket Club
CUF	Common University Fund
CUHC	Cambridge University Hockey Club
CUMS	Cambridge University Musical Society
CUNY	City University of New York
CUP	Cambridge University Press
CUPGRA	Cambridge University Postgraduate Research Association
CURUFC	Cambridge University Rugby Union Football Club
CV	Cross of Valour (Canada)
CVCP	Committee of Vice-Chancellors and Principals of the Universities of the United Kingdom (now see UUK)
CVO	Commander, Royal Victorian Order
CVS	Council for Voluntary Service

CVSNA	Council of Voluntary Service National Association
CWA	Crime Writers Association
CWGC	Commonwealth War Graves Commission
CWS	Co-operative Wholesale Society
CWU	Communication Workers Union

D

D	Duke
d	died; daughter
DA	Dame of St Andrew, Order of Barbados; Diploma in Anaesthesia; Diploma in Art; Doctor of Arts
DAA&QMG	Deputy Assistant Adjutant and Quartermaster-General
DAAD	Designers and Art Directors Association
DAAG	Deputy Assistant Adjutant-General
DA&QMG	Deputy Adjutant and Quartermaster-General
DAC	Development Assistance Committee; Diocesan Advisory Committee
DACG	Deputy Assistant Chaplain-General
DACOS	Deputy Assistant Chief of Staff
DAD	Deputy Assistant Director
DAdmin	Doctor of Administration
DADMS	Deputy Assistant Director of Medical Services
DADOS	Deputy Assistant Director of Ordnance Services
DADQ	Deputy Assistant Director of Quartering
DADST	Deputy Assistant Director of Supplies and Transport
DAEd	Diploma in Art Education
DAG	Deputy Adjutant-General
DAgr	Doctor of Agriculture
DAgrFor	Doctor of Agriculture and Forestry
DAMS	Deputy Assistant Military Secretary
D&AD	Designers and Art Directors Association
DAppSc	Doctor of Applied Science
DAQMG	Deputy Assistant Quartermaster-General
DArch	Doctor of Architecture
DArt	Doctor of Art
DArts	Doctor of Arts
DASc	Doctor in Agricultural Sciences
DASS	Diploma in Applied Social Studies
DATA	Draughtsmen's and Allied Technicians' Association (later AUEW(TASS))
DATEC	Art and Design Committee, Technician Education Council
DAvMed	Diploma in Aviation Medicine, Royal College of Physicians
DBA	Doctor of Business Administration
DBE	Dame Commander, Order of the British Empire
DBTS	Diploma in Biblical and Theological Studies
DC	District Council; District of Columbia
DCA	Doctor of Creative Arts; Department for Constitutional Affairs
DCAe	Diploma of College of Aeronautics
DCAS	Deputy Chief of the Air Staff
DCB	Dame Commander, Order of the Bath
DCC	Diploma of Chelsea College
DCCH	Diploma in Community Child Health
DCDS	Deputy Chief of Defence Staff
DCE	Diploma of a College of Education
DCG	Deputy Chaplain-General
DCGS	Deputy Chief of the General Staff
DCh	Doctor of Surgery
DCH	Diploma in Child Health
DCHS	Dame Commander, Order of the Holy Sepulchre
DCL	Doctor of Civil Law; Dr of Canon Law
DCLG	Department for Communities and Local Government
DCLI	Duke of Cornwall's Light Infantry
DCLJ	Dame Commander, Order of St Lazarus of Jerusalem
DCM	Distinguished Conduct Medal
DCMG	Dame Commander, Order of St Michael and St George
DCMS	Department for Culture, Media and Sport
DCnL	Doctor of Canon Law
DCNZM	Distinguished Companion, New Zealand Order of Merit
DCO	Duke of Cambridge's Own
DCom or **DComm**	Doctor of Commerce
DCP	Diploma in Clinical Pathology; Diploma in Conservation of Paintings
DCS	Deputy Chief of Staff; Doctor of Commercial Sciences
DCSG	Dame Commander, Order of St Gregory the Great
DCSO	Deputy Chief Scientific Officer
DCT	Doctor of Christian Theology
DCVO	Dame Commander, Royal Victorian Order
DD	Doctor of Divinity
DDAM	Diploma in Disability Assessment Medicine
DDes	Doctor of Design
DDGAMS	Deputy Director General, Army Medical Services
DDH	Diploma in Dental Health
DDL	Deputy Director of Labour
DDME	Deputy Director of Mechanical Engineering
DDMI	Deputy Director of Military Intelligence
DDMO	Deputy Director of Military Operations
DDMS	Deputy Director of Medical Services
DDMT	Deputy Director of Military Training
DDNI	Deputy Director of Naval Intelligence
DDO	Diploma in Dental Orthopaedics
DDPH	Diploma in Dental Public Health
DDPR	Deputy Director of Public Relations
DDPS	Deputy Director of Personal Services
DDR	Deutsche Demokratische Republik
DDRA	Deputy Director Royal Artillery
DDra	Doctor of Drama
DDS	Doctor of Dental Surgery; Director of Dental Services
DDSc	Doctor of Dental Science
DDSD	Deputy Director Staff Duties
DDSM	Defense Distinguished Service Medal
DDST	Deputy Director of Supplies and Transport
DDWE&M	Deputy Director of Works, Electrical and Mechanical
DE	Doctor of Engineering; Delaware (postal)
DEA	Department of Economic Affairs
DEc	Doctor of Economics
decd	deceased
DEconSc	Doctor of Economic Science
DEd	Doctor of Education
DEFRA	Department for Environment, Food and Rural Affairs
Deleg.	Delegate
DEME	Directorate of Electrical and Mechanical Engineering
DEMS	Defensively Equipped Merchant Ships
(DemU)	Democratic Unionist
DenD	Docteur en Droit
DEng	Doctor of Engineering
DenM	Docteur en Médicine
DEOVR	Duke of Edinburgh's Own Volunteer Rifles
DEP	Department of Employment and Productivity; European Progressive Democrats
Dep.	Deputy
DERA	Defence Evaluation and Research Agency
DES	Department of Education and Science (later DFE); Dr in Environmental Studies
DèsL	Docteur ès lettres
DèS or **DèsSc**	Docteur ès sciences
DesRCA	Designer of the Royal College of Art
DESU	Diplôme d'Etudes Supérieures d'Université
DETR	Department of the Environment, Transport and the Regions
DFA	Doctor of Fine Arts
DFAS	Decorative and Fine Art Society
DFC	Distinguished Flying Cross
DFE	Department for Education (later DFEE)
DFEE or **DfEE**	Department for Education and Employment (*now see* DFES)
DFES or **DfES**	Department for Education and Skills
DFFP	Diploma in Fertility and Family Planning
DFH	Diploma of Faraday House
DFID	Department for International Development
DFil	Doctor en Filosofia
DFLS	Day Fighter Leaders' School
DFM	Distinguished Flying Medal
DFPHM	Diplomate Member, Faculty of Public Health Medicine
DfT	Department for Transport
DG	Director General; Directorate General; Dragoon Guards
DGAA	Distressed Gentlefolks Aid Association
DGAMS	Director-General Army Medical Services
DGCHS	Dame Grand Cross, Order of the Holy Sepulchre
DGDP	Diploma in General Dental Practice, Royal College of Physicians

DGEME	Director General Electrical and Mechanical Engineering
DGLP(A)	Director General Logistic Policy (Army)
DGMS	Director-General of Medical Services
DGMT	Director-General of Military Training
DGMW	Director-General of Military Works
DGNPS	Director-General of Naval Personal Services
DGP	Director-General of Personnel
DGPS	Director-General of Personal Services
DGS	Diploma in Graduate Studies
DGStJ	Dame of Grace, Order of St John of Jerusalem (*now see* DStJ)
DGU	Doctor of Griffith University
DH	Doctor of Humanities
DHA	District Health Authority
Dhc	Doctor *honoris causa*
DHE	Defence Housing Executive
DHEW	Department of Health Education and Welfare (US)
DHL	Doctor of Humane Letters; Doctor of Hebrew Literature
DHLitt	Doctor of Humane Letters
DHM	Dean Hole Medal
DHMSA	Diploma in the History of Medicine (Society of Apothecaries)
DHQ	District Headquarters
DHS	Dame, Order of the Holy Sepulchre
DHSS	Department of Health and Social Security
DHum	Doctor of Humanities
DHumLit	Doctor of Humane Letters
DIA	Diploma in Industrial Administration
DIAS	Dublin Institute of Advanced Sciences
DIC	Diploma of the Imperial College
DICTA	Diploma of Imperial College of Tropical Agriculture
DIG	Deputy Inspector-General
DIH	Diploma in Industrial Health
DIMP	Darjah Indera Mahkota Pahang
DIntLaw	Diploma in International Law
Dio.	Diocese
DipA	Diploma of Arts in Theology
DipAA	Diploma in Applied Art
DipAD	Diploma in Art and Design
DipAE	Diploma in Adult Education
DipAe	Diploma in Aeronautics
DipAgr	Diploma in Agriculture
DipArch	Diploma in Architecture
DipASE	Diploma in Advanced Study of Education, College of Preceptors
DipASS	Diploma in Applied Social Studies
DipBA	Diploma in Business Administration
DipBS	Diploma in Fine Art, Byam Shaw School
DipCAM	Diploma in Communications, Advertising and Marketing of CAM Foundation
DipCC	Diploma of the Central College
DipCD	Diploma in Civic Design
DipCE	Diploma in Civil Engineering; Diploma of a College of Education (Scotland)
DipECLAM	Diplomate, European College of Laboratory Animal Medicine
DipEcon	Diploma in Economics
DipEd	Diploma in Education
DipEE	Diploma in Electrical Engineering
DipEl	Diploma in Electronics
DipESL	Diploma in English as a Second Language
DipEth	Diploma in Ethnology
DipEurHum	Diploma in European Humanities
DipEVPC	Diplomate, European Veterinary Parasitology College
DipFBOM	Diploma in Farm Business Organisation and Management
DipFD	Diploma in Funeral Directing
DipFE	Diploma in Further Education
DipFM	Diploma in Forensic Medicine
DipGSM	Diploma in Music, Guildhall School of Music and Drama
DipHA	Diploma in Hospital Administration
DipHE	Diploma in Higher Education
DipHSM	Diploma in Health Services Management
DipHIC	Diploma in Hospital Infection Control
DipHum	Diploma in Humanities
DipHV	Diploma in Health Visiting
DipICArb	Diploma in International Commercial Arbitration
DipIT	Diploma in Information Technology
DipLA	Diploma in Landscape Architecture
DipLib	Diploma of Librarianship
DipLLP	Diploma in Law and Legal Practice
DipLP	Diploma in Legal Practice
DipM	Diploma in Marketing
DipMed	Diploma in Medicine
DipN	Diploma in Nursing
DipNEC	Diploma of Northampton Engineering College (*now* City University)
DIPP	Diploma of Interventional Pain Practice
DipPA	Diploma of Practitioners in Advertising (*now see* DipCAM)
DipPE	Diploma in Physical Education
DipPSA	Diploma in Public Service Administration
DipPSW	Diploma in Psychiatric Social Work
DipRE	Diploma in Religious Education
DipREM	Diploma in Rural Estate Management
DipSMS	Diploma in School Management Studies
DipSoc	Diploma in Sociology
DipSocSc	Diploma in Social Science
DipSRAA	Diploma in the Study of Records and Administration of Archives
DipSW	Diploma in Social Work
DipTA	Diploma in Tropical Agriculture
DipT&CP	Diploma in Town and Country Planning
DipTh	Diploma in Theology
DipTMHA	Diploma in Training and Further Education of Mentally Handicapped Adults
DipTP	Diploma in Town Planning
DipTPT	Diploma in Theory and Practice of Teaching
DipTRP	Diploma in Town and Regional Planning
DipYCS	Diploma in Youth and Community Studies
DIS	Diploma in Industrial Studies
DistTP	Distinction in Town Planning
DIur	Doctor of Law
Div.	Division; Divorced
Div.Test	Divinity Testimonium (of Trinity College, Dublin)
DJAG	Deputy Judge Advocate General
DJPD	Dato Jasa Purba Di-Raja Negeri Sembilan (Malaysia)
DJStJ	Dame of Justice, Order of St John of Jerusalem (*now see* DStJ)
DJur	*Doctor Juris* (Doctor of Law)
DK	Most Esteemed Family Order (Brunei)
DL	Deputy Lieutenant; Democratie Libérale
DLAS	Diploma in Laboratory Animal Science, Royal College of Veterinary Surgeons
DLaws	Doctor of Laws
DLC	Diploma of Loughborough College
DLES	Doctor of Letters in Economic Studies
DLI	Durham Light Infantry
DLIS	Diploma in Library and Information Studies
DLit or DLitt	Doctor of Literature; Doctor of Letters
DLittS	Doctor of Sacred Letters
DLJ	Dame of Grace, Order of St Lazarus of Jerusalem
DLO	Diploma in Laryngology and Otology
DLP	Diploma in Legal Practice
DLR	Docklands Light Railway
DM	Doctor of Medicine
DMA	Diploma in Municipal Administration
DMCC	Diploma in the Medical Care of Catastrophe, Society of Apothecaries
DMD	Doctor of Medical Dentistry (Australia)
DME	Director of Mechanical Engineering
DMet	Doctor of Metallurgy
DMI	Director of Military Intelligence
DMin	Doctor of Ministry
DMiss	Doctor of Missiology
DMJ	Diploma in Medical Jurisprudence
DMJ(Path)	Diploma in Medical Jurisprudence (Pathology)
DMLJ	Dame of Merit, Order of St Lazarus of Jerusalem
DMO	Director of Military Operations
DMR	Diploma in Medical Radiology
DMRD	Diploma in Medical Radiological Diagnosis
DMRE	Diploma in Medical Radiology and Electrology
DMRT	Diploma in Medical Radio-Therapy
DMS	Director of Medical Services; Decoration for Meritorious Service (South Africa); Diploma in Management Studies

DMSc	Doctor of Medical Science
DMSSB	Direct Mail Services Standards Board
DMT	Director of Military Training
DMus	Doctor of Music
DN	Diploma in Nursing
DNB	Dictionary of National Biography
DNE	Director of Naval Equipment
DNH	Department of National Heritage
DNI	Director of Naval Intelligence
DNZM	Dame Companion, New Zealand Order of Merit
DO	Diploma in Ophthalmology
DOAE	Defence Operational Analysis Establishment
DObstRCOG	Diploma of Royal College of Obstetricians and Gynaecologists (now see DRCOG)
DOC	District Officer Commanding
DocArts	Doctor of Arts
DocEng	Doctor of Engineering
DoE	Department of the Environment
DoH	Department of Health
DoI	Department of Industry
DOL	Doctor of Oriental Learning
Dom.	Dominus (Lord)
DOMS	Diploma in Ophthalmic Medicine and Surgery
DOR	Director of Operational Requirements
DOrthRCS	Diploma in Orthodontics, Royal College of Surgeons
DOS	Director of Ordnance Services; Doctor of Ocular Science
Dow.	Dowager
DP	Data Processing
DPA	Diploma in Public Administration; Discharged Prisoners' Aid; Doctor of Public Administration
DPD	Diploma in Public Dentistry
DPEc	Doctor of Political Economy
DPed	Doctor of Pedagogy
DPH	Diploma in Public Health
DPh or DPhil	Doctor of Philosophy
DPharm	Doctor of Pharmacy
DPhilMed	Diploma in Philosophy of Medicine
DPhysMed	Diploma in Physical Medicine
DPLG	Diplômé par le Gouvernement
DPM	Diploma in Psychological Medicine; Diploma in Personnel Management
DPMS	Dato Paduka Mahkota Selangor (Malaysia)
DPMSA	Diploma in Philosophy and Ethics of Medicine, Society of Apothecaries
DPP	Director of Public Prosecutions
DPR	Director of Public Relations
DPS	Director of Postal Services; Director of Personal Services; Doctor of Public Service; Diploma in Pastoral Studies
DPSA	Diploma in Public and Social Administration
DPSE	Diploma in Professional Studies in Education
DPSM	Diploma in Public Sector Management
DPsych	Doctor of Psychology
DQMG	Deputy Quartermaster-General
Dr	Doctor
DRA	Defence Research Agency (now see DERA)
DRAC	Director Royal Armoured Corps
DRC	Diploma of Royal College of Science and Technology, Glasgow
DRCOG	Diploma of Royal College of Obstetricians and Gynaecologists
DRD	Diploma in Restorative Dentistry
Dr ing	Doctor of Engineering
Dr jur	Doctor of Laws
DrŒcPol	Doctor Œconomiæ Politicæ (Doctor of Political Economy)
Dr phil	Doctor of Philosophy
Dr rer. nat.	Doctor of Natural Science
Dr rer. pol.	Doctor of Political Science
DRS	Diploma in Religious Studies
Drs	Doctorandus
DRSAMD	Diploma of the Royal Scottish Academy of Music and Drama
DS	Directing Staff; Doctor of Science
DSA	Diploma in Social Administration
DSAC	Defence Scientific Advisory Council
DSAO	Diplomatic Service Administration Office
DSC	Distinguished Service Cross
DSc	Doctor of Science

DScA	Docteur en sciences agricoles
DSc(Eng)	Doctor of Engineering Science
DSCHE	Diploma of the Scottish Council for Health Education
DScMil	Doctor of Military Science
DSc (SocSci)	Doctor of Science in Social Science
DSD	Director Staff Duties; Diploma in Speech and Drama
DSF	Director Special Forces
DSG	Dame, Order of St Gregory the Great
DSIR	Department of Scientific and Industrial Research (later SRC; then SERC)
DSL	Doctor of Sacred Letters
DSLJ	Dato Seri Laila Jasa (Brunei)
DSM	Distinguished Service Medal
DSNB	Dato Setia Negara Brunei
DSNS	Dato Setia Negeri Sembilan (Malaysia)
DSO	Companion of the Distinguished Service Order
DSocSc	Doctor of Social Science
DSP	Director of Selection of Personnel; Docteur en sciences politiques (Montreal)
dsp	decessit sine prole (died without issue)
DSS	Department of Social Security; Doctor of Sacred Scripture
Dss	Deaconess
DSSc	Doctor of Social Science
DST	Director of Supplies and Transport
DStJ	Dame of Grace, Most Venerable Order of the Hospital of St John of Jerusalem; Dame of Justice, Most Venerable Order of the Hospital of St John of Jerusalem
DSTL	Defence Science and Technology Laboratory
DTA	Diploma in Tropical Agriculture
DTD	Dekoratie voor Trouwe Dienst (Decoration for Devoted Service)
DTech	Doctor of Technology
DTH	Diploma in Tropical Hygiene
DTh or DTheol	Doctor of Theology
DThPT	Diploma in Theory and Practice of Teaching
DTI	Department of Trade and Industry
DTLR	Department for Transport, Local Government and the Regions
DTM&H	Diploma in Tropical Medicine and Hygiene
DU or DUniv	Honorary Doctor of the University
Dunelm	Dunelmensis (of Durham)
DUP	Democratic Unionist Party; Docteur de l'Université de Paris
DVA	Diploma of Veterinary Anaesthesia
DVH	Diploma in Veterinary Hygiene
DVLA	Driver and Vehicle Licensing Authority
DVLC	Driver and Vehicle Licensing Centre
DVM or DVetMed	Doctor of Veterinary Medicine
DVMS or DVM&S	Doctor of Veterinary Medicine and Surgery
DVO	Driver, Vehicle and Operator
DVR	Diploma in Veterinary Radiology
DVSc	Doctor of Veterinary Science
DVSM	Diploma in Veterinary State Medicine
DWP	Department for Work and Pensions

E

E	East; Earl; England
e	eldest
EA	Environment Agency
EAA	Edinburgh Architectural Association
EACR	European Association for Cancer Research
EADS	European Aeronautics Defence and Space Company
EAF	East African Forces
EAGA	Energy Action Grants Agency
EAHY	European Architectural Heritage Year
EAP	East Africa Protectorate
EASD	European Association of Securities Dealers
EAW	Electrical Association for Women
EBC	English Benedictine Congregation
Ebor	Eboracensis (of York)
EBRD	European Bank for Reconstruction and Development
EBSQ-Vasc	European Board of Surgery Qualification in Vascular Surgery
EBU	European Broadcasting Union

EC	Etoile du Courage (Canada); European Community; European Commission; Emergency Commission
ECA	Economic Co-operation Administration; Economic Commission for Africa
ECAFE	Economic Commission for Asia and the Far East (*now see* ESCAP)
ECB	England and Wales Cricket Board
ECCTIS	Education Courses and Credit Transfer Information Systems
ECE	Economic Commission for Europe
ECGD	Export Credits Guarantee Department
ECHR	European Court of Human Rights
ECLA	Economic Commission for Latin America
ECLAC	United Nations Economic Commission for Latin America and the Caribbean
ECOSOC	Economic and Social Committee of the United Nations
ECSC	European Coal and Steel Community
ED	Efficiency Decoration; Doctor of Engineering (US); European Democrat
ed	edited
EdB	Bachelor of Education
EDC	Economic Development Committee
EdD	Doctor of Education
EDF	European Development Fund
EDG	European Democratic Group; Employment Department Group
Edin.	Edinburgh
Edn	Edition
EDP	Executive Development Programme
EdS	Specialist in Education
Educ	Educated
Educn	Education
EEA	European Environment Agency
EEC	European Economic Community (*now see* EC); Commission of the European Communities
EEF	Engineering Employers' Federation; Egyptian Expeditionary Force
EEIBA	Electrical and Electronic Industries Benevolent Association
EETPU	Electrical Electronic Telecommunication & Plumbing Union (later AEEU)
EETS	Early English Text Society
EFCE	European Federation of Chemical Engineering
EFIAP	Excellence, Fédération Internationale de l'Art Photographique
EFTA	European Free Trade Association
eh	ehrenhalber (honorary)
EI	East Indian; East Indies
EIA	Engineering Industries Association
EIB	European Investment Bank
EIEMA	Electrical Installation Equipment Manufacturers' Association
E-in-C	Engineer-in-Chief
EIS	Educational Institute of Scotland
EISCAT	European Incoherent Scatter Association
EIU	Economist Intelligence Unit
ELBS	English Language Book Society
ELDR	European Liberal, Democrat and Reform Party
ELSE	European Life Science Editors
ELT	English Language Teaching
EM	Edward Medal; Earl Marshal
EMBL	European Molecular Biology Laboratory
EMBO	European Molecular Biology Organisation
EMEA	European Medicines Agency (formerly European Agency for the Evaluation of Medical Products)
EMI	European Monetary Institute
EMP	Electro Magnetic Pulse; Executive Management Program Diploma
EMS	Emergency Medical Service
EMU	European Monetary Union
Eng.	England
Engr	Engineer
ENO	English National Opera
ENSA	Entertainments National Service Association
ENT	Ear Nose and Throat
ENTO	Employment National Training Organisation
EO	Executive Officer
EOC	Equal Opportunities Commission
EOPH	Examined Officer of Public Health

EORTC	European Organisation for Research on Treatment of Cancer
EP	European Parliament
EPICC	European Process Industries Competitiveness Centre
EPOS	Electronic Point of Sale
EPP	European People's Party
EPSRC	Engineering and Physical Sciences Research Council
EPsS	Experimental Psychology Society
er	elder
ER	Eastern Region (BR); East Riding
ERA	Electrical Research Association
ERC	Electronics Research Council
ERD	Emergency Reserve Decoration (Army)
ESA	European Space Agency
ESART	Environmental Services Association Research Trust
ESCAP	Economic and Social Commission for Asia and the Pacific
ESCP-EAP	Ecole Supérieure de Commerce de Paris-Ecole des Affaires de Paris
ESF	European Science Foundation
ESL	English as a Second Language
ESNS	Educational Sub-Normal Serious
ESOL	English for Speakers of Other Languages
ESPID	European Society for Paediatric Infectious Diseases
ESRC	Economic and Social Research Council; Electricity Supply Research Council
ESRO	European Space Research Organization (*now see* ESA)
ESTA	European Science and Technology Assembly
ESU	English-Speaking Union
ETA	Engineering Training Authority
ETH	Eidgenössische Technische Hochschule
ETU	Electrical Trades Union
ETUC	European Trade Union Confederation
ETUCE	European Trade Union Committee for Education
EU	European Union
EUDISED	European Documentation and Information Service for Education
Euratom	European Atomic Energy Community
EurBiol	European Biologist (*now see* EurProBiol)
EurChem	European Chemist
EurGeol	European Geologist
Eur Ing	European Engineer
EUROM	European Federation for Optics and Precision Mechanics
EurProBiol	European Professional Biologist
EUW	European Union of Women
eV	eingetragener Verein
Ext	Extinct

F

FA	Football Association
FAA	Fellow, Australian Academy of Science; Fleet Air Arm
FAAAI	Fellow, American Association for Artificial Intelligence
FAAAS	Fellow, American Association for the Advancement of Science
FAAO	Fellow, American Academy of Optometry
FAAP	Fellow, American Academy of Pediatrics
FAARM	Fellow, American Academy of Reproductive Medicine
FAAV	Fellow, Central Association of Agricultural Valuers
FAAVCT	Fellow, American Academy of Veterinary and Comparative Toxicology
FABE	Fellow, Association of Building Engineers
FACC	Fellow, American College of Cardiology
FACCA	Fellow, Association of Certified and Corporate Accountants (*now see* FCCA)
FACCP	Fellow, American College of Chest Physicians
FACD	Fellow, American College of Dentistry
FACDS	Fellow, Australian College of Dental Surgeons (*now see* FRACDS)
FACE	Fellow, Australian College of Educators (*formerly* of Education)
FACerS	Fellow, American Ceramic Society
FAChAM	Fellow, Australasian Chapter of Addiction Medicine, Royal Australian College of Physicians
FAChPM	Fellow, Australasian Chapter of Palliative Medicine, Royal Australian College of Physicians
FACHSE	Fellow, Australian College of Health Service Executives

FACI	Fellow, Australian Chemical Institute (*now see* FRACI)
FACM	Fellow, Associaton of Computing Machinery
FACMA	Fellow, Australian College of Medical Administrators (*now see* FRACMA)
FACMG	Fellow, American College of Medicinal Genetics
FACOG	Fellow, American College of Obstetricians and Gynæcologists
FACOM	Fellow, Australian College of Occupational Medicine
FACP	Fellow, American College of Physicians
FACPM	Fellow, American College of Preventive Medicine
FACR	Fellow, American College of Radiology
FACRM	Fellow, Australian College of Rehabilitation Medicine
FACS	Fellow, American College of Surgeons
FACVSc	Fellow, Australian College of Veterinary Scientists
FACVT	Fellow, American College of Veterinary Toxicology (*now see* FAAVCT)
FADM	Fellow, Academy of Dental Materials
FADO	Fellow, Association of Dispensing Opticians
FAEM	Faculty of Accident and Emergency Medicine (*now see* CEM)
FAeSI	Fellow, Aeronautical Society of India
FAFPHM	Fellow, Australian Faculty of Public Health Medicine
FAGO	Fellowship in Australia in Obstetrics and Gynaecology
FAGS	Fellow, American Geographical Society
FAHA	Fellow, Australian Academy of the Humanities; Fellow, American Heart Association
FAI	Fellow, Chartered Auctioneers' and Estate Agents' Institute (*now* (after amalgamation) *see* FRICS); Fédération Aéronautique Internationale
FAIA	Fellow, American Institute of Architects
FAIAA	Fellow, American Institute of Aeronautics and Astronautics
FAIAS	Fellow, Australian Institute of Agricultural Science (*now see* FAIAST)
FAIAST	Fellow, Australian Institute of Agricultural Science and Technology
FAIB	Fellow, Australian Institute of Bankers
FAIBF	Fellow, Australasian Institute of Bankers + Finance
FAIBiol	Fellow, Australian Institute of Biology
FAICD	Fellow, Australian Institute of Company Directors
FAIE	Fellow, Australian Institute of Energy
FAIEx	Fellow, Australian Institute of Export
FAIFST	Fellow, Australian Institute of Food Science and Technology
FAII	Fellow, Australian Insurance Institute
FAIM	Fellow, Australian Institute of Management
FAIMBE	Fellow, American Institute for Medical and Biological Engineering
FAIP	Fellow, Australian Institute of Physics
FAISB	Fellow, Society for the Study of Artificial Intelligence and the Simulation of Behaviour
FAM	Fellow, Academy of Marketing
FAMA	Fellow, Australian Medical Association
FAMI	Fellow, Australian Marketing Institute
FAMINZ(Arb)	Fellow, Arbitrators and Mediators Institute of New Zealand
FAMM	Fellow, Academy of Medicine, Malaysia
FAmNucSoc	Fellow, American Nuclear Society
FAMS	Fellow, Ancient Monuments Society; Fellow, Academy of Medicine, Singapore
F and GP	Finance and General Purposes
FANY	First Aid Nursing Yeomanry
FANZCA	Fellow, Australian and New Zealand College of Anaesthetists
FANZCP	Fellow, Australian and New Zealand College of Psychiatrists (*now see* FRANZCP)
FAO	Food and Agriculture Organization of the United Nations
FAOrthA	Fellow, Australian Orthopaedic Association
FAPA	Fellow, American Psychiatric Association
FAPHA	Fellow, American Public Health Association
FAPM	Fellow, Association of Project Managers
FAPS	Fellow, American Phytopathological Society
FAPT	Fellow, Association for Preservation Technology (US)
FArborA	Fellow, Aboricultural Association
FARE	Federation of Alcoholic Rehabilitation Establishments
FARELF	Far East Land Forces
FAS	Fellow, Antiquarian Society; Fellow, Nigerian Academy of Science; Funding Agency for Schools
FASA	Fellow, Australian Society of Accountants (*now see* FCPA)
FASc	Fellow, Indian Academy of Sciences
fasc.	fascicule
FASCE	Fellow, American Society of Civil Engineers
FASI	Fellow, Architects' and Surveyors' Institute
FASME	Fellow, American Society of Mechanical Engineers
FASPOG	Fellow, Australian Society for Psychosomatic Obstetrics and Gynaecology
FASSA	Fellow, Academy of the Social Sciences in Australia
FAusIMM	Fellow, Australasian Institute of Mining and Metallurgy
FAustCOG	Fellow, Australian College of Obstetricians and Gynæcologists (later FRACOG; *now see* FRANZCOG)
FAWT	Farm Animal Welfare Trust
FBA	Fellow, British Academy; Federation of British Artists
FBAHA	Fellow, British Association of Hotel Accountants
FBC	Fellow, Birmingham Conservatoire
FBCartS	Fellow, British Cartographic Society
FBCO	Fellow, British College of Optometrists (*formerly of* Ophthalmic Opticians (Optometrists)) (*now see* FCOptom)
FBC	Fellow, Birmingham Conservatoire
FBCS	Fellow, British Computer Society
FBCS CITP	Fellow, British Computer Society, with Chartered Professional Status
FBEC(S)	Fellow, Business Education Council (Scotland)
FBEng	Fellow, Association of Building Engineers
FBES	Fellow, Biological Engineering Society (*now see* FIPEM)
FBHA	Fellow, British Hospitality Association
FBHI	Fellow, British Horological Institute
FBHS	Fellow, British Horse Society
FBI	Federation of British Industries (*now see* CBI); Federal Bureau of Investigation
FBIA	Fellow, Bankers' Institute of Australasia
FBIAT	Fellow, British Institute of Architectural Technicians
FBIBA	Fellow, British Insurance Brokers' Association (*now see* FBIIBA)
FBID	Fellow, British Institute of Interior Design
FBIDA	Fellow, British Interior Design Association
FBIDST	Fellow, British Institute of Dental and Surgical Technologists
FBII	Fellow, British Institute of Innkeeping
FBIIBA	Fellow, British Insurance and Investment Brokers' Association
FBIM	Fellow, British Institute of Management (later FIMgt)
FBINZ	Fellow, Bankers' Institute of New Zealand
FBIPM	Fellow, British Institute of Payroll Management (*now see* FIPPM)
FBIPP	Fellow, British Institute of Professional Photography
FBIRA	Fellow, British Institute of Regulatory Affairs
FBIS	Fellow, British Interplanetary Society
FBKS	Fellow, British Kinematograph Society (*now see* FBKSTS)
FBKSTS	Fellow, British Kinematograph, Sound and Television Society
FBOA	Fellow, British Optical Association
FBOU	Fellow, British Ornithologists' Union
FBPharmacolS	Fellow, British Pharmacological Society
FBPICS	Fellow, British Production and Inventory Control Society
FBPsS	Fellow, British Psychological Society
FBritIRE	Fellow, British Institution of Radio Engineers (later FIERE)
FBS	Fellow, Building Societies Institute (later FCBSI; *now see* FCIB)
FBSI	Fellow, Boot and Shoe Institution (*now see* FCFI)
FBSM	Fellow, Birmingham School of Music (*now see* FBC)
FC	Football Club
FCA	Fellow, Institute of Chartered Accountants; Fellow, Institute of Chartered Accountants in Australia; Fellow, New Zealand Society of Accountants; Federation of Canadian Artists
FCAI	Fellow, New Zealand Institute of Cost Accountants; Fellow, Canadian Aeronautical Institute (*now see* FCASI)
FCAM	Fellow, CAM Foundation
FCAnaes	Fellow, College of Anaesthetists (*now see* FRCA)
FCA(SA)	Fellow, College of Anaesthetists (South Africa)
FCASI	Fellow, Canadian Aeronautics and Space Institute

FCBSI Fellow, Chartered Building Societies Institute (merged with Chartered Institute of Bankers; *now see* FCIB)

FCCA Fellow, Chartered Association of Certified Accountants

FCCEA Fellow, Commonwealth Council for Educational Administration

FCCS Fellow, Corporation of Secretaries (*formerly* of Certified Secretaries)

FCCT Fellow, Canadian College of Teachers

FCEC Federation of Civil Engineering Contractors

FCEM Fellow, College of Emergency Medicine

FCFI Fellow, Clothing and Footwear Institute

FCGA Fellow, Certified General Accountants of Canada

FCGI Fellow, City and Guilds of London Institute

FCGP Fellow, College of General Practitioners (*now see* FRCGP)

FChS Fellow, Society of Chiropodists

FCI Fellow, Institute of Commerce

FCIA Fellow, Corporation of Insurance Agents

FCIArb Fellow, Chartered Institute of Arbitrators

FCIB Fellow, Corporation of Insurance Brokers; Fellow, Chartered Institute of Bankers

FCIBS Fellow, Chartered Institution of Building Services (*now see* FCIBSE); Fellow, Chartered Institute of Bankers in Scotland

FCIBSE Fellow, Chartered Institution of Building Services Engineers

FCIC Fellow, Chemical Institute of Canada (*formerly* Canadian Institute of Chemistry)

FCIEH Fellow, Chartered Institute of Environmental Health

FCIH Fellow, Chartered Institute of Housing

FCII Fellow, Chartered Insurance Institute

FCIJ Fellow, Chartered Institute of Journalists

FCILA Fellow, Chartered Institute of Loss Adjusters

FCILT Chartered Fellow, Chartered Institute of Logistics and Transport

FCIM Fellow, Chartered Institute of Marketing; Fellow, Institute of Corporate Managers (Australia)

FCIOB Fellow, Chartered Institute of Building

FCIPA Fellow, Chartered Institute of Patent Agents (*now see* CPA)

FCIPD Fellow, Chartered Institute of Personnel and Development

FCIPR Fellow, Chartered Institute of Public Relations

FCIPS Fellow, Chartered Institute of Purchasing and Supply

FCIS Fellow, Institute of Chartered Secretaries and Administrators (*formerly* Chartered Institute of Secretaries)

FCISA Fellow, Chartered Institute of Secretaries and Administrators (Australia)

FCIT Fellow, Chartered Institute of Transport (*now see* FCILT)

FCIWEM Fellow, Chartered Institution of Water and Environmental Management

FCIWM Fellow, Chartered Institution of Wastes Management

FCLIP Fellow, Chartered Institute of Library and Information Professionals

FCM Faculty of Community Medicine

FCMA Fellow, Chartered Institute of Management Accountants (*formerly* Institute of Cost and Management Accountants); Fellow, Communications Management Association

FCMC Fellow grade, Certified Management Consultant

FCMI Fellow, Chartered Management Institute

FCMSA Fellow, College of Medicine of South Africa

FCNA Fellow, College of Nursing, Australia

FCO Foreign and Commonwealth Office

FCOG(SA) Fellow, South African College of Obstetrics and Gynæcology

FCollH Fellow, College of Handicraft

FCollP Fellow, College of Preceptors

FCommA Fellow, Society of Commercial Accountants (*now see* FSCA)

FCOphth Fellow, College of Ophthalmologists (*now see* FRCOphth)

FCOptom Fellow, College of Optometrists

FCP Fellow, College of Preceptors

FCPA Fellow, Australian Society of Certified Practising Accountants

FCPath Fellow, College of Pathologists (*now see* FRCPath)

FCPCH Fellow, College of Paediatrics and Child Health (*now see* FRCPCH)

FCPS Fellow, College of Physicians and Surgeons

FCP(SoAf) Fellow, College of Physicians, South Africa

FCPSO(SoAf) Fellow, College of Physicians and Surgeons and Obstetricians, South Africa

FCPS (Pak) Fellow, College of Physicians and Surgeons of Pakistan

FCRA Fellow, College of Radiologists of Australia (*now see* FRACR)

FCS Federation of Conservative Students

FCS or FChemSoc Fellow, Chemical Society (now absorbed into Royal Society of Chemistry)

FCSD Fellow, Chartered Society of Designers

FCSHK Fellow, College of Surgeons of Hong Kong

FCSLT Fellow, College of Speech and Language Therapists (*now see* FRCSLT)

FCSM Fellow, Cambridge School of Music

FCSP Fellow, Chartered Society of Physiotherapy

FCSSA or FCS(SoAf) Fellow, College of Surgeons, South Africa

FCSSL Fellow, College of Surgeons of Sri Lanka

FCST Fellow, College of Speech Therapists (later FCSLT; *now see* FRCSLT)

FCT Federal Capital Territory (*now see* ACT); Fellow, Association of Corporate Treasurers; Fellow, College of Teachers

FCTB Fellow, College of Teachers of the Blind

FCU Fighter Control Unit

FCWA Fellow, Institute of Costs and Works Accountants (*now see* FCMA)

FD Doctor of Philosophy

FDA Association of First Division Civil Servants

FDF Food and Drink Federation

FDI Fédération Dentaire Internationale

FDP Freie Demokratische Partei

FDS Fellow in Dental Surgery

FDSRCPSGlas Fellow in Dental Surgery, Royal College of Physicians and Surgeons of Glasgow

FDSRCS or FDS RCS Fellow in Dental Surgery, Royal College of Surgeons of England

FDSRCSE Fellow in Dental Surgery, Royal College of Surgeons of Edinburgh

FE Far East

FEA Fellow, English Association

FEAF Far East Air Force

FEANI Fédération Européenne d'Associations Nationales d'Ingénieurs

FEBS Federation of European Biochemical Societies

FECI Fellow, Institute of Employment Consultants

FECTS Fellow, European Association for Cardiothoracic Surgery

FEE Fédération des Expertes Comptables Européens

FEF Far East Fleet

FEFC or FEFCE Further Education Funding Council for England

FEFCW Further Education Funding Council for Wales

FEI Fédération Equestre Internationale; Fellow, Energy Institute

FEIDCT Fellow, Educational Institute of Design Craft and Technology

FEIS Fellow, Educational Institute of Scotland

FELCO Federation of English Language Course Opportunities

FEng Fellow, Royal Academy (*formerly* Fellowship) of Engineering (*now see* FREng)

FEPS Federation of European Physiological Societies

FES Fellow, Entomological Society; Fellow, Ethnological Society; Fellow, Society for the Environment

FESC Fellow, European Society of Cardiology

FETCS Fellow, European Board of Thoracic and Cardiovascular Surgeons

FF Fianna Fáil; Field Force

FFA Fellow, Faculty of Actuaries (in Scotland); Fellow, Institute of Financial Accountants

FFAEM Fellow, Faculty of Accident and Emergency Medicine (*now see* FCEM)

FFARACS Fellow, Faculty of Anaesthetists, Royal Australasian College of Surgeons (*now see* FANZCA)

FFARCS Fellow, Faculty of Anaesthetists, Royal College of Surgeons of England (*now see* FRCA)

FFARCSI Fellow, Faculty of Anaesthetists, Royal College of Surgeons in Ireland

FFAS Fellow, Faculty of Architects and Surveyors, London (*now see* FASI)

FFA(SA) Fellow, Faculty of Anaesthetists (South Africa) (*now see* FCA(SA))

FFB   Fellow, Faculty of Building
FFCM   Fellow, Faculty of Community Medicine (*now see* FFPH); Fellow, Faculty of Church Music
FFCMI   Fellow, Faculty of Community Medicine of Ireland
FFCS   Founding Fellow, Contemporary Scotland
FFDRCSI   Fellow, Faculty of Dentistry, Royal College of Surgeons in Ireland
FFFP   Fellow, Faculty of Family Planning & Reproductive Health Care of the Royal College of Obstetricians and Gynaecologists
FFGDP(UK) Fellow, Faculty of General Dental Practitioners of the Royal College of Surgeons
FFHC   Freedom from Hunger Campaign
FFHom   Fellow, Faculty of Homoeopathy
FFI   Finance for Industry; Fauna & Flora International
FFOM   Fellow, Faculty of Occupational Medicine
FFOMI   Fellow, Faculty of Occupational Medicine of Ireland
FFOP (RCPA) Fellow, Faculty of Oral Pathology, Royal College of Pathologists of Australasia
FFPath, RCPI Fellow, Faculty of Pathologists of the Royal College of Physicians of Ireland
FFPH   Fellow, Faculty of Public Health
FFPHM   Fellow, Faculty of Public Health Medicine (*now see* FFPH)
FFPHMI   Fellow, Faculty of Public Health Medicine of Ireland
FFPM   Fellow, Faculty of Pharmaceutical Medicine
FFPRHC   Faculty of Family Planning & Reproductive Health Care, Royal College of Obstetricians and Gynaecologists
FFPS   Fauna and Flora Preservation Society (*now see* FFI)
FFR   Fellow, Faculty of Radiologists (*now see* FRCR)
FFSEM   Fellow, Faculty of Sports and Exercise Medicine, Royal College of Physicians of Ireland and Royal College of Surgeons in Ireland
FG   Fine Gael
FGA   Fellow, Gemmological Association
FGCL   Fellow, Goldsmiths' College, London
FGCM   Fellow, Guild of Church Musicians
FGDS   Fédération de la Gauche Démocratique et Socialiste
FGGE   Fellow, Guild of Glass Engineers
FGI   Fellow, Institute of Certificated Grocers
FGMS   Fellow, Guild of Musicians and Singers
FGS   Fellow, Geological Society
FGSM   Fellow, Guildhall School of Music and Drama
FGSM(MT)   Fellow, Guildhall School of Music and Drama (Music Therapy)
FHA   Fellow, Institute of Health Service Administrators (*formerly* Hospital Administrators) (later FHSM)
FHAS   Fellow, Highland and Agricultural Society of Scotland
FHCIMA   Fellow, Hotel Catering and International (formerly Institutional) Management Association
FHKAES   Fellow, Hong Kong Academy of Engineering Sciences
FHKCP   Fellow, Hong Kong College of Physicians
FHKCS   Fellow, Hong Kong College of Surgeons
FHKIE   Fellow, Hong Kong Institution of Engineers
FHMAAAS   Foreign Honorary Member, American Academy of Arts and Sciences
FHS   Fellow, Heraldry Society; Forces Help Society and Lord Roberts Workshops (*now see* SSAFA)
FHSA   Family Health Services Authority
FHSM   Fellow, Institute of Health Services Management (later FIHM)
FH-WC   Fellow, Heriot-Watt College (*now* University), Edinburgh
FIA   Fellow, Institute of Actuaries
FIAA   Fellow, Institute of Actuaries of Australia
FIAAS   Fellow, Institute of Australian Agricultural Science
FIAA&S   Fellow, Incorporated Association of Architects and Surveyors
FIACM   Fellow, International Association of Computational Mechanics
FIAE   Fellow, Irish Academy of Engineering
FIAgrE   Fellow, Institution of Agricultural Engineers
FIAgrM   Fellow, Institute of Agricultural Management
FIAI   Fellow, Institute of Industrial and Commercial Accountants
FIAL   Fellow, International Institute of Arts and Letters
FIAM   Fellow, International Academy of Management
FIAMBE   Fellow, International Academy for Medical and Biological Engineering

FIAP   Fellow, Institution of Analysts and Programmers; Fellow, Indian Academy of Paediatrics
FIArb   Fellow, Institute of Arbitrators (*now see* FCIArb)
FIArbA   Fellow, Institute of Arbitrators of Australia
FIAS   Fellow, Institute of Aeronautical Sciences (US) (*now see* FAIAA)
FIASc   Fellow, Indian Academy of Sciences
FIASSID   Fellow, International Association for the Scientific Study of Intellectual Disability
FIAWS   Fellow, International Academy of Wood Sciences
FIB   Fellow, Institute of Bankers (*now see* FCIB)
FIBA   Fellow, Institute of Business Administration, Australia (*now see* FCIM)
FIBI   Fellow, Institute of Bankers of Ireland
FIBiol   Fellow, Institute of Biology
FIBiotech Fellow, Institute for Biotechnical Studies
FIBMS   Fellow, Institute of Biomedical Sciences
FIBP   Fellow, Institute of British Photographers
FIBScot   Fellow, Institute of Bankers in Scotland (*now see* FCIBS)
FIC   Fellow, Institute of Chemistry (then FRIC; *now see* FRSC); Fellow, Imperial College, London
FICA   Fellow, Commonwealth Institute of Accountants; Fellow, Institute of Chartered Accountants in England and Wales (*now see* FCA)
FICAI   Fellow, Institute of Chartered Accountants in Ireland
FICB   Fellow, Institute of Canadian Bankers
FICD   Fellow, Institute of Civil Defence (*now see* FICDDS); Fellow, Indian College of Dentists; Fellow, International College of Dentists
FICDDS   Fellow, Institute of Civil Defence and Disaster Studies
FICE   Fellow, Institution of Civil Engineers
FICeram   Fellow, Institute of Ceramics (later FIM)
FICES   Fellow, Institution of Chartered Engineering Surveyors
FICFM   Fellow, Institute of Charity Fundraising Managers (*now see* FInstF)
FICFor   Fellow, Institute of Chartered Foresters
FIChemE   Fellow, Institution of Chemical Engineers
FICM   Fellow, Institute of Credit Management
FICMA   Fellow, Institute of Cost and Management Accountants
FICOG   Fellow, Indian College of Obstetricians and Gynaecologists
FICorr   Fellow, Institute of Corrosion
FICorrST   Fellow, Institution of Corrosion Science and Technology (*now see* FICorr)
FICPD   Fellow, Institute of Continuing Professional Development
FICS   Fellow, Institute of Chartered Shipbrokers; Fellow, International College of Surgeons
FICT   Fellow, Institute of Concrete Technologists
FICW   Fellow, Institute of Clerks of Works of Great Britain
FIDA   Fellow, Institute of Directors, Australia (*now see* FAICD)
FIDCA   Fellow, Industrial Design Council of Australia
FIDDA   Fellow, Interior Decorators and Designers Association (*now see* FBIDA)
FIDE   Fédération Internationale des Echecs; Fellow, Institute of Design Engineers; Fédération Internationale pour le Droit Européen
FIDEM   Fédération Internationale de la Médaille
FIDM   Fellow, Institute of Direct Marketing
FIDPM   Fellow, Institute of Data Processing Management
FIEAust   Fellow, Institution of Engineers, Australia
FIEC   Fellow, Institute of Employment Consultants
FIED   Fellow, Institution of Engineering Designers
FIEE   Fellow, Institution of Electrical Engineers
FIEEE   Fellow, Institute of Electrical and Electronics Engineers (NY)
FIEEIE   Fellow, Institution of Electronics and Electrical Incorporated Engineers (*now see* FIIE)
FIEEM   Fellow, Institute of Ecology and Environmental Management
FIEHK   Fellow, Institution of Engineering, Hong Kong
FIEI   Fellow, Institution of Engineering Inspection (*now see* FIQA); Fellow, Institution of Engineers of Ireland
FIEIE   Fellow, Institution of Electronic Incorporated Engineers (later FIEEIE; *now see* FIIE)
FIEJ   Fédération Internationale des Editeurs de Journaux et Publications
FIEMA   Fellow, Institute of Environmental Management and Assessment
FIEnvSci   Fellow, Institution of Environmental Sciences

FIERE	Fellow, Institution of Electronic and Radio Engineers (*now see* FIEE)
FIES	Fellow, Illuminating Engineering Society (later FIllumES; *now see* FCIBSE); Fellow, Institution of Engineers and Shipbuilders, Scotland
FIET	Fédération Internationale des Employés, Techniciens et Cadres
FIEx	Fellow, Institute of Export
FIExpE	Fellow, Institute of Explosives Engineers
FIFA	Fédération Internationale de Football Association
FIFEM	Fellow, International Federation of Emergency Medicine
FIFF	Fellow, Institute of Freight Forwarders (*now see* FIFP)
FIFireE	Fellow, Institution of Fire Engineers
FIFM	Fellow, Institute of Fisheries Management
FIFor	Fellow, Institute of Foresters (*now see* FICFor)
FIFP	Fellow, Institute of Freight Professionals
FIFST	Fellow, Institute of Food Science and Technology
FIGasE	Fellow, Institution of Gas Engineers (*now see* FIGEM)
FIGCM	Fellow, Incorporated Guild of Church Musicians
FIGD	Fellow, Institute of Grocery Distribution
FIGEM	Fellow, Institution of Gas Engineers and Managers
FIGO	International Federation of Gynaecology and Obstetrics
FIH	Fellow, Institute of Housing (*now see* FCIH); Fellow, Institute of the Horse
FIHE	Fellow, Institute of Health Education
FIHEEM	Fellow, Institute of Healthcare Engineering and Estate Management
FIHM	Fellow, Institute of Housing Managers (later FIH; *now see* FCIH); Fellow, Institute of Healthcare Management
FIHort	Fellow, Institute of Horticulture
FIHospE	Fellow, Institute of Hospital Engineering
FIHT	Fellow, Institution of Highways and Transportation
FIHVE	Fellow, Institution of Heating & Ventilating Engineers (later FCIBS and MCIBS)
FIIA	Fellow, Institute of Industrial Administration (later CBIM and FBIM); Fellow, Institute of Internal Auditors
FIIB	Fellow, International Institute of Biotechnology
FIIC	Fellow, International Institute for Conservation of Historic and Artistic Works
FIIDA	Fellow, International Interior Design Association (*now see* FBIDA)
FIIE	Fellow, Institute of Incorporated Engineers in Electronic, Electrical and Mechanical Engineering
FIIM	Fellow, Institution of Industrial Managers
FIInfSc	Fellow, Institute of Information Scientists (*now see* FCLIP)
FIIP	Fellow, Institute of Incorporated Photographers (*now see* FBIPP)
FIIPC	Fellow, India International Photographic Council
FIIPE	Fellow, Indian Institution of Production Engineers
FIL	Fellow, Institute of Linguists
FILA	Fellow, Institute of Landscape Architects (*now see* FLI)
FILDM	Fellow, Institute of Logistics and Distribution Management (later FILog)
FilDr	Doctor of Philosophy
Fil.Hed.	Filosofie Hedersdoktor
FILLM	Fédération Internationale des Langues et Littératures Modernes
FIllumES	Fellow, Illuminating Engineering Society (*now see* FCIBSE)
FILog	Fellow, Institute of Logistics (later FILT)
FILT	Fellow, Institute of Logistics and Transport (*now see* FCILT)
FIM	Fellow, Institute of Materials (*formerly* Institution of Metallurgists, then Institute of Metals) (*now see* FIMMM)
FIMA	Fellow, Institute of Mathematics and its Applications
FIMarE	Fellow, Institute of Marine Engineers (*now see* FIMarEST)
FIMarEST	Fellow, Institute of Marine Engineering, Science and Technology
FIMatM	Fellow, Institute of Materials Management (later FILog)
FIMBRA	Financial Intermediaries, Managers and Brokers Regulatory Association
FIMC	Fellow, Institute of Management Consultants (*now see* FCMC)
FIMCB	Fellow, International Management Centre from Buckingham
FIMechE	Fellow, Institution of Mechanical Engineers
FIMfgE	Fellow, Institution of Manufacturing Engineers (*now see* FIEE)
FIMFT	Fellow, Institute of Maxillo-facial Technology
FIMgt	Fellow, Institute of Management (*now see* FCMI)
FIMGTechE	Fellow, Institution of Mechanical and General Technician Engineers
FIMH	Fellow, Institute of Materials Handling (later FIMatM); Fellow, Institute of Military History
FIMI	Fellow, Institute of the Motor Industry
FIMinE	Fellow, Institution of Mining Engineers (later FIMM)
FIMIT	Fellow, Institute of Musical Instrument Technology
FIMLS	Fellow, Institute of Medical Laboratory Sciences (*now see* FIBMS)
FIMLT	Fellow, Institute of Medical Laboratory Technology (later FIMLS)
FIMM	Fellow, Institution of Mining and Metallurgy (*now see* FIMMM)
FIMMA	Fellow, Institute of Metals and Materials Australasia
FIMMM	Fellow, Institute of Materials, Minerals and Mining
FIMS	Fellow, Institute of Mathematical Statistics
FIMT	Fellow, Institute of the Motor Trade (*now see* FIMI)
FIMTA	Fellow, Institute of Municipal Treasurers and Accountants (*now see* IPFA)
FIMunE	Fellow, Institution of Municipal Engineers (now amalgamated with Institution of Civil Engineers)
FIN	Fellow, Institute of Navigation (*now see* FRIN)
FINA	Fédération Internationale de Natation Amateur
FInstAM	Fellow, Institute of Administrative Management
FInstArb(NZ)	Fellow, Institute of Arbitrators of New Zealand
FInstB	Fellow, Institution of Buyers
FInstBiol	Fellow, Institute of Biology (*now see* FIBiol)
FInstCES	Fellow, Institution of Civil Engineering Surveyors
FInstD	Fellow, Institute of Directors
FInstE	Fellow, Institute of Energy (*now see* FEI)
FInstEnvSci	Fellow, Institute of Environmental Sciences
FInstF	Fellow, Institute of Fuel (later FInstE); Fellow, Institute of Fundraising
FInstFF	Fellow, Institute of Freight Forwarders Ltd (later FIFF)
FInstHE	Fellow, Institution of Highways Engineers (*now see* FIHT)
FInstLEx	Fellow, Institute of Legal Executives
FInstLM	Fellow, Institute of Leadership and Management
FInstM	Fellow, Institute of Meat; Fellow, Institute of Marketing (*now see* FCIM)
FInstMC	Fellow, Institute of Measurement and Control
FInstMSM	Fellow, Institute of Marketing and Sales Management (later FInstM; *now see* FCIM)
FInstMet	Fellow, Institute of Metals (later part of Metals Society; then FIM)
FInstNDT	Fellow, Institute of Non-Destructive Testing
FInstP	Fellow, Institute of Physics
FInstPet	Fellow, Institute of Petroleum (*now see* FEI)
FInstPI	Fellow, Institute of Patentees and Inventors
FInstPkg	Fellow, Institute of Packaging
FInstPS	Fellow, Institute of Purchasing and Supply (*now see* FCIPS)
FInstSM	Fellow, Institute of Sales Management (*now see* FInstSMM)
FInstSMM	Fellow, Institute of Sales and Marketing Management
FInstTT	Fellow, Institute of Travel & Tourism
FInstW	Fellow, Institute of Welding (*now see* FWeldI)
FINucE	Fellow, Institution of Nuclear Engineers
FIOA	Fellow, Institute of Acoustics
FIOB	Fellow, Institute of Building (*now see* FCIOB)
FIOH	Fellow, Institute of Occupational Hygiene
FIOM	Fellow, Institute of Office Management (*now see* FIAM)
FIOP	Fellow, Institute of Printing (*now see* FIP3)
FIOSH	Fellow, Institute of Occupational Safety and Health
FIP	Fellow, Australian Institute of Petroleum
FIPA	Fellow, Institute of Practitioners in Advertising
FIPAA	Fellow, Institute of Public Administration Australia
FIPD	Fellow, Institute of Personnel and Development (*now see* FCIPD)
FIPDM	Fellow, Institute of Physical Distribution Management (later FILDM)
FIPEM	Fellow, Institute of Physics and Engineering in Medicine
FIPENZ	Fellow, Institution of Professional Engineers, New Zealand
FIPG	Fellow, Institute of Professional Goldsmiths

FIPHE	Fellow, Institution of Public Health Engineers (later FIWEM)
FIPlantE	Fellow, Institution of Plant Engineers
FIPM	Fellow, Institute of Personnel Management (later FIPD)
FIPPM	Fellow, Institute of Payroll and Pensions Management
FIPR	Fellow, Institute of Public Relations (now see FCIPR)
FIProdE	Fellow, Institution of Production Engineers (later FIMfgE; now see FIEE)
FIPSM	Fellow, Institute of Physical Sciences in Medicine (now see FIPEM)
FIP3	Fellow, Institute of Paper, Printing and Publishing
FIQ	Fellow, Institute of Quarrying
FIQA	Fellow, Institute of Quality Assurance
FIQS	Fellow, Institute of Quantity Surveyors
FIRA	Furniture Industry Research Association
FIRI	Fellow, Institution of the Rubber Industry (later FPRI)
FIRM	Fellow, Institute of Risk Management
FIRSE	Fellow, Institution of Railway Signalling Engineers
FIRTE	Fellow, Institute of Road Transport Engineers
FIS	Fellow, Institute of Statisticians
FISA	Fellow, Incorporated Secretaries' Association; Fédération Internationale des Sociétés d'Aviron
FISE	Fellow, Institution of Sales Engineers; Fellow, Institution of Sanitary Engineers
FISITA	Fédération Internationale des Sociétés d'Ingénieurs des Techniques de l'Automobile
FISM	Fellow, Institute of Supervisory Managers (now see FInstLM); Fellow, Institute of Sports Medicine
FISOB	Fellow, Incorporated Society of Organ Builders
FIST	Fellow, Institute of Science Technology
FISTC	Fellow, Institute of Scientific and Technical Communicators
FISTD	Fellow, Imperial Society of Teachers of Dancing
FIStructE	Fellow, Institution of Structural Engineers
FISW	Fellow, Institute of Social Work
FITD	Fellow, Institute of Training and Development (later FIPD)
FITE	Fellow, Institution of Electrical and Electronics Technician Engineers
FITSA	Fellow, Institute of Trading Standards Administration
FIW	Fellow, Welding Institute (now see FWeldI)
FIWE	Fellow, Institution of Water Engineers (later FIWES)
FIWEM	Fellow, Institution of Water and Environmental Management (now see FCIWEM)
FIWES	Fellow, Institution of Water Engineers and Scientists (later FIWEM)
FIWM	Fellow, Institution of Works Managers (now see FIIM); Fellow, Institute of Wastes Management (now see FCIWM)
FIWO	Fellow, Institute of Water Officers
FIWPC	Fellow, Institute of Water Pollution Control (later FIWEM)
FIWSc	Fellow, Institute of Wood Science
FIWSP	Fellow, Institute of Work Study Practitioners (now see FMS)
FJI	Fellow, Institute of Journalists (now see FCIJ)
FJIE	Fellow, Junior Institution of Engineers (now see CIMGTechE)
FKC	Fellow, King's College London
FKCHMS	Fellow, King's College Hospital Medical School
FL	Florida (postal)
FLA	Fellow, Library Association (now see FCLIP)
Fla	Florida
FLAI	Fellow, Library Association of Ireland
FLAS	Fellow, Chartered Land Agents' Society (now (after amalgamation) see FRICS)
FLCM	Fellow, London College of Music
FLHS	Fellow, London Historical Society
FLI	Fellow, Landscape Institute
FLIA	Fellow, Life Insurance Association
FLLA	Fellow, Association of Lawyers and Legal Advisers
FLS	Fellow, Linnean Society
Flt	Flight
FM	Field-Marshal
FMA	Fellow, Museums Association
FMAAT	Fellow Member, Association of Accounting Technicians
FMedSci	Fellow, Academy of Medical Sciences
FMES	Fellow, Minerals Engineering Society
FMI	Foundation for Manufacturing and Industry

FMinSoc	Fellow, Mineralogical Society of Great Britain and Ireland
FMS	Federated Malay States; Fellow, Medical Society; Fellow, Institute of Management Services
FMSA	Fellow, Mineralogical Society of America
FNA	Fellow, Indian National Science Academy
FNAEA	Fellow, National Association of Estate Agents
FNCO	Fleet Naval Constructor Officer
FNECInst	Fellow, North East Coast Institution of Engineers and Shipbuilders
FNI	Fellow, Nautical Institute; Fellow, National Institute of Sciences in India (now see FNA)
FNIA	Fellow, Nigerian Institute of Architects
FNM	Free National Movement
FNMSM	Fellow, North and Midlands School of Music
FNZEI	Fellow, New Zealand Educational Institute
FNZIA	Fellow, New Zealand Institute of Architects
FNZIAS	Fellow, New Zealand Institute of Agricultural Science
FNZIC	Fellow, New Zealand Institute of Chemistry
FNZIE	Fellow, New Zealand Institution of Engineers (now see FIPENZ)
FNZIM	Fellow, New Zealand Institute of Management
FNZPsS	Fellow, New Zealand Psychological Society
FO	Foreign Office (now see FCO); Field Officer; Flag Officer; Flying Officer
FODA	Fellow, Overseas Doctors' Association
FODC	Franciscan Order of the Divine Compassion
FOIC	Flag Officer in charge
FOMA	Flag Officer, Maritime Aviation
FOMI	Faculty of Occupational Medicine of Ireland
FONA	Flag Officer, Naval Aviation
FONAC	Flag Officer, Naval Air Command
FOR	Fellowship of Operational Research
For.	Foreign
FOREST	Freedom Organisation for the Right to Enjoy Smoking Tobacco
FOX	Futures and Options Exchange
FPA	Family Planning Association
FPC	Family Practitioner Committee (later FHSA); Financial Planning Certificate
FPEA	Fellow, Physical Education Association
FPH	Faculty of Public Health
FPHM	Faculty of Public Health Medicine (see now FPH)
FPhS	Fellow, Philosophical Society of England
FPI	Fellow, Plastics Institute (later FPRI)
FPIA	Fellow, Plastics Institute of Australia; Fellow, Planning Institute of Australia
FPMI	Fellow, Pensions Management Institute
FPRI	Fellow, Plastics and Rubber Institute (later FIM)
FPS	Fellow, Pharmaceutical Society (now also FRPharmS); Fauna Preservation Society (later FFPS)
FPhysS	Fellow, Physical Society
f r	fuori ruole
FRA	Fellow, Royal Academy
FRAC	Fellow, Royal Agricultural College
FRACDS	Fellow, Royal Australian College of Dental Surgeons
FRACGP	Fellow, Royal Australian College of General Practitioners
FRACI	Fellow, Royal Australian Chemical Institute
FRACMA	Fellow, Royal Australian College of Medical Administrators
FRACO	Fellow, Royal Australian College of Ophthalmologists
FRACOG	Fellow, Royal Australian College of Obstetricians and Gynaecologists (now see FRANZCOG)
FRACP	Fellow, Royal Australasian College of Physicians
FRACR	Fellow, Royal Australasian College of Radiologists
FRACS	Fellow, Royal Australasian College of Surgeons
FRAD	Fellow, Royal Academy of Dancing
FRAeS	Fellow, Royal Aeronautical Society
FRAgS	Fellow, Royal Agricultural Societies (ie of England, Scotland and Wales)
FRAHS	Fellow, Royal Australian Historical Society
FRAI	Fellow, Royal Anthropological Institute of Great Britain & Ireland
FRAIA	Fellow, Royal Australian Institute of Architects
FRAIB	Fellow, Royal Australian Institute of Building
FRAIC	Fellow, Royal Architectural Institute of Canada
FRAIPA	Fellow, Royal Australian Institute of Public Administration
FRAM	Fellow, Royal Academy of Music

FRAME Fund for the Replacement of Animals in Medical Experiments

FRANZCOG Fellow, Royal Australian and New Zealand College of Obstetricians and Gynaecologists

FRANZCP Fellow, Royal Australian and New Zealand College of Psychiatrists

FRANZCR Fellow, Royal Australian and New Zealand College of Radiologists

FRAPI Fellow, Royal Australian Planning Institute (*now see* FPIA)

FRAS Fellow, Royal Astronomical Society; Fellow, Royal Asiatic Society

FRASE Fellow, Royal Agricultural Society of England

FRBS Fellow, Royal Society of British Sculptors; Fellow, Royal Botanic Society

FRCA Fellow, Royal College of Art; Fellow, Royal College of Anaesthetists

FRCCO Fellow, Royal Canadian College of Organists

FRCD(Can.) Fellow, Royal College of Dentists of Canada

FRCGP Fellow, Royal College of General Practitioners

FRCM Fellow, Royal College of Music

FRCN Fellow, Royal College of Nursing

FRCO Fellow, Royal College of Organists

FRCO(CHM) Fellow, Royal College of Organists with Diploma in Choir Training

FRCOG Fellow, Royal College of Obstetricians and Gynaecologists

FRCOphth Fellow, Royal College of Ophthalmologists

FRCP Fellow, Royal College of Physicians, London

FRCPA Fellow, Royal College of Pathologists of Australasia

FRCP&S (Canada) Fellow, Royal College of Physicians and Surgeons of Canada

FRCPath Fellow, Royal College of Pathologists

FRCPC Fellow, Royal College of Physicians of Canada

FRCPCH Fellow, Royal College of Paediatrics and Child Health

FRCPE or FRCPEd Fellow, Royal College of Physicians, Edinburgh

FRCPGlas Fellow, Royal College of Physicians and Surgeons of Glasgow

FRCPI Fellow, Royal College of Physicians of Ireland

FRCPSGlas Hon. Fellow, Royal College of Physicians and Surgeons of Glasgow

FRCPsych Fellow, Royal College of Psychiatrists

FRCR Fellow, Royal College of Radiologists

FRCS Fellow, Royal College of Surgeons of England

FRCSCan Fellow, Royal College of Surgeons of Canada

FRCSE or FRCSEd Fellow, Royal College of Surgeons of Edinburgh

FRCSGlas Fellow, Royal College of Physicians and Surgeons of Glasgow

FRCSI Fellow, Royal College of Surgeons in Ireland

FRCSLT Fellow, Royal College of Speech and Language Therapists

FRCSoc Fellow, Royal Commonwealth Society

FRCST Fellow, Royal College of Surgeons of Thailand

FRCUS Fellow, Royal College of University Surgeons (Denmark)

FRCVS Fellow, Royal College of Veterinary Surgeons

FREconS Fellow, Royal Economic Society

FREng Fellow, Royal Academy of Engineering

FRES Fellow, Royal Entomological Society of London

FRFPSG Fellow, Royal Faculty of Physicians and Surgeons, Glasgow (*now see* FRCPGlas)

FRG Federal Republic of Germany

FRGS Fellow, Royal Geographical Society

FRGSA Fellow, Royal Geographical Society of Australasia

FRHistS Fellow, Royal Historical Society

FRHS Fellow, Royal Horticultural Society (*now see* MRHS)

FRIAS Fellow, Royal Incorporation of Architects of Scotland; Royal Institute for the Advancement of Science

FRIBA Fellow, Royal Institute of British Architects (*and see* RIBA)

FRIC Fellow, Royal Institute of Chemistry (*now see* FRSC)

FRICS Fellow, Royal Institution of Chartered Surveyors

FRIH Fellow, Royal Institute of Horticulture (NZ)

FRIN Fellow, Royal Institute of Navigation

FRINA Fellow, Royal Institution of Naval Architects

FRIPA Fellow, Royal Institute of Public Administration (the Institute no longer has Fellows)

FRIPH Fellow, Royal Institute of Public Health

FRIPHH Fellow, Royal Institute of Public Health and Hygiene (*now see* FRIPH)

FRMCM Fellow, Royal Manchester College of Music

FRMedSoc Fellow, Royal Medical Society

FRMetS Fellow, Royal Meteorological Society

FRMIA Fellow, Retail Management Institute of Australia

FRMS Fellow, Royal Microscopical Society

FRNCM Fellow, Royal Northern College of Music

FRNS Fellow, Royal Numismatic Society

FRPharmS Fellow, Royal Pharmaceutical Society

FRPS Fellow, Royal Photographic Society

FRPSL Fellow, Royal Philatelic Society, London

FRS Fellow, Royal Society

FRSA Fellow, Royal Society of Arts

FRSAI Fellow, Royal Society of Antiquaries of Ireland

FRSAMD Fellow, Royal Scottish Academy of Music and Drama

FRSanI Fellow, Royal Sanitary Institute (*now see* FRSH)

FRSC Fellow, Royal Society of Canada; Fellow, Royal Society of Chemistry

FRS(Can) Fellow, Royal Society of Canada (used when a person is also a Fellow of the Royal Society of Chemistry)

FRSCM Hon. Fellow, Royal School of Church Music

FRSC (UK) Fellow, Royal Society of Chemistry (used when a person is also a Fellow of the Royal Society of Canada)

FRSE Fellow, Royal Society of Edinburgh

FRSGS Fellow, Royal Scottish Geographical Society

FRSH Fellow, Royal Society for the Promotion of Health

FRSL Fellow, Royal Society of Literature

FRSocMed Fellow, Royal Society of Medicine

FRSNZ Fellow, Royal Society of New Zealand

FRSSAf Fellow, Royal Society of South Africa

FRSTM&H Fellow, Royal Society of Tropical Medicine and Hygiene

FRSV Fellow, Royal Society of Victoria

FRTPI Fellow, Royal Town Planning Institute

FRTS Fellow, Royal Television Society

FRUSI Fellow, Royal United Services Institute

FRVA Fellow, Rating and Valuation Association (*now see* IRRV)

FRVC Fellow, Royal Veterinary College

FRWCMD Fellow, Royal Welsh College of Music and Drama

FRZSScot Fellow, Royal Zoological Society of Scotland

FS Field Security

fs Graduate, Royal Air Force Staff College

FSA Fellow, Society of Antiquaries; Financial Services Authority

FSAA Fellow, Society of Incorporated Accountants and Auditors

FSACOG Fellow, South African College of Obstetricians and Gynaecologists

FSAE Fellow, Society of Automotive Engineers; Fellow, Society of Art Education

FSAI Fellow, Society of Architectural Illustrators

FSAIEE Fellow, South African Institute of Electrical Engineers

FSArc Fellow, Society of Architects (merged with the RIBA 1952)

FSaRS Fellow, Safety and Reliability Society

FSAScot Fellow, Society of Antiquaries of Scotland

FSASM Fellow, South Australian School of Mines

fsc Foreign Staff College

FSCA Fellow, Society of Company and Commercial Accountants

FScotvec Fellow, Scottish Vocational Education Council

FSCRE Fellow, Scottish Council for Research in Education

FSDC Fellow, Society of Dyers and Colourists

FSE Fellow, Society of Engineers

FSG Fellow, Society of Genealogists

FSGD Fellow, Society of Garden Designers

FSGT Fellow, Society of Glass Technology

FSI Fellow, Chartered Surveyors' Institution (*now see* FRICS); Fellow, Securities Institute

FSIA Fellow, Securities Institute of Australia

FSIAD Fellow, Society of Industrial Artists and Designers (*now see* FCSD)

FSIP Fellow, Society of Investment Professionals

FSLAET Fellow, Society of Licensed Aircraft Engineers and Technologists

FSLCOG Fellow, Sri Lankan College of Obstetrics and Gynaecology

FSLCPaed Fellow, Sri Lanka College of Paediatricians

FSLTC	Fellow, Society of Leather Technologists and Chemists
FSMA	Fellow, Incorporated Sales Managers' Association (later FInstMSM, then FInstM)
FSMC	Freeman of the Spectacle-Makers' Company
FSME	Fellow, Society of Manufacturing Engineers
FSMPTE	Fellow, Society of Motion Picture and Television Engineers (US)
FSNAD	Fellow, Society of Numismatic Artists and Designers
FSNAME	Fellow, American Society of Naval Architects and Marine Engineers
FSOE	Fellow, Society of Operations Engineers
FSOGC	Fellow, Society of Obstetricians and Gynaecologists of Canada
FSPI	Fellow, Society of Practitioners of Insolvency
FSQA	Fellow, Scottish Qualifications Authority
FSRHE	Fellow, Society for Research into Higher Education
FSRP	Fellow, Society for Radiological Protection
FSS	Fellow, Royal Statistical Society
FSSI	Fellow, Society of Scribes and Illuminators
FSTD	Fellow, Society of Typographic Designers
FSVA	Fellow, Incorporated Society of Valuers and Auctioneers (*now see* RICS)
FT	Financial Times
FTAT	Furniture, Timber and Allied Trades Union
FTC	Flying Training Command; Full Technological Certificate, City and Guilds of London Institute
FTCD	Fellow, Trinity College, Dublin
FTCL	Fellow, Trinity College of Music, London
FTI	Fellow, Textile Institute
FTII	Fellow, Chartered Institute (*formerly* Incorporated Institute, then Institute) of Taxation
FTMA	Fellow, Telecommunications Managers Association (*now see* FCMA)
FTP	Fellow, Thames Polytechnic
FTS	Fellow, Australian Academy of Technological Sciences and Engineering (*now see* FTSE); Flying Training School; Fellow, Tourism Society
FTSC	Fellow, Tonic Sol-fa College
FTSE	Fellow, Australian Academy of Technological Sciences and Engineering
FUCEB	Fellow, University of Central England in Birmingham
FUCUA	Federation of University Conservative and Unionist Associations (*now see* FCS)
FUMDS	Fellow, United Medical and Dental Schools
FUMIST	Fellow, University of Manchester Institute of Science and Technology
FVCM	Fellow, Victoria College of Music
FVRDE	Fighting Vehicles Research and Development Establishment
FWAAS	Fellow, World Academy of Arts and Sciences
FWACP	Fellow, West African College of Physicians
FWCB	Fellow, Worshipful Company of Blacksmiths
FWCMD	Fellow, Welsh College of Music and Drama (*now see* FRWCMD)
FWeldI	Fellow, Welding Institute
FWSOM	Fellow, Institute of Practitioners in Work Study, Organisation and Method (*now see* FMS)
FZS	Fellow, Zoological Society
FZSScot	Fellow, Zoological Society of Scotland (*now see* FRZSScot)

G

GA	Geologists' Association; Gaelic Athletic (Club); Georgia (postal)
Ga	Georgia
GAI	Guild of Architectural Ironmongers
GAP	Gap Activity Projects
GAPAN	Guild of Air Pilots and Air Navigators
GATT	General Agreement on Tariffs and Trade (*now* World Trade Organisation)
GB	Great Britain
GBA	Governing Bodies Association
GBE	Knight or Dame Grand Cross, Order of the British Empire
GBGSA	Governing Bodies of Girls' Schools Association (*formerly* Association of Governing Bodies of Girls' Public Schools)
GBM	Grand Bauhinia Medal (Hong Kong)

GBS	Gold Bauhinia Star (Hong Kong)
GBSM	Graduate of Birmingham and Midland Institute School of Music
GC	George Cross
GCB	Knight or Dame Grand Cross, Order of the Bath
GCBS	General Council of British Shipping
GCC	General Chiropractic Council
GCCC	Gonville and Caius College, Cambridge
GCCS	Government Code and Cipher School
GCFR	Grand Commander, Order of the Federal Republic of Nigeria
GCH	Knight Grand Cross, Hanoverian Order
GCHQ	Government Communications Headquarters
GCIE	Knight Grand Commander, Order of the Indian Empire
GCLJ	Grand Cross, Order of St Lazarus of Jerusalem
GCLM	Grand Commander, Order of the Legion of Merit of Rhodesia
GCM	Gold Crown of Merit (Barbados)
GCMG	Knight or Dame Grand Cross, Order of St Michael and St George
GCON	Grand Cross, Order of the Niger
GCSE	General Certificate of Secondary Education
GCSG	Knight Grand Cross, Order of St Gregory the Great
GCSI	Knight Grand Commander, Order of the Star of India
GCSJ	Knight Grand Cross of Justice, Sovereign Order of St John of Jerusalem (Knights Hospitaller)
GCSL	Grand Cross, Order of St Lucia
GCStJ	Bailiff or Dame Grand Cross, Most Venerable Order of the Hospital of St John of Jerusalem
GCVO	Knight or Dame Grand Cross, Royal Victorian Order
gd	grand-daughter
GDBA	Guide Dogs for the Blind Association
GDC	General Dental Council
Gdns	Gardens
GDR	German Democratic Republic
GDST	Girls' Day School Trust
Gen.	General
Ges.	Gesellschaft
GFD	Geophysical Fluid Dynamics
GFS	Girls' Friendly Society
ggd	great-grand-daughter
ggs	great-grandson
GGSM	Graduate in Music, Guildhall School of Music and Drama
GHQ	General Headquarters
Gib.	Gibraltar
GIMechE	Graduate, Institution of Mechanical Engineers
GKT	Guy's, King's and St Thomas' (Medical and Dental School of King's College London)
GL	Grand Lodge
GLA	Greater London Authority
GLAA	Greater London Arts Association (*now see* GLAB)
GLAB	Greater London Arts Board
GLC	Greater London Council
Glos	Gloucestershire
GM	George Medal; Grand Medal (Ghana); genetically modified
GMB	(Union for) General, Municipal, Boilermakers
GMBATU	General, Municipal, Boilermakers and Allied Trades Union (*now see* GMB)
GmbH	Gesellschaft mit beschränkter Haftung
GMC	General Medical Council; Guild of Memorial Craftsmen; General Management Course (Henley)
GMWU	General and Municipal Workers' Union (later GMBATU; *now see* GMB)
GNC	General Nursing Council
GNVQ	General National Vocational Qualification
GNZM	Knight or Dame Grand Companion, New Zealand Order of Merit
GOC	General Officer Commanding
GOC-in-C	General Officer Commanding-in-Chief
GOE	General Ordination Examination
GOMLJ	Grand Officer of Merit, Order of St Lazarus of Jerusalem
GOQ	Grand Officer, National Order of Quebec
GOSK	Grand Officer, Order of the Star and Key (Mauritius)
Gov.	Governor
Govt	Government
GP	General Practitioner; Grand Prix
Gp	Group

GPDST	Girls' Public Day School Trust (*now see* GDST)
GPMU	Graphical, Paper and Media Union
GPO	General Post Office
GR	General Reconaissance
Gr.	Greek
GRSM	Graduate of the Royal Schools of Music
GS	General Staff; Grammar School
g s	grandson
GSA	Girls' Schools Association
GSD	Gibraltar Social Democrats
GSM	General Service Medal; (Member of) Guildhall School of Music and Drama
GSMD	Guildhall School of Music and Drama
GSO	General Staff Officer
GTCL	Graduate, Trinity College of Music
GTS	General Theological Seminary (New York)
GUI	Golfing Union of Ireland
GWR	Great Western Railway

H

HA	Historical Association; Health Authority
HAA	Heavy Anti-Aircraft
HAC	Honourable Artillery Company
HACAS	Housing Association Consultancy and Advisory Service
Hants	Hampshire
HARCVS	Honorary Associate, Royal College of Veterinary Surgeons
Harv.	Harvard
HAT	Housing Action Trust
HBM	His (or Her) Britannic Majesty (Majesty's); Humming Bird Gold Medal (Trinidad)
hc	*honoris causa* (honorary)
HCA	Hospital Corporation of America
HCEG	Honourable Company of Edinburgh Golfers
HCF	Honorary Chaplain to the Forces
HCIMA	Hotel, Catering and International (formerly Institutional) Management Association
HCO	Higher Clerical Officer
HCSC	Higher Command and Staff Course
HDA	Hawkesbury Diploma in Agriculture (Australia); Health Development Agency
HDD	Higher Dental Diploma
HDE	Higher Diploma in Education
HDFA	Higher Diploma in Fine Art
HDipEd	Higher Diploma in Education
HE	His (or Her) Excellency; His Eminence
HEA	Health Education Authority (*now see* HDA)
HEC	Ecole des Hautes Etudes Commerciales; Higher Education Corporation
HEFCE	Higher Education Funding Council for England
HEFCW	Higher Education Funding Council for Wales
HEH	His (or Her) Exalted Highness
Heir-pres.	Heir-presumptive
HEO	Higher Executive Officer
HEQC	Higher Education Quality Council (*now see* QAA)
HERDA-SW	Higher Education Regional Development Association - South West
HERO	Higher Education Research Opportunities
Herts	Hertfordshire
HFEA	Human Fertilisation and Embryology Authority
HG	Home Guard
HGTAC	Home Grown Timber Advisory Committee
HH	His (or Her) Highness; His Holiness; Member, Hesketh Hubbard Art Society
HHA	Historic Houses Association
HHD	Doctor of Humanities (US)
HI	Hawaii (postal)
HIH	His (or Her) Imperial Highness
HIM	His (or Her) Imperial Majesty
HIV	Human Immunodeficiency Virus
HJ	Hilal-e-Jurat (Pakistan)
HKIA	Hong Kong Institute of Architects
HKIPM	Hong Kong Institute of Personnel Management
HKSAR	Hong Kong Special Administrative Region
HLD	Doctor of Humane Letters
HLI	Highland Light Infantry

HM	His (or Her) Majesty, or Majesty's
HMA	Head Masters' Association
HMAS	His (or Her) Majesty's Australian Ship
HMC	Headmasters' and Headmistresses' (*formerly* Headmasters') Conference; Hospital Management Committee
HMCIC	His (or Her) Majesty's Chief Inspector of Constabulary
HMCS	His (or Her) Majesty's Canadian Ship
HMHS	His (or Her) Majesty's Hospital Ship
HMI	His (or Her) Majesty's Inspector
HMIED	Honorary Member, Institute of Engineering Designers
HMMTB	His (or Her) Majesty's Motor Torpedo Boat
HMNZS	His (or Her) Majesty's New Zealand Ship
HMOCS	His (or Her) Majesty's Overseas Civil Service
HMS	His (or Her) Majesty's Ship
HMSO	His (or Her) Majesty's Stationery Office
HNC	Higher National Certificate
HND	Higher National Diploma
H ofC	House of Commons
H of L	House of Lords
Hon.	Honourable; Honorary
HPA	Health Protection Agency
HPk	Hilal-e-Pakistan
HQ	Headquarters
HQA	Hilali-Quaid-i-Azam (Pakistan)
HR	Human Resources
HRGI	Honorary Member, The Royal Glasgow Institute of the Fine Arts
HRH	His (or Her) Royal Highness
HRHA	Honorary Member, Royal Hibernian Academy
HRI	Honorary Member, Royal Institute of Painters in Water Colours
HROI	Honorary Member, Royal Institute of Oil Painters
HRSA	Honorary Member, Royal Scottish Academy
HRSW	Honorary Member, Royal Scottish Water Colour Society
HRUA	Hon. Member, Royal Ulster Academy
HSC	Health and Safety Commission
HSE	Health and Safety Executive
HSH	His (or Her) Serene Highness
HSS	Health and Social Services
Hum.	Humanity, Humanities (Classics)
Hunts	Huntingdonshire
HVCert	Health Visitor's Certificate

I

I	Island; Ireland
IA	Indian Army; Iowa (postal)
IAA	International Academy of Architecture
IAAF	International Association of Athletics Federations (formerly International Amateur Athletic Federation)
IABSE	International Association of Bridge and Structural Engineers
IAC	Indian Armoured Corps; Institute of Amateur Cinematographers
IACP	International Association of Chiefs of Police
IACR	Institute of Arable Crops Research
IADB	Inter American Development Bank
IADR	International Association for Dental Research
IAEA	International Atomic Energy Agency
IAF	Indian Air Force; Indian Auxiliary Force
IAHM	Incorporated Association of Headmasters
IAHS	International Association of Hydrological Sciences
IAM	Institute of Advanced Motorists; Institute of Aviation Medicine
IAMAS	International Association of Meteorology and Atmospheric Sciences
IAMC	Indian Army Medical Corps
IAML	International Association of Music Libraries
IAMTACT	Institute of Advanced Machine Tool and Control Technology
IAO	Incorporated Association of Organists
IAOC	Indian Army Ordnance Corps
IAPS	Incorporated Association of Preparatory Schools
IAPSO	International Association for the Physical Sciences of the Oceans
IARO	Indian Army Reserve of Officers

IAS	Indian Administrative Service; Institute for Advanced Studies; International Academy of Science
IASC	International Arctic Science Committee
IASS	International Association for Scandinavian Studies
IATA	International Air Transport Association
IATUL	International Association of Technological University Libraries
IAU	International Astronomical Union
IAVCEI	International Assembly of Volcanology and Chemistry of the Earth's Interior
IAWPRC	International Association on Water Pollution Research and Control
ib. or **ibid.**	*ibidem* (in the same place)
IBA	Independent Broadcasting Authority; International Bar Association
IBBY	International Board for Books for Young People
IBCA	International Braille Chess Association
IBG	Institute of British Geographers (now part of RGS)
IBRD	International Bank for Reconstruction and Development (World Bank)
IBRO	International Bank Research Organisation; International Brain Research Organisation
IBTE	Institution of British Telecommunications Engineers
IBVM	Institute of the Blessed Virgin Mary
i/c	in charge; in command
ICA	Institute of Contemporary Arts; Institute of Chartered Accountants in England and Wales (now see ICAEW)
ICAA	Invalid Children's Aid Association
ICAC	Independent Commission Against Corruption, Hong Kong
ICAEW	Institute of Chartered Accountants in England and Wales
ICAI	Institute of Chartered Accountants in Ireland
ICAO	International Civil Aviation Organization
ICAS	Institute of Chartered Accountants of Scotland
ICBP	International Council for Bird Preservation
ICBS	Irish Christian Brothers' School
ICC	International Chamber of Commerce; International Cricket Council (formerly International Cricket Conference)
ICCA	International Council for Commercial Arbitration
ICCROM	International Centre for Conservation at Rome
ICD	*Iuris Canonici Doctor* (Doctor of Canon Law); Independence Commemorative Decoration (Rhodesia)
ICD.D	Institute of Corporate Directors Director (Canada)
ICE	Institution of Civil Engineers
ICED	International Council for Educational Development
ICEF	International Federation of Chemical, Energy and General Workers' Unions
Icel.	Icelandic
ICES	International Council for the Exploration of the Sea
ICF	International Federation of Chemical and General Workers' Unions (now see ICEF)
ICFC	Industrial and Commercial Finance Corporation (later part of Investors in Industry)
ICFTU	International Confederation of Free Trade Unions
ICHCA	International Cargo Handling Co-ordination Association
IChemE	Institution of Chemical Engineers
ICI	Imperial Chemical Industries
ICJ	International Commission of Jurists
ICL	International Computers Ltd
ICM	International Confederation of Midwives
ICMA	Institute of Cost and Management Accountants (now see CIMA)
ICME	International Commission for Mathematical Education
ICNL	International Center for Not for Profit Law
ICOM	International Council of Museums
ICOMOS	International Council on Monuments and Sites
ICorr	Institute of Corrosion
ICorrST	Institution of Corrosion Science and Technology (now see ICorr)
ICPO	International Criminal Police Organization (Interpol)
ICRC	International Committee of the Red Cross
ICRF	Imperial Cancer Research Fund (now see CRUK)
ICS	Indian Civil Service
ICSA	Institute of Chartered Secretaries and Administrators
ICSC	International Council of Shopping Centres
ICSD	International Council for Scientific Development
ICSID	International Council of Societies of Industrial Design; International Centre for Settlement of Investment Disputes
ICSM	Imperial College School of Medicine
ICSS	International Committee for the Sociology of Sport
ICSTIS	Independent Committee for Supervision of Telephone Information Services
ICSTM	Imperial College of Science, Technology and Medicine, London
ICSU	International Council for Science (formerly International Council of Scientific Unions)
ICT	International Computers and Tabulators Ltd (later ICL); Information and Communications Technology
ID	Independence Decoration (Rhodesia); Idaho (postal)
IDA	International Development Association
IDB	Internal Drainage Board; Industrial Development Board
IDC	Imperial Defence College (now see RCDS); Inter-Diocesan Certificate
idc	completed a course at, or served for a year on the Staff of, the Imperial Defence College (now see rcds)
IDDA	Interior Decorators and Designers Association (now see BIDA)
IDRC	International Development Research Centre
IDS	Institute of Development Studies; Industry Department for Scotland
IEA	Institute of Economic Affairs
IEC	International Electrotechnical Commission
IEE	Institution of Electrical Engineers
IEEE	Institute of Electrical and Electronics Engineers (NY)
IEEIE	Institution of Electrical and Electronics Incorporated Engineers (now see IIE)
IEETE	Institution of Electrical and Electronics Technician Engineers (now see IIE)
IEI	Institution of Engineers of Ireland
IEIE	Institution of Electronics and Electrical Incorporated Engineers (now see IIE)
IEME	Inspectorate of Electrical and Mechanical Engineering
IEng	Incorporated Engineer
IERE	Institution of Electronic and Radio Engineers
IES	Indian Educational Service; Institution of Engineers and Shipbuilders in Scotland; International Electron Paramagnetic Resonance Society
IExpE	Institute of Explosives Engineers
IFAC	International Federation of Automatic Control
IFAD	International Fund for Agricultural Development (UNO)
IFAW	International Fund for Animal Welfare
IFBWW	International Federation of Building Woodworkers
IFC	International Finance Corporation
IFIAS	International Federation of Institutes of Advanced Study
IFIP	International Federation for Information Processing
IFLA	International Federation of Library Associations
IFMGA	(Member of) International Federation of Mountain Guides Associations
IFOR	Implementation Force
IFORS	International Federation of Operational Research Societies
IFPI	International Federation of the Phonographic Industry
IFRA	World Press Research Association
IFS	Irish Free State; Indian Forest Service; Institute for Fiscal Studies
IG	Instructor in Gunnery
IGasE	Institution of Gas Engineers
IGPP	Institute of Geophysics and Planetary Physics
IGS	Independent Grammar School
IGU	International Geographical Union; International Gas Union
IHA	Institute of Health Service Administrators (later IHSM)
IHBC	(Member of) Institute of Historic Building Conservation
IHM	Institute of Healthcare Management
IHospE	Institute of Hospital Engineering
IHSM	Institute of Health Services Management (now see IHM)
IHVE	Institution of Heating and Ventilating Engineers (later CIBS)
IIE	Institution of Incorporated Engineers
IIExE	Institution of Incorporated Executive Engineers
IILS	International Institute for Labour Studies
IIM	Institution of Industrial Managers
IIMR	Institute of Investment Management and Research

IIMT	International Institute for the Management of Technology
IInfSc	Institute of Information Scientists
IIS	International Institute of Sociology
IISI	International Iron and Steel Institute
IISS	International Institute of Strategic Studies
IIT	Indian Institute of Technology
IL	Illinois (postal)
ILA	International Law Association
ILAC	International Laboratory Accreditation Co-operation
ILEA	Inner London Education Authority
ILEC	Inner London Education Committee
Ill	Illinois
ILO	International Labour Office; International Labour Organisation
ILP	Independent Labour Party
ILR	Independent Local Radio; International Labour Review
ILT	Institute for Learning and Teaching in Higher Education
ILTM	Member, Institute for Learning and Teaching in Higher Education
IM	Individual Merit
IMA	International Music Association; Institute of Mathematics and its Applications
IMC	Instrument Meteorological Conditions
IMCB	International Management Centre from Buckingham
IMCO	Inter-Governmental Maritime Consultative Organization (now see IMO)
IME	Institute of Medical Ethics
IMEA	Incorporated Municipal Electrical Association
IMechE	Institution of Mechanical Engineers
IMechIE	Institution of Mechanical Incorporated Engineers (now see IIE)
IMEDE	Institut pour l'Etude des Méthodes de Direction de l'Entreprise
IMF	International Monetary Fund
IMGTechE	Institution of Mechanical and General Technician Engineers
IMinE	Institution of Mining Engineers
IMM	Institution of Mining and Metallurgy (now see IMMM)
IMMLEP	Immunology of Leprosy
IMMM	Institute of Materials, Minerals and Mining
IMO	International Maritime Organization
Imp.	Imperial
IMRO	Investment Management Regulatory Organisation
IMS	Indian Medical Service; Institute of Management Services; International Military Staff
IMTA	Institute of Municipal Treasurers and Accountants (now see CIPFA)
IMU	International Mathematical Union
IMunE	Institution of Municipal Engineers (now amalgamated with Institution of Civil Engineers)
IN	Indian Navy; Indiana (postal)
INASFMH	International Sports Association for People with Mental Handicap
Inc.	Incorporated
INCA	International Newspaper Colour Association
Incog.	Incognito
Ind.	Independent
Inf.	Infantry
INFORM	Information Network Focus on New Religious Movements
INSA	Indian National Science Academy
INSEA	International Society for Education through Art
INSEAD or Insead	Institut Européen d'Administration des Affaires
Insp.	Inspector
INSS	Institute of Nuclear Systems Safety
Inst.	Institute
InstBE	Institution of British Engineers
Instn	Institution
InstSMM	Institute of Sales and Marketing Management
INTELSAT	International Telecommunications Satellite Organisation
IOC	International Olympic Committee; Intergovernmental Oceanographic Commission
IOCD	International Organisation for Chemical Science in Development
IoD	Institute of Directors
IODE	Imperial Order of the Daughters of the Empire
I ofM	Isle of Man
IOM	Isle of Man; Indian Order of Merit
IOP	Institute of Painters in Oil Colours
IOSCO	International Organisation of Securities Committees
IOTA	(Fellow of) Institute of Transport Administration
IoW	Isle of Wight
IP	Intellectual Property
IPA	International Publishers' Association
IPC	International Property Corporation
IPCIS	International Institute for Practitioners in Credit Insurance and Surety
IPCS	Institution of Professional Civil Servants
IPE	International Petroleum Exchange
IPFA	Member or Associate, Chartered Institute of Public Finance and Accountancy (now see CPFA)
IPHE	Institution of Public Health Engineers (later IWEM)
IPI	International Press Institute; Institute of Patentees and Inventors
IPlantE	Institution of Plant Engineers
IPM	Institute of Personnel Management (later CIPD)
IPPA	Independent Programme Producers' Association
IPPF	International Planned Parenthood Federation
IPPR	Institute for Public Policy Research
IPPS	Institute of Physics and The Physical Society
IPR	Institute of Public Relations (now see CIPR)
IPRA	International Public Relations Association
IProdE	Institution of Production Engineers (later Institution of Manufacturing Engineering; now see IEE)
IPS	Indian Police Service; Indian Political Service; Institute of Purchasing and Supply
IPSM	Institute of Public Sector Managers
IPU	Inter-Parliamentary Union
IRA	Irish Republican Army
IRAD	Institute for Research on Animal Diseases
IRC	Industrial Reorganization Corporation; Interdisciplinary Research Centre
IRCAM	Institute for Research and Co-ordination in Acoustics and Music
IRCert	Industrial Relations Certificate
IREE(Aust)	Institution of Radio and Electronics Engineers (Australia)
IRI	Institution of the Rubber Industry (now see PRI)
IRO	International Refugee Organization
IRPA	International Radiation Protection Association
IRRV	(Fellow/Member of) Institute of Revenues, Rating and Valuation
IRTE	Institute of Road Transport Engineers
IS	International Society of Sculptors, Painters and Gravers
Is	Island(s)
ISABE	International Society for Air Breathing Engines
ISAF	International Sailing Federation
ISBA	Incorporated Society of British Advertisers
ISC	Imperial Service College, Haileybury; Indian Staff Corps; Independent Schools Council
ISCis	Independent Schools Council Information Service
ISCM	International Society for Contemporary Music
ISCO	Independent Schools Careers Organisation
ISE	Indian Service of Engineers
ISI	International Statistical Institute; Independent Schools Inspectorate
ISIS	Independent Schools Information Service (see now ISCis)
ISJC	Independent Schools Joint Council (now see ISC)
ISM	Incorporated Society of Musicians
ISMAR	International Society of Magnetic Resonance
ISME	International Society for Musical Education
ISMP	International Senior Management Program
ISMRC	Inter-Services Metallurgical Research Council
ISO	Imperial Service Order; International Organization for Standardization
ISSA	International Social Security Association
ISSTIP	International Society for Study of Tension in Performance
ISTC	Iron and Steel Trades Confederation; Institute of Scientific and Technical Communicators
ISTD	Imperial Society of Teachers of Dancing; Institute for the Study and Treatment of Delinquency
IStructE	Institution of Structural Engineers
ISVA	Incorporated Society of Valuers and Auctioneers
IT	Information Technology; Indian Territory (US)
It. or Ital.	Italian
ITA	Independent Television Authority (later IBA)
ITAB	Information Technology Advisory Board

ITB	Industry Training Board
ITC	International Trade Centre; Independent Television Commission
ITCA	Independent Television Association (formerly Independent Television Companies Association Ltd)
ITDG	Intermediate Technology Development Group
ITEME	Institution of Technician Engineers in Mechanical Engineering
ITF	International Transport Workers' Federation
ITN	Independent Television News
ITO	International Trade Organization
ITSA	Information Technology Services Agency
ITU	International Telecommunication Union
ITV	Independent Television
ITVA	International Television Association
IUA	International Union of Architects
IUB	International Union of Biochemistry (now see IUBMB)
IUBMB	International Union of Biochemistry and Molecular Biology
IUC	Inter-University Council for Higher Education Overseas (now see IUPC)
IUCN	World Conservation Union (formerly International Union for the Conservation of Nature and Natural Resources)
IUCW	International Union for Child Welfare
IUGG	International Union of Geodesy & Geophysics
IUGS	International Union of Geological Sciences
IUHPS	International Union of the History and Philosophy of Science
IULA	International Union of Local Authorities
IUPAB	International Union of Pure and Applied Biophysics
IUPAC	International Union of Pure and Applied Chemistry
IUPAP	International Union of Pure and Applied Physics
IUPC	Inter-University and Polytechnic Council for Higher Education Overseas
IUPS	International Union of Physiological Sciences
IUSSP	International Union for the Scientific Study of Population
IUTAM	International Union of Theoretical and Applied Mechanics
IVF	In-vitro Fertilisation
IVS	International Voluntary Service
IWA	Inland Waterways Association
IWEM	Institution of Water and Environmental Management (now see CIWEM)
IWES	Institution of Water Engineers and Scientists (later IWEM)
IWGC	Imperial War Graves Commission (now see CWGC)
IWM	Institution of Works Managers (now see IIM)
IWO	Institution of Water Officers
IWPC	Institute of Water Pollution Control (later IWEM)
IWS	International Wool Secretariat
IWSA	International Water Supply Association
IWSOM	Institute of Practitioners in Work Study Organisation and Methods (now see IMS)
IWSP	Institute of Work Study Practitioners (now see IMS)
IYRU	International Yacht Racing Union (now see ISAF)
IZ	I Zingari

J

JA	Judge Advocate
JACT	Joint Association of Classical Teachers
JAG	Judge Advocate General
Jas	James
JCB	Juris Canonici (or Civilis) Baccalaureus (Bachelor of Canon (or Civil) Law)
JCR	Junior Common Room
JCS	Journal of the Chemical Society
JCD	Juris Canonici (or Civilis) Doctor (Doctor of Canon (or Civil) Law)
JCI	Junior Chamber International
JCL	Juris Canonici (or Civilis) Licentiatus (Licentiate in Canon (or Civil) Law)
JCO	Joint Consultative Organisation (of AFRC, MAFF, and Department of Agriculture and Fisheries for Scotland)
JD	Doctor of Jurisprudence
jd	jure dignitatis (by virtue of status)
JDipMA	Joint Diploma in Management Accounting Services

JG	Junior Grade
JILA	Joint Institute for Laboratory Astrophysics
JInstE	Junior Institution of Engineers (now see IMGTechE)
JISC	Joint Information Systems Committee, Higher Education Funding Council
jl(s)	journal(s)
JMB	Joint Matriculation Board
JMN	Johan Mangku Negara (Malaysia)
JMOTS	Joint Maritime Operational Training Staff
JNCC	Joint Nature Conservation Committee
Jno. or Joh.	John
JP	Justice of the Peace
Jr	Junior
jsc	qualified at a Junior Staff Course, or the equivalent, 1942–46
JSCSC	Joint Services Command and Staff College
JSD	Doctor of Juristic Science
JSDC	Joint Service Defence College
jsdc	completed a course at Joint Service Defence College
JSLS	Joint Services Liaison Staff
JSM	Johan Setia Mahkota (Malaysia); Master of the Science of Jurisprudence
JSPS	Japan Society for the Promotion of Science
JSSC	Joint Services Staff College
jssc	completed a course at Joint Services Staff College
JSU	Joint Support Unit
jt, jtly	joint, jointly
JUD	Juris Utriusque Doctor (Doctor of Both Laws (Canon and Civil))
Jun.	Junior
Jun.Opt.	Junior Optime
JWS or jws	Joint Warfare Staff

K

KA	Knight of St Andrew, Order of Barbados
Kans	Kansas
KAR	King's African Rifles
KBE	Knight Commander, Order of the British Empire
KC	King's Counsel
KCB	Knight Commander, Order of the Bath
KCC	Commander, Order of the Crown, Belgium and Congo Free State
KCGSJ	Knight Commander of Magisterial Grace, Order of St John of Jerusalem (Knights Hospitaller)
KCH	King's College Hospital; Knight Commander, Hanoverian Order
KCHS	Knight Commander, Order of the Holy Sepulchre
KCIE	Knight Commander, Order of the Indian Empire
KCL	King's College London
KCLJ	Knight Commander, Order of St Lazarus of Jerusalem
KCMG	Knight Commander, Order of St Michael and St George
KCN	Knight Commander, Most Distinguished Order of the Nation (Antigua and Barbuda)
KCSA	Knight Commander, Military Order of the Collar of St Agatha of Paternò
KCSG	Knight Commander, Order of St Gregory the Great
KCSHS	Knight Commander with Star, Order of the Holy Sepulchre
KCSI	Knight Commander, Order of the Star of India
KCSJ	Knight Commander, Sovereign Order of St John of Jerusalem (Knights Hospitaller)
KCSS	Knight Commander, Order of St Silvester
KCVO	Knight Commander, Royal Victorian Order
KDG	King's Dragoon Guards
KEO	King Edward's Own
KFOR	Kosovo Force
KG	Knight, Order of the Garter
KGB	Komitet Gosudarstvennoi Bezopasnosti (Committee of State Security, USSR)
KGCHS	Knight Grand Cross, Order of the Holy Sepulchre
KGCSS	Knight Grand Cross, Order of St Silvester
KGN	Knight Grand Collar, Most Distinguished Order of the Nation (Antigua and Barbuda)
KGSJ	Knight of Grace, Sovereign Order of St John of Jerusalem (Knights Hospitaller)
KGStJ	Knight of Grace, Order of St John of Jerusalem (now see KStJ)

KH	Knight, Hanoverian Order
KHC	Hon. Chaplain to the King
KHDS	Hon. Dental Surgeon to the King
KHNS	Hon. Nursing Sister to the King
KHP	Hon. Physician to the King
KHS	Hon. Surgeon to the King; Knight, Order of the Holy Sepulchre
K-i-H	Kaisar-i-Hind
KJStJ	Knight of Justice, Order of St John of Jerusalem (now see KStJ)
KLJ	Knight, Order of St Lazarus of Jerusalem
KM	Knight of Malta
KMJ	Knight, Supreme Military Order of the Temple of Jerusalem
KMLJ	Knight of Merit, Order of St Lazarus of Jerusalem
KNH	Knight Companion, Most Exalted Order of National Hero (Antigua and Barbuda)
KNZM	Knight Companion, New Zealand Order of Merit
KOM	Companion, National Order of Merit (Malta)
KORR	King's Own Royal Regiment
KOSB	King's Own Scottish Borderers
KOYLI	King's Own Yorkshire Light Infantry
KP	Knight, Order of St Patrick
KPM	King's Police Medal
KrF	Kristelig Folkeparti
KRRC	King's Royal Rifle Corps
KS	King's Scholar; Kansas (postal)
KSC	Knight of St Columba
KSG	Knight, Order of St Gregory the Great
KSJ	Knight, Sovereign Order of St John of Jerusalem (Knights Hospitaller)
KSLI	King's Shropshire Light Infantry
KSS	Knight, Order of St Silvester
KStJ	Knight, Most Venerable Order of the Hospital of St John of Jerusalem
KStJ(A)	Associate Knight of Justice, Most Venerable Order of the Hospital of St John of Jerusalem
KT	Knight, Order of the Thistle
Kt	Knight
KUOM	Companion of Honour, National Order of Merit (Malta)
KY	Kentucky (postal)
Ky	Kentucky

L

L	Liberal
LA	Los Angeles; Library Association; Liverpool Academy; Louisiana (postal)
La	Louisiana
LAA	Light Anti-Aircraft
Lab	Labour
LAC	London Athletic Club; Los Angeles County
LACSAB	Local Authorities Conditions of Service Advisory Board
LAE	London Association of Engineers
LAMDA	London Academy of Music and Dramatic Art
LAMSAC	Local Authorities' Management Services and Computer Committee
LAMTPI	Legal Associate Member, Town Planning Institute (now see LMRTPI)
Lance-Corp.	Lance-Corporal
Lancs	Lancashire
LAPADA	London & Provincial Antique Dealers' Association
LARSP	Language Assessment, Remediation and Screening Procedure
Lautro	Life Assurance and Unit Trust Regulatory Organisation
LBC	London Broadcasting Company; London Borough Council
LBHI	Licentiate, British Horological Institute
LC	Cross of Leo
LCA	Licensed Companies Auditor
LCAD	London Certificate in Art and Design (University of London)
LCC	London County Council (later GLC)
LCCI	London Chamber of Commerce and Industry
LCD	Lord Chancellor's Department
LCh	Licentiate in Surgery
LCJ	Lord Chief Justice

LCL	Licentiate of Canon Law
LCM	(Member of) London College of Music and Media
LCP	Licentiate, College of Preceptors
LCSP	London and Counties Society of Physiologists
LCST	Licentiate, College of Speech Therapists
LD	Liberal and Democratic; Licentiate in Divinity
LDC	Limited Duration Company (US)
LDDC	London Docklands Development Corporation
LDiv	Licentiate in Divinity
LDP	Liberal Democratic Party (Japan)
Ldr	Leader
LDS	Licentiate in Dental Surgery
LDV	Local Defence Volunteers
LEA	Local Education Authority
LEAD	Leadership in Environment and Development
LEADR	Lawyers Engaged in Alternative Dispute Resolution
LEDU	Local Enterprise Development Unit
LEP	Local Ecumenical Project
LEPRA	British Leprosy Relief Association
LèsL	Licencié ès lettres
LèsSc	Licencié ès Sciences
LG	Lady Companion, Order of the Garter
LGA	Local Government Association
LGSM	Licentiate, Guildhall School of Music and Drama
LGTB	Local Government Training Board
LH	Light Horse
LHD	Literarum Humaniorum Doctor (Doctor of Literature)
LHSM	Licentiate, Institute of Health Services Management
LI	Light Infantry; Long Island
LIBA	Lloyd's Insurance Brokers' Association
Lib Dem	Liberal Democrat
LIBER	Ligue des Bibliothèques Européennes de Recherche
LicMed	Licentiate in Medicine
Lieut	Lieutenant
LIFFE	London International Financial Futures and Options Exchange
LIFT	Local Improvement Finance Trust
LIMA	Licentiate, Institute of Mathematics and its Applications; International Licensing Industry Merchandisers' Association
Lincs	Lincolnshire
LIOB	Licentiate, Institute of Building
Lit.	Literature; Literary
LitD	Doctor of Literature; Doctor of Letters
Lit.Hum.	Literae Humaniores (Classics)
LittD	Doctor of Literature; Doctor of Letters
LJ	Lord Justice
LLB	Bachelor of Laws
LLC	Limited Liability Company
LLCM	Licentiate, London College of Music
LLD	Doctor of Laws
LLL	Licentiate in Laws
LLM	Master of Laws
LLP	Limited Liability Partnership
LLSC	Local Learning and Skills Council
LM	Licentiate in Midwifery
LMBC	Lady Margaret Boat Club
LMC	Local Medical Committee
LMCC	Licentiate, Medical Council of Canada
LMed	Licentiate in Medicine
LMH	Lady Margaret Hall, Oxford
LMR	London Midland Region (BR)
LMS	London, Midland and Scottish Railway; London Missionary Society; London Mathematical Society
LMSSA	Licentiate in Medicine and Surgery, Society of Apothecaries
LMRTPI	Legal Member, Royal Town Planning Institute
LNat	Liberal National
LNER	London and North Eastern Railway
LOB	Location of Offices Bureau
L ofC	Library of Congress; Lines of Communication
LP	Limited Partnership
LPh	Licentiate in Philosophy
LPO	London Philharmonic Orchestra
LPTB	London Passenger Transport Board (later LTE; now see LRT)
LRAD	Licentiate, Royal Academy of Dancing
LRAM	Licentiate, Royal Academy of Music

LRCP	Licentiate, Royal College of Physicians, London
LRCPE	Licentiate, Royal College of Physicians, Edinburgh
LRCPI	Licentiate, Royal College of Physicians of Ireland
LRCPSGlas	Licentiate, Royal College of Physicians and Surgeons of Glasgow
LRCS	Licentiate, Royal College of Surgeons of England
LRCSE	Licentiate, Royal College of Surgeons, Edinburgh
LRCSI	Licentiate, Royal College of Surgeons in Ireland
LRelSc	Licentiate in Religious Sciences
LRFPS(G)	Licentiate, Royal Faculty of Physicians and Surgeons, Glasgow (*now see* LRCPSGlas)
LRIBA	Licentiate, Royal Institute of British Architects (*now see* RIBA)
LRPS	Licentiate, Royal Photographic Society
LRSM	Licentiate, Royal Schools of Music
LRT	London Regional Transport
LSA	Licentiate, Society of Apothecaries; Licence in Agricultural Sciences
LSC	Learning and Skills Council
LSE	London School of Economics and Political Science
LSHTM	London School of Hygiene and Tropical Medicine
LSO	London Symphony Orchestra
LSS	Licentiate in Sacred Scripture
Lt	Lieutenant; Light
LT	Lady, Order of the Thistle; London Transport (*now see* LRT); Licentiate in Teaching
LTA	Lawn Tennis Association
LTB	London Transport Board (later LTE; *now see* LRT)
LTCL	Licentiate of Trinity College of Music, London
Lt Col	Lieutenant Colonel
LTE	London Transport Executive (*now see* LRT)
Lt Gen.	Lieutenant General
LTh	Licentiate in Theology
LTS	London Topographical Society
LU	Liberal Unionist
LUOTC	London University Officers' Training Corps
LVO	Lieutenant, Royal Victorian Order (*formerly* MVO (Fourth Class))
LWT	London Weekend Television
LXX	Septuagint

M

M	Marquess; Member; Monsieur
m	married
MA	Master of Arts; Military Assistant; Massachusetts (postal)
MAA	Manufacturers' Agents Association of Great Britain
MAAF	Mediterranean Allied Air Forces
MAAT	Member, Association of Accounting Technicians
MACE	Member, Australian College of Education; Member, Association of Conference Executives
MACI	Member, American Concrete Institute
MACM	Member, Association of Computing Machines
MACS	Member, American Chemical Society
MADO	Member, Association of Dispensing Opticians
MAE	Member, Academia Europaea
MAEE	Marine Aircraft Experimental Establishment
MAF	Ministry of Agriculture and Fisheries
MAFF	Ministry of Agriculture, Fisheries and Food
MAHL	Master of Arts in Hebrew Letters
MAI	*Magister in Arte Ingeniaria* (Master of Engineering)
MAIAA	Member, American Institute of Aeronautics and Astronautics
MAIBC	Member, Architectural Institute of British Columbia
MAICD	Member, Australian Institute of Company Directors
MAICE	Member, American Institute of Consulting Engineers
MAIChE	Member, American Institute of Chemical Engineers
Maj. Gen.	Major General
MALD	Master of Arts in Law and Diplomacy
Man	Manitoba
M&A	Mergers and Acquisitions
MAO	Master of Obstetric Art
MAOT	Member, Association of Occupational Therapists
MAOU	Member, American Ornithologists' Union
MAP	Ministry of Aircraft Production
MAPsS	Member, Australian Psychological Society
MARAC	Member, Australasian Register of Agricultural Consultants

MArch	Master of Architecture
MARIS	Multi-State Aquatic Resources Information System
Marq.	Marquess
MAS	Minimal Access Surgery
MASAE	Member, American Society of Agricultural Engineers
MASC	Member, Australian Society of Calligraphers
MASc	Master of Applied Science
MASCE	Member, American Society of Civil Engineers
MASME	Member, American Society of Mechanical Engineers
Mass	Massachusetts
MAT	Master of Arts and Teaching (US)
MATh	Master of Arts in Theology
Math.	Mathematics; Mathematical
MATSA	Managerial Administrative Technical Staff Association
MAusIMM	Member, Australasian Institute of Mining and Metallurgy
MB	Medal of Bravery (Canada); Bachelor of Medicine; Manitoba (postal)
MBA	Master of Business Administration
MBASW	Member, British Association of Social Workers
MBC	Metropolitan/Municipal Borough Council
MBCS	Member, British Computer Society
MBE	Member, Order of the British Empire
MBES	Member, Biological Engineering Society
MBFR	Mutual and Balanced Force Reductions (negotiations)
MBHI	Member, British Horological Institute
MBIFD	Member, British Institute of Funeral Directors
MBII	Member, British Institute of Innkeeping
MBIM	Member, British Institute of Management (later MIMgt)
MBKS	Member, British Kinematograph Society (*now see* MBKSTS)
MBKSTS	Member, British Kinematograph, Sound and Television Society
MBL	Master of Business Leadership
MBOU	Member, British Ornithologists' Union
MBPICS	Member, British Production and Inventory Control Society
MBritIRE	Member, British Institution of Radio Engineers (later MIERE; *now see* MIEE)
MBS	Member, Building Societies Institute (*now see* MCBSI)
MBSc	Master of Business Science
MC	Military Cross; Missionaries of Charity
MCAM	Member, CAM Foundation
MCB	Master in Clinical Biochemistry
MCBSI	Member, Chartered Building Societies Institute
MCC	Marylebone Cricket Club; Metropolitan County Council
MCCDRCS	Member in Clinical Community Dentistry, Royal College of Surgeons
MCD	Master of Civic Design
MCE	Master of Civil Engineering
MCFP	Member, College of Family Physicians (Canada)
MCGI	Member, City and Guilds of London Institute
MCh or **MChir**	Master in Surgery
MChD	Master of Dental Surgery
MChE	Master of Chemical Engineering
MChemA	Master in Chemical Analysis
MChOrth	Master of Orthopaedic Surgery
MCIArb	Member, Chartered Institute of Arbitrators
MCIBS	Member, Chartered Institution of Building Services (*now see* MCIBSE)
MCIBSE	Member, Chartered Institution of Building Services Engineers
MCIH	Member, Chartered Institute of Housing
MCIJ	Member, Chartered Institute of Journalists
MCIM	Member, Chartered Institute of Marketing
MCIMarE	Member, Canadian Institute of Marine Engineers
MCIOB	Member, Chartered Institute of Building
MCIPD	Member, Charted Institute of Personnel and Development
MCIPR	Member, Chartered Institute of Public Relations
MCIPS	Member, Chartered Institute of Purchasing and Supply
M.CIRP	Member, International Institution for Production Engineering Research
MCIS	Member, Institute of Chartered Secretaries and Administrators
MCIT	Member, Chartered Institute of Transport (*now see* CMILT)
MCIWEM	Member, Chartered Institution of Water and Environmental Management

MCIWM	Member, Chartered Institution of Wastes Management
MCL	Master in Civil Law
MCLIP	Member, Chartered Institute of Library and Information Professionals
MCMI	Member, Chartered Management Institute
MCollP	Member, College of Preceptors
MCom	Master of Commerce
MConsE	Member, Association of Consulting Engineers
MConsEI	Member, Association of Consulting Engineers of Ireland
MCOphth	Member, College of Ophthalmologists (now see MRCOphth)
MCP	Member of Colonial Parliament; Master of City Planning (US)
MCPA	Member, College of Pathologists of Australia (now see MRCPA)
MCPath	Member, College of Pathologists (now see MRCPath)
MCPP	Member, College of Pharmacy Practice
MCPS	Member, College of Physicians and Surgeons
MCS	Malayan Civil Service
MCSD	Member, Chartered Society of Designers
MCSEE	Member, Canadian Society of Electrical Engineers
MCSP	Member, Chartered Society of Physiotherapy
MCST	Member, College of Speech Therapists
MCT	Member, Association of Corporate Treasurers
MD	Doctor of Medicine; Military District; Maryland (postal)
Md	Maryland
MDC	Metropolitan District Council
MDes	Master of Design
MDiv	Master of Divinity
MDS	Master of Dental Surgery
MDSc	Master of Dental Science
ME	Mining Engineer; Middle East; Master of Engineering; Maine (postal); Myalgic Encephalomyelitis
MEAF	Middle East Air Force
MEC	Member of Executive Council; Middle East Command
MEc	Master of Economics
MECAS	Middle East Centre for Arab Studies
Mech.	Mechanics; Mechanical
MECI	Member, Institute of Employment Consultants
Med.	Medical
MEd	Master of Education
MED	Master of Environmental Design
MEdSt	Master of Educational Studies
MEF	Middle East Force
MEI	Member, Energy Institute
MEIC	Member, Engineering Institute of Canada
MELF	Middle East Land Forces
Mencap	Royal Society for Mentally Handicapped Children and Adults
MEng	Master of Engineering
MEnvS	Master of Environmental Studies
MEO	Marine Engineering Officer
MEP	Member of the European Parliament
MESc	Master of Engineering Science
MetR	Metropolitan Railway
MetSoc	Metals Society (formed by amalgamation of Institute of Metals and Iron and Steel Institute; now merged with Institution of Metallurgists to form Institute of Metals)
MEWI	Member, Expert Witness Institute
MEXE	Military Engineering Experimental Establishment
MF	Master of Forestry
MFA	Master of Fine Arts
MFC	Mastership in Food Control
MFCM	Member, Faculty of Community Medicine (later MFPHM)
MFFP	Member, Faculty of Family Planning, Royal College of Obstetricians and Gynaecologists
MFGB	Miners' Federation of Great Britain (now see NUM)
MFH	Master of Foxhounds
MFHom	Member, Faculty of Homoeopathy
MFOM	Member, Faculty of Occupational Medicine
MFPaed	Member, Faculty of Paediatrics, Royal College of Physicians of Ireland
MFPH	Member, Faculty of Public Health
MFPHM	Member, Faculty of Public Health Medicine (now see MFPH)
MFPHMI	Member, Faculty of Public Health Medicine of Ireland
MGA	Major General in charge of Administration
MGC	Machine Gun Corps
MGDSRCS	Member in General Dental Surgery, Royal College of Surgeons
MGGS	Major General, General Staff
MGI	Member, Institute of Certificated Grocers
MGO	Master General of the Ordnance; Master of Gynaecology and Obstetrics
Mgr	Monsignor
MHA	Member of House of Assembly
MHCIMA	Member, Hotel Catering and International (formerly Institutional) Management Association
MHK	Member of the House of Keys
MHort (RHS)	Master of Horticulture, Royal Horticultural Society
MHR	Member of the House of Representatives
MHRA	Modern Humanities Research Association
MHRF	Mental Health Research Fund
MHSM	Member, Institute of Health Services Management (now see MIHM)
MI	Military Intelligence; Michigan (postal)
MIAeE	Member, Institute of Aeronautical Engineers
MIAgrE	Member, Institution of Agricultural Engineers
MIAM	Member, Institute of Administrative Management
MIAS	Member, Institute of Aeronautical Science (US) (now see MAIAA); Member, Institute of Architects and Surveyors
MIBC	Member, Institute of Business Counsellors; Member, Institute of Building Control
MIBF	Member, Institute of British Foundrymen
MIBiol	Member, Institute of Biology
MIBritE	Member, Institution of British Engineers
MICE	Member, Institution of Civil Engineers
MICEI	Member, Institution of Civil Engineers of Ireland
MICeram	Member, Institute of Ceramics (later MIM)
MICFor	Member, Institute of Chartered Foresters
Mich	Michigan
MIChemE	Member, Institution of Chemical Engineers
MICM	Member, Institute of Credit Management
MICorr	Member, Institute of Corrosion
MICorrST	Member, Institution of Corrosion Science and Technology (now see MICorr)
MICS	Member, Institute of Chartered Shipbrokers
MIDPM	Member, Institute of Data Processing Management
MIE(Aust)	Member, Institution of Engineers, Australia
MIED	Member, Institution of Engineering Designers
MIEE	Member, Institution of Electrical Engineers
MIEEE	Member, Institute of Electrical and Electronics Engineers (NY)
MIEEM	Member, Institute of Ecology and Environmental Management
MIEI	Member, Institution of Engineering Inspection
MIEMA	Member, Institute of Environmental Management and Assessment
MIEMgt	Member, Institute of Environmental Management (now see MIEMA)
MIEnvSc	Member, Institute of Environmental Science
MIERE	Member, Institution of Electronic and Radio Engineers (now see MIEE)
MIES	Member, Institution of Engineers and Shipbuilders, Scotland
MIET	Member, Institute of Engineers and Technicians
MIEx	Member, Institute of Export
MIExpE	Member, Institute of Explosives Engineers
MIFA	Member, Institute of Field Archaeologists
MIFF	Member, Institute of Freight Forwarders (now see MIFP)
MIFireE	Member, Institution of Fire Engineers
MIFM	Member, Institute of Fisheries Management
MIFor	Member, Institute of Foresters (now see MICFor)
MIFP	Member, Institute of Freight Professionals
MIGasE	Member, Institution of Gas Engineers (now see MIGEM)
MIGEM	Member, Institution of Gas Engineers and Managers
MIGeol	Member, Institution of Geologists
MIH	Member, Institute of Housing (now see MCIH)
MIHM	Member, Institute of Housing Managers (later MIH); Member, Institute of Healthcare Management
MIHort	Member, Institute of Horticulture
MIHT	Member, Institution of Highways and Transportation
MIHVE	Member, Institution of Heating and Ventilating Engineers (later MCIBS)
MIIA	Member, Institute of Industrial Administration (later FBIM)
MIIM	Member, Institution of Industrial Managers

MIInfSc   Member, Institute of Information Sciences (*now see* MCLIP)
MIL   Member, Institute of Linguists
Mil.   Military
MILGA   Member, Institute of Local Government Administrators
MILocoE   Member, Institution of Locomotive Engineers
MILog   Member, Institute of Logistics (*now see* MILT)
MILT   Member, Chartered Institute of Logistics and Transport
MIM   Member, Institute of Materials (*formerly* Institution of Metallurgists, then Institute of Metals) (*now see* MIMMM)
MIMarE   Member, Institute of Marine Engineers (*now see* MIMarEST)
MIMarEST   Member, Institute of Marine Engineering, Science and Technology
MIMC   Member, Institute of Management Consultants
MIMechE   Member, Institution of Mechanical Engineers
MIMEMME   Member, Institution of Mining Electrical & Mining Mechanical Engineers (later MIMinE)
MIMgt   Member, Institute of Management (*see now* MCMI)
MIMGTechE   Member, Institution of Mechanical and General Technician Engineers
MIMI   Member, Institute of the Motor Industry
MIMinE   Member, Institution of Mining Engineers (later MIMM)
MIMM   Member, Institution of Mining and Metallurgy (*now see* MIMMM)
MIMMM   Member, Institute of Materials, Minerals and Mining
MIMunE   Member, Institution of Municipal Engineers (now amalgamated with Institution of Civil Engineers)
MIN   Member, Institute of Navigation (*now see* MRIN)
Min.   Ministry
Minn   Minnesota
MInstAM   Member, Institute of Administrative Management
MInstBE   Member, Institution of British Engineers
MInstCE   Member, Institution of Civil Engineers (*now see* FICE)
MInstD   Member, Institute of Directors
MInstE   Member, Institute of Energy (*now see* MEI)
MInstEnvSci   Member, Institute of Environmental Sciences
MInstF   Member, Institute of Fuel (later MInstE)
MInstHE   Member, Institution of Highway Engineers (*now see* MIHT)
MInstM   Member, Institute of Marketing (*now see* MCIM)
MInstMC   Member, Institute of Measurement and Control
MInstME   Member, Institution of Mining Engineers
MInstMet   Member, Institute of Metals (later part of Metals Society; then MIM)
MInstP   Member, Institute of Physics
MInstPet   Member, Institute of Petroleum (*now see* MEI)
MInstPI   Member, Institute of Patentees and Inventors
MInstPkg   Member, Institute of Packaging
MInstPS   Member, Institute of Purchasing and Supply
MInstR   Member, Institute of Refrigeration
MInstRA   Member, Institute of Registered Architects
MInstT   Member, Institute of Transport (later MCIT)
MInstTA   Member, Institute of Transport Administration
MInstTM   Member, Institute of Travel Managers in Industry and Commerce
MInstW   Member, Institute of Welding (*now see* MWeldI)
MInstWM   Member, Institute of Wastes Management (*now see* MCIWM)
MINucE   Member, Institution of Nuclear Engineers
MIOA   Member, Institute of Acoustics
MIOB   Member, Institute of Building (*now see* MCIOB)
MIOM   Member, Institute of Office Management (*now see* MIAM)
MIOSH   Member, Institution of Occupational Safety and Health
MIPA   Member, Institute of Practitioners in Advertising
MIPD   Member, Institute of Personnel and Development (now *see* MCIPD)
MIPlantE   Member, Institution of Plant Engineers
MIPM   Member, Institute of Personnel Management (later MIPD)
MIPR   Member, Institute of Public Relations (*now see* MCIPR)
MIProdE   Member, Institution of Production Engineers (*now see* MIEE)
MIQ   Member, Institute of Quarrying
MIQA   Member, Institute of Quality Assurance
MIRE   Member, Institution of Radio Engineers (later MIERE)
MIREE(Aust)   Member, Institution of Radio and Electronics Engineers (Australia)

MIRM   Member, Institute of Risk Management
MIRO   Mineral Industry Research Organisation
MIRT   Member, Institute of Reprographic Technicians
MIRTE   Member, Institute of Road Transport Engineers
MIS   Member, Institute of Statisticians
MISI   Member, Iron and Steel Institute (later part of Metals Society)
MIStructE   Member, Institution of Structural Engineers
MIT   Massachusetts Institute of Technology
MITA   Member, Industrial Transport Association
MITD   Member, Institute of Training and Development (later MIPD)
MITE   Member, Institution of Electrical and Electronics Technician Engineers
MITI   Member, Institute of Translation & Interpreting
MITSA   Member, Institute of Trading Standards Administration
MITT   Member, Institute of Travel and Tourism
MIWE   Member, Institution of Water Engineers (later MIWES)
MIWEM   Member, Institution of Water and Environmental Management (*now see* MCIWEM)
MIWES   Member, Institution of Water Engineers and Scientists (later MIWEM)
MIWM   Member, Institution of Works Managers (*now see* MIIM)
MIWPC   Member, Institute of Water Pollution Control (later MIWEM)
MIWSP   Member, Institute of Work Study Practitioners (*now see* MMS)
MJA   Medical Journalists Association
MJI   Member, Institute of Journalists (*now see* MCIJ)
MJIE   Member, Junior Institution of Engineers (*now see* MIGTechE)
MJS   Member, Japan Society
MJur   *Magister Juris* (Master of Law)
ML   Licentiate in Medicine; Master of Laws
MLA   Member of Legislative Assembly; Modern Language Association; Master in Landscape Architecture; Museums, Libraries and Archives Council
MLC   Member of Legislative Council; Meat and Livestock Commission
MLCOM   Member, London College of Osteopathic Medicine
MLI   Member, Landscape Institute
MLib   Master of Librarianship
MLitt   Master of Letters
Mlle   Mademoiselle
MLO   Military Liaison Officer
MLR   Modern Language Review
MLS   Master of Library Science
MM   Military Medal; Merchant Marine
MMA   Metropolitan Museum of Art
MMB   Milk Marketing Board
MMD   Movement for Multi-Party Democracy
MME   Master of Mining Engineering
Mme   Madame
MMechE   Master of Mechanical Engineering
MMet   Master of Metallurgy
MMGI   Member, Mining, Geological and Metallurgical Institute of India
MMin   Master of Ministry
MMM   Member, Order of Military Merit (Canada)
MMRS   Member, Market Research Society
MMS   Member, Institute of Management Services
MMSA   Master of Midwifery, Society of Apothecaries
MMus   Master of Music
MN   Merchant Navy; Minnesota (postal)
MNAS   Member, National Academy of Sciences (US)
MND   Motor Neurone Disease
MNECInst   Member, North East Coast Institution of Engineers and Shipbuilders
MNI   Member, Nautical Institute
MNIMH   Member, National Institute of Medical Herbalists
MNSE   Member, Nigerian Society of Engineers
MNZIS   Member, New Zealand Institute of Surveyors
MNZPI   Member, New Zealand Planning Institute
MO   Medical Officer; Military Operations; Missouri (postal)
Mo   Missouri
MoD   Ministry of Defence
Mods   Moderations (Oxford)
MOF   Ministry of Food
MOH   Medical Officer(s) of Health

MOI	Ministry of Information
MOM	Member, Order of Merit (Malta)
MOMA	Museum of Modern Art
MOMI	Museum of the Moving Image
Mon	Monmouthshire
Mont	Montgomeryshire
MOP	Ministry of Power
MOrthRCS	Member in Orthodontics, Royal College of Surgeons
MoS	Ministry of Supply
Most Rev.	Most Reverend
MoT	Ministry of Transport
MOV	Member, Order of Volta (Ghana)
MP	Member of Parliament
MPA	Master of Public Administration; Member, Parliamentary Assembly, Northern Ireland
MPAGB	Member, Photographic Alliance of Great Britain
MPBW	Ministry of Public Building and Works
MPH	Master of Public Health
MPhil	Master of Philosophy
MPIA	Master of Public and International Affairs
MPMI	Member, Property Management Institute
MPO	Management and Personnel Office
MPP	Member, Provincial Parliament; Master in Public Policy (Harvard)
MPRISA	Member, Public Relations Institute of South Africa
MPS	Member, Pharmaceutical Society (now see MRPharmS)
MR	Master of the Rolls; Municipal Reform
MRAC	Member, Royal Agricultural College
MRACP	Member, Royal Australasian College of Physicians
MRACS	Member, Royal Australasian College of Surgeons
MRad	Master of Radiology
MRAeS	Member, Royal Aeronautical Society
MRAIC	Member, Royal Architectural Institute of Canada
MRAS	Member, Royal Asiatic Society
MRC	Medical Research Council
MRCA	Multi-Role Combat Aircraft
MRCGP	Member, Royal College of General Practitioners
MRC-LMB	Medical Research Council Laboratory of Molecular Biology
MRCOG	Member, Royal College of Obstetricians and Gynaecologists
MRCOphth	Member, Royal College of Ophthalmologists
MRCP	Member, Royal College of Physicians, London
MRCPA	Member, Royal College of Pathologists of Australia
MRCPath	Member, Royal College of Pathologists
MRCPCH	Member, Royal College of Paediatrics and Child Health
MRCPE	Member, Royal College of Physicians, Edinburgh
MRCPGlas	Member, Royal College of Physicians and Surgeons of Glasgow
MRCPI	Member, Royal College of Physicians of Ireland
MRCPsych	Member, Royal College of Psychiatrists
MRCS	Member, Royal College of Surgeons of England
MRCSE	Member, Royal College of Surgeons of Edinburgh
MRCSI	Member, Royal College of Surgeons in Ireland
MRCVS	Member, Royal College of Veterinary Surgeons
MRD RCS	Member in Restorative Dentistry, Royal College of Surgeons
MRE	Master of Religious Education
MRHS	Member, Royal Horticultural Society
MRI	Magnetic Resonance Imaging; Member, Royal Institution
MRIA	Member, Royal Irish Academy
MRIAI	Member, Royal Institute of the Architects of Ireland
MRIC	Member, Royal Institute of Chemistry (now see MRSC)
MRICS	Member, Royal Institution of Chartered Surveyors
MRIN	Member, Royal Institute of Navigation
MRINA	Member, Royal Institution of Naval Architects
MRNZCGP	Member, Royal New Zealand College of General Practitioners
MRPharmS	Member, Royal Pharmaceutical Society
MRSanI	Member, Royal Sanitary Institute (now see MRSH)
MRSC	Member, Royal Society of Chemistry
MRSH	Member, Royal Society for the Promotion of Health
MRSL	Member, Order of the Republic of Sierra Leone
MRSocMed	Member, Royal Society of Medicine
MRST	Member, Royal Society of Teachers
MRTPI	Member, Royal Town Planning Institute
MRurSc	Master of Rural Science
MRUSI	Member, Royal United Service Institution
MRVA	Member, Rating and Valuation Association
MS	Master of Surgery; Master of Science (US); Mississippi (postal); Multiple Sclerosis
MS, MSS	Manuscript, Manuscripts
MSA	Master of Science, Agriculture (US); Mineralogical Society of America; Motor Sports Association
MSAAIE	Member, Southern African Association of Industrial Editors
MSAE	Member, Society of Automotive Engineeers (US)
MSAICE	Member, South African Institution of Civil Engineers
MSAInstMM	Member, South African Institute of Mining and Metallurgy
MS&R	Merchant Shipbuilding and Repairs
MSC	Manpower Services Commission; Missionaries of the Sacred Heart
MSc	Master of Science
MScD	Master of Dental Science
MScSoc	Master of Social Sciences
MScSocMed	Master of Science in Social Medicine
MSD	Meritorious Service Decoration (Fiji)
MSE	Master of Science in Engineering (US)
MSF	(Union for) Manufacturing, Science, Finance
MSFA	Member, Society of Financial Advisers
MSHyg	Master of Science in Hygiene
MSI	Member, Securities Institute
MSIA	Member, Society of Industrial Artists
MSIAD	Member, Society of Industrial Artists and Designers (now see MCSD)
MSIT	Member, Society of Instrument Technology (now see MInstMC)
MSLS	Master of Science in Library Science
MSM	Meritorious Service Medal; Madras Sappers and Miners; Master in Science Management
MSN	Master of Science in Nursing
MSocAdmin	Master of Social Administration
MSocIS	Member, Société des Ingénieurs et Scientifiques de France
MSocSc	Master of Social Sciences
MSocWork	Master of Social Work
MSoFHT	Member, Society of Food Hygiene Technology
MSP	Member, Scottish Parliament
MSR	Member, Society of Radiographers
MSRP	Member, Society for Radiological Protection
MSSc	Master of Social Sciences
MSt	Master of Studies
MSTD	Member, Society of Typographic Designers
MSW	Master of Social Work
MSzP	Magyar Szocialista Párt
MT	Mechanical Transport; Montana (postal)
Mt	Mount, Mountain
MTA	Music Trades Association
MTAI	Member, Institute of Travel Agents
MTB	Motor Torpedo Boat
MTCA	Ministry of Transport and Civil Aviation
MTD	Midwife Teachers' Diploma
MTech	Master of Technology
MTEFL	Master in the Teaching of English as a Foreign or Second Language
MTh	Master of Theology
MTIA	Metal Trades Industry Association
MTIRA	Machine Tool Industry Research Association (now see AMTRI)
MTPI	Member, Town Planning Institute (now see MRTPI)
MTS	Master of Theological Studies; Ministerial Training Scheme
MUniv	Honorary Master of the University
MusB	Bachelor of Music
MusD	Doctor of Music
MusM	Master of Music
MV	Merchant Vessel, Motor Vessel (naval)
MVB	Bachelor of Veterinary Medicine
MVEE	Military Vehicles and Engineering Establishment
MVO	Member, Royal Victorian Order
MVSc	Master of Veterinary Science
MW	Master of Wine
MWA	Mystery Writers of America
MWeldI	Member, Welding Institute
MWSOM	Member, Institute of Practitioners in Work Study Organisation and Methods (now see MMS)

N

N	Nationalist; Navigating Duties; North
n	nephew
NA	National Academician (America)
NAACP	National Association for the Advancement of Colored People
NAAFI	Navy, Army and Air Force Institutes
NAAS	National Agricultural Advisory Service
NAB	National Advisory Body for Public Sector Higher Education
NABC	National Association of Boys' Clubs (later NABC-CYP)
NABC-CYP	National Association of Boys' Clubs - Clubs for Young People
NAC	National Agriculture Centre
NACAB	National Association of Citizens' Advice Bureaux
NACCB	National Accreditation Council for Certification Bodies
NACETT	National Advisory Council for Education and Training Targets
NACF	National Art-Collections Fund
NACRO	National Association for the Care and Resettlement of Offenders
NADFAS	National Association of Decorative and Fine Arts Societies
NAE	National Academy of Engineering
NAEW	Nato Airborn Early Warning
NAHA	National Association of Health Authorities (now see NAHAT)
NAHAT	National Association of Health Authorities and Trusts
NAHT	National Association of Head Teachers
NALGO or Nalgo	National and Local Government Officers' Association
NAMAS	National Measurement and Accreditation Service
NAMCW	National Association for Maternal and Child Welfare
NAMH	MIND (National Association for Mental Health)
NAMMA	NATO MRCA Management Agency
NAPAG	National Academies Policy Advisory Group
NARM	National Association of Recording Merchandisers (US)
NAS	National Academy of Sciences
NASA	National Aeronautics and Space Administration (US)
NASDAQ	National Association of Securities Dealers Automated Quotation System
NASDIM	National Association of Security Dealers and Investment Managers (later FIMBRA)
NAS/UWT	National Association of Schoolmasters/Union of Women Teachers
NATCS	National Air Traffic Control Services (now see NATS)
NATFHE	National Association of Teachers in Further and Higher Education (combining ATCDE and ATTI)
NATLAS	National Testing Laboratory Accreditation Scheme
NATO	North Atlantic Treaty Organisation
NATS	National Air Traffic Services
Nat. Sci.	Natural Sciences
NATSOPA	National Society of Operative Printers, Graphical and Media Personnel (formerly of Operative Printers and Assistants)
NAYC	Youth Clubs UK (formerly National Association of Youth Clubs)
NB	New Brunswick; Nebraska (postal)
NBA	North British Academy
NBC	National Book Council (later NBL); National Broadcasting Company (US)
NBL	National Book League
NBPI	National Board for Prices and Incomes
NC	National Certificate; North Carolina
NCA	National Certificate of Agriculture
NCARB	National Council of Architectural Registration Boards
NCAS	Natural Environment Research Council Centres for Atmospheric Science
NCB	National Coal Board
NCC	National Computing Centre; Nature Conservancy Council (now see NCCE); National Consumer Council
NCCE	Nature Conservancy Council for England (English Nature)
NCCI	National Committee for Commonwealth Immigrants
NCCL	National Council for Civil Liberties
NCD	National Capital District, Papua New Guinea
NCDAD	National Council for Diplomas in Art and Design
NCEA	National Council for Educational Awards
NCET	National Council for Educational Technology
NCH	National Children's Homes
NCLC	National Council of Labour Colleges
NCOP	National Council of Provinces (South Africa)
NCOPF	National Council for One Parent Families
NCRI	National Cancer Research Institute
NCSE	National Council for Special Education
NCSS	National Council of Social Service
NCTA	National Community Television Association (US)
NCTJ	National Council for the Training of Journalists
NCU	National Cyclists' Union
NCVCCO	National Council of Voluntary Child Care Organisations
NCVO	National Council for Voluntary Organisations
NCVQ	National Council for Vocational Qualifications
NCYPE	National Centre for Young People with Epilepsy
ND	North Dakota
NDA	National Diploma in Agriculture
NDC	National Defence College; NATO Defence College
NDD	National Diploma in Dairying; National Diploma in Design
NDEA	National Defense Education Act
NDH	National Diploma in Horticulture
NDIC	National Defence Industries Council
NDP	New Democratic Party
NDTA	National Defense Transportation Association (US)
NE	North-east
NEAB	Northern Examinations and Assessment Board
NEAC	New English Art Club
NEAF	Near East Air Force
NEARELF	Near East Land Forces
NEB	National Enterprise Board
NEBSS	National Examinations Board for Supervisory Studies
NEC	National Executive Committee
NECCTA	National Education Closed Circuit Television Association
NECInst	North East Coast Institution of Engineers and Shipbuilders
NEDC	National Economic Development Council; North East Development Council
NEDO	National Economic Development Office
NEH	National Endowment for the Humanities
NEL	National Engineering Laboratory
NERC	Natural Environment Research Council
NESTA	National Endowment for Science, Technology and the Arts
NF	Newfoundland and Labrador (postal)
NFC	National Freight Consortium (formerly Corporation, then Company)
NFCG	National Federation of Consumer Groups
NFER	National Foundation for Educational Research
NFHA	National Federation of Housing Associations
NFMS	National Federation of Music Societies
NFS	National Fire Service
NFSH	National Federation of Spiritual Healers
NFT	National Film Theatre
NFU	National Farmers' Union
NFWI	National Federation of Women's Institutes
NGO	Non-Governmental Organisation(s)
NGTE	National Gas Turbine Establishment
NH	New Hampshire
NH&MRC	National Health and Medical Research Council (Australia)
NHBC	National House-Building Council
NHS	National Health Service
NHSU	National Health Service University
NI	Northern Ireland; Native Infantry
NIAB	National Institute of Agricultural Botany
NIACE	National Institute of Adult Continuing Education
NIACRO	Northern Ireland Association for the Care and Resettlement of Offenders
NIAE	National Institute of Agricultural Engineering
NIAID	National Institute of Allergy and Infectious Diseases
NICE	National Institute for Health and Clinical Excellence (formerly National Institute of Clinical Excellence)
NICEC	National Institute for Careers Education and Counselling
NICEIC	National Inspection Council for Electrical Installation Contracting

NICG	Nationalised Industries Chairmen's Group
NICRO	National Institute for Crime Prevention and Re-integration of Offenders
NICS	Northern Ireland Civil Service
NID	Naval Intelligence Division; National Institute for the Deaf; Northern Ireland District; National Institute of Design (India)
NIESR	National Institute of Economic and Social Research
NIH	National Institutes of Health (US)
NIHCA	Northern Ireland Hotels and Caterers Association
NIHEC	Northern Ireland Higher Education Council
NII	Nuclear Installations Inspectorate
NILP	Northern Ireland Labour Party
NIMR	National Institute for Medical Research
NISA	National Ice Skating Association of UK
NISTRO	Northern Ireland Science and Technology Regional Organisation
NISW	National Institute of Social Work
NIU	Northern Ireland Unionist
NJ	New Jersey
NL	National Liberal; No Liability
NLCS	North London Collegiate School
NLF	National Liberal Federation
NLYL	National League of Young Liberals
NM	New Mexico (postal)
NMR	Nuclear Magnetic Resonance
NMRS	National Monuments Record of Scotland
NMSI	National Museum of Science and Industry
NNMA	Nigerian National Merit Award
NNOM	Nigerian National Order of Merit
NODA	National Operatic and Dramatic Association
Northants	Northamptonshire
NOTB	National Ophthalmic Treatment Board
Notts	Nottinghamshire
NP	Notary Public
NPA	Newspaper Publishers' Association
NPFA	National Playing Fields Association
NPG	National Portrait Gallery
NPk	Nishan-e-Pakistan
NPL	National Physical Laboratory
NPQH	National Professional Qualification for Headship
NRA	National Rifle Association; National Recovery Administration (US); National Rivers Authority
NRAO	National Radio Astronomy Observatory
NRCC	National Research Council of Canada
NRD	National Registered Designer
NRDC	National Research Development Corporation
NRMA	National Roads and Motorists' Association
NRPB	National Radiological Protection Board
NRR	Northern Rhodesia Regiment
NRSA	National Research Service Award (US)
NS	Nova Scotia; New Style in the Calendar (in Great Britain since 1752); National Society; National Service
ns	Graduate of Royal Naval Staff College, Greenwich
NSA	National Skating Association (now see NISA)
NSAIV	Distinguished Order of Shaheed Ali (Maldives)
NSERC	Natural Sciences and Engineering Research Council, Canada
NSF	National Science Foundation (US)
NSM	Non-Stipendiary Minister
NSMHC	National Society for Mentally Handicapped Children (now see Mencap)
NSPCC	National Society for Prevention of Cruelty to Children
NSQT	National Society for Quality through Teamwork
NSRA	National Small-bore Rifle Association
N/SSF	Novice, Society of St Francis
NSTC	Nova Scotia Technical College
NSW	New South Wales
NT	New Testament; Northern Territory (Australia); Northwest Territories (Canada); National Theatre; National Trust
NT&SA	National Trust & Savings Association
NTDA	National Trade Development Association
NTO	National Training Organisation
NTUC	National Trades Union Congress
NUAAW	National Union of Agricultural and Allied Workers
NUBE	National Union of Bank Employees (later BIFU)

NUFLAT	National Union of Footwear Leather and Allied Trades (now see NUKFAT)
NUGMW	National Union of General and Municipal Workers (later GMBATU)
NUHKW	National Union of Hosiery and Knitwear Workers (now see NUKFAT)
NUI	National University of Ireland
NUJ	National Union of Journalists
NUJMB	Northern Universities Joint Matriculation Board
NUKFAT	National Union of Knitwear, Footwear and Apparel Trades
NUM	National Union of Mineworkers
NUMAST	National Union of Marine, Aviation and Shipping Transport Officers
NUPE	National Union of Public Employees
NUR	National Union of Railwaymen (now see RMT)
NUS	National Union of Students
NUT	National Union of Teachers
NUTG	National Union of Townswomen's Guilds
NUTGW	National Union of Tailors and Garment Workers
NUTN	National Union of Trained Nurses
NUU	New University of Ulster
NV	Nevada (postal)
NVQ	National Vocational Qualification
NW	North-west
NWC	National Water Council
NWFP	North-West Frontier Province
NWP	North-Western Province
NWT	North-Western Territories
NY	New York
NYC	New York City
NYO	National Youth Orchestra
NYT	National Youth Theatre
NZ	New Zealand
NZEF	New Zealand Expeditionary Force
NZIA	New Zealand Institute of Architects
NZRSA	New Zealand Retired Services Association

O

o	only
OA	Officier d'Académie
OAM	Medal of the Order of Australia
O&E	Operations and Engineers (US)
O&M	organisation and method
O&O	Oriental and Occidental Steamship Co.
OAS	Organisation of American States; On Active Service
OASC	Officer Aircrew Selection Centre
OAU	Organisation for African Unity
OB	Order of Barbados
ob	obiit (died)
OBC	Order of British Columbia
OBE	Officer, Order of the British Empire
OBI	Order of British India
OC	Officer, Order of Canada (equivalent to former award SM)
OC or **o/c**	Officer Commanding
oc	only child
OCC	Order of the Caribbean Community
OCDS or **ocds Can**	Overseas College of Defence Studies (Canada)
OCF	Officiating Chaplain to the Forces
OCPA	Office of the Commissioner for Public Appointments
OCS	Officer Candidates School
OCSS	Oxford and Cambridge Shakespeare Society
OCTU	Officer Cadet Training Unit
OCU	Operational Conversion Unit
OD	Officer, Order of Distinction (Jamaica); Order of Distinction (Antigua)
ODA	Overseas Development Administration
ODI	Overseas Development Institute
ODM	Ministry of Overseas Development
ODPM	Office of the Deputy Prime Minister
ODSM	Order of Diplomatic Service Merit (Lesotho)
OE	Order of Excellence (Guyana)
OEA	Overseas Education Association
OECD	Organization for Economic Co-operation and Development

OED	Oxford English Dictionary
OEEC	Organization for European Economic Co-operation (*now see* OECD)
OF	Order of the Founder, Salvation Army
OFCOM	Office of Communications
OFEMA	Office Française d'Exportation de Matériel Aéronautique
OFFER	Office of Electricity Regulation
Ofgem	Office of Gas and Electricity Markets
OFM	Order of Friars Minor (Franciscans)
OFMCap	Order of Friars Minor Capuchin (Franciscans)
OFMConv	Order of Friars Minor Conventual (Franciscans)
OFR	Order of the Federal Republic of Nigeria
OFS	Orange Free State
OFSTED	Office for Standards in Education
OFT	Office of Fair Trading
Oftel	Office of Telecommunications
Ofwat	Office of Water Services
OGS	Oratory of the Good Shepherd
OH	Ohio (postal)
OHMS	On His (or Her) Majesty's Service
O i/c	Officer in charge
OJ	Order of Jamaica
OK	Oklahoma (postal)
OL	Officer, Order of Leopold; Order of the Leopard (Lesotho)
OLJ	Officer, Order of St Lazarus of Jerusalem
OLM	Officer, Legion of Merit (Rhodesia)
OM	Order of Merit; Order of Manitoba
OMCS	Office of the Minister for the Civil Service
OMI	Oblate of Mary Immaculate
OMLJ	Officer, Order of Merit, Order of St Lazarus of Jerusalem
OMM	Officer, Order of Military Merit (Canada)
ON	Order of the Nation (Jamaica); Ontario (postal)
OND	Ordinary National Diploma
ONDA	Ordinary National Diploma in Agriculture
ONS	Office for National Statistics
Ont	Ontario
ONZ	Order of New Zealand
ONZM	Officer, New Zealand Order of Merit
OON	Officer, Order of the Niger
OOnt	Order of Ontario
OP	*Ordinis Praedicatorum* (of the Order of Preachers (Dominican)); Observation Post
OPCON	Operational Control
OPCS	Office of Population Censuses and Surveys (*now see* ONS)
OPRA	Occupational Pensions Regulatory Authority
OPS	Office of Public Service
OPSS	Office of Public Service and Science (*now see* OPS)
OQ	Officer, National Order of Quebec
OR	Order of Rorima (Guyana); Operational Research; Oregon (postal)
ORC	Orange River Colony
ORGALIME	Organisme de Liaison des Industries Métalliques Européennes
ORHA/CPA	Office of Reconstruction and Humanitarian Assistance/Coalition Provisional Authority
ORL	Otorhinolaryngology
ORS	Operational Research Society
ORSA	Operations Research Society of America
ORSL	Order of the Republic of Sierra Leone
ORT	Organization for Rehabilitation through Training
ORTF	Office de la Radiodiffusion et Télévision Française
o s	only son
OSA	Order of St Augustine (Augustinian); Ontario Society of Artists
OSB	Order of St Benedict (Benedictine)
osc	Graduate of Overseas Staff College
OSCE	Organisation for Security and Co-operation in Europe
OSFC	Franciscan (Capuchin) Order
O/Sig	Ordinary Signalman
OSMTH	Ordo Supremus Militaris Templi Hierosolymitani (Supreme Military Order of the Temple of Jerusalem)
OSNC	Orient Steam Navigation Co.
osp	*obiit sine prole* (died without issue)
OSRD	Office of Scientific Research and Development
OSS	Office of Strategic Services
OST	Office of Science and Technology
OStJ	Officer, Most Venerable Order of the Hospital of St John of Jerusalem
OSUK	Ophthalmological Society of the United Kingdom
OT	Old Testament
OTC	Officers' Training Corps
OTL	Officer, Order of Toussaint L'Ouverture (Haiti)
OTU	Operational Training Unit
OTWSA	Ou-Testamentiese Werkgemeenskap in Suider-Afrika
OU	Oxford University; Open University
OUAC	Oxford University Athletic Club
OUAFC	Oxford University Association Football Club
OUBC	Oxford University Boat Club
OUCC	Oxford University Cricket Club
OUDS	Oxford University Dramatic Society
OUP	Oxford University Press; Official Unionist Party
OURC	Oxford University Rifle Club
OURFC	Oxford University Rugby Football Club
OURT	Order of the United Republic of Tanzania
Oxon	Oxfordshire; *Oxoniensis* (of Oxford)

P

PA	Pakistan Army; Personal Assistant; Pennsylvania (postal)
PAA	President, Australian Academy of Science
pac	passed the final examination of the Advanced Class, The Military College of Science
PACE	Protestant and Catholic Encounter; Property Advisers to the Civil Estate
PACTA	Professional Associate, Clinical Theology Association
PAg	Professional Agronomist
PALS	Partnership for Active Leisure Scheme for Disabled Children
P&O	Peninsular and Oriental Steamship Co.
P&OSNCo.	Peninsular and Oriental Steam Navigation Co.
PAO	Prince Albert's Own
PASI	Professional Associate, Chartered Surveyors' Institution (later ARICS)
PASOK	Panhellenic Socialist Movement
PBS	Public Broadcasting Service
PC	Privy Counsellor; Police Constable; Perpetual Curate; Peace Commissioner (Ireland); Progressive Conservative (Canada)
pc	*per centum* (in the hundred)
PCC	Parochial Church Council; Protected Cell Company (Guernsey)
PCE	Postgraduate Certificate of Education
pce	passed command examinations
PCEF	Polytechnic and Colleges Employers' Forum
PCFC	Polytechnics and Colleges Funding Council
PCG	Primary Care Group
PCL	Polytechnic of Central London
PCMO	Principal Colonial Medical Officer
PCNZM	Principal Companion, New Zealand Order of Merit
PCS	Parti Chrétien-Social; Public and Commercial Services Union
PCT	Primary Care Trust
PdD	Doctor of Pedagogy (US)
PDG	Président Directeur Général
PDipHEd	Postgraduate Diploma in Health Education
PDR	People's Democratic Republic
PDRA	post doctoral research assistant
PDSA	People's Dispensary for Sick Animals
PDTC	Professional Dancer's Training Course Diploma
PDTD	Professional Dancer's Teaching Diploma
PE	Procurement Executive; Prince Edward Island (postal)
PEI	Prince Edward Island
PEN	Poets, Playwrights, Editors, Essayists, Novelists (Club)
PEng	Registered Professional Engineer (Canada); Member, Society of Professional Engineers
Penn	Pennsylvania
PEP	Political and Economic Planning (*now see* PSI)
PER	Professional and Executive Recruitment
PES	Party of European Socialists
PEST	Pressure for Economic and Social Toryism
PETRAS	Polytechnic Educational Technology Resources Advisory Service
PF	Procurator-Fiscal
PFA	Professional Footballers' Association

pfc	Graduate of RAF Flying College
PFE	Program for Executives
PFI	Private Finance Initiative
PGA	Professional Golfers' Association
PGCA	Post Graduate Certificate of Adjudication
PGCE	Post Graduate Certificate of Education
PGCTh	Postgraduate Certificate in Theology
PGDCCI	Postgraduate Diploma in Computing for Commerce and Industry
PGDPT	Postgraduate Diploma in Pastoral Theology
PGTC	Postgraduate Teaching Certificate
PH	Presidential Order of Honour (Botswana)
PHAB	Physically Handicapped & Able-bodied
PhB	Bachelor of Philosophy
PhC	Pharmaceutical Chemist
PhD	Doctor of Philosophy
Phil.	Philology, Philological; Philosophy, Philosophical
PhL	Licentiate in Philosophy
PHLS	Public Health Laboratory Service
PhM	Master of Philosophy (USA)
PhmB	Bachelor of Pharmacy
Phys.	Physical
PIA	Personal Investment Authority
PIARC	Permanent International Association of Road Congresses
PIB	Prices and Incomes Board (later NBPI)
PICAO	Provisional International Civil Aviation Organization (now ICAO)
pinx.	*pinxit* (he painted it)
PIRA	Paper Industries Research Association
PITCOM	Parliamentary Information Technology Committee
PJG	Pingat Jasa Gemilang (Singapore)
PJHQ	Permanent Joint Headquarters
PJK	Pingkat Jasa Kebaktian (Malaysia)
Pl.	Place; Plural
PLA	Port of London Authority
PLAB	Professional and Linguistic Assessments Board
PLC or plc	public limited company
Plen.	Plenipotentiary
PLI	President, Landscape Institute
PLP	Parliamentary Labour Party; Progressive Liberal Party (Bahamas)
PLR	Public Lending Right
PMA	Personal Military Assistant
PMC	Personnel Management Centre
PMD	Program for Management Development
PMedSci	President, Academy of Medical Sciences
PMG	Postmaster-General
PMN	Panglima Mangku Negara (Malaysia)
PMO	Principal Medical Officer; Princess Mary's Own
PMRAFNS	Princess Mary's Royal Air Force Nursing Service
PMS	Presidential Order of Meritorious Service (Botswana); President, Miniature Society
PNBS	Panglima Negara Bintang Sarawak
PNEU	Parents' National Educational Union
PNG	Papua New Guinea
PNP	People's National Party
PO	Post Office
POB	Presidential Order of Botswana
POMEF	Political Office Middle East Force
Pop.	Population
POST	Parliamentary Office of Science and Technology
POUNC	Post Office Users' National Council
POW	Prisoner of War; Prince of Wales's
PP	Parish Priest; Past President
pp	pages
PPA	Periodical Publishers Association
PPARC	Particle Physics and Astronomy Research Council
PPCLI	Princess Patricia's Canadian Light Infantry
PPCSD	Past President, Chartered Society of Designers
PPDF	Parti Populaire pour la Démocratie Française
PPE	Philosophy, Politics and Economics
PPInstHE	Past President, Institution of Highway Engineers
PPIStructE	Past President, Institution of Structural Engineers
PPITB	Printing and Publishing Industry Training Board
PPP	Private Patients Plan
PPRA	Past President, Royal Academy
PPRBA	Past President, Royal Society of British Artists

PPRBS	Past President, Royal Society of British Sculptors
PPRE	Past President, Royal Society of Painter-Printmakers (*formerly* of Painter-Etchers and Engravers)
PPRIBA	Past President, Royal Institute of British Architects
PPROI	Past President, Royal Institute of Oil Painters
PPRP	Past President, Royal Society of Portrait Painters
PPRSA	Past President, Royal Scottish Academy
PPRSW	Past President, Royal Scottish Society of Painters in Water Colours
PPRTPI	Past President, Royal Town Planning Institute
PPRWA	Past President, Royal Watercolour Association
PPS	Parliamentary Private Secretary
PPSIAD	Past President, Society of Industrial Artists and Designers
PQ	Province of Quebec
PQCCC	Post Qualification Certificate in Child Care
PQE	Professional Qualifying Examination
PR	Public Relations; Parti républicain
PRA	President, Royal Academy
PRASEG	Associate Parliamentary Renewable and Sustainable Energy Group
PRBS	President, Royal Society of British Sculptors
PRCA	Public Relations Consultants Association
PRCS	President, Royal College of Surgeons
PrD	Doctor of Professional Practice
PRE	President, Royal Society of Painter-Printmakers (*formerly* of Painter-Etchers and Engravers)
Preb.	Prebendary
PrEng.	Professional Engineer
Prep.	Preparatory
Pres.	President
PRHA	President, Royal Hibernian Academy
PRI	President, Royal Institute of Painters in Water Colours; Plastics and Rubber Institute
PRIA	President, Royal Irish Academy
PRIAS	President, Royal Incorporation of Architects in Scotland
Prin.	Principal
PRISA	Public Relations Institute of South Africa
PRL	Liberal Reform Party (Belgium)
PRO	Public Relations Officer; Public Records Office
Proc.	Proctor; Proceedings
Prof.	Professor; Professional
PROI	President, Royal Institute of Oil Painters
PRO NED	Promotion of Non-Executive Directors
PRORM	Pay and Records Office, Royal Marines
Pro tem.	*Pro tempore* (for the time being)
Prov.	Provost; Provincial
Prox.	*Proximo* (next)
Prox.acc.	*Proxime accessit* (next in order of merit to the winner)
PRS	President, Royal Society; Performing Right Society Ltd
PRSA	President, Royal Scottish Academy
PRSE	President, Royal Society of Edinburgh
PRSH	President, Royal Society for the Promotion of Health
PRSW	President, Royal Scottish Water Colour Society
PRUAA	President, Royal Ulster Academy of Arts
PRWA	President, Royal West of England Academy
PRWS	President, Royal Society of Painters in Water Colours
PS	Pastel Society; Paddle Steamer
ps	passed School of Instruction (of Officers)
PSA	Property Services Agency; Petty Sessions Area
psa	Graduate of RAF Staff College
psc	Graduate of Staff College († indicates Graduate of Senior Wing Staff College)
PSD	Petty Sessional Division; Social Democratic Party (Portugal)
PSE	Party of European Socialists
PSGB	Pharmaceutical Society of Great Britain (*now see* RPSGB)
PSI	Policy Studies Institute
PSIAD	President, Society of Industrial Artists and Designers
PSM	Panglima Setia Mahkota (Malaysia)
psm	Certificate of Royal Military School of Music
PSMA	President, Society of Marine Artists
PSNC	Pacific Steam Navigation Co.
PSO	Principal Scientific Officer; Personal Staff Officer
PSOE	Partido Socialista Obrero Espan˜ol
PSSC	Personal Social Services Council
PsyD	Doctor of Psychology
PTA	Passenger Transport Authority; Parent-Teacher Association

PTC	Personnel and Training Command
PTE	Passenger Transport Executive
Pte	Private
ptsc	passed Technical Staff College
Pty	Proprietary
PUP	People's United Party; Progressive Unionist Party
PVSM	Param Vishishc Seva Medal (India)
PWD	Public Works Department
PWE	Political Welfare Executive
PWO	Prince of Wales's Own
PWR	Pressurized Water Reactor
PYBT	Prince's Youth Business Trust

Q

Q	Queen
QAA	Quality Assurance Agency for Higher Education
QAIMNS	Queen Alexandra's Imperial Military Nursing Service
QALAS	Qualified Associate, Chartered Land Agents' Society (later, after amalgamation, ARICS)
QARANC	Queen Alexandra's Royal Army Nursing Corps
QARNNS	Queen Alexandra's Royal Naval Nursing Service
QBD	Queen's Bench Division
QC	Queen's Counsel; Quebec (postal)
QCA	Qualifications and Curriculum Authority
QCB	Queen's Commendation for Bravery
QCVS	Queen's Commendation for Valuable Service
QCVSA	Queen's Commendation for Valuable Service in the Air
QDR	Qualified in Dispute Resolution
QEH	Queen Elizabeth Hall
QEO	Queen Elizabeth's Own
QFSM	Queen's Fire Service Medal for Distinguished Service
QGM	Queen's Gallantry Medal
QHC	Honorary Chaplain to the Queen
QHDS	Honorary Dental Surgeon to the Queen
QHNS	Honorary Nursing Sister to the Queen
QHP	Honorary Physician to the Queen
QHS	Honorary Surgeon to the Queen
Qld	Queensland
Qly	Quarterly
QMAAC	Queen Mary's Army Auxiliary Corps
QMC	Queen Mary College, London (now see QMW)
QMG	Quartermaster-General
QMO	Queen Mary's Own
QMW	Queen Mary and Westfield College, London
QO	Qualified Officer
QOOH	Queen's Own Oxfordshire Hussars
Q(ops)	Quartering (operations)
QORWK	Queen's Own Royal West Kent Regiment
QOY	Queen's Own Yeomanry
QPM	Queen's Police Medal
QPSM	Queen's Public Service Medal (New Zealand)
Qr	Quarter
QRIH	Queen's Royal Irish Hussars
QS	Quarter Sessions; Quantity Surveying
qs	RAF graduates of the Military or Naval Staff College
QSM	Queen's Service Medal (NZ)
QSO	Queen's Service Order (NZ)
QTS	Qualified Teacher Status
QUB	Queen's University, Belfast
qv	quod vide (which see)
QVRM	Queen's Volunteer Reserve Medal
qwi	Qualified Weapons Instructor

R

(R)	Reserve
RA	Royal Academician; Royal Academy; Royal (Regiment of) Artillery
RAA	Regional Arts Association; Royal Australian Artillery
RAAF	Royal Australian Air Force
RAAMC	Royal Australian Army Medical Corps
RABI	Royal Agricultural Benevolent Institution
RAC	Royal Automobile Club; Royal Agricultural College; Royal Armoured Corps
RACDS	Royal Australian College of Dental Surgeons

RACGP	Royal Australian College of General Practitioners
RAChD	Royal Army Chaplains' Department
RACI	Royal Australian Chemical Institute
RACO	Royal Australian College of Ophthalmologists
RACOG	Royal Australian College of Obstetricians and Gynaecologists
RACP	Royal Australasian College of Physicians
RACS	Royal Australasian College of Surgeons; Royal Arsenal Cooperative Society
RAD	Royal Academy of Dance
RADA	Royal Academy of Dramatic Art
RADAR	Royal Association for Disability and Rehabilitation
RADC	Royal Army Dental Corps
RADIUS	Religious Drama Society of Great Britain
RAE	Royal Australian Engineers; Royal Aerospace Establishment (formerly Royal Aircraft Establishment); Research Assessment Exercise
RAEC	Royal Army Educational Corps
RAeS	Royal Aeronautical Society
RAF	Royal Air Force
RAFA	Royal Air Forces Association
RAFO	Reserve of Air Force Officers (now see RAFRO)
RAFR	Royal Air Force Reserve
RAFRO	Royal Air Force Reserve of Officers
RAFVR	Royal Air Force Volunteer Reserve
RAI	Royal Anthropological Institute of Great Britain & Ireland; Radio Audizioni Italiane
RAIA	Royal Australian Institute of Architects
RAIC	Royal Architectural Institute of Canada
RAM	(Member of) Royal Academy of Music
RAMC	Royal Army Medical Corps
RAN	Royal Australian Navy
R&D	Research and Development
RANR	Royal Australian Naval Reserve
RANVR	Royal Australian Naval Volunteer Reserve
RAOC	Royal Army Ordnance Corps
RAPC	Royal Army Pay Corps
RARDE	Royal Armament Research and Development Establishment
RARO	Regular Army Reserve of Officers
RAS	Royal Astronomical Society; Royal Asiatic Society; Recruitment and Assessment Services
RASC	Royal Army Service Corps (now see RCT)
RASE	Royal Agricultural Society of England
RAuxAF	Royal Auxiliary Air Force
RAVC	Royal Army Veterinary Corps
RB	Rifle Brigade
RBA	Member, Royal Society of British Artists
RBK&C	Royal Borough of Kensington and Chelsea
RBL	Royal British Legion
RBS	Royal Society of British Sculptors
RBSA	(Member of) Royal Birmingham Society of Artists
RBY	Royal Bucks Yeomanry
RC	Roman Catholic
RCA	Member, Royal Canadian Academy of Arts; Royal College of Art; (Member of) Royal Cambrian Academy
RCAC	Royal Canadian Armoured Corps
RCAF	Royal Canadian Air Force
RCamA	Member, Royal Cambrian Academy
RCAnaes	Royal College of Anaesthetists
RCAS	Royal Central Asian Society (now see RSAA)
RCCM	Research Council for Complementary Medicine
RCDS	Royal College of Defence Studies
rcds	completed a course at, or served for a year on the Staff of, the Royal College of Defence Studies
RCGP	Royal College of General Practitioners
RCHA	Royal Canadian Horse Artillery
RCHME	Royal Commission on Historical Monuments of England
RCM	(Member of) Royal College of Music
RCN	Royal Canadian Navy; Royal College of Nursing
RCNC	Royal Corps of Naval Constructors
RCNR	Royal Canadian Naval Reserve
RCNVR	Royal Canadian Naval Volunteer Reserve
RCO	Royal College of Organists
RCOG	Royal College of Obstetricians and Gynaecologists
RCP	Royal College of Physicians, London
RCPA	Royal College of Pathologists of Australia

RCPath	Royal College of Pathologists
RCPCH	Royal College of Paediatrics and Child Health
RCPE or **RCPEd**	Royal College of Physicians, Edinburgh
RCPI	Royal College of Physicians of Ireland
RCPSG	Royal College of Physicians and Surgeons of Glasgow
RCPsych	Royal College of Psychiatrists
RCR	Royal College of Radiologists
RCS	Royal College of Surgeons of England; Royal Corps of Signals; Royal College of Science
RCSE or **RCSEd**	Royal College of Surgeons of Edinburgh
RCSI	Royal College of Surgeons in Ireland
RCT	Royal Corps of Transport
RCVS	Royal College of Veterinary Surgeons
RD	Rural Dean; Royal Naval and Royal Marine Forces Reserve Decoration
Rd	Road
RDA	Diploma of Roseworthy Agricultural College, South Australia; Regional Development Agency
RDC	Rural District Council
RDF	Royal Dublin Fusiliers
RDI	Royal Designer for Industry (Royal Society of Arts)
RDS	Royal Dublin Society
RE	Royal Engineers; Fellow, Royal Society of Painter-Printmakers (*formerly* of Painter-Etchers and Engravers); Religious Education
REACH	Retired Executives Action Clearing House
react	Research Education and Aid for Children with potentially Terminal illness
Rear Adm.	Rear Admiral
REconS	Royal Economic Society
Regt	Regiment
REME	Royal Electrical and Mechanical Engineers
REngDes	Registered Engineering Designer
REOWS	Royal Engineers Officers' Widows' Society
REPC	Regional Economic Planning Council
RERO	Royal Engineers Reserve of Officers
Res.	Resigned; Reserve; Resident; Research
RETI	Association of Traditional Industrial Regions
Rev.	Reverend; Review
RFA	Royal Field Artillery
RFC	Royal Flying Corps (*now* RAF); Rugby Football Club
RFCA	Reserve Forces and Cadets Association
RFD	Reserve Force Decoration
RFH	Royal Festival Hall
RFN	Registered Fever Nurse
RFP	Registered Forensic Practitioner
RFPS(G)	Royal Faculty of Physicians and Surgeons, Glasgow (*now see* RCPSG)
RFR	Rassemblement des Français pour la République
RFU	Rugby Football Union
RGA	Royal Garrison Artillery
RGI	Royal Glasgow Institute of the Fine Arts
RGJ	Royal Green Jackets
RGN	Registered General Nurse
RGS	Royal Geographical Society
RGSA	Royal Geographical Society of Australasia
RHA	Royal Hibernian Academy; Royal Horse Artillery; Regional Health Authority
RHASS	Royal Highland and Agricultural Society of Scotland
RHB	Regional Hospital Board
RHBNC	Royal Holloway and Bedford New College, London
RHC	Royal Holloway College, London (later RHBNC)
RHF	Royal Highland Fusiliers
RHG	Royal Horse Guards
RHistS	Royal Historical Society
RHQ	Regional Headquarters
RHR	Royal Highland Regiment
RHS	Royal Horticultural Society; Royal Humane Society
RHUL	Royal Holloway, University of London
RHV	Royal Health Visitor
RI	(Member of) Royal Institute of Painters in Water Colours; Rhode Island
RIA	Royal Irish Academy
RIAI	Royal Institute of the Architects of Ireland
RIAM	Royal Irish Academy of Music
RIAS	Royal Incorporation of Architects in Scotland
RIASC	Royal Indian Army Service Corps
RIBA	(Member of) Royal Institute of British Architects
RIBI	Rotary International in Great Britain and Ireland
RIC	Royal Irish Constabulary; Royal Institute of Chemistry (*now see* RSC)
RICS	(Member of) Royal Institution of Chartered Surveyors
RIE	Royal Indian Engineering (College)
RIF	Royal Inniskilling Fusiliers
RIIA	Royal Institute of International Affairs
RILEM	Réunion internationale des laboratoires d'essais et de recherches sur les matériaux et les constructions
RIM	Royal Indian Marines
RIN	Royal Indian Navy
RINA	Royal Institution of Naval Architects
RINVR	Royal Indian Naval Volunteer Reserve
RIPA	Royal Institute of Public Administration
RIPH	Royal Institute of Public Health
RIPH&H	Royal Institute of Public Health and Hygiene (*now see* RIPH)
RIrF	Royal Irish Fusiliers
RLC	Royal Logistic Corps
RLSS	Royal Life Saving Society
RM	Royal Marines; Resident Magistrate; Registered Midwife
RMA	Royal Marine Artillery; Royal Military Academy Sandhurst (*now* incorporating Royal Military Academy, Woolwich)
RMB	Rural Mail Base
RMC	Royal Military College Sandhurst (*now see* RMA)
RMCM	(Member of) Royal Manchester College of Music
RMCS	Royal Military College of Science
RMedSoc	Royal Medical Society, Edinburgh
RMetS	Royal Meteorological Society
RMFVR	Royal Marine Forces Volunteer Reserve
RMIT	Royal Melbourne Institute of Technology
RMLI	Royal Marine Light Infantry
RMN	Registered Mental Nurse
RMO	Resident Medical Officer(s)
RMP	Royal Military Police
RMPA	Royal Medico-Psychological Association
RMS	Royal Microscopical Society; Royal Mail Steamer; Royal Society of Miniature Painters
RMT	National Union of Rail, Maritime and Transport Workers; Registered Massage Therapist
RN	Royal Navy; Royal Naval; Registered Nurse
RNAS	Royal Naval Air Service
RNAY	Royal Naval Aircraft Yard
RNC	Royal Naval College
RNCM	(Member of) Royal Northern College of Music
RNEC	Royal Naval Engineering College
RNIB	Royal National Institute of the Blind
RNID	Royal National Institute for Deaf People (*formerly* Royal National Institute for the Deaf)
RNLI	Royal National Life-boat Institution
RNLO	Royal Naval Liaison Officer
RNR	Royal Naval Reserve
RNRU	Royal Navy Rugby Union
RNS	Royal Numismatic Society
RNSA	Royal Naval Sailing Association
RNSC	Royal Naval Staff College
RNT	Registered Nurse Tutor; Royal National Theatre
RNTNEH	Royal National Throat, Nose and Ear Hospital
RNUR	Régie Nationale des Usines Renault
RNVR	Royal Naval Volunteer Reserve
RNVSR	Royal Naval Volunteer Supplementary Reserve
RNXS	Royal Naval Auxiliary Service
RNZA	Royal New Zealand Artillery
RNZAC	Royal New Zealand Armoured Corps
RNZAF	Royal New Zealand Air Force
RNZIR	Royal New Zealand Infantry Regiment
RNZN	Royal New Zealand Navy
RNZNVR	Royal New Zealand Naval Volunteer Reserve
ROC	Royal Observer Corps
ROF	Royal Ordnance Factories
R of O	Reserve of Officers
ROI	Member, Royal Institute of Oil Painters
RoSPA	Royal Society for the Prevention of Accidents
(Rot.)	Rotunda Hospital, Dublin (after degree)
RP	(Member of) Royal Society of Portrait Painters
RPC	Royal Pioneer Corps
RPE	Rocket Propulsion Establishment
RPF	Rassemblement pour la France

RPMS	Royal Postgraduate Medical School
RPO	Royal Philharmonic Orchestra
RPR	Rassemblement pour la République
RPS	Royal Photographic Society
RPSGB	Royal Pharmaceutical Society of Great Britain
RRC	Royal Red Cross; Rapid Reaction Corps
RRE	Royal Radar Establishment (later RSRE)
RRF	Royal Regiment of Fusiliers
RRS	Royal Research Ship
RSA	Royal Scottish Academician; Royal Society of Arts; Republic of South Africa
RSAA	Royal Society for Asian Affairs
RSAF	Royal Small Arms Factory
RSAI	Royal Society of Antiquaries of Ireland
RSAMD	Royal Scottish Academy of Music and Drama
RSanI	Royal Sanitary Institute (now see RSH)
RSAS	Royal Surgical Aid Society
RSC	Royal Society of Canada; Royal Society of Chemistry; Royal Shakespeare Company
RSCM	(Member of) Royal School of Church Music
RSCN	Registered Sick Children's Nurse
RSE	Royal Society of Edinburgh
RSF	Royal Scots Fusiliers
RSFSR	Russian Soviet Federated Socialist Republic
RSGS	Royal Scottish Geographical Society
RSH	Royal Society for the Promotion of Health
RSL	Royal Society of Literature; Returned Services League of Australia
RSM	Royal School of Mines
RSM or RSocMed	Royal Society of Medicine
RSMA	(Member of) Royal Society of Marine Artists
RSME	Royal School of Military Engineering
RSMHCA	Royal Society for Mentally Handicapped Children and Adults (see Mencap)
RSNC	Royal Society for Nature Conservation
RSO	Rural Sub-Office; Railway Sub-Office; Resident Surgical Officer
RSPB	Royal Society for Protection of Birds
RSPCA	Royal Society for Prevention of Cruelty to Animals
RSRE	Royal Signals and Radar Establishment
RSSAf	Royal Society of South Africa
RSSAILA	Returned Sailors, Soldiers and Airmen's Imperial League of Australia (now see RSL)
RSSPCC	Royal Scottish Society for Prevention of Cruelty to Children
RSTM&H	Royal Society of Tropical Medicine and Hygiene
RSUA	Royal Society of Ulster Architects
RSV	Revised Standard Version
RSW	Member, Royal Scottish Society of Painters in Water Colours
RTE	Radio Telefis Eireann
Rt Hon.	Right Honourable
RTL	Radio-Télévision Luxembourg
RTO	Railway Transport Officer
RTPI	Royal Town Planning Institute
RTR	Royal Tank Regiment
Rt Rev.	Right Reverend
RTS	Religious Tract Society; Royal Toxophilite Society; Royal Television Society
RTYC	Royal Thames Yacht Club
RU	Rugby Union
RUA	Royal Ulster Academy
RUC	Royal Ulster Constabulary
RUI	Royal University of Ireland
RUKBA	Royal United Kingdom Beneficent Association
RUR	Royal Ulster Regiment
RURAL	Society for the Responsible Use of Resources in Agriculture & on the Land
RUSI	Royal United Services Institute for Defence and Security Studies (formerly Royal United Service Institution)
RVC	Royal Veterinary College
RWA	(Member of) Royal West of England Academy
RWAFF	Royal West African Frontier Force
RWCMD	Royal Welsh College of Music and Drama
RWF	Royal Welch Fusiliers
RWS	(Member of) Royal Society of Painters in Water Colours
RYA	Royal Yachting Association
RYS	Royal Yacht Squadron
RZSScot	Royal Zoological Society of Scotland

S

(S)	(in Navy) Paymaster; Scotland
S	Succeeded; South; Saint
s	son
SA	South Australia; South Africa; Société Anonyme; Society of the Atonement
SAAF	South African Air Force
SABC	South African Broadcasting Corporation
SAC	Scientific Advisory Committee
sac	qualified at small arms technical long course
SACC	South African Council of Churches
SACEUR	Supreme Allied Commander Europe
SACIF	sociedad anónima commercial industrial financiera
SACLANT	Supreme Allied Commander Atlantic
SACRO	Scottish Association for the Care and Resettlement of Offenders
SACSEA	Supreme Allied Command, SE Asia
SA de CV	sociedad anónima de capital variable
SADF	Sudanese Auxiliary Defence Force
SADG	Société des Architectes Diplômés par le Gouvernement
SAE	Society of Automobile Engineers (US)
SAHFOS	Sir Alister Hardy Foundation for Ocean Science
SAMC	South African Medical Corps
SAN	Senior Advocate of Nigeria
SARL	Société à Responsabilité Limitée
Sarum	Salisbury
SAS	Special Air Service
Sask	Saskatchewan
SASO	Senior Air Staff Officer
SAT	Senior Member, Association of Accounting Technicians
SATB	Soprano, Alto, Tenor, Bass
SATRO	Science and Technology Regional Organisation
SB	Bachelor of Science (US)
SBAA	Sovereign Base Areas Administration
SBAC	Society of British Aerospace Companies (formerly Society of British Aircraft Constructors)
SBS	Special Boat Service
SBStJ	Serving Brother, Most Venerable Order of the Hospital of St John of Jerusalem
SC	Star of Courage (Canada); Senior Counsel; South Carolina
sc	student at the Staff College
SCA	Society of Catholic Apostolate (Pallottine Fathers); Société en Commandité par Actions
SCAA	School Curriculum and Assessment Authority
SCAO	Senior Civil Affairs Officer
SCAPA	Society for Checking the Abuses of Public Advertising
SCAR	Scientific Committee for Antarctic Research
ScD	Doctor of Science
SCDC	Schools Curriculum Development Committee
SCDI	Scottish Council for Development and Industry
SCF	Senior Chaplain to the Forces; Save the Children Fund
Sch.	School
SCI	Society of Chemical Industry
SCIE	Social Care Institute of Excellence
SCIS	Scottish Council of Independent Schools
SCL	Student in Civil Law
SCLC	Short Service Limited Commission
SCM	State Certified Midwife; Student Christian Movement
SCOB	Supreme Counsellor of Baobab (South Africa)
SCONUL	Standing Conference of National and University Libraries
SCOP	Standing Conference of Principals
Scot.	Scotland
ScotBIC	Scottish Business in the Community
SCOTMEG	Scottish Management Efficiency Group
SCOTVEC	Scottish Vocational Education Council
SCVO	Scottish Council for Voluntary Organisations
SD	Staff Duties; South Dakota (postal)
SDA	Social Democratic Alliance; Scottish Diploma in Agriculture; Scottish Development Agency
SDF	Sudan Defence Force; Social Democratic Federation
SDI	Strategic Defence Initiative
SDLP	Social Democratic and Labour Party
SDP	Social Democratic Party
SE	South-east
SEAC	South-East Asia Command

SEALF	South-East Asia Land Forces
SEATO	South-East Asia Treaty Organization
SEC	Security Exchange Commission
Sec.	Secretary
SED	Scottish Education Department
SEE	Society of Environmental Engineers
SEEDA	South East England Development Agency
SEFI	European Society for Engineering Education
SEN	State Enrolled Nurse; Special Educational Needs
SEP	Stanford Executive Program
SEPA	Scottish Environmental Protection Agency
SEPM	Society of Economic Palaeontologists and Mineralogists
SERC	Science and Engineering Research Council (*now see* EPSRC and PPARC)
SERT	Society of Electronic and Radio Technicians (later IEIE)
SESO	Senior Equipment Staff Officer
SF	Sinn Féin
SFA	Securities and Futures Authority
SFC	Scottish Funding Council NOTE: From Ian Cleland Ritchie's pr
SFOR	Stabilisation Force
SFTA	Society of Film and Television Arts (*now see* BAFTA)
SFTCD	Senior Fellow, Trinity College Dublin
SG	Solicitor-General
SGA	Member, Society of Graphic Art
Sgt	Sergeant
SHA	Secondary Heads Association; Special Health Authority
SHAC	London Housing Aid Centre
SHAEF	Supreme Headquarters, Allied Expeditionary Force
SHAPE	Supreme Headquarters, Allied Powers, Europe
SHEFC	Scottish Higher Education Funding Council
SHHD	Scottish Home and Health Department
SHND	Scottish Higher National Diploma
SHO	Senior House Officer
SIAD	Society of Industrial Artists and Designers (*now see* CSD)
SIAM	Society of Industrial and Applied Mathematics (US)
SIB	Shipbuilding Industry Board; Securities and Investments Board (*now see* FSA)
SICA-FICA	Foundation for International Commercial Arbitration
SICAV	Société d'Investissement à Capital Variable
SICOT	Société Internationale de Chirurgie Orthopédique et de Traumatologie
SID	Society for International Development
SIESO	Society of Industrial and Emergency Services Officers
SIMA	Scientific Instrument Manufacturers' Association of Great Britain
SIME	Security Intelligence Middle East
SIMG	*Societas Internationalis Medicinae Generalis*
SinDrs	Doctor of Chinese
SIROT	Société Internationale pour Recherche en Orthopédie et Traumatologie
SIS	Secret Intelligence Service
SITA	Société Internationale de Télécommunications Aéronautiques
SITPRO	Simpler Trade Procedures Board (*formerly* Simplification of International Trade Procedures)
SJ	Society of Jesus (Jesuits)
SJAB	St John Ambulance Brigade
SJD	Doctor of Juristic Science
SJJ	Setia Jubli Perak Tuanku Ja'afar
SK	Saskatchewan (postal)
SL	Serjeant-at-Law; Sociedad Limitada
SLA	Special Libraries Association
SLAC	Stanford Linear Accelerator Centre
SLAET	Society of Licensed Aircraft Engineers and Technologists
SLAS	Society for Latin-American Studies
SLD	Social and Liberal Democrats
SLP	Scottish Labour Party
SLS	Society of Legal Scholars
SM	Medal of Service (Canada) (*now see* OC); Master of Science; Officer qualified for Submarine Duties
SMA	Society of Marine Artists (*now see* RSMA)
SMB	Setia Mahkota Brunei
SMCC	Submarine Commanding Officers' Command Course
SME	School of Military Engineering (*now see* RSME)
SMEO	Squadron Marine Engineer Officer
SMHO	Sovereign Military Hospitaller Order (Malta)
SMIEE	Senior Member, Institute of Electrical and Electronics Engineers (New York)
SMIRE	Senior Member, Institute of Radio Engineers (New York)
SMMT	Society of Motor Manufacturers and Traders Ltd
SMN	Seri Maharaja Mangku Negara (Malaysia)
SMO	Senior Medical Officer; Sovereign Military Order
SMP	Senior Managers' Program
SMPTE	Society of Motion Picture and Television Engineers (US)
SMRTB	Ship and Marine Requirements Technology Board
SNAME	Society of Naval Architects and Marine Engineers (US)
SNCF	Société Nationale des Chemins de Fer Français
SND	Sisters of Notre Dame
SNH	Scottish Natural Heritage
SNP	Scottish National Party
SNTS	Society for New Testament Studies
SO	Staff Officer; Scientific Officer; Symphony Orchestra
SOAF	Sultan of Oman's Air Force
SOAS	School of Oriental and African Studies
Soc.	Society; Socialist (France)
SOCA	Serious and Organised Crime Agency
Soc & Lib Dem	Social and Liberal Democrats (*now see* Lib Dem)
SocCE(France)	Société des Ingénieurs Civils de France
SODEPAX	Committee on Society, Development and Peace
SOE	Special Operations Executive; Society of Operations Engineers
SOGAT	Society of Graphical and Allied Trades (*now see* GPMU)
SOLACE or Solace	Society of Local Authority Chief Executives
SOLT	Society of London Theatre
SOM	Society of Occupational Medicine
SOSc	Society of Ordained Scientists
SOTS	Society for Old Testament Study
sowc	Senior Officers' War Course
SP	Self-Propelled (Anti-Tank Regiment)
sp	*sine prole* (without issue)
SpA	Società per Azioni
SPAB	Society for the Protection of Ancient Buildings
SPARKS	Sport Aiding Medical Research for Children
SPCA	Society for the Prevention of Cruelty to Animals
SPCK	Society for Promoting Christian Knowledge
SPCM	Darjah Seri Paduka Cura Si Manja Kini (Malaysia)
SPD	Salisbury Plain District; Sozialdemokratische Partei Deutschlands
SPDK	Seri Panglima Darjal Kinabalu
SPG	Society for the Propagation of the Gospel (*now see* USPG)
SPk	Sitara-e-Pakistan
SPMB	Seri Paduka Makhota Brunei
SPMK	Darjah Kebasaran Seri Paduka Mahkota Kelantan (Malaysia)
SPMO	Senior Principal Medical Officer
SPNC	Society for the Promotion of Nature Conservation (*now see* RSNC)
SPNM	Society for the Promotion of New Music
SPR	Society for Psychical Research
SPRC	Society for Prevention and Relief of Cancer
sprl	société de personnes à responsabilité limitée
SPSO	Senior Principal Scientific Officer
SPTL	Society of Public Teachers of Law (*now see* SLS)
SPUC	Society for the Protection of the Unborn Child
Sq.	Square
sq	staff qualified
SQA	Sitara-i-Quaid-i-Azam (Pakistan)
Sqdn or Sqn	Squadron
SR	Special Reserve; Southern Railway; Southern Region (BR)
SRC	Science Research Council (later SERC); Students' Representative Council
SRCh	State Registered Chiropodist
SRHE	Society for Research into Higher Education
SRIS	Science Reference Information Service
SRN	State Registered Nurse
SRNA	Shipbuilders and Repairers National Association
SRO	Supplementary Reserve of Officers; Self-Regulatory Organisation
SRP	State Registered Physiotherapist
SRY	Sherwood Rangers Yeomanry
SS	Saints; Straits Settlements; Steamship
SSA	Society of Scottish Artists; Side Saddle Association
SSAC	Social Security Advisory Committee

SSAFA	Soldiers, Sailors, Airmens and Families Association-Forces Help (formerly Soldiers', Sailors', and Airmen's Families Association)
SSBN	Nuclear Submarine, Ballistic
SSC	Solicitor before Supreme Court (Scotland); Sculptors Society of Canada; *Societas Sanctae Crucis* (Society of the Holy Cross); Short Service Commission
SSEB	South of Scotland Electricity Board
SSEES	School of Slavonic and East European Studies
SSF	Society of St Francis
SSJE	Society of St John the Evangelist
SSLC	Short Service Limited Commission
SSM	Society of the Sacred Mission; Seri Setia Mahkota (Malaysia)
SSO	Senior Supply Officer; Senior Scientific Officer
SSR	Soviet Socialist Republic
SSRC	Social Science Research Council (*now see* ESRC)
SSSI	Sites of Special Scientific Interest
SSSR	Society for the Scientific Study of Religion
SSStJ	Serving Sister, Most Venerable Order of the Hospital of St John of Jerusalem
St	Street; Saint
STA	Sail Training Association
STB	*Sacrae Theologiae Baccalaureus* (Bachelor of Sacred Theology)
STC	Senior Training Corps
STD	*Sacrae Theologiae Doctor* (Doctor of Sacred Theology)
STETS	Southern Theological Education and Training Scheme
STh	Scholar in Theology
Stip.	Stipend; Stipendiary
STL	*Sacrae Theologiae Lector* (Reader or a Professor of Sacred Theology)
STM	*Sacrae Theologiae Magister* (Master of Sacred Theology)
STP	*Sacrae Theologiae Professor* (Professor of Divinity, old form of DD)
STSO	Senior Technical Staff Officer
STV	Scottish Television
SUNY	State University of New York
Supp. Res.	Supplementary Reserve (of Officers)
Supt	Superintendent
Surg.	Surgeon
Surv.	Surviving
SW	South-west
SWET	Society of West End Theatre (*now see* SOLT)
SWIA	Society of Wildlife Artists
SWO	Staff Warfare Officer
SWPA	South West Pacific Area
SWRB	Sadler's Wells Royal Ballet
Syd.	Sydney

T

T	Telephone; Territorial
TA	Telegraphic Address; Territorial Army
TAA	Territorial Army Association
TAF	Tactical Air Force
T&AFA	Territorial and Auxiliary Forces Association
T&AVR	Territorial and Army Volunteer Reserve
TANS	Territorial Army Nursing Service
TANU	Tanganyika African National Union
TARO	Territorial Army Reserve of Officers
TAS	Torpedo and Anti Submarine Course
TASS	Technical, Administrative and Supervisory Section of AUEW (now part of MSF)
TAVRA or TA&VRA	Territorial Auxiliary and Volunteer Reserve Association (*now see* RFCA)
TC	Order of the Trinity Cross (Trinidad and Tobago)
TCCB	Test and County Cricket Board (*now see* ECB)
TCD	Trinity College, Dublin (University of Dublin, Trinity College)
TCF	Temporary Chaplain to the Forces
TCPA	Town and Country Planning Association
TD	Territorial Efficiency Decoration; Efficiency Decoration (T&AVR) (since April 1967); Teachta Dala (Member of the Dáil, Eire)
TDD	Tubercular Diseases Diploma
TE	Technical Engineer
TEAC	Technical Educational Advisory Council

TEC	Technician Education Council (*now see* BTEC); Training and Enterprise Council
Tech(CEI)	Technician
TechRICS	Technical Member, Royal Institution of Chartered Surveyors
TEFL	Teaching English as a Foreign Language
TEFLA	Teaching English as a Foreign Language to Adults
TEM	Territorial Efficiency Medal
TEMA	Telecommunication Engineering and Manufacturing Association
Temp.	Temperature; Temporary
TEng(CEI)	Technician Engineer (*now see* IEng)
Tenn	Tennessee
TeolD	Doctor of Theology
TES	Times Educational Supplement
TESL	Teaching English as a Second Language
TESOL	Teaching English to Speakers of other Languages
TET	Teacher of Electrotherapy
Tex	Texas
TF	Territorial Force
TFR	Territorial Force Reserve
TFTS	Tactical Fighter Training Squadron
TGEW	Timber Growers England and Wales Ltd
TGO	Timber Growers' Organisation (*now see* TGEW)
TGWU	Transport and General Workers' Union
ThD	Doctor of Theology
THED	Transvaal Higher Education Diploma
THELEP	Therapy of Leprosy
THES	Times Higher Education Supplement
ThL	Theological Licentiate
ThM	Master of Theology
ThSchol	Scholar in Theology
TIMS	The Institute of Management Sciences
TLS	Times Literary Supplement
TMA	Theatrical Management Association
TMMG	Teacher of Massage and Medical Gymnastics
TN	Tennessee (postal)
TNC	Theatres National Committee
TOPSS	Training Organisation for the Personal Social Services
TOSD	Tertiary Order of St Dominic
TPI	Town Planning Institute (*now see* RTPI)
TPsych	Trainer in Psychiatry
TRA	Tenants' and Residents' Association
Trans.	Translation; Translated
Transf.	Transferred
TRC	Thames Rowing Club
TRE	Telecommunications Research Establishment (later RRE)
TRH	Their Royal Highnesses
TRIC	Television and Radio Industries Club
Trin.	Trinity
TRL	Transport Research Laboratory
TRRL	Transport and Road Research Laboratory (*now see* TRL)
TS	Training Ship
TSB	Trustee Savings Bank
tsc	passed a Territorial Army Course in Staff Duties
TSD	Tertiary of St Dominic
TSE	Transmissible Spongiform Encephalopathies
TSSA	Transport Salaried Staffs' Association
TSSF	Tertiary, Society of St Francis
TSWA	Television South West Arts
TTA	Teacher Training Agency
TUC	Trades Union Congress
TULV	Trade Unions for a Labour Victory
TUS	Trade Union Side
TV	Television
TVEI	Technical and Vocational Education Initiative
TWA	Thames Water Authority
TX	Texas (postal)

U

U	Unionist
u	uncle
UA	Unitary Authority
UACE	Universities Association for Continuing Education
UAE	United Arab Emirates

UAR	United Arab Republic
UAU	Universities Athletic Union
UBC	University of British Columbia
UBI	Understanding British Industry
UC	University College
UCAS	Universities and Colleges Admissions Service
UCCA	Universities Central Council on Admissions
UCCF	Universities and Colleges Christian Fellowship of Evangelical Unions
UCE	University of Central England
UCEA	Universities and Colleges Employers Association
UCET	Universities Council for Education of Teachers
UCH	University College Hospital (London)
UCL	University College London
UCLA	University of California at Los Angeles
UCLES	University of Cambridge Local Examinations Syndicate
UCMSM	University College and Middlesex School of Medicine
UCNS	Universities' Council for Non-academic Staff
UCNW	University College of North Wales
UCRN	University College of Rhodesia and Nyasaland
UCS	University College School
UCSB	University of California at Santa Barbara
UCSD	University of California at San Diego
UCSF	University of California at San Francisco
UCW	University College of Wales; Union of Communication Workers (now see CWU)
UDC	Urban District Council; Urban Development Corporation
UDF	Union Defence Force; Union pour la démocratie franc, aise
UDM	United Democratic Movement (South Africa)
UDR	Ulster Defence Regiment; Union des Démocrates pour la Vème République (now see RPR)
UDSR	Union Démocratique et Socialiste de la Résistance
UE	United Empire Loyalist
UEA	University of East Anglia
UED	University Education Diploma
UEFA	Union of European Football Associations
UEL	University of East London
UEMS	Union Européenne des Médecins Spécialistes
UF	United Free Church
UFAW	Universities Federation for Animal Welfare
UFC	Universities' Funding Council
UGC	University Grants Committee (later UFC)
UHI	University of Highlands & Islands Millennium Institute
UIAA	Union Internationale des Associations d'Alpinisme
UICC	Union Internationale contre le Cancer
UIE	Union Internationale des Etudiants
UISPP	Union Internationale des Sciences Préhistoriques et Protohistoriques
UITP	International Union of Public Transport
UJD	Utriusque Juris Doctor (Doctor of both Laws, Doctor of Canon and Civil Law)
UK	United Kingdom
UKAC	United Kingdom Automation Council
UKAEA	United Kingdom Atomic Energy Authority
UKCC	United Kingdom Central Council for Nursing, Midwifery and Health Visiting
UKCCCR	United Kingdom Co-ordinating Committee on Cancer Research
UKCICC	United Kingdom Commanders-in-Chief Committees
UKCIS	United Kingdom Chemical Information Service
UKCOSA	United Kingdom Council for Overseas Student Affairs
UKCP	United Kingdom Council for Psychotherapy
UKERNA	United Kingdom Education and Research Networking Association
UKIAS	United Kingdom Immigrants' Advisory Service
UKIC	United Kingdom Institute for Conservation
UKIP	United Kingdom Independence Party
UKISC	United Kingdom Industrial Space Committee
UKLF	United Kingdom Land Forces
UKMF(L)	United Kingdom Military Forces (Land)
UKMIS	United Kingdom Mission
UKOLN	United Kingdom Office of Library Networking
UKOOA	United Kingdom Offshore Operators Association
UKPIA	United Kingdom Petroleum Industry Association Ltd
UKSC	United Kingdom Support Command
UKSLS	United Kingdom Services Liaison Staff
UKU	United Kingdom Unionist
ULPS	Union of Liberal and Progressive Synagogues
UMDS	United Medical and Dental Schools
UMIST	University of Manchester Institute of Science and Technology
UMP	Union pour un Mouvement Populaire; Union pour une Majorité Présidentielle
UN	United Nations
UNA	United Nations Association
UNCAST	United Nations Conference on the Applications of Science and Technology
UNCIO	United Nations Conference on International Organisation
UNCITRAL	United Nations Commission on International Trade Law
UNCSTD	United Nations Conference on Science and Technology for Development
UNCTAD or Unctad	United Nations Commission for Trade and Development
UNDP	United Nations Development Programme
UNDRO	United Nations Disaster Relief Organisation
UNECA	United Nations Economic Commission for Asia
UNECE	United Nations Economic Commission for Europe
UNED	United Nations Environment and Development
UNEP	United Nations Environment Programme
UNESCO or Unesco	United Nations Educational, Scientific and Cultural Organisation
UNFAO	United Nations Food and Agriculture Organisation
UNFICYP	United Nations Force in Cyprus
UNHCR	United Nations High Commissioner for Refugees
UNICE	Union des Industries de la Communauté Européenne
UNICEF or Unicef	United Nations Children's Fund (formerly United Nations International Children's Emergency Fund)
UNIDO	United Nations Industrial Development Organisation
UNIDROIT	Institut International pour l'Unification du Droit Privé
UNIFEM	United Nations Development Fund for Women
UNIFIL	United Nations Interim Force in Lebanon
UNIPEDE	Union Internationale des Producteurs et Distributeurs d'Energie Electrique
UNISIST	Universal System for Information in Science and Technology
UNITAR	United Nations Institute of Training and Research
Univ.	University
UNO	United Nations Organization
UNRRA	United Nations Relief and Rehabilitation Administration
UNRWA	United Nations Relief and Works Agency
UNSCOB	United Nations Special Commission on the Balkans
UP	United Provinces; Uttar Pradesh; United Presbyterian
UPGC	University and Polytechnic Grants Committee
UPNI	Unionist Party of Northern Ireland
UPU	Universal Postal Union
UPUP	Ulster Popular Unionist Party
URC	United Reformed Church; Urban Regeneration Company
URSI	Union Radio-Scientifique Internationale
US	United States
USA	United States of America
USAAF	United States Army Air Force
USAF	United States Air Force
USAID	United States Agency for International Development
USAR	United States Army Reserve
USC	University of Southern California
USDAW	Union of Shop Distributive and Allied Workers
USM	Unlisted Securities Market
USMA	United States Military Academy
USMC	United States Marine Corps
USN	United States Navy
USNR	United States Naval Reserve
USPG	United Society for the Propagation of the Gospel
USPHS	United States Public Health Service
USPS	United States Postal Service
USS	United States Ship
USSR	Union of Soviet Socialist Republics
USVI	United States Virgin Islands
UT	Utah (postal)
UTC	University Training Corps
UTS	University of Technology, Sydney
UU	Ulster Unionist

UUK	Universities UK
UUUC	United Ulster Unionist Coalition
UUUP	United Ulster Unionist Party
UWCC	University of Wales College of Cardiff
UWCM	University of Wales College of Medicine
UWE	University of the West of England
UWIC	University of Wales Institute, Cardiff
UWIST	University of Wales Institute of Science and Technology
UWP	United Workers' Party (Dominica)
UWT	Union of Women Teachers

V

V	Five (Roman numerals); Version; Vicar; Viscount; Vice
v	*versus* (against)
v or vid.	*vide* (see)
VA	Virginia (postal)
Va	Virginia
VAD	Voluntary Aid Detachment
V&A	Victoria and Albert
VAT	Value Added Tax
VC	Victoria Cross; Voluntary Controlled
VCAS	Vice Chief of the Air Staff
VCDS	Vice Chief of the Defence Staff
VCGS	Vice Chief of the General Staff
VCNS	Vice Chief of the Naval Staff
VCT	Venture Capital Trust
VD	Royal Naval Volunteer Reserve Officers' Decoration (*now* VRD); Volunteer Officers' Decoration; Victorian Decoration
VDC	Volunteer Defence Corps
Ven.	Venerable
Vet.	Veterinary
VetMB	Bachelor of Veterinary Medicine
VG	Vicar-General
Vic	Victoria
Vice Adm.	Vice Admiral
Visc.	Viscount
VLSI	Very Large Scale Integration
VM	Victory Medal
VMA	Fixed Wing Marine Attack
VMH	Victoria Medal of Honour (Royal Horticultural Society)
VMI	Virginia Military Institute
VMSM	Voluntary Medical Services Medal
Vol.	Volume; Voluntary; Volunteers
VP	Vice-President
VPP	Volunteer Political Party
VPRP	Vice-President, Royal Society of Portrait Painters
VQMG	Vice-Quartermaster-General
VR	*Victoria Regina* (Queen Victoria); Volunteer Reserve
VRD	Royal Naval Volunteer Reserve Officers' Decoration
VRSM	Volunteer Reserves Service Medal
VSO	Voluntary Service Overseas
VT	Vermont (postal)
Vt	Vermont
VUP	Vanguard Unionist Party
VVD	Volkspartij voor Vrijheiden Democratie

W

W	West
WA	Western Australia; Washington (postal)
WAAF	Women's Auxiliary Air Force (later WRAF)
WACL	Women in Advertising and Communications, London
WAOS	Welsh Agricultural Organisations Society
Wash	Washington State
WCC	World Council of Churches
W/Cdr	Wing Commander
WCMD	Welsh College of Music and Drama (*now see* RWCMD)
WDA	Welsh Development Agency
WEA	Workers' Educational Association; Royal West of England Academy

WEU	Western European Union
WFEO	World Federation of Engineering Organisations
WFSW	World Federation of Scientific Workers
WFTU	World Federation of Trade Unions
WhF	Whitworth Fellow
WHO	World Health Organization
WhSch	Whitworth Scholar
WI	West Indies; Women's Institute; Wisconsin (postal)
Wilts	Wiltshire
WIPO	World Intellectual Property Organization
Wis	Wisconsin
Wits	Witwatersrand
WJEC	Welsh Joint Education Committee
WLA	Women's Land Army
WLD	Women Liberal Democrats
WLF	Women's Liberal Federation
Wm	William
WMA	World Medical Association
WMO	World Meteorological Organization
WNO	Welsh National Opera
WO	War Office; Warrant Officer
Worcs	Worcestershire
WOSB	War Office Selection Board
WR	West Riding; Western Region (BR)
WRAC	Women's Royal Army Corps
WRAF	Women's Royal Air Force
WRNS	Women's Royal Naval Service
WRVS	Women's Royal Voluntary Service
WS	Writer to the Signet
WSAVA	World Small Animal Veterinary Association
WSET	Wine and Spirits Educational Trust
WSPA	World Society for the Protection of Animals
WSPU	Women's Social and Political Union
WTO	World Trade Organisation
WUS	World University Service
WV	West Virginia (postal)
WVS	Women's Voluntary Services (*now see* WRVS)
WWF	World Wide Fund for Nature (*formerly* World Wildlife Fund)
WY	Wyoming (postal)

X

X	Ten (Roman numerals)
XO	Executive Officer

Y

y	youngest
YC	Young Conservative
YCNAC	Young Conservatives National Advisory Committee
Yeo.	Yeomanry
YES	Youth Enterprise Scheme
YHA	Youth Hostels Association
YMCA	Young Men's Christian Association
YOI	Young Offenders Institute
Yorks	Yorkshire
YPTES	Young People's Trust for Endangered Species
yr	younger
yrs	years
YT	Yukon Territory (postal)
YTS	Youth Training Scheme
YVFF	Young Volunteer Force Foundation
YWCA	Young Women's Christian Association

Z

ZANU PF	Zimbabwe African National Union Patriotic Front
ZAPU	Zimbabwe African People's Union

ADDENDA

The following biographies are of those whose deaths occurred before 31 December 2000, but were not reported until after the volume of *Who Was Who* covering the years 1996–2000 had been published.

ALLAN, (Charles) Lewis (Cuthbert), CEng, FICE, FIEE, FIMgt; Chairman, South of Scotland Electricity Board, 1967–73 (Deputy Chairman, 1964–67); Member, North of Scotland Hydro-Electric Board, 1967–73; *b* 22 July 1911; *s* of Charles W. Allan, Edinburgh, and Isabella H. Young; *m* 1938, Kathleen Mary Robinson, Chesterfield, Derbyshire; one *s* three *d. Educ:* Merchiston Castle School, Edinburgh; Pembroke College, Cambridge (Mechanical Sciences Tripos; MA). Bruce Peebles & Co. Ltd, Edinburgh, 1933–35; Balfour Beatty & Co. Ltd, 1935–38; Central Electricity Board, 1938–41; Ipswich Corp. Electric Supply and Transport Dept, 1941–44; North of Scotland Hydro-Electric Board, 1944–63 (Chief Electrical and Mechanical Engineer, 1954–63). *Publications:* articles in the electrical technical press and for World Power Conference. *Recreations:* gardening, walking, fishing, piping, Church work.
Died 9 Aug. 2000.

ALLAN, Lewis; *see* Allan, C. L. C.

ANDERSON, Hon. Sir Kevin (Victor); Kt 1980; Judge of the Supreme Court of Victoria, 1969–84; *b* 4 Sept. 1912; *s* of Robert Victor Anderson and Margaret Anderson (*née* Collins); *m* 1942, Claire Margaret Murphy; six *d. Educ:* Xavier Coll., Kew; Melbourne Univ. (LLB). Victorian Crown Law Dept, 1929–42: Courts Branch, 1929–35; Professional Asst, Crown Solicitor's Office, 1935–42; Lt, RAN, 1942–46; Victorian Bar, 1946–69; QC (Victoria) 1962. Chm., Bd of Inquiry into Scientology, 1963–65. Chm., Victorian Bar Council, 1966–67; Treasurer, Australian Law Council, 1966–68. Kt, Australian Assoc. of SMO of Malta, 1979. *Publications:* Stamp Duties in Victoria, 1949, 2nd edn 1968; joint author: Price Control, 1947; Landlord and Tenant Law, 1948, 3rd edn 1958; Victorian Licensing Law, 1952; Victoria Police Manual, 1956, 2nd edn 1969; Workers' Compensation, 1958, 2nd edn 1966; Fossil in the Sandstone: the Recollecting Judge, 1986; (ed) Victorian Law Reports, 1956–69. *Recreations:* yachting, woodworking. *Address:* PO Box 5081, Glenferrie South, Vic 3122, Australia. *Clubs:* Victoria Racing, Celtic, Essoign (Melbourne). *Died 14 Oct. 1999.*

ARMOUR, Mary Nicol Neill, RSA 1958 (ARSA 1940); RSW 1956; RGI 1977 (Vice-President, 1982; Hon. President, 1983); Teacher of Still Life, Glasgow School of Art, 1952–62 (Hon. Life President, 1982); *b* 27 March 1902; *d* of William Steel; *m* 1927, William Armour, RSA, RSW, RGI (*d* 1979). *Educ:* Glasgow Sch. of Art (Hon. Fellow 1993). Has exhibited at Royal Academy, Royal Scottish Academy, Soc. of Scottish Artists, and Royal Glasgow Institute. Work in permanent collections: Glasgow Municipal Gallery; Edinburgh Corporation; Art Galleries of Aberdeen, Perth, Dundee, Newport, Paisley, Greenock and Victoria (Australia). Fellow, Paisley Coll. of Technol., 1989; Hon. Life Vice Pres., Paisley Inst., 1983. Diploma, Paisley Art Inst., 1995. Hon. LLD Glasgow, 1980. *Recreations:* weaving, gardening. *Address:* Priory Park Private Residential Home, 19 Main Road, Castlehead, Paisley PA2 6AJ. *T:* (0141) 848 1718.
Died 5 July 2000.

BAKER, Wallis James, CB 1989; Chairman, Land Administration Commission, Queensland, 1983–89, retired; *b* 19 March 1931; *s* of James Campbell Baker and Doris Isabel (*née* Nowland); *m* 1960, Eileen Merle Seeney; one *s* one *d. Educ:* Downlands Coll., Toowoomba, Qld. Admitted Solicitor, Supreme Court of Qld, 1954, re-admitted, 1990; called to the Bar, Qld, 1969. Practised as Solicitor, Monto, Qld, 1955–68; entered Qld Public Service as career public servant, 1968. *Recreations:* tennis, ancient history, rock collecting. *Address:* 40 Hughes Avenue, Main Beach, Qld 4217, Australia. *T:* (7) 55280885. *Died 22 July 1999.*

BATE, Sir (Walter) Edwin, Kt 1969; OBE 1955; Barrister, Solicitor and Notary Public, Hastings, New Zealand, 1927-84; *b* 12 March 1901; *s* of Peter and Florence Eleanor Bate; *m* 1925, Louise Jordan; two *s* one *d. Educ:* Victoria Univ., Wellington (LLM (first class hons), 1922). Admitted Barrister and Solicitor, 1922; practised: Taumarunui, NZ, 1923-27; Hastings, NZ, 1927-84 (Partner, Simpson and Bate). Mayor, City of Hastings, NZ, 1953–59; Chm., Hawke Bay Hosp. Bd, 1941–74; Pres., Hosp. Bds Assoc. of NZ, 1953–74; Pres., Associated Trustee Savings Banks of NZ, 1968 and 1969. OStJ 1961. Grand Master of Freemasons in NZ, 1972–74. *Recreation:* gardening. *Address:* 38 Busby Hill, Havelock North, New Zealand. *T:* (6) 8777448. *Died 12 Sept. 1999.*

BELLAMY, Alexander William; Senior Legal Assistant, Council on Tribunals, 1967–76, retired (temporary Legal Assistant, 1963–67); *b* Aug. 1909; *m* 1931, Lena Marie Lauga Massy. *Educ:* Mill Hill Sch.; Clare Coll., Cambridge. Called to the Bar, Gray's Inn, 1934; practised at the Bar, London, 1934–38; Magistrate, Straits Settlements and FMS, 1938; Penang & Province Wellesley Volunteer Force, 1940–42; escaped from Singapore in 1942; seconded as District Magistrate, Gold Coast, 1942; legal staff, Malaya Planning Unit, WO, 1944; SO2 (Legal), SEAC, 1944; SO1 British Mil. Admin (Malaya), 1945; Pres., Superior Court, Penang, 1945; released from mil. service overseas, 1946, with Hon. rank of Lt Col; Crown Counsel, Singapore, 1946; District Judge (Civil), Singapore, 1948; District Judge and 1st Magistrate, Singapore, 1952; Actg Puisne Judge, Fedn of Malaya, 1953–54; Puisne Judge, Supreme Court, Nigeria, 1955; Actg Chief Justice, High Court of Lagos and Southern Cameroons, 1959, 1960; Actg Chief Justice, High Court of Lagos, 1961; a Judge of High Court of Lagos and Southern Cameroons, 1955–62. *Died 3 Dec. 1999.*

BIERICH, Marcus; Chairman, Supervisory Board, Robert Bosch GmbH, Stuttgart, since 1993 (Chairman, Board of Management, 1984–93); *b* 29 April 1926. *Educ:* Univs of Münster and Hamburg (PhD 1951; studies in mathematics, science and philosophy). Bankhaus Delbrück Schickler & Co., 1951–61; Director 1961–67; Mem. Bd of Management 1967–80, Mannesmann AG, Düsseldorf; Chief Financial Officer and Mem. Bd of Management, Allianz Versicherungs-AG, München, 1980–84. Hon. Dr rer. oec Univ. of Bochum, 1977. *Address:* Robert Bosch GmbH, PO Box 10 06 28, 70005 Stuttgart, Germany.
Died 25 Nov. 2000.

BISSELL, Claude Thomas, CC 1969; PhD; FRSC 1957; Professor, University of Toronto, 1971–83, then Emeritus (President of the University, 1958–71); *b* 10 Feb. 1916; *m* 1945, Christina Flora Gray; one *d. Educ:* Univ. of Toronto (BA 1936, MA 1937); Cornell Univ. (PhD 1940). Instructor in English, Cornell, 1938–41; Lecturer in

English, Toronto, 1941–42. Canadian Army, 1942–46; demobilised as Capt. University of Toronto: Asst Prof. of English, 1947–51; Assoc. Prof. of English, 1951–56; Prof. of English, 1962; Asst to Pres., 1948–52; Vice-Pres., 1952–56; Dean in Residence, University Coll., 1946–56; Pres., Carleton Univ., Ottawa, 1956–58. Chairman: The Canada Council, 1960–62; Canadian Universities Foundation, 1962–; President: Nat. Conference of Canadian Universities and Colleges, 1962–; World University Service of Canada, 1962–63. Vis. Prof. of Canadian Studies, Harvard, 1967–68. Aggrey-Fraser-Guggisberg Meml Lectr, Ghana Univ., 1976. Hon. DLitt: Manitoba, 1958; W Ontario, 1971; Lethbridge, 1972; Leeds, 1976; Toronto, 1977; Hon. LLD: McGill, 1958; Queen's, 1959; New Brunswick, 1960; Carleton, 1960; Montreal, 1960; St Lawrence, 1962; British Columbia, 1962; Michigan, 1963; Columbia, 1965; Laval, 1966; Prince of Wales Coll., 1967; Windsor, 1968; St Andrews, 1972. *Publications:* (ed) University College, A Portrait, 1853–1953, 1953; (ed) Canada's Crisis in Higher Education, 1957; (ed) Our Living Tradition, 1957; (ed) Great Canadian Writing, 1966; The Strength of the University, 1968; Halfway up Parnassus, 1974; The Humanities in the University, 1977; The Young Vincent Massey, 1981; The Imperial Canadian, 1986; Ernest Buckler Remembered, 1989; articles on literary subjects in Canadian and American jls. *Address:* 229 Erskine Avenue, Toronto, ON M4P 1Z5, Canada. *Clubs:* Arts and Letters, York (Toronto); Cercle Universitaire (Ottawa).
Died 21 June 2000.

BOTHA, Matthys Izak; South African Diplomat, retired; *b* 31 Oct. 1913; *s* of Johan Hendrik Jacobus Botha and Anna Botha (*née* Joubert); *m* 1940, Hester le Roux (*née* Bosman); two *s*. *Educ:* Selborne Coll.; Pretoria Univ. (BA, LLB). Called to the Transvaal Bar. Dept of Finance, Pretoria, 1931–44; S African Embassy, Washington, 1944–51; S African Permanent Mission to UN, NY, 1951–54; Head, Political Div., Dept of Foreign Affairs, Pretoria, 1955–59; Envoy Extraordinary and Minister Plenipotentiary, Switzerland, 1959–60; Minister, London, 1960–62; Ambassador and Permanent Rep., UN, NY, 1962–70; Ambassador to: Canada, 1970–73; Italy, 1973–77 (also to Costa Rica and El Salvador, 1973–74, and to Panama, 1973–76); UK, 1977–78; Ciskei, 1983–85. Member: Simon Vanderstel Foundn; Huguenot Soc. Knight of Grand Cross, Order of Merit (Italy), 1977. *Recreations:* swimming, golfing, cycling. *Club:* Somerset West Country (near Cape Town). *Died 1 June 1999.*

BRAY, Sir Theodor (Charles), Kt 1975; CBE 1964; Director, Queensland Arts Council, 1976–99; Chancellor, Griffith University, Brisbane, 1975–85; *b* 11 Feb. 1905; *s* of Horace and Maude Bray; *m* 1931, Rosalie (*d* 1988), *d* of Rev. A. M. Trengove; three *s* two *d* (and one *s* one *d* decd). *Educ:* state schs; Adelaide Univ. Apprentice Printer, Reporter, Register, Adelaide; Sub-editor, Chief Sub-editor, The Argus, Melbourne; Editor (26 yrs), Editor-in-Chief, Courier-Mail, Brisbane, 1942–68; Jt Man. Dir, Queensland Newspapers Pty Ltd, 1936–70, Dir, 1956–80; Chm., Australian Associated Press, 1968–70. Mem., Aust. Council for the Arts, 1969–73; Aust. Chm., Internat. Press Inst., 1962–70. Chm., Griffith Univ. Council, 1970–75. *Recreations:* bowls, travel. *Address:* 10/64 Macquarie Street, St Lucia, Qld 4067, Australia. *T:* (7) 38707442. *Clubs:* Queensland, Queensland University Staff (Brisbane).
Died 10 Aug. 2000.

BROUGHTON, Leonard; DL; Member, Lancashire County Council, 1974–89 (Chairman and Leader, 1974–81); *b* 21 March 1924; *s* of Charles Cecil Broughton and Florence (*née* Sunman); *m* 1949, Kathleen Gibson; one *d*. *Educ:* Kingston-upon-Hull. Served RASC, 1942–47. Estates Manager, Bedford Borough Council, 1957; businessman. Member: Blackpool County Borough Council, 1961–74 (Leader, 1968–73); Blackpool Bor. Council, 1974–79; NW Co. Boroughs' Assoc., 1968–74; NW Economic Planning Council, 1970–72; Assoc. of Co.

Councils, 1973–77; Board, Central Lancs Develt Corp., 1976–84. Mem. Court, Lancaster and Salford Univs, 1974–81; Vice-President: Lancs Youth Clubs Assoc., 1974–81; NW Arts Assoc., 1974–81; Blackpool Social Service Council, 1974–84; Chm., Blackpool and Fylde Civilian Disabled Soc., 1964–84. Freeman, Co. Borough of Blackpool, 1973. DL Lancs, 1975; High Sheriff of Lancashire, 1983–84. *Recreations:* gardening, overseas travel. *Address:* 14 The Grove, Cleveleys, Blackpool, Lancs FY5 2JD. *T:* (01253) 822886. *Died 29 May 2000.*

BROWN, Alexander Cosens Lindsay, CB 1980; Chief Veterinary Officer, Ministry of Agriculture, Fisheries and Food, 1973–80; *b* Glasgow, 30 Jan. 1920; *s* of William Tait Brown and Margaret Rae; *m* 1945, Mary McDougal Hutchison; two *s*. *Educ:* Hutchesons' Grammar Sch., Glasgow; Glasgow Veterinary Coll. Diploma of RCVS; FRCVS 1980. Ministry of Agriculture, Fisheries and Food: appointed Vet. Officer to Dorset, 1943; Divisional Vet. Officer, HQ Tolworth, 1955; Divisional Vet. Officer, Essex, 1958–62; Dep. Regional Vet. Officer, W Midland Region, Wolverhampton, 1962–63; Regional Vet. Officer, Eastern Region, Cambridge, 1963; HQ Tolworth, 1967; Dep. Dir, Veterinary Field Services, 1969–70, Dir, 1970–73. Mem. ARC, 1975–80. *Publications:* contribs to Jl of Royal Soc. of Medicine, Veterinary Record, State Veterinary Jl. *Recreations:* gardening, swimming, reading. *Address:* 29 Ashwood Park, Fetcham, Leatherhead, Surrey KT22 9NT. *T:* (01372) 457997. *Died 23 July 1999.*

BROWN, Robert Burnett; Associate, PE-International and Public Administration International, since 1996; *b* 10 Aug. 1942; *s* of late David Brown and of Isabella Dow; *m* 1972, Anne Boschetti. *Educ:* Kirkcaldy High Sch.; Edinburgh Univ. (1st cl. Hons BSc Chemistry). Min. of Social Security, 1967; DHSS, 1971–83; Cabinet Office and HM Treasury, 1983–87; DHSS and DSS, 1987–89; Under Sec., DSS, 1989–96. *Recreations:* jazz, rock and roll, football, Greece. *Died 11 Oct. 1998.*

BUCHANAN, Sir Charles Alexander James L.; see Leith-Buchanan.

BURDEN, 3rd Baron *cr* 1950, of Hazlebarrow, Derby; **Andrew Philip Burden;** *b* 20 July 1959; *e s* of 2nd Baron Burden and of Audrey Elsworth, *d* of Maj. W. E. Sykes; S father, 1995; *m* 1985, Jane Whaites (marr. diss. 1991). *Heir:* *b* Hon. Fraser William Elsworth Burden, *b* 6 Nov. 1964.
Died 23 April 2000.

BYERS, Sir Maurice (Hearne), Kt 1982; CBE 1978; QC (Aust.) 1960; barrister; Solicitor-General of Australia, 1973–83; Chairman, Australian Constitutional Commission, 1986–88; *b* 10 Nov. 1917; *s* of Arthur Tolhurst Byers and Mabel Florence Byers (*née* Hearne); *m* 1949, Patricia Therese Davis; two *s* one *d*. *Educ:* St Aloysius Coll., Milson's Point, Sydney; Sydney Univ. (LLB). Called to the Bar, NSW, 1944. Mem., Exec. Council, Law Council of Australia, 1966–68; Vice-Pres., NSW Bar Assoc., 1964–65, Pres., 1965–67. Leader, Australian delegations to: UN Commn on Internat. Trade Law, 1974, 1976–82; Diplomatic Conf. on Sea Carriage of Goods, Hamburg, 1979. Chm., Police Bd of NSW, 1984–88; Mem., Australian Law Reform Commn, 1984–85. Mem. Council, ANU, 1975–78. *Address:* 3 Kardinia Road, Clifton Gardens, NSW 2088, Australia. *T:* (2) 99698257. *Died 16 Jan. 1999.*

CHAYTOR, Sir George Reginald, 8th Bt *cr* 1831, of Croft, Yorkshire and Witton Castle, Durham; *b* 28 Oct. 1912; *s* of William Richard Carter Chaytor (*d* 1973) (*g s* of 2nd Bt) and Anna Laura (*d* 1947), *d* of George Fawcett; S cousin, Sir William Henry Clervaux Chaytor, 7th Bt, 1976. *Heir:* *cousin* Bruce Gordon Chaytor [*b* 31 July 1949; *m* 1969, Rosemary Lea, *d* of Reid Stephen; one *s* one *d*]. *Died 3 June 1999.*

COHEN, Lt-Col Nathan Leslie, OBE 1990; CPM 1956; TD 1949; JP; Judge of HM Court of Sovereign Base Areas of Akrotiri and Dhekalia, Cyprus, 1960–67; *b* 13 Jan. 1908; *s* of Reuben and Maud Cohen; unmarried. *Educ:* Stockton-on-Tees Grammar Sch.; Clifton Coll. In private practice as a Solicitor until 1939; called to the Bar, Lincoln's Inn, 1954. War Service, Aug. 1939–May 1945. Senior Legal Officer (Lt-Col), Military Govt, Carinthia, Austria, 1945–49; Pres. of Sessions Courts, Malaya, 1949–57; Justice of the Special Courts, Cyprus, 1958–59. Adjudicator under Immigration Appeals Act, 1970–71. Mem., Cleveland Co. Social Services Cttee 1978–80. Dist Hd, Forces Relief Soc., Stockton, 1975; Vice-President: Northern Area, Royal British Legion; Cleveland British Red Cross Soc.; Patron, Durham and Cleveland Royal British Legion, 1985–; President: Stockton Physically Handicapped Club, 1990–; St John Ambulance Assoc., Stockton and Thornaby. Hon. Mem., Stockton-on-Tees Rotary Club. JP Stockton-on-Tees, 1967. Freedom, Stockton-on-Tees, 1991. Diamond Jubilee Medal (Johore), 1955; Royal Brit. Legion Gold Badge, 1979; British Red Cross Badge of Honour, 1981, Voluntary Medical Service Medal, 1982; Service Medal, Order of St John, 1993; Paul Harris Fellowship Award, Rotary Club, 1997. SBStJ 1980. *Recreations:* travelling, reading. *Address:* 646 Yarm Road, Eaglescliffe TS16 0DH. *T:* (01642) 645485. *Club:* Royal Over-Seas League.

Died 27 Sept. 2000.

CONDON, Denis David, OBE 1964; Senior Representative at Lloyd's of London for Neilson McCarthy, Consultants, 1968–75; *b* 23 Oct. 1910; *s* of Capt. D. Condon and Mrs A. E. Condon; *m* 1933, Mary Marson; one *d. Educ:* Paston Grammar Sch., North Walsham, Norfolk. Journalist until 1939. War Service with Royal Artillery, UK and Burma (Major). Joined India Office, 1946; CRO, 1947; served India, Ceylon, Australia, Nigeria; Head of News Dept, CO, 1967–68. *Recreations:* fishing, bird-watching, gardening. *Address:* 3 Market Close, Brushford, Dulverton, Somerset TA22 9AG. *T:* (01398) 23309. *Clubs:* Gymkhana (Delhi); Australasian Pioneers (Sydney). *Died 6 June 2000.*

COPE, Hon. James Francis, CMG 1978; Speaker of the Australian House of Representatives, 1973–75; *b* 26 Nov. 1907; *s* of G. E. Cope; *m* 1931, Myrtle Irene, *d* of S. J. Hurst; one *d. Educ:* Crown Street Public Sch., NSW. Hon. Treaurer, NSW Br., Aust. Glass Workers' Union; Delegate to Federal Council, 1953–55. MHR (Lab) for divs of: Cook, 1955; Watson, 1955–69; Sydney, 1969–75. *Recreations:* billiards, horse racing, cricket, football. *Address:* 1/38–40 Fontainebleau Street, Sans Souci, NSW 2219, Australia. *Died 3 Feb. 1999.*

CRUMP, Rt Rev. William Henry Howes; Bishop of Saskatchewan, 1960–71; *b* London, Ontario, Canada, 13 March 1903; *m* 1st, 1932, Betty Margaret Dean Thomas; one *s* one *d*; 2nd, 1964, Rose (*d* 1992). *Educ:* London, Ontario; Univ. of Western Ontario; Huron Coll.; Trinity Coll., Toronto. Ordained Deacon, 1926, Priest, 1927. Curate, Wawanesa, Manitoba, 1926; Rector: Glenboro, Manitoba, 1927; Holland, Manitoba, 1931; Boissevain, Manitoba, 1933; St Aidan's, Winnipeg, 1933–44; Christ Church, Calgary, 1944–60; Canon of St Paul, Dio. of Calgary, 1949. *Died 1995.*

da COSTA, Harvey Lloyd, CMG 1962; Judge of Appeal, Court of Appeal for Bermuda, 1982–96; *b* 8 Dec. 1914; *s* of John Charles and Martha da Costa. *Educ:* Calabar High Sch., Jamaica; London Univ. (BA Hons 1938); St Edmund Hall, Oxford (Sen. Exhibnr; Rhodes Schol.; BA Hons 1942; MA, BLitt 1952). Called to the Bar, Gray's Inn, 1944; practised at Chancery Bar, 1950–52; Crown Counsel, Jamaica, 1952–54; Sen. Crown Counsel, Jamaica, 1954–56; Asst Attorney-Gen., Jamaica, 1956–59; QC Jamaica 1959; Attorney-Gen. of West Indies, 1959–62; practised Private Bar, Jamaica, 1962–77; Puisne Judge, 1978–80, Chief Justice, 1980–81, Bahamas Supreme Court; Judge of Appeal, Court of Appeal for Bahamas, 1982–85. Mem., Anguilla, British Virgin Is and Seychelles Commns. Hon. LLD Univ. of W Indies, 1990.

Recreation: swimming. *Address:* c/o Court of Appeal, Hamilton HM12, Bermuda. *Died 17 Sept. 2000.*

de PURY, David; Co-Founder and Chairman, de Pury, Pictet, Turrettini & Co. Ltd, since 1996; *b* 4 Dec. 1943; *s* of Jean Jacques de Pury and Marguerite de Pury (*née* Miescher); *m* 1991, Maria Eugenia Echeverria. *Educ:* Geneva Univ. (law degree). Attorney; Mem., Geneva Bar. Swiss Diplomatic Service, 1970–91: served in Washington, Mission to EC in Brussels, The Hague and Berne; Ambassador Plenipotentiary and Delegate of Swiss Govt for Trade Agreements, 1986–91; Chm., OECD Trade Cttee, 1989–91; Gov. for Switzerland, Inter-American Develt Bank, 1987–88. Co-Chm., ABB Asea Brown Boveri Gp, 1992–96; Chairman: Brown Boveri Ltd, 1992–96; EIC Electricity Investment Co., 1997–; Le Temps daily newspaper, 1998–; Electrowatt Engineering; Director: Ciba-Geigy, 1992–96; UNOTEC, 1992–97; Nestlé, 1993–; Gpe Schneider (Paris), 1997–; Jaakko Pöyry Gp (Helsinki); Zurich Financial Services Gp. Member, European Advisory Board: Schroders; Air Products. Member: Eur. Roundtable of Industrialists, 1994–96; Council, World Economic Forum; Exec. Cttee, Geneva Grad. Inst. for Internat. Studies, 1993–. Trustee, Internat. Crisis Gp, 1997–. Vice Chm., Internat. Fest. of Music, Lucerne. *Publications:* numerous articles in Swiss and internat. papers and jls. *Recreations:* ski-ing, tennis, music. *Address:* de Pury, Pictet, Turrettini & Co., Postfach 8242, 8050 Zurich, Switzerland. *T:* (1) 3183401, *Fax:* (1) 3183411. *Died 26 Dec. 2000.*

DICKINSON, Sir Ben; *see* Dickinson, Sir S. B.

DICKINSON, Sir Samuel Benson, (Sir Ben), Kt 1980; Chairman, Burmine Pty Ltd, 1985–88; Mining Advisor to South Australian Government, 1975–84; *b* 1 Feb. 1912; *s* of Sydney Rushbrook Dickinson and Margaret Dickinson (*née* Clemes); *m* 1960, Dorothy Joan Weidenhofer; three *s* one *d. Educ:* Haileybury Coll., Melbourne; Univ. of Melbourne (MSc). N Australia Aerial Geological and Geophysical Survey, 1935–36; geologist: Electrolytic Zinc, Mt Lyell, Mt Isa, mining cos, 1937–41; S Australian Geological Survey, 1941–42; Dir of Mines, Govt Geologist, Sec. to Minister of Mines, Dep. Controller, Mineral Production, Chm., Radium Hill Mines, 1943–56; Director: Rio Tinto Mining Co. of Australia, 1956–60; Sir Frank Duval's Gp of Cos, 1960–62; Chief Technical Advr, Pechiney Australia, 1962–65; Project Manager, Clutha Development Ltd and Daniel K. Ludwig Cos Australia, 1965–75. Chm., South Australian Govt Uranium Enrichment Cttee, 1979–84. *Publications:* technical reports for Australian Dept of Mines, Inst. of Mining and Metallurgy and mining jls and bulletins. *Recreations:* correspondence, media writing. *Address:* 21 Tiers Road, PO Box 321, Woodside, SA 5244, Australia. *T:* (8) 83899069. *Clubs:* Athenæum (Melbourne); American National (Sydney). *Died 2 Feb. 2000.*

DIXON, Stanley; Chairman, Midland-Yorkshire Tar Distillers Ltd, 1968–71; *b* 12 Aug. 1900; *m* 1936, Ella Margaret Hogg; two *s. Educ:* Leeds Grammar Sch.; Queen's Coll., Oxford. Articled to Leather & Veale, Chartered Accountants in Leeds, 1924–27; Manager, Leather & Veale (later Peat, Marwick, Mitchell & Co.), Leeds, 1927–35; Sec., Midland Tar Distillers Ltd, 1935–66; Dir, Midland Tar Distillers Ltd (later Midland-Yorkshire Holdings Ltd), 1943–71. Pres., Inst. of Chartered Accountants in England and Wales, 1968–69. Hon. DSocSc Birmingham, 1972. *Publications:* The Case for Marginal Costing, 1967; The Art of Chairing a Meeting, 1975. *Recreations:* Church affairs, gardening, music. *Address:* 83 Norton Road, Stourbridge, West Midlands DY8 2TB. *T:* (01384) 395672.

Died Sept. 2000.

DOCHERTY, Dr Daniel Joseph; JP; General Medical Practitioner, 1949–87, retired; Examining Medical Officer, Department of Health and Social Security, 1982–86; *b* 24 Oct. 1924; *s* of Michael Joseph Docherty and Ellen Stewart; *m* 1952, Dr Rosemary Catherine Kennedy; eight *s* two *d*. *Educ:* St Aloysius' Coll.; Anderson Coll. of Medicine; Glasgow Univ. LRCP, LRCS, LRFPS. MO, King's Flight, RAF Benson, 1950. Glasgow Town Councillor, 1959–75; Sen. Magistrate, City of Glasgow, 1964–65; Chairman: Police Cttee, 1967–68; Educn Cttee, 1971–74. Mem., MSC, 1974–77; Chm. in Scotland, Job Creation Programme, 1975–78. Member: Strathclyde Univ. Ct, 1971–72; Glasgow Univ. Ct, 1972–74; Council, Open Univ., 1972–75. JP Glasgow, 1961. *Recreation:* travel. *Address:* 1a Briar Gardens, Briar Road, Glasgow G43 2TF. *T:* (0141) 637 5005.   *Died 22 Aug. 1998.*

du PLESSIS, Prof. Daniel Jacob, FRCS; Vice-Chancellor and Principal, University of the Witwatersrand, 1978–83; *b* 17 May 1918; *s* of D. J. du Plessis and L. du Plessis (*née* Carstens); *m* 1946, Louisa Susanna Wicht; two *s*. *Educ:* Univ. of Cape Town (MB ChB 1941; Hon. Fellow, Smuts Hall, 1986); Univ. of the Witwatersrand (ChM 1951). Served, SA Medical Corps, 1942–46. Postgrad. study, 1947–51; Surgeon and Lectr, Univ. of Cape Town, 1952–58; Prof. of Surgery, Univ. of the Witwatersrand, 1958–77. Trustee, S African Blood Transfusion Service, 1985–. Pres., S Transvaal Br., Medical Assoc. of S Africa, 1986–87; Chairman of Council: B. G. Alexander Nursing Coll., 1985–95; Bonalesedi (formerly Natalspruit) Nursing Coll., 1985–92; Member: Council, Med. Univ. of Southern Africa, 1986–95; Adv. Council for Univs and Technikons, 1984–92; Council, Johannesburg Coll. of Educn, 1984–92; Council, Univ. of Transkei, 1989–94. Dir, Transvaal Bd, Provincial Bldg Soc., 1984–91. Governor, Amer. Coll. of Surgeons, 1988–94. Hon. Life Vice-President: Assoc. of Surgeons of S Africa; Surgical Res. Soc. of Southern Africa. Hon. FACS 1974; Hon. Fellow: Assoc. of Surgeons of GB and Ireland, 1979; Amer. Surgical Assoc., 1981; Hon. FCSSA 1982. Paul Harris Fellowship, Rotary Club, Orange Grove, Johannesburg, 1984. Hon. Mem., Alpha Omega Alpha Honor Med. Soc. (USA), 1986. Hon. LLD Witwatersrand, 1984; Hon. MD Cape Town, 1986; Hon. DSc Med. Univ. of Southern Africa, 1995. Order for Meritorious Service Cl. 1 (Gold), RSA, 1989. *Publications:* Principles of Surgery, 1968, 2nd edn 1976; Synopsis of Surgical Anatomy, 10th edn (with A. Lee McGregor) 1969, 11th edn 1975, 12th edn (with G. A. G. Decker) 1986; numerous articles in learned jls on surgical topics, esp. on diseases of parotid salivary gland and gastric ulcers. *Address:* 17 Chateau Road, Richmond, Johannesburg, 2092, South Africa.
      Died 11 Sept. 1999.

EKLUND, Dr (Arne) Sigvard; Director General, International Atomic Energy Agency, Vienna, 1961–81, then Emeritus; *b* Kiruna, Sweden, 19 June 1911; *m* 1941, Anna-Greta Johansson; one *s* two *d*. *Educ:* Uppsala Univ., Sweden (DSc 1946). Assoc. Prof. in Nuclear Physics, Royal Inst. of Technology, Stockholm, 1946–56; Dir of Research, 1950–56; Dir of Reactor Development Div., 1957–61, Swedish Atomic Energy Co., subseq. AB Atomenergi. Conference Sec.-Gen., 2nd Internat. UN Conf. on Peaceful Uses of Atomic Energy, 1958. Fellow, Amer. Nuclear Soc., 1961 (Hon. Life Mem., 1992); Member: Royal Swedish Acad. of Engineering Sciences, 1953; Royal Swedish Acad. of Sciences, 1972; New York Acad. of Scis, 1995; Hon. Member: British Nuclear Energy Soc., 1963; European Nuclear Soc., 1982; Assoc. for Nuclear Technique, Stockholm, 1992; For. Associate, Nat. Acad. of Engineering, USA, 1979. Dr *hc*: Univ. of Graz, 1968; Acad. of Mining and Metallurgy, Cracow, 1971; Univ. of Bucarest, 1971; Chalmers Inst. of Technol., Gothenberg, 1974; Buenos Aires, Budapest, Columbia and Moscow Univs, 1977; Dresden Technical and Yon-sei, Seoul Univs, 1978; Nat. Agrarian Univ. of La Molina, Peru, 1979; Royal Inst. of Technol., Stockholm, 1980. (Jointly) Atoms for Peace Award, 1968; Golden Medal of Honour, Vienna, 1971; Henry DeWolf Smyth Nuclear Statesman Award, 1976; Exceptional Service Award, Amer. Nuclear Soc., 1980; Swedish Energy Prize, 1991.

Hon. Senator, Univ. of Vienna, 1977. Comdr, Order of St Gregory, bestowed by His Holiness Pope John Paul II, 1982. Kt Comdr, Order of North Star, Sweden, 1971; Das Grosse Goldene Ehrenzeichen am Bande für Verdienste, Austria, 1981; Das Grosse Verdienstkreuz mit Stern und Schulterband, FRG, 1981; Aquila Azteca en el Grado de Banda, Mexico, 1981; SPk, 1987; Grand Cordon, Order of the Sacred Treasure, Japan, 1991. *Publications:* Studies in Nuclear Physics, 1946 (Sweden); preface to Light Water Reactor Safety, by Bengt Pershagen, 1989; (contrib.) Future of Nuclear Power, ed Bo Södersten, 1991; articles on peaceful uses of nuclear energy. *Address:* Krapfenwaldgasse 48, 1190 Vienna, Austria. *T:* (1) 3202424, *Fax:* (1) 3208492. *Club:* Sällskapet (Stockholm).
      Died 30 Jan. 2000.

ELSE, John, MBE 1946; TD 1946; Regional Chairman of Industrial Tribunals, Eastern Region, Bury St Edmunds, 1980–84; *b* 9 Aug. 1911; *s* of late Mr and Mrs A. G. Else; *m* 1937, Eileen Dobson; one *d*. *Educ:* Cowley Sch., St Helens; Liverpool Univ. (LLB 1930). Admitted as solicitor, 1932. Commnd TA, 1932; served War: UK and BEF, 1939–41 (despatches, 1940); Iraq, 1942; India, 1942–45 (ADS GHQ, 1944–45). Practised in St Helens, London and Birmingham, 1932–39; Partner, Beale & Co., London and Birmingham, 1946–61. Mem., Mental Health Review Tribunal, 1960–61; Chm., Traffic Comrs and Licensing Authority for Goods Vehicles, W Midlands Traffic Area, 1961–72; Indust. Tribunals Chm., Birmingham, 1972–76; Cambridge, 1976–80. *Recreations:* photography, gardening. *Address:* The Cottage, Long Lane, Fowlmere, Royston, Herts SG8 7TA. *T:* (01763) 208367.   *Died 8 Sept. 1996.*

ELYAN, Prof. Sir (Isadore) Victor, Kt 1970; Professor of Law, and Dean of the Faculty of Law, Durban-Westville University, 1973–77, retired; Chief Justice of Swaziland, 1965–70, retired; *b* 5 Sept. 1909; *s* of Jacob Elyan, PC, JP and Olga Elyan; *m* 1st, 1939, Ivy Ethel Mabel Stuart-Weir (*d* 1965); no *c*; 2nd, 1966, Rosaleen Jeanette O'Shea. *Educ:* St Stephen's Green Sch., Dublin; Trinity Coll., Dublin (BA 1929, LLB 1931, MA 1932). Admitted a Solicitor of Supreme Court of Judicature, Ireland, 1930; Barrister-at-Law, King's Inns 1949, Middle Temple, 1952. Resident Magistrate, HM Colonial Legal Service, Gold Coast, 1946–54, Senior Magistrate, 1954–55; Judge of Appeal of the Court of Appeal for Basutoland, the Bechuanaland Protectorate and Swaziland, 1955–66; Judge, High Courts of Basutoland and the Bechuanaland Protectorate, 1955–65; on occasions acted: as Judge between 1953 and 1955, Gold Coast; as Justice of Appeal, West African Court of Appeal; and as Chief Justice of Basutoland, the Bechuanaland Protectorate and Swaziland, also Pres. Court of Appeal, during 1956, 1961 and 1964; Judge of Appeal: Court of Appeal for Botswana, 1966–70; Court of Appeal for Swaziland, 1967–70; Court of Appeal, Lesotho, 1968–70. Served War, 1942–46; attached to Indian Army, 1944–46; GSO2 Military Secretary's Branch (DAMS), 1945–46 in rank of Major. Mem., Internat. Adv. Bd, The African Law Reports, 1969. *Publications:* (ed) High Commission Territories Law Reports, 1956, 1957, 1958, 1959, 1960. *Recreation:* sailing. *Address:* PO Box 22001, Fish Hoek 7975, Cape, South Africa.
      Died 16 Feb. 2000.

EVANS, John Marten Llewellyn, CBE 1956 (MBE 1945); JP; Official Solicitor to the Supreme Court of Judicature, 1950–70; *b* 9 June 1909; *s* of late Marten Llewellyn Evans, solicitor, and Edith Helena (*née* Lile); *m* 1943, Winifred Emily, *y d* of late Austin Reed; one *s* one *d*. *Educ:* Rugby Sch.; Trinity Coll., Oxford. Admitted solicitor, 1935; Legal Asst to the Official Solicitor, 1937. Served War of 1939–45, Major RA. Senior Legal Asst to the Official Solicitor, 1947; Asst Master in Lunacy, 1950. Vice-Chm., Austin Reed Group Ltd, 1969–77. Master of Worshipful Company of Cutlers, 1967–68. JP City of London, 1969. *Recreations:* the theatre, cricket, golf, tennis.
      Died 4 April 1995.

FAGGE, Sir John William Frederick, 11th Bt *cr* 1660; *b* 28 Sept. 1910; *s* of late William Archibald Theodore Fagge (*b* of 9th Bt) and Nellie (*d* 1924), *d* of H. T. D. Wise; *S* uncle, 1940; *m* 1940, Ivy Gertrude (*d* 1992), *d* of William Edward Frier, 15 Church Lane, Newington, Kent; one *s* one *d. Heir: s* John Christopher Fagge [*b* 30 April 1942; *m* 1974, Evelyn Joy Golding]. *Address:* c/o 11 Forbes Road, Faversham, Kent ME13 8QF.   *Died 5 Oct. 2000.*

FARRAR, Rex Gordon, LVO 1975; HM Diplomatic Service, retired; Consultant, De La Rue Co. plc, since 1990 (Regional Director (Tokyo), 1985–90); *b* 22 Aug. 1925; *s* of late John Percival Farrar and Ethel Florence Farrar (*née* Leader); *m* 1st, 1955, Mary Katharine Shutts (*d* 1977); 2nd, 1978, Masako (*née* Ikeda); one *s* one *d. Educ:* Latymer's Sch., Edmonton; London Univ. (BA Hons History). Served Royal Navy, 1944–47. Joined HM Diplomatic Service, 1947; served, New Orleans, 1953–57; Jakarta, 1960–63; Caracas, 1964–68; San Salvador, 1968–71; Tokyo, 1971–75; Rangoon, 1978–80; Consul-Gen. and Dir of Trade Promotion, Osaka, Japan, 1980–85. *Recreations:* golf, tennis, studying Japanese. *Club:* Kobe (Japan).   *Deceased.*

FAWKES, Sir Randol (Francis), Kt 1977; attorney-at-law, Bahamas, 1948–89; *b* 20 March 1924; *s* of Edward Ronald Fawkes and Mildred Fawkes (*née* McKinney); *m* 1951, Jacqueline Fawkes (*née* Bethel); three *s* one *d. Educ:* public schs in the Bahamas. Called to the Bar, Bahamas, 1948. A founder: Citizen Cttee, 1949; People's Penny Savings Bank, 1951. Elected Mem. (Progressive Liberal Party), House of Assembly, 1956; promoted law establishing Labour Day as Public Holiday, 1961. Founder, Pres. 1955, and then Vice Pres., Bahamas Fedn of Labour (led 19 day general strike which resulted in major labour and political reforms, 1958). Represented Labour Party at constitutional confs in London, 1963 and 1968; addressed UN Cttee of 24 on preparation of Bahamas for independence, 1966. Gen Sec., Bahamas Assoc. of former Mems of Parlt, 1990. *Publications:* You Should Know Your Government, 1949; The Bahamas Government, 1962; The New Bahamas, 1966; The Faith That Moved The Mountain: a memoir of a life and the times, 1977; Majority of One: the first 450 of the PLP–Labour Coalition, 1987. *Recreations:* swimming, music, Bible tract writing. *Address:* PO Box N-7625, John F. Kennedy Drive, Nassau, NP, Bahamas. *T:* (328) 3277.   *Died 14 June 2000.*

FERRALL, Sir Raymond (Alfred), Kt 1982; CBE 1969; Master Warden, Port of Launceston Authority, 1960–80; *b* 27 May 1906; *s* of Alfred C. Ferrall and Edith M. Ferrall; *m* 1st, 1931, Lorna (decd), *d* of P. M. Findlay; two *s* two *d*; 2nd, 1988, Sallie Sinclair Barnett. *Educ:* Launceston C of E Grammar Sch. Chairman: Launceston Bank for Savings, 1976–82; Tasmanian Colls of Advanced Educn, 1977–81; Launceston C of E Grammar Sch. Bd, 1956–73. Captain, Tasmanian Cricket team, 1934; Vice Captain, Tasmanian Amateur Football team, 1932. Freeman, City of Launceston, 1981. Hon. DLitt Tasmania, 1999. Silver Jubilee Medal, 1977. *Publications:* Partly Personal, 1976; Idylls of the Mayor, 1978; Notable Tasmanians, 1980; The Age of Chiselry, 1981; The Story of the Port of Launceston, 1984; A Proud Heritage, 1985. *Recreations:* writing, print collecting, sailing. *Address:* Elphin House, 3 Olive Street, Launceston, Tas 7250, Australia. *T:* (3) 63317122. *Clubs:* Launceston, Northern, Tamar Yacht (Tasmania).   *Died 1 June 2000.*

FIRTH, Andrew Trevor; Regional Chairman, Industrial Tribunals, Yorkshire/Humberside, 1982–88 (Chairman, Industrial Tribunals, 1972–82); *b* 4 June 1922; *s* of Seth Firth and Amy Firth; *m* 1946, Nora Cornforth Armitage; one *s* two *d. Educ:* Prince Henry's Grammar Sch.; Leeds Univ. (LLB). Served RA, 6th Airborne Div., Normandy, 1944, Lieut; Intelligence Officer, Potsdam Conf., 1945, Captain; Rhine Army Coll., 1946, Major. Partner, later Sen. Partner, Barret Chamberlain & McDonnell, Solicitors, Harrogate, Otley, Leeds, 1948–72. Pres., Harrogate and Dist Law Soc., 1965–66; Area Chm., Law

Soc. Legal Aid Cttee, Yorkshire, 1969–72. Bronze Star Medal, USA, 1945. *Recreations:* Chippendale Soc. (Chm., 1972–87; Pres., 1999–), golf, grandchildren. *Address:* Chevin Close, Birdcage Walk, Otley, West Yorkshire LS21 3HB. *Club:* Otley Golf.   *Died 8 April 1999.*

FISHER, Harold Wallace; Director, 1959–69, and Vice-President, 1962–69, Exxon Corporation (formerly Standard Oil Company (New Jersey)) New York, retired; *b* 27 Oct. 1904; *s* of Dean Wallace Fisher and Grace Cheney Fisher; *m* 1930, Hope Elisabeth Case (*d* 1989); one *s*; *m* 1989, Janet Wilson Sawyer. *Educ:* Massachusetts Institute of Technology (BSc). Joined Standard Oil Company (NJ), 1927; Dir, Esso Standard Oil Co. and Pres. Enjay Co. Inc., 1945; Resided in London, 1954–59; UK Rep. for Standard Oil Co. (NJ) and Chm. of its Coordination Cttee for Europe, 1954–57; Joint Managing Dir, Iraq Petroleum Co. Ltd and Associated Companies, 1957–59. Mem., Marine Bd, Nat. Acad. of Engineering, 1971–74; Vice-Chm., Sloan-Kettering Inst. for Cancer Research, 1974–75 (Chm., 1970–74); Mem., MIT Corp. Develt Cttee, 1975; Vice-Chm., and Chm. Exec. Cttee, Community Blood Council of Greater New York, 1969–71. Hon. DSc 1960, Clarkson Coll. of Technology, Nat. Acad. of Engrg. *Publications:* various patents and technical articles relating to the petroleum industry. *Recreations:* golf, photography, horology. *Address:* 68 Goose Point Lane, PO Box 1792, Duxbury, MA 02331, USA. *Club:* Duxbury Yacht.   *Died 8 Dec. 2000.*

FORBES of Craigievar, Sir John (Alexander Cumnock), 12th Bt *cr* 1630 (NS), of Craigievar, Aberdeenshire; JP; equestrian photo-journalist; *b* 29 Aug. 1927; *s* of Rear-Adm. the Hon. Arthur Lionel Ochoncar Forbes-Sempill (*d* 1962), *y s* of 17th Lord Sempill, and of Mary Cutting Holland (*d* 1940), *o d* of Arthur J. Cumnock; *S* kinsman, 1991; *m* 1st, 1956, Penelope Grey-Pennington (marr. diss. 1963); 2nd, 1966, Jane Carolyn, *o d* of C. Gordon Evans. *Educ:* Cheam; Stowe; Sandhurst. Captain, Seaforth Highlanders, 1945–49. Director: Garrick Theatre, 1951–65; The Cinema, Newton Stewart, 1966–94; Auchendon Centre of Equitation Ltd, later ACE, 1972–94. Scottish showjumping correspondent, Horse and Hound, 1994–. Baillie, Newton Stewart Town Council, 1965–76; Founder Convenor, Cree Valley Community Council, 1976. Chm. PR and Promotions, Scottish Br., BSJA. JP Wigtown, 1978. *Heir: kinsman* Andrew Iain Forbes [*b* 28 Nov. 1945; *m* 1984, Jane Elizabeth Dunbar-Nasmith; two *s* two *d*]. *Address:* Benevean, Kendoon, St John's Town of Dalry, Castle Douglas DG7 3UB. *Club:* Naval and Military.   *Died 9 Oct. 2000.*

FOSTER, Hon. Dennis (Haley), CVO 1983; CBE 1981; JP; Chief Secretary, Cayman Islands, 1976–86; *b* 26 March 1931; *s* of late Arnold and Agatha Foster; *m* 1955, Reba Raphael Grant; one *d. Educ:* Munro Coll., Kingston, Jamaica. Joined Cayman Is Civil Service, 1950; seconded as Asst Administrator, Turks and Caicos Is, 1959; Dist Comr, Lesser Is, 1960; Asst Administrator, Cayman Is, 1968. *Recreation:* gardening. *Address:* PO Box 860, George Town, Grand Cayman, Cayman Islands, WI. *T:* (94) 92236.   *Died 21 April 2000.*

FRY, Hon. Sir William Gordon, Kt 1980; JP; President, Legislative Council of Victoria, Australia, 1976–79; *b* 12 June 1909; *s* of A. G. Fry, Ballarat; *m* 1936, Lilian G., *d* of A. W. Macrae; four *s. Educ:* Ballarat High School; Melbourne Univ. Served War of 1939–45, 2nd AIF (Lt-Col, despatches). Education Dept of Victoria for 40 years; Headmaster of various schools, including Cheltenham East, Windsor, Cheltenham Heights. Councillor, City of Moorabbin; Mayor, 1968; MLC (L) for Higinbotham, Vic, 1967–79. Past Chm., Parly Select Cttee, Road Safety. Vice-Pres., Victoria League; Mem., RSL. Formerly Dep. Chm., World Bowls. Life Governor: Melbourne and Dist Ambulance Soc.; Royal Women's Hosp.; Royal Melbourne Hosp.; Gen. Management Cttee, Royal Victoria Eye and Ear Hosp.; Management Bd,

Cheltenham-Mordialloc Hosp. (18 years service); Committee Member: Melbourne Family Care Orgn; Richmond Foundn; Legacy Australia; Brighton Tech. Coll. JP Melbourne, 1968. *Recreations:* lawn bowls, golf, swimming. *Address:* 139 Atherton Road, Oakleigh, Vic 3166, Australia. *Clubs:* West Brighton, Royal Commonwealth Society (Victoria); Returned Services League (Cheltenham-Moorabbin).

Died 29 Sept. 2000.

FULTHORPE, Henry Joseph, FRINA; RCNC; General Manager, HM Dockyard, Portsmouth (Deputy Director of Naval Construction), 1967–75; *b* Portsmouth, 2 July 1916; *s* of Joseph Henry and Clarissa Fulthorpe; *m* 1939, Bette May Forshew; two *s* one *d*. *Educ:* Royal Naval Coll., Greenwich. Ship Design and Production, Admiralty, London and Bath, 1939–43; Principal (Ship) Overseer, Vickers, Barrow-in-Furness, 1943–46; Dep. Manager, HM Dockyard, Malta, 1946–49; Sec., Radiological Defence Panel, 1949–52; Staff Constr, first British atom bomb, Montebello Is, 1952–53; Constr i/c Minesweeper Design, Admty, Bath, 1953–54; Chief Constr, Maintenance, Bath, 1954–56; Dep. Manager, HM Dockyard, Portsmouth, 1956–58; Chief Constructor: HM Dockyard, Singapore, 1958–61; Dockyard Dept, Bath, 1961–63; Asst Dir of Naval Construction, Bath, 1963–64; Production Manager, HM Dockyard, Chatham, 1964–67; Manager, Constructive Dept, HM Dockyard, Portsmouth, 1967. *Address:* Apt 70, Holmbush Court, Queens Crescent, Southsea PO5 3HY. *T:* (023) 9275 0427.

Died 31 Jan. 1999.

GALES, Kathleen Emily, (Mrs Heinz Spitz); Senior Lecturer in Statistics, London School of Economics, 1966–90, retired; *b* 2 Dec. 1927; *d* of Albert Henry and Sarah Thomson Gales; *m* 1970, Heinz Spitz. *Educ:* Gateshead Grammar Sch.; Newnham Coll., Cambridge (Exhibnr; BA 1950); Ohio Univ. (Schol.; MA 1951). Asst Statistician, Foster Wheeler Ltd, 1951–53; Statistician, Municipal Statistical Office, Birmingham, 1953–55; Res. Asst and part-time Lectr, LSE, 1955–58; Asst Lectr in Statistics, LSE, 1958–60, Lectr, 1960–66. Vis. Associate Prof. in Statistics, Univ. of California, 1964–65. Statistical Consultant: Royal Commn on Doctors' and Dentists' Remuneration, 1959; WHO, 1960; Turkish Min. of Health, 1963. Mem., Performing Rights Tribunal, 1974–80. *Publications:* (with C. A. Moser and P. Morpurgo) Dental Health and the Dental Services, 1962; (with B. Abel-Smith) British Doctors at Home and Abroad, 1964; (with T. Blackstone et al.) Students in Conflict: LSE in 1967, 1970; articles in Jl RSS. *Recreations:* bridge, golf, travel. *Died 5 April 1995.*

GANDHI, Manmohan Purushottam, MA, FREconS, FSS; Editor, Major Industries of India Annual, since 1951 (vol. 34, 1988); Director: Indian Link Chain Manufacturers Ltd; Zenith Ltd; Orient General Industries Ltd; *b* 5 Nov. 1901; *s* of late Purushottam Kahanji Gandhi, of Limbdi (Kathiawad); *m* 1926, Rambhaben, BA (Indian Women's Univ.), *d* of Sukhlal Chhaganlal Shah of Wadhwan. *Educ:* Bahauddin Coll., Junagad; Gujerat Coll., Ahmedabad; Hindu Univ., Benares. BA (History and Econs), Bombay Univ., 1923; MA (Political Econ. and Political Philosophy), Benares Hindu Univ., 1925; Ashburner Prize of Bombay Univ., 1925. Statistical Asst, Govt of Bombay, Labour Office, 1926; Asst Sec., Indian Currency League, Bombay, 1926; Sec., Indian Chamber of Commerce, Calcutta, 1926–36; Sec., Indian Sugar Mills Assoc., 1932–36; Officer-in-Charge, Credit Dept, National City Bank of New York, Calcutta, 1936–37; Chief Commercial Manager, Rohtas Industries Ltd; Dalmia Cement Ltd, 1937–39; Dir, Indian Sugar Syndicate Ltd, 1937–39; Controller of Supplies, Bengal and Bombay, 1941–43; Secretary: Indian Nat. Cttee, Internat. Chamber of Commerce, Calcutta, 1929–31; Fedn of Indian Chambers of Commerce and Industry, 1928–29. Member: East Indian Railway Adv. Cttee, 1939–40; Bihar Labour Enquiry Cttee, 1937–39; UP and

Bihar Power Alcohol Cttee, 1938; UP and Bihar Sugar Control Board, 1938; Western Railway Adv. Cttee, Bombay, 1950–52; Small Scale Industries Export Prom. Adv. Cttee; Technical Adviser, Indian Tariff Board, 1947. Hon. Prof., Sydenham Coll. of Commerce, 1943–50. Member: All India Council of Tech. Educn, 1948–73; All India Bd of Studies in Commerce, 1948–70; All India Bd of Management Studies, 1978–84; Indian Merchants Chamber Cttee, 1945–83; Indian Council of Agriculture Res., 1959–66; Senate and Syndicate, Bombay Univ., 1957–69; Dean, Commerce Faculty, Bombay Univ., 1966–67. Director: E India Cotton Assoc., 1953–73 and 1983–84; Bombay Oils & Oilseeds Exchange, 1972–74; Bombay Yarn Exchange, 1972–75. Member: All-India Handloom Bd, 1952–58; Central Silk Bd, 1954–60; Handloom Export Adv. Council, 1965–68; Small-Scale Industries Bd, 1965–69. National FAO Liaison Cttee, 1974–76. Hon. Metropolitan Magistrate, Bombay, 1947–84; JP 1951–68. Swadeshi Prachar Sanuti, 1930–36. *Publications:* How to Compete with Foreign Cloth (with a foreword by Mahatma Gandhi), 1931; The Indian Sugar Industry: Its Past, Present and Future, 1934; The Indian Cotton Textile Industry-Its Past, Present and Future, 1937; The Indian Sugar Industry (annually, 1935–64); The Indian Cotton Textile Industry (annually, 1936–60); Centenary Volume of the Indian Cotton Textile Industry 1851–1950; Problems of Sugar Industry in India, 1946; Monograph on Handloom Weaving in India, 1953; Some Impressions of Japan, 1955; What I learnt from the Mahatma including the Twelve Letters of Mahatma Gandhi to M. P. Gandhi, 1930–32, with reminiscences, 1998. *Recreations:* tennis (name recorded for first time in Limca Book of Records, as oldest tennis player, playing tennis at 91, 1992), badminton, billiards, bridge, cricket. *Clubs:* Radio, National Sports, Rotary, Fifty-Five Tennis, Garden (Bombay).

GARRELS, John Carlyle; Chairman: Monsanto Chemicals Ltd, 1965–71; Monsanto Textiles Ltd, 1970–71; formerly Director: Forth Chemicals Ltd; Monsanto Australia Ltd; Monsanto Oil Co. of UK, Inc.; British Saccharin Sales Ltd; *b* 5 March 1914; *s* of John C. and Margaret Ann Garrels; *m* 1st, 1938, Valerie Smith; one *s* two *d*; 2nd, 1980, Isabelle Rogers Kehoe. *Educ:* Univ. of Michigan (BS (Chem. Eng.)); Harvard (Advanced Management Programme). Production Supervisor, Pennsylvania Salt Mfg Co., 1936–42; Monsanto Co.: various appts, 1942–54; Asst Gen. Manager, 1955; Monsanto Chemicals Ltd: Dep. Man. Dir, 1960; Man. Dir, 1961; Chm. and Man. Dir, 1965. Pres., British Plastics Fedn, 1970, 1971. Member: National Economic Development Cttee for Chemical Industry, 1971; Council, Chemical Industries Assoc. *Recreations:* golf, shooting, fishing. *Address:* 59 Commercial Wharf, Apt 7, Boston, MA 02110–3807, USA. *Clubs:* American; Sunningdale Golf; Yacht and Country (Stuart, Fla); Fishing of America (New York). *Died 28 Dec. 1995.*

GHIZ, Hon. Joseph Atallah; Justice of the Supreme Court, Prince Edward Island, since 1995; *b* 27 Jan. 1945; *s* of Atallah J. and Marguerite Farah (McKarris); *m* 1972, Rose Ellen, *d* of Douglas and Elizabeth McGowan; one *s* one *d*. *Educ:* Prince of Wales College; Dalhousie Univ. (BCom 1966, LLB 1969); LLM Harvard, 1981. Senior Partner, Scales, Ghiz, Jenkins & McQuaid, 1970–81; Crown Prosecutor, Queen's Co., 1970–72; Federal Narcotics Drug Prosecutor, 1970–79; Counsel to Commn of Inquiry into Charlottetown Police Force, 1977; private practice, 1981–86; QC (Can.) 1984. MLA (L) 6th Queens, 1982–93; Pres., Liberal Party of PEI, 1977–78, Leader, 1981–93; Premier, PEI, 1986–93. Dean, Faculty of Law, Dalhousie Univ., 1993–95. Chm., Bd of Advrs, Andersen Consulting, Canada, 1993–95; Dir, Guardian Insce Co. of Canada, 1994–95. Lectr, Univ. of Prince Edward Island, 1970–73. Mem., Canadian Council of Multiculturalism, 1972–75 (Past Regional Chm.); Dir, Canadian Civil Liberties Assoc., 1994–95. Member, Board of Directors: Canada's Nat. Hist. Soc., 1994–; Canadian Liver Foundn,

1994–95. Trustee, McGill Inst. for Study of Canada, 1993–. Hon. LLD Prince Edward Island, 1987. *Publications:* Towards a New Canada (jtly), 1978; Constitutional Impasse Over Oil and Gas, 1981. *Address:* Sir Louis Henry Davies Law Courts, 42 Water Street, PO Box 2000, Charlottetown, PE C1A 7N8, Canada. *T:* (902) 3686596, *Fax:* (902) 3686123. *Club:* Charlottetown.
Died 9 Nov. 1996.

GIDDEN, Barry Owen Barton, CMG 1962; *b* Southampton, 4 July 1915; *s* of late Harry William Gidden, MA, PhD. *Educ:* King Edward VI Sch., Southampton; Jesus Coll., Cambridge (Scholar; Class. Tripos Pts 1 and 2; BA). Served War of 1939–45: BEF, 1939–40, Major 1943. Apptd Asst Principal, HM Office of Works, 1939; Principal, Min. of Works, 1946; Private Sec. to Minister of Works, 1946–48; Principal, Colonial Office, 1949, Asst Sec., 1951; Counsellor, UK Mission to UN, New York, 1954–58; Establishment Officer, Colonial Office, 1958–65; Asst Sec., DHSS, 1965–75. *Recreation:* golf. *Address:* 15 Chesham Street, SW1X 8ND. *T:* (020) 7235 4185. *Club:* Walton Heath.
Died 29 Dec. 1997.

GLEESON, Most Rev. James William, AO 1979; CMG 1958; DD 1957; Archbishop of Adelaide, (RC), 1971–1985, then Emeritus; *b* 24 Dec. 1920; *s* of John Joseph and Margaret Mary Gleeson. *Educ:* St Joseph's Sch., Balaklava, SA; Sacred Heart Coll., Glenelg, SA. Priest, 1945; Inspector of Catholic Schs, 1947–52; Dir of Catholic Educn for South Australia, 1952–58; Auxiliary Bishop to the Archbishop of Adelaide and Titular Bishop of Sesta, 1957–64; Coadjutor Archbishop of Adelaide and Titular Archbishop of Aurusuliana, 1964–71. Episcopal Chm., Young Catholic Students Movement of Australia, 1958–65. FACE 1967. *Address:* Ennis, 28 Robe Terrace, Medindie, SA 5081, Australia. *T:* (8) 83443641.
Died 21 March 2000.

GORDON, Aubrey Abraham; a Recorder of the Crown Court, 1978–97; *b* 26 July 1925; *s* of Isaac and Fanny Gordon; *m* 1949, Reeva R. Cohen; one *s* twin *d. Educ:* Bede Collegiate Boys' Sch., Sunderland; King's Coll., Durham Univ., Newcastle upon Tyne (LLB 1945). Admitted solicitor, 1947. President: Houghton le Spring Chamber of Trade, 1955; Hetton le Hole Rotary Club, 1967; Sunderland Law Soc., 1976; NE Joel Intract Meml Home, 1990–93; Chairman: Houghton Round Table, 1959; Sunderland Victim Support Scheme, 1978–80; Sunderland Guild of Help, 1984–92. *Recreations:* local communal and religious interests, photography. *Address:* 1 Acer Court, Sunderland SR2 7EJ. *T:* (0191) 565 8993.
Died 11 Sept. 2000.

GRAHAM, Sir Samuel Horatio, Kt 1988; CMG 1965; OBE 1962; Chief Justice of Grenada, 1987–90; *b* Trinidad, 3 May 1912; *o s* of late Rev. Benjamin Graham and Mrs Graham, Trinidad; *m* 1943, Oris Gloria (*née* Teka); two *s* four *d. Educ:* Barbados; External Student, London Univ. (BA 1945, LLB 1949). Teacher and journalist until called to Bar, Gray's Inn, 1949. Private practice as Barrister in Grenada, 1949–53; Magistrate, St Lucia, 1953–57; Crown Attorney, St Kitts, 1957–59; Attorney-General, St Kitts, 1960–62; Administrator of St Vincent, 1962–66; Puisne Judge, British Honduras, 1966–69; Pres., Industrial Court of Antigua, 1969–70, Associate Pres., 1981–84; Puisne Judge, Supreme Court of the Commonwealth of the Bahamas, 1973–78. Acted Chief Justice: British Honduras, Feb.-May 1968; Bahamas, Oct. 1977; Temp. Judge, Belize Court of Appeal, 1980. Judicial Mem., Bermuda Constituencies Boundaries Commn, 1979. Chairman: Grenada Develt Bank, 1985–87; Grenada Industrial Develt Corp., 1985–87. Mem., Council of Legal Educn, WI, 1971–. Chairman Inquiries into: Income Tax Reliefs; Coconut Industry, St Lucia, 1955; Legislators' Salaries, St Kitts, 1962. Acted Administrator of St Lucia, St Kitts and Dominica on various occasions. CStJ 1964. *Recreations:* bridge, swimming. *Address:* PO Box 615, St George's, Grenada, West Indies. *Died 10 Aug. 1999.*

GRANADO, Donald Casimir, TC 1970; *b* 4 March 1915; *s* of Gregorio and Octavia Granado; *m* 1959, Anne-Marie Faustin Lombard; one *s* two *d. Educ:* Trinidad. Gen. Sec., Union of Commercial and Industrial Workers, 1951–53; Sec./Treas., Fedn of Trade Unions, 1952–53. Elected MP for Laventille, Trinidad, 1956 and 1961; Minister of: Labour and Social Services, 1956–61; Health and Housing, and Dep. Leader, House of Representatives, 1961–63. Ambassador to Venezuela, 1963–64; High Comr to Canada, 1964–69; Ambassador to Argentina and to Brazil, 1965–69; High Comr to London, 1969–71, and Ambassador to France, Germany, Belgium, Switzerland, Italy, Holland, Luxembourg and European Common Market, 1969–71. Led Trinidad and Tobago delegations to: India, Ceylon, Pakistan, 1958; CPA in Nigeria, Israel, Uganda, 1962; UN, 1965; St Lucia, 1966; attended Heads of Commonwealth Govts Conf., Singapore, 1971; rep. Trinidad and Tobago at missions to Grenada, Jamaica, France, and inaugurations of heads of govt of Chile and Brazil. First Gen. Sec., People's National Movement. Formerly: Vice-Chm., West India Cttee, London; Governor, Commonwealth Inst; Vice-Pres., Trinidad & Tobago Contract Bridge League. President: Fidelis Youth Club; National Golf Club; Vice-Pres., Trinidad & Tobago Golf Assoc.; Pres., Potentials Sports Club (also Manager, soccer team). National Father of the Year 1981. Spoke, read and wrote French and Spanish. *Recreations:* cricket, soccer, bridge and golf; music (tape-recording), writing.
Died 4 Sept. 1999.

GUDERLEY, Daisy Deborah, (Mrs C. Guderley); *see* Hyams, D. D.

HALL, Sir Robert de Zouche, KCMG 1953 (CMG 1952); resident in New Zealand; *b* 27 April 1904; *s* of late Arthur William Hall, Liverpool; *m* 1932, Lorna Dorothy (*née* Markham); one *s* one *d. Educ:* Willaston Sch.; Gonville and Caius Coll., Cambridge (MA 1932). Colonial Administrative Service, Tanganyika, 1926; Provincial Comr, 1947; Senior Provincial Comr, 1950; Mem. for Local Government, Tanganyika, 1950–53. Governor, Comdr-in-Chief, and Vice-Adm., Sierra Leone, 1953–56. Hon. Sec. Vernacular Architecture Group, 1959–72, Pres., 1972–73; Chm. Governing Body, Somerset County Museum, 1961–73; Mem. Gisborne Museum Staff, NZ, 1974–80. *Publication:* (ed) A Bibliography on Vernacular Architecture, 1973.
Died 20 March 1995.

HAMEED, A. C. Shahul; MP (United Nat. Party) Harispattuwa, Sri Lanka, since 1960; Minister of Foreign Affairs, Sri Lanka, 1977–89 and 1993–94; *b* 10 April 1929; *m*; two *s* one *d.* Former Dep. Chm., Public Accounts Cttee; concerned with foreign affairs, public finance and higher education; Minister of Higher Educn, Science and Technology, 1989–90; Minister of Justice and of Higher Educn, 1990–93. Chm., United Nat. Party, Sri Lanka, 1995. Leader of delegns to internat. confs, incl. UN; Chm., Ministerial Conf. of Non-Aligned Countries, 1977–79; Mem., Conf. of UN Cttee on Disarmament, 1989–93. Governor, Univ. of Sri Lanka. *Publications:* In Pursuit of Peace: on non-alignment and regional cooperation, 1983; Owl and the Lotus, 1986; Disarmament—a multilateral approach, 1988; Foreign Policy Perspectives of Sri Lanka, 1988; short stories and poems. *Address:* United National Party, 400 Kotte Road, Pitakotte, Sri Lanka. *Died 3 Sept. 1999.*

HANSON, Dr Bertram Speakman, CMG 1963; DSO 1942; OBE 194; ED; President, College of Radiologists of Australasia, 1961–62 (Gold Medal, 1990); *b* 6 Jan. 1905; *s* of William Speakman Hanson and Maggie Aitken Hanson; *m* 1932, Mayne, *d* of T. J. Gilpin; three *s* one *d. Educ:* St Peter's Coll., Adelaide; Univ. of Adelaide (MB, BS). War Service: Comd 2/8 Aust. Field Amb., 1940–43; ADMS, 9 Aust. Div., 1943–44. Hon. Radiotherapist, Royal Adelaide Hospital, 1952–64; Pres., SA Branch, BMA, 1952–53; Mem., Radiation Health Cttee, Nat. Health and Med. Research Coun., 1963–67. Pres., The Australian

Cancer Soc., 1964–67 (Gold Medal, 1979); Chairman: Exec. Board, Anti-Cancer Foundation, Univ. of Adelaide, 1955–74; Anti-Cancer Foundn, Univs of South Aust., 1980–86; Mem. Council, International Union Against Cancer, 1962–74. Pres., Nat. Trust of South Aust., 1979–82. FAMA 1967. Hon. FFR 1964; Hon. FRCR (Hon.) 1975. DUniv Adelaide, 1985. *Publications:* sundry addresses and papers in Med. Jl of Australia. *Recreation:* gardening. *Address:* 10 Rugby Street, Kingswood, SA 5062, Australia. *Club:* Adelaide. *Died 31 Dec. 1999.*

HEPTINSTALL, Leslie George; HM Diplomatic Service, retired; *b* 20 Aug. 1919; *s* of late Victor George Heptinstall and Maud Maunder; *m* 1949, Marion Nicholls (*d* 1986); one *d. Educ:* Thames Valley County Sch.; London Univ. (BSc Econ.). Served War of 1939–45: Capt., Royal Artillery; Middle East, Mediterranean, North-West Europe. Asst Principal, Colonial Office, 1948; Principal, 1951; seconded to West African Inter-Territorial Secretariat, Accra, 1955; Acting Chief Sec., 1958; Acting Administrator, W African Research Office, 1959; Principal, CRO, 1961; First Sec. on Staff of Brit. High Comr, Wellington, NZ, 1962–64; Dep. High Comr, Lahore, 1964–65; Head of South Asia Dept, ODM, 1966–68; Dep. Senior Trade Comr, Montreal, 1968–70; Internat. Coffee Orgn, 1971–73. *Recreations:* sailing, golf, tennis. *Address:* 34 Church Street, Leatherhead, Surrey KT22 8DW. *Died 21 Oct. 1996.*

HINDLEY, Prof. Colin Boothman; Director, Centre for Study of Human Development, 1967–88, and Professor of Child Development, 1972–84, then Professor Emeritus, Institute of Education, London; *b* Bolton, 1923; *m* 1945; two *s. Educ:* Bolton Sch.; Manchester Univ. (MB ChB 1946); University Coll., London (BSc 1949 (1st cl. Psychol.)). Asst Med. Officer, Hope Hosp., Salford; London University Institute of Education: Res. Psychologist, subseq. Sen. Lectr, 1949–72; Head of Adolescent Development Dip. Course, 1968–72. Psychol. Adviser, Internat. Children's Centre Growth Studies, Paris, 1954–84; Editor, Jl of Child Psychol. and Psychiatry, 1959–69; Mem. Council, Brit. Psychol. Soc., 1970–73; Mem. Cttee, Internat. Soc. for Study Behavioural Develt, 1969–75; Mem. Assoc. Child Psychol. and Psychiat. (Chm. 1967–68). FBPsS. *Publications:* Conceptual and Methodological Issues in the Study of Child Development, 1980; chapters in Child Development: International Method of Study, ed Falkner, 1960; Learning Theory and Personality Development, in Psychosomatic Aspects of Paediatrics, ed Mackeith and Sandler, 1961; The Place of Longitudinal Methods in the Study of Development, in Determinants of Behavioural Development, ed Mönks, Hartup and de Wit, 1972; (jt ed. and contrib.) Development in Adolescence, 1983; contribs to jls. *Recreations:* jazz, literature, gardening, walking, travel, cinema, modern art, science, philosophy. *Address:* Institute of Education, 20 Bedford Way, WC1H 0AL. *T:* (020) 7636 1500. *Died 12 May 2000.*

HOARE, Hon. Marcus Bertram, CMG 1965; Justice of Supreme Court of Queensland, 1966–80; *b* 3 March 1910; *s* of John George and Emma Hoare; *m* 1936, Eileen Parker; four *s. Educ:* Brisbane Grammar Sch. Solicitor, 1933; Barrister-at-Law, 1944; QC (Australia) 1960. *Address:* 13 Mortlake Road, Graceville, Brisbane, Qld 4075, Australia. *T:* (7) 33794181. *Died 11 July 1999.*

HOWD, Isobel; Regional Nursing Officer, Yorkshire Regional Health Authority, 1973–83; *b* 24 Oct. 1928; *née* Young; *m* 1951, Ralph Howd. SRN, RMN, BTA Cert. Matron, Naburn Hosp., York, 1960–63; Asst Regional Nursing Officer, Leeds Regional Hosp. Bd, 1963–70; Chief Nursing Officer, South Teesside Hosp. Management Cttee, 1970–73. Mem., Mental Health Act Commn, 1983–87. *Address:* Yew Tree Cottage, Upper Dunsforth, York YO26 9RU. *T:* (01423) 322534. *Died 11 Dec. 2000.*

HYAMS, Daisy Deborah, (Mrs C. Guderley), OBE 1974; *b* 25 Nov. 1913; *d* of Hyman Hyams and Annie Burnett; *m* 1936, Sidney Hart; no *c, m* 1975, Charles Guderley. *Educ:* Coborn Grammar Sch. for Girls, Bow. FGI. Joined Tesco, 1931; Man. Dir, Tesco (Wholesale) Ltd, 1965–82; Dir, Tesco Stores PLC, 1969–82. *Recreations:* travel, reading. *Address:* 10 Noblefield Heights, Great North Road, Highgate, N2 0NX. *T:* (020) 8348 1591. *Died 11 Sept. 1996.*

HYDE, W(illiam) Leonard, FCIB; Director, Leeds Permanent Building Society, 1972–90 (Chief General Manager, 1973–78; Vice-President, 1978–81; President, 1981–83); *b* 1914. Joined Leeds Permanent Building Soc., 1936. Member Council: Building Socs Assoc., 1973–78; Nat. House Builders, 1973–78; Chm., Yorkshire County Assoc. of Building Socs, 1978–80. *Recreations:* golf, walking. *Address:* 5 Burn Bridge Road, Harrogate, Yorks HG3 1NS. *T:* (01423) 871748. *Club:* Pannal Golf. *Died 11 Nov. 2000.*

JACKSON, Gerald Breck; Managing Director, NCB (Ancillaries) Ltd, 1972–1978; *b* 28 June 1916; *o s* of Gerald Breck Jackson and Mary Jackson, Paterson, NJ; *m* 1940, Brenda Mary, *o d* of William and Mary Titshall; one *s. Educ:* various schs in USA; Canford Sch., Dorset; Faraday House Engrg Coll. Graduate Trainee, Central Electricity Bd, 1938. HM Forces, RE, 1939–43. Various appts in HV transmission with CEB and BEA, 1943–55; Overhead Line Design Engr, BEA, 1955–61; Asst Regional Dir, CEGB, 1961–64; Chief Ops Engr, CEGB, 1964–66; Regional Dir, NW Region, CEGB, 1966–68; Dir Engineering, English Electric Co. Ltd, 1968–69; Sen. Exec., Thomas Tilling Ltd, and Dir subsid. cos, 1969–71; Man. Dir, John Mowlem & Co. Ltd, 1971–72. DFH, CEng, FIEE. *Publications:* Network for the Nation, 1960; Power Controlled, 1966. *Recreations:* photography, pen-and-ink drawing. *Address:* Larchwood, 1A Lansdowne Square, Tunbridge Wells, Kent TN1 2NF. *Died 1 Dec. 2000.*

JACKSON, Sir Robert, 7th Bt *cr* 1815, of Arlsey, Bedfordshire; *b* 16 March 1910; *s* of Major Francis Gorham Jackson (*d* 1942) (2nd *s* of 4th Bt) and Ana Maria Biscar Brennan; *S* kinsman, Sir John Montrésor Jackson, 6th Bt, 1980; *m* 1943, Maria E. Casamayou; two *d. Educ:* St George's College. Career on estancia. *Heir: kinsman* Keith Arnold Jackson [*b* 24 April 1921; *m* 1950, Pauline Mona, *d* of B. P. Climo, Wellington, NZ; four *s* one *d*]. *Address:* Boulevard Artigas 266, Flat 601, Montevideo, Uruguay. *T:* (2) 715032. *Club:* English (Montevideo). *Died 17 April 2000.*

JOHNSTON, John Douglas Hartley; Under Secretary (Legal), Solicitor's Office, Inland Revenue, 1986–95; Assistant Editor, Simon's Tax Cases; *b* 19 March 1935; *s* of John Johnston and Rhoda Margaret Hartley. *Educ:* Manchester Grammar Sch.; Jesus Coll., Cambridge (MA, LLB, PhD); Harvard Law Sch. (LLM). Called to the Bar, Lincoln's Inn, 1963. Practised at Bar, 1963–67; joined Solicitor's Office, Inland Revenue, 1968; Asst Solicitor, 1976–86. *Recreations:* reading, music, gardening. *Address:* Butterworths, Halsbury House, Chancery Lane, WC2A 1EL. *Died 10 March 2000.*

KAHURANANGA, Rt Rev. Musa; Archbishop of Tanzania, 1979–83; *b* 1921; *s* of Samweli and Mariamu Kahurananga; *m* 1941, Raheli Lutozi; three *s* four *d* (and one *s* decd). *Educ:* Teachers' Training College, Katoke Bukoba. Teacher; Deacon 1952, Priest 1953; Asst Bishop in Diocese of Central Tanganyika, 1962; Bishop of Western Tanganyika, 1966–83. *Recreation:* farming. *Address:* PO Box 13, Kasulu, Tanzania. *Died 30 Sept. 1997.*

KALO, Sir Kwamala, Kt 1983; MBE 1975; Director of Administrative College, Port Moresby, 1987–89; *b* 28 Feb. 1929; *s* of Kalo Navu and Navuga Kila; *m* 1951, Gimaralai Samuel (OBE 2000); two *s* two *d. Educ:* up to secondary level in Papua New Guinea. Govt Primary School teacher, 1949; served in Dept of Educn as classroom teacher, Headmaster, Inspector, Supt of Schools, Asst Sec. of Technical Educn, until 1979; represented Papua New Guinea in Trusteeship Council Meeting of UN, 1963; seconded to Public Services Commn as a Comr, 1979; High Comr for Papua New Guinea in New Zealand, 1983–86. Hon. Award, PNG Trng and Develt Soc., 1991. *Publication:* Sam Ila' Apa Gena Mari (Hymns by Sam Ila' Apa), 1989. *Address:* PO Box 8529, Boroko NCD, Port Moresby, Papua New Guinea.   *Died 17 Dec. 1995.*

KENNAWAY, Prof. Alexander, FIM; Senior Researcher and Lecturer, Conflict Studies Research Centre, Royal Military Academy, Sandhurst, since 1993; *b* 14 Aug. 1923; *s* of late Dr Noah Barou and Sophie Barou; *m* 1st, 1947, Xenia Rebel (marr. diss. 1970); one *s* one *d*; 2nd, 1973, Jean Simpson. *Educ:* Downsend Sch., Leatherhead; St Paul's Sch., London; Pembroke Coll., Cambridge (MA). CEng, FIMechE 1962; FIM (FPRI 1968). Engr Officer, Royal Navy: active list, 1942–47; reserve, 1970. Imperial Chemical Industries Ltd, 1947–58; Metal Box Co., 1958–60; Director: BTR Industries, 1960–66; Allied Polymer Gp, 1972–78; Thomas Jourdan, 1976–83; Imperial Polymer Technology, 1984–86. Chm., Terrafix, 1983–90. Mem. Bd, CAA, 1979–83. Hon. medical engrg consultant, various hosps and charities, 1950–. Mem., Standing Adv. Cttee on artificial limbs, DHSS, 1964–70. Vis. Prof. of Mech. Engrg, Imp. Coll. of Science and Technology, 1976–97. Interim Sec., Nat. Fedn of Zool Gardens of GB and Ireland, 1984–86. Pres., English Chess Assoc., 1988–92. For. Mem., Ukrainian Acad. of Transport, 1994. *Publications:* (contrib.) Advances in Surgical Materials, 1956; (contrib.) Polythene—technology and uses, 1958, 2nd edn 1960; Engineers in Industry, 1981; (contrib.) The British Malaise, 1982; some 30 papers on biomechanics, technology of use and production of rubbers and plastics, and on design of specific aids for disabled living; 55 papers on Soviet and Post-Soviet economy, defence industries, science, technologies, culture and history. *Recreations:* sailing, chess, music. *Address:* 12 Fairholme Crescent, Ashtead, Surrey KT21 2HN. *T:* (01372) 277678.   *Died 1 May 2000.*

KENNEDY, Eamon, PhD; Special Adviser, with rank of Ambassador, Permanent Mission of Ireland, United Nations, New York, since 1987; *b* 13 Dec. 1921; *s* of Luke William Kennedy and Ellen (*née* Stafford); *m* 1960, Barbara Jane Black, New York; one *s* one *d*. *Educ:* O'Connell Schools, Dublin; University Coll., Dublin (MA, BComm); National University of Ireland (PhD 1970). Entered Irish Diplomatic Service, 1943; 2nd Sec., Ottawa, 1947–49; 1st Sec., Washington, 1949–50; 1st Sec., Paris, 1950–54; Chief of Protocol, Dublin, 1954–56; Counsellor, UN Mission, New York, 1956–61; Ambassador to: Nigeria, 1961–64; Federal Republic of Germany, 1964–70; France, OECD and UNESCO, 1970–74; UN, 1974–78; UK, 1978–83; Italy, Turkey, Libya, and FAO Rome, 1983–86. Grand Cross: Order of Merit (German Federal Republic), 1970; Nat. Order of Merit (France), 1974. *Recreations:* golf, theatre, music. *Address:* 525 East 86th Street, Apartment 17-D, New York, NY 10028, USA; 6730 Nassau Point Road, Cutchogue, NY 11935, USA. *Club:* North Fork Country (Long Island, NY).   *Died 12 Dec. 2000.*

KITCHIN, Prof. Laurence Tyson; university teacher, translator and critic; *b* 21 July 1913; *s* of James Tyson Kitchin, MD Edin, and Eliza Amelia Kitchin (*née* Hopps); *m* 1955, Hilary Owen, artist; one step *s*. *Educ:* Bootham Sch.; King's Coll., London (BA 1934); Central Sch. of Speech and Drama (Acting Cert., 1st cl.). Served War, RAMC and briefly, RAEC, 1941–46. Mem., univ. debates team, USA, 1933; acted in Housemaster on stage and screen, 1936, and in films, incl. Pimpernel Smith; wrote extensively for BBC Third Prog., 1948–55; The Times corresp. and drama critic, 1956–62; numerous BBC talks on literature and drama, 1962–66; UK rep., Théâtre

dans le Monde, UNESCO, 1961–66; Lectr, Bristol Univ. and Tufts, London, 1966–70; Vis. Prof. of Drama, Stanford Univ., Calif, 1970–72; Vis. Prof. of Liberal Arts, City Univ. of NY, 1972–73, Prof., 1973–76; Vis. Prof. of Shakespeare Studies, Simon Fraser Univ., Canada, 1976–77. Renaissance verse translations from Italian, French and Spanish, BBC, 1978–79. Selected as one of Outstanding Educators of America, 1973. *Publications:* Len Hutton, 1953; Three on Trial: Byron, Bowdler and Machiavelli, 1959; Mid-Century Drama, 1960, 2nd edn 1962; Drama in the Sixties, 1966; Love Sonnets of the Renaissance (trans. from Italian, French, Spanish and Portuguese), 1990; radio scripts, incl.: The Trial of Lord Byron, 1948, Canada 1978; The Trial of Machiavelli, 1957; The Court Lady (trans. from Castiglione), 1954; The Elizabethan, Canada 1978; The Flaming Heart (Crashaw), 1981; contrib. Shakespeare Survey, Confronto Letterario, Mod. Lang. Rev., TLS, Encounter, Observer, Listener, THES. *Recreations:* tennis, televised soccer. *Address:* c/o National Westminster Bank, St James's & Piccadilly Branch, W1A 2DG. *Club:* Athenæum.
                Died 15 Sept. 1997.

KNOWLES, Sir Leonard (Joseph), Kt 1974; CBE 1963; barrister; Chief Justice of the Bahamas, 1973–78; *b* Nassau, 15 March 1916; *s* of late Samuel Joseph Knowles; *m* 1939, Harriet Hansen, *d* of John Hughes, Liverpool; two *s*. *Educ:* Queen's Coll., Nassau, Bahamas (first Bahamian student to take and pass Higher Sch. Certif. in Bahamas, 1934); King's Coll., London (LLB Hons 1937, 1st cl. in Final Bar Examinations); BD London, 1985. Served War of 1939–45, Royal Air Force (radar). Called to the Bar, Gray's Inn, London, 1939; Lord Justice Holker Scholar, Gray's Inn, 1940; practised law in Liverpool for some years; returned to Nassau, 1948, and was called to local Bar; Attorney-at-Law and Actg Attorney-Gen. of the Bahamas, 1949; Registrar-Gen., 1949–50; Past Stipendiary and Circuit Magistrate; returned to private law practice, 1978. Chm., Labour Board, Bahamas, 1953–63; MLC (Upper House of Legislature), 1960–63; President, Senate, 1964; re-elected, 1967, 1968, and continued to hold that office until 1972. Methodist local preacher. *Publications:* Elements of Bahamian Law, 1978, 2nd edn 1989; Financial Relief in Matrimonial Cases, 1980; Bahamian Real Property Law, 1989; My Life (autobiog.), 1989; Introduction to Bahamian Company Law, 1993; Law of Dower and Curtesy, 1994; Law of Executors and Administrators, 1996; Seven Greatest Events of All Time, 1998; Happy Birthday, Jesus; Stories From the Bahamas; compilations of Bahamian Statutes 1987–94. *Recreations:* music, motion photography, swimming. *Address:* 4684 South Beechwood Drive, Macon, GA 31210, USA. *Fax:* (912) 7410070.   *Died 23 Sept. 1999.*

KOLANE, John Teboho, ODSM, OL; LLD; Speaker of the National Assembly, Lesotho, 1973–86 and since 1990; *b* 22 Feb. 1926; *s* of Elizabeth and Zacharia Kolane; *m* 1955, Julia; two *s* three *d*. *Educ:* National University of Lesotho; Cambridge Univ.; BA South Africa; attorney's admission, Pretoria. Interpreter, District Comr's Court and Judicial Comr's Court, Lesotho, 1950–59; Registrar of Births, Marriages and Deaths, and Registrar of Deeds, 1959–63; Clerk of Senate, 1965–67; Permanent Secretary: Min. of Justice, 1967–69; Cabinet Office, 1969–70; Min. of Justice, 1970–73; High Comr to UK, 1986–89; Dir of Parly Affairs, Lesotho, 1990–92; Speaker of Constituent Assembly, 1992–93. LLD 1985. *Recreations:* golf, gardening, walking. *Address:* National Assembly, PO Box 190, Maseru, Lesotho. *Club:* Maseru Golf.
                Died 1999.

LEGGE, Rt Rev. William Gordon, DD; *b* 20 Jan. 1913; *s* of Thomas Legge and Jane (*née* Gill); *m* 1941, Hyacinth Florence Richards; one *s* one *d*. *Educ:* Bishop Feild and Queen's Colls, St John's, Newfoundland. Deacon 1938, priest 1939; Curate, Channel, 1938–41; Incumbent of Botwood, 1941–44; Rector, Bell Island, 1944–55; Sec., Diocesan Synod, 1955–68; Archdeacon of Avalon,

1955–68; Canon of Cathedral, 1955–76; Diocesan Registrar, 1957–68; Suffragan Bishop, 1968; Bishop of Western Newfoundland, 1976–78. DD *hc*, Univ. of King's College, Halifax, NS, 1973. *Address:* 52 Glenhaven Boulevard, Corner Brook, NF A2H 4P6, Canada.
Died 13 Jan. 1999.

LEGGETT, Sir Clarence (Arthur Campbell), Kt 1980; MBE (mil.) 1943; FRACS, FACS; Surgeon; Hon. Consulting Surgeon, Princess Alexandra Hospital, Brisbane, since 1968; *b* 24 July 1911; *s* of late A. J. Leggett; *m* 1939, Avril, *d* of late R. L. Bailey; one *s* two *d. Educ:* Sydney Univ. (MA, MB BS; 1st cl. Hons, Univ. Medallist, 1936); Queensland Univ. (MS). RMO, Royal Prince Alfred Hosp., Sydney, 1937–38; Asst Dep. Med. Supt, 1939. Major, AAMC, 1941–46. Asst Surgeon, Royal Brisbane Hosp., 1941–51; Junior Surg., 1951–56; Senior Surg., Princess Alexandra Hosp., Brisbane, 1956–68. University of Queensland: Hon. Demonstrator and Examiner, Anatomy Dept, 1941–47; Chief Asst, Dept of Surgery, 1947–51; Mem. Faculty Bd, 1947–51; Special Lectr, 1951–68. Member of Council: Queensland Inst. for Med. Research, 1948–65; RACS, 1966–75 (Gordon Craig Schol.; Chm. Court of Examiners, 1971–75; Junior Vice-Pres., 1973–75; Mem. Ct of Honour). FAMA 1985; Hon. FRCS 1983. *Publications:* numerous surgical and historical papers, orations and theses. *Recreations:* breeding Arabian horses and Hereford cattle; univ. blue, and mem., Australian hockey team, 1934. *Address:* Craigston, 217 Wickham Terrace, Brisbane, Queensland 4000, Australia. *T:* (7) 38310031. *Club:* Queensland (Brisbane).
Died 17 Sept. 1998.

LEITH-BUCHANAN, Sir Charles (Alexander James), 7th Bt *cr* 1775; President, United Business Machines Inc., Alexandria, Va, since 1978; *b* 1 Sept. 1939; *s* of John Wellesley MacDonald Leith-Buchanan (*g s* of 4th Bt) (*d* 1956) and Jane Elizabeth McNicol (*d* 1955), *d* of Ronald McNicol; *S* cousin, 1973; *m* 1962, Mary Anne Kelly (marr. diss. 1987); one *s* one *d*; *m* 1988, Janice J., *d* of Robert Granger Jenkins. *Heir: s* Gordon Kelly McNicol Leith-Buchanan, *b* 18 Oct. 1974. *Died 8 Feb. 1998.*

LEMIEUX, Prof. Raymond Urgel, CC 1994 (OC 1968); FRS 1967; Professor of Organic Chemistry, University of Alberta, 1961–80, University Professor, 1980–85, then Emeritus; *b* 16 June 1920; *s* of Octave Lemieux; *m* 1948, Virginia Marie McConaghie; one *s* five *d* (and one *s* decd). *Educ:* Edmonton, Alberta; Univ. of Alberta (BSc Hons Chem. 1943); McGill Univ. (PhD 1946). Research Fellow, Ohio State Univ., 1947; Asst Professor, Saskatchewan Univ., 1948–49; Senior Research Officer, National Research Council, Canada, 1949–54, Member, 1976–81; Professor, Ottawa Univ., 1954–61. Pres., Chem. Inst. of Canada, 1984–85. Rhône-Poulenc Lectr, RSC, 1989. FRSC 1955. Hon. FCIC 1992; Hon. Mem., Canadian Soc. for Chemistry, 1986. Hon. DSc: New Brunswick Univ., 1967; Laval Univ., 1970; Univ. de Provence, 1973; Univ. of Ottawa, 1975; Waterloo Univ., 1980; Meml Univ., Newfoundland, 1981; Quebec, 1982; Queen's Univ., Kingston, Ont, 1983; McGill, 1984; McMaster, 1986; Sherbrooke, 1986; Alberta, 1991; British Columbia, 1997; Hon. LLD: Calgary, 1979; Saskatchewan, 1993; Hon. PhD Stockholm, 1988. Chem. Inst. of Canada Medal, 1964; C. S. Hudson Award, Amer. Chem. Soc., 1966; W. N. Haworth Medal, Chem. Soc., 1978; Izaak Walton Killam Award, Canada Council, 1981; Diplôme d'Honneur, Groupe Français des Glucides, 1981; Sir Frederick Haultain Prize, Govt of Alberta, 1982; Tischler Award, Harvard Univ., 1983; Medal of Honor, CMA, 1985; Gairdner Foundn Internat. Award in Medical Science, 1985; LeSueur Award, SCI, 1989; King Faisal Internat. Prize for Science, 1990; Canada Gold Medal for Science and Engrg, 1991; E. C. Manning Nat. Award of Distinction, 1992; Medal of Honour, Pharmaceutical Manufacturers Assoc. of Canada Health Res. Foundn, 1992; Albert Einstein World Award of Sci., 1992; Alberta Sci. and Technol. Foundn Award, Alberta Pioneer, 1993;

Great Canadian Award, 1993; Wolf Foundn Prize in Chemistry, 1999. Eponymous lectures inaugurated at Ottawa Univ., 1972, and Alberta Univ., 1987; R. U. Lemieux Award for Organic Chm., Canadian Soc. for Chem., inaug. 1992; Strathcona County/R. U. Lemieux Chair in Carbohydrate Chemistry, Alberta Univ., 1999. Alberta Order of Excellence, 1990. *Publications:* over 200 research papers mainly in area of carbohydrate chemistry in Canadian Journal of Chemistry, etc. *Recreations:* golf, curling, fishing. *Address:* 7602, 119th Street, Edmonton, AB T6G 1W3, Canada. *T:* (403) 4365167. *Clubs:* University of Alberta Faculty (Edmonton); Lake Edith Golf (Jasper). *Died 22 July 2000.*

LEWIS, Roland Swaine, FRCS; Honorary Consultant Surgeon to the ENT Department, King's College Hospital, since 1973 (Consultant Surgeon, 1946–65, Senior Consultant Surgeon, 1965–73); Honorary Consultant ENT Surgeon: to Mount Vernon Hospital and The Radium Institute; to Norwood and District Hospital; *b* 23 Nov. 1908; *s* of Dr William James Lewis, MOH, and Constance Mary Lewis, Tyrwaun, Ystalyfera; *m* 1936, Mary Christianna Milne (Christianna Brand) (*d* 1988); one adopted *d. Educ:* Epsom Coll.; St John's Coll., Cambridge (BA 1929, MA 1945; MB BCh 1945); St George's Hospital. FRCS 1934. Surgical Chief Asst, St George's Hospital, 1935. Major, RAMC (ENT Specialist), 1939–45. *Publications:* papers to medical journals. *Recreations:* ornithology, fishing. *Address:* 88 Maida Vale, W9 1PR. *T:* (020) 7624 6253; Aberdar, Cwrt y Cadno, Llanwrda, Dyfed. *Died 24 Feb. 2000.*

LOW, Sir Alan (Roberts), Kt 1977; Governor, Reserve Bank of New Zealand, 1967–77, retired; *b* 11 Jan. 1916; 4th *s* of Benjamin H. Low and Sarah Low; *m* 1940, Kathleen Mary Harrow; one *s* two *d. Educ:* Timaru Main Sch.; Timaru Boys' High Sch.; Canterbury University College (MA 1937). Joined Reserve Bank of New Zealand, 1938; Economic Adviser, 1951; Asst Governor, 1960; Deputy Governor, 1962. Army Service, 1942–44; on loan to Economic Stabilisation Commission, 1944–46. Hon. Fellow, Bankers' Inst. of NZ, 1977. Hon. LLD Canterbury, 1977. *Publications:* No Free Lunch, 1983; Where DO We Go For Lunch, 1984; contributions to many economic and financial jls. *Recreations:* gardening, music, reading. *Address:* 171 Muritai Road, Eastbourne, Lower Hutt, New Zealand. *T:* 628861.
Died 18 April 1999.

LUPTON, Prof. Thomas; Professor of Organisational Behaviour, University of Manchester, 1966–86; Visiting Professor, Instituto de Estudios Superiores de la Empresa, Barcelona, 1987–94; Director of International Programmes, Escuela de Alta Dirección y Administración, Barcelona, 1990–95; *b* 4 Nov. 1918; *s* of Thomas Lupton, blacksmith, and Jane Lupton (*née* Vowell); *m* 1st, 1942, Thelma Chesney; one *d*; 2nd, 1963, Dr Constance Shirley Wilson; one *s* one *d*; 3rd, 1987, Dorothy Joyce Meredith. *Educ:* Elem. and Central Sch.; Technical Coll.; Ruskin Coll.; Oriel Coll., Oxford; Univ. of Manchester. DipEconPolSci (Oxon), MA (Oxon), PhD (Manch.). Served War, HM Forces, 1939–41 and 1944–46; Marine Engr, 1932–39, 1941–44. Research Posts: Liverpool Univ., 1951–54; Manchester Univ., 1954–57; Lectr in Sociology, Manchester Univ., 1957–59; Head of Dept of Industrial Admin, Coll. of Advanced Techn., Birmingham, 1959–64; Montague Burton Prof. of Ind. Rel., Univ. of Leeds, 1964–66; Dir, Manchester Business Sch., 1977–83. Gen. Editor, Jl of Management Studies, 1966–76; Dir, Pirelli General Cables Ltd, 1970–77; Member: Civil Service Arbitration Tribunal, 1967–70; Arbitration Panel, Dept of Employment, 1969–72; various official commns and tribunals, 1960–80. Hon. DSc Aston, 1987; Hon. DBA Manchester Metropolitan, 1997. *Publications:* On the Shop Floor, 1963; Industrial Behaviour and Personnel Management, 1964; Management and the Social Sciences, 1966, 3rd edn, 1983; Selecting a Wage Payment System (with D. Gowler),

1969; Job and Pay Comparisons (with A. M. Bowey), 1973; Wages and Salaries (with A. M. Bowey), 1974, rev. edn 1983; Achieving Change (with I. R. Tanner), 1987; articles in Jl of Management Studies, Manchester Sch., Production Engineer, etc. *Recreations:* golf, Association Football. *Address:* Foxhill, 106 Styal Road, Gatley, Cheadle, Cheshire SK8 4JR. *Died 16 May 2000.*

LUSH, Hon. Sir George (Hermann), Kt 1979; Justice, Supreme Court of Victoria, 1966–83; *b* 5 Oct. 1912; *s* of John Fullarton Lush and Dora Louise Emma Lush; *m* 1943, Winifred Betty Wragge; three *d*. *Educ:* Carey Grammar Sch.; Ormond Coll., Melbourne Univ. (LLM). Admitted, Victorian Bar, 1935; served War, Australian Imperial Forces, 1940–45; Lecturer, Mercantile Law, Melbourne Univ., 1947–55; QC: Victoria 1957, Tasmania 1958. Chairman, Victorian Bar Council, 1964–66; President: Medico-Legal Soc., Victoria, 1962–63; Australian Bar Assoc., 1964–66; Commnr, Overseas Telecommunications Commn, 1961–66. Chancellor, Monash Univ., 1983–92 (Mem. Council, 1969–74); Chm. Council, Ormond Coll., 1981–90. Hon. LLD Monash, 1993. *Recreations:* tennis, walking. *Address:* 37 Rochester Road, Canterbury, Vic 3126, Australia. *Clubs:* Melbourne, Melbourne Cricket (Melbourne); Lorne Country (Lorne, Vic). *Died 5 April 2000.*

LYONS, Sir Edward Houghton, Kt 1977; FAIM; Chairman, Totalisator Administration Board, Queensland, 1981–85. Formerly Chairman, Katies Ltd, and Gen. Manager, Industrial Acceptance Corp. Ltd; Dir, Bruck (Australia) Ltd. Trustee, National Party. *Address:* 47 Kneale Street, Holland Park Heights, Queensland 4121, Australia. *T:* (7) 33496461. *Died 13 Dec. 1999.*

McCALL, John Donald; Director, Consolidated Gold Fields Ltd, 1959–81 (Chairman, 1969–76); *b* 1 Feb. 1911; *s* of late Gilbert Kerr McCall; *m* 1942, Vere Stewart Gardner; one *s* one *d*. *Educ:* Clifton Coll.; Edinburgh Univ. Gold mining industry, S Africa, 1930–39. Served War of 1939–45, commnd Gordon Highlanders. Joined Consolidated Gold Fields Ltd, London, 1946 (Dir, 1959; Jt Dep. Chm., 1968). Dir, Ultramar plc, 1965–79. *Club:* Caledonian. *Died 25 Feb. 1999.*

MacDERMOTT, Edmond Geoffrey; Metropolitan Stipendiary Magistrate, 1972–84; *b* 29 July 1913. Called to Bar, Gray's Inn, 1935; Dept of Dir of Public Prosecutions, 1946–72, Asst Dir of Public Prosecutions, 1968–72. *Died 30 June 1988.*

MacGILL, (George) Roy (Buchanan), CBE 1965; General Manager, Cumbernauld Development Corporation, 1956–70; Deputy Chairman, Scottish Special Housing Association, 1971–76; *b* 20 Dec. 1905; *s* of George Buchanan MacGill; *m* 1934, Jean Ferguson Anderson (*d* 1995); two *d*. *Educ:* Glasgow High Sch. Chartered Accountant, 1928. FIMTA 1938. Town Chamberlain, Airdrie, 1932; Burgh Chamberlain, Dunfermline, 1947. *Recreations:* (from the sidelines) golf, music. *Address:* Buchanan House, 1 Grampian Way, Bearsden, Glasgow G61 4SP. *T:* (0141) 570 0160. *Died 14 Nov. 2000.*

MacGILL, Roy; *see* MacGill, G. R. B.

MACKLIN, Sir Bruce (Roy), Kt 1981; OBE 1970; FCA; company director; Chairman: Standard Chartered Bank Australia Ltd, since 1987; Hyundai Automotive Distributors Australia Pty, since 1990; *b* 23 April 1917; *s* of Hubert Vivian Macklin and Lillian Mabel Macklin; *m* 1944, Dorothy Potts, Tynemouth, England; two *s* one *d*. *Educ:* St Peter's Coll., Adelaide; St Mark's Coll., Univ. of Adelaide (Associate Univ. of Adelaide (Commerce)). Served RAAF (Aircrew), 1941–45. Practising chartered accountant, 1947–69. Pres., Aust. Chamber of Commerce, 1967–69. Hon. Consul in S Aust. for Fed. Republic of Germany, 1968–94; Leader, Aust. Govt Mission to Papua New Guinea, 1971. Mem. Council of Governors, St Peter's Coll., Adelaide, 1962–69; Mem.

Council, Univ. of Adelaide, 1965–71. A Founder, Adelaide Festival of Arts, 1958, Chm. Bd of Governors, 1972–78; Dep. Nat. Chm., Queen Elizabeth II Silver Jubilee Trust for Young Australians. Silver Jubilee Medal 1977. Commander's Cross, Order of Merit (Fed. Republic of Germany), 1986. *Recreations:* tennis, gardening, music. *Address:* Unit 221, 242–266 Greenhill Road, Glenside, SA 5065, Australia. *T:* (8) 83387848. *Clubs:* Adelaide, Naval, Military and Air Force (South Australia).
Died 29 Aug. 2000.

MAGUIRE, Rt Rev. Robert Kenneth, DD; Hon. Assisting Bishop: Diocese of Western New York, 1984–86; Diocese of Southeast Florida, 1984–89, retired; *b* 31 March 1923; *s* of late Robert Maguire and Anne Crozier; unmarried. *Educ:* Trinity Coll., Dublin (BA 1945; Divinity Testimonium, 1947). Deacon, 1947; priest, 1948; Curate of: St Mark, Armagh, 1947–49; St James the Apostle, Montreal, 1949–52; Dean of Residence, Trinity Coll., Dublin, 1952–60; Curate-in-charge of St Andrew's, Dublin, 1954–57; Minor Canon of St Patrick's Cathedral, Dublin, 1955–58; Dean and Rector of Christ Church Cathedral, Montreal, 1961–62; Bishop of Montreal, 1963–75. Co-ordinator: Canadian Conf., Theology '76, 1975–76; North American Consultation on the Future of Ministry, 1979–80. Assistant to the Primate, Anglican Church of Canada, 1980–84. DD (*jure dig.*): Dublin Univ., 1963; Montreal Diocesan Theol Coll., 1963; DCL (*hc*) Bishop's Univ., Lennoxville, Qué., 1963. *Address:* 4875 Dundas Street West, Apt 304, Islington, ON M9A 1B3, Canada. *Died 14 Oct. 2000.*

MAMALONI, Solomon Sunaone; MP (People's Alliance Party), Solomon Islands; Prime Minister of Solomon Islands, 1981–85, 1989–93 and 1994–97; *b* 21 June 1943. *Educ:* King George VI School; Te-Aute College, NZ. Exec. Officer, Civil Service, later Clerk to Legislative Council; MP Makira, 1970–76, West Makira, 1976–77 and 1980–; Chief Minister, British Solomon Islands, 1974–76; founder and leader, People's Progress Party (merged with Rural Alliance Party to form People's Alliance Party, 1979). Man. Dir, Patosha Co., 1977. *Address:* National Parliament Building, Honiara, Guadalcanal, Solomon Islands. *Died 11 Jan. 2000.*

MARTIN, Lt-Gen. Henry James, CBE 1943; DFC; Chief of Defence Staff, South African Defence Force, retired; *b* 10 June 1910; *s* of Stanley Charles Martin and Susan C. Fourie; *m* 1940, Renée Viljoen; one *s* two *d*. *Educ:* Grey Coll. Sch., Bloemfontein; Grey Univ. Coll., Bloemfontein. Joined S African Air Force, 1935, and played important rôle in British Empire Training Scheme in South Africa; commanded No 12 Sqdn in Western Desert (DFC, Croix Militaire de première classe Belgique); commanded No 3 Wing (a unit of Desert Air Force) and campaigned from El Alamein to Tunis; returned to Union, 1943. *Recreation:* rugger (represented Orange Free State, 1931–34, Transvaal, 1935–37, South Africa, 1937). *Address:* 42 Newlands Park, PO Box 370, Newlands Plaza, 0049, S Africa. *Died 19 Oct. 2000.*

MARTIN, Samuel Frederick Radcliffe, CB 1979; First Legislative Draftsman, 1973–79; *b* 2 May 1918; 2nd *s* of late William and Margaret Martin; *m* 1947, Sarah, *y d* of late Rev. Joseph and Margaret McKane; three *s*. *Educ:* Royal Belfast Academical Instn; Queen's Univ., Belfast (LLB). Called to the Bar, Gray's Inn, 1950. Examr, Estate Duty Office, NI, 1939; Professional Asst, Office of Parly Draftsmen, 1956. Legal Adviser to Examiner of Statutory Rules, NI, 1979–81; Asst Comr, Local Govt Boundaries' Commn, 1983–84. Northern Ireland Editor, Current Law, 1979–90. *Publications:* articles in NI Legal Qly and Gazette of Incorp. Law Soc. *Recreation:* golf. *Address:* Brynburn, 196 Upper Road, Greenisland, Carrickfergus, Co. Antrim BT38 8RW. *T:* (028) 9086 2417. *Died 20 Nov. 2000.*

MASSY, 9th Baron *cr* 1776 (Ire.); **Hugh Hamon John Somerset Massy;** *b* 11 June 1921; *o s* of 8th Baron, and

Margaret, 2nd *d* of late Richard Leonard, Meadsbrook, Ashbourne, Co. Limerick, and *widow* of Dr Moran, Tara, Co. Meath; *S* father, 1958; *m* 1943, Margaret, *d* of late John Flower, Barry, Co. Meath; four *s* one *d*. *Educ*: Clongowes Wood Coll.; Clayesmore Sch. Served War, 1940–45, Private, RAOC. *Heir*: *s* Hon. David Hamon Somerset Massy, *b* 4 March 1947. *Died 5 Aug. 1995.*

MURDOCH, William Ridley Morton, CBE 1963; DSC 1940 and Bar, 1942; VRD 1949; Sheriff of Grampian, Highland and Islands (formerly Ross and Cromarty), at Dingwall and Tain, 1971–78; *b* 17 May 1917; *s* of William Ridley Carr Murdoch and Margaret Pauline Mackinnon; *m* 1941, Sylvia Maud Pearson; one *s* one *d*. *Educ*: Kelvinside Academy, Glasgow; Glasgow Univ. (MA, LLB). War Service in Royal Navy, 1939–45; Captain, RNR, 1959. Solicitor in private practice, 1947–71. Dir, Glasgow Chamber of Commerce, 1955–71; Dean, Royal Faculty of Procurators in Glasgow, 1968–71. DL, County of City of Glasgow, 1963–75. OStJ 1976. *Recreations*: sailing, gardening. *Address*: Seaview, Shore Street, Gairloch, Ross-shire IV21 2BZ. *T*: (01445) 712481. *Died 31 July 2000.*

NATH, (Dhurma) Gian; *b* Triolet, Mauritius, 29 May 1934; *s* of Anmole Facknath, OBE and Mrs B. Facknath; *m* 1961, Chitralekha, *d* of Dr and Mrs Chiranji Lal Sud; two *s* one *d*. *Educ*: Delhi Univ. (BA Hons English 1960, MA 1962); Postgrad. Inst. of Internat. Affairs, New Delhi. Educn Officer, John Kennedy Coll., Mauritius, 1963–66 (Head of Dept of English, 1965–66); entered Diplomatic Service, Mauritius, as trainee, 1966; apptd to Mauritius High Commn, London, 1968; Head of Chancery, 1969; Counsellor, Mauritius Mission to EEC, 1972–76; Dep. High Comr, London, 1976–82; Ambassador in Cairo, 1982–83; High Comr in UK, 1983–87; Ambassador to Pakistan and (non-resident), to China, 1988–90; Ambassador to Australia, and concurrently to NZ, Brunei and Indonesia, 1990–92; Permt Rep. of Mauritius to UN, 1992–94; elected MP (Lab) Mauritius, 1995; Minister: of Trade and Shipping, Mauritius, 1995–96; of Arts, Culture and Leisure, 1996. Sec., OAU Gp, London, 1973–82. Mem., Television Bd, Mauritius Broadcasting Corp., 1965–66. Representative of Mauritius at various internat. meetings. Kt of Order of Pius IX (Vatican), 1987. *Recreations*: bridge, history of World War II, golf. *Address*: Rue de Chazal, Floreal, Mauritius.
Died 19 Oct. 1997.

NÉEL, Prof. Louis Eugène Félix; Grand Croix de la Légion d'Honneur; Croix de Guerre avec Palme; Président d'Honneur, Institut National Polytechnique de Grenoble (Président, 1971–76); *b* Lyon, 22 Nov. 1904; *s* of Louis Néel and Marie-Antoinette (*née* Hartmayer); *m* 1931, Hélène Hourticq; one *s* two *d*. *Educ*: Ecole Normale Supérieure; Agrégé de l'Université; DèsSc. Prof., Univ. of Strasbourg, 1937–45; Prof., Univ. of Grenoble, 1946–76; Dir, Centre d'Etudes Nucléaires, Grenoble, 1956–71, and Delegate of High Comr for Atomic Energy at the centre, 1971–76; rep. France at Scientific Council, NATO, 1960–83; Prés., Conseil Sup. Sûreté Nucléaire, 1973–86. Mem., Acad. of Science, Paris, 1953; Foreign Member: Acad. of Science, Russia (formerly USSR), 1959, Rumania, 1965, Poland, 1975; Royal Netherlands Acad., 1959; Deutsche Akademie der Naturforscher Leopoldina, 1964; Royal Society, 1966; Amer. Acad. of Arts and Sciences, 1966. Pres., Internat. Union of Pure and Applied Physics, 1963–66. Gold Medal, CNRS, 1965; Nobel Prize for Physics, 1970. Hon. Dr: Graz, 1948; Nottingham, 1951; Oxford, 1958; Louvain, 1965; Newcastle, 1965; Coïmbra, 1966; Sherbrooke, 1967; Madrid, 1978. *Publications*: numerous on magnetism. *Address*: 15 rue Marcel-Allégot, 92190 Meudon-Bellevue, France. *T*: 145343651. *Died 17 Nov. 2000.*

NISSAN, Prof. Alfred Heskel, PhD, DSc; FIChemE, FAIChE, FAIC; Consultant to WESTVACO (formerly West Virginia Pulp and Paper), New York (Vice-President, 1967–79, and Corporate Director of Research,

1962–79); Professor, College of Environmental Science and Forestry, Syracuse, New York, since 1979; *b* 14 Feb. 1914; *s* of Heskel and Farha Nissan, Baghdad, Iraq; *m* 1940, Zena Gladys Phyllis, *o d* of late Phillip and Lillian Frances Pursehouse-Ahmed, Birmingham; one *d*. *Educ*: The American Sch. for Boys, Baghdad, Iraq; Univ. of Birmingham (BSc 1st cl. Hons 1937, DSc Chem. Engrg). Instn of Petroleum Scholarship, 1936; Sir John Cadman Medal, 1937; Instn of Petroleum Medal and Prize and Burgess Prize, 1937; Research Fellow, 1937, Lectr, 1940, Univ. of Birmingham; Head of Central Research Labs, Bowater Paper Corporation Ltd, 1947; Technical Dir in charge of Research, Bowaters Development and Research Ltd, 1950; Research Prof. of Wool Textile Engineering, Univ. of Leeds, 1953; Prof. of Chemical Engrg, Rensselaer Polytechnic Inst., Troy, NY, USA, 1957. Hon. Vis. Prof., Uppsala Univ., 1974; ERCO Res. Fellow, Univ. of Toronto, 1987. Schwarz Memorial Lectr, Amer. Soc. of Mech. Engrs, 1967; Dow Dist. Lectr, Univ. of British Columbia, 1989. Member: Adv. Council for Advancement of Industrial R&D, State of NY, 1965–; Board of Directors: Technical Assoc. of Pulp & Paper Industry, 1968–71 (R&D Div. Award, 1976); Industrial Res. Inst., 1973–77. Bd of Trustees, Amer. Inst. of Chemists Foundn, 1989–91. Mem. Sigma XI. Alexander Mitscherlich Medal, Zellcheming, W Germany, 1980; Gold Medal, Technical Assoc. of Pulp and Paper Industry, 1982. *Publications*: (ed) Textile Engineering Processes, 1959; (ed) Future Technical Needs and Trends in the Paper Industry, 1973; Lectures on Fiber Science in Paper, 1977; papers on physical chemistry and chemical engrg problems of petroleum, paper and textile technology in scientific jls. *Address*: 6A Dickel Road, Scarsdale, NY 10583, USA. *Deceased.*

NORWOOD, Sir Walter (Neville), Kt 1971; former Chairman and Managing Director, C. B. Norwood Ltd; *b* 14 July 1907; *s* of late Sir Charles John Boyd Norwood and Rosina Ann, *d* of George Tattle, Wellington, NZ; *m* 1935, Rana Muriel, *d* of David Redpath; two *s* one *d*. *Educ*: Wellington and Wanganui. Chm., later Pres., NZ Motor Corp. Trustee: C. J. B. Norwood Crippled Children's Trust; Norwood Cricket Trust; Rana and Walter Norwood Charitable Trust. Past President: Wellington Rotary Club; Wellington Racing Club. *Recreations*: racing, farming, sailing. *Address*: Hillcrest, 24 Mataroa Avenue, Northland, Wellington, New Zealand. *Clubs*: Wellesley, Wellington (Wellington, NZ). *Died 1 April 2000.*

NSEKELA, Amon James, OURT 1985; Director: Tanzania–Zambia Railway Authority, since 1982; Computers and Telecoms Systems, since 1993; *b* 4 Jan. 1930; *s* of Ngonile Reuben Nsekela and Anyambilile Nsekela (*née* Kalinga); *m* 1957, Christina Matilda Nsekela (*née* Kyusa); two *s*. *Educ*: Rungwe Dist Sch.; Malangali Secondary Sch.; Tabora Govt Sen. Sec. Sch.; Makerere UC (DipEd); Univ. of Pacific (Scholar, MA). Schoolteacher, Rungwe Middle Sch. and Alliance Secondary Sch., 1954–57; entered Civil Service as DO, Moshi, 1960; Perm. Sec., Min. of External Affairs and Defence, 1963; Perm. Sec. to Min. of Commerce, 1964; Prin. Sec. to Treasury (also ex-officio Paymaster Gen.), 1966–67. MP 1973–75, and Mem. E African Legis. Assembly, 1967–70. High Comr, UK, 1974–81, and Ambassador Extraordinary and Plenipotentiary to Ireland, 1980–81. Chm. or Dir of many cos and corporations, 1967–, incl.: Chm., Nat. Insurance Corp. of Tanzania, 1967–72; Chm. and Man. Dir, Nat. Bank of Commerce, 1967–74 and 1981–94; Chm., Tanzania Investment Bank, 1982–91; Director: Nat. Develt Corp. (formerly Chm., Tanganyika Develt Corp.); Bd of Internal Trade; E African Airways Corp.; Bd, African Medical Res. Fund, 1986–. Mem./Sec., Presidential Commn on Estabt of Democratic One-Party State in Tanzania; Mem., Internat. Council of Trustees, Internat. Defence and Aid Fund for Southern Africa, 1985–. Chairman: Council, Inst. of Finance Management, 1971–; Inst. of Develt Management, 1982–; Public Service Salaries Review Commn, 1985–86. Pres.,

Tanzania Soc. for Internat. Develt; Past Pres., Economic Assoc. of Tanzania; Chm., Britain–Tanzania Soc., 1982–. Mem., TANU, 1955. Mem., NEC, Chama Cha Mapinduzi, 1987–. Chm. Council, Univ. of Dar es Salaam; Vice-Chm., Council, Sokoine Univ. of Agriculture, 1982–. *Publications:* Minara ya Historia ya Tanganyika: Tanganyika hadi Tanzania, 1965, new edns 1966 and 1971; Demokrasi Tanzania, 1973; (with A. L. Nhonoli) The Development of Health Services in Mainland Tanzania: Tumetoka Mbali, 1976; Socialism and Social Accountability in a Developing Nation, 1978; (ed) Southern Africa: toward economic liberation, 1981; Towards Rational Alternatives, 1984; A Time to Act, 1984; contribs to Jl of Administration Overseas (ODM), African Review, Development Dialogue. *Recreations:* swimming, darts, reading, writing. *Address:* 9 Lupa Way, Box 722, Mbeya, Tanzania. *Died 21 Sept. 1999.*

OLIVIER, Henry, CMG 1954; DScEng, PhD, DEng; FICE, FASCE; specialist consulting engineer in water resources engineering, Henry Olivier & Associates, since 1974; *b* 25 Jan. 1914; *s* of Jacobus Olivier, Umtali, S Rhodesia; *m* 1st, 1940, Lorna Renée Collier; one *d* (one *s* decd); 2nd, 1979, Johanna Cecilia van der Merwe. *Educ:* Umtali High Sch.; Cape Town Univ. (BSc 1936; MSc 1947); University College London (PhD 1953); DEng Witwatersrand, 1967. Beit Engineering Schol., 1932–38; Beit Fellow for two Rhodesias, 1939. Engineering post-grad. training with F. E. Kanthack & Partners, Consulting Engineers, Johannesburg, 1937; Sir Alex. Gibb & Partners, Cons. Engineers, London: training 1938, Asst Engineer, 1939; experience covers design and construction of steam-electric power-stations, hydro-electric, floating harbour, irrigation, and water resources development schemes in UK, Africa, Middle East, and USA; Chief Engineer in charge civil engineering contracts, Owen Falls Hydro-Electric Scheme, Uganda, 1950–54; Partner in firm of Sir Alexander Gibb and Partners (Africa), 1954–55; Resident Director and Chief Engineer (Rhodesia), in firm of Gibb, Coyne & Sogei (Kariba), 1955–60; Consultant (mainly in connection with Indus Basin Project in Pakistan) to Sir Alexander Gibb and Partners, London, 1960–69 (Sen. Consultant, 1967); Partner, Gibb Hawkins and Partners, Johannesburg, 1963–69, associated with design and construction of Hendrik Verwoerd and P. K. le Roux dams on Orange River, RSA; Chm. LTA Ltd and LTA Engineering Ltd, 1969–73; major projects: Cahora Bassa Hydro-electric Scheme in Mozambique as mem. of Internat. Consortium Zamco; Orange-Fish Tunnel in South Africa; Sen. Partner, Henry Olivier and Associates, 1974–86, acting for Dept of Water Affairs, RSA, on concept plans for water and power projects in Lesotho, Transkei, Swaziland and Botswana; major concept plans accepted and implemented Lesotho Highlands Water Scheme. Mem., Exec. Cttee, SA Nat. Cttee on Large Dams, 1972–81. FRSA. Hon. Fellow, SA Inst. of Civil Engineers (Pres., 1979). Hon. DSc: Cape, 1968; Rhodesia, 1977; Orange Free State, 1992. Order for Meritorious Service (Gold) (S Africa), 1992. *Publications:* Irrigation and Climate, 1960; Irrigation and Water Resources Engineering, 1972; Damit, 1975; Great Dams in Southern Africa, 1977; papers to Institution Civil Engineering Journal, Internat. Commn on Irrigation and Drainage, Water for Peace Conference, Washington, DC. *Recreation:* bowls. *Club:* Country (Johannesburg). *Died 6 Oct. 1994.*

ONGLEY, Hon. Sir Joseph (Augustine), Kt 1987; Judge of the High Court of New Zealand, 1975–86; *b* 5 Feb. 1918; *s* of Arthur Montague Ongley, OBE and Nora Crina Ongley; *m* 1943, Joan Muriel Archer; four *s* one *d*. *Educ:* St Patrick's Coll., Silverstream; Victoria Univ. of Wellington (LLB). Admitted Barrister and Solicitor of Supreme, later High, Court of NZ, 1939; Crown Solicitor, Palmerston North, 1960–75; retired, 1986, then served in temp. capacity until 1995. Life Mem., NZ Cricket Council (former Pres.); Patron, Central Dists Cricket Assoc., NZ, 1995. *Recreations:* formerly cricket

(represented NZ), golf. *Address:* 10 Lancaster Street, Karori, Wellington, New Zealand. *T:* (4) 4769585. *Clubs:* Wellington; Manawatu (Palmerston North). *Died 22 Oct. 2000.*

PEDLEY, Alan Sydney, DFC 1946; Lord Mayor of Leeds, 1975–76; District Insurance Manager, 1974–82, retired; *b* 16 Aug. 1917; *s* of Herbert Leonard Pedley and Edith Mary (*née* Skipsey); *m* 1st, 1949, Evelyn Anderson (*née* Scott) (*d* 1977); 2nd, 1981, Shirley Elizabeth (*d* 1995), widow of Reg Howard. *Educ:* Leeds Modern Sch. Entered Insurance, 1934; retd (Commercial Union), 1971; joined Barclays Insurance Services Co. Ltd, 1971. Member: Leeds CC, 1951–81; W Yorkshire Metropolitan CC, 1973–81; Dep. Lord Mayor, 1971–72. Hon. Alderman, City of Leeds, 1993. FCII 1949. *Recreations:* cricket, Association football, Rugby League, music, theatre, the Arts, after dinner speaking. *Address:* Whitelea, 8 Bentcliffe Close, Leeds LS17 6QT. *T:* Leeds (0113) 268 5424. *Died 10 Nov. 1999.*

PETERKIN, Sir Neville (Allan Mercer), Kt 1981; Chief Justice, West Indies Associated States, 1980–84; *b* 27 Oct. 1915; *s* of Joseph Allan Peterkin and Evelyn Peterkin; *m* 1942, Beryl Thompson; two *s* one *d*. *Educ:* Wellington Sch., Somerset. Called to Bar, Middle Temple, 1939. Registrar, St Lucia, 1943; Magistrate, Trinidad and Tobago, 1944; Resident Magistrate, Jamaica, 1954; High Court Judge: Trinidad, 1957; Associated States, 1967; Justice of Appeal, Associated States, 1975. *Recreations:* golf, bridge. *Address:* c/o Court of Appeal, PO Box 1093, Castries, St Lucia, West Indies. *Died 20 March 1998.*

POORE, Sir Herbert Edward, 6th Bt *cr* 1795; *b* April 1930; *s* of Sir Edward Poore, 5th Bt, and Amelia Guliemone; *S* father, 1938; *m. Heir: cousin* Roger Ricardo Poore [*b* 21 Oct. 1930; *m* Norma Naso]. *Deceased.*

RAFFERTY, Hon. Joseph Anstice, BA; FAIM, FID; JP; Agent General for Victoria in London, 1979–83; investor and primary producer, Australia, since 1983; *b* 10 Jan. 1911; *s* of late Col Rupert A. Rafferty, DSO, and Rose Sarah Anne Rafferty; *m* 1st, 1940, Miriam K. (decd), *d* of late Frank Richards, Devonport, Tas.; two *s*; 2nd, 1973, Lyn, *d* of Grace Jones, Brisbane, Qld. *Educ:* Christ Coll., Univ. of Tas. (BA); Univ. of Melbourne. FAIM 1954; FID 1960. Commonwealth Public Service, 1934–45; Personnel Manager, Australian National Airways, 1945–53; Personnel Management and Indust. Relations Consultant, 1953–70 (own practice; co. dir). MP (Lib) for: Caulfield, Vic, 1955–58; Ormond, Vic, 1958–67; Glenhuntly, Vic, 1967–79; Chm. Cttees and Dep. Speaker, Victorian Legislative Assembly, 1961–65; Parly Sec. for Cabinet, 1965–70; Minister for Labour and Industry, 1970–76; Asst Minister for Educn, 1970–72; Minister for Consumer Affairs, 1972–76; Minister for Fed. Affairs, 1974–76; Minister for Transport, 1976–78; Chief Sec. and Minister for Police and Emergency Services, 1978–79; Leader, Aust. Delegn to ILO Conf., Geneva, 1974. Pres., Melbourne Jun. Chamber of Commerce, 1950; Treasurer, Nat. Assoc. of Jun. Chambers of Commerce of Australia, 1951; Councillor: Melbourne Chamber of Commerce, 1950–76; Victorian Employers' Fedn, 1952–65. Dep. Leader, Aust. Delegn, 5th World Congress, Jun. Chamber of Commerce, Manila, 1950; Aust. Delegate, 6th World Congress, Jun. Chamber of Industry, Montreal, 1951; Delegate, 17th Triennial Congress, British Empire Chambers of Commerce, London, 1951. Mem. Council, La Trobe Univ., Vic, 1964–70; Trustee, Caulfield Racecourse Reserve, 1965–. Silver Jubilee Medal, 1977. Freeman, City of London, 1979. JP Victoria, 1970. *Recreations:* golf, swimming, walking, world travel, public speaking. *Address:* 8 Matlock Court, Caulfield North, Vic 3161, Australia. *T:* (3) 95000282. *Clubs:* Athenæum, Metropolitan Golf, MCC (Melbourne). *Died 14 June 2000.*

REVERDIN, Prof. Olivier, DrLitt; Professor of Greek, University of Geneva, 1958–83 (Hon. Professor, 1983);

Member, Consultative Assembly of Council of Europe, 1963–74 (President, 1969–72); Deputy (Liberal) for Geneva, Swiss National Council, 1955–71, Council of States (Senate), 1971–79; *b* 15 July 1913; *m* 1936, Renée Chaponnière; two *s* one *d. Educ:* Univ. of Geneva (LicLitt 1953; DrLitt 1945); Paris and Athens. Foreign Mem., French Sch. of Archaeology, Athens, 1936–38; Attaché Swiss Legation, Service of Foreign Interests, Rome, 1941–43; Privatdocent of Greek, Univ. of Geneva, 1945–57; Parly Redactor, 1945–54; Chief Editor 1954–59, Manager 1954–67, Pres., 1972–79, Journal de Genève. Mem. 1963–80, Pres. 1968–80, Swiss National Research Council; Mem., Swiss Science Council, 1958–80; Président: Fondation Hardt pour l'étude de l'antiquité classique, Geneva, 1959–96; Fondation Archives Jean Piaget, 1973–87; Vice-Pres., European Science Foundn, 1974–77, Mem. Exec. Council, 1977–80; Chm., Collections Baur, Geneva, 1984–. Hon. Mem., Soc. for Promotion of Hellenic Studies; Corresp. Mem., Acads of Athens and Vienna. Dr *hc*, Heidelberg, Strasbourg, Bucharest, Sorbonne, Zurich, Lausanne. *Publications:* La religion de la cité platonicienne, 1945; La guerre du Sonderbund, 1947, 2nd edn 1987; La Crète, berceau de la civilisation occidentale, 1960; Connaissance de la Suisse, 1966; Les premiers cours de Grec au Collège de France, 1984; Henri Estienne à Genève, 1988; Impressions grecques en Suisse au XVIᵉ et XVIIᵉ siècles, 1991. *Address:* 8 rue des Granges, 1204 Geneva, Switzerland. *T:* (22) 3115191.   *Died 16 June 2000.*

RHEA, Alexander Dodson, III; Executive Vice-President and Director, General Motors Overseas Corp., 1974–77; *b* 10 May 1919; *s* of Alexander D. Rhea, Jr and Annie Rhea; *m* 1945, Suzanne Menocal; one *s. Educ:* Princeton Univ. (BA Econs and Social Instns). Active service as Lt-Comdr USNR, 1941–45. Vice-Pres., Govt Employees Ins. Corp., Washington, DC, 1946–48; Treas. and Man. Dir, General Motors de Venezuela, Caracas, 1949–55; Vice-Pres., General Motors Overseas Corp., 1960–68; Regional Gp Dir, NY, 1960–66; Staff Man., 1966–67, General Motors Overseas Operations; Chm. and Man. Dir, General Motors-Holden's, Melbourne, 1968–70; Chm. and Man. Dir., Vauxhall Motors Ltd, 1970–74; Chm., European Adv. Council, General Motors Corp., 1974–77. Exec. Vice-Pres. and Dir, General Motors Overseas Corp., 1974–77. *Recreations:* reading, golf. *Address:* 580 Park Avenue, New York, NY 10021, USA. *Clubs:* Knickerbocker, Princeton, Colony (New York); Fort Worth, River Crest Country (Fort Worth, Texas); Melbourne (Melbourne); Greenbrier Golf and Tennis (White Sulphur Springs, West Virginia).
Died 1 Sept. 2000.

RINGADOO, Sir Veerasamy, GCMG 1986; Kt 1975; QC 1983; Officier de l'Ordre National Malgache 1969; President, Republic of Mauritius, 1992 (Governor-General and Commander-in-Chief of Mauritius, 1986–92); *b* 1920; *s* of Nagaya Ringadoo; *m* 1954, Lydie Vadamootoo; one *s* one *d. Educ:* Port Louis Grammar Sch.; LSE (LLB; Hon. Fellow, 1976). Called to Bar, 1949. Municipal Councillor, Port Louis, 1956; MLC for Moka-Flacq, 1951–67; Minister: Labour and Social Security, 1959–63; Education, 1964–67; Agriculture and Natural Resources, 1967–68; Finance, 1968–82; attended London Constitutional Conf., 1965; first MLA (Lab) for Quartier Militaire and Moka, 1967, re-elected 1976. Governor, IMF and African Develt Bank, 1970–82; Chm., Bd of Governors, African Develt Bank and African Develts Fund, 1977–78. Hon. DCL Mauritius, 1976; Hon. DLit Andhra, 1978; Dr *hc*: Bordeaux, 1988; Bharatidasan Univ., Tiruchirapalli, 1988. Médaille de l'Assemblée Nat. Française, 1971. *Address:* Cnr Antelme and Farquhar Streets, Quatre Bornes, Mauritius.
Died 9 Sept. 2000.

ROBERTS, Albert; JP; DL; *b* 14 May 1908; *s* of Albert Roberts and Annie Roberts (*née* Ward); *m* 1932, Alice Ashton (*d* 1989); one *s* one *d. Educ:* Woodlesford School;

Normanton and Whitwood Technical College, Yorks. Sec., Woodlesford Br., Yorks Miners Assoc., 1935–41; Safety Board, Mines Inspector, 1941–51. Mem., Rothwell UDC, 1937–52. MP (Lab) Normanton, 1951–83; Exec. Mem., British Group, Inter-Parly Union, 1955–83 (Chm., 1968–70). Exec. Mem., Yorkshire Area Heart Foundn; Vice-Pres., Yorkshire Soc. JP 1946, DL 1967, W Yorks. Order of Isabela la Católica (Spain), 1967; Diplomatic Order of Merit (Korean Republic), 1979. *Publication:* One of a Family (autobiog.), 1988. *Recreations:* cricket, bowls. *Address:* Cordoba, 14 Aberford Road, Oulton-Woodlesford, near Leeds LS26 8JR. *T:* (0113) 282 2303.
Died 11 May 2000.

ROBERTS, Sir (Edward Fergus) Sidney, Kt 1978; CBE 1972; former Federal President, Australian Country Party; grazier and manager of companies; *b* 19 April 1901; *s* of late E. J. Roberts. *Educ:* Scots Coll., Sydney. Gen. Manager, Ungra, Brisbane, 1957–70; owner, Boolaroo Downs, Clermont, Qld, 1928–63. Mem. Council, 1948–76, Vice-Pres., 1950–52, United Graziers' Assoc., Qld; Mem., 1954–63, Nat. Pres., 1962–63, Aust. Road Fedn. Mem. Bd, Queensland Country Life Newspaper, 1969–77; Pres., Aust. Country Party, Qld, 1967; Chm., Federal Council, ACP, 1969–74. Knighthood awarded for distinguished service to primary industry, Australia. *Address:* 53 Eldernell Avenue, Hamilton, Queensland 4007, Australia. *Club:* Queensland (Brisbane).
Died 5 Oct. 1998.

ROBERTS, (Herbert) John, CMG 1965; a Director, Rural Development Corporation of Zambia, 1980; *b* 22 Nov. 1919; *m* 1946, Margaret Pollard; three *s* one *d. Educ:* Holy Trinity, Weymouth; Milton, Bulawayo. Served War of 1939–45; Somaliland, Ethiopia, Burma. Elected MLC, Northern Rhodesia, 1954; Leader of Northern Rhodesia United Federal Party, 1959–63; Founder of National Progress Party, 1963; MP (Nat. Progress Party), Zambia, 1964–66, (Ind.), 1967–69; Minister of Labour and Mines, 1959–61; Leader of Opposition (NR), 1961–64; Leader of Opposition (Zambia), 1964–65; disbanded Nat. Progress Party, 1966. *Address:* Chanyanya Ranch, PO Box 32037, Lusaka, Zambia.   *Died 29 Dec. 1999.*

ROBERTS, John; *see* Roberts, H. J.

ROBERTS, Sir Sidney; *see* Roberts, Sir E. F. S.

ROSCOE, Sir Robert Bell, KBE 1981; FCPA; Director, Chase-NBA Group Ltd (Australia and New Zealand), 1969–80; Chairman: Melbourne Underground Rail Loop Authority, 1971–81; First Federation Discount Co. Ltd, 1975–84; *b* 7 Aug. 1906; *s* of T. B. Roscoe; *m* 1931, Daphne, *d* of G. Maxwell; one *d. Educ:* Central Tech. Coll., Brisbane. ABIA; ABINZ. Joined Qld Nat. Bank Ltd, 1921, Liquidator, 1949; State Manager, Qld, 1951–54; Nat. Bank of Australasia: State Manager, Victoria, 1954–60; Chief Inspector, 1960–65; Sen. Chief Inspector, 1965–66; Asst Chief Manager, 1966–69. Former Director: Hoechst Australia Ltd, 1970; All States Commercial Bills Ltd; Oceaniac Capital Corp. Ltd. *Address:* Unit 11, Camberwell Terrace, 22–24 Palmerston Street, Camberwell, Vic 3124, Australia. *Club:* Australian (Melbourne).   *Died 24 July 2000.*

ROWELL, Sir John (Joseph), Kt 1980; CBE 1974; Chairman, Legal Aid Commission of Queensland, 1979–90; Consultant, Neil O'Sullivan & Rowell, Solicitors, Brisbane (Senior Partner, 1968–88); *b* 15 Feb. 1916; *s* of Joseph Alfred Rowell and Mary Lilian Rowell (*née* Hooper), both born in England; *m* 1947, Mary Kathleen (*née* de Silva); three *s* two *d. Educ:* Brisbane Grammar School; Univ. of Queensland (BA). Served AIF, 1940–46; Captain 2/10 Fd Regt (Efficiency Medal, 1946). Admitted Solicitor, 1939; Notary Public, 1959. Pres., Queensland Law Soc. Inc., 1964–66 (Mem. Council, 1956–67); Treas., Law Council of Aust., 1961–63 (Mem. Exec., 1960–67); Mem. Bd, Faculty of Law, Univ. of Queensland, 1959–78; Chm., Legal Assistance Cttee of

Queensland, 1966–79; Member: Law Reform Commn of Qld, 1967–89; Commonwealth Legal Aid Commn, 1980–85. Chairman: Qld Bulk Handling Pty Ltd; Gas Corp. of Qld Ltd, 1974–90; Qld Bd, Capita Financial Gp (formerly City Mutual Life Assce Soc. Ltd), 1986–88 (Mem. Bd, 1971–88); Concrete Constructions (Qld) Pty, until 1993; Dir of Principal Bd, Boral Ltd and Boral Resources Ltd, 1974–87; Dir, Castlemaine Tooheys Ltd, 1980–85. Former Hon. Consul of Qld for Federal Repub. of Germany, 1963–86; Dean, Consular Corps of Qld, 1978–80. Pres., Qld Br., Australia-Britain Soc., 1988–94; Vice Pres., Qld Br., ESU, 1990–93. Officer's Cross, 1st class, 1979, Comdr's Cross, Order of Merit, 1986, FRG. *Recreations:* golf, fishing, reading. *Address:* Edgecliffe, 48 Walcott Street, St Lucia, Brisbane, Qld 4067, Australia. *T:* (7) 8709070. *Clubs:* Australian (Sydney); Brisbane, United Service, Tattersall's, Queensland Turf (Brisbane).

Died 5 May 1996.

RUBERTI, Prof. Antonio, FIEEE; MP (Left Democratic Party), Rome, since 1995; Professor of System Theory, La Sapienza University, Rome, since 1962; *b* Aversa, Italy, 24 Jan. 1927; *m* 1955, Luisa Andreozzi; one *s* three *d*. *Educ:* Naples Univ. (Laurea in electrical engrg). FIEEE 1985. La Sapienza University, Rome: Head, Engrg Faculty, 1973–76; Rector, 1976–87; Minister for Co-ordination of Scientific and Technol Research and for Research and Univs, 1987–92; MP (Italian Socialist Party), Rome-Latina-Frosinone-Viterbo, 1992; Mem., CEC, then Eur. Commn, 1993–95 (a Vice-Pres., 1993). Ordre National de la Légion d'Honneur (France), 1982; Leonardo da Vinci Medal (Italy), 1989. *Publications:* numerous scientific works on control and system theory, essays, books and encyclopedia articles on university policy concerning research and problems of technol innovation. *Address:* Via San Calepodio 36, 00152 Roma, Italy; Palazzo Montecitorio, Roma, Italy. *T:* (6) 67603905, *Fax:* (6) 67609948.

Died 4 Sept. 2000.

RUSSELL, Prof. Roger Wolcott; Vice Chancellor, and Professor of Psychobiology, Flinders University of South Australia, 1972–79, then Emeritus Professor (engaged in research, 1979–89); Research Psychobiologist, School of Biological Sciences, since 1990, Research Neurobiologist and Fellow of the Center for the Neurobiology of Learning and Memory, since 1991 (Lifetime Distinguished Fellow, 1994), University of California at Irvine; *b* 30 Aug. 1914; *s* of Leonard Walker and Sadie Stanhope Russell, Worcester, Mass, USA; *m* 1945, Kathleen Sherman Fortescue; one *s* one *d*. *Educ:* Worcester (Mass, USA) Public Schools; Clark Univ. (Livermore Schol., Clark Fellow in Psychology; BA 1935, MA 1936); Peabody Coll., Vanderbilt Univ. (Payne Schol.); University of Virginia (Du Pont Research Fellow; PhD 1939); DSc London, 1954. Instructor in Psychology: Univ. of Nebraska, 1939–41: Michigan State Coll., 1941; Research Psychologist, USAF Sch. of Aviation Medicine, 1941–42; Officer USAF, 1942–46; Asst Prof. in Psychol., Univ. of Pittsburgh, 1946–47; Assoc. Prof. of Psychol., Univ. of Pittsburgh and Res. Fellow in Neurophysiol., Western Psychiatric Inst., 1947–49; Fulbright Advanced Research Schol. and Director, Animal Research Lab., Institute of Psychiatry, Univ. of London, 1949–50; Prof. of Psychology and Head of Dept of Psychol., University Coll., London 1950–57 (on leave of absence, 1956–57); Dean of Advanced Studies, Indiana Univ., 1966–67 (Prof. and Chm. Dept of Psychology, 1959–66); Vice Chancellor, Academic Affairs, and Prof. of Psychology, Psycho-Biology and of Clinical Pharmacology and Therapeutics, Univ. of Calif, Irvine, 1967–72. Member: Australian Vice-Chancellors' Cttee, 1972–79; Bd of Dirs, Australian-American Educnl Foundn, 1972–79; Commonwealth Educnl R&D Cttee, 1974–79. Aust.-Amer. Educn Foundn Vis. Prof., Dept of Psychol., Univ. of Sydney, 1965–66; Vis. Erskine Fellow, Univ. of Canterbury, NZ, 1966; Visiting Professor: Sch. of Medicine, UCLA, 1976–77, 1980–90; Dept of Psychology, Univ. of Reading, 1977; Dept of Psychology,

Univ. of Stockholm, 1977. Executive Sec. of the American Psychological Assoc., 1956–59, Board of Directors, 1963–65, Pres. Div. 1, 1968–69; Mem., USPHS Adv. Cttee in Psychopharmacology, 1957–63, 1967–70, 1981–85; Member: Nat. Research Council, USA, 1958–61, 1963–65, 1967–71; Army Sci. Adv. Panel, USA, 1958–66; Sec.-Gen., Internat. Union of Psychological Science, 1960–66 (Vice-Pres., 1966–69; Pres., 1969–72; Mem. Exec. Cttee, 1972–80); Member, Scientific and Professional Socs in Europe, USA, Australia. FACE 1972; FASSA 1973. Hon. DSc: Newcastle, NSW, 1978; Flinders, 1979. Bronze Star Medal (USA), 1945; Army Commendation Medal (USA), 1946. *Publications:* (ed) Frontiers in Psychology, 1964; (ed) Frontiers in Physiological Psychology, 1966; (ed) Matthew Flinders: The Ifs of History, 1979; (ed) Behavioral Measures of Neurotoxicity, 1990; research papers on neurochemical bases of behaviour, experimental psycho-pathology, physiological, child and social psychology, psychopharmacology. *Recreation:* writing. *Address:* Center for the Neurobiology of Learning and Memory, University of California, Irvine, CA 92697–3800, USA; One Cherry North, Irvine, CA 92715. *T:* (714) 6510107.

Died 25 July 1998.

SAMARAKOON, Hon. Neville Dunbar Mirahawatte; Chief Justice, Democratic Socialist Republic of Sri Lanka, 1977–84; *b* 22 Oct. 1919; *s* of Alfred Charles Warnabarana Wickremasinghe Samarakoon and Rajapaksa Wasala Mudiyanselage Chandrawati Mirahawatte Kumarihamy; *m* 1949, Mary Patricia Mulholland; one *s* two *d*. *Educ:* Trinity Coll., Kandy; University Coll., Colombo; Law Coll., Colombo. Enrolled as Advocate, 1945; Crown Counsel, Attorney-General's Dept, 1948–51; reverted to Private Bar, 1951; QC 1968. Member: Bar Council, 1964–77; Disciplinary Bd for Lawyers 1971–74, 1976, 1977. Chairman: Judicial Service Commn, 1978–84; Council of Legal Educn.

Died 1990.

SEDOV, Leonid Ivanovich; 6 Orders of Lenin, Hero of Socialist Labour, USSR; Professor, Moscow University, since 1937; Chief of Department of Hydrodynamics, since 1941; Member, Russian Academy of Sciences; *b* 14 Nov. 1907; *m* 1931, Galya Tolstova; one *s* one *d*. *Educ:* Moscow University. Chief Engineer, Associate Chief lab., N.E. Zhukovsky Aerohydrodynamic Inst., Moscow, 1930–47; Vice-Pres., Internat. Astronautical Fedn, 1962–80 (Pres., 1959–61); Internat. Astronautical Acad., 1980–. Hon. Member: Amer. Acad. of Arts and Scis; Internat. Astronautical Acad.; Serbian Acad., Belgrade; Tech. Academy, Finland; For. Associate, Acad. of Scis, Paris; Academia Leopoldina. Hon. doctorates from many foreign universities. Medal of Obert; State Prize; Chaplygin Prize; Lomonosov Prize; Lyapunov Gold Medal, 1974; Guggenheim Award; Van Allen Award. Commandeur de la Légion d'Honneur (France). *Publications:* Theory of Plane Flow of Liquids, 1939; Plane Problems of Hydrodynamics and Aerodynamics, 1950, 1966, 1980; Similarity and Dimensional Methods in Mechanics, 1944, 1951, 1953, 1957, 1960, 1965, 1967, 1977, 1995; Introduction into the Mechanics of Continua, 1962; Mechanics of Continuous Media, 2 vols, 1970, 1973, 1976, 1983–84, 1996; Thoughts about Science and Scientists, 1980; (with A. G. Tsypkin) Fundamentals of Electromagnetical and Gravitational Macroscopic Theories, 1989; numerous articles. *Address:* Moscow University, Zone I, kv 84, Vorobrevy Gory, Moscow 119899, Russia.

Died 5 Sept. 1999.

SHERGOLD, Harold Taplin, CMG 1963; OBE 1958 (MBE 1945); served in Foreign and Commonwealth Office (formerly Foreign Office), 1954–80; *b* 5 Dec. 1915; *s* of late Ernest Henry Shergold; *m* 1949, Bevis Anael (*d* 1997), *d* of late William Bernard Reid; no *c*. *Educ:* Peter Symonds' School, Winchester; St Edmund Hall, Oxford; Corpus Christi Coll., Cambridge. Asst Master, Cheltenham Grammar Sch., 1937–40. Joined Hampshire Regt, 1940; transferred to Intelligence Corps, 1941; served in Middle East and Italy, 1941–46 (despatches). Joined Foreign Office, 1947; served in Germany, 1947–54. Chm., 1983–90, Pres., 1990–, Richmond, Twickenham & Dist Br., Guide Dogs for the Blind Assoc. *Address:* 1 Ancaster Court, Queens Road, Richmond, Surrey TW10 6JJ. *T:* (020) 8948 2048. *Died 25 Dec. 2000.*

SIMONET, Henri François; Commander, Order of Leopold, 1974; Member, Belgian Parliament, 1966–92; *b* Brussels, 10 May 1931; *m* 1960, Marie-Louise Angenent; one *s* one *d*. *Educ:* Univ. Libre de Bruxelles (DenD, DèsSc); Columbia Univ., USA. Asst, Univ. Libre de Bruxelles, 1956–58, then Prof.; Financial Adv., Inst. Nat. d'Etudes pour le Développement du Bas-Congo, 1958–59; Legal Adv., Commn of Brussels Stock Exchange, 1956–60; Dep. Dir, Office of Econ. Programming, 1961; Director of Cabinet: of Min. of Econ. Affairs and Power, 1961–65; of Dep. Prime Minister responsible for co-ordination of Econ. Policy, 1965; Minister of Econ. Affairs, 1972; Vice-Pres., Commn of the European Communities, 1973–77; Foreign Minister, Belgium, 1977–80; Sec. of State, Brussels Regional Economy, 1977–79. Mayor of Anderlecht, 1966–84. Comdr, Légion d'Honneur (France), 1985. *Publications:* various books and articles on economics, financial and political topics. *Died 15 Feb. 1996.*

SMART, Edwin; *see* Smart, L. E.

SMART, (Louis) Edwin, JD; Chairman and Chief Executive Officer, Trans World Corporation, 1978–87; Chairman of Executive Committee, Hilton International Co., since 1986 (Chairman of Board, 1978–86); *b* Columbus, Ohio, 17 Nov. 1923; *s* of Louis Edwin Smart and Esther Guthery; *m* 1st, 1944, Virginia Alice Knouff (marr. diss. 1958); one *s* one *d*; 2nd, 1964, Jeanie Alberta Milone; one *s*. *Educ:* Harvard Coll. (AB *magna cum laude* 1947); Harvard Law Sch. (JD *magna cum laude* 1949). Served to Lieut, USNR, 1943–46. Admitted to NY Bar, 1950; Associate, Hughes, Hubbard & Ewing, NYC, 1949–56; Partner, Hughes, Hubbard & Reed, NYC, 1957–64; Pres., Bendix Internat. and Dir, Bendix Corp. and foreign subsids, 1964–67; Trans World Airlines Inc.: Sen. Vice Pres., External Affairs, 1967–71, Corp. Affairs, 1971–75; Vice Chm. 1976; Chief Exec. Officer, 1977–78; Chm. of Bd, 1977–85; also Dir, Mem. Exec., and Mem. Finance Cttee. Chairman: Canteen Corp., 1973–; Spartan Food Systems Inc., 1979–; former Director: Sonat Inc.; The Continental Corp.; NY Stock Exchange; Trustee, Cttee for Econ. Develt, 1977–. Member: Conf. Bd, 1977–; Amer. Bar Assoc.; NY County Lawyers Assoc.; Phi Beta Kappa; Sigma Alpha Epsilon. *Address:* 535 E 86th Street, New York, NY 10028, USA. *Club:* Marco Polo (NYC). *Died 1 June 1998.*

SMITH, Sir Christopher Sydney Winwood, 5th Bt *cr* 1809; *b* 20 Sept. 1906; *s* of Sir William Sydney Winwood Smith, 4th Bt, and Caroline, *o d* of James Harris, Co. Cork; *S* father, 1953; *m* 1932, Phyllis Berenice, *y d* of late Thomas Robert O'Grady, Grafton, NSW, and Co. Waterford, Ireland; six *s* three *d* (and one *s* decd). *Heir: s* Robert Christopher Sydney Winwood Smith [*b* 1939; *m* 1971, Roslyn Nellie, *e d* of late James Keith McKensie; one *s* one *d*]. *Address:* Junction Road, via Grafton, New South Wales 2460, Australia. *Died 3 Dec. 2000.*

SMITH, Rev. Francis Taylor; Minister of St Paul's Parish Church, Dunfermline, since 1964; *b* 22 Jan. 1933; *s* of James William Smith and Jeannie Moir Catto Cockburn; *m* 1957, Jean Millar Wallace; three *s* one *d*. *Educ:* Aberdeen Grammar Sch.; Aberdeen Univ. (MA); Christ's Coll., Aberdeen (Licence to Preach). Student Assistant: Queen's Cross Church, Aberdeen, 1954–56; North Church, Aberdeen, 1956–57; Sen. Asst, Govan Old Church, Glasgow, 1957–58; Parish Minister, Aberlour, Banffshire, 1958–64. Chaplain: Dunfermline and West Fife Hosp., 1964–93; Dunfermline Maternity Hosp., 1988–93; Moderator of Dunfermline Presbytery, 1973–74; 1995–96. Councillor, Banff CC, 1964; Chairman: West

Fife Local Health Council, 1975–84; Queen Margaret Hosp. NHS Trust, Dunfermline, 1994–98; Vice Chm., Cttee on Ethical Med. Res., Fife Health Bd, 1996–99; Mem., Multi Centre Res. Ethics Cttee for Scotland, 1997–99; Vice-Pres., Assoc. of Scottish Local Health Councils, 1978–79, Pres., 1980, 1981; Crown Lay Nominee, General Medical Council, 1979–89. Chm., Fife Marriage Counselling Service, 1984–85. Governor, Aberlour Orphanage, 1964. *Recreations:* work, music, fishing, reading. *Address:* St Paul's Manse, 6 Park Avenue, Dunfermline, Fife KY12 7HX. *T:* (01383) 721124.
Died 25 Dec. 2000.

SOMERVILLE, Very Rev. Dr John Spenser, ONZ 1991; CMG 1978; MC 1945; Master, Knox College, Dunedin, 1963–78, retired; *b* 7 July 1910; *s* of James Cleland Hall Somerville and Grace Isabella (*née* Isherwood); *m* 1951, Janet Christina Macky (*d* 1988); four *s*. *Educ:* Univ. of Otago (MA 1934); Theol Hall, Knox Coll., Dunedin. Ordained Tapanui, 1938; Chaplain, 2 NZEF, 1942–45; Minister, St Andrews, Wellington, 1947–63. Moderator, Gen. Assembly of Presbyterian Church of NZ, 1960. Mem. Council, 1969–85, Chancellor, 1976–82, Univ. of Otago. Pres., Otago Early Settlers' Assoc., 1979–91. Hon. DD St Andrews, 1969; Hon. LLD Otago, 1979. *Publication:* Jack in the Pulpit (autobiog.), 1987. *Recreations:* cricket, bowls, reading, gardening. *Address:* 19 Constitution Street, Dunedin 9001, New Zealand. *T:* (3) 4779876. *Clubs:* Dunedin, University (Dunedin). *Died 5 Oct. 1999.*

SOUTHAM, Gordon Ronald, BSc; Headmaster, Ashville College, Harrogate, 1958–77; *b* 20 March 1918; *s* of late G. H. Southam, Brackley; *m* 1948, Joan, *d* of late W. Thompson; one *d*. *Educ:* Magdalen College School, Brackley; King's College, London (BSc (Gen. Hons) 1938, BSc (Special Physics) 1st Class Hons 1939); Westminster Coll., London (Teacher's diploma, 1947). AInstP 1947. Served Royal Air Force, 1940–46: Bomber Comd, 1940–43; Staff Officer in HQ, ACSEA, 1943–46 (Sqdn Ldr). Senior Physics Master, Culford School, 1947–49; Lecturer, 1950–52, Head of Department of Science, 1953–57, Royal Military Academy, Sandhurst. *Recreations:* motoring, electronics; formerly Rugby football, athletics. *Address:* Culford, 20 Oak Tree Drive, Bedale, N Yorks DL8 1UL. *Died 13 Aug. 2000.*

SPITZ, Kathleen Emily, (Mrs Heinz Spitz); *see* Gales, K. E.

STEAD, Ralph Edmund, FCA, FCMA; retired; Chairman, Eastern Region, British Gas Corporation, 1977–81; *b* 7 Jan. 1917; *s* of Albert Stead and Mabel Stead; *m* 1946, Evelyn Annie Ness (*d* 1997); two *s* two *d*. *Educ:* Manchester Grammar Sch.; Ilford County High Sch. FCA 1949; FCMA 1952. Served War, RASC, 1940–46. Asst Divl Accountant, Cambridge Div., Eastern Gas Bd, 1949–50; N Eastern Gas Board: Asst Chief Accountant, 1950–53; Group Accountant, Bradford Gp, 1953–57; N Western Gas Board: Gp Accountant, Manchester Gp, 1957–61; Gen. Man., West Lancs Gp, 1961–65; Head of Management Services, 1966–71; Dir of Finance, 1971–73; Dep. Chm., Eastern Reg., British Gas Corp., 1973–77. Member: Financial Instns Gp, DoE, 1981–82; Management Cttee, Lazards Property Unit Trust, 1979–92; Rent Assessment Panel for Scotland, 1983–87. *Recreations:* golf, gardening, reading. *Address:* 12 Abbotsford Court, Colinton Road, Edinburgh EH10 5EH. *Died 27 Sept. 2000.*

STEELE, Sir (Philip John) Rupert, Kt 1980; Director, Trust Company of Australia Ltd (formerly Union Fidelity Trustee Co. of Australia), 1984–91; *b* 3 Nov. 1920; *s* of late C. Steele; *m* 1946, Judith, *d* of Dr Clifford Sharp; one *s* two *d*. *Educ:* Melbourne C of E Grammar School. Served RAAF and 115 Sqdn (Lancaster), RAF; POW 1944. Director: Steele & Co. Ltd, 1949–59; Carlton Brewery Ltd, 1964–73; Carlton and United Breweries, 1973–84. Mem. Council, Royal Agr. Soc. of Victoria, 1961–74.

Pres., Prahan Football Club, 1980–85; Mem. Cttee, Victoria Racing Club, 1958–85, Hon. Treasurer, 1971–73, Vice-Chm., 1973–77, Chm., 1977–82; Mem., Racecourses Licensing Board, 1975–81. *Recreation:* racing thoroughbred horses. *Address:* 2/64 Irving Road, Toorak, Victoria 3142, Australia. *Died 20 Aug. 2000.*

STEELE, Sir Rupert; *see* Steele, Sir P. J. R.

SUTHERLAND, Ian, MA; Director of Education and Training, Health Education Council, 1971–86; *b* 7 July 1926; *m* 1951, Virginia Scovil Bliss (marr. diss. 1978); one *s* one *d. Educ:* Wyggeston Grammar School, Leicester; Sidney Sussex Coll., Cambridge (BA 1948, MA 1952). Asst Prof. of Classics, Univ. of New Brunswick, NB, Canada, 1949–50; Assistant Master: Christ's Hospital, 1951–52; Harrow School, 1952–60; Head Master, St John's School, Leatherhead, 1960–70; Dir of Educn, Health Educn Council, 1970–71. Mem., Wandsworth HA, 1986–89. Governor, Reeds Sch., 1980–93. *Publications:* From Pericles to Cleophon, 1954; (ed) Health Education: perspectives and choices, 1979; Health Education, Half a Policy: the rise and fall of the Health Education Council, 1987; Around the World by Train, 1991; Coastal Corners, 1997. *Recreations:* painting, cricket. *Address:* 14 The Green, Great Bowden, Market Harborough, Leics LE16 7EU. *Clubs:* Oxford and Cambridge, MCC, Free Foresters'. *Died Nov. 1999.*

SZWARC, Michael M., FRS 1966; Distinguished Professor of Chemistry, State University of New York, 1966–79, then Professor Emeritus; *b* 9 June 1909; Polish; *m* 1933, Marja Frenkel; one *s* two *d. Educ:* Warsaw Inst. of Technology (Chem. Eng. 1933); Hebrew Univ., Jerusalem (PhD 1942); Manchester Univ. (PhD (Phys. Chem.) 1947; DSc 1949). Lectr, Manchester Univ., 1945–52; State University College of Environmental Sciences, Syracuse, NY, 1952–82: Prof. of Physical and Polymer Chemistry; Research Prof.; Distinguished Prof. of Chemistry; Dir, Polymer Research Inst. Baker Lectr, Cornell Univ., 1972. Nobel Guest Prof., Univ. of Uppsala, 1969–72; Visiting Professor: Univ. of Leuven, 1974; Univ. of Calif, San Diego, 1979–80. Foreign Mem., Polish Acad. of Scis, 1988. Hon. Dr: Leuven, Belgium, 1974; Uppsala, Sweden, 1975; Louis Pasteur Univ., France, 1978. Amer. Chem. Soc. Award for Outstanding Achievements in Polymer Chemistry, 1969; Gold Medal, Soc. of Plastic Engrs, 1972; Gold Medal, Benjamin Franklin Inst., 1978; Herman Mark Award, Amer. Chem. Soc., 1990; Kyoto Award, 1991. *Publications:* Carbanions, Living Polymers and Electron Transfer Processes, 1968; Ions and Ion-pairs in Organic Chemistry, Vol. I, 1972, Vol. II, 1974; Ionic Polymerization and Living Polymers, 1993; Ionic Polymerization Fundamentals, 1996; numerous contribs to Jl Chem. Soc., Trans Faraday Soc., Proc. Royal Soc., Jl Amer. Chem. Soc., Jl Chem. Phys., Jl Phys. Chem., Jl Polymer Sci., Nature, Chem. Rev., Quarterly Reviews, etc. *Address:* 1176 Santa Luisa Drive, Solana Beach, CA 92075, USA. *T:* (619) 4811863. *Died Aug. 2000.*

TAVAIQIA, Ratu Sir Josaia (Nasorowale), KBE 1986; JP; First Vice President, Republic of Fiji, 1993 (Second Vice President, 1992–93); *b* 25 Dec. 1930; *s* of Ratu Josaia Tavaiqia and Adi Lusiana Ratu; *m* 1955, Adi Lady Merewalesi Naqei; three *d. Educ:* Queen Victoria Sch.; Natabua Indian Secondary Sch., Fiji (Sen. Cambridge Examination). Custom Officer, Custom Dept, Fiji, 1949–59; Hotel Manager, 1961–75; Minister of State for Forests, 1977–89. Pres., Rural Youth Council of Fiji, 1979–92. Traditional role as Tui (Chief) of Vuda, with tradit. title of Tui Vuda (Chief of Vuda). *Recreation:* Rugby management. *Address:* Viseisei, Vuda, Fiji. *T:* 661273. *Clubs:* Royal Commonwealth Society, Union. *Died 17 Nov. 1997.*

TAYLOR, Ronald Oliver; Managing Director, Vickers, 1988–90; *b* 12 Aug. 1931; *s* of Andrew James Taylor, CBE and late Mary Ann Symmers, *d* of George Cowie,

Aberdeen; *m* 1961, Frances Sylvia Howcroft; three *s* one *d. Educ:* Grove Academy, Dundee. Mem., Inst. of Chartered Accountants of Scotland. Vickers, 1958–90: Accountant, 1958; Managing Dir, Printing Machinery Group, 1969–72; Chief Exec., Howson-Algraphy Group, 1972–85; Director, 1977; Jt Dep. Managing Dir, 1984; Jt Managing Dir, 1987. Mem., CBI Europe Cttee, 1987–89. *Recreations:* golf, walking. *Address:* Ryburn, Crabtree Green, Collingham, near Wetherby, West Yorks LS22 5AB. *T:* (01937) 572135. *Died 13 Oct. 2000.*

TAYLOR, William Bernard; Public Sector Specialist Adviser: Invesco Asset Management Ltd (formerly MIM, subseq. Invesco MIM Ltd), 1986–97; Ivory & Sime (formerly Baronsmead PLC), 1993–97; Underwriting Member, Lloyd's, since 1988; *b* 13 Dec. 1930; *s* of Frank and Elizabeth Taylor; *m* 1956, Rachel May Davies; one *s* two *d. Educ:* Dynevor Sch., Swansea; Univ. of Kent (MA). CPFA. Nat. Service, RN, 1949–51; commnd RNVR; served in coastal forces. District Audit Service, 1951–61; Llwchwr UDC, 1961–70; Asst Educn Officer, Manchester Corp., 1970–72; Asst County Treasurer, 1972–73, Dep. County Treasurer, 1973–80, County Treasurer, 1980–86, Kent. Financial Adviser: Social Servs Cttee, ACC, 1983–86; Standing Conf. of Planning Auths in SE England, 1983–86; Hon. Treas., SE England Tourist Bd, 1980–86; Chm., wkg party of Council of Europe on borrowing by municipalities of member states, 1982–84; Dir, Interlake DRC Ltd, 1989–94. Public Sector Specialist Advisor: Ernst & Young (formerly Arthur Young), 1986–91; Lombard North Central, 1986–92; Sedgwick UK Ltd, 1986–95. Gov., and Chm. F and GP (formerly Finance Cttee), Kent Inst. of Art and Design, 1989–95; non-exec. Mem., and Chm. Finance and Rev. Cttee, Medway NHA, 1990–93; Vice-Chm., Medway NHS Trust, 1994–. Pres., Maidstone Rotary Club, 1995–96. FRSA. *Publications:* The Management of Assets: terotechnology in the pursuit of economic life cycle costs, 1980; The Financial Management of Local Authorities, 1993; contribs to local govt and other learned journals. *Recreations:* cricket, rugby, public speaking. *Address:* Selby Shaw, Heath Road, Boughton Monchelsea, near Maidstone, Kent ME17 4JE. *T:* (01622) 745022. *Died 5 March 1999.*

TENCH, William Henry, CBE 1980; Chief Inspector of Accidents, Department of Trade, 1974–81; *b* 2 Aug. 1921; *s* of Henry George Tench and Emma Rose Tench (*née* Orsborn); *m* 1944, Margaret Ireland; one *d. Educ:* Portsmouth Grammar School. CEng, FRAeS. Learned to fly in Fleet Air Arm, 1940; pilot with oil co. in S America, 1947 and 1948; joined KLM Royal Dutch Airlines, W Indies Div., 1948; transf. to Holland, 1951, flying N and S Atlantic, S African, ME and European routes; joined Min. of Transport and Civil Aviation as Inspector of Accidents, 1955. Consultant on aircraft accident investigation, MoD, 1986–87; Special Advr on air safety to EEC Comr for Transport, 1986–88. *Publication:* Safety is no Accident, 1985. *Recreations:* music, sailing. *Address:* Seaways, Restronguet Point, Feock, Cornwall TR3 6RB. *Died 20 Oct. 2000.*

THOMPSON, William Bell, PhD; Professor of Physics, University of California, 1965–90, then Emeritus; Chairman, Department of Physics, University of California at San Diego, 1969–72; *b* N Ireland, 27 Feb. 1922; *m* 1953, Gertrud Helene Goldschmidt, PhD (marr. diss. 1972); one *s* one *d*; *m* 1972, Johanna Elzelina Ladestein Korevaar. *Educ:* Univ. of British Columbia (BA 1945; MA 1947); PhD Toronto 1950. Senior Research Fellow, 1950, Deputy Chief Scientist, 1959, AERE Harwell; Head, Theoretical Physics Division, Culham Laboratory, UKAEA, 1961–63; Prof. of Theoretical Plasma Physics, Oxford Univ., 1963–65. Visiting Prof., Univ. of California, 1961. *Publications:* Introduction to Plasma Physics, 1962; numerous papers in learned journals, on controlled thermonuclear research, plasma physics, kinetic theory, etc. *Recreations:* music, walking. *Address:*

Physics Department, University of California at San Diego, La Jolla, CA 92093, USA.
Died 17 Oct. 1995.

THOMSON, Rt Hon. David Spence, CMG 1993; MC 1942; ED; PC 1981; *b* Stratford, NZ, 14 Nov. 1915; *s* of Percy Thomson, MBE; *m* 1942, June Grace Adams; one *s* three *d. Educ:* Stratford Primary and High Sch. Territorial Army, 1931–; served Middle East, 19th Inf. Bat. 1st Echelon, 1939–42; 2nd NZED, 1939–45; POW 1942; Hon. Col, 5 RNZIR, 1955–81; Brigadier (Reserve of Officers), 2nd Inf. Brig., 1959–60. Dairy farmer; Pres., NZ Federated Farmers Central Taranaki Exec., 1959–63. MP (Nat.) Stratford/Taranaki, 1963–84; Minister of Defence, War Pensions and Rehabilitation, 1966–72 and 1980–84; Minister of Tourism, 1966–69; Minister of Police, 1969–72; Minister of Labour and Immigration, 1972; Minister of Justice, 1975–78; Minister of State Services and Leader, House of Reps, 1978–84. *Recreations:* golf, gardening, classical music. *Address:* 22 Bird Road, Stratford, New Zealand. *Died 25 Oct. 1999.*

TURNER, Patricia, OBE 1981; Head of National Equal Rights Department, and National Industrial Officer, General, Municipal, Boilermakers and Allied Trades Union (formerly General and Municipal Workers' Union), 1971–89; Member, General Council, TUC, 1981–89; *b* 14 May 1927; *d* of John Richard and Maire Collins; *m* 1954, Donald Turner, BSc (Econ). *Educ:* London School of Economics (BSc (Econ), MSc (Econ)). Industrial sociology lectr, 1965–69; Consultant, Manpower and Productivity Service, Dept of Employment and Productivity, 1969–70; Sen. Industrial Relations Officer, Commn on Industrial Relations, 1970–71. Member: Confedn of Shipbuilding and Engineering Unions Exec. Council, 1971–89 (Pres., 1982–83); Engineering Industry Training Bd, 1971–89; Women's Nat. Commn, 1973–89; Central Arbitration Cttee, 1976–93; Dept of Employment Adv. Cttee on Women's Employment, 1980–89; Equal Opportunities Commn, 1985–91; Employment Appeal Tribunal, 1987–98. *Recreations:* reading, theatre. *Address:* 22 Kenilworth Road, Edgware, Middx HA8 8YG.
Died 22 July 2000.

VAI, Sir Mea, Kt 1996; CBE 1988; ISO 1980; retired public servant, Papua New Guinea; *b* 7 Aug. 1933; *s* of late Rev. Vai Hekure and Konio Toua; *m* 1956, Reia Gau; four *s* two *d. Educ:* Administrative Coll., PNG (matriculation). Started employment with Dept of Dist Services and Native Affairs, Australian Admin, 1949; served in Depts of Home Affairs, Education, Foreign Affairs and Trade, PNG; retired 1990. *Recreations:* reading, camping, hiking, swimming. *Address:* PO Box 240, Konedobu, Port Moresby, Papua New Guinea. *T:* 3212610. *Club:* Aviat Social (Port Moresby).
Died 26 Oct. 1996.

VERNON, Sir James, AC 1980; Kt 1965; CBE 1962 (OBE 1960); Director, O'Connell Street Associates Pty Ltd, since 1976; *b* 13 June 1910; *s* of Donald Vernon, Tamworth, New South Wales; *m* 1935, Mavis, *d* of C. Lonsdale Smith; two *d. Educ:* Sydney Univ. (BSc); University College, London (PhD). CSR Ltd: Chief Chemist, 1938–51; Senior Exec. Officer, 1951–56; Asst General Manager, 1956–57; Gen. Manager, 1958–72; Dir, 1958–82; Chm., 1978–80. Chairman: Commonwealth Cttee of Economic Enquiry, 1963–65; Australian Post Office Commn of Inquiry, 1973; Internat. Pres., Pacific Basin Econ. Council, 1980–82. FRACI; FAIM; FTSE. Hon. DSc: Sydney, 1965; Newcastle, 1969. Leighton Medal, Royal Australian Chemical Inst., 1965; John Storey Medal, Aust. Inst. of Management, 1971. Order of Sacred Treasure, 1st cl. (Japan), 1983. *Address:* 27 Manning Road, Double Bay, NSW 2028, Australia. *Clubs:* Australian, Union (Sydney). *Died 10 July 2000.*

WALLER, Sir Robert William, 9th Bt *cr* 1780, of Newport, Co. Tipperary; an Industrial Engineer, General Electric Co. of America, 1957–91; *b* 16 June 1934; *s* of Sir Roland Edgar Waller, 8th Bt, and Helen Madeline, *d* of Joseph Radl, Matawan, New Jersey, USA; *S* father, 1958; United States citizen; *m* 1960, Carol Anne (marr. diss. 1975; remarried 1997), *d* of J. E. Hines; two *s* two *d* (and one *s* decd). *Educ:* St Peter's Prep. Sch.; Newark Coll. of Engrg; Fairleigh Dickinson Univ. *Heir:* *s* John Michael Waller [*b* 14 May 1962; *m* 1986, Maria Renee Gonzalez; four *s* two *d*]. *Address:* 5 Lookout Terrace, Lynnfield, MA 01940, USA. *Died 12 Dec. 2000.*

WANSTALL, Hon. Sir Charles Gray, Kt 1974; Chief Justice of Queensland, Australia, 1977–82; *b* 17 Feb. 1912; *m* 1938, Olwyn Mabel, *d* of C. O. John; one *d. Educ:* Roma and Gympie State Schs; Gympie High Sch., Queensland, Australia. Called to Queensland Bar, 1933. High Court, 1942. MLA (Liberal) for Toowong, 1944–50; Pres., Liberal Party of Australia (Qld Div.), 1950–53. QC 1956; Judge, Supreme Court, Qld, 1958; Sen. Puisne Judge, 1971. *Recreations:* reading, photography. *Address:* 26/36 Jerdanefield Road, St Lucia, Brisbane, Queensland 4067, Australia. *Clubs:* Queensland (Brisbane); St Lucia Bowling. *Died 17 Oct. 1999.*

WELLS, Thomas Leonard, OOnt 1998; President, TLW Consulting, since 1993; *b* 2 May 1930; *s* of Leonard Wells and Lilian May Butler; *m* 1954, Audrey Alice Richardson; one *s* two *d. Educ:* University of Toronto. Advertising Manager: Canadian Hosp. Jl, 1951–61; Canadian Med. Assoc. Jl, 1961–67; Chm., Scarborough, Ont Bd of Educn, 1961, 1962. MLA (Progressive C) for Scarborough N, Ontario, 1963–85; Minister: without Portfolio (responsible for Youth Affairs), 1966–69; of Health, 1969–71; of Social and Family Services, 1971–72; of Education, 1972–78; of Intergovtl Affairs, 1978–85; Govt House Leader, Ont, 1980–85; Agent Gen. for Ont in UK, 1985–91; Comr, Expo 98 Canada Corp., 1991–92. Vice Chm., Bd, N York Performing Arts Centre, 1995–98; Mem., Bd of Dirs, Metro Toronto Convention Centre, 1995–. Hon. Fellow, Ont Teachers' Fedn, 1976. Hon. DLitt Univ. of Windsor, Ont, 1985. Freeman, City of London, 1985; Mem., Guild of Freemen of the City of London, 1987–. CLJ 1984. Confederation Medal, Canada, 1967; Silver Jubilee Medal, 1977; Confederation 125 Medal, 1992. *Recreations:* photography, walking, theatre, cinema. *Address:* 808–65 Spring Garden Avenue, Willowdale, ON M2N 6H9, Canada. *T:* (416) 2228914. *Clubs:* Royal Over-Seas League; Albany, Empire (Toronto). *Died 11 Oct. 2000.*

WHITE, John Sampson, AO 1982; CMG 1970; Secretary to the Governor, South Australia, 1976–82; *b* 9 June 1916; *s* of late W. J. White; *m* 1941, Dorothy G., *d* of late E. J. Griffin; one *s* one *d. Educ:* Black Forest Primary and Adelaide High Schs. AASA. Attorney-General's Dept, 1933–61. Served War, 2nd AIF, 1941–45, Captain. Asst Sec., Industries Develt Cttee, 1950, Sec., 1951–61; Sec., Land Agents' Bd, 1951–61; Sec. to Premier, SA, 1961–65; Mem., SA Superannuation Fund Bd, 1961–74; Comr of Charitable Funds, 1964–74; Sec., Premier's Dept, SA, 1965–74; Agent-Gen. for SA, 1974–76. Member: State Exec. Cttee, Meals on Wheels Inc., 1982–89 (Vice Pres., 1989–91); Pres., 1991–); Exec. Cttee, SA Br., Victoria League for Commonwealth Friendship, 1982–; Bd of Dirs, Service to Youth Council, 1982–84; Casino Supervisory Authy, 1983–86. Mem., Council of Governors, Presb. Girls' Coll., 1958–73. Freeman, City of London. *Recreations:* swimming, tennis. *Address:* 4 Evans Avenue, Mitcham, SA 5062, Australia. *Clubs:* Adelaide, Naval, Military and Air Force (Adelaide).
Died 23 Jan. 1999.

WOODRUFF, Harry Wells, CMG 1966; Assistant Secretary, Board of Trade, then Department of Trade and Industry, 1968–72, retired; *b* 31 Oct. 1912; *s* of Leonard Wells Woodruff and Rosina Woodruff; *m* 1938, Margaret Bradley; one *d. Educ:* Reigate Grammar Sch.; London Univ. Trade Comr, Johannesburg, 1946–51; Trade Comr and Economic Adviser to High Commissioner: Salisbury,

1951–55; Kuala Lumpur, 1957–61; Commercial Counsellor, Canberra, 1962–66; Economic Adviser to Foreign Office, 1966–68. *Publication:* (jtly) Economic Development in Rhodesia and Nyasaland, 1955. *Recreation:* painting. *Address:* 387 Sandbanks Road, Poole, Dorset.   *Died 19 June 2000.*

WOODS, Ivan; *see* Woods, W. I.

WOODS, (William) Ivan; Deputy Secretary, Department of Finance for Northern Ireland, 1973–76; 3rd *s* of late William and Anna Woods, Annaghmore, Co. Armagh; *m* 1st (wife *d* 1965); one *s* one *d*; 2nd, 1966, Florence Margaret, *o d* of late William and Florence Sloan, Ach-na-mara, Donaghadee, Co. Down; one *s* two *d*. *Educ:* Ranelagh Sch., Athlone; Mountjoy Sch., Dublin. Accountant, Min. of Finance for NI, 1962; NI Govt Liaison Officer in London, 1963; Director: Office of Parly Comr for Admin, NI, 1969; Office of Commissioner for Complaints, NI, 1969. Sec., Milibern Trust, 1976–79. *Address:* 112 Warren Road, Donaghadee, Co. Down BT21 0PQ. *T:* (028) 9188 3568. *Club:* Portaferry Sailing (Co. Down).   *Deceased.*

WOOTTON, Godfrey; *see* Wootton, N. G.

WOOTTON, (Norman) Godfrey; Stipendiary Magistrate for Merseyside, 1976–94; *b* 10 April 1926; *s* of H. N. and E. Wootton, Crewe, Cheshire. *Educ:* The Grammar Sch., Crewe; Liverpool Univ. (LLB). Called to Bar, Gray's Inn, 1951. Joined Northern Circuit, 1951. A Recorder of the Crown Court, 1972–96. *Recreations:* travel, photography. *Club:* Athenæum (Liverpool).
                                    Died 27 March 2000.

WRIGHT, Shirley Edwin McEwan; corporate consultant; *b* 4 May 1915; *s* of Alfred Coningsby Wright

and Elsie Derbyshire; *m* 1939, Dora Fentem; one *s* three *d*. *Educ:* Herbert Strutt Sch., Belper; Coll. of Technology, Manchester; Univ. of Sheffield (BEng). CEng, FIMechE. Metropolitan Vickers, 1932, ICI Explosives Div., 1938; Asst Chief Engr, ICI Nobel Div., 1955; Dir, Irvine Harbour Bd, 1962; Engrg and Techn Dir, ICI Nobel Div., 1965; Pres., Philippine Explosives Corp., 1970; Chief Exec., Livingston Develt Corp., 1972–77; Dir, Premix-Fibreglass, 1978–80. *Recreations:* cricket, golf. *Address:* 33 St Juliens Way, Cawthorne, near Barnsley S75 4ES. *T:* (01226) 792030.   *Died 26 Oct. 1999.*

YAMAZAKI, Toshio, Hon. KBE 1996; Adviser, Saison Foundation, since 1991; Japanese Ambassador to the Court of St James's, 1985–88, retired; *b* 13 Aug. 1922; *s* of Takamaro Yamazaki and Konoe Yamazaki; *m* 1955, Yasuko Arakawa; one *s* one *d*. *Educ:* Tokyo Univ. (Faculty of Law). 2nd Sec., Japanese Embassy, London, 1955–59; Dir, British Commonwealth Div., European and Oceanic Affairs Bureau, Min. of Foreign Affairs, 1962–64; Counsellor, Permt Mission to UN, NY, 1964–67; Dir, Financial Affairs Div., Minister's Secretariat, Min. of Foreign Affairs, 1967–70; Dep. Dir-Gen., Treaties Bureau, 1970; Minister, Washington, 1971–74; Dir-Gen., Amer. Affairs Bureau, Min. of Foreign Affairs, 1974–77; Dep. Vice-Minister for Admin, 1978–80; Ambassador to Egypt, 1980–82, to Indonesia, 1982–84. Chm., Japan-British Soc., Tokyo, 1988–94. Pres., Temple Univ., Japan, 1991–96. Grand Cordon, Order of Sacred Treasure (Japan), 1994; Banda 2nd cl., Orden del Aguila Azteca (Mexico), 1978; Grosses Verdienstkreuz mit Stern (FRG), 1979; Order of Republic, 1st cl. (Egypt), 1982. *Recreations:* theatre-going, golf. *Clubs:* Tokyo (Tokyo); Tokyo Golf.
                                    Died 7 June 2000.

A

AAGAARD, Robert, OBE 1993; Partner, R. & F. C. Aagaard, Designers and Decorators of Historic House Interiors, since 1980; *b* 27 June 1932; *s* of Villien Valdemar Aagaard and Florence (*née* Brooke); *m* 1960, Fiona Christine Drury; two *s* one *d*. *Educ:* Gresham's Sch., Holt. Man. Dir, 1960–80, Consultant, 1980–95, Robert Aagaard Ltd Antiques; Dir, Aagaard-Hanley Ltd, Fibrous Plasterers, 1970–80, Consultant, 1980–; Consultant, Robert Aagaard & Co., Period Chimneypieces. and Marble Processing, 1995–. Founder and Chm., Cathedral Camps, 1980–. Mem., Gen. Synod of C of E, 1995–. Chm., Ripon DAC, 1993–; Member: Ripon Cathedral Fabric Adv. Cttee, 1993–; Bradford Cathedral Fabric Adv. Cttee, 1997–; Cathedrals' Fabric Commn for England, 1995–; Ripon Dio. Redundant Churches Uses Cttee, 1984–. *Recreations:* gardening, walking. *Address:* Manor House, High Birstwith, Harrogate, N Yorks HG3 2LG. *T:* (01423) 770385. *Died 1 April 2001.*

ABEL SMITH, Henriette Alice, (Lady Abel Smith), DCVO 1977 (CVO 1964); JP; an Extra Lady-in-Waiting to the Queen (formerly as HRH Princess Elizabeth), since 1987 (a Lady-in-Waiting, 1949–87); *b* 6 June 1914; *d* of late Comdr Francis Charles Cadogan, RN, and late Ruth Evelyn (*née* Howard, *widow* of Captain Gardner Sebastian Bazley); *m* 1st, 1939, Sir Anthony Frederick Mark Palmer, 4th Bt (killed in action, 1941); one *s* one *d*; 2nd, 1953, Sir Alexander Abel Smith, KCVO, TD (*d* 1980); one *s* one *d*. JP Tunbridge Wells 1955, Gloucestershire 1971. *Address:* The Garden House, Quenington, Cirencester, Glos GL7 5BN. *T:* (01285) 750231. *Died 3 May 2005.*

ABEL SMITH, Col Richard Francis; Vice Lord-Lieutenant of Nottinghamshire, 1991–99; *b* 11 Oct. 1933; *s* of Col Sir Henry Abel Smith, KCMG, KCVO, DSO and late Lady May Cambridge, *o d* of Earl of Athlone, KG, GCB, GCMG, GCVO, DSO, PC, FRS and Princess Alice, Countess of Athlone, VA, GCVO, GBE; *m* 1960, Marcia Kendrew, JP, DL (High Sheriff, Notts, 1990–91); one *d*. *Educ:* Eton; RMA Sandhurst; Royal Agric. Coll., Cirencester. Commissioned, 1954, Royal Horse Guards (The Blues); Escort Comdr and ADC to Govs of Cyprus, 1957–60; Adjutant, 1960–61; Instr, Sandhurst, 1961–63. Comdr, Sherwood Rangers Sqn, Royal Yeomanry Regt, 1967–69, Hon. Col, 1979–89. Chm., Sports Aid Foundn (E Midlands), 1979–90. County Comr, Scouts (Notts), 1966–75. DL 1970, High Sheriff, 1978, Notts. *Recreations:* fishing, shooting. *Address:* Blidworth Dale, Ravenshead, Notts NG15 9AL. *Club:* Army and Navy. *Died 23 Dec. 2004.*

ABELL, John Norman; Chairman, Europe, CIBC Wood Gundy Inc., 1990–91; Vice-Chairman, Wood Gundy Inc., London, 1988–91; *b* 18 Sept. 1931; *s* of Sir George Edmond Brackenbury Abell; *m* 1957, Mora Delia (*née* Clifton-Brown); two *s* one *d*. *Educ:* Marlborough Coll.; Worcester Coll., Oxford (MA). Wood Gundy Ltd: joined in Vancouver, Canada, 1955; Internat. Man. Dir, Toronto, 1962; Dirr and Vice-Pres., 1966; Pres., Wood Gundy Inc., New York, 1966; Vice-Chm., Wood Gundy Ltd, Toronto, 1977; Dep. Chm. and Chief Exec., Orion Royal Bank Ltd, 1982, Chm. and Chief Exec. Officer, 1983–85; Vice-Chm., Wood Gundy Inc., Toronto, 1986–88; Director: Echo Bay Mines, Edmonton, Canada, 1980–; Minerals & Resources Corp. Ltd, 1985–89; First Australia Prime Income Investment Co. Ltd, 1986–92; Scotia Synfuels Ltd, Toronto, 1987–97; Euro-clear Clearance System, 1989–92; Stelco Inc., Hamilton, Ont, 1990–2002; A. T. Plastics Inc., Brampton, Ont, 1993–2001; Longwall Internat., 1993–95; Investec Bank (UK), 1993–. Mem., Securities and Investments Bd,

1985–86; Gov., Toronto Stock Exchange, 1987–88. Chairman: Arthritis Soc. of Canada, 1981–82; Canada Meml Foundn, 1992–. Mem. Council, GAP Activity Projects, 1983–98. Dir, London House for Overseas Graduates, 1984; Mem. Council, Reading Univ., 1984. *Address:* Whittonditch House, Ramsbury, Marlborough, Wilts SN8 2PZ. *T:* (01672) 520449. *Clubs:* Boodle's, MCC; Toronto, York (Toronto).
Died 26 May 2004.

ABERCONWAY, 3rd Baron *cr* 1911, of Bodnant; **Charles Melville McLaren;** Bt 1902; JP; President: John Brown & Co. Ltd, 1978–85 (Director, 1939–85; Chairman, 1953–78); English China Clays Ltd, since 1984 (Director, 1935–87; Chairman, 1963–84); President, Royal Horticultural Society, 1961–84, then President Emeritus; *b* 16 April 1913; *e s* of 2nd Baron Aberconway, CBE, LLD and Christabel (*d* 1974), *y d* of Sir Melville Macnaghten, CB; *S* father, 1953; *m* 1st, 1941, Deirdre Knewstub (marr. diss. 1949); one *s* two *d*; 2nd, 1949, Ann Lindsay Bullard, *o d* of Mrs A. L. Aymer, New York City; one *s*. *Educ:* Eton; New Coll., Oxford. Barrister, Middle Temple, 1937. Served War of 1939–45, 2nd Lieut RA. Deputy Chairman: Sun Alliance & London Insurance, 1976–85 (Dir, London Assurance, 1953); Westland Aircraft, 1979–84 (Dir, 1947–85); Dir, National Westminster Bank (formerly National Provincial Bank), 1953–83. Comr-Gen., Internat. Garden Fest., Liverpool, 1984; Director: Nat. Garden Fest. (Stoke on Trent) 1986 Ltd; Glasgow Garden Fest. Ltd, 1988; Gateshead Garden Fest. Ltd, 1990; Ebbw Vale Garden Fest. Ltd, 1992. JP 1946, High Sheriff, 1950, Denbighshire. *Recreations:* gardening, travel. *Heir: s* Hon. Henry Charles McLaren [*b* 26 May 1948; *m* 1981, Sally, *yr d* of Captain C. N. Lentaigne; one *s* one *d*]. *Address:* 25 Egerton Terrace, SW3 2DP; Bodnant, Tal-y-cafn, Colwyn Bay, Clwyd. *Died 4 Feb. 2003.*

ABERCROMBY, Sir Ian George, 10th Bt *cr* 1636, of Birkenbog; *b* 30 June 1925; *s* of Robert Ogilvie Abercromby (*g s* of 5th Bt); *S* kinsman, 1972; *m* 1st, 1950, Joyce Beryl (marr. diss. 1957), *d* of Leonard Griffiths; 2nd, 1959, Fanny Mary, *d* of late Dr Graham Udale-Smith; one *d*; 3rd, 1976, Diana Marjorie, *d* of H. G. Cockell, and *widow* of Captain Ian Charles Palliser Galloway. *Educ:* Lancing Coll.; Bloxham Sch. *Heir:* none. *Clubs:* Ski Club of Great Britain; Kandahar; Kildare Street (Dublin).
Died 16 May 2003 (ext).

ABERDARE, 4th Baron *cr* 1873, of Duffryn; **Morys George Lyndhurst Bruce,** KBE 1984; PC 1974; DL; *b* 16 June 1919; *s* of 3rd Baron Aberdare, GBE, and Margaret Bethune (*née* Black); *S* father 1957; *m* 1946, Maud Helen Sarah, *o d* of Sir John Dashwood, 10th Bt, CVO; four *s*. *Educ:* Winchester; New College, Oxford (MA). Welsh Guards, 1939–46. Minister of State, DHSS, 1970–74; Minister Without Portfolio, 1974; Chm. of Cttees, 1976–92, and a Dep. Speaker, 1976–2001, H of L; elected Mem., H of L, 1999. Chairman: Albany Life Assurance Co. Ltd, 1975–92; Metlife (UK) Ltd, 1986–92. Chm., The Football Trust, 1979–98; President: Welsh Nat. Council of YMCAs, 1963–2000; Kidney Res. Unit for Wales Foundn, 1970–2000; Tennis and Rackets Assoc., 1972–2004. Hon. LLD Wales, 1985. DL Dyfed, 1985. Bailiff Grand Cross, 1974, Prior for Wales, 1958–88, OStJ. *Publications:* The Story of Tennis, 1959; Willis Faber Book of Tennis and Rackets, 1980; J. T. Faber Book of Tennis and Rackets, 2002. *Recreations:* Real tennis, rackets. *Heir: s* Hon. Alastair John Lyndhurst Bruce [*b* 2 May 1947; *m* 1971, Elizabeth Mary Culbert, *d* of John Foulkes; one *s* one *d*]. *Address:* 26 Crown Lodge, 12 Elystan Street, SW3

3PP. *Clubs:* Boodle's, Lansdowne, MCC, Queen's (Pres., 1993–96). *Died 23 Jan. 2005.*

ABERDEEN AND TEMAIR, 6th Marquess of, *cr* 1916; **Alastair Ninian John Gordon;** Bt (NS) 1642; Earl of Aberdeen, Viscount Formartine, Lord Haddo, Methlic, Tarves and Kellie, 1682 (Scot.); Viscount Gordon 1814, Earl of Haddo 1916 (UK); painter; *b* 20 July 1920; *s* of 3rd Marquess of Aberdeen and Temair, DSO, and Cécile Elizabeth (*d* 1948), *d* of George Drummond, Swaylands, Penshurst, Kent; *S* brother, 1984; *m* 1950, Anne (ceramic sculptor), *d* of late Lt-Col Gerald Barry, MC; one *s* two *d*. *Educ:* Harrow; Camberwell Sch. of Art. Served War of 1939–45, Captain Scots Guards. Member: Internat. Assoc. of Art Critics; Bach Choir, 1939–82. Exhibitions of botanical painting in London, New York, Chicago, Sydney. *Recreations:* wine, women and song. *Heir: s* Earl of Haddo [*b* 31 March 1955; *m* 1981, Joanna Clodagh Houldsworth; three *s* one *d*]. *Address:* Quick's Green, near Pangbourne, Berks RG8 8SN. *Clubs:* Arts (Chm., 1966–76), MCC; Puffins (Edinburgh).
Died 19 Aug. 2002.

ABERGAVENNY, Marchioness of; Mary Patricia Nevill, DCVO 1981 (CVO 1970); an Extra Lady of the Bedchamber to the Queen, 1960–66 and since 1987 (a Lady of the Bedchamber, 1966–87); *b* 20 Oct. 1915; *d* of late Lt-Col John Fenwick Harrison, Royal Horse Guards, and Hon. Margery Olive Edith, *d* of 3rd Baron Burnham, DSO; *m* 1938, 5th Marquess of Abergavenny, KG, OBE; three *d* (and one *s* one *d* decd). *Address:* c/o Freemantle Farmhouse, North Oakley, Tadley, Hants.
Died 22 Feb. 2005.

ABERNETHY, William Leslie, CBE 1972; FCA, CPFA; Managing Trustee, Municipal Mutual Insurance Ltd, and Director of associated companies, 1973–87; Comptroller of Financial Services, Greater London Council, 1972–73 (Treasurer, 1964–72) and Chief Financial Officer, Inner London Education Authority, 1967–73; *b* 10 June 1910; *s* of Robert and Margaret Abernethy; *m* 1937, Irene Nobin (*d* 1998); one *s*. *Educ:* Darwen Grammar Sch., Lancs. Hindle & Jepson, Chartered Accts, Darwen, 1925–31; Borough Treasurer's Dept, Darwen, 1931–37; Derbyshire CC, Treasurer's Dept, 1937–48 (Dep. Co. Treas., 1944–48); 1st Treas., Newcastle upon Tyne Regional Hosp. Bd, 1948–50. LCC: Asst Comptroller, 1950–56; Dep. Comptroller, 1956–64; Comptroller, Sept. 1964–Mar. 1965. Chm. Exec. Council, RIPA, 1959–60. Mem. Council, IMTA, 1966–73. *Publications:* Housing Finance and Accounts (with A. R. Holmes), 1953; Internal Audit in Local Authorities and Hospitals, 1957; Internal Audit in the Public Boards, 1957; contribs professional jls. *Address:* 6 Thornhill Close, Port Erin, Isle of Man IM9 6NF. *T:* (01624) 835316. *Died 22 Sept. 2003.*

ABINGER, 8th Baron *cr* 1835; **James Richard Scarlett;** DL; Lieutenant-Colonel, late Royal Artillery; farmer and company director, retired; *b* 28 Sept. 1914; *e s* of 7th Baron and Marjorie (*d* 1965), 2nd *d* of John McPhillamy, Blair Athol, Bathurst, NSW; *S* father, 1943; *m* 1957, Isla Carolyn, *o d* of late Vice-Adm. J. W. Rivett-Carnac, CB, CBE, DSC; two *s*. *Educ:* Eton; Magdalene College, Cambridge (MA 1952). India, France, Airborne Corps, and attached RAF; RNXS, 1968. DL Essex, 1968. KStJ. *Heir: s* Hon. James Harry Scarlett [*b* 28 May 1959; *m* 1995, Tracy, *d* of N. Cloutier]. *Address:* Sheepcote House, Queen Street, Castle Hedingham, Halstead, Essex CO9 3HA. *T:* (01787) 460388. *Clubs:* Carlton, Royal Automobile. *Died 23 Sept. 2002.*

ABRAHAM, Maj.-Gen. Martin; *see* Abraham, Maj.-Gen. S. M. O'H.

ABRAHAM,   Maj.-Gen.   (Sutton)   Martin (O'Heguerty), CB 1973; MC 1942 and Bar, 1943; Secretary, Bedford College, University of London, 1976–82, retired; *b* 26 Jan. 1919; *s* of Capt. E. G. F. Abraham, CB, late Indian Civil Service, and Ruth Eostre

Abraham; *m* 1950, Iona Margaret (decd), *d* of Sir John Stirling, KT, MBE; two *s* one *d*. *Educ:* Durnford; Eton; Trinity Coll., Cambridge (BA Modern Languages). Commissioned in RA, 1939; transf. to 12th Royal Lancers, 1941; Egypt, 1941; Armoured Car Troop Leader, desert campaigns; Armoured Car Sqdn 2nd-in-Comd, Italian campaign; accepted surrender of Trieste (Sqdn Ldr); Mil. Asst to C-in-C Austria, and BAOR, 1946; psc 1948; Mem. Chiefs of Staff Secretariat, 1949–52; Sqdn Ldr 12th Lancers, Malaya, 1953–54; Mem. Staff Coll. Directing Staff, 1955–57; 2nd-in-Comd 12th Lancers, 1957–58; CO 12th Lancers, 1958–62 (Cyprus, 1959–60); Asst Mil. Sec., Southern Comd, 1960–62; GSO1, Staff Coll. (Minley Div.), 1960–62; Comdr RAC (Brig.), 1st Brit. Corps, Germany, 1964–66; idc 1967; Dir, Combat Develt (Army), MoD, 1968–71; Chief of Jt Services Liaison Orgn, BAOR, 1971–73; Mil. Adviser to Arms Control and Disarmament Res. Unit and Western Organisations Dept, FCO, 1973–76, retd. Col, 9/12 Royal Lancers, 1977–81. Governor, Bedford Coll., 1982–85. *Recreations:* painting, reading, sundry country pursuits. *Address:* c/o C. Hoare & Co., 37 Fleet Street, EC4P 4DQ. *Club:* Cavalry and Guards. *Died 15 May 2001.*

ACHESON, Prof. Roy Malcolm, ScD, DM; FRCP, FFCM, FFOM; Professor of Community Medicine, University of Cambridge, 1976–88, then Emeritus; Fellow, Churchill College, Cambridge, since 1976; *b* 18 Aug. 1921; *s* of Malcolm King Acheson, MC, MD and Dorothy Rennoldson; *m* 1950, Fiona Marigo O'Brien (marr. diss. 1990); two *s* one *d*. *Educ:* Merchiston Castle Sch., Edinburgh; TCD (MA, ScD); Brasenose Coll., Oxford (MA, DM); Radcliffe Infirmary, Oxford. FRCP 1973; FFCM 1972; FFOM (by distinction) 1984. Clin. and res. posts, Radcliffe Infirmary, Oxford; Rockefeller Trav. Fellow, Western Reserve and Harvard Univs, 1955–56; Radcliffe Trav. Fellow, Univ. of Oxford, 1955–57; Lectr in Social Med., Univ. of Dublin, 1955–59; FTCD, 1957–59; Sen. Lectr, then Reader in Social and Preventive Med., Guy's Hosp. Med. Sch. and London Sch. of Hygiene and Trop. Med., 1959–62; Yale University: Associate Prof. of Epidemiology, 1962; Prof. of Epidemiology, 1964–72; Fellow, Jonathan Edwards Coll., 1966–75; London Sch. of Hygiene and Tropical Medicine: Commonwealth Fund Sen. Trav. Fellow in Med., 1968–69; Dir, Centre for Extension Trng in Community Med., 1972–76. Hon. Cons. in Community Med., NE Thames RHA (formerly NE Metrop. RHB), 1972–76, E Anglian RHA, 1976–88; Prof. of Health Service Studies, Univ. of London, 1974–76. Samuel R. McLaughlin Vis. Prof. in Med., McMaster Univ., Hamilton, Ont, 1976. Member: Exec. Cttee and Council, Internat. Epidemiol Soc., 1964–75; Expert Cttee, Methods in Chronic Disease Epidemiol., WHO, 1966; GMC, 1979–88 (Mem. Exec. Cttee, 1979–88; Mem. Educn Cttee, 1979–86); GDC, 1985–88 (Mem. Educn Cttee, 1985–88); Cambridge HA, 1986–88. Cons., Argentina, Colombia, Guatemala, India, Venezuela, WHO, 1965–76; Rapporteur, Adv. Cttee on Med. Res., WHO, 1976–79. Faculty of Community Medicine: Mem. Bd, 1974–84; Sec. to Examrs, 1974–77; Vice Pres., 1986–88; and Mem., numerous cttees. Gov., Action in Internat. Medicine, 1989–92; Councillor, Oral and Dental Res. Trust, 1989–91. Hon. Fellow: Buenos Aires Acad. of Medicine, 1980; Singapore Acad. of Medicine, 1988. Hon. MA Yale, 1964. *Publications:* (ed) Comparability in International Epidemiology, 1965; Seminars in Community Medicine: (ed with L. Aird) I: Sociology, 1976; (ed with L. Aird and D. J. Hall) II: Health Information, Planning and Monitoring, 1971; (with S. Hagard) Health, Society and Medicine: an introduction to community medicine, 1985; (jtly) Costs and Benefits of the Heart Transplantation Programmes at Harefield and Papworth Hospitals, 1985; (jtly) History of Education in Public Health, 1991. *Recreations:* golf, choral singing, country matters, meditating in the bath. *Address:* 21 The Cliff, Brighton BN2 5RF. *T:* (01273) 698518. *Clubs:*

Oxford and Cambridge; Seaford Golf.
Died 2 April 2003.

ACKROYD, Rev. Prof. Peter Runham, PhD, DD; Samuel Davidson Professor of Old Testament Studies, University of London, 1961–82, then Emeritus Professor; *b* 15 Sept. 1917; *s* of Jabez Robert Ackroyd and Winifred (*née* Brown); *m* 1st, 1940, Evelyn Alice Nutt (*d* 1990), BSc (Manch.), *d* of William Young Nutt; two *s* three *d*; 2nd, 1991, Ann, MA (Oxon), *d* of James Golden. *Educ:* Harrow County School for Boys; Downing Coll., Cambridge (Open Exhibn in Modern Langs, 1935; Mod. and Med. Langs Tripos, Pt I, 1936, Pt II, 1938); Trinity Coll., Cambridge (Stanton Student, 1941–43; Dr Williams's Trust Exhibnr, 1941); BD Hons London, 1940; MTh London, 1942; PhD Cambridge, 1945; DD London, 1970. Minister of: Roydon Congregational Church, Essex, 1943–47; Balham Congregational Church, London, 1947–48; Lectr in Old Testament and Biblical Hebrew, Leeds Univ., 1948–52; Cambridge University: Univ. Lectr in Divinity, 1952–61; Select Preacher, 1955; Mem. Council of Senate, 1957–61; Hulsean Lectr, 1960–62; Select Preacher, Oxford, 1962, 1981 (McBride Sermon); Dean of Faculty of Theology, King's Coll., London, 1968–69; FKC 1969; Mem. Senate, London Univ., 1971–79; Dean, Univ. Faculty of Theology, 1976–80. Vis. Professor: Lutheran Sch. of Theology, Chicago, 1967 and 1976; Univ. of Toronto, 1972; Univ. of Notre Dame, Indiana, 1982; Emory Univ., Atlanta, 1984. Lectures: Selwyn, NZ, 1970; Ethel M. Wood, Univ. of London, 1982; (first) Walter S. Williams, Denver, 1982; Tübingen, 1983; Haskell, Oberlin, Ohio, 1984; series of lectures, Japan, 1983. External Examiner, Belfast, Bristol, Durham, Cambridge, Edinburgh, Leeds, Nottingham, Exeter, West Indies. Ordained deacon, 1957, priest, 1958; Hon. Curate, Holy Trinity, Cambridge, 1957–61. Proctor in Convocation, Cambridge Univ., 1960–64. Pres., Soc. for Old Testament Study, 1972 (Foreign Sec., 1986–89); Hon. Mem., Soc. of Biblical Literature, 1982–; Chairman: Council, British Sch. of Archaeology in Jerusalem, 1979–83; Palestine Exploration Fund, 1986–90 (Hon. Sec., 1962–70). Hon. DD St Andrews, 1970. *Publications:* Freedom in Action, 1951; The People of the Old Testament, 1959, new edn 1981; Continuity, 1962; The Old Testament Tradition, 1963; Exile and Restoration, 1968; Israel under Babylon and Persia, 1970; 1 & 2 Chronicles, Ezra, Nehemiah, Ruth, Jonah, Maccabees, 1970; 1 Samuel (Cambridge Bible Commentary), 1971; I & II Chronicles, Ezra, Nehemiah (Torch Bible Commentary), 1973; 2 Samuel, 1977; Doors of Perception, 1978, new edn 1983; Studies in the Religious Tradition of the Old Testament, 1987; The Chronicler in His Age, 1991; articles and reviews in various learned jls, dictionaries, etc; *translations:* E. Würthein's The Text of the Old Testament, 1957; L. Köhler's Hebrew Man, 1957, repr. 1973; O. Eissfeldt's The Old Testament: an introduction, 1965; *editor:* Bible Key Words, 1961–64; Society for Old Testament Study Book List, 1967–73; Palestine Exploration Quarterly, 1971–86; *joint editor:* SCM Press OT Library, 1960–80; Cambridge Bible Commentary, 1961–79; SCM Studies in Biblical Theol., 1962–77; Words and Meanings: essays presented to D. W. Thomas, 1968; Cambridge History of the Bible, vol. I, 1970; Oxford Bible Series, 1979–92; Cambridge Commentaries: Jewish and Christian Writings of the period 200 BC to AD 200, 1979–. *Recreations:* reading, music.
Died 23 Jan. 2005.

ACRES, Dr Douglas Ian, CBE 1987 (OBE 1981); JP; DL; Vice President, Magistrates' Association, since 1988 (Chairman of Council, 1984–87); *b* Brockley, 21 Nov. 1924; *y s* of Sydney Herbert and Hilda Emily Acres; *m* Joan Marjorie, *o d* of William Charles and Alice Emily Bloxham, Benfleet. *Educ:* Westcliff High Sch.; Borland's, Victoria; London Hosp. Med. Coll. MRCS, LRCP 1949; DMJ (Clin.); MRCGP 1968. House Surgeon and Casualty Registrar, King George Hosp., Ilford, 1949–51; RAF Med. Branch, 1951–53 (Dep. Pres., Air Crew Med. Bd,

Hornchurch; AOC's Commendation and Vote of Thanks, OStJ, East Coast Flood Disaster, 1953); gen. med. practice, Benfleet, 1953–84; MO, Remploy Ltd, 1965–99. Med. Adviser, Congregational Fedn, 1985–; Member: Cttee on Mentally Abnormal Offenders, 1972–75; Barclay Cttee on Role and Task of Social Worker, 1979; Parole Bd, 1984–87; Sec., Fedn of Alcohol Rehab. Estabts, 1980–82; Mem., Exec. Cttee, Alcohol Concern, 1983–87; Chairman: Essex Council on Alcoholism, 1981–86; Out of Court (Alt. for Drunkenness Offenders), 1982–89; Churches' Council on Alcohol and Drugs, 1986–89; Mem., Interdeptl Cttee on Alcoholism, 1975–78; Chm., Educn Cttee, Inst. for Study and Treatment and Delinquency, 1985–89. Cropwood Fellow, Inst. of Criminology, 1973; Mem., BMA (Chm., SE Essex Div., 1979). Magistrates' Association: Dep. Chm., 1983; Chm., Sentencing of Offenders Cttee, 1978–83; Chm., Essex and NE London Br., 1975–78; Chm., Trng Sub-Cttee, 1978–91. JP Essex, 1958; Chm., Rochford Bench, 1974–84; Member: Lord Chancellor's Essex Adv. Cttee, 1973–87; Essex Magistrates' Courts Cttee, 1973–92 (Chm., Trng Sub-Cttee, 1978–92); Essex Probation Cttee, 1972–92 (Chm., R&D Sub-Cttee, 1980–90); Pres., Essex Br., Nat. Assoc. of Probation Officers, 1983–89. Indep. Mem., Benfleet UDC, 1960–65 (Chm., Public Health Cttee). Mem., Board of Visitors, HM Borstal, Bullwood Hall, 1970–83 (Vice-Chm., 1976–82); Member, Governing Body: King John Sch., Thundersley, 1967–89 (Chm., 1971–89); SE Essex Sixth Form Coll., 1982–88. Lay Pastor: Battlesbridge Free Church, 1984–99, then Pastor Emeritus; Woodham Ferrers Congregational Church, 1984–92; Chaplain to Chm., Rochford DC, 1996–97. DL Essex 1978. CStJ. Med. corresp., SE Essex Evening Echo, 1968–95. *Publications:* articles and chapters on medico-legal matters. *Address:* Thundersley Lodge, Runnymede Chase, Thundersley, Benfleet, Essex SS7 3DB. *T:* (01268) 793241.
Died 2 Dec. 2001.

ADAM, Madge Gertrude, DPhil; FRAS; University Lecturer (Astronomy), Department of Astrophysics, University Observatory, Oxford, 1947–79; Research Fellow, St Hugh's College, Oxford, 1957–79, then Emeritus Fellow; *b* 6 March 1912; 2nd *d* of late John Gill Simpson and Gertrude Adam; unmarried. *Educ:* Municipal High School, Doncaster; St Hugh's College, Oxford (Scholar; MA). Research Scholar, Lady Margaret Hall, Oxford, 1935–37; Junior British Scholarship, 1936–37; Assistant Tutor of St Hugh's College and Research Assistant at Oxford University Observatory, 1937; lately Fellow and Tutor, St Hugh's College. *Publications:* papers in Monthly Notices of Royal Astronomical Society from 1937. *Address:* 17 Dove House Close, Upper Wolvercote, Oxford OX2 8BG.
Died 25 Aug. 2001.

ADAMS, Alec Cecil Stanley, CMG 1960; CBE 1952; HM Diplomatic Service, retired; *b* 25 July 1909; *e s* of late Stanley A. Adams. *Educ:* King's School, Canterbury; Corpus Christi Coll., Cambridge. One of HM Vice-Consuls in Siam, 1933; served in Portuguese East Africa (acting Consul at Beira, June 1936–Feb. 1937); local rank 2nd Secretary, Bangkok Legation, 1937; Acting Consul, Sourabaya, 1938; Bangkok Legation, 1939–40; Foreign Office, Ministry of Information, 1940; Consul, in Foreign Office, 1945; Bangkok, 1946, Acting Consul-Gen. and Chargé d'Affaires, 1948; Consul, Cincinnati, 1949; HM Chargé d'Affaires in Korea, 1950; HM Consul-Gen. at Houston, Texas, 1953–55; Counsellor and Consul-Gen. at HM Embassy, Bangkok, 1956–62; Dep. Comr-Gen. for South East Asia, 1962–63; Political Advisor to C-in-C (Far East) at Singapore, 1963–67; retired 1967. *Address:* Flat 513, 97 Southampton Row, WC1B 4HH. *Club:* Travellers.
Died 10 Feb. 2002.

ADAMS, Bernard Charles; architect; County Architect, Somerset County Council, 1960–80; *b* 29 Oct. 1915; *s* of late Charles Willoughby Adams and Emily Alice (*née* Ambrose); *m* 1st, 1942, Marjorie Barrett Weller (*d* 1986); one *d* (and two *d* decd); 2nd, 1989, Betty Isabel Tucker

(*née* Feist) (*d* 1992); 3rd, 1995, Ruth Atkinson, BSc (*née* Johnson). *Educ:* King James I Sch., Newport, IoW. ARIBA 1948, FRIBA 1968. TA, 1938–39; served 1939–41 (Battle of Britain), 219 Battery, 43 (Wessex) Div.; commissioned 1941; served 1941–46, 107 HAA Regt RA, France (Normandy), Belgium, Holland, Germany; Captain RA (despatches). Sen. Architect, Derbyshire CC, 1951–54; Asst County Architect, Kent CC, 1954–59; Dep. County Architect, Herts CC, 1959–60. Mem. Council, RIBA, 1963–69 and 1970–76 (Vice-Pres., 1970–72; Chm., SW Regional Council, 1972–74); Chm., Structure of the Profession Study, RIBA, 1976–79; Mem., Nat. Consultative Council for Building and Civil Engrg Industries, 1974–80; Pres., County Architects' Soc., 1973–74 (Vice-Pres., 1971–73); Hon. Mem., Soc. of Ch. Architects of Local Authorities (founded 1974), 1983 (Sen. Vice-Pres., 1974–75; Pres. 1975–76); Architect Adviser to ACC, 1971–80; Mem., Bd of Architectural Studies, Bristol Univ., 1964–74; Founder Chm., Architects' Cttee, Consortium for Method Building, 1961–68. Founder Mem., 1972, Chm., 1986–89, Taunton Theatre Trust, then Brewhouse Theatre and Arts Centre Co. (Hon. Life Mem., 1995). RIBA Architecture Award, 1970, and Commendation, 1974; Heritage Year Award, EAHY, 1975; Civic Trust Awards, 1962, 1968, 1971, and Commendation, 1965. FRSA 1972. *Publications:* contrib. Jl of RIBA and other jls. *Recreations:* arts, music, theatre, travel, languages. *Address:* Meadowside, Wild Oak Lane, Trull, Taunton, Somerset TA3 7JT. *T:* (01823) 272485.
Died 10 Sept. 2001.

ADAMS, Douglas Noël; author; *b* 11 March 1952; *s* of Christopher Douglas Adams and Janet Dora Adams (*née* Donovan, later Thrift); *m* 1991, Jane Belson; one *d. Educ:* Brentwood Sch., Essex; St John's Coll., Cambridge (BA, MA). Radio and TV writer, 1974–78; BBC Radio Producer, 1978; BBV TV Script Editor, 1978–80; novelist, 1979–. Dir and Chief Fantasist, The Digital Village, 1996–. Mem., Library and Information Commn, 1995–96. *Publications:* The Hitch Hiker's Guide to the Galaxy, 1979; The Restaurant at the End of the Universe, 1980; Life, the Universe and Everything, 1982; So Long, and Thanks for all the Fish, 1984; (with John Lloyd) The Meaning of Liff, 1984; The Original Hitch Hiker Radio Scripts, 1985; Dirk Gently's Holistic Detective Agency, 1987; The Long Dark Tea Time of the Soul, 1988; (with Mark Carwardine) Last Chance to See …, 1990; (with John Lloyd) The Deeper Meaning of Liff, 1990; Mostly Harmless, 1992; *posthumous publication:* The Salmon of Doubt: hitchhiking the galaxy one last time, 2002. *Recreations:* scuba diving, music, staring out of the window. *Address:* c/o The Digital Village, 11 Maiden Lane, WC2E 7NA. *T:* (020) 7543 1700; *e-mail:* askdna@tdv.com. *Club:* Groucho.
Died 11 May 2001.

ADAMS, Frederick Baldwin, Jr; Director, Pierpont Morgan Library, 1948–69, then Emeritus; *b* 28 March 1910; *s* of Frederick B. Adams and Ellen Walters Delano; *m* 1st, 1933, Ruth Potter (marr. diss.); 2nd, 1941, Betty Abbott (marr. diss.); four *d;* 3rd, 1969, Marie-Louise de Croy. *Educ:* St Paul's Sch.; Yale Univ. (BA). Air Reduction Co. Inc., 1933–48. President: New-York Historical Soc., 1963–71; Bd Governors, Yale University Press, 1959–71; Hon. Pres., Assoc. Internationale de Bibliophilie (Pres., 1974–83); Trustee, Yale Univ., 1964–71. Fellow: Amer. Acad. Arts and Sciences; Amer. Philosophical Soc.; Amer. Antiquarian Soc.; Mass Historical Soc.; Mem., Phi Beta Kappa. Hon. degrees: LittD: Hofstra Coll., 1959; Williams Coll., 1966; DFA, Union Coll., 1959; MA, Yale Univ., 1965; LHD, New York Univ., 1966. Chevalier, Légion d'Honneur (France), 1950; Comdr, Order of the Crown (Belgium), 1979. *Publications:* Radical Literature in America, 1939; One Hundred Influential American Books (with Streeter and Wilson), 1947; To Russia with Frost, 1963; contrib. to books and jls in bibliography, printing, collecting. *Address:* 208 rue de Rivoli, 75001 Paris, France. *Clubs:* Roxburghe;

Century, Grolier (NY); Cercle Interallié (Paris).
Died 7 Jan. 2001.

ADAMS, John Kenneth; Editor, Country Life, 1958–73; Editorial Director, Country Life Ltd, 1959–73; *b* 3 June 1915; *o c* of late Thomas John Adams and late Mabel Adams (*née* Jarvis), Oxford; *m* 1944, Margaret (*d* 2000), *o c* of late Edward Claude Fortescue, Banbury, Oxon. *Educ:* City of Oxford Sch.; Balliol Coll., Oxford (BA 1939). Asst Master, Stonyhurst Coll., 1939–40; served with RAFVR, 1940–41 (invalided); Asst Master, Wellington Coll., 1941–44; attached to Manchester Guardian as Leader-writer, 1942–44; Leader-writer, The Scotsman, 1944–46; joined editorial staff of Country Life, 1946; Asst Editor, 1952; Deputy Editor, 1956; Editor, 1958; Editorial Director, 1959. *Recreations:* gardening, ornithology, travel. *Address:* 95 Alleyn Park, West Dulwich, SE21 8AA. *T:* (020) 8693 1736. *Club:* Athenæum.
Died 23 Feb. 2003.

ADAMS, Norman (Edward Albert), RA 1972 (ARA 1967); ARCA 1951; artist (painter); Professor of Painting in Royal Academy Schools, 1995–2000; *b* 9 Feb. 1927; *s* of Albert Henry Adams and Winifred Elizabeth Rose Adams; *m* 1947, Anna Theresa; two *s. Educ:* Royal Coll. of Art. Head of Sch. of Painting, Manchester Coll. of Art and Design, 1962–70; Lectr, Leeds Univ., 1975–78; Prof. of Fine Art, and Dir of King Edward VII Coll. (formerly Sch.), Univ. of Newcastle upon Tyne, 1981–86; Keeper, Royal Acad., 1986–95. Exhibitions in America (New York, Pittsburgh); retrospective exhibitions: RCA, 1969; Whitechapel Gall., RA, 1988; Central Art Gall., Ashton-under-Lyne, 2003; Peter Scott Gall., Lancaster, 2005; solo exhibitions: RA Friends' Room, 2003; Way of the Cross drawings, Southwell Minster, 2003; Sailing to Byzantium drawings and paintings, Fine Art Soc., London, 2004. Paintings in collections of: most British provincial art galls; Tate Gall., London; Nat. Galls, New Zealand; Gulbenkian Mus., Lisbon; work purchased by: Arts Council of GB; Contemp. Art Soc.; Chantrey Bequest; various Educn Authorities. Murals at: Broad Lane Comprehensive Sch., Coventry; St Anselm's Church, S London; Our Lady of Lourdes, Milton Keynes; Stations of the Cross, St Mary's RC Church, Mulberry Street, Manchester, 1994–95. Decor for ballets, Covent Garden and Sadler's Wells. Kornferry Prize, RA Summer exhibn; RA Drawing Prize, 2003; Windsor & Newton Turner Watercolour Award, RA Summer exhibn, 2004. *Publications:* (with Glyn Hughes) Alibis and Convictions, 1978; A Decade of Painting 1971–81 (text by John Milner), 1981; (with A. Adams): Angels of Soho, 1988; Island Chapters, 1991; Life on Limestone, 1994. *Address:* Butts, Horton-in-Ribblesdale, Settle, North Yorks BD24 0HD. *T:* (01729) 860284; 6 Gainsborough Road, Chiswick, W4 1NJ.
Died 10 March 2005.

ADAMS, Sir Philip (George Doyne), KCMG 1969 (CMG 1959); HM Diplomatic Service, retired; *b* 17 Dec. 1915; *s* of late George Basil Doyne Adams, MD, and Arline Maud Adams (*née* Dodgson); *m* 1954, Hon. (Mary) Elizabeth Lawrence, *e d* of Baron Trevethin and Oaksey (3rd and 1st Baron respectively); two *s* two *d. Educ:* Lancing Coll.; Christ Church, Oxford. Entered Consular Service, 1939; served at: Beirut, 1939; Cairo, 1941; Jedda, 1945; FO, 1947; First Sec., 1948; Vienna, 1951; Counsellor, Khartoum, 1954; Beirut, 1956; FO, 1959; Chicago, 1963; Ambassador to Jordan, 1966–70; Asst Under-Sec., FCO, 1970; Dep. Sec., Cabinet Office, 1971–72; Ambassador to Egypt, 1973–75. Dir, Ditchley Foundn, 1977–82. Member: Board, British Council, 1977–82; Marshall Aid Commem. Commn, 1979–88. *Address:* 54 Sussex Square, W2 2SR. *Club:* Brooks's.
Died 14 Oct. 2001.

ADAMSON-MACEDO, Prof. Emeritus Colin, DSc; FIEE; engineering and higher education consultant; *b* 23 Nov. 1922; British; *m* 1946, Janet Marjory Conyers; one *d* (one *s* decd); *m* 1983, Dr Elvidina Nabuco Macedo; one *s* (two step *s* decd). *Educ:* Pocklington Sch., Yorks.

University of London (BSc 1947, MSc(Eng) 1952); University of Manchester (DSc 1961). REME (Capt.), 1942–46. Asst Lectr, then with A. Reyrolle & Co. (power systems analysis), 1946–52; Sen. Lectr, then Reader, in Electrical Power Systems Engrg, UMIST, 1952–61; Chm., Dept of Electrical Engrg and Electronics, UMIST, 1961–70; Rector, PCL, 1970–83; Overseas Adviser to Univ. of Salford, 1983–86. Mem., Conf. Internationale des Grands Réseaux Electriques; Chm. of Consultants, Educnl Overseas Services, 1975–90; Chm. of Panel 1 (and Mem. Council), British Calibration Service, 1969–83. Mem., Exec. Cttee, Inter-Univ. Council for Service Overseas, 1972–82. Mem., Bd of Trustees, Ecole Supérieure Interafricaine d'Electricité, Abidjan, 1979–90; UN Team leader for Yarmouk Univ. of Technology, Jordan, 1978–80. Vis. Professor: Univ. of Roorkee, India, 1954–55; Univs of Washington and Wisconsin, 1959; Middle East Techn. Univ., Ankara, 1967–68; Univ. of Technology, Baghdad, 1975–83; Fed. Univ. of Rio de Janeiro, 1983–93 (UNESCO Energy Conslt to Coordenação dos Programas de Pós-graduação de Engenharia, 1986); Advisor to Rector, Mahidol Univ., Thailand, 1984–92; NATO Fellow, Electrical/Electronics Res. Inst., ME Technical Univ., Ankara, 1987; Vis. Prof. and Energy Conslt, Inst. de Pesquisas Tecnológicas, Univ. of São Paulo, 1987–88; Consultant, Trng Policy Div., ILO, 1991–92. Mem. Governing Council, Polytechnic of Huddersfield HEC, 1989–92. Blumlein Meml Lectr, IEE, 1998. Bailie Meml Prize, IEE, 1948–49. *Publications:* (jtly) High Voltage Direct Current Power Transmission, 1960; High Voltage DC Power Convertors and Systems, 1963; University Perspectives, 1970; UNESCO reports: Higher Technical Education (Egypt), 1972; Alternative University Structures (UK), 1973, 3rd edn 1977; Technical Higher Education (Iraq), 1974; Post-secondary Education for Persons Gainfully-employed, 1976 and 1977; contribs to Proc. IEE and other learned jls. *Recreations:* yachting, oriental science and technology. *Address:* Yetts o' Huaxu, Glendevon by Dollar, Clackmannanshire FK14 7JY. *T:* (01259) 781641; Rua Tonelero 27/201, Edifício Yapa, Copacabana, 22030-000 Rio de Janeiro-RJ, Brazil. *Club:* Athenæum.   *Died 29 March 2005.*

ADLER, George Fritz Werner, OBE 1982; FREng; FIMechE; FICE; Director of Research, British Hydromechanics Research Association, 1971–86; *b* 12 Jan. 1926; *s* of Fritz Jacob Sigismund Adler and Hildegard Julie Adler (*née* Lippmann); *m* 1949, June Moonaheim Margaret Nash; three *d. Educ:* Penarth County School; Cardiff Technical Coll.; University Coll., Cardiff (Fellow 1984); Imperial Coll., London. BSc (Eng), DIC. FICE 1980; FREng (FEng 1981). Design Engineer, 1948, Chief, Mechanical Develt, 1953, English Electric, Rugby; Chief Mechanical Engineer, 1958, Gen. Manager Mech. Products, Marconi, 1962; Manager, Mech. Products Div., English Electric, 1966. Dir, Fluid Engineering Products Ltd, 1982–84. Vice-Pres., 1979, Pres., 1983, IMechE; Chm., CDRA (Fedn of Technology Centres), 1981–83; Vice-Pres., FEANI, 1987–89; Mem., Engineering Council, 1986–89; Treasurer, Fellowship of Engrg, 1988–91. FCMI (FBIM 1979); FInstD 1985. Eur Ing, FEANI, 1987. Freeman, City of London, 1984; Liveryman, Co. of Engrs, 1984–. *Publications:* chapter, Water Turbines (jtly), in Kempe's Engineers' Year Book, 1956; articles in technical jls. *Recreations:* gardening, swimming, music. *Address:* The Haining, Orchard Close, Longburton, Sherborne, Dorset DT9 5PP. *T:* (01963) 210641.   *Died 17 Nov. 2002.*

ADLER, Larry; see Adler, L. C.

ADLER, Lawrence Cecil, (Larry); mouth organist; *b* 10 Feb. 1914; *s* of Louis Adler and Sadie Hack; *m* 1st, 1938, Eileen Walser (marr. diss. 1961); one *s* two *d;* 2nd, 1969, Sally Cline (marr. diss. 1977); one *d. Educ:* Baltimore City Coll. Won Maryland Harmonica Championship, 1927; first stage appearance, 1928 (NY); first British appearance, 1934 (in C. B. Cochran's Streamline revue); first

appearance as soloist with Symphony Orchestra, Sydney, Australia, 1939; jt recital tours with dancer Paul Draper, US, 1941–49; soloist with NY Philharmonic and other major US Orchestras, also orchestras in England, Japan and Europe; war tours for Allied Troops, 1943, 1944, 1945; Germany, 1947, 1949; Korea (Brit. Commonwealth Div.), 1951; Israel (Six Day War), 1967, (Yom Kippur War), 1973; articles and book reviews in Sunday Times, New Statesman, Spectator, New Society, Observer, Punch; restaurant critic: Harpers & Queen, London Portrait; Boardroom; Chamber Life; columnist: What's On in London, Jazz Express, Jewish Gazette; numerous TV One Man Shows; soloist, Edinburgh Festival, playing first performance of unpublished Gershwin quartet (MS gift to Adler from I. Gershwin, 1963); works composed for Adler by: Dr Ralph Vaughan Williams, Malcolm Arnold, Darius Milhaud, Arthur Benjamin, Gordon Jacob, Cyril Scott, Francis Chagrin, Joaquin Rodrigo and others. Hon. Diploma: Peabody Conservatory of Music, Baltimore, 1986; City Coll., Baltimore, 1986. *Compositions:* film scores: Genevieve; King and Country; High Wind in Jamaica; The Great Chase, etc; TV scores: Midnight Men (BBC serial); various TV plays and documentaries; music for TV commercials, children's records, stage plays, etc; concert music: Theme and Variations; Camera III; One Man Show, From Hand to Mouth, Edinburgh Festival, 1965 (other festivals, 1965–). *Publications:* How I Play, 1937; Larry Adler's Own Arrangements, 1960; Jokes and How to Tell Them, 1963; It Ain't Necessarily So (autobiog.), 1985. *Recreations:* tennis, journalism, cycling, conversation; obsession: writing letters to Private Eye. *Address:* c/o MBA Literary Agents Ltd, 45 Fitzroy Street, W1P 5HR. *T:* (020) 7387 2076. *Clubs:* Groucho, Scribes; Paddington Tennis.   *Died 7 Aug. 2001.*

ADMANI, Dr (Abdul) Karim, OBE 1987; JP; consultant physician, with special interest in strokes and the elderly; *b* 19 Sept. 1937; *s* of late Haji Razzak Admani, Palitana, India, and of Hajiani Rahima Admani; *m* Seema, *d* of late Charles Robson, South Shields; one *s* one *d. Educ:* Gujarat Univ., India (BSc 1st cl. Hons); Karachi Univ., Pakistan (MB, BS); Univ. of London. DTM&H 1963; FRCP; FRCPE 1979; FRCPGlas 1988; FRSocMed 1988; FRIPH. Teacher, Trent RHA (formerly Sheffield AHA), 1970–; Clin. Lectr, Sheffield Med. Sch., 1972–; Clin. Dir of Medicine, Northern Gen. Hosp. Trust, 1990–92. Vis. Prof. of Medicine and Neurol., Quaide-Azam Med. Coll., Bahawalpur, Pakistan, 1990–. WHO External Examr, Coll. of Physicians and Surgeons of Bangladesh, 1990–93. Director: Ranmoor Grange Nursing Home Ltd, 1975–80; Sunningdale Yorks Ltd, 1983–. Overseas Doctors' Association in UK: Dir, 1976–; Chm., 1981–87; Pres., 1987–94; Chm., ODTS, 1979– (Chm., Educn and Postgrad. Trng Cttee, 1982–). General Medical Council: Mem., 1979–; Chm., L Cttee, 1990–92; Member: Prof. Conduct Cttee, 1979–91; Preliminary Proc. Council, 1991–; Educn Cttee, 1990–92 and 1994; Racial Equality Cttee, 1994–. Member: Exec. Cttee, BMA, Sheffield, 1974–; Central Cttee of Consultants and Specialists, 1979–93; Sheffield HA, 1977–82; Council, British Geriatric Soc., 1989–93 (Chm., Trent Region, 1989–93); Council, BRCS, 1991–94 (Chm., Region III, 1991–94; Pres., S Yorks 1982–); Exec. Cttee for Racial Equality in Sheffield, 1972–90 (Chm., 1978–); Exec. Cttee, Age Concern, Sheffield, 1982–90; Management Bd, Pakistan Muslim Centre, 1987–; NHS Nursing Home Tribunal, 1989–; Medico-Chirurgical Soc. of Sheffield. Chm., Inst. of Transcultural Health Care, 1991–. President: Muslim Council of Sheffield, Rotherham and Dists, 1978–; Union of Pakistani Orgns in UK and Europe, 1979–94. Chm., Pakistan Enterprise Center, 1993–. JP City of Sheffield, 1974. Member, Editorial Board: Pakistan Medical Bull., 1974–; Medi-Scene, 1981–; ODA News Rev., 1985–. *Publication:* (ed) Guidance for Overseas Doctors in National Health Service in UK, 1982, 1991. *Recreations:* tennis, table tennis, snooker, chess. *Address:* 1 Derriman Glen, Silverdale Road, Sheffield S11 9LQ. *T:* (0114) 236 0465; Northern General Hospital, Barnsley Road,

Sheffield. *Clubs:* Abbeydale Rotary (Pres., 1995), Conservative (Sheffield). *Died 18 June 2004.*

AGA KHAN, Prince Sadruddin, KBE 2002; Consultant and Chargé de Mission to the Secretary-General of the UN, since 1978; Founding Member and President, Bellerive Foundation and Groupe de Bellerive; Founding Member and Chairman, Independent Commission on Internal Humanitarian Issues, 1983; *b* 17 Jan. 1933; *s* of His late Highness Sir Sultan Mohamed Shah, Aga Khan III, GCSI, GCIE, GCVO and of Andrée Joséphine Caron; *m* 1957, Nina Sheila Dyer (marr. diss. 1962); *m* 1972, Catherine Aleya Sursock. *Educ:* Harvard Univ. (BA); Harvard Grad. Sch. Arts and Sciences; Centre of Middle Eastern Studies. Unesco Consultant for Afro-Asian Projects, 1958; Head of Mission and Adviser to UN High Comr for Refugees, 1959–60; Unesco Special Consultant to Dir-Gen., 1961; Exec. Sec., Internat. Action Cttee for Preservation of Nubian Monuments, 1961; UN Dep. High Comr for Refugees, 1962–65; UN High Comr for Refugees, 1965–77; Co-ordinator, UN Humanitarian and Econ. Assistance Progs relating to Afghanistan, 1988–90; Personal Rep. of UN Sec.-Gen. for Humanitarian Assistance relating to Iraq-Kuwait crisis, 1990–91. Vice Pres., WWF, 1986–. Hon. Fellow, Amer. Acad. of Arts and Scis. Dr *hc:* Fletcher Sch. of Law and Diplomacy, 1986; Univ. of Nice, 1988; Hon. LLD Leeds, 1992. Hon. Citizen Geneva, 1978. UN Human Rights Award, 1978; Hammarsköld Medal, German UN Assoc., 1979; Olympia Prize, Alexander S. Onassis Foundn, 1982; Man of Peace Award, Together for Peace Foundn, 1989; Freedom Award, Internat. Rescue Cttee, USA. Grand Cross: Order of St Silvestro (Papal), 1963; Order of Homayoun (Iran), 1967; Order of the Royal Star of Great Comoro (Comoro Is), 1970; Order of the Two Niles (First Class) Sudan, 1973; Commander's Cross with Star, Order of Merit of Polish People's Republic, 1977; Commandeur de la Légion d'Honneur (France), 1979; Hilal-e-Pakistan, 1991; Commander of Golden Ark (Netherlands). *Publications:* Lectures on refugee problems delivered to RSA and Acad. Internat. Law, The Hague; Violations of Human Rights and Mass Exodus, study for UN Commn on Human Rights, 1981. *Recreations:* Islamic art, sailing, ski-ing, hiking, kite-flying. *Address:* Château de Bellerive, 1245 Collonge-Bellerive, Canton of Geneva, Switzerland. *Clubs:* Travellers (Paris); Knickerbocker (New York). *Died 12 May 2003.*

AGLIONBY, His Honour Francis John; a Circuit Judge, 1980–97, a Deputy Circuit Judge, since 1997; *b* 17 May 1932; *s* of Francis Basil and Marjorie Wycliffe Aglionby; *m* 1967, Susan Victoria Mary Vaughan; one *s* one *d.* *Educ:* Charterhouse; Corpus Christi Coll., Oxford (MA). Nat. Service, 1950–52, commnd Nigeria Regt. Called to the Bar, Inner Temple, 1956, Bencher, 1976; a Recorder of the Crown Court, 1975–80. Chancellor of Diocese: of Birmingham, 1971–; of Portsmouth, 1978–; of Carlisle, 1991–. Mem., Adv. Bd for Redundant Churches, 1999–. Held Home Office enquiry into Horserace Totalisator Bd's bets transmissions procedures, 1979. *Recreations:* variable. *Address:* The Croft, Houghton, Carlisle, Cumbria CA3 0LD. *T:* (01228) 523747. *Club:* Brooks's. *Died 6 June 2002.*

AGNELLI, Dr Giovanni; industrialist; Chairman: Fiat, 1966–96 (Hon. Chairman, since 1996); Istituto Finanziario Industriale, since 1959; EXOR, SA, Luxembourg, since 1974; Giovanni Agnelli Foundation, since 1968; Chairman, Editrice La Stampa, since 1982; *b* Turin, Italy, 12 March 1921; *s* of Edoardo Agnelli, and *g s* of Giovanni Agnelli, founder of Fabbrica Italiana Automobili Torino (FIAT); *m* 1953, Princess Marella Caracciolo di Castagneto; one d (one *s* decd). *Educ:* Turin Univ. (DrJur 1943). Member Board: Italian Stock Cos Assoc.; Turin Industrial Assoc.; Member: Exec. Bd, Confedn of Italian Industry; Internat. Council, J. P. Morgan Chase, NY; Adv. Bd, Bilderberg Meetings. Hon. Chm., Council for US and Italy. Romanes Lectr, Univ. of Oxford, 1991. Hon. Fellow, Magdalen Coll., Oxford, 1991. Corresp. Mem., Moral and Political Scis Acad., Institut de France. Comdr, Légion d'Honneur (France), 2000. *Address:* c/o Fiat SpA, 250 via Nizza, Turin 10126, Italy. *T:* (11) 6861111. *Died 24 Jan. 2003.*

AIKEN, Joan Delano, (Mrs Julius Goldstein), MBE 1999; writer of historical, mystery and children's novels, plays and poetry; *b* 4 Sept. 1924; *d* of Conrad Potter Aiken and Jessie McDonald; *m* 1st, 1945, Ronald George Brown (*d* 1955); one *s* one *d*; 2nd, 1976, Julius Goldstein (*d* 2002). *Educ:* Wychwood Sch., Oxford. Inf. Officer, subseq. Librarian, UN London Inf. Centre, 1943–49; Features Editor, Argosy magazine, 1955–60; Copy-writer, J. Walter Thompson London office, 1960–61; time thereafter devoted to writing. Mem., Soc. of Authors. Guardian Award for Children's Literature, 1969; Lewis Carroll Award, 1970. *Publications:* (most also published in USA and as paperbacks): The Silence of Herondale, 1964; The Fortune Hunters, 1965; Trouble with Product X, 1966 (Beware of the Bouquet, USA 1966); Hate Begins at Home, 1967 (Dark Interval, USA 1967); The Ribs of Death, 1967 (The Crystal Crow, USA 1968); The Windscreen Weepers (stories), 1969; The Embroidered Sunset, 1970; The Butterfly Picnic, 1970 (A Cluster of Separate Sparks, USA 1972); Died on a Rainy Sunday, 1972; Voices in an Empty House, 1975; Castle Barebane, 1976; Last Movement, 1977; The Five-Minute Marriage, 1977; The Smile of the Stranger, 1978; A Touch of Chill (horror stories), 1979; The Lightning Tree, 1980 (The Weeping Ash, USA); The Girl from Paris, 1982; The Way to Write for Children, 1982; A Whisper in the Night, 1982; Foul Matter, 1983; Mansfield Revisited, 1984; Deception, 1987; Jane Fairfax, 1990; The Youngest Miss Ward, 1998; *for children:* (many also published in USA): All You've Ever Wanted (stories), 1953; More Than You Bargained For (stories), 1955; The Kingdom and the Cave, 1960; The Wolves of Willoughby Chase, 1962; Black Hearts in Battersea, 1964; Night Birds on Nantucket, 1966; The Whispering Mountain, 1968; A Necklace of Raindrops (stories), 1968; A Small Pinch of Weather (stories), 1969; Night Fall, 1969; Armitage, Armitage, Fly Away Home (stories), USA 1970; Smoke From Cromwell's Time, USA 1970; The Cuckoo Tree, 1971; The Kingdom Under the Sea (folktales), 1971; The Green Flash (fantasy and horror stories), USA 1971; A Harp of Fishbones (stories), 1972; Winterthing (play), USA 1972; The Mooncusser's Daughter (play), USA 1973; Winterthing & The Mooncusser's Daughter, 1973; Midnight is a Place, 1974; Arabel's Raven, USA 1974; Tales of Arabel's Raven, 1974; Not What You Expected (stories), USA 1974; Tale of a One-Way Street (stories), 1976; The Skin Spinners (poems), USA 1976; A Bundle of Nerves (horror stories), 1976; The Angel Inn (trans. from French), 1976; The Faithless Lollybird (stories), 1977; Mice and Mendelson, 1978; Go Saddle the Sea, 1978; Street (play), USA 1978; Arabel and Mortimer, 1979; The Shadow Guests, 1980; The Stolen Lake, 1981; Mortimer's Cross, 1983; Bridle the Wind, 1983; Up the Chimney Down and Other Stories, 1984; Fog Hounds, Wind Cat, Sea Mice, 1984, 2nd edn 1997; The Kitchen Warriors, 1984; The Last Slice of Rainbow, 1985; Mortimer Says Nothing, 1985; Dido and Pa, 1986; Past Eight O'Clock, 1986; A Goose on Your Grave, 1987; Beware of the Moon, 1987; The Teeth of the Gale, 1988; The Erl King's Daughter, 1988; Blackground, 1989; Give Yourself a Fright, 1989; Voices, 1989; A Foot in the Grave, 1990; A Fit of Shivers (horror stories), 1990; Morningquest, 1992; (with Lizza Aiken) Mortimer and Arabel, 1992; A Creepy Company, 1993; The Midnight Moropus, 1993; The Shoemaker's Boy, 1993; Is, 1993; Eliza's Daughter, 1994; The Winter Sleepwalker, 1994; Cold Shoulder Road, 1995; A Handful of Gold, 1995; The Cockatrice Boys, 1996; Emma Watson, 1996; The Jewel Seed, 1997; Mooncake, 1998; Limbo Lodge, 1999; Lady Catherine's Necklace, 2000; In Thunder's Pocket, 2001; The Scream, 2002; Ghostly Beasts, 2002; Midwinter Nightingale, 2003; The Wooden Dragon, 2004. *Recreations:* listening to music, looking at art, travel, reading, gardening, walking, talking to friends. *Address:* The Hermitage, East Street, Petworth, West Sussex GU28 0AB. *T:* (01798) 42279. *Clubs:* Society of Authors, Writers' Guild, Crime Writers' Association, PEN; Mystery Writers of America.

Died 4 Jan. 2004.

AIKEN, Air Chief Marshal Sir John (Alexander Carlisle), KCB 1973 (CB 1967); Director General of Intelligence, Ministry of Defence, 1978–81; *b* 22 Dec. 1921; *s* of Thomas Leonard and Margaret Aiken; *m* 1948, Pamela Jane (*née* Bartlett); one *s* one *d. Educ:* Birkenhead School. Joined RAF, 1941; Fighter Sqdns, Europe and Far East, 1942–45; Fighter Comd, 1946–47; CFS, 1948; Staff of RAF Coll., Cranwell, 1948–50; OC Univ. of Birmingham Air Sqdn, 1950–52; Staff Coll., 1953; HQ Fighter Comd, 1954–55; OC 29 Fighter Sqdn, 1956–57; jssc 1958; Headquarters AF North, 1958–60; Air Min., 1960–63; Station Comdr, RAF Finningley, 1963–64; Air Cdre Intelligence, Min. of Defence, 1965–67; idc 1968; Dep. Comdr, RAF, Germany, 1969–71; Dir-Gen. Training, RAF, 1971–72; Head of Economy Project Team (RAF), 1972–73; AOC-in-C, NEAF, Comdr British Forces Near East, and Administrator, Sovereign Base Areas, Cyprus, 1973–76; Air Member for Personnel, 1976–78. Pres., RAFA, 1984–85 and 1987–88 (Chm., Central Council, 1981–84); Member Council: RAF Benevolent Fund, 1988–; Chatham House, 1984–90. *Recreations:* walking, music. *Club:* Royal Air Force.

Died 31 May 2005.

AIKMAN, Colin Campbell, CBE 1990; PhD; *b* 24 Feb. 1919; *s* of Colin Campbell Aikman and Bertha Egmont Aikman (*née* Harwood); *m* 1952, Betty Alicia, *d* of R. Y. James; three *d* (one *s* decd). *Educ:* Palmerston North Boys' High Sch., Victoria University Coll., Wellington, NZ (LLM); London Sch. of Economics (PhD). Law Clerk in Legal Offices, 1935–41; Barrister and Solicitor of High Court of New Zealand, 1940–41; Prime Minister's Dept and Dept of External Affairs (Legal Adviser, 1949–55), 1943–55; Mem. NZ Delgn to San Francisco Conf., 1945; Prof. of Jurisprudence and Constitutional Law, Victoria Univ. of Wellington (Dean of Law Faculty, 1957–59, 1962–67), 1955–68; Mem. Council, NZ Inst. of Internat. Affairs (Nat. Pres., 1960–63, Dir. 1979–84), 1955–; Advr to NZ Govt on Constitutional Develt of Cook Is, Western Samoa and Niue, 1956–68, 1975; Vice-Chancellor, The Univ. of the South Pacific, Suva, Fiji, 1968–74; NZ High Comr to India, accredited also to Bangladesh and Nepal, 1975–78. Member: Council of Volunteer Service Abroad (Inc.) (Chm. 1962–65), 1962–68; Adv. Cttee on External Aid and Develt, 1980–88. Consultant, NZ Law Commn, 1988–91. Trustee, Norman Kirk Meml Trust, 1979– (Chm., 1994–99). Mem. Council, Nat. Univ. of Samoa, 1985–98. Hon. LLD Victoria Univ. of Wellington, 1992; DU Univ. of South Pacific, 1992; DUniv Nat. Univ. of Samoa, 1996. Silver Jubilee Medal, 1977; Western Samoa Order of Tiafau, 1993. *Publications:* (co-author): A Report to Members of the Legislative Assembly of the Cook Islands on Constitutional Development, 1963; New Zealand, The Development of its Laws and Constitution (ed Robson), 1967 (2nd edn); New Zealand's Record in the Pacific Islands in the Twentieth Century (ed Angus Ross), 1969; contribs to NZ Internat. Review, Victoria Univ. of Wellington Law Review. *Recreations:* golf, cricket, carpentry. *Address:* 7A/186 The Terrace, Wellington, New Zealand. *T:* (4) 4711602, *Fax:* (4) 4711630; *e-mail:* aikman@attglobal.net. *Clubs:* Wellington; Wellington Golf (Heretaunga).

Died 22 Dec. 2002.

AIREY, Sir Lawrence, KCB 1978 (CB 1976); Chairman of the Board of Inland Revenue, 1980–86, retired; Director (non-executive), 1987–94, and Deputy Chairman, 1988–94, Standard Life Assurance Co.; *b* 10 March 1926; *s* of late Lawrence Clark Airey and Isabella Marshall Pearson; *m* 1953, Patricia Anne, *d* of late Edward George Williams and Mary Selway; two *s* one *d. Educ:*

Royal Grammar Sch., Newcastle upon Tyne; Peterhouse, Cambridge. Served RM, 1945–47. Entered Civil Service, 1949; General Register Office, 1949–56; Cabinet Office, 1956–58; HM Treasury, 1958–79: Under-Sec., 1969–73; Dep. Sec., 1973–77; Second Perm. Sec., 1977–79. Research Fellow, Nuffield Coll., Oxford, 1961–62. Member: Bd of British Nat. Oil Corp., 1976–77; Govt Contracts Rev. Bd, 1986–99. *Recreations:* collecting books; music. *Address:* Lions House, Berwick-on-Tweed, Northumberland TD15 1JG. *T:* (01289) 304384.

Died 21 June 2001.

'AKAU'OLA, 'Inoke Fotu Faletau, CVO 1993; Governor of Vava'u, Tonga, since 2002; *b* 24 June 1937; 2nd *s* of 'Akau'ola (Sateki Faletau) and Celia Lyden; *S* brother, 1995; *m* 'Evelini Ma'ata Hurrell; three *s* three *d. Educ:* St Peter's, Cambridge, NZ; Tonga High Sch.; Auckland Grammar Sch.; UC Swansea (Hon. Fellow 1990); Manchester Univ. Joined Tonga Civil Service, 1958; Asst Sec., Prime Minister's Office, 1965; Sec. to Govt, 1969; seconded to Univ. of South Pacific, 1971; Sec. to Govt, 1972; High Comr, UK, 1972–82; Ambassador to: France, 1972–82; Germany, 1976–82; Belgium, Luxembourg, Netherlands, EEC, 1977–82; USA, 1979–82; USSR, 1980–82; Denmark, 1981–82; Director: Management Develt Programme, Commonwealth Secretariat, 1983–84; Commonwealth Foundn, 1985–93; Dep. Sec., Prime Minister's Office, Nuku'alofa, 1994–96; Sec. for Fisheries, Tonga, 1996–2002. *Recreations:* Rugby, tennis, reading, bridge, fishing. *Heir: s* Ahovaleamoemapa Faletau. *Address:* Teu Folau, Fanga-ò-Pilolevu, Nuku'alofa, Tonga. *Clubs:* Royal Over-Seas League; Royal Nuku'alofa.

Died 9 Oct. 2005.

ALBU, Marie, (Mrs A. H. Albu); see Jahoda, M.

ALDRIDGE, Frederick Jesse; Member, Public Health Laboratory Service Board, 1977–83; Under-Secretary and Controller of Supply, Department of Health and Social Security, 1968–75; *b* 13 Oct. 1915; *s* of late Jesse and Clara Amelia Aldridge; *m* 1940, Grace Hetty Palser (*d* 1999); two *d. Educ:* Westminster City Sch. Clerical Off., Air Min., 1933; Exec. Off., Min. of Health, 1935; RAF, 1940–46; Acct-General's Div., Min. of Health: Asst Acct-Gen., 1956; Dep. Acct-Gen., 1958; Asst Sec. for Finance and Dep. Acct-Gen., 1964; Asst Sec., Food, Health and Nutrition, also Civil Defence, 1966. *Recreation:* music. *Address:* 17 Tanglewood Close, Croydon CR0 5HX. *T:* (020) 8656 3623.

Died 20 Aug. 2003.

ALEXANDER OF WEEDON, Baron *cr* 1988 (Life Peer), of Newcastle-under-Lyme in the County of Staffordshire; **Robert Scott Alexander,** QC 1973; QC (NSW) 1983; *b* 5 Sept. 1936; *s* of late Samuel James and of Hannah May Alexander; *m* 1st, 1963, Frances Rosemary (*née* Pughe) (marr. diss. 1973); two *s* one *d*; one *d*; 2nd, 1978, Elizabeth (*née* Norman); (one *s* decd); 3rd, 1985, Marie Anderson (*née* Sugrue). *Educ:* Brighton Coll.; King's Coll., Cambridge (BA 1959; MA 1963; Hon. Fellow, 2001). Called to Bar, Middle Temple, 1961, Bencher, 1979, Master Treasurer, 2001; Vice Chm., 1984–85, Chm., 1985–86, of the Bar Council. Chm., Nat. Westminster Bank, 1989–99. Chm., Panel on Takeovers and Mergers, 1987–89; Dep. Chm., SIB, 1993–99; Mem., Govt Panel on Sustainable Develt, 1994–2000. Chairman: Delegated Powers and Deregulation Scrutiny Cttee, H of L, 1995–2002; H of L Audit Cttee, 2002–; Mem., Ind. Commn on Voting Reform, 1997–98. Non-executive Director: RTZ Corp., 1991–96; Internat. Stock Exchange of UK and Republic of Ireland, 1991–93; Total Elf Fina, 1996–2002. Chairman: Council, Justice, 1990–; Crisis, 1990–96. Trustee: National Gall., 1987–93; The Economist, 1990–. Governor, RSC, 1995– (Chm., 2000–04). Chancellor, Exeter Univ., 1998–. President: King's Coll. Assoc., 1980–81; Brighton Coll. 1993–; Mem., Council of Governors, Wycombe Abbey Sch., 1986–92. Presentation Fellow, KCL, 1995. FRSA 1991. Hon. LLD: Sheffield, 1991; Buckingham, 1992; Keele,

1993; Exeter, 1995; Warwick, 2003. *Publication:* The Voice of the People: a constitution for tomorrow, 1997. *Recreations:* theatre, cricket, tennis, painting. *Address:* House of Lords, SW1A 0PW. *Clubs:* Garrick, MCC (Mem. Cttee; Pres., 2000–01; Chm., 2002–).
Died 6 Nov. 2005.

ALEXANDER, Prof. John Malcolm, FREng; Emeritus Professor, University of Wales; *b* 14 Oct. 1921; *s* of Robert Henry Alexander and Gladys Irene Lightfoot Alexander (*née* Domville); *m* 1946, Margaret, *d* of F. A. Ingram; two *s. Educ:* Ipswich Sch.; City and Guilds Coll. DSc (Eng) London; PhD. FCGI; FICE; FIMechE; FIEE; FIMMM; FREng (FEng 1982). REME commn, 1942–47; Aluminium Labs Ltd, 1953–55; English Electric, 1955–57; London University: Reader in Plasticity, 1957–63; Prof. of Engrg Plasticity, 1963–69; Chm. Board of Studies in Civil and Mech. Engrg, 1966–68; Prof. of Applied Mechanics, Imperial Coll., 1969–78; Prof. and Head of Dept of Mech. Engrg, University Coll. of Swansea, 1978–83. Stocker Vis. Prof. in Engrg and Technol., 1985–87, Adjunct Prof., 1987–, Univ. of Ohio. Chm., Applied Mechanics Gp, IMechE, 1963–65; Mem., CIRP, 1965–; Vice-President: Inst. of Metals, 1968–71; Inst. of Sheet Metal Engrg, 1979–. Gov., Ipswich Sch., 1977–86. Chm., British Cold Forging Gp, 1973–79. Assessor, Sizewell 'B' Public Inquiry, 1983–85; Mem., Adv. Cttee on Safe Transport of Radioactive Materials, 1985–89. Series Editor, Ellis Horwood Ltd, 1970–91; Member Editorial Board: Internat. Jl Mech. Scis, 1968–91; Internat. Jl Machine Tool Design and Res., 1973–91. FRSA. Liveryman, Blacksmiths' Co., 1976. Joseph Bramah Medal, IMechE, 1970. *Publications:* Advanced Mechanics of Materials, Manufacturing Properties of Materials, 1963; Hydrostatic Extrusion, 1971; Strength of Materials, 1980; Manufacturing Technology, 1987; papers to Royal Soc., IMechE, Iron and Steel Inst., Inst. Metals, Metals Soc. *Recreations:* music, gardening, golf. *Address:* Rowan Cottage, Furze Hill Road, Headley Down, Hants GU35 8NP. *Club:* Army and Navy. *Died 6 April 2005.*

ALEXANDER, Sir Kenneth (John Wilson), Kt 1978; DL; FRSE 1978; Chancellor, University of Aberdeen, 1986–96; *b* Edinburgh, 14 March 1922; *o s* of late William Wilson Alexander; *m* 1949, Angela-May, *d* of late Capt. G. H. Lane, RN; one *s* four *d. Educ:* George Heriot's Sch., Edinburgh; Sch. of Economics, Dundee (BSc (Econ) London). Research Asst, Univ. of Leeds, 1949–51; Lectr, Univ. of Sheffield, 1951–56; Lectr, Univ. of Aberdeen, 1957–62; Dean of Scottish Business Sch., 1973–75 (Chm., Acad. Exec. Cttee, 1972–73); Prof. of Econs, Strathclyde Univ., 1963–80, on leave of absence, 1976–80; Chm., Highlands and Islands Develt Bd, 1976–80; Principal and Vice-Chancellor, Stirling Univ., 1981–86. Mem. Adv. Cttee on University of the Air, 1965. Director: Fairfields (Glasgow) Ltd, 1966–68; Upper Clyde Shipbuilders Ltd, 1968–71; Scottish Television, 1982–92; Stakis plc, 1987–93; Aberdeen Univ. Press, 1989–92 (Chm., 1990–92); Scottish Daily Record and Sunday Mail (1986) Ltd, 1990–92; Chairman: Govan Shipbuilders, 1974–76; Michael Kelly Associates, 1986–94; Scottish Industrial Exhibitions Ltd, 1991–99. Dir, Glasgow Chamber of Commerce, 1969–73; Economic Consultant to Sec. of State for Scotland, 1968–91; Chm., Cttee on Adult Educn in Scotland, 1970–73; Mem. Exec. Cttee, 1968–91, Dep. Chm. 1982–91, Scottish Council (Develt and Industry); Member: (part-time) Scottish Transport Gp, 1969–76; SSRC, 1975–76; Scottish Develt Agency, 1975–86; Bd, UK CEED, 1985. Governor: Technical Change Centre, 1981–87; Newbattle Abbey Coll., 1974–73; President: Section F, British Assoc., 1974; Saltire Soc., 1975–81; Scottish Section, Town and Country Planning, 1982–; Hon. Pres., The Highland Fund, 1983–; Chairman: John Muir Trust, 1985–88; Edinburgh Book Fest., 1987–91; Paxton Trust, 1989–94; Trustee, Nat. Museums of Scotland, 1985–87. CIMgt (CBIM 1980); FEIS 1983; FBEC(S) 1984; FRIAS 1988. DL Fife, 1992. Hon. DLitt: Aberdeen, 1987; Heriot–Watt, 1995; Hon. LLD: CNAA,

1976; Aberdeen, 1985; Strathclyde, 1986; Dundee, 1986; DUniv: Stirling, 1977; Open 1985. *Publications:* The Economist in Business, 1967; Productivity Bargaining and the Reform of Industrial Relations, 1969; (with C. L. Jenkins) Fairfields, a study of industrial change, 1971; (ed) The Political Economy of Change, 1976; articles in Oxford Econ. Papers, Quarterly Jl of Econ., Scottish Jl of Pol Econ., Economica, Yorkshire Bulletin Economics, and other jls. *Recreation:* Scottish antiquarianism. *Address:* 9 West Shore, Pittenweem, Fife KY10 2NV.
Died 27 March 2001.

ALEXANDER, Michael Charles; writer; *b* 20 Nov. 1920; *s* of late Rear-Adm. Charles Otway Alexander and Antonia Geermans; *m* 1963, Sarah Wignall (marr. diss.); one adopted *d. Educ:* Stowe; RMC, Sandhurst; Oflag IVC, Colditz. Served War: DCLI; 5 (Ski) Bn Scots Gds; 8 Commando (Layforce); HQ 70 Div. (Tobruk); HQ 13 Corps (GSO 3); SBS (POW, 1942–44); 2nd SAS Regt; War Office (Civil Affairs). Intergovtl Cttee on Refugees, 1946; Capt., retd, 1946. Editorial Director: Common Ground Ltd, 1946–50; OUP, 1950–51. Located Firuzkoh, Central Afghanistan, 1952; Himalayan Hovercraft Expedn, 1972; Yucatan Straits Hovercraft Expedn, 1975; Upper Ganges Hovercraft Expedn, 1980; Promoter, Scottish Highlands & Is Inflatable Boat Race; Founder and Hon. Pres., British Inflatable Boat Owners' Assoc., 1994. Dir, Adastra Productions. Founded: Woburn Safari Service, 1977; Chelsea Wharf Restaurant, 1983. Life Gov., RNLI. FZS, FRGS; Fellow, Royal Soc. for Asian Affairs. Co-publisher, Wildlife magazine, 1982–86. *Publications:* The Privileged Nightmare (with Giles Romilly), 1952 (republ., as Hostages at Colditz, 1975); Offbeat in Asia, 1953; The Reluctant Legionnaire, 1955; The True Blue, 1957; Mrs Fraser on the Fatal Shore, 1972, repr. 2001; Discovering the New World, 1976; Omai: noble savage, 1977; Queen Victoria's Maharajah, 1980, repr. 2001; Delhi-Agra: a traveller's companion, 1987. *Address:* 48 Eaton Place, SW1X 8AL. *T:* (020) 7235 2724. *Clubs:* Beefsteak, Chelsea Arts. *Died 19 Dec. 2004.*

ALEXANDER, Sir Michael (O'Donel Bjarne), GCMG 1992 (KCMG 1988; CMG 1982); HM Diplomatic Service, retired; Chairman, Royal United Services Institute for Defence Studies, since 1993; Director: Renaissance Capital (Moscow); RRC Bucharest, since 2000; *b* 19 June 1936; *s* of late Conel Hugh O'Donel Alexander, CMG, CBE, and Enid Constance Crichton Neate; *m* 1960, Traute Krohn; two *s* one *d. Educ:* Foyle Coll., Londonderry; Hall Sch., Hampstead; St Paul's Sch. (Schol.); King's Coll., Cambridge (Schol.; MA). Harkness Fellow (Yale and Berkeley) 1960–62; AM Yale 1962. Royal Navy, 1955–57. Entered HM Foreign (later Diplomatic) Service, 1962; Moscow, 1963–65; Office of Political Adviser, Singapore, 1965–68; FCO, 1968–72; Asst Private Sec. to Secretary of State (Rt Hon. Sir Alec Douglas-Home, MP, and Rt Hon. James Callaghan, MP) 1972–74; Counsellor (Conf. on Security and Co-operation in Europe) and later Head of Chancery, UK Mission, Geneva, 1974–77; Dep. Head, 1977–78, Head, 1978–79, Personnel Operations Dept, FCO; Private Sec. (Overseas Affairs) to the Prime Minister (Rt Hon. Margaret Thatcher, MP), 1979–81; Ambassador, Vienna, 1982–86; concurrently Hd of UK Delegn to the Negotiations on Mutual and Balanced Reduction of Forces and Armaments in Central Europe, 1985–86; Ambassador and UK Permanent Rep. on North Atlantic Council, Brussels, 1986–92 (Dean of Council, 1991–92). Dep. Chm., Wasserstein Perella Eastern Europe, 1992–97; Chairman: KINTO Securities, Kiev, 1994–97; Capital SA, Bucharest, 1995–2000 (co-founder; Dep. Chm., 1993–95); Bi-Link Capital Markets Ltd, 1998–99; Dir (and co-founder) Sector Capital, Moscow, 1995–96. Sen. Advr, Bain & Co., 1994–99. Organised: Britain in Vienna Fest., 1986; Grosses Goldenes Ehrenzeichen (Wien), 1986. Vice-Pres., Atlantic Council of UK, 1993–; Mem., Exec. Cttee, Anglo-Austrian Soc., 1992–. Former Public Schools', British Universities' and National Junior Foil

Champion; fenced for Cambridge Univ., 1957–60 (Captain, 1959–60); English Internat., 1958; Silver Medallist (Epée Team) Olympic Games, 1960; Gold Medallist, US Championships, 1961; Captained England, 1963; represented Cambridge in Field Events Match with Oxford, 1959, 1960. *Publications:* articles on East/West relations and international security. *Recreations:* reading history; watching or participating in sport of any kind. *Address:* c/o Renaissance Capital, 1 Angel Court, Copthall Avenue, EC2R 7HJ. *Clubs:* Garrick, Epée, All England Fencing; Hawks (Cambridge). *Died 1 June 2002.*

ALISON, Rt Hon. Michael James Hugh; PC 1981; *b* 27 June 1926; *m* 1958, Sylvia Mary Haigh; two *s* one *d*. *Educ:* Eton; Wadham Coll., Oxford. Coldstream Guards, 1944–48; Wadham Coll., Oxford, 1948–51; Lazard Bros & Co. Ltd, 1951–53; London Municipal Soc., 1954–58; Conservative Research Dept, 1958–64. MP (C) Barkston Ash, 1964–83, Selby, 1983–97. Parly Under-Sec. of State, DHSS, 1970–74; Minister of State: Northern Ireland Office, 1979–81; Dept of Employment, 1981–83; PPS to Prime Minister, 1983–87; Second Church Estates Comr, 1987–97. *Publication:* (ed jtly) Christianity and Conservatism, 1990. *Club:* Cavalry and Guards.
Died 28 May 2004.

ALISON, William Andrew Greig, FCLIP; Director of Libraries, City of Glasgow, 1975–81; *b* 23 Oct. 1916; *m* 1942, Jessie Youngson Henderson (decd); two *d*. *Educ:* Daniel Stewart's Coll., Edinburgh. Served War, RAF, 1940–46. Edinburgh Public Libraries, 1935–62: Assistant, 1935–46; Librarian, Fine Art Dept, 1946–55; Branch Librarian, 1955–61; Librarian, Scottish and Local History Depts, 1961–62; Glasgow City Libraries, 1962–81: Supt of District Libraries, 1962–64; Depute City Librarian, 1964–74; City Librarian, 1974–75. President: Scottish Library Assoc., 1975; Library Assoc., 1979 (also Mem. Council, 1979–82; Chm., Library Assoc. Publishing, 1981–82); Member: British Library Adv. Council, 1979–82; Nat. Library of Scotland Library Co-operation Cttee, 1974–81. British Council visits to: Zimbabwe, 1981; Bahrain, 1982; Syria, 1983. Silver Jubilee Medal, 1977. *Publication:* (associate ed.) New Library Buildings 1984–1989, 1990. *Recreations:* travel, philately. *Address:* St Mawgan, 103 Mossgiel Road, Glasgow G43 2BY. *T:* (0141) 632 6036. *Died 3 June 2005.*

ALIYEV, Heydar Alirza oglu; President, Republic of Azerbaijan, 1993–2003; Chairman, New Azerbaijan Party, since 1992; *b* 10 May 1923; *s* of Alirza Aliyev and Izzat Aliyeva; *m* Zarifa Aliyeva (*d* 1985); one *s* one *d*. *Educ:* Azerbaijan Inst. of Industry (Dip.); Azerbaijan State Univ. (Dip.). Various positions, Azerbaijan State Security Orgns, 1941–69; First Sec., Azerbaijan Communist Party, 1969–82; Mem. Politburo, CPSU, 1976–87; First Dep. Chm., Council of Ministers, USSR, in Moscow, 1982–87; retd from Communist Party, 1991; Chairman: Supreme Mejlis (Parlt), Nakhichevan Autonomous Republic, 1991–93; Supreme Soviet (Parlt), Azerbaijan, 1993. Hon. Dr: Baku State, 1994; Hojjat–Tapa, Turkey, 1994. Hero of Socialist Labour (USSR), 1979 and 1983. *Publications:* numerous articles on social, cultural, economic and political subjects published in foreign and domestic jls. *Recreations:* paintings, poetry, sport. *Address:* c/o Office of the President, 19 Istiglaliyyat Strasse, Baku 370001, Azerbaijan. *T:* (12) 988838, *Fax:* (12) 981414, 983328.
Died 12 Dec. 2003.

ALLAN, Colin Faulds, CB 1976; Chief Planning Inspector (Director of Planning Inspectorate), Department of the Environment, 1971–78, retired; *b* Newcastle upon Tyne, 1917; *s* of late Jack Stanley and Ruth Allan; *m* 1941, Aurea, 2nd *d* of Algernon Noble, Hexham; one *s* one *d*. *Educ:* Royal Grammar Sch., Newcastle upon Tyne; King's Coll. (Newcastle), Durham Univ. DipArch, ARIBA, DipTP (Distinction). Capt., RA, 1940–45; served in Iraq, India, Burma (despatches). Chief Asst to Dr Thomas Sharp, CBE, PPTPI, Planning Consultant, 1945–47; Area Planning Officer, Cumberland and Staffs CC, 1947–57;

joined Housing and Planning Inspectorate, 1957; Chief Housing and Planning Inspector, DoE (formerly Min. of Housing and Local Govt), 1967–71. *Recreations:* painting, bird-watching, eighteenth-century wineglasses. *Address:* Fieldfares, Chinthurst Lane, Shalford, Guildford, Surrey GU4 8JR. *T:* (01483) 561528. *Died 1 Aug. 2003.*

ALLAUN, Frank; *b* 27 Feb. 1913; *s* of Harry and Hannah Allaun; *m* 1st, 1941, Lilian Ball (*d* 1986); one *s* one *d*; 2nd, 1989, Millie Bobker. *Educ:* Manchester Grammar Sch. BA (Com). ACA. Town Hall Correspondent, and later Industrial Correspondent, Manchester Evening News; Northern Industrial Correspondent, Daily Herald; Editor, Labour's Northern Voice, 1951–67. Mem., NUJ; formerly Mem. AEU and Shop Assistants' Union; Vice President: Labour Action for Peace, 2001– (Pres., 1965–2001); Campaign for Nuclear Disarmament, 1983–; helped organise first Aldermaston march. MP (Lab) East Salford, 1955–83; PPS to the Secretary of State for the Colonies, Oct. 1964–March 1965, resigned. Mem., Labour Party National Executive, 1967–83, Dep. Chm., 1977–78, Chm., 1978–79. *Publications:* Stop the H Bomb Race, 1959; Heartbreak Housing, 1966; Your Trade Union and You, 1950; No Place Like Home, 1972; The Wasted '30 Billions, 1975; Questions and Answers on Nuclear Weapons, 1981; Spreading the News: a guide to media reform, 1989; The Struggle for Peace, 1992; numerous broadcasts. *Recreations:* walking, swimming. *Address:* 11 Eastleigh Road, Prestwich, Manchester M25 0BQ. *T:* (0161) 740 5085. *Died 26 Nov. 2002.*

ALLAWAY, Percy Albert, CBE 1973; FREng; Director, EMI Ltd, 1965–81; Chairman, EMI Electronics Ltd, 1968–81; Member, Executive Management Board, THORN EMI Ltd, 1980–81, Consultant, 1981–82; *b* 22 Aug. 1915; *s* of Albert Edward Allaway and Frances Beatrice (*née* Rogers); *m* 1959, Margaret Lilian Petyt. *Educ:* Southall Technical College. FIProdE, FIEE, FIQA. Trained EMI Ltd, 1930–35, returned 1940; Man. Dir, 1961–81, Chm., 1969–81, EMI Electronics Ltd; Chairman: EMI-Varian Ltd, 1969–81; EMI-MEC Ltd, 1968–81; Director: Nuclear Enterprises Ltd, 1961–81; SE Labs (EMI) Ltd, 1967–81. Pres., EEA, 1969–70 (former Mem. Council). Chm., Defence Industries Quality Assurance Panel, 1971–78; Past Chm. and Hon. Mem., NCQR; Member: Nat. Electronics Council, 1965–80; Raby Cttee, 1968–69; Parly and Scientific Cttee, 1976–82; Pres., IERE, 1975; a Vice-Pres., and Mem. Council, IQA; Member: Bd and Exec. Cttee, CEI, 1974–78 (Vice-Chm., 1979–80, Chm., 1980–81); Design Council, 1978–80; PO Engrg Adv. Cttee, 1977–81, British Telecom Engrg Adv. Cttee, 1981–82. Mem., Court and Council, Brunel Univ., 1976–82. FREng (FEng 1980); FRSA. Liveryman, 1978, and Mem. Court, 1981–86, Worshipful Co. of Scientific Instrument Makers. DTech (hc) Brunel, 1973. *Address:* Kroller, 54 Howards Wood Drive, Gerrards Cross, Bucks SL9 7HW. *T:* (01753) 885028. *Died 10 Sept. 2002.*

ALLEN, His Honour Anthony Kenway, OBE 1946; a Circuit Judge, 1978–90; *b* 31 Oct. 1917; *s* of Charles Valentine Allen and Edith Kenway Allen; *m* 1975, Maureen Murtough. *Educ:* St George's Coll., Weybridge, Surrey; St John's Coll., Cambridge (BA Hons); Freiburg and Grenoble Univs. Served War, RAF Special Intelligence, 1939–45 (Wing Comdr). Called to the Bar, Inner Temple, 1947. *Recreations:* gardening, walking, music. *Address:* 73 Downswood, Epsom Downs, Surrey KT18 5UJ. *Died 5 Jan. 2003.*

ALLEN, Arnold Millman, CBE 1977; Chairman, UKAEA, 1984–86; *b* 30 Dec. 1924; *s* of Wilfrid Millman and Edith Muriel Allen; *m* 1947, Beatrice Mary Whitaker; three *s* one *d*. *Educ:* Hackney Downs Secondary Sch.; Peterhouse, Cambridge (Scholar). Entered HM Treasury, 1945; Private Sec. to Financial Secretary, 1951–52; Principal, HM Treasury, 1953–55; Private Sec. to Chm. of UKAEA (Lord Plowden), 1956–57; HM Treasury, 1958; Dir of Personnel and Admin., Develt and Engrg Gp

(subseq. Reactor Gp), UKAEA, 1959–63; Gen. Manager, British Waterways Bd, 1963–68, and Mem. of Bd, 1965–68; UKAEA: Personnel Officer, 1968–69; Personnel and Programmes Officer, 1970; Secretary and Mem. for Administration, 1971; Mem. for Finance and Admin, 1976–84; Dep. Chm., 1981–84; Chief Exec., 1982–84. *Address:* Duntish Cottage, Duntish, Dorchester, Dorset DT2 7DR. *T:* (01300) 345258.
Died 22 Jan. 2005.

ALLEN, Hamish McEwan, CB 1984; Head of Administration Department, House of Commons, 1981–85; *b* 7 Sept. 1920; *s* of late Ernest Frank Allen and Ada Florence Allen (*née* Weeks); *m* 1951, Peggy Joan Fifoot; one *s*. *Educ:* City of Bath Sch.; Portsmouth Southern Secondary Sch. Served RAF, 1941–46. Air Ministry: Clerical Officer, 1938; Exec. Officer, 1948; House of Commons: Asst Accountant, 1959; Dep. Accountant, 1962; Head of Estabs Office, 1968. *Address:* 124 Ridge Langley, South Croydon, Surrey CR2 0AS.
Died 26 Sept. 2002.

ALLEN, Prof. John Frank, FRS 1949; Professor of Natural Philosophy in the School of Physical Sciences, University of St Andrews, 1947–78, then Honorary; *b* 6 May 1908; *s* of late Prof. Frank Allen, FRSC and Sarah Estelle, *d* of D. S. Harper, New Brunswick; *m* 1933, Elfriede Hiebert (marr. diss. 1951); one adopted *s*. *Educ:* Public schools of Winnipeg, Canada; University of Manitoba (BA 1928); University of Toronto (MA 1930, PhD 1933); MA Cantab 1936. Bursar, Student and Fellow of National Research Council of Canada, 1930–33; Fellow of National Research Council of USA, 1933–35; Research Assistant, Royal Society Mond Laboratory, Cambridge, 1935–44; Lecturer in Physics, Univ. of Cambridge and Fellow of St John's College, Cambridge, 1944–47. Hon. DSc: Manitoba, 1979; Heriot-Watt, 1984. *Publications:* numerous scientific papers and articles, mainly on experimental low temperature physics. *Recreation:* tracing the history of old St Andrews scientific instruments.
Died 22 April 2001.

ALLEN, John Piers, OBE 1979; Principal, Central School of Speech and Drama, 1972–78; *b* 30 March 1912; *s* of Percy Allen and Marjorie Nash; *m* 1st, 1937, Modwena Sedgwick; two *s*; 2nd, 1945, Anne Preston; two *s* two *d*; 3rd, 1982, Margaret Wootton. *Educ:* Aldenham Sch. Old Vic Theatre, 1933–35; Victor Gollancz Ltd, 1936–37; London Theatre Studio, 1937–39; RNVR, 1940–45; Dir, Glyndebourne Children's Theatre, 1945–51; writer-producer, BBC, 1951–61; Adjudicator, Dominion Drama Festival, Canada, 1956; UNESCO Drama Specialist. Australia, 1959, 1961; HM Inspector of Schs, 1961–72. Vis. Prof. of Drama, Westfield Coll., Univ. of London, 1979–83; Vis. Lectr, Centre for Arts, City Univ., 1979–83. Vice-Chm., British Theatre Assoc., 1978–83; Chairman: Accreditation Bd, Nat. Council of Drama Trng, 1979–83; Council of Dance Educn and Trng, 1982–95 (Chm., Accreditation Bd, 1979–82); Mem., CNAA Dance and Drama Panels, 1979–82; Vice-Pres., British Centre, Internat. Amateur Theatre Assoc., 1992–96. Chm., Old Meeting House Trust, Helmsley, 1993–. FGSM 1971; FRSAMD 1977; FRSA. *Publications:* Going to the Theatre, 1949; Great Moments in the Theatre, 1949; Masters of British Drama, 1957; Masters of European Drama, 1962; Drama in Schools, 1978; Theatre in Europe, 1981; A History of the Theatre in Europe, 1983; (ed) Three Medieval Plays, 1956. *Address:* Maple House, 2 Low Farm Close, Bolton Percy, York YO23 7HA. *T:* (01904) 744607.
Died 2 Jan. 2002.

ALLEN, Mark Echalaz, CMG 1966; CVO 1961; HM Diplomatic Service, retired; *b* 19 March 1917; *s* of late Lancelot John Allen and Eleanor Mary (*née* Carlisle); *m* 1948, Elizabeth Joan, *d* of late Richard Hope Bowdler and Elsie (*née* Bryning); two *s* one *d* (and one *d* decd). *Educ:* Charterhouse; Christ Church, Oxford (MA). Appointed Asst Principal, Dominions Office, 1939. Served War of 1939–45 in Western Desert, Sicily and Italy. Dublin, 1945;

Bombay, 1948; United Nations, New York, 1953; Madras, 1960; New Delhi, 1961; Diplomatic Service Inspector, 1964; Dep. Chief of Administration, DSAO, 1966; Minister (Econ. and Social Affairs), UK Mission to UN, New York, 1968; Ambassador to Zaïre and Burundi, 1971, and to Congo Republic, 1973; Permanent UK Rep. to Disarmament Conf., Geneva, 1974–77, retired from Diplomatic Service, 1977. Mem., Jt Inspection Unit, UN, 1978–84. *Address:* 1 Pemberton Place, Esher, Surrey KT10 9HU. *T:* (01372) 466902.
Died 15 March 2003.

ALLEN, Prof. William Sidney, MA, PhD (Cantab); FBA 1971; Professor of Comparative Philology in the University of Cambridge, 1955–82; Fellow of Trinity College, since 1955; *b* 18 March 1918; *er s* of late W. P. Allen and Ethel (*née* Pearce); *m* 1st, 1955, Aenea (*d* 1996), *yr d* of late Rev. D. McCallum and Mrs McCallum, Invergordon; 2nd, 2002, Diana, *y d* of late William R. Stroud and Catherine E. Stroud, Horse Pasture, St Helena Island. *Educ:* Christ's Hosp.; Trinity Coll., Cambridge (Classical Scholar); Porson Scholarship, 1939. War of 1939–45: RAC and General Staff (Int) (despatches). Lecturer in Phonetics, 1948–51, and in Comparative Linguistics, 1951–55, School of Oriental and African Studies, Univ. of London. Dialect research in India, 1952; Fellow, Rockefeller Foundation, USA, 1953; Brit. Council visitor, Univ. of W Indies, 1959. Linguistic Soc. of America's Professor, 1961; Collitz Professor, Linguistic Institute, USA, 1962; Ida Beam Lectr, Univ. of Iowa, 1983. Pres., Philological Soc., 1965–67. Hon. Fellow, Soc. for Cycladic Studies (Athens), 1977. Chm. Editorial Bd, CUP linguistic series, 1969–82; Editor, Lingua, 1963–85. *Publications:* Phonetics in Ancient India, 1953; On the Linguistic Study of Languages (inaugural lecture), 1957; Sandhi, 1962; Vox Latina, 1965; Vox Graeca, 1968, 3rd edn 1987; Accent and Rhythm, 1973; articles on general and comparative linguistics, phonetics, metrics, classical, Indian and Caucasian languages, Icelandic, Aegean cartography. *Address:* Trinity College, Cambridge CB2 1TQ. *T:* (01223) 366609.
Died 22 April 2004.

ALLENDALE, 3rd Viscount *cr* 1911; **Wentworth Hubert Charles Beaumont;** Baron 1906; DL; *b* 12 Sept. 1922; *e s* of 2nd Viscount Allendale, KG, CB, CBE, MC, and Violet (*d* 1979), *d* of Sir Charles Seely, 2nd Bt; *S* father, 1956; *m* 1948, Hon. Sarah Ismay (marr. diss. 1984), 2nd *d* of 1st Baron Ismay, KG, GCB, CH, DSO, PC; three *s*. *Educ:* Eton. RAFVR, 1940; Flight-Lieutenant 1943; ADC to Viceroy of India, 1946–47. DL Northumberland, 1961. *Heir: s* Hon. Wentworth Peter Ismay Beaumont [*b* 13 Nov. 1948; *m* 1975, Theresa Mary, *d* of F. A. More O'Ferrall; one *s* three *d*]. *Address:* Bywell Hall, Stocksfield on Tyne, Northumberland NE43 7AE. *T:* (01661) 843169; Allenheads, Hexham, Northumberland. *T:* (01434) 685205.
Died 27 Dec. 2002.

ALLIBONE, Thomas Edward, CBE 1960; DSc; FRS 1948; FREng; External Professor of Electrical Engineering, University of Leeds, 1967–79, then Emeritus; Visiting Professor of Physics, City University, since 1971; also Robert Kitchin (Saddlers) Research Professor, since 1983, and first Frank Poynton Professor, Physics Department, since 1984, City University; *b* 11 Nov. 1903; *s* of Henry J. Allibone; *m* 1931, Dorothy Margery, LRAM, ARCM (*d* 2001), *d* of Frederick Boulden, BSc, MEng, MIMechE; two *d*. *Educ:* Central Sch., Sheffield (Birley Scholar); Sheffield Univ. (Linley Scholar; PhD; DSc); Gonville and Caius Coll., Cambridge (Wollaston Scholar); PhD Cantab. 1851 Exhibition Sen. Student, Cavendish Laboratory, Cambridge, 1926–30; i/c High-Voltage Laboratory, Metropolitan-Vickers Electrical Co., Manchester, 1930–46; Director: Res. Laboratory, AEI, Aldermaston, 1946–63; AEI (Woolwich) Ltd, 1948–63; Scientific Adviser, AEI, 1963; Chief Scientist, Central Electricity Generating Bd, 1963–70. Mem., British Mission on Atomic Energy, Berkeley, Calif, and Oakridge, Tenn, 1944–45; Visitor: BISRA, 1949–55; ASLIB, 1955–62. Chm., Res. Cttee, British Electrical and

Allied Industries Res. Assoc., 1955–62. Member: Council, British Inst. of Radiology, 1935–38; Council, IEE, 1937–40, 1946–49, 1950–53; Cttee, Nat. Physical Laboratory, 1950–60; Govt Cttee on Copyright, 1951; DSIR (Mem., Industrial Grants Cttee, 1950–58); Council, Physical Soc., 1953–56; Council, Southern Electricity Bd, 1953–62; Adv. Council, Science Museum; Adv. Council, RMC; Adv. Court, AEA; Nuclear Safety Adv. Council, Min. of Power, 1959–88. Lectures: Faraday, 1946, 1956; Royal Instn Christmas, 1959; Wm Menelaus, 1959; Bernard Price, 1959; Trotter Patterson, 1963; Fison Memorial, 1963; Royal Soc. Rutherford Memorial, 1964 and 1972; Baird Memorial, 1967; Melchett, 1970. President: Section A, British Assoc., 1958; EIBA, 1958–59; Inst. of Information Scientists, 1964–67. Vice-President: Inst. of Physics, 1948–52; Royal Instn, 1955–57, 1970–72. Trustee, British Museum, 1968–74. Governor, Downe House, 1959–69; Chm. Governors, Reading Technical Coll., 1959–68. Lord of the Manor, Aldermaston, 1953–87. Mem. Court, Broderers' Co., 1985– (Liveryman, 1967). FInstP; FREng (Founder FEng 1976); Hon. FIEE; Fellow, Amer. Inst. of Electrical Engineers. Hon. DSc: Reading, 1960; City, 1970; Hon. DEng Sheffield, 1969. Röntgen Medal, British Inst. of Radiology; Thornton and Cooper Hill Medals, IEE; Melchett Medal, Inst. of Fuel. *Publications:* The Release and Use of Nuclear Energy, 1961; Rutherford: Father of Nuclear Energy (Rutherford Lecture 1972), 1973; The Royal Society and its Dining Clubs, 1975; Lightning: the long spark, 1977; Cockcroft and the Atom, 1983; Metropolitan-Vickers Electrical Co. and the Cavendish Laboratory, 1984; The Making of Physicists, 1987; papers on high voltage and transient electrical phenomena, fission and fusion. *Recreations:* photography, travel, gardening, philately. *Address:* York Cottage, Lovel Road, Winkfield, Windsor, Berks SL4 2ES. *T:* (01344) 884501.
Died 9 Sept. 2003.

ALLOTT, Prof. Antony Nicolas; Professor of African Law, University of London, 1964–86, then Professor Emeritus; *b* 30 June 1924; *s* of late Reginald William Allott and Dorothy Allott (*née* Dobson); *m* 1952, Anna Joan Sargant, OBE, *d* of late Tom Sargant, OBE, and Marie Černy; two *s* two *d*. *Educ:* Downside Sch.; New Coll., Oxford (BA 1st class Hons Jurisprudence, 1948); PhD London 1954. Lieut Royal Northumberland Fusiliers and King's African Rifles, 1944–46. Lectr in African Law, SOAS, London, 1948–60; Reader in African Law, Univ. of London, 1960–64; Prof. of African and Comparative Law, Birmingham Univ., 1987–91. Vis. Prof., Université de Paris I, 1984. Hon. Dir, Africa Centre, 1963–66; Pres., African Studies Assoc. of UK, 1969–70 (past Hon. Treas.); Vice-Pres., Internat. African Law Assoc., 1967. Académicien associé, Académie Internat. de Droit Comparé, 1982–; Hon. Corresp. Mem., Académie Royale des Sciences d'Outre-Mer, Belgium, 1980. Chm., Governing Body, Plater Coll., Oxford, 1993–98; formerly Gov., St Bartholomew's Hosp. Med. Sch. Member: Senate, Univ. of London, 1978–86; Council, Commonwealth Magistrates' and Judges' Assoc. (formerly Commonwealth Magistrates' Assoc.), 1972– (Hon. Life Vice-Pres., 1997); Chm., Mddx Magistrates' Cts Cttee, 1982–86. Chm., Barnet Petty Sessional Area, 1986; Dep. Chm., N Oxfordshire Magistrates' Court, 1993. JP: Middlesex 1969–86 (Chm., Gore Div., 1985–86); Oxfordshire 1987–94. KSG 1990. *Publications:* Essays in African Law, with special reference to the Law of Ghana, 1960; (ed) Judicial and Legal Systems in Africa, 1962, 2nd edn 1970; New Essays in African Law, 1970; The Limits of Law, 1980; (ed with G. Woodman) People's Law and State Law, 1985; articles in legal and other jls. *Recreations:* music, gardening. *Address:* Sorbrook Mill, Bodicote, Banbury, Oxon OX15 4AU.
Died 3 June 2002.

ALMENT, Sir (Edward) Anthony (John), Kt 1980; FRCOG; Consultant Obstetrician and Gynaecologist, Northampton, 1960–85, retired; *b* 3 Feb. 1922; *s* of Edward and Alice Alment; *m* 1946, Elizabeth Innes Bacon.

Educ: Marlborough Coll.; St Bartholomew's Hosp. Med. Coll. MRCS, LRCP 1945; FRCOG 1967 (MRCOG 1951). Served RAFVR, 1947–48. Training appointments: St Bartholomew's Hosp., 1945–46 and 1954–60; Norfolk and Norwich Hosp., 1948; Queen Charlotte's Hosp. and Chelsea Hosp. for Women, 1949–50; London Hosp., 1951–52. Royal Coll. of Obstetricians and Gynaecologists: Mem. Council, 1961–67, 1976–78; Hon. Sec., 1968–73; Pres., 1978–81. Chm., Cttee of Enquiry into Competence to Practise, 1973–76; Member: Oxford Reg. Hosp. Bd, 1968–74 (Chm., Med. Adv. Cttee, 1972–74); Oxford RHA, 1973–75; Central Midwives Bd, 1967–68; UK Central Council for Nursing, Midwifery and Health Visiting, 1980–83. Examiner: RCOG; Univs of Cambridge, Leeds and Dar-es-Salaam. Hon. Fellow, Amer. Assoc. of Obstetricians and Gynaecologists, 1973 (Joseph Price Oration, 1972); Hon. FRCPI 1979; Hon. FRCPE 1981; Hon. FRCGP 1982; Hon. FRACOG 1984; Hon. FRCPCH 1996. Hon. DSc Leicester, 1982. *Publications:* Competence to Practise, 1976; Overlap at the Intersecting Arcade: which way does it go?, 2002; contrib. to med. jls; articles on wine-related subjects. *Recreations:* wine, fishing, engineering, church architecture. *Address:* Winston House, Boughton, Northampton NN2 8RR.
Died 6 March 2002.

ALTRINCHAM, Barony of, *cr* 1945, of Tormarton; title disclaimed by 2nd Baron; *see under* Grigg, J. E. P.

AMIES, Sir (Edwin) Hardy, KCVO 1989 (CVO 1977); RDI 1964; Dressmaker by Appointment to HM The Queen, since 1955; Director, Hardy Amies Ltd, since 1946 (President, since 1996); Design Consultant to manufacturers in the UK, EEC, USA, Canada, Australia, New Zealand, Japan, and Korea; *b* 17 July 1909; *s* of late Herbert William Amies and Mary (*née* Hardy). *Educ:* Brentwood. Studied languages in France and Germany, 1927–30; trainee at W. & T. Avery Ltd, Birmingham, 1930–34; managing designer at Lachasse, Farm Street, W1, 1934–39. War Service, 1939–45: joined Intelligence Corps, 1939, becoming Lt-Col and head of Special Forces Mission to Belgium, 1944; founded dressmaking business, 1946. Chairman, Incorporated Society of London Fashion Designers, 1959–60 (Vice-Chm., 1954–56). FRSA 1965. Awards: Harper's Bazaar, 1962; Caswell-Massey, 1962, 1964, 1968; Ambassador Magazine, 1964; Sunday Times Special Award, 1965; Personnalité de l'Année (Haute Couture), Paris, 1986; Hall of Fame Award, British Fashion Council, 1989. Officier de l'Ordre de la Couronne (Belgium), 1946. *Publications:* Just So Far, 1954; ABC of Men's Fashion, 1964; Still Here, 1984; The Englishman's Suit, 1994. *Recreations:* gardening, opera, needlepoint. *Address:* The Old School, Langford, near Lechlade, Glos GL7 3LF; Hardy Amies Ltd, 14 Savile Row, W1X 2JN. *T:* (020) 7734 2436. *Clubs:* Queen's, Buck's.
Died 5 March 2003.

AMOS, Francis John Clarke, CBE 1973; ARIBA, PPRTPI; international consultant on institutional development; Chief Executive, Birmingham City Council, 1973–77; Senior Fellow, University of Birmingham, since 1977; *b* 10 Sept. 1924; *s* of late Frank Amos, FALPA (Director, H. J. Furlong & Sons, Ltd, London), and Alice Mary Amos; *m* 1956, Geraldine Mercy Sutton, MBE, JP, BSc (Econ), MRTPI; one *s* one *d* (and one *d* decd). *Educ:* Alleyn's Sch., and Dulwich Coll., London; Sch. of Architecture, The Polytechnic, London (DipArch); Sch. of Planning and Regional Research, London (SPDip); LSE and Birkbeck Coll., Univ. of London (BSc(Soc)). Served War: Royal Corps of Signals, 1942–44; RIASC, 1944–47. Harlow Develt Corp, 1951; LCC, Planning Div., 1953–58; Min. of Housing and Local Govt, 1958–59 and 1962–63; Adviser to Imperial Ethiopian Govt, 1959–62; Liverpool Corp. City Planning Dept, 1962–74, Chief Planning Officer 1966–74; Chairman: Planning Sub-Cttee, Merseyside Area Land Use/Transportation Study, 1967–73; Working Gp, Educnl Objectives in Urban and Regional Planning,

Centre for Environmental Studies, 1970–72; Examination in Public Buckinghamshire Structure Plan, 1981–82. Consultant, Halcrow Fox and Associates, 1984–. Member: Exec. Cttee, Internat. Centre for Regional Planning and Develt, 1954–59; various Cttees, Liverpool Council of Social Service, 1965–72; Exec. Cttee, Town and Country Planning Summer Sch., 1969–70; Planning, Architecture and Bldg Studies Sub-Cttee, UGC, 1968–74; Community Work Gp of Calouste Gulbenkian Foundn, 1970–82; Constitution Cttee, Liverpool Community Relations Council, 1970–73; Planning and Transport Res. Adv. Council, DoE, 1971–77; Town and Country Planning Council and Exec. Cttee, 1972–74; Adv. Cttee, Bldg Res. Estabt, 1972–77 (Chm., Planning Cttee, 1972–80); SSRC Planning and Human Geography and Planning Cttees, 1972–76; Social Studies Sub-Cttee, UGC, 1974–76; W Midlands Economic Planning Council, 1974–77; Environmental Bd, DoE, 1975–78; Trustee, Community Projects Foundn, 1978–88; Council of Management, Action Resource Centre, 1978–86; Study Commn on Family, 1978–83; Arts Council Regional Cttee, 1979–; Exec. Cttee, Watt Cttee on Energy, 1980–82; Planning Cttee, CNAA, 1980–83. Comr, London and Metropolitan Govt Staff Commn, 1984–87; Asst Comr, Local Govt Boundary Commn, 1986–. Chm., Birmingham Gp, Internat. Year for Shelter for the Homeless 1987. Special Prof. of Planning Practice and Management, Univ. of Nottingham, 1979–; Visiting Professor: Nottingham Univ., 1982–; QUB, 1991–. External Examiner in Planning: Univs of: Liverpool, 1967–70; Newcastle, 1968–71; Aston (Birmingham), 1970–71; Queen's (Belfast), 1972–74; Heriot-Watt, 1972–74; Nottingham, 1973–76; UCL 1975–77; Sheffield, 1979–82; Glasgow, 1979–82; Hong Kong, 1982–85; Polytechnics of: Leeds, 1967–68; Central London, 1967–70; Birmingham, 1975–79; Liverpool, 1977–82. From 1977, acted as adviser to govts in aid programmes: Bangladesh (UN); Barbados (IADB); Belize (World Bank); Bosnia (ODA); Dubai; Ghana (UN); Hong Kong (UK); Hungary; India (ODA); Iraq; Jordan; Laos; Latvia (EC); Mauritius; Poland; Tanzania (ODA); Trinidad and Tobago (UN); Turkey (OECD); Venezuela (IBRD); Kenya, Pakistan, Philippines, Romania and Zimbabwe (UN); Uganda (ODA); Ukraine (DFID); USSR (DFID); Zambia (British Council). Mem., County Exec. Cttee, Scout Assoc., 1977–85. Mem., Court, Univ. of Nottingham, 1975–. Chm., Sir Herbert Manzoni Scholarship Trust, 1975–95. Adviser to AMA Social Services Cttee, 1974–77; Chm., W Midlands Area, 1978–82, Mem. Nat. Exec., 1982–86, Nat. Assoc. of CAB. Member: Jt Land Requirements Cttee, 1983–; Nuffield Inquiry into Town and Country Planning, 1984–86. Pres., Royal Town Planning Inst., 1971–72 (AMTPI, 1955; Fellow 1967; Hon. Sec., 1979–90); Architect RIBA, 1951. FRSA 1977. Freeman of City of London, 1968. Publications: Education for Planning (CES Report), 1973; various reports on Liverpool incl.: Annual Reviews of Plans, Study of Social Malaise; RTPI Report on Future of Planning, 1971, 1977; (part) City Centre Redevelopment; (part) Low Income Housing in the Developing World; articles on Planning and Management in Local Govt in various professional jls. Recreations: travel; unsystematic philately and unskilled building. Address: The Coach House, Ashton Gifford, Codford, Warminster, Wilts BA12 0JX. T: (01985) 850610, Fax: (01985) 851170.   Died 20 May 2003.

ANDERSEN, Valdemar Jens, CMG 1965; OBE 1960 (MBE 1955); VRD 1962; Resident Commissioner, Gilbert and Ellice Islands Colony, 1962–70, retired; b 21 March 1919; 2nd s of Max Andersen, Maraenui, NZ; m 1946, Alison Leone, 2nd d of G. A. Edmonds, Remuera, Auckland, NZ; one s one d. Educ: Napier Boys High Sch., NZ; Auckland University Coll. (BSc). Lieutenant: RNZNVR, 1940–46; RANVR, 1947–62. British Solomon Islands Protectorate: Administrative Officer, 1947; Class A, Administrative Officer, 1954; Secretary

Protectorate Affairs, 1958. Recreation: gardening.
      Died 14 Nov. 2004.

ANDERSON, Sir Ferguson; see Anderson, Sir W. F.

ANDERSON, Rev. Prof. George Wishart, FRSE 1977; FBA 1972; Professor of Old Testament Literature and Theology, 1962–68, of Hebrew and Old Testament Studies, 1968–82, University of Edinburgh; b 25 Jan. 1913; s of George Anderson and Margaret Gordon Wishart; m 1st, 1941, Edith Joyce Marjorie Walter (decd); one s one d; 2nd, 1959, Anne Phyllis Walter (d 1999). Educ: Arbroath High Sch.; United Coll., St Andrews Univ. (Harkness Scholar; MA 1st Cl. Hons Classics, 1935); Fitzwilliam House and Wesley House, Cambridge Univ. (1st Cl. Theol Tripos Part I, 1937; 2nd Cl. Theol Tripos Part II, 1938; BA 1937; MA 1946). Chaplain, RAF, 1941–46. Asst Tutor, Richmond Coll., 1939–41; Tutor in OT Lang. and Lit., Handsworth Coll., 1946–56; Lecturer in OT Lit. and Theol., Univ. of St Andrews, 1956–58; Prof. of OT Studies, Univ. of Durham, 1958–62. Charles Ryder Smith Meml Lectr, 1964; Fernley-Hartley Lectr, 1969; Speaker's Lectr in Biblical Studies, Univ. of Oxford, 1976–80; Henton Davies Lectr, 1977; A. S. Peake Meml Lectr, 1984. Hon. Sec., Internat. Organization of Old Testament Scholars, 1953–71 (Pres., 1971–74); Society for Old Testament Study: Editor, Book List, 1957–66; Pres., 1963; Hon. Sec. (Foreign Correspondence), 1964–74. Mem. Editorial Bd of Vetus Testamentum, 1950–75. Hon. DD St Andrews, 1959; Hon. TeolD Lund, 1971. Burkitt Medal for Biblical Studies, British Acad., 1982. Publications: He That Cometh (trans. from Norwegian of S. Mowinckel), 1956; A Critical Introduction to the Old Testament, 1959, 2nd edn 1994; The Ras Shamra Discoveries and the Old Testament (trans. from Norwegian of A. S. Kapelrud, US 1963, UK 1965); The History and Religion of Israel, 1966 (trans. Chinese 1990); (ed) A Decade of Bible Bibliography, 1967; (ed) Tradition and Interpretation, 1979; articles in: The Old Testament and Modern Study (ed H. H. Rowley), 1951; The New Peake Commentary (ed M. Black and H. H. Rowley), 1962; The Cambridge History of the Bible, Vol. I (ed P. R. Ackroyd and C. F. Evans), 1970, and in various learned jls. Recreations: reading, music. Address: 51 Fountainhall Road, Edinburgh EH9 2LH.   Died 17 March 2002.

ANDERSON, H(ector) John, FRCP; Physician: St Thomas' Hospital, 1948–80 (Special Trustee, 1972–81); Lambeth Hospital, 1960–80; South Western Hospital, 1948–80; French Hospital, 1950–80; b Central Provinces, India, 5 Jan. 1915; s of H. J. Anderson; m 1st, 1940, Frances Pearce (marr. diss.), er d of Rev. W. P. Putt; one s one d; 2nd, 1956, Pauline Mary, d of A. Hammond; one d. Educ: Exeter Sch.; St Catharine's Coll., Cambridge (MA, MB); St Thomas' Hospital. FRCP 1950. Medical Registrar and Res. Asst Physician, St Thomas' Hospital, 1941 and 1942. Hon. Lt-Col RAMC; served MEF, 1944–47. Kitchener Scholar; Mead Prizeman, St Thomas' Hospital; Murchison Scholar, RCP, 1942; Goulstonian Lectr, RCP, 1951. Examiner: MB London; Medicine, Conjoint Bd, London and England; RCP. Mem. AHA, Lambeth, Southwark, Lewisham Area (T). Member: Assoc. of Physicians of Gt Britain; Thoracic Soc.; FRSoc.Med. Publications: Brim of Day, 1944; Poems, 1996; contrib. to medical literature. Address: 102 Lambeth Road, SE1 7PT. T: (020) 7928 1533.   Died 9 July 2002.

ANDERSON, Rev. Prof. Hugh, MA, BD, PhD; FRSE; Professor of New Testament Language, Literature and Theology, University of Edinburgh, 1966–85, then Professor Emeritus; b 18 May 1920; s of Hugh Anderson and Jeannie Muir; m 1945, Jean Goldie Torbit; one s one d (and one s decd). Educ: Galston Sch.; Kilmarnock Acad.; Univ. of Glasgow (MA (Hons Classics and Semitic Langs I), BD (Dist New Testament); PhD); post-doctoral Fellow, Univs of Oxford and Heidelberg. FRSE 1987. Chaplain, Egypt and Palestine, 1945–46; Lectr in Old Testament, Univ. of Glasgow, 1946–51; Minister, Trinity Presb. Church, Glasgow, 1951–57; A. B. Bruce Lectr,

Univ. of Glasgow, 1954–57; Prof. of Biblical Criticism, Duke Univ., N Carolina, 1957–66. Dir, Postgrad. Studies in Theology, Univ. of Edinburgh, 1968–72; Select Preacher, Oxford Univ., 1970; Haskell Lectr, Oberlin Coll., Ohio, 1971; McBride Vis. Prof. of Religion, Bryn Mawr Coll., Pa, 1974–75; Vis. Prof. of Religion, Meredith Coll., N Carolina, 1982; James A. Gray Lectr, 1982, Kenneth Willis Clark Meml Lectr, 1985, Duke Univ., N Carolina; Scholar-in-res., Florida Southern Coll., Lakeland, Fla, 1983; Warner Hall Lectr, St Andrews Presbyterian Coll., N Carolina, 1985; Bishop E. J. Pendergrass Prof. of Religion, Florida Southern Coll., 1986; J. Wallace Hamilton Lectr, Fla, 1988. Convener of Ch. of Scotland's Special Commn on Priorities of Mission in 70s and 80s, 1969–71; Chm., Internat. Selection Council for Albert Schweitzer Internat. Prizes, 1972–91. Hon. DD: Glasgow, 1970; Florida Southern Coll., 1986. *Publications:* Psalms I–XLV, 1951; Historians of Israel, 1957; Jesus and Christian Origins, 1964; The Inter-Testamental Period in The Bible and History (ed W. Barclay), 1965; (ed with W. Barclay) The New Testament in Historical and Contemporary Perspective, 1965; Jesus, 1967; The Gospel of Mark, 1976; Commentary on 3 and 4 Maccabees, Doubleday Pseudepigrapha Vol. 2, 1982; (with Walter Weaver) Perspectives on Christology, 1989; contribs to Religion in Life, Interpretation, Scottish Jl of Theology, Expos. Times, Anchor Bible Dictionary, Theologische Realenzyklopaedia. *Recreations:* golf, gardening, music. *Address:* Morningside Way, 23/13 Maxwell Street, Edinburgh EH10 5HT. *T:* (0131) 447 1401. *Clubs:* Greek (Edinburgh); Luffness Golf (E Lothian). *Died 14 Jan. 2003.*

ANDERSON, Prof. John, MD, FRCP; Professor of Medicine, King's College Hospital Medical School, 1964–86, then Emeritus; *b* 11 Sept. 1921; *s* of James and Margaret Anderson; *m* 1952, Beatrice May Venner; three *s. Educ:* Durham Univ. BA Hons, Dunelm (Mod. Hist.) 1942; MB, BS Hons, 1950; BSc Hons, 1952 (Physiology); MA (Mod. Hist.), MD. FRCP 1962. Served War, Lt, RA (Field) (Ayrshire Yeomanry), 1940–45. MRC Fellow in Clin. Med., UCH, London, 1952–55; Rockefeller Travelling Fellowship, 1956–57; Reader in Medicine, King's Coll. Hosp. Med. Sch., Med. Unit, 1962–64. WHO Consultant, medical educn, 1968. Mem., Med. Research Soc. FBCS 1969; FIBiol 1977. *Publications:* A New Look at Medical Education, 1965; Information Processing of Medical Records, 1970; articles in Lancet and BMJ, on: neutron activation, medical computing, cancer, endocrinology, med. educn. *Recreation:* computing. *Address:* 14 Styles Way, Park Langley, Beckenham, Kent BR3 3AJ. *Club:* University (Durham). *Died 26 June 2002.*

ANDERSON, Sir John (Muir), Kt 1969; CMG 1957; Commissioner of State Savings Bank of Victoria, 1962–81, Chairman of Commissioners, 1967; *b* 14 Sept. 1914; *s* of John Weir Anderson; *m* 1949, Audrey Drayton Jamieson; one *s* one *d. Educ:* Brighton Grammar Sch.; Melbourne Univ. 2/6th Commando Co., 1941; Lieut, 1st Australian Parachute Bn, 1944; served SE Asia, 1941–45. Established John M. Anderson & Co. Pty Ltd, Manufacturers, Agents and Importers, 1951; Managing Director, King Oscar Fine Foods Pty Ltd, 1956–92. Pres., Liberal and Country Party of Victoria, 1952–56 (Treasurer, 1957–61, 1978–80). Comr, Melbourne Harbour Trust, 1972–83. Trustee, Melbourne Exhibn, 1960, Chm. of Trustees, 1968. *Recreations:* swimming, fishing. *Address:* 25 Cosham Street, Brighton, Vic 3186, Australia. *Died 26 Sept. 2002.*

ANDERSON, Roy Arnold; Chairman Emeritus, Lockheed Corporation, since 1986; Chairman and Chief Executive, Weingart Foundation, 1994–98; *b* Ripon, Calif, 15 Dec. 1920; *s* of Carl Gustav Anderson and Esther Marie Johnson; *m* 1948, Betty Leona Boehme; two *s* two *d. Educ:* Ripon Union High Sch.; Humphreys Sch. of Business; Stanford Univ. AB 1947; MBA 1949; Phi Beta Kappa; CPA. Served War, USNR, 1942–46 and 1950–52.

Westinghouse Electric Corporation: Manager, Factory Accounting, 1952–56; Lockheed Missiles and Space Co.: Manager, Accounting and Finance, and Dir, Management Controls, 1956–65; Lockheed Georgia Co.: Dir of Finance, 1965–68; Lockheed Corporation: Asst Treas., 1968–69; Vice-Pres. and Controller, 1969–71; Sen. Vice-Pres., Finance, 1971–75; Vice-Chm. of Board, also Chief Financial and Admin. Officer, 1975–77; Chm. and Chief Exec. Officer, 1977–85; Chm., Exec. Cttee, Dir and Consultant, 1985–88. Director of cos in California. *Recreation:* golf. *Address:* c/o Lockheed-Martin Corporation, 606 South Olive Street, Los Angeles, CA 90014, USA. *T:* (213) 6898701. *Died 18 Oct. 2003.*

ANDERSON, Prof. Sir (William) Ferguson, Kt 1974; OBE 1961; David Cargill Professor of Geriatric Medicine, University of Glasgow, 1965–79; *b* 8 April 1914; *s* of James Kirkwood Anderson, Capt. 7th Scottish Rifles (killed on active service, Gaza, 1917) and late Sarah Barr Anderson; *m* 1940, Margaret Battison Gebbie; one *s* two *d. Educ:* Merchiston Castle Sch.; Glasgow Academy; Glasgow Univ. (MB Hons 1936; MD Hons 1942, with Bellahouston Gold Medal). FRCPGlas (FRFPSG 1939); FRCPE 1961; FRCP 1964; FRCPI 1975; FRCPC 1976. Med. Registrar, Glasgow Univ. Med. Clinic, 1939–41; Army Service, 1941–46, Major (Med. Specialist); Sen. Lectr, Dept of Materia Medica and Therapeutics, Univ. of Glasgow, and Asst Phys., Univ. Med. Clinic, Stobhill Hosp., Glasgow, 1946–49; Sen. Univ. Lectr, Medical Unit, also Hon. Cons. Phys., Cardiff Royal Infirmary, 1949–52; Physician in Geriatric Medicine, Stobhill Gen. Hosp., Adviser in Diseases of Old Age and Chronic Sickness, Western Reg. Hosp. Bd, Scotland, 1952–74. Mem., adv. panel on organization of medical care, WHO, 1973–83. Fogarty Internat. Scholar, Nat. Inst. on Aging, Bethesda, 1979. President: Royal Coll. of Phys and Surgs of Glasgow, 1974–76; British Geriatric Soc., 1975–78; BMA, 1977–78. Vice-President: Age Concern (Scotland); Marie Curie Meml Foundn. Hon. Vice-Pres., Scottish Retirement Council; Hon. Pres., Crossroads (Scotland) Care Attendant Schemes. Hon. Chairman: St Mungo's Old Folks' Club, Glasgow; European Clin. Sect., Internat. Assoc. Gerontology. Patron, Abbeyfield Soc. for Scotland. Fellow, Australasian Coll. of Biomedical Scientists (formerly Australasian Coll. of Technologists), 1971; Hon. Fellow, Amer. Coll. of Physicians, 1980. St Mungo Prize, Glasgow, 1968; Brookdale Award, Gerontological Soc. of America, 1984. KStJ 1974. *Publications:* Practical Management of the Elderly, 1967, 5th edn (with Dr B. Williams) 1989; (ed with Dr B. Isaacs) Current Achievements in Geriatrics, 1964; articles on geriatric medicine and preventive aspects of geriatrics in med. jls. *Recreation:* walking. *Address:* 11 Craigfern Drive, Blanefield, Glasgow G63 9DP. *T:* (01360) 770862. *Club:* University Staff (Glasgow). *Died 28 June 2001.*

ANDREW, Prof. (Edward) Raymond, PhD, ScD; FRS 1984; CPhys, EurPhys; FInstP; FRSE; Graduate Research Professor, University of Florida, 1983–98, then Emeritus; *b* Boston, Lincs, 27 June 1921; *s* of late Edward Richard Andrew and Anne (*née* Henderson); *m* 1948, Mary Farnham (*d* 1965); twin *d*; *m* 1972, Eunice Tinning. *Educ:* Wellingborough Sch.; Christ's (Open Scholarship) and Pembroke Colls, Univ. of Cambridge (MA, PhD, ScD). Scientific Officer, Royal Radar Establishment, Malvern, 1942–45; Cavendish Laboratory, Cambridge, 1945–48; Stokes Student, Pembroke Coll., Cambridge, 1947–49; Commonwealth Fund Fellow, Harvard Univ., 1948–49; Lectr in Natural Philosophy, Univ. of St Andrews, 1949–54; Prof. of Physics, University of Wales, Bangor, 1954–64; Lancashire-Spencer Prof. of Physics, 1964–83, and Dean of Faculty of Science, 1975–78, Univ. of Nottingham; Fellow, Christ's Coll., Cambridge, 1989. Vis. Prof. of Physics, Univ. of Florida, 1969–70; Vis. Fellow, Clare Hall, Cambridge, 1996. President: Groupement Ampère, 1974–80 (Hon. Pres., 1980–); Internat. Soc. of Magnetic Resonance, 1984–87; Chm., Standing Conf. of Profs of Physics, 1976–79; Mem.

Council, European Physical Soc., 1976–79; Chm., British Radio Spectroscopy Gp, 1981–83 (Founder-Chm., 1956–59); Mem., Bd of Trustees, Soc. of Magnetic Resonance in Medicine, 1983–91; Mem., Planning Cttee, US Nat. High Magnetic Field Lab., Fla, 1990–95. Selby Fellow, Aust. Academy of Sci., 1989; Fellow, Amer. Physical Soc., 1989. Hon. Mem., British Biophysical Soc., 1992. Hon. DSc: Univ. of Turku, Finland, 1980; Leipzig Univ., 1990; Wales, 1998; Dr *hc* Adam Mickiewicz Univ., Poznan, Poland, 1989. Wellcome Medal and Prize, Royal Soc., 1984; Distinguished Service Medal, Soc. of Magnetic Resonance in Med., 1991. Editor, Physics Reports, 1974–90; Editor-in-Chief, Magnetic Resonance in Medicine, 1983–91; Member, Editorial Board: Chemical Physics Letters, 1984–87; Solid State Nuclear Magnetic Resonance, 1991–. *Publications:* Nuclear Magnetic Resonance, 1955; (jtly) Clinical Magnetic Resonance, 1990; (jtly) Nuclear Magnetic Resonance at High Magnetic Fields, 1992; scientific papers in learned jls. *Recreation:* travel. *Address:* Department of Physics, University of Florida, Gainesville, FL 32611, USA. *T:* (352) 3926691. *Died 27 May 2001.*

ANDREW, Raymond; *see* Andrew, E. R.

ANDREWS, Hon. Sir Dormer (George), Kt 1987; Chief Justice of Queensland, 1985–89; *b* 8 April 1919; *s of* Miles Dormer Andrews and Margaret Mary Andrews (*née* Robertson); *m* 1943, Joan Merle Tear; three *s. Educ:* University of Queensland (BA, LLB). Flying Officer, RAAF, served UK and ME, 1940–44. Admitted Queensland Bar, 1947; District Court Judge, Queensland, 1959; Chm., District Courts, 1965; Judge, 1971, Senior Puisne Judge, 1982, Supreme Court of Queensland. Chm., Law Reform Commn, Queensland, 1973–82. *Recreations:* walking, reading. *Address:* 6 Jamieson Place, Brookfield, Brisbane, Qld 4069, Australia. *T:* (7) 33784298. *Clubs:* Queensland, Tattersalls, United Service (Brisbane). *Died 28 June 2004.*

ANDREWS, Brig. George Lewis Williams, CBE 1960; DSO 1944; Assistant Commandant, Royal Military Academy Sandhurst, 1957-60; *b* 1 July 1910; *o s of* Captain C. G. W. Andrews, The Border Regt (killed in action, 1914) and late Mrs Diana Gambier-Parry (*née* Norrington); *m* 1938, Marianne, *d* of late Carl Strindberg, Stockholm and Fru Greta Winbergh (*née* Skjöldebrand); one *s. Educ:* Haileybury; Sandhurst. Commissioned 2nd Lieut, The Seaforth Highlanders, 1930; active service, Palestine, 1936; served War of 1939–45: BEF, 1939, MEF, 1941–43, BLA, 1944–45; Command: 2nd Bn The Seaforth Highlanders, 1943–45; 1st Bn Seaforth Highlanders, 1953–54; 152nd Highland Infantry Brigade (TA), 1954–57. Hon. Col, 2nd Bn 51st Highland Volunteers, 1975–79. Lt-Col, 1953; Colonel, 1955; Hon. Brig., 1960; psc 1940; jssc 1948. Chevalier, Order of Leopold (Belgium), 1945; Croix de Guerre with palm (Belgium), 1945. *Address:* West Kingsteps, Nairn, Scotland IV12 5LF. *T:* (01667) 453231. *Died 27 Aug. 2001.*

ANDREWS, His Honour James Roland Blake F.; *see* Fox-Andrews.

ANGELES, Victoria de los; *see* de los Angeles.

ANGELL-JAMES, John, CBE 1967; MD, FRCP, FRCS; Hon. Consulting Surgeon in Otolaryngology, United Bristol Hospitals, 1966–87; *b* 23 Aug. 1901; *s of* Dr John Angell James, MRCS, LRCP and Emily Cormell (*née* Ashwin), Bristol; *m* 1930, Evelyn Miriam Everard (*d* 1998), *d* of Francis Over and Ada Miriam Everard, Birmingham; one *s* two *d. Educ:* Bristol Grammar Sch.; Univ. of Bristol (MB ChB 1st Cl. Hons 1924); London Hosp.; Guy's Hosp. MB BS Hons 1924, MD 1927, London. FRCS 1928; FRCP 1965. Res. appts, 1924–28, Bristol and London; Bristol Royal Infirmary: Hon. ENT Registrar, 1928–29; Hon. Asst ENT Surg., later Hon. ENT Surg., 1929–48; Hon. ENT Surg., Bristol Children's Hosp., 1928–48; Cons. ENT Surg., 1948–66; Clin. Tutor,

1928–55, Lectr and Head of Dept of Otolaryngology, 1955–66, Univ. of Bristol; Cons. ENT Surg., United Bristol Hosps, 1948–66. Lt-Col RAMC, 1942–46; Adviser in Otorhinolaryngol., MEF, 1945. Hunterian Prof., RCS, 1962; Semon Lectr in Laryngol., Univ. of London, 1965; James Yearsley Lectr, 1966; Sir William Wilde Meml Lectr, Irish Otolaryngol. Soc., 1966; Vis. Lectr, Univs of Toronto, Vermont, Cornell, Baylor, Chicago and Johns Hopkins Hosp. Royal Soc. of Medicine: Former Fellow, Hon. FRSocMed 1976; Hon. Mem., Sections of Laryngol. (Pres., 1955) and Otology. Member: SW Laryngolog. Assoc. (Chm. 1956); Brit. Medical Assoc. (Pres. Sect. of Otolaryngol., 1959; Chm. Bristol Div., 1966–67; Pres., Bath, Bristol and Som Br., 1968–69); Bristol Med.-Chirurg. Soc. (Pres., 1961); Visiting Assoc. of ENT Surgs of GB, 1948 (Pres., 1965–66); Brit. Assoc. of Otolaryngologists, 1942 (Pres., 1966–69); Collegium Oto-Rhino-Laryngologicum Amicitiae Sacrum, 1948 (Councillor, 1966–74; Pres., 1974); Barany Soc.; Pres., Otolaryngological Res. Soc., 1978. Extern. Examr, Univ. of Manchester, 1964. Hon. Member: Irish Otolaryngol. Soc.; S Africa Soc. of Otolaryngol.; Corresp. Mem., Deutsche Gesellschaft für Hals-Nasen-Ohren-Heilkunde Kopf-und Hals-Chirurgie. Hon. FRCSE 1971; Jobson Horne Prize, BMA, 1962; Colles Medal, RCSI, 1963; Dalby Prize, RSM, 1963; W. J. Harrison Prize in Laryngology, RSM, 1968. President: Gloucester Soc., 1977; Colston Soc., 1983–84. Chm. Editorial Cttee, Clinical Otolaryngology. *Publications:* chapters in: British Surgical Practice, 1951; Diseases of the Ear, Nose and Throat, 1952, 2nd edn 1966; Ultrasound as a diagnostic and surgical tool, 1964; Clinical Surgery, 1966; Ménière's Disease, 1969; Family Medical Guide, 1980; articles in learned jls in Eng., USA, Canada, Germany and Sweden. *Recreations:* farming; shooting. *Address:* The Leaze, Sundayshill Lane, Falfield, Wotton-under-Edge, Glos GL12 8DQ. *Died 19 June 2002.*

ANGUS, Rev. (James Alexander) Keith, LVO 1990; TD; Minister of Braemar and Crathie Parish Churches, 1979–95; an Extra Chaplain to the Queen, since 1996 (Domestic Chaplain, 1979–96); *b* 16 April 1929; *s of* late Rev. Walter C. S. Angus and Margaret I. Stephen; *m* 1956, Alison Jane Daly; one *s* one *d. Educ:* High School of Dundee; Univ. of St Andrews (MA). National Service, Army, 1947–49; served with TA, 1950–76; Captain RA (TA), 1955; Chaplain to 5, KOSB (TA), 1957–67, to 154 Regt, RCT (V), 1967–76. Assistant Minister, The Cathedral, Glasgow, 1955–56; Minister: Hoddam Parish Church, 1956–67; Gourock Old Parish Church, 1967–79. Convener, Gen. Assembly's Cttee on Chaplains to HM Forces, 1981–85. *Recreations:* fishing, hill walking, golf. *Address:* Darroch Den, Hawthorn Place, Ballater, AB35 5QH. *T:* (01339) 756260. *Club:* New (Edinburgh). *Died 22 Jan. 2002.*

ANNAND, Richard Wallace, VC 1940; ERD; DL; Personnel Officer at Finchale Abbey Training Centre for the Disabled, near Durham, 1948–79; late Captain Durham Light Infantry (RARO); *b* 5 Nov. 1914; *s of* Lt-Comdr Wallace Moir Annand, Royal Naval Division (killed Gallipoli 1915), and late Dora Elizabeth Chapman, South Shields; *m* 1940, Shirley Osborne, MBE 1978, JP 1957. *Educ:* Pocklington Sch., East Yorks. Staff of National Provincial Bank, 1933–37; commnd RNVR 1933 (Tyne and London Divisions), Midshipman, 1933, Sub-Lieut, 1936; transferred to Durham Light Infantry, Jan. 1938; served in France and Belgium, 1939–40 (wounded, VC (first Army VC of 2nd World War)). Invalided (severe deafness), Dec. 1948. President: N Eastern League of Hard of Hearing; Durham Co. Br., Normandy Veterans. Founder Member: British Assoc. of Hard of Hearing, 1946; Durham Co. Assoc. for Disabled, 1956. Hon. Freeman Co. Borough of South Shields, 1940. DL Co. Durham, 1956. *Recreation:* golf. *Address:* Springwell House, Whitesmocks, Durham DH1 4LL. *Clubs:* Royal Over-Seas League; County (Durham). *Died 24 Dec. 2004.*

ANNENBERG, Walter H., Hon. KBE 1976; US Ambassador to the Court of St James's, 1969–74; *b* 13 March 1908; *s* of M. L. Annenberg; *m* 1st, 1938, Veronica Dunkelman (marr. diss. 1950); one *d* (one *s* decd); 2nd, 1951, Leonore Rosensteil (*née* Cohn). *Educ:* Peddie Sch.; Univ. of Pennsylvania. President 1940, and former Chm., Triangle Publications Inc., Philadelphia, Pa; former Publisher: Philadelphia Inquirer; Seventeen Magazine; TV Guide; Daily Racing Form. Dir, New American Schools Develt Corp. Hon. Chm., Bd of Trustees, Eisenhower Med. Center. Hon. Bencher, Middle Temple, 1969; Hon. Old Etonian, 1990; Trustee, Winston Churchill Traveling Fellowships. Medal of Freedom, 1986; holds foreign decorations. *Address:* Llanfair Road, Wynnewood, PA 19096, USA; Suite A200, St David's Center, 150 Radnor-Chester Road, St Davids, PA 19087, USA. *Clubs:* White's; Racquet (Philadelphia); Lyford Cay (Bahamas); Swinley Forest Golf. *Died 1 Oct. 2002.*

ANNESLEY, 10th Earl *cr* 1789; **Patrick Annesley;** Baron Annesley, 1758; Viscount Glerawly, 1766; *b* 12 August 1924; *e s* of 9th Earl Annesley, and of Nora, *y d* of late Walter Harrison; *S* father, 1979; *m* 1947, Catherine, *d* of John Burgess, Edinburgh; four *d. Heir: b* Hon. Philip Harrison Annesley [*b* 29 March 1927; *m* 1951, Florence Eileen (*d* 1995), *o d* of late John Arthur Johnston]. *Died 2 Feb. 2001.*

ANNETT, David Maurice, MA; Headmaster of King's School, Worcester, 1959–79; *b* 27 April 1917; *s* of late M. W. Annett and Marguerite, *d* of Rev. W. M. Hobson; *m* 1953, Evelyn Rosemary (*d* 1996), *d* of late W. M. Gordon, Headmaster of Wrekin Coll., and *widow* of R. E. Upcott; one *d* (one step-*s* two step-*d*). *Educ:* Haileybury Coll.; Queens' Coll., Cambridge. Head of Classical Dept, 1939–53, Housemaster, 1948–53, Oundle Sch.; at Oundle Sch., 1939–53, and Housemaster, 1948–53; Headmaster , Marling Sch., Stroud, 1953–59. Served with 27th Field Regt, RA, in India and Burma (Capt.), 1941–45. *Address:* St Christopher, Beauchamp, Newland, Malvern, Worcs WR13 5AX. *T:* (01684) 565392. *Died 8 April 2004.*

ANNIS, David, MD; FRCS; Senior Research Fellow, University of Liverpool, since 1981 (Science and Engineering Research Council Senior Research Fellow, Institute of Medical and Dental Engineering, 1981–86); *b* 28 Feb. 1921; *s* of Harold and Gertrude Annis; *m* 1948, Nesta Roberts; three *s* one *d. Educ:* Manchester Grammar Sch.; Univ. of Liverpool (ChM 1953, MD 1959). FRCS 1946. Res. Fellow in Exptl Surgery, Mayo Clinic, Minn., 1949–51. Liverpool University: Sen. Lectr in Surgery, 1951–54; Dir of Studies, Surg. Sci., 1964–69; Dir, Bioengineering Unit, Dept of Surgery, 1969–85; Consultant Gen. Surgeon, Royal Liverpool Hosp., 1954–81. Member: Biomaterials Sub-Cttee, SRC, 1978–80; Physiolog. Systems and Disorders Bd, MRC, 1980–. Mem. Ct of Examrs, RCS, 1963–69; Examiner in Surgery, Univs of Leeds, Glasgow, Cardiff, Dundee, Liverpool and Lagos. Member, Editorial Committee: Bioengineering Jl, 1980–; British Jl of Surgery, 1965–80. *Publications:* contribs to: Wells and Kyle, Scientific Foundations of Surgery, 1967, 3rd edn 1982; Cuschieri, Moosa and Giles, Companion to Surgical Practice, 1982; papers on surgical and med. bioengrg subjects in learned jls. *Recreation:* countryside. *Address:* Little Hey, Dibbinsdale Road, Bromborough, Merseyside CH63 0HQ. *T:* (0151) 334 3422. *Died 3 Feb. 2003.*

ANSCOMBE, Elizabeth; *see* Anscombe, G. E. M.

ANSCOMBE, Prof. (Gertrude) Elizabeth (Margaret), FBA 1967; Professor of Philosophy, University of Cambridge, 1970–86, then Professor Emeritus; Fellow, New Hall, Cambridge, 1970–86, Hon. Fellow, since 1986; *b* 18 March 1919; *d* of late Allen Wells Anscombe and Gertrude Elizabeth Anscombe (*née* Thomas); *m* 1941, Prof. Peter Thomas Geach, FBA; three *s* four *d. Educ:* Sydenham High Sch.; St Hugh's Coll., Oxford (Schol. 2nd cl. Hon. Mods 1939, 1st cl. Greats 1941; Hon. Fellow, 1972);

Newnham Coll., Cambridge. Research studentships, Oxford and Cambridge, 1941–44; research fellowships, Somerville Coll., Oxford, 1946–64; Fellow, Somerville Coll., 1964–70, Hon. Fellow, 1970–. First Prince Franz Josef and Princess Gina Prof. of Ethics, Liechtenstein, 1996. Hon. Dr Laws Notre Dame Univ., 1986; Hon. DPhil and Letters Navarra Univ., 1989; Hon. DPhil Univ. of Louvain-la-Neuve, 1990. For. Hon. Mem., Amer. Acad. of Arts and Sciences, 1979. Ehrenkreuz Pro Litteris et Artibus (Austria), 1978; Forschungspreis, Alexander von Humboldt Stiftung, 1983. Papal order Pro Ecclesia et Pontifice, 1999. *Publications:* Intention, 1957; An Introduction to Wittgenstein's Tractatus, 1959; (with Peter Geach) Three Philosophers, 1961; Collected Papers: 1, Parmenides to Wittgenstein, 2, Metaphysics and the Philosophy of Mind, 3, Ethics, Religion and Politics, 1981; translator and co-editor of posthumous works of Ludwig Wittgenstein. *Address:* 3 Richmond Road, Cambridge CB4 3PP. *Died 5 Jan. 2001.*

ANSELL, Dr Barbara Mary, CBE 1982; Consultant Physician (Rheumatology), Wexham Park Hospital, Slough, 1985–88; Head of Division of Rheumatology, Clinical Research Centre, Northwick Park Hospital, Harrow, 1976–88; *b* 30 Aug. 1923; *m* A. H. Weston, MB, FRCGP (decd). *Educ:* Kings High Sch. for Girls, Warwick; Birmingham Univ. (MD 1969). MRCP 1951, FRCP 1967. Consultant Physician (Rheumatol.), Canadian Red Cross Hosp., Taplow, 1962–85. Mem., Cttee for the Review of Medicines, 1979–82. Member: British Assoc. for Rheumatism and Rehabilitation (Mem. Council, 1978–81); Arthritis and Rheumatism Council (Member: Educn Cttee, 1961–77 (Chm., 1966–68); Scientific Co-ordinating Cttee, 1981–; Exec. Cttee, 1987–); RCP Cttee on Rheumatology, 1972–82; Warnock Cttee of Enquiry into Educn of Handicapped Children, 1975; Exec. Cttee, British League Against Rheumatism, 1976–; Standing Cttee, European League Against Rheumatism, 1979–89 (Chm., Cttee on Paediatric Rheumatology, 1979–89); Heberden Soc. (Pres., 1976); Council, RCP, 1986–87 (2nd Vice-Pres., 1987–88); Rheumatology Chm., RCP Cttee on Higher Med. Trng, 1977–79. Hon. FRCS 1984; Hon. FRSocMed 1989; Hon. FRCPCH 1996. Hon. Member: Amer. Coll. of Physicians; American, Australian, Finnish, French, German and South African Rheumatism Associations; Spanish Soc. of Rheumatology. Editor, Medicine, 1974, 1976, 1978–79. *Publications:* (ed) Clinics in Rheumatic Diseases, 1976; Chronic Ailments in Childhood, 1976; (ed jtly) Surgical Management of Juvenile Chronic Polyarthritis, 1978; Rheumatic Disorders in Childhood, 1980; Inflammatory Disorders of Muscle, 1984; (ed jtly) Paediatric Rheumatology Update, 1990; (jtly) A Colour Atlas of Paediatric Rheumatology, 1991. *Recreations:* travelling, cooking. *Address:* Dumgoyne, Templewood Lane, Stoke Poges, Bucks SL2 4BG. *T:* (01753) 662321; (consulting rooms) 9 Beaumont Road, Windsor, Berks SL4 1HY. *Club:* Royal Society of Medicine. *Died 14 Sept. 2001.*

ANSTRUTHER of that Ilk, Sir Ralph (Hugo), 7th Bt *cr* 1694 (S), of Balcaskie, and 12th Bt *cr* 1700 (S), of Anstruther; GCVO 1992 (KCVO 1976; CVO 1967); MC 1943; DL; Hereditary Carver to the Queen; Equerry to the Queen Mother, 1959–98, also Treasurer, 1961–98, then Treasurer Emeritus; *b* 13 June 1921; *o s* of Capt. Robert Edward Anstruther (*d* 1921), MC, The Black Watch (*o s* of Sir Ralph Anstruther, 6th Bt), and Marguerite Blanche Lily (*d* 1992), *d* of Hugo de Burgh; *S* grandfather, 1934, and cousin, Sir Windham Eric Francis Carmichael-Anstruther, 11th Bt, 1980. *Educ:* Eton; Magdalene Coll., Cambridge (BA). Major (retd), Coldstream Gds. Served Malaya, 1950 (despatches). Mem. Queen's Body Guard for Scotland (Royal Co. of Archers). DL Fife, 1960–97, Caithness-shire, 1965. *Heir: cousin,* Ian Fife Campbell Anstruther, Capt. late Royal Corps of Signals [*b* 11 May 1922; *m* 1st, 1951, Honor (marr. diss. 1963), *er d* of late Capt. Gerald Blake, MC; one *d*; 2nd, 1963, Susan

Margaret Walker, *e d* of H. St J. B. Paten; two *s* three *d*]. *Address:* Balcaskie, Pittenweem, Fife KY10 2RD; Watten Mains, Caithness KW1 5UH. *Died 19 May 2002.*

ANTHONY, Metropolitan, of Sourozh; Head of the Russian Orthodox Patriarchal Church in Great Britain and Ireland (Diocese of Sourozh); *b* Lausanne, Switzerland, 19 June 1914; *o c* of Boris Edwardovich Bloom (Russian Imperial Diplomatic Service) and Xenia Nikolaevna Scriabin (sister of the composer Alexander Scriabin); *né* André Borisovich Bloom. *Educ:* Lycée Condorcet; Sorbonne, Paris (Dr of Med. 1943). Army service, med. corps French Army and Resistance, 1939–45. Gen. Practitioner, 1945–49. Took monastic vows, 1943; Priest, Russian Orthodox Church in Paris, 1948; Chaplain to Fellowship of St Alban and St Sergius, London, 1949–50; Vicar, Russian Orthodox Church of St Philip, London, 1950; apptd Hegumen, 1953, Archimandrite, 1956; consecrated Bishop of Sergievo, Suffragan Bishop, Exarchate of Western Europe, 1957; Archbishop of Sourozh, 1960, acting Exarch, 1962–65; Metropolitan of Sourozh and Exarch of the Patriarch of Moscow and All Russia in Western Europe, 1965–74. Member: Ecumenical Commn of Russian Orthodox Church; Central Cttee and Christian Medical Commn of World Council of Churches, 1968. Hulsean Preacher, Cambridge, 1972–73; Preacher, Lambeth Conf., 1978; Firth Lectures, Nottingham Univ., 1982; Eliot Lectures, Kent Univ., 1982; Constantinople Lecture, 1982. Hon. DD Aberdeen, 1973. Médaille de Bronze de la Société d'encouragement au bien (France), 1945; Browning Award (for spreading of the Christian gospel), USA, 1974. Orders of: St Vladimir 1st Cl. (Russia), 1962; St Andrew (Ecumenical Patriarchate), 1963; St Sergius (Russia), 1977. Lambeth Cross, 1975. *Publications:* Living Prayer, 1965; School for Prayer, 1970; God and Man, 1971; Meditations on a Theme, 1972; Courage to Pray, 1973; Essence of Prayer, 1986; Creative Prayer, 1987; *posthumous publication:* Encounter, 2005. *Address:* Russian Orthodox Cathedral, Ennismore Gardens, SW7 1NH. *T:* (020) 7584 0096. *Died 4 Aug. 2003.*

ANTICO, Sir Tristan, AC 1983; Kt 1973; President, Pioneer International Ltd (formerly Pioneer Concrete Services), since 1993 (Managing Director, 1949–88; Chairman, 1966–94); *b* 25 March 1923; *s* of Terribile Giovanni Antico and Erminia Bertin; *m* 1950, Dorothy Bridget Shields; two *s* four *d* (and one *s* decd). *Educ:* Sydney High Sch. Began career as Accountant; subseq. became Company Secretary, Melocco Bros; Founder of Pioneer Concrete Services Ltd. Chm., Tregoyd Holdings Pty Ltd, 1954; formerly Chairman: Ampol Ltd; Papuan Oil Search; formerly Director: Société Générale Australia Hldgs; Qantas Ltd. AC and Knighthood awarded for services to industry and the community. Comdr, Order of Star of Solidarity (Italy), 1967. *Recreations:* horse breeding and horse racing, swimming, yachting. *Clubs:* Tattersall's, Australian Jockey, Sydney Turf, American National, Royal Sydney Yacht Squadron (Sydney); Manly Golf. *Died 26 Dec. 2004.*

ANTROBUS, Sir Charles (James), GCMG 1996; OBE 1973; Governor-General, St Vincent and the Grenadines, since 1996; *b* 14 May 1933; *m* 1996, Gloria Janet Vena Ou Wai; one *s* two *d*. *Educ:* St Vincent Grammar Sch. Cable and Wireless: special assignment, Tortola, BVI, 1966–67; Relief Br. Manager, Montserrat, St Kitts and Dominica, 1967; Gen. Manager, St Vincent and the Grenadines, 1967–93. Mem. Bd, Duke of Edinburgh Award Scheme, St Vincent, 1972–. *Address:* Government House, Montrose, St Vincent and the Grenadines. *T:* 4561401. *Club:* St Vincent and the Grenadines Rotary (Past Pres.). *Died 3 June 2002.*

ANWYL-DAVIES, His Honour Marcus John, MA; QC 1967; a Circuit Judge, 1972–93; *b* 11 July 1923; *s* of late Thomas Anwyl-Davies and Kathleen Beryl Anwyl-Davies (*née* Oakshott); *m* 1st, 1954, Eva Hilda Elisabeth Paulson (marr. diss. 1974); one *s* one *d*; 2nd, 1983, Myrna Dashoff

(*d* 2002). *Educ:* Harrow Sch.; Christ Church, Oxford. Royal Artillery, including service with Hong Kong and Singapore RA, 1942–47 (despatches 1945). Called to Bar, Inner Temple, 1949. Legal Assessor, GMC and GDC, 1969–72; Liaison Judge to Herts Magistrates, 1972–82; Resident Judge, St Albans Crown Court, 1972–82. Vice-Pres., Herts Magistrates' Assoc., 1975; Pres., Council of HM's Circuit Judges, 1989. Member: Panel, Amer. Arbitration Assoc., 1993–; London Court of Internat. Arbitration, 1994–; Bd of Dirs, Center for Internat. Commercial Arbitration, 1994–; Nat. Assoc. of Securities Dealers Bd of Arbitrators, 1994–; Indian Council of Arbitration, 1999–; Public Arbitrator, Pacific Stock Exchange, 1995–2000; Arbitrator, Korean Commercial Arbitration Bd, 1996–. FCIArb 1992 (Mem. Cttee, N Amer. Br., 1993–96). United Grand Lodge of England: Grand Sword Bearer, 1990; Pres., Bd of Grand Stewards, 1990–91. *Recreation:* photography. *Address:* 39 Essex Street, WC2R 3AT. *T:* (020) 7353 4741; 16624 Calle Arbolada, Pacific Palisades, CA 90272–1934, USA. *T:* (310) 4599234, *Fax:* (310) 4598220; *e-mail:* marcusanwyldavies@verizon.net. *Club:* Reform. *Died 4 Oct. 2004.*

ap ROBERT, His Honour Hywel Wyn Jones; a Circuit Judge, 1975–94 (Judge of Cardiff County Court, 1993–94); *b* 19 Nov. 1923; *s* of Rev. Robert John Jones, BA, BD and Mrs Jones (*née* Evans); *m* 1956, Elizabeth Davies; two *d*. *Educ:* Cardiff High Sch.; Corpus Christi Coll., Oxford (MA). War Service, FO and Intell. Corps, 1942–46, in Britain and India. Called to the Bar, Middle Temple, 1950. A Recorder of the Crown Court, 1972–75; Stipendiary Magistrate, Cardiff, later S Glamorgan, 1972–75. Contested (Plaid Cymru) Cardiganshire, 1970. Hon. Mem., Gorsedd of Bards, 1973. Pres., Penarth Soc., 1995–. *Recreations:* Welsh literature, classical and modern languages. *Address:* Cefn Bryn, 56 Plymouth Road, Penarth, Vale of Glamorgan CF64 3DJ. *Club:* Cardiff and County (Cardiff). *Died 30 July 2001.*

AQUILECCHIA, Prof. Giovanni; Professor of Italian, University of London, 1970–89, then Emeritus (Bedford College, 1970–85; Royal Holloway and Bedford New College, 1985–89); Hon. Professor, University College London, since 1998 (Hon. Research Fellow, 1984–97); President, Centro Internazionale di Studi Bruniani, Naples, since 1996; *b* Nettuno, Rome, 28 Nov. 1923; *s* of late Gen. Vincenzo Aquilecchia and Maria L. Filibeck; *m* 1st, 1951, Costantina M. Bacchetta (marr. diss. 1973); two *s* one *d*; 2nd, 1992, Catherine M. Posford. *Educ:* Liceo T. Tasso, Rome; Univ. of Rome (DottLett 1946; Diploma di Perfezionamento in Filologia Moderna, 1948). Asst in Italian, Univ. of Rome, 1946–49; Boursier du Gouvernement Français at Collège de France, Univ. of Paris, 1949–50; British Council Scholar, Warburg Inst., Univ. of London, 1950–51; Asst, Dept of Italian Studies, Univ. of Manchester, 1951–53; Asst Lectr in Italian, University Coll. London, 1953–55, Lectr, 1955–59; Libero Docente di Letteratura Italiana, Univ. of Rome, 1958–; Lecturer in Italian, Univ. of London, at University Coll., 1959–61; Prof. of Italian Lang. and Lit., Univ. of Manchester, 1961–70. Corresp. Fellow, Arcadia Accademia Litterazia Italiana, 1961. Visiting Professor: Univ. of Melbourne, 1983; Univ. of Naples, 1990. Hon. MA Manchester, 1965. Serena Medal, British Acad., 1996. *Publications:* Giordano Bruno, 1971, 2nd edn, with Bibliography 1946–2000, 2001 (trans. French, 2000); Schede di italianistica, 1976; Le opere italiane di Giordano Bruno: critica testuale e oltre, 1991; Il dilemma matematico di Bruno tra atomismo e infinitismo, 1992; Schede bruniane, 1993; Nuove schede di italianistica, 1994; *critical editions of:* Giordano Bruno: La Cena de le Ceneri, 1955, 2nd edn (trans. French) 1994; Due Dialoghi sconosciuti, 1957; Dialoghi Italiani, 1958, repr. 1972, 1985; Praelectiones geometricæ e Ars deformationum, 1964; De la causa, principio et uno, 1973, 2nd edn (trans. French) 1996 (trans. Japanese, 1998); Candelaio, 1993 (trans. Chinese, 1999, Rumanian, 2000); Cabala del cavallo pegaseo, 1994; De l'infinito, universo e mondi, 1995; Spaccio de la bestia trionfante, 1999; De gli eroici furori, 1999; Pietro Aretino: Sei Giornate, 1969, 2nd edn with Introduction, 1975, 3rd edn (trans. French) vol. I 1998, vol. II 1999; Sonetti sopra i xvi modi, 1992; (co-editor) Poesie varie, 1992; Giovanni Villani: Cronica con le continuazioni di Matteo e Filippo, 1979; G. B. Della Porta: Metoposcopia, 1990; (co-editor) Collected essays on Italian Language and Literature, 1971; contrib. Atti dell'Accad. Nazionale Lincei, Bull. John Rylands Library, Nouvelles de la république des Lettres, Nuncius, etc. *Address:* Department of Italian, University College, Gower Street, WC1E 6BT. *Died 3 Aug 2001.*

ARAFAT, Yasser; President, Palestinian National Authority, since 1996; *b* 4 Aug. 1929; *m* 1991, Suha Tawil; one *d. Educ:* Cairo Univ. Joined League of Palestinian Students, 1944, Mem. Exec. Cttee, 1950, Pres., 1952–56; formed jointly, Fatah, 1956; engineer in Egypt, 1956, in Kuwait, 1957–65; Pres., Exec. Cttee, Palestine Nat. Liberation Movt, and Chm., Exec. Cttee, Palestine Liberation Orgn, 1968–; Pres., Central Cttee and Head, Political Dept, PLO, 1973–; Comdr Palestinian Revolutionary Forces; signed Declaration of Principles on Interim Self-Government, 1993, with Yitzhak Rabin. Joliot-Curie Gold Medal, 1975; (jtly) Nobel Peace Prize, 1994. *Address:* c/o Palestinian Delegation, 5 Galena Road, W6 0LT. *T:* (020) 8563 0008, *Fax:* (0181) 563 0058; (office) Al-Muntada, Al-Rimal, Gaza City, via Israel. *Died 11 Nov. 2004.*

ARAIN, Shafiq; Ugandan politician and diplomat; *b* 20 Nov. 1933; *s* of late Din Mohd Arain; *m* 1966, Maria Leana Godinho; one *s* two *d. Educ:* Government Sch., Kampala; Regent's Polytechnic, London; Nottingham Univ. MP (UPC), 1962–71; Mem., E African Legislative Assembly, 1963–71; E African Minister for Common Market and Economic Affairs, later E African Minister for Communications, Research and Social Services; Chairman: Minimum Wages Commn, 1964; Statutory Commn on Cooperative Movement, 1967. Uganda's Delegate to UN Gen. Assembly, 1965–66; Leader, Uganda Delegn to Canada and CPA Conf., Trinidad and Tobago, 1969. Mem. Governing Council, Univ. of Dar es Salaam, 1967–68; Chm., Commonwealth Parly Assoc., Uganda Br., 1969–70. Pres., Uganda Cricket Assoc., 1968–69. Left for exile in London following coup in 1971; returned to Uganda, 1979; elections were held in Dec. 1980; Minister without Portfolio, President's Office, and High Comr for Uganda to London, 1980–85. Dir, Equatorial Bank, 1989–94. *Recreations:* golf, walking, reading. *Clubs:* Uganda, Royal Over-Seas League, Mark's. *Died 20 March 2005.*

ARCHER, Bruce; *see* Archer, L. B.

ARCHER, John Norman; Managing Director, International Tanker Owners Pollution Federation Ltd, 1979–86; *b* 27 Feb. 1921; *s* of late Clifford Banks Archer and Grace Archer; *m* 1st, 1952, Gladys Joy (*née* Barnes) (*d* 1985); one step *d*; 2nd, 1986, Mrs Anne L. M. Appleby (*née* Padwick). *Educ:* Wandsworth School. Served with RA, 1939–46 (Major). Entered Civil Service, Board of Educn, 1937; Asst Principal 1947, Principal 1949, Min. of Educn; attended Admin. Staff Coll., Henley, 1960; Asst Sec. (Joint Head, Architects and Buildings Br.), 1962; technical assistance assignments in educn, Nigeria, Yugoslavia, Tunisia, 1961–63; Asst Sec., Treasury, O&M Div., 1964; Civil Service Department: Asst Sec., Management Services Development Div., 1968; Under-Sec., Management Services, 1970; Under-Sec., Marine Div., DTI, later Dept of Trade, 1972–79. Vice-Pres., Marine Soc. Freeman, City of London, 1985; Liveryman, Shipwrights' Co., 1986–. *Recreations:* lawn tennis, bridge, watching cricket. *Address:* 17 Sovereign House, Draxmont, Wimbledon Hill Road, SW19 7PG. *T:* (020) 8946 6429. *Clubs:* All England Lawn Tennis, Hurlingham, MCC; Kent CC; International Lawn Tennis of Great Britain. *Died 17 Aug. 2003.*

ARCHER, Prof. (Leonard) Bruce, CBE 1976; DrRCA; CEng, MIMechE; Professor, 1971–88, and Director of Research, 1985–88, Royal College of Art, then Emeritus Professor and Member of Court; Director and Secretary, Southwood House Estate Residents Co. Ltd, 1986–93; *b* 22 Nov. 1922; *s* of Leonard Castella Archer and Ivy Hilda Archer; *m* 1950, Joan Henrietta Allen (*d* 2001); one *d. Educ:* Henry Thornton Sch., London; City Univ., London. MIED. Served, Scots Guards, 1941–44. City Univ., 1946–50. Various posts in manufacturing industry, 1950–57; Lectr, Central Sch. of Art and Design, London, 1957–60; Guest Prof., Hochschule für Gestaltung, Ulm, 1960–61; Research Fellow, 1961–71; Hd of Dept of Design Research, 1968–85, RCA. Examiner res. degrees, various univs, 1985–. Various public appointments in design, educn and industrial and scientific policy, 1968–; Member: Design Council, 1972–80; Internat. Science Policy Foundn, 1979–96; Council, Assoc. of Art Instns, 1980–90; Res. Adv. Council, Derby Univ., 1993–96; Court, Derby Univ., 1995–; Chairman: Confedn of Art and Design Assocs, 1981–88; Adv. Bd, Res. Inst. Consumer Ergonomics, 1996–. Pres., Design Res. Soc., 1994–. Director: Gore Projects Ltd, 1982–90; Design Research Innovation Centre Ltd, 1982–86. Hon. FRCA 1988. Hon. DSc City, 1986. *Publications:* varied, on the theory and practice of research, design, develt and educn. *Recreations:* music, the theatre. *Address:* 15 Church Vale, N2 9PB. *T:* (020) 8444 4363, *Fax:* (020) 8883 0351. *Died 16 May 2005.*

ARCHER, Dr Mildred Agnes, (Mrs W. G. Archer), OBE 1979; in charge of Prints and Drawings Section, India Office Library, London, 1954–80; *b* 28 Dec. 1911; *d* of V. A. Bell, MBE; *m* 1934, William George Archer (*d* 1979); one *s* one *d. Educ:* St Hilda's College, Oxford (MA, DLitt 1978; Hon. Fellow 1978). Art historian (British period, India); resided India, 1934–47; revisited India (study tours), 1966, 1972, 1976, 1981–82, 1984, 1989. *Publications:* Patna Painting, 1947; (with W. G. Archer) Indian Painting for the British, 1955; Tippoo's Tiger, 1959; Natural History Drawings in the India Office Library, 1962; Indian Miniatures and Folk Paintings, 1967; Indian Architecture and the British, 1968; British Drawings in the India Office Library (2 vols), 1969; Indian Paintings from Court, Town and Village, 1970; Company Drawings in the India Office Library, 1972; Artist Adventurers in Eighteenth Century India, 1974; Indian Popular Painting, 1977; India and British Portraiture, 1770–1825, 1979; (with John Bastin) The Raffles Drawings in the India Office Library, 1979; Early Views of India, 1980; (with T. Falk) Indian Miniatures in the India Office Library, 1981; (with R. Lightbown) India Observed, 1982; Oil Paintings and Sculpture in the India Office Collection, 1986; Visions of India: the sketchbooks of William Simpson 1859–62, 1986; (with T. Falk) India Revealed: the art and adventures of James and William Fraser 1801–35, 1989; Company Drawings in the Victoria and Albert Museum, 1992; (with William Archer) India Served and Observed, 1994; articles in Country Life, Apollo, Connoisseur, History Today, Geographical Mag. *Recreations:* grandchildren, gardening, travel. *Address:* 5 Frog Meadow, Dedham, Colchester, Essex CO7 6AD. *T:* (01206) 323099. *Died 4 Feb. 2005.*

ARGYLL, 12th Duke of, *cr* 1701 (Scotland), 1892 (UK); **Ian Campbell;** JP; Marquess of Lorne and Kintyre; Earl of Campbell and Cowal; Viscount Lochow and Glenyla; Baron Inveraray, Mull, Morvern, and Tiry, 1701; Baron Campbell, 1445; Earl of Argyll, 1457; Baron Lorne, 1470; Baron Kintyre, 1633 (Scotland); Baron Sundridge, 1766; Baron Hamilton of Hameldon, 1776; Bt 1627; 36th Baron and 46th Knight of Lochow; Celtic title, Mac Cailein Mhor, Chief of Clan Campbell (from Sir Colin Campbell, knighted 1280); Hereditary Master of the Royal Household, Scotland; Hereditary High Sheriff of the County of Argyll; Admiral of the Western Coast and Isles; Keeper of the Great Seal of Scotland and of the Castles of Dunstaffnage, Dunoon, and Carrick and Tarbert; Lord-

Lieutenant of Argyll and Bute, since 1996 (Vice Lord–Lieutenant, 1994–96); *b* 28 Aug. 1937; *e s* of 11th Duke of Argyll, TD, and Louise (*d* 1970), *o d* of Henry Clews; *S* father, 1973; *m* 1964, Iona Mary, *d* of Captain Sir Ivar Colquhoun of Luss, 8th Bt; one *s* one *d*. *Educ:* Le Rosey, Switzerland; Glenalmond; McGill Univ., Montreal. Captain (retd) Argyll and Sutherland Highlanders. Member, Queen's Body Guard for Scotland, Royal Company of Archers, 1967–94. Chm., Beinn Bhuidhe Holdings, 1977–; Director: Campbell Distillers, 1982–; Aberlour Glenlivet Distillery Co.; White Heather Distillers; Muir, MacKenzie & Co., 1973–, and various other cos. President: Royal Caledonian Schs, 1972–96; Argyll Scouts Assoc., 1974–; Highland Soc. of London, 1986–87. Hon. Col, Argyll and Sutherland Highlanders Bn (ACF), 1981–91. DL 1987, JP 1996, Argyll and Bute. KStJ 1975. *Heir: s* Marquess of Lorne, *b* 29 May 1968. *Address:* Inveraray Castle, Inveraray, Argyll PA32 8XF. *T:* (01499) 302275, *Fax:* (01499) 302421. *Clubs:* White's; New (Edinburgh).   *Died 21 April 2001.*

ARGYRIS, Prof. John, CBE 2000; DScEng, DE Munich; FRS 1986; FREng; FRAeS; Professor of Aeronautical Structures in the University of London, at Imperial College of Science and Technology, 1955–75, Visiting Professor 1975–78, then Emeritus Professor; Director, Institute for Computer Applications, Stuttgart, 1984; *b* 19 Aug. 1916; *s* of Nicolas and Lucie Argyris; *m* 1953, Inga-Lisa (*née* Johansson); one *s*. *Educ:* 3rd Gymnasium, Athens; Technical Universities, Athens, Munich and Zurich. With J. Gollnow u. Son, Stettin, Research in Structures, 1937–39; Royal Aeronautical Soc., Research and Technical Officer, 1943–49; University of London, Imperial College of Science and Technology, Department of Aeronautics: Sen. Lectr, 1949; Reader in Theory of Aeronautical Structures, 1950; Hon. FIC 1985. Dir, Inst. for Statics and Dynamics, Stuttgart, 1959–84. Principal Ed., Jl of Computer Methods in Applied Mechanics and Engrg, 1972. Hon. Professor: Northwestern Polytech. Univ., Xian, China, 1980; Tech. Univ. of Beijing, 1983; Qinghua Univ., Beijing, 1984. Corresp. Mem., Acad. of Scis, Athens, 1973; Life Mem., ASME, 1981; Hon. Life Mem., NY Acad. of Scis, 1983; Foreign Associate, US Nat. Acad. of Engrg, 1986. FRAeS 1955; FAIAA 1983; FAAAS 1985; FREng (FEng 1990); FASCE 1991; Hon. Fellow, Groupe pour l'Avancement des Méthodes Numériques de l'Ingénieur, Paris, 1974; Hon. FCGI 1976; Hon. Fellow, Aeronautical Soc. of India, 1985; Hon. FRAeS 1986; Hon. Fellow, Romanian Acad., 1992; Hon. Mem., Greek Assoc. of Computational Mechs, 1994. Hon. Dott Ing Genoa, 1970; Hon. dr.tech Trondheim, 1972; Hon. Dr Ing Tech. Hanover, 1983; Hon. Tek. Dr Linköping, 1986; Hon. DSc (Maths) Athens, 1989; Hon. DSc (Mechs) Vilnius, 1991; Hon. DSc (Computer Mechs): Iasi, 1992; Tallinn, Estonia, 1993; Technical Univ., St Petersburg, 1993; Hon. DSc (phys, comput. and mechs) Tech. Univ. and Univ. of Timisoara, Romania, 1993; Hon. DSc (sci. of mechs) Technical Univ. of Athens, 1995; Hon. DSc (mechs and informatics) Univ. of Ioannina, 1995; Hon. DSc (engrg) Univ. of Thessaly in Volos, 1996. Silver Medal, RAeS, 1971; Von Kármán Medal, ASCE, 1975; Copernicus Medal, Polish Acad. of Scis, 1979; Timoshenko Medal, ASME, 1981; I. B. Laskowitz Award with Gold Medal in Aerospace Engrg, NY Acad. of Scis, 1982; World Prize in Culture, and election as Personality of the Year 1984, Centro Studi e Ricerche delle Nazione, Acad. Italia, 1983; Royal Medal, Royal Soc., 1985; Daidalus Gold Medal, Sir George Cayley Inst., 1988; Gold Medal, Bulgarian Acad. of Scis, 1991; Henri Coenda Medal in Gold, 1992. Gold Medal, Land Baden-Württemberg, 1980; Grand Cross of Merit, FRG, 1985; Grand Cross of Merit with Star, FRG, 1989; Grand Cross of the Phoenix, Greece, 1996; Gold Medal of Argonauts, Univ. of Thessaly in Volos, 1996. *Publications:* Handbook of Aeronautics, Vol. I, 1952; Energy Theorems and Structural Analysis, 1960; Modern Fuselage Analysis and the Elastic Aircraft, 1963; Recent Advances in Matrix Methods of Structural Analysis, 1964; Introduction into

the Finite Element Method, vols I, II and III, 1986–88; Dynamics of Structures, 1991; An overview of aerolasticity, 1992; An Exploration of Chaos, 1994; articles and publications in Ingenieur Archiv, Reports and Memoranda of Aeronautical Res. Council, Jl of RAeS and Aircraft Engineering, CMAME, Jl of AIAA, etc; over 490 scientific publications. *Recreations:* reading, music, hiking, archæology. *Address:* c/o Department of Aeronautics, Imperial College, Prince Consort Road, SW7 2BY. *T:* (020) 7589 5111. *Club:* English-Speaking Union.
Died 2 April 2004.

ARMITAGE, Henry St John Basil, CBE 1978 (OBE 1968); HM Diplomatic Service, retired; Middle East consultant; Honorary Secretary to British/Saudi Arabian Parliamentary Group, 1982–91; *b* 5 May 1924; *s* of Henry John Armitage and late Amelia Eleanor Armitage; *m* 1956, Jennifer Gerda Bruford, *d* of Prof. W. H. Bruford, FBA; one *s* one *d*. *Educ:* St Bede's and Bradford Grammar Schs; Lincoln Christ's Hosp.; Trinity Coll., Cambridge. Served Army, 1943–49; Arab Legion, 1946; British Mil. Mission to Saudi Arabia, 1946–49. Mil. Adviser to Saudi Arabian Minister of Defence, 1949–51; Desert Locust Control, Kenya and Aden Protectorates, 1952; in mil. service of Sultan of Muscat and Oman in Oman and Dhofar, 1952–59; Resident Manager, Gen. Geophysical Co. (Houston), Libya, 1959–60; Oil Consultant, Astor Associates, Libya, 1960–61; Business consultant, Beirut, 1962; joined HM Diplomatic Service, 1962; First Secretary (Commercial): Baghdad, 1963–67; Beirut, 1967–68; First Sec., Jedda, 1968 and 1969–74; Chargé d'Affaires: Jedda, 1969 and 1973; Abu Dhabi, 1975, 1976 and 1977; Counsellor and Consul Gen. in charge British Embassy, Dubai, 1974–78. Order of Abdul Aziz (Saudi Arabia), 2004. *Recreations:* reading, travel. *Address:* The Old Vicarage, East Horrington, Wells, Somerset BA5 3EA. *Club:* Travellers.   *Died 19 Oct. 2004.*

ARMITAGE, Kenneth; see Armitage, W. K.

ARMITAGE, (William) Kenneth, CBE 1969; RA 1994; sculptor; *b* 18 July 1916; *m* 1940, Joan Moore (*d* 1996). Studied at Slade Sch., London, 1937–39. Served War of 1939–45 in the Army. Teacher of Sculpture, Bath Academy of Art, 1946–56; Gregory Fellow in Sculpture, Leeds Univ., 1953–55. *One-man exhibitions:* Gimpel Fils, London, regularly 1952–; New York, 1954–58, the last at Paul Rosenberg & Co.; Marlborough Fine Art London, 1962, 1965; Arts Council Exhibn touring 10 English cities, 1972–73; Gall. Kasahara, Osaka, 1974, 1978 and Fuji Telecasting Gall., Tokyo, and Gal. Humanite, Nagoya, Stoke-on-Trent City Mus. and Art Gall., 1981; Sala Mendoza, Caracas, Venezuela, 1982; Taranman Gall., London, 1982; Retrospective Exhibn, Artcurial, Paris, 1985; Jonathan Clark Gall., London, 2001. *Guest Artist:* Caracas, Venezuela, 1963; City of Berlin, 1967–69. *Work shown in:* Exhibn of Recent Sculpture in British Pavilion at 26th Venice Biennale, 1952; Internat. Open-Air Exhibns of sculpture in Antwerp, London, Sonsbeek, Varese, and Sydney; British Council Exhibns of sculpture since 1952, which have toured Denmark, Germany, Holland, Norway, Sweden, Switzerland, Canada, USA, and S America; New Decade Exhibn, Museum of Modern Art, New York, 1955; British Section of 4th Internat. São Paulo Biennial, Brazil, 1957; 5th Internat. Exhibn of Drawings and Engravings, Lugano, 1958 (prize-winner); British Pavilion at 29th Venice Biennale, 1958; Art since 1945, Kassel Exhibition, 1959; work in British Sculpture in the 'Sixties' exhibition, Tate Gallery, 1965; Internat. Open-air Exhibn, Hakone, Japan, 1969, 1971; 24 English Sculptors, Burlington House, 1971; Jubilee sculpture exhibn, Battersea Park, 1977; World Expo 88, Brisbane; Seoul Olympic sculpture exhibn, 1988; Twelve Stars, Europ. Parlt Art Collection, 1992; Chelsea Harbour Sculpture, 1993; Yorkshire Sculpture Park, 1996; Friends' Room, RA, 1996; Millennium Sculpture Exhibn, Holland Park, 2000; Le corps mis à nus, Donjon de Vez (Oise), 2001. Work represented in: Victoria and Albert Museum,

Tate Gallery; Museum of Modern Art, New York; Musée d'Art Moderne, Paris; Galleria Nazionale d'Arti Moderne, Rome; Hakone Open-Air Sculpture Museum, Japan, and other galleries throughout the world. *Address:* c/o Director's Office, Tate Gallery, Millbank, SW1P 4RG.
Died 22 Jan. 2002.

ARNOLD, Rt Hon. Sir John Lewis, Kt 1972; PC 1979; President of the Family Division, 1979–88; a Judge in the Division, 1972–88; *b* 6 May 1915; *s* of late A. L. Arnold and E. K. Arnold; *m* 1st, 1940, Alice Margaret Dorothea (*née* Cookson) (marr. diss. 1963); one *s* one *d;* 2nd, 1963, Florence Elizabeth, *d* of H. M. Hague, Montreal; one *s* two *d. Educ:* Wellington Coll.; abroad. Called to Bar, Middle Temple, 1937; served War of 1939–45 in Army (despatches, 1945); resumed practice at Bar, 1946; QC 1958. Chairman: Bar Council, 1970–72; Plant Variety Rights Tribunal for proceedings in England and Wales, 1969–72. Hon. DLitt Reading, 1982. *Recreations:* cricket, travel. *Address:* Villa La Pergola, Via B. Bonci 14, Vagliagli 53010, Siena, Italy.
Died 18 Nov. 2004.

ARNOLD-FORSTER, David Oakley, OBE 1994; TD 1992; Chief Executive and Council Member, English Nature, since 2000; *b* 13 Sept. 1956; *s* of Thomas Edward Oakley Arnold-Forster and Elsie Margaret Arnold-Forster (*née* Brooksbank); *m* 1988, Anita Irene Stimpson. *Educ:* Rugby Sch.; Wye Coll., London Univ. (BSc 1978). Ministry of Defence, 1978–85, 1990–94: Admin. Trainee, 1978; Overseas Service, Germany, 1979–80; Private Sec. to Parly Under-Sec. of State (Armed Forces), 1981–84; Head, Chem. and Biol Arms Control Br., Defence Arms Control Unit, 1990–92; Overseas Services, Bosnia and Croatia, 1992–93; Richard Ellis, Chartered Surveyors, 1985–88; Dir, Richmount Enterprise Zone Managers Ltd, 1988–90; PA to R. A. Clegg (sometime Chm. and CEO, Mountleigh Gp), 1988–90; Chief Exec., N Yorks Moors Nat. Park, 1994–2000. Chm., MAFF Task Force for the Hills, 2000–01. Territorial Army, 1978–94: Sandhurst, 1980; 100 Regt, RA; HQ, 201, and OC 307 Battery (Major). Pres., Scarborough Cavaliers Rotary Club, 1999. *Recreations:* environment, walking, fly fishing, ski-ing, riding, American Civil War history. *Address:* c/o English Nature, Northminster House, Peterborough PE1 1UA. *T:* (01733) 455344. *Club:* Cavalry and Guards.
Died 29 Sept. 2002.

ARONSON, Theodore Ian Wilson; historical biographer; *b* 13 Nov. 1929; *s* of Philip Aronson and Hannah Wilson Aronson;; partner, Brian Roberts. *Educ:* Grey High Sch., Port Elizabeth, SA; Univ. of Cape Town (BA Fine Arts). *Publications:* The Golden Bees, 1964, 2nd edn 1975; Royal Vendetta, 1966, 2nd edn 1998; The Coburgs of Belgium, 1958, 4th edn 1996; The Fall of the Third Napoleon, 1970; The Kaisers, 1971, 2nd edn 1973; Queen Victoria and the Bonapartes, 1972; Grandmama of Europe, 1973, 5th edn 1998; Royal Ambassadors, 1975; A Family of Kings, 1975, 2nd edn 2000; Victoria and Disraeli, 1977, 2nd edn 1987; Kings over the Water, 1979, 2nd edn 1988; Princess Alice, 1981, 2nd edn 1988; Royal Family, 1983; Crowns in Conflict, 1986; The King in Love, 1988, 2nd edn 1989; Napoleon and Josephine, 1990; Heart of a Queen, 1991; Royal Family at War, 1993; Prince Eddy, 1994, 2nd edn 1996; Princess Margaret, 1997, 2nd edn 2001; Royal Subjects, 2001, 2nd edn 2002; various translations. *Recreations:* reading, travel, theatre. *Address:* 7 The Blue House, Market Place, Frome, Som BA11 1AP. *T:* (01373) 471581.
Died 13 May 2003.
[This entry did not appear in Who's Who.]

ASH, Maurice Anthony; Vice President, Town and Country Planning Association, since 1987 (Chairman of Executive, 1969–83; Chairman of Council, 1983–87); *b* 31 Oct. 1917; *s* of Wilfred Cracroft and Beatrice Ash; *m* 1947, Ruth Whitney Elmhirst (*d* 1986); three *d* (one *s* decd). *Educ:* Gresham's Sch., Holt; LSE (BSc (Econ)); Yale. Served War of 1939–45, armoured forces in Western Desert, Italy, Greece (despatches 1944). Mem., SW Regl

Economic Planning Council, 1965–68; Chm., Green Alliance, 1978–83. Trustee, Dartington Hall, 1964–92 (Chm., 1972–84); Mem., Henry Moore Foundn, 1980–89. *Publications:* The Human Cloud, 1962; Who are the Progressives Now?, 1969; Regions of Tomorrow, 1969; A Guide to the Structure of London, 1972; Green Politics, 1980; New Renaissance, 1987; Journey into the Eye of a Needle, 1989; Fabric of the World, 1992; articles on land use, education and environment. *Recreation:* applying Wittgenstein. *Address:* Sharpham House, Ashprington, Totnes, Devon TQ9 7UT. *T:* (01803) 732216, *Fax:* (01803) 732037.
Died 27 Jan. 2003.

ASHCROFT, David, TD 1957; MA; Headmaster, Cheltenham College, 1959–78; *b* 20 May 1920; *s* of late A. H. Ashcroft, DSO; *m* 1949, Joan Elizabeth Young; two *s* three *d. Educ:* Rugby Sch.; Gonville and Caius Coll., Cambridge (MA). War Service, 1940–46 (despatches). Asst Master, Rossall Sch., 1946–50; Asst Master, Rugby Sch., 1950–59. *Address:* London House, Ashton Keynes, Swindon, Wilts SN6 6NL. *T:* (01285) 861319.
Died 3 April 2003.

ASHENHURST, Maj.-Gen. Francis Ernest; Director, Defence Dental Services, 1990–92, retired; *b* 1 April 1933; *s* of Charles Ashenhurst and Margaret Jane (*née* MacLaine); *m* 1959, Hilary Chapman; two *d. Educ:* Methodist Coll., Belfast; Queen's Univ., Belfast (BDS); London Univ. (MSc). Commnd RADC, 1963; OC Rhine Area Dental Unit, 1964–66; Instr and Chief Instr, Depot and Trng Estabt, RADC, 1967–71; Commanding Officer: Army Dental Centres, Hong Kong, 1971–73; 6 Dental Gp, UKLF, 1973–76; postgrad. studies, 1976–77; Asst Dir, Army Dental Service, 1977–78; CO 1 Dental Gp, BAOR, 1978–81; Dep. Dir, Army Dental Service, 1981–84; Comdt, HQ and Central Gp, RADC, 1984; Dep. Comdr, Med. (Dentistry), BAOR, 1984–86; Comdr, HQ and Tech. Services, RADC, BAOR, 1986–88; Dir, Army Dental Service, 1989–90. QHDS, 1989–92. OStJ 1974. *Recreations:* gardening, listening to music, cooking. *Club:* Norfolk (Norwich).
Died 5 April 2004.

ASHFORD, Air Vice-Marshal Ronald Gordon, CBE 1978; *b* 2 May 1931; *s* of Richard Ashford and Phyllis Lancaster; *m* 1966, Patricia Ann Turner; two *d. Educ:* Ilfracombe Grammar Sch.; Bristol Univ. (LLB). Joined RAF, 1952; qualified as Navigator, 1953; OC No 115 Squadron, 1971–72; OC RAF Finningley, 1976–77; RCDS, 1978; Air Cdre Intelligence, 1979–83; Comdr, Southern Maritime Air Region, 1983–84; Dir Gen., Personal Services (RAF), MoD, 1984–85; retired. Chm., Metropolitan Traffic Comrs, 1985–91; Sen. Traffic Comr, Western Traffic Area and Licensing Authy, 1991–96. *Recreation:* golf. *Address:* Old Courthay, Church Lane, Brent Knoll, Som TA9 4DG. *Club:* Royal Air Force.
Died 2 Feb. 2003.

ASHMORE, Vice-Adm. Sir Peter (William Beckwith), KCB 1972 (CB 1968); KCVO 1980 (MVO (4th Class) 1948); DSC 1942; Extra Equerry to the Queen, since 1952; *b* 4 Feb. 1921; *yr s* of late Vice-Adm. L. H. Ashmore, CB, DSO and Tamara Vasilevna Schutt, St Petersburg; *m* 1952, Patricia Moray Buller, *o d* of late Admiral Sir Henry Buller, GCVO, CB and of Lady Hermione Stuart; one *s* three *d. Educ:* Yardley Court; RN Coll., Dartmouth. Midshipman, 1939. Served War of 1939–45, principally in destroyers (despatches); Lieut, 1941; Equerry (temp.) to King George VI, 1946–48; Extra Equerry, 1948; Comdr, 1951; Captain, 1957; Dep. Dir, RN Staff Coll., Greenwich, 1957; Captain (F) Dartmouth Training Squadron, 1960–61; Imperial Defence Coll., 1962; Admiralty, Plans Division, 1963; Rear-Adm. 1966; Flag Officer, Admiralty Interview Board, 1966–67; Chief of Staff to C-in-C Western Fleet and to NATO C-in-C Eastern Atlantic, 1967–69; Vice-Adm. 1969; Chief of Allied Staff, NATO Naval HQ, S Europe, 1970–72, retired 1972. Master of HM's Household, 1973–86. *Recreations:* fishing, golf. *Address:* Netherdowns,

Sundridge, near Sevenoaks, Kent TN14 6AR.
Died 31 July 2002.

ASHMORE, Prof. Philip George; Professor of Physical Chemistry, University of Manchester Institute of Science and Technology, 1963–81, then Professor Emeritus; *b* 5 May 1916; *m* 1943, Ann Elizabeth Scott; three *s* one *d*. *Educ:* Emmanuel Coll., Cambridge. Fellow, Asst Tutor and Dir of Studies of Natural Sciences, Emmanuel Coll., Cambridge, 1949–59; Lecturer in Physical Chem., Univ. of Cambridge, 1953–63; Fellow and Tutor to Advanced Students, Churchill Coll., Cambridge, 1959–63. Vice-Principal Acad. Affairs, UMIST, 1973, 1974. Course Consultant, Open Univ., 1981–85. *Publications:* The Catalysis and Inhibition of Chemical Reactions, 1963; (ed) Reaction Kinetics, 1975; RIC Monographs for Teachers: No 5 and No 9; many papers in TFS, International Symposium on Combustion, Jl of Catalysis. *Address:* 30 Queen Edith's Way, Cambridge CB1 4PN. *T:* (01223) 248225. *Died 8 March 2002.*

ASHTON, Anthony Southcliffe; *b* 5 July 1916; *s* of late Prof. Thomas Southcliffe Ashton, FBA and Marion Hague Ashton; *m* 1939, Katharine Marion Louise Vivian; two *d*. *Educ:* Manchester Grammar Sch.; Hertford Coll., Oxford (MA). Economist, Export Credits Guarantee Dept, 1937. Served War of 1939–45, as driver and Lt-Col, RASC. Asst Financial Editor, Manchester Guardian, 1945; Dep. Asst Dir of Marketing, NCB, 1947; Manager, various depts of Vacuum Oil Co. (later Mobil Oil Co.), 1949; attended Advanced Management Programme, Harvard Business Sch., 1961; Treasurer, 1961, Finance Director, 1967–69, Esso Petroleum Co.; Mem. Bd (Finance and Corporate Planning), Post Office Corp., 1970–73. Director: Tyzack and Partners Ltd, 1974–79; Provincial Insce Co., 1974–86. Member: Shipbuilding Industry Bd, 1967–71; Council of Manchester Business Sch., 1968–81; Dir, Oxford Univ. Business Summer Sch., 1974 (Mem., Steering Cttee, 1978–81). Trustee: PO Pension Fund, 1975–83; Tyzack Employee Trust, 1979–84; Dir, Exeter Trust, 1980–86 (Chm., 1982–86). Vice-Pres., Hertford Coll. Soc., 1977–. *Club:* Army and Navy. *Died 22 Nov. 2005.*

ASHTON, John Russell, CB 1988; retired engineer; *b* 28 Feb. 1925; *s* of Jessie Florence and John William Ashton; *m* 1951, Isobel Burbury; two *d*. *Educ:* Canberra Grammar School; Sydney University. BE (Civil Engineering). Hydro-Electric Commission, Tasmania: Engineer, 1947–54; System Development Engineer, 1954–71; Dep. Engineer for Civil Investigation, 1971–72; Asst to Comr, 1972–77; Commissioner, 1977–87. In-service training Fellowship, US Bureau of Reclamation, 1960. *Recreations:* golf, photography, carpentry, gardening. *Address:* 3 Lanrick Court, Lindisfarne, Tas 7015, Australia. *T:* (3) 62438758. *Died 14 Feb. 2003.*

ASHTON, Kenneth Bruce; General Secretary, National Union of Journalists, 1977–85; *b* 9 Nov. 1925; *m* 1955, Amy Anne Sidebotham; three *s* (and one *s* decd). *Educ:* Latymer Upper School. Served Army, 1942–46. Reporter: Hampstead and Highgate Express, 1947–50; Devon and Somerset News, Mansfield Reporter, Sheffield Star, 1950–58; Sub-Editor, Sheffield Telegraph, Daily Express, London and Daily Mail, Manchester, 1958–75. Nat. Exec. Cttee Mem., NUJ, 1968–75, Pres., 1975, Regional Organiser, 1975–77. Member: TUC Printing Industries' Cttee, 1975–86; Printing and Publishers' Industry Training Bd, 1977–83; British Cttee, Journalists in Europe, 1980–86; Communications Adv. Cttee, UK Nat. Commn for Unesco, 1981–86; consultative Mem., Press Council, 1977–80; Pres., Internat. Fedn of Journalists, 1982–86. *Died 8 Sept. 2002.*

ASHTON, Rt Rev. Leonard James, CB 1970; Bishop in Cyprus and The Gulf, 1976–83; Hon. Assistant Bishop, Diocese of Oxford, since 1984; *b* 27 June 1915; *s* of late Henry Ashton and Sarah Ashton (*née* Ing). *Educ:* Tyndale Hall, Bristol. Ordained deacon, 1942, priest, 1943; Curate, Cheadle, 1942–45; Chaplain, RAF, 1945–74: N Wales,

1945; AHQ Malaya and Singapore, 1946; BC Air Forces, Japan, 1947–48; Halton, 1948–49; Feltwell, 1949–50; Chap. and Lectr, RAF Chap. Sch., Cheltenham, 1950–53; Sen. Chap., AHQ Iraq, 1954–55; RAF Coll., Cranwell, 1956–60; British Forces Arabian Peninsular and Middle East Command, 1960–61; Asst Chap. Chief, Trng Commands, 1962–65; Resident Chap., St Clement Danes, Strand, 1965–69; Chaplain-in-Chief, (with relative rank of Air Vice-Marshal) RAF, and Archdeacon of RAF, 1969–73; QHC, 1967–73; Hon. Canon and Prebendary of St Botolph, Lincoln Cathedral, 1969–73, Canon Emeritus, 1973–; Asst Bishop in Jerusalem, 1974–76; Episcopal Canon: St George's Cathedral, Jerusalem, 1976–83; St Paul's Cath., Nicosia, Cyprus, 1989–; Commissary for Bishop in Iran and Bishop in Jerusalem, 1984–. ChStJ 1976. *Publication:* Winged Words, 1990. *Recreations:* gardening, photography. *Address:* 60 Lowndes Avenue, Chesham, Bucks HP5 2HJ. *T:* (01494) 782952. *Club:* Royal Air Force. *Died 19 Jan. 2001.*

ASHWORTH, James Louis, FIMechE, FIEE, ARTC (Salford); Full-Time Member for Operations, Central Electricity Generating Board, 1966–70, retired; *b* 7 March 1906; *s* of late James and Janet Ashworth; *m* 1931, Clara Evelyn Arnold (*d* 1992); one *s* two *d*. *Educ:* Stockport Grammar Sch.; Salford Royal Coll. of Technology. Apprenticeship with Mirrlees, Bickerton & Day Ltd, Stockport (Diesel Oil Engine Manufrs), 1924–29; Metro-Vickers Electrical Co. Ltd, 1929; Manchester Corp. Elec. Dept, Stuart Street Gen. Stn, 1930–32; Hull Corp. Elec. Dept, 1932–35; Halifax Corp. Elec. Dept, 1935–40; Mersey Power Co. Ltd, Runcorn, 1940–48; British Electricity Authority, North West: Chief Generation Engr (O), 1948–57; Dep. Divisional Controller, 1957–58; Central Electricity Generating Board, North West, Merseyside and North Wales Region: Dep. Regional Dir, 1958–62; Regional Dir, 1962–66. *Recreations:* gardening, photography, travel, reading. *Address:* Chase Cottage, 23 The Chase, Reigate, Surrey RH2 7DJ. *T:* (01737) 761279. *Died 7 Jan. 2005.*

ASHWORTH, Piers; QC 1973; a Recorder of the Crown Court, 1974–96; *b* 27 May 1931; *s* of late Tom and Mollie Ashworth; *m* 1st, 1959, Iolene Jennifer (marr. diss. 1978), *yr d* of late W. G. Foxley; three *s* one *d*; 2nd, 1980, Elizabeth, *er d* of late A. J. S. Aston. *Educ:* Christ's Hospital; Pembroke Coll., Cambridge (scholar; BA 1955). Commnd Royal Signals, 1951. Harmsworth Law Scholar, 1956; called to Bar, Middle Temple, 1956, Bencher, 1984; Midland and Oxford Circuit. Chm., Bar Mutual Indemnity Fund Ltd, 1987–98. Dir and Trustee, NADFAS, 2002–. Gov. and Almoner, Christ's Hosp, 1986–. *Recreations:* sailing, fine arts, bridge. *Address:* 2 Harcourt Buildings, Temple, EC4Y 9DB. *T:* (020) 7583 9020. *Died 16 April 2004.*

ASKE, Rev. Sir Conan, 2nd Bt *cr* 1922, of Aughton, East Riding of Yorkshire; Assistant Curate of St John-in-Bedwardine, Worcester, 1972–80; *b* 22 April 1912; *s* of Sir Robert William Aske, 1st Bt, TD, QC, LLD, and Edith (*d* 1918), *d* of Sir Walter Herbert Cockerline; S father 1954; *m* 1st, 1948, Vera Faulkner (*d* 1960); 2nd, 1965, Rebecca (*d* 1996), *d* of Hugh Grant, Wick, Caithness. *Educ:* Rugby; Balliol Coll., Oxford; Wycliffe Hall, Oxford. TA, London Irish Rifles, 1939; served, 1939–49, with East York Regt, Sudan Defence Force, Somalia Gendarmerie; Major, Civil Affairs Officer, Reserved Area of Ethiopia and The Ogaden, 1949–51; schoolmaster, Hillstone, Malvern, 1952–69; ordained deacon, 1970, priest, 1971; Asst Curate, Hagley, Stourbridge, 1970–72. Hon. Padre, Worcs Br., 1940 Dunkirk Veterans' Assoc., 1988–. *Heir: nephew* Robert John Bingham Aske, *b* 12 March 1941. *Address:* 167 Malvern Road, Worcester WR2 4NN. *T:* (01905) 422817. *Died 7 May 2001.*

ASTOR, Hon. (Francis) David (Langhorne), CH 1994; Editor of The Observer, 1948–75; Director, The Observer, 1976–81; *b* 5 March 1912; *s* of 2nd Viscount Astor and Nancy, Viscountess Astor, CH, MP (*d* 1964); *m*

1st, 1945, Melanie Hauser; one *d*; 2nd, 1952, Bridget Aphra Wreford; two *s* three *d*. *Educ:* Eton; Balliol, Oxford. Yorkshire Post, 1936. Served War of 1939–45, with Royal Marines, 1940–45 (Croix de Guerre, 1944). Foreign Editor of The Observer, 1946–48. *Publication:* (with V. Yorke) Peace in the Middle East: super powers and security guarantees, 1978. *Address:* 24 St Ann's Terrace, NW8 6PJ. *T:* (020) 7586 8689; Manor House, Sutton Courtenay, Oxon OX14 4AD. *T:* (01235) 848221. *Clubs:* Athenæum, Reform.   *Died 6 Dec. 2001.*

ATKINSON, Mary; *see* Hardwick, Mollie.

ATTENBOROUGH, John Philip, CMG 1958; CBE 1953 (OBE 1946); retired; *b* 6 Nov. 1901; *s* of late Frederick Samuel and Edith Attenborough; *m* 1947, Lucie Blanche Woods (*d* 1996), *y d* of late Rev. J. R. and Mrs Prenter and *widow* of late Dr P. P. Murphy; one step *s*. *Educ:* Manchester Grammar Sch.; Corpus Christi Coll., Oxford (MA). Superintendent of Education, Northern Nigeria, 1924–30; Lecturer and Senior Inspector, Education Dept, Palestine, 1930–37; Dir of Education, Aden, 1937–46; Deputy Dir of Education, Palestine, 1946–48; Asst Educational Adviser, Colonial Office, 1948; Dir of Education, Tanganyika, 1948–55; Mem. for Social Services, Tanganyika, 1955–57; Min. for Social Services, Tanganyika, 1957–58; Consultant: UNICEF, 1963–65; UNESCO, 1967; Devon CC, 1961–68; Mem., SW Regional Hosp. Bd, 1965–71. Pres. Torbay Conservative Assoc., 1967–79. *Address:* 6 Erith House, Lower Erith Road, Torquay, Devon TQ1 2PX.
                                          Died 24 Jan. 2002.

ATTERTON, David Valentine, CBE 1981; PhD; FREng; FIM; Chairman, TriVen VCT plc, 1999–2002; *b* 13 Feb. 1927; *s* of Frank Arthur Shepherd Atterton and Ella Constance (*née* Collins); *m* 1948, Sheila Ann McMahon; two *s* one *d*. *Educ:* Bishop Wordsworth's Sch., Salisbury; Peterhouse, Cambridge (MA, PhD). Post-doctorate research, Cambridge, 1950–52; joined Foundry Services Ltd, 1952; Managing Director: Foseco Ltd, 1966; Foseco Minsep Ltd, 1969; Chm., Foseco Minsep plc, 1979–86. Dep. Chm., Associated Engineering plc, 1979–86 (Dir 1972–); Director: Investors in Industry plc (formerly Finance Corp. for Industry and FFI), 1974–92; IMI plc, 1976–89; Barclays Bank UK Ltd, 1982–84; Bank of England, 1984–92; Barclays Bank, 1984–92; (part-time) British Coal, 1986–95; Marks and Spencer plc, 1987–92; Rank Organisation, 1987–97; Dimex Ltd, 1988–89; Chairman: Peripheral Vision Ltd, 1992–98; Guinness Mahon Holdings, 1993–98. Chm., NEDO Iron and Steel Sector Working Party, 1977–82; Member: ACARD, 1982–85; British N Amer. Assoc., 1982–92; Member, Board of Governors: United World Coll. of the Atlantic, 1968–85 (Chm., 1973–79); Wells Cathedral Sch., 1990–. Pres., Birmingham Chamber of Commerce and Industry, 1974–75. Pres., Inst. of Metals, 1987–88. Master, Founders' Co., 1994–95. *Publications:* numerous scientific papers in learned jls. *Recreations:* cartography, Japanese language, photography. *Address:* Cathedral Green House, Wells, Somerset BA5 2UB. *T:* (01749) 74907.
                                          Died 2 June 2002.

ATTYGALLE, Gen. Don Sepala, Hon. LVO 1954; Chairman and Managing Director, Air Lanka Ltd, 1993–95; High Commissioner for Democratic Socialist Republic of Sri Lanka in London, 1990–93; *b* 14 Oct. 1921; *m* 1958, Ithali Mercia Attygalle; one *s*. *Educ:* Royal College, Colombo; psc 1953, idc 1966. Commissioned into Army, 1940; Ceylon Light Infantry; Extra ADC to Governor-General of Ceylon, 1952–65; CO, Ceylon Armoured Corps, 1955; Comdr, Sri Lanka Army, 1967–77; Chief Co-Ordinating Authority, 1977, Sec., 1983–90, Min. of Defence. Deshamanya, 1990. *Recreations:* sports. *Address:* 6 Fairfield Gardens, Colombo 8, Sri Lanka.   *Died 15 Jan. 2001.*

ATWILL, Sir John; *see* Atwill, Sir M. J. N.

ATWILL, Sir (Milton) John (Napier), Kt 1979; Director, MEPC Australia Ltd, 1980–96; *b* 16 Jan. 1926; *s* of Milton Spencer Atwill and Isabella Caroline Atwill; *m* 1955, Susan Playfair; two *d*. *Educ:* Cranbrook Sch., Sydney; Geelong Church of England Grammar Sch.; Jesus Coll., Cambridge (MA). Called to the Bar, Gray's Inn, 1953, NSW Bar, 1953. President, NSW Division, Liberal Party of Australia, 1970–75 (Hon. Treas., 1968–69); Federal Pres., Liberal Party, 1975–82; Chm., Pacific Democrat Union, 1982; Vice-Chm., Internat. Democrat Union, 1983. *Recreations:* cricket, tennis. *Address:* 5 Chesterfield Street, 430 Edgecliff Road, Edgecliff, NSW 2027, Australia. *Clubs:* Australian, Union, Royal Sydney Golf, Melbourne.
                                          Died 27 Aug. 2001.

AUDU, Rev. Ishaya Shu'aibu, CFR 2001 (OFR 2000); FRCPE; Medical Director, Savannah Polyclinic, Zaria, since 1984; *b* 1 March 1927; *s* of Malam Bulus Audu and Malama Rakiya Audu; *m* 1958, Victoria Abosede Ohiorhenuan; two *s* five *d*. *Educ:* Ibadan and London Univs. House Officer, Sen. House Officer, Registrar in Surgery, Medicine, Obstetrics and Gynæcology and Pædiatrics, King's Coll. Hosp., London and Univ. Coll. Hosp., Ibadan, 1954–58; postgrad. studies, UK, 1959–60; Specialist Physician, Pædiatrician to Govt of Northern Nigeria and Personal Physician to Premier of North Region Govt, 1960–62; Lectr to Associate Professorship in Pæds, Univ. of Lagos Med. Sch., 1962–66; Vis. Res. Associate Prof., Univ. of Rochester Med. Sch., NY, 1964–65; Dep. Chm., Lagos Univ. Teaching Hosp. Man. Bd and Mem. Council, Univ. Lagos Med. Coll., 1962–66; Mem. Senate, Lagos Univ., 1963–66; Vice-Chancellor, Ahmadu Bello Univ., 1966–1975; Prof. of Medicine, 1967–77; Sen. Medical Officer, Ashaka Cement Co. Ltd, 1977–79; Minister of External Affairs, Fed. Republic of Nigeria, 1979–83; Ambassador and Perm. Rep. of Nigeria to UN, 1983–84. President: Christian Health Assoc. of Nigeria, 1986–93 (Trustee, 1993–); Leprosy Mission, Nigeria, 1998–; Chairman: Nat. Primary Health Care Develt Agency of Nigeria, 1992–94; Nat. Health Insurance Scheme, 2000–. Pro-Chancellor and Chairman of Council: Univ. of Nigeria, Nsukka, 1993–96; Univ. of Jos, 2000–. Ordained Minister, United Church of Christ in Nigeria, 1986. Hon. LHD Ohio, 1968; Hon DSc Nigeria, 1971; Hon. LLD Ibadan, 1973; FMC (Pæd) Nigerian Med. Council; FRSocMed. *Publications:* contribs to learned jls. *Recreations:* walking, table tennis. *Address:* (office) Basawa Road, Hayin Dogo, Samaru, Zaria, Nigeria; (home) 23a Circular Road, GRA, Zaria, Nigeria.
                                          Died 29 Aug. 2005.

AUSTIN, Prof. Colin Russell, FAA; Charles Darwin Professor of Animal Embryology, and Fellow of Fitzwilliam College, University of Cambridge, 1967–81, then Professor Emeritus; *b* 12 Sept. 1914; *s* of Ernest Russell Austin and Linda Mabel King; *m* 1941, Patricia Constance Jack; two *s*. *Educ:* Univ. of Sydney, Australia (BVSc 1936; DSc 1954); MA Cantab 1967. FAA 1987; FAIBiol 1987. Mem. Research Staff, CSIRO, Australia, 1938–54; Mem. Scientific Staff of MRC, UK, 1954–64; Head of Genetic and Develtl Disorders Res. Prog., Delta Regional Primate Res. Center, and Prof. of Embryology, Tulane Univ., New Orleans, 1964–67. F. R. Lillie Meml Fellow, Marine Biol Lab, Woods Hole, Mass, 1961. Visiting Professor: Florida State Univ., 1962; Univ. of Palermo, 1969; Univ. of NSW, 1974; Murdoch Univ., 1979; Univ. of Auckland, 1980; Chulalongkorn Univ., Bangkok, 1985; Goding Lectr, Australian Soc. for Reproductive Biol., 1991. Editor: Jl of Reproduction and Fertility, 1959–64; Reproduction in Mammals, 1972–86; Biological Reviews, 1981–84. Hon. Mem., Amer. Assoc. Anatomists, 1984; Hon. Member: Soc. Chilena Reprod. y Desarrollo, 1989; Eur. Soc. of Human Reproduction and Embryol., 1990. Medal and Citation, Istituto Sperimentale Italiano Lazzaro Spallanzani, 1972; Marshall Medal, Soc. for Study of Fertility, 1981; Pioneer Award, Internat. Embryo Transfer Soc., 1995. *Publications:* The Mammalian Egg, 1961; Fertilization, 1965; Ultrastructure of

Fertilization, 1968; Human Embryos: the debate on assisted reproduction, 1989; numerous research papers. *Recreations:* gardening, swimming, tennis. *Address:* 79 Dixon Road, Buderim, Qld 4556, Australia.

Died 29 June 2004.

AUSTIN, Vice-Adm. Sir Peter (Murray), KCB 1976; Director, Mastiff Electronic Systems, since 1987 (Managing Director, 1990–91); *b* 16 April 1921; *er s* of late Vice-Adm. Sir Francis Austin, KBE, CB, and late Lady (Marjorie) Austin (*née* Barker); *m* 1959, Josephine Rhoda Ann Shutte-Smith (*d* 2001); three *s* one *d. Educ:* RNC, Dartmouth. Cadet, Dartmouth, 1935. Served War of 1939–45: at sea in HMS Cornwall, 1939–40; destroyers, 1941–45. Qualif. as pilot in FAA, 1946; served in 807 Sqdn, 1947–49; CO 736 Sqdn, 1950–52; grad. from RAF Flying Coll., Manby, 1953; comd 850 Sqdn in HMAS Sydney, incl. Korea, 1953–54; Lt-Cmdr (Flying), HMS Bulwark, 1954–56; Comdr (Air), RNAS Brawdy, 1956–58; Comdr (Air), HMS Eagle, 1958–59; Captain, 1961; Captain F7 in HMS Lynx, 1963–65; CO, RNAS Brawdy, 1965–67; Staff of SACLANT, 1967–69; comd aircraft carrier, HMS Hermes, 1969–70; Rear-Adm., 1971; Asst Chief of Naval Staff (Ops and Air), 1971–73; Flag Officer, Naval Air Comd, 1973–74; retired; Vice-Adm., 1974. Operations Dir, Mersey Docks and Harbour Co., 1976–80; Dir, Avanova Internat. Consultants, 1980–89; Chm., Special Training Services, 1984–90. Vice-Chm. Council, Air League, 1987–95. Liveryman, GAPAN, 1987–. CCMI. *Recreations:* bicycling, swimming. *Club:* Army and Navy.

Died 13 May 2005.

AXELROD, Julius, PhD; Guest Researcher, Laboratory of Cell Biology, since 1984, Chief, Section on Pharmacology, Laboratory of Clinical Science, 1955–84 (Acting Chief, Jan.-Oct. 1955), National Institute of Mental Health, USA; Scientist Emeritus, National Institutes of Health, 1996; *b* NYC, 30 May 1912; *s* of Isadore Axelrod, Michaliev, Poland, and Molly Liechtling, Striej, Poland (formerly Austria); *m* 1938, Sally (*née* Taub) (*d* 1992); two *s. Educ:* George Washington Univ., Washington, DC (PhD); New York Univ. (MA); New York City Coll. (BS). Lab. Asst, Dept Bacteriology, NY Univ. Med. Sch., 1933–35; Chemist, Lab. Industrial Hygiene, 1935–46; Res. Associate, Third NY Univ.; Research Div., Goldwater Memorial Hosp., 1946–49; National Heart Institute, National Institutes of Health: Associate Chemist, Section on Chem. Pharmacology, 1949–50; Chemist, 1950–53; Sen. Chemist, 1953–55. Mem., Nat. Academy of Sciences, 1971; Fellow, Amer. Acad. of Arts and Sciences; Senior Mem., Amer. Inst. of Medicine, 1979. Thudicum Medal and Lecture, British Biochem Soc., 1989. Foreign Member: Royal Society, 1979; Deutsche Akademie der Naturforscher, 1984. Hon. LLD: George Washington, 1971; College City, NY, 1972; Hon. DSc: Chicago, 1966; Med. Coll., Wisconsin, 1971; New York, 1971; Pennsylvania Coll. of Med., 1973; Hahnemann Univ., 1987; McGill Univ., 1988; Doctor *hc* Panama, 1972; DPhil *hc:* Ripon Coll., 1984; Tel Aviv Univ., 1984. Nobel Prize (jtly) for Physiology-Medicine, 1970; winner of 15 awards; holds 23 hon. lectureships; Member: 13 editorial boards; 5 Sci. Adv. Cttees. *Publications:* (with Richard J. Wurtman and Douglas E. Kelly) The Pineal, 1968; numerous original papers and contribs to jls in biochem., pharmacol. and physiology. *Recreations:* reading and listening to music. *Address:* 10401

Grosvenor Place, Rockville, MD 20852, USA. *T:* (301) 4936376. *Died 29 Dec. 2004.*

AXISA, John Francis, MOM 1995; MBE 1950; *b* 20 Nov. 1906; *s* of late Emmanuel Axisa and Vincenzina (*née* Micallef); *m* 1939, Ariadne Cachia; three *s* one *d. Educ:* St Paul's Sch., Malta and privately. Joined Malta Civil Service, 1927; Dir of Emigration, 1947–56; Dir of Technical Education, 1956–59; Dir of Emigration, Labour and Social Welfare, 1959–60; Under-Sec., 1960–61; Commissioner-Gen. for Malta in London, 1961–64; Malta's first High Commissioner on Malta's Independence, 1964–69; Ambassador of Malta to: France, 1966–69; Fed. Republic of Germany, 1967–69; Libya, 1966–68; Belgium, 1967–68; Netherlands, 1968–69. Chm., Bd of Govs, St Edward's Coll., Malta, 1988–90 (Trustee, 1988–93). *Recreations:* woodwork, fishing, reading. *Address:* 5/8 Tower Road, Sliema, Malta, GC. *Club:* Union (Malta). *Died 11 April 2004.*

AXTON, Henry Stuart, (Harry), FCA; Chairman, Brixton Estate plc, 1983–93; *b* 6 May 1923; *s* of Wilfrid George Axton and Mary Louise Axton (*née* Laver); *m* 1947, Constance Mary Godefroy (*d* 1996); one *d. Educ:* Rock Ferry. RMC, Sandhurst, commissioned 1942; served: N Africa, Royal Tank Regt, NW Europe, Fife and Forfar Yeo.; wounded three times, invalided out, 1945. Articles, G. E. Holt & Son; Chartered Accountant 1948. Treas., United Sheffield Hosps and other hosp. appts, 1948–55; Company Sec., Midland Assurance, 1955–61; Brixton Estate, 1961–93: Man. Dir, 1964–83; Dep. Chm., 1971–83; Chm., Investment Cos in Australia and Switzerland. Pres., British Property Fedn, 1984–86 (Mem. Council, 1974–93; Vice-Pres., 1983–84; Hon. Life Mem., 1993). Dep. Chm., Audit Commn, 1987–91 (Mem., 1986–91). Chairman: Council, St George's Hosp. Med. Sch., 1977–92 (Mem., 1969–92; Dep. Chm. 1974–77; first Hon. Fellow 1992); St George's New Hosp. Bldg Cttee, 1972–92 (Mem., 1969–92); Nuffield Hosps, 1976–93 (Governor, 1968–93; Dep. Chm. 1975–76); BUPA Medical Centre, 1973–82 (Governor, 1970–82); Mem., Chichester HA, 1985–87; Governor: BUPA, 1969–80; St George's Hosp., 1970–74, Special Trustee, 1974–77. Chm., Chichester Festivities, 1989–98. Dir, Cathedral Works Organisation (Chichester), 1985–91. Mem., Archbp's Council for Church Urban Fund, 1990–94. Trustee, Chichester Fest. Theatre, 1995–2002. Chm., City of Chichester DFAS, 1999–2000 (Vice-Chm., 1995–99). Freeman, City of London, 1987. Lord of the Manor of Aldingbourne, 1993. *Recreations:* sailing, music. *Address:* Hook Place, Aldingbourne, Chichester, Sussex PO20 3TS. *T:* (01243) 542291. *Clubs:* Royal Thames Yacht, Royal Ocean Racing; Sussex. *Died 15 March 2002.*

AYLEN, Rear-Adm. Ian Gerald, CB 1962; OBE 1946; DSC 1942; CEng, FIMechE; *b* 12 Oct. 1910; *s* of late Commander A. E. Aylen, RN and Mrs S. C. M. Aylen; *m* 1937, Alice Brough Maltby (*d* 1995); one *s* two *d. Educ:* Blundell's, Tiverton. RNE Coll., Keyham, 1929–33; served in HMS Rodney; Curacoa; Galatea, 1939–40; Kelvin, 1940–42; 30 Assault Unit, 1945; Cossack; Fleet Engineer Officer, Home Fleet, 1957–58; CO HMS Thunderer, RNE Coll., 1958–60; Rear-Admiral, 1960; Admiral Superintendent, HM Dockyard, Rosyth, 1960–63; Dep. Sec., Instn Mechanical Engineers, 1963–65; Asst Sec., Council of Engineering Instns, 1966–71, retired 1971. *Died 5 Nov. 2003.*

B

BABCOCK, Horace Welcome; astronomer; Director, Mount Wilson and Palomar Observatories, 1964–78; *b* 13 Sept. 1912; *s* of Harold D. Babcock and Mary G. (*née* Henderson); *m* 1st, 1940; one *s* one *d*; 2nd, 1958; one *s*. *Educ:* California Institute of Technology (BS); Univ. of California (PhD). Instructor, Yerkes and McDonald Observatories, 1939–41; Radiation Laboratory, Mass Inst. of Tech., 1941–42; Calif Inst. of Tech., 1942–45; Staff Mem., Mount Wilson Observatory, 1946–51; Astronomer, Mount Wilson and Palomar Observatories, 1951–80; Founding Dir, Las Campanas Observatory, Chile, of Carnegie Instn, Washington, 1968–78. Elected to: National Acad. of Sciences, 1954 (Councillor, 1973–76); American Acad. of Arts and Sciences, 1959; American Philosophical Soc., 1966; Corres. Mem., Société Royale des Sciences de Liège, 1968; Associate, Royal Astronomical Soc., 1969; Member: American Astronomical Soc.; Astronomical Soc. of the Pacific; Internat. Astronomical Union. Hon. DSc Univ. of Newcastle upon Tyne, 1965. US Navy Bureau of Ordnance Development Award, 1945; Eddington Gold Medal, RAS, 1958; Henry Draper Medal of the National Acad. of Sciences, 1957; Bruce Medal, Astronomical Soc. of the Pacific, 1969; Gold Medal, RAS, 1970; Hale Prize, Amer. Astronomical Soc., 1992; Rank Prize in Opto-electronics, 1993. *Publications:* scientific papers in Astrophysical Jl, Publications of the Astronomical Soc. of the Pacific, Jl of Optical Soc. of America, etc, primarily on magnetic fields of the stars and sun, astrophysics, diffraction gratings, adaptive optics, and astronomical instruments. *Address:* The Observatories, Carnegie Institution of Washington, 813 Santa Barbara Street, Pasadena, CA 91101–1292, USA. *T:* (818) 5771122.

Died 29 Aug. 2003.

BABINGTON, His Honour Anthony Patrick; a Circuit Judge, 1972–87; *b* 4 April 1920; 2nd *s* of late Oscar John Gilmore Babington, MAI, AMICE, Monkstown, Co. Cork. *Educ:* Reading Sch. Served with Royal Ulster Rifles and Dorset Regt, 1939–45 (wounded twice); Croix de Guerre with Gold Star (France), 1944. Called to the Bar, Middle Temple, 1948; Bencher, 1977, Autumn Reader, 1994; South Eastern Circuit; Prosecuting Counsel to Post Office, SE Circuit (South), 1959–64; Metropolitan Stipendiary Magistrate, 1964–72. Mem., Home Office Working Party on Bail, 1971–73. Mem., Nat. Exec. Cttee. Internat. PEN English Centre, 1979–82. Trustee: New Bridge, 1985–2002; PEN Literary Foundn, 1990–2002. Hon. Bencher, King's Inns, Dublin, 1995. *Publications:* No Memorial, 1954; The Power to Silence, 1968; A House in Bow Street, 1969; The English Bastille, 1971; The Only Liberty, 1975; For the Sake of Example, 1983; Military Intervention in Britain, 1990; The Devil to Pay, 1991; Shell-Shock, 1997; An Uncertain Voyage, 2000. *Recreations:* music, theatre, reading. *Address:* Thydon Cottage, Chilham, near Canterbury, Kent CT4 8BX. *T:* (01227) 730300; (020) 7385 9925. *Clubs:* Garrick, Special Forces.

Died 10 May 2004.

BACK, Patrick; QC 1970; a Recorder of the Crown Court, 1972–89; *b* 23 Aug. 1917; *s* of late Ivor Back, FRCS, and Barbara Back (*née* Nash); *m* 1971, Rosina Hare, QC. *Educ:* Marlborough; Trinity Hall, Cambridge. Captain, 14th Punjab Regt, 1941–46. Called to Bar, 1940; Bencher, Gray's Inn, 1978. Commenced practice, Western Circuit, 1947, Leader, 1984–89; Dep. Chm., Devon QS, 1968. *Recreation:* fly-fishing. *Address:* Paddock Edge, Broadwindsor, Dorset. *T:* (01308) 868644; Flat 71, 8 New Crane Place, Garnet Street, Wapping, E1 9TT. *T:* (020) 7488 4371.

Died 26 April 2003.

BACON, Hon. James Alexander, AC 2004; MHA (Lab) Denison, Tasmania, 1996–2004; Premier of Tasmania, 1998–2004; *b* 15 May 1950; *m*; two *s*. Union official, 1973–79, State Sec., Tasmanian Br., 1980–89, Builders' Labourers' Fedn; Sec., Tasmanian Trades and Labor Council, 1989–95. Dir, Tasmanian Develt Authy, 1989–95. Member: Council, Trade Unions Exec., 1989–95; Nat. Labour Consultative Council, 1991–95. Leader, Parly Labor Party, Tas, 1997–. Delegate to: ILO Regl Conf., Bangkok, 1991; ILO Internat. Labor Conf., Geneva, 1994. *Address:* c/o Office of the Premier, 15 Murray Street, GPO Box 123, Hobart, Tas 7001, Australia. *T:* (3) 62333464.

Died 20 June 2004.

BADGER, Sir Geoffrey Malcolm, Kt 1979; AO 1975; PhD, DSc; FRSC, FRACI, FACE, FTSE, FAA; Chairman, Australian Science and Technology Council, 1977–82; *b* 10 Oct. 1916; *s* of J. McD. Badger; *m* 1941, Edith Maud, *d* of Henry Chevis. *Educ:* Geelong Coll.; Gordon Inst. of Technology; Univs of Melbourne, London (PhD), Glasgow (DSc). Instructor Lieut, RN, 1943–46. Finney-Howell Research Fellow, London, 1940–41; Research Chemist, ICI, 1941–43; Research Fellow, Glasgow, 1946–49. Univ. of Adelaide: Sen. Lectr, 1949–51; Reader, 1951–54; Prof. of Organic Chemistry, 1955–64, then Emeritus Professor; Dep. Vice-Chancellor, 1966–67; Vice-Chancellor, 1967–77; Res. Professor, 1977–79. Dir, Western Mining Corp., 1979–88. Mem. Executive, CSIRO, 1964–65. President: Aust. Acad. of Science, 1974–78; Aust. and NZ Assoc. for Advancement of Science, 1979–80; Chm., Order of Australia Assoc., 1989–92. DUniv Adelaide. H. G. Smith Medal, 1951, A. E. Leighton Medal, 1971, RACI; W. D. Chapman Medal, Instn of Engrs, Australia, 1974; ANZAAS Medal, 1981. *Publications:* Structures and Reactions of Aromatic Compounds, 1954; Chemistry of Heterocyclic Compounds, 1961; The Chemical Basis of Carcinogenic Activity, 1962; Aromatic Character and Aromaticity, 1969; (ed) Captain Cook, 1970; The Explorers of the Pacific, 1988; numerous papers in Jl Chem. Soc., etc. *Address:* 1 Anna Court, West Lakes, SA 5021, Australia. *T:* (8) 84494594. *Club:* Adelaide (Adelaide).

Died 23 Sept. 2002.

BADHAM, Douglas George, CBE 1975; JP; HM Lord-Lieutenant for Mid Glamorgan, 1985–89; company director; *b* 1 Dec. 1914; *s* of late David Badham, JP; *m* 1939, Doreen Spencer Phillips; two *d*. *Educ:* Leys Sch., Cambridge. CA. Exec. Director: Powell Duffryn Gp, 1938–69; Pascoe Hldgs, 1983–88; Alignrite, 1984–87; T. H. Couch, 1984–88; World Trade Centre Wales, 1984–; Chairman: Powell Duffryn Wagon Co., 1965–85; Hamell (West) Ltd, 1968–; T. T. Pascoe, 1983–89; Economic Forestry Gp PLC, 1981–88 (Dir, 1978–88); Novastar Internat. Ltd, 1996–. Chm., Nat. Health Service Staff Commn, 1972–75; Mem., 1978–84, Dep. Chm., 1980–84, Welsh Develt Agency. Member: Wales and the Marches Telecommunications Bd, 1973–80; British Gas Corp., 1974–83; Forestry Commn, S Wales Reg. Adv. Cttee, 1946–76 (Chm., 1973–76); Western Region Adv. Bd, BR, 1977–82; Welsh Council (Chm., Industry and Planning Panel), 1971–80; Nature Conservancy Council Adv. Cttee for Wales; Council, UWIST, 1975–80; Develt Corp. for Wales, 1965–83 (Chm., 1971–80). JP Glamorgan, 1962; DL, 1975–82, High Sheriff, 1976, Lieut, 1982, Mid Glamorgan. KStJ 1991. *Recreations:* forestry, trout breeding. *Address:* Swyn-y-Coed, Watford Road, Caerphilly, Mid Glamorgan CF8 1NE. *T:* (029) 2088 2094.

Died 7 Nov. 2003.

BAGNALL, Field Marshal Sir Nigel (Thomas), GCB 1985 (KCB 1981); CVO 1978; MC 1950 and Bar 1953; Chief of the General Staff, 1985–88; *b* 10 Feb. 1927; *s* of Lt-Col Harry Stephen Bagnall and Marjory May Bagnall; *m* 1959, Anna Caroline Church; two *d. Educ:* Wellington Coll. Joined Army, 1945; commnd Green Howards, 1946; Palestine, 1946–48, 8 Para Bn, 6th Airborne Div.; Malaya, 1949–53, Canal Zone and Cyprus, 1954–56, Green Howards; sc 1957, jssc 1962; GSO1 (Intell.), Dir of Borneo Ops, 1966–67; comd 4/7 Royal Dragoon Guards, NI and BAOR, 1967–69; Sen. Directing Staff (Army), Jt Services Staff Coll., 1970; comd Royal Armoured Corps HQ 1 (Br.) Corps, 1970–72; Defence Fellow, Balliol Coll., Oxford, 1972–73; Sec., Chief of Staff Cttee, 1973–75; GOC 4th Div., 1975–77; ACDS (Policy), MoD, 1978–80; Comdr, 1 (Br.) Corps, 1980–83; C-in-C BAOR and Comdr, Northern Army Gp, 1983–85. Col Comdt, APTC, 1981–88, RAC, 1985–88; ADC Gen. to the Queen, 1985–88. Hon. Fellow, Balliol Coll., Oxford, 1986. Co-Pres., Anglo-German Officers' Assoc., 1992–98. Comdr's Cross, Order of Merit (Germany), 1993. *Publication:* The Punic Wars, 1991 (trans. German 1995). *Recreations:* writing, reading, gardening, breeding water fowl. *Address:* c/o Royal Bank of Scotland, 49 Charing Cross Road, SW1A 2DX.   *Died 8 April 2002.*

BAGOT, 9th Baron *cr* 1780, of Bagot's Bromley, co. Stafford; **Heneage Charles Bagot;** Bt 1627; *b* 11 June 1914; *s* of Charles Frederick Heneage Bagot (*d* 1939) (4th *s* of *g s* of 1st Baron) and 2nd wife, Alice Lorina, *d* of Thomas Farr; *S* half-brother, 1979; *m* 1939, Muriel Patricia Moore, *y d* of late Maxwell James Moore Boyle; one *s* one *d. Educ:* Harrow. Formerly Major, QEO 6th Gurkha Rifles. *Recreations:* shooting, ski-ing, sailing. *Heir:* s Hon. Charles Hugh Shaun Bagot [*b* 23 Feb. 1944; *m* 1986, Mrs Sally A. Stone, *d* of D. G. Blunden; one *d*]. *Address:* Llithfaen, near Pwllheli, Gwynedd LL53 6PD; 16 Barclay Road, SW6 1EH. *Club:* Himalayan.
                                                          Died 19 Jan. 2001.

BAILEY, D(avid) R(oy) Shackleton, LittD; FBA 1958; Pope Professor of the Latin Language and Literature, Harvard University, 1982–88, later Emeritus; Adjunct Professor, University of Michigan, since 1989; *b* 10 Dec. 1917; *y s* of late Rev. J. H. Shackleton Bailey, DD, and Rosamund Maud (*née* Giles); *m* 1st, 1967, Hilary Ann (marr. diss. 1974), *d* of Leonard Sidney and Margery Bardwell; 2nd, 1994, Kristine Zvirbulis. *Educ:* Lancaster Royal Grammar Sch.; Gonville and Caius Coll., Cambridge (Hon. Fellow, 2000). Fellow of Gonville and Caius Coll., 1944–55, Praelector, 1954–55; Fellow and Dir of Studies in Classics, Jesus Coll., Cambridge, 1955–64; Visiting Lecturer in Classics, Harvard Coll., 1963; Fellow and Dep. Bursar, Gonville and Caius Coll., 1964; Senior Bursar 1965–68; Univ. Lectr in Tibetan, 1948–68; Prof. of Latin, Univ. of Michigan, 1968–74; Prof. of Greek and Latin, Harvard Univ., 1975–82. Andrew V. V. Raymond Vis. Prof., State Univ. of NY at Buffalo, 1973–74; Vis. Fellow of Peterhouse, Cambridge, 1980–81; Nat. Endowment of Humanities Fellowship, 1980–81. Mem., Amer. Philosophical Soc., 1977. Fellow, Amer. Acad. of Arts and Sciences, 1979. Hon. Mem., Soc. for Roman Studies, 1999. Editor, Harvard Studies in Classical Philology, 1978–84. Hon. LittD Dublin, 1984. Charles J. Goodwin Award of Merit, Amer. Philol Assoc., 1978; Kenyon Medal, British Acad., 1985. *Publications:* The Śatapañcāśatka of Mātrceta, 1951; Propertiana, 1956; Towards a Text of Cicero, ad Atticum; 1960; Ciceronis Epistulae ad Atticum IX-XVI, 1961; Cicero's Letters to Atticus, Vols I and II, 1965; Vol. V, 1966, Vol. VI, 1967, Vols III and IV, 1968, Vol. VII, 1970; Cicero, 1971; Two Studies in Roman Nomenclature, 1976; Cicero: Epistulae ad Familiares, 2 vols, 1977; (trans.) Cicero's Letters to Atticus, 1978; (trans.) Cicero's Letters to his Friends, 2 Vols, 1978; Towards a Text of Anthologia Latina, 1979; Selected Letters of Cicero, 1980; Cicero: Epistulae ad Q. Fratrem et M. Brutum, 1981; Profile of Horace, 1982; Anthologia Latina, I.1, 1982; Horatius, 1985; Cicero:

Philippics, 1986; (trans.) Cicero, Selected Letters, 1986; Ciceronis Epistulae, 4 vols, 1987–88; Lucanus, 1988; Onomasticon to Cicero's speeches, 1988; Quintilianus: *Declamationes minores*, 1989; Martialis, 1990; Back from Exile, 1991; Martial, 3 vols, 1993; Homoeoteleuton in Latin dactylic verse, 1994; Onomasticon to Cicero's Letters, 1994; Onomasticon to Cicero's Treatises, 1996; Selected Classical Papers, 1997; Cicero's Letters to Atticus, 4 vols, 1999; Valerius Maximus, 2000; Cicero's Letters to Friends, 3 vols, 2001; Cicero's Letters to Quintus and Brutus etc., 2002; Statius: Silvae, 2003; Statius: Thebaid, 2 vols, 2003; articles in Classical and Orientalist periodicals. *Recreation:* cat. *Address:* 303 North Division, Ann Arbor, MI 48104, USA.   *Died 28 Nov. 2005.*

BAILEY, Thomas Aubrey, MBE 1959; Senior Architect responsible for Ancient Monuments, Ministry of Public Building and Works, 1954–69; Director, Peter Cox Ltd, Building Restoration Specialists (Member of SGB Group of Cos), 1970–76; *b* 20 Jan. 1912; *o s* of late Thomas Edward Bailey and Emma Bailey; *m* 1944, Joan Woodman, *d* of late John Woodman Hooper; one *s. Educ:* Adams' Grammar Sch., Newport, Shropshire; Regent Street Polytechnic Sch. of Architecture. RIBA 1948. Entered HM Office of Works, Ancient Monuments Br., 1935; Asst Architect, 1945–49; Architect, London and E Anglia, 1949–54. Architectural Advr to Oxford Historic Bldgs Fund, 1963–69. Served on various cttees on stone decay and preservation; seconded to Sir Giles G. Scott, OM, RA, for Rebuilding of House of Commons, 1944–49. *Principal works:* Direction of MPBW Survey for Oxford Historic Bldg Appeal, 1957–62 and Cambridge Appeal, 1963; re-erection of fallen Trilithons at Stonehenge, 1958–64; Conservation of Claudian Aqueduct and Aurelian Wall, Brit. Embassy at Rome, 1957–69; etc. Resigned professional membership of RIBA and ARCUK, to enter specialised Bldg Industry, 1969. Mem. Conservation Cttee, for Council for Places of Worship, 1968; Mem. Council, 1970–, and Vice-Pres., Ancient Monuments Soc. FSA 1957; FRSA 1969; Fellow of Faculty of Bldg, 1970. Freeman of City of London, 1967; Freeman and Liveryman, Masons' Co., 1973 (Hon. Court of Assts). Hon. MA Oxon, 1963. *Publications:* (jtly) The Claudian Aqueduct in the Grounds of the British Embassy, Rome, 1966; many technical reports on conservation of Historic Monuments. *Recreations:* music, photography, travel, motoring. *Address:* 32 Anne Boleyn's Walk, Cheam, Sutton, Surrey SM3 8DF. *T:* (020) 8642 3185. *Club:* City Livery.   *Died 9 Dec. 2001.*

BAILLIE, Sir Gawaine George Hope, 7th Bt *cr* 1823, of Polkemmet, Linlithgowshire; *b* 8 March 1934; *s* of Sir Adrian Baillie, 6th Bt, and Hon. Olive Cecilia (*d* 1974), *d* of 1st Baron Queenborough, GBE; *S* father, 1947; *m* 1966, Margot, *d* of Senator Louis Beaubien, Montreal; one *s* one *d. Heir:* s Adrian Louis Baillie, *b* 26 March 1973. *Address:* Freechase, Warninglid, Sussex RH17 5SZ.
                                                          Died 21 Dec. 2003.

BAINES, Sir George G.; *see* Grenfell-Baines.

BAKER, Alex Anthony, CBE 1973; MD; FRCPsych; Consultant Psychiatrist with special interest in the elderly to Gloucestershire Clinical Area, 1973–77, retired; *b* 22 March 1922; *m* 1944; two *s* two *d. Educ:* St Mary's Hosp. Med. Sch. MD London, 1952; DPM 1946. MRCP 1971; FRCPsych 1971. Consultant Psychiatrist: Banstead Hosp., 1955; Mother and Baby Unit, Downview Hosp., 1958; St Mary Abbotts Hosp., 1967; Medical Administrator, Banstead Hosp., 1964; sometime Consultant to WHO; Sen. Principal Medical Officer, Dept of Health, 1968; Dir, NHS Hospital Adv. Service, 1969–73. *Publications:* (jtly) Social Psychiatry, 1952; (jtly) Psychiatric Services and Architecture, 1958; Psychiatric Disorders in Obstetrics, 1967; Comprehensive Psychiatric Care, 1976; chapters in sundry books; papers in numerous jls on research, psychiatric treatment, organisation of psychiatric services, etc. *Address:* Pineholm, High Close, Bovey Tracey, Devon TQ13 9EX.   *Died 8 Oct. 2001.*

BAKER, Anthony Baxter, CBE 1983; JP; Regional Administrator, Northern Regional Health Authority, 1973–83; *b* 12 June 1923; *s* of late Anthony Thurlbeck Baker and Robina Frances Jane (*née* Baxter); *m* 1st, 1946, Mary Margherita Patterson (*d* 1978); one *s* three *d*; 2nd, 1981, Judith Margaret Ayers, JP. *Educ:* Tynemouth High Sch.; Durham Univ. DPA; FHA. RAFVR, UK, Canada and Iceland, 1942–46. Admin. Asst, later Dep. Sec., SE Northumberland HMC, 1949–60; Asst Sec., later Principal Asst Sec., Newcastle Regional Hosp. Bd, 1960–73. JP Tynemouth 1965; former Chm., North Tyneside PSD. *Recreations:* Rugby football (PP Percy Park RFC; PP Northumberland RFU), golf. *Address:* 16 Dickson Drive, Highford Park, Hexham, Northumberland NE46 2RB.   *Died 19 Sept. 2003.*

BAKER, Maj.-Gen. Ian Helstrip, CBE 1977 (MBE 1965); rcds, psc; General Officer Commanding, North East District, 1980–82; Secretary, University College London, 1982–91; *b* 26 Nov. 1927; *e s* of late Henry Hubert Baker and Mary Clare Baker (*née* Coles); *m* 1956, Susan Anne, *y d* of late Major and Mrs Henry Osmond Lock; one *s* one *d* (and one *s* decd). *Educ:* St Peter's Sch., York; St Edmund Hall, Oxford; RMA, Sandhurst; Open Univ. (BA 1994). Commnd, 1948; 10th Fd Regt RA, 1949–51; 2nd Regt RHA, 1951–53; RAC Centre, 1953–55; transf. RTR, 1955; 4th Royal Tank Regt, 1955–57; HQ 10th Inf. Bde, 1957–58; Staff Coll., Camberley, 1959; DAAG HQ 17 Gurkha Div., Overseas Commonwealth Land Forces, Malaya and Singapore, 1960–62; OC Parachute Sqdn RAC (C Sqdn 2nd Royal Tank Regt), 1962–65; Instr Staff Coll., Camberley, and Bt Lt-Col, 1965; GSO1 and Asst Sec., Chiefs of Staff Cttee, MoD, 1966–67; Lt-Col 1966; CO, 1st Royal Tank Regt, UK and BAOR, 1967–69; Col 1970; Col, RTR, 1970–71; Brig. 1972; Comdr, 7th Armoured Bde, BAOR, 1972–74; RCDS, 1974; Brig. Gen. Staff, HQ UKLF, 1975–77; Services Fellow, St Catharine's Coll., Cambridge, 1977; Maj.-Gen., 1978; Asst Chief of the Gen. Staff, 1978–80. Col Comdt, Royal Tank Regt, 1981–86. Member: UK Conf. of Univ. Registrars and Secs, 1982–91; Organising Cttee for Internat. Confs of Univ. Administrators, 1983–91; Former UK Heads of Univ. Admin Soc., 1993– (Convener, 1998–2001). Mem., Univ. of London Mil. Educn Cttee, 1987–91. Elder, Crabtree Foundn, UCL, 1998– (Pres., 1995); Hon. President: Medical Students Soc., UCL, 1983–88; UCL Boat Club, 1986–93. Mem., RAC Benevolent Fund Cttee, 1985–89. Governor, Welbeck Coll., 1980–82. *Publications:* contribs to service and university papers and journals. *Address:* Owen's Farm, Hook, Hampshire RG27 9NG.   *Died 28 July 2005.*

BAKER, Stephen, OBE 1987; consultant; Managing Director, British Electricity International Ltd, 1978–86; *b* 27 March 1926; *s* of late Arthur and Nancy Baker; *m* 1950, Margaret Julia Wright; one *s* two *d*. *Educ:* Epsom Coll.; Clare Coll., Cambridge (MA). FIMechE. Engr Officer, RN, 1944–47; Apprentice, Davy United Engineering Co. Ltd, 1947–49; Works Engr, John Baker & Bessemer Ltd, 1949–51; Davy United Engineering Co. Ltd, 1951: Dir of Prodn, 1960; Gen. Man., 1961; Dir, Davy Ashmore Ltd, 1963; Dir of Ops, Davy-Ashmore Engrg Ltd, 1964; Chm. and Chief Exec. of Davy United Engrg Co. Ltd, Ashmore Benson Pease Ltd and Loewy Robertson Engrg Co. Ltd, 1968; Man. Dir, Kearney & Trecker Ltd, 1970; Co-ordinator of Industrial Advrs, Depts of Trade and Industry, 1974–78. *Recreations:* fishing, gardening. *Address:* 75 Slayleigh Lane, Sheffield S10 3RG.

    Died 23 April 2002.

BAKER, Wilson, PhD, DSc; FRS 1946; FRSC; retired; Alfred Capper Pass Professor of Organic Chemistry, University of Bristol, 1945–65 (Dean of the Faculty of Science, 1948–51; Emeritus Professor, University of Bristol, 1965); *b* 24 Jan. 1900; *yr s* of Harry and Mary Baker, Runcorn, Cheshire; *m* 1927, Juliet Elizabeth (*d* 1991), *d* of Henry and Julia R. Glaisyer, Birmingham; one *s* two *d*. *Educ:* Liverpool Coll. Upper Sch.; Victoria Univ. of Manchester (Mercer Schol., Baeyer Fellow and Dalton Scholar; BSc, MSc, PhD, DSc); MA Oxon. Asst Lecturer in Chemistry, Univ. of Manchester, 1924–27; Tutor in Chemistry, Dalton Hall, Manchester, 1926–27; Univ. Lecturer and Demonstrator in Chemistry, Univ. of Oxford, 1927–44; Fellow and Praelector in Chemistry, The Queen's Coll., Oxford, 1937–44. Vice-Pres. of the Chemical Society, 1957–60. *Publications:* (with T. W. J. Taylor) Prof. N. V. Sidgwick's The Organic Chemistry of Nitrogen, 2nd edn, 1937; numerous original papers on organic chemistry, dealing chiefly with the synthesis of natural products, the development of synthetical processes, compounds of abnormal aromatic type, organic inclusion compounds, and the preparation of large-ring compounds, and the chemistry of penicillin, published mainly in Jl of Chem. Soc. *Recreation:* music. *Address:* Lane's End, 54 Church Road, Winscombe, North Somerset BS25 1BJ. *T:* (01934) 843112.   *Died 3 June 2002.*

BALCHIN, John Alfred; General Manager, Stevenage Development Corporation, 1969–76, retired; *b* 8 Aug. 1914; *er s* of Alfred and Florence Balchin; *m* 1st, 1940, Elsie Dormer (*d* 1982); one *s* two *d*; 2nd, 1986, Edna Bilton (*née* Morgan). *Educ:* Sir Walter St John's Sch., Battersea; Sir John Cass Coll., City of London. DPA (London), DMA, FCIS, FCIH. LCC Clerk's Dept, 1932–38; civil defence co-ordination work, 1938–45; to Housing Dept, 1946–65; Principal Clerk, 1952; Asst Dir (Finance), 1960; Asst Dir (Housing Management), 1963; Sen. Asst Dir of Housing, GLC, 1965–69. Assoc. Sen. Lectr, for Housing Management and Administration, Brunel Univ., 1969–71. Member: Housing Services Adv. Gp, DoE, 1976–80; North British Housing Assoc., 1976–89; Auriol Housing Foundn, 1986–88. *Publications:* Housing: programming and development of estates, 1971, rev. edn 1978; Housing Management: history, principles and practice, 1972; Housing Studies, 1st series, 1979, 2nd series, 1980, rev. edn 1981; First New Town: an autobiography of the Stevenage Development Corporation, 1980; Sitting with Job: a Biblical study, 1998. *Address:* Rhoswiel Lodge, Weston Rhyn, Oswestry, Shropshire SY10 7TG. *T:* (01691) 773139.   *Died 9 Nov. 2003.*

BALDOCK, John Markham, MBE 2001; VRD 1949; Lieutenant Commander, RNVR, 1948; Chairman, Lenscrete Ltd, 1949–92; Director, CIBA-GEIGY (UK) Ltd, 1957–68; *b* 19 Nov. 1915; *s* of late Captain W. P. Baldock, and Mrs H. Chalcraft; *m* 1949, Pauline Ruth Gauntlett; two *s*. *Educ:* Rugby Sch.; Balliol Coll., Oxford. Agric. degree, 1937. Served War of 1939–45, with Royal Navy, Atlantic, Mediterranean, Indian Ocean; Russian convoys, 1942–43. Lloyds, EC3, 1945. Joined Board of Lenscrete, 1946. MP (C) Harborough Div. of Leics, 1950–59; former PPS to Rt Hon. D. Ormsby Gore (Minister of State, Foreign Office). Founder, Hollycombe steam collection. *Recreations:* country life, steam engines, industrial archæology. *Address:* The Old Stables, Hollycombe, Liphook, Hants GU30 7LR. *T:* (01428) 723233. *Club:* Farmers'.   *Died 3 Oct. 2003.*

BALDWIN, Captain George Clifton, CBE 1968; DSC 1941 and Bar 1944; RN (retd); Member: Press Council, 1973–78; Press Council Appointments Commission, 1978–90; *b* 17 Jan. 1921; *s* of late George and late Louisa Baldwin; *m* 1947, Hasle Mary McMahon; three *s*. *Educ:* Sleaford Grammar Sch., Lincs; Hitchin Grammar Sch., Herts. Served War: joined RN, 1939, Pilot in Fleet Air Arm; in comd: 807 Sqdn, 1943; No 4 Naval Fighter Wing, 1944–45. Qual. at Empire Test Pilots' Sch., 1946; in comd, 800 Sqdn, 1952; in comd, RN Air Station, Lossiemouth, 1961–62; Dir, Naval Air Warfare, MoD, 1964–66; in comd, RN Air Station, Yeovilton, 1966–68; ADC, 1967; retd, 1968. Chm., Fleet Air Arm Officers' Assoc., 1973–78 (Vice Pres., 1978–). *Address:* Applegarth, Church Lane, Lodsworth, Petworth, West Sussex GU28 9DD. *T:* (01798) 861236.   *Died 11 Nov. 2005.*

BALFOUR, 4th Earl of, *cr* 1922; **Gerald Arthur James Balfour;** Viscount Traprain 1922; JP; farmer; *b* 23 Dec. 1925; *er s* of 3rd Earl of Balfour and Jean (*d* 1981), 4th *d* of late Rev. Canon J. J. Cooke-Yarborough; *S* father, 1968; *m* 1956, Natasha Georgina (*d* 1994), *d* of late Captain George Anton. *Educ:* Eton; HMS Conway. Master Mariner's certificate. Mem., E Lothian CC, 1960–75. JP East Lothian, 1970. *Heir: cousin* Roderick Francis Arthur Balfour [*b* 9 Dec. 1948; *m* 1971, Lady Tessa Mary Isabel Fitzalan-Howard, *e d* of 17th Duke of Norfolk, KG, GCVO, CB, CBE, MC; four *d*]. *Address:* The Tower, Whittingehame, Haddington, Scotland EH41 4QA. *Clubs:* English-Speaking Union; International Association of Cape Horners. *Died 27 June 2003.*

BALFOUR, David Mathers, CBE 1970; CEng, MICE; Director, R. M. Douglas Construction Ltd, 1975–83; Chairman, Balfour, Beatty & Co. Ltd, 1971–74 (Managing Director, 1966–72); *b* 11 Jan. 1910; *s* of late George Balfour, MP and Margaret (*née* Mathers); *m* 1938, Elisabeth, *d* of John Murdoch Beddall; two *s* one *d*. *Educ:* Shrewsbury Sch.; Pembroke Coll., Cambridge (MA). Served War of 1939–45, Lt-Col RE. Joined Balfour, Beatty & Co. Ltd, as Civil Engineer, 1930 (Dir, 1942); Chairman: Power Securities Corporation Ltd, 1971–74; Balfour Kilpatrick Ltd, 1971–72 (Dir, 1971–75); Exec. Dir, British Insulated Callender's Cables Ltd, 1970–72. Chairman: Export Gp for the Constructional Industries, 1963–65; Fedn of Civil Engineering Contractors, 1966–67. *Recreations:* golf, shooting. *Address:* Little Garnstone Manor, Seal, Sevenoaks, Kent TN15 0HY. *T:* (01732) 761221. *Clubs:* East India, Devonshire, Sports and Public Schools; Rye Golf (Rye); Wildernesse Golf (Sevenoaks). *Died 21 Jan. 2001.*

BALFOUR, Michael John; JP; Director, IMI Bank (International), 1987–99 (Deputy Chairman, 1987–92); *b* 17 Oct. 1925; *s* of Duncan and Jeanne Germaine Balfour; *m* 1951, Mary Campbell Penney, *d* of Maj.-Gen. Sir (William) Ronald Campbell Penney, KBE, CB, DSO, MC; two *s* one *d* (and *e s* decd). *Educ:* Eton Coll.; Christ Church, Oxford (MA Hons Modern Languages 1949). War service, RAF, 1944–47. Entered Bank of England, 1950: Senior Adviser, European affairs, 1973, Chief Adviser, 1976; Asst Dir, 1980–85. Alternate Director, Bank for International Settlements, 1972–85; Mem., EEC Monetary Cttee, 1974–85. Dir, Balgonie Estates Ltd, 1955–; Chairman: IMI Capital Markets, later SIGECO (UK), Ltd, 1987–92 (Dir, 1987–95); IMI Securities Ltd, 1988–94. JP Roxburgh, 1988. *Recreations:* music, fishing, boating, etc. *Address:* Harrietfield, Kelso, Roxburghshire TD5 7SY. *T:* (01573) 224825. *Died 13 April 2004.*

BALL, Sir Charles (Irwin), 4th Bt *cr* 1911; Deputy Chairman, Associated British Ports Holdings, 1982–98; *b* 12 Jan. 1924; *s* of Sir Nigel Gresley Ball, 3rd Bt, and Florine Isabel (*d* 1992), *d* of late Col Herbert Edwardes Irwin; *S* father, 1978; *m* 1st, 1950, Alison Mary Bentley (marr. diss. 1983); one *s* one *d*; 2nd, 1994, Christine Trilby Knowles (*d* 2001), *d* of William Bedo Hobbs. *Educ:* Sherborne Sch. FCA 1960. Served RA, 1942–47. Chartered Accountant, 1950; Peat, Marwick, Mitchell & Co., 1950–54; joined Robert, Benson, Lonsdale & Co. Ltd (later Kleinwort, Benson Ltd), 1954; Director: Kleinwort, Benson Ltd, 1964–76 (Vice-Chm., 1974–76); Kleinwort, Benson, Lonsdale Ltd, 1974–76; Cadbury Schweppes Ltd, 1971–76; Chubb & Son Ltd, 1971–76; Sun Alliance and London Insurance Ltd, 1971–83; Telephone Rentals plc, 1971–89 (Vice-Chm., 1978–81, Chm., 1981–89); Tunnel Holdings Ltd, 1976–82; Barclays Bank Ltd, 1976–77 (Chm., Barclays Merchant Bank Ltd, 1976–77); Rockware Group plc, 1978–84; Peachey Property Corporation plc, 1978–88 (Chm., 1981–88); British Transport Docks Bd, 1971–82; Chm., Silkolene plc, 1989–94; Dep. Chm., Century Oils Group plc, 1991–94. Liveryman, 1960, Mem. Ct of Assts, 1979–87, Master, 1985, Clockmakers' Co. *Heir: s* Richard Bentley Ball [*b* 29 Jan. 1953; *m* 1991, Beverley Ann, *d* of late

Bertram Joffre Wright; one *d*]. *Address:* Killybegs, Eddystone Road, Thurlestone, Kingsbridge, Devon TQ7 3NU. *T:* (01548) 560062. *Died 8 Nov. 2002.*

BALLIN, Dame (Reubina) Ann, ONZ 2002; DBE 1993 (CBE 1981); Chairman (New Zealand), Australia New Zealand Council for the Care of Animals in Research and Teaching, 1993–97; *b* 20 Feb. 1932; *d* of late Jack Ballin and of Thelma Joyce (*née* Penberthy). *Educ:* St Hilda's Collegiate Sch.; Waikato Diocesan Sch.; Univ. of Auckland; Univ. of Canterbury (MA 1964). Vis. Psychologist, Princess Margaret Hosp., 1964–69; private Psychologist, Calvary Psychiatric Clinic, 1964–73; Student Counsellor, Univ. of Canterbury, 1974–86. Mem., Royal Commn on Social Policy, 1987–88; Nat. Chm., Internat. Year of Disabled People, 1979–82; Chm., NZ Council of Recreation and Sport, 1985–86; Mem., Hillary Commn for Sport and Recreation, 1986–88; Chm., Victims' Task Force, 1988–93. Pres., NZ Psychological Soc., 1978–79. Mem., Cambodia Trust, 1993–2000. Patron, Family Help Trust, 1993–2000. Hon. DLitt Canterbury, 2001. Sesquicentennial Medal, NZ, 1990. *Recreations:* sport, literature, food, embroidery, all broadcast media, gardens. *Address:* 3 Marblewood Drive, Papanui, Christchurch 8005, New Zealand. *T:* (3) 3521867; *e-mail:* aballin@clear.net.nz. *Died 2 Sept. 2003.*

BAMFORD, Joseph Cyril, CBE 1969; formerly Chairman and Managing Director: J. C. Bamford Excavators Ltd; JCB Farms Ltd; JCB Research Ltd; JCB Sales Ltd; JCB Service; JCB Earthmovers Ltd; *b* 21 June 1916; *s* of Cyril Joseph Bamford; *m* 1941, Marjorie Griffin; two *s*. *Educ:* St John's, Alton, Staffs; Stonyhurst Coll. Founded J. C. Bamford Excavators Ltd, 1945; more than seventy per cent of total production went to export market; initials JCB have entered the language as term for excavator. Hon. FICE 1998; Hon. FIMechE 1999. Hon. DTech Loughborough Univ. of Technol., 1983; Hon. DBA Buckingham, 1991; Hon. DEng Sheffield, 1992; Hon. DSc Warwick, 1998. *Recreations:* yacht designing, landscaping, landscape gardening. *Address:* Les Tourelles, Bon Port 15, 1820 Montreux-Territet, Switzerland. *Died 1 March 2001.*

BANANA, Rev. Dr Canaan Sodindo; President of Zimbabwe, 1980–87; *b* Esiphezini, Matabeleland, 5 March 1936; *s* of Aaron and Jese Banana; *m* 1961, Janet Mbuyazwe; three *s* one *d*. *Educ:* Mzinyati Mission; Tegwani Trng Inst.; Epworth Theol Coll., Salisbury; Kansai Industrial Centre, Japan; Wesley Theol Seminary, Washington, DC; Univ. of S Africa. Dip. in Urban and Industrial Mission, Kansai, 1970; MTS Hons, Wesley Theol Seminary, 1974; BA Hons Univ. of SA, 1980. Methodist Minister and Manager of Schools: Wankie Area, 1963–64; Plumtree Area, 1965–66 (Sch. Chaplain, Tegwani High Sch.); Methodist Minister, Fort Viet Area, 1967–68; Methodist Minister, Bulawayo and Chm., Bulaway Council of Churches, 1969–70; with Mambo Press as Promotion Officer for Moto, Catholic newspaper, 1971; Founder Mem. and first Vice Pres., ANC, Zimbabwe, 1971–73; ANC Rep. in N America and UN, 1973–75; Chaplain, American Univ., 1974–75; Publicity Sec., People's Movement Internal Co-ordinating Cttee (ZANU-PF), 1976–77; Reg. Co-ordinator, Matabeleland N and S Provinces, 1979–80. Chm., Southern Africa Contact Gp, 1970–73; Mem., Adv. Cttee, WCC, 1970–80. Hon. LLD: Amer. Univ., 1981; Univ. of Zimbabwe, 1983. *Publications:* The Zimbabwe Exodus, 1974; The Gospel According to the Ghetto, 1974, 3rd edn 1980; The Woman of my Imagination, 1980 (also in Ndebele and Shona versions); Theology of Promise, 1982; The Ethos of Socialism, 1988; various articles. *Recreations:* tennis, table tennis; soccer (player, referee and coach); volley ball (umpire); music. *Address:* c/o State House, Box 368, Harare, Zimbabwe. *T:* Harare (4) 26666. *Died 10 Nov. 2003.*

BANKS, Colin; Founder Partner, Banks and Miles, graphic designers, London, 1958–98 (Amsterdam, 1969–74,

Hamburg, 1990–93, and Brussels, 1991–93); *b* 16 Jan. 1932; *s* of late William James Banks and Ida Jenny (*née* Hood); *m* 1961, Caroline Grigson, PhD; one *s* (one *d* decd). Prodn Editor (with John Miles) of Which? and other Consumers' Assoc. magazines, 1964–93. Design Consultant to: Zool Soc., 1962–82; British Council, 1968–83; English National Opera, 1975–76; Direct Election Campaign, European Parlt, 1978, 1984; (new visual identity for) Post Office: Royal Mail, Telecommunications, etc, 1972–; British Telecom., 1980; Open Univ., 1980; US Govt Social Marketing Project, Family Planning, Indonesia, 1985; NERC, 1986; City Univ., 1987; CNAA, 1988; IMechE, 1988; Fondation Roi Baudouin, 1988–89; SERC, 1989. Designer/Design Adviser to: City and Guilds; Commn for Racial Equality; UN Univ., Japan, 1991–93; UNHCR, 1995–; other instns and commercial cos; Graphic Consultant to: London Transport, 1964–95; Mott MacDonald, 1989–; OUP, 1996–. Exhibitions: London, Paris, Amsterdam, Glasgow, Brussels, Kyoto, Hamburg; True To Type, Crafts Council, UK and Copenhagen, 1994–96. Vice-Pres., SIAD, 1974–76. Pres., Internat. Soc. of Typographic Designers, 1988–93 and 2000–; Design and Industries Assoc. Manager, Blackheath Sch. of Art, 1981–89; Gov., Bournemouth Coll. of Art, 1990–97; Mem. Bd, Internat. Inst. for Information Design, 1996–. Treas., Project Mala for children's educn and welfare, India, 1989–92. Vis. Prof., Royal Danish Acad., 1998–99. Lectured Europe, Asia, USA. FZS. Fifty Best German Printed Books, W Germany, 1989; Internationalen Buchkunst Ausstellung Medal, Leipzig, 1971, 1989; Gold Medal, Brno Biennale, 1986; RSA Green Award, 1989; BBC Envmtl Design Prize, 1990; Technol. and Creation Prize, Paris Cité, 1991; Internat. Award, Soc. of Typographic Designers, 1996; Ærespris, Danish Soc. for the Book, 1996. *Publications:* Social Communication, 1979; (with E. Schumacher Gebler) 26 Letters, Vol. I 1989, Vol. II 1992; London's Handwriting, 1995; contrib. jls, London, Budapest, Copenhagen, USA etc. *Recreation:* heuristics (productive laziness). *Address:* 29 Langton Way, SE3 7TJ. *Clubs:* Arts; Double Crown (Pres., 1989–90), Wynkyn de Worde (Chm., 1984–85); Rencontres Internationales de Lure. *Died 9 March 2002.*

BANNENBERG, Jon, RDI 1978; AMRINA; *b* Australia, 8 July 1929; *s* of Henryk and Kay Bannenberg; *m* 1960, Beaupré Robinson; two *s*. *Educ:* Canterbury High Sch., Sydney; Sydney Conservatorium of Music. RDI (Motor Yacht Design) 1978. Designed: 'Siècle d'Elégance' Exhibn, Louvre, Paris, 1959; CINOA Exhibn, V&A Museum, London, 1960; Eskenazi Gall., London, 1993; motor and sail boat designs include: Queen Elizabeth 2, 1967; Tiawana, Tamahine, 1968; Carinthia V, Anemos II, 1969; Benedic, 1970; Carinthia VI, Arjuna, Aetos, 1971; Blue Lady, Yellowbird, Firebird, Heron 21, 1972; Stilvi, Pegasus III, 1973; My Gail, Xiphias, Mediterranean Sky, 1974; Boule Dogue, Southern Breeze, 1975; Solitaire, 1976; Majestic, 1977; Rodis Island, Nabila, Cimba, 1979; My Gail II, Nahema, 1981; Acajou, Azteca, Paraiso, Bobbara, Three Y's, 1983; My Gail III, Cedar Sea, Shirley B, Highlander, Sterling One, Never Say Never, Garuda, 1985; Southern Cross III, Lady Ghislaine, 1987; Acharné, Starlight, 1988; Beaupré, Stefaren, G. Whiz, Mercedes, Mystique, 1989; Gee. Dee, Oceana, Opal C, 1991; Siran, Moecca, 1992; Coral Island, Kremlin Princess, 1994; Limitless, 1997; Thunder, 1998; Millennium, 1999; Multiple, 2002. Member, RYA. *Recreations:* running, swimming, sailing, music. *Address:* 35 Carlyle Square, Chelsea, SW3 6HA. *T:* (020) 7352 6129; 6 Burnsall Street, SW3 3ST. *T:* (020) 7352 4851, *Fax:* (020) 7352 8444. *Died 26 May 2002.*

BANNER, Josephina, (Mrs Delmar Banner); *see* Vasconcellos, J. de.

BANNON, John Kernan, ISO 1969; Director of Services, Meteorological Office, 1973–76; *b* 26 April 1916; *s* of Frederick J. Bannon, Clerk in Holy Orders and Eveline

Bannon, Muckamore, NI; *m* 1947, Pauline Mary Roch Thomas (*d* 2005), Pembroke; one *s* one *d*. *Educ:* Royal Sch., Armagh; Emmanuel Coll., Cambridge (Braithwaite Batty Scholar; BA (Wrangler) 1938). Technical Officer, Meteorological Office, 1938; commnd RAFVR, 1943–46 (Temp. Sqdn Ldr); Met. Office, 1946–76; idc 1963. *Publications:* some official scientific works; articles in meteorological jls. *Recreations:* walking, gardening. *Address:* 18 Courtenay Drive, Emmer Green, Reading RG4 8XH. *T:* (0118) 947 3696. *Died Oct. 2005.*

BARBARA, Agatha, KUOM 1990; social/welfare worker; President of the Republic of Malta, 1982–87; Chairperson, The Samaritans – Malta, since 1988; *b* Zabbar, 11 March 1923. *Educ:* Government Grammar School. ARP, 1940; Supervisor, Main Ammunition Depot, 1941–43. School teacher, 1944–46; entered politics, 1946; first woman Member of Parliament, 1947; became first woman Minister, in Labour Govt, 1955, as Minister of Education; also Minister of Educn, 1971–74; Minister of Labour, Culture, and Welfare, 1974–81. Was Acting Prime Minister of Malta on various occasions, and elected President of the Republic, 16 Feb. 1982. Patron: Ad Vitam St Michael's Band Club, Zabbar; Malta–China Friendship and Cultural Soc.; Boy Scouts Assoc., Malta, 1982 (Thanks Badge, 1986). Hon. Life Mem., Council of Women, Malta, 1986. Official Rep., World Inst. of Achievement, USA, 1992. Hon. Mem., European Community of Journalists, 1979. Hon. Academician: Accademia Universale A. Magno, Prato, Italy; Eur. Acad. of Lit., Sci. and Arts, Naples. Hon. PhD Univ. of Beijing, China, 1984. Keys and Freedom of: Lahore, Buenos Aires, Lima, San José, Bogotà and Montevideo, 1986; Aden, 1987. GCStJ 1996. Coronation Medal, 1953; Malta GC 50th anniv. medal for service in civil defence, 1992; 75th anniv. medal of re-introduction of self-govt in Malta, 1996. Stara Planina, 1st cl. with ribbon (Bulgaria), 1983; Order of National Flag 1st Class (Democratic People's Republic of Korea), 1985; Hishan-e-Pakistan (Islamic Republic of Pakistan), 1986; Sceptre of Authority of the Incas (Peru), 1986. *Recreations:* philately, classical and modern music. *Address:* Kenn Taghna, Wied Il-Ghajn Street, Zabbar, Republic of Malta.

Died 4 Feb. 2002.

BARBER, Baron *cr* 1974 (Life Peer), of Wentbridge, **Anthony Perrinott Lysberg Barber;** PC 1963; TD; DL; Chairman, Standard Chartered Bank plc, 1974–87; *b* 4 July 1920; *s* of John Barber, CBE, Doncaster; *m* 1st, 1950, Jean Patricia (*d* 1983), *d* of Milton Asquith, Wentbridge, Yorks; two *d*; 2nd, 1989, Mrs Rosemary Youens (*d* 2003), *d* of Rev. Canon Fearnly Youens. *Educ:* Retford Grammar Sch.; Oriel Coll., Oxford Univ. (PPE, MA) (Hon. Fellow 1971). Served War of 1939–45: commnd in Army (Dunkirk); seconded to RAF as pilot, 1940–45 (despatches; prisoner of war, 1942–45, took Law Degree with 1st Class Hons while POW, escaped from Poland, prisoner of the Russians). Barrister-at-law, Inner Temple, 1948 (Inner Temple Scholarship). MP (C): Doncaster, 1951–64; Altrincham and Sale, Feb. 1965–Sept. 1974; PPS to the Under-Sec. of State for Air, 1952–55; Asst Whip, 1955–57; a Lord Comr of the Treasury, 1957–58; PPS to the Prime Minister, 1958–59; Economic Sec. to the Treasury, 1959–62; Financial Sec. to the Treasury, 1962–63; Minister of Health and Mem. of the Cabinet, 1963–64; Chancellor of the Duchy of Lancaster, June-July 1970; Chancellor of the Exchequer, 1970–74. Chm., Conservative Party Organisation, 1967–70; Pres., Nat. Union of Cons. & Unionist Assocs, 1973. Dir, BP, 1979–88. Mem., Falkland Islands Inquiry (Franks Cttee), 1982. British Mem., Eminent Persons Gp on S Africa, 1986. Vice-Chm. Council, Charing Cross and Westminster Med. Sch., 1984–96 (Chm. Council, Westminster Med. Sch., 1975–84). Chm., RAF Benevolent Fund, 1991–95. DL W Yorks, 1987. *Publication:* Taking the Tide (memoirs), 1996. *Address:* House of Lords, SW1A 0PW. *Clubs:* Carlton, Royal Air Force. *Died 16 Dec. 2005.*

BARBER, John Norman Romney; company director and business consultant; *b* 22 April 1919; *s* of George Ernest and Gladys Eleanor Barber; *m* 1941, Babette Chalu (*d* 2003); one *s. Educ:* Westcliff. Served with Army, 1939–46 (Capt.). Min. of Supply, 1946–55 (Princ.); joined Ford Motor Co. Ltd, 1955, Finance Dir, 1962; Chm., Ford Motor Credit Co. Ltd, 1963; Dir, Henry Ford & Son Ltd, Cork, 1963; Dir, Autolite Motor Products Ltd, 1963; Finance Dir, AEI Ltd, 1965; Chm., Telephone Cables Ltd, 1967; Dir of Finance and Planning, 1968–71, Dep. Man. Dir, 1971–73, Dep. Chm. and Man. Dir, 1973–75, British Leyland Motor Corp. Ltd; Chairman, 1973–75: British Leyland International Ltd; Leyland Innocenti, SpA; Leyland Motor Corp. of Australia Ltd; Director: Leyland España SA; Automóviles de Turismo Hispano Ingleses SA; NZ Motor Corp. Ltd; British Leyland Motors Inc.; Metalurgica de Santa Ana SA. Chairman: Pullmaflex International Ltd, 1976–79; Aberhurst Ltd, 1976–88; A. C. Edwards Engineering Ltd, 1976–81; Cox & Kings Financial Services Ltd, 1980–85; C & K Executive Search Ltd, 1980–85; C & K Consulting Group Ltd, 1982–88; Director: Acrow plc, 1977–84; Good Relations Group plc, 1979–86; Amalgamated Metal Corp. Ltd, 1980–81; Spear & Jackson International plc, 1980–85; Economists Advisory Group Ltd, 1981–98; UK Investments Ltd, 1985–2001; The Communications Group Hldgs plc, 1990–; Deputy Chairman: Cox & Kings Ltd, 1980–81; John E. Wiltshier Group plc, 1980–88 (Dir, 1979–88). Mem., Royal Commn on Medical Educn, 1965–68; Chm., Adv. Cttee to BoT on Investment Grants, 1967–68; Mem., Adv. Council for Energy Conservation, 1974–75. Vice Pres., SMMT, 1974–76. CCMI (Mem. Council BIM, 1967–71). *Publications:* papers on management subjects in various jls. *Recreations:* motor sport, forestry, photography. *Address:* Woodpecker Lodge, Romsey Road, Ower, Romsey, Hants SO51 6AE. *Club:* British Automobile Racing. *Died 21 Oct. 2004.*

BARD, Dr Basil Joseph Asher, CBE 1968; innovation consultant, retired; Director, Scanning Technology Ltd, 1984–95; *b* London, 20 Aug. 1914; *s* of late Abram Isaac Bard and Anita Bard; *m* 1942, Ena Dora Birk; three *s. Educ:* Owen's Sch.; RCS (Imperial Coll.). BSc(Chem.), ARCS 1934, DIC (Chem. Engrg and Fuel Technology) 1935, PhD (Chem. Constitution of Coal) 1936, London; Bar Finals (1st cl. hons) and Studentship, Coun. of Legal Educn, 1937; called to Bar, Gray's Inn (Birkenhead and William Shaw Schol.), 1938. Practised at Bar, 1938–39; Legal Dept, Coal Commn, 1939–41; Explosives Prodn Dept, Min. of Supply, 1941–43; Materials Dept, Min. of Aircraft Production, 1943–45; Depts of Industrial Res., Educn, Design, etc, FBI, 1945–49; National Research Development Corporation, 1950–74: in turn, Commercial Man., Techn. Dir and Exec. Dir, Dept of Applied Science; Mem., 1956–73; Man. Dir, 1971–73; Exec. Dir, First National Finance Corp., 1974–76; Chm., Birmingham Mint Ltd, 1977–81. Director: Allied Insulators Ltd, 1975–77; Interflex Group, 1984–89; Chairman: NPM Gp, 1977–83; Xtec Ltd, 1983–86 (Dir, 1981–86); ProMicro Ltd, 1985–91. Founder and Chm., 1968–70, subsequently Vice-Pres., UK Licensing Execs Soc. (awarded Gold Medal 1973; Hon. Life Member, 1989). Consultant to UNIDO, 1972–74; Hon. Mem., Foundn for Sci. and Technol., 1990– (Hon. Treasurer, 1984–90); has served on various Govt Cttees. Pres., Jewish Meml Council, 1982–89; Vice-Pres., Anglo-Jewish Assoc., 1983– (Pres., 1977–83); Chm., Administration Cttee, UK Friends of Hebrew Univ. of Jerusalem, 1991– (Hon. Fellow, 1993; Life Gov., 1996). *Publications:* (ed) Industry and Research, 1947; (ed) The Patent System, 1975; various articles on science, technology, patents, industry, commerce and their inter-relationships. *Recreations:* music, bridge, chess, social life. *Address:* 23 Mourne House, Maresfield Gardens, Hampstead, NW3 5SL. *T:* (020) 7435 5340. *Club:* Athenæum. *Died 2 Feb. 2002.*

BARKER, Arthur Vincent, CBE 1974 (OBE 1955); Chartered Accountant; financial planning consultant; *b* 10 Nov. 1911; *e s* of late Arthur and Susannah Mary Barker; *m* 1936, Dorothy Drew; one *d. Educ:* Whitley and Monkseaton High Sch.; London Sch. of Economics. Qual. as CA, 1934; with Price Waterhouse & Co., 1934–35; with NAAFI in Middle East and UK, 1935–62 (Jt Gen. Man., 1955); British Railways: Member: Southern Region Bd, 1962–65; LMR Bd, 1965–68; Chm., Shipping and Internat. Services Div., 1968–69; Chairman: British Rail Hovercraft, 1970–71; British Transport Hotels Ltd, 1968–74; Mem., British Railways Bd, 1968–74. *Recreation:* fly-fishing. *Address:* 24 West Mount, The Mount, Guildford, Surrey GU2 5HL. *T:* (01483) 39524. *Died 4 March 2001.*

BARKER, Audrey Lilian; writer; *b* 13 April 1918; *d* of Harry and Elsie Barker; *m* 1942, Kenneth Bourne. *Educ:* County secondary schools in Beckenham, Kent and Wallington, Surrey. Editorial office, Amalgamated Press, 1936; Publisher's reader, Cresset Press, 1947; BBC, 1949–78. Mem. Exec. Cttee, PEN, 1981–85; Member Panel of Judges: Katherine Mansfield Prize, 1984; Macmillan Silver Pen Award for Fiction, 1986 and 1989. FRSL 1970. Atlantic Award in Literature, 1946; Somerset Maugham Award, 1947; Cheltenham Festival of Literature Award, 1963; SE Arts Creative Book Award, 1981. *Publications: collected stories:* Innocents, 1947; Novelette, 1951; Lost Upon the Roundabouts, 1964; Femina Real, 1971; Life Stories, 1981; No Word of Love, 1985; Any Excuse for a Party, 1991; Element of Doubt: ghost stories, 1992; *novels:* Apology for a Hero, 1950; The Joy-Ride (three novellas), 1963; A Case Examined, 1965; The Middling, 1967; John Brown's Body, 1969 (shortlisted for Booker Prize, 1969); A Source of Embarrassment, 1974; A Heavy Feather, 1978; Relative Successes, 1984; The Gooseboy, 1987; The Woman Who Talked to Herself, 1989; Zeph, 1992; The Haunt, 1999; *posthumous publication:* Submerged (collected stories), 2002. *Address:* Carshalton, Surrey. *Died 21 Feb. 2002.*

BARKER, Air Vice-Marshal John Lindsay, CB 1963; CBE 1946; DFC 1945; RAF (retired); *b* 12 Nov. 1910; *s* of Abraham Cockroft Barker and Lilian Alice (*née* Woods); *m* 1948, Eleanor Margaret Hannah (*d* 2001); one *s. Educ:* Trent Coll., Derbys; Brasenose Coll., Oxford. Called to the Bar, Middle Temple, 1947. RAFO, 1930, RAF, 1933. Served War of 1939–45: France, 1939–40; N Africa, 1942–44; Bomber Command, 1944–45; Far East, 1945–46; Palestine, 1946–48; Egypt, 1950–53; Air Attaché, Rome, 1955–58; Cmdr Royal Ceylon Air Force, 1958–63; Air Vice-Marshal, 1959; retd, 1963. Order of Merit, Italy, 1958. *Recreations:* golf, photography, sailing. *Address:* Wreyland Barn, Wreyland Way, Lustleigh, Devon TQ13 9TS. *T:* (01647) 277556. *Club:* Royal Air Force. *Died 7 May 2004.*

BARKER, Rear-Adm. John Perronet, CB 1985; RN retired, 1986; Administration Secretary, Missions to Seamen, 1987–93; *b* 24 June 1930; *s* of late Gilbert Barker and Dorothy G. Barker (*née* Moore); *m* 1955, Priscilla, *d* of late Sir William Christie, KCIE, CSI, MC; two *s. Educ:* Edgbaston Prep. Sch., Birmingham; Nautical Coll., Pangbourne; BRNC, Dartmouth. Entered RN, 1948; served, 1949–72: HMS King George V, Glory, Condor, Ceres, Lagos, Hampshire and Centurion; staff of C-in-C Home Fleet, of C-in-C Nore and of Comdr British Navy Staff, Washington; Sec. to ACNS (OR), MoD (Navy), to Flag Officer 2FEF, and to Flag Officer Plymouth; Sec. to Controller of the Navy, 1972–76; Student, RCDS, 1977; Dir, Fleet Supply Duties, MoD (Navy), 1978–80; Cdre, HMS Centurion, 1980–83; Chief of Staff to C-in-C, Naval Home Command, 1983–85. Member: IYRU World Youth Sailing, 1986–2002; Assoc. of RN Officers, 1987–; Sea Cadet Assoc., 1986–95; Life Rear Cdre, RNSA, 1986; Mgt Cttee, YMCA Fairthorne Manor, 1997–2002; Trustee, Whitby Mission and Seafarers' Trust, 1993–2003. Freeman, Co. of Shipwrights, 1983.

Recreations: sailing, gardening, DIY. *Address:* 25 Cambridge Road, Lee-on-the-Solent, Hants PO13 9DH. *Clubs:* Royal Yacht Squadron (Cowes); Royal Naval Sailing Association (Portsmouth); Midland Sailing (Birmingham). *Died 27 Dec. 2003.*

BARKER, Ronald William George, (Ronnie), OBE 1978; actor and writer; *b* 25 Sept. 1929; *s* of Leonard and Edith Barker; *m* 1957, Joy Tubb; two *s* one *d. Educ:* Oxford High Sch. Started acting career, Aylesbury Rep. Co., 1948. *Plays (West End):* Mourning Becomes Electra, 1955; Summertime, 1955; Listen to the Wind, 1955; Double Image, 1956; Camino Real, 1957; Lysistrata, 1958; Irma la Douce, 1958; Platanov, 1960; On the Brighter Side, 1961; Midsummer Night's Dream, 1962; Real Inspector Hound, 1968; The Two Ronnies, Palladium, 1978. *Films include:* Futtock's End, 1969; Robin and Marian, 1975; Picnic, 1975; Porridge, 1979; By the Sea, 1982; The Gathering Storm, 2002; My House in Umbria, 2004; *television: series:* Seven Faces of Jim, 1965; Frost Report, 1966–67; Hark at Barker, 1968–69; Six Dates with Barker, 1970; The Two Ronnies, 10 series, 1971–86; Twenty Years of the Two Ronnies, 1986; Porridge, 1974, 1975, 1976, 1977; Open All Hours, 1976, 1981, 1982; Going Straight, 1978; Clarence, 1987; *radio* includes: The Navy Lark, 1959–77. Scriptwriter as Gerald Wiley. Awards: Variety Club, 1969, 1974, 1980; SFTA, 1971; Radio Industries Club, 1973, 1974, 1977, 1981; Water Rats, 1975; British Acad. Award, 1975, 1977, 1978; Award for outstanding creative achievement, RTS, 1975; British Comedy Award for lifetime achievement, 1990; Lifetime Achievement Award, BBC, 1996. *Publications:* Book of Bathing Beauties, 1974; Book of Boudoir Beauties, 1975; It's Goodnight From Him, 1976; Sauce, 1977; Gentlemen's Relish, 1979; Sugar and Spice, 1981; Ooh-la-la!, 1983; Pebbles on the Beach, 1985; A Pennyworth of Art, 1986; Dancing in the Moonlight (autobiog.), 1993; All I Ever Wrote, 1999. *Recreations:* writing song lyrics, collecting postcards.
Died 3 Oct. 2005.

BARKER, Prof. Theodore Cardwell, PhD; FRHistS; Professor of Economic History, University of London, 1976–83, later Emeritus and engaged in research; *b* 19 July 1923; *s* of Norman Humphrey Barker and Louie Nettleton Barker (*née* Cardwell); *m* 1955, Joy Marie (Judith) Pierce. *Educ:* Cowley Sch., St Helens; Jesus Coll., Oxford (MA); Manchester Univ. (PhD). FRHistS 1963. Econ. History staff, LSE, 1953–64; first Prof. of Econ. and Social Hist., Univ. of Kent at Canterbury, 1964–76. President: Internat. Historical Congress, 1990–95 (Chm., British Nat. Cttee, 1978–93; Mem. Bureau, 1995–); Econ. Hist. Soc., 1986–89 (Hon. Sec., 1960–86); Railway and Canal Hist. Soc., 1986–88; Chairman: Management Cttee, Inst. of Historical Res., London Univ., 1977–88; Hist. Bd, CNAA, 1977–81; Management Cttee, London Univ. Business History Unit, 1979–86; Debrett's Business History Research Ltd, 1984–89; Athlone Press Adv. Cttee, 1988–. Chairman: Oral Hist. Soc., 1973–76; Transport History Res. Trust, 1991–97. Mem. Council, RHistS, 1967–70 and 1974–77. Hon. DLitt Manchester Metropolitan, 1998. *Publications:* A Merseyside Town in the Industrial Revolution (with J. R. Harris), 1954, repr. 1993; A History of the Girdlers Company, 1957; Pilkington Brothers and the Glass Industry, 1960; (with R. H. Campbell, Peter Mathias and B. S. Yamey) Business History, 1960, 2nd edn 1970; (with R. M. Robbins) A History of London Transport: Vol. I, 1963, Vol. II, 1974; (ed with J. C. McKenzie and John Yudkin) Our Changing Fare: two hundred years of British food habits, 1966; (with B. W. E. Alford) A History of the Worshipful Company of Carpenters, 1968; (ed) The Long March of Everyman, 1974; (with M. J. Hatcher) A History of British Pewter, 1974; (with C. I. Savage) An Economic History of Transport, 1975; The Glassmakers, 1977; The Transport Contractors of Rye, 1982; (ed with Michael Drake) The Population Factor, 1982; (ed) The Economic and Social Effects of the Spread of Motor Vehicles, 1987; Moving

Millions, 1990; (with Dorian Gerhold) The Rise and Rise of Road Transport 1700–1990, 1993; (ed with Anthony Sutcliffe) Megalopolis: the giant city in history, 1993; A Short, Illustrated and Updated History of Pilkington, 1994. *Recreations:* walking, motoring, visiting parts of Europe which many others do not reach. *Address:* Minsen Dane, Brogdale Road, Faversham, Kent ME13 8YA. *T:* (01795) 533523. *Club:* Reform (Mem., Gen. Cttee, 1997–). *Died 22 Nov. 2001.*

BARKSHIRE, Robert Hugh, CBE 1968; *b* 24 Oct. 1909; *yr s* of late Lt-Col Charles Robert Barkshire, OBE; *m* 1934, Sally (*d* 1992), *er d* of A. S. Blunt, Bedford; one *s. Educ:* King's Sch., Bruton. Bank of England, 1927–55: Private Sec. to the Governor (C. F. Cobbold, later Lord Cobbold), 1949–53; Sec. to Cttee of London Clearing Bankers, British Bankers' Assoc., Bankers' Clearing House, and Mem., various inter-Bank Cttees, 1955–70; Hon. Sec., Meetings of Officers of European Bankers' Assocs, 1959–72; Gen. Comr of Income Tax for City of London, 1969–78; Governor, NIESR, 1970–78. FCIB (FIB 1960). Freeman, City of London. *Address:* The Dower House, Headbourne Worthy, Winchester, Hants SO23 7LD. *Club:* Royal Thames Yacht.
Died 13 Nov. 2005.

BARLOW, Sir Thomas (Erasmus), 3rd Bt *cr* 1902; DSC 1945; DL; *b* 23 Jan. 1914; *s* of Sir Alan Barlow, 2nd Bt, GCB, KBE, and Nora (*d* 1989), *d* of late Sir Horace Darwin, KBE; *S* father, 1968; *m* 1955, Isabel, *d* of late Dr T. M. Body, Middlesbrough, Yorks; two *s* two *d. Educ:* Winchester College. Entered RN as cadet, 1932; qualified Submarines, 1937; served in Submarines in Atlantic, Mediterranean, Indian Ocean and Far East during War of 1939–45; Naval Staff Course, 1946; Joint Services Staff Course, 1947, Commander, 1950. British Joint Services Mission, Washington, 1950–53; Captain 1954; Imperial Defence Coll., 1957; Chief Staff Officer to Flag Officer Submarines, 1960–62; Commodore, HMS Drake, Devonport, 1962–64; retired, 1964. Actively concerned in Wildlife and Countryside Conservation: Berks, Bucks and Oxfordshire Wildlife Trust; Galapogos Conservation Trust. DL Bucks, 1977. Hon. DLitt Sussex, 1997. *Recreations:* bird watching, the countryside. *Heir: s* James Alan Barlow, *b* 10 July 1956. *Address:* 45 Shepherds Hill, Highgate, N6 5QJ. *T:* (020) 8340 9653. *Clubs:* Athenæum, Savile. *Died 12 Oct. 2003.*

BARNARD, Prof. Christiaan Neethling, MD, MMed, PhD; Professor of Surgical Science, Cape Town University, 1968–83, Professor Emeritus, 1984; Senior Consultant and Scientist in Residence, Oklahoma Heart Center, Baptist Medical Center, since 1985; *b* 8 Nov. 1922; *s* of Adam Hendrik Barnard and Maria Elizabeth Barnard (*née* De Swart); *m* 1st, 1948, Aletta Gertruida Louw (marr. diss. 1970); one *d* (one *s* decd); 2nd, 1970, Barbara Maria Zoellner (marr. diss. 1982; she *d* 1998); two *s*; 3rd, 1988, Karin Setzkorn (marr. diss. 1999); one *s* one *d. Educ:* Beaufort West High Sch.; Univ. of Cape Town (MB, ChB 1946, MD 1953; MMed); Univ. of Minnesota (MS, PhD 1958). Private practice, Ceres, CP, 1948–51; Sen. Resident MO, City Hosp., Cape Town, 1951–53; subseq. Registrar, Groote Schuur Hosp.; Registrar, Surgery Dept, Cape Town Univ.; Charles Adams Meml Schol., Univ. of Minnesota, and Dazian Foundn Bursary for study in USA; US Public Health Grant for further res. in cardiac surgery; Specialist Cardio-Thoracic Surgeon, Lectr and Dir of Surg. Res., Cape Town Univ. and Groote Schuur Hosp., 1958; Oppenheimer Meml Trust Bursary for overseas study, 1960; Head of Cardio-Thoracic Surgery, Cape Town Univ. Teaching Hosps, 1961; Assoc. Prof., Cape Town Univ., 1962. Performed world's first human heart transplant operation, 3 Dec. 1967, and world's first double-heart transplant, 25 Nov. 1974. Hon. fellow or member various colleges, societies, etc. FACS 1963; Fellow NY Cardiological Soc. 1965; FACC 1967. Numerous hon. doctorates, foreign orders and awards (incl. Dag Hammarskjöld Internat. Prize and Peace Prize,

Kennedy Foundn Award, Milan Internat. Prize for Science), hon. citizenships and freedoms, medallions, etc. *Publications:* (with V. Schrire) Surgery of Common Congenital Cardiac Malformations, 1968; One Life, 1969; Heart Attack: You Don't Have to Die, 1971; South Africa: Sharp Dissection, 1977; Best Medicine, 1979; Good Life—Good Death, 1980; (jtly) The Arthritis Handbook, 1984; The Best of Barnard, 1984; The Living Body, 1984; Your Healthy Heart, 1985; The Second Life, 1993; Fifty Ways to a Healthy Heart, 2000; *fiction:* The Unwanted, 1974; In the Night Season, 1977; The Faith, 1984; The Donor, 1996; numerous contribs to med. jls. *Recreations:* viticulture, ornithology, farming. *Address:* 9 Higgovale Close, Upper Kloof Street, Higgovale, Cape Town, 8001, South Africa. *Died 2 Sept. 2001.*

BARNARD, Prof. George Alfred, DSc; Emeritus Professor of Mathematics, University of Essex; *b* 23 Sept. 1915; *s* of Frederick C. and Ethel C. Barnard; *m* 1st, 1942, Helen J. B. Davies; three *s*; 2nd, 1949, Mary M. L. Jones; one *s*. *Educ:* Sir George Monoux Grammar Sch., Walthamstow; St John's Coll., Cambridge (Math. Trip., Pt III, 1936; MA; Res. Studentship, spent at Grad. Sch. Princeton, NJ, USA, 1937–39). Plessey Co., Ilford, as Math. Consultant, 1940–42; Ministry of Supply Adv. Unit, 1942–45; Maths Dept, Imperial Coll., London: Lectr, 1945–47; Reader in Math. Statistics, 1948–54; Professor, 1954–66; Prof. of Mathematics, Univ. of Essex, 1966–75; Prof. of Statistics, Univ. of Waterloo, 1975–81. Visiting Professor: Yale, 1966; Univ. of Waterloo, 1972–73; Univ. of Nottingham, 1975–77. Member: UGC, 1967–72; Computer Bd, 1970–72; SSRC, 1971–74. Royal Statistical Society: Council Mem. and Vice-Pres., 1952, 1962, Pres. 1971–72 (Chm. Res. Sect., 1958; Guy Medal in Silver, 1958, in Gold, 1975); Hon. Fellow, 1993. Mem. Internat. Statistical Inst., 1952 (Hon. Mem. 1996); Statistical Adviser, Brit. Standards Instn (with Prof. E. S. Pearson), 1954; Chm. Inst. of Statisticians, 1960–62; President: Operational Res. Soc., 1962–64; Inst. of Mathematics and its Applications, 1970–71 (Gold Medal, 1986); Fellow: Amer. Statistical Assoc.; Inst. of Mathematical Statistics; Amer. Assoc. for Advancement of Science. Hon. Dr Math. Waterloo, 1983; DUniv: Open, 1986; Essex, 1994; Hon. DSc City, 1991. Deming Medal, Amer. Soc. for Quality Control, 1991. *Publications:* (ed) The Foundations of Statistical Inference, 1962; papers in Jl Royal Statistical Society, Technometrics, Biometrika. *Recreation:* viola playing. *Address:* Mill House, Hurst Green, Brightlingsea, Essex CO7 0EH. *T:* (01206) 302388. *Died 30 July 2002.*

BARNES, Peter; dramatist; *b* 10 Jan. 1931; *s* of Frederick and Martha Barnes; *m* 1958, Charlotte (*née* Beck) (*d* 1995); *m* 1995, Christie (*née* Horn); two *s* two *d* (of whom two *s* one *d* are triplets). *Educ:* Stroud Grammar Sch. 1st Play, Sclerosis, 1965. Writer: The Ruling Class, 1969; Leonardo's Last Supper, 1970; Noonday Demons, 1970; adapted and co-directed: Wedekind's Lulu, 1972; The Bewitched, 1974; adapted and dir., Feydeau's The Purging, 1976; directed: Wedekind's The Singer, 1976; Jonson's Bartholomew Fair, 1978, 1987; Marston's Antonio, 1979; Wedekind's The Devil Himself, 1980; adapted Jonson's The Devil is an Ass, 1977; directed: For All Those Who Get Despondent, 1977; Laughter!, 1978; Somersaults, 1981; Red Noses (Laurence Olivier Award for Best Play), 1985; adapted Feydeau's Scenes from a Marriage, 1986; directed: The Spirit of Man (TV plays), 1989; Nobody Here But Us Chickens (TV plays) (RTS Award for Best TV Play), 1990; Sunsets and Glories, 1990; adapted Ninagawa's Tango at the End of Winter, 1991; dir, Bye Bye Columbus (TV play), 1992; adapted Enchanted April (film), 1993; adapted and dir., Hard Times (TV play), 1994; writer and dir, Dreaming (play), 1999; writer, Jubilee (play), 2001. *Radio plays include:* My Ben Jonson, 1973; The Two Hangmen, from Wedekind and Brecht, 1979; Barnes' People One, 1981; The Jumping Minuses of Byzantinium, 1981 (Giles Cooper Radio Award); A Mad World My Masters, from

Middleton, 1983; Barnes' People Two, 1983; The Primrose Path, from Feydeau, 1984; The Old Law, from Middleton, Rowley and Massinger, 1986; Barnes' People Three, 1986; Don Juan and Faust, from Grabbe, 1987; The Magnetic Lady, from Jonson, 1987; More Barnes' People, 1989. *Publications:* The Ruling Class, 1969 (John Whiting Award; Evening Standard Award); Leonardo's Last Supper, 1970; Noonday Demons, 1970; Lulu, 1971; The Bewitched, 1974; The Frontiers of Farce, 1976; Laughter!, 1978; The Collected Plays, 1981; Barnes' People Two, 1984; Red Noses, 1985; The Real Long John Silver (Barnes' People Three), 1986; The Collected Plays, 1989, vol. II, 1993, vol. III, 1996; The Spirit of Man, 1990; Nobody Here But Us Chickens, 1990; Sunsets and Glories, 1991; Dreaming, 1999; Jubilee, 2001; To Be Or Not To Be, 2002. *Address:* 7 Archery Close, Connaught Street, W2 2BE. *T:* (020) 7262 9205; (agent) Jeanne Casarotto, Casarotto Ramsay Ltd, National House, 60–66 Wardour Street, W1V 3HP. *T:* (020) 7287 4450. *Died 1 July 2004.*

BARRACLOUGH, Sir Kenneth (James Priestley), Kt 1978; CBE 1967 (OBE 1945); TD; JP; Chief Metropolitan Magistrate 1975–78, retired; *b* 22 March 1907; *s* of Herbert Barraclough, Leeds; *m* 1931, Gladys Evelyn (*d* 1996), *d* of Charles Henderson, Liverpool and Rio de Janeiro; two *s* one *d*. *Educ:* Oundle Sch.; Clare Coll., Cambridge. Barrister, Middle Temple, 1929 (Bencher, 1975); North Eastern Circuit. Inns of Court Regt, TA, 1938; Col 1945; HQ, 21st Army Group (despatches). Metropolitan Magistrate, 1954; Dep. Chm. Appeals Cttee, Hampshire QS, 1957–62; Chm., Home Office Poisons Board, 1958–76. Member: Adv. Cttee on Drug Dependence, 1966–70; Adv. Council on the Misuse of Drugs, 1972–73; Medicines Commn, 1969–75. JP Hampshire, 1957. *Address:* 18 Fitzroy Road, Fleet, Hants GU51 4JJ. *Died 3 April 2001.*

BARRAN, Sir David Haven, Kt 1971; Chairman, Midland Bank Ltd, 1980–82 (Deputy Chairman, 1975–80); *b* 23 May 1912; *s* of Sir John Barran, 2nd Bt and Alice Margarita (*née* Parks); *m* 1944, Jane Lechmere Macaskie; three *s* three *d* (and one *s* decd). *Educ:* Winchester; Trinity Coll., Cambridge (BA 1934). Joined Asiatic Petroleum Co., 1934; served in Egypt, Palestine, Sudan, India, 1935–46. Pres., Asiatic Petroleum Corp., New York, 1958; Man. Dir, Royal Dutch/Shell Group, 1961–72; Chm., Shell Oil Co., 1970–72; Director: Shell Transport and Trading Co. Ltd, 1961–83 (Dep. Chm., 1964–67; Chm., 1967–72; Man. Dir, 1964–73); General Accident Insurance; BICC; Glaxo Hldgs. Chairman: CBI Cttee on Inflation Accounting, 1973–74; Adv. Cttee on Appt of Advertising Agents, 1975–78 (Mem., 1973–78); Ct of Governors, Administrative Staff Coll., 1971–76; Governor, Centre for Environmental Studies, 1972–75. Pres., Embroiderers' Guild, 1982–87. Comdr, Order of Oranje Nassau, 1971; Comdr, Order of Merit, Fed. Repub. of Germany, 1980. *Address:* 36 Kensington Square, W8 5HP. *T:* (020) 7937 5664; Brent Eleigh Hall, Suffolk CO10 9NP. *T:* (01787) 247202. *Died 1 June 2002.*

BARRETT, Lt-Gen. Sir David William S.; *see* Scott-Barrett.

BARRETT, Spencer; *see* Barrett, W. S.

BARRETT, (William) Spencer, FBA 1965; Fellow, 1952–81 (Hon. Fellow, 1981), and Tutor in Classics, 1939–81, Keble College, Oxford; Reader in Greek Literature, University of Oxford, 1966–81; *b* 29 May 1914; *o s* of William Barrett and Sarah Jessie Barrett (*née* Robbins); *m* 1939, Georgina Margaret Elizabeth (*d* 1989), *e d* of William and Alma Georgina Annie Hill; one *s* one *d*. *Educ:* Derby Sch.; Christ Church, Oxford (Scholar; Ireland and Craven Schol. 1933; 1st Class Classical Hon. Mods 1934; Gaisford Prize for Greek Verse, 1934; de Paravicini Schol., 1934; 1st Class Lit. Hum. 1937; Derby Schol., 1937; Charles Oldham Prize, 1938). Lectr, Christ

Church, Oxford, 1938–39; Keble College, Oxford: Lectr, 1939–52; Librarian, 1946–66; Sub Warden, 1968–76; Univ. Lectr in Greek Literature, Oxford, 1947–66. Temp. Civilian Officer, Admty (Naval Intelligence Div.), 1942–45. *Publications:* (ed) Euripides, Hippolytos, 1964; Sophocles, Niobe (in Papyrus Fragments of Sophocles, ed R. Carden), 1974; articles in learned jls. *Address:* 8 The Avenue, Clifton, Bristol BS8 3HE. *T:* (0117) 974 3321.
Died 23 Sept. 2001.

BARRINGTON, Sir Alexander (Fitzwilliam Croker), 7th Bt *cr* 1831; *b* 19 Nov. 1909; *s* of Sir Charles Burton Barrington, 5th Bt, and Mary Rose (*d* 1943), *d* of Sir Henry Hickman Bacon, 10th and 11th Bt; *S* brother, 1980. *Educ:* Castle Park, Dalkey, Co. Dublin; Shrewsbury School; Christ Church, Oxford. Director of various private companies, 1932–39. Served in Army as Captain, Intelligence Corps, 1939–42; prisoner of war, Singapore and Thailand, 1942–45. Book publishers' executive, editor and production manager, 1946–72. *Recreations:* gardening, travel. *Heir: cousin* Benjamin Barrington [*b* 23 Jan. 1950; *m* 1980, Carola Christel Mogck; one *s* one *d*]. *Address:* Rush Court, Shillingford Road, Wallingford, Oxon OX10 8LL.
Died 6 Feb. 2003.

BARRON, (Thomas) Robert, CBE 1980; Member, British Railways Board, 1978–81; *b* 27 Dec. 1918; *s* of late Robert and Florence May Barron; *m* 1st, 1942, Constance Lilian Bolter (*d* 1997); one *s* three *d*; 2nd, 1997, Kathleen Lucy Corcoran. *Educ:* Dame Allan's Sch., Newcastle upon Tyne; King's Coll., Durham Univ. (BA 1st class Hons (Econ.)). Served RA and 1st Airborne Div., 1940–46. Joined LNER as Traffic Apprentice, 1946; Asst Gen. Manager, London Midland Region, 1966, Western Region, 1967; British Railways Board: Dir Management Staff, 1970; Controller of Corporate Planning, 1972; Dir of Planning and Investment, 1977. Exec. Dir, Channel Tunnel, 1981–82. Mem., NW Economic Planning Council, 1965–67. *Recreations:* music, fishing, watching sport. *Address:* 25 Shotford Road, Harleston, Norfolk IP20 9JN. *T:* (01379) 853625. *Died 9 April 2001.*

BARROW, John Frederick; HM Diplomatic Service, retired; *b* 28 Dec. 1918; *s* of Frederick William and Caroline Barrow; *m* 1947, Mary Roberta Young; two *d*. *Educ:* King Edward VII Sch., King's Lynn. Home Civil Service, 1936–39; war service in British and Indian Armies, 1939–46 (Major); rejoined Home Civil Service, 1946; Treasury, 1952–62; FCO, 1962; service overseas at Delhi, Kuala Lumpur, Jesselton, Prague, Washington, Hong Kong; retired as Counsellor, 1977.
Died 22 April 2004.

BARROWCLOUGH, Sir Anthony (Richard), Kt 1988; QC 1974; Parliamentary Commissioner for Administration, and Health Service Commissioner for England, Wales and Scotland, 1985–90; *b* 24 June 1924; *m* 1949, Mary Agnes Pery-Knox-Gore; one *s* one *d*. *Educ:* Stowe; New Coll., Oxford. Served RNVR, 1943–46 (Sub-Lieut and later Lieut). Called to the Bar, Inner Temple, 1949, Bencher 1982; Recorder, 1972–84. Part-time Mem., Monopolies Commn, 1966–69; Mem., Council on Tribunals (and Mem., Scottish Cttee), 1985–90; Indep. Mem. Council, FIMBRA, 1991–94. Chm., Dartmoor Steering Gp, 1990–99. *Recreation:* country pursuits. *Address:* The Old Vicarage, Winsford, near Minehead, Somerset TA24 7JF.
Died 3 June 2003.

BARTLEET, Rt Rev. David Henry; Bishop Suffragan of Tonbridge, 1982–93; *b* 11 April 1929; *s* of Edmund Arthur Bartleet and Helen Bartleet (*née* Holford); *m* 1956, Jean Mary (*née* Rees); one *s* two *d*. *Educ:* St Edward's School, Oxford; AA School of Architecture, London; St Peter's Hall, Oxford; Westcott House, Cambridge. Curate: St Mary-le-Tower, Ipswich, 1957–60; St George's, Doncaster (in charge of St Edmund's), 1960–64; Vicar: Edenbridge, Kent, 1964–73; Bromley, Kent, 1973–82. *Recreations:* music, architecture, icons. *Address:* 21 Lee

Road, Aldeburgh, Suffolk IP15 5EY. *T:* (01728) 452724.
Died 1 Nov. 2002.

BARTLETT, Maj.-Gen. John Leonard, CB 1985; Paymaster-in-Chief and Inspector of Army Pay Services, 1983–86, retired; *b* 17 Aug. 1926; *s* of late F. Bartlett and E. Bartlett; *m* 1952, Pauline (*née* Waite); two *s*. *Educ:* Holt Grammar Sch., Liverpool. MBCS, FCMI; jssc, psc, pfc. Commissioned Royal Army Pay Corps, 1946; served Hong Kong, Singapore, BAOR, War Office, Washington, Malta, Libya, HQ MELF, 1966–67 (despatches 1968); Staff Pmr and O i/c FBPO Berlin, 1968–69; GSO1 (Secretary) NATO Mil. Agency for Standardisation, 1969–71; Comd Pmr, Hong Kong, 1972–74; Col GS, MoD (ADP Coord.), 1974–76; Chief Pmr ADP and Station Comdr, Worthy Down, 1976–79; Chief Pmr, BAOR, 1980–82. Col Comdt, RAPC, 1987–90. Freeman, City of London, 1984. *Recreation:* golf. *Address:* c/o Lloyds TSB, The Square, Wickham, Hants PO17 5JQ. *Died 9 April 2004.*

BARTLETT, Prof. Maurice Stevenson, DSc; FRS 1961; Professor of Bio-mathematics in the University of Oxford, 1967–75, then Emeritus; *b* 18 June 1910; *s* of W. S. Bartlett, Scrooby; *m* 1957, Sheila (*d* 1998), *d* of C. E. Chapman; one *d*. *Educ:* Latymer Upper Sch.; Queens' Coll., Cambridge (Wrangler, 1932; Rayleigh Prize, 1934; MA 1936). DSc London. Asst Lectr in Statistics, University Coll., London, 1933–34; Statistician, Imperial Chemical Industries, Ltd, 1934–38; Lectr in Mathematics, Univ. of Cambridge, 1938–47; National Service, Min. of Supply, 1940–45; Professor of Mathematical Statistics, Univ. of Manchester, 1947–60; of Statistics, Univ. of London (University Coll.), 1960–67. Vis. Prof. of Mathematical Statistics, Univ. of NC, 1946. Mem. Internat. Statistical Institute, 1949, Hon. Mem., 1980; President: Manchester Statistical Soc., 1959–60; Biometric Soc. (Brit. Reg.), 1964–66; Internat. Assoc. Statistics Phys. Sci., 1965–67; Royal Statistical Society, 1966–67. Foreign Associate, Nat. Acad. of Scis, USA, 1993. Hon. DSc: Chicago, 1966; Hull, 1976. Gold Medal, Royal Statistical Soc., 1969; Weldon Prize and Medal, Oxford, 1971. *Publications:* An Introduction to Stochastic Processes, 1955; Stochastic Population Models in Ecology and Epidemiology, 1960; Essays in Probability and Statistics, 1962; Probability, Statistics and Time, 1975; Statistical Analysis of Spatial Pattern, 1976; Selected Papers, 3 vols, 1988; papers on statistical and biometrical theory and methodology. *Address:* Overcliff, 4 Trefusis Terrace, Exmouth, Devon EX8 2AX. *Died 8 Jan. 2002.*

BARTON, Maj.-Gen. Francis Christopher, CB 1966; CBE 1964 (OBE 1960); Commandant, Joint Warfare Establishment, Old Sarum, 1964–66, retired; *b* 17 Jan. 1916; *s* of Rev. John Bernard Barton, Elphinstone House, Hastings; *m* 1939, Olivia Mary Darroll-Smith; two *d*. *Educ:* Haileybury Coll. 2nd Lieut, Royal Marines, 1934; Lt-Col, 1956; Brig., 1961; Maj.-Gen., 1964. Comd 45 Commando, RM, 1958–60; Comd 3 Commando Brigade, RM, 1962–63. Voluntary Help Organiser, Royal Victoria Hospitals, Bournemouth, 1967–80; Chm., Standing Conf., Voluntary Help Organisers, 1971–72. *Address:* Moorhaven, Frogham, Fordingbridge, Hants SP6 2AJ. *Died 26 April 2001.*

BARTON-CHAPPLE, Dame Dorothy; *see* Tutin, Dame D.

BARWICK, David Robert, CBE 1976; QC 1977; Governor of British Virgin Islands, 1982–86; *b* 20 Oct. 1927; *s* of Jack Barwick and Kathleen Barwick (*née* Gould); *m* 1951, Margaret (*née* Funnell); one *s* two *d*. *Educ:* Christchurch Boys' High Sch.; Univ. of New Zealand (LLB). Barrister and Solicitor of the Supreme Court of New Zealand. Private practice, NZ, 1953–56; Asst Attorney-General, Judicial Comr, British Solomon Islands, 1956–62; Judge of the High Court of Western Pacific, Gilbert and Ellice Islands, 1962–67; Parliamentary Draftsman, Solicitor-General, Secretary for Justice, Actg

Attorney-General, Malaŵi, 1967–76; Attorney-General: Solomon Islands, 1976; Cayman Islands, 1976–82. *Recreations:* painting, conchology, music, golf. *Address:* PO Box 11557, Airport Post Office, Grand Cayman, Cayman Islands. *T:* 9457431. *Club:* Royal Commonwealth Society.
Died 25 April 2001.

BASHFORD, Humphrey John Charles, MA; Headmaster, Hessle High School, 1964–81, retired; *b* 5 Oct. 1920; *s* of late Sir Henry Bashford, MD, FRCP, and Margaret Eveline Sutton; *m* 1942, Alyson Margaret Liddle; one *s* three *d* (and one *s* decd). *Educ:* Sherborne Sch.; Clare Coll., Cambridge. MA Cambridge 1950. Served War of 1939–45: commissioned 2nd Bn Oxford Bucks LI, 1941; GSO3 HQ Airborne Corps 1944–46. Senior History Master, Leys Sch., Cambridge, 1947; Part-time Tutor, WEA, 1950; Headmaster, Wellingborough Sch., 1956–64. *Recreations:* gardening, fly-fishing. *Address:* 11 Cowgate, Welton, Brough, N Humberside HU15 1NB.
Died 2 Aug. 2004.

BASKERVYLE-GLEGG, Maj.-Gen. John, MBE 1974; Senior British Loan Service Officer, Oman, 1990–93; *b* 10 Nov. 1940; *s* of late Lt-Col John Baskervyle-Glegg and Ethne Baskervyle-Glegg (*née* Woollan); *m* 1974, Jane Van der Noot (*d* 2003). *Educ:* Eton; rcds, psc, osc. Grenadier Guards, 1960; served UK, Germany, Cyprus, Far East, Africa; Staff Coll., 1974; Comd 1st Bn Grenadier Guards, Berlin and UK, 1980–82; RCDS, 1982–84; Comdr 24 Inf. Bde, Catterick, 1984–86; Comdr British Mil. Adv. Training Team, Zimbabwe, 1987–89. *Recreations:* music, gardening, all sports, travel. *Address:* c/o National Westminster Bank, PO Box 11, 16 Library Place, St Helier, Jersey JE4 8PD. *Clubs:* Cavalry and Guards, MCC; I Zingari, Free Foresters. *Died 30 Nov. 2004.*

BASOV, Prof. Nikolai Gennadievich; Order of Lenin, 1967, 1969, 1972, 1975, 1982; Hero of Socialist Labour, 1969, 1982; Order of the Patriotic War, 1st degree, 1985; Physicist, Russia; Member of the Praesidium of the Russian Academy of Sciences, 1967–90, Adviser, since 1990; Director, Institute of Quantum Radiophysics (formerly Quantum Radiophysics Division), P. N. Lebedev Physical Institute, since 1989; Professor, Moscow Institute of Physical Engineers; *b* 14 Dec. 1922; *s* of Prof. Gennady Fedorovich Basov and Zinaida Andreevna Molchanova; *m* 1950, Ksenia Tikhonovna Nazarova; two *s. Educ:* secondary; Kiev Military-medical Sch.; Institute of Physical Engineers, Moscow. Joined the P. N. Lebedev Physical Institute, Moscow, 1948: Vice-Dir, 1958–73; Dir, 1973–89; Head, Lab. of Quantum Radiophysics, 1963–. Deputy, USSR Supreme Soviet, 1974–89 (Mem., Praesidium, 1982–89). Mem., Expert Council for President of Russian Fedn, 1991–93, for Prime Minister of Russian Fedn, 1993–. Hon. Chm., All-Union Soc., Znanie, 1990– (Chm. Bd, 1978–90); Vice-Pres., WFSW, 1983–90 (Hon. Mem., 1990–; Vice-Pres., Exec. Council, 1976–83). Editor-in-Chief: Priroda (Nature), Popular Sciences Magazine, 1967–90; Soviet Jl of Quantum Electronics, 1971–; Jl of Soviet Laser Res., 1980. Corresponding Mem., USSR Acad. of Sciences, 1962; Academician, 1966; Mem., Russian Optical Soc., 1991–. Fellow: Optical Soc. of America, 1974 (Mem. 1972); Indian Nat. Sci. Acad., 1987; Member: Acad. of Sciences of GDR, 1967; German Acad. of Natural Scis, Leopoldina, 1971; Bulgarian Acad. of Scis, 1974; Royal Swedish Acad. of Engineering Sciences, 1975; Polish Acad. of Scis, 1977; Czechoslovakian Acad. of Scis, 1977 (Gold Medal, 1975); Hon. Member: Bulgarian Phys. Soc., 1972; Urania Soc., GDR, 1980; Eur. Acad. of Arts, Scis and Humanities, 1980; TIT Soc. (Soc. for Dissemination of Natural Scis), Hungary, 1981; Internat. Acad. of Sciences, 1989; European Acad. of Sci. and Arts, Salzburg, 1991; Russian Acad. of Natural Scis, 1992; Acad. of Scis, Belorussia, 1995; Acad. of Scis, Georgia, 1996. Hon. Mem., Mark Twain Soc., USA, 1977. Hon. Dr: Polish Mil.-Tech. Acad., 1972; Jena Univ., 1974; Prague Polytechnic Inst., 1975; Pavia Univ., 1977; Madrid Polytechnic Univ., 1985;

Karl-Marx Stadt Technical Univ., 1988. Awarded Lenin Prize, 1959; Nobel Prize for Physics (jointly with Prof. A. M. Prokhorov of the P. N. Lebedev Physical Institute, Moscow, and Prof. C. H. Townes of MIT Cambridge, Mass, USA), 1964; A. Volta Gold Medal, Italian Physical Soc., 1977; E. Henkel Gold Medal, GDR, 1986; Kalinga Prize, UNESCO, 1986; Gold Medal, Slovakian Acad. of Sciences, 1988; M. V. Lomonosov Gold Medal, Acad. of Sciences of USSR, 1989; State Prize, USSR, 1989; Edward Teller Medal for Achievements in Fusion Energy, 1991. Order of Kirill and Mephodii (Bulgaria), 1981; Comdr's Cross, Order of Merit (Poland), 1986. *Address:* P. N. Lebedev Physical Institute, Russian Academy of Sciences, Lenin Prospekt 53, Moscow, Russia.
Died 1 July 2001.

BASS, Godfrey; see Bass, H. G. M.

BASS, (Harry) Godfrey (Mitchell), CMG 1972; HM Diplomatic Service, retired; *b* 26 Aug. 1914; *s* of late Rev. Arthur Edward Bass and Mildred Bass; *m* 1948, Monica Mary (*d* 2001), *d* of late Rev. H. F. Burroughs (and eponym of the orchid *Oncidium flexuosum* x *Rodriguezia fragrans*); two *s* one *d. Educ:* Marlborough Coll.; Gonville and Caius Coll., Cambridge (BA 1937, MA 1940); St John's Coll., Oxford (BA by incorp. 1937). British Museum, Dept of Egyptian and Assyrian Antiquities, 1939; Admiralty, 1940; Dominions Office, 1946; Asst Sec., Office of UK High Comr, Australia, 1948–51; Mem. of Secretariat, Commonwealth Economic Conference, 1952 and Meeting of Commonwealth Prime Ministers, 1953; Counsellor, Office of UK High Comr, Calcutta, 1954–57; Dep. UK High Comr, Fedn of Rhodesia and Nyasaland, 1959–61; British Minister (Pretoria and Cape Town) in the Republic of S Africa, 1961–62; seconded to Central African Office, 1963–64; British Dep. High Comr, Ibadan, 1965–67; Head of Consular Dept, FCO, 1967–70; High Comr in Lesotho, 1970–73. Chapter Clerk, St George's Chapel, Windsor, 1974–77. Compiled index of hatchment mottoes, 1998. Silver Jubilee Medal, 1977. *Recreation:* birdwatching. *Address:* Tyler's Mead, Reepham, Norfolk NR10 4LA. *Died 27 Feb. 2002.*

BATCHELOR, Sir Ivor (Ralph Campbell), Kt 1981; CBE 1976; FRCPE, DPM, FRCPsych; FRSE; Professor of Psychiatry, University of Dundee, 1967–82, then Emeritus Professor; *b* 29 Nov. 1916; *s* of Ralph C. L. Batchelor, FRCSE, FRCPE, and Muriel (*née* Shaw); *m* 1941, Honor Wallace Williamson; one *s* three *d. Educ:* Edinburgh Academy; Edinburgh Univ. (MB ChB). FRCPsych 1971 (Hon. 1984). RAFVR, 1941–46; Sqdn Ldr, Comd Neuro-psychiatrist, CMF. Asst Phys. and Dep. Phys. Supt, Royal Edinburgh Hosp., and Sen. Lectr in Psychiatry, Univ. of Edinburgh, 1947–56; Phys. Supt, Dundee Royal Mental Hosp., 1956–62; Prof. of Psychiatry, Univ. of St Andrews, 1962–67. Member: Gen. Nursing Council for Scotland (Chm. Educn Cttee), 1964–71; Standing Med. Adv. Cttee, Scotland, 1967–74; Adv. Cttee on Med. Research, Scotland, 1969–73; Scottish Council for Postgraduate Med. Educn, 1970–79; Chief Scientist Cttee, Scotland, 1973–82. Mem., Med. Services Review (Porritt) Cttee, 1958–62; Chm., Cttee on Staffing Mental Deficiency Hosps, 1967–70; Member: Cttee on Nursing (Briggs Cttee), 1970–72; Cttee on the Working of the Abortion Act (Lane Cttee), 1971–74; MRC, 1972–76 (Chm. Clinical Research Bd, 1973–74, Chm. Neuro-Sciences Bd, 1974–75); MRC Health Services Res. Panel, 1981–82; Royal Commn on the Nat. Health Service, 1976–79; Indep. Sci. Cttee on Smoking and Health, 1980–86; UK Central Council for Nursing, Midwifery and Health Visiting, 1980–83; Scottish Hosp. Endowments Res. Trust, 1984–90; Trustee, Tobacco Products Res. Trust, 1981–96. Chm. Trustees, Orchar Art Gall., Dundee, 1980–87. *Publications:* (with R. N. Ironside) Aviation Neuro-Psychiatry, 1945; Henderson and Gillespie's Textbook of Psychiatry, 8th edn 1956 to 10th edn 1969; papers on clinical psychiatry and health services. *Recreations:* rural rambles and natural history.

Address: 55 Hepburn Gardens, St Andrews, Fife KY16 9LS. *T:* (01334) 473130. *Clubs:* Athenæum; Royal and Ancient Golf (St Andrews).   *Died 24 April 2005.*

BATEMAN, Leslie Clifford, CMG 1965; FRS 1968; Secretary-General, International Rubber Study Group, 1976–83; *b* 21 March 1915; *s* of Charles Samuel Bateman; *m* 1st, 1945, Marie Louise Pakes (*d* 1967); two *s*; 2nd, 1973, Mrs Eileen Joyce Jones (*née* Henwood) (*d* 2002); one step *s* one step *d*. *Educ:* Bishopshalt Sch., Uxbridge; University Coll., London (BSc 1st cl. Hons Chem., 1935; PhD and Ramsey Memorial Medal, 1938; DSc 1955; Fellow, 1974). Oriel Coll., 1940–41; Chemist, Natural Rubber Producers Research Assoc., 1941–53; Dir of Research, 1953–62; Controller of Rubber Res., Malaysia, 1962–74; Chm., Internat. Rubber R&D Board, 1962–74. Mem., Malaysian Govt Task Force on Rubber Industry, 1983. Hon. DSc: Malaya, 1968; Aston, 1972. Colwyn Medal, 1963, and Jubilee Foundn Lectr, 1971, Inst. of Rubber Industry. Hon. PSM, Malaysia, 1974. *Publications:* (ed and contrib.) The Chemistry and Physics of Rubber-like Substances, 1963; numerous scientific papers in Jl Chem. Soc., etc, and articles on technical-economic status of natural rubber and its developments. *Recreations:* cricket, golf and other outdoor activities. *Address:* 3 Palmerston Close, Welwyn Garden City, Herts AL8 7DL. *T:* (01707) 322391.   *Died 12 Oct. 2005.*

BATES, Sir Alan (Arthur), Kt 2003; CBE 1995; actor; *b* 17 Feb. 1934; *m* 1970, Victoria Ward (*d* 1992); one *s* (one twin *s* decd). *Educ:* Herbert Strutt Grammar Sch., Belper, Derbyshire; RADA. *Theatre:* English Stage Co. (Royal Court Theatre, London): The Mulberry Bush; Cards of Identity; Look Back in Anger; The Country Wife; In Celebration; London (West End): Long Day's Journey into Night; The Caretaker; The Four Seasons; Hamlet; Butley, London and NY (Evening Standard Best Actor award, 1972; Antoinette Perry Best Actor award, 1973); Poor Richard, NY; Richard III and The Merry Wives of Windsor, Stratford, Ont.; Venice Preserved, Bristol Old Vic; Taming of the Shrew, Stratford-on-Avon, 1973; Life Class, 1974; Otherwise Engaged, Queen's, 1975 (Variety Club of GB Best Stage Actor award, 1975); The Seagull, Duke of York's, 1976; Stage Struck, Vaudeville, 1979; A Patriot for Me, Chichester, Haymarket, 1983, transf. Ahmanson, LA (Variety Club of GB Best Stage Actor award, 1983); Victoria Station, and One for the Road, Lyric Studio, 1984; The Dance of Death, Riverside Studios, Hammersmith, 1985; Yonadab, NT, 1985; Melon, Haymarket, 1987; Ivanov, and Much Ado About Nothing, Strand, 1989; Stages, NT, 1992; The Showman, Almeida, 1993; The Master Builder, Haymarket, 1995, Toronto, 1996; Simply Disconnected, and Fortune's Fool, Chichester, 1996; Life Support, Aldwych, 1997; Antony and Cleopatra, Timon of Athens, RSC, 1999; The Unexpected Man, NY, 2001; Fortune's Fool, NY, 2002. *Films:* The Entertainer, 1960; Whistle Down the Wind, 1961; A Kind of Loving, 1962; The Running Man, The Caretaker, 1963; Zorba the Greek, Nothing but the Best, 1964; Georgy Girl, 1966; King of Hearts, Far from the Madding Crowd, 1967; The Fixer (Oscar nomination), 1968; Women in Love, 1969; The Three Sisters (National Theatre Co.), 1970; A Day in the Death of Joe Egg, The Go-Between, 1971; Second Best (also prod.), 1972; Impossible Object, 1973; Butley, 1974; In Celebration, Royal Flash, 1975; An Unmarried Woman, 1977; The Shout, 1978; The Rose, 1979; Nijinsky, 1981; Quartet, 1982; The Return of the Soldier, 1983; The Wicked Lady, 1984; Duet for One, 1986; Prayer for the Dying, 1987; We Think the World of You, 1989; Mr Frost, Dr M, 1990; Hamlet, 1991; Losing Track, Secret Friends, 1992; Shuttlecock, 1994; Silent Tongue, 1994; The Grotesque, 1996; The Cherry Orchard, 2000; Gosford Park, The Mothman Prophecies, The Sum of All Fears, 2002; Evelyn, 2003. *Television:* various plays; Plaintiff and Defendant, Two Sundays, The Collection, 1977; The Mayor of Casterbridge, 1978; Very Like a Whale, The Trespasser, 1980; A Voyage Round my Father, Separate Tables, An Englishman Abroad, 1983 (BAFTA Best TV Actor award, 1984); Dr Fisher of Geneva, 1984; One for the Road, 1985; Pack of Lies, 1988; The Dog It Was that Died, 1988; 102 Boulevard Haussmann, 1991; Unnatural Pursuits, 1992; Hard Times, 1994; Oliver's Travels, 1995; Arabian Nights, In the Beginning, 2000; Love in a Cold Climate, Prince and the Pauper, 2001; Bertie and Elizabeth, 2002. *Recreations:* swimming, driving, riding, reading. *Address:* c/o Chatto & Linnit, 123A Kings Road, SW3 4PL. *T:* (020) 7352 7722, *Fax:* (020) 7352 3450.
                          Died 27 Dec. 2003.

BATES, Sir Geoffrey Voltelin, 5th Bt *cr* 1880; MC 1942; *b* 2 Oct. 1921; *s* of Major Cecil Robert Bates, DSO, MC (3rd *s* of 2nd Bt) and Hylda, *d* of Sir James Heath, 1st Bt; *S* uncle, 1946; *m* 1st, 1945, Kitty Kendall Lane (*d* 1956); one *s* (and one *s* decd); 2nd, 1957, Olivia Gwyneth Zoë (*d* 1969), *d* of Capt. Hon. R. O. FitzRoy (later 2nd Viscount Daventry); one *d* (and one *d* decd); 3rd, 1971, Mrs Juliet Eleanor Hugolyn Whitelocke-Winter (*d* 2003), *widow* of Edward Colin Winter and *d* of late Comdr G. C. A. Whitelocke, RN retd, and Mrs S. H. Whitelocke. *Educ:* Radley. High Sheriff, Flintshire, 1969. *Recreations:* hunting, shooting, fishing. *Heir:* *s* Edward Robert Bates, *b* 4 July 1946. *Address:* Gyrn Castle, Llanasa, near Holywell, Clwyd CH8 9BG. *T:* (01745) 853500.
                          Died 13 Feb. 2005.

BATES, James Patrick M.; *see* Martin-Bates.

BATES, Peter Edward Gascoigne, CBE 1987; Deputy Chairman, Plessey Electronic Systems Ltd, 1976–86; *b* 6 Aug. 1924; *s* of James Edward Bates and Esmé Grace Gascoigne Bates (*née* Roy); *m* 1947, Jean Irene Hearn, *d* of late Brig. W. Campbell Grant; two *s* one *d*. *Educ:* Kingston Grammar Sch.; School of Oriental and African Studies, Univ. of London; Lincoln Coll., Oxford. Served War, Intelligence Corps, SEAC and Japan, 1943–46; Captain 1945. Malayan CS, 1947–55; Rolls-Royce, Aero Engine Div., 1955–57; Bristol Aircraft (later British Aircraft Corp.), 1957–64, Special Director, 1963; joined Plessey Co., 1964: Gen. Man., Plessey Radar, 1967–71; Man. Dir, Radar Div., 1971–76. Mem., Adv. Cttee, Mitsubishi Electric Europe, 1991–99. Member: CBI Overseas Cttee, 1981–86; BOTB, 1984–87. Member: Council, Electronic Engrg Assoc., 1973–86 (Pres., 1976); Council, SBAC, 1978–86 (Pres., 1983–84); Pres., AECMA, 1985–86. *Publication:* Japan and the British Commonwealth Occupation Force 1946–1952, 1993. *Recreations:* golf, theatre, reading history and biography. *Address:* 22 Haygarth Place, Wimbledon, SW19 5BX. *T:* (020) 8946 0345. *Club:* Royal Wimbledon Golf.
                          Died 1 Sept. 2005.

BATH, Alan Alfred; Director, Education and Training, Commission of the European Communities, 1973–80; *b* 3 May 1924; *s* of Alfred Edward Bath and Doris Ellen Lawson; *m* 1st, 1946, Joy Roselle Thornton (*d* 1979), *d* of George Jeune, St Saviour, Jersey; one *s* two *d*; 2nd, 1987, Jill Diana Lesley Pearce, *d* of Eric and Nancy Douglas, Blandford Forum, Dorset. *Educ:* Frays Coll., Uxbridge; Queen's Univ., Belfast (BSc Econ). Commnd as pilot, RAF, 1942. Asst Lectr in Econs, QUB, 1950–53; Admin. Officer, Assoc. of Univs of British Commonwealth, 1953–58; Imperial Coll., Univ. of London, 1958–62 (Develt Sec., 1960–62); Sec., Cttee of Vice-Chancellors and Principals of Univs of UK, 1964–73; Sec., UK Nat. Delegn to Council of Europe Cttee for Higher Educn and Research, 1969–73. *Publication:* A Survey of the Work of the Winston Churchill Memorial Trust, 1985. *Recreations:* music, sailing, gardening. *Address:* 6 Sleepers Hill Gardens, Winchester, Hants SO22 4NT. *T:* (01962) 865848. *Clubs:* Athenæum, Royal Air Force.   *Died 8 July 2001.*

BATHURST, Sir Maurice (Edward), Kt 1984; CMG 1953; CBE 1947; QC 1964; *b* 2 Dec. 1913; *o* *s* of late Edward John James Bathurst and Annie Mary Bathurst; *m* 1941, Dorothy (marr. diss. 1963), *d* of late W. S. Stevens, LDS, RCS; one *s*; *m* 1968, Joan Caroline Petrie (*d* 1999).

Educ: Haberdashers' Aske's, Hatcham; King's Coll., London; Gonville and Caius Coll., Cambridge; Columbia Univ. LLB, First Class Hons. (London), 1937; University Law Schol. (London), 1937; Post-Grad. Research Studentship (London), 1938; Bartle Frere Exhibnr (Camb.), 1939; Tutorial Fellow (Chicago), 1939; Special Fellow (Columbia), 1940; LLM (Columbia), 1941; PhD (Camb.), 1949; LLD (London), 1966. Solicitor of Supreme Court, 1938–56. Called to Bar, Gray's Inn, 1957, Master of the Bench, 1970, Master of the Library, 1978–81. Legal Adviser: British Information Services, USA, 1941–43; British Embassy, Washington, 1943–46 (First Sec., 1944; Counsellor, 1946); Legal Mem., UK Delegation to United Nations, 1946–48; UK Rep., Legal Advisory Cttee, Atomic Energy Commission, 1946–48; Legal Adviser to British Chm., Bipartite Control Office, Frankfurt, 1949; Dep. Legal Adviser, CCG, 1949–51; Legal Adviser, UK High Commn, Germany, 1951–55; Judge, Supreme Court, British Zone, Germany, 1953–55; Legal Adviser, British Embassy, Bonn, 1955–57; British Judge, Arbitral Commn, Germany, 1968–69; Mem., Panel of Arbitrators, Internat. Centre for Settlement of Investment Disputes, 1968–87; a Pres., Arbitral Tribunals, Internat. Telecommunication's Satellite Orgn, 1974–78; Judge, Arbitral Tribunal and Mixed Commn for Agreement on German External Debts, 1977–88. Member UK Delegations to: UNRRA; United Nations San Francisco Conf.; Bermuda Civil Aviation Conf.; PICAO; Washington Financial Talks; UN Gen. Assembly; FAO; WHO; Internat. Tin Study Group; UK-US Double Taxation Treaty Negotiations; London Nine-Power Conf.; Paris Conf. on WEU; NATO Status of Forces Conf., Bonn. Internat. Vice-Pres., UN League of Lawyers; Vice President: Brit. Inst. of Internat. and Comparative Law; Acad. of Experts, 1988–92 (Hon. Fellow, 1992). Member: UK Cttee, UNICEF, 1959–84; Ct of Assistants, Haberdashers' Co. (Fourth Warden, 1973–74; Second Warden, 1978–79; First Warden, 1979–80; Master, 1980–81); Editorial Cttee, British Yearbook of International Law; *ad eundem,* Inner Temple; Gen. Council of the Bar, 1970–71; Senate of Inns of Court, 1971–73; Council of Legal Educn, 1971–79; Senate of the Inns of Court and the Bar, 1974–77. Hon. Vis. Prof. in Internat. Law, KCL, 1967–77; Hon. FKC. Chm. Governors, Haberdashers' Aske's Hatcham Schools, 1973–80. Pres., British Insurance Law Assoc., 1971–75. Freeman of the City of London and of the City of Bathurst, NB. Hon. DCL Sacred Heart, NB, 1946. *Publications:* Germany and the North Atlantic Community: a legal survey (with J. L. Simpson), 1956; (ed jtly) Legal Problems of an Enlarged European Community, 1972; notes and articles in British and American legal jls, etc. *Recreation:* theatre. *Address:* Airlie, The Highlands, East Horsley, Surrey KT24 5BG. *T:* (01483) 283269. *Club:* Garrick. *Died 28 Oct. 2004.*

BATTERSBY, Robert Christopher, CBE 1990 (MBE 1971); *b* 14 Dec. 1924; *s* of late Major Robert Luther Battersby, MM, RFA, late Indian Army, and Dorothea Gladys (*née* Middleton); *m* 1st, 1949, June Scriven (marr. diss.); one *d*; 2nd, 1955, Marjorie Bispham; two *s* one *d*. *Educ:* Firth Park Grammar Sch., Sheffield; Edinburgh Univ. (Gen Sciences); Fitzwilliam House, Cambridge (BA Hons Russian and Modern Greek 1950; Cert. of Educn 1952; MA 1954); Sorbonne; Toulouse Univ. (Cert. de Langue française, 1953); FIL 1958. Served Royal Artillery (Field) and Intelligence Corps, 1942–47 (Italian Campaign, Greece and Crete 1944, Central and Western Macedonia 1945–47); TA to 1952; Lieut RARO. Manager: Dowsett Gp of shipbuilding and civil engrg cos on major distant water trawler and pre-stressed concrete plant export contracts, 1953–63; Eastern Trade Dept, Glacier Metal Co. Ltd, 1963–66; Sales Dir, Associated Engrg Export Services Ltd, 1966–71; Sales Dir, GKN Contractors Ltd, 1971–73. Responsible for negotiating and installing USSR, Polish, Czechoslovak and Romanian plain bearing industries, Polish diesel engine component industry, and several other metallurgical and machining

plants in E Europe; Export, Financial and Commercial Adviser to various UK and USA cos. Mem. CBI and Soc. of British Engrs delegns to China, Poland, Yugoslavia and Singapore. Mem. Exec. Council, Russo-British Chamber of Commerce, and of London Chamber of Commerce Russian and Polish sections, 1968–73; Adviser to E European Trade Council, 1969–71. Principal Administrator: Credit and Investments Directorate-Gen., EEC Commn, Luxembourg, 1973–75; Agriculture Directorate-Gen., 1975–76; Fisheries Directorate-Gen., Brussels, 1976–79; Mem., first EEC Vice-Presidential delegn to Poland, 1977. MEP (C) Humberside, 1979–89; Mem., Agriculture and Budgetary Control Cttees, 1979; Chm., Fisheries Working Gp, 1979–84; Vice-Chairman: Fisheries Sub-Cttee, 1984–87; Budgetary Control, 1984–89; Vice-Pres., Eur. Parlt Delegn to China, 1981, 1984, and 1987, Eur. Parlt Delegn to USSR, 1987–89; Chief Whip, EDG, 1987–89. Contested (C) Humberside, Eur. Parly Elecn, 1989. Consultant on E Europe, 1990–; Special Advr on E Europe, Cons. Party, and Consultant to internat. orgns on E Europe, Russia and Central Asia, 1990–. Vice Pres., Yorkshire and Humberside Develt Assoc., 1980–87. Chm., Friends of Poland Assoc., Eur. Parlt, 1982–93. Occasional lectr at Farnham Castle and at American univs on East/West trade, and in Poland and USSR on automotive component manufg technology; broadcaster. Member: RIIA; Anglo-Hellenic Soc. FCMI (FBIM 1982). Order of European Merit, Luxembourg, 1981. KSG 1990. *Publications:* articles on fishing technology, shipbuilding and East/West trade; translations from Greek, Russian and other languages. *Recreations:* politics, European and Oriental languages, history, opera, music, travel. *Address:* 3 Ridgemount Way, Redhill, Surrey RH1 6JT. *T:* (01737) 213549, *Fax:* (01737) 213263. *Died 30 Sept. 2002.*

BATTY, Sir William (Bradshaw), Kt 1973; TD 1946; Chairman, Ford Motor Co. Ltd, 1972–75, retired (Managing Director, 1968–73); *b* 15 May 1913; *s* of Rowland and Nellie Batty; *m* 1946, Jean Ella Brice; one *s* one *d* (and one *s* decd). *Educ:* Hulme Grammar Sch., Manchester. Served War of 1939–45, RASC (Lt-Col). Apprentice toolmaker, Ford Motor Co. Ltd, Trafford Park, Manchester, 1930; Co. trainee, 1933; Press liaison, Advertising Dept, 1936; Service Dept, 1937; Tractor Sales Dept, 1945; Asst Man., Tractor Dept, 1948; Man., Tractor and Implement Product Planning, 1953; Man., Tractor Div., 1955; Gen. Man., Tractor Gp, 1961; Dir, Tractor Gp, 1963; Dir, Car and Truck Gp, 1964; Exec. Dir, 1963–75. Chairman: Ford Motor Credit Co. Ltd, 1968 (Dir, 1963–); Automotive Finance Ltd, 1970–75; Director: Henry Ford & Son Ltd, Cork, 1965–75; Ford Lusitana SARL, Portugal, 1973–75. Mem., Engineering Industries Council, 1975–76. Pres., SMMT, 1975–76. FCMI. Hon. LLD Manchester, 1976. *Recreations:* golf, sailing, gardening. *Club:* Royal Western Yacht. *Died 31 Oct. 2003.*

BAUER, Baron *cr* 1982 (Life Peer), of Market Ward in the City of Cambridge; **Peter Thomas Bauer,** DSc; FBA 1975; Professor of Economics, University of London, at the London School of Economics, 1960–83, then Emeritus Professor of Economics; Fellow of Gonville and Caius College, Cambridge, 1946–60, and since 1968; *b* 6 Nov. 1915; unmarried. *Educ:* Scholae Piae, Budapest; Gonville and Caius Coll., Cambridge (MA 1942). Reader in Agricultural Economics, University of London, 1947–48; University Lecturer in Economics, Cambridge Univ., 1948–56; Smuts Reader in Commonwealth Studies, Cambridge Univ., 1956–60. Hon. Fellow, LSE, 1997. *Publications:* The Rubber Industry, 1948; West African Trade, 1954; (with B. S. Yamey) The Economics of Underdeveloped Countries, 1957; Economic Analysis and Policy in Underdeveloped Countries, 1958; Indian Economic Policy and Devlopment, 1961; (with B. S. Yamey) Markets, Market Control and Marketing Reform, 1968; Dissent on Development, 1972; Aspects of Nigerian Development, 1974; Equality, the Third World and

Economic Delusion, 1981; Reality and Rhetoric: studies in the economics of development, 1984; articles on applied economics. *Address:* House of Lords, Westminster, SW1A 0PW. *Clubs:* Garrick, Beefsteak. *Died 3 May 2002.*

BAWN, Cecil Edwin Henry, CBE 1956; PhD; FRS 1952; Brunner Professor of Physical Chemistry in the University of Liverpool, 1969–Dec. 1973, then Emeritus (Grant-Brunner Professor of Inorganic and Physical Chemistry, 1948–69); *b* 6 Nov. 1908; British; *m* 1934, Winifred Mabel Jackson; two *s* one *d. Educ:* Cotham Grammar Sch., Bristol; Univ. of Bristol (BSc 1929; PhD in Chemistry, 1932). Asst Lectr in Chemistry, Univ. of Manchester, 1931–34; Lectr in Chemistry, 1934–38; Lectr in Physical Chemistry, Univ. of Bristol, 1938–45; Reader in Physical Chemistry, 1945–49. During War of 1939–45 was in charge of a Physico-Chemical Section in Armament Research Dept, Min. of Supply. Mem., Univ. Grants Cttee, 1965–74. Hon. DSc: Bradford, 1966; Birmingham, 1968; Bristol, 1974. Swinburne Gold Medal, 1966. *Publications:* The Chemistry of High Polymers, 1948; papers in chemical journals. *Address:* 1 Park Road, Crediton, Devon EX17 3BS. *Died 19 Sept. 2003.*

BAXTER, John Walter, CBE 1974; Consultant, G. Maunsell & Partners (Partner, 1955, Senior Partner, 1959–80); *b* 4 June 1917; *s* of late J. G. Baxter and late D. L. Baxter (*née* Phelps); *m* 1941, Jessie, *d* of late T. Pimblott; one *d. Educ:* Westminster City Sch.; City and Guilds Engrg College. BSc(Eng), FCGI, FEng, FICE, FRSA. Civil Engineer: Trussed Concrete Steel Co. Ltd, 1936–41; Shell Refining Co. Ltd, 1941–52; Maunsell Posford & Pavry, 1952–55. President: ICE, 1976–77 (Vice-Pres., 1973–76; Mem. Council, 1963–68 and 1970–79); Smeatonian Soc. of Civil Engrs, 1986; Vice-Chm., ACE, 1979–80, Chm., 1980–81. *Publications:* contrib. Proc. ICE. *Address:* The Check House, Beer Road, Seaton, Devon EX12 2PR. *T:* (01297) 24040. *Died 21 Oct. 2003.*

BAYLEY, Gordon Vernon, CBE 1976; FIA, FIMA, FSS; General Manager and Actuary, National Provident Institution, 1964–85; *b* 25 July 1920; *s* of late Capt. Vernon Bayley, King's Regt, and Mrs Gladys Maud Bayley; *m* 1945, Miriam Allenby, *d* of late Frederick Walter Ellis and Miriam Ellis, Eastbourne; one *s* two *d. Educ:* Abingdon. Joined HM Forces, 1940; commissioned Royal Artillery, Major 1945. Asst Actuary, Equitable Life Assurance Soc., 1949; Partner, Duncan C. Fraser and Co. (Actuaries), 1954–57; National Provident Institution: Assistant Sec., 1957, Joint Sec., 1959; Dir, 1970–94. Chm., Swiss Reinsurance Co. (UK), 1985–92; Dir, TR Industrial and Gen. Trust PLC, 1983–88. Mem., Occupational Pensions Bd, 1973–74. Member: Cttee to Review the Functioning of Financial Institutions, 1977–80; Companies House Steering Bd, 1988–90. Institute of Actuaries: Fellow, 1946; Hon. Sec., 1960–62; Vice-Pres., 1964–67; Pres., 1974–76; Chm., Life Offices Assoc., 1969–70 (Dep. Chm., 1967–68); Gold Medal, 1985. Chm., Bd of Governors, Abingdon Sch., 1979–83. *Publications:* contribs to Jl Inst. Actuaries, Jl Royal Statistical Soc. *Recreation:* sailing. *Address:* The Old Manor, Witley, Surrey GU8 5QW. *T:* (01428) 682301. *Clubs:* Athenæum, English Speaking Union; Sea View Yacht. *Died 25 March 2004.*

BAYNES, Sir John (Christopher Malcolm), 7th Bt *cr* 1801; Lieutenant-Colonel, retired; *b* 24 April 1928; *s* of Sir Rory Malcolm Stuart Baynes, 6th Bt and Ethel Audrey (*d* 1947), *d* of late Edward Giles, CIE; *S* father, 1979; *m* 1955, Shirley Maxwell, *o d* of late Robert Allan Dodds; four *s. Educ:* Sedbergh School; RMA Sandhurst; Edinburgh Univ. (MSc). Commissioned Cameronians (Scottish Rifles), 1949; served Malaya, 1950–53 (despatches); Aden, 1966; Defence Fellow, Edinburgh Univ., 1968–69; comd 52 Lowland Volunteers (TAVR), 1969–72; retired, 1972. Order of the Sword, 1st Class (Sweden), 1965. *Publications:* Morale, 1967, new edn 1987; The Jacobite Rising of 1715, 1970; History of the Cameronians, Vol. IV, 1971; The Soldier in Modern Society, 1971; Soldiers of Scotland, 1988; The Forgotten Victor, 1989; (ed jtly) A

Tale of Two Captains, 1990; No Reward but Honour?, 1991; Urquhart of Arnhem, 1993; Far from a Donkey: Gen. Sir Ivor Maxse, 1995; For Love of Justice, 1997; contribs to military and sporting jls. *Recreations:* shooting, fishing, golf. *Heir: s* Christopher Rory Baynes [*b* 11 May 1956; *m* 1992, Sandra Finuala Merriman; two *s* one *d*]. *Address:* Talwrn Bach, Llanfyllin, Powys SY22 5LQ. *T:* (01691) 648576. *Club:* Army and Navy. *Died 22 Jan. 2005.*

BEAGLEY, Thomas Lorne, CB 1973; Deputy Chief Executive, Property Services Agency, 1976–79; *b* 2 Jan. 1919; *s* of late Captain T. G. Beagley, Royal Montreal Regt; *m* 1942, Heather Blanche Osmond; two *s* one *d. Educ:* Bristol Grammar Sch.; Worcester Coll., Oxford (MA). Served War: 2nd Lieut, Northamptonshire Regt, 1940; Lt-Col, AQMG (Movements), AFHQ, Italy, 1945. Joined Min. of Transport, 1946; Cabinet Office, 1951–52; Min. of Defence, 1952–54; UK Delegn to NATO, 1954–57; UK Shipping Rep., Far East, 1960–63; Asst Under-Sec. of State, Dept of Economic Affairs, 1966–68; Under-Sec., Min. of Transport, 1968–71; Dep. Sec., Transport Industries, DoE, 1972–76. Member: Nat. Ports Council, 1979–81; Dover Harbour Bd, 1980–89. Chartered Institute of Transport: FCIT 1972; Pres., 1977; Award of Merit, 1988; Hon. Fellow, 1994. Pres., European Soc. of Transport Insts, 1984–90. Hon. FIRTE 1979. Viva Award for Transport Improvement, Carmen's Co., 1985. *Recreation:* galleries. *Address:* 3 Kings Ride House, 289 Sheen Road, Richmond, Surrey TW10 5AW. *T:* (020) 8876 1216. *Clubs:* Travellers; Richmond Golf. *Died 5 Jan. 2001.*

BEAL, Anthony Ridley; publishing consultant; Chairman: Heinemann Educational Books, 1979–84; Heinemann International, 1984–85; Managing Director, Heinemann Educational Books (International), 1979–84; *b* 28 Feb. 1925; *s* of Harold and Nesta Beal; *m* 1st, 1958, Rosemary Jean Howarth (*d* 1989); three *d*; 2nd, 1990, Carmen Dolores Carter (*née* Martinez). *Educ:* Haberdashers' Aske's Hampstead School; Downing College, Cambridge (scholar); 1st class English Tripos 1948. RNVR, 1943–46; Lectr in English, Eastbourne Training Coll., 1949; joined William Heinemann, 1949; Dep. Man. Dir, Heinemann Educational Books, 1962–73; Man. Dir, 1973–79; Dir, Heinemann Group of Publishers, 1973–85; Chairman: Heinemann Publishers (NZ), 1980–85; Heinemann Publishers Australia Pty, 1981–85; Ginn & Co., 1979–84. Chm., Educational Publishers' Council, 1980–83 (Vice-Chm., 1978–80); Mem. Council, Publishers' Assoc., 1982–86. *Publications:* D. H. Lawrence: Selected Literary Criticism, 1956; D. H. Lawrence, 1961; contrib to books on literature, education and publishing. *Recreations:* reading maps, travelling, thinking while gardening. *Address:* 19 Homefield Road, Radlett, Herts WD7 8PX. *T:* (01923) 854567. *Died 29 Oct. 2003.*

BEAMENT, Sir James (William Longman), Kt 1980; ScD; FRS 1964; Drapers Professor of Agriculture, University of Cambridge, 1969–89, then Emeritus; Life Fellow, Queens' College, Cambridge, since 1989; *b* 17 Nov. 1921; *o c* of late T. Beament, Crewkerne, Somerset; *m* 1962, Juliet, *y d* of late Prof. Sir Ernest Barker, Cambridge; two *s. Educ:* Crewkerne Grammar Sch.; Queens' Coll., Cambridge (Exhibnr 1941; BA 1943, MA 1946); London Sch. of Tropical Medicine; PhD London 1945; ScD Cantab 1960. Research Officer with Agricultural Research Council, Cambridge, 1946; Cambridge University: Univ. Lectr, 1961; Reader in Insect Physiology, 1966; Hd of Dept of Applied Biol., 1969–89; Queens' College, Cambridge: Fellow and Tutor, 1961; Vice-Pres., 1981–86. Member: Adv. Bd for the Res. Councils, 1977; NERC, 1970–83 (Chm., 1977–80). Mem., Composers' Guild of Great Britain, 1967. Scientific Medal of Zoological Soc., 1963. *Publications:* The Violin Explained, 1997; How We Hear Music, 2001; many papers on physiology in scientific jls; ed several review volumes; *music:* String Sextet, 1999.

Recreation: exposing musical fallacies. *Address:* 19 Sedley Taylor Road, Cambridge CB2 2PW. *T:* (01223) 562433; Queens' College, Cambridge CB3 9ET. *T:* (01223) 335511. *Died 10 March 2005.*

BEAMONT, Wing Comdr Roland Prosper, CBE 1969 (OBE 1953); DSO 1943, Bar 1944; DFC 1941, Bar 1943; DFC (US) 1946; FRAeS; author; *b* 10 Aug. 1920; *s* of Lieut-Col E. C. Beamont and Dorothy Mary (*née* Haynes); *m* 1st, 1942, Shirley Adams (*d* 1945); one *d*; 2nd, 1946, Patricia Raworth (*d* 1999); two *d*. *Educ:* Eastbourne Coll. Commissioned in RAF, 1939; served War of 1939–45, Fighter Command, RAF, BEF, Battle of Britain (despatches), Battle of France and Germany. Attached as Test Pilot to Hawker Aircraft Ltd during rest periods, in 1941 and 1943; Experimental Test Pilot, Gloster Aircraft Co. Ltd, 1946; Chief Test Pilot, English Electric Co., 1947–61; Special Dir and Dep. Chief Test Pilot, BAC, 1961–64; Director, Flight Operations, BAC Preston, later British Aerospace, Warton Division, 1965–78; Dir of Flight Operations, Panavia (Tornado testing), 1971–79. Events while Chief Test Pilot, English Electric Co. Ltd: 1st British pilot to fly at speed of sound (in USA), May 1948; 1st Flight of Britain's 1st jet bomber (the Canberra), May 1949; holder of Atlantic Record, Belfast-Gander, 4 hours 18 mins, Aug. 1951 and 1st two-way Atlantic Record, Belfast-Gander-Belfast, 10 hrs 4 mins Aug. 1952 (in a Canberra); first flight of P1, 1954 (Britain's first fully supersonic fighter); first British pilot in British aircraft to fly faster than sound in level flight, 1954, and first to fly at twice the speed of sound, Nov. 1958; first flight of Lightning supersonic all-weather fighter, 1957; first flight of TSR2, Sept. 1964 (Britain's first supersonic bomber). Britannia Trophy for 1953; Derry and Richards Memorial Medal, 1955; R. P. Alston Memorial Medal, RAeS, 1960; British Silver Medal for Aeronautics, 1965. Pres., Popular Flying Assoc., 1979–84. Master Pilot and Liveryman, Guild of Air Pilots. Hon. Fellow, Soc. of Experimental Testpilots, USA, 1985. DL Lancashire 1977–81. *Publications:* Phoenix into Ashes, 1968; Typhoon and Tempest at War, 1975; Testing Years, 1980; English Electric Canberra, 1984; English Electric P1 Lightning, 1985; Fighter Test Pilot, 1986; My Part of the Sky, 1989; Testing Early Jets, 1990; Tempest over Europe, 1994; Flying to the Limit, 1996; The Years Flew Past, 2001. *Recreation:* fly-fishing. *Address:* 5 Earls Manor Court, Winterbourne Earls, Salisbury, Wilts SP4 6EJ. *Club:* Royal Air Force. *Died 19 Nov. 2001.*

BEAN, Hugh (Cecil), CBE 1970; violinist (freelance); Professor of Violin, Royal College of Music, since 1954; *b* 22 Sept. 1929; *s* of Cecil Walter Claude Bean and Gertrude Alice Chapman; *m* 1963, Mary Dorothy Harrow; one *d*. *Educ:* Beckenham Grammar Sch. Studied privately, and at RCM, London (principal prize for violin) with Albert Sammons, 1938–57; Boise Trav. Schol., 1952; at Brussels Conservatoire with André Gertler (double premier prix for solo and chamber music playing), 1952–53. National Service, Gren. Gds, 1949–51. Formerly Leader of Harvey Phillips String Orch. and Dennis Brain Chamber Orch.; Leader of Philharmonia and New Philharmonia Orch., 1957–67; Associate Leader, BBC Symph. Orch., 1967–69; Co-Leader, Philharmonia Orch., 1990–94, Leader Emeritus, 1994–. Formerly Member: Bean-Parkhouse Duo; Music Gp of London. Has made solo commercial records, and has performed as soloist with many major orchestras. Hon. ARCM 1961, FRCM 1968; Hon. RAM 2002. *Recreations:* design and construction of flying model aircraft; steam-driven passenger hauling model railways; gramophone record collection. *Address:* Rosemary Cottage, 30 Stone Park Avenue, Beckenham, Kent BR3 3LX. *T:* (020) 8650 8774. *Died 26 Dec. 2003.*

BEAN, Dame Marjorie (Louise), DBE 1995 (OBE 1981; MBE 1968); Education Officer, Department of Education, Bermuda, 1949–74; *b* 25 May 1909; *d* of E. H. Stuart Bean and Josephine Augusta Bean (*née* Wentworth). *Educ:*

Berkeley Inst., Bermuda (Cambridge Sch. Cert. 1924); Wilberforce Univ., Ohio (BSc *cum laude* 1932, Hon. DHum 1950); London Univ. (DipEd 1946); Summer Courses, Teachers' Coll., Columbia Univ., NY, 1938 and 1939. Primary Teacher, Berkeley Prep. Sch., Bermuda, 1925–28; Principal, Sandys Secondary Sch., Bermuda, 1932–36 and 1963–65 (seconded); English and Geography Mistress, Berkeley Inst., 1938–49. First female MLA (Senate), Bermuda, 1981. Founder: Bermuda Nat. Trust; Berkeley Educnl Soc.; Cttee of Six; Queen's Birthday Ball and Presentation of Debutantes. Distinguished Service Award, Salvation Army Adv. Bd; many other local honours and awards. *Recreations:* travel, voluntary, civic and community activities: Church, school, clubs and charities. *Address:* 3 Berkeley Mews, Pembroke, Bermuda. *Clubs:* Royal Commonwealth Society (Hon. Pres., Bermuda Br.), Business and Professional Women's Association (Bermuda). *Died 16 March 2001.*

BEARDMORE, Alexander Francis, OBE 1987; FREng, FIMechE, FIEE; Engineer in Chief, Post Office, 1981–91, retired; *b* 20 Feb. 1931; *s* of Alexander Beardmore and Alice Beardmore (*née* Turner); *m* 1959, Pamela Anne Cozens; two *d*. *Educ:* Mitcham County Grammar School; London Univ. (BScEng, MSc). Nat. Service, Royal Signals, 1954–56. Post Office, 1948–91: Research Engineer, 1948–68; Controller Marketing, London Postal Region, 1972–77; Asst Dir, equipment provision, 1977–81. Chm., Unit Load Tech. Cttee, British Materials Handling Board, 1981–91. FCMI. *Recreations:* National Trust, gardening, DIY, walking. *Address:* Three Gables, Cheltenham Road, Baunton, Cirencester, Glos GL7 7BE. *T:* (01285) 654361. *Died 3 May 2005.*

BEARNE, Air Vice-Marshal Guy, CB 1956; *b* 5 Nov. 1908; *y s* of late Lieut-Col L. C. Bearne, DSO, AM; *m* 1933, Aileen Cartwright (decd), *e d* of late H. J. Randall, Hove; one *s* two *d*. Commissioned RAF, 1929; served in various Bomber Sqdns, 1930–33; specialist armament course, 1933; armament duties, 1934–44; Bomber Command, 1944–45 (despatches twice); Staff Officer i/c Administration, RAF Malaya, 1946; Joint Services Staff Coll., 1947; Dep. Dir Organisation (Projects), 1947–49; Command of Central Gunnery Sch., 1949–51; SASO, Rhodesian Air Training Gp, 1951–52; AOC Rhodesian Air Training Gp, 1953; Dir of Organisation (Establishments), Air Ministry, 1954–56; Air Officer in Charge of Administration, Technical Training Command, 1956–61; retd, 1961. *Address:* The Hollies, 6 Bradford Road, Corsham SN13 0QR. *T:* (01249) 713539. *Died 1 Nov. 2005.*

BEATTIE, Hon. Sir David (Stuart), GCMG 1980; GCVO 1981; QSO 1985; Governor-General of New Zealand, 1980–85; Chairman, New Zealand International Festival of the Arts, since 1987; *b* Sydney, Australia, 29 Feb. 1924; *s* of Joseph Nesbitt Beattie; *m* 1950, Norma Macdonald, QSO, *d* of John Macdonald; three *s* four *d*. *Educ:* Dilworth Sch.; Univ. of Auckland (LLB). Served War of 1939–45, Naval Officer. Barrister and Solicitor; President, Auckland Dist Law Soc., 1964; QC 1965; Judge of Supreme Court, 1969–80. Chairman, Royal Commission on the Courts, 1977–78; Mem., Commn on Courts of Fiji, 1993–94. Chm., NZ Meat Industry Assoc. (Inc.), 1988–90; Pres., NZ Olympic and Commonwealth Games Assoc., 1989–. Chm., Sir Winston Churchill Memorial Trust Board, 1975–80; Pres., NZ Sports Foundn, 1977–80, 1986–93 (Chm. of Trustees, 1977–80). Hon. LLD Auckland, 1983. *Publications:* legal articles. *Address:* 18 Golf Road, Heretaunga, Wellington, New Zealand. *Died 4 Feb. 2001.*

BEATTIE-MORIARTY, Brigid Mary, CBE 1998; Principal, Burntwood School for Girls, Wandsworth, since 1986; *b* 9 Nov. 1938; *d* of Richard Sydney Green and Eileen Mary Green; *m* 1st, 1962, Alan James Beattie (marr. diss. 1979); one *s*; 2nd, 1979, Denis Edmund Hugh Moriarty; one *s*, and one step *s* one step *d*. *Educ:* Convent of Holy Family, Littlehampton; London Sch. of Econs (BA

Hons Hist. 1960); London Inst. of Educn (PGCE 1969); Special Dip., Oxford Univ. Dept of Educn, 1984. History teacher: Parliament Hill Sch., 1961–70; Henley Grammar Sch., 1972–74; Sen. Teacher, William Forster Sch., Haringey, 1974–75; Dep. Headteacher, Holland Park Sch., 1975–83; Advisory Teacher: Equal Opportunities, ILEA, 1984–85; ILEA Secondary Mgt Trng Team, 1985–86. Head Teacher Fellow, Roehampton Inst. Higher Educn, 1988–92. Member: DFEE Steering Gp Anti-Bullying Project, 1991–93; Understanding British Industry, 1992–94; BBC Educn Broadcasting Council, 1993–96; FEFC (Gtr London), 1994–99. Non-exec. Dir, Wandsworth Community Health Trust, 1993–99. Member: Gtr London Arts Council, 1989–90; Gulbenkian SW Arts Project, 1990–91; Corp., Westminster Coll. Further Educn, 1999–; Educn Cttee, Goldsmiths' Co., 1999–. FRSA 1991. *Publications:* contrib. Arts Rev., Jl NFER, TES. *Recreations:* biography, art, architecture, theatre, opera, interiors, landscape, the aesthetic in general. *Address:* 74 Addison Gardens, W14 0DR. *T:* (020) 7603 6522. *Club:* Hurlingham. *Died 7 March 2001.*

BEAUMONT, Christopher; see Beaumont, H. C.

BEAUMONT, Christopher Hubert; a Recorder of the Crown Court, 1981–98; *b* 10 Feb. 1926; *s* of Hubert and Beatrix Beaumont; *m* 1st, 1959, Catherine Sanders Clark (*d* 1971); two *s*; 2nd, 1972, Sara Patricia Magee; one *d.* *Educ:* West Monmouth Sch., Pontypool; Balliol Coll., Oxford (MA). Served RN, 1944–47 (Sub-Lieut RNVR). Called to Bar, Middle Temple, 1950. Asst Dep. Coroner, Inner West London, 1963–81. Chm., Agricultural Land Tribunal, Eastern Area, 1985–98 (Dep. Chm., 1979–85). *Publications:* Law Relating to Sheriffs, 1968; Town and Country Planning Act 1968, 1969; Housing Act 1969, 1969; Town and Country Planning Acts 1971 and 1972, 1973; (with W. G. Nutley) Land Compensation Act 1973, 1973; (with W. G. Nutley) Community Land Act 1975, 1976; (ed) Planning Appeal Decisions, 1986– (with W. G. Nutley, 1986–98). *Address:* White Lodge, Crescent Road, Alverstoke, Gosport, Hants PO12 2DJ. *T:* (023) 9258 3184. *Died 11 June 2005.*

BEAUMONT, His Honour (Herbert) Christopher, MBE 1948; a Circuit Judge, 1972–85; *b* 3 June 1912; *s* of late Gerald Beaumont, MC and bar, and Gwendolene Beaumont (*née* Haworth); *m* 1940, Helen Margaret Gordon Smail (*d* 2000), *d* of William Mitchell Smail; one *s* two *d.* *Educ:* Uppingham Sch.; Worcester Coll., Oxford. Indian Civil and Political Services, 1936–47; Private Sec. to Lord Radcliffe, Chm. of Indo-Pakistan Boundary Commn, 1947; Foreign Office, 1948–52. Called to the Bar, Inner Temple, 1951; Metropolitan Magistrate, 1962–72. Chm. of the London Juvenile Courts, 1964; Dep. Chm., North Riding QS, 1966–71; temp. Resident Judge, Cyprus, 1986. Mem., Parole Bd, 1974–76; a Chm., Police (Disciplinary) Appeal Tribunal, 1988–96. *Recreations:* travel in Europe, growing vegetables. *Address:* Mead House Cottage, Mariners Lane, Southend, Bradfield, Berks RG7 6HU. *T:* (0118) 974 4064. *Club:* Brooks's. *Died 10 May 2002.*

BEAVEN, John Lewis, CMG 1986; CVO 1983 (MVO 1974); HM Diplomatic Service, retired; Ambassador to Sudan, 1986–90; *b* 30 July 1930; *s* of Charles and Margaret Beaven; *m* 1960, Jane Beeson (marr. diss.); one *s* one *d*; *m* 1975, Jean McComb Campbell. *Educ:* Newport (Gwent) High Sch. BoT, 1946; RAF, 1948–50; Asst Trade Comr, British High Commn, Karachi, 1956–60; Second Secretary (Commercial), British High Commn, Freetown, 1961–64; First Secretary (Commercial): British High Commn, Nicosia, 1964–66; Nairobi, 1966–68; FCO, 1969–72; Head of Chancery, British Embassy, Jakarta, 1972–74; Counsellor (Economic and Commercial), British High Commn, Lagos, 1975–77; Dep. Consul General and Dir, British Trade Develt Office, NY, 1978–82; Consul-General, San Francisco, 1982–86. *Recreations:* music, needlepoint, walking. *Address:* 230 Scannell Road, Ghent, NY 12075–0354, USA. *T:* (518)

3922152; *e-mail:* beaven@att.net.
Died 11 April 2004.

BEAZLEY, Peter George, CBE 1993; *b* 9 June 1922; *s* of Thomas Alfred and Agnes Alice Mary Beazley; *m* 1945, Joyce Marion Sulman; one *s* two *d* (and one *d* decd). *Educ:* Highgate Sch.; St John Baptist Coll., Oxford (Final Hons PPE, MA). Captain, Rifle Brigade, served in N Africa, Italy, Austria, 1942–47. Joined ICI, 1947; served in UK, Portugal, Germany, Belgium and S Africa as Manager, Gen. Manager, Divl Bd Dir, Vice Chm. and Man. Dir of associated cos, 1948–77; retd from ICI 1978. MEP (C) Bedfordshire, 1979–84, Bedfordshire South, 1984–94. Member: European Democratic Gp Bureau, 1982–83; Economic and Monetary Affairs and Industrial Policy Cttee, European Parlt, 1984–94 (Vice Chm., 1984–89); European Parlt Portuguese Parlt Jt delegn, 1979–84; European Parlt Japanese delegn, 1985–89; Vice Chm., SE Asia delegn, 1989–94. MRI; Mem., RIIA (Res. Fellow, 1977–78). *Publication:* The Role of Western Technology Transfer in the Development of the Soviet Union's Chemical Industry (with V. Sobeslavsky), 1979. *Recreations:* golf, gardening. *Club:* Oriental.
Died 23 Dec. 2004.

BECK, (James Henry) John; Director of Industries and Farms, Prison Department, Home Office, 1976–80; *b* 5 April 1920; *s* of James Henry and Elizabeth Kate Beck; *m* 1942, Doris Peacock (*d* 1995); one *d* (and one *d* decd). *Educ:* Polytechnic Secondary Sch., Regent Street, W1. Entered Home Office as Clerical Officer, 1937; HM Forces, 1939; returned to Home Office as Executive Officer, 1946; Higher Exec. Officer, 1950; Sen. Exec. Officer, 1958; Principal, 1963; Asst Sec., 1968. *Address:* Scarlet Oaks, Ridgway, Pyrford, Woking, Surrey GU22 8PN. *T:* (01932) 346064. *Died 11 Oct. 2001.*

BECK, John; see Beck, James H. J.

BECKETT, Sir Martyn Gervase, 2nd Bt *cr* 1921, of Kirkdale Manor, Nawton, N Riding of Yorkshire; MC 1945; RIBA; architect; *b* 6 Nov. 1918; *s* of Hon. Sir Gervase Beckett, 1st Bt, and Lady Marjorie Beckett (*d* 1964), *e d* of 5th Earl of Warwick; *S* father, 1937; *m* 1941, Hon. Priscilla Brett (*d* 2000), *y d* of 3rd Viscount Esher, GBE; two *s* one *d.* *Educ:* Eton; Trinity Coll., Cambridge (BA). DipArch 1951; ARIBA 1952. Enlisted in Green Howards, 1939; commnd Welsh Guards, 1940; served War of 1939–45 (MC); Lieut (temp. Captain). Built or reconstructed several country houses and housing estates, hotels, libraries etc; works to over 100 listed buildings and for National Trust. Architect to King's College Chapel, Cambridge, 1960– (internal alterations and renovations to the Chapel, 1968; repairs to the Ballustrade, 1978–91); Consulting Architect to: Gordonstoun, 1954–58; Savoy Hotel Gp, 1981–94; Temple Bar Trust, 1983–93; Charterhouse, 1983; Ampleforth Coll., 1984–; Eton Coll., 1986–92; Rank Labs, 1987–; BRCS, 1994–. Exhibited: RA, London, provinces; one man exhibitions: Clarges Gall., 1980 and 1983; Soar Gall., 1986, 1988, 1990, 1992, 1994 and 1995; Gall. 19, 1999. Trustee: Wallace Collection, 1972–92 (Chm. 1976–92); British Museum, 1978–88; CPRE Trust, 1983–90; Chm., Yorkshire Regional Cttee, Nat. Trust, 1980–85; Member: N York Moor Nat. Park Cttee, 1972–78; Council of Management, Chatsworth House Trust, 1981–; President: Ryedale Br., CPRE, 1964–; Friends of York Art Gall., 1970–83. Mem. Council, RSPB, 1985–87. Trustee, D'Oyly Carte Charity Trust, 1988–. FRSA 1982; FAMS 1955. Freeman, City of London, 1986. *Recreations:* painting, photography, piano. *Heir:* *s* Richard Gervase Beckett, QC [*b* 27 March 1944; *m* 1976, Elizabeth Ann, *d* of Major Hugo Waterhouse; one *s* three *d*]. *Address:* 3 St Albans Grove, W8 5PN. *T:* (020) 7937 7834; Kirkdale Farm, Nawton, Yorks. *Clubs:* Brooks's, MCC. *Died 5 Aug. 2001.*

BEDDINGTON, Dr Rosa Susan Penelope, (Mrs R. A. Denniston), FRS 1999; Head, Division of Mammalian Development, MRC National Institute for Medical

Research, since 1993; *b* 23 March 1956; 2nd *d* of late Roy Julian Beddington and Anna Dorothy Beddington; *m* 1987, Rev. Robin Alastair Denniston. *Educ:* Sherborne Sch. for Girls; Brasenose Coll., Oxford (BA 1977; DPhil 1981). Research Fellow, Lister Inst. for Preventive Medicine, Oxford, 1983–88; Res. Scientist, ICRF, Oxford, 1988–91; Sen. Res. Fellow, Centre for Genome Research, Edinburgh, 1991–93. Internat. Schol., Howard Hughes Med. Inst., 1993–98; Vis. Prof., Miller Inst., Berkeley, Calif, 1996. Mem., editl adv. bds, various internat. learned jls. Mem., scientific adv. bds, various Eur. sci. insts and biotechnol. cos. Mem., EMBO, 1998. Waddington Medal, Brit. Soc. for Develtl Biol., 1999. *Publications:* contribs to learned jls. *Recreations:* painting, gardening. *Address:* MRC National Institute for Medical Research, The Ridgeway, Mill Hill, NW7 1AA. *T:* (020) 8959 3666. *Died 18 May 2001.*

BEDFORD, 13th Duke of, *cr* 1694; **John Robert Russell;** Marquess of Tavistock, 1694; Earl of Bedford, 1550; Baron Russell of Chenies, 1540; Baron Russell of Thornhaugh, 1603; Baron Howland of Streatham, 1695; *b* 24 May 1917; *er s* of 12th Duke and Louisa Crommelin Roberta (*d* 1960), *y d* of Robert Jowitt Whitwell; *S* father 1953; *m* 1st, 1939, Clare Gwendolen Hollway (*née* Bridgman) (*d* 1945); two *s*; 2nd, 1947, Lydia (marr. diss. 1960), *widow* of Capt. Ian de Hoghton Lyle, 3rd *d* of 3rd Baron Churston and late Duchess of Leinster; one *s*; 3rd, 1960, Mme Nicole Milinaire, *d* of Paul Schneider. Coldstream Guards, 1939; invalided out, 1940. *Publications:* A Silver-Plated Spoon, 1959; (with G. Mikes) Book of Snobs, 1965; The Flying Duchess, 1968; (with G. Mikes) How to Run a Stately Home, 1971. *Heir: s* Marquess of Tavistock, *b* 21 Jan. 1940. *Address:* Château des Ligures, 2 rue Honoré Labande, Monte Carlo, MC 98000, Monaco. *Clubs:* Brooks's, Pratt's. *Died 25 Oct. 2002.*

BEDFORD, 14th Duke of, *cr* 1694; **Henry Robin Ian Russell;** Marquis of Tavistock, 1694; Earl of Bedford, 1550; Baron Russell, 1539; Baron Russell of Thornhaugh, 1603; Baron Howland of Streatham, 1695; DL; Director, London Pacific Group Ltd (formerly Berkeley Govett & Co. Ltd), since 1985; *b* 21 Jan. 1940; *s* of 13th Duke of Bedford and Clare Gwendolen Hollway (*née* Bridgman); *S* father, 2002; *m* 1961, Henrietta Joan, *d* of late Henry F. Tiarks; three *s*. *Educ:* Le Rosey, Switzerland; Harvard University. Partner, De Zoete and Bevan, 1970–82; Chairman: Cedar Investment Trust, 1977–82; Berkeley Develt Capital Ltd, 1984–92; TR Property Investment Trust, 1982–89 (Dir, 1982–91); Director: Touche, Remnant Holdings, 1977–88; Trafalgar House Ltd, 1977–91; United Racecourses, 1977–94. Hon. Trustee, Kennedy Memorial Trust (Chm., 1985–90). Pres., Woburn Golf and Country Club. DL Beds, 1985. *Heir: s* Marquess of Tavistock [*b* 30 March 1962; *m* 2000, Louise, *d* of late Donald Crammond and of Dowager Lady Delves Broughton; one *d*]. *Address:* Woburn Abbey, Woburn, Bedfordshire MK17 9WA. *T:* (01525) 290666. *Clubs:* White's; Jockey Club Rooms; The Brook (New York). *Died 13 June 2003.*

BEDFORD, Eric, CB 1959; CVO 1953; Chief Architect, Ministry of Works, 1952–70; *b* 23 Aug. 1909; *m* Elsie Winifred Maynard (*née* Steel) (*d* 1977); one *d*. *Educ:* Thornton Grammar Sch., Bradford. ARIBA 1933 (Grissell Gold Medal, 1934). Joined Ministry of Works, 1936; was responsible for Min. of Works decorations for the Coronation, 1953; Chief Architect, Directorate General of Works, MPBW, 1963–70. Design projects included: reconstruction of private chapel, Buckingham Palace, 1962; Post Office Tower, London, 1964; British High Commn, Ottawa, 1964; Marsham Street Develt, 1970. *Address:* Milestone Cottage, Hanley Swan, near Malvern, Worcs. *Died 28 July 2001.*

BEELEY, Sir Harold, KCMG 1961 (CMG 1953); CBE 1946; HM Diplomatic Service, retired; *b* 15 Feb. 1909; *s* of Frank Arthur Beeley; *m* 1st, 1933, Millicent Mary Chinn (marr. diss. 1953); two *d*; 2nd, 1958, Mrs Patricia

Karen Brett-Smith (*d* 1999); one *d*. *Educ:* Highgate; Queen's Coll., Oxford (1st Cl. in Modern History, 1930). Asst Lectr in Modern History, Sheffield Univ., 1930–31; University Coll., London, 1931–35; Junior Research Fellow and Lecturer, Queen's Coll., Oxford, 1935–38; Lecturer in Charge of History Dept, University Coll., Leicester, 1938–39; Mem. of wartime organisation of Royal Institute of International Affairs, and subsequently of Foreign Office Research Dept, 1939–45; Mem. of Secretariat of San Francisco Conf. and of Preparatory Commission of UN, 1945; Sec. of Anglo-American Cttee of Enquiry on Palestine, 1946; entered Foreign Service, 1946; Counsellor of Embassy, Copenhagen, 1949–50; Baghdad, 1950–53; Washington, 1953–55; Ambassador to Saudi Arabia, May–July 1955; Asst Under-Sec., Foreign Office, 1956–58; Dep. UK Representative to UN, New York, 1958–61; UK Representative, Disarmament Conf., Geneva, 1964–67; Ambassador to the United Arab Republic, 1961–64, 1967–69. Lectr in History, Queen Mary Coll., Univ. of London, 1969–75. Pres., Egypt Exploration Soc., 1969–88; Chairman: World of Islam Festival Trust, 1973–96; Egyptian-British Chamber of Commerce, 1981–92. *Club:* Reform.

Died 27 July 2001.

BEER, Prof. (Anthony) Stafford; international consultant, cybernetics in management; Partner, Cwarel Isaf Institute, since 1999; Visiting Professor of Cybernetics: University of Sunderland, since 1997; Business School, University of Northumbria, since 1998; University of Stockholm, since 1999; *b* London, 25 Sept. 1926; *er s* of late William John and Doris Ethel Beer; *m* 1st, 1947, Cynthia Margaret Hannaway (marr. diss. 1968); four *s* one *d*; 2nd, 1968, Sallie Steadman (*née* Child) (marr. diss. 1995); one *s* two *d*; partner, Allenna Leonard, PhD. *Educ:* Whitgift Sch.; University Coll., London; MBA Manchester, 1970; DSc Sunderland, 2000. Lieut, 9th Gurkha Rifles 1945; Captain, Royal Fusiliers 1947. Man. of Operational Res. and Prodn Controller, S. Fox & Co., 1949–56; Head of Op. Res. and Cybernetics, United Steel, 1956–61; Man. Dir, SIGMA Science in General Management Ltd and Dir, Metra International, 1961–66; Develt Dir, International Publishing Corp.; Dir, International Data Highways Ltd; Chm., Computaprint Ltd, 1966–69; Advisor in Cybernetics to Ernst and Whinney (Canada), 1970–87; Dir, Metapraxis Ltd (UK), 1984–87; Chairman: Syncho Ltd (UK), 1986–99; Viable Systems Internat. (USA), 1987–88; Team Syntegrity Inc. (Canada), 1992–99. Visiting Professor: of Gen. Systems, Open Univ., 1970–71; of Cybernetics: Manchester Univ. Business Sch., 1969–94; Durham Univ. Business Sch., 1990–93; Res. Prof. of Managerial Cybernetics, European Business Sch., UC of Swansea, 1990–97. Scientific Dir, Project Cybersyn, Chile, 1971–73; Adjunct Prof. of Stats and Operations Res., Pennsylvania Univ. (Wharton Sch.), 1972–81, and of Social Systems Scis, 1981–87; Co-Dir, Project Urucib, Uruguay, 1986–87. Ex-Pres., Operational Res. Soc.; Ex-Pres., Soc. for Gen. Systems Res. (USA); Pres., World Orgn of Systems and Cybernetics (formerly of Gen. Systems and Cybernetics), 1981–; Mem. UK Automation Council, 1957–69. Governor, Internat. Council for Computer Communication, 1973–93. Hon. Chm., The Stafford Beer Foundn, 1986–. Hon. Prof., Orgnl Transformation, Business Sch. (formerly Sch. of Inf. Sci. and Technol.), Liverpool John Moores Univ. (formerly Liverpool Poly.), 1990– (Hon. Fellow, 1996). Installation of Requiem (ten interactive paintings), Liverpool Metropolitan Cathedral, 1992–93. FWA 1986; FRSA 1991. Freeman, City of London, 1970. Hon. Fellow, St David's UC, Wales, 1989. Hon. LLD Concordia, Montreal, 1988; Dr Econ. Scis *hc* St Gallen, Switzerland, 2000. Silver Medal, Royal Swedish Acad. for Engrg Scis, 1958; Lanchester Prize (USA) for Ops Res., 1966; McCulloch Award (USA) for Cybernetics, 1970; Wiener Meml Gold Medal for Cybernetics, World Orgn of Gen. Systems and Cybernetics, 1984. *Publications:* Cybernetics and Management, 1959; Decision and Control, 1966;

Management Science, 1967; Brain of the Firm, 1972, new edn, 1981; Designing Freedom, 1974; Platform for Change, 1975; Transit (poems), 1977, extended edn 1983; The Heart of Enterprise, 1979; Diagnosing the System, for organizations, 1985; Pebbles to Computers: the thread, 1986; To Someone or Other (paintings), 1988; How Many Grapes Went into the Wine: Stafford Beer on the art and science of holistic management, ed Harnden and Leonard, 1994; Beyond Dispute: the invention of team syntegrity, 1994; chapters in numerous other books. *Recreations:* spinning, yoga, classics, staying put. *Address:* Cwarel Isaf, Pont Creuddyn, Llanbedr Pont Steffan, Ceredigion, Wales SA48 8PG; 34 Palmerston Square, Toronto, Ontario M6G 2S7, Canada. *Club:* Athenæum.
Died 23 Aug. 2002.

BEER, James Edmund; Consultant: Nelson Hirst Group, 1978–88; Co-operative Bank Ltd, 1982–85; *b* 17 March 1931; *s* of Edmund Huxtable Beer and Gwendoline Kate Beer; *m* 1953, Barbara Mollie (*née* Tunley); two *s* one *d*. *Educ:* Torquay Grammar; Leeds Univ. (BA Hons 1998). IPFA, FRVA, MBCS, MCMI. Torquay Borough Council, 1951–54; Chatham, 1954–56; Wolverhampton, 1956–58; Doncaster, 1958–60; Chief Accountant, Bedford, 1960–62; Asst Borough Treas., Croydon, 1963–65; Dep. Treas., Leeds, 1965; Chief Financial Officer, Leeds, 1968; Dir of Finance, Leeds City Council, 1973–78. Director: Short Loan and Mortgage Co. Ltd, 1978–88; Short Loan (Leasing) Ltd, 1979–88; London Financial Futures Co. Ltd, 1982–88. Mem. Local Govt Financial Exec., CIPFA, 1974–78; Financial Adviser to AMA, 1974–78; Treas., Soc. of Metropolitan Treasurers, 1974–78; Member: LAMSAC Computer Panel, 1972–78; Yorks and Humberside Develt Assoc. London Section, 1970–; Past Examr, CIPFA; Adviser on Rate Support Grant, AMA, 1974–78; Treas., Leeds Grand Theatre & Opera House Ltd, 1974–78; Governor, Leeds Musical Festival, 1979–84. Freeman, City of London, 1972; Liveryman, Basketmakers' Co., 1982–92. *Publications:* contrib. professional jls. *Recreations:* theatre, swimming, Rugby (past playing mem., Torquay Athletic RUFC). *Address:* 48 High Ash Avenue, Alwoodley, Leeds LS17 8RG. *T:* (0113) 268 3907.   *Died 18 Nov. 2005.*

BEER, Stafford; *see* Beer, A. S.

BEEZLEY, His Honour Frederick Ernest; a Circuit Judge, 1976–93; *b* 30 Jan. 1921; *s* of Frederick William Beezley and Lilian Isabel (*née* Markham); *m* 1969, Sylvia Ruth (*née* Locke). *Educ:* Acton County Sch. Served War, Royal Signals, Combined Operations, 1941–46. Called to Bar, Gray's Inn, 1947; Resident Judge, Cambridge Crown Court, 1987–93. *Recreations:* Freemasonry, fly-fishing, horse racing, musician with Ely Military Band. *Address:* White Lodge, 25 Northwold, Ely, Cambridge CB6 1BG.
Died 29 Aug. 2003.

BEGG, Robert William, CBE 1977; DL; CA; Partner, Mann Judd Gordon, Chartered Accountants, Glasgow, 1951–86 (Consultant, Mann Judd Gordon, then Moores Rowland, 1986–95); *b* 19 Feb. 1922; *s* of David Begg, CA, FFA, and Elizabeth Young Thomson; *m* 1948, Sheena Margaret Boyd; two *s*. *Educ:* Greenock Acad.; Glasgow Univ. (MA 1942). Served Royal Navy, 1942–46, Lieut RNVR (despatches). Mem., Institute of Chartered Accountants of Scotland, 1948. Member: Glasgow Univ. General Council Business Cttee, 1973–76; Court, Glasgow Univ., 1986–90. Hon. Treasurer: Royal Philosophical Soc. of Glasgow, 1952–62; Royal Glasgow Inst. of Fine Arts, 1975–86 (Pres., 1987–90); Mem. Bd of Governors, Glasgow School of Art, 1955–77, Chm., 1970–76; Trustee: RIAS Hill House Trust, 1977–82; Pollok Trust, 1987–2001; Member: Council, National Trust for Scotland, 1984–90 (Mem. Exec. Cttee, 1985–90); Museums and Galls Commn, 1988–91. Gov. of Patrons, Nat. Galls of Scotland, 1984–97 (Mem., 1974–91, Chm., 1980–87, Bd of Trustees). DL Glasgow, 1996. DUniv Glasgow, 1990. *Recreation:* painting. *Address:* 3 Colquhoun Drive, Bearsden, Glasgow G61 4NQ. *T:*

(0141) 563 5705. *Clubs:* Art, XIII (Glasgow).
Died 1 March 2001.

BEHR, Norman Isaac, FRICS; Vice President, London Rent Assessment Panel, 1988–93 (Valuer Member, 1983–87); *b* 28 Sept. 1922; *s* of Moses and Sarah Behr; *m* 1950, Anne Laurette Hilton (*d* 1999). *Educ:* Haberdashers' Aske's Sch.; College of Estate Management. Chartered Surveyor. Articled, De Groot & Co., 1939–42; served War, RAOC, REME, 1942–46; joined Valuation Office, 1948; District Valuer and Valuation Officer, Westminster, 1965–67, City of London, 1967–70; Superintending Valuer, 1970; Asst Chief Valuer, 1977; Dep. Chief Valuer (Rating), 1981–83. First Prize, Chartered Auctioneers and Estate Agents Inst., 1941; Wainwright Prize, Royal Instn of Chartered Surveyors, 1950. *Recreations:* opera, cooking, computers. *Address:* 43 Netherhall Gardens, NW3 5RL. *T:* (020) 7435 9391.   *Died 30 May 2001.*

BEILL, Air Vice-Marshal Alfred, CB 1986; Appeals Secretary, King Edward VII's Hospital for Officers, 1987–96; *b* 14 Feb. 1931; *s* of late Group Captain Robert Beill, CBE, DFC and Sophie Beill; *m* 1953, Vyvian Mary Crowhurst Archer; four *d*. *Educ:* Rossall Sch.; RAF Coll., Cranwell. Commnd RAF, 1952; served, 1952–64: RAF Marham, Stafford and Fauld; HQ Air Forces ME, Aden; RAF Supply Control Centre, Hendon; student, RAF Staff Coll., Andover, 1964; HQ FEAF, Singapore, 1965–67; student, JSSC, Latimer, 1968; OC Supply and Movements Sqdn, RAF Scampton, 1968–69; HQ Maintenance Comd, 1969–70; DS JSSC (later NDC), 1970–73; Comd Supply Officer, HQ NEAF, Cyprus, 1973–75; Dir of Engrg and Supply Policy (RAF), 1976–78; student, RCDS, 1978; Dir of Movements (RAF), 1979–82; Dir of Supply Policy and Logistics Plans (RAF), 1982–84; Dir Gen. of Supply (RAF), 1984–87, retired. ADC to the Queen, 1974–75. Life Vice Pres., RAF Swimming Assoc., 1987– (Pres., 1982–87). *Address:* c/o Lloyds TSB, Cox's & King's Branch, 7 Pall Mall, SW1Y 5NA. *Club:* Royal Air Force.   *Died 14 Nov. 2001.*

BEISHON, (Ronald) John, DPhil; CPsychol, CEng; Director, Consumers' Association, 1987–94; Chief Executive, Association for Consumer Research, 1987–94; *b* 10 Nov. 1930; *s* of Arthur and Irene Beishon; *m* 1955, Gwenda Jean Solway; two *s* two *d*. *Educ:* Battersea Polytechnic; Univ. of London (BSc); Univ. of Birmingham; Univ. of Oxford (DPhil). MIM, AFBPsS. National Service, RASC, 1951–53; Technical Officer, ICI Ltd, 1954–58; Section Leader, BICC Ltd, 1958–61; Sen. Res. Asst, Oxford Univ., 1961–64; Lectr, Bristol Univ., 1964–68; Reader, Sussex Univ., 1968–71; Professor of Systems, Open Univ., 1971–80; Dir, Poly. of South Bank, 1980–85 (Hon. Fellow, 1986); seconded as actg Dir, 1985, Permanent Dir, 1986–87, Poly. of North London. Bd Dir, Internat. Consumer Res. and Testing Ltd, 1990–94; Director: New Statesman and Soc., 1995–96; Beishon Publications Ltd, 1995–; Chm., Experts (UK) Ltd, 1999–. Member, Executive Committee: Internat. Organisation Consumer Unions, 1987–94 (Hon. Sec., 1991–94); Rep., FAO and Codex Alimentarius, 1988–95); NHBC, 1988–91; Mem., Gatwick Airport Consultative Cttee, 1993– (Mem., Passenger Services Sub-Cttee, 1993–); Chm., Southern Customer Services Cttee, Ofwat, 1996–. Mem., Governing Bd, Brighton Univ. (formerly Brighton Poly.), 1985– (Chm., Audit Cttee, 1990–92); Chm., Bd of Management, Co-operative Coll., 1995–96. FRSA. Hon. Fellow, N London Univ. 1993. DUniv Central England, 1993. *Publications:* (ed with G. Peters) Systems Behaviour, 1973, 2nd edn 1976; articles in various jls. *Recreation:* squash. *Address:* 421 Ditchling Road, Brighton, East Sussex BN1 6XB. *Club:* Wig and Pen.
Died 28 April 2001.

BELCHER, Ronald Harry, CMG 1958; Under-Secretary, Ministry of Overseas Development, 1965–75; *b* 5 Jan. 1916; *s* of Harry Albert Belcher; *m* 1948, Hildegarde (*née* Hellyer-Jones) (*d* 2000); one *s*. *Educ:* Christ's Hosp., Horsham; Jesus Coll., Cambridge (BA (Hons Classics)

1937; Dipl. Class. Arch. Cantab 1938); Brasenose Coll., Oxford (BA 1938). Indian Civil Service, Punjab, 1939–48; Commonwealth Relations Office, 1948–65; seconded to Foreign Office for service in British Embassy, Washington, 1951–53; Private Sec., 1953–54; Asst Sec., 1954; Deputy High Commissioner for the UK in S Africa, 1956–59; Asst Under Sec. of State, CRO, 1960–61; British Dep. High Comr, Delhi, 1961–65. *Address:* Fieldview, Lower Road, Fetcham, Surrey KT22 9EJ. *Died 11 Oct. 2002.*

BELHAM, David Ernest, CB 1975; Principal Assistant Solicitor (Under Secretary), Department of Employment, 1970–77, retired; *b* 9 Aug. 1914; *s* of Ernest George Belham and Grace Belham (*née* Firth); *m* 1938, Eunice Monica (*née* Vine); two *s* two *d*. *Educ:* Whitgift Sch.; Law Society's Sch. of Law. Solicitor (Hons), 1937. Private practice, 1937–39. Served War, RAFVR, 1940–46. Entered Solicitor's Department, Min. of Labour, 1946; Asst Solicitor, 1962. *Address:* 26 The Chase, Findon, Worthing, W Sussex BN14 0TT. *T:* (01903) 873771. *Died 30 Jan. 2002.*

BELL, Archibald Angus; QC (Scot.) 1961; Sheriff of Glasgow and Strathkelvin (formerly Lanark) at Glasgow, 1973–95; *b* 13 April 1923; *o s* of James Dunlop Bell, solicitor, Ayrshire, and Katherine Rachel Gordon Miller; *m* 1949, Dorothy (marr. diss. 1972), *d* of Dr Pollok Donald, Edinburgh, and Mrs Dorothy Donald; two *s*. *Educ:* The Leys Sch., Cambridge; Univ. of St Andrews (MA 1947); Univ. of Glasgow (LLB 1949). Admitted to Faculty of Advocates, 1949. Served War, Royal Navy, 1941–45; Sub-Lieut RNVR. Reporter, Court of Session Cases, 1952–55; Standing Junior Counsel in Scotland: to Board of Trade, 1955–57; to War Dept, 1957–61. Comr under NI (Emergency Provisions) Act, 1973–75; Advr to Sec. of State, NI, 1974–75. Mem. Court, St Andrews Univ., 1966–70. Pres., Scottish Cricket Union, 1975. Contested (C and U) Maryhill Div. of Glasgow, 1955. *Publications:* For a Shilling of Reward, 1999; Blowing Bubbles, 2001. *Recreations:* watching the sun rise, getting fun out of games; formerly hockey and cricket blue, St Andrews, and Pres. UAU and Dramatic Soc. *Clubs:* MCC; Royal Scots (Edinburgh); Royal and Ancient (St Andrews); RNVR (Scotland). *Died 2 Oct. 2001.*

BELL, Prof. Colin Roy, FRSE; Principal and Vice Chancellor, University of Stirling, since 2001; *b* 1 March 1942; *s* of late Ernest Arthur Bell and Annie Bell (*née* Chaplin); *m* 1st, 1964, Jocelyn Mumford (marr. diss. 1986); one *s* one *d*; 2nd, 1987, Janette Webb; two *d*. *Educ:* Judd Sch., Tonbridge; Univ. of Keele (BA 1964); Univ. of Wales (MSc Econs 1966). Lectr, 1968–71, Sen. Lectr, 1971–73, Reader, 1973–75, Univ. of Essex; Prof. of Sociology, Univ. of NSW, 1975–79; Prof. of Sociology, Univ. of Aston, 1980–84; Social Scientist, Univ. of Leicester Med. Sch., 1985–86; Res. Fellow, Centre for Educnl Sociology, Univ. of Edinburgh, 1986–88; Prof. of Sociology, 1988–98, Vice Principal, 1993–98, Univ. of Edinburgh; Vice Chancellor and Principal, Univ. of Bradford, 1998–2001. Mem., SHEFC, 1999–. FRSE 1992; FRSA 1998; Founding AcSS 1999. *Publications:* Middle Class Families, 1968; Community Studies, 1971; Power, Persistence and Change, 1975; Doing Sociological Research, 1977; Property, Paternalism and Power, 1977; Social Researching, 1984; articles in sociology and policy jls. *Recreations:* jazz, blues, domestic pursuits. *Address:* University of Stirling, Stirling FK9 4LA. *T:* (01786) 467011. *Died 24 April 2003.*

BELL, Edith Alice, OBE 1981; Chief Nursing Officer, Welsh Office, 1972–81; *b* 14 Sept. 1919; *d* of George and Alice Bell. *Educ:* Girls' Grammar Sch., Lancaster. SRN University Hosp., Leeds; SCM St Luke's Hosp., Bradford; Cert. Royal Medico Psychological Assoc., Westwood Hosp., Bradford; Registered Nurse, Mentally Subnormal, Aston Hall, Derby. Ward Sister, Aston Hall Hosp., Derby, 1941–43; Sen. Asst Matron, Royal Albert Hosp., Lancaster, 1943–46; Dep. Matron, Darenth Park Hosp., Dartford, 1946–48; Gp Matron, Fountain Gp HMC,

London, 1948–60; Management Services Officer, SE RHB, Scotland, 1960–63; Chief Regional Nursing Officer, E Anglian RHB, 1963–72. WHO Fellowship, 1951. Past Member: Gen. Nursing Council, England and Wales; Nat. Council of Nurses; Standing Nursing Adv. Cttee; Services Cttee, Internat. Council of Nurses; Jt Bd, Clinical Nursing Studies; Council, Queen's Inst. of Dist Nursing Service; SW Metrop. RHB: Nursing, Research and Trng Cttees. Chairman: Mental Nurses Cttee; Jt Organizations; Reg. Nursing Officers Gp; Royal Coll. of Nursing Br. Mem., NHS Reorganization Steering Cttee. Hon. Sec., Mental Hosp. Matrons Assoc.; Pres., Inst. of Religion and Medicine. Chm., CS Retirement Fellowship Gp, 1987– (Chm., N Lancs and S Cumbria Br., 1989–); Mem., Cttee of Management, 1988–93; Welfare Cttee, 1988–93, Standing Orders Cttee, 1993–99). Chm., Old Girls' Assoc., Girls' Grammar Sch., Lancaster, 1987–95 (Mem. Cttee, 1995–). *Publications:* contribs to professional jls. *Recreations:* reading, travel, gardening, supporting ecumenical activities. *Address:* Tyla Teg, 51 Farmdale Road, Newlands, Lancaster LA1 4JB. *Club:* Civil Service. *Died 6 July 2003.*

BELL, Sir Ewart; see Bell, Sir W. E.

BELL, Sir (George) Raymond, KCMG 1973; CB 1967; Vice-President, European Investment Bank, 1973–78, Hon. Vice-President, 1978; *b* 13 March 1916; *e s* of late William Bell and Christabel Bell (*née* Appleton); *m* 1944, Joan Elizabeth, *o d* of late W. G. Coltham and Christina Coltham; two *s* two *d*. *Educ:* Bradford Grammar Sch.; St John's Coll., Cambridge (Scholar). Served War 1941–44, Royal Navy (Lieut RNVR). Entered Civil Service, Assistant Principal, 1938; Min. of Health, 1938; transf. Treasury, 1939; Principal, Civil Service, 1945; Asst Sec., 1951; Under-Sec., 1960; Dep. Sec., 1966; Dep. Sec. HM Treasury, 1966–72. Sec. (Finance), Office of HM High Commissioner for the UK in Canada, 1945–48; Counsellor, UK Permanent Delegn to OEEC/NATO, Paris, 1953–56; Principal Private Sec. to Chancellor of Exchequer, 1958–60. Mem. UK Delegation to Brussels Conference, 1961–62 and 1970–72. *Recreations:* music, reading, travel. *Address:* Quartier des Bories, Aouste-sur-Sye, 26400 Crest, Drôme, France. *T:* 475252694. *Died 18 Feb. 2002.*

BELL, Rear-Adm. John Anthony, CB 1977; Research Fellow, Exeter University, 1986–89, retired; Director, Naval Education Service, 1975–78; Chief Naval Instructor Officer, 1978–79; *b* 25 Nov. 1924; *s* of Mathew Bell, Dundee, and Mary Ann Ellen Bell (*née* Goss), London; *m* 1946, Eileen Joan Woodman; two *d* (and one *d* decd). *Educ:* St Ignatius Coll., Stamford Hill; London Univ. BA, BSc, LLB. Barrister, Gray's Inn, 1970. RM 1943–45; Schoolmaster, RN, Instr Lt, Courses, Reserve Fleet, service with RAN, 1945–52; HMS Implacable, Theseus, Admiralty, HMS Excellent, 1952–59; HMS Centaur, RN Staff Course, Staff of SACLANT, USA, Directing Staff, RN Staff Course, Western Fleet, 1959–69; Naval Educn Service, Dir, Dept of Naval Oceanography and Meteorology, 1969–75; Instr Captain 1969, Rear-Adm. 1975. Educn Sec. of the BBC, 1979–83; Dep. Chairman: Police Complaints Bd, 1983–85; (Discipline), Police Complaints Authority, 1985–86; Vice Chm., Police Educn Foundn for Visual Aids, 1986–88; Member: BEC Educn Cttee, 1975–79; C&G Policy Cttee, 1975–79; TEC, 1976–79; Cert. of Extended Educn Cttee, DES, 1978–79; FEFCE SW Cttee, 1993–99. Pres., Sea Cadet Corps, Gravesend, 1982–84; Vice-Pres., United Services Catholic Assoc., 1979–; Nat. Vice-Pres., RN Assoc., 1983–96 (Dep. Pres., 1996–). Chairman: Kent EC Cttee, 1982–84; RNLI, Wellington, 1988–98 (Pres., 1998–). Vice-Chm., Bd (formerly Court) of Govs, London Guildhall Univ. (formerly City of London Poly.), 1984–95; Governor: SOAS, London Univ., 1975–79; Somerset Coll. of Art and Technology, 1987–95 (Vice-Chm. of Govs, 1989–95); London Coll. of Furniture, 1988–90. Editor-in-Chief, Education Media International, 1988–2000. Hon. LLD

London Guildhall, 1996. KSG 1983. *Recreations:* swimming, wines, travelling, France.
Died 30 April 2004.

BELL, Prof. Kathleen Myra, CBE 1978; Professor of Social Studies in the University of Newcastle upon Tyne, 1971–83, then Professor Emeritus; *b* 6 March 1920; *d* of late Walter Petty and Myra Petty; *m* 1945, Rev. Jack Martin Bell (*d* 1993); one *s* one *d. Educ:* St Joseph's Coll., Bradford; Univ. of Manchester (Prize in Public Admin 1940). Asst Personnel Officer, later Trng Officer, Min. of Supply ROF, 1942–45. Tutor and Lectr in Univ. Depts of Extra-Mural Studies, 1945–63; University of Newcastle upon Tyne: Lectr in Social Studies, 1963–67; Sen. Tutor, 1967–69; Sen. Lectr, 1969–71. Member: Lord Chancellor's Council on Tribunals, 1963–81 (Chm., Cttee on Functions of the Council, 1977–81); Social Admin. Cttee of Jt Univ. Council for Public and Social Admin., 1965–83; BBC Programmes Complaints Commn, 1978–81; Academic Adviser (apptd by Govt Chief Scientist) to DHSS Social Security Res. Policy Cttee, 1976–83; Expert Adviser to OECD Directorate for Social Affairs and Educn, for their project, Role of Women in the Economy, 1976–77; Member: AHA for N Tyneside, 1974–77; Davies Cttee on Hosp. Complaints Procedure, 1971–73. Member Editorial Board: Jl of Social Policy, 1971–78; Jl of Social Welfare Law, 1977–. *Publications:* Tribunals in the Social Services, 1969; Disequilibrium in Welfare, 1973; Research Study on Supplementary Benefit Appeal Tribunals—Review of Main Findings, Conclusions and Recommendations, 1975; The Functions of the Council on Tribunals, 1980; various papers in Jl of Social Policy, Econ. and Social Admin, and other jls. *Address:* Silverton, 86 Trinity Road, Edinburgh EH5 3JU. *Club:* Scottish Arts (Edinburgh). *Died 16 Dec. 2001.*

BELL, Sir Raymond; *see* Bell, Sir G. R.

BELL, Robert Donald Murray, CB 1966; Under-Secretary in Scottish Departments, 1959–76; *b* 8 Oct. 1916; *s* of Robert William and Mary Caroline Bell; *m* 1941, Karin Anna Smith (decd); one *d* (one *s* decd). *Educ:* Christ's Hosp.; Clare Coll., Cambridge (First Class Hons, Natural Sciences Tripos (Physics), 1938). Served War of 1939–45: RA, 1940–45 (Mil. Coll. of Science, Bury, 1943). Joined Scottish Office, 1938; Principal, Scottish Home Dept, 1946; Private Sec. to Sec. of State for Scotland, 1947–50. *Died 11 Nov. 2001.*

BELL, Walter (Fancourt), CMG 1967; *b* 7 Nov. 1909; *s* of Canon George Fancourt Bell; *m* 1948, Katharine Spaatz, Washington, DC, USA; no *c. Educ:* Tonbridge Sch. Barrister, Inner Temple. Vice-Consul (Acting): New York, 1935–40; Mexico City, 1940–41; New York, 1941–42; Foreign Office, London, 1942–45; 1st Sec., Brit. Embassy, Washington, DC, 1946–48; attached E Africa High Commn, Nairobi, Kenya, 1949–52; 1st Sec., Brit. High Commn, New Delhi, 1952–55; attached War Office, London, 1956–57; Adviser, Federal Govt, W Indies, 1957–60; attached Govt of Kenya, 1961–63; Counsellor, British High Commn, Nairobi, Kenya, 1963–67. US Medal of Freedom with Bronze Palm, 1946. *Recreation:* walking. *Address:* 6 Onslow Square, SW7 3NP. *Club:* Travellers. *Died 23 Jan. 2004.*

BELL, William Archibald Ottley Juxon; Founder, 1980, Chairman, 1980–96, and President, since 1996, Heritage of London Trust; *b* 7 July 1919; *s* of Maj. William Archibald Juxon Bell and Mary Isabel Maude Bell (*née* Ottley); *m* 1947, Belinda Mary (*née* Dawson) (*d* 2001); three *s* three *d. Educ:* Eton; Trinity College, Oxford (MA Hist.). Captain, Welsh Guards, 1940–45. Entered HM Foreign Service, 1945; Political Private Sec. to Sir Terence Shone, UK High Comr in India, 1946–47; Sec. to Exec. Dirs, British S Africa Co., 1947–50; Partner and Dir, King & Shaxson Ltd (Bill-brokers), 1950–90. Mem. of Lloyd's, 1970. Mem. for Chelsea, GLC and ILEA, 1970–86. Chairman: Diocesan Bd of Finance for Oxon, 1973–76; GLC Historic Bldgs Cttee, 1977–81; Oxfordshire

Buildings Trust, 1987–93; English Heritage Commemorative Plaques Working Gp, 1990–95; Member: Cttee, Oxfordshire Historic Churches Trust, 1970– (Pres., 1995–99); UK Cttee for European Architectural Heritage Year, 1973–75; London Adv. Cttee, English Heritage, 1986–90. High Sheriff, Oxon, 1978–79. *Recreations:* painting, shooting, golf, music. *Address:* 165 Cranmer Court, SW3 3HF. *T:* (020) 7589 1033. *Clubs:* White's, Pratt's, Beefsteak.
Died 10 March 2005.

BELL, Sir (William) Ewart, KCB 1982 (CB 1978); Head of Northern Ireland Civil Service, 1979–84 and Second Permanent Secretary, Northern Ireland Office, 1981–84, retired; *b* 13 Nov. 1924; *s* of late Rev. Dr Frederick G. Bell and Margaret Jane Ewart; *m* 1957, Kathleen Ross Boucher; two *d. Educ:* Methodist Coll., Belfast; Wadham Coll., Oxford (MA). Asst Master, Cheltenham Coll., 1946–48; Northern Ireland Civil Service, 1948–84: Min. of Health and Local Govt, 1948–52; Min. (later Dept) of Commerce, 1952–76; Asst Sec., 1963–70; Dep. Sec., 1970–73; Sec., 1973–76; Permanent Sec., Dept of Finance, 1976–79. Dir, Ulster Bank Ltd, 1985–95. Hon. Treas., QUB, 1985–93. Pres., Irish RFU, 1986–87; Chm., Rugby World Cup Ltd, 1993–95. *Recreations:* gardening, golf, Rugby football (Irish Rugby International, 1953).
Died 2 Jan. 2001.

BELLAMY, Prof. Edmund Henry, MA, PhD; Professor of Physics in the University of London, Westfield College, 1960–84, then Emeritus; *b* 8 April 1923; *s* of Herbert Bellamy and Nellie (*née* Ablett); *m* 1946, Joan Roberts; three *s. Educ:* Quarry Bank Sch., Liverpool; King's Coll., Cambridge. Lectr in Natural Philosophy, 1951–59, Sen. Lectr, 1959–60, Univ. of Glasgow; Vis. Physicist, Univ. of Pisa, 1960. Mem., Nuclear Physics Board, SRC, 1965–66. Visiting Professor: Univ. of Stanford, 1966–67; Univ. of Pisa, 1985–86; Emeritus Fellow, Leverhulme Trust, 1987–89; Consultant, Univ. of Florida, 1990; CERN Fellow, 1981–82. *Publications:* numerous scientific papers in Proc. Phys. Soc. and other journals. *Recreations:* ski-ing, squash, travel, football, golf. *Address:* 134 Main Road, Long Hanborough, Witney, Oxon OX29 8JY. *T:* (01993) 882227. *Died 11 Dec. 2005.*

BELLINGER, Sir Robert (Ian), GBE 1967; Kt 1964; Chairman: Kinloch (PM) Ltd, 1946–75; National Savings Committee, 1970–75 (also President, 1972–75); Director, Rank Organisation, 1971–83; *b* Tetbury, Glos, 10 March 1910; *s* of David Morgan Bellinger, Cardiganshire, and Jane Ballantine Deans, Edinburgh; *m* 1962, Christiane Marie Louise Janssens, Brussels; one *s* one *d. Educ:* Church of England sch. Elected Court of Common Council, 1953; Chm. City of London Freemen's Sch., 1957; Alderman for Ward of Cheap, 1958; Sheriff, City of London, 1962–63; Lord Mayor of London, 1966–67; one of HM Lieutenants, City of London, 1976–. Chairman: Panel for Civil Service Manpower Review, 1968–71; Adv. Cttee on Magistracy, City of London, 1968–76; Licensing Cttee, City of London; Finance Cttee, BBC; Governor, BBC, 1968–71; Trustee, St Paul's Cathedral Trust, 1977–96. Dir, Arsenal Football Club, 1960–96 (Life Pres., 1996). Chairman: Anglo-Danish Soc., 1976–83; Danish Trade Adv. Bd, 1979–82. Past Master, Broderers' Co.; Liveryman, Fletchers' Co. Hon. DSc City Univ., 1966. Gentleman Usher of the Purple Rod, Order of the British Empire, 1969–85. KStJ 1966; Commandeur, Ordre de Léopold, cl. III (Belgium), 1963; Comdr, Royal Order of the Phoenix (Greece), 1963; Officier, Ordre de la Valeur Camerounaise (Cameroons), 1963; Knight Comdr of the Order of Dannebrog (Denmark), 1977. *Recreations:* tennis, football, music, motoring. *Address:* Penn Wood, Fulmer, Bucks SL3 6JL. *T:* (01753) 662029. *Club:* City Livery.
Died 8 July 2002.

BELLO, Mohammed, CON 1965; Chief Justice of Nigeria, 1987–95; *b* 1930; *s* of Mallam Muhammadu Gidado; *m* 1962; many *c. Educ:* Harvard Law School. Called to the Bar, Lincoln's Inn. Northern Nigeria appointments: Crown Counsel, 1956; Magistrate, 1961; Dir of Public Prosecutions, 1964; Judge of the High Court, 1966; Senior Puisne Judge, North-Central and Kwara States, 1968; occasional Acting Chief Justice, Northern State, 1969–75; Justice of Supreme Court of Nigeria, 1975. Fellow, Nigerian Inst. of Advanced Legal Studies, 1984. Hon. LLD: Ibadan, 1987; Ahmadu Bello, 1990; Lagos, 1992. *Recreation:* rambling. *Address:* 4 Umaru Dallaje Road, PO Box 365, Katsina, Nigeria. *T:* (65) 34964. *Died 4 Nov. 2004.*

BELLOW, family name of **Baron Bellwin.**

BELLOW, Saul; American writer; *b* 10 June 1915; *s* of Abraham and Liza Gordon Bellow; *m* 1st, 1937, Anita Goshkin (marr. diss.); one *s*; 2nd, 1956, Alexandra Tschacbasov (marr. diss.); one *s*; 3rd, 1961, Susan Glassman (marr. diss.); one *s*; 4th, 1974, Alexandra Tuleca (marr. diss.); 5th, 1989, Janis Freedman; one *d. Educ:* Univ. of Chicago; Northwestern Univ. Hon. DLitt Northwestern, 1962. Nobel Prize for Literature, 1976; Malaparté Prize for Literature, Italy, 1984. Commander, Legion of Honour (France), 1983; Commander, Order of Arts and Letters (France), 1985 (Croix de Chevalier, 1968). *Publications:* Dangling Man, 1944 (reissued 1972); The Victim, 1947; The Adventures of Augie March, 1953 (National Book Award, 1954); Seize the Day, 1956; Henderson the Rain King, 1959; Herzog, 1964 (National Book Award, Internat. Literary Prize, 1965); Mosby's Memoirs and Other Stories, 1969; Mr Sammler's Planet, 1970 (National Book Award, 1970); Humboldt's Gift, 1975 (Pulitzer Prize 1976); To Jerusalem and Back, 1976; The Dean's December, 1982; (short stories) Him with His Foot in His Mouth, 1984; More Die of Heartbreak, 1987; A Theft, 1989; The Bellarosa Connection, 1989; Something to Remember Me By: three tales, 1991; It All Adds Up (essays), 1994; The Actual, 1997; Ravelstein, 2000; Collected Stories, 2001. *Address:* University Professors, Boston University, 745 Commonwealth Avenue, Boston, MA 02215, USA.

Died 5 April 2005.

BELLWIN, Baron *cr* 1979 (Life Peer), of the City of Leeds; **Irwin Norman Bellow;** JP; DL; *b* 7 Feb. 1923; *s* of Abraham and Leah Bellow; *m* 1948, Doreen Barbara Saperia; one *s* two *d. Educ:* Lovell Road; Leeds Grammar School; Leeds Univ. (LLB). Leader, Leeds City Council, 1975–79; Vice-Chm. Assoc. of Metropolitan Authorities, 1978–79. Parly Under Sec. of State, DoE, 1979–83; Minister of State, 1983–84. Mem., Commn for New Towns, 1985–95; Vice-Pres., Internat. New Towns Assoc, 1985. Non-executive Chairman: Programme Publications Ltd, 1996–; Bellow Machine Co. Ltd, 2000–. Non-executive Director: Taylor Woodrow, 1985–92; Sinclair Goldsmith Holding, 1986–93; Lewis Gp, 1993–; Stewart Title (UK), 1993–; Farr Brokers Ltd, 1994–96. Chm., N Hull HAT, 1993–99. Mem., Nat. Sports Council, 1972–75; Pres., English Basket Ball Assoc., 1972–75. Pres., Yorks Kidney Res. Fund, 1990–. Governor, Leeds Grammar Sch., 1966– (Vice Chm., 1994–). Master, Guild of World Traders in London, 1989. JP Leeds, 1969; DL W Yorks, 1991. *Recreation:* golf. *Address:* Woodside Lodge, Ling Lane, Scarcroft, Leeds LS14 3HX. *T:* (0113) 289 2908. *Club:* Moor Allerton Golf (Pres.). *Died 11 Feb. 2001.*

BELSTEAD, 2nd Baron *cr* 1938; **John Julian Ganzoni;** PC 1983; JP; Baron Ganzoni (Life Peer), 1999; Bt 1929; Lord-Lieutenant of Suffolk, 1994–2002; *b* 30 Sept. 1932; *o s* of 1st Baron Belstead and Gwendolen Gertrude Turner (*d* 1962); *S* father, 1958. *Educ:* Eton; Christ Church, Oxford (MA 1961). Parliamentary Under-Secretary of State: DES, 1970–73; NI Office, 1973–74; Home Office, 1979–82; Minister of State: FCO, 1982–83; MAFF, 1983–87; DoE, 1987–88; Dep. Leader, H of L, 1983–87; Leader, H of L and Lord Privy Seal, 1988–90; HM Paymaster General and Minister, NI Office, 1990–92. Chm., Parole Board, 1992–97. Chm., Assoc. of Governing Bodies of Public Schools, 1974–79. JP

Borough of Ipswich, 1962; DL Suffolk, 1979. *Heir:* none. *Address:* House of Lords, SW1A 0PW. *T:* (020) 7219 3000. *Clubs:* Boodle's, MCC; All England Lawn Tennis (Wimbledon). *Died 3 Dec. 2005 (ext).*

BENGOUGH, Sir Piers (Henry George), KCVO 1986; OBE 1973; DL; Her Majesty's Representative, Ascot, 1982–97 (Trustee, Ascot Racecourse, 1973–97); *b* 24 May 1929; *s* of Nigel and Alice Bengough; *m* 1952, Bridget Shirley Adams; two *s. Educ:* Eton. Commnd 10th Royal Hussars (PWO), 1948; commanded Royal Hussars (PWO), 1971–73, retired. Formerly amateur rider; wins incl. Grand Military Gold Cup (4 times). Member: Jockey Club, 1965– (Steward, 1974–77, 1990–92); Horserace Betting Levy Board, 1978–81; Director: Hereford Racecourse Co., 1974–2001; Cheltenham Steeplechase Co., 1977–90; Ludlow Race Club, 1979–2004; Chm., Compensation Fund for Jockeys, 1981–89. Mem., HM Bodyguard, Hon. Corps of Gentlemen-at-Arms, 1981–99 (Standard Bearer, 1997–99). Hon. Col The Royal Hussars (PWO), 1983–90. DL, 1987, High Sheriff, 2002, Hereford and Worcester. *Recreations:* shooting, fishing. *Address:* Great House, Canon Pyon, Hereford HR4 8PD. *Clubs:* Cavalry and Guards, Pratt's. *Died 18 April 2005.*

BENJAMIN, Prof. Bernard; Professor of Actuarial Science, The City University, London, 1973–75, later Emeritus; *b* 8 March 1910; *s* of Joseph and Lucy Benjamin, London; *m* 1937, May Pate (*d* 1977); Horsham, Suffolk; two *d. Educ:* Colfe Grammar Sch.; Sir John Cass Coll., London Univ. (BSc (Hons), PhD). Served War, 1943–46, RAF. LCC, 1928; statistician: Public Health Dept, 1940; General Register Office, 1952; Chief Statistician, 1954; Director: Statistics, Ministry of Health, 1963–65; Research and Intelligence, GLC, 1965–70; Statistical Studies, CS College, 1970–73; Hon. Cons. in Med. Stats to Army, 1966. Chm., Statistics Users Council (formerly Standing Cttee of Statistics Users), 1971–90. Fellow: Inst. of Actuaries (a Vice-Pres. 1963; Pres., 1966–68; Gold Medal, 1975); Royal Statistical Soc. (Pres. 1970–71; Guy Medal in Gold, 1986); Galton Inst. (formerly Eugenics Soc.) (Pres., 1982–87; Galton Lectr, 1981). Hon. DSc: City Univ., London, 1981; Kent Univ. 1987. Internat. Insurance Prize of Italy, 1985. *Publications:* Social and Economic Factors in Mortality, 1965; Health and Vital Statistics, 1968; Demographic Analysis, 1969; The Population Census, 1970; (with H. W. Haycocks) The Analysis of Mortality and Other Actuarial Statistics, 1971; Statistics in Urban Administration, 1976; (ed) Medical Records, 1977; General Insurance, 1977; (jtly) The Analysis of Mortality and Other Actuarial Statistics, 1980, 3rd edn 1993; (jtly) Pensions: the problems of today and tomorrow, 1987; Population Statistics, 1989; (with Amal Soliman) Mortality on the Move, 1993; numerous medical and population statistical papers and contribs to Jl of Royal Statistical Society and Jl of Inst. of Actuaries. *Recreations:* gardening, painting (both kinds), music. *Address:* c/o Institute of Actuaries, Staple Inn Hall, High Holborn, WC1V 7QJ. *Club:* Athenæum. *Died 15 May 2002.*

BENNETT, Rt Hon. Sir Frederic (Mackarness), Kt 1964; PC 1985; DL; *b* 2 Dec. 1918; 2nd *s* of late Sir Ernest Bennett and Lady (Marguerite) Bennett; *m* 1945, Marion Patricia, *e d* of Cecil Burnham, OBE, FRCSE. *Educ:* Westminster. Served War of 1939–45, enlisted Middx Yeo., 1939; commissioned RA, 1940; commended for gallantry, 1941; Military Experimental Officer in Petroleum Warfare Dept, 1943–46, when released with rank of Major. TA&VRA, 1973–83. Called to English Bar, Lincoln's Inn, 1946, Southern Rhodesian Bar, 1947. Observer, Greek Communist War, 1947–49; Diplomatic correspondent, Birmingham Post, 1950–52. Contested (C) Burslem, 1945, Ladywood Div. of Birmingham, 1950. MP (C): Reading N, 1951–55; Torquay, Dec. 1955–1974; Torbay, 1974–87. PPS to Under-Sec. of State, Home Office, 1953–55, to Minister of Supply, 1956–57, to Paymaster-Gen., 1957–59, and to Pres. of Bd of Trade, 1959–61. Chm. Exec. Cttee, CPA Gen. Council,

1971–73; Vice Pres., Council of Europe and WEU Assembly, 1979–87; Chairman, 1979–87: Pol Affairs Cttee, Council of Europe; Gen. Affairs Cttee, WEU; Federated Gp, Eur. Democrats and Christian Democrats. Lord of the Manor of Mawddwy. Co-Pres., ESU of Pakistan, 1988–. DL Greater London, 1990. Freeman, City of London, 1984. Hon. Dr of Law Istanbul, 1984. Comdr, Order of Phœnix, Greece, 1963; (Sithari) Star of Pakistan, 1st cl., 1964; Order of Al-Istiqlal, 1st cl., Jordan, 1980; Comdr, Order of Isabel la Católica, Spain, 1982; Order of Hilal-i-Quaid-i-Azam, Pakistan, 1983; Commander's Cross, Order of Merit, FRG, 1989; Order (first class) of Polonia Restituta, Poland, 1990 (Comdr, 1977; Grand Comdr's Cross, 1984); Knight of Vitezi, Hungary, 1990; Order of Cross of Terra Mariana (first class), Estonia, 1996; Knight's Cross, Order of Merit, Hungary, 2001. *Publications:* Speaking Frankly, 1960; Detente and Security in Europe, 1976; China and European Security, 1978; The Near and Middle East and Western European Security, 1979, 2nd edn 1980; Reds under the Bed, or the Enemy at the Gate—and Within, 1979, 3rd edn 1982; Impact of Individual and Corporate Incentives on Productivity and Standard of Living, 1980; Fear is the Key: Ulster; Kashmir Today, 1996. *Recreations:* shooting, fishing, yachting. *Address:* Cwmllecoediog, Aberangell, near Machynlleth, Powys SY20 9QP. *T:* (01650) 511430, *Fax:* (01650) 511469. *Clubs:* Carlton, Anglo-Belgian; Royal Torbay Yacht (Torquay).
Died 14 Sept. 2002.

BENNETT, Rt Rev. Manu Augustus, ONZ 1989; CMG 1981; DD; Bishop of Aotearoa, 1968–81; *b* 10 Feb. 1916; *s* of Rt Rev. F. A. Bennett, Bishop of Aotearoa, 1928–50, and Alice Rangioue Bennett; *m* 1944, Kathleen Clark; one *d*. *Educ:* Victoria Univ. Coll.; Univ. of Hawaii (BSc 1954). Ordained deacon, 1939, priest, 1940; Vicar of Tauranga, Te Puke Maori District, Dio. Waiapu, 1940–44; Chaplain to 2 NZEF, 1944–46; Pastor of Rangitikei South-Manawatu Pastorate, Dio. Wellington, 1946–52; Asst Vicar of Church of Holy Nativity, Honolulu, 1953–54; Pastor of Wellington Pastorate, 1952–57; Vicar of Ohinemutu Pastorate, Waikato, 1964–68. Nat. Council of Churches Chaplain, Dept of Justice. Mem., Waitangi Tribunal on Treaty Matters. Faculty Mem., Native Ministries Consortium, Vancouver Sch. of Theology, Univ. of BC; Kaumatua, Te Rau Kahikatea Unit, St John's Coll., Auckland. Hon. DD: Jackson Coll., 1964; Waikato, 1997. *Address:* 25c Eason Street, Rotorua, New Zealand. *Died 20 Dec. 2001.*

BENNETT, Mary Letitia Somerville, MA; Principal, St Hilda's College, Oxford, 1965–80, Hon. Fellow 1980; Pro-Vice-Chancellor, Oxford University, 1979–80; *b* 9 Jan. 1913; *o c* of Rt Hon. H. A. L. Fisher, OM, and Lettice Ilbert; *m* 1955, John Sloman Bennett, CMG (*d* 1990). *Educ:* Oxford High Sch.; Somerville Coll., Oxford (Schol.; 2nd Cl. Mods, 1st Cl. Lit. Hum.; Hon. Fellow, 1977). Jt Broadcasting Cttee, 1940–41; Transcription Service of BBC, 1941–45; Colonial Office, 1945–56. Mem., Hebdomodal Council, Oxford Univ., 1973–79. Hon. Sec., Society for the Promotion of Roman Studies, 1960–85. *Publications:* The Ilberts in India, 1995; Who was Dr Jackson?, 2002. *Address:* Rock Cottage, Thursley, Surrey GU8 6QJ; 25A Alma Place, Oxford OX4 1JW. *Club:* University Women's. *Died 1 Nov. 2005.*

BENNETT, Philip Hugh Penberthy, CBE 1972; FRIBA; FCIArb; Consultant, T. P. Bennett Partnership, architects, 1980–95 (Partner, 1948–80, Senior Partner, 1967–80); *b* 14 April 1919; *o s* of Sir Thomas Penberthy Bennett, KBE, FRIBA, and Mary Langdon Edis; *m* 1943, Jeanne Heal; one *s* one *d*. *Educ:* Highgate Sch.; Emmanuel Coll., Cambridge (MA). Lieut (G) RNVR, 1940–46. Principal works: town centres at Bootle and Stratford (London); head offices for Norwich Union Insce Socs, Ford Motor Co. and other commercial cos; dept stores for United Africa Co. in Ghana and Nigeria, Bentalls (Kingston) and Fenwicks (Newcastle); extensions to Middlesex Hosp.; hostel for Internat. Students Trust; Cunard Internat. Hotel; flats for local authorities and private developers; buildings for airfield and dock develt. Chm., Building Regulations Adv. Cttee (DoE), 1965–77; former RIBA rep. on Jt Contracts Tribunal (Chm., 1973–78) and Nat. Jt Consultative Cttee (Chm., 1970); Mem. other cttees of RIBA and NEDO; Governor: Sch. of Building, 1952–72; Vauxhall Coll. of Further Educn, 1972–77; Member: Home Office Deptl Cttee enquiring into Fire Service, 1967–70; Adv. Council for Energy Conservation, 1974–76. Dir, BEC Building Trust Ltd, 1984–91. *Publications:* Architectural Practice and Procedure, 1981; chapter on building, in Britain 1984, 1963; articles in Building, Financial Times, etc. *Recreations:* travel, drawing, theatre. *Address:* Grey Walls, Park Lane, Aldeburgh, Suffolk IP15 5PH. *T:* (01728) 452766.
Died 28 Sept. 2004.

BERESFORD, Prof. Maurice Warwick, FBA 1985; Professor of Economic History, University of Leeds, 1959–85, then Emeritus; *b* 6 Feb. 1920; *s* of late H. B. Beresford and Mrs N. E. Beresford. *Educ:* Boldmere and Green Lane Elementary Schs; Bishop Vesey's Grammar Sch., Sutton Coldfield; Jesus Coll., Cambridge (exhibnr and schol.; Goldsmiths' Co. Open Exhibnr; Historical Tripos, Pt I class I, 1940, Pt II class I, 1941; MA 1945). On Staff of Birmingham Univ. Settlement, 1941–42; Sub-warden, Percival Guildhouse, Rugby, 1942–43; Warden, 1943–48; University of Leeds: Lecturer, 1948–55; Reader, 1955–59; Dean, 1958–60; Chm., Sch. of Economic Studies, 1965–68, 1971–72, 1981–83; Chm. of Faculty Bd, 1968–70. Harrison Vis. Prof. of History, Coll. of William and Mary, Virginia, 1975–76; Vis. Prof. of History, Strathclyde Univ., 1987–90. Voluntary teacher, Wakefield Prison, 1975–92. Chairman: Yorks Citizens' Advice Bureaux Cttee, 1963–69; Parole Review Cttee, Leeds Prison, 1970–92; Northern Area Inst. for Study and Treatment of Delinquency, 1973–78; Co-opted Mem., City of Leeds Probation Cttee, 1972–78; SSRC, Economic and Social History Cttee, 1972–75. Minister's nominee, Yorkshire Dales National Park Cttee, 1964–71; Member: Consumer Council, 1966–71; Hearing Aids Council, 1969–71; Royal Commn on Historical Monuments (England), 1979–90. Hon. Vice-Pres., Yorks Archaeol Soc., 1986 (Medallist, 1989); Hon. Patron, Thoresby Soc., 1985. Hon. DLitt: Loughborough, 1984; Hull, 1986; Leicester, 2002; Leeds, 2004. *Publications:* The Leeds Chambers of Commerce, 1951; The Lost Villages of England, 1954, rev. edn 1998; History on the Ground, 1957, rev. edn 1998; (with J. K. S. St Joseph) Medieval England: an Aerial Survey, 1958, rev. edn 1979; Time and Place, 1962; New Towns of the Middle Ages, 1967, rev. edn 1988; (ed with G. R. J. Jones) Leeds and Its Region, 1967; (with J. G. Hurst) Deserted Medieval Villages, 1971, rev. edn 1989; (with H. P. R. Finberg) English Medieval Boroughs, 1973; (with B. J. Barber) The West Riding County Council 1889–1974, 1979; Walks Round Red Brick, 1980; Time and Place: collected essays, 1985; East End, West End, 1988; (with J. G. Hurst) Wharram Percy—Deserted Medieval Village, 1990; contribs to Oxford DNB, Economic History Review, Agricultural History Review, Medieval Archaeology, etc. *Recreations:* music, theatre, maps, delinquency. *Address:* 4 Claremont Avenue, Leeds LS3 1AT. *T:* (0113) 245 4563.
Died 15 Dec. 2005.

BERGER, Vice-Adm. Sir Peter (Egerton Capel), KCB 1979; LVO 1960; DSC 1949; MA; Bursar, 1981–91, and Fellow, Selwyn College, Cambridge, since 1981; *b* 11 Feb. 1925; *s* of late Capel Colquhoun Berger and Winifred Violet Berger (*née* Levett-Scrivener); *m* 1956, June Kathleen Pigou; three *d*. *Educ:* Harrow Sch. MA Cantab 1984. Served War of 1939–45: entered RN as a Cadet, 1943; Normandy and South of France landings in HMS Ajax, 1944; Sub-Lt, 1945; Lieut, 1946; Yangtse Incident, HMS Amethyst, 1949; Lt-Comdr, 1953; Comdr, 1956; Fleet Navigating Officer, Home Fleet, 1956–58; Navigating Officer, HM Yacht Britannia, 1958–60;

Commanded HMS Torquay, 1962–64; Captain, 1964; Defence, Naval and Military Attaché, The Hague, 1964–66; commanded HMS Phoebe, 1966–68; Commodore, Clyde, 1971–73; Rear-Adm., 1973; Asst Chief of Naval Staff (Policy), 1973–75; COS to C-in-C Fleet, 1976–78; Flag Officer Plymouth, Port Admiral Devonport, Comdr Central Sub Area Eastern Atlantic and Comdr Plymouth Sub Area Channel, 1979–81, retired 1981. *Recreations:* shooting, fishing, history. *Address:* Carl's Barn, Church Road, Carlton, near Newmarket, Suffolk CB8 9JZ. *T:* (01223) 290241. *Died 19 Oct. 2003.*

BERGSTRÖM, Prof. Sune, MD; Swedish biochemist; *b* 10 Jan. 1916; *s* of Sverker Bergström and Wera (*née* Wistrand); *m* Maj Gernandt; one *s. Educ:* Karolinska Inst (MD 1944, DMedSci 1944). Squibb Inst., USA, 1941–42; Med. Nobel Inst., Stockholm, 1942–46; Basle Univ., 1946–47; Prof. of Biochemistry, Lund Univ., 1947–58; Prof. at Karolinska Inst, 1958–80, Dean of Med. Faculty, 1963–66, Rector, 1969–77. Consultant to WHO. Chm., Board, Nobel Foundn, 1975–87 (and Chm., Adv. Council, Med. Research, 1977–82). Member: Swedish Acad. of Scis; Swedish Acad. of Engineering; Amer. Acad. of Arts and Scis; Nat. Acad. of Scis, USA; Acad. of Sci., USSR; Acad. of Med. Scis, USSR; Papal Acad. of Sci.; Hon. Mem., Amer. Soc. of Biol. Chemists. Albert Lasker Basic Med. Research Award, 1977; (jtly) Nobel Prize for Physiology or Medicine, 1982. *Publications:* papers on heparin, autoxidation, bile acids and chlorestrol, prostaglandins. *Address:* Karolinska Institutet, Nobel Forum, Box 270, 17177 Stockholm, Sweden.
Died 15 Aug. 2004.

BERIO, Luciano; composer; *b* 24 Oct. 1925; *s* of Ernesto Berio and Ada dal Fiume; *m* 1st, 1950, Cathy Berberian (marr. diss. 1964; she *d* 1983); one *d*; 2nd, 1964, Susan Oyama (marr. diss. 1971); one *s* one *d*; 3rd, 1977, Talia Pecker; two *s. Educ:* Liceo Classico, Oneglia; Conservatorio G. Verdi, Milan. A founder, Studio di Fonologia, Milan, 1955; teacher of composition, Juilliard Sch., NY, 1965–71; Hd, electro-acoustic dept, IRCAM, Paris, 1974–80; founder and Artistic Dir, Tempo Reale, Florence, 1987–. Hon. Dr Composition, City Univ., London, 1979; Hon. Dr Siena, 1995. Siemens Prize, Munich, 1989; Wolf Foundn Prize, Jerusalem, 1991; Praemium Imperiale, Japan, 1996. *Compositions include:* Differences, 1958; Epifanie, 1959–63, revised as Epiphanies, 1991; Circles, 1960; Passaggio, 1962; Laborintus II, 1965; Sinfonia, 1968; Concerto for 2 pianos, 1972; Opera, 1969–74; Sequenzas I–XI for solo instruments, and for female voice, 1958–88; A-Ronne for five actors, 1974–75; Coro for chorus and orchestra, 1975–76; La Ritirata Notturna di Madrid, 1975; Ritorno degli Snovidenia, 1977; La Vera Storia, 1981; Un Re in Ascolto, 1983; Voci, 1984; Requies, 1985; Formazioni, 1986; Ricorrenze, 1987; Concerto II (Echoing Curves), 1988; Ofanim, 1988; Canticum Novissimi Testamenti, 1989; Rendering (Schubert), 1990; Continuo, 1991; Cronaca del Luogo, 1999; SOLO, concerto for trombone, 2000. *Address:* Il Colombaio, Radicondoli (Siena), Italy.
Died 27 May 2003.

BERNARD, Daniel, Hon. CMG 1995; Hon. CBE 1992; Ambassador of France to the Court of St James's, 1998–2002; *b* 13 Sept. 1941; *m* 1964, Monique Beaumet; two *s* one *d. Educ:* Université de Lyon (LèsL (English)); Institut d'Etudes Politiques, Lyon (Dip.); Ecole Nationale d'Administration. Second Sec., Dublin, 1967–71; UN Directorate, Min. of Foreign Affairs, 1975–77; First Sec., Perm. Repn to EEC, 1977–81; Advr to Private Office of External Relations Minister, 1981–83; Deleg., Internat. Affairs Directorate, Industry and Res. Min., 1984; Diplomatic Advr to Prime Minister, 1984–86; Inspr, Min. of Foreign Affairs, 1986; seconded to EEC, 1987–88; Special Advr to Pres. of Nat. Assembly, 1988–90; Dir, Press Information and Communications Dept, and Min. Spokesman, Min. of Foreign Affairs, 1990–92; Prin. Private Sec. to Foreign Minister, 1992–93; Ambassador to Netherlands, 1993–95; Perm. Rep. to UN, Geneva, 1995–98. Chevalier: de l'Ordre National du Mérite (France), 1981; de la Légion d'Honneur (France), 1997. *Recreations:* music, sport. *Address:* c/o French Embassy, 58 Knightsbridge, SW1X 7JT. *T:* (020) 7201 1006, *Fax:* (020) 7201 1003. *Club:* Travellers.
Died 29 April 2004.

BERNSTEIN, Ronald Harold, DFC 1944; QC 1969; FCIArb; a Recorder of the Crown Court, 1974–90; *b* 18 Aug. 1918; *s* of late Mark and Fanny Bernstein; *m* 1955, Judy, *d* of David Levi, MS, and Vera Levi; three *s* one *d. Educ:* Swansea Grammar Sch.; Balliol Coll., Oxford. BA (Jurisprudence) 1939; FCIArb 1982. Served in RA, 1939–46, and in 654 Air OP Sqdn, RAF, 1942–46. Commanded 661 Air OP Sqdn, RAuxAF, 1954–56. Called to the Bar, Middle Temple, 1948, Bencher, 1975–. Mem., Gen. Council of the Bar, 1965–69; Vice-Pres., 1988–91, Vice-Pres. Emeritus, 1991–; CIArb. Pres., Highgate Soc., 1983–93. Hon. MRICS (Hon. ARICS 1986); Hon. FSVA 1987. *Publications:* (jointly) The Restrictive Trade Practices Act, 1956; Handbook of Rent Review, 1981, and subseq. edns to 1997; Handbook of Arbitration Practice, 1987, 3rd edn 1997; Joint Ventures in Property, 1993; Essentials of Rent Review, 1995. *Address:* (professional) Falcon Chambers, Falcon Court, EC4Y 1AA. *T:* (020) 7353 2484, (home) (020) 8340 9933, *Fax:* (020) 8348 7676; *e-mail:* rhbern@aol.com. *Club:* Athenæum.
Died 8 May 2004.

BERRY, John, CBE 1968; DL; PhD; FRSE 1936; consultant on water impoundment biology, 1968–90; Conservation and Fisheries Adviser to: North of Scotland Hydro-Electric Board, 1968–89; South of Scotland Electricity Board, 1973–89; *b* Edinburgh, 5 Aug. 1907; *o s* of late William Berry, OBE, DL, Tayfield, Newport, Fife; *m* 1936, Hon. Bride Fremantle, MA (Cantab), 3rd *d* of 3rd Baron Cottesloe, CB; two *s* one *d. Educ:* Eton; Trinity Coll., Cambridge (BA 1929 (Zoo. Chem. Phys. Pt I and Law Pt II); MA 1933); St Andrews Univ. (PhD 1935). Salmon research, Fishery Bd for Scotland, 1930–31; Res. Officer, 1932–36, Dir, 1937–39, Biological Research Station, University Coll., Southampton; Press Censor for Scotland, 1940–44; Biologist and Information Officer, North of Scotland Hydro-Electric Bd, 1944–49; Dir of Nature Conservation in Scotland, 1949–67. Consultant Ecologist, Scottish Landowners' Fedn, 1984–87. Chm., Interdepartmental Salmon Res. Gp (UK and Ireland), 1971–82; Dir, British Pavilion, Expo '71, Budapest. Mem., Scottish Marine Biology Assoc., 1947–71 (RSE rep., Exec. Cttee, 1947; Mem Council, 1948–54, 1957–66). Pres. 1954–56, Vice-Pres. 1956–60, and Mem., 1966–72, Commn on Ecology, Internat. Union for Conservation of Natural Resources; UK rep., Exec. Bd, Internat. Wildfowl Research Bureau, 1963–72; Vice-President; RZS Scotland, 1959–82 (Hon. Life Fellow and Hon. Vice-Pres., 1982); Scottish Wildlife Trust; Vice-Pres. and Mem. Council, Wildfowl Trust, 1969– (Hon. Life Fellow, 1983); Hon. Life Fellow, RSPB, 1984. Mem. Court, Dundee Univ., and Delegate to Commonwealth Univs Congress, 1970–78. DL Fife, 1969. Hon. LLD Dundee, 1970; Hon. DSc St Andrews, 1991. *Publications:* The Status and Distribution of Wild Geese and Wild Duck in Scotland, 1939; various papers and articles on freshwater fisheries, hydro-electric development and ornithology. *Recreations:* natural history (esp. wild geese and insects), music. *Address:* The Garden House, Tayfield, Newport-on-Tay, Fife DD6 8HA. *T:* (01382) 543118. *Club:* New (Edinburgh). *Died 16 Feb. 2002.*

BESCH, Anthony John Elwyn, FGSM; opera and theatre director, since 1950; Head of Opera Studies, Guildhall School of Music and Drama, 1986–89; *b* 5 Feb. 1924; *s* of late Roy Cressy Frederick Besch and Anne Gwendolen Besch. *Educ:* Rossall Sch., Lancs; Worcester Coll., Oxford (MA). FGSM 1989. Dir, opera and theatre, 1950–: Royal Opera House, Covent Garden; Glyndebourne Opera; English Nat. Opera, London Coliseum; Scottish Opera;

Opera North; New Opera Co., London; Handel Opera Soc.; Edinburgh Festival; Wexford Festival; Deutsche Oper, Berlin; Royal Netherlands Opera; Théâtre de la Monnaie, Brussels; Opéra de Lyon; Teatro Colon, Buenos Aires; New York City Opera; San Francisco Opera; Canadian Opera Co.; Nat. Arts Centre, Canada; Australian Opera; State Opera, S Australia; Victoria State Opera. *Recreation:* gardening. *Address:* 203 Ham Street, Ham, Richmond, Surrey TW10 7HF. *Club:* Garrick.

Died 23 Dec. 2002.

BESSBOROUGH, 11th Earl of, *cr* 1739 (Ire.); **Arthur Mountifort Longfield Ponsonby;** Baron Bessborough (Ire.) 1721; Viscount Duncannon (Ire.) 1722; Baron Ponsonby (GB) 1749; Baron Duncannon (UK) 1834; *b* 11 Dec. 1912; *s* of Hon. Cyril Myles Ponsonby (*d* 1915), 2nd *s* of 8th Earl, and Rita Narcissa Longfield (*d* 1977); *S* cousin, 1993; *m* 1st, 1939, Patricia (*d* 1952), *d* of Col Fitzhugh Minnigerode, Va, USA; one *s* one *d*; 2nd, 1956, Anne Marie Galitzine (marr. diss. 1963); 3rd, 1963, Madeleine Lola Margaret, *d* of Maj.-Gen. Laurence Grand, CB, CIE, CBE; two *s. Educ:* Harrow; Trinity Coll., Cambridge. Captain, Welsh Guards, 1940–46. *Heir: s* Viscount Duncannon [*b* 16 Feb. 1941; *m* 1972, Alison, *d* of William Storey, OBE; two *s* one *d*]. *Address:* Roche Court, Winterslow, Wilts SP5 1BG. *T:* (01980) 862204.

Died 5 April 2002.

BESSEY, Gordon Scott, CBE 1968; Director of Education, Cumberland, 1949–74, Cumbria, 1974–75; *b* 20 Oct. 1910; *s* of late Edward Emerson and Mabel Bessey, Great Yarmouth; *m* 1937, Cynthia (JP 1966), *d* of late William and Mary Bird, Oxford; one *s* three *d. Educ:* Heath Sch., Halifax; St Edmund Hall, Oxford (BA 1932, DipEd 1933, MA 1937). Teaching: Keighley and Cheltenham, 1933–37; Admin. Asst, Surrey, 1937–39; Asst, later Dep. Educn Officer, Norfolk, 1939–45; Dep. Educn Officer, Somerset, 1945–49. Mem., Youth Service Development Council, 1960–67; Chm., Working Party on part-time training of Youth Leaders, 1961–62; Pres., Assoc. of Chief Educn Officers, 1963; Treas., Soc. of Educn Officers, 1971–74; Chairman: Educnl Adv. Council of IBA (formerly ITA), 1970–74; County Educn Officers' Soc., 1969–70. Chairman: East Cumbria Community Health Council, 1974–79; Assoc. of Community Health Councils in England and Wales, 1977–79; Voluntary Action, Cumbria, 1975–84. Hon. DCL Newcastle upon Tyne, 1970. *Recreations:* fishing, golf, fell-walking, ornithology. *Address:* The Lawn, Holybourne, near Alton, Hants GU34 4ER. *T:* (01420) 544107.

Died 2 April 2001.

BEST, Prof. Ernest; Professor of Divinity and Biblical Criticism, University of Glasgow, 1974–82, then Professor Emeritus; Dean of the Faculty of Divinity, 1978–80; *b* 23 May 1917; *s* of John and Louisa Elizabeth Best; *m* 1949, Sarah Elizabeth Kingston (*d* 2002); two *d. Educ:* Methodist Coll., Belfast; Queen's Univ., Belfast (BA, MA, BD, PhD); Presbyterian Coll., Belfast. Asst Minister, First Bangor Presbyterian Church, 1943–49; Minister, Caledon and Minterburn Presbyterian Churches, 1949–63; Lectr (temp.), Presbyterian Coll., Belfast, 1953–54; Guest Prof., Austin Presbyterian Theol Seminary, Texas, 1955–57; Lectr in Biblical Lit. and Theol., St Andrews Univ., 1963–74 (Sen. Lectr 1971–74). Lectures: Nils W. Lund, Chicago, 1978; Manson Meml, Manchester Univ., 1978; Sprunt, Richmond, Va, 1985; Ethel M. Wood, London Univ., 1986. Vis. Prof. of New Testament Studies, Knox Coll., Dunedin, NZ, 1983; Vis. Fellow, Univ. of Otago, 1983; Gunning Fellow, New Coll., Edinburgh Univ., 1993. Jt Editor, Biblical Theology, 1962–72; Associate Editor, Irish Biblical Studies, 1978–. Hon. DD Glasgow, 1997. *Publications:* One Body in Christ, 1955; The Temptation and the Passion, 1965, 2nd edn 1990; The Letter of Paul to the Romans, 1967; 1 Peter, 1971; 1 and 2 Thessalonians, 1972; From Text to Sermon, 1977, 2nd edn 1988; (ed jtly) Text and Interpretation, 1979; Following Jesus, 1981; Mark: the Gospel as story, 1983;

Disciples and Discipleship, 1986; 2 Corinthians, 1987; Paul and His Converts, 1988; Interpreting Christ, 1993; Ephesians: a guide, 1993; Essays on Ephesians, 1997; Ephesians, 1998; Ephesians: a shorter introduction, 2003; contrib. Biblica, Ecumenical Review, Expository Times, Interpretation, Jl Theol Studies, New Testament Studies, Novum Testamentum, Scottish Jl Theology, Catholic Biblical Qly, Zeit. neu. test. Wiss. *Recreations:* vegetable growing, golf. *Address:* 13 Newmill Gardens, St Andrews, Fife KY16 8RY. *Died 1 Oct. 2004.*

BETHE, Prof. Hans Albrecht, PhD; Professor of Theoretical Physics, Cornell University, 1937–75, then Professor Emeritus; *b* Strassburg, Germany, 2 July 1906; *m* 1939, Rose Ewald; one *s* one *d. Educ:* Goethe Gymnasium, Frankfurt on Main; Univ. of Frankfurt; Univ. of Munich (PhD 1928). Instructor in Theoretical Physics, Univs of Frankfurt, Stuttgart, Munich and Tübingen, 1928–33; Lectr, Univs of Manchester and Bristol, 1933–35; Asst Prof., Cornell Univ., Ithaca, 1935–37; Dir, Theoretical Physics Div., Los Alamos Atomic Scientific Laboratory, 1943–46. Sabbatic leave to Cambridge Univ., academic year, 1955–56. Mem., President's Science Adv. Cttee, 1956–59. Member: Nat. Acad. Sciences; Amer. Physical Soc.; Amer. Astron. Soc.; For. Mem., Royal Society. Holds hon. doctorates in Science. US Medal of Merit, 1946; Planck Medal, German Physical Soc., 1955; Eddington Medal, Royal Astronomical Soc., 1961; Enrico Fermi Award, US Atomic Energy Commn, 1961; Nobel Prize for Physics, 1967. *Publications:* (jt author) Elementary Nuclear Theory, 1947; Mesons and Fields, 1955; Quantum Mechanics of One- and Two-Electron Atoms, 1957; Intermediate Quantum Mechanics, 1964; contributions to: Handbuch der Physik, 1933, 1954; Reviews of Mod. Physics, 1936–37, 1990; Physical Review; Astrophysical Jl. *Address:* Newman Laboratory of Nuclear Studies, Cornell University, Ithaca, NY 14853, USA. *Died 6 March 2005.*

BETHEL, David Percival; *see* Bethell, D. P.

BETHELL, David Percival, CBE 1983; Director, Leicester Polytechnic, 1973–87; *b* Bath, 7 Dec. 1923; *s* of William George Bethell and Elsie (*née* Cossins); formerly used surname spelling of Bethel; *m* 1943, Margaret Elizabeth (*d* 1998), *d* of late Alexander Wrigglesworth; one *s* one *d. Educ:* King Edward VI Sch., Bath; Crypt Grammar Sch., Glos; West of England Coll. of Art; Bristol Univ., 1946–51; NDD, ATD, FSAE, FCSD, RWA. Served with RN, Far East, 1943–45. Lectr, Stafford Coll. of Art, 1951–56; Deputy Principal, Coventry Coll. of Art, 1956–65; Principal, Coventry Coll. of Art, 1965–69; Dep. Dir, Leicester Polytechnic, 1969–73. Pres., Nat. Soc. for Art Educn, 1965–66; Member: Nat. Adv. Cttee for Art Educn, 1965–71; Jt Summerson Coldstream Cttee, 1968–70; The Design Council, 1980–88; Nat. Adv. Bd for Local Authority Higher Educn, 1983–87; OECD Directing Gp for Management of Higher Educn, 1984–87; Cttee for Internat. Co-operation in Higher Educn, British Council, 1981–88; Chairman: CNAA Cttee for Art and Design (and Research Degrees Sub-Cttee), 1975–81; Educn and Trng Bd, Chartered Soc. of Designers, 1987–91; Study Team on Delivery of Primary Health Care Services, 1987–88; Cttee of Dirs of Polytechnics, 1978–80; Vice-Chm., Inter-Univs and Polytechnics Council for Higher Educn Overseas. Sometime Design Consultant to Massey Ferguson, Van Heusen, Monotype Corp., etc. British Council Adviser to Hong Kong Govt, 1971; Chairman: UGC/NAB Town & Country Planning Courses Cttee, 1985–86; Hong Kong Planning Cttee for Academic Accreditation, 1986–89; Hong Kong Council for Acad. Accreditation, 1989–92; Member: Hong Kong UPGC, 1982–92; World Council, INSEA; Council of Europe; Assessor, Partnership Trust, 1991–93; Convenor, W Midlands Br., Conservative Acad. Liaison Forum, 1993–. Chairman: Cyril Wood Meml Trust; Leicester Haymarket Theatre, 1979–85; Frame-Work Knitters Educnl Bursary Awards Cttee, 1992–; Mem. Council,

RWA, 1993– (Sen. Vice-Pres., 1997–2002; Hon. Vice-Pres., 2002). Pres., Leicester Literary and Philosophical Soc., 2002–03. Paintings and prints in Glos Libraries, Stafford Art Gallery, Coventry, RWA, private collections. Liveryman, Co. of Frame-Work Knitters (Steward, 1994–97; Mem., Ct of Assts, 1997–). Aust. Commonwealth Travelling Fellowship, 1979. FRSA. Hon. LLD Leicester, 1982; Hon. DLitt Loughborough, 1987; Hon. DEd UWE, 1998; Hon. DDes Bournemouth, 2001. *Publications:* A Case of Sorts, 1991; An Industrious People, 1991; 120 Woodcuts & the Bard, 1994; Initial Influences, 1996. *Recreations:* travel; study of art, design, architecture; archæology, music. *Address:* 48 Holmfield Road, Stoneygate, Leicester LE2 1SA. *Club:* Athenæum.
Died 11 Dec. 2005.

BETHUNE, Hon. Sir (Walter) Angus, Kt 1979; pastoralist; *b* 10 Sept. 1908; *s* of Frank Pogson Bethune and Laura Eileen Bethune; *m* 1936, Alexandra P., *d* of P. A. Pritchard; one *s* one *d*. *Educ:* Hutchin's Sch., Hobart; Launceston Church of England Grammar Sch. Served War, RAAF Air Crew, Middle East, 1940–43. Member, Hamilton Municipal Council, 1936–56, resigned (Dep. Warden, 1955–56). MHA, Wilmot, Tasmania, 1946–75, resigned; Leader of Opposition, 1956–69; Premier and Treasurer, Tasmania, 1969–72. Leader of Liberal Party, 1960–72, resigned. President: Clarendon Children's Homes, 1977–83; St John's Ambulance Brigade (Tasmania), 1979–86. OStJ 1982. *Address:* 1 Quinn Court, Sandy Bay, Tas 7005, Australia. *Clubs:* Tasmanian; Naval, Military and Air Force; Royal Autocar of Tasmania.
Died 22 Aug. 2004.

BETTS, Prof. Alan Osborn, PhD, MA, BSc, MRCVS; Principal and Dean, The Royal Veterinary College, University of London, 1970–89, then Emeritus Professor; *b* 11 March 1927; *s* of late A. O. and D. S. A. Betts; *m* 1st, 1952, Joan M. Battersby (marr. diss. 1990; she *d* 1992); one *s* one *d*; 2nd, 1990, Jane Margaret Jones. *Educ:* Royal Veterinary Coll.; Magdalene Coll., Cambridge. Asst in Gen. Practice, 1949; Animal Health Trust Research Scholar, 1950–52; Demonstrator, Univ. of Cambridge, 1952–56; Commonwealth Fund Fellow, Cornell Univ., USA, 1955–56; University Lectr, Cambridge, 1956–64; Prof. of Veterinary Microbiology and Parasitology, Univ. of London, 1964–70; Vice-Chm., 1976–88, Acting Chm., 1989, Governing Body of Wye Coll.; Dep. Vice-Chancellor, Univ. of London, 1984–88. Leverhulme Vis. Fellow, Graduate Sch. of Admin, Univ. of Calif, Davis, 1982. Treasurer: BVA, 1967–70; RCVS, 1978–81; Pres., Vet. Res. Club, 1984–85. Member: Brit. Pharmacopoeia Commn 1978–93; EC Adv. Cttee on Veterinary Trng, 1980–90; Bucks FHSA, 1992–96; Complaints Convenor, Bucks HA, 1998–. Mem. Council, Imperial Cancer Research Fund, 1988–97. Vice-Chm., Comparative Clin. Studies Foundn, 2003–. Trustee, Hunterian Mus., RCSE, 1990–. Dalrymple-Champneys Cup and Medal of BVA, 1978; Faculty Medal, Vet. Faculty, Univ. of Munich, 1985. *Publications:* Viral and Rickettsial Infections of Animals, 1967; papers in microbiological, veterinary and management jls. *Recreations:* travel, gliding. *Address:* Clarissa House, High Street, Wappenham, Towcester, Northants NN12 8SN. *T:* and *Fax:* (01327) 860812. *Club:* Athenæum.
Died 25 Nov. 2005.

BETTS, Air Vice-Marshal (Charles) Stephen, CBE 1963; Head of Control and Inspection Division, Agency for the Control of Armaments, WEU, Paris, 1974–84; *b* 8 April 1919; *s* of H. C. Betts, Nuneaton; *m* 1st, 1943, Pauline Mary (deceased), *d* of Lt-Col P. Heath; two *d*; 2nd, 1964, Margaret Doreen (*d* 1993), *d* of Col W. H. Young, DSO; 3rd, 1996, Denys Mary, *d* of William de Montigny Clarke. *Educ:* King Edward's Sch., Nuneaton; Sidney Sussex Coll., Cambridge (MA). Joined RAF 1941; Air Cdre 1966; Asst Comdt (Eng.), RAF Coll., Cranwell, 1971–72; Air Vice-Marshal 1972; AOC No 24 Group, RAF, 1972–73, retired 1974. *Recreations:* travel, music. *Address:* Cranford, Weston Road, Bath BA1 2XX. *T:* and

Fax: (01225) 310995. *Club:* Royal Air Force.
Died 3 July 2002.

BETTS, Rt Rev. Stanley Woodley, CBE 1967; *b* 23 March 1912; *yr s* of Hubert Woodley and Lillian Esther Betts. *Educ:* Perse Sch.; Jesus Coll., Cambridge (MA 1937); Ridley Hall, Cambridge. Curate of St Paul's Cheltenham, 1935–38; Chaplain, RAF, 1938–47 (despatches); Sen. Chaplain of BAFO, Germany, 1946–47; Comdt, RAF Chaplains' Sch., Dowdeswell Court, 1947; Chaplain, Clare Coll., Cambridge, 1947–49; Chaplain, Cambridge Pastorate, 1947–56; Proctor in Convocation, 1952–59; Vicar of Holy Trinity Cambridge, 1949–56; Exam. Chaplain to Bishop of Southwell, 1947–56; Select Preacher to University of Cambridge, 1955; Suffragan Bishop of Maidstone, 1956–66; Archbishop of Canterbury's Episcopal Representative with the three Armed Forces, 1956–66; Dean of Rochester, 1966–77. Chm., Bd of the Church Army, 1970–80; Vice-President: Lee Abbey, 1977–; Wadhurst Coll., 1984–97 (Chm. Council 1976–84). *Address:* 2 King's Houses, Pevensey, Sussex BN24 5JR. *T:* (01323) 762421. *Club:* National.
Died 7 June 2003.

BETTS, Air Vice-Marshal Stephen; *see* Betts, Air Vice-Marshal C. S.

BEVAN, Walter Harold, CBE 1977; FCIS; Chairman, Gateshead District Health Authority (formerly of Gateshead Area Health Authority), 1977–84; *b* 22 May 1916; *s* of late Walter Bevan and Sarah (*née* Grainger); *m* 1958, Patricia Edna Sadler, *d* of late Sir Sadler Forster, CBE, DCL; twin *s* and *d*. *Educ:* Gateshead Sch. FCIS 1961. 5th Bn Royal Northumberland Fusiliers, TA, 1938–42; served War: commissioned RA; Arakan campaign, Burma, with 81st W African Div., 1942–46; 4/5 Bn Royal Northumberland Fusiliers, TA, 1947–52. Asst to Sec., North Eastern Trading Estates Ltd, 1937, Chief Accountant 1956; English Industrial Estates Corporation: Chief Accountant, 1960; Sec., 1966; Finance Dir and Sec., 1973; Chief Exec. and Chm., Management Bd, 1974–79. *Publications:* articles on industrial estates and distribution of industry. *Recreations:* listening to music, bowling, reading, Methodist Church. *Died 7 Nov. 2005.*

BEVINGTON, Eric Raymond, CMG 1961; *b* 23 Jan. 1914; *s* of late R. Bevington and N. E. Bevington (*née* Sutton); *m* 1939, Enid Mary Selina (*née* Homer); one *s* one *d*. *Educ:* Monkton Combe Sch.; Loughborough Coll.; Queens' Coll., Cambridge. CEng, MIMechE. Cadet, HM Overseas Service, Gilbert and Ellice Islands, 1937; District Officer, Fiji, 1942; Sec., Commn of Enquiry into Cost of Living Allowances, Nigeria, 1945–46; Admin. Officer Cl I, Fiji, 1950; Asst Col Sec. (Develt), Fiji, 1951; Develt Comr, Brunei, 1954; Financial Sec., Fiji, 1958–61; Development Commissioner, 1962–63; Mem., Executive Council, Fiji, 1958–63; Senior Project Engineer, Wrigh Rain Ltd, 1964–67; Appeals Inspector, Min. of Housing and Local Govt, 1967–70; Sen. Housing and Planning Inspector, DoE, 1970–78. Mem., New Forest DC, 1979–83. *Publication:* The Things We Do For England, 1990. *Address:* The Old Parsonage Court, Flat 7, Otterbourne, Winchester, Hants SO21 2EP. *T:* (01962) 712560. *Died 30 April 2004.*

BEVINS, Anthony John; Political Editor, The Express, 1998–2000; *b* 16 Aug. 1942; *s* of Rt Hon. John Reginald Bevins, PC and Mary Leonora (*née* Jones); *m* 1965, Ruchira Mishtuni (*née* Roy) (*d* 2001); one *s* one *d*. *Educ:* Liverpool Collegiate Grammar Sch.; LSE (BSc Econ). VSO, 1964–66; Sub-Editor, Liverpool Daily Post & Echo, 1967–69; Liverpool Daily Post: Dep. Chief Sub-Editor, 1969–70; Political Corresp., 1970–73; Political Staff, Sunday Express, 1973; Political Correspondent: The Sun, 1973–76; Daily Mail, 1976–81; The Times, 1981–86; Political Editor: The Independent, 1986–93 and 1996–98; The Observer, 1993–96. Political Reporter of the Year, Granada TV What the Papers Say, 1990; Jt Winner, British

Press Awards, Exclusive of the Year, 1993.
Died 23 March 2001.

BEVINS, Kenneth Milton, CBE 1973; TD 1951; Director: Royal Insurance Co. Ltd, then Royal Insurance plc, 1970–88; Royal Insurance Holdings, 1988–89; *b* 2 Nov. 1918; *yr s* of late John Milton Bevins and Grace Eveline Bevins, Liverpool; *m* 1st, 1940, Joan Harding (*d* 1969); two *d*; 2nd, 1971, Diana B. Sellers, *y d* of late Godfrey J. Sellers, Keighley. *Educ:* Liverpool Collegiate Sch. Served War, 1939–46: 136 Field Regt, RA, incl. with 14th Army in Burma, 1943–46 (Major). Joined Royal Insurance Co. Ltd, 1937; Sec., 1957; Gen. Manager, 1963; Dep. Chief Gen. Manager, 1966; Chief Gen. Manager, 1970–80; Director: Trade Indemnity Co. Ltd, 1970–80 (Chm., 1975–80); Mutual & Federal Insurance Co. Ltd, 1971–80; British Aerospace plc, 1981–87. Dir, Fire Protection Assoc., 1963–77 (Chm., 1966–68). Member: Jt Fire Research Organisation Steering Cttee, 1966–68; Home Secretary's Standing Cttee on Crime Prevention, 1967–73; Exec. Cttee, City Communications Centre, 1976–80; Bd, British Aerospace, 1980–81; Govt Cttee to review structure, functions and status of ECGD, 1983–84. Chm., British Insurance Assoc., 1971–73 (Dep. Chm., 1967–71). *Recreations:* travel, gardening, reading, painting. *Address:* Linton, The Drive, Sevenoaks, Kent TN13 3AF. *T:* (01732) 456909. *Clubs:* Oriental, Army and Navy.
Died 30 June 2001.

BIBBY, Sir Derek (James), 2nd Bt *cr* 1959, of Tarporley, Co. Palatine of Chester; MC 1945; DL; President, Bibby Line Group Ltd (formerly Bibby Line Ltd), since 1992 (Chairman, 1969–92); *b* 29 June 1922; *s* of Major Sir (Arthur) Harold Bibby, 1st Bt, DSO, DL, LLD, and of Marjorie, *d* of Charles J. Williamson; *S* father, 1986; *m* 1961, Christine Maud, *d* of late Rt Rev. F. J. Okell, MA, DD, Bishop of Stockport; four *s* one *d*. *Educ:* Rugby; Trinity Coll., Oxford (MA). Served War, Army, 1942–46. DL Cheshire, 1987. *Recreation:* gardening. *Heir: s* Michael James Bibby [*b* 2 Aug. 1963; *m* 1994, Beverley, *o d* of Donald Graham; two *s* (twins)]. *Address:* Willaston Grange, Willaston, Neston, Cheshire CH64 2UN. *T:* (0151) 327 4913.
Died 9 Oct. 2002.

BICKNELL, Claud, OBE 1946; a Law Commissioner, 1970–75; a part-time Chairman of Industrial Tribunals, 1975–83; *b* Rowlands Gill, near Newcastle upon Tyne, 15 June 1910; 2nd *s* of Raymond Bicknell and Phillis Bicknell (*née* Lovibond); *m* 1st, 1934, Esther Irene (*d* 1958), *e d* of Kenneth Bell; one *s* two *d* (and one *d* decd); 2nd, 1960, Christine Betty Reynolds, CBE (*d* 1999). *Educ:* Oundle Sch.; Queens' Coll., Cambridge (MA 1935). Pres., Cambridge Univ. Mountaineering Club, 1930–31. Admitted as a solicitor, 1934; Asst Solicitor, 1934–39, and partner, 1939–70, in firm of Stanton, Atkinson & Bird, Newcastle upon Tyne. Dir, Northern Corporation Ltd, 1939–53. Auxiliary Fire Service, Newcastle upon Tyne, 1939–41; Nat. Fire Service, 1941–45; Sen. Fire Staff Officer, Home Office, 1943–45. Mem. Planning Bd, Lake District Nat. Park, 1951–70 (Chm., Development Control Cttee, 1957–70). Chm., Newcastle upon Tyne Housing Improvement Trust Ltd, 1966–70. Pres., Newcastle upon Tyne Incorp. Law Soc., 1969. *Recreation:* mountains. *Address:* Aikrigg End Cottage, Burneside Road, Kendal LA9 6DZ. *Clubs:* Garrick, Alpine.
Died 18 March 2002.

BIDGOOD, John Claude, MIEx; Director, Bidgood Holdings Ltd, 1947–97; *b* 12 May 1914; *s* of late Edward Charles Bidgood, Leeds; *m* 1945, Sheila Nancy Walker Wood; one *s* two *d*. *Educ:* London Choir Sch.; Woodhouse Technical Sch. Served early part of War of 1939–45 as Pilot RAF. Mem. Leeds City Council, 1947–55 (late Chm. Works Cttee and City Architects Cttee). Contested (C) N E Leeds, 1950, 1951; MP (C) Bury and Radcliffe, 1955–64; PPS to Joint Parly Secs, Min. of Pensions and Nat. Insurance, 1957–58; Mem. Parly Select Cttee on Estimates, 1958–64. Formerly Chairman: Anglo-Dominion Finance Co. Ltd; Anglo

Dominion Construction Co. Ltd; Anglo-Dominion Trading Co. Ltd. Chm., Yorks Assoc. for the Disabled, 1950–58; Member: Inst. of Export; Leeds and Bradford Joint Aerodrome Cttee, 1951–55. Mayor, Chapeltown Corporation, 1987–88. Hon. Citizen, City of Atlanta, Georgia, 1960; Freeman, City of London, 1961; Liveryman and Mem., Worshipful Co. of Horners. *Recreations:* music, travel. *Address:* The Old Joinery, Walton, near Wetherby, W Yorks LS23 7DQ. *T:* (01937) 844028. *Club:* City Livery.
Died 17 Aug. 2001.

BIGGS, Vice-Adm. Sir Geoffrey (William Roger), KCB 1993; Military Adviser to Fujitsu, and to ICL, since 1995; *b* 23 Nov. 1938; *s* of Vice-Adm. Sir Hilary Biggs, KBE, CB, DSO and Lady Biggs; *m* 1st, 1968, Marcia (*née* Leask) (marr. diss. 1978); three *s*; 2nd, 1981, Caroline Ann (*née* Daly); one *d*, and two step *s*. *Educ:* St Andrews, Eastbourne; Charterhouse. Joined RN 1956, Submarine Service, 1960; commanded HM Ships: Otus, 1969–70; Superb, 1978–79; Brilliant, 1984–85; Broadsword, 1985–86; Capt. 2nd Frigate Sqn, 1985–86; Dir of Naval Ops, 1986–89; Flag Officer Gibraltar, 1990; Comdr British Forces Gibraltar, 1990–92; Dep. Comdr and C of S to C-in-C Fleet, 1992–94; retd, 1995. *Recreations:* lawnmowing, crosswords, family and friends. *Address:* c/o Naval Secretary, Victory Building, HM Naval Base, Portsmouth PO1 3LS.
Died 29 June 2002.

BILL, (Edward) Geoffrey (Watson), OBE 1991; FSA, FRHistS; Lambeth Librarian, 1958–91; Lecturer and Archivist, Christ Church, Oxford, 1950–91; *b* 19 Feb. 1924; *s* of Edward Richard Bill and Anne (*née* Greenwood); *m* 1951, Margaret Nancy Finch; one *s* one *d*. *Educ:* Kingston Grammar Sch.; Balliol Coll., Oxford (MA). FRHistS 1983; FSA 1984. Served Army, 1943–46 (Lieut). Dept of Western MSS, Bodleian Library, Oxford, 1954–58. DLitt Lambeth, 1983. *Publications:* Christ Church Meadow, 1965; (with Dr J. F. A. Mason) Christ Church and Reform 1850–1867, 1970; University Reform in Nineteenth Century Oxford, 1973; Education at Christ Church Oxford 1660–1800, 1988; Catalogue of MSS in Lambeth Palace Library, 1972–83. *Recreation:* avoiding gardening. *Address:* 22 Helme Lodge, Kendal, Cumbria LA9 7QA.
Died 2 Dec. 2001.

BILLINGHAM, Prof. Rupert Everett, MA, DPhil, DSc Oxon; FRS 1961; Professor and Chairman, Department of Cell Biology and Anatomy, Southwestern Medical School, University of Texas Health Science Center at Dallas, 1971–86, Professor Emeritus, 1990; *b* 15 Oct. 1921; *o s* of Albert Everett and Helen Louise Billingham, Oxford; *m* 1951, Jean Mary Morpeth; two *s* one *d*. *Educ:* City of Oxford High Sch.; Oriel Coll., Oxford. Served 1942–46, as Lieut RNVR. Asst Lectr, later Lectr in Zoology, University of Birmingham, 1947; Junior Research Fellow, British Empire Cancer Campaign, 1950; Intermediate Research Fellow, Brit. Emp. Cancer Campaign, 1953; Hon. Res. Asst, later Res. Associate, Dept of Zoology, University Coll., London, 1951; Wistar Prof. of Zoology, Univ. of Pennsylvania, USA, and Mem. of Wistar Institute of Anatomy and Biology, Philadelphia, 1957; Prof. and Chm., Dept of Medical Genetics, Univ. of Pennsylvania Med. Sch., Pa, 1965–71. Member: Allergy and Immunology Study Section, Nat. Insts of Health, US Public Health Service, 1958–62; Transplantation and Immunology Cttee, Nat. Insts of Health, 1968–70, 1971–73; Scientific Adv. Cttee, Massachusetts General Hospital, 1976–79; Nat. Allergy and Infectious Diseases Council, Nat. Insts of Health, 1980–83; Sigma Xi College of Nat. Lecturers, 1981–83; President: Transplantation Soc., 1974–76; Internat. Soc. for Immunology of Reproduction, 1983–86. Hon. Mem., British Transplantation Soc., 1988. Fellow, New York Acad. of Sciences, 1962; Fellow, Amer. Acad. of Arts and Sciences, 1965. Lectures: Herman Beerman, Soc. for Investigative Dermatology, 1963; I. S. Ravdin, Amer. College of Surgeons, 1964; *Sigma Xi*, Yale, 1965; Nat. Insts of Health, 1965; J. W. Jenkinson Meml, Oxford, 1965–66; Harvey,

NY, 1966; Kinyoun, Nat. Inst. of Allergy and Infectious Diseases, 1979; Dist. Guest, Soc. for Gyn. Investigation, 1982. Hon. DSc: Trinity Coll., Hartford, Conn, 1965; Univ. of Pennsylvania, 1992. Alvarenga Prize, Coll. Physicians, Philadelphia, 1963; Hon. Award Medal, Amer. Assoc. of Plastic Surgeons, 1964; Adair Award, Amer. Gynecological Soc., 1971; AOA Honor Med. Soc., 1974. *Publications:* The Immunobiology of Transplantation (with W. K. Silvers), 1971; The Immunobiology of Mammalian Reproduction (with A. E. Beer), 1976; contribs to scien. jls on biology of skin, immunology of tissue transplantation and immunology of mammalian reproduction. *Recreations:* woodwork, gardening. *Address:* RR3, Box 86P, Vineyard Haven, MA 02568, USA. *T:* (508) 6937939.

Died 16 Nov. 2002.

BINGLEY, Juliet Martin, (Lady Bingley), MBE 1991; Research Social Worker, City Corporation Social Services, based at St Mark's Hospital, EC1, 1990–96 (Senior Social Worker, 1973–90); *b* 18 July 1925; *d* of Reginald Vick, OBE, MCh, FRCS and Mary Kate Vick; *m* 1948, Adm. Sir Alexander Noel Campbell Bingley, GCB, OBE (*d* 1972); one *s* two *d*. *Educ:* King Alfred School, Hampstead; London Sch. of Economics. Associated Mem., Inst. of Medical Social Workers. Social Worker, St Bartholomew's Hosp., 1945–48. Chairman: Nat. Assoc. of Mental Health, 1979–84; Good Practices in Mental Health, 1989–93; Vice-Chm., Nat. Assoc. for Colitis and Crohn's Disease, 1989–97; Vice Pres., Mind, 1996–. Counsellor, Dr Aubrey and Partners, Welwyn, Herts, 1990–. CStJ 1962. Companion of Honour, Republic of Malta, 1976. *Publication:* What it Was and What it Was Not (poems), 2002. *Recreations:* music, gardening, reading, theatre, moving furniture, collecting Staffordshire figures, lawn mowing. *Address:* Hoddesdonbury Farm, Hoddesdon, Herts EN11 8LS. *T:* (01992) 463238. *Died 16 Jan. 2005.*

BIOBAKU, Dr Saburi Oladeni, CMG 1961; MA, PhD; research historian and management consultant; Research Professor and Director, Institute of African Studies, University of Ibadan, 1976–83; *b* 16 June 1918; *s* of late Chief S. O. Biobaku, Aré of Iddo, Abeokuta; *m* 1949, Muhabat Folasade, *d* of Alhaji L. B. Agusto, barrister-at-law, Lagos; one *s*. *Educ:* Govt Coll., Ibadan; Higher Coll., Yaba; University Coll., Exeter; Trinity Coll., Cambridge. BA London, 1945; BA Cantab, 1947, MA 1951; PhD London, 1951. Education Officer, Nigeria, 1947–53; Registrar, University Coll., Ibadan, 1953–57; Dir, Yoruba Historical Research Scheme, 1956–; Sec. to Premier and Executive Council, Western Nigeria, 1957–61; Pro-Vice-Chancellor, Univ. of Ife, Nigeria, 1961–65; Vice-Chancellor, Univ. of Lagos, 1965–72; Chairman, Management Consultant Services Ltd, Lagos, 1972–76, 1983–. Hon. DLitt. Created: Aré of Iddo, Abeokuta, 1958; Agbakin of Igbore, 1972; Maye of Ife, 1980; Baapitan of Egbaland, 1980. *Publications:* The Origin of the Yoruba, 1955; The Egba and Their Neighbours 1842–1872, 1957; Living Cultures of Nigeria, 1977; When We Were Young, 1993; A Window on Nigeria, 1996; When We Were No Longer Young, 1999; contribs to Africa, jl of Nigerian Historical Soc., Odu (Joint Ed.), etc. *Recreations:* soccer, tennis, badminton, swimming, walking. *Address:* PO Box 7741, Lagos, Nigeria. *T:* (home) (1) 4961430. *Clubs:* Metropolitan (Lagos); Dining (Ibadan). *Died 8 Feb. 2001.*

BIRCH, Robert Edward Thomas, CBE 1979; Director General, Federation Against Copyright Theft, 1982–85; *b* 9 May 1917; *s* of late Robert Birch and Edith Birch; *m* 1946, Laura Pia Busini; two *d*. *Educ:* Dulwich Coll. Served RA, 1940–46, Africa, Italy, NW Europe (Major). Admitted solicitor, 1942; joined Solicitors' Dept, New Scotland Yard, 1946; Dep. Solicitor, 1968; Solicitor, 1976–82. *Recreations:* swimming, travel.

Died 12 Oct. 2004.

BIRKMYRE, Sir Archibald, 3rd Bt *cr* 1921, of Dalmunzie, Co. Perth; *b* 12 Feb. 1923; *s* of Sir Henry

Birkmyre, 2nd Bt and Doris Gertrude Birkmyre (*née* Austen Smith); *S* father, 1992; *m* 1953, Gillian Mary, *o d* of late E. M. Downes, OBE; one *s* two *d*. *Educ:* Radley Coll. Served India and Burma, RA, 1942–45. Mem., London Stock Exchange, 1954–88. *Recreations:* golf, fishing, shooting. *Heir:* *s* James Birkmyre [*b* 29 Feb. 1956; *m* 1990, Leslie Amanda, *er d* of Richard Lyon, Seal Beach, Calif; one *s*]. *Address:* The Old Presbytery, Buckland, Faringdon, Oxon SN7 8QW. *T:* (01367) 870253. *Clubs:* Boodle's, MCC; Huntercombe Golf.

Died 7 May 2001.

BIRKS, Lt-Gen. Anthony Leonard, CB 1993; OBE 1985 (MBE 1977); Chief of Defence Force, New Zealand Defence Force, 1995–99; *b* 30 Dec. 1941; *s* of Clifford Birks and Maisie Lola Gapes (*née* Brown); *m* 1964, Georgina May Ball, Bedfordshire; two *s* one *d*. *Educ:* St Andrew Coll., Christchurch; Nelson Coll.; RMA Sandhurst. Commissioned 1961; Platoon Comdr, 1 RNZIR, Malaya and Borneo, 1963–65; 1 Australian Task Force, Vietnam, 1968; 11 Field Force, Vietnam, 1970; Chief Instructor, Tactical Sch., 1977–78; Staff Coll., Australia, 1974; CO 2/1 RNZIR, 1979–81; Dir of Plans, Army, 1981–82; JSSC 1983; Comdr 3TF, 1985–87; Asst Chief Ops HQ, NZ Defence Force, 1988–89; RCDS 1990; Dep. Chief of Defence Staff, HQ NZ Defence Force, 1991; CGS NZ Army, 1992–95. NZ Trustee, Prince's (formerly Prince of Wales') Trust, 2000–; Advr, Ngati Awa Service Acad., 2000–02. *Recreations:* golf, Harley-Davidson motor-cycling. *Address:* 208 Pohutukawa Avenue, Ohope Beach, Whakatane, Bay of Plenty, New Zealand. *Club:* Wellington (Wellington).

Died 21 Jan. 2002.

BIRKS, Dr Jack, CBE 1975; FREng; Life President, British Maritime Technology Ltd, since 1995 (Chairman, 1985–95); *b* 1 Jan. 1920; *s* of late Herbert Horace Birks and of Ann Birks; *m* 1st, 1948, Vere Elizabeth Burrell-Davis (*d* 1998); two *s* two *d*; 2nd, 2000, Margaret Lucy Stevens. *Educ:* Ecclesfield Grammar Sch.; Univ. of Leeds (BSc, PhD). Served with REME, Europe and India, 1941–46 (despatches, Captain). Exploration Research Div., Anglo Iranian Oil Co., 1948–57; Manager, Petroleum Engrg Research, BP Research Centre, Sunbury, 1957–59; Vice-Pres. Exploration, BP North America, NY, 1959–62; various techn. and managerial appts, subseq. Dir and Gen. Man., Iranian Oil Exploration & Producing Co., Teheran and Masjid-i-Sulaiman, 1962–70; Gen. Man., Exploration and Production Dept, British Petroleum Co. Ltd, London, 1970–72; Technical Dir, BP Trading Ltd, and Dep. Chm., BP Trading Exec. Cttee, 1972–77; a Man. Dir, British Petroleum, 1978–82; Chairman: BP Coal, 1981–82; Selection Trust, 1981–82; BP Minerals International, 1981–82; NMI Ltd, 1982–85; Charterhouse Petroleum, 1982–86; Schroder Energy, subseq. LAE Energy Inc., 1981–88; London American Energy NV, 1986–88 (Dir, 1981–88); Mountain Petroleum, 1988–90 (Dir, 1986–90); North American Gas Investment Trust plc, 1989–95; Director: Jebsens Drilling, subseq. Midland and Scottish Resources, 1982–97 (Chm., 1994–97); George Wimpey, 1982–90; Petrofina (UK), 1986–89; Bellwether Exploration Co., 1988–; Gulf Indonesia Resources Ltd, 1997–. Member: SRC, 1976–80; Meteorological Cttee, 1977–82; Adv. Council on R&D, Dept of Energy, 1978–82; Offshore Energy Technology Bd, Dept of Energy, 1978–82. Mem. Council, Royal Instn of GB, 1988–. President: Soc. for Underwater Technology, 1974; Pipeline Industries Guild, 1979–81; Inst. of Petroleum, 1984–86. FREng (FEng 1978). Hon. FIMechE 1987. Hon. LLD Aberdeen, 1981; DU Surrey, 1981. *Publications:* contribs to technical internat. oil jls, sci. papers on oilfields develts and North Sea oil. *Recreations:* tennis, cricket, golf. *Address:* High Silver, High Street, Holt, Norfolk NR25 6BN. *T:* (01263) 712847. *Clubs:* Athenæum; Norfolk (Norwich). *Died 27 June 2001.*

BIRKS, Prof. Peter Brian Herrenden, FBA 1989; Regius Professor of Civil Law, University of Oxford, and

Fellow of All Souls College, Oxford, since 1989; *b* 3 Oct. 1941; *e s* of Dr Peter Herrenden Birks and Mary (*née* Morgan); *m* 1984, Jacqueline S. Berrington (*née* Stimpson). *Educ:* Trinity Coll., Oxford (MA; Hon. Fellow, 1994); University Coll., London (LLM; Fellow, 1993). DCL Oxon, 1991; LLD Edin., 1991. Lectr in Laws, UCL, 1966–71; Law Fellow, Brasenose Coll., Oxford, 1971–81; Prof. of Civil Law, and Head of Dept of Civil Law, Edinburgh Univ., 1981–87; Prof. of Law, Southampton Univ., 1988–89. Wisselleerstoelhouder, Faculty of Law, Univ. of Nijmegen, 1994–96; Vis. Prof., Univ. of Texas at Austin, 2001. Hon. Sec., SPTL, later SLS, 1989–96 (Mem. Council, 1988–96; Pres., 2002–03); Member: Lord Chancellor's Adv. Cttee on Legal Educn, 1989–91; Social Sciences Cttee, Schs Exams and Assessment Council, 1989–91 (Chm., Law Cttee, 1988–89); Humanities Res. Bd, 1996–98; Sec., Standing Conf. on Legal Educn, 1991–94. Consultant Editor, Restitution Law Review, 1993–. Mem., Eur. Acad. of Private Lawyers, 1994–. Hon. QC 1995. FRSA 1992. Hon. DJur: Regensburg, 1996; Nijmegen, 2003; Hon. LLD De Montfort, 1999. *Publications:* Introduction to the Law of Restitution, 1985; (ed with D. N. MacCormick) The Legal Mind, 1986; (with G. McLeod) The Institutes of Justinian, 1987; (ed) New Perspectives on the Roman Law of Property, 1989; Restitution: the future, 1992; (ed) Frontiers of Liability, vols 1 and 2, 1994; (ed) Reviewing Legal Education, 1994; (ed) Laundering and Tracing, 1995; (ed) Wrongs and Remedies in 21st Century, 1996; (ed) What are Law Schools For?, 1996; (ed) Privacy and Loyalty, 1997; (ed) The Classification of Obligations, 1997; English Private Law, 2000; Unjust Enrichment, 2003; articles on Roman law, legal history, legal educn, and restitution. *Address:* Oak Trees, Sandy Lane, Boars Hill, Oxford OX1 5HN. *T:* (01865) 735625; All Souls College, Oxford OX1 4AL. *T:* (01865) 279338, *Fax:* (01865) 279299. *Club:* Athenæum.
Died 6 July 2004.

BIRLEY, Sir Derek (Sydney), Kt 1989; Vice-Chancellor, University of Ulster, 1984–91; *b* 31 May 1926; *s* of late Sydney John and Margaret Birley; *m* 1948, Margery Duckworth; two *s*; *m* 1990, Prof. Norma Reid. *Educ:* Hemsworth Grammar Sch.; Queens' Coll., Cambridge (BA 1950, MA 1954). Royal Artillery, 1944–48; Schoolmaster, Queen Elizabeth Grammar Sch., Wakefield, 1952–55; Admin. Asst, Leeds Educn Cttee, 1955–59; Asst Educn Officer: Dorset, 1959–61; Lancs, 1961–64; Dep. Dir of Educn, Liverpool, 1964–70; Rector, Ulster Polytechnic, 1970–84. Hon. Fellow, Sheffield Poly., 1991. Hon. LLD QUB, 1991. *Publications:* The Education Officer and his World, 1970; (with Anne Dufton) An Equal Chance, 1971; Planning and Education, 1972; The Willow Wand, 1979; Sport and the Making of Britain, 1993; Land of Sport and Glory, 1994; Playing the Game, 1996; A Social History of English Cricket (William Hill Sports Book of the Year, Cricket Soc. Literary Award), 1999. *Recreations:* books, cricket, jazz. *Address:* Min Dowr, Hodder's Way, Cargreen, Saltash, Cornwall PL12 6NY. *Died 14 May 2002.*

BIRT, Prof. (Lindsay) Michael, AO 1986; CBE 1980; FTS; Vice-Chancellor, University of New South Wales, 1981–92; Chairman, Australian Science and Technology Council, 1992–93; *b* 18 Jan. 1932; *s* of Robert Birt and Florence Elizabeth Chapman; *m* 1959, Jenny Tapfield; two *s*. *Educ:* Melbourne Boys' High Sch.; Univ. of Melbourne (BAgrSc, BSc, PhD); Univ. of Oxford (DPhil). FTS 1992. Univ. of Melbourne: Lectr in Biochemistry, 1960–63; Sen. Lectr in Biochem., 1964; Sen. Lectr in Biochem., Univ. of Sheffield, 1964–67; Foundn Prof. of Biochemistry, ANU, 1967–73; Emer. Prof.,1974; Vice-Chancellor designate, Wollongong Univ. Coll., Nov. 1973; Vice-Chancellor, Univ. of Wollongong, 1975–81. Hon. DLitt Wollongong, 1981; Hon. LLD Sheffield, 1988; Hon. DSc: New South Wales, 1992; Queensland, 1992; Dr (*hc*) Charles Sturt. *Publications:* Biochemistry of the Tissues (with W. Bartley and P. Banks), 1968 (London), 1970 (Germany, as Biochemie), 1972 (Japan);

Not an Ivory Tower: the making of an Australian Vice-Chancellor, 1997. *Recreations:* music, reading. *Address:* 85 Florida Road, Palm Beach, NSW 2108, Australia. *T:* (2) 99744651. *Clubs:* Union, University and Schools (Sydney); Melbourne Cricket, Sydney Cricket.
Died 28 Oct. 2001.

BIRT, Ven. Canon William Raymond; Archdeacon of Berkshire, 1973–77, Archdeacon Emeritus, since 1985; Hon. Canon of Christ Church Cathedral, Oxford, 1980; *b* 25 Aug. 1911; *s* of Rev. Douglas Birt, Rector of Leconfield with Scorborough, and Dorothy Birt; *m* 1st, 1936, Marie Louise Jeaffreson (*d* 1990); one *s* two *d*; 2nd, 1994, Diana Bronwen Warren (*née* Montgomery). *Educ:* Christ's Hospital; Ely Theological Coll. Served War of 1939–45, Major, 22nd Dragoons (RAC), 1941–46 (despatches). Schoolmaster, Trent Coll., 1929–31; sub-editor, Daily Sketch, 1933–34; asst editor, Play Rights Publications, 1934–39; Editor: Winchester Publications, 1946–49; Country Life Books, 1949–56. Ordained deacon, 1956, priest, 1957; Curate, Caversham, 1956–59; Vicar, St George, Newbury, 1959–71; Rector of West Woodhay, 1971–81, Asst Rector, 1981–91; Rural Dean of Newbury, 1969–73. *Recreations:* gardens and gardening. *Address:* 1 The Old Bakery, George Street, Kingsclere, Newbury, Berkshire RG20 5NQ. *T:* (01635) 297426.
Died 11 March 2002.

BISHOP, Sir Frederick (Arthur), Kt 1975; CB 1960; CVO 1957; Director-General of the National Trust, 1971–75; *b* 4 Dec. 1915; *o s* of A. J. Bishop, Bristol; *m* 1940, Elizabeth Finlay Stevenson (*d* 1999); two *s* one *d*. *Educ:* Colston's Hospital, Bristol; LLB (London). Inland Revenue, 1934. Served in RAF and Air Transport Auxiliary, 1942–46. Joined Ministry of Food, 1947, where Principal Private Secretary to Ministers, 1949–52; Asst Secretary, Cabinet Office, 1953–55; Principal Private Secretary to the Prime Minister, 1956–59; Deputy Secretary: of the Cabinet, 1959–61; Min. of Agriculture, Fisheries and Food, 1961–64; Perm. Sec., Min. of Land and Natural Resources, 1964–65, resigned. Chm., Home Grown Timber Advisory Cttee, 1966–73; Member: BBC Gen. Adv. Council, 1971–75; Crafts Adv. Council, 1973–75. Director: S. Pearson & Son Ltd, 1965–70; Pearson Longman, 1970–77; English China Clays Ltd, 1975–86; Devon and Cornwall Bd, Lloyds Bank, 1976–86. *Address:* Manor Barn, Church Road, Bramshott, Liphook GU30 7SQ. *Died 2 March 2005.*

BJELKE-PETERSEN, Hon. Sir Johannes, KCMG 1984; Premier of Queensland, 1968–87; *b* Dannevirke, NZ, 13 Jan. 1911; *s* of late C. G. Bjelke-Petersen, Denmark; *m* 1952, Florence Isabel (Senator for Queensland in Commonwealth Parliament, 1981–93), *d* of J. P. Gilmour; one *s* three *d*. *Educ:* Taabinga Valley Sch.; corresp. courses, and privately. MLA National Party (formerly Country Party): for Nanango, 1947–50; for Barambah, 1950–87; Minister for Works and Housing, Qld, 1963–68. *Address:* Bethany, Kingaroy, Queensland 4610, Australia. *Died 23 April 2005.*

BJØRNSON, Maria Elena; theatre designer, since 1969; *b* Paris, 16 Feb. 1949; *d* of Bjørn Bjørnson and Maria Prodan. *Educ:* Byam Shaw Sch. of Art (Pre-Dip); Central Sch. of Art and Design (MA). Ext. Examr, Central St Martin's Theatre Dept, 1993–. Designs include: *stage:* Scapino (costumes), NT, 1969; 13 productions for Citizens' Th., Glasgow; Antony and Cleopatra, Bankside Globe, 1973; Hedda Gabler, Duke of York's, 1977; Vieux Carré (costumes), Piccadilly, 1978; The Cherry Orchard, Chichester, 1981; The Lonely Road, Old Vic, 1985; Phantom of the Opera, Her Majesty's, 1986, NY and worldwide 1987 (numerous awards, UK and overseas, incl. Drama mag., 1987; Tony Award for Best Set and Best Costumes, 1987; Drama Critics' Award, LA, 1988); Follies, Shaftesbury, 1987 (Best Design award, Drama mag., 1988); Aspects of Love, Prince of Wales', 1989, NY, 1990; Phèdre, Aldwych, 1998; Britannicus, 1998, Plenty, 1999, Albery; The Cherry Orchard, RNT, 2000; Cat on a Hot Tin Roof, Lyric, 2001; *Royal Shakespeare Co.:* The Way of the World, 1978; Hamlet, 1984; Measure for Measure, 1974, 1991; A Midsummer Night's Dream, 1981; The Tempest, 1982; Camille, 1984; The Blue Angel, 1991; *Royal Ballet:* Sleeping Beauty, 1994; *opera:* Katya Kabanova, 1971; The Gambler, 1974, Wexford Fest.; Macbeth, La Scala, Milan, 1997; *Scottish Opera:* Rake's Progress (costumes), 1971; Tristan and Isolde (costumes), 1973; The Magic Flute (costumes), 1974; The Golden Cockerel (costumes), 1975; Die Meistersinger, 1976; Jenufa, Il Seraglio (costumes), The Bartered Bride (costumes), Hansel and Gretel (costumes), 1978; Don Giovanni, Katya Kabanova, 1979; The Cunning Little Vixen, 1980; House of the Dead, 1987; *Welsh National Opera:* Jenufa, 1975; Il Trovatore, 1976; The Makropulos Case, 1978; Ernani, 1979; Cunning Little Vixen, 1980; House of the Dead, 1982; *English National Opera:* Toussaint, 1977; Die Walkyrie, 1983; Carmen, 1986; Queen of Spades, 1987; Cunning Little Vixen, 1988; *Opera North:* Rigoletto, 1979; Don Giovanni, 1981; Werther, 1982; *Royal Opera:* Tales of Hoffman, 1980; Der Rosenkavalier (costumes), 1984; Donnerstag aus Licht, 1985; Katya Kabanova, 1994; Don Giovanni, 2002; *Glyndebourne:* Così fan tutte, 1991; also for productions in Sydney, Kassel, Houston, Geneva, Florence, Paris, Netherlands, Canada, and the provinces. *Recreations:* travel, running away. *Address:* c/o Judy Daish Associates, 2 St Charles Place, W10 6EG. *Club:* Peg's.

Died 13 Dec. 2002.

BLACK, Sir Douglas (Andrew Kilgour), Kt 1973; MD, FRCP; Professor of Medicine, Manchester University and Physician, Manchester Royal Infirmary, 1959–77, later Emeritus; Chief Scientist, Department of Health and Social Security, 1973–77; *b* 29 May 1913; *s* of late Rev. Walter Kilgour Black and Mary Jane Crichton; *m* 1948, Mollie Thorn; one *s* two *d. Educ:* Forfar Academy; St Andrews Univ. (BSc 1933; MB, ChB 1936; MD 1940). MRCP 1939; FRCP 1952; FACP, FRACP, FRCPGlas, 1978; FRCPath, FRCPI, FRCPE, 1979; FRCPsych, 1982; FRCGP, FRCOG, FFPHM (FFCM 1983); FFOM 1984. MRC Research Fellow, 1938–40; Beit Memorial Research Fellow, 1940–42. Major RAMC, 1942–46. Lecturer, then Reader, in Medicine, Manchester Univ., 1946–58. Horder Travelling Fellow, 1967; Sir Arthur Sims Commonwealth Travelling Prof., 1971; Rock Carling Fellow, 1984. Lectures: Goulstonian, RCP, 1953; Bradshaw, RCP, 1965; Lumleian, RCP, 1970; Harben, RIPH&H, 1973; Crookshank, RCR, 1976; Harveian Orator, RCP, 1977; Maurice Bloch, Glasgow, 1979; Linacre, St John's Coll., Cambridge, 1980; Lloyd Roberts, RSM, 1980; John Locke, Soc. of Apothecaries, 1990; Thomas Young, St George's Hosp. Med. Sch., 1990; Annual, Office of Health Econs., 1994. Secretary, Manchester Medical Soc., 1957–59. Member: Medical Research Council, 1966–70 and 1971–77 (Chm., Clinical Res. Bd, 1971–73); Assoc. of Physicians; Medical Research Soc.; Renal Assoc., etc. President: RCP, 1977–83; Section X, British Assoc., 1977; Medical Protection Soc., 1982–85; BMA, 1984–85; Hon. Mem., Manchester Lit. and Phil. Soc., 1991. Trustee, 1968–77, Chm., 1977–83, Smith Kline & French Foundn. Chm., Research Working Group on Inequalities in Health, 1977–80. Hon. FMedSci 2000. Hon. DSc: St Andrews, 1972; Manchester, 1978; Leicester, 1980; Cambridge, 1994; Hon. LLD Birmingham, 1984; Hon. MD Sheffield, 1984. KStJ 1989. *Publications:* Sodium Metabolism in Health and Disease, 1952; Essentials of Fluid Balance, 4th edn, 1967; The Logic of Medicine, 1968; (ed) Renal Disease, 4th edn, 1979; An Anthology of False Antitheses (Rock Carling Lecture), 1984; Invitation to Medicine, 1987; Recollections and Reflections, 1987; contributions to various medical journals. *Recreations:* reading and writing. *Address:* Upper House, Buildwas Road, Ironbridge, Shropshire TF8 7DW. *T:* (01952) 433930. *Club:* Athenæum.   *Died 13 Sept. 2002.*

BLACK, Prof. Archibald Niel; Professor of Engineering, University of Southampton, 1968–72, then Emeritus; *b* 10 June 1912; *s* of late Steuart Gladstone Black, Glenormiston, Victoria, Australia, and Isabella McCance (*née* Moat); *m* 1940, Cynthia Mary Stradling (*d* 1997); one *s* two *d. Educ:* Farnborough Sch.; Eton Coll.; Trinity Coll., Cambridge (1st cl. hons with distinction in Applied Mechanics in Mech. Sciences Tripos, 1934; MA 1938). Lectr and Demonstrator in Engrg Science, Oxford Univ., 1935; Donald Pollock Reader in Engrg Science, Oxford Univ., 1945–50; Prof. of Mech. Engrg, Southampton Univ., 1950–67. Dep. Chm., Universities Central Council on Admissions, 1964–72. Hon. DSc Southampton, 1975. *Publications:* (with K. Adlard Coles) North Biscay Pilot, 1970, rev. edn 1977; papers in Proc. Royal Soc. and technical jls. *Recreation:* sailing. *Address:* Little Pensbury, Compton Street, Compton, Winchester, Hants SO21 2AS. *T:* (01962) 712360. *Club:* Royal Cruising.

Died 14 Jan. 2001.

BLACKER, Gen. Sir (Anthony Stephen) Jeremy, KCB 1992; CBE 1987 (OBE 1979); FIMechE; Master-General of the Ordnance, Ministry of Defence, 1991–95; *b* 6 May 1939; *s* of late Kenneth Anthony Blacker, CBE and Louise Margaret Blacker (*née* Band); *m* 1973, Julia Mary (*née* Trew); two *d. Educ:* Sherborne School; RMA Sandhurst; Corpus Christi Coll., Cambridge (BA Hons). FIMechE 1990. Commnd Royal Tank Regt, 1959; Staff Coll., 1971; MA to VCGS, 1976–79; Comd 1 RTR, 1979–81; Mil. Dir of Studies, RMCS, 1981–82; Comd 11 Armd Brigade, 1982–84; Principal Staff Officer to Chief of Defence Staff, 1985–87; Comdt, RMCS, 1987–89; ACDS (Operational Requirements), Land Systems, MoD, 1989–91. Col Comdt, REME, 1987–92, RTR, 1988–95, RAC, 1993–95; Hon. Col, Royal Yeo. and Westminster Dragoons, 1997–2002. *Recreations:* ski-ing, tennis, golf, investment trusts.   *Died 17 March 2005.*

BLACKER, Gen. Sir Cecil (Hugh), GCB 1975 (KCB 1969; CB 1967); OBE 1960; MC 1944; Adjutant-General, Ministry of Defence (Army), 1973–76, retired; ADC (General) to the Queen, 1974–76; *b* 4 June 1916; *s* of Col Norman Valentine Blacker and Olive Georgina (*née* Hope); *m* 1947, Felicity Mary, *widow* of Major J. Rew and *d* of Major I. Buxton, DSO; two *s. Educ:* Wellington Coll. Joined 5th Royal Inniskilling Dragoon Guards, 1936; Commanded 23rd Hussars, 1945; Instructor, Staff Coll., Camberley, 1951–54; Commanded 5th Royal Inniskilling Dragoon Guards, 1955–57; Military Asst to CIGS, 1958–60; Asst Commandant, RMA, Sandhurst, 1960–62; Commander, 39 Infantry Brigade Group, 1962–64; GOC 3rd Div., 1964–66; Dir, Army Staff Duties, MoD, 1966–69; GOC-in-C Northern Command, 1969–70; Vice-Chief of the General Staff, 1970–73. Colonel Commandant: RMP, 1971–76; APTC, 1971–76; Col, 5th Royal Inniskilling Dragoon Guards, 1972–81. Member: Jockey Club, 1954– (Dep. Sen. Steward, 1984–86); Horserace Betting Levy Bd, 1981–84; President: BSJA, 1976–80; BEF, 1980–84. *Publications:* The Story of Workboy, 1960; Soldier in the Saddle, 1963; Monkey Business, 1993. *Recreations:* painting; amateur steeplechase rider, 1947–54; represented GB in World Modern Pentathlon Championships, 1951; represented GB in Showjumping, 1959–61. *Address:* Cowpasture Farm, Hook Norton, Banbury, Oxon OX15 5BY.

Died 18 Oct. 2002.

BLACKER, Gen. Sir Jeremy; *see* Blacker, Gen. Sir A. S. J.

BLACKHAM, Rear-Adm. Joseph Leslie, CB 1965; DL; *b* 29 Feb. 1912; *s* of Dr Walter Charles Blackham, Birmingham, and Margaret Eva Blackham (*née* Bavin); *m* 1938, Coreen Shelford Skinner, *er d* of Paym. Captain W. S. Skinner, CBE, RN; one *s* one *d. Educ:* West House Sch., Edgbaston; RNC Dartmouth. Specialised in Navigation; served war of 1939–45; JSSC 1950; Comdr, RNC Greenwich, 1953–54; Captain 1954; Admty. 1955–57; Sen. Officer, Reserve Fleet at Plymouth, 1957–59; Admty Naval Staff, 1959–61; Cdre. Supt, HM

Dockyard, Singapore, 1962–63; Rear-Adm. 1963; Admiral Supt, HM Dockyard, Portsmouth, 1964–66; retired. Mem., IoW Hosp. Management Cttee, 1968–74; Vice-Chm., IoW AHA 1974–82; Chm., Family Practitioners Cttee, IoW, 1974–85; Mem., Bd of Visitors, HM Prison, Parkhurst, 1967–82 (Chm., 1974–77). CC Isle of Wight, 1967–77 (Chm., 1975–77); DL Hants and IoW, 1970–87; High Sheriff, IoW, 1975. Mentioned in despatches for service in Korea, 1951. SBStJ 1991. *Address:* Trinity Cottage, Love Lane, Bembridge, Isle of Wight PO35 5NH. *T:* (01983) 874386.

Died 18 May 2004.

BLACKWELL, Sir Basil (Davenport), Kt 1983; FREng; Chief Executive, 1974–85, and Chairman, 1985, Westland PLC (formerly Westland Aircraft Ltd) (Vice-Chairman, 1974–84, Deputy Chairman, 1984); *b* Whitkirk, Yorks, 8 Feb. 1922; *s* of late Alfred Blackwell and Mrs H. Lloyd; *m* 1948, Betty Meggs, *d* of late Engr Captain Meggs, RN; one *d*. *Educ:* Leeds Grammar Sch.; St John's Coll., Cambridge (MA; Hughes Prize); London Univ. (BScEng). FIMechE; FRAeS (Gold Medal, 1982). Sci. Officer, Admiralty, 1942; Rolls-Royce Ltd, 1945; Engine Div., Bristol Aeroplane Co. Ltd, 1949; Bristol Siddeley Engines Ltd: Dep. Chief Engr, 1959; Sales Dir, 1963; Man. Dir, Small Engine Div., 1965 (subseq. Small Engines Div. of Rolls-Royce Ltd). Commercial Dir, Westland Aircraft Ltd, 1970–72; Westland Helicopters Ltd: Man. Dir, 1972; Chm., 1976–85; Chairman: British Hovercraft Corp., 1979–85; Normalair-Garrett Ltd, 1979–85. Member Council: BIM; CBI; NDIC; SBAC (Vice-Pres., 1978; Pres., 1979 and 1980; Dep. Pres., 1980); EEF (Vice-Pres., 1983–85); Bath Univ., 1986–95. Pres., AECMA, 1984–85 (Président d'honneur 1985); Chm., Astrid Trust, 1986–93. CCMI. Hon. DSc, 1994, Chancellor's Medal, 1997, Hon. Fellow, 2003, Bath Univ. *Publications:* (jtly) The Global Challenge of Innovation, 1991; contrib. professional jls. *Recreations:* gardens and gardening. *Address:* High Newland, Newland Garden, Sherborne, Dorset DT9 3AF. *T:* (01935) 813516. *Died 18 May 2003.*

BLAIKLEY, Robert Marcel; HM Diplomatic Service, retired; *b* 1 Oct. 1916; *s* of late Alexander John Blaikley and Adelaide Blaikley (*née* Miller); *m* 1942, Alice Mary Duncan; one *s* one *d*. *Educ:* Christ's Coll., Finchley; St John's Coll., Cambridge. Served HM Forces, 1940–46. Inland Revenue, 1946–48; General Register Office, 1948–65, Asst Secretary, 1958; transferred to Diplomatic Service as Counsellor, 1965; on loan to Colonial Office, 1965–66; Head of Aviation and Telecommunications Dept, CO, 1966–68; Counsellor, Jamaica, 1968–71; Ghana, 1971–73. *Recreations:* reading, growing shrubs. *Address:* 23 Deanery Walk, Avonpark, Winsley Road, Limpley Stoke, Bath BA2 7JQ. *Died 11 July 2003.*

BLAIR, Thomas Alexander; QC (NI) 1958; Chief Social Security (formerly National Insurance) Commissioner (Northern Ireland), 1969–83; *b* 12 Dec. 1916; *s* of late John Blair and Wilhelmina Whitla Blair (*née* Downey); *m* 1947, Ida Irvine Moore (decd); two *s* one *d*. *Educ:* Royal Belfast Academical Instn; Queen's Univ. Belfast (BA, LLB). Served War, RN, 1940–46 (commissioned, 1941). Called to Bar of N Ireland, 1946. Chairman: Wages Councils; War Pensions Appeal Tribunal. Sen. Crown Counsel for Co. Tyrone; Mem. Departmental Cttee on Legal Aid. Apptd Dep. Nat. Insurance Umpire, 1959; Pres., Industrial Tribunals (NI), 1967–69. *Recreations:* sport, reading. *Address:* Room 52, Colinton Nursing Home, 69 Spylaw Road, Edinburgh EH10 5BP.

Died 29 April 2005.

BLAIR-OLIPHANT, Air Vice-Marshal David Nigel Kington, CB 1966; OBE 1945; *b* 22 Dec. 1911; *y s* of Col P. L. K. Blair-Oliphant, DSO, Ardblair Castle, Blairgowrie, Perthshire, and Laura Geraldine Bodenham; *m* 1942, Helen Nathalie Donald (*d* 1983, *yr d* of Sir John Donald, KCIE; one *s* (and one *s* and one *d* decd). *Educ:* Harrow; Trinity Hall, Cambridge (MA). Joined RAF, 1934; Middle East and European Campaigns, 1939–45;

RAF Staff Coll., 1945–48; Group Capt. 1949; Air Cdre 1958; Dir, Weapons Engineering, Air Ministry, 1958–60; British Defence Staffs, Washington, 1960–63; Acting Air Vice-Marshal, 1963; Pres., Ordnance Board, 1965–66; Air Vice-Marshal, 1966. *Address:* 9 Northfield Road, Sherfield-on-Lodon, Hook, Hants RG27 0DR. *T:* (01256) 882724. *Club:* Royal Air Force.

Died 5 June 2005.

BLAKE, Baron *cr* 1971 (Life Peer), of Braydeston, Norfolk; **Robert Norman William Blake,** FBA 1967; JP; Provost, The Queen's College, Oxford, 1968–87, Hon. Fellow, 1987; a Pro-Vice-Chancellor, Oxford University, 1971–87; Joint Editor, Dictionary of National Biography, 1980–90; *b* 23 Dec. 1916; *er s* of William Joseph Blake and Norah Lindley Daynes, Brundall, Norfolk; *m* 1953, Patricia Mary (*d* 1995), *e d* of Thomas Richard Waters, Great Plumstead, Norfolk; three *d*. *Educ:* King Edward VI Grammar Sch., Norwich; Magdalen Coll., Oxford (MA; 1st Cl. Final Honour Sch. of Modern Greats, 1938; Eldon Law Scholar, 1938). Served War of 1939–45; Royal Artillery; North African campaign, 1942; POW in Italy, 1942–44; escaped, 1944; despatches, 1944. Oxford University: Student and Tutor in Politics, Christ Church, 1947–68; Censor, 1950–55; Senior Proctor, 1959–60; Mem., Hebdomadal Council, 1959–81; Ford's Lectr in English History for 1967–68; Centenary Romanes Lectr, 1992. Member: Royal Commn on Historical Manuscripts, 1975–97 (Chm., 1982–89); Bd of Trustees, BM, 1978–88; Bd, Channel 4, 1983–86. Chm., Hansard Soc. Commn on Electoral Reform, 1975–76; Pres., Electoral Reform Soc., 1986–93. Mem. (Conservative) Oxford City Council, 1957–64. Rhodes Trustee, 1971–87 (Chm., 1983–87). Prime Warden, Dyers' Co., 1976–77. High Bailiff of Westminster Abbey and Searcher of the Sanctuary, 1988–89; High Steward of Westminster Abbey, 1989–99. Hon. Student, Christ Church, Oxford, 1977; Hon. Fellow, Pembroke Coll., Cambridge, 1992. Hon. DLitt: Glasgow, 1972; East Anglia, 1983; Westminster Coll., Fulton, Mo, 1987; Buckingham, 1988. *Publications:* The Private Papers of Douglas Haig, 1952; The Unknown Prime Minister (Life of Andrew Bonar Law), 1955; A History of the Norwich Union Life Insurance Society, 1958; Disraeli, 1966, repr. 1998; The Conservative Party from Peel to Churchill, 1970, 2nd edn, The Conservative Party from Peel to Thatcher, 1985, 3rd edn, The Conservative Party from Peel to Major, 1997; The Office of Prime Minister, 1975; (ed with John Patten) The Conservative Opportunity, 1976; A History of Rhodesia, 1977; Disraeli's Grand Tour, 1982; (ed) The English World, 1982; The Decline of Power 1915–1964, 1985; (ed with Hugh Cecil) Salisbury: the man and his policies, 1987; (ed) Oxford Illustrated Encyclopaedia, Vol. 4, World History from 1800, 1989; (ed with Roger Louis) Churchill, 1993; Winston Churchill: a pocket biography, 1998; Jardine Matheson, Traders of the Far East, 1999. *Address:* Riverview House, Brundall, Norfolk NR13 5LA. *T:* (01603) 712133. *Clubs:* Beefsteak, Pratt's, Oxford and Cambridge; Vincent's (Oxford); Norfolk County.

Died 20 Sept. 2003.

BLAKE, Sir Peter (James), KBE 1995 (OBE 1991 MBE 1983); Chief Executive Officer, Team New Zealand Ltd, America's Cup Defence 2000, 1994–2000; Captain, Seamaster, blakexpeditions, since 2000; *b* 1 Oct. 1948; *m* 1979, Pippa Glanville; one *s* one *d*. *Educ:* Takapuna GS, Auckland; Auckland Tech. Inst. (NZCE (Mech.)). Began sailing at age of 5; first long ocean race, NZ to Pacific Islands (1200 miles), at age of 16; built own Van de Stadt 23 foot keelboat, Bandit, at age of 18; won NZ Jun. Offshore Gp Champ., Bandit, 1967–68; Watch Leader, Cape Town/Rio de Janeiro race, Ocean Spirit, 1971; Whitbread Round the World Yacht Race: Watch Leader: Burton Cutter, 1973–74; Heath's Condor, 1977–78; Skipper/Navigator: Ceramco NZ, 1981–82 (Southern Ocean Trophy); Lion NZ, 1985–86; Skipper/Project Manager, Steinlager 2, 1989–90 (Southern Ocean Trophy, Overall Race hons); Skipper, Miama/Montego Bay race,

Condor, 1979 (race record); Manager, NZ Admirals Cup Team in UK, 1982; winner: Around Australia 2-handed race, Steinlager 1, 1988; America's Cup, Black Magic, 1995 (with NZ team won NZ Supreme Sports Award); has taken part in most major ocean races around the world. With Sir Robin Knox-Johnson, set non–stop around the world sailing record, 74 days 22 hours 17 minutes 22 secs, Enza NZ, 1994. Captain, Antarctic Explorer, Cousteau Soc., 1997–2000. Life Mem., Royal NZ Yacht Squadron, 1995. Trustee, NZ Internat. Yachting Trust, 1985–; Mem., Assoc. of Cape Horners, 1978–; Pres., Jules Verne Assoc., 1995–. NZ Yachtsman of the Year, 1982, (jtly) 1989–90; NZ Sportsman of the Year, 1990; Hobson Medal, NZ Maritime Assoc., 1994; British Yachtsman of the Year, 1995; Sir Francis Chichester Trophy, RYS, 1995; Prix de l'Aventure Sportive, Académie des Sports, 1996. *Publications:* Blake's Odyssey, 1982; Peter Blake's Yachting Book, 1984; Lion New Zealand, 1986; Peter Blake: adventurer, 1996. *Recreations:* flying, scuba diving, piano, yachting. *Address:* Longshore, 3 Western Parade, Emsworth, Hants PO10 7HS. *T:* (01243) 377027. *Clubs:* West Mersea Yacht (Life Mem.), Ocean Cruising, Emsworth Sailing, Royal Southern Yacht (Hon. Mem.), Royal Southampton Yacht (Hon. Mem.), Royal Yacht Squadron (Hon. Mem.); Royal Port Nicholson Yacht (Wellington).   *Died 6 Dec. 2001.*

BLAKER, George Blaker, CMG 1963; Under-Secretary, HM Treasury, 1955–63, and Department of Education and Science, 1963–71 retired; *b* Simla, India, 30 Sept. 1912; *m* 1938, Richenda Dorothy Buxton (*d* 1987); one *d*. *Educ:* Eton; Trinity Coll., Cambridge. Private Sec. to Ministers of State in the Middle East, 1941–43; Cabinet Office, 1943; Private Sec. to Sec. of War Cabinet, 1944; Principal Private Sec. to Minister of Production and Presidents of the Board of Trade, 1945–47; accompanied Cabinet Mission to India, 1946; Sec. of UK Trade Mission to China, 1946; HM Treasury, 1947; UK Treasury Representative in India, Ceylon and Burma, 1957–63. President: Surrey Trust for Nature Conservation, 1969–80; Scientific and Medical Network, 1986– (Hon. Sec., 1973–86). Gold Medal, Royal Soc. for the Protection of Birds, 1934. *Address:* Lake House, Vann Lake Road, Ockley, Surrey RH5 5NS.
Died 28 Nov. 2001.

BLAMIRE, Roger Victor; veterinary consultant; Director of Veterinary Field Services, Ministry of Agriculture, Fisheries and Food, 1979–83; *b* 9 July 1923; *s* of Thomas Victor Blamire and Anetta Elizabeth (*née* Lawson); *m* 1947, Catherine Maisie Ellis Davidson; two *d*. *Educ:* Kendal Sch.; Royal (Dick) Veterinary Coll., Edinburgh. MRCVS, DVSM. RAVC, 1945–48 (Captain); served India, Burma and Malaya. MAF, 1949; Asst Vet. Officer, City of London, 1949; Dep. Chief Advr on Meat Inspection, MOF, 1952; Dep. Dir, Vet. Field Services, MAFF, 1968. Hon. FRSH, 1979. *Recreations:* walking, gardening, listening to music. *Address:* 5 Atbara Road, Teddington, Middx TW11 9PA. *T:* (020) 8943 4225.
Died 1 Aug. 2003.

BLATCH, Baroness *cr* 1987 (Life Peer), of Hinchingbrooke in the county of Cambridgeshire; **Emily May Blatch,** CBE 1983; PC 1993; *b* 24 July 1937; *d* of Stephen Joseph and Sarah Triggs; *m* 1963, John Richard Blatch, AFC; two *s* one *d* (of whom one *s* one *d* are twins) (and one *s* decd). *Educ:* Prenton, Birkenhead; Huntingdonshire College. WRAF, 1955–59; Ministry of Aviation, 1959–63. Member: Bd, Peterborough Develt Corp., 1984–89; Cambs CC, 1977–89 (Leader, 1981–85); ACC, 1981–85; European Econ. and Social Cttee, 1986–87; Cons. Nat. Local Govt Adv. Cttee, 1988–92. Baroness in Waiting (Govt Whip), H of L, 1990; Parly Under-Sec. of State for the Envmt, 1990–91; Minister of State: DoE, 1991–92; DFE, 1992–94; Home Office, 1994–97; Opposition front bench spokesman on educn and employment, 1997–2000; Dep. Leader of Opposition, H of L, 2000–. Vice Pres., LGA, 2000–. Chm., Anglo-American Community

Relations Cttee, RAF Alconbury, 1985–91. Pres., Nat. Benevolent Inst., 1989–. Member: Air League Council, 1998–; Air Cadet Council, 1998–; Trustee: Dorman Mus. Appeal, Middlesbrough, 1997–; RAF Mus., 1998–. Pres., Shakespeare at The George, Huntingdon, 1995–; Patron, Huntingdon Male Voice Choir, 1997–. FRSA 1985. Hon. LLD Teesside, 1997. Paul Harris Fellow, Rotary Club, 1992. *Recreations:* music, theatre. *Address:* House of Lords, SW1A 0PW. *Club:* Royal Air Force.
Died 31 May 2005.

BLEACKLEY, David, CMG 1979; DPhil; Head, Overseas Division, and Assistant Director, Institute of Geological Sciences, 1975–80; *b* 1 Feb. 1919; *s* of Alfred Mason and Hilda Gertrude Bleackley; *m* 1st, 1945, Peggy Florence Chill (*d* 1966); one *s* one *d*; 2nd, 1973, Patricia Clavell Strakosch (*née* Hore); two step *s* one step *d*. *Educ:* City of Oxford Sch.; The Queen's Coll., Oxford (BA 1939, MA 1942, DPhil 1960). Served War, Royal Engineers, 1939–45. Geologist: Shell Oil Co., 1946–50; Geological Survey, British Guiana, 1954–57, Dep. Dir, 1957–60; Overseas Geological Surveys, 1960–65; Dep. Head, Overseas Div., Inst. of Geological Sciences, 1965–75. FIMM 1969; FGS 1943. *Publications:* papers in various jls. *Recreation:* country pursuits. *Address:* Well Farm, Dagnall, near Berkhamsted, Herts HP4 1QU. *T:* (01442) 843232.
Died 17 June 2002.

BLOCK, Brig. David Arthur Kennedy William, CBE 1961; DSO 1945; MC 1943; Command 18th Training Brigade, Royal Artillery, 1958–61, retired; *b* 13 June 1908; *s* of late Col Arthur Hugh Block; *m* 1949, Elizabeth Grace (*d* 1975), *e d* of late Lt-Col E. G. Troyte-Bullock, CMG, Zeals House, Wiltshire, and *widow* of Major G. E. Sebag-Montefiore, D'Anvers House, Culworth, near Banbury; no *c*. *Educ:* Blundell's; RMA, Woolwich. Served War of 1939–45 (despatches, MC, DSO); CO 152nd (Ayrshire Yeomanry) Field Regt, RA, 1943–45; Coll. Comdr, RMA Sandhurst, 1947–50; CO 2nd Regt RHA, 1950–53; GSO1 Secretariat, SHAPE, 1953–54; CRA, 7th Armoured Div., 1954–57. ADC to the Queen, 1959–61. *Recreations:* hunting, shooting, golf. *Address:* Slades House, East Knoyle, Salisbury, Wilts SP3 6AB. *T:* (01747) 830234. *Club:* Army and Navy.   *Died 26 June 2001.*

BLOOD, Bindon, (Peter); Director, Western Marketing Consultants Ltd, since 1987; Senior Industrialist and Enterprise Counsellor for Department of Trade and Industry, 1986–94; *b* 24 Sept. 1920; *o s* of Brig. William Edmunds Robarts Blood, CBE, MC, Croix de Guerre, and Eva Gwendoline (*née* Harrison); *m* 1953, Elizabeth Ann, *d* of Harold Drummond Hillier, MC; one *s* one *d*. *Educ:* Imperial Service Coll., Windsor. Family public works and civil engineering business, 1938–41; served Royal Engineers, 1941–46 (despatches 1944); Engineering Div., Forestry Commn, 1946–48; regular commn, RE, 1948; Second i/c, RE Officer Training Unit, 1948–51; Staff Coll., Camberley, 1951; Sec., Army Bd, NATO Mil. Agency for Standardisation, 1952–53; invalided from service, 1953; Intelligence Co-ordination Staff, FO, 1953–58; Founder and formerly Managing Director: Isora Integrated Ceilings Ltd; Clean Room Construction Ltd; Mitchel and King (Sales) Ltd; Dep. Chm. and Group Marketing Dir, King Group. Institute of Marketing: Dir of Marketing Services, 1971; Dir-Gen., 1972–84. Chm., Industrial Market Research Ltd, 1984–87. Gov., Berks Coll. of Art and Design, 1975–89 (Chm. of Govs, 1981–86). FRSA, FInstM. *Recreations:* photography, furniture restoration, travel, music, local community activities. *Address:* 8 Woodhurst South, Ray Mead Road, Maidenhead, Berks SL6 8NZ. *T:* and *Fax:* (01628) 626600; *e-mail:* peterblood@UKonline.co.uk.
Died 13 Aug. 2004.

BLOOM, André Borisovich; *see* Anthony, Metropolitan.

BLOOMFIELD, Barry Cambray, MA, FLA; Director, Collection Development, Humanities and Social Sciences, British Library, 1985–90; *b* 1 June 1931; *s* of Clifford

Wilson Bloomfield and Eileen Elizabeth (*née* Cambray); *m* 1958, Valerie Jean Philpot. *Educ:* East Ham Grammar Sch.; University College of the South-West, Exeter; University Coll. London; Birkbeck Coll., London. Served in Intelligence Corps, Malaya, 1952–54. Assistant, National Central Library, 1955; Librarian, College of St Mark and St John, Chelsea, 1956–61; Asst Librarian, London Sch. of Economics, 1961–63; Dep. Librarian, 1963–72, Librarian, 1972–78, School of Oriental and African Studies; Dir, India Office Library and Records, British Library (formerly FCO), 1978–85 and concurrently Keeper, Dept of Oriental MSS and Printed Bks, British Library, 1983–85. Chm., SCONUL Group of Orientalist Libraries, 1975–80; President: Bibliographical Soc., 1990–92 (Vice-Pres., 1979–90); Private Libraries Assoc., 1998–2001; Assoc. of Independent Libraries, 2000–; Vice-Pres., Philip Larkin Soc., 1995–; Member: Council, Royal Asiatic Soc., 1980–84, 1996–2000; British Assoc. for Cemeteries in S Asia, 1980–90; Britain-Burma Soc., 1980–90; Exec. Cttee, Friends of the Nat. Libraries, 1981–96; Chm., Rare Books Gp, LA, 1991–95; International Federation of Library Associations: Chairman: Sect. on Bibliography, 1985–89; Div. of Bibliographic Control, 1985–89; Mem., Professional Bd, 1987–89. Trustee, Shakespeare Birthplace Trust, 1987–91. Vis. Professor, Univ. of Florida, 1963; Vis. Fellow, Univ. of Hawaii, 1977. FLA 1959 (Hon. FLA 1998). Hon. Mem., ABA, 1999. Walford Award, LA, 1998. *Publications:* New Verse in the '30s, 1960; W. H. Auden: a bibliography, 1964, 2nd edn 1972; (ed) Autobiography of Sir J. P. Kay Shuttleworth, 1964; (ed with V. J. Bloomfield, J. D. Pearson) Theses on Africa, 1964; (ed) Theses on Asia, 1967; (ed) The Acquisition and Provision of Foreign Books by National and University Libraries in the UK, 1972; An Author Index to Selected British 'Little' Magazines, 1976; Philip Larkin: a bibliography 1933–1976, 1979, 2nd edn 2001; (ed) Middle East Studies and Libraries, 1980; Brought to Book, 1995; (ed) A Directory of Rare Books and Special Collections in the United Kingdom and Ireland, 2nd edn, 1997; numerous articles in library and bibliog. jls. *Recreations:* reading, music. *Address:* Brambling, 24 Oxenturn Road, Wye, Kent TN25 5BE. *T:* (01233) 813038. *Club:* Civil Service.   *Died 26 Feb. 2002.*

BLOUNT, Sir Walter (Edward Alpin), 12th Bt *cr* 1642; DSC 1943 and two Bars 1945; farmer; *b* 31 Oct. 1917; *s* of Sir Edward Robert Blount, 11th Bt, and Violet Ellen (*d* 1969), *d* of Alpin Grant Fowler; *S* father, 1978; *m* 1954, Eileen Audrey, *d* of late Hugh B. Carritt; one *d*. *Educ:* Beaumont College; Sidney Sussex Coll., Cambridge (MA). Served RNVSR, 1939–47 (MTBs). Qualified as Solicitor, 1950; practised: Gold Coast, West Africa, 1950–52; London and Cambridge, 1952–76. Farmer, Tilkhurst, East Grinstead, Sussex, 1978–. *Recreation:* sailing. *Heir:* none. *Address:* Tilkhurst, Imberhorne Lane, East Grinstead, Sussex RH19 1TY. *T:* (01342) 323018; Regent House, Seaview, IoW PO34 5ET. *Clubs:* Bembridge Sailing, Seaview Yacht, Cambridge Cruising, RNVR Sailing, Island Sailing.

Died 18 Dec. 2004 (ext).

BLOW, Prof. David Mervyn, FRS 1972; Professor of Biophysics, 1977–94, then Emeritus, and Senior Research Fellow, since 1994, Imperial College, University of London; *b* 27 June 1931; *s* of Rev. Edward Mervyn and Dorothy Laura Blow; *m* 1955, Mavis Sears; one *s* one *d*. *Educ:* Kingswood Sch.; Corpus Christi Coll., Cambridge (MA, PhD). FInstP. Fulbright Scholar, Nat. Inst. of Health, Bethesda, Md, and MIT, 1957–59; MRC Unit for Study of Molecular Biological Systems, Cambridge, 1959–62; MRC Lab. of Molecular Biology, Cambridge, 1962–77; College Lectr and Fellow, Trinity Coll., Cambridge, 1968–77; Imperial College, London: Dean, Royal Coll. of Sci., 1981–84; Head, Dept of Physics, 1991–94. Pres., British Crystallographic Assoc., 1984–87. For. Associate Mem., Acad. des Scis, Paris, 1992. Mem. Governing Body, Imperial Coll., London, 1987–94. Social Colours, Imperial Coll. Students' Union, 1986, 1989.

Biochem. Soc. CIBA Medal, 1967; (jtly) Charles Léopold Meyer Prize, 1979; (jtly) Wolf Foundn Prize for Chemistry, 1987. *Publications:* (with K. C. Holmes) The Use of x-ray Diffraction in the Study of Protein and Nucleic Acid Structure, 1966; Outline of Crystallography for Biologists, 2002; papers and reviews in scientific jls. *Recreations:* walking, sailing. *Address:* Blackett Laboratory, Imperial College, University of London, SW7 2AZ.

Died 8 June 2004.

BLUNDELL, Commandant Daphne Mary, CB 1972; Director, WRNS, 1970–73; *b* 19 Aug. 1916. *Educ:* St Helen's Sch., Northwood; Bedford Coll., London. Worked for LCC as Child Care Organiser. Joined WRNS, Nov. 1942; commnd 1943; served in Orkneys, Ceylon, E Africa; Malta, 1954–56; Staff of Flag Officer Naval Air Comd, 1964–67; Staff of C-in-C Portsmouth, 1967–69; Supt WRNS Training and Drafting, 1969–70. Supt 1967; Comdt 1970, retd 1973; Hon. ADC to the Queen, 1970–73. *Address:* 15 Northbrook Drive, Northwood, Middx HA6 2YU.   *Died 24 May 2004.*

BLUNT, Maj.-Gen. Peter, CB 1978; MBE 1955; GM 1959; *b* 18 Aug. 1923; *s* of A. G. Blunt and C. M. Blunt; *m* 1949, Adrienne, *o d* of Gen. T. W. Richardson; three *s*. Joined Army aged 14 yrs, 1937; commnd Royal Fusiliers; served Duke of Cornwall's LI and Royal Scots Fusiliers, until 1946; foreign service, 1946–49; Staff Coll., 1957; Jt Services Staff Coll., 1963; RCDS, 1972; comd 26 Regt, Bridging, 1965; GSO 1 Def. Plans, FARELF, 1968; Comdr RCT 1 Corps, 1970; Dep. Transport Officer-in-Chief (Army), later Transp. Off.-in-Chief, 1973; Asst Chief of Personnel and Logistics (Army), MoD, 1977–78; Asst Chief of Defence Staff (Personnel and Logistics), MoD, 1978–79. Man. Dir, Earls Court Ltd, 1979–80; Exec. Vice-Chm., Brompton and Kensington Special Catering Co. Ltd, 1979–80; Jt Man. Dir, Angex-Watson, 1980–83; Dir, Associated Newspapers, 1984–90; Chm. and Man. Dir, Market Sensors, 1986–88; Man. Dir, 1980–88, non-exec. Chm., 1988–90, Angex Ltd; Chm., Argus Shield Ltd, 1988–89. Rep. Col Comdt, RCT, 1987–89 (Col Comdt, 1974–89). Specially apptd Comr, Royal Hosp., Chelsea, 1979–85. Exec. Mem., Caravan Club, 1989–. Liveryman, Co. of Carmen, 1973. *Recreations:* fishing, caravanning. *Address:* Harefield House, Crowood Lane, Ramsbury, Marlborough, Wilts SN8 2PT. *T:* (01672) 520296. *Club:* RCT Luncheon (Patron).

Died 8 Aug. 2003.

BOARDMAN, Baron *cr* 1980 (Life Peer), of Welford in the County of Northamptonshire; **Thomas Gray Boardman,** MC 1944; TD 1952; DL; Chairman, National Westminster Bank, 1983–89 (Director, 1979–89; Chairman, Eastern Region, 1979–83); *b* 12 Jan. 1919; *s* of John Clayton Boardman, late of Daventry, and Janet Boardman, formerly Houston; *m* 1948, (Norah Mary) Deirdre, *widow* of John Henry Chaworth-Musters, Annesley Park, Nottingham, and *d* of late Hubert Vincent Gough; two *s* one *d*. *Educ:* Bromsgrove. Served Northants Yeomanry, 1939–45 and subsequently; Commanding Northants Yeomanry, 1956. Qualified as a Solicitor, 1947. MP (C) Leicester SW, Nov. 1967–74, Leicester South Feb.–Sept. 1974; Minister for Industry, DTI, 1972–74; Chief Sec. to Treasury, 1974. Hon. Treas., Cons. Party, 1981–82. Chairman: Chamberlain Phipps Ltd, 1958–72; The Steetley Co. Ltd, 1978–83 (Dir, 1975–83); Heron Internat. NV, 1993–95; Director: Allied Breweries Ltd, 1968–72 and 1974–77 (Vice-Chm., 1975–76); MEPC, 1980–89; Mem. Adv. Bd, LEK Partnership, 1990–97. Pres., Assoc. of British Chambers of Commerce, 1977–80. Chm., Cttee of London and Scottish Bankers, 1987–89. Mem., Exec. Assoc. of Cons. Peers, 1981–84, 1991–95. Freeman, City of London, 1984; HM Lieut, City of London, 1989–; DL Northants, 1977, High Sheriff, Northants, 1979. *Recreation:* riding. *Address:* 29 Tufton Court, Tufton Street, SW1P 3QH. *T:* (020) 7222 6793; The Manor House, Welford, Northampton NN6 6HX.

T: (01858) 575235. *Club:* Cavalry and Guards.
Died 10 March 2003.

BODDY, Jack Richard, MBE 1973; JP; Group Secretary, Agricultural and Allied Workers Trade Group, Transport and General Workers Union, 1982–87 (General Secretary, National Union of Agricultural and Allied Workers, 1978–82); *b* 23 Aug. 1922; *s* of Percy James Boddy and Lucy May Boddy, JP; *m* 1943, Muriel Lilian (*née* Webb) (*d* 1987); three *s* one *d*; *m* 1990, (Margaret) Joan Laws. *Educ:* City of Norwich Sch. Agricultural worker, 1939; farm foreman, 1943. District Organiser: Lincolnshire NUAAW, 1953; Norfolk NUAAW, 1960. Mem., TUC Gen. Council, 1978–83. Leader, Workers' side, Agricl Wages Bd, 1978–87. Member: Agricl Cttee, EDC, 1978–88; Economic and Social Cttee, EEC, 1980–90; Food and Drink Cttee, EDC, 1984–87; Industrial Injuries Adv. Cttee, DHSS, 1983–87. Formerly member: St Andrews and Hellesdon HMC (Chm., 1969–74); Little Plumstead HMC; E Anglian RHB. Mem., Swaffham Town Council, 1987–2003 (Dep. Mayor, 1990–91; Mayor, 1991–92); Breckland District Council: Mem., 1987–99; Chm., Housing Cttee, 1995–98; Vice Chm., Planning Cttee, 1995–98; Chm., Eco-tech Cttee, 1995–98; Vice Chm., 1997–98; Chm., 1998–99. Pres., Mid Norfolk Mencap, 1988–91. Freeman, City of Norwich; Hon. Citizen, Swaffham, 2003. JP Swaffham, 1947. *Recreations:* caravanning, gardening. *Address:* The Brambles, 2b Spinners Lane, Swaffham, Norfolk PE37 7ND. *T:* (01760) 722916. *Died 9 March 2004.*

BOGGIS-ROLFE, Hume, CB 1971; CBE 1962; farmer; *b* 20 Oct. 1911; *s* of Douglass Horace Boggis-Rolfe and Maria Maud (*née* Bailey); *m* 1941, Anne Dorothea, *e d* of Capt. Eric Noble, Henley-on-Thames; one *s* one *d* (and one *s* decd). *Educ:* Paris and Berlin; Westminster Sch.; Freiburg Univ.; Trinity Coll., Cambridge. Called to Bar, Middle Temple, 1935. Army, Intelligence Corps, 1939–46 (Lieut-Col). Private Sec. to Lord Chancellor, 1949–50; Asst Solicitor in Lord Chancellor's Office, 1951–65; Sec. to Law Commn, 1965–68; Dep. Clerk of the Crown in Chancery, and Asst Perm. Sec. to Lord Chancellor, 1968–75, and Dep. Sec., Lord Chancellor's Office, 1970–75. Master, Merchant Taylors' Co., 1971–72. Chm., Friends of the Elderly and Gentlefolks' Help, 1977–84. *Recreations:* gardening, travelling. *Address:* The Grange, Wormingford, Colchester, Essex, CO6 3AU. *T:* (01787) 227303. *Club:* Athenæum.
Died 28 July 2002.

BOGSCH, Arpad, Dr jur; Director General, World Intellectual Property Organization, 1973–97 (Deputy Director General, 1963–73); *b* 24 Feb. 1919; *s* of Arpad Bogsch and Emilia Taborsky; *m* 1942, Pauline Takats; one *s* one *d*; *m* 1994, Adèle Fankhauser. *Educ:* Univ. of Budapest (Dr jur); Univ. of Paris (Dr jur); George Washington Univ. (LLM). Called to the Budapest Bar, 1940, to the Washington DC Bar, 1952. Private law practice, Budapest, 1940–48; Legal Officer, Unesco, Paris, 1948–54; Legal Adviser, Library of Congress, Washington DC, 1954–63. Hon. Prof. of Law, Peking Univ., 1991. LLD *hc*: Jabalpur, 1978; George Washington, 1985; Colombo, 1987; Kyung Hee, Korea, 1991; Eötvös Lóránd, Budapest, 1991; Bucharest, 1991; Delhi, 1991; Moscow, 1993; Charles Univ., Prague, 1994; Kiev, 1995; Mathias Bel, Slovakia, 1996; Tbilisi, 1996. Decorations from: Sweden, 1967; Austria, 1977; Spain, 1980; Senegal and Republic of Korea, 1981; Bulgaria, 1985; France, Japan and Thailand, 1986; Hungary, 1991; Colombia, France and Senegal, 1992; Germany, 1993; Tanzania, 1995; Hungary and Cuba, 1996; Sweden, 1997. *Address:* 12 chemin du Vieux-Bois, 1292 Chambesy, Switzerland. *T:* (22) 7582267. *Died 19 Sept. 2004.*

BOHUSZ-SZYSZKO, Dame Cicely (Mary Strode); *see* Saunders, Dame C. M. S.

BOLAND, John Anthony; Public Trustee and Accountant General, 1987–91 (Public Trustee, 1980–87); *b* 23 Jan. 1931; *s* of late Daniel Boland, MBE, and Hannah Boland (*née* Barton), Dublin; *m* 1972, Ann, *d* of late James C. Doyle and Maureen Doyle. *Educ:* Castleknock Coll.; Xavier Sch.; Christian Brothers, Synge Street; Trinity Coll., Dublin (MA, LLB). Called to the Bar, Middle Temple, 1956; called to Irish Bar, 1967. Joined Public Trustee Office, 1956; Chief Administrative Officer, 1974–79; Asst Public Trustee, 1979–80. Hon. Mem., College Historical Soc., TCD, 1954. Trustee, London Trust for TCD (formerly TCD (Univ. of Dublin) Trust), 1980–. Asst Editor, The Supreme Court Practice, 1984–91. *Recreations:* walking, foreign travel, theology. *Address:* 22 Waltham Terrace, Blackrock, Co. Dublin, Ireland. *T:* and *Fax:* (1) 278 0120. *Club:* Kildare Street and University (Dublin). *Died 14 Nov. 2001.*

BOLLAND, Group Captain Guy Alfred, CBE 1943; Chief Intelligence Officer, British Joint Services Mission, Washington, DC, USA, 1949 and 1956–59, retired; *b* 5 Nov. 1909; 3rd *s* of late Capt. L. W. Bolland; *m* 1935, Sylvia Marguerite, 2nd *d* of late Oswald Duke, Cambridge; one *s* three *d*. *Educ:* Gilbert Hannam Sch., Sussex. Commissioned RAF, 1930, Pilot Officer; No 1 (Fighter) Sqdn, 1931; 84 (Bomber) Sqdn, Iraq, 1932; CFS, 1934; Flying Instr, 1934–36; RAF Navigation Sch., 1937; No 228 Flying Boat Sqdn, 1937–39; Commanding Officer: RAF Hooton Park, 1939–40 (Sqdn Ldr); 217 Sqdn, St Eval, 1940–41 (Wing Comdr); Fleet Aviation Officer on battleship King George V (when Bismarck sunk), 1941–42; Commanding Officer: RAF Gibraltar, 1942–43 (despatches (N African landings); Gp Capt.); RAF Pembroke Dock, 1943–44; RAF Staff Coll., 1945; Dep. Dir Orgn and Estabt, Air Min., 1946; USAF Air War Coll., 1948; CO RAF Ballykelly, 1952; Dep. Dir Ops (Maritime), 1954. *Recreations:* golf, bowls, travel. *Address:* The Oaks, Shaftesbury Road, Woking, Surrey GU22 7DU. *T:* (01483) 760548. *Died 20 Jan. 2001.*

BOLT, David Ernest, CBE 1984; FRCS; President, British Medical Association, 1987–88; *b* 21 Sept. 1921; *s* of Rev. E. A. J. Bolt and Hilda I. Bolt; *m* 1955, Phyllis Margaret, (Peggy), Fudge; two *d*. *Educ:* Queen Elizabeth's Hosp., Bristol; Univ. of Bristol (MB ChB 1945). FRCS 1950. Senior Surgical Registrar, W Middx Hosp. and St Mary's Hosp., Paddington, 1955–60; Consultant Surgeon, W Middx Hosp., 1960–82; Hon. Lectr, Charing Cross Hosp., 1972–82. British Medical Association: Mem., Central Cttee for Hosp. Med. Service (Dep. Chm., 1975–79; Chm., 1979–83); Dep. Chm., Jt Consultants' Cttee, 1979–83; Mem. Council, 1975–83. Mem., GMC, 1979–89 (Chm., Professional Conduct Cttee). *Publications:* articles on surgical subjects in professional jls. *Recreations:* motor boat cruising, tree planting, reading, walking. *Address:* Feniton House, Feniton, Honiton, Devon EX14 0BE. *T:* (01404) 850921. *Club:* Royal Society of Medicine. *Died 21 March 2002.*

BOLTON, 7th Baron *cr* 1797, of Bolton Castle, co. York; **Richard William Algar Orde-Powlett;** *b* 11 July 1929; *s* of 6th Baron Bolton and Victoria Mary, *d* of Henry Montagu Villiers, MVO; *S* father, 1963; *m* 1st, 1951, Hon. Christine Helena Weld Forester (marr. diss. 1981), *e d* of 7th Baron Forester, and Marie Louise Priscilla, CStJ, *d* of Sir Herbert Perrott, 6th Bt, CH, CB; two *s* one *d*; 2nd, 1981, Masha Anne (marr. diss. 1990), *d* of Major F. E. Hudson, Winterfield House, Hornby, Bedale, Yorks; 3rd, 1991, Mrs Lavinia Fenton. *Educ:* Eton; Trinity Coll., Cambridge (BA). Chairman: Richmond Div., Conservative Assoc., 1957–60; Yorkshire Div., Royal Forestry Soc., 1962–64; Member Council, Timber Growers' Organization. Director: Yorkshire Insurance Co., 1964–70; General Accident Life Assurance Ltd, 1970–98. JP, North Riding of Yorkshire, 1957–80. FRICS. *Recreations:* shooting, fishing. *Heir: s* Hon. Harry Algar Nigel Orde-Powlett [*b* 14 Feb. 1954; *m* 1977, Philippa, *d* of Major P. L. Tapply; three *s*]. *Address:* Bolton Hall, Leyburn, North Yorkshire DL8 4UF. *T:* (01969) 22003. *Died 29 July 2001.*

BOLTON, Sir Frederic (Bernard), Kt 1976; MC 1945; FIMarEST; Chairman: The Bolton Group, 1953–91; Dover Harbour Board, 1982–88 (Member, 1957–62 and 1980–88); *b* 9 March 1921; *s* of late Louis Hamilton Bolton and Beryl Dyer; *m* 1st, 1950, Valerie Margaret Barwick (*d* 1970); two *s*; 2nd, 1971, Vanessa Mary Anne Robarts; two *s* two *d*. *Educ:* Rugby. Served War, Welsh Guards, 1940–46 (MC 1945, Italy); Northants Yeomanry, 1952–56. Member: Lloyd's, 1945–; Baltic Exchange, 1946–. Chm., Atlantic Steam Nav. Co. & Subs, 1960–71; Dir, B.P. Tanker Co., 1968–82; Mem., Brit. Rail Shipping & Int. Services Bd, 1970–82 (later Sealink UK Ltd). Mem., Lloyd's Register of Shipping Gen. Cttee, 1961–86; Chairman: Ship & Marine Technol. Requirements Bd, 1977–81; British Ports Assoc., 1985–88; Pilots' Nat. Pension Fund, 1991–94; Member: PLA, 1964–71; Nat. Ports Council, 1967–74; President: Chamber of Shipping of UK, 1966; Inst. of Marine Engineers, 1968–69 and 1969–70; British Shipping Fedn, 1972–75; Internat. Shipping Fedn, 1973–82; Gen. Council of British Shipping, 1975–76; British Maritime League, 1985–91. Hon. Treas., W Oxfordshire Cons. Assoc., 1991–95. Hon. FNI. Jt Master, 1956–67, Chm., 1967–72, Grafton Hunt. *Recreations:* country sports. *Address:* Pudlicote, near Charlbury, Oxon OX7 3HX. *Club:* City of London. *Died 27 July 2005.*

BOLTON, John Eveleigh, CBE 1972; DSC 1945; DL; Chairman and Managing Director, Growth Capital Ltd, since 1968; Chairman: Hall Bolton Estates Ltd; Riverview Investments Ltd; *b* 17 Oct. 1920; *s* of late Ernest and Edith Mary Bolton; *m* 1948, Gabrielle Healey Hall (*d* 1989), *d* of late Joseph and Minnie Hall; one *s* one *d*. *Educ:* Ilkley Sch.; Wolverhampton Sch.; Trinity Coll., Cambridge (Cassel Travelling Schol., 1948; BA Hons Econs 1948, MA 1953); Harvard Business School (Baker Schol., 1949; MBA with dist., 1950). Articled pupil to Chartered Acct, 1937–40; intermed. exam. of Inst. of Chartered Accts, 1940. Served War of 1939–45 (DSC): Destroyers, Lt RNVR, 1940–46. Research for Harvard in British Industry, 1950–51; Finance Dir, Solartron Laboratory Instruments Ltd, Kingston-upon-Thames, 1951–53 (Chm., 1953); Chm. and Man. Dir: Solartron Engineering Ltd, 1952; The Solartron Electronic Group Ltd, Thames Ditton and subseq. Farnborough, Hants, 1954–63 (Dep. Chm., 1963–65). Director or former Director: NCR Co. Ltd; Alphameric PLC; Black & Decker Group Inc.; Black & Decker Holdings Inc.; Black & Decker Investment Co.; Black & Decker Corp.; Plasmec PLC; Dawson International plc; Johnson Wax Ltd; Redland plc; Hoskyns plc; Business Advisers Ltd; Camperdowne Investment Holdings Ltd; Pres., Develt Capital Gp Ltd, 1984–88. A Gen. Comr of Income Tax, 1964–. British Institute of Management: Chm. Council, 1964–66; Bowie Medal 1969; Life Vice-Pres.; CCMI; Pres., Engrg Industries Assoc., 1981–84; Chm. and Founder Subscriber: Advanced Management Programmes Internat. Trust; Foundn for Management Educn; Business Grads Assoc.; Dir, Management Publications Ltd, 1966–73 (Chm., 1969); Mem. Exec. Cttee, AA; Hon. Treasurer, Surrey Univ., 1975–82 (Past Chm.); Member: Sub-Cttee on Business Management Studies, UGC; Council of Industry for Management Educn; Harvard Business Sch. Vis. Cttee, 1962–75; Adv. Cttee on Industry, Cttee of Vice-Chancellors, 1984; Business Educn Forum, 1969–74. Mem. Org. Cttee, World Research Hospital. Member: UK Automation Council, 1964–65; Adv. Cttee for Management Efficiency in NHS, 1964–65; Cttee for Exports to New Zealand, 1965–68; Adv. Cttee, Queen's Award to Industry, 1972–; Council, Inst. of Dirs; Chm., Economic Develt Cttee for the Rubber Industry, 1965–68; Vice-Chm., Royal Commn on Local Govt in England, 1966–69; Chm., Committee of Inquiry on Small Firms, 1969–71. Trustee, Small Business Research Trust. Life FRSA. DL Surrey, 1974; High Sheriff of Surrey, 1980–81. DUniv Surrey, 1982; Hon. DSc Bath, 1986. *Publications:* articles in newspapers and journals; various radio and TV broadcasts on industrial topics. *Recreations:*

shooting, swimming, gardening, opera, antiques. *Address:* Sunnymead, Tite Hill, Englefield Green, Surrey TW20 0NH. *T:* (01784) 435172. *Clubs:* Harvard Club of London, Institute of Directors. *Died 15 Feb. 2003.*

BOND-WILLIAMS, Noel Ignace, CBE 1979; Director, National Exhibition Centre Ltd, 1970–89; *b* 7 Nov. 1914; *s* of late W. H. Williams, Birmingham; *m* 1939, Mary Gwendoline Tomey (*d* 1989); one *s* two *d*. *Educ:* Oundle Sch.; Birmingham Univ. (BSc). FIMMM; FCMI. Pres. Guild of Undergrads 1936–37, Pres. Guild of Grads 1947, Birmingham Univ. Various appts in metal industry; Director: Enfield Rolling Mills Ltd, 1957–65; Delta Metal Co. Ltd, 1967–77; Vice-Chm., 1978–79, Chm., 1979–83, Remploy Ltd; Dir, 1972–85, and Vice-Chm., 1979–85, Lucas (Industries) Ltd. Industrial Adviser, DEA, 1965–67. Pres., Birmingham Chamber of Commerce, 1969. Member: Commn on Industrial Relations, 1971–74; Price Commn, 1977–79. Mem. Council, Industrial Soc., 1947–78; Pres., Brit. Non-ferrous Metals Fedn, 1974–75. Pro-Chancellor, Univ. of Aston in Birmingham, 1970–81. Hon. DSc Aston, 1975. *Publications:* papers and articles on relationships between people in industry. *Recreation:* sailing. *Address:* Courtyard House, High Street, Lymington, Hants SO41 9AH. *T:* (01590) 672593. *Clubs:* Royal Cruising, Royal Lymington Yacht. *Died 18 March 2003.*

BONDI, Prof. Sir Hermann, KCB 1973; FRS 1959; FRAS; Master of Churchill College, Cambridge, 1983–90, Fellow, since 1990; Professor of Mathematics, King's College, London, since 1954 (Titular, 1971–85, Emeritus, since 1985); *b* Vienna, 1 Nov. 1919; *s* of late Samuel and Helene Bondi, New York; *m* 1947, Christine M. Stockman, *d* of late H. W. Stockman, CBE; two *s* three *d*. *Educ:* Realgymnasium, Vienna; Trinity Coll., Cambridge (MA). Temporary Experimental Officer, Admiralty, 1942–45; Fellow, Trinity Coll., Cambridge, 1943–49, and 1952–54; Asst Lecturer, Mathematics, Cambridge, 1945–48; University Lecturer, Mathematics, Cambridge, 1948–54. Dir-Gen., ESRO, 1967–71; Chief Scientific Advr, MoD, 1971–77; Chief Scientist, Dept of Energy, 1977–80; Chm. and Chief Exec., NERC, 1980–84. Research Associate, Cornell Univ., 1951; Visiting Prof., Cornell Univ., 1960; Raman Prof., Indian Acad. of Scis, 1996. Lectures: Harvard Coll. Observatory, 1953; Lowell, Boston, Mass, 1953; Halley, Oxford, 1962; Tarner, Cambridge, 1965; Lees-Knowles, Cambridge, 1974; Conway Meml, London, 1992. Chairman: Space Cttee, MoD, 1964–65; Nat. Cttee for Astronomy, 1963–67; Adv. Council on Energy Conservation, 1980–82; IFIAS 1984–97. Secretary, Royal Astronomical Soc., 1956–64; Mem., SRC, 1973–80. President: Inst. of Mathematics and its Applications, 1974–75; British Humanist Assoc., 1982–99; Assoc. of British Science Writers, 1981–85; Soc. for Res. into Higher Educn, 1981–97; Assoc. for Science Educn, 1982; Hydrographic Soc., 1985–87; Rationalist Press Assoc., 1982–. Mem. Ct, London Univ., 1963–67. Hon. Fellow, Indian Acad. of Scis, 1996. FKC 1968. Hon. DSc: Sussex 1974; Bath 1974; Surrey 1974; York 1980; Southampton 1981; Salford, 1982; Birmingham, 1984; St Andrews, 1985; Hon. DTech Plymouth, 1995; Dr *hc* Vienna, 1993. Hon. FIEE 1979; Hon. FInstP 1992; Hon. FIMA 1993. Gold Medal: Einstein Soc., 1983; Inst. of Mathematics and its Applications, 1988; G. D. Birla Internat. Award for Humanism, 1990; Decoration of Honour for Sci. and Art, Austria, 1997; Gold Medal, RAS, 2001. *Publications:* Cosmology, 1952, 2nd edn 1960; The Universe at Large, 1961; Relativity and Commonsense, 1964; Assumption and Myth in Physical Theory, 1968; (with Dame Kathleen Ollerenshaw) Magic Squares of Order Four, 1982; Science, Churchill and me (autobiog.), 1990; papers on astrophysics, etc, in Proc. Royal Society, Monthly Notices, Royal Astronomical Society, Proc. Cam. Phil. Society, etc. *Recreations:* walking, travelling. *Address:* Churchill College, Cambridge CB3 0DS; 60 Mill Lane,

Impington, Cambridge CB4 9XN.
Died 10 Sept. 2005.

BONHAM CARTER, Hon. Raymond Henry; Executive Director, S. G. Warburg & Co. Ltd, 1967–77; retired in 1979 following disability; *b* 19 June 1929; *s* of Sir Maurice Bonham Carter, KCB, KCVO, and Lady Violet Bonham Carter, DBE (later Baroness Asquith of Yarnbury); *m* 1958, Elena Propper de Callejon; two *s* one *d*. *Educ:* Winchester Coll.; Magdalen Coll., Oxford (BA 1952); Harvard Business Sch. (MBA 1954). Irish Guards, 1947–49. With J. Henry Schröder & Co., 1954–58; acting Advr, Bank of England, 1958–63; Alternate Exec. Dir for UK, IMF, and Mem., UK Treasury and Supply Delegn, Washington, 1961–63; S. G. Warburg & Co. Ltd, 1964; Director: Transport Development Group Ltd, 1969–77; Banque de Paris et des Pays Bas NV, 1973–77; Mercury Securities Ltd, 1974–77; seconded as Dir, Industrial Develt Unit, DoI, 1977–79. Mem. Council, Internat. Inst. for Strategic Studies (Hon. Treasurer, 1974–84). *Address:* 7 West Heath Avenue, NW11 7QS.
Died 17 Jan. 2004.

BONNEY, James William; QC 1995; *b* 5 Sept. 1948; *s* of late James Henry Bonney, inshore fisherman, and of Alice Bonney (*née* Butler); *m* 1975, Judith Anne, *d* of Montague William Lacey; one *s* one *d*. *Educ:* St John the Divine C of E Sch.; King Edward VII Sch., Lytham; Keble Coll., Oxford (BA 1974; BCL 1975; MA 1983). Admitted Solicitor, 1970; Asst Solicitor, 1970–75; called to the Bar, Lincoln's Inn, 1975 (Jenkin's Schol.); Vis. Tutor in Jurisprudence, Keble Coll., Oxford, 1975–76; Mem., Northern Circuit, 1976–; a Dep. High Court Judge, Chancery Div., 1996–. Member: Chancery Bar Assoc., 1977–; Ecclesiastical Law Soc., 1988–; Assoc. of Contentious Trust and Probate Specialists, 1998–; Property Bar Assoc., 2000–; Professional Negligence Bar Assoc., 2001–; Bar European Gp, 2001–. Reader, St Cuthbert's Parish Church, Lytham, 1983–. *Recreation:* choral singing. *Address:* 10 Old Square, Lincoln's Inn, WC2A 3SU. *T:* (020) 7405 0758; 24 Norfolk Road, Lytham, Lancs FY8 4JG. *T:* (01253) 794259; Flat 5, 24 Old Buildings, Lincoln's Inn, WC2A 3UP. *T:* (020) 7404 8663. *Club:* Lytham Yacht. *Died 12 July 2003.*

BONSER, Rt Rev. David; Bishop Suffragan of Bolton, 1991–99; *b* 1 Feb. 1934; *s* of George Frederick and Alice Bonser; *m* 1960, Shirley Wilkinson (*d* 2004); one *s* two *d*. *Educ:* Hillhouse Secondary Sch., Huddersfield; King's Coll., London Univ. (AKC); Manchester Univ. (MA). Curate: St James's, Heckmondwike, 1962–65; St George's, Sheffield, 1965–68; Rector of St Clement's, Chorlton-cum-Hardy, 1968–82; Hon. Canon of Manchester Cathedral, 1980–82; Area Dean of Hulme, 1981–82; Archdeacon of Rochdale, 1982–91; Team Rector, Rochdale Team Ministry, 1982–91 (Vicar of St Chad's, 1982–86). *Recreations:* theatre, reading, walking, ski-ing, music, soup-making. *Address:* 82 Birchfield Drive, Marland, Rochdale OL11 4NY. *T:* (01706) 352522.
Died 20 March 2005.

BOORSTIN, Dr Daniel J., FRHistS; (12th) Librarian of Congress, 1975–87, then Emeritus; *b* 1 Oct. 1914; *s* of Samuel Boorstin and Dora (*née* Olsan); *m* 1941, Ruth Carolyn Frankel; three *s*. *Educ:* schs in Tulsa, Okla; Harvard Univ. (AB, summa cum Laude); Balliol Coll., Oxford (Rhodes Schol., BA Juris. 1st Cl. Hons, BCL 1st Cl. Hons); Yale Univ. Law Sch. (Sterling Fellow, JSD). Called to Bar, Inner Temple, 1937; admitted Mass Bar, 1942. Instr, tutor in history and lit., Harvard Univ. and Radcliffe Coll., 1938–42; Lectr, legal history, Law Sch., Harvard, 1939–42; Sen. Attorney, Office of Lend Lease Admin, Washington, DC, 1942–43; Office of Asst SG, USA, 1942–43; Asst Prof. of History, Swarthmore Coll., 1942–44; Univ. of Chicago, 1944–69: Asst Prof., 1944–49; Associate Prof., Preston and Sterling Morton Distinguished Prof. of Amer. History, 1956–69. During his 25 years tenure at Chicago, Visiting Lectr at Rome and Kyoto Univs, Sorbonne and Cambridge (Fellow, Trinity

Coll., and Pitt Prof. of Amer. History and Instns; LittD 1968). Smithsonian Institution: Dir, Nat. Museum History and Techn., 1969–73; Sen. Historian, 1973–75. Many public service membership assignments, trusteeships, and active concern with a number of Amer. Assocs, esp. those relating to Amer. history, educn and cultural affairs. Past Pres., American Studies Assoc. Hon. FAGS. Hon. LittD Sheffield, 1979; Hon. DLitt: Cambridge, 1968; East Anglia, 1980; Sussex, 1983; numerous other hon. degrees. Watson-Davis Prize of the History of Science, Soc. for Discoverers, 1986; Charles Frankel Prize, Nat. Endowment for the Humanities, 1989; Nat. Book Award Medal for Distinguished Contribution to American Letters, 1989; Jefferson Medal, Amer. Phil Soc., 1999. Officier de l'Ordre de la Couronne, Belgium, 1980; Chevalier, Légion d'Honneur, France, 1984; Grand Officer, Order of Prince Henry the Navigator, Portugal, 1985; First Class Order of the Sacred Treasure, Japan, 1986. *Publications: include:* The Mysterious Science of the Law, 1941; The Lost World of Thomas Jefferson, 1948; The Genius of American Politics, 1953; The Americans: The Colonial Experience, 1958 (Bancroft Prize); America and the Image of Europe, 1960; The Image, 1962; The Americans: The National Experience, 1965 (Parkman Prize); The Decline of Radicalism, 1969; The Sociology of the Absurd, 1970; The Americans: The Democratic Experience, 1973 (Pulitzer Prize for History and Dexter Prize, 1974); Democracy and Its Discontents, 1974; The Exploring Spirit (BBC 1975 Reith Lectures), 1976; The Republic of Technology, 1978; (with Brooks M. Kelley) A History of the United States, 1980; The Discoverers, 1984 (Watson-Davis Prize), illustrated edn 1991; Hidden History, 1987; The Creators, 1992; Cleopatra's Nose, 1994; The Daniel J. Boorstin Reader, 1996; The Seekers, 1998; *for young readers:* Landmark History of the American People, vol. I, From Plymouth to Appomattox, 1968; vol. II, From Appomattox to the Moon, 1970; New Landmark History of the American People, 1987; *edited:* Delaware Cases 1792–1830, 1943; An American Primer, 1966; American Civilization, 1971; The Chicago History of American Civilization (30 vols). *Address:* (home) 3541 Ordway Street, NW, Washington, DC 20016, USA. *T:* (202) 9661853; (office) Library of Congress, Washington, DC 20540, USA. *Clubs:* Cosmos (Washington); Elizabethan (Yale); International House (Japan).
Died 28 Feb. 2004.

BOOTH, Eric Stuart, CBE 1971; FRS 1967; FREng; Chairman, Yorkshire Electricity Board, 1972–79; *b* 14 Oct. 1914; *s* of Henry and Annie Booth; *m* 1945, Mary Elizabeth Melton (*d* 1987); two *d*; *m* 1988, Pauline Margaret Ford. *Educ:* Batley Grammar Sch.; Liverpool Univ. Apprentice, Metropolitan Vickers Electrical Co. Ltd, 1936–38; Technical Engineer, Yorks Electric Power Co., 1938–46; Dep., later City Electrical Engineer and Manager, Salford Corporation, 1946–48; various posts associated with construction of Power Stations with British, later Central Electricity Authority, 1948–57, Dep. Chief Engineer (Generation Design and Construction), 1957; Chief Design and Construction Engineer, 1958–59, Bd Mem. for Engrg, 1959–71, CEGB. Part-time Mem., UKAEA, 1965–72. Pres., IEE, 1976–77. Dir, British Electricity Internat., 1979–84; Consultant to Electricity Council, 1979–84. FREng (FEng 1976). Hon. FIEE 1986. Hon. DTech Bradford, 1980. *Address:* Pinecroft, Upper Dunsforth, York YO26 9RU. *T:* (01423) 322821.
Died 1 May 2005.

BOOTH, John Antony W.; *see* Ward-Booth.

BOOTH, John Barton, FRCS; Physician, St Bridget's Hospice, Douglas, since 2000; Consultant Otolaryngologist, London (later Royal London) Hospital, 1972–98, and Royal Hospital of St Bartholomew, 1995–98, then Hon. Consulting Otolaryngologist, Barts and the London (formerly Royal Hospitals) NHS Trust; *b* 19 Nov. 1937; *s* of (Percy) Leonard Booth and Mildred Amy (*née* Wilson); *m* 1966, Carroll Griffiths (*d* 2004); one *s. Educ:* Canford Sch., Dorset; King's Coll., London (AKC 1963); King's Coll. Hosp. Med. Sch. (MB, BS 1963). MRCS, LRCP, 1963; FRCS 1968. House Surgeon: Birmingham Accident Hosp., 1964; Hosp. for Sick Children, Gt Ormond St, 1965; House Surgeon, Registrar, Sen. Registrar, RNTNEH, 1966–70; Sen. Registrar, Royal Free Hosp., 1970–72; Clin. Asst, Neuro-Otology, Nat. Hosp. for Nervous Diseases, 1968, 1971; Consultant Surgeon, RNTNEH, 1973–78; Civil Consultant (Otology), RAF, 1983–2000, then Hon. Consultant; Hon. Consultant, St Luke's Hosp. for the Clergy, 1983–2000; Hon. Consultant Laryngologist: Musicians Benevolent Fund, 1974–2000; Royal Coll. of Music, 1974–2000; Newspaper Press Fund, 1982–2000; Royal Opera House, Covent Gdn, 1983–2000; Royal Soc. of Musicians of GB, 1987–2000; Concert Artists Assoc., 1987–2000; Webber-Douglas Acad. of Dramatic Art, 1987–2000. Hunterian Prof., RCS, 1980–81. Hon. Chm., IXth British Acad. Conf. in Otolaryngol., 1995. Vice-Chm., 1960–61, Chm., 1961–62, Vice-Pres., 1962–63, Fedn of Univ. Conservatives; Mem., Gen. Purposes and Exec. Cttees, Cons. Party, 1961–62. FRSocMed 1967 (Mem. Council, 1980–88 and 1993–96; Hon. Sec., 1996–2000; Sen. Vice-Pres., 2001–02; Pres., Otology Sect., 1996–97; Pres., United Services Section, 1999–2001; Vice-Pres., History of Medicine Section, 2000–). FRAeS 2004 (MRAeS (Medical Aviation Gp) 1990); Hon. Mem., Amer. Otological Soc., 1995. FZS 1996. Howell Head Prize (jtly), Univ. of London, 1988. Editor, Jl of Laryngology and Otology, 1987–92 (Asst Editor, 1979–87; Abstract Editor, 1987–94). *Publications:* (ed) Vol. 3, The Ear, of 5th edn of Scott-Brown's Otolaryngology, 1987, 6th edn 1997; chapters in: Rob and Smith, Operative Surgery, 3rd edn 1976; Audiology and Audiological Medicine, vol. I, 1981; Otologic Medicine and Surgery, 1988. *Recreations:* golf, music, the arts, gardening. *Address:* Crofton Lodge, 24 The Crofts, Castletown, Isle of Man IM9 1LZ. *T:* (01624) 823837. *Clubs:* Royal Automobile, MCC; Royal & Ancient Golf (St Andrews).   *Died 22 July 2005.*

BOOTH, John Dick L.; *see* Livingston Booth.

BOOTH, Martin, FRSL; writer; *b* 7 Sept. 1944; *s* of William John Kenneth Booth and Alice Joyce Booth (*née* Pankhurst); *m* 1968, Helen Barber; one *s* one *d. Educ:* Hong Kong and Kenya. Started writing at the age of 17, encouraged by Edmund Blunden and Robert Druce; addicted to the habit ever since. Fellow Commoner: St Peter's Coll., Oxford, 1972; Corpus Christi Coll., Cambridge, 1980. FRSL 1980. *Publications: include: fiction*: Hiroshima Joe, 1985; A Very Private Gentleman, 1991; Adrift in the Oceans of Mercy, 1996; The Industry of Souls, 1998; Islands of Silence, 2002; *children's fiction*: War Dog, 1997; Music on the Bamboo Radio, 1998; Panther, 1999; PoW, 2000; Dr Illuminatus, 2003; *Midnight Saboteur, 2004; Soul Stealer, 2004; non-fiction*: Carpet Sahib: a life of Jim Corbett, 1986; Rhino Road, 1992; The Dragon and the Pearl: a Hong Kong notebook, 1994; Opium: a history, 1996; The Doctor, The Detective and Arthur Conan Doyle, 1997; The Dragon Syndicates, 1999; A Magick Life: a biography of Aleister Crowley, 2000; Cannabis: a history, 2003; Gweilo, 2004; also film scripts, wildlife documentaries, feature films, verse, literary criticism and journalism. *Recreations:* puncturing pomposity, harpooning hypocrisy, Chinese history, big game tracking, archaeology. *Address:* c/o Gillon Aitken Associates, 18–21 Cavaye Place, SW10 9PT. *T:* (020) 7373 8672.   *Died 12 Feb. 2004.*

BOREEL, Sir Francis (David), 13th Bt, *cr* 1645; Counsellor, Netherlands Foreign Service, 1966–87 (Attaché, 1956), retired; *b* 14 June 1926; *s* of Sir Alfred Boreel, 12th Bt and Countess Reiniera Adriana (*d* 1957), *d* of Count Francis David Schimmelpenninck; *S* father 1964; *m* 1964, Suzanne Campagne; three *d. Educ:* Utrecht Univ. *Recreations:* tennis, sailing. *Heir: kinsman* Stephen Gerard Boreel [*b* 9 Feb. 1945; *m* Francien P. Kooyman;

one *s*]. *Address:* Kapellestraat 25, 4351 A. L. Veere, Netherlands.   *Died 24 March 2001.*

BOREHAM, Sir Leslie Kenneth Edward, Kt 1972; a Judge of the High Court, Queen's Bench Division, 1972–92; Presiding Judge, North Eastern Circuit, 1974–80; Deputy Chairman, Agricultural Lands Tribunal; *b* 19 Oct. 1917; *o s* of Harry Edward and Mary Amelia Boreham; *m* 1941, Rachel (*d* 1998), *o c* of Trevor Morgan and Elizabeth Harding; one *s* one *d. Educ:* Bungay Grammar Sch. Served War of 1939–45, RAF. Called to the Bar at Lincoln's Inn, Nov. 1947, Bencher 1972; admitted to Bar of St Helena, 1963. Joined South-Eastern Circuit. Dep. Chm. 1962–65, Chm. 1965–71, East Suffolk QS; QC 1965; Recorder of Margate, 1968–71. Chm., Lord Chancellor's Cttee on Trng of Magistrates, 1974–82; Pres., Central Council of Probation Cttees, 1976–82; Parole Bd, 1979–81 (Vice Chm., 1981). *Recreations:* gardening, golf. *Address:* c/o Royal Courts of Justice, Strand, WC2A 2LL.   *Died 2 May 2004.*

BORTHWICK, Sir John Thomas, 3rd Bt *cr* 1908, of Whitburgh, Humbie, Co. Haddington; MBE 1945; *b* 5 Dec. 1917; *o s* of Hon. James Alexander Borthwick (*d* 1961) and Irene, *d* of George Wise; *S* to Btcy of uncle (1st and last Baron Whitburgh), 1967; *m* 1st, 1939, Irene Sophie (marr. diss. 1961; she *d* 1978), *o c* of Joseph Heller; three *s*; 2nd, 1962, Irene, *d* of Leo Fink; two *s. Educ:* Eton; Trinity Coll., Oxford. Served War of 1939–45. Late Major, Rifle Bde, TA. *Heir: s* Antony Thomas Borthwick [*b* 12 Feb. 1941; *m* 1st, 1966, Gillian Deirdre Broke Thurston (marr. diss.); one *s* two *d*; 2nd, 1985, Jenny Lanning (marr. diss.)].   *Died 25 Oct. 2002.*

BOULIND, Mrs (Olive) Joan, CBE 1975; Fellow, 1973–79, and Tutor, 1974–79, Hughes Hall, Cambridge; *b* 24 Sept. 1912; *e d* of Douglas Siddall and Olive Raby; *m* 1936, Henry F. Boulind (decd), MA, PhD; one *s* (and one *s* one *d* decd). *Educ:* Wallasey High Sch., Cheshire; Univ. of Liverpool (BA 1st class Hons History, Medieval and Modern; DipEd); MA Cantab 1974. Teacher: Wirral Co. Sch. for Girls, 1934–36; Cambridgeshire High Sch. for Girls, 1963. Nat. Pres., Nat. Council of Women, 1966–68 (Sen. Vice-Pres., 1964–66); Co-Chm., Women's Consultative Council, 1966–68; Leader, British delegn to conf. of Internat. Council of Women, Bangkok, 1970; Co-Chm., Women's Nat. Commn, 1973–75; Co-Chm., UK Co-ordinating Cttee for Internat. Women's Year, 1975; Chm., Westminster College Management Cttee, 1980–88. Member: Commn on the Church in the Seventies, Congregational Church in England and Wales, 1970–72 (Vice-Chm., 1971–72); Ministerial Trng Cttee, United Reformed Church, 1972–79 and 1982–86 (Chm., 1982–86); East Adv. Council, BBC, 1976–84 (Chm. 1981–84). Deacon, Emmanuel Congregational Ch., Cambridge, 1958–66. Trustee, Homerton Coll. of Educn, 1955–94. *Recreations:* reading, travel, music.

                                    Died 29 July 2004.

BOULTING, Roy; Producer and Joint Managing Director, Charter Film Productions Ltd, since 1973; *b* 21 Nov. 1913; *s* of Arthur Boulting and Rose Bennett. *Educ:* HMS Worcester; Reading Sch. Formed independent film production company with twin brother John, 1937. Served War of 1939–45, RAC, finishing as Capt.; films directed for Army included Desert Victory (Oscar), Tunisian Victory and Burma Victory. Producer: Brighton Rock, 1947; Seven Days to Noon, 1950; Private's Progress, 1955; Lucky Jim (Edinburgh Festival), 1957; I'm All Right Jack, 1959; Heavens Above!, 1962. Director: Pastor Hall, 1939; Thunder Rock, 1942; Fame is the Spur, 1947; The Guinea Pig, 1948; High Treason, 1951; Singlehanded, 1952; Seagulls over Sorrento, Crest of the Wave, 1953; Josephine and Men, 1955; Run for the Sun, 1955; Brothers in Law, 1956; Happy is the Bride, 1958; Carlton-Browne of the FO, 1958–59; I'm All Right Jack, 1959; The Risk, 1960; The French Mistress, 1960; Suspect, 1960; The Family Way, 1966; Twisted Nerve, 1968; There's a Girl in My Soup, 1970; Soft Beds, Hard

Battles, 1974; Danny Travis, 1978; The Last Word, 1979; The Moving Finger, 1984. *Play:* (with Leo Marks) Favourites, 1977. Dir, British Lion Films Ltd, 1958–72. Mem. Adv. Council, Dirs' and Producers' Rights Soc., 1988–. Hon. Dr RCA, 1990. Evening Standard Award for outstanding contribn to British films, 1997. *Address:* Charter Film Productions Ltd, Twickenham Film Studios, St Margarets, Twickenham, Middlesex TW1 2AW. *Club:* Lord's Taverners. *Died 5 Nov. 2001.*

BOURDILLON, Mervyn Leigh; JP; Lord-Lieutenant of Powys, 1986–98; *b* 9 Aug. 1924; *s* of late Prebendary G. L. Bourdillon; *m* 1961, Penelope, *d* of late P. W. Kemp-Welch, OBE; one *s* three *d. Educ:* Haileybury. Served RNVR, 1943–46. Forestry Comr, 1973–76. Mem., Brecon County Council, 1962–73. DL 1962, JP 1970, High Sheriff 1970, Brecon; Vice Lord-Lieutenant, Powys, 1978–86. KStJ 1994. *Address:* Gilwern, Beulah, Llanwrtyd Wells, Powys LD5 4YG. *Died 11 Sept. 2002.*

BOVENIZER, Vernon Gordon Fitzell, CMG 1948; Assistant Under-Secretary of State, Ministry of Defence, 1964–68, retired; *b* 22 July 1908; *s* of Rev. Michael Fitzell Bovenizer and Mary Gordon; *m* 1937, Lillian Cherry (*d* 1970), *d* of John Henry Rowe, Cork; two *s* two *d. Educ:* Liverpool Coll.; Sidney Sussex Coll., Cambridge (Scholar). War Office, 1931–45; Control Commission for Germany, 1945, until return to War Office, 1948; Asst Private Sec. to Secretaries of State for War, 1936, and 1940–42; Resident Clerk, 1934–37; Asst Sec., 1942, civilian liaison with US Armies in the UK; Establishment Officer and Dir of Organisation, CCG, 1945–47; Asst Sec. and Dep. Comptroller of Claims, War Office, 1948–58; Counsellor, UK Delegation to NATO, 1958–60; Asst Under-Sec. of State, War Office, 1960–68. US Medal of Freedom, 1945. *Club:* Reform. *Died 22 Nov. 2005.*

BOWDEN, Rt Rev. David; *see* Bowden, Rt Rev. R. D.

BOWDEN, Sir Frank Houston, 3rd Bt *cr* 1915; MA Oxon; retired industrialist and landowner; *b* 10 Aug. 1909; *o s* of Sir Harold Bowden, 2nd Bt, GBE, and of Vera, *d* of Joseph Whitaker; *S* father 1960; *m* 1st, 1934, Marie-José, *d* of Charles Stiénon and Comtesse Laure de Messey; one *s*; 2nd, 1937, Lydia Eveline (*d* 1981), *d* of Jean Manolovici, Bucharest; three *s*; 3rd, 1989, Oriol Annette Mary, *d* of Charles Hooper Bath. *Educ:* Rugby; Merton Coll., Oxford. Served with RNVR, 1939–44. President: University Hall, Buckland, 1967–71; British Kendo Assoc., 1969; Thame Br., RN Assoc. Hon. Vice-Pres., 3rd World Kendo Championships, 1976. Vice-Pres., Oxfordshire County Scout Council, 1970–. Pres., Merton Soc., 1976–80. Order of the Rising Sun, Gold Rays with Rosette (Japan), 2000. *Recreation:* collecting weapons and armour, particularly Japanese (Vice-Chm., Japan Soc. of London, 1970–75, 1979–82, 1984–87, Vice-Pres., 1987–), photography, entomology. *Heir: s* Nicholas Richard Bowden, *b* 13 Aug. 1935. *Clubs:* White's, Royal Thames Yacht. *Died 1 Dec. 2001.*

BOWDEN, Rt Rev. (Raymond) David; Bishop of Bendigo, 1995–2002; *b* 31 July 1937; *s* of Raymond Bowden and Mona Lillian Bowden (*née* Blaxell); *m* 1962, Linda Elizabeth Kleinschafer; two *s* one *d. Educ:* Newcastle Boys' High Sch., NSW; St John's Coll., Morpeth, ACT (ThL 1960; ThSchol 1970). Assistant Curate: St Peter's Cathedral, Armidale, 1960–64; St Paul, W Tamworth, 1964–65; Vicar: Warialda, 1965–69; Good Shepherd, Savona, NY, USA, 1969–71; Assoc. Rector, St Clement, Berkeley, Calif, 1971–72; Chaplain, Armidale Sch., 1973–74; Vicar, Glen Innes, 1974–82; Rector, Terrigal, 1982–92 and Archdeacon, Central Coast, 1985–92; Canon, Christ Church Cathedral, Newcastle, 1992–95; Archdeacon of Newcastle, 1992–95. *Publication:* Heroes of the Faith, 1998. *Recreations:* watching cricket, classical music, escape literature. *Address:* Benenden, 23 Fremantle Drive, Woodrising, NSW 2284, Australia; *e-mail:* dlbowden@tpg.com.au. *Died 29 July 2004.*

BOWDEN, Prof. Ruth Elizabeth Mary, OBE 1980; DSc; FRCS; Professor of Anatomy, Royal Free Hospital School of Medicine, University of London, 1951–80, later Emeritus; Sir William Collins Professor of Human and Comparative Anatomy, Royal College of Surgeons of England, 1984–89; Hon. Research Fellow, Institute of Neurology, 1980–96; *b* 21 Feb. 1915; *o c* of late Frank Harold and Louise Ellen Bowden. *Educ:* Westlands Sch.; St Paul's Girls' Sch.; London (Royal Free Hospital) Sch. of Medicine for Women, University of London (MB, BS; DSc). House Surg. and later House Physician, Elizabeth Garrett Anderson Hosp. (Oster House branch), 1940–42; House Surg., Royal Cancer Hosp., 1942; Grad. Asst in Nuffield Dept of Orthopaedic Surgery, Peripheral Nerve Injury Unit, Oxford, 1942–45; Asst Lectr in Anatomy, Royal Free Hospital Sch. of Medicine, 1945, later Lectr, then Univ. Reader in Human Anatomy, 1949; Rockefeller Travelling Fellowship, 1949–50; Hunterian Prof., RCS, 1950; part-time Lectr, Dept of Anatomy, St Thomas's Hosp. Med. Sch., 1980–83. WHO Consultant in anatomy, Khartoum Univ., 1972, 1974, 1977. President: Anat. Soc. of GB and Ireland, 1970; Medical Women's Fedn, 1981. Member: Exec. Cttee, Women's Nat. Commn, 1984–89; Exec. Cttee, N London Hospice Gp, 1986–97 (Mem. Council, 1986–98; Chm. Professional Sub-Cttee, 1986–90); Exec. Cttee, 1988–97, and Med. Adv. Bd, 1992, LEPRA. Member, later Convenor: Acad. Awards Cttee, British Fedn of University Women, 1956–94; Cttee for Awards and Fellowships, Internat. Fedn of University Women, 1986–92. FRSocMed; Fellow: Brit. Orthopaedic Assoc.; Linnean Soc. Life Vice-President: Chartered Soc. of Physiotherapy (Chm., 1960–70); Inst. of Science Technology (Pres., 1960–65); Riding for the Disabled Assoc. DCLJ 1988, DMLJ 1984. Jubilee Medal, 1977; Wood Jones Medal, RCS, 1988. *Publications:* Peripheral Nerve Injuries, 1958; (contrib.) Surgery of the Spine, ed G. Findlay and R. Owen, 1992; contribs to Peripheral Nerve Injuries Report of Medical Research Council; contrib. to Oxford Companion to Medicine; contribs to medical and scientific jls. *Recreations:* reading, music, painting, walking, gardening, carpentry. *Address:* 6 Hartham Close, Hartham Road, N7 9JH. *T:* (020) 7607 3464. *Died 19 Dec. 2001.*

BOWEN, (Evan) Roderic; QC 1952; Master Emeritus of the Middle Temple; *b* 6 Aug. 1913; 2nd *s* of late Evan Bowen, JP, and Margaret Ellen Twiss, The Elms, Cardigan. *Educ:* Cardigan Schs; University Coll., Aberystwyth; St John's Coll., Cambridge (BA 1935; MA 1940). Practised at the Bar with chambers in Cardiff until 1940; served in HM Forces, 1940–45, in the ranks and subsequently as an officer on staff of Judge Advocate-Gen. Recorder of: Carmarthen, 1950; Merthyr Tydfil, 1953–60; Swansea, 1960–64; Cardiff, 1964–67; Chm., Montgomeryshire QS, 1959–71; Social Security (formerly Nat. Insurance) Comr, 1967–86. MP (L) County of Cardigan, 1945–66; Dep. Chm. of Ways and Means, 1965–66. Chm., Welsh Parliamentary Party, 1955. Pres., St David's UC, Lampeter, 1977–92; Member Governing Body: Nat. Museum of Wales, 1945–2001; Univ. of Wales, 1950–2001. Hon. Fellow, Trinity Coll., Carmarthen, 1992. Hon. LLD Wales, 1972. *Address:* 3 Maynard Court, Fairwater Road, Llandaff, Cardiff CF5 2LD. *T:* (029) 2056 3207. *Club:* County (Cardiff). *Died 18 July 2001.*

BOWEN, Roderic; *see* Bowen, E. R.

BOWMAN, Sir Paul Humphrey Armytage, 5th Bt *cr* 1884, of Holmbury St Mary, Surrey; *b* 10 Aug. 1921; *s* of Major Humphrey Ernest Bowman, CMG, CBE (*d* 1965), and Frances Guinevere Armytage (*d* 1923), and *great nephew* of Sir William Paget Bowman, 2nd Bt; *S* cousin, 1994; *m* 1st, 1943, Felicité Anne Araminta MacMichael (marr. diss. 1947); 2nd, 1947, Gabrielle May Currie (marr. diss. 1974); one *d*; 3rd, 1974, Elizabeth Deirdre Churchill (*d* 1993). *Educ:* Eton. Served War, 1940–46, Coldstream

Guards (Major); twice wounded. Dir, Hill Samuel Co. Ltd, 1962–78. *Died 6 Jan. 2003 (ext).*

BOWRING, Edgar Rennie Harvey, MC 1945; Chairman, C. T. Bowring & Co. Ltd, 1973–78; Director, Marsh & McLennan Cos Inc., New York, 1980–88, Advisory Director, 1988–95; *b* 5 Nov. 1915; *y s* of Arthur Bowring; *m* 1940, Margaret Grace (*née* Brook) (*d* 1999); two *s* one *d. Educ:* Eastbourne Coll.; Clare Coll., Cambridge (MA); Berkeley Coll., Yale, USA (Mellon Fellow). War of 1939–45: commissioned Kent Yeomanry, RA, 1939; served in Iceland, France and Germany (despatches, 1944); demobilised, 1946. Solicitor, 1949; Partner in Cripps Harries Hall & Co., 1950–55. Member of Lloyd's, 1962. Joined C. T. Bowring & Co. (Insurance) Ltd, 1956 (Dir, 1960); Dep. Chm., 1966, Chief Exec., 1970, Chm., 1973–77, C. T. Bowring (Insurance) Holdings Ltd. Chairman: English & American Insurance Co. Ltd, 1965–71; Crusader Insurance Co. Ltd, 1973–77; Bowmaker Ltd, 1973–77. Pres., Insurance Inst. of London, 1971–72 (Dep. Pres., 1970–71); Vice-Pres., Corporation of Insurance Brokers, 1970–77; Mem., Insurance Brokers Registration Council, 1979–81. Chm., City Cttee for Electoral Reform, 1978–82. Comdt, West Kent Special Constab., 1965–71. Trustee, Meml Univ. of Newfoundland Harlow Campus, 1979–97. CIMgt. *Recreations:* gardening, golf. *Address:* Leopards Mill, Horam, East Sussex TN21 0PD. *T:* (01435) 812687. *Clubs:* City University; Rye Golf; Piltdown Golf.
Died 29 June 2001.

BOX, John Allan Hyatt, OBE 1998; RDI 1992; free-lance production designer of films; *b* 27 Jan. 1920; *s* of late Allan Cyril Box and Bertha (*née* Storey); *m* 1st, 1944, Barbara Courtenay Linton (marr. diss. 1951); 2nd, 1953, Doris Lee (*d* 1992); two *d. Educ:* Ceylon; Highgate Sch.; Sch. of Architecture, London Poly. ARIBA 1948. Served RAC and RTR, 1940–46 (mentioned in despatches, Normandy, 1944). Entered film industry, 1948; films designed include: The Million Pound Note, 1954; The Inn of the Sixth Happiness, 1958; Our Man in Havana, 1959; The World of Suzie Wong, 1960; Lawrence of Arabia, 1961 (Academy Award 1962); Doctor Zhivago, 1965 (Academy Award 1966); A Man for All Seasons, 1966 (BAFTA Award 1967); Oliver!, 1967 (Academy Award 1968); Nicholas and Alexandra, 1970 (Academy Award 1970); Travels with My Aunt, 1972; The Great Gatsby, 1973 (BAFTA Award 1974); Rollerball, 1974 (BAFTA Award 1975); A Passage to India, 1984; Black Beauty, 1994; First Knight, 1995; produced: The Looking Glass War, 1969. FRSA 1993. Award for special contribution to films, BAFTA, 1991; Critics' Circle Award for Lifetime Achievement, 1999. *Recreations:* painting, visiting art galleries and exhibitions, interest in cricket and Rugby. *Address:* 5 Elm Bank Mansions, The Terrace, Barnes, SW13 0NS. *T:* (020) 8876 9125.
Died 7 March 2005.

BOXER, Air Cdre Henry Everard Crichton, CB 1965; OBE 1948; idc, ndc, psc; *b* 28 July 1914; *s* of late Rear-Adm. Henry P. Boxer; *m* 1st, 1938, Enid Anne Louise (*d* 1994), *d* of late Dr John Moore Collyns; two *s* one *d* (and one *d* decd); 2nd, 1996, Hope Poland (*d* 1998). *Educ:* Shrewsbury Sch.; RAF Coll., Cranwell. Commissioned RAF, 1935; No 1 Fighter Squadron, 1935–37; No 1 Flying Training Sch., 1937–39; Specialist Navigator, 1939. Served War of 1939–45, in UK, S Africa and Europe. BJSM, Washington, DC, 1945–48; directing Staff, RAF Staff Coll., 1949–50; Coastal Command, 1951–52; Nat. Defence Coll., Canada, 1952–53; Air Ministry, 1953–56; OC, RAF Thorney Island, 1956–58. ADC to the Queen, 1957–59; IDC, 1959; Sen. Air Liaison Officer and Air Adviser to British High Comr in Canada, 1960–62; AO i/c Admin, HQ Coastal Comd, 1962–65; Dir of Personnel (Air), MoD (RAF), 1965–67; retd, 1967. Counsellor (Defence Equipment), British High Commn, Ottawa, 1967–74; retd, 1975. *Address:* 42 Courtenay Place,

Lymington, Hants SO41 3NQ. *T:* (01590) 672584. *Club:* Royal Air Force. *Died 13 July 2005.*

BOYD, Christopher; *see* Boyd, T. C.

BOYD, Sir Robert (Lewis Fullarton), Kt 1983; CBE 1972; FRS 1969; Professor of Physics in the University of London, 1962–83, then Emeritus; Director, Mullard Space Science Laboratory of Department of Physics and Astronomy of University College, London, 1965–83; *b* 1922; *s* of late William John Boyd, PhD, BSc; *m* 1st, 1949, Mary (*d* 1996), *d* of late John Higgins; two *s* one *d*; 2nd, 1998, Betty, *d* of late Herbert Frank Chelmsford, *widow* of Stanley Robinson. *Educ:* Whitgift Sch.; Imperial Coll., London (BSc (Eng) 1943); University Coll., London (PhD 1949; Fellow 1988). FIEE 1967; FInstP 1972. Exp. Officer at Admty Mining Estabt, 1943–46; DSIR Res. Asst, 1946–49; ICI Res. Fellow, 1949–50, Maths Dept, UCL; ICI Res. Fellow, Physics Dept, UCL, 1950–52; Lectr in Physics, UCL, 1952–58, Reader in Physics, UCL, 1959–62. Prof. of Astronomy (part-time), Royal Institution, 1961–67; IEE Appleton Lectr, 1976; Bakerian Lectr, Royal Soc., 1978; Halley Lectr, Univ. of Oxford, 1981. Chairman: Meteorol Res. Cttee, MoD, 1972–75; Astronautics Cttee, MoD, 1972–77; Member: BBC Science Cons. Gp, 1970–79; SRC, 1977–81 (Chm., Astronomy, Space and Radio Bd, 1977–80); Council, Physical Soc., 1958–60; Council, RAS, 1962–66 (Vice-Pres., 1964–66); British Nat. Cttee on Space Res., 1976–87. Pres., Victoria Inst., 1965–76. Trustee, Nat. Maritime Museum, 1980–89. Governor: St Lawrence Coll., 1965–76; Croydon Coll., 1966–80; Southlands Coll., 1976–94; Chm., London Bible Coll., 1983–90. Hon. DSc Heriot-Watt, 1979. *Publications:* The Upper Atmosphere (with H. S. W. Massey), 1958; Space Research by Rocket and Satellite, 1960; Space Physics, 1975; papers in sci. jls on space sci. and other topics. *Recreations:* elderly Rolls Royce motors, model engineering. *Address:* 9 Cherwell Gardens, Chandlers Ford, Eastleigh SO53 2NH. *Died 5 Feb. 2004.*

BOYD, (Thomas) Christopher; farmer, 1963–96; *b* 14 Aug. 1916; *s* of Rev. William Grenville Boyd and Dorothy (*née* Clarke); *m* 1957, Anneliese Icking; one *s* two *d. Educ:* Marlborough; Hertford Coll., Oxford. Army, 1940–44; civil servant, 1939 and 1944–48 (Under-Sec. to Govt of India, 1944–46); with British Iron and Steel Fedn, 1948–51. Chelsea Borough Councillor, 1953–59. MP (Lab) Bristol NW, 1955–59; contested (Lab): Isle of Thanet, 1945, 1950; Harborough, 1951; Dumfriesshire, 1966. *Address:* The Quillet, Appledore, Kent TN26 2DD.
Died 15 March 2004.

BOYDELL, (The Worshipful Chancellor) Peter Thomas Sherrington; QC 1965; Leader, Parliamentary Bar, 1975–97; Chancellor of Dioceses of Oxford, since 1958, Truro, 1957–97, and Worcester, 1959–97; *b* 20 Sept. 1920; *s* of late Frank Richard Boydell, JP, and Frances Barton Boydell, Blenheim Lodge, Whitegate Drive, Blackpool; unmarried. *Educ:* Arnold Sch., Blackpool; Manchester Univ. (LLB 1940). Served War of 1939–45; Adjt, 17th Field Regt, RA, 1943; Bde Major, RA, 1st Armoured Div., 1944; Bde Major, RA, 10th Indian Div., 1945. Qualified as Solicitor, 1947. Called to the Bar, Middle Temple, 1948, Bencher, 1970, Dep. Treas., 1988, Treas., 1989; in practice at the Bar, 1948–97. Chm., Planning and Local Govt Cttee of the Bar, 1973–86; Founder Chm., Local Govt and Planning, Bar Assoc., 1986–90. Member: Legal Board of Church Assembly, 1958–71; Adv. Bd for Redundant Churches, 1993–99. Contested (C) Carlisle, 1964. Associate (by invitation and election) RICS, 1982; ACIArb 1985. *Recreations:* hill walking, music, travel. *Address:* 45 Wilton Crescent, SW1X 8RX. *T:* (020) 7235 5505. *Clubs:* Garrick, Royal Automobile; Climbers.
Died 23 Feb. 2001.

BOYES, James Ashley; Headmaster of City of London School, 1965–84; *b* 27 Aug. 1924; *s* of late Alfred Simeon

Boyes and of Edith May Boyes; *m* 1st, 1949, Diana Fay (*née* Rothera), MA Cantab; two *d*; 2nd, 1973, April Tanner (*née* Rothery). *Educ:* Rugby Sch.; Clare Coll., Cambridge. Lieut RNVR; N Russian convoys and Brit. Pacific Fleet, 1942–46. Cambridge Univ., 1942, 1946–48; 1st class Hons Mod. Hist., 1948; Mellon Fellowship, Yale Univ., 1948–50; MA Yale, 1950. Asst Master, Rugby Sch., 1950–55; Headmaster, Kendal Grammar Sch., Westmorland, 1955–60; Dir of Studies, Royal Air Force Coll., Cranwell, 1960–65. Since retirement engaged in work for the mentally ill; Vice-Chair, Nat. Schizophrenia Fellowship, 1989–. *Recreations:* squash racquets, sailing. *Address:* 12 Linver Road, SW6 3RB. *Clubs:* Royal Automobile, Hurlingham; Harlequins RUFC (Hon. Mem.); Hawks (Cambridge); Royal Windermere Yacht.
Died 6 July 2004.

BOYLAND, Prof. Eric, (Dick), PhD, DSc; Professor of Biochemistry, University of London, at Chester Beatty Research Institute, Institute of Cancer Research, Royal Marsden Hospital, 1948–70, then Emeritus Professor; Visiting Professor in Environmental Toxicology, London School of Hygiene and Tropical Medicine, 1970–76; *b* Manchester, 24 Feb. 1905; *s* of Alfred E. and Helen Boyland; *m* 1931, Margaret Esther (*d* 1985), *d* of late Maj.-Gen. Sir Frederick Maurice, KCMG, CB; two *s* one *d*. *Educ:* Manchester Central High Sch.; Manchester Univ. (BSc Tech. 1926; MSc 1928; DSc 1936); PhD London. Research Asst in Physiology, Manchester Univ., 1926–28; Grocers' Company Scholar and Beit Memorial Fellow for Med. Research at Lister Institute for Preventive Medicine, 1928–30, and Kaiser Wilhelm Institut für Medizinische Forschung, Heidelberg, 1930–31; Physiological Chemist to Royal Cancer Hosp., London, 1931; Reader in Biochemistry, University of London, 1935–47. Research Officer in Ministry of Supply, 1941–44; Ministry of Agriculture, 1944–45. Consultant to Internat. Agency for Research on Cancer, Lyon, 1970–72; Mem., WHO Panel on Food Additives. Hon. FFOM, RCP, 1982. Hon. PhD Frankfurt, 1982; Hon. MD Malta, 1985. Judd Award for Cancer Research, New York, 1948. *Publications:* The Biochemistry of Bladder Cancer, 1963; Modern Trends in Toxicology, vol. I, 1962, vol. II, 1974; scientific papers in biochemistry and pharmacology. *Recreation:* looking at paintings. *Clubs:* Athenæum; Rucksack (Manchester).
Died 31 May 2002.

BOYLES, Edgar William; Under Secretary, Inland Revenue, 1975–81; *b* 24 March 1921; *s* of William John Boyles and Jessie Louisa Boyles; *m* 1950, Heather Iris Hobart, SRN; three *s* one *d*. *Educ:* Bedford Modern Sch. RAF, 1940–46. Tax Officer, Inland Revenue, 1939; Principal Inspector of Taxes, 1962; Sen. Principal Inspector, 1967. *Recreations:* chess, gardening, watching cricket. *Address:* The Keeley, 155 Bedford Road, Wootton, Bedford MK43 9BA. *T:* (01234) 851875.
Died 7 May 2001.

BRABOURNE, 7th Baron *cr* 1880; **John Ulick Knatchbull,** CBE 1993; Bt 1641; film and television producer; Director, Thames Television, 1975–93 (Chairman, 1990–93); *b* 9 Nov. 1924; *s* of 5th Baron and Lady Doreen Geraldine Browne (daughter of the Crown of India; DStJ) (*d* 1979), *y d* of 6th Marquess of Sligo; *S* brother, 1943; *m* 1946, Lady Patricia Edwina Victoria Mountbatten (later Countess Mountbatten of Burma, CBE, CD); four *s* two *d* (and one *s* decd). *Educ:* Eton; Oxford. *Films produced:* Harry Black, 1958; Sink the Bismarck!, 1959; HMS Defiant, 1961; Othello, 1965; The Mikado, 1966; Romeo and Juliet; Up the Junction, 1967; Dance of Death, 1968; Tales of Beatrix Potter, 1971; Murder on the Orient Express, 1974; Death on the Nile, 1978; Stories from a Flying Trunk, 1979; The Mirror Crack'd, 1980; Evil Under the Sun, 1982; A Passage to India, 1984; Little Dorrit, 1987. *TV series:* National Gallery, 1974; A Much-Maligned Monarch, 1976; Leontyne, 1987. Director: Copyright Promotions Gp, 1974– (Vice Chm., 1995–); Thorn EMI, 1981–86.

Governor: BFI, 1979–94 (Fellow, 1985); National Film Sch., 1980–95; Mem., British Screen Adv. Council, 1985–97; Trustee: BAFTA, 1975–; Science Museum, 1984–94; Nat. Mus. of Photography, Film and Television, 1984–94. Pres., Kent Trust for Nature Conservation, 1958–97. Governor: Gordonstoun Sch., 1964–94; United World Colls, 1965–96; Norton Knatchbull Sch., 1969–95; Wye Coll., later Imperial Coll. at Wye, 1955–99 (Provost, 1994–99). University of Kent: Pro-Chancellor, 1992–98; Mem. Council, 1968–98. *Heir: s* Lord Romsey, *b* 8 Oct. 1947. *Address:* Newhouse, Mersham, Ashford, Kent TN25 6NQ. *T:* (01233) 503636, *Fax:* (01233) 502244.
Died 22 Sept. 2005.

BRADBURN, John; Chief Registrar of the High Court of Justice in Bankruptcy, 1984–88; Registrar of the Companies Court and Clerk of the Restrictive Practices Court, 1980–88; *b* 4 April 1915; *s* of Harold and Fanny Louise Bradburn; *m* 1948, Irène Elizabeth Norman, JP, *yr d* of Denham Grindley and Bertha Norman; two *s*. *Educ:* Repton; Trinity Coll., Oxford (MA). Served War, 1939–46, Oxfordshire and Bucks LI (Major). Called to the Bar, Inner Temple, 1939; practised at Chancery Bar, Lincoln's Inn, 1946–79 (Bencher, 1972–); a Conveyancing Counsel of the Supreme Court, 1977–80; Lord Chancellor's Legal Visitor, Ct of Protection, 1980–83. Mem., Gen. Council of the Bar, 1962–66. *Recreation:* freemasonry. *Address:* West Mews, 11 Calcot Court, Calcot Park, Reading, Berks RG31 7RW. *T:* (0118) 942 5418. *Club:* MCC.
Died 13 May 2005.

BRADBURY, Surgeon Vice-Adm. Sir Eric (Blackburn), KBE 1971; CB 1968; FRCS 1972; Medical Director-General of the Navy, 1969–72; Chairman, Tunbridge Wells District Health Authority, 1981–84; *b* 2 March 1911; *s* of late A. B. Bradbury, Maze, Co. Antrim; *m* 1939, Elizabeth Constance Austin (*d* 1991); three *d*. *Educ:* Royal Belfast Academical Instn; Queen's Univ., Belfast (MB, BCh 1934); DMRD (London) 1949. Joined RN (Medical Service), 1934; served at sea in HMS Barham, HMS Endeavour, HMS Cumberland, 1935–38 and in HMS Charybdis and HMHS Oxfordshire, 1941–45; served in RN Hospitals: Haslar, Chatham, Plymouth and Malta; Med. Officer-in-Charge, RN Hosp., Haslar, and Comd MO, Portsmouth, 1966–69. QHP 1966–72. Hon. LLD 1973.
Died 6 Jan. 2003.

BRADLEY, Thomas George; Director, British Section, European League for Economic Co-operation, 1979–91; *b* 13 April 1926; *s* of George Henry Bradley, Kettering; *m* 1953, Joy (*d* 1993), *d* of George Starmer, Kettering; two *s*. *Educ:* Kettering Central Sch., Northants. Elected to Northants County Council, 1952, County Alderman, 1961; Mem., Kettering Borough Council, 1957–61. Transport Salaried Staffs' Association: Branch Officer, 1946–58; Mem. Exec. Cttee, 1958–77; Treasurer, 1961–64; Pres., 1964–77; Acting Gen. Sec., 1976–77. MP Leicester NE, July 1962–1974, Leicester E, 1974–83 (Lab, 1962–81, SDP, 1981–83); PPS: to Minister of Aviation, 1964–65; to Home Secretary, 1966–67; to Chancellor of the Exchequer, 1967–70; Chm., Select Cttee on Transport, 1979–83. Vice-Chm., Labour Party, 1974–75; Chm., 1975–76; Mem., Labour Party NEC, 1966–81. Contested: (Lab) Rutland and Stamford, 1950, 1951 and 1955; (Lab) Preston S, 1959; (SDP) Leicester E, 1983. *Address:* The Orchard, 111 London Road, Kettering, Northants NN15 7PH. *T:* (01536) 513019.
Died 9 Sept. 2002.

BRADMAN, Sir Donald (George), AC 1979; Kt 1949; President of South Australian Cricket Association, 1965–73; Chairman, Australian Cricket Board, 1960–63 and 1969–72; *b* Cootamundra, NSW, 27 Aug. 1908; *s* of George and Emily Bradman; *m* 1932, Jessie Martha (*d* 1997), *d* of James Menzies, Mittagong, NSW; one *s* one *d* (and one *s* decd). *Educ:* Bowral Intermediate High Sch. Played for NSW, 1927–34; for S Australia, 1935–49; for Australia, 1928–48, Capt. 1936–48; records included: highest aggregate and greatest number of centuries in

England *v* Australia test matches; highest score for Australia *v* England in test matches (334 at Leeds, 1930). Formerly stock and share broker and Mem. Stock Exchange of Adelaide Ltd. *Publications:* Don Bradman's Book, 1930; How to Play Cricket, 1935; My Cricketing Life, 1938; Farewell to Cricket, 1950, repr. 1988; The Art of Cricket, 1958; The Bradman Albums, 1988; *relevant publications:* Bradman: The Great, by B. J. Wakley, 1959; Sir Donald Bradman, by Irving Rosenwater, 1978; Bradman—The Illustrated Biography, by Michael Page, 1983; The Don, by Roland Perry, 1996. *Recreations:* cricket, golf, tennis, billiards, squash. *Address:* 2 Holden Street, Kensington Park, SA 5068, Australia. *Clubs:* MCC (Hon. Life Mem. and Hon. Life Vice-Pres.); Commerce (Adelaide).
Died 25 Feb. 2001.

BRADY, Very Rev. Ernest William; Dean of Edinburgh, 1976–82 and 1985–86; *b* 10 Nov. 1917; *s* of Ernest and Malinda Elizabeth Brady; *m* 1948, Violet Jeanne Louise Aldworth (*d* 1993); one *s* one *d. Educ:* Harris Academy, Dundee (Dux and Classics Medallist, 1936); Univ. of St Andrews; Edinburgh Theological Coll. (Luscombe Schol. 1942); LTh (Dunelm) 1942. Deacon 1942, Priest 1943; Asst Curate, Christ Church, Glasgow, 1942; Asst Curate, St Alphage, Hendon, 1946; Rector, All Saints, Buckie, 1949; Rector, All Saints, Edinburgh, 1957; Chaplain, Royal Infirmary of Edinburgh, 1959–74; Priest-in-Charge, Priory Church of St Mary of Mount Carmel, South Queensferry, 1974–82; Canon of St Mary's Cathedral, Edinburgh, 1967, Hon. Canon, 1983–85, 1986–; Synod Clerk, Diocese of Edinburgh, 1969. Sub-dean, Collegiate Church of St Vincent, Edinburgh (Order of St Lazarus of Jerusalem), 1982–89. Kt of Holy Sepulchre of Jerusalem (Golden Cross with Crown), 1984. *Recreations:* Holy Land pilgrimage, choral music, ecclesiastical vestments and embroidery. *Address:* 44 Glendevon Place, Edinburgh EH12 5UJ. *T:* (0131) 337 9528. *Died 13 May 2003.*

BRAIN, Sir (Henry) Norman, KBE 1963 (OBE 1947); CMG 1953; HM Diplomatic Service, retired; *b* 19 July 1907; *s* of late B. Brain, Rushall, Staffs; *m* 1939, Nuala Mary (decd), *d* of late Capt. A. W. Butterworth; one *s* (and one *s* decd). *Educ:* King Edward's Sch., Birmingham; The Queen's Coll., Oxford (MA). Entered the Consular Service, 1930, and served at Tokyo, Kobe, Osaka, Tamsui, Manila, Mukden, Shanghai and Dairen; interned by Japanese, 1941–42; repatriated and served in Foreign Office, 1943; appointed to Staff of Supreme Allied Comdr, South-East Asia, 1944–46; Political Adviser to Saigon Control Commission, 1945; served with Special Commissioner in South-East Asia, at Singapore, 1946–48; Counsellor, Foreign Office, 1949; Inspector of HM Foreign Service Estabts, 1950–53; Minister, Tokyo, 1953–55; Ambassador to Cambodia, 1956–58; Asst Under-Sec. of State, FO, 1958–61; Ambassador to Uruguay, 1961–66, retired, 1966. Chairman: Royal Central Asian Soc., 1970–74; Japan Soc. of London, 1970–73; Pres., British Uruguayan Soc., 1974–. *Recreations:* music, golf. *Died 27 Dec. 2002.*

BRAININ, Norbert, OBE 1960; concert violinist; formed Amadeus Ensemble, incorporating Amadeus Trio, 1988; Professor of Chamber Music: Hochschule für Musik, Cologne, since 1976; Royal Academy of Music, since 1986; *b* Vienna, 12 March 1923; *s* of Adolph and Sophie Brainin; *m* 1948, Kathe Kottow; one *d. Educ:* High Sch., Vienna. Commenced musical training in Vienna at age of seven and continued studies there until 1938; emigrated to London in 1938 and studied with Carl Flesch and Max Rostal; won Carl Flesch prize for solo violinists at the Guildhall Sch. of Music, London, 1946. Formed Amadeus String Quartet, 1947, Leader until disbanded in 1987. Professor: (annual) Amadeus Quartet Course, RAM; of Violin, Scuola di Musica di Fiesole, 1974; of Violin, Hochschule für Musik Franz Liszt Weimar, 1995. DUniv York, 1968; Hon. DMus London, 1983; Dr *hc* Venezuela, 1996. Grosse Verdienstzeichen, Vienna, 1999. Grand

Cross of Merit, 1st cl. (FRG), 1972; Cross of Honour for Arts and Science (Austria), 1972. *Address:* 19 Prowse Avenue, Bushey Heath, Herts WD2 1JS. *T:* (020) 8950 7379, *Fax:* (020) 8209 1907. *Died 10 April 2005.*

BRAITHWAITE, Sir (Joseph) Franklin (Madders), Kt 1980; DL; Chairman: Baker Perkins Holdings plc, 1980–84; Peterborough Independent Hospital plc, 1981–87; *b* 6 April 1917; *s* of late Sir John Braithwaite and Martha Janette (*née* Baker); *m* 1939, Charlotte Isabel, *d* of late Robert Elmer Baker, New York; one *s* one *d. Educ:* Bootham Sch.; King's Coll., Cambridge, 1936–39 (BA 1939, MA 1955). Served Army, 1940–46 (Captain). Joined Baker Perkins Ltd, 1946, Dir 1950, Vice-Chm. 1956; Chm., Baker Perkins Exports Ltd, 1966; Man. Dir, Baker Perkins Holdings Ltd, 1971. Dir, Lloyds Bank Ltd, Eastern Counties Regional Board, 1979–87. Member: Mech. Engrg Industry Economic Development Cttee, 1974–79; Management Board, 1978–82, Commercial and Econ. Cttee, 1977–84, Engrg Employers' Fedn; Board of Fellows, 1974–79, Economic and Social Affairs Cttee, 1979–84, BIM. Mem., Peterborough Develt Corp., 1981–88, Dep. Chm. 1982–88. Pres., Process Plant Assoc., 1977–79, Hon. Life Vice-Pres., 1981. CCMI. DL Cambs, 1983. *Recreations:* music, golf. *Address:* 7 Rutland Terrace, Stamford, Lincs PE9 2QD. *T:* (01780) 751244. *Club:* Army and Navy. *Died 12 June 2005.*

BRANDO, Marlon; American actor, stage and screen; *b* Omaha, Nebraska, 3 April 1924; *s* of Marlon Brando; *m* 1957, Anna Kashfi (marr. diss. 1959); one *s. Educ:* Libertyville High Sch., Illinois; Shattuck Military Academy, Minnesota. Entered Dramatic Workshop of New School for Social Research, New York, 1943; has studied with Elia Kazan and Stella Adler. *Plays include:* I Remember Mama, Broadway, 1944; Truckline Café, 1946; Candida, 1946; A Flag is Born, 1946; The Eagle Has Two Heads, 1946; A Streetcar Named Desire, 1947. *Films include:* The Men, 1950; A Streetcar Named Desire, 1951; Viva Zapata!, 1952; Julius Cæsar, 1953; The Wild Ones, 1953; Désirée, 1954; On the Waterfront, 1954; Guys and Dolls, 1955; Tea House of the August Moon, 1956; Sayonara, 1957; The Young Lions, 1958; The Fugitive Kind, 1960; Mutiny on the Bounty, 1962; The Ugly American, 1963; Bedtime Story, 1964; The Saboteur, Code Name-Morituri, 1965; The Chase, 1966; Appaloosa, 1966; Southwest to Sonora, 1966; A Countess from Hong Kong, 1967; Reflections in a Golden Eye, 1967; Candy, 1968; The Night of the Following Day, 1969; Quiemad!, 1970; The Nightcomers, 1971; The Godfather, 1972; Last Tango in Paris, 1972; The Missouri Breaks, 1975; Apocalypse Now, 1977; Superman, 1978; The Formula, 1981; A Dry White Season, 1990; The Freshman, 1990; Christopher Columbus, 1992; Don Juan DeMarco, 1994; The Island of Doctor Moreau, 1996; The Score, 2001. Directed, produced and appeared in One-Eyed Jacks, 1959. Academy Award, best actor of year, 1954, 1972. *Publication:* Songs My Mother Taught Me (autobiog.), 1994; *posthumous publication:* (jtly) Fan Tan (novel), 2005. *Died 1 July 2004.*

BRANN, Col William Norman, OBE 1967; ERD; Lord Lieutenant for County Down, 1979–90, retired; *b* 16 Aug. 1915; *s* of Rev. William Brann, BA, LLB, and Francesca Brann; *m* 1950, Anne Elizabeth Hughes (*d* 2005); one *s* two *d. Educ:* Campbell Coll., Belfast. With Beck & Scott Ltd, Food Importers, Belfast, 1934–80, Chm., 1984–98. Served War of 1939–45, Army, France and Far East; TA, 1947–53. Hon. ADC to HE the Governor of N Ireland, 1952–72. Belfast Harbour Comr, 1960–79. Chm., Somme Hosp. for Ex Service Men and Women, retd; Pres., Burma Star Assoc., NI. County Down: DL 1974–79; JP 1980; High Sheriff, 1982. KStJ 1991. *Recreations:* gardening, hunting. *Address:* 23 Ballymoney Road, Craigantlet, Newtownards, Co. Down BT23 4TG. *T:* (028) 9042 2224. *Club:* Ulster Reform (Belfast).
Died 30 Dec. 2005.

BRASH, Rev. Alan Anderson, OBE 1962; Moderator, Presbyterian Church of New Zealand, 1978–79; *b* 5 June 1913; *s* of Thomas C. Brash, CBE, New Zealand, and Margaret Brash (*née* Allan); *m* 1938, Eljean Ivory Hill; one *s* one *d. Educ:* Dunedin Univ., NZ (MA); Edinburgh Univ. (BD). Parish Minister in NZ, 1938–46 and 1952–56; Gen. Sec., NZ Nat. Council of Churches, 1947–52 and 1957–64, East Asia Christian Conf., 1958–68; Dir, Christian Aid, London, 1968–70; Dir, Commn on Inter-Church Aid, Refuge and World Service, WCC, 1970–73; Dep. Gen. Sec., WCC, 1974–78. Hon. DD Toronto, 1971. *Address:* 8 Gatonby Place, Avonhead, Christchurch, New Zealand.
Died 24 Aug. 2002.

BRASHER, Christopher William, CBE 1996; President, London Marathon Ltd, since 1995 (Founder and Chairman, 1981–95); Chairman, Brasher Leisure Ltd, since 1977; *b* 21 Aug. 1928; *s* of William Kenneth Brasher, CBE and Katie Howe Brasher; *m* 1959, Shirley Bloomer; one *s* two *d. Educ:* Rugby Sch.; St John's Coll., Cambridge (MA); Pres., Mountaineering Club and Athletic Club, Cambridge Univ. Management Trainee and Jun. Executive, Mobil Oil Co., 1951–57; Sports Editor, 1957–61, columnist and Olympic Corresp., 1961–91, The Observer; BBC Television: Reporter, Tonight, 1961–65; Editor, Time Out, and Man Alive, 1964–65; Head of Gen. Features, 1969–72; reporter/producer, 1972–81. Man. Dir, Fleetfoot Ltd, 1979–95; Chairman: Reebok UK Ltd, 1990–92; Berghaus, 1993–98; The Brasher Boot Co., 1992–2001. Co-Founder and Chm., British Orienteering Fedn (formerly English Orienteering Assoc.), 1966–69 (Vice-Pres., 1984–). Trustee, London Marathon Charitable Trust, 1981–; Founder, 1983, and Trustee, 1983–92, 1996–, John Muir Trust; Chairman: Chris Brasher Trust, 1988–; Petersham Trust, 1999–. Rep. GB, Olympic Games, 1952 and 1956; Gold Medal for 3,000 metres Steeplechase, 1956. DUniv Stirling, 1989; Hon. DSc Kingston, 1996. Sports Writer of the Year (British Press Awards), 1968, 1976. OStJ 1995. National Medal of Honour, Finland, 1975. *Publications:* The Red Snows (with Sir John Hunt), 1960; Sportsmen of our Time, 1962; Tokyo 1964: a diary of the XVIIIth Olympiad, 1964; Mexico 1968: a diary of the XIXth Olympics, 1968; Munich 72, 1972; (ed) The London Marathon: the first ten years, 1991. *Recreations:* mountains, fishing, horse racing, orienteering, social running. *Address:* The White House, Chaddleworth, Berks RG20 7DY. *T:* (01488) 638498. *Clubs:* Travellers, Alpine, Hurlingham; Ranelagh Harriers (Petersham); Thames Hare and Hounds (Kingston Vale).
Died 28 Feb. 2003.

BRAY, Denis Campbell, CMG 1977; CVO 1975; JP; Chairman, Denis Bray Consultants Ltd, Hong Kong, since 1985; *b* 24 Jan. 1926; *s* of Rev. Arthur Henry Bray and Edith Muriel Bray; *m* 1952, Marjorie Elizabeth Bottomley; four *d* (one *s* decd). *Educ:* Kingswood Sch.; Jesus Coll., Cambridge (MA). BScEcon London. RN, 1947–49. Colonial Service Devonshire Course, 1949–50; Admin. Officer, Hong Kong, 1950; Dist Comr, New Territories, 1971; Hong Kong Comr in London, 1977–80; Sec. for Home Affairs, Hong Kong, 1973–77 and 1980–84, retd. Chairman: English Schools Foundn, Hong Kong, 1985–91; Jubilee Sports Centre, Hong Kong, 1985–89; Dir, Hong Kong Philharmonic, 1985–2003. Director: First Pacific Davies Ltd, 1986–99; Herald Holdings Ltd, 1987–; Leighton Asia Ltd, 1990–2000; Exec. Dir, Community Chest of Hong Kong, 1985–92. Pres., Hong Kong Yachting Assoc., 1989–91. JP 1960–85, and 1987. *Publication:* Hong Kong Metamorphosis, 2001. *Address:* 131 Lime Walk, Headington, Oxford OX3 7AD. *Clubs:* Travellers, London Rowing; Leander (Henley-on-Thames); Hong Kong, Hong Kong Jockey, Royal Hong Kong Yacht; Tai Po Boat. *Died 8 July 2005.*

BRAY, Jeremy William, PhD; *b* 29 June 1930; *s* of Rev. Arthur Henry Bray and Mrs Edith Muriel Bray; *m* 1953, Elizabeth (*née* Trowell); four *d. Educ:* Aberystwyth Grammar Sch.; Kingswood Sch.; Jesus Coll., Cambridge (PhD 1956). Researched in pure mathematics at Cambridge, 1953–55; Choate Fellow, Harvard Univ., USA, 1955–56; Technical Officer, Wilton Works of ICI, 1956–62. Contested (Lab) Thirsk and Malton, 1959. MP (Lab): Middlesbrough West, 1962–70; Motherwell and Wishaw, Oct. 1974–1983; Motherwell South, 1983–97. Parly Sec., Min. of Power, 1966–67; Jt Parly Sec., Min. of Technology, 1967–69; Opposition spokesman on science and technology, 1983–92. Member: Select Cttee on Nationalised Industries, 1962–64; Estimates Cttee, 1964–66 (Chm., Sub-cttee, 1964–66); Expenditure Cttee, 1978–79; Select Cttee on Treasury and Civil Service, 1979–83 (Chm., Sub-cttee, 1981–82); Select Cttee on Sci. and Technol., 1992–97; Bd, Parly Office of Sci. and Technol., 1993–97; Chairman: Labour, Science and Technol. Group, 1964–66; All-Party Parly Mental Health Gp, 1994–97; Vice Pres., Parlt and Sci. Cttee, 1993–97; Vice Chairman: Parly Engrg Gp, 1993–97; British-Chinese Parly Gp, 1987–95. Co-Dir, Programme of Res. into Econometric Methods, QMC and Imperial Coll., 1971–74. Dir, Mullard Ltd, 1970–73. Consultant, Battelle Res. Centre, Geneva, 1973; Sen. Res. Fellow, 1974, Vis. Prof., 1975–79, Univ. of Strathclyde; Vis. Res. Fellow, Imperial Coll., 1989–93. Mem. Adv. Council, Save British Science, 1993–. Dep. Chm., Christian Aid, 1972–84. Chm., Fabian Soc., 1971–72. Hon. DSc Leicester, 1995. *Publications:* Decision in Government, 1970; Production Purpose and Structure, 1982; Fabian pamphlets and articles in jls. *Recreation:* sailing. *Address:* 21 Horn Lane, Linton, Cambs CB1 6HT. *T:* (01223) 890424.
Died 31 May 2002.

BRAY, William John, CBE 1975; FREng; Director of Research, Post Office, 1966–75 (Dep. Director, 1965); *b* 10 Sept. 1911; British; *m* 1936, Margaret Earp (*d* 1998); one *d* (and one *d* decd). *Educ:* Imperial Coll., London Univ. Electrical engineering apprenticeship, Portsmouth Naval Dockyard, 1928–32; Royal and Kitchener Scholarships, Imperial Coll., 1932–34; entered PO Engineering Dept as Asst Engineer, 1934; Commonwealth Fund Fellowship (Harkness Foundation) for study in USA, 1956–57; Staff Engineer, Inland Radio Br., PO Engineering Dept, 1958. Vis. Prof., UCL, 1974–78. External Examr, MSc (Communications), Imperial Coll., London, 1976–80. Participation in work of International Radio Consultative Cttee of International Telecommunication Union and European Postal and Telecommunication Conferences; Consultant to UK Council for Educnl Technology, 1976–78. Associate Mem., World Innovation Foundn, 1999. MSc(Eng), FCGI, DIC, FIEE; FREng (FEng 1978). DUniv Essex, 1976. J. J. Thomson Medal, IEE, 1978. *Publications:* Memoirs of a Telecommunications Engineer, 1983; The Communications Miracle: telecommunication pioneers from Morse to the Information Superhighway, 1995; Then, Now and Tomorrow: the autobiography of a communications engineer, 1999; Innovation and the Communication Revolution, 2002; papers in Proc. IEE (IEE Ambrose Fleming Radio Sect. and Electronics Div. Premium Awards), IEE Review. *Recreation:* writing. *Address:* The Pump House, Bredfield, Woodbridge, Suffolk IP13 6AH. *T:* (01394) 385838; *e-mail:* bray@btinternet.com. *Died 6 Sept. 2004.*

BRAY, Winston, CBE 1970; Deputy Chairman and Deputy Chief Executive, BOAC, 1972–74; Member Board, BOAC, 1971–74; Member Board, BAAC Ltd (formerly BOAC (AC Ltd), 1969–74; *b* 29 April 1910; *s* of late Edward Bray and Alice Walker; *m* 1937, Betty Atterton Miller (*d* 1999); one *s* one *d* (and one *d* decd). *Educ:* Highgate Sch.; London Univ. (BCom). Missouri Pacific Railroad, USA, 1932; Asst to Traffic Manager, British Airways, 1938; Traffic Dept, BOAC, 1940; Sales Promotion Supt, 1946; Sales Manager, 1950; Sales Planning Manager, 1954; Dir of Planning, 1964; Planning Dir, 1969; Dep. Managing Dir, 1972. FCIT. *Recreations:* sailing, gardening. *Address:* Altenburg, Trafford Road,

Great Missenden, Bucks HP16 0BT.
Died 6 Nov. 2003.

BRAYBROOK, Edward John, CB 1972; *b* 25 Oct. 1911; *s* of late Prior Wormsley Braybrook and Kate Braybrook; *m* 1937, Eva Rosalin, (Peggy), Thomas; one *s* two *d. Educ:* Latymer Secondary Sch., Edmonton. Asst Naval Store Officer, Admty, Chatham, Malta and Devonport, 1930–37; Deputy Naval Store Officer, Admty, 1938–39; Naval Store Officer, Admty and Haslemere, 1940–43; Suptg Naval Store Officer, Levant, 1943; Comdr/Captain (SP) RNVR Suptg Naval Store Officer, Ceylon and Southern India, 1944–46; Supt, Perth, Scotland, 1946–47; Asst Director of Stores, Admty, 1947–53; Suptg Naval Store Officer, Chatham, 1953–55; Deputy Director of Stores, Admty, 1955–64; Director of Stores (Naval), MoD, 1964–70; Dir-Gen. Supplies and Transport (Naval), MoD, 1970–73. *Recreations:* gardening, photography, painting, handicrafts. *Address:* 22 Church Drive, North Harrow, Middx HA2 7NW. *T:* (020) 8427 0838.
Died 14 Sept. 2001.

BRAYBROOKE, Neville Patrick Bellairs; writer; *b* 30 May 1923; *s* of Patrick Philip William Braybrooke and Lettice Marjorie Bellairs; *m* 1953, June Guesdon Jolliffe (writer as Isobel English) (*d* 1994); one step *d. Educ:* Ampleforth. Ed., The Wind and the Rain (qly), 1941–51. *Publications:* This is London, 1953; London Green: the Story of Kensington Gardens, Hyde Park, Green Park and St James's Park, 1959; London, 1961; The Idler (novel), 1961; The Delicate Investigation (play for BBC), 1969; Four Poems for Christmas, 1986; Dialogue with Judas (long poem), 1989; Two Birthdays (poem), 1995; The Inward Star (poem), 1999; (with Isobel English) Olivia Manning (biog.), 2001; *edited:* T. S. Eliot: a symposium for his 70th birthday, 1958, 7th edn 1986; A Partridge in a Pear Tree: a celebration for Christmas, 1960; Pilgrim of the Future: a Teilhard de Chardin symposium, 1966, 2nd edn 1968; The Letters of J. R. Ackerley, 1975, 2nd edn 1977; Seeds in the Wind: 20th century juvenilia from W. B. Yeats to Ted Hughes, 1989, 3rd edn 1991; contrib. Independent, Guardian, New Statesman, New Yorker, Observer, The Tablet, Sunday Times, The Times, Times Lit. Suppl., Sunday Telegraph, Spectator. *Recreations:* animals, reading little reviews, hats. *Address:* Grove House, Castle Road, Cowes, IoW PO31 7QZ. *T:* (01983) 293950. *Club:* PEN.
Died 14 July 2001.

BRAYNE, Richard Bolding, MBE 1957; Clerk of the Worshipful Company of Ironmongers, 1973–90 (Assistant Clerk, 1971; Master, 1993–94); *b* 28 Oct. 1924; 3rd *s* of late Brig. Frank Lugard Brayne, MC, CSI, CIE, ICS, and Iris Goodeve Brayne, K-i-H; *m* 1947, Anne Stoddart Forrest; one *s* two *d. Educ:* Sherborne Sch.; Pembroke Coll., Cambridge. Indian Army, 3rd (Peshawar) Indian Mountain Battery, FF, India, Burma and Far East, 1942–46. Entered Colonial Service as DO, Tanganyika, 1948; Staff Officer to HRH The Princess Margaret's tour of Tanganyika, 1956; Dist Comr, 1957; Principal, Admin. Trng Centre and Local Govt Trng Centre, 1960. Prin. Asst Sec., Min. of Educn, 1963; Mem., E African UGC and Makerere Univ. College Council, 1963; retd from Colonial Service, 1964. Sec., Brit. Paper and Board Makers' Assoc., 1964; Trng Adviser and Develt Manager, CITB, 1966. Member: Exec. Cttee, Nat. Assoc. of Almshouses, 1972–2000 (Chm., 1981–87); Council, Royal Surgical Aid Soc., 1972–95 (Chm., 1982–87). *Recreations:* golf, bridge, gardening.
Died 24 Oct. 2004.

BRAZIER-CREAGH, Maj.-Gen. Sir (Kilner) Rupert, KBE 1962 (CBE 1947); CB 1954; DSO 1944; Secretary of the Horse Race Betting Levy Board, 1961–65; Director of Staff Duties, War Office, 1959–61, retired; *b* 12 Dec. 1909; 2nd *s* of late Lt-Col K. C. Brazier-Creagh; *m* 1st, 1938, Elizabeth Mary (*d* 1967), *d* of late E. M. Magor; one *s* two *d*; 2nd, 1968, Mrs Marie Nelson. *Educ:* Rugby; RMA, Woolwich. 2nd Lieut, 1929; served War of 1939–45 (despatches, DSO); Bde Major, 9th Armoured Div., 1941;

GSO1 12th Corps, 1943; Commanded 25th Field Regt, 1944; BGS 21st Army Group and BAOR, 1945–48 (CBE); idc 1949; DDRA, War Office, 1950; CRA 11th Armoured Div., 1951–52; Chief of Staff Malaya Command, 1952–55 (despatches, CB); Asst Comdt, Staff Coll., 1955–57; Chief of Staff, Eastern Command, 1957–59. Officer, American Legion of Merit, 1945. *Recreation:* racing. *Address:* Travis Corners Road, Garrison, NY 10524, USA.
Died 4 April 2002.

BREDIN, Maj.-Gen. Humphrey Edgar Nicholson, CB 1969; DSO 1944 (and bars, 1945 and 1957); MC 1938 (and bar, 1939); DL; Appeals Secretary, Cancer Research Campaign, Essex and Suffolk, 1971–83; *b* 28 March 1916; *s* of Lt-Col A. Bredin, late Indian Army, and Ethel Bredin (*née* Homan); *m* 1st, 1947, Jacqueline Geare (marr. diss. 1961; she *d* 1997); one *d*; 2nd, 1965, Anne Hardie (*d* 1995); two *d. Educ:* King's School, Canterbury; RMC, Sandhurst. Commnd Royal Ulster Rifles, 1936; commanded: 6th Royal Inniskilling Fusiliers, 1944; 2nd London Irish Rifles, 1945; Eastern Arab Corps, Sudan Defence Force, 1949–53; 2nd Parachute Regt, 1956–57; 99th Gurkha Infty Bde Group, 1959–62. Campaigns: Dunkirk, 1940; N Africa, 1943; Italy, 1943–45; Palestine, 1937–39 and 1946–47; Suez, 1956; Cyprus, 1956–57; Singapore-Malaya Internal Security, 1959–62; Chief of British Commander-in-Chief's Mission to Soviet Forces in Germany, 1963–65; comd 42nd Div. (TA), 1965–68; Brig. 1964; Maj.-Gen. 1965; Dir, Volunteers, Territorials and Cadets, 1968–71; retired 1971. Col Comdt, The King's Division, 1968–71; Col of the Regt, Royal Irish Rangers, 1979–85; Hon. Col D (London Irish Rifles) Co., 4th (V) Bn, The Royal Irish Rangers, 1980–86. Chm. Essex Co. Cttee, Army Benevolent Fund, 1983–92; President: Dunkirk Veterans Clacton and Colchester Assoc., 1983–99; 78th Div. Battleaxe Club, 1991–95. DL Essex, 1984. *Recreations:* shooting, fishing, gardening. *Address:* c/o Rodmead Farm, Maiden Bradley, Warminster, Wilts BA12 7HP. *T:* (01985) 844689.
Died 2 March 2005.

BRETT, Sir Charles (Edward Bainbridge), Kt 1990; CBE 1981; Consultant, L'Estrange & Brett, Solicitors, Belfast, 1994–98 (Partner, 1954–94); *b* 30 Oct. 1928; *s* of Charles Anthony Brett and Elizabeth Joyce (*née* Carter); *m* 1953, Joyce Patricia Worley; three *s. Educ:* Rugby Sch.; New Coll., Oxford (Schol.; MA History). Solicitor, 1953. Journalist, Radiodiffusion Française and Continental Daily Mail, 1949–50. Member: Child Welfare Council of Northern Ireland, 1958–61; Northern Ireland Cttee, National Trust, 1956–83 and 1985–93 (Mem. Council, 1975–89); Board, Arts Council of N Ireland, 1970–76, and 1994–98 (Vice-Chm., 1994–98); Chairman: N Ireland Labour Party, 1962; Ulster Architectural Heritage Soc., 1968–78 (Pres., 1979–); HEARTH Housing Assoc., 1978 and 1985–2000 (Vice-Pres., 2000–); NI Housing Exec., 1979–84 (Mem. Bd, 1971–77, Vice-Chm., 1977–78); Internat. Fund for Ireland, 1986–89. Mem. Bd, Irish Architectural Archive, Dublin, 1985–88. Hon. Mem., Royal Society of Ulster Architects, 1973; Hon. MRIAI 1988; Hon. FRIBA 1987. Hon. LLD QUB, 1989. *Publications:* Buildings of Belfast 1700–1914, 1967, rev. edn 1985; Court Houses and Market Houses of Ulster, 1973; Long Shadows Cast Before, 1978; Housing a Divided Community, 1986; Buildings of County Antrim, 1996; Five Big Houses of Cushendun, 1997; Buildings of County Armagh, 1999; Buildings of North County Down, 2002; Georgian Belfast, 2004; Towers of Crim Tartary, 2005; lists and surveys for Ulster Architectural Heritage Soc., National Trusts of Guernsey and Jersey, and Alderney Soc; (as Albert Rechts) Handbook to a Hypothetical City, 1986. *Club:* Oxford and Cambridge.
Died 19 Dec. 2005.

BRETT, Lionel; see Esher, 4th Viscount.

BRIDGE, Ronald George Blacker, CBE 1990 (OBE 1985); Hong Kong Civil Service, retired; *b* 7 Sept. 1932; *s* of Blacker Frank Bridge and Aileen Georgina Edith (*née*

Shaw); *m* 1956, Olive Tyrrell Brown; two *s* two *d*. *Educ:* Charterhouse; Lincoln Coll., Oxford (MA). National Service, 1954–56. Colonial Office Devonshire Course, 1956–57; Hong Kong Civil Service, 1957–89: language study, 1957–58; Resettlement Officer, 1958–61; Asst Sec. (Lands and Buildings), 1961–69; Asst Comr for Resettlement, 1969–72; Asst Colonial Sec. (Estabt), 1971–72; Dep. Sec. for the Civil Service, 1972–76; Dep. Sec. for Security, 1976–77; Sec. for the Civil Service, 1977–78; Dir of Immigration, 1978–83; Comr for Labour, 1983–86; Sec. for Educn and Manpower, 1986–89. Part-time: with Waltons & Morse, solicitors, 1989–94; with Nabarro Nathanson, solicitors, 1995–96. *Recreations:* St Helen's Church Bishopsgate, Scottish dancing, walking, reading. *Address:* 15 Lincoln Street, SW3 2TP. *T:* (020) 7581 8090. *Died 14 April 2001.*

BRIERLEY, Christopher Wadsworth, CBE 1987; Senior Adviser, Natural Gas Development Unit, World Bank, Washington, USA, 1990–94; Managing Director, Resources and New Business, 1987–89, and Member of the Board, 1985–89, British Gas plc (formerly British Gas Corporation); *b* 1 June 1929; *s* of Eric Brierley and Edna Mary Lister; *m* 1st, Dorothy Scott (marr. diss. 1980); two *d*; 2nd, 1984, Dilwen Marie Srobat (*née* Morgan). *Educ:* Whitgift Middle School, Croydon. FCMA, ACIS. Branch Accountant, Hubert Davies & Co., Rhodesia, 1953–56; private business, N Rhodesia, 1956–59; Accountant, EMI, 1960; Chief Accountant, EMI Records, 1965; Dir of Finance, Long & Hambly, 1968; Chief Accountant, E Midlands Gas Bd, 1970; Director of Finance: Eastern Gas Bd, 1974; British Gas, 1977; Dir, 1980, Man. Dir, 1982, Economic Planning, British Gas. *Recreation:* music. *Address:* 6 Digswell House, Monks Rise, Welwyn Garden City, Herts AL8 7NX. *Died 8 March 2002.*

BRIERLEY, John David, CB 1978; retired Civil Servant; *b* 16 March 1918; *s* of late Walter George Brierley and Doris Brierley (*née* Paterson); *m* 1956, Frances Elizabeth Davis; one adopted *s* one adopted *d*. *Educ:* elementary schools, London and Croydon; Whitgift Sch., Croydon; Lincoln Coll., Oxford (*Lit Hum*. BA Hons 1940). Served War, Army, RASC, 1940–46. Ministry of Education, later Department of Education and Science, 1946–77: Principal Finance Officer, 1969–75; Under Sec., 1969–77. Dean of Studies, Working Mens' Coll., NW1, 1978–81 (Mem. Corp., 1980–94); Governor, Croydon High Sch. (GPDST), 1980–91. *Recreations:* walking, photography, music. *Address:* Little Trees, Winterbourne, near Newbury, Berks RG20 8AS. *T:* (01635) 248870. *Died 29 April 2005.*

BRIGGS, Rt Rev. George Cardell, CMG 1980; Bishop of Seychelles, 1973–79; *b* Latchford, Warrington, Cheshire, 6 Sept. 1910; *s* of George Cecil and Mary Theodora Briggs; unmarried. *Educ:* Worksop Coll., Notts; Sidney Sussex Coll., Cambridge (MA); Cuddesdon Theological Coll. Deacon 1934; priest 1935; Curate of St Alban's, Stockport, 1934–37; Missionary priest, Diocese of Masasi, Tanzania, 1937; Archdeacon of Newala and Canon of Masasi, 1955–64; Rector of St Alban's, Dar-es-Salaam, 1964–69; Warden of St Cyprian's Theological Coll., Masasi, 1969–73; Asst Bishop, Diocese of Derby, and Assistant Priest, parish of St Giles, Matlock, 1979–80. *Recreations:* walking, reading, music. *Address:* College of St Barnabas, Blackberry Lane, Lingfield, Surrey RH7 6NJ. *T:* (01342) 870747. *Club:* Royal Commonwealth Society. *Died 15 March 2004.*

BRIGSTOCKE, Baroness *cr* 1990 (Life Peer), of Kensington in the Royal Borough of Kensington and Chelsea; **Heather Renwick Brigstocke,** CBE 2000; Chairman, English-Speaking Union of the Commonwealth, 1993–99; High Mistress of St Paul's Girls' School, 1974–89; *b* 2 Sept. 1929; *d* of late Sqdn-Ldr J. R. Brown, DFC and Mrs M. J. C. Brown, MA; *m* 1st, 1952, Geoffrey Brigstocke (*d* 1974); three *s* one *d*; 2nd, 2000, Baron Griffiths,MC, PC. *Educ:* Abbey Sch., Reading; Girton Coll., Cambridge (MA, Pt I Classics, Pt

II Archaeolog. and Anthropol.); Univ. Winchester Reading Prize, 1950. Classics Mistress, Francis Holland Sch., London, SW1, 1951–53; part-time Classics Mistress, Godolphin and Latymer Sch., 1954–60; part-time Latin Teacher, National Cathedral Sch., Washington, DC, 1962–64; Headmistress, Francis Holland Sch., London, NW1, 1965–74. Comr, Museums and Galls Commn, 1992–2000. Member: Council, London House for Overseas Graduates, 1965–91 (Vice-Chm., 1975–80); Council, Middlesex Hosp. Med. Sch., 1971–80; Cttee, AA, 1975–90; Council, RHC, 1977–85; Council, The City Univ., 1978–83; Pres., Girls' Schools Assoc., 1980–81; Vice Pres., C & G, 1993–. Member: Health Educn Authority, 1989–98; Modern Foreign Langs Wkg Gp, 1989–90. Non-exec. Dir, 1982–90, Mem., Programme Adv. Bd, 1990–93, LWT; Ind. Dir, The Times, 1990–; Associate Dir, Great Universal Stores, 1993–96; non-exec. Dir, Burberrys, 1993–96. Member Council: RSA, 1983–87; St George's House, Windsor, 1984–90; Pres., Bishop Creighton House Settlement, Fulham, 1977–; Chairman: Thames LWT Telethon Trust, 1990; Menerva Educnl Trust, 1991–93; Mem. Council, Nat. Literacy Trust, 1993–; Chm. of Trustees, Geffrye Mus., 1990–2000; Trustee: Nat. Gall., 1975–82; Kennedy Meml Trust, 1980–85; Technology Colls Trust (formerly City Technology Colls Trust), 1987–; GB Sasakawa Foundn, 1994–. Governor: Mus. of London, 1986–92; Wellington Coll., 1975–87; Royal Ballet Sch., 1977–92; United World College of the Atlantic, 1980–85; Forest Sch., 1982–90; Imperial Coll., 1991–98; Gordonstoun Sch., 1991–93; Chm. of Govs, Landau Forte Coll., Derby, 1993– (Gov., 1992–). Hon. Bencher, Inner Temple, 1992. *Address:* House of Lords, SW1A 0PW. *T:* (020) 7219 3000. *Died 30 April 2004.*

BRISTOW, Hon. Sir Peter (Henry Rowley), Kt 1970; a Judge of the High Court, Queen's Bench Division, 1970–85; *b* 1 June 1913; *s* of Walter Rowley Bristow, FRCS and Florence (*née* White); *m* 1st, 1940, Josephine Noel Leney (*d* 1969); one *s* (one *d* decd); 2nd, 1975, Elsa (*d* 2001), *widow* of H. B. Leney. *Educ:* Eton; Trinity College, Cambridge. Pilot, RAFVR, 1935–45; tutor, Empire Central Flying Sch., 1942–43. Called to the Bar, Middle Temple, 1936, Bencher 1961, Treasurer 1977; QC 1964; Mem., Inns of Court Senate, 1966–70 (Hon. Treas., 1967–70); Judge, Court of Appeal, Guernsey, and Court of Appeal, Jersey, 1965–70; Dep. Chm., Hants QS, 1964–71; Judge of the Commercial Court and Employment Appeals Tribunal, 1976–78; Vice-Chm., Parole Bd, 1977–78 (Mem. 1976); Presiding Judge, Western Circuit, 1979–82. *Publication:* Judge for Yourself, 1986. *Recreations:* fishing, gardening. *Address:* The Folly, Membury, Axminster, Devon EX13 7AG. *Died 1 Aug. 2002.*

BRITTON, Prof. Denis King, CBE 1978; Professor of Agricultural Economics at Wye College, University of London, 1970–83, then Emeritus Professor; Hon. Fellow, Wye College, 1986; *b* 25 March 1920; *s* of Rev. George Charles Britton and Harriet Rosa (*née* Swinstead); *m* 1942, Margaret Alice Smith; one *s* two *d*. *Educ:* Caterham School; London School of Economics, London University (BSc (Econ.)). Asst Statistician, Ministry of Agriculture and Fisheries, 1943–47; Lecturing and Research at University of Oxford, Agricultural Economics Res. Inst., 1947–52; MA Oxon 1948 (by decree); Economist, United Nations Food and Agriculture Organisation, Geneva, 1952–59; Gen. Manager, Marketing and Economic Res., Massey-Ferguson (UK) Ltd, 1959–61; Prof. of Agricultural Economics, Univ. of Nottingham, 1961–70; Dean, Faculty of Agriculture and Horticulture, Univ. of Nottingham, 1967–70. Member: EDC for Agriculture, 1966–83; Home Grown Cereals Authority, 1969–87; Adv. Council for Agriculture and Horticulture, 1973–80; Adv. Cttee, Nuffield Centre for Agric. Strategy, 1975–80; MAFF Gp to review Eggs Authority, 1985; Chairman: Council, Centre for European Agricl Studies, Wye Coll., 1974–79; Forestry Commn Rev. Gp on Integration of

Farming and Forestry, 1983–84; President: Internat. Assoc. of Agric. Economists, 1976–79; British Agric. Economics Soc., 1977–78; Special Adviser, House of Commons Select Cttee on Agric., 1980–83. Vis. Prof., Uppsala, 1973; Winegarten Lecture, NFU, 1981. Farmers' Club Cup, 1966. FSS 1943; FRAgS 1970; FRASE 1980. Hon. DAgric, Univ. of Bonn, 1975; Hon. DEcon, Univ. of Padua, 1982. *Publications:* Cereals in the United Kingdom, 1969; (with Berkeley Hill) Size and Efficiency in Farming, 1975; (with H. F. Marks) A Hundred Years of British Food and Farming: a statistical survey, 1989; (ed) Agriculture in Britain: changing pressures and policies, 1990; articles in Jl of Royal Statistical Society, Jl of Agricultural Economics, Jl of RSA, etc. *Recreation:* music. *Address:* 29 Chequers Park, Wye, Ashford, Kent TN25 5BB.

Died 12 Oct. 2005.

BRITTON, Sir Edward (Louis), Kt 1975; CBE 1967; General Secretary, National Union of Teachers, 1970–75; retired; *b* 4 Dec. 1909; *s* of George Edwin and Ellen Alice Britton; *m* 1936, Nora Arnald (*d* 1991); no *c. Educ:* Bromley Grammar School, Kent; Trinity College, Cambridge. Teacher in various Surrey schools until 1951; Headmaster, Warlingham County Secondary School, Surrey, 1951–60; Gen. Sec., Assoc. of Teachers in Technical Institns, 1960–68. Pres., National Union of Teachers, 1956–57. Sen. Res. Fellow, Educn Div., Sheffield Univ., 1975–79; Mem. of staff, Christ Church Coll., Canterbury, 1979–86. Vice-Pres., NFER, 1979–; Member: TUC General Council, 1970–74; Beloe Cttee on Secondary Schs Exams, 1960; Schools Council, 1964–75; Adv. Cttee for Supply and Trng of Teachers, 1973–75; Burnham Primary and Secondary Cttee, 1956–75 (Jt Sec. and Leader of Teachers' Panel, 1970–75); Burnham Further Educn Cttee, 1959–69 (Jt Sec. and Leader of Teachers' Panel, 1961–69); Officers' Panel, Soulbury Cttee (and Leader), 1970–75; Staff Panel, Jt Negotiating Cttee Youth Leaders (and Leader), 1970–75; Warnock Cttee on Special Educn, 1974–78; Council and Exec., CGLI, 1974–77; Central Arbitration Cttee, 1977–83. Chm., Nat. Centre for Cued Speech for the Deaf, 1986–88. FCP 1967; Hon. FEIS 1974. Hon. DEd CNAA, 1969. *Publications:* many articles in educational journals. *Address:* 40 Nightingale Road, Guildford, Surrey GU1 1ER. *Died 3 Jan. 2005.*

BRITZ, Jack; General Secretary, Clearing Bank Union, 1980–83; independent human resources consultant, since 1983; *b* 6 Nov. 1930; *s* of Alfred and Hetty Britz; *m* 1955, Thelma Salaver; one *s* two *d. Educ:* Luton Grammar School. Entered electrical contracting industry, 1944; various posts in industry; Director, Rolfe Electrical Ltd, 1964–65. National Recruitment Officer, EETPU, 1969–74; short period with Commission on Industrial Relations as sen. industrial relations officer, 1974; Personnel Manager, Courage Eastern Ltd, 1974–77; Gp Personnel Director, Bowthorpe Group Ltd, 1977–80. HR Interim Mgt, 1989–. Advr, Investors in People, 1998–. NVQ Assessor, mgt and trng, 1992–. *Recreations:* walking, history, wargaming, oil painting, etc. *Address:* Holmwood, Church Place, Pulborough, W Sussex RH20 1AF.

Died 29 Sept. 2005.

BROCKHOUSE, Dr Bertram Neville, CC 1995 (OC 1982); FRS 1965; Professor of Physics, McMaster University, Canada, 1962–84, then Emeritus; *b* 15 July 1918; *s* of Israel Bertram Brockhouse and Mable Emily Brockhouse (*née* Neville); *m* 1948, Doris Isobel Mary (*née* Miller); four *s* two *d. Educ:* University of British Columbia (BA); University of Toronto (PhD). Served War of 1939–45 with Royal Canadian Navy. Lectr, University of Toronto, 1949–50; Research Officer, Atomic Energy of Canada Ltd, 1950–59; Branch Head, Neutron Physics Br., 1960–62. Foreign Member: Royal Swedish Acad. of Sciences, 1984; Amer. Acad. of Arts and Sciences, 1990. Hon. DSc: Waterloo, 1969; McMaster, 1984; Toronto, 1995; UBC, and Dalhousie, 1996. Nobel Prize for Physics (jtly), 1994. *Publications:* some 75 papers in learned

journals. *Address:* PO Box 7338, Ancaster, Ontario L9G 3N6, Canada. *T:* (905) 648 6329.

Died 13 Oct. 2003.

BROCKINGTON, Prof. Colin Fraser; Professor of Social and Preventive Medicine, Manchester University, 1951–64, Emeritus, 1964; *b* 8 Jan. 1903; *s* of Sir William Brockington; *m* 1933, Dr Joyce Margaret Furze; three *s* one *d. Educ:* Oakham Sch.; Gonville and Caius Coll., Cambridge; Guy's Hosp., London. MD, MA, DPH, BChir Cantab, MSc Manchester. MRCS, MRCP. Called to the Bar, Middle Temple. Medical Superintendent, Brighton Infectious Diseases Hosp. and Sanatorium, 1929; Asst County Medical Officer, Worcs CC, 1930–33; general medical practice, Kingsbridge, Devon, 1933–36; Medical Officer of Health, Horsham and Petworth, 1936–38; Dep. County Medical Officer of Health, Warwickshire CC, 1938–42; County Medical Officer of Health: Warwickshire CC, 1942–46; West Riding CC, 1946–51. Member: Central Adv. Council for Educn (Eng.), 1945–56; Central Training Council in Child Care (Home Office), 1947–53; Adv. Council for Welfare of Handicapped (Min. of Health), 1949–54; Nursing Cttee of Central Health Services Council (Min. of Health), 1949–51; Council of Soc. of Med. Officers of Health, 1944–66; Public Health Cttee of County Councils Assoc., 1945–49. Chairman: WHO Expert Cttee on School Health, 1950; Symposium on "Mental Health–Public Health Partnership," 5th Internat. Congress on Mental Health, Toronto, 1954; WHO Research Study Group on Juvenile Epilepsy, 1955; UK Cttee of WHO, 1958–61. Took part as Expert in Technical Discussions on Rural Health at World Health Assembly, 1954; Far Eastern Lecture Tour for British Council, 1956–57; visited India, 1959, 1962, S America 1960, Jordan 1966–67, Spain 1967, Arabia 1968, Turkey 1955, 1969, 1970, 1972, Greece 1970, for WHO; Lecture Tour, S Africa and Middle East, 1964. *Publications:* Principles of Nutrition, 1952; The People's Health, 1955; A Short History of Public Health, 1956, 2nd edn 1966; World Health, 1958, 4th edn (electronic) 1996; The Health of the Community, 1955, 1960, 1965; Public Health in the Nineteenth Century, 1965; The Social Needs of the Over-Eighties, 1966; The Health of the Developing World, 1985; wide range of contribs to learned jls. *Recreations:* bookbinding, travel. *Address:* Werneth, Silverburn, Ballasalla, Isle of Man IM9 2DT. *T:* (01624) 3465. *Died 25 Nov. 2004.*

BRODIE OF BRODIE, (Montagu) Ninian (Alexander); JP; DL; Chief of Clan Brodie; landowner since 1953; *b* 12 June 1912; *s* of I. A. M. Brodie of Brodie (*d* 1943) and C. V. M. Brodie of Brodie (*née* Hope) (*d* 1958); *m* 1939, Helena Penelope Mills Budgen (*d* 1972); one *s* one *d. Educ:* Eton. Stage, films, TV, 1933–40 and 1945–49. Served Royal Artillery, 1940–45. JP Morayshire, 1958; Hon. Sheriff-Substitute, 1958; DL Nairn, 1970. *Recreations:* shooting, collecting pictures. *Heir:* s Alastair Ian Ninian Brodie, Younger of Brodie [*b* 7 Sept. 1943; *m* 1968, Mary Louise Johnson (marr. diss. 1986); two *s* one *d*]. *Address:* Brodie Castle, Forres, Moray IV36 2TE, Scotland. *T:* (01309) 641202. *Died 3 March 2003.*

BROKE, Maj.-Gen. Robert Straton, CB 1967; OBE 1946; MC 1940; *b* 15 March 1913; *s* of Rev. Horatio George Broke and Mary Campbell Broke (*née* Adlington); *m* 1939, Ernine Susan Margaret Bonsey (*d* 1997); two *s. Educ:* Eton College (KS); Magdalene College, Cambridge (BA). Commissioned Royal Artillery, 1933. Served War of 1939–45: France, 1940; Abyssinia, 1940–41 (despatches); Syria, 1941 (despatches); N Africa, 1942–43. Commander Royal Artillery: 5th Division, 1959; 1st Division, 1960; 1st (British) Corps 1961; Northern Army Group, 1964–66, retired. Col Comdt, RA, 1968–78; Representative Col Comdt, 1974–75. Dir, Wellman Engrg Corp., later Wellman plc, and Chm. of six cos within the Group, 1968–88. Chm., Iron and Steel Plant Contractors Assoc., 1972, 1977. Pres., Metallurgical Plantmakers' Fedn, 1977–79. Treas., London Appeals,

Macmillan Cancer Relief (formerly Cancer Relief Macmillan Fund), 1989–97. *Recreations:* country sports. *Address:* Ivy Farm, Holme Hale, Thetford, Norfolk IP25 7DJ. *T:* (01760) 440225. *Club:* Army and Navy.

Died 8 Jan. 2002.

BROME, Vincent; author; *b* 14 July 1916; *s* of Nathaniel Gregory and Emily Brome. *Educ:* Streatham Grammar School; Elleston School; privately. Formerly: Feature Writer; Editor, Menu Magazines; Min. of Information; Asst Editor, Medical World. Since then, author of biographies, novels, plays and essays; broadcaster. Mem., British Library Adv. Cttee, 1975–82. *Plays:* The Sleepless One (prod. Edin), 1962; BBC plays. *Publications:* Anthology, 1936; Clement Attlee, 1947; H. G. Wells, 1951; Aneurin Bevan, 1953; The Last Surrender, 1954; The Way Back, 1956; Six Studies in Quarrelling, 1958; Sometimes at Night, 1959; Frank Harris, 1959; Acquaintance With Grief, 1961; We Have Come a Long Way, 1962; The Problem of Progress, 1963; Love in Our Time, 1964; Four Realist Novelists, 1964; The International Brigades, 1965; The World of Luke Simpson, 1966; Freud and His Early Circle, 1967; The Surgeon, 1967; Diary of A Revolution, 1968; The Revolution, 1969; The Imaginary Crime, 1969; Confessions of a Writer, 1970; The Brain Operators, 1970; Private Prosecutions, 1971; Reverse Your Verdict, 1971; London Consequences, 1972; The Embassy, 1972; The Day of Destruction, 1975; The Happy Hostage, 1976; Jung—Man and Myth, 1978; Havelock Ellis—Philosopher of Sex, 1981; Ernest Jones: Freud's alter ego, 1983; The Day of the Fifth Moon, 1984; J. B. Priestley, 1988; The Other Pepys, 1992; Love in the Plague, 2001; Retribution, 2001; contrib. The Times, Sunday Times, Observer, Guardian, New Statesman, New Society, Encounter, Spectator, TLS etc. *Recreations:* writing plays and talking. *Address:* 45 Great Ormond Street, WC1N 3HZ. *T:* (020) 7405 0550. *Club:* Savile. *Died 16 Oct. 2004.*

BROOKES, Baron *cr* 1975 (Life Peer), of West Bromwich; **Raymond Percival Brookes,** Kt 1971; Life President, GKN plc (formerly Guest, Keen & Nettlefolds Ltd) (Group Chairman and Chief Executive, 1965–74); *b* 10 April 1909; *s* of William and Ursula Brookes; *m* 1937, Florence Edna Sharman; one *s.* Part-time Mem., BSC, 1967–68. First Pres., British Mechanical Engrg Confedn, 1968–70; a Vice-Pres., Engrg Employers' Fedn, 1967–75. Member: Council, UK S Africa Trade Assoc. Ltd, 1967–74; Council, CBI, 1968–75; BNEC, 1969–71; Wilberforce Ct of Inquiry into electricity supply industry dispute, Jan. 1971; Industrial Develt Adv. Bd, 1972–75. Member: Exec. Cttee, 1970–, Council, 1969–, Pres., 1974–75, Soc. of Motor Manufacturers & Traders Ltd; Court of Governors, Univ. of Birmingham, 1966–75; Council, Univ. of Birmingham, 1968–75. Pres., Motor Ind. Res. Assoc., 1973–75. Chm., Rea Bros (IoM) Ltd, 1976–89; Director: Plessey Co. Ltd, 1974–89; AMF Inc., 1975–78. *Recreations:* golf, fly-fishing. *Address:* GKN plc, PO Box 55, Redditch, Worcs B98 0TL; (private) Mallards, Santon, Isle of Man IM4 1EH.

Died 31 July 2002.

BROOKS, Caroline St J.; *see* St John-Brooks.

BROOKS, Prof. Christopher Leonard, DPhil; FSA; Professor of Victorian Culture, Exeter University, since 2001; *b* 23 Jan. 1949; *s* of Donald and Lilian Brooks; *m.* *Educ:* Grammar Sch., Plympton; Manchester Univ. (BA 1971); Lincoln Coll., Oxford (DPhil 1979). Exeter University: Lectr in English, 1976–92; Senior Lectr in Victorian Studies, 1992–98; Reader in Victorian Culture, 1998–2001; Hd, Sch. of English and American Studies, 1990–93. Victorian Society: Mem., Main Cttee, 1980–; Vice-Chm., 1987–93; Chm., 1993–2001. Member: Exeter DAC for Care of Churches, 1982–96; Technical Adv. Cttee, Exeter Cathedral, 1982–88; Wallpaintings Cttee, Council for Care of Churches, 1988–91; Fabric Cttee, Exeter Cathedral, 1990–; Fabric Cttee, Truro Cathedral, 1990–97; English Heritage: Adv. Cttee on

Cathedrals and Churches, 1993–2001; Places of Worship Panel, 2001–; Historic Settlements and Landscapes Adv. Cttee, 2001–. Sec., Devon Bldgs Gp, 1985–95; Mem., Kensal Green Cemetery Adv. Cttee, 1990–. Mem. Council, Royal Archaeol Inst., 1993–96. Mem., Steering Gp for Albert Meml, DNH, 1993–94; Trustee, Albert Meml Trust, 1994–99. Leverhulme Trust Res. Fellow, 1997–98. *Publications:* Signs for the Times: symbolic realism in the mid-Victorian world, 1984; (with D. Evans) The Great East Window of Exeter Cathedral, 1988; Mortal Remains: the history and present state of the Victorian and Edwardian cemetery, 1989; (ed with A. Saint) The Victorian Church: architecture and society, 1995; The Albert Memorial, 1995; (with P. Faulkner) The White Man's Burdens: an anthology of British Poetry of the Empire, 1996; The Gothic Revival, 1999; (ed) The Albert Memorial: The Prince Consort National Memorial, its history, contexts and conservation, 2000. *Recreations:* pubs, cricket. *Address:* 48 Park Street, Crediton, Devon EX17 3EH; Victorian Society, 1 Priory Gardens, Bedford Park, W4 1TT. *T:* (020) 8994 1019; School of English, Queen's Building, University of Exeter, Exeter, Devon EX4 4QH. *T:* (01392) 264265. *Died 23 Feb. 2002.*

BROOKS, Leslie James, CEng, FRINA; RCNC; Deputy Director of Engineering (Constructive), Ship Department, Ministry of Defence (Procurement Executive), 1973–76, retired; *b* 3 Aug. 1916; *s* of late C. J. D. Brooks and Lucy A. Brooks, Milton Regis, Sittingbourne, Kent; *m* 1941, Ruth Elizabeth Olver, Saltash, Cornwall; two *s.* *Educ:* Borden Grammar Sch., Sittingbourne, Kent; HM Dockyard Schs, Sheerness and Chatham; Royal Naval Engrg Coll., Keyham; RNC, Greenwich. War of 1939–45: Asst Constructor, Naval Construction Dept, Admty, Bath, 1941–44; Constr Lt-Comdr on Staff of Allied Naval Comdr, Exped. Force, and Flag Officer, Brit. Assault Area, 1944. Constr in charge Welding, Naval Constrn Dept, Admty, Bath, 1945–47; Constr Comdr, Staff of Comdr-in-Chief, Brit. Pacific Fleet, 1947–49; Constr in charge, No 2 Ship Tank, Admty Experiment Works, Haslar, Gosport, 1949–54. Naval Constrn Dept, Admty, Bath: Constr, Merchant Shipping Liaison, 1954–56; Chief Constr in charge of Conversion of First Commando Ships, and of Operating Aircraft Carriers, 1956–62; Dep. Supt, Admty Exper. Works, Haslar, 1962–64; Senior Officers War Course, RNC Greenwich, 1964–65; Ship Dept, Bath: Asst Dir of Naval Constrn, Naval Constrn Div., MoD(N), 1965–68; Asst Dir of Engrg (Ships), MoD(PE), 1968–73; Dep. Dir of Engrg/Constr., MoD(PE), 1973. Mem., Royal Corps of Naval Constructors. *Recreations:* walking, photography, natural history. *Address:* Merrymeet, Perrymead, Bath BA2 5AY. *T:* (01225) 832856. *Died 29 Nov. 2001.*

BROOM, Air Marshal Sir Ivor (Gordon), KCB 1975 (CB 1972); CBE 1969; DSO 1945; DFC 1942 (Bar to DFC 1944, 2nd Bar 1945); AFC 1956; international aerospace consultant, since 1977; Chairman: Gatwick Handling Ltd, 1982–93; Farnborough Aerospace Development Corporation, 1985–92; *b* Cardiff, 2 June 1920; *s* of Alfred Godfrey Broom and Janet Broom; *m* 1942, Jess Irene Broom (*née* Cooper); two *s* one *d.* *Educ:* West Monmouth Grammar Sch.; Pontypridd County Sch., Glam. Joined RAF, 1940; commissioned, 1941; 114 Sqdn, 107 Sqdn, 1941; CFS Course, 1942; Instructor on: 1655 Mosquito Trg Unit; 571 Sqdn, 128 Sqdn; commanded 163 Sqdn, 1943–45; HQ, ACSEA, 1944–46; commanded 28 (FR) Sqdn, 1946–48; RAF Staff Coll. Course, Bracknell, 1949; Sqdn Comdr, No 1 ITS, 1950–52; No 3 Flying Coll. Course, Manby, 1952–53; commanded 57 Sqdn, 1953–54; Syndicate Leader, Flying Coll., Manby, 1954–56; commanded Bomber Command Development Unit, Wittering, 1956–59; Air Secretary's Dept, 1959–62; commanded RAF Bruggen, 1962–64; IDC, 1965–66; Dir of Organisation (Establishments), 1966–68; Commandant, Central Flying School, 1968–70; AOC No 11 (Fighter) Gp, Strike Comd, 1970–72. Dep. Controller, 1972–74, Controller, 1974–77, Nat. Air

Traffic Services; Mem., CAA Bd, 1974–77. Dir, Plessey Airports Ltd, 1982–86. Pres., Mosquito Aircrew Assoc., 1993–. Vice–Pres., RAFA, 1981–. President: Pathfinder Assoc., 1990–93; Blenheim Soc., 1990–. QCVSA 1955. *Recreations:* golf, skiing. *Address:* Cherry Lawn, Bridle Lane, Loudwater, Rickmansworth, Herts WD3 4JB. *Clubs:* Royal Air Force; Moor Park Golf (Pres., 1992–97).
Died 24 Jan. 2003.

BROSAN, Dr George Stephen, CBE 1982; TD 1960; Director, North East London Polytechnic, 1970–82; *b* 8 Aug. 1921; *o s* of Rudolph and Margaret Brosan; *m* 1952, Maureen Dorothy Foscoe; three *d*. *Educ:* Kilburn Grammar Sch.; Faraday House; The Polytechnic; Birkbeck Coll., London. Faraday Scholar, 1939. PhD 1951; DFH 1957; CEng 1976, Eur Ing 1989, Hon. FIEE 1991 (FIEE 1964); CMath 1982; MRIN 1983. Teaching staff, Regent Street Polytechnic, 1950–58; Head of Dept, Willesden Coll. of Technology, 1958–60; Further Educn Officer, Middlesex CC, 1960–62; Principal, Enfield Coll. of Technology, 1962–70. Pres., Tensor Club of GB, 1973–82; Pres., IProdE, 1975–77 (Hon. FIProdE 1980–91); Mem. Council, BIM, 1975–79; Chairman: CEI Educn Cttee, 1978–79; Accountancy Educn Consultative Bd, 1979–82. Life Mem., ASME, 1977. Hon. MIED 1967; Hon. Mem., Council for Educn in the Commonwealth, 1983. CIMgt (FBIM 1975). Chevalier du Tastevin, 1976; Yachtmaster Ocean, 1986. *Publications:* (jtly) Advanced Electrical Power and Machines, 1966; (jtly) Patterns and Policies in Higher Education, 1971; numerous articles and papers in academic and professional press. *Recreation:* computing. *Address:* Winton Dene, Ashen, Sudbury, Suffolk CO10 8JN; Tartagli Alti, Paciano 06060, Province of Perugia, Italy. *Club:* Reform.
Died 31 Oct. 2001.

BROTHERHOOD, Air Cdre William Rowland, CBE 1952; Director, Guided Weapons (Trials), Ministry of Aviation (formerly Supply), 1959–61; *b* 22 Jan. 1912; *s* of late James Brotherhood, Tintern, Mon.; *m* 1939, Margaret (*d* 1981), *d* of late Ernest Sutcliffe, Louth, Lincs; one *s* one *d*. *Educ:* Monmouth School; RAF College, Cranwell. Joined RAF, 1930; Group Captain, 1943; Air Commodore, 1955; Director, Operational Requirements, Air Ministry, 1955–58. *Address:* Fisherman's Cottage, 25 Dial Close, Seend, Melksham, Wilts SN12 6NP. *T:* (01380) 828189.
Died 1 Aug. 2003.

BROUGH, Michael David, FRCS; Consultant Plastic Surgeon: University College London Hospitals, Royal Free and Whittington Hospitals, since 1982; St Luke's Hospital for the Clergy, since 1986; King Edward VII's Hospital for Officers, since 1992; *b* 4 July 1942; *s* of late Kenneth David Brough and Frances Elizabeth Brough (*née* Davies); *m* 1974, Dr Geraldine Moira Sleigh; two *s* two *d*. *Educ:* Westminster Sch.; Christ's Coll., Cambridge (MA); Middlesex Hosp. Med. Sch. (MB, BChir). Med. posts at Middlesex and Central Middlesex Hosps, 1968–71; Surgical trng posts, Birmingham Hosps, 1971–74; Plastic Surgery trng posts, Mount Vernon Hosp., London, Odstock Hosp., Salisbury, Withington Hosp., Manchester, 1975–80; Cons. Plastic Surg., St Andrews Hosp., Billericay, Queen Elizabeth Hosp., Hackney, Whipps Cross Hosp., 1980–82. Hon. Sen. Lectr in Plastic Surgery, London Univ., 1985–. Hon. Sec., Phoenix Appeal, 1988–95. President: Plastic Surg. Sect., RSM, 1990–91; BAPS, 2002. Vice-Pres., Healing Foundn, 2003–. *Publications:* chapters in books; contribs to med. jls on plastic and reconstructive surgery. *Recreations:* family, skiing, Modern Pentathlon Half-Blue, 1964. *Address:* The Consulting Suite, 82 Portland Place, W1B 1NS. *T:* (020) 7935 8910. *Club:* Hawks (Cambridge).
Died 18 Nov. 2004.

BROWN, Gen. Arnold, OC 1982; International Leader, and General, Salvation Army, 1977–81; *b* 13 Dec. 1913; *s* of Arnold Rees Brown and Annie Brown; *m* 1939, Jean Catherine Barclay; two *d*. *Educ:* Belleville Collegiate, Canada. Commnd Salvation Army Officer, 1935; Editor,

Canadian War Cry, 1937–47; Nat. Publicity Officer, Canada, 1947–62; Nat. Youth Officer, Canada, 1962–64; Head of Internat. Public Relations, Internat. HQ, London, 1964–69; Chief of Staff, 1969–74; Territorial Comdr, Canada and Bermuda, 1974–77. Freeman, City of London, 1978. Hon. LHD Asbury Coll., USA, 1972; Hon. DD Olivet Coll., USA, 1981. *Publications:* What Hath God Wrought?, 1952; The Gate and the Light, 1984; Fighting for His Glory, 1988; Yin: the mountain the wind blew here, 1988; With Christ at the Table, 1991; Occupied Manager—Unoccupied Tomb, 1994; Reading Between the Lines, 1997. *Recreations:* reading, writing, music. *Address:* 1200 Don Mills Road, Suite 416, North York, ON M3B 3N8, Canada. *Club:* Rotary of London and Toronto. *Died 26 June 2002.*

BROWN, Prof. Arthur Joseph, CBE 1974; FBA 1972; Professor of Economics, University of Leeds, 1947–79, then Emeritus (Head, Department of Economics and Commerce, 1947–65); Pro-Vice-Chancellor, Leeds University, 1975–77; *b* 8 Aug. 1914; *s* of J. Brown, Alderley Edge, Cheshire; *m* 1938, Joan H. M., *d* of Rev. Canon B. E. Taylor, Holy Trinity, Walton Breck, Liverpool; two *s* (and one *s* decd). *Educ:* Bradford Grammar Sch.; Queen's Coll., Oxford (BA 1st cl. Hons PPE 1936, MA 1939; Hon. Fellow, 1985); DPhil Oxon 1939. Fellow of All Souls Coll., Oxford, 1937–46; Lectr in Economics, Hertford Coll., Oxford, 1937–40; on staff of: Foreign Research and Press Service, 1940–43; Foreign Office Research Dept, 1943–45; Economic Section, Offices of the Cabinet, 1945–47. Visiting Professor: of Economics, Columbia Univ., City of New York, Jan.-June 1950; ANU, 1963. Member: East African Economic and Fiscal Commn, 1960; UN Consultative Group on Economic and Social Consequences of Disarmament, 1961–62; First Secretary of State's Adv. Gp on Central Africa, 1962; Hunt Cttee on Intermediate Areas, 1967–69; UGC, 1969–78 (Vice-Chm., 1977–78); Chm., Adv. Panel on Student Maintenance Grants, 1967–68; directing Regional Economics project, NIESR, 1966–72. President: Section F, British Assoc. for the Advancement of Science, 1958; Royal Economic Soc., 1976–78 (Vice-Pres., 1978–). Hon. DLitt: Bradford, 1975; Kent, 1979; Hon. LLD Aberdeen, 1978; Hon. LittD Sheffield, 1979. *Publications:* Industrialisation and Trade, 1943; Applied Economics-Aspects of the World Economy in War and Peace, 1948; The Great Inflation, 1939–51, 1955; Introduction to the World Economy, 1959; The Framework of Regional Economics in the United Kingdom, 1972; (with E. M. Burrows) Regional Economic Problems, 1977; (with J. Darby) World Inflation since 1950: a comparative international study, 1985; articles in various journals. *Recreations:* gardening, walking. *Address:* 24 Moor Drive, Leeds LS6 4BY. *T:* (0113) 275 5799. *Club:* Athenæum.
Died 28 Feb. 2003.

BROWN, Carter; *see* Brown, John C.

BROWN, David K.; *see* Kennett Brown.

BROWN, Vice-Adm. Sir David (Worthington), KCB 1984; *b* 28 Nov. 1927; *s* of late Captain J. R. S. Brown, RN and of Mrs D. M. E. Brown; *m* 1958, Etienne Hester Boileau; three *d*. *Educ:* HMS Conway. Joined RN, 1945; commanded HM Ships MGB 5036, MTB 5020, Dalswinton, Chailey, Cavendish, Falmouth, Hermione, Bristol; Dir, Naval Ops and Trade, 1971–72; Dir of Officers Appointments (Exec.), 1976–78; Asst Chief of Defence Staff (Ops), 1980–82; Flag Officer Plymouth, Port Adm. Devonport, 1982–85. Pres., Portsmouth Services Fly Fishing Assoc., 1995-2005. Younger Brother of Trinity House, 1965. *Recreation:* fishing. *Club:* Army and Navy. *Died 13 July 2005.*

BROWN, Prof. Fred, OBE 1999; FRS 1981; Professorial Fellow, Queen's University, Belfast, since 1986; *b* 31 Jan. 1925; *m* 1948, Audrey Alice Doherty; two *s*. *Educ:* Burnley Grammar Sch.; Manchester Univ. (BSc 1944, MSc 1946,

PhD 1948). Asst Lectr, Manchester Univ., 1946–48; Lectr, Bristol Univ. Food Preservation Res. Station, 1948–50; Senior Scientific Officer: Hannah Dairy Res. Inst., Ayr, 1950–53; Christie Hosp. and Holt Radium Inst., Manchester, 1953–55; Head, Biochemistry Dept, 1955–83, and Dep. Dir, 1980–83, Animal Virus Res. Inst., Pirbright, Surrey; Hd of Virology Div., Wellcome Res. Labs, Beckenham, Kent, 1983–90; Prof. of Microbiology, Univ. of Surrey, 1989–90; Adjunct Prof., Sch. of Epidemiology and Public Health, Yale Univ., 1990–95. Vis. Scientist, US Dept of Agric., Plum Is. Animal Disease Center, NY, 1995–. Mem., Spongiform Encephalopathy Adv. Cttee, 1990–98. Hon. DSc QUB, 1992. *Publications:* papers on viruses causing animal diseases, in scientific journals. *Recreations:* watching cricket, Association football, listening to classical music, fell walking. *Address:* Syndal, Glaziers Lane, Normandy, Surrey GU3 2DF. *T:* (01483) 811107. *Died 20 Feb. 2004.*

BROWN, Hanbury; *see* Brown, R. H.

BROWN, Harold Arthur Neville, CMG 1963; CVO 1961; HM Diplomatic Service, retired; *b* 13 Dec. 1914; *s* of Stanley Raymond and Gladys Maud Brown; *m* 1939, Mary McBeath Urquhart (*d* 1994); one *s* one *d*. *Educ:* Cardiff High School; University College, Cardiff. Entered Ministry of Labour as 3rd Class Officer, 1939; Asst Principal, 1943; Private Sec. to Permanent Sec. of Min. of Labour and Nat. Service, 1944–46; Principal, 1946; Labour Attaché, Mexico City (and other countries in Central America and the Caribbean), 1950–54; transferred to Foreign Office, 1955; Head of Chancery, Rangoon, 1958 and 1959; British Ambassador in Liberia, 1960–63; Corps of Inspectors, Foreign Office, 1963–66; Ambassador to Cambodia, 1966–70; Consul-General, Johannesburg, 1970–73; Minister, Pretoria, Cape Town, 1973–74. Knight Great Band of the Humane Order of African Redemption, 1962. *Address:* 14 Embassy Court, King's Road, Brighton BN1 2PX. *Died 31 Aug. 2004.*

BROWN, Prof. Herbert Charles, PhD; R. B. Wetherill Research Professor Emeritus, Purdue University, 1978–2003 (Professor, 1947–60, R. B. Wetherill Research Professor, 1960–78); *b* 22 May 1912; *s* of Charles Brown and Pearl (*née* Gorinstein); *m* 1937, Sarah Baylen; one *s*. *Educ:* Wright Jun. Coll., Chicago (Assoc. Sci. 1935); Univ. of Chicago (BS 1936; PhD 1938). University of Chicago: Eli Lilly Postdoctoral Res. Fellow, 1938–39; Instr, 1939–43; Wayne University: Asst Prof., 1943–46; Associate Prof., 1946–47. Member: Nat. Acad. of Sciences, USA, 1957–; Amer. Acad. of Arts and Sciences, 1966–; Hon. Mem., Phi Lambda Upsilon, 1961–; Hon. Fellow, Chem. Soc., London, 1978– (Centenary Lectr, 1955; C. K. Ingold Medal, 1978); Foreign Fellow, Indian Nat. Science Acad., 1978–. Hon. Dr of Science: Chicago, 1968; Wayne State, 1980; Hebrew Univ. Jerusalem, 1980; Pontifica Univ. Catolica de Chile, 1980; Wales, 1982; Purdue, 1982, etc. (Jtly) Nobel Prize in Chemistry, 1979. American Chemical Society: Harrison Howe Award, Rochester Sect., 1953; Nichols Medal, NY Sect., 1959; Linus Pauling Medal, Oregon and Puget Sound Sects, 1968; Roger Adams Medal, Organic Div., 1971; Priestley Medal, 1981; Oesper Award, Cincinnati Sect., 1990; Herbert C. Brown Medal and Award, 1998. Award for Creative Res. in Org. Chem., Soc. of Organic Chem. Mfg Assoc., 1960; Herbert Newby McCoy Award, Purdue Univ., 1965 (1st co-recipient); Nat. Medal of Science, US Govt, 1969; Madison Marshall Award, 1975; Allied Chemical Award for Grad. Trng and Innovative Chem., 1978 (1st recipient); Perkins Medal, Amer. Sect., Soc. of Chemical Industry, 1982; Gold Medal, Amer. Inst. Chem., 1985; Chem. Sci. Award, Nat. Acad. of Scis, 1987; G. M. Kossolopoff Medal, Auburn Sect., Amer. Chem. Soc., 1987. Order of the Rising Sun, Gold and Silver Star (Japan), 1989. *Publications:* Hydroboration, 1962; Boranes in Organic Chemistry, 1972; Organic Syntheses via Boranes, 1975; The Non-classical Ion Problem, 1977; (with A. Pelter and K. Smith) Borane Reagents, 1988;

(jtly) Organic Synthesis via Boranes: recent developments, 2002; (with A. Suzuki) Suzuki Coupling, 2003; over 1260 scientific articles in Jl Amer. Chem. Soc., Jl Org. Chemistry, Jl Organometal. Chemistry, and Synthesis. *Recreations:* travel, photography. *Address:* Department of Chemistry, Purdue University, West Lafayette, IN 47907, USA. *T:* (317) 4945316. *Died 19 Dec. 2004.*

BROWN, (John) Carter, Hon. CBE 1993; Director, National Gallery of Art, Washington, DC, 1969–92, then Director Emeritus; Chairman: US Commission of Fine Arts, since 1971; Ovation Inc., the Arts Network, since 1993; *b* 8 Oct. 1934; *s* of John Nicholas Brown and Anne Kinsolving Brown; *m* 1st, 1971, Constance Mellon (marr. diss. 1973); 2nd, 1976, Pamela Braga Drexel (marr. diss. 1991); one *s* one *d*. *Educ:* Harvard (AB *summa cum laude* 1956; MBA 1958); Inst. of Fine Arts, NY Univ. (Museum Trng Prog., Metropol. Museum of Art; MA 1961). Studied: with Bernard Berenson, Florence, 1958; Ecole du Louvre, Paris, 1958–59; Rijksbureau voor Kunsthistorische Documentatie, The Hague, 1960. National Gallery of Art: Asst to Dir, 1961–63; Asst Dir, 1964–68; Dep. Dir, 1968–69. Mem., Federal Council on Arts and Humanities, 1971–. Treas., White House Historical Assoc., 1969–; Mem., Cttee for Preservation of the White House. Mem. Bd of Govs, John Carter Brown Liby; Trustee: Doris Duke Charitable Foundn; John F. Kennedy Center for Performing Arts; Nat. Geographic Soc.; Storm King Art Center; World Monuments Fund; Newport Restoration Foundn. Chm., Pritzker Prize Jury, 1979–. Mem., Amer. Philosophical Soc., 1992; Fellow, Amer. Acad. of Arts and Scis, 1993; Hon. Mem., Amer. Inst. of Architects, 1975; Hon. FRA 1991. Holds 17 hon. degrees. Gold Medal of Honor, National Arts Soc., 1972; Gold Medal of Honor, Nat. Inst. of Social Sciences, 1987; Nat. Medal of Arts, USA, 1991. Commandeur, l'Ordre des Arts et des Lettres, France, 1975; Chevalier de la Légion d'Honneur, France, 1976; Knight, Order of St Olav, Norway, 1979; Comdr, Order of the Republic, Egypt, 1979; Comdr, Order of Orange-Nassau, Netherlands, 1982; Commendatore, Order of Merit of Italian Republic, 1984; Kt Comdr, Order of Isabel la Católica, Spain, 1985; Austrian Cross of Honor for Arts and Letters, 1986; Comdr, Royal Order of the Polar Star, Sweden, 1988; Grande Oficial, Order of Prince Henry the Navigator, Portugal, 1992. Phi Beta Kappa, 1956. Author/ Dir, (film), The American Vision, 1966; author and narrator, (TV), Rings of Passion: five emotions in world art, 1997–. *Publications:* Rings: five passions in world art, 1996; contrib. professional jls and exhibn catalogues. *Recreations:* sailing, photography. *Address:* (office) Suite 621, 1201 Pennsylvania Avenue NW, Washington, DC 20004, USA. *Clubs:* Knickerbocker, New York Yacht (New York). *Died 17 June 2002.*

BROWN, Sir John (Gilbert Newton), Kt 1974; CBE 1966; Vice President, Blackwell Group Ltd, since 1987 (Director, 1980–87); *b* 7 July 1916; *s* of John and Molly Brown, Chilham, Kent; *m* 1946, Virginia, *d* of late Darcy Braddell and Dorothy Braddell; one *s* two *d*. *Educ:* Lancing Coll.; Hertford Coll., Oxford (MA Zoology). Bombay Branch, Oxford University Press, 1937–40; commissioned Royal Artillery, 1941; served with 5th Field Regiment, 1941–46; captured by the Japanese at Fall of Singapore, 1942; prisoner of war, Malaya, Formosa and Japan, 1942–45; returned Oxford University Press, 1946; Sales Manager, 1949; Publisher, 1956–80; Chm., University Bookshops (Oxford) Ltd; Chm., 1980–83, Dep. Chm., 1983–87, Dir, 1980–87, B. H. Blackwell Ltd; Chm., 1983–85, Dir, 1983–87, Basil Blackwell Ltd (formerly Basil Blackwell Publisher Ltd); Director: Willshaw Booksellers Ltd, Manchester, 1966–89; Book Tokens Ltd, 1973–89; Archival Facsimiles Ltd, 1986–89; John Brown Publishing Ltd, 1989–. Pres., Publishers' Assoc., 1963–65. Member: Nat. Libraries Cttee; EDC for Newspapers, Printing and Publishing Industry, 1967–70; Adv. Cttee on Scientific and Technical Information, 1969–73; Communication Adv. Cttee for UK Nat. Cttee for

UNESCO; Royal Literary Fund (Asst Treasurer); Bd of British Library, 1973–79; Royal Soc. Cttee on Scientific Information; Bd, British Council, 1968–81; Open Univ. Visiting Cttee. Professorial Fellow, Hertford Coll., Oxford, 1974–80. FRSA 1964. *Address:* Milton Lodge, Great Milton, Oxford OX44 7NJ. *T:* (01844) 279217. *Club:* Garrick.   *Died 3 March 2003.*

BROWN, Ven. Michael René Warneford; Archdeacon of Nottingham, 1960–77, then Archdeacon Emeritus; *b* 7 June 1915; *s* of late George and Irene Brown; *m* 1978, Marie Joyce Chaloner, *d* of late Walter Dawson, and of Sarah Dawson, Burbage, Leics; three step *s. Educ:* King's School, Rochester; St Peter's College, Oxford; St Stephen's House, Oxford (MA). Deacon 1941; priest, 1942; Asst Master, Christ's Hospital, 1939–43; Curate of West Grinstead, 1941–43. Chap. RNVR, 1943–46; chaplain and Dean of St Peter's College and Curate of St Mary the Virgin, Oxford, 1946; Lecturer, RN College, Greenwich, 1946–47; Librarian, 1948–50 and Fellow, 1948–52, of St Augustine's Coll., Canterbury; Priest-in-charge of Bekesbourne, 1948–50; Asst Secretary, CACTM, 1950–60. Examining Chaplain: to Bishop of Southwell, 1954–77; to Archbishop of Canterbury, 1959–60; Commissary to Bishop of Waikato, 1958–70; Hon. Officiating Chaplain, RM, Deal, Kent, 1987–96. Member: Church of England Pensions Board, 1966–84; Church Commissioners' Redundant Churches Cttee, 1978–88; Chm., Redundant Churches' Uses Cttee in Canterbury Dio., 1980–89; Vice-Chm., Diocesan Adv. Cttee for the Care of Churches, 1980–93; Church Commissioner, 1968–78. *Recreations:* antiquarian and aesthetic, especially English paintings and silver. *Address:* Faygate, 72 Liverpool Road, Walmer, Deal, Kent CT14 7LR. *T:* (01304) 361326. *Club:* Athenæum.
       Died 14 Feb. 2004.

BROWN, Hon. Sir Ralph Kilner, Kt 1970; OBE (mil.) 1945; TD 1952; DL; a Judge of the High Court, Queen's Bench Division, 1970–84; a Judge of Employment Appeal Tribunal, 1976–84; *b* 28 Aug. 1909; *s* of Rev. A. E. Brown, CIE, MA, BSc; *m* 1943, Cynthia Rosemary Breffit; one *s* two *d. Educ:* Kingswood School; Trinity Hall, Cambridge (Squire Law Scholar; MA). TA 1938; War Service, 1939–46; DAQMG NW Europe Plans; DAAG HQ53 (Welsh) Div.; AQMG (Planning), COSSAC; Col Q (Ops) and Brig. Q Staff HQ 21 Army Group (despatches, OBE); Hon. Col, TARO, 1952. Barrister, Middle Temple (Harmsworth Scholar; Bencher, 1964; Master Reader, 1982); Midland Circuit, 1934 and Northern Circuit, 1975; QC 1958; Recorder of Lincoln, 1960–64; Recorder of Birmingham, 1964–65; Chairman, Warwicks QS, 1964–67 (Dep. Chm., 1954–64); a Judge of the Central Criminal Court, 1965–67; Recorder of Liverpool, and Judge of the Crown Court at Liverpool, 1967–69; Presiding Judge, N Circuit, 1970–75. Chairman, Mental Health Review Tribunal, Birmingham RHB Area, 1962–65. Contested (L):Oldbury and Halesowen, 1945 and 1950; South Bucks, 1959 and 1964. President: Birmingham Liberal Organisation, 1946–56; (and Chm.), W Midland Liberal Fedn, 1950–56; Mem., Liberal Party Exec., 1950–56. Pres., Birmingham Bn, Boys Bde, 1946–56; Mem., Exec., Boys Bde, 1950–55. Former Member: CCPR; Cttee of RNIB; Cttee of RNID. Former Mem., Governing Body, Kingswood Sch. DL Warwickshire, 1956. Guild of Freemen, City of London. *Publications:* The Office of Reader in the Middle Temple, 1982; Top Brass and No Brass, 1991. *Recreations:* watching athletics (represented Cambridge University and Great Britain; British AAA Champion 440 yds hurdles, 1934); cricket, Rugby football. *Address:* 174 Defoe House, Barbican, EC2Y 8ND. *Clubs:* Naval and Military; Hawks (Cambridge).   *Died 12 June 2003.*

BROWN, Prof. Robert Hanbury, AC 1986; FRS 1960; Professor of Physics (Astronomy), in the University of Sydney, 1964–81, then Emeritus Professor; *b* 31 Aug. 1916; *s* of Colonel Basil Hanbury Brown and Joyce Blaker;

m 1952, Hilda Heather Chesterman; twin *s* one *d. Educ:* Tonbridge School; Brighton Technical College; City and Guilds College, London. BSc (Eng), London (external), 1935; DIC, 1936; DSc Manchester, 1960. MIEE, 1938. Air Ministry, Bawdsey Research Station, working on radar, 1936–42; British Air Commission, Washington, DC, 1942–45; Principal Scientific Officer, Ministry of Supply, 1945–47; Consulting Engineer, Sir Robert Watson-Watt and partners, 1947–49; ICI Research Fellow of Manchester University, 1949; Professor of Radio-Astronomy in the University of Manchester, 1960–63. Pres., Internat. Astronomical Union, 1982–85. ARAS 1986; FAA 1967. Hon. Mem., Aust. Optical Soc., 1987; Hon. MRIN 1997; Hon. FNA 1975; Hon. FASc 1975; Hon. Fellow, Royal Astronomical Soc. of Canada, Astronomical Soc. of India, 1987. Hon. DSc: Sydney, 1984; Monash, 1984. Holweck Prize, 1959; Eddington Medal, 1968; Lyle Medal, 1971; Britannica Australia Award, 1971; Hughes Medal, 1971; Michelson Medal, Franklin Inst., 1982; ANZAAS Medal, 1987. *Publications:* The Exploration of Space by Radio, 1957; The Intensity Interferometer, 1974; Man and the Stars, 1978; Photons, Galaxies and Stars, 1985; Wisdom of Science, 1986; Boffin, 1991; publications in Physical and Astronomical Journals. *Address:* White Cottage, Penton Mewsey, Andover, Hants SP11 0RQ.   *Died 16 Jan. 2002.*

BROWN, Robert Ross Buchanan, CBE 1968; CEng, FIEE; Chairman, Southern Electricity Board, 1954–74; *b* 15 July 1909; 2nd *s* of Robert and Rhoda Brown, Sydney, Australia; *m* 1940, Ruth Sarah Aird; one *s* two *d. Educ:* The King's School, Sydney; Sydney Univ. (BSc); Emmanuel Coll., Cambridge Univ. (BA 1932). Captain 4th County of London Yeomanry, 1940–45. Dep. Gen. Manager, 1938, Gen. Manager, 1945, Wessex Electricity Co.; Dep. Chm., Southern Electricity Board, 1948. *Recreations:* gardening, golf. *Address:* Mumbery Lodge, School Hill, Wargrave, Reading, Berks RG10 8DY.
       Died 7 Sept. 2001.

BROWN, Ven. Robert Saville; Archdeacon of Bedford, 1974–79, Archdeacon Emeritus since 1979; *b* 12 Sept. 1914; *s* of late John Harold Brown and Frances May Brown; *m* 1947, Charlotte, *d* of late Percy John and Edith Furber; one *s. Educ:* Bedford Modern Sch.; Selwyn Coll., Cambridge (MA). Deacon 1940, priest 1941; Curate: Gt Berkhamsted, 1940–44; St Mary's, Hitchin, 1944–47; Vicar, Wonersh, 1947–53; Rector, Gt Berkhamsted, 1953–69; Canon of St Albans Cath., 1965; Vicar of St Paul's, Bedford, 1969–74; Priest-in-Charge of Old Warden, 1974–79. *Recreations:* reading, travel, chess. *Address:* The Rowans, 29 The Rise, Amersham, Bucks HP7 9AG. *T:* (01494) 728376.   *Died 20 April 2001.*

BROWN, Ronald William; JP; consultant, since 1991; Deputy Director General, Federation of Master Builders, 1987–91 (Director of Industrial Relations, 1984–87); *b* 7 Sept. 1921; *s* of George Brown; *m* 1944, Mary Munn; one *s* two *d. Educ:* Elementary School, South London; Borough Polytechnic. Sen. Lectr in Electrical Engineering, Principal of Industrial Training Sch. Leader of Opposition, Wanstead and Woodford BC, 1953–56; Leader, Camberwell Borough Council, 1956; Alderman and Leader, London Bor. of Southwark, 1964–74. MP Shoreditch and Finsbury, 1964–74, Hackney South and Shoreditch, 1974–83 (Lab, 1964–81, SDP, 1981–83); Asst Govt Whip, 1966–67; contested (SDP) Hackney South and Shoreditch, 1983. Member: Council of Europe Assembly and WEU, 1965–76; European Parlt, 1977–79. Chm., Energy Commn, Rapporteur on Science, Technology and Aerospace questions; Parly Advr to Furniture, Timber and Allied Trades Union, 1967–81. Member: Council of Europe, 1979–83; WEU, 1979–83. Member: Bldg Cttee, Construction ITB, 1985–90; NW Thames RHA, 1974–88; E London and City HA Local Res. and Ethics Cttee, 1994–. St Bartholomew's Hospital: Member: Bd of Govs, 1964–74; Jt Res. Bd, 1980–; Local Res. and Ethics Cttee, 1980–94 (Vice-Chm., 1992–94); St

Bartholomew's Hospital Medical College: Gov., 1974–95; Mem. Exec. Cttee, 1978–95; Treas., 1978–86. Trustee: St Mark's Res. Foundn, 1974–2001; St Mark's Educnl Trust, 1995–2001. Estate Gov., Alleyn's Coll. of God's Gift, 1961–82 (Chm., Bd of Govs, 1976–78). FCMI. JP Co. London, 1961. *Address:* 45 Innings Drive, Pevensey Bay, E Sussex BN24 6BH. *Died 27 July 2002.*

BROWN, Ronald William; Deputy Legal Adviser and Solicitor to Ministry of Agriculture, Fisheries and Food, to Forestry Commission and to (EEC) Intervention Board for Agricultural Produce, 1974–82; *b* 21 April 1917; *o s* of late William Nicol Brown and Eleanor Brown (*née* Dobson); *m* 1958, Elsie Joyce (*d* 1983), *er d* of Sir Norman Guttery, KBE, CB and Lady Guttery (*née* Crankshaw); two *s. Educ:* Dover Coll.; Corpus Christi Coll., Cambridge (MA). Served War, 1939–45, King's Own Royal Regt (Lancaster), France, W Desert, Burma (Chindits) (Major). Called to the Bar, Gray's Inn, 1946. Entered Legal Dept, Min. of Agric. and Fisheries, 1948; Asst Solicitor, MAFF, 1970. *Address:* 18 Tracery, Park Road, Banstead, Surrey SM7 3DD. *T:* (01737) 358569. *Club:* Royal Automobile. *Died 25 Jan. 2005.*

BROWN, Sir Thomas, Kt 1974; Chairman, Eastern Health and Social Services Board, Northern Ireland (formerly NI Hospitals Authority), 1967–84, retired; *b* 11 Oct. 1915; *s* of Ephraim Hugh and Elizabeth Brown; *m* 1988, Dr Eleanor A. Thompson. *Educ:* Royal Belfast Academical Institution. Admitted Solicitor, 1938. Mem., Royal Commn on NHS, 1976–79. *Recreation:* boating. *Died 8 Nov. 2003.*

BROWN, Dr William Christopher, OBE 1966; RDI 1977; Founder, Brown Beech & Associates, 1987; *b* 16 Sept. 1928; *s* of William Edward Brown and Margaret Eliza Brown; *m* 1964, Celia Hermione Emmett. *Educ:* Monmouth Sch.; University Coll., Southampton (BScEng); Imperial Coll. of Science and Technol., London (DIC); FIC 1987. Partner, Freeman, Fox & Partners, 1970–85. Principal designer for major bridges, incl.: Volta River, 1956; Forth Road, 1964; Severn and Wye, 1966; Auckland Harbour, 1969; Erskine, 1971; Bosporus, 1973; Avonmouth, 1975; Humber, 1981; Bosporus 2, 1988. Holds patents on new concepts for long-span bridges, incl. Messina Straits. Designer for radio telescopes in Australia and Canada, and for other special structures. Master, Faculty of RDI, 1983–85. Hon. FRIBA 1978. Hon. Dr: Bosporus Univ., 1988; RCA, 1998. McRobert Award, 1970; Construction Industry Award, Engrg News Record, 1989; Gustave Trasenster Medal, Liège Univ., 1992; UK and European steel design awards, 1968, 1971, 1976; John A. Roebling Medal, MSA, 2004. *Publications:* technical papers for engrg instns in UK and abroad. *Recreations:* archaeology, photography, motoring. *Address:* 1 Allen Mansions, Allen Street, W8 6UY. *T:* (020) 7937 6550. *Club:* Royal Over-Seas League.

Died 16 March 2005.

BROWN, Rev. William Martyn; *b* 12 July 1914; *s* of Edward Brown, artist; *m* 1939, Elizabeth Lucy Hill; one adopted *s. Educ:* Bedford School; Pembroke College, Cambridge (Scholar; 1st Class Honours in Modern Languages, 1936, MA 1947). Assistant Master, Wellington College, 1936–47; Housemaster 1943–47; Headmaster: The King's School, Ely, 1947–55; Bedford School, 1955–75. Commissioner of the Peace, 1954. Ordained 1976; Priest-in-charge, Field Dalling and Saxlingham, 1977–84; RD of Holt, 1984–88. *Recreation:* watercolour painting. *Address:* Lodge Cottage, Field Dalling, Holt, Norfolk NR25 7AS. *T:* (01328) 830403.

Died 14 Dec. 2005.

BROWNE, Andrew Harold; full-time Chairman of Industrial Tribunals, Nottingham Region, 1983–96 (part-time Chairman, 1975–83); *b* 2 Dec. 1923; *s* of late Harold and Ada Caroline Browne; *m* 1951, Jocelyn Mary Vade Ashmead; two *s* one *d. Educ:* Repton; Trinity Hall, Cambridge (MA). ACIArb 1983. Served Royal Navy,

1942–46; Lieut RNVR. Admitted Solicitor, 1950; Partner in firm of Wells & Hind, Nottingham, 1952–83. Dep. Clerk of the Peace, Nottingham QS, 1951–55. Chairman, National Insurance Local Tribunal, Nottingham, 1965–83; Member, E Midland Rent Assessment Panel, 1966–83 (Vice-Pres., 1972–83). Lay Chm., Bingham Deanery Synod, 1987–96. Chm., Reserve Forces Reinstatement Cttee, 1991–93. Hon. Mem., Notts Law Soc., 1996. *Recreations:* rural England, organ music. *Address:* The House in the Garden, Elton, near Nottingham NG13 9LA. *T:* (01949) 850419. *Club:* Aula.

Died 7 Aug. 2004.

BROWNE, Percy Basil; DL; retired farmer; Chairman, Devon & Exeter Steeplechases Ltd, 1990–96; *b* 2 May 1923; *s* of late Captain W. P. Browne, MC; *m* 1st, 1947, Pamela Exham (*d* 1951); one *s*; 2nd, 1953, Jenefer Petherick (marr. diss. 1991); two *s* one *d*; 3rd, 1991, Susan, *widow* of Rupert Arkell. *Educ:* The Downs, Colwall; Eton College. Served War of 1939–45 with Royal Dragoons in Italy and NW Europe. Rode in Grand National, 1953. MP (C) Torrington Division of Devon, 1959–64. Dir, Appledore Shipbuilders Ltd, 1965–72 (former Chm.); Chairman: N Devon Meat Ltd, 1982–86; Western Counties Bldg Soc., 1983–85; West of England Bldg Soc., 1987–89 (Vice-Chm., 1985–87); Vice-Chm., Regency & West of England Bldg Soc., 1989–90. Mem., SW Reg. Hosp. Bd, 1967–70. Chm., Minister of Agriculture's SW Regl Panel, 1985–88. High Sheriff, Devon, 1978; DL Devon, 1984. *Address:* Newtown Farm, Semington, Trowbridge BA14 6JU. *T:* (01225) 708082.

Died 5 March 2004.

BROWSE, Lillian Gertrude, CBE 1998; author; private archivist; *b* 21 April 1906; *d* of Michael Browse and Gladys Browse (*née* Meredith); *m* 1st, 1934, Ivan H. Joseph; 2nd, 1964, Sidney H. Lines (decd). *Educ:* Barnato Park, Johannesburg. Studied with Margaret Craske at Cecchetti Ballet Sch., London, 1928–30; joined Dolin-Nemtchinova ballet co., 1930; gave up ballet and worked at Leger Galls, London, 1931–39; organised war-time exhbns at Nat. Gall. and travelling exhibns for CEMA, 1940–45, also exhibns for Inst. of Adult Educn; Organising Sec., Red Cross picture sale, Christie's, 1942; founder partner, Roland, Browse & Delbanco, 1945; Founder Dir, Browse & Darby, 1977–81. Ballet Critic, Spectator, 1950–54. Organised: Sickert exhbn, Edinburgh, 1953; Sickert centenary exhbn, Tate Gall., 1960; exhibited own private collection at Courtauld Inst. Galls, 1983. Hon. Fellow, Courtauld Inst., 1986. *Publications:* Augustus John Drawings, 1941; Sickert, 1943; (ed) Ariel Books on the Arts, 1946; Degas Dancers, 1949; William Nicholson: Catalogue Raisonné, 1955; Sickert, 1960; Forain, 1978; Duchess of Cork Street: an autobiography of an art dealer, 1999; preface to Degas and the Dance, by Richard Kendall and Jill de Vonyar, 2002; contribs to Apollo, Sunday Times, Country Life, Burlington Magazine and various articles. *Recreation:* gardening.

Died 2 Dec. 2005.

BRUCE OF DONINGTON, Baron *cr* 1974 (Life Peer), of Rickmansworth; **Donald William Trevor Bruce;** economist; Chartered Accountant, Baker Tilly; writer; *b* 3 Oct. 1912; *s* of late W. T. Bruce, Norbury, Surrey; *m* 1st, 1939, Joan Letitia Butcher (marr. diss. 1980); one *s* two *d* (and one *d* decd); 2nd, 1981, Cyrena Shaw Heard. *Educ:* Grammar School, Donington, Lincs. FCA 1947. Re-joined Territorial Army, March 1939; commissioned, Nov. 1939; Major, 1942; served at home and in France until May 1945 (despatches). MP (Lab) for North Portsmouth, 1945–50; Parliamentary Private Sec. to Minister of Health, 1945–50; Member: Min. of Health delegn to Sweden and Denmark, 1946; House of Commons Select Cttee on Public Accounts, 1948–50. MEP, 1975–79. Opposition spokesman on Treasury, economic and industrial questions, House of Lords, 1979–83, on trade and industry, 1983–86, on Treasury and economic questions, 1986–90. *Publications:* (jtly) The State of the Nation, 1997; miscellaneous contributions on political science and economics to newspapers and periodicals. *Address:* Hobson House, 2 Bloomsbury Street, WC1B 3ST.   *Died 18 April 2005.*

BRUCE, George Robert, OBE 1984; poet and critic; *b* 10 March 1909; *s* of Henry George Bruce and Jeannie Roberta (*née* Gray); *m* 1935, Elizabeth Duncan (*d* 1994); one *s* one *d. Educ:* Fraserburgh Acad.; Aberdeen Univ. (MA 1st Cl. Hons English Lit. and Lang. 1932). Teacher of English and Hist., Dundee High Sch., 1933–46; gen. progs producer, Aberdeen, 1946–56, Features Producer, Edinburgh, 1956–70, BBC; Th. and Literary Critic, Sunday Times, 1964–76; (First) Fellow in Creative Writing, 1971–73, Extramural Lectr, 1973, Glasgow Univ. Visiting Professor: Union Theol Seminary, Richmond, Va, 1974; Coll. of Wooster, Ohio, 1976–77; St Andrews Presbyterian Coll., Laurinburg, N Carolina, 1985. Writer-in-Residence, Prescott Coll., Arizona, 1974; Scottish-Australian Writing Fellow, 1982. Hon. Member: Cockburn Assoc., 1975; Saltire Soc., 1986; Hon. Pres., Scottish Poetry Liby, 1991. Hon. DLitt: Coll. of Wooster, Ohio, 1977; Aberdeen, 2000. *Publications: poetry:* Sea Talk, 1944; Selected Poems, 1947; Landscapes and Figures, 1967; The Collected Poems of George Bruce, 1970; The Red Sky Poems, 1985; Perspective: poems 1970–1986, 1987; Pursuit: poems 1986–1998 (Scottish Book of Year, Saltire Soc.), 1999; Today Tomorrow: the collected poems of George Bruce 1933–2000, 2001; (with John Bellany) Woman of the North Sea (art/poetry), 2001; also ed anthologies of Scottish poetry; *non-fiction:* (with T. S. Halliday) Scottish Sculpture, 1946; Neil M. Gunn, 1971; Anne Redpath, 1974; The City of Edinburgh, 1974, rev. edn 1977; Festival in the North: the story of the Edinburgh Festival, 1975; William Soutar 1898–1943: the man and the poet, 1978; To Foster and Enrich: the first fifty years of the Saltire Society, 1986. *Recreation:* receiving and visiting friends. *Address:* 25 Warriston Crescent, Edinburgh EH3 5LB. *T:* (0131) 556 3848.   *Died 25 July 2002.*

BRUNT, Peter Astbury, FBA 1969; Camden Professor of Ancient History, Oxford University, and Fellow of Brasenose College, 1970–82; *b* 23 June 1917; *s* of Rev. Samuel Brunt, Methodist Minister, and Gladys Eileen Brunt. *Educ:* Ipswich Sch.; Oriel Coll., Oxford (Open Schol. in History, 1935; first classes in Class. Mods, 1937, and Lit. Hum., 1939; Craven Fellowship, 1939). Temp. Asst Principal and (later) Temp. Principal, Min. of Shipping (later War Transport), 1940–45. Sen. Demy, Magdalen Coll., Oxford, 1946; Lectr in Ancient History, St Andrews Univ., 1947–51; Fellow and Tutor of Oriel Coll., Oxford, 1951–67, Dean, 1959–64, Hon. Fellow, 1973; Fellow and Sen. Bursar, Gonville and Caius Coll., Cambridge, 1968–70. Editor of Oxford Magazine, 1963–64; Chm., Cttee on Ashmolean Museum, 1967; Deleg., Clarendon Press, 1971–79; Mem. Council, British Sch. at Rome, 1972–87; Pres., Soc. for Promotion of Roman Studies, 1980–83. *Publications:* Thucydides (selections in trans. with introd.), 1963; Res Gestae Divi Augusti (with Dr J. M. Moore), 1967; Social Conflicts in the Roman Republic, 1971; Italian Manpower 225 BC–AD 14, 1971, rev. edn 1987; (ed) Arrian's Anabasis (Loeb Classical Library), vol. I, 1976, vol. II, 1983; The Fall of the Roman Republic and related essays, 1988; Roman Imperial Themes, 1990; Studies in Ancient Greek History and Thought, 1992; articles in classical and historical jls. *Address:* 37 Woodstock Close, Woodstock Road, Oxford OX2 8DB. *T:* (01865) 553024.   *Died 5 Nov. 2005.*

BRYAN, Sir Paul (Elmore Oliver), Kt 1972; DSO 1943; MC 1943; *b* 3 Aug. 1913; *s* of Rev. Dr J. I. Bryan, PhD; *m* 1st, 1939, Betty Mary (*née* Hoyle) (*d* 1968); two *d* (and one *d* decd); 2nd, 1971, Cynthia, *d* of Sir Patrick Ashley Cooper and of Lady Ashley Cooper, Hexton Manor, Herts, and *widow* of Patrick Duncan. *Educ:* St John's School, Leatherhead (Scholar); Caius College, Cambridge (MA). Served War of 1939–45: enlisted, 6th Royal West Kent Regt, 1939; commissioned, 1940; Lieut-Col, 1943;

served in France, N Africa, Sicily, Italy; Comdt 164th Inf. OCTU (Eaton Hall), 1944. Sowerby Bridge UDC, 1947; contested Sowerby, March 1949, 1950 and 1951. MP (C), Howden Div. of ER Yorks, 1955–83; Boothferry, 1983–87. Assistant Government Whip, 1956–58; Parliamentary Private Secretary to Minister of Defence, 1956; a Lord Commissioner of the Treasury, 1958–61; Vice-Chairman, Conservative Party Organisation, 1961–65; Conservative Front Bench Spokesman on Post Office and broadcasting, 1965; Minister of State, Dept of Employment, 1970–72. Chm., All Party Hong Kong Parly Gp, 1974–84; Vice-Chm., Conservative 1922 Cttee, 1977–87. Chm., Croydon Cable Television, subseq. United Artists Cables Internat. (London South), 1985–; Director: Granada TV Rental Ltd, 1966–70; Granada Television, 1972–83; Granada Theatres, 1973–83; Greater Manchester Independent Radio Ltd, 1972–84; Scottish Lion Insurance Co. Ltd, 1981–95; Hewetson Holdings Ltd, 1983–91; (alternate) Port of Felixstowe, 1991–94; Dep. Chm., Furness Withy and Co. Ltd, 1984–89 (Dir, 1983–). *Publication:* Wool, War and Westminster, 1993. *Address:* Park Farm, Sawdon, near Scarborough, North Yorks YO13 9EB. *T:* (01723) 859370; 5 Westminster Gardens, Marsham Street, SW1P 4JA. *T:* (020) 7834 2050.
                                                  Died 11 Oct. 2004.

BRYANS, Dame Anne (Margaret), DBE 1957 (CBE 1945); DStJ; Chairman, Order of St John of Jerusalem and BRCS Service Hospitals Welfare and VAD Committee, 1960–89; Vice-Chairman, Joint Committee, Order of St John and BRCS, 1976–81; *b* 29 Oct. 1909; *e d* of Col Rt Hon. Sir John Gilmour, 2nd Bt, GCVO, DSO, MP, of Montrave and Mary Louise Lambert; *m* 1932, Lieut-Comdr J. R. Bryans, RN, retired (*d* 1990); one *s. Educ:* privately. Joined HQ Staff British Red Cross Society, 1938; Deputy Commissioner British Red Cross and St John War Organisation, Middle East Commission, 1943; Commissioner Jan.-June 1945. Dep. Chm., 1953–64, Vice-Chm., 1964–76, Exec. Cttee, BRCS; Lay Mem., Council for Professions Supplementary to Med., 1973–79. Member: Bd of Governors, Eastman Dental Hosp., 1973–79; Camden and Islington AHA, 1974–79; Vice-Pres., Open Sect., RSocMed, 1975, Pres. 1980–82; former Member: ITA, later IBA; Govt Anglo-Egyptian Resettlement Bd; BBC/ITA Appeals Cttee; Med. Sch. St George's Hosp.; Special Trustee and former Chm., Royal Free Hosp. and Friends of Royal Free Hosp.; former Chairman: Bd of Governors, Royal Free Hosp.; Council, Florence Nightingale Hosp.; Vice-Pres., Royal Coll. of Nursing; former Governor, Westminster Hosp. FRSocMed 1976; Hon. FRSocMed 1994. *Address:* 25 Links Road, Lundin Links, Leven, Fife KY8 6AT. *Club:* Royal Lymington Yacht.   *Died 21 April 2004.*

BRYANT, Rt Rev. Denis William, DFC 1942; retired; *b* 31 Jan. 1918; *s* of Thomas and Beatrice Maud Bryant; *m* 1940, Dorothy Linda (*née* Lewis); one *d. Educ:* Clark's Coll., Ealing; Cardiff Techn. Coll. Joined RAF; Wireless Operator/Air Gunner, 1936; Navigator, 1939; France, 1940 (despatches); Pilot, 1943; commn in Secretarial Br., 1948; Adjt, RAF Hereford, 1950; Sqdn-Ldr i/c Overseas Postings Record Office, Gloucester, 1951; Sqdn-Ldr DP7, Air Min., 1953. Ordinand, Queen's Coll., Birmingham, 1956; Deacon, 1958; Priest, 1959; Rector of Esperance, 1961–67; Archdeacon of Goldfields, 1966–67; Bishop of Kalgoorlie, 1967 until 1973 when Kalgoorlie became part of Diocese of Perth; Asst Bishop of Perth, and Archdeacon and Rector of Northam, 1973–75; Rector of Dalkeith, WA, 1975–85. Hon. Chaplain, Anglican Homes, 1985–2000. *Recreations:* squash, tennis, oil painting. *Address:* U3 Dorothy Genders Village, 99 McCabe Street, Mosman Park, WA 6012, Australia. *T:* (8) 93854515.
                                                  Died 9 Aug. 2005.

BRYANT, Michael Dennis, CBE 1988; actor; Royal National Theatre player, since 1977, Associate Director, since 1996; *b* 5 April 1928; *s* of William and Ann Bryant; *m* 1st, 1958, Josephine Martin (marr. diss. 1980); two *s* two *d*; 2nd, 1990, Judith Mary Coke. *Educ:* Battersea Grammar Sch. Merchant Navy, 1945; Army, 1946–49; drama sch., 1949–51; theatre and television, 1957–77; RSC, 1964–65. Rôles with National, subseq. Royal National, Theatre include: Hieronimo, in Spanish Tragedy; Iago, in Othello; Lenin, in State of Revolution (Best Actor, SWET awards, 1977); title rôle, in Mayor of Zalamea (Best Actor, British Theatrical Assoc. awards, 1981); Enobarbus, in Antony and Cleopatra, and Gloucester, in King Lear (Best Supporting Actor: Olivier awards, 1987; (for Enobarbus) London Critics awards, 1987); Prospero, in The Tempest, 1988; Polonius, in Hamlet, 1989; Racing Demon, 1990; The Wind in the Willows, 1990; Murmuring Judges, 1991; Doolittle, in Pygmalion, 1992; Trelawny of the Wells, 1993; The Absence of War, 1993; Johnny on a Spot, 1994; York, in Richard II, 1995; John Gabriel Borkman, 1996; Fool, in King Lear, 1997; Peter Pan, 1998; Money, Summerfolk, 1999; The Cherry Orchard, 2000. *Recreation:* rambling. *Address:* 19 Deanhill Court, Upper Richmond Road West, SW14 7DJ.

Died 25 April 2002.

BRYARS, John Desmond, CB 1982; Deputy Under Secretary of State (Finance and Budget), Ministry of Defence, 1979–84, retired; *b* 31 Oct. 1928; *s* of William Bryars, MD and Sarah (*née* McMeekin); *m* 1964, Faith (*d* 2000), *d* of Frederick Momber, ARCM and Anne Momber. *Educ:* St Edward's Sch., Oxford; Trinity Coll., Oxford (schol.; MA). Army, 1946–48. Entered Civil Service, Air Ministry, 1952; HM Treasury, 1960–62; Private Sec. to Sec. of State for Air, 1963–64, to Minister of Defence, RAF, 1964–65; Asst Sec., MoD, 1965–73; RCDS 1973; Asst Under-Sec. of State, MoD, 1973–75 and 1977–79; Under Sec., Cabinet Office, 1975–77. *Address:* 42 Osterley Road, Osterley, Isleworth, Middlesex TW7 4PN. *Club:* Royal Commonwealth Society.

Died 9 Nov. 2003.

BRYCE, Sir Gordon; *see* Bryce, Sir W. G.

BRYCE, Sir (William) Gordon, Kt 1971; CBE 1963; Chief Justice of the Bahamas, 1970–73; *b* 2 Feb. 1913; *s* of James Chisholm Bryce and Emily Susan (*née* Lees); *m* 1940, Molly Mary (*d* 2003), *d* of Arthur Cranch Drake; two *d*. *Educ:* Bromsgrove Sch.; Hertford Coll., Oxford (MA). Called to Bar, Middle Temple. War Service, 1940–46 (Major). Colonial Service: Crown Counsel, Fiji, 1949; Solicitor General, Fiji, 1953; Attorney General: Gibraltar, 1956; Aden, 1959; Legal Adviser, S Arabian High Commn, 1963; Attorney General, Bahamas, 1966. Comr, revised edn of Laws: of Gilbert and Ellice Islands, 1952; of Fiji, 1955; Comr, Bahamas Law Reform and Revision Commn, 1976. *Recreations:* riding, gardening. *Address:* Nevis, Broad Lane, Brancaster, Norfolk PE31 8AU.

Died 5 Jan. 2004.

BRYMER, Jack, OBE 1960; Principal Clarinettist, London Symphony Orchestra, 1972–87; *b* 27 Jan. 1915; *s* of J. and Mrs M. Brymer, South Shields, Co. Durham; *m* 1939, Joan Richardson, Lancaster; one *s*. *Educ:* Goldsmiths' Coll., London Univ. (FGCL 1991). Schoolmaster, Croydon, general subjects, 1935–40. RAF, 1940–45. Principal Clarinettist: Royal Philharmonic Orchestra, 1946–63; BBC Symphony Orchestra, 1963–72; Professor: Royal Acad. of Music, 1950–58; Royal Military Sch. of Music, Kneller Hall, 1969–73; Guildhall Sch. of Music and Drama, 1981–; Member of Wigmore, Prometheus and London Baroque ensembles; Dir, London Wind Soloists. Directed recordings of the complete wind chamber music of Mozart, Beethoven, Haydn and J. C. Bach. Presenter of several BBC music series, inc. At Home (nightly). Took a life-long interest in mainstream jazz, and in later life toured and performed as soloist with many of finest British and American players in that field. Pres., ISM, 1993. Hon. RAM 1955; FGSM 1986; FRNCM 1992. Hon. MA Newcastle upon Tyne, 1973; Hon. DMus: Kingston, 1993; de Montfort, 1995. Cobbett Medal, Worshipful Co. of Musicians, 1989. *Publications:* The Clarinet (Menuhin Guides), 1976; From Where I Sit (autobiog.), 1979; In the

Orchestra, 1987. *Recreations:* golf, tennis, swimming, carpentry, gardening, music. *Address:* 31 Sycamore Court, Hoskins Road, Oxted, Surrey RH8 9JQ. *T:* (01883) 712843. *Club:* Croham Hurst Golf.

Died 16 Sept. 2003.

BRYSON, Adm. Sir Lindsay (Sutherland), KCB 1981; FRSE 1984; FREng; Director, 1985–97, Chairman, 1990–97, ERA Technology; Lord Lieutenant of East Sussex, 1989–2000; *b* 22 Jan. 1925; *s* of James McAuslan Bryson and Margaret Bryson (*née* Whyte); *m* 1951, Averil Curtis-Willson; one *s* two *d*. *Educ:* Allan Glen's Sch., Glasgow; London Univ. (External) (BSc (Eng)). FIEE (Hon. FIEE 1991), FRAeS. Engrg Cadet, 1942; Electrical Mechanic, RN, 1944; Midshipman 1946; Lieut 1948; Comdr 1960; Captain 1967; comd HMS Daedalus, RNAS Lee-on-Solent, 1970–71; RCDS 1972; Dir, Naval Guided Weapons, 1973; Dir, Surface Weapons Project (Navy), 1974–76; Dir-Gen. Weapons (Naval), 1977–81, and Chief Naval Engr Officer, 1979–81; Controller of the Navy, 1981–84. Chm., Marine Technology Directorate, 1986–92; Dep. Chm., GEC-Marconi (formerly The Marconi Co. and GEC Avionics), 1987–90; Director (non-executive): Molins, 1988–99; Elswick, 1990–94. Pres., Sussex Sci. and Technol. Regl Orgn, 1990–94. Chairman: New Sussex Opera, 1990–99; Brighton Festival Trust, 1991–2000; Brighton West Pier Trust, 1995–. Institution of Electrical Engineers: Vice-Pres., 1982–84; Dep. Pres., 1984–85; Pres., 1985–86; Faraday Lectr, 1976–77. President: Soc. of Underwater Technol., 1989–91; Assoc. of Project Managers, 1991–95. Worshipful Co. of Cooks: Liveryman, 1964; Assistant, 1980; Warden, 1985; Second Master, 1986; Master, 1987; Liveryman, Worshipful Co. of Engrs, 1988. Chairman of Council: Sussex Univ., 1989–95 (Vice-Chm., 1988–89); Brighton Coll., 1990–98 (Governor, 1986–99). Chm., Old Market Trust (Hanover Band), 1996–2001. Hon. Fellow, Paisley Coll. of Technology, 1986; Hon. FIMechE, 1991; Hon. DSc Strathclyde, 1987; Hon DSc(Eng) Bristol, 1988; Hon LLD Sussex, 1995. KStJ 1990. *Publications:* contribs to Jl RAeS, Jl IEE, Trans RINA, Seaford Papers, Control Engineering. *Recreations:* opera, fair weather sailing, gardening. *Address:* 74 Dyke Road Avenue, Brighton BN1 5LE. *T:* (01273) 553638, *Fax:* (01273) 562478; *e-mail:* lbryson@aol.com.uk. *Clubs:* Army and Navy, MCC; Sussex; Sussex CC.

Died 24 March 2005.

BUCHAN, Ven. Eric Ancrum; Archdeacon of Coventry, 1965–77, Archdeacon Emeritus, since 1977; *b* 6 Nov. 1907; *s* of late Frederick Samuel and Florence Buchan. *Educ:* Bristol Grammar School; St Chad's College, University of Durham (BA). Deacon 1933, priest 1934; Curate of Holy Nativity, Knowle, Bristol, 1933–40; Chaplain RAFVR, 1940–45; Vicar of St Mark's with St Barnabas, Coventry, 1945–59; Hon. Canon of Coventry Cathedral, 1953; Chaplain, Coventry and Warwickshire Hospital, 1945–59; Sec., Laymen's Appeal, Dio. of Coventry, 1951–53; Rural Dean of Coventry, 1954–63; Rector of Baginton, 1963–70. Chm. Dio. Board of Finance, 1958–77; Organiser of Bishop's Appeal, 1958–61; Dio. Director of Christian Stewardship, 1959–65; Domestic Chaplain to Bishop of Coventry, 1961–65. Church Commissioner, 1964–78. Member: Central Board of Finance, 1953–80 (Chm., Develt and Stewardship Cttee, 1976–80; Mem., Church Comrs and Central Bd of Finance Joint Liaison Cttee, 1976–80); Schools Council, 1958–65. Member, Governing Body, St Chad's College, Durham University, 1966–83. Vice-Pres., Scouts of Wales, 1994–96. Awarded Silver Acorn for outstanding services to the Scout Movement, 1974. *Address:* College of St Barnabas, Blackberry Lane, Lingfield, Surrey RH7 6NJ. *T:* (01342) 870573.

Died 27 April 2001.

BUCHANAN, Prof. Sir Colin (Douglas), Kt 1972; CBE 1964; Lieutenant-Colonel; consultant with Colin Buchanan & Partners, 47 Princes Gate, London; *b* 22 Aug.

1907; s of William Ernest and Laura Kate Buchanan; m 1933, Elsie Alice Mitchell (d 1984); two s one d. Educ: Berkhamsted School; Imperial College, London. Sudan Govt Public Works Dept, 1930–32; Regional planning studies with F. Longstreth Thompson, 1932–35; Ministry of Transport, 1935–39. War Service in Royal Engineers, 1939–46 (despatches). Ministry of Town and Country Planning (later Ministry of Housing and Local Govt), 1946–61; Urban Planning Adviser, Ministry of Transport, 1961–63; Prof. of Transport, Imperial Coll., London, 1963–72; Prof. of Urban Studies and Dir, Sch. for Advanced Urban Studies, Bristol Univ., 1973–75. Vis. Prof., Imperial Coll., London, 1975–78. Member: Commn on Third London Airport, 1968–70; Royal Fine Art Commn, 1972–74. Pres., CPRE, 1980–85. Pres., Friends of the Vale of Aylesbury, 1985–94. Hon. DCL Oxon, 1972; Hon. DSc: Leeds, 1972; City, 1972. Publications: Mixed Blessing, The Motor in Britain, 1958; Traffic in Towns (Ministry of Transport report), 1963; The State of Britain, 1972; No Way to the Airport, 1981; numerous papers on town planning and allied subjects. Recreations: photography, carpentry, caravan touring. Address: Appletree House, Lincombe Lane, Boars Hill, Oxford OX1 5DU. T: (01865) 739458.

Died 6 Dec. 2001.

BUCHANAN, Sir Dennis; see Buchanan, Sir R. D.

BUCHANAN, John David, MBE 1944; ERD 1989; DL; Headmaster of Oakham School, Rutland, 1958–77; b 26 Oct. 1916; e s of late John Nevile Buchanan and Nancy Isabel (née Bevan); m 1st, 1946, Janet Marjorie (d 1990), d of late Brig. J. A. C. Pennycuick, DSO; three s four d (and one s decd); 2nd, 1992, Banoo Ramsamy. Educ: Stowe; Trinity College, Cambridge (MA). Served with Grenadier Guards, 1939–46; Adjutant, 3rd Bn Grenadier Guards, 1941–43 (despatches, 1943); Brigade Major, 1st Guards Bde, 1944–45; Private Secretary to Sir Alexander Cadogan, Security Council for the UN, 1946. Assistant Master, Westminster Under School, 1948; Assistant Master, Sherborne School, 1948–57. Administrator, Inchcape Educational Scholarship Scheme, 1978–94; Educnl Consultant to Jerwood Foundn, 1978–. FRSA 1991. DL Leics, 1980. Publications: Operation Oakham, 1984; Oakham Overture to Poetry, 1985; Oakham Orations, 1995. Recreation: gardening. Address: Rose Cottage, Owston, Leics LE15 8DN.

Died 26 July 2005.

BUCHANAN, Sir (Ranald) Dennis, Kt 1991; MBE 1976; Chairman and Managing Director, Flight West Airlines Pty Ltd, since 1987; b Sydney, 6 Nov. 1932; s of Stanley Brisbane Buchanan and Jessica (née Hall); m 1956, Della Agnes Brown; four s five d (and one s decd). Educ: All Saints Coll., Bathurst, NSW. Joined Gibbes Sepik Airways Ltd, Wewak, PNG, 1949; purchased Territory Airlines Ltd, 1957 (renamed Talair Pty Ltd, 1975), Chm. and Man. Dir, 1957–93. Recreation: farming. Address: PO Box 1580, Port Vila, Vanuata. T: 26481; Flight West Airlines, PO Box 1126, Eagle Farm, Qld 4009, Australia. T: (7) 32121201, Fax: (7) 32121522.

Died 28 Aug. 2001.

BUCHANAN, Richard; JP; b 3 May 1912; s of late Richard Buchanan and Helen Henderson; m 1st, 1938, Margaret McManus (d 1963); six s two d; 2nd, 1971, Helen Duggan, MA, DipEd. Educ: St Mungo's Boys' School; St Mungo's Academy; Royal Technical Coll. Councillor (Lab), City of Glasgow, 1949–64 (Past Chm. Libraries, Schools and Standing Orders Cttees); Hon. City Treasurer, 1960–63. MP (Lab) Springburn, Glasgow, 1964–79; PPS to Treasury Ministers, 1967–70; Mem. Select Cttees: Public Accounts; Services; Chm., H of C Library Cttee. Chm., West Day School Management, 1958–64; Governor, Notre Dame College of Education, 1959–64. Chm., Belvidere Hospital; Mem. Board of Managers, Glasgow Royal Infirmary. Hon. Pres., Scottish Library Assoc. (Pres., 1963); Life Mem., Scottish Secondary Teachers' Assoc., 1979; Chairman: Scottish

Central Library; Adv. Cttee. Nat. Library of Scotland; Cttee on Burrell Collection; St Mungo's Old Folks' Day Centre, 1979–85; Dir, Glasgow Citizens Theatre. Pres., Buchanan Soc., 1989–91. JP Glasgow, 1954. Hon. FCLIP (Hon. FLA, 1979). Recreations: theatre, walking, reading. Address: 18 Gargrave Avenue, Garrowhill, Glasgow G69 7LP. T: (0141) 771 7234. Club: St Mungo's Centenary (Glasgow).

Died 22 Jan. 2003.

BUCK, Sir (Philip) Antony (Fyson), Kt 1983; QC 1974; Barrister-at-Law; b 19 Dec. 1928; yr s of late A. F. Buck, Ely, Cambs; m 1st, 1955, Judy Elaine (marr. diss. 1989), o d of late Dr C. A. Grant, Cottesloe, Perth, W Australia, and Mrs Grant; one d; 2nd, 1990, Bienvenida Perez-Blanco (marr. diss. 1993); m 1994, Tamara Norashkaryan. Educ: King's School, Ely; Trinity Hall, Cambridge (BA History and Law, 1951; MA 1954). Chm., Cambridge Univ. Cons. Assoc. and Chm., Fedn of Univ. Conservative and Unionist Associations, 1951–52. Called to the Bar, Inner Temple, 1954; Legal Adviser, Nat. Association of Parish Councils, 1957–59 (Vice-Pres., 1970–74). MP (C) Colchester, 1961–83, Colchester North, 1983–92. PPS to Attorney-General, 1963–64; Parly Under-Sec. of State for Defence (Navy), MoD, 1972–74. Chm., Select Cttee on Parly Comr for Admin (Ombudsman), 1977–92; Sec., Conservative Party Home Affairs Cttee, 1964–70, Vice-Chm., 1970–72, Chm., Oct./Nov. 1972; Chm., Cons. Parly Defence Cttee, 1979–89; Mem. Exec., 1922 Cttee, Oct./Nov. 1972, 1977–92. Sponsored and piloted through the Limitation Act, 1963. Recreations: most sports, reading. Club: Oxford and Cambridge.

Died 6 Oct. 2003.

BUCKERIDGE, Anthony Malcolm, OBE 2003; writer; b 20 June 1912; m 1st, 1936, Sylvia Goulden Brown; one s one d; 2nd, 1962, Eileen Norah Selby; one s. Educ: Seaford Coll., Sussex; University Coll. London. Nat. Fire Service, 1940–45; Schoolmaster, St Lawrence Coll. Ramsgate, until 1950; writer of TV and radio plays and musicals; writer, Jennings plays, BBC Children's Hour, 1948–64. Publications: Jennings goes to School, 1950; Jennings follows a Clue, 1951; Jennings' Little Hut, 1951; Jennings and Darbishire, 1952; Jennings' Diary, 1953; A Funny Thing Happened, 1953; Rex Milligan's Busy Term, 1953; According to Jennings, 1954; Our Friend Jennings, 1955; Rex Milligan raises the Roof, 1955; Thanks to Jennings, 1957; Rex Milligan holds forth, 1957; (ed) Stories for Boys, 1957, vol. 2, 1965; Take Jennings, for instance, 1958; (ed) In and out of School, 1958; Jennings, as usual, 1959; The Trouble with Jennings, 1960; Just like Jennings, 1961; Rex Milligan reporting, 1961; Leave it to Jennings, 1963; Jennings, of course!, 1964; Especially Jennings!, 1965; A Bookful of Jennings, 1966, reissued as The Best of Jennings, 1972; Jennings abounding, 1967; Jennings in particular, 1968; Trust Jennings!, 1969; The Jennings Report, 1970; Typically Jennings!, 1971; Speaking of Jennings!, 1973; Jennings at large, 1977; Jennings abounding! (play), 1980; Jennings again!, 1991; That's Jennings, 1994; While I Remember (autobiog.), 1999; Introducing Rex Milligan, 2002; 5 volumes of plays for radio: Jennings sounds the Alarm, 1999; Jennings breaks the Record, 2000; Jennings joins the Search Party, 2001; Jennings to the Rescue, 2002; Jennings and the Roman Remains, 2002. Recreations: acting, directing plays. Address: East Crink, Barcombe Mills, Lewes, Sussex BN8 5BL. T: (01273) 400383.

Died 28 June 2004.

BUCKLE, (Christopher) Richard (Sandford), CBE 1979; writer; critic; exhibition designer; b 6 Aug. 1916; s of late Lieut-Col C. G. Buckle, DSO, MC, Northamptonshire Regt, and Mrs R. E. Buckle (née Sandford). Educ: Marlborough; Balliol. Served Scots Guards, 1940–46; in action in Italy (despatches, 1944). Founded "Ballet", 1939. started "Ballet" again, 1946 (continued for seven years); ballet critic: Observer, 1948–55; Sunday Times, 1959–75; advised: Canada Council on state of ballet in Canada, 1962; Sotheby & Co.

on their sales of Diaghilev Ballet material, 1967–69. Co-founder, Theatre Mus., 1968–83. First play, Gossip Column, prod Q Theatre, 1953; Family Tree (comedy), prod Connaught Theatre, Worthing, 1956. *Organised:* Diaghilev Exhibition, Edinburgh Festival, 1954, and Forbes House, London, 1954–55; The Observer Film Exhibition, London, 1956; Telford Bicentenary Exhibition, 1957; Epstein Memorial Exhibition, Edinburgh Festival, 1961; Shakespeare Exhibition, Stratford-upon-Avon, 1964–65 (smaller version, Edinburgh, 1965); Treasures from the Shakespeare Exhibition, NPG, London, 1964–65; The Communities on the March area in the Man in the Community theme pavilion, Universal and Internat. Exhibition of 1967, Montreal; Exhibition of Beaton Portraits, 1928–68, NPG, 1968; Gala of ballet, Coliseum, 1971; exhibn of Ursula Tyrwhitt, Ashmolean Mus., Oxford, 1974; exhibn Omaggio ai Disegnatori di Diaghilev, Palazzo Grassi, Venice, 1975; exhibn of ballet, opera and theatre costumes, Salisbury Fest., 1975; exhibn Happy and Glorious, 130 years of Royal photographs, NPG, 1977; presented Kama Dev in recital of Indian dancing, St Paul's Church, Covent Garden, 1970; *designed:* new Exhibition Rooms, Harewood House, Yorks, 1959; redesigned interior of Dundee Repertory Theatre, 1963 (burnt down 3 months later). *Publications:* John Innocent at Oxford (novel), 1939; The Adventures of a Ballet Critic, 1953; In Search of Diaghilev, 1955; Modern Ballet Design, 1955; The Prettiest Girl in England, 1958; Harewood (a guide-book), 1959 and (re-written and re-designed), 1966; Dancing for Diaghilev (the memoirs of Lydia Sokolova), 1960; Epstein Drawings (introd. only), 1962; Epstein: An Autobiography (introd. to new edn only), 1963; Jacob Epstein: Sculptor, 1963; Monsters at Midnight: the French Romantic Movement as a background to the ballet Giselle (limited edn), 1966; Nijinsky, 1971, 10th edn 1998; Nijinsky on Stage: commentary on drawings of Valentine Gross, 1971; (ed) U and Non-U revisited, 1978; Diaghilev, 1979; (ed) Self Portrait with Friends, selected diaries of Cecil Beaton, 1979; Buckle at the Ballet, 1980; (with Roy Strong and others) Designing for the Dancer, 1981; (contrib.) The Englishman's Room, ed A. Lees-Milne, 1986; (contrib.) Sir Iain Moncreiffe of that Ilk, ed J. Jolliffe, 1986; L'Après-midi d'un faune, Vaslav Nijinski (introd. only), 1983; (with John Taras) George Balanchine, Ballet Master, 1988; *autobiography:* 1, The Most Upsetting Woman, 1981; 2, In the Wake of Diaghilev, 1982. *Recreations:* caricature, light verse. *Address:* Roman Road, Gutch Common, Semley, Shaftesbury, Dorset SP7 9BE.
Died 12 Oct. 2001.

BUCKLE, Richard; *see* Buckle, C. R. S.

BUCKLEY, George Eric; Counsellor, Atomic Energy, British Embassy, Tokyo, 1976–81; *b* 4 Feb. 1916; *s* of John and Florence Buckley; *m* 1941, Mary Theresa Terry (*d* 1994); one *s* one *d*. *Educ:* Oldham High Sch.; Manchester Univ. BSc (Hons) Physics; MInstP. Lectr in Physics, Rugby Coll. of Technol., 1938. War service, Sqdn Ldr, RAF, 1940–46. Manager, Health Physics and Safety, Windscale Works, 1949; Works Manager, Capenhurst Works, 1952; Chief Ops Physicist, Risley, 1956; Chief Tech. Manager, Windscale and Calder Works, 1959; Superintendent: Calder Hall and Windscale Advanced Gas Cooled Reactors, 1964; Reactors, and Head of Management Services, 1974. *Recreations:* travel, good food, golf. *Address:* G10 Longueville Court, The Village Green, Orton Longueville, Peterborough PE2 7DN.
Died 30 Sept. 2003.

BUCKLEY, James Arthur, CBE 1975; *b* 3 April 1917; *s* of late James Buckley and of Elizabeth Buckley; *m* 1939, Irene May Hicks; two *s*. *Educ:* Christ's Hosp., Horsham, Sussex; Westminster Technical Coll.; Bradford Technical Coll. RAFVR, 1940–46. Gas Light & Coke Co.: Gas Supply Pupil, 1934; Actg Service Supervisor, 1939; Service Supervisor, 1946; North Thames Gas Board: Divisional Man., 1954; Commercial Man., 1962;

Commercial Man. and Bd Mem., 1964; East Midlands Gas Board: Dep. Chm., 1966–67; Chm., 1967–68; Mem., Gas Council, later British Gas Corp., 1968–76. Pres., IGasE, 1971–72.
Died Aug. 2004.

BUDD, Bernard Wilfred; QC 1969; *b* 18 Dec. 1912; *s* of late Rev. W. R. A. Budd; *m* 1944, Margaret Alison, MBE, *d* of late Rt Hon. Edward Leslie Burgin, PC, LLD, MP; two *s*. *Educ:* Cardiff High Sch.; W Leeds High Sch.; Pembroke Coll., Cambridge (schol. in natural scis; BA 1934, MA 1944). Joined ICS, 1935; various Dist appts incl. Dep. Comr, Upper Sind Frontier, 1942–43; Collector and Dist Magistrate, Karachi, 1945–46; cont. in Pakistan Admin. Service, 1947; Dep. Sec., Min. of Commerce and Works, Govt of Pakistan, 1947; Anti-corruption Officer and Inspector-Gen. of Prisons, Govt of Sind, 1949. Called to Bar, Gray's Inn, 1952; ceased practice, 1982. Contested (L), Dover, 1964 and 1966, Folkestone and Hythe, Feb. and Oct. 1974 and 1979. Chm., Assoc. of Liberal Lawyers, 1978–82. Vice-Pres., Internat. Assoc. for the Protection of Industrial Property (British Group), 1978–92. Methodist Local (lay) Preacher, 1933–2002. *Recreations:* birds, hill walking. *Address:* Highlands, Elham, Canterbury, Kent CT4 6UG. *T:* (01303) 840350. *Clubs:* Oxford and Cambridge, National Liberal.
Died 25 Aug. 2003.

BUDDEN, Kenneth George, FRS 1966; MA, PhD; Reader in Physics, University of Cambridge, 1965–82, then Emeritus; Fellow of St John's College, Cambridge, since 1947; *b* 23 June 1915; *s* of late George Easthope Budden and Gertrude Homer Rea; *m* 1947, Nicolette Ann Lydia de Longesdon Longsdon; no *c*. *Educ:* Portsmouth Grammar Sch.; St John's College, Cambridge (MA, PhD). Telecommunications Research Establishment, 1939–41; British Air Commn, Washington, DC, 1941–44; Air Command, SE Asia, 1945; Research at Cambridge, 1936–39 and from 1947. *Publications:* Radio Waves in the Ionosphere, 1961; The Wave-Guide Mode Theory of Wave Propagation, 1961; Lectures on Magnetoionic Theory, 1964; The Propagation of Radio Waves, 1985; numerous papers in scientific jls, on the propagation of radio waves. *Recreation:* gardening. *Address:* 15 Adams Road, Cambridge CB3 9AD. *T:* (01223) 354752.
Died 4 Sept. 2005.

BULL, Anthony, CBE 1968 (OBE 1944); Transport Consultant: Kennedy and Donkin, 1971–85; Freeman Fox and Partners, 1971–87; *b* 18 July 1908; 3rd *s* of Rt Hon. Sir William Bull, 1st Bt, PC, MP, JP, FSA (*d* 1931), and late Lilian, 2nd *d* of G. S. Brandon, Oakbrook, Ravenscourt Park; *m* 1946, Barbara (*d* 1947), *er d* of late Peter Donovan, Yonder, Rye, Sussex; one *d*. *Educ:* Gresham's Sch., Holt; Magdalene Coll., Cambridge (Exhibnr; MA). Joined Underground Group of Cos, 1929; served in Staff, Publicity and Public Relations Depts and Chairman's Office. Sec. to Vice-Chm., London Passenger Transport Board, 1936–39. Served War, 1939–45: RE; Transportation Br., War Office, 1939–42; Trans-Africa L of C, 1942–43; GHQ, Middle East, 1943; Staff of Supreme Allied Comdr, SE Asia (end of 1943); Col 1944; Transp. Div., CCG, 1945–46. Returned to London Transport as Chief Staff and Welfare Officer, 1946; Member: LTE, 1955–62; LTB, 1962–65; Vice-Chm., LTE (formerly LTB), 1965–71. Advr to House of Commons Transport Cttee, 1981–82. Institute of Transport: served on Council, 1956–59; Vice-Pres., 1964–66; Hon. Librarian, 1966–69; Pres., 1969–70. Mem. Regional Advisory Council for Technological Educn, 1958–62 (Transp. Adv. Cttee, 1950–62; Chm. Cttee, 1953–62). CStJ 1969. Bronze Star (USA), 1946. *Publications:* contribs to transport journals. *Recreation:* travel. *Address:* 35 Clareville Grove, SW7 5AU. *T:* (020) 7373 5647. *Club:* Oxford and Cambridge.
Died 23 Dec. 2004.

BULL, Anthony; *see* Bull, P. A.

BULL, George Anthony, OBE 1990; FRSL 1982; writer, translator and consultant; Director, Anglo-Japanese Economic Institute, since 1986; Editor, International

Minds, since 1989; President, Central Banking Publications, since 1990; Publisher: Insight Japan, since 1992; Euro–Japanese Journal, since 1994; Insight Europe, since 2000; innovation, since 2000; *b* 23 Aug. 1929; *s* of George Thomas Bull and Bridget Philomena (*née* Nugent); *m* 1957, Doreen Marjorie Griffin; two *s* two *d*. *Educ:* Wimbledon Coll.; Brasenose Coll., Oxford (MA). National Service, Royal Fusiliers, 1947–49. Reporter, Financial Times, 1952–56, Foreign News Editor, 1956–59; News Editor, London Bureau, McGraw-Hill World News, 1959–60; The Director, 1960–84: successively Dep. Editor, Editor, Editor-in-Chief. Dir 1971–98, and Trustee 1976–, The Tablet; Trustee, The Universe, 1970–86. Chm., Commn for Internat. Justice and Peace, Episcopal Conf. of England and Wales, 1971–74; Mem. Council, RSL, 1986– (Hon. Treas., 1992–98); Mem., UK Cttee, European Cultural Foundn, 1987–; Co-Founder and Dir, Inst. of Public Enterprise Studies, 1996–; Hon. Treasurer, Soc. for Renaissance Studies, 1967–88; Vice-Pres., British–Italian Soc., 1995–. Mem. Adv. Bd, Chesterton Rev., 1999–. Governor: St Mary's Coll., Strawberry Hill, 1976–87; Westminster Choir Sch., 1994–; Foundation Governor, St Thomas More Sch., 1980–87. KCSG 1999. Order of Sacred Treasure (Japan), 1999. *Publications:* (with A. Vice) Bid for Power, 1958, 2nd edn 1960; Vatican Politics, 1966; The Renaissance, 1968, new edn 1973; (ed) The Director's Handbook, 1969, 2nd edn 1978; (with E. D. Foster) The Director, his Money and his Job, 1970; (with Peter Hobday and John Hamway) Industrial Relations: the boardroom viewpoint, 1972; Venice: the most triumphant city, 1982 (Folio Society 1980, USA 1982); Inside the Vatican, 1982 (USA 1983, Italy 1983 (as Dentro il Vaticano), Germany and Japan 1987, Hungary, 1989); Michelangelo, 1995 (USA 1996); translations: Artists of the Renaissance, 1979–; (with Peter Porter) Life, Letters and Poetry of Michelangelo, 1987; The Travels of Pietro della Valle, 1989; translations for Penguin Classics: Life of Cellini, 1956; Machiavelli, The Prince, 1961; Vasari, Lives of the Artists, Vol. I, 1965, vol II, 1987; Castiglione, The Book of the Courtier, 1967; Aretino, Selected Letters, 1976. *Recreations:* book collecting, travelling. *Address:* 19 Hugh Street, SW1V 1QJ. *Clubs:* Garrick, Savile, Beefsteak. *Died 6 April 2001.*

BULL, (Peter) Anthony; JP; FRICS; Proprietor, Walter Bull & Co., 1987–97; *b* 8 July 1937; *s* of Sir Walter Edward Avenon Bull, KCVO; *m* 1964, Susan Mary Battersby. *Educ:* Rugby Sch.; Coll. of Estate Management. Partner, Vigers, 1965–87. City of London: Mem., Court of Common Council, 1968–; Alderman, Ward of Cheap, 1984–. Mem., City and Hackney Jt Consultative Cttee, 1998–2001. Church Comr, 1986–98; Churchwarden, St Lawrence Jewry, 1984–. Mem., ESU, 1984. Mem., Co. of Parish Clerks, 1993–; Liveryman: Merchant Taylors' Co., 1965; Chartered Surveyors' Co., 1977 (Master, 1990–91); Mem., Guild of Freemen, 1998. Vice Chm., City of London Br., RNLI, 1992–. Member, Council: City of London Br., Royal Soc. of St George; C&G, 1998–; Governor: Westminster City Sch.; Bridewell Royal Hosp., 1984–; Christ's Hosp., 1984–; Trustee, United Westminster Schs, 1992–. Patron, Ward of Cheap Club, 1984–; Pres., Associate Ward Clubs, 1997–. Mem., Assoc. of Lancastrians in London. Mem. Court, HAC, 1984–. JP City of London, 1984. *Recreations:* clocks, golf, wine, gardening, City of London. *Address:* 58 Burnt Ash Road, Lee, SE12 8PY. *T:* (020) 8852 0043. *Clubs:* Guildhall, City Livery, MCC, ESU. *Died 10 Oct. 2003.*

BULLOCK, Baron *cr* 1976 (Life Peer), of Leafield, Oxon; **Alan Louis Charles Bullock,** Kt 1972; FBA 1967; Founding Master, 1960, and Hon. Fellow, since 1980, St Catherine's College, Oxford (Master, 1960–80); Vice-Chancellor, Oxford University, 1969–73; *b* 13 Dec. 1914; *s* of Frank Allen Bullock; *m* 1940, Hilda Yates, *d* of Edwin Handy, Bradford; three *s* one *d* (and one *d* decd). *Educ:* Bradford Grammar Sch.; Wadham Coll., Oxford (Scholar). MA; 1st Class Lit Hum, 1936; 1st Class, Modern

Hist., 1938. DLitt Oxon, 1969. Fellow, Dean and Tutor in Modern Hist., New Coll., 1945–52; Censor of St Catherine's Soc., Oxford, 1952–62; Chairman: Research Cttee of RIIA, 1954–78; Nat. Advisory Council on the Training and Supply of Teachers, 1963–65; Schools Council, 1966–69; Cttee on Reading and Other Uses of English Language, 1972–74 (Report, A Language for Life, published 1975); Trustees, Tate Gallery, 1973–80; Friends of Ashmolean Museum; Cttee of Enquiry on Industrial Democracy, 1976 (Report publ. 1977); Member: Arts Council of Great Britain, 1961–64; SSRC, 1966; Adv. Council on Public Records, 1965–77; Organising Cttee for the British Library, 1971–72. Joined Social Democratic Party, 1981. Sen. Fellow, Aspen Inst., USA; Trustee: Aspen Inst., Berlin; The Observer, 1957–69; Dir, The Observer, 1977–81. Raleigh Lectr, British Acad., 1967; Stevenson Meml Lectr, LSE, 1970; Leslie Stephen Lectr, Cambridge, 1976. Hon. Fellow, Merton Coll., Wadham Coll., Linacre Coll., Wolfson Coll., New Coll. and St Antony's Coll., Oxford. For. Mem., Amer. Acad. Arts and Sciences, 1972; Mem., Academia Europaea, 1990. Hon. FRIBA; Hon. FRA. Hon. Dr Univ. Aix-Marseilles; Hon. DLitt: Bradford; Reading; Newfoundland; Leicester; Sussex; Warwick; Essex; DUniv Open; Hon. Dr Leeds, 2000. Chevalier Légion d'Honneur, 1970; Grosse Verdienstkreuz (Germany), 1995. *Publications:* Hitler, A Study in Tyranny, 1952, rev. edn 1964; The Liberal Tradition, 1956; The Life and Times of Ernest Bevin, Vol. I, 1960, Vol. II, 1967, Vol III (Ernest Bevin, Foreign Secretary), 1983; (ed) The Twentieth Century, 1971; (ed with Oliver Stallybrass) Dictionary of Modern Thought, 1977, new edn (with S. Trombley), 1999; (ed) The Faces of Europe, 1980; (ed with B. R. Woodings) Fontana Dictionary of Modern Thinkers, 1983; The Humanist Tradition in the West, 1985; Hitler and Stalin: parallel lives, 1991, rev. edn 1998; Building Jerusalem, 2000; Ernest Bevin, a Biography, 2002; Gen. Editor (with Sir William Deakin) of The Oxford History of Modern Europe. *Address:* St Catherine's College, Oxford OX1 3UJ. *Died 2 Feb. 2004.*

BULLOUGH, Prof. Donald Auberon, FSA, FRHistS; Professor of Mediaeval History, University of St Andrews, 1973–91, later Emeritus; *b* 13 June 1928; *s* of late William Bullough and Edith Shirley (*née* Norman); *m* 1st, 1963, Belinda Jane Turland (marr. diss.); two *d*; 2nd, 1995, Dr Alice Harting-Correa; one step *s* three step *d*. *Educ:* Newcastle-under-Lyme High Sch.; St John's Coll., Oxford (BA 1950, MA 1954). FRHistS 1958; FSA 1968; FRPSL 1993. National Service, 1946–48: commnd RA (attached RHA). Harmsworth Scholar, Merton Coll., Oxford, 1951; Medieval Scholar, British Sch. at Rome, 1951; Fereday Fellow, St John's Coll., Oxford, 1952–55; Lectr, Univ. of Edinburgh, 1955–66; Prof. of Med. History, Univ. of Nottingham, 1966–73; Dean, Faculty of Arts, Univ. of St Andrews, 1984–88. Vis. Prof., Southern Methodist Univ., Dallas, 1965–66; British Acad. Overseas Vis. Fellow, Max-Planck-Inst. für Gesch., 1972–73; Lilly Endowment Fellow, Pennsylvania Univ., 1980–81; Vis. Prof., Rutgers Univ., NJ, 1991–92, 1993–94; Visitor, IAS, Princeton, 1994–95; Vis. Prof., Univ. of Auckland, NZ, 1996. Lectures: Ford's, in English Hist., Univ. of Oxford, 1979–80; Scott-Hawkins, Southern Methodist Univ., Dallas, 1980; Andrew Mellon, Catholic Univ., Washington, 1980; Raleigh, British Acad., 1985; (Inaugural) Hector Munro Chadwick, Univ. of Cambridge, 1990. Corresponding Fellow, Monumenta Germaniae Historica, 1983–; Hon. Fellow, British Sch. at Rome, 1998 (Mem. Council, Exec., Finance Cttee, 1975–95; Acting Dir, 1984). Mem., Nottingham Univ. Hosp. Management Cttee, 1971–74. Dir, Paul Elek Ltd, 1968–79. Mem., Gen. Synod of Scottish Episcopal Church, 1998–2002. Major RA (TA); seconded OTC, 1957–67. *Publications:* The Age of Charlemagne, 1965 (2nd edn 1974; also foreign trans); (ed with R. L. Storey) The Study of Medieval Records, 1971; Carolingian Renewal: sources and heritage, 1991; contrib. Settimane di Studi del Centro ital. di St. sull'Alto Medioevo, TLS,

British and continental hist. jls, philatelic jls. *Recreations:* talk, looking at buildings, postal history, cooking. *Address:* 14 Queens Gardens, St Andrews, Fife KY16 9TA. *T:* (01334) 478802. *Club:* Athenæum.

Died 26 June 2002.

BULLUS, Wing Comdr Sir Eric (Edward), Kt 1964; journalist; *b* 20 Nov. 1906; 2nd *s* of Thomas Bullus, Leeds; *m* 1949, Joan Evelyn (*d* 1993), er *d* of H. M. Denny; two *d. Educ:* Leeds Modern Sch.; Univ. of Leeds. Commnd RAFVR, Aug. 1940; served War of 1939–45; Air Min. War Room, 1940–43; joined Lord Louis Mountbatten's staff in SE Asia, 1943; Wing Comdr, 1944; served India, Burma and Ceylon; demobilized, 1945. Journalist, Yorkshire Post, Leeds and London, 1923–46. Mem. Leeds City Council, 1930–40; Sec., London Municipal Soc., 1947–50; Mem., Harrow UDC, 1947–50; Vice-Pres., Assoc. of Municipal Corps, 1953. MP (C) Wembley N, 1950–Feb. 1974; PPS to Secretary for Overseas Trade, 1953, to Minister of State, BOT, 1954–56, to Minister of Aviation, 1960–62, to Secretary of State for Defence, 1962–64. FRGS 1947; Fellow Royal Statistical Society, 1949. Foundation Mem. of Brotherton Collection Cttee of Univ. of Leeds, 1935; Member: Archdeaconry Council of Delhi, 1944; Management Board, Cambridge Mission to Delhi, 1954; House of Laity, Church Assembly, 1960. Ripon Diocesan Reader, 1929; London Diocesan Reader, 1947; St Alban's Diocesan Reader, 1960; Canterbury Diocesan Reader, 1967; Central Readers' Board, 1960; London Readers' Board, 1954. Council, Westfield Coll., Univ. of London. Pres., Soc. of Yorkshiremen in London, 1969–70. *Publications:* History of Leeds Modern School, 1931; History of Church in Delhi, 1944; History of Lords and Commons Cricket, 1959. *Recreations:* played Headingley RU Football Club 15 years and Yorkshire Amateurs Assoc. Football Club; cricket, swimming (bronze and silver medallions). *Address:* Westway, Herne Bay, Kent CT6 8RL. *Clubs:* St Stephen's Constitutional, MCC. *Died 31 Aug. 2001.*

BULMER, Dr Gerald; Rector of Liverpool Polytechnic, 1970–85 (sabbatical leave, 1984–85), retired; *b* 17 Nov. 1920; *s* of Edward and Alice Bulmer; *m* 1943, Greta Lucy Parkes, MA; two *d. Educ:* Nunthorpe Sch., York; Selwyn Coll., Cambridge (BA 1941; PhD 1944; MA 1945). Asst Master, King's Sch., Canterbury, 1945–49; Sen. Lecturer, Woolwich Polytechnic, 1949–53; Head of Dept of Science and Metallurgy, Constantine Technical Coll., Middlesbrough, 1954–57; Vice-Principal, Bolton Technical Coll., 1958–59; Principal, West Ham Coll. of Technology, 1959–64; Dir, Robert Gordon's Inst. of Technology, Aberdeen, 1965–70. Mem. Council, CNAA, 1967–78. Freeman, City of York, 1952. Hon. DSc CNAA, 1986. *Publications:* papers on organic sulphur compounds in Jl Chem. Soc. and Nature. *Address:* 11 Capilano Park, Winifred Lane, Aughton, Ormskirk, Lancs L39 5HA. *Died 17 July 2004.*

BULPITT, Cecil Arthur Charles, (Philip Bulpitt); Director, BIM Foundation Ltd, 1977–84 (Chairman, 1979–82); *b* 6 Feb. 1919; *s* of A. E. Bulpitt; *m* 1943, Joyce Mary Bloomfield; one *s* one *d. Educ:* Spring Grove Sch., London; Regent Street Polytechnic. Territorial Army, to rank of Staff Capt., RA, 1937–45. Carreras Ltd: joined firm, 1935; Gen. Manager, 1960; Asst Managing Dir, 1962; Dep. Chm. and Chief Exec., 1968; Chm., 1969–70; Dir, Thomas Tilling, 1973–81; Chairman: Tilling Construction Services Ltd, 1978–81; InterMed Ltd, 1978–81; Graham Building Services Ltd, 1979–81; Newey & Eyre Gp Ltd, 1979–81. Member: London Reg. Council, CBI, 1978–81; BBC Consultative Gp on Industrial and Business Affairs, 1980–84. MIPM 1955; CCMI (FBIM 1963; Vice-Chm. Council, and Dir, Bd of Companions, BIM, 1979–83). Freeman, City of London, 1969. *Publication:* The Chief Executive, 1971. *Recreations:* golf, swimming, reading, travelling. *Address:* 15 The Manor, Badgers Holt, Tunbridge Wells, Kent TN2 3ET. *T:* (01892) 514394. *Clubs:* El Madronal Country, Las

Brisas Golf (Nueva Andalucia, Spain).

Died 11 May 2005.

BUNTING, Prof. Arthur Hugh, CMG 1971; Professor of Agricultural Development Overseas, Reading University, 1974–82, later Emeritus; *b* 7 Sept. 1917; *e s* of S. P. and R. Bunting; *m* 1941, Elsie Muriel Reynard; three *s. Educ:* Athlone High Sch., Johannesburg, S Africa; Univ. of the Witwatersrand, Johannesburg (BSc (Hons Botany), MSc 1938); Oriel Coll., University of Oxford (Rhodes Scholar for the Transvaal, 1938; DPhil 1941). CBiol, FIBiol; FLS 1993. Asst Chemist, Rothamsted Experimental Station, 1941–45; Member Human Nutrition Research Unit, Medical Research Council, 1945–47; Chief Scientific Officer, Overseas Food Corporation, 1947–51; Senior Research Officer, Sudan Min. of Agriculture, 1951–56; Prof. of Agricultural Botany, 1956–73, Dean, Faculty of Agriculture, 1965–71, Univ. of Reading. Foundn Mem., 1968–72, and Mem., 1974–80, Vice-Chm. 1975–77, and Chm. 1978–80, Board of Trustees, Internat. Inst. of Tropical Agriculture, Ibadan, Nigeria; Member: UK Council for Scientific Policy, 1970–72; UN Adv. Cttee on the Applications of Science and Technology to Develt (ACAST), 1972–75; Governing Bodies, Grassland Res. Inst., Hurley, 1959–77, Plant Breeding Inst., Cambridge, 1960–76; Consultant and then Mem., Scientific Cttee, Cotton Res. Corp., 1958–76 (Chm., 1972–76); Member: Panel of Scientific Advisers, CDC, 1967–94; Meteorological Cttee, MoD, 1973–88; Foundn Mem., Internat. Bd for Plant Genetic Resources, 1974–78. Pres., Assoc. of Applied Biologists, 1963–64, Hon. Mem., 1979–. Jt Editor, Journal of Applied Ecology, 1964–68. LLD *hc* Ahmadu Bello Univ., 1968. *Publications:* (ed) Change in Agriculture, 1970; (ed jtly) Policy and Practice in Rural Development, 1976; (ed jtly) Advances in Legume Science, 1980; (ed) Agricultural Environments, 1987; numerous papers in scientific and agricultural journals. *Recreation:* music. *Address:* 27 The Mount, Caversham, Reading, Berks RG4 7RU. *T:* (0118) 947 2487; *e-mail:* a.h.bunting@reading.ac.uk.

Died 8 May 2002.

BUNTING, Hugh; *see* Bunting, A. H.

BUNTING, John Reginald, CBE 1965; author and educational consultant, retired; *b* 12 Nov. 1916; *s* of John Henry and Jane Bunting, Mansfield; *m* 1940, (May) Hope Sturdy, Malvern, Jamaica; no *c. Educ:* Queen Elizabeth's Grammar Sch., Mansfield; Queen's Coll., Oxford (MA, DipEd). Sen. English Master and Housemaster, Munro Coll., Jamaica, 1939–42; Headmaster, Wolmer's Sch., Jamaica, 1943–49; Principal, King's Coll., Lagos, 1949–54; Actg Dir of Broadcasting, Nigeria, June–Oct. 1952; Actg Inspector of Educn, Western Region, Nigeria, April–Oct. 1954; Dep. Chief Federal Adviser on Educn, Nigeria, 1954–58; Chief Federal Adviser on Educn, Nigeria, 1958–61; Educn Adviser, W Africa, Brit. Council, 1961 and Head, Graduate VSO Unit, 1962; Asst Controller, Educn Div., 1964; Evans Bros Ltd: Editorial Consultant, 1965–68; Dir, Overseas Sales and Publications, 1969; Dir-Gen., Centre for Educnl Develt Overseas, 1970–74; Adviser on Educn to British Council, 1974–76. Hon. Jt Editor, W African Jl of Educn, 1956–61. *Publications:* Civics for Self-Government, 1956; New African English Course (Book 5), 1960; (jtly) Caribbean Civics, 1960; (jtly) Civics for East Africa, 1961; Primary English Course (Book 6): for Ghana, 1962, for Sierra Leone, 1969, for West Cameroon, 1971; Civics: a course in citizenship and character training, 1973; To Light a Candle, 1976. *Recreations:* golf, fishing, painting, bowls. *Address:* 2 Coach & Horses, The Street, Charmouth, Dorset DT6 6PN. *T:* (01297) 560127. *Club:* MCC. *Died 21 Sept. 2001.*

BURBIDGE, Sir Herbert (Dudley), 5th Bt *cr* 1916; *b* 13 Nov. 1904; *s* of Herbert Edward Burbidge (*d* 1945) 2nd *s* of 1st Bt, and Harriet Georgina (*d* 1952), *d* of Henry Stuart Hamilton, Londonderry; *S* cousin, 1974; *m* 1933, Ruby Bly (*d* 1994), *d* of Charles Ethelbert Taylor; one *s. Educ:* University Sch., Victoria, BC, Canada. Harrods Ltd,

Knightsbridge, 1923–28; R. P. Clarke (Stock Brokers), Vancouver, BC, 1929–31; Merchandising Manager, Silverwood Industries of Vancouver, BC, 1931–70; retired 1970. President: Vancouver Executive Club, 1942; Vancouver Sales Executive Club, 1948. Mem. Bd of Referees, Workmen's Compensation Bd, 1943–61. *Recreation:* landscape gardening. *Heir:* s Peter Dudley Burbidge [*b* 20 June 1942; *m* 1967, Peggy Marilyn, *d* of Kenneth Anderson, Ladner, BC; one s one d]. *Address:* 3809 West 24th Avenue, Vancouver, BC V6S 1L9, Canada. *Club:* Vancouver Executive.

Died 31 March 2001.

BURCH, Rt Rev. William Gerald, DD; *b* Winnipeg, Manitoba, 5 March 1911; *m* 1942, Carroll Borrowman (*d* 1995); four *d*. *Educ:* University of Toronto (BA); Wycliffe Coll., Toronto. Deacon, 1936; Priest, 1938. Curate, Christ Church, Toronto, 1936–40; Incumbent, Scarborough Junction with Sandown Park, 1940–42; Rector: St Luke, Winnipeg, 1942–52; All Saints, Windsor, 1952–56; Examining Chaplain to Bishop of Huron, 1955–56; Canon of Huron, 1956; Dean and Rector, All Saints Cathedral, Edmonton, 1956–60; Suffragan Bishop of Edmonton, 1960–61; Bishop of Edmonton, 1961–76. *Address:* 901 Richmond Avenue, Victoria, BC V8S 3Z4, Canada. *T:* (250) 5984369.   *Died 22 Oct. 2003.*

BURCHFIELD, Dr Robert William, CBE 1975; Editor, A Supplement to the Oxford English Dictionary, 1957–86; Chief Editor, The Oxford English Dictionaries, 1971–84; Senior Research Fellow, St Peter's College, Oxford, 1979–90, then Emeritus Fellow (Tutorial Fellow, 1963–79); *b* Wanganui, NZ, 27 Jan. 1923; *s* of Frederick Burchfield and Mary Burchfield (*née* Blair); *m* 1949, Ethel May Yates (marr. diss. 1976); one *s* two *d*; *m* 1976, Elizabeth Austen Knight. *Educ:* Wanganui Technical Coll., New Zealand, 1934–39; Victoria University Coll., Wellington, NZ, 1940–41, 1946–48; MA (NZ) 1948; Magdalen Coll., Oxford, 1949–53; BA (Oxon) 1951, MA 1955. Served War, Royal NZ Artillery, NZ and Italy, 1941–46. NZ Rhodes Scholar, 1949. Junior Lectr in English Lang., Magdalen Coll., Oxford, 1952–53; Lectr in English Lang., Christ Church, Oxford, 1953–57; Lectr, St Peter's Coll., Oxford, 1955–63. Hon. Sec., Early English Text Society, 1955–68 (Mem. Council, 1968–80); Editor, Notes and Queries, 1959–62; Pres., English Assoc., 1978–79. Hon. For. Mem., American Acad. of Arts and Scis, 1977–; Hon. Fellow, Inst. of Linguists, 1984–. Hon. DLitt, Liverpool, 1978; Hon. LitD Victoria Univ. of Wellington, NZ, 1983. Freedom of City of Wanganui, 1986. Shakespeare Prize, FVS Foundn, Hamburg, 1994. *Publications:* (with C. T. Onions and G. W. S. Friedrichsen) The Oxford Dictionary of English Etymology, 1966; A Supplement to the Oxford English Dictionary, vol. I (A–G), 1972, vol. II (H–N), 1976, vol. III (O–Scz), 1982, vol. IV (Se–Z), 1986; (with D. Donoghue and A. Timothy) The Quality of Spoken English on BBC Radio, 1979; The Spoken Language as an Art Form, 1981; The Spoken Word, 1981; The English Language, 1985; The New Zealand Pocket Oxford Dictionary, 1986; (ed) Studies in Lexicography, 1987; Unlocking the English Language, 1989; Points of View, 1992; (ed) The Cambridge History of the English Language, vol. V, 1994; The New Fowler's Modern English Usage, 3rd edn, 1996; contribs to: Times Lit. Supp., Trans Philological Soc., Encounter, etc. *Recreations:* investigating English grammar, travelling, gardening. *Address:* 14 The Green, Sutton Courtenay, Oxon OX14 4AE. *T:* (01235) 848645. *Club:* Athenæum.

Died 5 July 2004.

BURGE, Stuart, CBE 1974; freelance director and actor; *b* 15 Jan. 1918; *s* of late H. O. Burge and K. M. Haig; *m* 1949, Josephine Parker; three s two *d*. *Educ:* Eagle House, Sandhurst; Felsted Sch., Essex. Served War of 1939–45, Intell. Corps. Actor; trained Old Vic, 1936–37; Oxford Rep., 1937–38; Old Vic and West End, 1938–39; Bristol Old Vic, Young Vic, Commercial Theatre, 1946–49; 1st Dir, Hornchurch, 1951–53; productions for theatre and TV, 1953–; Dir, Nottingham Playhouse, 1968–74; Artistic Dir, Royal Court Theatre, 1977–80. *Theatre:* Lulu, 1970; Measure for Measure, The Devil is an Ass, Edinburgh Fest. and Nat. Theatre, 1977; Another Country, Greenwich 1981 and Queen's 1982; (actor) The Seagull, Royal Court, 1981; The London Cuckolds, Royal Court and Lyric Hammersmith, 1985; Curtains, Hampstead, 1987, Whitehall, 1988; The Black Prince, Aldwych, 1989; Sunsets and Glories, Leeds Fest., 1990; The Provoked Wife, Touring Partnership, 1994; Last Dance at Dum Dum, Royal Court at New Ambassadors, 1999; *opera:* La Colombe, Buxton and Sadler's Wells, 1983; *television:* Luther, Bill Brand, Sons and Lovers, The Old Men at the Zoo, Much Ado About Nothing (BBC Shakespeare), Breaking Up, Naming the Names, The Rainbow, House of Bernarda Alba, After the Dance, The Wexford Trilogy, The Writing Game, Talking Heads, etc; *films:* Othello, 1964; Julius Caesar, 1969. Vis. Prof., UC Davis, USA; Hon. Prof. of Drama, Nottingham Univ. *Publication:* (ed) King John (Folio Society), 1973. *Address:* c/o Harriet Cruickshank, 97 Old South Lambeth Road, SW8 1XU.

Died 24 Jan. 2002.

BURGES, Alan; *see* Burges, N. A.

BURGES, (Norman) Alan, CBE 1980; PhD; FIBiol; FLS; Vice-Chancellor, New University of Ulster, Coleraine, Northern Ireland, 1966–76; *b* 5 Aug. 1911; *s* of late Lieut J. C. Burges, East Maitland, NSW; *m* 1940, Florence Evelyn (*née* Moulton); three *d*. *Educ:* Sydney Univ., Australia (BSc Hons 1931, MSc 1932; represented Sydney and Combined Australian Univs at athletics, 1932); Emmanuel Coll., Cambridge (PhD 1937; Senior 1851 Scholar, 1937). Served War of 1939–45, RAF Bomber Command (despatches). Botanical Survey, Nauru Is, 1932; Research Fellow, Emmanuel Coll., 1938; Prof. of Botany, Sydney Univ., 1947–52; Dean of Faculty of Science and Fellow of Senate, 1949–52; Holbrook Gaskell Prof. of Botany, Univ. of Liverpool, 1952–66, Acting Vice-Chancellor, 1964–65; Pro-Vice-Chancellor, 1965–66. Chm., NI Adv. Council for Education, 1966–75; Member: Cttee, Nature Conservancy, England, 1959–66; Waste Management Adv. Council; Chm., Jt Malay/Japanese/UK Rainforest Res. Stn, Pasoh, Malaya, 1967. Chairman: Ulster American Folk Park, 1975–88; NI American Bicentennial Cttee, 1975–77; Scots Irish Trust, 1977–92; Nat. Trust NI Cttee, 1978–81. Mem., Acad. Adv. Cttee, Loughborough Univ., 1967–71. Joint Editor, Flora Europæa Project, 1956–. Hon. Gen. Sec., ANZAAS, 1947–52; President: British Ecological Soc., 1958, 1959; British Mycological Soc., 1962. Hon. LLD QUB, 1973; Hon. DTech Loughborough, 1975; Hon. DSc Ulster, 1977. *Publications:* Micro-organisms in the Soil, 1958; (with F. Raw) Soil Biology, 1967; reports: Primary Educn in Northern Ireland, 1968; Existing Selection Procedure for Secondary Educn in Northern Ireland, 1971; Reorganisation of Secondary Educn in Northern Ireland, 1973; various in scientific journals on plant diseases and fungi. *Recreation:* sailing. *Address:* Tokes Cottage, Semley, Wilts SP7 8BP. *T:* (01747) 830297. *Club:* Royal Air Force.   *Died 4 Oct. 2002.*

BURGES, Maj.-Gen. Rodney Lyon Travers, CBE 1963; DSO 1946; *b* 19 March 1914; *s* of Richard Burges and Hilda Christine Burges (*née* Lyon); *m* 1946, Sheila Marion Lyster Goldby (*d* 1991), *d* of H. L. Goldby; one *d* (one s decd). *Educ:* Wellington; RMA, Woolwich. 2nd Lieut RA, 1934; war service in Burma, 1942 and 1944–45; CO The Berkshire Yeomanry (145 Fd Regt, RA), 1945; Comdr, E Battery, RHA, 1949–51; Bt Lt-Col 1953; 2nd in comd, 1 RHA, 1954–55; CO 3 RHA, 1955–57; CRA 3 Div., 1958–59; IDC, 1960; Brig. Q (Ops) WO, 1961–63; CCRA, 1 Corps, BAOR, 1963–64; Maj.-Gen. 1964; GOC, Cyprus District, 1964–66; VQMG, MoD, 1966–67. Joined Grieveson, Grant & Co., 1968, Partner 1971, retd 1978; Consultant to Pat Simon Wines Ltd, 1978–85; Dir, Caroline Fine Wines Ltd, 1982–85.

Freeman and Liveryman, Fishmongers' Co., 1974. *Recreations:* racing, drinking wine in the sun. *Address:* Freemantle, Over Wallop, Hants SO20 8JE. *Clubs:* Buck's, Army and Navy. *Died 4 June 2002.*

BURGESS, Cyril Duncan, CB 1989; ERD 1970; Chairman, Council for Registered Gas Installers, 1991–94; *b* 18 Oct. 1929; *s* of John Arthur Burgess and Doris (*née* Sedgwick); *m* 1954, Jean Kathleen Whitney; one *s* one *d*. *Educ:* Southgate County Grammar Sch.; Univ. of London (BSc). CChem; MRSC. National Service, Royal Signals, 1950. Asst Engineer, English Electric Co., 1952; HM Factory Inspectorate, 1953; served in London and Huddersfield; Sup. Inspector, Scotland, 1974; Sec., Adv. Cttee on Asbestos, 1976; Dir, Hazardous Substances Div., HSE, 1978–89. Chm., Adv. Cttees on Dangerous Substances, 1982, on Toxic Substances, 1985. *Address:* 108 Gravel Lane, Hemel Hempstead, Herts HP1 1SB. *T:* (01442) 392734. *Died 17 Oct. 2005.*

BURGH, 7th Baron, *cr* 1529 (title called out of abeyance, 1916; by some reckonings he is 9th Baron (from a *cr* 1487) and his father was 8th and grandfather 7th); **Alexander Peter Willoughby Leith;** *b* 20 March 1935; *s* of 6th (or 8th) Baron Burgh; *S* father 1959; *m* 1st, 1957, Anita Lorna Eldridge (marr. diss. 1982); two *s* one *d*; 2nd, 1984, Wilma Schramm; one *d*. *Educ:* Harrow; Magdalene Coll., Cambridge (BA). *Heir: s* Hon. Alexander Gregory Disney Leith [*b* 16 March 1958; *m* 1st, 1984, Catherine Mary (marr. diss. 1999), *d* of David Parkes; two *s*; 2nd, 1999, Emma Jane Burdick]. *Died 14 July 2001.*

BURGNER, Thomas Ulric; Secretary, Committee of Vice Chancellors and Principals, 1989–95; *b* 6 March 1932; *s* of John Henry Burgner and Clara Doerte Burgner (*née* Wolff); *m* 1958, Marion (*née* Chasik) (*d* 1996); two *s*. *Educ:* Haberdashers' Aske's, Hampstead; St Catharine's Coll., Cambridge (BA Hons, MA); Dip. Personnel Management. Flying Officer, RAF, 1954–55. National Coal Board, 1955–61; Assoc. of Chemical and Allied Employers, 1961–65; Principal, Dept of Economic Affairs, 1965–69; HM Treasury: Principal, 1969–72; Asst Secretary, 1972–76; Head of Exchange Control Div., 1972–74; Head of General Aid Div., 1974–76; Under Secretary, 1976; on secondment as Sec., NEDC, 1976–80; Head of Public Enterprises Gp, 1980–85; Head, Industry, Agric. and Employment Gp, 1985–89. Mem., BSC, 1980–83. Consultant, LTW Ltd, 1995–99. Chairman: Independent Longcare Inquiry, 1995–96 (report published 1998); Inspection Adv. Panel, Soc. Services Cttee, Borough of Barnet, 1999– (Mem., 1997–99); Member: UKCC Finance Cttee, 1998–; Bd, Nat. Care Standards Commn, 2001–. Reviewer, Health Adv. Service, 1999–. Member Council: Univ. of London, 1997–; Inst. of Educn, 1999–; RSAS Agecare, 1999–. Vice-Chm., Relatives Assoc., 1997–. Trustee, Anna Freud Centre, 1994–99. *Publication:* The Regulation and Inspection of Social Services, 1996. *Address:* 12 Kingsley Place, Highgate, N6 5EA. *T:* and *Fax:* (020) 8340 9759. *Died 14 July 2001.*

BURKE, John Joseph, OBE 2004; Vice Lord–Lieutenant, County of Bristol, since 2002; Vice Chairman, Bristol & West plc, since 1999; *b* 18 Sept. 1942; *m* 1967, Sally Elliott; three *s*. *Educ:* Bridlington Grammar Sch.; Sutton High Sch., Plymouth. Family retail business, 1958–64; Bristol & West Building Society, subseq. Bristol & West plc, 1964–: Gen. Manager, Retail Ops, 1988–90, Business Develt, 1990–91; Main Bd Dir, 1991–; Business Develt Dir, 1991–93; Man. Dir and Chief Exec., 1993–99. Pres., Bristol Chamber of Commerce and Initiative, 2000–. DL Bristol, 2002. *Recreations:* fishing, Rugby supporter. *Address:* Bristol & West plc, PO Box 27, One Temple Quay, Bristol BS99 7AX; Lea Farm, Sutton Wick, Bishop Sutton, Bristol BS39 5XR. *T:* (01761) 221242. *Died 2 April 2004.*

BURKE-GAFFNEY, Michael Anthony Bowes; QC 1977; a Recorder, 1986–92; *b* Dar-es-Salaam, Tanzania, 1

Aug. 1928; *s* of late Henry Joseph O'Donnell Burke-Gaffney, OBE and Constance May (*née* Bishop); *m* 1961, Constance Caroline (*née* Murdoch); two *s* one *d*. *Educ:* Douai Sch.; RMA, Sandhurst. ACIArb. Commissioned Royal Irish Fusiliers, 1948; served with 1st Bn, Suez Canal Zone, Akaba, Gibraltar, BAOR and Berlin; served with Royal Ulster Rifles, Korean War, 1951, and in Hong Kong; qual. as interpreter in Turkish (studied at London Univ. and in Istanbul), 1955; Staff Captain, HQ 44 Div., 1956–58, when resigned commn and read for the Bar; joined Gray's Inn, 1956 (Lord Justice Holker Sen. Scholar); called to the Bar, 1959; Bencher, 1986. Jun. Counsel to HM Treasury in certain planning matters, 1974–77; a Legal Assessor to GMC and GDC, 1985. *Publications:* Three Lakes Inquiry Report, 1976; contrib. various articles in legal publications. *Recreations:* family, cricket, wildlife, painting, viniculture. *Address:* Durley, Savernake Forest, Marlborough, Wilts SN8 3AZ. *Club:* Naval and Military. *Died 3 June 2001.*

BURLEY, Sir Victor (George), Kt 1980; CBE 1969;FIEAust; FIEE, FIMechE, FIProdE; Chairman: Advisory Council of Commonwealth Scientific and Research Organization (CSIRO), 1979–81; Allied Industries Pty Ltd, 1984–2000; *b* 4 Dec. 1914; *s* of G. H. Burley and M. A. Luby; *m* 1941, Alpha Loyal Lord; one *s* three *d*. *Educ:* High Sch., Tasmania; Univ. of Tasmania (BE). FIFST; FInstD, FAIM. Cadbury-Fry-Pascall Pty Ltd, Australia, 1938–71: Chief Engr, Director and Vice-Chm.; Dir, Cadbury Schweppes Aust Ltd, 1971–78; Cons. Dir, Cadbury Fry Hudson NZ; Technical Cons., Cadbury Schweppes UK, 1978–82. Member, Adv. Council, CSIRO, 1961–78; Chm., State Cttee, Tas. CSIRO, 1964–78; Foundn Mem., Commonwealth Adv. Cttee on Advanced Educn, 1965–71; Foundn Chm., Council of Advanced Educn, Tasmania, 1968–76; Mem., Sci. and Industry Forum, Aust. Acad. of Science, 1967–81. Director: Productivity Promotion Council, Australia, 1983–88; University Research Co., 1985–90. University of Tasmania: Warden of Convocation, 1964–74; Mem., Faculty of Engrg, 1968–93; Mem. Council, 1982–84. *Recreations:* music, reading. *Address:* Montaigne, 553 Sandy Bay Road, Hobart, Tas 7005, Australia. *T:* (3) 62252583. *Clubs:* Melbourne (Melbourne); Tasmanian (Hobart). *Died 23 April 2003.*

BURNETT, Sir David Humphery, 3rd Bt *cr* 1913; MBE 1945; TD; one of HM Lieutenants of the City of London; *b* 27 Jan. 1918; *s* of Sir Leslie Trew Burnett, 2nd Bt, CBE, TD, DL, and Joan (*d* 1994), *d* of Sir John Humphery; *S* father, 1955; *m* 1948, Geraldine Elizabeth Mortimer, *d* of Sir Godfrey Arthur Fisher, KCMG; two *s* (and one *s* decd). *Educ:* Harrow; St John's Coll., Cambridge (MA). Served War of 1939–45 (despatches, MBE), in France, N Africa, Sicily and Italy; Temp. Lt-Col GSO1, 1945. Partner, David Burnett & Son, Chartered Surveyors, 1947–50; Director: Proprietors of Hay's Wharf Ltd, 1950–80 (Chm., 1965–80); Guardian Royal Exchange Assurance, 1967–88. Chm., London Assoc. of Public Wharfingers, 1964–71; Mem. PLA, 1962–75. Chm., 1976–81, Pres., 1985, S London Botanical Inst. Mem. Council, Brighton Coll., 1971–93. Master: Company of Watermen and Lightermen of the River Thames, 1964; Girdlers Company, 1970. FRICS 1970 (ARICS 1948); FCMI (FBIM 1968); FLS 1979. *Heir: s* Charles David Burnett [*b* 18 May 1951; *m* 1st, 1989, Victoria Joan (marr. diss.), *d* of James Simpson; one *d*; 2nd, 1998, Kay Rosemary Naylor]. *Address:* Tandridge Hall, near Oxted, Surrey RH8 9NJ; Twizel Millhouse, Cornhill-on-Tweed, Northumberland TD12 4UX. *Clubs:* Turf, Oxford and Cambridge. *Died 19 May 2002.*

BURNEY, Sir Cecil (Denniston), 3rd Bt *cr* 1921 of Preston House, Preston Candover, Southampton; *b* 8 Jan. 1923; *s* of Sir Charles Dennistoun Burney, 2nd Bt, CMG, and Gladys (*d* 1982), *d* of George Henry High; *S* father, 1968; *m* 1957, Hazel Marguerite de Hamel, *yr d* of late Thurman Coleman; two *s*. *Educ:* Eton; Trinity Coll., Cambridge. Man. Dir, 1951–68, Chm., 1968–72,

Northern Motors Ltd; Chairman: Hampton Trust PLC, 1975–87; JMD, subseq. Rhino, Group plc, 1988–92; Director: Security Building Soc., 1959–71; Mount Martin Gold Mines NL, 1985–87. Member of Legislative Council, N Rhodesia, 1959–64; MP Zambia, 1964–68; Chairman, Public Accounts Cttee, Zambia, 1963–67. *Recreations:* tennis, skiing. *Heir: s* Nigel Dennistoun Burney [*b* 6 Sept. 1959; *m* 1992, Lucy Brooks; two *s* one d]. *Address:* PO Box 32037, Lusaka, Zambia; 5 Lyall Street, SW1X 8DW. *T:* (020) 7235 4014. *Clubs:* White's, Carlton, Turf, Buck's; Leander; Harare, Bulawayo (Zimbabwe); Ndola (Zambia). *Died 19 April 2002.*

BURNHAM, 6th Baron *cr* 1903, of Hall Barn, Beaconsfield, Bucks; **Hugh John Frederick Lawson;** Bt 1892; *b* 15 Aug. 1931; *yr s* of 4th Baron Burnham, CB, DSO, MC, TD and (Marie) Enid Burnham, CBE (*d* 1979), *d* of Hugh Scott Robson, Buenos Aires; *S* brother, 1993; *m* 1955, Hilary Margaret, *yr d* of Alan Hunter, Perth; one *s* two *d*. *Educ:* Eton Coll.; Balliol Coll., Oxford (MA). Commissioned Scots Guards, 1950. Daily Telegraph, 1955–86 (Dep. Man. Dir, 1984–86). Dir Gen., King George's Fund for Sailors, 1988–93. A Dep. Speaker, H of L, 1995–2001, 2002–; Opposition spokesman on defence, H of L, 1997–2001; Opposition Dep. Chief Whip, H of L, 1997–2001; elected Mem., H of L, 1999. Younger Brother, Trinity House, 1998–. *Recreations:* Freemasonry, sailing, shooting. *Heir: s* Hon. Harry Frederick Alan Lawson, *b* 22 Feb. 1968. *Address:* Woodlands Farm, Beaconsfield, Bucks HP9 2SF. *Clubs:* Turf, Pratt's, Royal Ocean Racing; Royal Yacht Squadron.
Died 1 Jan. 2005.

BURNS, Anne, (Mrs D. O. Burns); British Gliding Champion (first woman), 1966; Principal Scientific Officer, Royal Aircraft Establishment, Farnborough, Hants, 1953–77; *b* 23 Nov. 1915; *d* of late Major Fleetwood Hugo Pellew, W Yorks Regt, and Violet Pellew (*née* Du Pré); *m* 1947, Denis Owen Burns (*d* 1990); no *c. Educ:* The Abbey Sch., Reading; St Hugh's Coll., Oxford (BA). Joined Min. of Supply, 1940; engaged in aircraft research at RAE, Farnborough, Hants, under various ministries, 1940–77. First woman glider pilot to cross Channel, 1957; international records: 4 gliding records in S Africa, 1961; records, S Africa, 1963, 1965; Colorado USA, 1967. Britannia Trophy (with Denis Burns), Royal Aero Club, 1961; Lilienthal Medal, Fédération Aéronautique Internationale, 1966. QCVSA, 1955 and 1963. *Publications:* contrib. scientific jls. *Recreations:* snooker, bowls. *Address:* Clumps End, Lower Bourne, Farnham, Surrey GU10 3HF.
Died 22 Jan. 2001.

BURNS, Dr B(enedict) Delisle, FRS 1968; Visitor, Divison of Neurobiology, University of Newcastle upon Tyne; *b* 22 Feb. 1915; *s* of C. Delisle Burns and Margaret Hannay; *m* 1st, 1938, Angela Ricardo; four *s*; 2nd, 1954, Monika Kasputis; one *d. Educ:* University Coll. Sch.; Tübingen Univ.; King's Coll., Cambridge; University Coll. Hospital. MRCS, LRCP 1939. Univ. extension lecturing for WEA, 1936–38; operational research, 1939–45; Research Asst, Nat. Inst. for Med. Research, 1945–49; Associate Prof. of Physiology, McGill Univ., Canada, 1950–58; Scientific Advisor to Dept of Veterans' Affairs, 1950–67; Prof. of Physiology, 1958–67, Chm., Dept of Physiology, 1965–67, McGill Univ., Canada; Head, Div. of Physiology and Pharmacology, Nat. Inst. of Medical Research, 1967–76; MRC External Staff, Anatomy Dept, 1976–80, Hon. Prof. of Neurobiology, 1977–80, Univ. of Bristol. *Publications:* The Mammalian Cerebral Cortex, 1958; The Uncertain Nervous System, 1968; about 100 articles on neurophysiology in scientific jls. *Recreations:* painting, interior decoration. *Address:* Division of Neurobiology, University of Newcastle upon Tyne, NE2 4HH. *T:* (0191) 222 6000, ext. 6948.
Died 6 Sept. 2001.

BURNS, Prof. Tom, FBA 1982; Professor of Sociology, University of Edinburgh, 1965–81; *b* 16 Jan. 1913; *s* of

John and Hannah Burns; *m* 1944, Mary Elizabeth Nora Clark; one *s* four *d. Educ:* Hague Street LCC Elementary Sch.; Parmiters Foundation Sch.; Univ. of Bristol (BA). Teaching in private schools in Tunbridge Wells and Norwich, 1935–39; Friends' Ambulance Unit, 1939–45 (POW, Germany, 1941–43); Research Asst, W Midland Gp on Post-war Reconstruction and Planning, 1945–49; Lectr, Sen. Lectr and Reader, Univ. of Edinburgh, 1949–65. Vis. Prof., Harvard, 1973–74. Mem., SSRC, 1969–70. *Publications:* Local Government and Central Control, 1954; (with G. M. Stalker) The Management of Innovation, 1961; (ed) Industrial Man, 1969; (ed with E. Burns) Sociology of Literature and Drama, 1973; The BBC: Public Institution and Private World, 1977; Erving Goffman, 1991; Description, Explanation and Understanding, 1994; articles in a number of jls in Britain, USA, France, etc. *Recreations:* music, gardening. *Address:* Inchgarvie Lodge, South Queensferry, West Lothian EH30 9JS. *Died 20 June 2001.*

BURNS, Prof. William, CBE 1966; Emeritus Professor of Physiology, University of London; Professor of Physiology, Charing Cross Hospital Medical School, 1947–77; Hon. Consultant Otologist, Charing Cross Group of Hospitals; *b* 15 Oct. 1909; *e s* of late Charles Burns, MB, ChB, JP and Mary Sillars, lately of Stonehaven, Scotland; *m* 1936, Margaret, *o d* of late W. A. Morgan, Glasgow; one *s* one *d. Educ:* Mackie Acad., Stonehaven; Aberdeen Univ. BSc 1932, MB ChB 1935, DSc 1943 Aberdeen. FRCP 1973. Asst in Physiology, Aberdeen, 1935; Lectr in Physiology, Aberdeen, 1936; War-time duty with Admiralty, 1942; established in RN Scientific Service, 1946; Supt RN Physiological Laboratory, 1947; Chm., Flying Personnel Res. Cttee, RAF, 1978–80; Emeritus Civil Consultant to RN in Audiology; Hon. Consultant to RAF in Acoustic Science; pt-time activity for MRC, 1977–84. Member: Council, BAAS, 1956–61 (Pres., Sect. I, Cardiff, 1960); Scientific Adv. Cttee, Inst. of Sound and Vibration Res., Univ. of Southampton, 1964–74; Noise Adv. Council, 1977–81; BMA; formerly: Mem., Cttee on Hearing, Bio-acoustics and Bio-mechanics, Nat. Res. Council, USA; Mem. or Chm., cttees of BSI, ISO, DHSS, MRC, on various aspects of hearing; Member: Physiol Soc.; British Inst. of Acoustics; Hon. Life Mem., British Soc. Audiology. *Publications:* Noise and Man, 1968, 2nd edn 1973; (with D. W. Robinson) Hearing and Noise in Industry, 1970; articles on various aspects of hearing, in Journal of the Acoustical Soc. of America, Annals of Occupational Hygiene, Proc. Assoc. of Industrial Med. Officers, etc. *Recreations:* working in wood and metal; interested in engineering in general. *Died 15 March 2004.*

BURROUGH, Alan, CBE 1970; Director, 1946–87, President, 1983–87, James Burrough plc (Chairman, 1968–82); Chairman: London Tideway Harbour Co. Ltd, since 1988; Albion Quay (1992) Ltd, since 1992; *b* 22 Feb. 1917; *s* of Ernest James Burrough and Sophie (*née* Burston); *m* 1st, 1939, Rosemary June Bruce (*d* 1993); two adopted *s* one adopted *d*; 2nd, 1995, Sheila Vivien van Dam. *Educ:* St Paul's Sch., London; Jesus Coll., Cambridge Univ. (MA). Joined James Burrough Ltd, 1935. War of 1939–45: 91st Field Regt, RA, and 5th RHA (Captain). Rejoined James Burrough Ltd, 1945: Director, 1946; Deputy Chairman, 1967; Chairman, 1968; Director: Corby Distilleries Ltd, Montreal, 1968–82; Hawks Co. Ltd, 1989–97. Dep. Pres., Oxon Br., British Red Cross, 1982–86. *Clubs:* Naval and Military; Hawks (Cambridge); Royal Channel Islands Yacht, Royal Lymington Yacht.
Died 23 July 2002.

BURROUGH, Rt Rev. John Paul, MBE 1946; Bishop of Mashonaland, 1968–81; *b* 5 May 1916; *s* of Canon E. G. Burrough; *m* 1962, Elizabeth, (Bess) (*d* 1991), *widow of* Stephen John White; one step *d. Educ:* St Edward's Sch.; St Edmund Hall, Oxford (BA 1937, MA); Ely Theol. College (DipTh 1938). Coach, Tigre Boat Club, Buenos Aires, 1938–39. Captain, Royal Signals, Malaya Campaign

(POW), 1940–45. Asst, Aldershot Parish Church, 1946–51; Mission Priest, Dio. of Korea, 1951–59; Anglican Chaplain to Overseas Peoples in Birmingham, 1959–68; Canon Residentiary of Birmingham, 1967–68; Rector of Empingham and Hon. Asst Bishop, Diocese of Peterborough, 1981–85. Chaplain and Sub-Prelate, Order of St John of Jerusalem, 1969–. *Publications:* Lodeleigh, 1946; God and Human Chance, 1984; Angels Unawares, 1988. *Recreation:* rowing (Oxford crews, 1937 and 1938). *Address:* 6 Mill Green Close, Bampton, Oxon OX18 2HF. *T:* (01993) 850952. *Clubs:* Leander (Henley); Vincent's (Oxford).   *Died 27 Jan. 2003.*

BURROWS, Sir Bernard (Alexander Brocas), GCMG 1970 (KCMG 1955; CMG 1950); *b* 3 July 1910; *s* of Edward Henry Burrows and Ione, *d* of Alexander Macdonald; *m* 1944, Ines (*d* 1997), *d* of late John Walter; one *s* one *d*. *Educ:* Eton; Trinity Coll., Oxford. Entered HM Foreign Service (later Diplomatic Service), 1934; served at HM Embassy, Cairo, 1938–45; Foreign Office, 1945–50; Counsellor HM Embassy, Washington, 1950–53; Political Resident in the Persian Gulf, 1953–58; Ambassador to Turkey, 1958–62; Dep. Under-Secretary of State, FO, 1963–66; Permanent British Representative to N Atlantic Council, 1966–70, retired 1970. Dir-Gen., Federal Trust for Educn and Res., 1973–76. *Publications:* (with C. Irwin) Security of Western Europe, 1972; (contrib.) The Third World War, 1978; Devolution or Federalism, 1980; (with G. Edwards) The Defence of Western Europe, 1982; Footnotes in the Sand, 1990; A Myth for our Time, 2001. *Address:* Durford Wood House, Upper Durford Wood, Petersfield GU31 5AN. *Club:* Travellers.   *Died 7 May 2002.*

BURROWS, Reginald Arthur, CMG 1964; HM Diplomatic Service, retired; *b* 31 Aug. 1918; *s* of late Arthur Richard Burrows, first Dir of Programmes, BBC; *m* 1952, Jenny Louisa Henriette Campiche (*d* 1985); one *s* one *d*. *Educ:* Mill Hill Sch.; St Catharine's Coll., Cambridge (Chancellor's Medal for English Verse, 1939; BA 1943, MA 1947). Served with Royal Air Force, Bomber Comd, SE Asia and Italy, 1941–45; comd No 13 (bomber) Sqdn, 1945. Entered the Foreign Service (later the Diplomatic Service), 1947; served in: Paris; Karachi; Tehran; Saigon; The Hague; Istanbul; Foreign Office; Minister, Islamabad, 1970–72; Univ. of Leeds, 1972–73; on secondment as Under-Sec., Civil Service Selection Bd, 1974–75; Asst Under-Sec. of State, 1975–78. *Recreations:* walking, studying Roman history. *Address:* Flat 9, Summer Court, Summer Hill, Harbledown, near Canterbury, Kent CT2 8NP. *T:* (01227) 457394.   *Died 10 Dec. 2002.*

BURSTEIN, Dame Rose; *see* Heilbron, Dame R.

BURT, Hon. Sir Francis (Theodore Page), AC 1988; KCMG 1977; QC 1960; Governor of Western Australia, 1990–93 (Lieutenant-Governor, 1977–90); *b* Perth, WA, 14 June 1918; *s* of A. F. G. Burt; *m* 1943, Margaret, *d* of Brig. J. E. Lloyd; two *s* two *d*. *Educ:* Guildford Grammar Sch.; Univ. of Western Australia (LLB, LLM); Hackett Schol., 1941; admitted to Bar of WA, 1941. Served War, RAN and RAAF, 1940–45. A Judge of Supreme Ct, WA, 1969–88; Chief Justice, WA, 1977–88. President: Law Soc. of WA, 1960–62; WA Bar Assoc., 1963–65. Visiting Lectr in Law, Univ. of WA, 1945–65. Chairman: Inst. of Radiotherapy, WA, 1960–62; Bd of Management, Sir Charles Gairdner Hosp., Hollywood, WA, 1962–72; Queen Elizabeth II Medical Centre Trust, 1966–85; Mem., Senate of Univ. of WA, 1968–76. Hon. LLD Univ. of WA, 1987. *Recreations:* tennis, fishing. *Address:* Unit 99, 4 Albert Street, Claremont, WA 6010, Australia. *Club:* Weld (Perth).   *Died 8 Sept. 2004.*

BURTON, Richard Hilary; Chairman, Cable Authority, 1984–90; *b* 28 Dec. 1923; *s* of Robert Claud and Theodora Constance Helen Burton; *m* 1962, Priscilla Jane Coode-Adams; one *s* one *d*. *Educ:* Lancing; Brasenose Coll., Oxford (MA 2nd Cl. Hons Jurisprudence). Served War, 1942–46, 60th Rifles, Captain (mentioned in

despatches); Mem., Military Courts, Palestine, 1946. Called to the Bar, Inner Temple, 1951; practised at Bar, 1951–54. Gillette Industries Ltd: Manager, Legal Dept, 1954–65; Legal Dir, 1965–78; Chm., 1978–84; Dep. to Chm., The Gillette Company (USA), 1984–88; Chm., Nestor-BNA plc, 1986–89. Chm., W Middlesex Arts Develt Trust, 1978–86. Freeman: City of London, 1974; Information Technologists' Co., 1988. FRSA. *Recreations:* cricket, real tennis, shooting, ornithology, lepidoptery. *Address:* Danmoor House, Heckfield, Hook, Hants RG27 0JY. *T:* (0118) 932 6233. *Clubs:* Boodle's, MCC (Mem. Cttee, 1989–92).   *Died 20 Sept. 2002.*

BURY, Air Cdre Thomas Malcolm Grahame, CB 1972; OBE 1962; retired as Head of Technical Training and Maintenance, British Aircraft Corporation, Saudi Arabia; *b* 11 Sept. 1918; *s* of late Ernest Bury, OBE; *m* 1951, Dillys Elaine Jenkins, MBE (*d* 2000), *d* of Dr Aneurin Jenkins, Swansea; two *s* one *d*. *Educ:* Forest Sch., E17. Served War, 1939–45, NW Europe, Arabia. Joined RAF, 1935; STSO, HQ, 1 Gp, 1961–64; DDME, MoD, 1965–66; Senior Engr Officer, Air Forces Gulf, 1967–68; Command Mech. Engr, HQ Strike Command, 1968–73; retired 1973. *Address:* 45 Abbey Mill, Church Street, Bradford on Avon, Wilts BA15 1AB.

                        Died 27 July 2002.

BUSHBY, Frederick Henry; Director of Services, Meteorological Office, 1978–84; *b* 10 Jan. 1924; *s* of Mr and Mrs Frederick George Bushby; *m* 1st, 1945, Joan Janet Gates (*d* 1996); one *s*; 2nd, 2000, Margaret Joan (*née* Atkins). *Educ:* Portsmouth Southern Secondary Sch.; Imperial Coll. of Science and Technol. (BSc 1st Cl. Hons Special Maths). ARCS. Meteorol Br., RAF, 1944–48; Meteorol Office, 1948–84; Asst Dir (Forecasting Res.), 1965–74; Dep. Dir (Dynamical Res.), 1974–77, (Forecasting), 1977–78. *Recreations:* bridge, bowls.

                        Died 22 Jan. 2004.

BUSVINE, Prof. James Ronald; Professor of Entomology as applied to Hygiene, University of London, 1964–76, Emeritus Professor 1977; *b* 15 April 1912; *s* of William Robert and Pleasance Dorothy Busvine; *m* 1960, Joan Arnfield; one *s* one *d*. *Educ:* Eastbourne Coll.; Imperial Coll. of Science and Technology, London Univ. (BSc Special (1st Cl. Hons) 1933); PhD 1938, DSc 1948, London. Imperial Chemical Industries, 1936–39; MRC Grants, 1940–42; Entomological Adviser, Min. of Health, 1943–45; London Sch. of Hygiene and Tropical Medicine: Lecturer 1946; Reader 1954; Professor 1964. Member: WHO Panel of Experts on Insecticides, 1956– (Cttee Chm. 1959 and 1968); FAO Panel of Experts on Pest Resistance, 1967– (Cttee Rapporteur). Travelled professionally in Malaya, Ceylon, Africa, USA, India, etc. *Publications:* Insects and Hygiene, 1951, 3rd edn 1980; A Critical Review of the Techniques for Testing Insecticides, 1957, 2nd edn 1971; Anthropod Vectors of Disease, 1975; Insects, Hygiene and History, 1976; I warmed both Hands, 1986; Discovery of Disease Transmission by Arthropods and 90 Years of Attempts to stop it, 1993; numerous scientific articles. *Recreations:* painting, bridge. *Address:* Musca, 26 Braywick Road, Maidenhead, Berks SL6 1DA. *T:* (01628) 622888.

                        Died 15 Jan. 2003.

BUTLER, Denis William Langford; Comptroller and City Solicitor to the City of London, 1981–89; *b* 26 Oct. 1926; *s* of late William H. Butler, Shrewsbury and Kitty Butler; *m* 1953, Marna (*née* Taylor); three *d*. *Educ:* Repton. RM, 1945–47. Admitted Solicitor, 1951. Assistant Solicitor: Norfolk CC, 1953–54; Shropshire CC, 1954–57; Sen. Asst Solicitor, Lindsey (Lincs) CC, 1957–60; Dep. Clerk, 1960–74; County Solicitor and Clerk, 1974–81; Wilts CC. Chm., County Secs Soc., 1974–76. Freeman, City of London, 1981; Liveryman, City of London Solicitors' Co., 1983–. *Recreations:* travel, gardening. *Club:* Guildhall.   *Died 20 Dec. 2004.*

BUTLER, George William P.; *see* Payne-Butler.

BUTLER, Ian Geoffrey, CBE 1990; FCA; Chairman, Cookson Group, 1976–May 1990 and Nov. 1990–July 1991; Director, Barclays Bank, 1985–91; *b* 12 April 1925; *s* of Hubert Desramaux Butler and Nita Butler (*née* Blake); *m* 1973, Anne Robertson; two *d. Educ:* Huyton Hill, Liverpool; Stowe Sch.; Trinity Coll., Oxford (MA). Commissioned Coldstream Guards, 1943–47. Tansley Witt & Co., 1948–55, Partner, 1951–55; Goodlass Wall & Lead Industries, subseq. named Cookson Group, 1956–98: Finance Dir, 1965; Managing Dir, 1973. Chm., Tioxide Gp, 1987–90. Treasurer and Mem. Exec. Cttee, Internat. Yacht Racing Union, 1977–90; Mem. Council, Royal Yachting Assoc., 1960–91 (former Hon. Treasurer). *Recreations:* sailing, ski-ing, fell walking. *Address:* Wyke House, Ellanore Lane, West Wittering, West Sussex PO20 8AN. *T:* (01243) 513269. *Clubs:* Royal Thames Yacht; Royal Yacht Squadron, Itchenor Sailing.
Died 4 March 2001.

BUTLER, John Manton, MSc; *b* 9 Oct. 1909; *m* 1940, Marjorie Smith, Melbourne; one *s* one *d. Educ:* Southland, NZ; Univ. of Otago (Sen. Schol., NZ, Physics; BSc 1929; Smeaton Schol. Chemistry, 1930, John Edmond Fellow, 1930; MSc 1st class Hons). Pres., Students' Union; Graduate Rep. Univ. Council. Joined Shell, NZ, 1934; served various Shell cos in UK, Australia and S Africa until 1957; Man. Dir, Lewis Berger (GB) Ltd, 1957; Dir, Berger, Jenson & Nicholson Ltd, 1969–74. Chm., BNEC Cttee for Exports to NZ, 1967 (Dep. Chm., 1965). Pres., NZ Soc., 1971. Member: Cttee, Spastics Soc.; St David's Cttee, Conservative Assoc., 1979–80; Aust. Inst. of Internat. Affairs, 1981–. Consultant. *Recreations:* travel, golf, photography. *Address:* Osborne, 28 Ranfurlie Crescent, Glen Iris, Victoria 3146, Australia. *T:* (3) 998859458. *Club:* Royal Melbourne Golf.
Died Sept. 2001.

BUTTERWORTH, Baron *cr* 1985 (Life Peer), of Warwick in the County of Warwickshire; **John Blackstock Butterworth,** CBE 1982; JP; DL; First Vice-Chancellor, University of Warwick, 1963–85; *b* 13 March 1918; *o s* of John William and Florence Butterworth; *m* 1948, Doris Crawford Elder; one *s* two *d. Educ:* Queen Elizabeth's Grammar Sch., Mansfield; The Queen's Coll., Oxford (MA 1946). Royal Artillery, 1939–46. Called to the Bar, Lincoln's Inn, 1947, Hon. Bencher, 1989. New College, Oxford: Fellow, 1946–63; Dean, 1952–56; Bursar, 1956–63; Sub Warden, 1957–58; Junior Proctor, 1950–51; Faculty Fellow, Nuffield Coll., 1953–58; Mem., Hebdomadal Council, Oxford Univ., 1953–63. Managing Trustee 1964–85, Trustee, 1985–, Nuffield Foundation; Pres., Foundn for Sci. and Technol., 1997– (Chm., 1990–97); Univ. Comr (under Educn Reform Act 1988), 1988–. Chairman: Inter-Univ. Council for Higher Educn Overseas, 1968–77; Univs Cttee for Non-teaching Staffs, 1970–85; Inquiry into work of Probation Officers and Social Workers in Local Authorities and Nat. Service, 1971–73; Standing Cttee on Internat. Co-operation in Higher Educn, British Council, 1981–85; Inter-Univ. and Polytechnic Council, 1981–85; Member: Royal Commn on the Working of the Tribunals of Inquiry (Act) 1921, 1966; Intergovtl Cttee on Law of Contempt in relation to Tribunals of Inquiry, 1968; Jarratt Cttee on University Efficiency, 1986; Cttee on the review of UGC, 1987;

Noise Adv. Council, 1974–81; Bd, British Council, 1981–85; British delegn to Commonwealth Educn Confs in Lagos, 1968, Canberra, 1971, Kingston, 1974, Accra, 1977, Colombo, 1980. Hon. Emeritus Governor, Royal Shakespeare Theatre (Governor, 1964–99). DL Warwickshire, 1967–74, DL West Midlands 1974; JP City of Oxford, 1962, Coventry, 1963. Hon. DCL Sierra Leone, 1976; Hon. DSc Aston, 1985; Hon. LLD Warwick, 1986. *Address:* The Barn, Barton, Guiting Power, Glos GL54 5US. *T:* (01451) 850297. *Club:* Athenæum.
Died 19 June 2003.

BUTTFIELD, Dame Nancy (Eileen), DBE 1972; Senator for South Australia, Oct. 1955–June 1965, July 1968–1974; *b* 12 Nov. 1912; *d* of Sir Edward Wheewall Holden and Hilda May Lavis; *m* 1936, Frank Charles Buttfield; two *s. Educ:* Woodlands Church of England Girls' Grammar Sch., Adelaide; Composenea; Paris; Univ. of Adelaide, SA. Exec. Mem., Commonwealth Immigration Adv. Council, 1955–; Vice-President: Good Neighbour Council of SA, 1956–62; Phoenix Soc. for the Physically Handicapped, 1959–. Dir, Co-operative Building Soc. of SA, 1959, then Emeritus Dir. Mem. Council, Bedford Industries, 1965–. Mem., Nat. Council of Women of SA. *Recreations:* farming, dress-making, gourmet cooking, music. *Address:* 52 Strangeways Terrace, North Adelaide, SA 5006, Australia. *Clubs:* Queen Adelaide, Lyceum, Royal Adelaide Golf (all SA).
Died 4 Sept. 2005.

BYWATERS, Eric George Lapthorne, CBE 1975; FRCP; Professor of Rheumatology, Royal Postgraduate Medical School, University of London, 1958–75, then Emeritus; Hon. Consultant Physician, Hammersmith Hospital and Wexham Park Hospital, Slough, Bucks; *b* 1 June 1910; *s* of George Ernest Bywaters and Ethel Penney; *m* 1935, Betty Euan-Thomas (*d* 1998); three *d. Educ:* Sutton Valence Sch., Kent; Middx Hosp. (Sen. Broderip Schol., Lyell Gold Medallist; MB BS 1933). FRCP 1950. McKenzie McKinnon Fellow, RCP, 1935; Asst Clin. Pathologist, Bland Sutton Inst., 1936; Rockefeller Travelling Fellow and Harvard Univ. Research Fellow in Med., 1937–39; Beit Memorial Fellow, 1939; Actg Dir, MRC Clin. Res. Unit (Shock), 1943; Lectr in Med., Postgrad. Med. Sch., 1945; Dir, MRC Rheumatism Res. Unit, Taplow, 1958–75; Sen. MRC Res. Fellow, Bone and Joint Unit, London Hosp., 1977–. Pres., European League against Rheumatism, 1977 (Hon. Mem. 1981); Councillor, Internat. League against Rheumatism. Hon. Librarian, Heberden Library, RCP, 1970–90 (Hon. Mem., Heberden Soc., 1977). Fellow, RPMS, 1993. Hon. FACP, 1973; Hon. FRCP&S (Canada), 1977; Hon. FRSocMed, 1983. Hon. MD Liège, 1973. Gairdner Foundation Medical Award, 1963; Heberden Orator and Medallist, 1966; Croonian Lectr, RCP, 1968; Bunim Lectr and Medallist, 1973; Ewart Angus Lectr, Toronto, 1974; Samuel Hyde Lectr, RSocMed, 1986. Hon. Mem. Dutch, French, Amer., German, Czech, Spanish, Portuguese, Aust., Indian, Canadian, Chilean, Peruvian, Jugoslav, Egyptian, Turkish, Greek, S African and Argentine Rheumatism Assocs. *Publications:* papers on rheumatism, crush syndrome, etc. *Recreations:* painting, gardening. *Address:* 53 Burkes Road, Beaconsfield, Bucks HP9 1PW.
Died 2 April 2003.

C

CABLE, Sir James (Eric), KCVO 1976; CMG 1967; HM Diplomatic Service, retired; writer; *b* 15 Nov. 1920; *s* of late Eric Grant Cable, CMG and Nellie Margaret, *o d* of Harry John Skelton Hythe; *m* 1954, Viveca Hollmerus; one *s*. *Educ*: Stowe; Corpus Christi Coll., Cambridge (PhD 1973). Served Royal Signals, 1941–46, Major. Entered Foreign (later Diplomatic) Service, 1947; 2nd Sec., 1948; Vice-Consul, Batavia, 1949; 2nd Sec., Djakarta, 1949; acted as Chargé d'Affaires, 1951 and 1952; Helsinki, 1952; FO, 1953; 1st Sec., 1953; Mem. of British Delegn to Geneva Conf. on Indo-China, 1954; 1st Sec. (Commercial), Budapest, 1956; Head of Chancery and Consul, Quito, 1959; acted as Chargé d'Affaires, 1959 and 1960; FO, 1961 and Head of SE Asia Dept, 1963–66; Counsellor, Beirut, 1966–69; acted as Chargé d'Affaires at Beirut, 1967, 1968 and 1969; Research Associate, Institute for Strategic Studies, 1969–70; Head of Western Organisations Dept, FCO, 1970–71; Counsellor, Contingency Studies, FCO, 1971; Head of Planning Staff, 1971–75, and Asst Under-Sec. of State, 1972–75, FCO; Ambassador to Finland, 1975–80. Leverhulme Res. Fellow, 1981–82. Member: Adv. Bd, Centre of Internat. Studies, Cambridge, 1994–; Conseil Scientifique, Institut de Stratégie Comparée, Paris, 1996–. *Publications*: Britain in Tomorrow's World, 1969 (as Grant Hugo); Appearance and Reality in International Relations, 1970 (as Grant Hugo); Gunboat Diplomacy, 1971, 3rd edn 1994; The Royal Navy and the Siege of Bilbao, 1979; Britain's Naval Future, 1983; Diplomacy at Sea, 1985; The Geneva Conference of 1954 on Indochina, 1986, 2nd edn 2000; Political Institutions and Issues in Britain, 1987; Navies in Violent Peace, 1989; Intervention at Abadan, 1991; The Political Influence of Naval Force in History, 1998; articles in British and foreign jls. *Address*: 8 Essex Close, Cambridge CB4 2DW.   *Died 27 Sept. 2001.*

CADIEUX, Hon. Léo Alphonse Joseph, OC 1975; PC 1965; Ambassador of Canada to France, 1970–75; *b* 28 May 1908; *s* of Joseph E. Cadieux and Rosa Paquette, both French Canadian; *m* 1962, Monique, *d* of Placide Plante; one *s*. *Educ*: Commercial Coll. of St Jerome and Seminary of Ste Thérèse de Blainville, Quebec. Editorial staff of La Presse, Montreal, Quebec, 1930–41; Associate Dir of Public Relations, Can. Army, 1941–44; War Corresp. for La Presse, Montreal, 1944; Mayor of St Antoine des Laurentides, Que., 1948. First elected to House of Commons, gen. elec., 1962; re-elected gen. elec., 1963, 1965, 1968; apptd Associate Minister of Nat. Defence, 1965; Minister of National Defence, Canada, 1967–70. *Address*: 20 Driveway, Appt 1106, Ottawa, ON K2P 1C8, Canada.   *Died 11 May 2005.*

CAIRNS, Dr James Ford; MHR (ALP) for Lalor, 1969–78 (for Yarra, 1955–69); *b* 4 Oct. 1914; *s* of James John Cairns and Letitia Cairns (*née* Ford); *m* 1939, Gwendolyn Olga Robb (d 2000); one *s* (and one *s* decd). *Educ*: Melton/Sunbury State Sch.; Northcote High Sch.; Melbourne Univ. MComm and PhD (Melb.). Australian Estates Co. Ltd, 1932; Victoria Police Force, 1935. Served War, AIF, 1945. Melbourne University: Sen. Tutor, Lectr, Sen. Lectr (Economic Hist.), 1946–55; Nuffield Dominion Fellow, Oxford Univ., 1951–52. Minister for Overseas Trade, 1972–74; Treasurer of Australia, 1974–75; Dep. Prime Minister, 1974–75; Minister for the Environment, Australia, 1975. Chifley Meml Lect., 2001. *Publications*: Australia, 1951 (UK); Living with Asia, 1965; The Eagle and the Lotus, 1969; Tariffs or Planning, 1970; Silence Kills, 1970; The Quiet Revolution, 1972; Oil in Troubled Waters, 1976; Vietnam: Scorched Earth Reborn, 1976; Growth to Freedom, 1979; Survival Now, the Human Transformation, 1983; Human Growth: its

source ... and potential, 1985; Strength Within: towards an end to violence, 1988; The Untried Road, 1990; Towards a New Society: a new day has begun, 1993; Reshaping the Future, 1997; On the Horizon, 1999; A New Day, 2002; numerous articles in jls and press, incl. title Australia: History in Enc. Brit. *Recreations*: sleeping, reading, listening to music.   *Died 12 Oct. 2003.*

CALCUTT, Sir David (Charles), Kt 1991; QC 1972; Chairman, City Panel on Takeovers and Mergers, 1989–2000; a Judge of the Courts of Appeal of Jersey and Guernsey, 1978–2000; Chancellor of the Dioceses of Exeter and of Bristol, since 1971 and in Europe (formerly Gibraltar in Europe), since 1983; *b* 2 Nov. 1930; *s* of late Henry Calcutt; *m* 1969, Barbara, JP and Freeman, City of London, *d* of late Vivian Walker. *Educ*: Christ Church, Oxford (chorister); Cranleigh Sch. (music schol.); King's Coll., Cambridge (choral schol.; Stewart of Rannoch Schol., 1952; prizeman; MA, LLB, MusB). Called to the Bar, Middle Temple, 1955 (Bencher, 1981; Treas., 1998); Harmsworth Law Schol., Garraway Rice Prize, 1956; Chm. of the Bar, 1984–85 (Vice-Chm., 1983–84). Dep. Chm., Somerset QS, 1970–71; a Recorder, 1972–89. Fellow Commoner, 1980–85, Master, 1986–94, Magdalene Coll., Cambridge (Hon. Fellow, 1994). Dept of Trade Inspector, Cornhill Consolidated Gp Ltd, 1974–77; Chairman: CS Arbitration Tribunal, 1979–94; Falkland Is Commn of Enquiry, 1984; Inst. of Actuaries' Appeal Bd, 1985–94; Dep. Pres., 1983–87, Pres., 1987–97, Lloyds of London Appeal Tribunal; Member: Criminal Injuries Compensation Bd, 1977–97; Council on Tribunals, 1980–86; conducted: Cyprus Service Police Inquiry, 1985–86; Review of Press Self-Regulation, 1992–93; Member: Interception of Communications Tribunal, 1986–2001 (Vice-Pres., 1996–2001); Investigatory Powers Tribunal, 2000–; Pres., Interception of Communications Tribunal (Guernsey), 1998–; Arbitrator, Internat. Centre for the Settlement of Investment Disputes, Washington, 1992–2004 (Conciliator, 1986–92); Indep. Mem., Diplomatic Service Appeal Bd, 1986–92; Assessor of Compensation for Miscarriages of Justice, Home Office, 1989–2001, MoD, 1993–; Chairman: Cttee on Privacy and Related Matters, 1989–90; Council of the Banking Ombudsman, 1994–2001; Judicial Chm., City Disputes Panel, 1994–; Chm., Legal Services Commn, IoM, 2000–01. UK Deleg., Consultative Cttee, Bars and Law Socs, EEC, 1979–83. Gresham Prof. of Law, 1992–95. Fellow, Internat. Acad. of Trial Lawyers (NY), 1978–; Hon. Member: American Bar Assoc., 1985–; Canadian Bar Assoc., 1985–; Cambridge Union Soc., 1994–. Dir, Edington Music Fest., 1956–64. Dep. Chm., RCM, 1988–90 (FRCM 1988). Chairman: Council, Cranleigh and Bramley Schs, 1987–93 (Vice-Chm., 1983–87); Septemviri, Cambridge Univ., 1988–95; Gov., Ditchley Foundn, 1992–. Trustee, Winchester Cathedral Trust, 1992–. Fellow, Winchester Coll., 1992–. Hon. LLD: Exeter, 1996; Staffordshire, 1997; Southampton, 1998; UWE, 1998. *Recreation*: living on Exmoor. *Address*: Outer Temple Chambers, The Outer Temple, 222 Strand, WC2R 1BA. *T*: (020) 7353 6381. *Clubs*: Athenæum; New (Edinburgh); Hawks (Cambridge).
               Died 11 Aug. 2004.

CALDOW, William James, CMG 1977; Consultant, ICI plc, 1981–86; *b* 7 Dec. 1919; *s* of William Caldow and Mary Wilson Grier; *m* 1950, Monique Henriette Hervé, *d* of Gaétan Hervé, Chevalier de la Légion d'Honneur and Croix de Guerre (member of French Resistance, executed 1944); one *s* (and one *s* decd). *Educ*: Marr College (Dux Medallist); Glasgow University (Scholar; MA Hons);

Sorbonne. Captain, Intelligence Corps, 1940–45. Colonial Administrative Service, Gold Coast, later Ghana, 1947–59; War Office, later Ministry of Defence, 1959–80. *Recreations:* reading, music, bird watching. *Address:* 3 Pilgrims Way, Guildford, Surrey GU4 8AB. *T:* (01483) 562183. *Died 27 May 2004.*

CALLAGHAN OF CARDIFF, Baron *cr* 1987 (Life Peer), of the City of Cardiff in the County of South Glamorgan; **Leonard James Callaghan,** KG 1987; PC 1964; *b* 27 March 1912; *s* of James Callaghan, Chief Petty Officer, RN; *m* 1938, Audrey Elizabeth Moulton (*d* 2005); one *s* two *d*. *Educ:* Elementary and Portsmouth Northern Secondary Schs. Entered Civil Service as a Tax Officer, 1929; Asst Sec., Inland Revenue Staff Fedn, 1936–47 (with an interval during the War of 1939–45, when served in Royal Navy). Joined Labour Party, 1931. MP (Lab): S Cardiff, 1945–50; SE Cardiff, 1950–83; Cardiff S and Penarth, 1983–87. Parly Sec., Min. of Transport, 1947–50; Chm. Cttee on Road Safety, 1948–50; Parliamentary and Financial Sec., Admiralty, 1950–51; Opposition Spokesman: Transport, 1951–53; Fuel and Power, 1953–55; Colonial Affairs, 1956–61; Shadow Chancellor, 1961–64; Chancellor of the Exchequer, 1964–67; Home Secretary, 1967–70; Shadow Home Sec., 1970–71; Opposition Spokesman on Employment, 1971–72; Shadow Foreign Sec., 1972–74; Sec. of State for Foreign and Commonwealth Affairs, 1974–76; Minister of Overseas Develt, 1975–76; Prime Minister and First Lord of the Treasury, 1976–79; Leader, Labour Party, 1976–80; Leader of the Opposition, 1979–80. Father, House of Commons, 1983–87. Deleg. to Council of Europe, Strasburg, 1948–50 and 1954. Mem., Labour Party NEC, 1957–80; Treasurer, Labour Party, 1967–76, Vice-Chm. 1973, Chm. 1974. Consultant to Police Fedn of England and Wales and to Scottish Police Fedn, 1955–64. President: Adv. Cttee on Protection (formerly Pollution) of the Sea, 1963–2001 (Chm., 1952–63); United Kingdom Pilots Assoc., 1963–76; Jt Pres., RIIA, 1983–2003. Hon. Pres., Internat. Maritime Pilots Assoc., 1971–76. Pres., Univ. of Wales, Swansea (formerly UC Swansea), 1986–95 (Hon. Fellow, 1993). Visiting Fellow, Nuffield Coll., Oxford, 1959–67, Hon. Life Fellow, 1967; Hon. Fellow: UC Cardiff, 1978; Portsmouth Polytechnic, 1981; Cardiff Inst. of Higher Educn, 1991. Hon. LLD: Wales, 1976; Sardar Patel Univ., India, 1978; Birmingham, 1981; Sussex, 1989; Westminster, 1993; Liverpool, 1996; Hon. PhD Meisei Univ., Tokyo, 1984; DUniv Open, 1996. Hon. Bencher, Inner Temple, 1976. Freeman: City of Portsmouth, 1991; City of Swansea, 1993; Hon. Freeman: City of Cardiff, 1974; City of Sheffield, 1979. Hubert H. Humphrey Internat. Award, 1978. Grand Cross, 1st class, Order of Merit of Federal Republic of Germany, 1979. *Publications:* A House Divided: the dilemma of Northern Ireland, 1973; Time and Chance (autobiog.), 1987. *Address:* House of Lords, SW1A 0PW.
Died 26 March 2005.

CALLAWAY, Sir Frank (Adams), Kt 1981; AO 1995; CMG 1975; OBE 1970; Professor and Head of Department of Music, University of Western Australia, 1959–84, Professor Emeritus, 1985; *b* 16 May 1919; *s* of Archibald Charles Callaway and Mabel Callaway (*née* Adams); *m* 1942, Kathleen Jessie, *d* of R. Allan; two *s* two *d*. *Educ:* West Christchurch High Sch.; Dunedin Teachers' Coll., NZ; Univ. of Otago, NZ (MusB); Royal Academy of Music. FRAM, ARCM, FTCL; FACE. Mem., RNZAF Band, 1940–42. Head, Dept of Music, King Edward Tech. Coll., Dunedin, NZ, 1942–53; Reader in Music, Univ. of WA, 1953–59. Conductor: King Edward Tech. Coll. Symphony Orchestra, 1945–53; Univ. of WA Orchestral Soc., 1953–64; Univ. of WA Choral Soc., 1953–79; Guest Conductor: WA Symphony Orchestra; S Australia Symphony Orchestra; Adelaide Philharmonic Choir; Orpheus Choir, Wellington, NZ. Member: Australian Music Exams Bd, 1955–84 (Chm., 1964–66 and 1977–79); Adv. Bd, Commonwealth Assistance to Australian Composers, 1966–72; Australian Nat. Commn

for UNESCO, 1968–82; Exec. Bd, Internat. Music Council of UNESCO, 1976–82 (Pres., 1980–81; Individual Mem., 1982–85, Life Mem. of Honour, 1986); Music Bd, Australia Council, 1969–74; Chairman: WA Arts Adv. Bd, 1970–73; WA Arts Council, 1973–79; Organizing Cttees, Aust. Nat. Eisteddfod 1979, Indian Ocean Fests, 1979, 1984; Indian Ocean Arts Assoc., 1980–85 (Pres., 1985–). Founding Pres. and Life Mem., Australian Soc. for Music Educn, 1966–71; Mem., Bd of Dirs, Internat. Soc. for Music Educn, 1958– (Pres., 1968–72, Treasurer, 1972–88, Hon. Pres., 1988–). External Examiner (Music), Kenyatta Univ., Nairobi, 1985–87; Consultant, Callaway Internat. Resource Centre for Music Educn, Univ. of WA, 1988–. Patron, Music Council of Australia, 1994. Foundn Mem., 1983, Pres., 1984–97, WA Br., Lord's Taverners Australia. Founding Editor: Australian Jl of Music Educn, 1967–82; Studies in Music, 1967–84; Internat. Jl of Music Educn, 1983–85; General Editor, Music Series and Music Monographs. W Australian Citizen of the Year, 1975. Hon. Fellowship in Music, Australian Music Exams Bd, 1997. Hon. MusD: W Australia, 1975; Melbourne, 1982. Aust. Nat. Critics' Circle Award for Music, 1977; Sir Bernard Heinze Award for Service to Australian Music, 1988; Internat. Percy Grainger Medal, 1991; Internat. Music Council/ UNESCO Music Prize, 1997. *Publications:* (General Ed.) Challenges in Music Education, 1975; (ed with D. E. Tunley) Australian Composition in the Twentieth Century, 1978; (compiled) Percy Grainger Symposium, 1982; (ed) Essays in Honour of David Evatt Tunley, 1995; articles on music and music education. *Recreations:* reading, gardening, cricket. *Address:* 64/177 Dampier Avenue, Kallaroo, WA 6025, Australia. *T:* and *Fax:* (8) 94015127.
Died 22 Feb. 2003.

CALTON, Patsy; MP (Lib Dem) Cheadle, since 2001; *b* 19 Sept. 1948; *d* of John Gordon and Joan Yeldon; *m* 1969, Clive Roger Calton; one *s* two *d*. *Educ:* Wymondham Coll., Norfolk; UMIST (BSc Biochem.); Univ. of Manchester (PGCE). Chemistry teacher, 1971–79 and 1987–2001. Mem. (Lib Dem) Stockport MBC, 1994– 2002 (Dep. Leader, 1999–2001). *Recreations:* running (London marathons, 1999, 2001–03), gardening, reading. *Address:* House of Commons, SW1A 0AA. *T:* (020) 7219 8471; 3 Gillbent Road, Cheadle Hulme, Cheadle SK8 7LE. *T:* (0161) 485 6560. *Club:* National Liberal.
Died 29 May 2005.

CALVERT, Florence Irene, (Mrs W. A. Prowse); Principal, St Mary's College, University of Durham, 1975–77; *b* 1 March 1912; *d* of Ernest William Calvert and Florence Alice (*née* Walton); *m* 1977, William Arthur Prowse (*d* 1981). *Educ:* Univ. of Sheffield (BA, 1st Cl. Hons French and Latin, MA). Asst Language Teacher, Accrington Grammar Sch., 1936–39; Head, Modern Langs Dept, Accrington Girls' High Sch., 1939–48; Univ. of Durham: Lectr in Educn, 1948; Sen. Lectr, 1964–75. *Publications:* French Plays for the Classroom, 1951; L'Homme aux Mains Rouges, 1954; Contes, 1957; French by Modern Methods in Primary and Secondary Schools, 1965. *Address:* 7 St Mary's Close, Shincliffe, Durham DH1 2ND. *T:* (0191) 386 5502.
Died 22 Dec. 2002.

CALVERT, Phyllis; actress; *b* 18 Feb. 1915; *d* of Frederick and Annie Bickle; *m* 1941, Peter Murray Hill (*d* 1957); one *s* one *d*. *Educ:* Margaret Morris Sch.; Institut Français. Malvern Repertory Company, 1935; Coventry, 1937; York, 1938. First London appearance in A Woman's Privilege, Kingsway Theatre, 1939; Punch Without Judy, Embassy, 1939; Flare Path, Apollo, 1942; Escapade, St James's, 1953; It's Never Too Late, Strand, 1954; River Breeze, Phoenix, 1956; The Complaisant Lover, Globe, 1959; The Rehearsal, Globe, 1961; Ménage à Trois, Lyric, 1963; Portrait of Murder, Savoy, Vaudeville, 1963; A Scent of Flowers, Duke of York's, 1964; Present Laughter, Queen's, 1965; A Woman of No Importance, Vaudeville, 1967; Blithe Spirit, Globe, 1970; Crown Matrimonial,

Haymarket, 1973; Dear Daddy, Ambassadors, 1976; Mrs Warren's Profession, Worcester, 1977; She Stoops to Conquer, Old World, Exeter, 1978; Suite in Two Keys, tour, 1978; Before the Party, Queen's, 1980; Smithereens, Theatre Royal, Windsor, 1985; The Heiress, Chichester Fest., 1989. First film appearance, 1939. *Films include:* Kipps, The Young Mr Pitt, Man in Grey, Fanny by Gaslight, Madonna of the Seven Moons, They were Sisters, Time out of Mind, Broken Journey, My Own True Love, The Golden Madonna, A Woman with No Name, Mr Denning Drives North, Mandy, The Net, It's Never Too Late, Child in the House, Indiscreet, The Young and The Guilty, Oscar Wilde, Twisted Nerve, Oh! What a Lovely War, The Walking Stick, Mrs Dalloway. *Television* series and serials: Kate, 1970; Cover her Face, 1985; All Passion Spent, 1986; A Killing on the Exchange, 1987; Boon, 1987; Sophia and Constance, 1988; The Woman He Loved, 1988; Capsticks Law, 1989; Victoria Wood, 1989; After Henry, 1990; Lime Grove, 1991; Jute City, 1991; Woof, 1991; House of Elliot, 1993; Sherlock Holmes, 1994; Casualty, 1996; Midsomer Murders, 1999; plays: Death of a Heart, 1985; Across the Lake, 1988. *Recreations:* swimming, gardening, collecting costume books. *Address:* 1 Sandringham Court, Westleigh Avenue, SW15 6RE. *Died 8 Oct. 2002.*

CAMERON OF LOCHIEL, Colonel Sir Donald (Hamish), KT 1973; CVO 1970; TD 1944; JP; 26th Chief of the Clan Cameron; Lord-Lieutenant of County of Inverness, 1971–85 (Vice-Lieutenant, 1963–70); Chartered Accountant; *b* 12 Sept. 1910; *s* of Col Sir Donald Walter Cameron of Lochiel, KT, CMG, 25th Chief of the Clan Cameron, and Lady Hermione Emily Graham (*d* 1978), 2nd *d* of 5th Duke of Montrose; *S* father, as 26th Chief, 1951; *m* 1939, Margaret, *o d* of Lieut-Col Hon. Nigel Gathorne-Hardy, DSO; two *s* two *d*. *Educ:* Harrow; Balliol Coll., Oxford. Joined Lovat Scouts, 1929; Major 1940; Lieut-Col 1945; Lieut-Col comdg 4/5th Bn (TA) QO Cameron Highlanders, 1955–57; Col 1957 (TARO). Hon. Colonel: 4/5th Bn QO Cameron Highlanders, 1958–67; 3rd (Territorial) Bn Queen's Own Highlanders (Seaforth and Camerons), 1967–69; 2nd Bn, 51st Highland Volunteers, 1970–75. Member (part-time): British Railways Bd, 1962–64; Scottish Railways Bd, 1964–72 (Chm. Scottish Area Bd, BTC, 1959–64); Transport Holding Co., 1962–65; Director: Royal Bank of Scotland, 1954–80 (Vice-Chm., 1969–80); Save & Prosper Gp, 1968–84; Culter Guard Bridge Holdings Ltd, 1970–77 (Chm., 1970–76); Scottish Widows Life Assurance Soc., 1955–81 (Chm., 1964–67). Crown Estate Comr, 1957–69. Chm., Scottish Cttee, Malcolm Sargent Cancer Fund for Children, 1975–91. President: Scottish Landowners Fedn, 1979–84; Royal Highland and Agricultural Soc. of Scotland, 1971, 1979 and 1987. Governor, Harrow Sch., 1967–77. *Heir: s* Donald Angus Cameron, younger of Lochiel,*b* 2 Aug. 1946. *Address:* Achnacarry, Spean Bridge, Inverness-shire PH34 4EJ. *T:* (01397) 712708. *Clubs:* Pratt's; New (Edinburgh).
Died 26 May 2004.

CAMERON, Ellen; *see* Malcolm, E.

CAMERON, Prof. J(ames) Malcolm, MD, PhD; FRCSGlas, FRCPath; Professor of Forensic Medicine, University of London, at The London Hospital Medical College, 1973–92, then Professor Emeritus; Consulting Editor, Medicine, Science and Law (Editor, 1970–95); *b* 29 April 1930; *s* of late James Cameron and Doris Mary Robertson; *m* 1956, Primrose Agnes Miller McKerrell, MCST (*d* 1999); one *d*. *Educ:* The High Sch. of Glasgow; Univ. of Glasgow (MB ChB 1954, MD 1959, PhD 1966); DMJ. FRCPath 1977; FRCSGlas 1983. Registrar in Lab. Med., 1959–60, Sen. Registrar in Path., 1960–62, Southern Gen. Hosp., Glasgow; Lectr in Path., Univ. of Glasgow, 1962; The London Hospital Medical College: Lectr in Forensic Med., 1963–65; Sen. Lectr in Forensic Med., 1965–70; Reader in Forensic Med., 1970–72; Sen. Lectr in Forensic Med. at St Bartholomew's Hosp. Med.

Coll., 1971–92; Ver Heyden De Lancey Reader in Forensic Medicine, Council of Legal Educn, 1978–92. Lectr, Metropolitan Police Detective Trng Sch., Detective Trng Sch., Bristol and Special Investigation Br., RMP, 1969–92. Hon. Consultant: London, subseq. Royal London Hosp., 1967–92; in Forensic Medicine, to Army, 1971–92, and RN, 1972–92; RAF, 1990–92; Emeritus Consultant to Army, 1999–; Hon. Med. Advr, Amateur Swimming Assoc., 1985-2000 (Hon. Life Mem., 1997). Formerly: Examiner in Forensic Med., Univ. of Dublin; Convenor for Exams of Dip. in Med. Jurisp., Hon. Soc. of Apothecaries of London. Chm. and Hon. Sec., Med. Cttee, Ligue Européenne de Natation, 1990–2000. Member: BMA; Council, RCPath; Council, Brit. Assoc. Forensic Med. (Pres., 1985–87); British Acad. of Forensic Scis (Sec. Gen., 1970–85; Pres., 1978–79); FINA Med. Cttee (Hon. Sec., 1986–2000); Assoc. of Police Surgeons of GB (Hon. Fellow); Forensic Science Soc.; Assoc. of Clinical Pathologists; Pathological Soc. of GB and Ire.; Research Defence Soc. Sen. Fellow, Amer. Acad. of Forensic Sciences; Mem., Academia Internationalis Medicinae Legalis et Medicinae Socialis. Hon. Dip. in Forensic Odontology, London Hosp. Med. Coll., 1985. *Publications:* scientific papers in numerous learned jls, both med. and forensic. *Recreations:* sports medicine and legal medicine. *Clubs:* Savage, Royal Naval Medical.
Died 14 June 2003.

CAMERON, Prof. Kenneth, CBE 1987; FBA 1976; Professor of English Language, 1963–87, then Professor Emeritus, and Head of Department of English Studies, 1984–87, University of Nottingham; *b* Burnley, Lancs, 21 May 1922; *s* of late Angus W. Cameron and E. Alice Cameron, Habergham, Burnley; *m* 1st, 1947, Kathleen (*d* 1977), *d* of late F. E. Heap, Burnley; one *s* one *d*; 2nd, 1998, Jean Phyllis Russell-Gebbett, *d* of late James Bremner. *Educ:* Burnley Grammar Sch.; Univ. of Leeds (BA Hons, Sch. of English Language and Literature); PhD Sheffield. Served War, 1941–45; Pilot, RAF. Asst Lectr in English Language, Univ. of Sheffield, 1947–50; Nottingham University: Lectr in English Language, 1950–59; Sen. Lectr, 1959–62; Reader, 1962–63. External Prof., Loughborough Univ., 1990–93; Leverhulme Emeritus Fellow, 1990–91. Sir Israel Gollancz Meml Lecture, British Academy, 1976; O'Donnell Lectr, 1979. Pres., Viking Soc., 1972–74; Hon. Dir, 1966–93, Hon. Sec., 1972–93, English Place-Name Soc.; Editor, Jl of the English Place-Name Soc., 1972–90; Gen. Editor, English Place-Name Survey, 1966–93. FRHistS 1970; FSA 1984. Hon. FilDr Uppsala, 1977; Hon. LittD Sheffield, 1991. Sir Israel Gollancz Meml Prize, British Academy, 1969; Jöran Sahlgren Prize, Royal Gustaf Adolfs Acad., Sweden, 1990. *Publications:* The Place-Names of Derbyshire, 1959; English Place-Names, 1961, rev. edn 1996; Scandinavian Settlement in the Territory of the Five Boroughs: the place-name evidence, 1965; The Meaning and Significance of OE *walh* in English Place-Names, 1980; The Place-Names of the County of the City of Lincoln, 1985; The Place-Names of Lincolnshire: Yarborough Wapentake, 1991; The Wapentake of Walshcroft, 1992; Stenton and Place-Names, 1994; The Wapentakes of Ludborough and Haverstoe, 1996; The Wapentake of Bradley, 1997; A Dictionary of Lincolnshire Place Names, 1998; The Wapentake of Manley, 2001; *festschrift:* Studies in Honour of Kenneth Cameron, 1987; contribs to Nottingham Medieval Studies, Medium Ævum, Mediaeval Scandinavia, Festschrifts, etc. *Recreations:* sports (supporting), home, "The Queens". *Address:* 16 The Cloisters, Beeston, Nottingham NG9 2FR. *T:* (0115) 925 4303. *Died 10 March 2001.*

CAMP, William Newton Alexander; writer and political and corporate adviser, retired; *b* 12 May 1926; *s* of I. N. Camp, OBE, Colonial Administrative Service, Palestine, and Freda Camp; *m* 1st, 1950, Patricia Cowan (marr. diss. 1973); two *s* one *d*; 2nd, 1975, Juliet Schubart, *d* of late Hans Schubart, CBE; four step *s*. *Educ:* Bradfield Coll.; Oriel Coll., Oxford (Classical Scholar, MA). Served in

Army, 1944–47. Asst Res. Officer, British Travel and Holidays Assoc., 1950–54; Assistant Secretary: Consumer Adv. Council, BSI, 1954–59; Gas Council, 1960–63; Public Relations Adviser, Gas Council (British Gas Corp.), 1963–67; Dir of Information Services, British Steel Corp., 1967–71; Mem., BNOC, 1976–78. Special Adviser: milling and baking industries, 1972–90; British Leyland Motor Corp., 1975; railway trades unions, 1975–76; C. A. Parsons & Co. Ltd, 1976–77; Prudential Corp. (formerly Prudential Assurance Co.), 1978–88; Northern Engineering Industries plc, 1978–84; Corporate Advr, British Railways Bd, 1977–90. Director: Quartet Books, 1973–76; Westminster Communications Gp Ltd, 1989–90; Chm., Camden Consultants Ltd, 1975–91. Mem. Exec. Cttee, Labour Euro-Safeguards Campaign, 1999–. Trustee, Transport 2000, 1997–. Mem. Cttee, Foundn for Al Quds Med. Sch., Jerusalem, 1997–. Chm., Oxford Univ. Labour Club, 1949; contested (Lab) Solihull, 1950; Mem., Southwark Borough Council, 1953–56; Press Adviser (unpaid) to Prime Minister, Gen. Election, 1970. Founder Mem., Public Enterprise Group. *Publications: novels:* Prospects of Love, 1957; Idle on Parade, 1958 (filmed, 1959); The Ruling Passion, 1959; A Man's World, 1962; Two Schools of Thought, 1964; Flavour of Decay, 1967; The Father Figures, 1970; Stroke Counterstroke, 1986; *biography:* The Glittering Prizes (F. E. Smith), 1960. *Address:* 61 Gloucester Crescent, NW1 7EG. *T:* (020) 7482 5112; Keeper's Cottage, Marshfield, near Chippenham, Wilts SN14 8PD. *T:* (01225) 891211. *Clubs:* Garrick, Beefsteak.   *Died 25 Jan. 2002.*

CAMPBELL OF CROY, Baron *cr* 1974 (Life Peer), of Croy in the County of Nairn; **Gordon Thomas Calthrop Campbell,** MC 1944, and Bar, 1945; PC 1970; DL; Vice-Lord-Lieutenant, Highland Region (Nairn), 1988–99; *b* 8 June 1921; *s* of late Maj.-Gen. J. A. Campbell, DSO and Bar; *m* 1949, Nicola Elizabeth Gina Madan; two *s* one *d. Educ:* Wellington and Hospital. Served War of 1939–45: commissioned in Regular Army, 1939; Captain, 1940; instructor OCTU, Larkhill; RA, Major, 1942; commanded 320 Field Battery in 15 Scottish Div.; wounded and disabled, 1945. Entered HM Foreign Service, 1946; served, until 1957, in FO, UK Delegn to the UN (New York), Cabinet Office (Private Sec. to Sec. of Cabinet) and Vienna; Sec., first Conf. of Privy Councillors on Security, 1955. MP (C) Moray and Nairn, 1959–Feb. 1974; Asst Govt Whip, 1961–62; a Lord Comr of the Treasury and Scottish Whip, 1962–63; Joint Parly Under-Sec. of State, Scottish Office, 1963–64; Opposition Spokesman on Defence and Scottish Affairs, 1966–70; Sec. of State for Scotland, 1970–74. Vice-Pres., Parly Maritime Gp, 1986–. Partner in Holme Rose Farms and Estate, 1969–; Chm. Scottish Bd, 1976–94, Dir, 1983–91, Alliance and Leicester (formerly Alliance) Building Soc.; Chm., Stoic Financial Services (formerly Stoic Insurance Services), 1979–93. Oil industry consultant, 1975–95; Advisory Committee on Pollution of Sea: Vice-Pres., 1976–84; Acting Chm., 1980–82; Chm., 1987–89. Chm., Scottish Cttee, Internat. Year of Disabled, 1981; Mem., RA Council, Scotland, 1980–91; Pres., Anglo-Austrian Soc., 1991–2003. Trustee, Thomson Foundn, 1980–2002; First Fellow, Nuffield Provincial Hospitals Trust Queen Elizabeth The Queen Mother Fellowship, 1980. DL Nairn, 1985. *Publication:* Disablement: problems and prospects in the UK, 1981. *Recreations:* music, birds. *Address:* House of Lords, SW1A 0PW.

Died 26 April 2005.

CAMPBELL, Prof. Alexander Elmslie, PhD; FRHistS; Professor of American History, University of Birmingham, 1972–87 (part-time, 1984–87); Director of American Studies, 1972–84); later Emeritus Professor; *b* 12 May 1929; *s* of Rev. John Young Campbell and Emma (*née* Wickert); *m* 1st, 1956, Sophia Anne Sonne (*d* 1972); one *s* one *d*; 2nd, 1983, Juliet Jeanne d'Auvergne Collings (CMG 1988). *Educ:* Paisley Grammar Sch.; Perse Sch., Cambridge; St John's Coll., Cambridge (MA; PhD 1956); MA Oxon 1959. FRHistS 1970. Smith-Mundt Student,

Harvard Univ., 1953–54; Fellow, King's Coll., Cambridge, 1955–59; Second Sec., HM Foreign Service, 1958–60; Fellow and Tutor in Mod. Hist., Keble Coll., Oxford, 1960–72, Emeritus Fellow 1981–. Vis. Professor: Hobart and William Smith Colls, NY, 1970; Columbia Univ., 1975; Univ. of Kansas, 1976; Stanford Univ., 1977. Mem., Inst. for Advanced Study, Princeton, 1975. *Publications:* Great Britain and the United States, 1895–1903, 1960; (ed) Expansion and Imperialism, 1970; America Comes of Age: the era of Theodore Roosevelt, 1971; (ed) The USA in World Affairs, 1974; articles and reviews in collections and jls. *Address:* 3 Belbroughton Road, Oxford OX2 6UZ. *T:* (01865) 558685. *Clubs:* Athenæum; Cosmos (Washington, DC).

Died 16 Aug. 2002.

CAMPBELL, Sir Donald, Kt 1994; CBE 1987; FRCA; FRCS; FRCSE; FFARCSI; FRCPGlas; FRCPE; Professor of Anaesthesia, University of Glasgow, 1976–92, thenEmeritus (Dean of Faculty of Medicine, 1987–91); President, Royal College of Physicians and Surgeons of Glasgow, 1992–94; *b* 8 March 1930; *s* of Archibald Peter and Mary Campbell; *m* 1st, 1954, Nancy Rebecca McKintosh (decd); one *s* one *d*; 2nd, 1975, Catherine Conway Bradburn; two *d. Educ:* Hutchesons' Boys' Grammar Sch.; Univ. of Glasgow (MB, ChB). Lectr in Anaesthesia, 1959–60, Cons. Anaesthetist, 1960–76, Royal Inf., Glasgow. Vice-Dean, 1981–82, Dean, 1982–85, Faculty of Anaesthetists, RCS; Vice-Pres., RCS, 1985–87; Visitor, RCPSG, 1990–92. Chm., Scottish Council for Postgrad. Med. Educn, 1985–90. FACP; FRACP. *Publications:* A Nurse's Guide to Anaesthetics, Resuscitation and Intensive Care, 1964, 7th edn 1983; Anaesthetics, Resuscitation and Intensive Care, 1965, 8th edn 1996; contribs to med. jls, mainly on anaesthesia and intensive therapy. *Recreation:* angling. *Address:* Novar, 27 Tannoch Drive, Milngavie, Glasgow G62 8AR. *T:* (0141) 956 1736.   *Died 14 Sept. 2004.*

CAMPBELL, Harold Edward; Director, Greater London Secondary Housing Association, 1978–83; Chairman, Sutton (Hastoe) Housing Association, 1975–85; *b* 28 Feb. 1915; *s* of Edward Inkerman Campbell and Florence Annie Campbell. *Educ:* Southbury Road Elementary Sch.; Enfield Central Sch. Asst Sec., 1946–64, Sec., 1964–67, Cooperative Party; Mem., 1967–73, Dep. Chm., 1969–73, Housing Corp.; Gen. Manager, Newlon Housing Trust, 1970–76; Chairman: Cooperative Planning Ltd, 1964–74; Co-Ownership Develt Soc. Ltd, 1966–76; Sutton Housing Trust, 1973–80 (Trustee, 1967–86); Dir, Co-op. Housing Centre, and S British Housing Assoc., 1976–78; Dep. Chm., Stevenage Develt Corp., 1968–80; Mem., Cooperative Develt Agency, 1978–81; Pres., Enfield Highway Cooperative Soc. Ltd, 1976–85 (Dir, 1965–85); Dir, CWS Ltd, 1968–73. Chairman: DoE Working Party on Cooperative Housing, 1973–75; DoE Working Group on New Forms of Housing Tenure, 1976–77; Housing Assoc. Registration Adv. Cttee, 1974–79; Hearing Aid Council, 1970–71. Borough Councillor, Enfield, 1959–63. *Recreations:* music, theatre, cinema. *Address:* 31 Epperstone Court, West Bridgford, Nottingham NG2 7QR.

Died 14 Jan. 2002.

CAMPBELL, Air Vice-Marshal Ian Robert, CB 1976; CBE 1964; AFC 1948; *b* 5 Oct. 1920; *s* of late Major and Hon. Mrs D. E. Campbell; *m* 1st, 1953, Beryl Evelyn Newbigging (*d* 1982); one *s*; 2nd, 1984, Elisabeth Lingard-Guthrie. *Educ:* Eton; RAF Coll., Cranwell. Anti-Shipping Ops, 1940–42; POW, Italy and Germany, 1942–45; 540 Sqdn, Benson, 1946; psa 1949; PSO to C-in-C Far East, 1950; 124 (F) Wing Oldenburg, 1953; OC, RAF Sandwich, 1956; pfc 1957; OC 213 Sqdn, Bruggen, 1958; ACOS Plans HQ 2ATAF, 1959; OC, RAF Marham, 1961; MoD (Air) DASB, 1964; SASO, HQ No 1 Group, 1965; Air Attaché, Bonn, 1968; Dir of Management and Support Intell., MoD, 1970–73; C of S, No 18 (M) Group, Strike Command, 1973–75, retired. *Recreations:*

shooting, travel. *Address:* Pike Farm, Fossebridge, Cheltenham, Glos GL54 3JR. *Clubs:* Boodle's, Royal Air Force.   *Died 18 Oct. 2001.*

CAMPBELL, Sir Niall (Alexander Hamilton), 8th Bt *cr* 1831, of Barcaldine and Glenure; 15th Chieftain, Hereditary Keeper of Barcaldine Castle; Clerk to Justices of N Devon Divisions of Barnstaple, Bideford and Great Torrington and South Molton, 1976–90; *b* 7 Jan. 1925; *o s* of late Ian Vincent Hamilton Campbell, 7th Bt, CB, and Madeline Lowe Reid (*d* 1929), *e d* of late Hugh Anglin Whitelocke, FRCS; *S* father, 1978; *m* 1st, 1949, Patricia Mary (marr. diss. on his petition, 1956), *d* of R. G. Turner; 2nd, 1957, Norma Joyce, *d* of W. N. Wiggin; two *s* one *d* (including twin *s* and *d*) (and one *d* decd). *Educ:* Cheltenham College (Scholar); Corpus Christi Coll., Oxford. Called to the Bar, Inner Temple. Served War, 1943–46, Lieut Royal Marines; in Inf. bn, NW Europe campaign and on staff of Comdr RM training bde. Appts as Hosp. Administrator, 1953–70, inside and outside NHS, including St Mary's, Paddington, London Clinic, and Royal Hosp. and Home for Incurables, Putney (Chief Exec.); Dep. Chief Clerk, Inner London Magistrates' Courts, 1970–76, and Dep. Coroner, Inner London (South), Southwark. Mem. Exec. Cttee, N Devon Community Health Council; Governor, Grenville Coll., Bideford; Mem. Management Cttee, N Devon Cheshire Home. *Publication:* Making the Best Use of Bed Resources—monograph based on lecture sponsored by King Edward's Hospital Fund, 1965. *Recreations:* garden labour; writing letters to the Times, with little success; keeping a golden retriever; birds. *Heir: er s* Roderick Duncan Hamilton Campbell, of Barcaldine, Younger [*b* 24 Feb. 1961; *m* 1989, Jean Caroline, *d* of Laurie Bicknell, Braunton, Devon; three *d*]. *Address:* Hillfoot, Moss Road, North Connel, Oban, Argyllshire PA37 1RX. *Club:* Marshalls (Barnstaple).   *Died 15 Nov. 2003.*

CAMPBELL, Prof. Peter Nelson; Courtauld Professor of Biochemistry, and Director of the Courtauld Institute, Middlesex Hospital Medical School, London University, 1976–87, then Emeritus Professor; Editor in Chief, Biotechnology and Applied Biochemistry, 1981–95; *b* 5 Nov. 1921; *s* of late Alan A. Campbell and Nora Nelson; *m* 1946, Mollie (*née* Manklow); one *s* one *d* (and one *s* decd). *Educ:* Eastbourne Coll.; University Coll. London (BSc, PhD, DSc; Fellow, 1981). FIBiol. Research and Production Chemist with Standard Telephones and Cables, Ltd, 1942–46; PhD student, 1946–47, Asst Lectr, 1947–49, UCL; staff of Nat. Inst. for Med. Research, Hampstead and Mill Hill, 1949–54; Asst, Courtauld Inst. of Biochem., Middx Hosp. Med. Sch., 1954–57; Sen. Lectr, Middx Hosp. Med. Sch., 1957–64; Reader in Biochem., Univ. of London, 1964–67; Prof. and Head of Dept of Biochem., Leeds Univ., 1967–75. Hon. Lectr, Dept of Biochem., UCL, 1954–67; Hon. Consulting Chemical Pathologist to Middlesex Hosp., 1987–. Butland Vis. Prof., Univ. of Auckland, 1988. Chm., Assoc. of Researchers in Medicine and Sci., 1987–95. Hon. Mem., Biochemical Soc., 1988. Convenor, FEBS Scientific Apparatus Recycling Scheme, 1990–. Foreign Mem., Lithuanian Acad. of Scis. Hon. DSc Sofia, and Tbilisi, 2002. Diplôme d'Honneur, FEBS, 1981; Dist. Service Award, IUBMB, 2000. *Publications:* Structure and Function of Animal Cell Components, 1966; (ed with B. A. Kilby) Basic Biochemistry for Medical Students, 1975; (ed) Biology in Profile, 1981; (with A. D. Smith) Biochemistry Illustrated, 1982, 4th edn 2000; (ed) Oxford Dictionary of Biochemistry and Molecular Biology, 1997, rev. edn 2000; A Biochemical Foreign Correspondent, 2003; many scientific papers in Biochem. Jl. *Recreations:* theatre, travelling, conversation. *Address:* Department of Biochemistry and Molecular Biology, University College London, WC1E 6BT. *T:* (020) 7679 2169; *e-mail:* pcampbell@biochemistry.ucl.ac.uk.
                                                Died 7 Feb. 2005.

CAMPBELL, Prof. Peter (Walter); Professor of Politics, Reading University, 1964–91, then Emeritus; *b* 17 June 1926; *o s* of late W. C. H. and L. M. Campbell. *Educ:* Bournemouth Sch.; New Coll., Oxford (2nd class PPE 1947; MA 1951). Research Student, Nuffield Coll., Oxford, 1947–49; Asst Lecturer in Govt, Manchester Univ., 1949–52, Lectr, 1952–60; Vice-Warden, Needham Hall, 1959–60; Reading University: Prof. of Political Economy, 1960–64; Dean, Faculty of Letters, 1966–69; Chm., Graduate Sch. of Contemporary European Studies, 1971–73. Vis. Lectr in Political Science, Victoria Univ. Coll., NZ, 1954. Hon. Sec. Political Studies Assoc., 1955–58; Chm., Inst. of Electoral Research, 1959–65; Mem. Council, Hansard Soc. for Parly Govt, 1962–77; Hon. Treas., Joint Univ. Council for Social and Public Administration, 1965–69; Chm., Reading Romilly Assoc., 1965–69; Vice-Chm., Reading and District Council of Social Service, 1966–71; Vice-Pres., Electoral Reform Soc., 1972–97; Mem., Nat. Cttee for Electoral Reform, 1976–93; Trustee, Ballot Services (ERS) Ltd, 1988–92; Hon. Treas., CAER, 1990–94. Member: Adv. Panel, Commonwealth Scholarship Commn, 1964–73; Political Science Cttee, SSRC, 1968–72; CNAA Bds and Panels, 1971–78; Social Studies Sub-Cttee, UGC, 1973–83. Co-Pres., Reading Univ. Cons. Assoc., 1961–91. Mem. Council, Campaign for Homosexual Equality, 1978–79; Convenor, Reading CHE, 1979–80; Mem. Council of Management, Albany Soc., 1988–91; Vice-Pres., Cons. Gp for Homosexual Equality, 1988–91 (Chm., 1982–88); Chm., Exec. Cttee, Soc. for Individual Freedom, 1992–93; Trustee, Civic Educn and Res. Trust, 1993–95. Patron, Univ. of Buckingham, 1984–. Editor, Political Studies, 1963–69. *Publications:* (with W. Theimer) Encyclopædia of World Politics, 1950; French Electoral Systems and Elections, 1789–1957, 1958; (with B. Chapman) The Constitution of the Fifth Republic, 1958; articles in British, French and New Zealand Jls of Political Science. *Recreations:* ambling, idling. *Address:* 6 Treyarnon Court, 37 Eastern Avenue, Reading RG1 5RX. *T:* (0118) 966 1888. *Club:* Athenæum.   *Died 21 April 2005.*

CAMPBELL, Hon. Sir Walter (Benjamin), AC 1989; Kt 1979; QC (Qld) 1960; Governor of Queensland, Australia, 1985–92; *b* 4 March 1921; *s* of Archie Eric Gordon Campbell and Leila Mary Campbell; *m* 1942, Georgina Margaret Pearce; one *s* one *d* (and one *s* decd). *Educ:* Univ. of Queensland (MA, LLB; Hon. LLD 1980). Served War, RAAF, 1941–46 (pilot). Called to the Qld Bar, 1948; Judge, Supreme Court, Qld, 1967; Chief Justice, Qld, 1982–85. Chairman: Law Reform Commn of Qld, 1969–73; Remuneration Tribunal (Commonwealth), 1974–82; sole Mem., Academic Salaries Tribunal (Commonwealth), 1974–78. President: Qld Bar Assoc., 1965–67; Australian Bar Assoc., 1966–67; Mem. Exec., Law Council of Aust., 1965–67. Dir, Winston Churchill Meml Trust, 1969–80; Chm., Utah Foundn, 1977–85. Mem. Senate 1963–85, and Chancellor 1977–85, Univ. of Qld. Hon. Life Vice Pres., Aircrew Assoc. (UK), 1993. Trustee, Gowrie Scholarship Trust Fund, 1984–. Patron, Soc. of St Andrew of Scotland, 1986–. Fellow Aust. Inst. Judicial Admin., 1986. KStJ 1986. Freeman, City of London, 1987; Liveryman, GAPAN, 1988. Hon. DLitt James Cook Univ., 1988; DUniv: Queensland Univ. of Technology, 1991; Griffith Univ., 1992. *Recreations:* golf, reading. *Address:* 6 Dennison Street, Ascot, Brisbane, Qld 4007, Australia. *Clubs:* Queensland, Brisbane (Hon. Life Mem.), United Service (Hon. Life Mem.), Royal Queensland Golf (Brisbane); Australasian Pioneers (Sydney).   *Died 4 Sept. 2004.*

CAMPOS, Roberto de Oliveira, Hon. GCVO 1976; *b* Cuiabá, Mato Grosso, 17 April 1917; *s* of Waldomiro and Honorina de Oliveira Campos; *m* Maria Stella Tambellini; two *s* one *d*. *Educ:* Catholic Seminaries: Guaxupé and Belo Horizonte, Brazil (grad. Philosophy and Theol.); George Washington Univ., Washington (MA Econs); Columbia Univ., NYC (Hon. Dr). Entered Brazilian Foreign Service, 1939; Economic Counsellor, Brazil-US EDC,

1951–53; Dir 1952, Gen. Man. 1955, Pres. 1959, Nat. Economic Develt Bank; Sec. Gen., Nat. Develt Council, 1956–59; Delegate to internat. confs, incl. ECOSOC and GATT, 1959–61; Roving Ambassador for financial negotiations in W Europe, 1961; Ambassador of Brazil to US, 1961–63; Minister of State for Planning and Co-ord., 1964–67; Ambassador to UK, 1975–82; Senator, 1982, then Deputy for Rio de Janeiro, House of Congress, Brazil. Prof., Sch. of Econs, Univ. of Brazil, 1956–61. Mem. or past Mem., Cttees and Bds on economic develt (particularly inter-Amer. econ. develt). *Publications:* Ensaios de História Econômica e Sociologia; Economia, Planejamento e Nacionalismo; A Moeda, o Govêrno e o Tempo; A Técnica e o Riso; Reflections on Latin American Development; Do outro lado da cerca; Temas e Sistemas; Ensaios contra a maré; (jtly) Política Econômica e Mitos Políticos; Trends in International Trade (GATT report); Partners in Progress (report of Pearson Cttee of World Bank); A Nova Economia Brasileira; Formas Criativas do Desenvolvimento Brasileiro; Omundo que vejo e náo desejo; Reflexões do Crepúsculo; O Século Esquisito; Guia Para os Perplexos; Ensaios Imprudentes; Além do Cotidiano; Antologia do bom senso; A Lanterna na popa (memoirs); technical articles and reports on develt and internat. econs, in jls. *Address:* Rua Francisco Otaviano 140, Ipanema 22080, Rio de Janeiro, Brazil.
Died 9 Oct. 2001.

CANN, James Charles; MP (Lab) Ipswich, since 1992; *b* 28 June 1946; *s* of Charles George Cann and Brenda Julia Cann; *m* 1970, Rosemary Lovitt; two *s*. *Educ:* Barton on Humber Grammar Sch.; Kesteven Coll. of Education. Schoolteacher, 1967–92; Dep. Head, Handford Hall Primary Sch., Ipswich, 1981–92. Leader, Ipswich Council, 1979–91. *Recreations:* snooker, squash, badminton, walking, reading, history. *Address:* 79 Woodbridge Road East, Ipswich IP4 5QL. *Clubs:* various Ipswich sports and social. *Died 15 Oct. 2001.*

CAPE, Maj.-Gen. Timothy Frederick, CB 1972; CBE 1966; DSO; idc, jssc, psc; *b* Sydney, 5 Aug. 1915; *s* of C. S. Cape, DSO, Edgecliff, NSW; *m* 1961, Elizabeth (*d* 1985), *d* of Brig. R. L. R. Rabett; one *d*. *Educ:* Cranbrook Sch., Sydney; RMC Duntroon. Served with RAA, 1938–41; Bde Major Sparrow Force, Timor, 1942; GSO1: (Air) New Guinea Force, 1942–43; (Ops) Melbourne, 1944; (Air) Morotai, 1945; (Ops) Japan, 1946–47; (Plans) Melbourne, 1948–49; Instructor, Staff Coll., Camberley, UK, 1950–52; Comdt, OCS, Portsea, 1954–56; Dep. Master-Gen. Ordnance, 1957–59; COS Northern Comd, Brisbane, 1961; Dir of Staff Duties, Army HQ, Canberra, 1962–63; Comdr, Adelaide, 1964; GOC Northern Comd, Brisbane, 1965–68; Master-General of the Ordnance, 1968–72; retd 1972. Nat. Chm., Royal United Services Inst. of Australia, 1980–83; Chm., Nat. Disaster Relief Cttee and Mem., Nat. Council, Australian Red Cross Soc., 1975–85. Bronze Star (US). *Address:* Unit 311, The Grange, 67 Macgregor Street, Deakin, ACT 2600, Australia. *Clubs:* Melbourne (Melbourne); Commonwealth (Canberra); Union (Sydney); Royal Sydney Golf. *Died 20 Dec. 2003.*

CAPEL CURE, (George) Nigel, TD; JP; DL; *b* 28 Sept. 1908; *o s* of late Major George Edward Capel Cure, JP, Blake Hall, Ongar; *m* 1935, Nancy Elizabeth, *d* of late William James Barry, Great Witchingham Hall, Norwich; two *s* one *d*. *Educ:* Eton; Trinity Coll., Cambridge. DL and JP, 1947, High Sheriff, 1951, Essex; Vice-Lieutenant, later Vice Lord-Lieutenant, Essex, 1958–78; late of Blake Hall, Ongar. *Recreations:* shooting, cricket. *Address:* Ashlings, Moreton Road, Ongar, Essex CM5 0EZ. *T:* (01277) 362634. *Clubs:* MCC, City University.
Died 8 Aug. 2004.

CAPLAN, Leonard; QC 1954; *b* 28 June 1909; *s* of late Henry Caplan, Liverpool; *m* 1st, 1942, Tania Finklestein, LLB Lond., BLitt Oxon (*d* 1974); two *d*; 2nd, 1977, Mrs Herskovits (marr. diss. 1989), NY. Served War of 1939–45, Royal Artillery (Anti-Tank): Staff Captain, 47th

Div.; Staff Captain ("Q" Operations), Southern Command, engaged in D-Day Planning; passed Staff Coll., Camberley; Major, DAAG and Lt-Col, AAG, HQ Allied Land Forces, South East Asia. Called to the Bar, Gray's Inn, 1935; Bencher, 1964; Vice-Treasurer, 1978; Treasurer, 1979; Master of the Library, 1980–86; joined South Eastern Circuit; Middle Temple, 1949; sometime Dep. High Ct Judge. Chm., Coll. Hall (Univ. of London), 1958–67. Chm., Mental Health Review Tribunal, SE Region, 1960–63; Vice-Chm., NI Detention Appeals Tribunal, 1973–75; Senate of Inns of Court and the Bar, 1975–81. Pres., Medico-Legal Soc., 1979–81. Contested (C): Pontypool, 1935; N Hammersmith, 1945; N Kensington, 1950, 1951. *Publications:* (with Marcus Samuel) The Great Experiment: a critical study of Soviet Five Year Plans, 1935; numerous historico-legal articles. *Recreation:* reading. *Address:* 1 Pump Court, Temple, EC4Y 7AB. *T:* (020) 7353 9332. *Died 18 Jan. 2001.*

CAPLAT, Moran Victor Hingston, CBE 1968; General Administrator, Glyndebourne Festival Opera, 1949–81; *b* 1 Oct. 1916; *s* of Roger Armand Charles Caplat and Norah Hingston; *m* 1943, Diana Murray Downton; one *s* two *d* (and one *s* decd). *Educ:* privately; Royal Acad. of Dramatic Art. Actor, etc., 1934–39. Royal Navy, 1939–45. Glyndebourne: Asst to Gen. Man., 1945; Gen. Man., later known as Gen. Administrator, 1949. *Publication:* Dinghies to Divas (autobiog.), 1985. *Address:* Mermaid Cottage, 6 Church Road, Newick, Lewes, East Sussex BN8 4JU. *T:* (01825) 722964. *Clubs:* Garrick, Royal Ocean Racing. *Died 19 June 2003.*

CAPSTICK, His Honour Brian Eric; QC 1973; a Circuit Judge, 1985–97, a Senior Circuit Judge, 1997–98; *b* 12 Feb. 1927; *o s* of late Eric and Betty Capstick; *m* 1960, Margaret Harrison; one *s* one *d*. *Educ:* Sedbergh; Queen's Coll., Oxford (Scholar) (MA). Served HM Forces, 1945–48: 17/21st Lancers, Palestine, 1947–48. Tancred Student, and called to Bar, Lincoln's Inn, 1952; Bencher, 1980; a Recorder, 1980–85. Dep. Chm., Northern Agriculture Tribunal, 1976–; Asst Boundary Comr, 1978–85; Member: Parole Bd, 1995–2001; Mental Health Review Tribunal, 1999–2000. Appeal Steward, British Board of Boxing Control, 1985–. *Recreations:* wine, reading, cooking. *Address:* 71 South End Road, NW3 2RJ. *Club:* Garrick. *Died 31 Dec. 2005.*

CARLESS, Prof. John Edward, PhD; FRPharmS; Professor and Head of Department of Pharmaceutics, School of Pharmacy, London University, 1977–83; Emeritus Professor, since 1984; *b* 23 Nov. 1922; *s* of Alfred Edward Carless and Frances Mary (*née* Smith); *m* 1950, Dorothy Litherland; one *d*, and two step *d*. *Educ:* Leominster Grammar Sch.; Leicester Coll. of Science and Technol. (BPharm); Univ. of Manchester (MSc, PhD). FPS 1947. Asst Lectr in Pharmacy, Univ. of Manchester, 1947–54; Chelsea College: Sen. Lectr in Pharmaceutics, 1954–61; Reader, 1961–67; Prof. of Pharmaceutics, 1967–77. Member: Cttee on Safety of Medicines, 1976–78 (Mem., Sub-Cttee on Chemistry, Pharmacy and Standards, 1973–92); Veterinary Products Cttee, 1978–85; Cttee on Review of Medicine, 1980–92; UK Working Gp on iodine prophylaxis following nuclear accidents, 1989–90; Chm., Pharmacy Bd, CNAA, 1978–85. Chm., Reigate Photographic Soc., 1984–86; Governor, Reigate Sixth Form Coll., 1986–93. Harrison Meml Medal, Royal Pharmaceutical Soc., 1980. *Publications:* (ed jtly) Advances in Pharmaceutical Sciences: Vol. 1, 1964–vol. 5, 1982; (contrib.) Bentley's Text Book of Pharmaceutics, 1977. *Recreations:* photography, listening to records, bowls, wood turning. *Address:* Manton, Colley Manor Drive, Reigate, Surrey RH2 9JS. *T:* (01737) 243670.
Died 12 Sept. 2001.

CARLISLE OF BUCKLOW, Baron *cr* 1987 (Life Peer), of Mobberley in the County of Cheshire; **Mark Carlisle;** PC 1979; QC 1971; DL; Chairman, Criminal Injuries Compensation Board, 1989–2000; a Judge of the Courts of Appeal, Jersey and Guernsey, 1990–99; *b* 7 July 1929; 2nd

s of late Philip Edmund and Mary Carlisle; *m* 1959, Sandra Joyce Des Voeux; one *d*. *Educ:* Radley Coll.; Manchester Univ. (LLB Hons 1952). Called to the Bar, Gray's Inn, 1953, Bencher 1980; Northern Circuit; a Recorder, 1976–79, 1981–98. Mem., Home Office Advisory Council on the Penal System, 1966–70. MP (C): Runcorn, 1964–83; Warrington S, 1983–87. Jt Hon. Sec., Conservative Home Affairs Cttee, 1965–69; Conservative front bench spokesman on Home Affairs, 1969–70; Parly Under-Sec. of State, Home Office, 1970–72; Minister of State, Home Office, 1972–74; Sec. of State for Educn and Science, 1979–81. Chairman: Cons. Home Affairs Cttee, 1983–87; Parole Review Cttee, 1987–88; Prime Minister's Adv. Cttee on Business Appts of Crown Servants, 1988–99; Soc. of Cons. Lawyers, 1996–2001. Treas., CPA, 1982–85, Dep. Chm., UK Br., 1985–87. Mem., Adv. Council, BBC, 1975–79. DL Cheshire, 1983. *Recreation:* golf. *Address:* House of Lords, SW1A 0PW; 3 Holt Gardens, Mobberley, Cheshire WA16 7LH. *T:* (01565) 872275. *Clubs:* Garrick; St James's (Manchester).
Died 14 July 2005.

CARLISLE, Brian Apcar, CBE 1974; DSC 1945; Chairman, Saxon Oil PLC, 1980–85; *b* 27 Dec. 1919; 2nd *s* of Captain F. M. M. Carlisle, MC; *m* 1953, Elizabeth Hazel Mary Binnie, 2nd *d* of Comdr J. A. Binnie, RN; one *s* three *d*. *Educ:* Harrow Sch.; Corpus Christi Coll., Cambridge. Royal Navy, 1940–46, served in N Atlantic, Channel and Mediterranean in HMS Hood and destroyers; Sudan Political Service, 1946–54, served in Kassala, Blue-Nile and Bahr-el-Ghazal Provinces; Royal Dutch/Shell Group, 1955–74: served in India with Burmah Shell, 1960–64; Regional Co-ordinator, Middle East, and Dir, Shell International Petroleum, 1970–74; participated in pricing negotiations with OPEC states, 1970–73; Dir, Home Oil Co. Ltd, 1977–80; Oil Consultant to Lloyds Bank International, 1975–81. Chm., Bd of Governors, Gordon's Sch. (formerly Gordon Boys' Sch.), 1985–95. Chm., Sudan Church Assoc., 1982–99. *Recreations:* gardening, crosswords, golf. *Address:* 39 Springfield Avenue, Hartley Wintney, Hook, Hants RG27 8SF. *T:* (01252) 842224.
Died 23 April 2005.

CARMAN, George Alfred; QC 1971; a Recorder, 1972–84; *b* 6 Oct. 1929; *o s* of late Alfred George Carman and Evelyn Carman; *m* 1st, 1955, Ursula Peer Groves (marr. diss. 1959); 2nd, 1960, Cecilia Sparrow (marr. diss. 1976); one *s*; 3rd, 1976, Frances Elizabeth Venning (marr. diss. 1984). *Educ:* St Joseph's Coll., Blackpool; Balliol Coll., Oxford (First Class, Final Hons Sch. of Jurisprudence, 1952). Captain RAEC, 1948–49. Called to the Bar (King George V Coronation Schol.), Lincoln's Inn, 1953, Bencher 1978; first practised on Northern Circuit. *Address:* c/o 5 Verulam Buildings, Gray's Inn, WC1R 5LY. *Club:* Garrick.   *Died 2 Jan. 2001.*

CARMICHAEL OF KELVINGROVE, Baron *cr* 1983 (Life Peer), of Camlachie in the District of the City of Glasgow; **Neil George Carmichael;** *b* Oct. 1921; *m* 1948, Catherine McIntosh Rankin (marr. diss. 1987); one *d*. *Educ:* Estbank Acad.; Royal Coll. of Science and Technology, Glasgow. Employed by Gas Board in Planning Dept. Past Member Glasgow Corporation. MP (Lab) Glasgow, Woodside, Nov. 1962–74, Glasgow, Kelvingrove, 1974–83; contested (Lab) Glasgow, Hillhead, 1983. PPS to Minister of Technology, 1966–67; Jt Parly Sec., Min. of Transport, 1967–69; Parly Sec., Min. of Technology, 1969–70; Parliamentary Under-Secretary of State: DoE, 1974–75; DoI, 1975–76. Mem., Select Cttee on Transport, 1980–83. Hon. Sec., Scottish Labour Gp of MPs, 1979–83. Opposition front bench spokesman, H of L, on Transport, 1987–97, on Scotland, 1987–97. *Address:* House of Lords, SW1A 0PW; 53 Partick Hill Road, Glasgow G11 5AB.   *Died 19 July 2001.*

CARNARVON, 7th Earl of, *cr* 1793; **Henry George Reginald Molyneux Herbert,** KCVO 1982; KBE 1976; DL; Baron Porchester 1780; *b* 19 Jan. 1924; *o s* of 6th Earl of Carnarvon and Catherine (*d* 1977), *d* of late Jacob

Wendell, New York; *S* father, 1987; *m* 1956, Jean Margaret, *e d* of Hon. Oliver Wallop, Big Horn, Sheridan Co., Wyoming, USA; two *s* one *d*. Late Lieut RHG; retired pay, 1947. Hon. Col, Hampshire Fortress Regt, RE (TA) 1963–67, retaining rank of Hon. Col. Racing Manager to the Queen, 1969–. Chairman: South East Economic Planning Council, 1971–79; ARC, 1978–82; Stallion Adv. Cttee to Betting Levy Bd, 1974–86; Standing Conf. on Countryside Sports, 1978–; Newbury Racecourse plc, 1985–98; London and SE Regl Planning Conf. (formerly Standing Conf. on London and SE Regl Planning Auths), 1989–2001; Vice-Pres., Game Conservancy (formerly Game Res. Assoc.), 1967– (Chm., 1960–67); President: Thoroughbred Breeders' Assoc., 1969–74, 1986–91 (Chm. 1964–66); RASE, 1980–81. Member: Hampshire Agriculture Exec. Cttee, 1955–65; Nature Conservancy, 1963–66; Sports Council, 1965–70 (Chm., Planning Cttee, 1965–70); Forestry Commission, 1967–70; President: Hampshire and IoW Naturalist Trust, 1987–95; Amateur Riders' Assoc., 1969–75; Hampshire County Cricket Club, 1966–68; Mem., Jockey Club, 1964– (Chm., Flat Pattern Cttee, 1967–85). CC Hants, 1954; County Alderman, 1965–74 (Hon. Alderman, 1997); Vice-Chm. County Council, 1971–74, Chm., New County Council, 1973–77; Vice-Chm., CC Assoc., 1972–74 (Chm. Planning Cttee, 1968–74); Member: Basingstoke Town Develt Jt Cttee, 1960–73; Andover Town Develt Jt Cttee, 1960–65. Chm., H of L All Pty London Gp, 1993–; elected Mem., H of L, 1999. Verderer of the New Forest, 1961–65. DL Hants 1965. High Steward of Winchester, 1977. Hon. Fellow, Portsmouth Polytech., 1976. Hon. DSc Reading, 1980. *Heir: s* Lord Porchester, *b* 10 Nov. 1956. *Address:* Milford Lake House, Burghclere, Newbury, Berks RG20 9EL. *T:* (01635) 253387. *Clubs:* White's, Portland.
Died 11 Sept. 2001.

CARPENTER, Ven. Frederick Charles; Archdeacon of the Isle of Wight, 1977–86, then Archdeacon Emeritus; Chaplain, Godolphin School, Salisbury, 1989–95; *b* 24 Feb. 1920; *s* of Frank and Florence Carpenter; *m* 1952, Rachel Nancy (*d* 1994), *widow* of Douglas H. Curtis; one step *s*. *Educ:* Sir George Monoux Grammar Sch., Walthamstow; Sidney Sussex Coll., Cambridge (BA 1947, MA 1949); Wycliffe Hall, Oxford; MPhil Exeter, 1993. Served with Royal Signals, 1940–46; Italy, 1944 (despatches). Ordained deacon, 1949, priest, 1950; Curate of Woodford, 1949–51; Asst Master, 1951–62, and Asst Chaplain, 1951–58, then Chaplain, 1958–62, Sherborne School, Dorset; Vicar of Moseley, Birmingham, 1962–68; Dir of Religious Educn, Dio. of Portsmouth, 1968–75; Canon Residentiary of Portsmouth, 1968–77; Priest-in-charge of the Holy Cross, Binstead, IoW, 1977–86. *Recreations:* music, conversation. *Address:* 21 Gracey Court, Woodland Road, Broadclyst, Exeter, Devon EX5 3GA. *T:* (01392) 462445.   *Died 19 Feb. 2003.*

CARPENTER, Humphrey William Bouverie, FRSL; author, broadcaster, musician; *b* 29 April 1946; *s* of late Rt Rev. Harry James Carpenter and Urith Monica Trevelyan; *m* 1973, Mari Christina Prichard; two *d*. *Educ:* Dragon Sch., Oxford; Marlborough Coll.; Keble Coll., Oxford (MA, DipEd). FRSL 1983. BBC general trainee, 1968–70; staff producer, BBC Radio Oxford, 1970–74; freelance writer and broadcaster, 1975–. Founded: 1983, the band Vile Bodies, playing 1920s and 1930s dance music and jazz, resident at the Ritz Hotel, London, 1987–94; 1984, Mushy Pea Theatre Co., children's theatre group. Prog. Dir, Cheltenham Fest. of Lit., 1994–96. *Plays:* Father Ignatius, Edinburgh Fest. fringe, 1974; Mr Majeika, the Musical, Oxford, 1991, Shaw Theatre, 1993; Secret Gardens trilogy, BBC Radio, 1992; Babes (musical), Oxford, 1992, Shaw Theatre, 1993; Over the Rainbow, BBC Radio, 1995; Gulliver's Travels, Theatr Clywd, 1995; (adapted) Listen to the Wind, King's Head, 1996. *Publications:* A Thames Companion (with Mari Prichard), 1975; J. R. R. Tolkien: a biography, 1977; The Inklings (Somerset Maugham Award), 1978; Jesus (Past

Masters series), 1980; (ed with Christopher Tolkien) The Letters of J. R. R. Tolkien, 1981; W. H. Auden: a biography, 1981 (E. M. Forster Award, Amer. Acad. of Arts and Letters, 1984); (with Mari Prichard) The Oxford Companion to Children's Literature, 1984; OUDS: a centenary history of the Oxford University Dramatic Society, 1985; Secret Gardens: the golden age of children's literature, 1985; Geniuses Together: American writers in Paris, 1987; A Serious Character: the life of Ezra Pound (Duff Cooper Meml Prize), 1988; The Brideshead Generation: Evelyn Waugh and his friends, 1989; Benjamin Britten: a biography, 1992 (Royal Philharmonic Soc. award); The Envy of the World: fifty years of the BBC Third Programme and Radio 3, 1996; Robert Runcie: the reluctant archbishop, 1996; Dennis Potter, a biography, 1998; That Was Satire That Was, 2000; The Angry Young Men, 2002; Spike Milligan, the biography, 2003; *children's books:* The Joshers, 1977; The Captain Hook Affair, 1979; Mr Majeika, 1984; Mr Majeika and the Music Teacher, 1986; Mr Majeika and the Haunted Hotel, 1987; The Television Adventures of Mr Majeika, 1987; More Television Adventures of Mr Majeika, 1988; Mr Majeika and the Dinner Lady, 1989; Further Television Adventures of Mr Majeika, 1990; Mr Majeika and the School Play, 1991; Mr Majeika and the School Book Week, 1992 (Mr Majeika books serialised on television, 1988–90); (with Jenny McDade) Wellington and Boot, 1991; What Did You Do At School Today?, 1992; Charlie Crazee's Teevee, 1993; Mr Majeika and the School Inspector, 1993; Mr Majeika and the Ghost Train, 1994; Shakespeare Without the Boring Bits, 1994; Mr Majeika and the School Caretaker, 1996; (ed) The Puffin Book of Classic Children's Stories, 1996; Mr Majeika Vanishes, 1997; More Shakespeare Without the Boring Bits, 1997; Mr Majeika and the School Trip, 1999; Mr Majeika on the Internet, 2000; Mr Majeika and the Last Spell Book, 2003. *Recreations:* sleep, exploring decayed railway junctions. *Address:* 6 Farndon Road, Oxford OX2 6RS; *e-mail:* humphrey@hcarpenter.demon.co.uk.

Died 4 Jan. 2005.

CARRINGTON, Walter Hadrian Marshall; Director, Constructive Teaching Centre Ltd, since 1960; Teacher, F. Matthias Alexander Technique, since 1939; *b* 4 May 1915; *s* of Rev. Walter Marshall Carrington and Hannah Carrington (*née* Robinson); *m* 1940, Dilys Mary Gwyneth Jones; three *s. Educ:* Choir Sch. of All Saints; St Paul's Sch.; completed F. Matthias Alexander's trng course for teachers of his Alexander Technique. Served War of 1939–45: RAF Pilot trng, 1941; with 614 (Pathfinder) Sqn, MAAF, 1944 (Pathfinder Award); Flight Lieut. Asst to F. Matthias Alexander, 1939–41, 1946–55. Mem., Pathfinder Assoc., 1945–. MInstD 1960. *Publications:* Explaining the Alexander Technique, 1992; Thinking Aloud, 1994; A Time to Remember, 1996; The Art of Living, 1999; Personally Speaking, 2001. *Recreations:* riding, dressage, classical horsemanship. *Address:* 18 Lansdowne Road, W11 3LL. *T:* (020) 7727 7222. *Died 7 Aug. 2005.*

CARRUTHERS, Colin Malcolm, CMG 1980; HM Diplomatic Service, retired; *b* 23 Feb. 1931; *s* of late Colin Carruthers and Dorothy Beatrice Carruthers; *m* 1954, Annette Audrey Buckton; three *s* one *d. Educ:* Monkton Combe School; Selwyn College, Cambridge (BA 1954, MA 1965). Royal Signals, 1950–51; joined HMOCS Kenya, 1955; District Officer, Kenya, 1955–63; Dep. Civil Sec., Rift Valley Region, Kenya, 1963–65; Field Dir, Oxfam, Maseru, Lesotho, 1965–67; joined HM Diplomatic Service, 1968; First Sec. (Economic), Islamabad, 1969–73; First Sec., Ottawa, 1973–77; Counsellor and Hd of Chancery, Addis Ababa, 1977–80 (Chargé d'Affaires, 1978–79); Asst Election Comr, Zimbabwe-Rhodesia elecns, 1980; Head of South Pacific Dept, FCO, 1980–83, retired. UK Comr, British Phosphate Comrs, 1981–87; Govt and Internat. Relns Consultant, World Vision Internat., 1985–97; Dir and Trustee, World Vision UK, 1997–2001. Governor, Monkton Combe Sch., 1984–91. Churchwarden, St

Alban's, Frant, 1992–97; Lay Reader, Chichester Dio., 1994–. *Recreations:* golf, family. *Address:* 6 Lime Close, Frant, near Tunbridge Wells, Kent TN3 9DP. *T:* (01892) 750238. *Club:* Hawks (Cambridge).

Died 7 May 2003.

CARTER, Bernard; *see* Carter, R. W. B.

CARTER, Sir Charles (Frederick), Kt 1978; FBA 1970; Vice-Chancellor, University of Lancaster, 1963–79; *b* Rugby, 15 Aug. 1919; *y s* of late Frederick William Carter, FRS; *m* 1944, Janet Shea (*d* 2000); one *s* two *d. Educ:* Rugby Sch.; St John's Coll., Cambridge. Friends' Relief Service, 1941–45; Lectr in Statistics, Univ. of Cambridge, 1945–51; Fellow of Emmanuel Coll., 1947–51 (Hon. Fellow, 1965); Prof. of Applied Economics, The Queen's Univ., Belfast, 1952–59; Stanley Jevons Prof. of Political Economy and Cobden Lectr, Univ. of Manchester, 1959–63. Chairman: Science and Industry Cttee, RSA, British Assoc. and Nuffield Foundn, 1954–59; Schools' Broadcasting Council, 1964–71; Joint Cttee of the Univs and the Accountancy Profession, 1964–70; Adv. Bd of Accountancy Educn, 1970–76; North-West Economic Planning Council, 1965–68; Centre for Studies in Social Policy, 1972–78; PO Rev. Cttee, 1976–77; NI Economic Council, 1977–87; Sec.-Gen., Royal Econ. Soc., 1971–75; Member: UN Expert Cttee on Commodity Trade, 1953; Capital Investment Advisory Cttee, Republic of Ireland, 1956; British Assoc. Cttee on Metric System, 1958; Council for Scientific and Industrial Research, 1959–63; Commn on Higher Education, Republic of Ireland, 1960–67; Heyworth Cttee on Social Studies, 1963; Advisory Council on Technology, 1964–66; North Western Postal Bd, 1970–73; President: Manchester Statistical Soc., 1967–69; BAAS, 1981–82; Pres., 1989–91, Jt Pres., 1991–97, PSI. Chm. Council, Goldsmiths' Coll., Univ. of London, 1988–94. Hon. MRIA; Comp OR; Trustee: Joseph Rowntree Meml Trust, 1966–94 (Vice-Chm., 1981–94); Sir Halley Stewart Trust, 1969– (Chm., 1986–97); Chairman: Rosehill Theatre Trust, 1984–98; Learning from Experience Trust, 1986–92 and 1994–98. Joint Editor: Journal of Industrial Economics, 1955–61; Economic Journal, 1961–70; Editor, Policy Studies, 1980–88. Hon. DEconSc, NUI, 1968; Hon. DSc: NUU, 1979; Lancaster, 1979; QUB, 1980; Hon. LLD: TCD, 1980; Liverpool, 1982. *Publications:* The Science of Wealth, 1960, 3rd edn 1973; (with W. B. Reddaway and J. R. N. Stone) The Measurement of Production Movements, 1948; (with G. L. S. Shackle and others) Uncertainty and Business Decisions, 1954; (with A. D. Roy) British Economic Statistics, 1954; (with B. R. Williams) Industry and Technical Progress, 1957; Investment in Innovation, 1958; Science in Industry, 1959; (with D. P. Barritt) The Northern Ireland Problem, 1962, 2nd edn 1972; Wealth, 1968; (with G. Brosan and others) Patterns and Policies in Higher Education, 1971; On Having a Sense of all Conditions, 1971; (with J. L. Ford and others) Uncertainty and Expectation in Economics, 1972; Higher Education for the Future, 1980; (with J. H. M. Pinder) Policies for a Constrained Economy, 1982; (with P. John) A New Accord, 1992; Members One of Another, 1996; articles in Economic Journal, etc. *Recreation:* gardening. *Address:* 86 Kirkintilloch Road, Lenzie, Glasgow G66 4LF. *T:* (0141) 776 6223; *e-mail:* sircart@aol.com. *Club:* National Liberal.

Died 27 June 2002.

CARTER, His Eminence G(erald) Emmett, Cardinal, CC 1983; Archbishop of Toronto, 1978–90, then Archbishop Emeritus; *b* Montreal, Quebec, 1 March 1912; *s* of Thomas Carter and Mary Kelty. *Educ:* Univ. of Montreal (BA, MA, PhD); Grand Seminary of Montreal (STL). Founder, Director and Teacher, St Joseph's Teachers' Coll., Montreal, 1939–61; Auxiliary Bishop of London, Ont., 1961; Bishop of London, 1964. Cardinal, 1979. Chm., Internat. Cttee for English in the Liturgy, 1971; Pres., Canadian Catholic Conf. of Bishops, 1975–77. Elected Member, Permanent Council of the

Synod of Bishops in Rome, 1977. Hon. LLD: W Ontario, 1964; Concordia, 1976; Windsor, 1977; McGill, 1980; Notre Dame, 1981; St Francis Xavier, 1998; Assumption, Windsor, 1999; Hon. DD Huron Coll., W Ont., 1978; Hon. DHL Duquesne, Pittsburgh, 1965; Hon. DLitt: St Mary's, Halifax, 1980; (in Medieval Studies), Pontifical Inst. of Medieval Studies, Toronto, 1995 (also Hon. Licence in Med. Studies); Hon. DSL Univ. of St Michael's Coll., Toronto, 1998. *Publications:* The Catholic Public Schools of Quebec, 1957; Psychology and the Cross, 1959; The Modern Challenge, 1961. *Recreations:* tennis, skiing. *Address:* Catholic Pastoral Centre, 1155 Yonge Street, Toronto, ON M4T 1W5, Canada. *T:* (416) 9340606, *Fax:* (416) 9343437. *Died 6 April 2003.*

CARTER, Godfrey James, CBE 1984; Parliamentary Counsel, 1972–79; *b* 1 June 1919; *s* of Captain James Shuckburgh Carter, Grenadier Guards (killed in action, 1918), and Diana Violet Gladys Carter (*née* Cavendish); *m* 1946, Cynthia, *e d* of Eric Strickland Mason; three *s. Educ:* Eton (KS); Magdalene Coll., Cambridge (BA 1945, MA 1948; LLB 1946, LLM 1948). War Service (Rifle Bde), Middle East, 1940–43 (twice wounded). Called to the Bar, Inner Temple, 1946; Asst Parly Counsel, 1949–56; commercial dept, Bristol Aeroplane Co. Ltd, and Bristol Siddeley Engines Ltd, 1956–64; re-joined Parly Counsel Office, 1964; Dep. Counsel, 1970. *Address:* Old Bournstream House, Wotton-under-Edge, Glos GL12 7PA. *T:* (01453) 843246. *Died 28 July 2003.*

CARTER, Sir John (Patrick Gregorio), Kt 1966; QC (Guyana) 1962; Guyana Diplomatic Service, retired; *b* 27 Jan. 1919; *s* of Kemp R. Carter; *m* 1st, Dorothy Frasier (marr. diss.); 2nd, 1959, Sara Lou (formerly Harris); two *s,* one step *d. Educ:* Univ. of London (BA, LLB). Called to the English Bar, Middle Temple, 1942; admitted to Guyana (formerly British Guiana) Bar, 1945; Member of Legislature of Guyana, 1948–53 and 1961–64; Pro-Chancellor, Univ. of Guyana, 1962–66; Ambassador of Guyana to US, 1966–70; High Comr for Guyana in UK, 1970–76; Ambassador to China and Korea, 1976–81 and to Japan, 1979–81; High Comr to Jamaica, 1981–83. *Recreations:* cricket, swimming. *Address:* 2008 Derby Ridge Lane, Silver Spring, MD 20910–2651, USA. *Clubs:* MCC; Georgetown (Guyana). *Died 23 Feb. 2005.*

CARTER, Peers Lee, CMG 1965; HM Diplomatic Service, retired; Member Committee, Afghanaid, 1984–95 (Trustee, 1984–92; Chairman, 1989–92); *b* 5 Dec. 1916; *s* of Peers Owen Carter; *m* 1940, Joan Eleanor Lovegrove; one *s. Educ:* Radley; Christ Church, Oxford. Entered HM Foreign Service, 1939. Joined the Army in 1940; served in Africa (with Gen. Leclerc) and Europe (SOE). HM Embassy, Baghdad, 1945; First Secretary, Commissioner-General's Office, Singapore, 1951; Counsellor, HM Embassy, Washington, 1958; (Temp. duty) UK Delegation to UN, New York, 1961; Head of UK Permanent Mission, Geneva, 1961; Inspector of Foreign Service Establishments, 1963–66; Chief Inspector of HM Diplomatic Service, 1966–68; Ambassador to Afghanistan, 1968–72; Ministerial Interpreter and Asst Under-Sec. of State, FCO, 1973–76; Dir, Afghanistan Support Cttee, 1981–84; Member: Bureau Internat. Afghanistan, Paris, 1985–97; Internat. Assoc. of Conference Interpreters, 1976–87. Sardar-e A'ala, Afghanistan, 1971. *Address:* Dean Land Shaw, by Jobes, Balcombe, West Sussex RH17 6HZ. *T:* (01444) 811205. *Club:* Special Forces. *Died 8 Feb. 2001.*

CARTER, Peter Basil; QC 1990; Emeritus Fellow, Wadham College, Oxford, since 1988 (Fellow, 1949–88); *b* 10 April 1921; *s* of Albert George Carter and Amy Kathleen FitzGerald (*née* Arthur); *m* 1st, 1960, Elizabeth Maxwell (*née* Ely) (decd); 2nd, 1982, Lorna Jean (*née* Sinclair). *Educ:* Loughborough GS; Oriel Coll., Oxford (BA 1st Cl. Hons Jurisprudence; BCL 1st Cl. Hons; Vinerian Scholar, 1949; MA). War Service, RAC, 1941–46 (Croix de Guerre, 1944). Called to the Bar, Middle Temple, 1947; Hon. Bencher, 1981. Curator,

Bodleian Library, Oxford, 1963–90; Sen. Bursar, Wadham Coll., Oxford, 1965–77. Inns of Court School of Law: Lectr in Conflict of Laws, 1960–89; Lectr in Evidence, 1971–95; Hon. Reader, 1985. Visiting Professor of Law: Univ. of Melbourne, 1953; Univ. of Florida, 1955; New York Univ., 1961 and 1969; Osgoode Hall Law Sch., Ont, 1971, 1973, 1978 and 1982; Walter S. Owen Prof., Univ. of British Columbia, 1986; Canada Commonwealth Vis. Fellow, Faculty of Law, Univ. of Toronto, 1970; delivered Gen. Course of Lectures on Private Internat. Law, The Hague Acad. of Internat. Law, 1981. Rapporteur, Cttee on Transnational Recognition and Enforcement of Foreign Public Laws, Internat. Law Assoc., 1984–88. Gen. Comr for Income Tax Appeals, E Oxfordshire, 1965–95 (Chm., 1991–95). Dir (non-exec.), University Life Assurance Soc., 1969–91 (Chm., 1980–91). FInstD 1984. Hon. LLD: Victoria (BC), 1995; Pace, NY, 1997. JP Oxon, 1959–88. Jt Editor, International and Comparative Law Qly, 1961–2000; Gen. Editor, Oxford Monographs in Private Internat. Law, 1992–2001. *Publications:* Essays on the Law of Evidence (with Sir Zelman Cowen), 1956; Cases and Statutes on Evidence, 1981, 2nd edn 1990, supplement 1992; articles, mostly on private internat. law or law of evidence, in British Yearbook of Internat. Law, Internat. and Comparative Law Qly, Law Qly Rev., Cambridge Law Jl, Modern Law Rev., etc. *Recreation:* appreciating architecture. *Address:* Wadham College, Oxford OX1 3PN. *T:* (01865) 277900. *Club:* Oxford and Cambridge. *Died 16 Sept. 2004.*

CARTER, (Robert William) Bernard, CMG 1964; HM Diplomatic Service, retired; *b* 1913; 3rd *s* of late William Joseph Carter and Lucy (*née* How); *m* 1945, Joan Violet, *o d* of Theodore and Violet Magnus; one *s* two *d* (and one *d* decd). *Educ:* St Bees Sch., Cumberland; Trinity Coll., Oxford (Scholar). Served with the Royal Navy, 1940–46; Lieut, RNVR. Asst Master, Glenalmond, Perthshire, 1936; Administrative Assistant, Newcastle upon Tyne Education Cttee, 1946; Principal, Board of Trade, 1949; Trade Commissioner: Calcutta, 1952; Delhi, 1955; Accra, 1956; Principal Trade Commissioner, Colombo (Assistant Secretary), 1959; Senior British Trade Commissioner in Pakistan, 1961; Minister (Commercial), Pakistan, and Dep. High Comr, Karachi, 1967–68; Dep. High Comr, 1969–73 and Consul-Gen., 1973, Melbourne. *Recreations:* reading, travelling, collecting beer-mugs. *Address:* The Old Parsonage, Heywood, Westbury, Wilts BA13 4NB. *T:* (01373) 822194. *Club:* Oriental. *Died 11 July 2001.*

CARTER, William Nicholas, (Will), OBE 1984; Founder, Rampant Lions Press, 1949 (Senior Partner, 1971–91); *b* 24 Sept. 1912; *s* of Thomas Buchanan Carter and Margaret Theresa Stone; *m* 1939, Barbara Ruth Digby (*d* 1994); one *s* three *d. Educ:* Sunningdale Sch.; Radley. Served War, RN, 1941–46: S Atlantic, Coastal Forces Eastern Med.; commnd 1943. Gen. career in printing, advertising, typography and inscriptional letter-carving. Artist-in-Residence, Dartmouth Coll., NH, USA, 1969. Member: Royal Mint Adv. Cttee, 1971–91; Arch. Adv. Panel, Westminster Abbey, 1979–92. Hon. Fellow, Magdalene Coll., Cambridge, 1977. Frederick W. Goudy Award, Rochester Inst. of Technol., New York State, 1975; Silver Jubilee Medal, 1977. *Publication:* (with Wilfrid Blunt) Italic Handwriting, 1954. *Address:* 12 Chesterton Road, Cambridge CB4 3AB. *T:* (01223) 357553. *Club:* Double Crown (Pres., 1961). *Died 17 March 2001.*

CARTER-JONES, Lewis, CBE 1995; *b* Gilfach Goch, S Wales, 17 Nov. 1920; *s* of Tom Jones, Kenfig Hill, Bridgend, Glam.; *m* 1945, Patricia Hylda, *d* of late Alfred Bastiman, Scarborough, Yorks; two *d. Educ:* Bridgend County Sch.; University Coll. of Wales, Aberystwyth (BA; Chm. Student Finance Cttee; Capt, Coll., Univ. and County Hockey XI). Served War of 1939–45 (Flight Sergeant Navigator, RAF). Head of Business Studies, Yale Grammar Technical Sch., Wrexham, 1950–64. Contested (Lab) Chester, by-election, 1956, and general election, 1959. MP (Lab) Eccles, 1964–87. Chairman: Cttee for

Research for Apparatus for Disabled, 1973–80; Anglo-Columbian Gp, 1975–87; PLP Disablement Gp, 1975–81; PLP Aviation Gp, 1978–87. Exec. Mem., UK Br., CPA, 1983–87; Secretary: Indo-British Parly Gp, 1966–87; All-Party BLESMA Gp, 1973–87; All Party Aviation Gp, 1980–87. Hon. Parliamentary Adviser: RNIB, 1973–87; British Assoc. of Occupational Therapists; Soc. of Physiotherapists, until 1987. Mem., Gen. Adv. Council, IBA, 1982–87. Chairman: British Cttee, Rehabilitation International, 1978–92; Adv. Gp on Artificial Limbs to DoH, 1993–; Vice-President: Wales Council for the Disabled, 1981–; RADAR, 1987– (Chm., Access to the Skies Cttee, 1992–); Member: Disablement Services Authority, 1987–91; Disabled Persons Transport Adv. Cttee, Dept of Transport, 1988– (Chm., Airport Sub Cttee, 1988–); Adv. Gp on Rehabilitation to Sec. of State for Health, 1991–; Trustee, Granada Telethon, 1987. Dir, Possum Controls Ltd, 1974–92. *Address:* Cader Idris, 5 Cefn Road, Rhosnesni, Wrexham, Clwyd LL13 9NF.
Died 26 Aug. 2004.

CARTER-RUCK, Peter Frederick; Founder, Senior Partner, 1981–98, and Media and Trust Consultant, 1998–2000, Peter Carter-Ruck and Partners, Solicitors; Trust and Media Consultant, Pellys, Bishop's Stortford, since 1999; *b* 26 Feb. 1914; *s* of Frederick Henry Carter-Ruck and Nell Mabel Carter-Ruck; *m* 1940, Pamela Ann (*d* 2003), *o d* of late Gp Capt. Reginald Stuart Maxwell, MC, DFC, AFC, RAF; one *d* (one *s* decd). *Educ:* St Edward's, Oxford; Law Society; Solicitor of the Supreme Court (Hons). Admitted Solicitor, 1937; served RA, 1939–44, Captain Instr in gunnery. Sen. Partner, Oswald Hickson, Collier & Co., 1945–81. Specialist Member, Council of Law Soc., 1971–84; Chairman: Law Soc. Law Reform Cttee, 1980–83; Media Cttee, Internat. Bar Assoc., 1983–85; Mem., Council of Justice (Internat. Commn of Jurists), 1968–; President: City of Westminster Law Soc., 1975–76; Council, Media Soc., 1981–82 and 1984–86 (Hon. Life Vice Pres., 1988). Fellow, Soc. for Advanced Legal Studies, 1998–. Governor, St Edward's Sch., Oxford, 1950–78; past Chm. and Founder Governor, Shiplake Coll., Henley, 1966–73; Gov., St Bartholomew Charitable Foundn, 1996–. Mem. Livery, City of London Solicitors' Co., 1949–. *Publications:* Libel and Slander, 1953, 5th edn 1997; (with Ian Mackrill) The Cyclist and the Law, 1953; (with Edmund Skone James) Copyright: modern law and practice, 1965; Memoirs of a Libel Lawyer, 1990. *Address:* Carlton Mansions, York Buildings, Adelphi, WC2N 6LS. *T:* (020) 7839 7515; Latchmore, Great Hallingbury, Bishop's Stortford, Herts CM22 7PE. *T:* (01279) 654357, *Fax:* (01279) 504921; *e-mail:* peter-carter-ruck@dial.pipex.com; Eilagadale, N Ardnamurchan, Argyll PH36 4LG. *T:* (01972) 510267. *Clubs:* Garrick, Press, Royal Ocean Racing; Royal Yacht Squadron, Lloyd's Yacht, Law Society Yacht (past Commodore), Ocean Cruising (past Commodore).
Died 19 Dec. 2003.

CARTIER-BRESSON, Henri; photographer, draughtsman; *b* France, 22 Aug. 1908; *m* 1970, Martine Franck; one *d*. Studied painting with André Lhote, 1927–28. Asst Dir to Jean Renoir, 1936–39; Co-founder, Magnum Photos, 1947. Photographs exhibited: Mexico; Japan; Mus. of Modern Art, NY, 1947, 1968, 1987; Villa Medicis, Rome; Louvre, 1955, 1967, Grand Palais, 1970, Paris; V&A, 1969; Manege, Moscow, 1972; Edinburgh Festival, 1978; Hayward Gall., London, 1978. Collection of 390 photographs at DeMenil Foundn, Houston, USA, V&A, Univ. of Fine Arts, Osaka, Japan, Bibliothèque Nationale, Paris. Drawings exhibited: Carlton Gall., NY, 1975; Bischofberger Gall., Zürich, 1976; Forcalquier Gall., France, 1976; Mus. of Modern Art, Paris, 1981; Mus. of Modern Art, Mexico, 1982; French Inst., Stockholm, 1983; Pavilion of Contemporary Art, Milan, 1983; Mus. of Modern Art, Oxford, 1984; Palace Liechtenstein, Vienna, Salzburg, 1985; Herstand Gall., NY, 1987; Ecole des Beaux Arts, Paris, 1989; Le Printemps, Tokyo, 1989; Fondation Gianadda, Switzerland, 1990; Villa Medicis,

Rome, 1990; Musée de Louvain, Belgium, 1991; Mus. of Modern Art, Taiwan, 1991; Palazzo Sanvitale, Parma, 1992; Museo Camon Aznar, Zaragoza, 1992; Hamburg, 1994; Tokyo, Barcelona, 1995; Minneapolis Art Inst., 1996; Berggruen Gall., 1996; Galerie Claude Bernard, Paris, 1997; RCA, 1998; Mus. of Contemporary Art, Kyoto, 1998; Hayward and Nat. Portrait Galls, 1998; Künsthaus, Zürich, 1998; Palazzo Medici Riccardi, Florence, then travelling, 1999–; Landscapes, Tokyo, Kyoto, 1999, Paris, 2000. Retrospectives (photographs and drawings): Bibliothèque Nationale, Paris, 2003; Barcelona, 2004. Documentary films: on hosps, Spanish Republic, 1937; (with J. Lemare) Le Retour, 1945; (with J. Boffety) Impressions of California, 1969; (with W. Dombrow) Southern Exposures, 1970. Mem., Amer. Acad. of Arts and Scis, 1974. Hon. Prof., Acad. of Fine Arts, China, 1996. Hon. DLitt Oxon, 1975. Awards: US Camera, 1948; Overseas Press Club of America, 1949; Amer. Soc. of Magazine Photography, 1953; Photography Soc. of America, 1958; Overseas Press Club, 1954 (for Russia), 1960 (for China), 1964 (for Cuba); German Photographic Soc.; Hasselblad, 1983; Novecento, Palermo, 1986; Japanese Photographic Soc., 1989. *Publications:* (ed) Images à la Sauvette (The Decisive Moment), 1952; The Europeans, Moscow, 1955; From One China to the Other, 1956; Photographs by Cartier-Bresson; Flagrants Délits (The World of Henri Cartier-Bresson, 1968); (with F. Nourrissier) Vive la France, 1970; Cartier-Bresson's France, 1971; (jtly) L'Homme et la Machine, 1972 (Man and Machine, 1969) for IBM; Faces of Asia, 1972; A Propos de l'URSS, 1973 (About Russia, 1974); Henri Cartier-Bresson Pocket Book, 1985; Henri Cartier-Bresson in India, 1988; Traits pour Traits (Line by Line), 1989 (drawings); L'Amérique Furtivement (America in Passing), 1991; A Propos de Paris, 1994 (also German, American and Japanese edns); Carnets mexicains (text by Carlos Fuentes), 1995 (also German and Italian edns); André Breton, roi soleil, 1995; L'imaginaire d'après nature, 1996 (also German and US edns); Dessins 1974–1997 (text by Jean Leymarie), 1997; Europeans, 1998; Tête à Tête (text by E. H. Gombrich), 1998 (also French, German and US edns); The Mind's Eye, 1999; *relevant publications:* Yves Bonnefoy, Henri Cartier-Bresson, Photographer, 1979, rev. edn 1992; André P. de Mandiargues, Photoportrait, 1985; Peter Galassi, Early Work, USA 1987 (French edn 1991), 2nd edn 2001, as Landscapes and Cityscapes; Jean Pierre Montier, L'Art sans Art, 1995; Henri Cartier-Bresson: the man, the image and the world: a retrospective, 2003. *Address:* c/o Magnum Photos, 19 rue Hégesippe Moreau, 75018 Paris, France; c/o Helen Wright, 135 East 74th Street, New York, NY 10021, USA.
Died 2 Aug. 2004.

CARVER, Baron *cr* 1977 (Life Peer), of Shackleford in the County of Surrey; **Field-Marshal (Richard) Michael (Power) Carver,** GCB 1970 (KCB 1966; CB 1957); CBE 1945; DSO 1943 and Bar 1943; MC 1941; designated British Resident Commissioner in Rhodesia, 1977–78a; *b* 24 April 1915; 2nd *s* of late Harold Power Carver and Winifred Anne Gabrielle Carver (*née* Wellesley); *m* 1947, Edith, *d* of Lt-Col Sir Henry Lowry-Corry, MC; two *s* two *d*. *Educ:* Winchester Coll.; Sandhurst. 2nd Lieut Royal Tank Corps, 1935; War of 1939–45 (despatches twice); GSO1, 7th Armoured Div., 1942; OC 1st Royal Tank Regt, 1943; Comdr 4th Armoured Brigade, 1944; Tech. Staff Officer (1), Min. of Supply, 1947; Joint Services Staff Coll., 1950; AQMG, Allied Land Forces, Central Europe, 1951; Col GS, SHAPE 1952; Dep. Chief of Staff, East Africa, 1954 (despatches); Chief of Staff, East Africa, 1955; ide 1957; Dir of Plans, War Office, 1958–59; Comdr 6th Inf. Brigade, 1960–62; Maj.-Gen. 1962; GOC, 3 Div., 1962–64, also Comdr Joint Truce Force, Cyprus, and Dep. Comdr United Nations' Force in Cyprus, 1964; Dir, Army Staff Duties, Min. of Defence, 1964–66; Lt-Gen. 1966; comd FE Land Forces, 1966–67; Gen., 1967; C-in-C, Far East, 1967–69; GOC-in-C, Southern Command, 1969–71; Chief of the General Staff, 1971–73; Field-

Marshal 1973; CDS, 1973–76. Col Commandant: REME 1966–76; Royal Tank Regt, 1968–72; RAC, 1974–77; ADC (Gen.) 1969–72. Hon. DLitt Southampton, 1991. *Publications:* Second to None (History of Royal Scots Greys, 1919–45), 1954; El Alamein, 1962; Tobruk, 1964; (ed) The War Lords, 1976; Harding of Petherton, 1978; The Apostles of Mobility, 1979; War Since 1945, 1980; A Policy for Peace, 1982; The Seven Ages of the British Army, 1984; Dilemmas of the Desert War, 1986; Twentieth Century Warriors, 1987; Out of Step: memoirs of Field-Marshal Lord Carver, 1989; Tightrope Walking: British defence policy since 1945, 1992; (ed) Letters of a Victorian Army Officer: Edward Wellesley 1840–1854, 1995; Britain's Army in the 20th Century, 1998; National Army Museum Book of the Boer War, 1999. *Address:* Wood End House, Wickham, Fareham, Hants PO17 6JZ. *T:* (01329) 832143. *Club:* Royal Anglo-Belgian.

Died 9 Dec. 2001.

CARVER, Peter William John; JP, DL; landowner and farmer; Commissioner-in-Chief, 1995–99, Chief Commissioner, Operations and Member, Board of Trustees, 1999–2000, St John Ambulance; *b* 18 June 1938; *s* of late John Henton Carver and Juliet Carver (*née* Clitherow); *m* 1963, Jacqueline Boyce; one *s*. *Educ:* Uppingham Sch. Nat. Service, 2nd Lt, DCLI, 1957–59. Staff broadcaster, British Forces Network, Germany and Radio Luxembourg, 1959–64. Mem., ER Yorks CC, 1971–74. Contested (C) Kingston-upon-Hull, Feb. and Oct. 1974. Chm. and Pres., Humberside Euro Constituency, 1979–88. County Commissioner: Humberside Scouts, 1983–90 (Chm., 1978–83; Pres., 1991–); St John Ambulance (Humberside), 1991–95; Mem. Council, Scout Assoc., 1986–90. Underwriting Mem., Lloyd's, 1971–98. Mem., Yorks Regl Cttee, NT, 1985–91. Patron, living of N Cave, E Yorks, 1969–. JP 1973, DL 1983, Humberside, later ER Yorks; High Sheriff, ER Yorks, 1997–98. KStJ 1995. *Recreations:* gardens, historic houses, Hull City FC (supporter for over 50 years). *Address:* Manor House, North Cave, E Yorks HU15 2LW. *T:* (01430) 422203.

Died 28 Feb. 2003.

CASH, Sir Gerald (Christopher), GCMG 1980; GCVO 1985 (KCVO 1977); OBE 1964; JP; Governor-General, Commonwealth of the Bahamas, 1979–88 (Acting Governor-General, 1976–79); Consultant Counsel, Cash, Fountain & Co., Nassau, since 1989; *b* Nassau, Bahamas, 28 May 1917; *s* of late Wilfred Gladstone Cash and of Lillian Cash; *m* Dorothy Eileen (*née* Long); two *s* one *d*. *Educ:* Govt High Sch., Nassau. Called to the Bar, Middle Temple, 1948. Counsel and Attorney, Supreme Court of Bahamas, 1940. Member: House of Assembly, Bahamas, 1949–62; Exec. Council, 1958–62; Senate, 1969–73 (Vice-Pres., 1970–72; Pres., 1972–73). Member: Bd of Educn, 1950–62; Immigration Cttee, 1958–62; Road Traffic Cttee, 1958–62; Police Service Commn, 1964–69. Rep. Bahamas, Independence Celebrations of Jamaica, Trinidad and Tobago, 1962. Chairman: Labour Bd, 1950–52; Vis. Cttee, Boys Indust. Sch., 1952–62; Bd of Governors, Govt High Sch., 1949–63 and 1965–76; Bahamas Nat. Cttee, United World Colls, 1977–. Formerly: Hon. Vice-Consul for Republic of Haiti; Vice-Chancellor, Anglican Dio.; Admin. Adviser, Rotary Clubs in Bahamas to Pres. of Rotary Internat.; Treasurer and Dir, YMCA; Treas., Bahamas Cricket Assoc.; Chm., Boy Scouts Exec. Council; Mem. Board: Dirs of Central Bank of Bahamas; Dirs of Bahamas Assoc. for Mentally Retarded. Formerly: President: Rotary Club of E Nassau; Gym Tennis Club; Florida Tennis Assoc.; Bahamas Lawn Tennis Assoc.; Bahamas Table Tennis Assoc.; Vice-President: Boy Scouts Assoc.; Olympic Assoc., Amateur Athletic Assoc., Swimming Assoc., Football Assoc., Bahamas. JP Bahamas, 1940. Coronation Medal, 1953; Silver Jubilee Medal, 1977; Silver Medal, Olympic Order, 1983. *Recreations:* golf, tennis, table tennis, swimming. *Address:* 4 Bristol Street, PO Box N-476, Nassau, Bahamas. *T:* 3934767, 3932062. *Clubs:* Royal

Commonwealth Society; Kingston Cricket (Jamaica); Lyford Cay, Gym Tennis (Nassau).

Died 6 Jan. 2003.

CASSEL, His Honour Sir Harold (Felix), 3rd Bt *cr* 1920, of Lincoln's Inn, City of London; TD 1975; QC 1970; a Circuit Judge, 1976–88; *b* 8 Nov. 1916; 3rd *s* of Rt Hon. Sir Felix Cassel, 1st Bt, PC, QC (*d* 1953), and Lady Helen Cassel (*d* 1947), *d* of 3rd Earl of Verulam; *S* brother, 1969; *m* 1st, 1940, Ione Jean Barclay (marr. diss. 1963); three *s* one *d*; 2nd, 1963, Mrs Eileen Elfrida Smedley (*d* 2001). *Educ:* Stowe; Corpus Christi Coll., Oxford. Served War of 1939–45, Captain, 1941, Royal Artillery. Called to the Bar, Lincoln's Inn, 1946. Dep. Chm., Herts QS, 1959–62; Recorder of Great Yarmouth, 1968–71 (Hon. Recorder, 1972); a Recorder, 1972–76. JP Herts, 1959–62. *Recreations:* shooting, scuba diving, travelling. *Heir: s* Timothy Felix Harold Cassel [*b* 30 April 1942; *m* 1st, 1971, Jenifer Puckle (marr. diss. 1976); one *s* one *d*; 2nd, 1979, Ann Mallalieu, QC (later Baroness Mallalieu); two *d*]. *Address:* 49 Lennox Gardens, SW1X 0DF. *T:* (020) 7584 2721. *Club:* Boodle's. *Died 17 Sept. 2001.*

CASSON, (Frederick) Michael, OBE 1983; self-employed potter, since 1945 (first workshop, 1952); *b* 2 April 1925; *s* of William and Dorothy Casson; *m* 1955, Sheila Wilmot; one *s* two *d*. *Educ:* Tollington Grammar Sch.; Hornsey Coll. of Art (Art Teachers Dip.). First pots made 1945; continued to make functional pots from opening of first workshop, 1952; later making stoneware and porcelain pots fired with wood. Teacher part-time, all ages, 1946–95: taught history of ceramics and lectured in USA. Founder member: Craftsmen Potters Assoc., 1958 (Chm., 1963–67); Harrow Studio Pottery Course, 1963; Vice-Chm., Crafts Council of GB, 1986–88. Presenter, The Craft of the Potter, BBC TV series, 1975. Hon. DA Wolverhampton, 2000. Gold Medal, Prague Internat. Acad. of Ceramic Art, 1964; Lifetime achievement award, Internat. Conf. on Ceramics, Aberystwyth, 2001. *Publications:* Pottery in Britain Today, 1967; The Craft of the Potter, 1976, 2nd edn, 1980; many articles in Crafts, Ceramic Review, Ceramics Monthly (USA). *Recreation:* history - particularly the history of crafts. *Address:* Wobage Farm, Upton Bishop, near Ross-on-Wye, Herefordshire HR9 7QP. *T:* (01989) 780233. *Died 12 Dec. 2003.*

CASSON, Michael; *see* Casson, F. M.

CASTLE OF BLACKBURN, Baroness *cr* 1990 (Life Peer), of Ibstone in the County of Buckinghamshire; **Barbara Anne Castle;** PC 1964; Member (Lab) Greater Manchester West, European Parliament, 1984–89 (Greater Manchester North, 1979–84); Leader, British Labour Group, 1979–85, Vice-Chairman of Socialist Group, 1979–86, European Parliament; *b* 6 Oct. 1910; *d* of Frank and Annie Rebecca Betts; *m* 1944, Edward Cyril Castle (later Baron Castle) (*d* 1979), no *c*. *Educ:* Bradford Girls' Grammar Sch.; St Hugh's Coll., Oxford (BA). Elected to St Pancras Borough Council, 1937; Member Metropolitan Water Board, 1940–43; Editor, Town and County Councillor, 1936–40; Administrative Officer, Ministry of Food, 1941–44; Housing Correspondent and Affairs Adviser, Daily Mirror, 1944–45. MP (Lab) Blackburn, 1945–50, Blackburn East, 1950–55, Blackburn, 1955–79. Minister of: Overseas Development, 1964–65; Transport, 1965–68; First Secretary of State and Sec. of State for Employment and Productivity, 1968–70; Sec. of State for Social Services, 1974–76. Labour Party: Mem., NEC, 1950–79; Vice-Chm., 1957–58, Chm., 1958–59. Hon. Fellow: St Hugh's Coll., Oxford, 1966; Bradford and Ilkley Community Coll., 1985; UMIST, 1991; Humberside Poly., 1991; York Univ., 1992. Hon. DTech: Bradford, 1968; Loughborough, 1969; Hon. LLD: Lancaster, 1991; Manchester, 1993; Cambridge, 1998; Hon. DLitt De Montfort, 1998; Hon. Dr North London, 1998. Cross of Order of Merit (FRG), 1990. *Publications:* part author of Social Security, ed Dr Robson, 1943; The Castle Diaries 1974–76, 1980, vol. II, 1964–70, 1984, repr. in one vol., 1990; Sylvia and Christabel Pankhurst, 1987;

Fighting All the Way (autobiog.), 1993. *Recreations:* poetry, walking. *Address:* House of Lords, SW1A 0PW.
Died 3 May 2002.

CATLING, Sir Richard (Charles), Kt 1964; CMG 1956; OBE 1951; KPM 1945; CPM 1942; *b* 22 Aug. 1912; *y s* of late William Catling, Leiston, Suffolk; *m* 1951, Mary Joan Feyer (*née* Lewis) (*d* 1974). *Educ:* The Grammar School, Bungay, Suffolk. Palestine Police, 1935–48; Federation of Malaya Police, 1948–54; Commissioner of Police, Kenya, 1954–63 (despatches); Inspector General of Police, Kenya, 1963–64; Police Advr to Jordan Govt, 1971–75. Security/Safety Consultant to Guthrie Corp., London, 1965–88. Officer Brother, OStJ, 1956. Freeman, City of London, 1979. *Recreations:* reading, gardening. *Address:* Hall Fen House, Irstead, Norfolk NR12 8XT. *Club:* East India.   *Died 22 March 2005.*

CATTO, 2nd Baron *cr* 1936, of Cairncatto, co. Aberdeen; **Stephen Gordon Catto;** Bt 1921; Chairman: Yule Catto & Co. plc, 1971–2000; Morgan Grenfell Group plc, 1980–87; Director, Times Newspapers Holdings Ltd, since 1981, and other companies; *b* 14 Jan. 1923; *o s* of 1st Baron Catto and Gladys Forbes (*d* 1980), *d* of Stephen Gordon; *S* father, 1959; *m* 1st, 1948, Josephine Innes (marr. diss. 1965), *er d* of G. H. Packer, Alexandria, Egypt; two *s* two *d*; 2nd, 1966, Margaret (*d* 1998), *d* of J. S. Forrest, Dilston, Tasmania; one *s* one *d*; 3rd, 2001, Diana Dumergue Clifford-Turner (*née* Brown). *Educ:* Eton; Cambridge Univ. Served with RAFVR, 1943–47. Dir, 1957, Chief Exec., 1973–74, and Chm., 1973–79, Morgan Grenfell & Co. Ltd; Chairman: Australian Mutual Provident Soc. (UK branch), 1972–91; Pearl Gp, 1989–91; Director: The General Electric Co. plc, 1959–93; News International plc, 1969–96. Member, Advisory Council, ECGD, 1959–65; part-time Mem., London Transport Bd, 1962–68; Mem., London Adv. Cttee, Hong Kong & Shanghai Banking Corp., 1966–80. Chm. Council, RAF Benevolent Fund, 1978–91; Trustee and Chm., Exec. Cttee, Westminster Abbey Trust, 1973–97. *Heir: s* Innes Gordon Catto, *b* 7 Aug. 1950. *Address:* (office) Clarebell House, 5–6 Cork Street, W1X 1PB; 41 William Mews, Lowndes Square, SW1X 9HQ. *Clubs:* Oriental; Melbourne (Australia).
Died 3 Sept. 2001.

CAULFIELD, Patrick Joseph, CBE 1996; RA 1993; artist; *b* London, 29 Jan. 1936; *s* of Patrick and Annie Caulfield; *m* 1st, 1968, Pauline Jacobs (marr. diss. 1999); three *s*; 2nd, 1999, Janet Nathan. *Educ:* Acton Central Secondary Modern Sch.; Chelsea Sch. of Art; RCA (Sen. FRCA 1993). Served RAF, 1953–56. Taught at Chelsea Sch. of Art, 1963–71. First exhibited, FBA Galls, 1961; group exhibitions include: Whitechapel, Tate, Hayward, Waddington and Tooth Galls, and ICA, in London; Walker Art Gall., Liverpool; and exhibns in Paris, Brussels, Milan, NY, São Paulo, Berlin, Lugano, Dortmund, Bielefeld and Helsinki. One-man exhibitions include: Robert Fraser Gall., London, 1965, 1967; Robert Elkon Gall., NY, 1966, 1968; Waddington Galls, 1969, 1971, 1973, 1975, 1979, 1981, 1985, 1997, 1998; Tate Gall. (retrospective), 1981; Serpentine Gall. (retrospective), 1992; Hayward Gall. (retrospective), 1999; also in Italy, France, Australia, Belgium, USA and Japan. Designs for ballets, Covent Garden: Party Game, 1984; Rhapsody, 1995. Work in public collections incl. Tate Gall.; V&A; Walker Art Gall., Liverpool; Whitworth Art Gall., and Manchester City Art Gall.; and museums and galls in GB, Australia, USA, W Germany and Japan. Hon. Fellow: London Inst., 1996; Bolton Inst., 1999. Hon. Dr Surrey, 2000; Hon. RI Portsmouth, 2002. *Address:* 19 Belsize Square, NW3 4HT; c/o Waddington Galleries, 2 Cork Street, W1X 1PA.   *Died 29 Sept. 2005.*

CAUSLEY, Charles Stanley, CBE 1986; CLit 2001; poet; broadcaster; *b* Launceston, Cornwall, 24 Aug. 1917; *o s* of Charles Causley and Laura Bartlett. *Educ:* Launceston National Sch.; Horwell Grammar Sch.; Launceston Coll.; Peterborough Training Coll. Served on lower-deck in

Royal Navy (Communications Branch), 1940–46. Literary Editor, 1953–56, of BBC's West Region radio magazines Apollo in the West and Signature. Awarded Travelling Scholarships by Society of Authors, 1954 and 1966. Mem., Arts Council Poetry Panel, 1962–66. Hon. Vis. Fellow in Poetry, Univ. of Exeter, 1973. FRSL 1958. Hon. DLitt Exeter, 1977; Hon. MA Open, 1982. Awarded Queen's Gold Medal for Poetry, 1967; Cholmondeley Award, 1971; Kurt Maschler Award, 1987; Ingersoll Prize, 1990. *Publications:* Hands to Dance (short stories), 1951, rev. edn as Hands to Dance and Skylark, 1979; *poetry:* Farewell, Aggie Weston, 1951; Survivor's Leave, 1953; Union Street, 1957; Peninsula (ed), 1957; Johnny Alleluia, 1961; Dawn and Dusk (ed), 1962; Penguin Modern Poets 3 (with George Barker and Martin Bell), 1962; Rising Early (ed), 1964; Modern Folk Ballads (ed), 1966; Underneath the Water, 1968; Figure of 8, 1969; Figgie Hobbin, 1971; The Tail of the Trinosaur, 1973; (ed) The Puffin Book of Magic Verse, 1974; Collected Poems 1951–1975, 1975; The Hill of the Fairy Calf, 1976; (ed) The Puffin Book of Salt-Sea Verse, 1978; The Animals', Carol, 1978; (ed) Batsford Book of Stories in Verse for Children, 1979; (trans.) 25 Poems by Hamdija Demirović, 1980; (ed) The Sun, Dancing, 1982; Secret Destinations, 1984; 21 Poems, 1986; (trans.) Kings' Children, 1986; Early in the Morning, 1986; Jack the Treacle Eater, 1987; A Field of Vision, 1988; The Young Man of Cury, 1991; Bring in the Holly, 1992; Collected Poems, 1992; All Day Saturday, 1994; Going to the Fair, 1994; Collected Poems for Children, 1996; (jtly) Penguin Modern Poets, 1996; Collected Poems 1951–1997, 1997; Selected Poems for Children, 1997; Collected Poems 1951–2000, 2000; *children's stories:* Three Heads made of Gold, 1978; The Last King of Cornwall, 1978; The Merrymaid of Zennor, 1999; *verse plays:* The Gift of a Lamb, 1978; The Ballad of Aucassin and Nicolette, 1981; *libretti:* Jonah (music by William Mathias), 1990; St Martha and the Dragon (music by Phyllis Tate), 1991; contrib. to many anthologies of verse in Great Britain and America. *Recreations:* the theatre; European travel; the re-discovery of his native town; playing the piano with expression. *Address:* 2 Cyprus Well, Launceston, Cornwall PL15 8BT. *T:* (01566) 772731.
Died 4 Nov. 2003.

CAVANAGH, John Bryan; dress designer; Chairman and Managing Director, John Cavanagh Ltd, retired 1974; *b* 28 Sept. 1914; *s* of Cyril Cavanagh and Anne (*née* Murphy). *Educ:* St Paul's School. Trained with Captain Edward Molyneux in London and Paris, 1932–40. Joined Intelligence Corps, 1940, Captain (GS, Camouflage), 1944. On demobilisation, 1946, travelled throughout USA studying fashion promotion; Personal Asst to Pierre Balmain, Paris, 1947–51; opened own business, 1952; opened John Cavanagh Boutique, 1959; took own complete Collection to Paris, 1953; designed clothes for late Princess Marina and wedding dresses for the Duchess of Kent and Princess Alexandra. Elected to Incorporated Society of London Fashion Designers, 1952 (Vice-Chm., 1956–59). Gold Medal, Munich, 1954. *Recreations:* the theatre, swimming, travelling. *Address:* Nazareth House, Hammersmith Road, W6 8DB.
Died 24 March 2003.

CAVE, Prof. Alexander James Edward, MD, DSc; FRCS; Emeritus Professor of Anatomy, University of London; *b* Manchester, 13 Sept. 1900; *e s* of late John Cave and Teresa Anne d'Hooghe; *m* 1st, 1926, Dorothy M. Dimbleby (*d* 1961); one *d*; 2nd, 1970, Catherine Elizabeth FitzGerald (*d* 1999). *Educ:* Manchester High Sch.; Victoria University of Manchester (MB, ChB (distinction Preventive Medicine) 1923; MD (commendation) 1937; DSc 1944); DSc London, 1967. FRCS 1959. Senior Demonstrator (later Lecturer) in Anatomy, University of Leeds, 1924–34; Senior Demonstrator of Anatomy and Curator of Anatomical Museum, University College, London, 1934–35; Asst Conservator of Museum, 1935–46, Arnott Demonstrator, 1936–46, Professor of Human and Comparative Anatomy, 1941–46, Royal

College of Surgeons; Prof. of Anatomy, St Bartholomew's Hospital Medical Coll., University of London, 1946–67. Morrison Watson Research Fellow, 1961–72. Arris and Gale Lectr, RCS, 1932, 1941; Stopford Lectr, Manchester Univ., 1967. Late Examiner in Anatomy, Universities of Cambridge, Malta, London and Ireland, Primary FRCS and English Conjoint Board; Hon. Fellow, Linnean Society (Pres., 1970–73); Fellow and Hon. Res. Associate (late Vice-Pres. and Council Mem.) and Silver Medallist, Zoological Society; Life-Member (late Council Mem., Hon. Secretary and Recorder, Vice-Pres.) Anatomical Soc.; Hon. Associate BM (Nat. Hist.). Liveryman, Soc. of Apothecaries. *Publications:* papers on human and mammalian morphology. *Address:* c/o Smith & Williamson, Prospect House, 2 Athenaeum Road, Whetstone, N20 9YU. *Died 17 May 2001.*

CAVENAGH, Prof. Winifred Elizabeth, OBE 1977; PhD, BScEcon; Professor of Social Administration and Criminology, University of Birmingham, 1972–76, then Emeritus; Barrister-at-Law; *b* 12 Nov. 1908; *d* of Arthur Speakman and Ethel Speakman (*née* Butterworth); *m* 1938, Hugh Cavenagh; one step *s. Educ:* London Sch. of Economics, Univ. of London (BSc Econ); PhD Birmingham. Called to the Bar, Gray's Inn, 1964. With Lewis's Ltd, 1931–38; Min. of Labour, 1941–45. Univ. of Birmingham, 1946–. Birmingham: City Educn Cttee (co-opted expert), 1946–66; City Magistrate, 1949– (Dep. Chm., 1970–78; supplemental list, 1978–); Police Authority, 1970–78. Governor, Birmingham United Teaching Hosps (Ministerial appt, 1958–64); W Midlands Economic Planning Council, 1967–71; Indep. Mem. of Wages Councils; Home Office Standing Advisory Cttee on Probation, 1958–67; Lord Chancellor's Standing Adv. Cttee: on Legal Aid, 1960–71; on Training of Magistrates, 1965–73. Nat. Chm., Assoc. of Social Workers, 1955–57; Council, Magistrates Assoc. (co-opted expert), 1965–78; BBC Gen. Adv. Council, 1977–80; Chm., Industrial Tribunal, 1974–77; Hon. Mem., Internat. Assoc. of Juvenile and Family Courts (Vice-Pres., 1978–91). Visiting Prof., Univ of Ghana, 1971; Eleanor Rathbone Meml Lectr, 1976; Moir Cullis Lectr Fellowship, USA, 1977, Canada, 1980. *Publications:* Four Decades of Students in Social Work, 1953; The Child and the Court, 1959; Juvenile Courts, the Child and the Law, 1967; contrib. articles to: Public Administration, Brit. Jl Criminology, Justice of the Peace, Social Work To-day, etc. *Recreations:* theatre, music, films. *Address:* 32 St James Road, Edgbaston, Birmingham B15 2NX. *Club:* University Women's. *Died 7 May 2004.*

CAVENAGH-MAINWARING, Captain Maurice Kildare, DSO 1940; RN; with Simpson (Piccadilly) Ltd, 1961–91; *b* 13 April 1908; *yr s* of Major James Gordon Cavenagh-Mainwaring, Whitmore Hall, Whitmore, Staffordshire; *m* Iris Mary, *d* of late Colonel Charles Denaro, OBE; one *s. Educ:* RN Coll., Dartmouth. Joint Services Staff College, 1951–52; HMS St Angelo and Flag Captain to Flag Officer, Malta, 1952–54; Pres., Second Admiralty Interview Bd, 1955–56; Naval Attaché, Paris, 1957–60; retired RN, 1960. ADC to the Queen, 1960. Cross of Merit, Sovereign Order, Knights of Malta, 1955; Comdr, Légion d'Honneur, 1960. *Address:* 47 Cadogan Gardens, SW3 2TH. *T:* (020) 7584 7870. *Club:* Naval and Military. *Died 9 Jan. 2003.*

CAWDRON, George Edward; District Judge (Magistrates' Courts) (formerly Provincial Stipendiary Magistrate), North East London, since 1993; *b* 24 Feb. 1943; 3rd *s* of William Edward Cawdron and Louise Kathleen (*née* Walker); *m* 1965, Linda Margaret Preest; two *d. Educ:* Arnos Sch. Called to the Bar, Inner Temple, 1974. Dep. Clerk to the Justices, Willesden Div., London, 1975–77; Clerk to the Justices, Dacorum Div., 1977–91; Dacorum and Watford Divs, 1991–93, Herts; County Trng Officer for magistrates and staff, Herts, 1980–93. *Recreations:* classic cars, swimming, golf, gardening. *Address:* Croft End, 23 Barncroft Road, Berkhamsted,

Herts HP4 3NL. *T:* (01442) 871112.
Died 4 Oct. 2002.

CAWLEY, 3rd Baron *cr* 1918; **Frederick Lee Cawley;** Bt 1906; *b* 27 July 1913; *s* of 2nd Baron Cawley and Vivienne (*d* 1978), *d* of Harold Lee, Broughton Park, Manchester; *S* father, 1954; *m* 1944, Rosemary Joan, *y d* of late R. E. Marsden; six *s* one *d. Educ:* Eton; New Coll., Oxford (BA Nat. Science (Zoology), 1935, MA 1942). Called to the Bar, Lincoln's Inn, 1938; practised at the Patent Bar, 1946–73. Served War of 1939–45 in Europe; Capt. RA Leicestershire Yeomanry (wounded). Mem. Woking UDC, 1949–57. Dep. Chm. of Cttees, House of Lords, 1958–67; Member, Joint Parliamentary Committees: Consolidation Bills, 1956–73; Delegated Legislation, 1972–73; Ecclesiastical, 1974–96; former Chm. of many Private Bill Select Cttees. *Recreation:* gardening. *Heir: s* Hon. John Francis Cawley [*b* 28 Sept. 1946; *m* 1979, Regina Sarabia, *e d* of late Marqués de Hazas, Madrid; three *s* one *d*]. *Address:* Bircher Hall, Leominster, Herefordshire HR6 0AX. *T:* (01568) 780218.
Died 13 April 2001.

CAWTHRA, Rear-Adm. Arthur James, CB 1966; Admiral Superintendent, HM Dockyard, Devonport, 1964–66; *b* 30 Sept. 1911; *s* of James Herbert Cawthra, MIEE, and Margaret Anne Cawthra; *m* 1959, Adrien Eleanor Lakeman Tivy (*d* 2000), *d* of Cecil B. Tivy, MCh, Plymouth; one *s* (and one *s* decd). *Educ:* abroad. Joined Royal Navy, 1930; Imperial Defence Course, 1956; HMS Fisgard, 1958–59; Dir Underwater Weapons, Admiralty, 1960–63. Capt. 1955; Rear-Adm. 1964.
Died 22 Sept. 2005.

CELA, Camilo José; Grand Cross, Order of Isabel la Católica; Spanish writer; *b* 11 May 1916; *s* of Camilo Cela and Camila (*née* Trulock Bertorini); *m* 1st, 1944, Maria del Rosario Conde Picavea (marr. diss.); one *s*; 2nd, 1991, Marina Castaño. *Educ:* Univ. of Madrid. Has held various jobs including those of actor, bull fighter, painter, journalist and civil servant. Senator, Cortés, 1977–78. Founder, 1956, and Editor, 1956–79, Papeles de Son Armadans (literary jl). Asturias Prize, 1987; Nobel Prize for Literature, 1989. Grand Cross, Order of the Sun (Peru). *Publications: fiction:* La familia de Pascal Duarte, 1942; Pabellón de reposo, 1943; Nuevas andanzas y desventuras del Lazarillo de Tormes, 1944; La colmena, 1951; Timoteo el incomprendido, 1952; Santa Balbina, 37, gas en cada piso, 1952; Mrs Cadwell habla con su hijo, 1952; Café des artistas, 1953; La catira, 1955; El molino de viento, 1956; Tobogán de hambrientos, 1962; El ciudadano Iscariote Reclús, 1965; La familia del héroe o Discurso histórico de los últimos restos, 1965; Víspera, festividad y octava de San Camilo 1936 en Madrid, 1969; Oficio de tinieblas 5, 1973; Mazurca para dos muertos, 1983 (Nat. Literature Prize, 1984); Cristo Versus Arizona, 1988; Los Caprichos de Francisco de Goya y Lucientes, 1989; El asesinato del perdedor, 1994; La cruz de San Andrés, 1994; Madera de boj, 1999; *short stories:* Esas nubes que pasan, 1945; El bonito crimen del carabinero, 1947; El gallego y su cuadrilla, 1949; Nuevo retablo de Don Cristobita, 1957; Los viejos amigos, 1960; Gavillas de fábulas sin amor, 1962; Toreo de salón: farsa con acompañamiento de clamor y murga, 1963; El solitario y los sueños de Quesada de Rafael Zabaleta, 1963; Once cuentos de fútbol, 1963; Izas, rabizas y colipoterras: drama con acompañamiento de cachondeo y dolor de corazón, 1964; Nuevas escenas matritenses, 1965; Rol de cornudos, 1976; El espejo y otros cuentos, 1981; La bandada de palomas, 1987; El hombre y el mar, 1990; La sima de las penúltimas inocencias, 1993; *poetry:* Pisando la dudosa luz del día, 1945; El monasterio y las palabras, 1945; Cancionero de la Alcarria, 1948; Tres poemas gallegos, 1957; Reloj de arena, reloj de sol, reloj de sangre, 1989; Poesía completa, 1996; *ballads:* La verdadera historia de Gumersinda Cosculluela, moza que prefirió la muerte a la deshonva, 1959; Encarnación Toledano o la Perdición de los hombres, 1959; Viaje a USA, 1965; *plays:* Maria Sabina, 1967; El carro de heno o el inventor de la guillotina, 1969; Homenaje al Bosco II, 1999; *travel:* Viaje a la Alcarria, 1948; Avila, 1952; Del Miño al Bidasoa, 1952; Judíos, moros y cristianos, 1956; Primer viaje andaluz, 1959; Páginas de geografía errabunda, 1965; Viaje al Pirineo de Lérida, 1965; Madrid, 1966; Barcelona, 1970; Nuevo viaje a la Alcarria, 1986; Galicia, 1990; *non-fiction:* Diccionario secreto, 1968; Enciclopedia del erotismo, 1976; Diccionario geográfico popular, vol. I, 1998; *essays:* Mesa revuelta, 1945; Cajón de sastre, 1957; La rueda de los ocios, 1957; Cuatro figuras del 98, 1959; Garito de hospicianos o guirigay de imposturas y bambollas, 1963; Las compañías convenientes y otros fingimientos y cegueras, 1963; Al servicio de algo, 1969; Los sueños vanos, los ángeles curiosos, 1979; Vuelta de hoja, 1981; Los vasos comunicantes, 1981; El juego de los tres madroños, 1983; El asno de Buridán, 1986; Cachondeos, escarceos y otros meneos, 1991; Desde el palomar de Hita, 1991; El camaleón soltero, 1992; El huevo del juicio, 1993; A bote pronto, 1994; *memoirs:* La rosa, 1959; Memorias, entendimientos y voluntades, 1993; *adaptations and translations:* Poema del Cid, Cantar 1, 1957–59; Ruperto de No la, Libro de guisados manjares y potajes, 1969; Bertolt Brecht, La resistible ascensión de Arturo Ui, 1975; La Celestina, 1979; El Quijote, 1981. *Address:* c/o Agencia Literaria Carmen Balcells, Diagonal 580, 08021 Barcelona, Spain.   *Died 17 Jan. 2002.*

CHADWICK, Gerald William St John, (John), CMG 1961; HM Diplomatic Service, retired; *b* 28 May 1915; *s* of late John F. Chadwick, solicitor; *m* 1938, Madeleine Renée Boucheron (*d* 1991); two *s* one *d.* Lancing; St Catharine's Coll., Cambridge (Open Exhibitioner). Asst Principal, Colonial Office, 1938; transf. Dominions Office, following demobilisation, 1940; Sec., Parly Mission to Newfoundland, 1943; further missions to Newfoundland and Bermuda, 1946 and 1947; attended United Nations, 1949; Office of UK High Commission, Ottawa, 1949–52; Counsellor, British Embassy, Dublin, 1952–53; UK Delegn to NATO, Paris, 1954–56; Asst Sec., CRO, 1956; Asst Under-Sec. of State, CRO, 1960–66; first Dir, Commonwealth Foundn, 1966–80. Governor, Commonwealth Inst., 1967–80. Certificate of Merit, Canadian Historical Soc., 1968. *Publications:* The Shining Plain, 1937; (contrib.) A Decade of the Commonwealth 1955–64, 1966; Newfoundland: Island into Province, 1967; International Organisations, 1969; (ed jtly) Professional Organisations in the Commonwealth, 1976; The Unofficial Commonwealth, 1982; numerous reviews and articles. *Recreation:* travel.   *Died 5 May 2001.*

CHADWICK, John; *see* Chadwick, G. W. St J.

CHADWICK, Lynn Russell, CBE 1964; RA 2001; sculptor since 1948; *b* 24 Nov. 1914; *s* of late Verner Russell Chadwick and Margery Brown Lynn; *m* 1942, Charlotte Ann Secord (marr. diss. 1959; she *d* 1997); one *s; m* 1959, Frances Mary Jamieson (*d* 1964); two *d; m* 1965, Eva Reiner; one *s. Educ:* Merchant Taylors' Sch. Architectural Draughtsman, 1933–39. Pilot, FAA, 1941–44. Exhibitions held in various London galleries by Arts Council and British Council; works also shown in numerous internat. exhibitions, incl. Venice Biennale, 1956 (Internat. Sculpture Prize). *Works in public collections:* Tate Gall., London; British Council, London; Arts Council of GB; Victoria and Albert Mus.; Pembroke Coll., Oxford; City Art Gall., Bristol; Art Gall., Brighton; Whitworth Art Gall., Univ. of Manchester; Musée National d'Art Moderne, Paris; Boymans van Beuningen Mus., Rotterdam; Municipality of Recklinghausen; Staatliche Graphische Sammlung, Munich; Staatische Kunstmuseum, Duisburg; Art Gall., Gothenburg; Musées Royaux des Beaux-Arts de Belgique, Brussels; Galleria d'Arte Moderna, Rome; Museo Civico, Turin; Nat. Gall. of SA, Adelaide; Nat. Gall. of Canada, Ottawa; Mus. of Fine Arts, Montreal; Mus. of Modern Art, NY; Carnegie Inst., Pittsburgh; Univ. of Michigan; Albright Art Gall.,

Buffalo; Art Inst., Chicago; Inst. de Artes Contemporáneas, Lima. Hon. Fellow: Cheltenham and Gloucester Coll. of Higher Educn, 1995; Bath Spa UC, 1998. Associate, Académie Royale de Belgique, 1995. Order of Andres Bello, 1st cl. (Venezuela), 1988; Commandeur des Arts et des Lettres (France), 1993. *Address:* Lypiatt Park, Stroud, Glos GL6 7LL.   *Died 25 April 2003.*

CHAKAIPA, Most Rev. Patrick Fani; Archbishop of Harare (formerly Salisbury), (RC), since 1976; *b* 25 June 1932; *s* of Chakaipa and Chokutaura. *Educ:* Chishawasha Minor and Regional Major Seminary, nr Harare; Kutama Teachers' Coll. Ecclesiastic qualifications in Philosophy and Theology; Teacher Training Cert. Asst priest, Makumbi Mission, 1967–69; Priest-in-Charge, All Souls Mission, Mutoko, 1969–73; Episcopal Vicar, Mutoko-Mrewa Area, 1970–73; Auxiliary Bishop of Salisbury, 1973–76. Pres., Inter-Regl Meeting of Bishops of Southern Africa, 1992–95. Chancellor, Catholic Univ. in Zimbabwe, 1998–. *Publications:* Karikoga, 1958; Pfumo reRopa, 1961; Rudo Ibofu, 1961; Garandichauya, 1963; Dzasukwa, 1967. *Recreation:* chess. *Address:* PO Box Cy 330, Causeway, Harare, Zimbabwe. *T:* 792125.   *Died 8 April 2003.*

CHALLENS, Wallace John, CBE 1967 (OBE 1958); Director, Atomic Weapons Research Establishment, Aldermaston, 1976–78; *b* 14 May 1915; *s* of late Walter Lincoln Challens and Harriet Sybil Challens (*née* Collins); *m* 1st, 1938, Winifred Joan Stephenson (*d* 1971); two *s*; 2nd, 1973, Norma Lane. *Educ:* Deacons Sch., Peterborough; University Coll., Nottingham; BSc (Hons) London. Research Dept, Woolwich, 1936; Projectile Develt Estabt, Aberporth, 1939. British Commonwealth Scientific Office, Washington, 1946; Armament Research Estabt, Fort Halstead, 1947; Atomic Weapons Research Estabt: Fort Halstead, 1954; Aldermaston, 1955–78 (Hd, Warhead Develt, 1959–65; Asst Dir, 1965–72; Dep. Dir, 1972–76). Scientific Dir of trials at Christmas Island, 1957. FInstP 1944. US Medal of Freedom (Bronze) 1946. *Recreation:* golf. *Address:* Far End, Crossborough Hill, Basingstoke, Hampshire RG21 4AG. *T:* (01256) 464986.   *Died 1 March 2002.*

CHALMERS, William Gordon, CB 1980; MC 1944; Crown Agent for Scotland, 1974–84; *b* 4 June 1922; *s* of Robert Wilson Chalmers and Mary Robertson Chalmers (*née* Clark); *m* 1948, Margaret Helen McLeod (*d* 1997); one *s* one *d. Educ:* Robert Gordon's Coll., Aberdeen; Aberdeen Univ. (BL). University, 1940–42 and 1947–48. Served with Queen's Own Cameron Highlanders, 1942–47. Solicitor in Aberdeen, 1948–50; Procurator Fiscal Depute at Dunfermline, 1950–59; Sen. Procurator Fiscal Depute at Edinburgh, 1959–63; Asst in Crown Office, 1963–67; Dep. Crown Agent, 1967–74. Jt Hd, War Crimes Enquiry in UK, 1988–89. *Recreations:* golf, bridge. *Address:* 3/4 Rocheid Park, East Fettes Avenue, Edinburgh EH4 1RP. *T:* (0131) 332 7937.   *Died 28 May 2003.*

CHAMBERLAIN, Richard, TD 1949; Chief Master of the Supreme Court, Chancery Division, 1985–86 (Master, 1964–84); *b* 29 Jan. 1914; *o s* of late John Chamberlain and Hilda (*née* Poynting); *m* 1938, Joan (*d* 1997), *d* of late George and Eileen Kay; two *s* one *d. Educ:* Radley Coll.; Trinity Coll., Cambridge (MA). Admitted Solicitor, 1938. Served War, 1939–45, Devon Regt, TJFF, Staff Coll., Haifa. Partner, Kingsford Dorman & Co., 1948–64. Worshipful Co. of Solicitors of the City of London: Asst, 1966; Warden, 1973–74; Master, 1975. *Publication:* (Asst Ed.) Supreme Court Practice, 1967. *Recreation:* grandparental duties. *Address:* Sunrise, Christchurch Road, Virginia Water, Surrey GU25 4BE. *T:* (01344) 843777.   *Died 23 March 2005.*

CHAMBERLAIN, William Richard Frank; DL; Chairman: Cricket Council, 1990–96; Test and County Cricket Board, 1990–94; *b* 13 April 1925; *s* of Lt-Comdr

Richard Chamberlain and Elizabeth Chamberlain (née Robson); *m* 1960, Gillian Diarmid Castle (*d* 2000); one *s* one *d*. *Educ*: Uppingham School. Served Fleet Air Arm 1943–46. Played cricket for Northants CCC, 1946. Joined W. W. Chamberlain (Assoc. Cos) Ltd, subseq. Chamberlain Phipps, 1947: Dir, 1953; Jt Man. Dir, 1957; Chm. and Jt Man. Dir, 1963–69; Dep. Chm. and Man. Dir, 1969, Chm. and Man. Dir, 1972, Chm., 1975–87, Chamberlain Phipps Ltd; Chm., Stead & Simpson, 1984–89; Regional Dir, Nat. Westminster Bank, 1983–90; Dir, Kingsgrange, 1989–91; Mem. Council, CBI, 1982–87. Pres., Northants CCC, 1990– (Chm., 1985–90). Freeman, City of London; Master, Patternmaker's Co., 1987. High Sheriff, 1990, DL 1991, Northants. *Recreations:* cricket, shooting. *Address:* Manor House, Swineshead, Bedford MK44 2AF. *T:* (01234) 708283. *Clubs:* Naval and Military, East India, MCC, Lord's Taverners.

Died 8 April 2004.

CHAN, Nai Keong, (Kenneth), CBE 1985; FREng; JP; Chairman, Leighton (Asia) Ltd, since 1997; Chairman Emeritus, Parsons Brinckerhoff (Asia) Ltd, since 1992; *b* 17 Nov. 1931; two *s* one *d*. FICE, FIStructE, FHKIE, FHKAES; FREng (FEng 1986). Public Works Dept, Hong Kong: pupil engineer, Roads Office, 1952; Civil Engineering Office, 1960; Sen. Engineer, 1964; Highways Office, 1969; Principal Govt Engineer, 1973, i/c Tuen Mun New Town develt; Dir, Engineering Dept, 1980; Dep. Dir, Public Works, 1981; Dep. Sec. for Lands and Works, 1982; Sec. for Lands and Works, 1983–86; Gp Man. Dir, Cavendish Internat. Holdings Ltd, 1987–89; Dir, Parsons Brinckerhoff (Asia) Ltd, 1989–92. JP Hong Kong, 1972. Hon. DTech Loughborough, 1984. *Recreations:* bridge, swimming, yoga, music. *Address:* c/o Parsons Brinckerhoff (Asia) Ltd, 23/F AIA Tower, 183 Electric Road, North Point, Hong Kong. *T:* 25798899, *Fax:* 28569908. *Clubs:* Hongkong, Hong Kong Jockey, Chinese, Chinese Recreation, China (Hong Kong).

Died 9 May 2003.

CHANDLER, Dr David Geoffrey; author; lecturer and military historian, Royal Military Academy Sandhurst; *b* 15 Jan. 1934; *s* of late Rev. Geoffrey Edmund Chandler and Joyce Mary Chandler; *m* 1961, Gillian Dixon; three *s*. *Educ*: Marlborough Coll.; Keble Coll., Oxford (BA 1955; Cert Ed 1956; MA 1960; DLitt 1991). Captain, RAEC, Royal W Africa Frontier Force, Nigeria, 1956–60; Royal Military Academy Sandhurst: Lectr, Dept of Modern Subjects, 1960–61; Lectr, 1961–64, Sen. Lectr, 1964–69, Dept of Mil. History; Dep. Head, 1969–80, Head, 1980–94, Dept of War Studies. Visiting Professor: Mershon, in Mil. History, Ohio State Univ., 1970; Mary Ann Northen, in Humanities, Virginian Mil. Inst., 1988; Mil. Studies, US Marine Corps Univ., 1991. Trustee, Royal Armouries, HM Tower of London, and Leeds, 1989–95. Hon. President: European Union of Re-enactments Soc., 1990–95 (Founder, 1990); Napoleonic Assoc. (UK), 1994–. Mil. advr, War and Peace, BBC TV, 1971–73; question setter, Mastermind, 1990–94; mil. history consultant, Great Military Leaders, Channel 4, 1992–93; Consultant, From Hoplites to Harrier—a Radio History of War, BBC, 1993–94. FRHistS 1966; FRGS 1971. Golden Cross of Merit (Polish govt in exile), 1979. *Publications* include: The Campaigns of Napoleon, 1967 (Internat. Napoleonic Soc. Lit. Award, 1995); The Marlborough Wars: Robert Parker and Count de Mérode-Westerloo, 1968; Marlborough as Military Commander, 1973; The Art of War on Land, 1973; The Art of Warfare in the Age of Marlborough, 1976; A Dictionary of the Napoleonic Wars, 1979; Waterloo: The Hundred Days, 1984; An Atlas of Military Strategy, 1618–1868, 1980; Sedgemoor, 1685, 1985; (ed) Napoleon's Marshals, 1987; (ed) Military Maxims of Napoleon, 1987; Battles and Battlescenes of World War Two, 1989; Austerlitz, 1805, 1990; The Illustrated Napoleon, 1990; (ed) The Great Battles of the British Army, 1991; (ed) Sandhurst—the Royal Military Academy: 250 years, 1991; Jena, 1806, 1993; (sen. ed.) D-Day Encyclopaedia, 1993; On the

Napoleonic Wars (Napoleonic Soc. of Amer. Lit. Award), 1994; (sen. ed.) The Oxford Illustrated History of the British Army, 1995; (ed) A Traveller's Guide to the Battlefields of Europe, 1998; Napoleon, 2001; Blenheim Preparation, 2004; Serjeant John Wilson's Diary (of the Fifteenth Foot), 2005; contribs to DNB. *Recreations:* battlefield visits, wargaming, military re-enactment societies, rowing, naval model-making, drawing. *Address:* Hindford, Monteagle Lane, Yateley, Hants GU46 6LT. *T:* (01252) 872175.

Died 10 Oct. 2004.

CHANDRASEKHAR, Prof. Sivaramakrishna, FRS 1983; Director, Centre for Liquid Crystal Research, Bangalore, since 1991; *b* 6 Aug. 1930; *s* of S. Sivaramakrishnan and Sitalaxmi; *m* 1954, Ila Pinglay; one *s* one *d*. *Educ:* Nagpur Univ. (MSc, DSc); Pembroke Coll., Cambridge (PhD 1958; ScD 1987). Res. Schol., Raman Res. Inst., Bangalore, 1950–54; 1851 Exhibn Schol., Cavendish Lab., Cambridge, 1954–57; DSIR Fellow, Dept of Crystallography, UCL, 1957–59; Res. Fellow, Davy Faraday Res. Lab., Royal Instn, 1959–61; Prof. and Hd of Dept of Physics, Univ. of Mysore, 1961–71; Prof., Raman Res. Inst., Bangalore, 1971–90. Nehru Vis. Prof., and Fellow Pembroke Coll., Cambridge, 1986–87; Bhatnagar Fellow, CSIR, 1990–95. India Corresp., 1987–, Royal Medal, 1994, Royal Soc.; Niels Bohr—UNESCO Gold Medal, 1998. Chevalier, Ordre des Palmes Académiques (France), 1999. *Publications:* Liquid Crystals, 1977, 2nd edn, 1992; editor of several books; contrib. scientific papers to learned jls. *Address:* Centre for Liquid Crystal Research, PO Box 1329, Jalahalli, Bangalore 560013, India.

Died 8 March 2004.

CHANEY, Hon. Sir Frederick (Charles), KBE 1982 (CBE 1969); AFC 1945; Chairman, Home Building Society, 1974–87; *b* 12 Oct. 1914; *s* of Frederick Charles Chaney and Rose Templar Chaney; *m* 1938, Mavis Mary (née Bond) four *s* three *d*. *Educ:* Aquinas Coll.; Claremont Coll. Served War, RAAF, 1940–45. Teacher, 1936–40 and 1946–55. MHR (L) Perth, 1955–69; Govt Whip, 1961–63; Minister for the Navy, 1963–66; Administrator, Northern Territory, 1970–73. Lord Mayor of Perth, WA, 1978–82. Dep. Pres., King's Park Bd, 1981–84. Freeman, City of Perth, 1998. *Address:* 9A Melville Street, Claremont, WA 6010, Australia. *T:* (9) 3840596. *Clubs:* West Australian Cricket Assoc., East Perth Football (Perth).

Died 17 Dec. 2001.

CHANNON, Prof. Derek French, DBA; FCIM; Professor of Management, Imperial College of Science, Technology and Medicine, 1990–97; *b* 4 March 1939; *s* of John French and Betty Blanche Channon; *m* 1963, Ann Lesley (marr. diss. 1986); one *s* one *d*. *Educ:* University Coll. London (BSc); Manchester Business Sch. (MBA); Harvard Graduate Sch. of Business (DBA). FCIM 1985. Marketing management, Royal Dutch Shell Gp, 1960–68; Lectr in Marketing, Manchester Business Sch., 1968–70; Ford Foundn European Doctoral Fellow, Harvard Bus. Sch., 1968–71; Manchester Business School: Sen. Res. Fellow, 1971–76; Prof. of Strategic Management and Marketing, 1977–89; Associate Dir, 1985–87. Jt Man. Dir, Evode Holdings PLC, 1976–77; Director: Bray Technologies, 1983–92; Royal Bank of Scotland, 1988–95. Pres., Strategic Management Soc., 1985–88 (Dir, 1982–). *Publications:* Strategy and Structure of British Enterprise, 1973; (with J. Stopford and B. Norburn) Business Policy, 1975; British Banking Strategy and the International Challenge, 1977; The Service Industries, 1978; (with R. M. Jalland) Multi-national Strategic Planning, 1979; British Transnational Bank Strategy, 1979; (with J. Stopford and J. Constable) Cases in Strategic Management, 1980; (with P. Rushton) Retail Electronic Banking and Point of Sale, 1982; Bank Strategic Management and Marketing, 1986; Global Banking Strategy, 1988; (ed) Blackwell Encyclopedic Dictionary of Strategic Management, 1997. *Recreations:* golf, tennis, painting.

Died 14 July 2003.

CHAPMAN, Prof. Garth; Professor of Zoology, Queen Elizabeth College, University of London, 1958–82, then Emeritus (Vice Principal, 1974–80; Acting Principal, Sept. 1977–March 1978; Fellow, 1984); *b* 8 Oct. 1917; *o s* of E. J. Chapman and Edith Chapman (*née* Attwood); *m* 1941, Margaret Hilda Wigley; one *s* one *d* (and one *s* decd). *Educ:* Royal Grammar Sch., Worcester; Trinity Hall, Cambridge (Major Scholar); ScD Cantab 1977. FIBiol 1963; FKC 1985. Telecommunications Research Establishment, Ministry of Aircraft Production, 1941–45; Asst Lectr in Zoology, 1945–46, Lectr in Zoology, 1946–58, QMC, Univ. of London; Dean, Faculty of Science, Univ. of London, 1974–78. Vis. Prof., Univ. of California, Berkeley, 1967, Los Angeles, 1970–71. Member: Cttee for Commonwealth Univ. Interchange, British Council, 1978–80; Inter-Univ. Council for Higher Educn Overseas, 1973–83; Council, Westfield Coll., Univ. of London, 1978–84; Central Research Fund Cttee B, 1978–82; Management Cttee of Univ. Marine Biological Station, Millport, 1975–82. *Publications:* Zoology for Intermediate Students (with W. B. Barker), 1964; Body Fluids and their Functions, 1967; various on structure and physiology of marine invertebrates. *Recreations:* gardening, wood-engraving. *Address:* The Grove, Callis Street, Clare, Suffolk CO10 8PX. *T:* (01787) 277235. *Club:* Athenæum.
Died 1 Nov. 2003.

CHAPMAN, Geoffrey Lloyd; Vice Judge Advocate General, 1984–94; *b* 20 Oct. 1928; *o s* of Sydney Leslie Chapman and Dora Chapman (*née* Lloyd); *m* 1958, Jean, *er d* of Valentine Harry Coleman and Marjorie Coleman (*née* Poston); one *s* two *d*. *Educ:* Latymer Upper School; Christ Church, Oxford (BCL, MA). National Service, 1947–49 (2nd Lieut, RASC). Called to the Bar, Inner Temple, 1953; practised London and Western Circuit; Legal Assistant: Min. of Labour and Nat. Service, 1957; JAG's Office, 1958; Dep. Judge Advocate, 1961 (Germany, 1963–66, Cyprus, 1969–72); Asst JAG, 1971 (Germany, 1972–76); Dep. JAG, British Forces in Germany, 1979–82. *Recreations:* beagling, reading. *Address:* The Myrtles, Alma Road, Reigate, Surrey RH2 0DH. *T:* (01737) 247860.
Died 28 Oct. 2004.

CHAPMAN NYAHO, Daniel Ahmling, CBE 1961; Director: Pioneer Tobacco Co. Ltd, Ghana (Member of British-American Tobacco Group), 1967–89; Standard Bank Ghana Ltd, 1970–75; *b* 5 July 1909; *s* of William Henry Chapman and Jane Atsiamesi (*née* Atriki); *m* 1941, Jane Abam (*née* Quashie); two *s* four *d* (and two *d* decd). *Educ:* Bremen Mission Schs, Gold Coast and Togoland; Achimota Coll., Ghana; St Peter's Hall, Oxford. Postgraduate courses at Columbia Univ. and New York Univ.; Teacher, Government Senior Boys' School, Accra, 1930; Master, Achimota Coll., 1930–33, 1937–46. Area Specialist, UN Secretariat, Lake Success and New York, 1946–54; Sec. to Prime Minister and Sec. of Cabinet, Gold Coast/Ghana, 1954–57; Ghana's Ambassador to USA and Permanent Representative at UN, 1957–59; Headmaster, Achimota Sch., Ghana, 1959–63; Dir, UN Div. of Narcotic Drugs, Geneva, 1963–66; Ambassador (Special Duties), Min. of External Affairs, Ghana, 1967. Gen. Sec., All-Ewe Conf., 1944–46; Commonwealth Prime Ministers' Conf., 1957; Mem., Ghana delegn to the conf. of indep. African States, Accra, 1958. First Vice-Chm., Governing Council of UN Special Fund, 1959; Chairman: Mission of Indep. African States to Cuba, Dominican Republic, Haiti, Venezuela, Bolivia, Paraguay, Uruguay, Brazil, Argentina, Chile, 1958; Volta Union, 1968–69. Vice-Chairman: Commn on Univ. Educn in Ghana, 1960–61; Ghana Constituent Assembly, 1978–79. Member: Board of Management, UN Internat. Sch., New York, 1950–54, 1958–59; UN Middle East and N Africa Technical Assistance Mission on Narcotics Control, 1963; Dir, UN Consultative Gp on Narcotics Control in Asia and Far East, Tokyo, 1964; Member: Political Cttee of Nat. Liberation Council, 1967; Board of Trustees of General Kotoka Trust Fund, 1967–83; Chairman: Arts Council of Ghana, 1968–69; Council of Univ. of Science

and Technology, Kumasi, 1972; Bd of Directors, Ghana Film Industry Corporation, 1979–80; Ghana National Honours and Awards Cttee, 1979–80. Darnforth Vis. Lectr, Assoc. Amer. Colls, 1969, 1970. Hon. LLD Greenboro Agric. and Techn. Coll., USA, 1958. Fellow, Ghana Acad. of Arts and Sciences. *Publications:* Human Geography of Eweland, 1946; Our Homeland—Book I: South-East Gold Coast, 1945; (Ed.) The Ewe News-Letter, 1945–46. *Recreations:* music, gardening, walking. *Address:* 7 Tenth Avenue, Tesano, Accra, Ghana. *T:* 227180.
Died 13 July 2001.

CHAPPLE, Baron *cr* 1985 (Life Peer), of Hoxton in Greater London; **Francis Joseph Chapple;** General Secretary, Electrical, Electronic, Telecommunication and Plumbing Union, 1966–84; *b* Shoreditch, 8 Aug. 1921; *m* 1st, 1944, Joan Nicholls (*d* 1994); two *s*; 2nd, 1999, Phyllis Luck. *Educ:* elementary school. Started as Apprentice Electrician; Electrical Trades Union: Mem., 1937–83; Shop Steward and Branch Official; Mem. Exec. Council, 1958; Asst Gen. Sec., 1963–66. Mem., Gen. Council of TUC, 1971–83, Chm. 1982–83; Gold Badge of Congress, 1983. Member: National Exec. Cttee of Labour Party, 1965–71; Cttee of Inquiry on Shipping, 1967; Royal Commn on Environmental Pollution, 1973–77; Horserace Totalisator Bd, 1976–90; Energy Commn, 1977–79; NEDC, 1979–83; Nat. Nuclear Corp., 1980–86; Southern Water Authority, 1983–89; Director: Inner City Enterprises, 1983–88; N. G. Bailey Orgn, 1989–99. *Publication:* (autobiog.) Sparks Fly, 1984. *Recreation:* racing pigeons. *Address:* c/o Amalgamated Engineering and Electrical Union, Hayes Court, West Common Road, Bromley BR2 7AU.
Died 19 Oct. 2004.

CHARD, Prof. Timothy, MD; FRCOG; Professor, Obstetrics and Gynaecology, Bart's and The London, Queen Mary's School of Medicine and Dentistry (formerly St Bartholomew's and Royal London School of Medicine and Dentistry, Queen Mary and Westfield College), University of London, since 1996; *b* 4 June 1937; *s* of Henry Francis and Dorothea Elaine Chard; *m* 1st, 1965, Marty Jane Batten (marr. diss.); two *s*; 2nd, 1977, Linda Kay Elmore (marr. diss.); 3rd, 2000, Mary Christina Munro Macintosh. *Educ:* Merchant Taylors' School; St Thomas's Hosp. Med. Sch. (MB BS 1960); MD 1968. FRCOG 1977. Junior med. posts, 1960–65; MRC Clinical Research Fellow, 1965–68; Sen. Lectr, St Bartholomew's Hosp. Med. Coll., 1968–73; Prof. of Reproductive Physiol., St Bartholomew's Hosp. Med. Coll., 1973–96. *Publications:* (jointly): Radioimmunoassay, 1978, 5th edn 1995; Placental Function Tests, 1982; Basic Sciences for Obstetrics, 1984, 5th edn 1998; Computing for Clinicians, 1988, 2nd edn 1995. *Recreations:* fine arts, venture capital. *Address:* 171 Lauderdale Tower, EC2Y 8BY. *T:* (020) 7628 5662; *e-mail:* timchard@ waitrose.com.
Died 21 July 2003.

CHARLEMONT, 14th Viscount *cr* 1665 (Ire.); **John Day Caulfeild;** Baron Caulfeild of Charlemont 1620 (Ire.); *b* 19 March 1934; *s* of Eric St George Caulfeild (*d* 1975) and Edith Evelyn, *d* of Frederick William Day, Ottawa; *S* uncle, 1985; *m* 1st, 1964, Judith Ann (*d* 1971), *d* of James E. Dodd; one *s* one *d*; 2nd, 1972, Janet Evelyn, *d* of Orville R. Nancekivell. *Heir: s* Hon. John Dodd Caulfeild [*b* 15 May 1966; *m* 1991, Nadea Stella, *d* of Wilson Fortin; one *s*]. *Address:* 820 Burnhamthorpe Road, Apt 1009, Etobicoke, Ontario M9C 4W2, Canada.
Died 10 Nov. 2001.

CHARLES, Dame Eugenia; see Charles, Dame M. E.

CHARLES, Dame (Mary) Eugenia, DBE 1991; OCC 2003; Prime Minister and Minister of Finance, Commonwealth of Dominica, 1980–95; MP (Dominica Freedom Party) Roseau, 1970–95 (Nominated MP, 1970–75); *b* 15 May 1919; *d* of John Baptiste Charles and Josephine (*née* Delauney). *Educ:* Convent High Sch., Roseau, Dominica; St Joseph's Convent, St George's, Grenada; University Coll., Univ. of Toronto (BA);

London Sch. of Econs and Pol. Science (Hon. Fellow 2002). Called to the Bar, Inner Temple, 1947; admitted to practice, Dominica, 1949. Entered Parlt, 1970; Leader of the Opposition, 1975–79; Minister of Foreign Affairs, 1980–90. *Recreations:* reading, gardening, travelling. *Address:* PO Box 121, 1 Cross Lane, Roseau, Commonwealth of Dominica. *T:* 4482855, *T:* (office) 4482876. *Died 6 Sept. 2005.*

CHARLESWORTH, Arthur Leonard, FCIOB; Joint Managing Director, John Mowlem Co., 1978–89; Non-Executive Director, John Mowlem Group, 1989–95; *b* 11 June 1927; *s* of William Henry and Florence Alice Charlesworth; *m* 1948, June Edith (*née* Sims); one *s* two *d*. *Educ:* Wandsworth Grammar Sch. Joined John Mowlem Co., 1941; Dir, Mowlem (Building), 1965, John Mowlem & Co., 1969; Man. Dir, John Mowlem & Co., 1978; Jt Man. Dir, Mowlem Group, 1986. FRSA. *Recreation:* golf. *Address:* 61 Vicarage Road, SW14 8RY. *T:* (020) 8876 6724. *Club:* Richmond Golf. *Died 16 Jan. 2001.*

CHATTEN, Harold Raymond Percy, CB 1975; RCNC; Chief Executive, Royal Dockyards, 1975–79, and Head of Royal Corps of Naval Constructors, Apr.-Sept. 1979, Ministry of Defence; *s* of Walter Henry Chatten, CBE, CEng, FIEE; *m* Eileen Mary (*d* 2001). *Educ:* Clare Coll., Cambridge (BA 1941, MA 1946). Production Manager, HM Dockyard, Chatham, 1967–70; General Manager, HM Dockyard, Rosyth, Fife, 1970–75. *Died 30 May 2005.*

CHATTY; *see* Hatty, Hon. Sir C. J.

CHEDLOW, Barry William; QC 1969; a Recorder of the Crown Court, 1974–96; Member, Criminal Injuries Compensation Board, 1976–96; *b* Macclesfield, 8 Oct. 1921; *m* Anne Sheldon, BA; one *s* one *d*. *Educ:* Burnage High Sch.; Manchester Univ.; Birkbeck Coll., London (BA Hons German 1997). Served RAF, 1941–46: USAAF, Flying Instructor, 1942; Flt-Lt 1943. Called to Bar, Middle Temple, 1947, Bencher, 1976; Prizeman in Law of Evidence. Practised in London, Midland and Oxford Circuit; arbitrator in aviation disputes. *Publications:* author and editor of various legal text-books. *Recreations:* flying (private pilot's licence, singles, twins, helicopters), languages, sailing. *Address:* Thatchers Hall, Hundon, Suffolk CO10 8EE. *T:* (01440) 786262. *Club:* Royal Air Force. *Died 5 May 2005.*

CHEETHAM, Francis William, OBE 1979; FMA; arts and museums consultant, since 1991; Director, Norfolk Museums Service, 1974–90; *b* 5 Feb. 1928; *s* of Francis Cheetham and Doris Elizabeth Jones; *m* 1954, Monica Fairhurst; three *s* one *d*. *Educ:* King Edward VII Sch., Sheffield; Univ. of Sheffield (MA). Dep. Art Dir and Curator, Castle Museum, Nottingham, 1960–63; Dir, City of Norwich Museums, 1963–74. Winston Churchill Fellow, 1967. Member: Management Cttee, Norfolk and Norwich Triennial Fest., 1966–89; Crafts Council, 1978–81; Management Cttee, Eastern Arts Assoc., 1978–79, 1987–89; Bd, Norwich Puppet Theatre, 1981–87; Founder Mem., National Heritage, 1970; Chairman: Norfolk and Norwich Film Theatre, 1968–70; Norfolk Contemporary Crafts Soc., 1972–85 and 1991–94 (Life Pres., 1985); Melton Mart Trust, 1990–92. Museums Association: AMA 1959; FMA 1966; Hon. Treasurer, 1970–73; Vice-Pres., 1977–78, 1979–80; Pres., 1978–79; Chm., Soc. of County Museum Dirs, 1974–77; Museum Advr to ACC, 1976–84. Member: Exec. Bd, ICOM (UK), 1981–84; Bd, Radio Broadland (ILR Station), 1983–96. FRSA 1986. *Publications:* Medieval English Alabaster Carvings in the Castle Museum, Nottingham, 1962, revd edn 1973; English Medieval Alabasters, 1984; The Alabaster Men: sacred images from Medieval England, 2001; Alabaster Images of Medieval England, 2003; Unearthed: Nottingham's Medieval alabasters, 2004; contrib. Jl of Museums Assoc. *Recreations:* hill-walking, listening to music, especially early and baroque. *T:* (01603) 434091. *Died 8 Nov. 2005.*

CHEETHAM, Sir Nicolas (John Alexander), KCMG 1964 (CMG 1953); HM Diplomatic Service, retired; *b* 8 Oct. 1910; *s* of Sir Milne Cheetham, KCMG, and Anastasia (*née* Mouravieff, later Mrs Nigel Law), CBE, DStJ; *m* 1st, 1937, Jean Evison Corfe (marr. diss. 1960); two *s*; 2nd, 1960, Lady Mabel Brooke (*née* Jocelyn) (*d* 1985). *Educ:* Eton College; Christ Church, Oxford. Entered HM Diplomatic Service, 1934; served in Foreign Office and at Athens, Buenos Aires, Mexico City and Vienna; UK Deputy Permanent Representative on North Atlantic Council, 1954–59; HM Minister to Hungary, 1959–61; Assistant Under-Secretary, Foreign Office, 1961–64; Ambassador to Mexico, 1964–68. *Publications:* A History of Mexico, 1970; New Spain, 1974; Mediaeval Greece, 1981; Keepers of the Keys: the Pope in history, 1982. *Address:* 50 Cadogan Square, SW1X 0JW. *T:* (020) 7589 5624. *Club:* Travellers. *Died 14 Jan. 2002.*

CHEEVERS, William Harold; Director of Engineering, Granada Television, 1970–73; *b* 20 June 1918; *m* 1964, Shirley Cheevers; one *s*; *m* 1999, Marion Cheevers. *Educ:* Christ's Coll., London. Engineer, BBC Television, 1938–39. War Service, Army, PoW, 1941–45. Sen. Engr, BBC Television, 1946–54; Planning Engr, Radio-Corp. of America, USA and Canada, 1954–55; Hd of Engineering, Associated Rediffusion, 1955–60; Gen. Manager, 1960–63; Jt Man. Dir, 1963–67, Man. Dir, 1967–70, Westward Television; Dir, ITN News and IT Publications, 1967–70; Director: Keith Prowse, 1963–70; Direct Line Services, 1964–87; Prowest, 1967–70; Penwell Ltd, 1971–88. Chm., British Regional Television Assoc., 1968–69. FBKS; MInstD; MCMI; AssIEE. *Publications:* articles for most TV jls, and symposiums, at home and abroad. *Recreations:* boating, golf, reading. *Address:* 52 Preston Down Road, Paignton, Devon TQ3 1DU. *T:* (01803) 524455. *Club:* Royal Western Yacht (Plymouth). *Died 23 Aug. 2002.*

CHESTERTON, Dame Elizabeth (Ursula), DBE 1987 (OBE 1977); architect and town planner; *b* 12 Oct. 1915; *d* of late Maurice Chesterton, architect, and Dorothy (*née* Deck). *Educ:* King Alfred Sch.; Queen's Coll., London; Architectural Assoc. Sch. of Architecture, London. AA Dipl. (Hons) 1939; ARIBA 1940; DistTP 1968; FRTPI 1967 (AMTPI 1943). Asst County Planning Officer, E Suffolk CC, 1940–47; Develt Control Officer, Cambs CC Planning Dept, 1947–51; Staff Member: Social Res. Unit, Dept of Town Planning, UCL, 1951–53; Architectural Assoc. Sch. of Architecture, 1954–61. Member: Council, Architectural Assoc., 1964–67; Royal Fine Art Commn, 1970–93; Historic Buildings Council, 1973–84; Royal Parks Review Gp, 1991–96. English Heritage: Member: Historic Bldgs Adv. Cttee, 1984–88; Historic Areas Adv. Cttee, 1984–91; Historic Bldgs and Areas Adv. Cttee, 1991–; British Rail: Member: Envmt Panel, 1983–88; Architecture Panel, 1988–91; Architecture and Design Panel, 1991–93; National Trust: Member: Architecture Panel, 1978–90; Council, 1984–90; Mem., Fabric Adv. Cttee, Exeter Cathedral, 1994–97. FRSA 1982. Reports prepared: Report on Local Land Use for the Dartington Hall Trustees, 1957; (jtly) The Historic Core of King's Lynn: study and plan, 1964; Plan for the Beaulieu Estate, 1966; North West Solent Shore Estates Report, 1969; (jtly) Snowdon Summit Report for Countryside Commission, 1974; Plans for Quarries and Rail Distribution Depots, Foster Yeoman and Yeoman (Morvern), 1974–81; Central Area Study, Chippenham, for North Wiltshire District Council, 1975–80; The Crumbles, Eastbourne, for Chatsworth Settlement, 1976; Aldeburgh, Suffolk, for Aldeburgh Soc., 1976; Old Market Conservation and Redevelopment Study, for City of Bristol and Bristol Municipal Charities, 1978; Uplands Landscape Study, for Countryside Commission, 1980. *Recreations:* gardening, travel. *Address:* 12 The Mount, NW3 6SZ. *T:* (020) 7435 0666. *Died 18 Aug. 2002.*

CHETWYND, Sir Arthur (Ralph Talbot), 8th Bt *cr* 1795; President, Brocton Hall Communications Ltd,

Toronto, 1978–88 (former Chairman); Chairman, Board of Directors, Chetwynd Productions Inc. (formerly Chetwynd Films Ltd), Toronto, 1977–90 (Founder, President and General Manager, 1950–76); *b* Walhachin, BC, 28 Oct. 1913; *o s* of Hon. William Ralph Talbot Chetwynd, MC, MLA (*d* 1957) (*b* of 7th Bt), and Frances Mary (*d* 1986), *d* of late James Jupe; *S* uncle, 1972; *m* 1940, Marjory May McDonald, *er d* of late Robert Bruce Lang, Vancouver, BC, and Glasgow, Scotland; two *s*. *Educ*: Vernon Prep. Sch., BC; Univ. of British Columbia (Physical Education and Recreation). Prior to 1933, a rancher in interior BC; Games Master, Vernon Prep. School, BC, 1936–39, also Instructor, Provincial Physical Education and Recreation; Chief Instructor, McDonald's Remedial Institute, Vancouver, 1939–42; Dir of Remedial Gymnastics, British Columbia Workmen's Compensation Board, 1942; Chief Instructor, Medical Reconditioning, RCAF, 1943–45; Associate in Physical and Health Educn, Univ. of Toronto, also Publicity Officer, Univ. of Toronto Athletic Assoc., 1946–52. Former Dir, NZ Lamb Co. Ltd. Former Chairman: Canterbury Cathedral Appeal in Canada; Codrington Coll. (Barbados) Appeal in Canada; Toronto Branch, Royal Commonwealth Soc.; Pres., Empire Club of Canada, 1974–75; Chairman: Nat. Council, Royal Commonwealth Soc. of Canada, 1993–95; Royal Commonwealth Soc. Toronto Foundn; Member: Monarchist League of Canada; Military and Hospitaller Order of St Lazarus in Jerusalem, Canada. Freedom, City of London, 1984. KCLJ; CMLJ. Hon. Mem., Order of Barbados (SCM), 1984. *Recreations:* photography, travelling, swimming. *Heir: er s* Robin John Talbot Chetwynd [*b* 21 Aug. 1941; *m* 1st, 1967, Heather Helen (marr. diss. 1986), *d* of George Bayliss Lothian; one *s* one *d*; 2nd, 1986, Donna (*née* Davey)]. *Address:* #1–117 King Street East, Cobourg, ON K9A 1L2, Canada. *Club:* Albany (Toronto).   *Died 11 July 2004.*

CHEUNG, Sir Oswald (Victor), Kt 1987; CBE 1976 (OBE 1972); QC (Hong Kong) 1965; Member, Executive Council, Hong Kong, 1974–86; *b* 22 Jan. 1922; *s* of Cheung U Pui and Elizabeth Ellis; *m* 1963, Pauline Cheng; one *s*. *Educ:* Diocesan Boys' Sch.; Hong Kong Univ.; University Coll., Oxford (BA 1949, MA 1963). Called to the Bar, Lincoln's Inn, 1951; Bencher, 1987. Magistrate, 1951–52; Hong Kong Bar, 1952–; Mem., Legislative Council, Hong Kong, 1970–81 (Senior Unofficial Mem., 1978–81); Chairman: Criminal Injuries Compensation Bd; Law Enforcement Injuries Compensation Bd. Director: Mass Transit Railway Corp., 1975–89; Hong Kong Electric (Holdings) Ltd, 1985–94; Ciba-Geigy (HK) Ltd, 1981–96; Wing On Company Internat. Ltd, 1994–. Member: Univ. and Polytechnic Grants Cttee, 1970–78; Court, Hong Kong Univ. Trustee, Croucher Foundn, 1986–92; Chm., Children's Meals Soc., 1966–81; Steward, Royal Hong Kong Jockey Club, 1977–92 (Chm. of Stewards, 1986–89). Captain, Royal Hong Kong Regt, 1956–62, Hon. Col, 1977–82. Fellow, Internat. Acad. of Trial Lawyers. Hon. LLD Hong Kong, 1979; Hon. DSocSc City Univ. of Hong Kong, 1999. *Recreations:* photography, racing, travel. *Address:* New Henry House, 10th Floor, 10 Ice House Street, Hong Kong. *T:* 25242156. *Clubs:* Hong Kong Jockey, Hong Kong, Hong Kong Golf, Chinese.   *Died 10 Dec. 2003.*

CHIANG KAI-SHEK, Madame, (Mayling Soong Chiang); Chinese sociologist; *y d* of C. J. Soong; *m* 1927, Generalissimo Chiang Kai-Shek (*d* 1975). *Educ:* Wellesley Coll., USA. First Chinese woman appointed Mem. Child Labor Commn; Inaugurated Moral Endeavor Assoc.; established schools in Nanking for orphans of Revolutionary Soldiers; former Mem. Legislative Yuan; served as Sec.-General of Chinese Commission on Aeronautical Affairs; formerly: Member Chinese Commission on Aeronautical Affairs; Director-General of the New Life Movement and Chairman of its Women's Advisory Council; Founder and Director: National Chinese Women's Assoc. for War Relief; National Assoc. for Refugee Children; Chinese Women's Anti-Aggression

League; Huashing Children's Home; Cheng Hsin Medical Rehabilitation Center for Post Polio Crippled Children. Chm., Fu Jen Catholic University. Governor, Nat. Palace Museum. Frequently made inspection tours to all sections of Free China where personally trained girl workers carry on war area and rural service work; accompanied husband on military campaigns; first Chinese woman to be decorated by National Govt of China. Recipient of highest military and Civil decorations; formerly: Hon. Chm., British United Aid to China Fund, China; Hon. Chm., Soc. for the Friends of the Wounded; Hon. President, American Bureau for Medical Aid to China; Patroness, International Red Cross Commn; Hon. President, Chinese Women's Relief Assoc. of New York; Hon. Chairman, Canadian Red Cross China Cttee; Hon. Chairman, Board of Directors, India Famine Relief Cttee; Hon. Mem., New York Zoological Soc.; Hon. Pres., Cttee for the Promotion of the Welfare of the Blind; Life Mem., San Francisco Press Club and Associated Countrywomen of the World; Mem., Phi Beta Kappa, Eta Chapter; first Hon. Member, Bill of Rights Commemorative Society; Hon. Member: Filipino Guerrillas of Bataan Assoc.; Catherine Lorillard Wolf Club. Hon. FRCS. Hon. LHD: John B. Stetson Univ., Deland, Fla, Bryant Coll., Providence, RI, Hobart and William Smith Colls, Geneva, NY; Hon. LLD: Rutgers Univ., New Brunswick, NJ, Goucher Coll., Baltimore, Wellesley Coll., Wellesley, Mass, Loyola Univ., UCLA, Russell Sage Coll., Troy, NY, Hahnemann Medical Coll., Philadelphia, Pa, Wesleyan Coll., Macon, Ga, Univ. of Michigan, Univ. of Hawaii, Boston Univ., Mass. Medal of Honour, New York City Federation of Women's Clubs; YWCA Emblem; Gold Medal, New York Southern Soc.; Chi Omega Nat. Achievement Award for 1943; Gold Medal for distinguished services, National Institute for Social Sciences; Distinguished Service Award, Altrusa Internat. Assoc.; Churchman Fifth Annual Award, 1943; Distinguished Service Citation, All-American Conf. to Combat Communism, 1958; Hon. Lieut-Gen. US Marine Corps. *Publications:* China in Peace and War, 1939; China Shall Rise Again, 1939; This is Our China, 1940; We Chinese Women, 1941; Little Sister Su, 1943; Ten Eventful Years, for Encyclopædia Britannica, 1946; Album of Reproduction of Paintings, vol. I, 1952, vol. II, 1962; The Sure Victory, 1955; Madame Chiang Kai-Shek Selected Speeches, 1958–59; Madame Chiang Kai-shek Selected Speeches, 1965–66; Album of Chinese Orchid Paintings, 1971; Album of Chinese Bamboo Paintings, 1972; Album of Chinese Landscape Paintings, 1973; Album of Chinese Floral Paintings, 1974; Conversations with Mikhail Borodin, 1977; Religious Writings 1934–63, 1964.   *Died 23 Oct. 2003.*

CHIASSON, Most Rev. Donat; Archbishop of Moncton, (RC), 1972–95; *b* Paquetville, NB, 2 Jan. 1930; *s* of Louis Chiasson and Anna Chiasson (*née* Godin). *Educ:* St Joseph's Univ., NB; Holy Heart Seminary, Halifax, NS; Theological and Catechetical studies, Rome and Lumen Vitae, Belgium. Ordained priest, Bathurst, NB, 1953. *Address:* PO Box 1010, Rogersville, NB E4Y 2W8, Canada.   *Died 8 Oct. 2003.*

CHIBA, Kazuo, Hon. KCMG 1998; Lecturer, Kitasato University, Japan, since 1999; *b* 19 April 1925; *s* of Shinichi and Miyoko Chiba; *m* 1954, Keiko Okamoto; one *s* one *d*. *Educ:* Univ. of Tokyo (LLB 1949); Fletcher Sch. of Law and Diplomacy, Medford, Mass, USA (MA 1951). Served in Imperial Japanese Navy, 1944–45. Joined Min. of Foreign Affairs, Tokyo, 1948: Geneva, 1956; Iran, 1958; Min. of For. Affairs, 1959; Washington, DC, 1964; Dir, N America Div., N American Affairs Bureau, Min. of For. Affairs, 1967; Minister, Moscow, 1972; Consul-Gen., Atlanta, Ga, 1974; Consul-Gen., W Berlin, 1976; Dir Gen., Middle Eastern and African Affairs Bureau, Min. of For. Affairs, 1978; Ambassador: to Sri Lanka, 1980; in Geneva (Perm. Mission of Japan to internat. orgns), 1982–87; to UK, 1988–91. Advr, 1991–96, Statutory Auditor, 1997–2001, Toshiba Corp.; Counselor, Mitsui &

Co. Ltd, 1991–98; Dir, Foreign & Colonial Pacific Investment Trust, London, 1993–97; Advr, Financial Times, 1995–2001; Auditor, Kitasato Univ., 1997–2003. Chairman: GATT Council, 1984–85; GATT Contracting Parties, 1985–86. Vis. Centennial Prof., LSE, 1992–94; Vis. Res. Fellow, Merton Coll., Oxford, 1992. Order of the Rising Sun (Japan), 1997. *Recreations:* reading (history), travel. *Address:* 3–11–7 Sekimachi-kita, Nerima-ku, Tokyo 177-0051, Japan. *Died 14 Sept. 2004.*

CHILVER, Brian Outram; Chairman, Eskmuir Properties Ltd, since 1990; *b* 17 June 1933; *s* of late Bertram Montagu Chilver and of Edith Gwendoline Chilver; *m* 1956, Erica Mary; two *s* two *d. Educ:* University College Sch. FCA 1965; FCMA 1993. Temple Gothard & Co., 1949–55 (articled clerk); National Service, RAF, 1955–57; Barton Mayhew & Co., 1957–59; Temple Gothard & Co., 1959–85 (Partner, 1960, Senior Partner, 1975); Chairman: Laing Properties plc, 1987–90; Seafield plc, 1990–96; Forward Technology Industries plc, 1991–2000; Dir (non-exec.), John Laing plc, 1988–2002. Chm., Tear Fund, 1990–99. *Recreations:* walking, swimming, reading, music. *Address:* Bretaye, Limbourne Lane, Fittleworth, West Sussex RH20 1HR; (office) 8 Queen Anne Street, W1G 9LD. *Died 5 July 2004.*

CHOLERTON, Frederick Arthur, CBE 1978; *b* 15 April 1917; *s* of Frederick Arthur Cholerton and Charlotte (*née* Wagstaffe); *m* 1939, Ethel (*née* Jackson); (one *s* decd). *Educ:* Penkhull Secondary Sch., Stoke-on-Trent. Locomotive driver, British Rail, 1934–77; Trade Union work with ASLEF, 1934–71. City of Stoke-on-Trent: Councillor, 1951–87; Leader of Council, 1976–81; Lord Mayor, 1971–72; Staffordshire County Council: Councillor, 1973–89; Vice-Chm., 1973–76; Chm., 1977 and 1981–89; Opposition Leader, 1977–81. Chm., Poplar Resource Management Co. Ltd, 1992–96; Director: North Staffordshire South Cheshire Broadcasting (Signal Radio), Ltd, 1982–88; Longton Enterprise Ltd, 1980–87; 1986 Nat. Garden Festival, Stoke-on-Trent, Staffordshire Ltd, 1983–88; W Midlands Industrial Develt Bd, 1983–89; Staffordshire Cable, 1988–93. Chairman: Bereavement Care Centre, Potteries and N Staffs, 1988–95; Staffs Sports for Disabled Trust, 1992–; Trustee, Central Telephon, 1990–. JP Stoke-on-Trent, 1956–74. MUniv Keele, 1988. *Recreations:* sports, gardening, politics, voluntary work for charities. *Died 15 March 2004.*

CHORLEY, Prof. Richard John; Professor of Geography, University of Cambridge, 1974–94, later Emeritus; Fellow of Sidney Sussex College, Cambridge, 1962–94, later Emeritus (Vice-Master, 1990–93); *b* 4 Sept. 1927; *s* of Walter Joseph Chorley and Ellen Mary Chorley; *m* 1965, Rosemary Joan Macdonald More; one *s* one *d. Educ:* Minehead Grammar Sch.; Exeter Coll., Oxford (MA); ScD Cantab. Lieut, RE, 1946–48. Fulbright Schol., Columbia Univ., 1951–52; Instructor: in Geography, Columbia Univ., 1952–54; in Geology, Brown Univ., 1954–57; Cambridge University: Demonstrator in Geography, 1958–62; Lectr in Geography, 1962–70, Reader, 1970–74. British rep. on Commn on Quantitative Techniques of Internat. Geographical Union, 1964–68; Dir, Madingley Geog. Courses, 1963–78. First Hon. Life Mem., British Geomorphological Res. Gp, 1974; Corresponding Mem., Italian Geographical Soc.; Emeritus Hon. Fellow, Internat. Assoc. of Geomorphologists, 1997. Hon. DSc Bristol, 1996. Gill Meml Medal, 1967, Patron's Medal, 1987, RGS; Hons Award, Assoc. of Amer. Geographers, 1981; David Linton Award, 1984. *Publications:* co-author of: The History of the Study of Landforms, Vols I, II and III, 1964, 1973, 1991; Atmosphere, Weather and Climate, 1968, 7th edn 1997; Network Analysis in Geography, 1969; Physical Geography, 1971; Environmental Systems, 1978; Geomorphology, 1984; co-editor of: Frontiers in Geographical Teaching, 1965; Models in Geography, 1967; editor of: Water, Earth and Man, 1969; Spatial Analysis in Geomorphology, 1972; Directions in

Geography, 1973; contribs to: Jl of Geology, Amer. Jl of Science, Bulletin of Geolog. Soc. of Amer., Geog. Jl, Geol. Magazine, Inst. of Brit. Geographers, etc. *Recreations:* theatre, grave renovation. *Address:* 76 Grantchester Meadows, Newnham, Cambridge CB3 9JL. *Died 12 May 2002.*

CHOUFFOT, Geoffrey Charles, CBE 1983 (MBE 1965); Deputy Chairman, Civil Aviation Authority, 1980–83; *m* 1941, June Catherine (decd), *d* of Rev. W. Peebles Fleming; one *s* two *d.* Gp Dir, Safety Services, CAA, 1978–80. Dir and Treas., St Wilfrid's Hospice (South Coast) Ltd, 1987–93. *Club:* Royal Air Force. *Died 24 Jan. 2003.*

CHRISTIAN, Prof. John Wyrill, FRS 1975; Professor of Physical Metallurgy, Oxford University, 1967–88, then Emeritus; Fellow of St Edmund Hall, Oxford, 1963–93, then Emeritus; *b* 9 April 1926; *e s* of John Christian and Louisa Christian (*née* Crawford); *m* 1949, Maureen Lena Smith; one *s* one *d* (and one *s* decd). *Educ:* Scarborough Boys' High Sch.; The Queen's Coll., Oxford (BA 1946, DPhil 1949, MA 1950). Oxford University: Pressed Steel Co. Ltd Research Fellow, 1951–55; Lectr in Metallurgy, 1955–58; George Kelley Reader in Metallurgy, 1958–67. Visiting Professor: Univ. of Illinois, 1959; Case Inst. of Technology, USA, 1962–63; MIT and Stanford Univ., 1971–72; Hon. Prof., Beijing Univ. of Sci. and Tech., 1987–. Lectures: Williams, MIT, 1971; Hume-Rothery Meml, 1976; Inst. of Metals, AIME, 1981; Campbell Meml, ASM, 1982. Hon. Member: India Materials Res. Soc., 1991–; Japan Inst. of Metals, 1991–. Rosenhain Medallist, Inst. of Metals, 1969; Mehl Medallist, AIME, 1981; Platinum Medallist, Metals Soc., 1984; Gold Medallist: Acta Metallurgica, 1984; Japan Inst. of Metals; Medal for Dist. Service, Univ. of Pennsylvania, 1996. Editor: Progress in Materials Science, 1970–; Jl Less Common Metals, 1976–85. *Publications:* Metallurgical Equilibrium Diagrams (with others), 1952; The Theory of Transformations in Metals and Alloys, 1965, 2nd rev. edn 1975; contribs to scientific jls. *Address:* 11 Charlbury Road, Oxford OX2 6UT. *T:* (01865) 558569. *Died 27 Feb. 2001.*

CHRISTIE, John Belford Wilson, CBE 1981; Sheriff of Tayside, Central and Fife (formerly Perth and Angus) at Dundee, 1955–83; *b* 4 May 1914; *o s* of late J. A. Christie, Advocate, Edinburgh; *m* 1939, Christine Isobel Syme, *o d* of late Rev. J. T. Arnott; four *d. Educ:* Merchiston Castle Sch.; St John's Coll., Cambridge; Edinburgh Univ. Admitted to Faculty of Advocates, 1939. Served War of 1939–45, in RNVR, 1936–48. Sheriff-Substitute of Western Div. of Dumfries and Galloway, 1948–55. Mem., Parole Bd for Scotland, 1967–73. Mem., Queen's Coll. Council, Univ. of St Andrews, 1960–67; University of Dundee: Mem. Court, 1967–75; Hon. Lectr, Dept of Private Law. Hon. LLD Dundee, 1977. KCHS 1994, with star, 2001 (KHS 1988). *Recreations:* curling, golf. *Address:* Glebe House, Ashlar Lane, Cupar, Fife KY15 5BA. *T:* (01334) 653999. *Clubs:* New (Edinburgh); Royal and Ancient (St Andrews). *Died 20 July 2002.*

CHRISTIE, John Rankin, CB 1978; Deputy Master and Comptroller of the Royal Mint, 1974–77; *b* 5 Jan. 1918; *s* of Robert Christie and Georgina (*née* Rankin); *m* 1941, Constance May, *d* of Henry Gracie; one *s* two *d. Educ:* Ormskirk Grammar Sch.; London Sch. of Economics. Royal Ordnance Factories, 1936–43; Royal Artillery, 1943–47 (Captain). Min. of Supply, 1947; Admin. Staff Coll., 1949; Air Ministry, 1954; Private Sec. to Ministers of Supply, 1955–57; Asst Sec., 1957; British Defence Staffs, Washington, 1962–65; Under-Sec., Min. of Aviation, 1965–67, Min. of Technology, 1967–70, Min. of Aviation Supply, 1970–71; Asst Under-Sec. of State, MoD, 1971–74. *Recreations:* travel, bird-watching. *Address:* Twitten Cottage, East Hill, Oxted, Surrey RH8 9AA. *T:* (01883) 713047. *Died 8 April 2003.*

CHRISTODOULOU, Anastasios, CBE 1978; Secretary-General, Association of Commonwealth Universities, 1980–96; Secretary-General (formerly Joint Secretary), UK Commonwealth Scholarship Commission, 1980–96; Executive Secretary, Marshall Scholarships Commemoration Commission, 1980–96; *b* Cyprus, 1 May 1932; *s* of Christodoulos and Maria Haji Yianni; *m* 1955, Joan P. Edmunds; two *s* two *d*. *Educ:* St Marylebone Grammar Sch.; The Queen's Coll., Oxford (MA). Colonial Administrative Service, Tanganyika (Tanzania), 1956–62; served as District Commissioner and Magistrate. Univ. of Leeds Administration, 1963–68: Asst Registrar, 1963–65; Dep. Sec., 1965–68; Secretary, Open Univ., 1969–80. Chm., Surrey Univ. Centre for Commonwealth and European Educnl Develt, 1990–96; Vice-Chm., Commonwealth Inst., 1981–89; Member: Bd of Trustees, Harlow Campus, Meml Univ. of Newfoundland, 1980–97; Exec. Cttee, Council for Educn in Commonwealth, 1980–99 (Chm., 1996–99); Fulbright Commn, 1980–96; Bd of Trustees, Richmond Coll., London, 1988–; Bd of Trustees, Internat. Extension Coll., 1994–99 (Chm., 1996–99); Bd of Govs, Commonwealth of Learning, 1988–93. Member, Court: Exeter Univ., 1980–96; Hull Univ., 1980–96; RCA, 1980–96. FRSA. Hon. Prof., Univ. of Mauritius, 1986; Hon. Vis. Prof., Surrey, 1991–. Hon. FCP 1995. DUniv: Open, 1981; Athabasca, 1981; Brunel, 1996; Ottawa, 1998; Hon. LLD Auckland, 1992; Hon. DCL Acadia, 1992. Univ. of Lesotho 50th Anniversary Award for Distinguished Service to African Educn, 1995. *Recreations:* sport, music, bridge; international and Commonwealth relations. *Address:* 246 Lauderdale Mansions, Lauderdale Road, W9 1NQ. *T:* (020) 7286 0011, *Fax:* (020) 7289 3309. *Club:* Royal Commonwealth Society. *Died 20 May 2002.*

CHRISTOPHERSON, Romola Carol Andrea, CB 1998; Associate Director, Media Strategy, since 1999; non-executive Director, Primary Care Group Ltd, since 1999; *b* 10 Jan. 1939; *d* of late Albert Edward Christopherson and Kathleen Christopherson (*née* Marfitt). *Educ:* Collegiate Sch. for Girls, Leicester; St Hugh's Coll., Oxford (BA Hons English). DSIR, Min. of Technology, 1962; DoE, 1970; MAFF, 1978; N Ireland Office, 1981; Dep. Press Sec. to Prime Minister, 1983; Head of Inf., Dept of Energy, 1984; Dir of Information, then of Press and Publicity, DHSS, later DoH, 1986–98. *Recreations:* amateur dramatics, antiques. *Address:* 28 Wharton Street, WC1X 9PJ. *Died 16 Jan. 2003.*

CHUBB, Andrew Vyvyan; His Honour Judge Chubb; a Circuit Judge, since 1999; *b* 5 April 1943; 2nd *s* of late Arthur Vyvyan Travers Chubb and Margaret Anis Chubb (*née* Elstone); *m* 1967, Jennifer Jane Houston Dalzell; two *s* one *d*. *Educ:* Nautical Coll., Pangbourne. Served RN, 1961–81. Called to the Bar, Middle Temple, 1975; Recorder, 1997–99. *Address:* Portsmouth Crown Court, Winston Churchill Avenue, Portsmouth, Hants PO1 2EB. *Club:* Royal Over-Seas League. *Died 27 July 2001.*

CHUBB, Dr Frederick Basil, MA, DPhil, LittD; Professor of Political Science, 1960–91, later Fellow Emeritus, Trinity College, Dublin; *b* 8 Dec. 1921; *s* of late Frederick John Bailey Chubb and Gertrude May Chubb, Ludgershall, Wilts; *m* 1st, 1946, Margaret Gertrude Rafther (*d* 1984); no *c*; 2nd, 1985, Orla, *d* of Seán and Veronica Sheehan; one *d*. *Educ:* Bishop Wordsworth's Sch., Salisbury; Merton Coll., Oxford (BA 1946; MA; DPhil 1950); MA, LittD 1976, Dublin. Lecturer in Political Science, Trinity Coll., Dublin, 1948; Fellow in Polit. Sci., 1952; Reader in Polit. Sci., 1955; Bursar, 1957–62. Chairman: Comhairle na n-Ospidéal, 1972–78; Employer-Labour Conf., 1970–. MRIA 1969. *Publications:* The Control of Public Expenditure, 1952; (with D. E. Butler (ed) and others) Elections Abroad, 1959; A Source Book of Irish Government, 1964, 2nd edn 1983; (ed with P. Lynch) Economic Development and Planning, 1969; The Government and Politics of Ireland, 1970, 3rd edn 1992; Cabinet Government in Ireland, 1974; The

Constitution and Constitutional Change in Ireland, 1978; The Politics of the Irish Constitution, 1991; articles in learned jls. *Recreation:* fishing. *Address:* 19 Clyde Lane, Ballsbridge, Dublin 4. *T:* (1) 6684625. *Died 8 May 2002.*

CHUMAS, Henry John, CMG 1991; TD 1969; Director General, Directorate General for Customs Union and Indirect Taxation, Commission of the European Communities, 1989–90 (Director, 1986–89); retired; *b* 21 Dec. 1933; *s* of Charles Savel Chumas and Bertha Emily Pratley; *m* 1956, Maureen Audry Collin; one *s* two *d* (and one *d* decd). *Educ:* Ealing Grammar Sch. for Boys; Sch. of Slavonic Studies, Cambridge Univ. Intelligence Corps, TA, 1957–71, Major and Co. Comdr, Intelligence and Security Gp, 1969–71. Immigration Officer, Home Office, 1955–61; HM Customs and Excise: Asst Principal, 1962–64; Principal, 1964–69; Sloan Fellow, London Grad. Sch. of Business Studies, 1969–70; Asst Sec., 1970–73; Dir, Customs Union service, Commn of EC, 1973–86. *Recreations:* ski-ing, sailing. *Address:* Les Peupliers, Chemin Perrey, 27680 Trouville la Haule, France. *T:* 232428831. *Died 27 June 2001.*

CHUNG Se Yung, Hon. CBE 1983; Hon. Chairman, Hyundai Development Co., since 1999; *b* 6 Aug. 1928; *m* 1958, Young Ja Park; one *s* two *d*. *Educ:* Korea Univ. (BA); Miami Univ. of Ohio (MA). Joined Hyundai Construction Co., 1957, Man. Dir, 1960–67; Pres., Hyundai Motor Co., 1967–86; Chm., Hyundai Motor Co. and Hyundai Business Gp, 1987–96; Hon. Chm., Hyundai Motor Co., 1996–99. Chairman: Korea-UK Econ. Co-operation Cttee, 1977–95; Korea-America Assoc., 1998–; Vice-Chairman: Korea-USA Econ. Assoc., 1986–91; Korea Traders Assoc., 1988–91; Korea-USA Business Council, 1990–97; Korea-Japan Econ. Assoc., 1994–; Adviser: Korea Employers Fedn (Vice-Chm., 1982–95); Fedn of Korea Industries (Vice-Chm., 1987–96). Pres., Korea Water-ski Assoc., 1979–98. Hon. LLD Miami Univ. of Ohio, 1983; Hon. Dr: Yonsei, 1996; Korea, 1997. Outstanding CEO Award, Korea Mgt Assoc., 1987, 1994. Order of Industrial Service Merit, Gold Tower (Korea), 1985; Order of Service Merit (Korea), 1998. *Address:* Hyundai Development Co., 679–4 Yoksam-dong, Kangnam-gu, Seoul 135–080, South Korea. *Died 21 May 2005.*

CLAPHAM, Sir Michael (John Sinclair), KBE 1973; Chairman: IMI Ltd, 1974–81; BPM Holdings Ltd, 1974–81; *b* 17 Jan. 1912; *s* of Sir John Clapham, CBE, FBA and Lady Clapham, Cambridge; *m* 1935, Hon. Elisabeth Russell Rea (*d* 1994), *d* of 1st Baron Rea; two *s* one *d* (and one *s* decd). *Educ:* Marlborough Coll.; King's Coll., Cambridge (BA 1933, MA 1938). Apprenticed as printer with University Press, Cambridge, 1933–35; Overseer and later Works Man., Percy Lund Humphries & Co. Ltd, Bradford, 1935–38; joined ICI Ltd as Man., Kynoch Press, 1938; seconded, in conseq. of developing a diffusion barrier, to Tube Alloys Project (atomic energy), 1941–45; Personnel Dir, ICI Metals Div., 1946; Midland Regional Man., ICI, 1951; Jt Man. Dir, ICI Metals Div., 1952, Chm. 1959; Dir, ICI, 1961–74, Dep. Chm. 1968–74; served as Overseas Dir; Dir, ICI of Austr. & NZ Ltd, 1961–74; Director: Imperial Metal Industries Ltd, 1962–70; Lloyds Bank Ltd, 1971–82 (Dep. Chm., 1974–80); Grindlay's Bank Ltd, 1975–84; Associated Communications Corp., 1982–88; Heytesbury (UK) Ltd, 1988–90; Mem., General Motors European Adv. Council, 1975–82. Dep. Pres., 1971–72, Pres., 1972–74, CBI. Member: Standing Adv. Cttee on Pay of Higher Civil Service, 1968–71; Review Body on Doctors' and Dentists' Remuneration, 1968–70; IRC, 1969–71. Member: Birmingham Educn Cttee, 1949–56; W Mids Adv. Coun. for Tech., Commercial and Art Educn, and Regional Academic Bd, 1952; Govt Youth Service Cttee (Albemarle Cttee), 1958; CNAA, 1964–77 (Chm., 1971–77); NEDC, 1971–76. Life Governor, Birmingham Univ., 1955 (Mem. Council, 1956–61); Mem. Court,

Univ. of London, 1969–85. Pres., Inst. of Printing, 1980–82. Hon. DSc Aston, 1973; Hon. LLD: CNAA, 1978; London, 1984. *Publications:* Printing, 1500–1730, in The History of Technology, Vol. III, 1957; Multinational Enterprises and Nation States, 1975; Perishable Collections, 1997; various articles on printing, personnel management and education. *Recreations:* sailing, cooking. *Address:* 26 Hill Street, W1J 5NN. *T:* (020) 7499 1240. *Clubs:* Naval, Royal Yacht Squadron.

Died 11 Nov. 2002.

CLARE, Herbert Mitchell N.; *see* Newton-Clare.

CLARK OF KEMPSTON, Baron *cr* 1992 (Life Peer), of Kempston in the County of Bedfordshire; **William Gibson Clark,** Kt 1980; PC 1990; *b* 18 Oct. 1917; *m* 1944, Irene Dorothy Dawson Rands (*d* 2003); two *s* (and one *s* one *d* decd). *Educ:* London. Mem., Chartered Association (formerly Association) of Certified Accountants, 1941. Served in Army, 1941–46, UK and India (Major). Mem., Wandsworth Borough Council, 1949–53 (Vice-Chm., Finance Cttee). Contested (C) Northampton, 1955; MP (C): Nottingham South, 1959–66; East Surrey, 1970–74; Croydon South, 1974–92. Opposition front bench spokesman on economics, 1964–66; Chairman: Select Cttee on Tax Credits, 1973; Cons. Back-bench Finance Cttee, 1979–92. Jt Dep. Chm., Cons. Party Organisation, 1975–77 (Jt Treas., 1974–75). Pres., City Gp for Smaller Cos, 1993–98. Chm., Anglo-Austrian Soc., 1983–98 (Patron, 1998–). Hon. Nat. Dir, Carrington £2 million Appeal, 1967–68. Freeman, City of London, 1987. Grand Gold Cross (Austria), 1989; Grand Decoration of Honour in Gold with Star (Austria), 1994. *Recreation:* reading. *Address:* The Clock House, Box End, Bedford MK43 8RT. *T:* (01234) 852361; 3 Barton Street, SW1P 3NG. *T:* (020) 7222 5759. *Clubs:* Carlton, Buck's.

Died 4 Oct. 2004.

CLARK, Rt Rev. Alan Charles; RC Bishop of East Anglia, 1976–94; Former Bishop, since 1995; *b* 9 Aug. 1919; *s* of William Thomas Durham Clark and Ellen Mary Clark (*née* Compton). *Educ:* Westminster Cathedral Choir Sch.; Ven. English Coll., Rome, Italy. Priest, 1945; Curate, St Philip's, Arundel, 1945–46; postgrad. studies, Rome, 1946–48 (Doctorate in Theol., Gregorian Univ., Rome, 1948); Tutor in Philosophy, English Coll., Rome, 1948–53, Vice-Rector, 1954–64; Parish Priest, St Mary's, Blackheath, SE3, 1965–69; Auxiliary Bishop of Northampton, 1969–76; Titular Bishop of Elmham, 1969–76. *Peritus* at Vatican Council, 1962–65; Jt Chm., The Anglican/Roman Catholic Internat. Commn, 1969–81 (Lambeth Cross); Chm., Dept for Mission and Unity, Bishops' Conf. of Eng. and Wales, 1984–94; Co-Moderator, Jt Working Group of RC Church and WCC, 1984–93. Freeman, City of London, 1969. *Recreation:* music. *Address:* 19 Upgate, Poringland, Norwich NR14 7SH. *Died 16 July 2002.*

CLARK, Desmond; *see* Clark, John D.

CLARK, Sir John (Allen), Kt 1971; retired; Chief Executive Officer, The Plessey Company plc, 1962–89; Chairman, GEC-Plessey Telecommunications Holdings, 1988–89; *b* 14 Feb. 1926; *e s* of late Sir Allen Clark and Lady (Jocelyn) Clark, *d* of late Percy and Madeline Culverhouse; *m* 1st, 1952, Deirdre Kathleen (marr. diss. 1962), *d* of Samuel Herbert Waterhouse and Maeve Murphy Waterhouse; one *s* one *d*; 2nd, 1970, Olivia, *d* of H. Pratt and of late Mrs R. S. H. Shepard; twin *s* one *d*. *Educ:* Harrow; Cambridge. Served War of 1939–45; commnd RNVR (2nd Lieut). Received early industrial training with Metropolitan Vickers and Ford Motor Co.; spent over a year in USA, studying the electronics industry. Asst to Gen. Manager, Plessey International Ltd, 1949; Dir and Gen. Man., Plessey (Ireland) Ltd, and Wireless Telephone Co. Ltd, 1950; appointed to main board, The Plessey Co. Ltd, 1953; Gen. Man., Plessey Components Group, 1957; Dep. Chm., The Plessey Co.

Ltd, 1967–70, Chm., 1970–89. Director: International Computers Ltd, 1968–79; Banque Nationale de Paris Ltd, 1976–89. Pres., Telecommunication Engineering and Manufacturing Assoc., 1964–66, 1971–73; Vice-President: Inst. of Works Managers; Engineering Employers' Fedn. Member: Nat. Defence Industries Council; Engineering Industries Council, 1975–89. CompIEE; FIM. Order of Henry the Navigator, Portugal, 1973. *Recreations:* horseriding, shooting. *Address:* Redenham Park, Redenham, near Andover, Hants SP11 9AQ. *Club:* Boodle's. *Died 3 Dec. 2001.*

CLARK, Prof. J(ohn) Desmond, CBE 1960; PhD; ScD; FBA 1961; FSA 1952; FRSSAf 1959; Professor of Anthropology, University of California, Berkeley, USA, 1961–86, then Emeritus Professor; *b* London, 10 April 1916; *s* of late Thomas John Chown Clark and Catharine (*née* Wynne); naturalised American, 1993; *m* 1938, Betty Cable, *d* of late Henry Lea Baume and Frances M. S. (*née* Brown); one *s* one *d*. *Educ:* Monkton Combe Sch.; Christ's Coll., Cambridge (PhD in Archaeology 1950; ScD 1975). Dir, Rhodes-Livingstone Museum, Livingstone, N Rhodesia, 1938–61. Conducted excavations in Southern, East and Equatorial Africa, the Sahara, Ethiopia, Syria, 1938–, India, 1980–82, China, 1990–. Military Service in East Africa, Abyssinia, The Somalilands and Madagascar, 1941–46. Founder Mem. and Sec., N Rhodesia Nat. Monuments Commn, 1948–61. Corr. Mem., Scientific Coun. for Africa South of the Sahara, 1956–64, etc. Lectures: Faculty Res. Berkeley, 1979; Raymond Dart, Johannesburg, 1979; Mortimer Wheeler, British Acad., 1981; John Mulvaney, ANU, 1991; Distinguished, Amer. Anthropol. Assoc., 1992. Fellow, Amer. Acad. of Arts and Sciences, 1965; Mem., Nat. Acad. of Science, USA, 1993. Hon. DSc: Univ. of the Witwatersrand, 1985; Univ. of Cape Town, 1985. Huxley Medal, RAI, 1974; Gold Medal, Soc. of Antiquaries of London, 1985; Fellows Medal, Calif. Acad. of Scis, 1987; Gold Medal, Archaeological Inst. of America, 1989; L. S. B. Leakey Prize, 1996; Grahame Clark Medal for Prehistory, British Acad., 1997. Comdr, Nat. Order of Senegal, 1968. *Publications:* The Prehistoric Cultures of the Horn of Africa, 1954; The Prehistory of Southern Africa, 1959; The Stone Age Cultures of Northern Rhodesia, 1960; Prehistoric Cultures of Northeast Angola and their Significance in Tropical Africa, 1963; (ed) Proc. 3rd Pan-African Congress on Pre-history, 1957; (comp.) Atlas of African Pre-history, 1967; (ed with W. W. Bishop) Background to Evolution in Africa, 1967; Kalambo Falls Prehistoric Site, vol. I, 1969, vol. II, 1973, vol. III, 2000; The Prehistory of Africa, 1970; (ed) Cambridge History of Africa, vol I, 1982; (ed with G. R. Sharma) Palaeoenvironment and Prehistory in the Middle Son Valley, India, 1983; (ed with Steven A. Brandt) From Hunters to Farmers: the causes and consequences of food production in Africa, 1984; (ed) Cultural Beginnings, 1991; 295 contribs to learned journals on prehistoric archaeology. *Recreations:* gardening, walking, photography. *Address:* Grand Lake Gardens, 401 Santa Clara Avenue, Apt 223–24, Oakland, CA 94610, USA. *T:* (510) 6250444, *Fax:* (510) 6250555. *Clubs:* Royal Commonwealth Society, Oxford and Cambridge.

Died 14 Feb. 2002.

CLARK, Prof. Jonathan William, (Jon), CBE 2004; Professor of Industrial Relations, University of Southampton, 1990–99, then Emeritus; *b* 1 June 1949; *s* of late Ernest Roy Clark and Hazel Lucy Clark (*née* Lucas). *Educ:* Royal Grammar Sch., High Wycombe; Univ. of Birmingham (BA); Free Univ. of West Berlin; Univ. of Bremen (DrPhil). Res. Officer, LSE, 1976–77; Res. Fellow, Groupe de Sociologie du Travail, Univ. of Paris VII, 1977–78; University of Southampton: Lectr, 1978–86; Sen. Lectr. 1986–90; Dean of Soc. Scis. 1994–97; Dir, New College, 1998; Professorial Res. Fellow, Univ. of Warwick, 1991–93. Chair: UK Police Negotiating Bd, 2000–04; Police Adv. Bd for England and Wales, 2001–04. Mem., ACAS Nat. Panel of Trade

Disputes Arbitrators, 1990–. Director: Bournemouth SO, 2000–03; New Ashgate Gall., 2003–. *Publications:* (with R. Lewis) Labour Law and Politics in the Weimar Republic, 1981; (with Lord Wedderburn and R. Lewis) Labour Law and Industrial Relations: building on Kahn-Freund, 1983; (jtly) The Process of Technological Change, 1988; (with I. McLoughlin) Technological Change at Work, 1988, 2nd edn 1994; (with R. Lewis) Employment Rights, Industrial Tribunals and Arbitration: the case for alternative dispute resolution, 1993; Human Resource Management and Technical Change, 1993; (with C. Barnard and R. Lewis) The Exercise of Individual Employment Rights in the Member States of the European Community, 1995; Managing Innovation and Change, 1995; James S Coleman, 1996. *Recreations:* classical music, opera, travel. *Address:* 16 Holt Road, Fitzhugh, Southampton, Hants SO15 2HU. *Died 21 Oct. 2005.*

CLARK, Rev. Canon Malcolm Aiken; Dean, Collegiate Church of St Vincent since 1982; Dean of Edinburgh, 1983–85, Hon. Canon, St Mary's Cathedral, since 1985; *b* 3 Oct. 1905; *s* of Hugh Aiken Clark, MB, CM, and Agnes Roberta Douglas Baxter; *m* 1936, Margherita Felicinna Columba Gannaway (*d* 1973); two *s* one *d*. *Educ:* Drax, Yorks; High Sch. of Glasgow; Lichfield Theol Coll. Deacon 1934, priest 1935, Glasgow; Curate, St John's, Greenock; Rector, All Saints, Lockerbie, 1938–49, with All Saints, Langholm, 1939–42. Chaplain, RAFVR, 1942–46. Priest-in-charge, St Mary's, Dalkeith, 1949–56; Rector, Good Shepherd, Murrayfield, 1956–77; retired; warrant to officiate, dio. Edinburgh; Chaplain of St Vincent, Edinburgh, Order of St Lazarus of Jerusalem, 1977–99; Canon 1980. FSA (Scot.) 1979. *Address:* 12 St Vincent Street, Edinburgh EH3 6SH. *T:* (0131) 557 3662. *Died 1 Dec. 2002.*

CLARK, Sir Thomas (Edwin), Kt 1986; retired director; farming since 1986; *b* 6 Aug. 1916; *s* of Thomas Edwin and Margaret Clark; *m* 1st, 1938, Joan Mary Hodgson (marr. diss. 1954); one *s* two *d* (and one *d* decd); 2nd, 1954, Josephine Mary Buckley (*d* 1962); one *s* two *d*; 3rd, 1963, Patricia Mary France; two *s* one *d*. *Educ:* King's College, Auckland. General labourer, Amalgamated Brick and Pipe Co., 1932; Asst Factory Manager, 1937; Associate Director, 1939; Manager, R&D, 1938; Gen. Manager, 1942; Director and Jt Gen. Manager, 1946 (with brother M. M. Clark); Jt Man. Dir, 1954; company name changed to Ceramco, 1964; Man. Dir, 1972, retired 1984. Chm., West Auckland Hospice Trust. *Recreations:* yachting, gardening. *Clubs:* Auckland; Royal NZ Yacht Squadron, Titirangi Golf, Helensville Golf. *Died 14 June 2005.*

CLARK HUTCHISON, Sir George Ian; *see* Hutchison.

CLARKE, Guy Hamilton, CMG 1959; HM Diplomatic Service, retired; Ambassador to Nepal, 1962–63; *b* 23 July 1910; 3rd *s* of late Dr and Mrs Charles H. Clarke, Leicester. *Educ:* Wyggeston Grammar Sch., Leicester; Trinity Hall, Cambridge. Probationer Vice-Consul, Levant Consular Service, Beirut, 1933; transf. to Ankara, 1936; Corfu, 1940; Adana, 1941; Baltimore, 1944; then served at: Washington, Los Angeles (Consul 1945), Bangkok, Jedda, Kirkuk (Consul 1949), Bagdad, Kirkuk (Consul-Gen. 1951); Ambassador to the Republic of Liberia, 1957–60, and to the Republic of Guinea, 1959–60; Mem. United Kingdom Delegation to United Nations Gen. Assembly, New York, 1960; HM Consul-General, Damascus, Feb. 1961, and Chargé d'Affaires there, Oct. 1961–Jan. 1962. *Address:* High Candovers, Hartley Mauditt, Alton, Hants GU34 3BP. *Died 20 June 2004.*

CLARKE, Norman, OBE 1982; first Secretary and Registrar, Institute of Mathematics and its Applications, 1964–87, then Emeritus; *b* 21 Oct. 1916; *o s* of late Joseph Clarke and of Ellen Clarke, Oldham; *m* 1940, Hilda May Watts; two *d*. *Educ:* Hulme Grammar Sch., Oldham; Univ. of Manchester (BSc; Pres. Univ. Union, 1938–39). FInstP; FIMA (Hon. FIMA 1990). External Ballistics Dept,

Ordnance Bd, 1939–42; Armament Res. Estabt, Br. for Theoretical Res., 1942–45; Dep. Sec., Inst. Physics, 1945–65. Hon. Sec., Internat. Commn on Physics Educn, 1960–66. Member: Southend-on-Sea CBC, 1961–74 (Alderman, 1964–74; Chm. of Watch Cttee, 1962–69 and of Public Protection Cttee, 1969–78); Southend-on-Sea BC, 1974–93 (Mayor, 1975–76; Chm., Highways Cttee, 1980–84; Leader, 1984–87, 1990–93; Leader, Cons. Gp, 1984–93); Vice-Chm., Essex Police Authority, 1969–85; Mem., Essex CC, 1973–85. Hon. Freeman, Southend-on-Sea, 1996. *Publications:* (editor and contributor): A Physics Anthology; (with S. C. Brown) International Education in Physics; Why Teach Physics?; The Education of a Physicist; (contributor): A Survey of the Teaching of Physics in Universities (Unesco); Metrication; papers on educn. *Recreations:* cricket, gastronomy, photography. *Address:* 106 Olive Avenue, Leigh-on-Sea, Essex SS9 3QE. *T:* (01702) 558056. *Club:* MCC. *Died 22 Nov. 2002.*

CLARKE, Robin Mitchell, MC 1944; JP; DL; Chairman, Gatwick Airport Consultative Committee, 1982–90; *b* 8 Jan. 1917; *e s* of Joseph and Mary Clarke; *m* 1946, Betty Mumford; twin *s* and *d*. *Educ:* Ruckholt Central Sch., Leyton. Middleton and St Bride's Wharf, Wapping, 1932–34; Town Clerk's Office, City of Westminster, 1935–40. War of 1939–45: 12th Regt, RHA (HAC) and 142 (Royal Devon Yeomanry) Fd Regt, RA; Major, 1944; served Sicily and Italy (wounded, despatches, MC). Town Clerk's Office, Westminster, 1946–48; Crawley Development Corporation, 1948–62; Manager, Crawley, Commn for the New Towns, 1962–78; Chief Exec., New Towns Commn, 1978–82. Vice-Pres., St Catherine's Hospice, Crawley, 1989– (Chm., 1983–89). Master, Worshipful Co. of Chartered Secs and Administrators, 1984–85. ACIS 1949; FCIS 1959 (Mem. Nat. Council, 1968–87; Pres., 1978). JP Crawley, 1971; DL West Sussex, 1982. FRSA 1980. *Address:* Mayford Cottage, 89 Golden Avenue, East Preston, W Sussex BN16 1QT. *T:* (01903) 771739. *Died 29 Jan. 2002.*

CLARKE, Major Sir Rupert William John, 3rd Bt *cr* 1882; AM 1999; MBE 1943; late Irish Guards; Chairman: United Distillers Co., 1960–88; National Australia Bank Ltd (formerly National Bank of Australasia), 1986–92 (Director, since 1955); International Ranch Management Services Pty Ltd; P & O Australia Ltd, 1983–96 (Director, since 1980; Hon. President, since 1996); *b* 5 Nov. 1919; *s* of 2nd Bt and Elsie Florence (who *m* 2nd, 1928, 5th Marquess of Headfort), *d* of James Partridge Tucker, Devonshire; *S* father, 1926; *m* 1st, 1947, Kathleen (*d* 1999), *d* of P. Grant Hay, Toorak, Victoria, Australia; two *s* one *d* (and one *s* decd); 2nd, 2000, Mrs Gillian de Zoete (formerly Lady Forres, *née* Grant). *Educ:* Eton; Magdalen Coll., Oxford (MA). Served War of 1939–45 (despatches, MBE). Chm., Cadbury Schweppes Australia Ltd (formerly Schweppes (Australia)), 1955–89; Dir, Cadbury Schweppes, 1977–85; Chairman: Bank of South Pacific, 1986–92; First National Ltd, 1986–92; Vice Chm., Conzinc, 1970–87; Director: Riotinto of Australia, 1962–87; Custom Credit Corp.; Morganite Australia Pty (Chm., 1976–84); National Australia Gp (UK), 1990–92. Vice Pres., Howard Florey Inst. of Exptl Physiology and Medicine, 1997–2000 (Mem. Bd, 1994–2000). Pres., Royal Humane Soc. of Australasia Inc., 1992–99. Mem. Cttee, Vic Amateur Turf Club (Chm., 1972–88); Councillor, Royal Agricl Soc. of Vic, 1965–. Hon. Consul General for Monaco, 1975–2002 (Hon. Consul, 1961). Hon. Fellow, Trinity Coll., Melbourne, 1981. Officier de la Légion d'Honneur, 1998; Comdr, Ordre des Grimaldi (Monaco); Officer, Order of Leopold (Belgium), 1989. *Publication:* At War with Alex (memoirs), 2000. *Heir: s* Rupert Grant Alexander Clarke, LLB (Hons) [*b* 12 Dec. 1947; *m* 1978, Susannah, *d* of Sir Robert Law-Smith, CBE, AFC; one *s* two *d*]. *Address:* Bolinda Vale, Clarkefield, Vic 3430, Australia; G4/1 Wallace Avenue, Toorak, Vic 3142, Australia. *Fax:* (3) 98268194, (office) (3) 96702629. *Clubs:* Cavalry and Guards, Lansdowne;

Melbourne, Athenæum, Australian (Melbourne); Union (Sydney). *Died 4 Feb. 2005.*

CLARKE, Stanley George, CBE 1975; Chief Inspector of the Prison Service, 1971–74; Member: Prisons Board, 1971–74; Parole Board, 1975–78; *b* Dunfermline, 5 May 1914; *s* of Stanley and Catherine Clarke; *m* 1940, Mary Preston Lewin; one *s* one *d. Educ:* Sutton High Sch., Plymouth (school colours: cricket, Rugby, soccer). Civil Service Clerk: Dartmoor Prison, 1931; Lowdham Grange Borstal, 1933; North Sea Camp, 1935; Borstal Housemaster: Portland, 1937; North Sea Camp, 1939. Served War, 1941–45 (despatches); Sqdn Ldr, RAF. Borstal Housemaster: Hollesley Bay Colony, 1945; Gaynes Hall, 1946; Dep. Governor, Manchester Prison, 1947; Governor: Norwich Prison, 1949; Nottingham Prison, 1952; Eastchurch Prison, 1955; Liverpool Prison, 1959; Asst Dir of Prisons, in charge of North Region, 1964; Asst Controller, Prison Dept, 1970. *Died 4 Feb. 2005.*

CLARKE, Sir Stanley (William), Kt 2001; CBE 1990; DL; Life President and non-executive Director, St Modwen Properties PLC, since 2004 (Chairman, 1986–2004); *b* 7 June 1933; *s* of Victor Raymond Clarke and Mabel Ellen Clarke (*née* Royall); *m* 1958, Hilda Joan Leavesley; one *s* three *d. Educ:* St Peter's Sch., Stapenhill, Burton upon Trent; Burton upon Trent Tech. High Sch.; Burton Tech. Coll. Founded plumbing business, 1954, later S. W. Clarke (Contractors) Ltd, then Clarke Homes; estabd St Modwen Properties Ltd, 1966 (all part of Clarke Gp); estabd St Modwen Properties PLC, 1986, following sale of Clarke Gp. Founder and Chm., Northern Racing Ltd, 1994–2004; Life Pres., Northern Racing plc, 2004. Mem., Jockey Club, 1991–. DL 2002, High Sheriff 2003–04, Staffs. DUniv Staffordshire, 1998. *Recreations:* horse racing, breeding racehorses. *Address:* The Knoll, Barton-under-Needwood, Staffs DE13 8AB. *T:* (01283) 712294. *Died 19 Sept. 2004.*

CLAYSON, Christopher William, CBE 1974 (OBE 1966); President, Royal College of Physicians of Edinburgh, 1966–70; retired; *b* 11 Sept. 1903; *s* of Christopher Clayson and Agnes Lilias Montgomerie Hunter; *m* 1st, 1933, Elsie Webster Breingan (decd); 2nd, 1988, Anne Dorothy Miller or Middlemiss. *Educ:* George Heriot's Sch.; Edinburgh University (MB, ChB 1926; DPH 1929; MD (Gold Medal) 1936). FRCPE 1951; FRCP 1967. Physician: Southfield Hosp., Edinburgh, 1931–44; Edinburgh City Hosp., 1939–44; Lectr in Tuberculosis Dept, Univ. of Edinburgh, 1939–44; Med. Supt, Lochmaben Hosp., 1944–48; Consultant Phys. in Chest Medicine, Dumfries and Galloway, 1948–68; retd from clinical practice, 1968. Served on numerous Govt and NHS cttees, 1948–; Chairman: Scottish Licensing Law Cttee, 1971–73; Scottish Council for Postgrad. Med. Educn, 1970–74. Hon. Mem., Scottish Soc. of Physicians; Mem., Thoracic Soc.; Hon. FACP 1968; Hon. FRACP 1969; Hon. FRCPGlas 1970; Hon. FRCGP 1971; Hon. FRCPE 1990. William Cullen Prize, RCPE, 1978. *Publications:* various papers on tuberculosis problem and on alcoholism in leading medical jls. *Recreations:* gardening, fishing. *Address:* Cockiesknowe, Lochmaben, Lockerbie, Dumfriesshire DG11 1RL. *T:* (01387) 810231. *Died 17 Jan. 2005.*

CLAYTON, Prof. George Scott; Newton Chambers Professor of Applied Economics, 1967–83, Pro-Vice-Chancellor, 1978–82, then Emeritus Professor, University of Sheffield; *b* 15 July 1922; *s* of late William Clayton and Gertrude Alison Clarke Clayton; *m* 1948, Rhiannon Jones, JP; two *s* two *d. Educ:* Liverpool Collegiate Sch.; King's Coll., Cambridge (Exhibnr). Served War of 1939–45: Pilot, RAF, 1941–45; Pilot, Fleet Air Arm, 1945. Univ. of Liverpool: Asst Lectr, 1947–50; Lectr, 1950–57; Sen. Lectr, 1957–60 and 1961–63; Sen. Simon Res. Fellow, Univ. of Manchester, 1960–61; Prof. and Head of Dept of Econs, UCW Aberystwyth, 1963–67. Luis Olariaga Lectr, Madrid Univ., 1959; Special Univ. Lectr, London, 1970; Page Fund Lectr, UC Cardiff, 1970. Member: Council,

Royal Econ. Soc., 1965–68; Commn on Rating and Taxation in IoM (report published, 1967); (part-time) East Midland Gas Bd, 1967–70; Crowther Cttee on Consumer Credit, 1968–70; Scott Cttee on Property Bonds and Equity-linked Insce, 1970–72; Econs Cttee, SSRC, 1978–82 (Vice-Chm., 1979–82). Non-exec. Dir, Pioneer Mutual Assurance Co., 1976–90; Consultant, Eastern Caribbean Central Bank, 1987–. Chm., British, Canadian and Amer. Mission to British Honduras, 1966; Economic Adviser: Govt of Tanzania, 1965–66; Govt of Gibraltar, 1974–82. Chm., Assoc. of Univ. Teachers of Economics, 1973–78. *Publications:* (contrib.) A New Prospect of Economics, ed G. L. S. Shackle, 1956; (contrib.) Banking in Western Europe, ed R. S. Sayers, 1959; Insurance Company Investment, 1965; Problems of Rail Transport in Rural Wales: two case studies, 1967; Monetary Theory and Monetary Policy in the 1970s, 1971; British Insurance, 1971; articles in Econ. Jl, etc. *Recreations:* tennis, sailing, theatre, fell walking. *Address:* 40 Ranmoor Crescent, Sheffield S10 3GW. *T:* (0114) 263 0531, *Fax:* (0114) 263 0386. *Club:* Hawks (Cambridge).

Died 16 April 2002.

CLEAVER, William Benjamin, CEng, FIMinE; JP; Deputy Director, South Wales Area, National Coal Board, 1969–85; *b* 15 Sept. 1921; *s* of David John Cleaver and Blodwen (*née* Miles); *m* 1943, Mary Watkin (*née* James); one *s* two *d. Educ:* Pentre (Rhondda) Grammar Sch.; University Coll. Cardiff (BSc Hons). National Coal Board: Manager: N Celynen Collieries, Gwent, 1947; Oakdale Colliery, Gwent, 1950; Production Manager (Group), S Wales, 1953; Area General Manager, No 2 S Wales Area, 1958. Sec., Contemporary Art Soc. for Wales, 1972–91; Member: Welsh Arts Council, 1977–83 (Vice-Chm., 1980–83); Arts Council of GB, 1980–83; Council, Nat. Museum of Wales, 1982–2000; Exec. Cttee, Council of Museums in Wales, 1983–97 (Chm., 1986–97). Founder Pres., Cardiff Jun. Ch. of Commerce, 1953. Rugby Union Football: Cardiff RFC, 1940–50; Welsh Rugby International, 1947–50 (14 caps); British Lion to NZ and Aust., 1950; Barbarian Rugby Club, 1946; Founder Chm., Welsh Youth Rugby Union, 1949–57. JP Cardiff 1973. OstJ 1961. *Recreations:* theatre, fine arts. *Address:* 29 Lon-y-deri, Rhiwbina, Cardiff CF14 6JN. *T:* (029) 2069 3242. *Club:* Cardiff and County (Cardiff).

Died 29 Sept. 2003.

CLEDWYN OF PENRHOS, Baron *cr* 1979 (Life Peer), of Holyhead in the Isle of Anglesey; **Cledwyn Hughes,** CH 1977; PC 1966; Leader of the Opposition, House of Lords, 1982–92 (Deputy Leader of the Opposition, 1981–82); *b* 14 Sept. 1916; *er s* of Rev. Henry David and Emily Hughes; *m* 1949, Jean Beatrice, *d* of Captain Jesse and Sarah Hughes; one *s* one *d. Educ:* Holyhead Grammar Sch.; University Coll. of Wales, Aberystwyth (LLB; Hon. Fellow, 1986). Solicitor, 1940. Served RAFVR, 1940–45. Mem., Anglesey County Council, 1946–52. Contested (Lab) Anglesey, 1945 and 1950; MP (Lab) Anglesey, 1951–79; Opposition spokesman for Housing and Local Govt, 1959–64; Minister of State for Commonwealth Relations, 1964–66; Sec. of State for Wales, 1966–68; Minister of Agriculture, Fisheries and Food, 1968–70; Opposition spokesman on Agriculture, Fisheries and Food, 1970–72; Commissioner of the House of Commons, 1979. Member: Cttee of Public Accounts, 1957–64; Cttee of Privileges, 1974–79. Chm., House of Lords Select Cttee on Agriculture and Food, 1980–83. Chairman: Welsh Parliamentary Party, 1953–54; Welsh Labour Group, 1955–56; Parly Labour Party, Oct. 1974–1979 (Vice-Chm., March–Oct. 1974); Welsh Cttee on Economic and Industrial Affairs, 1982–84; Jt Chm., TUC/Labour Party Liaison Cttee, 1974–79. Mem. Parly Delegn to Lebanon, 1957; represented British Govt at Kenya Republic Celebrations, 1964; led UK Delegn to The Gambia Independence celebrations, 1965; Mission to Rhodesia, July 1965; led UK Mission on Contingency Planning to Zambia, 1966; led Parliamentary Delegn to USSR, 1977; Prime Minister's Envoy to Southern Africa,

Nov.-Dec. 1978. Vice-Pres., Britain in Europe, 1975. Mem., Political Honours Cttee, 1992–98. Director: Shell UK Ltd, 1980–84; Anglesey Aluminium Ltd, 1980–; Holyhead Towing Ltd, 1980; a Regional Advr in Midland Bank, with special responsibilities for Wales, 1979–94. Member, County Councils' Assoc., 1980–; Chm., Welsh Theatre Co., 1981–85; President: Housing and Town Planning Council, 1980–92; Age Concern, Wales, 1980–85; Soc. of Welsh People Overseas, 1979–91; Assembly of Welsh Counties, 1990–. Pro-Chancellor, Univ. of Wales, 1985–94; President: UCW, Aberystwyth, 1976–85 (Fellow, 1988); Univ. of Wales, Bangor, 1995–. Fellow: UCW, Aberystwyth, 1988; Trinity Coll., Carmarthen, 1993. Hon. Freedom of Beaumaris, 1972; Freeman: Borough of Anglesey, 1976; City of Cardiff, 2000. Hon. LLD: Wales, 1970; Sheffield, 1992; Glamorgan, 1996. Alderman, Anglesey CC, 1973. *Publication:* Report on Conditions in St Helena, 1958. *Address:* Penmorfa, Trearddur, Holyhead, Gwynedd LL65 2YR. *T:* (01407) 860544. *Club:* Travellers.

Died 22 Feb. 2001.

CLEGG, Brian George Herbert; management consultant and company director; *b* 10 Dec. 1921; *s* of Frederic Bradbury Clegg and Gladys Butterworth; *m* 1st, 1949, Iris May Ludlow (marr. diss. 1976); one *s* one *d*; 2nd, 1976, Anne Elizabeth Robertson (marr. diss. 1996); one *s*; 3rd, 1997, Banjit, (Joom,) Sawaengdee (marr. diss. 1999); 4th, 1999, Christine Lawino. *Educ:* Manchester Grammar Sch.; Trinity Coll., Cambridge (Open Math. Schol., MA). FIS, FIM, CEng, FIGasE. Sci. Officer, Min. of Supply, 1942; Hon. Flt-Lt, RAFVR. Statistician, Liverpool Gas Co., 1946; Market and Operational Res. Man., Southern Gas Bd, 1957; Commercial Man., Southern Gas Bd, 1961; Dep. Dir of Marketing, Gas Council, 1968; Dir of Marketing, British Gas Corp., 1972; Chm., Northern Region of British Gas Corp., 1975–82, retired. Dir (nominee), Midland Montagu Ventures Ltd, 1984–92. *Publications:* numerous articles and papers on marketing and fuel matters. *Recreations:* swimming, ice-skating, electronic organ. *Address:* 30 The Pines, 40 The Avenue, Poole, Dorset BH13 6HJ.

Died 6 June 2001.

CLELAND, Dame Rachel, DBE 1980 (CBE 1966; MBE 1959); *b* Peppermint Grove, 19 Jan. 1906; *d* of W. H. Evans, Perth, WA; *m* 1928, Sir Donald Cleland, *s* of E. D. Cleland; two *s. Educ:* Methodist Ladies' Coll., Perth, WA; Kindergarten Training Coll. Pres., Girl Guide Assoc., Papua and New Guinea, 1952–66; President: Red Cross, Papua and New Guinea, 1952–66; Branch of Aust. Pre-Sch. Assoc. (TPNG), 1952–66. *Publications:* Pathways to Independence: official and family life in Papua New Guinea 1951–1976, 1984, 2nd edn 1985; Grassroots to Independence and Beyond: contribution by women in Papua New Guinea, 1996. *Recreations:* music, theatre, reading. *Address:* Unit 5, 4–6 Bell Street, Goondiwindi, Qld 4390, Australia. *Club:* Queen's (Sydney).

Died 18 April 2002.

CLELAND, William Paton, FRCP, FRCS, FACS; Consulting Surgeon, National Heart and Chest Hospital; Consulting Thoracic Surgeon, King's College Hospital; Emeritus Consultant to the Royal Navy; late Adviser in Thoracic Surgery to the Department of Health and Social Security; *b* 30 May 1912; *o s* of Sir John Cleland, CBE; *m* 1940, Norah (*d* 1994), *d* of George E. Goodhart; two *s* one *d. Educ:* Scotch Coll., Adelaide; Univ. of Adelaide, S Australia (MB, BS). FRCS 1946. Resident appts, Royal Adelaide and Adelaide Children's Hosps, 1935–36; MRCP 1939; House Physician and Resident Surgical Officer, Brompton Chest Hosp., 1939–41. Served in EMS as Registrar and Surgeon, 1939–45. Consultant Thoracic Surgeon, King's Coll. Hosp., 1948; Surgeon, Brompton Chest Hosp., 1948; Sen. Lectr in Thoracic Surgery, Royal Postgrad. Med. Sch., 1949; Dir, Dept of Surgery, Cardio-Thoracic Inst., Brompton Hosp. Member: Assoc. Thoracic Surgeons of Gt Brit. and Ire.; Thoracic Soc.; British Cardiac Soc.; Amer. Coll. of Surgeons. Editor, Jl of

Cardiovascular Surgery, 1978–83. Comdr, Order of Lion of Finland; Comdr, Order of Falcon of Iceland. *Publications:* (jt author) Medical and Surgical Cardiology, 1969; chapters on thoracic surgery in British Surgical Practice, Diseases of the Chest (Marshall and Perry), Short Practice of Surgery (Bailey and Love), and Operative Surgery (Rob and Rodney Smith); articles on pulmonary and cardiac surgery in medical literature. *Recreations:* fishing, gardening, beekeeping. *Address:* Green Meadows, Goodworth Clatford, Andover, Hants SP11 7HH. *T:* (01264) 324327.

Died 29 March 2005.

CLEMENT, David Morris, CBE 1971; FCA; Chairman, Joint Mission Hospital Equipment Board Ltd, 1978–85; *b* 6 Feb. 1911; 2nd *s* of Charles William and Rosina Wannell Clement, Swansea; *m* 1938, Kathleen Mary (*d* 1991), *o d* of Ernest George Davies, ACA, Swansea; one *d. Educ:* Bishop Gore's Grammar Sch., Swansea. Mem. Inst. Chartered Accountants, 1933. A. Owen John & Co., Swansea, and Sissons Bersey Gain Vincent & Co., London, Chartered Accts, 1928–35; ICI Ltd, Lime Gp, 1935–40; Chloride Electrical Storage Co. Ltd, 1941–46; National Coal Board: Sec., North Western Div., 1946–49; Chief Acct, Northern and Durham Divs, 1950–55; Dep. Dir-Gen. of Finance, 1955–61; Dir-Gen. of Finance, 1961–69; Bd Mem., 1969–76; Chairman: NCB (Ancillaries) Ltd, 1973–79; Redwood-Corex Services Ltd, 1978–82. Chairman: Staff and Mineworkers Pension Schemes Jt Investment Cttee, 1961–76; Public Corporations Finance Gp, 1975–76. Dep. Chm., Horizon Exploration Ltd, 1978–80. Underwriting Member of Lloyd's, 1978–96. Member: Aircraft and Shipbuilding Industries Arbitration Tribunals, 1980–83; Council, CIPFA, 1975–76; Council, CGLI (Hon. Treas.), 1978–82. Hon. FCGI. *Recreations:* golf, photography. *Address:* The Old Hall, Mulbarton, Norfolk NR14 8JS. *T:* (01508) 578655. *Clubs:* Directors'; Norfolk (Norwich).

Died 17 March 2002.

CLERK of Penicuik, Sir John Dutton, 10th Bt *cr* 1679; CBE 1966; VRD; FRSE 1977; JP; Lord-Lieutenant of Midlothian, 1972–92 (Vice-Lieutenant, 1965–72); *b* 30 Jan. 1917; *s* of Sir George James Robert Clerk of Penicuik, 9th Bt, and Hon. Mabel Honor (*d* 1974), *y d* of Col Hon. Charles Dutton and *sister* of 6th Baron Sherborne, DSO; *S* father, 1943; *m* 1944, Evelyn Elizabeth Robertson; two *s* two *d. Educ:* Stowe. Cdre RNR, retd. Brig., 1973–89, Ensign, 1989–96, Lieut, 1996–, Queen's Body Guard for Scotland, Royal Company of Archers. JP 1955, DL 1956, Midlothian. *Heir: s* Robert Maxwell Clerk, Younger of Penicuik OBE [*b* 3 April 1945; *m* 1970, Felicity Faye, *yr d* of George Collins, Bampton, Oxford; two *s* one *d*]. *Address:* Penicuik House, Penicuik, Midlothian EH26 9LA. *T:* (01968) 674318. *Clubs:* Royal Over-Seas League; New (Edinburgh).

Died 25 Oct. 2002.

CLIFFORD, Rev. Paul Rowntree, MA; President, Selly Oak Colleges, Birmingham, 1965–79; *b* 21 Feb. 1913; *s* of Robert and Harriet Rowntree Clifford; *m* 1st, 1947, Marjory Jean Tait (*d* 1988); one *s* one *d*; 2nd, 1989, Dorothy Marion White, OBE (*d* 2002). *Educ:* Mill Hill Sch.; Balliol Coll., Oxford (MA 1939); Mansfield and Regents Park Colls, Oxford. West Ham Central Mission, London: Asst Minister, 1938–43; Supt Minister, 1943–53; McMaster Univ., Hamilton, Canada: Asst Prof. of Homiletics and Pastoral Theology, 1953–59; Dean of Men and Chm., Dept of Religion, 1959–64; Prof. of Religion, 1964–65. Hon. Treas., Internat. Assoc. for Mission Studies, 1974–88; Sec., Foundn for Study of Christianity and Society, 1980–90. *Publications:* The Mission of the Local Church, 1953; The Pastoral Calling, 1959; Now is the Time, 1970; Interpreting Human Experience, 1971; The Death of the Dinosaur, 1977; Politics and the Christian Vision, 1984; Government by the People?, 1986; An Ecumenical Pilgrimage, 1994; The Reality of the Kingdom, 1996; Radical Politics, 1996; Expanding Horizons, 1997; articles in Jl of Religion, Metaphysical Rev., Dialogue, Canadian Jl of Theology, Scottish Jl of Theology, Foundations, Religious Studies. *Recreations:*

reading, writing. *Address:* Honeywood House, Rowhook, Horsham, West Sussex RH12 3QD. *Club:* Reform (Chm., 1987–89; Trustee, 1990–).

Died 18 Jan. 2003.

CLIVE, Nigel David, CMG 1967; OBE 1959; MC 1944; TD; HM Diplomatic Service, retired; *b* 13 July 1917; *s* of late Horace David and Hilda Mary Clive; *m* 1949, Maria Jeanne Tambakopoulou. *Educ:* Stowe; Christ Church, Oxford (Scholar). Commissioned 2nd Middx Yeomanry, 1939; served in Middle East and Greece. Joined Foreign Office, 1946; served Athens, 1946–48; Jerusalem, 1948; FO, 1948–50; Baghdad, 1950–53; FO, 1953–58; Tunis, 1958–62; Algiers, 1962–63; FO, 1964–65; Head of Information Research Dept, FCO (formerly FO), 1966–69; Adviser to Secretary-General of OECD, 1970–80. *Publications:* A Greek Experience 1943–1948, 1985; (trans.) M. Koromila, In the Trail of Odysseus, 1994. *Recreations:* reading, travel. *Address:* Flat 1, 37 Lowndes Square, SW1X 9JL. *T:* (020) 7235 1186. *Clubs:* Brooks's, Special Forces, MCC. *Died 6 May 2001.*

COATES, Michael Arthur, FCA; Chairman, Price Waterhouse, World Firm, 1982–88; *b* 12 May 1924; *yr s* of late Joseph Michael Smith Coates, OBE, Elmfield, Wylam, Northumberland, and Lillian Warren Coates (*née* Murray); *m* 1st, 1952, Audrey Hampton Thorne (marr. diss. 1970); one *s* two *d*; 2nd, 1971, Sally Rogers (marr. diss. 1980). *Educ:* Uppingham Sch. Admitted Mem., Inst. of Chartered Accountants, 1951. Served RA, mainly in ME and Italy, 1942–47. Articled with Price Waterhouse & Co., Newcastle, 1942; returned to Price Waterhouse, 1947; transf. to London, 1954; Price Waterhouse & Co.: Partner, 1959–82; Dep. Sen. Partner, 1974–75; Sen. Partner, 1975–82; Chm., Price Waterhouse Internat. Manpower Cttee, 1971–74; Mem., Policy Cttee, 1974–88. *Recreations:* diverse, including music, modern painting, antiques, gardens, reading, railways, photography. *Address:* 20 Wilton Crescent, SW1X 8SA. *T:* (020) 7235 4423; Cantray House, Croy, Inverness-shire IV2 5PW. *T:* (01667) 493204. *Died 17 Nov. 2004.*

COATES, Reginald Charles, FREng; Emeritus Professor of Civil Engineering, University of Nottingham, since 1983; *b* 28 June 1920; *s* of Wilfrid and Margaret Anne Coates; *m* 1942, Doris Sheila (*née* Sharrad) (*d* 1988); two *s* one *d*. *Educ:* New Mills Grammar Sch.; Herbert Strutt Sch., Belper; University Coll., Nottingham. Served War of 1939–45, Corps of Royal Engineers. University of Nottingham: Lectr in Civil Engineering, 1946; Sen. Lectr, 1953; Prof. and Head of Dept of Civil Engrg, 1958–82; Dep. Vice-Chancellor, 1966–69; Prof. and Hd, Dept of Civil Engrg, Papua New Guinea Univ. of Technol., 1982–85. Member: Council, ICE, 1967–72 (Vice-Pres., 1975–78, Pres., 1978–79); Sheffield Regional Hosp. Bd, 1971–74; Notts AHA, 1974–75; Council, Construction Industry Research and Information Assoc., 1978–82; Adv. Cttee, Books for Overseas, British Council, 1974–82; Construction and Housing Res. Adv. Council, DoE, 1976–79. FREng (FEng 1978). *Publications:* (with M. G. Coutie and F. K. Kong) Structural Analysis, 1972, 3rd edn 1987; occasional articles in technical press. *Recreations:* cooking and idling. *Died 22 Nov. 2004.*

COBB, Timothy Humphry, MA; Headmaster, Dover College, 1958–73; *b* 4 July 1909; *s* of Humphry Henry Cobb and Edith Muriel (*née* Stogdon); *m* 1952, Cecilia Mary Josephine, *d* of W. G. Chapman; two *s* one *d*. *Educ:* Harrow; Magdalene Coll., Cambridge. Asst Master, Middlesex Sch., Concord, Mass, USA, 1931–32; Bryanston Sch., Blandford, Dorset, 1932–47 (Housemaster, Head of Classics, Estate Bursar); Headmaster of King's Coll., Budo, Kampala, Uganda, 1947–58; formerly Sec., Uganda Headmasters' Association. *Publication:* Certificate English Language Practice, 1958. *Recreations:* music, railways, producing vegetables. *Address:* Parkgate Farm, Framlingham, Woodbridge, Suffolk IP13 9JH. *T:* (01728) 638672. *Clubs:*

MCC; Bluemantles Cricket (Tunbridge Wells and W Kent). *Died 27 April 2002.*

COCHRAN, William, PhD; FRS 1962; Professor of Natural Philosophy, University of Edinburgh, 1975–87, then Emeritus; *b* 30 July 1922; *s* of James Cochran and Margaret Watson Cochran (*née* Baird); *m* 1953, Ingegerd Wall; one *s* two *d*. *Educ:* Boroughmuir Sch., Edinburgh; Edinburgh Univ. (MA). Asst Lectr, Edinburgh Univ., 1943–46; Demonstrator and Lectr, Univ. of Cambridge, 1948–62; Reader in Physics, Univ. of Cambridge, 1962–64; Fellow, Trinity Hall, Cambridge, 1951–64; University of Edinburgh: Prof. of Physics, 1964–75; Dean, Faculty of Science, 1978–81; Vice-Principal, 1984–87. Research fellowships abroad, 1950–51, 1958–59, 1970. Hon. Fellow, Trinity Hall, Cambridge, 1982. Hon. DSc: Heriot-Watt, 1992; Edinburgh, 1994. Guthrie Medal, Inst. Physics and Phys. Soc., 1966; Hughes Medal, Royal Soc., 1978; Potts Medal, Franklin Inst., 1985. *Publications:* (with H. Lipson) The Crystalline State, vol. III, 1954, new edn 1966; Dynamics of Atoms in Crystals, 1973; (jtly) 20th Century Physics, 1995. *Recreations:* Scots verse, family history. *Address:* Department of Physics, The University, The King's Buildings, Edinburgh EH9 3JZ; 3 Rustic Cottages, Colinton Road, Edinburgh EH13 0LD. *Died 28 Aug. 2003.*

COCKS OF HARTCLIFFE, Baron *cr* 1987 (Life Peer), of Chinnor in the County of Oxfordshire; **Michael Francis Lovell Cocks;** PC 1976; *b* 19 Aug. 1929; *s* of late Dr H. F. Lovell Cocks; *m* 1st, 1954, Janet Macfarlane; two *s* two *d*; 2nd, 1979, Valerie Davis. *Educ:* Bristol University. Various posts in education, 1954–68; Lectr, Bristol Polytechnic, 1968. Contested (Lab): Bristol West, 1959; South Gloucestershire, 1964, 1966. MP (Lab) Bristol S, 1970–87. An Asst Govt Whip, 1974–76; Parly Sec. to the Treasury and Govt Chief Whip, 1976–79; Opposition Chief Whip, 1979–85; a Dep. Speaker, H of L, 1990–. Vice-Chm., Bd of Govs, BBC, 1993–98. *Publication:* Labour and the Benn Factor, 1989. *Recreations:* swimming, listening to music, reading. *Died 26 March 2001.*

CODRINGTON, Sir Simon (Francis Bethell), 3rd Bt *cr* 1876; *b* 14 Aug. 1923; *s* of Sir Christopher William Gerald Henry Codrington, 2nd Bt, and Joan Mary Hague-Cook (*d* 1961); *S* father, 1979; *m* 1st, 1947, Joanne (marr. diss. 1959), *d* of J. W. Molineaux and *widow* of William Humphrey Austin Thompson; 2nd, 1959, Pamela Joy Halliday Wise (marr. diss. 1979); three *s*; 3rd, 1980, Sarah Gwynne Gaze (*née* Pennell) (marr. diss. 1987); 4th, 1989, Shirley Ann, *d* of Percival Davis. *Educ:* Eton. Late Coldstream Guards. *Heir: s* Christopher George Wayne Codrington [*b* 20 Feb. 1960; *m* 1991, Noelle, *d* of Dale Leverson; one *s* one *d*]. *Address:* Dodington, Chipping Sodbury, Bristol BS37 6SD. *T:* (01454) 312354. *Died 17 Aug. 2005.*

COEN, Massimo (Aldo), Hon. CBE 1991; Cavaliere al Merito del Lavoro 1982; Grande Ufficiale nell'Ordine al Merito della Repubblica Italiana 1979; Hon. Life President, Italian Chamber of Commerce and Industry for the UK, 1994; President, Etrufin Reserco Ltd, since 1985; *b* Bologna, 29 July 1918; *s* of Cavaliere Ragioniere Terzo Coen and Delia Coen Guetta; *m* 1946, Thelma Doreen Kelley (*d* 1993); one *s* three *d*. *Educ:* Liceo Marco Foscarini, Venice (dipl. 1937); Padua University; London School of Economics. Came to London from Venice because of racial laws, 1939; interned in Isle of Man, June–Dec. 1940; Netherland Shipping & Trading Cttee Ltd, Jan.–April 1941; Italian Section, BBC External Services, 1941–46 (Shift Leader and Senior Announcer Translator); Chairman and Managing Director: Granosa Trading Co. Ltd and subsidiaries (dealing in textiles), 1946–92; Florence (Arts & Crafts) Ltd, 1946–92; Thames Rugs & Tweed Fabrics Ltd, 1959–92; Chm., Britalia Consultants Ltd, 1993–2001. Dir, Business Develt–Italy, Levy Gee Chartered Accountants, 1994–2001; Chief Advr, Internat. Affairs Italy, Simmons & Simmons Solicitors, 1993–2000. Vis. Prof., Dept of Italian, UCL, 1996–. Councillor,

1951–72, Vice-Pres., 1972–78, Pres., 1978–94, Italian Chamber of Commerce for GB; Chm., 1985–99, Life Hon. Chm., 1999, Club di Londra; Mem., Rotary Club, London, 1996–2001. Many radio plays, talks and commentaries during the war years. Acted in Snowbound, 1947, Hotel Sahara, 1951. Hon. LLD Warwick, 1997. Cavaliere 1956, Ufficiale 1968, Commendatore 1972, nell'Ordine al Merito della Repubblica Italiana. *Publications:* Four Lectures, 1996; Another Four Lectures, 1999; contrib. to Italian Studies, Raccordo. *Recreations:* shooting, fishing; formerly golf, competition skiing and fencing. *Address:* 14 Acacia Road, St John's Wood, NW8 6AN. *T:* (020) 7722 2459, *Fax:* (020) 7586 8595.

Died 13 Feb. 2004.

COFFIN, Cyril Edwin, CBE 1984; Director General, Food Manufacturers' Federation, 1977–84; *b* 29 June 1919; s of late Percy Edwin Coffin and Helena Constance Coffin; *m* 1947, Joyce Mary Tobitt; one *s* one *d* (and one *d* decd). *Educ:* King's Coll. Sch., Wimbledon; King's Coll., Cambridge. War service, 1939–45, Captain RIASC; jssc 1950. Civil servant, 1946–77, incl. Burma Office, 1946, and Min. of Food, later MAFF, 1947–63; Alternate UK Governor, Internat. Atomic Energy Agency, 1964; Under-Secretary: Min. of Technology, later DTI, 1966; Dept of Prices and Consumer Protection, 1974–77. FRSA 1979. *Publications:* Working with Whitehall, 1987; A Blackmore Vale Family, 1992; articles in various jls. *Recreations:* music, learning languages. *Address:* 54 Cambridge Avenue, New Malden, Surrey KT3 4LE. *T:* (020) 8942 0763. *Died 3 April 2005.*

COGMAN, Very Rev. Frederick Walter; Dean of Guernsey, 1967–78; Rector of St Peter Port, Guernsey, 1976–78; *b* 4 March 1913; *s* of William Frederick Cogman and Mabel Cozens; *m* 1940, Rose Hélène Mauger; one *s* one *d*. *Educ:* Rutlish Sch., Merton; King's Coll., London. Asst Priest, Upton-cum-Chalvey, Slough, 1938–42; Chaplain and Housemaster, St George's Sch., Harpenden, 1942–48; Rector of St Martin, Guernsey, 1948–76. *Recreation:* music. *Died 23 July 2005.*

COHEN, Michael Antony; housing consultant, since 2001; Chief Executive, The Guinness Trust, 1987–2001; *b* 18 April 1940; *s* of Gerald and Beatrice Cohen; *m* 1967, Jennifer Audrey Price; one *s* two *d*. *Educ:* Quarry Bank Grammar School, Liverpool; Univ. of Liverpool (BA Hons Econ.). FCA; MIH. Articled clerk, 1962–65; Accountant and Planning Manager, Bank of London & S America, 1965–72; posts in European and US banking, Lloyds Bank, 1972–78; Internat. Project Finance Manager, Lloyds Bank, 1978–82; Regional Dir, Housing Corp., 1982–87. Non-executive Director: Housing Forum Ltd, 1999–2001; Barnet Homes Ltd, 2004–; Royal Nat. Orthopaedic Hosp. Trust, 2004–. Mem. Council, London Borough of Barnet, 1972–78. Chairman: St Mungo Community Housing Assoc., 1991–; Barnet Housing Aid Centre, 1990–; Phoenix Cinema Trust Ltd, 1996–; Trustee, Prince's Foundn, 1999–2002. Chm. Govs, Christ's Coll., Finchley, 1996–2000. *Recreations:* walking, eating, France, theatre, finding time. *Address:* 6 Talbot Avenue, East Finchley, N2 0LS. *T:* (020) 8883 9433; *e-mail:* mike.cohen@tinyworld.co.uk.

Died 2 Sept. 2005.

COHEN, Her Honour Myrella; QC 1970; a Circuit Judge, 1972–95; *b* 16 Dec. 1927; *d* of late Samuel and Sarah Cohen, Manchester; *m* 1953, Lt-Col Mordaunt Cohen, TD; one *s* one *d*. *Educ:* Manchester High Sch. for Girls; Colwyn Bay Grammar Sch.; Manchester Univ. (LLB 1948). Called to the Bar, Gray's Inn, 1950. Recorder of Hull, 1971; Dep. High Court Judge, Family Div., 1975–95. Mem., Parole Bd, 1983–86. Dep. Pres., Internat. Assoc. of Jewish Lawyers and Jurists, 1996–; Chm., UK Assoc. of Jewish Lawyers, 1996–. Vice-Pres., N of England CRC, 1974–. Life Mem., Council, League of Jewish Women, 1991; Exec. Mem., Jewish Marriage Council, 1990–. Pres., 1968, 1988, Hon. Mem., 1989, Sunderland Soroptomists. Patron: Sunderland Council for the Disabled; Suzy Lamplugh Trust; Women of North Distaff Cttee; British Emunah. FRSA 1993. Hon. LLD Sunderland, 1992. *Address:* 1 Peters Lodge, 2 Stonegrove, Edgware, Middlesex HA8 7TY. *Club:* Soroptimist of Great Britain. *Died 25 Oct. 2002.*

COHEN, Stanley; *b* 31 July 1927; *s* of Thomas and Teresa Cohen; *m* 1954, Brenda P. Rafferty; three *s* one *d*. *Educ:* St Patrick's and St Charles' Schools, Leeds. Served in Royal Navy, 1947–49. Employed in Clothing Industry, 1943–47 and 1949–51; Clerical Officer with British Railways, 1951–70. Mem. Leeds City Council, 1952–71; elected Alderman, 1968. Contested (Lab) Barkston Ash, 1966; MP (Lab) Leeds South East, 1970–83. PPS to Minister of State, DES, 1976–79. Mem., Duke of Edinburgh's Commonwealth Study Conf. to Australia, 1968. *Recreations:* walking, camping, driving. *Address:* 9 Pendil Close, Whitkirk, Leeds LS15 0NE. *T:* (0113) 264 9568. *Clubs:* Crossgates Recreational; Irish Centre (Leeds). *Died 23 Feb. 2004.*

COKER, Peter Godfrey, RA 1972 (ARA 1965); ARCA 1953; artist; *b* 27 July 1926; *m* 1951, Vera Joyce Crook; one *s* decd. *Educ:* St Martin's Sch. of Art; Royal Coll. of Art (Royal Schol.). Brit. Inst. Schol., 1954. Arts Council Award to Artists, 1976. Hon. RE 1998. One-man Exhibitions: Zwemmer Gall., 1956, 1957, 1959, 1964, 1967; Magdalene Street Gall., Cambridge, 1968; Stone Gall., Newcastle, 1969; Thackeray Gall., London, 1970, 1972, 1974, 1975, 1976, 1978; Gallery 10, London, 1980, 1982, 1984, 1986, 1988; Flying Colours Gall., Edinburgh, 1990; Gainsborough's House, Sudbury, 2003; RA, 2004; Graves Art Gall., Sheffield, 2004–05. Retrospective Exhibitions: Minories, Colchester, 1972; Victoria Gall., Bath, 1972; Morley Gall., London, 1973; Mappin Art Gall., Sheffield, 1973; Chelmsford and Essex Museum, 1978; Royal Acad., 1979; Fitzwilliam Mus., Cambridge, 1989 (working drawings and sketchbooks, 1955–88); Kendal, 1992, then tour to Carlisle, Royal Acad. and Ipswich (landscapes 1956–90); Chris Beetles Gall., 2002. Represented in Group Exhibitions: Tate Gall., 1958; Jordan Gall., Toronto, 1958; John Moores, Liverpool, 1959, 1961; Northampton, 1960; Europaisches Forum, Alpbach, Austria, 1960; Neue Galerie, Linz, 1960; RCA, 1952–62; Painters in E Anglia, Arts Council, 1966; Bicentenary Exhibn, Royal Acad., 1768–1968, 1968; British Painting 1900–1960, Sheffield and Aberdeen, 1975–76; British Painting 1952–77, RA; Recent Chantrey Purchases, Tate Gall., 1981; Acquisitions since 1980, Tate Gall., 1982; The Forgotten Fifties, Sheffield and UK tour, 1984; Exhibition Road, RCA, 1988; The Kitchen Sink Painters, Mayor Gall., 1991; New Displays, Tate Gall., 1992. Works in permanent collections: Tate Gall.; British Museum; Scottish Nat. Gall. of Modern Art; Arts Council; Contemp. Art Soc., GB; Contemp. Art Soc., Wales; Chantrey Bequest; Nat. Portrait Gall.; V&A; Nat. Maritime Museum; Eastern Arts Assoc.; Rugby Library and Museum; Chelmsford and Essex Museum; Castle Museum, Norwich; Fitzwilliam Mus., Cambridge; Art Galls and Museums of Carlisle, Ipswich, Leicester, Rochdale, Doncaster; Art Galls of Bath (Victoria), Batley, Birmingham, Coventry (Herbert), Kendal (Abbot Hall), Kettering, Leeds City, Liverpool (Walker), Manchester City, Sheffield City, Southport (Atkinson), Salford; RCA; RA; Minories, Colchester; Beecroft Art Gall., Southend-on-Sea; Educn Cttees of Nottingham, Essex, Derbyshire, Lancs, ILEA; Liverpool Univ.; Stedelijk Mus., Ostend; Berardo Collection, Sintra, Portugal; Ashmolean Mus., Oxford; Bibliothèque nationale de France, Paris; École nationale supérieure des Beaux-Arts, Paris. *Publications:* Etching Techniques, 1976; *relevant publications:* Peter Coker RA, by David Wootton and John Russell Taylor, 2002; Peter Coker RA: new work, by Frances Spalding, 2003; The Old and the New, by Andrew Lambirth, 2004. *Recreations:* food and wine. *Address:* The Red House, Mistley, Manningtree, Essex CO11 1BX.

Died 16 Dec. 2004.

COLCHESTER, Tom; see Colchester, T. C.

COLCHESTER, Trevor Charles, (Tom), CMG 1958; HM Colonial Service, retired; *b* London, 18 April 1909; *s* of Charles Colchester; *m* 1937, Nancy Joan Russell; one *d*. *Educ:* Corpus Christi Coll., Cambridge (MA). HM Colonial Service, 1931–64; in Kenya, Zanzibar, and Northern Rhodesia; Sec. to Cabinet, Kenya, 1954–57; Permanent Sec., Kenya, 1957–61. Sec., Commonwealth Assoc. of Architects, 1964–74. Hon. FRIBA 1975. *Recreations:* conservation, gardening, fly-fishing, music. *Address:* Plomesgate, Aldeburgh, Suffolk IP15 5QB. *T:* (01728) 452871. *Died 26 Jan 2001.*

COLDSTREAM, Sir George (Phillips), KCB 1955 (CB 1949); KCVO 1968; QC 1960; *b* 20 Dec. 1907; *s* of late Francis Menzies Coldstream; *m* 1st, 1934, Mary Morna (marr. diss. 1948), *o d* of Major and Mrs A. D. Carmichael, Meigle, Perthshire; one *d* (and one *d* decd); 2nd, Sheila Hope, *widow* of Lt–Col J. H. H. Whitty, DSO, MC. *Educ:* Rugby; Oriel Coll., Oxford. Called to the Bar, Lincoln's Inn, 1930. Bencher, 1954; Asst to Parly Counsel to Treasury, 1934–39; Legal Asst, Lord Chancellor's Office, 1939–44; Dep. Clerk of the Crown, 1944–54; Clerk of the Crown in Chancery and Permanent Sec. to the Lord Chancellor, 1954–68. Member: British War Crimes Executive, 1944–46; Anglo-Amer. Legal Exchanges, 1961–69; Royal Commn on Assizes and Quarter Sessions, 1967–70; Top Salaries Review Body, 1971–82. Part-time Chm., Industrial Tribunals, 1975–80. Chm., Council of Legal Educn, 1970–73. Hon. LLD Columbia Univ., 1966. *Address:* The Gate House, Seaford, East Sussex BN25 2AH. *T:* (01323) 892801. *Clubs:* Athenæum; Royal Cruising. *Died 19 April 2004.*

COLDWELLS, Rev. Canon Alan Alfred; Canon of St George's Chapel, Windsor, 1987–95; *b* 15 Jan. 1930; *yr s* of late Alfred Carpenter Coldwells and of Leila Philis Eugenie Coldwells (*née* Livings); *m* 1963, Mary Patricia (*d* 2001), *d* of A. L. Hemsley; one *s* two *d*. *Educ:* Haileybury and ISC; University Coll., Oxford (MA); Wells Theological Coll. Deacon 1955, priest 1956; Curate, St Andrew's Parish, Rugby, 1955–62; Curate in charge, St George's, Rugby, 1956–62; Vicar of Sprowston and Rector of Beeston St Andrew, Norfolk, 1962–73; RD, Norwich North, 1970–72; Director, Samaritans, Norwich, 1970–72; Rector of Rugby, 1973–87; RD of Rugby, 1973–78; Hon. Canon, Coventry Cathedral, 1983–87, Canon Emeritus, 1988. Chaplain to Lord Mayor of London, 1999–2000. *Publications:* The Story of St Andrew's, Rugby, 1979; St George's Chapel, Windsor Castle, 1993; The Albert Chapel, Windsor Castle, 1995. *Recreations:* art, painting, local history. *Address:* 26 King Edward Street, Slough, Berks SL1 2QS. *T:* (01753) 538589. *Died 8 Feb. 2001.*

COLE, Sir (Alexander) Colin, KCB 1992; KCVO 1983 (CVO 1979); MVO 1977); TD 1972; Garter Principal King of Arms, 1978–92; *b* 16 May 1922; *er s* of late Capt. Edward Harold Cole and Blanche Ruby Lavinia (*née* Wallis); *m* 1944, Valerie, *o d* of late Capt. Stanley Walter Card; four *s* three *d* (and two *c* (twins) decd). *Educ:* Dulwich; Pembroke Coll., Cambridge; Brasenose Coll., Oxford (BCL, MA). Served War of 1939–45, Capt. Coldstream Guards. Barrister-at-law (Inner Temple), 1949, Hon. Bencher, 1988. Fitzalan Pursuivant of Arms Extraordinary, 1953; Portcullis Pursuivant of Arms, 1957; Windsor Herald of Arms, 1966. HAC (TA), 1956; Major: Inf. Bn, 1961; 6th (Volunteer) Bn, Queen's Regt, 1971–73; Lt–Col RARO (Brevet, 1973); Hon. Col, 6/7 Bn, Queen's Regt, 1981–86. Mem. Court of Common Council of City of London (Castle Baynard Ward), 1964–; Sheriff, City of London, 1976–77. Freeman of City of London; Freeman and Liveryman, Scriveners', Basketmakers' and Painter Stainers' Companies of London. Fellow, Heraldry Soc.; Hon. Heraldic Adviser, Monumental Brass Soc. Dep. Knight Principal, Imperial Soc. of Knights Bachelor, 1995–; Pres., Royal Soc. of St George, 1982–98. OStJ. *Publications:* articles on heraldry

and kindred subjects in their appropriate journals; illus. Visitations of London (1568) and Wiltshire (1623) (Harleian Soc.). *Recreations:* art, archæology, architecture, wine-bibbing. *Address:* Holly House, Burstow, Surrey RH6 9RG. *Clubs:* Cavalry and Guards, City Livery. *Died 18 Feb. 2001.*

COLE, (Claude Neville) David, CBE 1977; JP; Deputy Managing Director, International Thomson Organisation plc, 1985–86 (Joint Deputy Managing Director, 1980–84); Chairman of Trustees, Thomson Foundation, since 1986; *b* 4 June 1928; 2nd *s* of late W. J. Cole and of Mrs M. J. Cole; *m* 1951, Alma Gwlithyn Williams (*d* 1990); one *s* one *d* (and one *s* decd); *m* 1992, Mary Agnes Rose Symonds. *Educ:* Royal Masonic School; Harvard Business Sch. Journalist: Merthyr Express; South Wales Echo; Daily Graphic (Manchester); Daily Sketch (London); Daily Recorder; Empire News (Cardiff); Editor, Western Mail, Cardiff, 1956–59; Managing Director: Western Mail and Echo Ltd, 1959–67 (later Chm.); Newcastle Chronicle and Journal Ltd, 1967–69; Thomson Regional Newspapers Ltd: Asst Man. Dir and Editorial Dir, 1969–72; Man. Dir and Chief Exec., 1972–82; Chm., 1980–82; Chm. and Chief Exec., Thomson Information Services, 1982–84. Chairman: Rainbird Publishing Gp, 1980–85; Hamish Hamilton, 1982–85; Thomson Books, 1980–85; Janes Publishing Co., 1981–86; Celtic Press Ltd; Director: Thomson Organisation (Exec. Bd), 1973–80; Reuters Ltd, 1976–81. Chairman: Cole Cttee on Recruitment of Nurses in Wales, 1961–63; Working Party on Welsh Tourism, 1963–64; Barry Development Partnership, 1986–88; Civic Trust for Wales, 1986–96 (Pres., 1996–); Member: Aberfan Disaster Fund, 1966–67; Welsh Hospitals Bd, 1962–67. Director: Welsh Nat. Opera Co. Ltd, 1960–71; Welsh Develt Agency, 1987–90; Celtic Trees plc. Member: Council, Newspaper Soc., 1974–86 (Pres., 1982); Press Council, 1976–80; PIRA Council, 1984–86; Dir, Press Assoc. (Chm. 1976–77, 1977–78). Trustee, Reuters Ltd, 1983–. Chairman: Univ. of Wales Investment Cttee; Univ. of Wales Press, 1992–; Member: Court of Govs, Univ. of Wales, 1962–; Council, Univ. of Wales, 1962–; Governing Body, Cardiff Coll. of Music and Drama, 1963–67; Council, Welsh Nat. Sch. of Medicine, 1964–67; Council, Univ. of Wales Coll., Cardiff, 1988–92; Council, Cardiff New Theatre Trust, 1964–67; Welsh Nat. Theatre Cttee. Vice-Patron, Coun. for Wales, Brit. Empire and Commonwealth Games. Pres., Tenovus, 1963–. FCMI. Hon. LLD Wales, 1989. OStJ. *Publications:* This and Other Worlds (poems), 1975; Meeting Places and other poems, 1977; Mount of Angels (poems), 1978; The New Wales, 1991; Challenges to a Challenging Faith, 1995; The Wells of Life (poems), 1996. *Recreations:* two of the three R's. *Address:* Flat One, Gwentland, Marine Parade, Penarth, S Glam CF64 3BE. *T:* (029) 2070 3487. *Clubs:* East India, Devonshire, Sports and Public Schools; Cardiff and County (Cardiff). *Died 3 June 2003.*

COLE, Sir Colin; see Cole, Sir A. C.

COLE, David; see Cole, C. N. D.

COLE, Eileen Marie Lucy, CBE 1987; Chief Executive, Research International (Unilever Ltd), 1973–85 (in Rotterdam, 1973–77), retired 1985; *b* 22 April 1924; *d* of Arthur Walter Cole and Mary Agnes Boyd. *Educ:* grammar schs; Girton Coll., Cambridge (BA Hons Econ.). Joined Unilever as trainee, 1948; with associated cos and market res. div. of Unilever, 1948–60; Market Research Controller, Lever Bros Ltd, 1960–64; Research Bureau Ltd: Dir, 1964–67; Chm. and Man. Dir, 1967–72. Director: (non-exec.) Post Office, 1980–90; (part-time), LRT, 1984–88. Vice-Pres., 1979–, and Full Mem., UK Market Res. Soc. (Chm., 1977–79; Hon. Life Mem., 1985); Council Mem., Women in Management, 1971–; Mem., Careers Advisory Services: Cambridge Univ., 1968–75, 1979–83; Reading Univ., 1970–76, 1979–. FCMI; MInstD. Freeman: Marketors' Co., 1992; City of London, 1993. *Publications:* various in learned jls connected with market research. *Recreations:* gardening, cooking, reading, theatre. *Address:* Nicholas Farm, Lower Wield, Alresford, Hants SO24 9RX. *Died 31 March 2004.*

COLE, Humphrey John Douglas; Deputy Secretary and Chief Economic Adviser, Department of Transport, and Chief Economic Adviser, Department of the Environment, 1983–87; *b* 30 Jan. 1928; *s* of late G. D. H. Cole and Dame Margaret Cole, DBE; *m* 1955, Hilda Annette Robinson; two *s* one *d. Educ:* Winchester Coll.; Trinity Coll., Cambridge (BA 1948, MA 1953). Research, Oxford Inst. of Statistics, 1950–61; Head, Economic Indicators and Foreign Trade, OECD Statistics Div., 1961–66; Dept of Economic Affairs: Senior Economic Adviser (Regional), 1966–67; Asst Dir of Econs, 1967–69; Dir of Econs, Min. of Technology, 1969–70; Dir of Econs (Urban and Highways), DoE, 1970–72; Dir Gen., Econs and Resources, DoE, 1972–76; Chief Economic Advr, DoE and Dept of Transport, 1976–82. *Publications:* articles in Bulletin of Inst. of Statistics, 1950–61. *Recreation:* walking. *Address:* 3 The Mead, W13 8AZ. *T:* (020) 8997 8285. *Died 4 Jan. 2003.*

COLECLOUGH, Peter Cecil; Chairman, Howard Machinery Ltd, 1969–82 (Director, 1950–82); Director: NCR Ltd, 1971–87; National Westminster Bank (Chairman SE Region), 1976–86; *b* 5 March 1917; *s* of late Thomas James Coleclough and of Hilda Emma (*née* Ingram); *m* 1944, Pamela Beresford (*née* Rhodes); one *s* (and one *s* decd). *Educ:* Bradfield. Served War, Cheshire Yeomanry, 1939; commnd into Roy. Warwickshire Regt, 1940; served until 1946. Mem., FBI/CBI Council, 1962–72; Chairman: E Region, CBI, 1971–72; Meat and Livestock Commn, 1971–74. Leader, OECD/BIAC Investment Gp to Ceylon, 1968 and 1969. President: Agricl Engrs Assoc., 1971–72; Royal Warrant Holders Assoc., 1971–72. Chm., Appeals and Management Cttee, S Essex Medical Educn and Research Trust, 1969–75. *Recreation:* fishing. *Address:* Longlands Hall, Stonham Aspal, Stowmarket, Suffolk IP14 6AR. *T:* (01449) 711242. *Died 3 Feb. 2002.*

COLEGATE, Raymond, CBE 1982; FCIT, FRAeS; air transport consultant; *b* 31 Aug. 1927; *s* of Ernest William and Violet Colegate; *m* 1961, Sally Healy; one *s* one *d. Educ:* County Sch. for Boys, Gravesend; LSE (BA (Hons) History). Joined BoT, 1949; seconded to Central Statistical Office, 1952–53; Asst Private Sec. to President, 1955–56; seconded to Treasury, 1957–59; seconded to EFTA Secretariat, Geneva and Brussels, 1960–64; CRE Dept, BoT, 1964–67; Aviation Dept, BoT/DTI, 1967–72; Civil Aviation Authority: Mem., 1974–90; Head, Economic Policy and Licensing Div., 1972–75; Head, Economic Dept, 1975–77; Gp Dir, Econ. Services, later Economic Regulation, 1977–89; Man. Dir (Europe), Global Aviation Associates Ltd, 1991–95. FCIT 1983 (Vice-Pres., 1988–91); FRAeS 2000. *Publications:* articles. *Recreations:* music, travel, thinking. *Address:* 40 Lebanon Park, Twickenham TW1 3DG. *T:* (020) 8892 8272. *Died 10 July 2001.*

COLEMAN, Rt Rev. Peter Everard; Bishop Suffragan of Crediton, 1984–96; an Assistant Bishop, diocese of Bath and Wells, since 1996; *b* 28 Aug. 1928; *s* of Geoffrey Everard Coleman and Lilian Coleman; *m* 1960, HSH Princess Elisabeth-Donata Reuss; two *s* two *d. Educ:* Haileybury; King's Coll., London Univ. (LLB, AKC); Bristol Univ. (MLitt). Mil. Service, RHG and RA, 1947–49. Called to the Bar, Middle Temple, 1965. Ordained deacon, 1955, priest, 1956; Chaplain and Lectr, King's Coll., London, 1960–66; Vicar of St Paul's, Clifton, and Chaplain, Bristol Univ., 1966–71; Canon Residentiary and Dir of Training, Bristol, 1971–81; Archdeacon of Worcester, 1981–84. Clerical Member, Court of Arches, 1980–91; Mem. General Synod, 1974–81, 1990–95. Chm., British Trust for the Ecumenical Inst., Jerusalem, 1991–. Provost, Western Div., Woodard Corp., 1992– (Fellow, 1985–). OStJ 1993. Jt Editor, Theology, 1982–91. *Publications:* Experiments

with Prayer, 1961; A Christian Approach to Television, 1968; Christian Attitudes to Homosexuality, 1980; Gay Christians—a moral dilemma, 1989; The Ordination of Women to the Priesthood, 1990; *posthumous publication:* Christian Attitudes to Marriage: from ancient times to the third millennium, 2004. *Recreations:* film making, fishing. *Address:* Boxenwood Cottage, West Bagborough, Bishops Lydeard, Somerset TA4 3HQ. *T:* (01984) 618607. *Club:* Army and Navy. *Died 27 Dec. 2001.*

COLEMAN, Prof. Robert George Gilbert; Professor of Comparative Philology, University of Cambridge, 1985–97, then Emeritus; Fellow of Emmanuel College, Cambridge, since 1960; *b* 2 Oct. 1929; *s* of Thomas Lichfield Danks and Sheila Carr Bush; adopted 1934 by George Gilbert Coleman and Rosina Emily Warner; *m* 1st, 1958, Dorothy Gabe (marr. diss. 1992; she *d* 1992); one *s*; 2nd, 1992, Anne Thompson; two *s. Educ:* Rongotai and Wellington Colls, NZ; Victoria Univ. of Wellington (MA 1951); Emmanuel Coll., Cambridge (BA 1954; Burney Prize (shared), 1955; MA 1960). Lecturer: Dept of Humanity, Aberdeen Univ., 1955–60; Faculty of Classics, Cambridge Univ., 1960–85; Tutor, 1963–71, Librarian, 1980–85, Emmanuel Coll., Cambridge. *Publications:* A Commentary on Vergil's Eclogues, 1977; (ed) New Studies in Latin Linguistics, 1991; essays and papers in classical and philological jls. *Recreations:* music, conversation, exploring strange towns. *Address:* 7 Linton Road, Balsham, Cambridge CB1 6HA.
Died 18 Jan. 2001.

COLERIDGE, Lady (Marguerite) Georgina; Editor, Homes and Gardens, 1949–63; *b* 19 March 1916; *d* of 11th Marquess of Tweeddale; *m* 1941, Arthur Coleridge (*d* 1988), *yr s* of John Duke Coleridge; one *d. Educ:* home, abroad as a child. Freelance writer, Harpers Bazaar, etc, 1936; joined National Magazine Co.: Circulation Dept, 1937; Advertisement Dept, 1938; joined Country Life, 1945; Dir, Country Life Ltd, 1962–74; Dir, George Newnes Ltd, 1963–69; Publisher: Homes and Gardens; Woman's Journal, 1969–71; Ideal Home, 1970–71; Dir, Special Projects, IPC Women's Magazines, 1971–74; Consultant: IPC Women's Magazines, 1974–82; Public Relations Counsel Ltd, 1974–85 (Dir, 1978–85). Chairman: Inst. of Journalists (London Dist), 1954, Fellow 1970; Women's Press Club, 1959 (Pres., 1965–67); Mem., Internat. Assoc. of Women and Home Page Journalists, 1968–74; Associate, Women in Public Relations, 1972; Associate Mem., Ladies Jockeys Assoc. of GB, 1973; Founder Mem., Media Soc. Ltd (Inst. of Journalists Foundn), 1973–76. Member: Information Cttee, Brit. Nutrition Foundn, 1975–79; Information Cttee, RCP, 1977–81. Co-Founder, 1959, and Founder Vice-Pres., Women of the Year Lunch; Vice-Pres., Greater London Fund for the Blind, 1981; President: Dale Youth Club, N Kensington, 1978; Friends of Moorfields, 1981–92. Freeman, Stationers and Newspapermakers' Co., 1973. *Publications:* Grand Smashional Pointers (book of cartoons), 1934; I Know What I Like (clichés), 1959; That's Racing, 1978; many features for various jls. *Recreations:* racing, writing, cooking; nothing highbrow.
Died 25 March 2003.

COLES, His Honour Gerald James Kay, QC 1976; a Circuit Judge, 1985–2001; *b* 6 May 1933; *o s* of James William Coles and Jane Elizabeth Coles; *m* 1958, Kathleen Yolande, *e d* of Alfred John Hobson, FRCS, and Kathleen Elizabeth Hobson; three *s. Educ:* Coatham Sch., Redcar; Brasenose Coll., Oxford; Harvard Law Sch., Harvard Univ. Meritorious Award, Hastings Schol., Queen's Coll., Oxford, 1949; Akroyd Open Schol. 1950; BA 1954, BCL 1955, Oxon; Westengard Schol., Harvard Law Sch., 1955; LLM 1956. Called to Bar, Middle Temple, 1957; practised at Bar, London and NE Circuit, 1957–85; Prosecuting Counsel to Inland Revenue, 1971–76; a Recorder, 1972–85; Designated Family Judge, York, 1990–96; Resident Judge, Bradford Crown Court, 1992–2000. A Pres., Mental Health Review Tribunals, 1986–. Mem.,

Ethnic Minorities Adv. Cttee, Judicial Studies Bd, 1993–98. *Recreations:* Freemasonry (Provincial Grand Master and Grand Supt, Prov. of Yorks, N and E Ridings, 1995–), music, theatre, photography. *Address:* Redwood, Dean Lane, Hawksworth, Guiseley, Leeds, Yorks LS20 8NY. *Clubs:* Oxford and Cambridge; Bradford.

Died 3 Sept. 2002.

COLHOUN, Prof. John; Barker Professor of Cryptogamic Botany, University of Manchester, 1960–80, then Emeritus; Dean, Faculty of Science, 1974 and 1975, Pro-Vice-Chancellor, 1977–80, Univeristy of Manchester; *b* 15 May 1913; *yr s* of late James and Rebecca Colhoun, Castlederg, Co. Tyrone; *m* 1949, Margaret (*d* 1997), *e d* of late Prof. Gilbert Waterhouse, LittD, and Mary Elizabeth, *e d* of Sir Robert Woods; two *d* (and one *d* decd). *Educ:* Edwards Sch., Castlederg, Co. Tyrone; The Queen's Univ. of Belfast (BSc, MAgr); Imperial Coll. of Science, London Univ. (DIC; PhD, DSc); MSc Manchester. Min. of Agriculture for Northern Ireland: Research Asst, 1939–46; Senior Scientific Officer, 1946–50; Principal Scientific Officer, 1951–60; The Queen's Univ., Belfast: Asst Lecturer in Agricultural Botany, 1940–42; Asst Lectr 1942–45, Jun. Lectr 1945–46, Lectr 1946–54, Reader 1954–60, in Mycology and Plant Pathology. Warden of Queen's Chambers, 1942–49. FLS 1955. FIBiol 1963. President: British Mycological Soc., 1963; The Queen's Univ. Assoc., 1960–61; The Queen's Univ. Club, London, 1983–85. Chm., Fedn of British Plant Pathologists, 1968; Hon. Mem., British Soc. for Plant Pathology, 1989. Jt Editor, Jl of Phytopathology (Phytopath. Zeitschrift), 1973–91. *Publications:* Diseases of the Flax Plant, 1947; Club Root Disease of Crucifers caused by *Plasmodiophora brassicae* Woron, 1958; numerous papers in Annals of Applied Biology, Annals of Botany, Trans Brit. Mycological Soc., Nature, Phytopath. Z. *Address:* 12 Southdown Crescent, Cheadle Hulme, Cheshire SK8 6EQ. *T:* (0161) 485 2084. *Club:* Athenæum.

Died 5 Jan. 2002.

COLLINS, Dame Diana (Clavering), DBE 1999; *b* 13 Aug. 1917; *d* of Jan Lettsom Elliot and Florence Elizabeth Vere Elliot (*née* Fison); *m* 1939, Rev. Canon Lewis John Collins (*d* 1982); four *s*. *Educ:* Bedgebury Park Sch.; Lady Margaret Hall, Oxford. Trustee: Internat. Defence & Aid Fund for Southern Africa, 1982–91; Canon Collins Educn Trust for Southern Africa, 1991–. Hon. DLitt Bradford, 1996. *Publications:* Partners in Protest, 1992; Time and the Priestleys, 1994. *Recreations:* reading, gardening, concert and opera, theatre. *Address:* Mill House, Chappel Road, Mount Bures CO8 5AX. *T:* (01787) 227388.

Died 23 May 2003.

COLLINS, Henry Edward, CBE 1948; FREng; consulting mining engineer; *b* 4 Oct. 1903; *s* of James Collins; *m* 1934, Cecilia Harris (*d* 1975); no *c*. *Educ:* Rotherham Grammar Sch.; Univ. of Sheffield (MEng). Sen. Lectr in Mining, Univ. of Sheffield, 1935–38; Manager, Rossington Main Colliery, Doncaster, 1939–42; Agent, Markham Colliery, Doncaster, 1942–44; Chief Mining Agent, Doncaster Amalgamated Collieries Ltd, 1944–45; Dir Coal Production, CCG, 1945–47; British Chm., UK/US Coal Control Gp, Germany (later Combined Coal Control Gp), 1947–50; Production Dir, Durham Div., NCB, 1950–56; Dir-Gen. of Reconstruction, NCB, 1956–57; Board Mem. for Production, NCB, 1957–67; Consultant to NCB, 1967–69. Chairman: NCB Opencast Executive, 1961–67; NCB Brickworks Executive, 1962–67; Whittlesea Central Brick Co. Ltd, 1966–67; past Director: Omnia Concrete Sales Ltd; Bradley's (Concrete) Ltd; Powell Duffryn Technical Services Ltd; Inter-Continental Fuels Ltd. Chm., Field Res. Steering Cttee, Min. of Power, 1964–67; Member: Govtl Cttee on Coal Derivatives, 1959–60; Minister of Power's Adv. Council on Research and Develt, 1963–67; Min. of Power Nat. Jt Pneumoconiosis Cttee, 1964–67; Safety in Mines (Adv.) Bd; Mining Qualifications Bd, 1962–69. Pres., Inst. of

Mining Engineers, 1962, Hon. Fellow, 1988. FREng (FEng 1976). *Publications:* Mining Memories and Musings: the autobiography of a mining engineer, 1985; numerous papers on mining engineering subjects. *Address:* St Mary's Nursing Home, Ednaston, Brailsford, Derby DE6 3BA.

Died 12 Feb. 2003.

COLLUM, Sir Hugh (Robert), Kt 2004; FCA; Chairman, British Nuclear Fuels PLC, 1999–2004; *b* 29 June 1940; *s* of late Robert Archibald Hugh Collum and Marie Vivien Collum (*née* Skinner); *m* 1965, Elizabeth Noel Stewart; two *d*. *Educ:* Eton. FCA 1964. With Coopers & Lybrand, 1959–64; Dir, Plymouth Breweries Ltd and Courage Western, 1965–72; Financial Director: Courage Ltd, 1973–81; Cadbury Schweppes PLC, 1981–86; Beecham Gp, 1987–89; Exec. Vice Pres. and Chief Financial Officer, SmithKline Beecham, 1989–98. Non-executive Director: Imperial Tobacco, 1978–81; Sedgwick Gp, 1987–92; M & G Gp, 1992–98; Ladbroke Gp, 1994–96; Safeway, 1997–2004; Whitehead Mann Gp, 1997–2005; Invensys, 1998–2002; Celltech Gp, 1999–2003; S African Breweries, 1999–2002; Chm., Chiroscience Gp, 1998–99. Mem. Adv. Bd, Barclays Private Bank, 2001–. Chm., Hundred Gp of Finance Dirs, 1990–92. Member: Cadbury Cttee on Financial Aspects of Corporate Governance, 1991–95; CBI President's Cttee, 1999–2004. Japan 21 Century Gp, 1999–2004. Liveryman, Co. of Wax Chandlers, 1963–; Mem., Ct of Assts, Co. of Chartered Accountants, 1992– (Master, 2004-05). Founding Societies Award, 2002. *Recreations:* sport, opera, travel, shooting. *Address:* Clinton Lodge, Fletching, E Sussex TN22 3ST. *T:* (01825) 722952. *Clubs:* Boodle's, MCC.

Died 29 Aug. 2005.

COLTHURST, Sir Richard La Touche, 9th Bt *cr* 1744, of Ardrum, co. Cork; *b* 14 Aug. 1928; *er s* of Sir Richard St John Jefferyes Colthurst, 8th Bt, and Denys Maida Hanmer West (*d* 1966), *e d* of Augustus William West; *S* father, 1955; *m* 1953, Janet Georgina, *d* of L. A. Wilson-Wright, Coolcarrigan, Co. Kildare; three *s* one *d*. *Educ:* Harrow; Peterhouse, Cambridge (BA 1952, MA 1956). Host and Organiser, Blarney Castle Internat. Horse Trials, 1992– (Competition Complet Internat.). Mem., Internat. Dendrology Soc. Liveryman, Grocers' Co. *Recreations:* forestry, cricket, tennis, swimming. *Heir: s* Charles St John Colthurst [*b* 21 May 1955; *m* 1987, Nora Mary, *d* of Mortimer Kelleher, Dooniskey, Lissarda, Co. Cork; one *s* three *d*]. *Address:* Blarney Castle, Co. Cork, Eire; Ardrum, Inniscarra, Co. Cork, Eire. *Clubs:* MCC, I Zingari, Free Foresters; Hawks, Pitt (Cambridge).

Died 22 March 2003.

COLTMAN, Sir (Arthur) Leycester (Scott), KBE 1997; CMG 1993; HM Diplomatic Service, retired; Ambassador to Colombia, 1994–98; *b* 24 May 1938; *s* of late Arthur Cranfield Coltman and Vera Vaid; *m* 1969, Maria Piedad Josefina Cantos Aberasturi; two *s* one *d*. *Educ:* Rugby School; Magdalene Coll., Cambridge. Foreign Office, 1961–62; Third Secretary, British Embassy, Copenhagen, 1963–64; Second Secretary, Cairo 1964–65, Madrid 1966–69; Manchester Business School, 1969–70; Foreign Office, 1970–74; Commercial Secretary, Brasilia, 1974–77; Foreign Office, 1977–79; Counsellor, Mexico City, 1979–83; Counsellor and Hd of Chancery, Brussels, 1983–87; Head: Mexico and Central America Dept, 1987–90; Latin America Dept, 1990; Ambassador to Cuba, 1991–94. *Recreations:* squash, chess, bridge, music. *Address:* Flat 4, 37 de Vere Gardens, W8 5AW.

Died 31 March 2002.

COLVILLE, Lady Margaret, CVO 1994; an Extra Woman of the Bedchamber to HM Queen Elizabeth the Queen Mother, 1990–2002; *b* 20 July 1918; *d* of 4th Earl of Ellesmere, MVO; *m* 1948, Sir John Rupert Colville, CB, CVO (*d* 1987); two *s* one *d*. Served War of 1939–45 in ATS (Junior Subaltern). Lady in Waiting to the Princess Elizabeth, Duchess of Edinburgh, 1946–49. *Address:* The Close, Broughton, near Stockbridge, Hants SO20 8AA. *T:* (01794) 301331.

Died 3 May 2004.

COLVIN, John Horace Ragnar, CMG 1968; HM Diplomatic Service, retired; *b* Tokyo, 18 June 1922; *s* of late Adm. Sir Ragnar Colvin, KBE, CB and Lady Colvin; *m* 1st, 1948, Elizabeth Anne Manifold (marr. diss., 1963); one *s* one *d*; 2nd, 1967, Moranna Sibyl de Lerisson Cazenove; one *s* one *d*. *Educ:* RNC Dartmouth; University of London. Royal Navy, 1935–51. Joined HM Diplomatic Service, 1951; HM Embassies, Oslo, 1951–53 and Vienna, 1953–55; British High Commn, Kuala Lumpur, 1958–61; HM Consul-General, Hanoi, 1965–67; Ambassador to People's Republic of Mongolia, 1971–74; HM Embassy, Washington, 1977–80. Dir for Internat. Relations, Chase Manhattan Bank, 1980–86. Hon. Vis. Fellow, Sch. of E European Studies, 1995–. *Publications:* Twice Around the World, 1991; Not Ordinary Men, 1994; Volcano Under Snow, 1996; Lions of Judah, 1997; Nomonhan, 1999; Decisive Battles, 2003; contribs to British and US jls. *Address:* 12A Evelyn Mansions, Carlisle Place, SW1P 1NH. *Clubs:* Brooks's, Beefsteak. *Died 4 Oct. 2003.*

COLYER-FERGUSSON, Sir James Herbert Hamilton, 4th Bt *cr* 1866; *b* 10 Jan. 1917; *s* of Max Christian Hamilton Colyer-Fergusson (*d* on active service, 1940) and Edith Jane (*d* 1936), singer, *d* of late William White Miller, Portage la Prairie, Manitoba; *S* grandfather, 1951. *Educ:* Harrow; Balliol Coll., Oxford (BA 1939; MA 1945). Formerly Capt., The Buffs; served War of 1939–45 (prisoner-of-war, 1940). Entered service of former Great Western Railway Traffic Dept, 1947, later Operating Dept of the Western Region of British Rlys. Personal Asst to Chm. of British Transport Commission, 1957; Passenger Officer in SE Division of Southern Region, BR, 1961; Parly and Public Correspondent, BRB, 1967; Deputy to Curator of Historical Relics, BRB, 1968. *Heir:* none. *Address:* 61 Onslow Square, SW7 3LS. *Club:* Naval and Military. *Died 9 Jan. 2004 (ext).*

CONCANNON, Rt Hon. John Dennis, (Don), PC 1978; *b* 16 May 1930; *m* 1953, Iris May Wilson; two *s* two *d*. *Educ:* Rossington Sec. Sch. Coldstream Guards, 1947–53; Mem. Nat. Union of Mineworkers, 1953–66; Branch Official, 1960–65. Mem., Mansfield Town Council, 1962–66. MP (Lab) Mansfield, 1966–87. Asst Govt Whip, 1968–70; Opposition Whip, 1970–74; Vice-Chamberlain, HM Household, 1974; Parly Under-Sec. of State, NI Office, 1974–76; Minister of State, NI Office, 1976–79; Opposition Spokesman for Defence, 1979–80, for NI, 1980–83. Mem., Commonwealth War Graves Commn, 1986–94. *Recreations:* cricket, basket-ball. *Address:* 69 Skegby Lane, Mansfield, Notts NG19 6QS. *T:* (01623) 627235. *Died 14 Dec. 2003.*

CONNELL, Charles Percy; Puisne Judge, Kenya Colony, 1951–64; *b* 1 Oct. 1902; *s* of C. R. Connell, barrister-at-law and K. Adlard; *m* 1946, Mary O'Rourke (*d* 2001). *Educ:* Charterhouse; New Coll., Oxford (Hons, Jurisprudence). Called to the Bar, Lincoln's Inn, 1927. Joined Kenya Judicial Service, 1938 (Resident Magistrate). Served War of 1939–45 (8th Army Clasp and war medals); commnd King's African Rifles, 1941; British Military Administration (Legal and Judicial), Eritrea and Tripolitania, 1942–46. Acting Puisne Judge, Kenya, 1950; retired 1964. *Recreations:* tennis, cricket, trout fishing. *Address:* c/o Isle of Man Bank, Bowring Road, Ramsey, Isle of Man. *Died 29 Oct. 2002.*

CONNELL, Dame Ninette; *see* de Valois, Dame N.

CONSTANTINE OF STANMORE, Baron *cr* 1981 (Life Peer), of Stanmore in Greater London; **Theodore Constantine,** Kt 1964; CBE 1956; AE 1945; DL; *b* 15 March 1910; *er s* of Leonard and Fanny Louise Constantine; *m* 1935, Sylvia Mary (*d* 1990), *y d* of Wallace Henry Legge-Pointing; one *s* (one *d* decd). *Educ:* Acton Coll. Personal Asst to Chm. of public company, 1926–28; Executive in industry, 1928–38; Managing Dir of public company subsidiary, 1938–39. Served War of 1939–45, AAF (AEA 1945). Dir of Industrial Holding Company,

1956–59; Chm. of Public Companies, 1959–86. Organisational work for Conservative Party as Constituency Chm., Area Chm., Mem. Nat. Exec. Cttee, Policy Cttee, Nat. Advisory Cttee on Publicity. Chm., Nat. Union Cons. and Unionist Assocs, 1967–68, Pres. 1980. Trustee, Sir John Wolstenholme Charity; Master, Worshipful Co. of Coachmakers, 1975; Freeman of City of London, 1949. High Sheriff of Greater London, 1967; DL Greater London, 1967–85. *Recreations:* watching motor racing, reading, walking. *Address:* House of Lords, SW1A 0PW. *Club:* Carlton. *Died 13 Feb. 2004.*

COOK, Sir Alan (Hugh), Kt 1988; FRS 1969; Master of Selwyn College, Cambridge University, 1983–93; *b* 2 Dec. 1922; *s* of late Reginald Thomas Cook, OBE, and of Ethel Cook; *m* 1948, Isabell Weir Adamson; one *s* one *d*. *Educ:* Westcliff High Sch. for Boys; Corpus Christi Coll. Cambridge. MA, PhD, ScD. Admty Signal Estabt, 1943–46; Research Student, then Res. Asst, Dept of Geodesy and Geophysics, Cambridge, 1946–51; Metrology Div., Nat. Physical Laboratory, Teddington, 1952; Vis. Fellow, Jt Inst. for Laboratory Astrophysics, Boulder, Colorado, 1965–66; Supt, Standards (subseq. Quantum Metrology) Div., Nat. Physical Laboratory, 1966–69; Prof. of Geophysics, Univ. of Edinburgh, 1969–72; Cambridge University: Jacksonian Prof. of Natural Philosophy, 1972–90; Fellow, King's Coll., 1972–83; Head of Dept of Physics, 1979–84. Vis. Prof. and Green Schol., Univ. of Calif. at Los Angeles, Berkeley and San Diego, 1981–82; Vis. Fellow, Center of Theol Inquiry, Princeton, 1993. Member: NERC, 1974–80; SERC, 1984–88. Chm., Press Syndicate, Cambridge Univ. Press, 1988–93. FInstP; FRSE 1970; Foreign Fellow, Accad. Naz. dei Lincei, 1971. Pres., RAS, 1977–79. Fellow, Explorers' Club, NY, 1980. Humphry Davy Lectr, Royal Soc., 1994. C. V. Boys Prize, 1967, Charles Chree Medal and Prize, 1993, Inst. of Physics. *Publications:* Gravity and the Earth, 1969; Global Geophysics, 1970; Interference of Electromagnetic Waves, 1971; Physics of the Earth and Planets, 1973; Celestial Masers, 1977; Interiors of the Planets, 1980; The Motion of the Moon, 1988; Gravitational Experiments in the Laboratory, 1993; Observational Foundations of Physics, 1994; Edmond Halley: charting the heavens and the seas, 1998; many contribs learned jls on gravity, artificial satellites, precise measurement, fundamental constants of physics and astronomy, history of science. *Recreations:* amateur theatre, travel, painting, gardening. *Address:* 8 Wootton Way, Cambridge CB3 9LX. *T:* (01223) 356887. *Died 23 July 2004.*

COOK, Brian Hartley K.; *see* Kemball-Cook.

COOK, Charles Alfred George, MC 1945; GM 1945; FRCS; Consultant Ophthalmic Surgeon: Guy's Hospital, 1954–73; Moorfields Eye Hospital, 1956–73; Teacher of Ophthalmology, University of London (Guy's Hospital and Institute of Ophthalmology), 1955–73; *b* 20 Aug. 1913; *s* of late Charles F. Cook and Beatrice Grist; *m* 1939, Edna Constance Dobson; one *s* one *d*. *Educ:* St Edward's Sch., Oxford; Guy's Hospital. MRCS, LRCP 1939; DOMS (Eng.), 1946; FRCS 1950. Capt. and Major RAMC, 1939–45. Moorfields Eye Hospital: Clinical Asst, 1946–47; Ho. Surg., 1948–49; Sen. Resident Officer, 1950; Chief Clin. Asst, 1951–55. Sen. Registrar, Eye Dept, Guy's Hospital, 1951–55; Moorfields Research Fellow, Inst. of Ophthalmology, 1951–58; Ophthalmic Surg., West Middlesex Hospital, 1954–56. Mem., Court of Examrs, RCS; Examr for DOMS, RCP and RCS; Examr Brit. Orthoptic Board; Sec., Ophthalmological Soc. of UK, 1956–57. Member: Cttee of Management, Inst. of Ophthalmology, 1960–63 (Vice-Dean of Inst., 1959–62); Cttee of Management, London Refraction Hosp., 1983–88; Council, Coll. of Opth. Opticians, 1979–83 (Hon. Fellow 1982); Bd of Governors, Faculty of Dispensing Opticians, 1980–84. Governor: Royal Nat. Coll. for Blind, 1967–80; Moorfields Eye Hosp., 1962–65. Hon. DSc Aston, 1983. Renter Warden, Upper Warden, then Master, Worshipful Co. of Spectacle Makers, 1975–81. Freeman, City of London. *Publications:* (ed) S. Duke Elder, Embryology, vol. 3, 1963; (contrib.) Payling, Wright and Symers, Systematic Pathology, 1966; (jt) May and Worth, Diseases of the Eye, 1968; articles in Brit. Jl of Ophthalmology, Trans Ophthalmological Soc., Jl of Pathology and other Med. Jls. *Recreations:* swimming, reading; an interest in all outdoor recreations. *Address:* 13 Clarence Terrace, Regent's Park, NW1 4RD. *T:* (020) 7723 5111. *Clubs:* Athenæum, Garrick.

Died 24 Dec. 2003.

COOK, Frank Patrick, (Pat); Member, Commission for Local Administration in England and first Local Ombudsman for the North and North Midlands, 1974–85; *b* 28 March 1920; *o c* of Frank Cook, FRCS, FRCOG and Edith Harriet (*née* Reid); *m* 1st, 1945, Rosemary Eason (marr. diss. 1975); two *s* one *d*; 2nd, 1975, Margaret Rodgers, 2nd *d* of Dr J. W. Rodgers, PhD; one *s*. *Educ:* Rugby; Trinity Hall, Cambridge (Open Schol.); LSE (Personnel Management); ASC (Session 16). Royal Marines, 1939–46 (Major; despatches). Courtaulds Ltd, 1946–56; Nat. Coal Board, 1956–61; Venesta Ltd, 1961–64 (Dir, 1963); Principal, British Transport Staff Coll., 1964–69; First Chief Exec., English Tourist Board, 1970–74. Chm., Microtest Research Ltd, 1982–87; Dir and Sec., Mellory Ltd, 1993–99. Indep. Mem., Council, FIMBRA, 1988–90; a Vice President: IPM, 1965–67; RCN, 1973–95; Member: Nat. Nursing Staff Cttee, 1967–72; Brighton and Lewes HMC, 1972–74; Ombudsman Adv. Bd, Internat. Bar Assoc., 1975–85; Exec. Cttee, Fawcett Soc., 1975–77; Council, Univ. of York, 1979–85; Merchant Taylors' Co. of York, 1981–; N Yorks FPC, 1985–87. Conducted inquiry into provision for health care in St Helens and Knowsley, 1990. Governor: Martin House Hospice for Children, 1984–86; Bootham and The Mount Quaker Schs, 1987–89. Hon. LLD Hull, 1986. *Publications:* Shift Work, 1954; Ombudsman (autobiog.), 1981; articles on personnel management. *Address:* Mellory, Old Cleeve, near Minehead, Somerset TA24 6HS. *T:* (01984) 640176.

Died 8 July 2004.

COOK, Cdre Henry Home, RN; Vice-President, Chiltern Society, since 1994 (Chairman, 1988–93); Director of Public Relations, Scientific Exploration Society, 1984–88; *b* 24 Jan. 1918; *o s* of George Home Cook, Edinburgh; *m* 1943, Theffania, *yr d* of A. P. Saunders, Gerrards Cross; two *s* two *d*. *Educ:* St Lawrence Coll., Ramsgate; Pangbourne College. Entered RN as Paymaster Cadet, 1936; Comdr 1955; Captain 1963; Cdre 1970. Naval Sec. to Vice-Adm. Sir Guy Sayer, 1953–59; Sqdn Supply Officer, 1st S/m Sqdn, 1959; Comdr, RNC Greenwich, 1961; Naval Attaché, Ankara, 1964; Dir of Public Relations (RN), 1966; Defence Adviser to British High Comr, and Head of British Defence Liaison Staff, Ottawa, 1970–72; retired, 1973. ADC to HM the Queen, 1971–72. A Gen. Comr of Income Tax, 1983–92. Dir, Ellerman City Liners Ltd, 1973–80. Pres., Anchorites, 1978; Vice-Pres., Inst. of Admin. Management, 1983–. FInstAM 1973 (Chm., 1982). DipCAM 1975. *Recreations:* fencing, swimming, sailing. *Address:* Ramblers Cottage, Layters Green, Chalfont St Peter, Bucks SL9 8TH. *T:* (01753) 883724. *Club:* Army and Navy.

Died 9 Sept. 2003.

COOK, Joseph, CChem, FRSC; management consultant; *b* 7 April 1917; *y s* of Joseph Cook, MBE, JP, and Jane Cook (*née* Adams), Cumberland; *m* 1950, Betty (decd), *d* of James and Elizabeth Barlow, Standish, Lancs; two *d*. *Educ:* Whitehaven Grammar Sch.; Univ. of Liverpool (BSc, DipEd). RAF, 1939–40. Posts in Ministries of Supply, Aviation, Technology and Defence, 1941–59; Dir, ROF Burghfield, 1959–65; Gp Dir, Ammunition Factories, 1966; Dir Gen. (Prodn) ROF, 1966–74; Man. Dir, Millbank Tech. Services Ordnance Ltd, 1974–77 (on secondment from MoD). *Recreations:* gardening, golf. *Address:* Abbots-wood, Bramley Road, Pamber End, near

Basingstoke, Hants RG26 5QP. *T:* (01256) 850304.

Died 20 Oct. 2004.

COOK, Pat; *see* Cook, F. P.

COOK, Brig. Richard Arthur, CBE 1961; Brigadier General Staff, Southern Command, 1958–61, retired; *b* 26 May 1908; *s* of Capt. W. C. Cook; *m* 1940, Sheila Mary Ostell Prosser (*d* 2000); two *s*. *Educ:* St Paul's Sch.; RMA, Woolwich. Commissioned, Royal Artillery, 1928; posted to India, 1933; served War of 1939–45 in India and Burma: Staff Coll., 1941; Regimental Comd, 1943; Joint Services Staff Coll., 1947; Col, 1948; Col Administrative Plans, GHQ, MELF, 1948–51; CRA (Brig.) 16th Airborne Div., 1954–56; NATO Defence Coll., 1957. *Address:* 3 Meadow Court, Whiteparish, Wilts SP5 2SE. *T:* (01794) 884409. *Club:* Army and Navy.

Died 23 Sept. 2001.

COOK, Rt Hon. Robert Finlayson, (Rt Hon. Robin); PC 1996; MP (Lab) Livingston, since 1983 (Edinburgh Central, Feb. 1974–1983); Leader of the House of Commons and President of the Council, 2001–03; *b* 28 Feb. 1946; *s* of late Peter Cook, headmaster and Christina Cook (*née* Lynch); *m* 1969, Margaret K. Whitmore (marr. diss. 1998), medical consultant; two *s*; *m* 1998, Gaynor Regan. *Educ:* Aberdeen Grammar Sch.; Univ. of Edinburgh (MA Hons English Lit). Tutor-Organiser with WEA, 1970–74. Chm., Scottish Assoc. of Labour Student Organisations, 1966–67; Sec., Edinburgh City Labour Party, 1970–72; Mem., Edinburgh Corporation, 1971–74, Chm. Housing Cttee, 1973–74. An Opposition Treasury spokesman, 1980–83; opposition front bench spokesman on: European and community affairs, 1983–84; trade, 1986–87; health, 1987–92; trade and industry, 1992–94; foreign and commonwealth affairs, 1994–97; Sec. of State for Foreign and Commonwealth Affairs, 1997–2001. Labour's Campaigns Co-ordinator, 1984–86; Chm., Labour Party, 1996–97. Mem., Tribune Group. *Publication:* Point of Departure, 2003. *Recreations:* eating, reading, talking. *Address:* c/o House of Commons, SW1A 0AA. *T:* (020) 7219 4040.

Died 6 Aug. 2005.

COOK, Rt Hon. Robin; *see* Cook, Rt Hon. Robert F.

COOKE, (Alfred) Alistair, Hon. KBE 1973; journalist and broadcaster; *b* 20 Nov. 1908; *s* of Samuel Cooke and Mary Elizabeth Byrne; US citizen, 1941; *m* 1st, 1934, Ruth Emerson; one *s*; 2nd, 1946, Jane White Hawkes; one *d*. *Educ:* Blackpool Grammar Sch.; Jesus Coll., Cambridge (Scholar; Hon. Fellow, 1986); Yale Univ.; Harvard. Founded Cambridge University Mummers, 1928; First Class, English Tripos, 1929; Second Class, 1930. Editor, The Granta, 1931; Commonwealth Fund Fellow, 1932–34. BBC Film Critic, 1934–37; London Correspondent for NBC, 1936–37; Commentator on American Affairs for BBC, 1938–2004; broadcast American Letter, subseq. Letter from America, BBC, 1946–2004; Special Correspondent on American Affairs, The London Times, 1938–40; American Feature Writer, The Daily Herald, 1941–43; UN Correspondent of the Manchester Guardian (which changed name to Guardian, 1959), 1945–48; Chief Correspondent in US of The Guardian, 1948–72. Master of ceremonies: Ford Foundation's television programme, Omnibus, 1952–61; UN television programme, International Zone, 1961–67; Masterpiece Theatre, 1971–92. Wrote and narrated, America: a personal history of the United States, BBC TV, 1972–73 (Peabody Award for meritorious services to broadcasting, 1972; Writers' Guild of GB award for best documentary of 1972; Dimbleby Award, Soc. of Film and TV Arts, 1973; four Emmy awards of (US) Nat. Acad. of TV Arts and Sciences, 1973). Hon. LLD: Edinburgh, 1969; Manchester, 1973; Hon. LittD: St Andrews, 1975; Cantab, 1988. Peabody Award for internat. reporting, 1952 and 1983; Benjamin Franklin Medal, RSA, 1973; Howland Medal, Yale Univ., 1977. *Publications:* (ed) Garbo and the Night Watchmen, 1937, repr. 1972; Douglas Fairbanks: The Making of a Screen Character,

1940; A Generation on Trial: USA v Alger Hiss, 1950; Letters from America, 1951; Christmas Eve, 1952; A Commencement Address, 1954; (ed) The Vintage Mencken, 1955; Around the World in Fifty Years, 1966; Talk about America, 1968; Alistair Cooke's America, 1973, repr. 2002; Six Men, 1977, repr. 1995; The Americans: fifty letters from America on our life and times, 1979; (with Robert Cameron) Above London, 1980; Masterpieces, 1982; The Patient has the Floor, 1986; America Observed, 1988; Fun & Games with Alistair Cooke, 1994; Memories of the Great and the Good, 1999. *Recreations:* watching tennis, medical history, music, golf. *Address:* 1150 Fifth Avenue, New York City, NY 10128, USA; Nassau Point, Cutchogue, Long Island, NY, USA. *Clubs:* Lotos, Links (New York); San Francisco Golf.
Died 30 March 2004.

COOKE, Sir Charles Fletcher F.; *see* Fletcher-Cooke.

COOKE, Randle Henry, LVO 1971; Chairman, Randle Cooke and Associates, Recruitment Consultants, since 1992 (Managing Director, 1987–92); *b* 26 April 1930; *o s* of late Col H. R. V. Cooke, Dalicote Hall, Bridgnorth, Salop and Mrs E. F. K. Cooke, Brodawel, Tremeirchion, N Wales; *m* 1961, Clare, *d* of late C. J. M. Bennett, CBE; one *s* one *d*. *Educ:* Heatherdown, Ascot; Eton College. 2nd Lieut, 8th King's Royal Irish Hussars, 1949; served Korea, 1950–53 with Regt and USAF (POW); ADC to GOC 7th Armoured Div., 1955; Regimental Adjt, 1957; Instructor, RMA Sandhurst, 1960; Sqdn Comdr, QRIH, Malaya, Borneo and Germany, 1963; GSO3 (SD), HQ 1st Div., 1965. Equerry to the Duke of Edinburgh, 1968–71; Private Sec. to Lord Mayor of London, 1972–74. Dir, Personnel and Administration, Alginate Industries plc, 1974–78; Managing Director: ARA International Ltd, 1984–86; Mervyn Hughes International Ltd, 1986–87. Dep. Dir, Treasurers' Dept, Cons. Central Office, 1992–95; Fund-Raising Dir, Royal Botanic Gdns, Kew, 1995–97. Freeman of City of London, 1971. *Recreations:* most things to do with water. *Address:* Chess House, Green Lane, Prestwood, Great Missenden, Bucks HP16 0QA. *T:* (01494) 862147, *Fax:* (01494) 863632. *Clubs:* Cavalry and Guards; Caterpillar. *Died 27 April 2002.*

COOKE, Roy, MA; JP; Director of Coventry School Foundation, 1977–92, retired; *b* Manchester, 6 May 1930; *s* of Reginald Herbert Cooke and Alice Cooke; *m* 1957, Claire Marion Medlicott Woodward, *d* of Lt-Col C. S. Woodward, CBE, JP, DL and Irene Anne Woodward, Glamorgan; three *s*. *Educ:* Manchester Grammar Sch. (schol.); Trinity Coll., Oxford (schol.; BA 1951; MA 1955; DipEd). Army service, 1951–54; commnd RAEC; Staff Officer in Germany (Captain, actg Major). Assistant Master: Gillingham Grammar Sch., Kent, 1955–56; Woking Grammar Sch., Surrey, 1956–58; Manchester Grammar Sch., 1958–64; Head of For. Langs, Stockport Sch., 1964–68; Headmaster: Gravesend Sch. for Boys, 1968–74; King Henry VIII Sch., Coventry, 1974–77. JP Kent, 1972, W Midlands, 1976. *Recreations:* photography, travel, reading, music. *Address:* 10 Stivichall Croft, Coventry CV3 6GN. *Died 1 Aug. 2004.*

COOPER, Andrew Ramsden, CBE 1965; FREng, FIEE; industrial consultant, since 1966; Member for Operations and Personnel, Central Electricity Generating Board, 1957–66; *b* 1 Oct. 1902; *s* of Mary and William Cooper, Rotherham, Yorks; *m* 1922, Alice Robinson (marr. diss. 1982); one *s* two *d*; *m* 1982, Helen Louise Gordon (*d* 1997). *Educ:* Rotherham Grammar Sch.; Sheffield Univ. AssocEng; SFInstE. FIEE; FREng (FEng 1977). Colliery Engineer, Yorks and Kent, 1918–28; Chief Electrical Engineer, Pearson & Dorman Long, 1928; Personal Asst to G. A. Mower, London, 1934; joined Central Electricity Board Operation Dept as Chief of Control, NW England and N Wales, 1935; transf. to HQ, 1937; during War, evacuated to Surrey (formed Surrey Social Council for helping troops; introd. self-educn and entertainment for isolated army units; granted uniform rank of Capt.); Operation Engineeer, SE and E England, 1942; Chief Operation Engineer to Central Electricity Board, 1944; Controller, Merseyside and N Wales Div. (Central Electricity Authority), 1948–52; NW Div., 1952–54; N West, Merseyside and N Wales Reg., 1954–57; Bd Mem., Ops, Grid Control and Personnel, CEGB, 1957–66. Mem., GB-USSR Cttee, 1967–91. Internat. Pres., CIGRE, 1966–72. Inventor, ARCAID Deaf/Blind Conversation Machine. Faraday Lectr, 1952–53; Bernard Price Meml Lects, S African Inst. of Electr. Engrg, 1970. Mem., BBC Debating Soc., Manchester, 1952–55; Founder, Nasmyth Club, London and Manchester, 1936. Hon. Mem., Batti-Wallahs Assoc. Pres. Electricity Industries Benevolent Assoc., 1964–66; Companion, EEIBA, 1994. Hon. Life FIEEE. Hon. MEng Liverpool Univ., 1954. Meritorious Service Award, Power Engrg Soc. of America, 1972; Willans Medal, IEE, 1952; Thornton Medal, AMEME, 1961; Donor, Power/Life Award, Power Engrg Soc., IEEE, 1970; Centennial Award and Plaque, IEEE, 1984. *Publications: include:* (paper) Load Dispatching, with Special Reference to the British Grid System (John Hopkinson Award, 1948, Willans Medal, 1952, IEE); The Human Approach to Management, 1989, 3rd edn 1994. *Recreations:* golf, art, music, writing, broadcasting, lecturing. *Address:* Victoria Nursing Home, 81 Dyke Road Avenue, Hove, Sussex BN3 6DA. *Clubs:* Savile, Energy Industries (Hon. Mem.), 25 (Hon. Mem.), Dynamicables (Hon. Mem.). *Died 21 Dec. 2002.*

COOPER, Rt Hon. Sir Frank, GCB 1979 (KCB 1974; CB 1970); CMG 1961; PC 1983; Chairman, High Integrity Systems Ltd, 1986–95; Director: Babcock International Group, 1983–90; Morgan Crucible, 1983–94; N. M. Rothschild & Sons, 1983–96; *b* 2 Dec. 1922; *s* of late V. H. Cooper, Fairfield, Manchester; *m* 1948, Peggie, *d* of F. J. Claxton; two *s* one *d* (and one *s* decd). *Educ:* Manchester Grammar Sch.; Pembroke Coll., Oxford (Hon. Fellow, 1976). Served War of 1939–45, Pilot, RAF, 1941–46. Asst Principal, Air Ministry, 1948; Private Secretary: to Parly Under-Sec. of State for Air, 1949–51; to Permanent Under-Sec. of State for Air, 1951–53; to Chief of Air Staff, 1953–55; Asst Sec., Head of the Air Staff, Secretariat, 1955–60; Dir of Accounts, Air Ministry, 1961–62; Asst Under-Sec. of State, Air Min., 1962–64, Min. of Defence, 1964–68; Dep. Under-Sec. of State, Min. of Defence, 1968–70; Dep. Sec., CSD, 1970–73; Permanent Under-Secretary of State: NI Office, 1973–76; MoD, 1976–82. Hon. Consultant, RUSI, 1982–. Chm., United Scientific Hldgs, 1985–89. Mem., Adv. Council on Public Records, 1989–92. Chm., Inst. of Contemp. British Hist., 1986–92. Member Council: KCL, 1981–89; Imperial Coll., 1983–96 (Chm., 1988–96); Chm. Delegacy, King's Coll. Med. and Dental Sch., 1983–89; Visitor, Univ. of Loughborough, 1988–; Chm., Liddell Hart Trustees, 1987–; Gov., Cranbrook Sch., 1982–92 (Chm., 1984–92). FKC 1987; FIC 1988. *Recreation:* walking. *Address:* Apartment 2, Oaklands, Kemnal Road, Chislehurst, Kent BR7 6LZ. *T:* (020) 8467 1263. *Clubs:* Athenæum, Royal Air Force.
Died 26 Jan. 2002.

COOPER, George Edward; Chairman, North Thames Gas Region (formerly North Thames Gas Board), 1970–78; Part-time Member, British Gas Corporation, 1973–78; *b* 25 Jan. 1915; *s* of H. E. Cooper and R. A. Jones, Wolverhampton; *m* 1941, Dorothy Anne Robinson (*d* 1993); one *s*. *Educ:* Wolverhampton Municipal Grammar Sch. Wolverhampton and Walsall Corp., 1933–40. Served War, 1940–45, with RA in Middle East (Bimbashi Sudan Defence Force), Captain. Qualified as Accountant, Inst. of Municipal Treasurers and Accountants (later Chartered Inst. of Public Accountants), 1947; Hemel Hempstead Development Corp., 1948–50; W Midlands Gas Bd (finally Dep. Chm.), 1950–70. IPFA (FIMTA 1965); CIGEM (CIGasE 1968). Officer OStJ 1976. *Recreations:* photography, geology, golf. *Club:* City Livery. *Died Aug. 2004.*

COOPER, Joseph Elliott Needham, OBE 1982; pianist and broadcaster; *b* 7 Oct. 1912; *s* of Wilfrid Needham and Elsie Goodacre Cooper; *m* 1st, 1947, Jean (*d* 1973), *d* of late Sir Louis Greig, KBE, CVO; no *c*; 2nd, 1975, Carol (*d* 1996), *d* of Charles and Olive Borg. *Educ:* Clifton Coll. (music schol.); Keble Coll., Oxford (organ schol.; MA). ARCM (solo piano). Studied piano under Egon Petri, 1937–39. Served War, in RA, 1939–46. Solo pianist debut, Wigmore Hall, 1947 (postponed, Oct. 1939, owing to War); concerto debut, Philharmonia Orchestra, 1950; BBC debut Promenade Concerts, Royal Albert Hall, 1953; thereafter toured in British Isles, Europe, Africa, India, Canada. Many solo piano records. Chm., BBC TV prog., Face The Music, 1966–84. Found a solution to riddle of Elgar's Enigma Variations, 1991. Hon. Chm., Barclaycard Composer of the Year Competition, 1983. Liveryman, Worshipful Co. of Musicians, 1963–. Member: Music Panel of Arts Council (and Chm. piano sub-cttee), 1966–71; Council, Musicians Benevolent Fund, 1987–90; Trustee, Countess of Munster Musical Trust, 1975–80. Governor, Clifton College. Ambrose Fleming award, Royal Television Soc., 1961; Music Trades Assoc. Record Award, 1976. *Publications:* Hidden Melodies, 1975; More Hidden Melodies, 1976; Still More Hidden Melodies, 1978; Facing the Music (autobiog.), 1979; Arrangement of Vaughan Williams Piano Concerto for 2 pianos (in collab. with composer). *Recreations:* jigsaws, church architecture. *Address:* Octagon Lodge, Ranmore, near Dorking, Surrey RH5 6SX. *T:* (01483) 282658. *Club:* Garrick. *Died 4 Aug. 2001.*

COOPER, Sir Patrick Graham Astley, 6th Bt *cr* 1821, of Gadebridge, Herts; Director, Crendon Concrete Co. Ltd, Long Crendon, 1973–83; *b* 4 Aug. 1918; *s* of late Col C. G. A. Cooper, DSO, RA and I. M. M. A. Cooper, Abergeldie, Camberley, Surrey; *S* cousin, Sir Henry Lovick Cooper, 5th Bt, 1959; *m* 1942, Audrey Ann Jervoise, *d* of late Major D. P. J. Collas, Military Knight of Windsor; one *s* two *d. Educ:* Marlborough Coll. Served 1939–40, Gunner, RA, 52 AA Bde TA (invalided out). Qualified RICS, 1949; Sen. Asst Land Comr, Min. of Agric., Fisheries and Food, 1950–59. Joined Crendon Concrete Co. Ltd, 1959. *Recreations:* golf, tennis. *Heir: s* Alexander Paston Astley Cooper [*b* 1 Feb. 1943; *m* 1974, Minnie Margaret, *d* of Charles Harrison]. *Address:* White Cottage, 3 Townside, Haddenham, Aylesbury, Bucks HP17 8BG. *T:* (01844) 292305. *Died 15 June 2002.*

COOPER, Sir Robert (George), Kt 1998; CBE 1987; Chairman, Fair Employment Commission (formerly Agency) for Northern Ireland, 1976–99; Member, Northern Ireland Standing Advisory Commission on Human Rights, 1976–99; *b* 24 June 1936; *er s* of William Hugh Cooper and Annie (*née* Pollock); *m* 1974, Patricia, *yr d* of Gerald and Sheila Nichol, Belfast; one *s* one *d. Educ:* Foyle Coll., Londonderry; Queen's Univ., Belfast (LLB). Industrial Relations, International Computers Ltd, Belfast, 1958–63; Asst Sec., Engineering Employers' Fedn, NI, 1963–67; Sec. 1967–72; Gen. Sec., Alliance Party of Northern Ireland, 1972–73. Member (Alliance): West Belfast, NI Assembly, 1973–75; West Belfast, NI Constitutional Convention, 1975–76; Minister, Manpower Services, NI, 1974. Hon. LLD QUB, 1999. *Address:* Lynwood, 104 Bangor Road, Holywood, Co. Down, N Ireland BT18 0LR. *T:* (028) 9042 2071. *Died 16 Nov. 2004.*

COOPER, William, (Harry Summerfield Hoff), FRSL; novelist; *b* 4 Aug. 1910; *m* 1951, Joyce Barbara Harris (*d* 1988); two *d. Educ:* Christ's Coll., Cambridge. Assistant Commissioner, Civil Service Commission, 1945–58; Personnel Consultant to: UKAEA, 1958–72; CEGB, 1958–72; Commn of European Communities, 1972–73; Asst Dir, Civil Service Selection Bd, 1973–75; Mem. Bd of Crown Agents, 1975–77; Personnel Advr, Millbank Technical Services, 1975–77. Adjunct Prof. of English Lit., Syracuse Univ., 1977–90. FRSL 1971. *Publications:* (as H. S. Hoff) Trina, 1934; Rhéa, 1935; Lisa,

1937; Three Marriages, 1946; (as William Cooper) Scenes from Provincial Life, 1950; The Struggles of Albert Woods, 1952; The Ever-Interesting Topic, 1953; Disquiet and Peace, 1956; Young People, 1958; C. P. Snow (British Council Bibliographical Series, Writers and Their Work, No 115), 1959; Prince Genji (a play), 1960; Scenes from Married Life, 1961; Memoirs of a New Man, 1966; You Want The Right Frame of Reference, 1971; Shall We Ever Know?, 1971; Love on the Coast, 1973; You're Not Alone, 1976; Scenes from Metropolitan Life, 1982; Scenes from Later Life, 1983; From Early Life (autobiog.), 1990; Immortality at any Price, 1991; Scenes from Death & Life, 1999. *Address:* 22 Kenilworth Court, Lower Richmond Road, SW15 1EW. *T:* (020) 8788 8326. *Club:* Savile. *Died 5 Sept. 2002.*

COOPER, Maj.-Gen. William Frank, CBE 1971 (OBE 1965); MC 1945; *b* 30 May 1921; *s* of Allan Cooper, Officer of Indian State Railways, and Margaret Cooper; *m* 1945, Elisabeth Mary Finch (*d* 1999); one *s* one *d. Educ:* Sherborne Sch.; RMA Woolwich. Commnd in RE, 1940; served N Africa and Italy (MC; despatches 1944); Malaya, 1956–58 (despatches); S Arabia, 1963–65 (OBE); Chief Engr FARELF, 1968–70; Dep. Dir Army Staff Duties, MoD, 1970–72; Dir, Mil. Assistance Office, 1972–73; DQMG, 1973–76, retd. Col Comdt, RE, 1978–83. Dir, Gin Rectifiers and Distillers Assoc. and Vodka Trade Assoc., 1976–90. *Recreations:* fishing, birdwatching, theatre, gardening. *Address:* c/o Lloyds TSB, 118 High Street, Hungerford, Berks RG17 0LY. *Club:* Army and Navy. *Died 5 Jan. 2002.*

COPEMAN, Harold Arthur; Under-Secretary, HM Treasury, 1972–76; *b* 27 Jan. 1918; *s* of H. W. M. and G. E. Copeman; *m* 1948, Kathleen (Kay) Gadd (*d* 1992); one *s. Educ:* Manchester Grammar Sch.; The Queen's Coll., Oxford (BA, 1st Cl. Hons in PPE, 1939; MA). Served War, Army: Cheshire Regt, RA (Instructor in Gunnery) and Ordnance Board (Applied Ballistics Dept), 1940–45. HM Treasury, 1946–76. Consultant, Fiscal Affairs Dept, IMF, 1982. Vis. Fellow, Warwick Univ., 1976–84. *Publications:* (jtly) Health Care: priorities and management, 1980; The National Accounts: a short guide, 1981; Singing in Latin, 1990; The Pocket Singing in Latin, 1990; Singing the Meaning, 1996. *Recreations:* music, Latin pronunciation, photography. *Address:* 22 Tawney Street, Oxford OX4 1NJ. *T:* (01865) 243830. *Died 27 Nov. 2003.*

CORBETT, Rev. Canon (Charles) Eric; Canon-Treasurer, Liverpool Cathedral, 1979–83; *b* 6 Oct. 1917; *m* Sylvia Howe. *Educ:* Jesus College, Oxford (BA 1939; MA 1943); Wycliffe Hall, Oxford. Deacon 1940, priest 1941, St Asaph; Curate of Gresford, 1940–44; CF, 1944–47; Curate of Eglwys-Rhos, 1947–49; Rector of Harpurhey, 1949–54; Vicar of St Catherine's, Wigan, 1954–61; Vicar of St Luke, Farnworth, 1961–71; Rural Dean of Farnworth, 1964–71; Archdeacon of Liverpool, 1971–79. *Address:* 80 Latham Avenue, Helsby, Cheshire WA6 0EB. *T:* (01928) 724184. *Died 6 April 2002.*

CORBETT, Rev. Canon Eric; *see* Corbett, Rev. Canon C. E.

CORBETT, Lt-Col Uvedale, CBE 1984; DSO 1944; DL; *b* 12 Sept. 1909; *s* of Major C. U. Corbett, Stableford, Bridgnorth, Shropshire; *m* 1st, 1935, Veronica Marian Whitehead (marr. diss. 1952); two *s* one *d*; 2nd, 1953, Mrs Patricia Jane Walker (*d* 1985); 3rd, 1987, Mrs Peggy Roberts (*d* 1997). *Educ:* Wellington (Berks); RMA, Woolwich. Commissioned Royal Artillery, 1929; relinquished command 3rd Regt RHA 1945; retired. MP (C) Ludlow Div. of Shropshire, 1945–51. Chairman: Sun Valley Poultry Ltd, 1961–83; British Poultry Fedn, 1979–84. DL Hereford and Worcester, 1983. *Address:* Easthampton House, Leominster, Herefordshire HR6 9NZ. *T:* (01568) 708260. *Club:* Army and Navy. *Died 1 Sept. 2005.*

CORBY, George Arthur; international meteorological consultant, retired; *b* 14 Aug. 1917; *s* of Bertie John Corby and Agnes May (*née* Dale); *m* 1951, Gertrude Anne Nicoll; one *s* one *d*. *Educ:* St Marylebone Grammar Sch.; Univ. of London (BSc Special Maths 1st Cl.). Architect's Dept, LCC, 1936–42; entered Met. Office, 1942; Flt Lt, RAFVR, 1943; Sqdn Leader, Dep. Chief Met. Officer, ACSEA, 1945–46; Sen. Met. Officer, Northolt Airport, 1947–53; research, 1953–73; Dep. Dir for Communications and Computing, 1973–76; Dir of Services and Dep. Dir Gen., 1976–78. Vice-Pres., Royal Meteorol Soc., 1975–77. *Publications:* official scientific pubns and res. papers on mountain airflow, dynamical meteorol., and numerical forecasting. *Recreations:* music, photography. *Address:* Kings Barn, High Street, Harwell, Oxon OX11 0EY. *T:* (01235) 832883.
Died 11 July 2003.

CORDLE, John Howard; *b* 11 Oct. 1912; *s* of late Ernest William Cordle; *m* 1st, 1938, Grace (marr. diss. 1956); two *s* (and two *s* one *d* decd); 2nd, 1957, Venetia (marr. diss. 1971), *e d* of Col A. Maynard, OBE; one *s* three *d*; 3rd, 1976, Terttu, *y d* of Mikko Heikura, Finland; two *s*. *Educ:* City of London Sch. Served RAF (commissioned), 1940–45. Owner, Church of England Newspaper, 1960–71. Member: Archbishops of Canterbury and York Commission on Evangelism, 1945–46; Church Assembly, 1946–53; Oxford Churches Patronage Trust, 1947– (Chm., 1955–); Ecclesiastical Cttee of H of C, 1975–77; Hon. Treas., The World's Evangelical Alliance, 1949–53. Lay-Reader, Rochester, 1941–. Mem. of Lloyd's, 1952. Prospective Parly Cand. (C) NE Wolverhampton, 1949; contested (C) Wrekin Div., 1951; MP (C) Bournemouth E and Christchurch, Oct. 1959–1974, Bournemouth E, 1974–77; Chairman: West Africa Cttee, Conservative Commonwealth Council, 1962–77; Church and Parliament All-Party Gp, 1975–77; Sec., All Party Anglo-Libyan Gp, H of C, 1964–67. Member, UK Delegation to: Council of Europe, Strasbourg, 1974–77 (Vice-Chm., Parly and Public Relations Cttee, 1976–77); WEU, Paris, 1974–77; Rapporteur, 1976–77, to Cttee on Social and Health Questions, on the institution of Internat. Medical Card. Primrose League: Chm., Finance Cttee, 1964–67; Hon. Treas., 1964–67; Chm., Gen. Purposes Cttee, 1967–68. Chm., Wessex Aid to Addicts Gp, 1985–; Pres. Salisbury District Speech-impaired Children Trust, 1988–. Governor, London Coll. of Divinity, 1947–52; Life Governor: St Mary's and St Paul's Coll., Cheltenham; Epsom Coll.; Mem. Court, Univ. of Southampton, 1960–77. Freeman, City of London, 1956; Member: Founders' Livery Co. (Master, 1990–91); Consultative Livery Cttee, City of London, 1991–92. Gold Staff Officer, Coronation, 1953. Grand Band, Order of the Star of Africa (Liberia), 1964. *Recreations:* shooting, golf, gardening. *Address:* Malmesbury House, The Close, Salisbury, Wilts SP1 2EB. *Clubs:* Carlton, National (Trustee, 1946–), English-Speaking Union.
Died 22 Nov. 2004.

CORFIELD, Rt Hon. Sir Frederick (Vernon), Kt 1972; PC 1970; QC 1972; a Recorder of the Crown Court, 1979–87; *b* 1 June 1915; *s* of late Brig. F. A. Corfield, DSO, OBE, IA, and M. G. Corfield (*née* Vernon); *m* 1945, Elizabeth Mary Ruth Taylor; no *c*. *Educ:* Cheltenham Coll. (Scholar); RMA, Woolwich. Royal Artillery, 1935; 8th Field Regt, RA, India, 1935–39; served War of 1939–45: Actg Captain and Adjutant, 23rd Field Regt, BEF, 3rd Div., 1939; 51st (Highland) Div., 1940 (despatches); prisoner of war, Germany, 1940–45. Called to Bar, Middle Temple, 1945 (Bencher, 1980); JAG's Branch, WO, 1945–46; retired, 1946; farming, 1946–56. MP (C) South Glos, 1955–Feb. 1974; Jt Parly Sec., Min. of Housing and Local Govt, 1962–64; Minister of State, Board of Trade, June–Oct. 1970; Minister of Aviation Supply, 1970–71; Minister for Aerospace, DTI, 1971–72. Mem., British Waterways Bd, 1974–83 (Vice-Chm., 1980–83); Dir, Mid-Kent Water Co., 1975–91. Chm., London and Provincial Antique Dealers' Assoc., 1975–89.

Pres. Council, Cheltenham Coll., 1985–88. *Publications:* Corfield on Compensation, 1959; A Guide to the Community Land Act, 1976; (with R. J. A. Carnwath) Compulsory Acquisition and Compensation, 1978.
Died 25 Aug. 2005.

CORK AND ORRERY, 14th Earl of, *cr* 1620; **John William Boyle,** DSC 1945; VRD 1952; Baron Boyle of Youghal 1616; Viscount Dungarvan 1620; Baron Boyle of Broghill 1621; Viscount Boyle of Kinalmeaky and Baron of Bandon Bridge 1621; Earl of Orrery 1660 (all Ire.); Baron Boyle of Marston (GB) 1711; *b* 12 May 1916; *yr s* of Hon. Reginald Courtenay Boyle, MBE, MC (*d* 1946), *ggs* of 8th Earl, and Violet (*d* 1974), *d* of Arthur Flower; *S* brother, 1995; *m* 1943, Mary Leslie, *o d* of Gen. Sir Robert Gordon-Finlayson, KCB, CMG, DSO; three *s*. *Educ:* Harrow; King's Coll., London (BSc). FICE. Served War 1939–45, Home and Mediterranean Fleet; Lt-Comdr RNVR, 1939–54 (despatches twice). Formerly: Consultant: Sir Alexander Gibb and Partners, subseq. Gibb; PE Consulting Gp, etc; Chief Engr, Ind Coope Ltd. *Recreations:* home, family, country life, reading, making and mending. *Heir: s* Viscount Dungarvan,*b* 3 Nov. 1945. *Address:* Nether Craigantaggart, Dunkeld, Perthshire PH8 0HQ. *T:* and *Fax:* (01738) 710239. *Club:* Landsdowne.
Died 14 Nov. 2003.

CORK, Sir Roger (William), Kt 1997; FCA; Lord Mayor of London, 1996–97; Partner: Moore Stephens, 1994–99; Moore Stephens Booth White, 1995–99; *b* 31 March 1947; *s* of Sir Kenneth Cork, GBE and Nina (*née* Lippold); *m* 1970, Barbara Anita Pauline (*d* 1996), *d* of Reginald Harper; one *s* two *d*. *Educ:* St Martin's Sch., Northwood; Uppingham Sch. FICM, FIPA, FCIS. Partner, W. H. Cork Gully subseq. Cork Gully, 1970–93; associated with Coopers & Lybrand, 1980–93. Chm., Chester Boyd Ltd. President: City of London Br., Inst. of Dirs, 1991– (Chm., 1987–91); Soc. of Young Freemen, 1994–97; Inst. of Credit Management, 1999– (Chm., 1985–87; Vice Pres., 1989–99); Mem., Assoc. of Business Recovery Professionals. Governor, St Dunstan's Coll. Educnl Foundn, 1983– (Chm. of Govs, 1991–99). Chm., London and SE Reg., CRC, subseq. Cancer Res. UK, 1998–; Patron and Vice Pres., Iain Rennie Hospice at Home, 1998–; Trustee and Vice Pres., Scannappeal, 1998–; Patron, Northwich Park Inst. for Medical Res., 2001–; Vice-Pres., Bridewell Royal Hosp. and King Edwards, Witley, 2002–. Trustee and Mem. Council, Restoration of Appearance and Function Trust, 2000–; Pres., Wendover Arm Trust, 1992–. City of London: Freeman, 1972; Alderman, Tower Ward, 1983–; Sheriff, 1992–93; HM Lieutenant, 1997–. Master, Bowyers' Co., 1990–92; Freeman, Co. of Watermen and Lightermen; Member Court: Chartered Accountants' Co. (Jun. Warden, 2001–02); World Traders' Co. (Master, 1999–2000); Butchers' Co.; Chartered Secretaries' and Administrators' Co., 2001–; Hon. Liveryman: Envmntl Cleaners' Co. (Mem. Court, 1998–); Hon. Mem., Co. (formerly Guild) of Tax Advrs. City Fellow, Hughes Hall, Cambridge, 1998. Hon. DSc City, 1996. OStJ. Bintang Darjah Seri Paduka Makkota Brunei Yang Amat Mulia (Brunei), 1993; Order of Infante D. Henrique 3rd cl. (Portugal), 1993. *Recreations:* sailing, photography, DIY. *Address:* Rabbs, The Lee, Great Missenden, Bucks HP16 9NX. *T:* (01494) 837296. *Clubs:* East India (Hon. Mem.), City Livery, Tower Ward (Pres., 1984–), Billingsgate Ward (Master, 1980–81), Royal Yachting Association, Little Ship; Hardway Sailing.
Died 21 Oct. 2002.

CORLETT, Rev. Dr Ewan Christian Brew, OBE 1985; MA, PhD; FREng; Chairman and Managing Director, BCH Ltd (formerly Burness, Corlett & Partners Ltd), 1954–88, and since 1995; *b* 11 Feb. 1923; *s* of Malcolm James John and Catherine Ann Corlett; *m* 1946, Edna Lilian Büggs (*d* 2002); three *s*. *Educ:* King William's Coll., IOM; Oxford Univ. (MA Engrg Sci.); Durham Univ. (PhD Naval Architecture); Diocesan Training Inst., IOM. Dept of Director of Naval Construction, Admiralty, Bath,

1944–46; Tipton Engrg Co., Tipton, 1946–47; Aluminium Develt Assoc. Research Scholar, Durham Univ., 1947–50; Naval Architect, British Aluminium Co., 1950–53; Design Dir, Burness, Corlett & Partners Ltd, 1953–54, Man. Dir, 1954–88. Ordained deacon, 1991, priest, 1992; Asst Curate, Maughold Parish, IOM, 1991–2004. Chm. Council, RINA, 1977–79, Vice-Pres., 1971–82, Hon. Vice-Pres., 1982–. Home Office Assessor (Technical Inquiries), 1959–80; Assessor, Herald of Free Enterprise Inquiry, 1987. Originator and i/c salvage, SS Great Britain from Falkland Is, 1968–70; Hon. Naval Architect and Vice-Pres., SS Great Britain Project, 1970–. Mem. Board, Nat. Maritime Inst., 1978–82; Trustee, Nat. Maritime Museum, 1974–92. Mem. Court, Shipwrights' Co., 1976–, Prime Warden 1990. Pres., Ramsey Station, RNLI, 1994–. FRINA 1954; FIMarEST (FIMarE 1954); FREng (FEng 1978); Hon. FRIN 1980; Hon. FNI 1992. *Publications:* The Iron Ship, 1976, 4th edn 2002; The Revolution in Merchant Shipping 1950–1980, 1980; numerous papers to learned instns. *Recreations:* painting, astronomy, ship modelling. *Address:* Cottimans, Port-e-Vullen, Isle of Man IM7 1AP. *T:* (01624) 814009, *Fax:* (01624) 817248; *e-mail:* ecbc.cottimans@manx.net. *Club:* Manx Sailing and Cruising.   *Died 8 Aug. 2005.*

CORLEY, Sir Kenneth (Sholl Ferrand), Kt 1972; Chairman and Chief Executive, Joseph Lucas (Industries) Ltd, 1969–73; *b* 3 Nov. 1908; *s* of late S. W. Corley and Mrs A. L. Corley; *m* 1937, Olwen Mary Yeoman (*d* 1999); one *s* one *d. Educ:* St Bees, Cumberland. Joined Joseph Lucas Ltd, 1927; Director, 1948. President: Birmingham Chamber of Commerce, 1964; SMMT, 1971. Governor, Royal Shakespeare Theatre; Life Governor, Birmingham Univ.; Chm. Governors, St Bees Sch., 1978–84. Chevalier, Légion d'Honneur (France), 1975. *Recreations:* fell-walking, theatre. *Address:* Bradbury House, Gosforth, Cumbria CA20 1AU. *T:* (019467) 25987.
                                                  Died 6 March 2005.

CORNWELL, Roger Eliot; Chairman, Louis Dreyfus & Co. Ltd, since 1982 (Director since 1978); *b* 5 Feb. 1922; *s* of Harold and Kathleen Cornwell. *Educ:* St Albans Sch.; Jesus Coll., Oxford (MA). *Address:* 42 Brompton Square, SW3 2AF.   *Died 16 Nov. 2005.*

CORY, John; Vice Lord-Lieutenant of South Glamorgan, 1990–2003; Director, John Cory & Sons Ltd, 1949–91; *b* 30 June 1928; *s* of John and Cecil Cory; *m* 1965, Sarah Christine, *d* of John Meade, JP, DL; two *d. Educ:* Eton; Trinity College, Cambridge. Chm., Cardiff RDC, 1971–72. Member, Governing Body, 1957–74, Representative Body, 1960–99, Church in Wales. Pres., Nat. Light Horse Breeding Soc., 1977–78. Joint Master, Glamorgan Hounds, 1962–67. High Sheriff, 1959, JP 1961, DL 1968, Glamorgan. KStJ. *Address:* The Grange, St Brides-super-Ely, Cardiff CF5 6XA. *T:* (01446) 760211. *Clubs:* MCC; Cardiff and County (Cardiff).
                                                  Died 17 Dec. 2003.

COSGRAVE, Patrick John, PhD; writer; *b* 28 Sept. 1941; *s* of Patrick John Cosgrave and Margaret FitzGerald; *m* 1st, 1965, Ruth Dudley Edwards (marr. diss. 1974); 2nd, 1974, Norma Alicia Green (marr. diss. 1980); one *d;* 3rd, 1981, Shirley Ward. *Educ:* St Vincent's Sch., Dublin; University Coll., NUI, Dublin (BA, MA); Univ. of Cambridge (PhD). London Editor, Radio Telefis Eireann, 1968–69; Conservative Research Dept, 1969–71; Political Editor, The Spectator, 1971–75; Features Editor, Telegraph Magazine, 1974–76; Special Adviser to Rt Hon. Mrs Margaret Thatcher, 1975–79; Managing Editor, Quartet Crime (Quartet Books), 1979–81. *Publications:* The Public Poetry of Robert Lowell, 1970; Churchill at War: Alone, 1974; Cheyney's Law (novel), 1977; Margaret Thatcher: a Tory and her party, 1978, 2nd edn as Margaret Thatcher: Prime Minister, 1979; The Three Colonels (novel), 1979; R. A. Butler: an English Life, 1981; Adventure of State (novel), 1984; Thatcher: the First Term, 1985; Carrington: a life and a policy, 1985; The Lives of Enoch Powell, 1989; The Strange Death of Socialist Britain, 1992; contribs to

Proc. of Royal Irish Academy, Irish Historical Studies, Encounter, Policy Rev., New Law Jl, The Times, Daily Telegraph, Sunday Telegraph, The Independent, Sunday Tribune, New DNB. *Recreations:* thriller fiction, cooking, roses, cricket. *T:* (020) 7627 0306.
                                                  Died 15 Sept. 2001.

COSSERAT, Kay, RDI 1986; Director, Cosserat Design Ltd, since 1976; Part-time Lecturer, Royal College of Art, since 1990, and Chelsea School of Art, since 1985; *b* 24 Oct. 1947; *d* of Robert and Elizabeth Macklam; *m* 1972, Christopher Graham Peloquin Cosserat; two *s. Educ:* Cleveland Sch., Eaglescliffe; Goldsmiths' Sch. of Art (Dip AD 1st cl. Hons); Royal Coll. of Art (MA Textiles 1972); Sanderson Travel Scholarship, 1972. Formed Cosserat Design Partnership, 1974; Founder Mem., London Designer Collections, 1974; currently producing textile and garment designs on a consultancy basis. Mem., Fashion and Textile Bd, CNAA, 1978. Vis. Prof., London Inst., 1992–; Part-time Lecturer: St Martins Sch. of Art, 1972–80; RCA, 1976–79; External Assessor: Central Sch. of Art, 1982–85; Trent Poly., 1983–85; Liverpool Poly., 1985–87; Huddersfield Poly., 1985–88; QUB, 1990–92; Univ. of Ulster, 1990–93; Winchester Sch. of Art, 1991–93. *Recreations:* gardening, ski-ing, collecting '30s pottery.   *Died 9 Dec. 2003.*

COSTAIN, Noel Leslie, OBE 1964; Director of Works, University of Sheffield, 1964–78; *b* 11 Jan. 1914; *s* of George Wesley Costain and Minnie Grace Pinson; *m* 1945, Marie José Elizabeth (*née* Bishton); two *d. Educ:* King Edward's Sch., Five Ways, Birmingham; Univ. of Birmingham (BSc). CEng, MICE. Engineer with Sir R. MacAlpine & Sons, 1937–38; Epsom and Ewell BC, 1939; Air Min., Directorate-Gen. of Works; Section Officer, Orkneys and Shetlands, 1940–43; Prin. Works Officer, Sierra Leone, 1944–46; Superintending Engr, Air Ministry, 1946–51; RAF Airfield Construction Br.: Cmdg 5352 Wing, Germany, and OC, RAF Church Lawford, 1951–54; Superintending Engr, Works Area, Bristol, 1954–58; Chief Engr, MEAF, 1958–60; Chief Resident Engr, BMEWS, Fylingdales, 1960–63. Vice-Chm., Yorkshire Univs Air Squadron Cttee. FINucE 1959 (Mem. Council, 1965; Vice-Pres., 1969; Pres., 1972–76). *Recreations:* travel, gardening.   *Died 5 March 2004.*

COTTER, Lt-Col Sir Delaval James Alfred, 6th Bt *cr* 1763, of Rockforest, Cork; DSO 1944; late 13th/18th Royal Hussars; *b* 29 April 1911; *s* of Sir James Laurence Cotter, 5th Bt and Ethel Lucy (*d* 1956), *d* of Alfred Wheeler; *S* father, 1924; *m* 1st, 1943, Roma (marr. diss. 1949), *o d* of late Adrian Rome, Dalswinton Lodge, Salisbury, Southern Rhodesia, and *widow* of Sqdn Ldr K. A. K. MacEwen; two *d;* 2nd, 1952, Mrs Eveline Mary Paterson (*d* 1991), *d* of late E. J. Mardon, ICS (retired), and *widow* of Lt-Col J. F. Paterson, OBE, *Educ:* Malvern Coll.; RMC, Sandhurst. Served War of 1939–45 (DSO); retired, 1959. JP Wilts, 1962–63. *Heir: n* Patrick Laurence Delaval Cotter [*b* 21 Nov. 1941; *m* 1967, Janet, *d* of George Potter, Barnstaple; one *s* two *d*]. *Address:* Millbrook House Retirement Home, Childe Okeford, Blandford Forum, Dorset DT11 8EY.   *Died 2 April 2001.*

COTTON, Bernard Edward, CBE 1976; Chairman, South Yorkshire Residuary Body, 1985–89; *b* 8 Oct. 1920; *s* of Hugh Harry Cotton and Alice Cotton; *m* 1944, Stephanie Anne (*d* 2003), *d* of Rev. A. E. and Mrs Furnival; three *s. Educ:* Sheffield City Grammar Sch.; Sheffield Univ. Served Army, 1939–45, latterly as Lieut, Worcs Yeomanry (53rd Airlanding Light Regt RA). Joined Round Oak Steelworks, Brierley Hill, 1949, Sales Man., 1954–57; Gen. Man., Samuel Osborn (Canada) Ltd, Montreal, 1957–63; Samuel Osborn & Co. Ltd: Sales Dir, 1963–69; Man. Dir, 1969; Chm. and Chief Exec., 1969–78; Pres., 1978–80. Dir, Renold Ltd, 1979–84; Dep. Chm., Baker Perkins plc, 1983–86. Chairman: Yorks and Humberside Reg. Econ. Planning Council, 1970–79; Health Service Supply Council, 1980–85; Mem., BR Eastern Bd, 1977–85; Pres., Yorks and Humberside Develt

Assoc., 1973–84. Chm., BIM Working Party on Employee Participation, 1975. Pro Chancellor, Sheffield Univ., 1982–87. Master, Cutlers' Co. in Hallamshire, 1979–80. Hon. Fellow, Sheffield Hallam Univ. (formerly Sheffield City Poly.), 1980. CCMI (Hon. Life Mem.). Hon. LLD Sheffield, 1988. *Recreations:* gardening and other quiet pursuits. *Address:* 2 Hillcote Rise, Fulwood, Sheffield S10 3PW. *T:* (0114) 230 3082.
Died 15 June 2004.

COTTON, Sir John Richard, KCMG 1969 (CMG 1959); OBE 1947 (MBE 1944); HM Diplomatic Service, retired; Adjudicator, Immigration Appeals, 1970–81; *b* 22 Jan. 1909; *s* of late J. J. Cotton, ICS, and Gigia Ricciardi Arlotta; *m* 1937, Mary Bridget Connors (*d* 2000), Stradbally, County Waterford, Ireland; three *s. Educ:* Wellington Coll.; RMC, Sandhurst. Commissioned 1929; 8th King George's Own Light Cavalry (IA), 1930–34; transferred to Indian Political Service, 1934; served in Aden, Abyssinia (Attaché HM Legation, 1935), Persian Gulf, Rajputana, Hyderabad, Kathiawar, Baroda, New Delhi (Dep. Sec. Political Dept); transferred to HM Foreign Service, 1947; First Sec., Karachi, 1947–48; FO, 1949–51; Commercial Counsellor, HM Embassy, Madrid, 1951–54; Consul-Gen., Brazzaville, 1954–55, Leopoldville, 1955–57; Counsellor (Commercial), HM Embassy, Brussels, 1957–62; Consul-Gen., São Paulo, Brazil, 1962–65; Ambassador to Kinshasa, Congo Republic (later Zaire), and to Burundi, 1965–69. *Address:* Lansing House, Hartley Wintney, Hants RG27 8RY. *T:* (01252) 842681.
Died 23 Dec. 2001.

COULSON, His Honour (James) Michael; a Circuit Judge, Midland and Oxford Circuit, 1983–90; a Deputy Circuit Judge, 1990–98; *b* 23 Nov. 1927; *s* of William Coulson, Wold Newton Hall, Driffield, E Yorks; *m* 1st, 1955, Dilys Adair Jones (marr. diss.; she *d* 1994); one *s*; 2nd, 1977, Barbara Elizabeth Islay, *d* of Dr Roland Moncrieff Chambers; one *s* one *d. Educ:* Fulneck Sch., Yorks; Merton Coll., Oxford; Royal Agricultural Coll., Cirencester. Served E Riding Yeomanry (Wenlocks Horse); Queen's Own Yorks Yeomanry (Major). Called to Bar, Middle Temple, 1951; Mem. North Eastern Circuit; Asst Recorder of Sheffield, 1965–71; Dep. Chm., NR of Yorks QS, 1968–71; a Regl Chm. of Industrial Tribunals, 1968–83; a Recorder of the Crown Court, 1981–83. Dep. Chm., Northern Agricl Land Tribunal, 1967–73. MP (C) Kingston-upon-Hull North, 1959–64; PPS to Solicitor Gen., 1962–64; Mem., Executive Cttee, Conservative Commonwealth Council. Former Mem., Tadcaster RDC. Sometime Sec., Bramham Moor and York and Ainsty Point to Point Race Meetings. *Recreations:* hunting, reading, travel. *Address:* The Tithe Barn, Wymondham, Melton Mowbray, Leics LE14 2AS. *Club:* Cavalry and Guards.
Died 18 June 2002.

COULSON, Michael; *see* Coulson, J. M.

COULTHARD, Air Vice-Marshal Colin Weal, CB 1975; AFC 1953 (Bar 1958); retired; *b* 27 Feb. 1921; *s* of late George Robert Coulthard and Cicely Eva Coulthard (*née* Minns); *m* 1st, 1941, Norah Ellen Creighton (marr. diss.); one *s* two *d*; 2nd, 1957, Eileen Pamela (*née* Barber); one *s. Educ:* Watford Grammar Sch.; De Havilland Aeronautical Tech. Sch. Commissioned RAF, 1941; Fighter Pilot, 1942–45 (despatches, 1945); HQ Fighter Comd, 1948–49; RAF Staff Coll., 1950; OC 266 Sqn, Wunstorf, 1952–54, DFLS, CFE, 1955; OC Flying, 233(F) OCU, 1956–57; OC AFDS, CFE, 1957–59; HQ Fighter Comd, 1959–60; Stn Cdr, Gutersloh, 1961–64; MoD, 1964–66; SOA, AHQ Malta, 1966–67; DOR 1(RAF), MoD, 1967–69; Air Attaché, Washington, DC, 1970–72; Mil. Dep. to Head of Defence Sales, MoD, 1973–75. Governor, Truro Sch., 1981–91. Hon. FRAeS 1975. *Recreations:* walking, shooting, motor sport. *Address:* Fiddlers, Old Truro Road, Goonhavern, Truro TR4 9NN. *T:* (01872) 540312. *Club:* Royal Air Force.
Died 15 Nov. 2004.

COUPER, Sir Nicholas; *see* Couper, Sir R. N. O.

COUPER, Sir (Robert) Nicholas (Oliver), 6th Bt *cr* 1841; *b* 9 Oct. 1945; *s* of Sir George Robert Cecil Couper, 5th Bt, and Margaret Grace (*d* 1984), *d* of late Robert George Dashwood Thomas; *S* father, 1975; *m* 1st, 1972, Curzon Henrietta MacKean (marr. diss. 1986); one *s* one *d*; 2nd, 1991, Katrina Frances, *d* of Sir Michael Walker, GMCG. *Educ:* Eton; RMA, Sandhurst. Major, Blues and Royals; retired, 1975. Worked as property consultant. *Heir: s* James George Couper, *b* 27 Oct. 1977. *Address:* 79 Devonshire Road, W4 2HU.
Died 9 May 2002.

COUTTS, Prof. John Archibald; Professor of Jurisprudence in the University of Bristol, 1950–75, then Emeritus; Pro-Vice Chancellor, 1971–74; *b* 29 Dec. 1909; *e s* of Archibald and Katherine Jane Coutts; *m* 1940, Katherine Margaret Alldis (*d* 1998); two *s. Educ:* Merchant Taylors', Crosby; Downing Coll., Cambridge (MA, LLB). Called to the Bar, Gray's Inn, 1933; lectured in Law: University Coll., Hull, 1934–35; King's Coll., London, 1935–36; Queen's Univ., Belfast, 1936–37; Trinity Coll., Dublin, 1937–50; Prof. of Laws, University of Dublin, 1944–50. Fellow, Trinity College, Dublin, 1944–50. Visiting Professor: Osgoode Hall Law Sch., Toronto, 1962–63; Univ. of Toronto, 1970–71, 1975–76. *Publications:* The Accused (ed); contributions to legal journals. *Address:* 22 Hurle Crescent, Clifton, Bristol BS8 2SZ. *T:* (0117) 973 6984.
Died 23 July 2002.

COUZENS, Sir Kenneth (Edward), KCB 1979 (CB 1976); Chairman, Crédit Lyonnais Capital Markets, 1991–96 (Director, 1989–98; Vice-Chairman, 1996–98); *b* 29 May 1925; *s* of Albert Couzens and May Couzens (*née* Biddlecombe); *m* 1947, Muriel Eileen Fey; one *d* (one *s* decd). *Educ:* Portsmouth Grammar Sch.; Caius Coll., Cambridge. Inland Revenue, 1949–51; Treasury, 1951–68, and 1970–82; Civil Service Dept, 1968–70. Private Sec. to Financial Sec., Treasury, 1952–55, and to Chief Sec., 1962–63; Asst Sec., 1963–69; Under-Secretary: CSD, 1969–70; Treasury, 1970–73; Dep. Sec., Incomes Policy and Public Finance, 1973–77; Second Perm. Sec. (Overseas Finance), 1977–82; Perm. Under-Sec. of State, Dept of Energy, 1983–85. Dep. Chm., NCB, subseq. British Coal, 1985–88; Chm., Coal Products, 1988–92 (Dir, 1986–92). Vice-Chm., Monetary Cttee, European Community, 1982; Member: UK Adv. Bd, Nat. Econ. Res. Assocs, 1986–98; Local Govt Commn, 1993–95. *Address:* Coverts Edge, Woodsway, Oxshott, Surrey KT22 0ND. *T:* (01372) 843207. *Club:* Reform.
Died 4 Aug. 2004.

COVEN, Major Edwina Olwyn, CBE 1988; JP; DL; HM Lieutenant, City of London, since 1981; Director, Capital Corporation (formerly Crockfords) Plc, 1993–98; *b* 23 Oct. 1921; *d* of Sir Samuel Instone, DL, and Lady (Alice) Instone; *m* 1951, Frank Coven (*d* 2001). *Educ:* Queen's Coll., London; St Winifred's, Ramsgate; Lycée Victor Duruy, Paris; Marlborough Gate Secretarial Coll., London (1st Cl. Business Diploma). Volunteered for Mil. Service, Private ATS; commnd ATS (subseq. WRAC); Army Interpreter (French); served UK and overseas, incl. staff appts, Plans and Policy Div., Western Union Defence Org. and NATO, Directorate Manpower Planning, WO, 1942–56. 1959–: Children's Writer, Fleetway Publications; Gen. Features Writer, National Magazine Co.; Reporter, BBC Woman's Hour; performer and adviser, children's and teenage progs, ITV. Mem. Adv. Council, Radio London (BBC), 1978–81. Dir, 1985–93, Dep. Chm., 1990–93, TV-am. Chm., Davbro Chemists, 1967–71; stores consultant on promotion and fashion, 1960–77; Mem., Women's Adv. Cttee (Clothing and Footwear Sub-Cttee), BSI, 1971–73. Caseworker, Soldiers', Sailors' and Airmen's Assoc., 1995–99. JP Inner London, North Westminster, 1965–72 (Dep. Chm., 1971–72); JP City of London Commn, 1969–88 (Dep. Chm., 1971–88); Greater London: DL 1987, Rep. DL Hammersmith and Fulham, 1989–94; Mem., Central Council Probation and After-Care Cttee, 1971; Chm.,

City of London Probation and After-Care Cttee, 1971–77; Chm, City of London Police Cttee, 1984–87 (Dep. Chm., 1983–84); Mem., Police Cttee, AMA, 1985–97. Mem., Jt Cttee of Management, London Court of Internat. Arbitration 1983–89. Dowgate Ward, City of London: Court of Common Council, 1972–99; elected Alderman, 1973 and 1974; Deputy, 1975–. Chief Commoner, City of London, 1987–88. Freedom, City of London, 1967; Mem., Guild of Freemen, City of London, 1971; Freeman, Loriners' Co., 1967; Liveryman, Spectacle Makers' Co., 1972; Hon. Liveryman, Lightmongers' Co., 1990. Member: Council, WRAC Assoc., 1973–90 (Vice Pres., 1984–88; Vice-Chm., 1985–89; Chm., 1989–90); TAVRA, City of London, 1979–86; Associated Speakers, 1975–; London Home Safety Council, 1980–84; Vice Chm., Cities of London and Westminster Home Safety Council, 1984–89; Vice President: Nat. Org. for Women's Management Educn, 1983–90; FANY, 1989–; Operation Raleigh, 1989–95; Chm., Cttee for Celebration of 800th Year of Mayoralty, Corp. of London, 1988–90. Member: Court, Sussex Univ., 1994–; Bd of Governors, City of London Sch., 1972–77; Chm., Bd of Governors, City of London Sch. for Girls, 1978–81; Mem., Royal Soc. of St George, 1972–; Chm., Vintry and Dowgate Wards Club, 1977. FRSA 1988. Hon. Captain of Police, Salt Lake City, 1986; Order of Wissam Alouite (Morocco), 1987. OStJ 1987. *Publication:* Tales of Oaktree Kitchen, 1959 (2nd edn 1960; adapted for ITV children's educnl series). *Recreations:* homemaking, lawn tennis, watching a variety of spectator sports. *Address:* 23 Tavistock, Devonshire Place, Eastbourne, Sussex BN21 4AG. *Clubs:* Hurlingham; Devonshire (Eastbourne).

Died 15 Dec. 2005.

COVEN, Frank; London and European Director, The Nine Television Network of Australia, 1974; *b* 26 April 1910; *s* of Isaac L. Coven and Raie Coven; *m* 1951, Major Edwina Olwyn Coven (*née* Instone), CBE. *Educ:* The Perse Sch., Cambridge; France and Germany. Studied film prodn, Universal Film Company and EFA Studios, Berlin. TA (Ranks), 1938; War Service, 1939–45 (commnd 1941). Film admin and prodn, Gaumont British Studies, 1932; Studio Manager, Gainsborough Pictures, 1935; TV prodn, BBC/Daily Mail, 1937–38; Jt Dep. Organiser, Daily Mail Ideal Home Exhibition (radio, television, special features), 1945; Manager, Public Relations, Associated Newspapers, 1949; interviews, Wimbledon tennis commentaries, children's series "Write it Yourself" BBC TV, 1949–54 (subseq. ITV); TV Adviser, Bd of Associated Newspapers, 1953, Associated Rediffusion, 1954; London Rep., Television Corporation Ltd, Sydney, and Herald-Sun Pty, Melbourne, 1954; Dir, Compagnie Belge Transmarine SA and Imperial Stevedoring Co. SA, 1959; Head of Publicity and Promotions, Associated Newspapers, 1961; 1962: Director: Associated Newspapers Gp; Bouverie Investments Ltd; Managing Director: Northcliffe Developments Ltd; Frank Coven Enterprises Ltd, presenting (with John Roberts) plays in London, incl. The Professor, How's the World Treating You? and, with London Traverse Theatre Co., works by Saul Bellow and others, 1964–69; Gen. Man., United Racecourses Ltd (Epsom, Sandown Park, Kempton Park), 1970, Man. Dir 1970, Vice-Chm. 1972. Mem., Variety Club of GB. Mem., Royal Soc. of St George, 1972. *Publications:* various Daily Mail Guides to Television Development in UK. *Recreations:* lawn tennis, swimming, study of varied media (current affairs). *Address:* 23 Tavistock, Devonshire Place, Eastbourne, Sussex BN21 4AG. *Clubs:* Saints and Sinners; Hurlingham, Queen's; Devonshire (Eastbourne).   *Died 7 Sept 2001.*

COVENTRY, 11th Earl of, *cr* 1697; **George William Coventry;** Viscount Deerhurst, 1697; *b* 25 Jan. 1934; *o s* of 10th Earl and Hon. Nesta Donne Philipps, *e d* of 1st Baron Kylsant; *S* father, 1940; *m* 1st, 1955, Marie Farquhar-Medart (marr. diss. 1963); (one *s* decd); 2nd, 1969, Ann (marr. diss. 1975), *d* of F. W. J. Cripps, Bickley, Kent; 3rd, 1980, Valerie Anne Birch (marr. diss. 1988);

4th, 1992, Rachel Wynne, *d* of J. Mason. *Educ:* Eton; RMA, Sandhurst. *Heir: cousin* Francis Henry Coventry [*b* 27 Sept. 1912; *m* 1945, Yolande Lucienne, *yr d* of Lucien P. di Benedetto; one *d*]. *Address:* Earls Croome Court, Earls Croome, Worcester WR8 9DE.

Died 14 June 2002.

COVENTRY, 12th Earl of *cr* 1697; **Francis Henry Coventry;** Viscount Deerhurst 1697; *b* 27 Sept. 1912; *yr s* of Col the Hon. Charles John Coventry, CB and Lily (*née* Whitehouse); *S* cousin, 2002; *m* 1945, Yolande Lucienne, *yr d* of Lucien P. di Benedetto; one *d*. *Educ:* Eton; New Coll., Oxford. *Heir: cousin* Victor Gerald Coventry [*b* 4 Oct. 1917; *m* 1943, Constance Hilda Green; one *d* (one *s* decd)].   *Died 13 March 2004.*

COWAN, Dr William Maxwell, FRS 1982; Vice President and Chief Scientific Officer, Howard Hughes Medical Insitute, 1988–2000; *b* 27 Sept. 1931; *s* of Adam Cowan and Jessie Sloan Cowan (*née* Maxwell); *m* 1956, Margaret Sherlock; two *s* one *d*. *Educ:* Univ. of the Witwatersrand, S Africa (BSc Hons); Hertford Coll., Oxford Univ. (MA, DPhil, BM, BCh; Hon. Fellow, 1997). University Lecturer in Anatomy, Oxford, 1958–66; Fellow of Pembroke Coll., Oxford, 1958–66 (Hon. Fellow, 1986); Associate Prof., Univ. of Wisconsin, 1966–68; Washington University, St Louis: Professor and Head of Dept of Anatomy, Sch. of Medicine, 1968–80; Director, Div. of Biological Sciences, 1975–80; Salk Institute for Biological Studies: non-resident Fellow, 1977–80; Professor, 1980–86; Vice Pres. and Dir, Develtl Neurobiol., 1980–86; Provost and Exec. Vice-Chancellor, Washington Univ., St Louis, 1986–87. Mem., Amer. Philosophical Soc., 1987. Fellow, Amer. Acad. of Arts and Scis, 1975; For. Mem., Norwegian Acad. of Scis, 1980; Foreign Associate: US National Academy of Sciences, 1981; Royal Soc. of S Africa, 1986. Hon. DSc: Northwestern, 1994; Emory, 1994. *Publications:* The Use of Axonal Transport for Studies of Neuronal Connectivity, 1975; Aspects of Cellular Neurobiology, 1978; Studies in Developmental Neurobiology, 1981; Molecular and Cellular Approaches to Neural Development, 1998; Annual Reviews of Neuroscience, Vol. 1 1978, Vols 2–22, 1979–2000. *Recreations:* photography, reading, travel. *Address:* 6337 Windermere Circle, North Bethesda, MD 20852, USA. *T:* (301) 4939097.   *Died 30 June 2002.*

COWLEY, Maj.-Gen. John Cain, CB 1971; DL; Paymaster-in-Chief and Inspector of Army Pay Services, Ministry of Defence, 1967–72, retired; with de Zoete and Bevan, Stockbrokers, 1972–79; *b* 17 July 1918; *er s* of late Philip Richard and Eleanor Cowley, Ballaquane, Peel, Isle of Man; *m* 1948, Eileen Rosemary, CBE 1982, *d* of late George Percival Stewart, Aigburth, Liverpool; three *s*. *Educ:* Douglas Sch., Isle of Man. War of 1939–45: commissioned, RAPC, 1940; served: Palestine, Western Desert, Italy, France, Belgium, Holland, Germany. Dep. Asst Adj.-Gen., Middle East, 1949–51; GSOI, with Permanent Under Sec., War Office, 1952–54; West African Frontier Force, 1956–59; Dep. Paymaster-in-Chief: War Office, 1960–63; BAOR, 1963–65; Chief Paymaster, Eastern Command, 1965–67. Capt. 1946, Maj. 1953, Lt-Col 1955, Col. 1960, Brig. 1963, Maj.-Gen. 1967; psc, 1948; jssc, 1955; Administrative Staff Coll., 1960. Col Comdt, RAPC, 1974–79. Chm., W Sussex, Duke of Edinburgh's Award Scheme, 1986–95; Vice-Pres., W Sussex Scouts, 1992–. Vice-Pres., St Catherine's Hospice, 1981–. Governor, St Michaels, Burton Park, 1982–88 (Chm. of Govs, 1986–88). High Sheriff, W Sussex, 1984–85; DL W Sussex, 1986. *Recreations:* shooting, fishing, ornithology. *Address:* The Old Post Office, Nuthurst, Horsham, West Sussex RH13 6LH. *T:* (01403) 891266. *Club:* Army and Navy.

Died 18 Nov. 2002.

COWLEY, Dr John Maxwell, FRS 1979; FAA; Galvin Professor of Physics, Arizona State University, USA, since 1970 (Regents' Professor, 1988–94, Emeritus, since 1994); *b* 18 Feb. 1923; *s* of Alfred E. and Doris R. Cowley; *m*

1951, Roberta J. (*née* Beckett); two *d*. *Educ:* Univ. of Adelaide (BSc 1942, MSc 1945, DSc 1957); MIT (PhD 1949). FAA 1961. Res. Officer, CSIRO, Australia, 1945–62; Prof. of Physics, Univ. of Melbourne, 1962–70. International Union of Crystallography: Mem. Exec. Cttee, 1963–69; Chm., Commn on Electron Diffraction, 1987–93; Ewald Prize, 1987. *Publications:* Diffraction Physics, 1975; approx. 500 articles in learned jls. *Recreations:* painting, music. *Address:* 2625 E Southern Avenue C-90, Tempe, AZ 85282, USA. *T:* (480) 8313123. *Died 18 May 2004.*

COWLING, Maurice John; Fellow of Peterhouse, Cambridge, 1963–93, then Emeritus; *b* 6 Sept. 1926; *s* of Reginald Frederick Cowling and May (*née* Roberts); *m* 1996, Patricia Gale (*née* Holley). *Educ:* Battersea Grammar Sch.; Jesus Coll., Cambridge (Historical Tripos, Pt I 1948, Pt II 1949). Served British and Indian Armies (Captain Queen's Royal Regt), 1944–48. Fellow, Jesus Coll., Cambridge, 1950–53; Res. Fellow, Univ. of Reading, 1953–54; FO, 1954; Member, Editorial Staff: The Times, 1955–56; Daily Express, 1957–58; Fellow, Jesus Coll., Cambridge, 1961–63; Lectr in History, then Reader in Modern English History, Univ. of Cambridge, 1961–88. Olin Vis. Prof. of Religion, Columbia Univ., 1989; Vis. Prof., Adelphi Univ., 1993–97. Literary Editor, The Spectator, 1970–71. Dir, Politeia, 1998–. Contested (C) Bassetlaw, 1959; Mem., Cambs and Isle of Ely CC, 1966–70. *Publications:* The Nature and Limits of Political Science, 1963; Mill and Liberalism, 1963, 2nd edn 1989; Disraeli, Gladstone and Revolution, 1967; The Impact of Labour, 1971; The Impact of Hitler, 1975; (ed) Conservative Essays, 1978; Religion and Public Doctrine in Modern England, vol. i 1980, vol. ii 1985, vol. iii 2001; A Conservative Future, 1997. *Address:* 10a Redcliffe, Caswell Bay, Swansea SA3 3BT.
Died 24 Aug. 2005.

COX, Alan Seaforth; Clerk to the Grocers' Company, 1965–81; Secretary, Grocers' Trust Company Ltd, 1968–81; *b* 15 Oct. 1915; *m* 1st, 1944, Jean Heriot-Maitland (marr. diss. 1952); one *s*; 2nd, 1954, Mary Thornton (*d* 1990); three *s* one *d*. Served War: London Scottish and Gold Coast Regt, 1939–45; Staff Officer, WO, 1945–46. Farming and banking, Argentine (Patagonia), 1947–52; joined Grocers' Co., 1954. Sec., Governing Body of Oundle Sch., 1965–81. Hon. Mem. Ct, Grocers' Co., 1981–. *Recreations:* bridge, cribbage, dining and wining. *Address:* The Mount, Winchelsea, East Sussex TN36 4EG. *T:* (01797) 226543.
Died 6 Sept. 2004.

COX, His Honour Anthony; see Cox, His Honour J. A.

COX, Prof. Archibald; Carl M. Loeb University Professor, Harvard University, 1976–84, then Emeritus; *b* 17 May 1912; *s* of Archibald Cox and Frances Bruen (*née* Perkins); *m* 1937, Phyllis Ames; one *s* two *d*. *Educ:* St Paul's Sch., Concord; Harvard Univ. AB 1934, LLB 1937. Admitted to Mass Bar, 1937. Gen. practice with Ropes, Gray, Best, Coolidge & Rugg, 1938–41; Office of Solicitor-Gen., US Dept of Justice, 1941–43; Assoc. Solicitor, Dept of Labor, 1943–45; Lectr on Law, Harvard, 1945–46, Prof. of Law, 1946–61; Solicitor-Gen., US Dept of Justice, 1961–65; Williston Prof. of Law, Harvard Law Sch., 1965–76. Pitt Prof., Univ. of Cambridge, 1974–75; Vis. Prof. of Law, Boston Univ., 1984–97. Co-Chm., Constrn Industry Stablizn Commn, 1951–52; Chm., Wage Stablzn Bd, 1952; Mem. Bd Overseers, Harvard, 1962–65. Special Watergate Prosecutor, 1973. Hon. LLD: Loyola, 1964; Cincinnati, 1967; Rutgers, Amherst, Denver, 1974; Harvard, 1975; Michigan, 1976; Wheaton, 1977; Northeastern, 1978; Clark, 1980; Notre Dame, 1983; Hon. LHD: Hahnemann Med. Coll., 1980; Univ. of Mass, 1981; Illinois, 1985. *Publications:* Cases on Labor Law, 9th edn 1981; (jtly) Law and National Labor Policy, 1960; Civil Rights, the Constitution and the Courts, 1967; The Warren Court, 1968; The Role of the Supreme Court in American Government, 1976; Freedom of Expression, 1981; The Court and the Constitution, 1987; miscellaneous articles. *Address:* 78 Condon Point, Brooksville, MA 04617, USA; (office) Harvard Law School, Cambridge, MA 02138, USA. *T:* (617) 4953133. *Clubs:* Somerset (Boston, Mass); Century Association (New York). *Died 29 May 2004.*

COX, Arthur George Ernest S.; *see* Stewart Cox.

COX, Major Horace Brimson T.; *see* Trevor Cox.

COX, His Honour (James) Anthony; a Circuit Judge, 1976–94; *b* 21 April 1924; *s* of Herbert Sidney Cox and Gwendoline Margaret Cox; *m* 1950, Doris Margaret Fretwell; three *s* one *d*. *Educ:* Cotham Sch., Bristol; Bristol Univ. (LLB Hons 1948). War Service, Royal Marines, 1943–46. Called to the Bar, Gray's Inn, 1949; a Recorder of the Crown Court, 1972–76. Pres., Anchor Soc., 1985–86. *Recreations:* watching cricket, the arts. *Address:* Haldonhay, Lower Court Road, Newton Ferrers, Plymouth, Devon PL8 1DE. *Clubs:* MCC; Royal Western Yacht (Plymouth); Yealm Yacht. *Died 3 Jan. 2002.*

COX, Peter Denzil John H.; *see* Hippisley-Cox.

COX, Peter Richmond, CB 1971; Deputy Government Actuary, 1963–74; *b* 3 Sept. 1914; *s* of Richard R. Cox, civil servant, and Nellie (*née* Richmond); *m* 1971, Faith Blake Schenk. *Educ:* King's Coll. Sch., Wimbledon. Entered Government Actuary's Dept, 1933. Qualified as Fellow, Institute of Actuaries, 1939. Joint Hon. Sec., Institute of Actuaries, 1962–64 (Vice-Pres., 1966–68). Pres., Eugenics Soc., 1970–72. Chm., CS Insurance Soc., 1973–78. Silver Medal, Inst. of Actuaries, 1975. *Publications:* Demography, 1950 (5 edns); (with R. H. Storr-Best) Surplus in British Life Assurance, 1962; (ed jtly) Population and Pollution, 1972; Resources and Population, 1973; Population and the New Biology, 1974; Equalities and Inequalities in Education, 1975; various papers on actuarial and demographic subjects. *Recreations:* music, painting, gardening. *Address:* The Level House, Mayfield, East Sussex TN20 6BW. *T:* (01435) 872217. *Club:* Actuaries. *Died 1 Sept. 2001.*

COXETER, Harold Scott Macdonald, (Donald), CC 1997; PhD; FRS 1950; Professor of Mathematics, University of Toronto, 1948–80, then Emeritus Professor; *b* 9 Feb. 1907; *s* of Harold Samuel Coxeter and Lucy (*née* Gee); *m* 1936, Hendrina Johanna Brouwer (*d* 1999), The Hague; one *s* one *d*. *Educ:* King Alfred Sch., London; St George's Sch., Harpenden; Trinity Coll., Cambridge (Entrance Scholar, 1926; BA 1929; Smith's Prize, 1931; Hon. Fellow, 2001); PhD Cantab 1931. Fellow, Trinity Coll., Cambridge, 1931–36; Rockefeller Foundn Fellow, 1932–33, Procter Fellow, 1934–35, Princeton; Asst Prof., 1936–43, Associate Prof., 1943–48, Univ. of Toronto. Visiting Professor: Notre Dame, 1947; Columbia, 1949; Dartmouth Coll., 1964; Amsterdam, 1966; Edinburgh, 1967; UEA, 1968; ANU, 1970; Sussex, 1972; Warwick, Utrecht, 1976; CIT, 1977; Bologna, 1978. Editor, Canadian Jl of Mathematics, 1948–57. President: Canadian Mathematical Congress, 1965–67; Internat. Mathematical Congress, 1974. Foreign Mem., Koninklijke Nederlandse Akademie van Wetenschappen, 1975; Hon. Member: Mathematische Gesellschaft, Hamburg, 1977; Wiskundig Genootschap, Amsterdam, 1978; London Mathematical Soc., 1978. Hon. LLD: Alberta, 1957; Trent, 1973; Toronto, 1979; Hon. DMath Waterloo, 1969; Hon. DSc: Acadia, 1971; Carleton, 1984; McMaster, 1988; York, 1994; Hon. Dr rer. nat. Giessen, 1984. Sylvester Medal, Royal Soc., 1997. *Publications:* Non-Euclidean Geometry, 1942, 6th edn 1998; Regular Polytopes, 1948, 3rd edn 1973; The Real Projective Plane, 1949, 3rd edn 1992; (with W. O. J. Moser) Generators and Relations, 1957, 4th edn, 1980; Introduction to Geometry, 1961 and 1969; Projective Geometry, 1964, 2nd edn, revd 1987; (with S. L. Greitzer) Geometry Revisited, 1967; Twelve Geometric Essays, 1968; Regular Complex Polytopes, 1974, 2nd edn 1990; (with W. W. Rouse Ball)

Mathematical Recreations and Essays, 11th edn 1939, 13th edn 1987; (with R. W. Frucht and D. L. Powers) Zero-symmetric Graphs, 1981; Kaleidoscopes, 1995; various mathematical papers. *Recreation:* music. *Address:* 67 Roxborough Drive, Toronto, ON M4W 1X2, Canada.
Died 31 March 2003.

CRABBE, Kenneth Herbert Martineau, TD; Deputy Chairman, The Stock Exchange, 1970–73; *b* 4 Nov. 1916; *m* 1st, 1940, Rowena Leete (*d* 1981); one *s*; 2nd, 1982, Belinda V. Fitzherbert (*née* Batt); three step *s* one step *d*. *Educ:* Stowe Sch. Commnd TA, 1937; psc; Major, RA. Member, Stock Exchange, London, 1937–; Mem. Council, The Stock Exchange, 1963–78. *Recreations:* golf, fishing, shooting, painting. *Address:* Spandrels, Walliswood, Dorking, Surrey RH5 5RJ. *T:* (01306) 627275. *Clubs:* Boodle's; West Sussex Golf.
Died 17 Nov. 2001.

CRABTREE, His Honour Jonathan; a Circuit Judge, 1986–2003; *b* 17 April 1934; *s* of Charles H. Crabtree and Elsie M. Crabtree; *m* 1st, 1957, Caroline Ruth Keigwin (*née* Oliver) (marr. diss. 1976); one *s* three *d* (and one *s* decd); 2nd, 1980, Wendy Elizabeth Hudson (*née* Ward). *Educ:* Bootham; St John's Coll., Cambridge (MA, LLM). Called to Bar, Gray's Inn, 1958. A Recorder, 1974–86. *Recreations:* cricket, cooking, history, archaeology. *Address:* 204 Mount Vale, York YO24 1DL. *T:* (01904) 646609.
Died 11 Feb. 2005.

CRACROFT, Air Vice-Marshal Peter Dicken, CB 1954; AFC 1932; *b* 29 Nov. 1907; *s* of Lt-Col H. Cracroft, Bath; *m* 1932, Margaret Eliza Sugden Patchett (*d* 2001); two *s*. *Educ:* Monkton Combe Sch., Bath. Commissioned RAF 1927; Fleet Air Arm, 1928–31; Central Flying Sch. Instructors' Course, 1931; Flying Instructor, Leuchars, 1931–35; Adjt HMS Courageous, 1936–37; Chief Flying Instructor, Oxford Univ. Air Sqdn, 1937–39; RAF Stn Mount Batten, 1939–40; Air Staff, Coastal Command, 1940–41; OC RAF Station, Chivenor, 1941–43; SASO 19 Gp (later 17 Gp), 1943–44; OC 111 Op. Trg Unit, Bahamas, 1944–45; SASO HQ Air Comd, SE Asia, Mil. Gov. Penang, 1945; AOC Bombay, 1945–46; SASO, HQ 19 Gp, 1946–48; RAF Dir and CO, Jt Anti-Submarine Sch., Londonderry, 1948–50; Sen. Air Liaison Officer, S Africa, 1950–52; AOC 66 Gp, Edinburgh, 1952–53; Senior Air Staff Officer, Headquarters Coastal Command, 1953–55; AOC Scotland and 18 Group, 1955–58; retired from RAF, Dec. 1958. *Address:* The Hyde, Walditch, Bridport, Dorset DT6 4LB. *T:* (01308) 427694.
Died 27 July 2003.

CRADOCK, John Anthony, CB 1980; MBE 1952; Deputy Secretary, Ministry of Defence, 1981–82; *b* 19 Oct. 1921; *o s* of John Cradock and Nan Cradock (*née* Kelly); *m* 1948, Eileen (*née* Bell); one *s* one *d*. *Educ:* St Brendan's Coll., Bristol; Bristol Univ. (BA 1946). Military service, 1941–46 (Captain Royal Signals). Malayan Civil Service, 1946–57; War Office, 1957–67; MoD, 1967–75; Under Sec., N Ireland Office, 1975–77; MoD, 1977–82. *Address:* c/o Lloyds TSB, Morpeth, Northumberland NE61 1AN.
Died 7 March 2003.

CRAIB, Douglas Duncan Simpson, CBE 1974; FRAgS 1971; farmer, 1937–83; Member, Potato Marketing Board of Great Britain, 1968–83; *b* 5 April 1914; *s* of Peter Barton Salsbury Simpson and Helen Duncan; changed name by deed poll, 1930; *m* 1939, Moyra Louise Booth (decd); one *s* one *d*. *Educ:* Aberdeen Grammar Sch.; Dundee High School. Commerce, 1934. Captain, 7th Bn Seaforth Highlanders, 1939–42. Dir, NALCO Ltd, Aberdeen, 1956–68. Chm., Elec. Cons. Council, N Scotland Area, 1971–79; Mem., N of Scotland Hydro-Elec. Bd, 1971–79. Dir, Royal Highland and Agric. Soc. of Scotland, 1961–74 (Chm., 1967–69; Hon. Sec. and Hon. Treas., 1970–74; Hon. Vice-Pres., 1978–79, 1987–88); Member: Highland Agric. Exec. Cttee, 1958–72 (Chm., 1970–72); Scottish Agric. Consultative Panel, 1963–87; Scottish Council of Technical Educn, 1973–85 (Assessor, 1981–85). President:

Moray Area, NFU, 1945; Moray Farmers' Club, 1950; Governor: N of Scotland Coll. of Agriculture, 1970–84; Rowett Res. Inst., Aberdeen, 1973–86; Trustee, The MacRobert Trusts, Scotland, 1970–84. DL Moray, 1974–90. *Address:* The Old School, Mosstodloch, Fochabers, Morayshire IV32 7LE. *T:* (01343) 820733. *Clubs:* Farmers'; Elgin (Elgin, Morayshire).
Died 9 June 2001.

CRAIG, Mrs Barbara Denise, MA Oxon; Principal of Somerville College, Oxford, 1967–80, Honorary Fellow, 1980; *b* 22 Oct. 1915; *o d* of John Alexander Chapman and Janie Denize (*née* Callaway); *m* 1942, Wilson James Craig, CBE (*d* 1989); no *c*. *Educ:* Haberdashers' Aske's Girls' Sch., Acton; Somerville Coll., Oxford. Craven Fellow, 1938; Goldsmiths' Sen. Student, 1938; Woolley Fellow in Archæology, Somerville Coll., 1954–56. Temp. Asst Principal, Mins of Supply and Labour, 1939–40; Asst to Prof. of Greek, Aberdeen Univ., 1940–42; Temp. Asst Principal, Min. of Home Security, 1942; Temp. Principal, Min. of Production, 1943–45. Unofficial work as wife of British Council officer in Brazil, Iraq, Spain, Pakistan, 1946–65; from 1956, archæological work on finds from British excavations at Mycenae. *Recreation:* bird-watching (Mem., Brit. Ornithologists' Union). *Address:* The Wynd, Gayle, Hawes, North Yorkshire DL8 3SD. *T:* (01969) 667289.
Died 25 Jan. 2005.

CRAM, Prof. Donald James; University Professor Emeritus, University of California, Los Angeles, since 1990; *b* 22 April 1919; *s* of William Moffet and Joanna Shelley Cram; *m* 1st, 1940, Jean Turner (marr. diss. 1968); 2nd, 1969, Jane L. Maxwell (*d* 2000); 3rd, 2000, Caroline Cook (*née* Collett). *Educ:* Rollins Coll., Fla (BS); Univ. of Nebraska (MS); Harvard Univ. (PhD). Chemist, Merck & Co., 1942–45; University of California, LA, 1947–90: Instr, ACS Fellow, 1947–48; Asst Prof., 1948–51; Associate Prof., 1951–56; Prof. of Chemistry, 1956; S. Winstein Prof. of Chemistry, 1985–95; Univ. Prof., 1988–90. Guggenheim Fellow, 1955. Centenary Lectr, London, 1976. Chemical Consultant: Upjohn Co., 1952–88; Union Carbide Corp., 1961–82; Eastman Kodak, 1982–91; Technicon Co., 1984–91; Istituto Guido Donegani, Milan, 1988–91. MACS 1945; MRSC 1955; MNAS 1961; Mem., Amer. Acad. of Arts and Scis, 1967; Sigma Xi, Phi Beta Kappa (Hon.). Hon. FRSC 1989. Hon. Dr: Uppsala, 1977; Rollins, 1988; Hon. DSc: S California, 1983; Nebraska, 1989; Western Ontario, 1990; Sheffield, 1991. (Jtly) Nobel Prize for Chemsitry, 1987; American Chemical Society Awards: Creative Work in Org. Chem., 1965; Arthur C. Cope, for Dist Achievement, 1974; Roger Adams, in Org. Chem., 1985; Willard Gibbs Medal, 1985; Richard Tolman Medal,1985; Calif. Scientist of the Year, 1974; Armand Hammer Award, Nat. Acad. of Scis, 1992; President's Medal of Science, 1993. Fields of interest in organic chemistry: molecular complexation, stereochemistry, carbanions, carbonium ions, organosulfur chemistry, paracyclophanes, mold metabolites. *Publications:* (jtly) Organic Chemistry, 1959, 4th edn (jtly), 1980 (trans. into 12 langs); Carbanions, 1965; (jtly) Elements of Organic Chemistry, 1967; (jtly) Essence of Organic Chemistry, 1978; From Design to Discovery, 1990; (jtly) Container Molecules and Their Guests, 1994; numerous articles in ACS Jl, Jl Org. Chem., Chemical Communications, Angewandte Chemie, Tetrahedron. *Recreations:* surfing, ski-ing, tennis, guitar, reading. *Clubs:* Ironwood Country; San Onofre Surfing, Surfers' Medical Association (California).
Died 17 June 2001.

CRAMOND, Dr William Alexander, AO 1994; OBE 1960; FRSE; Professor of Clinical Psychiatry, Flinders University, South Australia, 1983–92, Emeritus Professor of Psychiatry, 1993; *b* 2 Oct. 1920; *er s* of William James Cramond, MBE and of May Battisby, Aberdeen; *m* 1949, Bertine J. C. Mackintosh, MB, ChB, FRANZCP, Dornoch; one *s* one *d*. *Educ:* Robert Gordon's Coll., Aberdeen; Aberdeen Univ. MB, ChB, MD, FRCPsych,

FRANZCP, FRACP, DPM. Physician Supt, Woodilee Mental Hosp., Glasgow, 1955–61; Dir of Mental Health, S Australia, 1961–65; Prof. of Mental Health, Univ. of Adelaide, 1963–71; Principal Medical Officer in Mental Health, Scottish Home and Health Dept, 1971–72; Dean of Faculty of Medicine and Prof. of Mental Health, Univ. of Leicester, 1972–75; Principal and Vice-Chancellor, Stirling Univ., 1975–80; Dir of Mental Health Services, NSW, 1980–83; Clinical Dir, Cleland House, Glenside Hosp., SA, 1983–85; Chm., Bd of Dirs, SA Mental Health Services, 1993–95. Hon. Prof., Clinical Psychiatry, Sydney, 1980–83. DUniv Stirling, 1984. *Publications:* papers on psychosomatic medicine and on care of dying in Brit. Jl Psychiat., Lancet, BMJ. *Recreations:* reading, theatre. *Address:* 28 Tynte Street, North Adelaide, SA 5006, Australia. *Club:* Adelaide (Adelaide).
Died 7 June 2004.

CRANE, Prof. (Francis) Roger; Professor of Law, Queen Mary College, University of London, 1965–78, then Emeritus; *b* 19 Dec. 1910; *s* of Francis Downing Crane and Elizabeth Mackintosh; *m* 1938, Jean Berenice Hadfield (*d* 1986); two *s* one *d*. *Educ:* Highgate Sch.; University Coll., London (LLB 1933). Solicitor, 1934, Clifford's Inn Prize. Lecturer in Law, King's Coll. and private practice, 1935–38; Lecturer in Law, University of Manchester, 1938–46; Prof. of Law, University of Nottingham, 1946–52; Prof. of English Law, King's Coll., London, 1952–65; Dean of the Faculty of Law, QMC, London, 1965–76. University of London: Mem. Senate, 1969–71, 1973–78; Chm. Academic Council, 1975–78; Mem. Court, 1975–78. Visiting Professor: Tulane Univ., 1960; University of Khartoum, 1963; Dean of the Faculty of Law and Visiting Prof., University of Canterbury (New Zealand), 1964; Visiting Professor: Univ. of Melbourne, 1972; Monash Univ., 1972; Univ. of Sydney, 1980. Pres., Soc. of Public Teachers of Law, 1975–76. FKC 1976; Fellow QMW (Fellow QMC 1980). Served War of 1939–45: Royal Corps of Signals, Major, 1944. *Publications:* (jointly) A Century of Family Law, 1957; articles and notes in legal periodicals. *Address:* 25 Winston Drive, Isham, Kettering, Northants NN14 1HS. *T:* (01536) 723938.
Died 12 Jan. 2001.

CRANE, Roger; *see* Crane, F. R.

CRAVEN, Air Marshal Sir Robert Edward, KBE 1970 (OBE 1954); CB 1966; DFC 1940; *b* 16 Jan. 1916; *s* of Gerald Craven, Port Elizabeth, S Africa, and Edith Craven, York; *m* 1940, Joan Peters (*d* 1991); one *s* one *d*. *Educ:* Scarborough Coll. MN, 1932–37; Pilot Officer, RAF, 1937; 201, 210, 228 Sqdns, 1937–41; RAF Staff Coll., 1942; Staff Appts: Coastal Command, 1942 (despatches thrice); Directing Staff, RAF Staff Coll., 1944; HQ, Mediterranean and Middle East, Cairo, 1945; CO Eastleigh, Kenya, 1946; RN Staff Coll., 1948; Directing Staff, Joint Services Staff Coll., 1949; Standing Group, NATO Washington, 1951; RAF St Eval, 1954; Directing Staff, RAF Staff Coll., 1957; Group Capt. 1957; CO RAF Lyneham, 1959; Dir, Personal Services, RAF, 1961; Air Cdre 1961; Air Officer Admin., Transport Comd, 1964; Air Vice-Marshal, 1965; SASO, Flying Training Comd, 1967–68; Training Comd, 1968–69; Commander, Maritime Air Forces, NATO Air Comdr Eastern Atlantic, Channel and North Sea, 1969–72, retired. Order of Menelik (Ethiopia), 1955. *Recreations:* water fowl breeding, antique furniture restoration and reproduction. *Address:* Letcombe House, Letcombe Regis, Oxon OX12 9LD. *Club:* Royal Air Force.
Died 20 Feb. 2003.

CRAWFORD, Douglas; *see* Crawford, G. D.

CRAWFORD, (George) Douglas; author; *b* 1 Nov. 1939; *s* of Robert and Helen Crawford; *m* 1964, Joan Burnie (marr. diss. 1984); one *s* one *d*. *Educ:* Glasgow Academy; St Catharine's Coll., Cambridge (MA). Features Editor, Business, 1961–63; Industrial Corresp., Glasgow Herald, 1963–66; Editor, Scotland Magazine, 1966–70; Dir, Polecon Gp of Cos, 1970–89; journalist, Glasgow Herald, subseq. The Herald, 1989–95; Editor, Business and Finance, 1993–95. MP (SNP) Perth and East Perthshire, Oct. 1974–1979; contested (SNP) Perth and Kinross, 1983. *Recreations:* hill-walking, swimming, playing piano and clavichord, watching cricket. *Address:* Flat 3/1, 8 Hall Street, Campbeltown PA28 6BU.
Died 17 April 2002.

CRAWFORD, Sir (Robert) Stewart, GCMG 1973 (KCMG 1966; CMG 1951); CVO 1955; HM Diplomatic Service, retired; *b* 27 Aug. 1913; *s* of Sir William Crawford, KBE; *m* 1938, Mary Katharine (*d* 1992), *d* of late Eric Corbett, Gorse Hill, Witley, Surrey; three *s* one *d* (and one *s* decd). *Educ:* Gresham's Sch., Holt; Oriel Coll., Oxford. Home Civil Service (Air Ministry), 1936; Private Sec. to Chief of Air Staff, 1940–46; Asst Sec., Control Office for Germany and Austria, 1946; Foreign Office, 1947; Counsellor, British Embassy, 1954–56; Counsellor, later Minister, British Embassy, Baghdad, 1957–59; Dep. UK Delegate to OEEC Paris, 1959–60; Asst Under Sec., Foreign Office, 1961–65; Political Resident, Persian Gulf, 1966–70; Dep. Under-Sec. of State, FCO, 1970–73. Mem., BBC Gen. Adv. Council, 1976–84; Chairman: Cttee on Broadcasting Coverage, 1973–74; Broadcasters' Audience Res. Bd, 1980–88. *Address:* 19 Adam Court, Bell Street, Henley-on-Thames, Oxon RG9 2BJ. *T:* (01491) 574702. *Club:* Phyllis Court (Henley-on-Thames).
Died 11 Oct. 2002.

CRAWFORD, Sir Stewart; *see* Crawford, Sir R. S.

CRAWFORD, Vice-Adm. Sir William (Godfrey), KBE 1961; CB 1958; DSC 1941; *b* 14 Sept. 1907; *s* of late H. E. V. Crawford, Wyld Court, Axminster, and Mrs M. E. Crawford; *m* 1939, Mary Felicity Rosa (*d* 1995), *d* of Sir Philip Williams, 2nd Bt; three *s* one *d*. *Educ:* RN Coll., Dartmouth. Lieut RN, 1929; specialised in gunnery, 1932; Lieut-Comdr, 1937; Gunnery Officer, HMS Rodney, 1940–42; Comdr, Dec. 1941; SO to 2nd i/c, Eastern Fleet, 1942–44; Exec. Officer, HMS Venerable, 1944–46; Capt. 1947; in comd HMS Pelican and 2nd Frigate Flotilla, Med., 1948–49; Dep.-Dir RN Staff Coll., 1950–52; in comd HMS Devonshire, 1952–53; in comd RN Coll., Dartmouth, 1953–56; Rear-Adm. 1956; Imperial Defence Coll., 1956–58; Flag Officer, Sea Training, 1958–60; Vice-Adm. 1959; Comdr British Navy Staff and Naval Attaché Washington, 1960–62; retired list, 1963. Dir, Overseas Offices, BTA, 1964–72. *Recreations:* sailing, fishing. *Address:* Broadlands, Whitchurch Canonicorum, Bridport, Dorset DT6 6RJ. *T:* (01297) 489591. *Club:* Cruising.
Died 16 June 2003.

CREAGH, Maj.-Gen. Sir Kilner Rupert B.; *see* Brazier-Creagh.

CREAMER, Brian; Consulting Physician, St Thomas's Hospital, London, 1991 (Physician, 1959–91); Senior Lecturer in Medicine, United Medical and Dental Schools (St Thomas's), 1959–91; Hon. Consultant in Gastroenterology to the Army, 1970–90; *b* 12 April 1926; *s* of late L. G. Creamer, Epsom; *m* 1953, Margaret Holden Rees; two *s* one *d*. *Educ:* Christ's Hosp.; St Thomas's Hosp. MB, BS Hons London, 1948; MD London, 1952. FRCP 1966 (MRCP 1950). Research Asst, Mayo Clinic, Rochester, USA, 1955–56; Dean: St Thomas's Hosp. Med. Sch., 1979–84; UMDS of Guy's and St Thomas's Hosps, 1984–86. Vis. Prof., Shiraz Univ., Iran, 1977–78. Sir Arthur Hurst Memorial Lectr, 1968; Watson Smith Lectr, RCP, 1971. Member: SE Thames RHA, 1982–85; Medway DHA, 1987–89; W Lambeth DHA, 1989–90. Member: British Soc. of Gastroenterology; Assoc. of Physicians of GB and NI; Exec. Subcttee, Univ. Hosps Assoc., 1981–86. Chm. Council, Trinity Hospice, 1987–92. Member: Collegiate Council, Univ. of London, 1980–86; Senate, Univ. of London, 1981–86; Council of Almoners, Christ's Hosp., 1986–98. *Publications:* (ed) Modern Trends in Gastroenterology, vol. 4, 1970; (ed) The Small Intestine, 1974; contribs to med. jls. *Recreations:* grappling with drawing and painting, listening to music.

Address: Ashfold, Old Lane Gardens, Effingham, Surrey KT11 1NN. *T:* (01483) 283320.   *Died 23 June 2005.*

CREEK, Malcolm Lars, LVO 1980; OBE 1985; HM Diplomatic Service, retired; Consul-General, Auckland, 1988–90; *b* 2 April 1931; *s* of Edgar Creek and Lily Creek (*née* Robertshaw); *m* 1st, 1953, Moira Pattison (marr. diss. 1970); one *d* (one *s* decd); 2nd, 1970, Gillian Bell; one *s* one *d* (and one *d* decd). *Educ:* Belle Vue Sch., Bradford. BA Hons London. Nat. Service, 1950–52. Foreign Office, 1953; served Mogadishu, Harar, Mexico City, Abidjan, Chile; First Sec., San José, 1968; Havana, 1971; FCO, 1974; Head of Chancery, Tunis, 1978; Lima, 1981; High Comr, Vanuatu, 1985. *Recreations:* reading, family history, cricket. *Address:* 17 Bertram Drive North, Meols, Wirral, Merseyside L47 0LN. *T:* (0151) 632 5520.
Died 21 May 2003.

CREIGHTON, Harold Digby Fitzgerald; Editor, The Spectator, 1973–75 (Chairman, 1967–75); *b* 11 Sept. 1927; *s* of late Rev. Digby Robert Creighton and Amy Frances Rohde; *m* 1964, Harriett Mary Falconer Wallace, *d* of late A. L. P. F. Wallace of Candacraig, Mem., Queen's Body Guard for Scotland; four *d. Educ:* Haileybury. Consolidated Tin Smelters, Penang, 1950–52; Dir, machine tool companies, London, 1952–63; Dir, machine tool companies, London, 1952–63; Chm., Scottish Machine Tool Corp. Ltd, Glasgow, 1963–68. *Address:* 18 St James Chambers, Ryder Street, SW1Y 6QA. *Clubs:* Beefsteak, Brooks's.
Died 3 July 2003.

CRESSWELL, Helen; freelance author and television scriptwriter; *b* 11 July 1934; *d* of Annie Edna Clarke and Joseph Edward Cresswell; *m* 1962, Brian Rowe (marr. diss. 1995); two *d. Educ:* Nottingham Girls' High Sch.; King's College, London (BA English Hons). Member: Soc. of Authors; BAFTA; RTS. Children's Writer's Award (jtly), BAFTA, 2000. *Television series:* Lizzie Dripping, 1973–75; Jumbo Spencer, 1976; The Bagthorpe Saga, 1980; The Secret World of Polly Flint, 1985; Moondial, 1988; The Return of the Psammead, 1993; The Watchers, 1994; The Famous Five, 1995; The Demon Headmaster, 1995; *adaptations:* Five Children and It, 1990; The Phoenix and the Carpet, 1997; Little Grey Rabbit, 2000; numerous TV plays. *Publications:* Sonya-by-the-Shire, 1961; Jumbo Spencer, 1963; The White Sea Horse, 1964; Pietro and the Mule, 1965; Jumbo Back to Nature, 1965; Where the Wind Blows, 1966; Jumbo Afloat, 1966; The Piemakers, 1967; A Tide for the Captain, 1967; The Signposters, 1968; The Sea Piper, 1968; The Barge Children, 1968; The Night-watchman, 1969; A Game of Catch, 1969; A Gift from Winklesea, 1969; The Outlanders, 1970; The Wilkses, 1970; The Bird Fancier, 1971; At the Stroke of Midnight, 1971; The Beachcombers, 1972; Lizzie Dripping, 1972; The Bongleweed, 1972; Lizzie Dripping Again, 1974; Butterfly Chase, 1975; The Winter of the Birds, 1975; My Aunt Polly, 1979; My Aunt Polly By the Sea, 1980; Dear Shrink, 1982; The Secret World of Polly Flint, 1982; Ellie and the Hagwitch, 1984; The Bagthorpe Saga: Pt 1, Ordinary Jack, 1977; Pt 2, Absolute Zero, 1978; Pt 3, Bagthorpes Unlimited, 1978; Pt 4, Bagthorpes *v* The World, 1979; Pt 5, Bagthorpes Abroad, 1984; Pt 6, Bagthorpes Haunted, 1985; Pt 7, Bagthorpes Liberated, 1988; Pt 8, The Bagthorpe Triangle, 1992; Moondial, 1987; Time Out, 1987; Rosie and the Boredom Eater, 1989; Whatever Happened in Winklesea?, 1989; Meet Posy Bates, 1990; Posy Bates Again, 1991; Lizzie Dripping and the Witch, 1991; The Return of the Psammead, 1992; Posy Bates and the Bag Lady, 1992; The Watchers, 1993; (ed) Puffin Book of Funny Stories, 1993; Classic Fairy Tales, 1993; Polly Thumb, 1994; Stonestruck, 1995; Bagthorpes Besieged, 1995; Mystery at Winklesea, 1995; Giant, 1995; Birdspell, 1995; (ed) Mystery Stories, 1996; Bag of Bones, 1997; Snatchers, 1998. *Recreations:* watercolour painting, collecting books, antiques and coincidences, sundial watching. *Address:* Old Church Farm, Eakring, Newark, Notts NG22 0DA. *T:* (01623) 870401.   *Died 26 Sept. 2005.*

CREW, Air Vice-Marshal Edward Dixon, CB 1973; DSO 1944 and Bar 1950; DFC 1941 and Bar 1942; FRAeS; Planning Inspectorate, Department of the Environment, 1973–87; *b* 24 Dec. 1917; *er s* of F. D. Crew, MB, MRCS, LRCP; *m* 1945, Virginia Martin; one *s. Educ:* Felsted Sch.; Downing Coll., Cambridge (MA). Commissioned RAFVR, 1939; served War of 1939–45: night fighter sqdns; 604 Sqdn, 85 Sqdn; Comd 96 Sqdn; permanent commission, 1945. Malayan Emergency, Comd No 45 Sqdn, 1948–50; on exchange, RCAF, 1952–54; CFE, 1954–56; Comd RAF Brüggen, Germany, 1959–62; Comdr, Air Forces Borneo, 1965–66; AOC Central Reconnaissance Estabt, 1968; Dep. Controller, Nat. Air Traffic Services, 1969–72; various Air Staff jobs at Air Min. and MoD; retd 1973. Mem., Cotswold DC, 1991–95. FRAeS 1972. *Recreation:* golf. *Address:* National Westminster Bank, 10 Benet Street, Cambridge CB2 3PU. *Club:* Royal Air Force.   *Died 18 Aug. 2002.*

CRICHTON, Col Richard John Vesey, CVO 1986; MC 1940; *b* 2 Nov. 1916; *s* of Col Hon. Sir George Crichton, GCVO, and Lady Mary Crichton; *m* 1948, Yvonne Avril Catherine, *d* of late Dr and Mrs H. E. Worthington; three *s. Educ:* Eton; RMC, Sandhurst. Commissioned 2/Lieut Coldstream Guards, 1936; served War of 1939–45, Belgium, 1940, Italy, 1943–44 (twice wounded, MC, despatches); Commanded: 1st Bn Coldstream Guards, 1954–57; Coldstream Guards, 1958–61, retired 1961. Comptroller, Union Jack Services Clubs, 1964–66; Member, HM Body Guard, Hon. Corps of Gentlemen at Arms, 1966–86; Clerk of the Cheque and Adjutant, 1979–81; Lieutenant, 1981–86. Mem., Hants CC and Police Authority, 1964–67. *Publication:* The Coldstream Guards 1946–1970, 1972. *Address:* Derwent House, Hartley Wintney, Hampshire RG27 8RE. *Club:* Cavalry and Guards.   *Died 30 Jan. 2002.*

CRICK, Francis Harry Compton, OM 1991; FRS 1959; J. W. Kieckhefer Distinguished Professor, The Salk Institute for Biological Studies, since 1977 (President, 1994–95); Adjunct Professor of Psychology, University of California, San Diego; *b* 8 June 1916; *e s* of late Harry Crick and late Annie Elizabeth (*née* Wilkins); *m* 1st, 1940, Ruth Doreen Dodd (marr. diss. 1947); one *s*; 2nd, 1949, Odile Speed; two *d. Educ:* Mill Hill Sch.; University Coll., London (BSc; Fellow, 1962); Caius Coll., Cambridge (PhD; Hon. Fellow, 1976). Scientist in Admiralty, 1940–47; Strangeways Laboratory, Cambridge, 1947–49; MRC Lab. of Molecular Biology, Cambridge, 1949–77; Brooklyn Polytechnic, NY, USA, 1953–54. Vis. Lectr Rockefeller Inst., NY, USA, 1959; Vis. Prof., Chemistry Dept, Harvard, 1959; Fellow, Churchill Coll., Cambridge, 1960–61 (Hon. Fellow, 1965); Vis. Biophysics Prof., Harvard, 1962; Non-resident Fellow, Salk Inst. for Biological Studies, San Diego, 1962–73; Ferkhauf Foundn Visiting Prof., Salk Inst., 1976–77. For. Hon. Mem., Amer. Acad. of Arts and Sciences, 1962; Hon. Mem., Amer. Soc. Biological Chem., 1963; Hon. MRIA, 1964; FAAAS 1966; Fellow, INSA, 1982; Hon. FRSE, 1966; Hon. FIBiol, 1995; Hon. Fellow: Indian Acad. of Scis, 1985; Tata Inst. of Fundamental Res., Bombay, 1996; For. Associate, US Nat. Acad. of Sciences, 1969; Mem., German Acad. of Science, Leopoldina, 1969; MAE 1998; For. Mem., American Philos. Soc., Philadelphia, 1972; Hon. Mem., Hellenic Biochem. and Biophys. Soc., 1974. Associate For. Mem., French Acad. of Scis, 1978. 60 named lectures, 1959–94. Warren Triennial Prize, Boston, USA (with J. D. Watson), 1959; Lasker Award (jointly), 1960; Prix Charles Léopold Mayer, French Académies des Sciences, 1961; Research Corp. Award (with J. D. Watson), 1961; Gairdner Foundation Award, Toronto, 1962; Nobel Prize for Medicine (jointly), 1962; Royal Medal, Royal Soc., 1972; Copley Medal, Royal Soc., 1975; Michelson-Morley Award, Cleveland, 1981; Benjamin P. Cheney Medal, Spokane, Washington, 1986; Golden Plate Award, Phoenix, 1987; Albert Medal, RSA, 1987; Wright Prize VIII, Harvey Mudd Coll., Calif., 1988; Joseph Priestly Award, Dickinson Coll., Pennsylvania,

1988; Distinguished Achievement Award, Oregon State Univ., 1995. Friends of the Library. *Publications:* Of Molecules and Men, 1966; Life Itself, 1981; What Mad Pursuit: a personal view of scientific discovery, 1988; The Astonishing Hypothesis: The scientific search for the soul, 1994; papers and articles on molecular and cell biology and on neurobiology in scientific journals. *Address:* The Salk Institute for Biological Studies, PO Box 85800, San Diego, CA 92186–5800, USA; 1792 Colgate Circle, La Jolla, CA 92037, USA.   *Died 28 July 2004.*

CRILL, Sir Peter (Leslie), KBE 1995 (CBE 1980); Kt 1987; Bailiff of Jersey, and President of the Court of Appeal of Jersey, 1986–95; Judge, Court of Appeal of Jersey and Guernsey, 1986–98; *b* 1 Feb. 1925; *s* of S. G. Crill, and Olive Le Gros; *m* 1953, A. F. R. Dodd, MB, *d* of E. A. Dodd, JP, Dromara, NI; two *d* (and one *d* decd). *Educ:* Victoria Coll., Jersey; Exeter Coll., Oxford (King Charles I Scholar; MA; Hon. Fellow, 1991). Called to the Bar, Middle Temple, 1949; called to the Jersey Bar, 1949. In private practice in Jersey, 1949–62. States of Jersey Deputy for St Clement, 1951–58; States of Jersey Senator, 1960–62; Solicitor General, Jersey, 1962–69; Attorney General, Jersey, 1969–75; Dep. Bailiff, 1975–86. Mem. Council, University of Buckingham, 1981–96. Pres., La Société Jersiaise, 1980–85; Chairman: Jersey Arts Trust, 1995–2002; Alliance Française (Jersey), 1996–2003; Mem., Conseil de la Fédération Britannique des Comités de l'Alliance Française, 1998–2000. Liveryman, Glass Sellers' Co., 1995. Hon. LLD Buckingham, 1997. CStJ 1994. *Recreations:* books, pottering about. *Address:* Beechfield House, Trinity, Jersey, Channel Islands JE3 5JU. *T:* (01534) 20270. *Clubs:* Athenæum; Royal Channel Islands Yacht.   *Died 3 Oct. 2005.*

CRIPPIN, Harry Trevor, FCIS; Chief Executive and Town Clerk, Cardiff City Council, 1979–88; *b* 14 May 1929; *s* of Harry and Mary Elizabeth Crippin; *m* 1959, Hilda Green, JP; one *s* one *d*. *Educ:* Leigh Grammar Sch., Lancs. DMA; FCIS 1975. Asst Town Clerk, Manchester, 1970–74; City Sec., Cardiff CC, 1974–79. FCMI. OStJ 1986. *Address:* 23 Greenwood Road, Llandaff, Cardiff CF5 2QD. *T:* (029) 2056 4103.   *Died 22 Feb. 2001.*

CRISP, Sir (John) Peter, 4th Bt *cr* 1913; *b* 19 May 1925; *o s* of Sir John Wilson Crisp, 3rd Bt, and Marjorie (*d* 1977), *d* of F. R. Shriver; *S* father, 1950; *m* 1954, Judith Mary (*d* 1998), *d* of late H. E. Gillett; three *s* one *d*. *Educ:* Westminster. *Heir:* *s* John Charles Crisp [*b* 10 Dec. 1955; *m* 1992, Mary Jo, *er d* of Dr and Mrs D. MacAuley]. *Address:* Crabtree Cottage, Drungewick Lane, Loxwood, Billingshurst, West Sussex RH14 0RP. *T:* (01403) 752374.   *Died 20 March 2005.*

CRITCHETT, Sir Ian (George Lorraine), 3rd Bt *cr* 1908; HM Diplomatic Service, retired; Counsellor, Foreign and Commonwealth Office, 1977–80; *b* 9 Dec. 1920; *s* of Sir Montague Critchett, 2nd Bt, and Innes (*d* 1982), 3rd *d* of late Col F. G. A. Wiehe, The Durham Light Infantry; *S* father, 1941; *m* 1st, 1948, Paulette Mary Lorraine (*d* 1962), *e d* of late Col H. B. Humfrey; 2nd, 1964, Jocelyn Daphne Margret, *e d* of late Comdr C. M. Hall; one *s* one *d*. *Educ:* Harrow; Clare Coll., Cambridge (BA). RAFVR, 1942–46. Joined Foreign Office, 1948; 3rd Sec. (Commercial), at Vienna, 1950–51; 2nd Sec. (Commercial) at Bucharest, 1951–53; 2nd Sec. at Cairo, 1956; First Sec., FO, 1962. *Publication:* Selected Poems, 1998. *Heir:* *s* Charles George Montague Critchett, *b* 2 April 1965. *Address:* Uplands Lodge, Pains Hill, Limpsfield, Oxted, Surrey RH8 0RF. *Clubs:* Travellers, MCC.   *Died 19 June 2004.*

CROCKER, Sir Walter (Russell), KBE 1978 (CBE 1955); Lieutenant-Governor of South Australia, 1973–82; *b* 25 March 1902; *e s* of Robert Crocker and Alma Bray, Parnaroo, SA; *m* 1951, Claire (marr. diss. 1968), *y d* of F. J. Ward, Headmaster of Prince Alfred Coll., Adelaide, and *widow* of Dr John Gooden, physicist; two *s*. *Educ:* Univ. of Adelaide; Balliol Coll., Oxford; Stanford Univ., USA.

Entered Colonial Administrative Service (Nigeria), 1930; transf. to League of Nations, 1934, and to ILO (Asst to Dir-Gen). Served War, 1940–45 (Lt-Col). Farming at Parnaroo, 1946; UN Secretariat (Chief of Africa Sect.), 1946–50; Prof. of Internat. Relations, ANU, 1950–52 (Actg Vice-Chancellor, 1951); High Comr for Australia to India, 1952–55; Ambassador to Indonesia, 1955–57; High Comr to Canada, 1957–58; High Comr to India and Ambassador to Nepal, 1958–62; Ambassador to the Netherlands and Belgium, 1962–65; Ambassador to Ethiopia and High Comr to Kenya and Uganda, 1965–67; Ambassador to Italy, 1967–70. Hon. Col, Royal South Australia Regt, 1977–. Croix de Guerre avec palme, l'Ordre royal du Lion (Belgium), 1945; Cavaliere di Gr. Croce dell'Ordine al Merito (Italy), 1970; Order of Malta (Grand' Uffiziale del Merito Melitense), 1975. *Publications:* The Japanese Population Problem, 1931; Nigeria, 1936; On Governing Colonies, 1946; Self-Government for the Colonies, 1949; Can the United Nations Succeed?, 1951; The Race Question as a factor in International Relations, 1955; Nehru, 1965; Australian Ambassador, 1971; Memoirs, 1981; Sir Thomas Playford, 1983. *Recreations:* gardening, walking, music; previously ski-ing, tennis. *Address:* 624 Seaview Road, Grange, SA 5022, Australia. *Club:* Adelaide.   *Died 14 Nov. 2002.*

CROFTON, Sir (Henry Edward) Melville, 6th Bt *cr* 1838, of Longford House, Sligo; MBE 1970; *b* 15 Aug. 1931; *s* of Brig. Roger Crofton, CIE, MC and Dorothy (*née* Hatchell); *S* cousin, Sir Malby Crofton, 5th Bt, 2002; *m* 1955, Mary Brigid Riddle; two *s* one *d*. *Educ:* Hilton Coll., Natal; Trinity Coll., Cambridge (BA Engrg 1954). Cadet, HMOCS, 1955; Asst Dist Comr, Nyasaland, 1956; Clerk to the Cabinet, 1966, Principal Admin. Officer, 1968, Malaŵi; Industrial Trng Advr, ODA, London, 1974–91. Vis. Consultant, UNIDO, Vienna, 1979; Consultant, FO Know How Fund for Central and Eastern Europe and former Soviet Union, 1991–2001. *Publications:* UNIDO background papers for First and Second World Consultations on Training of Industrial Manpower, 1982 and 1987. *Recreations:* history, travel. *Heir:* *s* Julian Malby Crofton [*b* 26 Nov. 1958; *m* 1989, Hilary Twort; two *s* one *d*]. *Address:* Haldon, St Giles Hill, Winchester, Hampshire SO23 0JH. *T:* (01962) 852408, *Fax:* (01962) 842741; *e-mail:* mel.crofton@btinternet.com.
                              Died 24 June 2003.

CROFTON, Sir Malby (Sturges), 5th Bt *cr* 1838 (orig. *cr* 1661), of Longford House, Sligo; Partner, Messrs Fenn & Crosthwaite; Member of the London Stock Exchange, 1957–75; *b* 11 Jan. 1923; *s* of Sir Malby Richard Henry Crofton, 4th Bt, DSO and Bar, and Katharine Beatrix Pollard; *S* father, 1962; *m* 1st, 1961, Elizabeth Madeline Nina (*née* Mansel) (marr. diss. 1966); 2nd, 1998, Sally Eden; one step *s*. *Educ:* Eton (King's Scholar); Trinity Coll., Cambridge (scholar). Served with Life Guards, 1942–46, in Middle East and Italy. Kensington Borough Council: Mem., 1962; Leader, 1968–77; Mayor, Kensington and Chelsea, 1978; Member: GLC, 1970–73; ILEA, 1970–73; Ealing N, GLC, 1977–81; Leader, GLC Scrutiny Cttee, 1977–78. Vice-Chm., NW Thames RHA, 1980–85. Hon.Treasurer, Marie Curie Meml Foundn; Dir, St Edward's Housing Assoc.; Chm., Kensington and Chelsea, Age Concern, 1987–. Pres., Ealing N Cons. Assoc. Freeman, Royal Bor. of Kensington and Chelsea, 1983. Hon. Fellow, Chelsea Coll. *Recreations:* tennis, swimming, motoring, planting trees, farming. *Heir:* kinsman Henry Edward Melville Crofton [*b* 15 Aug. 1931; *m* 1955, Brigid, twin *d* of Gerald K. Riddle; two *s* one *d*]. *Address:* 12 Caithness Road, W14 0JB; Longford House, Beltra, Co. Sligo, Eire. *Clubs:* Cavalry and Guards, Hurlingham.   *Died 20 Jan. 2002.*

CROFTON, Sir Melville; *see* Crofton, Sir H. E. M.

CROOK, 2nd Baron *cr* 1947, of Carshalton, Surrey; **Douglas Edwin Crook,** CEng, MICE; *b* 19 Nov. 1926; *s* of 1st Baron Crook and Ida Gertrude (*d* 1985), *d* of Joseph Haddon; *S* father, 1989; *m* 1954, Ellenor (*d* 1998),

d of late Robert Rouse; one *s* one *d*. *Educ:* Whitgift School, Croydon; Imperial Coll., London (BSc Eng, DIC, ACGI). *Heir: s* Hon. Robert Douglas Edwin Crook, BSc, MBA [*b* 19 May 1955; *m* 1981, Suzanne Jane Robinson, BA, LLB; two *s*]. *Address:* 15 Cordova Court, Earls Avenue, Folkestone, Kent CT20 2HQ.
Died 18 June 2001.

CROOK, Arthur Charles William; Editor, The Times Literary Supplement, 1959–74; *b* 16 Feb. 1912; *m* 1948, Sarita Mary Vivien Bushell (marr. diss.); one *s* two *d*; *m* 2002, Juliet Diana Wrightson. Editorial staff of The Times; Asst Editor, The Times Literary Supplement, 1951–59. Pres. and Chm., Royal Literary Fund, 1984–90. *Recreation:* theatre. *Address:* 70 Regent's Park Road, NW1 7SX. *T:* (020) 7722 8446. *Club:* Garrick.   *Died 15 July 2005.*

CROOK, Brig. Paul Edwin, CBE 1965 (OBE 1946); DSO 1957; *b* 19 April 1915; *s* of late Herbert Crook and Christine Crook, Lyme Regis; *m* 1st, 1944, Joan (marr. diss. 1967), *d* of late William Lewis; one *d*; *m* 2nd, 1967, Betty, *d* of late John William Wyles. *Educ:* Uppingham Sch.; Emmanuel Coll., Cambridge (BA 1936, MA 1956). Commnd into QORWK Regt, 1935; served: India and Palestine, 1937–39; War of 1939–45, Africa, NW Europe, Burma; Chief Civil Affairs Officer (Col), Netherlands East Indies, 1946; comd 3rd Bn The Parachute Regt, 1954–57; Suez Ops, 1956; comd Army Airborne Trng and Develt Centre, 1959–62; Comdr and Chief of Staff, Jamaica Defence Force, 1962–65; Security Ops Advisor to High Comr for Aden and S Arabia, 1965–67; Comdr, Rhine Area, 1969–70. Col, 1959; Brig., 1963; retired 1971. ADC to The Queen, 1965. Hon. Col, 16 Lincoln Co. Parachute Regt (VR), 1974–79; Dep. Hon. Col, The Parachute Regt (TAVR): 15th (Scottish) Bn, 1979–83; 4th Bn, 1984–85. Chm., Lincs County Scouts, 1975–88. Bronze Star (US), 1945. *Publication:* Came the Dawn, 1989. *Recreations:* cricket, golf, jazz. *Address:* The Longhouse, Diptford, Totnes, Devon TQ9 7LY. *T:* (01548) 821609. *Clubs:* Naval and Military, MCC; Jamaica (W Indies).
Died 20 Oct. 2004.

CROOKENDEN, Maj.-Gen. George Wayet Derek; DL; Emeritus Fellow, Peterhouse, Cambridge, since 1989; *b* 11 Dec. 1920; *o s* of late Lt-Col John Crookenden and Iris Margherita Gay; *m* 1948, Elizabeth Mary Angela Bourke (decd); one *s* one *d*. *Educ:* Winchester Coll.; Christ Church, Oxford. Commnd RA, 1941; GSO1, SHAPE, 1961–62; CO, 19 Field Regt, RA, 1962–64; Comdr, 7 Artillery Bde, 1964–67; Exercise Controller, CICC (West), 1969–71; Chief, British Commanders-in-Chief Liaison Mission, 1971–72; C of S, Contingencies Planning, SHAPE, 1972–75. Col Comdt, RA, 1977–82. Fellow and Sen. Bursar, Peterhouse, Cambridge, 1975–88. DL Cambs, 1984. *Club:* Army and Navy.
Died 11 Jan. 2005.

CROOKENDEN, Lt-Gen. Sir Napier, KCB 1970 (CB 1966); DSO 1945; OBE 1954; DL; Lieutenant, HM Tower of London, 1975–81; *b* 31 Aug. 1915; 2nd *s* of late Col Arthur Crookenden, CBE, DSO; *m* 1948, Patricia Nassau, *d* of 2nd Baron Kindersley, CBE, MC, and of Nancy Farnsworth, *d* of Dr Geoffrey Boyd; two *s* two *d*. *Educ:* Wellington Coll.; RMC, Sandhurst. Commissioned, Cheshire Regt, 1935; Bde Major, 6th Airlanding Bde, 1943–44; CO, 9th Bn, The Parachute Regt, 1944–46; GSO1 (Plans) to Dir of Ops, Malaya, 1952–54; Comdr, 16th Parachute Bde, 1960–61; idc 1962; Dir, Land/Air Warfare MoD (Army Dept), 1964–66; Commandant, RMCS, Shrivenham, 1967–69; GOC-in-C, Western Comd, 1969–72. Col, The Cheshire Regt, 1969–71; Col Comdt, The Prince of Wales Div., 1971–74. Director: SE Regional Bd, Lloyds Bank Ltd, 1973–86; Flextech Ltd, 1978–86. A Trustee, Imperial War Museum, 1973–83. Chm., SSAFA, 1974–85; a Vice-Pres., RUSI, 1978–85. DL Kent, 1979. *Publications:* Dropzone Normandy, 1976; Airborne at War, 1978; Battle of the Bulge 1944, 1980. *Club:* Army and Navy.   *Died 31 Oct. 2002.*

CROPPER, Dame Hilary (Mary), DBE 2004 (CBE 1999); non-executive Chairman, Xansa plc (formerly FI Group), 2002–03 (Chief Executive, 1985–2000; Executive Chairman, 2000–02); *b* 9 Jan. 1941; *d* of Arnold Trueman and Madeline Emily Trueman (*née* Sutton); *m* 1963, Peter John Cropper; one *s* two *d*. *Educ:* Univ. of Salford (BSc Hons Maths). Sen. management positions, ICL, 1970–85. Non-executive Director: TSB, 1987–90; London First, 1996–99; Barclays plc, 1998–; Barclays Bank plc, 1998–. Member: Financial Reporting Council, 1997–2003; New Deal Taskforce, 2000–01; Nat. Employment Panel, 2001–; Security Commn, 2002–. Non-exec. Member: POB, 1990–96; BOTB, 1992–96. External Advr, Civil Service Sen. Appts, 2000–. Gov., Univ. of Hertfordshire, 1995–2000. Freeman, City of London, 1987. CCMI; FBCS; FRSA.
Died 26 Dec. 2004.

CROSS, 3rd Viscount *cr* 1886; **Assheton Henry Cross;** late Lieutenant Scots Guards; *b* 7 May 1920; *e s* of 2nd Viscount and Maud Evelyn (who *m* 2nd, 1944, Guy Hope Coldwell (*d* 1948), Stoke Lodge, Ludlow, Salop; she *d* 1976), *d* of late Maj.-Gen. Inigo Jones, CB, CVO, Kelston Park, Bath; *S* father, 1932; *m* 1952, Patricia Mary (marr. diss. 1957; she *m* 1960, Comdr G. H. H. Culme-Seymour), *e d* of E. P. Hewetson, JP, The Craig, Windermere, Westmorland; two *d*; *m* 1972, Mrs Victoria Webb (marr. diss. 1977; she *d* 1997); *m* 1983, Mrs Patricia J. Rossiter (marr. diss. 1987). *Educ:* Shrewsbury; Magdalene Coll., Cambridge. *Heir:* none. *Club:* Cavalry and Guards.   *Died 5 Dec. 2004 (ext).*

CROSS, Clifford Thomas, CB 1977; Commissioner, Customs and Excise, 1970–79; *b* 1 April 1920; *o s* of late Arthur and Helena Cross; *m* 1942, Ida Adelaide Barker; one *s* two *d*. *Educ:* Latymer Upper Sch., Hammersmith; Univ. of London (LLB). Joined Inland Revenue, 1939; Customs and Excise, 1946–79: Asst Sec. 1959; Comr 1970. *Recreations:* gardening, crosswords, watching television, etc. *Address:* Longacre, 101 Histon Road, Cottenham, Cambs CB4 8UQ. *T:* (01954) 250757.
Died 30 Jan. 2002.

CROSS, Air Chief Marshal Sir Kenneth (Brian Boyd), KCB 1959 (CB 1954); CBE 1945; DSO 1943; DFC 1940; *b* 4 Oct. 1911; *s* of Pembroke H. C. Cross and Mrs Jean Cross; *m* 1945, Brenda Megan (*d* 1991), *d* of Wing-Comdr F. J. B. Powell; two *s* one *d*. *Educ:* Kingswood Sch., Bath. Pilot Officer, RAF, 1930; Flying Badge, 1931; 25 Fighter Sqdn, 1931; Flying Officer, 1932; Flying Instructor, No 5 FTS Sealand and Cambridge Univ. Air Sqdn, 1934; Flt Lt 1935; Sqdn Ldr 1938; commanded No 46 Fighter Sqdn UK, Norway, 1939–40; Wing Comdr 1940; posted Middle East, 1941; Actg Group Capt. 1941; Actg Air Commodore, 1943; Director Overseas Operations, Air Ministry, 1944; Imperial Defence Coll., 1946; reverted Group Capt., 1946; Group Capt. Operations HQ BAFO Germany, 1947; OC Eastern Sector Fighter Command, 1949; Dir of Weapons, Air Ministry, 1952; subs. Air Cdre, 1953; Dir of Ops, Air Defence, 1954–Dec. 1955; Air Vice-Marshal, 1956; AOC No 3 (Bomber) Group, 1956–59; Air Marshal, 1961; AOC-in-C, Bomber Comd, 1959–63; AOC-in-C, Transport Comd, 1963–66; Air Chief Marshal, 1967; retd, 1967. Dir, Suffolk Br., 1968, London Br., 1974, British Red Cross Soc. War Cross (Norway), 1941; Legion of Merit (USA), 1944; Legion of Honour, 1944, Croix de Guerre, 1944 (France); Order of Orange Nassau (Netherlands), 1945. *Publication:* Straight and Level, 1993. *Recreations:* Rugby football and golf (colours RAF). *Address:* c/o Gorseway Retirement Community, 354 Seafront, Hayling Island, Hants PO11 0BA. *Clubs:* Royal Air Force; Royal Mid Surrey Golf.
Died 18 June 2003.

CROSSLEY, Sir Julian (Charles), 5th Bt *cr* 1909, of Glenfield, Dunham Massey, co. Chester; production manager, screen writer and consultant, film industry; *b* 11 Dec. 1964; *yr s* of Sir Christopher John Crossley, 3rd Bt and of his 1st wife, Carolyne Louise (*née* Sykes, later

Murray); *S* brother, 2000. *Educ:* Marymount Palos Verdes Coll. (AA Pre-Business); Northern Arizona Univ. (BA Business Mgt). *Recreations:* golf, tennis, snow ski-ing, scuba diving. *Heir: cousin* Sloan Nicholas Crossley, *b* 20 March 1958. *Address:* 2829 Ocean Park Boulevard #4, Santa Monica, CA 90405, USA. *T:* (310) 392 8873.

Died 5 Dec. 2003.

CRUTCHLEY, Brooke, CBE 1954; Printer of the University of Cambridge, 1946–74; Fellow of Trinity Hall, 1951–73, Emeritus Fellow, 1977 (Vice-Master, 1966–70); Honorary Fellow of St Edmund's College (formerly St Edmund's House), Cambridge, since 1980; *b* 31 July 1907; *yr s* of late Ernest Tristram Crutchley, CB, CMG, CBE, and Anna, *d* of James Dunne; *m* 1936, Diana, *d* of late Lt-Col Arthur Egerton Cotton, DSO, and Beryl Marie (who *m* 2nd, John Lee Booker); two *s* one *d. Educ:* Shrewsbury; Trinity Hall, Cambridge. Editorial Staff of Yorkshire Post, 1929–30; Asst Univ. Printer at Cambridge, 1930–45; Secretary's Dept of the Admiralty, 1941–45. Pres., Inst. of Printing, 1972–74. Hon. Col, Commonwealth of Kentucky, 1974. Bicentenary Medal, RSA, 1977. *Publication:* To be a printer (autobiog.), 1980. *Address:* The Hope Residential and Nursing Care Home, Brooklands Avenue, Cambridge CB2 2BQ. *Club:* Double Crown. *Died 31 Aug. 2003.*

CRUTTWELL, Hugh (Percival); Principal of Royal Academy of Dramatic Art, 1966–84, retired; *b* Singapore, 31 Oct. 1918; *s* of Clement Chadwick Cruttwell and Grace Fanny (*née* Robin); *m* 1953, Geraldine McEwan, actress; one *s* one *d. Educ:* King's Sch., Bruton; Hertford Coll., Oxford. Schoolteacher; Asst Stage Manager, subseq. Dir, Theatre Royal, Windsor; Teacher, LAMDA, 1959–65. Consultant to Kenneth Branagh, 1984–.

Died 24 Aug. 2002.

CUDLIPP, Michael John; Chief Executive (formerly Secretary), The History of Advertising Trust, since 1994 (Governor, 1984–86); Hon. Secretary and Administrator, 1986–94); *b* 24 April 1934; *o s* of late Percy Cudlipp and Mrs Gwendoline May Cudlipp; *m* 1st, 1957, Margaret Susannah Rees (marr. diss. 1975); one *d*; 2nd, 1985, Jane Gale; two step *d. Educ:* Tonbridge Sch., Kent. Trainee reporter, feature writer, gossip columnist, sub-editor, South Wales Echo, Cardiff, 1953–57; Sub-editor, Evening Chronicle, Manchester (various freelance jobs on daily and Sunday newspapers in Manchester), 1957–58; News Editor and Asst Editor (News), Sunday Times, 1958–67; Asst Editor (Night), Jt Man. Editor and sen. Dep. Editor, The Times, 1967–73; Chief Editor, London Broadcasting Co., 1973–74; Consultant on Public Relations to NI Office (temp. Civil Servant with rank of Under-Sec.), 1974–75; Dir of Information, Nat. Enterprise Bd, 1975–78; Director: External and Internal Communications, Internat. Thomson Orgn, 1979–85; The Georgian Gp, 1992–94. Mem., Consumer and Advertising Studies Course Adv. Cttee, Univ. of East London, 1992–. Exhibitions directed: The Image of Women in Advertising from Victorian Times to Today, Royal Instn and various mus, 1995–2001; Gilroy is good for you, Laing Gall., Newcastle upon Tyne, and RCA, 1998; From Ephesus to e-commerce: 2010 years of advertising, London Coll. of Printing and various mus, 2000–01. Mem., UK Futurists Network, 2001–. Mem., Soc. of Archivists, 1995–. FRSA 2001. US State Dept Leader Grant (to study race relations in the US), 1962. Ampleforth Sch. Headmaster's Lecture, on Prejudice, 1997. *Publication:* The Thirty Club of London: free speech within four walls, 1999. *Recreations:* boats, conservation, English cricket, Rugby football. *Address:* Stepping Hill House, 25 Ballygate, Beccles, Suffolk NR34 9ND; *e-mail:* archive@hatads.demon.co.uk. *Died 25 Oct. 2004.*

CUDLIPP, Reginald; writer specialising on Japan; Director, Anglo-Japanese Economic Institute, London, 1961–86, retired; *b* Cardiff, 11 Dec. 1910; *s* of William and Mrs B. A. Cudlipp, Cardiff; *m* 1945, Rachel Joyce Braham. *Educ:* Cardiff Technical Coll. Began journalistic career on Penarth News, Glamorgan; Sub-Ed., Western Mail, Cardiff; joined News of the World Sub-Editorial Staff, 1938; served War, 1940–46; rejoined News of the World and became Special Correspondent in USA, 1946–47, Features Ed., 1948–50, Dep. Ed., 1950–53, Ed., 1953–59; Dir, News of the World Ltd, 1955–60. Extensive industrial tours and on-the-spot economic study of Japan, regularly, 1962–86. Completed 60 years in active journalism, 1926–86. Life Mem., NUJ, 1929. Lecturer and writer on Japan's past, present and future; also first-hand research on developing nations and economic co-operation, especially in Africa and Asia; invited to Japan, 1989, to brief businessmen on the Japan/EEC partnership after 1992. Editor, Japan (quarterly review and monthly survey), and special pubns on the Japanese scene, 1961–86. Order of the Sacred Treasure, Japan, 1982. *Publications:* numerous contribs to newspapers and periodicals, on Japan and Anglo-Japanese affairs. *Recreations:* music, travel, and reading, writing and talking about Japan. *Address:* 42 Martlets Court, Queen Street, Arundel, West Sussex BN18 9NZ. *Died 21 Jan. 2005.*

CULLEN, Raymond; Chairman, The Calico Printers' Association Ltd and subsidiaries, 1964–68; *b* 27 May 1913; *s* of late John Norman Cullen and Bertha (*née* Dearden); *m* 1940, Doris (*d* 1984), *d* of A. W. Paskin; two *d. Educ:* King's Sch., Macclesfield; St Catharine's Coll., Cambridge (Scholar, MA). Joined The Calico Printers' Assoc. Ltd Commn Printing, 1934; transf. overseas, 1938; service in India and China; Chairman and Managing Director: W. A. Beardsell & Co. (Private) Ltd, Madras, 1949–55 (Dir, 1946); Mettur Industries Ltd, 1949–55; Marshall Fabrics Ltd, 1955–62; Director: Calico Printers' Assoc. Ltd, 1962–68; Barclays Bank Ltd Manchester Local Bd, 1965–69. Member: Textile Council, 1967–69; Council, Inst. of Directors, 1967–69; NW Economic Planning Council, 1968–69; Governor, Manchester Grammar Sch., 1968–83. *Recreations:* fishing, golf (Pres., Cheshire Union of Golf Clubs, 1977–78). *Address:* Cranford, Ladybrook Road, Bramhall, Cheshire SK7 3NB. *T:* (0161) 485 3204.

Died 9 Dec. 2001.

CULLINGWORTH, Prof. (John) Barry; Emeritus Professor of Urban Affairs and Public Policy, University of Delaware, since 1994; *b* 11 Sept. 1929; *s* of Sidney C. and Winifred E. Cullingworth; *m* 1951, Betty Violet (*née* Turner); one *s* two *d. Educ:* High Pavement Sch., Nottingham; Trinity Coll. of Music, London; London Sch. of Economics. Research Asst, Asst Lectr and Lectr, Univ. of Manchester, 1955–60; Lectr, Univ. of Durham, 1960–63; Sen. Lectr and Reader, Univ. of Glasgow, 1963–66; Dir, Centre for Urban and Regional Studies, Univ. of Birmingham, 1966–72; Dir, Planning Exchange, Scotland, 1972–75; Official Historian, Cabinet Office, 1975–77; Prof. and Chm., Dept of Urban and Regional Planning, 1977–80, Res. Prof., Centre for Urban and Community Studies, 1980–82, Prof. of Planning, 1982–83, Univ. of Toronto; Unidel Prof. of Urban Affairs and Public Policy, Univ. of Delaware, 1983–94; Sen. Res. Fellow, Dept of Land Economy, Univ. of Cambridge, 1994–99. Vis. Prof., Univ. of Strathclyde, 1980–86. Vice-Chm., Scottish Housing Adv. Cttee; Chairman: Cttee on Community Facilities in Expanding Towns (report, The Needs of New Communities, 1967); Cttee on Unfit Housing in Scotland (report, Scotland's Older Houses, 1967); Cttee on Allocation of Council Houses (report, Council Housing: purposes, procedures and practices, 1968); Adv. Cttee on Rent Rebates and Rent Allowances, 1973–77. Mem., Ont. Council of Health, 1979–83; Vice-Pres., Housing Centre Trust, 1972–. FRSA 1974; Hon. MRTPI. *Publications:* Housing Needs and Planning Policy, 1960; Housing in Transition, 1963; Town and Country Planning in England and Wales, 1964; English Housing Trends, 1965; Housing and Local Government, 1966; Scottish Housing in 1965, 1967; A Profile of Glasgow Housing, 1968; (with V. Karn) Ownership and Management of Housing in New Towns, 1968; Housing and Labour Mobility, (Paris) 1969; Town and Country

Planning in Britain, 1972, 13th edn (with V. Nadin) as Town and Country Planning in the UK, 2001; Problems of an Urban Society (3 vols), 1973; Environmental Planning—Reconstruction and Land Use Planning, 1975; Essays on Housing Policy, 1979; New Towns Policy, 1980; Canadian Housing Policy Research, 1980; Land Values, Compensation and Betterment, 1981; Rent Control, 1983; Canadian Planning and Public Participation, 1984; Urban and Regional Planning in Canada, 1987; Energy, Land and Public Policy, 1990; The Political Culture of Planning, 1993; Planning in the USA, 1997, 2nd edn (with Roger Caves) 2003; British Planning: 50 years of urban and regional policy, 1999. *Address:* 102 Thornton Road, Girton, Cambridge CB3 0NN. *T:* (01223) 277170. *Died 6 Feb. 2005.*

CULLIS, Michael Fowler, CVO 1955; HM Diplomatic Service, retired; Director, UK Committee, European Cultural Foundation, Amsterdam, 1983–92; *b* 22 Oct. 1914; *s* of Emeritus Prof. Charles Gilbert Cullis, Imperial Coll. of Science and Technology, London Univ., and Winifred Jefford, *d* of Sir George Fowler; *m* 1968, Catherine Cameron (*d* 2001), *d* of Alexander Robertson, Arbroath, Scotland; no *c. Educ:* Wellington Coll. (scholar); Brasenose Coll., Oxford (Hulme Open Scholar; MA Classics). Law (Lincoln's Inn), and journalism, 1938–39. Military Intelligence, Gibraltar, 1939–40; served Min. of Economic Warfare (London, Spain and Portugal), 1940–44; joined FO as head of Austrian Section, 1945; Political Adviser on Austrian Treaty negotiations (London, Moscow, Vienna, Paris, New York), 1947–50; Special Asst, Schuman Plan, 1950; First Sec., British Embassy, Oslo, 1951–55; Regional (Information) Counsellor for the five Nordic countries, British Embassy, Copenhagen, 1955–58; Dep. Gov. of Malta, 1959–61; Sen. Research Associate, Atlantic Institute, Paris, 1962–65; writing, lecturing, etc, at various European centres, 1965–66; Dir, Arms Control and Disarmament Res., FO, then FCO, 1967–74; Advr on relations with non-govtl bodies, FCO, 1974–79. Unsuccessful candidate (C), European Elections, 1979. Vice-Pres., Inst. of Linguists, 1984–89. Chevalier (1st cl.) Order of Dannebrog, 1957. *Publications:* (contrib.) The Price of Victory, 1983; (contrib.) Festschrift for Gerald Stourzh, 1990; articles and broadcasts, mainly on international affairs. *Recreations:* music, theatre. *Address:* Peel House, Buntingford, Herts SG9 9AE. *T:* (01763) 272209. *Died 27 June 2004.*

CUMMINGS, Constance, CBE 1974; actress; *b* Seattle, USA, 15 May 1910; *d* of Kate Cummings and Dallas Vernon Halverstadt; *m* 1933, Benn Wolfe Levy, MBE (*d* 1973); one *s* one *d. Educ:* St Nicholas Girls' Sch., Seattle, Washington, USA. Began stage work, 1932; since then has appeared in radio, television, films and theatre; joined National Theatre Co., 1971. Member: Arts Council, 1965–71; Council, English Stage Co., 1978–; Chm., Young People's Theatre Panel, 1966–70. *Plays include:* Goodbye, Mr Chips, 1938; The Taming of the Shrew, 1938; The Good Natured Man, 1939; St Joan, 1939; Romeo and Juliet, 1939; The Petrified Forest, 1942; Return to Tyassi, 1952; Lysistrata, 1957; The Rape of the Belt, 1957; JB, 1961; Who's Afraid of Virginia Woolf?, 1964; Justice is a Woman, 1966; Fallen Angels, 1967; A Delicate Balance, 1969; Hamlet, 1969; Children, 1974; Stripwell, 1975; All Over, 1976; Wings, 1978 (televised, USA, 1982); Hay Fever, 1980; The Chalk Garden, NY, 1982; Mrs Warren's Profession, Vienna, 1982; Eve, 1984; The Glass Menagerie, USA, then London, 1985; Crown Matrimonial, 1988; Tête à Tête, USA, 1989; Uncle Vanya, Chichester, 1996; *National Theatre:* Coriolanus, Amphitryon 38, 1971; A Long Day's Journey into Night, 1972; The Cherry Orchard, The Bacchae, 1973; The Circle, 1974–75. Fanny Kemble at Home, one woman show, 1986; has appeared Albert Hall, performing with orchestra Peter and the Wolf and Honegger's Jeanne d'Arc au Bûcher. *Recreations:* anthropology and music. *Died 23 Nov. 2005.*

CUNNANE, Most Rev. Joseph; Archbishop of Tuam, (RC), 1969–87, then Archbishop Emeritus; *b* 5 Oct. 1913; *s* of William and Margaret Cunnane, Knock, Co. Mayo. *Educ:* St Jarlath's Coll., Tuam; St Patrick's Coll., Maynooth. BA 1st Hons, Ancient Classics, 1935; DD 1941; Higher Dip. Educn 1941. Ordained priest, 1939; Prof. of Irish, St Jarlath's Coll., 1941–57; Curate: Balla, Co. Mayo, 1957–67; Clifden, Co. Galway, 1967–69. Cross of Chaplain Conventual, SMO Malta, 1970. *Publications:* Vatican II on Priests, 1967; contribs to Irish Ecclesiastical Record, Furrow, Doctrine and Life, Studies in Pastoral Liturgy, etc. *Address:* Bon Secours Hospital, Tuam, Co. Galway, Ireland. *Died 8 March 2001.*

CUNNINGHAM, Group Captain John, CBE 1963 (OBE 1951); DSO 1941 (Bars 1942, 1944); DFC 1941 (Bar); AE 1941; DL; Executive Director, British Aerospace, Hatfield, 1978–80; *b* 27 July 1917; *s* of late A. G. Cunningham and of E. M. Cunningham. *Educ:* Whitgift. Joined AAF, 1935; called up Aug. 1939; commanded 604 Sqdn, 1941–42; Staff job, 1942–43; commanded 85 Sqdn, 1943–44; Group Capt. Night Operations HQ 11 Group, 1944. Apprenticed to De Havilland Aircraft Co., Hatfield, 1935–38; employed, 1938–Aug. 1939, with De Havillands, Light Aircraft Development and Test Flying; Chief Test Pilot, de Havilland Aircraft Co., 1946–77; Exec. Dir, Hawker Siddeley Aviation, 1963–77. International Record Flight, 16 Oct. 1957: London to Khartoum direct; distance 3,064 statute miles in 5 hrs 51 mins, by Comet 3; average speed 523 statute mph. Derry and Richards Memorial Medal, GAPAN, 1965; Segrave Trophy, 1979; Air League Founders' Medal, 1979. DL: Middx, 1948; Greater London, 1965. Russian Order of Patriotic War 1st cl., 1944; USA Silver Star, 1945. *Address:* Canley, Kinsbourne Green, Harpenden, Herts AL5 3PE. *Died 21 July 2002.*

CURE, (George) Nigel C.; *see* Capel Cure.

CURRALL, Alexander, CB 1970; CMG 1965; Managing Director, Post Office, 1972–77; *b* 30 Jan. 1917; *s* of late R. T. Currall, Edinburgh; *m* 1940, Madeleine Crombie Saunders; one *s. Educ:* George Watson's Coll., Edinburgh; Edinburgh Univ. Min. of Supply, 1939–40; Royal Artillery and Indian Artillery, 1940–46. Successively in Min. of Supply, Min. of Materials and Board of Trade, concerned mainly with internat. economic negotiations, excepting the period 1950–54, when responsible for public trading in non-ferrous metals, and 1954–55, when holding a Commonwealth Fellowship for travel and study in USA. Seconded to Foreign Office as Dep. Consul-Gen., New York, 1960–62; Minister (Commercial), British High Commn, Ottawa, 1962–66; Under-Secretary: Board of Trade, 1966–67; DEA, 1967–68; Dir, Dept for Nat. Savings, 1968–72. Director: Renold, 1977–84; National Counties Building Soc., 1977–87 (Chm., 1984–86); Applied Photophysics Ltd, 1980–86 (Chm., 1981–86); Photophysics Research Ltd, 1980–86 (Chm., 1981–86); Grantham House Ltd, 1980–86 (Chm., 1981–86); The Pryors Ltd, 1983–87. Manager, Royal Instn, 1972–75, 1977–80, 1981–84. *Address:* Fairlawn, Buckden, Skipton, North Yorkshire BD23 5JA. *Club:* Caledonian. *Died 29 Oct. 2005.*

CURTIS, Sir (Edward) Leo, Kt 1965; Lord Mayor of Melbourne, Australia, 1963–64 and 1964–65; *b* London, 13 Jan. 1907; *s* of P. Curtis; *m* 1938, Elvira Lillian Prahl; two *s* three *d. Educ:* St Edmund's Coll., Ware; St Patrick's Coll., Goulburn, NSW. Joined Melbourne City Council, Dec. 1955; retired March 1975. President of Retail Traders Association of Victoria, 1962–63. *Address:* 4 Armadale Street, Armadale, Vic 3143, Australia. *Clubs:* Athenæum, Kelvin (Melbourne); various sporting. *Died 20 Feb. 2001.*

CURTIS, Very Rev. Frank; *see* Curtis, Very Rev. W. F.

CURTIS, Sir Leo; *see* Curtis, Sir E. L.

CURTIS, Michael Howard; Executive Aide to HH The Aga Khan, 1959–86; Director, Aga Khan Health and Education Services, Geneva, 1985–92; Chairman, Nation Printers and Publishers, Nairobi, Kenya, 1972–77; Director, Nation Newspapers, 1959–94 (Managing Director and Chief Executive, 1959, retired); *b* 28 Feb. 1920; *e s* of late Howard and Doris May Curtis; *m* 1st, 1947, Barbara Winifred Gough (marr. diss. 1961); two *s* two *d*; 2nd, 1961, Marian Joan Williams (*d* 1984); two step *s*. *Educ:* St Lawrence Coll.; Sidney Sussex Coll., Cambridge (MA). Eastern Daily Press, Norwich, 1945; News Chronicle: Leader Writer, 1946; Dep. Editor, 1952; Editor, 1954–57; Dir, News Chronicle Ltd, 1954–57; Personal Aide to HH The Aga Khan, 1957–59. *Clubs:* Garrick; Muthaiga (Nairobi). *Died 3 July 2004.*

CURTIS, Very Rev. (Wilfred) Frank; Provost of Sheffield, 1974–88, Provost Emeritus since 1988; *b* 24 Feb. 1923; *s* of W. A. Curtis, MC and Mrs M. Curtis (*née* Burbidge); *m* 1951, Muriel (*née* Dover); two *s* two *d*. *Educ:* Foster's Sch., Sherborne; Bishop Wordsworth's Sch., Salisbury; King's Coll., London (AKC). Served in RA, 1942–47; Major 1946. London Univ., 1947–52; Curate of High Wycombe, 1952–55; Church Missionary Society, 1955–74: Area Sec., Devon and Cornwall, 1955–65; Adviser in Rural Work, 1957–65; SW Regional Sec., 1962–65; Home Sec., 1965–74; Vice-Pres., 1977–. Rural Dean of Okehampton, 1989–92. Mem., Gen. Synod of C of E, 1977–85. Chm., Community Action Panel (S Yorks Police), 1983–86; Mem., Sheffield Council Voluntary Service, 1978–88; Chm., Radio Sheffield Religious Adv. Panel, 1985–88. Chaplain to Master Cutler, 1976, 1978, 1982, 1984. Hon. Fellow, Sheffield City Polytechnic, subseq. Sheffield Hallam Univ., 1980. Hon. Canon, 1982–93, and Bishop's Commissary, 1983–93, Maseno North Diocese, Kenya; Bishop's Commissary, Nambale, Kenya, 1988–93. *Recreations:* walking, photography, nature study. *Address:* 17 Norwood Avenue, Exeter, Devon EX2 4RT. *T:* (01392) 432642.
Died 25 May 2005.

CURZON, Leonard Henry, CB 1956; *b* 4 Jan. 1912; *s* of late Frederick Henry Curzon; *m* 1935, Greta, *e d* of late Willem and Anny van Praag; (one *s* decd). *Educ:* Sir Walter St John's Sch.; Jesus Coll., Cambridge (Scholar, BA, LLB). Civil Servant, 1934–72: Import Duties Adv. Cttee; Air Ministry, Ministries of Aircraft Production, Supply, Aviation and Defence. IDC 1947. *Address:* Southease, Derringstone Hill, Barham, Kent CT4 6QD. *T:* (01227) 831449. *Died 5 Feb. 2004.*

CUSDIN, Sidney Edward Thomas, OBE 1946; DSc (Hong Kong); FRIBA, AADip; *b* 28 July 1908; *s* of Sidney Herbert Cusdin, London; *m* 1936, Eva Eileen (Peggy) (*d* 1997), *d* of F. P. Dorizzi, London; no *c*. *Educ:* Municipal School of Arts and Crafts, Southend-on-Sea, Essex; Architectural Assoc., London. AA Holloway Scholarship, 1927; Fifth Year Travelling Studentship, 1929; joined staff of Stanley Hall & Easton and Robertson: British Pavilions at Brussels Internat. Exhibition and Johannesburg Exhibition; elected Member of AA Council, 1937, and worked on RIBA Cttees. Served War of 1939–45, RAF, on staff of HQ, No. 26 Group (despatches twice, OBE). Re-joined firm of Easton & Robertson, 1946; firm later known as Easton & Robertson, Cusdin, Preston and Smith, until 1965 when this partnership was dissolved; Sen. Partner, Cusdin, Burden and Howitt, until 1976. Pres. AA, 1950–51; Mem. Council RIBA, 1950–51. Awarded Henry Saxon Snell Prize and Theakston Bequest, 1950; Principal works: London: Development of the Hosp. for Sick Children, Great Ormond Street, British Postgraduate Medical Fedn, and London Univ., Inst. of Child Health; Medical Coll. of St Bartholomew's Hosp., New Hostel and Labs; Middlesex Hosp. Medical Sch.; New Sch. Buildings and Astor Coll.; National Inst. for Medical Research Develt, Mill Hill; Cambridge: Dept of Engineering, New Workshops and Laboratories; Univ.

Chemistry Laboratories; United Cambridge Hosps, Addenbrooke's Hosp., Hills Rd, New Develt; MRC, extension of Lab. of Molecular Biology; Harlow: Princess Alexandra Hosp.; Belfast: Queen's Univ. of Belfast, Inst. of Clin. Science; Royal Victoria Hosp. Develt; Royal Belfast Hosp. for Sick Children, alterations and additions; Malaya: plans for Develt of Univ. of Malaya; Hong Kong; plans for develt of Univ. of Hong Kong; Cons. Architect for: Queen Elizabeth Hosp., Hong Kong (awarded RIBA Bronze Medal); Faculty of Medicine, Univ. of Riyadh, Saudi Arabia. Chm., British Consultants Bureau, 1972–74. Gov., Brendoncare Foundn, 1987–94 (Dir, 1992; Vice Patron, 1993). Hon. Freeman, Apothecaries' Soc., 1981. *Publications:* (with James Crooks) Suggestions and Demonstration Plans for Hospitals for Sick Children, 1947. *Recreations:* theatre, travel, fishing; spending time in believing that "WS" was Shakespeare. *Clubs:* Savile, Royal Air Force, The Sette of Odd Volumes.
Died 8 Dec. 2005.

CUTHBERT, Betty Wake, (Lady Cuthbert), CBE 1946 (OBE 1943); *b* 20 Jan. 1904; *d* of Guy Shorrock and Emma Wake; *m* 1928, Vice-Adm. Sir John Cuthbert, KBE, CB (*d* 1987); no *c*. Joined Auxiliary Fire Service, London, as driver, 1938; Fire Staff, Home Office, 1941; Chief Woman Fire Officer, National Fire Service, 1941–46. Nat. Chm., Girls' Venture Corps, 1946–67 (Pres., 1967). Mem., Hampshire CC, 1967–74. Chm. Govs, Cricklade Coll., Andover, 1973–81. OStJ 1944. *Address:* Ibthorpe Manor Farm, Hurstbourne Tarrant, Andover, Hants SP11 0BY. *Died 1 Sept. 2005.*

CUTLER, Sir (Arthur) Roden, VC 1941; AK 1981; KCMG 1965; KCVO 1970; CBE 1957; Governor of New South Wales, 1966–81; company director; Chairman, State Bank of New South Wales, 1981–86; *b* 24 May 1916; *s* of Arthur William Cutler and Ruby Daphne (*née* Pope); *m* 1st, 1946, Helen Gray Annetta (*née* Morris), AC 1980 (*d* 1990); four *s*; 2nd, 1993, Joan Edith (*née* Goodwin). *Educ:* Sydney High Sch.; University of Sydney (BEc). Public Trust Office (NSW), 1935–42; served War of 1939–45 (VC). State Secretary, RSS & AILA (NSW), 1942–43; Mem., Aliens Classification and Adv. Cttee to advise Commonwealth Govt, 1942–43; Asst Dep. Dir, Security Service, NSW, 1943; Asst Comr Repatriation, 1943–46; High Commissioner for Australia: to New Zealand, 1946–52; to Ceylon, 1952–55; HM's Australian Minister to Egypt, 1955–56; Secretary General, SEATO Conference, 1957; Chief of Protocol, Dept of External Affairs, Canberra, 1957–58; State President of RSL, formerly RSSAILA (ACT), 1958; Australian High Comr to Pakistan, 1959–61; Australian Representative to Independence of Somali Republic, 1960; Australian Consul-General, New York, 1961–65; Ambassador to the Netherlands, 1965. Delegate to UN General Assembly, and Australian Rep., Fifth Cttee, 1962–63–64. Chairman: Ansett Express (formerly Air New South Wales), 1981–92; First Australia Fund, 1985–95; First Australia Prime Income Fund, 1986–95; First Australia Prime Income Investment Co., 1986–95; Rothmans Foundn, 1987–93; Occidental Life Assurance Co. of Australia, 1987–90; First Commonwealth Fund, 1992–95; Director: Rothmans Hldgs Ltd (formerly Rothmans of Pall Mall), 1981–93; Permanent Trustee Co., 1981–92; Rothsay Property Investments Ltd, 1991–. Dep. Pres., VC and GC Assoc., 1991–. Hon. Colonel: Royal New South Wales Regt, 1966–85; Sydney Univ. Regt, 1966–85; Hon. Air Cdre RAAF. Hon. LLD, Univ. of Sydney; Hon. DSc: Univ. of New South Wales; Univ. of Newcastle; Hon. DLitt: Univ. of New England; Univ. of Wollongong. KStJ 1965. *Address:* 12A Karoola, 442 Edgecliff Road, Edgecliff, NSW 2027, Australia. *T:* (2) 93261233, *Fax:* (2) 93273563. *Clubs:* Australian, Union (Sydney); Royal Sydney Yacht Squadron, Royal Prince Alfred Yacht (Sydney), Royal Sydney Golf. *Died 21 Feb. 2002.*

CUTLER, Sir Roden; *see* Cutler, Sir A. R.

D

d'ABO, Jennifer Mary Victoria; Chairman: Moyses Stevens Investments, 1990–99; Moyses Stevens Ltd, 1989–99; *b* 14 Aug. 1945; *d* of Michael Hammond-Maude and Rosamond Hammond-Maude (*née* Patrick); *m* 1st, David Morgan-Jones (marr. diss.); one *d*; 2nd, 1970, Peter Cadbury (marr. diss. 1976); one *s*; 3rd, Robin d'Abo (marr. diss. 1987). *Educ:* Hatherop Castle, Glos. Chairman: Ryman Ltd, 1981–87; Roffey Brothers Ltd, 1988; Director: Burlingtons Furnishing Co., 1977–80; Jean Sorelle, 1980–83; Stormgard plc, 1985–87; London Docklands Develt Corp., 1985–88; Channel Four Television, 1986–87; (non.-exec.) Pentos plc, 1987–88. Member: Doctors' and Dentists' Remuneration Review Body, 1989–92; Industrial Develt Bd for NI, 1992–94. Imperial Cancer Research Fund, subseq. Cancer Research UK: Mem. Council, 1994–; Pres., Nat. Events Cttee, 1993–99. Trustee, BM (Natural History), 1988–99. *Publication:* Jennifer d'Abo at Home, 1999. *Address: e-mail:* JENdABO@aol.com. *Died 30 April 2003.*

DACIE, Prof. Sir John (Vivian), Kt 1976; MD, FRCP; FRS 1967; Professor of Haematology, Royal Postgraduate Medical School of London, University of London, 1957–77, then Emeritus; *b* 20 July 1912; British; *s* of John Charles and Lilian Maud Dacie, Putney; *m* 1938, Margaret Kathleen Victoria Thynne; two *s* two *d* (and one *s* decd). *Educ:* King's Coll. Sch., Wimbledon; King's Coll. Hospital, London (MB, BS 1935; MD 1952). MRCP 1936, FRCP 1956; FRCPath (Pres., 1973–75). Various medical appointments, King's Coll. Hospital, Postgraduate Medical Sch. and Manchester Royal Infirmary, 1936–39. Pathologist, EMS, 1939–42; Major, then Lieut-Col, RAMC, 1943–46. Senior Lecturer in Clinical Pathology, then Reader in Haematology, Postgraduate Medical Sch., 1946–56. Chm., Med. and Scientific Adv. Panel, Leukaemia Research Fund, 1975–85. Hon. FRSocMed 1984 (Pres., 1977). Hon. MD: Uppsala, 1961; Marseille, 1977. *Publications:* Practical Haematology, 1950, 2nd edn 1956, 8th edn (jtly) 1995; Haemolytic Anaemias, 1954: 2nd edn, Part I, 1960, Part II, 1962, Parts III and IV, 1967; 3rd edn, Part I, 1985, Part II, 1988, Part III, 1992, Part IV, 1995, Part V, 1999; various papers on anaemia in medical journals. *Recreations:* music, entomology, gardening. *Address:* 10 Alan Road, Wimbledon, SW19 7PT. *T:* (020) 8946 6086. *Died 12 Feb. 2005.*

da COSTA, Sergio Corrêa, Hon. GCVO 1968; Brazilian diplomat, retired; *b* 19 Feb. 1919; *s* of Dr I. A. da Costa and Lavinia Corrêa da Costa; *m* 1st, 1943, Zazi Aranha; one *s* two *d*; 2nd, 1991, Michèle Stemer-Sursock. *Educ:* Law Sch., Univ. of Brazil; post grad. UCLA; Brazilian War Coll. Career diplomat; Sec. of Embassy, Buenos Ayres, then Washington, 1944–48; Acting Deleg., Council of OAS, Wash., 1946–48; Inter-American Econ. and Social Council, Washington, 1946–48; Dep. Head, Economic Dept, Min. of Ext. Relations, 1952; Actg Pres., Braz. Nat. Techn. Assistance Commn, 1955–58; Minister-Counsellor, Rome, 1959–62; Permanent Rep. to FAO, Rome, 1960; Mem., Financial Cttee of FAO, 1962–63; Ambassador to Canada, 1962–65; Asst Sec.-Gen. for Internat. Organizations at Min. Ext. Relations, 1966; Sec.-Gen., Min. of Ext. Relations, 1967–68; Acting Minister for External Relations, 1967–68; Ambassador to UK, 1968–75; Permanent Rep. to UN in NY, 1975–83; Ambassador to USA, 1983–86. Member: Brazilian Acad. of Letters; Brazilian Hist. and Geographical Inst.; Brazilian Soc. of Internat. Law; American Soc. of Internat. Law. Grand Officer: Military Order of Aeronautical Merit, Brazil, 1967; Order of Naval Merit, Brazil, 1967; also numerous Grand Crosses, etc, of Orders, from other countries, 1957–. *Publications:* (mostly in Brazil): As 4

Coroas de Pedro I, 1941; Pedro I e Metternich, 1942; Diplomacia Brasileira na Questao de Leticia, 1943; A Diplomacia do Marechal, 1945; Every Inch a King—A biography of Pedro I, Emperor of Brazil, 1950 (NY 1964, London 1972); Mots sans frontières, 1999 (Paris; trans. Portuguese, 2000); Brasil Segredo de Estado, 2002; Brésil, Les Silences de l'Histoire, 2003 (Paris); Crônica de uma guerra secreta—Nazismo na América: a conexão argentina, 2004. *Recreations:* reading, writing, boating. *Address:* Apartment 404, Avenida Atlântica 1782, 22021–001 Rio de Janeiro, Brazil. *Clubs:* White's, Travellers; Rideau, Country (Ottawa); Circolo della Caccia (Rome). *Died 29 Sept. 2005.*

DACRE OF GLANTON, Baron *cr* 1979 (Life Peer), of Glanton in the County of Northumberland; **Hugh Redwald Trevor-Roper;** Master of Peterhouse, Cambridge, 1980–87 (Hon. Fellow, 1987); *b* 15 January 1914; *er s* of late Dr B. W. E. Trevor-Roper, Glanton and Alnwick, Northumberland; *m* 1954, Lady Alexandra Howard-Johnston (*d* 1997), *e d* of Field-Marshal 1st Earl Haig, KT, GCB, OM, GCVO, KCIE; two step *s* one step *d*. *Educ:* Charterhouse; Christ Church, Oxford. Served War of 1939–45, British Intelligence. Res. Fellow, Merton Coll., Oxford, 1937–39 (Hon. Fellow, 1980). Student of Christ Church, Oxford, 1946–57; Censor, 1947–52; Hon. Student, 1979; Regius Prof. of Modern Hist., and Fellow of Oriel Coll., Oxford Univ., 1957–80 (Hon. Fellow, 1980). Dir, Times Newspapers Ltd, 1974–88. Chevalier, Legion of Honour (France), 1975. *Publications:* Archbishop Laud, 1940; The Last Days of Hitler, 1947; The Gentry, 1540–1640, 1953; (ed) Hitler's Table Talk, 1953; (ed with J. A. W. Bennett) The Poems of Richard Corbett, 1955; Historical Essays, 1957; (ed) Hitler's War Directives, 1939–45, 1964; (ed) Essays in British History Presented to Sir Keith Feiling, 1964; The Rise of Christian Europe, 1965; Religion, The Reformation and Social Change, 1967; (ed) The Age of Expansion, 1968; The Philby Affair, 1968; The European Witch-Craze of the 16th and 17th Centuries, 1970; The Plunder of the Arts in the Seventeenth Century, 1970; Princes and Artists, 1976; A Hidden Life, 1976; (ed) The Goebbels Diaries, 1978; Renaissance Essays, 1985; Catholics, Anglicans and Puritans, 1987; From Counter-Reformation to Glorious Revolution, 1992. *Address:* The Old Rectory, Didcot, Oxon OX11 7EB. *Clubs:* Beefsteak, Garrick. *Died 26 Jan. 2003.*

DAICHES, David, CBE 1991; DPhil, PhD; FRSL; FRSE; Director, Institute for Advanced Studies in the Humanities, Edinburgh University, 1980–86; Professor of English, 1961–77, and Dean of the School of English Studies, 1961–68, University of Sussex, then Emeritus Professor; *b* 2 Sept. 1912; *s* of late Rabbi Dr Salis Daiches and Flora Daiches (*née* Levin); *m* 1st, 1937, Isobel J. Mackay (*d* 1977); one *s* two *d*; 2nd, 1978, Hazel Neville (*née* Newman) (*d* 1986). *Educ:* George Watson's Coll., Edinburgh; Edinburgh Univ. (Vans Dunlop Schol., Elliot Prize; MA); Balliol Coll., Oxford (Elton Exhibnr; MA, DPhil); PhD Cantab. Asst in English, Edinburgh Univ., 1935–36; Andrew Bradley Fellow, Balliol Coll., Oxford, 1936–37; Asst Prof. of English, Univ. of Chicago, 1939–43; Second Sec., British Embassy, Washington, 1944–46; Prof. of English, Cornell Univ., USA, 1946–51; University Lecturer in English at Cambridge, 1951–61; Fellow of Jesus Coll., Cambridge, 1957–62. Visiting Prof. of Criticism, Indiana Univ., USA, 1956–57; Hill Foundation Visiting Prof., Univ. of Minnesota, Spring 1966. Lectures: Elliston, Univ. of Cincinnati, 1960; Whidden, McMaster Univ., Canada, 1964; Ewing, Univ. of Calif., 1967; Carpenter Meml, Ohio Wesleyan Univ.,

1969; Alexander, Univ. of Toronto, 1980; Gifford, Univ. of Edinburgh, 1983. Hon. Prof., Stirling Univ., 1980; Sen. Mellon Fellow, Nat. Humanities Center, USA, 1987–88. Fellow, Centre for the Humanities, Wesleyan Univ., Middletown, Conn, 1970. Hon. Fellow, Sunderland Polytechnic, 1977. Hon. LittD Brown Univ.; Docteur *hc* Sorbonne; Hon. DLitt: Edinburgh, 1976; Sussex, 1978; Glasgow, 1987; Guelph, 1990; DUniv Stirling, 1980; Dott. *in honorem* Bologna, 1989. Lifetime Achievement Award, 18th Century Scottish Studies Soc., 1988; Fletcher of Saltoun Award for Services to Scotland, 1988. *Publications:* The Place of Meaning in Poetry, 1935; New Literary Values, 1936; Literature and Society, 1938; The Novel and the Modern World, 1939, new edn 1960; Poetry and the Modern World, 1940; The King James Bible: a study of its sources and development, 1941; Virginia Woolf, 1942; Robert Louis Stevenson, 1947; A Study of Literature, 1948; Robert Burns, 1950, new edn 1966; Willa Cather: a critical introduction, 1951; Critical Approaches to Literature, 1956; Two Worlds (autobiog.), 1956; Literary Essays, 1956; John Milton, 1957; The Present Age, 1958; A Critical History of English Literature, 1960; George Eliot's Middlemarch, 1963; The Paradox of Scottish Culture, 1964; (ed) The Idea of a New University, 1964; English Literature (Princeton Studies in Humanistic Scholarship), 1965; More Literary Essays, 1968; Some Late Victorian Attitudes, 1969; Scotch Whisky, 1969; Sir Walter Scott and his World, 1971; A Third World (autobiog.), 1971; (ed) The Penguin Companion to Literature: Britain and the Commonwealth, 1971; Robert Burns and his World, 1971; (ed with A. Thorlby) Literature and Western Civilization, vol. I, 1972, vols II and V, 1973, vols III and IV, 1975, vol. VI, 1976; Charles Edward Stuart: the life and times of Bonnie Prince Charlie, 1973; Robert Louis Stevenson and his World, 1973; Was, 1975; Moses, 1975; James Boswell and his World, 1976; Scotland and the Union, 1977; Glasgow, 1977; Edinburgh, 1978; (with John Flower) Literary Landscapes of the British Isles: a narrative atlas, 1979; (ed) Selected Writings and Speeches of Fletcher of Saltoun, 1979; (ed) Selected Poems of Robert Burns, 1979; (ed) A Companion to Scottish Culture, 1981; Literature and Gentility in Scotland, 1982; Robert Fergusson, 1982; Milton's Paradise Lost, 1983; God and the Poets, 1984; Edinburgh, A Travellers' Companion, 1986; A Wee Dram, 1990; A Weekly Scotsman and Other Poems, 1994; Gen. Editor, Studies in English Literature, 1961–85. *Recreations:* talking, music. *Address:* 22 Belgrave Crescent, Edinburgh EH4 3AL.
Died 15 July 2005.

DAIN, Rt Rev. Arthur John, OBE 1979; Senior Assistant Bishop and Chief Executive Officer, Diocese of Sydney, 1980–82; *b* 13 Oct. 1912; *s* of Herbert John Dain and Elizabeth Dain; *m* 1st, 1938, Edith Jane Stewart, MA, *d* of Dr Alexander Stewart, DD; four *d*; 2nd, 1986, Hester A. Quirk, BSc. *Educ:* Wolverhampton Grammar Sch.; Ridley Coll., Cambridge. Missionary in India, 1935–40; 10th Gurkha Rifles, 1940–41; Royal Indian Navy, 1941–47; Gen. Sec., Bible and Medical Missionary Fellowship, formerly Zenana Bible and Medical Mission, 1947–59; Overseas Sec., British Evangelical Alliance, 1950–59; Federal Sec., CMS of Australia, 1959–65; Hon. Canon of St Andrew's Cathedral, 1963; Asst Bishop, Dio. of Sydney, 1965–82. *Publications:* Mission Fields To-day, 1956; Missionary Candidates, 1959. *Recreation:* sport. *Address:* 1 Green Meadows, The Welkin, Lindfield, West Sussex RH16 2PE. *T:* (01444) 482736. *Died 3 March 2003.*

DAISLEY, Paul; MP (Lab) Brent East, since 2001; *b* 20 July 1957; *s* of Peter A. Daisley and late B. Joan Daisley; *m* 1984, Lesley Jordan. Accounting Officer, Texaco, 1976–84; Dir of Finance and Admin, Daisley Associates, 1984–96. Mem. (Lab), Brent BC, 1990– (Leader, 1996–2001). Mem., MSF, 1976–; Br. Sec., ASTMS, 1979–84. *Recreation:* Leicester City FC supporter. *Address:* (office) 102 Liddell Gardens, NW10 3QE; c/o House of Commons, SW1A 0AA. *Died 18 June 2003.*

DAKERS, Lionel Frederick, CBE 1983; FRCO; Director, Royal School of Church Music, 1972–89 (Special Commissioner, 1958–72); Examiner to the Associated Board of the Royal Schools of Music, 1958–94; Director: Hymns Ancient and Modern, since 1976; SCM Press, 1998–2001; *b* Rochester, Kent, 24 Feb. 1924; *o s* of late Lewis and Ethel Dakers; *m* 1951, Mary Elisabeth (*d* 1997), *d* of Rev. Claude Williams; four *d*. *Educ:* Rochester Cathedral Choir Sch. Studied with H. A. Bennett, Organist of Rochester Cathedral, 1933–40, with Sir Edward Bairstow, Organist of York Minster, 1943–45, and at Royal Academy of Music, 1947–51. Organist of All Saints', Frindsbury, Rochester, 1939–42. Served in Royal Army Educational Corps, 1943–47. Cairo Cathedral, 1945–47; Finchley Parish Church, 1948–50; Asst Organist, St George's Chapel, Windsor Castle, 1950–54; Asst Music Master, Eton Coll., 1952–54; Organist of Ripon Cathedral, 1954–57; Conductor, Ripon Choral Soc. and Harrogate String Orchestra, 1954–57; Hon. Conductor, Exeter Diocesan Choral Assoc., 1957–72; Lectr in Music, St Luke's Coll., Exeter, 1958–70; Organist and Master of the Choristers, Exeter Cathedral, 1957–72; Conductor: Exeter Musical Soc., 1957–72; Exeter Chamber Orchestra, 1959–65. President: Incorporated Assoc. of Organists, 1972–75; London Assoc. of Organists, 1976–78; ISM, 1990–91; Mem. Council, Royal Coll. of Organists, 1967– (Pres., 1976–78; Dep. Pres., 1996–99); Vice-President: Friends of Cathedral Music, 1977–; Fedn of Cathedral Old Choristers' Assocs, 1980–; Herbert Howells Soc., 1987–; Church Music Soc., 1990–; Sec., Cathedral Organists' Assoc., 1972–88. Chairman: Organs Adv. Cttee of Council for Care of Churches of C of E, 1974–96; Nat. Learn the Organ Year, 1989–90; Friends of the Musicians' Chapel, 1988–; Salisbury DAC, 1990–98; Nat. Organ Teachers' Encouragement Scheme, 1990–92. Member: Archbishops' Commn in Church Music, 1988–92; Salisbury Diocesan Liturgical Adv. Cttee, 1992–95; Editl Cttee, Common Praise, 1996–2000. Lay Canon, Salisbury Cathedral, 1993–98, Emeritus, 1998. Gov., Godolphin Sch., 1990–94. Trustee, Ouseley Trust, 1990–2001. Hon. Mem., US Assoc. of Anglican Musicians, 1978; Hon. Life Mem., Methodist Church Music Soc., 1990. ARCO 1944; FRCO 1945; ADCM 1952; BMus Dunelm, 1951; ARAM 1955; FRAM 1962; FRSCM 1969; FRCM 1980. Fellow, St Michael's Coll., Tenbury, 1973. Hon. Fellow, Westminster Choir Coll., USA, 1975. Hon. DMus: Lambeth, 1979; Exeter, 1990. Composer of church music, etc. *Publications:* Church Music at the Crossroads, 1970; A Handbook of Parish Music, 1976; Making Church Music Work, 1978; (ed) Music and the Alternative Service Book, 1980; (ed) The Choristers Companion, 1980; (ed) The Psalms—their use and performance today, 1980; The Church Musician as Conductor, 1982; Church Music in a Changing World, 1984; Choosing and Using Hymns, 1985; (ed) New Church Anthem Book, 1992; The Church Anthem Handbook, 1994; Places Where They Sing, 1995; (with E. Routley) A Short History of English Church Music, 1997; (ed) Ash Wednesday to Easter for Choirs, 1998; A Miscellany of Thoughts, 1999; Beauty beyond Words, 2000; (jtly) Beneath a Travelling Star, 2001. *Recreations:* book collecting, gardening, continental food, travel. *Address:* 6 Harcourt Terrace, Salisbury, Wilts SP2 7SA. *T:* (01722) 324880. *Clubs:* Athenæum; St Wilfrid's (NY) (Hon. Mem.). *Died 10 March 2003.*

DALE, David Kenneth Hay, CBE 1976; Governor, Montserrat, West Indies, 1980–85, retired 1988; *b* 27 Jan. 1927; *s* of Kenneth Hay Dale and Francesca Sussana Hoffman; *m* 1956, Hanna Szydlowska; one *s*. *Educ:* Dorchester Grammar Sch. Joined Queen's Royal Regt, 1944; 2/Lieut 8th Punjab Regt, 1945; Lieut 4 Bn (PWO) 8th Punjab Regt, 1946; Lieut Royal Regt of Artillery, 1948, Captain 1955: served Kenya and Malaya (despatches); Dist Officer, Kenya, 1960, Dist Comr, 1962; Admin Officer Cl. B, subseq. Cl. A, Anglo-French Condominium, New Hebrides, W Pacific, 1965–73; Perm. Sec., Min. of Aviation, Communications and

Works, Seychelles, 1973–75; Dep. Governor, Seychelles, 1975; Sec. to Cabinet, Republic of Seychelles, 1976; FCO, 1977–80. Clerk, Shipwrights' Co., 1986–87. Pres., Somerton Frome Constit. Cons. Assoc., 1994–97 (Vice-Chm., Finance, 1990–94). *Recreations:* birdwatching, walking, colonial and military history. *Address:* Chatley Cottage, Batcombe, near Shepton Mallet, Somerset BA4 6AF. *T:* (01749) 850449. *Club:* East India.

Died 8 Nov. 2001.

DALRYMPLE-HAY, Sir James Brian, 6th Bt *cr* 1798; estate agent, retired; *b* 19 Jan. 1928; *e s* of Lt-Col Brian George Rowland Dalrymple-Hay (*d* on active service, 1943) and Beatrice (*d* 1935), *d* of A. W. Inglis; *S* cousin, 1952; *m* 1958, Helen Sylvia, *d* of late Stephen Herbert Card and Molly M. Card; three *d. Educ:* Hillsbrow Preparatory Sch., Redhill; Blundell's Sch., Tiverton, Devon. Royal Marine, 1946–47; Lieut Royal Marine Commando, 1947–49. Estate Agent and Surveyor's Pupil, 1949; Principal, 1955–67; Partner, Whiteheads PLC, Estate Agents, 1967, Dir, 1983–85; Principal, Dalrymple-Hay Overseas, 1985–87. *Heir: b* John Hugh Dalrymple-Hay [*b* 16 Dec. 1929; *m* 1962, Jennifer, *d* of late Brig. Robert Johnson, CBE; one *s*]. *Address:* The Red House, Church Street, Warnham, near Horsham, W Sussex RH12 3QW. *Died 21 Sept. 2005.*

DALSAGER, Poul Christian; Member, Commission of the European Communities, 1981–84; *b* 5 March 1929; *m* 1951, Betty Jørgensen; two *s. Educ:* grammar sch. Bank employee, .1945–64; Mem. (Social Democrat), Danish Parliament, 1964–81; Minister for: Agriculture and Fisheries, 1975–77 and 1979–81, for Agriculture, 1977–78. Chairman: Market Cttee of Parlt, 1971–73; Social-Democratic Gp in Parlt, 1978–79. Mem. and Vice Pres., European Parlt, 1973 and 1974. Delegate to UN Gen. Assembly, 1969–71. Mayor, Hjørring, 1990–95 (Dep. Mayor, 1986–90). *Address:* Nørregade 4-3, 9800 Hjørring, Denmark. *Died 2 May 2001.*

DALTON, Peter Gerald Fox, CMG 1958; HM Diplomatic Service, retired; *b* 12 Dec. 1914; *s* of Sir Robert (William) Dalton, CMG; *m* 1944, Josephine Anne Helyar; one *s* one *d. Educ:* Uppingham Sch.; Oriel Coll., Oxford. HM Embassy, Peking 1937–39; HM Consulate-Gen., Hankow, 1939–41; HM Embassy, Chungking, 1941–42; Foreign Office, 1942–46; HM Legation, Bangkok, 1946; HM Embassy, Montevideo, 1947–50; Foreign Office, 1950–53; Political Adviser, Hong Kong, 1953–56; Foreign Office, 1957–60; HM Embassy, Warsaw, 1960–63; HM Consul-General: Los Angeles, 1964–65; San Francisco, 1965–67; Minister, HM Embassy, Moscow, 1967–69. *Address:* North Lodge, North Street, Mayfield, Sussex TN20 6AN. *T:* (01435) 873421.

Died 15 July 2003.

DALY, Carol Yvonne; Headmistress, St Albans High School for Girls, since 1994; *b* 3 April 1950; *d* of Ronald D. Meeks and Irene M. A. Meeks (*née* Wright); *m* 1972, Nicholas John Peter Daly; one *d. Educ:* Nottingham Univ. (BSc Hons Geol. and Chem.; PGCE). Housemistress and Hd of Chemistry, King's Sch., Ely, 1973–85; Sen. Mistress, Netherhall Sch., Cambridge, 1985–90; Headmistress, Forest Girls' Sch., Snaresbrook, 1990–94. Chm., Professional Develt, GSA. Inspector, ISI. FRSA 1992. *Recreations:* gardening, travel, reading. *Address:* St Albans High School for Girls, Townsend Avenue, St Albans, Herts AL1 3SJ. *T:* (01727) 853800.

Died 28 Sept. 2005.

DALY, Michael de Burgh, MD, ScD; FRCP; Emeritus Professor of Physiology in the University of London, since 1984; Distinguished Visitor (formerly Visiting Scientist), Department of Physiology, Royal Free and University College Medical School, Royal Free Campus (formerly Royal Free Hospital School of Medicine), London, since 1984; *b* 7 May 1922; *s* of Dr Ivan de Burgh Daly, CBE, FRS; *m* 1948, Beryl Esmé, *y d* of late Wing Commander A. J. Nightingale; two *s. Educ:* Loretto Sch., Edinburgh;

Gonville and Caius Coll., Cambridge (Nat. Science Tripos Part I, 1943, Part II, 1944, Physiology with Pharmacology; MA; ScD 1960; MD 1963); St Bartholomew's Hosp. House-physician, St Bartholomew's Hospital, 1947; Asst Lecturer, 1948–50, and Lecturer, 1950–54, in Physiology, UCL; Rockefeller Foundation Travelling Fellowship in Medicine, 1952–53; Locke Research Fellow of Royal Soc., 1955–58; St Bartholomew's Hospital Medical College: Prof. and Hd of Dept of Physiology, 1958–84; Governor, 1975–95; Treas., 1983–84. Vis. Prof. of Physiology, Univ. of NSW, 1966; Vis. Lectr, Swedish Univs, 1959–60; G. L. Brown Lectr, Physiological Soc., 1985–86. Member: Personnel Res. Ethics Cttee, MoD (Navy) (formerly Adv. Panel for Underwater Physiological Res., MoD), 1975– (Chm., 1990–); MRC/RN Personnel Res. Cttee, Underwater Physiology Sub-Cttee, 1975–94; Res. Funds Cttee, British Heart Foundn, 1982–85; Armed Services Consultant Approval Bd in Applied Physiology/ Aviation Medicine, MoD, 1989–. Mem., 1981–84, Chm., 1984–, Editorial Bd of Monographs of Physiological Soc.; Co-Editor of Journal of Physiology, 1956–63, 1984–89. FRSocMed 1959. Member: Soc. of Experimental Biol., 1965–; Physiological Soc., 1951–86 (Hon. Mem., 1986); Osler Med. Club, 1974–87; European Underwater Biomed. Soc., 1971–; Undersea Med. Soc. Inc., 1971–88. Schafer Prize in Physiology, University Coll., London, 1953; Thruston Medal, Gonville and Caius Coll., 1957; Sir Lionel Whitby Medal, Cambridge Univ., 1963; Gold Medal (jtly), BMA, 1972. *Publications:* Peripheral Arterial Chemoreceptors and Respiratory-Cardiovascular Integration, 1997; contributor to: Lippold and Winton, Human Physiology; Starling, Principles of Human Physiology; Emslie-Smith, Paterson, Scratcherd and Read, Textbook of Physiology; papers on the integrative control of respiration and the cardiovascular system in Journal of Physiology; contrib. to film on William Harvey and the Circulation of the Blood. *Recreation:* model engineering. *Address:* 7 Hall Drive, Sydenham, SE26 6XL. *T:* (020) 8778 8773. *Died 1 March 2002.*

DALY, Lt-Gen. Sir Thomas (Joseph), KBE 1967 (CBE 1953; OBE 1944); CB 1965; DSO 1945; Chief of the General Staff, Australia, 1966–71; *b* 19 March 1913; *s* of late Lt-Col T. J. Daly, DSO, VD, Melbourne; *m* 1946, Heather, *d* of late James Fitzgerald, Melbourne; three *d. Educ:* St Patrick's Coll., Sale; Xavier Coll., Kew, Vic; RMC, Duntroon (Sword of Honour). 3rd LH, 1934; attached for training 16/5 Lancers, India, 1938; 3rd Carabiniers, 1939; Adjt, 2/10 Aust. Inf. Bn, 1939; Bde Major, 18 Inf. Bde, 1940 (despatches); GSO2 6 Aust. Div., 1941; GSO1 5 Aust. Div., 1942 (despatches); Instructor, Staff Sch. (Aust.), 1944; CO 2/10 Inf. Bn, AIF, 1944; Instr, Staff Coll., Camberley, UK, 1946; Joint Services Staff Coll., Latimer, 1948; Dir of Mil. Art, RMC Duntroon, 1949; Dir of Infantry, AHQ, 1951; Comd 28 Brit. Commonwealth Inf. Bde, Korea, 1952; Dir, Ops and Plans, AHQ, 1953; IDC, London, 1956; GOC Northern Command, Australia, 1957–60; Adjt Gen., 1961–63; GOC, Eastern Command, Australia, 1963–66. Col Comdt, Royal Australian Regt, and Pacific Is Regt, 1971–75. Director: Jennings Industries Ltd, 1974–85; Fruehauf Australia Ltd, 1974–88; Associated Merchant Bank (Singapore), 1975–77. Mem., Nat. Council, Australian Red Cross, 1972–75; Chm., Council, Australian Nat. War Memorial, 1974–82 (Mem., 1966–74); Councillor, Royal Agricl Soc. of NSW, 1972–85. Legion of Merit (US), 1953. *Recreations:* golf, watching football, cricket. *Address:* 16 Victoria Road, Bellevue Hill, NSW 2023, Australia. *Clubs:* Australian (Sydney); Royal Sydney Golf. *Died 5 Jan. 2004.*

DAMERELL, Derek Vivian; Governor, 1974–88, and Deputy Chairman, 1984–88, BUPA (Chief Executive, 1974–84); *b* 4 Aug. 1921; *s* of William James Damerell (Lt-Col), MBE and Zoe Damerell; *m* 1942, Margaret Isabel Porritt (*d* 2003), *d* of Prof. B. D. Porritt; three *s* three *d. Educ:* ISC; Edinburgh Univ.; Harvard Business Sch. Parent Bd, BPB Industries, 1953–64; Regional Dir, Internat.

Wool Secretariat, 1965–73. Dir, Murrayfield plc, 1982–87. Governor, Nuffield Nursing Homes Trust, 1974–80; Founder, Ind. Hosp. Gp (Chm., 1975–80); Internat. Fedn of Voluntary Health Service Funds: Mem. Council, 1976–; Dep. Pres., 1980–81, Pres., 1981–84; Mem. Bd of Governors, Assoc. Internat. de la Mutualité, 1974–83. *Recreations:* sailing (jt founder, BCYC, 1947), travel. *Clubs:* various yacht. *Died 26 Oct. 2004.*

DAMMERS, Very Rev. Alfred Hounsell, (Horace); Dean of Bristol, 1973–87; *b* 10 July 1921; *s* of late B. F. H. Dammers, MA, JP; *m* 1947, Brenda Muriel, *d* of late Clifford Stead; two *s* two *d. Educ:* Malvern Coll. (Schol.); Pembroke Coll., Cambridge (Schol., MA); Westcott House, Cambridge. Served RA (Surrey and Sussex Yeo.), 1941–44. Asst Curate, Adlington, Lancs, 1948; Asst Curate, S Bartholomew's, Edgbaston, Birmingham, and Lectr at Queen's Coll., Birmingham, 1950; Chaplain and Lectr at S John's Coll., Palayamkottai, S India, 1953; Vicar of Holy Trinity, Millhouses, Sheffield, and Examining Chaplain to Bishop of Sheffield, 1957; Select Preacher at Univ. of Cambridge, 1963; Select Preacher at Univ. of Oxford, 1975, 1989; Chairman, Friends of Reunion, 1965; Canon Residentiary and Director of Studies, Coventry Cathedral, 1965. Founder, The Life Style Movement, 1972. Companion, Community of the Cross of Nails, 1975. *Publications:* Great Venture, 1958; Ye Shall Receive Power, 1958; All in Each Place, 1962; God is Light, God is Love, 1963; AD 1980, 1966; Lifestyle: a parable of sharing, 1982, 2nd edn 2001; A Christian Lifestyle, 1986; Lord Make Us One, 1988; (ed) Preaching from the Cathedrals, 1998; St John's Gospel: a study guide, 1999; Thank You, Holy Spirit, 2004. *Recreations:* campaigning on peace and justice issues, visiting friends and relations. *Address:* 4 Bradley Avenue, Shirehampton, Bristol BS11 9SL. *Died 23 Aug. 2004.*

DANIEL, Gerald Ernest, CPFA, FCA; County Treasurer, Nottinghamshire County Council, 1974–84; *b* 7 Dec. 1919; *s* of Ernest and Beata May Daniel; *m* 1942, Ecila Roslyn Dillow; one *s* one *d. Educ:* Huish's Grammar Sch., Taunton. Served War, 1939–46, Somerset LI. Various appts in Borough Treasurers' Depts at Taunton, Scunthorpe and Bexhill, 1935–50; Cost and machine accountant, subseq. Chief Accountant, City Treasury, Bristol, 1950–60; Dep. Borough Treasurer, Reading, 1960–64; Borough Treasurer, West Bromwich, 1965–68; City Treasurer, Nottingham, 1968–74. Public Sector Advr, Pannell Kerr Forster, Chartered Accountants, 1984–93; Financial Advr, British Assoc. of Med. Managers, 1995–97. Sec., 1971–76, Chm., 1976–81, Officers Side, Jt Negotiating Cttee for Chief Officers in Local Govt. Dir, Horizon Travel, 1975–85. Treasurer: E Midlands Airport, 1968–84; E Midlands Arts Assoc., 1969–84. President: Nottingham Soc. of Chartered Accountants, 1976; Assoc. of Public Service Finance Officers, 1978; Soc. of County Treasurers, 1979; Chartered Inst. of Public Finance and Accountancy, 1983–84 (Mem. Council, 1971–85; Vice-Pres., 1982). FMAAT (Mem. Council, 1981–83). FRSA. Organist, St Bartholomew's Church, Cross-in-Hand, E Sussex, 1986–99. *Recreations:* gardening, music. *Address:* Brookvale, Star Lane, Blackboys, Uckfield, East Sussex TN22 5LD. *T:* (01825) 890712. *Died 1 Feb. 2004.*

DANIEL, Sir Goronwy Hopkin, KCVO 1969; CB 1962; DPhil; HM Lieutenant for Dyfed, 1978–89; *b* Ystradgynlais, 21 March 1914; *s* of David Daniel; *m* 1940, Lady Valerie, (*d* 2000), *d* of 2nd Earl Lloyd George of Dwyfor; one *s* two *d. Educ:* Pontardawe Secondary Sch.; Amman Valley County Sch.; University Coll. of Wales, Aberystwyth; Jesus Coll., Oxford (Meyricke Scholar; Hon. Fellow, 1979); DPhil Oxon. Oxford Institute of Statistics, 1937–40; Lecturer, Dept of Economics, Bristol Univ., 1940–41; Clerk, House of Commons, 1941–43; Ministry of Town and Country Planning, 1943–47; Chief Statistician, Ministry of Fuel and Power, 1947–55; Under-Sec., Coal Div., 1955–62, Gen. Div., 1962–64; Permanent

Under-Sec. of State, Welsh Office, 1964–69; Principal, Aberystwyth UC, 1969–79; Vice-Chancellor, Univ. of Wales, 1977–79; Chm., Welsh Fourth Channel Authority, 1981–86. Dir, Bank of Wales, 1972–90 (Dep. Chm., 1985–90). Member: Welsh Language Council, 1974–78; Gen. Adv. Council, BBC, 1974–79; Adv. Council on Energy Conservation, 1977–79; SSRC, 1980–83; Dep. Chm., Prince of Wales' Cttee, 1980–86. Chairman: Home-Grown Timber Adv. Cttee, 1974–81; Cttee on Water Charges in Wales, 1974–75; Welsh Congregational Meml Coll., 1985–90; Working Gp on Powers and Functions of Univ. of Wales, 1988–89. Pres., West Wales Assoc. for the Arts, 1971–85. Hon Mem., Gorsedd of Bards, 1966. Hon. Freeman, City of London, 1982. Fellow, Univ. of Wales. Hon. LLD, Univ. of Wales, 1980. *Publications:* papers in statistical, fuel and power, and other js. *Recreations:* country pursuits, sailing. *Address:* Cae Ffynnon, 67 St Michaels Road, Cardiff CF5 2AN. *T:* (029) 2055 3150. *Died 17 Jan. 2003.*

DANIELL, Brig. (Averell) John, CBE 1955 (MBE 1939); DSO 1945; *b* 19 June 1903; *s* of late Lt-Col Oswald James Daniell, QO Royal West Kent Regt, and May Frances Drummond Daniell (*née* Adams); *m* 1934, Phyllis Kathleen Rhona Grove-Annesley (*d* 2002); two *s* one *d. Educ:* Wellington Coll.; RM Acad., Woolwich. Commissioned, Royal Field Artillery, 1923; Captain, RA, 1936; Major, 1940; Lt-Col, 1943. Served War of 1939–45; Middle East, Iraq, Burma. Col, 1948; Brig., 1952; retired, 1955. Administrative Officer, Staff Coll., Camberley, 1955–61. Col Comdt, Royal Artillery, 1956–66. *Address:* c/o 46 Carson Road, West Dulwich SE21 8HU.

Died 4 Oct. 2002.

DANIELL, Sir Peter (Averell), Kt 1971; TD 1950; DL; Senior Government Broker, 1963–73; *b* 8 Dec. 1909; *s* of R. H. A. Daniell and Kathleen Daniell (*née* Monsell); *m* 1935, Leonie Mayne Harrison (*d* 1997); two *s* one *d. Educ:* Eton Coll.; Trinity Coll., Oxford (MA). Joined Mullens & Co., 1932, Partner, 1945; retd 1973. Served KRRC, 1939–45, Middle East and Italy. Master, Drapers' Co., 1980–81. DL Surrey 1976. *Recreations:* shooting, fishing, golf. *Address:* Glebe House, Buckland, Betchworth, Surrey RH3 7BL. *T:* (01737) 842320. *Clubs:* Brooks's, Alpine. *Died 27 May 2002.*

DANINOS, Pierre; French author; *b* Paris, 26 May 1913; *m* 1st, 1942, Jane Marrain (marr. diss.); one *s* two *d*; 2nd, 1968, Marie-Pierre Dourneau. *Educ:* Lycée Janson de Sailly, Paris. Began to write for newspapers, 1931; reporter for French press in England, USA, etc. Liaison agent with British Army, Dunkirk, 1940. Published first book in Rio de Janeiro, 1940; returned to France, 1941, Chronicler for Le Figaro. *Publications:* Le Sang des Hommes, 1940; Meridiens, 1945; Les Carnets du Bon Dieu (Prix Interallié 1947); L'Eternel Second, 1949; Sonia, les autres et moi (Prix Courteline, 1952) (English trans., Life with Sonia, 1958); Les Carnets du Major Thompson, 1954 (English trans., Major Thompson Lives in France, 1955); Le Secret du Major Thompson, 1956 (English trans., Major Thompson and I, 1957); Vacances à Tous Prix, 1958; Un certain Monsieur Blot, 1960 (English trans., 1961); Le Jacassin, 1962; Snobissimo, 1964; Le 36ème dessous, 1966; Le Major Tricolore, 1968; Ludovic Morateur, 1970; Le Pyjama, 1972; La Première Planète à Droit en Sortant par la Voie Lactée, 1973; Les Touristocrates, 1974; Made in France, 1977; La Composition d'Histoire, 1979; Le Veuf Joyeux, 1981; La Galerie des Glaces, 1983; La France dans tous ses états, 1985; La France Prise aux Mots, 1986; Profession: écrivain (autobiog.), 1988; Candidement Vôtre, 1992; Quarante Ans de Vacances, 1993; Ah, vous écrivez toujours?, 1999; Les Derniers Carnets de Major Thompson, 2001. *Recreations:* tennis, ski-ing, collecting British hobbies. *Address:* 15 rue Chauveau, 92200 Neuilly, France. *Died 7 Jan. 2005.*

DANKERT, Pieter, Kt, Order of Netherlands Lion; Commander, Order of Orange Nassau; *b* Jan. 1934; *m* 1962, Paulette Puig; one *s* two *d. Educ:* Amsterdam Free

Univ. Member (Partij van de Arbeid) Tweede Kamer, Dutch Parlt, 1968–81; Sec. of State for Foreign Affairs, 1989–94. Mem., Adv. Cttee Internat. Questions, Min. of Foreign Affairs, Netherlands. Formerly Internat Sec., Partij van de Arbeid. MEP, 1977–87 and 1994–99 (Pres., 1982–84). Member: NATO Assembly, WEU Assembly and Assembly of Council of Europe, 1971–77; Expert Cttee on Charter Regl and Minority Langs, Council of Europe. *Address:* Hoogstraat 1, 1135 BZ Edam, Netherlands. *Died 21 June 2003.*

DARGIE, Sir William Alexander, Kt 1970; CBE 1969 (OBE 1960); artist; portrait, figure and landscape painter; Chairman, Commonwealth Art Advisory Board, Prime Minister's Department, 1969–73 (Member, 1953–73); *b* 4 June 1912; *s* of Andrew and Adelaide Dargie; *m* 1937, Kathleen, *d* of late G. H. Howitt; one *s* one *d*. Official War Artist (Capt.) with AIF in Middle East, Burma, New Guinea, India, 1941–46. Dir, National Gall. of Victoria Art Schs, 1946–53. Member: Interim Council of Nat. Gallery Canberra, 1968–72; Nat. Capital Planning Cttee, Canberra, 1970–73; Aboriginal Arts Adv. Cttee, 1970–72; Trustee: Native Cultural Reserve, Port Moresby, Papua-New Guinea, 1970–73; Museum of Papua-New Guinea, 1970–73; Mem. Council, Nat. Museum, Victoria, 1978–83; Chm., Bd of Trustees, McClelland Gall., 1981–87. FRSA 1951. MA *hc* Footscray Inst. of Technol., 1986. Archibald Prize for portraiture, 1941, 1942, 1945, 1946, 1947, 1950, 1952, 1956; Woodward Award, 1940; McPhillimy Award, 1940; McKay Prize, 1941. *Portraits* include: Duke of Gloucester, 1947; The Queen, for Commonwealth of Aust., 1954; Duke of Edinburgh, for City of Melbourne, 1956; Sir Macfarlane Burnet, Sir William Ashton, Sir Lionel Lindsay, acquired for Commonwealth Nat. Collection. Rep. in public and private collections in Aust., NZ, England and USA. One-man exhbn, Leger Galls, London, 1958. Exhibited with RA and Royal Soc. of Portrait Painters. *Publication:* On Painting a Portrait, 1956. *Recreations:* books, chess, tennis. *Address:* 19 Irilbarra Road, Canterbury, Victoria 3126, Australia. *T:* (3) 98363396. *Clubs:* Melbourne, Melbourne Savage (Melbourne). *Died 26 July 2003.*

DARLING, 2nd Baron *cr* 1924, of Langham; **Robert Charles Henry Darling;** DL; Major retired, Somerset Light Infantry; *b* 15 May 1919; *s* of late Major Hon. John Clive Darling, DSO; *S* grandfather, 1936; *m* 1942, Bridget Rosemary Whishaw (*d* 1997), *d* of Rev. F. C. Dickson; one *s* two *d*. *Educ:* Wellington Coll.; RMC Sandhurst. Somerset LI, retired, 1955. Sec., later Chief Executive, Royal Bath and West and Southern Counties Soc., 1961–79, Pres., 1989. DL Somerset 1972, Avon 1974, Somerset 1996. *Recreations:* fishing, gardening. *Heir: s* Hon. Robert Julian Henry Darling, FRICS [*b* 29 April 1944; *m* 1970, Janet, *yr d* of Mrs D. M. E. Mallinson, Richmond, Yorks; two *s* one *d*]. *Died 16 Oct. 2003.*

DARNLEY-THOMAS, Rita; *see* Hunter, R.

DARVALL, Sir (Charles) Roger, Kt 1971; CBE 1965; former company director; *b* 11 Aug. 1906; *s* of late C. S. Darvall; *m* 1931, Dorothea May (*d* 1997), *d* of late A. C. Vautier; two *d*. *Educ:* Burnie, Tasmania. FASA. Gen. Manager, Australia & New Zealand Bank Ltd, Melbourne, 1961–67; former Director: Broken Hill Pty; Rothmans of Pall Mall Aust.; H. C. Sleigh Ltd; Australia New Guinea Corp.; Electrolux Pty; L. M. Ericsson Pty; Munich Re-Insurance Co. of Aust.; Australian Eagle Insurance Co. Comr, State Electricity Commn of Vic, 1969–79. *Recreations:* motoring, gardening, outdoors. *Address: c/o* 33 Albion Street, South Yarra, Vic 3141, Australia. *Club:* Athenæum (Melbourne). *Died 20 Aug. 2002.*

DARVALL, Sir Roger; *see* Darvall, Sir C. R.

da SILVA, John Burke, CMG 1969; HM Diplomatic Service, retired; Adviser, Commercial Union Assurance Co., 1973–84; *b* 30 Aug. 1918; *o s* of late John Christian da Silva and Gabrielle Guittard; *m* 1st, 1940, Janice (decd),

d of Roy Mayor, Shrewsbury, Bermuda; one *d*; 2nd, 1963, Jennifer, *yr d* of late Capt. the Hon. T. T. Parker, DSC, RN, Greatham Moor, Hants; one *s* two *d*. *Educ:* Stowe Sch.; Trinity Coll., Cambridge (BA 1939, MA 1962). Commnd Intell. Corps 1940, served with 1st Airborne Div., N Africa and Italy, GS02 SHAEF, France and Germany (despatches); Control Commn Germany and Austria. Joined Foreign Service, 1948; served Rome, Hamburg, Bahrain, Aden; Counsellor, Washington, 1966; FCO, 1969; retired 1973. A Vice-Pres., Royal Soc. for Asian Affairs, 1983–86. Chm., Governors, Virginia Water Junior Sch., 1973–83. Hon. Life Mem., Oriental Ceramic Soc., 1994. *Publications:* contrib. Oriental Art, Trans OCS, Asian Affairs, etc. *Recreation:* oriental art. *Address:* Copse Close, Virginia Water, Surrey GU25 4PH. *T:* (01344) 842342. *Club:* Travellers. *Died 9 May 2003.*

DATE, William Adrian, CBE 1973; Puisne Judge, Supreme Court of British Guiana, 1956–64; *b* 1 July 1908; *er s* of James C. Date; *m* 1st, 1933, Dorothy MacGregor Grant (*d* 1979); two *d*; 2nd, 1981, Rhoda Elaine Minors (*d* 1989). *Educ:* Queen's Royal Coll., Trinidad; Grenada Boys' Secondary Sch.; Lodge Sch., Barbados; Middle Temple, London. Magistrate and District Govt Officer, St Lucia, 1933–39; Crown Attorney, St Vincent, 1939–44; Legal Draughtsman, Jamaica, 1944–47; Chief Secretary, Windward Islands, 1947–50; Puisne Judge of the Supreme Court of the Windward and Leeward Islands, 1950–56. *Recreation:* bridge. *Address:* PO Box 123, St George's, Grenada, West Indies. *Died 14 Sept. 2004.*

DAVIDSON, Alan Eaton; author; HM Diplomatic Service, retired; Managing Director, Prospect Books Ltd, 1982–2000; *b* 30 March 1924; *s* of William John Davidson and Constance (*née* Eaton); *m* 1951, Jane Macatee; three *d*. *Educ:* Leeds Grammar Sch.; Queen's Coll., Oxford. 1st class hons Class. Mods and Greats. Served in RNVR (Ordinary Seaman, later Lieut) in Mediterranean, N Atlantic and Pacific, 1943–46. Member of HM Foreign Service, 1948; served at: Washington, 1950–53; The Hague, 1953–55; FO, 1955–59; First Secretary, British Property Commission, and later Head of Chancery, British Embassy, Cairo, 1959–61; Head of Chancery and Consul, Tunis, 1962–64; FO, 1964; Counsellor, 1965; Head, Central Dept, FO, 1966–68; Head of Chancery, UK Delegn to NATO, Brussels, 1968–71; seconded, as Vis. Fellow, Centre for Contemporary European Studies, Univ. of Sussex, 1971–72; Head of Defence Dept, FCO, 1972–73; Ambassador to Vientiane, 1973–75. CMG 1975. *Publications:* Seafish of Tunisia and the Central Mediterranean, 1963; Snakes and Scorpions Found in the Land of Tunisia, 1964; Mediterranean Seafood, 1972; The Role of the Uncommitted European Countries in East-West Relations, 1972; Fish and Fish Dishes of Laos, 1975; Seafood of South East Asia, 1976; (with Jane Davidson) Dumas on Food, 1978; North Atlantic Seafood, 1979; (with Jennifer Davidson) Traditional Recipes of Laos, 1981; On Fasting and Feasting (annotated anthology), 1988; A Kipper with My Tea, 1988; (with Charlotte Knox) Seafood, 1989; (with Charlotte Knox) Fruit, 1991; Something Quite Big (novel), 1993; The Oxford Companion to Food, 1999; (with Helen Saberi) Trifle, 2001; The Wilder Shores of Gastronomy (anthology), 2002. *Address:* 45 Lamont Road, World's End, SW10 0HU. *T:* (020) 7352 4209. *Died 2 Dec. 2003.*

DAVIDSON, Alfred Edward; international lawyer; Vice-President and General Counsel, Technical Studies, 1957–70, and 1973–91; *b* New York, 11 Nov. 1911; *s* of Maurice Philip Davidson and Blanche Reinheimer; *m* 1934, Claire H. Dreyfuss (*d* 1981); two *s*. *Educ:* Harvard Univ. (AB); Columbia Law Sch. (LLB). Advocate, Bar of New York, 1936; of Dist of Columbia, 1972; Asst to Gen. Counsel, US Dept of Labor, Wash., 1938–40; review section, Solicitor's Office, 1940–41; Legis. Counsel, Office of Emergency Management, in Exec. Office of President, 1941–43; Asst Gen. Counsel, Lend-Lease Admin (later Foreign Economic Admin), 1943–45; Gen. Counsel,

1945–; Gen. Counsel, UNRRA, Nov. 1945; Counsel, Preparatory Commn for Internat. Refugee Org., 1947; Dir, European Headqrs of UNICEF, 1947–51; Advisor, Office of Sec.-Gen. of UN, 1951–52; Gen. Counsel, UN Korean Reconstr. Agency, 1952–54; Exec. Asst to Chm., Bd of Rio Tinto of Canada, 1955–58; European Representative, Internat. Finance Corp., 1970–72; Counsel to Wilmer, Cutler & Pickering, Attorneys at Law, 1972–75. Dir, Channel Tunnel Study Gp, 1960–70; Hon. Chm., Democratic Party Abroad, 1989. Co-Founder, Assoc. for Promotion of Humor in Internat. Affairs; Hon. Chm., Common Cause Overseas. *Publications:* contribs various periodicals and newspapers. *Recreations:* tennis, bridge, chess, reading. *Club:* Standard Athletic (France).
Died 15 Feb. 2002.

DAVIDSON, Ian Robert, RIBA; Director, Lifschutz Davidson Ltd, since 1986; *b* 3 June 1954; *s* of Sir Robert (James) Davidson and Barbara Elsie (*née* Eagles); *m* 1977, Lenaura Mary Nelmes; one *s* one *d*. *Educ:* Leamington Coll. for Boys; Leicester Poly. (DipArch with Commendation 1978). Registered Architect 1979; RIBA 1979. With Richard Rogers Partnership, 1978–81, Foster Associates, 1981–86; with Alex Lifschutz, founded Lifschutz Davidson Ltd, 1986. *Projects* include: Richard Rogers & Partners' office ext., Thames Wharf Studios, 1991 (RIBA Award, 1992); Broadwall Community Housing, London, 1994 (Royal Fine Arts Commn/ Sunday Times Bldg of Year, RIBA Award, 1995; DoE Nat. Housing Design Award, Civic Trust Housing Award, 1996); develt at Oxo Tower Wharf, 1996 (Royal Fine Art Commn Urban Regeneration Award, RIBA Award, 1997; Civic Trust Award, 1998; Waterfront Center Honor Award, 2000); Royal Victoria Dock Bridge, 1999 (Royal Acad./A. J. Bovis Award, 1997; ICE Award of Merit, RIBA Arch. Award, Design Council Millennium Product, 1999). Chm., RIBA Awards Gp, 2000–; Mem. Bd, Architects' Registration Bd, 2000–. FRSA 1993. *Recreations:* my children, sailing, travel. *Address:* Lifschutz Davidson Ltd, Thames Wharf Studios, Rainville Road, W6 9HA. *Died 6 Feb. 2003.*

DAVIDSON, His Honour Ian Thomas Rollo; QC 1977; a Circuit Judge, 1984–97; *b* 3 Aug. 1925; *s* of late Robert Davidson and Margaret Davidson; *m* 1954, Gyöngyi (marr. diss. 1982), *d* of Prof. C. Anghi; one *s* one *d*; *m* 1984, Barbara Ann Watts; one *s*. *Educ:* Fettes Coll.; Corpus Christi Coll., Oxford (Schol.; MA Lit.Hum.). Royal Armoured Corps, 1943–47, Lt Derbs Yeomanry. Called to Bar, Gray's Inn, 1955. Asst Lectr, University Coll., London, 1959–60; Deputy Recorder, Nottingham, 1971; a Recorder of the Crown Court, 1974. *Recreations:* music, golf, photography. *Address:* c/o Crown Court, Canal Street, Nottingham NG1 7EJ.
Died 17 April 2005.

DAVIDSON, James Alfred, OBE 1971; retired RN and Diplomatic Service; *b* 22 March 1922; *s* of Lt-Comdr A. D. Davidson and Mrs (Elizabeth) Davidson; *m* 1955, Daphne (*née* While); two *d*, and two step *s*. *Educ:* Christ's Hospital; RN Coll., Dartmouth. Royal Navy, 1939–60 (war service Atlantic, Mediterranean and Far East); commanded HM Ships Calder and Welfare; Comdr 1955; retd 1960. Holds Master Mariner's Cert. of Service. Called to the Bar, Middle Temple, 1960. Joined CRO (later FCO) 1960; served Port of Spain, Phnom Penh (periods as Chargé d'Affaires 1970 and 1971); Dacca (Chargé d'Affaires, later Dep. High Comr, 1972–73); Vis. Scholar, Univ. of Kent, 1973–74; British High Comr, Brunei, 1974–78; participated, Sept. 1978, in finalisation of Brunei Independence Treaty; Governor, British Virgin Islands, 1978–81. Vis. Fellow, LSE Centre for Internat. Studies, 1982–84. Legal Mem. and Pres., Mental Health Review Tribunal, 1982–95; a Chm., Pensions Appeals Tribunals, 1984–95. *Publications:* Brunei Coinage, 1977; Indo-China: Signposts in the Storm, 1979. *Address:* Little Frankfield, Seal Chart, near Sevenoaks, Kent TN15 0HA. *T:* (01732) 761600. *Club:* Army and Navy. *Died 6 May 2004.*

DAVIDSON, Air Vice-Marshal Rev. Sinclair Melville, CBE 1968; Priest-in-charge, Holy Trinity, High Hurstwood, 1982–88; *b* 1 Nov. 1922; *s* of late James Stewart Davidson and Ann Sinclair Davidson (*née* Cowan); *m* 1944, Jean Irene, *d* of late Edward Albert Flay; one *s* (and one *s* decd). *Educ:* Bousfield Sch., Kensington; RAF Cranwell; RAF Tech. Coll.; Chichester Theol Coll. CEng, FRAeS, FIEE. War service with 209, 220 and 53 Sqdns RAF, 1941–45 (despatches); Staff RAF Coastal and Fighter Comds, 1946–53; Air Staff, Egypt, Iraq and Cyprus, 1954–55; psa 1956; Air Staff, Air Min., 1957–60; jssc 1960; Dirg Staff, RAF Staff Coll., Bracknell, 1961–63; Asst Comdt, RAF Locking, 1963–64; Chm. Jt Signal Bd (Middle East), 1965; Chief Signal Officer and Comd Electrical Engr, Near East Air Force, 1966–67; idc 1968; Dir of Signals (Air), MoD, 1969–71; AO Wales and Stn Comdr, RAF St Athan, 1972–74; Asst Chief of Defence Staff (Signals), 1974–77. Sec., IERE, 1977–82. Deacon 1981, priest 1982. *Address:* Trinity Cottage, High Hurstwood, E Sussex TN22 4AA. *T:* (01825) 732151. *Club:* Royal Air Force. *Died 24 Jan. 2003.*

DAVIES, (Albert) Meredith, CBE 1982; Principal, Trinity College of Music, 1979–88; Guest Conductor, Royal Opera House, Covent Garden, and Sadler's Wells, 1960–72, also BBC; *b* 30 July 1922; 2nd *s* of Rev. E. A. Davies; *m* 1949, Betty Hazel, *d* of late Dr Kenneth Bates; two *s* one *d* (and one *s* decd); one *d* (one *s* decd) with Cara Lancaster. *Educ:* Royal College of Music (Jun. Exhibnr, 1930); Stationers' Company's Sch.; Keble Coll., Oxford; Accademia di S. Cecilia, Rome. Organist to Hurstpierpoint Coll., Sussex, 1939; elected Organ Scholar, Keble Coll., 1940. Served War of 1939–45, RA, 1942–45. Conductor, St Albans Bach Choir, 1947; Organist and Master of the Choristers, Cathedral Church of St Alban, 1947–49; Musical Dir, St Albans Sch., 1948–49; Organist and Choirmaster, Hereford Cathedral, and Conductor, Three Choirs' Festival (Hereford), 1949–56; Organist and Supernumerary Fellow of New Coll., Oxford, 1956–59; Associate Conductor, City of Birmingham Symphony Orchestra, 1957–59, Dep. Musical Dir, 1959–60; Conductor, City of Birmingham Choir, 1957–64; Musical Director; English Opera Group, 1963–65; Vancouver Symphony Orchestra, 1964–71; Chief Conductor, BBC Trng Orchestra, 1969–72; Music Dir, Royal Choral Soc., 1972–85; Conductor, Leeds Phil. Soc., 1975–84. Pres., ISM, 1985–86. Chm., Delius Trust, 1991–97. *Address:* 10 Mallard Close, New Alresford, Hants SO24 9BX.
Died 9 March 2005.

DAVIES, Very Rev. Alun Radcliffe; Dean of Llandaff, 1977–93; *b* 6 May 1923; *s* of Rev. Rhys Davies and Jane Davies; *m* 1952, Winifred Margaret Pullen (*d* 1999); two *s* one *d*. *Educ:* Cowbridge Grammar Sch.; University Coll., Cardiff (BA 1945; Fellow, 1983); Keble Coll., Oxford (BA 1947, MA 1951); St Michael's Coll., Llandaff. Curate of Roath, 1948–49; Lecturer, St Michael's Coll., Llandaff, 1949–53; Domestic Chaplain to Archbishop of Wales, 1952–57, to Bishop of Llandaff, 1957–59; Chaplain RNR, 1953–60; Vicar of Ystrad Mynach, 1959–75; Chancellor of Llandaff Cathedral, 1969–71; Archdeacon of Llandaff, 1971–77; Residentiary Canon of Llandaff Cathedral, 1975–77. Chaplain, Lieutenancy of S Glam, 1994–. *Address:* 15 Sinclair Drive, Penylan, Cardiff CF23 9AH. *T:* (029) 2045 6149. *Died 8 June 2003.*

DAVIES, Andrew Owen Evan; Consultant, Lee Bolton & Lee, since 2001 (Senior Partner, 1987–2000); Legal Adviser of Dean and Chapter of Canterbury Cathedral, 1984–2002 (Registrar and Legal Adviser of the Diocese of Canterbury, 1982–96); *b* 12 Jan. 1936; *s* of late Ninian Rhys Davies and Gweneth Elizabeth Davies; *m* 1963, G. Margaret Stephens; one *s* two *d*. *Educ:* Shrewsbury Sch. Solicitor, Notary Public. National Service, Royal Fusiliers, 1954–56. Law studies and articles, 1956–62; admitted Solicitor, 1962; Partner, Evan Davies & Co., 1964–80; Evan Davies & Co. amalgamated with Lee Bolton & Lee, 1980; Partner, Lee Bolton & Lee, 1980–83, Dep. Sen.

Partner, 1983–87. *Recreations:* country pursuits, golf, reading, family. *Address:* (office) 1 The Sanctuary, Westminster, SW1P 3JT. *T:* (020) 7222 5381. *Club:* Boodle's. *Died 12 Oct. 2005.*

DAVIES, Rear-Adm. Anthony, CB 1964; CVO 1972; RN, retired; *b* 13 June 1912; *s* of late James Arthur and Margaret Davies; *m* 1940, Lilian Hilda Margaret (*d* 1980), *d* of Admiral Sir Harold Martin Burrough, GCB, KBE, DSO, and Lady (Nellie Wills) Burrough; two *s* two *d.* *Educ:* Royal Naval Coll., Dartmouth; Open Univ. (BA 1983). Midshipman, HMS Danae, 1930–32; Sub-Lieut, HMS Despatch, 1934; Lieut, HMS Duncan, 1935–37; Gunnery course, 1938; HMS Repulse, 1939; HMS Cossack, 1940–41; Lieut-Comdr, HMS Indefatigable, 1943–45; Comdr, HMS Triumph, 1950; HMS Excellent, 1951–54; Capt., HMS Pelican, 1954–55; Dep. Dir, RN Staff Coll., 1956–57; Far East Fleet Staff, 1957–59; Dep. Dir, Naval Intelligence, 1959–62; Rear-Adm., 1963; Head of British Defence Liaison Staff, Canberra, Australia, 1963–65. Warden, St George's House, Windsor Castle, 1966–72. *Address:* Witts Piece, 11A South Street, Aldbourne, Marlborough, Wilts SN8 2DW. *T:* (01672) 540418. *Died 14 Jan. 2003.*

DAVIES, Christopher Evelyn K.; *see* Kevill-Davies.

DAVIES, (Claude) Nigel (Byam); *b* 2 Sept. 1920; unmarried. *Educ:* Eton; studied at Aix en Provence University, 1937, and at Potsdam, 1938; PhD London (archaeology). Entered Sandhurst, 1939, later commissioned Grenadier Guards. Served Middle East, Italy and Balkans, 1942–46. Formerly Managing Dir of Windolite Ltd. MP (C) Epping Div. of Essex, 1950–51. *Publications:* Los Señoríos Independientes del Imperio Azteca, 1968; Los Mexicas: primeras pasos hacia el imperio, 1973; The Aztecs, 1973; The Toltecs, 1977; Voyagers to the New World: fact and fantasy, 1979; The Toltec Heritage, 1980; Human Sacrifice, 1981; The Ancient Kingdoms of Mexico, 1983; The Rampant God, 1984; The Aztec Empire, 1987; The Incas, 1995; The Ancient Kingdoms of Peru, 1997. *Recreation:* travel. *Address:* Sonora 75, Colonia Chapultepec, Tijuana, Baja California, Mexico. *T:* (66) 861036. *Club:* Carlton. *Died 25 Sept. 2004.*

DAVIES, George Raymond, (Gerry), OBE 1977; FCLIP; Director, The Booksellers Association of Great Britain and Ireland, 1964–66 and 1970–81 (Hon. Life Member, 1981); *b* 3 Oct. 1916; *s* of George John Davies and Eva Florence Davies; *m* 1945, Sylvia Newling (*d* 1998); one *s* one *d.* *Educ:* East Ham Grammar Sch. FCLIP (FLA 1948). Local govt service, 1934–40; land reclamation, 1940–45; estate under-bailiff, 1945–46; W Suffolk and Cambridge Public Libraries, 1947–54 (Dep. City Librarian, 1953); Gen. Sec., Booksellers Assoc., 1955–64; Man. Dir, Bowker Publishing Co. Ltd, 1966–67; Editor, Publishers Inf. Card Services Ltd, 1968–69; Jt Dep. Editor, The Bookseller, 1969–70. Founder-Mem., Internat. Community of Booksellers Assocs, 1956 (Mem. Council, 1972–78); Mem. Council, Internat. Booksellers Fedn, 1978–85 (Pres. 1978–81; Editor, Booksellers International, 1982–88; Hon. Life Mem., 1989); Chm., BA Service House Ltd, 1977–82; Patron, Book Trade Benevolent Soc., 1989– (Chm., 1974–86; Pres., 1986–89). *Publications:* (ed jtly) Books are Different, 1966; A Mortal Craft, 1980; One Hundred Years: the history of the Booksellers Association, 1995; (contrib.) The Book of Westminster, 1964; (contrib.) Books and Their Prices, 1967; The End Game (poems), 1999; About and Roundabout (poems), 2001; Out in the Open (poems), 2002; Persons and Passions (poems), 2003; contrib. to Logos, Library Rev., Library World, Year's Work in Librarianship, DNB, Canadian Bookseller, American Bookseller, Australian Bookseller and Publisher, Publishers Weekly, and The Bookseller. *Recreations:* estate management, writing words and music. *Address:* Crotchets, Rotherfield Lane, Mayfield, East Sussex TN20

6AS. *T:* (01435) 872356. *Club:* Savile. *Died 10 Feb. 2004.*

DAVIES, Handel, CB 1962; FREng; FRAeS; FAIAA; aeronautical engineering consultant; *b* 2 June 1912; *m* 1942, Mary Graham Harris (*d* 2003). *Educ:* Aberdare Grammar Sch.; Univ. of Wales (MSc). Royal Aircraft Establishment and Min. of Aircraft Production, 1936–47; Hd of Aerodynamics Flight Div., RAE, 1948–52; Chief Superintendent, Aeroplane and Armament Experimental Establishment, Boscombe Down, 1952–55; Scientific Advr to Air Ministry, 1955–56; Dir-Gen., Scientific Research (Air), Min. of Supply, 1957–59; Dep. Dir, RAE, Farnborough, 1959–63. Dep. Controller of Aircraft, (R&D), Min. of Aviation, 1963–67, Min. of Technology, 1967–69. Tech. Dir, British Aircraft Corp., 1969–77. Chm., Standing Conf. on Schools Sci. and Technology, 1978–82. Fellow, University Coll., Cardiff, 1981. Wilbur and Orville Wright Meml Lectr, 1979. Hon. FRAeS 1982 (FRAeS 1948; Pres., 1977–78; Gold Medal, 1974). *Publications:* papers in Reports and Memoranda of ARC and Jl of RAeS. *Recreation:* sailing. *Address:* Keel Cottage, Woodham Road, Horsell, Woking, Surrey GU21 4DL. *T:* (01483) 714192. *Club:* Royal Air Force Yacht (Hamble). *Died 28 April 2003.*

DAVIES, His Honour Ian Hewitt, TD; a Circuit Judge, 1986–2000; *b* 13 May 1931; *s* of late Rev. J. R. Davies; *m* 1962, Molly Cecilia Vaughan Vaughan. *Educ:* Kingswood Sch.; St John's Coll., Cambridge (MA). Nat. Service, commnd KOYLI; served with 3rd Bn Parachute Regt, 1950–51; TA, 1952–71 (Lt-Col). Called to the Bar, Inner Temple, 1958. *Clubs:* Boodle's, Royal Automobile, MCC, Hurlingham. *Died 28 July 2002.*

DAVIES, John; *see* Davies, L. J.

DAVIES, His Honour (Lewis) John; QC 1967; a Circuit Judge (Official Referee), 1984–93; *b* 15 April 1921; *s* of William Davies, JP, and Esther Davies; *m* 1956, Janet Mary Morris; one *s* two *d.* *Educ:* Pontardawe Grammar Sch.; University College of Wales, Aberystwyth (LLB Wales (1st cl.) 1942); Trinity Hall, Cambridge (Common Law Prizeman, 1943; Scholar, 1943–44; BA 1st cl.; LLB 1st cl.). Asst Principal, HM Treasury, 1945–46; Senior Law Lecturer, Leeds Univ., 1946–48; Administrative Asst, British Petroleum, 1949–52. Called to the Bar, Middle Temple, 1948, Bencher, 1973 (Emeritus, 1993); a Recorder, 1974–84. Mem., Bar Council, 1969–71; Mem., Senate, 1976–78. Mem., Council of Legal Educn, 1976–79. Inspector, DoT, 1977. Mem., Gorsedd, 1986–. *Recreations:* gardening, golf. *Address:* Old Manor Cottage, 24 Park Road, Teddington, Middx TW11 0AQ. *T:* (020) 8977 3975. *Club:* Travellers. *Died 4 Dec. 2005.*

DAVIES, Marcus John A.; *see* Anwyl-Davies.

DAVIES, Meredith; *see* Davies, Albert Meredith.

DAVIES, Nigel; *see* Davies, Claude N. B.

DAVIES, Ven. Philip Bertram; Archdeacon of St Albans, 1987–98, then Emeritus; *b* 13 July 1933; *s* of Rev. Bertram Davies and Nancy Jonsson Davies (*née* Nicol); *m* 1963, (Elizabeth) Jane, *d* of late Ven. John Farquhar Richardson; two *s* one *d* (and one *d* decd). *Educ:* Lancing Coll.; Cuddesdon Theol Coll. Travancore Tea Estates Ltd, 1954–58; Lewis's Ltd, 1959–61. Ordained deacon, 1963, priest, 1964; Curate, St John the Baptist, Atherton, 1963–66; Vicar, St Mary Magdalene, Winton, Eccles, 1966–71; Rector, St Philip with St Stephen, Salford, 1971–76; Vicar, Christ Church, Radlett, 1976–87; RD of Aldenham, 1979–87. *Recreations:* gardening, fishing. *Address:* Stone Cottage, 34 School Road, Finstock, Oxon OX7 3DJ. *T:* (01993) 868207. *Died 1 Feb. 2005.*

DAVIES, Sir Rees; *see* Davies, Sir Robert R.

DAVIES, Robert David, CB 1982; CVO 1977; RD 1963; JP; Director, Office of the Premier, Department of the Premier and Cabinet, Western Australia, 1983 and Clerk of Executive Council, 1975–83; *b* 17 Aug. 1927; *s* of late William Harold Davies and of Elsie Davies; *m* 1948, Muriel Patricia Cuff; one *s* one *d*. *Educ*: Fremantle Boys High Sch.; Perth Technical Coll. Senior AASA. Defence Service, 1945–47; Asst Comr, State Taxation Dept, 1973; Under Sec., Premier's Dept, WA, 1975. Comdr, RANR, 1972. JP 1970. *Recreations*: fishing, sailing. *Address*: 68 Beazley Road, Leeming, WA 6149, Australia. *T*: (9) 3324041. *Died 20 July 2001.*

DAVIES, Rt Rev. Robert Edward, CBE 1981; MA, ThD; Bishop of Tasmania, 1963–81; *b* Birkenhead, England, 30 July 1913; *s* of late R. A. Davies, Canberra; *m* 1953, Helen M., *d* of H. M. Boucher; two *d*. *Educ*: Cessnock High School; Queensland University; St John's Theological College, Morpeth, NSW. Assistant Priest, Christ Church Cathedral, Newcastle, NSW, 1937–41. War of 1939–45: Toc H Army Chaplain, 1941–42; Chaplain, Royal Australian Air Force, Middle East and Mediterranean, 1942–46. Vice-Warden, St John's College, University of Queensland, Brisbane, 1946–48; Archdeacon of Canberra and Rector of Canberra, 1949–53; Archdeacon of Wagga Wagga, NSW, 1953–60; Assistant Bishop of Newcastle and Warden of St John's Theological College, Morpeth, NSW, 1960–63. *Recreations*: golf, tennis. *Address*: 12 Elboden Street, Hobart, Tasmania 7000, Australia. *Clubs*: Tasmanian, Naval Military and Air Force of Tas (Tas). *Died 17 May 2002.*

DAVIES, Robert Henry, MBE 1962; DFC 1943; HM Diplomatic Service, retired; *b* 17 Aug. 1921; *s* of John and Lena Davies; *m* 1st, 1945, Marion Ainsworth (marr. diss. 1973); one *s* one *d*; 2nd, 1973, Maryse Deuson. *Educ*: John Bright County Sch., Llandudno. RAF, 1940–46; flew with S African Air Force, N Africa, 1942–43. Joined Min. of Food, 1946; transf. to CRO, 1954; served in India, 1954–57 and Canada, 1959–62; HM Diplomatic Service, 1965; served in Brussels, 1967–70; Consul-Gen. and Counsellor (Admin), Moscow, 1973–75; FCO, 1975–76; Counsellor, Paris, 1976–81. *Recreations*: golf, birdwatching, reading. *Address*: 16 Beechcroft Drive, Guildford, Surrey GU2 5SA. *Club*: Bramley Golf. *Died 17 Feb. 2001.*

DAVIES, Sir (Robert) Rees, Kt 2005; CBE 1995; DPhil; FBA 1987; Chichele Professor of Medieval History, University of Oxford, 1995–2004; Fellow of All Souls College, 1995–2004, then Emeritus; *b* 6 Aug. 1938; *s* of William Edward Davies and Sarah Margaret Williams; *m* 1966, Carys Lloyd Wynne; one *s* one *d*. *Educ*: University Coll. London (BA; Hon. Fellow, 1998); Merton Coll., Oxford (DPhil; Hon. Fellow, 2004). FRHistS 1968. Asst Lectr, UC, Swansea, 1961–63; Lectr, UCL, 1963–76; Prof. of History, 1976–95, British Academy Wolfson Res. Prof. in Humanities, 1993–95, and Vice-Principal, 1988–91, Univ. (formerly Univ. Coll.) of Wales, Aberystwyth. Wiles Lectr, QUB, 1988; James Ford Special Lectr, Univ. of Oxford, 1988; Vis. Fellow, Magdalen Coll., Oxford, 1992; Special History Lectr, Univ. of Newcastle upon Tyne, 1994; Ford Lectures, Univ. of Oxford, 1998. Chm., Nat. Curriculum History Cttee for Wales, 1989–91; Mem., Res. Gp, HEFCW, 1993–94. Convenor, History at Univs Defence Gp, 1991–92. Chm., Ancient Monuments Bd for Wales, 1995–2005 (Mem., 1977–; Dep. Chm., 1993–95); Member, Council: Nat. Museum of Wales, 1987–90; Historical Assoc., 1991–93; President: RHistS, 1992–96 (Mem. Council, 1979–82; Vice Pres., 1987–91); Assoc. of History Teachers of Wales, 1994–2004; Chm., Cttee on Acad. Res. Projects, British Acad., 1997–2002. Pres., Hon. Soc. of Cymmrodorion, 2002–; Mem., Welsh Acad., 1990. Hon. Fellow: UC of Swansea, 1993; Univ. of Wales, Aberystwyth, 1996. Hon. DLitt Wales, 2000. Wolfson Literary Award for History, 1987; Norton Medlicott Medal, Historical Assoc., 1994. Asst Editor and Review Editor, History, 1963–73. *Publications*: Lordship and Society in the March of Wales 1282–1400, 1978; (ed) Welsh Society and Nationhood,

1984; Conquest, Co-existence and Change: Wales 1063–1415, 1987; (ed) The British Isles 1100–1500, 1988; Domination and Conquest: the experience of Ireland, Scotland and Wales 1100–1300, 1990; The Revolt of Owain Glyn Dwr, 1995; The First English Empire: power and identities in the British Isles 1093–1343, 2000 ((jtly) British Academy Book Prize, 2001); numerous contribs to learned jls. *Recreations*: walking, music. *Address*: 9 Dale Close, Oxford OX1 1TU. *T*: (01865) 242816. *Died 16 May 2005.*

DAVIS, Brian Michael; consultant and adviser, oil industry, since 1994; Chairman and Chief Executive, Mobil Oil Company Ltd, 1990–92; *b* 28 May 1937; *s* of Frederick Thomas Davis and Irene Florence (*née* Burgess); *m* 1962, Patricia Ann Wilkinson; three *s*. *Educ*: London Univ., LSE (BSc Econs). FCMA. Joined Mobil Oil Co. Ltd, 1958: various positions in accounting and finance systems, marketing, planning and supply in UK, Europe and USA, 1958–77; Gen. Manager, Mobil Kenya Gp, 1977–79; Strategic/Marketing Planning, Mobil South Inc./Mobil Europe Inc., 1979–84; Pres., Mobil Oil Portuguesa, 1984–86; Area Exec., Mobil Europe, 1986–87; Pres., Mobil Oil Italiana, 1987–90. Dir, Petrola UK, 1995–. *Recreations*: golf, tennis, music, theatre. *Died 23 Jan. 2001.*

DAVIS, Sir (Ernest) Howard, Kt 1978; CMG 1969; OBE 1960; Deputy Governor, Gibraltar, 1971–78; *b* 22 April 1918; *m* 1948, Marie Davis (*née* Bellotti); two *s*. *Educ*: Christian Brothers Schs, Gibraltar and Blackpool; London Univ. (BA 1st cl. hons). Gen. Clerical Staff, Gibraltar, 1936–46; Asst Sec. and Clerk of Councils, 1946–54; seconded Colonial Office, 1954–55; Chief Asst Sec., Estabt Officer and Public Relations Officer (responsible for opening Radio Gibraltar), Gibraltar, 1955–62; Director of Labour and Social Security, 1962–65; Financial and Development Secretary, 1965–71; Acting Governor, various periods, 1971–77. Chairman, Committee of Enquiry: PWD, 1980–81; Electricity Dept, 1982; Chm., Gibraltar Broadcasting Corp., 1982–83. Pres., Calpe Rowing Club, 1985–92. *Recreations*: cricket, gardening, bridge. *Address*: Flat 7/6, Jumpers Building, Witham's Road, Gibraltar. *T*: 70358. *Died 28 Oct. 2003.*

DAVIS, Sir Howard; see Davis, Sir E. H.

DAVIS, Ivor John Guest, CB 1983; Director, Common Law Institute of Intellectual Property, 1986–91; *b* 11 Dec. 1925; *s* of Thomas Henry Davis and Dorothy Annie Davis; *m* 1954, Mary Eleanor Thompson; one *s* one *d*. *Educ*: Devonport High Sch.; HM Dockyard Sch., Devonport. BSc London (ext.). Apprentice, HM Dockyard, Devonport, 1941–45; Draughtsman, 1946–47; Patent Office, Department of Trade: Asst Examr, 1947; Asst Comptroller, 1973; Comptroller Gen., Patents, Designs and Trade Marks, 1978. Pres., Administrative Council, European Patent Office, 1981–85. Mem. Adv. Panel, Centre d'études de la propriété industrielle, Strasbourg, 1979–85. Mem. Council, Inst. of Intellectual Property, 1991–99. Mem., Editorial Adv. Bd, World Patent Information Jl, 1979–85. *Recreations*: crosswords, music, gardening. *Address*: 5 Birch Close, Eynsford, Dartford DA4 0EX. *Died 8 Dec. 2004.*

DAVIS, John Darelan R.; see Russell-Davis.

DAVIS, Leslie Harold Newsom, CMG 1957; *b* 6 April 1909; *s* of Harold Newsom Davis and Aileen Newsom Davis (*née* Gush); *m* 1950, Judith Anne, *d* of L. G. Corney, CMG; one *s* two *d*. *Educ*: Marlborough; Trinity Coll., Cambridge (BA 1930, MA 1946). Apptd to Malayan Civil Service, 1932; Private Sec. to Governor and High Comr, 1938–40; attached to 22nd Ind. Inf. Bde as Liaison Officer, Dec. 1941; interned by Japanese in Singapore, 1942–45; District Officer, Seremban, 1946–47; British Resident, Brunei, 1948; Asst Adviser, Muar, 1948–50; Sec. to Mem. for Education, Fed. of Malaya, 1951–52; Mem. for Industrial and Social Relations, 1952–53; Sec. for Defence and Internal Security, Singapore, 1953–55; Permanent Sec., Min. of Communications and Works, Singapore, 1955–57. Special Rep., Rubber Growers' Assoc. in Malaya, 1958–63. *Recreation:* golf. *Address:* Berrywood, Heyshott, near Midhurst, West Sussex GU29 0DH. *Club:* Oxford and Cambridge. *Died 16 June 2003.*

DAVSON, Sir Christopher (Michael Edward), 3rd Bt *cr* 1927, of Berbice, British Guiana; *b* 26 May 1927; *yr s* of Sir Edward Rae Davson, 1st Bt, KCMG (*d* 1937) and Margot Elinor (*née* Glyn) (*d* 1966), OBE; *S* brother, Sir Anthony Glyn, 2nd Bt, 1998; *m* 1st, 1962, Evelyn Mary (marr. diss. 1971), *o d* of James Wardrop; one *s*; 2nd, 1975, Kate, *d* of Ludovic Foster. *Educ:* Eton Coll. FCA. Articled Price Waterhouse & Co., London, 1948–51; sugar planter, British Guiana, 1951–55; (last) Chm., S. Davson & Co. Ltd (founded 1816), 1955; Dir, Bookers Sugar Co. Ltd, 1956–65; Finance Director: Bookers Engineering Holdings Ltd, 1957–65; Bookers Agricultural Holdings Ltd, 1958–65; Founder Dir, The Nigerian Sugar Co. Ltd, 1962–65. Captain, late Welsh Guards, 1945–48, RARO, 1949–77. Liveryman, Musicians' Co., 1969–. *Publication:* I Merlin—an Historical Recreation, 2000. *Recreations:* archaeology, history, opera. *Heir: s* George Trenchard Simon Davson [*b* 5 June 1964; *m* 1985, Joanna (marr. diss. 1996), *e d* of Rev. Dr James Bentley; one *s* one *d*]. *Address:* 4 Mermaid Street, Rye, East Sussex TN31 7ET. *T:* (01797) 222661, *Fax:* (01797) 224424. *Club:* Lansdowne. *Died 21 Dec. 2004.*

DAWSON, (Joseph) Peter; Consultant, Education International, since 1998 (Co-ordinator for Europe, 1993–98); *b* 18 March 1940; *s* of Joseph Glyn and Winifred Olwen Dawson; *m* 1964, Yvonne Anne Charlton Smith; one *s* one *d*. *Educ:* Bishop Gore Grammar Sch., Swansea; University College of Swansea (BSc, DipEd). Asst Master, Chiswick Grammar Sch., 1962; Field Officer, 1965, Sen. Field Officer, 1966, NUT; Asst Sec., 1969, Negotiating Sec., 1974, ATTI; Negotiating Sec., 1976, Gen. Sec., 1979–89, Asst Sec. (Pensions and Memship Services) and Internat. Rep., 1989–93, NATFHE. Gen. Sec., ETUCE, 1991–93 (Mem. Exec. Bd, 1984–93; Chm., Higher Educn Working Gp, 1989–93). Vice-Pres., 1962–64, Sen. Treas., 1965–68, NUS. Member: Teachers' Panel, Teachers' Superannuation Working Party, 1969–93 (Chm., 1979–93); Eur. Cttee, World Confedn of Organisations of Teaching Profession, 1983–93; Cttee on Workers' Capital, ICFTU, 2000–. Mem. (Lab) Lewisham BC, 2002– (Vice-Chairman: Governance Select Cttee, 2002–03; Public Accounts Select Cttee, 2003–). Sec., Horniman, subseq. Forest Hill, Br., W Lewisham Lab. Party, 1999–. Gov., Holy Trinity Sch., Forest Hill, 1989–93, 1998– (Vice-Chm., 2001–). Hon. FCP 1984. *Recreations:* football, cricket, theatre. *Address:* 3 Westwood Park, Forest Hill SE23 3QB. *T:* and *Fax:* (020) 8291 6200. *Club:* Surrey County Cricket. *Died 19 Jan. 2005.*

DAWSON, Peter; see Dawson, J. P.

DAWSON, Air Vice-Marshal Reginald Thomas, CBE 1987; Director of Legal Services, Royal Air Force, 1989–92, retired; *b* 6 Aug. 1930; *s* of Herbert James and Lilian Ethel Dawson; *m* 1963, Geraldine Sandra Peters; one *s* one *d*. *Educ:* Hastings Grammar Sch.; Skinners' Sch., Tunbridge Wells. Qualified as solicitor, 1953. Nat. service, RAF, as pilot, 1953–55; in private practice as solicitor, 1955–57; RAF Reserve, 1955–57; rejoined RAF, 1957; Flt Lt, later Sqn Ldr, RAF Legal Branch, 1957–68; Wing Comdr, 1968; Dep. Dir of Legal Services, NEAF, 1968–71; UK Legal Officer, Australian, NZ and UK Force, Singapore, 1971–74; Gp Captain, 1974; Dep. Dir of Legal Services, RAF Germany, 1974–78; Legal Services 1, RAF, 1978–82, Dep. Dir, 1982–89; Air Cdre, 1982; Air Vice-Marshal, 1989. *Recreations:* game shooting, golf, sailing, walking, gardening, reading. *Address:* The Minstrels, Netherfield Hill, Battle, E Sussex TN33 0LH. *T:* (01424) 772186. *Club:* Royal Air Force.
Died 17 May 2004.

DEAKIN, Sir (Frederick) William (Dampier); see Deakin, Sir William.

DEAKIN, George Anthony Hartley, (Tony), CBE 1996; Chairman, Addenbrooke's NHS Trust, 1996–2002; *b* 4 June 1937; *s* of Capt. George Deakin, MC and Bar, and Winsome Deakin, MBE (*née* Combe); *m* 1962, Daphne Caroline Gill; two *s* two *d*. *Educ:* Dragon Sch., Oxford; Sherborne Sch., Dorset; Trinity Coll., Oxford (MA Hons); MBA INSEAD. 2nd Lieut, 13/18 Royal Hussars, 1956–57; Exercise Whiteshod, Norway, 1957; Lieut and Capt., AER, 1957–66. Called to the Bar, Gray's Inn, 1963. Joined British Petroleum Co. Ltd, 1961: Pres., BP N America Trading, 1979–82; Man. Dir, BP Africa, 1982–86; Pres., BP Belgium, 1987–88; Head, IT Gp Centre, 1989–90; Chm. and Chief Exec., BP Southern Africa, 1990–95; Head, Africa Reg., BP Oil Internat., 1993–95. Mem. Cttee, Assoc. of MBAs (East), 1997–2002. Trustee, Fund for Addenbrooke's, 1997–. Mem., HAC, 1983–. *Recreations:* Laser sailing, ski-ing (haute route Chamonix to Zermatt, 2000), bridge, reading Trollope and Schlink. *Address:* Manting House, Meldreth, Royston, Herts SG8 6NU. *T:* (01763) 260276. *Clubs:* Farmers', Ski of GB; Overy Staithe Sailing (Norfolk); Zeekoevlei Yacht (Cape Town). *Died 11 April 2003.*

DEAKIN, Sir William, Kt 1975; DSO 1943; MA; Warden of St Antony's College, Oxford, 1950–68, retired; Hon. Fellow, 1969; *b* 3 July 1913; *e s* of Albert Witney Deakin, Aldbury, Tring, Herts; *m* 1st, 1935, Margaret Ogilvy (marr. diss. 1940), *d* of late Sir Nicholas Beatson Bell, KCSI, KCIE; two *s*; 2nd, 1943, Livia Stela (*d* 2001), *d* of Liviu Nasta, Bucharest. *Educ:* Westminster Sch.; Christ Church, Oxford (1st Class, Modern History, 1934; Amy Mary Preston Read Scholar, 1935; Hon. Student, 1979). Fellow and Tutor, Wadham Coll., Oxford, 1936–49, Research Fellow, 1949, Hon. Fellow, 1961. Served War of 1939–45: with Queen's Own Oxfordshire Hussars, 1939–41; seconded to Special Operations, War Office, 1941; led first British Military Mission to Tito, May 1943. First Secretary, HM Embassy, Belgrade, 1945–46. Hon. FBA, 1980. Russian Order of Valour, 1944; Chevalier de la Légion d'Honneur, 1953; Grosse Verdienstkreuz, 1958; Yugoslav Partisan Star (1st Class), 1969. *Publications:* The Brutal Friendship, 1962; (with G. R. Storry) The Case of Richard Sorge, 1964; The Embattled Mountain, 1971. *Address:* 83330 Le Castellet Village, Var, France. *Clubs:* White's, Brooks's. *Died 22 Jan. 2005.*

DEAN, His Honour (Charles) Raymond; QC 1963; a Circuit Judge (formerly Judge of County Courts), 1971–88; Senior Circuit Judge, 1985–88; *b* 28 March 1923; *s* of late Joseph Irvin Gledhill Dean and late Lilian Dean (*née* Waddington); *m* 1948, Pearl Doreen (*née* Buncall); one *s* one *d*. *Educ:* Hipperholme Grammar Sch.; The Queen's Coll., Oxford (1941–42 and 1945–47). RAF Flying Duties, 1942–45 (Flt Lieut). BA (Jurisprudence) 1947, MA 1948; called to Bar, Lincoln's Inn, 1948; Deputy Chairman, West Riding QS, 1961–65; Recorder: of Rotherham, 1962–65; of Newcastle upon Tyne, 1965–70; of Kingston-upon-Hull, 1970–71. *Recreations:* fishing, motoring, reading, Rugby Union (latterly non-playing), golf. *Address:* Inner Court, 3 Hudson Mews, Boston Spa, West Yorks LS23 6AD. *T:* (01937) 844155. *Club:* Leeds. *Died 3 Oct. 2003.*

DEAN, Raymond; see Dean, C. R.

DEBENHAM, Sir Gilbert Ridley, 3rd Bt *cr* 1931, of Bladen, co. Dorset; *b* 28 June 1906; 2nd *s* of Sir Ernest Ridley Debenham, 1st Bt, JP and Cecily, *d* of Rt Hon. William Kenrick, PC; *S* brother, Sir Piers Debenham, 2nd Bt, 1964; *m* 1935, Violet Mary (*d* 1994), *e d* of late His Honour Judge (George Herbert) Higgins; two *s* one *d* (and one *s* decd). *Educ:* Eton; Trinity Coll., Cambridge (BA 1928; BChir 1935). DPM 1946; MRCPsych 1971. *Heir: g s* Thomas Adam Debenham, *b* 28 Feb. 1971. *Address:* Tonerspuddle Farm, Dorchester, Dorset.
Died 3 June 2001.

DEBREU, Prof. Gerard; Professor of Economics, 1962–91, Professor of Mathematics, 1975–91, and University Professor, 1985–91, then Emeritus, University of California, Berkeley; *b* 4 July 1921; *s* of Camille Debreu and Fernande (*née* Decharne); US citizen, 1975; *m* 1945, Françoise Bled; two *d. Educ:* Ecole Normale Supérieure, Paris; Agrégé de l'Université, Paris, 1946; DSc Univ. de Paris, 1956. Research Associate: CNRS, Paris, 1946–48; Cowles Commn for Research in Economics, Univ. of Chicago, 1950–55; Associate Prof. of Economics, Cowles Foundn for Research in Economics, Yale Univ., 1955–61. President: Econometric Soc., 1971; American-Economic Assoc., 1990. Member: Nat. Acad. of Sciences, USA, 1977; Amer. Philos. Soc., 1984; Fellow, Amer. Acad. of Arts and Scis, 1970; Dist. Fellow, Amer. Economic Assoc., 1982; For. Associate, French Acad. of Scis, 1984. Hon. degrees: Bonn, 1977; Lausanne, 1980; Northwestern, 1981; Toulouse, 1983; Yale, 1987; Université de Bordeaux I, 1988. Nobel Prize in Economic Sciences, 1983. Officier de la Légion d'Honneur, 1993 (Chevalier, 1976); Comdr de l'Ordre National du Mérite, 1984. *Publications:* Theory of Value: an axiomatic analysis of economic equilibrium, 1959, 2nd edn 1971 (trans. into French, Spanish, German and Japanese); Mathematical Economics: twenty papers, 1983; contribs to Econometrica, Procs of Nat. Acad. of Scis, Review of Economic Studies, Economie Appliquée, Procs of Amer. Math. Soc., Internat. Economic Review, Review of Economic Studies, La Décision, Jl of Mathematical Economics, Amer. Economic Review. *Address:* Department of Economics, University of California, Berkeley, CA 94720–3880, USA. *T:* (510) 6427284; *e-mail:* debreu@econ.berkeley.edu.
Died 31 Dec. 2004.

DE BUTTS, Brig. Frederick Manus, CMG 1967; OBE 1961 (MBE 1943); DL; *b* 17 April 1916; *s* of late Brig. F. C. De Butts, CB, DSO, MC, and K. P. M. O'Donnell; *m* 1944, Evelyn Cecilia, *d* of Sir Walter Halsey, 2nd Bt; one *s* one *d. Educ:* Wellington Coll.; Oriel Coll., Oxford. Commissioned into Somerset LI, 1937. Served War of 1939–45, in Middle East, Italy, France and Germany (despatches, 1941, 1944). Staff Coll., 1944; Malaya (despatches, 1950); Joint Services Staff Coll., 1954; Bt Lieut-Colonel, 1957; comd 3rd Bn Aden Protectorate Levies, 1958–60; Bde Colonel, Light Infantry, 1961–64; Comdr, Trucial Oman Scouts, 1964–67; HQ Home Counties District, Shorncliffe, Kent, 1967–68; Defence Attaché, Cairo, 1968–71; retired 1971; employed on contract as COS (Brig.), MoD, United Arab Emirates, 1971–73; Hon. Brig. 1973. Mem., Dacorum DC, 1976–83. Hon. Dir, Herts Soc., 1981–91. County Chm., 1973–76, County Comr, 1976–81, Vice-Pres., 1981–89, Pres., 1989–97, Herts Scouts; Vice-Pres., Herts Girl Guides, 1981–; Governor, Abbot's Hill School, 1971–92 (Chm., 1975–84). DL Herts 1975. *Publication:* Now the Dust has Settled: memories of war and peace 1939–1994, 1995. *Recreations:* tennis, hill-walking, ski-ing. *Address:* Church Cottage, Hoggeston, Buckingham, Bucks MK18 3LL. *T:* (01296) 713811. *Died 24 Aug. 2005.*

de COURCY LING, John, CBE 1990; HM Diplomatic Service, 1959–78; politician, publisher and writer, since 1978; *b* 14 Oct. 1933; *s* of Arthur Norman Ling, Warwick, and Veronica de Courcy, Painestown, Co. Kildare; *m* 1959, Jennifer Rosemary Haynes, 2nd *d* of Stanley Haynes, Denham and Margaret McLurg, Vancouver; one *s* three *d. Educ:* King Edward's Sch., Edgbaston; Clare Coll., Cambridge (BA 1955; MA 1989). 2nd Lieut, Royal Ulster Rifles, 1956; Lieut on active service, Cyprus, 1957–58. Res. Dept, ME Sect., FO, 1959; a private sec. to Ministers of State for Foreign Affairs, Lord Harlech, 1960–61, to Joseph Godber, 1961–63; 2nd Sec., Santiago, 1963–66; 1st Sec., Nairobi, 1966–69; Rhodesia Dept, FO, 1969; American Dept, FO, 1970–71; Asst Hd, W African Dept, 1971–74; Chargé d'Affaires, Chad, 1973; Counsellor, HM Embassy, Paris, 1974–77; resigned, 1978, to enter politics. MEP (C) Midlands Central, 1979–89.

European Parliament: Cons. Chief Whip, 1979–82; Chm., EU Parly Delegn to Israel, 1979–83; Vice-Chm., Develt Aid Cttee, 1983–89. Mem., Council of Lloyds, 1986–88. Mem., Catholic Bishops' Cttee on Europe, 1983–2001. Mem. Council, RIIA, 1990–93. *Publications:* (with T. R. McK. Sewell) Famine and Surplus, 1985; Empires Rise and Sink, 1996; contribs to the Tablet and various political papers. *Recreations:* racing, ski-ing, yachting, sociable golf. *Address:* Coutts & Co., 440 Strand, WC2 0QS. *Clubs:* Beefsteak, Special Forces; Leander (Henley-on-Thames); Chipping Norton Golf. *Died 10 Nov. 2005.*

DEEDES, Maj.–Gen. Charles Julius, CB 1968; OBE 1953; MC 1944; *b* 18 Oct. 1913; *s* of General Sir Charles Deedes, KCB, CMG, DSO; *m* 1939, Beatrice Murgatroyd (decd), Brockfield Hall, York; three *s. Educ:* Oratory Sch.; Royal Military Coll., Sandhurst. Served War of 1939–45 (despatches); Asst Military Sec., GHQ Middle East, 1945; Officer Comdg Glider Pilot Regt, 1948; GSO1 War Office, 1950; Officer Comdg 1st Bn KOYLI, 1954 (despatches); Col Gen. Staff, War Office, 1956; comd 146 Infantry Brigade (TA), 1958; Dep. Dir, MoD, 1962; Chief of Staff: HQ Eastern Comd, 1965; HQ Southern Comd, 1968. Col, KOYLI, 1966–68; Dep. Col, The Light Infantry (Yorks), 1968–72. Military Cross (Norway), 1940. *Recreations:* riding, tennis. *Address:* Lea Close, Brandsby, York YO61 4RW. *T:* (01347) 888239.
Died 7 May 2005.

de la MARE, Prof. Albinia Catherine, OBE 1993; FBA 1987; Professor of Palaeography, King's College, London, 1989–97; *b* 2 June 1932; *d* of Richard Herbert Ingpen de la Mare and Amy Catherine Donaldson. *Educ:* Queen's Coll., Harley St, W1; Lady Margaret Hall, Oxford (MA); Warburg Inst., London (PhD). FRHistS; FSA. Dept of Western MSS, Bodleian Liby, 1962–88, Asst Librarian, 1964–88. Susette Taylor Fellow, 1964, Hon. Res. Fellow, 1979, Hon. Fellow, 1989, Lady Margaret Hall, Oxford; Guest Scholar, J. Paul Getty Museum, Malibu, 1992; Sen. Res. Fellow, Center for Advanced Study in the Visual Arts, Nat. Gall. of Art, Washington, 1998. Mem., Comité Internat. de Paléographie Latine, 1986–. *Publications:* Catalogue of the Italian manuscripts of Major J. R. Abbey (with J. J. G. Alexander), 1969; Catalogue of the Lyell Manuscripts, Bodleian Library, Oxford, 1971; The Handwriting of Italian Humanists, 1973; New Research on Humanistic Scribes in Florence, in Miniatura Fiorentina del Rinascimento, ed A. Garzelli, 1985; articles in learned periodicals, etc. *Recreations:* music, gardening, travel. *Address:* Tithe Barn House, 11 High Street, Cumnor, Oxford OX2 9PE. *T:* (01865) 863916.
Died 19 Dec. 2001.

De-la-NOY, Michael; author; *b* 3 April 1934; *yr s* of late Eric De-la-Noy Walker and Kathleen Harvard (*née* Johnson). *Educ:* Bedford Sch. Commnd RAC; served in Egypt, 1952–54. Member, editorial staff: Bedfordshire Times, 1954–57; Brighton & Hove Herald, 1958–60; Editor, Richard Thomas & Baldwin, 1961–62; Religious Editor, Prism Pubns, 1962–65; Editor, Pergamon Press, 1966–67; Press Officer to Archbp of Canterbury and Asst Information Officer, Church Inf. Office, 1967–70; Dir, Albany Trust and Sec., Sexual Law Reform Soc., 1970–71; Editor, Open Univ., 1975–77. Member: House of Laity, Church Assembly, 1965–67; Steering Cttee on Liturgical Revision, 1965–67. *Publications:* Before the Storm (poems), 1958; A Child's Life of Christ, 1964; Young Once Only: a study of boys on probation, 1965; The Fields of Praise: an anthology of religious poetry, 1968; A Day in the Life of God, 1971; Elgar: the man, 1983; (ed) The Journals of Denton Welch, 1984; Denton Welch: the making of a writer, 1984; The Honours System, 1985, rev. edn 1992; Acting as Friends: the story of the Samaritans, 1987; (ed) Fragments of a Life Story: the collected short writings of Denton Welch, 1987; Eddy: the life of Edward Sackville-West, 1988; Michael Ramsey: a portrait, 1990; Windsor Castle: past and present, 1990; Exploring Oxford, 1991; The Church of England: a portrait, 1993; The Queen Behind the Throne, 1994; The King who never was: the story of Frederick, Prince of Wales, 1996; Mervyn Stockwood: a lonely life, 1996; Scott of the Antarctic, 1997; George IV, 1998; Bedford School: a history, 1999; The House of Hervey: a history of tainted talent, 2001; Queen Victoria at Home, 2002; contrib. DNB. *Recreation:* going for very short walks. *Address:* c/o Hodson-Margetts, 65 Brook Street, Raunds, Wellingborough, Northants NN9 6LL. *Club:* Wig and Pen.   *Died 12 Aug. 2002.*

de LISLE, Everard John Robert March Phillipps; stockbroker; Vice Lord-Lieutenant of Leicestershire, 1990–2003; *b* 8 June 1930; *s* of late Maj. J. A. F. M. P. de Lisle, DL and Elizabeth Muriel de Lisle; *m* 1959, Hon. Mary Rose Peake, *d* of 1st Viscount Ingleby, PC; two *s* one *d*. *Educ:* Eton; RMA Sandhurst. Commnd RHG, 1950; Captain, 1954; Major, 1960; retired 1962. Member: London Stock Exchange, 1965–; Securities Inst. High Sheriff, 1974–75, DL 1980, Leics. *Recreations:* shooting, country pursuits. *Address:* Stockerston Hall, Oakham, Leics LE15 9JD; 11 Buckingham Court, Kensington Park Road, W11 3BP. *Clubs:* Pratt's; Leicestershire Far and Near.   *Died 30 April 2003.*

de los ANGELES, Victoria, Cross of Lazo de Dama of Order of Isabel the Catholic, Spain; Condecoracíon Banda de la Orden de Civil de Alfonso X (El Sabio), Spain; opera and concert-artiste (singing in original languages), lyric-soprano, since 1944; *b* Barcelona, Spain, 1 Nov. 1923; *m* 1948, Enrique Magriñá (decd); two *s*. *Educ:* Escoles Milà i Fontanals de la Generalitat de Catalunya, Barcelona; Conservatorium of Barcelona; University of Barcelona (Hon. Dr). Studied until 1944 at Conservatorium, Barcelona; first public concert, in Barcelona, 1944; début at Gran Teatro del Liceo de Barcelona, in Marriage of Figaro, 1945; concert and opera tours in Spain and Portugal, 1945–49; winner of first prize at Concours Internat. of Geneva, 1947; first appearances at Paris Opéra, Stockholm Royal Opera, Copenhagen Royal Opera, and début at La Scala, Milan, also South-American and Scandinavian concert tours, 1949; first appearance at Covent Garden, and Carnegie Hall Début, 1950; first United States concert tour, and Metropolitan Opera of New York season, first appearances at La Monnaie, Brussels, Holland and Edinburgh Festivals, 1951; first appearances at Teatro Colón, Buenos Aires, and Teatro Municipal, Rio de Janeiro, 1952. Since 1952 has appeared at the most important opera theatres and concert halls of Europe, North, South and Central America and Canada; first tour in S Africa, 1953; first tour in Australia and New Zealand, 1956; first appearance, Vienna State Opera, 1957; opening Festival, Bayreuth, with Tannhäuser, 1961; first tour in Japan and Far East, 1964. Gold Medal, Barcelona, 1958; Silver Medal, province of Barcelona, 1959; Premio Nacional de Música, Spain; Medal Premio Roma, 1969, and various French, Italian, Dutch and American awards; Gold Disc for 5 million copies sold, UK.   *Died 15 Jan. 2005.*

de MARÉ, Eric, RDI 1997; RIBA; writer and photographer; *b* 10 Sept. 1910; *s* of Bror and Ingrid de Maré; *m* 1st, 1936, Vanessa Burrage (*d* 1972); 2nd, 1974, Enid Verity. *Educ:* St Paul's Sch., London; Architectural Assoc., London (Dip.). RIBA 1934. Asst in several arch. practices, 1933–36; in private practice, 1936–40. War Service, survived, with spell in Home Guard designing frondy camouflage. Editor, Architects' Jl, 1942–46; freelance writer and photographer, mostly on architectural, topographical and photographic subjects, 1946–. Has travelled extensively in British Isles, Europe and USA in search of freelance fodder; much lecturing. Hon. Treasurer, Social Credit Party, 1938–46. Hon. Mem., Glos Architectural Assoc., 1986. Photography exhibitions: Architectural Assoc., 1990; Glasgow Sch. of Architecture, 1991. *Publications:* Britain Rebuilt, 1942; The Canals of England, 1950, 2nd edn 1952, repr. 1987; Scandinavia, 1952; Time on the Thames, 1952; The

Bridges of Britain, 1954, 3rd edn 1989; Gunnar Asplund, 1955; Penguin Photography, 1957, 7th edn 1980; London's Riverside: past, present and future, 1958; (with Sir James Richards) The Functional Tradition in Early Industrial Buildings, 1958; Photography and Architecture, 1961; Swedish Cross Cut: the story of the Göta Canal, 1964; London's River: the story of a city, 1964, 2nd edn 1975 (Runner-up for 1964 Carnegie Award); The City of Westminster: heart of London, 1968; London 1851: the year of the Great Exhibition, 1972; The Nautical Style, 1973; The London Doré Saw: a Victorian evocation, 1973, repr. as Victorian London Observed, 2001; Wren's London, 1975; Architectural Photography, 1975; The Victorian Wood Block Illustrators, 1980 (Yorkshire Post Award for best book on art, 1980); A Matter of Life or Debt, 1983, 4th edn 1986; contrib. Arch. Rev., TLS, Illustrated London News, etc; *relevant publication:* Eric de Maré, Builder with Light, 1990 (Architectural Association monograph of selected photographs, with text by Andrew Higgott and bibliography). *Recreations:* talking to friends, reading history, philosophizing, looking at trees, preaching Douglas Social Credit and the Age of Leisure. *Address:* Dynevor House, New Street, Painswick, Glos GL6 6UN. *T:* (01452) 812543.   *Died 22 Jan. 2002.*

de MAULEY, 6th Baron *cr* 1838; **Gerald John Ponsonby;** *b* 19 Dec. 1921; *er s* of 5th Baron de Mauley and Elgiva Margaret (*d* 1987), *d* of Hon. Cospatrick Dundas and Maud Dundas (later Lady Cordeaux); *S* father, 1962; *m* 1954, Helen Alice, *d* of late Hon. Charles W. S. Douglas and *widow* of Lieut-Col B. L. L. Abdy Collins, OBE, MC, RE; two step *s*. *Educ:* Eton; Christ Church, Oxford (MA). Served War of 1939–45, France; Lieut Leics Yeo., Captain RA. Called to Bar, Middle Temple, 1949. *Heir: nephew* Rupert Charles Ponsonby, *b* 30 June 1957. *Address:* Langford House, Little Faringdon, Lechlade, Glos GL7 3QN.   *Died 17 Oct. 2002.*

de MONTMORENCY, Sir Arnold (Geoffroy), 19th Bt *cr* 1631; President, Contemporary Review Co. Ltd, since 1995 (Literary Editor 1960–90; Chairman, 1962–95); *b* 27 July 1908; *s* of Prof. James Edward Geoffrey de Montmorency (*d* 1934) and Caroline Maud Saumarez (*d* 1973), *d* of Maj.-Gen. James de Havilland; *S* cousin, 1979; *m* 1949, Nettie Hay Anderson (marr. annulled 1953, remarried 1972), *d* of late William Anderson and Janet Hay, Morayshire; no *c*. *Educ:* Westminster School (Triplett Exhibn); Peterhouse, Cambridge (BA 1930, LLM 1931, MA 1934). Harmsworth Law Scholar. Called to the Bar, 1932. Served War, RASC and staff in ME, Italy and Yugoslavia, 1940–45. Contested (L) Cambridge, 1959, Cirencester and Tewkesbury, 1964. Chm. (pt-time), Industrial Tribunals, 1975–81. Member, RIIA; Pres., Friends of Peterhouse. *Publication:* Integration of Employment Legislation, 1984. *Heir:* none. *Club:* National Liberal.   *Died 23 Dec. 2003. (ext).*

DENBIGH, Prof. Kenneth George, FRS 1965; MA Cantab, DSc Leeds; Principal of Queen Elizabeth College, University of London, 1966–77; Professor Emeritus in the University of London, 1977; *b* 30 May 1911; *s* of late G. J. Denbigh, MSc, Harrogate; *m* 1935, Kathleen Enoch; two *s*. *Educ:* Queen Elizabeth Grammar Sch., Wakefield; Leeds University. Imperial Chemical Industries, 1934–38, 1945–48; Lecturer, Southampton Univ., 1938–41; Ministry of Supply (Explosives), 1941–45; Lecturer, Cambridge Univ., Chemical Engineering Dept, 1948–55; Professor: of Chemical Technology, Edinburgh, 1955–60, of Chemical Engineering Science, London Univ., 1960–61; Courtauld's Prof., Imperial Coll., 1961–66. Dir, Council for Science and Society, 1977–83. Fellow, Imperial Coll., 1976; FKC, 1985. Hon. DèsSc Toulouse, 1960; Hon. DUniv. Essex, 1967. *Publications:* The Thermodynamics of the Steady State, 1951; The Principles of Chemical Equilibrium, 1955; Science, Industry and Social Policy, 1963; Chemical Reactor Theory, 1965; An Inventive Universe, 1975; Three Concepts of Time, 1981; (with J. S. Denbigh) Entropy in Relation to Incomplete

Knowledge, 1985; various scientific papers. *Address:* 19 Sheridan Road, Merton Park, SW19 3HW.
Died 23 Jan. 2004.

DENBY, Patrick Morris Coventry, CMG 1982; Assistant Director-General (Treasurer and Financial Comptroller), International Labour Office, Geneva, 1976–81; *b* 28 Sept. 1920; *s* of Robert Coventry Denby and Phyllis Denby (*née* Dacre); *m* 1950, Margaret Joy, *d* of Lt-Col C. L. Boyle; one *d* (and two *d* decd). *Educ:* Bradford Grammar Sch.; Corpus Christi Coll., Oxford (Open Scholar; Honour Mods, Cl. II; MA). War service with Intelligence Corps, as Temp. Lieut RNVR, and with Foreign Office (GCHQ), 1941–46. Unilever Ltd, UK and Australia, management trainee and product manager, 1946–51; joined International Labour Office, 1951: Professional Officer, 1951; Chief of Budget and Control Div., 1959; Chief of Finance and General Services Dept, Treasurer and Financial Comptroller, 1970; Chm., Investments Cttee; Mem., UN Pension Board, 1971–75. Chm., WIPO Appeal Bd, 1985–91. *Recreations:* ski-ing, mountain walking, tennis. *Address:* 7 Framers Court, Ellis Way, Lane End, High Wycombe, Bucks HP14 3LL. *Club:* Stoke Poges Lawn Tennis. *Died 3 July 2001.*

DENHAM, Maurice, OBE 1992; actor since 1934; *b* 23 Dec. 1909; *s* of Norman Denham and Winifred Lillico; *m* 1936, Margaret Dunn (*d* 1971); two *s* one *d*. *Educ:* Tonbridge Sch. Hull Repertory Theatre, 1934–36; theatre, radio and television, 1936–39. Served War of 1939–45: Buffs, 1939–43; Royal Artillery, 1943–45; despatches, 1946. Theatre, films, radio and television, 1946–. *Radio includes:* ITMA, 1939–40; Much Binding in the Marsh, 1946; Winston, 6 series, 1986–93; Tale of Two Cities, 1988; The Sitter, 1990; Forsyte Chronicles, 1990; Six P. G. Wodehouse stories, 1995; The Oldest Member, 1998. *Theatre includes:* The Andersonville Trial, Mermaid, 1960; Macbeth, King John, Old Vic, 1961; The Apple Cart, Mermaid, 1970; Uncle Vanya, Hampstead, 1979; Incident at Tulse Hill, Hampstead, 1981. *Films include:* The Purple Plain, 1954; Doctor at Sea, 1955; Day of the Jackal, 1972; 84 Charing Cross Road, 1986. *Television includes:* Talking to a Stranger, 1968; All Passion Spent, 1986; Klaus Barbie, 1987; Behaving Badly, 1988; Inspector Morse, 1991; La Nonna, 1991; You Rang M'Lord, 1992; Lovejoy, 1992; Memento Mori, 1992; Sherlock Holmes, 1992; Peak Practice, 1993; Bed, 1994; Pie in the Sky, The Last Journey of Robert Rylands, 1995; Casualty, The Beggar Bride, 1997. *Recreations:* conducting gramophone records, golf. *Clubs:* Garrick, Green Room; Stage Golfing.
Died 24 July 2002.

DENNISON, Stanley Richard, CBE 1990; PhD; FRSC; Group Chief Executive, ECC Group (formerly English China Clays) plc, 1988–90; *b* 28 May 1930; *s* of Arthur and Ellen Dennison; *m* 1955, Margaret Janet Morrison; two *s* two *d*. *Educ:* Latymer's Sch., Edmonton; University Coll. London (BSc, PhD). CBIM 1988. Chemist, Min. of Supply, 1954; English China Clays: Res. Chemist, 1956; Res. Man., 1970; Res. Dir, Clay Div., 1980; Man. Dir, Clay Div., 1984; Dir, English China Clays PLC, 1984. Dir, Devon and Cornwall TEC, 1990–91. Chm., Cornwall and Is of Scilly HA, 1994–98. *Publications:* contribs to pubns on industrial minerals, their technology and application in paper. *Recreations:* music, walking. *Address:* Lower Colvreath Farm, Roche, St Austell, Cornwall PL26 8LR. *Died 22 Sept. 2002.*

DENNISS, Gordon Kenneth, CBE 1979; Consultant Chartered Surveyor, Eastman & Denniss, Surveyors, 1983–88 (Senior Partner, 1945–83); Senior Partner, G. K. Denniss Farms, since 1990; *b* 29 April 1915; *e s* of late Harold W. Denniss; *m* 1939, Violet Fiedler, Montreal; one *s* two *d*. *Educ:* Dulwich Coll.; Coll. of Estate Management. FRICS. Articled to uncle, Hugh F. Thoburn, Chartered Surveyor, Kent, developing building estates, 1935, professional asst 1938; Eastman & Denniss: Junior Partner, 1943; sole principal, 1945. Crown Estate Comr, 1965–71. Farming 2500 acres in E Sussex and Kent. Hon. Life

Mem., Ashurst CC, Kent (Pres., 1989–97). *Recreations:* farming, cricket, political economy, golf. *Address:* Evans Leap, Withyham, Hartfield, E Sussex TN7 4DA. *T:* (01892) 770720; 4 Winterhaldenweg, 79856 Hinterzarten, Black Forest, Germany. *Clubs:* Farmers', MCC; Surrey County Cricket. *Died 10 July 2005.*

DENNISTON, Rosa Susan Penelope; *see* Beddington, R. S. P.

DENT, Sir John, Kt 1986; CBE 1976 (OBE 1968); Chairman, Civil Aviation Authority, 1982–86; *b* 5 Oct. 1923; *s* of Harry F. Dent; *m* 1954, Pamela Ann, *d* of Frederick G. Bailey; one *s*. *Educ:* King's Coll., London Univ. (BSc(Eng)). FREng (FEng 1980); FRAeS, FIMechE, FIEE, FCMI. Admty Gunnery Estabs at Teddington and Portland, 1944–45; Chief Engr, Guided Weapons, Short Bros & Harland Ltd, Belfast, 1955–60; Chief Engr, Armaments Div., Armstrong Whitworth Aircraft, Coventry, 1961–63; Dir and Chief Engr, Hawker Siddeley Dynamics Ltd, Coventry, 1963–67; Director: Engrg Gp, Dunlop Ltd, Coventry, 1968–76; Dunlop Holdings Ltd, 1970–82; Industrie Pirelli SpA, 1978–81; Dunlop AG, 1979–82; Pirelli Gen. plc, 1980–92; Pirelli Ltd, 1985–92; Man. Dir, Dunlop Ltd, 1978–82. President: Coventry and District Engrg Employers' Assoc., 1971 and 1972; Engrg Employers' Fedn, 1974–76 (1st Dep. Pres., 1972–74); Inst. of Travel Managers, 1986–94; Internat. Fedn of Airworthiness, 1987–89; Chm., Nationalized Industries' Chairman's Group, 1984–85. Member: Engineering Industries Council, 1975–76; Review Bd for Government Contracts, 1976–82; Royal Dockyards Policy Bd, 1976–82; NCB, 1980–82. *Recreations:* gardening, fishing, cabinet-making. *Address:* Helidon Grange, Helidon, near Daventry, Northants NN11 6LG.
Died 16 June 2002.

DENTON OF WAKEFIELD, Baroness *cr* 1991 (Life Peer), of Wakefield in the County of West Yorkshire; **Jean Denton**, CBE 1990; *b* 29 Dec. 1935; *d* of late Charles J. Moss and Kathleen Moss (*née* Tuke); *m* 1958, Dr A. A. Denton, CBE (marr. diss. 1974; he *d* 2001). *Educ:* Rothwell Grammar Sch.; LSE (BScEcon). Procter & Gamble, 1959–61; EIU, 1961–64; IPC, 1964–66; Hotel and Catering Dept, Univ. of Surrey, 1966–69; racing/rally driver, 1969–72; Marketing Director: Huxford Gp, 1972–78; Heron Motor Gp, 1978–80; Man. Dir, Herondrive, 1980–85; External Affairs Dir, Austin Rover, 1985–86; Dep. Chm., Black Country Dev' Corp., 1987–91. Director: Ordnance Survey, 1985–88; British Nuclear Fuels, 1987–92; Burson-Marsteller, 1987–92; London & Edinburgh Insce Group, 1989–92; Triplex Lloyd, 1990–92; Think Green, 1989–92. Baroness in Waiting (Govt Whip), 1991–92; Parliamentary Under-Secretary of State: DTI, 1992–93; DoE, 1993–94; NI Office, 1994–97. Opposition spokesman on Trade and Industry, H of L, 1998–. Pres., Forum UK, 1991– (Chm., 1989–92); Chairman: Marketing Gp of GB, 1987, 1988; Women on the Move against Cancer, 1979–92 (Pres., 1992–); Member: Board, UK 2000, 1986–88; Engrg Council, 1986–91; Teachers' Pay Review, 1989, 1990 and 1991; NHS Policy Bd, 1990–91. Mem. Adv. Bd, Royal Acad., 1986–87; Mem. Council, RSA, 1991; Governor, LSE, 1982–91; Trustee, Brooklands Museum, 1987–88. *Recreation:* talking shop. *Address:* House of Lords, SW1A 0PW. *Fax:* (020) 7735 2642. *Club:* British Women Racing Drivers. *Died 5 Feb. 2001.*

DENTON, Dr Anthony Albert, CBE 1997; FREng, FIMechE; FRINA; Senior Consultant, Noble Denton Group (Marine and Engineering Consultants); *b* 14 March 1937; *s* of Walter Granville Denton and Evelyn Truelove Denton; *m* 1st, 1959, Jean Moss, later Baroness Denton of Wakefield, CBE (marr. diss. 1974; she *d* 2001); 2nd, 1974, Anthea Philippa Hilda Wood. *Educ:* Queen Elizabeth Grammar Sch., Wakefield; Downing Coll., Cambridge (MA 1958); Imperial Coll. London (PhD 1966; DIC). FIMechE 1980; FRINA 1982; FREng (FEng 1983); Hon. FIMechIE 1997; Hon. FIIE 1998. Graduate apprentice,

Quasi Arc Co., 1958–60; Consultant, W. D. Noble & Co., 1960–71 (put first oil rig into North Sea, 1964); Lectr, Imperial Coll., London, 1963–66; Technical Dir, 1971–77, Chm., 1977–97, Noble Denton Gp. Mem., Defence Scientific Adv. Council, 1992–95; Chm., Marine Technol. Bd, MoD, 1992–94. Chm., UK Nat. Co-ordinating Cttee, Internat. Decade for Natural Disaster Reduction, 1995–2000. Mem., Bd of Mgt, Marine Technol. Directorate, 1996–; Independent Advr, Inter-Agency Cttee on Marine Sci. and Technol., 1994–2000. Chm., Sea Ops Gp, Commn on Concrete Sea Structures, Fédération Internat. de la Précontrainte (FIP), 1974–89. President: IMechE, 1993–94; IMechIE, 1996–98; IIE, 1998–; Vice-Pres. and Hon. Sec., Internat. Affairs, Royal Acad. Engrg, 1992–95; Mem. Council, Inst. Materials, 1995–99. Hon. Vis. Prof., City Univ., 1986–. Freeman, City of London, 1995. Hon. DSc City, 1998. *Publications:* numerous technical papers, mainly on offshore oil and gas develt. *Recreations:* Rugby football, motor racing, desultory Munro bagging, fine wine appreciation. *Address:* Noble House, 131 Aldersgate Street, EC1A 4EB. *T:* (020) 7606 4961. *Clubs:* Oriental; Royal Northern and University (Aberdeen).   *Died 3 March 2001.*

de OLIVEIRA CAMPOS, Roberto; *see* Campos.

de PIRO, His Honour Alan Caesar Haselden; QC 1965; FCIArb 1978; a Circuit Judge, 1983–91; *b* Singapore, 31 Aug. 1919; *e s* of late J. W. de Piro and Louise Bell Irvine; *m* 1947, Mary Elliot (marr. diss.; decd); one *s* (and one *s* decd); *m* 1964, Mona Addington (*d* 1998) (Baroness and Bohemian); one step *s* one step *d. Educ:* Repton; Trinity Hall, Cambridge (Sen. Scholar; CUAC (¼ mile) 1939; BA 1945 (1st cl. Hons Nat. Sci. and Law); Blackstone Schol.; MA 1947). Royal Artillery, 1940–45 (Capt.), West Africa. Called to the Bar, Middle Temple, 1947; Inner Temple, 1962; Bencher, Middle Temple, 1971, Reader, 1988; in practice at the Bar, London and Midlands, 1947–83; Deputy Chairman: Beds QS, 1966–71; Warwicks QS, 1967–71; a Recorder of the Crown Court, 1972–83. Inspector, Canvey Island (Liquid Natural Gas) Public Local Inquiry, 1981–82. Member: Gen. Council of the Bar, 1961–65, 1966–70, 1971–73; Senate of the Inns of Court and the Bar, 1976–81; Council, Internat. Bar Assoc., 1967–86 (Chm., Human Rights Cttee, 1979–82); Editorial Advisory Cttee, Law Guardian, 1965–73; Law Panel, British Council, 1967–74. Vice-Pres., L'Union Internat. des Avocats, 1968–73, Co-Pres., 1969. Legal Assessor, Disciplinary Cttee, RCVS, 1970–83. *Publications:* Mona, a life, 1999; Mona and Alan, 2000. *Recreations:* waterway canals, gardens, conversation. *Address:* 206 Mountjoy House, Barbican, EC2Y 8BP. *Club:* Hawks (Cambridge).   *Died 29 May 2005.*

DERMOTT, William, CB 1984; Under Secretary, Head of Agricultural Science Service, Agricultural Development and Advisory Service, Ministry of Agriculture, Fisheries and Food, 1976–84; *b* 27 March 1924; *s* of William and Mary Dermott; *m* 1946, Winifred Joan Tinney; one *s* one *d. Educ:* Univ. of Durham (BSc, MSc). Agricl Chemist, Univ. of Durham and Wye Coll., Univ. of London, 1943–46; Soil Scientist, Min. of Agriculture, at Wye, Bangor and Wolverhampton, 1947–70; Sen. Sci. Specialist, and Dep. Chief Sci. Specialist, MAFF, 1971–76; Actg Dir Gen., ADAS, 1983–84. Pres., British Soc. of Soil Science, 1981–82. *Publications:* papers on various aspects of agricultural chemistry in scientific jls. *Recreations:* gardening, the countryside. *Address:* 22 Chequers Park, Wye, Ashford, Kent TN25 5BB. *T:* (01233) 812694.   *Died 25 Nov. 2002.*

DERRIDA, Jacques; writer; *b* 15 July 1930; *s* of Aimé Derrida and Georgette Safar; *m* 1957, Marguerite Aucouturier; one *s,* and one *s* with Sylviane Agacinski. *Educ:* Ecole Normale Supérieure, Paris. Taught at Sorbonne, 1960–64; at Ecole Normale Supérieure, 1965–84. Hon. DLitt Cambridge, 1992. *Publications:* La voix et le phénomène, 1967; De la grammatologie, 1967; L'écriture et la différence, 1967; Marges, 1972; La

dissémination, 1972; Glas, 1974; La vérité en peinture, 1979; La carte postale, 1980; Positions, 1981; Spurs: Nietzsche's styles, 1981; Archaeology of the Frivolous, 1987; Psyché, 1987; De l'esprit, 1987; Mémoires: pour Paul De Man, 1988; Du droit à la philosophie, 1990; Mémoires d'aveugle, 1990; Le problème de la genèse dans la philosophie de Husserl, 1990; L'autre cap, 1991; Donner le temps, 1991; Qu'est-ce que la poésie?, 1991; Reader, 1991; Acts of Literature, 1992; Cinders, 1992; Spectres de Marx, 1993; Aporias, 1994; De l'hospitalité, 1997; Politiques de l'amitié, 1997; Demeure: fiction and testimony, 1998; Donner la mort, 1999; The Work of Mourning, 2001; Papier Machine, 2001. *Address:* Ecole des Hautes Etudes en Sciences Sociales, 54 boulevard Raspail, 75006 Paris, France.   *Died 8 Oct. 2004.*

DERRY, Thomas Kingston, OBE 1976; MA, DPhil; Assistant Master, St Marylebone Grammar School, 1945–65; *b* 5 March 1905; *y s* of late Rev. W. T. Derry, Wesleyan Minister; *m* 1930, Gudny (*d* 1989), *e d* of late Hjalmar Wesenberg, Commander of Order of Vasa, Oslo, Norway. *Educ:* Kingswood Sch., Bath; Queen's Coll., Oxford (Bible Clerk and Taberdar; 1st Cl., Classical Mods, 1925; 1st Cl., Final Sch. of Modern History, 1927; Sen. George Webb Medley Scholar, 1927; Gladstone Prizeman, 1928; MA, DPhil). Sixth Form Master and Chief History Master, Repton Sch., 1929–37; Headmaster, Mill Hill School, 1938–40; Political Intelligence Dept of Foreign Office, 1941–45. Visiting Prof., Wheaton Coll., Mass, 1961–62. Kt, Order of St Olav (Norway), 1981. *Publications:* (with T. L. Jarman) The European World, 1950, rev. and extended edn 1975; The Campaign in Norway (official military history), 1952; (with T. L. Jarman and M. G. Blakeway) The Making of Britain, 3 vols, 1956–69; A Short History of Norway, 1957; (with T. I. Williams) A Short History of Technology, 1960; The United Kingdom Today, 1961; A Short Economic History of Britain, 1965; (with E. J. Knapton) Europe 1815–1914, 1965; Europe 1914 to the Present, 1966; A History of Modern Norway, 1814–1972, 1973; A History of Scandinavia, 1979; (with T. L. Jarman) Modern Britain, 1979; A History of St Edmund's Church, Oslo, 1884–1994, 1994. *Address:* Nils Lauritssons vei 27A, 0854 Oslo, Norway. *T:* (2) 23009647.   *Died 11 July 2001.*

DESIO, Prof. Ardito, Dr nat. sci.; FRGS; Professor of Geology (and Past Director of Institute of Geology), at the University of Milan, and of Applied Geology, at the Engineering School of Milan, 1931–72, then Emeritus; *b* Palmanova, Frioul, 18 April 1897; *s* of Antonio Desio and Caterina Zorzella; *m* 1932, Aurelia Bevilacqua; one *s* one *d. Educ:* Udine and Florence. Grad. Univ. of Florence in Nat. Sciences, 1920. Volunteer, 1st World War, 1915, Lieut, Alpine Troops, 1916–17, POW, 1917–18; Captain, 1924–53; Major, 1954. Asst, University of Florence, 1922, and of Pavia, 1923, also Univ. and Engineering Sch., Milan, 1924–25 to 1930–31; Lectr in Geology, Phys. Geography, University of Milan, 1929–30 and in Palaeontology there until 1935. Geol Consultant, Edison Co. and Public Power Corp. of Greece, 1948–79. Pres., Italian Geological Cttee, 1966–73; Dir, Rivista Italiana di Paleontologia e Stratigrafia, 1942–95; Past Dir, Geologia Tecnica. Past Pres., Ital. Geolog. Soc.; Mem. (Hon. Pres.), Ital. Assoc. of Geologists; Past Pres., Ital. Order of Geologists; Mem., Ital. Order of Journalists; Hon. Member: Ital. Paleont. Soc.; Gesellschaft für Erdkunde zu Berlin, 1941; Italian Geog. Soc., 1955; Faculty of Sciences University of Chile, 1964; Geological Soc. of London, 1964; Indian Paleont. Soc.; Soc. Ital. Progresso delle Scienze, 1978; Ist. per il Medio ed Estremo Oriente, 1979; Assoc. Mineraria Subalpina, 1985; Corresp. Member: Soc. Géol. Belgique, 1952; Explorer Club, USA, 1987; Life Mem., Geog. Soc., USA, 1955; Member: Institut d'Egypte, 1936; Accademia Naz. Lincei, 1948; Inst. Lombardo Accad. Scienze Lettere, 1949. In 1938 discovered first deposits of natural oil and gas in subsoil of Libya and Mg-K salt deposit in Marada Oasis; led expedition to K2 (8611m, 2nd highest peak in the World;

reached for 1st time on 31 July 1954), and 18 expeditions in Africa (Libya, Ethiopia) and Asia (Iran, Afghanistan, Pakistan, Nepal, Burma, Philippines, Tibet); in summer 1987 organised expedition which re-measured height of two highest mts in the world, Mt Everest and K2; in summer 1988 expedition visited the northern slope of Karakorum as far as the Kun Lun mountain range; in summers 1989 and 1990 organised a permanent scientific lab. (a glass and aluminium pyramid) in Nepal below the top of Everest at 5050m; also organised every year until 1993 a dozen ambient expeditions in the Himalaya and Karakorum, concerning geodesy, geophysics, geology, ethnography, physiology, and medicine of high altitude. Santoro Prize, 1931; Royal Prize, 1934, Royal Acad. Lincei; Gold Medal of the Republic of Pakistan, 1954; Gold Medal of the Sciences, Letters and Arts, of Italy, 1956; Patrons medal of Royal Geog. Soc. of London, 1957; USA Antarctic Service Medal, 1974; Gold Lion of Lion's Club, Udine, 1976; Paul Harris Award, Internat. Rotary Club, 1986; Gold Medal of Ital. Geol. Soc., 1988; Gold Medal of Rotary Club, 1988. Kt Grand Cross, Order of Merit, Italy, 1955. *Publications:* about 440, among them: Le Isole Italiane dell'Egeo, 1931; La spedizione geografica Italiana al Karakoram 1929, 1936; scientific reports of his expedns to Libyan Sahara, 7 vols, 1938–42; Le vie della sete, 1950; Geologia applicata all'ingegneria, 1949, 3rd edn 1973–89; Ascent of K2, 1956 (11 languages, 15 editions); Geology of the Baltoro Basin (Karakorum), 1970; Results of half-a-century investigation on the glaciers of the Ortler-Cevedale, 1973; La Geologia dell'Italia, 1973; Geology of Central Badakhshan (NE Afghanistan), 1975; Geology of the Upper Shaksgam Valley, Sinkiang, China, 1980; L'Antartide, 1985; Sulle Vie della Sete, dei Ghiacci e dell'Oro, 1987; Which is the highest mountain in the world?, 1988; Geographic features of the Karakorum, 1991; some 250 articles in newspapers and magazines of different countries. *Recreation:* alpinist. *Address:* Via S. Andrea delle Fratte 38/A, 00186 Roma, Italy. *Clubs:* Italian Alpine; Touring (Italy); Hon. Member: Alpine; Andino Venezolano (Caracas); Internat. Rotary; Panatlon; Himalayan; Excursionista Carioca (Brazil); Alpin Français.
Died 12 Dec. 2001.

de VALOIS, Dame Ninette, (Dame Ninette Connell), OM 1992; CH 1982; DBE 1951 (CBE 1947); Founder and Director of the Royal Ballet, 1931–63 (formerly the Sadler's Wells Ballet, Royal Opera House, Covent Garden, and the Sadler's Wells Theatre Ballet, Sadler's Wells Theatre); Founder, 1926 and Head, 1926–70, The Royal Ballet School (originally Academy of Choreographic Art, subseq. The Sadler's Wells School of Ballet); *b* Baltiboys, Blessington, Co. Wicklow, 6 June 1898; *née* Edris Stannus; 2nd *d* of Lt-Col T. R. A. Stannus, DSO, Carlingford; *m* 1935, Dr Arthur B. Connell. Première danseuse British National Opera Company, 1918; Prima ballerina the Royal Opera Season Covent Garden (International), May to July 1919 and again in 1928; Mem., The Diaghileff Russian Ballet, 1923–26; choreographic dir to the Old Vic, the Festival Theatre, Cambridge, and The Abbey Theatre, Dublin, 1926–30. Founder of The National Sch. of Ballet, Turkey, 1947. Principal choreographic works: Job, 1931; The Rake's Progress, 1935; Checkmate; Don Quixote. FRAD 1963. Hon. MusDoc London, 1947; Hon. DLitt: Reading, 1951; Oxford, 1955; New Univ. of Ulster, 1979; Hon. DMus: Sheffield, 1955; Durham, 1982; Hon. MusD Trinity Coll., Dublin, 1957; Hon. DFA Smith Coll., Mass, USA, 1957; Hon. LLD: Aberdeen, 1958; Sussex, 1975. Gold Albert Medal, RSA, 1964; (jtly) Erasmus Prize Foundn Award (first woman to receive it), 1974; Irish Community Award, 1980. Chevalier of the Legion of Honour (France), 1950. *Publications:* Invitation to the Ballet, 1937; Come Dance with Me (autobiog.), 1957; Step By Step, 1977. *Address:* c/o Royal Ballet School, 153 Talgarth Road, W14.
Died 8 March 2001.

de VILLIERS, 3rd Baron *cr* 1910; **Arthur Percy de Villiers;** retired; *b* 17 Dec. 1911; *s* of 2nd Baron and Adelheid, *d* of H. C. Koch, Pietermaritzburg, Natal; *S* father, 1934; *m* 1939, Lovett (marr. diss. 1958), *d* of Dr A. D. MacKinnon, Williams Lake, BC; one *s* two *d*. *Educ:* Magdalen Coll., Oxford. Called to the Bar, Inner Temple, 1938. Farming in New Zealand. Admitted as a barrister to the Auckland Supreme Court, 1949. *Recreations:* gardening, golf. *Heir:* s Hon. Alexander Charles de Villiers [*b* 29 Dec. 1940; *m* 1966 (marr. diss)]. *Address:* PO Box 66, Kumeu, Auckland 1250, NZ. *T:* (9) 4118173. *Club:* Royal Commonwealth Society (Auckland).
Died 23 March 2001.

DEVONSHIRE, 11th Duke of, *cr* 1694; **Andrew Robert Buxton Cavendish,** KG 1996; MC; PC 1964; Baron Cavendish, 1605; Earl of Devonshire, 1618; Marquess of Hartington, 1694; Earl of Burlington, 1831; Baron Cavendish (UK) 1831; Vice-Lord-Lieutenant of the County of Derby, 1957–87; Chancellor of Manchester University, 1965–86; *b* 2 Jan. 1920; *o* surv. *s* of 10th Duke of Devonshire, KG, and Lady Mary Cecil, GCVO, CBE (*d* 1988), *d* of 4th Marquess of Salisbury, KG, GCVO; *S* father, 1950; *m* 1941, Hon. Deborah Vivian Freeman-Mitford; one *s* two *d*. *Educ:* Eton; Trinity Coll., Cambridge. Served War of 1939–45, Coldstream Guards (MC). Contested (C) Chesterfield Div. of Derbyshire, 1945 and 1950. Parliamentary Under-Sec. of State for Commonwealth Relations, Oct. 1960–Sept. 1962; Minister of State, Commonwealth Relations Office, Sept. 1962–Oct. 1964 and for Colonial Affairs, 1963–Oct. 1964. Steward of the Jockey Club, 1966–69. Mem., Horserace Totalisator Board, 1977–86; a Trustee, Nat. Gallery, 1960–68; President: The Royal Hosp. and Home, Putney, 1954–91; Lawn Tennis Assoc., 1955–61; RNIB, 1979–85; Nat Assoc. for Deaf Children, 1978–95; Building Societies Assoc., 1954–61; Vice-Pres., London Library, 1993–; Chairman: Grand Council, British Empire Cancer Campaign, 1956–81; Throughbred Breeders' Assoc., 1978–81. Mayor of Buxton, 1952–54. Hon. Col, Manchester and Salford Univs OTC, 1981–85. Freeman, Borough of Eastbourne, 2002. Hon. LLD: Manchester; Sheffield; Liverpool; Hon. Dr Law, Memorial Univ. of Newfoundland. *Publication:* Park Top: a romance of the Turf, 1976. *Heir:* s Marquess of Hartington,*b* 27 April 1944. *Address:* Chatsworth, Bakewell, Derbyshire DE45 1PP. *T:* (01246) 582204; 4 Chesterfield Street, W1J 5JF. *T:* (020) 7499 5803. *Clubs:* Brooks's, Jockey, White's.
Died 3 May 2004.

de WINTON, Michael Geoffrey, CBE 1960 (OBE 1952); MC 1944; Assistant Legal Secretary to the Law Officers, 1972–80; *b* 17 Oct. 1916; *s* of John Jeffreys de Winton and Ida de Winton; *m* 1948, Ursula Mary, *d* of E. E. Lightwood, MB; two *s* one *d*. *Educ:* Monmouth School. Admitted Solicitor, 1939. War service, 1939–46: commnd S Wales Borderers, 1940; Company Comdr 2nd Punjab Regt, Indian Army, in India, Middle East and Burma, 1942–45 (despatches twice). Administrative officer, Nigeria, 1946–48; Crown Counsel, 1948–53; called to the Bar, Gray's Inn, 1953; Principal Legal Draftsman, W Nigeria, 1954; Solicitor General and Permanent Sec. to Min. of Justice, W Nigeria, 1957–61; retired from HMOCS and re-admitted solicitor, 1961; Asst Legal Adviser, Colonial Office, 1961–66, CRO 1967, FCO 1968; Asst Solicitor, Law Officers Dept (Internat. and Commonwealth affairs), 1969; Under Secretary, 1974; retired, 1980. Legal consultant to overseas govts and internat. organizations; Principal Legal Adviser, British Indian Ocean Territory, 1982–83. *Recreations:* music, art. *Address:* Stable Cottage, Church Walk, Stalbridge, Dorset DT10 2LR. *T:* (01963) 62834.
Died 23 April 2001.

DIAMOND, Baron *cr* 1970 (Life Peer), of the City of Gloucester; **John Diamond;** PC 1965; FCA; Chairman: Royal Commission on Distribution of Income and Wealth, 1974–79; Industry and Parliament Trust, 1976–82; Trustee, Social Democratic Party, 1981–82; Leader of SDP in House of Lords, 1982–88; *b* Leeds, 30 April 1907; *s* of Henrietta and Rev. S. Diamond, Leeds; *m*

1st, 1932, Sadie Lyttleton (marr. diss. 1947); two *s* one *d*; 2nd, 1948, Julie Malamuth (marr. diss.); one *d*; 3rd, 1976, Barbara Jean Kagan (*née* Blower). *Educ:* Leeds Grammar Sch. Qualified as Chartered Accountant, 1931, and commenced practice as John Diamond & Co. MP (Lab) Blackley Div. of Manchester, 1945–51, Gloucester, 1957–70; Chief Secretary to the Treasury, 1964–70 (in the Cabinet, 1968–70); formerly PPS to Minister of Works; Deputy Chm. of Cttees, House of Lords, 1974. Chm., Prime Minister's Adv. Cttee on Business Appts of Crown Servants, 1975–88. Chm. of Finance Cttee, Gen. Nursing Council, 1947–53; Dir of Sadler's Wells Trust Ltd, 1957–64; Hon. Treas., Fabian Soc., 1950–64. Hon. LLD Leeds, 1978. *Publications:* Socialism the British Way (jtly), 1948; Public Expenditure in Practice, 1975. *Recreations:* music, gardening, reading the classics. *Address:* Aynhoe, Doggetts Wood Lane, Chalfont St Giles, Bucks HP8 4TH.
Died 3 April 2004.

DIBELA, Sir Kingsford, GCMG 1983 (CMG 1978); Governor-General of Papua New Guinea, 1983–89; *b* 16 March 1932; *s* of Norman Dibela and Edna Dalauna; *m* 1952, Winifred Tomolarina; two *s* four *d*. *Educ:* St Paul's Primary Sch., Dogura. Qualified as primary school teacher; teacher, 1949–63. Pres., Weraura Local Govt Council, 1963–77; MP, PNG, 1975–82; Speaker of Nat. Parlt, 1977–80. *Recreations:* golf, cricket. *Address:* PO Box 113, Port Moresby, Papua New Guinea. *Club:* Port Moresby Golf. *Died 22 March 2002.*

DICK, Kay; writer; *b* 29 July 1915; *o d* of Mrs Kate Frances Dick. *Educ:* Geneva, Switzerland; Lycée Français de Londres, S Kensington. Worked in publishing and bookselling; edited (as Edward Lane) 13 issues of magazine, The Windmill. *Publications: fiction:* By the Lake, 1949; Young Man, 1951; An Affair of Love, 1953; Solitaire, 1958; Sunday, 1962; They (South-East Arts Literature Prize), 1977; The Shelf, 1984; *non-fiction:* Pierrot, 1960; Ivy and Stevie, 1971; Friends and Friendship, 1974; *edited:* London's Hour: as seen through the eyes of the fire-fighters, 1942; Late Joys at the Players Theatre, 1943; The Mandrake Root, 1946, At Close of Eve, 1947, The Uncertain Element, 1950 (three vols of strange stories); Bizarre and Arabesque (anthology from Edgar Allan Poe), 1967; Writers at Work, 1972. *Recreations:* friends, gardening, walking the dog. *Address:* Flat 5, 9 Arundel Terrace, Brighton, East Sussex BN2 1GA. *T:* (01273) 697243. *Died 19 Oct. 2001.*

DICKEN, Air Vice-Marshal Michael John Charles Worwood, CB 1990; Private Secretary to Lord Mayor of London, 1992–99; Air Officer Administration and Air Officer Commanding Support Group, RAF Support Command, 1989–92; *b* 13 July 1935; *s* of late Air Cdre Charles Worwood Dicken, CBE and Olive Eva Dicken (*née* Eustice); *m* 1962, Jennifer Ann Dore; two *d* (one *s* decd). *Educ:* Sherborne; St Peter's Hall, Oxford; RAF College, Cranwell. Commissioned 1958; served Cyprus, Borneo and UK to 1970; RAF Staff College, 1971; Asst Defence Advr, Canberra, 1972–74; RAF Uxbridge, 1975–76; NDC, 1976; RAF Coningsby, 1977–79; Staff Coll. Directing Staff and Dir, Comd and Staff Training, 1980–82; OC RAF Hereford, 1982–83; HQ 1 Gp, 1984–85; Dir of Personnel Management (Airmen), 1986–88. Liveryman, Scriveners' Co., 1991–. *Recreations:* golf, light aircraft, field sports. *Club:* Royal Air Force.
Died 23 Dec. 2005.

DICKENS, Prof. Arthur Geoffrey, CMG 1974; FBA 1966; Director, Institute of Historical Research and Professor of History in the University of London, 1967–77, then Emeritus Professor; *b* 6 July 1910; *er s* of Arthur James Dickens and Gertrude Helen Dickens (*née* Grasby), both of Hull, Yorks; *m* 1936, Molly (*d* 1978), *er d* of Walter Bygott; two *s. Educ:* Hymers Coll., Hull; Magdalen Coll., Oxford (Demy, 1929–32, Senior Demy, 1932–33; BA with 1st Class Hons in Mod. Hist., 1932; MA 1936); DLit London, 1965. Served in RA, 1940–45; demobilised as Staff Capt. Fellow and Tutor of Keble

Coll., Oxford, 1933–49, Hon. Fellow, 1971; Oxford Univ. Lecturer in Sixteenth Century English History, 1939–49; University of Hull: G. F. Grant Prof. of History, 1949–62; Dep. Principal and Dean of Faculty of Arts, 1950–53; Pro-Vice-Chancellor, 1959–62; Prof. of History, King's Coll., Univ. of London, 1962–67; FKC, 1977. Mem. Senate and Academic Council, Univ. of London, 1974–77. Pres., Ecclesiastical History Soc., 1966–68. Member: Advisory Council on Public Records, 1968–76; Adv. Council on Export of Works of Art, 1968–76; Records Cttee, Essex CC, 1965–71; History of Medicine Adv. Panel, Wellcome Trust, 1974–79; Steering Cttee, Business History Unit, LSE, 1978–85. Chm., Victoria History of the Counties of England, 1967–68. Sec., 1967–73, Chm. and Gen. Sec., 1973–79, British Nat. Cttee of Historical Sciences; Foreign Sec., British Acad., 1969–79 (Vice-Pres., 1971–72); Vice-Pres., British Record Soc., 1978–80; Hon. Vice-President: RHistS, 1977– (Vice-Pres., 1969–73); Historical Assoc., 1977– (Pres., Central London Branch, 1982–); Sec., Anglo-German Group of Historians, 1969–76; Pres., German History Soc., 1979–89. Editor, Bulletin of the Inst. of Historical Research, 1967–77. Visiting Prof., Univ. of Rochester, NY, 1953–54; Fellow, 1954, Vis. Prof., 1972, Folger Library, Washington, DC; Strassberg Vis. Prof., Univ. of Western Australia, 1981; Hon. Professorial Fellow, Univ. of Wales, Aberystwyth, 1979–. Lectures: Birkbeck, Trinity Coll., Cambridge, 1969–70; James Ford Special, Univ. of Oxford, 1974; Neale, UCL, 1977; Bithell, Inst. of Germanic Studies, 1978; Stenton, Reading, 1980. Governor, Highgate Sch., 1976–86. FRHistS 1947; FSA 1962. Medlicott Medal, Historical Assoc., 1985 (first recipient). Hon. DLitt: Kent, 1976; Hull, 1977; Leicester, 1978; Sheffield, 1978; Hon. LittD Liverpool, 1977. Comdr's Cross, Order of Merit (Fed. Repub. of Germany), 1980. *Publications:* Lübeck Diary, 1947; The Register of Butley Priory, 1951; The East Riding of Yorkshire, 1954; Lollards and Protestants, 1959; Thomas Cromwell, 1959; Tudor Treatises, 1960; Clifford Letters, 1962; The English Reformation, 1964, 2nd edn 1989; Reformation and Society in 16th Century Europe, 1966; Martin Luther and the Reformation, 1967; (ed jtly) The Reformation in England to the Accession of Elizabeth I, 1967; The Counter-Reformation, 1968; The German Nation and Martin Luther, 1974; The Age of Humanism and Reformation, 1977; (ed and contrib.) The Courts of Europe, 1977; Reformation Studies, 1982; (with J. M. Tonkin) The Reformation in Historical Thought, 1985; Late Monasticism and the Reformation, 1994; (jtly) Erasmus the Reformer, 1994; (Gen. Editor) Documents of Modern History Series, 1966–; (Gen. Editor) A New History of England Series, 1975–; about 60 articles in English Historical Review, Church Quarterly Review, Yorkshire Archæological Jl, Cambridge Antiquarian Jl, Bodleian Library Record, Archiv für Reformationsgeschichte, Britain and the Netherlands, Victoria County History, York, Trans Royal Hist. Soc.; Jl of Ecclesiastical History, Archæological Jl, Encycl. Britannica, Chambers's Encycl., etc; *Festschrift:* Reformation Principle and Practice: essays in honour of A. G. Dickens, ed P. N. Brooks, 1980. *Recreations:* travel, 20th Century British art. *Address:* 401 Carole House, Oldfield Estate, Fitzroy Road, NW1 8UA.
Died 31 July 2001.

DICKENSON, Lt-Col Charles Royal, CMG 1965; Postmaster-General of Rhodesia, 1964–68; *b* 17 June 1907; *e s* of Charles Roland and Gertrude Dickenson; *m* 1950, Hendrika Jacoba Margaretha Schippers; three *d. Educ:* Shaftesbury Grammar Sch., Dorset. Entered British Post Office as Engineering Apprentice, 1923; BPO HQ, 1932–39. Served War in Royal Signals, 1939–45 (Lt-Col). Asst Controller of Telecommunications, BPO NW Regional HQ, 1945–47; BPO HQ, London, 1947–50; loaned to S Rhodesia Govt, 1950–54; Controller of Telecommunications, Ministry of Posts, Fedn of Rhodesia and Nyasaland, 1954–57; Regl Controller for N Rhodesia, Fedn of Rhodesia and Nyasaland, 1957–61; Dep.

Postmaster-Gen., 1961–62, Postmaster-Gen., 1962–63, Rhodesia and Nyasaland. Hon. Mem., S Africa Inst. of Electronic and Radio Engineers, 1966. ICD, OLM (Rhodesia), 1979. *Recreations:* growing orchids, photography. *Address:* 4600 Gatlin Oaks Lane, Orlando, FL 32806, USA.　　　　　　　　　*Died 6 Feb. 2003.*

DICKINSON, John Lawrence, (Bob), CBE 1973; DL; FCA; Chairman: SKF Steel Ltd, 1974–82; Bofors Cos (UK), 1974–83; General Manager, SKF Holding Co. (Holland), 1975–83; *b* 16 Nov. 1913; *s* of Tom Dickinson and Jennie Louise Dickinson; *m* 1937, Bettine Mary Jenkins; two *d. Educ:* Taunton Sch. Qual. as Chartered Accountant, 1937; Chief Accountant, Lucas Industries, 1937–44; SKF (UK) Ltd: Finance Dir and Sec., 1944–62; Sales Dir, 1962–66; Man. Dir, 1967–75, retired. Chairman: Sheffield Twist Drill & Steel Co. Ltd, 1978–81 (Dep. Chm., 1974–78); Weyroc Ltd (subsid. of Swedish Match Co.), 1975–82; British Rail (Eastern) Bd, 1970–81. Mem., National Enterprise Bd, 1975–79; Chm., NEDO Industrial Engines Sector Working Party, 1976–79; Mem. Gen. Council, also Finance and Gen. Purposes Cttee, CBI, until 1977; first Chm., Eastern Regional Council. Dep. Chm., Cranfield Inst., retd 1983. Hon. Life Vice-Pres., Luton and District Chamber of Commerce and Industry. High Sheriff, Bedfordshire, 1972–73; DL Beds 1976. Gold Medal, Royal Patriots Soc. (Sweden), 1975. *Recreations:* gardening, National Hunt racing. *Address:* Arkle House, Upton End, Shillington, Hitchin, Herts SG5 3PG. *T:* (01462) 711554.　　　　　　　　　*Died 1 Sept. 2001.*

DICKSON, Leonard Elliot, CBE 1972; MC 1945; TD 1951; Solicitor, Dickson, Haddow & Co., 1947–84; *b* 17 March 1915; *s* of Rev. Robert Marcus Dickson, DD, Lanark, and Cordelia Elliot; *m* 1950, Mary Elisabeth Cuthbertson; one *s* one *d. Educ:* Uppingham, Rutland; Univ. of Cambridge (BA 1936); Univ. of Glasgow (LLB 1947). Served War, with 1st Bn Glasgow Highlanders, HLI, 1939–46. Clerk to Clyde Lighthouses Trust, 1953–65. Chm., Lowland TAVR, 1968–70; Vice-Chm. Glasgow Exec. Council, NHS, 1970–74. DL Glasgow, 1963–98. *Publication:* Historical Sketch of Glasgow Society of Sons of the Clergy, 1990. *Recreations:* travel, gardening. *Address:* Bridge End, Gartmore, by Stirling FK8 3RR. *T:* (01877) 382220. *Club:* Royal Scottish Automobile (Glasgow).　　　　　　　　　*Died 24 Feb. 2002.*

DIGBY, Adrian, CBE 1964; FSA; Keeper, Department of Ethnography, British Museum, 1953–69; excavated Maya site of Las Cuevas, British Honduras, 1957; *b* 13 June 1909; *s* of late William Pollard Digby, FInstP, MIME, MIEE; *m* 1939, Sylvia Mary, *d* of late Arnold Inman, OBE, KC; two *d. Educ:* Lancing; Brasenose Coll., Oxford (MA). Entered British Museum as Asst Keeper, 1932. Served War of 1939–45: Intelligence Division Naval Staff, Admiralty, 1942–44; Hydrographic Dept, Admiralty, 1944–45. Vis. Prof. in Archaeology, Univ. de Los Andes, Bogota, 1970. Pres. Sect. H, BAAS, 1962; Vice-Pres. Royal Anthropological Inst., 1962–66. Hon. Asst Sec. of International Congress of Anthropological and Ethnological Sciences, London, 1934; Hon. Sec. of International Congress of Americanists, Cambridge, 1952. Granted patent for a walking stick with pick-up device, 2000. *Publications:* Ancient American Pottery (with G. H. S. Bushnell), 1955; Maya Jades, 1964; articles on anthropological subjects in Man and in Chambers's Encyclopædia. *Recreation:* sundials. *Address:* Greentrees, Eastcombe, Stroud, Glos GL6 7DR. *T:* (01452) 770409.　　　　　　　　　*Died 29 Nov. 2001.*

DILLON, Hon. Sir Brian; *see* Dillon, Hon. Sir G. B. H.

DILLON, C(larence) Douglas; Chairman, US & Foreign Securities Corporation, 1967–84; Managing Director, Dillon, Read & Co. Inc., 1971–83; *b* Geneva, Switzerland, 21 Aug. 1909; *s* of Clarence Dillon; *m* 1st, 1931, Phyllis Ellsworth (*d* 1982); two *d*; 2nd, 1983, Susan Sage. *Educ:* Groton Sch.; Harvard Univ. (AB). Served US Naval Reserve, 1941–45 (Lieut-Comdr; Air Medal, Legion of

Merit). Mem., NY Stock Exchange, 1931–36; US and Foreign Securities Corporation and US and International Securities Corporation, 1937–53 (Dir, 1938–53; Pres., 1946–53); Dir, Dillon, Read & Co. Inc., 1938–53 (Chm. of Bd, 1946–53); American Ambassador to France, 1953–57; Under-Sec. of State for Economic Affairs, USA, 1957–59; Under-Sec. of State, USA, 1959–61; Sec. of the Treasury, USA, 1961–65. Dir, Council on Foreign Relations, 1965–78 (Vice-Chm. 1977–78); Pres., Board of Overseers, Harvard Coll., 1968–72; Chm., Rockefeller Foundn, 1971–75; Chm., Brookings Instn, 1971–75. Trustee Emeritus, Metropolitan Museum of Art (President, 1970–77; Chm., 1977–83). Hon. Dr of Laws: New York Univ., 1956; Lafayette Coll., 1957; Univ. of Hartford, Conn, 1958; Columbia Univ., 1959; Harvard Univ., 1959; Williams Coll., 1960; Rutgers Univ., 1961; Princeton Univ., 1961; Univ. of Pennsylvania, 1962; Bradley Univ., 1964; Middlebury Coll., 1965; Tufts Univ., 1982; Marymount Manhattan Coll., 1984. US Presidential Medal of Freedom, 1989.

　　　　　　　　　Died 10 Jan. 2003.

DILLON, Rt Hon. Sir (George) Brian (Hugh), Kt 1979; PC 1982; a Lord Justice of Appeal, 1982–94; *b* 2 Oct. 1925; *s* of late Captain George Crozier Dillon, RN; *m* 1954, Alison, *d* of late Hubert Samuel Lane, MC and Dr Isabella Lane, MB, ChB Edin.; two *s* two *d. Educ:* Winchester Coll.; New Coll., Oxford. Called to the Bar, Lincoln's Inn, 1948; QC 1965; a Judge of the High Court of Justice, Chancery Division, 1979–82. *Address:* Tanyard House, 17 Station Road, Woodbridge, Suffolk IP12 4AU. *T:* (01394) 386458.　　　　　　　　　*Died 22 June 2003.*

DINGWALL-SMITH, Ronald Alfred, CB 1977; *b* 24 Feb. 1917; 2nd *s* of Robert Frederick Sydney Smith (*d* in action 1917) and Alice Olive Brookman; *m* 1946, Margaret Eileen Dingwall; adopted surname Dingwall-Smith; one *s* one *d. Educ:* Alleyn's Sch., Dulwich; London School of Economics (evening classes). Entered Civil Service as Clerical Officer, Ministry of Transport, 1934; Exchequer and Audit Dept, 1935–47; Scottish Development Dept, 1947–65; Scottish Development Dept, 1965–70; Under-Sec. (Principal Finance Officer), Scottish Office, 1970–78. Sen. Res. Fellow, Glasgow Univ., 1979–81. Director: St Vincent Drilling Ltd, 1979–80; Hanover (Scotland) Housing Assoc. Ltd, 1979–92 (Chm., 1988–92); Heritage Housing Ltd, 1982–92 (Chm., 1988–92); Hanover (Caol) Housing Assoc. Ltd, 1986–92 (Chm., 1988–92). Mem., Commn for Local Authy Accts in Scotland, 1980–85. Governor, Moray Hse Coll. of Educn, Edinburgh, 1980–87. *Recreations:* golf, bowls (Pres., Braid Bowling Club, Edinburgh, 1990 (Hon. Sec., 1980–89)), gardening. *Address:* 14 Mains Grove, Davidson's Mains, Edinburgh EH4.

　　　　　　　　　Died 28 Sept. 2004.

DISBREY, Air Vice-Marshal William Daniel, CB 1967; CBE 1945 (OBE 1943); AFC 1939; *b* London, 23 Aug. 1912; *s* of Horace William Disbrey; *m* 1939, Doreen Alice, *d* of William Henry Ivory, Stevenage; two *d. Educ:* Minchenden Sch. Joined RAF as an Apprentice, 1928; gained Cadetship to RAF Coll., Cranwell, 1931; No 3 Fighter Sqdn, 1933–34; Fleet Air Arm, 1934–37; Engr Specialist Course, Henlow, 1937–39; Engr Officer, No 13 Group HQ, 1940–41; Engr Officer, HQ Fighter Comd, 1941–43; Chief Engr Officer, 2nd TAF, 1943–46; Staff Coll. Course, 1946; CO, No 12 Sch. of Technical Training, 1946–48; Sen. Technical Officer, Royal Indian Air Force, 1948–51; Min. of Supply, 1951–54; Chief Engr Officer, Bomber Comd, 1954–57; Imperial Defence Coll., 1957; Dir of Research and Development, Bombers, Min. of Aviation, 1958–61; Comdt, No 1 Radio Sch., Locking, 1961–64; Dir-Gen. of Engineering (RAF), 1964–67; AO Engineering, Bomber Comd, 1967, Strike Comd, 1968–70, retired. Manager, Tech. Trng Inst., Airwork Services, Saudi Arabia, 1970. CEng; FIMechE; FRAeS. *Recreations:* golf, sailing. *Address:* Flat 20, Swallowfield

Park, Reading RG7 1TG. *Club:* Royal Air Force.
Died 26 June 2001.

DIX, Alan Michael, OBE 1985; Director General, Motor Agents' Association Ltd, 1976–85; *b* 29 June 1922; *s* of late Comdr Charles Cabry Dix, CMG, DSO, RN, and Ebba Sievers; *m* 1955, Helen Catherine McLaren; one *s* one *d*. *Educ:* Stenhus Kostskole, Denmark. Escaped Nazi occupied Denmark to Scotland, 1943; joined RAF, commissioned 1944. President, Capitol Car Distributors Inc., USA, 1958–67; Gp Vice-Pres., Volkswagen of America, USA, 1967–68; Man. Dir, Volkswagen (GB) Ltd, London, 1968–72; Pres., Mid Atlantic Toyota Inc., USA, 1972–73; Dir Marketing, British Leyland International, 1973–74; Proprietor, Alan M. Dix Associates, 1974–76. Chm., Motor Agents Pensions Administrators Ltd, 1976–85; Dir, Hire Purchase Information Ltd, 1977–85. Freeman and Liveryman, Coachmakers' and Coach Harness Makers' Co., 1980. FIMI, FInstM, FIMH, FIMgt. King Christian X war medal (Denmark), 1947. *Publications:* contribs to automotive trade jls. *Recreations:* yachting, photography; the study of professional management (internat. speaker on management and organisation). *Address:* Hillside, Peebles, Letham Grange, Arbroath, Angus DD11 4QA. *T:* (01241) 890421. *Clubs:* Danish, Royal Air Force, Burkes; Royal Air Force Yacht (Hamble). *Died 24 Oct. 2001.*

DIXON, Sir Ian (Leonard), Kt 1996; CBE 1991; Chairman, Willmott Dixon Ltd, 1991–98; *b* 3 Nov. 1938; *s* of late Leonard Dixon and Constance Dixon (*née* Holroyd); *m* 1961, Valerie Diana Barclay; two *s* one *d*. *Educ:* SW Essex Tech. Coll.; Harvard Business Sch. FCIOB 1980. Trainee estimator/surveyor, C. S. Foster & Sons Ltd, 1956–62; Gen. Manager, John Corby & Sons Ltd, 1962–67; Man. Dir, Willmott Dixon Ltd, 1967–91. Chairman: Construction Ind. Council, 1991–94; Construction Ind. Bd, 1996–97; Partnership Sourcing Ltd, 1998–2000. Mem., Nat. Council, CBI, 1984–96 (Chm., E Reg., 1988–90). Mem., Beds CC, 1977–85. Chm., Beds TEC, 1990–91. Chairman: N Herts HA, 1984–87; Riverside HA, 1991–92. Mem. Council, UCL, 1992–96; Pro-Chancellor and Chm., Bd of Govs, Univ. of Luton, 1998–2000 (Vice Chm. Govs, 1996–98); Gov., Anglia Poly. Univ., 1992–95. Liveryman: Co. of Painter-Stainers; Co. of Constructors. Pres., CIOB, 1989–90. Hon. FIStructE 1995; Hon. FCIPS 1997; Hon. RICS 2001; Hon. Mem., Amer. Inst. of Constructors, 1989. Hon. PhD Anglia Poly. Univ., 1992. *Recreations:* Rugby football, stamp collecting. *Address:* Chestnut Spinney House, Church End, Haynes, Beds MK45 3RJ.
Died 20 July 2001.

DIXON, Peter Vibart; Chairman, Merton Crossroads Care Attendant Scheme Ltd, since 1996; *b* 16 July 1932; *s* of late Meredith Vibart Dixon and Phyllis Joan (*née* Hemingway); *m* 1955, Elizabeth Anne Howie Davison; three *s*. *Educ:* Summer Fields; Radley Coll.; King's Coll., Cambridge (BA Classics and Law 1955, MA 1959). Royal Artillery, 1951–52. Asst Principal, HM Treasury, 1955; Office of Lord Privy Seal, 1956; HM Treasury, 1956–62: Private Sec. to Economic Sec., 1959; Principal, 1960; Colonial Office, 1963; CS Selection Bd, 1964–65; HM Treasury, 1965–72, Asst Sec., 1969; Counsellor (Economic), HM Embassy, Washington, 1972–75; HM Treasury, 1975–82: Press Sec., 1975–78; Under Sec., Industrial Policy, 1978–82; Sec., NEDC, 1982–87; Dir of Planning and Admin, Turner Kenneth Brown, solrs, 1988–92. Mem., 1994, Chm., 1995–96, Merton, Sutton and Wandsworth FHSA. Mem. Council, RIPA, 1976–82. Gov., Streatham Hill and Clapham High Sch., 1996–99. Pastoral Auxiliary, Dio. of Southwark, 1994–. FRSA 1984. *Address:* 23 Spencer Hill, Wimbledon, SW19 4PA. *T:* (020) 8946 8931. *Club:* Oxford and Cambridge.
Died 11 June 2001.

DIXON-WARD, Frank, CBE 1979; Member, Board of Overseers, Massachusetts SPCA, since 1988; *b* 28 June 1922; *s* of late Cecil Ward, LRAM, and Helen Cecilia

Ward (*née* Woodward), Eastbourne; *m* 1960, Claire Collasius (*d* 1985); one *s* one *d*. *Educ:* Eastbourne Grammar Sch. Admitted Solicitor (Hons), 1948. Articled to Town Clerk, Eastbourne, 1940. Served War, RAF, 1941–46. Solicitor posts, Peterborough, 1948–51, West Ham, 1952–54; Deputy Town Clerk, Hove, 1954–62; Town Clerk: Camberwell, 1963–65; Southwark, 1964–70; Chief Exec., Lambeth, 1970–81; Consultant, 1982; Exec. Dir, RSPCA, 1982–87. Lawyer/Chm., London Rent Assessment Cttees, 1982, 1986–93. Hon. Clerk: South London Housing Consortium, 1965–70; Social Service Cttee, London Boroughs Assoc., 1966–82; Hon. Legal Adviser: Age Concern (Gtr London), 1965–82; Eurogroup for Animal Welfare, 1986–92; Hon. Vice-Pres., WSPA, 1998 (Mem., Bd of Dirs, 1986–98). Member official committees: London Welfare Services, 1963–65; NHS Reorganisation, 1969–74; Homelessness, 1970–72; Citizens Advice Bureaux, 1973–74; Jt Approach to Social Policies, 1975–76; Exec. Cttee, SOLACE, 1975–81. Chairman: Local Govt Legal Soc., 1957; Hove Round Table, 1961–62; Mem. Council, Sussex LTA, 1957–62. Chm., St Dunstan's College Soc., 1975–78. Eurogroup Medal, 1992. *Recreations:* music, lawn tennis. *T:* (020) 7727 9396. *Club:* Royal Over-Seas League.
Died 5 Nov. 2002.

DOBBS, Joseph Alfred, CMG 1972; OBE 1957 (MBE 1945); TD 1945; HM Diplomatic Service, retired; *b* Abbeyleix, Ireland, 22 Dec. 1914; *s* of John L. Dobbs and Ruby (*née* Gillespie); *m* 1949, Marie, *d* of Reginald Francis Catton, Sydney; four *s*. *Educ:* Worksop Coll.; Trinity Hall, Cambridge (Schol.); BA 1936, MA 1946). Pres., Cambridge Union Soc., 1936. Served War of 1939–45, Major, Royal Artillery (despatches). Joined Foreign Office, 1946; served Moscow, 1947–51, 1954–57 and 1965–68; FO, 1951–54; Delhi, 1957–61; Warsaw, 1961–64; Rome, 1964–65; Consul-Gen., Zagreb, 1969–70; Minister, Moscow, 1971–74. *Recreations:* reading, conversation. *Address:* The Old House, Wyhe Hall, Gillingham, Dorset SP8 5NS. *T:* (01747) 823440.
Died 28 Sept. 2002.

DOBBS, Captain Sir Richard (Arthur Frederick), KCVO 1991; Lord-Lieutenant of County Antrim, 1975–94 (HM Lieutenant for County Antrim, 1959–75); *b* 2 April 1919; *s* of Senator Major Arthur F. Dobbs, DL, of Castle Dobbs, and Hylda Louisa Dobbs; *m* 1953, Carola Day, *d* of Christopher Clarkson, Old Lyme, Conn, USA; four *s* one *d*. *Educ:* Eton; Magdalene Coll., Cambridge (MA). Served War: 2nd Lieut Irish Guards (Supp. Reserve), 1939; Captain 1943. Called to Bar, Lincoln's Inn, 1947; Member, Midland Circuit, 1951–55. *Address:* Castle Dobbs, Carrickfergus, County Antrim, N Ireland BT38 9BX. *T:* (028) 9337 2238. *Club:* Cavalry and Guards. *Died 8 July 2004.*

DOBSON, Christopher Selby Austin, CBE 1976; FSA; Librarian, House of Lords, 1956–77; *b* 25 Aug. 1916; *s* of late Alban Tabor Austin Dobson, CB, CVO, CBE; *m* 1941, Helen Broughton (*d* 1984), *d* of late Capt. E. B. Turner, Holyhead; one *d* (one *s* decd). *Educ:* Clifton Coll.; Emmanuel Coll., Cambridge (BA). With National Council of Social Service, 1938–39. Served War of 1939–45, Lieut Middx Regt (despatches). Asst Principal (Temp.), Ministry of Education, 1946–47; Asst Librarian, House of Lords, 1947–56. *Publication:* (ed) Oxfordshire Protestation Returns 1641–42, 1955. *Recreations:* collecting books, stamps, etc. *Address:* Swan House, Symonds Lane, Linton, Cambridge CB1 6HY. *T:* (01223) 893796. *Clubs:* Roxburghe; (Hon.) Rowfant (Cleveland).
Died 22 Dec. 2005.

DODD, William Atherton, CMG 1983; *b* 5 Feb. 1923; *s* of Frederick Dodd and Sarah Atherton; *m* 1949, Marjorie Penfold; two *d*. *Educ:* Chester City Grammar Sch.; Christ's Coll., Cambridge (MA, CertEd). Served War, 1942–45: Captain, 8 Gurkha Rifles. Sen. History Master, Ipswich Sch., 1947–52; Educn Officer, Dept of Educn, Tanganyika, 1952–61; Sen. Educn Officer, Min. of Educn,

Tanzania, 1961–65; Lectr, Dept of Educn in Developing Countries, Univ. of London Inst. of Educn, 1965–70; Educn Adviser, ODM, 1970–77; Chief Educn Advr, 1978–83, and Under Sec. (Educn Div.), 1980–83, ODA. Consultant: UC Cardiff, 1983–87; Inst. of Educn, Univ. of London, 1983–91; Child-to-Child Trust, 1988–91. UK Mem., Unesco Exec. Bd, 1983–85. Chm., Christopher Cox Meml Fund, 1983–96. Trustee, Internat. Extension Coll., 1987–96. *Publications:* A Mapbook of Exploration, 1965; Primary School Inspection in New Countries, 1968; Education for Self-Reliance in Tanzania, 1969; (with J. Cameron) Society, Schools and Progress in Tanzania, 1970; (ed) Teacher at Work, 1970; (with C. Criper) Report on the Teaching of the English Language in Tanzania, 1985. *Recreations:* music, cricket. *Address:* 20 Bayham Road, Sevenoaks, Kent TN13 3XD. *T:* (01732) 454238. *Clubs:* MCC; Sevenoaks Vine, Sevenoaks Probus.
Died 5 Feb. 2004.

DODDERIDGE, Morris, CBE 1974 (OBE 1962); British Council Representative, Rome, 1970–75; *b* 17 Oct. 1915; *s* of Reginald William Dodderidge and Amy Andrew; *m* 1941, Esme Williams (*d* 1997); one *s* one *d* (and one *s* decd). *Educ:* Hertford Grammar Sch.; King's Coll., London (BA 1st cl. hons English 1937; Brewer Prize for Lit.); Inst. Educn, London (Teachers Dip. 1938); DipEd 1952. Asst Master, Hele's Sch., Exeter, 1938–40. War of 1939–45, Royal Signals; served N Africa, Italy, Austria (Captain, despatches). Joined British Council, 1946: Dir of Studies, Milan, 1947–53; Rep., Norway, 1953–57; Teaching of English Liaison Officer, 1957–59; Dir, Recruitment Dept, 1959–64; Controller: Recruitment Div., 1964–66; Overseas Div. A, 1966–67; Home Div. I, 1967–68; Appts Div., 1968–70. *Publications:* Man on the Matterhorn, 1940; (with W. R. Lee) Time for a Song, 1965.
Died 3 Feb. 2003.

DODDS, Denis George, CBE 1977; FIEE; solicitor; Chairman, British Approval Service for Electricity Cables Ltd, 1982–93; *b* 25 May 1913; *s* of Herbert Yeaman Dodds and Violet Katharine Dodds; *m* 1st, 1937, Muriel Reynolds Smith (*d* 1989); two *s* three *d*; 2nd, 1995, Penelope Jane Tuohy. *Educ:* Rutherford Coll., Newcastle upon Tyne; King's Coll., Durham Univ. ; LLB London. Served Royal Navy (Lieut RNVR), 1941–46. Asst Solicitor and Asst Town Clerk, Gateshead, 1936–41; Dep. Town Clerk and Dep. Clerk of the Peace, City of Cardiff, 1946–48; Sec., S Wales Electricity Board, 1948–56; Chief Industrial Relns Officer, CEA and Industrial Relns Advr, Electricity Council, 1957–59; Dep. Chm., 1960–62, Chm., 1962–77, Merseyside and N Wales Electricity Bd. Chairman: Merseyside Chamber of Commerce and Industry, 1976–78; Port of Preston Adv. Bd, 1978; Assoc. of Mems of State Industry Bds, 1976–89. Member: CBI Council for Wales, 1960–78; NW Economic Planning Council, 1971; Dir, Development Corporation for Wales, 1970–83. Mem., Nat. Adv. Council for Employment of the Disabled, 1978–91. *Recreations:* music, gardening. *Address:* Corners, 28 Grange Park, Westbury on Trym, Bristol BS9 4BP. *T:* (0117) 962 1440.
Died 16 July 2003.

DODSON, Sir Derek (Sherborne Lindsell), KCMG 1975 (CMG 1963); MC 1945; DL; HM Diplomatic Service, retired; Special Representative of Secretary of State for Foreign and Commonwealth Affairs, 1981–95; *b* 20 Jan. 1920; *e* and *o* surv. *s* of late Charles Sherborne Dodson, MD, and Irene Frances Lindsell; *m* 1st, 1952, Julie Maynard Barnes (*d* 1992); one *s* one *d*; 2nd, 1997, Urania Massouridis (*née* Papadam); two step *s*. *Educ:* Stowe; RMC Sandhurst. Commissioned as 2nd Lieut in Royal Scots Fusiliers, 1939, and served in Army until Feb. 1948. Served War of 1939–45 (MC): India, UK, Middle East, and with Partisans in Greece and N Italy. Mil. Asst to Brit. Comr, Allied Control Commn for Bulgaria, July 1945–Sept. 1946; GSO 3, War Office, Oct. 1946–Nov. 1947; apptd a Mem. HM Foreign Service, 1948; 2nd Sec., 1948; Acting Vice-Consul at Salonika, Sept. 1948; Acting

Consul Gen. there in 1949 and 1950; Second Sec., Madrid, 1951; promoted First Sec., Oct. 1951; transferred to Foreign Office, Sept. 1953; apptd Private Sec. to Minister of State for Foreign Affairs, 1955; First Sec. and Head of Chancery, Prague, Nov. 1958; Chargé d'Affaires there in 1959, 1960, 1961, 1962; promoted and apptd Consul at Elisabethville, 1962; Transf. FO and apptd Head of the Central Dept, 1963; Counsellor, British Embassy, Athens, 1966–69; Ambassador: to Hungary, 1970–73; to Brazil, 1973–77; to Turkey, 1977–80. Chm., Beaver Guarantee Ltd, 1984–86; Consultant, Benguela Rly Co. (Director, 1984–92). Chm., Anglo-Turkish Soc., 1982–95. Mem., Bd of Governors, United World College of the Atlantic, 1982–95. DL Lincoln, 1987. Order of the Southern Cross, Brazil. *Recreations:* reading, walking. *Address:* 47 Ovington Street, SW3 2JA. *T:* (020) 7589 5055; Gable House, Leadenham, Lincoln LN5 0PN. *T:* (01400) 272212. *Clubs:* Boodle's, Travellers.
Died 22 Nov. 2003.

DOHERTY, Arthur; Member (SDLP) Londonderry East, Northern Ireland Assembly, 1998–2002; *b* 19 Jan. 1932; *s* of Michael Doherty and Mary Doherty (*née* Devlin); *m* 1956, Mary Farrell; one *s* two *d*. *Educ:* Barrack Street Primary Sch., Strabane; St Columb's Coll., Derry; St Joseph's Coll. of Education, Belfast (Teacher's Cert. 1956; ATC 1956); Univ. of Ulster (BEd Hons Educn and Art 1981). Teacher, St Columba's Primary Sch., Derry, 1953–57; Principal, Duncrun Primary Sch., Derry, 1957–69; Head of Art and Design, St Mary's High Sch., Limavady, Co. Derry, 1969–89. Mem., NI Forum for Political Dialogue, 1996. Mem. (SDLP), Limavady BC, 1977–; Mayor, Limavady, 1993–94. Member: NW Reg. Cross-Border Gp, 1989– (former Chair); Western Educn and Liby Bd, 1993–; Council for Nature Conservation and the Countryside, 1995–; Chair, Forum for Local Govt and the Arts, 1995–. Contested (SDLP) Londonderry E, UK parly elecns, 1983, 1987, 1992, 1997. *Recreations:* wife and family, reading, crosswords, galleries and museums, physical recreation no longer possible except for gentle walking, gardening, swimming. *Address:* Gartan, 30 Tircreven Road, Magilligan, Limavady BT49 0LN.
Died 6 Feb. 2003.

DOLL, Prof. Sir (William) Richard (Shaboe), CH 1996; Kt 1971; OBE 1956; DM, MD, DSc; FRCP, FMedSci; FRS 1966; Hon. Consultant, Cancer Research UK (formerly ICRF) Cancer Studies Unit, Radcliffe Infirmary, Oxford, since 1983; first Warden, Green College, Oxford, 1979–83 (Hon. Fellow, 1983); *b* Hampton, 28 Oct. 1912; *s* of Henry William Doll and Amy Kathleen Shaboe; *m* 1949, Joan Mary Faulkner, MB, BS, MRCP, DPH (*d* 2001); one *s* one *d*. *Educ:* Westminster Sch. (Hon. Fellow, 1991); St Thomas's Hosp. Med. Sch., London. MB, BS 1937; MD 1945; DSc London 1958. FRCP 1957. RAMC, 1939–45. Appts with MRC, 1946–69: Mem., Statistical Research Unit, 1948; Dep. Dir, 1959; Dir, 1961–69; Hon. Associate Physician, Central Middlesex Hosp., 1949–69; Teacher in Medical Statistics and Epidemiology, UCH Med. Sch., 1963–69; Regius Prof. of Medicine, and Student of Christ Church, Oxford Univ., 1969–79 (Hon. Student, 1998). Member: MRC, 1970–74; Royal Commn on Environmental Pollution, 1973–79; Standing Commn on Energy and the Environment, 1978–81; Scientific Council of Internat. Cancer Res. Agency, 1966–70 and 1975–78; Council, Royal Society, 1970–71, 1996–98 (a Vice-Pres., 1970–71); Chairman: Adverse Reaction Sub-Cttee, Cttee on Safety of Medicines, 1970–77; UK Co-ordinating Cttee on Cancer Research, 1972–77. William Julius Mickle Fellow, Univ. of London, 1955. Hon. Lectr, LSHTM, 1956–62 (Hon. Fellow 1982); Milroy Lectr, 1953, Marc Daniels Lectr, 1969, Harveian Orator, 1982, RCP. Founder FMedSci 1998. Emeritus Mem., Academia Europaea, 1990; Hon. Fellow: FPHM, 1974; RCGP, 1978; FOM, 1987; RCOG, 1992; UMDS, 1992; RCR, 1993; RCS, 1997; Hon. FIA 1999. Hon. Foreign Member: Norwegian Acad. of Scis, Amer. Acad. of Arts and Scis. Hon DSc: Newcastle, 1969; Belfast, 1972; Reading, 1973; Newfoundland, 1973; Stony Brook, 1988; Harvard, 1988; London, 1988; Oxon, 1989; Oxford Brookes, 1994; Kingston, 1996; Aberdeen, 2003; Hon. DM Tasmania, 1976; Hon. MD: Birmingham, 1994; Bergen, 1996. David Anderson Berry Prize (jtly), RSE 1958; Bisset Hawkins Medal, RCP, 1962; UN award for cancer research, 1962; Gairdner Award, Toronto, 1970; Buchanan Medal, Royal Soc., 1972; Presidential award, NY Acad. Sci., 1974; Prix Griffuel, Paris, 1976; Gold Medal, RIPH&H, 1977; Mott Award, Gen. Motors' Cancer Res. Foundn, 1979; Bruce Medal, Amer. Coll. of Physicians, 1981; National Award, Amer. Cancer Soc., 1981; Gold Medal, BMA, 1983; Conrad Röntgen Prize, Accad. dei Lincei, 1984; Johann-Georg-Zimmermann Prize, Hanover, 1985; Royal Medal, Royal Soc., 1986; Ettore Majorana Erice Science for Peace Prize, 1990; first Helmut Horten Award, Lugano, 1991; first Prince Mahidol Award, Bangkok, 1992; Gold Medal, RSocMed, 1997; British Thoracic Soc. Medal, 1998; Hewitt Award, RSocMed, 1999; Dr Nathan Davis Internat. Award, Amer. Med. Assoc., 2001; (jtly) King Olav V Prize, Norwegian Cancer Soc., 2002; (jtly) Tyler Prize, 2003. *Publications:* Prevention of Cancer: pointers from epidemiology, 1967; (jtly) Causes of Cancer, 1982; (jtly) Cancer Incidence and Mortality in England and Wales, 2001; articles in scientific journals on aetiology of lung cancer, leukaemia and other cancers, also aetiology and treatment of peptic ulcer, effects of smoking, ionizing radiations, oral contraceptives; author (jtly) Med. Research Council's Special Report Series, 1951, 1957, 1964. *Recreations:* food and conversation. *Address:* Green College, Oxford OX2 6HG.						*Died 24 July 2005.*

DOLLEY, Christopher; Chairman, Damis Agencies Ltd, since 1983; *b* 11 Oct. 1931; *yr s* of late Dr Leslie George Francis Dolley and of Jessie, Otford, Kent; *m* 1966, Christine Elizabeth Cooper; three *s*. *Educ:* Bancroft's Sch.; Corpus Christi Coll., Cambridge. Joined Unilever, 1954; with Unilever subsidiaries, 1954–62: G. B. Ollivant Ltd, 1954–59; United Africa Co., 1959–62; joined Penguin Books Ltd as Export Manager, 1962; became Dir, 1964, Man. Dir, 1970–73, Chm., 1971–73; Dir for Book Develt, IPC, 1973–77. Exec. Vice-Pres., Penguin Books Inc., Baltimore, 1966; Director: Penguin Publishing Co., 1969–73 (Jt Man. Dir, 1969); Pearson Longman Ltd, 1970–73; The Hamlyn Group, 1971–81; Globalscan Ltd, 1997–. Mem., Nat. Film Finance Corp., 1971–81; Dir, Nat. Film Trustee Corp., 1971–81. *Publication:* (ed) The Penguin Book of English Short Stories, 1967. *Recreations:* golf, gardening, collecting. *Clubs:* Savile; 14 West Hamilton Street (Baltimore, Md).						*Died 1 Feb. 2004.*

DOLTON, David John William; management consultant, since 1989; *b* 15 Sept. 1928; *e s* of late Walter William and Marie Frances Duval Dolton; *m* 1959, Patricia Helen Crowe (marr. diss. 1985); one *s* one *d*; *m* 1986, Rosalind Jennifer Chivers. *Educ:* St Lawrence Coll., Ramsgate. FCIS, FCIPD, FCMI. 2nd Lt RA, 1946–48. Various appointments in Delta Metal Co. Ltd, 1950–76, incl. Commercial Director, Extrusion Division, and Director of Administration and Personnel, Rod Division, 1967–76; Chief Exec., Equal Opportunities Commn, 1976–78; Asst Gen. Manager, Nat. Employers Mutual Gen. Insce Assoc. Ltd, 1979–89. Governor, The Queen's Coll., Birmingham, 1974–88. Reader Emeritus, Dio. Gloucester. Liveryman, Worshipful Co. of Gold and Silver Wyre Drawers. *Recreations:* music, reading, walking, travel, photography. *Address:* Arrabon, Cirencester Road, South Cerney, Cirencester, Glos GL7 6HT. *T:* (01285) 862600; *e-mail:* daviddolton@aol.com.				*Died 15 Jan. 2004.*

DOMINGO SOLANS, Dr Eugenio; Member, Executive Board, European Central Bank, 1998–2004; *b* Barcelona, 26 Nov. 1945. *Educ:* French Lycée, Barcelona; Univ. of Barcelona (BEc 1968); Autonomous Univ. of Madrid (DEc 1975). Professor of Public Finance: Univ. of Barcelona, 1968–70; Autonomous Univ. of Madrid,

1970–; economist: Banco Atlántico, 1970, 1973–77, 1978–79; Res. Gp, Spanish Govt's Econ. and Social Develt Plan Dept, 1970–73; Econ. Advr, Min. of Economy, 1977–78; Manager, Res. Dept, Inst. of Econ. Studies, 1979–86; Asst Pres., 1986–94, Mem. Bd and Exec. Commn, 1988–94, Banco Zaragozano; Mem. Governing Council and Exec. Commn, Bank of Spain, 1994–98. Prof. of Monetary Policy and Spanish Tax System, UC of Financial Studies, Complutense Univ. of Madrid, 1996–. Member Board: BZ Gestión, 1987–91; Banco de Toledo, 1988–94 (Sec. Bd, 1990–94). *Address:* c/o European Central Bank, Kaiserstrasse 29, 60311 Frankfurt am Main, Germany.				*Died 9 Nov. 2004.*

DONALD, Dr Alastair Geoffrey, CBE 1993 (OBE 1982); FRCGP, FRCPE, FRCPSGlas; General Medical Practitioner, 1952–92; Assistant Director, Edinburgh Postgraduate Board for Medicine, 1970–91; Regional Adviser in General Practice, SE Scotland, 1972–91; President, Royal College of General Practitioners, 1992–94; *b* 24 Nov. 1926; *s* of Dr Pollok Donald and Henrietta Mary (*née* Laidlaw); *m* 1st, 1952, Patricia Ireland (marr. diss. 1998); two *s* one *d*; 2nd, 2003, Gladys Leslie. *Educ:* Edinburgh Academy; Corpus Christi Coll., Cambridge (MA); Edinburgh Univ. (MB, ChB). Mem., Cambridge and Edinburgh Univ. Athletic Teams. RAF Medical Branch, 1952–54; general medical practice, Leith and Cramond (Edin.), 1954–92; Lectr, Dept of General Practice, Univ. of Edinburgh, 1960–70. Royal College of General Practitioners: Vice-Chm. of Council, 1976–77; Chm., 1979–82; Chm., Bd of Censors, 1978–79; past Chm. and Provost, SE Scotland Faculty. Chairman: UK Conf. of Postgrad. Advisers in Gen. Practice, 1978–80; Jt Cttee on Postgrad. Trng for Gen. Practice, 1982–85; Armed Services Gen. Practice Approval Bd, 1987–98. Vice-Chm., Medical and Dental Defence Union of Scotland, 1992–97 (Hon. Fellow, 1998). Specialist Advr, H of C Social Services Select Cttee, 1986–87. Radio Doctor, BBC (Scotland), 1976–78. Chm., Scottish Cttee, ASH, 1985–92. Chm. Court of Directors, Edinburgh Acad., 1978–85 (Dir, 1955–85); President: Edinburgh Academical Club, 1978–81; Rotary Club of Leith, 1957–58. Lectures: James Mackenzie, RCGP, 1985; David Bruce, RAMC, 1987; Robert Campbell, Ulster Med. Soc., 1989; Ian Murray Scott, 1991, Pinsent, 1993, Fulton, 1994, RCGP; Richard Scott, Edinburgh Univ., 1996. James Mackenzie Medal, RCPE, 1983; Defence Med. Services Medal, 1993; Hippocrates Medal, SIMG, 1994; Foundn Council Award, RCGP, 1997; Paul Harris Fellow, Rotary Internat., 1996. *Publications:* contribs to medical jls. *Recreations:* golf, family life, reading The Times. *Address:* 2 Northlawn Terrace, Easter Park Drive, Edinburgh EH4 6SD. *T:* (0131) 336 3824. *Clubs:* Royal Air Force; Hawks (Cambridge).				*Died 5 June 2005.*

DONALD, Craig Reid Cantlie, CMG 1963; OBE 1959; MLC Uganda, 1954–62; *b* 8 Sept. 1914; *s* of Rev. Francis Cantlie and Mary Donald, Lumphanan, Aberdeenshire; *m* 1945, Mary Isabel Speid (*d* 1989); one *d*. *Educ:* Fettes; Emmanuel Coll., Cambridge (Scholar; BA 1937, MA 1947). Administrative Officer, Cyprus, 1937; Military Service, 1940–46, Lieut.-Col. Commissioner, Famagusta, 1948; Registrar, Cooperative Societies, 1951; Deputy Financial Sec., Uganda, 1951; Sec. to the Treasury, 1956–63. Fellow, Econ. Develt Inst., World Bank, 1956. Bursar, Malvern Coll., 1964–79. Governor: Hillstone Sch., 1979–86; Ellerslie, 1979–93; Downs Sch., Colwall, 1979–92. *Recreation:* country pursuits. *Address:* 55 Geraldine Road, Malvern WR14 3NU. *T:* (01684) 561446. *Club:* Travellers.				*Died 30 Jan. 2002.*

DONALDSON OF LYMINGTON, Baron *cr* 1988 (Life Peer), of Lymington in the County of Hampshire; **John Francis Donaldson,** Kt 1966; PC 1979; Master of the Rolls, 1982–92; *b* 6 Oct. 1920; *er s* of late Malcolm Donaldson, FRCS, FRCOG, and Evelyn Helen Marguerite Maunsell; *m* 1945, Dorothy Mary Warwick (Dame Mary Donaldson, GBE) (*d* 2003); one *s* two *d*.

Educ: Charterhouse; Trinity Coll., Cambridge (BA Hons 1946, MA 1959; Hon. Fellow, 1983); MA Oxon 1982. Sec. of Debates, Cambridge Union Soc., 1940; Chm., Fedn of Univ. Conservative and Unionist Assocs, 1940. Commnd Royal Signals, 1941; served with: Guards Armoured Divisional Signals, UK and NW Europe, 1942–45; Military Govt, Schleswig-Holstein, 1945–46; Hon. Lieut-Col, 1946. Called to the Bar, Middle Temple, 1946 (Harmsworth Law Scholar, 1946; Bencher 1966; Treas. 1986); Jun. Counsel to Registrar of Restrictive Trading Agreements, 1959–61; QC 1961; Dep. Chm., Hants QS, 1961–66; Mem., Council on Tribunals, 1965–66; Judge of the High Court, Queen's Bench Div., 1966–79; Pres., Nat. Industrial Relations Court, 1971–74; a Lord Justice of Appeal, 1979–82. Chairman: inquiry into prevention of pollution from merchant shipping, 1993–94; MV Derbyshire Assessment, 1995; Review of Salvage and Intervention and their Command and Control, 1999; Review of Five Year Strategy for HM Coastguard, 1999. Mem., Gen. Council of the Bar, 1956–61, 1962–66; Pres. Council, Inns of Court, 1987–90. Mem., Procedure Cttee, H of L, 2003–; Pres., Parly Maritime Gp, 2003–. Mem., Croydon CBC, 1949–53. President: Carthusian Soc., 1978–82; British Maritime Law Assoc., 1979–95 (Vice-Pres., 1969–78); British Insurance Law Assoc., 1979–81 (Dep. Pres., 1978–79); British Records Assoc., 1982–92; Chairman: Adv. Council on Public Records, 1982–92; Magna Carta Trust, 1982–92; Financial Law Panel, 1992–2002; Appeals Panel, London Metal Exchange, 2003–. Appeals Comr, Direct Marketing Assoc., 1998–. FCIArb 1980 (Pres., 1980–83). Hon. Member: Assoc. of Average Adjusters, 1966 (Chm., 1981); Grain and Feed Trade Assoc., 1979; Liverpool Cotton Assoc., 1979; Law Soc., 1994. Governor, Sutton's Hosp. in Charterhouse, 1981–84. Visitor: UCL, 1982–92; Nuffield Coll., Oxford, 1982–92; London Business Sch., 1986–92. Hon. Freeman, 1984, Hon. Liveryman, 2000, Worshipful Co. of Drapers. DU Essex, 1983; Hon. LLD: Sheffield, 1984; Nottingham Trent, 1992; Southampton, 1998. Silver Medal, Thomas Gray Meml Trust, 1995. *Publications:* Jt Ed., Lowndes and Rudolf on General Average and the York-Antwerp Rules, 8th edn 1955, 9th edn 1964, 10th edn 1975; contrib. to title Insurance, in Halsbury's Laws of England, 3rd edn 1958. *Recreations:* travel, do-it-yourself. *Address:* House of Lords, SW1A 0PW. *T:* (home) (01590) 675716. *Clubs:* Royal Cruising, Royal Lymington Yacht.

Died 31 Aug. 2005.

DONALDSON OF LYMINGTON, Lady; *see* Donaldson, Dame D. M.

DONALDSON, Dame (Dorothy) Mary, GBE 1983; JP; Lord Mayor of London for 1983–84; Alderman, City of London Ward of Coleman Street, 1975–91; *b* 29 Aug. 1921; *d* of late Reginald George Gale Warwick and Dorothy Alice Warwick; *m* 1945, John Francis Donaldson (*see* Rt Hon. Baron Donaldson of Lymington, PC); one *s* two *d*. *Educ:* Portsmouth High Sch. for Girls (GPDST); Wingfield Morris Orthopædic Hosp.; Middlesex Hosp., London. SRN 1946. Chairman: Women's Nat. Cancer Control Campaign, 1967–69; Interim Licensing Authy for Human In Vitro Fertilisation and Embryol., 1985–91; Vice-Pres., British Cancer Council, 1970; Member: NE Met. Regional Hosp. Bd, 1970–74; NE Thames RHA, 1976–81. Governor: London Hosp., 1971–74; Gt Ormond Street Hosp. for Sick Children, 1978–80; Member: Cities of London and Westminster Disablement Adv. Cttee, 1974–79; Inner London Educn Authority, 1968–71; City Parochial Foundn, 1969–75; Cttee, Royal Humane Soc., 1968–83; Cttee, AA, 1985–89; Press Complaints Commn, 1991–; Chm. Council, Banking Ombudsman, 1985–94; Vice-Pres., Counsel and Care for the Elderly, 1980–; Pres., BACUP, 1985–93. Governor: City of London Sch. for Girls, 1971–83; Berkhamsted Schools, 1976–80; Mem., Governing Body, Charterhouse Sch., 1980–85; Mem., Court of Common Council, 1966–75, Sheriff, 1981–82, HM Lieutenant, 1983, City of London; Mem. Guild of Freemen, City of London, 1970

(Mem. Court, 1983–86); Liveryman, Gardeners' Co., 1975; Hon. Freeman, Shipwrights' Co., 1985. JP Inner London, 1960; Mem., Inner London Juvenile Court Panel, 1960–65. Hon. Mem., CIArb, 1981; Hon. Fellow: Girton Coll., Cambridge, 1983; Portsmouth Univ. (formerly Poly.), 1984. FRSH 1984; Hon. FRCOG 1991. Hon. DSc City, 1983. DStJ 1984. Freedom, City of Winnipeg, 1968. Order of Oman, 1982; Order of Bahrain, 1984. Grand Officier, Ordre Nat. du Mérite, 1984. *Recreations:* gardening, travelling. *T:* (home) (01590) 675292. *Clubs:* Reform; Royal Cruising, Royal Lymington Yacht.

Died 4 Oct. 2003.

DONALDSON, Dame Mary; *see* Donaldson, Dame D. M.

DONIACH, Prof. Israel, MD; FRCPath 1963; FRCP 1968; Professor of Morbid Anatomy in University of London, London Hospital, 1960–76, then Emeritus Professor; Hon. Lecturer in Histopathology, St Bartholomew's Hospital Medical School, since 1976; *b* 9 March 1911; *yr s* of late Aaron Selig and Rahel Doniach; *m* 1933, Deborah Abileah; one *s* (one *d* decd). *Educ:* University Coll. and Hosp., London; MD London, 1936. Asst Pathologist, St Mary's Hosp., London, 1935–37; Clinical Pathologist and Cancer Research Asst, Mount Vernon Hosp., Northwood, 1937–43; Senior Lecturer in Morbid Anatomy, Postgraduate Medical Sch. of London, 1943–59, Reader, 1959–60. Hon. FRSocMed 1990; Hon. Member: Pathol. Soc., 1987; Soc. for Endocrinol., 1985. *Publications:* papers in morbid anatomy and experimental pathology in various journals. *Address:* 25 Alma Square, NW8 9PY. *T:* (020) 7286 1617. *Died 11 Feb. 2001.*

DONKIN, Alexander Sim; HM Diplomatic Service, retired; Counsellor (Administration), UK Mission to United Nations, and Deputy Consul-General, New York, 1977–82; *b* 14 July 1922; *s* of Matthew Henderson Donkin and Margaret Donkin; *m* 1944, Irene Florence (*née* Willis) (*d* 1988); two *d*. *Educ:* Monkwearmouth Sch., Co. Durham. Served War, RAF, 1941–46; Sqdn Ldr. Civil Service, 1947–66; HM Diplomatic Service, 1966: FCO, 1966–70; Washington, 1970–74; FCO, 1974–77. *Recreations:* music, walking, photography, gliding. *Address:* 1 Amberley Road, Eastbourne, East Sussex BN22 0EH.

Died 11 Sept. 2001.

DOOKUN, Sir Dewoonarain, Kt 1984; Chairman, State Bank of Mauritius Ltd; Chairman and Managing Director, Mauritius Cosmetics Ltd, since 1966; *b* 7 Dec. 1929; *s* of Jadoonath Dookun; *m* 1959, Henriette Keupp; two *s*. *Educ:* St Joseph College; Univ. of Edinburgh. Manufacturing, marketing, business administration and accounts, Mainz, West Germany; founder of: Mauritius Cosmetics, 1966; Paper Converting Co., 1967; Jet Industries, 1967; FDG Garments Industries, 1968; Agri-Pac, 1979; Deramann, 1979; Gumboots Manufacturers, 1976; DG Rubber, 1979; Elite Textiles, 1982; Deodan Textile, 1984. *Recreations:* reading, walking, golf. *Address:* (office) No 1 Queen Elizabeth II Avenue, Port Louis, Mauritius; Queen Mary Avenue, Floreal, Mauritius. *T:* 6862361; *telex:* 4239 Dookun IW. *Clubs:* Institute of Directors; Mauritius Gymkhana; Swastika.

Died 24 July 2004.

DORMAND OF EASINGTON, Baron *cr* 1987 (Life Peer), of Easington in the county of Durham; **John Donkin Dormand;** *b* 27 Aug. 1919; *s* of Bernard and Mary Dormand; *m* 1963, Doris Robinson; one step *s* one step *d*. *Educ:* Bede Coll., Durham; Loughborough Coll.; St Peter's Hall, Oxford (Hon. Fellow, St Peter's Coll., 1993); Univ. of Harvard. Teacher, 1940–48; Education Adviser, 1948–52 and 1957–63; District Education Officer, Easington RDC, 1963–70. MP (Lab) Easington, 1970–87. An Asst Govt Whip, 1974; a Lord Comr of HM Treasury, 1974–79; Chm., PLP, 1981–87. *Recreations:* music, sport, films. *Died 18 Dec. 2003.*

DORNHORST, Antony Clifford, CBE 1977; MD, FRCP; Professor of Medicine, St George's Hospital Medical School, 1959–80; Civilian Consultant in Aviation Medicine to RAF, 1973–85; *b* 2 April 1915; *s* of Ernst Dornhorst and Florence, *née* Partridge; *m* 1946, Helen Mary Innes; three *d*. *Educ*: St Clement Danes Sch.; St Thomas's Hosp. Medical Sch.; MB BS London 1937; MD London 1939. FRCP 1955. Junior appts, St Thomas' Hosp., 1937–39. Served with RAMC, mostly in Mediterranean theatre, 1940–46. Reader in Medicine, St Thomas's Hosp. Med. Sch., 1949–59. Member: MRC, 1973–77; SW Thames RHA, 1974–82. *Publications*: papers in various jls on normal and abnormal physiology. *Recreation*: music. *Address*: 8 Albert Place, W8 5PD. *T*: (020) 7937 8782. *Died 9 March 2003.*

DORRELL, Ernest John; Secretary, Headmasters' Conference, 1975–79; General Secretary, Secondary Heads Association, 1978–79 (Secretary, Incorporated Association of Headmasters, 1975–77); *b* 31 March 1915; *s* of John Henry Whiting Dorrell and Amy Dorrell (*née* Roberts); *m* 1940, Alwen Irvona Jones (decd); one *s* (one *d* decd). *Educ*: Taunton Sch.; Exeter Coll., Oxford (Exhibr). Hon. Mods and Lit. Hum., MA. Served with 71 Field Regt and HQ 46 Div. RA, 1940–46. Asst Master, Dauntsey's Sch., 1937–40 and 1946–47; Admin. Asst, WR Educn Dept, 1947–50; Dep. Dir of Educn, 1950–70, Dir of Educn, 1970–74, Oxfordshire CC. Report on Educn in St Helena, 1974. Member: BBC Schs Broadcasting Council, 1975–79; Thames TV Educn Adv. Council, 1976–79. *Recreations*: walking, travel, golf. *Address*: Lynfield, 2 Gravel Lane, Warborough, Wallingford, Oxon OX10 7SD. *T*: (01865) 858342. *Died 11 March 2002.*

DORWARD, David Keay; Director of Finance, Dundee City Council, since 1995; *b* 24 May 1954; *s* of David Dorward and Christina Dorward (*née* Keay); *m* 1977, Gail Elizabeth Bruce; three *d*. *Educ*: Kinross High Sch.; Perth High Sch.; Glasgow Coll. of Technology. CPFA 1982. Trainee Accountant, Perth and Kinross Jt CC, 1971–75; Tayside Regional Council: Trainee Accountant, 1975–82; Sen. Accountant, 1982–83; Principal Accountant, 1983–84; Financial Planning Officer, 1984–86; Chief Financial Planning Officer, 1986–93; Depute Dir of Finance, 1993–95. *Recreations*: golf, supporting Dundee United, bowls, going to the theatre. *Address*: 4 Norrie Street, Broughty Ferry, Dundee DD5 2SD. *T*: (01382) 739006. *Clubs*: Dundee United Businessmen's (Dundee); Broughty Bowling; Abertay Golf. *Died 24 Dec. 2003.*

DOUGLAS, Prof. Charles Primrose, FRCOG; Professor of Obstetrics and Gynæcology, University of Cambridge, 1976–88, then Emeritus; Fellow, Emmanuel College, Cambridge, 1979–88; *b* 17 Feb. 1921; *s* of Dr C. Douglas, Ayr, Scotland; *m* 1948, Angela Francis; three *s* one *d*. *Educ*: Loretto Sch.; Peterhouse, Cambridge; Univ. of Edinburgh. Surg. Lieut RNVR, 1944–47. Registrar and Sen. Registrar, Victoria Infirmary, Glasgow, 1950–59; William Waldorf Astor Foundn Fellow, 1957; Vis. Fellow, Duke Univ., NC, 1957; Sen. Lectr, Univ. of the West Indies, 1959–65; Prof. of Obst. and Gyn., Royal Free Hosp. Sch. of Medicine, 1965–76. Member: Bd of Governors, Royal Free Hosp., 1972–74; Camden and Islington AHA, 1974–76; Cambridge AHA, 1981–82; Cambridge DHA, 1983–88. Mem. Council, RCOG, 1980–86. Hon. FACOG 1983. *Publications*: contribs to BMJ, Amer. Heart Jl, Jl of Obst. and Gynæcol. of Brit. Commonwealth, etc. *Recreations*: golf, travel, art. *Address*: 32 Lorimer Street, Bathurst, NSW 2795, Australia. *Died 23 Aug. 2005.*

DOUGLAS, Rt Hon. Sir William (Randolph), KCMG 1983; Kt 1969; PC 1977; High Commissioner for Barbados in London, 1991–93; *b* Barbados, 24 Sept. 1921; *e s* of William P. Douglas and Emily Frances Douglas (*née* Nurse); *m* 1st, 1951, Thelma Ruth (*née* Gilkes) (*d* 1992); one *s* one *d*; 2nd, 1997, Denise Alva (*née* Hope). *Educ*:

Bannatyne Sch. and Verdun High Sch., Verdun, Que., Canada; McGill Univ. (BA Hons); London Sch. of Economics (LLB). Private Practice at Barbados Bar, 1948–50; Dep. Registrar, Barbados, 1950; Resident Magistrate, Jamaica, 1955; Asst Attorney-Gen., Jamaica, 1959; Solicitor-Gen., Jamaica, 1962; Puisne Judge, Jamaica, 1962; Chief Justice of Barbados, 1965–86; Ambassador to USA, 1987–91. Chairman: Commonwealth Caribbean Council of Legal Education, 1971–77; ILO Fact-Finding and Conciliation Commn to S Africa, 1993; Commn of Inquiry into three Crown Corps, Bahamas, 1993–96; ILO Cttee of Experts on the Application of Conventions and Recommendations, 1995–2001 (Mem., 1975–2001); ILO Commn of Enquiry on Forced Labour in Myanmar, 1997–98. Pres., ILO Administrative Tribunal, 1994–98 (Judge, 1982–98). *Clubs*: Barbados Yacht; Pau Golf (France). *Died 12 Aug. 2003.*

DOWLING, Dame Jean (Elizabeth), DCVO 1978 (CVO 1976; MVO 4th cl. 1971, 5th cl. 1964); *b* 7 Nov. 1916; *d* of Captain William Taylor (killed in action, 1917) and Margery Hooper Alchin; *m* 1993, Ambrose Francis Dowling, MVO, MBE, TD. *Educ*: Tunbridge Wells High Sch. (GPDST). Entered Office of Private Secretary to the Queen, 1958; Chief Clerk, 1961–78. *Recreations*: music, walking, looking at old buildings. *Address*: Church Cottage, Frittenden, Cranbrook, Kent TN17 2DD. *Died 22 Dec. 2002.*

DOWLING, Kenneth, CB 1985; Deputy Director of Public Prosecutions, 1982–85; *b* 30 Dec. 1933; *s* of Alfred and Maria Dowling; *m* 1957, Margaret Frances Bingham; two *d*. *Educ*: King George V Grammar Sch., Southport. RAF, 1952–54. Called to the Bar, Gray's Inn, 1960. Immigration Branch, Home Office, 1954–61; joined DPP Dept: Legal Asst, 1961; Sen. Legal Asst, 1966; Asst Solicitor, 1972; Asst Dir, 1976; Princ. Asst Dir, 1977. *Recreations*: reading, golf. *Died 11 March 2003.*

DOWN, Sir Alastair (Frederick), Kt 1978; OBE 1944 (MBE 1942); MC 1940; TD 1951; Chairman, The Burmah Oil Co. PLC, 1975–83 (Chief Executive, 1975–80); *b* 23 July 1914; *e s* of Frederick Edward Down and Margaret Isobel Down (*née* Hutchison); *m* 1947, Maysie Hilda, (Bunny), Mellon; two *s* two *d*. *Educ*: Edinburgh Acad.; Marlborough Coll. CA 1938. Commissioned in 7th/9th Bn, The Royal Scots (TA), 1935. Joined British Petroleum Co. Ltd in Palestine, 1938. Served War of 1939–45 (despatches twice, MC, MBE, OBE, Kt Comdr, Order of Orange Nassau, with swords, 1946), Middle East, N Africa, Italy and Holland, with Eighth Army and 1st Canadian Army as Lt-Col and full Col. Rejoined BP, in Iran, 1945–47; Head Office, 1947–54; Canada, 1954–62 (Chief Rep. of BP in Canada, 1954–57; Pres., BP Group in Canada, 1957–62); Pres., BP Oil Corp., 1969–70; Man. Dir, 1962–75 and Dep. Chm., 1969–75, British Petroleum Co. Ltd. Director: TRW Inc., USA, 1977–86; Scottish American Investment Co. Ltd, 1980–85; Royal Bank of Canada, 1981–85; Chairman: British-North American Res. Assoc., 1980–84; London American Energy NV, 1981–85. Member: Review Body for pay of doctors and dentists, 1971–74; Television Adv. Cttee, 1971–72; Council, Marlborough Coll., 1979–87 (Chm. Council, 1982–87); Hon. Treasurer, Field Studies Council, 1977–81. FRSA 1970; FCMI (FBIM 1972); JDipMA (Hon.), 1966. Hambro British Businessman of the Year Award, 1980; Cadman Meml Medal, Inst. of Petroleum, 1981. *Recreations*: shooting, golf, fishing. *Address*: Greystones, Newland, Sherborne, Dorset DT9 3AG. *Club*: New (Edinburgh). *Died 22 Oct. 2004.*

DOWNE, 11th Viscount, *cr* 1680; **John Christian George Dawnay;** Bt 1642; Baron Dawnay of Danby (UK) *cr* 1897; DL; technology manager; *b* Wykeham, 18 Jan. 1935; *s* of 10th Viscount Downe, OBE and Margaret Christine (*d* 1967), *d* of Christian Bahnsen, NJ; *S* father, 1965; *m* 1965, Alison Diana, *d* of I. F. H. Sconce, OBE; one *s* one *d*. *Educ*: Eton Coll.; Christ Church, Oxford. 2nd Lieut,

Grenadier Guards, 1954–55. Non-marine broker at Lloyd's, 1958–65. Part-time Mem., Electronics Res. Gp, J. J. Thomson Physical Lab., Univ. of Reading, 1964–78; Brookdeal Electronics Ltd: Man. Dir. 1965–68; Vice-Chm., 1968–71; Chm., 1971–84; Director: Dawnay Faulkner Associated Ltd (Consultants), 1968–; Allen Bradley Electronics Ltd, 1970–81; George Rowney & Co. Ltd, 1978–83; York Ltd, 1980–99 (Chm., 1980–93; Pres., 1993–); Yorkshire Bank PLC, 1990–96; SensorDynamics Ltd, 1990–; Aaston Ltd, 1992–; Aaston Inc., 1992–. Dir, Scarborough Theatre Trust, 1981– (Vice-Chm., 1986–). Member: CLA Yorks Br. Cttee, 1966– (Chm., 1988–90); CLA Exec. Cttee, 1990–94; N Yorks Moors Nat. Park Cttee, 1969–97 (Vice-Chm., 1982–85); N Riding/N Yorks County Council, 1969–85; Nat. Railway Mus. Cttee, 1974– (Chm., 1985–97); N Yorks and ER Rural Develt Cttee (formerly N Yorks Rural Develt Commn County Cttee), 1978– (Chm., 1986–99); President: N York Moors Hist. Railway Trust, 1970–; Yorks Rural Community Council, 1977–; Aston Martin Owners Club, 1980–; Friends of the Nat. Railway Mus., 1988–; Trustee: Nat. Mus. of Science and Industry, 1985–97; Burton Constable Foundn, 1992–2000. Hon. Col, 150 (Yorkshire) Regt RLC(V) (formerly 150 (Northumbrian) Regt RCT(V)), 1984–95. Freeman, Co. of the Staple of England, 1979; Liveryman, Co. of Scientific Instrument Makers, 1991–. DL N Yorks, 1981. *Publications:* contributions to various journals. *Recreations:* linear circuit design, railways (selectively). *Heir:* s Hon. Richard Henry Dawnay, *b* 9 April 1967. *Address:* Wykeham Abbey, Scarborough, North Yorks YO13 9QS. *T:* (01723) 862404; 5 Douro Place, W8 5PH. *T:* (020) 7937 9449. *Club:* Pratt's.   *Died 15 March 2002.*

DOWNES, George Stretton, CBE 1976; Deputy Receiver for the Metropolitan Police District, 1973–76; *b* London, 2 March 1914; *e s* of late George and Rosalind S. Downes; *m* 1st, 1939, Sheilah Gavigan (*d* 1986); two *s* two *d*; 2nd, 1991, Barbara (*née* Rudge). *Educ:* Cardinal Vaughan Sch., Kensington. Joined Metropolitan Police Office, 1934; Secretary, 1969. *Recreations:* golf, gardening. *Address:* 13 Ember Gardens, Thames Ditton, Surrey KT7 0LL.   *Died 19 Feb. 2002.*

DOWNEY, Anne Elisabeth; Her Honour Judge Downey; a Circuit Judge, since 1986; *b* 22 Aug. 1936; *d* of John James Downey and Ida May Downey. *Educ:* Notre Dame Convent, Liverpool; Liverpool Univ. (LLB (Hons.)). Called to the Bar, Gray's Inn, 1958. A Recorder, 1980–86. *Recreations:* antiques, reading. *Address:* Copperfield, 4 Pine Walks, Prenton, Birkenhead L42 8LQ. *T:* (0151) 608 2404.   *Died 24 June 2002.*

DOWNING, David Francis, PhD; Head of Land Systems Group, British Defence Staff, British Embassy, Washington, 1983–87; *b* 4 Aug. 1926; *e s* of late Alfred William and Violet Winifred Downing; *m* 1948, Margaret Joan Llewellyn; one *s* one *d*. *Educ:* Bristol Grammar Sch.; Univ. of Bristol (BSc 1952, PhD 1955); BA Open, 1996. Served Coldstream Gds and Royal Welch Fusiliers, 1944–48 (Lieut RWF, 1947). Student Mem. of delegn from Brit. univs to Soviet univs, 1954; Eli Lilley Res. Fellow, Univ. of Calif, LA, and Fulbright Travel Scholarship, 1955–56; Long Ashton Res. Stn, Univ. of Bristol, 1957–58; Chem. Defence Estabt, 1958–63; Defence Res. Staff, Washington, 1963–66; Chem. Defence Estabt, 1966–68; Counsellor (Scientific), British High Commn, Ottawa, 1968–73; Head, Management Services, 1973–75, Head, Pyrotechnics Br., 1975–78, RARDE; Counsellor (Scientific), British Embassy, Moscow, 1978–81; Asst Dir, Resources and Programmes B, MoD, 1981–83. Pt-time Chm., CS Sci. Recruitment Bds, 1988–95. Reader, Salisbury Cathedral, 1990– (Archbishops' Diploma for Readers, 1995). Governor: Salisbury and Wells Theological Coll., 1987–94 (Chm., 1990–94); Sarum Coll., 1994–. FRSA 1969. *Publications:* scientific papers, mainly in Jl of Chem. Soc., and Qly Reviews of Chem. Soc. *Recreations:* cathedral music,

Arctic and Antarctic travel, bird watching, ski-ing. *Address:* 13 The Close, Salisbury, Wilts SP1 2EB. *T:* (01722) 323910. *Club:* Army and Navy.   *Died 30 July 2005.*

DOWNS, Rosalyn, (Mrs George Wallingford Downs); *see* Tureck, R.

DOWNSHIRE, 8th Marquess of, *cr* 1789 (Ire.); **Arthur Robin Ian Hill;** Viscount Hillsborough, Baron Hill 1717; Earl of Hillsborough, Viscount Kilwarlin 1751; Baron Harwich (GB) 1756; Earl of Hillsborough, Viscount Fairford (GB) 1772; Hereditary Constable of Hillsborough Fort; farmer, since 1963; *b* 10 May 1929; *s* of Lord Arthur Francis Henry Hill (*d* 1953) (*yr s* of 6th Marquess) and Sheila (*d* 1961), *d* of Col Stewart MacDougall of Lunga; *S* uncle, 1989; *m* 1st, 1957, Hon. Juliet Mary (*d* 1986), *d* of 7th Baron Forester; two *s* one *d*; 2nd, 1989, Mrs Diana Hibbert (*née* Cross; *d* 1998); 3rd, Tessa, *widow* of Vere Fane. *Educ:* Eton. 2nd Lieut Royal Scots Greys, 1948–50. Articled clerk, 1950–55; Chartered Accountant (ACA 1959). *Recreations:* shooting, travel. *Heir:* s Earl of Hillsborough, *b* 4 Feb. 1959. *Address:* High Burton House, Masham, Ripon, North Yorks HG4 4BS. *T:* (01765) 689326. *Clubs:* White's, Pratt's.   *Died 18 Dec. 2003.*

DOWNWARD, Sir William (Atkinson), Kt 1977; JP; Lord-Lieutenant of Greater Manchester, 1974–87; *b* 5 Dec. 1912; *s* of late George Thomas Downward; *m* 1946, Enid (*d* 2001), *d* of late Ald. Charles Wood. *Educ:* Manchester Central High Sch.; Manchester Coll. of Technology. Councillor, Manchester City Council, 1946–75; Lord Mayor of Manchester, 1970–71, Alderman, Manchester, 1971–74. Dir, Royal Exchange Theatre Co., 1976–89; Chairman: Manchester Overseas Students Welfare Conf., 1972–87; Peterloo Gall., 1974–76. Chm., Pat Seed Appeal Fund, 1977–98; President: Manchester Opera Soc., 1977–; Gtr Manchester Fedn of Boys' Clubs, 1978–2002; Broughton House Home for Disabled Ex-Servicemen, 1978–98. Member, Court of Governors: Manchester Univ., 1969–96; Salford Univ., 1974–87. FRSA 1978; Hon. RNCM 1982. DL Lancs, 1971; JP Manchester, 1973. Hon. LLD Manchester, 1977. KStJ 1974. *Address:* 23 Kenmore Road, Northenden, Manchester M22 4AE. *T:* (0161) 998 4742.   *Died 1 Jan. 2005.*

DOYLE, Brian André; Judge, Botswana Court of Appeal, 1973–79 and 1988–91; *b* 10 May 1911; *s* of John Patrick Doyle, ICS and Louise Doyle (*née* Renard); *m* 1937, Nora (*née* Slattery) (*d* 1992); one *s* one *d*. *Educ:* Douai Sch.; Trinity Coll., Dublin (BA, LLB). British Univs and Hosps Boxing Champion, 1929, 1930, 1931 (Flyweight), 1932 (Bantamweight); Irish Free State Army Boxing Champion, 1930 (Flyweight). Called to Irish Bar, 1932; Magistrate, Trinidad and Tobago, 1937; Resident Magistrate, Uganda, 1942; Solicitor-Gen., Fiji, 1948; Attorney-Gen., Fiji, 1949; KC (Fiji), 1950, later QC; Attorney-Gen., N Rhodesia, 1956; Minister of Legal Affairs and Attorney-Gen., Northern Rhodesia (Zambia), 1964), 1959–65, retired as minister, 1965; Chm., Local Govt Service Commn, Zambia, 1964; Justice of Appeal, 1965; Chief Justice and Pres., Supreme Court of Zambia, 1969–75. Dir, Law Develt Commn, Zambia, 1976–79; Chm., Delimitation Commn, Botswana, 1981–82. *Recreations:* fishing, golf. *Address:* 26 Choumert Square, Peckham Rye, SE15 4RE.   *Died 30 Oct. 2004.*

DRAPER, (John Haydn) Paul; Senior Planning Inspector, Department of Environment, 1977–86, retired; *b* 14 Dec. 1916; *o c* of late Haydn Draper, clarinet player, and Nan Draper; *m* 1941, Nancy Allum (*d* 1998), author and journalist; one *s* one *d* (and one *d* decd). *Educ:* LCC primary sch.; Bancroft's Sch.; University Coll. London. Engr in Post Office, 1939–48; Royal Signals, Signalman to Major, Middle East, N Africa, Sicily, NW Europe (despatches), 1940–46; MoT, 1948–64 and 1968–70; Jt Principal Private Sec. to Minister, 1956–58; Asst Sec., 1959; Counsellor (Shipping), British Embassy, Washington, 1964–67; BoT, 1967–68; Under-Sec., 1968;

DoE, 1970–74; Senior Planning Inspector, 1973–74; Resident Chm., Civil Service Selection Bd, 1975–76.
Died 11 Nov. 2002.

DRAPER, Paul; *see* Draper, J. H. P.

DREW, Joanna Marie, CBE 1985; Director, Hayward and Regional Exhibitions, South Bank Centre, 1987–92; *b* Naini Tal, India, 28 Sept. 1929; *d* of Brig. Francis Greville Drew, CBE, and Sannie Frances Sands. *Educ:* Dartington Hall; Edinburgh Univ. (MA Hons Fine Art); Edinburgh Coll. of Art (DA). Arts Council of GB, 1952–88: Asst Dir of Exhibns, 1970; Dir of Exhibns, 1975; Dir of Art, 1978–86. Mem. Council, RCA, 1979–82. Officier: l'Ordre des Arts et Lettres (France), 1988 (Chevalier, 1979); l'Ordre Nat. du Mérite (France), 1994 (Chevalier, 1990). *Died 20 April 2003.*

DREYER, Adm. Sir Desmond (Parry), GCB 1967 (KCB 1963; CB 1960); CBE 1957; DSC 1940; JP; DL; *b* 6 April 1910; *yr s* of Adm. Sir Frederic Dreyer, GBE, KCB; *m* 1st, 1934, Elisabeth (*d* 1958), *d* of Sir Henry Chilton, GCMG; one *s* one *d* (and one *s* decd); 2nd, 1959, Marjorie Gordon (*d* 1997), *widow* of Hon. R. G. Whiteley. *Educ:* RN Coll., Dartmouth. Joined RN 1924. Served War of 1939–45. Captain, 1948; Cdre First Class, 1955; Chief of Staff, Mediterranean, 1955–57; Asst Chief of Naval Staff, 1958–59; Flag Officer (Flotillas) Mediterranean, 1960–61; Flag Officer Air (Home), 1961–62; Comdr, Far East Fleet, 1962–65; Second Sea Lord, 1965–67; Chief Adviser (Personnel and Logistics) to Sec. of State for Defence, 1967–68. Principal Naval ADC to the Queen, 1965–68. Gentleman Usher to the Sword of State, 1970–80. Member: Nat. Bd for Prices and Incomes, 1968–71; Armed Forces Pay Review Body, 1971–79. President: RN Benevolent Trust, 1970–78; Not Forgotten Assoc., 1973–91; Officers' Pension Soc., 1978–84; Regular Forces Employment Assoc., 1978–82. JP 1968, High Sheriff, 1977–78, DL 1985, Hants. *Recreations:* fishing, golf. *Address:* Brook Cottage, Cheriton, near Alresford, Hants SO24 0QA. *T:* (01962) 771215. *Club:* Army and Navy. *Died 15 May 2003.*

DREYFUS, John Gustave, FIOP; typographical consultant and historian; *b* 15 April 1918; *s* of late Edmond and Marguerite Dreyfus; *m* 1948, Irène Thurnauer; two *d* (one *s* decd). *Educ:* Oundle Sch.; Trinity Coll., Cambridge (BA 1939, MA 1945). FIOP 1977. Served War, Army, 1939–45. Joined Cambridge University Press as graduate trainee, 1939; Asst Univ. Printer, 1949–56; Typographical Adviser, 1956–82; Typographical Adviser to Monotype Corp., 1955–82; European Consultant to Limited Editions Club, USA, 1956–77; Dir, Curwen Press, 1970–82; Sandars Reader in Bibliography, Univ. of Cambridge, 1979–80. Helped plan exhibn, Printing and the Mind of Man, 1963 (also designed catalogues). President: Assoc. Typographique Internationale, 1968–73 (organised internat. congresses for Assoc.); Printing Historical Soc., 1991 (org. Caxton Internat. Congress, 1976). FRSA. Sir Thomas More Award, Univ. of San Francisco, 1979; Laureate, Amer. Printing Historical Soc., 1984; Frederic W. Goudy Award, Rochester Inst. of Technology, NY, 1984; Gutenberg Prize, Mainz, 1996. *Publications:* The Survival of Baskerville's Punches, 1949; The Work of Jan van Krimpen, 1952; (ed series) Type Specimen Facsimiles, 1963–71; Italic Quartet, 1966; (ed with François Richaudeau) La Chose Imprimée (French encyc. on printing), 1977; A History of the Nonesuch Press, 1981; French Eighteenth Century Typography, 1982; A Typographical Masterpiece, 1990; Into Print, 1994; contrib. The Library. *Recreations:* travel, theatre-going. *Address:* 38 Lennox Gardens, SW1X 0DH. *T:* (020) 7584 3510. *Club:* Garrick. *Died 29 Dec. 2002.*

DRIVER, Sir Antony (Victor), Kt 1986; Chairman, South West Thames Regional Health Authority, 1982–88; *b* London, 20 July 1920; *s* of late Arthur William Driver and Violet Clementina Driver (*née* Browne); *m* 1948, Patricia (*née* Tinkler); three *s*. *Educ:* King's Coll., Univ. of

London (BScEng Hons); Dip., Graduate Sch. of Industrial Admin., Carnegie-Mellon Univ., Pittsburgh. CEng; FIMechE, FInstPet; FIMgt. In oil industry with Shell-Mex and BP Ltd, until 1975, and BP Oil Ltd, 1976–80: seconded to British Petroleum Co., as Marketing Manager, N Europe, 1969–71; General Manager, Sales, 1971–78; Dir, Personnel and Admin, 1979–80. Non-executive Director: Candles Ltd, 1976–80; Rockwool Ltd, 1978–80; Baxter Fell & Co. Ltd, 1980–85; Chm., Hoogovens (UK) Ltd, 1985–88. Director: Inst. of Cancer Research, 1981–95; Breakthrough Breast Cancer, 1995–; Oil Industries Club Ltd, 1981–; Surrey Assoc. of Youth Clubs and Surrey PHAB Ltd, 1991–. Liveryman, Tallow Chandlers' Co., 1977–; Freeman, City of London. *Recreations:* travel, gardening, wine, pyrotechnics. *Address:* Winterdown, Holmbury St Mary, Dorking, Surrey RH5 6NL. *T:* (01306) 730238. *Died 7 Jan. 2002.*

DRUCKER, Henry Matthew, PhD; Chairman, Oxford Philanthropic, since 1999 (Managing Director, 1994–99); *b* 29 April 1942; *s* of Arthur and Frances Drucker; *m* 1975, Nancy Livia Newman. *Educ:* Allegheny Coll., Meadville, Penn (BA Philosophy); London Sch. of Economics (PhD PolPhil). Lectr in Politics, 1964–76, Sen. Lectr in Politics, 1976–86, Univ. of Edinburgh; Director: Univ. Develt Office, Oxford Univ., 1987–93; Campaign for Oxford, 1988–93. Mem., British Museum Develt Trust, 2000–. Vis. Prof. of Govt, LSE, 1994–99. *Publications:* Political Uses of Ideology, 1974; (ed with M. G. Clarke) Our Changing Scotland, 1977; Breakaway—The Scottish Labour Party, 1978; (ed with Nancy Drucker) Scottish Government Yearbook, 1978–82; Doctrine and Ethos in the Labour Party, 1979; (ed) Multi-Party Britain, 1979; (with Gordon Brown) The Politics of Nationalism and Devolution, 1980; (ed) John P. Mackintosh on Scotland, 1982; (general ed.) Developments in British Politics, 1983; (general ed.) Developments in British Politics 2, 1986, rev. edn 1988. *Recreations:* reading aloud to wife, walking. *Address:* 33 Bainton Road, Oxford OX2 7AG.
Died 30 Oct. 2002.

DRUCKER, Prof. Peter (Ferdinand); writer and consultant; Clarke Professor of Social Science and Management, Claremont Graduate School, Claremont, Calif, 1971–2002; *b* 19 Nov. 1909; *s* of Adolph B. Drucker and Caroline (*née* Bond); *m* 1937, Doris Schmitz; one *s* three *d*. *Educ:* Austria, Germany, England. Investment banker, London, 1933–36; newspapers, 1937–41; Professor of Philosophy and Politics, Bennington Coll., Bennington, Vt, USA, 1942–49; Prof. of Management, NY Univ., 1950–71; Professorial Lectr in Oriental Art, Claremont Colls, 1980–86. Management Consultant (internat. practice among businesses and govts) (as well as Professorships), 1943–. Has recorded audio-cassettes and video cassettes on management practice. Holds hon. doctorates from univs in Belgium, Czech Republic, GB, Japan, Spain, Switzerland, USA. Hon. FCMI; FAAAS; Fellow: Amer. Acad. of Management; Internat. Acad. of Management. Godkin Lectr, Harvard Univ., 1994. US Presidential Medal of Freedom, 2002. Order of Sacred Treasure, Japan; Grand Cross, Austria. *Publications:* End of Economic Man, 1939, new edn 1995; Future of Industrial Man, 1942, new edn 1994; Concept of the Corporation, 1946, new edn 1992; The New Society, 1950, new edn 1992; Practice of Management, 1954, new edn 1996; America's Next Twenty Years, 1959; Landmarks of Tomorrow, 1960, new edn 1996; Managing for Results, 1964, new edn 1996; The Effective Executive, 1966, new edn 1996; The Age of Discontinuity, 1969, new edn 1992; Technology, Management and Society, 1970; Men, Ideas and Politics, 1971; The New Markets . . . and other essays, 1971; Management: tasks, responsibilities, practices, 1974, new edn 1996; The Unseen Revolution: how pension fund socialism came to America, 1976, 2nd edn 1995; Adventures of a Bystander, 1979, new edn 1998; Managing in Turbulent Times, 1980, new edn 1996; Toward the New Economics, 1981; The Changing World of the Executive (essays), 1982; Innovation and

Entrepreneurship, 1985, new edn 1996; The Frontiers of Management, 1986; The New Realities, 1989, new edn 2003; Managing the Non-Profit Organisation, 1990, new edn 1996; Managing for the Future, 1992; The Ecological Vision, 1993; Post Capitalist Society, 1993; Managing at a Time of Great Change, 1995; Drucker on Asia: a dialogue with Isao Nakauchi, 1997; Peter Drucker on the Profession of Management, 1998; Management Challenges for the 21st Century, 1999; The Essential Drucker (anthology), 2001; Managing in the Next Society, 2002; A Functioning Society (anthology), 2002; The Daily Drucker, 2004; *novels:* The Last of All Possible Worlds, 1982; The Temptation to Do Good, 1984. *Recreations:* mountaineering; Japanese history and paintings. *Died 11 Nov. 2005.*

DUCHÊNE, Louis-François; author; Director, European Research Centre, Sussex University, 1974–82, then Emeritus Professor; *b* 17 Feb. 1927; *s* of Louis Adrien Duchêne and Marguerite Lucienne Duchêne (*née* Lainé); *m* 1952, Anne Margaret Purves (*d* 1997); one *d*. *Educ:* St Paul's Sch.; London Sch. of Economics. Leader writer, Manchester Guardian, 1949–52; Press attaché, High Authority, European Coal and Steel Community, Luxembourg, 1952–55; Correspondent of The Economist, Paris, 1956–58; Dir, Documentation Centre of Action Cttee for United States of Europe (Chm. Jean Monnet), Paris, 1958–63; Editorial writer, The Economist, London, 1963–67; Ford Foundn Fellow, 1967–69; Dir, IISS, 1969–74. *Publications:* (ed) The Endless Crisis, 1970; The Case of the Helmeted Airman: a study of W. H. Auden, 1972; New Limits on European Agriculture, 1985; (ed with G. Shepherd) Managing Industrial Change in Western Europe, 1987; Jean Monnet: first statesman of interdependence, 1994. *Address:* 3 Powis Villas, Brighton, East Sussex BN1 3HD. *T:* (01273) 329258. *Died 12 July 2005.*

DUCKWORTH, Sir Edward Richard Dyce, 4th Bt *cr* 1909, of Grosvenor Place, City of Westminster; *b* 13 July 1943; *er s* of Sir Richard Dyce Duckworth, 3rd Bt and Violet Alison (*d* 1996), *d* of Lt-Col G. B. Wauchope, DSO; *S* father, 1997, but his name does not appear on the Official Roll of the Baronetage; *m* 1976, Patricia, *o d* of Thomas Cahill; one *s* one *d*. *Educ:* Marlborough; Cranfield. *Heir: s* James Dyce Duckworth, *b* 20 Dec. 1984. *Died 7 Oct. 2005.*

DUDGEON, Air Vice-Marshal Antony Greville, CBE 1955; DFC 1941; *b* 6 Feb. 1916; *s* of late Prof. Herbert William Dudgeon, Guy's Hosp. and Egyptian Government Service; *m* 1942, Phyllis Margaret (*d* 1994), *d* of late Group Capt. John McFarlane, OBE, MC, AFC, Lowestoft, Suffolk; one *s* one *d*. *Educ:* Eton; RAF Cranwell. RAF Service, 1933–68, in UK, Europe, Near, Middle and Far East, USA; personnel work, training, operations, flight safety, organisation of new formations, liaison with civilian firms and youth organisations; courses at Staff Coll., Flying Coll., and London Polytechnic (Dip.); NATO Staff; 6 command appointments; over 100 operational sorties; 3,500 hours on over 70 types of aircraft as pilot. Manager, Professional Staff Services, McKinsey & Co., Paris, 1968–78; representative, France, Grangersol Ltd, 1978–81. *Publications: autobiographical works:* A Flying Command (under pen-name Tom Dagger), 1962; The Luck of the Devil (1929–41), 1985, rev. edn as Delightful and Dangerous, 2002; Wings Over North Africa (1941–4), 1987, rev. edn as A North African Pilot, 2002; The War That Never Was (1941), 1991; Hidden Victory (1941), 2000; stories and articles contributed to Blackwood's Magazine and to other jls. *Recreations:* writing, lecturing, photography, swimming; languages (French, Egyptian). *Address:* 155 Rivermead Court, Ranelagh Gardens, SW6 3SF. *Clubs:* Royal Air Force, Hurlingham. *Died 5 Jan. 2004.*

DUDLEY, Baroness (14th in line), *cr* 1439–1440 (called out of abeyance, 1916); **Barbara Amy Felicity Hamilton;** *b* 23 April 1907; *o d* of 12th Baron Dudley and Sybil Augusta

(*d* 1958), *d* of late Rev. Canon Henry William Coventry; *S* brother, 1972; *m* 1st, 1929, Guy Raymond Hill Wallace (*d* 1967), *s* of late Gen. Hill Wallace, CB, RHA; three *s* one *d*; 2nd, 1980, Charles Anthony Crosse Hamilton. *Recreations:* floral water-colours (has exhibited Royal Watercolour Society); gardening. *Heir: e s* Hon. Jim Anthony Hill Wallace [*b* 9 Nov. 1930; *m* 1962, Nicola Jane, *d* of Lt-Col Philip William Edward Leslie Dunsterville; two *s*]. *Address:* Hill House, Kempsey, Worcestershire WR5 3PY. *T:* (01905) 820253. *Died 27 May 2002.*

DUE, Ole, Grand Cross, Order of Dannebrog, 1994 (Kt 1970); President, Court of Justice of European Communities, 1988–94; *b* 10 Feb. 1931; *s* of Stationmaster H. P. Due and Jenny Due (*née* Jensen); *m* 1954, Alice Maud Halkier Nielsen; three *s* one *d*. *Educ:* Copenhagen Univ. (Law degree, 1955). Ministry of Justice, Copenhagen: civil servant, 1955; Head of Div., 1970; Head of Dept, 1975; Appeal Court Judge *ai*, 1978; Judge, Court of Justice of EC, 1979–88. Legal Counsellor to Danish Delegn, negotiations of adhesion to EC, 1970–72; Mem., Danish Delegn to Hague Conf. on private internat. law, 1964–76. Chm., Danish Inst. of Internat. Affairs, 1995–2002. Joint Ed., series, EF-Karnov, 1973–98. Hon. Member: Gray's Inn; King's Inns, Dublin. Hon. Prof., Copenhagen, 1994. Dr *hc* Stockholm, 1991. *Publications:* (ed) EF-lovregister, 1973–75; (jtly) Juridisk Grundbog, 1975; (jtly) Kommenteret færdselslov, 1979; articles on community law, private internat. law and legal technique. *Recreation:* hiking. *Address:* Mördrupvej 116, 3060 Espergärde, Denmark. *Died 21 Jan. 2005.*

DUFFUS, Sir Herbert (George Holwell), Kt 1966; Chief Justice of Jamaica, 1968–73; *b* 30 Aug. 1908; *e s* of William Alexander Duffus, JP, and Emily Henrietta Mary (*née* Holwell); *m* 1939, Elsie Mary (*née* Hollinsed); no *c*. *Educ:* Cornwall Coll., Jamaica. Admitted as solicitor: Jamaica, 1930, England, 1948; called to the Bar, Lincoln's Inn, 1956. Resident Magistrate, Jamaica, 1946–58; acted as Puisne Judge, Jamaica, 1956–58; Puisne Judge, Jamaica, 1958–62; Judge of Appeal, Jamaica, 1962–64; Pres. Court of Appeal, 1964–67; Acting Governor General of Jamaica, 1968, 1973. Chm., Police Service Commn (Jamaica), 1958–68. Chairman: Commn of Enquiry into Prisons of Jamaica, 1954; Commn of Enquiry into the admin of justice and police brutality in Grenada, WI, 1974; Sole Commissioner, Enquiries into: Maffesanti Affair, 1968; Operations of Private Land Developers in Jamaica, 1975–76; Barbados Govt's Private Enterprises, 1977–78; Electoral Malpractices (Jamaican Local Govt Elecns), 1986. Pres., Boy Scouts Assoc., Jamaica, 1967–70. Chm., Western Regl Council, Cheshire Homes, 1975–89. Chancellor of the Church (Anglican) in Jamaica, 1973–76. *Address:* 6 Braywick Road, PO Box 243, Liguanea PO, Kingston 6, Jamaica. *T:* 9279980; 119 Main Street, Witchford, Ely, Cambs CB6 2HQ. *T:* (01353) 663281. *Died 22 Oct. 2002.*

DUFFY, Daniel; Chairman, Transport and General Workers' Union, 1988–96; *b* 3 Oct. 1929; *s* of late William and Mary Duffy; *m* Susan (*née* Salton). *Educ:* St Mungo's Academy. Transport Driver, 1947; joined S. H. & M. Assoc., 1947. Member: Exec. Council, Scottish Commercial Motormen's Union, 1960–71 (Pres., 1969–71); TGWU Exec. Council, 1971–96; TUC General Council, 1988–96. *Recreation:* bowls. *Address:* c/o TGWU, Transport House, 128 Theobalds Road, Holborn WC1X 8TN. *Died 16 March 2004.*

DUGDALE, Kathryn Edith Helen, (Lady Dugdale), DCVO 1984 (CVO 1973); JP; DL; a Lady-in-Waiting to the Queen, 1985–2002; *b* 4 Nov. 1923; *d* of Rt Hon. Oliver Stanley, PC, MC, MP and Lady Maureen Vane-Tempest Stewart; *m* 1956, Sir John Robert Stratford Dugdale, KCVO; two *s* two *d*. *Educ:* many and varied establishments. Served with WRNS. Temp. Woman of the Bedchamber to The Queen, 1955–60, Extra Woman of the Bedchamber 1960–72; Woman of the Bedchamber,

1972–2002. Pres., Shropshire Community Council. JP Salop, 1964; DL Shropshire, 1995. Employee of Greater London Fund for the Blind. *Recreations:* gardening, reading. *Address:* Tickwood Hall, Much Wenlock, Salop TF13 6NZ. *T:* (01952) 882644.
Died 12 March 2004.

DUISENBERG, Willem Frederik, (Wim); President, European Central Bank, 1998–2003; *b* 9 July 1935; *m* 1st, 1960, Tine Stelling; two *s* one *d*; 2nd, 1987, Gretta Nieuwenhuizen. *Educ:* State Univ. of Groningen (PhD 1965). Scientific Asst, State Univ. of Groningen, 1961–65; IMF, 1965–69; Special Advr, 1969–70; Exec. Dir, 1981–82, Pres. and Governor, 1982–97, De Nederlandsche Bank NV; Prof. of Macro-Economics, Univ. of Amsterdam, 1970–73; Minister of Finance, Netherlands, 1973–77; MP (Socialist Party), 1977–78; Mem. and Vice-Chm. Exec. Bd, Rabobank Nederland, 1978–81; President: BIS, 1988–90, 1994–97 (also Dir); European Monetary Inst., 1997–98. Hon. Dr New Univ. of Lisbon. Commander: Order of Orange-Nassau (Netherlands); Order of Netherlands Lion; Legion of Honour (France), 1998; Grand Cross: Order of Merit (Luxembourg); Order of Merit (Senegal); Order of the Crown (Belgium); Knight Grand Cross, Royal Order of North Star (Sweden). *Publications:* Economic Consequences of Disarmament, 1965; The IMF and the International Monetary System, 1966; The British Balance of Payments, 1969; Some Remarks on Imported Inflation, 1970. *Address:* c/o European Central Bank, Kaiserstrasse 29, 60311 Frankfurt-am-Main, Germany. *T:* (69) 13440.
Died 31 July 2005.

DUKE, Cecil Howard Armitage; Director of Establishments and Organisation, Ministry of Agriculture, Fisheries and Food, 1965–71; *b* 5 May 1912; *s* of late John William Duke and Gertrude Beatrice (*née* Armitage); *m* 1st, 1939, Eleanor Lucy (*née* Harvie) (*d* 1992); one *s* one *d*; 2nd, 1994, Joan Gladys Haig Daly (*née* Seymour) (*d* 1997). *Educ:* Selhurst Grammar Sch.; LSE. RNVR, 1942–45 (Corvettes). Entered Civil Service, 1929; Asst Princ., 1940; Princ., 1945; Private Sec. to Lord Presidents of the Council, 1951–53; Asst Sec., Land Drainage Div. and Meat Div., 1953; Under-Sec., 1965. *Recreations:* walking, gardening, watching Sussex cricket. *Address:* Boucherne Residential Home, Holloway Road, Heybridge, Maldon, Essex CM9 4SQ. *Died 19 May 2004.*

DUMMETT, George Anthony, FREng; FIChemE; Chairman, Council of Engineering Institutions, 1976–77 (Vice-Chairman, 1975); *b* 13 Oct. 1907; *s* of George Herbert Dummett and Gertrude (*née* Higgins); *m* 1st, 1931, Peggy Schaeffer; 2nd, 1939, Ursula Margarete Schubert; two *s* one *d*. *Educ:* Rugby Sch.; Birmingham Univ.; Pembroke Coll., Cambridge (MA). Research in phys. chem., Cambridge Univ., 1930–32; Research Asst, Thorncliffe Coal Distillation Ltd, 1932–35; APV Co. Ltd, then Aluminium Plant and Vessel Co. Ltd: Technical Res. Asst, 1935; Laboratory Manager, 1943; Chem. Engrg Dept Manager, 1948; Scientific Manager, 1949; Res. Dir, 1956; Dep. Man. Dir, 1965–72; Dir, APV (Holdings) Ltd, 1962–72; Dep. Chm., APV Internat., 1965–72. Chm., Res. Cttee, FBI, 1958–65; Pres., IChemE, 1968–69, Hon. Fellow, 1981. Chm., European Fedn Chemical Engrng, 1977–78. Hon. Member: Soc. de Chimie Ind., 1969; Dechema, 1976. FREng (FEng 1977). *Publications:* From Little Acorns: a history of the APV company, 1981; numerous papers on chemical and biochemical engrg, metallurgy, etc. *Recreations:* music, mountaineering, gardening, stamp collecting. *Address:* 10 Priory Crescent, Lewes, East Sussex BN7 1HP. *T:* (01273) 473731. *Clubs:* Alpine, Climbers. *Died 13 June 2001.*

DUNBOYNE, 28th Baron by Prescription, 18th Baron by Patent; Patrick Theobald Tower Butler; His Honour The Lord Dunboyne, VRD; a Circuit Judge, 1972–86; *b* 27 Jan. 1917; *e s* of 27th Baron Dunboyne and Dora Isolde Butler (*d* 1977), *e d* of Comdr F. F. Tower; *S* father, 1945; *m* 1950, Anne Marie, *d* of late Sir Victor Mallet,

GCMG, CVO; one *s* three *d*. *Educ:* Winchester; Trinity Coll., Cambridge (MA). Pres. of Cambridge Union. Lieut Irish Guards (Suppl. Res.); served European War, 1939–44 (King's Badge) (prisoner, then repatriated); Foreign Office, 1945–46. Barrister-at-Law, Middle Temple (Harmsworth Scholar), Inner Temple, South-Eastern Circuit, King's Inns, Dublin. In practice 1949–71. Recorder of Hastings, 1961–71; Dep. Chm., Quarter Sessions: Mddx, 1963–65; Kent, 1963–71; (full-time) Inner London 1971–72. Legal Aid No 2 Area Cttee, 1954–64. Commissary Gen., Diocese of Canterbury, 1959–71. Home Sec's Ward-boundaries Comr, 1960–70. Irish Genealogical Research Society: Fellow, 1982; Pres., 1971–91; Vice-Pres., 1992–; Founder Hon. Sec., Bar Lawn Tennis Soc., 1950 (Vice-Pres. 1963–), and of Irish Peers Assoc., 1963–71 (Chm., 1987–90); Pres., Wireless Telegraphy Appeal Tribunal for Eng. and Wales, 1967–70. Mem. Council, Friends of Canterbury Cathedral, 1953–71. Lt, RNVR, 1951–58, RNR, 1958–60. *Publications:* The Trial of J. G. Haigh, 1953; (with others) Cambridge Union, 1815–1939, 1953; Butler Family History, 1966, 7th edn 1990; When the States were Young, 1997. *Recreations:* rowing, lawn tennis, chess. *Heir: s* Hon. John Fitzwalter Butler [*b* 31 July 1951; *m* 1975, Diana Caroline, *yr d* of Sir Michael Williams, KCMG; one *s* three *d*]. *Address:* 36 Ormonde Gate, SW3 4HA. *T:* (020) 7352 1837. *Clubs:* Irish; International Lawn Tennis of Great Britain (Vice-Pres., Pres. 1973–83) and (hon.) of Australia, France, Germany, Monaco, Netherlands and USA; Forty Five Lawn Tennis (Pres., 1974–91); All England Lawn Tennis (Wimbledon); Pitt, Union (Cambridge). *Died 19 May 2004.*

DUNCAN, Dr George Douglas; Regional Medical Officer, East Anglian Regional Health Authority, 1973–85; *s* of late George Forman Duncan and of Mary Duncan (*née* Davidson); *m* 1949, Isobel (*née* Reid); two *s* one *d*. *Educ:* Robert Gordon's Coll., Aberdeen; Aberdeen Univ. MB, ChB 1948; DPH 1952; FFCM 1972; BA (Hons) Open Univ., 1992. Various hosp. appts; Asst MOH Stirlingshire, Divisional MO Grangemouth, 1953–57; Asst Sen. MO, Leeds RHB, 1957–60; Dep. Sen. Admin. MO, Newcastle RHB, 1960–68; Sen. Admin. MO, East Anglian RHB, 1968–73. Member: Nat. Nursing Staff Cttee and Nat. Staff Cttee for Nurses and Midwives, 1970–74; PHLS Bd, 1973–75; Central Cttee for Community Medicine, 1974–81; Chm., English Regl MOs Gp, 1981–83; Vice-Pres., FCM RCP, 1979–83. QHP 1984–87. Hon. Mem., BPA, 1988–96; Hon. Founder Fellow, RCPCH, 1996. Hon. MA Cambridge, 1986. *Address:* 12 Storey's Way, Cambridge CB3 0DT. *T:* (01223) 701409. *Died 5 May 2004.*

DUNHAM, Sir Kingsley (Charles), Kt 1972; PhD; SD; FRS 1955; FRSE; FGS; FREng; Director, Institute of Geological Sciences, 1967–75; *b* Sturminster Newton, Dorset, 2 Jan. 1910; *s* of Ernest Pedder and Edith Agnes Dunham; *m* 1936, Margaret (*d* 1998), *d* of William and Margaret Young, Choppington, Northumberland; (one *s* decd). *Educ:* Durham Johnston Sch.; Hatfield Coll., Durham Univ. (PhD 1932; Sen. Fellow, 1990); Adams House, Harvard Univ. (SD 1935). Temporary Geologist, New Mexico Bureau of Mines, 1934; HM Geological Survey of Great Britain: Geologist, 1935–45; Senior Geologist, 1946; Chief Petrographer, 1948; Prof. of Geology, Univ. of Durham, 1950–66, Emeritus, 1968–; Sub-Warden of Durham Colls, 1959–61. Miller Prof., University of Ill, 1956. Director: Weardale Minerals Ltd, 1982–86; Blackdene Minerals Ltd, 1983–86. Member: Council, Royal Society, 1965–66 (Foreign Sec., a Vice-Pres., 1971–76; Royal Medal, 1970); Council for Scientific Policy (Min. of Educn and Sci.), 1965–66. President: Instn of Mining and Metallurgy, 1963–64 (Gold Medal, 1968); Yorks Geological Soc., 1958–60 (Sorby Medal, 1964); Internat. Union of Geological Sciences, 1969–72; Geological Soc. of London, 1966–68 (Council, 1949–52, 1960–64; Bigsby Medal, 1954; Murchison Medal, 1966; Wollaston Medal, 1976); BAAS, 1972–73; Mineralogical Soc., 1975–77; NE Region, Inst. of

Geologists, 1981–; Founder Mem., Instn of Geology, 1976 (Fellow, 1985; Aberconway Medal, 1986). Trustee, British Museum (Natural History), 1963–66. Member, Geology-Geophysics Cttee, NERC, 1965–70; Chairman: Internat. Geol. Correlation Project, IUGS-UNESCO, 1973–76; Council for Environmental Science and Engineering, 1973–75. Mem. Council and UK Rep., 1972–77, Hon. Scholar, 1977–, Internat. Inst. for Applied Systems Analysis, Laxenburg, Vienna. President: Durham Univ. Soc., 1973–75; City, Dunelm and Palatinate Probus; Hon. Pres., Friends of Killhope, 1985–. FREng (Founder FEng, 1976). Hon. FIMM. Hon. Member: Royal Geol Soc. Cornwall (Bolitho Medal, 1972); Geol Soc. of India, 1972; Hon. Foreign Fellow, Geol Soc. of America; Corr. Foreign Mem., Austrian Acad. of Scis, 1971; Hon. Foreign Member: Société Géologique de Belge, 1974; Bulgarian Geological Soc., 1975. Fellow, Imperial Coll., 1976; Hon. Fellow, St John's Coll., Durham, 1991. Hon. DSc: Dunelm, 1946; Liverpool, 1967; Birmingham, 1970; Illinois, 1971; Leicester, 1972; Michigan, 1973; Canterbury, 1973; Edinburgh, 1974; Exeter, 1975; Hull, 1978; Hon. ScD Cantab, 1973; DUniv Open, 1982. Mitchell Meml Medal, City of Stoke on Trent, 1974; Haidinger Medaille der Geologischen Bundesanstalt, 1976; von Buch Medal, Deutsche Geologische Gesellschaft, 1981. Hon. Citizen of Texas, 1975. *Publications:* Geology of the Organ Mountains, 1935; Geology of the Northern Pennine Orefield, Vol. 1, 1948, 2nd edn 1990, Vol. 2 (with A. A. Wilson), 1985; (ed) Symposium on the Geology, Paragenesis and Reserves of the Ores of Lead & Zinc, 2nd edn 1950; Fluorspar, 1952; (with F. W. Anderson) Geology of Northern Skye, 1966; (with W. C. C. Rose) Geology and Hermatite Deposits of South Cumbria, 1977; articles in Quarterly Jl of Geological Soc., Mineralogical Magazine, Geological Magazine, American Mineralogist, etc. *Recreations:* music (organ and pianoforte), gardening. *Address:* Charleycroft, Quarryheads Lane, Durham DH1 3DY. *T:* (0191) 348977. *Club:* Geological Society.   *Died 5 April 2001.*

DUNKEL, Arthur; Chairman, Arthur Dunkel consultancy, Geneva, since 1993; *b* 28 Aug. 1932; *s* of Walter Dunkel and Berthe Lerch; *m* 1957, Christiane Müller-Cerda (decd); one *s* one *d*. *Educ:* Univ. of Lausanne (LèsSc écon. et comm.). Federal Office for external economic affairs, 1956: successively Head of sections for OECD matters, 1960; for cooperation with developing countries, 1964; for world trade policy, 1971; Permanent Representative of Switzerland to GATT, 1973; Delegate of Federal Council for Trade Agreements, rank of Ambassador, 1976; in this capacity, head of Swiss delegations to multilateral (GATT, UNCTAD, UNIDO, etc) and bilateral negotiations in the fields of trade, development, commodities, transfer of technology, industrialisation, agriculture, etc; Dir Gen., GATT, 1980–93. Prof. at Univs of Geneva, 1983, 1997, and Fribourg, 1987. Dr *hc* rer. pol.: Fribourg, 1980; Basle, 1992. Freedom Prize, Max Schmidheiny Foundn, 1989; Consumers Prize for World Trade, USA, 1990; Assoc. of Swiss Holding Cos Prize, 1993; Prize, Max Petitpierre Foundn, 1993. *Publications:* various articles and studies in economic, commercial, agricl and develt fields. *Address:* 56 rue du Stand, 1204 Geneva, Switzerland.
Died 8 June 2005.

DUNLAP, Air Marshal Clarence Rupert, CBE 1944; CD; RCAF retired; *b* 1 Jan. 1908; *s* of late Frank Burns Dunlap, Truro, Nova Scotia; *m* 1935, Hester, *d* of late Dr E. A. Cleveland, Vancouver, BC; one *s*. *Educ:* Acadia Univ.; Nova Scotia Technical Coll. Joined RCAF 1928 as Pilot Officer; trained as pilot and specialised in aerial survey; later specialised in armament; Dir of Armament, RCAF HQ Ottawa on outbreak of War; commanded: RCAF Station, Mountain View, Ont., Jan.-Oct. 1942; RCAF Station, Leeming, Yorks, Dec. 1942–May 1943; 331 Wing NASAF, Tunisia, May-Nov. 1943; 139 Wing TAF, Nov. 1943–Feb. 1945; 64 Base, Middleton St George, Feb.-May 1945; Dep., AMAS, AFHQ, Ottawa, 1945–48; Air Mem. for Air Plans, AFHQ, Ottawa,

1948–49; AOC North-West Air Command, Edmonton, Alberta, 1949–51; Commandant of National Defence Coll., Kingston, Ont., 1951–54; Vice Chief of the Air Staff, AFHQ, Ottawa, 1954–58; Dep. Chief of Staff, Operations, SHAPE, Paris, 1958–62; Chief of Air Staff, AFHQ, Ottawa, 1962–64; Dep. C-in-C, N Amer. Air Def. Comd, 1964–67. Hon. DCL Acadia Univ., 1955; Hon. DEng Nova Scotia Technical Coll., 1967. USA Silver Star; Croix de Guerre (with Gold Palm). *Address:* 203–1375 Newport Avenue, Victoria, BC V8S 5E8, Canada. *Clubs:* Union (Victoria); Victoria Golf.
Died 20 Oct. 2003.

DUNN, John Churchill; broadcaster; *b* 4 March 1934; *s* of late John Barrett Jackson Dunn and of Dorothy Dunn (*née* Hiscox); *m* 1958, Margaret Jennison; two *d*. *Educ:* Christ Church Cathedral Choir School, Oxford; The King's School, Canterbury. Nat. Service, RAF, 1953–55. Joined BBC as studio manager, External Service, 1956; announcer/newsreader, Gen. Overseas Service, 1958, Domestic Services, 1959; worked all radio networks before joining Light Programme/Radio 2, and subseq. freelance; *radio series include:* Just For You; Housewives' Choice; Music Through Midnight; Roundabout; Jazz at Night; Saturday Sport; Sunday Sport; 4th Dimension; Breakfast Special; It Makes Me Laugh; Nat. and European Brass Band Championships; Light Music Festivals; The John Dunn Show, 1972–98; Friday Night is Music Night; numerous TV appearances. Freeman, City of London, 1985. TV and Radio Industries Club Personality of the Year, 1971, 1984, 1986; Variety Club of GB Radio Personality of the Year, 1983; Daily Mail Silver Microphone, 1988; Sony Award, 1998. *Publications:* John Dunn's Curious Collection, 1982; Answers Please, 1994, rev. and expanded edn 1995. *Recreations:* music, wine, sitting in the sun. *Address:* c/o Jo Gurnett Personal Management, 45 Queen's Gate Mews, SW7 5QN. *T:* (020) 7584 7642.   *Died 28 Nov. 2004.*

DUNN, Air Marshal Sir Patrick Hunter, KBE 1965 (CBE 1950); CB 1956; DFC 1941; FRAeS; *b* 31 Dec. 1912; *s* of late William Alexander Dunn and Jean MacFarlane Dunn (*née* Metcalfe), Ardentinny, Argyllshire; *m* 1939, Diana Ledward Smith; two *d*. *Educ:* Glasgow Academy; Loretto; Glasgow Univ. Commissioned, 1933, Pre-war service in flying boats; as flying instructor 500 (County of Kent) Sqdn, AAF; with the Long Range Development Unit and as instructor at the Central Flying Sch. War service included command of 80 and 274 Fighter Squadrons and 71 OTU, all in Middle East (1940–42); at Air Ministry, and in Fighter Command, Sector Commander, 1945–46. Post-war service in Air Ministry, 1947–48; Malaya, 1949–50; NATO Defence Coll., 1950–52; Fighter Command, 1953–56; ADC to the Queen, 1953–58. AOC and Commandant, RAF Flying Coll., 1956–58; Deputy Air Sec., 1959–61; AOC No. 1 Group, Bomber Command, 1961–64; AOC-in-Chief, Flying Training Command, 1964–66; retired from RAF, 1967. Director i/c Management Services, British Steel Corp., 1967–68; resigned to become Dep. Chm., British Eagle Internat. Airlines Ltd; Chm., Eagle Aircraft Services, 1969; Aviation Consultant, British Steel Corporation, 1969–76. Mem. Council, Air League, 1968–73 and 1975–79 (Dep. Chm., 1972–73; Chm., Defence Cttee, 1968–73); Member: British Atlantic Cttee, 1976–93; Atlantic Council, 1993–. Dir, Gloucester, Coventry, Cricklewood and Kingston Industrial Trading Estates, 1969–75 and 1977–81. A Trustee and Governor of Loretto, 1959–81; President: Fettesian-Lorettonian Club, 1972–75; Lorettonian Soc., 1980–81; Mem. Cttee, Assoc. of Governing Bodies of Public Schs, 1976–79. *Recreations:* tennis, sailing, shooting. *Address:* Little Hillbark, Hockett Lane, Cookham Dean, Berks SL6 9UF. *Clubs:* Royal Air Force, Hurlingham; Royal Air Force Yacht.
Died 17 June 2004.

DUNN, Robert John; *b* 14 July 1946; *s* of late Robert and of Doris Dunn, Swinton, Lancs; *m* 1976, Janet Elizabeth

Wall, BD, d of late Denis Wall, Dulwich; two s. Educ: State schs. BA (Politics and History); Dip. Mgt Studies. Senior Buyer, J. Sainsbury Ltd, 1973–79. Councillor, London Borough of Southwark, 1974–78 (Opposition Minority Gp spokesman on Housing and Finance Matters); Mem. (C), Dartford BC, 1999–. MP (C) Dartford, 1979–97. PPS to Parly Under-Secs of State at DES, 1981–82, to Paymaster General and Chancellor of the Duchy of Lancaster, 1982–83; Parly Under-Sec. of State, DES, 1983–88. Mem., Parly Select Cttee on the Environment, 1981–82, on Selection, 1991–97; Jt Sec., Cons backbench Educn Cttee, 1980–81; Chairman: Cons. backbench Social Security Cttee, 1988–89; Cons. backbench Transport Cttee, 1992–97; Vice-Chm., Cons. backbench Party Organization Cttee, 1989–97; Mem. Exec. Cttee, 1922 Cttee, 1988–97. Contested (C): Eccles, Feb. and Oct. 1974; Dartford, 1997 and 2001. Vice-Pres., Eccles Conservative Assoc., 1974; President: Dartford Conservative Future (formerly Dartford Young Conservatives), 1976–; Kent Gp Young Conservatives, 1982–85; SE Area Young Conservatives, 1989–; SE Area Educn Adv. Cttee, 1982–93; Dartford br., Kent Assoc. for the Disabled, 1983–. Recreations: canvassing, American politics. Club: Dartford Rotary (Hon. Mem.).
Died 24 April 2003.

DUNNETT, Dorothy, (Lady Dunnett), OBE 1992; portrait painter, since 1950, and novelist, since 1961; b 25 Aug. 1923; d of Alexander Halliday and Dorothy Eveline Millard; m 1946, Sir Alastair MacTavish Dunnett (d 1998); two s. Educ: James Gillespie's High Sch., Edinburgh. British Civil Service, 1940–55. Non-exec. Dir, Scottish Television plc, 1979–92. Trustee: Scottish Nat. War Meml, 1962–96; Nat. Library of Scotland, 1986–. Bd Mem., Edinburgh Book Fest., 1988–95; Hon. Vice-Pres., Scottish PEN, 1997–. FRSA 1986. Literature Award, St Andrews Presbyterian Coll., Laurinburg, USA, 1993. *Publications: historical novels:* King Hereafter, 1982; *Lymond Chronicle:* The Game of Kings, 1961; Queens' Play, 1964; The Disorderly Knights, 1966; Pawn in Frankincense, 1969; Ringed Castle, 1971; Checkmate, 1975; *House of Niccolò:* Niccolò Rising, 1986; The Spring of the Ram, 1987; Race of Scorpions, 1989; Scales of Gold, 1991; The Unicorn Hunt, 1993; To Lie with Lions, 1995; Caprice and Rondo, 1997; Gemini, 2000; *mysteries:* Dolly and the Singing Bird, 1968; Dolly and the Cookie Bird, 1970; Dolly and the Doctor Bird, 1971; Dolly and the Starry Bird, 1973; Dolly and the Nanny Bird, 1976; Dolly and the Bird of Paradise, 1983; Moroccan Traffic, 1991; *non-fiction:* (with Alastair M. Dunnett and David Paterson) The Scottish Highlands, 1988. *Recreations:* travel, orchestral music, opera, ballet. *Address:* 87 Colinton Road, Edinburgh EH10 5DF. *Clubs:* Caledonian; New (Edinburgh). *Died 9 Nov. 2001.*

DUNSTAN, Rev. Prof. Gordon Reginald, CBE 1989; F. D. Maurice Professor of Moral and Social Theology, King's College, London, 1967–82, then Emeritus; Chaplain to the Queen, 1976–87; b 25 April 1917; yr s of late Frederick John Menhennet and Winifred Amy Dunstan (née Orchard); m 1949, Ruby Maud (née Fitzer); two s one d. Educ: Plymouth Corp. Gram. Sch.; University of Leeds (BA, 1st cl. Hist., 1938, Rutson Post-Grad. Schol. 1938, MA w dist. 1939); College of the Resurrection, Mirfield. FSA 1957; FKC 1974. Deacon 1941, priest 1942; Curate, King Cross, Halifax, 1941–45; Huddersfield, 1945–46; Sub Warden, St Deiniol's Library, Hawarden, 1945–49; Vicar of Sutton Courtney with Appleford, 1949–55; Lecturer, Wm Temple Coll., 1947–49; Ripon Hall, Oxford, 1953–55; Minor Canon, St George's Chapel, Windsor Castle, 1955–59; Westminster Abbey, 1959–67; Canon Theologian, Leicester Cathedral, 1966–82, Canon Emeritus, 1982–. Hon. Res. Fellow, Exeter Univ., 1984–2002. Sec., C of E Council for Social Work, 1955–63; Sec., Church Assembly Jt Bd of Studies, 1963–66; Editor of Crucible, 1962–66; Editor of Theology, 1965–75; Dep. Priest in Ordinary to the Queen, 1959–64, Priest in Ordinary, 1964–76; Select

Preacher: University of Cambridge 1960, 1977; Leeds, 1970; Hulsean Preacher, 1977. Lectures: Prideaux, Univ. of Exeter, 1968; Moorhouse, Melbourne, 1973; Stephenson, Sheffield, 1980; Gresham's Prof. in Divinity, City Univ., 1969–71. Consultant, Lambeth Conf., 1988. Mem. Council, Canterbury and York Soc., 1950–85 (Vice-Pres., 1985–). Mem. or Sec. cttees on social and ethical problems; Vice-Pres., 1965–66, and Chm. Brit. Cttee, of Internat. Union of Family Organizations, 1964–66; Vice-Pres., London Medical Gp and Inst. of Medical Ethics, 1985–2001; Pres., Tavistock Inst. of Med. Psychology, 1991–; Member: Adv. Gp on Transplant Policy, Dept of Health, 1969; Council of Tavistock Inst. of Human Relations (Vice-Pres., 1977–82), and Inst. of Marital Studies, 1969–88; Adv. Gp on Arms Control and Disarmament, FCO, 1970–74; Adv. Cttee on Animal Experiments, Home Office, 1975–89; Council, Advertising Standards Auth., 1981–93; MRC/RCOG Voluntary Licensing Authority, 1985–91; Cttee on Ethics of Gene Therapy, DoH, 1989–93; Nuffield Council on Bioethics, 1991–95; Unrelated Live Transplant Regulatory Authy, 1990–97. Pres., Devon and Cornwall Record Soc., 1984–87; Vice-Pres., UFAW, 1985–. Founder FMedSci 1998. Hon. FRSocMed 1985; Hon. MRCP 1987; FRCOG ad eundem 1991; Hon. FRCGP 1993; Hon. FRCP 1995; Hon. FRCPCH 1996. Hon. DD Exeter, 1973; Hon. LLD Leicester, 1986. *Publications:* The Family Is Not Broken, 1962; The Register of Edmund Lacy, Bishop of Exeter 1420–1455, 5 vols, 1963–72; A Digger Still, 1968; Not Yet the Epitaph, 1968; The Sacred Ministry, 1970; The Artifice of Ethics, 1974; A Moralist in the City, 1974; (ed) Duty and Discernment, 1975; (ed with M. J. Seller) Consent in Medicine, 1983; (ed with M. J. Seller) The Status of the Human Embryo: perspectives from moral tradition, 1988; (ed with D. Callahan) Biomedical Ethics: an Anglo-American dialogue, 1988; (ed with E. A. Shinebourne) Doctors' Decisions: ethical conflicts in medical practice, 1989; (ed) The Human Embryo: Aristotle and the Arabic and European Traditions, 1990; (ed with P. J. Lachmann) Death, Dying and the Medical Duty, 1996. *Recreations:* small islands, domus and rus. *Address:* Flat 33, Mapledene, 10 St Agnes Road, Birmingham B13 9PW. *Died 15 Jan. 2004.*

DURBIN, Leslie Gordon James, CBE 1976; MVO 1943; silversmith; b 21 Feb. 1913; s of late Harry Durbin and of Lillian A. Durbin; m 1940, Phyllis Ethel Ginger, RWS; one s one d. Educ: Central Sch. of Arts and Crafts, London. Apprenticed to late Omar Ramsden, 1929–39; full-time schol., 1938–39, travelling schol., 1939–40, both awarded by Worshipful Co. of Goldsmiths. Started working on own account in workshop of Francis Adam, 1940–41. RAF, Allied Central Interpretation Unit, 1941–45. Wkg partnership with Leonard Moss, 1945–75. Commissioned by Jt Cttee of Assay Offices of GB to design Silver Jubilee Hall Mark; designed regional variants of pound coin for Royal Mint, 1983. Retrospective exhibn, Leslie Durbin, 50 years of Silversmithing, Goldsmiths' Hall, 1982. Hon. LLD Cambridge, 1963. Council of Industrial Design Awards for Silver for the 70's; MVO awarded for work on Stalingrad Sword. *Died 24 Feb. 2005.*

DURBIN, Phyllis Ethel, (Mrs Leslie Durbin); see Ginger, P. E.

DURHAM, Sir Kenneth, Kt 1985; Chairman: Unilever, 1982–86; Kingfisher (formerly Woolworth Holdings) plc, 1986–90 (non-executive Deputy Chairman, 1985–86); Deputy Chairman, British Aerospace, 1986–90 (Board Member, 1980–90); b 28 July 1924; s of late George Durham and Bertha (née Aspin); m 1946, Irene Markham; one s one d. Educ: Queen Elizabeth Grammar Sch., Blackburn; Univ. of Manchester (Hatfield Schol.; BSc Hons Physics). Flight Lieut, RAF, 1942–46. ARE, Harwell, 1950; Unilever: joined Res. Lab., Port Sunlight, 1950, Head of Lab., 1961; Head, Res. Lab., Colworth, Bedford, 1965; assumed responsibility for animal feed interests, 1970; Chm., BOCM Silcock Ltd, 1971; Dir,

Unilever Ltd, 1974, Vice-Chm., 1978; Dir, Unilever NV, 1974–86. Board Mem., Delta PLC, 1984–; Dir, Morgan Grenfell Hldgs, 1986–90. Chairman: Food, Drink and Packaging Machinery EDC, NEDO, 1981–86; Trade Policy Res. Centre, 1982–89; Industry and Commerce Liaison Cttee, Royal Jubilee Trusts, 1982–87; Economic and Financial Policy Cttee, CBI, 1983–86; Priorities Bd for Govt Agricl Depts and AFRC, 1984–87; Member: British-N America Cttee, 1982–87; British Shippers Council, 1982–86; Bd, British Exec. Service Overseas, 1982–86; Adv. Cttee, CVCP, 1984–; Governing Body, ICC UK, 1984–88; ACARD, 1984–86; European Adv. Council, NY Stock Exchange, 1985–; Council for Industry and Higher Educn, 1985–; Adv. Panel, Science Policy Res. Unit, Sussex Univ., 1985–; Adv. Bd, Industrial Res. Labs, Durham Univ., 1985–; President: ABCC, 1986–87; BAAS, 1986–87. Attended Harvard Advanced Management Program, 1962; Member: Council, PSI, 1978–85; Council, Royal Free Hosp. Sch. of Med., 1984–. Vice-President: Liverpool Sch. of Tropical Medicine, 1982–; Opportunities for the Disabled, 1982–88; Help the Aged, 1986–; Trustee: Leverhulme Trust, 1974–98; Civic Trust, 1982–. Governor, NIESR, 1983–. CCMI (CBIM 1978); FIGD 1983. Hon. FBA 1997. Hon. LLD Manchester, 1984; Hon. DSc: Loughborough, 1984; QUB. Comdr, Order of Orange Nassau (Netherlands), 1985. *Publications:* Surface Activity and Detergency, 1960; various scientific papers. *Recreations:* walking, golf. *Club:* Athenæum.
Died 17 Feb. 2005.

DURIE, Sir Alexander (Charles), Kt 1977; CBE 1973; Vice-President, The Automobile Association, since 1977 (Director-General, 1964–77); *b* 15 July 1915; *er s* of late Charles and Margaret Durie (*née* Gardner), Shepton Mallet, Somerset; *m* 1941, Joyce, *o c* of late Lionel and Helen Hargreaves (*née* Hirst), Leeds and Bridlington, Yorks; one *s* one *d*. *Educ:* Queen's Coll., Taunton. Served War of 1939–45, Royal Artillery; Gunnery Staff Course (IG), 1941; Lt-Col 1945. Joined Shell-Mex and BP Ltd, 1933; Dir, Shell Co. of Australia Ltd, 1954–56; Dir, 1962, Man. Dir, 1963–64, Shell-Mex and BP Ltd; Director: Mercantile Credit Co. Ltd, 1973–80; Thomas Cook Group Ltd, 1974–79; Private Patients Plan Ltd, 1977–87 (a Vice-Pres., 1987–); H. Clarkson (Holdings) Ltd, 1978–85; Chelsea Building Soc., 1979–87. Gen. Commissioner of Income Tax, 1960–85; Member, Government Inquiries into: Civilianisation of Armed Forces, 1964; Cars for Cities, 1964; Road Haulage Operators' Licensing, 1978. FCIT; FIMgt (FBIM 1959; Council Mem., 1962–73; Chm. Exec. Cttee, 1962–65; Vice-Chm. Council, 1962–67; Chm., Bd of Fellows, 1970–73; Verulam Medal 1973); Member: Nat. Road Safety Adv. Council, 1965–68; Adv. Council on Road Res., 1965–68; Brit. Road Fedn Ltd, 1962 (Vice-Pres., 1978); Council, Internat. Road Fedn Ltd, London, 1962–64; Council, Motor and Cycle Trades Benevolent Fund, 1959–73; Marketing Cttee, BTA, 1970–77; Adv. Cttee on Traffic and Safety, TRRL, 1973–77; Vice-President: British Assoc. of Industrial Editors, 1959–71; Alliance Internationale de Tourisme, 1965–71 (Pres., 1971–77); Chm., Indep. Schs Careers Orgn, 1969–73 (Vice-Pres., 1973–). Governor: Ashridge Coll., 1963–78 (Vice Pres., 1978–93); Queen's Coll., Taunton, 1969–83. Chm. Council, Imperial Soc. of Knights Bachelor, 1986–88 (Mem., 1978–). Pres., Surrey CCC, 1984–85 (Mem. Cttee, 1970–80; Vice-Pres., 1980–84, 1985–); Vice-Pres., Hampshire CCC, 1984–. Freeman of City of London and Liveryman, Worshipful Co. of Paviors, 1965. Hon. FInstHE 1969. Spanish Order of Touristic Merit Silver Medal, 1977. *Recreations:* cricket, golf, racing. *Address:* The Garden House, Windlesham, Surrey GU20 6AD. *T:* (01276) 472035. *Clubs:* MCC; Royal and Ancient; Berkshire Golf. *Died 5 Jan. 2001.*

DURIE, Rev. Ian Geoffrey Campbell, CBE 1991 (OBE 1987); Curate, St Mark's, Battersea Rise, since 1998; *b* 21 Aug. 1944; *s* of late Frederick Robert Edwin Durie and of Joan Elizabeth Campbell Durie (*née* Learoyd); *m* 1968, Carolyn Jane Whitehead; one *d*. *Educ:* Fettes Coll., Edinburgh; RMA, Sandhurst; St John's Coll., Cambridge (MA Mech. Sci.); St John's Theol Coll., Nottingham (MTh). Commnd RA; Adjt, 27 Field Regt, RA, 1973; sc 1974; Battery Comd, 29 Commando Regt, RA, 1979; SO1 Plans, Falklands Is, 1984; CO, 29 Commando Regt, RA, 1984; Instr, Staff Coll., 1987; Chief Instr, Tactics, Royal Sch. of Artillery, 1988; Commander: RA 1st Armd Div., 1989; RA 1st (UK) Armd Div. Artillery Gp, Op. Desert Sabre (Gulf War), 1991; rcds, 1992; Dir, Land Warfare, 1992; Dir, RA, 1994–96, retired in rank of Maj.-Gen. Col Comdt, RA, 1996–2002; Rep. Col Comdt, RA, 2001–02. Ordained deacon, 1998, priest, 1999. Hon. Exec. Chm., ACCTS Mil. Ministries Internat. (formerly Assoc. of Christian Confs and Teaching Services), 1998–; Patron, Christian Discovery Trust, Scotland, 1995–2003. *Recreations:* the ethics of war and revolution, golf (of sorts), garden, fishing, family. *Address:* c/o St Mark's Church, Battersea Rise, SW11 1EJ. *Died 21 April 2005.*

DURKIN, Air Marshal Sir Herbert, KBE 1976; CB 1973; CEng, FIEE; Controller of Engineering and Supply (RAF), 1976–78; *b* 31 March 1922; *s* of Herbert and Helen Durkin, Burnley, Lancs; *m* 1951, Dorothy Hope, *d* of Walter Taylor Johnson, Burnley; one *s* two *d*. *Educ:* Burnley Grammar Sch.; Emmanuel Coll., Cambridge (MA). Commissioned into Tech. Br., RAF, Oct. 1941. Served War, with No 60 Gp, until 1945. India, 1945–47, becoming ADC to AOC-in-C India; Central Bomber Estabt, 1947–50; Sqdn Ldr, 1950; Atomic Weapons Research Estabt, 1950–52; RAF Staff Coll., 1953; Chief Signals Officer, AHQ, Iraq, 1954–56; Wing Comdr, Chief Instr of Signals Div. of RAF Tech. Coll., 1956–58; Air Ministry, 1958–60; jssc, 1961; HQ, 2 ATAF, 1961–63; Gp Capt 1962; Sen. Tech. Staff Officer, HQ Signals Command, 1964–65; Comdt, No 2 Sch. of Tech. Trg, Cosford, 1965–67; Air Cdre, 1967; Director of Eng (Policy), MoD, 1967–69; IDC, 1970; Air Vice Marshal, 1971; AOC No 90 Group, RAF, 1971–73; Dir-Gen. Engineering and Supply Management, 1973–76. Pres., IEE, 1980 (Dep. Pres., 1979). Pres., Assoc. of Lancastrians in London, 1988–90. Freeman, City of London, 1988. *Recreation:* golf. *Address:* Willowbank, Drakes Drive, Northwood, Middlesex HA6 2SL. *T:* (01923) 823167. *Clubs:* Royal Air Force; Moor Park Golf (Capt., 1988). *Died 12 April 2004.*

DUTHIE, Prof. Robert Buchan, CBE 1984; MA Oxon; MB, ChM; FRCSE, FRCS; Nuffield Professor of Orthopædic Surgery, Oxford University, 1966–92, then Emeritus; Professorial Fellow, Worcester College, Oxford, 1966–92, then Emeritus Fellow; Surgeon, Nuffield Orthopædic Centre, Oxford, 1966–92; Civilian Consultant Adviser in Orthopaedic Surgery to Royal Navy, since 1976; *b* 4 May 1925; 2nd *s* of late James Andrew Duthie and late Elizabeth Jean Duthie, Edinburgh; *m* 1956, Alison Ann Macpherson Kittermaster, MA; two *s* two *d*. *Educ:* Aberdeen Grammar Sch.; King Edward VI Gram. Sch., Chelmsford; Heriot-Watt Coll., Edinburgh; University of Edinburgh Med. Sch. Robert Jones Prize 1947, MB, ChB 1948, ChM (with dist.) (Gold Medal for Thesis) 1956, University of Edinburgh; FRCSE 1953; Hon. FACS 1987. Ho. Surg., Royal Infirmary, 1948–49; Ho. Phys., Western Gen. Hosp., Edinburgh, 1949. Active service in Malaya, RAMC, 1949–51. Registrar, Royal Infirmary, Edinburgh, 1951–53; David Wilkie Res. Schol. of University of Edinburgh, 1953; Res. Fellow of Scottish Hosps Endowment Research Trust, Edinburgh, 1953–56; Res. Fellow, Nat. Cancer Inst., Bethesda, USA, 1956–57; Extern. Mem. of MRC in Inst. of Orthopædics, London and Sen. Registrar, 1957–58; Prof. of Orthopædic Surg., University of Rochester Sch. of Medicine and Dentistry and Orthopædic Surg.-in-Chief, University of Rochester Med. Centre, 1958–66. Consultant Adviser in Orthopaedics and Accident Surgery to DHSS, 1971–80. Mem., Royal Commn on Civil Liability and Compensation for Personal Injury, 1973–78;

Chairman: Adv. Cttee of Res. in Artificial Limbs and Appliances, DHSS, 1975; Working Party on Orthopaedic Services to Sec. of State for Social Services, 1980–81. Governor, Oxford Sch. for Boys, 1967–91 (Chm., 1986–91). Fellow Brit. Orthopædic Assoc. (Pres., 1983–84); Pres., Internat. Soc. of Research in Orthopaedics and Trauma, 1987–90; Member: Internat. Soc. for Orthopædic Surgery and Traumatology; Orthopædic Research Soc.; Inter-urban Orthopædic Club: Internat. Orthopædic Club. Amer. Rheumatism Assoc.; Hon. Member: Portuguese Soc. of Orthopaedic Surgery and Traumatology; Japanese Orthopaedic Assoc.; Corresponding Member: Assoc. of Orthopaedic Surgery and Traumatology, Yugoslavia; German Soc. of Orthopaedics and Traumatology; Hon. Fellow, Austrian Traumatology Assoc. Hon. DSc Rochester, NY, 1982. President's Prize, Soc. Internat. de Chirurgie, 1957. Commander, SMO, Malta. *Publications:* (co-author) Textbook of Orthopædic Surgery, 8th edn, 1983, 9th edn, 1996; contribs to med. and surg. jls relating to genetics, histochemistry, transplantation, pathology, neoplasia of musculo-skeletal tissues, and clinical subjects. *Recreations:* writing, stained glass. *Address:* Apartment 14, Prebendal Court, Station Road, Shipton-under-Wychwood, Oxon OX7 6BB. *T:* (01993) 831593.   *Died 25 Dec. 2005.*

DYMOKE, Rear-Adm. Lionel Dorian, CB 1974; *b* 18 March 1921; *s* of Henry Lionel Dymoke and Dorothy (*née* Briscoe); *m* 1st, 1952, Patricia Pimlott (*d* 1968); one *s*; 2nd, 1970, Iris Hemsted (*née* Lamplough). *Educ:* Nautical Coll., Pangbourne. Entered Royal Navy, 1938; Comdr 1953; Captain 1961; Rear-Adm. 1971; retired 1976. *Address:* 3 Woodland Place, Bath BA2 6EH. *T:* (01225) 464228.   *Died 8 Jan. 2004.*

DYMOND, Michael John; Chief Executive (formerly Director General), Defence Accounts Agency, Ministry of Defence, 1989–95; *b* 11 Aug. 1936; *s* of Archibald William John Dymond and Violet Eileen Mary Dymond (*née* Young); *m* 1963, Angela Rosalind Terry; one *s* one *d.* *Educ:* Colston's Sch., Bristol; Merton Coll., Oxford (BA Jurisp. 1960; MA). ACA 1963, FCA 1973. Chartered Accountant and Auditor, Deloitte & Co., 1960–66; Passenger Fares Officer, Audit, British Railways, 1966–70; Group Financial Controller, Metals Research Ltd, 1970–73; Asst Dir, Audit, MoD, 1973–76; Careers Officer for Accountants, DTI, 1976–81; Dep. Dir Gen. Management Audit, MoD, 1981–88. *Recreations:* singing, music, cricket, stamps. *Address:* Laburnum Cottage, 4 Hughes Court, High Street, Rode, Bath BA3 6NX. *T:* (01373) 830149.   *Died 21 Feb. 2001.*

DYSART, Countess of (11th in line), *cr* 1643; **Rosamund Agnes Greaves;** Baroness Huntingtower, 1643; *b* 15 Feb. 1914; *d* of Major Owain Greaves (*d* 1941), RHG, and Wenefryde Agatha, Countess of Dysart (10th in line); *S* mother, 1975. *Heir: sister* Lady Katherine Grant of Rothiemurchus [*b* 1 June 1918; *m* 1941, Colonel John Peter Grant of Rothiemurchus, MBE (*d* 1987); one *s* one *d*]. *Address:* Bryn Garth, Grosmont, Abergavenny, Gwent NP7 8LS.   *Died Dec. 2003.*

E

EABORN, Prof. Colin, PhD, DSc (Wales); FRS 1970; FRSC; Professor of Chemistry, University of Sussex, 1962–88, then Emeritus; *b* 15 March 1923; *s* of Tom Stanley and Caroline Eaborn; *m* 1949, Joyce Thomas. *Educ:* Ruabon Grammar Sch., Denbighshire; U C of N Wales, Bangor (Hon. Fellow, 2000). Asst Lecturer, 1947, Lecturer, 1950, and Reader 1954, in Chemistry, Univ. of Leicester. Research Associate, Univ. of California at Los Angeles, 1950–51; Robert A. Welch Visiting Scholar, Rice Univ., Texas, 1961–62; Erskine Fellow, Univ. of Canterbury (NZ), 1965; Pro-Vice Chancellor (Science), Univ. of Sussex, 1968–72; Dist. Prof., New Mexico State Univ., 1973; Canadian Commonwealth Fellow, Univ. of Victoria, BC, 1976; Lectures: Riccoboni, Univ. of Padua, 1977; Gilman, Iowa State Univ., 1978; R. A. Welch Vis., Texas, 1983. Hon. Sec., Chemical Society, 1964–71; Vice-Pres., Dalton Div., 1971–75: Mem. Council, Royal Soc., 1978–80, 1988–89; Chm., British Cttee on Chemical Educn, 1967–69; Mem., Italy/UK Mixed Commn, 1972–80. Mem., Editl Adv. Bd, Organometallics, 1999–2002. Hon. DSc Sussex, 1990. F. S. Kipping Award, Amer. Chem. Soc., 1964; Organometallic Award, Chem. Soc., 1975; Ingold Lectureship and Medal, Chem. Soc., 1976; Main Gp Award, Chem. Soc., 1989. *Publications:* Organosilicon Compounds, 1960; Organometallic Compounds of the Group IV Elements, Vol. 1, Part 1, 1968; numerous research papers, mainly in Jl of Chem. Soc., Organometallics and Jl of Organometallic Chemistry (Regional Editor, 1963–95). *Address:* 3 Ridgeway Paddock, Kingston, Lewes BN7 3LA. *T:* (01273) 473680; *e-mail:* c.eaborn@sussex.ac.uk.   *Died 22 Feb. 2004.*

EADIE, Ellice Aylmer, CBE 1966; Standing Counsel to General Synod of Church of England, 1972–80; *b* 30 June 1912; *d* of late Rt Rev. R. T. Hearn, LLD, sometime Bishop of Cork, and Dr M. E. T. Hearn, MD, FRCPI; *m* 1946, John Harold Ward Eadie (*d* 1995). *Educ:* Cheltenham Ladies' Coll.; St Hugh's Coll., Oxford. Called to the Bar, Gray's Inn, 1936. Flt Officer, WAAF, 1941–46. Parliamentary Counsel Office, 1949–72, Parly Counsel, 1968–72.   *Died 31 March 2001.*

EARLE, Very Rev. George Hughes, SJ; MA; project worker, Jesuit Refugee Service, since 2000; *b* 20 Sept. 1925; *s* of late Lieut-Col F. W. Earle, DSO, JP, Morestead House, Winchester, and late Marie Blanche Lyne-Stevens. *Educ:* Pilgrims' Sch., Winchester; Westminster Sch.; Peter Symonds' Sch., Winchester; Balliol Coll., Oxford. Served with RAF, 1943–47. Joined Soc. of Jesus, 1950. Taught at Beaumont Coll., 1955–57, and Stonyhurst Coll., 1962–63; Headmaster, Stonyhurst Coll., 1969–72; Superior of Southwell House, 1972–75; Educnl Asst to Provincial, 1972–75; Co-editor, The Way, 1974–78; Rector of St Aloysius, Glasgow, 1978–81; Superior, English Province, SJ, 1981–87; Dean of Studies, St Joseph's Theol Inst., Cedara, Natal, 1990–92; Co-ordinator of Seminaries, S African Bishops' Conf., 1993–94; Bursar, Murray House, Johannesburg, 1998–99. *Recreations:* none; wasting time. *Address:* 112 Thornbury Road, Osterley, Middx TW7 4NN.   *Died 10 Oct. 2003.*

EASTWOOD, John Stephen; a Recorder, 1987–92; Regional Chairman of Industrial Tribunals, Nottingham Region, 1983–92; *b* 27 April 1925; *s* of Rev. John Edgar Eastwood and Elfreda Eastwood; *m* 1949, Nancy (*née* Gretton); one *s* two *d*. *Educ:* Denstone College, Uttoxeter. Solicitor. RN (Coder), 1943–46. Articles, and Asst Sol. to Leics CC, 1946–50; Asst Sol., Salop CC, 1950–53; Sen. Asst Sol., Northants CC, 1953–58; Partner, Wilson & Wilson, Solicitors, Kettering, 1958–76; Chm., Industrial Tribunals, 1976–83; Asst Recorder, 1983–87. *Recreations:* music, painting, photography, walking, gardening, exploring British Isles, grandchildren. *Address:* 59 Beatrice Road, Kettering, Northants NN16 9QS. *T:* (01536) 514906.   *Died 19 Sept. 2003.*

EAYRS, Prof. John Thomas, PhD, DSc; Sands Cox Professor of Anatomy, University of Birmingham, 1968–77; *b* 23 Jan. 1913; *e s* of late Thomas William Eayrs, AMICE, and Florence May (*née* Clough); *m* 1941, Frances Marjorie Sharp; one *s* two *d*. *Educ:* King Edward's, Birmingham; University of Birmingham. In industry until 1938. War service: Pte Royal Warwicks Regt, 1939–40; 2nd Lieut Manchester Regt, 1940; Lieut 1940; Capt. 1941; Major 1942; Worcester Regt, 1943; sc Staff Coll., Camberley, 1944. University of Birmingham: Peter Thompson Prize, 1947; John Barritt Melson Memorial Gold Medal, 1947; Lectr in Anatomy, 1948; Bertram Windle Prize, 1950; Sen. Lectr 1955; Research Fellow, Calif. Inst. of Technology, 1956–57; Reader in Comparative Neurology, Birmingham, 1958; Henry Head Research Fellow, Royal Society, London, 1957–62; Prof. of Neuroendocrinology, Birmingham, 1961; Fitzmary Prof. of Physiology, BPMF, London Univ., 1963–68. Governor, King Edward's Foundn, Birmingham, 1968–77. *Publications:* scientific papers dealing with developmental neuroendocrinology and behaviour in Jl Endocrin., Jl Anat. (London), Anim. Behav., etc. *Recreations:* genealogy, foreign travel and languages. *Address:* 51 Old Street, Upton upon Severn, Worcester WR8 0HN.   *Died 16 Aug. 2001.*

EBAN, Abba; a Member of the Knesset, 1959–88; Minister of Foreign Affairs, Israel, 1966–74; *b* 2 Feb. 1915, Cape Town, SA; *s* of Avram and Alida Solomon; *né* Aubrey Solomon; *m* 1945, Susan Ambache; one *s* one *d*. *Educ:* Queens' Coll., Cambridge (Triple First; BA 1937; MA 1941; Hon. Fellow, 1998). Res. Fellow and Tutor for Oriental Langs, Pembroke Coll., Cambridge, 1938. Liaison officer of Allied HQ with Jewish population in Jerusalem, 1942–44; Chief Instructor, Middle East Arab Centre, Jerusalem, 1944–46; Jewish Agency, 1946–47; Liaison Officer with UN Special Commn on Palestine, 1947; UN: Representative of provisional govt of Israel, 1948; Permanent rep., 1949–59; Vice-Pres., General Assembly, 1953; Ambassador to USA, 1950–59; Minister without Portfolio, 1959–60; Minister of Educn and Culture, 1960–63; Dep. Prime Minister, 1963–66. Pres., Weizmann Inst. of Science, 1958–66; Vice-Pres., UN Conf. on Sci. and Technol. in Advancement of New States, 1963; Mem., UN Adv. Cttee on Sci. and Technol. for Develt. Fellow: World Acad. of Arts and Scis; Amer. Acad. of Arts and Scis; Amer. Acad. of Pol Science. Hon. Doctorates include: New York; Boston; Maryland; Cincinnati; Temple; Brandeis; Yeshiva; Aberdeen. TV series: Personal Witness, 1992; Civilization and the Jews, 1994; TV prog., Brink of Peace, 1997. *Publications:* The Modern Literary Movement in Egypt, 1944; Maze of Justice, 1946; Social and Cultural Problems in the Middle East, 1947; The Toynbee Heresy, 1955; Voice of Israel, 1957; Tide of Nationalism, 1959; Chaim Weizmann: a collective biography, 1962; Reality and Vision in the Middle East (Foreign Affairs), 1965; Israel in the World, 1966; My People, 1968; My Country, 1972; An Autobiography, 1978; The New Diplomacy: international affairs in the modern age, 1983; Heritage, Civilisation and the Jews, 1985; Personal Witness: Israel through my eyes, 1993; Diplomacy for the Next Century, 1998; articles in English, French, Hebrew and Arabic. *Address:* PO Box 394, Herzliya 46747, Israel.   *Died 17 Nov. 2002.*

EBERHART, Richard (Ghormley); Professor Emeritus of English and Poet in Residence, Dartmouth College, USA; Florida Ambassador of the Arts, since 1984; *b* Austin, Minn, 5 April 1904; *s* of late Alpha La Rue Eberhart and Lena Eberhart (*née* Lowenstein); *m* 1941, Helen Elizabeth Butcher (*d* 1993), Christ Church, Cambridge, Mass; one *s* one *d*. *Educ:* Dartmouth Coll., USA (AB); St John's Coll., Cambridge Univ., England (BA, MA; Hon. Fellow, 1986); Harvard Univ. Grad. Sch. of Arts and Sciences. Taught English, 1933–41, also tutor to son of King Prajadhipok of Siam for a year. Served War in USN Reserve finishing as Lieut-Comdr, 1946; subseq. entered Butcher Polish Co., Boston, Mass, as Asst Man., finishing as Vice-Pres. (subseq. Hon. Vice-Pres. and Mem. Bd of Directors). Founder (and first Pres.) Poets' Theatre Inc., Cambridge, Mass, 1950. Called back to teaching, 1952, and has served as Poet in Residence, Prof., or Lecturer at Univ. of Washington, Univ. of Conn., Wheaton Coll., Princeton; Prof. of English and Poet in Residence at Dartmouth Coll., 1956, Class of 1925 Chair, 1968 (on leave of absence as Consultant in Poetry to the Library of Congress, 1959–61). Visiting Professor: Univ. of Washington, 1967, Jan.–June 1972; Columbia Univ., 1975; Distinguished Vis. Prof., Florida Univ., 1974– (President's Medallion, 1977); Regents Prof., Univ. of California, Davis, 1975; First Wallace Stevens Fellow, Timothy Dwight Coll., Yale, 1976. Advisory Cttee on the Arts, for the National Cultural Center (later John F. Kennedy Memorial Center), Washington, 1959; Member: Amer. Acad. and Inst. of Arts and Letters, 1960; Nat. Acad. of Arts and Sciences, 1967; Amer. Acad. of Arts and Letters, 1982. Elliston Lecturer on Poetry, University of Cincinnati, 1961. Fellow, Acad. of Amer. Poets, 1969 (Nat. Book Award, 1977). Poet Laureate of New Hampshire, 1979–84. Apptd Hon. Consultant in American Letters, The Library of Congress, 1963–66; reapptd, 1966–69. Hon. Pres., Poetry Soc. of America, 1972. Participant, Poetry International, London, 1973; Exhibn, Dartmouth Coll. Library, 1984. Hon. LittD: Dartmouth Coll., 1954; Skidmore Coll., 1966; Coll. of Wooster, 1969; Colgate Univ., 1974; St Lawrence Univ., 1985; Hon. DHL, Franklin Pierce, 1978. Shelley Meml Prize; Bollingen Prize, 1962; Pulitzer Prize, 1966; Phi Beta Kappa poem, Harvard, 1967; Hon. Mem., Alpha Chapter, Mass, 1967; New York Qly Poetry Day Award, 1980; Sarah Josepha Hale Award, Richards Library, Newport, NH, 1982; Robert Frost Medal, Poetry Soc. of America, 1986. Diploma: World Acad. of Arts and Culture, Republic of China, 1981; Internat. Poets Acad., Madras, India, 1987. Richard Eberhart Day: 14 July 1982, RI; 14 Oct. 1982, Dartmouth; Eberhart at Eighty, celebration at Univ. of Florida, 4–6 April 1984. *Publications:* (concurrently in England and America): A Bravery of Earth, 1930; Reading the Spirit, 1936; Selected Poems, 1951; Undercliff, Poems, 1946–53, also Great Praises, 1957; Collected Poems 1930–1960, 1960; Collected Verse Plays, 1962; The Quarry, 1964; Selected Poems 1930–1965, New Directions, 1965; Thirty One Sonnets, 1967; Shifts of Being, 1968; Fields of Grace, 1972 (Nat. Book Award nominee, 1973); Poems to Poets, 1975; Collected Poems 1930–1976, 1976; To Eberhart from Ginsberg: a letter about 'Howl', 1956, 1976; Of Poetry and Poets (criticism), 1979; Ways of Light, 1980; Survivors, 1980; Four Poems, 1980; New Hampshire/ Nine Poems, 1980; Chocorua, 1981; Florida Poems, 1981; The Long Reach, 1984; Collected Poems 1930–1986, 1988; Maine Poems, 1989; New and Collected Poems, 1990; Recorded Readings of his Poetry, 1961, 1968; four documentary films, 1972, 1975, 1986, 1987; *Festschriften:* (in New England Review, 1980) Richard Eberhart: a celebration; (in Negative Capability, 1986) Richard Eberhart. *Recreations:* swimming, cruising, tennis, flying 7-ft kites. *Address:* 80 Lyme Road #161, Hanover, NH 03755-1230, USA. *Clubs:* Century (New York); Buck's Harbor Yacht (S Brooksville, Maine); Signet (Harvard). *Died 9 June 2005.*

EBSWORTH, Hon. Dame Ann (Marian), DBE 1992; a Judge of the High Court of Justice, Queen's Bench Division, 1992–2001; *b* 19 May 1937; *d* of late Arthur E. Ebsworth, OBE, BEM, RM and Hilda Mary Ebsworth. *Educ:* Notre Dame Convent, Worth, Sussex; Portsmouth High Sch., GPDST; Royal Holloway Coll., London Univ. (BA Hons (History)). Called to Bar, Gray's Inn, 1962; Bencher, 1992. A Recorder of the Crown Court, 1978–83; a Circuit Judge, 1983–92. Member: Mental Health Review Tribunal, 1975–83, 1984–90; Parole Bd, 1989–92; Civil and Family Cttee, Judicial Studies Bd, 1991–92. *Recreations:* Italian travel, medieval history, needlework. *Died 4 April 2002.*

ECCLES, Geoffrey, OBE 1986; CEng; Regional Chairman, British Gas plc, Eastern, 1987–90; *b* 25 Dec. 1925; *s* of George William Eccles and Elsie Eccles (*née* Hepworth); *m* 1946, Marjorie Jackson; one *s*. *Educ:* Halifax and Bradford Colls of Technol. MIGEM (MIGasE 1961). West Midlands Gas Board: various technical and managerial appts, incl. Asst Regl Distribution Engr, 1964; Grid Engr, 1967; Dep. Pipelines Engr, Gas Council, 1971; Pipelines Engr, British Gas Corp., 1980; Dep. Chm., Eastern Gas, 1984. *Recreations:* hill walking, reading, music. *Address:* 3 Little Gaddesden House, Little Gaddesden, Berkhamsted, Herts HP4 1PL. *T:* (01442) 842731. *Died 15 Sept. 2005.*

EDDEY, Prof. Howard Hadfield, CMG 1974; FRCS, FRACS, FACS; Foundation Professor of Surgery, University of Melbourne, at Austin Hospital and Repatriation General Hospital, 1967–75, then Emeritus; also Dean of Austin Hospital and Repatriation General Hospital Clinical School, 1971–75; *b* Melbourne, 3 Sept. 1910; *s* of Charles Howard and Rachel Beatrice Eddey; *m* 1940, Alice Paul (decd); two *s* one *d*. *Educ:* Melbourne Univ.; St Bartholomew's Hosp. Med. Sch. (BSc, MB BS, 1934). FRCS 1938 (Hallett Prize); FRACS 1941; FACS 1964. Served War, 1941–45: AAMC, Major and Surgical Specialist; served in PoW camps: Changi (Singapore); Sandakan and Kuching (Borneo). Hon. Surgeon: Prince Henry Hosp., Melbourne, 1946–47; Alfred Hosp., Melbourne, 1947; Royal Melbourne Hosp., 1947–67; Peter MacCallum Clinic; Cons. Surg., Royal Melbourne and Royal Women's Hosps, 1967; Mem., Faculty of Med., Univ. of Melbourne, 1950–75 (Mem. Convocation, 1965–67); Indep. Lectr in Surgical Anatomy, Univ. of Melb., 1950–65; Dean, Royal Melb. Hosp. Clin. Sch., 1965–67. Colombo Plan Visitor to India, 1960–65; Cons. in Surg., Papuan Med. Coll., 1965–68. Member: Cancer Inst. Bd, 1958–67; Med. and Sci. Cttee, Anti-Cancer Council of Vic., 1958–67; Chm., Melb. Med. Postgrad. Cttee, 1963–71; Vice-Pres., Aust. Postgrad. Fedn in Med., 1965–71 (Life Governor, 1972). Member: AMA, 1935; Council, RACS, 1967–75 (Mem. Bd of Examrs, 1958–75, Chm. Bd, 1968–73; Hon. Librarian, 1968–75). Member: Med. Bd of Vic., 1968–77; Austin Hosp. Bd of Management, 1971–77 (Vice-Pres., 1975–77; Life Governor, 1977). Hunterian Prof., RCS, 1960; Vis. Prof. of Surg., 1962, External Examr in Surg., 1970, Univ. of Singapore; Leverhulme Fellow, Univ. of Melb., 1974; Vis. Prof. of Surg., Univ. of Hong Kong, 1974. Howard Eddey Medal, named in 1982 by RACS and awarded to most successful cand., Part I exam (surgery) for FRACS in SE Asia, in recognition of dist. service to RACS. Hon. Surgeon to HRH Prince Charles on his visit to Victoria, 1974. Melbourne and Australian Universities Lacrosse Blue. *Publications:* many, in sci. jls, particularly in relation to diseases of salivary glands and cancer of mouth. *Recreation:* reading. *Died 16 Sept. 2004.*

EDIE, His Honour Thomas Ker; a Circuit Judge, South Eastern Circuit, 1972–84; *b* 3 Oct. 1916; *s* of H. S. Ker Edie, Kinloss, Morayshire; *m* 1945, Margaret, *d* of Rev. A. E. Shooter, TD; four *s* one *d*. *Educ:* Clifton; London Univ. Called to Bar, Gray's Inn, 1941. Metropolitan Magistrate, 1961–70; Dep. Chm. Middlesex QS, 1970–71. *Died 28 March 2002.*

EDIS, Richard John Smale, CMG 1994; HM Diplomatic Service; Ambassador to Algeria, since 2001; *b* 1 Sept. 1943; *s* of late Denis Edis and of Sylvia (*née* Smale); *m* 1971, Geneviève Cérisoles; three *s*. *Educ:* King Edward's Sch., Birmingham (schol.); St Catharine's Coll., Cambridge (Exhibnr; MA). British Centre, Stockholm, 1965–66; entered HM Diplomatic Service, 1966; FO, 1966–68; Third, later Second Sec., Nairobi, 1968–70; Second, later First Sec., Lisbon, 1971–74; FCO, 1974–77; First Sec., UK Mission to UN, New York, 1977–80; Alternate UK Rep. to UN Human Rights Commn, 1978–81; Asst Head of Southern African Dept, FCO, 1981–82; Counsellor 1982; on secondment to Northern Ireland Office as Asst Sec., 1982–84; Dep. Leader, UK Disarmament Delegn, Geneva, 1984–88; Comr, British Indian Ocean Territory, and Head, E Africa Dept, FCO, 1988–91; Vis. Fellow, Centre of Internat. Studies, Univ. of Cambridge, 1991–92; Ambassador to Mozambique, 1992–95; Ambassador to Tunisia, 1995–98, and Co-ordinator, EU–Mediterranean Affairs, 1997–98; Sen. Dir (Civil), RCDS, 1999–2001. Served Metropolitan Special Constabulary, 1975–92 (Special Constabulary Medal, 1991). Officer, Military Order of Christ, Portugal, 1973. *Publications:* Peak of Limuria, 1993; (with J. Baker) The Story of St Catharine's College, 1997; Byzantine Tunisia, 1998; contrib. Cambridge Review of Internat. Affairs, and other academic jls. *Recreations:* history, reading. *Address:* c/o Foreign and Commonwealth Office, SW1A 2AH. *Clubs:* Travellers; The Union (Cambridge).
Died 10 April 2002.

EDMOND, Prof. John Marmion, PhD; FRS 1986; Professor of Marine Geochemistry, Massachusetts Institute of Technology, since 1970; *b* 27 April 1943; *s* of late Andrew John Shields Edmond and Christina Marmion Edmond; *m* 1978, Massoudeh Vafai; two *s*. *Educ:* Univ. of Glasgow (BSc 1st class Hons, Pure Chemistry, 1965); Univ. of California at San Diego, Scripps Instn of Oceanography (PhD, Marine Chemistry, 1970). Massachusetts Institute of Technology: Asst Prof., 1970; Associate Prof., 1975; Full Prof., 1981. Fellow: American Geochemical Soc., 1996; European Geochemical Soc., 1996 (Urey Medal, 1999). Mackelwane Award, Amer. Geophysical Union, 1976. *Publications:* over 150 scientific papers in professional jls. *Recreations:* reading, gardening. *Address:* E34-201, Massachusetts Institute of Technology, Cambridge, MA 02139, USA. *T:* (617) 2535739, *Fax:* (617) 2538630; *e-mail:* jedmond@mit.edu.
Died 10 April 2001.

EDMONDS, Sheila May, PhD; Fellow, and Lecturer in Mathematics, Newnham College, Cambridge, 1945–82, then Fellow Emerita; *b* 1 April 1916; *d* of late Harold Montagu Edmonds and Florence Myra Edmonds (*née* Lilley). *Educ:* Wimbledon High Sch.; Newnham Coll., Cambridge (MA; PhD 1944). Research Student, Westfield Coll., 1939–40; Newnham College, Cambridge: Res. Student, 1940–41; Res. Fellow, 1941–43; Asst Lectr, 1943–45; Vice-Principal, 1960–81. *Publications:* papers in mathematical journals. *Recreations:* travel, photography.
Died 2 Sept. 2002.

EDMONDS, Winston Godward, CBE 1966; ERD 1945; Managing Director, Manchester Ship Canal Co., 1961–70; *b* 27 Nov. 1912; *s* of Wilfred Bell Edmonds and Nina (*née* Godward); *m* 1st, 1940, Sheila Mary (*née* Armitage) (*d* 1990); one *s*; 2nd, 1995, Alice Teresa (*née* Verity). *Educ:* Merchant Taylors'. Joined LNER, first as traffic apprentice and then in various positions, 1930–46; Manchester Ship Canal Co.: Commercial Manager, 1947–58; Manager, 1959–61. *Recreations:* golf, philately. *Address:* Silvermead, 17 Thatcher Avenue, Torquay, Devon TQ1 2PD. *T:* (01803) 293401.
Died 21 July 2005.

EDWARDS, Douglas John; Consultant, Argyll Foods Ltd (formerly Louis C. Edwards & Sons (Manchester) Ltd), 1979–84 (Joint Chairman and Managing Director, 1966–79); Chairman and Managing Director, Imexport Meats Ltd, 1979–82; *b* 18 March 1916; *s* of Louis Edwards

and Catherine Edwards; *m* 1st, 1941, Emmeline H. Haslam (*d* 1964); two *s*; 2nd, 1973, Valerie Barlow-Hitchen. *Educ:* De La Salle Coll., Salford. Served in Grenadier Guards, 1940–45. Member of Lloyd's, 1965–. Joined Manchester Conservative Party, 1947; Mem. Manchester City Council, 1951–74; Alderman, 1967–74; Lord Mayor of City of Manchester, 1971–72; Greater Manchester Metropolitan CC, 1974–78; High Sheriff, 1975–76. President: Manchester Cttee, Grenadier Guards Assoc., 1968–81 (Life Mem.); Greater Manchester Youth Assoc., 1973–80; Chairman: Manchester Br., Variety Club of GB, 1969–70; Northern Cttee, Hotel and Catering Benev. Assoc., 1976–81. Governor: De La Salle Teacher Training Coll., Greater Manchester, 1972–81; De La Salle Coll., Salford, 1972–81. DL Greater Manchester, 1979–81. Freeman and Liveryman, Makers of Playing Cards Co., 1974. KCHS (Papal knighthood) 1993 (KHS 1986). Polonia Restituta, First Cl., 1972. *Recreations:* golf, sailing, shooting. *Address:* Apt 10A, The Marbella, 250 South Ocean Boulevard, Boca Raton, FL 33432, USA. *T:* (561) 3928203. *Clubs:* Carlton; Royal Thames Yacht; Lloyd's Yacht; Lancs County Cricket (Life Mem.); Cheshire Polo; Altrincham Rifle; Antibes Yacht; St Francis Yacht (Hon. Mem.), Royal Palm Yacht and Country (Boca Raton, Florida).
Died 8 Nov. 2005.

EDWARDS, Sir George (Robert), OM 1971; Kt 1957; CBE 1952 (MBE 1945); FRS 1968; FREng; DL; Chairman, British Aircraft Corporation 1963–75; Pro-Chancellor, University of Surrey, 1964–79, then Pro-Chancellor Emeritus; *b* 9 July 1908; *m* 1935, Marjorie Annie (*née* Thurgood) (*d* 1994); one *d*. *Educ:* S West Essex Tech Coll.; London Univ. (BScEng). Gen. engineering, 1928–35; joined Design Staff, Vickers-Aviation Ltd, Weybridge, 1935; Experimental Manager, Vickers-Armstrongs Ltd, Weybridge Works, 1940; Chief Designer, Weybridge Works, 1945; Dir, Vickers Ltd, 1955–67. Pres., RAeS, 1957–58; Vice-Pres., Royal Soc. of Arts, 1958–61. MRI, 1971–. Pres., Surrey CCC, 1979 (Vice-Pres., 1974). DL Surrey, 1981. Hon. Fellow, Manchester Coll. of Sci. and Technol.; Hon. FRAeS 1960; Hon. FIMechE; Hon. FAIAA. Hon. DSc: Southampton, 1962; Salford, 1967; Cranfield, 1970; City, 1975; Stirling, 1979; Surrey, 1979; Hon. DSc(Eng) London, 1970; Hon. LLD Bristol, 1973. George Taylor Gold Medal, 1948; British Gold Medal for Aeronautics, 1952; Daniel Guggenheim Medal, 1959; Air League Founders Medal, 1969; Albert Gold Medal RSA, 1972; Royal Medal, Royal Soc., 1974. *Publications:* various papers and lectures in Jl RAeS, Amer. Inst. of Aeronautical Scis and Amer. Soc. of Automotive Engrs. *Recreation:* painting. *Address:* Albury Heights, White Lane, Guildford, Surrey GU4 8PR. *T:* (01483) 504488. *Club:* Athenæum.
Died 2 March 2003.

EDWARDS, Jack Trevor, CBE 1985; CEng, FICE, FCIT; Chairman, Halcrow Fox and Associates, 1986–92; Consultant, Freeman Fox & Partners, since 1986 (Senior Partner, 1979–86); *b* 23 June 1920; *s* of late Col Cyril Ernest Edwards, DSO, MC, JP, and Jessie Boyd; *m* 1959, Josephine, (Sally), *d* of late S. W. Williams; one *d*. *Educ:* Felsted Sch.; City and Guilds Coll., Imperial Coll. London (BScEng, FCGI). RAF Armament and Airfield Construction Branches, Sqdn Ldr, 1941–46. Civil Engr on hydro-electric and thermal power stations, James Williamson and Partners, 1946–50; Freeman Fox & Partners: Engineer, 1951–64; Partner, 1965–79; special field: civil engrg and building works associated with thermal power stations and railways at home and overseas; major projects: Hong Kong Mass Transit Railway, opened 1980; Baghdad and Taipei Metros; Engineer to Dean and Chapter of St Paul's Cathedral, 1969–86. Mem. Council, British Consultants Bureau, 1979–85 (Chm., 1982–83). Liveryman, Painter-Stainers' Co., 1969–. *Publications:* Civil Engineering for Underground Rail Transport, 1990; contrib. Proc. Instn of Civil Engrs. *Recreation:* sailing. *Address:* Keepers, 77 Brentwood Road, Ingrave, Brentwood, Essex CM13 3NU. *T:* (01277) 810285. *Clubs:*

Royal Cruising, Royal Burnham Yacht.
Died 6 Nov. 2002.

EDWARDS, Linda Kay; Director, National Osteoporosis Society, since 1986; *b* 13 Feb. 1948; *d* of Richard Waldemar Sinclair Wallis (name changed by deed poll to stage name, Don Ricardo) and Evelyn Lily Wallis (*née* Ross McCandie); *m* 1972, Anthony John Edwards; one *s* one *d*. *Educ:* Maidenhead High Sch.; London Univ. (BA Hons English Lit. 1969). DipCAM 1972; MIPR 1972. Advertising and PR, Beechams UK Ltd, 1969–70; PR, N Thames Gas Bd, 1970–71; Regl Press and Publicity Officer, Post Office, 1971–82; PR consultant, 1982–86 (clients incl. major retailers, solicitors, architects, small businesses, charities). Trustee: Internat. Osteoporosis Foundn, 1997–; Long-Term Med. Conditions Alliance, 1999–. Hon. MA Bristol, 2001. *Recreations:* theatre, ski-ing, chess, sheep. *Address:* National Osteoporosis Society, Camerton, Bath BA2 0PJ. *T:* (01761) 471771, *Fax:* (01761) 471104; (home) Cariad, Kilmersdon, Bath BA3 5SU.   *Died 16 Dec. 2002.*

EDWARDS, Stewart Leslie, CMG 1967; Under-Secretary, Department of Trade and Industry, later Department of Trade, 1970–74; *b* 6 Nov. 1914; *s* of late Walter James and Lilian Emma Edwards; *m* 1940, Dominica Jeanne Lavie, *d* of Joseph Lavie and Jeanne Jauréguiberry; two *s*. *Educ:* King's Sch., Canterbury; Corpus Christi Coll., Cambridge (Foundn Scholar; BA 1936; MA 1943). Appointed to War Office, 1937. Military service, 1942–44. Called to the Bar, Inner Temple, 1947. Seconded from War Office to OEEC, 1948–51; Board of Trade, 1951–65; Minister (Economic), Bonn, 1965–70. *Recreations:* music, reading, hill-walking, wine. *Address:* B51 Résidence La Pastourelle, Bât. A, 20 Avenue Daniel-Hedde, 17200 Royan, France. *T:* 546392203.
Died 1 May 2002.

EGAN, Hon. Seamus; Judge of the Supreme Court of Ireland, 1991–96; *b* 1923; *m* Ada Leahy; two *s* five *d*. *Educ:* Blackrock College; University Coll. Dublin. Called to the Bar, 1945; practised on Western Circuit; Judge of the High Court, Ireland, 1984. Chm., Hepatitis C Compensation Tribunal, 1997–2003. *Recreations:* golf, classical music, theatre; represented Connaught at tennis and table tennis. *Address:* Killowen, Shrewsbury Road, Dublin 4, Ireland.
Died 23 Jan. 2004.

EGGLESTON, Prof. (Samuel) John, BScEcon, MA, DLitt; Professor, 1985–96, then Emeritus, and Chairman, 1985–91, Department of Education, University of Warwick; *b* 11 Nov. 1926; *s* of Edmund and Josephine Eggleston, Dorchester; *m* 1957, Greta Patrick; two *s* two *d*. *Educ:* Chippenham Grammar Sch.; LSE (BScEcon 1957); Univ. of London Inst. of Educn (MA 1965); DLitt Keele, 1977. Teacher, Suffolk and Worcs, 1950–54; Leverhulme Scholarship, LSE, 1954–57; Teacher, Beds, and Headteacher, Oxfordshire, 1957–60; Lectr, Loughborough Coll. of Educn, 1960–63; Lectr, later Sen. Lectr, Leicester Univ., 1963–67; Keele University: Prof. and Head of Dept of Educn, 1967–84; Chm., Bd of Soc. Scis, 1976–79; Chm., Higher Degree and Res. Cttee, 1981–84. Vis. Commonwealth Fellow, Canada, 1973–74; Leverhulme Fellow, 1994–97; Vis. Res. Prof., Univ. of Central England, 1994–; Vis. Prof., Middlesex Univ., 1995–. Director: DES Res. Project, Structure and Function of Youth Service, 1968–74; Schs Council Project, Design and Craft Educn, 1968–74; DES Research Projects: Training for Multi-Racial Educn, 1978–80; Minority Gp Adolescence, 1981–84. Chairman: Council of Europe Workshop on Multi-Cultural Higher Educn, 1981–86; Education Cttee, Central Television, 1987–; Technol. Exams Cttee, RSA, 1993–; Trustees and Judges, Young Electronic Designer Awards, 1988–; Vice-Chm., Design & Technology Assoc., 1992–; Member: Council of Europe Working Party, Diversif. of Tertiary Educn, 1972–78; Cheshire Educn Cttee, 1981–83; Council, Eur. Inst. of Educn and Social Policy, 1983–93; Educnl Res. Bd, SSRC, 1973–77; Panel on Public Disorder and

Sporting Events, SSRC, 1976–77; Assessment of Performance Unit, DES, Consultative Cttee, 1980–88; Res. Consultancy Cttee, DES, 1981–83; Arts Council Cttee on Trng for the Arts, 1982–87; Academic Adv. Cttee, EEC Erasmus Project, 1990–92. Editor: Design and Technology Teaching (formerly Studies in Design Education and Craft), 1968–96; Sociological Rev., 1982–95 (Chm., Editorial Bd, 1970–82); Mentoring and Tutoring, 1993–97; Chm., Editorial Bd, European Jl of Educn (formerly Paedagogica Europaea), 1976– (Editor in Chief, 1968–76); Founding Chm., Editorial Bd, Multicultural Teaching, 1982–. Hon. FCollH 1968; Hon. FEIDCT 1987; Hon. FCP. DUniv Middlesex, 1994; Hon. DEd Sunderland, 1999. *Publications:* The Social Context of the School, 1967; (with G. N. Brown) Towards an Education for the 21st Century, 1969; (ed with A. R. Pemberton) International Perspectives of Design Education, 1973; (ed) Contemporary Research in the Sociology of Education, 1974; Adolescence and Community, 1976; New Developments in Design Education, 1976; The Sociology of the School Curriculum, 1977; The Ecology of the School, 1977; (ed) Experimental Education in Europe, 1978; Teacher Decision Making in the Classroom, 1979; School Based Curriculum Development, 1980; Work Experience in Secondary Schools, 1982; Education for Some, 1986; The Challenge for Teachers, 1992; Teaching Design & Technology, 1992, 3rd edn 2001; (ed) Re-education for Employment, 1992; Arts Education for a Multicultural Society, 1995; Staying on at School, 2000; (ed) Teaching Design and Technology: a guide to recent research, 2001; articles in books and jls, incl. Sociol., Brit. Jl of Sociol., New Soc., Educnl Res. *Recreations:* work in design and craft, ski-ing, travel. *Address:* Institute of Education, University of Warwick, Coventry CV4 7AL. *T:* (024) 7652 4104.   *Died 12 Dec. 2001.*

EGMONT, 11th Earl of, *cr* 1733; **Frederick George Moore Perceval;** Bt 1661; Baron Perceval, 1715; Viscount Perceval, 1722; Baron Lovell and Holland (Great Britain), 1762; Baron Arden, 1770; Baron Arden (United Kingdom), 1802; *b* 14 April 1914; *o s* of 10th Earl and Cecilia (*d* 1916), *d* of James Burns Moore, Montreal; *S* father, 1932; *m* 1932, Ann Geraldine, *d* of D. G. Moodie; one *s* one *d* (and two *s* decd). *Heir: s* Viscount Perceval, *b* 17 Aug. 1934. *Address:* Two-dot Ranch, Nanton, Alberta, Canada.   *Died 10 Dec. 2001.*

EHRLICH, Prof. Cyril, PhD; Professor of Economic and Social History, Queen's University, Belfast, 1974–86, then Emeritus; *b* London, 13 Sept. 1925; *s* of Henry Ehrlich and Dinah (*née* Jacobs); *m* 1954, Felicity Ruth Bell-Bonnett; two *s* one *d*. *Educ:* several grammar schools; London Sch. of Econs (BSc Econ 1950; PhD 1958). Served RAF and Army, 1943–47. Res. Asst, LSE, 1950–52; Lectr, then Sen. Lectr, Makerere Coll., Uganda, 1952–61; Queen's University, Belfast: Lectr, then Sen. Lectr and Reader, 1961–74; Dean, Econs Faculty, 1979–81. Visiting Professor in Music: Royal Holloway, London Univ., 1995–; Goldsmiths Coll., London Univ., 1998–. *Publications:* The Uganda Company, 1953; The Piano: a history, 1976, 2nd edn 1990; (contrib.) Oxford History of East Africa, Vol. II 1965, Vol. III 1976; The Music Profession in Britain since the 18th Century: a social history, 1985; Harmonious Alliance: a history of the Performing Right Society, 1989; First Philharmonic: a history of the Royal Philharmonic Society, 1995; (contrib.) The Blackwell History of Music in Britain: the Twentieth Century, 1995; (contrib.) Wigmore Hall 1901–2001: a celebration, 2001; contrib. reviews and articles in Econ. Hist. Rev., Jl African Hist., Music and Letters, Musical Times, The Times, TLS, New Grove. *Recreations:* piano, opera. *Address:* 1 St Andrew's Lane, Old Headington, Oxford OX3 9DP. *T:* (01865) 760585.
Died 29 May 2004.

ELCOAT, Rev. Canon George Alastair; Vicar of Tweedmouth, Berwick-upon-Tweed, 1987–91 (Priest-in-charge, 1981–87); Chaplain to The Queen, 1982–92; Rural Dean of Norham, 1982–91; *b* 4 June 1922; *s* of George Thomas Elcoat and Hilda Gertrude Elcoat. *Educ:* Tynemouth School; Queen's College, Birmingham. Served RAF, 1941–46. Asst Master, Newcastle Cathedral Choir School, 1947–48. Deacon 1951, priest 1952; Asst Curate, Corbridge, 1951–55; Vicar: Spittal, 1955–62; Chatton with Chillingham, 1962–70; Sugley, 1970–81; RD, Newcastle West, 1977–81; Hon. Canon, Newcastle, 1979–91, Hon. Canon Emeritus, 1991–. *Recreations:* fell walking, photography, gardening, music. *Address:* 42 Windsor   Crescent,   Berwick-upon-Tweed, Northumberland TD15 1NT.   *Died 12 Feb. 2004.*

ELKIN, Alexander, CMG 1976; international law consultant, retired; *b* St Petersburg, 2 Aug. 1909; *o c* of Boris and Anna Elkin; *m* 1937, Muriel Solomons, Dublin. *Educ:* Grunewald Gymnasium and Russian Academic Sch., Berlin; Univ. of Berlin; Kiel Univ. (DrJur 1932); London Univ. (LLM 1935). Called to the Bar, Middle Temple, 1937; practised at English Bar, 1937–39; BBC Monitoring Service, 1939–42; war-time govt service, 1942–45; Associate Chief, Legal Service, UN Interim Secretariat, London, 1945–46; Asst Dir, UN European Office, Geneva, 1946–48; Legal Adviser to UNSCOB, Salonica, 1948; Dep. Legal Adviser, later Legal Adviser, OEEC, then OECD, Paris, 1949–61; UNECA Legal Consultant, formation of African Devolt Bank and Econ. Council for Africa, 1962–64; Actg Gen. Counsel of ADB, 1964–65; UNDP Legal Consultant, formation of Caribbean Devolt Bank, 1967–68; Special Adviser on European Communities Law, FCO, 1970–79. Legal consultancies for: WHO, 1948; IBRD, 1966; W Afr. Regional Gp, 1968; OECD, 1975. Lectured: on Europ. payments system and OEEC/OECD activs, Univ. of the Saar, 1957–60, and Univ. Inst. of Europ. Studies, Turin, 1957–65; on drafting of treaties, UNITAR Seminars, The Hague, Geneva and NY, for legal advisers and diplomats, 1967–84; on language and law, Univ. of Bath, 1979–96; Univ. of Bradford, 1979–84. Hon. Vis. Prof., Bradford Univ., 1982–84. Mem., RIIA. Hon. LLD Bath, 1990. Ford Foundn Leadership Grant, 1960. *Publications:* contrib. European Yearbook, Jl du Droit Internat., Revue Générale de Droit Internat. Public, Survey of Internat. Affairs 1939–1946, Travaux pratiques de L'Institut de Droit Comparé de la Faculté de Droit de Paris, etc. *Recreations:* reading, visiting art collections, travel. *Address:* 70 Apsley House, Finchley Road, NW8 0NZ. *Club:* Travellers.   *Died 22 Nov. 2001.*

ELLERTON, Sir Geoffrey (James), Kt 1992; CMG 1963; MBE 1956; Chairman, Local Government Boundary Commission for England, 1983–92; *b* 25 April 1920; *er s* of Sir Cecil Ellerton; *m* 1946, Peggy Eleanor, *d* of late F. G. Watson; three *s*. *Educ:* Highgate Sch.; Hertford Coll., Oxford (MA). Military Service, 1940–45. Apptd Colonial Administrative Service as District Officer, Kenya, 1945; acted as Minister for Internal Security and Defence, 1960 and 1962; retired as Permanent Sec., Prime Minister's Office and Sec. to the Cabinet, at time of Kenya's Independence, Dec. 1963. Sec. to the Maud and Mallaby Cttees on Management and Staffing in Local Government, 1964. Joined Elder Dempster Lines, 1965, Chm., 1972–74; an Exec. Dir, Ocean Transport & Trading Ltd, 1972–80; Dir, Overseas Containers Ltd, 1975–80; Chm., Globe Management Ltd, 1981–83; Dir, Globe Investment Trust PLC, 1983–86. Mem. Council, Liverpool Univ., 1974–78; a Vice-Pres., Liverpool Sch. of Tropical Medicine, 1978–87; Hakluyt Society: Mem. Council, 1984–86; Hon. Treas., 1986–94; Trustee, 1994–2003. *Recreations:* opera, books. *Address:* Briar Hill House, Broad Campden, Chipping Campden, Glos GL55 6XB. *T:* (01386) 841003. *Clubs:* Royal Over-Seas League (Chm., Central Council, 1995–2000; Vice-Pres., 2000–), MCC.   *Died 31 May 2005.*

ELLIOT, Aydua Helen S.; *see* Scott-Elliot.

ELLIOTT, Frank Abercrombie, MD, FRCP; Emeritus Professor of Neurology, University of Pennsylvania, since 1979; Consultant, Elliott Neurology Centre, Pennsylvania Hospital, Philadelphia, since 1975; *b* 18 Dec. 1910; *s* of Arthur Abercrombie Elliott and Kathleen Gosselin; *m* 1st, 1940, Betty Kathleen Elkington; two *d*; 2nd, 1970, Mrs Josiah Marvel (*née* Hopkins). *Educ:* Rondebosch; Univ. of Cape Town (Univ. entrance schol., 1928; Lewis Meml schol., 1930–34; MB, ChB with Hons and Gold Medal); Hiddingh Travelling Fellowship, 1936–39. FRCP 1948; FACP 1973. House Surg. and House Phys. to professorial units, Cape Town; House Physician, British Postgrad. Sch. of Medicine and Nat. Hosp. for Nervous Diseases, London; Resident MO, Nat. Heart Hosp. RAMC, 1943–48, Lt-Col; Adviser in Neurology, India and War Office. Physician to Charing Cross Hosp., 1947–58, to Moorfields Eye Hospital, 1949–58; Prof. of Neurology, Univ. of Pennsylvania, 1963–78. Lectr and Examiner, London Univ. Member: Assoc. of British Neurologists; Assoc. of British Physicians; Internat. Soc. of Internal Medicine; Amer. Acad. of Neurology; Philadelphia Neurol Soc. *Publications:* (ed) Clinical Neurology, 1952; Clinical Neurology, 1964, 2nd edn, 1971; papers on neurol subjects and origins of aggressive behaviour. *Address:* 3339 Schoolhouse Lane, Philadelphia, PA 19144, USA. *Club:* Philadelphia.   *Died 28 May 2003.*

ELLIOTT, Hugh Percival, CMG 1959; retired, 1967; *b* 29 May 1911; *s* of late Major P. W. Elliott, IA; *m* 1951, Bridget Rosalie (*d* 1981), *d* of late Rev. A. F. Peterson. *Educ:* St Lawrence Coll., Ramsgate; Hertford Coll., Oxford. Joined Colonial Administrative Service, Nigeria, 1934; seconded Colonial Office, 1946; Supervisor, Colonial Service Courses, London, 1948–50; Senior District Officer, 1954; Permanent Sec., 1956; Adviser, Govt of Eastern Nigeria, 1962–67. Many visits to Ethiopia, Zimbabwe, Kenya, Uganda and Nigeria to support the initiatives for Moral Re-Armament by African friends, 1968–. Companion, Order of the Niger, Nigeria, 1964. *Publications:* Darkness and Dawn in Zimbabwe, 1978; Dawn in Zimbabwe, 1980. *Recreations:* the countryside, watercolour painting, Africa. *Address:* Hall Grange, Shirley Church Road, Croydon CR9 5AL.

Died 28 April 2004.

ELLIOTT, Sir Ronald (Stuart), Kt 1981; Director: International Board, Security Pacific National Bank, USA, 1983–91; Security Pacific Australia Ltd, 1985–91; *b* 29 Jan. 1918; *s* of Harold J. W. Elliott and Mercedes E. Manning; *m* 1944, Isabella Mansbridge Boyd; one *s* one *d*. *Educ:* C of E Grammar Sch., Ballarat, Victoria. ABIA; FAIM. Commonwealth Banking Corporation: Sec., 1960–61; Dep. Manager for Queensland, 1961–63; Chief Manager, Foreign Div., 1963–64; Chief Manager, Queensland, 1964–65; Gen. Manager, Commonwealth Devolt Bank of Australia, 1966–75; Dep. Man. Dir, 1975–76, Man. Dir, 1976–81, Commonwealth Banking Corp.; Chm., Australian European Finance Corp. Ltd, 1976–81. Director: Australian Bd, Internat. Commodities Clearing House Ltd, 1981–88; Brambles Industries, 1981–90. Mem., Sci. and Industry Forum, Australian Acad. of Sci., 1978–81. Dir, Australian Opera, 1980–87; Mem., Australian Film Devolt Corp., 1970–75. *Recreations:* golf, reading, music, particularly opera. *Address:* PO Box 1401, Armidale, NSW 2350, Australia. *T:* (2) 67722387. *Clubs:* Union, Australian Golf (Sydney) (Pres., 1982–87, Capt., 1987–88); Armidale Golf.   *Died 18 Oct. 2001.*

ELLIS, Alice Thomas; *see* Haycraft, A. M.

ELLIS, His Honour Arthur Robert Malcolm; DL; a Circuit Judge (formerly Judge of County Courts), 1971–86; *b* 27 June 1912; *s* of David and Anne Amelia Ellis, Nottingham; *m* 1938, Brenda Sewell (*d* 1983); one *d*. *Educ:* Nottingham High Sch. Admitted Solicitor, 1934; called to the Bar, Inner Temple, 1953. Chm., Nottingham Council of Social Service, 1950–55; Dep. Chm., E Midland Traffic Area, 1955–71; Chm., Min. of Pensions and Nat. Insce Tribunal, Sutton-in-Ashfield, 1961–64,

Notts, 1964–71; Chm., Medical Appeals Tribunal, 1971–76. Chm., Notts QS, 1963–71 (Dep.-Chm., 1962–63); Chm., Derbyshire QS, 1966–71 (Dep.-Chm., 1965–66). DL Notts, 1973. *Recreations:* golf, bridge, reading. *Address:* Byways, 5 Manvers Grove, Radcliffe-on-Trent, Notts NG12 2FT. *Club:* United Services (Nottingham). *Died 28 Feb. 2003.*

ELLIS, Rear-Adm. Edward William, CB 1974; CBE 1968; *b* 6 Sept. 1918; *s* of Harry L. and Winifred Ellis; *m* 1945, Dilys (*née* Little); two *s*. Joined RN, 1940; War service afloat in HM Ships Broadwater and Eclipse, and liaison duties in USS Wichita and US Navy destroyer sqdn; psc 1952; Comdr 1953; Staff of Flag Officer Flotillas, Mediterranean, 1954–55; Sec. to 4th Sea Lord, 1956–58; Sec. to C-in-C South Atlantic and South America, 1959–60; HM Ships Bermuda and Belfast, 1960–62; Captain 1963; Head of C-in-C Far East Secretariat, 1963–65; Sec. to C-in-C Portsmouth and Allied C-in-C Channel, 1965–66; Sec. to Chief of Naval Staff and 1st Sea Lord, 1966–68; Cdre RN Barracks Portsmouth, 1968–71; Rear-Adm. 1972; Adm. Pres., RNC Greenwich, 1972–74. Private Sec. to Lord Mayor of London, 1974–82. Freeman of the City of London, 1974; Liveryman, Shipwrights' Co., 1980. OStJ 1981. Commander, Royal Order of Dannebrog (Denmark), 1974. *Recreations:* fishing, gardening. *Address:* South Lodge, Minstead, Lyndhurst, Hants SO43 7FR. *Club:* Army and Navy. *Died 13 Jan. 2002.*

ELLIS, Mary; actress; singer; authoress; *b* New York City, 15 June 1897; took British citizenship, 1946; *m* 1st, 1919, L. A. Bernheimer (decd); 2nd, Edwin Knopf (marr. diss.); 3rd, Basil Sydney (marr. diss.); 4th, J. Muir Stewart Roberts (decd). *Educ:* New York. Studied art for three years; studied singing with Madame Ashforth. First stage appearance, Metropolitan Opera House, NY, in Sœur Angelica, 1918; with Metropolitan Opera, 1918–22; first appearance dramatic stage, as Nerissa in The Merchant of Venice, Lyceum, NY, 1922; was the original Rose Marie (in the musical play, Rose Marie), Imperial, 1924; The Dybbuk, NY, 1925–26; many NY leads followed incl. Taming of the Shrew, 1927, Becky Sharp, 1929; first appearance on London stage, as Laetitia in Knave and Queen, Ambassadors', 1930; Strange Interlude, Lyric, 1932; Double Harness, Haymarket, 1933; Music in the Air, His Majesty's, 1934; Glamorous Night, Drury Lane, 1935; Innocent Party, St James's, 1937; Dancing Years, Drury Lane, 1939. From 1939–43 worked in hospital welfare and gave concerts for troops. Re-appeared on stage as Marie Foret in Arc de Triomphe, Phœnix, London, 1943; Old Vic (at Liverpool Playhouse), 1944 : Ella Rentheim in John Gabriel Borkman; Linda Valaine in Point Valaine; Lady Teazle in The School for Scandal; Maria Fitzherbert in The Gay Pavilion, Piccadilly, 1945; Mrs Dane's Defence, Embassy, 1946, also première and tour of Hattie Stowe, 1946–47; post-war successes included: Playbill (Harlequinade and The Browning Version), Phœnix, 1949; Man in the Raincoat, Edinburgh, 1949; If this be Error, Hammersmith, 1950; Volumnia in Coriolanus, RSC, Stratford, 1952; After the Ball (Oscar Wilde-Noel Coward), Globe, 1954–55; Mourning Becomes Electra, Arts, 1955–56; Dark Halo, Arts, 1959; Look Homeward Angel, Pembroke Th., Croydon, 1960; Phœnix, 1962; Yvonne Arnaud Th., Guildford: Silver Cord (revival), 1971; Mrs Warren's Profession, 1972. *Films:* Bella Donna, 1934; Hollywood, 1935–36: Paris in Spring; All The King's Horses; Fatal Lady; Glamorous Night, 1937; Gulliver's Travels, 1961. After 1972 devoted time to writing, radio and television; made several major television appearances, also many radio programmes and interviews; television, 1956–: Shaw's Great Catherine, Van Druten's Distaff Side, Memoirs of Sherlock Holmes and numerous others. Theatre lectures in USA, 1977. *Publications:* Those Dancing Years (autobiog.), 1982; Moments of Truth, 1986. *Recreations:* painting, travel, writing. *Address:* c/o Chase Manhattan Bank, 125 London Wall, EC2Y 5AJ. *Died 30 Jan. 2003.*

ELLIS, Sir Ronald, Kt 1978; FREng, FIMechE; Chairman, EIDC Ltd, 1981–93; *b* 12 Aug. 1925; *s* of William Ellis and Besse Brownbill; *m* 1st, 1956, Cherry Hazel Brown (*d* 1978); one *s* one *d*; 2nd, 1979, Myra Ann Royle. *Educ:* Preston Grammar Sch.; Manchester Univ. (BScTech Hons 1949). FIMechE 1949; FREng (FEng 1981). Gen. Man., BUT Ltd, 1954; Gen. Sales and Service Man., 1962, Gen. Man., 1966, Leyland Motors Ltd; Man. Dir, British Leyland Truck and Bus, 1968; Dir, British Leyland Motor Corp. Ltd, 1970. Head of Defence Sales, MoD, 1976–81. Chm., Bus Manufacturers Hldg Co., 1972–76. Dir of corp. develt, Wilkinson Sword Gp, 1981–82; Pres. and Man. Dir, Industrial Div., 1982–85, Dir, Internat. Gp, 1981–86, Allegheny International. Director: Yarrow & Co., 1981–86; Redman Heenan Internat., 1981–86; Bull Thompson Associates, 1987–89; IDRH Ltd, 1987–89; R. L. Holdings Ltd, 1989–90. Vice-Pres., SMMT, 1972–73; Dir, ROFs, 1976–81. Mem., Engineering Council, 1988–92. Governor, UMIST, 1970–92, Vice-Pres., 1983–92, Hon. Fellow, 1981. Freeman, City of London, 1984. *Recreation:* fishing. *Died 10 Nov. 2005.*

ELMES, Dr Peter Cardwell, MBE 2003; Director, Medical Research Council Pneumoconiosis Unit, Llandough Hospital, Penarth, 1976–81, retired from MRC 1982; Consultant in Occupational Lung Diseases, since 1976; *b* 12 Oct. 1921; *s* of Florence Romaine Elmes and Lilian Bryham (*née* Cardwell); *m* 1957, Margaret Elizabeth (*née* Staley); two *s* one *d*. *Educ:* Rugby; Oxford Univ. (BM, BCh 1945); Western Reserve Univ., Cleveland, Ohio (MD 1943). MRCP 1951. Mil. Service, RAMC, 1946–48. Trng posts, Taunton and Oxford, 1948–50; Registrar, then Sen. Registrar in Medicine, Hammersmith Hosp., 1950–58; Dept of Therapeutics, Queen's Univ., Belfast: Sen. Lectr, 1959–63; Reader, 1963–67; Prof. of Therapeutic Sciences, 1967–71; Whitla Prof. of Therapeutics and Pharmacology, 1971–76. Member: Medicines Commn, 1976–79; Industrial Injuries Adv. Council, 1982–87; Indep. Scientific Cttee on Smoking and Health, 1982–92. Chm., Ruperra Castle Conservation Trust, 1997–2002; Vice Chm., Welsh Historic Gardens Trust, 1997–2003. *Publications:* contrib. med. jls on chronic chest disease, treatment and control of infection, occupational lung disease asbestosis, and mesothelioma. *Recreations:* working on house and garden, saving castles and historic gardens. *Address:* Dawros House, St Andrews Road, Dinas Powys, Vale of Glamorgan CF64 4HB. *T:* (029) 2051 2102, *Fax:* (029) 2051 5975. *Died 19 Nov. 2003.*

ELMSLIE, Maj.-Gen. Alexander Frederic Joseph, CB 1959; CBE 1955; psc; FCIT; *b* 31 Oct. 1905; *er s* of Captain A. W. Elmslie, RAEC and Florence Edith Elmslie (*née* Kirk); *m* 1931, Winifred Allan Wright (decd); one *d* (one *s* decd). *Educ:* Farnham Grammar Sch.; RMC Sandhurst; Staff Coll., Camberley. Commissioned in Royal Army Service Corps, 29 Jan. 1925, and subsequently served in Shanghai, Ceylon, E Africa and Singapore; served War of 1939–45 (despatches) in Madagascar, India (Combined Ops) and Europe (SHAEF); Dep. Dir of Supplies and Transport, War Office, 1953–55; Dir of Supplies and Transport, GHQ Far East Land Forces, 1956–57; Inspector, RASC, War Office, 1957–60, retired. Chairman Traffic Commissioners: NW Traffic Area, 1962–64; SE Traffic Area, 1965–75. Hon. Col 43 (Wessex) Inf. Div. Coln, RASC, TA, 1960–64; Col Comdt, RASC, 1964–65; Col Comdt, Royal Corps of Transport, 1965–69. Fellow, Royal Commonwealth Soc. *Address:* 9 Stanmer House, Furness Road, Eastbourne, E Sussex BN21 4EY. *Died 13 Sept. 2005.*

ELPHICK, Michael John; actor; *b* 19 Sept. 1946; *s* of Herbert Frederick Elphick and Joan Mary (*née* Haddow); partner, Julia Alexander (*d* 1996); one *d*. *Educ:* Lancastrian Sch. for Boys, Chichester; Central Sch. of Speech and Drama. *Theatre* includes: The Changing Room, Royal Court; Hamlet, Royal Court; The Ticket of Leave Man,

National; Pygmalion, Albery, 1997; *films* include: Blind Terror; Phyliss Dixie; The Knowledge; The Elephant Man; Quadrophenia; The Curse of the Pink Panther; Gorky Park, 1983; Privates on Parade, 1983; Little Dorritt, 1987; The Krays; Buddy's Song, 1992; *television* includes: The Nearly Man; Holding On; Blue Remembered Hills; Bloomfield; Oxbridge Blues, 1984; David Copperfield, 1999; *series:* Private Schultz, 1981; Smiley's People, 1981–82; Pull the Other One, 1984; Three Up, Two Down, 1985–88; Boon, 1986–93; Harry, 1993–94; EastEnders, 2001. *Publication:* Absolute Beginner's Guide to Cookery. *Recreation:* boats. *Address:* c/o ICM, Oxford House, 76 Oxford Street, W1D 1BS. *T:* (020) 7636 6565, *Fax:* (020) 7323 0101. *Clubs:* Groucho, Gerry's.
Died 7 Sept. 2002.

ELSTOB, Peter (Frederick Egerton); Vice-President: International PEN, since 1981 (Secretary-General, 1974–81); English PEN, since 1978; Managing Director, Archive Press Ltd, since 1964 (co-founder 1963); writer and entrepreneur; *b* London, 22 Dec. 1915; *e s* of Frederick Charles Elstob, chartered accountant, RFC, and Lillian Page, London; *m* 1st, 1937, Medora Leigh Smith (marr. diss. 1953); three *s* one *d* (and one *d* decd); 2nd, 1953, Barbara Zacheisz (*d* 1992); one *s* one *d*. *Educ:* private schs, London, Paris, Calcutta; state schs, NY and NJ; Univ. of Michigan, 1934–35. Reporter, salesman, tourist guide, 1931–36. Volunteer, Spanish Civil War, 1936 (imprisoned and expelled); served War of 1939–45, RTR, 1940–46 (despatches). Founded Yeast-pac Co. Ltd with A. B. Eiloart, 1938, Dir, 1938–70, Man. Dir, 1970–93; with A. B. Eiloart: bought Arts Theatre Club, London, 1941; founded Peter Arnold Studios (artists' and writers' colony, Mexico), 1951–52, and Archives Designs Ltd, 1954–62; Director: MEEC Prodns (Theatre), 1946–54; Peter Arnold Properties, 1947–61; City & Suffolk Property Ltd, 1962–70; ABC Expedns, 1957–61; Manager, Small World Trans-Atlantic Balloon Crossing, 1958–59. Chm., Dorking Divl Lab. Party, 1949–50. Mem., Burley Br., RBL, 1996–. Bulgarian Commemorative Medal, 1982; Normandy Freedom Medal, 1994. *Publications:* (autobiog.) Spanish Prisoner, 1939; (with A. B. Eiloart) The Flight of the Small World, 1959; *novels:* Warriors for the Working Day, 1960; The Armed Rehearsal, 1964; Scoundrel, 1986; *military history:* Bastogne the Road Block, 1968; The Battle of the Reichswald, 1970; Hitler's Last Offensive, 1971; Condor Legion, 1973; (ed) The Survival of Literature, 1979; (ed series) PEN International Books; PEN Broadsheet, 1977–82. *Recreations:* playing the Stock Exchange, travelling. *Address:* Ponds Cottage, Burley Lawn, Ringwood, Hants BH24 4DL. *T:* (01425) 403406. *Clubs:* Savage, Garrick, PEN, Society of Authors.
Died 21 July 2002.

ELVIN, Prof. (Herbert) Lionel; Director of the University of London Institute of Education, 1958–73 (Professor of Education in Tropical Areas, 1956–58, Emeritus Professor of Education, 1973; Hon. Fellow, 1993); *b* 7 Aug. 1905; *e s* of late Herbert Henry Elvin; *m* 1934, Mona Bedortha (*d* 1997), *d* of Dr C. S. S. Dutton, San Francisco; one *s*. *Educ:* elementary schs; Southend High Sch.; Trinity Hall, Cambridge (1st cl. Hons, History and English; Hon. Fellow, 1980). Commonwealth Fellow, Yale Univ., USA, Fellow of Trinity Hall, Cambridge, 1930–44; Temporary Civil Servant (Air Min., 1940–42, MOI, 1943–45); Principal, Ruskin Coll., Oxford, 1944–50; Dir, Dept of Educn, UNESCO, Paris, 1950–56. Parliamentary candidate (Lab), Cambridge Univ., 1935. Formerly: Pres., English New Education Fellowship; Pres., Council for Education in World Citizenship; Chm., Commonwealth Educn Liaison Cttee; Member: Cttee on Higher Education; Govt of India Educn Commn; University Grants Cttee, 1946–50; Central Advisory Council for Education (England) and Secondary School Examinations Council. *Publications:* Men of America, 1941; An Introduction to the Study of Literature (Poetry), 1949; Education and Contemporary Society, 1965; The Place of Commonsense in Educational Thought, 1977;

(ed) The Educational Systems in the European Community, 1981; Encounters with Education, 1987. *Recreations:* formerly most games indifferently, athletics (half-mile, Cambridge *v* Oxford, 1927).
Died 14 June 2005.

ELWORTHY, Sir Peter (Herbert), Kt 1988; farmer; *b* 3 March 1935; *s* of Harold Herbert Elworthy and June Mary Elworthy (*née* Batchelor); *m* 1960, Fiona Elizabeth McHardy; two *s* two *d*. *Educ:* Waihi Prep. Sch.; Christ's Coll.; Lincoln Agric. Coll. Nuffield Scholarship, UK, 1970; McMeekan Meml Award, 1978; Bledisloe Award, Lincoln, 1987. FNZIAS. Director: Reserve Bank of NZ, 1985–99; Landcorp, 1986–88; BP NZ Ltd, 1986–; Ascot Management Corp. (NZ) Ltd, 1991–94; Enerco NZ Ltd, 1992–95; Huttons Kiwi Ltd, 1992–96; Skellerup Gp Ltd, 1993–96; Chm., Timaru Port Co., 1988–97. Mem., NZ Adv. Cttee on Overseas Aid, 1986–89 (Chm., 1988–89). President: NZ Deer Farmers Assoc., 1974–81; Federated Farmers of NZ, 1984–87; Chairman: Ravensdown Co-op, 1977–82; NZ Farmlands Ltd, 1989–92; Electricity Distribution Reform Unit, 1990–92; The Power Co., 1990–97; Rural Electrical Reticulation Council, 1990–96; Southland Electric Power Supply, 1990–97; QEII National Trust, 1987–93; NZ Rural Property Trust, 1988–89; Opihi (SC) River Develt Co, 1992–; NZ Rural Properties Ltd, 1992–2000; Seabil (NZ) Ltd, 1994–96; Dir, Sky City Ltd, 1992–. Trustee: Lincoln Univ. Foundn, 1989–; Waitingi Foundn, 1990–; NZ Inst. Econ. Res. (Inc.), 1991–; Allan Duff Charitable Foundn, 1994–; Chm., Salvation Army Inaugural Community Support Cttee, 1994–96; Patron, Internat. Organic Agric. Conf., Lincoln, 1994–. NZ Commemoration Medal, 1990. *Recreations:* riding, fishing, flying (licensed pilot), tennis, reading. *Address:* Craigmore Farm, Maungati, 2RD, Timaru, New Zealand. *T:* (3) 6129809. *Clubs:* Farmers'; Christchurch (Canterbury, NZ); Wellington (Wellington).
Died 11 Jan. 2004.

EMBLING, John Francis, CB 1967; Deputy Under-Secretary of State, Department of Education and Science, 1966–71; *b* 16 July 1909; *m* 1940, Margaret Gillespie Anderson; one *s*. *Educ:* University of Bristol. Teaching: Dean Close, 1930; Frensham Heights, 1931; Lecturer: Leipzig Univ., 1936; SW Essex Technical Coll., 1938 (Head of Dept, 1942); Administrative Asst, Essex LEA, 1944; Ministry of Education: Principal, 1946; Asst Secretary, 1949; Under-Secretary of State for Finance and Accountant-General, Dept of Education and Science, 1960–66. Research Fellow in Higher Educn, LSE, 1972–73, Univ. of Lancaster, 1974–76. Mem. Council, Klagenfurt Univ., 1972–. Grand Cross, Republic of Austria, 1976.
Died 26 May 2003.

EMERY, Rt Hon. Sir Peter (Frank Hannibal), Kt 1982; PC 1993; MA; FCIPS; *b* 27 Feb. 1926; *s* of late F. G. Emery, Highgate; *m* 1st, 1954, Elizabeth Nicholson (marr. diss.); one *s* one *d*; 2nd, 1972, Elizabeth, *y d* of late G. J. R. Monnington; one *s* one *d*. *Educ:* Scotch Plains, New Jersey, USA; Oriel Coll., Oxford (MA). Joint Founder and First Secretary of the Bow Group. MP (C): Reading, 1959–66; Honiton, March 1967–1997; Devon E, 1997–2001. Parly Private Sec. in Foreign Office, War Dept and Min. of Labour, 1960–64; Opposition front bench spokesman for Treasury, Economics and Trade, 1964–66; Parliamentary Under-Secretary of State: DTI, 1972–74; Dept of Energy, 1974. Member: Select Cttee on Industry and Trade, 1979–87; Select Cttee on Procedure, 1972–97 (Chm., 1983–97); Select Cttee on Modernisation of H of C, 1997–2001; Select Cttee on Foreign Affairs, 1997–2001. Jt Hon. Sec., 1922 Cttee, 1964–65 (Treas., 1997–2001); Jt Vice-Chm., Conservative Finance Cttee, 1970–72; Chm., Cons. Housing and Construction Cttee, 1974–75. Member, Delegation to CPA Conference: Westminster, 1961; Canada, 1962; Fiji, 1981; Leader, Delegn to Kenya, 1977; Delegate: Council of Europe and WEU, 1962–64, 1970–72; North Atlantic Assembly, 1983–2001 (Chairman: Science and Technology Cttee,

1985–89; Sup. Cttee on Mil. Technol.; Rapporteur, 1989–93; Vice Chm., 1993–97); Deleg. and Treas., OSCE (formerly CSCE), 1992–2000. Chm., Winglaw Gp, 1984–2000; Director: Property Growth Insurance, 1966–72; Phillips Petroleum-UK Ltd, 1963–72; Institute of Purchasing and Supply, 1961–72; Sec.-Gen., European Federation of Purchasing, 1962–72; Chm., Consultative Council of Professional Management Organisations, 1968–72. Founding Chm., Nat. Asthma Campaign, 1990–. Mem. Adv. Bd, Center for Strategic and Internat. Studies, Washington DC, 1990–. *Recreations:* sliding down mountains, tennis, cricket, golf, bridge (Capt., H of C team, 1984–). *Address:* Tytherleigh Manor, near Axminster, Devon EX13 7BD. *T:* (01460) 220309; 8 Ponsonby Terrace, SW1P 4QA. *T:* (020) 7222 6666. *Clubs:* Carlton (Chm., Political Cttee, 2002–), Portland; Leander (Henley-on-Thames).   *Died 9 Dec. 2004.*

EMSLIE, Baron *cr* 1980 (Life Peer), of Potterton in the District of Gordon; **George Carlyle Emslie,** MBE 1946; FRSE 1987; PC 1972; Lord Justice-General of Scotland and Lord President of the Court of Session, 1972–89; *b* 6 Dec. 1919; *s* of late Alexander and Jessie Blair Emslie; *m* 1942, Lilias Ann Mailer Hannington (*d* 1998); three *s. Educ:* High Sch. of Glasgow; Univ. of Glasgow (MA, LLB). Served War of 1939–45 (despatches); commnd A and SH, 1940; North Africa, Italy, Greece, Austria, 1942–46; psc Haifa, 1944; Bde Major (Infantry), 1944–46. Advocate, 1948; Advocate Depute (Sheriff Courts), 1955; QC (Scotland) 1957; Sheriff of Perth and Angus, 1963–66; Dean, Faculty of Advocates, 1965–70; Senator of Coll. of Justice in Scotland and Lord of Session, 1970–72. Chm., Scottish Agricultural Wages Bd, 1969–73; Mem., Council on Tribunals (Scottish Cttee), 1962–70. Vice-Chm., Bd of Trustees, Nat. Library of Scotland, 1975–2001. Hon. Bencher: Inner Temple, 1974; Inn of Court of N Ireland, 1981. Hon. LLD Glasgow, 1973. *Recreation:* golf. *Address:* 47 Heriot Row, Edinburgh EH3 6EX. *T:* (0131) 225 3657. *Clubs:* New (Edinburgh); Honourable Company of Edinburgh Golfers.   *Died 21 Nov. 2002.*

EMSLIE, Prof. Ronald Douglas, FDSRCS; Dean of Dental Studies, Guy's Hospital Medical and Dental Schools, 1968–80; Professor of Periodontology and Preventive Dentistry, University of London, 1970–80, then Emeritus; *b* 9 March 1915; *s* of late Alexander G. H. Emslie and Elizabeth Spence; *m* 1951, Dorothy, *d* of William A. Dennis, Paris, Ill, USA; three *s* (and one *s* decd). *Educ:* Felsted Sch.; Guy's Hosp. Dental Sch., London (BDS); Univ. of Illinois, Chicago (MSc). FDSRCS 1950; DRD (Edin.), 1978. Served War: Surg. Lt (D) RNVR, 1943–46; Surg. Lt Comdr (D) RNVR, 1946. Half-time Asst in Dept of Preventive Dentistry, Guy's Hosp., 1946–48, also in private practice with Mr E. B. Dowsett; Research Fellow, Univ. of Illinois, Chicago, 1948–49; Head of Dept of Preventive Dentistry, Guy's Hosp., 1949–55; Reader in Preventive Dentistry, 1956–62, Prof. of Preventive Dentistry, 1963–70, Univ. of London (Guy's Hosp. Dental Sch.). Vis. Lectr, Univ. of Illinois, 1956; Nuffield Grant to study dental aspects of facial gangrene, in Nigeria, Sept.–Dec. 1961. Sci. Advr, Brit. Dental Jl, 1961–80 (Sci. Asst Ed., 1951–61). Consultant in Periodontology to RN, 1971–80. Chm., Dental Health Cttee of BDA, 1963–69; Member: Internat. Dental Fedn; Internat. Assoc. for Dental Research; Dental Educn Adv. Council (Chm., 1978–80); Bd of Faculty of Dental Surgery, RCS, 1966–81 (Vice-Dean, 1976–77); Fluoridation Soc. (Chm. 1970–80); Bd of Studies in Dentistry, Univ. of London (Chm., 1975–77). Past Pres., Odontological Section, RSM; Pres., Brit. Soc. of Periodontology, 1959–60. Fellow, BDA. Hon. Fellow, UMDS, 1995. *Publications:* various contribs to dental literature. *Recreation:* old motor cars. *Address:* Amberwood, 3 Summerlay Close, Kingswood, Surrey KT20 6HE. *T:* (01737) 352640.   *Died 31 May 2002.*

ENGLISH, Cyril; President, Nationwide Housing Trust, 1991–97 (Chairman, 1987–90); Director, Nationwide Building Society, 1978–90 (Deputy Chairman, 1989–90); *b* 18 Feb. 1923; *s* of Joseph and Mary Hannah English; *m* 1945, Mary Brockbank; two *d. Educ:* Ashton-under-Lyne Grammar School. ALCM. Joined Nationwide Building Society, 1939; Asst Secretary, 1961; Asst General Manager, 1967; General Manager, 1971; Deputy Chief General Manager, 1974; Chief Gen. Manager, 1981–85. CCMI. *Recreations:* golf, music. *Address:* Ashton Grange, Cedar Drive, Pangbourne, Berks RG8 7BH. *T:* (0118) 984 3841. *Club:* Calcot Park Golf (Reading).

Died 9 April 2005.

ENRIGHT, Dennis Joseph, OBE 1991; CLit 1998; freelance writer; *b* 11 March 1920; *s* of late George and Grace Enright; *m* 1949, Madeleine Harders; one *d. Educ:* Leamington Coll.; Downing Coll., Cambridge (BA 1943, MA 1946); DLitt Alexandria. Lectr in English, Univ. of Alexandria, 1947–50; Organising Tutor, Univ. of Birmingham Extra-Mural Dept, 1950–53; Vis. Prof., Kōnan Univ., Japan, 1953–56; Vis. Lectr, Free Univ. of Berlin, 1956–57; British Council Prof., Chulalongkorn Univ., Bangkok, 1957–59; Prof. of English, Univ. of Singapore, 1960–70; Hon. Prof. of English, Univ. of Warwick, 1975–80. Dir, Chatto and Windus, 1974–82. Co-Editor, Encounter, 1970–72. FRSL 1961. Hon. DLitt Warwick, 1982; DUniv Surrey, 1985. Cholmondeley Poetry Award, 1974; Queen's Gold Medal for Poetry, 1981. *Publications: poetry:* The Laughing Hyena, 1953; Bread Rather Than Blossoms, 1956; Some Men Are Brothers, 1960; Addictions, 1962; The Old Adam, 1965; Unlawful Assembly, 1968; Selected Poems, 1969; Daughters of Earth, 1972; The Terrible Shears, 1973; Rhyme Times Rhyme (for children), 1974; Sad Ires, 1975; Paradise Illustrated, 1978; A Faust Book, 1979; Collected Poems, 1981; Instant Chronicles, 1985; Collected Poems 1987, 1987; Selected Poems 1990, 1990; Under the Circumstances, 1991; Old Men and Comets, 1993; Collected Poems 1948–1998, 1998; *novels:* Academic Year, 1955; Heaven Knows Where, 1957; Insufficient Poppy, 1960; Figures of Speech, 1965; The Way of the Cat, 1992; *novels for children:* The Joke Shop, 1976; Wild Ghost Chase, 1978; Beyond Land's End, 1979; *non-fiction:* The Apothecary's Shop, 1957; (co-ed.) English Critical Texts, 1962; Conspirators and Poets, 1966; Shakespeare and the Students, 1970; Man is an Onion, 1972; (ed) A Choice of Milton's Verse, 1975; Samuel Johnson: Rasselas, 1976; A Mania for Sentences, 1983; (ed) Fair of Speech: the uses of euphemism, 1985; The Alluring Problem: an essay on irony, 1986; Fields of Vision: essays on literature, language and television, 1988; Interplay: a kind of commonplace book, 1995; Play Resumed: a journal, 1999; Signs and Wonders: selected essays, 2001; *travel:* The World of Dew: Japan, 1955; Memoirs of a Mendicant Professor, 1969; *translations:* (co-ed.) The Poetry of Living Japan, 1957; The Sayings of Goethe, 1996; *anthologies:* (ed) The Oxford Book of Contemporary Verse 1945–1980, 1980; (ed) The Oxford Book of Death, 1983; (ed) The Faber Book of Fevers and Frets, 1989; (ed jtly) The Oxford Book of Friendship, 1991; The Oxford Book of the Supernatural, 1994; contributor to: Scrutiny, Encounter, London Review of Books, TLS, etc; *posthumous publication:* Injury Time, 2003. *Recreations:* reading, writing, television, listening to music. *Address:* 35A Viewfield Road, SW18 5JD.   *Died 31 Dec. 2002.*

ERDMAN, Edward Louis, FSVA; Founder, 1934, Chairman, 1934–74, and Senior Consultant, 1974–2000, Edward Erdman, Surveyors, later Erdman Lewis International, then Colliers Erdman Lewis; *b* 4 July 1906; *s* of David and Pauline Erdman; *m* 1949, Pamela (*née* Mason); one *s. Educ:* Grocers' Co. Sch. TA KRRC, 1937; war service, N Africa and Italy, 1939–45. Re-opened practice, 1945. WPHT Housing Association (subseq. Sanctuary Housing Association): Mem., Central Council, 1974–87; Chm., 1978–87; Pres. 1987, then Hon. Pres. Mem., Property Adv. Panel to Treasury, 1975–77. FRSA

1957. *Publication:* People and Property, 1982.
Died 28 Jan. 2003.

ERICKSON, Prof. John, FRSE 1982; FBA 1985; University Endowment Fellow, and Director, Centre for Defence Studies, University of Edinburgh, 1988–96 (Hon. Fellow, Defence Studies and Professor Emeritus, since 1996); *b* 17 April 1929; *s* of Henry Erickson and Jessie (*née* Heys); *m* 1957, Ljubica (*née* Petrović); one *s* one *d*. *Educ:* South Shields High Sch.; St John's Coll., Cambridge (MA). Research Fellow, St Anthony's Coll., Oxford, 1956–58; Lectr, Dept of History, St Andrews Univ., 1958–62; Lectr, Sen. Lectr and Reader, Dept of Government, Univ. of Manchester, 1962–67; Edinburgh University: Reader, Lectr in Higher Defence Studies, 1967; Prof. of Politics (Defence Studies), 1969–88. Visiting Professor: Russian Res. Center, Univ. of Indiana, 1967; Texas A&M Univ., 1981; Dept. of History, Yale Univ., 1987. Pres., Assoc. of Civil Defence and Emergency Planning Officers, 1981–. FRSA 1991; Hon. Fellow, Aerospace Acad., Ukraine, 1995. *Publications:* The Soviet High Command 1918–1941, 1962, repr. 2001; Storia dello Stato Maggiore Sovietico, 1963; (ed) The Military-Technical Revolution, 1966; (ed) The Armed Services and Society, 1970; Soviet Military Power, 1971; The Road to Stalingrad, 1975 (repr 1998); (ed) Soviet Military Power and Performance, 1979; The Road to Berlin, 1983; (ed) Barbarossa, The Axis and the Allies, 1994; (jtly) The Soviet Armed Forces 1918–1992: a research guide to Soviet sources, 1996; (jtly) The Russian Front 1941–1945, 1999; (introd) Invasion 1940, 2000; (jtly) The Eastern Front in Photographs 1941–1945, 2001. *Recreations:* military models and music. *Address:* 13 Ravelston House Road, Edinburgh EH4 3LP. *T:* (0131) 332 1787. *Club:* Scottish Arts (Edinburgh).
Died 10 Feb. 2002.

ERRÁZURIZ, (Talavera) Hernán; Senior Partner, Errázuriz and Co., Attorneys at Law, since 1972; Professor of Law, University of Chile, since 1996; *b* 14 Feb. 1941; *s* of Ladislao Errázuriz Pereira and Amelia Talavera Balmaceda; *m* 1964, Carmen Cruzat Amunategui; three *s* five *d*. *Educ:* German Sch. and Military Sch. Santiago; Univ. of Chile (Law degree, 1965); New York Sch. of Law. Admitted to legal practice, 1965; Sen. Partner, Errázuriz & Co. (estab. 1905 by grandfather); Legal Advr, Chilean Copper Corp., 1962–68; University of Chile: Prof. of Economic law, 1968–93; Dir, Inst. of Internat. Studies, 1974–83; Ambassador to UK, 1993–96. Legal Advr to Confedn of Chilean Entrepeneurs, 1973–76. President: Assoc. of Chilean Industries, 1968–73; Latin American Assoc. of Industries, 1970–72; Chilean Council of Econ. Law, 1988–; Mem., Cttee of Foreign Investment of Chile, 1968–73. Mem., Internat. Gp of Lawyers, SGL, 1988–93. President: Liberal Youth Party, 1960–64; Chilean Liberal Party (PAC), 1991–93. *Publications:* Chilean Economic Law 1968–1974; The Chilean Economy in a Democratic Framework, 1984. *Recreations:* horse riding, theatre, opera. *Address:* Burgos 88, Santiago, Chile. *Clubs:* Royal Automobile; De La Union (Santiago); Los Leones Golf (Santiago).
Died 21 April 2003.

ERRITT, (Michael) John (Mackey), CB 1991; Deputy Director, Central Statistical Office, 1989–91; *b* 15 Feb. 1931; *s* of late William Albert Erritt, MBE, and Anna Erritt; *m* 1957, Marian Elizabeth Hillock; two *s*. *Educ:* St Andrews Coll., Dublin; Prince of Wales Sch., Nairobi; Queen's Univ., Belfast (BSc (Econ)). Res. Officer, Science and Industry Cttee, 1953; Asst Statistician, CSO, 1955; Statistician: BoT, 1960; Treasury, 1964; BoT, 1967; Chief Statistician: Inland Revenue, 1968; CSO, 1973; Depts of Industry, Trade and Prices and Consumer Protection, 1975; MoD, 1979; Asst Under-Sec. of State (Statistics), MoD, 1981; Asst Dir, CSO, 1985. *Publications:* articles in official, academic and trade jls. *Recreations:* gardening, travel, grandfathering. *Address:* Green Tiles, 14 Brook

Lane, Lindfield, Sussex RH16 1SG.
Died 3 Oct. 2002.

ERSKINE, Ralph, CBE 1978; architect; own practice (in Sweden, since 1939); *b* 24 Feb. 1914; *s* of late George and Mildred Erskine; *m* 1939, Ruth Monica Francis (decd); one *s* two *d* (and one *d* decd). *Educ:* Friends' Sch., Saffron Walden, Essex; Regent Street Polytechnic (architecture). ARIBA 1936; AMTPI 1938; SAR 1965. Won number of prizes in architectl comps in Sweden; one year's study at Academy for Fine Arts, Sweden, 1945. *Work executed:* town plans; workers' houses; co-operative housing and industrial housing; flats; hostels; factories; ski-hotel; shopping centre; school; town hall; hall of residence at Clare Coll., Cambridge; churches; housing estates at Newmarket and Killingworth; clearance scheme, Byker, Newcastle upon Tyne; design of new town, Resolute Bay, Canada; University Library, Allhuset and Sports Hall, Stockholm Univ.; London Ark, Hammersmith. Lecturing: in America, Canada, Japan and many countries in Europe. For. Mem., Royal Acad. of Arts, Sweden, 1972; Hon. Mem., Bund Deutscher Architekten, 1983. Hon. Fellow, AIA, 1966; Hon. RA 1984. Hon. Dr Lund, Sweden, 1975; Hon. DLitt Heriot-Watt, 1982. SAR's Kasper Sahlin prize for 1971 and 1981; Ytong Prize, 1974; Guld medal, Litteris et Artibus, 1980; Canadian Gold Medal, RAIC, 1983; Wolf Prize for Architecture, 1984; Royal Gold Medal, RIBA, 1987. *Publications:* for several architectl magazines, on building in northern climates, etc. *Relevant publication:* Ralph Erskine, by Mats Egelius, 1978. *Recreations:* ski-ing, skating, swimming, yachting, ice yachting. *Address:* Box 156, Gustav III's väg 4, 17802 Drottningholm, Sweden. *T:* 7590352.
Died 16 March 2005.

ERZINÇLIOĞLU, Dr Zakaria; forensic entomologist; writer and scientific consultant, since 1995; *b* 30 Dec. 1951; *s* of Zakaria Ahmet Erzinçlioğlu and Kadria Sanna Erzinçlioğlu (*née* Shuhdi); *m* 1984, Sharon Wynne Davies; one *s* two *d*. *Educ:* Wolverhampton Poly. (BSc 1975); Univ. of Durham (PhD 1984). Zool Recorder, Zool Soc. of London, 1976–81; mature res. student and part-time demonstrator, Dept of Zool., Univ. of Durham, 1981–84; Department of Zoology, University of Cambridge: Field Studies Council Res. Associate, 1984–88; Field Studies Council Res. Officer, 1988–90; Sen. Res. Associate, 1990–92; Independent Investigator, 1992–94; Affiliated Researcher, 1995–; Dir, Forensic Sci. Res. Centre, Univ. of Durham, 1994–95. Hon. Lectr, Univ. of London, 1990–. Member, Council: Linnean Soc., 1990–93; Zool Soc., 1997–98; Sec. and Co-Founder, British Zool Soc., 1999–. Mem., NT Wicken Fen Mgt Cttee, 1991–94. Campaigner for criminal justice reform. Trustee, Bosnia-Herzegovina Heritage Rescue Foundn, 1995–96; Mem., Adv. Cttee, Centre for Albanian Studies, 1998–. John Hull Grundy Medal for Medical Entomology, RAMC, 1994. *Publications:* Blowflies, 1996; (jtly) Suspicious Death Scene Investigation, 1996; Maggots, Murder and Men, 2000; Every Contact Leaves a Trace, 2001; contrib. numerous papers to learned jls. *Recreations:* reading history and biography, visiting sites of historical interest. *Address:* 28 Harlton Road, Little Eversden, Cambridge CB3 7HB. *T:* (01223) 263897.
Died 26 Sept. 2002.

ESHER, 4th Viscount *cr* 1897; **Lionel Gordon Baliol Brett,** CBE 1970; MA; PPRIBA; DistTP; Baron 1885; Rector and Vice-Provost, Royal College of Art, 1971–78; *b* 18 July 1913; *o s* of 3rd Viscount Esher, GBE; *S* father, 1963; *m* 1935, Christian, *e d* of late Col Ebenezer Pike, CBE, MC; five *s* one *d*. *Educ:* Eton (Scholar); New Coll., Oxford (Scholar); BA (1st Class), 1935; Hon. Fellow, 1980; RIBA Ashpitel Prizeman, 1939. Served War in RA, 1940–45; France and Germany, 1944–45 (despatches); Major. Architect Planner, Hatfield New Town, 1949–59; major housing projects: Hatfield, Stevenage, Basildon; consultant architect: Downside Abbey; Maidenhead Town Centre; Abingdon Town Centre; Portsmouth City

Centre; York City Centre; Santiago, Chile and Caracas, Venezuela (both for UNDP); principal buildings include: (with Francis Pollen): High Comr's House, Lagos; 82 and 190 Sloane St, London; Pall Mall Ct, Manchester; Downside Sch. extensions; Exeter Coll., and Oxenford Hall, Oxford; (with Teggin & Taylor) Civic Offices, Portsmouth. Lecture tours: USA 1953; India, 1954; Australia, 1959; S America, 1970. Governor, Museum of London, 1970–77; Member: Royal Fine Art Commn, 1951–69; Adv. Bd for Redundant Churches (Chm., 1977–83); Advisory Council, Victoria and Albert Museum, 1967–72; Arts Council of GB, 1972–77 (Chm., Art Panel); Environment Panel, British Rail, 1977–85; National Trust (Chm., Thames and Chilterns Reg., 1979–83); Vice-Pres., RIBA, 1962–65; Pres., 1965–67; Trustee, Soane Museum, 1976–94. Hon. DLitt Strathclyde Univ., 1967; Hon. DUniv York, 1970; Hon. DSc Edinburgh, 1981. Hon. Fellow: Amer. Inst. of Architects, 1967; Portsmouth Polytechnic, subseq. Portsmouth Univ., 1984; Chartered Inst. of Designers, 1975. *Publications:* Houses, 1947; The World of Architecture, 1963; Landscape in Distress, 1965; York: a study in conservation, 1969; Parameters and Images, 1970; (with Elisabeth Beazley) Shell Guide to North Wales, 1971; A Broken Wave, 1981; The Continuing Heritage, 1982; Our Selves Unknown (autobiog.), 1985; The Glory of the English House, 1991; Collected Poems, 2000. *Recreation:* landscapes. *Heir: s* Hon. Christopher Lionel Baliol Brett [*b* 23 Dec. 1936; *m* 1st, 1962, Camilla Charlotte (marr. diss. 1970), *d* of Sir (Horace) Anthony Rumbold, 10th Bt, KCMG, KCVO, CB; one *s* two *d*; 2nd, 1971, Valerie Harrington; two *s* twin *d*]. *Address:* Snowball Hill, Russell's Water, Henley on Thames RG9 6EU. *Club:* Arts. *Died 9 July 2004.*

ESPIE, Sir Frank (Fletcher), Kt 1979; OBE 1971; FTS, FIMMM, MAIMM, MAIME; company director, retired; *b* 8 May 1917; *s* of late Frank Fancett Espie and Laura Jean Espie; *m* 1st, 1941, Madeline Elizabeth Robertson (decd); one *s* three *d*; 2nd, 1985, Jean Primrose Angove. *Educ:* St Peter's Coll., Adelaide; Univ. of Adelaide (BEng). FTS 1978; FIMMM (FIMM 1958). CRA Ltd: Dir, 1968; Dep. Chm., 1974–79; non-exec. Dir, 1979–85; Bougainville Copper Ltd: Gen. Man., 1965; Man. Dir, 1969; Chm., 1971–79; non-exec. Dir, 1979–85. Director: ICI Aust. Ltd, 1979–87; Tubemakers of Australia, 1980–87; Westpac Banking Corporation, 1981–90; Woodside Petroleum, 1981–89. Chairman: Nat. Petroleum Adv. Cttee, 1979–87; Australian Mineral Foundn Inc., 1988–91. Member: Exec. Cttee, Aust. Mining Industry Council, 1973–81 (Pres., 1978–80); Council: Australasian Inst. of Mining and Metallurgy, 1970–88 (Pres., 1975; Inst. Medal, 1980); Aust. Acad. of Technological Scis, 1980–90. *Recreations:* swimming, golf. *Address:* 31 Grandview Grove, Toorak Gardens, SA 5065, Australia. *Clubs:* Melbourne, Athenæum, Royal Melbourne Golf (Melbourne); Union (Sydney); Adelaide (Adelaide). *Died 11 Jan. 2004.*

ESSEX, 10th Earl of, *cr* 1661; **Robert Edward de Vere Capell;** Baron Capell, 1641; Viscount Malden, 1661; *b* 13 Jan. 1920; *s* of Arthur Algernon de Vere Capell (*d* 1924) and Alice Mabel (*d* 1951), *d* of James Currie, Wimbledon; S kinsman, 1981; *m* 1942, Doris Margaret, *d* of George Frederick Tomlinson, Morecambe; one *s*. *Heir: s* Viscount Malden, *b* 29 May 1944. *Died 5 June 2005.*

ESSLIN, Martin Julius, OBE 1972; Professor of Drama, Stanford University, California (for two quarters annually), 1977–88, then Emeritus; *b* 8 June 1918; *s* of Paul Pereszlenyi and Charlotte Pereszlenyi (*née* Schiffer); *m* 1947, Renate Gerstenlang; one *d*. *Educ:* Gymnasium, Vienna; Vienna Univ.; Reinhardt Seminar of Dramatic Art, Vienna. Joined BBC, 1940; Producer and Scriptwriter, BBC European Services, 1941–55; Asst Head, BBC European Productions Dept, 1955; Asst Head, Drama (Sound), BBC, 1961; Head of Drama (Radio), BBC, 1963–77. Awarded title Professor by Pres. of Austria, 1967; Vis. Prof. of Theatre, Florida State Univ.,

1969–76. Hon. DLitt Kenyon Coll., Ohio, 1978. Ehrenkreuz für Kunst und Wissenschaft, 1st cl. (Austria), 1998. *Publications:* Brecht, A Choice of Evils, 1959; The Theatre of the Absurd, 1962, 8th edn 2001; (ed) Beckett (anthology of critical essays), 1965; Harold Pinter, 1967; The Genius of the German Theatre, 1968; Reflections, Essays on Modern Theatre (NY), 1969 (UK, as Brief Chronicles, 1970); The Peopled Wound: the plays of Harold Pinter, 1970, rev. edn as Pinter: a study of his plays, 1973, 4th edn as Pinter: the Playwright, 1982, 6th edn 2000; (ed) The New Theatre of Europe, 1970; Artaud, 1976; An Anatomy of Drama, 1976; (ed) Illustrated Encyclopaedia of World Theatre, 1977; Mediations, Essays on Brecht, Beckett and the Media, 1981; The Age of Television, 1982; The Field of Drama, 1987; trans. Horváth, Judgement Day, 1986. *Recreations:* reading, book collecting. *Address:* 64 Loudoun Road, NW8 0NA. *T:* (020) 7722 4243; Ballader's Plat, Winchelsea, Sussex TN36 4EN. *T:* (01797) 226392. *Club:* Garrick. *Died 24 Feb. 2002.*

ESTEY, Hon. Willard Zebedee, CC 1990; Counsel, McCarthy Tétrault, Toronto, since 1988; Chancellor, Wilfrid Laurier University, Waterloo, Ont, 1990–95; *b* 10 Oct. 1919; *s* of James Wilfred Estey and Muriel Baldwin Estey; *m* 1946, Marian Ruth McKinnon; three *s* one *d*. *Educ:* Univ. of Saskatchewan (BA, LLB); Harvard Law Sch. (LLM). Served Canadian Army and RCAF, 1939–45. Mem., Bar of Sask., 1942 and of Ont, 1947; QC Ont 1960. Prof., Coll. of Law, Univ. of Sask., 1946–47; Lectr, Osgoode Hall Law Sch., 1947–51. Practised law, Toronto, 1947–72. Pres., Canadian Bar Assoc., Ont, 1972. Mem. Court of Appeal, 1973, and Chief Justice of High Court, Supreme Court of Ont, 1975; Chief Justice of Ontario, 1976; Justice of Supreme Court of Canada, 1977–88. Commissioner: Steel Profits Inquiry, Royal Commn of Inquiry, 1974; Air Canada Inquiry, 1975; Inquiry into certain banking operations, 1985–86. Special Advr to Chm., Bank of Nova Scotia, 1990–94. Pres., Ballard Foundn. Formerly: Chm., Press Council of Ontario; Hockey Canada. Hon. LLD: Wilfrid Laurier Univ., Waterloo, Ont, 1977; Univ. of Toronto, 1979; Univ. of W Ont, 1980; Law Soc. of Upper Canada, 1981; Univ. of Saskatchewan, 1984; Univ. of Lethbridge, 1985. *Address:* 70 Rosehill Avenue, Toronto, ON M4T 2W7, Canada. *Died 25 Jan. 2002.*

EVANS, A. Briant; Hon. Consulting Gynæcological Surgeon, Westminster Hospital and Chelsea Hospital for Women; Hon. Consulting Obstetric Surgeon, Queen Charlotte's Maternity Hospital; *b* 26 June 1909; *e s* of late Arthur Evans, OBE, MD, MS, FRCS; *m* 1939, Audrey Marie (*d* 2003), *er d* of late Roland Eveleigh Holloway; three *s*. *Educ:* Westminster Sch.; Gonville and Caius Coll., Cambridge; Westminster Hosp. MA, MB, BCh Cantab. FRCS; FRCOG. Sometime Examiner in Obstetrics to Univs of Cambridge and London and to RCOG. Temp. Lieut-Col RAMC, served in Egypt, Italy and Austria; OC No. 9 Field Surgical Unit. *Address:* Chilton House, Chilton, Aylesbury, Bucks HP18 2LR. *Died 3 March 2005.*

EVANS, Alun S.; *see* Sylvester-Evans.

EVANS, (Arthur) Mostyn; General Secretary, Transport and General Workers Union, 1978–85; Member, TUC General Council, 1977–85; *b* 13 July 1925; *m* 1947, Laura Bigglestone; two *s* three *d* (and one *s* decd). *Educ:* Cefn Coed Primary Sch., S Wales; Church Road Secondary Modern Sch., Birmingham. Transport and General Workers Union: District Officer, Birmingham, Chem. and Engrg Industries, 1956; Regional Officer, Midlands, 1960; Nat. Officer, Engrg, 1966; National Secretary: Chem., Rubber, and Oil Industries, 1969; Engineering Industries, 1969; Automotive Section, 1969–73; Nat. Organiser, 1973–78. Part-time Mem., Nat. Bus Co., 1976–78; Member: BOTB, 1978–79; NEDC, 1978–84; Exec., ITF, 1980–; Council, ACAS, 1982–; Pres., ICEF, 1982– (Vice-Pres., 1980–82). Councillor (Lab), Borough of Kings Lynn and W Norfolk, 1991– (Mayor, 1996–97; Hon. Alderman, 2000). *Recreation:* music. *Address:* Cheney House, Cheney Hill, Heacham, King's Lynn, Norfolk PE31 7BX. *T:* (01485) 70477. *Died 12 Jan 2002.*

EVANS, Briant; see Evans, A. B.

EVANS, Emrys; see Evans, W. E.

EVANS, Gwynfor, Honorary President, Plaid Cymru, since 1982 (President, 1945–81, Vice-President, 1943–45); *b* 1 Sept. 1912; *s* of Dan Evans and Catherine Mary Richard; *m* 1941, Rhiannon Prys Thomas; four *s* three *d. Educ:* Gladstone Road Elementary Sch.; County Sch., Barry; Univ. of Wales, Aberystwyth (Fellow, 1994); St John's Coll., Oxford. Qual. Solicitor, 1939. Hon. Sec., Heddychwyr Cymru (Welsh Pacifist movement), 1939–45; Chm., Union of Welsh Independents, 1954. MP (Plaid Cymru) Carmarthen, July 1966–1970 and Oct. 1974–1979. Contested (Plaid Cymru) Carmarthen, 1979 and 1983. Mem., Carmarthen CC, 1949–74. Past Mem. Welsh Broadcasting Council. Hon. Fellow, Trinity Coll., Carmarthen, 1997. Hon. LLD Wales, 1973. Soc. of Cymmrodorion Medal, 1984. *Publications:* Plaid Cymru and Wales, 1950; Rhagom i Ryddid, 1964; Aros Mae, 1971; Wales can Win, 1973; Land of My Fathers, 1974; A National Future for Wales, 1975; Diwedd Prydeindod, 1981; Bywyd Cymro, 1982; Seiri Cenedl, 1986; Welsh Nation Builders, 1987; Pe Bai Cymru'n Rhydd, 1989; Fighting for Wales, 1990; Heddychiaeth Gristnogol yng Nghymru, 1991; Cymru o Hud, 1992; For the Sake of Wales, 1996; The Fight for Freedom, 2000; Gwlad yr Hud, 2000; External Wales, 2002. *Address:* Talar Wen, Pencarreg, Llanybydder, Dyfed SA40 9QQ. *T:* (01570) 480907. *Died 21 April 2005.*

EVANS, Huw Prideaux, CB 1993; Financial Advisor, International Monetary Fund, since 2000; *b* 21 Aug. 1941; *s* of late Richard Hubert Evans and Kathleen Annie Evans; *m* 1st, 1966, Anne (*née* Bray) (marr. diss.); two *s*; 2nd, 2002, Polly King. *Educ:* Cardiff High Sch.; King's Coll., Cambridge (MA); London Sch. of Econs and Polit. Science (MSc). Economist: HM Treasury, 1964–72; European Commn, 1972–73; Asst Econ. Sec., Hong Kong Govt, 1973–75; Sen. Econ. Adviser, 1976–79, Under Sec., 1980–89, Dep. Sec., 1989–94, HM Treasury; UK Exec. Dir, IMF and World Bank, and Econ. Minister, Washington, 1994–97; Special Adviser: Bank of England, 1997–98; FSA, 1998–99. *Address:* International Monetary Fund, 700 19th Street NW, Washington, DC 20007, USA. *Club:* Oxford and Cambridge. *Died 15 Feb. 2002.*

EVANS, Michael Nordon, CMG 1964; Permanent Secretary, Ministry of Health and Housing, Kenya, 1960–64; Vice-Consul (Commercial), Cape Town, 1965–82; *b* 27 April 1915; *s* of late Christmas and Lilian Margaret Louise Evans; *m* 1st, 1939, Mary Stockwood; one *d*; 2nd, 1951, Mary Josephine Suzette van Vloten; one *d. Educ:* Eastbourne Coll.; Queens' Coll., Cambridge (BA 1938). District Officer, Colonial Administrative Service, Kenya, 1939; African Courts Officer, Kenya, 1953; Dep. Comr for Local Govt, 1954; Permanent Sec., 1958. *Recreation:* latterly reading only. *Address:* Hugon Lodge, 13 Hugon Road, Claremont, Western Cape, 7700, Republic of South Africa. *Clubs:* Hawks (Cambridge); Kelvin Grove (Cape Town). *Died 22 April 2003.*

EVANS, Mostyn; see Evans, Arthur M.

EVANS, (William) Emrys, CBE 1981; Senior Regional Director, Wales, Midland Bank Ltd, 1976–84; *b* 4 April 1924; *s* of late Richard and Mary Elizabeth Evans; *m* 1946, Mair Thomas; one *d. Educ:* Llanfair Caereinion County Sch. FCIB. Served War, RN, 1942–46 (despatches 1944). Entered Midland Bank Ltd, 1941; Asst Gen. Manager (Agric.), 1967–72; Reg. Dir, S Wales, 1972–74; Reg. Dir, Wales, 1974–76. Director: Executive Secondment Ltd, 1983–90 (Vice Chm., 1983–90); Align-Rite Ltd, 1984–2001; Chm., Menter a Busnes, 1988–99; Chm. and

Founder Trustee, Sefydliad Addysg Menter a Busnes, 1998–. Chairman: Welsh Cttee for Economic and Industrial Affairs, 1984–91; Midland Bank Adv. Council for Wales, 1984–. Director: Develt Corp. for Wales, 1973–77; Welsh Industrial Develt Adv. Bd, 1975–86; Develt Bd for Rural Wales, 1976–89; Royal Welsh Agricl Soc., 1973– (Chm., Mgt Bd, 1999–); Mem. Council, CBI, Wales, 1975–86 (Chm., 1979–81). Pres., Royal Nat. Eisteddfod of Wales, 1980–83 (Fellow, 1997). Vice President: Tenovus Cancer Res. Unit, 1980–; Kidney Res. Unit for Wales Foundn, 1980–; Barnardos, 1989– (Chm., Dr Barnardo's Centenary in Wales Appeal, 1988); Trustee: Catherine and Lady Grace James Foundn, 1973–; John and Rhys Thomas James Foundn, 1973–; Welsh Sports Aid Trust, 1980–98 (Vice Chm., 1988–98); Llandovery Coll., 1982–93; Council for the Protection of Rural Wales, 1991–; Children's Hosp. for Wales Appeal Ltd, 1999–; Treas., Lloyd George Statue Appeal Trust, 1998–. Pres., Welsh Sports Aid Foundn, 1996– (Gov., 1980–; Chm., 1988–94); Member: Council for the Welsh Lang., 1973–78; Design Council Wales Adv. Cttee, 1981–86; Prince of Wales Cttee, 1975–87; Dairy Produce Quota Tribunal, 1984–92; NPFA, Cymru, 1998–2002. Vice Pres., Cardiff Business Club, 1975–; Pres., Cwlwm Busnes, 1995–. Pres., Welsh Congregational Church in Wales, 1989 (Treasurer, 1975–86); Sec., Ebenezer Welsh Cong. Ch, Cardiff, 1990–. Treasurer, Mansfield Coll., Oxford, 1977–89 (Trustee, 1989–95); Member, Court and Council: UC Swansea (later Univ. of Wales, Swansea), 1972–96 (Chm. Council, 1982–96; Fellow, 1997; Life Mem. Ct, 1998); UC Aberystwyth, 1979–84 (Fellow, 2001); Univ. of Wales, 1980– (Treas., 1998–99). Hon. LLD Wales, 1983. FRSA 1982. High Sheriff, S Glamorgan, 1985–86. *Recreations:* golf, gardening, music. *Address:* Maesglas, Pen-y-turnpike, Dinas Powis, Vale of Glamorgan CF64 4HH. *T:* (029) 2051 2985, *Fax:* (029) 2051 1091. *Club:* Cardiff and County (Cardiff). *Died 18 July 2004.*

EVANS O'ROURKE, Sarah Louise; Director for Resources and General Affairs, Secretariat General of European Commission, since 2000; *b* 3 Jan. 1948; *d* of John Desmond O'Rourke and Margaret Brenda (*née* Shelley, later Camou); *m* 1974, Richard Frederick Evans; one *s* one *d. Educ:* University Coll. London (LLB Hons 1969); Univ. of Notre Dame du Lac, USA (Cert. Amer. Law 1970). Trainee, Bank of America, London, 1971–72; Res. Asst, Brunel Univ., 1973; joined European Commn, 1974: DG XV Financial Instns and Fiscal Affairs, 1974–78; DG V Employment, Social Affairs and Educn, 1983–88; Asst to Head of Service, Task Force Human Resources, Educn, Trng and Youth, 1989–93; Head of Unit for Personnel and Admin, DG V Employment, Indust. Relns and Social Affairs, 1994–96; Dir for Rights and Obligations, DG IX Personnel and Admin, 1996–99; Principal Advr and Mem. of Cabinet of Pres., Eur. Commn, 1999–2000. *Recreations:* reading, swimming, gardening. *Address:* European Commission, Rue de la Loi 200, 1049 Brussels, Belgium. *Died 9 Jan. 2003.*

EVELEIGH, Air Vice-Marshal Geoffrey Charles, CB 1964; OBE 1945; RAF retired; *b* 25 Oct. 1912; *s* of Ernest Charles Eveleigh, Henley-on-Thames; *m* 1939, Anthea Josephine (*d* 1998), *d* of F. H. Fraser, Ceylon; one *s* one *d. Educ:* Brighton Coll.; RAF Coll., Cranwell. Joined RAF, 1932; served War of 1939–45 in Bomber Command and No 2 Group; Dep. Chief of Air Staff, Royal New Zealand Air Force, 1955–57; Air Commodore, 1957; Dir-Gen. of Signals, Air Ministry, 1959–61; Air Vice-Marshal, 1961; Air Officer, Administration, Fighter Command, 1961–64; retd 1965. *Address:* 22 Rosehill Park, Emmer Green, Reading RG4 8XE. *Club:* Royal Air Force. *Died 20 Dec. 2005.*

EVERARD, Simon, TD 1968; DL; Chairman, Alliance and Leicester plc (formerly Alliance and Leicester Building Society), 1994–98; *b* 30 Oct. 1928; *s* of Charles Miskin Everard and Monica Mary Everard (*née* Barford); *m* 1955,

Joceline Margaret Holt (*d* 2000); three *s* one *d*. *Educ:* Uppingham Sch.; Clare Coll., Cambridge (Hons History). Served TA, Leics Yeomanry, subseq. Leics and Derbys Yeomanry. Ellis & Everard: joined 1952; Chm., 1980–90 and 1991–92; joined Leicester Temperance Building Soc., 1967; merged with Leicester Permanent Bldg Soc., 1974, with Alliance Bldg Soc., 1984; Dep. Chm., 1984–94. Non-exec. Dir, Croda International, 1991–98. DL Leics, 1984. *Recreations:* shooting, tennis, golf, bridge. *Address:* South View Farm, Main Street, Tur Langton, Leics LE8 0PJ. *Club:* Cavalry and Guards. *Died 17 Jan. 2005.*

EVERETT, Douglas Hugh, MBE 1946; FRS 1980; Leverhulme Professor of Physical Chemistry, 1954–82, then Emeritus, Dean of Faculty of Science, 1966–68, Pro-Vice-Chancellor, 1973–76, University of Bristol; *b* 26 Dec. 1916; *e s* of late Charles Everett and Jessie Caroline; *m* 1942, Frances Elizabeth Jessop (*d* 1999); two *d*. *Educ:* Grammar Sch., Hampton-on-Thames; University of Reading (Wantage Scholar, 1935–38; Kitchener Scholar, 1936–39; BSc 1938); Balliol Coll., Oxford (Ramsay Fellow, 1939–41; DPhil 1942; MA 1947); DSc Reading 1956. Special Scientific Duties, WO, 1942–45. ICI Fellow, Oxford Univ., 1945–47; Chemistry Lecturer, Dundee Univ. Coll., 1947; Fellow, Lecturer and Tutor, Exeter Coll., Oxford, 1947–48; Prof. of Chemistry, Dundee Univ. Coll., University of St Andrews, 1948–54. Chm., IUPAC Commn on Colloid and Surface Chemistry, 1969–73. Mem., Building Research Board, DSIR, 1954–61; a Vice-Pres., Faraday Soc., 1958–61, 1963–65, 1968–70, Pres., 1976–78; Mem. Chemical Soc. Council, 1961–64, 1972–74 (Tilden Lectr, 1955; Award in Colloid and Surface Chemistry, 1971); Pres., Section B, BAAS, 1979–80; a Vice-Pres. and Gen. Sec., BAAS, 1983–88; Pres., Internat. Assoc. of Colloid and Interface Scientists, 1988–90. FRSE 1950. *Publications:* Introduction to Chemical Thermodynamics, 1959, 2nd edn, 1971; Basic Principles of Colloid Science, 1988; (with W. Rudzinski) Adsorption of Gases on Heterogeneous Surfaces, 1991; papers on physical chemistry in scientific jls. *Recreations:* walking, painting. *Address:* School of Chemistry, The University, Bristol BS8 1TS; 35 Downleaze, Bristol BS9 1LX. *Died 25 June 2002.*

EVERSON, Sir Frederick (Charles), KCMG 1968 (CMG 1956); HM Diplomatic Service, retired; *b* 6 Sept. 1910; *s* of Frederick Percival Everson; *m* 1937, Linda Mary Clark (*d* 1984); two *s* one *d* (and one *s* decd). *Educ:* Tottenham County Sch., Middlesex; BSc (Econ.) London. Entered Civil Service, 1928; Consular Service, 1934; Chief Administrative Officer, British Embassy, Bonn, Germany, 1953–56; Ambassador to El Salvador, 1956–60; Commercial Counsellor, British Embassy, Stockholm, 1960–63; Minister (Economic), British Embassy, Paris, 1963–68. *Died 27 May 2001.*

EVETTS, Prof. Jan Edgar, PhD; Professor of Device Materials, University of Cambridge, 1998–2004, then Emeritus Professor and Distinguished Research Fellow; *b* 31 March 1939. *Educ:* Pembroke Coll., Cambridge (BA 1961; MA 1965; PhD 1966). Department of Materials Science and Metallurgy, University of Cambridge: formerly Lectr; Reader in Device Materials, 1993–98; Fellow, Pembroke Coll., 1965–96. Royal Soc. Armourers and Brasiers' Co. Award (jtly), 1993. *Publications:* (ed) High Temperature Superconductivity, 1991; (ed) Critical Currents: symposium proceedings, 1992; (ed) Concise Encyclopaedia of Magnetic and Superconducting Materials, 1992. *Address:* Department of Materials Science and Metallurgy, University of Cambridge, Pembroke Street, Cambridge CB2 3QZ. *Died 18 Aug. 2005.*

EWBANK, Prof. Inga-Stina; Professor of English Literature, University of Leeds, 1985–97, then Emeritus; *b* 13 June 1932; *d* of Gustav and Ingeborg Ekeblad; *m* 1959, Roger Ewbank; one *s* two *d*. *Educ:* Högre Allänna Läroverket för Flickor, Gothenburg; Univs of Carleton (BA), Gothenburg (Fil.kand.), Sheffield (MA) and Liverpool (PhD). William Noble Fellow, Univ. of

Liverpool, 1955–57; Res. Fellow at Shakespeare Inst., Univ. of Birmingham, 1957–60; Univ. of Liverpool: Asst Lectr, 1960–63; Lectr, 1963–70; Sen. Lectr, 1970–72; Reader in English Literature, Bedford Coll., Univ. of London, 1972–74, Hildred Carlile Prof., 1974–84. Vis. Lectr, Univ. of Munich, 1959–60; Vis. Assoc. Prof., Northwestern Univ., 1966; Visiting Professor: Harvard Univ., 1974; Univ. of Maryland, 1981; Georgetown Univ., 1982; Columbia Univ., 1984, 1987. Mem., Univ. Grants Cttee, Hong Kong, 1982–97. Hon. DPhil: Oslo, 1997; Gothenburg, 2001; Hon. Dr jur Lingnan (Hong Kong), 1999. Bauhinia Silver Star (Hong Kong), 1999. *Publications:* Their Proper Sphere: A Study of the Brontë Sisters as Early-Victorian Female Novelists, 1966; Shakespeare, Ibsen and the Unspeakable (Inaugural Lecture), 1975; (with Peter Hall) Ibsen's John Gabriel Borkman: An English Version, 1975; The Wild Duck, 1991; (ed jtly) Shakespeare's Styles, 1980; The Arts of Performance in Elizabethan Drama, 1991; Three Chamber Plays by August Strindberg, 1997; Anglo-Scandinavian Cross-currents, 1999; Five Ibsen Plays (trans.), 2001; chapters in: A New Companion to Shakespeare Studies, 1971; The Cambridge Companion to Shakespeare Studies, 1986; The Cambridge Companion to Ibsen Studies, 1994, and other books; contrib. Shakespeare Survey, Ibsen Yearbook, Rev. Eng. Studies, Mod. Lang. Rev., English Studies, etc. *Recreations:* same as work: reading, theatre; children. *Address:* 19 Woodfield Road, Ealing, W5 1SL. *T:* (020) 8997 2895. *Died 7 June 2004.*

EWIN, Sir David Ernest Thomas F.; see Floyd Ewin.

EYNON, Prof. John Marles, OBE 1990; RIBA; FSA; Professor of Architecture, University of Wales, and Head, Welsh School of Architecture, 1980–87, then Professor Emeritus; *b* 3 Jan. 1923; *s* of Philip Stanley Eynon and Gwendoline Eynon (*née* Marles); *m* 1950, Yvonne Marie, *e d* of Claire Faber (*née* Vermuse) and Vivian Valdemar Faber. *Educ:* Welsh Sch. of Architecture, Univ. of Wales (MA, Dip. Arch.) ARIBA 1950, FRIBA 1963, FSA 1974. Military service: Captain RE, regtl duties, wounded, training, staff work. Chartered and Registered Architect, 1950; with Alwyn Lloyd & Gordon, later Alex Gordon & Partners, 1950–70; private practice and consultancy (historic buildings and conservation), 1970–. Lectr, Sen. Lectr, Prof. of Architecture, Welsh Sch. of Architecture, Univ. of Wales, 1956–87. Member: Historic Buildings Council for Wales, 1970–95; Welsh Arts Council, 1978–89; Craft Cttee for Wales (Chm.), Craft Council, 1970–89; Cambrian Archaeol. Assoc., 1969–; Assoc. of Artists and Designers in Wales, 1970–98; Royal Welsh Agricl Soc., 1977; Llandaff Diocesan Adv. Cttee, Church in Wales, 1988–; Cardiff Castle Management Cttee, 1990–. Prince of Wales Awards, 1976, 1977; Europa Nostra Award, 1985. *Publications:* contribs to learned jls. *Recreation:* painter (retrospective exhibition, Cardiff, 1976). *Address:* 39 Waterloo Road, Penylan, Cardiff CF23 9BJ. *T:* (029) 2048 5098. *Died 18 Feb. 2004.*

EYRE, Maj.-Gen. Sir James (Ainsworth Campden Gabriel), KCVO 1986 (CVO 1978); CBE 1980 (OBE 1975); *b* 2 Nov. 1930; *s* of late Edward Joseph Eyre and Hon. Dorothy Elizabeth Anne Pelline (*née* Lyon-Dalberg-Acton); *m* 1967, Monica Ruth Esther Smyth; one *s* one *d*. *Educ:* Harvard Univ. (BA, LLB). Commissioned RHG, 1955; Commanding Officer, The Blues and Royals, 1970–73; GSO 1 HQ London District, 1973–75; Officer Commanding Household Cavalry and Silver Stick, 1975–78; Col GS HQ Northern Ireland, 1978–80; Sec., Chiefs of Staff Cttee, MoD, 1980–82; Dir of Defence Programmes Staff (Concepts), MoD, 1982–83; GOC London Dist and Maj. Gen. Comdg Household Div., 1983–86. Comdr SMO Malta Pro Merito Militensis with Swords, 1999. *Recreations:* racing, shooting. *Address:* Somerville House, East Garston, Berks RG17 7EX. *Club:* Turf. *Died 3 Jan. 2003.*

F

FABER, Julian Tufnell; Chairman: Willis Faber Ltd, 1972–77; Cornhill Insurance plc, 1986–88 (Director, 1972–88); *b* 6 April 1917; *s* of late Alfred and Edith Faber; *m* 1944, Lady (Ann) Caroline, *e d* of 1st Earl of Stockton, OM, PC, FRS, and late Lady Dorothy Macmillan; three *s* one *d* (and one *s* decd). *Educ:* Winchester; Trinity Coll., Cambridge. Joined Willis, Faber & Dumas Ltd, 1938. Served Welsh Guards (Major 2nd Bn), 1939–45. Director: Willis, Faber & Dumas Ltd, 1952; Willis, Faber & Dumas (Agencies) Ltd, 1965; Taisho Marine & Fire Insurance Co. (UK) Ltd, 1972 (Chm.); Willis Faber (Middle East) SAL, 1973; Morgan Grenfell Ltd, 1974–77; Allianz International Insurance Co., 1974. Former Mem. Bd of Governors, Summer Fields Sch., Oxford. Member: MCC Cttee, 1981–84; Kent CCC Cttee, 1977–84. *Address:* Fisher's Gate, Withyham, E Sussex TN7 4BB; Flat 4, 17 Sloane Court West, SW3 4TD. *Clubs:* White's, City of London, MCC. *Died 11 Jan. 2002.*

FABER, Thomas Erle, PhD; Chairman, Geoffrey Faber Holdings Ltd (formerly Faber & Faber (Publishers) Ltd), since 1977 (Director since 1969); Fellow of Corpus Christi College, Cambridge, since 1953; *b* 25 April 1927; *s* of Sir Geoffrey Faber; *m* 1st, 1959, Penelope (*d* 1983), *d* of Clive Morton, actor; two *s* two *d*; 2nd, 1986, Dr Elisabeth van Houts; one *s* one *d*. *Educ:* Oundle Sch.; Trinity Coll., Cambridge (MA, PhD). University of Cambridge: Res. Fellow, Trinity Coll., 1950–53; Univ. Demonstr, 1953–58; Armourers' and Brasiers' Fellow, 1958–59; Lectr in Physics, 1959–93; Treasurer, Corpus Christi Coll., 1963–76. *Publications:* Introduction to the Theory of Liquid Metals, 1972; Fluid Dynamics for Physicists, 1995; papers on superconductivity, liquid metals and liquid crystals. *Recreations:* walking, local history. *Address:* The Old Vicarage, Thompson's Lane, Cambridge CB5 8AQ. *T:* (01223) 356685. *Died 27 July 2004.*

FAGE, Prof. John Donnelly, MA, PhD; Professor of African History, 1963–84, then Emeritus, Pro-Vice-Chancellor, 1979–84, and Vice-Principal 1981–84, University of Birmingham; *b* 3 June 1921; *s* of late Arthur Fage, CBE, FRS, and Winifred Eliza Donnelly; *m* 1949, Jean, *d* of late Fred Banister, MBE; one *s* one *d*. *Educ:* Tonbridge Sch.; Magdalene Coll., Cambridge (scholar, MA, PhD). Served War, Pilot with RAFVR (Flt Lt), 1941–45. Bye-Fellow, Magdalene Coll., Cambridge, 1947–49; Lectr and Sen. Lectr, 1949–55; Prof. of History, 1955–59, and Dep. Principal, 1957–59, UC of the Gold Coast; Lectr in African History, SOAS, Univ. of London, 1959–63; University of Birmingham: Dir, Centre of West African Studies, 1963–82; Dep. Dean, Faculty of Arts, 1973–75, Dean, 1975–78. Visiting Professor: Univ. of Wisconsin, Madison, 1957; Smith Coll., Northampton, Mass, 1962. Founding Hon. Sec., African Studies Assoc. of the UK, 1963–66 (Vice-Pres. 1967–68, Pres. 1968–69); Council Mem., Internat. African Inst., 1965–75, and Consultative Dir, 1975–80; Member: UNESCO Scientific Cttee for Gen. History of Africa, 1971–80; Culture Adv. Cttee of UK Nat. Commn for UNESCO, 1967–85 (Chm., 1978–85); Co-ordinating Council of Area Studies Associations, 1980–86 (Vice-Chm. 1980–84, Chm., 1984–86); Chm., Birmingham Jt Cttee for Adult Educn Inf. and Advice Services, 1985–88. FRHistS. Hon. Fellow, SOAS, Univ. of London. Editor (with Roland Oliver), The Jl of African History, 1960–73; Gen. Editor (with Roland Oliver), The Cambridge History of Africa, 8 vols, 1975–86. *Publications:* An Introduction to the History of West Africa, 1955, 3rd edn 1962; An Atlas of African History, 1958, 2nd edn 1978; Ghana, a Historical Interpretation, 1959; (with Roland Oliver) A Short History of Africa, 1962, 6th edn 1988; A History of West Africa, 1969, reprinted 1993; (ed) Africa Discovers Her Past, 1970; (ed with Roland Oliver) Papers on African Prehistory, 1970; A History of Africa, 1978, 3rd edn 1995; A Guide to Sources for Western Africa, 1987, 2nd edn 1994; To Africa and Back (memoirs), 2002; articles in historical and Africanist jls. *Recreations:* doing things to houses and gardens. *Address:* Hafod Awel, Pennal, Machynlleth, Powys SY20 9DP. *T:* (01654) 791207. *Club:* Athenæum. *Died 6 Aug. 2002.*

FAIR, Donald Robert Russell, OBE (mil.) 1945; Board Member, Central Electricity Generating Board, 1975–77; *b* 26 Dec. 1916; *s* of Robert Sidney Fair and Mary Louie Fair; *m* 1941, Patricia Laurie Rudland; one *s*. *Educ:* Roan Sch., Blackheath; King's Coll., London Univ. (BSc, AKC). CEng, FInstE; CPhys, FInstP. Served War of 1939–45, RAF (Wing Comdr; despatches 1944; USAAF Commendation 1944). Lectr, RMA Sandhurst, 1948–50; UKAEA, 1950–62; Central Electricity Generating Bd, 1962–77. *Recreations:* sailing, cricket. *Address:* 22 Carlton Leas, The Leas, Folkestone, Kent CT20 2DJ. *T:* (01303) 250573. *Died 19 Aug. 2001.*

FAIRCLOUGH, Rt Hon. Ellen Louks, PC (Can.) 1957; CC 1995 (OC 1979); FCA 1965; UE; Member of Progressive Conservative Party, Canada; *b* Hamilton, Ont, 28 Jan. 1905; *d* of Norman Ellsworth Cook and Nellie Bell Louks; *m* 1931, David Henry Gordon Fairclough (decd); (one *s* decd). *Educ:* Hamilton Public and Secondary Schs. Certified Public Accountant, public practice, 1935–57 (Fellow, Chartered Accountants of Ontario, 1965). Hamilton City Council: Alderman, 1946–49; Controller, 1950. Elected to House of Commons as Progressive Conservative mem. for Hamilton West, 1950; re-elected at gen. elections, 1953, 1957, 1958, 1962, defeated in 1963 election. Sec. of State for Canada, 1957–58; Minister of Citizenship and Immigration, 1958–62; Postmaster-Gen., 1962–63. Chancellor, Royal Hamilton Coll. of Music, 1978–80. Mem. Bd, Ontario Bicentennial Commn, 1983–84; Hon. Treas. and Exec. Dir, Chedoke-McMaster Hosps Foundn, 1982–86; Patron: Huguenot Soc. of Canada, 1979–; United Empire Loyalists Assoc., Hamilton Br., 1980–. Internat. Treasurer, Zonta Internat. HQ, Chicago, 1972–76 (Hon. Life Mem.). Ontario Govt Bldg named Ellen Fairclough Bldg, 1982. LLD (*hc*) McMaster, 1975; Hon. LLD Brock, 1996. *Publication:* Saturday's Child (memoirs), 1996. *Recreations:* music, reading and photography. *Clubs:* Albany (Toronto); Hamilton, Zonta I (Hamilton); Faculty (McMaster). *Died 13 Nov. 2004.*

FAIRCLOUGH, Sir John (Whitaker), Kt 1990; FREng, FBCS; Chief Scientific Adviser to Cabinet Office, 1986–90; *b* 23 Aug. 1930; *m* 1st, 1954, Margaret Ann (*d* 1996); two *s* one *d*; 2nd, 2000, Karen Jefferson. *Educ:* Manchester Univ. (BScTech). Ferranti, 1954; IBM: Poughkeepsie Lab., US, 1957; Hursley Lab., UK, 1958; Dir of Develt, IBM UK Ltd, 1964; Asst Gen. Manager and Dir Data Processing, IBM UK, 1968; Dir, Raleigh Development Lab., USA, 1970; System Develt Div. Vice Pres., Raleigh, USA, 1972; System Communication Div. Vice Pres. and Man. Dir, Dir of Develt, Hursley Lab., UK, 1974; System Product Div. Vice Pres. and Man. Dir, Hursley Lab., UK, 1982; Dir of Manufacturing & Develt, IBM UK Ltd, and Chm., IBM UK Laboratories Ltd, 1983. Chairman: Systematica Ltd, 1990–92; Rothschild Ventures Ltd, 1990–98; Southampton Holdings Ltd, 1996–; Smart Chemical Co. Ltd, 1998–; Opsys plc, 1998–; non-executive Director: Oxford Instruments Gp, 1990–98; N. M. Rothschild & Sons Ltd, 1990–97; Infolink plc, 1991–93; DSC (Europe), 1992–98; DSC

Communication Corp., 1992–98; Lucas Industries, 1992–96; Psion plc, 1995–2000; Southampton Innovation Ltd, 1996–; Southampton Hldgs Ltd, 1997–. Chairman: Engineering Council, 1991–96 (Mem., 1982–90); CEST, 1990–95; Prince Charles' Innovation Initiative, 1991–97. Pres., BCS, 1987. Vice Pres., UMIST, 1992–95; Dep. Chm., Council, Southampton Univ., 1996–2001. Trustee, Mental Health Foundn, 1997–98. FCGI 1997. Freeman, City of London, 1989. Fellow, Nat. Acad. of Engrg, USA, 1990. Hon. FICE 1995; Hon. FIEE 1996; Hon. FIMechE 1996. Hon. Fellow: Portsmouth Polytech., 1991; Manchester Metropolitan Univ., 1992. Hon. DSc: Southampton, 1983; Cranfield, 1987; Manchester, 1988; Aston, 1990; Polytech. of Central London, 1991; City, 1992; Hon. DTech Loughborough, 1990. Mensford Gold Medal, IProdE, 1989; Gold Medal Award of Merit, Carmen's Co., 1995; President's Award, Engrg Council, 1996. *Recreations:* gardening, carpentry. *Address:* 3 Clockhouse Close, SW19 5NT.

Died 5 June 2003.

FAIRWEATHER, Brig. Claude Cyril, CB 1967; CBE 1965 (OBE 1944); TD 1944; JP; Vice Lord-Lieutenant, County of Cleveland, 1977–82; Chairman, North of England TA&VRA, 1968–71; *b* 17 March 1906; *s* of Nicholas Fairweather, Middlesbrough; *m* 1930, Alice Mary, *e d* of late Sir William Crosthwaite; one *s* one *d*. *Educ:* St Peter's Sch., York. 2nd Lieut, Royal Corps of Signals, 1928; Lt-Col 1941; Col 1943; Brig. 1945. Chm., North Riding T&AFA, 1950–53 and 1962–68; Mem., TA Advisory Cttee and TA Exec. Cttee, 1968–71. Chm., St John Council, N Yorks (Vice-Pres., N Yorks St John Amb. Bde); Hon. Col, 34 (N) Signal Regt (V), 1967–75; Chairman: N Riding Co. Cadet Cttee, 1947–52; St Luke's HMC, Middlesbrough, 1959–74; Cleveland AHA, 1973–76. Retd Company Dir. Hon. Trust Representative for Cleveland, Royal Jubilee Trusts, 1977–81. DL 1949, JP 1963, NR Yorks. KStJ 1978. *Recreations:* golf, cricket, Rugby football. *Address:* Broomcroft House, Eccleshall Road South, Sheffield S11 9PY. *T:* (0114) 235 2352, *Fax:* (0114) 235 2351. *Clubs:* Army and Navy; Cleveland (Middlesbrough); Royal and Ancient (St Andrews).

Died 17 May 2003.

FALCONER, Prof. Douglas Scott, FRS 1973; FRSE 1972; *b* 10 March 1913; *s* of Gerald Scott Falconer and Lillias Harriet Gordon Douglas; *m* 1942, Margaret Duke; two *s*. *Educ:* Edinburgh Academy; Univ. of St Andrews (BSc); Univ. of Cambridge (PhD, ScD). Scientific Staff of Agricultural Research Council, 1947–68; Prof. of Genetics, Univ. of Edinburgh, and Dir, ARC Unit of Animal Genetics, 1968–80. *Publications:* Introduction to Quantitative Genetics, 1960, 4th edn 1996; papers in scientific jls. *Died 23 Feb. 2004.*

FALCONER, Peter Serrell, FRIBA; Founder of The Falconer Partnership, Architects and Consultants, and of Handling Consultants Ltd, Stroud and Johannesburg; *b* 7 March 1916; *s* of Thomas Falconer, FRIBA, and Florence Edith Falconer; presumed heir to the Barony (1206) and Lordship (1646) of Halkerton, vacant since 1966; *m* 1941, Mary Hodson; three *s* one *d*. *Educ:* Bloxham Sch., Banbury. Commenced practice in Stroud, as partner in Ellery Anderson Roiser & Falconer, 1944; Sen. Partner of Peter Falconer and Partners, 1959–82 (with br. office in Adelaide, SA, 1970). Specialist in materials handling and industrial architecture. Mem., Materials Handling Inst. FRSA. *Publications:* Building and Planning for Industrial Storage and Distribution, 1975; contributor to: Architectural Review; Architects' Jl; Material Handling magazines. *Recreations:* restoring historic buildings, garden planning, motor sport. *Address:* St Francis, Lammas Park, Minchinhampton, Stroud, Glos GL6 9HA. *T:* (01453) 882188. *Died 29 Jan. 2003.*

FALETAU, 'Inoke Fotu; *see* 'Akau'ola.

FALKINGHAM, Ven. John Norman; Warden, Community of the Holy Name, 1969–85; *b* 9 Feb. 1917;

2nd *s* of Alfred Richard Falkingham and Amy Grant (*née* Macallister); *m* 1947, Jean Dorothy Thoren; two *d*. *Educ:* Geelong Grammar Sch., Corio, Vic; Trinity Coll., Univ. of Melbourne. BA (Hons) Melbourne 1940; ThL (1st Cl. Hons), ThD 1978, Australian Coll. of Theol.; prizes for Divinity and Biblical Greek. Deacon, 1941; priest, 1942. Curate of Holy Trinity, Surrey Hills, Vic, 1941–44; Chaplain, Trinity Coll., Univ. of Melbourne, 1944–50; Incumbent, St Paul's, Caulfield, Vic, 1950–61; Exam. Chaplain to Archbishop of Melbourne, 1947–61; Lectr in Theol. Faculty, Trinity Coll., Melbourne, 1950–60; Canon of St Paul's Cath., Melbourne, 1959–61; Dean of Newcastle, NSW, 1961–75; Rector of St Paul's, Manuka, ACT, 1975–82; Canon of St Saviour's Cath., Goulburn, 1976–81; Archdeacon of Canberra, 1981–82, Archdeacon Emeritus, 1982. Sec., Liturgical Commn of Gen. Synod, 1966–78; Mem. Bd of Delegates, Aust. Coll. of Theology, 1962–88; Lecturer: Canberra Coll. of Ministry, 1975–84; St Mark's Library, Canberra, 1982–87; Chm., Bd of Dirs, Canberra C of E Girls' Grammar Sch., 1983–90. *Publications:* articles in various jls. *Recreation:* walking. *Address:* 4 Serra Place, Stirling, ACT 2611, Australia. *Died 22 March 2005.*

FALLA, Paul Stephen; Deputy Director of Research, Foreign Office, 1958–67; *b* 25 Oct. 1913; *s* of Norris Stephen Falla and Audrey Frances Stock, Dunedin, New Zealand; *m* 1958, Elizabeth Shearer; one *d*. *Educ:* Wellington and Christ's Colls, NZ; Balliol Coll., Oxford (Scholar). Appointed to Foreign Office, 1936; served HM Embassies, Warsaw, 1938–39, Ankara, 1939–43, Tehran, 1943; Foreign Office, 1943–46; UK Delegn to UN, New York, 1946–49; Foreign Office, 1949–67. Member: Exec. Cttee, Translators' Assoc., Soc. of Authors, 1971–73 and 1984–86 (Vice-Chm., 1973); Council, Inst. Linguists, 1975–81; Cttee, Translators' Guild, 1975–81. FIL 1984; Fellow, Inst. of Translation and Interpreting, 1989. Scott Moncrieff Prize, 1972 and 1981; Schlegel-Tieck Prize, 1983. *Publications:* (ed) The Oxford English-Russian Dictionary, 1984; about 50 book translations from French, German, Dutch, Russian, Polish and other languages, 1967–. *Recreation:* reading (history, philosophy, poetry, language matters). *Address:* 63 Freelands Road, Bromley, Kent BR1 3HZ. *T:* (020) 8460 4995. *Club:* Travellers. *Died 9 Aug. 2003.*

FANSHAWE OF RICHMOND, Baron *cr* 1983 (Life Peer), of South Cerney in the County of Gloucestershire; **Anthony Henry Fanshawe Royle,** KCMG 1974; *b* 27 March 1927; *s* of Sir Lancelot Royle, KBE; *m* 1957, Shirley Worthington; two *d*. *Educ:* Harrow; Sandhurst. Captain, The Life Guards (Germany, Egypt, Palestine and Transjordan), 1945–48; 21st SAS Regt (TA), 1948–51, M Sqn, 1950–51. Joined Sedgwick Collins, 1948; Dir, 1984–99, Chm., 1993–97, Sedgwick Gp. MP (C) Richmond, 1959–83; Parliamentary Private Secretary: to Under-Sec. of State for the Colonies, 1960; to Sec. of State for Air, 1960–62; to Minister of Aviation, 1962–64; Vice-Chm., Cons. Parly Foreign Affairs Cttee, 1965–67; Tory Whip, 1967–70; Parly Under-Sec. of State for Foreign and Commonwealth Affairs, 1970–74. Vice-Chm., Cons. Party Orgn, 1979–84 (Chm., Internat. Office, 1979–84). Mem., Assembly of Council of Europe and WEU, 1965. Chm., Wilkinson Sword Gp, 1980–83; Director: Westland Gp, 1985–94; Xerox UK (formerly Rank Xerox UK), 1988–2001; TI Group, 1990–99. Vice Pres., Franco-British Council, 1975–99. Develt Trustee, Nat. Army Mus., 1981–. Esteemed Family Order (1st cl.), Brunei, 1975. *Address:* House of Lords, SW1A 0PW. *Clubs:* Pratt's, White's, Brooks's. *Died 28 Dec. 2001.*

FARMER, Frank Reginald, OBE 1967; FRS 1981; Director, Safety Reliability Directorate, Department of Atomic Energy, then Atomic Energy Authority, 1947–79, retired; *b* 18 Dec. 1914; *s* of Frank Henry Farmer and Minnie Godson; *m* 1939, Betty Smart; one *s* two *d*. *Educ:* St John's Coll., Cambridge (scholar; BA). Kestner Evaporator & Engineering Co., 1936–46. Editor,

Reliability Engineering, 1980. FInstP 1965; Hon. FSE 1974; Foreign Associate, Nat. Acad. of Engineers, USA, 1980. Churchill Gold Medal, Soc. of Engrs, 1974. *Publication:* Nuclear Reactor Safety, 1977. *Recreations:* golf, books. *Address:* The Long Wood, Lyons Lane, Appleton, Warrington WA4 5ND. *T:* (01925) 262503.
Died 10 June 2001.

FARMER, Hugh Robert Macdonald, CB 1967; *b* 3 Dec. 1907; *s* of late Charles Edward Farmer and late Emily (*née* Randolph); *m* 1st, 1934, Penelope Frances (*d* 1963), *d* of late Capt. Evelyn Boothby, RN; one *s* three *d*; 2nd, 1966, Jean (*d* 1988), *widow* of Peter Bluett Winch. *Educ:* Cheam Sch.; Eton Coll.; New Coll., Oxford. House of Commons: Asst Clerk, 1931; Sen. Clerk, 1943; Clerk of Private Bills and Taxing Officer, and Examr of Petitions for Private Bills, 1958–60; Clerk of Cttees, 1960–65; Clerk/Administrator, 1965–72, retired 1972. *Recreation:* reading. *Address:* Redcot, Three Gates Lane, Haslemere, Surrey GU27 2LL. *T:* (01428) 656367. *Club:* MCC.
Died 26 May 2004.

FARMER, Robert Frederick, OBE 1985; General Secretary, Institute of Journalists, 1962–87; Member of Council, Media Society, 1982–90 (Secretary, 1973–82); *b* 19 Aug. 1922; *s* of Frederick Leonard Farmer and Gladys Farmer (*née* Winney); *m* 1958, Anne Walton. *Educ:* Saltley Grammar Sch., Birmingham. Served War of 1939–45, Royal Armoured Corps, 1941–52 (commnd 3rd Carabiniers, despatches, Burma campaign). Secretariat: Instn of Plant Engineers, 1952–59; Instn of Civil Engineers, 1959–62. Consultative Mem., Press Council, 1962–87; Mem., Cttee on Defamation, 1971–75. *Recreation:* art history. *Address:* c/o Chartered Institute of Journalists, Suite 2, Dock Offices, Surrey Quays, Lower Road, SE16 2XL. *Died 27 July 2003.*

FARNDON, Prof. John Richard, MD; FRCS; Professor of Surgery, University of Bristol, since 1988; Hon. Consultant Surgeon, Bristol Royal Infirmary, since 1988; *b* 16 Feb. 1946; *s* of George Arthur Farndon and Margaret Cooper; *m* 1972, Christine Brenda Louet; two *s* one *d*. *Educ:* Woodhouse Grammar Sch., Sheffield; Univ. of Newcastle upon Tyne (BSc, MB BS, MD). Surgical training posts in Newcastle upon Tyne, 1971–79; Peel Travelling Fellow and Internat. Res. Fellow, Duke Univ., USA, 1979–81; Sen. Lectr in Surgery, Univ. of Newcastle upon Tyne and Consultant to Royal Infirmary, Newcastle, 1981–88. James IV Travelling Fellow, 1984; Hunterian Prof., RCS, 1985; Travelling Fellow, Australasian Coll. of Surgeons, 1985; British Council Scholar to India, 1991; Dist. Visitor, RCS of Australia, 1993; Penman Vis. Prof., Univ. of Cape Town, 1995. Ext. Examiner, Chinese Univ. of Hong Kong, 1994. Vice-Pres-designate, Assoc. of Surgeons of GB and Ireland. Hon. Fellow, Assoc. of Surgeons in India, 1997; Hon. FRCSE. Consultant to World Jl of Surgery, 1991–; Editor, British Jl of Surgery, 1992– (Chm.-designate, Editl Bd). *Publications:* (ed with G. Keen) Operative Surgery and Management, 3rd edn 1992; (ed) Breast and Endocrine Surgery, 1997; numerous papers and chapters on surgical endocrinology and oncology. *Recreations:* gardening, Betjeman Society (founder member), classical music. *Address:* Department of Surgery, Bristol Royal Infirmary, Marlborough Street, Bristol BS2 8HW. *T:* (0117) 926 0601. *Clubs:* Royal Society of Medicine; Clifton (Bristol).
Died 6 Feb. 2002.

FARNHAM, 12th Baron, *cr* 1756; **Barry Owen Somerset Maxwell;** Bt (NS) 1627; Chairman, Avon Rubber plc, 1978–97 (Director, 1966–97); Director, General Accident Life Assurance Ltd, 1996–97; *b* 7 July 1931; *s* of Hon. Somerset Arthur Maxwell, MP (died of wounds received in action, 1942), and Angela Susan (*d* 1953), *o d* of late Capt. Marshall Owen Roberts; *S* grandfather, 1957; *m* 1959, Diana Marion (CVO 1998), *er d* of Nigel Gunnis; two adopted *d*. *Educ:* Eton; Harvard Univ. Chairman: Brown, Shipley & Co. Ltd (Merchant Bankers), 1984–91 (Dir, 1959–91); Brown Shipley Hldgs plc, 1976–91; Dir,

1967–95, Dep. Chm., 1987–89, Chm., 1989–95, Provident Mutual Life Assce Assoc. Pres., Tree Council, 1992–. Pro Grand Master, United Grand Lodge of England, 1991–2001. *Heir: b* Hon. Simon Kenlis Maxwell [*b* 12 Dec. 1933; *m* 1964, Karol Anne, *d* of Maj.-Gen. G. E. Prior-Palmer, CB, DSO, and Katherine Edith Bibby; two *s* one *d* (of whom one *s* one *d* are twins)]. *Address:* 11 Earl's Court Gardens, SW5 0TD; Farnham, Co. Cavan. *Clubs:* Boodle's, City of London; Kildare Street and University (Dublin). *Died 22 March 2001.*

FARNINGHAM, (Alexander) Ian, DSC; Managing Director, Industrial Relations and Personnel, British Shipbuilders, 1977–80; *b* 3 Nov. 1923; *s* of Alexander Farningham and Janet Leask Broadley; *m* 1st, 1949, Lois Elizabeth Halse (marr. diss. 1981); one *s* two *d*; 2nd, 1981, Susan Wyllie. *Educ:* Glebelands Primary Sch., Dundee; Morgan Academy, Dundee; St Andrews Univ. (MA). Served FAA, 1941–46 (Lieut (A); DSC), RNVR. *Recreations:* walking, birdwatching, photography. *Address:* 1 John Smith Place, Kintyre Street, Tarbert, Argyll PA29 6UW. *T:* (01880) 820029. *Died 16 Nov. 2001.*

FARNINGHAM, Ian; *see* Farningham, A. I.

FARQUHARSON, Sir James (Robbie), KBE 1960 (CBE 1948; OBE 1944); retired, subsequently farming; *b* 1 Nov. 1903; *s* of Frank Farquharson, Cortachy, Angus, Scotland, and Agnes Jane Robbie; *m* 1933, Agnes Binny Graham (*d* 1992); two *s*. *Educ:* Royal Technical College, Glasgow; Glasgow Univ. (BSc 1923). Assistant Engineer: LMS Railway, 1923–25; Kenya and Uganda Railway, 1925–33; Sen. Asst Engr, Kenya and Uganda Railway, 1933–37; Tanganyika Railways: Asst to Gen. Manager, 1937–41; Chief Engr, 1941–45; Gen. Manager, 1945–48; Dep. Gen. Manager, East African Railways, 1948–52; General Manager: Sudan Railways, 1952–57; East African Railways and Harbours, 1957–61; Asst Crown Agent and Engineer-in-Chief of Crown Agents for Overseas Govts and Admins, 1961–65. Chm., Millbank Technical Services Ordnance Ltd, 1973–75. Fellow, Scottish Council for Develt and Industry, 1986. *Publication:* Tanganyika Transport, 1944. *Recreation:* cricket. *Address:* Kinclune, by Kirriemuir, Angus DD8 5HX. *T:* (01575) 574710. *Club:* Nairobi (Kenya). *Died 17 Feb. 2005.*

FARQUHARSON, Robert Alexander, CMG 1975; HM Diplomatic Service, retired; *b* 26 May 1925; *s* of late Captain J. P. Farquharson, DSO, OBE, RN, and Mrs Farquharson (*née* Prescott-Decie); *m* 1955, Joan Elizabeth, *o d* of Sir (William) Ivo Mallet, GBE, KCMG; two *s* one *d* (and one *s* decd). *Educ:* Harrow; King's Coll., Cambridge. Served with RNVR, 1943–46. Joined Foreign (later Diplomatic) Service, 1949; 3rd Sec., Moscow, 1950; FO, 1952; 2nd Sec., Bonn, 1955; 1st Sec., Panama, 1958; Paris, 1960; FO, 1964; Counsellor, Dir of British Trade Develt, S Africa, 1967; Minister, Madrid, 1971; Consul-Gen., San Francisco, 1973; Ambassador to Yugoslavia, 1977–80. Lay Canon of Salisbury Cathedral, 2000–. Lord of the Manor of Bockleton. *Address:* Church House, Donhead St Andrew, Shaftesbury SP7 9EB. *Club:* Flyfishers'. *Died 28 Sept. 2005.*

FARRER, William Oliver, CVO 1991; Senior Partner, Farrer & Co., Solicitors, 1976–91 (Partner, 1955–91); *b* 23 June 1926; *s* of John Oliver Farrer, MC, and Winifred Millicent Farrer; *m* 1st, 1955, Margery Hope Yates (*d* 1976); two *s* one *d*; 2nd, 1979, Hazel Mary Andrew. *Educ:* Eton Coll.; Balliol Coll., Oxford (MA). Lieut, Coldstream Guards, 1945–48. Admitted a Solicitor, 1953; Solicitor to the Duchy of Lancaster, 1984–91; Mem., Solicitors' Disciplinary Tribunal, 1986–94. Dir, Sotheby's, 1992–96. Mem. Council, Inst. of Cancer Res., 1994–2001. *Recreations:* golf, music. *Address:* Popmoor, Fernhurst, Haslemere, Surrey GU27 3LL. *T:* (01428) 642564. *Clubs:* Brooks's, MCC; Royal and Ancient (St Andrews); Honourable Company of Edinburgh Golfers. *Died 27 Feb. 2004.*

FARRINGTON, Sir Henry Francis Colden, 7th Bt *cr* 1818; RA retired; *b* 25 April 1914; *s* of Sir Henry Anthony Farrington, 6th Bt, and Dorothy Maria (*d* 1969), *o d* of Frank Farrington; *S* father, 1944; *m* 1947, Anne, *e d* of late Major W. A. Gillam, DSO; one *s* one *d*. *Educ*: Haileybury. Retired from Army, 1960 (Major; then Hon. Col). *Heir: s* Henry William Farrington, MRICS [*b* 27 March 1951; *m* 1979, Diana Donne Broughton, *yr d* of Geoffrey Broughton, Somerset; two *s*]. *Address*: Higher Ford, Wiveliscombe, Taunton, Somerset TA4 2RL. *T*: (01984) 623219. *Died 11 March 2004.*

FARVIS, Prof. (William) Ewart (John), CBE 1978 (OBE 1972); BSc, BSc(Eng); CEng,FRSE; engineering consultant; Professor of Electrical Engineering, University of Edinburgh 1961–77, then Emeritus; *b* 12 Dec. 1911; *o s* of late William Henry Farvis and Gertrude Anne Farvis; *m* 1939, Margaret May Edmonstone Martin; one *s* one *d*. *Educ*: Queen Elizabeth's Hosp., Bristol; Bristol and London Univs. Lectr, University Coll., Swansea, 1937–40 and 1945–48; Air Ministry, Telecommunications Res. Estab., 1940–45; Lectr/Sen. Lectr, Edinburgh Univ., 1948–61, Prof. and Head of Dept of Electrical Eng., 1961–77, Chairman, Sch. of Engineering Sci. 1972–75. Mem., British Nat. Cttee for Radio Science, 1960–66; Science Research Council: Mem., Electrical and Systems Cttee, 1968–72; Engineering Board, 1972–75 and 1976–81; Polytechnics Cttee, 1975–78; Chm., Solid-state Devices Panel, 1972–75; Electrical and Systems Cttee 1972–75; Advanced Ground Transport Panel 1975–80; Mem. Council, 1976–81. Mem. Council, IEE, 1972–75 and 1976–79; Hon. FIEE 1987. Editor, Microelectronics Journal, 1976–78. *Recreation*: music. *Address*: 14 Cluny Terrace, Edinburgh EH10 4SW. *T*: (0131) 447 4939. *Club*: Athenæum. *Died 12 Oct. 2005.*

FATAYI-WILLIAMS, Hon. Atanda, GCON 1983; CFR 1980; Chief Justice of Nigeria, 1979–83; *b* 22 Oct. 1918; *s* of Alhaji Issa Williams and Alhaja Ashakun Williams; *m* 1948, Irene Violet Lofts; three *s*. *Educ*: Methodist Boys' High Sch., Lagos, Nigeria; Trinity Hall, Cambridge (BA 1946, LLM 1947, MA 1949; Hon. Fellow 1983). Called to the Bar, Middle Temple, 1948. Private practice, Lagos, 1948–50; Crown Counsel, Lagos, 1950–55; Dep. Comr for Law Revision, Western Nigeria, 1955–58; Chief Registrar, High Court of Western Nigeria, 1958–60; High Court Judge, 1960–67; Justice of Appeal, Western State Court of Appeal, 1967–69; Justice, Supreme Court of Nigeria, 1969–79. Mem., Council of State, 1983–84, 1990–. Chairman: Ports Arbitration Bd, 1971; All Nigeria Law Reports Cttee, 1972–75; Body of Benchers, 1979–80; Legal Practitioners' Privileges Cttee, 1979–83; Federal Judicial Service Commn, 1979–83; Judiciary Consultative Cttee, 1979–83; National Archives Cttee, 1979–83; Presidential Cttee on Medical Doctors' Remuneration, 1990; Bd of Trustees, The Van Leer Nigerian Educn Trust, 1973–85; Crescent Bearers, Lagos, 1978–84; Council of Legal Educn, 1984–. Mem., Nigerian Inst. of Internat. Affairs, 1972–97. Trustee, Nigerian Youth Trust, 1979–84. Hon. Fellow, Nigerian Inst. of Advanced Legal Studies, 1983; Life FRSA 1949. Presidential Award for outstanding service to the Judiciary, Nigeria, 1992. *Publications*: (ed) Western Nigeria Law Reports, 1955–58; (with Sir John Verity) Revised Laws of the Western Region of Nigeria, 1959; Sentencing Processes, Practices and Attitudes, as seen by an African Court Judge, 1970; Faces, Cases and Places (autobiog.), 1983. *Recreations*: reading, swimming, walking. *Address*: 8 Adetokunbo Ademola Street, Victoria Island, Lagos, Nigeria. *T*: (1) 611315. *Clubs*: Athenæum, Oxford and Cambridge; Metropolitan (Lagos). *Died 9 April 2002.*

FAULL, David Wenlock, OBE 1993; Consultant, Winckworth & Pemberton, 1990–98 (Senior Partner, 1985–90); *b* 25 Feb. 1929; *s* of Eldred Faull and Mary Jessie Faull (*née* Wenlock). *Educ*: Taunton School. Qualified solicitor, 1954; joined Winckworth & Pemberton, 1978;

Diocesan Registrar: St Albans, 1960–79; Chelmsford, 1960–89; Southwark, 1960–93; London, 1969–97; Rochester, 1997–98; Dep. Registrar, Dio. of Europe, 1980; Legal Sec., Bishop of Rochester, 1960–98; Chapter Clerk and Solicitor to St Paul's Cathedral, 1981–2000. Mem., Legal Adv. Commn, C of E, 1988–94. Mem., Solicitors' Disciplinary Tribunal, 1992–2001. Chm., Ecclesiastical Law Assoc., 1988–90; Treasurer, Ecclesiastical Law Soc., 1986–95. Founder Mem., Paddington Church's Housing Assoc., 1964; Board Member: Hastoe (formerly Sutton and Hastoe) Housing Assoc., 1987–2004; Wyvern Housing Assoc., 2000–05. Chm., Christian Children's Fund (GB), 1992–98; Vice Chm. Trustees, Bishop's Palace, Wells, 2000. Mem., Co. of Parish Clerks, 1991. MA Lambeth 1997. *Recreations*: walking, theatre, Cornish history. *Address*: Lanteglos House, St Thomas Street, Wells BA5 2UZ. *T*: (01749) 675334. *Club*: Athenæum. *Died 28 March 2005.*

FAUVELLE, Major Michael Henry; barrister-at-law; *b* 12 Aug. 1920; *s* of Victor Edmond Fauvelle and Brigid Mary Fauvelle (*née* Westermann); *m* 1964, Marie-Caroline (*d* 2004), *e d* of Count and Countess Stanislas d'Orsetti, Château de la Grènerie, Jarzé, France; one *s* one *d*. *Educ*: Stonyhurst Coll.; Royal Military Coll., Sandhurst. Commissioned, 2/Lieut The South Lancashire Regt, 1939, T/Major 1944; active service in N Africa, Italy and Palestine (wounded three times, arguably five); Staff employment as GSO 3 (Ops), Gibraltar, 1947; Staff Captain Q HQ Palestine, 1947–48; Staff Captain A HQ BMM to Greece and HQ 2 Inf. Bde, 1948–50; Adjt 1st Bn, 1951; Major 1952; retired, 1953. Called to the Bar, Lincoln's Inn, 1955; Western Circuit and Hampshire Sessions, 1955–; Dep. Recorder, Oxford, Bournemouth and Reading, 1971; a Dep. Circuit Judge, 1972–79; a Recorder, 1979–92; Hd of Chambers at 17 Carlton Crescent, Southampton, 1975–82. Pres., Pensions Appeal Tribunals for England and Wales, 1987–93 (a Chm., 1983–93; Dep. Pres., 1984–87). Lord Chancellor's Legal Visitor, 1983–90. *Recreations*: travel by sea, forestry, avoiding stress. *Address*: Tadley Cottage, Wherwell, Hampshire SP11 7JU. *T*: (01264) 860217, *Fax*: (01264) 861254. *Club*: Home Guard (Wherwell, Hants). *Died 8 Oct. 2005.*

FAWCUS, Sir (Robert) Peter, KBE 1964 (OBE 1957); CMG 1960; Overseas Civil Service, retired; *b* 30 Sept. 1915; *s* of A. F. Fawcus, OBE; *m* 1943, Isabel Constance (*née* Ethelston) (*d* 2001); one *s* one *d*. *Educ*: Charterhouse; Clare Coll., Cambridge (BA 1937). Served RNVR, 1939–46 (Lt-Comdr). Joined Colonial Service as District Officer, Basutoland, 1946; Bechuanaland Protectorate: Govt Sec., 1954; Resident Comr, 1959; HM Comr, 1963–65; retd 1965. *Publication*: Botswana: the road to independence, 2000. *Address*: Dochart House, Killin, Perthshire FK21 8TN. *Died 22 April 2003.*

FEILDEN, Geoffrey Bertram Robert, CBE 1966; FRS 1959; FREng, FIMechE; Principal Consultant, Feilden Associates, since 1981; *b* 20 Feb. 1917; *s* of Robert Humphrey Feilden, MC, and Olive Feilden (*née* Binyon); *m* 1st, Elizabeth Ann Gorton; one *s* two *d*; 2nd, Elizabeth Diana Angier (*née* Lloyd). *Educ*: Bedford Sch.; King's Coll., Cambridge (Scholar; MA). Lever Bros. and Unilever Ltd, 1939–40; Power Jets Ltd, 1940–46; Ruston and Hornsby Ltd, 1946–59; Chief Engineer, Turbine Dept, 1949; Engineering Dir, 1954; Man. Dir, Hawker Siddeley Brush Turbines Ltd, and Dir of Hawker Siddeley Industries Ltd, 1959–61; Gp Technical Dir, Davy-Ashmore Ltd, 1961–68; Dep. Dir Gen., British Standards Instn, 1968–70, Dir Gen. 1970–81. Director: Averys Ltd, 1974–79; Plint & Partners Ltd, 1982–2001. Member: Cttees and Sub-Cttees of Aeronautical Research Council, 1947–62; BTC Res. Adv. Council, 1956–61; Council for Sci. and Indust. Res. of DSIR, 1961–65; Design Council (formerly CoID), 1966–78 (Dep. Chm., 1977–78); Central Adv. Council for Science and Technology, 1970–71; Vis. Cttee to RCA, 1968–84 (Chm., 1977–84);

Res. Develt and Engrg Cttee, Industrial Develt Bd for NI, 1983–86; Chm., UK Panel for CODATA (formerly British Nat. Cttee on Data for Sci. and Technol.), 1988–97 (UK Deleg. to CODATA, 1989–97); Pres., European Cttee for Standardisation, 1977–79. Member, Royal Society Delegation: to USSR, 1965; Latin America, 1968; People's Republic of China, 1975; Leader, BSI Delegn to People's Republic of China, 1980. Technical Adviser to Govt of India, 1968. DSIR Visitor to Prod. Engineering Res. Assoc. of Gt Brit., 1957–65, and to Machine Tool Industry Res. Assoc., 1961–65. Member Council: Royal Society (a Vice-Pres., 1967–69); IMechE, 1955–61, 1969–80; Univ. of Surrey, 1977–78. Trustee: Maurice Lubbock Meml Fund, 1973–2001; Smallpeice Trust, 1981–88. Hon. Freedom, City of Lincoln, 2003. FREng (Founder FEng 1976); Senior Fellow, RCA, 1986. Hon. FIStructE; Hon. FIQA; Hon. MIED. Hon. DTech: Loughborough, 1970; Lincoln, 2003; Hon. DSc QUB, 1971. MacRobert Award for innovation (jt winner), 1983; Hodgson Prize, RAeS, 1994. *Publications:* Gas Turbine Principles and Practice (contributor), 1955; First Bulleid Memorial Lecture (Nottingham Univ.), 1959; Report, Engineering Design, 1963 (Chm. of Cttee); numerous papers and articles on engineering subjects. *Recreations:* sailing, ski-ing, driving kitchen and garden machines. *Address:* 1 Hambutts Mead, Painswick, Glos GL6 6RP. *T:* (01452) 812112. *Club:* Athenæum.

Died 1 May 2004.

FEILDEN, Richard John Robert, OBE 1998; Senior Partner, Feilden Clegg Bradley (formerly Feilden Clegg), Architects, since 1995; *b* 29 March 1950; *s* of late Geoffrey Bertram Robert Feilden, CBE, FRS and of Elizabeth Feilden; *m* 1975, Patricia Nelson; two *s* one *d. Educ:* Rugby Sch.; King's Coll., Cambridge (MA 1972); Architectural Assoc. (AA Dip. 1975); Bristol Univ. (DipArch Cons.). Founded Feilden Clegg Design, 1975; co. became Feilden Clegg, Architects, 1995, then Feilden Clegg Bradley, Architects, 1999. Vis. Prof., UCE, 2000–. Mem., CABE, 2000–03. Special Advr, Urban Task Force, 1999. Chm., Higher Educn Design Quality Forum, 1995–2000. Royal Institute of British Architects: Chm., Community Architecture Gp, 1990–93; Mem., 1994–2000, Vice-Chm., 1998–2000, Council. *Recreations:* forestry, cycling, walking, sailing. *Address:* Sheephouse Farm Barn, Bathford, Bath BA1 8EE; *e-mail:* feildens@sheephouse.demon.co.uk. *Died 3 Jan. 2005.*

FEINBERG, Peter Eric; QC 1992; a Recorder, since 1994; *b* 26 Oct. 1949; *s* of Leon and May Feinberg; *m* 1988, Tini Flannery (marr. diss.); two *s. Educ:* Bradford Grammar Sch.; University Coll. London (LLB Hons). Called to the Bar, Inner Temple, 1972; Asst Recorder, 1990. Pres., Mental Health Tribunals, 1995–. *Recreations:* opera, music, jogging, Czech Republic. *Address:* No 5 Chambers, 199 Strand, WC2R 1DR. *Club:* Lambs.

Died 4 Nov. 2004.

FEINSTEIN, Prof. Charles Hilliard, PhD; FBA 1983; Professor of Economic History, University of Oxford, 1989–99, then Emeritus; Fellow, All Souls College, Oxford, 1989–99, then Emeritus; *b* 18 March 1932; *s* of Louis and Rose Feinstein; *m* 1st, 1958, Ruth Loshak; one *s* three *d*; 2nd, 1980, Anne Digby. *Educ:* Parktown Boys' High Sch., Johannesburg; Univ. of Witwatersrand (BCom 1950); Fitzwilliam Coll., Cambridge (PhD 1958). CA (SA) 1954. Cambridge University: Research Officer, Dept of Applied Econs, 1958–63; Univ. Lectr in Faculty of Econs, 1963–78; Clare College: Fellow, 1963–78, Hon. Fellow, 1994; Sen. Tutor, 1969–78; Prof. of Econ. and Social History, 1978–87, and Head, Dept of Econ. and Related Studies, 1981–86, Univ. of York; Reader in Recent Social and Econ. History, and Professorial Fellow, Nuffield Coll., 1987–89, Univ. of Oxford. Harvard University: Vis. Res. Fellow, Russian Res. Centre, 1967–68; Vis. Scholar, Dept of Econ., 1986–87; Vis. Lectr, Univ. of Delhi, 1972; W. D. Wilson Vis. Fellow, Univ. of Cape Town, 1994; Visiting Professor: Univ. of Cape Town, 1995–2002; CIT,

1997; Univ. of Keio, 2001. Vice-Pres., British Acad., 1991–93 (Mem. Council, 1990–93); Member Council: Royal Economic Soc., 1980–94; Economic History Soc., 1980–99; Mem., Economic Affairs Cttee, SSRC, 1982–86 (Chm., 1985–86). Governor, NIESR, 1985–. Man. Editor, The Economic Jl, 1980–86. *Publications:* Domestic Capital Formation in the United Kingdom 1920–1938, 1965; (ed) Socialism, Capitalism and Economic Growth, essays presented to Maurice Dobb, 1967; National Income, Expenditure and Output of the United Kingdom 1855–1965, 1972; (ed) York 1831–1981, 1981; (jtly) British Economic Growth 1856–1973, 1982; (ed) The Managed Economy: essays in British economic policy and performance since 1929, 1983; Studies in Capital Formation 1750–1920, 1988; (ed) New Directions in Economic and Social History, vol. I, 1989, vol. II, 1992; (ed) Banking, Currency and Finance in Europe between the Wars, 1995; (jtly) The European Economy between the Wars, 1997; (ed) Chinese Technology Transfer in the 1990s, 1997; The Economic Development of the United Kingdom since 1870, 1997; (jtly) Making History Count, 2002. *Recreations:* reading, looking for second-hand books. *Address:* Treetops, Harberton Mead, Headington, Oxford OX3 0DB. *Died 27 Nov. 2004.*

FELD, Valerie, (Val); Member (Lab) Swansea East, National Assembly for Wales, since 1999; *b* 29 Oct. 1947; *d* of Jim Breen Turner and late Evelyn Breen Turner; *m* 1969, John Feld (marr. diss. 1979); two *d. Educ:* Hillgrove Sch., Bangor; Abbey Sch., Malvern Wells; University Coll., Cardiff (MSc Econ). Researcher and copywriter, 1969–73; voluntary, community and parental activities, 1973–78; housing advice worker and co-ordinator, Chorley Rights Centre, 1978–81; Director: Shelter Cymru, 1981–89; EOC Wales, 1989–99. Chm., Econ. Develt Cttee, Nat Assembly for Wales, 1999–. Treas., Yes for Wales, 1997–99. FRSA 1995. *Publications:* various articles and reports on housing, equal opportunities and devolution issues. *Recreations:* gentle walking, choral music, Turkish baths. *Address:* National Assembly for Wales, Cardiff Bay, Cardiff CF99 1NA.

Died 17 July 2001.

FERGUSSON, Sir James Herbert Hamilton C.; *see* Colyer-Fergusson.

FERMAN, James Alan; Director (formerly Secretary), British Board of Film Classification (formerly British Board of Film Censors), 1975–99; *b* New York, 11 April 1930; *m* 1956, Monica Sophie (*née* Robinson); one *s* one *d. Educ:* Great Neck High Sch., NY; Cornell Univ. (BA Hons); King's Coll., Cambridge (BA Hons 1955, MA 1971). Actor, writer and univ. lectr until 1957; author/adaptor, Zuleika (musical comedy), Saville Theatre, 1957; television director of drama and documentaries, 1957–75: trained on Armchair Theatre, then 7½ years in ITV, then freelance, chiefly at BBC, 1965–75; principal director: The Planemakers (SFTA Award, 1963); Miss Hanago; The Pistol; Kafka's America (Critics' Circle Award, 1966); Before the Party (BAFTA Award, 1970); also stage producer; wrote and dir., Drugs and Schoolchildren, documentary film series for teachers and social workers. Part-time Lectr in Community Studies, Polytech. of Central London, 1973–76 (Dir and Chm., Community Mental Health Prog., in-service trng for social workers, health workers, teachers, etc, organised jtly with MIND); Educn Advr, Standing Conf. on Drug Abuse; Vice-Pres., Assoc. for Prevention of Addiction. Chm. and organiser, internat. confs on standards in screen entertainment, BBFC, 1982–97. *Recreations:* theatre, music, reading, hill-walking. *Died 24 Dec. 2002.*

FEWSON, Prof. Charles Arthur, OBE 2001; PhD; FRSE; FIBiol; Professor of Microbial Biochemistry, University of Glasgow, 1982–2001 (Director, Institute of Biomedical and Life Sciences, 1994–2000); *b* 8 Sept. 1937; *s* of Arthur Fewson and Brenda Margaret Fewson; *m* 1965, Margaret Christina Rose Moir; two *d. Educ:* Hymers Coll., Hull; Nottingham Univ. (BSc 1958); Bristol Univ. (PhD

1961). FRSE 1979; FIBiol 1983. Res. Fellow, Cornell Univ., NY, 1961–63; Department of Biochemistry, University of Glasgow: Lectr, 1963–68; Sen. Lectr, 1968–79; Reader, 1979–82. *Publications:* numerous scientific papers and reviews on microbial and plant biochemistry. *Recreations:* hill-walking, gardening. *Address:* Branxholm, Trinity Lane, Innellan, Dunoon, Argyll and Bute PA23 7SP. *T:* (01369) 830059.

Died 29 Aug. 2005.

FFITCH, George Norman; Managing Director, London Broadcasting Company and Independent Radio News, 1979–85; *b* 23 Jan. 1929; *s* of late Robert George Ffitch; *m* 1958, Pamela Mary Lyle (*d* 1990); one *s* one *d*. *Educ:* state schools and London Univ. Industrial Correspondent, Political Correspondent and Output Editor, Independent Television News, 1955–62; interviewer and presenter, ITV, 1962–67; Political Editor and an Asst Editor, The Economist, 1967–74; Associate Editor, Daily Express, 1974–76; columnist and broadcaster, 1976–79. *Recreation:* playing at playing golf. *Address:* 11 Exeter House, Putney Heath, SW15 3SU. *T:* (020) 8785 2460. *Club:* Reform.

Died 5 July 2001.

FIELD, Arnold, OBE 1965; aerospace consultant/technical journalist; Joint Field Commander, National Air Traffic Services, 1974–77; *b* 19 May 1917; *m* 1943, Kathleen Dulcie Bennett; one *s* one *d*. *Educ:* Sutton Coldfield Royal Sch.; Birmingham Technical Coll. RAF, 1940–46 (Sqdn Ldr). Civil Air Traffic Control Officer, 1946; Centre Supt, Scottish Air Traffic Control Centre, 1954; Centre Supt, London Air Traffic Control Centre, 1957; Divisional Air Traffic Control Officer, Southern Div., 1963; Dir, Civil Air Traffic Ops, 1969. Master, Guild of Air Traffic Control Officers, 1958; Pres., Internat. Fedn of Air Traffic Control Officers, 1970; Mem., Aviation/Space Writers' Assoc., 1986–. Gp Editor, Internat. Defence Newsletter, Law Enforcement Industry Digest, 1988–. *Publications:* The Control of Air Traffic, 1981; International Air Traffic Control, 1985; From Take-off to Touchdown—A Passenger's Guide, 1984; articles in Interavia, Times Supplement, Flight, Controller. *Recreations:* vintage cars, flying. *Address:* Footprints, Stoke Wood, Stoke Poges, Bucks SL2 4AU. *T:* (01753) 642710. *Club:* Bentley Drivers (Long Crendon).   *Died 19 Dec. 2003.*

FIELD, William James; *b* 22 May 1909; *s* of late Frederick William Field, solicitor; unmarried. *Educ:* Richmond County Sch.; London Univ; abroad. Volunteered for Army, Sept. 1939 and served in ranks and as officer in Intelligence Corps and RASC. Joined Labour Party, 1935; Chm., South Hammersmith Divisional Labour Party, 1945–46; contested Hampstead Div., General Election, 1945; MP (Lab) North Paddington, Nov. 1946–Oct. 1953. PPS to Sec. of State for War, May-Oct. 1951 (to Under-Sec. for War, 1950–51). Mem., Hammersmith Borough Council, 1945–53 (Leader, 1946–49). A Vice-Pres., Assoc. of Municipal Corporations, 1952–53; for several years, Mem., Metropolitan Boroughs' Standing Jt Cttee and of many local govt bodies.

Died 11 Oct. 2002.

FIELD-FISHER, Thomas Gilbert, TD 1950; QC 1969; a Recorder of the Crown Court, 1972–87; *b* 16 May 1915; *s* of Caryl Field-Fisher, Torquay; *m* 1945, Ebba (*d* 2003), *d* of Max Larsen, Linwood, USA. *Educ:* King's Sch., Bruton; Peterhouse, Cambridge (BA 1937, MA 1942). Served Queen Victoria's Rifles, KRRC, 1939–47; BEF 1940 (POW; despatches). Called to Bar, Middle Temple, 1942, Bencher, 1976. Judge Advocate Gen.'s Dept, 1945–47 (i/c War Crimes Dept, CMF); joined Western Circuit, 1947. Mem., Bar Council, 1962–66. Deputy Chairman: SW Agricultural Land Tribunal, 1967–82; Cornwall QS, 1968–71; Chm., Maria Colwell Inquiry, 1973–74. Actg Deemster, IOM, 1989–90. Vice-Chm., London Council of Social Service, 1966–79; Vice-Pres., London Voluntary Service Council, 1979–. Mem., Home Secretary's Adv. Cttee on Animal Experiments, 1980–89. Vice-President:

UFAW, 1989–99; Dogs' Home, Battersea, 1995– (Chm., 1982–95); Founder and Chm., Assoc. of British Dogs' Homes, 1985–. Pres., Cornwall Magistrates' Assoc., 1985–97. Autumn Reader, Middle Temple, 1991. *Publications:* Animals and the Law, 1964; Rent Regulation and Control, 1967; Dog Problem: a lawyer's view, 1989; A Dog's Life–Sam, 1997; contribs to Halsbury's Laws of England, 3rd and 4th edns, Law Jl, and other legal publications. *Recreations:* tennis, dogs, collecting watercolours, MG cars, gardening. *Address:* 38 Hurlingham Court, SW6 3UW. *T:* (020) 7736 4627; 2 King's Bench Walk, Temple, EC4Y 7DE. *T:* (020) 7353 1746. *Clubs:* Hurlingham, International Lawn Tennis of Great Britain.   *Died 8 June 2003.*

FIELDEN, Frank; Secretary, Royal Fine Art Commission, 1969–79; *b* 3 Oct. 1915; *s* of Ernest and Emma Fielden, Greenfield, Yorks; *m* 1939, Margery Keeler; two *d*. *Educ:* University of Manchester (graduated, 1938); MA Dunelm. Served War of 1939–45 with Royal Engineers (Special Forces), France, N Africa, Italy, Germany. Town Planning Officer to Nigerian Government, 1945–46; Lectr and Sen. Lectr, Univ. of Durham, 1946–59; Prof. of Architecture, Univ. of Strathclyde, 1959–69. Mem., Royal Fine Art Commn for Scotland, 1965–69. RIBA Athens Bursar, 1950, Bronze Medallist 1960. Chairman: Soc. of Architectural Historians of Great Britain, 1965–67; Richmond Soc., 1971–74. *Publications:* articles in professional journals and national press. *Recreations:* music, gardening. *Address:* 28 Caledonian Road, Chichester, W Sussex PO19 2LQ.   *Died 31 July 2001.*

FIELDING, Prof. Kenneth Joshua, DPhil; Saintsbury Professor of English Literature, 1966–84, part-time 1984–87, then Emeritus, and Fellow, since 1984, University of Edinburgh; *b* 10 July 1924; *s* of Joshua Douglas Fielding and Edith Llewelyn Fielding; *m* 1956, Jean Arnold Ferguson (*d* 1994); one *d* decd. *Educ:* Gt Yarmouth Grammar Sch.; University Coll., Oxford (Open Schol.; MA 1948; DPhil 1953). Served Royal Signals, 1943–46. William Noble Fellow, Univ. of Liverpool, 1951–53; Lectr, 1954, Sen. Lectr, 1956–57, Malayan Coll. of Educn, Kirkby, Liverpool; Cheshire Coll. of Educn, Alsager; Vice Principal, City of Liverpool Coll. of Educn, 1957–66. Bobst Vis. Prof., New York Univ., 1973. Sen. Ed., Collected Letters of Thomas and Jane Welsh Carlyle, 30 vols, 1970–; Ed., The Carlyle Newsletter, 1–9, 1979–88. *Publications:* Charles Dickens: a survey, 1954; Charles Dickens: a critical introduction, 1958, enlarged edn 1965; (ed) The Speeches of Charles Dickens, 1960, enlarged edn 1985; (ed jtly) The Letters of Charles Dickens, vol. 1, 1970, vol. 5, 1981; Joint Editor: Carlyle Past and Present: original essays, 1976; Carlyle's The French Revolution, 1989; Carlyle's Reminiscences, 1997; Jane Carlyle, The Simple Story of My Own First Love, 2001; Jane Carlyle: newly selected letters, 2004; contribs to numerous books and jls, on Dickens, Carlyle and other Victorians. *Recreation:* reading. *Address:* 67 Grange Loan, Edinburgh EH9 2EG. *T:* (0131) 667 5154; University of Edinburgh, 22A Buccleuch Place, Edinburgh EH8 9JX.   *Died 20 May 2005.*

FILLEUL, Peter Amy, MA; Head Master, William Hulme's Grammar School, Manchester, 1974–87; *b* 7 Aug. 1929; *s* of J. C. Filleul and L. A. Mundy; *m* 1963, Elizabeth Ann Talbot; one *s* one *d*. *Educ:* Victoria Coll., Jersey; Bedford Sch.; (Exhibnr) Exeter Coll., Oxford (MA, DipEd). Royal Air Force, 1952–55 (Sword of Merit, RAF Spitalgate, 1952). Portsmouth GS, 1955–65; Stationers' Company's Sch., 1965–68; Cardiff High Sch. (Head Master), 1969–74. *Recreations:* rifle shooting, fishing. *Address:* Kirkliston, Midvale Close, Upper Midvale Road, St Helier, Jersey, Channel Islands JE2 3ZJ. *T:* (01534) 759941.   *Died 2 Jan. 2004.*

FINCHAM, Prof. John Robert Stanley, FRS 1969; FRSE 1978; Arthur Balfour Professor of Genetics, University of Cambridge, 1984–91, then Emeritus;

Professorial Fellow, Peterhouse, Cambridge, 1984–91, then Emeritus Fellow; Hon. Fellow, Division of Biology, University of Edinburgh, since 1992; *b* 11 Aug. 1926; *s* of Robert Fincham and Winifred Emily Fincham (*née* Western); *m* 1950, Ann Katherine Emerson; one *s* three *d*. *Educ*: Hertford Grammar Sch.; Peterhouse, Cambridge (BA 1946, PhD 1950, ScD 1964). Bye-Fellow of Peterhouse, 1949–50; Lectr in Botany, University Coll., Leicester, 1950–54; Reader in Genetics, Univ. of Leicester, 1954–60; Head of Dept of Genetics, John Innes Inst., 1960–66; Prof. of Genetics, Leeds Univ., 1966–76; Buchanan Prof. of Genetics, Univ. of Edinburgh, 1976–84. Vis. Associate Prof. of Genetics, MIT, 1960–61. Pres., Genetical Soc., 1978–81. Editor, Heredity, 1971–78. *Publications*: Fungal Genetics (with P. R. Day), 1963, 4th edn 1979; Microbial and Molecular Genetics, 1965; Genetic Complementation, 1966; Genetics, 1983; (jtly) Genetically Engineered Organisms, 1991; Genetic Analysis, 1995; papers in Biochemical Jl, Jl Gen. Microbiol., Jl Biol. Chem., Heredity, Jl Molecular Biol., Genet. Res. *Recreations*: listening to music, walking. *Address*: 20 Greenbank Road, Edinburgh EH10 5RY. *Died 9 Feb. 2005.*

FINDLAY, Ian Herbert Fyfe; Chairman, Lloyd's, 1978 and 1979 (Deputy Chairman, 1977); *b* 5 Feb. 1918; *s* of Prof. Alexander Findlay, CBE, Aberdeen, and Alice Mary (*née* de Rougement); *m* 1950, Alison Mary Ashby; two *s* one *d*. *Educ*: Fettes Coll., Edinburgh. Served War, Royal Artillery, 1939–46. Mem. of Lloyd's, 1946. Chairman: Price Forbes (Holdings) Ltd, 1967; Sedgwick Forbes Holdings Ltd, 1974–77 (Dep. Chm., 1972). Mem. Cttee, Lloyd's Insurance Brokers Assoc., 1961–65 and 1966–69 (Chm., Non-Marine Cttee, 1967–68; Chm. of Assoc., 1969–70); Mem., Cttee of Lloyd's, 1971–74, 1976–79; Chm., British Insurance Brokers Assoc., 1980–82. Trustee, St George's English Sch., Rome, 1980–91; Vice-Pres., Guide Dogs for the Blind, 1987– (Chm., 1981–87); Governor, Brighton Coll., 1981–88. Pres., Senior Golfers' Soc., 1990–93. *Recreations*: golf, postal history. *Address*: West Cottage, 1 The Close, Eliot Vale, Blackheath, SE3 0UR. *T*: (020) 8318 4644. *Clubs*: City of London; Royal and Ancient Golf (St Andrews); Royal St George's (Sandwich); Addington (Surrey). *Died 29 Dec. 2001.*

FINGLAND, Sir Stanley (James Gunn), KCMG 1979 (CMG 1966); HM Diplomatic Service, retired; High Commissioner to Kenya, 1975–79; UK Permanent Representative to the UN Environment Programme 1975–79, and to UN Centre for Human Settlements, 1979; *b* 19 Dec. 1919; *s* of late Samuel Gunn Fingland and late Agnes Christina (*née* Watson); *m* 1946, Nellie (*née* Lister); one *s* one *d*. *Educ*: Royal High Sch., Edinburgh. TA 1938. War service, 1939–46 as Major, Royal Signals; served N Africa, Sicily, Italy, Egypt. Commonwealth Relations Office, 1948; British High Commn, India, 1948–51; Australia, 1953–56; Advr on Commonwealth and External Affairs to Governor-Gen., Nigeria, 1958–60; British High Commn, Nigeria, 1960; Advr on Commonwealth and External Affairs to Governor-Gen., Fedn of The W Indies, 1960–61, and to Governor of Trinidad and Tobago, 1962; British Dep. High Commissioner: Trinidad and Tobago, 1962–63; Rhodesia, 1964–66; High Comr, Sierra Leone, 1966–69; Asst Under-Sec. of State, FCO, 1969–72; Ambassador to Cuba, 1972–75. *Recreation*: fishing.
Died 20 Jan. 2003.

FINLAYSON, Maj.-Gen. Robert G.; *see* Gordon-Finlayson.

FINNEY, James; Chairman, Staff Commission for Education and Library Boards, 1981–85; Permanent Secretary, Department of Manpower Services for Northern Ireland, 1976–80, retired; *b* 21 Jan. 1920; *s* of James and Ellen Finney, Co. Armagh; *m* 1956, Barbara Ann Bennett, Wargrave, Berks; one *s* three *d*. *Educ*: Royal Belfast Academical Instn; Trinity Coll., Dublin Univ. BA

1st cl. Mods 1942. Royal Engrs, 1943–46. Min. of Educn for N Ireland, 1946–76. *Recreation*: gardening. *Address*: 2A Fort Road, Dundonald, Belfast, N Ireland BT16 1XR. *T*: (028) 9048 3428. *Died 30 July 2003.*

FIRMSTON-WILLIAMS, Peter, CBE 1987 (OBE 1979); Chairman, Flowers and Plants Association, 1984–89; *b* 30 Aug. 1918; *s* of late Geoffrey and Muriel Firmston-Williams; *m* 1944, Margaret Beaulah; one *s* one *d*. *Educ*: Harrow. Served War, Infantry, Green Howards Regt, 1939–45 (Captain). J. Lyons & Co. Ltd, 1945–53; Marketing Director, United Canners Ltd, 1953–55; Associated British Foods Ltd, Director, Store Operations, Fine Fare, 1958–61; Fitch Lovell Ltd, Man. Dir, Key Markets Ltd, 1962–71; Associated Dairies Group Ltd, Man. Dir, ASDA Stores, and Dir, Associated Dairies, 1971–81. Director: Woolworth Hdgs (formerly Paternoster Stores), 1981–85 (non-exec. Dir, 1985–86; Dep. Chm., 1982–85); Bredero Properties Ltd, 1986–; Chm., Bayfleet Hldgs Ltd, 1988–. Chairman: Covent Garden Market Authority, 1982–88; Retail Consortium, 1984–86. *Recreations*: golf, water skiing, gardening. *Address*: Oak House, 12 Pembroke Road, Moor Park, Northwood, Middx HA6 2HR. *T*: (01923) 823052.
Died 16 Jan. 2002.

FIRTH, Prof. Sir Raymond (William), Kt 1973; CNZM 2001; MA; PhD; FBA 1949; Professor of Anthropology, University of London, 1944–68, then Emeritus; *b* 25 March 1901; *s* of late Wesley Hugh Bourne Firth and Marie Elizabeth Jane Cartmill; *m* 1936, Rosemary (*d* 2001), *d* of Sir Gilbert Upcott, KCB; one *s*. *Educ*: Auckland Grammar Sch.; Auckland University College; London School of Economics (Hon. Fellow, 1970). Anthropological research in British Solomon Islands, including one year on Tikopia, 1928–29; Lecturer in Anthropology, 1930–31, Acting Professor of Anthropology, 1931–32, University of Sydney; Lecturer in Anthropology, 1932–35, Reader, 1935–44, LSE. Hon. Sec., Royal Anthropological Institute, 1936–39 (President 1953–55); Research in peasant economics and anthropology in Malaya, as Leverhulme Research Fellow, 1939–40; served with Naval Intelligence Division, Admiralty, 1941–44; Secretary of Colonial Social Science Research Council, Colonial Office, 1944–45; Academic Advr, ANU, 1948–52; Fellow, Center for Advanced Study in the Behavioral Sciences, Stanford, 1958–59; Prof. of Pacific Anthropology, Univ. of Hawaii, 1968–69. Visiting Professor: British Columbia, 1969; Cornell, 1970; Chicago, 1971; Graduate Center, City Univ. of New York, 1971; Univ. of California, Davis 1974, Berkeley 1977; Auckland, 1978. Life Pres., Assoc. of Social Anthropologists, 1975. Foreign Hon. Mem., Amer. Acad. of Arts and Sciences, 1963; Hon. Mem., Royal Society NZ, 1964; Foreign Member: American Philosophical Society, 1965; Royal Soc. NSW; Royal Danish Academy of Sciences and Letters, 1966; Internat. Union of Anthropol and Ethnol Sciences, 1983; European Assoc. of Social Anthropologists, 1990. Social research surveys: W Africa, 1945; Malaya, 1947, 1963; New Guinea, 1951; Tikopia, 1952, 1966. Hon. degrees: DPh Oslo, 1965; LLD Michigan, 1967; LittD East Anglia, 1968; Dr Letters ANU, 1969; DHumLett Chicago, 1968; DSc British Columbia, 1970; DLitt Exeter, 1972; DLit Auckland, 1978; PhD Cracow, 1984; DSc Econ London, 1984. *Publications*: The Kauri Gum Industry, 1924; Primitive Economics of the New Zealand Maori, 1929, new edn 1959; Art and Life In New Guinea, 1936; We, The Tikopia: a sociological study of kinship in primitive Polynesia, 1936; Human Types, 1938, new edn 1975; Primitive Polynesian Economy, 1939, new edn 1964; The Work of the Gods in Tikopia, 1940, new edn 1967; Malay Fishermen: their peasant economy, 1946, enlarged edn 1966; Elements of Social Organization, 1951, new edn 1971; (ed) Two Studies of Kinship in London, 1956; (ed) Man and Culture: an evaluation of the work of Malinowski, 1957; Social Change in Tikopia, 1959;

History and Traditions of Tikopia, 1961; Essays on Social Organization and Values, 1964; (with B. S. Yamey) Capital Saving and Credit in Peasant Societies, 1964; Tikopia Ritual and Belief, 1967; Rank and Religion in Tikopia, 1970; (with J. Hubert and A. Forge) Families and Their Relatives, 1970; Symbols Public and Private, 1973; Tikopia-English Dictionary, 1985; Tikopia Songs, 1990; Religion: a humanist interpretation, 1996. *Recreations:* Romanesque art, early music. *Address:* 33 Southwood Avenue, N6 5SA. *Club:* Athenæum.

Died 22 Feb. 2002.

FISHER OF REDNAL, Baroness *cr* 1974 (Life Peer), of Rednal, Birmingham; **Doris Mary Gertrude Fisher;** JP; Member of the European Parliament, 1975–79; Member, Warrington and Runcorn (formerly Warrington) Development Corporation, 1974–89; *b* 13 Sept. 1919; *d* of late Frederick J. Satchwell, BEM; *m* 1939, Joseph Fisher (*d* 1978); two *d*. *Educ:* Tinker's Farm Girls' Sch.; Fircroft Coll.; Bournville Day Continuation Coll. Member: Birmingham City Council, 1952–74; Labour Party, 1945–; UNESCO study group; Nat. Pres. Co-operative Women's Guild, 1961–62. Contested Ladywood, Birmingham, 1969 by-election; MP (Lab) Birmingham, Ladywood, 1970–Feb. 1974. Member: Gen. Medical Council, 1974–79; New Towns Staff Commn, 1976–79; Birmingham Civic Housing Assoc. Ltd, 1982–; Vice-President: Assoc. of Municipal Authorities, 1980–97; Assoc. of Dist Councils, 1982–97; Inst. of Trading Standards Admin. Pres., Birmingham Royal Inst. for the Blind, 1980–; Chm., W Midlands Macmillan Fund, 1995. Patron, St Basil's Centre for Young Homeless, Birmingham. Guardian, Birmingham Assay Office, 1979–89; Mem., Hallmarking Council, 1989–94. Chm. Governors, Baskerville Special Sch., 1981–87; Governor, Hunter's Hill Special Sch., 1988–94. JP Birmingham, 1961. Hon. Alderman, 1974, Birmingham District Council. DUniv UCE, 1998. *Recreations:* swimming, walking. *Died 18 Dec. 2005.*

FISHER, Rt Rev. Edward George K.; *see* Knapp-Fisher.

FISHER, Hon. Sir Henry (Arthur Pears), Kt 1968; President, Wolfson College, Oxford, 1975–85, Hon. Fellow, 1985; *b* 20 Jan. 1918; *e s* of Lord Fisher of Lambeth, PC, GCVO; *m* 1948, Felicity (BA Hons Open Univ., 1987), *d* of late Eric Sutton; one *s* three *d*. *Educ:* Marlborough; Christ Church, Oxford (Schol.; Gaisford Greek Prose Prize, 1937; 1st cl. Hons Mods 1938; BA 1942; MA 1943). Served War, Leics Regt, 1940–46: Staff Coll., Quetta, 1943; GSO2, 1943–44; GSO1 HQ 14th Army, 1945; Hon. Lieut-Col 1946 (despatches). All Souls College, Oxford: Fellow, 1946–73, 1991– (Emeritus, 1976–91); Estates Bursar, 1961–66; Sub-Warden, 1965–67. Called to the Bar, Inner Temple, 1947, Bencher, 1966; QC 1960; Recorder of Canterbury, 1962–68; a Judge of the High Court of Justice, Queen's Bench Div., 1968–70. Director: J. Henry Schroder Wagg & Co. Ltd, 1970–75; Schroder International Ltd, 1973–75; Thomas Tilling plc, 1970–83; Equity and Law Life Assurance Soc. plc, 1975–87; Equity and Law plc, 1987. Mem., Gen. Council of the Bar, 1959–63, 1964–68, Vice-Chm., 1965–66, Chm., 1966–68; Vice-President: Senate of the Four Inns of Court, 1966–68; Bar Assoc. for Commerce, Finance and Industry, 1973–. Pres., Howard League, 1983–91; Chairman: Cttee of Inquiry into Abuse of the Social Security System, 1971; City Cttee on Company Law, 1974–76; Cttee of Inquiry into self-regulation at Lloyd's, 1979–80; Appeal Cttee, Panel on Take-overs and Mergers, 1981–87; Jt Commn on the Constitution (set up by Social Democratic and Liberal Parties), 1981–83; (founder) Investment Management Regulatory Orgn, 1986–88. Conducted inquiry into Confait case, 1976–77. Member: Private Internat. Law Cttee, 1961–63; Council on Tribunals, 1962–65; Law Reform Cttee, 1963–66; BBC Progs Complaints Commn, 1972–79. Mem. Council, Marlborough Coll., 1967–83 (Chm., 1977–82);

Mem. Governing Body, Imperial Coll., 1973–88 (Chm., 1975–88) (FIC 1974); Trustee, Pilgrim Trust, 1965–92 (Chm., 1979–83, 1989–92). Hon. Mem., Lloyd's, 1983. Hon. Fellow, Darwin Coll., Cambridge, 1984. Hon. LLD Hull, 1979. *Recreation:* music. *Address:* Garden End, Cross Lane, Marlborough, Wilts SN8 1LA. *T:* (01672) 515420. *Club:* Travellers. *Died 10 April 2005.*

FISHER, Rev. James Atherton; Canon of St George's, Windsor, 1958–78, Treasurer, 1962–77; *b* 1 May 1909; *s* of Rev. Legh Atherton Fisher and Beatrice Edith Fisher; *m* 1938, Joan Gardiner Budden; two *s* one *d*. *Educ:* Haileybury; Sidney Sussex Coll., Cambridge (Scholar; 1st cl. Theological Tripos Pts I and II (Senior Scofield Prize); BA 1932, MA 1945). Cuddesdon Theological Coll. Deacon 1933; priest, 1934; Assistant Curate: St Matthew's, Oxhey, 1933–36; The Priory Church, Dunstable, 1936–39; Chaplain of Bedford Sch., 1939–43; Vicar of St Paul's, Peterborough, 1943–53; Religious Broadcasting Asst, BBC, 1953–58; Chaplain of St Christopher's Coll., Blackheath, 1954–58; Chaplain of Heathfield Sch., Ascot, 1959–64. Founder Mem., Council of St George's House, Windsor Castle, 1966–78 (resp. for Clergy trng, 1966–74). *Address:* 1 Thames Close, Charfield, Wotton-under-Edge, Glos GL12 8UA. *Died 12 Feb. 2001.*

FISHER, Rt Rev. Brother Michael, SSF, **(Reginald Lindsay Fisher);** Assistant Bishop, Diocese of Ely, 1985–96; *b* 6 April 1918; *s* of late Reginald Watson Fisher and Martha Lindsay Fisher. *Educ:* Clapham Central School; Bolt Court; Westcott House, Cambridge. Member, Society of St Francis, 1942. Deacon 1953, priest 1954, dio. Ely; Licence to officiate: Diocese of Ely, 1954–62; Newcastle, 1962–67; Sarum, 1967–79; Bishop Suffragan of St Germans, 1979–85; Bishop to HM Prisons, 1985. Minister Provincial, 1967–79, Minister-Gen., 1985–91, SSF. MA Lambeth, 1978. *Publications:* For the Time Being (autobiog.), 1993; A Word In Time (sermons and addresses), 1997. *Recreations:* painting, music, cinema, people. *Address:* Hope Residential and Nursing Care Home, Brooklands Avenue, Cambridge CB2 2BQ.

Died 5 Dec. 2003.

FISHER, Nancy Kathleen; *see* Trenaman, N. K.

FISHER, Thomas Gilbert F.; *see* Field-Fisher.

FITT, Baron *cr* 1983 (Life Peer), of Bell's Hill in the County of Down; **Gerard Fitt;** *b* 9 April 1926; *s* of George Patrick and Mary Ann Fitt; *m* 1947, Susan Gertrude Doherty (*d* 1996); five *d* (and one *d* decd). *Educ:* Christian Brothers' Sch., Belfast. Merchant Seaman, 1941–53; various positions, 1953–. Councillor, later Alderman, Belfast Corp., 1958–81; MP (Eire Lab) Parlt of N Ireland, Dock Div. of Belfast, 1962–72; Mem. (SDLP) N Belfast, NI Assembly, 1973–75, NI Constitutional Convention, 1975–76; Dep. Chief Exec., NI Exec., 1974; elected MP (Repub. Lab) Belfast West, 1966; a founder and Leader, Social Democratic and Labour Party, and MP (SDLP), 1970–79, when resigned Leadership; MP (Socialist), 1979–83. Contested (Socialist) Belfast West, 1983. *Recreation:* full-time politics. *Address:* House of Lords, SW1A 0PW. *Died 26 Aug. 2005.*

FITTER, Richard Sidney Richmond; author and naturalist; *b* 1 March 1913; *o s* of Sidney and Dorothy Fitter; *m* 1938, Alice Mary, (Maisie), Stewart (*d* 1996), *e d* of Dr R. S. Park, Huddersfield; two *s* one *d*. *Educ:* Eastbourne Coll.; LSE (BSc (Econ)). Research staff: PEP, 1936–40; Mass-Observation, 1940–42; Operational Research Section, Coastal Command, 1942–45; Sec., Wild Life Cons. Special Cttee, Hobhouse Cttee on Nat. Parks, 1945–46; Asst Editor, The Countryman, 1946–59; Open Air Corresp., The Observer, 1958–66; Dir, Intelligence Unit, Council for Nature, 1959–63; Editor, Kingfisher, 1965–72. Vice-Pres., Fauna and Flora Preservation Soc., 1988– (Hon. Sec., 1964–81; Chm., 1983–87); Member: Species Survival Commn (formerly

Survival Service Commn), Internat. Union for Cons. of Nature, 1963– (Chm., Steering Cttee, 1975–88); Scientific Authy for Animals, DoE, 1965–81; Conservation Adv. Cttee, World Wildlife Fund Internat., 1977–79; Trustee, World Wildlife Fund, UK, 1977–83; Past Pres., Berks, Bucks and Oxfordshire Naturalists' Trust; Chm., Council for Nature, 1979; Vice Chm., Falkland Is Foundn, later Falklands Conservation, 1986–94 (Vice Pres., 1994–2005); Vice-Pres., Galapagos Conservation Trust, 1995–; President: London Natural Hist. Soc., 1998–2000; Wild Flower Soc., 2000–02; Minister's Rep., Southern Council for Sport and Recreation, 1980–82; formerly Hon. Treas. and Hon. Sec., British Trust for Ornithology; Chm., Gen. Purposes Cttee, Royal Soc. for Protection of Birds; and council or cttee mem. of numerous nat. history and conservation bodies. Editor, The London Naturalist. Scientific FZS. Christopher Cadbury Medal, RSNC, 1998; Peter Scott Medal, British Naturalists' Assoc., 1998. Officer, Order of the Golden Ark (The Netherlands), 1978. *Publications:* London's Natural History, 1945; London's Birds, 1949; Pocket Guide to British Birds, 1952; Pocket Guide to Nests and Eggs, 1954; (with David McClintock) Pocket Guide to Wild Flowers, 1956; The Ark in Our Midst, 1959; Six Great Naturalists, 1959; Guide to Bird Watching, 1963; Wildlife in Britain, 1963; Britain's Wildlife: rarities and introductions, 1966; (with Maisie Fitter) Penguin Dictionary of Natural History, 1967; Vanishing Wild Animals of the World, 1968; Finding Wild Flowers, 1972; (with H. Heinzel and J. Parslow) Birds of Britain and Europe, with North Africa and the Middle East, 1972; (with A. Fitter and M. Blamey) Wild Flowers of Britain and Northern Europe, 1974; (with Sir Peter Scott) The Penitent Butchers, 1979; (with M. Blamey) Handguide to the Wild Flowers of Britain and Northern Europe, 1979; (with M. Blamey) Gem Guide to Wild Flowers, 1980; (with N. Arlott and A. Fitter) The Complete Guide to British Wildlife, 1981; (ed with Eric Robinson) John Clare's Birds, 1982; (with A. Fitter and J. Wilkinson) Collins Guide to the Countryside, 1984; (with A. Fitter and A. Farrer) Grasses, Sedges, Rushes and Ferns of Britain and Northern Europe, 1984; (ed) The Wildlife of the Thames Counties, 1985; Wildlife for Man, 1986; (with R. Manuel) Field Guide to the Freshwater Life of Britain and NW Europe, 1986; (with A. Fitter) Guide to the Countryside in Winter, 1988; (with A. Fitter and M. Blamey) Wild Flowers of Britain and Ireland, 2003. *Recreations:* botanising, observing wild and human life, exploring new habitats, reading. *Address:* Danewood, 9 Coppice Avenue, Great Shelford, Cambridge CB2 5AQ. *T:* (01223) 843573. *Club:* Athenæum.

Died 3 Sept. 2005.

FitzGERALD, Sir George (Peter Maurice), 5th Bt *cr* 1880, of Valencia, Co. Kerry; 23rd Knight of Kerry; MC 1944; Major, Army, retired; *b* 27 Feb. 1917; *s* of Sir Arthur Henry Brinsley FitzGerald, 4th Bt, and Mary Eleanor (*d* 1967), *d* of late Capt. Francis Forester; *S* father, 1967; *m* 1939, Angela Dora Mitchell; one *s* one *d. Educ:* Harrow; RMC, Sandhurst. Commnd into Irish Guards, 1937; 2nd in comd, 1st Bn, 1944; 2nd in comd, 2nd Bn, 1946; retired, 1948. *Heir: s* Adrian James Andrew Denis FitzGerald, *b* 24 June 1940. *Address:* Colin's Farm House, 55 High Street, Durrington, Salisbury, Wilts SP4 8AQ. *Club:* Army and Navy.   *Died 6 April 2001.*

FITZGERALD, Kaarene Noelle, AC 1999; Executive Director, Sudden Infant Death Research Foundation, Australia, since 1977; *b* 12 Dec.; *d* of Leslie George Stout and Muriel Joyce Stout (*née* Larsen); *m* (marr. diss. 1992); two *s* two *d* (and one *s* decd). *Educ:* Mt Maunganui Coll., NZ; PioPio High Sch., NZ. Director: SIDSaustralia, 1986–2001; SIDS Internat., 1987–94 and 1998–; Chm./ Founder, SIDS Global Strategy Task Force, 1992–. Mem., Women Chiefs of Enterprises, 2001–. Trustee, Monash Inst. Reproduction and Develt, 1993–. Mem. Bd and Newsletter Ed., Order of Australia Cttee (Vic Br.), 1999–.

Speaker in many countries on infant mortality, mktg and mgt. *Publications:* contrib. to jls on infant mortality, mktg and mgt. *Recreations:* Formula One motor racing, horse racing, polo. *Address:* 26 Washington Avenue, East Malvern, Vic 3145, Australia; SIDS and Kids, 1227 Malvern Road, Malvern, Vic 3144, Australia. *T:* (3) 98229611; *e-mail:* kaarene@sidsaustralia.org.au. *Clubs:* Melbourne Racing, Victoria Racing, Victoria Polo (Mem. Bd, 1997–; Pres., 2001–) (Melbourne).

Died 24 May 2003.

FitzGIBBON, Louis Theobald Dillon; Comte Dillon in France; political writer; *b* 6 Jan. 1925; *s* of Comdr Francis Lee-Dillon FitzGibbon, RN, and Kathleen Clare (*née* Atchison), *widow* of Hon. Harry Lee-Dillon; *m* 1st, 1950, Josephine Miriam Maud (*née* Webb) (marr. diss. 1962); 2nd, 1962, Madeleine Sally (*née* Hayward-Surry) (*d* 1980); one *s* two *d*; 3rd, 1980, Joan Elizabeth Jevons (marr. diss. 1994). *Educ:* St Augustine's Abbey Sch.; Royal Naval Coll., Dartmouth. Royal Navy, 1942–54 (incl. War of 1939–45 and service in ex-German U-1171); Polish interpreter's course, 1950–52. Dir, De Leon Properties Ltd, 1954–72. Solicitor's articled clerk, 1960–63; Anglo-Polish Conf., Warsaw, 1963. Personal Asst to Rt Hon. Duncan Sandys, MP (later Lord Duncan-Sandys), 1967–68; Gen. Sec., British Council for Aid to Refugees, 1968–72; United Nations (UNHCR) Mission to South Sudan, 1972–73; Dir of a medical charity, 1974–76; Exec. Officer, Nat. Assoc. for Freedom, 1977–78; Gen. Sec. of a trade assoc., 1978–80; Hon. Sec., British Horn of Africa Council, 1984–92. Mem., RIIA, 1982, 1988. Won first Airey Neave Meml Scholarship (proj. on Somalia), 1981. Hon. Secretary: Jt Cttee for Preservation of Historic Portsmouth, 1956–61; Katyn Memorial Fund, 1971–77; Area Pres., St John Amb. Brigade (Hants East), 1974–76. Katyn Meml Medal Bronze (USA), 1977; Laureate van de Arbeid (Netherlands), 1982. Polish Gold Cross of Merit, 1969; Kt Comdr, Order of Polonia Restituta (Polish Govt in Exile), 1976 (Officer, 1971; Comdr, 1972); Kt of Honour and Devotion and Officer of Merit, SMHO (Malta), 1985; Officer, Order of Merit (FRG), 1990. *Publications:* Katyn—A Crime without Parallel, 1971; The Katyn Cover-up, 1972; Unpitied and Unknown, 1975; Katyn—Triumph of Evil (Ireland), 1975; The Katyn Memorial, 1976; Katyn Massacre (paper) 1977, 3rd edn 1989; Katyn (USA), 1979; Katyn (in German), 1979; The Betrayal of the Somalis, 1982 (commnd by Japan-Somalia Friendship Assoc. in Japanese, 1989); Straits and Strategic Waterways in the Red Sea, 1984; Ethiopia Hijacks the Hijack, 1985; The Evaded Duty, 1985. *Recreations:* politics, writing, reading, history, languages. *Address:* Flat 2, 8 Portland Place, Brighton BN2 1DG. *T:* (01273) 685661.   *Died 31 Jan. 2003.*

FITZPATRICK, Gen. Sir (Geoffrey Richard) Desmond, GCB 1971 (KCB 1965; CB 1961); GCVO 1997; DSO 1945; MBE 1943; MC 1939; *b* 14 Dec. 1912; *o s* of Brig.-Gen. Sir Richard Fitzpatrick, CBE, DSO, and Lady (Georgina Ethel) Fitzpatrick; *m* 1st, 1944, Mary Sara (*d* 1996), *o d* of Sir Charles Campbell, 12th Bt; one *s* one *d*; 2nd, 1998, Lettice, *o d* of late Capt. Edward Stafford-King-Harman and *widow* of Major George Errington. *Educ:* Eton; RMC Sandhurst. Commnd The Royal Dragoons, 1932; served in Palestine, 1938–39; served War of 1939–45 (despatches), in Middle East, Italy, NW Europe. Bt Lieut-Col 1951; Col 1953; ADC to the Queen, 1959; Maj.-Gen. 1959; Asst Chief of Defence Staff, MoD, 1959–61; Dir Mil. Ops, War Office, 1962–64; Chief of Staff, BAOR, 1964–65; Lt-Gen. 1965; GOC-in-C, N Ire., 1965–66; Vice-Chief of Gen. Staff, 1966–68; Gen. 1968; C-in-C, BAOR, and Commander N Army Gp 1968–70; Dep. Supreme Allied Comdr, Europe, 1970–73; ADC (General) to the Queen, 1970–73. Lieut-Governor and C-in-C, Jersey, 1974–79. Col, The Royal Dragoons, 1964–69; Dep. Col, 1969–74, Col, 1979–98, The Blues and Royals, and Gold Stick to the Queen, 1979–98; Col Comdt, RAC, 1971–74. *Address:* Belmont,

Otley, Suffolk IP6 9PF. *Clubs:* Cavalry and Guards; Royal Yacht Squadron. *Died 12 Oct. 2002.*

FITZWALTER, 21st Baron *cr* 1295; **(Fitzwalter) Brook Plumptre;** JP; Hon. Captain, The Buffs; *b* 15 Jan. 1914; *s* of late George Beresford Plumptre, Goodnestone, Canterbury, Kent; *S* uncle, 1943 (FitzWalter Barony called out of abeyance in his favour, 1953); *m* 1951, Margaret Melesina, *yr d* of (Herbert) William Deedes, JP, Galt, Hythe, Kent; five *s*. *Educ:* Diocesan Coll., Rondebosch, Cape; Jesus Coll., Cambridge. Served War of 1939–45, with the Buffs (Royal East Kent Regt) in France, Belgium, UK and India; attached RIASC, as Capt. Landowner and farmer; succeeded to family estate, 1943. JP Kent, 1949. *Heir: s* Hon. Julian Brook Plumptre [*b* 18 Oct. 1952; *m* 1988, Sally, *o d* of late I. M. T. Quiney; three *s*]. *Address:* Goodnestone Park, Canterbury, Kent CT3 1PL. *T:* (01304) 840218. *Died 14 Oct. 2004.*

FLEMING, John, FRSL; writer; *b* 12 June 1919; *s* of Joseph Fleming and Elizabeth Stawart. *Educ:* Rugby Sch.; Trinity Coll., Cambridge (BA). FRSL 1963. Editor of Style & Civilisation, Art in Context, and, Architect and Society, for Penguin Books, 1964–. *Publications:* Robert Adam and his Circle in Edinburgh and Rome, 1962; (with Sir Nikolaus Pevsner and Hugh Honour) The Penguin Dictionary of Architecture, 1966, 5th rev. edn, as Penguin Dictionary of Architecture and Landscape Architecture, 1998; (with Hugh Honour) The Penguin Dictionary of Decorative Arts, 1977, rev. edn 1989; (with Hugh Honour) A World History of Art, 1982 (Mitchell Prize, 1982), 5th edn 1999 (US edn, The Visual Arts: a history); (with Hugh Honour) The Venetian Hours of Henry James, Whistler and Sargent, 1991. *Recreation:* gardening. *Died 29 May 2001.*

FLEMMING, John Stanton, CBE 2001; FBA 1991; Warden, Wadham College, Oxford, 1993–2003; *b* 6 Feb. 1941; *s* of Sir Gilbert Nicolson Flemming, KCB, and late Virginia Coit; *m* 1963, Jean Elizabeth (*née* Briggs); three *s* one *d*. *Educ:* Rugby Sch.; Trinity Coll., Oxford (BA 1962, MA 1966; Hon. Fellow, 1994); Nuffield Coll., Oxford. Lecturer and Fellow, Oriel Coll., Oxford, 1963–65 (Hon. Fellow, 1993); Official Fellow in Economics, 1965–80, Emeritus Fellow, 1980, and Bursar, 1970–79, Nuffield Coll., Oxford. Bank of England: Chief Advr, 1980–84; Economic Advr to the Governor, 1984–88; Exec. Dir, 1988–91; Chief Economist, EBRD, 1991–93. Member: Nat. Freight Corp., 1978–80; Adv. Bd on Research Councils, 1986–91; Royal Commn on Envmtl Pollution, 1995–; Chairman: Economic Affairs Cttee, SSRC, 1981–84; Hansard Soc./Eur. Policy Forum Commn on Regulation of Privatised Utilities, 1995–96; Mgt Cttee, NIESR, 1996–2002. Vice-Pres., Royal Economic Soc., 1998– (Mem. Council, 1980–98; Treas., 1993–98); British Academy: Mem. Council, 1993–2002; Vice Pres., 1994–95; Hon. Treas., 1995–2002. Associate Editor: Oxford Economic Papers, 1970–73; Review of Economic Studies, 1973–76; Editor, Economic Jl, 1976–80. Hon. DSocSc Brunel, 2003. *Publications:* Inflation, 1976; contrib. economic jls. *Address:* 6 Polstead Road, Oxford OX2 6TN. *Died 5 Aug. 2003.*

FLETCHER, Alan Philip; QC 1984; *b* 28 June 1914; *s* of late Philip Cawthorne Fletcher, MC and Edith Maud Fletcher; *m* 1945, Annette Grace Wright (*d* 2004); three *s* one *d*. *Educ:* Marlborough Coll.; Trinity Coll., Oxford (MA). Hockey blue, 1936 and 1937. Served War, Army, England and India, 1939–45, ending as acting Lt-Col. Called to the Bar, Inner Temple, 1940; bencher; Junior Counsel, Inland Revenue (Rating Valuation), 1969–84. Member (C): Hendon BC, 1954–65; Barnet LBC, 1964–74 (Leader, 1965–73). *Recreation:* architectural and garden history. *Address:* 26 Hollies Close, Royston, Herts SG8 7DZ. *T:* (01763) 248580. *Died 22 Nov. 2004.*

FLETCHER, Geoffrey Scowcroft; artist and author; *b* 3 April 1923; *o s* of Herbert Fletcher and Annie Talence

Fletcher; *m* 1953, Mary Jean Timothy. *Educ:* University Coll., London (Dip. in Fine Art); British Sch. at Rome (Abbey Major Schol., 1948). Drawings appeared in Manchester Guardian, 1950; London drawings and articles featured in The Daily Telegraph, 1958–. Author of television features on unusual aspects of London; instrumental in saving a number of metropolitan buildings from demolition. Drawings and paintings in various public and private collections in England and abroad, including: exhibn of paintings and drawings in possession of Islington Council, 1972, 1978; exhibs of drawings and paintings, 1981, 1986, Lancashire industrial drawings and paintings, 1992–93, paintings, drawings and pubns, 1996, Bolton Art Gall.; collection of English watercolours and drawings presented to Bury Art Gall., 2003; *acquisitions:* drawings and sketchbooks, British Museum, 1990; oil paintings and sketchbooks, Guildhall Art Gall., 1990–97; drawings and sketchbooks, Ashmolean Mus., 1991–92; oil paintings and drawings, Bury Art Gall., 1993–94; watercolours, Whitworth Art Gall., Manchester, 1996; London and Continental oil paintings, Guildhall Art Gall., 1998; oil paintings and drawings, Blackpool Art Gall., 1999–2000; recent watercolours, Oldham Art Gall., 2004. Geoffrey Fletcher Room, decorated with the artist's drawings, opened Selfridge Hotel, London, 1973. Designed enamel box for St Paul's Cathedral Appeal, 1972; *exhibitions:* drawings, Miles Gall., St James's, 1980; East End Drawings and Paintings, Limehouse, 1984; London drawings, Guildhall, City of London, 1988; Genoese drawings, for City of Genoa promotion, London, 1988; paintings, Guildhall Art Gall., 1999–2000. *Publications:* The London Nobody Knows, 1962, 3rd edn 1996 (filmed, 1968); City Sights, 1963; Pearly Kingdom, 1965; London's River, 1966; Elements of Sketching, 1966 (Amer. edn, 1968); Down Among the Meths Men, 1966; London's Pavement Pounders, 1967; Geoffrey Fletcher's London, 1968; London After Dark, 1969; Changing London (Drawings from The Daily Telegraph), 1969; The London Dickens Knew, 1970; London Souvenirs, 1973; Paint It In Water Colour, 1974; Italian Impressions, 1974; Sketch It In Black and White, 1975; London: a private view, 1989; The Spitalfields Prints, 1990; Daily Telegraph Series: London Prints, 1975; London Colour Prints, 1978; London Portraits, 1978; London at My Feet, 1979; London Alleys, 1980. *Address:* c/o Cassell plc, Wellington House, 125 Strand, WC2R 0BB; c/o R. Davis-Poynter, 118 St Pancras, Chichester, W Sussex. *Died 22 June 2004.*

FLETCHER, Major John Antony, MBE 1953; Royal Artillery, retired; Secretary, Institute of Road Transport Engineers, 1963–85; *b* 4 May 1918; *s* of Alexander Ernest Fletcher and Abbie (*née* Wheeler); *m* 1st, 1951, Elizabeth Cross (marr. diss. 1979; she *d* 1992); one *s* three *d*; 2nd, 1980, Susan Mary Brown. *Educ:* Cheltenham Coll. Jun. Sch.; Abingdon Sch.; RMA, Woolwich; Army and RAF Staff Colls (psc, pac). 2nd Lieut, RA, 1938; war service, Malta, Middle East, Malaya and Burma; Korea Commonwealth Div.; retired 1960. Secretariat, Powell Duffryn Gp, 1960–63. Chm., Assoc. of Care-Takers and Care-Seekers, 1985–88. Hon. FIRTE 1985. *Publications:* article in Gunner Jl; eight letters (out of twelve!) to The Times. *Recreations:* being ex!: ex-playing mem., MCC; ex-Stragglers of Asia; ex-United Hunts Club; ex-Sherringham and many other golf clubs; ex-FRSA. *Address:* Milford Cottage, 10 Cudnall Street, Charlton Kings, Cheltenham, Glos GL53 8HT. *T:* (01242) 522367.
Died 20 Aug. 2001.

FLETCHER, Sir Leslie, Kt 1983; DSC 1945; FCA; Deputy Chairman, RMC Group, 1991–96 (Director, 1983–96); *b* 14 Oct. 1922; *s* of Ernest and Lily Fletcher; *m* 1947, Audrey Faviell Jackson; one *s* one *d*. *Educ:* Nether Edge Secondary Sch., Sheffield. FCA 1952. Served War, RNVR (FAA), 1942–46 (Lieut). Helbert Wagg & Co. Ltd (subseq. J. Henry Schroder Wagg & Co. Ltd), 1955–71, Dir 1966–71; Chm., Glynwed Internat., 1971–86; Dep. Chm., Standard Chartered PLC, 1983–89 (Dir, 1972–89);

Chairman: Westland Group, 1989–94; Rank Orgn, 1992–95 (Dir, 1984–95). Mem. Council, CBI, 1976–86. *Recreations:* gardening, golf, photography. *Address:* Hafod, The Green, Sherfield-on-Loddon, Hook, Hants RG27 0EN. *Clubs:* Brooks's, MCC, Royal Automobile; Royal & Ancient Golf (St Andrews). *Died 19 May 2002.*

FLETCHER-COOKE, Sir Charles (Fletcher), Kt 1981; QC 1958; *b* 5 May 1914; *yr s* of late Capt. C. A. and Gwendolen May Fletcher-Cooke; *m* 1959, Diana Lady Avebury (marr. diss. 1967; she *d* 1993), *d* of late Capt. Edward King and of Mrs J. St Vincent Hand. *Educ:* Malvern Coll. (Scholar); Peterhouse, Cambridge (Schol.; MA 1940). FCIArb 1981. Pres., Cambridge Union, 1936; Editor, The Granta, 1936. Called to the Bar, Lincoln's Inn, 1938 (1st Class Hons, Bar Final Examination; Studentship and Certificate of Honour); Bencher 1969. Mem. Senate, Four Inns of Court, 1970–74. Served War of 1939–45, in Naval Intelligence Div. and on Joint Intelligence Staff, with rank of Lt-Comdr, RNVR. MP (C) Darwen, Lancs, 1951–83; Joint Parly Under-Sec. of State, Home Office, 1961–63; Chm., Select Cttee on Parly Comr for Admin, 1974–77. Mem., Statute Law Cttee, 1955–61, 1970–83. Legal Adviser to British Delegation, Danube Conf., Belgrade, 1948; Deleg. to Consultative Assembly of Council of Europe, 1954–55. Mem., European Parlt, 1977–79. Dato SPMB, Brunei, 1978. *Publications:* (with others) The Rule of Law; (with M. J. Albery) Monopolies and Restrictive Trade Practices. *Recreation:* fishing. *Address:* The Red House, Clifton Hampden, Oxon OX14 3EW. *T:* (01865) 407754. *Clubs:* Garrick, Pratt's. *Died 24 Feb. 2001.*

FLOWER, Rear-Adm. (Edward) James (William), CB 1980; Director, Post-Design (Ships), Ministry of Defence (Navy), 1977–80; *b* 5 July 1923; *m* Martha Pyman; three *d. Educ:* Blundell's Sch. Joined RN, 1941; served in HM Ships Norfolk, Duke of York, Liverpool, Whitby, Urchin and Tenby; Canadian Nat. Defence Coll., 1966; Fleet Marine Engineering Officer, Western Fleet, 1967–69; commanded RN Nuclear Propulsion Test and Trng Estab., 1970–71; MoD (Navy), 1971–75; Flag Officer Portsmouth, and Port Admiral, Portsmouth, 1975–76; Dir of Engrg (Ships), MoD, 1976–77. *Address:* Fairmount, Hinton Charterhouse, Bath BA3 6AZ. *Died 19 Dec. 2002.*

FLOYD EWIN, Sir David Ernest Thomas, Kt 1974; LVO 1954; OBE 1965; MA; Lay Administrator, 1939–44, Registrar and Receiver, 1944–78, Consultant to the Dean and Chapter, since 1978, St Paul's Cathedral; Notary Public; *b* 17 Feb. 1911; 7th *s* of late Frederick P. Ewin and Ellen Floyd; *m* 1948, Marion Irene, *d* of William R. Lewis; one *d. Educ:* Eltham. MA (Lambeth) 1962. Chairman: Tubular Exhibn, subseq. Tubular Edgington, Group, 1978–91; Stonebert Ltd and subsids, 1985–91. Freeman, City of London, 1948; Member of Court of Common Council for Ward of Castle Baynard, 1963–96 (Dep., 1972–96); Vice-Pres., Castle Baynard Ward Club, 1972–96 (Chm. 1962 and 1988); Chm., Gresham Cttee, 1975–76, Benevolent Cttee, 1991–96, Corp. of London; Member: Lord Mayor and Sheriffs Cttee, 1976, 1978, 1984 (Chm., 1987); Court of Assts, Hon. Irish Soc., 1976–79; Surrogate for Province of Canterbury; Trustee: City Parochial Foundn, 1967–90 (Chm., Pensions Cttee, 1978–90); St Paul's Cathedral Trust, 1978–; Temple Bar Trust, 1979–96; Dep. Chm., City of London's Endowment Trust for St Paul's Cathedral, 1982–. Hon. Dir, British Humane Assoc.; Governor and Member of Court: Sons of the Clergy Corp.; St Gabriel's Coll., Camberwell, 1946–72. Senior Past Master: Scriveners' Co.; Guild of Freemen of the City of London; Liveryman, Wax Chandlers' Co.; Gold Staff Officer at Coronation of HM Queen Elizabeth, 1953. KStJ 1970 (OStJ 1965). *Publications:* A Pictorial History of St Paul's Cathedral, 1970; The Splendour of St Paul's, 1973; numerous papers and articles. *Recreations:* tennis, gardening, fishing. *Address:*

13 Seaborne Court, Alta Vista Road, Paignton, S Devon TQ4 6DP. *T:* (01803) 523993; Chapter House, St Paul's Churchyard, EC4M 8AD. *T:* (020) 7248 2705. *Clubs:* City Livery, Guildhall. *Died 11 Nov. 2003.*

FOGARTY, Christopher Winthrop, CB 1973; Deputy Secretary, Overseas Development Administration, Foreign and Commonwealth Office, (formerly Ministry of Overseas Development), 1976–81; *b* 18 Sept. 1921; *s* of late Philip Christopher Fogarty, ICS, and Hilda Spenser Fogarty; *m* 1961, Elizabeth Margaret Ince (*d* 1972). *Educ:* Ampleforth Coll.; Christ Church, Oxford. War Service (Lieut RA), 1942–45. Asst Principal, 1946, Principal, 1949, HM Treasury; Permanent Sec., Min. of Finance of Eastern Nigeria, 1956; Asst Sec., HM Treasury, 1959, Under-Sec., 1966; Treasury Rep., S Asia and FE, 1967–72; Dep. Sec., HM Treasury, and Dir, European Investment Bank, 1972–76. *Address:* 4 Greenwood Court, 7/9 The Parade, Epsom, Surrey KT18 5DP. *Clubs:* Royal Commonwealth Society, Travellers. *Died 23 Sept. 2005.*

FOGARTY, Michael Patrick; Director, Institute for Family and Environmental Research, 1981–84; *b* 3 Oct. 1916; *s* of late Philip Christopher Fogarty, ICS, and Mary Belle Pye, Galway; *m* 1939, Phyllis Clark (*d* 1998); two *s* two *d. Educ:* Ampleforth Coll.; Christ Church, Oxford. Lieut RA, 1940 (wounded, Dunkirk). Nuffield Coll., Oxford, 1941–51 (Fellow, 1944); Montague Burton Prof. of Industrial Relations, University Coll. of S Wales and Mon, 1951–66; Dir and Prof., Econ. and Social Res. Inst., Dublin, 1968–72; Centre for Studies in Social Policy: Sen. Fellow, 1973; Dep. Dir, 1977–78; Dep. Dir, PSI, 1978–82. Also held posts in Administrative Staff Coll., Oxford Institute of Statistics, Nat. Institute of Economic and Social Research, Ministry of Town and Country Planning, and as Asst Editor, The Economist. Chairman: Cttee on Industrial Relations in the Electricity Supply Bd (Ireland), 1968–69; Banks Inquiry, 1970–71; Member: Commn on the Status of Women (Ireland), 1970–72; Commn on Insurance Industry (Ireland), 1970–72; Cttee on Aid to Political Parties, 1975–76. President: Newman Assoc., 1957–59; Movement for Christian Democracy, 1995–; Chm., Catholic Social Guild, 1959–63; Mem., Social Welfare Commn, RC Bishops' Conf. (England and Wales); Vice-Pres. Assoc. of University Teachers, 1964–66. Prospective Parly candidate (Lab) Tamworth, 1938–44; contested (L): Devizes, 1964 and 1966; Abingdon, Feb. and Oct. 1974. Vice-Pres. of the Liberal Party, 1964–66. Contested (L) Thames Valley, European Parlt, 1979. District Councillor, Vale of White Horse, 1973–87; CC Oxfordshire, 1981–89 (Vice-Chm., 1985–86; Chm., 1986–87). Hon. Dr of Political and Social Science, Louvain, 1963. *Publications:* Prospects of the Industrial Areas of Great Britain, 1945; Plan Your Own Industries, 1947; (ed) Further Studies in Industrial Organisation, 1948; Town and Country Planning, 1948; Economic Control, 1955; Personality and Group Relations in Industry, 1956; Christian Democracy in Western Europe, 1820–1953, 1957; The Just Wage, 1961; Under-Governed and Over-Governed, 1962; The Rules of Work, 1963; Company and Corporation—One Law?, 1965; Companies Beyond Jenkins, 1965; Wider Business Objectives, 1966; A Companies Act 1970?, 1967; (with Allen, Allen and Walters) Women in Top Jobs, 1971; (with Rapoport and Rapoport) Sex, Career and Family, 1971; Women and Top Jobs: the next move, 1972; Irish Entrepreneurs Speak For Themselves, 1974; Forty to Sixty, 1975; Company Responsibility and Participation—A New Agenda, 1975; Pensions—where next?, 1976; (with Eileen Reid) Differentials for Managers and Skilled Manual Workers in the UK, 1980; Retirement Age and Retirement Costs, 1980; (with Allen and Walters) Women in Top Jobs 1968–79, 1981; (ed) Retirement Policy: the next fifty years, 1982; (with Ryan and Lea) Irish Values and Attitudes, 1984; (with D. Brooks) Trade Unions and British Industrial Development, 1986; (with Ian Christie)

Companies and Communities, 1990; (jtly) More Than Money, 1993; Phoenix or Cheshire Cat, 1995; Motorways Merge, 1999; My Life and Ours, 1999. *Recreations:* swimming, walking. *Died 20 Jan. 2001.*

FOGG, Prof. Gordon Elliott, (Tony), CBE 1983; FRS 1965; Professor and Head of the Department of Marine Biology, University College of North Wales, Bangor, 1971–85, then Professor Emeritus; *b* 26 April 1919; *s* of Rev. L. C. Fogg; *m* 1945, Elizabeth Beryl Llechid-Jones (*d* 1997); one *s* one *d*. *Educ:* Dulwich Coll.; Queen Mary Coll., London (BSc 1939); St John's Coll., Cambridge (PhD 1943; ScD 1966). Sea-weed Survey of British Isles, 1942; Plant Physiologist, Pest Control Ltd, 1943–45; successively Asst Lectr, Lectr and Reader in Botany, University Coll. London, 1945–60; Rockefeller Fellow, 1954; Prof. of Botany, Westfield Coll., Univ. of London, 1960–71. Member: Royal Commn on Environmental Pollution, 1979–85; NERC, 1981–82. Royal Soc. Leverhulme Vis. Prof., Kerala, 1969–70; Leverhulme Emeritus Fellow, 1986. Botanical Sec., Soc. for Experimental Biology, 1957–60; President: British Phycological Soc., 1961–62; International Phycological Soc., 1964; Inst. of Biology, 1976–77; Chm. Council, Freshwater Biol Assoc., 1974–85; Joint Organizing Sec., X International Botanical Congress. Visiting research worker, 1966, 1974, 1979, Chm., Scientific Adv. Cttee, 1971–84, British Antarctic Survey; Biological Gen. Sec., 1967–72, Pres., Section K, 1973, BAAS. Chm., Menai Members' Assoc., NT, 2003–. Trustee: BM (Natural Hist.), 1976–85; Royal Botanic Gardens, Kew, 1983–89. Fellow, Queen Mary and Westfield Coll., London (formerly QMC), 1976. Hon. LLD Dundee, 1974. *Publications:* The Metabolism of Algae, 1953; The Growth of Plants, 1963; Algal Cultures and Phytoplankton Ecology, 1965, 3rd edn (with B. Thake) 1987; Photosynthesis, 1968; (jointly) The Blue-green Algae, 1973; (with D. Smith) The Explorations of Antarctica, 1990; A History of Antarctic Science, 1992; The Biology of Polar Habitats, 1998; papers in learned jls. *Recreations:* water colour painting, walking. *Address:* Bodolben, Llandegfan, Menai Bridge, Isle of Anglesey LL59 5TA. *T:* (01248) 712916. *Club:* Athenæum.

Died 30 Jan. 2005.

FOLEY, Maurice (Anthony), CMG 1987; Deputy Director General, Directorate General for Development, Commission of the European Communities, 1973–86; *b* 9 Oct. 1925; *s* of Jeremiah and Agnes Foley; *m* 1952, Katherine, *d* of Patrick and Nora O'Riordan; three *s* one *d*. *Educ:* St Mary's Coll., Middlesbrough. Formerly: electrical fitter, youth organiser, social worker. Member: ETU, 1941–46; Transport and General Workers Union, 1948–; Royal Arsenal Co-operative Soc. MP (Lab) West Bromwich, 1963–73; Joint Parliamentary Under-Sec. of State, Dept of Economic Affairs, 1964–66; Parliamentary Under-Secretary: Home Office, 1966–67; Royal Navy, MoD, 1967–68; FCO, 1968–70. *Died 8 Feb. 2002.*

FOLEY, Sir Noel; see Foley, Sir T. J. N.

FOLEY, Sir (Thomas John) Noel, Kt 1978; CBE 1967; Chairman: CSR Ltd, 1980–84; Allied Manufacturing and Trading Industries (AMATIL) Ltd, 1955–79 (retired); *b* 1914; *s* of late Benjamin Foley, Brisbane. *Educ:* Brisbane Grammar Sch., Queensland; Queensland Univ. (BA, BCom). Chairman: Bank of NSW, 1978–82; Westpac Banking Corp., 1982–87. Founding Pres., WWF, Australia, 1978–80. DUniv Sydney. *Address:* 15 Bass Place, St Ives, NSW 2075, Australia. *Died 30 Jan. 2005.*

FOOT, Paul Mackintosh; writer; journalist; with Private Eye, since 1993; *b* 8 Nov. 1937; *e s* of Baron Caradon (Life Peer), GCMG, KCVO, OBE, PC; *m* 1st, 1962, Monica Beckinsale (marr. diss. 1970); two *s*; 2nd, 1971, Roseanne Harvey (marr. diss. 1995); one *s*, partner, Clare; one *d*. *Educ:* University Coll., Oxford. Editor of Isis, 1961; President of the Oxford Union, 1961. TUC delegate from

Nat. Union of Journalists, 1967 and 1971. Contested (Socialist Workers Party) Birmingham, Stechford, March 1977. Editor, Socialist Worker, 1974–75; with The Daily Mirror, 1979–93. What The Papers Say Awards: Journalist of the Year, 1972, 1989; Journalist of the Decade (1990s), 2000; Campaigning Journalist of the Year, British Press Awards, 1980; (with Tim Laxton) George Orwell Prize for Journalism, 1994. *Publications:* Immigration and Race in British Politics, 1965; The Politics of Harold Wilson, 1968; The Rise of Enoch Powell, 1969; Who Killed Hanratty?, 1971; Why You Should Be a Socialist, 1977; Red Shelley, 1981; The Helen Smith Story, 1983; Murder at the Farm: who killed Carl Bridgewater?, 1986; Who Framed Colin Wallace?, 1989; Words as Weapons, 1990; Articles of Resistance, 2000; contrib. Counterblasts, 1989. *Address:* c/o Private Eye, 6 Carlisle Street, W1V 5RG. *Died 18 July 2004.*

FORAY, Prof. Cyril Patrick; High Commissioner for Sierra Leone in the United Kingdom, 1993–95 and 1996–2000; *b* 16 March 1934; *s* of Michael Kelema Foray and Mary Bridget Foray (*née* Alie); *m* 1958, Arabella Williams; two *s* two *d*. *Educ:* St Edward's Secondary Sch., Freetown, Sierra Leone; Fourah Bay Coll., Freetown; St Cuthbert's Soc., Durham Univ.; UCLA. Asst Master, St Edward's Secondary Sch., Freetown, 1958–60, Sen. Asst Master, 1960–62; part-time Lectr, Dept of Hist., Fourah Bay Coll., 1959–60; Lectr, Njala UC, 1964–67; Department of History, Fourah Bay College: Temp. Lectr, 1968–69 and 1972–73; Lectr, 1973–77; Actg Hd, 1975–77; Hd of Dept, 1977–85; Sen. Lectr, 1977–81; Associate Prof., 1981–85; Vice Principal, 1984–85; Prof. and Principal, 1985–93. University of Sierra Leone: Public Orator, 1976–85; Dean, Faculty of Arts, 1978–82; Pro-Vice Chancellor, 1988–90. MP Bo Town I constituency, Sierra Leone, 1969–73; Minister of: Ext. Affairs, 1969–71; Health, May–Sept. 1971. *Publications:* Historical Dictionary of Sierra Leone, Vol. 12, 1977; articles on Sierra Leone in Encyclopaedia Africana, 1979; The Road to the One Party—The Sierra Leone Experience, 1988. *Recreations:* cricket, lawn tennis. *Address:* 2 Leicester Road, Freetown, Sierra Leone. *Died 31 July 2003.*

FORBES, Hon. Sir Alastair (Granville), Kt 1960; President, Courts of Appeal for St Helena, Falkland Islands and British Antarctic Territories, 1965–88, and British Indian Ocean Territory, 1986–88; *b* 3 Jan. 1908; *s* of Granville Forbes and Constance Margaret (*née* Davis); *m* 1936, Constance Irene Mary Hughes-White (*d* 1995); two *d*. *Educ:* Blundell's Sch.; Clare Coll., Cambridge. Called to the Bar, Gray's Inn, 1932; Magistrate and Govt Officer, Dominica, BWI, 1936; Crown Attorney, Dominica, 1939; Resident Magistrate, Fiji, 1940; Crown Counsel, Fiji, 1942; Solicitor-Gen., Fiji, and Asst Legal Adviser, Western Pacific High Commission, 1945; Legal Draftsman, Federation of Malaya, 1947; Solicitor-Gen., Northern Rhodesia, 1950; Permanent Sec., Ministry of Justice, and Solicitor-Gen., Gold Coast, 1951; Puisne Judge, Kenya, 1956; Justice of Appeal, Court of Appeal for Eastern Africa, 1957; Vice-Pres., Court of Appeal for Eastern Africa, 1958; Federal Justice, Federal Supreme Court of Rhodesia and Nyasaland, 1963–64; Pres., Ct of Appeal: for Seychelles, 1965–76; for Gibraltar, 1970–83. Chairman: Constituencies Delimitation Commissions, N Rhodesia, 1962 and 1963, and Bechuanaland, 1964; Gibraltar Riot Inquiry, 1968. Mem., Panel of Chairmen of Industrial Tribunals (England and Wales), 1965–73; Pres., Pensions Appeal Tribunals for England and Wales, 1973–80 (Chm., 1965–73). *Publications:* Index of the Laws, Dominica, 1940; Revised Edition of Laws of Fiji, 1944. *Address:* Badgers Holt, Church Lane, Sturminster Newton, Dorset DT10 1DH. *T:* (01258) 473268.

Died 19 July 2001.

FORD, His Honour Peter; a Circuit Judge, 1990–2000; *b* 30 Sept. 1930; *s* of late Rev. Cecil Henry Ford and Gwyneth Kathleen Ford (*née* Hall); *m* 1961, Jenifer

Dekenah, Cape Town; one *d. Educ:* Ellesmere Coll.; Univ. of Manchester (LLB). Called to the Bar, Gray's Inn, 1952. In practice as barrister, Northern Circuit, 1952–55; legal advr in industry, 1956–59; in practice as barrister, Patent Bar, 1959–79; Mem., Bds of Appeal, European Patent Office, Munich, 1979–90; Chm., Legal Bd of Appeal, 1985–90; nominated Judge of Patents County Court, 1990. Reader in C of E, 1955–. MRI 1958; FRSA 1953. *Publications:* various articles in legal jls. *Recreations:* music, foreign languages, travel. *Died 9 March 2003.*

FORDE, Hon. Harold McDonald, CH (Barbados) 1994; MD; consultant physician; High Commissioner for Barbados in UK, 1984–86; *b* 10 Jan. 1916; *s* of Gertrude and William McDonald Forde; *m* 1949, Alice Leslie; one *s* two *d. Educ:* Harrison College, Barbados; University College London; University College Hospital (MB BS 1942; MD); DPH, DTM&H. MO, Colonial Med. Service, Belize, 1947–52; First Lectr, Dept. of Medicine, Univ. of West Indies, Jamaica, 1952–57; Consultant Physician, Barbados, 1957–78; Med. Supt, Barbados Gen. Hosp., 1961–64; Senior Lectr, Dept of Medicine, Univ. of West Indies, 1967–78 (Associate Dean, 1967–73); Mem. Senate, Univ. of W Indies, 1973–75; Chief Med. Officer, Commonwealth of Bahamas, 1978–79; Consultant Physician, Barbados, 1980–84; Chief Med. Officer, Life of Barbados, 1973–84. Mem. Privy Council, Barbados, 1980–85; Senior Fellow, Commonwealth Fund, 1976; Tech. Expert, Commonwealth Fund for Tech Co-Opn, 1978–79; Governor, Commonwealth Foundn, 1984. Hon. Vice-President: West India Cttee; Commonwealth Inst. Past Dist Gov., Lions Clubs Internat., 1973 (Life Mem., 1988; Melvin Jones Fellow, 1992). Mem., NY Acad. of Scis. Hon. FRCP 1971; Hon. FRCPE 1972; Hon. FACP 1975. Silver Jubilee Medal, 1977. *Publications:* articles in WI med. jls. *Recreations:* cricket, soccer, bridge, chess, athletics, music. *Club:* Royal Commonwealth Society. *Died 20 Jan. 2004.*

FORDER, Kenneth John; Registrar of the Architects Registration Council of the United Kingdom (established under Architects Registration Acts 1931 to 1969), 1977–90; *b* 11 June 1925; *s* of late James A. Forder and Elizabeth Forder (*née* Hammond); *m* 1948, Dorothy Margôt Burles; two *d. Educ:* Westcliff Sch.; Hertford Coll., Oxford (MA); Queens' Coll., Cambridge. Called to the Bar, Gray's Inn, 1963. RAF, Flt Lieut, Aircrew Navigator, 1943–47. District Officer, N Rhodesia, 1951–61; District Commissioner, N Rhodesia, 1962–64; General Secretary, National Federation of Meat Traders, 1964–73; Bar Practice, 1973–77. Freeman of the City of London, 1966. *Publications:* Architects in Europe, 1987; The Chittenden Legend, 1994; Fifty True Stories from Life, Never Before Told, 1995. *Recreations:* tennis, bridge, chess. *Address:* Napier Cottage, Napier Avenue, SW6 3NJ. *T:* (020) 7736 3958. *Club:* Hurlingham. *Died 13 July 2001.*

FORESTER, 8th Baron *cr* 1821; **George Cecil Brooke Weld Forester;** DL; Director: Linley Farms, since 1974; Sipolilo Estates, since 1977; *b* 20 Feb. 1938; *s* of 7th Baron Forester and Marie Louise Priscilla (*d* 1988), *d* of Col Sir Herbert Perrott, 6th Bt, CH, CB; *S* father, 1977; *m* 1967, Hon. Elizabeth Catherine Lyttelton, 2nd *d* of 10th Viscount Cobham, KG, PC, GCMG, GCVO, TD; one *s* three *d. Educ:* Eton; Royal Agricultural College, Cirencester (MRAC). Director: Pett Hammett, 1977–99; Lady Forester Hosp. Trust, 1994–; Bridgnorth Home Care Co-op., 1994–2002; Callkilo, 1996–99; Telford Drive, 1996–2002. Member: CLA (Mem. Minerals Working Party, 1980–98); Mem. Council, 1987–96; Mem. Exec., 1990–95); W Midlands Council for Sport and Recreation, 1991–95. President: The Greenwood Trust, 1990–; Shropshire Farming and Wildlife Adv. Gp, 1991–97; Midlands Flyfishers, 1999; Shropshire Cricket League, 1999. Former Chairman: Shropshire CLA; Shropshire Tree Council; Forestry Commn Regl Adv. Cttee. DL Shropshire, 1995. *Recreations:* fishing, silviculture, fine arts,

the environment. *Heir: s* Hon. Charles Richard George Weld Forester, *b* 8 July 1975. *Address:* Willey Park, Broseley, Salop TF12 5JJ. *T:* (01952) 882146.

Died 4 Feb. 2004.

FORGE, Andrew Murray; artist, writer; Professor of School of Art, University of Yale, Conn, USA (Dean, 1975–83); *b* Hastingleigh, Kent, 10 Nov. 1923; *s* of Sidney Wallace Forge and late Joanna Ruth Forge (*née* Bliss); *m* 1st, 1950, Sheila Deane (marr. diss.); two *d* (and one *d* decd); 2nd, 1974, Ruth Miller. *Educ:* Downs Sch.; Leighton Park; Camberwell Sch. of Art (NDD). Sen. Lectr, Slade Sch., UCL, 1950–64; Head of Dept of Fine Art, Goldsmith's Coll., 1964–70. Trustee: Tate Gallery, 1964–71 and 1972–74; National Gallery, 1966–72; Member: Nat. Council for Diplomas in Art and Design, 1964–72; Jt NCDAD/NACEA Cttee, 1968–70; Calouste Gulbenkian Foundn Cttee to report on future of conservation studies in UK, 1970–72; Pres., London Group, 1964–71. Trustee, Amer. Acad. in Rome, 1983–. *Publications:* Klee, 1953; Vermeer, 1954; Soutine, 1965; Rauschenberg, 1972; (with C. Joyes) Monet at Giverny, 1975; (ed) The Townsend Journals, 1976; (with Robert Gordon) Monet, 1983; (with Dawn Adès) Francis Bacon, 1985; (jtly) The Last Flowers of Manet, 1986; (with R. Gordon) Degas, 1988. *Recreation:* travel. *Address:* Malthouse, Elmsted, near Ashford, Kent TN25 5JZ.

Died 4 Sept. 2002.

FORMAN, Michael Bertram, TD 1945; Director of Personnel and Organisation, TI Group plc, 1973–84; *b* 28 March 1921; *s* of late Rev. A. Forman, CBE, and Flora Smith; *m* 1947, Mary Railston-Brown, *d* of late Rev. W. R. Railston-Brown; four *d. Educ:* Loretto Sch., Musselburgh; Manchester Coll. of Technology. TA commn, 7th KOSB, 1939; served War, 1939–46, Inf. and Airborne Forces, UK, Holland, Germany (POW), India. Labour Management, Courtaulds Ltd, 1946–53; Dir, Inst. of Personnel Management, 1953–56; Head of Staff Planning, NCB, 1956–59; Chief Staff Officer, SW Div., NCB, 1959–62; TI Group plc (formerly Tube Investments Ltd): Personnel Relations Adviser and Dep. Dir of Personnel, 1962–68; Personnel Dir, Steel Tube Div., 1968–73. Mem., NBPI, 1968–70; Chm., CSAB, 1984–90. CCIPD; FRSA. *Recreations:* reading, gardening, fishing, shooting. *Address:* Meikleholmside, Annan Water, Moffat, Dumfriesshire DG10 9LS. *T:* (01683) 220376. *Clubs:* Savile; New (Edinburgh).

Died 15 March 2005.

FORREST, Rear-Adm. Sir Ronald (Stephen), KCVO 1975; JP; DL; *b* 11 Jan. 1923; *s* of Stephen Forrest, MD, and Maud M. McKinstry; *m* 1st, 1947, Patricia (*d* 1966), *e d* of Dr and Mrs E. N. Russell; two *s* one *d*; 2nd, 1967, June (*née* Weaver), *widow* of Lieut G. Perks, RN; one step *s* one step *d. Educ:* Belhaven Hill; RNC, Dartmouth. Served War of 1939–45 at sea, Lieut 1943 (despatches 1944); CO HMS Teazer, 1956; on loan to Pakistan Navy, 1958–60; jssc 1963; Chief Staff Officer to Adm. Comdg Reserves, 1964; comd Dartmouth Trng Sqdn, 1966; Dir, Seaman Officers Appts, 1968; CO, HMS London, 1970; Rear-Adm. 1972; Defence Services Secretary, 1972–75. Chm. Council, Devon Co. Agricl Assoc., 1991–98 (Pres., 1990–91). County Comr, St John Amb. Bde, Devon, 1976–81, Comdr, 1981–87. JP Honiton, 1978; DL Devon, 1985. Naval Gen. Service Medal, 1949. Chevalier, Ordre du Mérite Agricole (France), 1990. KStJ 1987 (CStJ 1983). *Recreation:* gardening. *Address:* Higher Seavington, Stockland, near Honiton, Devon EX14 9DE. *Clubs:* Naval, Army and Navy. *Died 25 March 2005.*

FORREST, Surgeon Rear-Adm. (D) William Ivon Norman, CB 1970; Director of Naval Dental Services, Ministry of Defence, 1968–71; *b* 8 June 1914; *s* of late Eng. Lt James Forrest; *m* 1942, Mary Margaret McMordie Black (*d* 1996); three *s. Educ:* Christ's Hospital; Guy's Hospital. LDS RCS. Dental House Surgeon, Guy's Hosp., 1936–37; Royal Navy: Surg. Lieut (D), 1937; Surg. Lt-Comdr (D),

1943; Surg. Comdr (D), 1950; Surg. Capt. (D), 1960; Surg. Rear-Adm. (D), 1968; Consultant in Dental Surgery, 1963. *Recreations:* gardening, photography, bewilderment. *Address:* 32 St Peters Court, Hylton Road, Petersfield, Hants GU32 3JH. *T:* (01730) 260041.
Died 12 July 2002.

FORSHAW, Brig. Peter, CBE 1984 (OBE 1980); FCIPS; Under Secretary, HM Treasury, 1990–94 (Director of Purchasing Group); *b* 12 June 1936; *s* of Alfred Ogden Forshaw and Florence Clara Vera (*née* Taylor); *m* 1960, Helen Patricia Talbot Cliff; two *d*. *Educ:* Wimborne, Dorset; RMCS Shrivenham and Staff Coll., Camberley. FCIPS (FInstPS 1990). National Service, 1954; served Army, 1954–90: Cyprus, 1957–59; Hong Kong, 1965–67; Army Staff Course, 1967; Comd, Germany, 1974–76; on Staff, RMCS, 1976–79; DCS Cyprus, 1982–84; Commander Supply Germany, 1987–89; retired 1990. Mem., Bd of Management, CIPS, 1992–94. FIMgt (FBIM 1986). Liveryman, Broderers' Co. *Recreations:* field sports, glass engraving, water colours. *Address:* New Barn House, Ansty, Salisbury SP3 5PX. *T:* (01747) 828338. *Club:* Army and Navy.
Died 6 Aug. 2001.

FORSTER, Sir Archibald (William), Kt 1987; FREng, FIChemE, FInstPet; Chairman and Chief Executive: Esso UK plc, 1983–93; Esso Petroleum Co. Ltd, 1980–93; Esso Exploration & Production UK Ltd, 1983–93; *b* 11 Feb. 1928; *s* of William Henry and Matilda Forster; *m* 1954, Betty Margaret Channing; three *d*. *Educ:* Tottenham Grammar Sch.; Univ. of Birmingham (BSc (Hons) ChemEng 1949, Cadman Medallist). Served Royal Air Force, Pilot (FO), 1949–51. Joined Esso Petroleum Co. Ltd, 1951; Refinery Manager, Milford Haven, 1962–63; Supply Manager, London, 1963–64; Refinery Manager, Fawley, 1964–69; Manager, Refining Dept, Esso Europe Inc., 1969–71; Exec. Dir, Esso Petroleum Co. Ltd, 1971–73; Exec. Asst to Chm., Exxon Corp., 1973–74; Manager, Corporate Planning Co-ordination, Exxon Corp., 1974–75; Vice-Pres., Esso Europe Inc., 1975–78; Dir, Exxon Research & Engineering Co., 1975–78; Man. Dir, Esso Petroleum Co. Ltd, 1979–80; Chm., Esso Pension Trust, 1980–93 (Dir, 1979–80); Director: Esso Europe Inc., 1980–87; Esso Africa Inc., 1980–86; Rover Group, 1986–88; Midland Bank, 1986–98; Esso Europe-Africa Services Inc., 1987–93; Trafalgar House, 1992–96; United News and Media (formerly United Newspapers), 1993–96; HSBC Private Equity (formerly Montagu Private Equity), 1993–98; Engen Ltd, 1994–98. Exec. Bd Mem., Lloyd's Register of Shipping, 1981–94; Mem., Competition (formerly Monopolies and Mergers) Commn, 1993–99. President: Oil Industries Club, 1982–83; IChemE, 1985; Inst. of Petroleum, 1988–90. Governor, ESU, 1981–87. FREng (FEng 1983). Hon. DSc: Birmingham, 1981; Loughborough, 1986; Southampton, 1988.
Died 14 Feb. 2001.

FORSTER, Charles Ian Kennerley, CBE 1964; Under-Secretary, Department of Trade and Industry, 1970–72; *b* 18 July 1911; *s* of Douglas Wakefield Forster; *m* 1942, Thelma Primrose Horton (marr. diss. 1974); one *s* one *d*; *m* 1975, Mrs Loraine Huxtable. *Educ:* Rossall Sch. FIA 1936. Served RA, 1939–45. With Sun Life Assurance Soc., 1928–39, and 1946. Statistics Branch, Admty, 1946–54; Ministry of Power, 1954 (Chief Statistician, 1955–65, Dir of Statistics, 1965–69); Min. of Technology, 1969. Energy consultant to NCB, 1972–81, retd. *Publications:* contribs to Jls of Inst. of Actuaries and Inst. of Actuaries Students Soc., Trans VII World Power Conf., Trans Manchester Statistical Soc., Statistical News. *Recreations:* bridge, stamps. *Address:* 140 Watchfield Court, Chiswick, W4 4NE. *T:* (020) 8994 3128.
Died 6 Jan. 2003.

FORSTER, David Oakley A.; *see* Arnold-Forster.

FORSYTH, Jennifer Mary; Under-Secretary, HM Treasury and Department of Transport, 1975–83, retired;

Councillor (Lab) Kensington and Chelsea, 1986–98 (Dep. Mayor, 1997–98); *b* 7 Oct. 1924; *o d* of late Matthew Forsyth, theatrical director, and Marjorie Forsyth. *Educ:* Frensham Heights; London Sch. of Economics and Political Science (Pres. of Students' Union, 1944–45) (BScEcon). Joined Home Finance Div., HM Treasury, 1945; UN Economic Commn for Europe, 1949–51; Information Div., HM Treasury, 1951–53; Principal, Estabts, Overseas Finance and Planning Divs, 1954–62; UK Treasury Delegn, Washington, 1962–64; Assistant Secretary: DEA, 1965–69; Social Services Div., HM Treasury, 1969–75; Under Secretary: Home, Transport and Education Gp, HM Treasury, 1975–80; Dept of Transport (Roads), 1980–83. Governor: Frensham Heights, 1965–76; Thomas Jones Primary Sch., 1990–2001. *Recreations:* going to the theatre and to the Mediterranean.
Died 29 Nov. 2005.

FORTESCUE, Sir (John) Adrian, KCMG 2004; LVO 1972; Director General, Justice and Home Affairs, European Commission, 1999–2003; Visiting Fellow, Harvard University, 2003–04; *b* 16 June 1941; *s* of T. V. N. Fortescue, CBE; *m* 1st, 1978, Jillian Sarah Montague-Evans (marr. diss. 1987); one *s*; 2nd, 1989, Marie Wolfcarius. HM Diplomatic Service, 1964–94: MECAS, 1964; served Amman, FCO and Paris, 1966–72; on loan to EC, 1973–75; FCO, 1976–79; Washington, 1979–81; Head of Presidency Unit, ECD, FCO, 1981–82; Counsellor, Budapest, 1983–84; on loan to Commn of Eur. Communities, 1985–94 (Chef de Cabinet to Lord Cockfield, Vice-Pres., 1985–88); Dep. Dir Gen., Secretariat Gen., EC, 1994–99.
Died 17 Aug. 2004.

FORTIER, Most Rev. Jean-Marie; Archbishop of Sherbrooke (RC), 1968–96, then Emeritus; *b* 1 July 1920. *Educ:* Laval University, Quebec. Bishop Auxiliary, La Pocatière, PQ, 1961–65; Bishop of Gaspé, PQ, 1965–68. Elected Pres., Canadian Catholic Conference, 1973–75. Prés. de l'Assemblée des Evêques du Québec, 1984–89. *Publication:* (contrib.) Dictionnaire d'Histoire et de Géographie. *Address:* 2 rue Port-Dauphin, QC G1R 5K5, Canada. *T:* (418) 6923935.
Died 31 Oct. 2002.

FORWOOD, Sir Dudley (Richard), 3rd Bt *cr* 1895, of The Priory, Gateacre, Childwall, co. Palatine of Lancaster; Member of Lloyd's; *b* 6 June 1912; *s* of Sir Dudley Baines Forwood, 2nd Bt, CMG, and Norah Isabella (*née* Lockett) (*d* 1962); *S* father, 1961; *m* 1952, Mary Gwendoline (*d* 1999) (who *m* 1st, Viscount Ratendone, later 2nd Marquis of Willingdon; 2nd, Robert Cullingford; 3rd, Col Donald Croft-Wilcock), *d* of Basil S. Foster. *Educ:* Stowe Sch. Attaché, British Legation, Vienna, 1934–37; Equerry to the Duke of Windsor, 1937–39. Served War of 1939–45, Scots Guards (Major). Master, New Forest Buckhounds, 1956–65; Official Verderer of the New Forest, 1974–82; Chairman: New Forest and Hampshire County Show, 1964–78; New Forest Consultative Panel, 1970–82; Crufts, 1973–87; Hon. Vice Pres., RASE (Hon. Dir, 1973–78; Vice-Pres., 1979). *Recreation:* hunting. *Heir:* cousin Peter Noel Forwood [*b* 15 Oct. 1925; *m* 1950, Roy Murphy; six *d*]. *Address:* Uppacott, Bagnum, near Ringwood, Hants BH24 3BZ. *T:* (01425) 471480.
Died 25 Jan. 2001.

FOSKETT, Douglas John, OBE 1978; FCLIP; Director of Central Library Services and Goldsmiths' Librarian, University of London, 1978–83; *b* 27 June 1918; *s* of John Henry Foskett and Amy Florence Foskett; *m* 1948, Joy Ada (*née* McCann); one *s* two *d*. *Educ:* Bancroft's Sch.; Queen Mary Coll., Univ. of London (BA 1939); Birkbeck Coll., Univ. of London (MA 1954). Ilford Municipal Libraries, 1940–48; RAMC and Intell. Corps, 1940–46; Metal Box Co. Ltd, 1948–57; Librarian, Univ. of London Inst. of Educn, 1957–78. Chairman of Council, Library Assoc., 1962–63, Vice-Pres., 1966–73, Pres., 1976; Hon. Library Adviser, RNID, 1965–90; Mem., Adv. Cttee on Sci. and Techn. Information, 1969–73; Mem. and Rapporteur, Internat. Adv. Cttee on Documentation,

Libraries and Archives, UNESCO, 1968–73; Cons. on Documentation to ILO and to European Packaging Fedn; Cttee Mem., UNISIST/UNESCO and EUDISED/Council of Europe Projects; Member: Army Educn Adv. Bd, 1968–73; Library Adv. Council, 1975–77. Visiting Professor: Univ. of Michigan, 1964; Univ. of Ghana, 1967; Univ. of Ibadan, 1967; Brazilian Inst. for Bibliography and Documentation, 1971; Univ. of Iceland, 1974. Hon. FCLIP (FLA 1949, Hon. FLA, 1975); Hon. Fellow, Polytechnic of North London, 1981. *Publications:* Assistance to Readers in Lending Libraries, 1952; (with E. A. Baker) Bibliography of Food, 1958; Information Service in Libraries, 1958, 2nd edn 1967; Classification and Indexing in the Social Sciences, 1963, 2nd edn 1974; Science, Humanism and Libraries, 1964; Reader in Comparative Librarianship, 1977; Pathways for Communication, 1984; contrib. to many professional jls. *Recreations:* books, travel, writing, cricket. *Address:* 23 St Helen's Court, St Helen's Parade, Southsea, Portsmouth PO4 0RR. *T:* (023) 9282 9808. *Clubs:* MCC; Sussex CC.
Died 7 May 2004.

FOSS, Kathleen, (Kate); Member of Board, since 1983 and Chairman, since 1989, Direct Mail Services Standards Board; *b* 17 May 1925; *d* of George Arden and May Elizabeth Arden; *m* 1951, Robert Foss; one *s*. *Educ:* Northampton High Sch.; Whitelands Coll. (Teaching Dip.). Teacher: Northants, 1945–47; Mddx, 1947–53 (Dep. Head); Westmorland, 1953–60 (History specialist). Chairman: Consumers in European Community Gp (UK), 1979–82; Insurance Ombudsman Bureau, 1986– (Mem. Council, 1984–91); Member: Nat. Consumer Council, 1980–83; Consumers' Consultative Cttee, Brussels, 1981–86; Law Commn Standing Cttee on Conveyancing, 1985–88; Data Protection Tribunal Panel, 1986–99; Council for Licensed Conveyancers, 1986–88. Vice Pres., Keep Britain Tidy Gp, 1982–88 (Vice-Chm., 1979–82); Mem. Exec., National Fedn of Women's Insts, 1969–81 (National Treasurer, 1974–78); Chm., Bd of Dirs, WI Books Ltd, 1981–89. *Recreations:* golf, bridge. *Address:* 1 Elbow Lane, Undercliffe, Bradford BD2 4PB. *T:* (01274) 630442.
Died 4 March 2002.

FOSTER; see Hylton-Foster.

FOSTER, Sir Richard (Anthony), Kt 2000; DL; FSA, FMA; Director, National Museums and Galleries on Merseyside, since 1986; *b* 3 Oct. 1941; *s* of late Eric Kenneth Foster and Sylvia Renee Foster; *m* 1964, Mary Browning James; two *s* one *d*. *Educ:* Kingswood Sch., Bath; London Sch. of Economics (BSc Econ 1963); Manchester Univ. (MA 1968). Student Asst, Leicester Museum, 1964–66; Museum Asst, Bowes Museum, Barnard Castle, 1967–68; Keeper in Charge, Durham Light Infantry Museum and Arts Centre, Durham, 1968–70; Dir, Oxford City and County Museum, Woodstock, 1970–74; Dir, Museum Services, Oxfordshire County Museum Service, Woodstock, 1974–78; Dir of Museums, Merseyside County Museums, Liverpool, 1978–86. Mem., Museums and Galls Commn, 1993–. Vice-Pres., NADFAS, 1998–. Hon. Fellow, Liverpool John Moores Univ., 1993. Hon. LLD Liverpool, 1999. DL Merseyside, 1997. *Recreations:* sailing, watching football. *Address:* National Museums and Galleries on Merseyside, Liverpool Museum, William Brown Street, Liverpool L3 8EN. *T:* (0151) 207 0001.
Died 8 March 2001.

FOSTER, Sir Robert (Sidney), GCMG 1970 (KCMG 1964; CMG 1961); KCVO 1970; Governor-General and Commander-in-Chief of Fiji, 1970–73 (Governor and C-in-C, 1968–70); retired 1973; *b* 11 Aug. 1913; *s* of late Sidney Charles Foster and Jessie Edith (*née* Fry); *m* 1947, Margaret (*née* Walker) (*d* 1991); no *c*. *Educ:* Eastbourne Coll.; Peterhouse, Cambridge (MA). Appointed Cadet, Administrative Service, Northern Rhodesia, 1936; District Officer, N Rhodesia, 1938. War Service, 2nd Bn Northern Rhodesia Regt, 1940–43, Major. Provincial Commissioner, N Rhodesia, 1957; Sec., Ministry of Native Affairs, N Rhodesia, 1960; Chief Sec., Nyasaland, 1961–63; Dep. Governor, Nyasaland, 1963–64; High Comr for W Pacific, 1964–68. KStJ 1968. Officer of the Legion of Honour, 1966. *Recreation:* self-help. *Address:* 18 Windmill Lane, Histon, Cambridge CB4 9JF. *Clubs:* Royal Over-Seas League; Leander (Henley); Hawks (Cambridge).
Died 12 Oct. 2005.

FOSTER, Thomas Ashcroft; Director of Social Services, Lancashire County Council, 1986–90; *b* 27 May 1934; *s* of Thomas Lawrence Foster and Ada May Foster (*née* Ashcroft); *m* 1959, Beryl Wilson; two *d*. *Educ:* Rivington and Blackrod Grammar Sch.; Univ. of Leicester (Dip. Social Studies 1957); University Coll. of South Wales and Momouthshire (Dip. Applied Social Studies 1963); Univ. of Sheffield (MA 2001). Youth Employment Asst, Derbyshire CC, 1957–59; Child Care Officer, Manchester City Council, 1959–62; Senior Mental Welfare Officer, Carlisle City Council, 1963; Student Supervisor, Children's Dept, Glamorgan CC, 1963–67; Area Children's Officer, Lancs CC, 1967–71; Divl Dir, Social Services, Cheshire CC, 1971–73; Dir, Social Services, Tameside MBC, 1973–86. Mem., Cttee of Inquiry into Mental Handicap Nursing and Care, 1975–79; Social Services Adviser, AMA, 1983–86. Sen. Vice-Pres., Assoc. of Dirs of Social Servs, 1990 (Hon. Sec., Mental Health sub-cttee, 1991–95). Hon. Lectr, Univ. of Lancaster, 1990–2000. *Recreations:* theatre, archaeology, walking.
Died 30 May 2002.

FOTHERGILL, Richard Humphrey Maclean; Director, The Ceres Trust, 1988–97; *b* 21 March 1937; *s* of late Col C. G. Fothergill, RM, and Mrs E. G. Fothergill; *m* 1962, Angela Cheshire Martin; three *d*. *Educ:* Sandle Manor, Fordingbridge; Clifton Coll., Bristol; Emmanuel Coll., Cambridge (BA Hons Nat. Sci. Tripos, 1958). Commnd RASC, National Service, 1959–61. Contemporary Films Ltd, 1961; Head of Biology, SW Ham Technical Sch., 1961–69; Res. Fellow, Nat. Council for Educnl Technol., 1970–72; Founder and Head of PETRAS (Educnl Devlt Unit), Newcastle upon Tyne Polytechnic, 1972–80; Director: Microelectronics Educn Prog., DES, 1980–86; CET, 1986–87. Co-founder, Sec. and Treasurer, Standing Conf. on Educnl Devlt Services in Polytechnics, 1974–80; Member: London GCE Bd and Schools Council Science Cttee, 1968–72; Standards and Specifications Cttee, CET, 1972–80. *Publications:* A Challenge for Librarians, 1971; Resource Centres in Colleges of Education, 1973; (with B. Williams) Microforms in Education, 1977; Child Abuse: a teaching package, 1978; (with I. Butchart) Non-book Materials in Libraries: a practical guide, 1978, 3rd edn 1990; (with J. S. A. Anderson) Microelectronics Education Programme: policy and guidelines, 1983; Implications of the New Technology for the School Curriculum, 1988; The Fothergills: a first history, 1998; The Fothergills: a second history, 2001; articles in Visual Educn, Educn Libraries Bull., Educnl Media Internat., and Educnl Broadcasting Internat. *Recreations:* reading, television, films, walking. *Address:* 17 Grenville Drive, Brunton Park, Newcastle upon Tyne NE3 5PA. *T:* (0191) 236 3380. *Club:* National Film Theatre.
Died 28 Oct. 2004.

FOWLER, Richard Nicholas; QC 1989; *b* 12 Oct. 1946; 2nd *s* of late Ronald Hugh Fowler and Winifred Mary Fowler (*née* Hull). *Educ:* Bedford Sch.; Brasenose Coll., Oxford (BA). Called to the Bar, Middle Temple, 1969, Bencher, 2000. Liveryman, Goldsmiths' Co., 1989–. *Recreations:* walking, opera, dogs. *Address:* 20 Ennismore Gardens Mews, SW7 1HY. *T:* (020) 7589 7279; 4 Raymond Buildings, Gray's Inn, WC1R 5BP. *T:* (020) 7405 7211.
Died 11 April 2005.

FOWLER HOWITT, William; see Howitt.

FOWLES, John; writer; *b* 31 March 1926; *s* of Robert John Fowles and Gladys May Richards; *m* 1st, 1956, Elizabeth Whitton (*d* 1990); 2nd, 1998, Sarah Smith. *Educ:* Bedford

Sch.; New Coll., Oxford (Hon. Fellow, 1997). English Centre PEN Silver Pen Award, 1969; W. H. Smith Award, 1970. *Publications:* The Collector, 1963; The Aristos, 1965; The Magus, 1966, rev. edn 1977; The French Lieutenant's Woman, 1969; Poems, 1973; The Ebony Tower, 1974 (televised, 1984); Shipwreck, 1975; Daniel Martin, 1977; Islands, 1978; (with Frank Horvat) The Tree, 1979; (ed) John Aubrey's Monumenta Britannica, parts 1 and 2, 1980, part 3 and Index, 1982; The Enigma of Stonehenge, 1980; Mantissa, 1982; Thomas Hardy's England, 1984; Land, 1985; A Maggot, 1985; Wormholes: essays and occasional writings, 1998; Lyme Worthies, 2000; John Fowles, Journals, vol. 1, 2003, vol. 2, 2005. *Recreations:* mainly Sabine. *Address:* c/o Anthony Sheil, Gillon Aitken Associates Ltd, 18–21 Cavaye Place, SW10 9PT.   *Died 5 Nov. 2005.*

FOX, Rt Hon. Sir (John) Marcus, Kt 1986; MBE 1963; PC 1996; *b* 11 June 1927; *s* of late Alfred Hirst Fox; *m* 1954, Ann, *d* of F. W. J. Tindall; one *s* one *d. Educ:* Wheelright Grammar Sch., Dewsbury. Mem., Dewsbury County Borough Council, 1957–65; contested (C): Dewsbury, 1959; Huddersfield West, 1966. MP (C) Shipley, 1970–97; contested (C) same seat, 1997. An Asst Govt Whip, 1972–73; a Lord Comr, HM Treasury, 1973–74; Opposition spokesman on Transport, 1975–76; Parly Under-Sec. of State, DoE, 1979–81. Mem., Parly Select Cttee on Race Relations and Immigration, 1970–72; Sec., Cons. Party's Transport Industries Cttee, 1970–72; a Vice-Chm., Cons. Party Orgn, 1976–79; Chairman: Cttee of Selection, 1984–92; 1922 Cttee, 1992–97 (a Vice-Chm., 1983–92). Chm., Nat. Assoc. of Cons. Clubs, 1988–98. *Recreations:* reading, tennis, walking. *Address:* 10 Woodvale Crescent, Oakwood Park, Bingley, West Yorks BD16 4AL.

                                                    Died 16 March 2002.

FOX, Rt Hon. Sir Marcus; *see* Fox, Rt Hon. Sir J. M.

FOX-ANDREWS, His Honour James Roland Blake; QC 1968; a Circuit Judge (Official Referee), 1985–94; *b* 24 March 1922; step *s* of late Norman Roy Fox-Andrews, QC; *m* 1950, Angela Bridget Swift (*d* 1991); two *s. Educ:* Stowe; Pembroke Coll., Cambridge. FCIArb. Served War, RNVR, 1940–46. Called to the Bar, Gray's Inn, 1949, Bencher, 1974. Dep. Chm., Devon QS, 1970–71; Recorder of Winchester, 1971, Hon. Recorder, 1972–2000; a Recorder of the Crown Court, 1972–85. Leader, Western Circuit, 1982–84. Member: Gen. Council of the Bar, 1968–72; Senate of Inns of Court and the Bar, 1976–79. Chartered Arbitrator, 1998–2001. Editor, Inst. of Arbitrators Jl, 1950–54. *Publications:* (jtly) Leasehold Property (Temporary Provisions) Act, 1951; contrib. Halsbury's Laws of England, 3rd edn, building contracts, architects and engineers; (jtly) Landlord and Tenant Act, 1954; Business Tenancies, 1970, 6th edn 2001; (jtly) Assured Tenancies, 1989, 2nd edn 1998. *Address:* 20 Cheyne Gardens, SW3 5QT. *T:* (020) 7352 9484; Lepe House, Exbury, Hants SO45 1AD. *T:* (023) 8089 1648. *Club:* Hurlingham.   *Died 15 Sept. 2002.*

FOXLEE, James Brazier; Under Secretary, Ministry of Agriculture, Fisheries and Food, 1971–81, retired; *b* 20 Nov. 1921; *s* of late Arthur Brazier Foxlee and Mary Foxlee (*née* Fisher); *m* 1952, Vera June (*née* Guiver); one *s* two *d. Educ:* Brentwood Sch. Entered Min. of Agric. and Fisheries (later MAFF) as Clerical Officer, 1938. Served War, RNVR, Ordinary Seaman, 1941; commissioned, 1942; Lieut, in comd Light Coastal Forces craft and mine-sweepers. MAFF: Exec. Officer, 1946; HEO, 1948; SEO, 1950; Principal, 1955 (Welsh Dept); 1955–57; Treas., 1961–62); Asst Sec., 1965 (Regional Controller, Leeds, 1965–69). Hon. Fellow, NIAB, 1982; Hon. Mem., Arable Res. Inst. Assoc., 1990. *Recreations:* watching cricket, camping, oenology. *Address:* Wyton, Huntingdon, Cambs.
                                                    Died 30 Nov. 2005.

FOXLEY-NORRIS, Air Chief Marshal Sir Christopher (Neil), GCB 1973 (KCB 1969; CB 1966); DSO 1945; OBE 1956; President, Cheshire Foundation, since 2002 (Vice Chairman, 1972–74; Chairman, 1974–82; Chairman Emeritus, 1982–2002); Chairman, Battle of Britain Fighter Association, since 1978; *b* 16 March 1917; *s* of Major J. P. Foxley-Norris and Dorothy Brabant Smith; *m* 1948, Joan Lovell Hughes; no *c. Educ:* Winchester (schol.); Trinity Coll., Oxford (schol.; Hon. Fellow, 1973); Middle Temple (Harmsworth Schol.). Commissioned RAFO, 1936; France, 1940; Battle of Britain, 1940; various operational tours of duty in wartime. MA 1946. ACDS, 1963; AOC No 224 Gp, FEAF, 1964–67; Dir-Gen., RAF Organization, MoD, 1967–68; C-in-C, RAF Germany and Comdr, NATO 2nd Tactical Air Force, 1968–70; Chief of Personnel and Logistics, MoD, 1971–74; retd. Vice Pres., RUSI, 1979. Chairman: Trinity Coll. Oxford Soc., 1984–86; Ex RAF and Dependants Severely Disabled Holiday Trust, 1984. Pres., Leonard Cheshire Housing Assoc., 1978–. CCMI. *Publications:* A Lighter Shade of Blue, 1978; various in RUSI and other service jls. *Recreations:* writing, broadcasting. *Address:* Tumble Wood, Northend Common, Henley-on-Thames RG9 6LJ. *T:* (01491) 638457. *Clubs:* Royal Air Force; Phyllis Court (Henley-on-Thames).   *Died 28 Sept. 2003.*

FOXON, David Fairweather, FBA 1978; Reader in Textual Criticism, University of Oxford, and Fellow of Wadham College, Oxford, 1968–82, then Emeritus Fellow; *b* 9 Jan. 1923; *s* of late Rev. Walter Foxon and Susan Mary (*née* Fairweather); *m* 1947, Dorothy June (marr. diss. 1963; she *d* 1988), *d* of late Sir Arthur Jarratt, KCVO; one *d. Educ:* Kingswood Sch., Bath; Magdalen Coll., Oxford (BA 1948, MA 1953). Foreign Office, 1942–45; Asst Keeper, Dept of Printed Books, British Museum, 1950–65; Professor of English, Queen's Univ., Kingston, Ontario, 1965–67. Harkness Fellow, 1959–61; Guggenheim Fellow, 1967–68; Sen. Res. Fellow, Clark Library, UCLA, 1974–75; Lyell Reader in Bibliography, Oxford, 1975–76; Sandars Reader in Bibliography, Cambridge, 1977–78. Pres., Bibliographical Soc., 1980–81 (Gold Medal, 1985). Hon. Mem., Bibliographical Soc. of America, 1986. John H. Jenkins Award for Bibliography, 1977. *Publications:* T. J. Wise and the Pre-Restoration Drama, 1959; Libertine Literature in England, 1660–1745, 1964; (ed) English Bibliographical Sources, 1964–67; English Verse 1701–1750: a catalogue, 1975; Pope and the Early Eighteenth-century Book Trade (ed J. McLaverty), 1991; contribs to bibliographical jls. *Recreation:* music. *Address:* 7 Fane Road, Marston, Oxford OX3 0RZ. *T:* (01865) 248350.   *Died 5 June 2001.*

FOXON, (Harold) Peter, OBE 1976; Group Managing Director, Inchcape plc, 1981–84 (Director, 1971; a Managing Director, 1978); *b* 7 April 1919; *s* of William Henry Foxon and Kathleen Avis (*née* Perry); *m* 1948, Elizabeth Mary Butterfield; one *s* three *d. Educ:* Bancroft's. Served War, 1939–46, Royal Signals, Captain. Insurance, 1935–39; Smith Mackenzie & Co. Ltd (East Africa), 1946–69; Chm., Mackenzie Dalgety Ltd, 1966–69; Man. Dir, Gilman & Co. Ltd, Hong Kong, and Chm., Inchcape Hong Kong Ltd, 1969–77. Director: Dodwell & Co., Ltd, 1978–81; Anglo-Thai Corp., 1978–82; Berry Trust Ltd, 1977–88; Member: Hong Kong Trade Adv. Gp, 1978–84; South East Asia Trade Adv. Gp, 1978–82. Master, Barbers' Co., 1986–87. *Recreation:* golf. *Address:* 48 Abingdon Court, Abingdon Villas, W8 6BT. *T:* (0171) 937 8713; Tanglin, Second Avenue, Frinton-on-Sea, Essex CO13 9LX. *T:* (01255) 672208. *Clubs:* City of London, Oriental; Muthaiga (Kenya); Hong Kong (Hong Kong).
                                                    Died 19 Jan. 2001.

FOXON, Peter; *see* Foxon, H. P.

FRANCIS, Ven. Edward Reginald; Archdeacon of Bromley, 1979–94, Emeritus since 1994; *b* 31 Jan. 1929; *s* of Alfred John and Elsie Hilda Francis; *m* 1st, 1950, Joyce

Noreen Atkins (*d* 1997); three *s*; 2nd, 2001, Maureen Joan Chadwick. *Educ*: Maidstone and Dover Grammar Schools; Rochester Theological College. National Service, RAF, 1947–49. Insurance, including period at Chartered Insurance Inst. (ACII), 1950–59. Ordained, 1961; Chaplain, Training Ship Arethusa, and Curate of All Saints, Frindsbury, 1961–64; Vicar of St William's, Chatham, 1964–73; Vicar and Rural Dean of Rochester, 1973–78. Mem., General Synod of C of E, 1981–94. Mem., Kent Industrial Mission, 1979–89; Jt Chm., Council for Social Responsibility, Dioceses of Canterbury and Rochester, 1983–89; Dir of Continuing Ministry Educn, dio. of Rochester, 1989–94. *Recreations*: ornithology, walking, music. *Address*: 3 Powell Close, Aylesford, Kent ME20 7BW. *T*: (01622) 718729.
Died 16 May 2004.

FRANCIS, Owen, CB 1960; Chairman, London Electricity Board, 1972–76; *b* 4 Oct. 1912; *yr s* of Sidney and Margaret Francis, The White House, Austwick, Yorks; *m* 1938, Joan St Leger (*née* Norman) (*d* 2003); two *d*. *Educ*: Giggleswick Sch., Yorks. Entered Civil Service as Asst Auditor, Exchequer and Audit Dept, 1931; Asst Principal, Mines Dept, 1937; Principal, 1940; Asst Sec., Ministry of Fuel and Power, 1943; Under-Sec., Ministry of Power, 1954–61; Mem., 1962–64, Dep. Chm., 1965–72, CEGB. *Address*: Meadow Cottage, Stanford Dingley, Berks RG7 6LT. *T*: (0118) 974 4394. *Clubs*: Royal Yacht Squadron; Seaview Yacht; St Moritz Tobogganing. *Died 26 July 2005.*

FRANK, Air Vice-Marshal Alan Donald, CB 1967; CBE 1962; DSO 1943; DFC 1941; Bursar, St Antony's College, Oxford, 1970–74; *b* 27 July 1917; *s* of late Major N. G. Frank and M. H. Frank (*née* Donald); *m* 1941, Jessica Ann Tyrrell; two *s* two *d*. *Educ*: Eton; Magdalen Coll., Oxford. Commanded 51 Squadron Bomber Command, 1943; RAF Staff Coll., 1944; OC 83 Sqdn, 1957; OC RAF Honington, 1958–60; Group Captain Ops, Bomber Comd, 1960–62; Dir Operational Requirements, MoD, 1962–65; Air Attaché and OC, RAF Staff, Washington, 1965–68; SASO, RAF Air Support Command, 1968–70. *Recreations*: music, gardening. *Address*: Roundway House, Devizes, Wilts SN10 2EG. *Died 6 Oct. 2001.*

FRANK, Sir Douglas (George Horace), Kt 1976; QC 1964; Deputy Judge of the High Court, Queen's Bench Division, 1976–89; *b* 16 April 1916; *s* of late George Maurice Frank and Agnes Winifred Frank; *m* 1st; one *s* one *d* (and one *d* decd); 2nd, 1963, Sheila Frances (*née* Beauchamp); two *d*; 3rd, 1979, Audrey (MA Cantab), *yr d* of late Charles Leslie Thomas, solicitor, Neath, Glam. Served war in Royal Artillery (TA); BEF, France, 1939–40. Called to the Bar, Gray's Inn, 1946 (Bencher, 1970; Master of Moots, 1978–83; Master of Estate, 1982–84); established first Barristers' Chambers in Gray's Inn, 1966. Formerly Asst Comr, Parly Boundary Commn for England; Civil Service Comr, DoE, 1971–74; Pres., Lands Tribunal, 1974–88. Mem., Cttee Public Participation in Planning (Min. Housing and Local Govt), 1968; conducted Brixham Marina Inquiry, 1987. Founder Chm., Planning and Local Govt Cttee of the Bar, 1971–74; Mem., Senate of Inns of Court and Bar, 1984–85. Leader, Bar Delegn to IBA Conf., Tokyo, 1970. Hon. Pres., Anglo-American Real Property Inst., 1980–90. *Publications*: various legal. *Recreations*: theatre, music, walking. *Address*: Old Farm House, Middleton, Rhossili SA3 1PJ. *T*: and *Fax*: (01792) 392980; 10 South Square, Gray's Inn, WC1R 5EU. *T*: and *Fax*: (020) 7242 2937. *Died 30 Oct. 2004.*

FRANKLIN, Albert Andrew Ernst, CVO 1965; CBE 1961 (OBE 1950); HM Diplomatic Service, retired; *b* 28 Nov. 1914; *s* of Albert John Henry Franklin; *m* 1944, Henrietta Irene Barry (decd); two *d*. *Educ*: Merchant Taylors' Sch.; St John's Coll., Oxford. Joined HM Consular Service, 1937; served in Peking, Kunming, Chungking, Calcutta, Algiers, Marseilles, Kabul, Basle,

Tientsin, Formosa, Düsseldorf and in the FO; HM Consul-General, Los Angeles, USA, 1966–74. Member of Kitchener Association. FRSA 1971. *Recreation:* chinese ceramics and paintings. *Address:* 5 Dulwich Wood Avenue, SE19 1HB. *T:* (020) 8670 2769. *Died 5 Sept. 2002.*

FRANKLIN, Andrew; *see* Franklin, Albert A. E.

FRASER, Sir Angus (McKay), KCB 1985 (CB 1981); TD 1965; Adviser to the Prime Minister on Efficiency and Effectiveness in Government, 1988–92; *b* 10 March 1928; *s* of late Thomas Douglas Fraser; *m* 1st, 1955, Margaret Neilson (marr. diss. 1968); one *s* (one *d* decd); 2nd, 1991, Gillian Fenwick (*née* Manning); one step *d*. *Educ:* Falkirk High Sch.; Bordeaux Univ.; Glasgow Univ. (MA 1950; DLitt 1993). Nat. Service in RA, 1950–52; 44 Parachute Bde (TA), 1953–66. Entered HM Customs and Excise, 1952; HM Treasury, 1961–64; Under-Sec. and Comr of Customs and Excise, 1972; Under-Sec., CSD, 1973; Comr of Customs and Excise, 1976; Dep. Chm., Bd of Customs and Excise, 1978; Dep. Sec., CSD, subseq. MPO, 1980–83; First CS Comr, 1981–83; Chm., Bd of Customs and Excise, 1983–87. Advr, European Patent Office, 1988–. Chm., Civil Service, PO and BT Lifeboat Fund, 1986–98; Vice-Pres., 1994–, and Mem., Cttee of Management, 1986–, RNLI; President: Electronic Commerce Assoc., 1988–97; George Borrow Soc., 1991–; British Internat. Freight Assoc., 1993–95; Vice-Pres., RIPA, 1985–92. Trustee: Bethlem Art and History Collections Trust, 1992–; CS Benevolent Fund, 1991–98. FSA 1991; FRSA 1985; Hon. FCIPS 1993. *Publications:* (ed) A Journey to Eastern Europe in 1841, 1981; (ed) George Borrow's Letters to John Hasfeld 1835–1839, 1982, 1841–1846, 1984; George Borrow, a Bibliographical Study, 1984; The Gypsies, 1992, 2nd edn 1995; articles and reviews in jls and encyclopedias, 1950–. *Recreations:* literary research, book collecting. *Address:* 84 Ennerdale Road, Kew, Richmond, Surrey TW9 2DL. *T:* (020) 8940 9913. *Clubs:* Reform, Caledonian; Norfolk (Norwich). *Died 27 May 2001.*

FRASER, Maj.-Gen. Colin Angus Ewen, CB 1971; CBE 1968 (MBE 1941); General Officer Commanding, Southern Command, Australia, 1971–74; retired March 1974; *b* Nairobi, Kenya, 25 Sept. 1918; *s* of A. E. Fraser, Rutherglen, Vic.; *m* 1942, Dorothy, *d* of A. Champion; two *s* one *d*. *Educ:* Johannesburg; Adelaide High Sch.; RMC, Duntroon (grad. 1938); Melbourne Univ. (BA). Served War of 1939–45: UK, Middle East, Pacific. Staff Coll., Camberley, 1946; Dep. Comdr, Commonwealth Div., Korea, 1955–56; Dir, Military Trng, 1957–58; Services Attaché, Burma, 1960–62; Chief of Staff, Northern Command, Brisbane, 1964–68; Commandant, Royal Military Coll., Duntroon, 1968–69; Commander, Australian Force, Vietnam, 1970–71. *Address:* 65/1 Moore Street, Taringa, Qld 4068, Australia. *Club:* Tasmanian (Hobart). *Died 29 Sept. 2001.*

FRASER, Air Marshal Rev. Sir (Henry) Paterson, KBE 1961 (CBE 1945); CB 1953; AFC 1937; RAF, retired; concrete consultant; Auxiliary Pastoral Minister, Ramsey Deanery, Isle of Man; *b* 15 July 1907; *s* of late Harry Fraser, Johannesburg, South Africa; *m* 1933, Avis Gertrude Haswell; two *s*. *Educ:* St Andrews Coll., Grahamstown, South Africa; Pembroke Coll., Cambridge (MA). RAFO, and Pres. University Air Sqdn, Cambridge; joined RAF, 1929; served in India; RAF Engineering Course, Henlow, 1933–34; Aerodynamic Flight, RAE, Farnborough, 1934–38; RAF Staff Coll., 1938; Directorate of War Organization, Air Ministry, 1939–40; commanded Experimental Flying Section, RAE, Farnborough, 1941; Mem. RAF Element, Combined Chiefs of Staff, Washington DC, 1942; Dep. Dir of War Organization, Air Ministry, 1943; Senior Administrative Planner, 2nd Tactical Air Force, 1943–44, and Dep. Air Officer in Charge of Administration, 2nd TAF, 1944–45; commanded Aircraft and Armament Experimental Establishment, Boscombe Down, 1945–46; Dep. Dir (Air

Staff) Policy, Air Ministry, 1947–48; Defence Research Policy Staff, Ministry of Defence, 1948–51; idc 1951; Senior Air Staff Officer, Headquarters Fighter Command, 1952–53; Chief of Staff, Headquarters Allied Air Forces, Central Europe, 1954–56; AOC No 12 Group, Fighter Command, 1956–58; Dir, RAF Exercise Planning, 1959; UK Representative on Permanent Military Deputies Group of Cento, 1959–62; Inspector-Gen., RAF, 1962–64. Ordained deacon, 1977, priest, 1978; Hon. Curate, Ramsey, 1977. Taylor Gold Medal, RAeS, 1937; FRAeS. *Address:* 803 King's Court, Ramsey, Isle of Man IM8 1LP. *T:* (01624) 813069.   *Died 4 Aug. 2001.*

FRASER, Sir Ian (James), Kt 1986; CBE 1972; MC 1945; Chairman, Lazard Brothers, 1980–85; Deputy Chairman: Vickers Ltd, 1980–89; TSB Group plc, 1985–91; *b* 7 Aug. 1923; 2nd *s* of late Hon. Alastair Thomas Joseph Fraser and Lady Sibyl Fraser (*née* Grimston); *m* 1st, 1958, Evelyn Elizabeth Anne Grant (*d* 1984); two *s* two *d*; 2nd, 1993, Fiona Margaret Douglas-Home. *Educ:* Ampleforth Coll.; Magdalen Coll., Oxford. Served War of 1939–45: Lieut, Scots Guards, 1942–45 (despatches). Reuter Correspondent, 1946–56; S. G. Warburg & Co. Ltd, 1956–69; Dir-Gen., Panel on Take-overs and Mergers, 1969–72; Director: BOC International Ltd, 1972–85; Davy International Ltd, 1972–84; Chloride Gp Ltd, 1976–80; S. Pearson & Son Ltd, 1977–89; EMI Ltd, 1977–80; Eurafrance SA, 1979–85; Pearson-Longman Ltd, 1980–83; Chairman: Rolls-Royce Motors, 1971–80; Datastream Ltd, 1976–77. Part-time Mem., CAA, 1972–74. Chairman, City Capital Markets Cttee, 1974–78; Accepting Houses Cttee, 1981–85; Member: Exec. Cttee, City Communications Centre, 1976–85; Cttee on Finance for Industry, NEDC, 1976–79; President's Cttee, CBI, 1979–81; Exec. Cttee, Jt Disciplinary Scheme of Accountancy Insts, 1979–81; Vice-Pres., BBA, 1981–85. Chm., Lloyd's Syndicate 90 (1982) Names Assoc., 1990–96. Mem. Exec., Help the Hospices, 1985–90. Trustee, Tablet Trust, 1976–90 (Chm., Finance Cttee, 1985–90). Governor, More House Sch., 1970–75. FRSA 1970; CCMI (FBIM 1974). Kt of Honour and Devotion, SMO of Malta, 1971. *Publication:* The High Road to England (autobiog.), 1999. *Recreations:* fishing, gardening, Scottish history. *Address:* South Haddon, Skilgate, Taunton, Somerset TA4 2DR. *T:* (01398) 331247.   *Died 8 May 2003.*

FRASER, Air Marshal Rev. Sir Paterson; *see* Fraser, Air Marshal Rev. Sir H. P.

FRASER McLUSKEY, Very Rev. James; *see* McLuskey.

FREDERICK, Sir Charles Boscawen, 10th Bt *cr* 1723, of Burwood House, Surrey; *b* 11 April 1919; *s* of Sir Edward Boscawen Frederick, 9th Bt, CVO and Edith Katherine, (Kathleen), Cortlandt (*d* 1970), *d* of late Col W. H. Mulloy, RE; *S* father, 1956; *m* 1949, Rosemary, *er d* of late Lt-Col R. J. H. Baddeley, MC; two *s* two *d*. *Educ:* Eton. 2nd Lieut Grenadier Guards, 1942; served N Africa and Italy, 1943–45 (despatches); Capt. 1945; Palestine, 1946–47 (despatches); Malaya, 1948–49; Egypt, 1952–53; Major, 1953. Member: London Stock Exchange, 1954–62; Provincial Brokers Stock Exchange, 1962 (Mem. Council, 1966; Chm. 1972); Stock Exchange Council, and Chm., Provincial Unit, 1973–75. General Commissioner of Income Tax, 1966. JP 1960. *Heir:* *s* Christopher St John Frederick [*b* 28 June 1950; *m* 1990, Camilla, *o d* of Sir Derek Gilbey, 3rd Bt; one *s* one *d*]. *Address:* 18 Esplanade, Fowey, Cornwall PL23 1HY.   *Died 21 March 2001.*

FREELAND, Mary Graham, (Mrs J. M. Freeland); *see* McGeown, M. G.

FREELING, Nicolas; writer since 1960; *b* 3 March 1927, of English parents; *m* 1954, Cornelia Termes; four *s* one *d*. *Educ:* primary and secondary schs. Hotel-restaurant cook, throughout Europe, 1945–60; novelist, 1960–.

Publications: (numerous trans.) Love in Amsterdam, 1961; Because of the Cats, 1962; Gun before Butter, 1962; Valparaiso, 1963; Double Barrel, 1963; Criminal Conversation, 1964; King of the Rainy Country, 1965; Dresden Green, 1966; Strike Out Where Not Applicable, 1967; This is the Castle, 1968; Tsing-Boum, 1969; Kitchen Book, 1970; Over the High Side, 1971; Cook Book, 1971; A Long Silence, 1972; Dressing of Diamond, 1974; What Are the Bugles Blowing For?, 1975; Lake Isle, 1976; Gadget, 1977; The Night Lords, 1978; The Widow, 1979; Castang's City, 1980; One Damn Thing After Another, 1981; Wolfnight, 1982; Back of the North Wind, 1983; No Part in Your Death, 1984; A City Solitary, 1985; Cold Iron, 1986; Lady Macbeth, 1987; Not as far as Velma, 1989; Sandcastles, 1989; Those in Peril, 1990; The Pretty How Town, 1992; You Who Know, 1993; Criminal Convictions, 1994; The Seacoast of Bohemia, 1994; A Dwarf Kingdom, 1996; One More River, 1997; Some Day Tomorrow, 1999; Village Book, 2001; The Janeites, 2002. *Address:* 24 avenue de Général de Gaulle, 67190 Mutzig, France.

Died 20 July 2003.

FREEMAN, John Allen, OBE 1958; PhD; FRES, CBiol, FIBiol; Director, PestInfestation Control Laboratory, Ministry of Agriculture, Fisheries and Food, 1977–79; *b* 30 Sept. 1912; *s* of Laurence Freeman and Maggie Rentoul Freeman; *m* 1945, Hilda Mary Jackson; one *s* one *d*. *Educ:* City of London Sch. (Jun. Corp. Scholar, Travers Scholar); Imperial Coll. of Science and Technol., London Univ. (BSc Special 1st Cl. Hons 1933, PhD 1938). ARCS; FRES 1943; FIBiol 1963. Min. of Agric. Scholar in Entomology, 1934–37: Hull University Coll., 1934–35; Rothamsted Exper. Stn, 1936; Cornell Univ., USA, 1936–37; Vineland Exper. Stn, Ont, Canadian Dept of Agric., 1937. Res. Asst, Imp. Coll., London, 1938–40; Jun. Scientific Officer, Dept of Science and Indust. Res. Pest Infestation Lab., 1940; seconded Min. of Food Infest. Control, 1940–47; Chief Entomologist, 1944; Sen. Sci. Officer, 1946; transf. Min. of Agric., 1947; Principal Sci. Off., 1947; seconded OECD, 1954–55, and CENTO, 1957–58; Sen. Principal Sci. Off., 1958; Dep. Chief Sci. Off., and Dep. Dir Pest Infest. Control Lab., 1971; Chief Sci. Off., 1977. Member: British Ecol Soc.; Assoc. of Applied Biol. Treasurer, Royal Entomol Soc. of London, 1977–84; Hon. Treas., Inst. of Biol, 1965–69. Pres., Royal Coll. of Science Union and Imp. Coll. Union, 1934. Has travelled professionally in N and S America, Europe, Africa, ME and Far East. Freeman of City of London, 1947. *Publications:* scientific articles, mainly on pests of stored foods. *Recreations:* gardening, photography, travel, DIY. *Address:* 5 Woodmere Way, Park Langley, Beckenham, Kent BR3 6SJ. *T:* (020) 8658 6970.   *Died 23 Dec. 2003.*

FREEMAN, Joseph William, OBE 1968; Director of Social Service, Leeds, 1970–78; *b* 8 April 1914; *s* of Thomas and Emma Freeman; *m* 1939, Louise King (*d* 1986); one *s* one *d*. *Educ:* sch. in Liverpool; Liverpool Univ. (BSc Econ. 1938); Morley Coll. and Toynbee Hall, London; BA Hons Open Univ. 1983. CQSW 1970. Qual. social worker; Probation Service, Birmingham, 1938; served War of 1939–45: Army, 1940, commnd RA, 1941; Probation Service, Liverpool, 1946; Children's Officer: Warrington, 1948; Bolton, 1951; Sheffield, 1955. Organist Emeritus, St James Parish Church, Eccleston Park, 1995. *Publications:* (contrib.) Child Care Revisited, 1998; papers in social work jls. *Recreation:* music. *Address:* 15 Fairfield Gardens, Crank Road, St Helens WA11 7SL.

Died 14 Nov. 2003.

FREETH, Hon. Sir Gordon, KBE 1978; Chairman, Australian Consolidated Minerals, 1981–90; *b* 6 Aug. 1914; *s* of late Rt Rev. Robert Evelyn Freeth and Gladys Mary Snashall; *m* 1939, Joan Celia Carew Baker; one *s* two *d*. *Educ:* Sydney Church of England Grammar Sch.; Guildford Grammar Sch.; Univ. of Western Australia. Rowed for Australia in British Empire Games, Sydney,

1938. Admitted as Barrister and Solicitor, WA, 1938; practised law at Katanning, WA, 1939–49. Served as Pilot, RAAF, 1942–45. Elected to House of Representatives as Member for Forrest, 1949; MP 1949–69; Minister: for Interior and Works, 1958–63; for Shipping and Transport, 1963–68; Assisting Attorney-Gen., 1962–64; for Air, and Minister Assisting the Treasurer, 1968; for External Affairs, 1969; Ambassador to Japan, 1970–73; practised law in Perth, WA, 1973–77; High Comr for Australia in UK, 1977–80. *Recreations:* gardening, golf. *Address:* Tingrith, 25 Owston Street, Mosman Park, WA 6012, Australia. *Club:* Weld (Perth).   *Died 27 Nov. 2001.*

FRENCH, Sir Christopher (James Saunders), Kt 1979; Judge of the High Court of Justice, Queen's Bench Division, 1982–97 (Family Division, 1979–82); Judge of Employment Appeals Tribunal, 1985–97; *b* 14 Oct. 1925; 2nd *s* of late Rev. Reginald French, MC, MA, Hon. Chaplain to the Queen, and Gertrude Emily Mary (*née* Haworth); *m* 1957, Rosina Philippa, (Wendy) (*d* 2000), *d* of Philip Godfrey Price, Abergavenny; one *s* one *d*. *Educ:* Denstone Coll. (scholar); Brasenose Coll., Oxford (scholar). Coldstream Guards, 1943–48 (Capt.). Called to the Bar, Inner Temple, 1950, Bencher, 1975; QC 1966. Dep. Chm., Bucks QS, 1966–71. Recorder of Coventry, 1971–72; a Recorder, and Hon. Recorder of Coventry, 1972–79; Presiding Judge, SE Circuit, 1982–85. Member: Gen. Council of the Bar, 1963–67; Senate of Inns of Court and Bar, 1978–79; Lord Chancellor's Adv. Cttee on Trng Magistrates, 1974–80. *Publication:* (contrib.) Agency, in Halsbury's Laws of England, 4th edn, 1973. *Recreations:* walking, music, painting, fishing. *Address:* c/o Royal Courts of Justice, Strand, WC2A 2LL. *Clubs:* Garrick, Pilgrims.   *Died 14 March 2003.*

FRENCH, Henry William, CBE 1971; CEng, FIEE; CPhys, FInstP; FCP; Senior Chief Inspector (Deputy Secretary), Department of Education and Science, 1972–74; *b* 14 Feb. 1910; *s* of Henry Moxey French and Alice French (*née* Applegate); *m* 1936, Hazel Anne Mary Ainley (*d* 2000); two *s*. *Educ:* Varndean School, Brighton; Woolwich Polytechnic (Fellow, 1966); BSc London. Engineering Technician, 1925–27; Armed Forces (Royal Corps of Signals, Army Educational Corps), 1927–38; Lecturer, Radar Engineering, Mil. Coll. of Science, 1938–46; Dep. Dir, Educn and Training, Electric and Musical Industries, 1946–48; HM Inspector of Schools (Further Education), 1948–56; Regional Staff Inspector (NW), 1956–59; Staff Inspector (Engineering), 1956–65; Chief Inspector for Further Educn for Industry and Commerce, DES, 1965–72. Pro-Chancellor, 1978–81, Sen. Pro-Chancellor and Chm. Council, 1981–86, Loughborough Univ.; Mem. Council, Brighton Polytechnic, 1976–87 (Hon. Fellow, 1987). Hon. Fellow, Sheffield Polytechnic, 1975. Hon. DSc Loughborough Univ. of Technology, 1966. *Publications:* Technician Engineering Drawing 1, 1979; Engineering Technicians: some problems of nomenclature and classification, 1980. *Recreations:* polyphonic music, opera, travel. *Address:* Furze Hill Lodge, Furze Hill, Kingswood, Surrey KT20 6EP. *T:* (01737) 360146.   *Died 3 July 2001.*

FREND, Rev. Prof. William Hugh Clifford, TD 1959 (Clasp, 1966); DD; FRSE, FSA, FBA 1983; Hon. Assistant Priest, Fulbourn group of parishes, since 1990; Professor of Ecclesiastical History, 1969–84, then Professor Emeritus, and Dean of Divinity Faculty, 1972–75, Glasgow University; *b* 11 Jan. 1916; 2nd *s* of late Rev. E. G. C. Frend, Shottermill, Surrey and Edith (*née* Bacon); *m* 1951, Mary Grace (*d* 2002), *d* of late E. A. Crook, FRCS; one *s* one *d*. *Educ:* Fernden Sch.; Haileybury Coll. (Schol.); Keble Coll., Oxford (Schol.; 1st cl. Hons Mod. Hist., 1937; Craven Fellow, 1937; DPhil 1940); BD Cantab 1964; DD Oxon 1966. Asst Princ., War Office, 1940; seconded Cabinet Office, 1941; FO (Pol Intell.), 1942; service in N Africa, Italy and Austria, 1943–46 (Gold Cross of Merit with Swords, Polish Forces); commn Queen's

Royal Regt (TA), 1947–67. Ed. Bd, German Foreign Min. Documents, 1947–51; Res. Fellow, Nottingham Univ., 1951; Gonville and Caius College, Cambridge: S. A. Cook Bye-Fellow, 1952; Fellow, 1956–69; Dir Studies, Archaeology, 1961–69; Bye-Fellow, 1997; Cambridge University: Asst Lectr, 1953, Lectr in Divinity, 1958–69; Birkbeck Lectr in Ecclesiastical History, 1967–68. Lay Mem., CSSB 1970–72. Chm., AUT (Scotland), 1976–78. Pres., Ecclesiastical History Soc., 1972; Vice-Pres., Assoc. internat. d'Etudes patristiques, 1983–87; Président d'Honneur, Internat. Commn for Comparative Study of Ecclesiastical History (CIHEC), 1983 (Vice-Pres. 1975–80, Pres. 1980–83). Associate Dir, Egypt Exploration Soc. excavations at Q'asr Ibrim, Nubia, 1963–64; Guest Scholar at Rhodes Univ., 1964, and Peter Ainslie Meml Lecturer; Guest Prof., Univ. of S Africa, 1976; Vis. Prof. of Inter-religious Studies (Walter and Mary Tuohy Chair), John Carroll Univ., Cleveland, 1981; Vis. Fellow, Harvard Univ. Center for Byzantine Studies, Dumbarton Oaks, 1984. Licensed Lay Reader, 1956, Deacon, 1982, Priest, 1983, serving in Aberfoyle parish; Priest-in-Charge, Barnwell with Thurning and Luddington, 1984–90. Mem., Peterborough Diocesan Synod, 1988–90. Editor, Modern Churchman, 1963–82; British Mem., Editl Bd, Coptic Encyclopædia, 1980–91. Member: NY Acad. of Scis, 1994; AAAS, 1995. FSA 1952 (Mem. Council, 1992–94); FRHistS 1954; FRSE 1979. Hon. DD Edinburgh, 1974. *Publications:* The Donatist Church, 1952; Martyrdom and Persecution in the Early Church, 1965; The Early Church, 1965; (contrib.) Religion in the Middle East, 1968; The Rise of the Monophysite Movement, 1972; Religion Popular and Unpopular in the Early Christian Centuries, 1976; (contrib.) Cambridge History of Africa, vol. ii, 1978; Town and Country in the Early Christian Centuries, 1980; The Rise of Christianity, 1984; Saints and Sinners in the Early Church, 1985; History and Archaeology in the Study of Early Christianity, 1988; (contrib.) Agostino d'Ippona: quaestiones disputatae, 1989; The Archaeology of Early Christianity: a history, 1996; Orthodoxy, Paganism and Dissent in the Early Christian Centuries, 2002; From Dogma to History: how our understanding of the early Church developed, 2003; (contrib.) Cambridge History of Christianity, vol. 1, 2006; articles in Jl Theol Studies, Jl Roman Studies, Jl Eccles. History, Jahrbuch für Antike und Christentum, etc. *Recreations:* archæology, gardening, writing, collecting old coins and stamps. *Address:* Clerk's Cottage, Little Wilbraham, Cambridge CB1 5LB. *Club:* Authors' (Dist. Mem., 2000).   *Died 1 Aug. 2005.*

FRESHWATER, Prof. Donald Cole, FREng; Professor, Louisiana State University, 1986–96; Professor Emeritus, University of Technology, Loughborough, 1987; *b* 21 April 1924; *s* of Thomas and Ethel May Freshwater; *m* 1948, Margaret D. Worrall (marr. diss. 1977); one *s* three *d*; *m* 1980, Eleanor M. Lancashire (*née* Tether). *Educ:* Brewood Grammar Sch.; Birmingham Univ. (BSc, PhD); Sheffield Univ.; Loughborough Coll. (DLC). Fuel Engineer, Min. of Fuel and Power, 1944; Chemical Engr: APV Co. Ltd, 1948; Midland Tar Distillers Co. Ltd, 1950; Lectr, Dept of Chem. Engrg, Univ. of Birmingham, 1952–57; Loughborough College (later University) of Technology: Hd, Dept of Chem. Engrg, 1957–86; Dean of Pure and Applied Science, 1982–85; Sen. Pro Vice-Chancellor, 1972–74. Visiting Professor: Univ. of Delaware, USA, 1962; Georgia Inst. of Technology, 1980–81. Chm., Chem. Engrg Gp, Soc. of Chemical Industry, 1973–75; Mem. Council, IChemE, 1982–87 (Vice Pres., 1985–87). FREng (FEng 1986). Hon. DSc Loughborough, 1989. Dow Award for Excellence in Teaching, 1996; Council Medal, IChemE, 1998. *Publications:* Chemical Engineering Data Book, 1959; People, Pipes & Processes: a history of chemical engineering, 1997; numerous papers on mass transfer, particle technology and educn in chem. engrg jls. *Recreations:* sailing, collecting watercolours. *Address:* 15 Halstead Road, Mountsorrel, Loughborough LE12 7HD.

Clubs: Athenæum; Mountsorrel Working Men's.
Died 2 Aug. 2004.

FRIEDLANDER, Frederick Gerard, (Friedrich Gerhart), PhD; FRS 1980; Reader Emeritus, University of Cambridge, since 1982; Hon. Research Fellow, Department of Mathematics, University College London; *b* Vienna, 25 Dec. 1917; *oc* of Paul Friedländer and Elfriede (*née* Eisler), (Ruth Fischer); *m* 1944, Yolande Morris Moden (*d* 1968); two *s* one *d*. *Educ:* Univ. of Cambridge (BA, PhD). Fellow of Trinity Coll., Cambridge, 1940; Temporary Experimental Officer, Admiralty, 1943; Faculty Asst Lectr, Cambridge, 1945; Lecturer: Univ. of Manchester, 1946; Univ. of Cambridge, 1954; Fellow of St John's Coll., Cambridge, 1961; Fellow of Wolfson Coll., Cambridge, 1968; Reader in Partial Differential Equations, Univ. of Cambridge, 1979. *Publications:* Sound Pulses, 1958; The Wave Equation on a Curved Space-Time, 1975; Introduction to the Theory of Distributions, 1982, 2nd edn (with M. Joshi); 1999; papers in mathematical jls. *Address:* 28 Greenlands, Cambridge CB2 2QY. *Died 20 May 2001.*

FRISBY, Roger Harry Kilbourne; QC 1969; a Recorder, 1972–78 and 1986–95; *b* 11 Dec. 1921; 2nd *s* of late Herbert Frisby and Hylda Mary Frisby; *m* 1961, Audrey Mary Jennings (marr. diss. 1980), Metropolitan Stipendiary Magistrate; two *s* one *d* (and one *s* one *d* by previous marriage); *m* 1998, Mrs Muriel Wilkinson. *Educ:* Bablake Sch.; Christ Church, Oxford; King's Coll., Univ. of London. Called to the Bar, Lincoln's Inn, 1950. *Address:* Queen Elizabeth Building, Temple, EC4Y 9BS. *T:* (020) 7583 5766. *Club:* Hurlingham. *Died 3 Dec. 2001.*

FRITH, Hon. Royce (Herbert), CM 2001; QC (Can.) 1974; Consultant, Borden Ladner Gervais, Barristers and Solicitors, 1996–2005; High Commissioner for Canada in the United Kingdom, 1994–96; *b* 12 Nov. 1923; *s* of George Harry Frith and Annie Beatrice (*née* Royce); *m* 1948, Elizabeth Mary Davison (*d* 1976); one *d* (one *s* decd). *Educ:* Lachine High Sch., Quebec; Parkdale Coll. Inst., Toronto; Victoria Coll., Univ. of Toronto (BA); Osgoode Hall Law Sch. (LLB); Univ. of Ottawa (Dip. d'etudes supérieures). Practised law, Toronto and Perth, 1949–89. Mem. (L) Senate, Ontario, 1977–94; Dep. Govt Leader, 1980–84; Dep. Leader of Opposition in Senate, 1984–91, Leader, 1991–93. Comr, Royal Commn on Bilingualism and Biculturalism, 1963–70; Legal Advr to Comr of Official Langs, 1971–77. Pres., Ontario Liberal Assoc., 1961–62. Life Mem., Law Soc. of Upper Canada. Part-time broadcaster. *Publications:* Hoods on the Hill, 1991; The Show Must Not Go On, 1993. *Recreations:* music, theatre, golf, tennis, squash. *Address:* 510–4101 Yew Street, Vancouver, BC V6L 3B7, Canada; Borden Ladner Gervais, Barristers and Solicitors, Box 48600, Vancouver, BC V7X 1T2, Canada.
Died 17 March 2005.

FRÖHLICH, Prof. Albrecht, PhD; FRS 1976; Professor of Pure Mathematics, King's College, University of London, 1962–81, then Emeritus; Senior Research Fellow, Imperial College, University of London, 1982–96; Emeritus Fellow, Robinson College, Cambridge (Fellow 1982–84); *b* 22 May 1916; *s* of Julius Fröhlich and Frida Fröhlich; *m* 1950, Dr Evelyn Ruth Brooks; one *s* one *d*. *Educ:* Realgymnasium, Munich; Bristol Univ. (BSc 1948, PhD 1951). Asst Lectr in Maths, University Coll., Leicester, 1950–52; Lectr in Maths, University Coll. of N Staffs, 1952–55; King's College, London: Reader in Pure Maths, 1955–62; Hd, Dept of Maths, 1971–81. Vis. Royal Soc.-Israeli Acad. Research Prof., 1978; George A. Miller Prof., Univ. of Illinois, 1981–82; Gauss Prof., Göttingen Acad. of Scis, 1983; vis. prof. at other univs in USA, Canada, Germany, France, Switzerland, China and India. Corres. Mem., Heidelberg Acad. of Scis, 1982. FKC 1977. Hon. DSc: Bordeaux, 1986; Bristol, 1998. Senior Berwick Prize, 1976, de-Morgan Medal, 1992, London Math. Soc.; Res. Prize, Alexander von Humboldt Foundn, 1992.

Publications: Formal Groups, 1968; Galois Module Structure of Algebraic Integers, 1983; Class Groups and Hermitian Modules, 1984; (with M. J. Taylor) Algebraic Number Theory, 1991; papers in math. jls. *Recreations:* cooking, eating, walking, music. *Address:* Robinson College, Cambridge CB3 9AN. *Died 8 Nov. 2001.*

FROST, Sir Terence Ernest Manitou, (Sir Terry), Kt 1998; RA 1992; artist; Professor of Painting, University of Reading, 1977–81 (formerly Reader in Fine Art), Professor Emeritus 1981; *b* 13 Oct. 1915; *m* 1945, Kathleen Mary Clarke; *five s* one *d*. *Educ:* Leamington Spa Central Sch. Exhibitions: Leicester Galls, 1952–58; Waddington Galls, 1958–; B. Schaeffer Gall., NY, 1960–62; Plymouth 1976; Bristol 1976; Serpentine Gall., 1977; Paris, 1978; Norway, 1979; Austin/Desmond Fine Art, 1989; Adelson Gall., NY, 1992–94; Mayor Gall., London, 1994; McGeary Gall., Brussels, 1995; Green on Red Gall., Dublin, 1995; Belgrave Gall., London, 1997; (retrospective) RA, 2000; Tate, St Ives, 2003. Oil paintings acquired by Tate Gall., Nat. Gall. of Canada, Nat. Gall. of NSW; also drawing acquired by Victoria and Albert Mus. Other work in public collections: Canada, USA, Germany, Australia, and in Edinburgh, Dublin, Leeds, Hull, Manchester, Birmingham, Liverpool, Bristol, etc. First glass sculpture made in Murano, Italy, 1998. Gregory Fellow in Painting, Univ. of Leeds, 1954–56. Hon. LLD CNAA, 1978. *Publications:* (illus.) 11 Poems by Federico Garcia Lorca, 1989; (jtly) Terry Frost, 1994. *Address:* Gernick Field Studio, Tredavoe Lane, Newlyn, Penzance TR18 5DL. *T:* (01736) 365902.
Died 1 Sept. 2003.

FRY, Christopher; dramatist; *b* 18 Dec. 1907; *s* of Charles John Harris and Emma Marguerite Hammond, *d* of Emma Louisa Fry; *m* 1936, Phyllis Marjorie Hart (*d* 1987); one *s*. *Educ:* Bedford Modern Sch. Actor at Citizen House, Bath, 1927; Schoolmaster, Hazlewood Preparatory Sch., Limpsfield, Surrey, 1928–31; Dir, Tunbridge Wells Repertory Players, 1932–35; life too complicated for tabulation, 1935–39; The Tower, a pageant-play, produced at Tewkesbury Fest., 1939; Dir, Oxford Repertory Players, 1940 and 1944–46, directing at Arts Theatre, London, 1945; Staff dramatist, Arts, 1947. FRSL. Hon. Fellow, Manchester Metrop. Univ. (formerly Manchester Poly.), 1988. DLitt Lambeth, 1988; Hon. DLitt: Sussex, 1994; De Montfort, 1994. Queen's Gold Medal (for Poetry), 1962; Benson Medal, RSL, 2001. *Plays:* A Phoenix Too Frequent, Mercury, 1946, St George's Theatre, 1983; The Lady's Not for Burning, Arts, 1948, Globe, 1949, Chichester, 1972; The Firstborn, Edinburgh Festival, 1948; Thor, with Angels, Canterbury Festival, 1949; Venus Observed, St James's, 1950, Chichester, 1992; The Boy with a Cart, Lyric, Hammersmith, 1950; Ring Round the Moon (translated from French of Jean Anouilh), Globe, 1950; A Sleep of Prisoners, produced St Thomas' Church, Regent Street, W1, 1951; The Dark is Light Enough, Aldwych, 1954; The Lark (trans. from French of Jean Anouilh), Lyric, Hammersmith, 1955; Tiger at the Gates (trans. from French of Jean Giraudoux), Apollo, 1955; Duel of Angels (trans. from Pour Lucrèce, of Jean Giraudoux), Apollo, 1958; Curtmantle, Edinburgh Festival, 1962; Judith (trans. from Giraudoux), Her Majesty's, 1962; A Yard of Sun, National, 1970; Peer Gynt (trans.), Chichester, 1970; Cyrano de Bergerac (trans.), Chichester, 1975; One Thing More, or Caedmon Construed, Chelmsford Cathedral, 1986. *TV:* The Brontës of Haworth, four plays, 1973 (also performed on stage, 1985); Sister Dora, 1977; The Best of Enemies, 1977. *Film Commentary* for The Queen is Crowned (Coronation film, 1953); *Film scripts:* (participation) Ben Hur; Barabbas; The Bible; The Beggar's Opera. *Publications:* The Boy with a Cart, 1939; The Firstborn, 1946; A Phoenix Too Frequent, 1946; The Lady's Not for Burning, 1949; Thor, with Angels, 1949; Venus Observed, 1950, rev. edn 1992; (trans.) Ring Round the Moon, 1950; A Sleep of Prisoners, 1951; The

Dark is Light Enough, 1954; (trans.) The Lark, 1955; (trans.) Tiger at The Gates, 1955; (trans.) Duel of Angels, 1958; Curtmantle, 1961 (Heinemann Award of RSL); (trans.) Judith, 1962; A Yard of Sun, 1970; (trans.) Peer Gynt, 1970 (this trans. included in The Oxford Ibsen, vol. III, Brand and Peer Gynt, 1972); Four Television Plays: the Brontës at Haworth, 1954; (trans.) Cyrano de Bergerac, 1975; Can You Find Me: a family history, 1978; (ed and introd) Charlie Hammond's Sketch Book, 1980; Selected Plays, 1985; Genius, Talent and Failure, 1986 (Adam Lecture); One Thing More, or Caedmon Construed, 1987; Looking for a Language (lecture), 1992; A Ringing of Bells, 2000. *Address:* The Toft, East Dean, Chichester, West Sussex PO18 0JA. *Club:* Garrick.

Died 30 June 2005.

FRY, Richard Henry, CBE 1965; Financial Editor of The Guardian (formerly Manchester Guardian), 1939–65; *b* Berlin, 3 Sept. 1900; *né* Richard Freund; *m* 1929, Katherine (*née* Maritz) (*d* 2000); no *c*. *Educ:* Berlin and Heidelberg Univs. *Publications:* Zero Hour, 1936; Watch Czechoslovakia, 1938; A Banker's World: the revival of the City, 1957–70, 1970; Bankers in West Africa, 1976. *Address:* Balint House, The Bishops Avenue, N2 0BG. *T:* (020) 8458 1392. *Club:* Reform.　　*Died 28 Jan. 2002.*

FUGARD, Maj.-Gen. Michael Teape, CB 1990; an Adjudicator of Immigration Appeals, 1990–95 (full-time, 1991–95); a Recorder, 1992–95; *b* Chester, 27 March 1933; *s* of Rev. Theodore Teape Fugard and Lilian Teape Fugard (*née* Baker); *m* 1961, Theresia Hollensteiner; two *s* two *d*. *Educ:* Chester Cathedral Sch.; Sherborne Sch. Admitted Solicitor, 1957. Enlisted Army, RASC, 1957; commnd, Captain Army Legal Services (later Army Legal Corps), 1958; OC (Major) Army Legal Aid, Far East Land Forces, 1960, Lt-Col 1971; Asst Dir Army Legal Services, MoD, 1973–78; Col Legal Staff, HQ UKLF, 1979; Comdr Army Law Trng and Pubns Br., 1980; Comdr Army Legal Aid, BAOR, 1982; Comdr (Brig.) Army Legal Gp UK, 1983; Maj.-Gen. 1986; Dir, Army Legal Services, 1986–90. An Asst Recorder, 1986–92. Mem., Lord Chancellor's Panel of Independent Inspectors, 1990–91. Associate, Council of Immigration Judges, 1997. Governor, Royal Sch., Bath, 1985–92; Chm., Leaden Hall Sch., Salisbury, 1988–95 (Gov. Emeritus, 1996). *Address:* 5 Elm Grove, Salisbury, Wilts SP1 1NQ.

Died 25 March 2001.

FULTON, Hon. Davie; see Fulton, Hon. E. D.

FULTON, Hon. (Edmund) Davie, OC 1992; PC (Canada) 1957; QC (BC) 1957; barrister and solicitor; Associate Counsel, Swinton & Company, Vancouver, 1983–90, retired; *b* 10 March 1916; *s* of Frederick John Fulton, KC, and Winifred M. Davie; *m* 1946, Patricia Mary, *d* of J. M. Macrae and Christine Macrae (*née* Carmichael), Winnipeg; three *d*. *Educ:* St Michael's Sch., Victoria, BC; Kamloops High Sch.; University of British Columbia (BA); St John's Coll., Oxford (BA; Rhodes Scholar, elected 1936). Admitted to Bar of British Columbia, 1940. Served in Canadian Army Overseas as Company Comdr with Seaforth Highlanders of Canada and as DAAG 1st Canadian Inf. Div., 1940–45, including both Italian and Northwest Europe campaigns (despatches); transferred to R of O with rank of Major, 1945. Practised law with Fulton, Verchere & Rogers, Kamloops, BC, 1945–68, and with Fulton, Cumming, Richards & Co., Vancouver, 1968–73; Judge, Supreme Court of British Columbia, 1973–81. A Comr, 1986–92, Chm., 1990–92, Canadian Sect., Internat. Jt Commn, Ottawa. Elected to House of Commons of Canada, 1945; re-elected in 1949, 1953, 1957, 1958, 1962, 1965. Acting Minister of Citizenship and Immigration, June 1957–May 1958; Minister of Justice and Attorney Gen., Canada, June 1957–Aug. 1962; Minister of Public Works, Aug. 1962–April, 1963. Mem., Vancouver Adv. Cttee, Guaranty Trust Co. of Canada, 1983–86. Member: Law Soc. of BC, 1940–; Law Soc. of Upper Canada, 1957–;

Canadian Bar Assoc., 1940–. Mem. Senate, Univ. of British Columbia, 1948–57, 1969–75. Dir, Western Recovery Foundn, Vancouver, 1985–; Hon. Dir, Physical Medicine Res. Foundn, 1993– (Dir, 1987–93). Hon. Colonel: Rocky Mountain Rangers, 1959; 419 Sqdn, RCAF, 1993–96. Hon. LLD: Ottawa, 1960; Queen's, 1963. Human Relns Award, Canadian Council of Christians and Jews, 1985; Citation for meritorious service to country and profession, Trial Lawyers Assoc. of BC, 1986. *Address:* 4716 Paton Street, Vancouver, BC V6L 2J1, Canada. *Clubs:* Vancouver, Shaughnessy Golf and Country (Vancouver).　　*Died 22 May 2001.*

FUNG, Hon. Sir Kenneth Ping-Fan, Kt 1971; CBE 1965 (OBE 1958); JP; Chairman, KPFF Holding Ltd, since 1972; Director, The Bank of East Asia Ltd, Hong Kong, 1947–97 (Chief Manager, 1963–69); Senior Consultant for External Economy, Chongqing, Sichuan Province, China, since 1985; *b* 28 May 1911; *yr s* of late Fung Ping Shan, JP; *m* 1933, Ivy (*née* Kan) Shiu-Han, OBE, JP (*d* 2001), *d* of late Kan Tong-Po, JP; four *s* one *d*. *Educ:* Government Vernacular Sch.; Sch. of Chinese Studies, Univ. of Hong Kong. Unofficial Mem., Urban Council, 1951–60; Unofficial MLC, 1959–65, MEC, 1962–72. Hon. Chairman: Sui Fung Consultants Ltd; Dransfield Hldgs Ltd (Chm., 1993–2000); Hon. Dir, Beijing Municipal Develt Centre of Sci. and Technol. of Agric., Forestry and Animal Husbandry. Pres., Chm., Mem. etc of numerous social organisations, both present and past, including: Pres., WWF, Hong Kong; Hon. Chm., Hong Kong Nat. Cttee, United World Colleges; Member: HK Br., CPA; Bd of Trustees, Duke of Edinburgh Award; Rotary Internat. (Paul Harris Fellow; 50-Year Membership Award, 1985); Internat. Council, Asia Soc., NY; Overseer Emer., Univ. of Calif. Hosp. Med. Sch., San Francisco. Comr St John Ambulance Bde (first Chinese to serve), 1953–58; first Chinese Hon. ADC to 4 successive Governors and Officers Admin. Govt (rep. StJAB). Life Mem. Court, Univ. of Hong Kong; formerly Mem. Council, Chinese Univ. of Hong Kong. JP Hong Kong, 1952. Founder Mem., Royal Asiatic Soc.; Mem. other Socs and Assocs; FRGS, Hong Kong. Hon. degrees: LLD, Chinese Univ. of Hong Kong, 1968; DSocSc, Univ. of Hong Kong, 1969. Silver Acorn, Commonwealth Scout Council (UK), 1976; Gold Dragon, Scout Assoc. of Hong Kong, 1985. KStJ 1958. Order of the Sacred Treasure, II Class (Japan), 1985; Knight Grand Officer, 1984 (Knight Commander, 1979), Internat. Order of St Hubert (Austria). *Recreations:* racing, golf, swimming. *Address:* (home) Apt 24B, 101 Repulse Bay Road, Repulse Bay, Hong Kong; (office) KPFF Holding Ltd, 620 Prince's Building, 10 Chater Road, Hong Kong. *T:* 25220311. *Clubs:* Hong Kong, Hong Kong Jockey (Hon. Steward), Hong Kong Golf, Hongkong Country, Hongkong Squash (Life Mem.), Chinese Recreation (Hon. Pres.), American, Rotary (Hong Kong); Knickerbocker, Sky, Explorers' (New York); Bohemian (San Francisco); Tokyo, Hodogaya Country (Japan).　　*Died 16 May 2002.*

FURLONG, Monica; writer; *b* 17 Jan. 1930; *d* of Alfred Gordon Furlong and Freda Simpson; *m* 1953, William John Knights (marr. diss. 1977); one *s* one *d*. *Educ:* Harrow County Girls' Sch.; University College London. Truth, Spectator, Guardian, 1956–61; Daily Mail, 1961–68; Producer, BBC, 1974–78. Moderator, Movement for the Ordination of Women, 1982–85. Hon. DD Gen. Theol Seminary, NY, 1986; Hon. DLitt Bristol, 1995. *Publications:* Travelling In, 1971; Contemplating Now, 1971; God's A Good Man (poems), 1974; Puritan's Progress, 1975; Christian Uncertainties, 1975; The Cat's Eye (novel), 1976; Merton (biog.), 1980; Cousins (novel), 1983; (ed) Feminine in the Church, 1984; Genuine Fake: a biography of Alan Watts, 1986; Thérèse of Lisieux (biog.), 1987; Wise Child (novel), 1987; (ed) Mirror to the Church, 1988; A Year and a Day (novel), 1990; A Dangerous Delight, 1991; Bird of Paradise (memoir), 1995; Flight of the Kingfisher: a journey among the

Kukatja Aborigines, 1996; Visions & Longings: medieval women mystics, 1996; C of E, The State It's In, 2000; (ed jtly) Reflections on Forgiveness and Spiritual Growth, 2001. *Address:* c/o Sinclair-Stevenson, 3 South Terrace, SW7 2TB. *T:* (020) 7581 2550.   *Died 14 Jan. 2003.*

FURLONG, Ronald (John), FRCS; Hon. Consulting Orthopædic Surgeon: St Thomas' Hospital; King Edward VII Hospital for Officers; Queen Victoria Hospital, East Grinstead; and lately to the Army; *b* 3 March 1909; *s* of Frank Owen Furlong and Elsie Muriel Taffs, Woolwich; *m* 1st, 1936, Elva Mary Ruth Lefeaux (marr. diss. 1947); one *s* three *d*; 2nd, 1948, Nora Christine Pattinson (marr. diss. 1969); one *d*; 3rd, 1970, Eileen Mary Watford. *Educ:* Eltham Coll.; St Thomas's Hosp. (MB, BS London 1931). MRCS, LRCP, 1931; FRCS 1934. Served with Royal Army Medical Corps, 1941–46. Home Commands, North Africa and Italy; Brigadier, Consulting Orthopædic Surgeon to the Army, 1946, Hon. Consulting Orthopædic Surgeon 1951; Orthopædic Surgeon, St Thomas' Hosp., 1946. Introd. Muller Total Hip Replacement to England, 1969; established: surgical co., Jt Replacement Instrumentation Ltd, 1970; JRI (Manufacturing) Ltd, 1974; designed and implanted first in the world Hydroxy-apatite ceramic coated total hip replacement, Queen's Award for Technol Achievement, 1993; inaug. Furlong Research Foundn, 1988. *Publications:* Injuries of the Hand, 1957; (trans.) Pauwel's Atlas of the Biomechanics of the Normal and Diseased Hip, 1978; (trans.) Pauwel's Biomechanics of the Locomotor Apparatus, 1980; (trans.) W. Braun, O. Fischer, On the Centre of Gravity of the Human Body, 1986; contrib. Jl of Bone and Joint Surgery. *Recreations:* reading, history, archæology. *Address:* Lister House, 11–12 Wimpole Street, W1N 7AB. *T:* (020) 7637 1844. *Club:* Athenæum.   *Died 12 Aug. 2002.*

FURNISS, Air Vice-Marshal Peter, DFC 1944; TD 1964; Director of Legal Services, RAF, 1978–82; *b* 16 July 1919; *s* of John and Mary Furniss; *m* 1954, Denise Cotet; one *s* two *d*. *Educ:* Sedbergh School. Commissioned 1st Bn The Liverpool Scottish TA, Queen's Own Cameron Highlanders, 1939; seconded to RAF, 1942; Comd No 73 Fighter Sqdn, 1945–46; demobilised 1946; admitted as Solicitor, 1948; commissioned in Legal Branch, RAF, 1950; Director of Legal Services: HQ Air Forces Middle East, Aden, 1961–63; HQ Far East Air Force, Singapore, 1969–71; HQ RAF Germany, 1973–74; Dep. Dir of Legal Services (RAF), 1975–78. *Recreations:* shooting, gardening, fishing. *Address:* 18 Sevington Park, Loose, Maidstone, Kent ME15 9SB. *T:* (01622) 744620. *Club:* Royal Air Force.   *Died 11 Dec. 2005.*

G

GALBRAITH, Neil, CBE 1975; QPM 1959; DL; HM Inspector of Constabulary, 1964–76, retired; *b* 25 May 1911; *s* of late Peter and Isabella Galbraith; *m* 1942, Catherine Margaret Thornton; one *s* one *d*. *Educ:* Kilmarnock Academy. Constable to Inspector, Lancs Constabulary, 1931–46. Chief Supt, Herts Constabulary, 1946–51; Asst Chief Constable, Monmouthshire Constabulary, 1951–55; Chief Constable, Leicester City Police, 1956; Chief Constable, Monmouthshire Constabulary, 1957–64. DL Gwent (formerly Monmouth), 1973. *Recreation:* living. *Address:* 7 Caringal Place, St Ives, Sydney, NSW 2075, Australia. *T:* (2) 94494404. *Died 29 April 2004.*

GALBRAITH, William Campbell; QC 1977; *b* 25 Feb. 1935; *s* of William Campbell Galbraith and Margaret Watson or Galbraith; *m* 1959, Mary Janet Waller; three *s* (and one *s* decd). *Educ:* Merchiston Castle Sch.; Pembroke Coll., Cambridge (MA); Edinburgh Univ. (LLB). Teacher, Turkey, 1959–61; Lectr, Meshed Univ., Iran, 1961–62; admitted to Faculty of Advocates, 1962; in practice at Scottish Bar, 1962–67; Sen. State Counsel, Malaŵi, 1967–70; Parly Draftsman, London, 1970–74; Parly Counsel, Canberra, 1974; returned to practice, 1975; Parly Counsel, Scottish Law Commn, 1975–95; Counsel to Lord Pres., 1975–89. Chm., Nat. Health Tribunal (Scotland), 1987–95. *Recreations:* fishing, music, travel. *Died 4 April 2005.*

GALE, Prof. Ernest Frederick, PhD, ScD; FRS 1953; Professor of Chemical Microbiology, University of Cambridge, 1960–81, then Emeritus; Fellow of St John's College, Cambridge, 1949–88; *b* 15 July 1914; *s* of Nellie Annie and Ernest Francis Edward Gale; *m* 1937, Eiry Mair Jones (decd); one *s*. *Educ:* St John's Coll. Cambridge (Scholar); BSc London; BA, PhD, ScD Cantab. Research in biochemistry, Cambridge, 1936–83; Senior Student, Royal Commn for Exhibition of 1851, 1939; Beit Memorial Fellow, 1941; Scientific Staff of MRC, 1943; Reader in Chemical Microbiology, Univ. of Cambridge, 1948–60; Dir, MRC Unit for Chemical Microbiology, 1948–62. Herter Lectr, Johns Hopkins Hosp., Baltimore, USA, 1948; Commonwealth Travelling Fellow, Hanna Lectr, Western Reserve Univ., 1951; Harvey Lectr, New York, 1955; Leeuwenhoek Lectr, Royal Society, London, 1956; Malcolm Lectr, Syracuse Univ., 1967; M. Stephenson Meml Lectr, 1971; Linacre Lectr, St John's Coll., Cambridge, 1973; Squibb Lectr, Nottingham Univ., 1986. Visiting Fellow, ANU, 1964–65. Member: Food Investigation Bd, 1954–58; Internat. Union of Biochemistry Commn on Enzymes, 1957–61. Hon. Mem., Soc. for Gen. Microbiology, 1978 (Meetings Sec., 1954–58; Internat. Rep., 1963–67; Pres., 1967–69). *Publications:* Chemical Activities of Bacteria, 1947; The Molecular Basis of Antibiotic Action, 1972, 2nd edn 1981; scientific papers in Biochem. Jl, Jl of Gen. Microbiology, Biochimica et Biophysica Acta, etc. *Recreations:* photography, wood carving. *Address:* 59 Blake Court, Winchmore Hill, N21 1SQ. *T:* (020) 7263 0228. *Died 7 March 2005.*

GALE, Michael Sadler, MC 1945; Assistant Under-Secretary of State, Prison Department, Home Office, 1972–79; *b* 5 Feb. 1919; *s* of Rev. John Sadler and Ethel Gale; *m* 1950, Philippa, *d* of Terence and Betty Ennion; two *s* one *d* (and one *s* decd). *Educ:* Tonbridge Sch.; Oriel Coll., Oxford (Scholar, MA). Served War of 1939–45: enlisted 1939, Royal Fusiliers; commnd 1940, Queen's Own Royal W Kent Regt, Major 1944; served N Africa and NW Europe. Housemaster, HM Borstal, Rochester, 1946–48; Dep. Governor, HM Prison, Durham, 1948–49;

Staff Course Tutor, Imperial Trng Sch., Wakefield, 1949–50; Principal, 1950–52; Governor, HM Prison: The Verne, 1952–57; Camp Hill, 1957–62; Wandsworth, 1962–66; Asst Dir, Prison Dept, Home Office, 1966–69; Controller, Planning and Develt, 1969–75; Controller, Operational Administration, 1975–79; Mem. Prisons Board, 1969–79. *Recreations:* walking, reading, gardening. *Address:* 5A Christchurch Road, Winchester, Hants SO23 9SR. *T:* (01962) 853836. *Died 29 April 2004.*

GALLACHER, Baron *cr* 1982 (Life Peer), of Enfield in Greater London; **John Gallacher;** *b* 7 May 1920; *s* of William Gallacher and Janet Stewart; *m* 1947, Freda Vivian Chittenden; one *s*. *Educ:* St Patrick's High School, Dumbarton; Co-operative College, Loughborough. Chartered Secretary. President: Enfield Highway Co-operative Soc., 1954–68; Inst. of Meat, 1983–86; Secretary, International Co-operative Alliance, 1963–67; Parliamentary Sec., Co-operative Union, 1974–83; Mem., Select Cttee on the European Communities, 1983–89. Chief opposition spokesman on agriculture and food, 1989–92. *Publication:* Service on the Board (a handbook for directors of retail co-operatives), 1974, 2nd edn 1976. *Address:* House of Lords, SW1A 0PW. *T:* (020) 7219 3000. *Died 4 Jan. 2004.*

GALLEY, Robert Albert Ernest, PhD; FRSC; Director, Shell Research Ltd, Woodstock Agricultural Research Centre, Sittingbourne, Kent, 1960–69; *b* 23 Oct. 1909; *s* of John and Jane A. Galley; *m* 1st 1933, Elsie Marjorie Walton (*d* 1985); one *s* two *d*; 2nd 1988, Ann Louise Grundy (*née* Dale). *Educ:* Colfe's Grammar Sch.; Imperial Coll., London (BSc 1930, PhD 1932). FRIC 1944. Research Chemist, Wool Industries Research Assoc., 1932–34; Chemist, Dept of War Department Chemist, 1934–37; Lectr, Sir John Cass Coll., 1937–39; Prin. Exper. Officer, Min. of Supply, Chemical Inspectorate, 1939–45, Flax Establishment, 1945–46; Sen. Prin. Scientific Officer, Agric. Research Council (Sec. Interdepartmental Insecticides Cttees), 1946–50; seconded to Scientific Secretariat, Office of Lord Pres. of Council, 1950–52; Dir, Tropical Products Institute, Dept of Scientific and Industrial Research (formerly Colonial Products Laboratory), 1953–60. *Publications:* papers in Journal of Chem. Soc., Chemistry and Industry, World Crops, etc. *Recreations:* tennis, gardening, sailing. *Address:* Riversdale, 26 River Reach, Teddington, Middx TW11 9QL. *Died 2 Dec. 2001.*

GAM, Rt Rev. Sir Getake, KBE 1995; Head Bishop, Evangelical Lutheran Church of Papua New Guinea, 1982–98; *b* 12 Aug. 1943; *s* of Getanuka Gam and Maluave Gam; *m* 1975, Anna Goba; two *s* three *d* and one adopted *s*. *Educ:* Martin Luther Seminary, Lae, PNG (BTh). Pastoral Ministry, Finschhafen and Panguna, Bougainville, 1971–75; teacher, Martin Luther Seminary, 1976–78; Dir, Evangelism Dept, Evangelical Lutheran Ch of PNG, 1978–81. Sec. and Treas., Lae Soccer Referees Assoc. Independence Medal (PNG), 1975. *Recreation:* football (formerly played soccer and Australian rules football). *Address:* Evangelical Lutheran Church of Papua New Guinea, Box 80, Lae, Papua New Guinea. *T:* 4723711, *Fax:* 4721056. *Died 11 Aug. 2003.*

GAMMIE, Gordon Edward, CB 1981; QC 1989; Counsel to the Speaker (European Legislation etc), House of Commons, 1983–93; *b* 9 Feb. 1922; *s* of Dr Alexander Edward Gammie and Ethel Mary Gammie (*née* Miller); *m* 1949, Joyce Rust; two *s*. *Educ:* St Paul's Sch.; The Queen's Coll., Oxford (MA). War service, 1941–45; Captain, 1st Bn Argyll and Sutherland Highlanders. Called to the Bar, Middle Temple, 1948. Entered Govt Legal Service, 1949;

Asst Solicitor, Mins of Health and of Housing and Local Govt, 1967; Under-Sec. (Principal Asst Solicitor), Min. of Housing and Local Govt, later DoE, 1969–74; Under-Sec., Cabinet Office, 1975–77; Dep. Treasury Solicitor, 1977–79; Legal Advr and Solicitor to MAFF, 1979–83. *Recreations:* reading, listening to music. *Address:* Ty Gwyn, 52 Sutton Lane, Banstead, Surrey SM7 3RB. *T:* (01737) 355287. *Died 19 July 2001.*

GANDY, Ronald Herbert; Treasurer to the Greater London Council, 1972–77; *b* 22 Nov. 1917; *s* of Frederick C. H. Gandy and Olive (*née* Wilson); *m* 1942, Patricia M. Turney; two *s* one *d*. *Educ:* Banister Court Sch.; Taunton's Sch., Southampton. Town Clerk's Dept, Civic Centre, Southampton CBC, 1936; London County Council: Admin. Officer, Comptroller's Dept, 1937; Asst Comptroller, 1957; Dep. Comptroller, 1964; Dep. Treasurer, GLC, 1965; Dep. Chief Financial Officer, ILEA, 1967. Mem. CIPFA. *Address:* 15 Lynbury Court, Watford, Herts WD18 7HL. *T:* (01923) 224215.
Died 4 Nov. 2002.

GARDINER, Duncan; *see* Gardiner, J. D. B.

GARDINER, Sir George (Arthur), Kt 1990; *b* 3 March 1935; *s* of Stanley and Emma Gardiner; *m* 1st, 1961, Juliet Wells (marr. diss. 1980); two *s* one *d*; 2nd, 1980, Helen Hackett. *Educ:* Harvey Grammar Sch., Folkestone; Balliol Coll., Oxford (1st cl. hons PPE). Sec., Oxford Univ. Conservative Assoc., 1957. Chief Political Corresp., Thomson Regional Newspapers, 1964–74. Contested (C) Coventry South, 1970. MP (C) Reigate, Feb. 1974–1997; contested (Referendum) same seat, 1997. Member: Select Cttee on Home Affairs and its Sub-Cttee on Race Relns and Immigration, 1979–82; Exec., 1922 Cttee, 1987–93; Sec., Cons. European Affairs Cttee, 1976–79, Vice-Chm., 1979–80, Chm., 1980–87; Chm., 92 Gp, 1984–96; Vice-Chm., Cons. Foreign and Commonwealth Affairs Cttee, 1988–97. Mem. Council, Cons. Way Forward, 1991–97 (Editor, FORWARD, 1991–97). *Publications:* The Changing Life of London, 1973; Margaret Thatcher: from childhood to leadership, 1975; A Bastard's Tale, 1999. *Address:* 16 Acris Street, SW18 2QP.
Died 16 Nov. 2002.

GARDINER, (John) Duncan (Broderick); author and broadcaster; Editor, Western Mail, 1974–81; *b* 12 Jan. 1937; *s* of late Frederick Keith Gardiner and Ruth Dixon; *m* 1965, Geraldine Mallen; one *s* one *d*. *Educ:* St Edward's School, Oxford. Various editorial positions in Sheffield, Newcastle, and Cardiff; Sunday Times in London, 1963–64, 1966–73. *Recreations:* travel, all sport, wine and food, crosswords. *Died March 2003.*

GARDNER, Sir Edward (Lucas), Kt 1983; QC 1960; a Recorder of the Crown Court, 1972–85; *b* 10 May 1912; *s* of late Edward Walker Gardner, Fulwood, Preston, Lancs; *m* 1st, 1950, Noreen Margaret (marr. diss. 1962), *d* of late John Collins, Moseley, Birmingham; one *s* one *d*; 2nd, 1963, Joan Elizabeth (*d* of late B. B. Belcher, Bedford; one *s* one *d*. *Educ:* Hutton Grammar Sch. Served War of 1939–45: joined RNVR as ordinary seaman, 1940; served in cruisers, Mediterranean; commnd RNVR; Chief of Naval Information, E Indies, 1945. Journalist (freelance; Lancashire Daily Post, then Daily Mail) prior to 1940; broadcasting and freelance journalism, 1946–49; called to the Bar, Gray's Inn, 1947, Bencher, 1968; admitted to Nigerian and British Guianan Bars, 1962; also appeared in Courts of Goa, High Court of Singapore, and Supreme Court of India. Deputy Chairman of Quarter Sessions: East Kent, 1961–71; County of Kent, 1962–71; Essex, 1968–71. Contested (C) Erith and Crayford, April 1955; MP (C): Billericay Div. of Essex, 1959–66; S Fylde, 1970–83; Fylde, 1983–87. PPS to Attorney-General, 1962–63. Chm., Select Cttee on Home Affairs, 1984–87. Chairman: Justice Working Party on Bail and Remands in Custody, 1966; Bar Council Cttee on Parly Privilege, 1967; Exec. Cttee, Justice, 1968. Chm., Soc. of Cons. Lawyers, 1975–85 (Chm. Exec. Cttee, 1969–75; Chm.,

Cttee responsible for pamphlets, Rough Justice, on future of the Law, 1968, Crisis in Crime and Punishment, 1971, The Proper Use of Prisons, 1978, Who Do We Think We Are?, 1980, on need for new nationality law). Member: Departmental Cttee on Jury Service, 1963; Cttee on Appeals in Criminal Cases, 1964; Commonwealth War Graves Commn, 1971–87. Governor: Thomas Coram Foundn for Children, 1962–97; Queenswood Sch., 1975–87. Steward, British Boxing Bd of Control, 1975–84. *Publication:* (part author) A Case for Trial (pamphlet recommending procedural reforms for committal proceedings implemented by Criminal Justice Act, 1967). *Recreation:* walking. *Address:* Sparrows, Hatfield Broad Oak, Bishop's Stortford, Herts CM22 7HN. *T:* (01279) 718265. *Clubs:* Garrick, United and Cecil (Chm. 1970). *Died 22 Aug. 2001.*

GARDNER, Prof. John William; Consulting Professor, School of Education, Stanford University, since 1996; *b* 8 Oct. 1912; *s* of William Frederick and Marie (Flora) Gardner; *m* 1934, Aida Marroquin; two *d*. *Educ:* Stanford Univ. (AB 1935, AM 1936); Univ. of Calif. (PhD 1938). 1st Lt-Captain, US Marine Corps, 1943–46. Teaching Asst in Psychology, Univ. of Calif., 1936–38; Instructor in Psychology, Connecticut Coll., 1938–40; Asst Prof. in Psychology, Mt Holyoke Coll., 1940–42; Head of Latin Amer. Section, Federal Communications Commn, 1942–43; Carnegie Corporation of New York: Staff Mem., 1946–47; Exec. Associate, 1947–49; Vice-Pres., 1949–55; Pres., 1955–67; Pres., Carnegie Foundn for Advancement of Teaching, 1955–67; Sec. of Health, Education and Welfare, 1965–68; Chairman: Urban Coalition, 1968–70; Common Cause, 1970–77; Independent Sector, 1980–83; US Adv. Commn on Internat. Educational and Cultural Affairs, 1962–64; Pres. Johnson's Task Force on Educn, 1964; White House Conf. on Educn, 1965; President's Commn on White House Fellowships, 1977–81; Senior Fellow, Aspen Inst., 1981–; Miriam and Peter Haas Prof. in Public Service, Stanford Univ., 1989–96. Dir, Amer. Assoc. for Advancement of Science, 1963–65. Director: New York Telephone Co., 1962–65; Shell Oil Co., 1962–65; Time Inc., 1968–71; American Airlines, 1968–71; Rockefeller Brothers Fund, 1968–77; New York Foundn, 1970–76. Trustee: Metropolitan Museum of Art, 1957–65; Stanford Univ., 1968–82; Chm., Nat. Civic League, 1994–96. Benjamin Franklin Fellow, RSA, 1964. Holds hon. degrees from various colleges and univs. USAF Exceptional Service Award, 1956; Presidential Medal of Freedom, 1964; Public Welfare Medal, Nat. Acad. of Science, 1967. *Publications:* Excellence, 1961, rev. edn 1984; (ed) Pres. John F. Kennedy's book, To Turn the Tide, 1961; Self-Renewal, 1964, rev. edn 1980; No Easy Victories, 1968; The Recovery of Confidence, 1970; In Common Cause, 1972; Know or Listen to Those who Know, 1975; Morale, 1978; Quotations of Wit and Wisdom, 1980; On Leadership, 1990. *Address:* 836 Lathrop Drive, Stanford, CA 94305, USA.
Died 16 Feb. 2002.

GARDNER, Philip John, VC 1941; MC 1941; Chairman, J. Gardner Holdings Ltd, 1955–2001; *b* 25 Dec. 1914; *s* of Stanley John Gardner and Mable (*née* Puttick); *m* 1939, Renee Sherburn; one *s*. *Educ:* Dulwich Coll. Westminster Dragoons, TA, 1938–39; served 4th RTR, N Africa, 1939–42, when captured at Tobruk. Dir, J. Gardner Hldgs Ltd, 1946. *Died 15 Feb. 2003.*

GARING, Air Commodore William Henry, CBE 1943; DFC 1940; *b* Corryong, Victoria, 26 July 1910; *s* of late George Garing, retired grazier, and Amy Evelyn Garing; *m* 1st, 1940 (marr. diss); one *s* one *d*; 2nd, 1954, Marjorie Irene Smith, Preston, England; two *d*. *Educ:* Corryong Higher Elementary School; Royal Melbourne Inst. of Technol.; Royal Military Coll., Duntroon, ACT. Began career as Electrical and Mechanical Engineer, 1928; entered RMC, Duntroon, 1929, as specially selected RAAF Cadet; Flying Training: Point Cook, Australia,

1931; Sch. of Air Pilotage and Specialist Navigation Sch., UK 1934–35; Seaplane Flying Instructor and Chief Navigation Instructor, Point Cook, Victoria, 1936; commanded Seaplane Squadron, Point Cook; conducted first Specialist Air Navigation Course in Australia, 1938; posted to United Kingdom in 1939; served with No 10 Aust. Sunderland Squadron, RAAF, as Flt Commander in Coastal Command, RAF, 1939; operations in N Atlantic, France and Mediterranean (DFC); flew Lord Lloyd to France for discussions with Pétain Government prior to collapse of France, 1940, and subsequently was pilot to the late Duke of Kent and to Mr Eden (later Earl of Avon), and others (Atlantic Star; despatches); arrived Australia, 1941; Senior Air Staff Officer, HQ Northern Area (extended from Neth. Indies through New Guinea, British Solomons to New Caledonia), 1941; commanded No 9 (Operational) Group RAAF, New Guinea, 1942; Milne Bay Campaign, 1942; Buna Campaign, 1942–43 (American DSC, awarded by Gen. MacArthur); 1943 (CBE, awarded for air operations SW Pacific); commanded No 1 Operational Training Unit, E Sale, Victoria, 1943–44; Director Operational Requirements, 1944; SASO to RAAF Rep., Washington, 1945–46, subseq. RAAF Rep. (1939–45 star); OC Western Area, 1947; JSSC, 1948; ADC to the King, 1951; Commandant School Land/Air Warfare, NSW, 1950; AOC Amberley, Qld, 1951; Imperial Defence Coll., London, 1952; AOC Overseas HQ, and RAAF Rep., London, 1953; AOC RAAF, Richmond, NSW, 1953–55; AOC RAAF and Commandant RAAF Staff Coll., Point Cook, Victoria, 1955–60; Air Officer, South Australia, and OC, RAAF, Edinburgh Field, Salisbury, SA, 1960–64, retired. Exec. Dir, Rothmans Nat. Sport Foundn, Sydney, Australia, 1964; Commercial Relations Manager, Alfred Dunhill Ltd, 1971–75. Holds No 1 1st cl. Air Navigators' Certificate (Australia); Air Master Navigator (RAF). Bd, Royal Freemasons Benevolent Inst.; Co-ordinator, Masonic Internat. Fest., 1977–79. FAIM 1964. *Recreations:* Alpine ski-ing, water ski-ing, yachting, shooting, flying, carpentry, landscape painting, gardening. *Clubs:* Imperial Service, Royal Automobile, New South Wales Leagues, Tattersall's (Sydney).   *Died 1 Jan. 2004.*

GARLICK, Sir John, KCB 1976 (CB 1973); Permanent Secretary, Department of the Environment, 1978–81; *b* 17 May 1921; *m* 1945, Frances Esther Munday (*d* 1992); three *d. Educ:* Westcliff High Sch., Essex; Univ. of London. Entered Post Office Engineering Dept, 1937; Ministry of Transport, 1948; Private Sec. to Rt Hon. Ernest Marples, 1959–60; Asst Sec., 1960; NEDO, 1962–64; Under-Sec., Min. of Transport, 1966, later DoE; Dep. Sec., DoE, 1972–73; Dir-Gen., Highways, DoE, 1973–74; Second Permanent Sec., Cabinet Office, 1974–77. Mem., LDDC, 1981–92. Dir, Abbey National plc (formerly Abbey National Building Soc.), 1981–92. Chm., Alcohol Concern, 1985–96. *Address:* 16 Astons Road, Moor Park, Northwood, Middx HA6 2LD. *T:* (01923) 824628.   *Died 17 Aug. 2005.*

GARNER, Frederick Leonard; Chairman, Pearl Assurance Company Ltd, 1977–83, President, and President, Pearl Group, 1983–88, retired; *b* 7 April 1920; *s* of Leonard Frank Garner and Florence Emily Garner; *m* 1953, Giovanna Maria Anzani, Italy. *Educ:* Sutton County Sch., Surrey. Served War, RA, 1940–46. Joined Pearl Assurance Co., 1936; rejoined, 1946; sole employment, 1946–83. Director: Schroder Global Trust, 1971–89; Kleinwort Development Fund, 1981–. *Address:* 98 Tudor Avenue, Worcester Park, Surrey KT4 8TU. *T:* (020) 8337 3313. *Club:* Royal Automobile.   *Died 9 Jan. 2004.*

GARRETT, Thomas John; Principal, Royal Belfast Academical Institution, 1978–90; *b* 13 Sept. 1927; *s* of late Mr and Mrs T. J. Garrett; *m* 1958, Sheenah Agnew (*d* 1991), *o d* of late Mr and Mrs G. Marshall, Drymen, Stirlingshire; one *d. Educ:* Royal Belfast Acad. Instn; QUB (BA); Heidelberg Univ. Asst Master: Royal Belfast Acad. Instn, 1951–54; Nottingham High Sch. for Boys,

1954–56; Sen. German Master, 1956–73, Housemaster, 1968–73, Campbell Coll., Belfast; Headmaster, Portora Royal Sch., Enniskillen, 1973–78. Member: Broadcasting Council for N Ireland, 1982–84; Northern Ireland Partnership, 1987–; Ind. Commn for Police Complaints (NI), 1990–97. Mem., Mus. and Arts Cttee, Down DC, 1996–2001. Mem., Bd of Govs, Bloomfield Collegiate Sch., 1992–2001. Pres., Old Instonians Assoc., 1996–97. *Publications:* Modern German Humour, 1969; Two Hundred Years at the Top—a dramatised history of Portora Royal School, 1977. *Recreations:* writing, hill-walking, ornithology. *Address:* Carnbeg, 44 Dunmore Road, Spa, Ballynahinch, Co. Down BT24 8PR. *T:* (028) 9756 2399. *Club:* East India.   *Died 13 Feb. 2003.*

GARTON, John Leslie, CBE 1974 (MBE (mil.) 1946); President, Henley Royal Regatta, since 1978; *b* 1 April 1916; *er s* of late C. Leslie Garton and Madeline Laurence; *m* 1939, Elizabeth Frances (*d* 2002), *d* of Sir Walter Erskine Crum, OBE; one *s* (and two *s* decd). *Educ:* Eton; Magdalen Coll., Oxford (MA). Commissioned TA, Royal Berkshire Regt, 1938. Served War, in France, 1940; psc 1943; Gen. Staff Ops Br., First Canadian Army HQ, in Europe, 1944–46; transf. to RARO, Scots Guards, 1951. Chm., Coca-Cola Bottling Co. (Oxford) Ltd, 1951–65, Coca-Cola Western Bottlers Ltd, 1966–71. Henley Royal Regatta: Steward, 1960; Mem. Cttee of Management, 1961–77; Chm., 1966–77. Amateur Rowing Association: Exec. Cttee and Council, 1948–77; Pres., 1969–77; Hon. Life Vice-Pres., 1978. Hon. Sec. and Treas., OUBC Trust Fund, 1959–69; Mem., Finance and Gen. Purposes Cttee, British Olympic Assoc., 1969–77; Thames Conservator, 1970–74; Chm., World Rowing Championships, 1975; Trustee, Leander Trust, 1982– (Chm., 1982–96). Liveryman, Grocers' Company, 1947–. High Sheriff, Bucks, 1977. *Recreations:* supporting the sport of rowing (rowed in Eton VIII, 1934, 1935, Captain of Boats, 1935; rowed in the Boat Race for Oxford, 1938, 1939, Pres. OUBC, 1939), shooting (particularly deer-stalking), fishing. *Address:* Mill Green House, Church Street, Wargrave, Berkshire RG10 8EP. *T:* (0118) 940 2944. *Club:* Leander (elected 1936, Life Mem., 1953, Cttee, 1956, Chm. Executive, 1958–59, Pres., 1980–83).   *Died 23 May 2002.*

GARTON, Prof. William Reginald Stephen, FRS 1969; Professor of Spectroscopy, University of London, Imperial College, 1964–79, then Professor Emeritus; Associate Head, 1970–79, and Senior Research Fellow, since 1979, Department of Physics, Imperial College; *b* Chelsea, 7 March 1912; *s* of William and Gertrude Emma Caroline Garton; *m* 1st, 1940, Margarita Fraser Callingham (marr. diss. 1976); four *d*; 2nd, 1976, Barbara Lloyd (*née* Jones) (*d* 2000). *Educ:* Sloane Sch.; Chelsea Polytechnic; Imperial Coll. (BSc, ARCS 1936; DSc 1958; Hon. Fellow 1983). Demonstrator in Physics, Imperial Coll., 1936–39. Served in RAF, 1939–45. Imperial College, London University: Lectr in Physics, 1946–54; Sen. Lectr, 1954–57; Reader, 1957–64. External Examiner: Univ. of Singapore, 1972–75; Univ. of Malaya, 1986–89. Associate, Harvard Coll. Observatory, 1963–; Nuffield Fellow, Univ. of Western Ontario, 1964; Hertz Fellow, Univ. of Bonn, 1984; Leverhulme Trust Emeritus Fellow, 1987–89. W. F. Meggers Award, 1976, Fellow, 1979, Optical Soc. of America. Hon. DSc York Univ., Toronto, 1972. *Publications:* contrib. on spectroscopy in Advances in Atomic and Molecular Physics (ed D. R. Bates), 1966 (New York); numerous papers on spectroscopy and atomic physics. *Recreations:* gardening, Oriental history. *Address:* Blackett Laboratory, Imperial College, SW7 2AZ. *T:* (020) 7589 5111; Chart House, Great Chart, Ashford, Kent TN23 3AP. *T:* (01233) 621657.

          Died 28 Aug. 2002.

GASK, Daphne Irvine Prideaux, (Mrs John Gask), OBE 1976; JP; Member, Inner London Commission of the Peace, 1982–88; *b* 25 July 1920; *d* of Roger Prideaux Selby and Elizabeth May (*née* Stirling); *m* 1945, John Gask,

MA, BM, BCh; one *s* one *d. Educ:* St Trinnean's, Edinburgh; Tolmers Park, Herts; Collège Brillantmont, Lausanne, Switzerland. BA Open Univ., 1979. CAB worker, 1985–2003. Member: Shropshire Probation and After-Care Cttee, 1960–80 (Chm., 1978–80); Exec. Cttee, Central Council of Probation and After-Care Cttees, 1964–80 (Vice-Chm., 1977–80); Royal Commn on Criminal Procedure, 1978–80; Council, Magistrates' Assoc., 1968–80 (Mem. Exec. Cttee, 1976–80); Sports Council Adv. Gp, 1978–80; NACRO, 1982–; Asst Sec., L'Association Internationale des Magistrats de la Jeunesse et de la Famille, 1979–86 (Hon. Mem., 1986–; Mem., Gen. Purposes Cttee, 1986–). Served on Salop CC, 1965–77; Chm., Leisure Activities Cttee, 1974–77. Mem., W Midland Reg. Sports Council (Vice-Chm., 1970–77). Member: Council of Management, Stonham Housing Assoc., 1994–99; Family Courts' Consortium, 1996–. JP Salop, 1952. Mello Matlos medal, Brazil, 1986. *Publication:* Juvenile Delinquents and Young People in Danger in an Open Environment (research project), 1996. *Recreations:* travel, gardening, photography. *Address:* The Old School House, Garrett Street, Cawsand, near Torpoint, Cornwall PL10 1PD. *T:* (01752) 822136. *Died 18 Nov. 2004.*

GASKELL, (John) Philip (Wellesley), PhD, LittD; Fellow of Trinity College, Cambridge, since 1967 (Librarian, 1967–86; Tutor, 1973–83); *b* 6 Jan. 1926; *s* of John Wellesley Gaskell and Olive Elizabeth, *d* of Philip B. Baker; *m* 1st, 1948, Margaret (marr. diss. 1984), *d* of late H. S. Bennett, FBA, and Joan Bennett; two *s* one *d*; 2nd, 1984, Annette Ursula Beighton (marr. diss.); one *d. Educ:* Dragon Sch., Oxford; Oundle Sch.; King's Coll., Cambridge (MA; PhD 1956; LittD 1980). Served War, 1943–47, Lance-Bombardier RA: BLA, 1944–45; Radio SEAC, 1946–47. Fellow of King's Coll., Cambridge, 1953–60, Dean, 1954–56, Tutor, 1956–58; Head of English Dept, and Librarian, Oundle Sch., 1960–62; Keeper of Special Collections, Glasgow Univ. Library, 1962–66; Warden of Maclay Hall, 1962–64, of Wolfson Hall, 1964–66, Glasgow Univ. Sandars Reader in Bibliography, Cambridge Univ., 1978–79; Part-time Prof. of Literature, CIT, 1983–88. Editor, The Book Collector, 1952–54. *Publications:* The First Editions of William Mason, 1951; John Baskerville, a bibliography, 1959, rev. edn 1973; Caught!, 1960; A Bibliography of the Foulis Press, 1964, rev. edn 1986; Morvern Transformed, 1968, rev. edn 1980; (with R. Robson) The Library of Trinity College, Cambridge, 1971; A New Introduction to Bibliography, 1972, rev. edn 1974, 1979, 1985; (ed and trans with P. Bradford) The Orthotypographia of Hieronymus Hornschuch, 1972; From Writer to Reader, 1978; Trinity College Library, the first 150 years, 1980; (with Clive Hart) Ulysses: a review of three texts, 1989; Landmarks in English Literature, 1998; Standard Written English: a guide, 1998; Landmarks in European Literature, 1999; Landmarks in Classical Literature, 1999; contrib. The Library, Jl Printing Historical Soc., etc. *Recreations:* jazz, teaching, writing. *Address:* Primrose Cottage, Mawgan, Helston, Cornwall TR12 6AB. *T:* (01326) 221314; *e-mail:* philip.gaskell@exeter.ac.uk.

Died 31 July 2001.

GASKELL, Philip; *see* Gaskell, J. P. W.

GATEHOUSE, Sir Robert Alexander, Kt 1985; a Judge of the High Court, Queen's Bench Division, 1985–96; *b* 30 Jan. 1924; *s* of late Major-Gen. A. H. Gatehouse, DSO, MC; *m* 1st, 1951, Henrietta Swann; 2nd, 1966, Pamela Fawcett. *Educ:* Wellington Coll.; Trinity Hall, Cambridge (BA 1949). Served War of 1939–45: commnd into Royal Dragoons; NW Europe. Called to the Bar, Lincoln's Inn, 1950; Bencher, 1977; QC 1969. Governor, Wellington Coll., 1970–94. *Recreations:* music, wood sculpture. *Address:* Cross Farm, Frimley Green, Surrey GU16 6LS; Flat 9, Elm Quay Court, SW8 5DE.

Died 30 Oct. 2002.

GAUDRY, Roger, CC (Canada) 1968; DSc; FRSC; President, Jules & Paul-Emile Léger Foundation, 1983–95;

b 15 Dec. 1913; *m* 1941, Madeleine Vallée; two *s* three *d. Educ:* Laval Univ. (BA 1933; BSc 1937; DSc 1940); Oxford Univ. (Rhodes Schol., 1937–39). Organic Chemistry, Laval University: Lectr, 1940; Prof., 1945; Full Prof., 1950. Ayerst Laboratories: Asst Dir of Research, 1954; Dir of Research, 1957; Vice-Pres. and Dir of Research, 1963–65; Rector, Univ. of Montreal, 1965–75; Dir, 1975–88, Chm., 1984–88, Bio-Research Labs; Chm., Nordic Labs, 1975–91. Director: Corby Distilleries, 1975–89; Bank of Montreal, 1975–84; Alcan Aluminium, 1976–86; Hoechst Canada, 1977–87; SKW Canada, 1978–88; St Lawrence Starch, 1983–89. Chm., Science Council of Canada, 1972–75; President: Internat. Assoc. of Univs, 1975–80; Sci., Technology and Industry Centre of Montreal, 1988–90. Chm. Bd, UN Univ., 1974–76; Dir, Inst. de recherches cliniques, Montreal, 1975–96; Chm., Network for Neural Regeneration and Functional Recovery, 1990–94. Hon. FRCP&S (Canada), 1971. Hon. doctorates: (Laws): Univ. of Toronto, 1966; McGill Univ., 1967; Univ. of Clermont-Ferrand, France, 1967; St Thomas Univ., 1968; Brock Univ., 1969; Concordia Univ., 1980; (Science): RMC of Kingston, 1966; Univ. of BC, 1967; Univ. of Saskatchewan, 1970; Univ. of Western Ontario, 1976; (Civil Laws) Bishop's Univ., 1969. Parizeau Medal from Assoc. Canadienne Française pour l'Avancement des Sciences, 1958. KM 1976; Silver Jubilee Medal, 1977; Compagnon de Lavoisier, 1985; Grand Officier de l'Ordre du Québec, 1992; Medal of 125th Anniversary of Confederation, 1992; World Award of Educn, World Cultural Council, Mexico, 1996. *Publications:* author and co-author of numerous scientific papers in organic and biological chemistry. *Address:* 6100 chemin Deacon, apt 03-L, Montréal, QC H3S 2V6, Canada. *Died 7 Oct. 2001.*

GAULD, William Wallace; Under-Secretary, Department of Agriculture and Fisheries for Scotland, 1972–79; *b* 12 Oct. 1919; *e s* of late Rev. W. W. Gauld, DD, of Aberdeen, and Charlotte Jane Gauld (*née* Reid); *m* 1943, Jean Inglis Gray (*d* 1999); three *d. Educ:* Fettes; Aberdeen Univ. (MA 1st Cl. Hons Classics). Served Pioneer Corps, 1940–46 (Major 1945). Entered Dept of Agriculture for Scotland, 1947; Private Sec. to Secretary of State for Scotland, 1955–57; Asst Sec., 1958; Scottish Development Dept, 1968–72; Mem. Agricultural Research Council, 1972–79. Pres., Botanical Soc., Edinburgh, 1978–80. *Address:* 1 Banks Crescent, Crieff, Perthshire PH7 3SR.

Died 2 June 2002.

GAY, Rear-Adm. George Wilsmore, CB 1969; MBE 1946; DSC 1943; JP; Director-General of Naval Training, 1967–69; retired; *b* 2 Oct. 1913; *s* of late Engr Comdr George Murch Gay and Mrs O. T. Gay (*née* Allen); *m* 1941, Nancy Agnes Clark; two *s* one *d. Educ:* Eastman's Sch., Southsea; Nautical Coll., Pangbourne. Entered RN, 1930; Cadet Trng, 1930–32; RNEC, Keyham, 1932–35; HMS Glorious, 1935–37; Engr Off., HMS Porpoise, 1939–41, HMS Clyde, 1941–43; HMS Dolphin, 1938 and 1943–46; HM Dockyard, Portsmouth, 1946–47; Comdr 1947; HMS Euryalus, 1947–49; Sqdn Engr Off., 1st Submarine Sqdn, HMS Forth, 1949–50; Trng Comdr, HMS Raleigh, 1951–53; Admiralty Engr Overseer, Vickers Armstrong Ltd, 1953–55; HMS Dolphin, 1956–58; Capt. 1958; Senior Officer, War Course, Royal Naval Coll., Greenwich, 1958; HM Dockyard, Malta, 1959–60; CO, HMS Sultan, Gosport, 1960–63; Chief Staff Off. Material to Flag Off. Submarines, 1963–66; Admty Interview Bd, 1966; Rear-Adm. 1967. FIMechE (MIMechE 1958). JP Plymouth 1970. *Recreations:* fishing, sailing, gardening. *Died 15 Nov. 2001.*

GAYDON, Prof. Alfred Gordon, FRS 1953; Warren Research Fellow of Royal Society, 1945–74; Professor of Molecular Spectroscopy, 1961–73, then Emeritus, and Fellow, since 1980, Imperial College of Science and Technology, London; *b* 26 Sept. 1911; *s* of Alfred Bert Gaydon and Rosetta Juliet Gordon; *m* 1940, Phyllis Maude Gaze (*d* 1981); one *s* one *d. Educ:* Kingston

Grammar Sch., Kingston-on-Thames; Imperial Coll., London (BSc (Physics) 1932; DSc London 1942. Worked on molecular spectra, and on measurement of high temperatures, on spectra and structure of flames, and shock waves. Hon. Dr (University of Dijon), 1957. Rumford Medal, Royal Society, 1960; Bernard Lewis Gold Medal, Combustion Inst., 1960. *Publications:* Identification of Molecular Spectra (with Dr R. W. B. Pearse), 1941, 1950, 1963, 1965, 1976; Spectroscopy and Combustion Theory, 1942, 1948; Dissociation Energies and Spectra of Diatomic Molecules, 1947, 1953, 1968; Flames, their Structure, Radiation and Temperature (with Dr H. G. Wolfhard), 1953, 1960, 1970, 1979; The Spectroscopy of Flames, 1957, 1974; The Shock Tube in High-temperature Chemical Physics (with Dr I. Hurle), 1963. *Recreations:* wild-life photography; formerly rowing.

Died 16 April 2004.

GEACH, Gertrude Elizabeth Margaret; see Anscombe, G. E. M.

GEDDES, Ford Irvine, MBE 1943; Chairman, P&O Steam Navigation Co., 1971–72 (Director, 1960–72; a Deputy Chairman, 1968–71); *b* 17 Jan. 1913; *e s* of Irvine Campbell Geddes and Dorothy Jefford Geddes (*née* Fowler); *m* 1945, Barbara Gertrude Vere Parry-Okeden; one *s* four *d. Educ:* Loretto Sch.; Gonville and Caius Coll., Cambridge (BA 1934). Joined Anderson Green & Co. Ltd, London, 1934. Served War RE, 1939–45 (Major). Director: Bank of NSW (London Adv. Bd), 1950–81; Equitable Life Assce Soc., 1955–76 (Pres. 1963–71); British United Turkeys Ltd, 1962–69, 1976–78 (Chm., 1976–78). Chm., British Shipping Fedn, 1965–68; Pres., Internat. Shipping Fedn, 1967–69. *Address:* 8 Kensington Court Gardens, Kensington Court Place, W8 5QE. *Clubs:* City of London; Union (Sydney).   *Died 2 Oct. 2002.*

GELL, Prof. Philip George Houthem, FRS 1969; Professor and Head of Department of Experimental Pathology, Birmingham University, 1968–78, retired; *b* 20 Oct. 1914; *s* of late Major P. F. Gell, DSO, and Mrs E. Lewis Hall; *m* 1941, Albinia Susan Roope Gordon; one *d* (one *s* decd). *Educ:* Stowe Sch.; Trinity Coll., Cambridge (MB, BChir 1940); University Coll. Hosp. MRCS, LRCP 1939; FRCPath 1969. Ho. Phys. to Med. Unit, UCH, 1939; Emergency Public Health Laboratory Service, 1940–43; on staff of Nat. Inst. for Med. Research, 1943–48; Reader, 1948–60, Prof. (Personal) of Immunological Pathology, 1960–68, Dept of Exptl Pathology, Birmingham Univ. *Publications:* (ed with R. R. A. Coombs and P. J. Lachmann) Clinical Aspects of Immunology, 1968, 3rd edn 1974; contribs to Jl of Experimental Med., Immunology, 1960–. *Recreations:* gardening, painting, philosophy of science. *Address:* Wychwood, Cranes Lane, Kingston, Cambridge CB3 7NJ. *T:* (01223) 262714.   *Died 3 May 2001.*

GELLHORN, Peter, FGSM; Professor, Guildhall School of Music and Drama, 1981–92; *b* 24 Oct. 1912; *s* of late Dr Alfred Gellhorn, and Mrs Else Gellhorn; *m* 1943, Olive Shirley (*née* Layton), 3rd *d* of 1st Baron Layton, CH, CBE; two *s* two *d. Educ:* Schiller Realgymnasium, Charlottenburg; University of Berlin; Berlin Music Acad. FGSM 1989. After passing final exams (with dist.) as pianist and conductor, left Germany 1935. Musical Dir, Toynbee Hall, London, E1, 1935–39; Asst Conductor, Sadler's Wells Opera, 1941–43. On industrial war service, 1943–45; Conductor, Royal Carl Rosa Opera (115 perfs), 1945–46; Conductor and Head of Music Staff, Royal Opera House, Covent Garden (over 260 perfs), 1946–53; Conductor and Chorus Master, Glyndebourne Festival Opera, 1954–61, rejoined Glyndebourne Music Staff, 1974 and 1975; Dir, BBC Chorus, 1961–72; Conductor, Elizabethan Singers, 1976–80. Has also worked at National Sch. of Opera, annually at Summer Sch. of Music at Dartington Hall; composes; wrote and arranged music for silhouette and puppet films of Lotte Reiniger (at intervals, 1933–57). Mem., Music Staff, London Opera Centre, 1973–78; Conductor: Morley Coll. Opera Gp, 1974–79;

Barnes Choir, 1982–2000; Music Dir, Opera Players Ltd, 1950–2000; Mem. Staff, Opera Sch., RCM, 1980–88, conducting its opera perfs, 1981. Lectures on courses arranged by various County Councils and adult colleges; frequently adjudicated at music fests in UK and overseas. Musical Dir, Opera Barga, Italy, from foundn, 1967–69. *Recreations:* reading, walking and going to plays. *Address:* 33 Leinster Avenue, East Sheen, SW14 7JW. *T:* (020) 8876 3949. *Club:* BBC.   *Died 13 Feb. 2004.*

GEORGES, Rt Hon. (Philip) Telford; PC 1986; Judge of the Court of Appeal, Grand Cayman, 1985–2000; *b* Dominica, 5 Jan. 1923; *s* of John Georges and Milutine Cox; *m* 1945, Grace Glasgow (marr. diss.); *m* 1981, Joyce Cole. *Educ:* Dominica Grammar Sch.; Toronto Univ. (BA). Called to the Bar, 1949; in private practice, Trinidad and Tobago, 1949–62; Judge of the High Court, Trinidad and Tobago, 1962–74; on secondment as Chief Justice of Tanzania, 1965–71; acting Justice of Appeal, Trinidad and Tobago, 1972; Judge of the Courts of Appeal of Bahamas, 1975–81, of Bermuda, 1975–81 and 1990–94, of Belize, 1975–81 and 1993–97; Judge of the Supreme Court, 1981–83, Chief Justice, 1983, Zimbabwe; Chief Justice of the Bahamas, 1984–89. Law Reform Comr, Bahamas, 1989–95. Prof. of Law, 1974–81, and Dean of the Faculty of Law, 1977–79, Univ. of WI at Cave Hill. Vice-Chm., Trinidad and Tobago Constitutional Reform Commn, 1971–74; Chm., Crime Commn, Bermuda, 1977–78; Mem., Admin. Tribunal, Inter-American Develt Bank, 1993–98. Mem., Judicial Cttee, OAS, 1992–95. Hon. LLD: Toronto; Dar-es-Salaam; West Indies, 1985; Dalhousie, 1995. Order of Caribbean Community, 1994; Award of Dominica, 1996. *Recreation:* walking. *Address:* Newcastle, St John, Barbados.   *Died 13 Jan. 2005.*

GERAINT, Baron *cr* 1992 (Life Peer), of Ponterwyd in the County of Dyfed; **Geraint Wyn Howells;** farmer; an Extra Lord-in-Waiting to the Queen, since 1998; *b* 15 April 1925; *s* of David John Howells and Mary Blodwen Howells; *m* 1957, Mary Olwen Hughes Griffiths; two *d. Educ:* Ponterwyd Primary Sch.; Ardwyn Grammar School. MP Cardigan, Feb. 1974–1983, Ceredigion and Pembroke North, 1983–92 (L 1983–88, Lib Dem 1988–92). Leader, Welsh Lib Dems, 1979–85. Dep. Speaker, H of L, 1994–99. Former Mem., British Wool Marketing Bd (Vice-Chm., 1971–83); Chm., Wool Producers of Wales Ltd, 1977–87. Pres., Royal Welsh Agricl Show Soc., 1983. Life Mem., Farmers' Union of Wales, 2004. FRAgS 1980. Fellow, Univ. of Wales, Aberystwyth, 2002. Sec., Ponterwyd Eisteddfod, 1944–2001; Mem., Gorsedd y Beirdd, 1976. *Recreations:* walking, sport. *Address:* Glennydd, Ponterwyd, Cardiganshire SY23 3LB. *T:* (01970) 890258.

Died 17 April 2004.

GERHARD, Dr Derek James, (Jeremy), CB 1986; Deputy Master and Comptroller, Royal Mint, 1977–88, retired; *b* 16 Dec. 1927; *s* of late F. J. Gerhard, Banstead; *m* 1952, Dr Sheila Cooper, *d* of late Dr G. K. Cooper; three *s* two *d. Educ:* Highgate Sch.; Fitzwilliam Coll., Cambridge (MA; Hon. Fellow 1986); Reading Univ. (PhD). Commnd 3rd Carabiniers (Prince of Wales DG), 1945–48. Dept of Scientific Adviser, Air Ministry, 1952–57; transf. to DSIR, 1957; Sec., British Commonwealth Scientific Cttee, 1959–60; Asst Sci. Attaché, British Embassy, Washington, 1961–64; transf. to Admin. CS, 1964; Board of Trade, latterly leader UK Delegn to Internat. Consultative Shipping Gp, 1964–69; Head of Management Services, BoT, 1969–71; loaned to CSD (Personnel Management), 1971–73; Dept of Industry, leader UK Delegn to Internat. Tin Council, 1973–75; Air Div., DoI, 1975–77. Pres., Mint Dir's Conf., 1982–84. Mem., Welsh Council, CBI, 1984–87. Hon. Treas., CTBI (formerly CCBI), 1992–2000. *Publications:* various scientific papers. *Recreations:* gardening, woodwork. *Address:* Little Dowding, Dorking Road, Walton-on-the-Hill, Surrey KT20 7TJ. *T:* (01737) 813045.   *Died 18 Sept. 2004.*

GEROSKI, Dr Paul Andrew; Chairman, Competition Commission, since 2004 (Deputy Chairman, 2001–04); *b* 18 Oct. 1952; *m* Alice Sampson; one *s* one *d. Educ:* Bard Coll., USA (BA); Univ. of Warwick (MA, PhD). Lectr, Univ. of Southampton, 1977–89; London Business School: Sen. Lectr, 1989–91; Prof. of Economics, 1991–2004. Council Mem., REconS. Fellow, Centre for Econ. Policy Research. Mem., editl bds of several jls. *Publications:* (jtly) Entry and Market Contestability: an international comparison, 1991; Market Dynamics and Entry, 1991; (with G. K. Knight) Targeting Competitive Industries, 1991; Market Structure, Corporate Performance and Innovative Activity, 1995; (with P. Gregg) Coping with Recession: UK company performance in adversity, 1997; The Evolution of Markets, 2003; (with C. Markides) Fast Second: how smart companies bypass radical innovation to enter and dominate new markets, 2004; numerous papers in learned jls. *Recreations:* music, reading, watching Charlton Athletic FC. *Address:* Competition Commission, Victoria House, Southampton Row, WC1B 4AD.
Died 28 Aug. 2005.

GERRARD, John Henry, CBE 1981 (OBE 1972); MC 1944; QPM 1975; Assistant Commissioner, Metropolitan Police, 1978–81; *b* 25 Nov. 1920; *s* of Archie Reginald and Evelyn Gerrard; *m* 1943, Gladys Hefford; two *s. Educ:* Cordwainers' Technical Coll. Served War, Army, 1939–46: Iceland, 1940–42; commissioned 1st Mddx Regt, 1943; NW Europe, 1944–46 (Captain). Constable to Commander, 1946–65; Comdr, West End Central, 1965–68; Comdr 'A' Dept (Public Order/Operations), 1968–70; Deputy Assistant Commissioner: 'A' (Operations), 1970–74; No 1 Area, 1974–78. Chm., Met. Police Museums Adv. Bd, 1975–81. Freeman, City of London, 1978. Comr, London Dist, SJAB, 1983–88. KStJ 1986. *Recreations:* philately, history.
Died 2 June 2003.

GERSHEVITCH, Dr Ilya, FBA 1967; Fellow of Jesus College, Cambridge, 1962, then Emeritus; Reader in Iranian Studies, University of Cambridge, 1965–82, then Emeritus; *b* Zürich, 24 Oct. 1914; *o s* of Arkadi and Mila Gershevitch, Smolensk, Russia; *m* 1951, Lisbeth, *d* of Josef Syfrig, Lucerne; one *d. Educ:* Swiss schools at Locarno and Lugano; Univ. of Rome (classics) (Dottore in Lettere 1937); Univ. of London (Oriental studies) (PhD 1943); MA Cantab, 1948. Monitored foreign broadcasts, London, 1942–47; Lecturer in Iranian Studies, Univ. of Cambridge, 1948–65. First European to penetrate into certain areas of Western Makran (dialect field-work), 1956. Vis. Prof. at Columbia Univ., New York, 1960–61 and 1965–66; Univ. Exchange Visitor, USSR, 1965; Ratanbai Katrak Lecturer, Univ. of Oxford, 1968. Pres., Philological Soc., 1980–84. Foreign Fellow: Danish Acad., 1982; Accademia dei Lincei, Rome, 1987; Acad. of Scis of Russian Fedn, Moscow, 1992. Hon. PhD Berne, 1971. *Publications:* A Grammar of Manichean Sogdian, 1954; The Avestan Hymn to Mithra, 1959; Philologia Iranica, 1985; articles in specialist jls, encyclopaedias and collective books. *Recreation:* music. *Address:* Jesus College, Cambridge CB5 8BL. *T:* (01223) 314552; 54 Owlstone Road, Cambridge CB3 9JH. *T:* (01223) 357996. *Died 11 April 2001.*

GERSTENBERG, Richard Charles; Chairman, General Motors Corporation, 1972–74 (a Director, 1967–79); *b* Little Falls, NY, 24 Nov. 1909; *s* of Richard Paul Gerstenberg and Mary Julia Booth; *m* 1934, Evelyn Josephine Hitchingham; one *s* one *d. Educ:* Univ. of Michigan (AB). General Motors Corporation: Asst Comptroller, 1949–55; Treasurer, 1956–60; Vice-Pres., in charge of financial staff, 1960–67; Exec. Vice-Pres. in charge of Finance, 1967–70; Vice-Chm. Bd and Chm. Finance Cttee, 1970–72. *Clubs:* Bloomfield Hills Country; Paradise Valley Country (Scottsdale, Arizona); Mohawk (NY) Fish and Game. *Died 11 July 2002.*

GETTY, Sir (John) Paul, KBE 1986; *b* 7 Sept. 1932; adopted British nationality, 1998; *s* of J. Paul Getty and Ann (*née* Rork); *m* 1st, 1956, Gail (marr. diss. 1966), *d* of

Judge Harris; two *s* two *d*; 2nd, 1966, Talitha (*d* 1971), *d* of William Pol; one *s*; 3rd, 1994, Victoria, *d* of late Comdr Gerald Holdsworth. Worked in Getty Oil, Italia, 1959–70. *Recreations:* watching cricket and old movies, bibliophily. *Address:* PO Box 8799, SW1A 1ZD. *Clubs:* Garrick, Pratt's, MCC; Royal Yacht Squadron.
Died 17 April 2003.

GIBBS, Rt Hon. Sir Harry (Talbot), AC 1987; GCMG 1981; KBE 1970; PC 1972; Chief Justice of Australia, 1981–87; *b* 7 Feb. 1917; *s* of late H. V. Gibbs, formerly of Ipswich, Qld; *m* 1944, Muriel Ruth (*née* Dunn); one *s* three *d. Educ:* Ipswich Grammar Sch., Qld; Univ. of Queensland (BA, LLM). Served War, Australia and New Guinea, 1939–45, Major (despatches). Admitted as Barrister, Qld, 1939; QC 1957; Judge of Supreme Court of Qld, 1961; Judge of Federal Court of Bankruptcy and of Supreme Court of Australian Capital Territory, 1967; Justice of High Court of Australia, 1970. Hon. Bencher, Lincoln's Inn, 1981. Hon. LLD Queensland, 1980; DUniv Griffith, 1987. *Address:* 30 Lodge Road, Cremorne, NSW 2090, Australia. *T:* (2) 99091844. *Clubs:* Australian (Sydney); Queensland (Brisbane).
Died 25 June 2005.

GIBBS, Field Marshal Sir Roland (Christopher), GCB 1976 (KCB 1972); CBE 1968; DSO 1945; MC 1943; Lord-Lieutenant for Wiltshire, 1989–96; Chief of the General Staff, 1976–79; ADC General to the Queen, 1976–79; *b* 22 June 1921; *yr s* of late Maj. G. M. Gibbs, Parkleaze, Ewen, Cirencester; *m* 1955, Davina Jean Merry; two *s* one *d. Educ:* Eton Coll.; RMC Sandhurst. Commnd into 60th Rifles, 1940; served War of 1939–45 in N Africa, Italy and NW Europe; comd 3rd Bn Parachute Regt, 1960–62; GSO1, Brit. Army Staff, Washington, 1962–63; Comdr 16 Para. Bde, 1963–66; Chief of Staff, HQ Middle East, 1966–67; IDC 1968; Commander, British Forces, Gulf, 1969–71; GOC 1 (British) Corps, 1972–74; C-in-C, UKLF, 1974–76. Colonel Commandant: 2nd Bn The Royal Green Jackets, 1971–78; Parachute Regt, 1972–77. Constable, HM Tower of London, 1985–90. Salisbury Regional Dir, Lloyds Bank, 1979–91. Chm., Nat. Rifle Assoc., 1984–90. DL, 1980, Vice Lord-Lieutenant, 1982–89, Wilts. KStJ 1990. *Recreation:* out-of-door sports. *Address:* Patney Rectory, Devizes, Wilts SN10 3QZ. *Clubs:* Turf, Cavalry and Guards.
Died 31 Oct. 2004.

GIBBS, Stephen, CBE 1981; Chairman: Turner & Newall Ltd, 1979–82; Gibbs Associates Ltd (formerly Gibbs Littlewood Associates), 1984–91; *b* 12 Feb. 1920; *s* of Arthur Edwin Gibbs and Anne Gibbs; *m* 1941, Louie Pattison; one *s* one *d. Educ:* Oldbury Grammar Sch.; Birmingham Univ. (part-time). FIMMM. British Industrial Plastics Ltd, Oldbury, Warley, W Midlands, 1936–39. Served RASC, 1939–46. British Industrial Plastics Ltd: Technical Dept, 1946–52; Gen. Sales Manager, 1952–56; Dir, and Chm. of subsidiary cos, 1956–68; Turner & Newall Ltd, Manchester: Dir, 1968–72; Man. Dir, 1972–76; Dep. Chm., 1976–79; Chm., Gascoigne Moody Associates, 1984–87; Dir, Whitford Hall & Dodderhill (formerly Whitford Hall Ltd), 1990–95. Chm., Energy Policy Cttee, CBI, 1981–83. *Address:* Corner House, 11 Dodderhill Road, Droitwich Spa, Worcs WR9 8QN. *Died 9 April 2003.*

GIBSON, Baron *cr* 1975 (Life Peer); of Penn's Rocks; **Richard Patrick Tallentyre Gibson;** Chairman, National Trust, 1977–86; *b* 5 Feb. 1916; *s* of Thornely Carbutt Gibson and Elizabeth Anne Augusta Gibson; *m* 1945, Elisabeth Dione Pearson; four *s. Educ:* Eton Coll.; Magdalen Coll., Oxford (Hon. Fellow, 1977). London Stock Exchange, 1937. Served with Mddx Yeo, 1939–46; N Africa, 1940–41; POW, 1941–43; Special Ops Exec., 1943–45; Political Intell. Dept, FO, 1945–46. Westminster Press Ltd, 1947–78 (Dir, 1948); Director: Whitehall Securities Corp. Ltd, 1948–60, 1973–83; Financial Times Ltd, 1957–78 (Chm., 1975–77); Economist Newspaper Ltd, 1957–78; Pearson PLC (formerly S. Pearson & Son Ltd), 1960–88 (Dep. Chm., 1969; Exec. Dep. Chm., 1975; Chm., 1978–83); Royal Exchange Assce, 1961–69; Chm., Pearson Longman Ltd, 1967–79. Hon. Treas. Commonwealth Press Union, 1957–67. Chm., Arts Council, 1972–77. Vice-Pres., RSA, 1986–90; Chm., RSA Environment Cttee, 1986–90. Trustee, Historic Churches Preservation Trust, 1958; Member: Exec. Cttee, National Trust, 1963–72; Council, Nat. Trust, 1966–86; Adv. Council, V&A Museum, 1968–75 (Chm., 1970); UK Arts Adv. Commn, Calouste Gulbenkian Foundn, 1969–72; Redundant Churches Fund, 1970–71; Exec. Cttee, Nat. Art Collections Fund, 1970–91; Bd, Royal Opera House, 1977–87; Treasurer, Sussex Univ., 1983–87; Trustee, Glyndebourne Fest. Opera, 1965–72 and 1977–86. Hon. DLitt: Reading, 1980; Keele, 1992; DUniv Sussex, 1989. *Recreations:* music, gardening, architecture. *Address:* Penn's Rocks, Groombridge, Tunbridge Wells TN3 9PA. *T:* (01892) 864244. *Clubs:* Garrick, Brooks's.

Died 20 April 2004.

GIBSON, John Walter; Chief of Operational Research, SHAPE Technical Centre, 1977–84; *b* 15 Jan. 1922; *s* of late Thomas John Gibson and Catherine Gibson (*née* Gregory), Bamburgh, Northumberland; *m* 1951, Julia (*d* 2000), *d* of George Leslie Butler, Buxton, Derbyshire; two *s* one *d*. *Educ:* A. J. Dawson Sch., Durham; Sheffield Univ.; University Coll., London. RNVR, 1942–46. Sheffield Univ., 1940–42, 1946–47 (BSc); University Coll., London, 1947–48. Safety-in-Mines Research Estabt, 1948–53; BJSM, Washington, DC, 1953–56; Royal Armament Research and Develt Estabt, 1957–60; Head of Statistics Div., Ordnance Bd, 1961–64; Supt, Assessment Br., Royal Armament Research and Develt Estabt, 1964–66, Prin. Supt, Systems Div., 1966–69; Asst Chief Scientific Adviser (Studies), MoD, 1969–74; Under-Secretary: Cabinet Office, 1974–76; MoD, 1976–77. FSS 1953. *Address:* 7 Islestone Court, Bamburgh, Northumberland NE69 7BQ. *T:* (01668) 214501.

Died 31 Aug. 2004.

GIBSON, Rear-Adm. Peter Cecil, CB 1968; *b* 31 May 1913; 2nd *s* of Alexander Horace Cecil Gibson and Phyllis Zeline Cecil Gibson (*née* Baume); *m* 1938, Phyllis Anna Mary Hume, *d* of late Major N. H. Hume, IMS, Brecon; two *s* one *d*. *Educ:* Ealing Priory; RN Engrg Coll., Keyham. RN, 1931; HMS Norfolk, EI, 1936–38; maintenance test pilot, RN Aircraft Yard, Donibristle, 1940–41; Air Engr Officer, RNAS, St Merryn, 1941–42; Staff of RANAS, Indian Ocean, E Africa, 1942–43, Ceylon, 1943–44; Staff Air Engr. Off., British Pacific Fleet, 1945–46; Aircraft Maintenance and Repair Dept, 1946–49; loan service RAN, 1950–52; Trng Off., RNAS, Arbroath, 1952–54; Engr Off., HMS Gambia, 1954–56 and as Fleet Engr. Off., E Indies, 1955–56; Staff Engr. Off., Flag Off. Flying Trng, 1957–60; Dep. Dir Service Conditions, 1960–61; Dir Engr Officers' Appts, 1961–63; Supt RN Aircraft Yard, Fleetlands, 1963–65; Dep. Controller Aircraft (RN), Min. of Aviation, 1966–67, Min. of Technology, 1967–69, retired, 1969. ADC, 1965–66. Comdr 1946; Capt. 1957; Rear-Adm. 1966. Chm. United Services Catholic Assoc., 1966–69. *Recreation:* bridge. *Address:* Pangmere, Hampstead Norreys, Thatcham, Berks RG18 0TE.

Died 10 Dec. 2005.

GIBSON, Rt Hon. Sir Ralph (Brian), Kt 1977; PC 1985; a Lord Justice of Appeal, 1985–94; *b* 17 Oct. 1922; 2nd *s* of Roy and Emily Gibson; *m* 1949, Ann Chapman Ruether, Chicago; one *s* two *d*. *Educ:* Charterhouse; Brasenose Coll., Oxford (MA 1948; Hon. Fellow 1986). Army Service, 1941–45: Lieut, 1st KDG; Captain, TJFF. Called to Bar, Middle Temple, 1948, Bencher 1974; QC 1968. A Recorder of the Crown Court, 1972–77; Judge of the High Court of Justice, Queen's Bench Div., 1977–85. Chm., Law Commn, 1981–85. Bigelow Teaching Fellow, University of Chicago, 1948–49. Member: Council of Legal Educn, 1971–86; Parole Bd, 1979–81; Court of

Ecclesiastical Causes Reserved, 1986–96; Chm., Fees Adv. Commn, C of E, 1986–97. Pres., Central Council of Probation Cttees, 1982–86. Hon. LLD Dalhousie, 1983. *Address:* 8 Ashley Gardens, SW1P 1QD. *T:* (020) 7828 9670. *Club:* Emsworth Sailing. *Died 30 Oct. 2003.*

GIBSON, Wilford Henry, CBE 1980; QPM 1976; Assistant Commissioner (Administration and Operations), Metropolitan Police, 1977–84, retired; *b* 12 Oct. 1924; *s* of late Ernest Gibson and Frances Mary (*née* Kitching); *m* 1949, Betty Ann Bland; two *d*. Served War, Signaller, RAF, 1943–47. Joined Metropolitan Police as Constable, 1947; Inspector 1960; Supt 1965; Comdr 1971; Dep. Asst Comr, A Dept (Operations), 1974. Chm., Met. Police Flying Club and Met. Police Modern Pentathlon Club, 1976–84. Chm., British Home and Hosp. for Incurables, 1989–99, Vice Pres., 2000–. OStJ 1977. *Recreations:* reading, travelling, watching sport.

Died 30 July 2001.

GIBSON-WATT, Baron *cr* 1979 (Life Peer), of the Wye in the District of Radnor; **James David Gibson-Watt,** MC 1943 and 2 Bars; PC 1974; DL; a Forestry Commissioner, 1976–86; Chairman, Timber Growers United Kingdom, 1987–90 (Hon. President, 1993–98); *b* 11 Sept. 1918; *er s* of late Major James Miller Gibson-Watt, DL, JP; *m* 1942, Diana (*d* 2000), 2nd *d* of Sir Charles Hambro; two *s* two *d* (and one *s* decd). *Educ:* Eton; Trinity Coll (BA). Served War of 1939–45: Welsh Guards, 1939–46; N African and Italian campaigns. Contested (C) Brecon and Radnor constituency, 1950 and 1951; MP (C) Hereford, Feb. 1956–Sept. 1974; a Lord Commissioner of the Treasury, 1959–61; Minister of State, Welsh Office, 1970–74. FRAgS; Pres., Royal Welsh Agric. Soc., 1976 (Chm. Council, 1976–94). Chm., Council on Tribunals, 1980–86. Mem., Historic Buildings Council, Wales, 1975–79. DL Powys, 1968; JP Rhayader, retd 1989. *Address:* Doldowlod, Llandrindod Wells, Powys. *T:* (01597) 860208. *Club:* Boodle's. *Died 7 Feb. 2002.*

GICK, Rear-Adm. Philip David, CB 1963; OBE 1946; DSC and Bar, 1942; Chairman, Emsworth Shipyard Group, 1965–90; *b* 22 Feb. 1913; *s* of late Sir William John Gick, CB, CBE; *m* 1938, Aylmer Rowntree (*d* 1993); one *s* three *d*. *Educ:* St Lawrence Coll., Ramsgate. Joined RN, 1931; qualified as Pilot, 1936; Capt. 1952; Comd HMS Daring, RNAS, Lossiemouth, HMS Bulwark, 1952–58; Rear-Adm. 1961; Flag Officer, Naval Flying Training, 1961–64, retd. *Recreation:* sailing. *Address:* Furzefield, Bosham Hoe, West Sussex PO18 8ET. *T:* (01243) 572219. *Died 16 Jan. 2002.*

GIFFORD, Prof. (Charles) Henry, FBA 1983; Winterstoke Professor of English, University of Bristol, 1967–75, Professor of English and Comparative Literature, Jan.-July 1976, retired; *b* 17 June 1913; *s* of Walter Stanley Gifford and Constance Lena Gifford (*née* Henry); *m* 1938, Mary Rosamond van Ingen; one *s* one *d*. *Educ:* Harrow Sch.; Christ Church, Oxford (BA 1936, MA 1946). War Service, 1940–46, Royal Armoured Corps. Univ. of Bristol: Asst Lectr, 1946; Sen. Lectr, 1955; Prof. of Modern English Literature, 1963. Clark Lectr, Trinity Coll., Cambridge, 1985. Gen. Editor, Cambridge Studies in Russian Literature, 1980–84. *Publications:* The Hero of his Time, 1950; (with Charles Tomlinson) Castilian Ilexes: versions from Antonio Machado, 1963; The Novel in Russia, 1964; Comparative Literature, 1969; Tolstoy: a critical anthology, 1971; Pasternak: a critical study, 1977; Tolstoy, 1982; Poetry in a Divided World (1985 Clark Lectures), 1986; articles and reviews on English and comparative literature. *Address:* 10 Hyland Grove, Bristol BS9 3NR. *T:* (0117) 950 2504. *Died 23 Nov. 2003.*

GILBERT, Sir Arthur, Kt 1999; President, Gilbert Financial Co., since 1950; *b* 16 May 1913; *s* of Lazarus and Bella Bernstein; adopted surname of Gilbert; *m* 1st, 1934, Rosalinde Gilbert (*d* 1995); one *s*; 2nd, 1997, Marjorie W. Haworth. Private ownership, Rosalinde Gilbert Ltd, 1934–48; real estate developer and investor, 1950–. Gilbert

Collection, incl. silver, mosaics and portrait miniatures, donated to UK, 1996. Hon. Dr Technion Inst. Technol., Israel, 1998; Hon. PhD Hebrew Univ. of Jerusalem, 1999. *Recreations:* tennis, art collector. *Address:* 9536 Wilshire Boulevard, # 420, Beverly Hills, CA 90212–2434, USA. *T:* (310) 2472966. *Club:* Beverly Hills Tennis (Calif).
Died 2 Sept. 2001.

GILBERT, Prof. Geoffrey Alan, FRS 1973; Professor of Biochemistry, University of Birmingham, 1969–85, then Emeritus; *b* 3 Dec. 1917; *s* of A. C. Gilbert and M. M. Gilbert (*née* Cull); *m* 1948, Lilo M. Gilbert (*née* Czigler de Egerszalok); two *s. Educ:* Kingsbury County Sch., Middx; Emmanuel Coll., Cambridge (MA, PhD, ScD). Research Fellow, Medical Sch., Harvard Univ., 1946–47. University of Birmingham Chemistry Department: Lectr, 1943–46; Sen. Lectr, 1947–61; Reader, 1961–69. Chm., British Biophysical Soc., 1974. Mem., Editorial Bd, Jl of Molecular Biol., 1972–87. *Publications:* articles and papers in scientific jls. *Recreations:* photography, gardening, fox-watching. *Address:* 194 Selly Park Road, Birmingham B29 7HY. *T:* (0121) 472 0755. *Died 1 March 2005.*

GILBERT, Maj.-Gen. Glyn Charles Anglim, CB 1974; MC 1944; *b* 15 Aug. 1920; *s* of late C. G. G. Gilbert, OBE, MC, and H. M. Gilbert, MBE, Bermuda; *m* 1943, Heather Mary Jackson (*d* 2000); three *s* one *d. Educ:* Eastbourne Coll.; RMC Sandhurst. Commnd 1939; served with 2nd Lincolns, 1940–47, NW Europe and Palestine; Instructor, Sch. of Infantry, 1948–50; 3rd Bn Para. Regt, 1951; Staff Coll., 1952; staff and regimental appts in MoD, Airborne Forces, Royal Lincolns and Para. Regt, 1952–66; Cyprus, Egypt and Malaya; idc 1966; comd Sch. of Infantry, 1967–70; GOC 3rd Div., 1970–72; Comdt, Joint Warfare Estab., 1972–74, retired. Dir, Fitness for Industry Ltd, 1980–96. *Recreation:* following the sun. *Club:* Army and Navy. *Died 26 Sept. 2003.*

GILBERT, Ronald Stuart J.; see Johnson-Gilbert.

GILDER, Robert Charles, FIA; Directing Actuary, Government Actuary's Department, 1979–83; *b* 22 April 1923; *s* of Charles Henry Gilder and Elsie May (*née* Sayer); *m* 1954, Norah Mary Hallas; two *s. Educ:* Brentwood School. Served War, RAF, 1941–46. Liverpool Victoria Friendly Soc., 1940–41 and 1946–48; Government Actuary's Dept, 1948–83; Actuary, 1959; Principal Actuary, 1973. FIA 1951. *Recreations:* cricket, golf, music.
Died 7 May 2004.

GILES, Air Comdt Dame Pauline; see Parsons, Air Comdt Dame P.

GILES, Robert Frederick; Senior Clerk, House of Commons, 1979–83; *b* 27 Dec. 1918; *s* of Robert and Edith Giles; *m* 1948, Mabel Florence Gentry; two *d. Educ:* Drayton Manor Sch., Hanwell. Min. of Agriculture, 1936–39. Royal Navy, 1939–45: CO, HMS Tango, 1942–44. Various assignments, MAF, from 1945; Regional Controller, Northern Region MAFF, 1963–68; Head, Food Standards/Food Science Div., 1968–74; Under Sec., MAFF, 1975–78; Food Standards and Food Subsidies Gp, 1975; Food Feedingstuffs and Fertilizer Standards Gp, 1977. *Recreations:* walking, theatre. *Address:* 8 The Ridings, Copthill Lane, Kingswood, Surrey KT20 6HJ. *Club:* Civil Service. *Died 18 Dec. 2005.*

GILL, (James) Kenneth; President, Saatchi and Saatchi Company PLC, 1985–94; *b* 27 Sept. 1920; *s* of late Alfred Charles and Isabel Gill; *m* 1948, Anne Bridgewater; one *s. Educ:* Highgate Sch. Served RAC, 24th Lancers and Intelligence Corps, GSO II, 1939–45. Copywriter, S. T. Garland Advertising Service, 1938–39; Chm., Garland-Compton Ltd, 1970–76; Saatchi and Saatchi Company: Chm., 1976–85; Pres. and Dir, 1985–89. FIPA. *Recreations:* the theatre, the cinema, cricket. *Address:* Davenport House, Duntisbourne Abbots, Cirencester, Glos GL7 7JN. *T:* (01285) 821468.
Died 3 Sept. 2005.

GILLAM, Stanley George, MA, MLitt; Librarian, The London Library, 1956–80; *b* 11 Aug. 1915; *s* of Harry Cosier Gillam, Oxford; *m* 1950, Pauline, *d* of Henry G. Bennett, Oxford; one *s. Educ:* Southfield Sch.; Saint Catherine's Coll., Oxford. Bodleian Library, Oxford, 1931–40 and 1946–54. Oxfordshire and Bucks Light Infantry (1st Bucks Bn), 1940–46. Asst Sec. and Sub-Librarian, The London Library, 1954–56. *Publications:* The Building Accounts of the Radcliffe Camera, 1958; The Divinity School and Duke Humfrey's Library at Oxford, 1988; The Radcliffe Camera, 1992; articles in The Bodleian Library Record and other periodicals. *Address:* c/o Mrs P. Gillam, 47 Welcombe Grove, Solihull, W Midlands B91 1PD. *T:* (0121) 704 4802.
Died 29 April 2004.

GILLANDERS, Prof. Lewis Alexander; Clinical Professor in Radiology, University of Aberdeen, and Consultant in Charge, Radiology Services (Grampian Health Board), 1964–88, then Professor Emeritus in Radiology; *b* 7 Feb. 1925; *s* of Kenneth John Alexander Gillanders and Nellie May Sherris; *m* 1960, Nora Ellen Wild, MB, ChB; one *s* one *d. Educ:* Dingwall Acad.; Univ. of Glasgow (MB ChB 1947). Commnd, RAMC, 1948–50; gen. medical practice, Scottish Highlands, 1950–52; trained in Diagnostic Radiology, Glasgow Royal Infirmary and United Birmingham Hosps, 1953–58; Consultant Radiologist, Aberdeen Teaching Hosps, 1958. Examiner in Radiology for: RCR, 1969–79, and DMRD, Univ. of Aberdeen, 1969–89; Faculty of Radiologists, RCSI, 1975–77; Univ. of Nairobi, 1978–80; Univ. of Wales, 1981–83. Member, GMC, 1979–84; Vice-Pres., RCR, 1981–83. *Publications:* chapter in Pye's Surgical Handicraft (1st edn 1884), 19th edn 1969, 20th edn 1977; papers in gen. med. and radiol literature, students' magazines, etc. *Recreations:* derivations and meanings; golf, do-it-yourself. *Address:* 17 Denhead, Kirk Brae, Cults, Aberdeen AB15 9QT. *Died 24 Dec. 2002.*

GILLESPIE, William Hewitt, MD; FRCP, FRCPsych; Emeritus Physician, Maudsley Hospital (Physician, 1936–70); *b* 6 Aug. 1905; *s* of Rev. W. H. Gillespie, Manchuria and Co. Down, and Isabella B. Gillespie (*née* Grills), Co. Down, N Ireland; *m* 1st, 1932, Dr Helen Turover (*d* 1975); one *s* one *d*; 2nd, 1975, Sadie Mervis. *Educ:* George Watson's Coll.; Univ. of Edinburgh (1st pl. Open Bursary Exam., 1924; MB, ChB (hons) 1929; Dip. in Psychiatry, 1931; MD 1934); Univ. of Vienna. MRCP 1936; FRCP 1962. McCosh Travelling Scholarship, in Vienna, 1930–31; LCC Mental Hosps Service, 1931–36; Lecturer, Inst. of Psychiatry, 1944–70; Dir, London Clinic of Psychoanalysis, 1944–47. Freud Meml Vis. Prof. of Psychoanalysis, University Coll. London, 1976–77. Trng Sec., 1947–50, Chm., 1954–56, Inst of Psychoanalysis; President: British Psychoanalytical Soc., 1950–53 and 1971–72 (Hon. Mem., 1975); Internat. Psychoanalytic Assoc., 1957–61 (Hon. Vice-Pres., 1991). FRSocMed. *Publications:* Life, Sex and Death: selected writings, ed M. D. A. Sinason, 1995; contributed to: Recent Advances in Psychiatry, 1944; Psychiatrie sociale de l'enfant, 1951; Psychoanalysis and the Occult, 1953; The Sexual Perversions, 1956; The Pathology and Treatment of Sexual Deviation, 1964; Foundations of Child Psychiatry, 1968; various articles in medical, psychiatric and psychoanalytic jls. *Recreations:* music, reading, walking. *Address:* 4 Eton Villas, NW3 4SX.

Died 30 June 2001.

GILLICK, Rev. John, SJ; MA; Spiritual Director, St Peter's National Seminary, Hammanskraal, S Africa, 1986–90, retired; *b* Wallasey, 27 March 1916; 2nd *s* of Laurence Gillick and Catherine Devine. *Educ:* St Francis Xavier's Coll., Liverpool; Heythrop and Campion Hall, Oxford (1st Cl. Hons Mod. History; MA). Asst Master at Mount St Mary's and Beaumont. Two years writing and photography in Italy and Africa. Headmaster, Beaumont Coll., 1964–67; studied psychology at Loyola Univ., Chicago, 1967–68 (MA); Dir, Laboratories for the

Training of Religious Superiors in S Africa, 1969; Dir, Fons Vitae (Pastoral Institute for Religious), 1970–84. Chm., Catholic AIDS Network, Cape Town, 1992–2004. *Publications:* Teaching the Mass, 1961; Baptism, 1962; Teaching the Mass: African, 1963; Teaching the Sacraments: African, 1964; Teaching Confirmation, 1964, etc; *illustrations for:* The Breaking of Bread, 1950; The Pilgrim Years, 1956; Our Faith, 1956; The Holy Mass, 1958; Christ Our Life, 1960; Catholic Encyclopedia, 1965. *Address:* 8 The Elms, York Road, Rosebank, 7700, South Africa; c/o 114 Mount Street, W1Y 6AH.

Died 5 May 2005.

GILLING, Lancelot Cyril Gilbert, OBE 1985; CBiol, FIBiol; FRAgS; Member, Royal Commission on Environmental Pollution, 1984–89; *b* 7 March 1920; *s* of Gilbert Joseph Gilling and Esther Marianne Gilling (*née* Clapp); *m* 1951, Brenda Copp; two *d. Educ:* Shebbear Coll., N Devon; Reading Univ. (BSc Agr). Pres. Union, Reading Univ., 1948–49. Lectr, Dorset Coll. of Agric., 1949–51; Head of Agric. Dept, Writtle Coll. of Agric., Essex, 1951–57; Principal, Askham Bryan Coll. of Agric. & Hortic., 1957–84. Regular lecturer, Internat. Centre for Agricl Educn, Berne, 1968–76. Member: Technical Develt Cttee and Educn and Gen. Purposes Cttee, Royal Agricl Soc., 1970–85; Northern Regional Panel, MAFF, 1982–88; Adv. Cttee on Agric. and Vet. Sci., British Council, 1972–86; Chm., York Agricl Soc., 1983–92 (Pres., 1981–82; Vice-Chm., 1992–98; Chm. Finance Cttee, 1995–2000). Chm. and Life Vice-Pres., Yorks Philosophical Soc., 1982–88; Mem. Sub-Cttee, Yorkshire Mus., 1982–96. Chairman: Yorks Wildlife Trust, 1992–94 (Mem. Council and Chm., F and GP Cttee, 1985–92); York Centre, Nat. Trust, 1989–91. Gov., Univ. Coll. of Ripon and York St John, 1976–99. Hon. Mem., CGLI. *Publications:* contribs to Agricultural Progress, Jl of Agricl Educn Assoc. and Jl of Royal Agricl Soc. *Recreations:* ornithology, travel, choral music. *Address:* The Spinney, Brandsby, York YO61 4RQ.   *Died 17 Sept. 2004.*

GILMOUR, Dr Alan Breck, CVO 1990; CBE 1984; FRCGP; Director, National Society for the Prevention of Cruelty to Children, 1979–89, retired; *b* 30 Aug. 1928; *er* surv. *s* of late Andrew Gilmour, CMG and Nelle Twigg; *m* 1957, Elizabeth, *d* of late H. and L. Heath; two *d. Educ:* Clayesmore Sch.; King's Coll., London; King's Coll. Hosp. (Raymond Gooch Schol.; MB BS 1956). LMSSA 1956; FRCGP 1974 (MRCGP 1965). General medical practitioner, 1958–67; during this period served as Member: Standing Med. Adv. Cttee, Min. of Health; Working Party on General Practice; Educn Cttee, RCGP; BMA Council, and others. British Medical Association Secretariat, 1967–79: Asst Sec., 1967; Under Sec., 1972; Dep. Sec., 1977; appts included: Overseas Sec. and Med. Dir, Commonwealth Med. Adv. Bureau, 1967–72; Med. Dir, Career Service, 1967–76; Sec., Bd of Sci. and Educn, 1972–76 (Commonwealth Med. Assoc. meetings, Singapore/Malaysia, Jamaica, Ghana; Observer, Commonwealth Med. Conf., Mauritius, 1971); Jt Sec., Med. Sci. meetings, Vancouver, Jamaica, Dublin; Dep. Sec., Jt Consultants Cttee, 1976–79. Chairman: Internat. Alliance on Child Abuse and Neglect, 1983–90; Michael Sieff Foundn, 1990–96 (Trustee Emeritus, 1996–); Mem., Health Educn Authority, 1989–95; Hon. Treas., Assoc. for Study of Med. Educn, 1975–80; Vice-Pres., Sect. Med. Educn, RSM, 1979–82. Pres., Bridport Br., Parkinson's Disease Soc. Trustee: Kidscape, 1991–93 (Chm., 1992–93); Faithfull Foundn, 1992–94 (Patron, 1994–). Gov., Sir John Colfox Sch. (formerly Colfox Sch.), 1994– (Chm., 1995–); Mem. Council, Clayesmore Sch., 1995–2000 (Dep. Chm.). MInstD. Liveryman, Worshipful Soc. of Apothecaries of London, 1973–. *Publications:* Innocent Victims: the question of child abuse, 1988; Child Abuse Enquiry reports, and various articles on child abuse and on med. educn, careers in medicine, gen. practice; ed or ed jtly, Care of the Elderly, Primary Health Care Teams, Competence to Practise, and other reports. *Recreations:* gardening, walking, music. *Address:* 106 Crock

Lane, Bothenhampton, Bridport, Dorset DT6 4DH. *T:* (01308) 423116. *Club:* Royal Society of Medicine.

Died 18 July 2001.

GILMOUR, Colonel Sir Allan (Macdonald), KCVO 1990; OBE 1961; MC 1942, and Bar 1943; Lord-Lieutenant of Sutherland, 1972–91; Chairman, Highland River Purification Board, 1994–96 (Vice-Chairman, 1986–94); *b* 23 Nov. 1916; *o s* of late Captain Allan Gilmour, of Rosehall, Sutherland, and Mary H. M. Macdonald, of Viewfield, Portree, Skye; *m* 1941, Jean Wood; three *s* one *d. Educ:* Winchester Coll. Gazetted, The Seaforth Highlanders, Jan. 1939; served War, in Middle East, France and Germany (despatches, 1945). Staff Coll., 1946; Regimental and Staff Service in: Germany, Middle East, UK, Pakistan and Africa, 1946–67, incl. Instructor, Staff Coll., Quetta, on loan to Pakistan Army, 1952–54; Chief of Gen. Staff, Ghana Armed Forces, 1959–62; service in Congo, 1961–62; retired from Army, 1967. Pres., Highland TA&VRA, 1989–91 (Vice-Pres., 1972–89). Chm., East Sutherland Council of Social Service, 1973–77; Mem., Highland Health Bd, 1974–81 (Chm., 1981–83); Pres., Voluntary Gps Sutherland, 1993–96. Mem., Highlands and Is Develt Consultative Council, 1975–87. Member: Highland Regl Council, 1977–96; Sutherland DC, 1978–86 (Chm., 1974–78); Sutherland CC, 1970–74. DL Sutherland, 1971. DSC (USA) 1945. *Recreations:* fishing, local government. *Address:* Invernauld, Rosehall, Lairg, Sutherland IV27 4EU. *T:* (01549) 441204.   *Died 22 Sept. 2003.*

GIMSON, (George) Stanley; QC (Scot.) 1961; Sheriff Principal of Grampian, Highland and Islands, 1975–82; *b* 6 Sept. 1915. *Educ:* High Sch. of Glasgow; Glasgow Univ. TA, 1938–46; commnd, RA, 1941; attached Indian Artillery, 1941–46; POW, Singapore, River Kwai. Advocate, 1949; Standing Jun. Counsel, Dept of Agriculture for Scotland and Forestry Commn, 1956–61; Sheriff Principal of Aberdeen, Kincardine and Banff, 1972–74. Chairman: Pensions Appeals Tribunals, Scotland, 1971–95 (Pres., 1971–75); Medical Appeal Tribunals, 1985–91. Member, Board of Management: Edinburgh Central Hosps, 1960–70 (Chm., 1964–70); Edinburgh Royal Victoria Hosps, 1970–74 (Vice-Chm.). Dir, Scottish Nat. Orchestra Soc. Ltd, 1962–80; Trustee, Nat. Library of Scotland, 1963–76; Chm., RSSPCC, Edinburgh, 1972–76. Hon. Advr, RBL, Scotland, on captivity in FE during War of 1939–45; Chm., Scottish FE POW Assoc., 1996–. Hon. LLD Aberdeen, 1981. *Address:* 16 Royal Circus, Edinburgh EH3 6SS. *T:* (0131) 225 8055. *Club:* Royal Northern and University (Aberdeen).

Died 30 Aug. 2003.

GINGER, Phyllis Ethel, (Mrs Leslie Durbin), RWS 1958 (ARWS 1952); freelance artist, since 1940; *b* 19 Oct. 1907; *m* 1940, Leslie Durbin, CBE, MVO (*d* 2005); one *s* one *d. Educ:* Tiffin's Girls' Sch., Kingston on Thames. LCC three years' scholarship at Central School of Arts and Crafts, 1937–39. Water colours for Pilgrim Trust Recording Britain Scheme, 1941–42; Royal Academy Exhibitor; drawings and lithographs purchased by: Washington State Library, 1941; Victoria and Albert Museum, 1952; London Museum, 1954; South London Art Gallery, 1960. *Publications:* Alexander the Circus Pony, 1941; book jacket designs; book illustrations include: London by Mrs Robert Henrey, 1948; The Virgin of Aldemanbury, by Mrs Robert Henrey, 1960. *Address:* 298 Kew Road, Kew, Richmond, Surrey TW9 3DU. *T:* (020) 8940 2221.   *Died 3 May 2005.*

GIULINI, Carlo Maria; conductor; Music Director, Los Angeles Philharmonic Orchestra, 1978–84; *b* 9 May 1914; *m* Marcella de Girolami (*d* 1994); three *s. Educ:* Accademia Santa Cecilia, Rome. Début as conductor, Rome, 1944; formed Orchestra of Milan Radio, 1950; Principal Conductor, La Scala, Milan, 1953–55; début in Great Britain, conducting Verdi's Falstaff, Edinburgh Festival, 1955; closely associated with Philharmonia Orchestra, 1955–; début at Royal Opera House, Covent Garden,

Don Carlos, 1958; Principal Guest Conductor, Chicago Symphony Orch., 1969–78; Music Dir, Vienna Symphony Orch., 1973–76; conducted new prodn of Falstaff in Los Angeles, at Covent Garden, and at Teatro Comunale, Florence, 1982, after 14 year absence from opera. Laureate Conductor, Swedish Radio Orch. Hon. Mem., Ges. der Musikfreunde, Vienna, 1978; Hon. DHL DePaul Univ., Chicago, 1979. Gold Medal: Bruckner Soc., 1978; International Mahler Soc.; Una Vita Nella Musica. *Recreation:* sailing. *Address:* c/o Signor Francesco Giulini, Via Bonnet 7, 20121 Milan, Italy.

Died 14 June 2005.

GLADWIN OF CLEE, Baron *cr* 1994 (Life Peer), of Great Grimsby in the County of Humberside; **Derek Oliver Gladwin,** CBE 1979 (OBE 1977); JP; Regional Secretary (Southern Region), General and Municipal Workers' Union, 1970–90; Member, Post Office Board (formerly Post Office Corporation), 1972–94; *b* 6 June 1930; *s* of Albert Victor Gladwin and Ethel Gladwin (*née* Oliver); *m* 1956, Ruth Ann Pinion; one *s. Educ:* Carr Lane Junior Sch., Grimsby; Wintringham Grammar Sch.; Ruskin Coll., Oxford; London Sch. of Economics. British Railways, Grimsby, 1946–52; fishing industry, Grimsby, 1952–56; Regl Officer 1956–63, Nat. Industrial Officer 1963–70, Gen. and Municipal Workers' Union. Chm., Labour Party's Conf. Arrangements Cttee, 1974–90. Bd Mem., BAe, 1977–91. Mem., Employment Appeal Tribunal, 1992–2002. Member: Council, Industrial Soc., 1968 (Mem. Exec. Cttee, 1968–91); Bd of Trustees, Diabetes UK (formerly British Diabetic Assoc.), 1995–2001; Armed Forces Pay Review Body, 1998–. Pres., Holiday Care Service, 1998–. Hon. Pres., Ruskin Coll., Oxford, 2000– (Chm., Governing Council, 1979–99). Vis. Fellow, Nuffield Coll., Oxford, 1978–86. JP Surrey, 1969. *Address:* 2 Friars Rise, Woking, Surrey GU22 7JL. *T:* (01483) 714591; House of Lords, SW1A 0PW. *Died 10 April 2003.*

GLASS, John Basil Caldwell; Master, Supreme Court of Judicature of Northern Ireland, 1987–98; *b* 21 May 1926; *s* of John Glass and Muriel Florence Glass (*née* Caldwell); *m* 1st, 1952, Elizabeth Charlotte Caldwell (marr. diss. 1980); four *s*; 2nd, 1980, Mary Burnell Clark (*née* Chubb). *Educ:* Methodist Coll., Belfast; Queen's Univ., Belfast (Rowing Blue, 1947) (LLB 1947). Articled to J. B. McCutcheon, Solicitor, Belfast, 1947; admitted as solicitor, 1950; in private practice as solicitor, Belfast, 1950–87. Observer of legal, political, economic and social conditions in Haiti under rule of Pres. Duvalier, 1962. Founder Mem., Alliance Party of NI, 1970 (Chm., 1970–72; Pres., 1972–74; Dep. Leader, 1976–80). Mem. (Alliance) for S Belfast, NI Assembly, 1973–74; Mem., NI Constnl Convention, 1975; Belfast City Council: Mem. for S Belfast, 1977–81; Chm., Community Services Cttee, 1977–79. Member: Belfast Educn and Library Bd, 1977–81; NI Consumer Council, 1977–85 (Chm., Legal Affairs Cttee, 1982–85); Council Mem., NI Chamber of Commerce and Industry, 1986–87. Rep. of Methodist Ch in Ireland on Exec. Cttee, World Methodist Council, visiting Jamaica, Norway, W Germany and Sweden, 1961–65. Pres., QUB Assoc., 1996–98. Founder Mem., Corrymeela Community, Ballycastle, 1965. *Publication:* contrib. A Handbook of Consumer Law, 1982. *Recreations:* reading, music, theatre, sailing, hill-walking, cycling, gardening. *Died 30 Sept. 2005.*

GLEGG, Maj.-Gen. John B.; *see* Baskervyle-Glegg.

GLEN, Sir Alexander (Richard), KBE 1967 (CBE 1964); DSC 1942 (and Bar), 1945); Vice President, British Air Line Pilots' Association, 1994–2002 (President, 1982–94); *b* 18 April 1912; *s* of late R. Bartlett Glen, Glasgow; *m* 1st, 1936, Nina Nixon (marr. diss. 1945); one *s* decd; 2nd, 1947, Baroness Zora de Collaert (*d* 2003). *Educ:* Fettes Coll.; Balliol Coll., Oxford (BA Hons Geography). Travelled on Arctic Expeditions, 1932–36; Leader, Oxford Univ. Arctic Expedition, 1935–36; Banking, New York and London, 1936–39. RNVR, 1939–59, Capt. 1955.

Export Council for Europe: Dep. Chm., 1960–64; Chm., 1964–66; Chairman: H. Clarkson & Co., 1965–73; Anglo World Travel, 1978–81; Dep. Chm., British Transport Hotels, 1978–83; Director: BICC, 1964–70; Gleneagles Hotels, 1980–83. Chm., BTA, 1969–77; Member: BNEC, 1966–72; Board of BEA, 1964–70; Nat. Ports Council, 1966–70; Horserace Totalisator Bd, 1976–84. Chm., Adv. Council, V&A Museum, 1978–84; Mem., Historic Buildings Council, 1976–80. Awarded Cuthbert Peek Grant by RGS, 1933; Bruce Medal by RSE, 1938; Andrée Plaque by Royal Swedish Soc. for Anthropology and Geography, 1939; Patron's Gold Medal by RGS, 1940. Polar Medal (clasp Arctic 1935–36), 1942; Norwegian War Cross, 1943; Chevalier (1st Class), Order of St Olav, 1944; Czechoslovak War Cross, 1946. *Publications:* Young Men in the Arctic, 1935; Under the Pole Star, 1937; Footholds Against a Whirlwind (autobiog.), 1975; Target Danube: a river finally not too far, 2002. *Recreations:* friends old and new, the arts, the world today. *Address:* The Dower House, Stanton, Broadway, Worcs WR12 7NE. *Clubs:* City of London; Explorers (NY). *Died 6 March 2004.*

GLENDINING, Rev. Canon Alan, LVO 1979; Chaplain to the Queen, 1979–94; Hon. Canon of Norwich Cathedral, since 1977; *b* 17 March 1924; *s* of late Vincent Glendining, MS, FRCS and Freda Alice; *m* 1948, Margaret Locke, *d* of Lt-Col C. M. Hawes, DSO and Frances Cooper Richmond; one *s* one *d* (and one *d* decd). *Educ:* Radley; Westcott House, Cambridge. Newspaper publishing, 1945–58. Deacon, 1960; Priest, 1961. Asst Curate, South Ormsby Group of Parishes, 1960–63; Rector of Raveningham Group of Parishes, 1963–70; Rector, Sandringham Group of Parishes, and Domestic Chaplain to the Queen, 1970–79; Rural Dean of Heacham and Rising, 1972–76; Rector of St Margaret's, Lowestoft, and Team Leader of Lowestoft Group, 1979–85; Vicar of Ranworth with Panxworth with Woodbastwick, Bishop's Chaplain for the Broads and Senior Chaplain for Holidaymakers, 1985–89; RD of Blofield, 1987–89. *Recreation:* writing. *Address:* 7 Bellfosters, Kings Staithe Lane, Kings Lynn, Norfolk PE30 1LZ.

Died 6 Aug. 2004.

GLOVER, Anthony Richard Haysom; Chief Executive Officer, City Council of Norwich, 1980–88; *b* 29 May 1934; 2nd *s* of late Arthur Herbert Glover and late Marjorie Florence Glover; *m* 1960, Ann Penelope Scupham, *d* of late John Scupham, OBE; two *s* one *d. Educ:* Culford Sch., Bury St Edmunds; Emmanuel Coll., Cambridge (BA). HM Customs and Excise: Asst Principal, 1957; Principal, 1961; on secondment to HM Treasury, 1965–68; Asst Sec., 1969; Asst Sec., HM Treasury, 1972–76; Dep. Controller, HM Stationery Office, 1976–80. Sec., Norfolk Historic Bldgs Trust, 1991–95. University of East Anglia: Mem. Council, 1984–88; part-time Tutor, Dept. of Extra-Mural Studies, 1991–; part-time Tutor: WEA, 1991–; Norfolk CC, 1991–. *Recreations:* music, reading, writing, alpine gardening. *Address:* 7 Hillside Road, Thorpe St Andrew, Norwich NR7 0QG. *T:* (01603) 433508. *Died 15 April 2004.*

GLOVER, Robert Finlay, TD 1954; Headmaster, Monmouth School, 1959–76; *b* 28 June 1917; *yr s* of T. R. Glover, Public Orator in University of Cambridge, and Alice, *d* of H. G. Few; *m* 1941, Jean, *d* of late N. G. Muir, Lincoln; one *s* two *d. Educ:* The Leys Sch.; Corpus Christi Coll., Oxford. Served in Royal Artillery (TA), 1939–46; Staff Coll., Camberley, 1944; Major, 1944. Asst Master, Ampleforth Coll., 1946–50; Head of Classics Dept, King's Sch., Canterbury, 1950–53; Headmaster, Adams' Grammar Sch., Newport, Salop, 1953–59; Dep. Sec., Headmasters' Conference and Assoc., 1977–82. Fellow, Woodard Corp., 1982–87. *Publications:* Notes on Latin, 1954; (with R. W. Harris) Latin for Historians, 1954. *Recreations:* normal. *Address:* Brockhill Lodge, West Malvern Road, The Wyche, Malvern, Worcs WR14 4EJ.

T: (01684) 564247. *Club:* East India, Devonshire, Sports and Public Schools. *Died 2 May 2001.*

GOAVA, Sir Sinaka (Vakai), KBE 1998 (CBE 1984; MBE 1975); Government service, Papua New Guinea and Australia, 1946–84; a part-time consultant to the Motu-Koitabu on Land Group Incorporations, since 1997; *b* 5 July 1927; *s* of James Goava Oa and Mea Tapo Dai; *m* 1949, (Hekure) Naomi Vaieke; two *s* five *d* (and twin *s* decd). *Educ:* LMS Primary Sch., Hanuabada; Administrative Coll., Port Moresby (matric. 1967). Trainee clerk and broadcaster, 1946–48; radio announcer and translator, Depts of Educn, of Dist Services and Native Affairs, and of the Administrator, PNG, 1948–63; Sen. Interpreter, House of Assembly, 1964–65; Sen. Magistrate, Local, Dist and Children's Courts, 1967–75; Sec., Land Courts Secretariat, Dept of Justice, 1976–81; Chairman: Commn of Inquiry into Land Matters, PNG, 1973–74; Commn of Inquiry into suitable form of govt for NCD, 1981; NCD Interim Commn, 1982–83 (Mem., 1982–85); 10th Independence Anniv. Cttee, PNG, 1985. Consultant, Hanuabada Village project, NCD Interim Commn and Motu-Koitabu Interim Assembly, 1986. Mem., Hanuabada Local Govt Council, 1952–54; Vice Pres., Fairfax Local Govt Council, 1954–57. Mem. Bd of Trustees, Peace Foundn Melanesia (formerly Foundn for Law, Order and Justice), 1991–. Life Mem., Public Employees Assoc. (Hon. Mem., Life Mems Gp). Public Service and Community Service Medal, PNG, 1975; Long Service and Good Conduct Medal, PNG, 1983; PNG Independence Medal, 1975, PNG 10th Independence Anniv. Medal, 1985; Silver Jubilee Medal, 1977. *Publications:* A Cross Road to Justice, 2000; judicial and govt reports; contribs to PNG press. *Recreations:* cricket, fishing, singing, dancing, reading, writing, stamp collecting. *Address:* (home) PO Box 689, Port Moresby, National Capital District, Papua New Guinea.
Died 9 May 2003.

GODFREY, Norman Eric; *b* 16 Aug. 1927; *s* of Cecil and Beatrice Godfrey. *Educ:* Northampton Grammar Sch.; London Sch. of Econs (BScEcon). Career mainly in HM Customs but also served in Min. of Transport/DoE, 1968–71, and Price Commn, 1976–79; Comr, HM Customs and Excise, 1979–86. *Recreations:* music, especially opera, composing, theatre, travel. *Address:* 2 Belsize Avenue, NW3 4AU. *T:* (020) 7435 6085; *e-mail:* normanegodfrey@yahoo.co.uk. *Died 6 March 2004.*

GODWIN, Fay S.; photographer; *b* 17 Feb. 1931; *d* of Sidney Simmonds and Stella MacLean; *m* 1961, Anthony Godwin (marr. diss.); two *s*. Writer, lecturer, and tutor of photographic workshops. *Solo exhibitions* include: Land, Serpentine Gall., and UK tour, 1985–87, Yale Center for British Art, USA, and Stanford Mus. of Art, USA; British Council internat. tour, 1984–94; Photographers' Gall., London, 1985; Nat. Mus. of Photography, Bradford, 1986, 1988; Royal Photographic Soc., Bath, 1990; Glassworks & Secret Lives, Mead Gall., Warwick Arts Centre and tour, 1995–97; A Perfect Republic of Shepherds, Wordsworth Trust, 1997; *retrospectives:* Barbican, 2001; Landmarks, Scottish NPG, 2003–04; *work in public and private collections* including: Nat. Mus. of Photography, Bradford; British Council; Nat. Portrait Gall.; British Library; Nat. Portrait Gall., Scotland; V&A Mus.; Stanford Mus. of Art, USA. Joined: Photographers' Gall. (Print Room), 1976; Zelda Cheatle Gall., 1989; Network Photographers, 1991; Collections, 1994; Focus Gall., 2001. Pres., Ramblers' Assoc., 1987–90 (Life Vice Pres., 1990). Fellow, Nat. Mus. of Film, Photography and TV, Bradford, 1986–87. Hon. FRPS 1990; Hon. FRIAS 1992. Hon. DrArts De Montfort, 2002. Arts Council of GB Award, 1978; Award, Erna & Victor Hasselbad Foundn, 1995. *Publications:* (jtly) The Oldest Road, 1975; (jtly) The Oil Rush, 1976; (jtly) The Drovers' Roads of Wales, 1977; (jtly) Islands, 1978; (jtly) Remains of Elmet, 1979; (jtly) Romney Marsh and the Royal Military Canal, 1980; (jtly) Tess: the story of a guide dog, 1981; (jtly) The

Whisky Roads of Scotland, 1982; Bison at Chalk Farm, 1982; (jtly) The Saxon Shore Way from Gravesend to Rye, 1983; (jtly) National Trust Book of Wessex, 1985; Land, 1985; The Secret Forest of Dean, 1986; Our Forbidden Land (Green Book of the Year), 1990; Elmet, 1994; The Edge of the Land, 1995; Glassworks & Secret Lives, 1999; Landmarks, 2001. *Recreations:* walking, reading, painting, looking at art and modern architecture. *Address:* c/o Photographers' Gallery, 5/8 Great Newport Street, WC2H 7HY. *Died 27 May 2005.*

GODWIN, Peter Raymond, CBE 1992; Chairman, Compton Capital Ltd, since 2000; Senior Adviser, Standard Bank London Ltd, since 2000; *b* 16 May 1942; *s* of Percy Raymond Godwin and Ethel Ellen May Godwin (*née* Dowse); *m* 1967, Wendy Dorothy Slater; one *s* one *d*. *Educ:* Harrow Co. Grammar Sch. ACIB 1965. Joined Lazard Brothers & Co. Ltd, 1958: Exec. Dir, 1979–86; Divl Dir, 1986–89; Man. Dir, 1989–97, Standard Chartered Merchant Bank Ltd (later Chartered West LB Ltd, then West Merchant Bank Ltd); Hd of Export Finance, Commerzbank AG, London, 1997–99. Non-executive Director: Korea Merchant Banking Corp., Seoul, 1976–86; Internat. Investment Corp. for Yugoslavia, SA, 1981–86; Standard Chartered Merchant Bank Zimbabwe Ltd, 1986–90; Financial Merchant Bank Nigeria Ltd, 1987–89; Korea-Europe Fund Ltd, 1996–. Chairman: Compton Plough Ltd, 1995–; Global Energy and Environment Ltd, 1999–; Fifth World Productions Ltd, 2000; Director: Swindon Town FC, 1995–; CEENET, 1996–98. Member: BOTB, 1995–99 (Vice-Chm., Markets Gp, 1998–); Singapore British Business Council, 1996–; Korea Trade Adv. Gp, 1974–92; Anglo-Taiwan Trade Cttee, 1975–92 (Pres., 1986–92); Tropical Africa Adv. Gp, 1982–95; Chm., Asia Pacific Adv. Gp, 1992–. Chm., Anglo-Ghanaian Business Assoc., 1991–95. Mem., Academic Council, Wilton Park, 1999–; Gov., Latymer Foundn at Hammersmith, 1986–92. Organist, St Andrew's Church, Roxbourne, Harrow. Mem., Cinema Organ Soc. FRSA 1998; MInstD 1999. *Address:* 16 Newquay Crescent, Harrow, Middx HA2 9LJ. *T:* (020) 8422 1801, *Fax:* (020) 8426 8540; *e-mail:* PRGodwin@aol.com. *Club:* Oriental. *Died 26 April 2001.*

GOLD, Sir Arthur (Abraham), Kt 1984; CBE 1974; Chairman, Commonwealth Games Council for England, 1979–90; Honorary Secretary, British Amateur Athletic Board, 1965–77 (Life Vice President, 1977); Vice President, British Olympic Association, since 1992 (Chairman, 1988–92); *b* 10 Jan. 1917; *s* of late Mark and Leah Gold; *m* 1942, Marion Godfrey (*d* 2002), *d* of late N. Godfrey; one *s*. *Educ:* Grocers' Company's Sch. Inst. of Motor Industry Wakefield Gold Medallist, 1945. Internat. high jumper, 1937; Athletics Team Leader Olympic Games: Mexico, 1968; Munich, 1972; Montreal, 1976; Commandant, English Commonwealth Games Team: Brisbane, 1982; Edinburgh, 1986; Auckland, 1990; Comdt, British Olympic Team, Albertville and Barcelona, 1992. Chm., Drug Abuse Adv. Cttee, Eur. Sports Conf., 1985–91; Vice-Chm., Cttee on Doping in Sport, Council of Europe, 1983–90; Member: Sports Council, 1980–88 (Chm., Drug Abuse Adv. Gp, 1981–92); Exec. Cttee, CCPR, 1982–90. President: Eur. Athletic Assoc., 1976–87 (Hon. Life Pres., 1988; Mem. Council, 1966–76); Counties Athletic Union, 1978–; UAU, 1984–; AAA, 1995–; Past President: London Athletic Club; Middlesex Co. Amateur Athletic Assoc. Hon. FCP 1987. Hon. DTech Loughborough, 1989; Hon. LLD Sheffield, 1991. Olympic Order (Silver), 1991. *Publications:* Ballet Training Exercises for Athletes, 1960; various contribs to technical books on athletics. *Recreations:* walking, talking, reading, weeding. *Address:* 49 Friern Mount Drive, Whetstone, N20 9DJ. *T:* (020) 8445 2848. *Clubs:* City Livery, MCC; London Athletic. *Died 25 May 2002.*

GOLD, Prof. Thomas, FRS 1964; John L. Wetherill Professor of Astronomy, Cornell University, 1971–86, Professor Emeritus of Astronomy, 1987; *b* 22 May 1920; *s*

of Max and Josefine Gold; *m* 1st, 1947, Merle E. Gold (*née* Tuberg); three *d*; 2nd, 1972, Carvel B. Gold (*née* Beyer); one *d*. *Educ:* Zuoz Coll., Switzerland; Trinity Coll., Cambridge (BA Mechanical Sciences, 1942; MA Mechanical Sciences, 1946; ScD, 1969). Fellow, Trinity Coll., Cambridge, 1947–51. British Admiralty, 1942–46; Cavendish Laboratory, Cambridge, 1946–47 and 1949–52; Med. Research Council, Zoological Lab., Cambridge, 1947–49; Sen. Principal Scientific Officer (Chief Asst), Royal Greenwich Observatory, 1952–56; Prof. of Astronomy, 1957–58, Robert Wheeler Willson Prof. of Applied Astronomy, 1958–59, Harvard Univ. Dir, Center for Radio-Physics and Space Research, Cornell Univ., 1959–81. Hon. Fellow, Trinity Coll., Cambridge, 1986. Hon. MA (Harvard), 1957. Member: Amer. Philosophical Soc.; Nat. Acad. of Sciences; Fellow, Amer. Acad. of Arts and Sciences. Gold Medal, RAS, 1985. *Publications:* Power from the Earth, 1987; The Deep Hot Biosphere, 1999; contribs to learned journals in astronomy, physics, biophysics, geophysics. *Recreations:* ski-ing, travelling. *Address:* 63 Waterwagon Road, Ithaca, NY 14850, USA. *Died 22 June 2004.*

GOLDIE, Ven. David; Archdeacon of Buckingham, since 1998; *b* 20 Dec. 1946; *s* of Frederick and Margaret Goldie; *m* 1969, (Emily) Rosemary Robson; three *d*. *Educ:* Glasgow Acad.; Glasgow Univ. (MA); Fitzwilliam Coll., Cambridge (MA); Westcott House, Cambridge. Ordained deacon, 1970, priest, 1971; Curate: Christ Church, Swindon, 1970–73; Troon, 1973–75; Mission Priest, Irvine and Rector, Ardrossan, 1975–82; Milton Keynes: Priest Missioner, 1982–86; Vicar, Christ the Cornerstone, 1986–98; RD, 1986–90; Borough Dean, and Canon of Christ Church, Oxford, 1990–98. Mem., Gen. Synod, C of E, 1990–. *Recreations:* dog-walking, organ playing, exploring France. *Address:* 60 Wendover Road, Aylesbury, Bucks HP21 9LW. *T:* (01296) 423269.

Died 7 April 2002.

GOLDS, Anthony Arthur, CMG 1971; LVO 1961; HM Diplomatic Service, retired; Director, British National Committee, International Chamber of Commerce, 1977–83; *b* 31 Oct. 1919; *s* of late Arthur Oswald Golds and Florence Golds (*née* Massey); *m* 1944, Suzanne Macdonald Young; one *s* one *d*. *Educ:* King's Sch., Macclesfield; New Coll., Oxford (Scholar). HM Forces (Royal Armoured Corps), 1939–46. CRO, 1948; 1st Sec., Calcutta and Delhi, 1951–53; Commonwealth Office, 1953–56; Head of Chancery, British Embassy, Ankara, 1957–59; Karachi, 1959–61; Counsellor, Commonwealth Office and Foreign Office, 1962–65; Head of Joint Malaysia/Indonesia Dept, 1964–65; Counsellor, Rome, 1965–70; Ambassador to the Republics of Cameroon, Gabon and Equatorial Guinea, 1970–72; High Comr to Bangladesh, 1972–74; Senior Civilian Instructor, RCDS, 1975–76. *Recreations:* music, cricket, golf, literature. *Address:* 4 Oakfield Gardens, SE19 1HF. *T:* (020) 8670 7621. *Club:* Dulwich & Sydenham Hill Golf.

Died 6 May 2003.

GOLDSTEIN, Joan Delano, (Mrs Julius Goldstein); see Aiken, J. D.

GOLLIN, Prof. Alfred Manuel, DLitt; FRSL; Professor of History, University of California, Santa Barbara, 1967–94, then Professor Emeritus (Chairman, Department of History, 1976–77); *b* 6 Feb. 1926; 2nd *s* of Max and Sue Gollin; *m* 1st, 1951, Gurli Sørensen (marr. diss.; she *d* 2003); two *d*; 2nd, 1975, Valerie Watkins (*née* Kilner) (*d* 2001). *Educ:* New York City Public Schs; City College of New York; Harvard Univ.; New Coll., Oxford (BA); St Antony's Coll., Oxford (MA); DPhil Oxon 1957; DLitt Oxon 1968. Served US Army, 1943–46; taught history at New Coll., Oxford, 1951–54; official historian for The Observer, 1952–59; Lectr, City Coll. of New York, 1959; Univ. of California, Los Angeles: Acting Asst Prof., 1959–60; Research Associate, 1960–61; Associate Prof., Univ. of California, Santa Barbara, 1966–67. Dir, Study Center of Univ. of California, UK and Ire., 1971–73;

Mem., US-UK Educnl Commn, 1971–72. Fellow: J. S. Guggenheim Foundn, 1962, 1964, 1971; Amer. Council of Learned Socs, 1963, 1975; Nat. Endowment for Humanities, 1989; FRHistS 1976; FRSL 1986. *Publications:* The Observer and J. L. Garvin, 1960; Proconsul in Politics: a study of Lord Milner, 1964; From Omdurman to V. E. Day: the Life Span of Sir Winston Churchill, 1964; Balfour's Burden, 1965; Asquith, a New View, in A Century of Conflict, Essays for A. J. P. Taylor, 1966; Balfour, in The Conservative Leadership (ed D. Southgate), 1974; No Longer an Island, 1984; The Impact of Air Power on the British People and their Government 1909–14, 1989; articles and reviews in various jls. *Recreation:* swimming. *Address:* 3775 Modoc Road, Santa Barbara, CA 93105, USA. *Died 30 Oct. 2005.*

GOMBRICH, Sir Ernst (Hans Josef), OM 1988; Kt 1972; CBE 1966; PhD; FBA 1960; FSA; Director of the Warburg Institute and Professor of the History of the Classical Tradition, University of London, 1959–76, then Emeritus Professor; *b* Vienna, 30 March 1909; *s* of Dr Karl B. Gombrich, Vice-Pres. of Disciplinary Council of Lawyers' Chamber, Vienna, and Prof. Leonie Gombrich (*née* Hock), pianist; *m* 1936, Ilse Heller; one *s*. *Educ:* Theresianum, Vienna; Vienna Univ. (PhD); MA Oxon 1950; MA 1961, LittD 1970, Cantab. FSA 1961; FRSL 1975. Research Asst, Warburg Inst., 1936–39. Served War of 1939–45 with BBC Monitoring Service. Senior Research Fellow, 1946–48, Lectr, 1948–54, Reader, 1954–56, Special Lectr, 1956–59, Warburg Inst., Univ. of London; Durning-Lawrence Prof. of the History of Art, London Univ., at University Coll., 1956–59. Slade Prof. of Fine Art in the University of Oxford, 1950–53; Visiting Prof. of Fine Art, Harvard Univ., 1959; Slade Prof. of Fine Art, Cambridge Univ., 1961–63; Lethaby Prof., RCA, 1967–68; Andrew D. White Prof.-at-Large, Cornell, 1970–77. A Trustee of the British Museum, 1974–79; Mem., Museums and Galleries Commn (formerly Standing Commn on Museums and Galleries), 1976–82. Hon. Fellow: Jesus Coll., Cambridge, 1963; UCL, 1992. Foreign Hon. Mem., American Academy of Arts and Sciences, 1964; For. Mem., Amer. Philosophical Soc., 1968; Hon. Member: American Acad. and Inst. of Arts and Letters, 1985; Akad. der Wissenschaften zu Göttingen, 1986; Modern Lang. Assoc. of America, 1988; Deutsche Akademie für Sprache und Dichtung, 1988; Austrian Acad. of Scis, 1991; Corresponding Member: Accademia delle Scienze di Torino, 1962; Royal Acad. of Arts and Sciences, Uppsala, 1970; Koninklijke Nederlandse Akademie van Wetenschapen, 1973; Bayerische Akad. der Wissenschaften, 1979; European Acad. of Arts, Scis and Humanities, 1980; Royal Swedish Acad. of Sciences, 1981; Accademia Nazionale dei Lincei, 1983; Royal Belgian Acad. of Science, Letters and Fine Arts, 1989. Hon. FRIBA, 1971; Hon. Fellow: Royal Acad. of Arts, 1982; Bezalel Acad. of Arts and Design, 1983; Akademie der bildenden Künste, Vienna, 1989. Hon. DLit: Belfast, 1963; London, 1976; Richmond Coll., London, 1993; Hon. LLD St Andrews, 1965; Hon. LittD: Leeds, 1965; Cambridge, 1970; Manchester, 1974; Hon. DLitt: Oxford, 1969; Harvard, 1976; New York, 1986; Urbino, 1992; Hon. Dr Lit. Hum.: Chicago, 1975; Pennsylvania, 1977; DU Essex, 1977; Hon. DHL: Brandeis, 1981; Emory, 1991; Hon. DPhil Vienna, 1999; Hon. Dr RCA, 1984; Hon. Dr in Geography and History, Universidad Complutense de Madrid, 1992. W. H. Smith Literary Award, 1964; Medal of New York Univ. for Distinguished Visitors, 1970; Erasmus Prize, 1975; Ehrenkreuz für Wissenschaft und Kunst, 1st cl., Austria, 1975; Hegel Prize, 1976; Medal of Collège de France, 1977; Orden Pour le Mérite für Wissenschaften und Künste, 1977; Ehrenzeichen für Wissenschaft und Kunst, Austria 1984; Premio Rosina Viva of Anacapri, 1985; Internat. Balzan Prize, 1985; Kulturpreis der Stadt Wien, 1986; Ludwig Wittgenstein-Preis der Österreichischen Forschungsgemeinschaft, 1988; Britannica Award, Encyclopedia Britannica, 1989; Goethe Medaille, 1989; Austrian Auslands Kulturpreis, 1993; Goethe Prize,

Frankfurt, 1994; Golden Medal, Vienna, 1994; Agnes and Elizabeth Mongan Prize, Villa I Tatti, 1996. Hon. Citizen, City of Mantova, 1998. *Publications:* Weltgeschichte für Kinder, 1936, rev. and enl. edn 1985; (with E. Kris) Caricature, 1940; The Story of Art, 1950, 16th edn 1995; Art and Illusion (The A. W. Mellon Lectures in the Fine Arts, 1956), 1960; Meditations on a Hobby Horse, 1963; Norm and Form, 1966; Aby Warburg, an intellectual biography, 1970; Symbolic Images, 1972; In Search of Cultural History, 1972; (jtly) Art, Perception and Reality, 1973; (ed jtly) Illusion in Nature and Art, 1973; Art History and the Social Sciences (Romanes Lect.), 1975; The Heritage of Apelles, 1976; Means and Ends (W. Neurath Lect.), 1976; The Sense of Order (Wrightsman Lect.), 1979; Ideals and Idols, 1979; The Image and the Eye, 1982; Tributes, 1984; New Light on Old Masters, 1986; Oskar Kokoschka in his Time, 1986; Reflections on the History of Art (ed R. Woodfield), 1987; Topics of Our Time, 1991; Styles of Art and Styles of Life (Reynolds Lect.), 1991; (with D. Eribon) Ce que l'image nous dit: entretiens sur l'art et la science, 1991; Gastspiele: zur Deutschen Sprache und Germanistik, 1992; On Pride and Prejudice in the Arts, 1992; Künstler, Kenner, Kunden (Wiener Vorlesungen im Rathaus), 1993; Das forschende Auge, 1994; Anthony Gormley, 1995; The Essential Gombrich (ed R. Woodfield), 1996; Shadows, 1996; Speis der Malerknaben (Wiener Vorlesungen 2), 1997; The Uses of Images, 1999; contributions to learned journals; *relevant publication:* E. H. Gombrich: a bibliography, ed J. B. Trapp, 2000. *Address:* 19 Briardale Gardens, NW3 7PN. *T:* (020) 7435 6639. *Died 3 Nov. 2001.*

GOOCH, Sir Peter; see Gooch, Sir T. S.

GOOCH, Sir Trevor Sherlock, 5th Bt *cr* 1866, of Clewer Park, Berkshire; *b* 15 June 1915; *s* of Charles Trevor Gooch (*d* 1963; *g s* of Sir Daniel Gooch, 1st Bt), and Hester Stratford (*d* 1957), *d* of late Lt-Col Wright Sherlock; *S* kinsman, 1989; *m* 1st, 1956, Denys Anne (*d* 1976), *o d* of late Harold Victor Venables; one *s* four *d*; 2nd, 1978, Jean, *d* of late Joseph Wright. *Educ:* Charterhouse. Flt Lt, RAFVR, 1939–46. *Heir: s* Miles Peter Gooch [*b* 3 Feb. 1963; *m* 2000, Louise Spiret; one *d*]. *Address:* Jardin de la Rocque, Mont de la Rocque, St Aubin, Jersey, CI. *T:* (01534) 742980. *Club:* Royal Channel Islands Yacht (Jersey). *Died 26 May 2003.*

GOODACRE, Kenneth, TD 1952; DL; Deputy Clerk to GLC, 1964–68; Clerk and Solicitor of Middlesex CC, 1955–65; Clerk of the Peace for Middlesex, 1959–65; *b* 29 Oct. 1910; *s* of Clifford and Florence Goodacre; *m* 1936, Dorothy (*d* 1992), *d* of Harold Kendall, solicitor, Leeds; one *s. Educ:* Doncaster Grammar Sch. Admitted solicitor, 1934; Asst Solicitor: Doncaster Corp., 1934–35; Barrow-in-Furness Corp., 1935–36; Sen. Solicitor, Blackburn Corp., 1936–39; served War of 1939–45, TA with E Lancs Regt and Staff 53 Div. (Major), and 2nd Army (Lieut-Col); released from Army Service, 1945, and granted hon. rank of Major; Deputy Town Clerk: Blackburn, 1945–49; Leicester, 1949–52; Town Clerk, Leicester, 1952–55. Partner, Gillhams, Solicitors, 1968–71; practised under name of K. Goodacre & Co., Solicitors, 1971–89. DL Middx, 1960–65, Greater London, 1965. *Club:* Hurlingham. *Died 10 Dec. 2004.*

GOODALL, His Honour Anthony Charles, MC 1942; DL; a Circuit Judge (formerly a Judge of County Courts), 1968–86; *b* 23 July 1916; *er s* of late Charles Henry and Mary Helen Goodall, The Manor House, Sutton Veny, Wilts; *m* 1947, Anne Valerie, *yr d* of late John Reginald Chichester and of Audrey Geraldine Chichester, Lurley Manor, Tiverton, Devon; one *s* two *d. Educ:* Eton; King's Coll., Cambridge. Called to the Bar, Inner Temple, 1939 (Certif. of Honour). Served War of 1939–45, 1st Royal Dragoons; taken prisoner (twice), 1944. Practised at the Bar, 1946–67. Pres., Plymouth Magistrates' Assoc., 1976–84; Mem., County Court Rule Cttee, 1978–83; Jt Pres., Council of HM Circuit Judges, 1986 (Jt Vice-Pres., 1985). DL Devon, 1987. *Publications:* (ed jtly) Faraday on

Rating; contrib. to Encycl. Court Forms and Precedents. *Address:* Hunts Meadow, Moretonhampstead, Devon TQ13 8PA. *T:* (01647) 440239. *Died 3 Feb. 2001.*

GOODDEN, Robert Yorke, CBE 1956; RDI 1947; architect and designer; Professor, School of Silversmithing and Jewellery, 1948–74, and Pro-Rector, 1967–74, Royal College of Art; *b* 7 May 1909; 2nd *s* of late Lieut-Col R. B. Goodden, OBE and Gwendolen Goodden; *m* 1st, 1936, Kathleen Teresa Burrow; 2nd, 1946, Lesley Macbeth Mitchell; two *s* two *d. Educ:* Harrow Sch. Trained AA Sch. of Architecture, 1926–31; AA Diploma 1932; ARIBA 1933. Served War of 1939–45, RAFVR, 1940–41, RNVR, 1941–45. Private practice as architect and designer, 1932–39; resumed private practice, 1946. Joint architect and designer: Lion and Unicorn Pavilion, South Bank Exhibition, 1951; Western Sculpture Rooms, Print Room Gall. and Gall. of Oriental Art, British Museum, 1969–71; designer of: domestic pressed glassware for Chance Brothers, 1934–48; Asterisk Wallpapers, 1934; sports section, Britain Can Make It Exhbn, 1946; Coronation hangings for Westminster Abbey, 1953; gold and silver plate in collections: Victoria and Albert Museum; Worshipful Co. of Goldsmiths; Royal Society of Arts; Downing Coll. and Sidney Sussex Coll., Cambridge; Royal Coll. of Art; glass for King's Coll., Cambridge, Grosvenor House, Min. of Works, and others; metal foil mural decorations in SS Canberra, 1961. Consulting Architect to Board of Trade for BIF, Olympia, 1947, Earls Ct, 1949, Olympia, 1950 and 1951. Member: Council of Industrial Design, 1955; National Council for Diplomas in Art and Design, 1961; Adv. Council, V&A Museum, 1977; Chm., Crafts Council, 1977–82. Mem. Council, Essex Univ., 1973. FSIA, 1947; Hon. Fellow, Sheffield Polytechnic, 1971. Hon. DesRCA, 1952; Hon. Dr RCA, 1974; Sen. Fellow, RCA, 1981. Master of Faculty, RDI, 1959–61. Liveryman, Worshipful Co. of Goldsmiths; Prime Warden 1976. SIAD Design Medal, 1972. *Publication:* (with P. Popham) Silversmithing, 1972. *Recreation:* daydreaming. *Address:* 16 Hatfield Buildings, Widcombe Hill, Bath, Somerset BA2 6AF.
Died 24 March 2002.

GOODING, Air Vice-Marshal Keith Horace, CB 1966; OBE 1951; *b* 2 Sept. 1913; *s* of late Horace Milford Gooding, Romsey, Hants; *m* 1st, 1943, Peggy Eileen (*d* 1962), *d* of late Albert William Gatfield, Guildford, Surrey; one *s*; 2nd, 1968, Jean, *d* of late Maurice Stanley Underwood, Andover, Hants; two *s* one *d* (incl. twin *s* and *d*). *Educ:* King Edward VI Sch., Southampton. Joined RAF, 1938; served Aden, Fighter Comd, 1939–45; Germany, 1945–47; NATO, 1953–55; Bomber Comd, 1958–61; AOA Maintenance Comd, 1965–68; Dir-Gen. of Supply (RAF), 1968–71, retired. *Recreations:* tennis, bridge. *Club:* Royal Air Force. *Died 4 March 2001.*

GOODPASTER, Gen. Andrew Jackson; United States Army, retired; US Medal of Freedom, 1984; DSC (US); DSM (Def.) (Oak Leaf Cluster); DSM (Army) (3 Oak Leaf Clusters); DSM (Navy); DSM (Air Force); Silver Star; Legion of Merit (Oak Leaf Cluster); Purple Heart (Oak Leaf Cluster); Superintendent, United States Military Academy, West Point, New York (in grade of Lt-Gen.), 1977–81; *b* 12 Feb. 1915; *s* of Andrew Jackson Goodpaster and Teresa Mary Goodpaster (*née* Mrovka); *m* 1939, Dorothy Anderson Goodpaster (*née* Anderson); two *d. Educ:* McKendree Coll., Lebanon, Ill; US Mil. Academy, 1935–39 (BS); Princeton Univ., 1947–50 (MSE, MA, PhD). 11th Eng. Panama, 1939–42; Ex O, 390th Eng. Gen. Svc Regt, Camp Claiborne, La, 1942–43; Comd and Gen. Staff Sch., Ft Leavenworth, Kansas, Feb.-April 1943; CO, 48th Eng. Combat Bn, II Corps, Fifth Army, 1943–44; Ops Div., Gen. Staff, War Dept (incl. It War Plans Cttee, JCS, 1945–46), 1944–47; Student, Civil Eng. Course and Polit. Sci. Grad. Sch., Princeton Univ., 1947–50; Army Mem., Jt Advanced Study Cttee, JCS, 1950–51; Special Asst to Chief of Staff, SHAPE, 1951–54; Dist Eng., San Francisco Dist, Calif, July-Oct. 1954; Def.

Liaison Officer and Staff Sec. to President of US, 1954–61; Asst Div. Comdr, 3rd Inf. Div., April–Oct. 1961, and CG, 8th Inf. Div., 1961–62, USAREUR; Sp. Asst (Policy) to Chm., JCS, Washington, DC, 1962–64; Asst to Chm., JCS, Washington, DC, 1964–66; Dir Joint Staff, JCS, Washington, DC, 1966–67; Dir of Sp. Studies, Office Chief of Staff, USA, Washington, DC, April–July 1967; Senior US Army Mem., Mil. Staff UN, 1967–68; Comdt. Nat. War Coll., Washington, DC, 1967–68; Mem., US Delegn for Negotiations with N Vietnam, Paris (additl duty), April–July 1968; Dep. Comdr, US Mil. Assistance Comd, Vietnam, 1968–69; Supreme Allied Commander Europe, 1969–74; C-in-C, US European Command, 1969–74. Sen. Fellow, Woodrow Wilson Internat. Center for Scholars, Washington, DC, 1975–76; Prof. of Govt and Internat. Studies, The Citadel, Charleston, SC, 1976–77; Sen. Fellow, Eisenhower World Affairs Inst., 1998–. Pres., Inst. for Defence Analyses, Alexandria, Va, 1983–85; Chairman: American Battle Monuments Commn, 1985–90; Atlantic Council of the US, 1985–97; George C. Marshall Foundn, 1993–2000. *Publication:* For the Common Defense, 1977. *Recreations:* golf, fishing, music. *Address:* Apt 345, 6200 Oregon Avenue NW, Washington, DC 20015, USA. *Died 16 May 2005.*

GOODRICH, David, CEng, RCNC; FRINA; Chairman, British Maritime Technology Ltd, since 1997 (Chief Executive, 1986–2002; Deputy Chairman, 1995–97); *b* 15 April 1941; *s* of William B. Goodrich and Florence B. Goodrich; *m* 1965, Margaret R. Riley; one *s* three *d*. *Educ:* MBA. Shipbuilding management apprentice, 1958–63; shipbuilding designer/estimator, 1963–65; Constructor, RCNC, 1965–77; Manager, Shipbuilding Technology, 1977–79, Man. Dir, 1979–85, BSRA. Chm., Soc. of Maritime Industries, 2002–; Bd Mem., AIRTO. Pres., RINA, 1999–2002. *Publication:* paper to Royal Soc. *Recreations:* squash, walking, family. *Address:* British Maritime Technology Ltd, Orlando House, 1 Waldegrave Road, Teddington, Middx TW11 8LZ.
Died 30 Oct. 2005.

GOODRICH, Rt Rev. Philip Harold Ernest; Bishop of Worcester, 1982–96; *b* 2 Nov. 1929; *s* of late Rev. Canon Harold Spencer Goodrich and Gertrude Alice Goodrich; *m* 1960, Margaret Metcalfe Bennett; four *d*. *Educ:* Stamford Sch.; St John's Coll., Cambridge (MA); Cuddesdon Theological Coll. Deacon 1954, priest 1955; Curate, Rugby Parish Church, 1954–57; Chaplain, St John's Coll., Cambridge, 1957–61; Rector of the South Ormsby Group of Parishes, 1961–68; Vicar of Bromley, 1968–73; Diocesan Director of Ordinands, Rochester, 1974–82; Bishop Suffragan of Tonbridge, 1974–82. *Recreations:* gardening, music, walking, looking at buildings. *Address:* Ordis Farm, Sutton St Nicholas, Hereford HR1 3AY. *T:* (01432) 880603.
Died 22 Jan. 2001.

GOODWIN, Dr Eric Thomson, CBE 1975; *b* 30 July 1913; *s* of John Edward Goodwin and Florence Goodwin; *m* 1st, 1940, Isobel Philip (*d* 1976); two *s*; 2nd, 1977, Avis Mary (*née* Thomson) (*d* 2002). *Educ:* King Edward VI Sch., Stafford; Harrow County Sch.; Peterhouse, Cambridge (BA 1934, Rayleigh Prize 1936, MA 1937, PhD 1938). Asst Lectr, Sheffield Univ., 1937–39; war service: Mathematical Lab., Cambridge, 1939–43; Admty Signal Estabt, Witley, 1943–44; Admty Computing Service, Bath, 1945; Maths Div., Nat. Physical Lab., 1945–71 (Supt 1951–71); Dep. Dir, Nat. Phys. Lab., 1971–74, retd. *Publications:* papers in learned jls on theoretical physics and numerical analysis. *Recreations:* music, reading, the countryside, philately. *Address:* 20 Consort Court, 5 York Road, Woking GU22 7XP. *T:* (01483) 729006.
Died 18 Dec. 2003.

GOODWIN, Prof. John Forrest, MD, FRCP; Professor of Clinical Cardiology, Royal Postgraduate Medical School, London, 1963–84, then Emeritus; Consulting Physician, Hammersmith Hospital, since 1949; Hon. Consulting Cardiologist, St George's Hospital, since 1986;

Emeritus Consultant Cardiologist, Cromwell Hospital, since 1996; *b* 1 Dec. 1918; *s* of late Col William Richard Power Goodwin, DSO, RAMC, and Myrtle Dale Goodwin (*née* Forrest); *m* 1943, Barbara Cameron Robertson; one *s* one *d*. *Educ:* Cheltenham Coll.; St Mary's Hosp. Medical Sch. (Univ. of London); MD London, 1946. FRCP 1957. Med. Registrar, St Mary's Hosp., 1943–44; Physician, Anglo-Iranian Oil Co., Abadan, 1944–45; Med. 1st Asst, Royal Infirmary, Sheffield, 1946–49; Lectr in Medicine and Cons. Physician, Postgraduate Med. Sch., London, 1949–59, Sen. Lecturer, 1959–63. Visiting Professor: Univ. of California at Los Angeles, 1966; Georgetown Univ. Sch. of Med., Washington, 1973; Mayo Clinic, 1985; Pfizer Vis. Prof., Massachusetts Gen. Hosp., 1987; Lectures: Watson Smith, RCP, 1967; St Cyres, Nat. Heart Hosp., 1970; Lumleian, RCP, 1980. Mem., Expert Cttee on Cardiovascular Diseases, WHO, 1979. FRSocMed 1943. Member: Brit. Cardiac Soc., 1950 (Pres., 1972–76); Med. Res. Soc., 1952; Assoc. of Physicians of Great Britain and Ireland, 1953; Council, Brit. Heart Foundation, 1964; Past Pres., Internat. Soc. and Fedn of Cardiology (Pres., 1977–81); Pres., Hypertrophic Cardiomyopathy Assoc., 1991–; 2nd Vice-Pres., RCP, 1979–80; Vice Pres., Coronary Prevention Gp, 1988– (Chm., 1985–88); Chm., Nat. Forum for the Prevention of Coronary Heart Disease, 1987–93. Member: Società Italiana di Cardiologia, 1964; Assoc. of European Pædiatric Cardiologists, 1967; Cardiac Soc. of Australia and NZ, 1974; Venezuelan Soc. of Cardiology, 1969; Burma Medical Assoc., 1987; Academy of Experts, 1996; Hon. Member: Swiss Cardiol. Soc.; Cardiac Soc., Ecuador; Hellenic Cardiac Soc., 1974; Cardiac Soc. of Mexico, 1977; Fellow: Amer. Coll. of Cardiology, 1967; Council on Clinical Cardiology, Amer. Heart Assoc., 1970; European Soc. of Cardiology, 1988; Hon. FACP 1985. Dr *hc* Lisbon, 1985. Gifted Teacher Award, Amer. Coll. of Cardiol., 1984. SPk 1968. Commander, Order of the Falcon (Iceland), 1972. *Publications:* (ed with R. Daley and R. E. Steiner) Clinical Disorders of the Pulmonary Circulation, 1960; (with W. Cleland, L. McDonald, D. Ross) Medical and Surgical Cardiology, 1969; (ed) Heart Muscle Disease, 1985; (ed with G. Baroldi and F. Camerini) Advances in Cardiomyopathies, 1990; (ed with E. Olsen) Cardiomyopathies—Realisation and Expectation, 1993; (ed with P. Yu) Progress in Cardiology, annually 1973–88; papers on diagnosis and treatment of congenital and acquired heart disease in British and foreign cardiac and other journals. *Recreations:* writing novels, photography, history, travel, watching Formula 1 motor racing. *T:* (020) 8977 5311. *Clubs:* Athenæum, Royal Society of Medicine.
Died 7 June 2001.

GOODWIN, Peter Austin, CBE 1986; Secretary, Public Works Loan Commission, 1979–87; Comptroller General, National Debt Office, 1980–87; Director, National Investment and Loans Office, 1980–87; *b* 12 Feb. 1929; *s* of late Stanley Goodwin and Louise Goodwin; *m* 1950, Audrey Vera Webb; one *d*. *Educ:* Harrow County Sch. Served RAF, 1947–49. Exec. Officer, Public Works Loan Commn, 1950; Principal, Civil Aviation Authority, 1973–76; Asst Secretary and Establishment Officer, Public Works Loan Commn, 1976–79. UK Mem., Gp of Experts advising on mgt of Pension Reserve Fund, Europ. Patent Office, 1986–87. *Recreations:* theatre, opera, ballet, country dancing, model railways. *Address:* 87 Woodmansterne Road, Carshalton Beeches, Surrey SM5 4JW. *T:* (020) 8643 3530. *Died 22 May 2002.*

GOONERATNE, Tilak Eranga; Ambassador of Sri Lanka to the Commission of the European Communities, and concurrently to Belgium, 1975–78; *b* 27 March 1919; *m* 1st, 1948, Pamela J. Rodrigo (*d* 1978); two *d*; 2nd, 1986, Ina Heyn. *Educ:* London Univ. (BA); Ceylon Law Coll. Advocate, Supreme Ct of Ceylon. Joined Ceylon Civil Service, 1943; Asst Sec., Min. of External Affairs, 1947–51; Govt Agent: Trincomalee, 1951–54; Matara, 1954–56; Registrar Gen., Marriages, Births and Deaths,

1956–58; Dir-Gen. of Broadcasting and Dir of Information, Ceylon, 1958–60; Comr, Co-operative Develt, 1960–63; Dir of Economic Affairs, 1963; Dep. Sec. to Treasury, 1963–65; Pres., Colombo Plan Council for Technical Co-operation in S and SE Asia, 1964–65; Ceylon deleg. to UN Gen. Assembly, 1964–65; Dep. Sec.-Gen., Commonwealth Secretariat, London, 1965–70; High Comr in UK, 1970–75. Commonwealth Fund for Technical Co-operation: Chm., Bd of Representatives, 1975–76; Chm., Review Gp of Experts. *Publications:* An Historical Outline of the Development of the Marriage and Divorce Laws of Ceylon; An Historical Outline of the Development of the Marriage and Divorce Laws Applicable to Muslims in Ceylon; Fifty Years of Co-operative Development in Ceylon; Mrs Sirima R. D. Bandaranaike, first woman Prime Minister in the world: as I knew her. *Address:* 51 Lapworth Court, Blomfield Villas, W2 6NN. *T:* (020) 7286 4675.   *Died 4 Feb. 2003.*

GOPAL, Dr Sarvepalli; Professor of Contemporary History, Jawaharlal Nehru University, New Delhi, 1972–83, then Emeritus; Fellow of St Antony's College, Oxford, 1966–95, Hon. Fellow, 1995; *b* 23 April 1923; *y c* and *o s* of Sir Sarvepalli Radhakrishnan, Hon. OM, Hon. FBA. *Educ:* Mill Hill School; Madras Univ. (MA, BL); Balliol Coll., Oxford (MA, DPhil, DLitt). Lecturer and Reader in History, Andhra Univ., Waltair, 1948–52; Asst Dir, Nat. Archives of India, 1952–54; Dir, Historical Div., Min. of Extl Affairs, New Delhi, 1954–66; Commonwealth Fellow, Trin. Coll., Cambridge, 1963–64; Reader in S Asian History, Oxford Univ., 1966–71. Vis. Prof., Leeds, 1977; Guest Scholar, Woodrow Wilson Center, Washington, 1992; Vis. Fellow, All Souls Coll., Oxford, 1992. Chairman: Nat. Book Trust, India, 1973–76; Indian Inst. of Advanced Study, 1992–; Madras Inst. of Develt Studies, 1995–97; Indian Inst. of Social Studies, 1995–98; Member: Indian UGC, 1973–79; UNESCO Exec. Bd, 1976–80. Pres., Indian History Congress, 1978. Corresp. FRHistS. Hon. Professor: Tirupati, 1971; Hyderabad, 1990. Hon. DLitt: Andhra, 1975; Tirupati, 1979; Banaras, 1984; Hyderabad, 1993. Sahitya Akademi award, 1976. *Publications:* The Permanent Settlement in Bengal, 1949; The Viceroyalty of Lord Ripon, 1953; The Viceroyalty of Lord Irwin, 1957; British Policy in India, 1965; Modern India, 1967; Jawaharlal Nehru, vol. 1, 1975, vol. 2, 1979, vol. 3, 1984; Radhakrishnan, 1989; general editor, Selected Works of Jawaharlal Nehru; contrib. articles to historical jls. *Recreations:* good food and travel. *Address:* 97 Radhakrishna Salai, Mylapore, Madras 4, India. *Club:* Oxford and Cambridge.   *Died 20 April 2002.*

GORDON, Prof. Cyrus H(erzl); Director, Center for Ebla Research, New York University, since 1982 (Gottesman Professor of Hebrew, 1973–89, then Emeritus Professor of Hebrew and other Near East Languages and Literatures); *b* 29 June 1908; *s* of Dr Benjamin Lee Gordon and Dorothy Cohen Gordon; *m* 1st, 1946, Joan Elizabeth Kendall (*d* 1985); two *s* three *d*; 2nd, 1986, Constance Victoria Wallace. *Educ:* Univ. of Pennsylvania (AB, MA, PhD). Harrison Schol., Univ. of Pennsylvania 1928–29, and Harrison Fellow, 1929–30. US Army Officer on active duty, 1942–46 (Col, US Air Force Reserve, retired). Instructor of Hebrew and Assyrian, University of Penn, 1930–31; Fellow and Epigrapher, American Schs of Oriental Research in Jerusalem and Baghdad, 1931–35; Teaching Fellow, Oriental Seminary, Johns Hopkins Univ., 1935–38; Lecturer in Hebrew and Ancient History, Smith Coll., 1938–39 and 1940–41; Mem., Institute for Advanced Study, Princeton, NJ, 1939–40 and 1941–42; Professor of Assyriology and Egyptology, Dropsie Coll., 1946–56; Joseph Foster Prof. of Near Eastern Studies, and Chm., Dept of Mediterranean Studies, Brandeis Univ., 1956–73, then Emeritus (Dean of Graduate Sch. and Associate Dean of Faculty, 1957–58). Fellow, Amer. Council of Learned Socs, 1932–33; Mem. Managing Cttee, Amer. Sch. of Classical Studies, Athens, 1958–73. Vis. Fellow in Humanities, Univ. of Colorado, 1967;

Visitor's Fellowship, Japan Foundn, 1974; Visiting Professor: New York Univ., 1970–73; in History and Archaeology, Univ. of New Mexico at Las Cruces, 1976; in Asian Studies, Dartmouth Coll., 1990; Distinguished Visiting Professor: in Humanities, SW Missouri State Univ., 1977–79; in Archaeology, New Mexico State Univ., 1979; in Maritime Civilizations, Haifa Univ., 1993. Lectures: Gay, Simmons Coll., 1970; Dal Grauer Meml, Univ. of British Columbia, 1988; University, Cornell Univ., 1992. Fellow: Amer.–Scandinavian Foundn, 1939; Amer. Acad. of Arts and Sciences, 1968–; Explorers Club, 1968–; Amer. Acad. of Jewish Res., 1981–; Japan Soc. for Promotion of Science, 1989; Hon. Fellow, Royal Asiatic Soc., 1975–. Member: Amer. Oriental Soc.; Soc. of Biblical Literature; Archæological Inst. of America; Amer. Historical Assoc.; Amer. Philological Assoc.; Amer. Assoc. of Univ. Professors. Corresp. Mem., Inst. for Antiquity and Christianity, Claremont Graduate Sch. and University Center, 1967–. Trustee: Boston Hebrew Coll., 1965–; Internat. Council for Etruscan Studies, Jerusalem, 1970–; Fenster Gallery of Jewish Art, Tulsa, Oklahoma, 1977–. Hon. Dr of Hebrew Letters, Baltimore Hebrew Coll., 1981; Hon. DHL Hebrew Union Coll., 1985; Hon. DLitt Boston Hebrew Coll., 1995; Hon. Dr of Hebrew Laws, Gratz Coll., 1996. Alumni Award, Gratz Coll., 1961; Directory of Educational Specialists Award, 1970; elected to Soc. of Scholars, Johns Hopkins Univ., 1990. *Publications:* Nouns in the Nuzi Tablets, 1936; Lands of the Cross and Crescent, 1948; Ugaritic Literature, 1949; Smith College Tablets, 1952; Ugaritic Manual, 1955; Adventures in the Nearest East, 1957; Hammurapi's Code, 1957; World of the Old Testament, 1958, rev. edn, The Ancient Near East, 1965; Before the Bible, 1962, rev. edn, The Common Background of Greek and Hebrew Civilizations, 1965; Ugaritic Textbook, 1965, 2nd edn 1998; Ugarit and Minoan Crete, 1966; Evidence for the Minoan Language, 1966; Forgotten Scripts: how they were deciphered and their impact on contemporary culture, 1968, rev. edn, Forgotten Scripts: their ongoing discovery and decipherment, 1982; Poetic Legends and Myths from Ugarit, 1977; The Pennsylvania Tradition of Semitics, 1986; (ed and contrib.) Publications of the Center for Ebla Research, vol. I, Eblaitica: essays on the Ebla archives and Eblaite Language, 1987, vol. II, 1990, vol. III, 1992, vol. IV, 2000; The Background to Jewish Studies in the Bible and in the Ancient East, 1994; A Scholar's Odyssey (autobiog.), 2000 (First Prize, Nat. Jewish Book Council, 2001); some works translated other languages; numerous articles in learned jls dealing with Near East, Mediterranean, OT and Egypto-Semitic philology; *relevant publications:* Orient and Occident: essays presented to Cyrus H. Gordon on the occasion of his Sixty-Fifth Birthday, 1973; The Bible World: essays in honor of Cyrus H. Gordon, 1980; A Synthesis of Cultures: essays on Cyrus H. Gordon's major contributions to Near East cultures, 1996; Boundaries of the Ancient Near Eastern World: a tribute to Cyrus H. Gordon, 1998. *Address:* (office) Department of Classical Studies, Brandeis University, Rabb 141, Waltham, MA 02254-9110, USA. *T:* (617) 7362180; (home) 130 Dean Road, Brookline, MA 02445, USA. *T:* (617) 7343046.

Died 30 March 2001.

GORDON, Giles Alexander Esmé; Literary Agent, Curtis Brown, since 1995; *b* 23 May 1940; *s* of late Alexander Esmé Gordon, RSA, FRIBA, FRIAS and Betsy Gordon (*née* McCurry); *m* 1st, 1964, Margaret Anna Eastoe (*d* 1989); one *s* one *d* (and one *s* decd); 2nd, 1990, Margaret Anne McKernan; one *s* two *d*. *Educ:* Edinburgh Academy; (briefly) Edinburgh College of Art. FRSL 1990. Trainee publisher, Oliver & Boyd, Edinburgh, 1959–63; advertising manager, Secker & Warburg, 1963–64; editor, Hutchinson, 1964–66; plays editor, Penguin Books, 1966–67; editl dir, Victor Gollancz, 1967–73; Literary Agent, Anthony Sheil Associates, later Sheil Land Associates, 1973–95. C. Day Lewis Fellow in Writing, KCL, 1974–75. Sec. and Chm., Soc. of Young Publishers; Member: Literature Panel, Arts Council, 1968–72; Cttee

of Management, Soc. of Authors; Cttee, Assoc. of Authors' Agents; Council, RSL, 1992–94; Cttee, Authors' Club, 1992–; Cttee, Soc. of Authors in Scotland, 1996–99. Lectr, Tufts Univ. in London, 1970–74; Lectr, Hollins Coll. in London, 1983–86. Theatre critic: Spectator; London Daily News; Drama; books columnist, The Times, 1993–95; columnist, Edinburgh Evening News, 1999–2001; restaurant critic, Caledonia, 1999–2001; Editor, Drama, 1984–86. Series Editor: Bloomsbury Classics short stories, 1995–99; Clarion Tales, 1996–99. *Publications:* Pictures from an Exhibition, 1970; The Umbrella Man, 1971; About a Marriage, 1972; Girl with Red Hair, 1974; (ed with A. Hamilton) Factions, 1974; (with Margaret Gordon) Walter and the Balloon (for children), 1974; (ed) Beyond the Words, 1975; Farewell, Fond Dreams, 1975; (ed) Prevailing Spirits, 1976; 100 Scenes from Married Life, 1976; (ed with Dulan Barber) Members of the Jury, 1976; (ed jtly) You Always Remember the First Time, 1976; (ed) A Book of Contemporary Nightmares, 1977; Enemies, 1977; The Illusionist, 1978; (ed with Fred Urquhart) Modern Scottish Short Stories, 1978; Ambrose's Vision, 1980; (ed) Shakespeare Stories, 1982; (ed) English Short Stories 1940–1980, 1982; (ed with David Hughes) Best Short Stories (annually), 1986–95; (ed) English Short Stories: 1900 to the present, 1988; (ed) The Twentieth Century Short Story in English: a bibliography, 1989; Aren't We Due a Royalty Statement?, 1993; (ed with David Hughes) The Best of Best Short Stories, 1986–1995, 1995; Scotland from the Air, 1996. *Recreations:* theatre, opera, walking, travelling, eating, drinking, book collecting. *Address:* Curtis Brown, 37 Queensferry Street, Edinburgh EH2 4QS. *Clubs:* Garrick, PEN, Useless Information Society.
Died 14 Nov. 2003.

GORDON, Prof. Ian Alistair, CBE 1971; PhD; Professor of English Language and Literature, University of Wellington, NZ, 1936–74, then Emeritus; *b* Edinburgh, 30 July 1908; *e s* of Alexander and Ann Gordon; *m* 1936, Mary Ann McLean Fullarton (decd), Ayr; one *s* three *d*. *Educ:* Royal High Sch., Edinburgh; University of Edinburgh (Bruce of Grangehill Bursar, Sloan Prizeman, Gray Prizeman, Scott Travelling Scholar (Italy), Dickson Travelling Scholar (Germany), Elliot Prizeman in English Literature, Pitt Scholar in Classical and English Literature; MA (Hons Classics) 1930, (Hons English) 1932; PhD 1936). Asst Lectr in English language and lit., Edinburgh Univ., 1932; Sub-Ed., Scot. Nat. Dictionary, 1930–36; Dean: Faculty of Arts, Victoria Univ. Coll., Wellington, 1944–47, 1952, 1957–61; Faculty of Languages, 1965–68; Vice-Chancellor, Univ. of New Zealand, 1947–52; Chm., Academic Bd, 1954–61. Visiting Professor: KCL 1954; Univ. of Edinburgh, 1962; Univ. of South Pacific, Fiji, 1972; France and Belgium, 1976; Univ. of Waikato, 1980; Res. Associate, UCL, 1969; Res. Fellow, Auckland Univ., 1993; Vis. Fellow, Edinburgh Univ., 1974–75; Vis. Fellow in Commonwealth Literature, Univ. of Leeds, 1975. Columnist, NZ Listener, 1977–88. Member: Copyright Cttee and Tribunal, 1958; UGC, 1960–70; Chairman: English Language Institute, 1961–72; NZ Literary Fund, 1951–73; Exec. Council, Assoc. of Univs of Br. Commonwealth, 1949–50. NZ representative at international conferences: Utrecht, 1948; Bangkok, 1960; Kampala, 1961; Karachi, 1961. Army Educn Service, 2 NZEF, Hon. Major. Hon. LLD Bristol, 1948; Hon. DLitt NZ, 1961; DUniv Stirling, 1975. Massey Univ. Medal, 1995. *Publications:* John Skelton, Poet Laureate, 1943; New Zealand New Writing, 1943–45; The Teaching of English, a study in secondary education, 1947; English Prose Technique, 1948; Shenstone's Miscellany 1759–1763, 1952; Katherine Mansfield, 1954; The Movement of English Prose, 1966; John Galt (biog.), 1972; Word (festschrift), 1974; Undiscovered Country, 1974; Katherine Mansfield's Urewera Notebook, 1979; Word Finder, 1979; A Word in Your Ear, 1980; (ed) Collins Concise English Dictionary, NZ edn, 1982; (ed) Collins Compact New Zealand Dictionary, 1985; Take My Word For It, 1997; Victorian Voyage, 2000; edited the

following works of John Galt: The Entail, 1970; The Provost, 1973; The Member, 1975; The Last of the Lairds, 1976; Short Stories, 1978; part-author: Edinburgh Essays in Scottish Literature, 1933; Essays in Literature, 1934; The University and the Community, 1946; John Galt (bicent. vol.), 1980; Lexicographical and Linguistic Studies, 1988; The Fine Instrument, 1989; articles in research journals and other periodicals. *Address:* Sarah Selwyn House, Selwyn Village, Point Chevalier, Auckland, New Zealand. *T:* (9) 8494325. *Club:* Aorangi Ski, New Zealand (former Pres.).
Died 26 Sept. 2004.

GORDON, Sir Keith (Lyndell), Kt 1979; CMG 1971; Chairman, Public Service Board of Appeal, St Lucia, 1978–88; Justice of Appeal, West Indies Associated States Supreme Court, 1967–72; *b* 8 April 1906; 3rd *s* of late George S. E. Gordon, journalist, and Nancy Gordon; *m* 1947, Ethel King; one *d*. *Educ:* St Mary's Coll., St Lucia, WI. Called to the Bar, Middle Temple, 1935. Magistrate, Grenada, 1938; Crown Attorney, Dominica, 1942; Trinidad and Tobago: Magistrate, 1943–46 and 1949–53; Exec. Officer, Black Market Board, 1946–48; Puisne Judge, Windward Islands and Leeward Islands, 1954–59; Puisne Judge, British Guiana, 1959–62; Chief Justice, West Cameroon, 1963–67. *Recreation:* gardening. *Address:* PO Box 505, Vigie, Castries, St Lucia.
Died 29 March 2003.

GORDON, Patrick W.; *see* Wolrige-Gordon.
Died 22 May 2002.

GORDON-CUMMING, Alexander Roualeyn, CMG 1978; CVO 1969; Director, Invest in Britain Bureau, Department of Industry, 1979–84; *b* 10 Sept. 1924; *s* of late Lt-Comdr R. G. Gordon-Cumming and Mrs M. V. K. Wilkinson; *m* 1st, 1965, Beryl Joyce Macnaughton Dunn (*d* 1973); one *d*; 2nd, 1974, Elizabeth Patricia Blackley (*d* 1983); one *d*; 3rd, 1999, Rosalind Diana Lynch Jones. *Educ:* Eton Coll. RAF, 1943; retd with rank of Gp Captain, 1969. Board of Trade, 1969; Dept of Trade and Industry, 1973; seconded HM Diplomatic Service, 1974–78. *Recreations:* gardening, ski-ing, fell walking, ballet. *Address:* Woodstock, West Way, West Broyle, Chichester, Sussex PO19 3PW. *T:* (01243) 776413. *Club:* Royal Air Force. *Died 24 Oct. 2004.*

GORDON CUMMING, Sir William Gordon, 6th Bt *cr* 1804; Royal Scots Greys; *b* 19 June 1928; *s* of Major Sir Alexander Penrose Gordon Cumming, 5th Bt, MC, and of Elizabeth Topham, *d* of J. Topham Richardson, Harps Oak, Merstham; *S* father, 1939; *m* 1953, Elisabeth (marr. diss. 1972), *d* of Maj.-Gen. Sir Robert Hinde, KBE, CB, DSO; one *s* three *d*; *m* 1989, Sheila Bates. *Educ:* Eton; RMC, Sandhurst. Late Royal Scots Greys; retired 1952. *Heir: s* Alexander Penrose Gordon Cumming [*b* 15 April 1954; *m* 1991, Louisa, *e d* of E. G. Clifton-Brown; two *s* one *d*]. *Address:* Altyre, Forres, Morayshire.
Died 10 Jan. 2002.

GORDON-FINLAYSON, Maj.-Gen. Robert, OBE 1957 (MBE 1945); DL; *b* 28 Oct. 1916; *yr s* of late Gen. Sir Robert Gordon-Finlayson, KCB, CMG, DSO, DL and Mary Leslie, *d* of James Richmond, Kincairney, Perthshire; *m* 1945, Alexandra, *d* of late John Bartholomew, Rowde Court, Rowde, Wilts; two *s*. *Educ:* Winchester Coll.; RMA, Woolwich. 2 Lieut RA, 1936; Major, BEF, 1940; Staff Coll., 1941; Middle East, 1942–43; NW Europe, 1944–45; India and Burma, 1945–47; GSO 1 1945; RHA, 1952–53; JSSC, 1953; Bt Lt-Col, 1955; AA&QMG, 3 Inf. Div., 1955–57; Near East (Suez Ops), 1956; Middle East, 1958; Lt-Col 1958; Comdr, 26 Field Regt RA, 1958–59; Col 1959; GSO 1, Staff Coll., 1960–62; Brig. CRA, 49 Div. TA, 1962–64; Brig. DQMG, HQ, BAOR, 1964–66; GOC 49 Inf. Div., TA/N Midland Dist, 1966–67; GOC E Midland District, 1967–70; retd, 1970. Hon. Col, 3rd (Volunteer) Bn The Worcestershire and Sherwood Foresters Regt, TAVR, 1971–78; Chm., Notts Co. Army Benevolent Fund,

1970–85; Mem., Notts Co. and E Midlands TAVR Assocs, 1971–85. Branch Patron, Notts Co. Dunkirk Veterans Assoc., 1990–; Pres., Notts Co. Royal British Legion, 1971–79; Vice-President: Notts Co. SSAFA, 1970–99; Notts Co. PDSA, 1970–87; Central Notts Scout Assoc., 1971–80. JP 1972–86. High Sheriff 1974, DL 1974, Notts. *Recreations:* shooting, fishing, ski-ing, gardening, walking. *Address:* 4 The Mews, Sutton Manor, Sutton Scotney, Winchester, Hants SO21 3JX. *T:* (01962) 760270; c/o Lloyds TSB, Cox's & King's Branch, 7 Pall Mall, SW1Y 5NA.   *Died 19 June 2001.*

GORDON LENNOX, Lord Nicholas Charles, KCMG 1986 (CMG 1978); KCVO 1989 (LVO 1957); HM Diplomatic Service, retired; a Governor, BBC, 1990–98; director of companies, since 1990; *b* 31 Jan. 1931; *yr s* of 9th Duke of Richmond and Gordon and of Elizabeth Grace, *y d* of late Rev. T. W. Hudson; *m* 1958, Mary (LVO 2001), *d* of late Brig. H. N. H. Williamson, DSO, MC; one *s* three *d*. *Educ:* Eton; Worcester Coll., Oxford (Scholar). 2nd Lieut KRRC, 1950–51. Entered HM Foreign Service, 1954; FO, 1954–57; Private Sec. to HM Ambassador to USA, 1957–61; 2nd, later 1st Sec., HM Embassy, Santiago, 1961–63; Private Sec. to Perm. Under-Sec., FO, 1963–66; 1st Sec. and Head of Chancery, HM Embassy, Madrid, 1966–71; seconded to Cabinet Office, 1971–73; Head of News Dept, FCO, 1973–74, Head of N America Dept, 1974–75; Counsellor and Head of Chancery, Paris, 1975–79; Asst Under-Sec. of State, FCO, 1979–84; Ambassador to Spain, 1984–89. Director: Foreign and Colonial Investment Trust; Sothebys; Plus Ultra Seguros (Spain); MGM Assurance. Vice-Chm., Canada Blanch Foundn, 1996–; Chm., Exec. Cttee, Historic Churches Preservation Trust, 1997–; Trustee, Pallant House Gallery, 1994–. Hon. Col, 4th Bn Royal Green Jackets, TA, 1990–95. Medal of Honour, Univ. of Madrid, 1988. Grand Cross, Order of Isabel la Católica (Spain), 1986. *Clubs:* Boodle's, Beefsteak.
                                   Died 11 Oct. 2004.

GORE-BOOTH, Hon. Sir David (Alwyn), KCMG 1997 (CMG 1990); KCVO 1997; Special Adviser to Chairman of HSBC Holdings plc, since 1999; *b* 15 May 1943; twin *s* of late Baron Gore-Booth, GCMG, KCVO; *heir-presumptive* to Sir Josslyn Gore-Booth, 9th Bt; *m* 1st, 1964, Jillian Sarah (*née* Valpy) (marr. diss. 1970); one *s*; 2nd, 1977, Mary Elisabeth Janet, *d* of Sir David Muirhead, KCMG, CVO; one step *s*. *Educ:* Eton Coll.; Christ Church, Oxford (MA Hons). HM Diplomatic Service, 1964–98: Middle East Centre for Arab Studies, 1964; Third Sec., Baghdad, 1966; Third, later Second Sec., Lusaka, 1967; FCO, 1969; Second Sec., Tripoli, 1969; FCO, 1971; First Sec., UK Permanent Representation to European Communities, Brussels, 1974; Asst Head of Financial Relations Dept, FCO, 1978; Counsellor, Jedda, 1980; Counsellor and Hd of Chancery, UK Mission to UN, NY, 1983; Hd of Policy Planning Staff, FCO, 1987; Asst Under Sec. of State (ME), FCO, 1989; Ambassador, Saudi Arabia, 1993; High Comr, New Delhi, 1996–98. Director: HSBC Bank Middle East, 1999–; British Arab Commercial Bank, 1999–; HSBC Bank Egypt, 1999–; Middle East Internat., 1999–; Saudi-British Bank, 2000–; Group 4 Falck, 2000; Vedanta Resources plc, 2003–. Co-Chairman: Dubai/UK Trade and Economic Cttee, 2000–; Qatar/Britain Assoc. of Businessmen, 2001–; Dir, Arab-British Chamber of Commerce, 2002–; Member: Moroccan-British Business Council, 2001–; Egyptian-British Business Council, 2003–; Vice-Pres., Middle East Assoc., 2002–. Trustee: Next Century Foundn, 1997–; Medical Aid for Palestinians, 2001–. Mem. Adv. Bd, Centre for Internat. Studies and Diplomacy, Birmingham Univ., 1999–. *Recreations:* tennis, current affairs, the island of Hydra (Greece). *Address:* 27 Wetherby Mansions, Earl's Court Square, SW5 9BH. *T:* (020) 7373 1767, *Fax:* (020) 7373 5313. *Clubs:* MCC, Travellers, Garrick, Hurlingham; Bill's Bar (Hydra).   *Died 31 Oct. 2004.*

GORMAN, William Moore, FBA 1978; Emeritus Fellow, Nuffield College, Oxford, since 1990 (Fellow, 1962–67 and 1979–90); *b* 17 June 1923; *s* of late Richard Gorman, Lusaka, Northern Rhodesia, and Sarah Crawford Moore, Kesh, Northern Ireland; *m* 1950, Dorinda Scott. *Educ:* Foyle Coll., Derry; Trinity Coll., Dublin (Hon. Fellow 1990). Asst Lectr, 1949, Lectr, 1951, and Sen. Lectr, 1957, in Econometrics and Social Statistics, Univ. of Birmingham; Prof. of Economics, Univ. of Oxford, 1962–67; Prof. of Economics, London Univ., at LSE, 1967–79. Fellow, 1961, European Econ., 1971–73, Pres. 1972, Econometric Soc. Mem., Academia Europaea, 1990; Hon. Foreign Member: Amer. Acad. of Arts and Scis, 1986; Amer. Economic Assoc., 1987. Hon. DSocSc Birmingham, 1973; Hon. DSc(SocSc) Southampton, 1974; Hon. DEconSc NUI, 1986; Hon. DSc (Econ) London, 1998. *Publications:* Separability and Aggregation, 1995; articles in various economic journals. *Address:* 32 Victoria Road, Oxford OX2 7QD.
                                   Died 13 Jan. 2003.

GORTON, Rt Hon. Sir John (Grey); PC 1968; GCMG 1977; AC 1988; CH 1971; Prime Minister of Australia, 1968–71; *b* 9 Sept. 1911; *m* 1st, 1935, Bettina (*d* 1983), *d* of G. Brown, Bangor, Maine, USA; two *s* one *d*; 2nd, 1993, Nancy, *widow* of John Home; five step *s* one step *d*. *Educ:* Geelong Grammar Sch.; Brasenose Coll., Oxford (MA; Hon. Fellow, 1968). Orchardist. Enlisted RAAF, Nov. 1940; served in UK, Singapore, Darwin, Milne Bay; severely wounded in air ops; discharged with rank of Flt-Lt, Dec. 1944. Councillor, Kerang Shire, 1947–52 (Pres. of Shire); Mem., Lodden Valley Regional Cttee. Senator for State of Victoria, Parlt of Commonwealth of Australia, 1949–68 (Govt Leader in Senate, 1967–68); Minister for Navy, 1958–63; Minister Assisting the Minister for External Affairs, 1960–63 (Actg Minister during periods of absence overseas of Minister); Minister in Charge of CSIRO, 1962–68; Minister for Works and, under Prime Minister, Minister in Charge of Commonwealth Activities in Educn and Research, 1963–66; Minister for Interior, 1963–64; Minister for Works, 1966–67; Minister for Educn and Science, 1966–68; MHR (L) for Higgins, Vic, 1968–75; Minister for Defence, and Dep. Leader of Liberal Party, March-Aug. 1971; Mem. Parly Liberal Party Exec., and Liberal Party Spokesman on Environment and Conservation and Urban and Regional Develt, 1973–75; Dep. Chm., Jt Parly Cttee on Prices, 1973–75. Contested Senate election (Ind.), ACT, Dec. 1975. *Address:* 32 Parsley Road, Vaucluse, NSW 2030, Australia.
                                   Died 19 May 2002.

GORTVAI, Dame Rosalinde; *see* Hurley, Dame R.

GOSCHEN, Sir Edward (Christian), 3rd Bt *cr* 1916, of Beacon Lodge, Highcliffe, co. Southampton; DSO 1944; Rifle Brigade; *b* 2 Sept. 1913; *er s* of Sir Edward Henry Goschen, 2nd Bt, and Countess Mary, 7th *d* of Count Danneskiold Samsoe, Denmark; *S* father, 1933; *m* 1946, Cynthia, *d* of late Rt Hon. Sir Alexander Cadogan, OM, GCMG, KCB, PC (*y s* of 5th Earl Cadogan), and Lady Theodosia Cadogan (*d* of 4th Earl of Gosford); one *s* one *d*. *Educ:* Eton; Trinity Coll., Oxford. Mem., Stock Exchange Council (Dep. Chm., 1968–71). Commonwealth War Graves Comr, 1977–86. *Heir:* *s* Edward Alexander Goschen [*b* 13 March 1949; *m* 1976, Louise Annette, *d* of Lt-Col R. F. L. Chance, MC, and Lady Ava Chance (*d* of 1st Viscount Stonehaven and Countess of Kintore (11th in line)); one *d*]. *Address:* Lower Farm House, Hampstead Norreys, Newbury, Berks RG16 0SG. *T:* (01635) 201270.   *Died 8 March 2001.*

GOULD, Donald (William), MRCS, DTM&H; writer and broadcaster on medical and scientific affairs; *b* 26 Jan. 1919; *s* of late Rev. Frank J. Gould; *m* 1st, 1940, Edna Forsyth (marr. diss. 1969); three *s* four *d*; 2nd, 1969, Jennifer Goodfellow; one *s* one *d*. *Educ:* Mill Hill Sch.; St Thomas's Hosp. Med. Sch., London (BSc Physiol.). Orthopædic House Surg., Botley's Park Hosp., 1942; Surg. Lieut, RNVR, 1942–46; Med. Off., Hong Kong

Govt Med. Dept, 1946–48; Lectr in Physiol., University of Hong Kong, 1948–51, Sen. Lectr, 1951–57; King Edward VII Prof. of Physiol., University of Malaya (Singapore), 1957–60; Lectr in Physiol., St Bartholomew's Hosp. Med. Coll., London, 1960–61, Sen. Lectr, 1961–63; External Examr in Physiol., University of Durham (Newcastle), 1961–63; Dep. Ed., Medical News, 1963–65; Editor: World Medicine, 1965–66; New Scientist, 1966–69; Med. Correspondent, New Statesman, 1966–78. Chm., Med. Journalists' Assoc., 1967–71; Vice-Chm., Assoc. of British Science Writers, 1970–71. *Publications:* The Black & White Medicine Show, 1985; The Medical Mafia, 1987; Nurses, 1988; Examining Doctors, 1991; contributions to: Experimentation with Human Subjects, 1972; Ecology, the Shaping Enquiry, 1972; Better Social Services, 1973; scientific papers in physiological jls; numerous articles on medical politics, ethics and science in lay and professional press. *Recreations:* writing poems nobody will publish, listening, talking, and walking. *Address:* Taunton Cottage, Wroslyn Road, Freeland, Witney OX29 8AQ. *T:* (01993) 880280; *e-mail:* gouldilocks@amserve.net.
Died 13 Feb. 2002.

GOULD, Prof. Stephen Jay, PhD; Professor of Geology, and Curator of Invertebrate Palaeontology, Museum of Comparative Geology, since 1973, and Alexander Agassiz Professor of Zoology, since 1982, Harvard University; *b* NYC, 10 Sept. 1941; *m* 1st, 1965, Deborah Lee (marr. diss.); two *s*; 2nd, 1995, Rhonda Roland Shearer. *Educ:* Antioch Coll. (AB 1963); Columbia Univ. (PhD 1967). Instr in Geology, Antioch Coll., 1966; Harvard University: Asst Prof., 1967–71, Associate Prof., 1971–73, of Geology; Asst Curator, 1967–71, Associate Curator, 1971–73, of Invertebrate Palaeontology, Mus. of Comparative Zoology; Mem., Cttee of Profs, Dept of Biology, 1973–; Adjunct Mem., Dept of History of Sci., 1973–. Vincent Astor Vis. Res. Prof. of Biology, NY Univ., 1996–. Tanner Lectures, Cambridge Univ., 1984, Stanford Univ., 1989; Terry Lectures, Yale Univ., 1986; Lilly Lectr, RCP, 1993. Member: Space Exploration Council, NASA, 1989–91; Bd, British Mus. (Natural History) Internat. Foundn, 1992–; Commn on the Future, Smithsonian Instn, 1992–94; Bd of Trustees, Rockefeller Foundn, 1994–. President: Palaeontological Soc., 1985–86 (Golden Trilobite Award for excellence in palaeontological writing, 1992); Soc. for the Study of Evolution, 1990–91 (Vice Pres., 1975–76). Member: Nat. Acad. of Scis, 1989; Associé, Mus. Nat. d'Histoire Naturelle, Paris, 1989; FAAAS 1975 (Mem. Council, 1974–76); Fellow, Amer. Acad. of Arts and Scis, 1983; FRSE 1990. Mem., Bd of Editors, Science, 1986–91. Numerous hon. doctorates. Medal of Excellence, Columbia Univ., 1982; Silver Medal, Zoological Soc. of London, 1984; Distinguished Service Award, Amer. Geological Inst., 1986; Gold Medal for Service to Zoology, Linnean Soc. of London, 1992; UCLA Medal, 1992. *Publications* include: Ontogeny and Phylogeny, 1977; Ever since Darwin, 1977; The Panda's Thumb, 1980; The Mismeasure of Man, 1981 (Nat. Book Critics Circle Award, 1982); A View of Life, 1981; Hen's Teeth and Horse's Toes, 1983; The Flamingo's Smile, 1985; Illuminations: a bestiary, 1986; Time's Arrow, Time's Cycle, 1987; An Urchin in the Storm, 1987; Wonderful Life, 1989 (Rhône-Poulenc Prize, 1991); Bully for Brontosaurus, 1991; Eight Little Piggies, 1993; Dinosaur in a Haystack, 1995; Full House, 1995; Questioning the Millennium, 1997; Rocks of Ages, 1999; The Lying Stones of Marrakech, 2000; The Structure of Evolutionary Theory, 2002; I Have Landed: splashes and reflections in natural history, 2002. *Address:* Harvard University Museum of Comparative Zoology, Cambridge, MA 02138, USA. *Died 20 May 2002.*

GOULD, Thomas William, VC 1942; Lieutenant RNR retired; *b* 28 Dec. 1914; *s* of late Reuben Gould (killed in action, 1916) and Mrs C. E. Cheeseman; *m* 1941, Phyllis Eileen Eldridge (*d* 1985); one *s*. *Educ:* St James, Dover, Kent. Royal Navy, 1933–37; Submarines, 1937–45

(despatches); invalided Oct. 1945. Business consultant, 1965–; company director. Pres., Internat. Submarine Assoc. of GB. *Address:* 6 Howland, Orton Goldhay, Peterborough, Cambs PE2 5QY. *T:* and *Fax:* (01733) 238918. *Died 6 Dec. 2001.*

GOW, Dame Wendy; *see* Hiller, Dame Wendy.

GOYDER, Daniel George, CBE 1996; solicitor; Consultant: Birketts, Ipswich, since 1983 (Partner, 1968–83); Linklaters (formerly Linklaters & Paines, then Linklaters & Alliance), 1997–2003; *b* 26 Aug. 1938; *s* of George Armin Goyder, CBE; *m* 1962, Jean Mary Dohoo; two *s* two *d*. *Educ:* Rugby Sch.; Trinity Coll., Cambridge (MA, LLB); Harvard Law Sch. (Harkness Commonwealth Fund Fellow, LLM). Admitted Solicitor, 1962; Asst Solicitor, Messrs Allen & Overy, 1964–67. Pt-time Lectr in Law, 1981–91, Vis. Prof., 1991–97, Univ. of Essex; Vis. Prof., KCL, 1991–; Sen. Fellow, Centre for European Legal Studies, Univ. of Cambridge, 2001–. Chm., St Edmundsbury and Ipswich Diocesan Bd of Finance, 1977–85; Hon. Lay Canon, St Edmundsbury Cathedral, 1987–93. Dep. Chm., Monopolies and Mergers Commn, 1991–97 (Mem., 1980–91). Leverhulme Trust Res. Grant, for research into EC competition law, 1986. Trustee, British Liver Trust, 1996–2002. *Publications:* The Antitrust Laws of the USA (with Sir Alan Neale), 3rd edn 1981; EEC Competition Law, 1988, 4th edn, as EC Competition Law, 2003. *Recreations:* choral singing, tennis, sport. *Address:* Manor House, Old London Road, Capel St Mary, Ipswich, Suffolk IP9 2JU. *T:* (01473) 310583. *Clubs:* Law Society; Ipswich and Suffolk (Ipswich). *Died 17 Feb. 2004.*

GRAHAM, John, CB 1976; Fisheries Secretary, Ministry of Agriculture, Fisheries and Food, 1967–76; *b* 17 March 1918; *s* of late John Graham; *m* 1940, Betty Ramage Jarvie; two *s* two *d* (and one *d* decd). *Educ:* Fettes Coll., Edinburgh; Trinity Coll., Cambridge (Schol.). Classical Tripos, MA Cantab. Entered Post Office as Asst Principal, 1939; Min. of Food, 1940. *Died 3 June 2004.*

GRAHAM, Kenneth, CBE 1987 (OBE 1971); Deputy General Secretary, Trades Union Congress, 1985–87 (Assistant General Secretary, 1977–85); Member Council, Institute for Employment Studies (formerly of Manpower Studies), 1975–97; *b* 18 July 1922; *er s* of late Ernest Graham and Ivy (*née* Hutchinson), Cleator, Cumbria; *m* 1945, Ann Winifred Muriel Taylor. *Educ:* Workington Tech. Sch.; Leyton Tech. Coll.; Univ. of London (external). Engrg apprentice, 1938–42; Wartime Radar Research Unit, 1942–45; Air Trng Sch., qual. licensed engr, Air Registration Bd, 1947; employed in private industry, Mins of Aircraft Prodn and Supply, BOAC, and RN Scientific Service. Joined AEU, 1938, Mem. Final Appeal Court, Nat. Cttee, Divisional Chm., District Pres., etc, 1947–61; Tutor (part-time) in Trade Union Studies, Univ. of Southampton and WEA, 1958–61; joined TUC Organisation Dept, 1961, Head of TUC Organisation and Industrial Relations Dept, 1966–77. Comr, MSC, 1974–87; Member: Bd, European Foundn for Improvement of Living and Working Conditions, 1976–87; Adv. Cttee, European Social Fund, 1976–87; Council, Templeton Coll. (Oxford Centre for Management Studies), 1984–95; NCVQ, 1986–92; Board, Open Coll., 1987–97; Interim Adv. Cttee to Sec. of State for Educn and Sci., on Teachers' Pay and Conditions, 1987–89; Employment Appeal Tribunal, 1989–93; Management Bd, Univs' Staff Develt and Trng Unit, subseq. Univs' Staff Develt Unit, 1989–93; Professional Conduct Cttee, Gen. Council of the Bar, 1990–95. Mem. Bd, Remploy Ltd, 1987–92. A Vice-Pres., Airborne Forces Charities Appeal, 1990–; Hon. Friend, Airborne Forces Charitable Trust, 1996–. FRSA 1987. Hon. LLD CNAA, 1986. Special Award of Merit, AEU, 1981; TUC Trades Councils Silver Badge for Merit, 1987; TUC Congress Gold Badge, 1987. *Publication:* (contrib.) Job Satisfaction: challenge and response in modern Britain, 1976. *Recreations:* music, military history. *Address:* 90

Springfield Drive, Ilford, Essex IG2 6QS. *T:* (020) 8554 0839. *Died 15 July 2005.*

GRAHAM, Winston Mawdsley, OBE 1983; FRSL; *b* Victoria Park, Manchester, 30 June 1910; *m* 1939, Jean Mary Williamson (*d* 1992); one *s* one *d.* Chm., Soc. of Authors, 1967–69. Books trans. into 17 languages. *Publications:* some early novels (designedly) out of print, and: Night Journey, 1941, rev. edn 1966; The Merciless Ladies, 1944, rev. edn 1979; The Forgotten Story, 1945 (ITV prodn, 1983); Ross Poldark, 1945; Demelza, 1946; Take My Life, 1947 (filmed 1947); Cordelia, 1949; Night Without Stars, 1950 (filmed 1950); Jeremy Poldark, 1950; Fortune is a Woman, 1953 (filmed 1956); Warleggan, 1953; The Little Walls, 1955; The Sleeping Partner, 1956 (filmed 1958; ITV prodn, 1967); Greek Fire, 1957; The Tumbled House, 1959; Marnie, 1961 (filmed 1963); The Grove of Eagles, 1963 (Book Society Choice); After the Act, 1965; The Walking Stick, 1967 (filmed 1970); Angell, Pearl and Little God, 1970; The Japanese Girl (short stories), 1971; The Spanish Armadas, 1972; The Black Moon, 1973; Woman in the Mirror, 1975; The Four Swans, 1976; The Angry Tide, 1977; The Stranger from the Sea, 1981 (televised, 1996); The Miller's Dance, 1982; Poldark's Cornwall, 1983; The Loving Cup, 1984; The Green Flash, 1986; Cameo, 1988; The Twisted Sword, 1990; Stephanie, 1992; Tremor, 1995; The Ugly Sister, 1998; Bella Poldark, 2002; Memoirs of a private Man, 2003. BBC TV Series Poldark (the first four Poldark novels), 1975–76, second series (the next three Poldark novels), 1977; Circumstantial Evidence (play), 1979. *Recreation:* gardening. *Address:* Abbotswood House, Buxted, East Sussex TN22 4PB. *Clubs:* Savile, Beefsteak, Pratt's. *Died 10 July 2003.*

GRAHAM HALL, Jean; *see* Hall.

GRAHAM-HARRISON, Francis Laurence Theodore, CB 1962; Deputy Under-Secretary of State, Home Office, 1963–74; *b* 30 Oct. 1914; *s* of Sir William Montagu Graham-Harrison, KCB, KC, and Lady Graham-Harrison, *d* of Sir Cyril Graham, 5th and last Bt, CMG; *m* 1941, Carol Mary St John, 3rd *d* of Sir Francis Stewart, CIE; one *s* three *d. Educ:* Eton; Magdalen Coll., Oxford. Entered Home Office, 1938. Private Secretary to Parliamentary Under-Secretary of State, 1941–43; Asst Private Secretary to Prime Minister, 1946–49; Secretary, Royal Commission on Capital Punishment, 1949–53; Asst Secretary, Home Office, 1953–57; Asst Under-Secretary of State, Home Office, 1957–63. Chm., Nat. Sound Archive Adv. Cttee, British Library, 1984–88; Trustee: Tate Gallery, 1975–82; Nat. Gallery, 1981–82. Gov., Thomas Coram Foundn, 1975–95. Chm., Exec. Finance Cttee, Dr Barnardo's, 1978–81. *Address:* 32 Parliament Hill, NW3 2TN. *T:* (020) 7435 6316.
Died 7 Dec. 2001.

GRAINGER, Leslie, CBE 1976; FREng; Chairman, Mountain Petroleum PLC, 1984–88; *b* 8 Aug. 1917; *m* 1941, Lynn. *Educ:* BSc. MInstF. Mem. for Science, NCB, 1966–77; Chairman: NCB (Coal Products) Ltd, 1975–78; NCB (IEA Services) Ltd, 1975–79; Man. Dir, Branon PLC, 1981–83; Dir, Cavendish Petroleum Plc, 1982–85 (Chm., 1982–84). *Publication:* (with J. G. Gibson) Coal Utilisation: Technology, Economics and Policy, 1981. *Address:* 16 Blackamoor Lane, Maidenhead, Berks SL6 8RD. *T:* (01628) 623923. *Died 24 July 2003.*

GRANDY, Marshal of the Royal Air Force Sir John, GCB 1967 (KCB 1964; CB 1956); GCVO 1988; KBE 1961; DSO 1945; RAF; Constable and Governor of Windsor Castle, 1978–88; *b* Northwood, Middlesex, 8 Feb. 1913; *s* of late Francis Grandy and Nell Grandy (*née* Lines); *m* 1937, Cecile Elizabeth Florence Rankin, CStJ (*d* 1993), *yr d* of Sir Robert Rankin, 1st and last Bt; two *s. Educ:* University College Sch., London. Short service commn, RAF, 1931 (perm. commn, 1936); No 54 (Fighter) Sqdn, 1932–35; Asst Adjt and Flying Instr, 604 (Middx) Sqdn., RAuxAF, 1935–36; Adjt and Flying Instr,

London Univ. Air Sqdn, 1937–39; Comd No 249 (Fighter) Sqdn during Battle of Britain; Staff Duties, HQ Fighter Comd, and Wing Comdr Flying RAF Coltishall, 1941; commanded: RAF Duxford, 1942 (First Typhoon Wing); HQ No 210 Group, No 73 Op Training Unit, and Fighter Conversion Unit at Abu Sueir, 1943–44; No 341 Wing (Dakotas), SE Asia Comd, 1944–45; DSO 1945, despatches 1943 and 1945. SASO No 232 Gp, 1945; *psc* 1946; Dep. Dir Operational Training, Air Min., 1946; Air Attaché, Brussels, 1949; Comd Northern Sector, Fighter Comd, 1950; Air Staff HQ Fighter Comd, 1952–54; Comdt, Central Fighter Estab., 1954–57; *idc* 1957; Comdr, Task Force Grapple (British Nuclear Weapon Test Force), Christmas Is., 1957–58; Assistant CAS (Ops), 1958–61; Commander-in-Chief, RAF, Germany and Comdr, Second Allied TAF, 1961–63; AOC-in-C, Bomber Command, 1963–65; C-in-C, British Forces, Far East, and UK Mil. Adviser to SEATO, 1965–67; Chief of the Air Staff, 1967–71; Governor and C-in-C, Gibraltar, 1973–78. Dir, Brixton Estate Ltd, 1971–73, 1978–83; Trustee, Imperial War Museum, 1971–78 (Chm., 1978–89); Dep. Chm. Council, RAF Benevolent Fund, 1980–96; Trustee: Burma Star Assoc., 1979–96 (Vice-Pres.); Shuttleworth Remembrance Trust, 1978–88 (Chm., Aerodrome Cttee, 1980–88); RAF Church, St Clement Danes, 1971–97; Prince Philip Trust Fund, Windsor and Maidenhead, 1982–92; Past President: Officers' Assoc.; Air League; Vice-President: Officers' Pension Soc., 1971–; Nat. Assoc. of Boys' Clubs, 1971–; Life Vice-Pres., RNLI, 1988– (Vice-Pres., 1986–88); Mem. Management Cttee, 1971–); Friends of Gibraltar Heritage Soc., 1986–; Mem. Cttee, Royal Humane Soc., 1978–95; Patron, Polish Air Force Assoc. in GB, 1979–2000. PMN 1967. Hon. Liveryman, Haberdashers' Co., 1968. Freeman, City of London, 1968. KStJ 1974. *Clubs:* White's, Pratt's, Royal Air Force; Royal Yacht Squadron (Cowes); Swinley Forest Golf.
Died 2 Jan. 2004.

GRANT, Sir Alistair; *see* Grant, Sir M. A.

GRANT, David James, CBE 1980; Lord-Lieutenant and Custos Rotulorum of County Durham, 1988–97; *b* 18 Jan. 1922; *s* of late Frederick Grant, MC, QC and Grace Winifred Grant (*née* McLaren); *m* 1949, Jean Margaret, *d* of Gp Capt. T. E. H. Birley, OBE; two *s* one *d. Educ:* Fettes Coll., Edinburgh; Oriel Coll., Oxford (Open Schol.; MA). Served War of 1939-45, RAFVR, Bomber Command and overseas 1940–45 (Flight Lieut). Chm., Darchem Ltd, 1963–92 (Chief Exec., 1959–88); Dep. Chm., William Baird plc, 1981–92. Chairman: Teesside Productivity Assoc., 1965–68; Northern Regl Council, CBI, 1973–75; Northern Regl Council, BIM, 1982–87; Member: Northern Econ. Planning Council, 1968–79; NE Industrial Develt Bd, 1975–84. President: N of England TA&VRA, 1990–93; N of England Anglo-Japanese Soc., 1990–97; Co. Durham, RBL, 1997–. Chm., Council, Univ. of Durham, 1985–92 (Hon. DCL 1988); Visitor, Teeside Univ., 1995–2000. Hon. DCL Newcastle upon Tyne, 1989. Co. Durham: DL 1982; High Sheriff, 1985–86; Vice Lord-Lieut, 1987–88. KStJ 1988. CIMgt. *Recreations:* gardening, golf. *Address:* Aden Cottage, Durham DH1 4HJ. *T:* (0191) 386 7161. *Club:* Durham County. *Died 23 March 2002.*

GRANT, John James, CBE 1960; Director, University of Durham Institute of Education, 1963–77; *b* 19 Oct. 1914; *s* of John and Mary Grant; *m* 1945, Jean Graham Stewart; two *s. Educ:* Shawlands Academy, Glasgow; Univ. of Glasgow (MA, EdB). Supply teaching, Glasgow, 1939–40. Served War: UK, India, Burma, 1940–46. Mod. Lang. Master, High Sch. of Glasgow, 1946–48; Lectr in Educn, Univ. of Durham, 1948–52; Vice-Principal, Fourah Bay Coll., Sierra Leone, 1953–55, Principal, 1955–60; Principal, St Cuthbert's Soc., Univ. of Durham, 1960–63. Hon. DCL Durham, 1960. *Recreations:* theatre, gardening. *Address:* Stokeleigh Residential Home, 19 Stoke Hill, Stoke Bishop, Bristol BS9 1JN. *Died 6 July 2004.*

GRANT, Sir (Matthew) Alistair, Kt 1992; DL; Governor, Bank of Scotland, 1998–99 (Director, since 1992); Deputy Chairman, Scottish & Newcastle plc, since 2000 (Chairman, 1997–2000); *b* 6 March 1937; *s* of John and Jessie Grant; *m* 1963, Judith Mary Dent; two *s* one *d*. *Educ:* Woodhouse Grove School, Yorks. 2nd Lieut Royal Signals, 1955–57. Unilever, 1958–63; J. Lyons, 1963–65; Connell May & Steavenson, 1965–68; Dir, Fine Fare, 1968–72; Managing Dir, Oriel Foods, 1973–77; Argyll Group, then Safeway, 1977–97: Chief Exec., 1986–93; Dep. Chm., 1986–88; Chm., 1988–97. Dir, Land Securities, 1996–. Chm., AFRC, later BBSRC, 1990–98. Visiting Professor: Retail, Stirling Univ., 1984–91; Marketing, Strathclyde Univ., 1991–. Chm., Food Policy Cttee, Retail Consortium, 1986–89; Dir, Marketing Council, 1995– (Vice Chm., 1996–). President: Nat. Grocers' Benevolent Fund, 1987–89; Inst. of Grocery Distribution, 1992–94; Advertising Assoc., 1989–93; RASE, 1993–94. Member: Listed Companies Adv. Cttee, 1990–93; Council, Scottish Council Develt and Industry, 1994–99; Conseil de Surveillance, Casino, Guichard-Perrachon SA (France), 1994–95. Mem. Bd of Trustees, Nat. Museums of Scotland, 1991–99; Trustee, Nat. Heritage Meml Fund, 1997–99. Regent, RCSE, 1994. FRSA 1988; FRAgS 1993; FRSE 1997. DL East Lothian, 1997. Hon. DBA: Strathclyde, 1992; Napier, 1994; Robert Gordon, 1998; Hon. DSc: Cranfield, 1993; Warwick, 1997; De Montfort, 1997; Dr *hc* Edinburgh, 1993. KStJ 1993. *Recreations:* books, paintings, horses, friends. *Address:* Bank of Scotland, PO Box 5, The Mound, Edinburgh EH1 1YZ. *Clubs:* Farmers', Beefsteak; New (Edinburgh). *Died 22 Jan. 2001.*

GRANT, Michael, CBE 1958 (OBE 1946); MA, LittD (Cambridge); *b* 21 Nov. 1914; *s* of late Col Maurice Harold Grant and Muriel, *d* of C. Jörgensen; *m* 1944, Anne-Sophie Beskow, Norrköping, Sweden; two *s*. *Educ:* Harrow Sch.; Trinity Coll., Cambridge (Porson Prizeman, First Chancellor's Classical Medallist, Craven Student). Fellow, Trinity Coll., Cambridge, 1938–49. Served War of 1939–45, Army, War Office, 1939–40, Actg Capt.; first British Council Rep. in Turkey, 1940–45. Prof. of Humanity at Edinburgh Univ., 1948–59; first Vice-Chancellor, Univ. of Khartoum, 1956–58; Pres. and Vice-Chancellor, QUB, 1959–66. J. H. Gray Lectr, Cambridge, 1955. Chm., Nat. Council for the Supply of Teachers Overseas, 1963–66. Pres., 1953–56, Medallist, 1962, and Hon. Fellow, 1984, Royal Numismatic Soc.; Huntington Medalist, American Numismatic Soc., 1965. President: Virgil Soc., 1963–66; Classical Assoc., 1977–78. Chm., Commonwealth Conf. on Teaching of English as 2nd Language, Makerere, Uganda, 1961. FSA. Hon. LittD Dublin, 1961; Hon. LLD QUB, 1967. Gold Medal for Educn, Sudan, 1977; Premio Internazionale Le Muse, Florence, 1989. *Publications:* From Imperium to Auctoritas, 1946; Aspects of the Principate of Tiberius, 1950; Roman Anniversary Issues, 1950; Ancient History, 1952; The Six Main Aes Coinages of Augustus, 1953; Roman Imperial Money, 1954; Roman Literature, 1954; translations of Tacitus and Cicero; Roman History from Coins, 1958; The World of Rome, 1960; Myths of the Greeks and Romans, 1962; (ed) Birth of Western Civilization, 1964 (new edn as Greece and Rome, 1986); The Civilizations of Europe, 1965; The Gladiators, 1967; The Climax of Rome, 1968; The Ancient Mediterranean, 1969 (Premio del Mediterraneo, Mazara del Vallo, 1983, for Italian edn); Julius Caesar, 1969; The Ancient Historians, 1970; The Roman Forum, 1970; Nero, 1970; Cities of Vesuvius, 1971; Herod the Great, 1971; Roman Myths, 1971; Cleopatra, 1972; The Jews in the Roman World, 1973; (with J. Hazel) Who's Who in Classical Mythology, 1973 (Premio Latina for Italian edn, 1986); The Army of the Caesars, 1974; The Twelve Caesars, 1975; (ed) Greek Literature, 1976; The Fall of the Roman Empire, 1976; Saint Paul, 1976; Jesus, 1977; History of Rome, 1978; (ed) Latin Literature, 1978; The Etruscans, 1980; Greek and Latin Authors 800 BC-AD 1000, 1980;

The Dawn of the Middle Ages, 1981; From Alexander to Cleopatra, 1982; History of Ancient Israel, 1984; The Roman Emperors, 1985; A Guide to the Ancient World, 1986; The Rise of the Greeks, 1987; (ed with R. Kitzinger) Civilization of the Ancient Mediterranean, 1988; The Classical Greeks, 1989; The Visible Past, 1990; Short History of Classical Civilization, 1991 (US edn, The Founders of the Western World); Greeks and Romans: a social history, 1992; Readings in the Classical Historians, 1992; The Emperor Constantine, 1993; Sayings of the Bible, 1994; Saint Peter, 1994; My First Eighty Years, 1994; The Antonines, 1994; Art in the Roman Empire, 1995; The Severans, 1996; From Rome to Byzantium: the Fifth Century, 1998; The Collapse and Recovery of the Roman Empire, 1998; Sick Caesars, 2000. *Club:* Athenæum. *Died 4 Oct. 2004.*

GRANVILLE SLACK, George; *see* Slack.

GRAVES, 9th Baron *cr* 1794 (Ire.); **Evelyn Paget Graves;** farmer, retired; *b* 17 May 1926; *s* of Alweyn Montague Graves (*d* 1956), and Kathleen Eleanor Cowle Priest (*d* 1974), and *g g s* of 2nd Baron Graves; *S* kinsman, 1994; *m* 1957, Marjorie Ann (OAM 1992), *d* of late Dr Sidney Ernest Holder; one *s* two *d* (and one *s* decd). *Heir: s* Hon. Timothy Evelyn Graves, *b* 27 March 1960. *Address:* Woodlands, 405 Mole Creek Road, Deloraine, Tas 7304, Australia. *T:* (3) 63622009. *Died 6 Dec. 2002.*

GRAY, 22nd Lord *cr* 1445; **Angus Diarmid Ian Campbell-Gray;** *b* 3 July 1931; *s* of Major Hon. Lindsay Stuart Campbell-Gray, Master of Gray, MC (*d* 1945), and Doreen (*d* 1948), *d* of late Cyril Tubbs, Thedden Grange, Alton, Hants; *S* grandmother, 1946; *m* 1959, Patricia Margaret (*d* 1987), *o d* of late Capt. Philip Alexander, Kilmorna, Lismore, Co. Waterford; one *s* three *d*; *m* 1994, Mrs Paul Williams (*née* Cecilia Wilfrida Dimsdale). *Heir: s* Master of Gray, *b* 3 Sept. 1964. *Address:* Airds Bay, Taynuilt, Argyll PA35 1JR. *Clubs:* Carlton, MCC. *Died 29 April 2003.*

GRAY, Hugh, PhD; former International Secretary, Theosophical Society; *b* 19 April 1916; *s* of William Marshall Kemp Gray; *m* 1954, Edith Esther (*née* Rudinger) (*d* 1998); no *c*. *Educ:* Battersea Grammar Sch.; London Sch. of Economics (BSc (Soc)). Army Service, Intelligence Corps. UNRRA and Internat. Refugee Organisation, 1945–52; Social Worker; Lectr at SOAS, University of London, 1962–66 and 1970–81; Chm., Centre for S Asian Studies, 1980–81; Gen. Sec., Theosophical Soc. in England, 1983–89. MP (Lab) Yarmouth, 1966–70. *Publications:* various articles on Indian politics and philosophy. *Died 1 April 2002.*

GRAY, Prof. Jeffrey Alan, PhD; Professor of Psychology, Institute of Psychiatry, University of London, 1983–99, then Emeritus Professor; *b* 26 May 1934; *s* of Maurice and Dora Gray; *m* 1961, Venus; two *s* two *d*. *Educ:* Magdalen Coll., Oxford (BA Hons Mod. Langs 1957; BA Hons Psychology 1959); Univ. of London (DipPsych 1960; PhD 1964). FBPsS 1993. Research Worker, Inst. of Psychiatry, 1960–64; Lectr in Psychol., Dept of Exp. Psych., Oxford, 1964–83; Fellow, University Coll., Oxford, 1965–83; Travelling Fellow, MRC, and Guest Investigator, Rockefeller Univ., NY, 1968–69; Soc. Sci. Res. Fellow, Nuffield Foundn, 1975–76; Associate Prof., Univ. of Paris VI, 1979–80; Mary Morten Moody Vis. Prof., VMI, Va, 1983; Vis. Prof., Collège de France, Paris, 1999; Fellow, Center for Advanced Study in Behavioral Scis, Stanford Univ., 2001–02. Director: Psychology at Work Ltd, 1989–; ReNeuron Ltd, 1997–2000. Mem., Gambling Review Body, Home Office, 1999–2001. Pres., Exptml Psychol. Soc., 1996–98. Ed., Behav. Brain Sci., 2002–. Hon. Fellow, Goldsmiths Coll., London Univ., 2002. Hon. Dr Washington and Lee, Va, 2000. Presidents' Award, BPsS, 1983; Kenneth Craik Award, St John's Coll., Cambridge, 1995. *Publications:* Pavlov's Typology, 1964; The Psychology of Fear and Stress, 1971, 2nd edn

1987; The Biological Bases of Individual Behaviour, 1972; Elements of a Two-Process Theory of Learning, 1975; Pavlov, 1979; The Neuropsychology of Anxiety, 1982, 2nd edn 2000; *posthumous publication:* Consciousness: creeping up on the hard problem, 2004; and other works. *Recreation:* ski-ing. *Address:* Department of Psychology, Institute of Psychiatry, De Crespigny Park, Denmark Hill, SE5 8AF. *T:* (020) 7919 3245.　　　*Died 30 April 2004.*

GRAY, Prof. (John) Richard; Professor of African History, University of London, 1972–89, then Emeritus; *b* 7 July 1929; *s* of Captain Alfred William Gray, RN and of Christobel Margaret Gray (*née* Raikes); *m* 1957, Gabriella, *d* of Dr Camillo Cattaneo; one *s* one *d*. *Educ:* Charterhouse; Downing Coll., Cambridge (Richmond Schol.; BA 1951); PhD London 1957. Lectr, Univ. of Khartoum, 1959–61; Res. Fellow, 1961–63, Reader, 1963–72, SOAS, Univ. of London. Vis. Prof., UCLA, 1967. Chairman: Africa Centre, Covent Garden, 1967–72; Britain-Zimbabwe Soc., 1981–84. Mem., Pontifical Cttee of Historical Sciences, 1982–. Ed., Jl African History, 1968–71. Order of St Silvester, 1966. *Publications:* The Two Nations: aspects of the development of race relations in the Rhodesias and Nyasaland, 1960; A History of the Southern Sudan 1839–1889, 1961; (with D. Chambers) Materials for West African History in Italian Archives, 1965; (ed with D. Birmingham) Pre-Colonial African Trade, 1970; (ed) The Cambridge History of Africa, vol. 4, 1975; (ed with E. Fasholé-Luke and others) Christianity in Independent Africa, 1978; Black Christians and White Missionaries, 1990; (ed with Yusuf Fadl Hasan) Religion and Conflict in Sudan, 2002. *Recreation:* things Italian. *Address:* 39 Rotherwick Road, NW11 7DD. *T:* (020) 8458 3676.　　　*Died 7 Aug. 2005.*

GRAY, Sir John (Walton David), KBE 1995; CMG 1986; HM Diplomatic Service, retired; Chairman: Financial Board (formerly Consultancy Board), Spadel UK, since 1997; Deffrainc Ltd, since 1998; *b* Burry Port, Carmarthenshire, 1 Oct. 1936; *s* of Myrddin Gray and Elsie Irene (*née* Jones), Llanelli, Carms; *m* 1957, Anthoula, *e d* of Nicolas Yerasimou, Nicosia, Cyprus; one *s* two *d*. *Educ:* Blundell's Sch.; Christ's Coll., Cambridge (Scholar and Tancred Student; BA 1959, MA 1963); ME Centre, Oxford; Amer. Univ., Cairo. Nat. Service, 1954–56. Joined Foreign Service, 1962; served: Mecas, 1962; Bahrain Agency, 1964; FO, 1967; Geneva, 1970; Sofia, 1974; Counsellor (Commercial), 1978, Counsellor and Hd of Chancery, 1980, Jedda; Hd of Maritime, Aviation and Environment Dept, FCO, 1982–85; Ambassador to Lebanon, 1985–88; Ambassador and UK Perm. Rep. to OECD, Paris, 1988–92; Ambassador to Belgium, 1992–96. Chm., OECD Information Policy Wkg Gp, 1980–82; Rapporteur, Study Team on Performance of OECD's Centre for Co-operation with Eur. Econs in Transition, 1994. Chm., Vandemoortele UK, 2000–02; Adviser: Hyder plc, 1996–99; Fortis Bank, 1998–; Burwood Corp., 1998–2002; MEM Group, 1999–2000. Member: Commonwealth War Graves Commn, 1997–; Cardiff Bay Develt Corp., 1998–2000. Trustee, Nat. Botanic Gdn of Wales, 1998–2002; Chm., Co-ordinating Cttee, Welsh Internat. Trust, 1997–2003. President: Wales Council Eur. Movt, 1997–; Inst. of Dirs, Wales, 2000–; Hon. Pres., Paris Chapter, Inst. of Welsh Affairs, 1992; Member: Cttee, Anglo-Belgian Soc., 1996–; Council, Belgium–Luxemburg Chamber of Commerce, 1997–; Cttee, ME Assoc., 1998–2000; Cttee, British–Lebanese Assoc., 1999–; RIIA. Hon. Consul of Belgium, Cardiff, 2000–. Vice-President: Cardiff Business Club, 1995; Crawshays Welsh Rugby Club, 1996–; WEA, Llanelli, 1997–. Mem. Council, Cheltenham Coll., 1994–97; Gov., Univ. of Glamorgan, 2000–. Hon. Fellow: Cardiff Univ., 1998; UWIC, 2000. Freeman, City of London, 1997; Hon. Freeman, Gardeners' Co., 1996. *Publications:* (jtly) Wales in Europe, 1997; (contrib.) Agenda for the Assembly, 1998. *Recreations:* watching Rugby football, light history, things Welsh, public speaking (Internat.

Toastmasters' After Dinner Speaker of the Year, 1993). *Address:* 10 Marine Parade, Penarth, Vale of Glamorgan CF64 3BG. *Clubs:* Royal Commonwealth Society, Royal Anglo-Belgian (Chm., 1998–); Cardiff and County (Cardiff); Llanelli Rugby Football.
　　　Died 1 Sept. 2003.

GRAY, Richard; see Gray, J. R.

GRAY, Robert Walker; see Gray, Robin.

GRAY, Robin, (Robert Walker Gray), CB 1977; Deputy Secretary, Department of Trade, 1975–84; *b* 29 July 1924; *s* of Robert Walker Gray and Dorothy (*née* Lane); *m* 1955, Shirley Matilda (*née* Taylor); two *s* one *d*. *Educ:* John Lyon Sch., Harrow; London Sch. of Economics (BScEcons 1946; Farr Medal in Statistics). Air Warfare Analysis Sect., Air Min., 1940–45; BoT, 1947; UK Delegn to OEEC, 1950–51; BoT, 1952–66; Commercial Counsellor, British High Commn, Ottawa, 1966–70; Under-Secretary: DTI, 1971–74; Dept of Prices and Consumer Protection, 1974–75; Dep. Sec., DoI, 1975. *Address:* Tansy, Brook Road, Wormley, Godalming, Surrey GU8 5UA. *T:* (01428) 682486.
　　　Died 17 July 2003.

GRAYSTON, Rev. Prof. Kenneth, MA, DLitt; Professor of Theology, Bristol University, 1965–79, then Emeritus Professor; Pro-Vice-Chancellor, Bristol University, 1976–79; *b* Sheffield, 8 July 1914; *s* of Ernest Edward and Jessie Grayston; *m* 1942, Elizabeth Alison (*d* 1995), *d* of Rev. Walter Mayo and Beatrice Aste, Elsfield, Oxon; no *c*. *Educ:* Colfe's Grammar Sch., Lewisham; Univs of Oxford and Cambridge; DLitt Bristol 1991. Ordained Methodist Minister, 1942; Ordnance Factory Chaplain, 1942–44; Asst Head of Religious Broadcasting, BBC, 1944–49; Tutor in New Testament Language and Literature, Didsbury Coll., 1949–64; Bristol University: Special Lecturer in Hellenistic Greek, 1950–64; Dean, Faculty of Arts, 1972–74; Hon. Fellow, 1992. Select Preacher to Univ. of Cambridge, 1952, 1962, to Univ. of Oxford, 1971. Sec., Studiorum Novi Testamenti Societas, 1955–65; Chairman: Theol Adv. Gp, British Council of Churches, 1969–72; Christian Aid Scholarships Cttee, 1973–78. *Publications:* The Epistles to the Galatians and to the Philippians, 1957; The Letters of Paul to the Philippians and the Thessalonians, 1967; The Johannine Epistles, 1984; Dying, We Live, 1990; The Gospel of John, 1990; The Epistle to the Romans, 1997; The New Testament: which way in?, 2000; contributions to: A Theological Word Book of the Bible, 1950; The Teacher's Commentary, 1955; The Interpreter's Dictionary of the Bible, 1962; A New Dictionary of Christian Theology, 1983, etc; contrib. to Expository Times, New Testament Studies, Theology, Scottish Jl Theology, Epworth Review, etc. *Recreation:* music. *Address:* 11 Rockleaze Avenue, Bristol BS9 1NG. *T:* (0117) 968 3872.
　　　Died 10 June 2005.

GREBENIK, Eugene, CB 1976; Consultant, Office of Population Censuses and Surveys, 1977–84; *b* 20 July 1919; *s* of S. Grebenik and E. Lopatitskaya; *m* 1946, Virginia, *d* of James D. Barker; two *s* one *d*. *Educ:* abroad; LSE (MSc (Econs)). Statistician, Dept of Economics, Univ. of Bristol, 1939–40; London Sch. of Economics: Asst 1940–44 and Lecturer, 1944–49, in Statistics (on leave, 1944–46; served in RN, 1944; Temp. Statistical Officer, Admiralty, 1944–45; Secretariat, Royal Commn on Population, 1945–46); Research Sec., Population Investigation Cttee, 1947–54; Reader in Demography, Univ. of London, 1949–54; Prof. of Social Studies, Univ. of Leeds, 1954–69; Principal, Civil Service Coll., 1970–76 and Dep. Sec., Civil Service Dept, 1972–76. Mem., Impact of Rates Cttee, Ministry of Housing, 1963–64. Social Science Research Council: Statistics Cttee, 1966–69; Cttee on Social Science and Government, 1968–72; Population Panel, 1971–73; Member: Cttee on Governance of London Univ., 1970–72; Council,

RHBNC (formerly RHC), Univ. of London, 1971–90. Pres., British Soc. for Population Studies, 1979–81. Sec.-Treasurer, Internat. Union for Scientific Study of Population, 1963–73. Hon. Fellow, LSE, 1969; Vis. Fellow, ANU, 1982–83; Hon. Vis. Prof., City Univ., 1986–89. Managing Ed., Population Studies, 1978–96 (Jt Ed., 1954–78). Olivia Schieffelin Nordberg Award, Population Council, 1997. *Publications:* (with H. A. Shannon) The Population of Bristol, 1943; (with D. V. Glass) The Trend and Pattern of Fertility in Great Britain; A Report on the Family Census of 1946, 1954; various articles in statistical and economic journals. *Address:* 16 Spindlers, Kidlington, Oxon OX5 2YP. *T:* (01865) 842697.　　　　　　　　　　　　　*Died 14 Oct. 2001.*

GREEN, Barry Spencer; QC 1981; **His Honour Judge Green;** a Circuit Judge, since 1993; *b* 16 March 1932; *s* of Lionel Maurice Green, FRCS and Juliette Green; *m* 1st, 1960, Marilyn Braverman (marr. diss. 1987); two *s*; 2nd, 1988, Muriel Coplan. *Educ:* Westminster Sch.; Christ Church, Oxford (MA, BCL). Called to the Bar, Inner Temple, 1954, Bencher, 1987; a Recorder, 1979–93. Legal Mem., Mental Health Review Tribunal, 1983–93; Mem., Criminal Injuries Compensation Bd, 1988–93. Gov., City Literary Inst., 1996–. *Recreation:* tennis. *Clubs:* Garrick, Roehampton.　　　　　　　　*Died 11 Feb. 2004.*

GREEN, Dame Mary Georgina, DBE 1968; BA; Head Mistress, Kidbrooke School, SE3, 1954–73; Chairman, BBC London Local Radio Council, 1973–78; Chairman, General Optical Council, 1979–85 (Member, 1977–79); *b* 27 July 1913; *er d* of late George Green and Rose Margaret Green (*née* Gibbs). *Educ:* Wellingborough High Sch.; Westfield Coll., University of London (Hon. Fellow, 1976; Fellow, QMW, 1989; Hon. Fellow, QMW, 1995). Assistant Mistress: Clapham High Sch., 1936–38; Streatham Hill and Clapham High Sch., 1938–40; William Hulme's Sch., Manchester, 1940–45; Head Mistress, Colston's Girls' Sch., Bristol, 1946–53. Member: Central Advisory Council for Education (Eng.), 1956–63; Church of England Board of Education, 1958–65; Council King George's Jubilee Trust, 1963–68; Court of Governors, London Sch. of Economics and Political Science, 1964–83; Royal Commission on Trade Unions and Employers' Assocs, 1965–68; Council, City University, 1969–78; Cttee of Inquiry into Nurses' Pay, 1977; Press Council, 1976–79; Review Body on Doctors' and Dentists' Remuneration, 1976–79. Dep. Chm., E-SU, 1976–82 (Governor, 1974–82); a Governor: BBC, 1968–73; Royal Ballet Sch., 1969–72; Centre for Educnl Develt Overseas, 1970–74; Rachel McMillan Coll. of Educn, 1970–73; Ditchley Foundn, 1978–97. Hon. DSc: City, 1981; Bradford, 1986. Hon. MADO 1985; Hon. FBCO 1985. *Address:* 45 Winn Road, SE12 9EX. *T:* (020) 8857 1514.　　　　　　　　　*Died 20 April 2004.*

GREEN, Brig. Percy William Powlett, CBE 1960 (OBE 1956); DSO 1946; *b* 10 Sept. 1912; *er s* of late Brig.-Gen. W. G. K. Green, CB, CMG, DSO, Indian Army; *m* 1943, Phyllis Margery Fitz Gerald May (*d* 1995), *d* of late Lieut-Col A. H. May, OBE; one *s* one *d*. *Educ:* Wellington Coll.; RMC. Commnd Northamptonshire Regt, 1932; Op. NW Frontier, India, 1936–37; BEF 1939–40; Lt-Col Comdg 2nd W Yorks Regt, 1945–46; Burma, 1944–45; Lt-Col Comdg 1 Malay Regt, 1946–47; Comd 4th King's African Rifles, 1954–56; Op. against Mau Mau; Col, Gen. Staff, War Office, 1956–57; Chief of Staff (Brig.) E Africa Comd, 1957–60; DDMI, War Office, 1961–63; Chief of Staff, N Ireland Command, 1963–65; Dep. Comdr, Aldershot District, 1965–67; retired, 1967. ADC to the Queen, 1965–67. Dep. Colonel, Royal Anglian Regt, 1966–76. *Recreations:* field sports. *Address:* Grudds, South Warnborough, Hook, Hants RG29 1RW. *T:* (01256) 862472.　　　　　　　　　　　*Died 23 Feb. 2004.*

GREEN, Lt-Col Sir Simon (Lycett), 5th Bt *cr* 1886, of Wakefield, Yorkshire and Ken Hill, Norfolk; TD 1947; DL; Chairman, Green's Economiser Group plc, 1956–83;

b 11 July 1912; *s* of Sir Edward Arthur Lycett Green, 3rd Bt and Elizabeth Green (*née* Williams); *S* brother, 1996; *m* 1st, 1935, Gladys (marr. diss. 1971), *d* of Arthur Ranicar; one *d*; 2nd, 1971, Mary, *d* of George Ramsden. *Educ:* Eton; Magdalene Coll., Cambridge (BA). Served War, 1939–45. Lt-Col comdg Queen's Own Yorkshire Dragoons Yeomanry, 1947–51. DL WR Yorks, 1952; JP Wakefield, 1959. *Recreations:* shooting, racing. *Heir: cousin* Edward Patrick Lycett Green [*b* 14 Oct. 1950; *m* 1st, 1971, Corden Sarah (marr. diss. 1975), *d* of C. B. Stretton Wilson; 2nd, 1977, Annette Patricia Josephine, *d* of O. P. J. Rochfort; two *d*].　　　　　　　　*Died 5 Nov. 2003.*

GREEN, Rev. Vivian Hubert Howard, DD, FRHistS; Fellow and Tutor in History, 1951–83, Rector, 1983–87, Hon. Fellow, 1987, Lincoln College, Oxford; *b* 18 Nov. 1915; *s* of Hubert James and Edith Eleanor Playle Green; unmarried. *Educ:* Bradfield Coll., Berks; Trinity Hall, Cambridge (Schol.; Goldsmiths' Exhibnr; 1st cl. Hist. Tripos, Parts I and II; Lightfoot Schol. in Ecclesiastical Hist.; Thirlwall Medal and Prize, 1941; MA 1941); MA Oxon by incorp., 1951; DD Cambridge, 1958; DD Oxon by incorp., 1958. Gladstone Research Studentship, St Deiniol's Library, Hawarden, 1937–38; ordained deacon, 1939, priest, 1940; Fellow, St Augustine's Coll., Canterbury, 1939–48; Chaplain, Exeter Sch. and St Luke's Training Coll., Exeter, 1940–42; Chaplain and Asst Master, Sherborne Sch., Dorset, 1942–51; Lincoln College, Oxford: Chaplain, 1951–69; Sen. Tutor, 1953–62 and 1974–77; Sub-Rector, 1970–83; acting Rector, 1972–73. Select Preacher, Oxford, 1959–60, 1992. Vis. Prof. of History, Univ. of S Carolina, 1982. *Publications:* Bishop Reginald Pecock, 1945; The Hanoverians, 1948; From St Augustine to William Temple, 1948; Renaissance and Reformation, 1952; The Later Plantagenets, 1955; Oxford Common Room, 1957; The Young Mr Wesley, 1961; The Swiss Alps, 1961; Martin Luther and the Reformation, 1964; John Wesley, 1964; Religion at Oxford and Cambridge (historical survey), 1964; The Universities, 1969; Medieval Civilization in Western Europe, 1971; A History of Oxford University, 1974; The Commonwealth of Lincoln College 1427–1977, 1979; Love in a Cool Climate: the letters of Mark Pattison and Meta Bradley 1879–1884, 1985; (ed) Memoirs of an Oxford Don: Mark Pattison, 1988; (with William Scoular) A Question of Guilt: the murder of Nancy Eaton, 1988; The Madness of Kings, 1993; A New History of Christianity, 1996; The European Reformation, 1998; contributor to: Dictionary of English Church History (ed Ollard, Crosse and Bond); The Oxford Dictionary of the Christian Church (ed Cross); European Writers, The Middle Ages and Renaissance (ed W. T. H. Jackson and G. Stade), vols I and II, 1983; The History of the University of Oxford, vol. V, The Eighteenth Century (ed L. S. Sutherland and L. G. Mitchell), 1986. *Address:* Lincoln College, Oxford OX1 3DR. *T:* (01865) 279830; Calendars, Burford, Oxon OX8 4LS. *T:* (01993) 823214.　　　　　　　*Died 18 Jan. 2005.*

GREENE OF HARROW WEALD, Baron *cr* 1974 (Life Peer), of Harrow; **Sidney Francis Greene,** Kt 1970; CBE 1966; Director: Trades Union Unit Trust, 1970–80; RTZ Corporation, 1975–80; Times Newspapers Holdings Ltd, 1980–82 (Times Newspapers Ltd, 1975–80); *b* 12 Feb. 1910; *s* of Frank James Greene and Alice (*née* Kerrod); *m* 1936, Masel Elizabeth Carter; three *d*. *Educ:* elementary. Joined Railway Service, 1924; appointed Union Organiser, 1944, Asst Gen. Sec., 1954, Gen. Sec., Nat. Union of Railwaymen, 1957–75. Mem., TUC Gen. Council, 1957–75 (Chm., 1969–70); Chm., TUC Economic Cttee, 1968–75. Member: National Economic Development Council, 1962–75; Advisory Council, ECGD, 1967–70; part-time Member: Southern Electricity Board, 1964–77; Nat. Freight Corp., 1973–77; a Dir, Bank of England, 1970–78. JP London, 1941–65. FCIT. *Recreations:* reading, gardening. *Address:* 26 Kynaston

Wood, Boxtree Road, Harrow Weald, Middx HA3 6UA.
Died 26 July 2004.

GREENE, Sir (John) Brian M.; *see* Massy-Greene.

GREENFIELD, Prof. (Archibald) David (Mant), CBE
1977; FRCP; Foundation Dean of the Medical School,
1966–81 and Professor of Physiology, 1966–82, then
Professor Emeritus, University of Nottingham; *b* 31 May
1917; *s* of late A. W. M. Greenfield, MA, and Winifred
(*née* Peck), Parkstone, Dorset; *m* 1943, Margaret (*née*
Duane) (*d* 1999); one *s* one *d. Educ:* Poole Grammar Sch.;
St Mary's Hospital Medical Sch. (BSc London, 1st class
hons Physiology, 1937; MB, BS 1940, MSc 1947, DSc
1953, London). FRCP 1973. Dunville Prof. of Physiology
in the Queen's Univ. of Belfast, 1948–64; Prof. of
Physiology in the Univ. of London, at St Mary's Hosp.
Med. Sch., 1964–67. Sometime Examr, Oxford,
Cambridge and 21 other Univs, RCS and RCSI; Chm.,
Special Trustees, Nottingham Univ. Hosps, 1984–90.
Member: Physiol. Systems Bd, MRC, 1976–77; UGC,
1977–82 (Chm. Med. and Dental Sub-Cttees, Assessor to
MRC); UPGC, Hong Kong, 1984–89 (Mem. 1981–89
and Chm. 1985–89, Med. Sub-Cttee); GMC and GMC
Educn Cttee, 1979–82; Med. Acad. Adv. Cttee, Chinese
Univ., Hong Kong, 1976–80; Foundn Cttee, Sultan
Qaboos Univ., Oman, 1981–86; Sheffield RHB,
1968–74; Nottingham Univ. HMC, 1969–74; Notts
AHA(T), 1974–79. Pres., Sect. of Biomed. Scis, British
Assoc. for Advancement of Sci., 1972; Mem., Biochemical
and Medical Research Societies. Hon. Mem.,
Physiological Soc., 1987. Chm., Editorial Bd,
Monographs of the Physiological Soc., 1975–79; Member,
Editorial Board: Amer. Heart Jl, 1959–66; Clinical
Science, 1960–65; Cardiovascular Research, 1966–79;
Circulation Res., 1967–73. OStJ 1978. Hon. LLD
Nottingham, 1977; Hon DSc QUB, 1978. Order of Sultan
Qaboos of Oman, 2nd Class, 1986. *Publications:* papers on
control of circulation of the blood, mainly in Lancet,
Journal of Physiology, Clinical Science, and Journal of
Applied Physiology. *Recreations:* sketching, bird watching,
travel. *Address:* 25 Sutton Passeys Crescent, Nottingham
NG8 1BX. *T:* (0115) 978 2424.   *Died 17 Nov. 2005.*

GREENHILL, Dr Basil Jack, CB 1981; CMG 1967;
FRHistS; FSA; author; Vice President, SS Great Britain
Project, since 1992 (Chairman, 1982–92); Chairman,
Centre for Maritime Historical Studies, University of
Exeter, 1991–98; Consultant, Chatham Publishing, since
1996; *b* 26 Feb. 1920; *o c* of B. J. and Edith Greenhill; *m*
1st, 1950, Gillian (*d* 1959), *e d* of Capt. Ralph Tyacke
Stratton, MC; one *s*; 2nd, 1961, Ann, *d* of Walter Ernest
Giffard; one *s. Educ:* Bristol Grammar Sch.; Bristol Univ.
(T. H. Green Scholar; PhD 1980). Served War of
1939–45: Lieut RNVR (Air Br.). Diplomatic Service,
1946–66; served: Pakistan; UK Delegn, New York;
Tokyo; UK Delegate to Conf. on Law of the Sea, Geneva;
Dep. High Comr in Pakistan; Ottawa. Dir, Nat. Maritime
Mus., Greenwich, 1967–83. Mem., Ancient Monuments
Bd for England, 1972–84; Vice Chm. Bd, Trustees of the
Royal Armouries, 1984–88; First Pres., Internat. Congress
of Maritime Museums, 1975–81. President: Devonshire
Assoc., 1984; Devon Hist. Soc., 1993–96; Trustee: Royal
Naval Museum, Portsmouth, 1973–83; Mary Rose Trust,
1979–83; RAF Museum, 1987–96; Univ. of Hull
Maritime Hist. Trust, 1997–. Governor, Dulwich Coll.,
1974–88; Chairman: Dulwich Picture Gall., 1977–88;
Nat. Museums' Directors' Conf., 1980–83; Govt Adv.
Cttee on Historic Wreck Sites, 1986–96. Principal
Advisor: BBC TV series: The Commanding Sea, 1980–82;
Trade Winds, 1984–85; BBC Radio series: The British
Seafarer, 1980–82; The Sea, The Sea, 1991. Hon. Fellow:
Univ. of Exeter, 1985; Univ. of Hull, 2001. Hon. DLitt:
Plymouth, 1996; Hull, 2002. Kt Comdr, Order of White
Rose, Finland, 1980. *Publications:* The Merchant
Schooners, vol. I, 1951, vol. II, 1957, rev. edns 1968,
1978, 1988; (ed and prefaced) W. J. Slade's Out of

Appledore, 1959, rev. edns 1972, 1974, 1980; Sailing For
A Living, 1962; (with Ann Giffard) Westcountrymen in
Prince Edward's Isle, 1967, 3rd edn 1974 (Amer. Assoc.
Award) (filmed 1975); (with Ann Giffard) The Merchant
Sailing Ship: a photographic history, 1970; (with Ann
Giffard) Women under Sail, 1970; Captain Cook, 1970;
Boats and Boatmen of Pakistan, 1971; (with Ann Giffard)
Travelling by Sea in the Nineteenth Century, 1972; (with
Rear-Adm. P. W. Brock) Sail and Steam, 1973; (with W.
J. Slade) West Country Coasting Ketches, 1974; A
Victorian Maritime Album, 1974; A Quayside Camera,
1975; (with L. Willis) The Coastal Trade: sailing craft of
British waters 900–1900, 1975; Archaeology of the Boat,
1976; (with Ann Giffard) Victorian and Edwardian Sailing
Ships, 1976, rev. edns 1981, 1982, 1987; (with Ann
Giffard) Victorian and Edwardian Ships and Harbours,
1978; (ed and prefaced) Georg Kåhrés The Last Tall Ships,
1978 (trans. Norwegian, 1980); (with Ann Giffard)
Victorian and Edwardian Merchant Steamships, 1979;
Schooners, 1980; The Life and Death of the Sailing Ship,
1980; (with Michael Mason) The British Seafarer, 1980;
(with Denis Stonham) Seafaring Under Sail, 1981;
Karlsson, 1982; The Woodshipbuilders, 1986; The Grain
Races, 1986; (with Ann Giffard) The British Assault on
Finland 1854–55, 1988; The Evolution of the Wooden
Ship, 1988; (with John Hackman) The Herzogin Cecilie,
1991 (trans. Swedish, 1991, German, 1993); (ed jtly and
contrib.) The New Maritime History of Devon, vol. 1,
1993, vol. 2, 1994; (ed and contrib.) The Advent of Steam,
1993; (ed and contrib.) The Last Century of Sail, 1993;
(with Owain Roberts) The Årby Boat, 1993; (with Ann
Giffard) Steam, Politics and Patronage, 1994; The Bertha
L. Downs, 1995; The Archaeology of Boats and Ships: an
introduction, 1995; (ed and prefaced) The Evolution of
the Sailing Ship 1250–1580, 1995; (with Peter Allington)
Paddle Wheel, Sail and Screw, 1996; (ed and contrib.) The
Chatham Directory of Inshore Craft, 1997; numerous
articles, reviews and broadcasts. *Recreations:* boating, travel,
coarse gardening. *Address:* West Boetheric Farmhouse, St
Dominic, Saltash, Cornwall PL12 6SZ. *Clubs:* Arts (Hon.
Mem.); Karachi Yacht (Karachi); Åland Nautical
(Mariehamn).   *Died 8 April 2003.*

GREENWOOD, 3rd Viscount *cr* 1937, of Holbourne, co.
London; **Michael George Hamar Greenwood;** Baron
Greenwood 1929; Bt 1915; *b* 5 May 1923; *yr s* of 1st
Viscount Greenwood, PC, KC and Margery, DBE, 2nd *d*
of Rev. Walter Spencer; *S* brother, 1998. *Educ:* Eton;
Christ Church, Oxford; Webber-Douglas Sch. of Singing
and Dramatic Art. Served War of 1939–45, RCS. With
Cazenove & Co., 1944–47; actor, 1947–. *Theatre* incl.
King of France in Joan of Arc at the Stake, 1947; *films:* The
Big Money; House in the Woods; The Bank Raiders;
Poor Cow; The Insomniac; *television* includes: The
Appleyards, Emergency Ward 10, Falstaff, Great
Expectations, Androcles and the Lion, Charlie Drake
Show, Dixon of Dock Green, Rob Roy, Adam Adamant
Lives, Honey Lane, Gnomes of Dulwich, Eric Sykes
Show. *Heir:* none. *Address:* 63 Portsea Hall, Portsea Place,
W2 2BY. *T:* (020) 7402 2975.

Died 7 July 2003 (ext).

GREENWOOD, His Honour Peter Bryan; a Circuit
Judge, 1972–99. Called to the Bar, Gray's Inn, 1955; Dep.
Chm., Essex QS, 1968–71. *Address:* c/o The Crown
Court, PO Box 9, Chelmsford, Essex CM1 1EL.
Died 4 June 2002.

GREETHAM, John Francis, CBE 1994; Chairman,
Whitewater Leisure Group, since 1993; *b* 17 July 1939; *s*
of Francis Greetham and Marjorie Greetham (*née* Seal); *m*
1977, Jill Herring; three *s* one *d. Educ:* Nunthorpe
Grammar Sch., York. Served RE, 1957–59. Dental equipt
mfr and designer, 1959–77; dairy farmer, 1977–87; Chief
Exec., Whitewater Leisure Gp, 1987–93. N Yorkshire
County Council: Member: (Independent), 1978–82; (C),
1982–86; Vice-Chm., Children and Young Persons Cttee,

1978–82; Mem., N Yorks Moors Cttee, 1978–86; Mem., Social Services Cttee, 1978–86. Member: N Yorks FPC, 1979–83; Scarborough DHA, 1980–84; Yorks RHA, 1984–90 (Vice-Chm., 1987–90); York DHA, 1990–91; Chairman: St James's Univ. Teaching Hosp. NHS Trust, 1991–94; Northern and Yorks RHA, later Northern and Yorks Region, NHS Exec., 1994–97. Founder Chm., NHS Trust Fedn, 1991–93; Council Mem., NAHAT, 1992–94; Member: NHS Audit Cttee, 1993–94; Private Sector Finance Gp, NHS, 1994; Bd, NHS Estates, 1994–98; NHS Policy Bd, 1994–97. Mem. Court Leeds Univ., 1991–98; Gov., Leeds Metropolitan Univ., 1991–. CIMgt; FInstD. *Recreations:* golf, swimming, walking, horse-riding, shooting, music. *Address:* The Old Rectory, Lockton, Pickering, York YO18 7PZ. *T:* (01751) 460253.
Died 16 April 2001.

GREGG, Hubert Robert Harry, MBE 2002; actor, composer, lyric writer, author, playwright and director; *b* London, 19 July 1914; *s* of Robert Joseph Gregg and Alice Maud (*née* Bessant); *m* 1st, 1943, Zoe Gail (marr. diss. 1950); one *d*; 2nd, 1956, Pat Kirkwood (marr. diss. 1979); 3rd, 1980, Carmel Lytton; one *s* one *d. Educ:* St Dunstan's Coll.; Webber-Douglas Sch. of Singing and Dramatic Art; BA Hons Open 1997. Served War, 1939–44: private, Lincs Regt, 1939; commnd 60th Rifles, 1940; transf. Intell.; with Polit. Warfare Exec., 1942 (duties included broadcasting in German). *Stage:* 1st London appearance, Julien in Martine, Ambassadors', 1933; Birmingham Rep., 1933–34; Shakespearean roles, Open Air Theatre, Regent's Park and at Old Vic, 1934, 1935; 1st New York appearance, Kit Neilan in French without Tears, 1937 (and London, 1938–39); London appearances include: Pip in The Convict, 1935; roles in classics (Orlando, Henry V, Hamlet), 1935–36; Frederick Hackett in Great Possessions, 1937; Peter Scott-Fowler in After the Dance, 1939; Polly in Men in Shadow, 1942; Michael Caraway in Acacia Avenue, 1944; Earl of Harpenden in While the Sun Shines, 1945, 1946; Tom D'Arcy in Off the Record, 1947; Gabriel Hathaway in Western Wind, 1949; (1st musical), John Blessington-Briggs in Chrysanthemum, 1958; Lionel Toope in Pools Paradise, 1961. *Chichester Festival Theatre:* Alexander MacColgie Gibbs in The Cocktail Party, Antonio in The Tempest, and Announcer in The Skin of our Teeth, 1968; Sir Lucius O'Trigger in The Rivals, Britannus in Caesar and Cleopatra, and Marcellin in Dear Antoine (also London), 1971. *Directed, London:* The Hollow (Agatha Christie's 1st stage success), 1951; re-staged To Dorothy - a Son, 1952 (subseq. toured in play, 1952–53); The Mousetrap (for 7 yrs from 1953); Speaking of Murder, 1958; The Unexpected Guest, 1958; From the French, 1959; Go Back for Murder, 1960; Rule of Three, 1962; re-staged The Secretary Bird, 1969 (subseq. toured in play, 1969–70). 1st solo performance, Leicester, 1970; subseq. performances in Britain and America (subjects include Shakespeare, Shaw, Jerome K. Jerome, the London Theatre, and the 20s, 30s and 40s); solo perf., Words by Elgar, Music by Shaw, Malvern Fest., 1978, Edinburgh Fest., 1979. *Films include:* In Which We Serve; Flying Fortress; Acacia Avenue (USA as The Facts of Love); The Root of all Evil; Vote for Huggett; Once upon a Dream; Robin Hood (Walt Disney); The Maggie (USA as High and Dry); Svengali; Doctor at Sea (also wrote music and lyrics); Simon and Laura; Speaking of Murder; The Third Visitor; Final Appointment; Room in the House; Stars in Your Eyes (also co-dir. and wrote music and lyrics). *Author of plays:* We Have Company (played in tour, 1953); Cheque Mate (dir. and appeared in); Villa Sleep Four (played in tour, 1965); From the French (written under pseudonym of Jean-Paul Marotte); Who's Been Sleeping . . . ? (also appeared in); The Rumpus (played in tour, 1967); Dear Somebody (perf. Germany as Geliebtes Traumbild, 1984); (screenplay) After the Ball (adapted from own television biog. of Vesta Tilley). *Songs:* Author of over 200, including: I'm going to get lit up; Maybe it's because I'm a Londoner. BBC broadcasts in drama, revue, poetry, etc, 1933–; announcer, BBC Empire

Service, 1934–35; radio musical of Three Men in a Boat, 1962 (adapted, wrote music and words, and appeared in); weekly radio progs with accent on nostalgia, 1965– (A Square Deal, I Remember it Well, Now and Then, Thanks for the Memory); Chairman: BBC TV Brains Trust, 1955; Youth Wants to Know, ITV, 1957; 40 week radio series on London theatres, 1974–75; biog. series: I Call it Genius, 1980–81; I Call it Style, 1981–; Hubert Gregg Remembers, ITV solo series, 1982–; 50 Years of Broadcasting, BBC celebration prog. Maybe It's Because …, 1984 (Sony Radio Award, 1985); Hubert Gregg Remembers (series for BBC World Service), 1985–; (wrote book, music and lyrics, and appeared in) Sweet Liza (radio musical play), 1985; (wrote script, music and lyrics for, and presented) My London (radio), 1986; (wrote and presented) Sounds and Sweet Airs (celebration of 60 yrs at the microphone), 1993; (wrote music and lyrics for) Sherry (musical play), 1993; (wrote and presented) Hubert Gregg and the Forties (commemorating 50th anniversary of D-Day), 1994; (wrote and presented) Hubert Gregg and the Twenties, Hubert Gregg and the Thirties, (radio), 1995; Hubert Gregg and the Fifties, 1996. Has dir., lectured and adjudicated at Webber-Douglas Sch., Central Sch. of Speech Trng and RADA. Patron, Cinema Theatre Assoc., 1973–; President: Northern Boys' Book Club, 1975– (succeeded P. G. Wodehouse); Concert Artists Assoc., 1979–80. Freedom of City of London, 1981. Gold Badge of Merit, British Acad. of Composers, Authors and Song Writers, 1982. *Publications:* April Gentleman (novel), 1951; We Have Company (play), 1953; A Day's Loving (novel), 1974; Agatha Christie and all that Mousetrap, 1980; Thanks for the Memory (biographies collected from radio series I Call it Genius and I Call it Style), 1983; Geliebtes Traumbild (play), 1984; music and lyrics. *Recreation:* nostalgia. *Address:* c/o Broadcasting House, W1A 1AA. *Club:* Garrick. *Died 29 March 2004.*

GRENFELL-BAINES, Prof. Sir George, Kt 1978; OBE 1960; DL; FRIBA; FRTPI; consultant architect-planner; consultant to Building Design Partnership; *b* Preston, 30 April 1908; *s* of Ernest Charles Baines and Sarah Elizabeth (*née* Grenfell); *m* 1st, 1939, Dorothy Hodson (marr. diss. 1952); two *d*; 2nd, 1954, Milena Ruth Fleischmann; one *s* one *d. Educ:* Roebuck Street Council Sch.; Harris Coll., Preston; Manchester Univ. (DipTP). RIBA Dist Town Planning, 1963. Commenced architectural practice, 1937; founded: Grenfell Baines Gp, 1940; Building Design Partnership, a multi-disciplinary practice covering all aspects of built environment, 1959 (Partner/Chm.), retired 1974; The Design Teaching Practice, 1974, retired 1979. Prof. and Head of Dept of Architecture, Univ. of Sheffield, 1972–75, Emeritus, 1976. Lectr/critic, 14 USA and Canadian univs, 1966; initiated own lecture tour USSR, visiting 19 cities, 1971; expert adviser: UNESCO Conf. Bldgs; Higher Educn, Chile, 1968; Conescal, Mexico City, 1973. RIBA: Mem. Council (nationally elected), 1952–70; Vice-Pres., 1967–69; Ext. examr, 12 Schs of Architecture, 1953–70; Chm. Cttees on Professional Practice, Town Planning, Gp Practice and Consortia; Architectural Competition Assessor 8 times; several competition awards: first place in 7 (one internat.); 18 premiums (four internat.). Hon. Fellow: Manchester Poly., 1974; Lancashire Poly., 1985. Hon. Vice-Pres., N Lancs Soc. Architects, 1977. Hon. Fellow, Amer. Inst. of Architects, 1982; Hon. Mem., IAA (Moscow Br.), 1998. Broadcaster, UK and Canada. Hon. DLitt Sheffield, 1981. DL Lancs, 1982. *Publications:* contribs to tech. jls. *Recreations:* brooding: on economics and alternative medicine; walking: on hills and by sea-shore. *Address:* 56 & 60 West Cliff, Preston, Lancs PR1 8HU. *T:* (01772) 252131, 555824. *Died 9 May 2003.*

GRENSIDE, Sir John (Peter), Kt 1983; CBE 1974; Senior Partner, Peat, Marwick, Mitchell & Co., Chartered Accountants, 1977–86; *b* 23 Jan. 1921; *s* of late Harold Cutcliffe Grenside and late Muriel Grenside; *m* 1946, Yvonne Thérèse Grau; one *s* one *d. Educ:* Rugby School.

ACA 1948, FCA 1960. War Service, Royal Artillery, 1941–46 (Captain). Joined Peat, Marwick, Mitchell & Co., 1948, Partner, 1960, Senior Partner, 1977; Chm., Peat Marwick Internat., 1980–83. Inst. Chartered Accountants: Mem. Council, 1966–83; Chm. of Parliamentary and Law Cttee, 1972–73; Vice-Pres., 1973–74; Dep. Pres., 1974–75; Pres., 1975–76; Chm., Overseas Relations Cttee, 1976–78; UK Rep. on Internat. Accounting Standards Cttee, 1976–80. Jt Vice-Pres., Groupe d'Etudes des Experts Comptables de la CEE, 1972–75; Chm., Review Bd for Govt Contracts, 1983–86; Mem. Panel of Judges for Accountants' Award for Company Accounts, 1973–77. Director: Allied-Lyons plc, 1986–93; Nomura Bank Internat. plc, 1987–96. Master, Worshipful Co. of Chartered Accountants in England and Wales, 1987–88. *Publications:* various articles for UK and US accountancy jls. *Recreations:* tennis, bridge. *Address:* 51 Cadogan Lane, SW1X 9DT. *T:* (020) 7235 3372. *Clubs:* Pilgrims, MCC, All England Lawn Tennis, Hurlingham.
Died 28 May 2004.

GRIBBLE, Rev. Canon Arthur Stanley, MA; Canon Residentiary and Chancellor of Peterborough Cathedral, 1967–79, then Canon Emeritus; *b* 18 Aug. 1904; *er s* of J. B. Gribble; *m* 1938, Edith Anne, *er d* of late Laurence Bailey; one *s*. *Educ:* Queens' Coll. and Westcott House, Cambridge (Burney Student, Univ. of Cambridge); Univ. of Heidelberg. Ordained deacon, 1930, priest, 1931; Curate: St Mary, Windermere, 1930–33; Almondbury, 1933–36; Chaplain, Sarum Theological Coll., 1936–38; Rector of Shepton Mallet, 1938–54; Principal, Queen's Coll., Birmingham and Recognised Lectr, Univ. of Birmingham, 1954–67. Examining Chaplain to Bp of Bath and Wells, 1947–54; Proctor in Convocation, diocese Bath and Wells, 1947–54; Rural Dean of Shepton Mallet, 1949–54; Prebendary of Wiveliscombe in Wells Cathedral, 1949–54; Hon. Canon, Birmingham Cathedral, 1954–67; Examng Chaplain to Bishop of Peterborough, 1968–84. Visiting Lectr, Graduate Theological Union, Berkeley, USA, 1970. Commissary for the Bishop of Kimberley and Kuruman, 1964–66. *Recreation:* mountaineering. *Address:* 2 Coylton Terrace, Bayford Hill, Wincanton, Somerset BA9 9LQ. *T:* (01963) 33678. *Died 9 March 2002.*

GRIEVE, Hon. Lord; William Robertson Grieve, VRD 1958; a Senator of the College of Justice in Scotland, 1972–88; *b* 21 Oct. 1917; *o s* of William Robertson Grieve (killed in action 1917); *m* 1947, Lorna St John (*d* 1989), *y d* of late Engineer Rear-Adm. E. P. St J. Benn, CB; one *s* one *d*. *Educ:* Glasgow Acad.; Sedbergh; Glasgow Univ. (John Clark (Mile-end) Schol., 1939; MA 1939, LLB 1946). Pres., Glasgow Univ. Union, 1938–39. RNVR: Sub-Lt 1939; Lieut 1942; Lt-Comdr 1950; served with RN, 1939–46. Admitted Mem., Faculty of Advocates, 1947; QC (Scot.) 1957. Junior Counsel in Scotland to Bd of Inland Revenue, 1952–57; Advocate-Depute (Home), 1962–64; Sheriff-Principal of Renfrew and Argyll, 1964–72. Procurator of the Church of Scotland, 1969–72; a Judge of the Courts of Appeal of Jersey and Guernsey, 1971. Independent Chm., Fish Farming Adv. Cttee, 1989. Chairman of Governors: Fettes Trust, 1978–86; St Columba's Hospice, 1981–99. *Recreations:* golf, painting. *Address:* 20 Belgrave Crescent, Edinburgh EH4 3AJ. *T:* (0131) 332 7500. *Clubs:* New (Edinburgh); Hon. Co. of Edinburgh Golfers; West Sussex Golf; Queen's Park Rangers Football. *Died 10 July 2005.*

GRIEVE, William Robertson; see Grieve, Hon. Lord.

GRIFFIN, Sir (Charles) David, Kt 1974; CBE 1972; *b* 8 July 1915; *s* of Eric Furnival Griffin and Nellie Clarendon Griffin (*née* Devenish-Meares); *m* 1941, Jean Falconer Whyte; two *s*. *Educ:* Cranbrook Sch., Sydney; Univ. of Sydney (LLB and Golf Blue). 8th Aust. Div. 2nd AIF, 1940–45; POW Changi, Singapore, 1942–45. Associate to Sir Dudley Williams and Mem. Bar NSW, 1946–49; Solicitor, Sydney, 1949–64. Alderman, Sydney City

Council, 1962–74, Chm. Finance Cttee, 1969–72; Lord Mayor of Sydney, 1972–73. Hon. Chm., Nabalco Pty Ltd, 1980–; Director: Lawpoint Pty Ltd, 1985–98 (Chm., 1985–88); OTC/Lawpoint, 1988–. Mem. Council, Royal Agricl Soc.; Mem. Nat. Council, Scout Assoc. of Australia (Life Councillor, NSW Br.); Dir, Nat. Seniors' Assoc. of Aust., 1991–. *Publications:* The Happiness Box (for children); The Will of the People; sundry speeches and short stories. *Recreations:* golf, fly-fishing. *Clubs:* Union (Sydney); Royal Sydney Golf, Pine Valley Golf (NJ, USA). *Died 25 March 2004.*

GRIFFITH, Owen Glyn, CBE 1980 (OBE 1969); MVO 1954; HM Diplomatic Service, retired; High Commissioner in Lesotho, 1978–81; *b* 19 Jan. 1922; *s* of late William Glyn Griffith and Gladys Glyn Griffith (*née* Picton Davies); *m* 1949, Rosemary Elizabeth Cecil Earl; two *s*. *Educ:* Oundle Sch.; Trinity Hall, Cambridge. Commnd in Welsh Guards (twice wounded in N Africa), 1941–43; Colonial Service (later HMOCS), Uganda, 1944–63: District Officer, 1944–51; Private Sec. to Governor, 1952–54; Dist Comr, 1954–61; Perm. Sec., Min. of Commerce and Industry, 1961–63; Principal, CRO, 1963; 1st Sec. and Head of Chancery, British Embassy, Khartoum, 1965; 1st Sec. (Commercial), British Embassy, Stockholm, 1969; Dep. British High Comr, Malaŵi, 1973; Inspector, 1976–78. *Recreations:* golf, fishing. *Address:* The Sundial, 10 Marsham Way, Gerrards Cross, Bucks SL9 8AD. *Club:* Denham Golf.
Died 16 June 2001.

GRIFFITHS, Lady; see Brigstocke, Baroness.

GRIFFITHS, Air Vice-Marshal Arthur, CB 1972; AFC 1964; *b* 22 Aug. 1922; *s* of late Edward and Elizabeth Griffiths; *m* 1950, Nancy Maud Sumpter; one *d*. *Educ:* Hawarden Grammar Sch. Joined RAF, 1940; war service with No 26 Fighter Reconnaissance Sqdn; post-war years as Flying Instructor mainly at CFS and Empire Flying Sch.; psc 1954; comd No 94 Fighter Sqdn Germany, 1955–56; Dirg Staff, RCAF Staff Coll., Toronto, 1956–59; HQ Bomber Comd, 1959–61; comd No 101 Bomber Sqdn, 1962–64; Gp Captain Ops, Bomber Comd, 1964–67; comd RAF Waddington, 1967–69; AOA and later Chief of Staff, Far East Air Force, 1969–71; Head of British Defence Liaison Staff, Canberra, 1972–74; Dir Gen., Security (RAF), 1976–77, and Comdt-Gen. RAF Regt, 1975–77. *Address:* Water Lane House, Castor, Peterborough PE5 7BJ. *T:* (01733) 380742. *Club:* Royal Air Force. *Died 13 Feb. 2003.*

GRIFFITHS, His Honour David John; a Circuit Judge, 1984–2000; Resident Judge, Maidstone Crown Court, 1995–2000; *b* 18 Feb. 1931; *m* Anita; three *s* one *d*. *Educ:* St Dunstan's Coll., Catford, SE6. Admitted to Roll of Solicitors, 1957; apptd Notary Public, 1969; Principal: D. J. Griffiths & Co., Bromley, 1960–84; Harveys, Lewisham, 1970–84. A Recorder, 1980–84. Mem., Scriveners' Co., 1983. *Recreations:* riding, music (male voice choir). *Club:* Farmers. *Died 4 Dec. 2004.*

GRIFFITHS, Islwyn Owen; QC 1973; a Recorder of the Crown Court, 1972–84; *b* 24 Jan. 1924; *m* 1951, Pamela Norah Blizard. *Educ:* Swansea Grammar Sch.; Christ Church, Oxford (MA, BCL). Army (Royal Artillery), 1942–47; TA (RA), 1947–51; TARO, 1951. Called to the Bar, Lincoln's Inn, 1953; Dep. Chm., Bucks QS, 1967–71. Comr, 1979–84, Chief Comr, 1981–84, National Insurance, later Social Security, Commn. *Recreation:* sailing. *Address:* Kings Farm House, Wimland Road, Faygate, near Horsham, Sussex RH12 4SS.
Died 5 May 2001.

GRIGG, John Edward Poynder, FRSL; writer; *b* 15 April 1924; *s* of 1st Baron Altrincham, KCMG, KCVO, DSO, MC, PC and Hon. Joan Dickson-Poynder, *o c* of 1st Baron Islington, GCMG, GBE, PC; *S* to father's barony, 1955, but did not apply for Writ of Summons to House of Lords;

discalimed title, 31 July 1963; *m* 1958, Patricia, *d* of late H. E. Campbell and Marion Wheeler; two adopted *s*. *Educ*: Eton; New Coll., Oxford (Exhibitioner; MA, Modern History; Gladstone Memorial Prize). Grenadier Guards, 1943–45. Editor, National and English Review, 1954–60; Columnist for The Guardian, 1960–70; with The Times, 1986–93. Pres., The London Library, 1996– (Chm., 1985–91). Pres., Blackheath Soc. Contested (C) Oldham West, 1951 and 1955. *Publications*: Two Anglican Essays, 1958; The Young Lloyd George, 1973; Lloyd George: the People's Champion, 1978 (Whitbread Award); 1943: The Victory That Never Was, 1980; Nancy Astor: Portrait of a Pioneer, 1980; Lloyd George: From Peace to War 1912–1916, 1985 (Wolfson Literary Prize); The History of The Times, Vol. 6: the Thomson Years, 1993; *posthumous publication*: Lloyd George: War Leader, 2002; contribs to other books, incl. DNB; articles and reviews. *Heir: Heir* (to disclaimed peerage): *b* Anthony Ulick David Dundas Grigg [*b* 12 Jan. 1934; *m* 1965, Elaine, *d* of Marquis de Miramon; two *s* one *d*]. *Address*: 32 Dartmouth Row, SE10 8AW. *T*: (020) 8692 4973. *Clubs*: Garrick, Beefsteak. *Died 31 Dec. 2001.*

GRIMSEY, Colin Robert; JP; consultant; *b* Manchester, 24 Dec. 1943; *yr s* of Arthur and Joan Grimsey; *m* 1976, Elizabeth Sermon; one *s* one *d*. *Educ*: Dartford Grammar Sch.; King's Coll., London (BSc Hons Physics 1964). Asst Principal, MoT, 1968–72; Principal, DoE, 1972–75; CSSB, 1975; DoE, 1976–79; Asst Sec., Dept of Transport, 1979–89; Under Sec., seconded to LRT, 1989–91; Dir of Finance, 1991–93, Head of Railways Directorate, 1993–96, Dept of Transport. JP NW Surrey, 1997. *Recreations*: family, choral singing, opera and theatre going, walking. *Died 6 April 2002.*

GRIMSTON OF WESTBURY, 2nd Baron *cr* 1964; **Robert Walter Sigismund Grimston;** Bt 1952; Director: Gray's Inn (Underwriting Agencies) Ltd, 1965–90 (Chairman, 1970–88); River Clyde Holdings, 1986–88; *b* 14 June 1925; *s* of 1st Baron Grimston of Westbury and Sybil Edith Muriel Rose (*d* 1977), *d* of Sir Sigismund Neumann, 1st Bt; *S* father, 1979; *m* 1949, Hon. June Mary Ponsonby, *d* of 5th Baron de Mauley; two *s* one *d*. *Educ*: Eton. Served Scots Guards, 1943–47 (Lt); NW Europe, 1944–45. Oil Industry, 1948–53; Sales Dir, Ditchling Press, 1953–61; Dir, Hinton Hill & Coles Ltd, 1962–83. Freeman, City of London, 1981; Liveryman, Gold and Silver Wyre Drawers' Co., 1981. *Recreations*: tennis, shooting, golf, walking. *Heir: s* Hon. Robert John Sylvester Grimston [*b* 30 April 1951; *m* 1984, Emily Margaret, *d* of Major John Shirley; two *d*]. *Address*: The Old Rectory, Westwell, near Burford, Oxon OX18 4JT. *Club*: Boodle's. *Died 16 June 2003.*

GRIMTHORPE, 4th Baron *cr* 1886; **Christopher John Beckett,** OBE 1958; Bt 1813; DL; Deputy Commander, Malta and Libya, 1964–67; *b* 16 Sept. 1915; *e s* of 3rd Baron Grimthorpe, TD, and Mary Lady Grimthorpe (*d* 1962); *S* father, 1963; *m* 1954, Lady Elizabeth Lumley (Lady Grimthorpe, DCVO); two *s* one *d*. *Educ*: Eton. 2nd Lieut, 9 Lancers, 1936; Lt-Col, 9 Lancers, 1955–58; AAG, War Office, 1958–61; Brigadier, Royal Armoured Corps, HQ, Western Command, 1961–64. Col, 9/12 Royal Lancers, 1973–77. ADC to the Queen, 1964–67. Director: Standard Broadcasting Corp. of Canada (UK), 1972–86; Thirsk Racecourse Ltd, 1972–; Yorkshire Post Newspapers, 1973–86; Pres., London Metropolitan Region YMCA, 1972–86. Mem., Jockey Club. DL North Yorkshire, 1969. *Recreations*: travel, horse sports. *Heir: s* Hon. Edward John Beckett [*b* 20 Nov. 1954; *m* 1992, Mrs Carey Elisabeth McEwen, *d* of Robin Graham; one *s*]. *Address*: Westow Hall, York YO60 7NE. *T*: (01653) 618225. *Clubs*: Cavalry and Guards, Portland. *Died 6 July 2003.*

GRINDON, John Evelyn, CVO 1957; DSO 1945; AFC 1948; Group Captain, RAF retired; *b* 30 Sept. 1917; *s* of Thomas Edward Grindon (killed in action, Ypres, Oct.

1917), and Dora (*née* Eastlake), Corisande, East Pentire, Cornwall; *m* 1st, 1937, Marion Hubber (marr. diss.); two *s*; 2nd, 1960, Marianne Jeanette Cheetham-Hill; one *s* one *d*. *Educ*: Dulwich College. Flight Cadet at RAF College, Cranwell, 1935–37; served in Advanced Air Striking Force, BEF, France, 1939–40 (No 150 Sqdn) and in No 5 Group Bomber Command (Nos 106, 630 and 617 Sqdns) during War of 1939–45, as Flight and Sqdn Comdr; Chief Instructor, Long Range Transport Force, 1946–49; Commanded The Queen's Flight, 1953–56; V-bomber captain and Station Comdr, 1956–57; retired at own request 1959. Dir/Gen. Manager in printing/publishing, 1961–71; Metropolitan Police, New Scotland Yard, 1976–81. *Recreations*: opera, ocean surf, racing. *Club*: Royal Air Force. *Died 11 Nov. 2001.*

GRINDROD, Helen Marjorie; QC 1982; a Recorder of the Crown Court, 1981–95; *b* 28 Feb. 1936; *d* of late Joseph and Marjorie Pritchard; *m* 1958, Robert Michael Grindrod; one *s*. *Educ*: Liverpool Inst. High Sch. for Girls; St Hilda's Coll., Oxford (MA; Hon. Fellow). Teacher, 1957–59. Called to the Bar, Lincoln's Inn, 1966, Bencher, 1990; Northern Circuit, 1966–2000. *Address*: Cerin Amroth, Beechfield Road, Alderley Edge SK9 7AU. *Died 11 July 2002.*

GRINT, Edmund Thomas Charles, CBE 1960; *b* 14 Feb. 1904; *e s* of Edmund Albert Grint; *m* 1930, Olive Maria (*d* 1991), *d* of Albert Cheyne Sherras; one *s* two *d*. *Educ*: London Univ. (Dip. Econs). Joined ICI, 1929; Commercial Dir, Nobel Div., 1946; Director: Billingham Div., 1952–61; Alkali Div., 1961–63; Mond Div., 1964; Dep. Chief Labour Officer, 1951; Chief Labour Officer, 1952–63; Gen. Manager Personnel, 1963–65. Chm., Nat. Dock Labour Board, 1966–69; Pres., Midland Iron and Steel Wages Bd, 1971–79. *Recreations*: golf, gardening. *Address*: Old Walls, Seal, Sevenoaks, Kent TN15 0JB. *T*: (01732) 61364. *Died 8 Feb. 2001.*

GRIST, Ian; Chairman, South Glamorgan Health Authority, 1992–96; *b* 5 Dec. 1938; *s* of late Basil William Grist, MBE and Leila Helen Grist; *m* 1966, Wendy Anne (*née* White), BSc; two *s*. *Educ*: Repton Sch.; Jesus Coll., Oxford (Schol.). Plebiscite Officer, Southern Cameroons, 1960–61; Stores Manager, United Africa Co., Nigeria, 1961–63; Wales Information Officer, Conservative Central Office, 1963–74; Conservative Research Dept, 1970–74. MP (C) Cardiff North, Feb. 1974–1983, Cardiff Central, 1983–92; contested (C) Cardiff Central, 1992. PPS to Secretary of State for Wales, 1979–81; Parly Under Sec. of State, Welsh Office, 1987–90. Member Select Committee on: Violence in the Family, 1977–79; Welsh Affairs, 1981–83 and 1986–87; Register of Members' Interests, 1983–87. Chm., Cons. W African Cttee, 1977–87 and 1991–92. Vice-Chm., Assoc. of Conservative Clubs, 1978–82. *Recreations*: reading, listening to music. *Address*: 1 Heol Ifor, Rhiwbina, Cardiff CF14 1SZ. *T*: (029) 2062 7483. *Died 2 Jan. 2002.*

GROVE, Maj.-Gen. David Anthony, OBE 1985; DL; retired, 1993; *b* 26 Aug. 1941; *s* of Lancelot Townley Grove and Joan Blanche Grove (*née* Hill); *m* 1971, Olivia Mary Crook; one *s* one *d*. *Educ*: Charterhouse Sch.; Univ. of Alberta (BSc Hons Physics). psc† 1974, RCDS 1988. Commissioned Royal Engineers, 1965; served BAOR, 1965–68; UKLF, 1969–70; Instructor, RSME, 1971–72; Staff Coll.; DAA&QMG, 24 Airportable Bde, 1975–76; BAOR, 1977–78; Instructor, Staff College, 1983; MA to VCGS, 1983–84; ASD, 1985; Comdt, RSME, 1986–87; Dep. Mil. Sec. (A), 1989–90; DGPS (Army), 1991–92; led Study into Future Career Structures for Army Officers and Soldiers, 1992–93. Col Comdt, RE, 1995–2003. Chm., RE Assoc., 1997–2000. Trustee, Haig Homes, 1998–2003. Comr, Duke of York's Royal Mil. Sch., 1998– (Chm. of Comrs, 2000–02). Chm., Stelling Minnis Parish Council, 1999–2002. Churchwarden, St Mary's, Stelling, 1999–. DL Kent, 2001. *Recreations*: golf, gardening, ski-ing. *Died 31 Dec. 2005.*

GROVE, Dennis; see Grove, W. D.

GROVE, (William) Dennis; Chairman, North West Water Group, 1989–93; *b* 23 July 1927; *s* of late William Grove and Elizabeth Charlotte Grove (*née* Bradley); *m* 1953, Audrey Irma Saxel; one *s* one *d. Educ:* Gowerton School; King's College, London (BSc). Joined Dunlop Group, 1951, subseq. Overseas Gen. Manager, to 1970; Chm. and Chief Exec., TPT, 1970–85; Vice-Pres., Sonoco International, 1978–85; Chm., NW Water Authy, 1985–89. *Recreations:* sports bystander, travel, golf. *Address:* Alderley Edge, Cheshire SK9 7XD. *Club:* Bramall Park Golf.   *Died 11 April 2004.*

GROVES, Ronald Edward, CBE 1972; Chairman, 1982–87, and Managing Director, 1984–86, Meyer International plc (following merger of International Timber with Montague L. Meyer in 1982); *b* 2 March 1920; *s* of Joseph Rupert and Eva Lilian Groves; *m* 1940, Beryl Doris Lydia Collins (*d* 2000); two *s* one *d. Educ:* Watford Grammar School. Joined J. Gliksten & Son Ltd. Served War of 1939–45, Flt-Lt RAF, subseq. Captain with BOAC. Re-joined J. Gliksten & Son Ltd, 1946: Gen. Works Man. 1947; Dir 1954; Jt Man. Dir 1964; Vice-Chm. 1967; Dir, Gliksten (West Africa) Ltd, 1949; Vice-Chm., International Timber Corp. Ltd, 1970 (name of J. Gliksten & Son Ltd changed to International Timber Corp. Ltd, 1970 following merger with Horsley Smith & Jewson Ltd); Chief Exec., 1973, Chm., 1976, Internat. Timber. Dir, Nat. Building Agency, 1978–82; Mem., EDC for Building, 1982–86; President: London and District Sawmill Owners Assoc., 1954–56; Timber Trade Fedn of UK, 1969–71; Nat. Council of Building Material Producers, 1987–90 (Mem., Cttee of Mgt, 1982–94); Timber Res. and Develt Assoc., 1990–98; Chm., Nat. Sawmilling Assoc., 1966–67. Mem., London and Regional Affairs Cttee, 1980–95, and Mem. Council, 1982–95, London Chamber of Commerce and Industry; Mem., London Regl Council, CBI, 1983–87; Dir, Business in the Community, 1984–87. Chairman: Rickmansworth UDC, 1957–58, 1964–65 and 1971–72 (Mem., 1951–74); W Herts Main Drainage Authority, 1970–74; Three Rivers District Council, 1977–78 (Mem., 1974–96); Mem., Herts CC, 1964–74. Pres., SW Herts Conservative Assoc., 2000–. Chairman of Governors: Watford Grammar Sch. for Girls, 1980–98; Watford Grammar Sch. for Boys, 1980–98. *Recreations:* visiting theatre and opera; local community work. *Address:* 8 Pembroke Road, Moor Park, Northwood, Middx HA6 2HR. *T:* (01923) 823187.   *Died 24 Feb. 2003.*

GRUNFELD, Prof. Cyril; Professor of Law, London School of Economics and Political Science, 1966–82, then Emeritus; *b* 26 Sept. 1922; *o s* of Samuel and Sarah Grunfeld; *m* 1945, Phyllis Levin; one *s* two *d. Educ:* Canton High Sch., Cardiff; Trinity Hall, Cambridge (MA, LLB). Called to the Bar, Inner Temple. British Army, 1942–45; Trinity Hall (Studentship), 1946–48; London School of Economics and Political Science: Asst, 1946–47; Asst Lectr, 1947–49; Lectr, 1949–56; Reader in Law, 1956–66; Pro-Dir, 1973–76; Convener, Law Dept, 1976–79; Dean, Faculty of Law, Univ. of London, 1978–80. Part-time Lectr in Trade Union Law, Ruskin Coll., Oxford, 1954–64; Vis. Research Fellow, ANU, 1970–71. Legal Adviser: to Commn on Industrial Relations, 1971–74; to Industrial Soc., 1982–87; to Nat. Assoc. of Port Employers, 1988–89. Mem., Trade Union Reform Cttee, Centre for Policy Studies, 1982–85. *Publications:* Modern Trade Union Law, 1966; The Law of Redundancy, 1971, 3rd edn 1989; contrib. to books and learned jls. *Recreations:* reading, walking. *Address:* c/o London School of Economics and Political Science, Houghton Street, WC2A 2AE.   *Died 20 Sept. 2001.*

GRUNSELL, Prof. Charles Stuart Grant, CBE 1976; PhD; Professor of Veterinary Medicine, University of Bristol, 1957–80, then Emeritus; *b* 6 Jan. 1915; *s* of Stuart and Edith Grunsell; *m* 1939, Marjorie Prunella Wright

(decd); one *s* two *d. Educ:* Shanghai Public Sch.; Bristol Grammar Sch.; The Royal (Dick) Veterinary Coll., Edinburgh (MRCVS 1937); PhD Edinburgh 1952. FRCVS 1971. In general practice at Glastonbury, Som, 1939–48; Senior Lecturer in Veterinary Hygiene and Preventive Medicine, Univ. of Edinburgh, 1952. Pro-Vice-Chancellor, Univ. of Bristol, 1974–77. Chm., Veterinary Products Cttee, 1970–80. Mem., General Synod of C of E, 1980–85; a Diocesan Reader. Defence Medal, 1946. *Publications:* papers on the erythron of ruminants, on vital statistics in veterinary medicine, on preventive medicine, and on veterinary education. *Recreation:* gardening. *Address:* Greenleaves, Mead Lane, Sandford, Bristol BS19 5RG. *T:* (01934) 822461.
                                         Died 27 May 2005.

GRYLLS, Sir Michael; see Grylls, Sir W. M. J.

GRYLLS, Sir (William) Michael (John), Kt 1992; *b* 21 Feb. 1934; *s* of late Brig. W. E. H. Grylls, OBE; *m* 1965, Sarah Smiles Justice, *d* of Captain N. M. Ford and Patricia, later Lady Fisher; one *s* one *d. Educ:* RN College, Dartmouth; Univ. of Paris. Lieut, Royal Marines, 1952–55. Mem., St Pancras Borough Council, 1959–62; Mem. GLC, 1967–70; Dep. Leader, ILEA, 1969–70; Chm., Further and Higher Educn, 1968–70. Contested (C) Fulham, 1964 and 1966. MP (C): Chertsey, 1970–74; NW Surrey, 1974–97. Mem., Select Cttee on Overseas Develt, 1970–78; Chairman: Cons. Trade and Industry Cttee, 1981–97 (Vice-Chm., Cons. Industry Cttee, 1975–81); Small Business Bureau, 1979–97. *Recreations:* sailing, riding, gardening, reading. *Address:* Winterborne Zelston House, near Blandford, Dorset DT11 9EU. *Clubs:* Carlton, Beefsteak; Royal Yacht Squadron (Cowes).
                                         Died 7 Feb. 2001.

GUAZZELLI, Rt Rev. Victor; Emeritus Auxiliary Bishop of Westminster (RC); Titular Bishop of Lindisfarne, since 1970; *b* 19 March 1920; *s* of Cesare Guazzelli and Maria (*née* Frepoli). *Educ:* Parochial Schools, Tower Hamlets; English Coll., Lisbon. Priest, 1945. Asst, St Patrick's, Soho Square, 1945–48; Bursar and Prof. at English Coll., Lisbon, 1948–58; Westminster Cathedral: Chaplain, 1958–64; Hon. Canon, 1964; Sub-Administrator, 1964–67; Parish Priest of St Thomas', Fulham, 1967–70; Vicar General of Westminster, 1970–1998; Aux. Bishop of Westminster (Bishop in E London), 1970–97. President: Pax Christi, 1975–2001; Apostleship of the Sea, 1993–2003; Chm., Cttee, Faith and Cultures, 1980–2001. *Address:* St Peter's Residence, 2A Meadow Road, South Lambeth, SW8 1QH. *T:* (020) 7735 0788.   *Died 1 June 2004.*

GUEST, George Howell, CBE 1987; FRCO; FRSCM; Organist of St John's College, Cambridge, 1951–91 (Fellow, since 1956); University Organist, Cambridge University, 1974–91; *b* 9 Feb. 1924; *s* of late Ernest Joseph Guest and late Gwendolen (*née* Brown); *m* 1959, Nancy Mary, *o d* of late W. P. Talbot; one *s* one *d. Educ:* Friars Sch., Bangor; King's Sch., Chester; St John's Coll., Cambridge (BA 1949, MusB 1950, MA 1954). FRCO 1942; FRSCM 1973. Served in RAF, 1942–46. Chorister: Bangor Cath., 1933–35; Chester Cath., 1935–39; Sub-Organist, Chester Cath., 1946–47; Organ Student, St John's Coll., Cambridge, 1947–51; John Stewart of Rannoch Scholar in Sacred Music, 1948; University Asst Lectr in Music, Cambridge, 1953–56, Univ. Lectr, 1956–82; Prof. of Harmony and Counterpoint, RAM, London, 1960–61. Director: Berkshire Boy Choir, USA, 1967, 1970; Arts Theatre, Cambridge, 1977–90. Concerts with St John's Coll. Choir in USA, Canada, Japan, Aust., Brazil, Hong Kong, most countries in W Europe; concerts and choral seminars in the Philippines and in S Africa; concerts with Community of Jesus Choir, USA, in Hungary, Yugoslavia and USSR; fests adjudicator in GB, Ire., Hong Kong and Patagonia. Mem. Council: RCO, 1964– (Pres., 1978–80); RSCM, 1983–98; President: Cathedral Organists' Assoc., 1980–82; IAO, 1987–89. Examiner to Associated Bd of Royal Schs of Music,

1959–92. Aelod er Anrhydedd, Gorsedd y Beirdd, Eisteddfod Genedlaethol Cymru, 1977; Dir, Côr Cenedlaethol Ieuenctid Cymru, 1984; Artistic Dir, Llandaf Festival, 1985. Hon. RAM 1984; Hon. FRCCO 1991; Hon. Fellow: UCNW, 1989; Univ. of Wales, Aberystwyth, 1999; Hon. FWCMD 1992. Hon. DMus Wales, 1989; MusD Lambeth 1977. John Edwards Meml Award, Guild for Promotion of Welsh Music, 1986. *Publication:* A Guest at Cambridge, 1994. *Recreation:* the Welsh language. *Address:* 9 Gurney Way, Cambridge CB4 2ED. *T:* (01223) 354932.   *Died 20 Nov. 2002.*

GUNN, Prof. Sir John (Currie), Kt 1982; CBE 1976; FRSE, FIMA; FInstP; Cargill Professor of Natural Philosophy, 1949–82, Head of Department, 1973–82 and Dean of Faculties, 1989–91, University of Glasgow; *b* 13 Sept. 1916; *s* of Richard Robertson Gunn and Jane Blair Currie; *m* 1944, Betty Russum (OBE 1984) (decd); one *s*. *Educ:* Glasgow Acad.; Glasgow Univ.(MA); St John's Coll., Cambridge (MA). Engaged in Admiralty scientific service, first at Admiralty Research Laboratory, later at Mine Design Dept, 1939–45; Research Fellow of St John's Coll., Cambridge, 1944; Lecturer in Applied Mathematics: Manchester Univ., 1945–46; University Coll., London, 1946–49. Member: SRC, 1968–72; UGC, 1974–81. Hon. DSc: Heriot-Watt, 1981; Loughborough, 1983; DUniv Open, 1989. *Publications:* papers on mathematical physics in various scientific journals. *Recreations:* golf, music, chess. *Address:* 32 Beaconsfield Road, Glasgow G12 0NY. *T:* (0141) 357 2001.   *Died 26 July 2002.*

GUNN, Thomson William, (Thom); poet; Senior Lecturer, English Department, University of California (Berkeley), 1990–99; *b* 29 Aug. 1929; *s* of Herbert Smith Gunn, and Ann Charlotte Gunn (*née* Thomson); unmarried. *Educ:* University Coll. Sch., Hampstead; Trinity Coll., Cambridge. British Army (National Service), 1948–50; lived in Paris six months, 1950; Cambridge, 1950–53; lived in Rome, 1953–54; lived in California from 1954. Lectr, later Associate Prof., English Dept, University of Calif (Berkeley), 1958–66, Vis. Lectr, 1975–90. (Jtly) David Cohen British Literature Prize for Lifetime Achievement, Arts Council, 2003. *Publications:* Poetry from Cambridge, 1953; Fighting Terms, 1954; The Sense of Movement, 1957; My Sad Captains, 1961; Selected Poems (with Ted Hughes), 1962; Five American Poets (ed with Ted Hughes), 1962; Positives (with Ander Gunn), 1966; Touch, 1967; Poems 1950–1966: a selection, 1969; Moly, 1971; Jack Straw's Castle and other poems, 1976; Selected Poems, 1979; The Passages of Joy, 1982; The Occasions of Poetry (ed Clive Wilmer), 1982; The Man with Night Sweats, 1992; Collected Poems, 1993; Shelf Life, 1993; Boss Cupid, 2000. *Recreations:* cheap thrills. *Address:* 1216 Cole Street, San Francisco, CA 94117, USA.   *Died 25 April 2004.*

GUNN, Sir William (Archer), AC 1990; KBE 1961; CMG 1955; JP; Australian grazier and company director; Chairman, International Wool Secretariat, 1961–73; *b* Goondiwindi, Qld, 1 Feb. 1914; *s* of late Walter and Doris Isabel Gunn, Goondiwindi; *m* 1939, Mary (Phillipa) (*d* 2002), *d* of F. B. Haydon, Murrurundi, NSW; one *s* one*d* (and one *d* decd). *Educ:* The King's Sch., Parramatta, NSW. Director: Rothmans of Pall Mall (Australia) Ltd; Grazcos Co-op. Ltd; Clausen Steamship Co. (Australia) Pty Ltd; Walter Reid and Co. Ltd; Gunn Rural Management Pty Ltd; Chairman and Managing Director: Moline Pastoral Co. Pty Ltd; Roper Valley Pty Ltd; Coolibah Pty Ltd; Mataranba Pty Ltd; Unibeef Australia Pty Ltd; Gunn Development Pty Ltd. Chm., Qld Adv. Bd, Develt Finance Corp., 1962–72; Member: Commonwealth Bank Bd, 1952–59; Qld Bd, Nat. Mutual Life Assoc., 1955–67; Reserve Bank Bd, 1959–. Chm., Australian Wool Bd, 1963–72; Member: Exec. Council, United Graziers Assoc. of Qld, 1944–69 (Pres., 1951–59; Vice-Pres., 1947–51); Aust. Wool Growers Council, 1947–60 (Chm. 1955–58); Graziers Federal Council of Aust., 1950–60 (Pres. 1951–54); Aust. Wool Bureau,

1951–63 (Chm. 1958–63); Aust. Meat Bd, 1953–66; Aust. Wool Testing Authority, 1958–63; Aust. Wool Growers and Graziers Council, 1960–65; Export Develt Council, 1962–65; Australian Wool Corp., 1973. Member: Council, NFU of Aust., 1951–54; CSIRO State Cttee, 1951–68; Faculty of Veterinary Science, Univ. of Qld, 1953–; Chm., The Wool Bureau Inc., New York, 1962–69; Trustee: Qld Cancer Fund; Australian Pastoral Research Trust, 1959–71. Coronation Medal, 1953; Golden Fleece Achievement Award (Bd of Dirs of Nat. Assoc. of Wool Manufrs of America), 1962; Award of Golden Ram (Natal Woolgrowers Assoc. of SA), 1973. *Address:* Goondiwindi, Qld 4390, Australia. *Clubs:* Queensland, Tattersalls, Queensland Turf (Brisbane); Union (Sydney); Australian (Melbourne).
          Died 17 April 2003.

GUNTON, Rev. Prof. Colin Ewart, DPhil, DD; Professor of Christian Doctrine, King's College, University of London, since 1984; *b* 19 Jan. 1941; *s* of Herbert Ewart Gunton and Mabel Priscilla Gunton; *m* 1964, Jennifer Mary Osgathorpe; two *s* two *d*. *Educ:* Nottingham High Sch.; Hertford Coll., Oxford (Schol; BA Lit Hum. 1964); Mansfield Coll., Oxford (BA Theol. 1966; MA 1967; DPhil 1973; DD London 1993. Ordained Minister, United Reformed Ch., 1972; Associate Minister, Brentwood URC, 1975–. King's College, London: Lectr in Philosophy of Religion, 1969–80; Lectr in Systematic Theol., 1980–83; Sen. Lectr, 1983–84; Dean, Faculty of Theol. and Religious Studies, 1988–90; Head, Dept of Theol. and Religious Studies, 1993–96. Bampton Lectr, Univ. of Oxford, 1992; Warfield Lectr, Princeton Theol Seminary, 1993. Pres., Soc. for Study of Theol., 1993–94. Hon. DD Aberdeen, 1999. Jt Editor, Internat. Jl of Systematic Theology, 1999–. *Publications:* Becoming and Being: the doctrine of God in Charles Hartshorne and Karl Barth, 1978; Yesterday and Today: a study of continuities in Christology, 1983, 2nd edn 1997; Enlightenment and Alienation: an essay towards a Trinitarian Theology, 1985; The Actuality of Atonement: a study of metaphor, rationality and the Christian Tradition, 1989; (ed with D. W. Hardy) On Being the Church: essays on the Christian Community, 1989; The Promise of Trinitarian Theology, 1991, 2nd edn 1997; (ed with C. Schwoebel) Persons, Divine and Human: King's College essays in theological anthropology, 1992; Christ and Creation: the 1990 Didsbury Lectures, 1993; The One, the Three and the Many: God, Creation and the Culture of Modernity (Bampton Lectures), 1993; A Brief Theology of Revelation (Warfield Lectures), 1995; (ed) God and Freedom: essays in historical and systematic theology, 1995; Theology through the Theologians, 1996; (ed) Cambridge Companion to Christian Doctrine, 1997; (ed) The Doctrine of Creation: essays in dogmatics, history and philosophy, 1997; The Triune Creator: a historical and systematic study, 1998; Intellect and Action, 2000; (ed) Trinity, Time and Church: a response to the theology of Robert W. Jenson, 2000; Theology through Preaching: sermons for Brentwood, 2001; The Christian Faith: an introduction to Christian doctrine, 2001; (ed jtly) The Practice of Theology, 2001; (ed jtly) The Lectionary Commentary, 2002; Act and Being: towards a theology of the divine attributes, 2003; Father, Son and Holy Spirit: towards a fully Trinitarian theology, 2003; contrib. to Scottish Jl of Theol., Jl of Theol Studies, Religious Studies, Mod. Theol., Theol., Expository Times, Theol. Today, Neue Zeitschrift für Systematische Theologie und Religionsphilosophie, Internat. Jl of Systematic Theol. *Recreations:* music, gardening, walking. *Address:* Department of Theology and Religious Studies, King's College, Strand, WC2R 2LS. *T:* (020) 7848 2459; 7 Oxford Court, Brentwood, Essex CM14 5EU. *T:* (01277) 221585.   *Died 6 May 2003.*

GURNEY, Prof. Oliver Robert, DPhil; FBA 1959; Shillito Reader in Assyriology, Oxford University, 1945–78; Titular Professor, 1965–78, then Professor

Emeritus; Fellow of Magdalen College, Oxford, 1963–78, then Emeritus; *b* 28 Jan. 1911; *s* of Robert Gurney, DSc, and Sarah Gamzu, MBE, *d* of Walter Garstang, MD, MRCP; *m* 1957, Mrs Diane Hope Grazebrook (*née* Esencourt); no *c. Educ:* Eton Coll.; New Coll., Oxford (MA, DPhil). Served War of 1939–45, in Royal Artillery and Sudan Defence Force. Freeman of City of Norwich. For. Mem., Royal Danish Acad. of Sciences and Letters, 1976. Pres., British Institute of Archaeology at Ankara, 1983–2000. Hon. DHL Chicago, 1991. *Publications:* The Hittites, 1952, repr. 1990; (with J. J. Finkelstein and P. Hulin) The Sultantepe Tablets, 1957; (with John Garstang) The Geography of the Hittite Empire, 1959; Ur Excavations, Texts, VII, 1974; Oxford Editions of Cuneiform Texts V (with S. N. Kramer), 1976, XI, 1989; Some Aspects of Hittite Religion (Schweich Lectures, 1976), 1977; The Middle Babylonian Legal and Economic Texts from Ur, 1983; articles in Annals of Archæology and Anthropology (Liverpool), Anatolian Studies, etc. *Recreation:* golf. *Address:* Fir Tree House, 10 Milton Lane, Steventon, Abingdon, Oxon OX13 6SA. *T:* (01235) 831212.   *Died 11 Jan. 2001.*

GUY, (Leslie) George; Assistant Secretary, Craft Sector, Amalgamated Union of Engineering Workers/Technical Administrative and Supervisory Section, 1983–84, retired; *b* 1 Sept. 1918; *s* of Albert and Annie Guy; *m* 1940, Audrey Doreen (*née* Symonds); two *d. Educ:* secondary modern school. National Union of Sheet Metal Workers: shop steward; Member: Branch and District Cttees; Nat. Executive Cttee; National President, June 1972–74; Asst General Secretary, 1974–77; Gen. Sec., Nat. Union of Sheet Metal Workers, Coppersmiths, Heating and Domestic Engrs, 1977–83, when Union transferred its engagements to AEUW/TASS. Member: General Council, TUC, 1977–83; Exec., CSEU, 1977–84; Engrg Industry Trng Bd, 1979–84; Council, Marine Training Assoc., 1983–. *Recreations:* work, politics.
Died 4 Dec. 2005.

GUY, Gen. Sir Roland (Kelvin), GCB 1987 (KCB 1981); CBE 1978 (MBE 1955); DSO 1972; Governor, Royal Hospital, Chelsea, 1987–93; *b* 25 June 1928; *s* of Lt-Col Norman Greenwood Guy and Edna Guy; *m* 1957, Dierdre, *d* of Brig. P. H. Graves Morris, DSO, MC, and Auriol Graves-Morris; two *d. Educ:* Wellington Coll.; RMA Sandhurst. Commnd KRRC, 1948; 1950–71: Signals Officer, Germany; Adjt Kenya Regt, and 2 KRRC; Weapon Trng Officer 1 KRRC; Staff Coll., Camberley; MoD; Co. Comdr 2 RGJ; DS Staff Coll.; Bn 2 i/c; Mil. Asst to Adjt Gen.; CO 1 RGJ; Col GS HQ Near East Land Forces, 1971; Comd 24 Airportable Bde, 1972; RCDS, 1975; Principal SO to CDS, 1976–78; Chief of Staff, HQ BAOR, 1978–80; Mil. Sec., 1980–83; Adjt Gen., 1984–86; ADC Gen. to the Queen, 1984–87; served in Kenya, Libya, British Guiana, Cyprus, Malaysia, W Germany, Berlin and NI. Colonel Commandant: 1st Bn Royal Green Jackets, 1981–86 (Rep. Col Comdt, 1985–86); Small Arms School Corps, 1981–87; Kenya Regt Assoc., 1988–2003. Chairman: Army Benevolent Fund, 1987–93; Royal Cambridge Home for Soldiers' Widows, 1987–93; Mem. Council of Management, PDSA, 1987–2001 (Chm. Council of Mgt, 1994–98). Dir, Corps of Commissionaires, 1988–94. Trustee, Nuffield Trust for Armed Forces, 1989–98. Governor: Wellington Coll., 1987–98 (Vice Pres., 1990–98); Milton Abbey Sch., 1987–2000. *Recreations:* playing the piano, painting, cooking. *Address:* c/o NatWest Bank, 25 Market Place, Blandford Forum, Dorset DT11 7AQ. *Club:* Army and Navy.   *Died 13 Dec. 2005.*

H

HABAKKUK, Sir (Hrothgar) John, Kt 1976; FBA 1965; FRHistS; Fellow, All Souls College, Oxford, 1950–67 and 1988–2001 (Hon. Fellow, 2001); Principal of Jesus College, Oxford, 1967–84, Hon. Fellow, 1984; *b* 13 May 1915; *s* of Evan Guest and Anne Habakkuk; *m* 1948, Mary Richards (*d* 2002); one *s* three *d*. *Educ:* Barry County Sch.; St John's Coll., Cambridge (scholar and Strathcona student; Historical Tripos: Part I, First Class, 1935; Part II, First Class (with distinction), 1936; Hon. Fellow 1971); MA 1940. Pembroke College, Cambridge: Fellow, 1938–50, Hon. Fellow 1973; Dir of Studies in History and Librarian, 1946–50; Temporary Civil Servant: Foreign Office, 1940–42, Board of Trade, 1942–46; Univ. Lectr, Faculty of Economics, Cambridge, 1946–50; Chichele Prof. of Economic History, Oxford Univ., 1950–67; Vice-Chancellor, Oxford Univ., 1973–77, a Pro Vice-Chancellor, 1977–83; Pres, UC Swansea, 1975–84 (Hon. Fellow, 1991). Vis. Lectr, Harvard Univ., 1954–55; Ford Res. Prof., Univ. of California, Berkeley, 1962–63; Ford Lecturer, 1984–85. Member: Grigg Cttee on Departmental Records, 1952–54; Adv. Council on Public Records, 1958–70; SSRC, 1967–71; Nat. Libraries Cttee, 1968–69; Admin. Bd, Internat. Assoc. of Univs, 1975–85; Royal Commn on Historic Manuscripts, 1978–90. Chairman: Cttee of Vice Chancellors and Principals of Univs of UK, 1976–77; Adv. Gp on London Health Servs, 1980–81; Oxfordshire DHA, 1981–84. Pres., RHistS, 1976–80. Foreign Member: Amer. Phil. Soc.; Amer. Acad. of Arts and Sciences. Hon. DLitt: Wales, 1971; Pennsylvania, 1975; Kent, 1978; Ulster, 1988; Hon. LittD Cambridge 1973. *Publications:* American and British Technology in the Nineteenth Century, 1962; Population Growth and Economic Development since 1750, 1971; Landowners: marriage, debt and the estates system 1650–1950, 1994; articles and reviews. *Address:* 28 Cunliffe Close, Oxford OX2 7BL. *T:* (01865) 556583.
Died 3 Nov. 2002.

HACKETT, John Charles Thomas; Director General, Federation of Civil Engineering Contractors, 1992–96; *b* 4 Feb. 1939; *s* of late Thomas John Hackett and Doris Hackett; *m* 1958, Patricia Margaret, *d* of late Eric Ronald Clifford and Margaret Tubb. *Educ:* Glyn Grammar Sch., Epsom, Surrey; London Univ. (LLB Hons, external). Prodn Planning Manager, Rowntree Gp, 1960–64; Prodn Controller, Johnson's Wax, 1964; Commercial Sec., Heating and Ventilating Contractors' Assoc., 1964–70; Sec., Cttee of Assocs of Specialist Engrg Contractors, 1968–79; Dep. Dir, 1970–79, Dir, 1980–84, British Constructional Steelwork Assoc.; Dir Gen., BIBA, subseq. BIIBA, 1985–91. Member: Council, CBI, 1980–88 and 1992–96; CBI Gp of Chief Execs of Major Sector Assocs, 1980–84 and 1992–96. FIMgt (FBIM 1981). *Publication:* BCSA Members' Contractual Handbook, 1972, 2nd edn 1979. *Recreations:* music, reading, walking, motoring. *Address:* 15 Downsway Close, Tadworth, Surrey KT20 5DR. *T:* (01737) 813024. *Died 2 June 2001.*

HADINGHAM, Reginald Edward Hawke, CBE 1988 (OBE 1971); MC 1943 and Bar 1943; TD 1946; Life President, Sparks, the sportsman's charity, 1995 (Chairman, 1968–94); *b* 6 Dec. 1915; *s* of Edward Wallace Hadingham and Ethel Irene Penelope Gwynne-Evans; *m* 1940, Lois Pope, *d* of Edward and Nora Pope; two *d*. *Educ:* Rokeby Prep. Sch., Wimbledon; St Paul's Sch. Joined Slazengers, 1933, European Sales Manager, 1936. Joined TA, 57th Anti-Tank Regt, 1938, commnd into 67th Anti-Tank Regt, 1938; served War of 1939–45 with 67th Anti-Tank Regt, RA; comd 302 Battery, 1942–45 (MC, Salerno 1943, and Bar, Garigliano 1943); CO 67 Regt, 1945, until disbanded, Oct. 1945. Returned to Slazengers as Asst Export Manager, Jan. 1946; Export Manager, 1949; Gen. Sales Manager, 1951; Sales Dir, 1952; Man. Dir, 1969; Chm. and Man. Dir, 1973; Chm. (non-exec.), 1976–83. All England Lawn Tennis Club: Mem. Cttee, 1976–84; Chm. of Club, and of Cttee of Management, The Championships, Wimbledon, 1984–89; Vice-Pres., 1990–; Pres., Internat. Lawn Tennis Club of GB, 1991–. Thrice Pres., Sette of Odd Volumes (Treas., 1953–). *Recreations:* reading, writing verse. *Address:* Westminster Beaumont, 35 Arteberry Road, Wimbledon, SW20 8AG. *Clubs:* Queen's, All England Lawn Tennis, Hurlingham, International Lawn Tennis of GB; Fitzwilliam Lawn Tennis (Dublin). *Died 27 Dec. 2004.*

HAIGH, Clement Percy, PhD; CPhys; FInstP; scientific and engineering consultant; *b* 11 Jan. 1920; *m* 1945, Ruby Patricia Hobdey; three *s*. *Educ:* Univ. of Leeds (BSc); King's Coll., London (PhD). Radiochemical Centre, Thorium Ltd, 1943–49; Medical Physicist, Barrow Hosp., Bristol, 1949–56; joined CEGB, 1956: Director, Berkeley Nuclear Laboratories, 1959–73; Dep. Director-General, Design and Construction Div., Gloucester, 1973–78; Dir of Research, BNOC, 1978–81. Dir, South Western Industrial Res., 1981–86. Assessor, Nuclear Safety Adv. Cttee, 1972–76; Member: BBC West Adv. Council, 1972–76; Mechanical Engrg and Machine Tools Requirements Bd, 1973–76; Off-Shore Energy Technology Bd, 1978–81; Board, National Maritime Inst., 1981–82; UK Chm., Joint UK/USSR Working Gp on Problems of Electricity Supply, 1974–78; Chm., Programme Steering Cttee, UK Offshore Steels Res. Project, 1981–87. Distinguished Lectr, American Nuclear Soc., San Francisco, 1965. FRSA. *Publications:* various papers on applied nuclear physics and on nuclear energy. *Recreations:* music, study of magnificent failures in technology. *Address:* Painswick, Old Sneed Park, Bristol, Avon BS9 1RG. *T:* (0117) 968 2065. *Club:* Savile.
Died 25 Feb. 2001.

HAILEY, Arthur; author; *b* 5 April 1920; *s* of George Wellington Hailey and Elsie Mary Wright; *m* 1st, 1944, Joan Fishwick (marr. diss. 1950); three *s*; 2nd, 1951, Sheila Dunlop; one *s* two *d*. *Educ:* English elem. schs. Pilot, RAF, 1939–47; Air Ministry staff officer, 1945–47; first ed., aircrew trng mag., Air Clues (Flt-Lt; AE); RCAF (R) (Flt-Lt 1951). Emigrated to Canada, 1947; became Canadian citizen, with dual nationality, 1952; various positions in industry and sales until becoming free-lance writer, 1956. Member: Authors League of America; (Emeritus), Alliance of Canadian Cinema, Television and Radio Artists; (Life), Writers Guild, Canada. *Films:* Time Lock, 1957; The Young Doctors, 1961. *Publications:* (in 40 countries and 38 languages): Flight into Danger (with John Castle), 1958 (also a play, and filmed 1956 as Zero Hour), US edn as Runway Zero-Eight; The Final Diagnosis, 1959; Close-Up (collected plays), 1960; In High Places, 1962; Hotel, 1965 (filmed, 1966, also television series); Airport, 1968 (filmed, 1970); Wheels, 1971 (filmed 1978); The Moneychangers, 1975 (filmed, 1976); Overload, 1979; Strong Medicine, 1984 (filmed, 1986); The Evening News, 1990; Detective, 1997 (filmed, 2004). *Address:* (home) Lyford Cay, PO Box N7776, Nassau, Bahamas; (office) Nancy Stauffer Associates, PO Box 1203, Darien, CT 06820, USA. *Club:* Lyford Cay (Life Mem.) (Bahamas). *Died 24 Nov. 2004.*

HAILSHAM, 2nd Viscount, *cr* 1929, of Hailsham; Baron, *cr* 1928 [disclaimed his peerages for life, 20 Nov. 1963]; *see under* Baron Hailsham of St Marylebone.

HAILSHAM OF SAINT MARYLEBONE, Baron *cr* 1970 (Life Peer), of Herstmonceux; **Quintin McGarel**

Hogg, KG 1988; CH 1974; PC 1956; FRS 1973; Editor, Halsbury's Laws of England, 4th edition, 1972–98; *b* 9 Oct. 1907; *er s* of 1st Viscount Hailsham, PC, KC, and Elizabeth (*d* 1925), *d* of Judge Trimble Brown, Nashville, Tennessee, USA, and *widow* of Hon. A. J. Marjoribanks; *S* father, 1950, as 2nd Viscount Hailsham, but disclaimed his peerages for life, 20 Nov. 1963 (Baron *cr* 1928, Viscount *cr* 1929); *m* 1st, 1931, Natalie Sullivan (marr. diss. 1943; she *d* 1987); 2nd, 1944, Mary Evelyn (*d* 1978), *d* of late Richard Martin of Ross; two *s* three *d*; 3rd, 1986, Deirdre Shannon (*d* 1998). *Educ*: Eton (Schol., Newcastle Schol.); Christ Church, Oxford (Scholar; First Class Hon. Mods, 1928; First Class Lit. Hum., 1930; Hon. Student, 1962). Pres., Oxford Union Soc., 1929. Served War of 1939–45: commissioned Rifle Bde Sept. 1939; served Middle East Forces, Western Desert, 1941 (wounded); Egypt, Palestine, Syria, 1942; Temp. Major, 1942. Fellow of All Souls Coll., Oxford, 1931–38, 1961–; Barrister, Lincoln's Inn, 1932; a Bencher of Lincoln's Inn, 1956, Treasurer, 1975; QC 1953. MP (C) Oxford City, 1938–50, St Marylebone, Dec. 1963–1970; Jt Parly Under-Sec. of State for Air, 1945; First Lord of the Admiralty, 1956–57; Minister of Education, 1957; Dep. Leader of the House of Lords, 1957–60; Leader of the House of Lords, 1960–63; Lord Privy Seal, 1959–60; Lord Pres. of the Council, 1957–59 and 1960–64; Minister for Science and Technology, 1959–64; Minister with special responsibility for: Sport, 1962–64; dealing with unemployment in the North-East, 1963–64; higher education, Dec. 1963–Feb. 1964; Sec. of State for Education and Science, April–Oct. 1964; Lord High Chancellor of GB, 1970–74 and 1979–87. Chm. of the Conservative Party Organization, Sept. 1957–Oct. 1959. Rector of Glasgow Univ., 1959–62; Chancellor, Univ. of Buckingham, 1983–92. Pres., Classical Assoc., 1960–61. Lectures: John Findley Green Foundation, 1960; Richard Dimbleby, 1976; Hamlyn, 1983; Granada, 1987; Warburton, 1987, F. A. Mann, 1988, Lincoln's Inn. Hon. Bencher, Inn of Court of NI, 1981; Hon. FICE 1963; Hon. FIEE 1972; Hon. FIStructE 1960. Hon. Freeman, Merchant Taylors' Co., 1971. Hon. DCL: Westminster Coll., Fulton, Missouri, USA, 1960; Newcastle, 1964; Oxon, 1974; Hon. LLD: Cambridge, 1963; Delhi, 1972; St Andrews, 1979; Leeds, 1982; Hon. DLitt Ulster, 1988. *Publications*: The Law of Arbitration, 1935; One Year's Work, 1944; The Law and Employers' Liability, 1944; The Times We Live In, 1944; Making Peace, 1945; Case for Conservatism, 1947; The Law of Monopolies, Restrictive Practices and Resale Price Maintenance, 1956; The Conservative Case, 1959; Interdependence, 1961; Science and Politics, 1963; The Devil's Own Song, 1968; The Door Wherein I Went, 1975; Elective Dictatorship, 1976; The Dilemma of Democracy, 1978; Hamlyn Revisited: the British legal system (Hamlyn Lectures), 1983; A Sparrow's Flight (autobiog.), 1990; On The Constitution, 1992; Values: collapse and cure, 1994. *Heir*: (*to disclaimed viscountcy*): *s* Rt Hon. Douglas Martin Hogg, QC, MP [*b* 5 Feb. 1945; *m* 1968, Sarah Boyd-Carpenter; one *s* one *d*]. *Address*: House of Lords, SW1A 0PW. *Clubs*: Carlton, Alpine, MCC.
Died 12 Oct. 2001.

HAINING, Thomas Nivison, CMG 1983; HM Diplomatic Service, retired; writer and lecturer on international affairs and Mongolian history; *b* 15 March 1927; *m* 1955, Dorothy Patricia Robson; one *s*. *Educ*: Edinburgh Univ.; Göttingen Univ. Foreign Office, 1952; served Vienna, Moscow, Rome and New York; Counsellor, FCO, 1972–79; Ambassador and Consul-Gen. to the Mongolian People's Republic, 1979–82. Aberdeen University: Hon. Res. Associate, 1988–90, Hon. Res. Fellow, 1991–2001, Dept of History; Hon. Pres., Chinese Studies Gp, 1989–2001. *Publications*: (contrib.) Mongolia Today, 1989; (trans. and ed) Ratchnevsky, Genghis Khan: his life and legacy, 1991; (contrib.) Legacy of the Mongol Empire, 1993; (contrib.) The Mongols of the 13th century through the eyes of early European travellers, 1995. *Address*: Carseview, 7 The

Banks, Brechin, Angus DD9 6JD. *T*: (01356) 622584. *Club*: Royal Northern and University (Aberdeen).
Died 17 July 2005.

HAINSWORTH, Gordon, MA; public sector consultant, since 1992; Chief Executive, Manchester, 1988–92; *b* 4 Nov. 1934; *s* of Harry and Constance Hainsworth; *m* 1962, Diane (*née* Thubron); one *s* one *d*. *Educ*: Leeds Modern Sch.; Trinity Coll., Cambridge (MA). Teaching, Leeds, Birmingham and West Riding, 1958–65; Admin. Assistant, Leeds, 1965–69; Asst Education Officer, Manchester, 1969–74; Under-Secretary (Education), Assoc. of Metropolitan Authorities, 1974–76; Dep. Educn Officer, Manchester, 1976–80; Director of Education, Gateshead, 1980–83; Chief Educn Officer, Manchester, 1983–88. Registered Inspector (Schs), OFSTED, 1992–99; Schs Adjudicator, 1999–. *Recreations*: family, golf, bridge, walking. *Address*: 14 Oldham Road, Denshaw, Oldham OL3 5SL. *T*: (01457) 820398.
Died 31 Aug. 2002.

HAINWORTH, Henry Charles, CMG 1961; HM Diplomatic Service, retired; *b* 12 Sept. 1914; *o s* of late Charles S. and Emily G. I. Hainworth; *m* 1944, Mary, *yr d* of late Felix B. and Lilian Ady; two *d*. *Educ*: Blundell's Sch.; Sidney Sussex Coll., Cambridge. Entered HM Consular Service, 1939; HM Embassy, Tokyo, 1940–42; seconded to Ministry of Information (Far Eastern Bureau, New Delhi), 1942–46; HM Embassy, Tokyo, 1946–51; Foreign Office, 1951–53; HM Legation, Bucharest, 1953–55; NATO Defence Coll., Paris, 1956; Political Office, Middle East Forces (Nicosia), 1956; Foreign Office, 1957–61 (Head of Atomic Energy and Disarmament Dept, 1958–61); Counsellor, UK Delegn to the Brussels Conf., 1961–63; HM Minister and Consul-Gen., Vienna, 1963–68; Ambassador to Indonesia, 1968–70; Ambassador and Perm. UK Rep. to Disarmament Conf., Geneva, 1971–74. Chm., Anglo-Indonesian Soc., 1992–99. *Publication*: A Collector's Dictionary, 1980. *Recreations*: reading, fishing. *Address*: 23 Rivermead Court, Ranelagh Gardens, SW6 3RU.
Died 28 Jan. 2005.

HALABY, Najeeb Elias; President, Halaby International Corporation, since 1973; Chairman, National Center for Atmospheric Research Foundation, since 1985; *b* 19 Nov. 1915; *s* of late Najeeb Elias Halaby and of Laura Wilkins Halaby; *m* 1st, 1946, Doris Carlquist (marr. diss. 1976); one *s* two *d*; 2nd, 1980, Jane Allison Coates (*d* 1996); *m* 1997, Libby Anderson Cater. *Educ*: Stanford Univ. (AB); Yale Univ. (LLB); Bonar Law Coll., Ashridge, (Summer) 1939. Called to the Bar: California, 1940; District of Columbia, 1948; NY, 1973. Practised law in Los Angeles, Calif, 1940–42, 1958–61; Associate, Laurance and Nelson Rockefeller, 1954–57. Air Corps Flight Instructor, 1940; Test pilot for Lockheed Aircraft Corp., 1942–43; Naval aviator, established Navy Test Pilot Sch., 1943; formerly Chief of Intelligence Coordination Div., State Dept; Foreign Affairs Advisor to Sec. of Defense; Chm., NATO Military Production and Supply Board, 1950; Asst Administrator, Mutual Security Economic Cooperation Administration, 1950–51; Asst Sec. of Defense for Internat. Security, 1952–54; Vice-Chm., White House Adv. Group whose report led to formation of Federal Aviation Agency, 1955–56, Administrator of the Agency, 1961–65; Pan American World Airways: Dir, 1966–72; Pres., 1968–71; Chief Exec., 1969–72; Chm., 1970–72; past Exec. Vice-Pres. and Dir, Servomechanisms Inc. Sec.-Treas., Aerospace Corp., 1959–61; Pres., American Technology Corp.; Chm., Dulles Access Rapid Transit Inc., 1985–98. Founder-Chm., US-Japan Econ. Council, 1971–73; Trustee: Aspen Inst., Aspen, Colo; Eisenhower Exchange Fellowships, Inc.; Wolf Trap Foundn; Amer. Univ. of Beirut; Coll. of William and Mary; Governor, Flight Safety Foundn. Member: Smithson Soc.; Brookings Council; Madison Council. Chm., SCF, 1992, then Emeritus. Fellow, Amer. Inst. of Aeronautics and Astronautics. Hon. LLB: Allegheny Coll., Pa, 1967;

Loyola Coll., LA, 1968. Monsanto Safety Award; FAA Exceptional Service Medal; G. L. Cabot Medal, Aero Club of New England, 1964; Gilbert Award, Air Traffic Controllers' Assoc., 1989. *Publications:* Crosswinds (memoir), 1979; First Forty Years of Jet Aviation, 1979. *Recreations:* golf, skiing, flying. *Address:* 175 Chain Bridge Road, McLean, VA 22101–1907, USA. *Clubs:* Alibi, Metropolitan, Chevy Chase (Washington); Bohemian (California); Tower (Virginia). *Died 2 July 2003.*

HALE, John Hampton; Director: Pearson plc, 1983–93 (Managing Director, 1983–86); Pearson Inc. (USA), 1983–93 (Chairman, 1983–86); *b* 8 July 1924; *s* of Dr John Hale and Elsie (Coles) Hale; *m* 1st, 1950; one *s* two *d*; 2nd, 1980, Nancy Ryrie Birks. *Educ:* Eton College (King's Scholar); Magdalene Coll., Cambridge (Mech. Scis Tripos, BA, MA); Harvard Grad. Sch. of Business Admin (Henry Fellow, 1948). RAF and Fleet Air Arm Pilot, 1943–46. Alcan Aluminium Ltd, Montreal, NY and London, 1949–83: Exec. Vice-Pres., Finance, 1970–82, Dir, Alcan Aluminium, 1970–85; Dir, Aluminium Co. of Canada, 1970–85 (Chm., 1979–83). Director: Nippon Light Metal Co., Japan, Indian Aluminium Co. and Alcan Australia, 1970–83; Canadian Adv. Bd, Allendale Mutual Insurance Co., 1977–83; Scovill Inc. (USA), 1978–85; Ritz-Carlton Hotel, Montreal, 1981–83; Concordia Univ. Business Sch., 1981–83; Bank of Montreal, 1985–95 (Mem., Internat Adv. Council, 1986–89); The Economist Newspaper, 1984–95; SSMC Inc. (USA), 1986–89; Chm., Fairey Holdings, 1983–87. Member: Lloyds, 1960–91; Exec. Cttee, British-North American Cttee, 1980–90; Council, Industry for Management Educn, 1983–87; Lay Mem., Stock Exchange Council, London, 1987–91. Chairman: Chambly County Protestant Central Sch. Bd, 1957–60; Business Graduates Assoc., 1967–70; Mem., Accounting Research Adv. Bd, Canadian Inst. of Chartered Accountants, 1975–81 (Chm., 1978–81). Director: Mont St Hilaire Nature Conservation Assoc., 1977–83 (Pres., 1980–83); Foundn for Canadian Studies, 1988–98; Governor, Stratford Festival, Ontario, 1981–83. Trustee, Royal Armouries, 1992–95. Mem., Court of Assts, Armourers' & Brasiers' Co., 1985– (Master, 1990 and 1998). *Recreations:* ski-ing, sailing, fishing, shooting, old Canadian books. *Address:* 71 Eaton Terrace, SW1W 8TN. *T:* (020) 7730 2929. *Clubs:* Royal Thames Yacht; Mount Royal (Montreal); Toronto.

Died 8 Jan. 2002.

HALES, Prof. (Charles) Nicholas, PhD, MD; FRCPath, FRCP, FMedSci; FRS 1992; Professor of Clinical Biochemistry, Department of Clinical Biochemistry, University of Cambridge, 1977–2002, then Professor Emeritus; Fellow, Downing College, Cambridge, 1964–70 and 1977–2002; *b* 25 April 1935; *s* of late Walter Bryan Hales and Phyllis Marjory Hales; *m* 1st, 1959, Janet May Moss; one *s* (and one *s* decd); 2nd, 1978, Margaret Griffiths; one *d*. *Educ:* King Edward VI Grammar Sch., Stafford; Univ. of Cambridge (BA 1956, MB, BChir, MA 1959, PhD 1964, MD 1971). MRCPath 1971, FRCPath 1980; MRCP 1971, FRCP 1976. House Surgeon, UCH, 1959, House Physician, 1960; Stothert Res. Fellow, Royal Soc., 1963–64; Lectr, Dept of Biochem., Univ. of Cambridge, 1964–70; Clinical Asst, Addenbrooke's Hosp., Cambridge, 1961–68, Hon. Consultant in Clin. Biochem., 1968–70; Prof. of Med. Biochem., Welsh National Sch. of Medicine, Cardiff, and Hon. Consultant in Med. Biochem., University Hosp. of Wales, Cardiff, 1970–77. Consultant in Med. Biochem., South Glam Health Authority (T). Mem., MRC, 1988–90. Founder FMedSci 1998. Lectures: Banting Meml, British Diabetic Assoc., 1991; Croonian, RCP, 1992; Kroc, Center for Diabetes Res., Univ. of Uppsala, 1992; Dale, Nat. Inst. for Biol Standards & Control, 1992; Kettle, RCPath, 1993; W. H. S. George Meml, Derby City Gen. Hosp., 1993; George Frederic Still Meml, RCPCH, 1999; Dorothy Hodgkin, Diabetes UK Annual Professional Conf., Birmingham, 2002. Medal, Soc., for Endocrinology, 1981; Foundn Award, Assoc. of Clin. Biochemists, 1991; Zeneca

Award in Analytical Biochem., Biochemical Soc., 1994; Baly Medal, RCP, 1995; Kone Award, Assoc. of Clinical Biochemists, 1999; Dist. Clinical Chemist Award, Internat. Fedn of Clinical Chemistry, 2002. *Recreations:* music, fishing. *Address:* Department of Clinical Biochemistry, Addenbrooke's Hospital, Hills Road, Cambridge CB2 2QR. *T:* (01223) 336787.

Died 15 Sept. 2005.

HALL, Arthur Herbert; Librarian and Curator, Guildhall Library and Museum, and Director of Guildhall Art Gallery, 1956–66; *b* 30 Aug. 1901; *y s* of Henry and Eliza Jane Hall, Islington, London; *m* 1927, Dorothy Maud (*née* Barton); two *s* one *d*. *Educ:* Mercers' Sch., Holborn, London. Served with RAOC, 1942–46. Entered Guildhall Library as junior asst, 1918; Dep. Librarian, 1943–56. Hon. Librarian, Clockmakers' and Gardeners' Companies, 1956–66. Chm. Council, London and Middlesex Archæological Soc., 1957–64, Vice-Pres., 1962–; Member: Council, London Topographical Soc., 1960–67; Exec. Cttee, Friends of Nat. Libraries, 1965–69. Hon. Secretary: Middlesex Victoria County History Council, 1966–78; Enfield Archaeological Soc., 1966–71. Master, 1974–75, Hon. Clerk, 1965–74, Asst Hon. Clerk, 1975–86, Civic Guild of Old Mercers; Liveryman, Clockmakers' Co. Pres., Upper Norwood Athenæum, 1993–96. FLA 1930; FSA 1963.

Died 16 March 2002.

HALL, Sir Douglas (Basil), 14th Bt *cr* 1687; KCMG 1959 (CMG 1958); *b* 1 Feb. 1909; *s* of late Capt. Lionel Erskine Hall and Jane Augusta Hall (*née* Reynolds); *S* brother, Sir Neville Hall, 13th Bt, 1978; *m* 1933, Rachel Marion Gartside-Tippinge (*d* 1990); one *s* two *d* (and one *s* decd). *Educ:* Radley Coll.; Keble Coll., Oxford (MA). Joined Colonial Admin. Service, 1930; posted to N Rhodesia as Cadet; District Officer, 1932; Senior District Officer, 1950; Provincial Commr, 1953; Administrative Sec., 1954; Sec. for Native Affairs to Government of Northern Rhodesia, 1956–59, Acting Chief Sec. for a period during 1958; Governor and C-in-C, Somaliland Protectorate, 1959–60. JP Co. Devon, 1964, Chm., Kingsbridge Petty Sessional Div., 1971–79. *Publications:* various technical articles. *Recreation:* vintage cars. *Heir:* s John Douglas Hoste Hall [*b* 7 Jan. 1945; *m* 1972, Angela Margaret, *d* of George Keys; two *s*]. *Died 8 April 2004.*

HALL, Prof. Edward Thomas, CBE 1988; Professor, Research Laboratory for Archaeology and the History of Art, Oxford University, 1975–89, then Emeritus Professor of Archaeological Sciences (Director 1954–89); Fellow of Worcester College, Oxford, 1969–89, then Emeritus; *b* 10 May 1924; *s* of late Lt-Col Walter D'Arcy Hall, MC, and Ann Madelaine Hall; *m* 1957, Jennifer, (Jeffie), Louise de la Harpe; two *s*. *Educ:* Eton; New Coll., Oxford (BA 1948, MA 1953, DPhil 1953; Hon. Fellow, 1994). FPhysS 1951. Served RNVR, 1942–45. Dir, GEC plc, 1988–90. Designer and manufacturer of scientific apparatus, Littlemore, Oxford, 1952–. Vis. Prof., UCL, 1995. Member: Science Mus. Adv. Council, 1979–84; Ancient Monuments Adv. Cttee, 1984–90; Hon. Scientific Cttee, Nat. Gall., 1970–99 (Chm., 1978–84); Council, Internat. Inst. of Conservation, 1971–94 (Pres., 1989–92); Expert Panel on Museums for Heritage Lottery Fund, 1995–99; Trustee: British Mus., 1973–95; Nat. Gall., 1977–84; Science Mus., 1984–92. Mem. Court, Goldsmiths' Co., 1976– (Prime Warden, 1985–86); Chm., Goldsmiths' Antique Plate Cttee, 1987–99. FSA. Hon. FBA 1984. *Publications:* contrib. Archaeometry, various jls concerning science applied to archaeology. *Address:* Beenhams, Railway Lane, Littlemore, Oxford OX4 4PY. *T:* (01865) 777800; Lawnfield, Holbeton, Devon PL8 1JL. *T:* (01752) 830226. *Clubs:* Beefsteak; Lucretians.

Died 11 Aug. 2001.

HALL, Rear-Adm. Geoffrey Penrose Dickinson, CB 1973; DSC 1943; DL; Hydrographer of the Navy, 1971–75; *b* 19 July 1916; *er s* of late Major A. K. D. Hall and Mrs P. M. Hall; *m* 1945, Mary Ogilvie Carlisle; two *s*

(one *d* decd). *Educ:* Haileybury. Cadet, RN, 1934; served in American waters, 1935–37 and on Nyon Patrol during Spanish Civil War; joined surveying service, 1938, served in Indian Ocean until 1939 when transf. to minesweeping in Far East; hydrographic duties, home waters, Iceland, W Africa; navigational and minesweeping duties, Icelandic waters; transf. to Combined Ops, SE Asia; subseq. comd frigate, British Pacific Fleet; from 1947, hydrographic work: with RNZN, 1949–51; subseq. five comds i/c surveys at home and abroad; served ashore and in Atlantic, Indian Ocean, Antarctic waters (Cuthbert Peek Grant, RGS, for work in furtherance of oceanographical exploration); twice Asst Hydrographer; surveyed between S Africa and Iceland, 1965–67; Asst Dir (Naval), Hydrographic Dept, Taunton, 1970; Rear-Adm. 1971. Pres., Hydrographic Soc., 1975. DL Lincs, 1982. *Publications:* Sailor's Luck (autobiog.), 1999; contribs to Nature, Deep Sea Research, Internat. Hydrographic Review, Navy International. *Recreation:* country pursuits. *Address:* Manby House, Manby, Louth, Lincs LN11 8UF. *T:* (01507) 327777. *Clubs:* Naval and Military, Royal Navy.   *Died 18 Jan. 2005.*

HALL, Prof. Geoffrey Ronald, CBE 1985; FREng, CChem, FRSC, SFInstE; Director, 1970–90, and Professor, 1986–90, Brighton Polytechnic, then Professor Emeritus and Hon. Fellow, University of Brighton; *b* 18 May 1928; *er s* of late Thomas Harold Hall, JP, and Muriel Frances Hall, Douglas, IoM; *m* 1950, Elizabeth Day Sheldon; two *s* one *d*. *Educ:* Douglas High Sch., IoM; Univ. of Manchester (BSc). Research in Nuclear Science and Engineering at AERE, Harwell, 1949–56; sabbatical at Oxford Univ., 1955; Colombo Plan Expert to Indian Atomic Energy Commn, 1956–58; Reader in Nuclear Technology, Imperial Coll., London, 1958–63; Prof. of Nuclear Technology, Imperial Coll., 1963–70. Member: CNAA, 1977–82; Engineering Council, 1981–86 (Vice-Chm., 1984–85); SERC, 1982–86 (Mem., Engrg Bd, SRC, later SERC, 1978–83); NCVQ, 1986–89; Chm., Engrg Working Gp, Nat. Adv. Body for Local Authority Higher Educn, 1982–84. Mem., Educnl Counselling Service, British Council, 1988–91 (Chm., 1989–91). Dir, Macmillan Intek, 1985–89. President: British Nuclear Energy Soc., 1970–71; Inst. of Fuel, 1976–77; Chm., Lewis Cohen Urban Studies Centre Support Trust, 1993–95; Founder Fellow, 1976, Fellowship of Engineering, then Royal Acad. of Engrg. *Publications:* papers related to nuclear science, fuels and engineering. *Recreations:* travel, bridge, golf. *Address:* 23 Firsdown Road, Worthing BN13 3BG.   *Died 3 Feb. 2001.*

HALL, Harold Percival, CMG 1963; MBE 1947; Director of Studies, Royal Institute of Public Administration, 1974–85; *b* 9 Sept. 1913; *s* of late Major George Charles Hall; *m* 1939, Margery Hall, *d* of late Joseph Dickson; three *s* (including twin *s*). *Educ:* Portsmouth Grammar Sch.; Royal Military College, Sandhurst (Prize Cadet; King's India Cadet; Hockey Blue Cricket Cap). Commnd Indian Army, 1933. Indian Political Service, 1937–47: Private Sec. to Resident, Central India States, 1937; Magistrate and Collector, Meerut, 1938–39. Military Service, 1938–43 (Major); Staff Coll., Quetta, 1941. Asst Political Agent, Loralai, 1943, Nasirabad, 1944; Dir, Food and Civil Supplies, and Dep. Sec., Revenue, Baluchistan, 1945–46; Colonial Office: Principal, 1947; Asst Sec. (Head of Pacific and Indian Ocean Dept), 1955–62; Sec., Commonwealth Royal Commn on Fedn of Malaya's independence, 1956; seconded to Office of UK Comr-Gen. for SE Asia, 1962–63; British Dep. High Comr for Eastern Malaysia, Kuching, Sarawak, 1963–64; Asst Sec., Colonial Office, 1965–66; Assistant Under-Secretary of State: Commonwealth Office, 1966–68; MoD, 1968–73. Mem. Governing Body, SOAS, 1971–74. *Recreation:* gardening. *Address:* Robina, The Chase, Ringwood, Dorset BH24 2AN. *T:* (01425) 479880.   *Died 30 Oct. 2004.*

HALL, Her Honour Jean Graham; a Circuit Judge (formerly Deputy Chairman, South-East London Quarter Sessions), 1971–89; *b* 26 March 1917; *d* of Robert Hall and Alison (*née* Graham). *Educ:* Inverkeithing Sch., Fife; St Anne's Coll., Sanderstead; London Sch. of Economics (Social Sci. Cert., 1937). Gold Medal (Elocution and Dramatic Art), Incorporated London Acad. of Music, 1935; Teacher's Dipl., Guildhall Sch. of Music, 1937; LLB Hons, 1950, LLM, London. FCIArb 1990. Club Leader and subseq. Sub-Warden, Birmingham Univ. Settlement, 1937–41; Sec., Eighteen Plus (an experiment in youth work), 1941–44; Probation Officer, Hants, subseq. Croydon, 1945–51. Called to the Bar, Gray's Inn, 1951. Metropolitan Stipendiary Magistrate, 1965–71. Pres., Gray's Inn Debating Soc., 1953; Hon. Sec., Soc. of Labour Lawyers, 1954–64; Pres., British Soc. of Criminology, 1971–74. Chm., Departmental Cttee on Statutory Maintenance Limits, 1966–68. Contested (Lab) East Surrey, 1955. FRSA 1994; Mem., Academy of Experts, 1991. Hon. LLD Lincoln, USA, 1979. *Publications:* Towards a Family Court, 1971; (jtly) Child Abuse: procedure and evidence, 1978, 3rd edn 1993; (jtly) The Expert Witness, 1992, 3rd edn 2001; (jtly) Crimes Against Children, 1992; (jtly) Haldane: statesman, lawyer, philosopher, 1996; (jtly) A Perfect Judge, 1999; (jtly) Oscar Wilde: the tragedy of being earnest, 2001. *Recreations:* travel, congenial debate, writing. *Club:* University Women's.   *Died 14 March 2005.*

HALL, John Anthony Sanderson, DFC 1943; QC 1967; FCIArb 1982; *b* 25 Dec. 1921; *s* of late Rt Hon. W. Glenvil Hall, PC, MP, andRachel Ida Hall (*née* Sanderson); *m* 1st, Nora Ella Hall (*née* Crowe) (marr. diss. 1974); one *s* two *d*; 2nd, Elizabeth Mary, widow of Alan Riley Maynard. *Educ:* Leighton Park Sch.; Trinity Hall, Cambridge (MA). Served RAF, 1940–46, 85 Squadron and 488 (NZ) Squadron (Squadron Leader; DFC and Bar). Called to Bar, Inner Temple, 1948, Master of the Bench, 1975; Western Circuit; Dep. Chm., Hants Quarter Sessions, 1967; Recorder of Swindon, 1971; a Recorder of the Crown Court, 1972–78. Member: Gen. Council of the Bar, 1964–68, 1970–74; Senate of the Four Inns of Court, 1966–68, 1970–74; Council of Legal Educn, 1970–74. Mem., 1972–79, Chm., 1978–79, UK Deleg. to Consultative Cttee, Bars and Law Socs of EEC; Mem., Foreign Compensation Commn, 1983–91. Dir Gen., Internat. Fedn of Producers of Phonograms and Videograms, 1979–81; Dir, City Disputes Panel, 1994–99. Governor, St Catherine's Sch., Bramley, 1967–88. *Recreation:* fly fishing. *Address:* 2 Dr Johnson's Buildings, Temple, EC4Y 7AY; Swallows, Blewbury, Oxon. *Club:* Royal Air Force.   *Died 5 Jan. 2004.*

HALL, Michael Kilgour H.; *see* Harrison-Hall.

HALL, Prof. William Bateman, FREng; Professor of Nuclear Engineering, University of Manchester, 1959–86, then Emeritus; *b* 28 May 1923; *s* of Sidney Bateman Hall and Doris Hall; *m* 1950, Helen Mary Dennis; four *d*. *Educ:* Urmston Grammar Sch.; College of Technology, Manchester. Engineering apprenticeship, 1939–44; Royal Aircraft Establishment, 1944–46; United Kingdom Atomic Energy Authority (formerly Dept of Atomic Energy, Min. of Supply), 1946–59: Technical Engineer, 1946–52; Principal Scientific Officer, 1952–56; Senior Principal Scientific Officer, 1956–58; Dep. Chief Scientific Officer, 1958. Mem., Adv. Cttee on Safety of Nuclear Installations, 1972–83. Pro-Vice-Chancellor, Univ. of Manchester, 1979–82. FREng (FEng 1986). *Publications:* Reactor Heat Transfer, 1958; papers to scientific and professional institutions. *Recreations:* music, designing and making steam engines. *Address:* High Raise, Eskdale, Holmrook, Cumbria CA19 1UA. *T:* (01946) 723275.   *Died 6 Aug. 2003.*

HALL, Willis; writer; *b* 6 April 1929; *s* of Walter and Gladys Hall; *m* 1962, Jill Bennett (marr. diss. 1965; she *d* 1990); *m* 1966, Dorothy Kingsmill Lunn; *m* 1973, Valerie Shute; one *s*, and three *s* by previous marriages. *Educ:* Cockburn High Sch., Leeds. Member: The Magic Circle; Internat. Brotherhood of Magicians; Soc. of Amer. Magicians;

Malta Magicians Soc. TV plays include: The Villa Maroc; They Don't all Open Men's Boutiques; Song at Twilight; The Road to 1984; TV series: The Fuzz, 1977; The Danedyke Mystery, 1979; Stan's Last Game, 1983; The Bright Side, 1985; The Return of the Antelope, 1986; The Reluctant Dragon, 1988; (with Keith Waterhouse): The Upper Crusts, 1973; Billy Liar, 1974; Worzel Gummidge, 1979 (adapted as stage musical, 1981). *Publications:* (with Michael Parkinson) The A–Z of Soccer, 1970; Football Report, 1973; Football Classified, 1974; My Sporting Life, Football Final, 1975; *children's books:* The Royal Astrologer, 1960; The Gentle Knight, 1967; The Incredible Kidnapping, 1975; The Summer of the Dinosaur, 1977; The Last Vampire, 1982; The Inflatable Shop, 1984; The Return of the Antelope, 1985; Dragon Days, 1985; Spooky Rhymes, 1987; The Antelope Company at Large, 1987; Dr Jekyll and Mr Hollins, 1988; Henry Hollins and the Dinosaur, 1988; The Vampire's Holiday, 1991; The Vampire's Revenge, 1993; The Vampire's Christmas, 1994; The Vampire Vanishes, 1995; Vampire Park, 1996; The Vampire Hunt, 1998; Vampire Island, 1999; *plays:* The Long and the Short and the Tall, 1959; A Glimpse of the Sea, 1969; Kidnapped at Christmas, 1975; Walk on, Walk on, 1975; Stag Night, 1976; Christmas Crackers, 1976; A Right Christmas Caper, 1977; (with Keith Waterhouse): Billy Liar, 1960; Celebration, 1961; All Things Bright and Beautiful, 1962; England Our England, 1962; Squat Betty and The Sponge Room, 1963; Say Who You Are, 1965; Whoops-a-Daisy, 1968; Children's Day, 1969; Who's Who, 1972; *adaptations:* (with Keith Waterhouse): de Filippo, Saturday, Sunday, Monday, 1973; de Filippo, Filumena, 1977; (with Denis King) A. A. Milne, The Wind in the Willows (musical), 1985; (with John Cooper) Charles Kingsley, The Water Babies (musical), 1987; Charlotte Brontë, Jane Eyre, 1992; Jane Austen, Mansfield Park, 1993; Alexandre Dumas, The Three Musketeers, 1994; *musicals:* (with Keith Waterhouse): The Card, 1973; Budgie, 1989; (with Denis King) Treasure Island, 1985; (with George Stiles and Anthony Drewe) J. M. Barrie, Peter Pan, 2000. *Recreation:* magic. *Address:* c/o Alexandra Cann representation, 12 Abingdon Road, W8 6AF. *Clubs:* Garrick, Lansdowne; Yorks CC. *Died 7 March 2005.*

HALL WILLIAMS, John Eryl; see Williams, John Eryl H.

HALLIBURTON, Rev. Canon (Robert) John; Priest-in-Charge, St Andrew's, Pau, France, since 2003; Canon Residentiary and Chancellor, St Paul's Cathedral, 1989–2003, then Canon Emeritus; *b* 23 March 1935; *s* of Robert Halliburton and Katherine Margery Halliburton (*née* Robinson); *m* 1968, Jennifer Ormsby Turner; one *s* two *d* (and one *s* one *d* decd). *Educ:* Tonbridge Sch.; Selwyn Coll., Cambridge (MA); Keble Coll., Oxford (DPhil); St Stephen's House, Oxford. Curate, St Dunstan and All Saints, Stepney, 1961; Tutor, 1967, Vice-Principal, 1971, St Stephen's House, Oxford; Lectr, Lincoln Coll., Oxford, 1973; Principal, Chichester Theol Coll., 1975–82, Canon and Prebend of Chichester Cathedral, 1976–82, Canon Emeritus, 1982–88; Canon and Preb. of Wightring and Theol Lectr, 1988–90; Priest-in-Charge, All Souls, St Margaret's-on-Thames, 1982–89. Lecturer: Southwark Ordination Course, 1984–89; Missionary Inst., Mill Hill, 1984–89. Select Preacher, Oxford Univ., 1976–77. Consultant, ARCIC, 1971–81; Mem., Doctrinal Commn of C of E, 1978–86. Examining Chaplain to Bishop of Kensington, 1983. Chm., Anglo-Catholic Ordination Candidates' Fund, 1996–. Pres., Sion Coll., 1998–99. *Publications:* The Authority of a Bishop, 1986; Educating Rachel, 1987; contributions to: The Eucharist Today, ed R. C. D. Jasper, 1974; The Study of Liturgy, ed C. P. M. Jones, 1978; Confession and Absolution, ed G. Rowell and M. Dudley, 1990; The Oil of Gladness, ed G. Rowell and M. Dudley, 1992; reports of C of E Doctrinal Commn, Believing in the Church, 1982, We Believe in God, 1987; articles in Studia Patristica, La Revue des Etudes Augustiniennes, Faith and Unity. *Recreations:* music, gardening. *Address:* chemin de

l'Eglise, 64350 Aurions Idernes, Pau, France. *T:* (5) 59040091. *Club:* Athenæum. *Died 26 Sept. 2004.*

HALLIDAY, Ian Francis, FCA; Finance Director, Lowndes Lambert Group Ltd, 1981–87; *b* 16 Nov. 1927; *s* of Michael and Jean Halliday; *m* 1952, Mary Busfield; one *s* two *d*. *Educ:* Wintringham Grammar Sch., Grimsby; Lincoln Coll., Oxford (MA Mathematics). Armitage & Norton, Chartered Accountants, 1951–69; qual. as Chartered Accountant, 1954; Partner, 1957; Finance Dir, Allied Textile Co. Ltd, 1970–74; on secondment as Dep. Director of Industrial Development Unit, Dept of Industry, 1974–77; Finance Dir, Leslie & Godwin (Holdings) Ltd, internat. insce and re-insce Lloyd's Brokers, 1977–80; Chief Exec., NEB, 1980. Mem., PLA, 1984–97. *Recreation:* gardening. *Address:* Blackmore Farm, Broadway, Bourn, Cambs CB3 7TA.
Died 14 June 2004.

HALLSWORTH, Prof. Ernest Gordon, DSc, FRSC; scientific consultant and author; Chairman of Directors, Hallsworth and Associates; *b* 1913; *s* of Ernest and Beatrice Hallsworth, Ashton-under-Lyne, Lancs; *m* 1st, 1943, Elaine Gertrude Seddon (*d* 1970), *d* of R. C. Weatherill, Waverley, NSW; two *s* one *d*,and one step *s*; 2nd, 1976, Merrily Ramly; one step *d*. *Educ:* Ashton Grammar Sch., Ashton-under-Lyne, Lancs; Univ. of Leeds (First Cl. Hons in Agric. Chem.; PhD 1939; DSc 1964). Sir Swire Smith Fellow and Asst Lectr in Agric. Chem., Univ. of Leeds, 1936; Lectr in Agric. Chem., Univ. of Sydney, 1940–51; Prof. of Soil Science, Univ. of West Australia, 1960–61; Prof. of Agric. Chem. and Head Dept Agric. Sci., Univ. Nottingham, 1951–64 (Dean, Faculty of Agric. and Hort., 1951–60); Chief of Div. of Soils, CSIRO, 1964–73; Chm., Land Resources Labs, CSIRO, 1973–78; Hon. Professorial Fellow, Science Policy Res. Unit, Sussex Univ., 1979–85. Pres. Lecturers' Assoc., Sydney Univ., 1946–49. Treas., Aust. Assoc. of Scientific Workers, 1943; Member: Pasture Improvement Cttee, Australian Dairy Produce Bd (NSW), 1948–51; Science Adv. Panel, Australian Broadcasting Commn, 1949–51; Chm. Insecticides and Fungicides Cttee, Australian Standards Inst., 1949–51. President: Internat. Soc. of Soil Science, 1964–68; Sect. 13, Aust. and NZ Assoc. for the Advancement of Science, 1976. Mem. Council, Flinders Univ., 1967–79; Chief Scientific Liaison Officer (Aust.), London, 1971. FTSE 1976; Fellow, World Acad. of Art and Science, 1989–; Mem., Académie d'Agriculture de France, 1983–; Hon. Member: Aust. Soc. of Soil Sci., 1984; Internat. Soc. of Soil Sci., 1990. Prescott Medal, Aust. Soc. Soil Science, 1984; Dokuchaev Medal, All-Union Soc. of Soil Sci., 1990. *Publications:* (ed) Nutrition of the Legumes, 1958; (ed with D. V. Crawford) Experimental Pedology, 1964; (with others) Handbook of Australian Soils, 1968; (with others) Principles of a Balanced Land Use Policy for Australia, 1976; Where Shall We Build Our New Cities?, 1978; Land and Water Resources of Australia, 1979; Socio-economic Effects and Restraints in Tropical Forest Management, 1982; The Anatomy, Physiology and Psychology of Erosion, 1987; contribs to: Aust. Jl Science, Jl Soc. Chem. Indust., Experimental Agric., Jl Agric. Science, Aust. Medical Jl, Jl Soil Science. *Recreations:* talking, pedology. *Address:* 8 Old Belair Road, Mitcham, SA 5062, Australia. *T:* (8) 82716423; 1 Bellevue Cottages, Blackboys, near Uckfield, Sussex. *T:* (01825) 890606. *Club:* Farmers'.
Died 14 Feb. 2002.

HALLWARD, Bertrand Leslie, MA; *b* 24 May 1901; *er s* of late N. L. Hallward, Indian Educational Service, and Evelyn A. Gurdon; *m* 1926, Catherine Margaret (*d* 1991), 2nd *d* of late Canon A. J. Tait, DD; four *d*. *Educ:* Haileybury Coll. (Scholar); King's Coll., Cambridge (Scholar). Fellow of Peterhouse, 1923–39 (Hon. Fellow, 1956), and Univ. Lectr, 1926–39, Cambridge; Headmaster of Clifton Coll., 1939–48; Vice-Chancellor, Nottingham Univ., 1948–65 (Hallward Library named at Nottingham Univ., 1989). Editor, Classical Qly, 1935–39. Hon. LLD:

Chattanooga, USA, 1958; Sheffield, 1964; Nottingham, 1965. *Publications:* Chapters II, III, IV, and part of VII (the Second and Third Punic Wars) in Cambridge Ancient History, Vol. VIII, 1930; *relevant publication:* Bertrand Hallward, by Derek Winterbottom, 1996. *Address:* 5 High Street, Chesterton, Cambridge CB4 1NQ.

Died 17 Nov. 2003.

HAMBRO, Baron *cr* 1994 (Life Peer), of Dixton and Dumbleton, in the County of Gloucester; **Charles Eric Alexander Hambro;** Chairman: Hambros PLC, 1983–97; Guardian Royal Exchange Assurance, 1988–99 (Director, 1968–99; Deputy Chairman, 1974–88); *b* 24 July 1930; *s* of late Sir Charles Hambro, KBE, MC, and Pamela Cobbold; *m* 1st, 1954, Rose Evelyn (marr. diss. 1976), *d* of Sir Richard Cotterell, 5th Bt, CBE; two *s* one *d*; 2nd, 1976, Cherry Felicity, *d* of Sir John Huggins, GCMG, MC. *Educ:* Eton. Served Coldstream Guards, 1949–51; joined Hambros Bank Ltd, 1952: Man. Dir, 1957; Dep. Chm., 1965; Chm., 1972–83; Director: Taylor Woodrow, 1962–97; P&OSN Co., 1987–2001; NHS-Nuova Holding Sanpaolo SpA (formerly Istituto Bancario San Paolo di Torino, then San Paolo Bank Hldgs), 1989–98. Chm., Royal Nat. Pension Fund for Nurses, 1968–2000. Trustee, British Museum, 1984–94. *Recreations:* shooting, farming, forestry. *Address:* Dixton Manor, Gotherington, Cheltenham, Glos GL52 9RB. *T:* (01242) 672011. *Clubs:* White's, MCC.

Died 7 Nov. 2002.

HAMBURGER, Sir Sidney (Cyril), Kt 1981; CBE 1966; JP; DL; Chairman, North Western Regional Health Authority, 1973–82; *b* 14 July 1914; *s* of Isidore and Hedwig Hamburger; *m* 1940, Gertrude, *d* of Morris Sterling; three *s*. *Educ:* Salford Grammar Sch. Served in Army, 1940–46, Capt. Salford City Council: Mem., 1946–70; Alderman, 1961–70; Mayor of Salford, 1968–69. Pres., Gtr Manchester Area CAB, 1990— (Chm., 1985–90); Chairman: NE Manchester Hosp. Management Cttee, 1970–74; NW ASH, 1977—; Age Concern, Salford, 1984—; Manchester Council for Soviet Jewry, 1984–97; Manchester Friends of Lithuanian Jewry, 1997—; Member: NW Electricity Bd Consultative Council, 1953–59 (Chm. Manchester Cttee, 1963–68); Manchester Regional Hosp. Bd, 1966–74 (Chm. Finance Cttee); Supplementary Benefits Commn, 1967–77; BBC NW Adv. Cttee, 1970–73; Manchester Univ. Court, 1973–84. President: Council, Manchester-Salford Jews, 1962–65; Jt Israel Appeal, Manchester, 1984—; Life-President: Manchester Jewish Homes for the Aged, 1965—; Zionist Central Council of Greater Manchester; Vice-Pres., Friends of Israel Assoc., Manchester; Nat. Pres., Trades Advisory Council, 1984—; Pres., Motability NW, 1989—; Vice-Pres., British Lung Foundn, 1987—. Governor; Ben Gurion Univ., Israel, 1979—. Hon. Fellow, Bar-Ilan Univ., Israel, 1979; Hon. MA Salford, 1987; Hon. LLD Manchester, 1983. Pro Ecclesia, Papal Award, 1982. JP Salford, 1957; DL Greater Manchester, 1981. *Recreation:* football. *Address:* 26 New Hall Road, Salford M7 0JU.

Died 6 June 2001.

HAMER, Hon. Sir Rupert (James), AC 1992; KCMG 1982; ED; LLM (Melb.); FAIM; Premier of Victoria, Australia, and Treasurer, 1972–81; *b* 29 July 1916; *s* of H. R. Hamer; *m* 1944, April F., *d* of N. R. Mackintosh; two *s* two *d*. *Educ:* Melbourne Grammar and Geelong Grammar Schs; Trinity Coll., Univ. of Melbourne (LLM; Fellow, 1982). Solicitor, admitted 1940. Served War of 1939–45: 5½ years, AIF, Tobruk, Alamein, NG, Normandy. MLC (L) E Yarra, 1958–71; MLA (L) Kew, Vic, 1971–81; Minister for: Immigration, 1962–64; Local Govt, 1964–71; Chief Sec. and Dep. Premier, Victoria, 1971–72; Minister for: the Arts, 1972–79; State Develt, Decentralization and Tourism, 1979–81. Chairman: Vic. State Opera, 1982—; Friends of Royal Botanic Gdns, Melbourne, 1992—; Nat. Inst. of Circus Arts, 1999—. Vice-Chm., Cttee of Management, Werribee Park; Nat. Pres., Save the Children Fund (Australia), 1989—; President: Vic.

Coll. of the Arts, 1982—; Melbourne Internat. Chamber Music Festival, 1989—; Greenhouse Action, Australia, 1989—; Melbourne Foundn Day Cttee, 1992—; Consultative Council on Cancer & Heart Disease, 1994—; Nat. Heritage Foundn, 1997—. Mem., Melbourne Scots Council, 1981—. Chieftain, Vic. Pipe Bands Assoc., 1976—; Trustee: Yarra Bend Park, 1974—; Melbourne Cricket Ground, 1976—. CO, Vic. Scottish Regt, CMF, 1954–58. Hon. LLD Univ. of Melbourne, 1982; DUniv Swinburne, 1995. *Recreations:* tennis, Australian Rules football, walking, music. *Address:* 35 Heather Grove, Kew, Victoria 3101, Australia.

Died 26 March 2004.

HAMILTON, Adrianne Pauline U.; *see* Uziell-Hamilton.

HAMILTON, Rt Rev. Alexander Kenneth, MA; Hon. Assistant Bishop, Diocese of Bath and Wells, since 1988; *b* 11 May 1915; *s* of Cuthbert Arthur Hamilton and Agnes Maud Hamilton; unmarried. *Educ:* Malvern Coll.; Trinity Hall, Cambridge (MA 1941); Westcott House, Cambridge. Ordained deacon, 1939, priest, 1940; Assistant Curate: Birstall, Leicester, 1939–41; Whitworth with Spennymoor, 1941–45; Chaplain, RNVR, 1945–47; Vicar: St Francis, Ashton Gate, Bristol, 1947–58; St John the Baptist, Newcastle upon Tyne, 1958–65; Rural Dean of Central Newcastle, 1962–65; Bishop Suffragan of Jarrow, 1965–80. *Publication:* Personal Prayers, 1963. *Recreations:* golf, trout fishing. *Address:* 3 Ash Tree Road, Burnham-on-Sea, Somerset TA8 2LB. *Clubs:* Naval; Burnham and Berrow Golf.

Died 22 Dec. 2001.

HAMILTON, Prof. George Heard; Director, Sterling and Francine Clark Art Institute, 1966–77, then Emeritus; Professor of Art, Williams College, Williamstown, Massachusetts, 1966–75, then Emeritus; Director of Graduate Studies in Art History, Williams College, 1971–75; *b* 23 June 1910; *s* of Frank A. Hamilton and Georgia Neale Heard; *m* 1945, Polly Wiggin; one *s* one *d*. *Educ:* Yale Univ. BA 1932; MA 1934; PhD 1942. Research Asst, Walters Art Gallery, Baltimore, 1934–36; Mem. Art History Faculty, Yale Univ., 1936–66 (Prof., 1956–66); Robert Sterling Clark Prof. of Art, Williams Coll., 1963–64; Slade Prof. of Fine Art, Cambridge Univ., 1971–72; Kress Prof. in Residence, Nat. Gall. of Art, Washington, DC, 1978–79. FRSA 1973; Fellow, Amer. Acad. of Arts and Science, 1979. Hon. LittD Williams Coll., 1977; Wilbur Lucius Cross Medal, Yale Grad. Sch., 1977; Amer. Art Dealers' Assoc. award for excellence in art hist., 1978. *Publications:* (with D. V. Thompson, Jr) De Arte Illuminandi, 1933; Manet and His Critics, 1954; The Art and Architecture of Russia, 1954; Monet's Paintings of Rouen Cathedral, 1960; European Painting and Sculpture 1880–1940, 1967; (with W. C. Agee) Raymond Duchamp-Villon, 1967; 19th and 20th Century Art: Painting, Sculpture, Architecture, 1970; Articles in Burlington Magazine, Gazette des Beaux-Arts, Art Bulletin, etc. *Recreations:* music, gardening. *Address:* 121 Gale Road, Williamstown, MA 01267, USA. *T:* (413) 4588626. *Clubs:* Century Association (New York); Elizabethan (New Haven); Edgartown Yacht (Mass).

Died 29 March 2004.

HAMILTON, Brig. Hugh Gray Wybrants, CBE 1964 (MBE 1945); DL; Chairman, Forces Help Society and Lord Roberts Workshops, 1976–91; *b* 16 May 1918; *s* of Lt-Col H. W. Hamilton, late 5th Dragoon Guards; *m* 1944, Claire Buxton; two *d*. *Educ:* Wellington Coll., Berks; Peterhouse, Cambridge; Royal Mil. Academy. Commnd Royal Engineers, 1938; served War of 1939–45, in BEF, BNAF, BLA; post-war service in Australia, BAOR, France and UK; Instructor, Army Staff Coll., Camberley, 1954–56; Student, IDC, 1965; retired, 1968. Gen. Manager, Corby Develt Corp., 1968–80. DL Northants, 1977. *Recreations:* riding, sailing, DIY. *Address:* Cherwell House, Hogg End, Chipping Warden, Banbury OX17 1LY. *T:* (01295) 660656.

Died 17 June 2005.

HAMILTON, Ian; *see* Hamilton, R. I.

HAMILTON, James, CBE 1979; *b* 11 March 1918; *s* of George Hamilton and Margaret Carey; *m* 1945, Agnes McGhee; one *s* three *d* (and one *s* decd). *Educ:* St Bridget's, Baillieston; St Mary's, High Whifflet. District Councillor, 6th Lanarks, 1955–58; Lanarks County Council, 1958–64. Mem. Nat. Exec., Constructional Engrg Union, 1958–71, Pres., 1968–69; Chm., Trade Union Group, Parly Labour Party, 1969–70. MP (Lab): Bothwell, 1964–83; Motherwell N, 1983–87. Asst Govt Whip, 1969–70; an Opposition Whip, 1970–74; a Lord Comr of the Treasury and Vice-Chamberlain of the Household, 1974–78; Comptroller of HM Household, 1978–79. *Recreations:* tennis, badminton, golf. *Address:* 12 Rosegreen Crescent, North Road, Bellshill, Lanarks ML4 1NT. *T:* (01698) 842071. *Died 11 April 2005.*

HAMILTON, Loudon Pearson, CB 1987; Chairman, Hanover (Scotland) Housing Association, since 1998; *b* 12 Jan. 1932; *s* of Vernon Hamilton and Jean Mair Hood; *m* 1st, 1956, Anna Mackinnon Young (*d* 1993); two *s*; 2nd, 1997, Rosemary Hutton (*née* Griffiths). *Educ:* Hutchesons' Grammar Sch., Glasgow; Glasgow Univ. (MA Hons Hist.). National Service, 2nd Lieut RA, 1953–55. Inspector of Taxes, Inland Revenue, 1956–60; Asst Principal, Dept of Agriculture and Fisheries for Scotland, 1960; Private Sec. to Parly Under-Sec. of State for Scotland, 1963–64; First Sec., Agriculture, British Embassy, Copenhagen and The Hague, 1966–70; Asst Sec., Dept of Agriculture and Fisheries for Scotland, 1973–79; Principal Estabt Officer, Scottish Office, 1979–84; Sec., Scottish Office Agriculture and Fisheries Dept, 1984–92. Mem., AFRC, 1984–92; Chairman: Scottish Food Quality Certification Co., 1995–2001; Scottish Agricl and Rural Develt Centre, 1992–2002. *Address:* Old Lyne Station, near Peebles, EH45 8NP. *T:* (01721) 740393. *Died 23 March 2005.*

HAMILTON, Mary Margaret; *see* Kaye, M. M.

HAMILTON, Sir Richard; *see* Hamilton, Sir Robert C. R. C.

HAMILTON, Sir (Robert Charles) Richard (Caradoc), 9th Bt *cr* 1647, of Silvertonhill, Lanarkshire; *b* 8 Sept. 1911; *s* of Sir Robert Caradoc Hamilton, 8th Bt, and Irene (*d* 1969), *d* of Sir Charles Mordaunt, 10th Bt; *S* father, 1959; *m* 1952, Elizabeth Vidal Barton; one *s* three *d*. *Educ:* Charterhouse; St Peter's Coll., Oxford (MA). Served in the Intelligence Corps, 1940–45. Schoolmaster at Ardingly Coll., Sussex, 1946–60. Owner, Walton Estate, Warwick; Mem., Warwickshire Br., CLA, 1962– (Chm., 1979–83). *Publications:* (trans.) de Luze, A History of the Royal Game of Tennis, 1979; (trans.) Pierre Barcellon, Rules and Principles of Tennis, 1987. *Recreations:* dramatist, Real tennis. *Heir: s* Andrew Caradoc Hamilton [*b* 23 Sept. 1953; *m* 1984, Anthea Jane Huntingford; three *d*]. *Address:* Walton, Warwick CV35 9HX. *T:* (01789) 840460. *Died 27 Sept. 2001.*

HAMILTON, (Robert) Ian; poet; *b* 24 March 1938; *s* of Robert Tough Hamilton and Daisy McKay; *m* 1st, 1963, Gisela Dietzel (marr. diss.); one *s*; 2nd, 1981, Ahdaf Soueif; two *s*; one *s* one *d* by Patricia Wheatley. *Educ:* Darlington Grammar Sch.; Keble Coll., Oxford (BA Hons). Editor, Review, 1962–72; Poetry and Fiction Editor, Times Literary Supplement, 1965–73; Lectr in Poetry, Univ. of Hull, 1972–73; Editor, The New Review, 1974–79. Presenter, Bookmark (BBC TV series), 1984–87. E. C. Gregory Award, 1963; Malta Cultural Award, 1974. *Publications:* (ed) The Poetry of War 1939–45, 1965; (ed) Alun Lewis: poetry and prose, 1966; (ed) The Modern Poet, 1968; The Visit (poems), 1970; A Poetry Chronicle, 1973; (ed) Robert Frost: selected poems, 1973; The Little Magazines, 1976; Returning (poems), 1976; Robert Lowell: a biography, 1983; (ed) Yorkshire in Verse, 1984; (ed) The New Review Anthology, 1985; Fifty Poems, 1988; In Search of J. D. Salinger, 1988; (ed) Soho Square, 1989; Writers in Hollywood, 1990; (ed) The Faber Book of Soccer, 1992; Keepers of the Flame: literary estates and the rise of biography, 1992; (ed) The Oxford Companion to Twentieth Century Poetry in English, 1994; Walking Possession: essays and reviews, 1994; Gazza Italia, 1994; Steps (poems), 1997; A Gift Imprisoned: the poetic life of Matthew Arnold, 1998; The Trouble with Money, and other essays, 1998; Sixty Poems, 1999; (ed) The Penguin Book of Twentieth Century Essays, 1999; *posthumous publication:* Against Oblivion: some lives of the twentieth-century poets, 2002. *Address:* c/o Gillon Aitken Associates, 29 Fernshaw Road, SW10 0TG. *Died 27 Dec. 2001.*

HAMLYN, Baron *cr* 1998 (Life Peer), of Edgeworth in the co. of Gloucestershire; **Paul Bertrand Hamlyn,** CBE 1993; Founder and Chairman: Octopus Publishing Group (London, New York and Sydney), 1971–97 (part of Reed International plc, from 1987); Mandarin Offset Ltd (formerly Mandarin Publishers) (Hong Kong), 1971–97; Chairman: Heinemann Publishers (Oxford) Ltd (formerly Heinemann Group of Publishers Ltd), 1985–97; Hamlyn Publishing Group, 1986–97 (Director, Paul Hamlyn Ltd, 1970–97); Book Club Associates, 1993–97; Co-founder (with Sir Terence Conran), Co-Chairman and Director, Conran Octopus, 1983–97; *b* Berlin, 12 Feb. 1926; 2nd *s* of late Prof. Richard Hamburger and Mrs L. Hamburger (*née* Hamburg); *m* 1st, 1952, Eileen Margaret, (Bobbie) (marr. diss. 1969), *d* of Col Richard Watson; one *s* one *d*; 2nd, 1970, Mrs Helen Guest. *Educ:* St Christopher Sch., Letchworth, Herts. Founder of Hamlyn Publishing Gp, 1953, which he re-purchased from Reed International, 1986; formed: Books for Pleasure, 1949; Prints for Pleasure, 1960; Records for Pleasure, marketing long-playing classical records, and Golden Pleasure Books (jt co. with Golden Press Inc., NY), 1961; Music for Pleasure (with EMI), 1965. Paul Hamlyn Gp acquired by Internat. Publishing Corp, 1964; joined IPC Bd with special responsibility for all Corporation's book publishing activities; Butterworth & Co. acquired 1968; Director, IPC, 1965–70; Chm., IPC Books, controlling Hamlyn Publishing Gp, 1965–70 (formerly Chm., Paul Hamlyn Holdings Ltd, and associated Cos); Jt Man. Dir, News International Ltd, 1970–71; set up Paul Hamlyn Foundn, 1972; Co-founder (with David Frost) and Dir, Sundial Publications, 1973–86; Co-founder (with Doubleday & Co., NY) and Dir, Octopus Books Internat. BV (Holland), 1973–86; Director: News International, 1971–86; Reed Book Publishing, 1971–97; Octopus Books Ltd, 1979–91; TV am, 1981–83; Reed Internat. Books, 1983–97; Michelin House Develt, 1985–; Bibendum Restaurant, 1986–; Reed Internat., 1987–97; Brandchart, 1987–; Chateau de Bagnols, 1988–; Michelin House Investment Co., 1989–; Reed Elsevier, 1993–98. Chm. Trustees, Public Policy Centre, 1985–87. Chancellor, Thames Valley Univ., 1993–99. Hon. FRCSI 1993. Hon. DLitt: Keele, 1988; Warwick, 1991. Albert Medal, RSA, 1993. *Address:* (office) 18 Queen Anne's Gate, SW1H 9AA. *T:* (020) 7227 3500. *Died 31 Aug. 2001.*

HAMMERSLEY, Dr John Michael, FRS 1976; Reader in Mathematical Statistics, University of Oxford, and Professorial Fellow, Trinity College, Oxford, 1969–87, then Emeritus Fellow; part-time Consultant, Oxford Centre for Industrial and Applied Mathematics, 1987–2000; *b* 21 March 1920; *s* of late Guy Hugh Hammersley and Marguerite (*née* Whitehead); *m* 1951, Shirley Gwendolene (*née* Bakewell); two *s*. *Educ:* Sedbergh Sch.; Emmanuel Coll., Cambridge. MA, ScD (Cantab); MA, DSc (Oxon). War service in Royal Artillery, Major, 1940–45. Graduate Asst, Design and Analysis of Scientific Experiment, Univ. of Oxford, 1948–55; Principal Scientific Officer, AERE, Harwell, 1955–59; Sen. Research Officer, Inst. of Economics and Statistics, Univ. of Oxford, 1959–69; Sen. Research Fellow, Trinity Coll., Oxford, 1961–69. FIMS 1959; FIMA 1964; Fulbright Fellow, Princeton, 1955; Erskine Fellow, 1978; Rouse Ball Lectr, Univ. of Cambridge, 1980. Mem., ISI, 1961. Von Neumann Medal for Applied Maths, Brussels, 1966; IMA Gold Medal, 1984; Pólya Prize, London Math. Soc., 1997. *Publications:* (with D. C. Handscomb) Monte Carlo

Methods, 1964, rev. edn 1966, 5th edn 1984, trans. as Les Méthodes de Monte Carlo, 1967; papers in scientific jls. *Address:* 11 Eynsham Road, Oxford OX2 9BS. *T:* (01865) 862181.   *Died 2 May 2004.*

HAMMOND, Prof. Nicholas Geoffrey Lemprière, CBE 1974; DSO 1944; DL; FBA 1968; Henry Overton Wills Professor of Greek, University of Bristol, 1962–73; a Pro-Vice-Chancellor, 1964–66; *b* 15 Nov. 1907; *s* of late Rev. James Vavasour Hammond, Rector of St Just-in-Roseland, Cornwall, and Dorothy May; *m* 1938, Margaret Campbell, *d* of James W. J. Townley, CBE, MIEE; two *s* two *d* (and one *d* decd). *Educ:* Fettes Coll. (schol.); Caius Coll., Cambridge (schol.); 1st Cl. Classical Tripos Pts I and II, dist. in Hist., Pt II). Montagu Butler Prize; Sandys Student; Pres. CU Hockey Club; Treas. Union Soc. Fellow, Clare Coll., Cambridge, 1930 (Hon. Fellow, 1974), Sen. Tutor, 1947–54; University Lectr in Classics, Cambridge, 1936; Junior Proctor, 1939; Headmaster, Clifton Coll., 1954–62. Johnson Prof., 1973–74, Brittingham Prof., 1977, Wisconsin Univ.; Mellon Prof., Reed Coll., Oregon, 1975–76; Leverhulme Prof., Univ. of Ioannina, 1978; Cornell Prof., Swarthmore Coll., Pennsylvania, 1983; Benedict Prof., Carleton Coll., Minnesota, 1987; Visiting Professor: Haverford Coll., 1978; Univ. of Auckland, 1980; St Olaf Coll., Minnesota, 1981; Pennsylvania Univ., 1982; Trinity Coll., Hartford, 1984; Adelaide Univ., 1984; Nat. Hellenic Res. Foundn, Athens, 1985; Nat. Humanities Center, N Carolina, 1986; Newcastle Univ., NSW, 1988, 1990, 1992. Chm., Managing Cttee, British Sch. at Athens, 1972–75. Pres., Hellenic Soc., 1965–68. Mem., Acad. of Athens, 1993; Foreign Mem., Amer. Acad. of Arts and Scis, 1996. DL Glos, 1968, Cambs. 1973. Hon. DLett: Wisconsin, 1981; St Olaf Coll., 1982; Carleton Coll., 1988; Ioannina, 1996. Steven Runciman Award, Anglo-Hellenic League, 1989. Officer, Order of the Phœnix (Greece), 1946; Companion, Soc. of Friends of the Greek People, 1992. Served War of 1939–45, as Lt-Col, campaigns in Greece, Crete, Syria, and Mem. Allied Mil. Mission, Greece, 1943–44 (despatches twice, DSO). *Publications:* Memoir of Sir John Edwin Sandys, 1933; History of Greece, 1959, 3rd edn 1986; Epirus, 1967; A History of Macedonia, Vol. 1, Historical Geography and Prehistory, 1972, Vol. 2 (with G. T. Griffith) 550–336 BC, 1974, Vol. 3 (with F. W. Walbank) 336–167 BC, 1988 (Vols 1–3 Greek edn 1996); Studies in Greek History, 1973; The Classical Age of Greece, 1976, new edn 1999; Migrations and Invasions in Greece, 1976; Alexander the Great: King, Commander and Statesman, 1981, 2nd edn 1989 (Spanish edn 1992); Venture into Greece: with the guerillas, 1943–44, 1983 (Greek trans., 1986); Three Historians of Alexander the Great, 1983; The Macedonian State, 1989 (Polish edn 1999); The Miracle that was Macedonia, 1991; West Macedonia: Resistance and Allied Military Mission 1943–44, 1993 (Greek edn 1994); Sources for Alexander the Great, 1993; Collected Studies, Vol. 1, 1993, Vol. 2, 1994, Vol. 3, 1994, Vol. 4, 1997; Philip of Macedon, 1994 (Greek edn 1997); The Genius of Alexander the Great, 1997 (Greek edn 1997); edited: Clifton Coll. Centenary Essays, 1962; Cambridge Ancient History, 3rd edn, vols I, II, III and IV; Oxford Classical Dictionary, 2nd edn 1970; Atlas of the Greek and Roman World in Antiquity, 1981; articles and reviews in learned jls. *Address:* 4 Barrington House, Southacre Park, Chaucer Road, Cambridge CB2 2TY. *T:* (01223) 357151.   *Died 24 March 2001.*

HAMPSHIRE, Margaret Grace, MA; JP; Principal of Cheltenham Ladies' College, 1964–79; *b* 7 Sept. 1918; *o d* of Dr C. H. Hampshire, CMG, MB, BS, BSc, sometime Sec. of British Pharmacopœia Commission, and Grace Mary Hampshire. *Educ:* Malvern Girls' Coll.; Girton Coll., Cambridge (BA 1941; MA 1945). Entered Civil Service, Board of Trade, 1941. Joined Staff of Courtaulds, 1951. Head of Government Relations Department, 1959–64. Member: Board of Governors, University Coll. Hosp., 1961–64; Marylebone Borough Council, 1962–64; SW Regional Hosp. Board, 1967–70; Midlands Electricity

Consultative Council, 1973–80; Vice-Pres., Intensive Care Trust, Cheltenham Hosp., 1985– (Chm., 1982–85). Reader, Painswick, Sheepscombe and Cranham, dio. of Gloucester, 1987–. County Sec., Gloucestershire Girl Guides, 1980–85; Governor, Alice Ottley Sch., Worcester, 1979–92. JP Cheltenham, 1970. *Recreations:* music, reading, foreign travel. *Address:* Ringwood, 9 The Croft, Painswick, Glos GL6 6QP.   *Died 6 June 2004.*

HAMPSHIRE, Sir Stuart (Newton), Kt 1979; FBA 1960; Warden of Wadham College, Oxford University, 1970–84; *b* 1 Oct. 1914; *s* of G. N. Hampshire and Marie West; *m* 1st, 1961, Renee Ayer (*d* 1980); 2nd, 1985, Prof. Nancy Lynn Delaney Cartwright,FBA; two *d*. *Educ:* Repton; Balliol Coll., Oxford. 1st Cl. Lit Hum, Oxford, 1936. Fellow of All Souls Coll., and Lectr in Philosophy, Oxford, 1936–40. Service in Army, 1940–45. Personal Asst to Minister of State, Foreign Office, 1945; Lectr in Philosophy, University Coll., London, 1947–50; Fellow of New Coll., Oxford, 1950–55; Domestic Bursar and Research Fellow, All Souls Coll., 1955–60; Grote Prof. of Philosophy of Mind and Logic, Univ. of London, 1960–63; Prof. of Philosophy, Princeton Univ., 1963–70; Prof., Stanford Univ., 1985–91. Fellow, Amer. Acad. of Arts and Sciences, 1968. Hon. DLitt Glasgow, 1973. *Publications:* Spinoza, 1951; Thought and Action, 1959; Freedom of the Individual, 1965; Modern Writers and other essays, 1969; Freedom of Mind and other essays, 1971; (ed jtly) The Socialist Idea, 1975; Two Theories of Morality, 1977; (ed) Public and Private Morality, 1978; Morality and Conflict, 1983; Innocence and Experience, 1989; Justice is Conflict, 1999; articles in philosophical journals. *Address:* 7 Beaumont Road, The Quarry, Headington, Oxford OX3 8JN. *T:* (01865) 761688.   *Died 13 June 2004.*

HAMPSON, Caroline; *see* St John-Brooks, C.

HAMPTON, 6th Baron *cr* 1874; **Richard Humphrey Russell Pakington;** Bt 1846; *b* 25 May 1925; *s* of 5th Baron Hampton, OBE, and Grace Dykes (*d* 1959), 3rd *d* of Rt Hon. Sir Albert Spicer, 1st Bt; *S* father, 1974; *m* 1958, Jane Elizabeth Farquharson, *er d* of late T. F. Arnott, OBE, TD, MB, ChB; one *s* two *d*. *Educ:* Eton; Balliol Coll., Oxford. RNVR, 1944–47. Varied employment, with advertising agencies, 1949–58; Worcestershire Branch, CPRE, 1958–71. Liberal Party Spokesman on NI, H of L, 1977–87. President: S Worcs Liberal Assoc., 1978–88; Upton-on-Severn Civic Soc., 1986–93. A Liberal Democrat. *Publication:* (with his father, Humphrey Pakington) The Pakingtons of Westwood, 1975. *Heir: s* Hon. John Humphrey Arnott Pakington [*b* 24 Dec. 1964; *m* 1996, Siena, *yr d* of Remo Caldato].
                                             Died 9 July 2003.

HAMPTON, Antony Barmore, TD 1954; DL; President, Record Marples Tools Ltd (formerly Bahco Record Tools), since 1981 (Chairman, 1958–81); President, Engineering Employers Federation, 1980–82; *b* 6 March 1919; *s* of Charles William Hampton and Winifred Elizabeth Hampton; *m* 1948, Helen Patricia Lockwood; five *s*. *Educ:* Rydal Sch.; Christ's Coll., Cambridge (MA). Served War, Indian Army, 1941–46 (despatches). C. and J. Hampton Ltd, 1947, until merger with Ridgway, 1972 (Chm. of both, 1958–81); Lloyds Bank Ltd: Chm., Yorkshire Board, 1972–84 (Mem., 1961–85); Dir, UK Board, 1972–85; Dir, Black Horse Agencies Ltd, 1983–85. Mem., Engrg Industry Trng Bd, 1979–82. Master Cutler of Hallamshire, 1966–67. Chm., Crucible Theatre Trust, Sheffield, 1970–82. DL S Yorkshire (previously W Riding), 1972. *Recreations:* sailing, fishing. *Address:* Tideway, 20 Wittering Road, Hayling Island, Hants PO11 9SP. *T:* (023) 9246 4361. *Club:* Little Ship (Hon. Life Mem., 1998).   *Died 15 May 2005.*

HANCOCK, Norman, CB 1976; CEng, FRINA; RCNC; Director of Warship Design, and Project Director, Invincible and Broadsword, Ministry of Defence, 1969–76; *b* 6 March 1916; *o s* of Louis Everard

Hancock, Plymouth; *m* 1940, Marie E., *d* of William E. Bow; two *s*. *Educ*: Plymouth Grammar Sch.; RNC Greenwich. Asst Constructor, AEW, Haslar, 1940; Constructor, Naval Construction Dept, 1944; British Services Observer (Constructor Comdr), Bikini, 1946. HM Dockyard, Singapore, 1949; Frigate design, Naval Construction Dept, 1952; Chief Constructor in charge of R&D, 1954; Prof. of Naval Architecture, RNC, Greenwich, 1957–62; Asst Dir of Naval Construction, in charge of Submarine Design and Construction, 1963–69. Past Mem. Council, RINA. Liveryman, Shipwrights' Co. *Recreations*: organ music, cabinet making, travel. *Address*: 41 Cranwells Park, Bath, Somerset BA1 2YE. *T*: (01225) 426045. *Died 5 Aug. 2003.*

HANCOCK, P(ercy) E(llis) Thompson, FRCP; former Hon. Consultant Physician: The Royal Free Hospital; The Royal Marsden Hospital; Potters Bar and District Hospital; National Temperance Hospital; Bishop's Stortford and District Hospital; *b* 4 Feb. 1904; *s* of Frank Hancock; *m* 1932, Dorothy Barnes (*d* 1953); two *d*; *m* 1955, Laurie Newton Sharp (*d* 1999). *Educ*: Wellington Coll., Berks; Caius Coll., Cambridge; St Bartholomew's Hospital. MB 1937, BCh 1930, Cantab; FRCP 1944. Formerly: Senior Examiner in Medicine, Univ. of London; Dir of Dept of Clinical Res., Royal Marsden Hosp. and Inst. of Cancer Res. Member: Council, Imperial Cancer Res. Fund; Grand Council, Cancer Research Campaign; Mem. Exec. Cttee, Action on Smoking and Health; Sen. Mem., Assoc. of Physicians, GB and Ireland. Hosp. Visitor, King Edward's Hosp. Fund for London. FRSocMed (Pres., Section of Oncology, 1974–75); Fellow, Assoc. Européene de Médecine Interne d'Ensemble. Corresp. Mem., Società Italiana de Cancerologia. Hon. Member: American Gastroscopic Soc., 1958; Sociedad Chilena de Cancerología; Sociedad Chilena de Hematología; Sociedad Médica de Valparaíso; Medal, Societa Medica Chirurgica di Bologna, 1964. *Publications*: (joint) Cancer in General Practice; The Use of Bone Marrow Transfusion with massive Chemotherapy, 1960; (joint) Treatment of Early Hodgkin's Disease, 1967. *Recreations*: dining and wining. *Died 8 Jan. 2004.*

HANDLEY-TAYLOR, Geoffrey, FRSL 1950; writer; Hon. Home and Overseas Information Correspondent, John Masefield Research and Studies, 1958–93; *b* 25 April 1920; 2nd *s* of Walter Edward Taylor and Nellie Hadwin (*née* Taylor), Horsforth. *Educ*: widely. Served War of 1939–45, Duke of Wellington's Regt and War Office. Literary and ballet lecture tours, UK and overseas, 1946–57. Chm., British Poetry-Drama Guild, 1948–52; Vice-Pres., Leeds Univ. Tudor Players, 1948–50; Publisher, Leeds University Poetry, 1949; featured in NBC-TV (USA) People series, 1955; Founder, Winifred Holtby Meml Collection, Fisk Univ., Nashville, 1955; Hon. Gen. Sec., Dumas Assoc., 1955–57; Donor, Sir Ralph Perring City of London Collection, Fisk Univ., 1962–65; Pres., St Paul's Literary Soc., Covent Garden, 1966–68; Chm. Gen. Council, Poetry Soc., 1967–68; served on PCC, St Paul's, Covent Garden, 1967–68; Mem. Gen. Council, NBL, 1968; Pres., Lancashire Authors' Assoc., 1969–72; a Trustee, Gladstone Meml Library, London, 1974–78; Jt Literary Trustee, Estate of Vera Brittain, 1979–90; (with Corliss Lamont) Hon. Founder Mem., John Masefield Soc., 1993–97. Several foreign decorations and awards. *Publications*: Mona Inglesby, Ballerina and Choreographer, 1947; Italian Ballet Today, 1949; (foreword to) Stars of the Opera, ed Frank Granville Barker, 1949; New Hyperion, 1950; Literary, Debating and Dialect Societies of GB, Ireland and France, 5 pts, 1950–54; A Selected Bibliography of Literature Relating to Nursery Rhyme Reform, 1952; Winifred Holtby Bibliography and Letters, 1955; (with Frank Granville Barker) John Gay and the Ballad Opera, 1956; (with Thomas Rae) The Book of the Private Press, 1958; John Masefield, OM, The Queen's Poet Laureate, 1960; (with Vera Brittain) Selected Letters of Winifred Holtby and Vera Brittain 1920–1935, 1961, 2nd edn 1970;

Bibliography of Monaco, 1961, 2nd edn 1968; Bibliography of Iran, 1964, 5th edn 1969; (with Timothy d'Arch Smith) C. Day Lewis, Poet Laureate, 1968; ed, County Authors Today Series, 9 vols, 1971–1973; Pogg (a satire), 1980; (with John Malcolm Dockeray) Vera Brittain, Occasional Papers, 1983; also contributions to: Encycl. Britannica; Hinrichsen Music Book, 1949–1958; Airs from The Beggar's Opera, arr. Edith Bathurst, 1953; The Beggar's Opera, ed Edward J. Dent, 1954; Kathleen: the life of Kathleen Ferrier 1912–1953, ed Maurice Leonard, 1988; (foreword to) John Masefield: a bibliographical description of his first, limited, signed and special editions, ed Crocker Wight, 1992; Markova: the legend, ed Maurice Leonard, 1995; Montgomery Clift, ed Maurice Leonard, 1997; John Masefield Bibliography, ed Philip W. Errington, 2004. *Died 27 May 2005.*

HANLEY, Howard Granville, CBE 1975; MD, FRCS; Consulting Urologist, King Edward VII's Hospital for Officers, London; Dean, 1968–72, Chairman, 1972–80, President, 1980–88, Institute of Urology, University of London; *b* 27 July 1909; *s* of F. T. Hanley; *m* 1939, Margaret Jeffrey; two *s*. *Educ*: St Bees Sch., Cumberland; Univ. of Liverpool (MB 1932; MD 1934). FRCS 1937. Urologist: St Peter's Hosps Gp, 1947–75; Royal Masonic Hosp., London, 1960–77; Urol Consultant to Army, 1951–75; Hon. Consulting Urologist, Royal Hosp., Chelsea, 1951–75. Visiting Professor of Urology: University of Calif, Los Angeles, 1958; Ohio State Univ., Columbus, 1961; University of Texas Southwestern Medical Sch., 1963; Tulane University, New Orleans, 1967. Royal College of Surgeons: Hunterian Prof., 1955; Dean, Inst. of Basic Med. Scis, 1972–76; Mem. Council, 1969–81; Vice-Pres., 1979–81; Royal Society of Medicine: Pres., Urol Sect., 1969–81; Hon. Librarian. Trustee, St Peter's Research Trust for the Cure of Kidney Disease, 1970–86. Fellow, Assoc. of Surgeons of GB and Ireland; Past Pres. (formerly Sec. and Treasurer), British Assoc. Urological Surgeons; Past Sec., Hunterian Soc.; Past Pres., Chelsea Clinical Soc. Member: Internat. Soc. Urology; German Urol Soc.; Soc. Française d'Urologie; European Assoc. of Urology. Corresponding Member: Amer. Assoc. Genito-urinary Surgeons; Western Sect., Amer. Urological Assoc. Liveryman, Worshipful Soc. of Apothecaries of London. Hon. FACS; Hon. FRSocMed 1991. *Publications*: chapters in: British Surgical Practice, 1957; Recent Advances in Urology, 1960; contribs to: A Textbook of Urology, 1960; Modern Trends in Urology, 1960; contribs to jls on surgery and urology. *Recreation*: gardening. *Address*: Brandon House, North End Avenue, NW3 7HP. *T*: (020) 8458 2035. *Club*: Athenæum. *Died 18 Feb. 2001.*

HANLEY, Sir Michael (Bowen), KCB 1974; *b* 24 Feb. 1918; *s* of late Prof. James Alec Hanley, PhD, ARCS; *m* 1957, Hon. Lorna Margaret Dorothy, *d* of late Hon. Claude Hope-Morley (2nd *s* of 1st Baron Hollenden); one adopted *s* one adopted *d*. *Educ*: Sedbergh School; Queen's Coll., Oxford (MA). Served War of 1939–45. Asst Mil. Attaché, Budapest, 1946–48; joined Security Service, 1948; Dep. Dir Gen., 1971–72, Dir Gen., 1972–78, MI5. *Address*: c/o Ministry of Defence, SW1. *Died 1 Jan. 2001.*

HANN, Sir James, Kt 1996; CBE 1977; Chairman: Hickson International plc, 1994–99; Bath Press Group plc, 1997–99; *b* 18 Jan. 1933; *s* of Harry Frank and Bessie Gladys Hann; *m* 1958, Jill Margaret Howe (*d* 1999); one *s* one *d*. *Educ*: Peter Symonds Sch., Winchester; IMEDE, Lausanne, Switzerland. FCIM, FInstPet. James Hann & Sons, 1950–52; Royal Artillery, 1952–54; United Dairies, 1954–65; IMEDE, 1965–66; Managing Director: Hanson Dairies, Liverpool, 1966–72; Seaforth Maritime, Aberdeen, 1972–86; Chairman: Bauteil Engineering, Glasgow, 1986–88; Exacta Holdings, Selkirk, 1986–90; Associated Fresh Foods, Leeds 1987–89; Strathclyde Inst., Glasgow, 1987–90; Scottish Nuclear, 1990–95; Eurotherm plc, 1996–98; Dep. Chm., Scottish Transport

Gp, 1987–90. Director: William Baird, 1991–2001; NFU Mutual and Avon Gp, 1993–98. Comr, Northern Lighthouse Bd, 1990–95 (Chm., 1993–94). Member: Offshore Energy Technology Bd, 1982–85; Offshore Tech. Adv. Gp, 1983–86; Nationalised Industries Chairman's Gp, 1990–95. Life Mem., Beaver Club, Montreal, 1981 (for services to Canadian offshore industry). Burgess of Guild, Aberdeen, 1982–. CCMI. Hon. FINucE 1993; Hon. Fellow European Nuclear Soc., 1994. *Recreations:* sailing, reading, music. *Address:* Wrington, N Somerset. *Died 14 Feb. 2004.*

HANSON, Baron *cr* 1983 (Life Peer), of Edgerton in the County of West Yorkshire; **James Edward Hanson,** Kt 1976; Chairman, Hanson PLC, 1965–97; Director: Hanson Transport Group Ltd, since 1946 (Chairman, 1965–96); Hanson Capital Ltd, since 2000; *b* 20 Jan. 1922; *s* of late Robert Hanson, CBE and Louisa Ann (Cis) (*née* Rodgers); *m* 1959, Geraldine (*née* Kaelin) (*d* 2004); one *s*, and one adopted *s* one step *d*. Served War, 1939–46. Mem., Ct of Patrons, RCS, 1991–; Trustee, Hanson Fellowship of Surgery, Oxford; Fellow, Cancer Res. Campaign. Life Mem., Royal Dublin Soc., 1948; Life Trustee, Univ. of Southern California, 2002. Freeman, City of London, 1964; Hon. Liveryman, Worshipful Co. of Saddlers, 1965. FRSA; CCMI. Hon. FRCR 1998. Hon. Fellow, St Peter's Coll., Oxford, 1996. Hon. LLD Leeds, 1984; Hon. DBA Huddersfield, 1991. *Address:* 28 Old Brompton Road, (Box 164), SW7 3SS. *T:* (020) 7245 6996. *Clubs:* Brooks's; Huddersfield Borough; The Brook (NY); Toronto. *Died 1 Nov. 2004.*

HARBERTON, 10th Viscount *cr* 1791; **Thomas de Vautort Pomeroy;** Baron Harberton 1783; *b* 19 Oct. 1910; *s* of 8th Viscount Harberton, OBE, and Mary Katherine (*d* 1971), *d* of A. W. Leatham; *S* brother, 1980; *m* 1st, 1939, Nancy Penoyer (marr. diss. 1946); 2nd, 1950, Pauline Stafford (*d* 1971); 3rd, 1978, Vilma (*d* 2000), *widow* of Sir Alfred Butt, 1st Bt. *Educ:* Eton. Joined Welsh Guards, 1932; transferred to RAOC, 1939; served BEF, then in India; retired, 1952. *Heir: nephew* Henry Robert Pomeroy [*b* 23 April 1958; *m* 1990, Caroline Mary, *d* of Jeremy Grindle; two *s*]. *Club:* Cavalry and Guards.
Died 12 March 2004.

HARBORNE, Prof. Jeffrey Barry, PhD, DSc; FRS 1995; Professor of Botany, University of Reading, 1976–93, then Emeritus; *b* 1 Sept. 1928; *s* of late Frank Percy Harborne, Bristol, and Phyllis Maud (*née* Sherriff); *m* 1953, Jean Charlotte, *d* of late Dr John Buchanan; two *s*. *Educ:* Wycliffe Coll., Stonehouse, Glos; Univ. of Bristol (BSc; PhD 1953; DSc 1966). Biochemist, John Innes Inst., 1955–65; Res. Fellow, Univ. of Liverpool, 1965–68; Reader, Univ. of Reading, 1968–76. Visiting Professor: Univ. of Texas, 1976; Univ. of Calif, 1977; Plenary Lectr, IUPAC Nat. Prods Symposium, 1976. Editor-in-Chief, Jl Phytochemistry, 1972–98. Member: RSC, 1956; Biochemical Soc., 1957. FLS 1986; FIBiol 1994. Gold Medal in Botany, Linnean Soc., 1985; Silver Medal: Phytochemical Soc. of Europe, 1986; Internat. Soc. of Chemical Ecology, 1993. *Publications:* Biochemistry of Phenolic Compounds, 1964; Comparative Biochemistry of the Flavonoids, 1967; Phytochemical Phylogeny, 1970; Phytochemical Ecology, 1972; Phytochemical Methods, 1973, 3rd edn 1998; Introduction to Ecological Biochemistry, 1977, 4th edn 1993; Phytochemical Aspects of Plant and Animal Coevolution, 1978; Plant Chemosystematics, 1984; Phytochemical Dictionary, 1993, 2nd edn 1999; The Flavonoids: advances in research since 1986, 1994; Dictionary of Plant Toxins, 1996; The Handbook of Natural Flavonoids, 1999; Chemical Dictionary of Economic Plants, 2001. *Recreations:* rambling, classical music. *Address:* School of Plant Sciences, Plant Science Laboratories, University of Reading, Reading RG6 6AS. *T:* (0118) 931 8162.
Died 21 July 2002.

HARDCASTLE, Sir Alan (John), Kt 1992; FCA; Chairman, Board of Banking Supervision, since 1998

(Member, since 1986); Chief Accountancy Adviser to HM Treasury and Head of Government Accountancy Service, 1989–93; *b* 10 Aug. 1933; *s* of late William and of Catherine Hardcastle; *m* 1st, 1958, Dinah (*née* Beattie) (marr. diss. 1983); two *s*; 2nd, 1983, Ione Marguerite (*née* Cooney); two step *d*. *Educ:* Haileybury Coll. Articled to B. W. Brixey, 1951–56; qualified, 1956; Nat. Service as Sub-Lieut RNVR, 1956–58. Joined Peat, Marwick, Mitchell & Co. (later Peat Marwick McLintock, then KPMG), 1958; Partner 1967; Gen. Partner 1972–88. DoT Inspector into affairs of St Piran Ltd (reported 1981). Non-exec. Dir, Chelsfield, 1994–. Inst. of Chartered Accountants in England and Wales: Mem. Council, 1974–94; Pres., 1983–85; Pres., Chartered Accountants Students' Soc. of London, 1976–80. Chm., Regulatory Bd and Dep. Chm. of Council, Lloyd's, 1993–97 (Mem. Council, 1987–88). Master, Co. of Chartered Accountants in England and Wales, 1978–79. Hon. Treas., Berkeley Square Charitable Trust; Trustee, Thalidomide Trust, 1997–. Life Gov. and Mem. Council, Haileybury Coll., 1995–; Chm. Govs, Lambrook Haileybury Sch., 1998–. Speaker and author of papers on accountancy topics. *Recreations:* music, theatre, fishing, the company of family and friends. *Address:* 53 Wynnstay Gardens, Allen Street, W8 6UU. *Clubs:* Athenæum, Naval. *Died 23 March 2002.*

HARDIE, Sir Douglas (Fleming), Kt 1990; CBE 1979; JP; non-executive Chairman, DDS Medicines Research Ltd, since 1997; Chairman, Edward Parker & Co. Ltd, 1960–98 (Managing Director, 1960–90); *b* 26 May 1923; *s* of late James Dunbar Hardie, JP, and of Frances Mary (*née* Fleming); *m* 1945, Dorothy Alice Warner; two *s* one *d*. *Educ:* Arnhall and Seafield House Prep. Schs; Trinity Coll., Glenalmond, Perthshire. Trooper, 58 Trng Regt, RAC, Bovington, 1941; commnd RMA, Sandhurst, 1942; 1st Fife and Forfar Yeomanry, NW Europe, 1942–46 (despatches); demobilised rank of Major. Dir 1964–84, Chm. 1984–85, H. & A. Scott (Holdings) Ltd; Chairman: A. G. Scott (Textiles) Ltd, 1985–88; Grampian TV, 1989–93 (Dir, 1984–93); Director: Dayco Rubber (UK) Ltd, 1956–86; Clydesdale Bank, 1981–92; Alliance Trust, 1982–93; Second Alliance Trust, 1982–93. Dep. Chm., SDA, 1978–91. Chm., CBI Scotland, 1976–78; Member: N of Scotland Hydro Elec. Bd, 1977–83; Scottish Econ. Council, 1977–91; Vice Chm., Prince's Scottish Youth Business Trust, 1987–2002. Mem. Council, Winston Churchill Meml Trust, 1985–2002. Deacon Convener, Nine Incorporated Trades (Dundee), 1951–54. FRSA 1988; CCMI (CBIM 1990). JP Dundee, 1971. Hon. LLD Dundee, 1992. Order of the Rising Sun (Japan), 2001. *Recreations:* golf, fishing. *Address:* The Anchorage, 8 Bingham Terrace, Dundee DD4 7HH. *T:* (01382) 456772. *Clubs:* Caledonian; Royal & Ancient Golf (St Andrews); Blairgowrie Golf; Panmure Golf (Barry).
Died 7 July 2005.

HARDIE, Miles Clayton, OBE 1988; Director General, International Hospital Federation, 1975–87; *b* 27 Feb. 1924; *s* of late Frederick Hardie and Estelle (*née* Clarke); *m* 1st, 1949, Pauline (marr. diss. 1974), *d* of late Sir Wilfrid Le Gros Clark, FRS; two *s*; 2nd, 1974, Melissa (marr. diss. 1984), *d* of late James Witcher, Houston, Texas; 3rd, 1985, Elizabeth, *d* of late Dudley Ash, *widow* of H. Spencer Smith. *Educ:* Charterhouse; Oriel Coll., Oxford (MA). Served War, RAF, 1943–46. Admin. Asst, Hosp. for Sick Children, London, 1949–51; Sec., Victoria Hosp. for Children, 1951–55; Sec., Bahrain Govt Med. Dept, 1956–58; joined staff of King Edward's Hosp. Fund for London, 1958, Dep. Dir, King's Fund Centre, 1963–66; Dir, 1966–75. Member: British Hosps Export Council, later Assoc. of British Health-Care Industries, 1967–75, 1987– (Hon. Sec., 1964–67); Council of Mgt, MIND/ Nat. Assoc. for Mental Health, 1967–86; Council, Nat. Assoc. of Leagues of Hosp. Friends, 1970–75; Adv. Council, Nat. Corp. Care of Old People, 1973–76; Man. Cttee of Spinal Injuries Assoc., 1975–79; Bd of Governors, Volunteer Centre, 1977–80; Council, Appropriate Health Resources and Technologies Action Gp, 1977–89.

Adviser to WHO, 1978– (WHO Health for All by the year 2000 Medal, 1987). Hon. Member: Amer. Hosp. Assoc., 1983–; Polish Hosp. Assoc., 1985–. Mem., Ct Assts, Salters' Co., 1969–79. *Recreations:* gardening, walking. *Address:* Tallow Cottage, Fishers Lane, Charlbury, Oxford OX7 3RX. *T:* (01608) 810088. *Died 25 Oct. 2002.*

HARDING, Roger John, CMG 1986; Chairman: Sujanara Ltd, since 1991; Bill Hill & Partners Ltd, since 1996; Director, ITT Defence Ltd, since 1993; *b* 7 April 1935; *s* of Charles William Harding and Lilian Mabel (*née* Trowbridge); *m* 1960, June Elizabeth Tidy; four *d*. *Educ:* Price's Sch., Fareham, Hants; Southern Grammar Sch., Portsmouth, Hants. Board of Trade, 1954–74; War Office, then Min. of Defence, 1974–91: Head of Defence Secretariat 8, 1979–82; Counsellor, Defence Supply, 1982–86, Minister, Defence Material, 1986–88, Washington; Dir Gen., Marketing, MoD, 1988–91. *Recreations:* soccer, cricket, golf, following fortunes of Portsmouth FC. *Club:* St John's Village (Woking). *Died 14 Oct. 2003.*

HARDINGE, 6th Viscount *cr* 1846, of Lahore and of King's Newton, Derbyshire; **Charles Henry Nicholas Hardinge;** Bt 1801; Senior Manager, Global Private Banking, Royal Bank of Canada Europe Ltd; *b* 25 Aug. 1956; *s* of 5th Viscount Hardinge and of Zoë Anne, *d* of Hon. Hartland de Montarville Molson, OBE, Montreal; *S* father, 1984; *m* 1985, Julie Therese Sillett, *d* of Joan Sillett of Sydney, Australia; two *d* one step *s*. Heir: *b* Hon. Andrew Hartland Hardinge [*b* 7 Jan. 1960; *m* 1990, Sophia Mary, *e d* of Capt. W. D. A. Bagnell; two *s* one *d*]. *Address:* Broadmere House, Broadmere, Farleigh Wallop, Basingstoke, Hants RG25 2JA. *Died 18 Jan. 2004.*

HARDMAN, Sir Henry, KCB 1962 (CB 1956); *b* 15 Dec. 1905; *s* of late Harry Hardman and Bertha Hardman; *m* 1937, Helen Diana (*d* 1996), *d* of late Robert Carr Bosanquet and Ellen Sophia Bosanquet; one *s* two *d*. *Educ:* Manchester Central High Sch.; University of Manchester. Lecturer for Workers' Educational Association, 1929–34; Economics Tutor, University of Leeds, 1934–45; joined Ministry of Food, 1940; Deputy Head, British Food Mission to N America, 1946–48; Under-Sec., Ministry of Food, 1948–53; Minister, UK Permanent Delegation, Paris, 1953–54; Dep. Sec., Ministry of Agriculture, Fisheries and Food, 1955–60; Dep. Sec., Ministry of Aviation, 1960, Permanent Sec., 1961–63; Permanent Sec., Ministry of Defence, 1963–64, Permanent Under Sec. of State, 1964–66. Mem., Monopolies Commn, 1967–70 (Dep. Chm., 1967–68); Chm., Cttee of enquiry into the Post Office pay dispute, 1971; Consultant to CSD on dispersal of govt work from London, 1971–73 (report published, 1973). Chairman: Covent Garden Mkt Authority, 1967–75; Home-Grown Cereals Authority, 1968–77. Governor and Trustee, Reserve Bank of Rhodesia, 1967–79. Hon. LLD Manchester, 1965. *Address:* 9 Sussex Square, Brighton BN2 1FJ. *T:* (01273) 688904. *Died 17 Jan. 2001.*

HARDWICK, Prof. James Leslie, PhD, DDS; FDSRCS; Professor of Preventive Dentistry, University of Manchester, 1960–78, then Emeritus; *b* 27 March 1913; *o s* of George Hardwicke Hardwick and Mary Ann Hardwick; *m* 1954, Eileen Margaret Isobel Gibson; two *s* two *d*. *Educ:* Rugby Sch.; Birmingham Univ. (MDS 1948, PhD 1950, DDS 1984); MSc 1964. FDSRCS 1954. Private and hospital dental practice, 1935–39. Served War of 1939–45, Army Dental Corps. University of Birmingham: Lecturer, 1945–48, Sen. Lecturer in Operative Dental Surgery, 1948–52; Reader in Dental Surgery, 1952–60. *Publications:* editor of, and contributor to, dental and other scientific jls and textbooks. *Address:* 2 Brook Court, Burcot Lane, Bromsgrove, Worcs B60 1AD. *T:* (01527) 570344. *Died 12 Nov. 2004.*

HARDWICK, Mary, (Mollie); author; *b* Manchester; *d* of Joseph Greenhalgh and Anne Frances Atkinson; *m* 1961, Michael John Drinkrow Hardwick (*d* 1991); one *s*. *Educ:*

Manchester High Sch. for Girls. Announcer, BBC (Radio) N Region, 1940–45; BBC (Radio) Drama Dept, 1946–62; freelance, 1963–. FRSA 1966. *Publications:* Stories from Dickens, 1968; Emma, Lady Hamilton, 1969; Mrs Dizzy, 1972; Upstairs Downstairs: Sarah's Story, 1973, The Years of Change, 1974, The War to end Wars, 1975, Mrs Bridges' Story, 1975, The World of Upstairs Downstairs, 1976; Alice in Wonderland (play), 1975; Beauty's Daughter, 1976 (Elizabeth Goudge Award for best historical romantic novel of year); The Duchess of Duke Street: The Way Up, 1976, The Golden Years, 1976, The World Keeps Turning, 1977; Charlie is my Darling, 1977; The Atkinson Heritage, 1978; Thomas and Sarah, 1978; Thomas and Sarah: Two for a Spin, 1979; Lovers Meeting, 1979; Sisters in Love, 1979; Dove's Nest, 1980; Willowwood, 1980; Juliet Bravo 1, 1980; Juliet Bravo 2, 1980; Monday's Child, 1981; Calling Juliet Bravo: New Arrivals, 1981; I Remember Love, 1982; The Shakespeare Girl, 1983; By the Sword Divided, 1983; The Merrymaid, 1984; Girl with a Crystal Dove, 1985; Malice Domestic, 1986; Parson's Pleasure, 1987; Uneaseful Death, 1988; Blood Royal, 1988; The Bandersnatch, 1989; Perish in July, 1989; The Dreaming Damozel, 1990; Come away Death, 1997; *with Michael Hardwick:* The Jolly Toper, 1961; The Sherlock Holmes Companion, 1962; Sherlock Holmes Investigates, 1963; The Man Who Was Sherlock Holmes, 1964; Four Sherlock Holmes plays, 1964; The Charles Dickens Companion, 1965; The World's Greatest Sea Mysteries, 1967; Writers' Houses: a literary journey in England, 1968; Alfred Deller: A Singularity of Voice, 1968, rev. edn 1980; Charles Dickens As They Saw Him, 1969; The Game's Afoot (Sherlock Holmes Plays), 1969; Plays from Dickens, 1970; Dickens's England, 1970; The Private Life of Sherlock Holmes, 1970; Four More Sherlock Holmes Plays, 1973; The Charles Dickens Encyclopedia, 1973; The Bernard Shaw Companion, 1973; The Charles Dickens Quiz Book, 1974; The Upstairs Downstairs Omnibus, 1975; The Gaslight Boy, 1976; The Hound of the Baskervilles and Other Sherlock Holmes Plays, 1982; numerous plays and scripts for radio and TV; contribs to women's magazines. *Died 13 Dec. 2003.*

HARDY OF WATH, Baron *cr* 1997 (Life Peer), of Wath upon Dearne in the co. of South Yorkshire; **Peter Hardy;** DL; *b* 17 July 1931; *s* of Lawrence Hardy and of Mrs I. Hardy, Wath upon Dearne; *m* 1954, Margaret Anne Brookes; two *s*. *Educ:* Wath upon Dearne Grammar Sch.; Westminster Coll., London (Teacher's Cert., London Univ.); Sheffield Univ. (DipEd). LCP. RAF, 1949–51. Schoolmaster in S Yorkshire, 1953–70. Member: Wath upon Dearne UDC, 1960–70 (Chm. Council, 1968–69); Governing Body of Wath Grammar Sch., 1960–71 (Chm. of Governors, 1967–68). Pres., Wath upon Dearne Labour Party, 1960–68. Contested (Lab): Scarborough and Whitby, 1964; Sheffield, Hallam, 1966. MP (Lab) Rother Valley, 1970–83, Wentworth, 1983–97. PPS to Sec. of State for the Environment, 1974–76; PPS to Foreign Sec., 1976–79. Chm., Defence Studies Gp, H of L, 2001–; Hon. Sec., All-Party Gp for Energy Studies, 1992–97; Vice-Chm., All-Party Conservation Cttee, 1972–97; Chm., PLP Energy Cttee, 1974–92; Parly attachment to RAF, 1992–93. Member: CSCE Assembly, 1992–97; UK delegn, 1976–97, and Lab. delegn (Leader, 1983–95) to Council of Europe and WEU; Chm., Cttee on Environment, Council of Europe, 1986–89 (Chm., Sub Cttee on Natural Envmt, 1978–86 and 1990–94; Vice-Chm., Socialist Gp, 1983–96); Chm., All Pty Conservation Gp, 2000–02. Member: Council, RSPB, 1984–89; Central Exec. Cttee, NSPCC, 1985–94; Bd, Landscape Foundn, 1996–2000. Vice-Pres., S Yorks Foundn, 1993; Jt Pres., Coalfield Communities Gp, 2000–; Patron, Yorkshire Wildlife Trust. President: Peak Dist and S Yorks Br., CPRE, 1998–2003; Rotherham ATC. DL S Yorks, 1997. *Publications:* A Lifetime of Badgers, 1975; various articles on educational and other subjects. *Recreations:* watching wild life, dogs. *Address:* 2 Gorse Close, Brampton, Bierlow, Rotherham, South

Yorkshire S63 6HW. *T:* (01709) 874590. *Clubs:* Royal
Air Force, Kennel (Hon. Mem.).
Died 16 Dec. 2003.

HARE, Prof. (Frederick) Kenneth, CC 1987 (OC 1978);
OOnt 1989; PhD; FRSC 1968; Professor of Geography
and Physics, 1969–84, and Director, Institute for
Environmental Studies, 1974–79, then University
Professor Emeritus in Geography, University of Toronto;
b Wylye, Wilts, 5 Feb. 1919; *s* of Frederick Eli Hare and
Irene Smith; *m* 1st, 1941, Suzanne Alice Bates (marr. diss.
1952); one *s*; 2nd, 1953, Helen Neilson Morrill; one *s* one
d. Educ: Windsor Grammar Sch.; King's Coll., University
of London (BSc; FKC 1967); Univ. of Montreal (PhD).
War service in Air Min., Meteorological Office, 1941–45.
Lectr in Geography, Univ. of Manchester, 1940–41;
McGill University: Asst and Assoc. Prof. of Geography,
1945–52; Prof. of Geography and Meteorology, 1952–64;
Chm. of Dept, 1950–62; Dean, Faculty of Arts and
Science, 1962–64; Prof. of Geography, King's Coll., Univ.
of London, 1964–66; Master, Birkbeck Coll., Univ. of
London, 1966–68; Pres., Univ. of British Columbia,
1968–69; Provost, Trinity Coll., Toronto, 1979–86;
Chancellor, Trent Univ., 1988–95; Chm., Adv. Bd on
Internat. Progs, Univ. of Toronto, 1990–94. Vis.
Centenary Prof., Univ. of Adelaide, 1974. Chm. Bd,
Arctic Inst. of N America, 1963; Dir, Resources for the
Future, 1968–80; Sci. Advr, Dept of the Environment,
Canada, 1972–74. Member: Nat. Research Council of
Canada, 1962–64; NERC, 1965–68; SSRC, Canada,
1974–76; Adv. Council, Electric Power Res. Inst.,
1978–80. Chairman: Adv. Cttee on Canadian
Demonstration Projects, 1974–75, for 1976 UN Conf. on
Human Settlements; Special Prog. Panel on Ecoscis,
NATO, 1975; Federal Study Gp on Nuclear Waste
Disposal, 1977; Climate Programme Planning Bd, Govt of
Canada, 1979–90; Commn on Lead in the Environment,
RSC, 1984–86; Section W, AAAS, 1985–86; Technical
Adv. Panel on Nuclear Safety, Ontario Hydro, 1990–94
(Mem., 1994–99); Comr, Ontario Nuclear Safety Review,
1987–88. President: Canadian Assoc. of Geographers,
1963–64; RMetS, 1967–68 (Vice-Pres., 1968–70); Sigma
Xi, 1986–87; Hon. Pres., Assoc. of Amer. Geographers,
1964. Fellow, Amer. Meteorological Soc., 1969 (Emeritus
Fellow, 1994); Hon. Fellow: Amer. Geographical Soc.,
1963; Royal Canadian Geographical Soc., 1997. Hon. Life
Mem., Birkbeck Coll., 1969; Hon. Fellow, Trinity Coll.,
Toronto, 1990. Hon. LLD: Queen's (Canada) Univ.,
1964; Univ. of W Ontario, 1968; Trent Univ., 1979;
Memorial Univ., 1985; Toronto, 1987; Hon. DSc:
McGill, 1969; York (Canada), 1978; Windsor, 1988;
Guelph, Ontario, 1996; DSc *ad eund.* Adelaide, 1974;
Hon. DSLitt Thorneloe Coll., Sudbury (Canada), 1984.
Hon. Cert. Graduation, Nat. Defence Coll., Kingston,
Canada, 1986. Meritorious Achievement Citation, Assoc.
Amer. Geographers, 1961; President's Prize, RMetS
(Can.), 1961, 1962; Patterson Medal, Can. Met. Service,
1973; Massey Medal, Royal Can. Geographical Soc.,
1974; Patron's Medal, RGS, 1977; Award for Scholarly
Distinction, Canadian Assoc. of Geographers, 1979; Univ.
of Toronto Alumni Assoc. Faculty Award, 1982; Sir
William Dawson Medal, RSC, 1987; Cullum Medal,
Amer. Geographical Soc., 1987; Internat. Meteorol Orgn
Prize, 1988. *Publications:* The Restless Atmosphere, 1953;
On University Freedom, 1968; (with M. K. Thomas)
Climate Canada, 1974, 2nd edn 1979; numerous articles in
Quarterly Jl Royal Meteorological Soc., Geography, and
other learned jls. *Recreation:* music. *Address:* 301 Lakeshore
Road West, Oakville, ON L6K 1G2, Canada. *Clubs:*
McGill Faculty (Montreal) (Hon. Life Mem.); Toronto
Faculty, York (Toronto).   *Died 23 Sept. 2002.*

HARE, Kenneth; *see* Hare, F. K.

HARE, Prof. Richard Mervyn, FBA 1964; White's
Professor of Moral Philosophy, University of Oxford, and
Fellow of Corpus Christi College, Oxford, 1966–83 (Hon.
Fellow, 1983); *b* 21 March 1919; *s* of late Charles Francis

Aubone Hare and Louise Kathleen (*née* Simonds); *m* 1947,
Catherine, *d* of Sir Harry Verney, 4th Bt, DSO; one *s* three
d. Educ: Rugby (Schol.); Balliol Coll., Oxford (Schol.; 1st
Lit. Hum., MA 1947). Commissioned Royal Artillery,
1940; Lieut, Indian Mountain Artillery, 1941; Prisoner of
War, Singapore and Siam, 1942–45. Fellow and Tutor in
Philosophy, Balliol Coll., Oxford, 1947–66, Hon. Fellow,
1974; Wilde Lectr in Natural Religion, Oxford, 1963–66.
Graduate Res. Prof. of Phil., Univ. of Florida at
Gainesville, 1983–94. Visiting Fellow: Princeton, 1957;
ANU, 1966; Center for Advanced Study in Behavioral
Sciences, Stanford, 1980; Visiting Professor: Univ. of
Michigan, 1968; Univ. of Delaware, 1974. Pres.,
Aristotelian Soc., 1972–73. Member: Nat. Road Safety
Advisory Council, 1966–68; C of E Working Parties on
Medical Questions, 1964–75. Hon. Fellow, Inst. of Life
Scis, Hastings Center, 1974; For. Hon. Mem., American
Acad. of Arts and Sciences, 1975. Hon. PhD Lund, 1991.
Tanner Award, 1979. *Publications:* The Language of
Morals, 1952; Freedom and Reason, 1963; Essays on
Philosophical Method, 1971; Practical Inferences, 1971;
Essays on the Moral Concepts, 1972; Applications of
Moral Philosophy, 1972; Moral Thinking, 1981; Plato,
1982; Hare and Critics, 1988; Essays in Ethical Theory,
1989; Essays on Political Morality, 1989; Essays on
Religion and Education, 1992; Essays on Bioethics, 1993;
Zum Moralischen Denken, 1994; Sorting Out Ethics,
1997; Objective Prescriptions and Other Essays, 1999.
Recreations: music, gardening. *Address:* Bywater, The
Street, Ewelme, near Wallingford, Oxon OX10 6HQ.
Died 29 Jan. 2002.

HARES, Phillip Douglas George, CBE 1985; Chairman
and Chief Executive, 1986–87, and Board Member for
Finance, 1981–86, British Shipbuilders (Deputy Chief
Executive, 1983–86); *b* 31 Dec. 1926; *s* of Edgar Sidney
George and Edith Winifred Frances Hares; *m* 1955, Violet
May Myers; one *s* one *d. Educ:* Richmond and East Sheen
Grammar Sch. Involved with management sciences and
computing in various commercial, industrial, and
consulting organisations, 1952–69, dating from early
application of computers in 1952 with J. Lyons & Co. Ltd;
Asst Man. Dir (Ops), British Mail Order Corp. Ltd (Great
Universal Stores), 1969–77; Man. Dir (Finance), British
Shipbuilders, 1978–81, Corporate Man. Dir, 1982–83;
Chairman: Falmouth Shiprepair Ltd, 1983–85; Vosper
Shiprepairers Ltd, 1983–85; Dir, Iron Trades Insce Gp,
1985–97. Member Council: CBI, 1983–87 (Mem.,
Economic Situation Cttee, 1983–87); Amer. Bureau of
Shipping, 1986–87. FRSA 1987–91. Freeman, City of
London, 1983; Liveryman, Worshipful Co. of
Shipwrights, 1984–94. *Recreations:* reading, music,
genealogy. *Address:* Leverets, 8 Downside Close,
Charmouth, Dorset DT6 6BH. *T:* (01297) 560042; *e-mail:*
philliphares@clara.net.   *Died 22 July 2004.*

HARIRI, Rafiq Bahaa Edine; MP Lebanon, since 1996;
Prime Minister of Lebanon, 1992–98 and 2000–04; *b* 1
Nov. 1944; *m* Nazek Audeh; five *s* two *d. Educ:* Arab
Univ. of Beirut (Commerce). Teacher; Civil Construction
Establishment, 1970–78; formed Saudi Oger, 1978; Oger
Co., 1979. Founder, Hariri Foundn, 1979–. Doctor *hc*:
Boston, 1986; Nice, 1988; Arabic Univ. of Beirut, 1993;
Georgetown Univ., Washington, 1996; Ottawa, 1997;
Montreal, 1997; Hon. DHL Lebanese American Univ.,
Beirut, 2002; Orient Doctorate, Moscow State Inst. for
Internat. Relns, 2003. Cedars Nat. Medal, 1983; St Peter
and St Paul Medal, 1983; 50th Anniv. Award, Save the
Children, 1983; Golden Key of Beirut, 1983; Medal of
Liberator of Argentina, Gen. José St Martin, 1995; Prix
Louis Michel, France, 1995; Al Nahda Medal, 1st
category, Jordan, 2001. Chevalier des Arts et des Lettres
(France), 1983; Grand Croix de la Légion d'Honneur
(France), 1996 (Chevalier, 1981; Officier, 1986); Grand
Gwang Hwa Medal, Order of Diplomatic Service (Korea),
1997; Le Grand Collier du Trône (Morocco), 1997;
Cavaliere di Gran Croce (Italy), 1997; Grand Cross, Star of
Romania, 2002. *Publication:* Statesmanship in

Government, 1999. *Recreation:* reading. *T:* (961) 1785011, *Fax:* (961) 1785014; *e-mail:* ipo@cyberia.net.lb.
Died 14 Feb. 2005.

HARKINS, His Honour Gerard Francis Robert; a Circuit Judge, 1986–2001; *b* 13 July 1936; *o s* of Francis Murphy Harkins and Katherine Harkins (*née* Hunt). *Educ:* Mount St Mary's College, Spinkhill, near Sheffield; King's College in University of Durham (later Univ. of Newcastle upon Tyne). LDS Dunelm 1961. Dental surgeon in general practice, Yorks, 1961–70; called to the Bar, Middle Temple, 1969; practised NE Circuit, 1970–86. Mem., Northumbria Probation Cttee, 1993–97. Pres., Mount Assoc., 1991–92. Governor, Mount St Mary's, 1990–93. *Address:* 34 Wyncote Court, Jesmond Park East, Newcastle upon Tyne NE7 7BG. *Club:* Lansdowne. *Died 21 March 2004.*

HARLE, James Coffin, DPhil, DLitt; Keeper, Department of Eastern Art, Ashmolean Museum, Oxford, 1967–87; Student of Christ Church, Oxford, 1970–87, then Emeritus; *b* 5 April 1920; *s* of James Wyly Harle and Elfrieda Frances (*née* Baumann); *m* 1st, 1949, Jacqueline Thérèse Ruch (marr. diss. 1966, she *d* 1968); 2nd, 1967, Mrs Carola Sybil Mary Fleming (*d* 1971); 3rd, 1973, Lady (Betty) Hulbert. *Educ:* St George's Sch., Newport, RI; Princeton Univ. (BA 1942, Phi Beta Kappa); Oxford Univ. (BA 1st cl. Sanskrit and Pali, 1956; DPhil 1959; DLitt 1989). Served War, 1942–46, USNR (Aviation Br.), retd as Lieut; DFC (US). Asst to Dean of the College, Princeton, 1947; Part-time instructor in English, Princeton, 1948–49; Fulbright Lectr, Philippines, 1953–54; Ashmolean Museum: Asst Keeper, 1960; Sen. Asst Keeper, 1962. Pres., Soc. for S Asian Studies (British Acad.), 1990–95. *Publications:* Tower Gateways in South India, 1963; Gupta Sculpture, 1974; The Art and Architecture of the Indian Subcontinent, 1986; articles in periodicals on Indian Art. *Address:* Hawkswell, 34 Portland Road, Oxford OX2 7EY. *T:* (01865) 515236. *Club:* Princeton (New York). *Died 27 June 2004.*

HARRIS OF GREENWICH, Baron *cr* 1974 (Life Peer), of Greenwich in Greater London; **John Henry Harris;** PC 1998; director of companies; *b* Harrow, Middlesex, 5 April 1930; *s* of late Alfred George and May Harris; *m* 1st, 1952, Patricia Margaret Alstrom (marr. diss. 1982); one *s* one *d*; 2nd, 1983, Angela Smith. *Educ:* Pinner County Grammar Sch., Middlesex. Journalist on newspapers in Bournemouth, Leicester, Glasgow and London. National Service with Directorate of Army Legal Services, WO. Personal assistant to Rt Hon. Hugh Gaitskell when Leader of the Opposition, 1959–62; Director of Publicity, Labour Party, 1962–64; Special Assistant: to Foreign Secretary, 1964–65; to Rt Hon. Roy Jenkins as Home Secretary, 1965–Nov. 1967, and as Chancellor, Nov. 1967–1970. Staff of Economist newspaper, 1970–74. Minister of State, Home Office, 1974–79. Spokesman on home affairs, Lib Dem, House of Lords, 1988–94; Lib Dem Chief Whip, H of L, 1994–. Mem., H of L Select Cttee on Murder and Life Imprisonment, 1988–89, on Public Service, 1996. Mem. Exec. Cttee, Britain in Europe, referendum campaign, 1975 (Jt Chm., Publicity Cttee). Chm., Parole Bd for England and Wales, 1979–82; Pres., Nat. Assoc. of Senior Probation Officers, 1983–92; Trustee, Police Foundn (Chm., Exec. Cttee), 1980. Eisenhower Exchange Fellow from UK, 1972. Mem., Harlow Council, Essex, 1957–63 (Chm., 1960–61); Leader of Labour Gp, 1961–63). *Address:* House of Lords, SW1A 0PW. *Clubs:* Reform, MCC. *Died 11 April 2001.*

HARRIS, (David) Kenneth, CBE 1992; journalist, author and broadcaster; Chairman, George Outram & Co. Ltd, later Caledonian Newspaper Publishing, 1981–92; Director, The Observer Ltd, 1978–93; *b* 11 Nov. 1919; *s* of David and Kathleen Harris; *m* 1st, 1949, Doris Young-Smith (*d* 1970); 2nd, 1987, Jocelyn Rymer; two *d*. *Educ:* Trowbridge High Sch.; Wadham Coll., Oxford. Served War, RA, 1940–45. Sheffield Telegraph, 1948–50; The Observer: Washington Corresp., 1950–53; Editl Staff,

1953–76; Associate Editor, 1976–84. Freelance TV and radio broadcaster, BBC and ITV, 1957–85. Debating tour for Oxford Union, USA, 1947; Founder, Observer Mace Debating Tournaments, 1953; Chm., ESU Overseas Debating Selection Cttee, 1960–95. *Publications:* Travelling Tongues, 1949; About Britain, 1967; Conversations, 1967; Talking To …, 1971; Attlee (authorised biog.), 1982; David Owen Personally Speaking, 1987; Thatcher, 1988; The Queen, 1994. *Recreations:* walking, horse racing, fishing, reading. *Address:* 4 Mill Lane, Donington, Lincs PE11 4TL. *T:* (01775) 822207. *Died 24 June 2005.*

HARRIS, Prof. James William, DCL, PhD; FBA 2001; Professor of Law, Oxford University, since 1996; Fellow, Keble College, Oxford, since 1973; *b* 17 March 1940; *s* of James Harris and Jessica (*née* Wentworth); *m* 1968, Prof. Jose Ferial Chambers , PhD, FBA; one *s*. *Educ:* Worcester Coll.; Wadham Coll., Oxford (MA; PhD 1973; DCL 2001). Admitted solicitor, 1965; Lectr, LSE, 1966–73. Mellon Res. Fellow, Princeton Univ., 1985; Allen, Allen & Hemsley Vis. Prof., Univ. of Sydney, 1987; Dist. Vis. Prof., Univ. of Hong Kong, 1994; Leverhulme Major Res. Fellow, 2000–03; Visiting Professor: Univ. of Jilin, China, 2002; ANU, Canberra, 2002. British Acad. Maccabean Lectr in Jurisprudence, 2001. *Publications:* Variation of Trusts, 1975; Law and Legal Science, 1979; Legal Philosophies, 1980, 2nd edn 1997; (with Sir Rupert Cross) Precedent in English Law, 4th edn 1991; Property and Justice, 1996; Property Problems: from genes to pension funds, 1997; contrib. articles to Oxford Jl Legal Studies, Cambridge Law Jl, Law Qly Rev., Ratio Juris. *Recreations:* walking, Shakespeare, Wagner. *Address:* Keble College, Oxford OX1 3PG. *T:* (01865) 272748.
Died 22 March 2004.

HARRIS, Kenneth; *see* Harris, D. K.

HARRIS, Brig. Lewis John, CBE 1961 (OBE 1949; MBE 1943); consultant, surveys and mapping; *b* 19 Dec. 1910; *e s* of David Rees Harris and Cecilia Harris; *m* 1975, (Thelma) Opal, *d* of James Marshall Carr and Zettie Lou Witt, and *widow* of Lt-Col A. L. Nowicki, US Corps of Engineers. *Educ:* Christ Coll., Brecon; RMA, Woolwich; Pembroke Coll., Cambridge (Exhibitioner; Mech. Sci. Tripos; MA). Commissioned RE, 1930; Triangulation of Jamaica, 1937–39; served War of 1939–45: British Expeditionary Force, 1939–40 (despatches); First Army in North Africa, 1942–43, AFHQ and American Seventh Army, Italy, 1944; Land Forces SE Asia, India, Burma and Malaya, 1944–46; Chief Instructor, Sch. of Mil. Survey, 1946–49; War Office, Geog. Section Gen. Staff, 1949–52; Ordnance Survey, 1952–53; Dir, Survey GHQ, Middle East, and GHQ, E Africa, 1953–55; Land Survey Adviser, Allied Forces, Mediterranean, 1954–55; Ordnance Survey of Great Britain, 1955–61; Brig. 1956; Dir, Map Production and Publication, 1956–59; Dir, Field Surveys, 1959–61; Dir of Mil. Survey, MoD and Chief of Geographical Section Gen. Staff, 1961–65. Consultant, Federal Surveys and Mapping, Canada, 1967–85. Hon. Col 135 Survey Engineer Regt, TA, 1965–67. Chm., Nat. Cttee for Cartography, Royal Society, 1961–67. Hon. Foreign Sec., Royal Geographical Soc., 1964–67; Vice-Pres., Internat. Cartographic Assoc., 1958–61. Hon. Vice-Pres., Army Rugby Union. FRAS, FRGS, FRICS. *Publications:* various papers on cartography in learned jls. *Recreations:* music, outdoor sports, travelling. *Address:* 12410 Hound Ears Point, Fox Den, PO Box 22129, Knoxville, TN 37933, USA. *Clubs:* Naval and Military, MCC; Hawks (Cambridge); Royal Ottawa Golf; I Zingari, Band of Brothers, Free Foresters.
Died 24 Jan. 2001.

HARRIS, Martin Richard; Director, National Westminster Bank PLC, 1977–93; *b* 30 Aug. 1922; *m* 1952, Diana Moira (*née* Gandar Dower), JP, Mayor of Merton, 1985–86; four *s*. *Educ:* Wellington Coll. FCA. Captain, RE, ME and Italy, 1941–46. Joined Price Waterhouse & Co., 1946, Partner, 1956–74; Dir Gen.,

Panel on Take-Overs and Mergers, 1974–77; Director: Reckitt and Colman, 1977–82 (Dep. Chm., 1979–82); County Bank, then NatWest Investment Bank, 1977–92; Inmos International, 1980–84; Equity & Law Life Assce Soc., 1981–87 (Dep. Chm., 1983–87); Westland plc, 1981–85; De La Rue Co. plc, 1981–93; TR Industrial & General Trust plc, 1983–86; Chm. and Dir, Nineteen Twenty-Eight Investment Trust plc, 1984–86; Dir, NatWest Smaller Cos Investment Trust, 1991–98. Institute of Chartered Accountants in England and Wales: Mem. Council, 1971–79; Chm., Parly and Law Cttee, 1973–74; Chm., Prof. Standards Cttee, 1977–79; Mem., Accountants Internat. Study Gp, 1972–74. Mem., DTI's Company Law Consultative Gp, 1972–74. Member: Court, Drapers' Co., 1978– (Master, 1987); Court, Co. of Chartered Accountants, 1977–90 (Master, 1983). Mem. Council, RCM, 1985–95 (Chm. Development Fund, 1984–92); Governor, QMC, London Univ., 1979–89; Chm. Council, Queen Mary and Westfield Coll., London Univ., 1989–95 (Hon. Fellow, 1997). FRCM 1988. US Silver Star 1945. *Recreations:* music and opera, philately, antique furniture and china, keeping busy. *Address:* 101 Church Road, Wimbledon, SW19 5AL. *T:* (020) 8946 0951. *Clubs:* Carlton, MCC. *Died 20 Sept. 2001.*

HARRIS, Prof. Peter Charles, MD, PhD; FRCP; Simon Marks Professor of Cardiology, University of London, 1966–88, then Emeritus; Consultant Physician, National Heart and Chest Hospitals; *b* 26 May 1923; *s* of late David Jonathan Valentine and Nellie Dean Harris; *m* 1st, 1952, Felicity Margaret Hartridge (marr. diss. 1982); two *d*; 2nd, 1989, Frances Monkarsh. *Educ:* St Olave's Grammar Sch.; Univ. of London (MB, BS 1946; MD (Univ. medal) 1951; PhD 1955). FRCP 1965 (MRCP 1950). House appts at King's Coll. Hospital, and elsewhere, 1946–55; Nuffield Fellow, Columbia Univ., New York, 1955–57; Lectr, Sen. Lectr then Reader in Medicine, Univ. of Birmingham, 1957–66; Dir, Inst. of Cardiology, Univ. of London, 1966–73. Pres., Internat. Soc. for Heart Research, 1981–83. Mem., Instituto Veneto, 1994. Hon. FACC, 1976. Editor, Cardioscience, 1990–96. *Publications:* (with D. Heath) The Human Pulmonary Circulation, 1962, 3rd edn 1986; articles to jls, etc, on cardio-pulmonary physiology and biochemistry. *Recreation:* chamber music. *Address:* 42 Great Percy Street, WC1X 9QR. *T:* (020) 7278 2911; 2089 Gulf of Mexico Drive #209, Longboat Key, FL 34228, USA. *T:* (941) 3831067. *Died 11 Dec. 2002.*

HARRIS, Richard Travis; Director, Burton Group plc, 1984–92; *b* 15 April 1919; 2nd *s* of Douglas Harris and Emmeline Harris (*née* Travis); *m* 1st, 1941, June Constance Rundle (marr. diss. 1953); two *d*; 2nd, 1953, Margaret Sophia Nye (*née* Aron); one *s* one *d*. *Educ:* Charterhouse; RMA Woolwich. Served War of 1939–45, France, Western Desert, Tunisia, Italy (despatches twice); BAOR, 1945–46; Sudan Defence Force Signal Regt, 1947–50 (CO, 1948–50); retired from Royal Signals, 1950, Lt-Col. Man. Dir, Rediffusion (Nigeria) Ltd and Gen. Manager, Rediffusion in Africa, 1951–54; Dep. Gen. Manager, Associated-Rediffusion Ltd, 1954–57; Man. Dir, Coates & Co. (Plymouth) Ltd, 1957–64 (Dir, 1957–68); Man. Dir, 1964–78, Chm., 1970–78, Dollond & Aitchison Ltd; Chm., Dollond & Aitchison Group Ltd (formerly TWW Enterprises Ltd), 1970–78 (Dir, 1968–85); Director: Gallaher Ltd, 1970–87 (Dep. Chm., 1978–84); Dollond International Ltd, 1973–83; Filotecnica Salmoiraghi SpA, 1974–83; Istituto Ottico Vigano SpA, 1974–83; Saunders Valve Co. Ltd, 1978–84; Mono Pumps Ltd, 1978–84; Formatura Iniezione Polimeri SpA, 1978–84; Tobacco Kiosks Ltd, 1978–84; Gallaher Pensions Ltd, 1975–84. Chairman: Fedn of Optical Corporate Bodies, 1970–82; Fedn of Ophthalmic & Dispensing Opticians, 1985–87 (Vice-Pres., 1987–97); Vice-Pres., Inst. of Dirs, 1985–89 (Chm. Council, 1982–85); Mem. Exec. Cttee, Wider Share Ownership Council, 1987–91; Mem. Council, Univ. of Birmingham, 1978–93, Life Mem., Court, 1981. Governor, Royal Shakespeare Theatre, 1980–94. Master,

Coachmakers' and Coach Harness Makers Co., 1963–64. *Publication:* Memoirs and Some Thoughts of an Unqualified Clunk, 2001. *Recreation:* fishing. *Address:* Woodpeckers, The Mount, Newcastle Road, Congleton SW12 4FD. *Died 24 Nov. 2003.*

HARRIS, Sir William (Gordon), KBE 1969; CB 1963; FREng, FICE; Director-General, Highways, Ministry of Transport, later Department of the Environment, 1965–73; *b* 10 June 1912; *s* of late Capt. James Whyte Harris, Royal Naval Reserve, and Margaret Roberta Buchanan Forsyth; *m* 1st, 1938, Margaret Emily Harvie (*d* 1991); three *s* one *d*; 2nd, 1992, Mrs Rachel Bishop (*née* Goucher). *Educ:* Liverpool Coll.; Sidney Sussex Coll., Cambridge (Mechanical Sciences Tripos, BA 1932; MA 1937). London Midland & Scottish Railway, 1932–35; Sudan Irrigation Dept, 1935–37; joined Civil Engineer in Chief's Dept, Admiralty, 1937; Asst Civil Engineer in Chief, 1950; Dep. Civil Engineer in Chief, 1955; Civil Engineer in Chief, 1959; Dir-Gen., Navy Works, 1960–63; Dir-Gen. of Works, MPBW, 1963–65. Partner, Peter Fraenkel & Partners, 1973–78; Chm., B & CE Holiday Management Co. & Benefit Trust Co., 1978–87. Dir, British Sch. of Osteopathy, 1982–92 (Chm., 1990–92). Chief British Delegate to: Perm. Internat. Assoc. of Navigation Congresses, 1969–85 (Vice-Pres., 1976–79); Perm. Internat. Assoc. of Road Congresses, 1970–73; Mem., Dover Harbour Bd, 1959–82 (Dep. Chm., 1975–79; Chm., 1980–82); Chm., Construction Industry Manpower Bd, 1976–79. Commonwealth Fund (of New York) Fellowship, 1950–51. A Vice-Pres., ICE, 1971–74, Pres. 1974–75. FREng (FEng 1977). Mem., Smeatonian Soc. of Civil Engineers, 1966– (Pres., 1984). Hon. DSc City, 1977. Hon. Seabee, US Navy, 1961. Decoration for Distinguished Civilian Service to US Army, 1985. *Recreations:* gardening, 16 grandchildren, five great-grandchildren. *Address:* Ninesprings, 10 Church Lane, East Carlton, Market Harborough, Leics LE16 8YA. *T:* (01536) 771307. *Died 20 Feb. 2005.*

HARRISON, Sir Donald (Frederick Norris), Kt 1990; MD, MS, PhD; FRCS; Professor of Laryngology and Otology University of London, 1963–90, and Dean, 1989–90, Institute of Laryngology and Otology, Gray's Inn Road, WC1, Emeritus Professor, 1990; Emeritus Surgeon, Moorfields Eye Hospital, 1991; Surgeon, Royal National Throat, Nose and Ear Hospital, 1962–90; *b* 9 March 1925; *s* of Frederick William Rees Harrison, OBE, JP, and Florence, *d* of Robert Norris, Portsmouth, Hants; *m* 1949, Audrey (*d* 2000), *o d* of Percival Clubb, Penarth, Glam; two *d*. *Educ:* Newport High Sch., Mon; Guy's Hosp. (MS 1959, MD 1960); PhD (London) 1983. FRCS 1955; FRCOphth 1993. House Surg., Guy's Hosp. and Royal Gwent Hospital, Newport; Surg. Registrar, Shrewsbury Eye and Ear Hosp.; Sen. Registrar, Throat and Ear Dept, Guy's Hosp.; Univ. Reader in Laryngology, Inst. of Laryngol. and Otol. Civilian Consultant on ENT to RN. Former Chairman: Special Adv. Cttee on Human Communication; Bd Postgrad. Med. Studies, London Univ. Member: Cttee of Management, Institute of Cancer Research; Internat. Cttee for Cancer of Larynx; Chm., NE Thames Region Postgrad. Cttee. Hunterian Prof., RCS, 1962; Eramus Wilson Demonstrator, RCS, 1971; Wellcome Prof., S Africa, 1988. Lectures: Chevalier Jackson, 1964; Yearsley, 1972; Wilde, 1972; Litchfield, 1973; Semon, 1974; Colles, RCSI, 1977; Jobson Horne, BMA, 1979; Conacher, Toronto, 1978; Harris, USA, 1984; Putney, USA, 1985; Baker, USA, 1986; Bryce, Toronto, 1987; McBride, Edinburgh, 1987; Douglas J. Guthrie, Edinburgh, 1988; Bob Owen (first), Cardiff, 1988; Ogura, USA, 1990; Som, USA, 1991; Stirk Adams, Birmingham, 1992; Watson-Williams, Bristol, 1994. Mem. Court of Examiners, RCS; Examr, NUI; External Examr, Univs of Melbourne, Southampton, Sydney, Manchester, Liverpool, Glasgow, Hong Kong, Belfast, Oxford and Cambridge. Scientific Fellow, Royal Zool Soc. of London; FRSM (Pres., 1994–96; Pres., Sect. of Laryngology, 1984 (former Vice-Pres.); Mem. Council,

Sect. of Oncology; Hon. Sec., 1987–93); Member Council: Brit. Assoc. of Otolaryngologists; Brit. Assoc. of Head and Neck Oncologists (Pres.); Asst Sec., Collegium Oto-Rhino-Laryngologium; Sen. Mem., Anatomical Soc. of Great Britain. Chm., Centennial Conf., Laryngeal Cancer, 1974; Master, British Acad. Conf. on ENT, 1991; Pres., World Congress Laryngeal Cancer, 1994. Hon. Fellow: Acad. ENT, America, 1976; Triol. Soc., USA, 1977; Amer. Laryngol Assoc., 1979; Hon. FRACS 1977; Hon. FRCSE 1981; Hon. FCSSA 1988; Hon. FACS 1990; Hon. FRSocMed 1991; Hon. FRCSI 1991; Hon. FACR 1995. Hon. Member: NZ ENT Soc.; Jamaican ENT Soc.; Polish ENT Soc.; Egyptian ENT Soc.; Otolaryngological Soc., Australia; Yugoslavian ENT Soc.; Spanish ENT Soc.; Philippine ENT Soc.; Hong Kong ENT Soc.; Amer. Head and Neck Soc.; Soc. Française d'Otorhinolaryngologie; Otolaryngological Soc., Denmark; Amer. Acad. of Facial Plastic Reconstr. Surgery; Pacific Coast Oto-Ophthalmological Soc.; Amer. Laryngological Soc.; For. Mem., Internat. Broncho-oesophagological Soc. Yeoman, Soc. of Apothecaries. W. J. Harrison Prize, RSM, 1978; Medal of Paris, 1988; Gold medal, Internat. Fedn of Oto Rhino Laryngological Socs, 1985; Gold Medal, NY Eye & Ear Alumni Assoc., 1988; Gold Medal, Joshi Meml Lecture, Indian ENT Soc., 1990; Holmgren Medal, Sweden, 1993. Editorial Board: Acta Otolaryngologica; Practica Oto-Rhino-Laryngologica; Annals of Oto-Rhino-Laryngology; Excerpta Medica (Sect. II); Otolaryngological Digest. *Publications:* (ed jtly) Scientific Basis of Otolaryngology, 1976; Dilemmas in ENT, 1990; Neoplasms of the Upper Jaw, 1993; Comparative Anatomy of Mammalian Larynx, 1995; Sir Felix Semon: Victorian laryngologist (1849–1921), 2000; articles on familial hæmorrhagic telangiectases, meatal oseomata, cancer chemotherapy, head and neck surgery in learned jls; chapters in text books on ent. and gen. surgery. *Recreations:* heraldry, radio control models. *Address:* Springfield, 6 Fisher's Farm, Horley, Surrey RH6 9DQ. *T:* (01293) 784307.   *Died 12 April 2003.*

HARRISON, Sir Francis Alexander Lyle, (Sir Frank), Kt 1974; MBE 1943; DL; QC (NI); President, Lands Tribunal for Northern Ireland, 1964–83; District Electoral Areas Commissioner, 1984; *b* 19 March 1910; *s* of Rev. Alexander Lyle Harrison and Mary Luise (*née* Henderson), Rostrevor, Co. Down; *m* 1940, Norah Patricia (*née* Rea) (*d* 1999); two *d. Educ:* Campbell Coll., Belfast; Trinity Coll., Dublin (BA (Moderator in Legal Sci.), LLB (Hons)). Called to Bar of NI, 1937, Bencher, 1961. Served War: commissioned Gen. List, Oct. 1939; ADC to GOC, NI, 1939–40; Major, Dep. Asst Adjt-Gen., HQ, NI, 1941–45 (MBE). Apptd to determine Industrial Assurance disputes in NI, 1946–62; Counsel to Attorney-Gen., NI, 1946–48; KC 1948; Legal Adviser to Min. of Home Affairs, 1949–64; Sen. Crown Prosecutor, Co. Fermanagh, 1948–54, subseq. for Counties Tyrone, Londonderry and Antrim, 1954–64; Chm., Mental Health Review Tribunal, 1948–64; Counsel to the Speakers of House of Commons and Senate of NI, 1953–64. Mem. Statute Law Cttee, NI, 1953–64; Chm., Advisory Cttee under Civil Authorities Special Powers Acts (NI), 1957–62; Chm., Shaftesbury Sq. HMC, 1964–73; Founder Mem., NI Assoc. of Mental Health, 1959. Boundary Comr under Local Govt (Boundaries) Act (NI), 1971 and 1982–84. DL Co. Down, 1973. *Publications:* Report of Working Party on Drug Dependence, 1968; Recommendations as to Local Government Boundaries and Wards in Northern Ireland, 1972, 1984; Recommendations as to District Electoral Areas in Northern Ireland, 1985. *Recreations:* hybridisation of narcissi, country pursuits, social service. *Address:* Ballydorn Hill, Killinchy, Newtownards, Co. Down, Northern Ireland BT23 6QB. *T:* (028) 9754 1250.   *Died 13 Aug. 2002.*

HARRISON, Francis Anthony Kitchener; Assistant Director, Civil Service Selection Board, 1967–79; *b* 28 Aug. 1914; *s* of late Fred Harrison, Headmaster of Newcastle High Sch., Staffs, and Mrs M. M. Harrison (*née*

Mitchell); *m* 1955, Sheila Noëlle, *d* of late Lt-Col N. D. Stevenson and of Lady Nye; three *s* one *d. Educ:* Winchester; New Coll., Oxford (MA 1942). Asst Principal, India Office, Nov. 1937; 1st Sec., UK High Commn, New Delhi, 1949–51; Commonwealth Relations Office, 1951–56; Asst Sec., 1954; Dep. High Comr for the UK at Peshawar, 1956–59; Asst Sec., CRO, 1959–61; British Dep. High Comr, New Zealand, 1961–64; Asst Sec., Cabinet Office, 1965–67. *Recreations:* reading, writing. *Address:* Lea Farm, Bramley, near Guildford, Surrey GU5 0LR. *T:* (01483) 893138.   *Died 10 March 2003.*

HARRISON, Sir Frank; *see* Harrison, Sir Francis A. L.

HARRISON, George, MBE 1965; musician, composer, film producer; *b* 25 Feb. 1943; *s* of Harold and Louise Harrison; *m* 1966, Patricia Ann Boyd (marr. diss. 1977); *m* 1978, Olivia Arias; one *s*. Member: The Rebels, 1956–58; The Quarrymen, 1958–60; The Beatles, 1960–70; Traveling Wilburys, 1987–90; solo performer, 1970–; *songs* composed include: (Beatles songs): Blue Jay Way; I Want To Tell You; Taxman; Here Comes the Sun; Something; Within You Without You; (solo): My Sweet Lord; Give Me Love (Give Me Peace On Earth); Bangladesh; Dark Horse; Living in the Material World; All Those Years Ago; Mind Set On You; *films* (performer, with The Beatles): A Hard Day's Night, 1964; Help!, 1965; Magical Mystery Tour (TV film), 1967; Yellow Submarine, 1968; Let It Be, 1970. Jt Founder, Handmade Films; *films* produced include: Life of Brian, 1979; Time Bandits, 1981; The Missionary, 1982; Privates on Parade, 1984; A Private Function, 1985; Mona Lisa, 1986; Withnail and I, 1987. *Publications:* (ed) Raga Mala: the autobiography of Ravi Shankar, 1999; (with Sir Paul McCartney and Ringo Starr) The Beatles Anthology, 2000. *Address:* Harrisongs Ltd, PO Box 16115, SW3 1ZL.   *Died 29 Nov. 2001.*

HARRISON, Hon. Sir (John) Richard, Kt 1980; ED; grape grower; *b* 23 May 1921; *s* of William Harrison and Jean (*née* Bell); *m* 1948, Margaret Kelly; three *s* one *d. Educ:* Wanganui Collegiate Sch.; Canterbury University Coll. (BA). CO, Hawke's Bay Regt, 1956–59. MP (Nat) for Hawke's Bay, 1963–84; Govt Whip, 1970–71; Opposition Whip, 1974–75; Chm. of Cttees, 1972, 1976–77; Speaker, House of Representatives, 1978–84. Pres., Commonwealth Parly Assoc., 1978–79. Pres., Nat. Soc. on Alcoholism and Drug Dependence, 1986–89; Patron, Prison Fellowship, NZ, 1988–. *Recreations:* gardening, classical music. *Address:* Springfield, RD2, Takapau, New Zealand.   *Died 5 Sept. 2003.*

HARRISON, Mrs Molly, MBE 1967; Curator, Geffrye Museum, 1941–69; *b* Stevenage, 23 Sept. 1909; *d* of late late Ernest Charles and Ethel Hodgett; *m* 1940, Gordon Frederick Harrison; three *d. Educ:* Friends Sch., Saffron Walden; Convent in Belgium; Sorbonne. Teaching in various schs, 1934–39; Asst to Curator, Geffrye Museum, 1939–41. FMA 1952; Member: Council Museums Assoc., 1953–56; Council of Industrial Design, 1958–61; Cttee of Management, Society of Authors, 1967. Lectr on varied educational topics. FRSA 1968. Editor, Local Search Series, 1969–77. *Publications:* Museum Adventure, 1950; Picture Source Books for Social History, 1951, 1953, 1955, 1957, 1958, 1960 and 1966; Furniture, 1953; Learning out of School, 1954; Food, 1954; Homes, 1960; Children in History, 1958, 1959, 1960, 1961; Your Book of Furniture, 1960; Shops and Shopping, 1963; How They Lived, 1963; Changing Museums, 1967; Hairstyles and Hairdressing, 1968; The English Home, 1969; People and Furniture, 1971; The Kitchen in History, 1972; Homes, 1973; Museums and Galleries, 1973; On Location: museums, 1974; People and Shopping, 1975; Home Inventions, 1975; Homes in Britain, 1975; Markets and Shops, 1979; Growing Up in Victorian Times, 1980; Homes in History, 1983; The Story of Travelling (4 vols), 1983, 1984; numerous articles and reviews. *Recreations:* reading, gardening. *Address:* New Place, High Street,

Whitchurch-on-Thames, Oxon RG8 7ET. *T:* (0118) 984 3736. *Died 7 Aug. 2002.*

HARRISON, Hon. Sir Richard; *see* Harrison, Hon. Sir J. R.

HARRISON, William Robert; Partner, Compass Partners Advisers, since 2002; *b* 5 Oct. 1948; *s* of William Harrison and Catherine Harrison; *m* 1970, Jacqueline Ann Brown; one *s* one *d. Educ:* London Sch. of Econs (BSc Econ, MSc Econ). Associate Dir, Mfrs Hanover Ltd, London, 1971–75; Sen. Finance Dir, BNOC, 1975–78; Dep. Man. Dir, Lehman Bros Kuhn Loeb, NY and London, 1978–81; Gp Treas., and Hd, Corporate Finance, Tricentrol Oil Corp., 1981–83; Dir, Corporate Finance, J. Henry Schroder Wagg & Co. Ltd, 1983–86; Lehman Brothers, London: Man. Dir, 1986–93; Vice-Chm. and Head, European Investment Banking, Lehman Bros Internat. Ltd, 1986–93; Robert Fleming, London: Chief Exec., Global Investment Banking, 1993–96; Mem., Gp Exec. and Gp Hldg Bd, 1993–96; Chief Exec., BZW, 1996–97; Dir, Barclays Bank, 1996–97; Vice-Chm., Global Corporates and Instns, Deutsche Morgan Grenfell, then Deutsche Bank, 1998–99; Jt Founder and Sen. Partner, Harrison Lovegrove, 1999–2001. Non-exec. Dir, Pilkington plc, 1998–; Mem., Adv. Council, Pinsents & Co., 2000–; Chm., Adv. Bd (UK), ING, 2005–. High Sheriff, Gtr London, 1997–98. Hon. Trustee, Foundn & Friends, Royal Botanic Gdns, Kew, 1996–. *Recreations:* sport, travel, gardening. *Died 15 Nov. 2005.*

HARRISON-HALL, His Honour Michael Kilgour; DL; a Circuit Judge, 1972–97; *b* 20 Dec. 1925; *s* of late Arthur Harrison-Hall, Oxford; *m* 1951, Jessie Margaret (*d* 2000), *d* of late Rev. Arthur William Brown, Collingbourne Ducis, Wilts; two *s* two *d. Educ:* Rugby; Trinity College, Oxford. Called to the Bar, Inner Temple, 1949. Dep. Chm., Warwickshire QS, 1968–71; a Recorder of the Crown Court, 1972. DL Warwicks, 1985. *Address:* Ivy House, Church Street, Barford, Warwick CV35 8EN. *T:* (01926) 624272. *Clubs:* Oxford and Cambridge; Leander. *Died 24 April 2005.*

HART, F(rancis) Dudley, MD; FRCP; Physician, and Physician-in-charge Rheumatism Unit, Westminster Hospital, SW1, 1946–74; Emeritus Physician: Hospital of St John and St Elizabeth, London; Westminster Hospital; lately Consulting Rheumatologist, The Star and Garter Home for Disabled Sailors, Soldiers and Airmen, Richmond; lately Hon. Consulting Physician (Civilian) to the Army; *b* 4 Oct. 1909; *s* of Canon C. Dudley Hart and Kate Evelyn Bowden; *m* 1944, Mary Josephine (*d* 2002), *d* of late Luke Tully, Carrigaline, Co. Cork; one *s* two *d. Educ:* Grosvenor Sch., Nottingham; Edinburgh Univ. MB, ChB Edinburgh 1933, MD 1939; MRCP 1937, FRCP 1949. House physician and clinical asst, Brompton Hosp., 1937; Med. Registrar, Royal Northern Hosp., 1935–37; Med. Registrar, Westminster Hosp., 1939–42; Med. Specialist and Officer i/c Med. Div., RAMC, 1942–46. Mem., Cttee on Review of Medicines, 1975–82. Ex-Pres. Heberden Soc.; Member: BMA; Med. Soc. of London. Arris and Gale Lectr, RCS, 1955; Ellman Lectr, RCP, 1969; Stanley Davidson Lectr, Univ. of Aberdeen, 1970; Bradshaw Lectr, RCP, 1975; Alexander Brown Meml Lectr, Univ. of Ibadan, Nigeria, 1979; Bernadine Becker Lectr, NY, 1984. Exec. Mem. and Vice-Pres., Arthritis Res. Campaign (formerly Arthritis and Rheumatism Council); Hon. FRSocMed. Hon. Member: British Soc. for Rheumatology; Ligue Française contre le Rheumatisme; La Societa di Rheumatologia Italia; American Rheumatism Association; Australian Rheumatism Association. *Publications:* (co-author) Drugs: actions, uses and dosage, 1963; (ed) French's Differential Diagnosis, 10th edn 1973, 12th edn 1985; (ed) The Treatment of Chronic Pain, 1974; Joint Disease: all the arthropathies, 4th edn 1987; (ed) Drug Treatment of the Rheumatic Diseases, 1978, 3rd edn 1987; (ed) Clinical Rheumatology Illustrated, 1987; (ed) Diagnostic Features of Disease, 1987; Colour Atlas of Rheumatology, 1987;

(jtly) Clinical Problems in Rheumatology, 1993; contributions to: Pye's Surgical Handicraft, 1939–72; Cortisone and ACTH, 1953; Miller's Modern Medical Treatment, 1962; Copeman's Textbook of the Rheumatic Diseases (ed J. T. Scott), 3rd edn 1964, 5th edn 1978; Encyclopedia of General Practice, 1964; Chambers's Encyclopædia, 1964; Drug Treatment, 1976; Butterworth's Medical Dictionary (all rheumatological sections), 1978; Overcoming Arthritis, 1981; articles and broadcasts on general medicine and rheumatism. *Recreations:* multi-track recording, travelling. *Address:* 19 Ranulf Road, Hampstead, NW2 2BT. *T:* (020) 7794 2525. *Died 10 April 2004.*

HART, Thomas Mure, CMG 1957; Financial Secretary, Singapore, 1954–59, retired; *b* 1 March 1909; *s* of late Maxwell M. Hart and Elizabeth Watson, Aiknut, West Kilbride; *m* 1936, Eileen Stewart Lawson; one *s* one *d. Educ:* Strathallan; Glasgow Univ.; Brasenose Coll., Oxford. Colonial Administrative Service, 1933; seconded Colonial Office, 1933–36; Malayan Civil Service, 1936; Dir of Commerce and Industry, Singapore, 1953. Bursar, Loretto Sch., Musselburgh, 1959–69. *Recreation:* golf. *Address:* Charlton Down Cottage, Charlton Down, Andover, Hants SP11 0HZ. *T:* (01264) 735590. *Club:* Honourable Company of Edinburgh Golfers. *Died 16 Jan. 2001.*

HARTHAN, John Plant, FLA; Keeper of the Library, Victoria and Albert Museum, 1962–76; *b* 15 April 1916; *y s* of late Dr George Ezra Harthan, Evesham, Worcs, and Winifred May Slater. *Educ:* Bryanston; Jesus Coll., Cambridge (MA); University Coll., London. Asst-Librarian, Southampton Univ., 1940–43; Royal Society of Medicine Library, 1943–44; Asst Under-Librarian, Cambridge Univ. Library, 1944–48; Asst-Keeper of the Library, Victoria and Albert Museum, 1948. FLA 1939. *Publications:* Bookbindings in the Victoria and Albert Museum, 1950, 3rd edn 1985; (ed jtly) F.D. Klingender, Animals in Art and Thought, 1971; Books of Hours, 1977, 3rd edn 1988; The History of the Illustrated Book, 1981; Introduction to Illuminated Manuscripts, 1983. *Recreations:* history of religion, royalty, music, botany, writing. *Address:* The Cotswold Home, Woodside Drive, Bradwell Grove, Burford, Oxon OX18 4XA. *Died 9 Jan. 2002.*

HARTWELL, Baron *cr* 1968 (Life Peer), of Peterborough Court in the City of London; **(William) Michael Berry;** MBE 1944; TD; Bt 1921; Chairman and Editor-in-Chief: The Daily Telegraph, 1954–87; Sunday Telegraph, 1961–87; *b* 18 May 1911; 2nd *s* of 1st Viscount Camrose and Mary Agnes, *e d* of late Thomas Corns, London; *S* brother, 1995 as 3rd Viscount Camrose but disclaimed his peerages for life (Viscount *cr* 1941, Baron *cr* 1929); *m* 1936, Lady Pamela Margaret Elizabeth Smith (*d* 1982), *yr d* of 1st Earl of Birkenhead, GCSI, PC, KC; two *s* two *d. Educ:* Eton (Captain of Oppidans; Editor of Chronicle); Christ Church, Oxford (MA). 2nd Lieut 11th (City of London Yeo.) Light AA Bde, RA (TA), 1938; served War of 1939–45; Capt. and Major, 1940; Lt-Col 1944 (despatches twice, MBE). Editor, Sunday Mail, Glasgow, 1934–35; Managing Editor, Financial Times, 1937–39; Chm. Amalgamated Press Ltd, 1954–59. Dir. and subseq. Dep. Chm., LWT, 1968–81. Trustee, Reuters, 1962–89. Jt Hon. Sec., Other Club, 1970–95. *Publications:* Party Choice, 1948; William Camrose, Giant of Fleet Street, 1992. *Heir: (to disclaimed Viscountcy) s* Hon. Adrian Michael Berry [*b* 15 June 1937; *m* 1967, Marina Beatrice, *d* of Cyrus Sulzberger; one *s* one *d*]. *Address:* 18 Cowley Street, Westminster, SW1P 3LZ. *T:* (020) 7222 4673; Oving House, Whitchurch, near Aylesbury, Bucks HP22 4HN. *T:* (01296) 641307; (office) 36 Broadway, SW1 0BH. *T:* (020) 7222 3833. *Clubs:* White's, Beefsteak; Royal Yacht Squadron. *Died 3 April 2001.*

HARTWELL, Eric, CBE 1983; Vice-Chairman, Forte plc (formerly Trusthouse Forte plc), 1972–93 (Chief Executive, 1979–82, Joint Chief Executive, 1982–83); *b*

10 Aug. 1915; *m* 1st, 1937, Gladys Rose Bennett (marr. diss.); one *s* one *d*; 2nd, 1952, Dorothy Maud Mowbray; one *s* one *d*. *Educ:* Mall Sch., Twickenham; Worthing High School. FHCIMA; CIMgt; FBHA. Electrical industry, 1932–37; Dir, Fortes & Co. Ltd, 1938; HM Forces, 1940–45; Jt Man. Dir, Forte Holdings Ltd, 1962; Dep. Man. Dir, Trust Houses Forte Ltd, 1970; Dep. Chief Exec., Trust Houses Forte Ltd, 1972–75; Jt Chief Exec., 1975–78. Chm., BHRCA, 1981–85. Mem. Nat. Council, CBI, 1971–86 (Chm., Finance Sub-Cttee, 1981–86). Mem. Council, Thames Heritage Trust Ltd, 1981 (Vice-Chm., 1983–87); Mem. Cttee, Nuffield Hosp., Enfield, 1984–87; Dir, LV Catering Educn Trust Ltd, 1965–87. Liveryman, Upholders' Co., 1952–. FRSA 1984. *Recreations:* yachting, painting, photography, golf. *Address:* Tall Trees, 129 Totteridge Lane, N20 8NS. *T:* (020) 8445 2321. *Clubs:* River Emergency Service Association, Inner Magic Circle; Thames Motor Yacht; South Herts Golf.
Died 11 Feb. 2001.

HARVEY, Bryan Hugh, CBE 1978; Adviser, Ministry of Defence, 1985–94; Chairman, Advisory Committee on Major Hazards, 1974–83; *b* 17 Oct. 1914; *y s* of late Oliver Harvey and Ellen Harvey (*née* Munn); *m* 1st, 1941, Margaret (*d* 1986), 2nd *d* of late E. G. Palmer; one *d*; 2nd, 1989, Christiane, *widow* of Maj. John Walton. *Educ:* KES Birmingham; Bristol Grammar Sch.; Corpus Christi Coll., Oxford; Harvard Univ. BA 1936; MA 1945; MSc 1953 (Industrial Hygiene). RAFVR, 1943–45. Printing industry until 1938, when joined Inspectorate of Factories; Dep. Chief Inspector, 1965; Chief Inspector, 1971–74; Dep. Dir Gen. (Dep. Sec.), Health and Safety Exec., 1975–76. Advr to Employment Cttee, H of C, 1980–83. Rockefeller Foundn Fellow, 1952–53; Hon. Lectr, Dept of Occupational Health, Univ. of Manchester, 1954–59; Vis. Prof., Univ. of Aston in Birmingham, 1972–79; External Examiner, Loughborough Univ. of Technology, 1984–89. Hon. Mem., British Occupational Hygiene Soc. (Pres. 1976–77). FSA 1964; Hon. Fellow, Instn of Occupational Safety and Health. *Publications:* (with R. Murray) Industrial Health Technology, 1958; (ed) Handbook of Occupational Hygiene, 1980; many articles in jls on industrial safety and hygiene, and industrial archaeology. *Recreations:* industrial archaeology, Georgian architecture, cabinet making. *Address:* 12 Memorial Place, Harpsden Way, Henley-on-Thames, Oxon RG9 1EP. *T:* (01491) 576474. *Clubs:* Leander, Phyllis Court (Henley-on-Thames). *Died 22 Feb. 2004.*

HARVEY, Rt Rev. Philip James Benedict, OBE 1973; Auxiliary Bishop of Westminster (RC) (Bishop in North London), 1977–91; Titular Bishop of Bahanna; *b* 6 March 1915; *s* of William Nathaniel and Elizabeth Harvey. *Educ:* Cardinal Vaughan Sch., Kensington; St Edmund's Coll., Ware, Herts. Ordained Priest, Westminster, 1939; Assistant Priest: Cricklewood, 1939–45; Kentish Town, 1945–46; Fulham, 1946–53; Asst Administrator, Crusade of Rescue, 1953–63, Administrator 1963–77. *Address:* Flat 1, 8 Morpeth Terrace, SW1P 1EQ. *T:* (020) 7798 9018. *Died 2 Feb. 2003.*

HARVEY, Major Thomas Cockayne, CVO 1951; DSO 1945; ERD 1990; Extra Gentleman Usher to the Queen, since 1952 (to King George VI, 1951–52); *b* 22 Aug. 1918; *s* of late Col John Harvey, DSO; *m* 1940, Lady (Katharine) Mary Coke (*d* 1993), (Woman of the Bedchamber to Queen Elizabeth the Queen Mother, 1961–63), *yr d* of 4th Earl of Leicester; one *s* two *d*. *Educ:* Radley; Balliol Coll., Oxford. Joined Scots Guards SRO, 1938; served Norway, 1940, Italy, 1944. Private Sec. to the Queen, 1946–51. *Recreations:* golf, shooting. *Address:* Warham House, Warham, Wells, Norfolk NR23 1NG. *T:* (01328) 710457. *Clubs:* White's, Beefsteak. *Died 11 June 2001.*

HASELGROVE, Dennis Cliff, CB 1963; FSA; Under Secretary, Department of the Environment, 1970–75; *b* 18 Aug. 1914; *s* of late H. Cliff Haselgrove, LLB, Chingford; *m* 1941, Evelyn Hope Johnston, MA, *d* of late R. Johnston, Edinburgh; one *s*. *Educ:* Uppingham Sch.;

King's Coll., Cambridge (1st Class, Classical Tripos, Parts I and II; BA 1936, MA 1943). Served in Intelligence Corps and 10th Baluch Regt, IA, 1941–45. Entered Ministry of Transport, Oct. 1937; Private Sec. to Permanent Sec., and Asst Priv. Sec. to Minister, 1941; Asst Sec., 1948; Under-Sec., 1957–70. Govt Delegate to: ILO Asian Maritime Conf., 1953; Internat. Conf. on Oil Pollution of the Sea, 1954, 1962; Internat. Lab. Conf. (Maritime Session), 1958; Internat. Conf. on Safety of Life at Sea, 1960. Imperial Defence Coll., 1955. *Recreations:* archæology, travel, philately. *Address:* 10 Church Gate, SW6 3LD. *T:* (020) 7736 5213. *Died 6 Sept. 2003.*

HASLAM, Baron *cr* 1990 (Life Peer), of Bolton in the County of Greater Manchester; **Robert Haslam,** Kt 1985; CEng, FInstME; Chairman, Wasserstein Perella & Co. Ltd, 1991–99; *b* 4 Feb. 1923; *s* of Percy and Mary Haslam; *m* 1st, 1947, Joyce Quin (*d* 1995); two *s*; 2nd, 1996, Elizabeth, *widow* of Hon. Michael Sieff, CBE. *Educ:* Bolton Sch.; Birmingham Univ. (BSc Coal Mining, 1st Cl.). Joined Manchester Collieries Ltd, 1944; National Coal Board, Jan. 1947; Mining Engr, Oct. 1947, Personnel Dir, 1960, ICI Nobel Div.; Dir, 1963, Dep. Chm., 1966, ICI Plastics Div.; Dep. Chm., 1969, Chm., 1971, ICI Fibres Div.; Dir, ICI Ltd, 1974–83; Chm., ICI Americas Inc., 1978–81; Dep. Chm., ICI plc, 1980–83; Chairman: British Steel Corporation, 1983–86; Tate & Lyle plc, 1983–86 (non-exec. Dep. Chm., 1982; Dir, 1978–86); British Coal, 1986–90 (non-exec. Dep. Chm., 1985–86; Dep. Chm., 1986); Bechtel Ltd, 1991–94; Director: Fibre Industries, Inc., 1971–75; Imperial Metal Industries, 1975–77; AECI Ltd, 1978–79; Carrington Viyella, 1982–83; Cable and Wireless, 1982–83; Bank of England, 1985–93; Adv. Dir, Unilever, 1986–93. Chairman: Man-Made Fibres Producers Cttee, 1972–74; Nationalized Industries Chairmen's Group, 1985–86 (Mem., 1983–90); British Occupl Health Res. Foundn, 1991–2000; Member: BOTB, 1981–85 (Chm., N America Adv. Gp, 1982–85); NEDC, 1985–89. Pres., IMinE, 1989–90. Chairman: Council, Manchester Business Sch., 1985–90; Governors, Bolton Sch., 1990–97; Michael Sieff Foundn, 1995–; Mem. Council, RHBNC, 1992–96. Freeman, City of London, 1985. Hon. FIMinE 1987. Hon. DTech Brunel, 1987; Hon. DEng Birmingham, 1987. *Publication:* (*posthumous*) An Industrial Cocktail (memoirs), 2003. *Recreations:* golf, travel. *Address:* c/o House of Lords, SW1A 0PW. *Club:* Wentworth. *Died 2 Nov. 2002.*

HASTINGS, Rev. Prof. Adrian Christopher; Professor of Theology, University of Leeds, 1985–94, then Emeritus; *b* 23 June 1929; *s* of late William George Warren Hastings and Mary Hazel Hastings (*née* Daunais); *m* 1979, Elizabeth Ann Spence. *Educ:* Worcester Coll., Oxford (MA 1953); Christ's Coll., Cambridge (PGCE 1958); Urban Univ., Rome (DTheol 1958). Ordained priest, 1955; Diocesan Priest, Masaka, Uganda, 1958–66; Editor, Post-Vatican II, Tanzania, 1966–68; Mindolo Ecumenical Foundn, Zambia, 1968–70; Res. Officer, SOAS, 1973–76; Fellow, St Edmund's House, Cambridge, 1974–76; Lectr and Reader in Religious Studies, Univ. of Aberdeen, 1976–82; Prof. of Religious Studies, Univ. of Zimbabwe, 1982–85. Fellow Commoner, St Edmund's Coll., Cambridge, 1998–. Birkbeck Lectr in Ecclesiastical Hist., Trinity Coll., Cambridge, 2001. Editor, Jl of Religion in Africa, 1985–99. Hon. DD Edinburgh Univ., 1992. *Publications:* Prophet and Witness in Jerusalem, 1958; (ed) The Church and the Nations, 1959; One and Apostolic, 1963; Church and Mission in Modern Africa, 1967; A Concise Guide to the Documents of the Second Vatican Council, 2 vols, 1968–69; Mission and Ministry, 1971; Christian Marriage in Africa, 1973; Wiriyamu, 1974; The Faces of God, 1975; African Christianity, 1976; (ed) Bishops and Writers, 1977; In Filial Disobedience, 1978; A History of African Christianity 1950–1975, 1979; In the Hurricane, 1986; A History of English Christianity 1920–1985, 1986, 4th edn 2001; African Catholicism, 1989; The Theology of a Protestant Catholic, 1990; Robert Runcie, 1991; (ed) Modern Catholicism, 1991;

Church and State: the English Experience, 1991; SOS Bosnia, 1993; The Church in Africa 1450–1950, 1994; The Shaping of Prophecy, 1995; Elias of Dereham, 1997; The Construction of Nationhood, 1997; (with E. Carpenter) Cantuar, 1997; (ed) A World History of Christianity, 1998; (ed) The Oxford Companion to Christian Thought, 2000; Oliver Tomkins: the ecumenical enterprise, 2001. *Recreations:* walking, visiting historic buildings, cutting hedges. *Address:* c/o Department of Theology and Religious Studies, The University, Leeds LS2 9JT. *T:* (0113) 233 3640; 3 Hollin Hill House, 219 Oakwood Lane, Leeds LS8 2PE. *T:* (0113) 240 0154.   *Died 30 May 2001.*

HASTINGS, Sir Stephen (Lewis Edmonstone), Kt 1983; MC 1944; *b* 4 May 1921; *s* of late Lewis Aloysius MacDonald Hastings, MC, and of Edith Meriel Edmonstone; *m* 1st, 1948, Harriet Mary Elisabeth (marr. diss. 1971), *d* of Col Julian Latham Tomlin, CBE, DSO; one *s* one *d*; 2nd, 1975, Hon. Elisabeth Anne, Lady Naylor-Leyland (*d* 1997), *yr d* of late Viscount FitzAlan of Derwent and of Countess Fitzwilliam. *Educ:* Eton; RMC, Sandhurst. Gazetted Ensign, Scots Guards, 1939; served: 2nd Bn, Western Desert, 1941–43 (despatches); SAS Regt, 1943; No 1 Special Force (SOE), Italy, 1944 (MC). Joined Foreign Office, 1948; British Legation, Helsinki, 1950–52; British Embassy, Paris, 1953–58; First Sec., Political Office, Middle East Forces, 1959–60. MP (C) Mid-Bedfordshire, Nov. 1960–1983. Partner and Manager, Milton Park Stud, 1985–. Chm., British Field Sports Soc., 1982–88; Mem. Council, Thoroughbred Breeders Assoc., 1989–91. Pres., Peterborough Cathedral Develt and Preservation Trust, 2001–. *Publications:* The Murder of TSR2, 1966; The Drums of Memory: an autobiography, 1995. *Recreations:* fieldsports, skiing, painting. *Address:* Stibbington House, Wansford, Peterborough PE8 6JS; 12A Ennismore Gardens, SW7 1AA. *Clubs:* White's, Pratt's.   *Died 10 Jan. 2005.*

HATFIELD, Rt Rev. Leonard Fraser; Bishop of Nova Scotia, 1980–84; *b* 1 Oct. 1919; *s* of Otto Albert Hatfield and Ada Hatfield (*née* Tower). *Educ:* Port Greville and Amherst High School; King's and Dalhousie Univ., Halifax (BA 1940, MA 1943, Sociology). Deacon 1942, priest 1943; Priest Assistant, All Saints Cathedral, Halifax, NS, 1942–46; Rector of Antigonish, NS, 1946–51; Asst Sec., Council for Social Service of Anglican Church of Canada, 1951–54; Gen. Sec., 1955–61; Rector: Christ Church, Dartmouth, NS, 1961–71; St John's, Truro, NS, 1971–76; Bishop Suffragan of NS, 1976, Bishop Co-adjutor, 1979. Canon of All Saints Cathedral, Halifax, 1969. Has served: Dio. Council, NS Synod; Corpn of Anglican Dio. Centre; Dean and Chapter, All Saints Cathedral; Bd of Governors, King's Coll.; Program Cttee and Unit of Public Social Responsibility, Gen. Synod; Council of Churches on Justice and Corrections; Anglican Cons. Council, and various cttees of WCC; Organizing Sec., Primate's World Relief and Develt Fund; founding mem., Vanier Inst. of the Family, Ottawa; convened Primate's Task Force on Ordination of Women to the Priesthood; rep. Anglican Church of Canada at Internat. Bishops' Seminar, Anglican Centre in Rome, 1980. Hon. DD: Univ. of King's Coll., Halifax, NS, 1956; Atlantic Sch. of Theology, Halifax, NS, 1985. *Publications:* He Cares, 1958; Simon Gibbons (First Eskimo Priest), 1987; Sammy the Prince, 1990; Great Fun with Organists, 1995. *Recreations:* fishing, gardening, travelling, playing bridge. *Address:* Port Greville, Site 31, Box O, RR#3, Parrsboro, NS B0M 1S0, Canada.   *Died 14 Sept. 2001.*

HATTY, Hon. Sir Cyril (James), Kt 1963; Minister of Finance, Bophuthatswana, 1979–82; *b* 22 Dec. 1908; *o s* of James Hatty and Edith (*née* Russen); *m* 1937, Doris Evelyn, *o d* of James Lane Stewart and Mable Grace Stewart; two *s*. *Educ:* Westminster City Sch. Deputy Dir, O & M Division, UK Treasury, until Jan. 1947; emigrated to S Africa, in industry, Feb. 1947; moved to Bulawayo, Southern Rhodesia, in industry, 1948. MP for Bulawayo

North, Sept. 1950–Dec. 1962; Minister of Treasury, 1954–62, also Minister of Mines, 1956–62. FCIS; Fellow, Inst. of Chartered Management Accountants; FIMgt. *Publications:* as Chatty: Digest of SR Company Law, 1952; (also illus.) There's Peace in Baobabwe, 1987; (also illus.) Zimbaby, Her Birth, Career and Comments, 2001; Digests on the Factories Act, etc. *Recreations:* painting, music. *Address:* Merton Park, PO Box 5, Norton, Zimbabwe. *Club:* Harare (Harare, Zimbabwe).

Died 19 Aug. 2001.

HAVELOCK, Sir Wilfrid (Bowen), Kt 1963; *b* 14 April 1912; *s* of late Rev. E. W. Havelock and Helen (*née* Bowen); *m* 1st, 1938, Mrs M. E. Pershouse (*née* Vincent) (marr. diss. 1967); one *s*; 2nd, 1972, Mrs Patricia Mumford, *widow* of Major Philip S. Mumford. *Educ:* Imperial Service Coll., Windsor, Berks. Elected to Kenya Legislative Council, 1948; Chm., European Elected Members, 1952; Mem., Kenya Executive Council, 1952; Minister for Local Govt, Kenya, 1954; Minister for Agriculture, 1962–63. Dep. Chm., Agricl Finance Corp., Kenya, 1964–84; Member: Nat. Irrigation Bd, 1974–79; Hotels and Restaurant Authority, 1975–81. Dir, Baobab Farm Ltd, 1980–96. Chm., Kenya Assoc. of Hotelkeepers and Caterers, 1974, 1975, 1976. Chm. Trustees, Gertrude's Children's Hosp., 1984–. Badge of Honour and Hon. Vice-Pres., BRCS, 1961. *Address:* PO Box 30181, Nairobi, Kenya. *T:* 762835. *Clubs:* Royal Commonwealth Society; Muthaiga Country, Nairobi, Mombasa, Mount Kenya Safari (Kenya).   *Died 6 April 2003.*

HAVELOCK-ALLAN, Sir Anthony James Allan, 4th Bt *cr* 1858; film producer; *b* 28 Feb. 1904; *s* of Allan Havelock-Allan (2nd *s* of Sir Henry Havelock-Allan, 1st Bt, VC, GCB, MP), and Annie Julia, *d* of Sir William Chaytor, 3rd Bt; *S* brother, 1975; *m* 1st, 1939, Valerie Louise Hobson, actress (marr. diss. 1952; she *d* 1998), *d* of late Comdr Robert Gordon Hobson, RN; one *s* (and one *s* decd); 2nd, 1979, Maria Theresa Consuela (Sara) Ruiz de Villafranca, *d* of late Don Carlos Ruiz de Villafranca (formerly Ambassador to Chile and to Brazil), and Doña Julia Ruiz de Villafranca y Osuña, Villafranca, prov. Madrid. *Educ:* Charterhouse; Switzerland. Artists and Recording Manager, Brunswick Gramophone Co., London and Vox AG, Berlin, 1924–29; entered films as Casting Dir and Producer's Asst, 1933; produced quota films for Paramount; produced for Pinebrook Ltd and Two Cities Films, 1938–40; Assoc. Producer to Noel Coward, 1941; with David Lean and Ronald Neame, formed Cineguild, 1942; Producer, Assoc. Producer or in charge of production for Cineguild, 1942–47; formed Constellation Films, independent co. producing for Rank Org. and British Lion, 1949; with Lord Brabourne and Major Daniel Angel formed British Home Entertainment to introduce Pay TV, 1958. Mem. Home Office Cttee on Employment of Children in Entertainment. Member: Cinematographic Films Council and Nat. Film Production Council, 1948–51; Nat. Film Archive Cttee; US Acad. of Motion Pictures Arts and Sciences, 1970; Chairman: British Film Academy, 1952; Council, Soc. of Film and Television Arts (later BAFTA), 1962, 1963. A Governor, British Film Inst. (and Mem. Production Cttee), 1958–65. *Films include:* This Man is News, 1939; This Man in Paris, 1939; The Lambeth Walk, 1940; Unpublished Story, 1942; From the Four Corners (documentary prod and dir); This Happy Breed (and writer), 1944; Brief Encounter (shared Academy script nomination), 1945; Blithe Spirit (writer), 1945; Great Expectations (shared Academy script nomination), 1946; Take my Life, 1948; Blanche Fury, 1948; Interrupted Journey, 1949; Oliver Twist, 1951; Never Take No for an Answer, 1951; The Young Lovers (dir Anthony Asquith), 1954; Shadow of the Eagle, 1955; Orders to Kill (dir Anthony Asquith), 1958; Meet Me Tonight; The Quare Fellow,1962; An Evening with the Royal Ballet (dir two ballets); (for television) Nat. Theatre's Uncle Vanya; Olivier's Othello, 1965; Zeffirelli's Romeo and Juliet, 1968; Up the Junction, 1968; David Lean's Ryan's Daughter, 1970. *Heir: s*

(Anthony) Mark David Havelock-Allan, QC, *b* 4 April 1951. *Address:* Flat 4, 77 Warwick Square, SW1V 2AR.
Died 11 Jan. 2003.

HAWKER, Rt Rev. Dennis Gascoyne; Hon. Assistant Bishop, diocese of Norwich, since 1993; *b* 8 Feb. 1921; *o s* of late Robert Stephen and Amelia Caroline Hawker; *m* 1944, Margaret Hamilton, *d* of late Robert and Daisy Henderson; one *s* one *d. Educ:* Addey and Stanhope Grammar Sch.; Queens' Coll., Cambridge (BA 1948, MA 1953); Cuddesdon Theol Coll., Oxford. Served War, Commnd Officer, Royal Marines, 1940–46 (War Substantive Major). Lloyds Bank, 1939–40. Deacon, 1950; Priest, 1951; Asst Curate, St Mary and St Eanswythe, Folkestone, 1950–55; Vicar, St Mark, South Norwood, 1955–60; St Hugh's Missioner, Dio. Lincoln, 1960–65; Vicar, St Mary and St James, Gt Grimsby, 1965–72; Bishop Suffragan of Grantham, 1972–87. Canon and Prebendary of Clifton, in Lincoln Cath., 1964–87; Proctor in Convocation, 1964–74. Hon. Chaplain, RNR, 1979–. *Address:* Pickwick Cottage, Hall Close, Heacham, Kings Lynn, Norfolk PE31 7JT. *T:* (01485) 570450. *Club:* Army and Navy.
Died 31 Jan. 2003.

HAWKES, Raymond; Deputy Director, Naval Ship Production, 1977–78; *b* 28 April 1920; *s* of Ernest Hawkes; *m* 1951, Joyce Barbara King; one *s* one *d. Educ:* RNC Greenwich. 1st cl. Naval Architecture, RCNC; CEng; FRINA. Ship design, Bath, 1942–45 and 1954–56; aircraft carrier research at RAE Farnborough, 1945–49; hydrodynamic research at AEW (Admiralty Experiment Works) Haslar, 1949–54; Principal Admty Overseer, Birkenhead, 1956–58; ship prodn, Bath, 1958–62; Chief Cons. Design, assault ships, survey fleet, small ships and auxiliaries, 1962–69; Senior Officers War Course 1966; Asst Dir Warship Design and Project Man. for Through Deck Cruiser, 1969–72; Dep. Dir, Warship Design, 1972–77. *Recreation:* golf. *Address:* Wood Meadow, Beechwood Road, Combe Down, Bath BA2 5JS. *T:* (01225) 832885.
Died 30 Dec. 2002.

HAWKESWORTH, John Stanley; film and television producer and dramatist; *b* 7 Dec. 1920; *s* of Lt-Gen. Sir John Hawkesworth, KBE, CB, DSO, and Lady (Helen Jane) Hawkesworth; *m* 1943, Hyacinthe Gregson-Ellis; one *s. Educ:* Rugby Sch.; Oxford Univ. (BA war degree). Joined Grenadier Guards, 1940; commnd 1941; demobilised 1946 (Captain). Entered film industry as Designer: The Third Man, The Man Who Never Was, The Prisoner, Father Brown; became Producer/Dramatist, Tiger Bay; TV creations include: Upstairs, Downstairs; The Duchess of Duke Street; Danger UXB; The Flame Trees of Thika; The Tale of Beatrix Potter; By the Sword Divided; Oscar; Sherlock Holmes, The Return of Sherlock Holmes and The Sign of Four; Campion; Chelworth; screenplay: Mrs 'Arris Goes to Paris, 1992. One man show (paintings), The Studio, Glebe Place, London, 1989, 1995, 1997, 1999 and 2001; exhibn, film designs, Austin/Desmond Fine Art, London, 1991; exhibn, paintings of Pembrokeshire, Newport, 1994. Many television awards, incl. Peabody Award, Univ. of Georgia, 1977. *Publications:* Upstairs, Downstairs, 1972; In My Lady's Chamber, 1973. *Recreations:* golf, gardening. *Address:* Fishponds House, Knossington, Oakham, Rutland LE15 8LX. *T:* (01664) 454339.
Died 30 Sept. 2003.

HAWKINS, Sir Paul (Lancelot), Kt 1982; TD 1945; FRICS; *b* 7 Aug. 1912; *s* of L. G. Hawkins and of Mrs Hawkins (*née* Peile); *m* 1st, 1937, E. Joan Snow (*d* 1984); two *s* one *d*; 2nd, 1985, Tina Daniels. *Educ:* Cheltenham Coll. Joined family firm, 1930; Chartered Surveyor, 1933. Served in TA, Royal Norfolk Regt, 1933–45; POW Germany, 1940–45. MP (C) SW Norfolk, 1964–87. An Asst Govt Whip, 1970–71; a Lord Comr of the Treasury, 1971–73; Vice-Chamberlain of HM Household, 1973–74. Mem., H of C (Services) Select Cttee, 1976–87. Mem., Delegn to Council of Europe and WEU, 1976–87; Chm., Agricl Cttee, Council of Europe, 1985–87. Dir (non-

exec.), Gorham Bateson (Agriculture) Seed Specialists, 1989–. CC Norfolk, 1949–70, Alderman, 1968–70. *Recreations:* walking, gardening, travel. *Address:* Stables, Downham Market, Norfolk PE38 9NL.
Died 29 Dec. 2002.

HAWTHORNE, Sir Nigel (Barnard), Kt 1999; CBE 1987; DL; self-employed actor and writer; *b* Coventry, 5 April 1929; *s* of Charles Barnard Hawthorne and Agnes Rosemary (*née* Rice). *Educ:* Christian Brothers' Coll., Cape Town, S Africa. Entered theatre professionally, 1950; returned to England, 1951, where he has worked ever since, with the exception of a small number of engagements abroad. *Stage:* Otherwise Engaged, 1976; Privates on Parade, 1978 (Best Supporting Actor, SWET and Clarence Derwent awards); Peer Gynt, and Tartuffe, with RSC, 1983–84 (Tartuffe televised 1985); Across from the Garden of Allah, 1986; Jacobowski and the Colonel, NT, 1986; The Magistrate, NT, 1986; Hapgood, Aldwych, 1988; Shadowlands, Queen's, 1989, Broadway, 1990–91 (Tony Award for Best Actor, 1991); The Madness of George III, NT, 1992 (Olivier Award for Best Actor, 1992; Evening Standard Best Actor Award, 1992), American tour, 1993, European tour, 1994; The Clandestine Marriage (also dir), Queen's, 1994; King Lear, RSC, and Japan, 1999; *television:* Marie Curie, 1977; Destiny, 1978; Edward and Mrs Simpson, 1978; The Knowledge, 1979; Yes Minister (series), annually 1980–83, 1985–86, Yes, Prime Minister (series), 1986, 1987 (Broadcasting Press Guild Award, 1980; BAFTA Best Light Entertainment Performance, 1981, 1982, 1986, 1987); The Critic, 1982; The Barchester Chronicles, 1982; Mapp and Lucia, 1984–86; The Miser, 1988; The Shawl, 1989; Relatively Speaking, 1989; The Trials of Oz, 1991; Flea-Bites, 1992; Late-Flowering Lust, 1994; The Fragile Heart, 1996 (BAFTA Best TV Actor, 1997); Forbidden Territory, 1997; Victoria and Albert, 2001; Call Me Claus, 2001; *films:* Firefox, Gandhi, Golda, 1981; John Paul II, 1983; The House, 1984; The Chain, 1985; Demolition Man, 1993; The Madness of King George, 1994; Richard III, Inside, Twelfth Night, 1996; Murder in Mind, Amistad, Madeline, The Object of My Affection, 1997; At Sachem Farm, The Clandestine Marriage, A Reasonable Man, The Big Brass Ring, 1998; The Winslow Boy, 1999. DL Herts, 1999. Hon. MA: Sheffield, 1987; Leicester, 1994; Hon. DLitt: Hertfordshire, 1992; Keele, 1999. *Posthumous publication:* Straight Face (autobiog.), 2002. *Recreations:* swimming, gardening, painting.
Died 26 Dec. 2001.

HAWTREY, John Havilland Procter, CBE 1958; FICE; Crown Agent and Engineer-in-Chief, 1965–69; *b* 16 Feb. 1905; *e s* of late Edmond Charles Hawtrey and Helen Mary Hawtrey (*née* Durand); *m* 1947, Kathleen Mary (*d* 1992), *d* of late Captain M. T. Daniel, RN, Henley-on-Thames; one *s* one *d. Educ:* Eton; City and Guilds Engineering Coll., London (BSc 1927). Asst Engineer, later Dist Engineer, Burma Railways, 1927–47. Served War of 1939–45: with RE, 1940–46; Major 1942, in India and Burma, 1942–46 (despatches). Entered office of Crown Agents for Oversea Govts and Administrations, 1948; Chief Civil Engineer, 1956. *Address:* Glyn Nest Residential Home, Ebenezer Street, Newcastle Emlyn, SA38 9BW.
Died 11 Feb. 2003.

HAY, Prof. John Duncan, MA, MD, FRCP; Professor of Child Health, University of Liverpool, 1957–74, then Professor Emeritus; *b* 6 Feb. 1909; *s* of late Prof. John Hay; *m* 1936, Jannett Ceridwen Evans (decd); one *s* two *d. Educ:* Liverpool Coll.; Sidney Sussex Coll., Cambridge; Liverpool Univ. MB, ChB, 1st Cl. Hons, Liverpool, 1933; MA 1934, MB 1935, Cambridge; MD Liverpool, 1936; DCH London, MRCP 1939; FRCP 1951. Holt Fellowship in Pathology, Liverpool, 1935; Cons. Pædiatrician to: Royal Liverpool Children's Hospital, 1939–74; Royal Liverpool Babies' Hospital, 1939–61; Birkenhead Children's Hosp., 1937–54; Liverpool Maternity Hosp. 1946–74; Lancashire County Hosp.,

Whiston, 1942–51; Liverpool Open-Air Hospital, Leasowe, and Mill Road Maternity Hosp., 1947–74; Alder Hey Children's Hosp., 1957–74; Liverpool Education Cttee, 1951–72. Demonstrator in Pathology, University of Liverpool, 1935 and 1938; Asst Lectr in Clinical Pædiatrics, University of Liverpool, 1948–57. Brit. Paediatric Association: Treasurer, 1964–71; Pres., 1972–73; Hon. Mem., 1973; President: Liverpool Med. Instn, 1972–73; Liverpool Paediatric Club, 1975–; Hon. Mem. Assoc. European Paediatric Cardiologists, 1975–. RAMC (Major and Lieut-Col), 1942–46. Publications: contribs to Archives of Disease in Childhood, British Heart Journal, BMJ, Lancet, Practitioner, Brit. Encyclopædia of Medical Practice, Medical Progress, 1957, Cardiovascular Diseases in Childhood. Recreations: music, fell walking. Address: c/o The Croft, Packhorse Lane, Marcham, Abingdon, Oxon OX13 6NT. T: (01865) 391216. Died 5 Dec. 2003.

HAYCRAFT, Anna Margaret, FRSL; writer; b 9 Sept. 1932; d of John and Alexandra Lindholm; m 1956, Colin Haycraft (d 1994); four s one d (and one s one d decd). Educ: Bangor County Grammar School for Girls; Liverpool School of Art. Fiction editor, Gerald Duckworth & Co., 1970; Columnist: The Spectator, 1985–89; The Universe, 1989–91; The Catholic Herald, 1991–96, 1998–; The Oldie, 1996–. FRSL 1999. Publications: as Anna Haycraft: Natural Baby Food, 1977; (with Caroline Blackwood) Darling, You Shouldn't Have Gone to So Much Trouble, 1980; as Alice Thomas Ellis: The Sin Eater, 1977; The Birds of the Air, 1980; The Twenty-Seventh Kingdom, 1982; The Other Side of the Fire, 1983; Unexplained Laughter, 1985 (Yorkshire Post Novel of the Year, 1985); (with Tom Pitt-Aikens) Secrets of Strangers, 1986; Home Life, 1986; More Home Life, 1987; The Clothes in the Wardrobe, 1987, The Skeleton in the Cupboard, 1988, The Fly in the Ointment, 1989, trilogy; Home Life Three, 1988; (with Tom Pitt-Aikens) The Loss of the Good Authority, 1989; (ed) Wales: an anthology, 1989; Home Life Four, 1989; A Welsh Childhood (autobiog.), 1990; The Inn at the Edge of the World, 1990 (Writers' Guild Award, 1990); Pillars of Gold, 1992; The Serpent on the Rock, 1994; The Evening of Adam, 1994; Cat Among the Pigeons: collection of 'Catholic Herald' essays, 1994; Fairy Tale, 1996; (ed) Valentine's Day, 2000; Gardening in the Dark/God does not Change: collection of 'Oldie' essays, 2004; Fish, Flesh and Good Red Herring, 2004. Address: c/o Peters Fraser & Dunlop, Drury House, 34–43 Russell Street, W2B 5HA. Died 8 March 2005.

HAYES, Colin Graham Frederick, MA; RA 1970 (ARA 1963); painter; b 17 Nov. 1919; s of Gerald Hayes and Winifred (née Yule); m 1st, 1949, Jean Westbrook Law (d 1988); three d; 2nd, 1992, Marjorie Christensen. Educ: Westminster Sch.; Christ Church, Oxford. Served Royal Engineers, 1940–45 (Middle East) (Capt.). Ruskin Sch. of Drawing, 1946–47. Tutor, Sen. Tutor and Reader, Royal College of Art, 1949–84; Hon. ARCA, 1960; Fellow, RCA, 1960–84 (Hon. Fellow, 1984). Pres., Royal Soc. of British Artists, 1993–98. Work in Collections: Arts Council; British Council; Carlisle Museum, etc. Publications: include: Renoir, 1961; Stanley Spencer, 1963; Rembrandt, 1969; many articles on painting in jls. Address: 2 Annandale Road, W4 2HF. T: (020) 8994 8762. Died 1 Nov. 2003.

HAYES, (John) Philip, CB 1984; Assistant Under-Secretary of State (Economics), Foreign and Commonwealth Office, 1975–84, retired; b 1924; s of late Harry Hayes and Mrs G. E. Hayes (née Hallsworth); m 1956, Susan Elizabeth, d of Sir Percivale Liesching, GCMG, KCB, KCVO; one s one d. Educ: Cranleigh Sch.; Corpus Christi Coll., Oxford. RAFVR, 1943–46. Barnett Memorial Fellowship, 1948–49; Political and Economic Planning, 1950–53; OEEC, 1953–58; Internat. Bank for Reconstruction and Develt, 1958–64; Head, Economic Develt Div., OECD, 1964–67; Dir, World Economy

Div., Economic Planning Staff, ODM, 1967–69; Dep. Dir Gen. of Economic Planning, ODM, later ODA, 1969–71; Dir, Econ. Program Dept, IBRD, 1971–73; Dir, Trade and Finance Div., Commonwealth Secretariat, 1973–75. Sen. Fellow, Trade Policy Res. Centre, 1984–89. Publications: Economic Effects of Sanctions on Southern Africa, 1987; Making Trade Policy in the European Community, 1993. Recreations: music, writing. Address: 223 Hoylake Crescent, Ickenham, Middx UB10 8JL. T: (01895) 633023. Died 25 Feb. 2001.

HAYES, John Trevor, CBE 1986; PhD; FSA; Director of the National Portrait Gallery, London, 1974–94; b 21 Jan. 1929; er s of late Leslie Thomas Hayes and Gwendoline (née Griffiths), London. Educ: Ardingly; Keble Coll. Oxford (Open Exhibnr; MA; Hon. Fellow, 1984); Courtauld Inst. of Art, London (PhD); Inst. of Fine Arts, New York. Asst Keeper, London Museum, 1954–70, Dir, 1970–74. Commonwealth Fund Fellow, NY Univ., 1958–59; Vis. Prof. in History of Art, Yale Univ., 1969. Chm., Walpole Soc., 1981–96. Publications: London: a pictorial history, 1969; The Drawings of Thomas Gainsborough, 1970; Catalogue of Oil Paintings in the London Museum, 1970, 2nd edn (with Mireille Galinou), 1996; Gainsborough as Printmaker, 1971; Rowlandson: Watercolours and Drawings, 1972; Gainsborough: Paintings and Drawings, 1975; The Art of Graham Sutherland, 1980; The Landscape Paintings of Thomas Gainsborough, 1982; The Art of Thomas Rowlandson, 1990; The Portrait in British Art, 1991; Catalogue of the British Paintings in the National Gallery of Art, Washington, 1992; Gainsborough and Rowlandson: a New York private collection, 1998; (ed) The Letters of Thomas Gainsborough, 2001; various London Museum and Nat. Portrait Gall. pubns; catalogues of Gainsborough exhibns for Tate Gall., Grand Palais and Ferrara Arte; numerous articles in The Burlington Magazine, Apollo and other jls. Recreations: ballet, opera, European travel. Address: 61 Grantham Road, Chiswick, W4 2RT. T: (020) 8747 9768. Club: Garrick. Died 25 Dec. 2005.

HAYES, Philip; see Hayes, J. P.

HAYR, Air Marshal Sir Kenneth (William), KCB 1988 (CB 1982); KBE 1991 (CBE 1976); AFC 1963 and Bar 1972; Deputy Chief of Defence Staff (Commitments), Ministry of Defence, 1989–92; retired in rank of Air Marshal, 1993; b 13 April 1935; s of late Kenneth James and Jeanie Templeton Hayr; m 1961, Joyce Gardner (d 1987); three s. Educ: Auckland Grammar Sch.; RAF Coll. Cranwell. Served Hunter and Lightning Sqns, 1957–64; Central Fighter Estabt/Fighter Comd Trials Unit, 1964–67; Phantom OCU Sqn Comdr, 1968–69; OC 1(F) Sqn (Harriers), 1970–71; RAF Staff Coll., 1972; OC RAF Binbrook (Lightnings), 1973–76; Inspector of Flight Safety (RAF), 1976–79; RCDS 1980; Asst Chief of Air Staff (Ops), 1980–82; AOC No 11 Group, RAF, 1982–85; Comdr British Forces Cyprus and Administrator Sovereign Base Areas, 1985–88; COS UK Air Forces and Dep. C-in-C, Strike Comd, 1988–89. Chm., NZ Aviation Heritage Trust Bd, 1993–. Freeman, City of London, 1984. Kuwait Liberation Order (1st Grade), 1991. Recreations: display aerobatics, wave ski-ing, wind surfing, paragliding, ski-ing, tennis. Clubs: Royal Air Force; Colonels'. Died 2 June 2001.

HAYTER, 3rd Baron cr 1927 of Chislehurst, Kent; George Charles Hayter Chubb, KCVO 1977; CBE 1976; Bt 1900; a Deputy Chairman, House of Lords, 1981–95; Managing Director, 1941–71, Chairman, 1957–81, Chubb & Son's Lock & Safe Co. Ltd; b 25 April 1911; e s of 2nd Baron Hayter and Mary (d 1948), d of J. F. Haworth; S father, 1967; m 1940, Elizabeth Anne Rumbold, MBE 1975; three s one d. Educ: Leys Sch., Cambridge; Trinity Coll., Cambridge (BA 1932, MA 1960). Chairman: Royal Society of Arts, 1965–66; Mgt Cttee, King Edward's Hospital Fund for London, 1965–82; Duke of Edinburgh's Countryside in 1970

Cttee. President: Business Equipment Trades Association, 1954–55; Canada-United Kingdom Chamber of Commerce, 1966–67; Royal Warrant Holders Association, 1967. Mem., CoID, 1964–71. Chairman: Executives Assoc. of GB, 1960; EDC International Freight Movement, 1972–79; British Security Industry Assoc., 1973–77. Liveryman, Weavers' Co., 1934–(Upper Bailiff, 1961–62). *Publication:* Security offered by Locks and Safes (Lecture, RSA), 1962. *Heir: s* Hon. (George) William (Michael) Chubb [*b* 9 Oct. 1943; *m* 1983, Waltraud, *yr d* of J. Flackl, Sydney, Australia; one *s*]. *Address:* Ashtead House, Ashtead, Surrey KT21 1LU. *T:* (01372) 273476.
Died 2 Sept. 2003.

HAYWOOD, Thomas Charles Stanley, OBE 1962; JP; Lieutenant of Leicestershire, 1974–84 (Lord Lieutenant of Rutland, 1963–74); *b* 10 March 1911; *s* of late Charles B. Haywood, Woodhatch, Reigate, Surrey; *m* 1937, Anne, *d* of J. B. A. Kessler, London; ones one *d* (and one *s* decd). *Educ:* Winchester; Magdalene Coll., Cambridge (BA 1932). Served 1939–42 with Leics Yeomanry, Capt. 1940, Hon. Col, 1970–77. Chm. Trustees, Oakham Sch., 1964–81. DL 1962, JP 1957, High Sheriff 1952, County of Rutland. *Address:* Gunthorpe, Oakham, Rutland LE15 8BE. *T:* (01572) 737203.
Died 24 Jan. 2003.

HAZLERIGG, 2nd Baron *cr* 1945, of Noseley; **Arthur Grey Hazlerigg,** MC 1945; TD 1948; JP, DL; Bt 1622; *b* 24 Feb. 1910; *e s* of 1st Baron Hazlerigg and Dorothy Rachel (*d* 1972), *e d* of John Henry Buxton, Easneye, Ware, Herts; *S* father, 1949; *m* 1945, Patricia (*d* 1972), *e d* of late John Pullar, High Seat, Fields Hill, Kloof, Natal, SA; one *s* two *d. Educ:* Eton; Trinity Coll., Cambridge (BA 1932). FRICS 1946. Served War of 1939–45, Leics Yeomanry; Major, 1941; served in Italy. DL Leics 1946; JP 1946. *Recreation:* golf. *Heir: s* Hon. Arthur Grey Hazlerigg [*b* 5 May 1951; *m* 1986, Laura (marr. diss. 1998), *e d* of Sir William Dugdale, 2nd Bt, CBE, MC; one *s* three *d* (incl. twin *d*); *m* 1999, Mrs Shan Chichester, *d* of Alastair McIndoe]. *Address:* Noseley Hall, Leicester LE7 9EH. *Clubs:* MCC; XL.
Died 30 Sept. 2002.

HEAD, Dennis Alec, CBE 1979; CEng, FRAeS; Divisional Director (Northern Ireland), STC, 1986–91; *b* 8 Nov. 1925; *s* of late Alec Head and Florence Head; *m* 1966, Julia Rosser-Owen, BA; one *s. Educ:* Whitgift Sch.; Peterhouse, Cambridge (Mech. Sciences Tripos, MA); Royal Naval Engrg Coll., Manadon. Served FAA, RN, 1943–47: Sub-Lt (A) RNVR, 1945; Air Engr Officer. Rolls-Royce Ltd: grad. apprentice, 1949; Manager, Design Services, Aero Engine Div., 1962; Dir of Personnel and Admin, 1967; Dir and Gen. Man., subseq. Man. Dir, Derby Engine Div., 1973; Man. Dir Aero Div., 1976; Man. Dir Operations, 1980–82; Member Board: Rolls-Royce Ltd, 1973–82; Rolls-Royce Turbomeca, 1973–82 (Chm., 1981–82); Turbo-Union, 1979–82; Chm., Rolls-Royce & Associates, 1981–82; Mem. Bd and Dir Operations, Short Brothers, 1982–86. Member: Reg. Adv. Council for Further Educn, 1968–73; Engrg Employers' Fedn Policy Cttee, 1978–82. *Recreations:* photography, history, music. *Address:* Ash Grove House, 6 Merebrook Close, Welland, Malvern, Worcs WR14 4JW. *T:* (01684) 569867.
Died 17 Nov. 2003.

HEAD, Major Sir Francis (David Somerville), 5th Bt *cr* 1838; late Queen's Own Cameron Highlanders; *b* 17 Oct. 1916; *s* of Sir Somerville Head, 4th Bt, FRGS and Grace Margaret (*d* 1967), *d* of late David Robertson; *S* father, 1924; *m* 1st, 1950, Susan Patricia (marr. diss. 1965), *o d* of A. D. Ramsay, OBE; one *s* one *d*; 2nd, 1967, Penelope, *d* of late Wilfred Alexander. *Educ:* Eton; Peterhouse, Cambridge (BA 1937). Served War of 1939–45 (wounded and prisoner); retired 1951. *Heir: s* Richard Douglas Somerville Head [*b* 16 Jan. 1951; *m* 1991, Edwina (marr. diss. 1998), *d* of late Edward Mansell. *Educ:* Eton; Magdalene Coll., Cambridge]. *Address:* 63 Chantry View Road, Guildford, Surrey GU1 3XU.
Died 16 Dec. 2005.

HEAD, Mildred Eileen, OBE 1971; owner, director and partner in several furniture and drapery shops, 1950–83; *b* 13 June 1911; *d* of Philip Strudwick Head and Katie Head. *Educ:* Sudbury Girls' Secondary Sch.; Chelsea Coll. of Physical Educn (Dipl.). MCSP. Teacher, Lectr and Organiser of Physical Educn, 1933–50. Comr of Inland Revenue, 1959–86. Member: Price Commn, 1973–77; Nat. Economic Cttee for Distributive Trades, 1974–84; Retail Consortium, 1971–83; Davignon/Narjes Cttee for Commerce and Distribution (EEC), 1979–86; Discip. Cttee, Assoc. of Certified Accountants, 1980–83. Assessor, Auld Cttee of Inquiry into Shops Hours, 1984–85. President: Nat. Fedn of Business and Professional Women of Gt Britain and N Ireland, 1966–69; Nat. Chamber of Trade, 1977–79 (Chm. Bd of Management, 1971–77); Internat. Fedn of Business and Professional Women, 1977–80 (first Vice-Pres., 1974–77). Mayor of Borough of Sudbury, 1970–71. Chm., Mgt Cttee, Quay Theatre, Sudbury, 1982–87. *Address:* Melford Court Nursing Home, Hall Street, Long Melford, Sudbury, Suffolk CO10 9JA. *T:* (01787) 880545.
Died 21 June 2003.

HEADFORT, 6th Marquis of, *cr* 1800; **Thomas Geoffrey Charles Michael Taylour,** FRICS; Bt 1704; Baron Headfort, 1760; Viscount Headfort, 1762; Earl of Bective, 1766; Baron Kenlis (UK), 1831; *b* 20 Jan. 1932; *o s* of 5th Marquis and Elsie Florence (*d* 1972), *d* of J. Partridge Tucker, Sydney, NSW, and widow of Sir Rupert Clarke, 2nd Bt of Rupertswood; *S* father, 1960; *m* 1st, 1958, Hon. Elizabeth Nall-Cain (from whom he obtained a divorce, 1969), *d* of 2nd Baron Brocket; one *s* two *d*; 2nd, 1972, Virginia, *d* of late Mr Justice Nable, Manila. *Educ:* Stowe; Christ's Coll., Cambridge (MA; Cert. of Proficiency in Rural Estate Management). 2nd Lieut Life Guards, 1950; acting Pilot Officer, RAFVR, 1952. Dir, Bective Electrical Co. Ltd, 1953; Sales Manager and Chief Pilot, Lancashire Aircraft Co. Ltd, 1959. Freeman, Guild of Air Pilots and Air Navigators, 1958. Piloted Prospector aircraft around Africa, 1960, etc. FRICS; FCIArb; Mem., Irish Auctioneers and Valuers Inst. Council, Royal Agricultural Society of England, 1961. Inspector, Royal Hong Kong Police, 1977. Commercial Pilot's Licence, 1967. *Heir: s* Earl of Bective, *b* 10 Feb. 1959; *m* 1987, Susan Jane, *er d* of late C. A. Vandervell and of Mrs Vandervell; two *s* two *d*. *Clubs:* Cavalry and Guards, Little Ship, House of Lords Yacht, Kildare Street and University (Dublin); Manila, Manila Yacht (Philippines); Hong Kong, Foreign Correspondents, Aberdeen Boat, Royal Hong Kong Jockey (Hong Kong).
Died 21 Oct. 2005.

HEALD, Mervyn; QC 1970; a Social Security Commissioner, 1988–2002; a Child Support Commissioner, 1993; *b* 12 April 1930; *s* of Rt Hon. Sir Lionel Heald, QC, and of Daphne Constance, CBE 1976, *d* of late Montague Price; *m* 1954, Clarissa Bowen; one *s* three *d. Educ:* Eton College; Magdalene College, Cambridge. Called to the Bar, Middle Temple, 1954; Bencher, 1978; Autumn Reader, 1997. A Recorder, 1985–88. *Recreations:* country pursuits. *Address:* Colhook Lodge, Colhook Common, Petworth, W Sussex GU28 9LE. *T:* (01428) 708198.
Died 1 March 2004.

HEALEY, Deryck John, FRSA 1978; FCSD; artist, sculptor; *b* 30 Jan. 1937; *s* of Leonard Melvon Healey and Irene Isabella Healey (*née* Ferguson); *m* 1962, Mary Elizabeth Pitt Booth (decd); two *s. Educ:* Northlands High Sch., Natal, SA (Victoria League Empire Scholar; DipAD, SA, 1955; Golden Jubilee Cert. of Merit, 1957); Manchester Polytechnic (DipAd 1958, Textile Design Prize, 1957, 1958; Design Travel Bursary, 1958; Royal Manch. Inst. Cert. of Merit, 1958; Calico Printers' Assoc. Fellow, 1961–62). Design Man., Good Hope Textiles, SA, 1959–66; Chairman: Deryck Healey Associates, London, 1966–85; Deryck Healey International, 1969–85; Dreamshire, 1985–87; Design Man., WPM London (Wallpaper mfrs), 1966–68; ICI Design Studio Manager, Asst to Elsbeth Juda, 1968–80; Consultant, D. H. I. Interiors Ltd, 1983–85; Design Consultant, Wedgwood,

1984–88. Chm., CNAA Textile and Fashion Bd, 1971–81; Member: CNAA Art and Design Cttee, 1971–81; Design Council Textile Design Selection Cttee, 1978–87; Craft Council Bd, 1983–85 (Textile Panel, 1980; Finance and Gen. Purposes Cttee, 1983–85; Chairman: Textile Develt Group, 1982–84; Projects and Organisations Cttee, 1983–85). RSA: Annual Sponsor, D. Healey Fashion and Colour Bursaries, 1978–85; Mem. Bursary Bd, 1982–88. Patron, New Art Tate Gall., 1983–. Member: Contemp. Art Soc., 1982–; ICA, 1970–; Chelsea Arts Club, 1982–88; Friend of RA, 1980–. SIAD: Mem., British Design Export Gp, 1980; Chm., Textile and Fashion Gp, 1966–67. External Examiner, Textile and Fashion courses: CNAA BA and MA; Liverpool, BA, 1978–80; Manchester, MA, 1976–79; Kingston, BA, 1978–80; St Martin's, BA, 1978–80; Glasgow, BA, 1979–82; RCA, Textiles, 1980; Adviser and External Examiner, Middx Polytechnic, BA, 1982–86; External Examiner: London Coll. of Furniture, BTEC, 1985–86; BA Fashion, St Martin's Sch. of Art, 1985–87. Vis Prof., RCA. Exhibitions: Salama-Caro Gall., London, 1990, 1991, 1994; Frankfurt Internat. Art Fair, 1990; Venice, 1990; Internat. Art Fairs, Cologne and Chicago, 1990; Phoenix Univ., Arizona, 1991; Fosbury, UK, 1991; Santa Fé, Mexico, 1992; Galerie Langer Fain, Paris, 1992; Koplin Gall., LA, 1993; Art of Concern, Base, London, 1994; Deaf, Edinburgh, 1996; Behind Walls, RSA, 1997; Back to Front, Natal Soc. of Art Gall., Durban, 1998; Blue Gall., London, 1998; Fragments, Natal Soc. of Art Gall., Durban, 2001; Words, Les Livres Gall., Colchester, 2001; Beach, Bean Bag Bohemia, Durban, 2002, Assoc. of Visual Arts, Cape Town, 2003; Portrait Drawings, Artist Space, Durban, 2004; retrospective: Manchester Metropolitan Univ., 2003. Installation, Seamen's Mission, Glasgow, 1992; special commn sculpture, Manchester Internat. Concert Hall, 1996. FCSD (FSIAD 1964). Hon. FRCA 2000. CoID Design Award, 1964; Queen's Award to Industry for Export, 1974; RSA Bicentenary Medal, 1981; Textile Institute Design Medal, 1982. *Publications:* Colour, 1980 (Mem. Editorial Bd and contrib.); Living with Colour, 1982; The New Art of Flower Design, 1986; Big Names, 1991; Open Studio, 1994; Our Island Garden Project, 1995; Beach 2003. *Address:* Ballast Quay House, Ballast Quay Road, Wivenhoe CO7 9JT. *Clubs:* various. *Died 12 Nov. 2004.*

HEANEY, Leonard Martin, CMG 1959; Overseas Civil Service, retired; *b* 28 Nov. 1906; *s* of Alexander John and Lilian Heaney; *m* 1947, Kathleen Edith Mary Chapman (*d* 2000); no *c. Educ:* Bristol Grammar Sch.; Oriel Coll., Oxford. Joined Colonial Service on leaving Oxford, 1929; served in Tanganyika, retiring as a Senior Provincial Commissioner, 1959. Military service with East African Forces in Abyssinia, Madagascar, Ceylon, Burma, 1940–45. *Recreation:* reading. *Address:* Royal Star and Garter Home, Richmond Hill, Richmond, Surrey TW10 6RR. *Died 16 July 2001.*

HEATH, (Edward) Peter, OBE 1946; a Deputy Chairman, Inchcape & Co. Ltd, 1976–79; *b* 6 June 1914; *m* 1953, Eleanor Christian Peck; one *s* three *d. Educ:* St Lawrence Coll., Ramsgate. Joined Borneo Co. Ltd, 1934; interned in Thailand, 1941–45. Gen. Manager, Borneo Co. Ltd, 1953–63; a Man. Dir, 1963–67; a Man. Dir, Inchcape & Co. Ltd, 1967–75. Director: Inchcape Far East Ltd, 1972–79; Mann Egerton & Co. Ltd, 1973–79; Dodwell & Co. Ltd, 1974–79; Chairman: Toyota GB and Pride & Clark, 1978–79; Anglo-Thai Corp. Ltd, 1978–79; Dep. Chm., Bewac Motor Corp., 1970–79. Consultant, Matheson & Co. Ltd, 1980–83; Director: Matheson Motor Hldgs, 1981–83; Lancaster Gp Hldgs, 1981–83. Deputy Chairman: Hong Kong Assoc., 1975–79; Anglo Thai Soc., 1975–85. Order of White Elephant (5th Cl.) (Thailand); Officer, Order of Orange Nassau (Netherlands). *Recreations:* hunting, gardening, motoring. *Address:* Cooks Place, Albury, Guildford, Surrey GU5 9BJ. *T:* (01483) 202698. *Died 12 Jan. 2003.*

HEATH, Rt Hon. Sir Edward (Richard George), KG 1992; MBE 1946; PC 1955; Member, Public Review Board, Arthur Andersen & Co., 1978–98; *b* Broadstairs, Kent, 9 July 1916; *s* of late William George and Edith Anne Heath. *Educ:* Chatham House Sch., Ramsgate; Balliol Coll., Oxford (Scholar; Hon. Fellow, 1969). Scholar, Gray's Inn, 1938 (Hon. Bencher, 1972). Pres., Oxford Univ. Conservative Assoc., 1937; Chm., Fedn of Univ. Conservative Assocs, 1938; Pres., Oxford Union, 1939; Oxford Union debating tour of American Univs, 1939–40; Pres., Fedn of Univ. Conservative and Unionist Assocs, 1959–77, Hon. Life Patron, 1977. Served War of 1939–45 (despatches, MBE): in Army, 1940–46, in France, Belgium, Holland and Germany; gunner in RA, 1940; Major 1945. Lieut-Col comdg 2nd Regt HAC, TA, April 1947–Aug. 1951; Master Gunner within the Tower of London, 1951–54. Administrative Civil Service, 1946–47, resigning to become prospective candidate for Bexley. MP (C): Bexley, 1950–74; Bexley, Sidcup, 1974–83; Old Bexley and Sidcup, 1983–2001. Asst Conservative Whip, Feb. 1951; Lord Comr of the Treasury, Nov. 1951, and Joint Dep. Govt Chief Whip, 1952, and Dep. Govt Chief Whip, 1953–55; Parliamentary Sec. to the Treasury, and Government Chief Whip, Dec. 1955–Oct. 1959; Minister of Labour, Oct. 1959–July 1960; Lord Privy Seal, with Foreign Office responsibilities, 1960–63; Sec. of State for Industry, Trade, Regional Development and Pres. of the Board of Trade, Oct. 1963–Oct. 1964; Leader of the Opposition, 1965–70; Prime Minister and First Lord of the Treasury, 1970–74; Leader of the Opposition, 1974–75; Father of the H of C, 1992–2001. Chm., Commonwealth Parly Assoc., 1970–74. Mem., Ind. Commn on Internat. Development Issues, 1977–79. Mem. Council, Royal College of Music, 1961–70; Chm., London Symphony Orchestra Trust, 1963–70 (Hon. Mem., LSO, 1974–); Vice-Pres., Bach Choir, 1970–; Pres., European Community Youth Orchestra, 1977–80; has made orchestral recordings. Smith-Mundt Fellowship, USA, 1953; Vis. Fellow, Nuffield Coll., Oxford, 1962–70, Hon. Fellow, 1970; Chubb Fellow, Yale, 1975; Montgomery Fellow, Dartmouth Coll., 1980. Lectures: Cyril Foster Meml, Oxford, 1965; Godkin, Harvard, 1966; Montagu Burton, Leeds, 1976; Edge, Princeton, 1976; Romanes, Oxford, 1976; Ishizaka, Japan, 1979; Felix Neuberg, Gothenburg, 1979; 10th STC Communication, London, 1980; Noel Buxton, Univ. of Essex, 1980; Alastair Buchan Meml, London, 1980; Hoover, Univ. of Strathclyde, 1980; Stanton Griffis Disting., Cornell Univ., 1981; Edwin Stevens, RSM, 1981; William Temple, York, 1981; City of London, Chartered Insce Inst., 1982; John Findlay Green, Westminster Coll., Missouri, 1982; Mizuno, Tokyo, 1982; ITT European, Brussels, 1982; Bruce Meml, Keele Univ., 1982; Gaitskell, Univ. of Nottingham, 1983; Trinity Univ., San Antonio, 1983; lect. to mark opening Michael Fowler Centre, Wellington, NZ, 1983; Bridge Meml, Guildhall, 1984; David R. Calhoun Jr Meml, Washington Univ., St Louis, 1984; Corbishley Meml, RSA, 1984; John Rogers Meml, Llandudno, 1985; George Woodcock, Univ. of Leicester, 1985; RIIA, 1985; John F. Kennedy Meml, Oxford, 1986; Edward Boyle Meml, RSA, 1988. Deroy Prof., Univ. of Michigan, 1990. Liveryman, Goldsmiths' Co., 1966; Hon. Freeman, Musicians' Co., 1973. Hon. FRCM; Hon. FRCO; Hon. Fellow, Royal Canadian Coll. of Organists. Hon. DCL: Oxon, 1971; Kent, 1985; Hon. DTech Bradford, 1971; Hon. LLD: Westminster Coll., Salt Lake City, 1975; Greenwich, 2001; Dr *hc* Univ. of Paris, Sorbonne, 1976; Hon. Dr of Public Admin, Wesleyan Coll., Macon, Ga, 1981; Hon. DL Westminster Coll., Fulton, Missouri, 1982; Hon. HLD Bellarmine Coll., Kentucky, 1994; DUniv Open, 1997. Charlemagne Prize, 1963; Estes J. Kefauver Prize 1971; Stresseman Gold Medal, 1971; Freiherr Von Stein Foundn Prize, 1972; Gold Medal of City of Paris, 1978; World Humanity Award, 1980; Gold Medal: European Parlt, 1981; Fondation du Mérite Européen, 1994; Jean Monnet Foundn, 1999. Grand

Cross: Order of Merit (Germany), 1993; Order of Liberty and Unity (Latin America), 1994; Order of the Aztec Eagle (Mexico), 1994; Grand Cordon, Order of the Rising Sun (Japan), 1998. Winner, Sydney to Hobart Ocean Race, 1969; Captain: Britain's Admiral's Cup Team, 1971, 1979; Britain's Sardinia Cup Team, 1980. *Publications:* One Nation—a Tory approach to social problems (jtly), 1950; Old World, New Horizons: Britain, Europe, and the Atlantic Alliance (Godkin Lectures), 1970; Sailing: a course of my life, 1975; Music: a joy for life, 1976, 2nd edn 1996; Travels: people and places in my life, 1977; Carols: the joy of Christmas, 1977; Music, 1997; The Course of My Life (autobiog.), 1998. *Recreations:* sailing, music. *Clubs:* Carlton, St Stephen's (Jt Pres., 1979–88), Buck's; Royal Yacht Squadron.   *Died 17 July 2005.*

HEATH, Henry Wylde Edwards, CMG 1963; QPM 1957; CPM 1953; Commissioner of Police, Hong Kong, 1959–67, retired; *b* 18 March 1912; *s* of late Dr W. G. Heath and Mrs L. B. Heath; *m* 1945, Joan Mildred Critchett; two *s* one *d. Educ:* Dean Close Sch.; HMS Conway. Probationer Sub-Inspector of Police, Leeward Islands, 1931; Asst Supt, Hong Kong, 1934; Superintendent, 1944, Asst Commissioner, 1950. *Recreations:* golf, ski-ing. *Address:* Quintynes Cottage, 4 Firle Drive, Seaford, Sussex BN25 2HT. *Clubs:* Seaford Golf; Kandahar Ski.   *Died 29 July 2002.*

HEATH, Sir Mark (Evelyn), KCVO 1980; CMG 1980; Minister, then Ambassador, to the Holy See, 1980–85; *b* 22 May 1927; *s* of late Captain John Moore Heath, RN; *m* 1954, Margaret Alice, *d* of Sir William Lawrence Bragg, CH, OBE, MC, FRS; two *s* one *d. Educ:* Marlborough; Queens' Coll., Cambridge. RNVR, 1945–48. HM Foreign (subseq. Diplomatic) Service, 1950–85: served in Indonesia, Denmark, Bulgaria, Canada;Dep. Hd, UK Delegn to OECD, 1971–74; seconded to Cabinet Office, 1974–75; Hd of W African Dept, FCO and Ambassador to Chad, 1975–78; Inspector, 1978–80. Dir of Protocol, Hong Kong Government, 1985–88. Chm., Friends of Anglican Centre, Rome, 1984–90. *Address:* St Lawrence, Lansdown Road, Bath BA1 5TD.
Died 28 Sept. 2005.

HEATH, Peter; see Heath, E. P.

HEAVENER, Rt Rev. Robert William; Bishop of Clogher, 1973–80, retired; *b* 28 Feb. 1905; *s* of Joseph and Maria Heavener; *m* 1936, Ada Marjorie, *d* of Rev. Chancellor Thomas Dagg; one *s* one *d. Educ:* Trinity Coll., Dublin (MA). Ordained, 1929; Curate, Clones; Diocesan Curate, 1930; Curate-in-charge, Lack, 1933–38; Rector: Derryvullen N, 1938–46; Monaghan, 1946–73; Rural Dean, 1946. Examining Chaplain and Canon of Clogher, 1951–62; Canon of St Patrick's Cathedral, Dublin, 1962–68; Archdeacon of Clogher, 1968–73. OCF, 1938–43; Mem. Staff of Command Welfare Officer, NI District, 1938–43. *Publications:* Co. Fermanagh, 1940 (a short topographical and historical account of NI); Diskos, 1970 (a collection of material for Adult Education); (as Robert Cielou) Spare My Tortured People, 1983 (an attempt to understand the Ulster situation today); Credo, 1993 (local history viewed in context of past and present). *Recreations:* tennis, rare book collecting. *Address:* 12 Church Avenue, Newtownabbey, Co. Antrim BT37 0PJ. *T:* (028) 9086 3242. *Club:* Friendly Brother House (Dublin).   *Died 8 March 2005.*

HECTOR, Gordon Matthews, CMG 1966; CBE 1961 (OBE 1955); Secretary to the Assembly Council, General Assembly of the Church of Scotland, 1980–85; *b* 9 June 1918; *s* of G. P. Hector, DSc, Aberdeen; *m* 1954, Mary Forrest, MB, ChB, *o d* of late Robert Gray, Fraserburgh, Aberdeenshire; one *s* two *d. Educ:* Edinburgh Academy; Lincoln Coll., Oxford. Military Service with East Africa Forces, 1940–45. Apptd Dist Officer, Kenya, 1946, Asst Sec., 1950; Sec. to Kenya Road Authority, 1951; Sec. to Govt of Seychelles, 1952, Acting Governor, 1953; Dep. Resident Comr and Govt Sec., Basutoland, 1956; Chief

Sec., Basutoland, 1964; Deputy British Government Representative, Lesotho (lately Basutoland), 1965–66. Sec., Basutoland Constitutional Commn, 1957–58. Clerk to the Univ. Court, Aberdeen, 1967–76; Dep. Sec. and Establishment Officer, Aberdeen Univ., 1976–80. Fellow of the Commonwealth Fund, 1939. Chm., Council of Victoria League in Scotland, 1983–88; Vice-Pres., St Andrew Soc., 1983–93. Chm., Great N of Scotland Rly Assoc., 1989–92. Mem., West End Community Council, 1983–89 (Chm., 1986–89). Member: Ct of Dirs, Edinburgh Acad., 1967–75; Bd of Governors, Oakbank D List Sch., 1969–90. Founding Fellow, Inst. of Contemporary Scotland. Cdre, Royal Wajir Yacht Club, 1948–49. Burgess of Guild, Aberdeen City. *Recreations:* railways ancient and modern, grandchildren. *Address:* 4 Montgomery Court, 110 Hepburn Gardens, St Andrews, Fife KY16 9LT. *Clubs:* Royal Over-Seas League; Vincent's (Oxford).   *Died 4 Oct. 2001.*

HEILBRON, Dame Rose, DBE 1974; a Judge of the High Court of Justice, Family Division, 1974–88; *b* 19 Aug. 1914; *d* of late Max and Nellie Heilbron; *m* 1945, Dr Nathaniel Burstein; one *d. Educ:* Belvedere Sch., GPDST; Liverpool Univ. (LLB 1st Class Hons, 1935; LLM 1937). Lord Justice Holker Scholar, Gray's Inn, 1936; called to Bar, Gray's Inn, 1939, Bencher, 1968, Treasurer, 1985; joined Northern Circuit, Leader, 1973–74, Presiding Judge, 1979–82; QC 1949; Recorder of Burnley, 1956–71, a Recorder, and Hon. Recorder of Burnley, 1972–74. Mem., Bar Council, 1973–74. Chm., Home Sec's Adv. Gp on Law of Rape, 1975–. Hon. Fellow: Lady Margaret Hall, Oxford, 1976; UMIST, 1986; Hon. LLD: Liverpool, 1975; Warwick, 1978; Manchester, 1980; CNAA, 1988. Formerly Hon. Col, WRAC(TA).
Died 8 Dec. 2005.

HEIM, Most Rev. Bruno Bernard, PhD, JCD; Apostolic Nuncio to the Court of St James's, 1982–85 (Apostolic Delegate, 1973–82); *b* Olten, Switzerland, 5 March 1911; *s* of Bernard and Elisabeth Heim-Studer. *Educ:* Olten, Engelberg and Schwyz; St Thomas of Aquino Univ.; Gregorian Univ.; Univ. of Fribourg; Papal Acad. of Diplomacy. Priest 1938; Vicar in Basle and Arbon, 1938–42; Chief Chaplain for Italian and Polish Internees in Switzerland, 1943–45; Sec., Papal Nunciature in Paris; Auditor at Nunciature in Vienna; Counsellor and Chargé d'affaires at Nunciature in Germany; titular Archbp of Xanthos, 1961; Apostolic Delegate to Scandinavia, 1961–69; Apost. Nuncio (Ambassador): to Finland, 1966–69; to Egypt, 1969–73; President of Caritas Egypt, 1969–73. Lauréat, French Acad.; Corresp. Mem., Real Academia de la Historia, Madrid, 1950; Mem. Council, Internat. Heraldic Acad.; Patron, Cambridge Univ. Heraldic and Genealogical Soc. Grand Cross: Order of Malta, 1950; Teutonic Order, 1961; Order of Finnish Lion, 1969; Order of St Maurice and Lazarus, 1973; (1st Class) Order of the Republic, Egypt, 1975; Bailiff Grand Cross and Grand Prior, Constantinian Order of St George; Sub-Prelate, Order of St John; Comdr, Order of Isabel la Catolica; Gr. Officer Order of Holy Sepulchre; Orders of Merit: Germany, Italy, Austria; Officier Légion d'honneur, etc. *Publications:* Die Freundschaft nach Thomas von Aquin, 1934; Wappenbrauch und Wappenrecht in der Kirche, 1947; Coutumes et droit héraldiques de l'Eglise, 1949; L'oeuvre héraldique de Paul Boesch, 1973; Heraldry in the Catholic Church, 1978, rev. and enlarged edn 1981; Kerkeleijke Heraldiek Averbode, 1980; Armorial Liber Amicorum, 1981; Or and Argent, 1994; L'araldila nella Chiesa Cattolica Vaticano, 2000; contrib. Adler, Zeitschrift f. Heraldik und Genealogie, Heraldisk Tidskrift. *Recreations:* heraldry, heraldic painting, cooking, gardening. *Address:* Zehnderweg 31, 4600 Olten, Switzerland.   *Died 18 March 2003.*

HEISKELL, Andrew; Chairman Emeritus, New York Public Library (Chairman, 1981–90; Director, since 1978); Chairman of the Board, 1960–80, and Chief Executive Officer, 1969–80, Time Inc., retired; *b* Naples, 13 Sept.

1915; *s* of Morgan Heiskell and Ann Heiskell (*née* Hubbard); *m* 1937, Cornelia Scott (marr. diss.); one *s* one *d*; *m* 1950, Madeleine Carroll (marr. diss.); *m* 1965, Marian, *d* of Arthur Hays Sulzberger, and *widow* of Orvil E. Dryfoos. *Educ:* Switzerland; France; University of Paris. Science teacher, Ecole du Montcel, Paris, 1935. Life Magazine: Science and Medicine Editor, 1937–39; Asst Gen. Manager, 1939–42; Gen. Manager, 1942–46; Publisher, 1946–60; Vice-Pres., Time, Inc., 1949–60. Overseer, Harvard Univ., 1973–79 (Pres., Bd of Overseers, 1977); Fellow, Harvard Coll., 1979–89. Chm., President's Cttee on Arts and Humanities, 1982–90; Vice-Chm., Vivian Beaumont Theater; Director: Enterprise Foundn; Bryant Park Restoration Corp.; Mem. Bd of Visitors, Graduate Sch. and University Center, City Univ. of New York; Trustee: People for the American Way; Amer. Acad. in Rome; Inst. of Internat. Educn; eponymous Andrew Heiskell Library for Blind and Physically Handicapped, opened 1991. Gold Medal Award of Merit, Wharton Sch. Alumni Soc., Univ. of Pennsylvania, 1968; John W. Gardner Leadership Award. Hon. LLD: Shaw Univ., 1968; Lake Erie Coll., 1969; Hofstra Univ., 1972; Hobart and William Smith Colls, 1973; Harvard, 1989; Hon. DLitt Lafayette Coll., 1969. *Address:* Time and Life Building, Rockefeller Center, New York, NY 10020; 870 United Nations Plaza, New York, NY 10017; Darien, CT, USA.

Died 6 July 2003.

HELEY, (Neil) Patrick; a District Judge (Magistrates' Courts) (formerly Stipendiary Magistrate), Norfolk, since 1994; *b* 25 April 1949; *s* of John William Heley and late Hilary Heley (*née* Stretton); *m* 1975, Jane Louise Holliday-Rhodes; one *s* one *d*. *Educ:* Leeds Univ. (LLB). Qualified as solicitor, 1973; Asst Solicitor, W Yorks County Prosecuting Solicitor's Office, 1974–82; Partner, Green Williamson & Way, Wakefield, 1984–93. Member: Bd of Visitors, Wakefield Prison, 1984–91; Duty Solicitor Cttee, Legal Aid Bd, 1992–94. *Recreations:* opera, music, literature, the countryside, small French restaurants. *Address:* The Magistrates' Court, Bishopsgate, Norwich NR3 1UP. *T:* (01603) 679500.   *Died 7 May 2004.*

HELLABY, Sir Alan; see Hellaby, Sir F. R. A.

HELLABY, Sir (Frederick Reed) Alan, Kt 1981; Managing Director, 1963–83, and Chairman, 1983–87, R. & W. Hellaby Ltd; Chairman, P&O New Zealand, 1986–94; Director, Bank of New Zealand, 1993–97; *b* 21 Dec. 1926; *s* of Frederick Allan Hellaby and Mavis Reed; *m* 1954, Mary Dawn Trotter; three *s* one *d*. *Educ:* King's Coll., Auckland; Auckland Univ. Joined R. & W. Hellaby Ltd, 1948: Dir, 1960–87; Dep. Chm., 1969–87. Chairman: NZ Insurance Co., 1979–81 (Dir, 1966–81); NZI Corp. (formed from merger of NZ Insurance and S British Insurance Gp), 1981–87 (Dir, 1981–89); NZ Steel Ltd, 1974–86 (Dir, 1964–86); Director: NZ Steel Develt Co. Ltd, 1981–86; Rheem NZ Ltd, 1979–88; IBM (NZ) Ltd, 1981–94; Alcan NZ Ltd, 1985–88; P&O Australia, 1986–94; NZ Guardians Trust, 1987–98; Alcan Australia Ltd, 1988–93; NZI Bank Ltd, 1989–90; Nat. Australia Bank NZ Ltd, 1991–93; former Director: NZ Steel Mining Ltd; Pacific Steel Ltd. Mem., Commn of Inquiry into Meat Industry, 1973. Chm., NZ Export Year Cttee, 1978–79. President: Auckland Chamber of Commerce, 1985–87 (Mem., 1984–95); NZ Chamber of Commerce, 1990–93 (Mem., 1987–93; Life Mem., 1993). Life Mem., King's Coll. Old Collegians' Bd, 1994 (Pres., 1962–63); Trustee, 1964–97; Chm. Bd of Governors, 1973–97; King's Coll.; Director: King's Sch.; St Cuthbert's Coll. Chm. and Trustee, NZ Police Centennial Trust, 1986; former Trustee: Massey Univ. Agricl Res. Foundn; NZ Red Cross Foundn. Hon. DSc Massey, 1982. *Recreation:* weekend farming. *Address:* 519 Remuera Road, Auckland, New Zealand. *T:* (9) 5247423, *Fax:* (9) 5244245. *Clubs:* Northern, Royal NZ Yacht Squadron (Auckland).

Died 19 May 2001.

HEMLOW, Prof. Joyce; Professor Emerita, McGill University, Montreal, Canada, since 1975; author; *b* 30 July 1906; *d* of William Hemlow and Rosalinda (*née* Redmond), Liscomb, NS. *Educ:* Queen's Univ., Kingston, Ont (MA; Hon. LLD 1967); Harvard Univ., Cambridge, Mass (AM, PhD). Preceding a univ. career, period of teaching in Nova Scotia, Canada; Lecturer in English Language and Literature at McGill Univ.; Prof. of English Language and Literature, McGill Univ., 1955, Greenshields Professor 1965. FRSC 1960. Guggenheim Fellow, 1951–52, 1960–62 and 1966. Member, Phi Beta Kappa, The Johnsonians, and of other literary and professional organizations. Hon. LLD Dalhousie, 1972. Brit. Academy Award (Crawshay Prize), 1960. *Publications:* The History of Fanny Burney, 1958 (James Tait Black Memorial Book Prize, 1958); A Catalogue of the Burney Family Correspondence, 1749–1878, 1971; (ed with others) The Journals and Letters of Fanny Burney (Madame d'Arblay), vols i-xii, 1972–84; (ed) Fanny Burney: selected letters and journals, 1986; articles in learned jls on Fanny Burney's novels and unpublished plays and on NS history. *Address:* Halifax, NS, Canada. *Club:* English-Speaking Union (Canadian Branch).

Died 3 Sept. 2001.

HEMMING, Air Commodore Idris George Selvin, CB 1968; CBE 1959 (OBE 1954); *b* 11 Dec. 1911; *s* of late George Hemming, Liverpool; *m* 1939, Phyllis, *d* of Francis Payne, Drogheda, Eire; two *s*. *Educ:* Chalford, Glos.; Wallasey, Cheshire. Joined RAF, 1928; served War of 1939–45, UK, India and Burma; Gp Capt. 1957; Air Cdre 1962; Dir of Equipment (Pol.) (RAF), MoD, 1962–66; Dir of Equipment (1) (RAF), MoD, Harrogate, 1966–68. *Recreations:* cricket, golf. *Address:* Ash House, St Chloe Green, Amberley, near Stroud, Glos GL5 5AP. *T:* (01453) 873581.   *Died 28 March 2005.*

HEMMINGS, David Leslie Edward; actor, director and producer; engaged in entertainment industry since 1949; watercolour painter; *b* 18 Nov. 1941; *m* 1st, 1960, Genista Ouvry (marr. diss. 1964); one *d*; 2nd, 1969, Gayle Hunnicutt (marr. diss. 1975); one *s*; 3rd, 1976, Prudence J. de Casembroot (marr. diss. 1997); two *s*; 4th, 2002, Lucy Williams; two *d*. *Educ:* Glyn Coll., Epsom, Surrey. Miles, in The Turn of the Screw, English Opera Group, 1954; Five Clues to Fortune, 1957; Saint Joan, 1957; The Heart Within, 1957; Men of Tomorrow, 1958; In the Wake of a Stranger, 1958; No Trees in the Street, 1959; Some People, 1962; Play it Cool, 1962; Live it Up, 1963; Two Left Feet, 1963; The System, 1964; Be my Guest, 1965; Eye of the Devil, 1966; Blow Up, 1966; Camelot, 1967; Barbarella, 1967; Only When I Larf, 1968; The Charge of the Light Brigade, 1968; The Long Day's Dying, 1968; The Best House in London, 1968; Alfred the Great, 1969; Fragment of Fear, 1970; The Walking Stick, 1970; Unman, Wittering & Zigo, 1971; The Love Machine, 1971; Voices, 1973; Don't Worry Momma, 1973; Juggernaut, 1974; Quilp, 1974; Profundo Rosso, 1975; Islands in the Stream, 1975; The Squeeze, 1976; Jeeves (musical), Her Majesty's, 1975; Power Play, 1978; Thirst, 1979; Beyond Reasonable Doubt, 1980; Jekyll and Hyde, 1980; Harlequin, 1980; The Rainbow, 1989; Gladiator, 2000; Spy Game, 2001; Last Orders, Mean Machine, Gangs of New York, 2002; League of Extraordinary Gentlemen, 2003. BBC TV, Scott Fitzgerald, 1975; ITV, The Rime of the Ancient Mariner, 1978; ITV, Charlie Muffin, 1979. Directed: Running Scared, 1972; The 14, 1973 (Silver Bear Award, Berlin Film Festival, 1973); Disappearance, 1977; Power Play, 1977; Just a Gigolo, 1978; David Bowie Stage, 1979; Murder By Decree, 1979; Survivor, 1979; Race to the Yankee Zephyr, 1980; also in Australia, NZ etc. Produced: Strange Behaviour, 1981; Turkey Shoot, 1981. Director: International Home Video FGH Pty Ltd (Melbourne); Film and General Holdings Inc. (California). *Recreation:* painting. *Clubs:* Chelsea Arts, Magic Circle.   *Died 3 Dec. 2003.*

HEMP, Prof. William Spooner, FRAeS; Stewarts and Lloyds Professor of Structural Engineering, Oxford University, 1965–83; Emeritus Fellow, Keble College, Oxford, since 1984 (Professorial Fellow, 1965–83); *b* 21 March 1916; *s* of late Rev. William James Hemp and Daisy Lilian Hemp; *m* 1938, Dilys Ruth Davies; one *s*. *Educ*: Paston Grammar Sch., North Walsham; Jesus Coll., Cambridge (Scholar, BA 1937, MA 1941). Aeronautical Engineer, Bristol Aeroplane Co., 1938–46. Coll. of Aeronautics: Sen. Lectr, 1946–50; Prof. of Aircraft Structures and Aeroelasticity, 1950–65; Head of Dept of Aircraft Design, 1951–65; Dep. Principal, 1957–65. Mem. various Aeronautical Res. Council cttees, 1948–. Vis. Prof., Stanford Univ., Calif, 1960–61. *Publications:* Optimum Structures, 1973; res. papers in the Theory of Structures, Solid Mechanics and Applied Mathematics. *Recreations:* mountain walking, music. *Address:* Duffryn House, Church Lane, Horton-cum-Studley, Oxford OX33 1AW. *Died 27 Feb. 2003.*

HENBEST, Harold Bernard; *see* Herbert, H. B.

HENDERSON, Prof. George Patrick, FRSE 1980; Professor of Philosophy in the University of Dundee (formerly Queen's College, Dundee), 1959–80, Dean, Faculty of Arts and Social Sciences, 1973–76; *b* 22 April 1915; *e s* of Rev. George Aitchison Henderson, MA, and Violet Margaret Mackenzie; *m* 1939, Hester Lowry Douglas McWilliam, BSc (*d* 1978), *d* of Rev. John Morell McWilliam, BA. *Educ:* Elgin Academy; St Andrews Univ. (Harkness Scholar; MA 1st Class Hons in Philosophy, 1936); Miller Prize and Ramsay Scholarship; Balliol Coll., Oxford (Ferguson Scholarship in Philosophy, 1936; BA 2nd Class Lit Hum, 1938; MA 1943). Asst in Logic and Metaphysics, University of St Andrews, 1938; Shaw Fellow in Mental Philosophy, University of Edinburgh, 1938. Army Service, 1940–46; Royal Artillery (commissioned 1940, Adjutant 1942–43) and Gen. Staff (GSO 3 1945); served in UK, Italy and Greece. Lecturer in Logic and Metaphysics, 1945, Sen. Lectr, 1953, University of St Andrews. Corresp. Member: Acad. of Athens, 1973; Ionian Acad., 1975. Editor of the Philosophical Quarterly, 1962–72. *Publications:* The Revival of Greek Thought 1620–1830, 1970 (trans. Greek, 1994); The Ionian Academy (trans. Greek), 1980; E. P. Papanoutsos, 1983; The Ionian Academy, 1988 (2nd edn, trans. Greek, 1994); numerous articles and reviews in learned jls. *Recreations:* modern Greek studies, gardening. *Died 12 May 2004.*

HENDERSON, John Ronald, CVO 1985; OBE 1985 (MBE 1945); Lord-Lieutenant of Berkshire, 1989–95; Chairman, Henderson Administration (Group), 1983–90; *b* 6 May 1920; *s* of Major R. H. W. Henderson and Mrs Marjorie Henderson (*née* Garrard); *m* 1st, 1949, Sarah Katherine Beckwith-Smith (*d* 1972); two *s* one *d*; 2nd, 1976, Catherine Christian; one step *s* two step *d*. *Educ:* Eton; Cambridge Univ. Served War: ADC to Field Marshal Montgomery, 1942–46; retd Major, 12th Royal Lancers, 1946. Trustee, Winston Churchill Meml Trust, 1985–. Vice Lord-Lieutenant, Berks, 1979–89. KStJ 1989. *Recreations:* racing, shooting, golf, tennis. *Address:* Bennetts Farm, West Woodhay, Newbury, Berks RG20 0BL. *T:* (01488) 668271. *Club:* White's. *Died 16 Dec. 2003.*

HENDERSON, Robert Brumwell, CBE 1979; Managing Director, 1959–83, Chairman, 1983–91, Ulster TV; *b* 28 July 1929; *s* of late Comdr Oscar Henderson, CVO, CBE, DSO, RN; *m* 1st, 1953, Joy Frances Duncan (marr. diss. 1969); two *d*; 2nd, 1970, Patricia Ann Davison. *Educ:* Brackenber House Sch., Belfast; Bradfield Coll., Berks; Trinity Coll., Dublin (BA Hons 1951, MA 1959). Journalism, London, Liverpool, Glasgow and Belfast, 1951–59. Director: ITN, 1964–68; Independent Television Publications, 1969–86; Dep. Chm., Powerscreen Internat., 1989–92; Director: Ulster Cablevision, 1985–93; Laganside Corp., 1988–92; Airtronics Internat., 1990–95, etc. Chm., Publicity Assoc. of NI, 1959–60; Vice-Pres., Co-operation North,

1979–99; President: Radio Industries Club of NI, 1963–70, 1972–80; Assoc. of Ulster Drama Fests, 1978–98; NI Chamber of Commerce and Industry, 1980–81; NI Chartered Inst. of Marketing, 1984–92; Chairman: NI Millennium Bid Cttee, 1994; Murals Make Ballynahinch Beautiful, 1995–2002. Member: Exec. Council, Cinema and Television Benevolent Fund, 1980–84; Council for Continuing Educn, 1975–85; Cttee to Review Higher Educn in NI, 1964; various cttees of TCD, Univ. of Ulster; Senate, QUB, 1980–2001; Council, Inst. of Dirs, 1973–93 (Chm., NI Br., 1973–79); Design Council (NI), 1980–92. Governor, Ulster Polytechnic, 1979–84. FRTS 1977 (Mem. Council, 1981–84, Chm., 1982–84, Vice Pres., 1986–91). Hon. DLitt Ulster, 1982; DUniv QUB, 2002. *Publications:* Midnight Oil, 1961; A Television First, 1977; Amusing, 1984; Brum: a life in television (autobiog.), 2003. *Recreations:* reading, theatre and cinema, golf. *Clubs:* Royal County Down Golf; Malone Golf. *Died 29 July 2005.*

HENLEY, Sir Douglas (Owen), KCB 1973 (CB 1970); Comptroller and Auditor General, 1976–81; *b* 5 April 1919; *m* 1942, June Muriel Ibbetson; four *d*. *Educ:* Beckenham County Sch.; London Sch. of Economics (Hon. Fellow, 1974). BSc (Econ.), 1939; Gerstenberg Studentship and Leverhulme Res. Studentship (not taken up). Served Army, 1939–46; Queen's Own Royal West Kent Regt and HQ 12th Inf. Bde (despatches twice, Italy, 1945). Treasury, 1946; Treas. rep. (Financial Counsellor) in Tokyo and Singapore, 1956–59; Asst Under-Sec. of State, DEA, 1964–69, Dep. Under-Sec. of State, 1969; Second Permanent Sec., HM Treasury, 1972–76. Mem. Council, GDST (formerly GPDST), 1982–2000 (Hon. Vice Pres., 2000–). Hon. LLD Bath, 1981. *Address:* Walwood House, Park Road, Banstead, Surrey SM7 3ER. *T:* (01737) 352626. *Died 1 Oct. 2003.*

HENNESSY, Christopher; journalist; Chairman, Associated Catholic Newspapers (1912) Ltd, 1970–79; Editor, 1954–72, Trustee, 1979–87, The Universe; *b* 29 Dec. 1909; *e s* of Daniel and Anne Hennessy; *m* 1942, Kathleen Margaret Cadley, Liverpool. *Educ:* St Edward's Coll., Liverpool. Served War of 1939–45 as Commissioned Officer in British and Indian Armies; commanded a Territorial Army Unit in the North-West, 1950–55. KCSG 1975. *Recreation:* travel. *Address:* Flat 49, The Metropole, The Leas, Folkestone, Kent CT20 2LU. *Died 5 Sept. 2004.*

HENNIKER, 8th Baron *cr* 1800; **John Patrick Edward Chandos Henniker-Major,** KCMG 1965 (CMG 1956); CVO 1960; MC 1945; Bt 1765; Baron Hartismere (UK) 1866; DL; Director, Wates Foundation, 1972–78; *b* 19 Feb. 1916; *s* of 7th Baron Henniker, and Molly (*d* 1953), *d* of Sir Robert Burnet, KCVO; *S* father, 1980; *m* 1st, 1946, Margaret Osla Benning (*d* 1974); two *s* one *d*; 2nd, 1976, Julia Marshall Poland (*née* Mason). *Educ:* Stowe; Trinity Coll., Cambridge. HM Foreign Service, 1938; served 1940–45, Army (Major, The Rifle Brigade). HM Embassy Belgrade, 1945–46; Asst Private Secretary to Secretary of State for Foreign Affairs, 1946–48; Foreign Office, 1948–50; HM Embassy, Buenos Aires, 1950–52; Foreign Office, 1952–60 (Counsellor and Head of Personnel Dept, 1953); HM Ambassador to Jordan, 1960–62; to Denmark, 1962–66; Civil Service Commission, 1966–67; Asst Under-Secretary of State, FO, 1967–68. Dir-Gen., British Council, 1968–72. Lay Mem., Mental Health Review Tribunal (Broadmoor), 1975–81; Member: Parole Bd, 1979–83; Council, Univ. of E Anglia, Norwich, 1979–86; Council, Toynbee Hall, 1978–90, Dep. Chm., 1982–86; Chm., Intermediate Treatment Fund, Rainer Foundn, 1985–90. Chairman: Suffolk Community Alcohol Services, 1983–93; Suffolk Rural Housing Assoc., 1984–; Pres., Suffolk Agricl Assoc., 1989. Trustee: City Parochial Foundn, 1973–90; London Festival Ballet, 1975–85. Governor: Cripplegate Foundn, 1979–90; Stowe Sch., 1982–90. Hon. (Lay) Canon of St

Edmundsbury Cathedral, 1986–92. DL Suffolk, 1988. Hon. DCL UEA, 1989; Hon. LLD New England Coll., NH, 1993. *Publication:* Painful Extractions (memoir), 2002. *Recreations:* gardening, ornithology. *Heir: s* Hon. Mark Ian Philip Chandos Henniker-Major [*b* 29 Sept. 1947; *m* 1973, Lesley Antoinette Masterton-Smith (marr. diss. 1995); two *s* three *d*; *m* 1996, Bente Toft]. *Address:* Red House, Thornham Magna, Eye, Suffolk IP23 8HH. *Club:* Special Forces.   *Died 29 April 2004.*

HENRY, David; Senior Director, Postal Services, 1978–82; *b* 19 April 1925; *s* of Thomas Glanffrwd Henry and Hylda Frances Henry. *Educ:* Midhurst Grammar Sch.; St John's Coll., Cambridge (BA Hons 1948, MA 1953). Asst Postal Controller, 1950; Head Postmaster, Norwich, 1961; Postal Controller, 1966; Controller Operations, 1968; Dir, Midlands Postal Region, 1969; Chm., Midlands Postal Board, 1974; Dir, London Postal Region, 1977. Freeman, City of London, 1978. JP Birmingham, 1972–77. *Recreations:* Rugby football, cricket.
          Died 6 Nov. 2002.

HENSLEY, John; Under Secretary, Ministry of Agriculture, Fisheries and Food, 1957–70; *b* 28 Feb. 1910; *s* of late Edward Hutton and Marion Hensley; *m* 1st, 1940, Dorothy Betty (*d* 1969), *d* of Percy George and Dorothy Coppard; one *s*; 2nd, 1971, Elizabeth, *widow* of Charles Cross and *d* of Harold and Jessie Coppard. *Educ:* Malvern; Trinity Coll., Cambridge (Chancellor's Classical Medal, BA 1931, MA 1935). Entered Min. of Agriculture and Fisheries, 1933; Priv. Sec. to Chancellor of Duchy of Lancaster and Minister of Food, 1939; Priv. Sec. to Minister of Agriculture and Fisheries, 1945; Asst Sec., 1946–57. Member: ARC, 1957–59; Council, Nat. Inst. of Agricultural Botany, 1970–73; Sec., Cttee of Inquiry into Veterinary Profession, 1971–75. *Recreations:* theatre, opera, genealogy. *Address:* 109 Markfield, Courtwood Lane, Croydon CR0 9HP. *T:* (020) 8657 6319.
          Died 15 Dec. 2002.

HEPBURN, Katharine; actress; *b* 12 May 1907; *d* of late Dr Thomas N. Hepburn and Katharine Houghton; *m* 1928, Ludlow Ogden Smith (marr. diss. 1934). *Educ:* Hartford; Bryn Mawr College. *Stage:* First professional appearance on stage, Baltimore, 1928, in Czarina; first New York appearance, 1928, in Night Hostess (under name Katharine Burns); The Warrior's Husband, 1932; The Philadelphia Story, 1939; Without Love, 1942; As You Like It, 1950; The Millionairess, New Theatre, London, 1952; Taming of the Shrew; Merchant of Venice; Measure for Measure, Australia, 1955; Coco, 1970; A Matter of Gravity, NY, 1976, tour, 1977; The West Side Waltz, NY, 1981. *Film:* Entered films, 1932; notable films: A Bill of Divorcement, 1932; Morning Glory, 1933 (Acad. Award); Little Women, 1933; The Little Minister, 1934; Alice Adams, 1935; Mary of Scotland, 1936; Quality Street, 1937; Stage Door, 1937; Bringing Up Baby, 1938; The Philadelphia Story, 1940; Woman of the Year, 1942; Keeper of the Flame, 1942; Dragon Seed, 1944; Without Love, 1945; Undercurrent, 1946; The Sea of Grass, 1947; Song of Love, 1947; State of the Union, 1948; Adam's Rib, 1949; The African Queen, 1951; Pat and Mike, 1952; Summer Madness, 1955; The Rainmaker, 1956; The Iron Petticoat, 1956; His Other Woman, 1957; Suddenly, Last Summer, 1959; Long Day's Journey into Night, 1962; Guess Who's Coming to Dinner, 1967 (Acad. Award); The Lion in Winter, 1968 (Acad. Award); The Madwoman of Chaillot, 1969; The Trojan Women, 1972; A Delicate Balance, 1973; Rooster Cogburn, 1975; On Golden Pond, 1981(Acad. Award). *Publications:* The Making of The African Queen, 1987; Me: stories of my life, 1991.   *Died 29 June 2003.*

HEPPEL, Peter John Merrick; QC 1992; **His Honour Judge Heppel;** a Circuit Judge, since 1998; *b* 31 March 1948; *s* of late John Edward Thomas and Ida Florence Heppel, Romford, Essex; *m* 1980, Janice Coulton (marr. diss. 1995); two *s* two *d*. *Educ:* Royal Liberty Sch., Romford; Univ. of Hull (LLB Hons); University Coll.

London (LLM). Called to the Bar, Middle Temple, 1970 (Harmsworth Scholar); in practice, NE Circuit, 1972–98; a Recorder, 1988–98; authorised to sit as High Court Judge. Designated Civil Judge: Hull Combined Court Centre, 2000–; Grimsby Combined Court Centre, 2000–; Magistrates' Liaison Judge, Hull Combined Court Centre, 1999–2001. Course Tutor, Judicial Studies Bd, 2003–. Fellow, Soc. for Advanced Legal Studies. Mem. Court, Univ. of Hull. *Recreations:* music, cricket, flat mountain biking. *Address:* Warriston, Parkfield Avenue, North Ferriby, East Yorks HU14 3AL; Hull Combined Court Centre, Lowgate, Hull HU1 2EZ. *T:* (01482) 586161. *Club:* Sloane.   *Died 13 March 2004.*

HERBERT, Prof. Harold Bernard; consultant, holistic learning; *b* 10 March 1924; *s* of late A. Bernard Henbest and Edith Winifred Henbest (*née* Herbert); *m* 1948, Rosalind Eve Skone James; two *s* one *d*. *Educ:* Barking Abbey Sch.; Imperial Coll. of Science, London. Beit Research Fellow, 1947–48; Lectr, University of Manchester, 1948–56; Research Fellow, Harvard Univ., 1953–54; Vis. Prof., UCLA, 1954; Reader, KCL, 1956–57; Prof of Organic Chemistry, QUB, 1958–73. Founder, The Learning Soc., 1988. *Publications:* Organic Chemistry (with M. F. Grundon), 1968; contribs to Jl of Chemical Soc. *Address:* 5 Witley Court, Coram Street, WC1N 1HD. *T:* (020) 7278 0888.
          Died 16 Feb. 2004.

HERBERT, Jocelyn, RDI 1971; designer; *b* 22 Feb. 1917; *d* of Sir Alan Patrick Herbert, CH, and Gwendolen (*née* Quilter); *m* 1937, Anthony Lousada (marr. diss. 1960); one *s* three *d*. *Educ:* St Paul's Girls' Sch.; Paris and Vienna; London Theatre Studio; Slade School of Art. Started painting at André L'Hote's Sch., Paris, 1932–33; studied drawing and painting with Leon Underwood, 1934; trained as theatre designer with Michel St Denis and George Devine, London Th. Studio, 1936–37; joined staff of English Stage Co., Royal Court Th., 1956; became freelance designer, 1958, centred largely on Royal Court. Hon. ARCA 1964; Hon. FRA, 1991. *Plays designed*, 1957–: *Royal Court Theatre:* Ionesco: The Chairs, The Lesson, Exit the King; W. B. Yeats: Purgatory; Ann Jellico: Sport of My Mad Mother; Samuel Beckett: Krapp's Last Tape, Happy Days, Not I, Footfalls, That Time; Arnold Wesker: Roots, The Kitchen, I'm Talking about Jerusalem, Chips with Everything; Arden: Serjeant Musgrave's Dance; Christopher Logue: Trials by Logue, Antigone, The Trial of Cob and Leach; Middleton: The Changeling; Shakespeare: Midsummer Night's Dream, Julius Caesar; John Osborne: Luther, A Patriot for Me, Inadmissible Evidence; Barry Reckford: Skyvers; W. Solvonka: The Lion and the Jewel; O'Neil and Seabrook: Life Price; Donald Howarth: Three Months Gone; David Storey: Home, The Changing Room, Cromwell, Life Class; Christopher Hampton: Savages, The Portage to San Cristobal of A. H.; Joe Orton: What the Butler Saw; David Hare: Teeth 'n' Smiles; Mustapha Matura: Rum and Coca Cola; *RSC:* Richard III; Ibsen's Ghosts; *Phoenix:* Brecht's Baal; Ronald Harwood's J. J. Fahr; *National Theatre:* Othello; Brecht's Mother Courage and Life of Galileo; A Woman Killed with Kindness; Adrian Mitchell's Tyger; Aeschylus' The Oresteia; Tony Harrison: The Trackers of Oxyrhynchus; Square Rounds; David Storey: Early Days; The March on Russia; Stages; *Queen's:* The Seagull; Brecht's Joan of the Stockyard; *Round House:* Hamlet; *Albery:* Pygmalion; *Aldwych:* Saratoga; (New York) Wesker's The Merchant; *Haymarket:* Heartbreak House; *Lyric, Hammersmith:* The Devil and the Good Lord; *Lyric, Shaftesbury Ave:* Gigi; *Haymarket, Leicester:* Timon of Athens; Julius Caesar; Sophocles' Creon; also Tony Harrison: The Kaisers of Carnuntum, Austria, 1995; The Labourers of Herakles, Delphi, 1995. *Opera*, 1967, and 1975–: Sadler's Wells: Gluck's Orpheus and Euridice; Paris Opera: Verdi's The Force of Destiny, 1975; Metropolitan, NY: Alban Berg's Lulu, 1977; Mozart's The Abduction, 1979; Brecht and Weil's Rise and Fall of the City of Mahagonny, 1979; Coliseum: Birtwistle's The Mask of

Orpheus, 1986. *Films:* Tony Richardson: (colour cons. and costumes) Tom Jones, 1961, (prodn designer) Hamlet, 1969, Ned Kelly, 1970, Hotel New Hampshire, 1983; Karel Reisz: (prodn designer) Isadora, 1968; Lindsay Anderson: (prodn designer) If . . . , 1969, O Lucky Man!, 1972; Whales of August, 1987; Tony Harrison: (prodn designer) Prometheus, 1999. Retrospective exhibn of theatre work, Royal Nat. Theatre, 1993. *Relevant publication:* Jocelyn Herbert: a theatre workbook, ed Cathy Courtney, 1993. *Recreations:* the country, painting. *Address:* 45 Pottery Lane, W11 4LY. *T:* (020) 7727 1104.
Died 6 May 2003.

HEREFORD, 18th Viscount *cr* 1550; **Robert Milo Leicester Devereux;** Bt 1611; Premier Viscount of England; *b* 4 Nov. 1932; *o s* of Hon. Robert Godfrey de Bohun Devereux (*d* 1934) and Audrey Maureen Leslie, DStJ 1963 (*d* 1978) (she *m* 2nd 1961, 7th Earl of Lisburne, who *d* 1965); *y d* of late James Meakin, Westwood Manor, Staffs and of late Countess Sondes; *S* grandfather, 1952; *m* 1969, Susan Mary (marr. diss. 1982), *o c* of Major Maurice Godley, Ide Hill, Sevenoaks, Kent, and of Mrs Glen Godley, Ascott, Shipston-on-Stour, Warwicks; two *s*. *Educ:* Eton. Served Royal Horse Guards (The Blues), 1960–63. Member: Royal Philharmonic Soc.; Royal Philharmonic Orchestra Assoc. OStJ. *Heir:* s Hon. Charles Robin de Bohun Devereux, *b* 11 Aug. 1975.
Died 25 Feb. 2004.

HERN, Major William Richard, (Dick), CVO 1980; CBE 1998; racehorse trainer; *b* Holford, Somerset, 20 Jan. 1921; *m* 1956, Sheilah Joan Davis (*d* 1998). Served War of 1939–45, North Irish Horse. Asst Trainer to Major M. B. Pope, MC, 1952–57; licence to train under Jockey Club rules, 1957–97; leading trainer on the flat, 1962, 1972, 1980, 1983. Races won include: Derby, 1979, 1980, 1989 (Troy, Henbit, Nashwan); 2,000 Guineas, 1971, 1989 (Brigadier Gerard, Nashwan); 1,000 Guineas, 1974, 1995 (Highclere, Harayir); St Leger, 1962, 1965, 1974, 1977, 1981, 1983 (Hethersett, Provoke, Bustino, Dunfermline, Cut Above, Sun Princess); Epsom Oaks, 1977, 1980, 1983 (Dunfermline, Bireme, Sun Princess); King George VI and Queen Elizabeth Diamond Stakes, 1972, 1979, 1980, 1985, 1989 (Brigadier Gerard, Troy, Ela-Mana-Mou, Petoski, Nashwan); Champion Stakes, 1971, 1972 (Brigadier Gerard); Eclipse Stakes, 1972, 1980, 1989, 1990 (Brigadier Gerard, Ela-Mana-Mou, Nashwan, Elmaamul); Coronation Cup, 1974, 1975 (Buoy, Bustino). *Address:* The Old Rectory, West Ilsley, Newbury, Berks RG20 7AR. *T:* (01635) 281251. *Died 22 May 2002.*

HERRON, Very Rev. Andrew; Clerk to the Presbytery of Glasgow, 1959–81; Editor, Church of Scotland Year Book, 1961–92; *b* 29 Sept. 1909; *s* of John Todd Herron and Mary Skinner Hunter; *m* 1935, Joanna Fraser Neill; four *d* (one *s* decd). *Educ:* Glasgow Univ. (MA, BD, LLB). ATCL 1930. Minister: at Linwood, 1936–40, at Houston and Killellan, 1940–59; Clerk to the Presbytery of Paisley, 1953–59; Moderator of General Assembly of Church of Scotland, 1971–72. Convener: Dept of Publicity and Publications, 1959–68; Gen. Admin Cttee; Business Cttee; Gen. Assembly, 1972–76, 1978; Gen. Trustee, Church of Scotland. Barclay Trust Lectr, 1989. Hon. DD: St Andrews, 1975; Glasgow, 1989; Hon. LLD Strathclyde, 1983. *Publications:* Record Apart, 1974; Guide to the General Assembly of the Church of Scotland, 1976; Guide to Congregational Affairs, 1978; Guide to Presbytery, 1983; Kirk by Divine Right (Baird lectures), 1985; A Guide to the Ministry, 1987; A Guide to Ministerial Income, 1987; Minority Report, 1990; Houston and Killellan: a handful of yesterdays, 1993; The Law and Practice of the Kirk: a guide and commentary, 1995; Inter Alia, 1995; Kirk Lore, 1999; Laughing Matters, 2000.
Died 27 Feb. 2003.

HERSHMAN, David Allan; QC 2002; a Recorder, since 2001; a Deputy High Court Judge, since 2003; *b* 6 Nov. 1958; *s* of Maurice Hershman, FRCS, and Patricia Hershman; *m* 1986, Abigail Goucher; four *d*. *Educ:* King's Sch., Worcester; King's Coll., London (LLB (Hons)). Called to the Bar, Gray's Inn, 1981. Chm., Care Standards (formerly Registered Homes) Tribunal, 1996–. Hon. Legal Advr to Acorns Children's Hospice, 1998–. *Publications:* (jtly) Children: law and practice, 1991; Child Protection: training and resources pack, 1991; (contrib.) The Family Court Practice, annually 1992–2002; The Family Law Directory, 1993; contrib. numerous articles to Family Law and other pubns. *Recreations:* tennis, travel. *Address:* 1 King's Bench Walk, Temple, EC4Y 7BD. *T:* (020) 7936 1500. *Died 4 Sept. 2004.*

HESLOP, Philip Linnell; QC 1985; *b* 24 April 1948; *s* of late Richard Norman Heslop and of Ina Winifred Heslop, Merstham, Surrey. *Educ:* Haileybury; Christ's Coll., Cambridge (schol.; BA Hons (Law Tripos) 1970; LLM 1971). Called to the Bar, Lincoln's Inn, 1970, Bencher, 1993; Jt Jun. Counsel (Chancery), DTI, 1979–85. Called to Bars of Hong Kong, Bermuda and Gibraltar for specific cases. Dep. Chm., Membership Tribunal, IMRO, 1988–; DTI Inspector, Consolidated Goldfields PLC. Chm., CU Cons. Assoc., 1969; Pres., Cambridge Union Soc., 1971; Chm., Coningsby Club, 1976; contested (C) Lambeth Vauxhall, 1979. *Publication:* (ed jtly) Crew on Meetings, 1975. *Recreations:* travel, sailing, ski-ing, history. *Address:* 4 Stone Buildings, Lincoln's Inn, WC2A 3XT. *T:* (020) 7242 5524. *Died 11 July 2003.*

HETHERINGTON, Sir Arthur (Ford), Kt 1974; DSC 1944; FREng; Chairman, British Gas Corporation, 1973–76 (Member 1961, Deputy Chairman 1967–72, Chairman 1972, Gas Council); *b* 12 July 1911; *s* of Sir Roger Hetherington CB, OBE and Honoria, *d* of Arthur Ranken Ford; *m* 1937, Margaret Lacey; one *s* one *d*. *Educ:* Highgate Sch.; Trinity Coll., Cambridge (BA). Joined staff of Gas Light & Coke Company, 1935. Served War, RNVR, 1941–45. North Thames Gas Board, 1945–55; joined staff of Southern Gas Board, 1955, Deputy Chairman, 1956, Chairman 1961–64; Chairman, E Midlands Gas Board, 1964–66. FREng (FEng 1976). Hon. FIGasE. Hon. DSc London, 1974. *Address:* 32 Connaught Square, W2 2HL. *T:* (020) 7723 3128. *Club:* Athenæum. *Died 16 Feb. 2002.*

HEWETT, Sir Peter (John Smithson), 6th Bt *cr* 1813, of Nether Seale, Leicestershire; MM 1956; a Judge of the High Court, Kenya, since 2000; *b* 27 June 1931; *s* of Sir John George Hewett, 5th Bt, MC and Yuilleen Maude (*d* 1980), *d* of late Samuel Frederick Smithson; *S* father, 1990; *m* 1958, Jennifer Ann Cooper, *o c* of late Emrys Thomas Jones, OBE; two *s* one *d*. *Educ:* Bradfield Coll.; Jesus Coll., Cambridge (BA). Called to the Bar, Gray's Inn, 1954; Advocate in Kenya. *Heir:* s Richard Mark John Hewett, *b* 15 Nov. 1958. *Address:* PO Box 15231, Nairobi, Kenya. *Died 1 June 2001.*

HEWISON, William Coltman; freelance illustrator, caricaturist and writer, since 1950; *b* 15 May 1925; *s* of Ralph Hewison and Mary Hewison; *m* 1950, Elsie Hammond; one *s* one *d*. *Educ:* S Shields High Sch.; S Shields Art Sch. (Bd of Educn Drawing Cert.); Regent St Poly. Art Sch. (Nat. Dip. in Painting); London Univ. (Art Teachers' Dip.). Enlisted in RAC, 1943; Gunner/Wireless Operator in 1st RTR, Normandy to Holland, 1944; casualty, Nov. 1944, evacuated to UK hosp.; GHQ Egypt, 1945–47. Part-time art teacher, 1950–57; Punch: contributor, 1950–92; Dep. Art Editor, 1957–60; Art Editor, 1960–84; Art Critic, 1984–87; contributor, The Times, 1992–2002. Drawings in collections: V&A Mus., 1976; British Museum, 1991; Karikatur & Cartoon Mus., Basel, 1994; Graphic Arts Collection, Princeton Univ., 1997. *Publications:* Types Behind the Print, 1963; Mindfire (novel), 1973; The Cartoon Connection, 1977; (with Ross Thomson) How to Draw & Sell Cartoons, 1985; ed and introduced twenty-two Punch cartoon collections, 1979–90. *Recreations:* open air drawing. *Address:* 5 Southdown Drive, Wimbledon, SW20 8EZ.
Died 7 April 2002.

HEWITT, Eric John, PhD, DSc; FRS 1982; Head of Biochemistry Group in Plant Sciences Division, Long Ashton Research Station, and Reader in Plant Physiology, University of Bristol, 1967–84; *b* London, 27 Feb. 1919; *s* of Harry Edward Hewitt, OBE, MD, DPH, and Blanche (*née* Du Roveray); *m* 1943, Hannah Eluned (*née* Williams); one *s*. *Educ:* Whitgift Sch., S Croydon; King's Coll., Univ. of London (BSc 1st Cl., AKC; DipEd); PhD, DSc Bristol. FIBiol. Asst Chemist/Chemist, MoS, 1940–42; Long Ashton Research Station: ARC Res. Grant Research Asst, 1942–45; Sen. Plant Physiologist, 1945–84; seconded to ARC Unit of Plant Nutrition (Micronutrients), 1952–59; SPSO (merit promotion), 1967. *Publications:* Sand and Water Culture Methods Used in the Study of Plant Nutrition, 1952, 2nd edn 1966; (with T. A. Smith) Plant Mineral Nutrition, 1975; (ed with C. V. Cutting): symposia, Nitrogen Metabolism in Plants, 1968; Nitrogen Assimilation of Plants, 1979; approx. 150 research contribs to jls. *Recreations:* gardening, reading, news, records. *Address:* Langdales, 63 Ridgeway Road, Long Ashton, Bristol BS41 9EZ. *T:* (01275) 392274.

Died 31 Dec. 2001.

HEYERDAHL, Thor; author and anthropologist, since 1938; *b* Larvik, Norway 6 Oct. 1914; *s* of Thor Heyerdahl and Alison Heyerdahl (*née* Lyng); *m* 1st, 1936, Liv Coucheron Torp (*d* 1969); two *s*; 2nd, 1949, Yvonne Dedekam-Simonsen; three *d*; 3rd, 1995, Jacqueline Beer. *Educ:* University of Oslo. Researches: in the Marquesas Islands (Pacific), 1937–38; among Coast Indians of Brit. Columbia, 1939–40. Active service Free Norwegian Army-Air Force parachute unit, 1942–45. Organised and led Kon-Tiki expedition, 1947; continued research in USA and Europe, with authorship, 1948–; organised and led Norwegian Archæological Expedition to the Galapagos Islands, 1952; experiments revealing tacking principles of balsa raft in Ecuador, 1953; field research, Bolivia, Peru, Colombia, 1954; organised and led Norwegian Archæological Expedition to Easter Island and the East Pacific, 1955–56; continued research, 1957–59; made crossing from Safi, Morocco, to W Indies in papyrus boat, Ra II, 1970; sailed from Qurna, Iraq, to Djibouti in reed boat, Tigris, 1977–78; organised and led two archaeol expedns to Maldive Islands, 1983–84; leader, organiser jt Norwegian/Chilean archaeol expedn, Easter Island, 1986–88; organiser Kon-Tiki Mus.—Museo Brüning archaeol project, Tucume, Peru, 1988–92; organiser, archaeol project, Tenerife, Canary Is, 1991–; orgainser and leader, archaeol project, Asov, Russia, 1991. Participation in: Internat. Congress of Americanists, 1952–; Pacific Science Congresses, 1961–, all with lectures subseq. publ. in Proc. Congress. Vice-President: World Assoc. of World Federalists, 1966–; Foundn for Exploration and Research on Cultural Origins, 1990–; Trustee, Internat. Bd, World Wildlife Fund, 1977–; Internat. Patron, United World Colls, 1980. Mem., Royal Norwegian Acad. of Science, 1958; Fellow: New York Acad. of Sciences, 1960; Amer. Anthropological Assoc., 1966. Hon. Prof., Inst. Politecnico Nacional, Mexico, 1972. Hon. Dir, Explorers' Club, NY, 1982. Hon. Member Geographical Society: Peru, 1953; Norway, 1953; Brazil, 1954; USSR, 1964. Hon. Doctor: Oslo, 1961; USSR Acad. of Scis, 1980; Lima, 1990; Havana, 1992; Maine, 1998; Hartford, 1998; Latvian Acad. of Scis, 1998. Retzius Medal, Swedish Soc. for Anthropology and Geography, 1950; Mungo Park Medal, Royal Scottish Geographical Society, 1951; Prix Bonaparte-Wyse from Société de Géographie, Paris, 1951; Elish Kent Kane Gold Medal, Geog. Soc. of Philadelphia, 1952; Vega Medal, Swedish Soc. of Anthropology and Geography, 1962; Lomonosov Medal, Moscow Univ., 1962; Royal Gold Medal, RGS, London, 1964; Gold Medal, City of Lima; Internat. Pahlavi Envmt Prize, UN, 1978; Bradford Washburn Award, Boston Mus. of Science, USA, 1982; Internat. Prize, Spanish Geog. Soc., 1998. Officer of El Orden por Méritos Distinguidos, Peru, 1953; Gr.-Officer, Order Al Merito della Repubblica Italiana, Italy, 1965; Comdr, Knights of Malta, 1970; Comdr with Star, Order of St Olav, Norway, 1970; Order of Merit, Egypt, 1971; Grand Officer, Royal Alaouites Order, Morocco, 1971; Hon. Citizen, Larvik, Norway, 1971; Kiril i Metodi Order, Bulgaria, 1972; Order of Golden Ark, Netherlands, 1980. *Films:* The Kon-Tiki Expedition (Oscar award for camera achievement, Nat. Acad. Motion Picture Arts and Scis, 1951); Galapagos Expedition; Aku-Aku, The Secret of Easter Island; The Ra Expeditions; The Tigris Expedition; The Maldive Mystery. *Publications:* Paa Jakt efter Paradiset, 1938; The Kon-Tiki Expedition, 1948; American Indians in the Pacific: the theory behind the Kon-Tiki expedition, 1952; (with A. Skjolsvold) Archæological Evidence of Pre-Spanish Visits to the Galapagos Islands, 1956; Aku-Aku: the secrets of Easter Island, 1957; (ed with E. N. Ferdon, Jr) Reports of the Norwegian Achæological Expedition to Easter Island and the East Pacific, Vol. I: The Archæology of Easter Island, 1961, vol. II: Miscellaneous Papers, 1965; Navel of the World (Chapter XIV) in Vanished Civilizations, 1963; Indianer und Alt-Asiaten im Pazifik: Das Abenteuer einer Theorie, 1965 (Vienna); Sea Routes to Polynesia, 1968; The Ra Expeditions, 1970; Chapters in Quest for America, 1971; Fatu-Hiva Back to Nature, 1974; Art of Easter Island, 1975; Zwischen den Kontinenten, 1975; Early Man and the Ocean, 1978; The Tigris Expedition, 1980; The Maldive Mystery, 1986; Easter Island: the mystery solved, 1989; (jtly) Pyramids of Tucume, 1995; Green was the Earth on the Seventh Day, 1996; I Adams Fotspor (autobiog), 1998; (jtly) The Hunt for Odin, 2001; contrib. National Geographical Magazine, Royal Geographical Journal, The Geographical Magazine, Archiv für Völkerkunde, Ymer, Swedish Geogr. Year-book, South-western Journal of Anthropology, Russian Academy of Sciences Yearbook, American Antiquity, Antiquity (Cambridge); works trans. into numerous languages; *relevant publications:* Senor Kon-Tiki, by Arnold Jacoby, 1965; The Kon-Tiki Man, by Christopher Ralling, 1990; Thor Heyerdahl the Explorer, by Snorre Evensberget, 1994. *Recreations:* outdoor life, travelling. *Address:* Kon-Tiki Museum, Bygdøynesveien 36, 0286 Oslo, Norway. *Died 18 April 2002.*

HEYMANN, Prof. Franz Ferdinand, PhD; CPhys, FInstP; Quain Professor of Physics, and Head of Department of Physics and Astronomy, University College, University of London, 1975–87, then Professor Emeritus; *b* 17 Aug. 1924; *s* of Paul Gerhard Heymann and Magdalena Petronella Heymann; *m* 1950, Marie Powell. *Educ:* Univ. of Cape Town (BScEng with Distinction, 1944); Univ. of London (PhD 1953). FInstP 1966. Engr, Cape Town, 1944–45; Jun. Lectr in Engrg, Univ. of Cape Town, 1945–47; Special Trainee, Metropolitan Vickers, Manchester, 1947–50; University College London: Asst Lectr in Physics, 1950–52; Lectr, 1952–60; Reader, 1960–66; Prof. of Physics, 1966–75; Fellow, 1987. *Publications:* scientific papers on res. done mainly in fields of particle accelerators and elementary particle physics. *Recreations:* music, philately, gardening. *Address:* Sunnybank, Gayle, Hawes, N Yorks DL8 3RS.

Died 28 March 2005.

HEYTESBURY, 6th Baron *cr* 1828; **Francis William Holmes à Court;** Bt 1795; *b* 8 Nov. 1931; *s* of 5th Baron Heytesbury and Beryl (*d* 1968), *y d* of late A. E. B. Crawford, LLD, DCL, Aston Clinton House, Bucks; *S* father, 1971; *m* 1962, Alison, *e d* of Michael Graham Balfour, CBE; one *s* one *d*. *Educ:* Bryanston; Pembroke College, Cambridge (BA 1954). *Heir:* *s* Hon. James William Holmes à Court [*b* 30 July 1967; *m* 1995, Polly Jane, *d* of A. G. Kendrick]. *Died 5 Oct. 2004.*

HEYWARD, Rt Rev. Oliver Spencer; Bishop of Bendigo, 1975–91; Assistant to Primate of Anglican Church of Australia, 1991–95; *b* Launceston, Tasmania, 16 March 1926; *s* of Harold and Vera Heyward; *m* 1952, Peggy Butcher; four *s*. *Educ:* Church Grammar Sch., Launceston; Univ. of Tasmania (BA Hons 1949); Oriel Coll., Univ. of Oxford (BA 1953, MA 1956); Cuddesdon Coll., Oxford. RAAF, 1944–46. Rhodes Scholar, 1949.

Deacon 1953, priest 1954, dio. Chichester; Asst Curate, St Peter's, Brighton, 1953–56; Rector of Sorell, Tasmania, 1956–60; Rector of Richmond, Tasmania, 1960–62; Precentor, St David's Cathedral, Hobart, 1962–63; Warden, Christ Coll., Univ. of Tasmania, 1963–74. Chm., Brotherhood of St Laurence, 1993–96. Pres., Bendigo Coll. of Advanced Educn, 1976–86; Comr, Victorian Post-Secondary Educn Commn, 1982–93. *Recreation:* gardening. *Address:* 7 Waltham Street, Richmond, Vic 3121, Australia. *Died 15 Dec. 2003.*

HEYWOOD, David George, CBE 1999; Chairman, Nestor Healthcare Group plc, 1994–2001; *b* 21 Aug. 1935; *s* of Samuel George Heywood and Hilda Kathleen Heywood (*née* Lamey); *m* 1960, Pamela Moore Chamings; two *s* one *d*. *Educ:* Kingswood Sch., Bath; Magdalene Coll., Cambridge (BA). ACCA 1964. With British American Tobacco Co. plc, 1960–91 (Dep. Chm., 1988–91); Chairman: Q. S. Hldgs plc, 1993–99; Remploy Ltd, 1994–2000. Non-exec. Dir, Rentokil Initial plc, 1991–98. *Recreations:* golf, foreign travel. *Address:* Logie, Cedar Road, Woking, Surrey GU22 0JH. *T:* (01483) 773188. *Clubs:* Worplesdon Golf (Woking); Royal North Devon Golf (Westward Ho!). *Died 8 Nov. 2004.*

HIBBERT, Sir Jack, KCB 1990; Director, Central Statistical Office, and Head of Government Statistical Service, 1985–92; *b* 14 Feb. 1932; *s* of late William Collier Hibbert and Ivy Annie (*née* Wigglesworth); *m* 1957, Joan Clarkson; two *s* one *d*. *Educ:* Leeds Grammar Sch.; London Sch. of Economics (BScEcon). Served RAF, 1950–52. Exchequer and Audit Dept, 1952–60; Central Statistical Office, 1960–65; LSE, 1965–66; CSO, 1966; Chief Statistician, 1970; Asst Dir, 1977; Under Sec., DTI, 1982–85. OECD and EUROSTAT Consultant, 1981 and 1993. *Publications:* Measuring the Effects of Inflation on Income, Saving and Wealth (OECD), 1983; articles in economic and statistical pubns. *Recreations:* golf, bridge. *Club:* Reform. *Died 23 Aug. 2005.*

HIBBERT, Sir Reginald (Alfred), GCMG 1982 (KCMG 1979; CMG 1966); HM Diplomatic Service, retired; *b* 21 Feb. 1922; *s* of late Alfred Hibbert, MBE, Sawbridgeworth, Herts; *m* 1949, Ann Alun Pugh, *d* of late Sir Alun Pugh; two *s* one *d*. *Educ:* Queen Elizabeth's Sch., Barnet; Worcester Coll., Oxford (Hon. Fellow, 1991). Served with SOE and 4th Hussars in Albania and Italy, 1943–45. Entered Foreign Service, 1946; served in Bucharest, Vienna, Guatemala, Ankara, Brussels; Chargé d'Affaires, Ulan Bator, 1964–66; Res. Fellow, Leeds Univ., 1966–67; Political Adviser's Office, Singapore, 1967–69; Political Adviser to C-in-C Far East, 1970–71; Minister, Bonn, 1972–75; Asst Under-Sec. of State, FCO, 1975–76; Dep. Under-Sec. of State, FCO, 1976–79; Ambassador to France, 1979–82; Dir, Ditchley Foundn, 1982–87. Vis. Fellow, Nuffield Coll., Oxford, 1984–88; Sen. Associate Mem., St Antony's Coll., Oxford, 1983–88; Hon. Res. Fellow, UC, Swansea, 1988–. Chm., Franco-British Soc., 1990–95; President: Fédn Britannique des Alliances Françaises, 1997–99; Albania Soc. of Britain, 1996–2000. Commandeur, Légion d'Honneur (France), 1995. *Publication:* The Albanian National Liberation Struggle: the bitter victory, 1991. *Address:* Frondeg, Pennal, Machynlleth, Powys SY20 9JX. *T:* (01654) 791220. *Club:* Reform. *Died 5 Oct. 2002.*

HICKEY, Sir Justin, Kt 1979; Chairman and Managing Director, Hickey Group; *b* 5 April 1920; *s* of Hon. Simon Hickey, Speaker, New South Wales Parliament, and Hilda Ellen Hickey (*née* Dacey); *m* 1964, Barbara Standish Thayer; one *s* two *d*. *Educ:* De La Salle College, Sydney. Chairman: Australian Family Trust, 1965; Thayer Foundation (US), 1972; Director: Biocom Internat. Ltd (Bermuda), 1987–; Chemical Fuels Corp. (Atlanta, Ga), 1987–. Mem., Lloyd's of London, 1979. FRSA 1978. JP 1950. *Publication:* Just-In Business, 1998. *Recreations:* yachting, art collection. *Address:* 36 Cypress Drive, Broadbeach Waters, Qld 4218, Australia.
Died 21 Aug. 2005.

HICKMAN, John Kyrle, CMG 1977; HM Diplomatic Service, retired; Director, Anaconda (South America) Inc., since 1988; *b* 3 July 1927; *s* of late J. B. Hickman and Joan Hickman; *m* 1956, Jennifer Love; two *s* one *d*. *Educ:* Tonbridge; Trinity Hall, Cambridge. Served in RA, 45th Field Regt, Commonwealth Bde, 1948–50. Asst Principal, WO, 1950; Principal, 1955; transf. to CRO, 1958; UK High Commn, Wellington, 1959–62; HM Diplomatic Service, 1965; British Embassy, Madrid, 1966; Consul-General, Bilbao, 1967; Dep. High Comr, Singapore, 1969–71; Head of SW Pacific Dept, FCO, 1971–74; Counsellor, Dublin, 1974–77; Ambassador to Ecuador, 1977–81, to Chile, 1982–87. Chm., Belize Independence Conf., 1981. Chairman: Anglo-Ecuadorian Soc., 1988–91; Anglo-Chilean Soc., 1991–95. Grand Cross, Order of Merit (Chile), 1992. *Publications:* The Enchanted Islands: the Galápagos Discovered, 1985; News from the End of the Earth: a portrait of Chile, 1998. *Recreations:* history, golf. *Address:* Ivy Bank, Oare, near Marlborough, Wilts. *Club:* Garrick. *Died 23 Feb. 2001.*

HIGGINS, Colin Kirk; Sheriff for North Strathclyde at Paisley, since 1990; *b* 9 Nov. 1945; *s* of late William Higgins and Janet Currie (*née* Lenney); *m* 1971, Anne McMahon; one *s* two *d*. *Educ:* St Patrick's High Sch., Coatbridge; Glasgow Univ. (LLB). Apprenticed to Town Clerk, Coatbridge, 1967–69; Legal Asst, 1969–70; Assistant, 1970–73; Partner, 1974–90; James Bell & Sons, later Bell, Russell & Co. Dean, Airdrie Soc. of Solicitors, 1989–90. *Recreations:* walking, travel, theatre, racquet sports. *Address:* Paisley Sheriff Court, St James' Street, Paisley, Strathclyde PA3 2HW. *T:* (0141) 887 5291.
Died 25 Jan. 2002.

HIGGINS, Michael Anthony, (Tony); Chief Executive, Universities and Colleges Admissions Service, 1993–2003; *b* 24 June 1944; *s* of Walter Higgins and late Marjorie (*née* Dandy); *m* 1st, 1969, Hilary Patricia Noble (marr. diss. 1978); one *s* one *d*; 2nd, 1978, Janet Iris Dutnall Sadow (*née* Foreman) (marr. diss. 1998). *Educ:* Wyggeston Boys' Sch., Leicester; Univ. of Newcastle upon Tyne (BA). Admin. Asst, then Asst Registrar, Univ. of Leicester, 1967–78; seconded, part-time, to BAAS, 1970–72; Sen. Asst Registrar, Loughborough Univ. of Technol., 1979–84; Chief Exec., Polytechnics Central Admissions System, 1984–93. Chairman: Conf. of Univ. Administrators, 1982–84; Higher Educn Inf. Services Trust, 1991–93; Member: PCFC and HEFCE Cttees on Performance Indicators, 1989–94; FEFC Widening Participation Cttee, 1994–97; Bd, Nat. Adv. Cttee on Careers Educn and Guidance, 1998–; Council of Europe Devel Project on Access to Higher Educn, 1993–96. Chief Officer, Higher Educn Business Enterprises Ltd, 1995–2001; Chm., Cheltenham Business Partnership, 2002–; Member: Bd, ECCTIS 2000 Ltd, 1990–98; Local Govt Commn on sch. year, 1999–2000; Bd, HERO, 2000–01. Chairman: Educate Ltd, 2001–; Sheffield Data Services Ltd, 2001–; Educnl Websites Ltd, 2001–; Director: HE in the UK Ltd, 2001–; FE in the UK Ltd, 2001–; Post 16 Educn in the UK Ltd, 2001–; Board Member: Student UK Ltd, 1999–; Swotbooks Ltd, 2000–. Res. Associate, Univ. of Oxford, 1998–. Overseas consultancies to govts and univs of Sweden, Uganda, BC, Slovenia, Taiwan, S Africa and Czech Republic. Chm., BBC Radio Leicester Adv. Council, 1980–84; Mem., BBC Midlands and E Adv. Council, 1992–95; Chm., Leicester Haymarket Theatre, 1986–91; Vice-Chm., Glos Everyman Theatre, 1991–93; Chm., Develt Cttee, Cheltenham Internat. Fests of Music, Literature and Jazz, 1988–2000. Chm., Governing Body, Glos Coll. of Arts and Technol., 2003– (Vice-Chm., 1993–2000); Mem. Council, Cheltenham Coll., 1997–2000. FCMI (FIMgt 1986); FRSA 1995. Hon. Fellow, Glos Univ. (formerly Cheltenham and Glos Coll. of Higher Educn), 1998. Hon. DEd West of England, 1993. *Publications:* Young People's Knowledge of Higher Education, 1990; Getting into Polytechnic, 1991; How to Complete your UCCA/PCAS Form, 1991, 1992; Higher Education: the student experience, 1992; Adults' Knowledge of Higher Education, 1992; How to Complete your UCAS Form, annually 1993–; (ed) Student Mobility in the European Community, 1993; Clearing the Way, annually 1994–; Higher Education Sans Frontières: policy practice and the European student market, 1994; The Careers Adviser/Higher Education Interface, 1994; Higher Education: the international student experience, 1995; Practical Progression: matching advanced GNVQs to higher education programmes, 1995; chapters and articles in books, jls and newspapers. *Recreations:* golf, cooking, Rugby Union. *Address:* 32 East Approach Drive, Cheltenham, Glos GL52 3JE. *Died 16 April 2004.*

HIGGINS, Tony; *see* Higgins, M. A.

HIGHAM, John Drew, CMG 1956; Head, Development Control Division, Department of the Environment, 1970–74; *b* 28 Nov. 1914; *s* of Richard and Margaret Higham, Pendleton, Lancs; *m* 1st, 1936, Mary Constance Bromage (*d* 1974); three *d*; 2nd, 1976, Katharine Byard Pailing, FRTPI. *Educ:* Manchester Grammar Sch.; Gonville and Caius Coll., Cambridge (Scholar). Admiralty: Asst Principal, 1936; Asst Private Sec. to First Lord, 1939; Private Sec. to Parliamentary Sec. and Parliamentary Clerk, 1940; Principal, 1941; transferred to Colonial Office, 1946; Asst Sec., Colonial Office, 1948; seconded to Singapore as Under Sec., 1953, and as Dir of Personnel, 1955–57 (acted on various occasions as Chief Sec.); Asst Sec., Min. of Housing and Local Govt, 1965. Vice-Chm., Bredon Parish Council, 1985–87. Chevalier 1st Cl. Order of St Olaf (Norway), 1948. *Address:* 17 Bannister Close, Oxford OX4 1SH. *T:* (01865) 251311. *Club:* National Liberal. *Died 5 Feb. 2002.*

HIGSON, Gordon Robert, PhD; medical technologist; *b* 10 June 1932; *s* of Robert and Agnes Higson; *m* 1955, Eileen Mary Warrington; two *s* one *d*. *Educ:* Thornleigh Coll., Bolton; Manchester Univ. (BSc 1954); Aberdeen Univ. (PhD 2000). FInstP 1968; FIEE 1978. Fairey Aviation Co., 1954–59; NCB Mining Res. Estabt, 1959–68; Department of Health and Social Security: Scientific and Tech. Services Br., 1969; Dir of Scientific and Tech. Services, 1980–84; Controller of Supply, 1984–85; Dir, Supplies Technology Div., 1986–88; Sec. Gen., Internat. Assoc. of Med. Prosthesis Manufacturers, 1988–90; Chm., Medical Technology Consultants Europe, 1989–95. Maynerod Lectr, BIR, 1986. *Publications:* The Medical Devices Directives—a Manufacturers' Handbook, 1994; Medical Device Safety: the regulation of medical devices for public health and safety, 2001; papers in scientific and tech. jls. *Recreations:* walking, theatre. *Address:* Burnden, Bridge of Canny, Banchory, Aberdeenshire AB31 4AT. *T:* (01330) 824952. *Died 9 Aug. 2001.*

HILD, Maj.-Gen. Henry; *see* Hild, Maj.-Gen. J. H.

HILD, Maj.-Gen. (John) Henry, MBE 1969; CEng, FIEE; Director: Siemens (UK) plc, 1984–97; Siemens Plessey Electronic Systems Ltd, 1989–95; consultant, since 1984; *b* 28 March 1931; *m* 1954, Janet Macdonald Brown; one *s* one *d*. *Educ:* Blackfriars, Laxton; Sandhurst. Joined Army, 1949; commissioned, 1952; Korea, 1952–53; sc 1961; MoD, DAQMG, 1962–64; Borneo, 1965; Hong Kong, 1966–67; 1 (BR) Corps, DAQMG, 1968–69; CO 18 Sig. Regt, 1969–71; DS, Staff Coll., 1972–73; Comd 1 Sig. Gp, 1974–76; Comdt, Sch. of Sigs, 1976–78; RCDS 1979; HQ BAOR, DQMG and CSO, 1980–84. Col Comdt, RCS, 1984–90. Dir, RCS Assoc. Trustee Ltd, 1989–97. Mem., Caravan Club Council, 1985–95. FIMgt. Princess Mary Medal, Royal Signals Inst., 1996. *Recreations:* entertaining friends, travel, sport. *Address:* c/o Lloyds TSB, 5 The Square, Petersfield, Hants GU32 3HL. *Clubs:* Army and Navy; Royal Signals Yacht (Adm., 1984–89). *Died 5 Dec. 2001.*

HILL, 8th Viscount *cr* 1842; **Antony Rowland Clegg-Hill;** Bt 1726–27; Baron Hill 1814; *b* 19 March 1931; *s* of 7th Viscount Hill and Elisabeth Flora (*d* 1967), *d* of Brig.-Gen. George Nowell Thomas Smyth-Osbourne, CB, CMG, DSO; *S* father, 1974; *m* 1st, 1963, Juanita Phyllis (marr. diss. 1976), *d* of John W. Pertwee, Salfords, Surrey; 2nd, 1989, Elizabeth Harriett, *d* of Ronald L. Offer, Salisbury, Wilts. *Educ:* Kelly Coll.; RMA, Sandhurst. Formerly Captain, RA. Freeman of Shrewsbury, 1957. *Heir: cousin* Peter David Raymond Charles Clegg-Hill [*b* 17 Oct. 1945; *m* 1973, Sharon Ruth Deane (marr. diss. 2000), Kaikohe, NZ; two *s* five *d*]. *Died 12 March 2003.*

HILL, Christopher; *see* Hill, J. E. C.

HILL, Prof. David Keynes, ScD; FRS 1972; Professor of Biophysics, Royal Postgraduate Medical School, University of London, 1975–82, then Professor Emeritus; *b* 23 July 1915; *s* of late Prof. Archibald Vivian Hill, CH, OBE, ScD, FRS, and Margaret Neville, *d* of late Dr J. N. Keynes; *m* 1949, Stella Mary Humphrey; three *d*, and one step *d*. *Educ:* Highgate Sch.; Trinity Coll., Cambridge; ScD Cantab 1965. Fellow, Trinity Coll., Cambridge, 1940–48; Physiologist on staff of Marine Biological Assoc., Plymouth, 1948–49; Sen. Lectr, 1949–62, Reader in Biophysics, 1962–75, Vice-Dean, 1969–74, Royal Postgrad. Med. Sch., London Univ. Physiological Society: Ed., Jl, 1969–76; Chm., Bd of Monographs, 1979–81. *Publications:* scientific papers in Jl Physiology. *Address:* Ivy Cottage, Winksley, Ripon, N Yorks HG4 3NR. *T:* (01765) 658562. *Died 18 Aug. 2002.*

HILL, (Eliot) Michael; QC 1979; QC (NSW) 1991; *b* 22 May 1935; *s* of Cecil Charles Hill and Rebecca Betty Hill; *m* 1965, Kathleen Irene (*née* Hordern); one *s* two *d*. *Educ:* Bancroft's Sch., Essex; Brasenose Coll., Oxford (MA). Called to the Bar, Gray's Inn, 1958, Bencher, 1986; South-Eastern Circuit. Prosecuting Counsel to Crown, Inner London Sessions, 1969–74; Jun. Pros. Counsel to Crown, Central Criminal Court, 1974–77; a Sen. Pros. Counsel to Crown, 1977–79; a Recorder, 1977–97. Chairman: Criminal Bar Assoc., 1982–86 (Sec., 1973–75; Vice-Chm., 1979–82); Inns of Court Advocacy Training Cttee, 1995–99; Member: Senate of the Inns of Court and the Bar, 1976–79 and 1982–86; Council of Legal Educn, 1977–86; Criminal Law Revision Cttee, 1983–; Bar Council, 1986–87 and 1989–90; Bd of Dirs, Internat. Soc. for Reform of Criminal Law, 1988– (Chm., Management Cttee, 1991–95; Pres., 1999–). Dir, Bar Mutual Indemnity Fund Ltd, 1987– (Chm., Investment Cttee, 1991–). *Recreations:* family, friends, riding, fishing and just living. *Address:* (chambers) 23 Essex Street, WC2R 3AS. *T:* (020) 7413 0353, (020) 8287 9005, *Fax:* (020) 7413 0374, (020) 8287 9005; *e-mail:* michaelhill@23essexstreet.co.uk; michaelhillqc@cs.com. *Club:* Garrick. *Died 19 Aug. 2003.*

HILL, John Andrew Patrick, CMG 2001; CBE 1978; Chairman, British Arab Commercial Bank, 1996–2003; *b* 8 Feb. 1936; *s* of Henry Wilfred Hill and Beatrice Rose Hill; *m* 1960, Barbara Anne Knifton; two *s* one *d*. *Educ:* Ealing Tech. Coll.; MECAS. British Bank of Middle East: Exec. (posts in India and ME), 1957–72; Area Manager, Saudi Arabia, 1972–77; Man. Dir, Saudi British Bank, 1978–79; Hongkong and Shanghai Banking Corporation: Asst Gen. Manager, 1979–82; CEO, 1982–86; Gen. Manager, 1986–90. Director: HSBC Bank ME, 1980–2003; HSBC Republic Bank (Cyprus), 1986–2003; Arabian Gulf Investments (FE) Ltd, 1986–2003; Cyprus Popular Bank, 1986–2003; Jabah Investments Ltd, 1987–2003; Arab British Chamber of Commerce, 1996–2002. Chm., Cttee for ME Trade, 1992–2000. Chm., Eric Thompson Charitable Trust, 1993–; Dir, Jerusalem and East Mission Trust, 1996–. FInstD 1996. *Recreations:* family, music, travel. *Address:* Hawkwood Manor, Sible Hedingham, Essex CO9 3RG. *T:* (01787) 460613. *Clubs:* Oriental, London Capital. *Died 6 Dec. 2004.*

HILL, (John Edward) Christopher, DLitt; FBA 1966; Master of Balliol College,'Oxford, 1965–78; *b* 6 Feb. 1912; *m* 1st, 1944, Inez Waugh; (one *d* decd); 2nd, 1956, Bridget Irene Sutton (*d* 2002); one *s* one *d* (and one *d* decd). *Educ:* St Peter's Sch., York; Balliol Coll., Oxford (BA 1931); DLitt 1965. Fellow of All Souls Coll., Oxford, 1934; Asst Lectr, University Coll., Cardiff, 1936; Fellow and Tutor in Modern History, Balliol Coll., Oxford, 1938. Private in Field Security Police, commnd Oxford and Bucks Light Inf., 1940, Major; seconded to Foreign Office, 1943. Returned to Balliol, 1945; University Lectr in 16th- and 17th-century history, 1959; Ford's Lectr, 1962. Vis. Prof., Open Univ., 1978–80. Hon. Fellow, Lancs Polytechnic, 1988. Hon. DLitt: Hull, 1966; E Anglia, 1968; Glasgow, 1976; Exeter, 1979; Wales, 1979; Leicester, 1996; King Alfred's Coll., Winchester, 1996; Hon. LittD Sheffield, 1967; Hon. LLD Bristol, 1976; DUniv: York, 1978; Open, 1982; Hon. Dr Sorbonne Nouvelle, 1979. Foreign Hon. Member: Amer. Acad. of Sciences, 1973; Hungarian Acad. of Sciences, 1982; Acad. of Sciences, GDR, 1988. *Publications:* The English Revolution 1640, 1940; (under name K. E. Holme) Two Commonwealths, 1945; Lenin and the Russian Revolution, 1947; The Good Old Cause (ed jtly with E. Dell), 1949; Economic Problems of the Church, 1956; Puritanism and Revolution, 1958; Oliver Cromwell, 1958; The Century of Revolution, 1961; Society and Puritanism in Pre-Revolutionary England, 1964; Intellectual Origins of the English Revolution, 1965; Reformation to Industrial Revolution, 1967; God's Englishman, 1970; Antichrist in 17th Century England, 1971; The World Turned Upside Down, 1972; ed, G. Winstanley, The Law of Freedom and other writings, 1973; Change and Continuity in Seventeenth Century England, 1975; Milton and the English Revolution, 1978 (Heinemann award; Milton Soc. of America award); Some Intellectual Consequences of the English Revolution, 1980; (with B. Reay and W. M. Lamont) The World of the Muggletonians, 1983; The Experience of Defeat: Milton and some contemporaries, 1984; Collected Essays Vol. I: Writing and Revolution in 17th Century England, 1985, Vol. II: Religion and Politics in 17th Century England, 1986, Vol. III: People and Ideas in 17th Century England, 1986; A Turbulent, Seditious, and Factious People: John Bunyan and his Church, 1988 (W. H. Smith Literary Award, 1989); A Nation of Change and Novelty: radical politics, religion and literature in 17th century England, 1990; The English Bible and the 17th Century Revolution, 1993; Liberty Against the Law, 1996; The Origins of the English Revolution Revisited, 1997; articles in learned jls, etc. *Address:* Woodway House, Sibford Ferris, Banbury, Oxon OX15 5RA.

Died 24 Feb. 2003.

HILL, Sir John (Maxwell), Kt 1974; CBE 1969; DFC 1945; QPM; Chief Inspector of Constabulary, Home Office, 1972–75; *b* 25 March 1914; *s* of late L. S. M. Hill, Civil Servant, Plymouth; *m* 1939, Marjorie Louisa (*d* 1992), *d* of late John Oliver Reynolds, Aylesbury, Bucks; one *s* one *d*. *Educ:* Plymouth Coll. Metropolitan Police Coll., Hendon, 1938–39; joined Metropolitan Police, 1933. Served with RAF, 1942–45. Dep. Comdr, New Scotland Yard, 1959; Metropolitan Police: Comdr, No 3 District, 1963, Comdr, No 1 District, 1964; HM Inspector of Constabulary, 1965; Asst Comr (Administration and Operations), 1966–68; Asst Comr (Personnel and Training), 1968–71; Dep. Comr, 1971–72. *Recreations:* walking, golf. *Address:* 7 Killasser Court, Tadworth, Surrey KT20 5AN. *Clubs:* Royal Automobile, Royal Air Force.

Died 6 May 2004.

HILL, Michael; *see* Hill, E. M.

HILL, Dr Polly; Fellow, Clare Hall, Cambridge, 1965–81, then Emeritus; *b* 10 June 1914; *née* Mary Eglantyne Hill; *d* of Prof. A. V. Hill, CH, OBE, FRS, and Margaret, *d* of Dr J. N. Keynes and F. A. Keynes; *m* 1953, Kenneth Humphreys (marr. diss. 1961; he *d* 1985); one *d*. *Educ:* Newnham Coll., Cambridge (PhD 1967). Editorial Asst,

REconS, 1936–38; research, Fabian Soc., 1938–39; temp. civil servant, 1940–51; editorial staff, West Africa (weekly), 1951–53; Res. Fellow, then Sen. Res. Fellow, Econs Dept, followed by Inst. of African Studies, Univ. of Ghana, 1954–65; financed by Center for Research on Econ. Devof, Univ. of Mich, Ann Arbor, mainly working in Cambridge and northern Nigeria, 1965–70, and by SSRC, mainly working in northern Nigeria, 1970–72; Smuts Reader in Commonwealth Studies, Cambridge Univ., 1973–79; fieldwork in villages in Karnataka, S India, 1977–78, and (as Leverhulme Emeritus Fellow) in Kerala, S India, 1981–82. Hon. Fellow, SOAS, 1998. *Publications:* The Unemployment Services, 1940; The Gold Coast Cocoa Farmer, 1956; The Migrant Cocoa-Farmers of Southern Ghana, 1963, 3rd edn 1977, repr. 1997; Rural Capitalism in West Africa, 1970, 2nd edn 1976; Rural Hausa, 1972; Population, Prosperity and Poverty: rural Kano, 1900 and 1970, 1977 (Amaury Talbot prize for African anthropology, 1977); Dry Grain Farming Families, 1982; Development Economics on Trial, 1986, 6th edn 1995; (ed with R. Keynes) Lydia and Maynard: letters between Lydia Lopokova and J. M. Keynes, 1989; Who were the Fen People? (Proc. Cambridge Antiquarian Soc.), 1993; articles on rural W Africa, India, and the earliest Cambridge women students, in learned jls; monographs and chapters in books. *Recreation:* poetry writing. *Address:* 4 Coates Drive, Isleham, Ely, Cambs CB7 5SJ.

Died 21 Aug. 2005.

HILL-NORTON, Baron *cr* 1979 (Life Peer), of South Nutfield, Surrey; **Admiral of the Fleet Peter John Hill-Norton,** GCB 1970 (KCB 1967; CB 1964); Chairman, Military Committee of NATO, 1974–77; *b* 8 Feb. 1915; *s* of Capt. M. J. Norton and Mrs M. B. Norton; *m* 1936, Margaret Eileen Linstow; one *s* one *d*. *Educ:* RNC Dartmouth. Went to sea, 1932; commnd, 1936; specialised in Gunnery, 1939; War of 1939–45: Arctic Convoys; NW Approaches; Admiralty Naval Staff. Comdr 1948; Capt. 1952; Naval Attaché, Argentine, Uruguay, Paraguay, 1953–55; comd HMS Decoy, 1956–57; comd HMS Ark Royal, 1959–61; Asst Chief of Naval Staff, 1962–64; Flag Officer, Second-in-Command, Far East Fleet, 1964–66; Dep. Chief of the Defence Staff (Personnel and Logistics), 1966; Second Sea Lord and Chief of Naval Personnel, Jan.-Aug. 1967; Vice-Chief of Naval Staff, 1967–68; C-in-C Far East, 1969–70; Chief of the Naval Staff and First Sea Lord, 1970–71; Chief of the Defence Staff, 1971–73. President: Sea Cadets Assoc., 1977–84; Defence Manufacturers' Assoc., 1980–84; British Maritime League, 1982–85; Vice-Pres., RUSI, 1977–90. Liveryman, Shipwrights' Co., 1973, Mem. Court, 1979; Freeman, City of London, 1973. *Publications:* No Soft Options, 1978; Sea Power, 1982. *Recreations:* gardening, foreign travel. *Address:* Cass Cottage, Hyde, Fordingbridge, Hants SP6 2QH. *Clubs:* Army and Navy; Royal Navy of 1765 and 1785.

Died 16 May 2004.

HILL-WOOD, Sir David (Basil), 3rd Bt *cr* 1921, of Moorfield, Glossop, co. Derby; Consultant, Investec, since 1998; *b* 12 Nov. 1926; *s* of Sir Basil Samuel Hill Hill-Wood, 2nd Bt, and Hon. Joan Louisa Brand (*d* 1996), *e d* of 3rd Viscount Hampden; *S* father, 1954; *m* 1970, Jennifer, 2nd *d* of late Peter McKenzie Strang, Adelaide; two *s* one *d*. *Educ:* Eton. Served in Army (Grenadier Guards), 1945–48. Morgan Grenfell & Co. Ltd, 1948–55; Myers & Co., Stockbrokers, 1955–71, Sen. Partner, 1971–74; Director: Capel-Cure Myers Ltd, 1974–77; Guinness Mahon & Co. Ltd (Bankers), 1977–98. Aust. Rep., FA Council, 1978–. Chm., Royal Merchant Navy Foundn, 1975–. High Sheriff, Berks, 1982. *Recreations:* soccer, golf. *Heir: s* Samuel Thomas Hill-Wood, *b* 24 Aug. 1971. *Address:* Dacre Farm, Farley Hill, Reading, Berks RG7 1XJ. *T:* (01734) 733185. *Clubs:* White's; Melbourne (Australia).

Died 12 April 2002.

HILLER, Dame Wendy, DBE 1975 (OBE 1971); actress; *b* 15 Aug. 1912; *d* of Frank Watkin and Marie Hiller, Bramhall, Cheshire; *m* 1937, Ronald Gow (*d* 1993); one *s*

one d. Educ: Winceby House, Bexhill. Manchester Repertory Theatre; Sir Barry Jackson's tour of Evensong, 1932; Sally Hardcastle in Love on the Dole, Garrick, 1935, NY, 1936; leading parts in Saint Joan and Pygmalion at Malvern Festival, 1936. Plays include: Twelfth Night, war factory tour, 1943; Cradle Song, Apollo, 1944; The First Gentleman, Savoy, 1945; Tess of the d'Urbervilles, Piccadilly, 1947; The Heiress, Biltmore, NY, 1947, Haymarket, London, 1950; Ann Veronica, Piccadilly, 1949; Waters of the Moon, Haymarket, 1951–53; The Night of the Ball, New, 1955; Old Vic Season, 1955–56; Moon for the Misbegotten, NY, 1957; Flowering Cherry, Haymarket, 1958; Toys in the Attic, Piccadilly, 1960; Aspern Papers, NY, 1962; The Wings of the Dove, Lyric, 1963; The Sacred Flame, Duke of York's, 1967; When We Dead Awaken, Edinburgh Festival, 1968; The Battle of Shrivings, Lyric, 1970; Crown Matrimonial, Haymarket, 1972; John Gabriel Borkman, National, 1975; Lies!, Albery, 1975; Waters of the Moon, Chichester, 1977, Haymarket, 1978; The Old Jest, 1980; The Importance of Being Earnest, Watford, 1981, Royalty, 1987; The Aspern Papers, Haymarket, 1984; Driving Miss Daisy, Apollo, 1988. Films: Pygmalion, 1938; Major Barbara, 1941; I Know Where I'm Going, 1946; Outcast of the Islands; Separate Tables, 1958 (Academy Award); Sons and Lovers, 1960; Toys in the Attic, 1963; A Man for All Seasons, 1966; David Copperfield, 1970; Murder on the Orient Express, 1974; The Elephant Man, 1980; The Lonely Passion of Judith Hearne,1987. TV: When We Dead Awaken, 1968; Peer Gynt, 1972; Clochemerle, 1973; Last Wishes, 1978; Richard II, 1979; Miss Morison's Ghosts, 1981; The Kingfisher, Witness for the Prosecution, Attracta, 1982; The Comedy of Errors, 1983; Death of the Heart, 1985; Darley's Folly, All Passion Spent, The Importance of Being Earnest, 1986; Ending Up, 1989; The Best of Friends, 1991; The Countess Alice, 1992. Hon. LLD Manchester, 1984. Address: c/o Chatto & Linnit, 123A King's Road, SW3 4PL.

Died 14 May 2003.

HILTON, Prof. Rodney Howard, FBA 1977; Professor of Medieval Social History, University of Birmingham, 1963–82, then Emeritus; b 17 Nov. 1916; s of John James Hilton and Anne Hilton; m 1st, Margaret Palmer (marr. diss.); one s; 2nd, Gwyn Evans (marr. diss.); one s one d; 3rd, 1971, Jean Birrell. Educ: Manchester Grammar Sch.; Balliol Coll., Oxford (BA 1938); Merton Coll., Oxford (DPhil). Army, 1940–46. University of Birmingham: Lectr and Reader in Medieval History, 1946–63; Dir, Inst. for Advanced Res. in the Humanities, 1984–87. Publications: The Economic Development of Some Leicestershire Estates in the 14th and 15th Centuries, 1947; (with H. Fagan) The English Rising of 1381, 1950; (ed) Ministers' Accounts of the Warwickshire Estates of the Duke of Clarence, 1952; (ed) The Stoneleigh Leger Book, 1960; A Medieval Society, 1966, rev. edn 1983; The Decline of Serfdom in Medieval England, 1969, rev. edn 1983; Bondmen Made Free, 1973; The English Peasantry in the Later Middle Ages, 1975; (ed) Peasants, Knights and Heretics, 1976; (ed) The Transition from Feudalism to Capitalism, 1976; (ed with T. H. Aston) The English Rising of 1381, 1984; Class Conflict and the Crisis of Feudalism, 1985; English and French Towns in Feudal Society 1992; articles and reviews in Past and Present, English Historical Review, Economic History Review, etc. Address: School of History, University of Birmingham, Birmingham B15 2TT. T: (0121) 414 5736.

Died 7 June 2002.

HINDLEY-SMITH, David Dury, CBE 1972; Registrar, General Dental Council (formerly Dental Board of the UK), 1947–81; b 20 Feb. 1916; e s of late James Dury Hindley-Smith; m 1947, Dorothy Westwood Legge (d 1987), e d of Arthur Collins and Mary Fielding; two step d. Educ: Uppingham; King's Coll., Cambridge (MA); Paris and Vienna. Passed examination for Diplomatic Service, 1939. War Service: Artists' Rifles, 1939; commissioned Royal Fusiliers, 1940; Liaison Officer to Gén. Leclerc,

1942, to Gén. de Gaulle's first administration, 1944; Acting Col. Mem., W Suffolk HA, 1982–86; Chm., Mental Health Cttee, W Suffolk HA, 1982–86. Mem. Council, Royal Dental Hosp., London Sch. of Dental Surgery, 1976–84 (Chm., 1981–84). Vice-Chm., Surrey Assoc. of Youth Clubs, 1950–70 (Vice-Pres., 1970–); Executive Chm., Nat. Assoc. of Youth Clubs, 1970–74 (Vice-Pres., 1974–); Chm., Sembal Trust, 1972–81; Vice-Pres., Suffolk Assoc. of Youth, 1984– (Chm., 1982–84). Hon. Mem., BDA, 1975; Hon. FDSRCSE 1977; Hon. FDSRCS 1980. Cecil Peace Prize, 1938. Recreations: gardening, cooking. Address: The Ark House, Whepstead, Bury St Edmunds, Suffolk IP29 4UB. T: (01284) 735351. Club: Royal Society of Medicine.

Died 23 April 2001.

HINDMARSH, Frederick Bell; Under-Secretary, Department of Health and Social Security, 1973–79, retired; b 31 Jan. 1919; yr s of Frederick Hindmarsh and Margaret May Hindmarsh; m 1947, Mary Torrance Coubrough; one d. Educ: County Grammar Sch., Acton. Clerical Officer, Min. of Health, 1936; Exec. Officer, 1937. Served war, Army, 1939–46. Min. of Pensions and Nat. Insurance and Min. of Social Security: Higher Exec. Officer, 1946; Sen. Exec. Officer, 1947; Chief Exec. Officer, 1951; Sen. Chief Exec. Officer, 1959; Prin. Exec. Officer, 1964; Asst Sec., DHSS, 1969. Recreation: music.

Died 1 April 2002.

HIPPISLEY-COX, Peter Denzil John; Partner: Dyson Bell Martin (formerly Dyson, Bell & Co.), London, 1953–92; Bircham & Co., 1989–92; b 22 May 1921; s of late Col Sir (Edward) Geoffrey Hippisley Cox, CBE, and Lady Hippisley Cox; m 1st, 1948, Olga Kay (marr. diss. 1956); one d; 2nd, 1956, Frieda Marion Wood; two d. Educ: Stowe; Trinity Coll., Cambridge (MA). Served War, RAF (Signals), 1941–46 (Flt Lieut). Admitted a solicitor, 1949. Dir, Equity & Law Life Assurance Soc., 1965–87 (Dep. Chm. 1973; Chm., 1977–85). Member: Council, Law Soc., 1956–81; Court, Drapers' Co., 1972– (Master, 1983–84). Governor, Bancroft's Sch., 1975–93. Recreation: music. Address: 48D Whistlers Avenue, SW11 3TS. T: (020) 7585 2142. Club: Carlton. Died 21 June 2001.

HIRD, Dame Thora, (Dame Thora Scott), DBE 1993 (OBE 1983); actress; b 28 May 1911; d of James Henry Hird and Mary Jane Mayor; m 1937, James Scott (d 1994); one d. Educ: The Misses Nelson's Prep Sch., Morecambe, Lancs. Royalty Theatre Repertory Co., Morecambe, 1931; first appeared in West End of London, 1940–42; No Medals, Vaudeville, 1944; The Queen Came By, Duke of York's, 1949; Tobacco Road, Playhouse, 1949; The Trouble-Makers, Strand, 1952; The Same Sky, Duke of York's, 1952; The Love Match, Palace, 1953. Film contract, Ealing Studios, 1940; many films include: Blacksheep of Whitehall; They Came in Khaki; A Kind of Loving; Once a Jolly Swagman; Maytime in Mayfair; Wide-eyed and Legless; TV series and serials: Meet the Wife; The First Lady; In Loving Memory; Hallelujah!; Last of the Summer Wine; Flesh and Blood; Praise Be!; Thora on the Straight and Narrow; Goggle Eyes; many plays, incl. Cream Cracker under the Settee (BAFTA Award for Best TV Actress, 1988); Waiting for the Telegram (BAFTA Award for Best TV Actress, 1999); Lost for Words, 1999 (BAFTA Award for Best TV Actress, 2000; US Internat. Emmy Award). Pye Female Comedy Star Award, 1984. Hon. DLitt Lancaster, 1989; DUniv 1997. Publications: Scene and Hird (autobiog.), 1976; Praise Be Notebook, 1991; Praise Be Year Book, 1991; Praise Be Christmas Book, 1991; Praise Be Book of Prayers, 1992; Praise Be I Believe, 1993; Is it Thora?, 1996; Not in the Diary, 2000; Nothing Like a Dame, 2001. Recreations: reading, gardening, travelling. Address: c/o Felix de Wolfe, Manfield House, 376–378 Strand, WC2R 0LR. T: (020) 7723 5561. Died 15 March 2003.

HITCH, Brian, CMG 1985; CVO 1980; HM Diplomatic Service, retired; Director, Diploma in European Studies, and Fellow of Kellogg College (formerly Rewley House),

University of Oxford, 1991–96, then Fellow Emeritus; *b* 2 June 1932; *m* 1954, Margaret Kathleen Wooller; two *d*. *Educ:* Wisbech Grammar Sch. (FRCO, LRAM); Magdalene Coll., Cambridge. Joined FO, 1955; 3rd/2nd Sec., Tokyo, 1955–61; FO, 1961–62; 2nd/1st Sec., Havana, 1962–64; 1st Sec., Athens, 1965–68; 1st Sec. and Head of Chancery, Tokyo, 1968–72; Asst Head, Southern European Dept, FCO, 1972–73; Dep. Head, later Head, Marine and Transport Dept, FCO, 1973–75; Counsellor, Bonn, 1975–77 and Algiers, 1977–80; Consul-Gen., Munich, 1980–84; Minister, Tokyo, 1984–87; High Comr to Malta, 1988–91. *Recreation:* music. *Address:* 19 Moreton Road, Oxford OX2 7AX. *T:* (01865) 556764.
Died 3 Aug. 2004.

HNATYSHYN, Rt Hon. Ramon John, CC 1990; CMM 1990; CD 1990; PC (Can.) 1979; QC (Can.) 1988; Governor General and Commander-in-Chief of Canada, 1990–95; Senior Partner, Gowling Lafleur Henderson LLP (formerly Gowling, Strathy & Henderson), since 1989; *b* 16 March 1934; *s* of John Hnatyshyn and Helen Constance Hnatyshyn (*née* Pitts); *m* 1960, Karen Gerda Nygaard Andreasen; two *s*. *Educ:* Victoria Public Sch.; Nutana Collegiate Inst., Univ. of Saskatchewan (BA 1954; LLB 1956). Royal Canadian Air Force: trng, 1951–56; 23 Wing Auxiliary, 1956–58. Called to the Bar, Saskatchewan, 1957, Ontario, 1986; QC Sask, 1973; practised to 1990. Private Sec. and Exec. Asst to Senate Leader of Govt, 1958–60; Lectr in Law, Univ. of Saskatchewan, 1966–74. MP (PC Party) Saskatoon-Biggar, 1974, Saskatoon West, 1979, 1980, 1984 elections; Dep. House Leader of Official Opposition, 1976; Minister of State for Science and Technology, 1979; Minister of Energy, Mines and Resources, 1979–80; Opposition Critic for Justice, 1980–84, and Solicitor Gen., 1984; Govt House Leader, 1984–86; Minister responsible for Regulatory Affairs, 1986; Minister of Justice and Attorney General of Canada, 1986–88. Pres., Queen's Privy Council for Canada, 1985–86. KStJ (Prior for Canada, 1990–95). *Address:* (office) Suite 2600, 160 Elgin Street, Ottawa, ON K1P 1C3, Canada.
Died 18 Dec. 2002.

HOARE, Sir Peter Richard David, 8th Bt *cr* 1786; *b* 22 March 1932; *s* of Sir Peter William Hoare, 7th Bt, and Laura Ray (*d* 1992), *o d* of Sir John Esplen, 1st Bt, KBE; *S* father, 1973; *m* 1st, 1961, Jane (marr. diss. 1967), *o d* of late Daniel Orme; 2nd, 1978, Katrin Alexa, Lady Hodson (marr. diss. 1982), *o d* of late Erwin Bernstiel; 3rd, 1983, Angela Francesca Ayarza Valdovinos de la Claustra, *d* of late Fidel Fernando Ayarza. *Educ:* Eton. *Recreations:* travelling, shooting, skiing. *Heir:* *b* David John Hoare,[*m* 1st, 1965, Mary Vanessa Cardew (marr. diss. 1978; one *s*; 2nd, 1984, Virginia Victoria Graham Labes]. *Address:* c/o Crèdit Andorrà, Avinguda Princep Benlloch 25, Andorra la Vella, Principality of Andorra. *Club:* Royal Automobile.
Died 26 June 2004.

HOBAN, (Brian) Michael (Stanislaus); Head Master of Harrow, 1971–81; *b* 7 Oct. 1921; 2nd *s* of late Capt. R. A. Hoban; *m* 1947, Jasmine, 2nd *d* of J. C. Holmes, MC, Charterhouse, Godalming; one *s* one *d* (and one *d* decd). *Educ:* Charterhouse (Scholar); University Coll., Oxford (Sch.; 2nd Cl. Hon. Mods, 1947; 2nd Cl. Lit. Hum., 1949); BA 1949, MA 1957). Served War of 1939–45: Capt., Westminster Dragoons; NW Europe, 1944–45 (despatches); demobilised, Nov. 1945. Capt. Northants Yeomanry, TA, 1950–56. Assistant Master: Uppingham Sch., 1949–52; Shrewsbury Sch., 1952–59; Headmaster, St Edmund's Sch., Canterbury, 1960–64; Head Master, Bradfield Coll., 1964–71. Pt-time Chm., CSSBs, 1984–91. Hon. Associate Mem., HMC, 1981– (Hon. Treasurer, 1975–80). Sometime CACTM and ACCM Lay Selector for dios of Canterbury and London. Sometime Mem., Central Adv. Bd, RAF Coll., Cranwell; Governor: Wellington Coll., 1981–92; St Edmund's Sch., Canterbury, 1975–96; St Margaret's Sch., Bushey, 1975–97. Pres., The Carthusian Soc., 1987–92. JP Berks, 1967–71. *Publication:* (with Donald Swann) Jesu Parvule,

1965. *Recreations:* music, reading. *Address:* St Luke's Wing, St Katherine's House, Ormond Road, Wantage OX12 8EA. *Clubs:* East India, Devonshire, Sports and Public Schools; Vincent's (Oxford).
Died 6 July 2003.

HOBAN, Michael; *see* Hoban, B. M. S.

HOBBS, Herbert Harry, CB 1956; CVO 1972; Director, Ancient Monuments and Historic Buildings, 1970–72, retired; *b* 7 Nov. 1912; *s* of late Bertie Hobbs and Agnes Dora (*née* Clarke); *m* 1937, Joan Hazel Timmins (*d* 1979); two *s* one *d*. *Educ:* Bedford Sch.; Corpus Christi Coll., Oxford. Entered War Office, 1935; Comptroller of Lands and Claims, 1956–60; Asst Under-Sec. of State (Works), War Office, 1960–63; Under-Sec., MPBW, later DoE, 1963–72. Medal of Freedom with bronze palm (USA), 1946. *Recreation:* music. *Address:* Blenheim Lodge Residential Home, North Road, Minehead, Somerset TA24 5QB. *T:* (01643) 705350.
Died 8 Aug. 2002.

HOBBS, John Charles; Chief Insurance Officer, Department of Health and Social Security, 1971–76; *b* 28 May 1917; British; *m* 1961, Doris Gronow. *Educ:* Portsmouth Southern Grammar Sch.; Portsmouth Coll. of Technology (BSc 1st cl. Hons 1936; BSc (Spec.) Maths, 1st cl. Hons, 1944). FIS 1950. Asst Principal, 1946; Principal, 1947; Asst Sec., 1957.
Died 6 April 2002.

HOBBS, Rev. Canon Keith; Archdeacon of Chichester, 1981–91; Canon Residentiary of Chichester Cathedral, 1981–91, then Canon Emeritus; *b* 3 March 1925; *s* of late Percival Frank and Gwennyth Mary Hobbs; *m* 1950, Mary (*d* 1998), *d* of late Louis Lingg and Mary Elizabeth Ruderman; one *s* (and one *s* decd). *Educ:* St Olave's Grammar School; Exeter Coll., Oxford (MA); Wells Theological Coll. Instr Branch, RN, 1946; retired (Lt Comdr), 1956. Deacon 1958, priest 1959; Curate, St Stephen, Clewer, 1958–60; Soho, 1960–62; St Stephen, S Kensington, 1962–78; Lectr and Co-ordinator of Counselling, Borough Road Coll., 1964–77; Actg Gen. Secretary, Church Union, 1977–78; Chaplain to Bishop of Chichester, 1978–81. *Address:* 10 St Martin's Square, Chichester, W Sussex PO19 1NR. *T:* (01243) 784260.
Died 11 June 2001.

HOBHOUSE OF WOODBOROUGH, Baron *cr* 1998 (Life Peer), of Woodborough in the co. of Wiltshire; **John Stewart Hobhouse,** Kt 1982; PC 1993; a Lord of Appeal in Ordinary, 1998–2004; *b* 31 Jan. 1932; *s* of Sir John Hobhouse, MC; *m* 1959, Susannah Sibyl Caroline, *d* of Sir Ashton Roskill, QC; two *s* one *d*. *Educ:* Christ Church, Oxford (BCL 1958; MA 1958). Called to the Bar, Inner Temple, 1955; QC 1973; a Judge of the High Court, Queen's Bench Div., 1982–93; a Lord Justice of Appeal, 1993–98. *Address:* House of Lords, SW1A 0PW.
Died 15 March 2004.

HOBMAN, David Burton, CBE 1983; Director, Age Concern England (National Old People's Welfare Council), 1970–87; *b* 8 June 1927; *s* of J. B. and D. L. Hobman; *m* 1954, Erica Irwin; one *s* one *d*. *Educ:* University College Sch.; Blundell's. Community work, Forest of Dean, 1954–56; British Council for Aid to Refugees, 1957; Nat. Council of Social Service, 1958–67; Visiting Lectr in Social Admin, Nat. Inst. for Social Work, 1967; Dir, Social Work Adv. Service, 1968–70. Vis. Prof., Sch. of Social Work, McGill Univ., Montreal, 1977; Vis. Fellow, Univ. of Sussex, 1994–97. Member: BBC/ITA Appeals Adv. Council, 1965–69; Steering Cttee, Enquiry into Homelessness, Nat. Asstce Bd, 1967–68; Adv. Council, Nat. Corp. for Care of Old People, 1970–74; Metrication Bd, 1974–80; Lord Goodman's Cttee Reviewing Law of Charity, 1975–76; Chairman: Social Welfare Commn Conf. of Bishops, 1968–71; Family Housing Assoc., 1969–70; Oftel Adv. Cttee for Disabled and Elderly Persons, 1984–92; Home Concern Housing Assoc., 1985–87; Jt Chm., Age Concern Inst. of Gerontology, KCL, 1986–87; Consultant, UN Div. of Social Affairs, 1968–69; Observer, White House Congress

on Ageing, 1971–; Pres., Internat. Fedn on Ageing, 1977–80, 1983–87 (Vice-Pres., 1974–77); Member: Personal Social Services Council, 1978–80; Exec. Cttee, Nat. Council of Voluntary Orgns, 1981–83; Anchor Housing, 1984–86; Exec. Sec., Charities Effectiveness Review Trust, 1987–92. Producer, Getting On (television programme), 1987–88. Special Advr, British delegn to World Assembly on Ageing, 1982. Mem. Adv. Bd, Saga Magazine, 1985–98; Dir, Cinetel Ltd. Governor: Newman Comp. Sch., Hove, 1971–76 (Chm.); Volunteer Centre, 1975–79; Conciliator, Sheltered Housing Adv. and Conciliation Service, 1990–94; Counsellor, Helen Hamlyn Foundn, 1991–98; Company Ombudsman, Peverel Gp, 1995–. President's Medal, British Geriatrics Soc., 1998. KSG. *Publications:* A Guide to Voluntary Service, 1964, 2nd edn 1967; Who Cares, 1971; The Social Challenge of Ageing, 1978; The Impact of Ageing, 1981; The Coming of Age, 1989; Planning Your Retirement, 1990; Intergenerational Solidarity—fact and fiction, 1993; The More We Are Together: a study of partnerships in later life, 1995; numerous papers, broadcasts. *Recreations:* reading, writing, grandchildren. *Address:* Robinswood, George's Lane, Storrington, Pulborough, W Sussex RH20 3JH.
Died 24 Dec. 2003.

HOBSON, Peter; Chairman, Business Task Force, Objective One Partnership for Cornwall and Scilly, 2000–02; *b* 2 Oct. 1944; *er s* of late William Hobson and Sheila (*née* Surtees); *m* 1st, 1976, Amanda Rosemary (marr. diss. 1997), *d* of Michael Thomas Emilius Clayton, CB, OBE; 2nd, 2003, Joan Goodwill (*née* Wharton). *Educ:* Rossall Sch.; Queen's Coll., Oxford (Fletcher Exhibnr; BA LitHum 1967; MA 1972). Wellington College: Classics Dept, 1968–86; Housemaster, 1971–86; Industrial Liaison Officer, 1978–86; Headmaster: Giggleswick Sch., 1986–93; Charterhouse, 1993–95. Chairman: ISIS N, 1991–93; ISIS London and SE, 1995. Schoolmaster Fellow, Queen's Coll., Oxford, 1982. *Recreations:* travel, life in Cornwall, reading biography, watching sport. *Address:* Chy-Pedyr, Commercial Road, St Keverne, Helston, Cornwall TR12 6LY. *Died 24 Aug. 2003.*

HOCKADAY, Sir Arthur (Patrick), KCB 1978 (CB 1975); CMG 1969; Secretary and Director-General, Commonwealth War Graves Commission, 1982–89; *b* 17 March 1926; *s* of late William Ronald Hockaday and Marian Camilla Hockaday, *d* of Rev. A. C. Evans; *m* 1955, Peggy (*d* 1998), *d* of late H. W. Prince. *Educ:* Merchant Taylors' Sch.; St John's Coll., Oxford (BA (1st cl. Lit. Hum.) 1949, MA 1952). Apptd to Home Civil Service, 1949; Admty, 1949–62; Private Sec. to successive Ministers of Defence and Defence Secretaries, 1962–65; NATO Internat. Staff, 1965–69 (Asst Sec. Gen. for Defence Planning and Policy, 1967–69); Asst Under-Sec. of State, MoD, 1969–72; Under-Sec., Cabinet Office, 1972–73; Dep. Under-Sec. of State, MoD, 1973–76; 2nd Permanent Under-Sec. of State, MoD, 1976–82. Chm., British Group, Council on Christian Approaches to Defence and Disarmament, 1989–99. Chm., Gallipoli Meml Lecture Trust, 1990–93. *Publications:* (contrib.) Ethics and Nuclear Deterrence, 1982; The Strategic Defence Initiative, 1985; (contrib.) Ethics and European Security, 1986; (contrib.) Ethics and International Relations, 1986; (contrib.) Just Deterrence, 1990; (contrib.) The Crescent and the Cross, 1998; occasional articles and reviews. *Recreation:* fell-walking. *Address:* 11 Hitherwood Court, Hitherwood Drive, SE19 1UX. *T:* (020) 8670 7940. *Clubs:* Naval and Military, Civil Service.
Died 21 Aug. 2004.

HOCKENHULL, Arthur James Weston, OBE 1966; HM Diplomatic Service, retired; *b* 8 Aug. 1915; *s* of late Frederick Weston Hockenhull and Jessie Gibson Kaye Hockenhull (*née* Mitchell); *m* 1955, Rachel Ann Kimber; two *d. Educ:* Clifton Coll.; Exeter Coll., Oxford (MA). HM Overseas Civil Service: various appts in Far East, Cyprus and British Guiana, 1936–57. Interned by

Japanese, in Singapore, 1942–45. First Sec., UK Commn, Singapore, 1958–63; Counsellor, British High Commn, Malaysia, 1964–68; HM Consul-Gen., Houston, 1969–74. *Recreations:* golf, gardening, swimming. *Club:* Oxford and Cambridge. *Died 30 Jan. 2002.*

HODDINOTT, Sir John (Charles), Kt 1998; CBE 1994; QPM 1988; DL; Chief Constable, Hampshire Constabulary, 1988–99; *b* 21 Sept. 1944; *s* of Leslie Charles and Olive Muriel Hoddinott; *m* 1967, Avril Petheram; two *d. Educ:* Trinity Coll., Cambridge (MA). Metropolitan Police, 1963–81; Asst Chief Constable, Surrey Police, 1981–83; Dep. Chief Constable, Hampshire Constabulary, 1983–88. DL Hampshire, 1999. FRSA 1996. Hon. LLM Southampton Inst., 1996; Hon. LLD Portsmouth, 1997. *Recreations:* sailing, Rugby, gardening.
Died 13 Aug. 2001.

HODGE, Sir Julian Stephen Alfred, Kt 1970; merchant banker; Chairman: Avana Group Ltd, 1973–81; Carlyle Trust (Jersey) Ltd, since 1977; St Aubins Investment Co. Ltd, since 1986; Founder and Chairman, Bank of Wales, 1971–85; Chairman, Bank of Wales (Jersey) Ltd, 1974–87; Director, Bank of Wales (IoM) Ltd, 1974–85; *b* 15 Oct. 1904; *s* of late Alfred and Jane Hodge; *m* 1951, Moira (*née* Thomas); two *s* one *d. Educ:* Cardiff Technical Coll. Certified Accountant, 1930. Founded Hodge & Co., Accountants and Auditors; Man. Dir, 1963–75, Exec. Chm., 1975–78, Hodge Group Ltd; former Chairman: Julian S. Hodge & Co. Ltd; Gwent Enterprises Ltd; Hodge Finance Ltd; Hodge Life Assurance Co. Ltd; Carlyle Trust Ltd, 1962–85; Dir, Standard Chartered Bank, 1973–75. Founder and Chairman: The Jane Hodge Foundation, 1962; Sir Julian Hodge Charitable Trust, 1964; Chairman: Aberfan Disaster Fund Industrial Project Sub-Cttee; Member: Welsh Economic Council, 1965–68; Welsh Council, 1968–79; Council, Univ. of Wales Inst. of Science and Technology (Treasurer, 1968–76; Pres., 1981–85); Foundation Fund Cttee, Univ. of Surrey; Duke of Edinburgh Conf., 1974; Prince of Wales Cttee, 1979–85. Pres., S Glamorgan Dist, St John Ambulance Bde; Trustee, Welsh Sports Trust. Former Governor, All Hallows (Cranmore Hall) Sch. Trust Ltd. FTII 1941. FRSA. Fellow, UWCC, 1989. Hon. LLD Univ. of Wales, 1971. KStJ 1977 (CStJ 1972); KSG 1978. *Publication:* Paradox of Financial Preservation, 1959. *Recreations:* golf, walking, reading, gardening. *Address:* Clos des Seux, Mont du Coin, St Aubin, St Brelade, Jersey, JE3 8BE. *Clubs:* Victoria (St Helier, Jersey); La Moye Golf (Jersey).
Died 18 July 2004.

HODGES, C(yril) Walter; free-lance writer, book illustrator, theatrical historian and designer; *b* 18 March 1909; *s* of Cyril James and Margaret Mary Hodges; *m* 1936, Greta (*née* Becker) (*d* 1999); two *s. Educ:* Dulwich Coll.; Goldsmiths' Coll. Sch. of Art. Commenced as stage designer, 1929, then illustrator for advertising, magazines (esp. Radio Times) and children's books; began writing, 1937; served with Army, 1940–46 (despatches); has designed stage productions (Mermaid Theatre, 1951, 1964), permanent Elizabethan stage, St George's Theatre, 1976; exhibns (Lloyds, UK Provident Instn; retrospective of theatre designs, Folger Shakespeare Library, Washington, 1988); mural decorations painted for Chartered Insce Inst., UK Provident Instn; Art Dir, Encyclopædia Britannica Films, 1959–61; reconstruction drawings for model of excavated Elizabethan Rose Theatre, Museum of London, 1989–91; consultant designer, Globe Theatre, Alexander Mills, N Carolina, USA, 1993–. Judith E. Wilson Lectr in Poetry and Drama, Cambridge, 1974; Co-ordinator, Symposium for the Reconstruction of Globe Playhouse, 1979, Adjunct Prof. of Theatre, 1980–83, Wayne State Univ., USA; Vis. Scholar, Univ. of Maryland, 1983. Hon. DLitt Sussex, 1979. Kate Greenaway Medal for illustration, 1965; Hons List, Hans Christian Andersen Internat. Award, 1966. *Publications:* Columbus Sails, 1939; The Flying House, 1947; Shakespeare and the Players, 1948; The Globe

Restored, 1953, rev. edn 1968; The Namesake, 1964; Shakespeare's Theatre, 1964; The Norman Conquest, 1966; Magna Carta, 1966; The Marsh King, 1967; The Spanish Armada, 1967; The Overland Launch, 1969; The English Civil War, 1972; Shakespeare's Second Globe, 1973; Playhouse Tales, 1974; The Emperor's Elephant, 1975; Plain Lane Christmas, 1978; The Battlement Garden, 1979; (ed) The Third Globe, 1981; Enter the Whole Army: the presentation of Shakespeare's plays in the theatres of his time, 1999; contributor: Shakespeare Survey; Theatre Notebook; (illus.) The New Cambridge Shakespeare, 1984–. *Recreations:* music (listening), letters (writing), museums (visiting). *Address:* c/o 18 Parkhouse Road, Minehead, Somerset TA24 8AD. *T:* (01643) 704629.   *Died 26 Nov. 2004.*

HODGES, Elaine Mary, OBE 1975; HM Diplomatic Service, retired; Counsellor, Foreign and Commonwealth Office, 1981–83; *b* 12 Nov. 1928; *d* of late Lancelot James Hodges and Edith Mary (*née* Crossland). *Educ:* Nottingham High School for Girls; St Anne's Coll., Oxford (BA Hons, MA). Joined Foreign Office, 1952; served in: Germany, 1952–53; Switzerland, 1955–56; Warsaw, 1959; New Delhi, 1963–64; Paris, 1967–69; Brussels, 1974–79. *Recreations:* gardening, antiques, travel. *Address:* 46 Westbridge Road, SW11 3PW. *T:* (020) 7228 3771.   *Died 12 Oct. 2003.*

HODGES, Mark Willie; Head of the Office of Arts and Libraries, 1982–84; *b* 23 Oct. 1923; *s* of William H. and Eva Hodges; *m* 1948, Glenna Marion (*née* Peacock); one *s* one *d*. *Educ:* Cowbridge Grammar Sch.; Jesus Coll., Oxford (MA 1948). Served War, RN, 1942–45. Lectr, Univ. of Sheffield, 1950–54; DSIR, 1954–56; Asst Scientific Attaché, Washington, 1956–61; Office of Minister for Science, 1961–64; Sec., Royal Commn on Med. Educn, 1965–68; Asst Sec., DES, 1968–79 (Arts and Libraries Br., 1977–79); Office of Arts and Libraries, 1979–84, Under Sec., 1982, Dep. Sec., 1983. Member: South Bank Theatre Bd, 1982–93 (Chm., 1984–93); Council, Royal Albert Hall, 1983–93; Council and Management Cttee, Eastern Arts Assoc., 1986–89. *Recreations:* woodwork, computer programming, listening to music. *Address:* The Corner Cottage, Church Way, Little Stukeley, Cambs PE28 4BQ. *T:* (01480) 459266.   *Died 19 Nov. 2005.*

HODGSON, Hon. Sir Derek; *see* Hodgson, Hon. Sir W. D. T.

HODGSON, George Charles Day, CMG 1961; MBE 1950; Permanent Secretary, Ministry of Transport and Communications, Nyasaland, 1963–64; *b* 21 Sept. 1913; *s* of late P. J. Hodgson and of A. E. Joubert; *m* 1st, 1940, Edna Orde (*d* 1977), *d* of late G. H. Rushmere; one *s*; 2nd, 1978, Cecile Paston Dewar (*née* Foster). *Educ:* Diocesan Coll., Rondebosch, Capetown, S Africa; Rhodes Univ., Grahamstown, S Africa; Cambridge Univ. Joined Colonial Administrative Service as Cadet, 1939. Military Service, 1940–42, Lieut, 1st Bn King's African Rifles. Returned to duty as Distr. Officer, Nyasaland, 1943; seconded for special famine relief duties in Nyasaland, 1949–50; Provincial Commissioner, 1952; Adviser on Race Affairs to Govt of Federation of Rhodesia and Nyasaland, 1958–59; Nyasaland Govt Liaison Officer to Monckton Commn, 1960; Permanent Sec., Ministry of Natural Resources and Surveys, Nyasaland, 1961–62; retired from HMOCS, Nov. 1964. Sec., 1964–86, Patron, 2001, Old Diocesans' Union, Diocesan Coll., Rondebosch, SA. *Recreations:* Rugby football, cricket, golf. *Address:* 308 Grosvenor Square, College Road, Rondebosch, 7700, South Africa. *Clubs:* Royal Cape Golf, Western Province Cricket (Cape Town).   *Died 2 Jan. 2002.*

HODGSON, Stanley Ernest, CBE 1974 (OBE 1966); Education Adviser, British High Commission, New Delhi, 1971–77; *b* 11 July 1918; *s* of Harold Frederick Hodgson, MPS, and Winifred Caroline (*née* Gale); *m* 1945, Joan Beryl (*née* Ballard); two *d*. *Educ:* Brentwood Grammar

Sch.; London Univ. (Teacher's Certif., 1941; BA Hons Russian, 1949). RA, 1941–46. British Council: India, 1949–54; Uganda, 1956–60; Reg. Rep., South India, 1965–68; Controller Estabts, 1969–71. Dir, Fest. of India in Britain ,1982. *Recreations:* reading, gardening, walking. *Address:* Clarendon, Netherfield Road, Battle, East Sussex TN33 0HJ. *T:* (01424) 772631. *Club:* Royal Commonwealth Society.   *Died 28 April 2001.*

HODGSON, Col Terence Harold Henry, DSO 1945; MC 1944; TD 1953; DL; FSVA; Vice Lord-Lieutenant of Cumbria, 1983–91; *b* 10 Dec. 1916; *s* of late Michael C. L. Hodgson, Grange-over-Sands; *m* 1st, 1942, Joan Winsome Servant (marr. diss. 1969; she *d* 1974); 2nd, 1972, Doreen Jacqueline Pollit Brünzel (*d* 1985); two *s* three *d* (and one *s* decd); 3rd, 1985, Elizabeth Robinson. *Educ:* Kendal Grammar Sch. FRICS 2001 (FSVA 1953); FRSH 1954. Served War with Border Regt, Ceylon, India and Burma; Comdr, 4th Bn Border Regt, TA, 1953–56; Dep. Comdr, 126 Inf. Bde, TA, 1956–59; Col TA, 1959; Hon. Colonel: King's Own Royal Border Regt, 1976–82; Cumbria Cadet Force, 1977–86. Dir, Cartmel Steeplechasers Ltd, 1959–98; Local Dir, Royal Insurance, 1960–. Chairman: Governors, Kirkbie Kendal Sch., 1970–86; Kendal Almshouse Charities, 1975–86; Cumbria Appeal Cttee, Army Benevolent Fund, 1987–93. Past Pres., Cumberland and Westmorland Rugby Union. DL Westmorland, 1958. *Recreations:* Rugby football, horse racing. *Address:* The Esplanade, Abbotsrood, Grange-over-Sands, Cumbria LA11 7HH. *T:* (015395) 32843. *Club:* Army and Navy.   *Died 3 Aug. 2004.*

HODGSON, Hon. Sir (Walter) Derek (Thornley), Kt 1977; a Judge of the High Court of Justice, Queen's Bench Division, 1977–92; *b* 24 May 1917; *s* of late Walter Hodgson, Whitefield, Manchester; *m* 1951, Raymonde Valda (*née* de Villiers) (*d* 1965); no *c*. *Educ:* Malvern Coll.; Trinity Hall, Cambridge (Scholar; 1st Cl. Law Tripos, Part II, 1938; 1st Cl. LLB, 1939). Served throughout War 1939–46, Royal Artillery; Burma 1942–45; released with rank of Captain, 1946. Called to Bar, Middle Temple, 1946 (Harmsworth Scholar; Bencher, 1967); QC 1961. Member: Gen. Council of the Bar, 1965–69; Senate of Inns of Court, 1966–69. Judge of the Salford Hundred Court of Record, 1965–71; a Law Comr, 1971–77; a Recorder of the Crown Court, 1972–77. Member: Lord Chancellor's Cttees on: Legal Educn, 1968–71; Contempt of Court, 1971–74; Butler Cttee on Mentally Abnormal Offenders, 1973–75; Parole Board, 1981–83 (Vice-Chm., 1982–83). Chm., Howard League Wkg Pty on Forfeiture (report published as The Profits of Crime and their Recovery, 1984). *Recreation:* travel. *Address:* Carpmael Building, Middle Temple Lane, EC4Y 7AT. *T:* (020) 7583 1613. *Clubs:* Oxford and Cambridge, MCC; Tennis and Racquets (Manchester); Hawks (Cambridge).   *Died 10 Oct. 2002.*

HODSON, Prof. Frank, PhD; Professor of Geology in the University of Southampton, 1958–81, then Emeritus; *b* 23 Nov. 1921; *s* of late Matthew and Gertrude Hodson; *m* 1945, Ada Heyworth; three *d*. *Educ:* Burnley Grammar Sch.; London Univ. (external student; BSc 1949); Reading Univ. (PhD 1951). Demonstrator, 1947–49, Lectr, 1949–58, Reading Univ.; Dean, Faculty of Science, 1972–74 and 1976–77, Public Orator, 1970–73, Univ. of Southampton. Murchison Fund, Geol. Soc., 1962. Founder Mem. and first Hon. Sec., Palaeontol. Assoc., 1957; Pres. Sect. C (geology), British Assoc. for Adv. of Science, 1975. Hon. Mem. Geol. Soc. de Belg. *Publications:* geol papers in pubns of learned socs. *Recreation:* book collecting.   *Died 27 Oct. 2002.*

HOFF, Harry Summerfield; *see* Cooper, William.

HOGARTH, (Arthur) Paul, OBE 1989; RA 1984 (ARA 1974); RE 1988; RDI 1979; painter, illustrator and draughtsman; *b* Kendal, Cumbria, 4 Oct. 1917; *s* of Arthur Hogarth and Janet Bownass; *m* 1st, 1940, Doreen (*d* 1948), *d* of Albert Courtman, Alderley Edge, Cheshire; 2nd,

1949, Phyllis (née Pamplin) (d 1962); one s; 3rd, 1963, Patricia Morgan Graham (née Douthwaite) (d 1981); 4th, 1989, Diana Marjorie (née Cochran). Educ: St Agnes Sch., Manchester; Coll. of Art, Manchester; St Martin's Sch. of Art, London. Travels in: Poland and Czechoslovakia, 1953; USSR and China, 1954; Rhodesia and S Africa, 1956; Ireland, with Brendan Behan, 1959; USA, 1961–79. Senior tutor of Drawing: Cambridge Sch. of Art, 1959–61; RCA, 1964–71; Associate Prof., Philadelphia Coll. of Art, 1968–69; Vis. Lectr, RCA, 1971–81. Hon. Pres., Assoc. of Illustrators, 1982. Exhibitions: one-man: Leicester Gall., London, 1955; Agnews, London, 1957; Amer. Embassy, London, 1964; retrospectives: Time-Life Bldg, London, 1968; World of Paul Hogarth, Arts Council, RCA Gall., 1970; Travels through the Seventies, Kyle Gall., London; The Other Hogarth, Northern Arts Council, 1985–86; Paul Hogarth at 80, RA, 1997; Cold War Reports: drawings 1947–67, Norfolk Inst. of Art & Design, Eastern Arts Council, 1989–90; Escape to the Sun: the travels of D. H. Lawrence, Univ. of Nottingham Arts Centre, 1996; exhibits regularly at Francis Kyle Gall., London. Sen. Fellow, RE, 1991. FRSA 1984. Dr RCA, 1971. Hon. DArts Manchester Metropolitan, 1999. Publications: Defiant People, 1953; Looking at China, 1956; People Like Us, 1958; (illus.) Brendan Behan's Island, 1962; Creative Pencil Drawing, 1964, 6th edn 1979; (illus.) Brendan Behan's New York, 1964; (with Robert Graves) Majorca Observed, 1965; (with M. Muggeridge) London à la Mode, 1966; Artist as Reporter, 1967, revised and enlarged edn, 1986; (with A. Jacob) Russian Journey, 1969; Drawing People, 1971; Artists on Horseback, 1972; Drawing Architecture, 1973; Paul Hogarth's American Album, 1974; Creative Ink Drawing, 1974, 5th edn 1979; Walking Tours of Old Philadelphia, 1976; Walking Tours of Old Boston, 1978; (with Stephen Spender) America Observed, 1979; Arthur Boyd Houghton, 1982; (with Graham Greene) Graham Greene Country, 1986; (with Laurence Durrell) The Mediterranean Shore, 1988; (with Peter Mayle) Illustrated Year in Provence, 1992; (with John Betjeman) In Praise of Churches, 1996; Drawing on Life (autobiog.), 1997. Address: c/o Royal Academy of Arts, Piccadilly, W1V 0DS. Club: Arts.

Died 27 Dec. 2001.

HOGARTH, Paul; see Hogarth, A. P.

HOGG, Vice-Adm. Sir Ian (Leslie Trower), KCB 1968 (CB 1964); DSC 1941, and Bar 1944; b 30 May 1911; 3rd s of Col John M. T. Hogg, IA, and Elma (née Brand); m 1945, Mary G. J., e d of Col and Mrs Marsden; two s. Educ: Cheltenham Coll. Entered Royal Navy, 1929; specialised in Navigation, 1937; HMS Cardiff, 1939; HMS Penelope, 1940; HMAS Napier, 1941–43; HMS Mauritius, 1944–45; Master of the Fleet, 1946–47; British Admiralty Delegn, Washington, DC, 1948–49; HMS Sluys, in comd, 1950–51; Staff of C-in-C Med., 1952–53; Captain RN, Dec. 1953; Brit. Joint Staff, Washington, DC, 1955–57; idc 1958; Staff of Chief of Defence Staff, 1959–60; Cdre, Cyprus, 1961–62; Dir, Chief of Defence Staff's Commonwealth Exercise, 1962–63; Rear-Adm. 1963; Flag Officer, Medway, and Admiral Superintendent, HM Dockyard, Chatham, 1963–66; Vice-Adm. 1966; Defence Services Sec., 1966–67; Vice-Chief of the Defence Staff, 1967–70, retired. Comptroller, Royal Soc. of St George, 1971–74; Dir, Richard Unwin Internat. Ltd, 1975–86. Address: 21 Chapel Side, Titchfield, Hants PO14 4AP. T: (01329) 847515. *Died 3 March 2003.*

HOGG, Sir Michael (David), 8th Bt cr 1846, of Upper Grosvenor Street, Middlesex; b 19 Aug. 1925; e s of Sir Arthur Ramsay Hogg, 7th Bt, MBE and Mary Aileen Hester Lee Evans (d 1980); S father, 1995; m 1956, Elizabeth Anne Thérèse, e d of Sir Terence Falkiner, 8th Bt; three s. Educ: Sherborne; Christ Church, Oxford (BA 1950; MA 1953). Served World War II; Captain, Grenadier Guards, 1943–47. Journalist, The Daily Telegraph, 1951–87: editor, Peterborough, 1971–79; asst editor, 1976; arts editor, 1979–86; letters editor, 1986–87.

Recreations: reading, painting, gossip. Heir: s Piers Michael James Hogg [b 25 April 1957; m 1982, Vivien (marr. diss. 1996), y d of Dr Philip Holman; one s one d].

Died 12 July 2001.

HOGGE, Maj.-Gen. (Arthur) Michael (Lancelot), CB 1979; DL; b 4 Aug. 1925; s of late Lt-Col A. H. F. Hogge, Punjab Regt, Indian Army, and Mrs K. M. Hogge; m 1952, Gunilla Jeane Earley; two s. Educ: Wellington Coll.; Brasenose Coll., Oxford. Commissioned, Oct. 1945; 6th Airborne Armoured Recce Regt and 3rd Hussars, Palestine, 1945–48; regimental appts, 3rd Hussars, BAOR, 1948–58; Queen's Own Hussars, BAOR, and Staff appts, 1958–65; comd Queen's Own Hussars, UK and Aden, 1965–67; Col GS, Staff Coll., 1969–71; Royal Coll. of Defence Studies, 1972; Dir of Operational Requirements, MoD, 1973–74, rank of Brig.; Dir Gen. Fighting Vehicles and Engineer Equipment, 1974–77; Dep. Master-General of the Ordnance, 1977–80. Gen. Man., Regular Forces Employment Assoc., 1981–87. Vice-Pres., Surrey Branch, SSAFA, 1996– (Chm., 1992–96). DL Surrey, 1993. Recreations: sailing, horticulture. *Died 13 July 2005.*

HOHLER, Henry Arthur Frederick, CMG 1954; HM Diplomatic Service, retired; Ambassador to Switzerland, 1967–70; b 4 Feb. 1911; e s of late Lt-Col Arthur Preston Hohler, DSO; m 1st, 1932, Mona Valentine (d 1944), d of late Lt-Col Arthur Murray Pirie, DSO; two s; 2nd, 1945, Eveline Susan, d of late Lt-Col Hon. Neville Albert Hood, CMG, DSO; two d. Educ: Eton; Sandhurst. 2nd Lieut Grenadier Guards, 1931. 3rd Sec. in Foreign Office, 1934; Budapest, 1936; 2nd Sec., 1939; Foreign Office, 1941; 1st Sec., 1945; Berne, 1945; Helsinki, 1948; Moscow, 1949; Counsellor, 1950; Head of Northern Dept, Foreign Office, 1951; Minister in Rome, 1956–60; Ambassador in Saigon, 1960–63; Minister in Paris, 1963–65; Asst Under-Sec., Foreign Office, 1966–67. Liveryman, Grocers' Company. Clubs: Boodle's; Metropolitan (Washington).

Died 19 May 2001.

HOLDEN, Sir Edward, 6th Bt cr 1893; Consultant Anæsthetist, Darlington and Northallerton Group Hospitals, 1957–74; b 8 Oct. 1916; s of Sir Isaac Holden Holden, 5th Bt, and Alice Edna Byrom (d 1971); S father, 1962; m 1942, Frances Joan, e d of John Spark, JP, Ludlow, Stockton-on-Tees; two adopted s. Educ: Leys Sch., Cambridge; Christ's Coll., Cambridge; St Thomas's Hosp. DA Eng., 1946. MRCS; LRCP 1942; FRCA (FFARCS, 1958). Formerly Vis. Anæsthetist, Cumb. Infirm., Carlisle; Cons. Anæsthetist, W Cumb. Hospital Group. Mem. Council, Harlow Car Gardens. Recreations: fishing, gardening. Heir: b Paul Holden [b 3 March 1923; m 1950, Vivien Mary Oldham; one s two d]. Address: 40 South End, Osmotherley, Northallerton, N Yorks DL6 3BL. Club: Farmers'. *Died 22 July 2003.*

HOLDER, Air Marshal Sir Paul (Davie), KBE 1965; CB 1964; DSO 1942; DFC 1941; Air Officer Commanding-in-Chief, RAF Coastal Command, NATO Commander Maritime Air, Channel Command, and Commander Maritime Air, Eastern Atlantic Area, 1965–68, retired; b 2 Sept. 1911; s of Hugh John and Frances Rhoda Holder; m 1940, Mary Elizabeth Kidd; two s. Educ: Bristol Univ. (MSc 1933; Robert Blair Fellow, 1934; PhD 1935); Univ. of Illinois, USA. Commissioned RAF, 1936; Flt Comdr 84 Sqdn, Iraq, 1938–39; Stn Admin. Officer, Habbiniya, Iraq, 1940–41; OC 218 Sqdn Bomber Comd, 1941–42 (1st thousand bomber raid, Cologne); SASO Force 686, Ankara, Turkey, 1943; Group Capt. Plans, MEAF; formed Marshal Tito's first Hurricane Fighter Sqdn, Benina, Libya, 1944; DS RAF Staff Coll., 1945; CO RAF Broadwell, Transport Comd, 1946; Vice-Pres., RAF Selection Bd, 1947–48; Student, Admin. Staff Coll., Henley-on-Thames, 1947; Chief Instr, RAF Officer Cadet Training Sch., 1948–49; CO, RAF, Shallufa, Egypt, 1950–51; CO, RAF, Kabrit, Egypt, 1952; Dep. Dir, Air Staff Policy, Air Min., 1953–55; Student, Imperial Defence Coll., 1956; AOC, Singapore, 1957; AOC, Hong Kong, 1958–59; ACAS (Trng), Air Min., 1960–62; AOC No 25 Gp, RAF

Flying Trng Comd, 1963–64. FRAeS 1966. *Recreations:* gardening, bridge. *Address:* Innisfree, Bramshott Chase, Hindhead, Surrey GU26 6DG. *T:* (01428) 604579. *Club:* Royal Air Force. *Died 22 April 2001.*

HOLDERNESS, Baron *cr* 1979 (Life Peer), of Bishop Wilton in the County of Humberside; **Richard Frederick Wood;** PC 1959; DL; *b* 5 Oct. 1920; 3rd *s* of 1st Earl of Halifax, KG, PC, OM, GCSI, GCMG, GCIE, TD; *m* 1947, Diana, *d* of late Col E. O. Kellett, DSO, MP, and Hon. Mrs W. J. McGowan; one *s* one *d. Educ:* Eton; New College, Oxford. Hon. Attaché, British Embassy, Rome, 1940; served War of 1939–45 as Lieutenant, KRRC, 1941–43; retired, wounded, 1943; toured US Army hospitals, 1943–45; New College, Oxford, 1945–47. MP (C) Bridlington, Yorkshire, 1950–79; Parliamentary Private Secretary: to Minister of Pensions, 1951–53; to Minister of State, Board of Trade, 1953–54; to Minister of Agriculture and Fisheries, 1954–55; Joint Parliamentary Secretary: Ministry of Pensions and National Insurance, 1955–58; Ministry of Labour, 1958–59; Minister of Power, October 1959–63, of Pensions and National Insurance, Oct. 1963–64; Minister of Overseas Develt, ODM, June–Oct. 1970, FCO, 1970–74. Dir, Hargreaves Group Ltd, 1974–86; Regional Dir, Yorkshire and Humberside regional board, Lloyds Bank, 1981–90. Chairman: Disablement Services Authy, 1987–91; Adv. Gp on Rehabilitation, DoH, 1991–96. Pres., Queen Elizabeth's Foundn for the Disabled, 1983–96. DL E Riding Yorks, 1967. Hon. LLD: Sheffield Univ., 1962; Leeds, 1978; Hull, 1982. Hon. Colonel: Queen's Royal Rifles, 1962; 4th (Volunteer) Bn Royal Green Jackets, 1967–89. *Address:* Hernes Keep, Winkfield, Berks SL4 4SY. *T:* (01344) 882416.

Died 11 Aug. 2002.

HOLGATE, Dr Sidney, CBE 1981; PhD; Founder Master of Grey College, University of Durham, 1959–80; Member, Academic Advisory Committee, Open University, 1969–81 (Vice-Chairman, 1972–75; Chairman, 1975–77); *b* Hucknall, Notts, 9 Sept. 1918; *e s* of late Henry and Annie Elizabeth Holgate; *m* 1942, Isabel Armorey; no *c. Educ:* Henry Mellish Sch., Nottingham; Durham Univ. (Open Scholar, Hatfield Coll., Durham, 1937; Univ. Mathematical Scholarship, 1940; BA (1st Cl. Hons Mathematics) 1940; DThPT 1941; MA 1943; PhD 1945). Commnd RAFVR (Trng Br.), 1942–45. Asst Master, Nottingham High Sch., 1941–42; University of Durham: Lectr in Mathematics, 1942–46; Sec. of the Durham Colls, 1946–59; Pro-Vice-Chancellor, 1964–69. Mem., Schools Council Gen. Studies Cttee, 1967–70; Chm., BBC Radio Durham Council, 1968–72; Vice-Chm., BBC Radio Newcastle Council, 1972–74. DUniv. Open, 1980. *Publications:* mathematical papers in Proc. Camb. Phil. Soc. and Proc. Royal Soc. *Recreations:* cricket and other sports, railways, bridge. *Address:* Rookstone, 46 North End, Durham DH1 4LW.

Died 17 May 2003.

HOLLAND, Arthur David, CB 1973; TD 1947; Chief Highway Engineer, Department of the Environment, 1970–74; *b* 1 Nov. 1913; *o s* of Col Arthur Leslie Holland, MC, TD, and Dora Helena Hassé; *m* 1938, Jean Moyra Spowart (decd); two *s. Educ:* Malvern Coll.; University of Bristol (BSc(Eng) Hons). Asst Engineer, Great Western Railway Co., 1935–36; N Devon CC, 1936–37; Ministry of Transport: Manchester, 1937–38; London, 1938–39; served War with RE, 1939–46: in Air Defence Gt Britain, 1939–42; with Middle East Forces, 1942–46, finally as Lt-Col RE (latterly Hon. Lt-Col), Sen. Staff Officer to Chief Engineer, Italy; Min. of Transport, Nottingham, 1946–47; Bridge Section, London, 1947–61; Divl Road Engr, E Midland Div., Nottingham, 1961–63; Asst Chief Engr (Bridges), 1963–65; Dep. Chief Engr, HQ London, 1965–70. FICE, FIStructE, FInstHE; Mem., Smeatonian Soc. of Civil Engrs, 1972– (Pres., 1991). *Publications:* contribs to Proc. Instn of Civil Engineers and Instn of Highway Engineers. *Address:* Pine Tree Cottage,

Pembroke Road, Woking, Surrey GU22 7DS. *T:* (01483) 762403. *Died 4 Sept. 2001.*

HOLLAND, Edward Richard Charles, OBE 1983 (MBE 1969); HM Diplomatic Service, retired; *b* 26 March 1925; *s* of Cecil Francis Richard Holland and Joyce Mary (*née* Pyne); *m* 1952, Dorothy Olive Branthwaite (*d* 1997); two *s. Educ:* Launceston Coll. Served RAF, 1943–48. Joined FO, 1948; served in Batavia, Bangkok, Oslo, Prague and Helsinki, 1949–57; Consul, Saigon, 1957; FO, 1959; Cape Town, 1962; First Sec., Monrovia, 1964; Consul: Stuttgart, 1969; Düsseldorf, 1971; FCO, 1972; First Sec., Islamabad, 1977; Consul-Gen., Alexandria, 1981–82. *Recreations:* gardening, playing with computer, reading. *Address:* 25 Stafford Road, Seaford, E Sussex BN25 1UE. *T:* (01323) 897631. *Clubs:* Civil Service; Seaford Constitutional. *Died 18 July 2005.*

HOLLAND, Sir Kenneth (Lawrence), Kt 1981; CBE 1971; QFSM 1974; Consultant, Fire Safety Engineering, since 1981; Director: Gent Ltd, 1981–93; Bas/Firelaw Ltd, since 1993; *b* 20 Sept. 1918; *s* of Percy Lawrence and Edith Holland; *m* 1941, Pauline Keith (*née* Mansfield); two *s* one *d. Educ:* Whitcliffe Mount Grammar Sch., Cleckheaton, Yorks. Entered Fire Service, Lancashire, 1937; Divisional Officer: Suffolk and Ipswich, 1948; Worcestershire, 1952; Dep. Chief Fire Officer, Lancashire, 1955; Chief Fire Officer: Bristol, 1960; West Riding of Yorkshire, 1967; HM Chief Inspector of Fire Services, 1972–80. Chm., Firelaw Ltd, 1988–93. Chm., British Fire Services Assoc., 1964–65; President: Fire Brigade Soc., 1969; IFireE, 1969; Commonwealth Overseas Fire Services Assoc., 1983–90; Assoc. of Structural Fire Protection Contractors and Manufacturers, 1986–90; Nat. Assoc. for Safety in the Home, 1988–90. Chairman: ISO Technical Cttee TC/21 Fire Equipment, 1983–94; Loss Prevention Certification Bd, 1984–92; Multi-technics Council, BSI, 1984–90; Visitor, Fire Res. Station, 1984–90. Vice Pres., Fire Services Nat. Benevolent Fund, 1973–. Trustee: Fire Services Res. Trng Trust, 1983–2003; Ivy Owen Award Trust, 1989–2000. Hon. Treasurer, Poole Arts Fedn, 1985–88. Pres., Past Rotarians Club, Bournemouth, 1995. Freeman, City of London, 1981. Defence Medal; Fire Brigade Long Service and Good Conduct Medal. OStJ 1964. *Recreations:* sports, gardening, the Arts. *Club:* Royal Over-Seas League. *Died 3 June 2001.*

HOLLAND, Brother Tristam (Keith), SSF; Anglican Franciscan friar; *b* 20 March 1946; *s* of late George Holland and Eva Holland (*née* Pinion-Clark). *Educ:* Eastwood Hall Park Sch.; Trinity Coll., Cambridge (BA 1988, MA 1992). Joined Society of St Francis, 1967; Guardian, Fiwila Friary and Leprosarium, Zambia, 1973–76; Provincial Sec., 1976–83, Gen. Sec., 1983–97, SSF. Member: Liturgical Commn of C of E, 1991–; Gen. Synod, C of E, 1995–. Editor, Franciscan Qly Magazine, 1994–. Mem., Labour Party. *Publications:* Celebrating Common Prayer, 1992; The Daily Office SSF, 1992; Exciting Holiness, 1997; The Word of the Lord, 4 vols, 1998–2001; The Gospel of the Lord, 1999; A Sense of the Divine, 2001. *Recreations:* reading novels, music, travel. *Address:* Hilfield Friary, Dorchester, Dorset DT2 7BE. *T:* (01300) 341166, *Fax:* (01300) 341293; *e-mail:* tristam@ssf.orders.anglican.org. *Died 28 Dec. 2002.*

HOLLAND-MARTIN, Rosamund Mary, (Lady Holland-Martin), DBE 1983 (OBE 1947); DL; Member, Central Executive Committee, National Society for the Prevention of Cruelty to Children, since 1947 (Chairman of the Society, 1969–87); *b* 26 June 1914; *d* of Charles Harry St John Hornby and Cicely Rachel Emily Barclay; *m* 1951, Adm. Sir Deric Holland-Martin, GCB, DSO, DSC (*d* 1977), Lord Lieutenant of Hereford and Worcester; one *s* one *d. Educ:* privately. WVS Administrator, South East, 1946–51; Vice-Chm., WRVS, 1978–81; Pres., Friends of Worcester Cathedral, 1978–98; Pres., Worcester Sea Cadets, 1978–. DL Hereford and Worcester, 1983. *Recreations:* needlework, photography, collecting things. *Address:* Bells Castle, Kemerton,

Tewkesbury, Glos GL20 7JW. *T:* (01386) 725333.
Died 18 June 2001.

HOLLEY, (William) Stephen, CBE 1979; General Manager, Washington Development Corporation, 1965–80; *b* 26 March 1920; *m* 1947, Dinah Mary Harper; three *s. Educ:* King William's Coll. Student Accountant, 1937–39. War service, RA (TA), 1939–45 (Major). Colonial Service, and Overseas Civil Service, 1945–64; Mem. Legislature and State Sec., Head of Civil Service, Sabah, Malaysia, 1964. DL Tyne and Wear, 1975–81. Hon. ADK (Malaysia). *Publications:* Washington—Quicker by Quango, 1983; Entente Cordiale, 1990; Godverse and Oddverse, 1998; White Headhunter in Borneo, 2004; contribs to Sarawak Museum Jl and press articles on New Town develt. *Recreations:* writing, gardening, theatre. *Address:* Forge Cottage, The Green, Abthorpe, Northants NN12 8QP. *Club:* Royal Commonwealth Society.
Died 4 July 2005.

HOLLIS, Sir Anthony Barnard, Kt 1982; a Judge of the High Court of Justice, Family Division, 1982–97; *b* 11 May 1927; *er s* of late Henry Lewis Hollis and of Gladys Florence Hollis (*née* Barnard); *m* 1956, Pauline Mary (*née* Skuce); one step *d. Educ:* Tonbridge Sch.; St Peter's Hall, Oxford (Hon. Fellow, St Peter's Coll., 1993). Called to the Bar, Gray's Inn, 1951 (Bencher, 1979); QC 1969; a Recorder of the Crown Court, 1976–82. Chm., Family Law Bar Assoc., 1974–76. *Recreation:* golf. *Address:* Hook Hill, Hook Hill Lane, Woking, Surrey GU22 0QB. *Clubs:* Garrick; Woking Golf; Royal St George's Golf (Sandwich).
Died 24 Nov. 2003.

HOLLIS, Ven. Gerald; Archdeacon of Birmingham, 1974–84; *b* 16 May 1919; *s* of Canon Walter Hollis and Enid (*née* Inchbold); *m* 1946, Doreen Emmet Stancliffe; one *s* three *d. Educ:* St Edward's Sch., Oxford; Christ Church, Oxford (MA); Wells Theological College. RNVR, 1940–45. Ordained deacon 1947, priest 1948; Curate: All Saints, Stepney, E1, 1947–50; i/c St Luke's, Rossington, 1950–55; Rector, Armthorpe, 1955–60; Vicar of Rotherham and Rural Dean, 1960–74. Hon. Canon, Birmingham Cathedral, 1984–. Mem. Gen. Synod, C of E, 1975–84. *Publication:* Rugger: do it this way, 1946. *Recreation:* gardening. *Address:* 68 Britford Lane, Salisbury, Wilts SP2 8AH. *T:* (01722) 338154. *Club:* Vincent's (Oxford).
Died 25 Nov. 2005.

HOLM, Sir Carl Henry, (Sir Charles Holm), Kt 1987; OBE 1975; land developer, dairy farmer, cane farmer; *b* 1 Aug. 1915; *s* of Frederick Otto Holm and Johanna Jamieson (formerly Stickens); *m* 1st, 1938, Myrtle Phyllis Murtha (*d* 1987); one *s*; 2nd, 1988, Joyce Elaine Blackbeard (*née* Shell). *Educ:* Baralaba State Sch.; Ipswich Boys' Sch.; Pimpana State Sch.; Coomera State Sch. Sgt, Volunteer Defence Corp., 1942–45. Albert Shire Council: Councillor, 1967–82; Mem., Town Planning Cttee, 1975–82; Chm., Works Cttee, 1975–82; National Party of Australia: first Sen. Vice-Pres., Qld, 1972–90; Federal Sen. Vice-Pres., 1975–; past Chm., Transport Cttee; past Chm., Conservation Cttee. Queensland Dairymen's Organisation: Mem., 1946–96; Chm., SE District Council, 1961–96; Mem., State Council, 1972–96; Mem., State Milk Exec., 1967–; Chm., United Milk Producers Co-operative Assoc., 1972–96; Pres., Metrop. Milk Producers Co-operative Assoc., 1976–79, Dir, 1979–96. *Recreation:* riding horses. *Address:* 4919 The Parkway, Sanctuary Cove, Qld 4212, Australia. *T:* (7) 55779085. *Club:* National (Southport, Qld) (Foundn Mem. and Chm., 1973–91).
Died 23 Nov. 2001.

HOLME, Maj.-Gen. Michael Walter, CBE 1966; MC 1945; *b* 9 May 1918; *s* of Thomas Walter Holme and Ruth Sangster Holme (*née* Rivington); *m* 1948, Sarah Christian Van Der Gucht; one *s* two *d. Educ:* Winchester College. Directing Staff, Staff Coll., Camberley, 1952–55; Comdr 1st Bn 3rd East Anglian Regt, 1960–62; Comdr Land Forces Persian Gulf, 1963–66; Chief of Staff, Western Comd, 1966–67; Divisional Brig., The Queen's Div.,

1968–69; GOC Near East Land Forces, 1969–72, retired. Dep. Col, The Royal Anglian Regiment, 1970–77. *Recreations:* various. *Address:* Glen Cottage, 145 Park Road, Camberley, Surrey GU15 2LL. *Club:* Army and Navy.
Died 5 Dec. 2004.

HOLMES, Barry Trevor; HM Diplomatic Service, retired; business development and public relations consultant, since 1993; *b* 23 Sept. 1933; *s* of Edwin Holmes and Marion (*née* Jones); *m* 1st, 1956, Dorothy Pitchforth (marr. diss. 1989); three *d*; 2nd, 1992, Sherie Shortridge (marr. diss. 2001). *Educ:* Bishopshalt Grammar School. Nat. Service, RA, Egypt, 1953–55 (Capt.). Entered HM Foreign Service, 1950; Personnel Services Dept, 1950–53; Foreign Office, 1955–58; Quito, 1958–62; FO, 1962–65; Vancouver, 1965–68; First Sec., FCO, 1968–72; Nairobi, 1972–75; FCO, 1975–80; Commercial Counsellor, Helsinki, 1980–85; Consul-Gen., Atlanta, 1985–92. Dir, British Amer. Business Gp, Atlanta, 1994–99. Pres., ESU Atlanta Br., 1996–97. Internat. Vice-Pres., Rotary Club of Atlanta, 2001–02. *Recreations:* chess, light opera, walking. *Address:* 2097R Lake Park Drive, Smyrna, GA 30080, USA.
Died 17 Nov. 2004.

HOLMES, Sir Peter (Fenwick), Kt 1988; MC 1952; Managing Director, 1982–93 and Chairman, Committee of Managing Directors, 1992–93, Royal Dutch/Shell Group; Director, Shell Transport and Trading Co., 1982–2001 (Chairman, 1985–93); *b* 27 Sept. 1932; *s* of Gerald Hugh Holmes and Caroline Elizabeth Holmes; *m* 1st, 1955, Judith Millicent (*née* Walker) (marr. diss. 1999); three *d*; 2nd, 1999, Mary Lois Holmes; one step *d. Educ:* Trinity Coll., Cambridge (MA). Various posts in Royal Dutch/Shell Group, 1956–93, including: Gen. Man., Shell Markets, ME, 1965–68; Chief Rep., Libya, 1970–72; Man. Dir, Shell-BP, Nigeria, 1977–81; Pres., Shell Internat. Trading, 1981–83. Pres., Hakluyt Foundn, 1997–. Trustee, WWF–UK, 1989–96. FRGS. Hon. DSc Cranfield, 1993. *Publications:* Mountains and a Monastery, 1958; Nigeria, Giant of Africa, 1985; Turkey, A Timeless Bridge, 1988. *Recreations:* mountaineering, ski-ing, travel to remote areas, fishing, photography, 19th century travel books. *Address:* c/o Shell Centre, SE1 7NA. *T:* (020) 7934 5611. *Clubs:* Athenæum, Alpine, Himalayan, Climbers, Kandahar.
Died 8 March 2002.

HOLT, Richard Anthony Appleby; Chairman, 1959–78, Managing Director, 1978–80, Hutchinson Ltd; Chairman: Hutchinson Publishing Group, 1965–80; Hutchinson Printing Trust, 1957–80; *b* 11 March 1920; *s* of Frederick Appleby Holt and Rae Vera Franz (*née* Hutchinson); *m* 1945, Daphne Vivien Pegram; three *s* two *d. Educ:* Harrow Sch.; King's Coll., Cambridge. Served War of 1939–45, commissioned 60th Rifles, 1941; demobilised, 1946 (Major). Admitted Solicitor, 1949. Dir, Constable & Co., 1968–90. Gov., Harrow Sch., 1952–82. *Recreation:* lawn tennis. *Address:* 55 Queen's Gate Mews, SW7 5QN. *T:* (020) 7589 8469. *Clubs:* All England Lawn Tennis & Croquet (Vice-Pres., 1982–), MCC.
Died 18 May 2001.

HOLT, Prof. Stephen Campbell, OBE 2000; PhD; Rector and Chief Executive, Roehampton Institute, London, 1988–99, then Emeritus Professor, University of Surrey Roehampton; *b* 27 Sept. 1935; *s* of late E. S. Holt and E. C. Holt; *m* 1st, 1959, Moira Jill Ditchburn (marr. diss.); two *s* one *d*; 2nd, 1989, Anne Ashcroft; two step *d. Educ:* Mill Hill Sch.; Emmanuel Coll., Cambridge (MA); PhD Manchester 1966. Nat. Service, RM, 1954–56, 2nd Lieut. Worked in family hosiery business, The Holt Hosiery Co., 1959–61; research, Dept of Govt, Univ. of Manchester, 1961–63; Asst Lectr and Lectr, Dept of Political Theory and Instns, Univ. of Sheffield, 1963–69; Vis. Prof., Univ. of Colorado, 1969–70; University of Bradford: Prof. of Eur. Studies, 1970–80; Pro Vice-Chancellor, 1976–78; University of Kent at Canterbury: Prof. of Eur. Studies, 1980–88; Pro Vice-Chancellor, 1986–88. Vis. Prof., Coll. of Europe, Bruges, 1984–88. CEDR Registered Mediator, 2001. Chm., Horsham Dist

Community Mediation Service. Hon. Fellow, St Mary's Coll., Twickenham, 2000. DUniv Surrey, 1999. *Publications:* The Common Market, 1967; Six European States, 1970; (with J. E. Farquharson) Europe from Below, 1975; articles in acad. jls. *Recreations:* reading, cosmology, theology. *Club:* Oxford and Cambridge.

Died 4 Dec. 2001.

HOLTBY, Very Rev. Robert Tinsley, FSA; Dean of Chichester, 1977–89, Dean Emeritus, 1989; *b* 25 Feb. 1921; *o s* of William and Elsie Holtby, Thornton-le-Dale, Yorkshire; *m* 1947, Mary, *er d* of late Rt Rev. Eric Graham; one *s* two *d*. *Educ:* York Minster Choir Sch.; Scarborough Coll. and High School; St Edmund Hall, Oxford, 1939 (MA 2nd Class Mod. Hist., 1946; BD 1957); Choral Scholar, King's Coll., Cambridge, 1944 (MA (2nd Class Theol.), 1952). Cuddesdon Theological Coll. and Westcott House, Cambridge, 1943–46. FSA 1990. Deacon, 1946; Priest, 1947. Curate of Pocklington, Yorks, 1946–48. Chaplain to the Forces, 1948–52: 14/20th King's Hussars, Catterick; Singapore; Priest-in-charge, Johore Bahru. Hon. CF, 1952–; Acting Chaplain, King's Coll., Cambridge, 1952; Chaplain and Asst Master, Malvern Coll., 1952–54; Chaplain and Assistant Master, St Edward's Sch., Oxford, 1954–59; Canon Residentiary of Carlisle and Diocesan Dir of Educn, 1959–67, Canon Emeritus, 1967–; Gen. Sec., Nat. Soc. for Promoting Religious Education, 1967–77; Sec., Schs Cttee, 1967–74, Gen. Sec., 1974–77, Church of England Bd of Educn. Vis. Fellow, W Sussex Inst. of Higher Educn, 1990–93. Select Preacher: Cambridge, 1984; Oxford, 1989. Chm., Cumberland Council of Social Service, 1962–67. Chaplain to High Sheriff of Cumberland, 1964, 1966. *Publications:* Daniel Waterland, A Study in 18th Century Orthodoxy, 1966; Carlisle Cathedral Library and Records, 1966; Eric Graham, 1888–1964, 1967; Carlisle Cathedral, 1969; Chichester Cathedral, 1980; Robert Wright Stopford, 1988; Bishop William Otter, 1989; Eric Milner-White, 1991; The Minster School, York, 1994. *Recreations:* music, walking, history. *Address:* 4 Hutton Hall, Huttons Ambo, York YO60 7HW. *T:* (01653) 696366.

Died 13 March 2003.

HOOD, Sir Harold (Joseph), 2nd Bt *cr* 1922, of Wimbledon, Co. Surrey; TD; Circulation Director: Universe, 1953–60; Catholic Herald, 1961–87; *b* 23 Jan. 1916; *e s* of Sir Joseph Hood, 1st Bt, and Marie Josephine (*d* 1956), *e d* of Archibald Robinson, JP, Dublin; *S* father, 1931; *m* 1946, Hon. Ferelith Rosemary Florence Kenworthy (*d* 2003), *o d* of 10th Baron Strabolgi and Doris, *o c* of late Sir Frederick Whitley-Thomson, MP; two *s* two *d* (and one *s* decd). *Educ:* Downside Sch. Mem. Editorial Staff, The Universe, 1936–39; Asst Editor, The Catholic Directory, 1950, Managing Ed., 1959–60; Editor, The Catholic Who's Who, 1952 Edition. 2nd Lieutenant 58th Middx Battalion RE (AA) (TA) 1939; Lieut RA, 1941. GCSG (Holy See) 1986; (KSG 1964; KCSG 1978); Kt of Magistral Grace, SMO Malta, 1972. *Heir:* *s* John Joseph Harold Hood, *b* 27 Aug. 1952. *Address:* 31 Avenue Road, NW8 6BS. *T:* (020) 7722 9088.

Died 5 Sept. 2005.

HOOKER, Michael Ayerst, PhD; Development Director, Newton Prep (school for intellectually gifted children), since 1998; *b* 22 Jan. 1923; *s* of late Albert Ayerst Hooker, late of Broomsleigh Park, Seal Chart, Kent, and Marjorie Mitchell Hooker (*née* Gunson). *Educ:* Marlborough; St Edmund Hall, Oxford (MA 1944); Univ. of the Witwatersrand (PhD 1952). Home Guard, Oxford Univ. Sen. Trng Corps and Army Cadet Force (TARO), 1940–48. British Council, 1945–47; Schoolmaster, England and S Africa, 1947–51; London Diocesan Bd of Educn, 1952–66; Visual Aids and Public Relations, 1953–59. Chm., Fedn of Conservative Students, 1944; Parly Candidate (C) Coventry East, 1955; various offices, Conservative Commonwealth Council, 1955–60. Wells Organisation, fund raising in UK and NZ, 1957–58; Man. Dir, Hooker Craigmyle & Co. Ltd (first institutional fund raising consultants in UK), 1959–72; Man. Dir, Michael Hooker and Associates Ltd, 1972–79; Develt Dir, The Look Wide Trust, 1979–80; Chief Exec. Gov., Truman and Knightley Educn Trust, 1981–87 (Gov., 1977–87); Exec. Dir, 1988–91, Sen. Educnl Advr, 1991–92, Jerwood Award; Dir, Donnington Grove Inter-Faith Prog., 1992–2001; Cultural Dir, Shi-tennoji International, 1992–98. From 1957, has helped to raise nearly £70 million for various good causes, incl. 13 historic cathedrals, univs, colleges, schools, medical causes, welfare charities, etc. Mem., Adv. Cttee on Charitable Fund Raising, Nat. Council of Social Service, 1971–73. Jt Founder and Chm., Friends of Friends, subseq. Routledge Soc., 1985–90; Chm., Dame Flora Robson Meml Cttee, 1994–96; Vice-Pres., Donnington Grove Soc., 1999–; Trustee: Ross McWhirter Foundn, 1976–98 (a Vice-Pres., 1999–); Dicey Trust, 1978–93; Police Convalescence and Rehabilitation Trust, 1981–92; Hon. Councillor, NSPCC, 1981–; Governor: Oakham Sch., 1971–83; Shi-tennoji Sch., 1986–2001; All Hallows House, 1991–98; Newton Prep. 1991–93. Patron: Elton John AIDS Foundn, 1993–98; Martlets Hospice, 1997–. Hon. Dir, Newton Inter-Faith Gp, 2002–. *Publications:* various pamphlets and broadcasts on charities, historic churches, educnl issues, law and taxation, Christian stewardship of money. *Address:* Flat 8, 85 Marine Parade, Brighton BN2 1AJ. *T:* (01273) 624265, *Fax:* (01273) 624304.

Died 26 Jan. 2004.

HOPE, Bob, (Leslie Townes Hope), Hon. KBE 1998 (Hon. CBE 1976); film, stage, radio, TV actor; *b* England, 29 May 1903; family migrated to US, 1907; *m* 1934, Dolores Reade; two adopted *s* two adopted *d*. *Educ:* Fairmont Gram Sch. and High Sch., Cleveland, Ohio. Started career as dance instructor, clerk, amateur boxer; formed dancing act for Fatty Arbuckle review. After Mid-West tours formed own Company in Chicago; toured New York and joined RKO Vaudeville and Keith Circuit; first important stage parts include: Ballyhoo, 1932; Roberta, 1933; Ziegfield Follies, 1935; first radio part, 1934. Entered films, 1938. *Films include:* Big Broadcast of 1938; Some Like It Hot, 1939; The Cat and the Canary, 1939; Road to Singapore, 1940; The Ghost Breakers, 1940; Road to Zanzibar, 1941; Nothing but the Truth, 1941; Louisiana Purchase, 1941; Star Spangled Rhythm, 1942; My Favorite Blonde, 1942; Road to Morocco, 1942; Let's Face It, 1943; They Got Me Covered, 1943; The Princess and the Pirate, 1944; Road to Utopia, 1945; Monsieur Beaucaire, 1946; My Favorite Brunette, 1947; Road to Rio, 1947; Where There's Life, 1947; The Great Lover, 1949; My Favorite Spy, 1951; The Lemon Drop Kid, 1951; Road to Bali, 1952; Son of Paleface, 1952; Here Come the Girls, 1953; Casanova's Big Night 1954; The Seven Little Foys, 1955; The Iron Petticoat, 1956; That Certain Feeling, 1956; Beau James, 1957; The Facts of Life, 1960; Bachelor in Paradise, 1961; The Road to Hong Kong, 1962; Call Me Bwana, 1963; A Global Affair, 1964; Boy, Did I Get a Wrong Number!, 1966; Eight on the Run, 1967; How to Commit Marriage, 1969; Cancel My Reservation, 1972. *TV series:* The Bob Hope Show, 1950–93; numerous guest appearances. Five Royal Command Performances. Awarded 44 honorary degrees; more than a thousand awards and citations for humanitarian and professional services. Congressional Gold Medal, US, 1963. KCSG 1998. *Publications:* They've Got Me Covered, 1941; I Never Left Home, 1944; So This is Peace, 1946; This One's on Me, 1954; I Owe Russia $1200, 1963; Five Women I Love, 1966; The Last Christmas Show, 1974; Road to Hollywood, 1977; Confessions of a Hooker, 1985; Don't shoot, it's only me, 1990. *Address:* Hope Enterprises, Inc., 210 North Pass Avenue, Suite 101, Burbank, CA 91505, USA.

Died 27 July 2003.

HOPKINS, Keith; *see* Hopkins, M. K.

HOPKINS, Prof. (Morris) Keith, FBA 1984; Professor of Ancient History, University of Cambridge, 1985–2001;

Fellow, since 1985, and Vice-Provost, since 2000, King's College, Cambridge; *b* 20 June 1934; *s* of late Albert Thomas Hopkins and Hélène Dorothy Pratt; *m* 1st, 1963, Juliet (marr. diss. 1989), *d* of Sir Henry Phelps Brown, MBE, FBA; two *s* one *d*; 2nd, 1991, Jennifer Simmons, two *d*. *Educ:* Brentwood School; King's College, Cambridge (BA 1958; MA 1961). Asst Lectr in Sociology, Leicester Univ., 1961–63; Research Fellow, King's College, Cambridge, 1963–67; Lectr and Senior Lectr in Sociology, LSE, 1963–67, 1970–72; Prof. of Sociology: Univ. of Hong Kong, 1967–69; Brunel Univ., 1972–85 (Dean, Faculty of Social Sciences, 1981–85). Mem., Inst. for Advanced Study, Princeton, 1969–70, 1974–75, 1983. *Publications:* Hong Kong: The Industrial Colony (ed), 1971; Conquerors and Slaves, 1978; Death and Renewal, 1983; A World Full of Gods, 1999. *Recreations:* drinking wine, gardening. *Address:* King's College, Cambridge CB2 1ST. *T:* (01223) 331100. *Died 8 March 2004.*

HORNER, Douglas George; Chairman, Mercantile Credit Company, 1980–84; Vice-Chairman, 1979–81, Director, 1975–84, Barclays Bank UK Limited; *b* 19 Dec. 1917; *s* of Albert and Louise Horner; *m* 1941, Gwendoline Phyllis Wall; one *s*. *Educ:* Enfield Grammar Sch. Commissioned, Royal Norfolk Regt, 1940. Barclays Bank: Asst Manager/Manager at various bank branches, 1954–71; Local Dir, Lombard Street, 1971; Regional Gen. Manager, London, 1973; Gen. Man., 1975; Senior Gen. Man., 1977; Dir Barclays Bank plc, 1977–83. *Recreations:* golf, gardening. *Died 10 Oct. 2001.*

HORRELL, John Ray, CBE 1979; TD; DL; farmer; *b* 8 March 1929; *er s* of late Harry Ray Horrell and of Phyllis Mary Horrell (*née* Whittome); *m* 1951, Mary Elizabeth Noëlle Dickinson; one *s* one *d*. Dir, Horrell's Farmers Ltd. Mem., Board, Peterborough New Town Develt Corp., 1970–88; formerly Mem. Oakes and Taylor Cttees of Enquiry. Member: Cambs (formerly Huntingdon and Peterborough) CC, 1963–97 (Chm., 1971–77; Chm., Educn Cttee; Leader, 1989–93); Peterborough City Council, 1996– (Mayor, City of Peterborough, 2005–); Chairman: Council of Local Educn Authorities, 1976–79; ACC, 1981–83 (Vice-Chm., 1979–81); E of England Agricl Soc., 1984–87. Mem. Council, CGLI, later C&G, 1975–96. Major, TA; a Vice-Chm., 1977–86, Chm., 1986–91, E Anglia TA&VRA. FRSA 1981. High Sheriff, Cambs, 1981–82; DL Cambs, 1973. *Address:* The Grove, Longthorpe, Peterborough PE3 6LZ. *T:* (01733) 262618. *Died 17 Dec. 2005.*

HORSFALL, Sir John (Musgrave), 3rd Bt *cr* 1909; MC 1946; TD 1949 and clasp 1951; JP; *b* 26 Aug. 1915; *s* of Sir (John) Donald Horsfall, 2nd Bt, and Henrietta (*d* 1936), *d* of William Musgrave; *S* father, 1975; *m* 1940, Cassandra Nora Bernardine, *d* of late G. E. Wright; two *s* one *d*. *Educ:* Uppingham. Major, Duke of Wellington's Regt. Dir, Skipton Building Society, 1960–85. Mem., Skipton RDC, 1952–74; Pres., Skipton Divl Conservative Assoc., 1966–79. Pres., Worsted Spinners Fedn, 1961–64. JP North Yorks, 1959. *Heir: s* Edward John Wright Horsfall [*b* 17 Dec. 1940; *m* 1965, Rosemary, *d* of Frank N. King; three *s*]. *Address:* Greenfield House, Embsay, Skipton, North Yorkshire BD23 6SD. *T:* (01756) 794560. *Died 12 Jan. 2005.*

HORSLEY, Air Marshal Sir (Beresford) Peter (Torrington), KCB 1974; CBE 1964; LVO 1956; AFC 1945; idc; psc; pfc; *b* 26 March 1921; *s* of late Capt. Arthur Beresford Horsley, CBE; *m* 1st, 1943, Phyllis Conrad Phinney (marr. diss. 1976); one *s* one *d*; 2nd, 1976, Ann MacKinnon, *d* of Gareth and Frances Crwys-Williams; two step *s* two step *d*. *Educ:* Wellington Coll. Joined Royal Air Force, 1940; served in 2nd TAF and Fighter Command. Adjt Oxford Univ. Air Sqdn, 1948; Commands: No 9 and No 29 Sqdns, RAF Wattisham, RAF Akrotiri; Equerry to Princess Elizabeth and to the Duke of Edinburgh, 1949–52; Equerry to the Queen, 1952–53; Equerry to the Duke of Edinburgh, 1953–56; Dep. Comdt, Jt Warfare Establishment, RAF Old Sarum,

1966–68; Asst CAS (Operations), 1968–70; AOC No 1 (Bomber) Gp, 1971–73; Dep. C-in-C, Strike Comd, 1973–75; retired RAF, 1975. Chairman: National Printing Ink Co., 1987–; Osprey Aviation Ltd, 1991–; Director: Horsley Hldgs, 1985–; RCR Internat., 1984–. Pres., Yorkshire Sports, 1986–. Croix de Guerre, 1944. Holds Orders of Christ (Portugal), North Star (Sweden), and Menelik (Ethiopia). *Publications:* (as Peter Beresford) Journal of a Stamp Collector, 1972; Sounds From Another Room (autobiog.), 1997. *Recreations:* ski-ing, philately. *Address:* c/o Barclays Bank, High Street, Newmarket CB8 8NH. *Club:* Hopetown Sailing. *Died 20 Dec. 2001.*

HORSLEY, (George) Nicholas (Seward); Chairman, 1970–86, Deputy Chairman, 1986–88, Northern Foods plc, retired; non-executive Chairman, Millway Foods Limited, 1988–89; *b* 21 April 1934; *s* of Alec Stewart Horsley and Ida Seward Horsley; *m* 1st, 1958, Valerie Anne Edwards (marr. diss. 1975); two *s* one *d*; 2nd, 1975, Sabita Sarkar (marr. diss. 1987); three *d*; 3rd, 1988, Alwyne Marjorie Law. *Educ:* Keswick Grammar Sch.; Bootham Sch., York; Worcester Coll., Oxford (BA). Freelance journalist, 1957–58. Northern Dairies Ltd: Trainee Manager, 1958; Director, 1963; Vice-Chairman, 1968–70 (Northern Dairies Ltd changed its name to Northern Foods Ltd in 1972). Chm., News on Sunday Publishing, 1986–87. Pres., Dairy Trade Fedn, 1975–77 and 1980–85. Chm., BBC Consultative Group on Industrial and Business Affairs, 1980–83; Mem., BBC Gen. Adv. Council, 1980–83. *Recreations:* music, bridge, watching cricket, reading. *Address:* Barbados, West Indies.
Died 18 Jan. 2004.

HORSLEY, Sir Peter; *see* Horsley, Sir B. P. T.

HORTON, Dr Eric William; livestock farmer, 1983–93; Director of Regulatory Affairs, Glaxo Group Research Ltd, 1980–83, Member Board, 1982–83; Director, Willow & Wicket Computer Cricket Ltd, 1994–2000; *b* 20 June 1929; *e s* of late Harold and Agnes Horton; *m* 1956, Thalia Helen (*d* 1999), *er d* of Sir George Lowe; two *s* one *d*. *Educ:* Sedbergh; Edinburgh Univ. (BSc 1953, MB ChB 1955, PhD 1958, DSc 1968, MD). FRCPE 1970. Mem. Scientific Staff, MRC, Nat. Inst. for Med. Res., London, 1958–60; Dir of Therapeutic Res. and Head of Pharmacology, Miles Labs Ltd, Stoke Poges, 1960–63; Sen. Lectr in Physiology, St Bartholomew's Hosp., London, 1963–66; Wellcome Prof. of Pharmacology, Sch. of Pharmacy, Univ. of London, 1966–69; Prof. of Pharmacology, Univ. of Edinburgh, 1969–80. Hon. Lectr in Pharmacol., Royal Free Hosp. Med. Sch., London, 1960–63; Hon. Sen. Res. Fellow, Med. Coll. of St Bartholomew's Hosp., London, 1980. Member: Adv. Cttee on Pesticides, MAFF, 1970–73; Biological Research and Cell Boards, MRC, 1973–75; Pharmacy Panel, SRC, 1980–81. Non-executive Director: Inveresk Res. Internat. Ltd, 1977–80; GLP Systems Ltd, 1978–80. Mem. Governing Body, Inveresk Res. Foundn (formerly International), 1971–80. Hon. Treas., Brit. Pharmacological Soc., 1976–80. Hon. Sec., Edin. Univ. RFC, 1949–50. Baly Medal, RCP, 1973. Member, Editorial Board: British Jl of Pharmacology, 1960–66; Pharmacological Reviews, 1968–74. *Publications:* Prostaglandins, 1972; papers in learned jls on peptides and prostaglandins. *Recreations:* listening to music, computer programming. *Died 11 Jan. 2003.*

HOTTER, Hans; bass-baritone opera and concert singer, retired 1972, but gave occasional concert performances until 1994; teaches masterclasses in USA, Japan, Great Britain, Austria, Germany and other countries; *b* Offenbach, Germany, 19 Jan. 1909; *m* 1936, Helga Fischer; one *s* one *d*. *Educ:* Munich. Concert career began in 1929 and opera career in 1930; sang his first Wotan, Munich State Opera, 1937. Prof. at Vienna Musik-Hochschule, 1977–80. Mem. of Munich, Vienna and Hamburg State Operas; guest singer in opera and concerts in all major cities of Europe and USA; concert tours in Australia; for 10 years, connected with Columbia

Gramophone Co., England; guest singer, Covent Garden Opera, London, 1947–72. Festivals: Salzburg, Edinburgh and Bayreuth. *Relevant publication:* Hans Hotter: man and artist, by Penelope Turing, 1984. *Address:* Bayerische Staatsoper, 80539 München, Germany.
Died 6 Dec. 2003.

HOUGHTON, Herbert; Director: Stenhouse Holdings Ltd, 1979–83; Reed Stenhouse Cos Ltd, 1977–86; Chancellor Insurance Co. Ltd, 1984; *b* 4 Oct. 1920; *s* of Herbert Edward and Emily Houghton; *m* 1st, 1939, Dorothy Ballantyne (*d* 1981); one *s* one *d*; 2nd, 1991, Catharine W. Duffy. *Educ:* William Hulmes' Grammar School. Director, Cockshoots Ltd, 1955; Man. Dir, Stenhouse Northern Ltd, 1968; Chairman: Sir Wm Garthwaite (Holdings) Ltd, 1973; Sten-Re Ltd, 1973; Director and Chief Executive, A. R. Stenhouse & Partners Ltd, 1977; Dir, British Vita Co. Ltd, 1969–84. *Recreations:* overseas travel, golf, reading, gardening. *Address:* 2 Orchard Court, Grindleford, Sheffield S30 1JH. *T:* (01433) 631142; 554 Palm Way, Gulf Stream, FL 33483, USA. *Died 12 March 2002.*

HOUNSFIELD, Sir Godfrey (Newbold), Kt 1981; CBE 1976; FRS 1975; Consultant to Laboratories, Central Research Laboratories of EMI Group (formerly Thorn EMI Central Research Laboratories), Hayes, Middx, since 1986 (Head of Medical Systems section, 1972–76; Chief Staff Scientist, 1976–77, Senior Staff Scientist, 1977–85); Consultant (part-time), National Heart & Chest Hospitals, Chelsea, since 1986; *b* 28 Aug. 1919; *s* of Thomas Hounsfield, Newark, Notts. *Educ:* Magnus Grammar Sch., Newark; City and Guilds Coll., London (Radio Communications qualif.); Faraday House Electrical Engineering Coll. (Diploma); grad. for IEE. Volunteered for RAF, 1939; served 1939–46 (incl. period as Lectr at Cranwell Radar Sch.); awarded Certificate of Merit (for work done in RAF), 1945. Attended Faraday House, where he studied elec. and mech. engrg, 1947–51. Joined EMI Ltd, 1951, working initially on radar systems and, later, on computers; led design team for the first large, all transistor computer to be built in Great Britain, the EMIDEC 1100, 1958–59; invented the EMI-scanner computerised transverse axial tomography system for X-ray examination, 1969–72 (first used at Atkinson Morley's Hosp., Wimbledon, and then used at leading hosps throughout the world, known as CAT or CT scanning); the technique can be applied to cranial examinations and the whole of the body; the system has overcome obstacles to the diagnosis of disease in the brain which have continued since Roentgen's day (1895); it includes a patient-scanning unit; developer of a new X-ray technique (the EMI-scanner system) which won the 1972 MacRobert Award of £25,000 for the invention, and a Gold Medal for EMI Ltd; working on Nuclear Magnetic Resonance Imaging, 1976–; Magnetic Resonance Imaging Advr, Nat. Heart Hosp. and Brompton Hosp.; formerly Professorial Fellow in Imaging Sciences, Manchester Univ. Hon. FRCP 1976; Hon. FRCR 1976; Hon. FREng (Hon. FEng 1994). Dr Medicine (*hc*) Universität Basel, 1975; Hon. DSc: City, 1976; London, 1976; Hon. DTech Loughborough, 1976. Wilhelm-Exner Medal, Austrian Industrial Assoc., 1974; Ziedses des Plantes Medal, Physikalisch Medizinische Gesellschaft, Würzburg, 1974; Prince Philip Medal Award, CGLI, 1975; ANS Radiation Industry Award, Georgia Inst. of Technology, 1975; Lasker Award, Lasker Foundn, 1975; Duddell Bronze Medal, Inst. Physics, 1976; Golden Plate Award, Amer. Acad. of Achievement, 1976; Reginald Mitchell Gold Medal, Stoke-on-Trent Assoc. of Engrs, 1976; Churchill Gold Medal, 1976; Gairdner Foundn Award, 1976; (jtly) Nobel Prize for Physiology or Medicine, 1979; Ambrogio d'Oro Award, City of Milan, 1980; Deutsche Roentgen Plakette, Deutsche Roentgen Museum, 1980. *Publications:* contribs: New Scientist; Brit. Jl of Radiology; Amer. Jl of Röntgenology. *Recreation:* mountain walking. *Address:* Central Research Laboratories, Dawley Road, Hayes, Middx UB3 1HH. *T:* (020) 8848 6404; 15 Crane Park Road, Twickenham TW2 6DF. *T:* (020) 8894 1746.
Died 12 Aug. 2004.

HOUSE, Ven. Francis Harry, OBE 1955; MA; Archdeacon of Macclesfield, 1967–78, then Archdeacon Emeritus; Rector of St James, Gawsworth, 1967–78; *b* 9 Aug. 1908; *s* of late Canon William Joseph House, DD; *m* 1938, Margaret Neave; two *d*. *Educ:* St George's Sch., Harpenden; Wadham Coll., Oxford; Cuddesdon Theological Coll. Sec. of Student Christian Movement of Gt Britain and Ireland, 1931–34; Deacon, 1936; Priest, 1937; Asst Missioner, Pembroke Coll. (Cambridge) Mission, Walworth, 1936–37; Travelling Sec. of World's Student Christian Federation, Geneva, 1938–40; Curate of Leeds Parish Church, 1940–42; Overseas Asst, Religious Broadcasting Dept, BBC, London, 1942–44; representative of World Student Relief in Greece, 1944–46; Sec. Youth Dept World Council of Churches, Geneva, and World Conference of Christian Youth, Oslo, 1946–47; Head of Religious Broadcasting BBC, London, 1947–55; Associate Gen. Sec. of the World Council of Churches, Geneva, 1955–62; Vicar of St Giles, Pontefract, 1962–67. Select Preacher, Cambridge Univ., 1949. Member: Gen. Synod of Church of England, 1970–78; Gen. Synod's Commn on Broadcasting, 1971–73; Bd for Mission and Unity, 1971–80 (Vice-Chm., 1971–75). Officer Royal (Hellenic) Order of Phoenix, 1947. *Publications:* The Russian Phoenix, 1988; articles contributed to: The Student Movement, The Student World, East and West, the Ecumenical Review, Theology, Crucible, One in Christ, etc. *Address:* The College of St Barnabas, Blackberry Lane, Lingfield, Surrey RH7 6NJ. *T:* (01342) 870186. *Died 1 Sept. 2004.*

HOWARD, Hon. Edmund Bernard Carlo, CMG 1969; LVO 1961; HM Diplomatic Service, retired; *b* 8 Sept. 1909; *s* of 1st Baron Howard of Penrith, GCB, GCMG, CVO, PC, and Lady Isabella Giustiniani-Bandini (*d* of Prince Giustiniani-Bandini, 8th Earl of Newburgh); *m* 1936, Cécile Geoffroy-Dechaume; three *s* one *d* (and one *d* decd). *Educ:* Downside Sch.; Newman Sch., Lakewood, NJ; New Coll., Oxford. Called to the Bar, 1932; Sec., Trustees and Managers, Stock Exchange, 1937. Served War, KRRC, 1940–45. Joined HM Diplomatic Service, 1947; served in: Rome, 1947–51; FO, 1951–53; Madrid, 1953–57; Bogotá, 1957–59; Florence, 1960–61; Rome, 1961–65; Consul-Gen., Genoa, 1965–69. Comdr, Order of Merit (Italy), 1973. *Publications:* Genoa: history and art in an old seaport, 1971 (Duchi di Galliera prize, 1973); trans. The Aryan Myth, 1974; Italia: the art of living Italian style, 1996. *Recreations:* travel, gardening. *Address:* Jerome Cottage, Marlow Common, Bucks SL7 2QR. *T:* (01628) 482129. *Died 4 June 2005.*

HOWARD, Sir Edward; *see* Howard, Sir H. E. de C.

HOWARD, Sir (Hamilton) Edward (de Coucey), 2nd Bt *cr* 1955, of Great Rissington, co. Gloucester; GBE 1972; Director of Stockbroking firm of Charles Stanley and Company Ltd; *b* 29 Oct. 1915; *s* of Sir (Harold Walter) Seymour Howard, 1st Bt, and Edith M. (*d* 1962), *d* of Edward Turner; *S* father, 1967; *m* 1943, Elizabeth Howarth Ludlow; two *s*. *Educ:* Le Rosey, Rolle, Switzerland; Radley Coll., Abingdon; Worcester Coll., Oxford. Mem. of the Stock Exchange, London, 1946. Sheriff of the City of London, 1966 (Common Councilman, 1951; Alderman, 1963); Lord Mayor of London, 1971–72; one of HM Lieutenants, City of London, 1976–90. Master of the Gardeners' Company, 1961. Hon. DSc City Univ., 1971. KStJ 1972. *Recreation:* gardening. *Heir:* *s* David Howarth Seymour Howard [*b* 29 Dec. 1945; *m* 1968, Valerie Picton Crosse; two *s* two *d*]. *Address:* Courtlands, Bishops Walk, Shirley Hills, Surrey CR0 5BA. *T:* (020) 8656 4444. *Clubs:* Guildhall, City Livery, United Wards. *Died 16 March 2001.*

HOWARD, Michael Stockwin; organ recitalist and recording artist; *b* London, 14 Sept. 1922; *er s* of Frank Henry Howard (viola, Internat. String Quartet; Foundn principal, Beecham's Philharmonic) and Florence Mabel Howard; *m* 6th, Elisabeth (*née* Fletcher); five *c* from former marriages. *Educ:* Ellesmere; Royal Acad. of Music; privately. Organist, Tewkesbury Abbey, 1943–44; Dir of Music, Ludgrove; Founder, Renaissance Society, and conductor, Renaissance Singers, 1944–64; Organist and Magister Choristarum, Ely Cath., 1953–58; Dir, Cantores in Ecclesia, 1964–86; Dir of Music, St Marylebone Parish Church, 1971–79; Organist to the Franciscans of Rye, 1979–83; Rector Chori, St Michael's Abbey, Farnborough, 1984–86. Performer at: Proms; Bath Fest.; Cheltenham Fest.; internat. fests incl. Czechoslovakia; broadcaster and writer. Hon. ARAM 1976. Prix Musicale de Radio Brno, 1967; Charpentier Grand Prix du Disque, 1975. Cavaillé-Coll organ recordings incl. principal works of César Franck. *Publications:* A Tribute to Cavaillé-Coll, 1985; Thine Adversaries Roar . . . (autobiographical observations), 2001. *Recreations:* steam railway traction, listening, reading. *Address:* 1 Somerset Villas, Corseley Road, Groombridge, Tunbridge Wells, Sussex TN3 9RR.   *Died 4 Jan. 2002.*

HOWARD, William Brian; Deputy Chairman, Northern Foods plc, 1988–97 (Director, 1987–97); Deputy Chairman, 1984–87, Joint Managing Director, 1976–86, Marks & Spencer plc; *b* 16 July 1926; *s* of William James and Annie Howard; *m* 1952, Audrey Elizabeth (*née* Jenney); one *s* one *d*. *Educ:* Revoe Junior Sch., Blackpool; Blackpool Grammar Sch.; Manchester Univ. (BA (Hons) Mod. Hist., Economics and Politics); Harvard Graduate Business Sch., 1973. Royal Signals, 1944–47. Marks & Spencer Ltd, 1951–87; Dir, 1973–87. A Church Comr, 1977–93. *Address:* Crawley Farm, Ballinger, Great Missenden, Bucks HP16 9LQ. *Club:* MCC.
Died 14 Oct. 2005.

HOWARTH, Prof. Leslie, OBE 1955; PhD; FRS 1950; FRAeS; CMath; Henry Overton Wills Professor of Mathematics, University of Bristol, 1964–76, then Emeritus; *b* 23 May 1911; *s* of late Fred and Elizabeth Ellen Howarth; *m* 1934, Eva Priestley; two *s*. *Educ:* Accrington Grammar Sch.; Manchester Univ. (BSc); Gonville and Caius Coll., Cambridge (Mathematical tripos, 1933; Smith's Prize, 1935; MA; PhD 1936). FRAeS 1951. Berry-Ramsey Research Fellow, King's Coll., Cambridge, 1936–45; Lecturer in Mathematics in the University of Cambridge, 1936–49; Fellow of St John's Coll., Cambridge, 1945–49; Prof. of Applied Mathematics, University of Bristol, 1949–64. Adams Prize, 1951. Worked at External Ballistics Dept, Ordnance Board, 1939–42, and at Armament Research Dept, 1942–45. Hon. FIMA 1979. *Publications:* (ed) Modern Developments in Fluid Dynamics: High Speed Flow; papers on aerodynamics. *Address:* Boucherne Residential Home, Holloway Road, Maldon, Essex CM9 4SQ.
Died 22 Sept. 2001.

HOWE, Jack, RDI 1961; FRIBA 1953; architect and industrial designer; *b* 24 Feb. 1911; *s* of Charles Henry and Florence Eleanor Howe; *m* 1939, Carmen Smith (marr. diss. 1959); one *s* one *d*; *m* 1960, Margaret Crosbie Corrie (*d* 1979); one *s* one *d* by former marriage; *m* 1981, Jennifer Mary Dixon (*née* Hughes D'Aeth). *Educ:* Enfield Grammar Sch.; Polytechnic Sch. of Architecture. FSIAD 1955. Asst to E. Maxwell Fry, 1933–37; Chief Asst to Walter Gropius and Maxwell Fry, 1937–39; Drawing Office Manager to Holland, Hannan & Cubitts Ltd for Royal Ordnance Factories at Wrexham and Ranskill, 1939–43; Associate Partner, Arcon, 1944–48; private practice, 1949; Partnership with Andrew Bain, 1959–76. Architectural work includes: Highbury Quadrant Primary School, (LCC); Windmill House, Lambeth (LCC Housing Scheme); Television Research Lab. for AEI Ltd; Kodak Pavilion, Brussels Exhibn, 1958; Official Architects for British Trade Fair, Moscow, 1961; Industrial Designs include: Diesel Electric Locomotives and Express Pullman Trains; also Rly equipment. Industrial Design Consultant to various large firms and to BR Board. Mem. Design

Index Cttee and Street Furniture Cttee, Design Council (formerly CoID), 1956–; Member: Cttee on Traffic Signs, Min. of Transport, 1962, 1963; Nat. Council for Diplomas in Art and Design. Pres., SIAD, 1963–64; Master of Faculty, RDI, 1975–77. Duke of Edinburgh's design prize, 1969. *Publications:* articles for various architectural and design jls. *Recreations:* music, theatre. *Address:* 4 Leopold Avenue, Wimbledon, SW19 7ET. *T:* (020) 8946 7116.
Died 3 Dec. 2003.

HOWE, Rt Rev. John William Alexander; Assistant Bishop, diocese of Ripon, 1985–91; *b* 14 July 1920; *s* of Frederic Arthur Howe and Elsie Howe (*née* Garner). *Educ:* Westcliff High Sch.; St Chad's Coll., Durham Univ. (BA 1943; MA, BD 1948). Ordained deacon, 1943, priest, 1944; Curate, All Saints, Scarborough, 1943–46; Chaplain, Adisadel Coll., Gold Coast, 1946–50; Vice-Principal, Edinburgh Theological Coll., 1950–55; Hon. Chaplain, St Mary's Cathedral, Edinburgh, 1951–55; Bishop of St Andrews, Dunkeld and Dunblane, 1955–69; Hon. Canon, St Mary's Cath., Glasgow, 1969; Exec. Officer of the Anglican Communion, 1969–71; Secretary General, Anglican Consultative Council, 1971–82; Research Fellow of the Research Project, ACC, 1983–85, retd. Hon. DD General Theological Seminary, NY, 1974; DD Lambeth, 1978. *Publication:* Highways and Hedges: Anglicanism and the Universal Church, 1985. *Address:* Churchfield Christian Care Centre, Millers Court, Radford, Nottingham NG7 3DP. *T:* (0115) 942 2317.
Died 26 April 2001.

HOWITT, Fowler; *see* Howitt, W. F.

HOWITT, W(illiam) Fowler, DA (Dundee); FRIBA; architect and hospital planning consultant, retired; *b* Perth, Scotland, May 1924; *s* of late Frederick Howitt, Head Postmaster, Forfar; *m* 1951, Ann Elizabeth, *o d* of late A. J. Hedges, Radipole, Dorset; three *s* one *d*. *Educ:* Perth Acad.; Sch. of Architecture, Dundee. RIBA Victory Schol., 1949. Served War, Royal Marines, 1943–46. Asst, Louis de Soissons, London (housing and flats), 1949–52; Prin. Asst to Vincent Kelly, Dublin (hosps and offices), 1952–55; Architect to St Thomas's Hosp. (hosp. rebuilding schemes, flats, offices), 1955–64; Partner, Cusdin Burden and Howitt, Architects, 1965–90. Projects include: design and supervision of Coll. of Medicine and King Khalid Hosp., King Saud Univ., Riyadh, Saudi Arabia; design of teaching hospitals: Abuja city and Niger State, Nigeria; children's hospitals, Anambra and Imo States, Nigeria; Addenbrooke's Hosp., Cambridge; Royal Victoria Hosp., Belfast; planning consultancy, 1980–92; gen. hosps, Sharjah and Fujairah, UAE; King Fahad Medical City, Riyadh, Saudi Arabia; Policlinico Teaching Hosp., Milan; private hosp., Milan; gen. hosps, Como and Varese. *Recreations:* reading, golf. *Address:* 32 Gloucester Road, Teddington, Middx TW11 0NU. *T:* (020) 8977 5772.   *Died 17 Feb. 2005.*

HOWKINS, John, MD; FRCS; Gynæcological Surgeon to St Bartholomew's Hospital, 1946–69 (Hon. Consultant Gynæcologist since 1969), to Hampstead General Hospital 1946–67 (Hon. Consultant Gynæcologist, since 1968), and to Royal Masonic Hospital, 1948–73; *b* 17 Dec. 1907; *m* 1940, Lena Brown; one *s* two *d*. *Educ:* Shrewsbury Sch.; London Univ. (Arts Scholar, Middlesex Hospital, 1926; MRCS, LRCP 1932; MB, BS London, 1933; MS London, 1936; MD (Gold Medal) London, 1937). FRCS 1936; MRCOG 1937, FRCOG 1947. House Surgeon and Casualty Surgeon, Middlesex Hosp., 1932–34; RMO, Chelsea Hosp. for Women, 1936; Gynæcological Registrar, Middlesex Hosp., 1937–38; Resident Obstetric Surg., at St Bartholomew's Hosp., 1938 and 1945. Temp. Wing-Comdr, RAFVR Med. Br., 1939–45. Hunterian Prof., RCS 1947; William Meredith Fletcher Shaw Lectr, RCOG, 1975. Sometime Examiner in Midwifery to Univs of Cambridge and London, RCOG, Conjoint Bd of England. Mem., Gynaecological Travellers' Club. *Publications:* Shaw's Textbook of Gynæcology, 7th edn 1956 to 9th edn 1971; Shaw's Textbook of Operative

Gynaecology, 2nd edn 1960 to 5th edn (jtly) 1983; (jtly) Bonney's Textbook of Gynæcological Surgery, 7th edn 1964, 8th edn 1974. *Recreations:* ski-ing, salmon fishing, sheep farming. *Address:* Caen Hen, Abercegir, Machynlleth, Powys, Wales SY20 8NR. *Clubs:* Ski Club of Great Britain (Chm. Council, 1964–67; Hon. Life Mem., 1968; Trustee, 1969–); Wilks XV (Hon. Mem.).
Died 6 May 2003.

HOWLETT, Anthony Douglas, RD 1971; Remembrancer of the City of London, 1981–86; *b* 30 Dec. 1924; *s* of late Ernest Robert Howlett and Catherine (*née* Broughton), Grantham, Lincs; *m* 1952, Alfreda Dorothy Pearce, *yr d* of Arthur W. Pearce, Hove, Sussex. *Educ:* King's Sch., Rochester; Wellingborough; King's Sch., Grantham; Trinity Coll., Cambridge (BA Hons 1948, LLB 1949, MA 1950). Served War, 1939–46, RNVR; RNVSR, 1951–60; RNR, 1960–75 (Lt Comdr 1968). Hon. Mem., HMS President. Called to the Bar, Gray's Inn, 1950; joined Legal Br., BoT, 1951; Sen. Legal Asst, 1960; Asst Solicitor, 1972, i/c Export Credit Guarantees Br., 1972–75, i/c Merchant Shipping Br., 1975–81. UK delegate: London Diplomatic Conf. on Limitation of Liability for Maritime Claims, 1976; Geneva Diplomatic Conf. on Multi-Modal Transport, 1980, and other internat. maritime confs. Vice-Chm., Enfield HA, 1987–93; Chm., Enfield Dist Res. Ethics Cttee, 1990–93. Founder Mem., Sherlock Holmes Soc. of London, 1951 (Chm., 1960–63, 1986–89; Pres., 1992–); Trustee, Crowborough Conan Doyle Trust Ltd, 1997–2001. Member: City Pickwick Club, 1988–; James Hilton Soc., 2001–. Freedom, City of London, 1981; Liveryman, Scriveners' Co., 1981–. OStJ 1986. Order of King Abdul Aziz (II) (Saudi Arabia), 1981; Order of Oman (III), 1982; Comdr, Order of Orange-Nassau (Netherlands), 1982; Officier, Légion d'Honneur (France), 1984; Comdr, Order of the Lion of Malaŵi, 1985; Order of Qatar (III), 1985. *Publications:* articles on Conan Doyle and Holmesiana. *Recreations:* book browsing, Sherlock Holmes, opera, photography, sailing and maritime history, foreign travel. *Address:* Rivendell, 37 Links Side, Enfield, Middlesex EN2 7QZ. *T:* (020) 8363 5802. *Club:* Naval.
Died 21 Aug. 2003.

HOYLE, Prof. Sir Fred, Kt 1972; FRS 1957; Hon. Research Professor: Manchester University, since 1972; University College, Cardiff, since 1975; Visiting Associate in Physics, California Institute of Technology, since 1963; *b* 24 June 1915; *s* of Ben Hoyle, Bingley, Yorks; *m* 1939, Barbara Clark; one *s* one *d. Educ:* Bingley Grammar Sch.; Emmanuel Coll., Cambridge (MA; Mayhew Prizeman, Mathematical Tripos, 1936; Smith's Prizeman, Goldsmith Exhibnr, Senior Exhibnr of Royal Commn for Exhibn of 1851, 1938; Hon. Fellow, 1983). War Service for British Admiralty, 1939–45. Fellow, St John's Coll., Cambridge, 1939–72 (Hon. Fellow, 1973); University Lecturer in Mathematics, Cambridge, 1945–58; Plumian Prof. of Astronomy and Exptl Philosophy, Cambridge Univ., 1958–72; Dir, Inst. of Theoretical Astronomy, Cambridge, 1967–73; Prof. of Astronomy, Royal Instn of GB, 1969–72; Staff Mem., Mount Wilson and Palomar Observatories, 1957–62. California Institute of Technology: Vis. Prof. of Astrophysics, 1953, 1954; Vis. Prof. of Astronomy, 1956; Sherman Fairchild Scholar, 1974–75; Addison White Greenaway Vis. Prof. of Astronomy; Andrew D. White Prof.-at-Large, Cornell Univ., 1972–78. Mem., SRC, 1967–72. Vice-Pres., Royal Society, 1970–71; Pres., Royal Astronomical Soc., 1971–73. Hon. MRIA (Section of Science), 1977; Mem., Amer. Philos. Soc., 1980; Hon. Member: Amer. Acad. of Arts and Sciences, 1964; Mark Twain Soc., 1978; Foreign Associate, US Nat. Acad. of Sciences, 1969. Hon. Fellow, Inst. of Astronomy, Cambridge Univ., 1996. Hon. ScD E Anglia, 1967; Hon DSc: Leeds, 1969; Bradford, 1975; Newcastle upon Tyne, 1976. Royal Astronomical Soc. Gold Medal, 1968; UN Kalinga Prize, 1968; Bruce Gold Medal, 1970, Klumphe-Roberts Award, 1977, Astronomical Soc. of Pacific; Royal Medal, Royal Soc.,

1974; Dag Hammarskjöld Gold Medal, Académie Diplomatique de la Paix, 1986; Karl Schwarzehild Medal, German Astronomical Soc., 1992; Balzan Prize, Fondation Internat. Balzan, 1994; Annenberg Award, Astronomy Educn, AAS, 1996; Crafoord Prize, Royal Swedish Acad. of Scis, 1997. *Publications:* Some Recent Researches in Solar Physics, 1949; The Nature of the Universe, 1951; A Decade of Decision, 1953; Frontiers of Astronomy, 1955; Man and Materialism, 1956; Astronomy, 1962; Star Formation, 1963; Of Men and Galaxies, 1964; Encounter with the Future, 1965; Galaxies, Nuclei and Quasars, 1965; Man in the Universe, 1966; From Stonehenge to Modern Cosmology, 1972; Nicolaus Copernicus, 1973; The Relation of Physics and Cosmology, 1973; (with J. V. Narlikar) Action-at-a-Distance in Physics and Cosmology, 1974; Astronomy and Cosmology, 1975; Astronomy Today, 1975 (US, as Highlights in Astronomy, 1975); Ten Faces of the Universe, 1977; On Stonehenge, 1977; Energy or Extinction, 1977; The Cosmogony of the Solar System, 1978; (with G. Hoyle) Commonsense and Nuclear Energy, 1979; (with J. V. Narlikar) The Physics-Astronomy Frontier, 1980; Ice, 1981; The Intelligent Universe, 1983; Comet Halley, 1985; (with G. Burbidge and J. V. Narlikar) A Differernt Approach to Cosmology, 2000; *with N. C. Wickramasinghe:* Lifecloud, 1978; Diseases from Space, 1979; Space Travellers: the Bringers of Life, 1981; Evolution from Space, 1981; Archaeopteryx, the Primordial Bird: a case of fossil forgery, 1986; Cosmic Life Force, 1988; The Theory of Cosmic Grains, 1991; Our Place in the Cosmos, 1993; *novels:* The Black Cloud, 1957; Ossian's Ride, 1959; (with J. Elliot) A for Andromeda, 1962; (with J. Elliot) Andromeda Breakthrough, 1964; October the First is Too Late, 1966; Element 79, 1967; *novels with G. Hoyle:* Fifth Planet, 1963; Rockets in Ursa Major, 1969; Seven Steps to the Sun, 1970; The Molecule Men, 1971; The Inferno, 1973; Into Deepest Space, 1974; The Incandescent Ones, 1977; The Westminster Disaster, 1978; *children's stories with G. Hoyle:* The Energy Pirate, 1982; The Giants of Universal Park, 1982; The Frozen Planet of Azuron, 1982; The Planet of Death, 1982; *autobiography:* The Small World of Fred Hoyle, 1986; Home is Where the Wind Blows, 1994; *play:* Rockets in Ursa Major, 1962; *libretto:* The Alchemy of Love; space serials for television; scientific papers. *Address:* c/o The Royal Society, 6 Carlton House Terrace, SW1Y 5AG.
Died 20 Aug. 2001.

HOYOS, Hon. Sir Alexander; *see* Hoyos, Hon. Sir F. A.

HOYOS, Hon. Sir (Fabriciano) Alexander, Kt 1979; former Lecturer, Cave Hill, University of the West Indies; retired History Teacher, Lodge School, St John; *b* Brazil, 5 July 1912; *s* of Emigdio and Adelina Hoyos, Peru; *m* 1st, 1940, Kathleen Carmen (*d* 1970); three *s* one *d*; 2nd, 1973, Gladys Louise. *Educ:* Wesley Hall Boys' School; Harrison Coll.; Codrington Coll., Durham Univ. (Sen. Island Schol.; BA 1936; MA 1943; Hon. MEd 1963); DLitt UWI, 1982. Taught at: Combermere Sch., Barbados; St Benedict's Coll., Trinidad; Lodge Sch., 1943–72; Moderator, Caribbean History Survey Course, Cave Hill, UWI, 1963–70. Leader-writer of Daily Advocate, 1937–43; Correspondent, London Times, 1938–65. Chm., Nat. Adv. Commn on Educn, 1983–86; Member: Barbados Christian Council, 1976–80; Privy Council for Barbados, 1977–86; Constitution Review Commn, 1977–78. Queen's Jubilee Medal, 1977. *Publications:* Some Eminent Contemporaries, 1944; Two Hundred Years, 1945; Story of Progressive Movement, 1948; Our Common Heritage, 1953; Memories of Princess Margaret and Our Past, 1955; Road to Responsible Government, 1960; Barbados, Our Island Home, 1960, 4th edn 1989; Rise of West Indian Democracy, 1963; Background to Independence, 1967; Builders of Barbados, 1972; Grantley Adams and the Social Revolution, 1974; Barbados: from the Amerindians to Independence, 1978; Visitor's Guide to Barbados, 1982; The Quiet Revolutionary (autobiog.), 1984; Tom Adams (biog.), 1988. *Recreations:* gardening, walking, talking, swimming. *Address:* Beachy Crest, Belair

Cross Road, Falmouth, St Philip, Barbados, WI. *T:* 4236323. *Club:* Barbados Yacht.   *Died 23 Aug. 2001.*

HOYTE, (Hugh) Desmond; SC; MP (People's National Congress), Guyana, since 1968; Leader of the Opposition, since 1992; Leader, People's National Congress; *b* 9 March 1929; *s* of George Alphonso Hoyte and Gladys Marietta Hoyte; *m* Joyce Hoyte; (two *d* decd). *Educ:* St Barnabas Anglican Sch.; Progressive High Sch.; Univ. of London (BA ext. 1950, LLB 1959). Called to the Bar, Middle Temple, 1959. QC 1970, later SC. Civil servant and teacher; practised at Guyana Bar, 1960–; Chm., Legal Practitioners' Cttee, 1964; Mem., Nat. Elections Commn, 1966. Minister: Home Affairs, 1969–70; Finance, 1970–72; Works and Communications, 1972–74; Economic Develt, 1974–80; People's National Congress: Vice-Pres., Economic Planning and Finance, 1980–83, Production, 1983–84; and Prime Minister, 1984; Pres., Co–op. Republic of Guyana, 1985–92. *Recreations:* reading, music, swimming, walking. *Address:* 14 North Road, Bourda, Georgetown, Guyana.
                                                                Died 22 Dec. 2002.

HUBBARD-MILES, Peter Charles, CBE 1981; self-employed small businessman, 1948–95; *b* 9 May 1927; *s* of Charles Hubbard and Agnes (*née* Lewis); *m* 1948, Pamela Wilkins; two *s* three *d.* *Educ:* Lewis' Sch., Pengam. Served RAF, 1945–48. County Councillor, Mid Glamorgan CC (formerly Glamorgan CC), 1967 (Leader, Conservative Group, 1974–83); Leader, Cons. Gp, Ogwr Borough Council, 1974–83, first Cons. Mayor 1979–80. Chm., Wales Cons. Local Govt Adv. Council, 1979–83. Contested (C) Bridgend, 1987. MP (C) Bridgend, 1983–87. PPS to Sec. of State for Wales, 1985–87. Chm. Governors, Bridgend Tech. Coll., 1977–81. *Recreations:* theatre, showbusiness. *Address:* 1 Cleviston Gardens, Newton, Porthcawl CF36 5RW.   *Died 1 Oct. 2005.*

HUDSON, Frank Michael Stanislaus; a Recorder of the Crown Court, 1981–87; *b* 28 Sept. 1916; *s* of Frederick Francis Hudson and Elizabeth Hudson (*née* O'Herlihy); *m* 1947, Jean Colburn (*née* Gordon); one *d.* *Educ:* Wimbledon Coll.; London Univ. (BA). Served War: 77th Field Regt RA, 1939–42; Glider Pilot Regt, 1942–45. Post-war employment in local govt and in trade assocs; called to the Bar, Middle Temple, 1961; practised Northern Circuit, 1969–86; Dep. Circuit Judge, 1977–80.
                                                                Died 13 April 2001.

HUDSON, James Ralph, CBE 1976; FRCS; Surgeon, Moorfields Eye Hospital, 1956–81, then Honorary Consulting Surgeon; Ophthalmic Surgeon, Guy's Hospital, 1963–76; Hon. Ophthalmic Surgeon: Hospital of St John and St Elizabeth, 1953–86; King Edward VII Hospital for Officers, 1970–86; Teacher of Ophthalmology, Guy's Hospital, 1964–76, Institute of Ophthalmology, University of London, 1961–81; Consultant Adviser in Ophthalmology, Department of Health and Social Security, 1969–82; *b* 15 Feb. 1916; *o s* of late William Shand Hudson and Ethel Summerskill; *m* 1946, Margaret May Oulpé; two *s* two *d.* *Educ:* The King's Sch., Canterbury; Middlesex Hosp. (Edmund Davis Exhibnr), Univ. of London. MRCS, LRCP 1939; MB, BS London 1940; DOMS (England) 1948; FRCS 1949; FRCOphth (FCOphth 1988; Hon. FCOphth 1990). Res. Med. Appts, Tindal House Emergency Hosp. (Middx Hosp. Sector), 1939–42. RAFVR Med. Service, 1942–46; Sqdn Ldr, 1944–46. Moorfields Eye Hosp., Clin. Asst, 1947, Ho. Surg., 1947–49, Sen. Resident Officer, 1949, Chief Clin. Asst, 1950–56; Middlesex Hosp., Clin. Asst Ophth. Outpatients, 1950–51; Ophth. Surg., W Middlesex Hosp., 1950–56, Mount Vernon Hosp., 1953–59. Civil Consultant in Ophthalmology to RAF, 1970–82. Examr in Ophthalmology (Dipl. Ophth. of Examg Bd of Eng., RCP and RCS, 1960–65; Mem. Court of Examrs, RCS, 1966–72). FRSocMed 1947 (Vice-Pres. Sect. of Ophthalmology, 1965); Member: Ophthal Soc. UK, 1948–88 (Hon. Sec. 1956–58, Vice-Pres., 1969–71, Pres., 1982–84); Faculty of Ophthalmologists, 1950–88

(Mem. Council, 1960–82; Hon. Sec. 1960–70; Vice-Pres., 1970–74; Pres., 1974–77; Rep. on Council of RCS, 1968–73; Hon. Mem., 1982–); Soc. Française d'Ophtal., 1950– (membre délégué étranger, 1970–92); Cttee d'Honneur Les Entretiens Annuels d'Ophtalmologie, 1970–; Internat. Council of Ophthalmology, 1978–86; UK Rep., Union Européenne des Médecins Spécialistes (Ophthalmology Section), 1973–91 (Pres., 1982–86); Hon. Fellow, Royal Aust. Coll. Ophthalmologists; Pilgrims of Gt Britain; Hon. Steward, Westminster Abbey, 1972–88. Liveryman, Soc. of Apothecaries, and Freeman of City of London. *Publications:* (with T. Keith Lyle) chapters in Matthews's Recent Advances in the Surgery of Trauma; contrib. to chapters in Rob and Rodney Smith's Operative Surgery, 1969; articles in: Brit. Jl of Ophthalmology; Trans Ophth. Soc. UK; Proc. Royal Soc. Med. *Recreations:* motoring, travel. *Address:* Flat 2, 17 Montagu Square, W1H 1RD. *T:* (020) 7487 2680.
                                                                Died 30 Dec. 2003.

HUDSON, John Arthur, CB 1970; Deputy Under-Secretary of State, Department of Education and Science, 1969–80; *b* 24 Aug. 1920; *s* of Francis Reginald Hudson and Dorothy Mary (*née* Crabbe); *m* 1960, Dwynwen Davies; one *s* one *d.* *Educ:* City of London Sch.; Jesus Coll., Oxford. Served War, Royal Corps of Signals, 1941–45 (despatches). Entered Ministry of Education, 1946. Mem., South Bank Theatre Bd, 1967–89. *Address:* The Rosary, Green Lane, Leominster, Herefordshire HR6 8QN. *T:* (01568) 614413.   *Died 18 Oct. 2004.*

HUDSON, Prof. Liam, PhD; psychologist and writer; partner, Balas Co-partnership, since 1987; *b* 20 July 1933; *er s* of Cyril and Kathleen Hudson; *m* 1st, 1955, Elizabeth Ward (marr. diss. 1965; she *d* 1965); 2nd, 1965, Bernadine Jacot de Boinod; three *s* one *d* (and one *d* decd). *Educ:* Whitgift Sch.; Exeter Coll., Oxford (MA). Post-graduate and post-doctoral research, Psychological Laboratory, Cambridge, 1957–65, and Research Centre, King's Coll., Cambridge, 1965–68; Fellow, King's Coll., Cambridge, 1966–68; Bell Prof. of Educnl Scis, Univ. of Edinburgh, 1968–77 and Dir, Res. Unit on Intellectual Develt, 1964–77; Prof. of Psychology, Brunel Univ., 1977–87. Mem., Inst. for Advanced Study, Princeton, 1974–75; Vis. Prof., Tavistock and Portman Clinics, London, 1987–96. Tanner Lectures, Yale Univ., 1997. Maurice Hille Award, SIAD, 1983. *Publications:* Contrary Imaginations, 1966; Frames of Mind, 1968; (ed) The Ecology of Human Intelligence, 1970; The Cult of the Fact, 1972; Human Beings, 1975; The Nympholepts, 1978; Bodies of Knowledge, 1982; Night Life, 1985; The Way Men Think, 1991; Intimate Relations, 1995. *Recreations:* painting and photography, making things, otherwise largely domestic. *Address:* Flat 6, 42 Upper Brook Street, W1K 7QP.   *Died 19 Feb. 2005.*

HUGHES, Sir David (Collingwood), 14th Bt *cr* 1773; sculptor; Managing Director, Louis Lejeune Ltd, 1978–1998; *b* 29 Dec. 1936; *s* of Sir Richard Edgar Hughes, 13th Bt and Angela Lilian Adelaide Pell (*d* 1967); *S* father, 1970; *m* 1964, Rosemary Ann Pain, MA, LLM, *d* of late Rev. John Pain; three *s* (and one *s* decd). *Educ:* Oundle; Magdalene Coll., Cambridge (BA 1960, MA 1967). National Service, RN, 1955–57. United Steel Cos Ltd, 1960–65; Unicam Instruments Ltd (subsequently Pye Unicam Ltd), export exec., 1965–70, E Europe manager, 1970–73. Builder, 1974–76. *Recreations:* shooting, fishing. *Heir: s* Thomas Collingwood Hughes, MSc, MBA, MRCP, FRCS [*b* 16 Feb. 1966; *m* 1996, Marina Louise Barbour, DPhil, MRCP, FRACP, *d* of Richard Barbour, Albany, WA]. *Address:* The Berristead, Wilburton, Ely, Cambs CB6 3RP. *T:* (01353) 740770. *Clubs:* Flyfishers'; Cambridge County (Cambridge).

                                                                Died 13 May 2003.

HUGHES, David John, FRSL; writer; *b* 27 July 1930; *o s* of late Gwilym Fielden Hughes and of Edna Frances Hughes; *m* 1st, 1958, Mai Zetterling (marr. diss. 1976; she *d* 1994); 2nd, 1980, Elizabeth Westoll; one *s* one *d.* *Educ:*

Eggar's Grammar Sch., Alton; King's College Sch., Wimbledon; Christ Church, Oxford (MA; Editor, Isis). FRSL 1986. Editorial Asst, London Magazine, 1953–55; Reader with Rupert Hart-Davis, 1956–60; Editor, Town magazine, 1960–61; script-writer and stills photographer of BBC documentaries and Scandinavian feature-films directed by Mai Zetterling, 1960–72; Editor, New Fiction Soc., 1975–78, 1981–82. Assistant Visiting Professor: Writers' Workshop, Univ. of Iowa, 1978–79, 1987; Univ. of Alabama, 1979; Vis. Associate Prof., Univ. of Houston, 1986. Film Critic, Sunday Times, 1982–83; Fiction Critic, 1982–99, Theatre Critic, 1996, Mail on Sunday. Mem. Council, RSL, 1989–96 (Life Vice Pres., 1998). Editor, Letters, jl of RSL, 1992–96. *Publications: fiction:* A Feeling in the Air, 1957; Sealed with a Loving Kiss, 1958; The Horsehair Sofa, 1961; The Major, 1964; The Man Who Invented Tomorrow, 1968; Memories of Dying, 1976; A Genoese Fancy, 1979; The Imperial German Dinner Service, 1983; The Pork Butcher, 1984 (Welsh Arts Council Fiction Prize, 1984; W. H. Smith Literary Award, 1985; filmed as Souvenir, 1989); But for Bunter, 1985; The Little Book, 1996; (ed) Winter's Tales: New Series I, 1985; (ed with Giles Gordon): Best Short Stories, annually 1986–95; The Best of Best Short Stories 1986–1995, 1995; *non-fiction:* J. B. Priestley, an informal study, 1958; The Road to Stockholm (travel), 1964; The Seven Ages of England (cultural history), 1967; The Rosewater Revolution, 1971; Evergreens, 1976; Himself & Other Animals: a portrait of Gerald Durrell, 1997; The Lent Jewels, 2002; The Hack's Tale, 2004. *Address:* 163 Kennington Road, SE11 6SF. *Clubs:* Savile; Surrey CC.
Died 11 April 2005.

HUGHES, Hon. Sir Davis, Kt 1975; Agent-General for New South Wales, in London, 1973–78; *b* 24 Nov. 1910; *m* 1940, Joan Philip Johnson; one *s* two *d*. *Educ:* Launceston High Sch., Tasmania; Phillip Smith Teachers' Coll., Hobart, Tas. Teacher, Tasmania, incl. Friends' Sch., Hobart, 1930–35; Master, Caulfield Grammar Sch., Melbourne, 1935–40. Served War, Sqdn Ldr, RAAF, Australia and overseas, 1940–45. Dep. Headmaster, Armidale Sch., Armidale, NSW, 1946–49; Mayor of Armidale, 1953–56. MLA, NSW, 1950–53 and 1956–65; Minister for Public Works, NSW, 1965–73. Aust. Rep., 1978–83, Dir, 1980–83, Société Génerale Australia Ltd; Rep., Derek Crouch Aust. Ltd, 1978–84. Hon. DEd Newcastle, NSW, 1996. Freeman: City of Armidale, NSW, 1965; City of London, 1975. *Recreations:* tennis, golf, fishing, racing. *Address:* 53 The Manor, 6 Tarragal Glen Road, Erina, NSW 2250, Australia. *Club:* Australasian Pioneers (Sydney).   *Died 16 March 2003.*

HUGHES, Rt Rev. John Taylor, CBE 1975; an Assistant Bishop, Diocese of Southwark, since 1986; *b* 12 April 1908; *s* of Robert Edward and Annie Hughes. *Educ:* Castle Hill Sch., Ealing; Uxbridge County Sch.; Bede Coll., University of Durham (BA 1931; MA 1935). Ordained deacon, 1931, priest, 1932; Asst Chaplain and Tutor, Bede Coll., Durham, 1931–34; Lecturer, Bede Coll., 1934–35; Curate, St John's, Shildon, Co. Durham, 1934–37; Vicar, St James, West Hartlepool, 1937–48; Canon Residentiary and Missioner of Southwark Cathedral and Warden of Diocesan Retreat House, Southwark, 1948–56; Bishop Suffragan of Croydon, 1956–77; Archdeacon of Croydon, 1967–77; Bishop to the Forces, 1966–75; an Asst Bishop, Diocese of Canterbury, 1977–86. *Recreations:* music, reading. *Address:* The Hospital of the Holy Trinity, North End, Croydon CR0 1UB. *T:* (020) 8686 8313.
Died 21 July 2001.

HUGHES, Major Richard Charles, MBE 1951; TD 1945; Director, Federation of Commodity Associations, 1973–78; *b* 24 Dec. 1915; *s* of late Frank Pemberton Hughes and Minnie Hughes, Northwich. *Educ:* Wrekin Coll., Wellington, Telford. TA commn, 4/5th (E of C) Cheshire Regt, 1935; regular commn, 22nd (Cheshire) Regt, 1939. Served War of 1939–45: 2 i/c 5th, 2nd and 1st Bns 22nd (Cheshire) Regt; served Palestine, 1945–47;

S/Captain MS and DAAG Western Comd, 1948–51; Korea, 1954; GSO2 Sch. of Infantry, 1955–56; Sec. of Sch. of Inf. Beagles, 1955–56; retd pay, 1958. Sec. to Sugar Assoc. of London, British Sugar Refiners Assoc. and Refined Sugar Assoc., 1958–78; formed British Sugar Bureau and apptd Sec., 1964–66. Hon. Treas., W Kensington Environment Cttee, 1974–75; Mem., Barons Keep Management Cttee, 1975. Member: City Liaison Cttee, Bank of England and City EEC Cttee, 1975; City Adv. Panel to City Univ., and Adviser to City of London Polytechnic, 1975; City Communications Consultative Gp, 1976. *Recreations:* travel, sailing, antiques. *Address:* Stone Cottage, 3 Bell Meadow Court, Tarporley, Cheshire CW6 0DT.   *Died 15 Feb. 2002.*

HUGHES, William, CB 1953; Chairman, Tooting Youth Project, 1981–87; *b* 21 Aug. 1910; *o s* of late William Hughes, Bishop's Stortford, Herts, and of Daisy Constance, *y d* of Charles Henry Davis; *m* 1941, Ilse Erna, *o d* of late E. F. Plohs; one *s* one *d*. *Educ:* Bishop's Stortford Coll.; Magdalen Coll., Oxford (demy). Entered Board of Trade, 1933; Asst Sec., 1942; Under-Sec., 1948–63 (Sec., Monopolies and Restrictive Practices Commission, 1952–55); Second Sec., 1963–70; Dep. Sec., 1970–71; Consultant to British Overseas Trade Bd, 1972–73; Under-Sec., Prices Commn, 1973–75. *Recreation:* music. *Address:* 250 Trinity Road, SW18 3RQ. *T:* (020) 8870 3652; Page's, Widdington, Essex CB11 3SN. *Clubs:* Reform; Leander.   *Died 24 July 2003.*

HUMPHREY, (Arthur) Hugh (Peters), CMG 1959; OBE 1952; Controller of Special Projects, Overseas Development Administration, Foreign and Commonwealth Office, 1961–71; Malayan Civil Service, 1934–60, retired; *b* 18 June 1911; *s* of late Arthur George Humphrey, bank manager; *m* 1948, Mary Valentine, *d* of late Lt-Col J. E. Macpherson; three *d*. *Educ:* Eastbourne Coll.; Merton Coll., Oxford (Open Exhbr 1930; 1st class Maths, 1933; MA 1948). Appointed Malayan Civil Service, 1934; Private Sec. to Governor of Straits Settlements and High Comr for Malay States, 1936–38; Resident, Labuan, 1940–42; interned by Japanese in Borneo, 1942–45; idc 1948; Sec. for Defence and Internal Security, Fedn of Malaya, 1953–57; Mem. of Federal Legislative and Executive Councils, 1953–56; Sec. to the Treasury, Federation of Malaya, 1957–59; Director of Technical Assistance, Commonwealth Relations Office, 1960–61; Controller of Special Projects, ODM, 1961. Official Leader, United Kingdom delegations at Colombo Plan conferences, Tokyo, 1960, and Kuala Lumpur, 1961. Coronation Medal, 1953. Hon. PMN 1958. *Recreations:* music, tennis. *Address:* 14 Ambrose Place, Worthing, Sussex BN11 1PZ. *T:* (01903) 233339. *Club:* East India, Devonshire, Sports and Public Schools.
Died 10 Sept. 2001.

HUMPHREY, Hugh; *see* Humphrey, A. H. P.

HUMPHREYS, Arthur Leslie Charles, CBE 1970; Director: Knowledge Engineering (UK) Ltd (formerly Computer Associated Systems Ltd), since 1982; Charles Babbage Institute, since 1978; *b* 8 Jan. 1917; *s* of late Percy Stewart Humphreys and late Louise (*née* Weston); *m* 1st, 1943, Marjorie Irene Murphy-Jones (*d* 1970); two *s* one *d*; 2nd, 1975, Audrey Norah Urquhart (*née* Dunningham) (*d* 1985); 3rd, 1994, Marion Terry Rushton (*née* Greest). *Educ:* Catford Grammar Sch.; Administrative Staff Coll., Henley. International Computers & Tabulators Ltd: Dir, 1963–83; Dep. Man. Dir, 1964; Man. Dir, 1967; ICL Ltd: Dir, 1968–82; Man. Dir, 1968–72; Dep. Chm., 1972–77; Dir, Data Recording Instrument Co. Ltd, 1957–84. *Recreations:* table tennis, bridge, music. *Address:* 24 Middle Street, Thriplow, Royston, Herts SG8 7RD. *T:* (01763) 208594.   *Died 29 Aug. 2003.*

HUNT, Arthur James, OBE 1971; FRTPI, FRICS; Chief Reporter for Public Inquiries, Scottish Office, 1974–79; *b* 18 Nov. 1915; *s* of Edward Henry and Norah Hunt; *m* 1946, Fanny Betty Bacon; one *s* three *d*. *Educ:* Tauntons

Sch., Southampton. Ordnance Survey, 1938–44; Planning Officer with West Sussex, Kent and Bucks County Councils, 1944–48; Asst County Planning Officer, East Sussex CC, 1948–52; Town Planning Officer, City of Durban, SA, 1953–61; Sen. and Principal Planning Inspector, Min. of Housing and Local Govt, 1961–68; Mem., Roskill Commn on the Third London Airport, 1968–70; Superintending Inspector, Dept of the Environment, 1971–74. *Recreations:* sailing, gardening, caravan touring. *Address:* Pentlands, 4 West Avenue, Middleton-on-Sea, West Sussex PO22 6EF.

Died 17 Jan. 2002.

HUNT, Brig. Kenneth, OBE 1955; MC 1943; Vice-President, International Institute for Strategic Studies, 1988–2000 (Deputy Director, 1967–77); *b* 26 May 1914; *s* of late John Hunt and Elizabeth Hunt; *m* 1939, Mary Mabel Crickett (*d* 1995); two *s* (and one *d* decd). *Educ:* Chatham House Sch., Ramsgate; sc Camberley; idc. Commissioned into Royal Artillery, 1940; served, Africa, Italy, Austria, with HAC, 1 RHA and 2 RHA, 1942–46 (despatches thrice); Bt Lt-Col 1955; CO 40 Fd Regt RA, 1958–60; CRA 51 Highland Div., 1961–63; IDC 1963; Dep. Standing Gp Rep. to N Atlantic Council, 1964–66; resigned commission, 1967. Dir, British Atlantic Cttee, 1978–81. Specialist Adviser to House of Commons Defence Cttee, 1971–84. Visiting Professor: Fletcher Sch. of Law, Cambridge, Mass, 1975; Univ. of S California, 1978–79; Univ. of Surrey, 1978–87. Mem. Council, RUSI, 1977; Fellow, Inst. of Security, Tokyo, 1979–. Freeman, City of London, 1977; Mem., HAC. Hon. Dr (PolSci), Korea Univ., 1977. Order of Rising Sun (Japan), 1984. *Publications:* NATO without France, 1967; The Requirements of Military Technology, 1967; Defence with Fewer Men, 1973; (ed) The Military Balance, annually, 1967–77; (jtly) The Third World War, 1978; (jtly) Asian Security, annually, 1979–89; Europe in the Western Alliance, 1988; contribs to learned jls, and chapters in books, in UK, USA, E Asia. *Recreations:* fly-fishing, listening to music. *Address:* 6 Canal Walk, Hungerford, Berkshire RG17 0EQ. *T:* (01488) 683996. *Clubs:* Army and Navy; International House of Japan (Tokyo). *Died 27 March 2004.*

HUNT, Prof. Norman Charles, CBE 1975; Professor of Business Studies, 1967–84, Vice-Principal, 1980–84, University of Edinburgh, then Emeritus Professor; *b* 6 April 1918; *s* of Charles Hunt and Charlotte (*née* Jackson), Swindon, Wilts; *m* 1942, Lorna Mary, 2nd *d* of Mary and William Arthur Mann, Swindon, Wilts; two *s. Educ:* Commonweal Sch.; Swindon Coll.; University of London (Sir Edward Stern Schol., BCom 1st cl. hons); PhD (Edinburgh). On Staff (Research Dept and Personal Staff of Chief Mechanical Engineer), GWR Co., 1934–45; University of Edinburgh: Lectr in Organisation of Industry and Commerce, 1946–53; Dir of Studies in Commerce, 1948–53; Prof. of Organisation of Industry and Commerce, 1953–66; Dean, Faculty of Social Scis, 1962–64. Member: Departmental Cttee on Fire Service, 1967–70; Rubber Industry NEDC, 1968–71; ODM Working Party on Management Educn and Training in Developing Countries, 1968–69; UGC, 1969–78 (Vice-Chm., 1974–76); Bd of Governors (and Chm., Mgt Develt Cttee), Council for Technical Educn and Training in Overseas Countries, 1971–75; Police Adv. Bd for Scotland, 1971–75; Council for Tertiary Educn in Scotland, 1979–84; CNAA, 1979–84. Consultant: UNIDO, 1973–85; Hong Kong Baptist Coll., 1984–87; Hong Kong Management Assoc., 1986–98. Chairman: R. and R. Clark Ltd, 1967–70; William Thyne Ltd, 1967–70; Director: William Thyne (Holdings) Ltd, 1963–70; William Thyne (Plastics) Ltd, 1967–70; INMAP Ltd, 1984–86; UnivEd Technologies Ltd, 1984–98 (Chm. 1984–86); Edinburgh Res. and Innovation Ltd, 1998–2000. Hon. DLitt Loughborough, 1975. *Publications:* Methods of Wage Payment in British Industry, 1951; (with W. D. Reekie) Management in the Social and Safety Services, 1974; articles in econ. and mgt

jls on industrial orgn, industrial relations, and mgt problems. *Recreations:* photography, motoring, foreign travel. *Address:* 65 Ravelston Dykes Road, Edinburgh EH4 3NU. *Died 7 April 2003.*

HUNT, Sir Robert (Frederick), Kt 1979; CBE 1974; DL; Chairman, Dowty Group PLC, 1975–86; Deputy Chairman, Rover Group (formerly BL plc), 1982–90 (Director, 1980–90); Director, Charter Consolidated, 1983–90; *b* 11 May 1918; *s* of late Arthur Hunt, Cheltenham and Kathleen Alice Cotton; *m* 1st, 1947, Joy Patricia Molly (*d* 1984), *d* of late Charles Leslie Harding, Cheltenham; four *d*; 2nd, 1987, Joyce Elizabeth Baigent, *d* of Otto Leiske. *Educ:* Pates Grammar Sch., Cheltenham; N Glos Techn. Coll. Apprenticed Dowty Equipment Ltd, 1935; Chief Instructor to Co.'s Sch. of Hydraulics, 1940; RAF Trng Comd, 1940; Export Man., Dowty Equipment Ltd, 1946; Vice-Pres. and Gen. Man., 1949, Pres., 1954, Dowty Equipment of Canada Ltd; Dir, Dowty Gp Ltd, 1956, Dep. Chm., 1959–75, Chief Exec., 1975–83. Dir, Eagle Star Hldgs plc, 1980–87. Chm., Bd of Trustees, Improvement District of Ajax, Ont, 1954; Dir, Ajax and Pickering Gen. Hosp., 1954; Chm., Cheltenham Hosp. Gp Man. Cttee, 1959; Chm., Glos AHA, 1974–81; Pres., 1967–68, Treas., 1973, Vice-Pres., 1976, Pres., 1977–78, SBAC. FREng (FEng 1982); FCASI 1976; FRAeS 1968, Hon. FRAeS 1981. Hon. DSc Bath, 1979. DL Glos, 1977; Hon. Freeman of Cheltenham, 1980. *Recreations:* family interests, golf, gardening. *Address:* Maple House, Withington, Glos GL54 4DA. *T:* (01242) 890344. *Club:* New (Cheltenham). *Died 17 Sept. 2004.*

HUNTER, Rt Rev. Anthony George Weaver; Assistant Bishop, 1976–80, Supernumerary Bishop, 1980–81, Diocese of Newcastle; *b* 3 June 1916; *s* of Herbert George Hunter and Ethel Frances Weaver; *m* 1st, 1948, Joan Isobel Marshall (*d* 1981); 2nd, 1982, Emlyn Marianne Garton (*née* Dent) (*d* 2001). *Educ:* Wanstead; Leeds Univ. (BA); Coll. of the Resurrection, Mirfield. Deacon, 1941; Priest, 1942; Curate of St George's, Jesmond, 1941–43; Orlando Mission Dist, 1943–47; Johannesburg Coloured Mission, 1947–48; Curate of St George's, Jesmond, 1948–49; Vicar of Ashington, 1949–60; Proctor in Convocation, 1959–60; Vicar of Huddersfield, 1960–68; Rural Dean of Huddersfield, 1960–68; Hon. Canon of Wakefield, 1962–68; Proctor in Convocation, 1962–68; Bishop of Swaziland, 1968–75; Rector of Hexham, Dio. Newcastle, 1975–79; Acting Archdeacon of Lindisfarne, 1981; retd Oct. 1981. OStJ. *Recreations:* walking, gardening, travel. *Address:* The West Wing, Sandwood House, Spaldington, East Yorks DN14 7NG. *T:* (01420) 422424.

Died 8 June 2002.

HUNTER, Evan; writer; *b* New York, 15 Oct. 1926; *s* of Charles F. Lombino and Marie Lombino; *né* Salvatore Albert Lombino; *m* 1st, 1949, Anita Melnick (marr. diss.); three *s*; 2nd, 1973, Mary Vann Finley (marr. diss.); one step *d*; 3rd, 1997, Dragica Dimitrijevic. *Educ:* Cooper Union; Hunter Coll. (BA 1950). Served USNR. Literary Father of the Year, 1961; Phi Beta Kappa. Grand Master Award, Mystery Writers of America, 1986; Cartier Diamond Dagger Award, CWA, 1998. *Publications include: as Evan Hunter:* The Blackboard Jungle, 1954; Second Ending, 1956; Strangers When We Meet, 1958; A Matter of Conviction, 1959; The Remarkable Harry, 1960; The Wonderful Button, 1961; Mothers and Daughters, 1961; Happy New Year, Herbie, 1963; Buddwing, 1964; The Paper Dragon, 1966; A Horse's Head, 1967; Last Summer, 1968; Sons, 1969; Nobody Knew They Were There, 1971; Every Little Crook and Nanny, 1972; The Easter Man, 1972; Seven, 1972; Come Winter, 1973; Streets of Gold, 1974; The Chisholms, 1976; Me and Mr Stenner, 1977; Walk Proud, 1978; Love, Dad, 1981; Far From the Sea, 1983; Lizzie, 1984; Criminal Conversation, 1994; Privileged Conversation, 1996; Candyland, 2001; The Moment She Was Gone, 2002; *as Ed McBain:* Cop Hater, 1956; The Mugger, 1956; The Pusher, 1956; The Con Man, 1957; Killer's Choice, 1958; Killer's Payoff, 1958;

Lady Killer, 1958; Killer's Wedge, 1959; 'Til Death, 1959; King's Ransom, 1959; Give the Boys a Great Big Hand, 1960; The Heckler, 1960; See Them Die, 1960; Lady, Lady, I Did It, 1961; The Empty Hours, 1962; Like Love, 1962; Ten Plus One, 1963; Ax, 1964; The Sentries, 1965; He Who Hesitates, 1965; Doll, 1965; Eighty Million Eyes, 1966; Fuzz, 1968; Shotgun, 1969; Jigsaw, 1970; Hail, Hail, the Gang's All Here!, 1971; Sadie When She Died, 1972; Let's Hear It for the Deaf Man, 1972; Death of a Nurse, 1972; Hail to the Chief, 1973; Bread, 1974; Where There's Smoke, 1975; Blood Relatives, 1975; So Long as You Both Shall Live, 1976; Guns, 1976; Long Time No See, 1977; Goldilocks, 1978; Calypso, 1979; Ghosts, 1980; Even the Wicked, 1980; Rumpelstiltskin, 1981; Heat, 1981; Beauty and the Beast, 1982; Ice, 1983; Jack and the Beanstalk, 1984; Lightning, 1984; Snow White and Rose Red, 1985; Eight Black Horses, 1985; Cinderella, 1986; Another Part of the City, 1986; Poison, 1987; Tricks, 1987; Puss in Boots, 1987; McBain's Ladies, 1988; The House that Jack Built, 1988; Lullaby, 1989; McBain's Ladies, Too, 1989; Downtown, 1989; Vespers, 1990; Mary, Mary, 1992; Mischief, 1993; There was a Little Girl, 1994; Romance, 1995; Gladly the Cross-Eyed Bear, 1996; Nocturne, 1997; The Last Best Hope, 1998; The Big Bad City, 1999; The Last Dance, 2000; Candyland, 2001; Money, Money, Money, 2002; Fat Ollie's Book, 2003; The Frumious Bandersnatch, 2004; Hark!, 2004; *screenplays:* Strangers When We Meet, 1959; The Birds, 1962; Fuzz, 1972; Walk Proud, 1979; Dream West (TV mini-series), 1986; *plays:* The Easter Man, 1964; The Conjuror, 1969. *Recreation:* travelling. *Address:* Curtis Brown, 28/29 Haymarket, SW1Y 4SP.

Died 6 July 2005.

HUNTER, Sir Ian (Bruce Hope), Kt 1983; MBE (mil.) 1945; Impresario; President, Askonas Holt Ltd, since 1998; Chairman, Tempo Video Ltd, since 1984; *b* 2 April 1919; *s* of late W. O. Hunter; *m* 1st, 1949, Susan (*d* 1977), *d* of late Brig. A. G. Russell; four *d*; 2nd, 1984, Lady Showering, *widow* of Sir Keith Showering. *Educ:* Fettes Coll., Edinburgh; abroad as pupil of Dr Fritz Busch and at Glyndebourne. Served War of 1939–45, Lt-Col. Asst to Artistic Dir, Edinburgh Festival, 1946–48; Artistic Administrator, Edinburgh Festival, 1949–50; Artistic Dir, Edinburgh Festival, 1951–55; Chm. and Chief Exec., 1953–88, Pres. and Dir, 1988–98, Harold Holt Ltd. Director, Bath Festivals, 1948, 1955, 1958–68; Adviser, Adelaide Festivals, 1960–64; Dir-Gen., Commonwealth Arts Festival, 1965; Artistic Director: Festivals of the City of London, 1962–80; Brighton Festivals, 1967–83; (with Yehudi Menuhin) Windsor Festivals, 1969–72; Hong Kong Arts Festivals, 1973–75; Malvern Festival, 1977–82; American Festival, 1985; Festival of German Arts, London, 1987. Dir, British Nat. Day Entertainment, Expo' 67. Dir, Live Music Now, 1983–. Member: Opera/Ballet Enquiry for Arts Council, 1967–69; Arts Administration Course Enquiry for Arts Council, 1970–71; Arts Council Trng Cttee, 1974–76; Centenary Appeal Cttee, RCM, 1982–; Adv. Cttee, Britain Salutes New York, 1983; Chairman: Entertainments Cttee, Queen's Silver Jubilee Appeal; Musicians' Benevolent Fund, 1987–95; Royal Concert Cttee, 1988–93. Pres., British Arts Festivals Assoc., 1978–81; Dep. Chm., Stravinsky Festival Trust; Trustee, Chichester Festival Theatre Trust, until 1988; Founder and Trustee, Young Concert Artists Trust, 1984–; Chm. of Governors, London Festival Ballet (later English National Ballet), 1984–89; Vice-Chm., Japan Fest. UK 1991, 1989–92; Mem. Cttee, Spanish Arts Festival, London, 1994; Vice-Pres., Yehudi Menuhin Sch. R. B. Bennett Commonwealth Prize for 1966. FRCM 1991 (Hon. RCM 1984); Hon. Mem., GSMD, 1975. FRSA (Mem. Council, 1968–73, 1976–83; Chm. Council, 1981–83; a Vice-Pres., 1981–). Mem. Ct of Assistants, Musicians' Co., 1981–84. Hon. DMus Bath, 1996. *Recreations:* gardening, painting. *Address:* Balcombe Place, Haywards Heath Road, Balcombe, West Sussex RH17 6QJ. *T:* (01444) 811066. *Club:* Garrick.

Died 5 Sept. 2003.

HUNTER, Surg. Rear-Adm. (D) John, CB 1973; OBE 1963; Director of Naval Dental Services, Ministry of Defence, 1971–74; *b* 21 Aug. 1915; *s* of Hugh Hunter and Evelyn Marian Hunter (*née* Jessop), Hale, Cheshire; *m* 1947, Anne Madelaine Hardwicke, Friarmayne, Dorset; three *s* two *d*. *Educ:* Bowdon Coll., Cheshire; Manchester Univ. LDS 1939. Surg. Lieut (D) RNVR 1940; HMS Kenya and 10th Cruiser Sqdn, 1941–42; HMS Howe, British Pacific Fleet, 1944–47; transf. to RN; HMS Forth on Staff of Rear-Adm. Destroyers, Mediterranean (Surg. Lt-Comdr), 1948–50; Dartmouth, Royal Marines; Surg. Comdr, Staff of Flag Officer Flotillas Mediterranean, 1956; service ashore in Admty., 1960–63; Surg. Captain (D), Staff of C-in-C Mediterranean, 1965–66; Staff of C-in-C Plymouth Comd, 1967–68; Fleet Dental Surgeon on Staff of C-in-C Western Fleet, 1969–70. QHDS 1971–74. Mem., South Hams DC, 1979–83. Chm., River Yealm Harbour Authority, 1982–85. *Recreations:* ocean racing, cruising, shooting. *Address:* Horsewells, Newton Ferrers, Plymouth PL8 1AT. *T:* (01752) 872254. *Clubs:* Royal Ocean Racing; Royal Western Yacht.

Died 1 April 2004.

HUNTER, Dame Pamela, DBE 1981; Vice-President, National Union of Conservative and Unionist Associations, since 1985 (Vice-Chairman, 1981–84; Chairman, 1984–85); *b* 3 Oct. 1919; *d* of late Col Thomas George Greenwell, TD, JP, DL, and Mabel Winifred Greenwell; *m* 1942, Gordon Lovegrove Hunter (*d* 1997); one *s* one *d*. *Educ:* Westonbirt Sch., Tetbury; Eastbourne Sch. of Domestic Economy. Served WRNS, 1942–45. Mem., Conservative Nat. Union Exec. Cttee, 1972–88; Chairman: Northern Area Cons. Women's Adv. Cttee, 1972–75; Cons. Women's Nat. Adv. Cttee, 1978–81; Mem., Cons. Party Policy Cttee, 1978–85. President: Berwick-upon-Tweed Cons. Assoc., 1986–89; N Area Cons. Council, 1986–89. Mem., Northumbrian Water Authority, 1973–76. Member: Berwick-upon-Tweed Borough Council, 1973–83; Chatton Parish Council 1987–95 (Chm., 1993–95); Lay Chm., Parish of Chatton with Chillingham PCC, 1989–92, and 1993–97, also formerly Church warden. *Recreations:* charity work for NSPCC, RNLI and N Northumberland Day Hospice; antiques. *Address:* The Coach House, Chatton, Alnwick, Northumberland NE66 5PY. *T:* (01668) 215259. *Club:* Lansdowne.

Died 30 May 2001.

HUNTER, Rita Nellie, CBE 1980; prima donna; leading soprano, Australian Opera, since 1981; *b* 15 Aug. 1933; *d* of Charles Newton Hunter and Lucy Hunter; *m* 1960, John Darnley-Thomas (*d* 1994); one *d*. *Educ:* Wallasey. Joined: Carl Rosa Opera Co., 1950; Sadler's Wells as leading soprano, 1958, and sang Brünnhilde in first complete Ring cycle, 1973; début: Berlin, 1970; Covent Garden, 1972; Metropolitan, NY, 1972; Munich, 1973; Australia, 1978 (returned 1980 and 1981); Seattle Wagner Fest., 1980; first perf. of Norma, San Francisco, then NY Metropolitan, 1975; first perf. of Tosca, Canberra, Aust., 1988; leading roles in Aida, Trovatore, Masked Ball, Cavalleria Rusticana, Lohengrin, Flying Dutchman, Idomeneo, Don Carlos, Turandot, Nabucco, Macbeth, Tristan and Isolde, Electra. Founded, 1986, and ran with husband, Maduo Sch. of Singing, Aust.; school renamed John Darnley-Thomas Singing Acad. and was run with daughter; also world-wide master classes. Many recordings, including complete Ring, complete Euryanthe, and several recital discs. Hon. DLitt Warwick, 1978; Hon. DMus Liverpool, 1983. RAM 1978. *Publication:* Wait till the Sun Shines, Nellie (autobiog.), 1986. *Recreations:* sewing, swimming, oil painting, reading, gardening (Mem. Royal Nat. Rose Soc.), caravanning (Mem. Caravan Club), swimming. *Address:* 305 Bobbin Head Road, North Turramurra, NSW 2074, Australia. *T:* (2) 99445062, *Fax:* (2) 94887526. *Club:* White Elephant.

Died 29 April 2001.

HURLEY, Dame Rosalinde, (Dame Rosalinde Gortvai), DBE 1988; LLB, MD; FRCPath; Professor of

Microbiology, University of London, at Institute of Obstetrics and Gynaecology (Royal Postgraduate Medical School), 1975–95, then Professor Emeritus, Imperial College School of Medicine; Consultant Microbiologist, Queen Charlotte's Maternity Hospital, 1963–95, then Hon. Consultant; *b* 30 Dec. 1929; *o d* of late William Hurley and Rose Clancey; *m* 1964, Peter Gortvai, FRCS (decd). *Educ:* Academy of the Assumption, Wellesley Hills, Mass, USA; Queen's Coll., Harley St, London; Univ. of London; Inns of Court. Called to the Bar, Inner Temple, 1958. House Surg., Wembley Hosp., 1955; Ho. Phys., W London Hosp., 1956; Sen. Ho. Officer, 1956–57, Registrar, 1957–58, Lectr and Asst Clin. Pathologist, 1958–62, Charing Cross Hosp. and Med. Sch. Chm., Medicines Commn, 1982–93; Mem., PHLS Bd, 1982–90 (Chm., Ethics Cttee, 1983); Chm., Nuffield Council on Bioethics Working Gp on Human Tissues (report published, 1995). EP Rep., Management Bd, European Medicines Evaluation Agency. Examiner, RCPath, and univs at home and abroad; Mem. Council, 1977–, Asst Registrar, 1978–, and Vice-Pres., 1984–87, RCPath; Royal Society of Medicine: Pres., Section of Pathology, and Vice-Pres., 1979–; Mem. Council, 1980–; Hon. Sec., 1984–90; Chm., 1980–82, formerly Vice-Chm., Cttee on Dental and Surgical Materials; Pres., Assoc. of Clinical Pathologists, 1984– (Pres.-elect, 1983–84); Chm., Assoc. of Profs of Medical Microbiol., 1987–94; Chm. Board, Therapeutic Res. and Educn Orgn, 1994–. Mem. Governing Body, Postgrad. Med. Fed., 1985–90. FRCOG 1993. Hon. FFPM 1990; Hon. FRSM 1995; CBiol, Hon. FIBiol 1998. DUniv Surrey, 1984. C. ver Heyden de Lancey Prize, RSM, 1991; Medal, RCPath, 1999. *Publications:* (jtly) Candida albicans, 1964; (jtly) Symposium on Candida Infections, 1966; (jtly) Neonatal and Perinatal Infections, 1979; chapters in med. books; papers in med. and sci. jls. *Recreations:* gardening, reading. *Address:* 2 Temple Gardens, Temple, EC4Y 9AY. *T:* (020) 7353 0577.   *Died 30 June 2004.*

HURST, John Gilbert, FBA 1987; FSA 1958; Assistant Chief Inspector of Ancient Monuments, English Heritage (formerly Department of the Environment), 1980–87; *b* 15 Aug. 1927; *s* of late Charles Chamberlain and Rona Hurst; *m* 1955, Dorothy Gillian Duckett (*d* 1971); two *d*. *Educ:* Harrow; Trinity Coll., Cambridge (BA Hons Archaeol. 1951; MA 1954). Joined Ancient Monuments Inspectorate, Min. of Works, 1952; Asst Inspector, 1954, Inspector, 1964 (Medieval rescue excavations); Principal Inspector (rescue excavations), 1973–80; directed excavations: Northolt Manor, 1950–70; Norwich, 1951–55; Dir, Wharram Res. Project, 1953–90. Sec., (Deserted) Medieval Village Res. Gp, 1952–86; British Association for Advancement of Science (Sect. H Anthrop.): Sec., 1954–57; Recorder, 1958–62; Pres., 1974; Society for Medieval Archaeology: Treas., 1957–76; Pres., 1980–83; Hon. Vice-Pres., 1983–; Vice-Pres., Soc. of Antiquaries of London, 1969–73; President: Soc. for Post-Medieval Archaeology, 1970–72 (Hon. Life Mem., 1993); Medieval Pottery Res. Gp, 1977–80; Southwark and Lambeth Arch. Soc., 1982–84; Hon. Vice-Pres., Medieval Settlement Res. Gp, 1986–. Hon. MRIA 1991. DUniv York 1995. Hon. Mem., Asoc. Española de Arqueología Medieval, Madrid, 1993. Gen. Editor, Wharram Research Project Monographs, 1979–. Legal and General Silver Trowel Award, Archaeologist of the Year, 1990. *Publications: include:* Deserted Villages of Oxfordshire, 1965 and Deserted Villages of Northamptonshire, 1966 (both with K. J. A. Allison and M. W. Beresford); (with M. W. Beresford) Deserted Medieval Villages: studies, 1971, 2nd edn 1989; (ed) B. Rackham, Medieval English Pottery, 2nd edn 1972; (ed with H. Hodges and V. Evison) Medieval Pottery from Excavations, 1974; (with D. S. Neal and H. J. E. Van Beuningen) Pottery Produced and Traded in North West Europe 1350–1650, 1986; (with M. W. Beresford) Wharram Percy: deserted medieval village, 1990; numerous contribs to learned jls. *Recreations:* listening to music, gardening. *Address:* The Old Dairy, 14 Main Street,

Great Casterton, Stamford, Lincs PE9 4AP. *T:* (01780) 757072.   *Died 29 April 2003.*

HUSKISSON, Robert Andrews, CBE 1979; Chairman, Lloyd's Register of Shipping, 1973–83 (Deputy Chairman, 1972–73); *b* 2 April 1923; *y s* of Edward Huskisson and Mary Huskisson (*née* Downing); *m* 1969, Alice Marian Swaffin. *Educ:* Merchant Taylors' Sch.; St Edmund Hall, Oxford. Served Royal Corps of Signals, 1941–47 (Major). Joined Shaw Savill & Albion Co. Ltd 1947; Dir 1966–72; Dep. Chief Exec., 1971–72; Director: Overseas Containers Ltd, 1967–72; Container Fleets Ltd, 1967–72; Cairn Line of Steamships Ltd, 1969–72. Director: SMIT Internat. Gp (UK) Ltd, 1982–87; Harland and Wolff plc, 1983–87; Lloyd's of London Press, 1983–89. President: British Shipping Fedn, 1971–72 (Chm. 1968–71); International Shipping Fedn, 1969–73; Chairman: Hotels and Catering EDC, 1975–79; Marine Technology Management Cttee, SRC, 1977–81. Dir, Chatham Historical Dockyard Trust, 1984–91; Chm., Essex Nuffield Hosp. Local Adv. Cttee, 1987–91. *Recreations:* golf, music. *Address:* Lanterns, Luppitt Close, Hutton Mount, Brentwood, Essex CM13 2JU. *Clubs:* Vincent's (Oxford); Thorndon Park Golf.   *Died 16 June 2004.*

HUTCHISON, Douglas; *see* Hutchison, J. D.

HUTCHISON, Lt-Comdr Sir (George) Ian Clark, Kt 1954; Royal Navy, retired; Member of the Queen's Body Guard for Scotland, Royal Company of Archers; *b* 4 Jan. 1903; *e s* of Sir George Clark Hutchison, KC, MP, Eriska, Argyllshire; *m* 1926, Sheena (*d* 1966), *o d* of late A. B. Campbell, WS; one *d*. *Educ:* Edinburgh Academy; RN Colleges, Osborne and Dartmouth. Joined Navy as Cadet, 1916; Lieut 1926; Lieut-Comdr 1934; specialised in torpedoes, 1929; emergency list, 1931; rejoined Navy Sept. 1939; served in Naval Ordnance Inspection Dept, 1939–43. Mem., Edinburgh Town Council, 1935–41; Chm., Public Assistance Cttee, 1937–39. Contested Maryhill Div. of Glasgow, 1935; MP (U) for West Div. of Edinburgh, 1941–59. Member: National Executive Council of British Legion (Scotland), 1943–51; Cttee on Electoral Registration, 1945–46; Scottish Leases Cttee, 1951–52. Gov., Donaldson's Sch. for the Deaf, Edinburgh, 1937–75. DL County of City of Edinburgh, 1958–84. *Recreations:* golf, fishing, walking, philately. *Address:* 16 Wester Coates Gardens, Edinburgh EH12 5LT. *T:* (0131) 337 4888. *Club:* New (Edinburgh).

Died 2 Feb. 2002.

HUTCHISON, Lt-Comdr Sir Ian Clark; *see* Hutchison, Sir G. I. C.

HUTCHISON, (Joseph) Douglas, CBE 1972; MC 1944; TD 1952; Director, Ranks Hovis McDougall Ltd, 1956–83; *b* 3 April 1918; *s* of late John K. Hutchison, Kinloch, Collessie, Fife and Ethel Rank, OBE; unmarried. *Educ:* Loretto; Clare Coll., Cambridge (BA Agric. 1939). Served Fife and Forfar Yeomanry, TA, 1939–46 (Major); comd Regt, 1951–53. Director: R. Hutchison & Co. Ltd, 1951–73; Ranks Ltd (later RHM), 1956. Mem., ARC, 1973–78. Pres., Nat. Assoc. British and Irish Millers, 1963–64 and 1974–75; Pres., Research Assoc. Flour Millers and Bakers, 1967–72; Chm., Game Conservancy, 1970–75. *Recreations:* gardening, music. *Address:* Bolfracks, Aberfeldy, Perthshire PH15 2EX. *Club:* New (Edinburgh).   *Died 6 Oct. 2001.*

HUTTON-WILLIAMS, Derek Alfred, MBE 1947; CEng, FIMechE; Director-General, Royal Ordnance Factories, 1969–75, retired; *b* 26 April 1914; *s* of William Hutton-Williams and Violet Woodfall Hutton-Williams; *m* 1936, Albrée Freeman; two *d*; *m* 1948, Yvonne Irene Anthony; one *s* one *d*. *Educ:* Oundle Sch.; London Univ. (Kitchener Scholar; BSc); AGGI; grad. NATO Defence Coll., Paris. MIEE. Pupil, Winget Ltd, Rochester, 1935; Techn. Asst, Royal Arsenal, Woolwich, 1938; Asst to Director, Small Arms and Fuzes, Ordance Factories, in charge of UK production of Sten carbine, 1939; Manager,

Royal Ordnance Factory, Theale, Berks, 1942; Dep.-Dir, Housing Supplies, Ministry of Supply, 1945; Partner, Hutton-Williams and Partners (Industrial Consultant), 1946; Supt, Royal Ordnance Factory, Maltby, Yorks, 1949; NATO Defence Coll., 1957; Asst Dir, Guided Weapons Production, Min. of Aviation, 1958; Dir, Inspectorate of Armaments, 1959; Dir, Royal Small Arms Factory, Enfield, 1964. *Recreations:* gardening, building, clock repair, music, recognising and accepting the inevitable, admiring craftsmanship. *Address:* 2 The Grove, Mount Street, Diss, Norfolk IP22 3QQ.
Died 22 Feb. 2001.

HUWS JONES, Robin; *see* Jones.

HUXLEY, Rev. Keith; Rector of Gateshead, Diocese of Durham, 1983–97; Chaplain to the Queen, 1981–98; *b* 17 Sept. 1933; *s* of George and Eluned Huxley. *Educ:* Birkenhead Sch.; Christ's Coll., Cambridge (MA); Cuddesdon Theol Coll. Ordained deacon, 1959, priest, 1960; Curate: St Mary's, Bowdon, 1959–61; Christ Church, Crewe, 1961–62; Chester Diocesan Youth Chaplain, 1962–68; Leader, Runcorn Ecumenical Team Ministry, 1968–75; Vicar, St Andrew's, Runcorn, 1968–73; Rector, East Runcorn Team Ministry, 1973–77; Home Secretary, Bd for Mission and Unity, C of E, 1977–83; RD of Gateshead, 1988–93. Secretary: NE Ecumenical Gp, 1983–94; Durham Ecumenical Relations Gp, 1985–97. Mem., Rotary Club, Gateshead, 1983–. *Recreation:* ornithology. *Address:* 2 Chaucer Close, Gateshead, Tyne and Wear NE8 3NG. *T:* (0191) 477 3094. *Died 14 April 2002.*

HYAM, Michael Joshua; His Honour Judge Hyam; Recorder of London, since 1998; a Senior Circuit Judge, since 1998; *b* 18 April 1938; *s* of Isaac J. Hyam and Rachel Hyam; *m* 1968, Diana Mortimer; three *s*. *Educ:* Westminster Sch.; St Catharine's Coll., Cambridge (MA). Called to Bar, Gray's Inn, 1962, Bencher, 1999; a Recorder, 1983–84; practised on SE Circuit, 1962–84; a Circuit Judge, 1984–98; Resident Judge, and Designated Family Judge, Norwich, 1991–98. Member: Council of Legal Education, 1980–86; Ethical Cttee, Cromwell Hosp., 1983–92; Chm., Area Criminal Justice Liaison Cttee, 1992–98. Gov., Dulwich Coll. Prep. Sch., 1986–92. HM Lieut, City of London, 1999–; Liveryman, Curriers' Co., 1998–; Hon. Liveryman, Fruiterers' Co., 1999. *Publication:* Learning the Skills of Advocacy, 1990, 4th edn 1999. *Recreations:* book collecting, cricket, gardening, yeast cookery. *Address:* Central Criminal Court, EC4M 7EH. *T:* (020) 7248 3277, *Fax:* (020) 7489 8451. *Clubs:* Garrick, MCC. *Died 8 July 2004.*

HYLTON-FOSTER, Baroness *cr* 1965, of the City of Westminster (Life Peer); **Audrey Pellew Hylton-Foster,** DBE 1990; British Red Cross Society: Director, Chelsea Division, 1950–60; President and Chairman, London Branch, 1960–83, Patron, since 1984; Hon. Consultant, National Headquarters, 1984–86; *b* 19 May 1908; *d* of 1st Viscount Ruffside, PC, DL (*d* 1958), and Viscountess Ruffside (*d* 1969); *m* 1931, Rt Hon. Sir Harry Hylton-Foster, QC (*d* 1965); no *c*. *Educ:* St George's, Ascot; Ivy House, Wimbledon. Pres., Research into Blindness Fund, 1965–76. Convenor, Cross Bench Peers, 1974–95. BRCS Queen's Badge of Honour. *Recreations:* gardening, fishing. *Address:* The Coach House, Tanhurst, Leith Hill, Holmbury St Mary, Dorking, Surrey RH5 6LU. *T:* (01306) 711975. *Died 31 Oct. 2002.*

I

IDALIE, Zoë, (Mme Heinric Idalie); *see* Oldenbourg-Idalie, Z.

IDDESLEIGH, 4th Earl of, *cr* 1885; **Stafford Henry Northcote;** Bt 1641; Viscount St Cyres, 1885; Vice Lord-Lieutenant of Devon, 1999–2002; Director, Devon & Exeter Steeplechases Ltd, since 1975 (Vice Chairman, 1990–98); *b* 14 July 1932; *er s* of 3rd Earl of Iddesleigh and Elizabeth (*d* 1991), *er d* of late F. S. A. Lowndes and Marie Belloc; *S* father, 1970; *m* 1955, Maria Luisa Alvarez-Builla y Urquijo (Condesa del Real Agrado in Spain), OBE, DL, *d* of late Don Gonzalo Alvarez-Builla y Alvera and Viscountess Exmouth, *widow* of 9th Viscount Exmouth; one *s* one *d. Educ:* Downside. 2nd Lieut, Irish Guards, 1951–52. Director: Television South West, 1982–92; Gemini Radio Ltd, 1993–98; Orchard Media Ltd, 1996–98; UDT, 1983–87; TSB Gp, 1986–87; TSB Commercial Hldgs, 1987; Mem., SW Region, TSB GP Bd (Chm., 1983–87). DL Devon, 1979. Kt SMO Malta. *Heir: s* Viscount St Cyres,*b* 15 Feb. 1957. *Address:* Shillands House, Upton Pyne Hill, Exeter, Devon EX5 5EB. *T:* (01392) 258916. *Club:* Army and Navy.
Died 8 July 2004.

INGE-INNES-LILLINGSTON, George David, CVO 1993; CBE 1986; DL; a Crown Estates Commissioner, 1974–93; *b* 13 Nov. 1923; *s* of late Comdr H. W. Innes-Lillingston, RN, formerly of Lochalsh House, Balmacara, Kyle, Ross-shire; *m* 1st, 1946, Alison Mary (*d* 1947), *er d* of late Canon F. W. Green, MA, BD, Norwich; one *d*; 2nd, 1955, Elizabeth Violet Grizel Thomson-Inge, *yr d* of Lt-Gen. Sir William Thomson, KCMG, CB, MC; two *s* one *d. Educ:* Stowe, Buckingham; Merton Coll., Oxford (MA Hons Agric.). Served War as Lieut RNVR, 1942–45; Lt-Comdr RNR, 1966. Member: Agricultural Land Tribunal, 1962–72; Minister's Agricultural Panel for W Midlands, 1972–76; Council for Charitable Support, 1985–90; Chairman: N Birmingham and District Hosps, 1968–74; Agric. and Hort. Cttee, BSI, 1980–86; President: Staffs Agricultural Soc., 1970–71; CLA, 1979–81 (Pres., Staffs Br., 1983–94). Dir, Lands Improvement Gp Ltd, and associated cos, 1983–91; Chm., Croxden Horticultural Products Ltd, 1986–91. Chm., Midland Reg., STA, 1983–94. Trustee, Lichfield Cathedral, 1980–99. FRAgS 1986. JP 1967–74, DL 1969, High Sheriff, 1966, Staffs. Bledisloe Gold Medal for Landowners, RASE, 1991. *Recreation:* growing trees. *Address:* The Old Kennels, Thorpe Constantine, Tamworth, Staffs B79 0LH. *T:* (01827) 830224. *Clubs:* Boodle's, Farmers', Royal Thames Yacht; Royal Highland Yacht (Oban).
Died 14 March 2002.

INGLIS, James Craufuird Roger, WS; Partner, Shepherd & Wedderburn, WS, 1976–89; Chairman, British Assets Trust plc, 1978–95; *b* 21 June 1925; *s* of Lt-Col John Inglis and Helen Jean Inglis; *m* 1952, Phoebe Aeonie Murray-Buchanan; two *s* four *d. Educ:* Winchester Coll.; Cambridge Univ. (BA); Edinburgh Univ. (LLB). Director: Scottish Provident Institution, 1962–95; Selective Assets Trust plc, 1988–95; Royal Bank of Scotland, 1967–89; Royal Bank of Scotland Gp plc, 1985–90. Chairman: European Assets Trust NV, 1972–95; Investors Capital Trust, 1985–94; Ivory & Sime Optimum Income Trust, 1989–95. *Recreation: golf. Address:* Lammerview, 1 Letham Mains Holdings, Haddington EH41 4NN. *T:* (01620) 810339. *Clubs:* New (Edinburgh); Royal and Ancient Golf (St Andrews); Hon. Company of Edinburgh Golfers.
Died 26 May 2001.

INGRAM, Prof. David John Edward, CBE 1991; DPhil, DSc; CPhys, FInstP; Vice-Chancellor, University of Kent at Canterbury, 1980–94, Emeritus Professor of Physics, since 1994; *b* 6 April 1927; *s* of late J. E. Ingram and Marie Florence (*née* Weller); *m* 1952, Ruth Geraldine Grace, *d* of late Donald McNair; two *s* one *d. Educ:* King's Coll. Sch., Wimbledon; New Coll., Oxford (MA); DSc Oxon 1960. Postgraduate research at Oxford Univ., 1948–52; Research Fellow and Lectr, University of Southampton, 1952–57; Reader in Electronics, University of Southampton, 1957–59; Prof. and Head of Dept of Physics, Univ. of Keele, 1959–73; Dep. Vice-Chancellor, University of Keele, 1964–65, 1968–71; Principal, Chelsea Coll., London Univ., 1973–80 (Fellow, 1984). Mem., UGC, Physical Sciences Cttee, 1971–74. British Council: Mem. Bd, 1992–95; Chm., Cttee on Higher Educn, 1991–95. Chairman: London Univ. Cttee for Non-Teaching Staff, 1979–80; London Univ. Central Coordinating Cttee for Computers, 1978–80; Standing Conf. on Univ. Admissions, 1982–89; Kent County Consultative Cttee Industry Year, 1986; Hon. Treas., CVCP, 1987–94 (Chm., Sub-Cttee on Staff and Student Affairs, 1986–89; Chm., Universities Staff Develt Trng Unit, 1989–94). Member: Carnegie UK Trust, 1980– (Chm., Cttee on Community Service, 1996–); Camberwell DHA, 1982–85; Thanet Health Care Trust, 1992–94; Somerset and Taunton NHS Trust, 1995–98; Esso Trust for Tertiary Educn, 1978–88; Univs Authorities Panel for Staff Salaries, 1987–89; Member Council: SPCK, 1980–93; CNAA, 1983–89; CET, 1983–85; UCCA, 1984–94 (Chm., 1991–94); UCAS, 1994–. Pres., Victoria Inst., 1986–. Member, Governing Body: Wye Coll., London Univ., 1975–94; King's Sch., Canterbury, 1983–96; St Lawrence Coll., 1980–89 (a Vice-Pres., 1989–); Cobham Hall, 1989–92; King's Coll. Hosp. Medical Sch., 1982–95; Roehampton Inst., 1978–88; London Sch. of Contemporary Dance, 1983–85; South Bank Univ. (formerly Poly.), 1989–96; West Heath Sch., 1990–94. DL Kent, 1992–95. FKC 1986; Hon. Fellow, Roehampton Inst., 1988. Hon. DSc: Clermont-Ferrand, 1965; Keele, 1983; Hon. DCL Kent, 1994. *Publications:* Spectroscopy at Radio and Microwave Frequencies, 1955, 2nd edn, 1967; Free Radicals as Studied by Electron Spin Resonance, 1958; Biological and Biochemical Applications of Electron Spin Resonance, 1969; Radiation and Quantum Physics, 1973; Radio and Microwave Spectroscopy, 1976; various papers in Proc. Royal Soc., Proc. Phys. Soc., etc. *Recreations:* sailing, debating, DIY. *Address:* Cordwainers Cottage, Maundown, Wiveliscombe, Somerset TA4 2BU. *Club:* Athenæum (Mem., Gen. Cttee, 1985–89).
Died 15 Jan. 2001.

INGRAMS, Leonard Victor, OBE 1980; Partner, L.V. Ingrams & Co. Ltd, since 1998; *b* 1 Sept. 1941; *s* of late Leonard St Clair Ingrams and Victoria Susan Beatrice (*née* Reid); *m* 1964, Rosalind Ann Moore; one *s* three *d. Educ:* Stonyhurst Coll.; Corpus Christi Coll., Oxford (1st cl. Classics (Mods) 1961; 1st cl. Lit.Hum. 1963; MA; Derby Schol. 1963; Sen. Schol. 1964; BLitt). Asst Lectr, QMC, 1965–67; joined Baring Bros, 1967, Man. Dir, 1975–81; Sen. Advr, Saudi Arabian Monetary Agency, 1974–79, Chief Advr to Gov., 1981–84; Dir, Robert Fleming Hldgs, 1985–96; Sen. Vice-Pres., Arab Banking Corp, 1996–98. Director: Deutschland Investment Corp., 1996–99 (Chm., 1990–96); Czech and Slovak Investment Corp., 1996– (Chm., 1992–96). Chm., Garsington Opera Ltd, 1990–; Mem., Mozart 2006 Cttee, Salzburg, 2000–. FRSA 1997. Pro Europa Foundn of Culture Prize, 2000. *Publications:* (ed) International Bond Portfolio

Management, 1988; contribs to various vols of Oxyrhynchus Papyri. *Recreations:* gardening, music. *Address:* (office) Suite 3, 32 Davies Street, W1K 4ND; Garsington Manor, Garsington, Oxford OX44 9DH. *T:* (01865) 361234. *Club:* Beefsteak. *Died 27 July 2005.*

INGROW, Baron *cr* 1982 (Life Peer), of Keighley in the County of West Yorkshire; **John Aked Taylor,** Kt 1972; OBE 1960; TD 1951; DL; JP; Life President, Timothy Taylor & Co. Ltd, since 1995 (Chairman and Managing Director, 1954–95); Lord-Lieutenant and Custos Rotulorum of West Yorkshire, 1985–92 (Vice Lord-Lieutenant, 1976–85); *b* 15 Aug. 1917; *s* of Percy Taylor, Knowle Spring House, Keighley, and Gladys Broster (who *m* 2nd, 1953, Sir (John) Donald Horsfall, 2nd Bt); *m* 1949, Barbara Mary (*d* 1998), *d* of Percy Wright Stirk, Keighley; two *d.* *Educ:* Shrewsbury Sch. Served War of 1939–45: Duke of Wellington's Regt and Royal Signals, Major; Norway, Middle East, Sicily, NW Europe and Far East. Mem., Keighley Town Council, 1946–67 (Mayor, 1956–57; Chairman: Educn Cttee, 1949–61; Finance Cttee, 1961–67); Mem. Council, Magistrates' Assoc., 1957–86 (Vice-Chm., Exec. Cttee, 1975–76; Chm., Licensing Cttee, 1969–76; Hon. Treasurer, 1976–86; Vice-Pres., 1986–; Past Pres. and Chm., WR Br.); Life Vice-Pres., W Yorks Br.); Chairman: Keighley Conservative Assoc., 1952–56 and 1957–67 (Pres., 1971–76; Jt Hon. Treas., 1947–52, and Chm., Young Conservatives, 1946–47); Yorkshire West Conservative European Constituency Council, 1978–84 (Pres., 1984–85); National Union of Conservative and Unionist Associations: Mem. Exec. Cttee, 1964–83, Chm., 1971–76; Vice-Chm., 1965–66, Chm., 1966–71; Yorkshire Area; Hon. Vice-Pres., 1976–, Pres., 1982–83. Gen. Comr of Income Tax, 1965–92. Vice-Pres., Yorks and Humberside TAVRA, 1985–88, and 1991–92 (Pres., 1988–91). Mem. Court, Univ. of Leeds, 1986–92. Pres., Council of Order of St John, S and W Yorks, 1985–92; KStJ 1986. JP Borough of Keighley 1949; DL West (formerly WR) Yorks, 1971. DUniv Bradford, 1990. *Address:* Fieldhead, Keighley, West Yorkshire BD20 6LP. *T:* (01535) 603895. *Died 7 Feb. 2002.*

INMAN, Herbert, CBE 1977; Regional Administrator, Yorkshire Regional Health Authority, 1973–77; Hon. Adviser to the Sue Ryder Foundation, since 1977, and Member of Council, 1986–89; Member, Executive Committee, Sue Ryder Homes, 1983–88 (Chairman, 1983–87); *b* 8 Jan. 1917; *s* of Matthew Herbert Inman and Rose Mary Earle; *m* 1939, Beatrice, *d* of Thomas Edward Lee and Florence Lee; twin *s.* *Educ:* Wheelwright Grammar Sch., Dewsbury; Univ. of Leeds. DPA. FHSM (Nat. Pres. 1968–69). Various hosp. appts, Dewsbury, Wakefield and Aylesbury, 1933–48; Dep. Gp Sec., Leeds (A) Gp HMC and Dep. Chief Admin. Officer, 1948–62; Gp Sec. and Chief Admin. Officer, Leeds (A) Gp HMC, 1962–70; Gp Sec. and Chief Admin. Officer, Leeds (St James's) Univ. HMC, 1970–73. *Publications:* occasional articles in hospital and health services jls. *Recreations:* Rugby and cricket (spectator), travel, gardening, swimming. *Address:* 7 Potterton Close, Barwick in Elmet, Leeds LS15 4DY. *T:* (0113) 281 2538.
Died 26 March 2002.

INNES, Maughan William; Controller Finance, National Research Development Corporation, 1965–77; *b* 18 Nov. 1922; *s* of Leslie W. Innes and Bridget Maud (*née* Humble-Crofts); *m* 1950, Helen Mary, *d* of Roper Spyers; one *s* (and one *s* decd). *Educ:* Marlborough College; BA Open Univ., 1988. Chartered Accountant, 1949; FCA 1960. RAF, 1941–46. Canada, 1953–60. *Recreations:* music, theatre. *Address:* Brook Cottage, Four Elms, Edenbridge, Kent TN8 6PA. *T:* (01732) 700232. *Club:* MCC.
Died 1 April 2001.

IRVINE, Very Rev. (John) Murray; Provost and Rector of Southwell Minster, 1978–91, then Emeritus; Priest-in-

Charge: of Edingley and Halam, 1978–91; of Rolleston with Fiskerton and Morton and Upton, 1990–91; *b* 19 Aug. 1924; *s* of Andrew Leicester Irvine and Eleanor Mildred (*née* Lloyd); *m* 1st, 1961, Pamela Shirley Brain (*d* 1992); one *s* three *d*; 2nd, 2000, Miriam Ruth van Laun (*née* Davis). *Educ:* Charterhouse; Magdalene Coll., Cambridge (BA 1946, MA 1949); Ely Theological Coll. Ordained deacon, 1948, priest, 1949; Curate of All Saints, Poplar, 1948–53; Chaplain of Sidney Sussex Coll., Cambridge, 1953–60; Selection Sec. of CACTM, 1960–65; Canon Residentiary, Prebendary of Hunderton, Chancellor and Librarian of Hereford Cathedral, and Dir of Ordination Training, Diocese of Hereford, 1965–78; Warden of Readers, 1976–78. *Address:* 9 Salston Barton, Strawberry Lane, Ottery St Mary, Devon EX11 1RG. *T:* (01404) 815901. *Died 14 Sept. 2005.*

IRVINE, Very Rev. Murray; see Irvine, Very Rev. J. M.

IRVINE, Norman Forrest; QC 1973; a Recorder of the Crown Court, 1974–86; *b* 29 Sept. 1922; *s* of William Allan Irvine and Dorcas Forrest; *m* 1964, Mary Lilian Patricia Edmunds (*née* Constable); (one *s* decd). *Educ:* High Sch. of Glasgow; Glasgow Univ. BL 1941. Solicitor (Scotland), 1943. Served War, 1942–45: Lieut Royal Signals, Staff Captain. HM Claims Commn, 1945–46; London Claims Supt, Provincial Insurance Co. Ltd, 1950–52. Called to Bar, Gray's Inn, 1955. *Recreations:* reading, piano, writing. *Address:* 11 Upland Park Road, Oxford OX2 7RU. *Died 31 Oct. 2005.*

IRVING, Clifford; see Irving, E. C.

IRVING, (Edward) Clifford, CBE 1981; Member, Legislative Council, Isle of Man, 1987–95; *b* 24 May 1914; *s* of late William Radcliffe Irving and Mabel Henrietta (*née* Cottier); *m* 1941, Nora, *d* of Harold Page, Luton; one *s* one *d.* *Educ:* Isle of Man; Canada. Member: House of Keys, 1955–61, 1966–81, 1984–87 (Acting Speaker, 1971–81); Executive Council, IOM Govt, 1968–81 (Chm., 1977–81). Member, Isle of Man Government Boards: Airports, 1955–58; Assessment, 1955–56; Social Security, 1956; Local Govt, 1956–62; Tourist, 1956–62; Finance, 1966–71. Member: Industrial Adv. Council, 1961–62, 1971–81, 1987–94; CS Commn, 1976–81. Chairman: IOM Tourist Bd, 1971–81; IOM Sports Council, 1971–81; IOM Harbours Bd, 1985–87. Chairman: Bank of Wales (IOM), 1985–87; Etam (IOM), 1985–; Refuge (IOM) Ltd, 1988–92; Director: Bank of Scotland (IOM) Ltd, 1987–95 (Chm., 1987–89); Bank of Scotland Nominees (IOM) Ltd, 1987–95 (Chm., 1987–89). President: Wanderers Male Voice Choir; Manx Nat. Powerboat Club; Manx Parachute Club; IOM Angling Assoc.; Douglas Br., RNLI; Douglas and Dist Angling Club; Douglas Bay Yacht Club; Past Rotarians' Club of IOM, 1996–97; Past Patron: Manx Variety Club; IOM TT Races. *Recreations:* powerboating, angling. *Address:* Highfield, Belmont Road, Douglas, Isle of Man IM1 4NR. *T:* (01624) 673652. *Clubs:* Douglas and District Angling; Douglas Bay Yacht. *Died 13 July 2004.*

ISAAC, Prof. Peter Charles Gerald; Professor of Civil and Public Health Engineering, 1964–81, then Emeritus, and Head of Department of Civil Engineering, 1970–81, University of Newcastle upon Tyne; Partner, Watson Hawksley (consulting engineers), 1973–83; *b* 21 Jan. 1921; *s* of late Herbert George Isaac and Julienne Geneviève (*née* Hattenberger); *m* 1950, Marjorie Eleanor White; one *s* one *d.* *Educ:* Felsted Sch.; London and Harvard Univs; BSc(Eng), SM; DLitt Newcastle, 1997. Asst Engineer, GWR, 1940–45; Lecturer in Civil Engineering, 1946; Senior Lecturer in Public Health Engineering, 1953, Reader, 1960, Univ. of Durham; Dean of Faculty of Applied Science, Univ. of Newcastle upon Tyne, 1969–73; Sandars Reader in Bibliography, Univ. of Cambridge, 1983–84. Member: Industrial Health Adv. Cttee, Min. of Lab. and Nat. Service, 1959–66; Working

Party on Sewage Disposal, 1969–70; WHO Expert Adv. Panel on Environmental Health, 1976–87; specialist advr, House of Lords Select Cttee on Sci. and Technol. II (Hazardous Waste), 1980–81 and House of Lords Select Cttee on Sci. and Technol. I (Water), 1982; DoE Long-Term Water-Research Requirements Cttee. Member of Council: ICE, 1968–71, 1972–75, 1977–80; IPHE, 1973–87 (Pres., 1977–78); Pres., British Occupational Hygiene Soc., 1962–63 (Hon. Mem., 1993); Mem. Bd, CEI, 1978–79. Trustee, Asian Inst. Technology, Bangkok, 1968–82 (Vice-Chm., 1979–82). Bibliographical Society: Mem. Council, 1970–74, 1979–83; Vice-Pres., 1984–94; Pres., 1994–96; Hon. Editor of Monographs, 1982–89. Chairman: History of the Book Trade in the North, 1965–; British Book Trade Index; Printing Historical Soc., 1989–91; Pres., Assoc. of Indep. Libraries, 1997–2000. Hon. Mem., Lit. and Philos. Soc., Newcastle upon Tyne. Director: Thorne's Students' Bookshop Ltd, 1969–74; Environmental Resources Ltd, 1972–74. Freeman, Co. of Stationers and Newspaper Makers, 1984, Liveryman, 1986, Renter Warden, 1998–99. FSA 1987; FICE 1956 (AMICE 1946); Hon. FIPHE 1986. Clemens Herschel Prize in Applied Hydraulics, 1952; Telford Premium, 1957; Thomas Bedford Award, 1978; Gold Medal, IPHE, 1987. *Publications:* Electric Resistance Strain Gauges (with W. B. Dobie), 1948; Public Health Engineering, 1953; Trade Wastes, 1957; Waste Treatment, 1960; River Management, 1967; William Davison of Alnwick: pharmacist and printer, 1968; Farm Wastes, 1970; Civil Engineering-The University Contribution, 1970; Management in Civil Engineering, 1971; Davison's Halfpenny Chapbooks, 1971; (ed) The Burman Alnwick Collection, 1973; William Davison's New Specimen, 1990; Six Centuries of the Provincial Book Trade in Britain, 1990; William Bulmer: the fine printer in context, 1993; (ed) Newspapers in the Northeast, 1999; (edited with B. McKay): Images and Texts, 1997; The Reach of Print, 1998; The Human Face of the Book Trade, 1999; The Mighty Engine, 2000; The Moving Market, 2001; contribs to various learned and technical jls. *Recreations:* bibliography, printing, book-trade history. *Address:* 10 Woodcroft Road, Wylam, Northumberland NE41 8DJ. *T:* (01661) 853174; *e-mail:* peterisaac@britishlibrary.net. *Clubs:* Royal Commonwealth Society, Penn.
Died 15 June 2002.

ISAAC, Rear-Adm. Robert Arthur, CB 1989; Director General Marine Engineering, Ministry of Defence (Procurement Executive), 1986–89; consultant (business with Japan), 1989–97; *b* 21 Feb. 1933; *s* of Frank and Florence Isaac; *m* 1960, Joy Little; one *s* one *d. Educ:* Oakham Sch.; Royal Naval Engrg Coll. (Dartmouth Special Entry). Entered RN, 1951; HMS Albion, 1957–59; HM Submarines Scotsman, Aurochs, nuclear trng, and HM Submarine Warspite, 1959–69; Dir Gen. Ships, MoD, 1970–74; HMS Blake, 1974–76; 2nd Sea Lord's Dept, MoD, 1976–78; Captain 1977; Naval Attaché, Tokyo and Seoul, 1979–81; Project Dir, Surface Ships, MoD (PE), 1981–84; HMS Thunderer, RNEC in comd, 1984–86; Rear-Adm. 1986. *Recreations:* sport, gardening. *Clubs:* Naval, Army and Navy.
Died 21 Sept. 2005.

ISHIHARA, Takashi, First Class, Order of the Rising Sun (Japan), 1991; Hon. KBE 1990; Counsellor, Nissan Motor Co., Ltd, since 1992 (Chairman, 1985–92); *b* 3 March 1912; *s* of Ichiji and Shigeyo Ishihara; *m* 1943, Shizuko Nakajo; one *s. Educ:* Law Dept, Tohoku Univ. (grad 1937). Joined Nissan Motor Co., Ltd, 1937; promoted to Gen. Man. of Planning and Accounting Depts respectively; Dir of Finance and Accounting, 1954; Man. Dir, 1963; Exec. Man. Dir, 1969; Exec. Vice Pres., 1973; Pres., 1977; Pres., Nissan Motor Corp. in USA, 1960–65; Chm., Nissan Motor Manufacturing Corp., USA, 1980–82. Exec. Dir, Keidanren (Fedn of Econ. Orgns), 1977–85; Chm., Keizai Doyukai (Japan Assoc. of

Corporate Execs), 1985–91; Dir, Nikkeiren (Japan Fedn of Employers Assocs), 1978–85; President: Japan Automobile Manufacturers Assoc., Inc., 1980–86; Japan Motor Industrial Fedn, Inc., 1980–86. Hon. DCL Durham, 1987. Blue Ribbon Medal (Japan), 1974; First Order of Sacred Treasure (Japan), 1983; Grand Cross (Spain), 1985. *Recreations:* reading, golf, ocean cruising. *Address:* Nissan Motor Co., 17–1 Ginza 6–chome, Chuo-ku, Tokyo 104, Japan; 20–3, 2–chome, Shiroganedai, Minato-ku, Tokyo 108, Japan.
Died 31 Dec. 2003.

ISLWYN, Baron *cr* 1997 (Life Peer), of Casnewydd in the co. of Gwent; **Royston John Hughes;** DL; *b* 9 June 1925; *s* of John Hughes, coal miner; *m* 1957, Florence Marion Appleyard; three *d. Educ:* Ruskin Coll., Oxford. Mem. Coventry City Council, 1962–66; various offices in Transport and General Workers' Union, 1959–66. MP (Lab): Newport, Gwent, 1966–83; Newport E, 1983–97. PPS to Minister of Transport, 1974–75; Mem., Speaker's panel, 1982–84, 1991–97; opposition frontbench spokesman on Welsh affairs, 1984–88. Joint Chairman: All Party Roads Gp, 1983–97; All Party Motors Gp, 1986–97; Chairman: PLP Sports Gp, 1974–83; PLP Steel Group, 1978–87, 1994–97; Parly Gp, TGWU, 1979–82. Chm., Welsh Grand Cttee, 1982–84, 1991–97. Exec. Mem., IPU, 1987–97 (Treas., 1990–92). Deleg., Council of Europe and WEU, 1991–97. Jt Chm., Rugby Union Gp, 1993–97; Pres., Newport Athletic Club, 1997–; Vice President: Crawshays RFC; Glamorgan CCC. DL Gwent, 1992. *Publication:* Seek Fairer Skies, 2003. *Recreations:* gardening, watching Rugby and cricket. *Address:* Chapel Field, Chapel Lane, Abergavenny, Gwent NP7 7BT. *T:* (01873) 856502. *Clubs:* Royal Automobile (Mem., Public Policy Cttee, 1983–97); Pontllanfraith Workingmen's Social.
Died 19 Dec. 2003.

ISOLANI, Casimiro Peter Hugh Tomasi, CBE 1975 (OBE 1960; MBE (mil.) 1945); LVO 1961; HM Diplomatic Service, retired; *b* 2 Sept. 1917; *s* of late Umberto Tomasi Isolani, Bologna, and Georgiana Eleanor Lyle-Smyth, Great Barrow, Ches; *m* 1943, Karin Gunni Signe Zetterström (*d* 1996), *d* of Henry Zetterström, Gothenburg; one *s. Educ:* Aldenham Sch.; Clare Coll., Cambridge (Major open schol., 1936, 1st cl. Mod. and Med. Lang. Tripos 1; Sen. Foundn schol., 1937; BA 1939). Served War, commnd RA 1940, Intell. Corps 1941; attached 1st Canadian Div., 1943 (Sicily, Italy landings); Psychol Warfare Br., 1944; GS1 (Civil Liaison, Liaison Italian Resistance), 1945; Hon. Partisan, Veneto Corpo Volontari della Liberta. FO 1946; Vice-Consul, Bologna, 1946; Attaché, later 1st Sec. (Information), British Embassy, Rome, 1947–61; resigned Foreign Service; Dep. Dir, Inst. for Strategic Studies, 1961–63; rejoined Foreign Service; Regional Information Officer, Paris, 1963–72; Counsellor (Information), British Embassy (and UK delegn NATO and UK Representation, EEC), Brussels, 1972–77. United Nations University: Rep. (Europe), 1978–85; Sen. Consultant, 1985–87. *Address:* 44 Pont Street, SW1X 0AD. *T:* (020) 7584 1543. *Club:* Special Forces.
Died 10 Sept. 2004.

IVAMY, Prof. Edward Richard Hardy; Professor of Law, University of London, 1960–86, then Emeritus; *b* 1 Dec. 1920; *o s* of late Edward Wadham Ivamy and Florence Ivamy; *m* 1965, Christine Ann Frances, *o d* of late William and Frances Culver; one *s. Educ:* Malvern Coll.; University Coll. London (LLB 1st cl. Hons 1947). PhD 1953; LLD 1967. Served War of 1939–45, RA: 67 Field Regt, N Africa, Italy and Middle East; 2nd Lieut 1942; Temp. Capt. 1945; Staff Capt., GHQ, Cairo, 1946. Called to the Bar, Middle Temple, 1949. University College London: Asst Lectr in Laws, 1947–50; Lectr, 1950–56; Reader in Law, 1956–60; Dean of Faculty of Laws, 1964 and 1965; Fellow, 1969. Hon. Secretary: Bentham Club, 1953–58; Soc. of Public Teachers of Law, 1960–63. Governor, Malvern Coll., 1982–. *Publications:* Show Business and the Law, 1955; (ed) Payne and Ivamy's

Carriage of Goods by Sea, 7th edn 1963–13th edn 1989; Hire-Purchase Legislation in England and Wales, 1965; Casebook on Carriage of Goods by Sea, 1965, 6th edn 1985; Casebook on Sale of Goods, 1966, 5th edn 1987; (ed) Chalmers's Marine Insurance Act 1906, 6th edn 1966–10th edn 1993; General Principles of Insurance Law, 1966, 6th edn 1993; (ed) Topham and Ivamy's Company Law, 13th edn 1967–16th edn 1978; Casebook on Commercial Law, 1967, 3rd edn 1979; Fire and Motor Insurance, 1968, 5th edn 1997; Casebook on Insurance Law, 1969, 4th edn 1984; Marine Insurance, 1969, 4th edn 1985; Casebook on Shipping Law, 1970, 4th edn 1987; Casebook on Partnership, 1970, 2nd edn 1982; Casebook on Agency, 1971, 3rd edn 1987; Personal Accident, Life and Other Insurances, 1973, 2nd edn 1980; (ed) Underhill's Partnership, 10th edn 1975–12th edn 1985; (ed) Halsbury's Laws of England, 4th edn 1978, vol. 25 (Insurance), 1977 and 1994, vol. 43 (Shipping and Navigation), 1983 and 1997; Dictionary of Insurance Law, 1981; Dictionary of Company Law, 1983, 2nd edn 1985; Insurance Law Handbook, 1983; Dictionary of Shipping Law, 1984; Encyclopaedia of Shipping Law Sources (UK), 1985; Encyclopedia of Oil and Natural Gas Law, 1986; Encyclopedia of Carriage Law Sources, 1987; Merchant Shipping (Liner Conferences) Act 1982, 1987; Merchant Shipping Act 1970, 1987; Merchant Shipping Act 1979, 1987; (ed) Mozley and Whiteley's Law Dictionary, 10th edn 1988 and 11th edn 1993; contribs to Encyclopædia Britannica, Chambers's Encyclopædia, Current Legal Problems, Jl of Business Law; Annual Survey of Commonwealth Law, 1967–77. *Recreations:* railways, cricket, tennis. *Address:* 7 Egliston Mews, SW15 1AP. *T:* (020) 8785 6718.   *Died 8 Sept. 2005.*

IVENS, Michael William, CBE 1983; Consultant, Aims of Industry, 1994–2001 (Director, 1971–94); Director, Foundation for Business Responsibilities, 1967–92; *b* 15 March 1924; *s* of Harry Guest Ivens and Nina Ailion; *m* 1st, 1950, Rosalie Turnbull (marr. diss. 1971); two *s* one *d* (and one *s* decd); 2nd, 1971, Katherine Laurence; two *s*. Jt Editor, Twentieth Century, 1967; Hon. Vice-Pres., Junior Hosp. Doctors Assoc., 1969; Director: Standard Telephone, 1970; Working Together Campaign, 1972–73. Jt Founder and Vice-Pres., Freedom Assoc.; Jt Founder and Trustee, Foundn for the Study of Terrorism, 1986; Member: Adv. Bd, US Industrial Council Educn Foundn, 1980–; Council and Hon. Treas., Poetry Soc., 1989–91; Adv. Cttee, Airey Neave Foundn, 1990–. *Publications:* Practice of Industrial Communication, 1963; Case Studies in Management, 1964; Case Studies in Human Relations, 1966; Case for Capitalism, 1967; Industry and Values, 1970; Which Way?, 1970; Prophets of Freedom and Enterprise, 1975; (ed jtly) Bachman's Book of Freedom Quotes, 1978; *poetry:* Another Sky, 1963; Last Waltz, 1964; Private and Public, 1968; Born Early, 1975; No Woman is an Island, 1983; New Divine Comedy, 1990; columns and articles under pseudonym Yorick. *Recreation:* campaigning. *Address:* 2 Mulgrave Road, NW10 1BT.   *Died 4 Nov. 2001.*

J

JACKSON, (Audrey) Muriel W.; *see* Ward-Jackson.

JACKSON, Dirik George Allan; His Honour Judge Dirik Jackson; a Circuit Judge, since 2000; *b* 10 June 1946; *s* of Allan Jackson and Catharina Maria Anna Jackson (*née* de Boer); *m* 1984, Nicola Bryant; two *s* one *d*. *Educ:* Tonbridge Sch.; Trinity Coll., Cambridge (BA, LLB). Called to the Bar, Lincoln's Inn, 1969; in practice, 1970–2000; Asst Recorder, 1987–92; Recorder, 1992–2000. *Recreations:* music, exploring the Internet, roller-blading, windsurfing in warm waters. *Address:* Woolwich Crown Court, 2 Belmarsh Road, SE28 0EY.
Died 18 Feb. 2004.

JACKSON, Sir Edward; *see* Jackson, Sir J. E.

JACKSON, Ian Macgilchrist, FRCS, FRCOG; Obstetric and Gynæcological Surgeon, Middlesex Hospital, 1948–79; Gynæcological Surgeon: Chelsea Hospital for Women, 1948–79; King Edward VII Hospital for Officers, 1961–84; Royal Masonic Hospital, 1963–79; Consulting Gynæcologist, King Edward VII Hospital, Midhurst, 1959; Consultant Obstetrician and Gynæcologist, RAF, 1964–83; *b* Shanghai, 11 Nov. 1914; *s* of Dr Ernest David Jackson; *m* 1943 (marr. diss. 1967); two *s* one *d*; *m* 1970, Deirdre Ruth Heitz. *Educ:* Marlborough Coll.; Trinity Hall, Cambridge (scholar; BA double 1st cl. hons, Nat. Sci. tripos pts I, II, 1936; MB BChir 1939). London Hospital: open scholarship, 1936; house appointments, 1939; First Asst, Surgical and Obstetric and Gynæcol Depts, 1940–43. Served as Surgical Specialist, RAMC, 1943–47 (Major); Parachute Surgical Team, 224 Para. Field Amb.; Mobile Surgical Unit, 3 Commando Brigade. Royal College of Obstetricians and Gynæcologists: Council, 1951–61, 1962–70; Hon. Sec., 1954–61; Chm., Examination Cttee, 1962–65, Hon. Treas., 1966–70; Hon. Librarian, RSM, 1969–75. Examiner for Univs of Cambridge, Oxford, and London, Conjoint Bd and RCOG. Mem., Court of Assts, Worshipful Soc. of Apothecaries, 1966, Senior Warden 1977, Master 1978, Hon. Treas., 1985–89; President: Chelsea Clinical Soc., 1979; Sydenham Medical Club, 1987–90. Order of the Star of Africa (Liberia), 1969; Grand Officer of Order of Istiqlal, Jordan, 1970. *Publications:* (jtly) British Obstetric and Gynæcological Practice, 1963; (jtly) Obstetrics by Ten Teachers, 1966, 2nd edn 1972; (jtly) Gynæcology by Ten Teachers, 1971; numerous contribs to medical literature. *Recreations:* fishing, golf, photography. *Address:* 23 Springfield Road, NW8 0QJ. *T:* (020) 7624 3580. *Died 24 June 2002.*

JACKSON, Sir (John) Edward, KCMG 1984 (CMG 1977); HM Diplomatic Service, retired; *b* 24 June 1925; *s* of late Edward Harry Jackson and Margaret Jackson; *m* 1952, Evelyn Stainton Harris, *d* of late George James Harris, MC and Mrs Friede Rowntree Harris, York; two *s* one *d*. *Educ:* Ardingly; Corpus Christi Coll., Cambridge. Served War of 1939–45, RNVR (Sub-Lt), 1943–46. Joined Foreign (later Diplomatic) Service, 1947; FO, 1947–49; 3rd Sec., Paris, 1949–52; 2nd Sec., FO, 1952–56; 1st Sec., Bonn, 1956–59; Guatemala City, 1959–62; FO, 1963–68; Counsellor, 1968; NATO Defence Coll., Rome, 1969; Counsellor (Political Adviser), British Mil. Govt, Berlin, 1969–73; Head of Defence Dept, FCO, 1973–75; Ambassador to Cuba, 1975–79; Head of UK Delegn to Negotiations on Mutual Reduction of Forces and Armaments and Associated Measures in Central Europe, with personal rank of Ambassador, 1980–82; Ambassador to Belgium, 1982–85. Chm., Brecon Beacons Natural Waters Ltd, later Spadel Ltd, 1985–96 (Vice-Chm., Consultancy Bd, 1997–2000); Dir, Herbert Mueller Ltd and associated cos, 1987–90. Dir, Armistice Festival, 1986–89. Chm., Anglo-Belgian Soc.,

1987–2001; Dep. Chm., Belgo-Luxembourg Chamber of Commerce, 1987–. Trustee, Imperial War Museum, 1986–95. Vice-Pres., Internat. Yehudi Menuhin Foundn (formerly Internat. Menuhin Assoc.), 1991–99. *Recreations:* the arts. *Address:* 17 Paultons Square, SW3 5AP. *Clubs:* Royal Anglo-Belgian (Dir, 1993–), Hurlingham.
Died 8 May 2002.

JACKSON, Very Rev. Lawrence; Provost of Blackburn, 1973–92, Provost Emeritus 1992; *b* Hessle, Yorks, 22 March 1926; *s* of Walter and Edith Jackson; *m* 1955, Faith Anne, *d* of Philip and Marjorie Seymour; four *d*. *Educ:* Alderman Newton's Sch.; Leicester Coll. of Technology; King's Coll., Univ. of London (AKC 1950); St Boniface Coll., Warminster. Asst Curate, St Margaret, Leicester, and Asst Chaplain, Leicester Royal Infirmary, 1951–54; Vicar of: Wymeswold, Leicester, 1954–59; St James the Greater, Leicester, 1959–65; Coventry (Holy Trinity), 1965–73. Canon of Coventry Cath., 1967–73; Rural Dean of Coventry N, 1969–73. Senior Chaplain: Leicester and Rutland ACF, 1955–65; Warwickshire ACF, 1965–73; Chaplain, Coventry Guild of Freemen, 1968–73; Dio. Chaplain, CEMS, 1969–71. Mem., Gen. Synod of C of E, 1975–92; a Church Comr, 1981–92. Dir, The Samaritans of Leicester, 1960–65; Pres., Coventry Round Table, 1968; Governor, Queen Elizabeth Grammar Sch., Blackburn, 1973–92. Pres., Midlands Club Cricket Conf., 1995. Freeman, City of London, 1982; Liveryman, Fruiterers' Co., 1982. *Publication:* Services for Special Occasions, 1982. *Recreations:* music, archæology, architecture, countryside, after dinner speaking. *Address:* Northcot, Brook Lane, Newbold-on-Stour, Stratford-upon-Avon, Warwicks CV37 8UA. *T:* (01789) 450721. *Clubs:* Forty, Lighthouse; Lord's Taverners'.
Died 15 Nov. 2002.

JACKSON, Muriel W.; *see* Ward-Jackson.

JACKSON, Oliver James V.; *see* Vaughan-Jackson.

JACKSON, Peter John Edward; His Honour Judge Jackson; a Circuit Judge, since 1992; *b* 14 May 1944; *s* of late David Charles Jackson and Sarah Ann Jackson (*née* Manester); *m* 1967, Ursula, *y d* of late Paul and Henny Schubert, Hamburg, Germany; two *d*. *Educ:* Brockley County Grammar Sch.; Sprachen und Dolmetscher Inst., Hamburg; London Univ. (LLB Hons 1967); Tübingen Univ., Germany (Dr jur. 1987). Called to the Bar, Middle Temple, 1968 (Blackstone Scholar; Churchill Prize; Bencher, 1999); called to the Bar of NI, 1982. Dep. Circuit Judge, 1979–81; Asst Recorder, 1982–83; a Recorder, 1983–92; Attorney Gen.'s List of Prosecuting Counsel, 1985–92; Partner, Campbell and Jackson Internat. Arbitral and Legal Consultants, Brussels, Stuttgart, Paris, 1985–90; Overseas Mem., Law Offices of Dr Brauner and Colleagues, Stuttgart, 1982–92. Mem., Arbitration Panel, ICC, 1990–92; Co-opted Mem., Internat. Practice Cttee, Bar Council, 1991–92; Trainer, Middle Temple Advocacy, 1998–. Approved Supervisor, Judicial and Legal Trainees in England, German Ministries of Justice and German Attorneys' Assoc., 1987–. Speaker/ Chm., legal seminars in England and overseas, 1987–; speaker, German Judges Acad., Berlin and Trier, 1994–. Chm., St Leonard's Soc., Ilford, 1993–2001. Gov., Newbold Coll., Bracknell, 1991–95. ACIArb 1983. *Recreations:* gardens, German Law, the German language, travel. *Address:* 3 Pump Court, Temple, EC4Y 7AJ. *T:* (020) 7353 0711; Southwark Crown Court, 1 English Grounds, SE1 2HU. *T:* (020) 7522 7200; 70372 Stuttgart (Bad Cannstatt), Seelbergstrasse 8, Germany. *T:* (0711) 954646-0, *Fax:* (0711) 954646-46.
Died 14 Nov. 2005.

JACKSON, Sir Thomas; *see* Jackson, Sir W. T.

JACKSON, Thomas; General Secretary, Union of Communication Workers (formerly Post Office Workers), 1967–82; antiquarian bookseller, 1982–97; *b* 9 April 1925; *s* of George Frederick Jackson and Ethel Hargreaves; *m* 1st, 1947, Norma Burrow (marr. diss. 1982); one *d*; 2nd, 1982, Kathleen Maria Tognarelli; one *d*. *Educ:* Jack Lane Elementary Sch. Boy Messenger, GPO, 1939; Royal Navy, 1943; Postman, 1946; Executive Mem., Union of Post Office Workers, 1955; Asst Sec., Union of Post Office Workers, 1964. Member: Gen. Council of TUC, 1967–82 (Chm., 1978–79; Chm., Internat. Cttee, 1978–82); Press Council, 1973–76; Annan Cttee on the Future of Broadcasting, 1974–77; CRE, 1977–78; Broadcasting Complaints Commn, 1982–87; Yorks Water Authority, 1983–89. HM Government Dir, British Petroleum, 1975–83; non-exec. Dir, Yorks Water plc, 1989–94. A Governor: BBC, 1968–73; NIESR, 1974–85. Member: Court and Council, Sussex Univ., 1974–78; Council, Bradford Univ., 1987–90. Chm., Ilkley Literature Fest., 1984–87. Hon. LLD Leeds, 1995. *Recreations:* cooking, photography. *Address:* 22 Parish Ghyll Road, Ilkley, West Yorks LS29 9NE.

Died 6 June 2003.

JACKSON, William Theodore, CBE 1967 (MBE 1946); ARIBA; MRTPI; Director of Post Office Services, Ministry of Public Building and Works, 1969–71, retired; *b* 18 July 1906; *y s* of Rev. Oliver Miles Jackson and Emily Jackson; *m* 1932, Marjorie Campbell; one *s* two *d*. *Educ:* Cheltenham Grammar Sch.; Regent St Poly. ARIBA 1931; MRTPI 1942. Dublin Chief Asst, 1932–36; Chief Architect, Iraq Govt, i/c of design and construction of Mausoleum for King Feisal, and other projects, 1936–39; Dir, Special Repair Service, Min. of Works, 1940–45; Ministry of Public Building and Works, 1946–71: Dir, Mobile Labour Force, 1946–50; Dir of Maintenance, 1950–56; seconded to World Bank as Advr to Development Plan organisation, 1957–59; Regional Dir, Home Counties, 1959–61; Dir, Headquarters Services, 1962–69. *Recreations:* gardening, painting. *Address:* 26 Roding Close, Elmbridge Road, Cranleigh, Surrey GU6 8TE. *T:* (01483) 276273. *Died 30 March 2002.*

JACKSON, Sir (William) Thomas, 8th Bt *cr* 1869; farmer, declined 1990; *b* 12 Oct. 1927; *s* of Sir William Jackson, 7th Bt, and Lady Ankaret Jackson (*d* 1945), 2nd *d* of 10th Earl of Carlisle; *S* father, 1985; *m* 1951, Gilian Malise, *d* of John William Stobart, MBE; three *s*. *Educ:* Mill Hill School; Royal Agricultural Coll., Cirencester. Qualified Associate Chartered Land Agents Soc., later ARICS; resigned, 1969. Nat. Service, 1947–49, 2/Lt Border Regt; Gen. Reserve as Lieut. Land Agent in various firms and on private estates till 1969, when he left the profession and started farming. Chairman: Cumberland Branch, CLA, 1984–86; Whitehaven Branch, NFU, 1983–85. *Recreation:* painting. *Heir: e s* (William) Roland Cedric Jackson, PhD [*b* 9 Jan. 1954; *m* 1977, Nicola Mary, *yr d* of Prof. Peter Reginald Davis, PhD, FRCS; three *s*]. *Address:* Fell End, Mungrisdale, Penrith, Cumbria CA11 0XR. *Died 13 March 2004.*

JACOB, Frederick Henry, CBiol; Director, Pest Infestation Control Laboratory, Ministry of Agriculture, Fisheries and Food, 1968–77; *b* 12 March 1915; *s* of Henry Theodore and Elizabeth Jacob; *m* 1941, Winifred Edith Sloman (decd); one *s* one *d*. *Educ:* Friars Sch., Bangor; UC North Wales. BSc, MSc; CBiol, FIBiol. Asst Entomologist: King's Coll., Newcastle upon Tyne, 1942–44; Sch. of Agriculture, Cambridge, 1944–45; Adviser in Agric. Zoology, UC North Wales, 1945–46; Adv. Entomologist, Min. of Agriculture and Fisheries, Nat. Agric. Adv. Service, N Wales, 1946–50; Head of Entomology Dept, MAFF, Plant Pathology Lab., 1950–68. Pres., Assoc. of Applied Biologists, 1976–77. *Publications:* papers mainly on systematics of Aphididae in learned jls. *Recreations:* hill walking, fishing, gardening. *Address:* Hillside, Almondbury Common, Huddersfield

HD4 6SN. *Clubs:* Climbers; Wayfarers (Liverpool).

Died 5 Feb. 2004.

JACOBS, Prof. John Arthur; Hon. Professor, Institute of Geography and Earth Sciences, University of Wales (formerly University College of Wales), Aberystwyth, since 1989; Professor of Geophysics, 1974–83, and Fellow, Darwin College, since 1976 (Vice Master, 1978–82), University of Cambridge; *b* 13 April 1916; *m* 1st, 1941, Daisy Sarah Ann Montgomerie (*d* 1974); two *d*; 2nd, 1974, Margaret Jones (marr. diss. 1981); 3rd, 1982, Ann Grace Wintle. *Educ:* Univ. of London. BA 1937, MA 1939, PhD 1949, DSc 1961. Instr Lieut RN, 1941–46; Lectr, Royal Holloway Coll., Univ. of London, 1946–51; Assoc. Prof., Univ. of Toronto, 1951–57; Prof., Univ. of British Columbia, 1957–67; Dir, Inst. of Earth Sciences, Univ. of British Columbia, 1961–67; Killam Meml Prof. of Science, Univ. of Alberta, 1967–74; Dir, Inst. of Earth and Planetary Physics, Univ. of Alberta, 1970–74. Res. Fellow, RHBNC, 1987–89. Sec., Royal Astronomical Soc., 1977–82; Harold Jeffreys Lectr, RAS, 1983. FRSC 1958; DSc *hc* Univ. of BC, 1987. Centennial Medal of Canada, 1967; Medal of Canadian Assoc. of Physicists, 1975; J. Tuzo Wilson Medal, Canadian Geophys. Union, 1982; John Adam Fleming Medal, Amer. Geophys. Union, 1994; Price Medal, RAS, 1994; Gold Medal, RAS (Geophysics), 2002. *Publications:* (with R. D. Russell and J. T. Wilson) Physics and Geology, 1959, 2nd edn 1974; The Earth's Core and Geomagnetism, 1963; Geomagnetic Micropulsations, 1970; A Textbook on Geonomy, 1974; The Earth's Core, 1975, 2nd edn 1987; Reversals of the Earth's Magnetic Field, 1984, 2nd edn 1994; Deep Interior of the Earth, 1992. *Recreations:* walking, music. *Address:* Institute of Geography and Earth Sciences, University of Wales, Aberystwyth, Dyfed SY23 3DB. *T:* (01970) 622646. *Died 13 Dec. 2003.*

JAHODA, Prof. Marie, (Mrs A. H. Albu); CBE 1974; DPhil; Professor Emeritus, University of Sussex; *b* 26 Jan. 1907; *d* of Carl Jahoda and Betty Jahoda; *m* 1st, 1927, Paul F. Lazarsfeld (marr. diss.); one *d*; 2nd, 1958, Austen Harry Albu (*d* 1994), sometime MP for Edmonton. *Educ:* Univ. of Vienna (DPhil). Prof. of Social Psychology, NY Univ., 1949–58; Res. Fellow and Prof. of Psychol., Brunel Univ., 1958–65; Prof. of Social Psychol., Sussex Univ., 1965–73. Sen. Res. Consultant to Sci. Policy Res. Unit, Sussex Univ., 1971–83. Hon. DLit: Sussex, 1973; Leicester, 1973; Bremen, 1984; Stirling, 1988; Hon. DPhil: Vienna, 1998; Linz, 1998. Grosse Silberne Ehrenzeichen für Verdienste (Austria), 1993. *Publications:* Die Arbeitslosen von Marienthal, 1933 (Eng. trans. 1971); Research Methods in Human Relations, 1953; Current Concepts of Positive Mental Health, 1958; Freud and the Dilemmas of Psychology, 1977; (ed) World Futures: the great debate, 1977; Employment and Unemployment, 1982. *Recreations:* cooking, chess. *Address:* 17 The Crescent, Keymer, West Sussex BN6 8RB. *T:* (01273) 842267.

Died 28 April 2001.

JAMES, Aubrey Graham Wallen; Deputy Chief Land Registrar, 1975–81; *b* 5 Jan. 1918; *s* of Reginald Aubrey James and Amelia Martha James; *m* 1952, Audrey Elizabeth, *er d* of Dr and Mrs A. W. F. Edmonds; two *s*. *Educ:* Nantgyle Grammar Sch.; London Univ. (LLB 1939). Solicitor, 1940. Served Second World War, 1940–46, Major, Cheshire Regt. Legal Asst, HM Land Registry, 1948; Asst Land Registrar, 1954; Land Registrar, 1963; Dist Land Registrar, Nottingham, 1963. Chm., E Midlands Region, CS Sports Council, 1970–75. *Recreations:* having had a life-long interest in several sporting activities, developed, in latter years, a latent interest in art, and was Chairman of a thriving local art group. *Address:* 11 Playle Chase, Great Totham, Maldon CM9 8UT. *Died 26 Aug. 2005.*

JAMES, Edward Foster, CMG 1968; OBE 1946; HM Diplomatic Service, retired; *b* 18 Jan. 1917; *s* of late Arthur Foster James; *m* 1985, Janet Mary Walls; one *s* two *d* by a previous marriage. *Educ:* Chiswick Grammar Sch. Served

HM Forces, 1939–46, India, Burma, Malaya, Indonesia; Lieut-Colonel (GSO1) (OBE, despatches twice). Joined HM Diplomatic Service, 1947; Rangoon, 1948; Hong Kong, 1951; FO, 1953; Rome, 1955; FO, 1958; Berlin, 1960; FO (later FCO), 1961–74. Exec. Dir, Inst. of Directors, 1975–76; Dep. Dir-Gen., CBI, 1976–83. Chm., Coastal Pollution Control plc, 1984–85; Dir, Tace plc, 1984–91. *Address:* 95 Gloucester Terrace, W2 3HB. *T:* (020) 7262 0139. *Club:* Boodle's.

Died 23 Jan. 2002.

JAMES, John A.; *see* Angell-James.

JAMES, Prof. John Ivor Pulsford, FRCS, FRCSE; George Harrison Law Professor of Orthopædic Surgery, Edinburgh University, 1958–79, then Emeritus Professor; Consultant in Orthopædic Surgery to the Navy, 1956–84; Head of Orthopaedic Services, Kuwait, 1980–83; *b* 19 Oct. 1913; *s* of late Stanley B. James and Jessica Heley; *m* 1968, Margaret Eiriol Samuel, MB, ChB; one *s* one *d.* *Educ:* Eggars Grammar Sch., Alton, Hants; University Coll. and Hosp., London (Hampshire County Schol., 1932–38; Ferrière Schol., University Coll., 1935; Goldsmid Schol., 1935, Magrath Schol., 1937, University Coll. Hosp.; MB BS 1940; MS 1942). Rockefeller Travelling Fellowship, 1947–48. Consultant Orthopædic Surgeon, Royal National Orthopædic Hospital, 1946–58; Asst Dir of Studies, Institute of Orthopædics, University of London, 1948–58. Fellow Univ. Coll., London. Hunterian Prof., RCS, 1957; Past Pres., British Orthopædic Assoc. (Fellow); Past Pres., British Soc. for Surgery of the Hand; Mem. Société Internationale de Chirurgie Orthopédique et de Traumatologie; Corresp. Member: Amer. Orthopædic Assoc.; Aust. Orthopædic Assoc.; Scandinavian Orthopædic Assoc.; Hon. Member: Amer. Acad. of Orthopædic Surgeons; Dutch Orthopædic Assoc.; Assoc. for Orthopædic Surgery and Traumatology of Yugoslavia; Canadian Orthopædic Assoc.; New Zealand Orthopædic Assoc.; Hellenic Assoc. of Orthopædics and Traumatology; Société Française d'Orthopédie et de Traumatologie. Hon. FRACS. Late Temp. Lt-Col RAMC (SOE). Named Pioneer of Hand Surgery, Internat. Soc. of Hand Surgery, 1995. Golden Star, Order of Service to the Yugoslav People, 1970. *Publications:* Scoliosis, 1967, 2nd edn 1976; Poliomyelitis, 1987; A Surgeon in Yugoslavia in World War II, BMJ, 1992; articles relating to curvature of the spine and surgery of the hand in medical journals, etc. *Recreations:* beekeeping, gardening. *Address:* Abbey Farm, The Vatch, Slad Valley, Glos GL6 7LE. *T:* (01453) 764986.

Died 11 July 2001.

JAMES, Prof. Philip Seaforth; Professor of English Law and Head of the Department of Law, University College at Buckingham, 1975–81; Professor Emeritus, University of Buckingham, since 1989; *b* 28 May 1914; *s* of Dr Philip William James, MC, and Muriel Lindley James; *m* 1954, Wybetty, *d* of Claas P. Gerth, Enschede, Holland; two *s.* *Educ:* Charterhouse; Trinity Coll., Oxford (MA). Research Fellow, Yale Univ., USA, 1937–38. Called to the Bar, Inner Temple, 1939. Served War of 1939–45, in Royal Artillery, India, Burma (Major; despatches). Fellow of Exeter Coll., Oxford, 1946–49; Prof. and Hd of Dept of Law, Leeds Univ., 1952–75. Visiting Professor: Univs of Yale and of Louisville, Kentucky, USA, 1960–61; Univ. of South Carolina, 1972–73; NY Law Sch., 1981–83. Chairman: Yorks Rent Assessment Panel, 1966–75; Thames Valley Rent Assessment Panel, 1976–80; Assessor to County Court under Race Relations Acts. Pres., SPTL, 1971–72. Governor, Swinton Conservative College, 1961–73. Hon. LLD Buckingham, 1986. Hon. Mem., Mark Twain Soc., 1979. *Publications:* An Introduction to English Law, 1950 (trans. Japanese, 1985); General Principles of the Law of Torts, 1959; Shorter Introduction to English Law, 1969; Six Lectures on the Law of Torts, 1980 (trans. Spanish); various articles, notes and reviews on legal and political subjects. *Address:* Chestnut View, Mill

Road, Whitfield, near Brackley, Northants NN13 5TQ. *Club:* National Liberal.

Died 5 May 2001.

JAMES, Prof. Dame Sheila (Patricia Violet); *see* Sherlock, Prof. Dame S. P. V.

JAMES, William Seymour; Chief Registrar in Bankruptcy, Royal Courts of Justice, since 2001 (Registrar in Bankruptcy, 1991–2001); *b* 11 Dec. 1945; *s* of late Arthur Dyfrig James and of Ann Pamela Mary James (*née* Pincham); *m* 1st, 1973, Pamela Margaret Lord (marr. diss. 1986); one *d*; 2nd, 1989, Susan Amy Barr (*née* Jones); two step *s.* *Educ:* St Edward's Sch., Oxford; College of Law, Guildford. Articled to L. W. S. Parry-Williams, Solicitor, Middlewich, 1966–71; Solicitor in private practice, 1971–91; Under-Sheriff, City of Gloucester, 1988–89. Asst Editor, Muir Hunter on Personal Insolvency, 1996–; Adv. Editor, Butterworths Encyclopaedia of Forms and Precedents, 1999–. *Recreations:* tennis, ski-ing, sailing. *Address:* Royal Courts of Justice, Strand, WC2A 2LL. *T:* (020) 7936 7319.

Died 21 Aug. 2003.

JAMES-MOORE, Jonathan Guy; Managing Director, Commedia, since 1999; *b* 22 March 1946; *s* of Wilfred Seward and Alana James-Moore; *m* 1975, Jenny Baynes; one *d.* *Educ:* Bromsgrove Sch.; Emmanuel Coll., Cambridge (MA). Founder Dir, Oxford & Cambridge Shakespeare Co., 1968–71; Gen. Manager, Sir Nicholas Sekers Theatre at Rosehill, 1971–72; Administrator: Mermaid Theatre, 1972–74; St George's Theatre, 1975–76; BBC Radio Light Entertainment, 1978–99: Hd of Light Entertainment, BBC Radio, later of Light Entertainment Radio, BBC Prodn, 1991–99. Co-Dir, VoiceQuality, 2003–. Chm., Radio Gp, Directors' Guild of Great Britain, 2003–. Mem. Council, Liverpool Inst. of Performing Arts, 1999–. *Recreations:* collecting wine labels, escaping to Umbria. *Address:* 120 Pembroke Road, Muswell Hill, N10 2JD. *T:* (020) 8883 9248. *Club:* Garrick.

Died 20 Nov. 2005.

JAMIESON, Major David Auldjo, VC 1944; CVO 1990; Member of HM Bodyguard, Hon. Corps of Gentlemen at Arms, 1968–90, Lieutenant, 1986–90; *b* 1 Oct. 1920; *s* of late Sir Archibald Auldjo Jamieson, KBE, MC and 1st wife, Doris, *d* of Capt. Henry Pearce, RN; *m* 1st, 1948, Nancy Elwes (*d* 1963), *y d* of Robert H. A. Elwes, Congham, King's Lynn; one *s* two *d*; 2nd, 1969, Joanna, *e d* of Edward Woodall. *Educ:* Eton Coll. Commissioned Royal Norfolk Regt, May 1939; served War of 1939–45, incl. Normandy, 1944 (VC); retired, 1948. Director: Australian Agricultural Co., 1949–78 (Governor, 1952–76); UK Branch, Australian Mutual Provident Society, 1963–89 (Dep. Chm., 1973–89); National Westminster Bank PLC, 1983–87; Steetley plc, 1976–86 (Dep. Chm., 1983–86). Clerk of the Cheque and Adjutant, Hon. Corps of Gentlemen at Arms, 1981–86. High Sheriff of Norfolk, 1980. *Address:* St Andrew's House, Burnham Market, King's Lynn, Norfolk PE31 8HH. *T:* (01328) 730606.

Died 5 May 2001.

JAMIESON, Rear-Adm. Ian Wyndham, CB 1970; DSC 1945; Emeritus Fellow, Jesus College, Oxford, 1986 (Home Bursar and Fellow, 1972–86); *b* 13 March 1920; *s* of late S. W. Jamieson, CBE; *m* 1949, Patricia Wheeler, Knowle, Warwickshire; two *s* one *d.* *Educ:* RNC, Dartmouth. Served War of 1939–45: Anti Submarine Warfare Specialist, 1943. Comdr, 1953; Staff of RN Tactical Sch., 1953–56; HMS Maidstone, 1956–58; Dir, Jt Tactical Sch., Malta, 1958; Capt. 1959; Asst Dir, Naval Intelligence, 1959–61; Comd HMS Nubian and 6th Frigate Sqdn, 1961–64; Dir, Seaman Officers Appts, 1964–66; Comd Britannia RN Coll., Dartmouth, 1966–68; Rear-Adm. 1968; Flag Officer, Gibraltar, and Admiral Superintendent, HM Dockyard, Gibraltar; also NATO Comdr, Gibraltar (Mediterranean Area), 1968–69; C of S to C-in-C Western Fleet, 1969–71; retired. Mem., Southern Arts Council, 1985–91. Hon. MA Oxon, 1973. *Recreations:* hockey (Scotland and Combined Services), cricket, golf, tennis. *Address:* 7 Leicester Close, Henley-on-Thames, Oxon RG9 2LD.   *Died 28 April 2005.*

JANES, (John) Douglas (Webster), CB 1975; Secretary, The Bach Choir, 1981–89; Deputy Secretary, Northern Ireland Office, 1974–79; *b* 17 Aug. 1918; *s* of late John Arnold Janes and Maud Mackinnon (*née* Webster); *m* 1st, 1943, Margaret Isabel Smith (*d* 1978); one *s* two *d*; 2nd, 1986, Mrs Joan Walker (*née* Bentley). *Educ:* Southgate County Sch., Mddx; Imperial Coll. of Science and Technology. 1st cl. BSc (Eng) London, ACGI, DIC. Entered Post Office Engineering Dept, Research Branch, 1939. Served Royal Signals, RAOC, REME, 1939–45: War Office, 1941–45; Major. Min. of Town and Country Planning, 1947; Min. of Housing and Local Govt, 1951; seconded to Min. of Power, 1956–58; HM Treasury, 1960–63; Min. of Land and Natural Resources, 1964–66; Prin. Finance Officer and Accountant Gen., Min. of Housing and Local Govt, 1968–70; Prin. Finance Officer (Local Govt and Develt), DoE, 1970–73; Dep. Sec., 1973; Chief Executive, Maplin Develt Authority, 1973–74. Chm., Home Grown Timber Adv. Cttee, 1981–93 (Mem., 1979–93); various management and organisation reviews, 1979–81. *Recreations:* singing, do-it-yourself.
          Died 1 Nov. 2003.

JAQUES, Prof. Elliott; Research Professor in Management Sciences, George Washington University, since 1989; *b* 18 Jan. 1917; *m* 1953, Kathleen (*née* Walsh); one *d*. *Educ:* Univ. of Toronto (BA, MA); Johns Hopkins MedSch. (MD); Harvard Univ. (PhD). Qual. Psychoanalyst (Brit. Psycho-Analysis Soc.) 1951. Rantoul Fellow in Psychology, Harvard, 1940–41; Major, Royal Can. Army Med. Corps, 1941–45; Founder Mem., Tavistock Inst. of Human Relations, 1946–51; private practice as psycho-analyst and industrial consultant, 1952–65; Brunel University: Head of Sch. of Social Sciences, 1965–70; Prof. of Sociology, 1970–82; Dir, Inst. of Orgn and Social Studies, 1970–85, then Prof. Emeritus of Social Sciences. Hon. Prof., Dept of Economics, Buenos Aires Univ., 1994–. Adviser to BoT on organisation for overseas marketing, 1965–69; Mem. Management Study Steering Cttee on NHS Reorganisation, 1972; consultant on leadership develt, US Army, 1979–90; mgt consultancy res., 1990–. Harry Levinson Award, Amer. Psychol Assoc., 2000. *Publications:* The Changing Culture of a Factory, 1951; Measurement of Responsibility, 1956; Equitable Payment, 1961; (with Wilfred Brown) Product Analysis Pricing, 1964; Time-Span Handbook, 1964; (with Wilfred Brown) Glacier Project Papers, 1965; Progression Handbook, 1968; Work, Creativity and Social Justice, 1970; A General Theory of Bureaucracy, 1976; Health Services, 1978; Levels of Abstraction and Logic in Human Action, 1978; The Form of Time, 1982; Free Enterprise, Fair Employment, 1982; Requisite Organisation, 1989, 2nd edn 1996; Executive Leadership, 1991; Human Capability, 1994; The Life and Behavior of Living Organisms, 2001; The Great Social Power of the CEO, 2001; articles in Human Relations, New Society, Internat. Jl of Psycho-Analysis, etc. *Recreations:* art, music, ski-ing. *Address:* 6 Raven Lane, Gloucester, MA 01930, USA.
          Died 8 March 2003.

JARRING, Gunnar V., PhD; Grand Cross, Order of the North Star, Sweden; Swedish Ambassador and Special Representative of the Secretary-General of the United Nations on the Middle East question, 1967–91; *b* S Sweden, 12 Oct. 1907; *s* of Gottfrid Jönsson and Betty Svensson; *m* 1932, Agnes, *d* of Prof. Carl Charlier, Lund; one *d*. *Educ:* Lund; Univ. of Lund (PhD). Family surname changed to Jarring, 1931. Associate Prof. of Turkish Langs, Lund Univ., 1933–40; Attaché, Ankara, 1940–41; Chief, Section B, Teheran, 1941; Chargé d'Affaires *ad interim:* Teheran and Baghdad, 1945; Addis Ababa, 1946–48; Minister: to India, 1948–51, concurrently to Ceylon, 1950–51; to Persia, Iraq and Pakistan, 1951–52; Dir, Polit. Div., Min. of Foreign Affairs, 1953–56; Permanent Rep. to UN, 1956–58; Rep. on Security Council, 1957–58;

Ambassador: to USA, 1958–64; to USSR, 1964–73, and to Mongolia, 1965–73. *Publications:* Studien zu einer osttürkischen Lautlehre, 1933; The Contest of the Fruits – An Eastern Turki Allegory, 1936; The Uzbek Dialect of Quilich, Russian Turkestan, 1937; Uzbek Texts from Afghan Turkestan, 1938; The Distribution of Turk Tribes in Afghanistan, 1939; Materials to the Knowledge of Eastern Turki (vols 1–4), 1947–51; An Eastern Turki-English Dialect Dictionary, 1964; Literary Texts from Kashghar, 1980; Return to Kashghar, 1986; Prints from Kashghar, 1991; Central Asian Turkic Place-names, 1997. *Address:* Pontus Ols väg 7, 26040 Viken, Sweden.
          Died 29 May 2002.

JASPER, Robin Leslie Darlow, CMG 1963; HM Diplomatic Service, retired; *b* 22 Feb. 1914; *s* of T. D. Jasper, Beckenham; *m* 1st, 1940, Jean Cochrane (marr. diss.; she *d* 2001); one *d*; 2nd, 1966, Diana Speed (*née* West); two step *d*. *Educ:* Dulwich; Clare Coll., Cambridge. Apprentice, LNER Hotels Dept, 1936–39; Bursar, Dominion Students Hall Trust (London House), 1939–40; RAFVR (Wing Comdr), 1940–45; Principal, India Office (later Commonwealth Relations Office), 1945; concerned with resettlement of the Sec. of State's Services in India, 1947–48; British Dep. High Commissioner, Lahore, Pakistan, 1949–52; Adviser to London Conferences on Central African Federation, and visited Central Africa in this connection, 1952–53; Counsellor, HM Embassy, Lisbon, 1953–55; visited Portuguese Africa, 1954; Commonwealth Relations Office, 1955–60 (Head of Information Policy Dept, 1958–60); attached to the United Kingdom delegation to the United Nations, 1955 and 1956; British Dep. High Commissioner, Ibadan, Nigeria, 1960–64; Counsellor, Commonwealth Office, 1965–67; Consul-Gen., Naples, 1967–71, retired 1972. Lived in Almuñécar, Granada, Spain, 1971–79. *Recreations:* tennis, Rugby fives, wind music, 17th Century Church Sculpture, claret, madrigals, mainstream jazz, psychotherapy. *Address:* Ashburnham Lodge, 62 London Road, St Leonard's-on-Sea, East Sussex TN37 6AS. *T:* (01424) 438575. *Clubs:* MCC, Jesters.
          Died 14 June 2004.

JEFFARES, Prof. Alexander Norman, (Derry), Hon. AM 1988; MA, PhD, DPhil; FRSL; FRSE; Professor of English Studies, Stirling University, 1974–86, Hon. Professor, since 1986; Managing Director, Academic Advisory Services Ltd, since 1975; Director, Colin Smythe Ltd, since 1978; *b* 11 Aug. 1920; *s* of late C. Norman Jeffares, Dublin; *m* 1947, Jeanne Agnès, *d* of late E. Calembert, Brussels; one *d*. *Educ:* The High Sch., Dublin; Trinity Coll., Dublin (Hon. Fellow, 1978); Oriel Coll., Oxford. Lectr in Classics, Univ. of Dublin, 1943–44; Lector in English, Univ. of Groningen, 1946–48; Lectr in English, Univ. of Edinburgh, 1949–51; Jury Prof. of English Language and Literature, Univ. of Adelaide, 1951–56; Prof. of English Lit., Leeds Univ., 1957–74. Sec., Australian Humanities Res. Council, 1954–57; Corresp. Mem. for GB and Ireland, 1958–70; Hon. Fellow, Aust. Acad. of the Humanities, 1970–. Mem. Council, RSE, 1985– (a Vice-Pres., 1988–89); Scottish Arts Council: Mem., 1979–84; Vice-Chm., 1980–84; Chm., Literature Cttee, 1979–83; Chm., Touring Cttee, 1983–84; Chm., Housing the Arts, 1980–84; Mem., Arts Council of GB, 1980–84. Chm., Book Trust Scotland (formerly NBL (Scotland)), 1984–89; Mem. Exec. Cttee, NBL, 1984–86; Mem. Bd, Book Trust, 1987–88. Pres., Internat. PEN Scottish Centre, 1986–89; Mem., Exec. Cttee, Scots Australian Council, 1992–. Vice-Pres., Film and Television Council of S Aust., 1951–56; Chairman: Assoc. for Commonwealth Literature and Language Studies, 1966–68 (Hon. Fellow 1971); Internat. Assoc. for Study of Anglo-Irish Literature, 1968–70 (Co-Chm., 1971–73; Hon. Life Pres., 1973–); Dir, Yeats Internat. Summer Sch., Sligo, 1969–71. Hon. Res. Fellow, Royal Holloway, Univ. of London, 1996. General Editor: Writers and Critics, 1960–73; New Oxford English Series, 1963–; Macmillan History of Literature, 1983–; (with

Michael Alexander) Macmillan Anthologies of English Literature, 1989; York Classics, 1988–; York Insights, 1989–; Joint Editor, Biography and Criticism, 1963–73; Literary Editor, Fountainwell Drama Texts, 1968–75; Co-Editor, York Notes, 1980–; Editor: A Review of English Literature, 1960–67; Ariel, A Review of Internat. English Literature, 1970–72; York Handbooks, 1984–. FRSL 1965; FRSE 1981; FRSA 1963; FAHA 1970. Dr de l'Univ. *hc* Lille, 1977; Hon. DLitt Ulster, 1990; DUniv Stirling, 2002. *Publications:* Trinity College, Dublin: drawings and descriptions, 1944; W. B. Yeats: man and poet, 1949, rev. edn 1996; Seven Centuries of Poetry, 1955, rev. edn 1960; (with M. Bryn Davies) The Scientific Background, 1958; The Poetry of W. B. Yeats, 1961; (ed with G. F. Cross) In Excited Reverie: centenary tribute to W. B. Yeats, 1965; Fair Liberty was All His Cry: a tercentenary tribute to Jonathan Swift 1667–1743, 1967; A Commentary on the Collected Poems of W. B. Yeats, 1968; (ed) Restoration Comedy, 4 vols, 1974; (with A. S. Knowland) A Commentary on the Collected Plays of W. B. Yeats, 1975; (ed) Yeats: the critical heritage, 1977; A History of Anglo-Irish Literature, 1982; A New Commentary on the Poems of W. B. Yeats, 1984; Brought up in Dublin (poems), 1987; Brought up to Leave (poems), 1987; (ed with Antony Kamm) An Irish Childhood, 1987; (ed with Antony Kamm) A Jewish Childhood, 1988; W. B. Yeats: a new biography, 1988, rev. edn 2001; (ed) Yeats's Poems, 1989, rev. edn 1996; (ed) W. B. Yeats: the love poems, 1990; (ed) W. B. Yeats: A Vision and related writings, 1990; (ed) W. B. Yeats: poems of place, 1991; (ed with Anna White) Always Your Friend: the Gonne-Yeats letters 1893–1938, 1992; (ed) Jonathan Swift: the selected poems, 1992; (with Brendan Kennelly) (ed) Joycechoyce, 1992; (ed jtly) Ireland's Women: writings past and present, 1994; (ed with Anna White) Maud Gonne, a Servant of the Queen, 1994; Images of Imagination: Irish essays, 1996; (ed with Martin Gray) The Collins Dictionary of Quotations, 1995; (ed) Victorian Love Poems, 1996; A Pocket History of Irish Literature, 1997; (ed) Irish Love Poems, 1997; The Irish Literary Movement: character sketches, 1998; (ed) The Secret Rose: love poems by W. B. Yeats, 1998; (ed) Ireland's Love Poems: wonder and a wild desire, 2000; (ed) Oliver St John Gogarty: poems and plays, 2001; (ed jtly) Letters to W. B. Yeats and Ezra Pound from Iseult Gonne, a girl that knew all Dante once, 2003; (ed jtly) Irish Literature, 4 vols, 2005; also: edns of works by Congreve, Farquhar, Goldsmith, Sheridan, Cowper, Maria Edgeworth, Disraeli, Whitman and Yeats; edns of criticisms of Swift, Scott and Yeats; various monographs on Swift, Goldsmith, George Moore, Yeats, Oliver St John Gogarty; contribs to learned jls. *Recreations:* drawing, motoring. *Address:* Craighead Cottage, Fife Ness, Crail, Fife KY10 3XN. *Clubs:* Athenæum, Royal Commonwealth Society. *Died 1 June 2005.*

JEFFREYS, Mrs Judith Diana; Assistant Director (Keeper), the Tate Gallery, 1975–83; *b* 22 Sept. 1927; *d* of Prof. Philip Cloake, FRCP and Letitia Blanche (*née* MacDonald); *m* 1968, William John Jeffreys (*d* 2004). *Educ:* Bedales; Courtauld Inst. of Art, Univ. of London (BA Hons History of Art). Tate Gallery: Asst Keeper, 1951–64; Publications Manager, 1960–65; Dep. Keeper, 1964–75. *Recreations:* reading, music, landscape gardening, water-colour painting. *Address:* Oak Ridge House, Sutton Mandeville, Salisbury, Wilts SP3 5LT.

Died 6 Feb. 2005.

JENKIN, Ian (Evers) Tregarthen, OBE 1984; Principal, Camberwell School of Art and Crafts, 1975–85; *b* 18 June 1920; *s* of Henry Archibald Tregarthen Jenkin, OBE and Dagmar Leggott. *Educ:* Stowe; Camberwell Sch. of Art and Crafts; Trinity Coll., Cambridge (MA Econ.); Slade Sch., University Coll. London. Served with Royal Artillery, 1939–46. Sec. and Tutor, Slade School, 1949–75; Curator, RA Schools, 1985–86; Co-founder (with Lord Young of Dartington), 1986, Dir, 1986–89, Pres., 1989–91, Vice-Pres., 1991–, Open Coll. of the Arts.

Chm., Craft Initiative Wkg Pty, Gulbenkian Foundn, 1985–89; Member: Art Panel, Arts Council (Vice-Chm.), 1979–82; Crafts Council, 1981–84 (Chm., Educn Cttee); Art and Design Working Gp, Nat. Adv. Body for Public Sector Higher Educn, 1982–85; Council, British Sch. at Rome, 1981–90 (Mem. Mgt Cttee, 1990–95; Chm., Painting Faculty, 1981–86; Chm., 1986–90, Mem., 1994–98, Fine Art Faculty); Cttee for Paintings in Hosps, 1982–97; Exec. Cttee, 1985–2001, Bd of Dirs, 2001–03, C&G Art Sch. Advisor, Member, Trustee, examiner, numerous educnl, art and conservation bodies; Trustee, Sir Stanley Spencer Meml Trust, 1982–2004; Chairman: E. Vincent Harris Fund for Mural Decoration, 1993–2001; Edwin Austin Abbey Meml Trust Fund for Mural Painting in GB, 1993–2001; Edwin Austin Abbey Meml Scholarships Council, 1994–98 (Mem., 1985–94 and 1998–2001). Pres., Dulwich Br., NADFAS, 1984–95; Vice-Pres., Nine Elms Gp of Artists, 1990–; Dir, Guild of St George, 1986–99 (Companion, 1984). Hon. Fellow, W Surrey Coll. of Art and Design, 1994; Hon. Mem., C&G, 1995. FRSA. Hon. Dr Arts CNAA 1987. *Publications:* Disaster Planning and Preparedness: a survey of practices and procedures (British Liby R&D report), 1986; An Outline Disaster Control Plan (British Liby Inf. Guide), 1987; contribs to DNB. *Recreations:* gardening, painting. *Address:* Barn Cottage, Grove Farm, Fifield, Maidenhead, Berks SL6 2PF. *Club:* Athenæum.

Died 5 Sept. 2004.

JENKINS OF HILLHEAD, Baron *cr* 1987 (Life Peer), of Pontypool in the County of Gwent; **Roy Harris Jenkins,** OM 1993; PC 1964; FBA; Chancellor, University of Oxford, since 1987; President, Royal Society of Literature, since 1988; Leader, Social and Liberal Democratic Peers, 1988–98; First Leader, Social Democratic Party, 1982–83 (Member of Joint Leadership, 1981–82); *b* 11 Nov. 1920; *o s* of late Arthur Jenkins, MP, and of Hattie Jenkins; *m* 1945, (Mary) Jennifer Morris, (Dame (Mary) Jennifer Jenkins); two *s* one *d*. *Educ:* Abersychan Grammar Sch.; University Coll., Cardiff (Hon. Fellow 1982); Balliol Coll., Oxford (First Cl. in Hon. Sch. of PPE 1941; Hon. Fellow 1969); DCL Oxford, 1987. Sec. and Librarian, Oxford Union Soc.; Chm., Oxford Univ. Democratic Socialist Club. Served War of 1939–45, in RA, 1942–46; Captain, 1944–46. Mem. of Staff, Industrial and Commercial Finance Corp. Ltd, 1946–48. MP (Lab): Central Southwark, 1948–50; Stechford, Birmingham, 1950–76; MP (SDP) Glasgow Hillhead, March 1982–1987. PPS to Sec. of State for Commonwealth Relations, 1949–50; Minister of Aviation, 1964–65; Home Secretary, 1965–67, 1974–76; Chancellor of the Exchequer, 1967–70; Dep. Leader, Labour Party, 1970–72. UK Deleg. to Council of Europe, 1955–57. Pres., European Commn, 1977–81. Contested: (Lab) Solihull Div. of Warwicks, 1945; Warrington by-election as first Social Democratic candidate, July 1981; Glasgow Hillhead (SDP/Alliance), 1982. Chm., Indep. Commn on the Voting System, 1997–98. Mem. Exec. Cttee, Fabian Soc., 1949–61 (Chm.,1957–58); Mem. Cttee of Management, Soc. of Authors, 1956–60; Governor, British Film Institute, 1955–58. Adviser to John Lewis Partnership, 1954–62; Dir of Financial Operations, 1962–64; Dir, Morgan Grenfell Hldgs Ltd, 1981–82. Vice-Pres., Inst. of Fiscal Studies, 1970–. Formerly: Dep. Chm. Federal Union; Chm., Labour European Cttee. Pres., Britain in Europe, Referendum Campaign, 1975; a Pres., UK Council of European Movt; Co-Pres., RIIA, 1993–2001. Pres., UWIST, 1975–81. Trustee, Pilgrim Trust, 1973–98. Lectures: G. M. Young, Oxford, 1963; Henry L. Stimson, Yale, 1971; Jean Monnet, Florence, 1977; Dimbleby, 1979; Churchill, Luxembourg, 1980, 2002; Rede, Cambridge, 1988; George Ball, Princeton, 1989; Goodman, 1989; Leverhulme, Liverpool, 1990; Stephenson, Glasgow, 1992; Paul-Henri Spaak, Harvard, 1994; Romanes, Oxford, 1996; Nobel, Oslo, 1997; Eleanor Rathbone, Durham, 1998; Jean Monnet, Hull, 2000; Lenihan Meml, Dublin, 2000; Churchill Meml, Westminster Coll., Fulton, 2002. Liveryman, Goldsmiths'

Co.; Freeman, City of London, 1965. Freeman, City of Brussels, 1980. Hon. Foreign Mem., Amer. Acad. Arts and Scis, 1973. Hon. FBA 1993; Hon. Fellow: Berkeley Coll., Yale, 1972; St Antony's Coll., Oxford, 1987. Hon. LLD: Leeds, 1971; Harvard, 1972; Pennsylvania, 1973; Dundee, 1973; Loughborough, 1975; Bath, 1978; Michigan, 1978; Wales, 1979; Bristol, 1980; Hon. DLitt: Glasgow, 1972; City, 1976; Warwick, 1978; Reading, 1979; London, 2000; Hon. DCL: Oxford, 1973; Kent, 1992; Hon. DSc Aston, 1977; DUniv: Keele, 1977; Essex, 1978; Open, 1979; Hon. DPhil Katholieke Univ., Leuven, 1979; Hon. doctorates: Urbino, 1979; TCD, 1979; Georgetown, 1988; W Virginia, 1992; Glamorgan, 1994; Bologna, 1994; Sofia, 1998. Charlemagne Prize, 1972; Robert Schuman Prize, 1972; Prix Bentinck, 1978. Order of European Merit (Luxemburg), 1976; Grand Cross: Legion of Honour of Senegal, 1979; Legion of Honour of Mali, 1979; Order of Charles III (Spain), 1980; Order of Merit (Italy), 1990; Order of Infante D. Henrique (Portugal), 1993; Comdr, Legion of Honour (France), 1999. *Publications:* (ed) Purpose and Policy (a vol. of the Prime Minister's Speeches), 1947; Mr Attlee: an Interim Biography, 1948; (contrib.) New Fabian Essays, 1952; Pursuit of Progress, 1953; Mr Balfour's Poodle, 1954; Sir Charles Dilke: A Victorian Tragedy, 1958; The Labour Case (Penguin Special), 1959; Asquith, 1964; (contrib.) Hugh Gaitskell: a memoir, 1964; Essays and Speeches, 1967; Afternoon on the Potomac?, 1972; What Matters Now, 1972; Nine Men of Power, 1975; Partnership of Principle, 1985; Truman, 1986; Baldwin, 1987; Gallery of Twentieth Century Portraits, 1988; European Diary 1977–81, 1989; A Life at the Centre (autobiog.), 1991; Portraits and Miniatures, 1993; Gladstone (Whitbread Biography Award), 1995; The Chancellors, 1998; Churchill, 2001; Twelve Cities, 2002. *Address:* 11 Hereford Mansions, Hereford Road, W2 5BA; St Amand's House, East Hendred, Oxon OX12 8LA. *Clubs:* Athenæum, Brooks's, Pratt's, Reform, Beefsteak, Oxford and Cambridge.   *Died 5 Jan. 2003.*

JENKINS OF PUTNEY, Baron *cr* 1981 (Life Peer), of Wandsworth in Greater London; **Hugh Gater Jenkins;** *b* 27 July 1908; *s* of Joseph Walter Jenkins and Florence Emily (*née* Gater), Enfield, Middlesex; *m* 1st, 1936, Marie (*née* Crosbie) (*d* 1989), *d* of Sqdn Ldr Ernest Crosbie and Ethel (*née* Hawkins); 2nd, 1991, Helena Maria (*d* 1994), *d* of Nicolas and Katerina Pavlidis, Athens. *Educ:* Enfield Grammar Sch. Personal exploration of employment and unemployment, and political and economic research, 1925–30; Prudential Assce Co., 1930–40. ROC, 1938; RAF: Fighter Comd, 1941; became GCI Controller (Flt Lt); seconded to Govt of Burma, 1945, as Dir Engl. Programmes, Rangoon Radio. Nat. Union of Bank Employees: Greater London Organiser, 1947; Res. and Publicity Officer; Ed., The Bank Officer, 1948; British Actors' Equity Assoc.: Asst Sec., 1950; Asst Gen. Sec., 1957–64. LCC: Mem. for Stoke Newington and Hackney N, 1958–65 (Public Control and Town Planning Cttees). Fabian Soc. lectr and Dir of Summer Schools in early post-war years; Chairman: H Bomb Campaign Cttee, 1954; Campaign for Nuclear Disarmament, 1979–81 (Vice-Pres., 1981–); CND, Aldermaston Marcher, 1957–63; Chm. Victory for Socialism, 1956–60; Mem. Exec. Cttee Greater London Labour Party. Contested (Lab): Enfield W, 1950; Mitcham, 1955; MP (Lab) Wandsworth, Putney, 1964–79; Minister for the Arts, 1974–76. Former Mem., Public Accounts Cttee. Member: Arts Council, 1968–71; Drama Panel, 1972–74; Nat. Theatre Bd, 1976–80; Dep. Chm., Theatres Trust, 1977–79; Dir, 1979–86, Consultant, 1986–, Life Pres., 1995. Theatres' Advisory Council: Jt Sec., 1963; Chm., 1964–74, 1976–86; Vice-Pres., 1986–95; Pres., 1996–. Occasional broadcasts and lectures on communications, theatrical and disarmament subjects. *Radio plays:* series, Scenes from an Autobiography: Solo Boy, 1983; When You and I Were Seventeen, 1985; A Day in September, 1986; In Time of War, 1986; Lost Tune from Rangoon, 1987; View to a Death, 1989. *Publications:* Essays in Local Government

Enterprise (with others), 1964; The Culture Gap, 1979; Rank and File, 1980; various pamphlets; contrib. to Tribune, New Statesman, Guardian, etc. *Recreations:* reading, writing, talking, viewing, listening, avoiding retirement. *Address:* House of Lords, SW1A 0PW. *T:* (020) 7219 6706, (office) (020) 7836 8591.
                                Died 26 Jan. 2004.

JENKINS, Rev. Dr Daniel Thomas; Free Church Minister and theologian; *b* 9 June 1914; *s* of Evan and Eleanor Jenkins; *m* 1942, Agatha Helen Mary Cree; two *s* three *d*. *Educ:* Merthyr Tydfil Schs; Edinburgh Univ. (MA, BD); Yorkshire United Coll.; Mansfield Coll., Oxford (BA). Ordained, 1940; Minister, Vineyard Congregational Ch, Richmond, Surrey, 1940–42; SCM, Univ. of Birmingham, 1942–45; Asst Editor, Christian Newsletter, London, 1945–48; Commonwealth Fund Fellow, NY, 1948–49; Minister: Oxted Congregational Ch, 1950–56; Kings Weigh House Congregational Ch, London, 1956–62; Chaplain and Reader, Univ. of Sussex, 1963–73; Minister, Regent Sq. URC, London, 1972–81; Weyerhaueser Prof., Princeton Theol Seminary, USA, 1981–84. Associate Prof. of Theol., Univ. of Chicago, 1950–62; Vis. Prof., KCL, 1973–75. Hon. DD: Knox Coll., Toronto, 1957; Edinburgh, 1964. *Publications:* The Nature of Catholicity, 1942; Prayer and the Service of God, 1945; The Gift of Ministry, 1947; The Doctors' Profession, 1948; Tradition and the Spirit, 1950; Europe and America, 1951; Congregationalism, 1954; The Strangeness of the Church, 1955; The Protestant Ministry, 1958; Equality and Excellence, 1961; Beyond Religion, 1962; The Christian Belief in God, 1964; The Educated Society, 1966; The British: their identity and their religion, 1975; Christian Maturity and Christian Success, 1982. *Address:* 301 Willoughby House, Barbican, EC2Y 8BL.   *Died 22 June 2002.*

JENKINS, David, CBE 1977; MA; Librarian, National Library of Wales, 1969–79; *b* 29 May 1912; *s* of late Evan Jenkins and Mary (*née* James), Blaenclydach, Rhondda; *m* 1948, Menna Rhys, *o d* of late Rev. Owen Evans Williams, Penrhyn-coch, Aberystwyth; one *s* one *d*. *Educ:* Ardwyn Grammar Sch., Aberystwyth; UCW, Aberystwyth (BA Hons Welsh Lit. 1936, MA 1948; W. P. Thomas (Rhondda) Schol. 1936; Sir John Williams Research Student, 1937–38; Hon. Fellow). Served War of 1939–45, Army: Major, 1943; NW Europe. National Library of Wales: Asst, Dept MSS, 1939–48; Asst Keeper, Dept of Printed Books, 1949, Keeper, 1957, Sen. Keeper, 1962. Professorial Fellow, UCW Aberystwyth, 1971–79. Gen. Comr of Income Tax, 1968–87; Chairman: Mid-Wales HMC, 1969–70; Welsh Books Council, 1974–80 (Vice-Chm. 1971–74); Library Adv. Council (Wales), 1979–82; Member: Adv. Council, British Library, 1975–82; BBC Archives Adv. Cttee, 1976–79; Court of Governors, Univ. of Wales; Ct and Council, UC Aberystwyth and Lampeter; Hon. Soc. of Cymmrodorion; Pantyfedwen Trust, 1969–95; Coll. of Librarianship Wales. Governor: Ardwyn Grammar Sch., 1963–72; Penweddig Compreh. Sch., 1973–77. Editor: NLW Jl, 1968–79; Jl Welsh Bibliog. Soc., 1964–79; Ceredigion, Trans Cards Antiq. Soc., 1973–84. JP Aberystwyth 1959–82: Chm. Llanbadarn Bench 1965–69; Vice-Chm., Aberystwyth Bench, 1980; Member: Dyfed Magistrates' Courts Cttee, 1975–79; Dyfed-Powys Police Authority, 1977–81. Hon. DLitt Wales, 1979. Sir Ellis Griffith Meml Prize, Univ. of Wales, 1975. *Publications:* Cofiant Thomas Gwynn Jones, 1973, 2nd edn 1994 (Welsh Arts Council Prize, 1974); (ed) Erthyglau ac Ysgrifau Kate Roberts, 1978; Bardd a Bro: T. Gwynn Jones, Cyngor y Celfyddydau, 1984; Bro Dafydd ap Gwilym, 1992; O Blas Gogerddan i Horeb, 1993; (with G. Morgan) History of National Library of Wales to 1952, 2000; articles in NLW Jl, Bull. Bd of Celtic Studies and many other jls; contrib. Dictionary of Welsh Biography, Cydymaith i lenyddiaeth Cymru, DNB. *Recreation:* walking. *Address:* Maesaleg, Penrhyn-coch, Aberystwyth, Dyfed SY23 3EH. *T:* (01970) 828766.   *Died 6 March 2002.*

JENKINS, (Gilbert) Kenneth; Keeper, Department of Coins and Medals, British Museum, 1965–78; *b* 2 July 1918; *s* of late Kenneth Gordon Jenkins and of Julia Louisa Jenkins (*née* Colbourne); *m* 1939, Cynthia Mary (*d* 1985), *d* of late Dr Hugh Scott, FRS; one *s* two *d*. *Educ:* All Saints Sch., Bloxham; Corpus Christi Coll., Oxford (Open Classical Schol., 1936; 1st cl. Hons Mods, 1938; BA 1946). Served War, Royal Artillery, 1940–46 (SE Asia, 1944–46). Asst Keeper, 1947, Dep. Keeper, 1956, British Museum. An Editor of Numismatic Chronicle, 1964. Mem., German Archaeological Inst., 1967; Corresp. Mem., Amer. Numismatic Soc., 1958; Hon. Mem., Swiss Numismatic Soc., 1979; Hon. FRNS, 1980. Akbar Medal, Numismatic Soc. of India, 1966; Royal Numismatic Soc. Medal, 1975; Archer Huntington Medal, Amer. Numismatic Soc., 1976. *Publications:* Carthaginian Gold and Electrum Coins (with R. B. Lewis), 1963; Coins of Greek Sicily, 1966; Sylloge Nummorum Graecorum (Danish Nat. Museum), part 42, N Africa (ed), 1969, part 43, Spain-Gaul (ed), 1979; The Coinage of Gela, 1970; Ancient Greek Coins, 1972; (with U. Westermark) The Coinage of Kamarina, 1980; (jtly) A Catalogue of the Calouste Gulbenkian Collection of Greek Coins, part II, 1989; articles in numismatic periodicals. *Recreations:* music, cycling. *Address:* Cecil Court, 2–4 Priory Road, Kew, Richmond, Surrey TW9 3DG. *Died 22 May 2005.*

JENKINS, Dr Ivor, CBE 1970; FREng; freelance consultant, since 1979; Group Director of Research, Delta Metal Co. Ltd, 1973–78; Managing Director, 1973–77, Deputy Chairman, 1977–78, Delta Materials Research Ltd; *b* 25 July 1913; *m* 1941, Caroline Wijnanda James; two *s*. *Educ:* Gowerton Grammar Sch.; Univ. of Wales, Swansea (BSc, MSc, DSc; Hon. Fellow, UC Swansea, 1986). Bursar, GEC Research Labs, Wembley, 1934; Mem. Scientific Staff, GEC, 1935; Dep. Chief Metallurgist, Whitehead Iron & Steel Co., Newport, Mon, 1944; Head of Metallurgy Dept, 1946, Chief Metallurgist, 1952, GEC, Wembley; Dir of Research, Manganese Bronze Holdings Ltd, and Dir, Manganese Bronze Ltd, 1961–69; Dir of Research, Delta Metal Co., and Dir, Delta Metal (BW) Ltd, 1969–73. Vis. Prof., Univ. of Surrey, 1978–90. FIMMM (FIM 1948; Pres. 1965–66); Fellow, Amer. Soc. of Metals, 1974; Pres., Inst. of Metals, 1968–69; Mem., Iron and Steel Inst., 1937– (Williams Prize, 1946); FREng (FEng 1979). Platinum Medallist, Metals Soc., 1978. *Publications:* Controlled Atmospheres for the Heat Treatment of Metals, 1946; (ed jtly) Selected Case Studies in Powder Metallurgy, 1991; (ed jtly) Powder Metallurgy: an overview, 1991; contribs to learned jls at home and abroad on metallurgical and related subjects. *Recreations:* music, gardening, swimming. *Address:* 31 Trotyn Croft, Aldwick Felds, Aldwick, Bognor Regis, Sussex PO21 3TX. *T:* (01243) 828749. *Died 15 Aug. 2003.*

JENKINS, John Robin, OBE 1999; writer; *b* Cambuslang, Lanarks, 11 Sept. 1912; *s* of late James Jenkins and Annie Robin; *m* 1937, Mary McIntyre Wyllie; one *s* two *d*. *Educ:* Hamilton Academy; Glasgow Univ. (MA Hons). *Publications:* (as Robin Jenkins) Happy for the Child, 1953; The Thistle and the Grail, 1954; The Cone-Gatherers, 1955; Guests of War, 1956; The Missionaries, 1957; The Changeling, 1958; Some Kind of Grace, 1960; Dust on the Paw, 1961; The Tiger of Gold, 1962; A Love of Innocence, 1963; The Sardana Dancers, 1964; A Very Scotch Affair, 1968; The Holy Tree, 1969; The Expatriates, 1971; A Toast to the Lord, 1972; A Far Cry from Bowmore, 1973; A Figure of Fun, 1974; A Would-be Saint, 1978; Fergus Lamont, 1979; The Awakening of George Darroch, 1985; Just Duffy, 1988; Poverty Castle, 1991; Willie Hogg, 1993; Leila, 1996; Lunderston Tales, 1996; Matthew and Sheila, 1998; Poor Angus, 2000; Childish Things, 2001; Lady Magdalen, 2002. *Recreations:* travel, golf. *Address:* Fairhaven, Toward, by Dunoon, Argyll PA23 7UE. *T:* (01369) 870288. *Died 24 Feb. 2005.*

JENKINS, Kenneth; *see* Jenkins, G. K.

JENKINS, Robin; *see* Jenkins, J. R.

JENKS, Sir (Maurice Arthur) Brian, 3rd Bt *cr* 1932, of Cheape in the City of London; chartered accountant in sole practice, 1993–2002; *b* 28 Oct. 1933; *er s* of Sir Richard Atherley Jenks, 2nd Bt and Marjorie Suzanne Arlette Jenks, *d* of Sir Arthur du Cros, 1st Bt; *S* father, 1993; *m* 1962, Susan Lois Allen; one *d*, and one adopted *s*. *Educ:* Charterhouse. Qualified chartered accountant, 1956; Partner, Mann Judd & Co., subseq. Touche Ross & Co., 1960–93. Mem. Ct of Assts, Haberdashers' Co., 1961– (Master, 1988–89 and 1992–93). *Publication:* Small Businesses: how to survive and succeed, 1989. *Recreations:* wine, racing. *Heir:* *b* Richard John Peter Jenks [*b* 28 June 1936; *m* 1963, Juniper Li-Yung, *e d* of Tan Sri Y. C. Foo; one *s* two *d*]. *Address:* Warren House, Savernake, Marlborough, Wilts SN8 3BQ. *T:* (01672) 870442. *Died 2 Oct. 2004.*

JENNINGS, Elizabeth Joan, CBE 1992; author; *b* 18 July 1926; *d* of Dr H. C. Jennings, Oxon. *Educ:* Oxford High Sch.; St Anne's Coll., Oxford. Asst at Oxford City Library, 1950–58; Reader for Chatto & Windus Ltd, 1958–60. *Publications: poetry:* Poems (Arts Council Prize), 1953; A Way of Looking, 1955 (Somerset Maugham Award, 1956); A Sense of the World, 1958; (ed) The Batsford Book of Children's Verse, 1958; Song for a Birth or a Death, 1961; a translation of Michelangelo's sonnets, 1961; Recoveries, 1964; The Mind Has Mountains (Richard Hillary Prize), 1966; The Secret Brother (for children), 1966; Collected Poems, 1967; The Animals' Arrival (Arts Council Bursary), 1969; (ed) A Choice of Christina Rossetti's Verse, 1970; Lucidities, 1970; Relationships, 1972; Growing Points, 1975; Consequently I Rejoice, 1977; After the Ark (for children), 1978; Selected Poems, 1980; Moments of Grace, 1980; (ed) The Batsford Book of Religious Verse, 1981; Celebrations and Elegies, 1982; In Praise of Our Lady (anthology), 1982; Extending the Territory, 1985; (contrib.) A Quintet (for children), 1985; Collected Poems 1953–1986, 1986 (W. H. Smith Award, 1987); Tributes, 1989; Times and Seasons, 1992; Familiar Spirits, 1994; A Spell of Words, 1997; Praises, 1998; Timely Issues, 2001; *prose:* Let's Have Some Poetry, 1960; Every Changing Shape, 1961; Robert Frost, 1964; Christianity and Poetry, 1965; Seven Men of Vision, 1976; also poems and articles in: New Statesman, New Yorker, Botteghe Oscure, Observer, Spectator, Listener, Vogue, The Independent, etc. *Recreations:* travel, looking at pictures, the theatre, the cinema, music, collecting, conversation. *Address:* c/o David Higham Associates Ltd, 5–8 Lower John Street, W1R 4HA. *Club:* Society of Authors. *Died 26 Oct. 2001.*

JENNINGS, Sir Robert (Yewdall), Kt 1982; QC 1969; a Judge, 1982–95, and President, 1991–94, the International Court of Justice; *b* 19 Oct. 1913; *o s* of Arthur Jennings; *m* 1955, Christine, *yr d* of Bernard Bennett; one *s* two *d*. *Educ:* Belle Vue Secondary Sch., Bradford; Downing Coll., Cambridge (scholar; 1st cl. pts I & II Law Tripos; LLB; MA; Hon. Fellow, 1982). Served War, Intelligence Corps, 1940–46; Hon. Major, Officers' AER. Called to the Bar, Lincoln's Inn, 1943 (Hon. Bencher, 1970). Whewell Scholar in Internat. Law, Cambridge, 1936; Joseph Hodges Choate Fellow, Harvard Univ., 1936–37; Asst Lectr in Law, LSE, 1938–39; Jesus College, Cambridge: Fellow, 1939, Hon. Fellow, 1982; Sen. Tutor, 1949–55; sometime Pres.; Whewell Prof. of Internat. Law, Cambridge Univ., 1955–81; Reader in Internat. Law, Council of Legal Educn, 1959–70. Pres., Eritrea/Yemen Arbitration, 1996–99; Appointing Authy, Iran–US Claims Tribunal, The Hague, 1999–. Member: Permanent Court of Arbitration, 1982–; Inst. of Internat. Law, 1967– (Vice-Pres., 1979; Pres., 1981–83; Hon. Mem., 1985–); Hon. Mem., Indian Soc. of Internat. Law; Hon. Life Mem., Amer. Soc. of Internat. Law (Manley O. Hudson Medal, 1993). Hon. LLD: Hull, 1987; Cantab, 1993; Leicester, 1995; Hon. Dr jur: Saarland, W Germany, 1988; La

Sapienza, Rome, 1990; Hon. DCL Oxon, 1996. Joint Editor: International and Comparative Law Quarterly, 1956–61; British Year Book of International Law, 1960–82. *Publications:* The Acquisition of Territory, 1963; General Course on International Law, 1967; Collected Writings of Sir Robert Jennings, 2 vols, 1998; articles in legal periodicals. *Address:* Jesus College, Cambridge CB5 8BL. *T:* (01223) 39339. *Clubs:* Oxford and Cambridge; Haagsche (The Hague). *Died 4 Aug. 2004.*

JEPHCOTT, Sir (John) Anthony, 2nd Bt *cr* 1962; *b* 21 May 1924; *s* of Sir Harry Jephcott, 1st Bt, and Doris (*d* 1985), *d* of Henry Gregory; *S* father, 1978; *m* 1st, 1949, Sylvia Mary, *d* of Thorsten Frederick Relling, Wellington, NZ; two *d*; 2nd, 1978, Josephine Agnes Sheridan. *Educ:* Aldenham; St John's Coll., Oxford; London School of Economics (BCom). Served with REME and RAEC, 1944–47. Longworth Scientific Instrument Co. Ltd: Dir, 1946; Man. Dir and Chm., 1952–73; Man. Dir and Chm., Pen Medic Ltd (NZ), 1973–78. Hon. FFARACS 1990. *Publications:* A History of Longworth Scientific Instrument Co. Ltd, 1988; correspondence in Anaesthesia (UK), and Anaesthesia and Intensive Care (Australia). *Recreations:* gardening, photography. *Heir: b* Neil Welbourn Jephcott [*b* 3 June 1929; *m* 1st, 1951, Mary Denise (*d* 1977), *d* of Arthur Muddiman; two *s* one *d*; 2nd, 1978, Mary Florence Daly]. *Address:* 26 Sage Road, Kohimarama, Auckland 5, New Zealand. *Died 7 Aug. 2003.*

JEROME, Hon. James Alexander; PC (Can.) 1981; Associate Chief Justice, Federal Court of Canada, 1980–98; lawyer, since 1958; *b* Kingston, Ont, 4 March 1933; *s* of Joseph Leonard Jerome and Phyllis Devlin; *m* 1958, Barry Karen Hodgins; two *s* two *d* (and one *s* decd). *Educ:* Our Lady of Perpetual Help Sch., Toronto; St Michael's Coll. High Sch., Toronto; Univ. of Toronto (BA 1954); Osgoode Hall. Alderman, Sudbury, Ont, 1966–67. MP, Sudbury, 1968–80; Parly Sec. to President of Privy Council, 1970–74; Speaker of the House of Commons, 1974–80. QC (Can.) 1976. Pres., Commonwealth Parly Assoc., 1976. *Recreations:* golf, piano. *Died 21 Aug. 2005.*

JOBERT, Michel; Commandeur de la Légion d'Honneur; Croix de Guerre (1939–45); politician, writer and lawyer; Founder and Leader, Mouvement des Démocrates, since 1974; *b* Meknès, Morocco, 11 Sept. 1921; *s* of Jules Jobert and Yvonne Babule; *m* Muriel Frances Green (decd); one *s. Educ:* Lycées de Rabat and Meknès; Dip. de l'Ecole libre des sciences politiques; Ecole nationale d'Administration. Cour des comptes: Auditor, 1949; Conseiller Référendaire, 1953. Member of Ministerial Cabinets: Finance, Labour and Social Security, President of the Council, 1952–56; Director of the Cabinet of the High Comr of the Republic in French West Africa, 1956–58; Dir of Cabinet of Minister of State, 1959–61; Jt Dir, 1963–66, then Dir, 1966–68, of the Prime Minister's Cabinet (Georges Pompidou); Pres., Council of Admin of Nat. Office of Forests, 1966–73; Administrator of Havas, 1968–73; Secretary-Gen., Presidency of the Republic, 1969–73; Minister for Foreign Affairs, 1973–74; Minister of State and Minister for Overseas Trade, 1981–83. Conseiller-maître, Cour des comptes, 1971– (Hon. Conseiller-maître, 1986). Arbitrator, Nat. Cttee, Internat. Chamber of Commerce, 1991. Former Board Member: SOFIRAD, Radio Monte-Carlo; French Radio and TV Organisation. Editor, La Lettre de Michel Jobert, 1974–84; Editorialiste, Paris ce Soir, Jan.–Feb. 1985. Prix de la Langue de France, 1989. *Publications:* Mémoires d'avenir, 1974; L'autre regard, 1976; Lettre ouverte aux femmes politiques, 1976; Parler aux Français, 1977; La vie d'Hella Schuster (novel), 1977; Maroc: extrême Maghreb du soleil couchant, 1978; La rivière aux grenades, 1982; Chroniques du Midi Libre, 1982; Vive l'Europe Libre, 1984; Par Trente-six chemins, 1984; Maghreb, à l'ombre de ses mains, 1985; Les Américains, 1987; Journal immédiat ... et pour une petite éternité, 1987; Vandales!,

1990; Journal du Golfe, 1991; Ni dieu ni diable, 1993; Chroniques de l'Espérance 1988–1992, 1993; L'aveuglement du monde occidental, Chroniques de politique internationale 1993–1996, 1997; Les illusions immobiles, Chroniques de politique internationale 1996–1998, 1999. *Address:* (home) 21 quai Alphonse-Le Gallo, 92100 Boulogne-sur-Seine, France; (office) 108 quai Louis Blériot, 75016 Paris, France. *Died 25 May 2002.*

JOHANSON, Rev. Dr Brian; Minister of Christ Church, United Reformed Church, Tonbridge, 1987–94; *b* 8 March 1929; *s* of Bernard Johanson and Petra Johanson; *m* 1st, 1955, Marion Shirley Giles (*d* 1994); one *s* two *d*; 2nd, 1995, Maureen Linnea Henderson. *Educ:* Univ. of South Africa (BA, DD); Univ. of London (BD). Parish Minister, S Africa, 1956–63; Sen. Lectr in Theology, 1964–69, Prof. of Theol., 1970–76, Univ. of SA; Minister of the City Temple, London, 1976–85; Dir of Ministerial Training, Presbyterian Church of Southern Africa, Johannesburg, 1985–86. Vis. Res. Fellow: Princeton Theol Seminary, 1970; Univ. of Aberdeen, 1976. *Publications:* univ. pubns in S Africa; booklets; essays in collections; articles in theol jls. *Address:* PO Box 5, Bodalla, NSW 2545, Australia; *e-mail:* beejay@hendersonuk.com. *Died 26 Oct. 2003.*

JOHN PAUL II, His Holiness Pope, (Karol Jozef Wojtyla); *b* Wadowice, Poland, 18 May 1920; *s* of Karol Wojtyla and Emilia Kaczorowska. *Educ:* Jagiellonian Univ., Cracow (Dr 1954); Pontificio Ateneo 'Angelicum' (Dr in Theology). Ordained priest, 1946; Prof. of Moral Theology, Univs of Lublin and Cracow, 1954–58; titular Bishop of Ombi, and Auxiliary Bishop of Cracow, 1958; Vicar Capitular, 1962; Archbishop and Metropolitan of Cracow, 1964–78. Cardinal, 1967; elected Pope, 16 Oct. 1978. Formerly Mem., Congregations Pro Institutione Catholica, Pro Sacramentis et Cultu Divino, and Pro Clero. Charlemagne Prize, 2004. *Publications:* The Goldsmith Shop (play), 1960; Love and Responsibility, 1962; Person and Act, 1969; The Foundations of Renewal, 1972; Sign of Contradiction, 1976; The Future of the Church, 1979; Easter Vigil and other poems, 1979; Collected Poems (trans. Jerzy Peterkiewicz), 1982; Crossing the Threshold of Hope (essays), 1994; The Place Within (trans. Jerzy Peterkiewicz), 1995; Gift and Mystery (autobiog.), 1996; Agenda for the Third Millennium, 1999; Roman Triptych (poem), 2003; Get Up, Let Us Go, 2004; Memory and Identity (memoirs), 2005. *Address:* Apostolic Palace, 00120 Vatican City. *Died 2 April 2005.*

JOHNSON, Prof. Barry Edward, PhD; FRS 1978; Professor of Pure Mathematics, University of Newcastle upon Tyne, 1969–2001; *b* 1 Aug. 1937; *s* of Edward Johnson and Evelyn May (*née* Bailey); *m* 1st, 1961, Jennifer Pat (*née* Munday) (marr. diss. 1979); two *s* one *d*; 2nd, 1990, Margaret Jones (*née* Brown). *Educ:* Epsom County Grammar Sch.; Hobart State High Sch.; Univ. of Tasmania (BSc 1956); Cambridge Univ. (PhD 1961). Instr, Univ. of Calif, Berkeley, 1961–62; Vis. Lectr, Yale Univ., 1962–63; Lectr, Exeter Univ., 1963–65; University of Newcastle upon Tyne: Lectr, 1965–68; Reader, 1968–69; Head of Dept of Pure Maths, 1976–83; Head of Sch. of Maths, 1983–86; Dean, Faculty of Sci., 1986–89. Vis. Prof., Yale Univ., 1970–71. Auditor, HEQC, 1993–. Mem., London Math. Soc. (Mem. Council, 1975–78; Pres., 1980–82). *Publications:* Cohomology of Banach Algebras, 1972; papers in Jl of London Math. Soc. and Amer. Jl of Maths. *Recreations:* reading, travel. *Address:* 63 Montagu Court, Gosforth, Newcastle upon Tyne NE3 4JL. *T:* (0191) 213 1013. *Died 5 May 2002.*

JOHNSON, Donald Edwin, RIBA, FRTPI; Under Secretary, 1978–80, and Deputy Chief Planner, 1975–80, Department of the Environment; *b* 4 July 1920; *s* of Henry William Johnson and Ann Catherine (*née* Lake); *m* 1947,

Thérèse Andrée Simone Marquant; two *s* one *d*. *Educ:* Haberdashers' Aske's, Hatcham; School of Architecture, Regent Polytechnic; APRR School of Planning. Served War, Royal Artillery and Royal Engineers, 1940–45. Planning Officer, Min. of Town and Country Planning, 1947; Sen. Planning Officer, 1950, Principal Planner, 1965, Asst Chief Planner, 1972. *Publications: fiction:* Project 38, 1963; Crooked Cross, 1964; Flashing Mountain, 1965; Devil of Bruges, 1966. *Address:* Flat D, 1 Morpeth Terrace, SW1P 1EW. *T:* (020) 7834 7300.

Died 10 Sept. 2005.

JOHNSON, Prof. Douglas William John; Professor of French History, University College London, 1968–90, then Emeritus; Visiting Professor, French Department, King's College, London, since 1993; *b* Edinburgh, 1 Feb. 1925; *o s* of John Thornburn Johnson and Christine Douglas Mair; *m* 1950, Madeleine Rébillard; one *d*. *Educ:* Royal Grammar Sch., Lancaster; Worcester Coll., Oxford (BA, BLitt); Ecole Normale Supérieure, Paris. Birmingham University: Lectr in Modern History, 1949; Prof. of Modern History and Chm. of Sch. of History, 1963–68; University College London: Head of Dept of History, 1979–83; Dean, Faculty of Arts, 1979–82. Vis. Prof., Univs of Aix-en-Provence, Nancy, Paris, British Columbia, Toronto, Caen, Lyons, Montreal, Texas. Lectures: Zaharoff, Oxford Univ., 1989; Simon Cohen Meml, Kent Univ., 1990; Creighton, London Univ., 1991; Stenton, Reading Univ., 1995; Centenary, Univ. of Aston, 1996. Chm. Bd of Examrs in History, Univ. of London, 1973–75; Member: CNAA, 1974–79; Franco–British Council, 1976–; Scientific Council, Fondation Charles de Gaulle, 1993–. FRHistS. Hon. DSc Aston, 1996. Ordre Nat. du Mérite (France), 1980; Commandeur des Palmes Académiques (France), 1987; Officier de la Légion d'Honneur (France), 1997 (Chevalier, 1990). *Publications:* Guizot: aspects of French history 1787–1874, 1963; France and the Dreyfus Affair, 1966; France, 1969; Concise History of France, 1970; The French Revolution, 1970; (ed) French Society and the Revolution, 1976; (ed jtly) Britain and France: ten centuries, 1980; (with Richard Hoggart) An Idea of Europe, 1987; (with Madeleine Johnson) The Age of Illusion, 1987; (with Geoffrey Best) The Permanent Revolution, 1988; Michelet and the French Revolution, 1990; How European are the French?, 1996; (ed with Anne Corbett) A Day in June: Britain and de Gaulle 1940, 2001; (ed with Richard Mayne and Robert Tombs) Cross-Channel Currents: 100 years of the Entente Cordiale, 2004; General Editor: The Making of the Modern World, 1971; The Fontana History of Modern France, 1983. *Recreations:* music, French politics. *Address:* 29 Rudall Crescent, NW3 1RR; 12 rue Delambre, Paris 75014, France. *Club:* Travellers. *Died 28 April 2005.*

JOHNSON, Air Vice-Marshal James Edgar, (Johnnie), CB 1965; CBE 1960; DSO 1943 and Bar, 1943, 1944; DFC 1941 and Bar, 1942; DL; Consultant, 'Johnnie' Johnson Housing; Director of companies in Canada, South Africa and UK; *b* 9 March 1916; *m* 1942, Pauline Ingate; two *s*. *Educ:* Loughborough Sch.; Nottingham Univ. Civil Engr and Mem. of RAFVR until 1939; served with 616 Sqdn AAF, 1940–42; 610 Sqdn AAF, 1943; Wing Comdr Flying: Kenley, 1943; 127 Wing, 1944; Officer Commanding: 125 Wing (2nd TAF), 1944–45; 124 Wing (2nd TAF), 1945–46; RCAF Staff Coll., 1947–48; USAF (Exchange Officer), 1948–50; served Korea (with USAF), 1950–51; OC, RAF Wildenrath (2nd TAF), 1952–54; Air Ministry, 1954–57; Officer Commanding, RAF Cottesmore, Bomber Command, 1957–60; idc 1960; Senior Air Staff Officer, No 3 Group, Bomber Command, Mildenhall, Suffolk, 1960–63; AOC, Air Forces Middle East, Aden, 1963–65; retired. DL Leicester, 1967. Order of Leopold, 1945, Croix de Guerre, 1945 (Belgium); Legion of Merit, 1950, DFC 1943, Air Medal, 1950 (USA); Légion d'Honneur (France), 1988. *Publications:* Wing Leader, 1956; Full Circle, 1964; The Story of Air Fighting, 1985; (jtly) Glorious Summer, 1990; (jtly) Courage in the Skies, 1992; (jtly) Winged Victory, 1995. *Recreations:* shooting, golf. *Address:* The Stables, Hargate, Buxton, Derbyshire SK17 8TA. *Club:* Royal Air Force.

Died 30 Jan. 2001.

JOHNSON, Air Vice-Marshal Johnnie; *see* Johnson, Air Vice-Marshal James E.

JOHNSON, Sir Peter (Colpoys Paley), 7th Bt *cr* 1755, of New York in North America; author; publishing consultant; *b* 26 March 1930; *s* of Sir John Paley Johnson, 6th Bt, MBE, and of Carol, *d* of late Edmund Haas; *S* father, 1975; *m* 1st, 1956, Clare (marr. diss. 1973), *d* of late Dr Nigel Bruce; one *s* two *d*; 2nd, 1973, Caroline Elisabeth, *d* of Sir John Hodsoll, CB; one *s*. *Educ:* Wellington Coll.; Royal Military Coll. of Science. Served RA, 1949; retired 1961, Captain. Dir, Sea Sure Ltd, 1965–73; Dir and Editor, Nautical Publishing Co. Ltd, 1970–81; Publishing Dir, Nautical Books, London, 1981–86. British Delegate, Internat. Offshore (Yachting) Council, 1970–79 (Chm. Internat. Technical Cttee, 1973–76); Ocean Racing Correspondent, Yachting World, London, 1971–81. Hon. Col, King's Royal Regt of NY (Canada), 1988–. *Publications:* Ocean Racing and Offshore Yachts, 1970, 2nd edn 1972; Boating Britain, 1973; Guinness Book of Yachting Facts and Feats, 1975; Guinness Guide to Sailing, 1981; This is Fast Cruising, 1985; The Encyclopedia of Yachting, 1989; Whitbread Round the World 1973–93, 1993; Yacht Clubs of the World, 1995; Yacht Rating, 1997; World Sailing Records, 2002; Maritime Flags, 2002. *Recreation:* sailing. *Heir: s* Colpoys Guy Johnson [*b* 13 Nov. 1965; *m* 1990, Marie-Louise, *d* of John Holroyd; three *s*]. *Address:* Dene End, Buckland Dene, Lymington, Hampshire SO41 9DT. *T:* (01590) 675921, *Fax:* (01590) 672885. *Clubs:* Royal Ocean Racing; Royal Yacht Squadron.

Died 24 May 2003.

JOHNSON, Philip Cortelyou; architect, with own firm, 1953–67, with Johnson/Burgee Architects, since 1967; *b* Cleveland, Ohio, 8 July 1906; *s* of Homer H. Johnson and Louise Pope Johnson. *Educ:* Harvard (AB 1927, *cum laude*); Graduate Sch. of Design, Harvard (BArch 1943). Dir, Dept of Architecture, Museum of Modern Art, New York, 1932–54, Trustee, 1958–. Has taught and lectured at: Yale Univ.; Cornell Univ.; Pratt Inst. (Dr Fine Arts, 1962). Member: AIA (NY Chapter); Architectural League, NY. Hon. Dr Fine Arts Yale, 1978. Gold Medal, AIA, 1978; Pritzker Architecture Prize, 1979. *Publications:* Machine Art, 1934; Mies van der Rohe, 1st edn 1947, 2nd edn 1953; (with Henry-Russell Hitchcock) The International Style, Architecture since 1922, 1932, new edn 1966; (jtly) Modern Architects, 1932; Architecture 1949–1965, 1966; Philip Johnson Writings, 1979; contrib. to Architectural Review. *Clubs:* Athenæum; Century.

Died 25 Jan. 2005.

JOHNSON, (Reginald) Stuart, CBE 1985; Director of Education, Leeds City Council, 1973–93; *b* 12 April 1933; *s* of late Reginald Johnson and Sarah Anne Johnson; *m* 1960, Dr Jennifer Johnson (*née* Craig); one *s* one *d*. *Educ:* Durham Univ. (BSc Hons); London Univ. (PGCE DipEd). Deputy Education Officer, Leeds CC, 1968–73. Member: UGC, 1979–89 (Chm., Educn Sub-Cttee, 1985–89); Advisory Cttee on Supply and Educn of Teachers, 1980– (Chm., Teacher Trng Sub-Cttee, 1981–); PPITB, 1977–80 (Chm., Trng Cttee, 1978–80). Member: BBC Schools and Further Educn Broadcasting Council, 1976–82; Social Security Tribunal. Adviser to Burnham Cttee, 1984. Administrator, Leeds International Pianoforte Competition, 1978–81. Mem. Council, Leeds Univ., 1986–; Gov., Leeds Girls' High Sch., 1990–; Chm., Leeds Coll. of Art and Design, 2000–. *Publications:* frequent articles in educnl press. *Recreations:* golf, cricket, fishing. *Address:* Mickleber House, Gargrave Road,

Gargrave, Skipton, N Yorks BD23 3AQ. *T:* (01756) 748423. *Club:* Leeds (Leeds). *Died 22 June 2001.*

JOHNSON, Stuart; *see* Johnson, R. S.

JOHNSON, Walter Hamlet; *b* Hertford, 21 Nov. 1917; *s* of John Johnson; *m* 1945, Anne. *Educ:* Devon House Sch., Margate. Councillor, Brentford and Chiswick for 6 years. Nat. Treasurer, 1965–77, Pres., 1977–81, Transport Salaried Staffs' Assoc. Joined Labour Party, 1945. Contested (Lab): Bristol West, 1955; South Bedfordshire, 1959; Acton, March 1968, in by-election. MP (Lab) Derby South, 1970–83; an Assistant Govt Whip, 1974–75. Chm., PLP Aviation Cttee, 1979–83. Particularly interested in welfare services, transport, labour relations and aviation matters. Principal Executive Asst, London Transport, 1980–83 (formerly a Sen. Exec., Staff Trng). Governor, Ruskin Coll., Oxford, 1966–85. *Recreation:* sport. *Address:* 9 Milton Court, Haywards Heath RH16 1EY. *T:* (01444) 412629. *Died 12 April 2003.*

JOHNSON-GILBERT, Ronald Stuart, OBE 1976; Secretary, Royal College of Surgeons of England, 1962–88; *b* 14 July 1925; *s* of Sir Ian A. Johnson-Gilbert, CBE and Rosalind Bell-Hughes; *m* 1951, Ann Weir Drummond; three *d. Educ:* Edinburgh Acad.; Rugby; Brasenose Coll., Oxford (Classical Exhbnr and Open Schol., 1943; MA). Intelligence Corps, 1943–46. Trainee, John Lewis Partnership, 1950–51; Admin. Staff, RCS, 1951–88; Secretary: Faculties of Dental Surgery and of Anaesthetists, 1958; Jt Conf. of Surgical Colls, 1963–88; Internat. Fedn of Surgical Colls, 1967–74; Hon. Sec., Med. Commn on Accident Prevention, 1984–88. Mem. Ct of Patrons, RCS, 1990–; Hunterian Trustee, RCS, 1989–2000. Hon. FFARCS 1983; Hon. FRCS 1987; Hon. FDSRCS 1987; Hon. FRCSI 1989. John Tomes Medal, BDA, 1980; McNeill Love Medal, RCS, 1981; Royal Australasian Coll. of Surgeons Medal, 1982. *Recreations:* music, painting, literature, golf. *Address:* Home Farm, Castle Rising, near King's Lynn, Norfolk PE31 6AE. *Died 23 April 2003.*

JOHNSTON OF ROCKPORT, Baron *cr* 1987 (Life Peer), of Caversham in the Royal County of Berkshire; **Charles Collier Johnston,** Kt 1973; TD; *b* 4 March 1915; *e s* of late Captain Charles Moore Johnston and Muriel Florence Mellon; *m* 1st, 1939, Audrey Boyes Monk, LLB; two *s;* 2nd, 1981, Mrs Yvonne Shearman. *Educ:* Tonbridge Sch., Kent. Commissioned TA, 1938; served War of 1939–45 (TD); Major RA, retd 1946. Managing Dir, 1948–76, Chm., 1951–77, Standex International Ltd (formerly Roehlen-Martin Ltd), Engravers and Engineers, Ashton Road, Bredbury, Cheshire; Chairman: Thames & Kennet Marina Ltd, 1982–94; James Burn International, 1986–; Standex Holdings Ltd, 1986– (Dir 1983). Jt Hon. Treas., Conservative Party, 1984–87. Chm., Macclesfield Constituency Conservative Assoc., 1961–65; Hon. Treas., NW Conservatives and Mem. Conservative Bd of Finance, 1965–71; Chm., NW Area Conservatives, 1971–76; Pres., Nat. Union of Conservative and Unionist Assocs, 1986–87 (Mem. Exec. Cttee, 1965–98, Chm. 1976–81). Nat. Chm., Cons. Friends of Israel, 1983–86. Mem., Boyd Commn, as official observers of elecns held in Zimbabwe/Rhodesia, April 1980. *Recreations:* spectator sports, travelling, gardening. *Address:* House of Lords, SW1A 0PW. *Died 30 April 2002.*

JOHNSTON, Most Rev. Allen Howard, CMG 1978; LTh; *b* Auckland, NZ, 1912; *s* of Joseph Howard Johnston; *m* 1937, Joyce Rhoda, *d* of John A. Grantley, Auckland; four *d. Educ:* Seddon Memorial Technical College; St John's College, Auckland; Auckland Univ. College. Deacon, 1935; Priest, 1936. Assistant Curate of St Mark's, Remuera, 1935–37; Vicar of Dargaville, 1937–42; Vicar of Northern Wairoa, 1942–44; Vicar of Otahuhu, 1944–49; Vicar of Whangarei, 1949–53; Archdeacon of

Waimate, 1949–53; Bishop of Dunedin, 1953–69; Bishop of Waikato, 1969–80; Primate and Archbishop of New Zealand, 1972–80. Fellow, St John's Coll., Auckland, 1970. Hon. LLD Otago, 1969. ChStJ 1974. *Address:* 207 Riddell Road, Auckland, New Zealand. *Died 22 Feb. 2002.*

JOHNSTON, Hon. Hugh de Beauchamp L.; *see* Lawson Johnston.

JOHNSTON, Ian Henderson, CB 1981; Deputy Controller Aircraft, Procurement Executive, Ministry of Defence, 1982–84; *b* 29 April 1925; *s* of late Peter Johnston and Barbara Johnston (*née* Gifford); *m* 1949, Irene Blackburn; two *d. Educ:* George Heriot's Sch., Edinburgh; Edinburgh Univ. (BSc Eng); Imperial Coll., London (DIC Aeronautics). D. Napier & Sons, 1945–46; National Gas Turbine Estabt, 1947–64; Ramjet Project Officer, Min. of Aviation, 1964–66; Exchange Officer to Wright Patterson Air Force Base, Ohio, 1966–68; Asst Dir (Engine Develt), Min. of Technology, 1968–70; Dep. Dir, National Gas Turbine Estabt, 1970–73; Ministry of Defence: Dir-Gen., Multi-Role Combat Aircraft, (PE), 1973–76; Dir, Mil. Vehicles and Engrg Estabt, 1976–78; Dep. Controller, Estabts and Res. B, and Chief Scientist (Army), 1978–80; Dep. Controller, Estabt Resources and Personnel, MoD, 1980–82. *Publications:* papers on turbine research in Aeronautical Research Council Reports and Memoranda Series. *Recreations:* golf, bridge. *Died 13 Sept. 2001.*

JOHNSTON, Sir John (Baines), GCMG 1978 (KCMG 1966; CMG 1962); KCVO 1972; HM Diplomatic Service, retired; *b* 13 May 1918; *e s* of late Rev. A. S. Johnston, Banbury, Oxon; *m* 1969, Elizabeth Mary (*d* 2004), *d* of late J. F. Crace; one *s. Educ:* Banbury Grammar Sch.; Queen's Coll., Oxford (Eglesfield Scholar). Served War, 1940–46: Adjt 1st Bn Gordon Highlanders, 1944; DAQMG HQ 30 Corps District, 1945. Asst Principal, Colonial Office, 1947; Principal, 1948; Asst Sec., West African Council, Accra, 1950–51; UK Liaison Officer with Commission for Technical Co-operation in Africa South of the Sahara, 1952; Principal Private Sec. to Sec. of State for the Colonies, 1953; Asst Sec., 1956; Head of Far Eastern Dept, Colonial Office, 1956; transferred to Commonwealth Relations Office, 1957; Dep. High Commissioner in S Africa, 1959–61; British High Commissioner: in Sierra Leone, 1961–63; in the Federation of Rhodesia and Nyasaland, 1963, Rhodesia, 1964–65; Asst, later Dep. Under-Secretary of State, FCO, 1968–71; British High Commissioner: in Malaysia, 1971–74; in Canada, 1974–78. A Governor, BBC, 1978–85. Chm., ARELS Exams Trust, 1982–94. Mem., Disasters Emergency Cttee, 1985–92. *Address:* 5 Victoria Road, Oxford OX2 7QF. *T:* (01865) 556927. *Died 16 Oct. 2005.*

JOHNSTON, Margaret; *see* Parker, M. A. McC. J.

JOHNSTON, Robert Smith; *see* Kincraig, Hon. Lord.

JOHNSTON, Very Rev. William Bryce; Minister of Colinton Parish Church, Edinburgh, 1964–91; an Extra Chaplain to the Queen in Scotland, since 1991 (Chaplain-in-Ordinary, 1981–91); *b* 16 Sept. 1921; *s* of William Bryce Johnston and Isabel Winifred Highley; *m* 1947, Ruth Margaret, *d* of Rev. James Arthur Cowley, ISO; one *s* two *d. Educ:* George Watson's Coll., Edinburgh; Edinburgh Univ. (MA Hons Classics 1942); New Coll., Edinburgh (BD (Dist.) 1945). Ordained as Chaplain to HM Forces, 1945; served in Germany and as Staff Chaplain, PoW Directorate, War Office, 1945–48; Minister: St Andrew's, Bo'ness, 1949; St George's, Greenock, 1955. Moderator of General Assembly of Church of Scotland, 1980–81. Convener: Board of St Colm's Coll., 1966–70; General Assembly: Cttee on Adult Educn, 1970; Church and Nation Cttee, 1972; Inter-Church Relations Cttee, 1978; Cttee on Role of Men and

Women, 1976; Chm., Judicial Commn, 1988–93. Mem., British Council of Churches, 1970–90 (Chm., Exec. Cttee, 1981–84); Delegate to 5th Assembly of World Council of Churches, 1975. Cunningham Lectr, New Coll., 1968–71; Vis. Lectr in Social Ethics, Heriot-Watt Univ., 1966–88. Mem., Broadcasting Council for Scotland, 1983–87. Pres., Edinburgh Rotary Club, 1975–76; Paul Harris Fellow, 2003. Trustee, Scottish Nat. War Memorial, 1981–94. Hon. DD Aberdeen, 1980; Hon. DLitt Heriot-Watt, 1989. *Publications:* (jtly) Devolution and the British Churches, 1978; (ed) Davies, Ethics and Defence, 1986; *translations:* K. Barth, Church Dogmatics, vol. 2, 1955; Calvin, Commentaries on Hebrews, 1 Peter, 1960; various Bible study pamphlets and theological articles for SCM, Scottish Jl of Theology. *Recreations:* organ music, bowls. *Address:* 15 Elliot Road, Edinburgh EH14 1DU. *T:* (0131) 441 3387. *Club:* New (Edinburgh). *Died 22 May 2005.*

JOHNSTONE, Michael Anthony Harry; a District Judge (Magistrates' Courts) (formerly Metropolitan Stipendiary Magistrate), 1980–2001; *b* 12 June 1936; *s* of late Thomas Johnstone and Violet Johnstone. *Educ:* St Edmund's College, Ware. Called to the Bar, Inner Temple, 1968; formerly Solicitor of the Supreme Court, admitted 1960; former Dep. Circuit Judge. Member: Soc. for Nautical Res.; Navy Records Soc.; Army Records Soc. Mem., Campaign for Real Ale. *Recreations:* real ale (weight permitting), the study and collection of books on military and naval history. *Address:* c/o Highbury Corner Magistrates' Court, 51 Holloway Road, N7 8JA. *Died 10 Oct. 2001.*

JOHNSTONE, William, CBE 1981; *b* 26 Dec. 1915; *s* of late David Grierson Johnstone and Jessie Lang Johnstone (*née* Malcolm); *m* 1942, Mary Rosamund Rowden; one *s* two *d*. *Educ:* Dalry High Sch.; Glasgow Univ. (BSc (Agric)). NDA, NDD. Technical Officer, Overseas Dept of Deutches Kalisyndikat, Berlin, 1938–39; joined ICI, 1940; seconded to County War Agricl Exec. Cttees in SE England on food prodn campaigns, 1940–45; Reg. Sales Management, ICI, 1950–61; Commercial Dir, Plant Protection Ltd, 1961–63; Man. Dir, 1963–73; Dir, ICI Billingham/Agricl Div., 1961–73; Dep. Chm., ICI Plant Protection Div., 1974–77. Chm. Subsid. Cos: Solplant (Italy), 1967–73; Sopra (France), 1971–75; Zeltia Agraria (Spain), 1976–77; Vis. Dir, ICI (United States) Inc., 1974–77; retd from ICI, 1977. Chairman: Meat and Livestock Commn, 1977–80; British Agricl Export Council, 1977–84; Member: European Trade Cttee, BOTB, 1982–85; Sino-British Trade Council, 1983–85. *Address:* The Long House, Oxenbourne Farm, East Meon, Petersfield, Hants GU32 1QL. *T:* (01730) 823216. *Club:* Farmers'. *Died 19 Nov. 2005.*

JONES, Prof. Albert Stanley, PhD; DSc; Professor of Chemistry, University of Birmingham, 1969–87, then Emeritus; *b* 30 April 1925; *s* of Albert Ernest Jones and Florence Jones (*née* Rathbone); *m* 1st, 1950, Joan Christine Gregg (*d* 1992); one *s* one *d*; 2nd, 1996, Rev. Gillian Linda Gibson, BEd. *Educ:* Waverley Grammar Sch.; Univ. of Birmingham (BSc (1st Cl. Hons) 1944, PhD 1947, DSc 1957). Beit Meml Fellow for Medical Res., 1949–52; University of Birmingham: Lectr in Chemistry, 1952–61; Sen. Lectr, 1961–63; Reader in Organic Chemistry, 1963–69. Chemical Society London: Birmingham Rep., 1959–62; Mem. Council, 1966–69; Chm., Nucleotide Group, 1967–72. *Publications:* 183 papers, incl. three review articles, in scientific jls, on various aspects of organic chemistry and biological chemistry, particularly concerning nucleic acid derivatives. *Recreations:* church activities, walking, music, reading. *Address:* Waverley, 76 Manor House Lane, Yardley, Birmingham B26 1PR. *T:* (0121) 743 2030. *Died 6 Jan. 2003.*

JONES, Rt Hon. Aubrey; PC 1955; Director: Thomas Tilling Ltd, 1970–82; Cornhill Insurance Company Ltd,

1971–82 (Chairman, 1971–74); *b* 20 Nov. 1911; *s* of Evan and Margaret Aubrey Jones, Merthyr Tydfil; *m* 1948, Joan, *d* of G. Godfrey-Isaacs, Ridgehanger, Hillcrest Road, Hanger Hill, W5; two *s*. *Educ:* Cyfarthfa Castle Secondary Sch., Merthyr Tydfil; London School of Economics (BSc (Econ.) 1st Cl. Hons 1933, Gladstone Memorial Prizewinner; Hon. Fellow, 1959). Gerstenberg Post-grad. Schol., LSE. On foreign and editorial staffs of The Times, 1937–39 and 1947–48. Joined British Iron and Steel Federation, 1949; General Dir, June-Dec. 1955. Served War of 1939–45, Army Intelligence Staff, War Office and Mediterranean Theatre, 1940–46. Contested (C): SE Essex, 1945; Heywood and Radcliffe (by-election), 1946. MP (U) Birmingham, Hall Green, 1950–65; PPS to Minister of State for Economic Affairs, 1952, and to Minister of Materials, 1953; Minister of Fuel and Power, Dec. 1955–Jan. 1957; Minister of Supply, 1957–Oct. 1959. Joined Liberal Party, 1981. Chairman: Staveley Industries Ltd, 1964–65 (Dir, 1962–65); Laporte Industries (Holdings) Ltd, 1970–72; Director: Guest, Keen & Nettlefolds Steel Co. Ltd, 1960–65; Courtaulds Ltd, 1960–63; Black & Decker, 1977–81. Chm., Nat. Bd for Prices and Incomes, 1965–70; Vice-Pres., Consumers' Assoc., 1967–72. Mem., Plowden Cttee of Inquiry into Aircraft Industry, 1965–66. Leading consultant to: Nigerian Public Service Commn, 1973–74; Iranian Govt, 1974–78; Plessey Ltd, 1978–80. Mem. Panel of Conciliators, Internat. Centre for Settlement of Investment Disputes, 1974–81. Pres., Oxford Energy Policy Club, 1976–88. Regent Lectr, Univ. of California at Berkeley, 1968. Visiting Fellow: New Coll., Oxford, 1978; Sci. Policy Res. Unit, Univ. of Sussex, 1986–, Hon. Fellow, 1993; Sen. Res. Associate, St Antony's Coll., Oxford, 1979–82; Guest Scholar, Brookings Instn, Washington, DC, 1982. Fellow Commoner, Churchill Coll., Cambridge, 1972 and 1982–86. Mem., Court of Governors, LSE, 1964–87. Hon. DSc Bath, 1968. Winston Churchill Meml Trust Award, 1985. *Publications:* The Pendulum of Politics, 1946; Industrial Order, 1950; The New Inflation: the politics of prices and incomes, 1973; (ed) Economics and Equality, 1976; (contrib.) My LSE, 1977; (contrib.) The End of the Keynesian Era, 1977; Oil: the missed opportunity, 1981; Britain's Economy: the roots of stagnation, 1985. *Address:* Arnen, 120 Limmer Lane, Felpham, Bognor Regis, West Sussex PO22 7LP. *T:* (01243) 582722. *Died 10 April 2003.*

JONES, Clement; *see* Jones, John C.

JONES, Rt Rev. Derwyn Dixon, DD; Bishop of Huron, 1984–90; *b* 5 Aug. 1925; *s* of Rev. Walter Jones, DD, and Mary Rosalie Jones (*née* Dixon); *m* 1960, Arline Carole Dilamarter; one *s* one *d*. *Educ:* Univ. of Western Ontario (BA); Huron College (LTh, DD). Deacon 1946, priest 1947; Curate: Holy Trinity, Winnipeg, 1946–48; All Saints', Windsor, 1948–49; Rector, St Andrew's, Kitchener, 1949–52; Asst Rector, St Paul's Cathedral, London, Ont, 1952–55; Rector: Canon Davis Memorial Church, Sarnia, 1955–58; St Barnabas, Windsor, 1958–66; St Peter's, Brockville, 1966–69; St James, Westminster, London, Ont, 1969–82; Archdeacon of Middlesex, 1978–82; Suffragan Bishop of Huron, 1982; Coadjutor Bishop, 1983. *Recreation:* music. *Address:* 3–515 Proudfoot Lane, London, ON N6H 5N9, Canada. *T:* (519) 6575068. *Club:* London (London, Ont). *Died 8 March 2005.*

JONES, Rev. Prof. Douglas Rawlinson; Lightfoot Professor of Divinity, University of Durham, 1964–85, then Emeritus; Residentiary Canon of Durham Cathedral, 1964–85, then Emeritus; *b* 11 Nov. 1919; *s* of Percival and Charlotte Elizabeth Jones; *m* 1946, Hazel Mary Passmore (*d* 2005); three *s* two *d*. *Educ:* Queen Elizabeth's Hosp., Bristol; St Edmund Hall, Oxford (Squire Scholar, 1938; BA 1941; MA 1945); Wycliffe Hall, Oxford. Ordained deacon, 1942, priest, 1943; Curate of St Michael and All Angels, Windmill Hill, Bristol, 1942–45; Lectr, Wycliffe

Hall, Oxford, 1945–50; Chaplain, Wadham Coll., Oxford, 1945–50; Lectr in Divinity, 1948–50; University of Durham: Lectr, 1951; Sen. Lectr, 1963. Mem., Gen. Synod of C of E, 1970–80 and 1982–85. Chairman of the Liturgical Commn, 1981–86. DD Lambeth, 1985. *Publications:* Haggai, Zechariah and Malachi, 1962; Isaiah, 56–66 and Joel, 1964; Instrument of Peace, 1965; Jeremiah, 1992; contrib. to: Peake's Commentary on the Bible, 1962; Hastings' Dictionary of the Bible, 1963; The Cambridge History of the Bible, 1963; Thomas Cranmer, 1990; Sacrifice and Redemption, 1991; articles in Jl of Theolog. Studies, Zeitschrift für die Alttestamentliche Wissenschaft, Vetus Testamentum, Theology, Scottish Jl of Theology. *Recreation:* carpentry. *Address:* Whitefriars, Kings Road, Longniddry, E Lothian EH32 0NN. *T:* (01875) 852149.   *Died 24 Nov. 2005.*

JONES, Eric S.; *see* Somerset Jones.

JONES, Ewan Perrins W.; *see* Wallis-Jones.

JONES, Sir Ewart (Ray Herbert), Kt 1963; DSc, PhD; FRS 1950; FRSC; Waynflete Professor of Chemistry, University of Oxford, 1955–78, then Emeritus; Fellow of Magdalen College, 1955–78, Hon. Fellow, 1978; *b* Wrexham, Denbighshire, 16 March 1911; *m* 1937, Frances Mary Copp (*d* 1999); one *s* two *d*. *Educ:* Grove Park Sch., Wrexham; UCNW, Bangor; Univ. of Manchester (DSc); PhD Wales; MA Oxon. Fellow of Univ. of Wales, 1935–37; Lecturer, Imperial Coll. of Science and Technology, 1938 (FIC 1967); Reader in Organic Chemistry, Univ. of London, and Asst Prof., 1945; Sir Samuel Hall Prof. of Chemistry, Manchester Univ., 1947–55. Arthur D. Little Visiting Prof. of Chemistry, MIT, 1952; Karl Folkers Lectr at Univs of Illinois and Wisconsin, 1957; Andrews Lectr, Univ. of NSW, 1960. Mem. Council for Scientific and Industrial Research, and Chm., Research Grants Cttee, 1961–65; Mem. SRC and Chm., Univ. Science and Technology Bd, 1965–69; Mem., Science Bd, 1969–72. Chemical Society: Tilden Lectr, 1949; Pedler Lectr, 1959; Robert Robinson Lectr, 1978; Dalton Lectr, 1985; Award for Service to the Society, 1973; Award in Natural Product Chem., 1974. President: Chemical Soc., 1964–66; RIC, 1970–72 (Chm., Chem. Soc./RIC Unification Cttee, 1975–80); Royal Soc. of Chemistry, 1980–82 (Millennium Fellow, 2000). Foreign Mem. Amer. Acad. of Arts and Sciences, 1967. Chm., Anchor and Guardian Housing Assocs, 1979–84. Hon. DSc: Birmingham, 1965; Nottingham, 1966; New South Wales, 1967; Sussex, 1969; Salford, 1971; Wales, 1971; East Anglia, 1978; Ulster, 1978; Hon. LLD Manchester, 1972. Meldola Medal, RIC, 1940; Fritzsche Award, Amer. Chem. Soc., 1962; Davy Medal, Royal Soc., 1966. *Publications:* scientific papers in Jl Chem. Soc. *Address:* 6 Sandy Lane, Yarnton, Kidlington, Oxon OX5 1PB. *T:* (01865) 372581.   *Died 7 May 2002.*

JONES, Francis John; Chairman, Telford Development Corporation, 1987–91; Chairman, Shropshire Health Authority, 1979–90; *b* 28 June 1928; *s* of John Francis and Mary Emma Jones; *m* 1st, 1953, Angela Mary Kelly (marr. diss.); one *s* one *d*; 2nd, 1970, Jean Elsie Sansome; two step *s* two step *d*. *Educ:* Manchester Grammar Sch.; Manchester Univ. Various marketing and sales positions; West African Colonies, 1950–52; Proctor & Gamble, 1952–54; Beecham Group, 1954–57; Crosse & Blackwell/Nestlé, 1957–64; W. Symington, 1964–69; Chm., Telford Foods, 1970–84, retired. *Recreations:* reading, music, opera. *Address:* 2 Swan Hill Gardens, Shrewsbury SY1 1NT. *T:* (01743) 362159.   *Died 8 Dec. 2005.*

JONES, Geoffrey Rippon R.; *see* Rees-Jones.

JONES, George Briscoe, CBE 1988; Director: Job Ownership Ltd, 1983–95; Partnership in Business Ltd, 1988–95; *b* 1 June 1929; *s* of late Arthur Briscoe Jones and Mary Alexandra Jones (née Taylor); *m* 1955, Audrey

Patricia Kendrick (*d* 1999); two *d*. *Educ:* Wallasey and Caldy Grammar Schools. Army, 1947–49; Unilever, 1949–84 (on secondment to CDA, 1982–84); Dir, BOCM Silcocks, 1974–82; Chm., Unitrition, 1977–82; Director: Co-op. Develt Agency, 1982–90; Chrisamer Ltd, 1989–93. Mem., Plunkett Foundn, 1985–92. Governor: QMW, 1993–95; Fort Hill Sch., 1993–95. *Recreations:* painting, sculpture, chess, bridge. *Address:* 32 Cleveland Drive, Little Sutton, South Wirral, Cheshire CH66 4XY.   *Died 20 March 2003.*

JONES, Rt Rev. Haydn Harold; Bishop of Venezuela, 1976–86; actor in films, television soap operas and commercials, for Venezuelan and international film companies, 1985–98; *b* 22 Aug. 1920; *s* of Charles Samuel and Blodwen Jones (née Williams), Penarth, Glam. *Educ:* Ordination training, Brotherhood of Saint Paul, Barton, Yorks. Served War of 1939–45, RAF, 1941–44. Ordained deacon 1947, priest 1948, Diocese of Bradford; Curate of St Barnabas, Heaton, Bradford, 1947–49; Tor Mohun, Torquay, 1949–51; Chaplain RN, 1951–53; Licence to Officiate, Diocese of London, 1954–62, Diocese of Coventry, 1962–63; Curate of St Peter's, Coventry, 1963–64; Rector of Clutton, Diocese of Bath and Wells, 1964–76, with Cameley, 1975–76; Surrogate, 1972–76; Dean of St Mary's Cathedral, Caracas, 1976–85. *Recreations:* formerly tennis (rep. RN 1952), bridge, films, theatre. *Address:* College of St Barnabas, Blackberry Lane, Lingfield, Surrey RH7 6NJ. *T:* (01342) 870107.
                          Died 16 June 2002.

JONES, Henry Arthur, CBE 1974; Vaughan Professor of Education, 1967–81, then Emeritus, Head of the Department of Adult Education, 1967–78, Pro-Vice-Chancellor, 1978–81, University of Leicester; *b* 7 March 1917; *er s* of Henry Lloyd Jones; *m* 1st, 1942, Molly (*d* 1971), 4th *d* of Richard Shenton; two *s*; 2nd, 1972, Nancy Winifred (née Cox), *widow* of Lt R. B. B. Jack, RN. *Educ:* Chorlton Grammar Sch.; Manchester Univ. (George Gissing Prizeman, 1936; Graduate Research Fellow, 1937, MA 1938). Served War of 1939–45 with Lancs Fusiliers and DLI, 1940–42. Sen. English Master, Chorlton Grammar Sch., 1942–47; Resident Staff Tutor, Manchester Univ., 1947–49; Asst Dir of Extra-Mural Studies, Liverpool Univ., 1949–52, Dep. Dir 1953–57; Principal, The City Literary Institute, 1957–67. Chairman: Assoc. for Adult Education, 1964–67; Adult Educn Cttee, IBA, 1973–77; Vice-Pres., Nat. Inst. of Adult Education (Exec. Chm., 1976–84); Member: Library Adv. Council, DES, 1965–68; Sec. of State's Cttee on Adult Educn, DES, 1968–72; Adv. Council for Adult and Continuing Educn, DES, 1977–83. Chm., Leics Consultative Cttee for Voluntary Orgns, 1974–77. Hon. Life Mem., Educnl Centres Assoc.; Vice-Pres., Pre-retirement Assoc. Editor: Vaughan Papers in Educn, 1967–82; Studies in Adult Education, 1974–82. *Publications:* Adult Literacy: a study of the impact, 1978; The Concept of Success in Adult Literacy, 1978; Adult Literacy: the UK experience, 1978; Education and Disadvantage, 1978; Stage by Stage, 1993; Great Bowden: a village and its people, 1999. *Address:* Stokes House, Great Bowden, Market Harborough, Leics LE16 7HF. *T:* (01858) 462846.   *Died 14 April 2002.*

JONES, Rt Rev. Hywel James; Bishop of British Columbia, 1980–84; *b* Wales, 4 March 1918; *s* of Ifor James and Ann Jones; *m* 1946, (Dorothy) Margaret Wilcox (*d* 1985); one *s* one *d*. *Educ:* Emmanuel Coll., Univ. of Saskatchewan (LTh). Deacon, then priest, 1942; Curate, Tofield, 1942; travelling priest, 1942–44; Incumbent of Parksville–Qualicum Beach, 1944–47; Colwood–Langford, 1947–56; Rector, St Mary the Virgin, Oak Bay, 1956–80. Hon. Canon of BC, 1959–68; Archdeacon of Quatsino, 1968–71, of Victoria, 1971–77; Archdeacon Emeritus, 1977–80. DD (*hc*) Emmanuel Coll., Univ. of Saskatchewan, 1980. *Recreations:* reading, music, gardening. *Address:* 2028 Frederick Norris Road, Victoria,

BC V8P 2B2, Canada. *T:* (250) 5927658. *Club:* Union (Victoria, BC).   *Died 23 April 2003.*

JONES, Ilston Percival Ll.; *see* Llewellyn-Jones.

JONES, (John) Clement, CBE 1972; writer, broadcaster, technical adviser to developing countries; *b* 22 June 1915; *o s* of Clement Daniel Jones; *m* 1939, Marjorie (*d* 1991), *d* of George Gibson, Llandrindod Wells; three *s. Educ:* Ardwyn, Aberystwyth; BA (Hons) Open Univ., 1983. Various journalistic positions; Express and Star, Wolverhampton: News Editor, 1955; Editor, 1960–71; Editorial Dir, 1971–74; Exec. Dir, Beacon Broadcasting, Wolverhampton, 1974–83. Pres., Guild of British Newspaper Editors, 1966–67, Hon. Life Vice-Pres., 1972 (Hon. Fellow, 1997). Member: Press Council, 1965–74; Adv. Bd, Thomson Foundn, 1965–87; BBC W Midlands Adv. Council, 1971–75; (part-time) Monopolies and Mergers Commn (Newspaper Panel), 1973–86; W Midlands Arts Assoc., 1973–78; Exec. Cttee, Soc. Internat. Develt, 1974–78; Vice Chm., Lichfield Dio. Media Council, 1976–82; Mem. Council, and Chm. Press Freedom Cttee, Commonwealth Press Union, 1975–80; Chm., Media Panel, Commn for Racial Equality, 1981–84. Vice-Chm., British Human Rights Trust, 1975–78. Governor, British Inst. Human Rights, 1971–82. Mem. Senate, Open Univ., 1983–86. Founder Mem., Circle of Wine Writers, 1966. Pres., Staffordshire Soc., 1971–74. Founder and Pres., Frinton and Walton Heritage Trust, 1984–. FRSA 1970. *Publications:* UNESCO World Survey of Media Councils and Codes of Ethics, 1976; Racism and Fascism, 1981; Race and the Media: thirty years on, 1982; A History of the First Fifty Years of the Guild of Editors, 1995; pamphlets on local history, NE Anglia. *Recreations:* travel, gardening. *Address:* Sandy Cross, Ridgeway Road, Dorking, Surrey RH4 3AY. *T:* (01306) 877691; *e-mail:* clement.jones@ btopenworld.com. *Club:* Athenæum.

         Died 5 Nov. 2002.

JONES, Sir Kenneth (George Illtyd), Kt 1974; a Judge of the High Court, Queen's Bench Division, 1974–89; *b* 26 May 1921; *s* of late Richard Arthur Jones and Olive Jane Jones, Radyr, Cardiff; *m* 1st, 1947, Dulcie (*d* 1977); one *s* two *d*; 2nd, 1978, June Patricia (prev. marr. diss.), *o d* of late Leslie Arthur and Winifred Doxey, Harrogate. *Educ:* Brigg Grammar Sch.; University Coll., Oxford (1939–41, 1945–46), MA. Treas., Oxford Union Society, 1941. Served in Shropshire Yeo. (76th Medium Regt RA), 1942–45; Staff Captain, HQ 13th Corps, 1945 (despatches). Called to Bar, Gray's Inn, 1946; joined Oxford Circuit, 1947; QC 1962; Mem. Gen. Council of the Bar, 1961–65, 1968–69; Bencher, 1969, Treas., 1987, Gray's Inn. Recorder of: Shrewsbury, 1964–66; Wolverhampton, 1966–71; the Crown Court, 1972; Dep. Chm., Herefordshire QS, 1961–71; a Circuit Judge, 1972–73. Dep. Chm., Boundary Commn for Wales, 1984–88. *Recreations:* theatre, opera, travel, sculpture, woodcarving, fishing. *Address:* 7 Radnor Close, Henley-on-Thames, Oxon RG9 2DA.   *Died 12 July 2004.*

JONES, Lewis C.; *see* Carter-Jones.

JONES, Penry; Chief Assistant (Television) (formerly Deputy Head of Programme Services), IBA (formerly ITA), 1971–82, retired; *b* 18 Aug. 1922; *s* of Joseph William and Edith Jones; *m* Beryl Joan Priestley; two *d. Educ:* Rock Ferry High Sch.; Liverpool Univ. Gen. Sec., YMCA, Altrincham, 1940; Sec., SCM, Southern Univs, 1945; Industrial Sec., Iona Community, 1948; Religious Programmes Producer, ABC Television, 1958; Religious Programmes Officer of ITA, 1964; Head of Religious Broadcasting, BBC, 1967. Chm., Dept of Communication, WCC, 1968–75. Chm., Iona Heritage Trust, 1997–. *Recreations:* hill-walking, swimming, watching Rugby football. *Address:* Erraid House, Isle of

Iona, Argyll PA76 6SJ. *T:* (01681) 700448.

         Died 25 Jan. 2004.

JONES, Rachel Marianne; National Governor for Wales of BBC, and Chairman of Broadcasting Council for Wales, 1960–65; *b* 4 Aug. 1908; *d* of John Powell Jones Powell, solicitor, Brecon, and Kathleen Mamie Powell; *m* 1935, Very Rev. William Edward Jones (*d* 1974); one *s* three *d. Educ:* Princess Helena Coll.; Bedford Coll., University of London. Subwarden, Time and Talents Settlement, Bermondsey, 1931–32. Member: Bd of Governors, Fairbridge Farm Sch., Western Australia, 1945–49; Council for Wales and Mon, 1959–66; Governing Body of the Church in Wales, 1953–78; Court and Council of Nat. Museum of Wales, 1962–78; St Fagan's Welsh Folk Museum Cttee, 1978–83; Pres., St David's Diocesan Mothers' Union, 1965–70. *Recreations:* music, gardening.

         Died 19 March 2001.

JONES, Air Vice-Marshal Rhys Tudor Brackley, CB 1990; FRCS; Senior Consultant, Royal Air Force Medical Branch, 1988–90; *b* 16 Nov. 1925; *s* of Sir Edgar Rees Jones, KBE and Lilian May Jones; *m* 1953, Irene Lilian, *d* of late Peter Valentine Spain Gammon; two *s. Educ:* King's Coll. Sch., Wimbledon; St Mary's Hosp., London (qualified 1950). House Surgeon to Mr Dickson-Wright and J. C. Goligher; joined RAF, 1952; Specialist in Surgery; Consultant, 1964; Hosp. service, Aden, Singapore, Germany, as gen. surgeon, special interest oncology; Hon. Consultant, Westminster Hosp., 1982; Cade Prof., RCS, 1981; Consultant Adviser in Surgery, 1982; Dean of Air Force Medicine, 1987. QHS, 1987–90. CStJ 1986. Lady Cade Medal, RCS, 1988. *Publications:* contribs to learned jls. *Address:* Westfield, Common Lane, Bale, near Fakenham, Norfolk NR21 0QD. *Club:* Royal Air Force.   *Died 8 Dec. 2003.*

JONES, Robert Gwilym L.; *see* Lewis-Jones.

JONES, R(obin) Huws, CBE 1969; Associate Director, Joseph Rowntree Memorial Trust, 1972–76, Consultant, 1976–78; *b* 1 May 1909; *s* of Edward Jones; *m* 1944, Enid Mary Horton; one *s* two *d. Educ:* Liverpool Univ. Lectr, Social Science Dept, Liverpool Univ., 1937–39; Staff Tutor (City of Lincoln) Oxford Univ. Extra-mural Delegacy, 1939–47; Dir of Social Science Courses, University Coll., Swansea, 1948–61; Principal, Nat. Inst. for Social Work Training, 1961–72. Visiting Prof., University of Minnesota, 1964; Heath Clark Lectr, University of London, 1969. Member: Cttee on Local Authority and Allied Personal Social Services, 1965–68; NE Metropolitan Regl Hosp. Bd, 1967–72; Chief Scientist's Cttee, DHSS, 1971–77; Scientific Advr to DHSS and to Welsh Office, 1977–82. Mem., Ciba Foundn Cttee on Compensation in Biomedical Research, 1979–80. Pres., Internat. Assoc. of Schools of Social Work, 1976–80. Founder Mem., Swansea Valley Project Cttee, 1961. Hon. Fellow, UC Swansea, 1986. Hon. LLD Wales, 1982. Frances Wood Prizeman, Royal Statistical Society. *Publications:* The Doctor and the Social Services, 1971; contributions to journals. *Address:* 46 Lucombe Way, Hartrigg Oaks, New Earswick YO32 4DS. *T:* (01904) 750763.   *Died 16 June 2001.*

JONES, Group Captain Royden Anthony; RAF retired; Regional Chairman of Industrial Tribunals, London (Central) Region, 1975–86; *b* 11 June 1925; *s* of Daniel Richard Glyndwr Jones and Hilda Margaret Jones (*née* Carruthers); *m* 1st, 1948, Krystyna Emilia Kumor (decd); one *s*; 2nd, 1955, Peggy Elizabeth Martin; one *s. Educ:* Torquay Grammar Sch. Trooper, Household Cavalry, 1943; RMC, Sandhurst, 1944; Captain, Arab Legion armoured car squadron, 1945–48. Qualified as solicitor, 1949; joined RAF Legal Services as prosecuting officer, 1950; RAF Staff Coll., 1961; served as Dep. Dir of Legal Services (RAF), in Cyprus and Germany, retiring as Gp Captain, 1975. *Publication:* Manual of Law for Kenya

Armed Forces, 1971. *Recreations:* country pursuits, reading, house maintenance, photography. *Address:* Hill Top House, Staunton Harold, Ashby-de-la-Zouch, Leics LE65 1RW. *T:* (01332) 862583. *Club:* Royal Air Force.

Died 3 Jan. 2005.

JONES, Most Rev. Walter Heath; Archbishop and Metropolitan of Rupert's Land, 1987–94; *b* 25 Dec. 1928; *s* of Harry Heath Jones and Anne Grace Evelyn Jones (*née* Stoddart); *m* 1951, L. Marilyn Jones (*née* Lunney); one *s* three *d*. *Educ:* Univ. of Manitoba (BA); St John's Coll. (LTh); Nashotah House (STM). Received into Episcopal Church of USA, 1958; Rector, St Mary's Church, Mitchell, S Dak, 1958–62; Vice-Pres. of Chapter, 1962–67; Dean of Calvary Cathedral, Sioux Falls, S Dak, 1968–70; Bishop of South Dakota, Sioux Falls, 1970–83; Bishop of Rupert's Land, 1983. Chancellor, St John's Coll., 1983–94 (Hon. Fellow, 1993). Hon. DD: St John's Coll., 1970; Nashotah House; Trinity Coll., 1990. Hon. Citizen of St Boniface, 1966; Bush Fellow, 1978. *Address:* 3782 Olympic Court, Rapid City, SD 57702, USA. *T:* (605) 3990921. *Died 22 March 2003.*

JONES-WILLIAMS, Dafydd Wyn, OBE 1970; MC 1942; TD 1954; DL; Commissioner for Local Administration for Wales (Local Ombudsman), 1974–79; *b* 13 July 1916; *s* of late J. Jones-Williams, Dolgellau; *m* 1945, Rosemary Sally, *e d* of late A. E. Councell, Blaenau Hall, Rhydymain; two *d*. *Educ:* Dolgellau Grammar Sch.; UCW Aberystwyth (LLB). Served 1939–45 with HAC and X Royal Hussars (Western Desert). Formerly comdg 446 (Royal Welch) AB, LAA Regt, RA (TA). Solicitor, 1939. Clerk of County Council, Clerk of Peace, and Clerk to Lieutenancy, Merioneth, 1954–70; Circuit Administrator, Wales and Chester Circuit, 1970–74. Member: Hughes-Parry Cttee on Legal Status of Welsh Language, 1963–65; Lord Chancellor's Adv. Cttee on Trng of Magistrates, 1974–81; Council on Tribunals, 1980–86; BBC Gen. Adv. Council, 1979–85. Formerly: Mem., Nature Conservancy (Chm., Cttee for Wales); Mem., Nat. Broadcasting Council for Wales; Chm., Merioneth and Montgomeryshire T&AFA. DL Merioneth, 1958. *Recreations:* golf, snooker, reading. *Address:* Bennar, Felin Isaf, Dolgellau, Gwynedd LL40 1ES. *T:* (01341) 422303. *Club:* Royal St Davids Golf. *Died 24 Dec. 2005.*

JORDAN, Francis Leo, (Frank), CBE 1989; QPM 1982; Chief Constable of Kent, 1982–89; *b* 15 June 1930; *s* of Leo Thomas and Mary Jordan; *m* 1951, Ruth Ashmore; one *s* two *d*. *Educ:* St Joseph's Coll., Trent Vale, Stoke-on-Trent. Staffordshire Police to rank of Chief Supt, 1950; seconded to Cyprus Police during EOKA emergency, 1956–58; Sen. Course in Criminology, Cambridge Univ., 1972; Sen. Comd Course, Police Staff Coll., 1973; Staff Officer to Home Office Police Inspectorate, 1975; Asst Chief Constable, West Midlands Police, 1976; Dep. Chief Constable of Kent, 1979. Mem., Parole Bd, 1990–93. Mem., Kent County Cttee, SSAFA, 1985–89. CBIM. FRSA 1990. OStJ 1988. *Recreations:* walking, old buildings, churches, etc, travel. *Club:* Royal Over-Seas League. *Died 17 Dec. 2002.*

JOSS, William Hay; a Recorder of the Crown Court, 1982–96; *b* 20 May 1927; *s* of William Taylor Barron Joss and Elizabeth Lindsay Lillie Joss; *m* 1961, Rosemary Sarah Joss; two *s*. *Educ:* Worksop Coll., Notts; Exeter Coll., Oxon (BA Jurisprudence). Served Army, commissioned into 14th/20th King's Hussars, 1945–48. Industry, production management, 1950–62; called to the Bar, Gray's Inn, 1957; practising barrister, 1962–96. *Recreations:* golf, music, literature. *Address:* 49 Village Road, Clifton Village, Nottingham NG11 8NP. *T:* (0115) 921 1894. *Club:* Nottingham and Notts United Services.

Died 29 Oct. 2004.

JOWETT, Very Rev. Alfred, CBE 1972; Dean of Manchester, 1964–83; *b* 29 May 1914; *s* of Alfred Edmund Jowett; *m* 1939, Margaret, *d* of St Clair Benford; one *s* three *d*. *Educ:* High Storrs Grammar Sch., Sheffield; St Catharine's Coll., Cambridge; Lincoln Theological Coll. BA 1935; Certif. Educn 1936; MA 1959. Deacon 1944; Priest 1945. Curate of St John the Evangelist, Goole, 1944–47; Sec., Sheffield Anglican and Free Church Council and Marriage Guidance Council, 1947–51; Vicar of St George with St Stephen, Sheffield, 1951–60; Part-time Lecturer, Sheffield Univ. Dept of Education, 1950–60; Vicar of Doncaster, 1960–64; Hon. Canon of Sheffield Cathedral, 1960–64. Select Preacher, Oxford Univ., 1964 and 1979. Mem., Community Relations Commn, 1968–77 (Dep. Chm., 1972–77). A Church Comr, 1978–80. Hon. Fellow, Manchester Polytechnic, 1972. OStJ 1979. Hon. LittD Sheffield, 1982. Hon. Freeman, City of Manchester, 1984. *Publication:* (part-author) The English Church: a New Look, 1966. *Recreation:* living with disablement by reading theology and fiction (ancient and modern). *Address:* 37 Stone Delf, Sheffield S10 3QX. *T:* (0114) 230 5455.

Died 28 July 2004.

JOY, Thomas Alfred, LVO 1979; President, Hatchards Ltd, 1985 (Managing Director, 1965–85); *b* 30 Dec. 1904; *s* of Alfred Joy and Annie Carpenter; *m* 1932, Edith Ellis. *Educ:* privately; Bedford House Sch., Oxford. Jun. Assistant, Bodleian Library, Oxford, 1919; indentured apprentice, 1919–25, buyer and cataloguer, 1925–35, J. Thornton & Son, University Booksellers, Oxford; Manager, Circulating Library, 1935–45, and Manager, Book Dept, 1942–45, Harrods; Army & Navy Stores: Manager, Book Dept, and founder of Library, 1945–56; Merchandise Manager, 1956; Dep. Managing Dir, 1956–65. Began Hatchards Authors of the Year parties, 1966. Employers' rep., Bookselling and Stationery Trade Wages Council, 1946–79, leader of employers' side, 1957; Member: Nat. Chamber of Trade, 1946–51; Wholesale Trades Adv. Cttee, 1946–51; 1948 Book Trade Cttee; Arts Council working party on obscene pubns, 1968–69, and sub-cttee on Public Lending Rights, 1970. President: Booksellers Assoc. of GB and Ire, 1957–58 (Hon. Life Pres., 1989); Book Trade Benevolent Soc., 1974–86 (Patron, 1986). Inaugurated Nat. Book Sale (first Chm. of Cttee, 1954–65). Hon. Life Mem., Soc. of Bookmen. FRSA 1967. Jubilee Medal, 1977. *Publications:* The Right Way to Run a Library Business, 1949; Bookselling, 1953; The Truth about Bookselling, 1964; Mostly Joy (autobiog.), 1971; The Bookselling Business, 1974; contribs to Bookseller and other trade jls. *Recreations:* reading, gardening. *Address:* 13 Cole Park Gardens, Twickenham, Middlesex TW1 1JB. *T:* (020) 8892 5660.

Died 15 April 2003.

JUDD, Eric Campbell, CBE 1974; LVO 1956; Chairman, West Africa Committee, 1976–85 (Vice-Chairman, 1963–76); *b* St Thomas, Ont, 10 Aug. 1918; *s* of Frederick William Judd, PhmB (Canada), and Marjorie Katherine (*née* Bell); *m* 1947, Janet Creswell (*née* Fish); two *s* one *d*. *Educ:* Wellington, Canada; St Thomas Collegiate; Toronto Univ. Trainee Manager, Cities Service Oil Co., Canada, 1937–40. Served War of 1939–45, RCAF and RAF, 1940–45: Canada, N Atlantic Ferry Comd, Europe, Malta, Middle East, Far East, W Indies; retd Sqdn Ldr RCAF Reserve, 1945. Joined Unilever Ltd, 1946; United Africa Co. Ltd, Nigeria, 1946–60, Chm., 1957–60; Dir, UAC Ltd London, 1960, Man. Dir, 1968; Dep. Chm. and Jt Man. Dir, UAC International, 1969–77. Mem. House of Assembly, Western Nigeria, 1955–56; Chairman: BNEC Africa, 1969–72; Adv. Gp Africa BOTB, 1972–74. Mem. Council, 1975–88, a Vice-Pres., 1983–88, Royal African Soc. *Recreations:* golf, tennis, theatre, music, reading. *Address:* 2 Gerard Court, Hitherfield Lane, Lydekker Park, Harpenden, Herts AL5 4JA. *T:* (01582) 712617. *Club:* MCC. *Died 24 Oct. 2001.*

JUPP, Sir Kenneth Graham, Kt 1975; MC 1943; a Judge of the High Court, Queen's Bench Division, 1975–90; *b* 2 June 1917; *s* of Albert Leonard and Marguerite Isabel Jupp; *m* 1947, Kathleen Elizabeth (*née* Richards); two *s* two *d*. *Educ:* Perse Sch., Cambridge; University Coll., Oxford (Sen. Class. Schol., 1936; 1st Cl. Hon. Mods (Classics) 1938; College Prize for Greek, 1939; MA Oxon (War Degree), 1945, avoided Finals by joining Army, 1939); Lincoln's Inn (Cholmeley Schol., 1939; Cassel Schol., 1946). Regimental Service in France, Belgium, N Africa and Italy, 1939–43; War Office Selection Board, 1943–46. Called to Bar, Lincoln's Inn, 1945, Bencher, 1973; QC 1966; Dep. Chm., Cambridge and Isle of Ely QS, 1965–71; a Recorder of the Crown Court, 1972–75; Presiding Judge, NE Circuit, 1977–81. Chm., Independent Schs Tribunal, 1964–67; conducted MAFF inquiry into Wool Marketing Scheme, 1965; Chm., Public Inquiry into Fire at Fairfield Home, Nottingham, 1975. *Publications:* Stealing Our Land, 1997; (trans. and ed) Anne-Robert Turgot, The Formation and Distribution of Wealth: reflections on capitalism, 1999; various pamphlets on theol and econ. subjects. *Recreations:* playing flute and piano, singing, language. *Address:* Farrar's Building, Temple, EC4Y 7BD.   *Died 15 March 2004.*

JURY, Archibald George, CBE 1961; FRIBA; FRIAS; City Architect, Glasgow, 1951–72; *b* 23 June 1907; *s* of late George John Jury and Mabel Sophie Jury (*née* Fisher); *m* 1931, Amy Beatrice Maw (MBE 1983); one *d*. *Educ:* Mount Radford, Exeter; SW School of Art. Architect to Council, Taunton, 1938–40, and 1945. Served War, 1940–45, with Corps of Royal Engineers (rank of Major). Chief Housing Architect, Liverpool, 1946–49; Dir of Housing, Glasgow, 1949–51; Dir of Planning, Glasgow, 1951–66. Organised the building of 100,000 houses, 100,000 school places and numerous civic buildings; responsible for the Glasgow Devpt Plan, 1960–80, and implementation of urban renewal programme and official architecture. Several Saltire Soc. awards for best-designed flats in Scotland. Chairman: Technical Panel, Scottish Local Authorities Special Housing Group, 1965–72; Technical Panel, Clyde Valley Planning Adv. Cttee, 1960–70. Pres., Glasgow Inst. of Architects, 1970–72. *Publications:* contrib. professional and technical journals.   *Died 25 Feb. 2003.*

K

KADIRGAMAR, Hon. Lakshman; President's Counsel, 1991; MP Sri Lanka; Minister of Foreign Affairs, Sri Lanka, 1994–2001 and since 2004; *b* 12 April 1932; *m* 1956, Angela Mireille, *d* of Rev. Malik; one *s* one *d*. *Educ:* Univ. of Ceylon (LLB Hons); Balliol Coll., Oxford (BLitt; Hon. Fellow, 2004). Called to the Bar, Inner Temple, 1958 (Hon. Bencher); Advocate, Supreme Court of Ceylon; Attorney, Sri Lanka; in legal practice, 1960–73; ILO, Geneva, 1973–75; WIPO, Geneva, 1976–88 (Dir, 1983); legal practice, Sri Lanka, 1988–94. *Recreation:* watching sports. *Address:* c/o Ministry of Foreign Affairs, Republic Building, Colombo 1, Sri Lanka. *Club:* National Liberal.
Died 12 Aug. 2005.

KANT, Krishan; Vice-President of India, since 1997; *b* Amritsar, 28 Feb. 1927; *s* of Lala Achint Ram, sometime MP; *m* 1958, Suman Kant; two *s* one *d*. *Educ:* Banaras Hindu Univ. (MSc Technol). Scientist, Council of Scientific and Industrial Res., New Delhi. Member: Rajya Sabha, 1966–77; Lok Sabha, 1977–80. Congress Party, subseq. Janata Party: former Sec. of Parly Party and of Exec. Cttee; Mem., Nat. Exec., 1977–88. Founder Gen. Sec., People's Union of Civil Liberties and Democratic Rights, 1976; former Mem. Exec. Council, Inst. of Defence Studies and Analysis. *Publications:* contrib. to newspapers and periodicals on national and international politics, culture and science policy. *Address:* Office of the Vice-President, 6 Maulana Azad Road, New Delhi 110011, India. *Died 27 July 2002.*

KARK, (Arthur) Leslie, MA (Oxon); FRSA; author, barrister; President, Lucie Clayton Colleges, 1951–95; Founder, Lucie Clayton Secretarial College, 1965; Chairman, Chartmill Roche Ltd; *b* 12 July 1910; *s* of Victor and Helena Kark, Johannesburg; *m* 1st, 1935, Joan Tetley (marr. diss., 1956); two *d*; 2nd, 1956, Evelyn Gordine, (Lucie Clayton) (*d* 1997); one *s* one *d*. *Educ:* Clayesmore; St John's Coll., Oxford. Called to Bar, Inner Temple, 1932; Features Editor of World's Press News, 1933; Editor of Photography, 1934; Public Relations Officer to Advertising Association, 1935; Features Editor News Review, 1936–39; London Theatre Critic, New York Herald Tribune; News Editor, Ministry of Information, 1940. Served War of 1939–45, RAF, 1940–46; Air-gunner; Wing Commander in Command of Public Relations (Overseas) Unit; author, Air Ministry's official book on Air War, Far East. Associate Editor, Courier Magazine, 1947–51; Dir of Public Relations for Australian Trade Comr, 1959–63. Short stories and novels translated into French, Swedish, German, Polish, etc. *Publications:* The Fire Was Bright, 1944; Red Rain, 1946; An Owl in the Sun, 1948; Wings of the Phœnix, 1949; On the Haycock, 1957. *Recreations:* fly-fishing, golf. *Address:* 9 Clareville Grove, SW7 5AU. *T:* (020) 7370 6349; Roche House, Sheep Street, Burford, Oxon OX18 4LS. *T:* (01993) 823007. *Club:* Oxford and Cambridge.
Died 23 Feb. 2004.

KARK, Austen Steven, CBE 1987; Managing Director, External Broadcasting (later World Service), BBC, 1985–86; *b* 20 Oct. 1926; *s* of late Major Norman Kark and Ethel Kark, formerly of Eaton Place, London, and Johannesburg; *m* 1st, 1949, Margaret Solomon (marr. diss. 1954); two *d*; 2nd, 1954, Nina Mary Bawden, CBE; one *d*, and one step *s* (and one step *s* decd). *Educ:* Upper Canada Coll., Toronto; Nautical Coll., Pangbourne; RNC; Magdalen Coll., Oxford (MA). Served RN and RIN, 1943–46. Directed first prodn in UK of Sartre's The Flies, Oxford, 1948; trained in journalism, Belfast Telegraph, L'Illustré, Zofingen, Switzerland; Courier, Bandwagon, London Mystery Magazine; free-lance journalist and broadcaster, London and New York, 1952–54; joined BBC, 1954; scriptwriter; Producer, External Services; Head of S European Service, 1964; Head of E European (and Russian) Service, 1972; Editor, World Service, 1973; Controller, English Services, and Editor, World Service, 1974; advised Lord Soames on election broadcasting, Rhodesia, and chaired enquiry into future of radio and television in Zimbabwe, 1980; Dep. Man. Dir, External Broadcasting, BBC, 1981–85. Broadcasting consultant, 1987–; Chm., CPC Guidebooks, 1988–. Mem. UK Delegn, CSCE London Information Forum, 1989. Trustee, Commonwealth Journalists Assoc. Trust., 1992–. Member: RIIA; Soc. of Authors. *Publications:* Attic in Greece, 1994; The Forwarding Agent, 1999. *Recreations:* Real tennis, mosaics, The Ægean, grandchildren. *Address:* 22 Noel Road, N1 8HA; 19 Kapodistriou, Nauplion 21100, Greece. *Clubs:* Oriental, MCC, Queen's, Royal Tennis Court, Bushmen (ex-Chairman). *Died 10 May 2002.*

KARK, Leslie; see Kark, A. L.

KARSH, Yousuf, CC 1990 (OC 1968); portrait photographer, since 1932; *b* Mardin, Armenia-in-Turkey, 23 Dec. 1908; parents Armenian; Canadian citizen; *m* 1939, Solange Gauthier (*d* 1961); *m* 1962, Estrellita Maria Nachbar. *Educ:* Sherbrooke, PQ Canada; studied photography in Boston, Mass, USA. Portrayed: Winston Churchill in Canada's Houses of Parliament, 1941; King George VI, 1943; HM Queen (then Princess) Elizabeth and the Duke of Edinburgh, 1951; HH Pope Pius XII, 1951; also portrayed, among many others: Shaw, Wells, Einstein, Sibelius, Somerset Maugham, Picasso, Eden, Eisenhower, Tito, Eleanor Roosevelt, Thomas Mann, Bertrand Russell, Attlee, Nehru, Ingrid Bergmann, Lord Mountbatten of Burma, Augustus John, Pope John Paul II; 20 portraits used on postage stamps of 15 countries. One man exhibitions: Men Who Make our World, Pav. of Canada, Expo 67; Montreal Mus. of Fine Arts, 1968; Boston Mus. of Fine Arts, 1968; Corning Mus., 1968; Detroit Inst. of Arts, 1969; Corcoran Gall. of Art, Washington, 1969; Macdonald House, London, 1969; Seattle Art Museum; Japan (country-wide), and Honolulu, 1970; in Europe and USA annually, 1971–; exhibn acquired in toto by: Museum of Modern Art, Tokyo; Nat. Gall. of Australia; Province of Alberta, Canada, 1975–76; numerous exhibns throughout US, 1971–75, 1976–77; Ulrich Museum, Wichita, Kansas, 1978; Museum of Science and Industry, Chicago, 1978; Evansville Museum, Ind., 1979; Palm Springs Desert Museum, 1980; inaugural exhibn, Museum of Photography, Film and TV, Bradford, 1983; NY, 1983; Nat. Portrait Gall., 1983, 1991; Edinburgh, 1984; Internat. Center of Photography, NY, 1983; Helsinki, 1984; Minneapolis Museum, 1985; Syracuse Museum, 1985; Sarasota (Florida) Museum, 1986; 80th birthday gala exhibn, Barbican, London, and in France, Germany, Spain, Switzerland, 1988; Muscarelle Mus. of Art, William and Mary Coll., Williamsburg, Virginia, 1987; Castle Buda Palace, Budapest, 1989; Nat. Gall. of Canada, 1989; Gulbenkian Foundn, Lisbon, 1989; Copenhagen, Brussels, Zurich, 1989; Vancouver Art Mus., 1990; Vero Beach, Fla, 1991; Montreal Mus. of Fine Arts, 1992; Internat. Centre of Photography, NY, 1992; Corcoran Gall., Washington, 1993; Minton Mus., Charlotte, NC, 1993; Tribute Exhibn, Bradford, 1993; Canadian Embassy, Washington, 1994; Mus. of Fine Arts, Boston, 1996; Detroit Art Inst., 1996–97; Canadian Embassy, London, 1998; Charlottetown Fest., PEI, 1998; Nat. Portrait Gall. of Australia, 1999; Boston-Nagoya Mus. of Fine Arts, Japan, 2000; German Historical Mus., Berlin, 2000 (catalogue pub. as Heroes of Light and

Shadow, 2001); Canadian Cultural Center, Rio de Janeiro, 2000. Visiting Professor: Ohio Univ., 1967–69; Emerson Coll., Boston, 1972–73, 1973–74; Photographic Advisor, Internat. Exhibn, Expo '70, Osaka, Japan; Judge, UN 40th anniversary internat. poster contest, 1985. Trustee, Photographic Arts and Scis Foundn, 1970. FRPS; Fellow Rochester Sci. Mus. RCA 1975. Gift of portfolio of artists' photographs to Bretholtz Center for patients and families, Brigham and Women's Hosp., Boston. Eponymous annual lect. inaugurated at Mus. of Fine Arts, Boston, 1998; established: annual Karsh Prize for Photography, Sch. of Mus. of Fine Arts, Boston, 1999; annual Mary Fay Essence of Nursing Award, Brigham and Women's Hosp., Boston, 1999. Holds 27 hon. degrees. Canada Council Medal, 1965; Centennial Medal, 1967; Master of Photographic Arts, Prof. Photogrs of Canada, 1970; First Gold Medal, Nat. Assoc. Photog. Art, 1974; Life Achievement Award, Encyclopaedia Britannica, 1980; Silver Shingle Award, Law Sch., Boston Univ., 1983; Lotos Medal of Merit, Lotos Club of NY, 1989; first Creative Edge Award, NY Univ., 1989; Gold Medal, Americas Soc., 1989; Master Photographer, Internat. Center of Photography, 1990; Jerusalem Prize in the Arts, Bezalel Acad., Israel, 1997; Fox-Talbot Award, British Inst. of Prof. Photography, 1998. *Publications:* Faces of Destiny, 1947; (co-author) This is the Mass, 1958; Portraits of Greatness, 1959; (co-author) This is Rome, 1960; (co-author) This is the Holy Land, 1961; (autobiog.) In Search of Greatness, 1962; (co-author) These are the Sacraments, 1963; (co-author) The Warren Court; Karsh Portfolio, 1967; Faces of our Time, 1971; Karsh Portraits, 1976; Karsh Canadians, 1979; Karsh: a fifty year retrospective, 1983, rev. edn, a sixty year retrospective, 1996; American Legends, 1992; Heroes of Light and Shadow, 2001. *Recreations:* tennis, bird-watching, archæology, music. *Address:* 2 Commonwealth Avenue, Boston, MA 02116, USA. *T:* (J. Fielder) (831) 3734569. *Clubs:* Garrick; Rideau (Ottawa); Century, Dutch Treat (NY).   *Died 13 July 2002.*

KATZ, Sir Bernard, Kt 1969; FRS 1952; Professor and Head of Biophysics Department, University College, London, 1952–78, then Emeritus, Hon. Research Fellow, 1978; *b* Leipzig, 26 March 1911; *s* of M. N. Katz; *m* 1945, Marguerite (*d* 1999), *d* of W. Penly, Sydney, Australia; two *s*. *Educ:* Univ. of Leipzig (MD 1934); University Coll., London (PhD and Beit Memorial Res. Fellow, 1938; DSc 1943). Biophysical research, University Coll., London, 1935–39; Carnegie Res. Fellow, Sydney Hospital, Sydney, 1939–42. Served War of 1939–45 in Pacific with RAAF, 1942–45; Flt-Lt, 1943. Asst Dir of Research, Biophysics Research Unit, University Coll., London, and Henry Head Research Fellow (Royal Society), 1946–50; Reader in Physiology, 1950–51. Lectures: Herter, Johns Hopkins Univ., 1958; Dunham, Harvard Coll., 1961; Croonian, Royal Society, 1961; Sherrington, Liverpool Univ., 1967; Fenn, IUPS, Glasgow, 1993. A Vice-Pres., Royal Society, 1965, Biological Sec. and Vice-Pres., 1968–76. Mem., Agric. Research Council, 1967–77. Foreign Member: Royal Danish Acad. Science and Letters, 1968; Accad. Naz. Lincei, 1968; Amer. Acad. of Arts and Sciences, 1969; For. Assoc., Nat. Acad. of Scis, USA, 1976; Hon. Member: Japanese Pharmacol. Soc., 1977; American Physiolog. Soc., 1985; Assoc. Mem., European Molecular Biol. Orgn, 1978; Corresp. Mem., Australian Acad. of Science, 1987. Fellow, University Coll., London. FRCP, 1968. Hon. FIBiol, 1978. Hon. DSc: Southampton, 1971; Melbourne, 1971; Cambridge, 1980; Hon. PhD Weizmann Inst., Israel, 1979; Hon. MD Leipzig, 1990. Feldberg Foundation Award, 1965; Baly Medal, RCP, 1967; Copley Medal, Royal Society, 1967; Nobel Prize (jtly) for Physiology and Medicine, 1970; Cothenius Medal, Deutsche Akademie der Wissenschaften, Leopoldina, 1989. Foreign Mem., Orden Pour le Mérite für Wissenschaften und Künste, 1982. *Publications:* Electric Excitation of Nerve, 1939; Nerve, Muscle and Synapse, 1966; The Release of Neural Transmitter Substances, 1969; papers on nerve and muscle physiology in Jl of

Physiol., Proc. Royal Society, etc. *Recreation:* chess. *Address:* University College, WC1E 6BT.
                    Died 20 April 2003.

KAUNTZE, Ralph, MBE 1944; MD; FRCP; Physician to Guy's Hospital, 1948–71, Consultant Physician Emeritus since 1971; *b* 5 June 1911; *s* of Charles Kauntze and Edith, *d* of Ralph Bagley; *m* 1st, 1935, Katharine Margaret (*d* 1993), *yr d* of late Ramsay Moodie; two *s* one *d*; 2nd, 1994, Enid M., *widow* of Lt-Col F. J. P. Dewhurst, RTR. *Educ:* Canford Sch.; Emmanuel Coll., Cambridge; St George's Hosp., London. William Brown Sen. Schol., St George's Hosp. 1932; MRCS, LRCP 1935; MA, MB, BCh Cantab 1937; MRCP 1939; MD Cantab 1946; FRCP 1950. Served, 1939–45, RAMC, chiefly Mediterranean area, Lt-Col O i/c Med. Div. Asst Dir of Dept of Med., Guy's Hosp., 1947–48, Physician to Cardiac Dept, 1956–71; Cons. Phys. to High Wycombe War Memorial Hosp., 1948–50; Dir Asthma Clinic, 1948–52, and of Dept of Student Health, 1950–63, Guy's Hosp.; Physician to Royal Masonic Hospital, 1963–76. Former Senior Cons. Phys. to: Commercial Union Assurance Co. Ltd; British & European Assurance Co.; European Assurance Co. Ltd. Hon. Vis. Phys., Johns Hopkins Hosp., Baltimore, 1958. Examiner in Medicine: RCP; London Univ. Mem. Brit. Cardiac Soc.; Mem. Assoc. of Physicians. *Publications:* contrib. med. jls. *Recreations:* farming, walking. *Address:* Arran House, rue de la Forge, St Martin, Jersey JE3 6BD. *T:* (01543) 854162.   *Died 3 Jan. 2004.*

KAY, Bernard Hubert Gerard; HM Diplomatic Service, retired; *b* 7 July 1925; *s* of William and Alice Kay; *m* 1957, Teresa Jean Dyer; three *d*. *Educ:* St Bede's, Bradford; Wadham Coll., Oxford (MA, MLitt). Royal Navy, 1943–46. Foreign Office, 1955; served: Hong Kong, 1958–62; Singapore, 1964; Manila, 1965; New Delhi, 1967; Vientiane, 1968; Dacca, 1972; Ulan Bator, 1973; FCO, 1973–80. *Recreations:* Asia, books, mountains, the sea. *Address:* 6 Savona Close, Wimbledon, SW19 4HT.
                    Died 19 July 2002.

KAY, Prof. Harry, CBE 1981; PhD; Vice-Chancellor, University of Exeter, 1973–84 (Hon. Professor, 1984); *b* 22 March 1919; *s* of late Williamson T. Kay; *m* 1941, Gwendolen Diana, *d* of Charles Edward Maude; one *s* one *d*. *Educ:* Rotherham Grammar Sch.; Trinity Hall, Cambridge (1938–39, 1946–51). Served War of 1939–45 with Royal Artillery. Research with Nuffield Unit into Problems of Ageing, Cambridge, 1948–51; Psychologist of Naval Arctic Expedition, 1949. Lecturer in Experimental Psychology, Univ. of Oxford, 1951–59; Prof. of Psychology, Univ. of Sheffield, 1960–73. Visiting Scientist, National Institutes of Health, Washington, DC, 1957–58. Pro-Vice-Chancellor, University of Sheffield, 1967–71. Pres., British Psychological Soc., 1971–72. Hon. Director: MRC Unit, Dept of Psychology, Sheffield; Nat. Centre of Programmed Instruction for Industry, Sheffield. Member: SSRC, 1970–73; MRC, 1975–77 (Chm.), Environmental Medicine Res. Policy Cttee, 1975–77); CNAA, 1974–79; Open Univ. Acad. Adv. Cttee; BBC Continuing Educn Adv. Cttee; Southern Univs Jt Bd (Chm., 1978–80); UCCA (Chm., 1978–84); NATO Human Factors Panel, 1972–75; GMC, 1984–89. Chairman: Central Council for Educn and Trng in Social Work, 1980–84; Bd of Management, Northcott Theatre, 1973–84. Hon. DSc: Sheffield, 1981; Exeter, 1985. Vernon Prize, 1962. *Publication:* (with B. Dodd and M. Sime) Teaching Machines and Programmed Instruction, 1968. *Recreations:* Sir Walter Raleigh, listening. *Address:* Coastguard House, 18 Coastguard Road, Budleigh Salterton EX9 6NU.   *Died 14 Dec. 2005.*

KAY, Rt Hon. Sir John (William), Kt 1992; PC 2000; Rt Hon. Lord Justice Kay; a Lord Justice of Appeal, since 2000; *b* 13 Sept. 1943; *y s* of late C. Herbert Kay and Ida Kay; *m* 1966, Jeffa Connell; one *s* two *d*. *Educ:* Denstone; Christ's Coll., Cambridge (MA). Called to Bar, Gray's Inn, 1968, Bencher, 1992. Tutor in Law, Liverpool Univ., 1968–69; in practice on Northern Circuit,

1968–92; a Recorder, 1982–92; QC 1984; a Judge of the High Court of Justice, QBD, 1992–2000. Presiding Judge, Northern Circuit, 1994–97. Member: Gen. Council of Bar, 1988–92; Crown Ct Rules Cttee, 1995–; Judicial Studies Bd, 1998–2001 (Chm., Criminal Cttee); Nat. Criminal Justice Bd, 2003–; Chairman: Criminal Justice Consultative Council, 2001–03; Criminal Justice Council, 2003–; Sentencing Guidance Council, 2004–. *Recreations:* Rugby, genealogy, horse racing. *Address:* c/o Royal Courts of Justice, Strand, WC2A 2LL. *Club:* Waterloo Rugby Football (Pres., 1995–97).   *Died 2 July 2004.*

KAYE, Mary Margaret, (Mrs G. J. Hamilton), FRSL; authoress and illustrator; *b* 6 Jan. 1916; *d* of late Sir Cecil Kaye, CSI, CIE, CBE, and Lady Kaye; *m* 1942, Maj.-Gen. G. J. Hamilton, CB, CBE, DSO (*d* 1985); two *d.* *Publications: historical novels:* Shadow of the Moon, 1957, rev. edn 1979; Trade Wind, 1963, revd edn 1981; The Far Pavilions, 1978 (televised 1984); *detective novels:* Six Bars at Seven, 1940; Death Walks in Kashmir, 1953 (republished as Death in Kashmir, 1984); Death Walks in Berlin, 1955; Death Walks in Cyprus, 1956 (republished as Death in Cyprus, 1984); Later Than You Think, 1958 (republished as Death in Kenya, 1983); House of Shade, 1959 (republished as Death in Zanzibar, 1983); Night on the Island, 1960 (republished as Death in the Andamans, 1985); Death in Berlin, 1985; *for children:* The Potter Pinner Books (series), 1937–41; The Ordinary Princess, 1980, US 1984 (shown on BBC TV Jackanory, 1983, 1984); Thistledown, 1981; *autobiography:* Vol. I, The Sun in the Morning, 1990; Golden Afternoon: being the second part of Share of Summer, her autobiography, 1997; Vol. 3, Enchanted Evening, 1997; *edited:* The Golden Calm, 1980; Moon of Other Days, a personal choice of Kipling's verse, 1988; *illustrated:* The Story of St Francis; Children of Galilee; Adventures in a Caravan. *Recreation:* painting. *Club:* Army and Navy.   *Died 29 Jan. 2004.*

KAZAN, Elia; author; independent producer and director of plays and films; *b* Constantinople, 7 Sept. 1909; *s* of George Kazan and Athena Sismanoglou; *m* 1st, 1932, Molly Thacher (*d* 1963); two *s* two *d;* 2nd, 1967, Barbara Loden (*d* 1980); one *s;* 3rd, 1982, Frances Rudge. *Educ:* Williams Coll. (AB); 2 years postgraduate work in Drama at Yale. Actor, Group Theatre, 1932–39; first London appearance as Eddie Fuseli in Golden Boy, St James, 1938. Directed *plays:* Skin of Our Teeth, 1942; All My Sons, A Streetcar Named Desire, 1947; Death of a Salesman, 1949; Camino Real, Tea and Sympathy, 1953; Cat on a Hot Tin Roof, 1955; Dark at Top of the Stairs, JB, 1958; Sweet Bird of Youth, 1959; After the Fall, 1964; But For Whom Charlie, 1964; The Changeling, 1964; Four times won best stage Director of Year, 1942, 1947, 1948, 1949. Directed *films:* Streetcar named Desire, 1951; Viva Zapata, 1952; Pinky, 1949; Gentleman's Agreement, 1948 (won Oscar, best Dir); Boomerang, 1947; A Tree Grows in Brooklyn, 1945; On the Waterfront, 1954 (won Oscar, best Dir); East of Eden, 1954; Baby Doll, 1956; A Face in the Crowd, 1957; Wild River, 1960; Splendour in the Grass, 1962; America, America, 1964; The Arrangement, 1969; The Visitors, 1972; The Last Tycoon, 1977. Three times won Best Picture of Year from New York Film Critics, 1948, 1952, 1955. Academy Award for Lifetime Achievement, 1999. *Publications:* America, America (novel), 1963; The Arrangement (novel), 1967; The Assassins, 1972; The Understudy, 1974; Acts of Love, 1978; The Anatolian, 1982; Elia Kazan, A Life (autobiog.), 1988; Beyond the Aegean, 1994; magazine articles in New York Times, Theatre Arts, etc. *Recreation:* tennis.
Died 28 Sept. 2003.

KEANE, Desmond St John; QC 1981; QC (Hong Kong) 1982; QC (NSW) 1986; QC (NI) 1993; *b* 21 Aug. 1941; *er s* of late Henry Keane, MB, BCh, and Patricia Keane; one *d; m* 1st, 1968, Susan Mary Little (marr. diss. 1987); two *s* one *d;* 2nd, 2001, Rachel Cheung Man Ching, barrister. *Educ:* Downside Sch.; Wadham Coll., Oxford (Schol.; MA Mod. Hist.). Called to the Bar, Middle

Temple, 1964; a Recorder, 1979–91. Dep. Judge, High Court of Hong Kong, 1983 and 1986. Hon. Lectr, Faculty of Law, Hong Kong Univ., 1982–88. *Recreations:* cricket umpiring, bridge. *Address:* Victoria Chambers, 177 Corporation Street (3rd Floor), Birmingham B4 6RG. *T:* (0121) 236 9900, *Fax:* (0121) 233 0675.
Died 21 June 2002.

KEANE, John B.; writer; *b* 21 July 1928; *s* of William B. Keane and Hannah (*née* Purtill); *m* Mary O'Connor; three *s* one *d. Educ:* Listowel Nat. Sch.; St Michael's Coll., Listowel, Co. Kerry. Chemist's asst, 1946–51; various jobs in UK, 1951–55; pub owner, Listowel, 1955–. Pres., Irish PEN, 1973–74. Life Mem., RDS, 1991. Hon. DLitt TCD, 1984; Hon. DFA Marymount Manhattan Coll. Independent Irish Life Award, 1986; Sunday Tribune Award, 1986; Fresh Amer. Lit. Award, 1988; Person of Year Award, 1991. *Publications:* include: Sive, 1959; The Street and Other Poems, 1961; Year of the Hiker, 1962; The Field, 1965 (filmed 1990); Big Maggie, 1967; The Crazy Wall, 1971; Letters Series of Books, 1967–91; *novels:* The Bodhran Makers, 1986; The Contractors; The High Meadow; Durango. *Recreations:* Gaelic football, Rugby, reading, walking. *Address:* 37 William Street, Listowel, Co. Kerry, Ireland. *Club:* Listowel GAA.
Died 30 May 2002.

KEAR, Dr Janet, (Mrs J. V. N. Turner), OBE 1993; ornithologist; Director of Centres, Wildfowl and Wetlands Trust, 1991–93, retired; *b* 13 Jan. 1933; *d* of Harold Kear and Constance May Kear (*née* Betteridge); *m* 1st, 1963, Geoffrey Vernon Townsend Matthews (marr. diss. 1977); 2nd, 1993, John V. N. Turner. *Educ:* Walthamstow Hall, Sevenoaks; Caspar Jun. Coll., Caspar, Wyoming; King's Coll., London (BSc 1956); Girton Coll., Cambridge (PhD 1959). Wildfowl and Wetlands Trust: Research Scientist, 1959–74; PSO 1974; Avicultural Co-ordinator, 1974–77; Curator, Martin Mere Centre, 1977–90; Asst Dir, 1978–90; Mem., Mgt Cttee, 1988–93. Fellow, Zool Dept, Liverpool Univ., 1978–92. Wildlife Inspector, Scientific Authy for Animals, DoE, 1977–81. Council Mem., NCC, later NCCE, 1990–97. Mem. Council, 1965–76, Sec., 1966–73, Assoc. for Study of Animal Behaviour; Zoological Society of London International Zoo Yearbook: Mem., Editl Bd, 1974–79 and 1989–2003; Chm., 1980–88; Mem. 1974, Chm. 1975–83, Breeding and Conservation Sub-cttee, Zoo Fedn; Member: Avicl Soc. Council, 1975–77; British Trust for Ornithology Council, 1983–86; Res. Adv. Cttee, 1977–83, Council 1994–99, RSPB; International Union for Conservation of Nature: Chm., Endangered Waterfowl Gp, 1976–87; Mem., Captive Breeding Specialist Gp, 1979–92; Jersey Wildlife Preservation Trust: Mem., Scientific Adv. Cttee, 1979–2001; Dir, Summer Sch., 1993; Council Mem., 1994–2003; British Ornithologists' Union: Mem. Council, 1980–88, Vice-Pres., 1989–91, Pres., 1991–95 (Medal, 1998); Mem., Internat. Ornithol Cttee, 1982– (Vice-Pres., XXII Internat. Ornith. Congress, Durban, 1998); Pres., Devon Bird Watching and Preservation Soc., 1995–2004. Trustee, Nat. Mus and Galls on Merseyside, 1997–. Editor: Ibis, BOU Jl, 1980–88; Wildfowl, Jl of Wildfowl and Wetlands Trust, 1989–96. Hon. Fellow, Manchester Metropolitan Univ. (formerly Manchester Poly.), 1983; Hon. Prof., Liverpool John Moores Univ. (formerly Liverpool Poly.), 1990–. Hon. DSc Liverpool Poly., 1990. *Publications:* (ed with N. Duplaix-Hall) Flamingos, 1975; (with A. J. Berger) The Hawaiian Goose, 1980; Eric Hosking's Wildfowl, 1985; The Mute Swan, 1989; Man and Wildfowl (Natural World's Book of the Year), 1990; Swans, 1990; Ducks of the World, 1991. *Recreations:* reading, gardening, walking. *Address:* Jewells Lodge, Umberleigh, Devon EX37 9EY. *T:* (01769) 580057. *Club:* Naval and Military.
Died 24 Nov. 2004.

KEE, His Honour William; a Circuit Judge, 1972–90; *b* 15 Oct. 1921; *yr s* of Robert and Dorothy Kee; *m* 1953, Helga Wessel Eckhoff (*d* 2004); one *s* three *d. Educ:*

Rottingdean Sch.; Stowe Sch. Served War, Army, 1941–46: attached 9th Gurkha Rifles, Dehra Dun, 1943; Staff Captain, Area HQ, 1945–46. Called to the Bar, Inner Temple, 1948; Principal Judge for County Courts in Kent, 1985–90. Jt Chm., Independent Schools' Tribunal, 1971–72. *Publications:* (jtly) Divorce Case Book, 1950; contributor to: titles in Atkin's Encyclopaedia of Court Forms; Halsbury's Laws of England. *Recreations:* listening to music, walking.   *Died 2 Dec. 2004.*

KEEBLE, Major Robert, (Peter), DSO 1940; MC 1945; TD 1946; Director: Associated Portland Cement Manufacturers Ltd, 1970–74; Aberthaw & Bristol Channel Portland Cement Co. Ltd, 1970–74; engaged in cement manufacture; *b* 20 Feb. 1911; *s* of late Edwin Percy and Alice Elizabeth Keeble; unmarried. *Educ:* King Henry VIII's Sch., Coventry. Comd Royal Engineer Field Company; Territorial Army Commn, passed Staff Coll., Camberley, 1939; served in War of 1939–45 (despatches twice, twice wounded, DSO, MC, 1939–45 Star, African Star, France-Germany Star and Defence Medal, TD). Mem., Inst. Quarrying. Governor, Hull Univ. Hon. Brother, Hull Trinity House. Freeman, City of London and Liveryman, Fanmakers' Co. *Recreation:* fishing. *Address:* 15 Fernhill Close, Kenilworth CV8 1AN. *T:* (01926) 855668. *Club:* Army and Navy.
       Died 23 Aug. 2004.

KEELING, Robert William Maynard; a Recorder of the Crown Court, 1980–89; *b* 16 Dec. 1917; *s* of Dr George Sydney Keeling, MD, and Florence Amy Keeling (*née* Maynard); *m* 1942, Kathleen Busill-Jones (*d* 1997); one *s* two *d*. *Educ:* Uppingham; Corpus Christi Coll., Cambridge (BA 1939). Served War, RASC, 1939–46: Western Desert, Libya, Palestine, Jordan, Italy, Greece (despatches 1944), Berlin. FO, 1946–47. Solicitor 1950; Partner in Monier-Williams & Keeling, 1956–80; Solicitor to Vintners' Company, 1953–79. Director, Sherry Producers Committee Ltd, 1967–80, Chairman 1980–. Diplôme de Grande Médaille d'Argent, Corporation des Vignerons de Champagne, 1988. Knight Comdr, Order of Civil Merit (Spain), 1967; Chevalier de la Légion d'Honneur (France), 1993. *Recreations:* travel, painting, music. *Address:* Vale Bank, Chadlington, Chipping Norton, Oxon OX7 3LZ.   *Died 16 March 2001.*

KEITH OF CASTLEACRE, Baron *cr* 1980 (Life Peer), of Swaffham in the County of Norfolk; **Kenneth Alexander Keith,** Kt 1969; merchant banker and industrialist; *b* 30 Aug. 1916; *er s* of late Edward Charles Keith, Swanton Morley House, Norfolk; *m* 1st, 1946, Lady Ariel Olivia Winifred Baird (marr. diss., 1958; she *d* 2003), 2nd *d* of 1st Viscount Stonehaven, PC, GCMG, DSO, and Countess of Kintore; one *s* one *d*; 2nd, 1962, Mrs Nancy Hayward (marr. diss. 1972; she *d* 1990), Manhasset, New York; 3rd, 1973, Mrs Marie Hanbury (*d* 2001), Burley-on-the-Hill, Rutland; 4th, 2002, Mrs Penelope de Laszlo. *Educ:* Rugby Sch. Trained as a Chartered Accountant. 2nd Lt Welsh Guards, 1939; Lt-Col 1945; served in North Africa, Italy, France and Germany (despatches, Croix de Guerre with Silver Star). Asst to Dir Gen. Political Intelligence Dept, Foreign Office, 1945–46. Partner, 1946, Dir, 1948, Man. Dir, 1951, Philip Hill & Partners Ltd; Chairman: Philip Hill Investment Trust Ltd, 1967–87; Hill Samuel Group Ltd, 1970–80; Chm. and Chief Exec., Rolls Royce Ltd, 1972–80; Vice-Chm., BEA, 1964–71; Director: Beecham Gp Ltd, 1949–87 (Vice-Chm., 1970–87, Chm., 1986–87); Eagle Star Insurance Co., 1955–75; Nat. Provincial Bank, 1967–69; Times Newspapers Ltd, 1967–81; British Airways, 1971–72; Standard Telephones and Cables, subseq. STC, 1977–89 (Chm., 1985–89); Bank of Nova Scotia Ltd, 1978–87. Member: NEDC, 1964–71; CBI/NEDC Liaison Cttee, 1974–78; Pres., BSI, 1989–94; Vice-Pres., EEF. Chairman: Economic Planning Council for East Anglia, 1965–70; Governor, Nat. Inst. of Economic and Social Research. Council Mem. and Dir, Manchester Business Sch. President: Royal Norfolk Agricl

Assoc., 1989; RoSPA, 1989–93. FCMI; FRSA. Hon. Companion, RAeS. *Recreations:* shooting, golf. *Address:* The Wicken House, Castle Acre, King's Lynn, Norfolk PE32 2BP. *T:* (01760) 755225. *Club:* White's.
       Died 1 Sept. 2004.

KEITH OF KINKEL, Baron *cr* 1977 (Life Peer), of Strathtummel; **Henry Shanks Keith,** GBE 1997; PC 1976; a Lord of Appeal in Ordinary, 1977–96; *b* 7 Feb. 1922; *s* of Baron Keith of Avonholm, PC; *m* 1955, Alison Hope Alan Brown, JP, MA; four *s* (including twin *s*) one *d*. *Educ:* Edinburgh Academy; Magdalen Coll., Oxford (MA; Hon. Fellow 1977); Edinburgh Univ. (LLB). Served War of 1939–45 (despatches); Scots Guards, 1941–45. Advocate, Scottish Bar, 1950; Barrister, Gray's Inn, 1951, Bencher 1976; QC (Scotland), 1962. Standing Counsel to Dept of Health for Scotland, 1957–62; Sheriff Principal of Roxburgh, Berwick and Selkirk, 1970–71; Senator of Coll. of Justice in Scotland, 1971–77. Chairman: Scottish Valuation Adv. Coun., 1972–76 (Mem., 1957–70); Cttee on Powers of Revenue Depts, 1980–83; Dep. Chm., Parly Boundary Commn for Scotland, 1976; Member: Law Reform Cttee for Scotland, 1964–70; Cttee on Law of Defamation, 1971–74; Panel of Arbiters: European Fisheries Convention, 1964–71; Convention for Settlement of Investment Disputes, 1968–71. *Address:* House of Lords, SW1A 0PW. *Club:* Flyfishers'.
       Died 21 June 2002.

KELBIE, Sheriff David; Sheriff of Grampian, Highland and Islands, at Aberdeen, since 1986; *b* 28 Feb. 1945; *s* of Robert Kelbie and Monica Eileen Pearn; *m* 1966, Helen Mary Smith; one *s* one *d*. *Educ:* Inverurie Acad.; Aberdeen Univ. (LLB Hons). Advocate; called to the Scottish Bar, 1968; Sheriff of N Strathclyde, 1979–86. Associate Lectr, Heriot-Watt Univ., 1971–75; Hon. Sec., Scottish Congregational Coll., 1975–82; Mem., UK/Ireland Cttee, 1986–90, Scotland Cttee, 1990–95, Christian Aid. Ed., Scottish Civil Law Reports, 1996–98. *Publications:* Small Claims Procedure in the Sheriff Court, 1994; articles in legal jls. *Recreations:* sailing, music, reading. *Address:* 38 Earlspark Drive, Bieldside, Aberdeen AB15 9AH. *T:* (01224) 868237.   *Died 30 May 2001.*

KELLEY, Joanna Elizabeth, OBE 1973; Assistant Director of Prisons (Women), 1967–74; *b* 23 May 1910; *d* of late Lt-Col William Beadon, 51st Sikhs; *m* 1934, Harper Kelley (*d* 1962); no *c*. *Educ:* Hayes Court; Girton Coll., Cambridge (MA; Hon. Fellow, 1968). Souschargé, Dept of Pre-History, Musée de l'Homme, Paris, 1934–39; Mixed Youth Club Leader, YWCA, 1939–42; Welfare Officer, Admiralty, Bath, 1942–47; Prison Service, 1947–74; Governor of HM Prison, Holloway, 1959–66. Member: Council, St George's House, Windsor, 1971–77; Redundant Churches Cttee, 1974–79; Scott Holland Trust, 1978–86; Sponsor, YWCA of GB, 1979–. FSA. Hon. LLD Hull Univ., 1960. *Publications:* When the Gates Shut, 1967; Who Casts the First Stone, 1978. *Recreation:* reading. *Address:* 31 Westmoreland Terrace, SW1V 4AQ.
       Died 12 April 2003.

KELLGREN, Prof. Jonas Henrik, FRCS, FRCP; Professor of Rheumatology, 1953–76, then Emeritus, Dean of Medical School, 1970–73, University of Manchester; *b* 11 Sept. 1911; *s* of Dr Harry Kellgren and Vera (*née* Dumelunksen); *m* 1st, 1934, Ruth Rushton (marr. diss. 1940); one *d*; 2nd, 1942, Thelma Marian Reynolds; four *d*. *Educ:* Bedales Sch.; University Coll., London (MB, BS, 1934). FRCS 1936; FRCP 1951. Junior clinical appointments, University Coll. Hosp., 1934–42 (Beit Memorial Fellow 1938–39); served War, 1942–46, as surgical and orthopædic specialist, RAMC; Mem. Scientific Staff, MRC, Wingfield Morris Orthopædic Hosp., Oxford, 1946–47; first Dir, Centre for Res. into Chronic Rheumatism, Univ. of Manchester, 1947–53. Expert Advr, WHO, 1961. Pres. Heberden Soc., 1958–59. *Publications:* numerous articles in medical and scientific jls. *Recreation:* landscape painting. *Address:*

Beckside Cottage, Rusland, Ulverston, Cumbria LA12
8JY. *T:* (01229) 84244. *Died 22 Feb. 2002.*

KEMBALL-COOK, Brian Hartley, MA; Headmaster,
Bedford Modern School, 1965–77; *b* 12 Dec. 1912; *s* of Sir
Basil Alfred Kemball-Cook, KCMG, CB, and Lady
(Nancy Annie) Kemball-Cook (*née* Pavitt); *m* 1947,
Marian, *d* of R. C. R. Richards, OBE; three *s* one *d. Educ:*
Shrewsbury Sch. (Sidney Gold Medal for Classics); Balliol
Coll., Oxford (Scholar; First Class Classical Honour Mods,
1933; First Class, Litt. Hum., 1935; MA). Sixth Form
Classics Master, Repton Sch., 1936–40. Served War of
1939–45: Intelligence Corps, 1940–46 (despatches);
Regional Intelligence Officer and Political Adviser to
Regional Comr, Hanover, 1946; Principal, Min. of
Transport, 1946–47. Sen. Classics Master, Repton Sch.,
1947–56; Headmaster, Queen Elizabeth's Grammar Sch.,
Blackburn, 1956–65. Chm., Bedfordshire Musical Festival,
1967–77. Croix de Guerre with Palm, 1946. *Publications:*
(ed) Shakespeare, Coriolanus, 1954; (contrib.) Education:
threatened standards, 1972; translated: Homer, Odyssey,
1994; Homeric Hymn to Hermes, 2000; Homeric Hymn
to Demeter, 2001. *Recreations:* mountaineering, music.
Address: 12 Francis Close, Hitchin, Herts SG4 9EJ. *T:*
(01462) 438862. *Club:* Climbers.
Died 19 Sept. 2002.

KEMP, Arnold; Foreign News Editor, The Observer, since
1999; *b* 15 Feb. 1939; *s* of Robert Kemp and Meta
Strachan; *m* 1963, Sandra Elizabeth Shand (marr. diss.);
two *d. Educ:* Edinburgh Academy; Edinburgh Univ.
(MA). Sub-Editor, Scotsman, 1959–62, Guardian,
1962–65; Production Editor, Scotsman, 1965–70, London
Editor, 1970–72, Dep. Editor, 1972–81; Editor, Glasgow
Herald, then The Herald, 1981–94; Consultant Editor,
Caledonian Publishing, 1994–97; contributor and desk
editor, The Observer, 1996–99. Chm., Commn on Future
of Voluntary Sector in Scotland, 1995–97. Dr *hc*
Edinburgh, 1992; Hon. DLitt Strathclyde, 1993; DUniv
Paisley, 1993. *Publication:* The Hollow Drum: Scotland
since the war, 1993. *Recreations:* jazz, reading, theatre.
Address: 8 Buckingham Court, 2 Queen Margaret Drive,
Glasgow G12 8DQ. *Club:* Caledonian.
Died 9 Sept. 2002.

KEMP, David Ashton McIntyre; QC 1973; a Recorder
of the Crown Court, 1976–96; *b* 14 Oct. 1921; *s* of late Sir
Kenneth McIntyre Kemp and Margaret Caroline Clare
Kemp; *m* 1st, 1949, Margaret Sylvia Jones (*d* 1971); 2nd,
1972, Maureen Ann Frances Stevens, widow. *Educ:*
Winchester Coll.; Corpus Christi Coll., Cambridge (BA
1st cl. hons Law 1948). Called to the Bar, Inner Temple,
1948, Bencher, 1980. *Publications:* (with M. S. Kemp) The
Quantum of Damages, Personal Injuries Claims, 1954, 4th
edn 1975; (with M. S. Kemp) The Quantum of Damages,
Fatal Accident Claims, 1956, 4th edn 1975). *Recreations:*
ski-ing, tennis, gardening. *Address:* 63 Brixton Water Lane,
SW2 1PH. *T:* (020) 7267 3295. *Clubs:* Hurlingham, Ski
Club of Great Britain; Kandahar Ski.
Died 28 June 2003.

KEMP, Hubert Bond Stafford, FRCS, FRCSE; Hon.
Consultant Orthopaedic Surgeon, since 1992; Consultant
Orthopaedic Surgeon: Royal National Orthopaedic
Hospital, London and Stanmore, 1974–92; The Middlesex
Hospital, 1984–90; Hon. Consultant Orthopaedic
Surgeon, St Luke's Hospital for the Clergy, 1975–90;
University Teacher in Orthopaedics; *b* 25 March 1925; *s*
of John Stafford Kemp and Cecilia Isabel (*née* Bond); *m*
1967, Moyra Ann Margaret Odgers; three *d. Educ:* Cardiff
High Sch.; Univ. of South Wales; St Thomas's Hosp.,
Univ. of London (MB, BS 1949; MS 1969). MRCS,
LRCP 1947; FRCSE 1960; FRCS 1970. Hon.
Consultant, Royal Nat. Orthopaedic Hosp., London and
Stanmore, 1965–74; Sen. Lectr, Inst. of Orthopaedics,
1965–74, Hon. Sen. Lectr, 1974–90. Hunterian Prof.,
RCS, 1969. Vis. Prof., VII Congress of Soc. Latino Amer.
de Orthopedia y Traumatologica, 1971. Member: MRC
Working Party on Tuberculosis of the Spine, 1974–;

MRC Working Party on Osteosarcoma, 1985–94; Chm.,
London Bone Tumour Unit, 1985–91. Member: Brit.
Orthopaedic Research Soc., 1967–; Internat. Skeletal
Soc., 1977–. Fellow, Brit. Orthopaedic Assoc., 1972–.
Robert Jones Gold Medal and Assoc. Prize, 1969 (Proxime
Accessit, 1964). *Publications:* (jtly) Orthopaedic Diagnosis,
1984; chapter in: A Postgraduate Textbook of Clinical
Orthopaedics, 1983, 2nd edn 1995; Baillière's Clinical
Oncology, Bone Tumours, 1987; (contrib.) Essential
Surgical Practice, 3rd edn, 1995; papers on diseases of the
spine, the hip, bone tumours. *Recreations:* fishing, painting.
Address: 55 Loom Lane, Radlett, Herts WD7 8NX. *T:* and
Fax: (01923) 854265; 45 Bolsover Street, W1P 8AQ. *T:*
(020) 7391 4255, (020) 7387 5070, *Fax:* (020) 7391 4288.
Died 28 Nov. 2004.

KEMP, Prof. Kenneth Oliver, FREng; Chadwick
Professor of Civil Engineering, 1970–84, then Emeritus,
and Fellow, 1984, University College London; *b* 19 Oct.
1926; *s* of Eric Austen Kemp; *m* 1952, Josephine Gloria
(*née* Donovan); no *c. Educ:* University College London
(BSc(Eng), PhD). FICE, FIStructE; FREng (FEng 1988).
Surveyor, Directorate of Colonial Surveys, 1947–49; Asst
Engr, Collins and Mason, Consulting Engrs, 1949–54.
University College London: Lectr, Sen. Lectr, Dept of
Civil Engrg, 1954–69; Reader in Structural Engrg,
1969–70; Hd of Civil Engrg Dept, 1970–84. *Publications:*
papers in: Proc. Instn of Civil Engrs; The Structural Engr;
Magazine of Concrete Research; Internat. Assoc. of
Bridge and Structural Engrg. *Address:* Rowan Cottage,
Brinton, Melton Constable, Norfolk NR24 2QF. *T:*
(01263) 860631. *Died 8 Aug. 2002.*

KEMP, Thomas Arthur, MD; FRCP; Physician: St
Mary's Hospital, 1947–75; Paddington General Hospital,
1950–75; *b* 12 Aug. 1915; *s* of Fred Kemp and Edith
Peters; *m* 1942, Ruth May Scott-Keat; one *s* one *d. Educ:*
Denstone Coll.; St Catharine's Coll., Cambridge
(Exhibnr); St Mary's Hosp., London (Schol.; MB, BChir
1940); MD 1953. MRCP 1941; FRCP 1949. Served in
Middle East, 1944–47; Lt-Col RAMC Officer i/c Medical
Div.; Hon. Cons. Physician to the Army, 1972–75.
Examiner in Medicine, Univs of London and Glasgow.
Pres., Brit. Student Health Assoc., 1962–63; Chm., Brit.
Student Tuberculosis Foundn, 1963–65. FRSocMed (Jt
Hon. Sec., 1961–67). Fellow, Midland Div., Woodard
Schs, 1962–85; Commonwealth Travelling Fellowship,
1967. *Publications:* papers in medical jls. *Recreations:* games,
especially Rugby football (played for Cambridge, 1936, for
Barbarians, 1936–49, for St Mary's Hosp., 1937–43, for
England, 1937–48 (Captain, 1948, Selector, 1954–61);
President: RFU, 1971–72; Students' RFU, 1980–97).
Address: 2 Woodside Road, Northwood, Middx
HA6 3QE. *T:* (01923) 821068. *Club:* Hawks
(Cambridge). *Died 26 Nov. 2004.*

KEMPSON, Rachel, (Lady Redgrave); actress; *b* Devon,
28 May 1910; *d* of Eric William Edward Kempson and
Beatrice Hamilton Ashwell Kempson; *m* 1935, Sir Michael
Redgrave, CBE (*d* 1985); one *s* two *d. Educ:* St Agnes
Convent, East Grinstead; Colchester County High Sch.;
Oaklea, Buckhurst Hill; RADA. First stage appearance in
Much Ado About Nothing, Stratford, 1933; first London
appearance in The Lady from Alfaqueque, Westminster,
1933; Stratford season, 1934; Liverpool Playhouse,
1935–36; Love's Labour's Lost, Old Vic, 1936; Volpone,
Westminster, 1937; Twelfth Night, Oxford, 1937; The
School for Scandal, Queen's, 1937; The Shoemaker's
Holiday, Playhouse, 1938; Under One Roof, Richmond,
1940; The Wingless Victory, Phoenix, 1943; Uncle Harry,
Garrick, 1944; Jacobowsky and the Colonel, Piccadilly,
1945; Fatal Curiosity, Arts, 1946; The Paragon, Fortune,
1948; The Return of the Prodigal, Globe, 1948; Candida,
Oxford, 1949; Venus Observed, Top of the Ladder, St
James's, 1950; The Happy Time, St James's, 1952;
Shakespeare Meml Theatre Co., 1953; English Stage Co.,
1956; The Seagull, St Joan of the Stockyards, Queen's,
1964; Samson Agonistes, Lionel and Clarissa, Guildford,

1965; A Sense of Detachment, Royal Court, 1972; The Freeway, NT, 1974; A Family and a Fortune, Apollo, 1975; The Old Country, Queen's, 1977; Savannah Bay, Royal Court, 1983; Chekhov's Women, Queen's, 1986; The Cocktail Party, Phoenix, 1986; Uncle Vanya, Vaudeville, 1988; Coriolanus, Young Vic, 1989. *Films* include: The Captive Heart, 1945; Georgy Girl, 1966; The Jokers; Charge of the Light Brigade, 1968; The Virgin Soldiers, 1969; Jane Eyre; Out of Africa, 1985; The Understanding, 1985. Frequent *television* appearances include series and serials: Elizabeth R; Jennie; Love for Lydia; The Bell, 1981; The Jewel in the Crown, 1984; The Black Tower, 1985; Small World, 1988; plays: Winter Ladies, Sweet Wine of Youth, 1979; Kate, the Good Neighbour, Getting On, The Best of Everything, and Jude, 1980; Blunt Instrument, Bosom Friends, and The Boxwallah, 1981; World's Beyond, 1986; Boon, She's been away, 1989; Lorna Doone, For the Greater Good, Uncle Vanya, 1990; *radio:* Hester, in The Forsyte Saga, 1990. *Publication:* A Family and its Fortunes (autobiog.), 1986. *Recreations:* gardening, letter writing. *Address:* c/o Creative Artists Management Ltd, 19 Denmark Street, WC2H 8NA. *Died 23 May 2003.*

KENDALL, Henry Walter George, OBE 1979; Director, British Printing Industries Federation, 1972–81; *b* 21 Dec. 1916; *s* of Henry Kendall and Beatrice (Kerry) Kendall; *m* 1945, Audrey Alison Woodward; two *s* one *d. Educ:* Archbishop Temple's Sch., Lambeth. FCMA. Training with Blades, East & Blades Ltd, 1933–40. War service, RAOC; special duties, War Office, London, 1941; Mil. Coll. of Science, Inspecting Ordnance Officer Western Comd, HQ Allied Land Forces SE Asia, 1940–46. Cost accountant, British Fedn of Master Printers, 1947–55; Chief Cost Accountant, 1955; Head of Management Services, 1967. Member Council: CBI, 1972–81; Printing Industry Research Assoc., 1972–81; Inst. of Printing, 1972–81. *Recreations:* theatre, gardening, travel. *Died 10 Nov. 2002.*

KENDELL, Dr Robert Evan, CBE 1992; FRCP, FRCPE, FRCPsych, FMedSci; FRSE; President, Royal College of Psychiatrists, 1996–99; *b* 28 March 1935; *s* of Robert Owen Kendell and Joan Evans; *m* 1961, Ann Whitfield; two *s* two *d. Educ:* Mill Hill School; Peterhouse, Cambridge (BChir 1959, MB 1960, MA 1964, MD 1967). FRCP 1974; FRCPE 1977; FRCPsych 1979; FRSE 1993. KCH Med. School, 1956–59; Maudsley Hosp., 1962–68; Vis. Prof., Univ. of Vermont Coll. of Medicine, 1969–70; Reader in Psychiatry, Inst. of Psychiatry, 1970–74; Prof. of Psychiatry, 1974–91, Dean, Faculty of Medicine, 1986–90, Univ. of Edinburgh; CMO, Scottish Office Home and Health Dept, 1991–96. Vis. Prof., Univ. of WA, 2001. Chm., WHO Expert Cttee on Alcohol Consumption, 1979; Mem., MRC, 1984–88, 1991–96. Founder FMedSci 1998. Hon. FRCSE 1995; Hon. FRCPSG, 1995. Gaskell Medal, RCPsych, 1967; Paul Hoch Medal, Amer. Psychopathol Assoc., 1988; Medal, Marcé Soc., 1994. *Publications:* The Classification of Depressive Illnesses, 1968; The Role of Diagnosis in Psychiatry, 1975; (ed) Companion to Psychiatric Studies, 3rd edn 1983 to 5th edn 1993. *Recreations:* overeating and walking up hills. *Address:* 3 West Castle Road, Edinburgh EH10 5AT. *T:* (0131) 229 4966, *Fax:* (0131) 228 7547. *Club:* Climbers'. *Died 19 Dec. 2002.*

KENNAN, Prof. George Frost; Professor, Institute for Advanced Study, Princeton, NJ, 1956–74, then Professor Emeritus; *b* 16 Feb. 1904; *m* 1931, Annelise Sorensen; one *s* three *d. Educ:* Princeton Univ. (AB); Seminary for Oriental Languages, Berlin. Foreign Service of the USA; many posts from 1926–52; US Ambassador to the USSR, 1952–53; Institute for Advanced Study, Princeton, 1953–61; US Ambassador to Yugoslavia, 1961–63. George Eastman Vis. Prof., Oxford, 1957–58; Reith Lectr, BBC, 1957; Prof., Princeton Univ., 1963 and 1964. President: Nat. Inst. of Arts and Letters, 1965–68; Amer. Acad. of Arts and Letters, 1968–72. Benjamin Franklin Fellow,

RSA, 1968; Corresp. FBA, 1983. Hon. LLD: Dartmouth and Yale, 1950; Colgate, 1951; Notre Dame, 1953; Kenyon Coll., 1954; New School for Social Research, 1955; Princeton, 1956; Michigan and Northwestern, 1957; Brandeis, 1958; Wisconsin, 1963; Harvard, 1963; Denison, 1966; Rutgers, 1966; Marquette, 1972; Catholic Univ. of America, 1976; Duke, 1977; Ripon Coll., 1978; Dickinson Coll., 1979; Lake Forest Coll., 1982; Clark, 1983; Oberlin Coll., 1983; Brown, 1983; New York, 1985; William and Mary Coll., and Columbia, 1986; Rider Coll., 1988; Hon. DCL Oxford, 1969; Dr of Politics *hc* Univ. of Helsinki, 1986. Pour le Mérite (Germany), 1976; Albert Einstein Peace Prize, Albert Einstein Peace Prize Foundn of Chicago, 1981; Grenville Clark Prize, Grenville Clark Fund at Dartmouth Coll., Inc., 1981; Börsenverein Peace Prize, Frankfurt, 1982; Gold Medal for History, AAIL, 1984; Creative Arts Award for Nonfiction, Brandeis Univ., 1986; Freedom from Fear Award, FDR Foundn, 1987; Physicians for Social Responsibility Award, 1988; Toynbee Prize, 1988; Encyclopaedia Britannica Award, 1989; Presidential Medal of Freedom, 1989; Governor's Award of NJ, 1990. *Publications:* American Diplomacy, 1900–1950, 1951 (US); Realities of American Foreign Policy, 1954 (US); Amerikanisch Russische Verhältnis, 1954 (Germany); Soviet-American Relations, 1917–1920: Vol. I, Russia Leaves the War, 1956 (Nat. Book Award; Pulitzer Prize 1957); Vol. II, The Decision to Intervene, 1958; Russia, the Atom and the West, 1958; Soviet Foreign Policy, 1917–1941, 1960; Russia and the West under Lenin and Stalin, 1961; On Dealing with the Communist World, 1964; Memoirs: vol. 1, 1925–1950, 1967 (Nat. Book Award 1968; Pulitzer Prize 1968); vol. 2, 1950–1963, 1973; From Prague after Munich: diplomatic papers 1938–1940, 1968; Democracy and the Student Left, 1968; The Marquis de Custine and his 'Russie en 1839', 1972; The Cloud of Danger, 1977; The Decline of Bismarck's European Order, 1979; The Nuclear Delusion, 1982; The Fateful Alliance: France, Russia and the coming of the First World War, 1985; Sketches from a Life, 1989; Around the Cragged Hill: a personal and political philosophy, 1993; At a Century's Ending: reflections 1982–1995, 1996; *relevant publication:* George F. Kennan and the Origins of Containment 1944–1946, 1997. *Club:* Century (New York City). *Died 17 March 2005.*

KENNEDY, Edward Arthur Gilbert; *b* Dublin, 5 May 1920; *s* of Captain Edward H. N. Kennedy, RN, and Frances A. Gosling, Bermuda; *m* 1944, Margarita Dagmara Hofstra; two *s* two *d. Educ:* Oundle; Pembroke Coll., Cambridge (BA Mod Langs 1946). Served War, RNVR, 1941–46. Joined Northern Ireland Civil Service, 1947; served mainly in Dept of Commerce until 1970, then in Office of NI Ombudsman (Sen. Dir, 1973–83); Vice-Chm., Music Cttee, N Ireland Arts Council, 1978–83; Hon. Pres., Belfast Ballet Club, 1970–82; Chm., Belfast Picture Borrowing Gp, 1970–84. *Recreation:* interest in the arts. *Address:* 29 Tweskard Park, Belfast BT4 2JZ. *T:* (028) 9076 3638. *Died 2002.*

KENNETT BROWN, David; a District Judge (Magistrates' Courts) (formerly Metropolitan Stipendiary Magistrate), since 1982; a Recorder, since 1989; *b* 29 Jan. 1938; *s* of late Thomas Kennett Brown, solicitor, and Vanda Brown; *m* 1966, Wendy Margaret Evans; one *s* two *d. Educ:* Monkton Combe Sch.; Lincoln Coll., Oxford. FCIArb 1982. Admitted Solicitor, 1965. Partner, Kennett Brown & Co., 1965–82. Chm., Family Proceedings and Youth Courts, 1983–. Chm., London Rent Assessment Panel, 1979–82; Pres., Central and S Mddx Law Soc., 1982. JP Willesden, 1975–82. *Recreations:* escaping to Cornwall, gardening. *Address:* c/o Marylebone Magistrates' Court, 181 Marylebone Road, NW1 5QJ. *Died 27 March 2003.*

KENNY, Anthony Marriott; His Honour Judge Kenny; a Circuit Judge, since 1987; *b* 24 May 1939; *o s* of late Noel Edgar Edward Marriott Kenny, OBE, and

Cynthia Margaret Seton Kenny (*née* Melville); *m* 1969, Monica Grant Mackenzie, *yr d* of late H. B. Grant Mackenzie, Pretoria; three *s*. *Educ:* St Andrew's Coll., Grahamstown, Cape Province; Christ's Coll., Cambridge (MA). Called to the Bar, Gray's Inn, 1963; South Eastern Circuit. A Recorder, 1980–87; Principal Judge in Civil Matters, Berks and Bucks, 1992–98; designated Family Judge: Reading, 1991–2000; Truro, 2000. *Recreations:* music, reading, tennis, ski-ing. *Address:* c/o SE Circuit Administator, 18 Maltravers Street, WC2R 3EU.
Died 14 Aug. 2002.

KERMODE, Hon. Sir Ronald (Graham Quayle), KBE 1986 (CBE 1975); Judge of the Court of Appeal, Republic of Fiji, 1988–91; *b* 26 June 1919; *s* of George Graham Kermode and Linda Margaret (*née* McInnis); *m* 1945, Amy Rivett Marr; two *s* two *d*. *Educ:* Whangarei High Sch., NZ; Auckland University Coll. (LLB). Served War, NZ and Fiji Mil. Forces, 1939–45. In private legal practice, 1945–75; Puisne Judge, Supreme Court of Fiji, 1976–86; Judge of the Court of Appeal: Kiribati, 1983–86; Fiji, 1985–87. Tribunal, Fiji Sugar Industry, 1985–92. Elected European MLC, Fiji, 1958, and served for 15 years as Mem. of Council and Parliament; first elected Speaker of the House of Representatives, 1968–73. *Address:* 44A Cook Street, Howick, Auckland, New Zealand. *T:* (9) 5375102.
Died 18 June 2004.

KERR, Clark; educator; *b* 17 May 1911; *s* of Samuel W. and Caroline Clark Kerr; *m* 1934, Catherine Spaulding; two *s* one *d*. *Educ:* Swarthmore Coll. (AB); Stanford Univ. (MA); Univ. of Calif., Berkeley (PhD). Actg Asst Prof., Stanford Univ., 1939–40; Asst Prof., later Assoc. Prof., Univ. of Washington, 1940–45; Prof., Dir, Inst. of Industrial Relations, Univ. of Calif, Berkeley, 1945–52; Chancellor, Univ. of Calif at Berkeley, 1952–58; Pres., Univ. of Calif, 1958–67, then Emeritus President. Chairman: Carnegie Commn on Higher Educn, 1967–74; Carnegie Council on Policy Studies in Higher Educn, 1974–80; Bd, Work in America Inst., 1975–98; Bd, Global Perspectives in Educn, 1976–85, then Chm. Emeritus. Govt service with US War Labor Board, 1942–45. Mem. Pres. Eisenhower's Commn on Nat. Goals, President Kennedy and President Johnson Cttee on Labor-Management Policy; Program Dir, Strengthening Presidential Leadership Project, Assoc. of Governing Bds of Univs and Colls, 1982–86; Contract Arbitrator for: Boeing Aircraft Co. and Internat. Assoc. of Machinists, 1944–45; Armour & Co. and United Packinghouse Workers, 1945–47, 1949–52; Waterfront Employers' Assoc. and Internat. Longshoremen's and Warehousemen's Union, 1946–47, etc. Member: Amer. Acad. of Arts and Sciences; Royal Economic Society; Amer. Econ. Assoc.; Nat. Acad. of Arbitrators, etc. Phi Beta Kappa, Kappa Sigma. Trustee, Rockefeller Foundation, 1960–75; Chm., Armour Automation Cttee, 1959–79. Hon. Fellow, LSE, 1977. Hon. LLD: Swarthmore, 1952; Harvard, 1958; Princeton, 1959; Notre Dame, 1964; Chinese Univ. of Hong Kong, 1964; Rochester, 1967; Hon. DLitt, Strathclyde, 1965; Hon. Dr, Bordeaux, 1962, etc. Harold W. McGraw, Jr, Prize in Educn, 1990. *Publications:* (jtly) Unions, Management and the Public, 1948, rev. edns 1960, 1967; (jtly) Industrialism and Industrial Man, 1960, rev. edns 1964, 1973; The Uses of the University, 1963, 5th edn 2001; Labor and Management in Industrial Society, 1964, rev. edn 1972; Marshall, Marx and Modern Times, 1969; (jtly) Industrialism and Industrial Man Reconsidered, 1975; Labor Markets and Wage Determination, 1977; Education and National Development, 1979; The Future of Industrial Societies, 1983; (jtly) The Many Lives of Academic Presidents, 1986; (ed jtly) Industrial Relations in a New Age, 1986; (ed jtly) Economics of Labor in Industrial Society, 1986; (jtly) How Labor Markets Work, 1988; (jtly) The Guardians: boards of trustees of American colleges and universities, 1989; The Great Transformation in Higher Education 1960–1980, 1991; Troubled Times for American Higher Education, 1993; Higher Education

Cannot Escape History: issues for the twenty-first century, 1993; (ed jtly) Labor Economics and Industrial Relations: markets and institutions, 1994; The Gold and the Blue: a personal memoir of the University of California 1949–67, Vol. I, Academic Triumphs, 2001, Vol. II, Political Turmoil, 2003; contribs to American Economic Review, Review of Economics and Statistics, Quarterly Jl of Economics, etc. *Recreation:* gardening. *Address:* 8300 Buckingham Drive, El Cerrito, CA 94530, USA. *T:* (510) 2339651; (office) Institute of Industrial Relations, University of California, Berkeley, CA 94720-5555, USA. *T:* (510) 6428106, *Fax:* (510) 6435528.
Died 2 Dec. 2003.

KERR, Rt Hon. Sir Michael (Robert Emanuel), Kt 1972; PC 1981; a Lord Justice of Appeal, 1981–89; *b* 1 March 1921; *s* of Alfred Kerr; *m* 1st, 1952, Julia (marr. diss. 1982), *d* of Joseph Braddock; two *s* one *d*; 2nd, 1983, Diana, *yr d* of H. Neville Sneezum; one *s* one *d*. *Educ:* Aldenham Sch.; Clare Coll., Cambridge (BA (1st cl. Hons Law) 1947, MA 1952; Hon. Fellow, 1986). Served War, 1941–45 (Pilot; Flt-Lt). Called to the Bar, Lincoln's Inn, 1948, Bencher 1968, Treas., 1989; QC 1961. Dep. Chm., Hants QS, 1961–71; Mem., Vehicle and General Enquiry Tribunal, 1971–72; a Judge of the High Court of Justice, Queen's Bench Div., and of the Commercial and Admiralty Cts, 1972–78; Chm., Law Commn of England and Wales, 1978–81. Pres., London Court of Internat. Arbitration, 1985–94, Hon. Pres., 1994; Chm. Comr, UN Compensation Commn, 1996–. Member: Bar Council, 1968–72; Senate, 1969–72. Mem. Council of Management: British Inst. of Internat. and Comparative Law, 1973–; Inst. of Advanced Legal Studies, 1979–85; Chairman: Lord Chancellor's inter-deptl cttee on Foreign Judgments, 1974–81; Cttee of Management, Centre of Commercial Law Studies, QMC, 1980–89; Supreme Court Procedure Cttee, 1982–86; Chairman, Appeal Committee: ICAEW (formerly ICA), 1990–; SFA, 1991–; Takeover Panel, 1993–2001; Arbitration Council, WIPO, 1993–; Mem., Internat. Adv. Cttee, British Columbia Internat. Arbitration Centre, 1986–. Vice-Pres., British Maritime Law Assoc., 1977–; President: CIArb, 1983–86; British-German Jurists Assoc., 1986–91; Euro-Arab Assoc. for Internat. Arbitration, 1997–. Hon. Mem., Amer. Law Inst., 1985; Hon. Life Mem., Amer. and Canadian Bar Assocs, 1976. Chorley Lectr, LSE, 1977; Alexander Lectr, CIArb, 1984. Governor, Aldenham Sch., 1959–87. Hon. Fellow, QMC, 1986. Knight Comdr, Grand Cross of Order of Merit (Germany), 1991. *Publications:* McNair's Law of the Air, 1953, 1965; The Macao Sardine Case, 1989; As Far As I Remember, 1995; articles and lectures on commercial law and arbitration. *Recreations:* travel, music, trying to work less, a second edition of children. *Address:* Essex Court Chambers, 24 Lincoln's Inn Fields, WC2A 3AD. *T:* (020) 7813 8000; 10 Peterborough Villas, SW6 2AT. *T:* (020) 7736 2144/6655. *Clubs:* Garrick, Pilgrims.
Died 14 April 2002.

KERR, Thomas Henry, CB 1983; Director, Royal Aircraft Establishment, 1980–84; *b* 18 June 1924; *s* of late Albert Edward Kerr and Mrs Francis Jane Kerr (*née* Simpson); *m* 1946, Myrnie Evelyn Martin Hughes; two *d*. *Educ:* Magnus Grammar, Newark; University Coll., Durham Univ. (BSc 1949); Diplôme Paul Tissendier 1957. CEng; FRAeS. RAFVR pilot, 1942–46. Royal Aircraft Establishment: Aero Flight, 1949–55; Head of Supersonic Flight Group, 1955–59; Scientific Adviser to C-in-C Bomber Comd, High Wycombe, 1960–64; Head of Assessment Div., Weapons Dept, RAE, 1964–66; Dep. Dir and Dir of Defence Operational Analysis Estabt, 1966–70; Head of Weapons Research Gp, Weapons Dept, RAE, 1970–72; Dir Gen. Establishments Resources Programmes (C), MoD (PE), 1972–74; Dir, Nat. Gas Turbine Estabt, 1974–80. R&D Dir, Royal Ordnance plc, 1984–86; Dir, Hunting Engineering, 1986–94 (Technical Dir, 1986–88). Consultant, Systems Designers Scientific, 1985–88. Mem. Council, RAeS, 1979, Pres., 1985–86. Freeman, City of London, 1996; Liveryman, GAPAN,

1996–2004. *Publications:* Always a Challenge: an RAF scientist in the Cold War years – a first hand account, 2002; reports and memoranda of Aeronautical Research Council, lectures to RAeS and RUSI. *Recreations:* bridge, water ski-ing, tennis, badminton. *Address:* Bundu, 013 Kingsley Avenue, Camberley, Surrey GU15 2NA. *T:* (01276) 25961. *Died 9 Sept. 2004.*

KERRUISH, Sir (Henry) Charles, Kt 1979; OBE 1964; President of Tynwald and of Legislative Council, Isle of Man, 1990–2000; Speaker, House of Keys, 1962–90; *b* 23 July 1917; *m* 1st, 1944, Margaret Gell (*d* 1970); one *s* three *d*; 2nd, 1975, Kay Warriner. *Educ:* Ramsey Grammar Sch. Farmer. Mem., House of Keys, 1946–90; ex-officio MLC, 1990–2000. Pres., CPA, 1983–84 (Regional Councillor for British Isles and Mediterranean, 1975–77). Mem. Court, Liverpool Univ., 1974–90. Hon. LLD Lancaster, 1990. *Recreations:* horse breeding, motor cycling. *Address:* Ballafayle, Maughold, Isle of Man. *T:* (01624) 812293. *Club:* Farmers'. *Died 23 July 2003.*

KERWIN, Prof. Larkin, CC 1980 (OC 1977); FRSC; Professor Emeritus, Laval University, since 1991; *b* 22 June 1924; *s* of T. J. Kerwin and Catherine Lonergan-Kerwin; *m* 1950, Maria Guadalupe Turcot; five *s* three *d*. *Educ:* St Francis Xavier Univ. (BSc 1944); Massachusetts Inst. of Technol. (MSc 1946); Université Laval (DSc 1949). FAIP. Laval University: Asst Prof., 1946; full Prof. of Physics, 1956; Dir, Dept of Physics, 1961–67; Vice-Dean, Faculty of Sciences, 1967–68; Vice-Rector, Academic, 1969–72; Rector, 1972–77. President: Royal Soc. of Canada, 1976–77; National Res. Council of Canada, 1980–89; IUPAP, 1988–91 (Sec.-Gen., 1972–84; First Vice-Pres., 1984–87); Canadian Space Agency, 1989–92. Mem., Académie des Grands Québecois, 1995. Hon. LLD: St Francis Xavier, 1970; Toronto, 1973; Concordia, 1976; Alberta, 1983; Dalhousie, 1983; Hon. DSc: British Columbia, 1973; McGill, 1974; Memorial, 1978; Ottawa, 1981; Royal Military Coll., Canada, 1982; Hon. DCL Bishop's, 1978; DSc (*hc*): Winnipeg, 1983; Windsor, 1984; Moncton, 1985; Montreal, 1991. Médaille de l'Assoc. Canadienne des Physiciens, 1969; Médaille Pariseau, 1965; Laval Alumni Medal, 1978; Gold Medal, Canadian Council of Professional Engineers, 1978; Rousseau Medal, l'ACFAS, 1983. Canadian Centennial Medal, 1967; Jubilee Medal, 1977, 2002. Kt Comdr with star, Holy Sepulchre of Jerusalem, 1974; Medal of Centenary of Roumania, 1977; Officier de la Légion d'Honneur (France), 1989. *Publications:* Atomic Physics, 1963 (trans. French, 1964, Spanish, 1970); papers in jls. *Recreation:* sailing. *Address:* 2166 Parc Bourbonnière, Sillery, QC G1T 1B4, Canada. *T:* (418) 5277949. *Died 1 May 2004.*

KESSEL, Prof. William Ivor Neil, MD; FRCP, FRCPE, FRCPsych; Professor of Psychiatry, 1965–90, and Dean of Postgraduate Studies, Faculty of Medicine, 1982–90, University of Manchester; *b* 10 Feb. 1925; *s* of Barney Kessel and Rachel Isabel Kessel; *m* 1958, Pamela Veronica Joyce (*née* Boswell); one *s* one *d*. *Educ:* Highgate Sch.; Trinity Coll., Cambridge (MA, MD); UCH Med. Sch.; Inst. of Psychiatry; MSc Manchester. FRCP 1967; FRCPE 1968; FRCPsych 1972. Staff, Inst. of Psych., 1960; scientific staff, MRC Unit for Epidemiol. of Psych. Illness, 1961, Asst Dir 1963; Hon. Sen. Lectr, Edinburgh Univ., 1964; Dean, Faculty of Med., Univ. of Manchester, 1974–76. Member: NW RHA, 1974–77; GMC, 1974–95; Adv. Council on Misuse of Drugs, 1972–80; Health Educn Council, 1979–86; Chm., Adv. Cttee on Alcoholism, DHSS, 1975–78; Cons. Adviser on alcoholism to DHSS, 1972–81, 1983–86. *Publications:* Alcoholism (with Prof. H. J. Walton), 1965, 3rd edn 1975, rev. edn 1989; articles on suicide and self-poisoning, alcoholism, psych. in gen. practice, psychosomatic disorders, psych. epidemiol., genius and mental illness, philosophy of uniform. *Address:* 24 Lees Road, Bramhall, Stockport, Cheshire SK7 1BT. *T:* (0161) 439 5121. *Club:* Athenæum. *Died 30 Dec. 2003.*

KEVILL-DAVIES, Christopher Evelyn, CBE 1973; JP; DL; *b* 12 July 1913; 3rd *s* of William A. S. H. Kevill-Davies, JP, Croft Castle, Herefordshire; *m* 1938, Virginia (*d* 2004), *d* of Adm. Ronald A. Hopwood, CB; one *s* one *d*. *Educ:* Radley College. Served War, Suffolk Yeomanry, 1939–43 and Grenadier Gds, 1943–45, France, Belgium and Germany. Mem., Gt Yarmouth BC, 1946–53; Chm., Norfolk Mental Deficiency HMC, 1950–69; Mem., East Anglian Regional Hosp. Bd, 1962 (Vice-Chm. 1967); Vice-Chm., E Anglian RHA, 1974–82. JP 1954, DL 1974–83, Norfolk; High Sheriff of Norfolk, 1965. *Address:* 11 Hale House, 34 De Vere Gardens, Kensington, W8 5AQ. *T:* (020) 7937 5066. *Clubs:* Cavalry and Guards, Royal Automobile; Norfolk (Norwich). *Died 24 Nov. 2004.*

KEYES, 2nd Baron *cr* 1943, of Zeebrugge and of Dover; **Roger George Bowlby Keyes;** Bt 1919; RN, retired; *b* 14 March 1919; 2nd *s* of Admiral of the Fleet Baron Keyes, GCB, KCVO, CMG, DSO and Eva Mary Salvin Bowlby (*d* 1973), Red Cross Order of Queen Elisabeth of Belgium, *d* of late Edward Salvin Bowlby, DL, of Gilston Park, Herts, and Knoydart, Inverness-shire; *S* father, 1945; *m* 1947, Grizelda Mary (*d* 1993), 2nd *d* of late Lieut-Col William Packe, DSO; three *s* two *d*. *Educ:* King's Mead Sch., Seaford; RNC, Dartmouth. Great Officer, Order of Leopold (Belgium), 2000. *Publication:* Outrageous Fortune, 1984 (SE Arts Literary Prize). *Heir: s* Hon. Charles William Packe Keyes [*b* 8 Dec. 1951; *m* 1978, Sadiye Yasmin Coskun, *e d* of late Mahir Coskun, Istanbul; *m* 1984, Sally Jackson; one *d*]. *Address:* St George's Lodge, Malling Road, Teston, Kent ME18 5AU. *Died 4 March 2005.*

KIDD, Sir Robert (Hill), KBE 1979; CB 1975; Head of Northern Ireland Civil Service, 1976–79; *b* 3 Feb. 1918; *s* of Andrew Kidd and Florence (*née* Hill), Belfast; *m* 1942, Harriet Moore Williamson; three *s* two *d*. *Educ:* Royal Belfast Academical Instn; Trinity Coll., Dublin (BA 1940, BLitt 1941). Army, 1941–46: commnd 1942, Royal Ulster Rifles, later seconded to Intell. Corps. Entered Northern Ireland Civil Service, 1947; Second Sec., Dept of Finance, NI, 1969–76. Allied Irish Banks: Dir, 1979–85; Mem., NI Local Bd, 1979–85 (Chm., 1980–85); Mem., NI Adv. Bd, 1985–88. Chairman: Ireland Co-operation North (UK) Ltd, 1982–85 (Bd Mem., 1985–89); Belfast Car Ferries Ltd, 1983–88. Board Mem., Irish Amer. Partnership, 1988–91. Governor, Royal Belfast Academical Inst., 1967–76, 1979–83; a Pro-Chancellor and Chm. Council, New Univ. of Ulster, 1980–84; Pres., TCD Assoc. of NI, 1981–83; Trustee: Scotch-Irish Trust of Ulster, 1980–96; Ulster Historical Foundn, 1981–95 (Chm., 1987–95). Hon. DLitt Ulster, 1985. *Recreation:* gardening. *Address:* 24 Massey Court, Belfast BT4 3GJ. *T:* (028) 9076 8694. *Died 28 Feb. 2004.*

KIDD, Ronald Alexander; HM Diplomatic Service, retired; *b* 19 June 1926; *s* of Alexander and Jean Kidd; *m* 1st, 1954, Agnes Japp Harrower (marr. diss. 1985); two *d*; 2nd, 1985, Pamela Dempster. *Educ:* Robert Gordon's College, Aberdeen; Queens' College, Cambridge (BA Hons 1951, MA 1956). Royal Air Force, 1944–48. Foreign Office, 1951; served at Singapore, Djakarta, Osaka and Macau, 1952–56; FO, 1956–60; Second, later First Sec., Seoul, 1961–62; Djakarta, 1962–63; Tokyo, 1964–68; FCO, 1968–71; Dar Es Salaam, 1971–72; Tokyo, 1972–77; Counsellor, FCO, 1977–81. Jubilee Medal, 1977. *Recreation:* golf. *Address:* 41 Princess Road, NW1 8JS. *T:* (020) 7722 8406; Apdo 159, Lista de Correíos, Sóller, Mallorca, Spain. *Club:* Royal Air Force. *Died 8 June 2002.*

KILBURN, Prof. Tom, CBE 1973; FRS 1965; FREng; Professor of Computer Science, University of Manchester, 1964–81, then Emeritus; *b* 11 Aug. 1921; *o s* of John W. and Ivy Kilburn, Dewsbury; *m* 1943, Irene (*née* Marsden); one *s* one *d*. *Educ:* Wheelwright Grammar Sch., Dewsbury; Sidney Sussex Coll., Cambridge (MA 1944); Manchester Univ. (PhD 1948; DSc 1953). FIEE; FBCS

1970 (Distinguished Fellow, 1974); FREng (FEng 1976). Telecommunications Research Estab., Malvern, 1942–46; Manchester Univ., 1947–81: Lecturer, 1949; Senior Lecturer, 1951; Reader in Electronics, 1955; Prof. of Computer Engineering, 1960. Foreign Associate, Nat. Acad. of Engrg, USA, 1980. Hon. FUMIST, 1984. DU Essex, 1968; DUniv Brunel, 1977; Hon. DSc Bath, 1979; Hon. DTech CNAA, 1981. McDowell Award, 1971, Computer Pioneer Award, 1982, IEEE; John Player Award, BCS, 1973; Royal Medal, Royal Society, 1978; Eckert Mauchly Award, ACM-IEEE, 1983. Mancunian of the year, Manchester Junior Chamber of Commerce, 1982. *Publications:* papers in Jl of Instn of Electrical Engineers, etc. *Address:* 11 Carlton Crescent, Urmston, Greater Manchester M31 1HZ. *T:* (0161) 748 3846.
Died 17 Jan. 2001.

KILBY, Jack St Clair; consultant, since 1970; *b* 11 Aug. 1923; *s* of Hubert and Vina Kilby; *m* 1958, Barbara Annegers (*d* 1981); two *d. Educ:* Univ. of Illinois (BS Electrical Engrg); Univ. of Wisconsin (MS Electrical Engrg). FIEEE 1966. Centralab. Div., Globe-Union Inc., 1948–58; Texas Instruments, Dallas, 1958–70 (invented first microchip); independent inventor, 1970–78; Dist. Prof. of Electrical Engrg, Texas A&M Univ., 1978–84. Holds numerous US patents. Mem., NAE, 1967. Nat. Medal of Sci., 1970; (jtly) Nobel Prize for Physics, 2000. *Address:* 6600 Lyndon B. Johnson Freeway, Dallas, TX 75240-6531, USA; *e-mail:* Kilby@71.cdm.
Died 20 June 2005.

KILLICK, Sir John (Edward), GCMG 1979 (KCMG 1971 CMG 1966); HM Diplomatic Service, retired; *b* 18 Nov. 1919; *s* of late Edward William James Killick and Doris Marjorie (*née* Stokes); *m* 1st, 1949, Lynette du Preez (*née* Leach) (*d* 1984); no *c*; 2nd, 1985, Irene M. H. Easton, OBE (*d* 1995). *Educ:* Latymer Upper Sch.; University Coll., London(Fellow 1973); Bonn Univ. Served with HM Forces, 1939–46: Suffolk Regt, W Africa Force and Airborne Forces. Foreign Office, 1946–48; Control Commn and High Commn for Germany (Berlin, Frankfurt and Bonn), 1948–51; Private Sec. to Parly Under-Sec., Foreign Office, 1951–54; British Embassy, Addis Ababa, 1954–57; Canadian Nat. Def. Coll., 1957–58; Western Dept, Foreign Office, 1958–62; Imp. Def. Coll., 1962; Counsellor and Head of Chancery, British Embassy, Washington, 1963–68; Asst Under-Sec. of State, FCO, 1968–71; Ambassador to USSR, 1971–73; Dep. Under-Sec. of State, FCO and Permanent Rep. on Council of WEU, 1973–75; Ambassador and UK Permanent Rep. to NATO, 1975–79. Dir, Dunlop South Africa, 1980–85. Pres., 1985–92, Vice-Pres., 1992–93, GB Atlantic Cttee; Vice-Pres., Atlantic Treaty Assoc., 1992–94. *Recreations:* reading, writing. *Address:* 5 Norstead Gardens, Southborough, Kent TN4 0DE. *Club:* East India.
Died 12 Feb. 2004.

KILNER BROWN, Hon. Sir Ralph; see Brown.

KILPATRICK, Dame Judith (Ann Gladys), DBE 2000; Headteacher, City of Portsmouth Girls' School, since 1995; *b* 20 Feb. 1952; *d* of James Foxley and late Kathleen Alice Foxley (*née* Kingdon); *m* 1994, Andrew Kelvin Kilpatrick (marr. diss. 1998). *Educ:* Cowley Grammar Sch. for Girls, St Helens; Univ. of Kent (BA Hons); Univ. of Southampton (PGCE). Teacher of History and English and Integrative Studies, 1974–85; Hd of Careers, 1985–86; Regents Park Girls' Sch., Southampton; Schools/Industry Liaison Officer, SE Hants, 1987–89; Dep. Headteacher, King Richard Sch., Portsmouth, 1989–93; Headteacher, The Wavell Sch., Farnborough, 1993–95. *Recreations:* opera, classical music, theatre, reading, travel. *Address:* 2 Rushmere Gate, Green Lane, Hambledon, Hants PO7 4SS. *T:* (023) 9263 2079.
Died 5 Sept. 2002.

KIMBERLEY, 4th Earl of, *cr* 1866; **John Wodehouse;** Bt, 1611; Baron Wodehouse, 1797; Lt Grenadier Guards; *b* 12 May 1924; *o s* of 3rd Earl Kimberley and Margaret (*d* 1950), *d* of late Col Leonard Howard Irby; *S* father, 1941;

m 1st, 1945, Diana Evelyn (marr. diss. 1948; she *d* 2000), *o d* of Lt-Col Hon. Sir Piers Walter Legh, GCVO, CMG, CIE, OBE; 2nd, 1949, Mrs Carmel June Dunnett (marr. diss. 1952; she *d* 1992); one *s*; 3rd, 1953, Mrs Cynthia Westendarp (marr. diss. 1960; she *d* 1999); two *s*; 4th, 1961, Margaret Simons (marr. diss. 1965); one *s*; 5th, 1970, Mrs Gillian Raw (marr. diss. 1982); 6th, 1982, Sarah Jane Hope Consett, *e d* of Colonel Christopher D'Arcy Preston Consett, DSO, MC. *Educ:* Eton; Cambridge. Lieut, Grenadier Guards, 1942–45; active service, NW Europe. Member: House of Lords All Party Defence Study Gp, 1976–99 (Sec., 1978–92; Pres., 1992–99); House of Lords All Party UFO Study Gp, 1979–99; former Liberal Spokesman on: aviation and aerospace; defence; voluntary community services; left Liberal Party, May 1979, joined Cons. Party. Chm., Foreign Affairs Cttee, Monday Club, 1979–82; Mem. Exec. Cttee, Assoc. of Cons. Peers, 1981–84; Pres., Cricklade and Latton Cons. Assoc., 1988– (Chm., 1986–88). Member: Council, The Air League; Council, British Maritime League; RUSI; IISS; British Atlantic Cttee. Delegate to N Atlantic Assembly, 1981–93. Vice-Pres., World Council on Alcoholism; Chm., Nat. Council on Alcoholism, 1982–85. Mem., British Bobsleigh Team, 1949–58. ARAeS 1977. *Publication:* The Whim of the Wheel (memoirs), 2001. *Recreations:* shooting, fishing, all field sports, gardening, bridge. *Heir:* s Lord Wodehouse [*b* 15 Jan. 1951; *m* 1973, Hon. Carol Palmer, *er d* of 3rd Baron Palmer, OBE; one *s* one *d*]. *Address:* Hailstone House, Cricklade, Swindon, Wilts SN6 6JP. *T:* (01793) 750344. *Clubs:* White's, Naval and Military, MCC; House of Lords' Yacht; Falmouth Shark Angling (Pres.).
Died 26 May 2002.

KIMBLE, George (Herbert Tinley), PhD; Professor of Geography, 1957–66, Chairman, Department of Geography, 1957–62, Indiana University; Research Director, US Geography Project, Twentieth Century Fund, 1962–68; *b* 2 Aug. 1908; *s* of John H. and Minnie Jane Kimble; *m* 1935, Dorothy Stevens Berry; one *s* one *d. Educ:* Eastbourne Grammar Sch.; King's Coll., London (MA); Univ. of Montreal (PhD). Asst Lectr in Geography, Univ. of Hull, 1931–36; Lectr in Geography, Univ. of Reading, 1936–39. Served War as Lt and Lt-Comdr, British Naval Meteorol Service, 1939–44. Prof. of Geography and Chm., Dept of Geography, McGill Univ., 1945–50; International Georgraphical Union: Sec.-Treasurer, 1949–56; Chm., Commn on Humid Tropics, 1956–61. Director: Amer. Geog. Soc., 1950–53; Survey of Tropical Africa, Twentieth Century Fund, NY, 1953–60. Lectures: Rushton, 1952; Borah, Univ. of Idaho, 1956; Haynes Foundn, Univ. of Redlands, 1966; Visiting Professor: Univ. of Calif. (Berkeley), 1948–49; Stanford Univ., 1961; Stockholm Sch. of Economics, 1961. Governor, Eastbourne Sixth Form Coll., 1980–81. FRGS 1931. Hon. Mem., Inst. British Geographers. Editor, Weather Res. Bulletin, 1957–60. *Publications:* Geography in the Middle Ages, 1938; The World's Open Spaces, 1939; The Shepherd of Banbury, 1941; (with Raymond Bush) The Weather, 1943 (Eng.), 1946 (Amer.), (author) 2nd (Eng.) edn 1951; Military Geography of Canada, 1949; (with Sir Dudley Stamp) An Introduction to Economic Geography, 1949; (with Sir Dudley Stamp) The World: a general geography, 1950; The Way of the World, 1953; Our American Weather, 1955; Le Temps, 1957; Tropical Africa (2 vols), 1960; Ghana, 1960; Tropical Africa (abridged edition), 1962; (with Ronald Steel) Tropical Africa Today, 1966; Hunters and Collectors, 1970; Man and his World, 1972; Herdsmen, 1973; From the Four Winds, 1974; This is our World, 1981; (ed for Hakluyt Soc.) Esmeraldo de Situ Orbis, 1937; (ed for American Geographical Soc. with Dorothy Good) Geography of the Northlands, 1955; articles in: Geog. Jl, Magazine, Review; Canadian Geog. Jl; Bulletin Amer. Meteorol Soc.; The Reporter; Los Angeles Times; The New York Times Magazine. *Recreations:* music, gardening. *Address:* 32 Heath Hill Lodge, Brighton BN2 4FH.
Died 14 Oct. 2004.

KINCHIN SMITH, Michael, OBE 1987; Chairman, Banburyshire Community Transport Association Ltd, 1993–98; *b* 8 May 1921; *s* of Francis John Kinchin Smith, Lectr in Classics, Inst. of Educn, London, and Dione Jean Elizabeth, *d* of Sir Francis Henry May, GCMG, sometime Governor of Hong Kong; *m* 1947, Rachel Frances, *er d* of Rt Hon. Sir Henry Urmston Willink, 1st Bt, MC, QC, Master of Magdalene Coll., Cambridge; four *s* two *d. Educ:* Westminster Sch. (King's Schol.); Christ Church, Oxford (Schol.; BA 1st cl. hons Mod. History); Pres. Oxford Union, 1941. Served with 2nd and 3rd Bns, Coldstream Guards in Italian Campaign (Captain; despatches). Commercial and Admin. Trainee, ICI Ltd, 1947; admin. posts with BBC, 1950–78: Asst, Staff Admin, 1950; Admin Officer, Talks (Sound), 1954; Asst Estabt Officer, TV, 1955; Estabt Officer, Programmes, TV, 1961; Staff Admin Officer, 1962; Asst Controller, Staff Admin, 1964; Controller, Staff Admin, 1967; Controller, Development, Personnel, 1976. Lay Assistant to Archbishop of Canterbury, 1979–84; Appointments' Sec. to Archbishops of Canterbury and York, and Sec., Crown Appts Commn, 1984–87. Lay Selector, ACCM, 1963–73 (Mem. Candidates Cttee, 1966–69); Lay Chm., Richmond and Barnes Deanery Synod, 1970–76; Mem. General Synod, C of E, 1975–78. Chm., Diocesan Trustees (Oxford) Ltd, 1991–98. Chm. Exec. Council, RIPA, 1975–77; CIPD; Vice Pres. (Pay and Employment Conditions), IPM, 1978–80. 1st Chm., Mortlake with East Sheen Soc., 1969–71; Chm., Assoc. of Amenity Societies in Richmond-upon-Thames, 1973–77. *Publication:* (jtly) Forward from Victory, 1943. *Recreations:* walking, local history. *Address:* Pitts Orchard, Cumberford, Bloxham, Banbury, Oxon OX15 4QG. *Club:* Oxford and Cambridge. *Died 30 Oct. 2002.*

KINCRAIG, Hon. Lord; Robert Smith Johnston; a Senator of the College of Justice in Scotland, 1972–87; Chairman, Review of Parole and related matters in Scotland, since 1988; *b* 10 Oct. 1918; *s* of W. T. Johnston, iron merchant, Glasgow; *m* 1st, 1943, Joan (decd), *d* of late Col A. G. Graham, Glasgow; one *s* one *d*; 2nd, 2003, Mrs Margaret Ogg. *Educ:* Strathallan, Perthshire; St John's Coll., Cambridge; Glasgow Univ. BA (Hons) Cantab, 1939; LLB (with distinction) Glasgow, 1942. Mem. of Faculty of Advocates, 1942; Advocate-Depute, Crown Office, 1953–55; QC (Scotland) 1955; Home Advocate Depute, 1959–62; Sheriff Principal of Roxburgh, Berwick and Selkirk, 1964–70; Dean of the Faculty of Advocates of Scotland, 1970–72. Contested (U) Stirling and Falkirk Burghs General Election, 1959. *Recreations:* gardening, golf. *Address:* Westwood Cottage, Longniddry, East Lothian EH32 0PL. *T:* (01875) 853583. *Club:* Hon. Company of Edinburgh Golfers (Edinburgh).
Died 19 Sept. 2004.

KING OF WARTNABY, Baron *cr* 1983 (Life Peer), of Wartnaby in the County of Leicestershire; **John Leonard King,** Kt 1979; President Emeritus, British Airways Plc, since 1997 (Chairman, 1981–93; President, 1993–97); President, Babcock International Group plc, since 1994 (Chairman, 1970–94); *b* 29 Aug. 1917; *yr s* of Albert John King and Kathleen King; *m* 1st 1941, Lorna Kathleen Sykes (*d* 1969); three *s* one *d*; 2nd, 1970, Hon. Isabel Monckton, *y d* of 8th Viscount Galway. Founded Ferrybridge Industries Ltd and Whitehouse Industries Ltd, subseq. Pollard Ball & Roller Bearing Co. Ltd, 1945 (Man. Dir 1945, Chm., 1961–69); Chairman: Dennis Motor Hldgs Ltd, 1970–72; Babcock & Wilcox Ltd, subseq. Babcock International plc, later FKI Babcock plc, then Babcock Internat. Gp, 1970–94; Dir, David Brown Corp. Ltd, 1971–75. Current chairmanships and directorships include: The Daily Telegraph plc; Short Brothers plc; Norman Broadbent International; Wide Range Engineering Services Ltd; The Spectator (1828), 1993–2004; Gartland Whalley Barker Plc, 1997–; former directorships include: Dick Corp. (USA); Royal Ordnance plc (Dep. Chm.); Clogau Gold Mines; National Nuclear Corp.; British Nuclear Associates Ltd; Tyneham

Investments; Babcock (Plant Leasing); 1928 Investment Trust; SKF (UK); Sabena World Airlines; First Union Corp. (USA). Member: Engineering Industries Council, 1975; NEDC Cttee on Finance for Investment, 1976–78; Grand Council and Financial Policy Cttee, CBI, 1976–78; Chairman: City and Industrial Liaison Council, 1973–85; Review Bd for Govt Contracts, 1975–78; British Olympic Appeals Cttee, 1975–78; Macmillan Appeal for Continuing Care, 1977–78; NEB, 1980–81 (Dep. Chm., 1979–80); Alexandra Rose Day Foundn, 1980–85; Mem. Cttee, Ranfurly Library Service; Vice-Pres., Cancer Relief Macmillan Fund (formerly Nat. Soc. for Cancer Relief), 1988; Trustee, Liver Res. Unit Trust, 1988–. Dir, Royal Opera Trust. Master of Foxhounds: Badsworth Foxhounds, 1949–58; Duke of Rutland's Foxhounds (Belvoir), 1958–72; Chm., Belvoir Hunt, 1972. Farms his estate in Leics. Freeman, City of London, 1984. FIMgt (FBIM 1978); FCILT (FCIT 1982). Hon. CRAeS, 1986. Hon. Dr Gardner-Webb Coll., USA, 1980; Hon. DSc Cranfield Inst. of Technology, 1989. Comdr, Royal Order of Polar Star (Sweden), 1983. Nat. Free Enterprise Award, 1987. *Recreations:* hunting, field sports, racing, painting. *Address:* Wartnaby, Melton Mowbray, Leics LE14 3HY. *Clubs:* White's, Pratts'; Brook (New York).
Died 12 July 2005.

KING, Charles Andrew Buchanan, CMG 1961; MBE 1944; HM Diplomatic Service, retired; *b* 25 July 1915; *s* of late Major Andrew Buchanan King, 7th Argyll and Sutherland Highlanders and of Evelyn Nina (*née* Sharpe). *Educ:* Wellington Coll.; Magdalene Coll., Cambridge (BA 1936, MA 1940). Vice-Consul: Zürich, 1940, Geneva, 1941; Attaché, HM Legation, Berne, 1942; transf. to FO, 1946; 2nd Sec., Vienna, 1950; transf. to FO 1953; to Hong Kong, 1958; to FO 1961; retired, 1967. Head of W European Div., Overseas Dept, London Chamber of Commerce, 1968–70. *Recreation:* travel. *Club:* Naval and Military. *Died 18 Oct. 2002.*

KING, Prof. Edmund James, PhD, DLit; Professor of Education, King's College, London, 1975–79, then Emeritus; *b* 19 June 1914; *s* of James and Mary Alice King; *m* 1939, Margaret Mary Breakell; one *s* three *d. Educ:* Univ. of Manchester (BA, MA); Univ. of London (PhD, DLit). Taught in grammar schs, 1936–47; Asst, then Sen. Asst to Dir of Extra-Mural Studies, Univ. of London, 1947–53; Lectr, subseq. Reader, KCL, 1953–75, also Dir, Comparative Research Unit, 1970–73. Visiting appts at Amer., Canadian and Chinese univs; also in Melbourne, Tokyo, Tehran, etc; lecturing and adv. assignments in many countries. Editor, Comparative Education, 1978–92. *Publications:* Other Schools and Ours, 1958, 5th edn 1979; World Perspectives in Education, 1962, 2nd edn 1965; (ed) Communist Education, 1963; Society, Schools and Progress in the USA, 1965; Education and Social Change, 1966; Comparative Studies and Educational Decision, 1968; Education and Development in Western Europe, 1969; (ed) The Teacher and the Needs of Society, 1970; The Education of Teachers: a comparative analysis, 1970; (with W. Boyd) A History of Western Education, 1972, 12th edn 1995; Post-compulsory Education, vol. I: a new analysis in Western Europe, 1974; vol. II: the way ahead, 1975 (both with C. H. Moor and J. A. Mundy); (ed) Reorganizing Education, 1977; (ed) Education for Uncertainty, 1979; Technological/occupational Challenge, Social Transformation and Educational Response, 1986. *Recreations:* gardening, music, writing. *Address:* 40 Alexandra Road, Epsom, Surrey KT17 4BT.
Died 8 Feb. 2002.

KING, Henry Edward St Leger; Chairman: Rentokil Initial plc (formerly Rentokil Group), since 1994 (Director, since 1985); GKR Group Ltd, 1995–2000; *b* 11 Oct. 1936; *s* of Robert James King and Dorothy Louisa Marie (*née* Wickert); *m* 1st, 1964, Kathleen Bridget Wilcock (marr. diss. 1989); one *d* (one *s* decd); 2nd, 1990, Susan Amy Goldsmith (marr. diss. 1994); 3rd, 1996,

Margaret Evelyn Empson Cox. *Educ:* Whitgift Middle Sch.; Fitzwilliam Coll., Cambridge (MA, LLB). Nat. Service, 1955–57. Solicitor, England, 1964 and Hong Kong, 1977. Joined Denton Hall, 1964: solicitor, 1964–67; Partner, 1967–96; Chm., 1993–96; Consultant, 1996–. Director: City Centre Restaurants plc, 1986–2001 (Chm., 1996–2001); Brambles Investments PLC, 1988–; TotalFinaElf Exploration UK (formerly Total Oil Marine) plc, 1997–. *Recreations:* travel, theatre, music. *Address:* 1 Fleet Place, EC4M 7WS. *T:* (020) 7245 7015. *Club:* Riverside Racquet.   *Died 16 March 2002.*

KING, Hilary William, CBE 1964 (MBE 1944); HM Diplomatic Service, retired; *b* 10 March 1919; *s* of Dr W. H. King, Fowey, Cornwall; *m* 1947, Dr Margaret Helen Grierson Borrowman; one *s* three *d*. *Educ:* Sherborne; Corpus Christi Coll., Cambridge (BA 1946). Served War of 1939–45; Signals Officer, mission to Yugoslav Partizan GHQ, 1943–45. Apptd Mem. Foreign (subseq. Diplomatic) Service, Nov. 1946; a Vice-Consul, Yugoslavia, 1947–48; transferred to Foreign Office, 1949; promoted 1st Sec., 1950; transf. to Vienna as a Russian Sec., 1951; Washington, 1953; transf. Foreign Office, 1958; Commercial Counsellor, Moscow, 1959; acted as Chargé d'Affaires, 1960; Ambassador to Guinea, 1962–65; St Antony's Coll., Oxford, Oct. 1965–June 1966; Counsellor of Embassy, Warsaw, 1966–67; Head of UN (Economic and Social) Dept, FCO, 1968–71; Consul-Gen., Hamburg, 1971–74. *Recreations:* sailing, amateur radio, Cold War history. *Address:* Fuaim an Sruth, South Cuan, Oban, Argyll PA34 4TU.   *Died 17 Feb. 2003.*

KING, Dame Ruth; *see* Railton, Dame R.

KINGHORN, Squadron Leader Ernest; *b* 1 Nov. 1907; *s* of A. Kinghorn, Leeds; *m* 1942, Eileen Mary Lambert Russell (*d* 1980); one *s* (and one *s* one *d* decd). *Educ:* Leeds, Basel and Lille Universities. Languages Master, Ashville Coll., Doncaster Grammar Sch. and Roundhay Sch., Leeds. Served in Intelligence Branch, RAF. British Officer for Control of Manpower, SHAEF, and Staff Officer CCG. MP (Lab) Great Yarmouth, 1945–50, Yarmouth Division of Norfolk, 1950–51. *Address:* 59 Queens Avenue, Hanworth, Middx TW13 7NT.

Died 15 Jan. 2001.

KINGSALE, 35th Baron *cr* 1223 (by some reckonings 30th Baron); **John de Courcy;** Baron Courcy and Baron of Ringrone; Premier Baron of Ireland; President, Impex Consultants Ltd, since 1988; Director: Marquis de Verneuil Trust, since 1971; de Courcy, Daunt Professional & Executive Agencies (Australia), since 1987; Kinsale Development Co., since 1989; Chairman, National Association for Service to the Realm; *b* 27 Jan. 1941; *s* of Lieutenant-Commander the Hon. Michael John Rancé de Courcy, RN (killed on active service, 1940), and Joan (*d* 1967), *d* of Robert Reid; *S* grandfather, 1969. *Educ:* Stowe; Universities of Paris and Salzburg. Short service commission, Irish Guards, 1962–65. At various times before and since: law student, property developer, film extra, white hunter, bingo caller, etc. Patron, L'Orchestre du Monde, 1988–. *Recreations:* shooting, food and drink, palaeontology, venery. *Heir: cousin* Nevinson Mark de Courcy, *b* 11 May 1958. *Address:* 15 Dallimore Mead, Nunney, Frome, Somerset BA11 4NB. *Club:* Cavalry and Guards.   *Died 15 Sept. 2005.*

KINGSTON, 11th Earl of, *cr* 1768 (Ire.); **Barclay Robert Edwin King-Tenison;** Bt 1682; Baron Kingston, 1764; Viscount Kingsborough, 1766; Baron Erris, 1800; Viscount Lorton, 1806; formerly Lieutenant, Royal Scots Greys; *b* 23 Sept. 1943; *o s* of 10th Earl of Kingston and Gwyneth, *d* of William Howard Evans (she *m* 2nd, 1951, Brig. E. M. Tyler (marr. diss.), DSO, MC, late RA and 3rd, 1963, Robert Woodford); *S* father, 1948; *m* 1st, 1965, Patricia Mary (marr. diss. 1974), *o d* of E. C. Killip, Llanfairfechan, N Wales; one *s* one *d*; 2nd, 1974, Victoria (marr. diss. 1979), *d* of D. C. Edmonds; 3rd, 1990, Corleen Jennifer Rathbone; 4th, 2000, Jane Sutherland. *Educ:*

Winchester. *Heir: s* Viscount Kingsborough [*b* 20 March 1969; *m* 1994, Ruth Margaret Buckner; one *s* one *d*].
Died 19 March 2002.

KINSMAN, Surgeon Rear-Adm. Francis Michael, CBE 1982 (OBE 1972); Surgeon Rear Admiral (Ships and Establishments), 1980–82, retired; *b* 5 May 1925; *s* of Oscar Edward Kinsman and Margaret Vera Kinsman; *m* 1st, 1949, Catherine Forsyth Barr; one *s*; 2nd, 1955, Margaret Emily Hillier; two *s*. *Educ:* Rydal Sch., Colwyn Bay; St Bartholomew's Hosp. DA. MRCS, LRCP, MFCM. Joined RN, 1952; served, 1952–66: HMS Comus, HMS Tamar, HMS Centaur; RN Hosp. Malta, RN Air Med. Sch., RNAS Lossiemouth; Pres., Central Air Med. Bd, 1966–69; Jt Services Staff Coll., 1969; Staff, Med. Dir Gen. (Naval), 1970–73; Dir, Naval Med. Staff Trng, 1973–76; Comd MO to C-in-C Naval Home Comd, 1976–79; MO i/c RN Hosp. Gibraltar, 1979–80. QHP 1980–82. OStJ 1977. *Recreations:* music, painting, fishing, woodwork. *Address:* Pound House, Meonstoke, Southampton, Hants SO32 3NP.

Died 17 Aug. 2005.

KINTORE, 13th Earl of, *cr* 1677 (Scot.); **Michael Canning William John Keith;** Lord Keith of Inverurie and Keith Hall, 1677 (Scot.); Bt 1897; Baron 1925; Viscount Stonehaven 1938; *b* 22 Feb. 1939; *s* of 12th Earl of Kintore, and of Delia Virginia, *d* of William Loyd; assumed surname of Keith in lieu of Baird, 1967; *S* father, 1989; *m* 1972, Mary Plum, *d* of late Sqdn Leader E. G. Plum, Rumson, NJ, and of Mrs Roy Hudson; one *s* one *d*. *Educ:* Eton; RMA Sandhurst. Lately Lieutenant, Coldstream Guards. President: Westminster Exams plc, 1996–; Inst. of Certified Book-Keepers, 1997–. ACII. Hon. Fellow, Internat. Assoc. of Book-Keepers, 1994– (Pres., 1994–96). Hon. LLD Aberdeen, 1993. *Heir: s* Lord Inverurie, Master of Kintore, *b* 15 April 1976. *Address:* The Stables, Keith Hall, Inverurie, Aberdeenshire AB51 0LD. *T:* (01467) 620495.   *Died 30 Oct. 2004.*

KIRALFY, Prof. Albert Kenneth Roland; Professor of Law, King's College, London, 1964–81, then Emeritus Professor; *b* Toronto, 5 Dec. 1915; *s* of Bolossy Kiralfy, theatrical impresario, and Helen Dawnay; *m* 1960, Roberta Ann Routledge. *Educ:* Streatham Grammar Sch.; King's Coll., London Univ. (LLB 1935, LLM 1936, PhD 1949). Served War of 1939–45. Called to the Bar, Gray's Inn, 1947. King's College, London: Asst Lectr, 1937–39 and 1947–48; Lectr, 1948–51; Reader, 1951–64; Dean of College Law Faculty, 1974–77; FKC 1971. Chm., Bd of Studies in Laws, London Univ., 1971–74; Dean of Univ. Law Faculty, 1980–81. Vis. Prof., Osgoode Hall Law Sch., Toronto, 1961–62; Exchange Scholar, Leningrad Law Sch., 1964, Moscow Law Sch., 1970; Prague Acad. of Sciences, 1975. Dir, Comparative Law Course, Luxembourg, 1968. Chm., Council of Hughes Parry Hall, London Univ., 1970–82. Editor, Journal of Legal History, 1980–90; Mem. Editorial Bd, Internat. and Comparative Law Quarterly, 1956–86; Reviser, English trans., Polish Civil Code, 1981. *Publications:* The Action on the Case, 1951; The English Legal System, 1954 (and later edns; 8th edn 1990); A Source Book of English Law, 1957; Potter's Historical Introduction to English Law, 4th edn 1958; (with Prof. G. Jones) Guide to Selden Society Publications, 1960, reissued as part of Selden Soc. Centenary Guide, 1987; Translation of Russian Civil Codes, 1966; chapter, English Law, in Derrett, Introduction to Legal Systems, 1968; (with R. A. Routledge) Guide to Additional MSS at Gray's Inn Library, 1971; General Editor, Comparative Law of Matrimonial Property, 1972; (ed jtly): New Perspectives in Scottish Legal History, 1984; Custom, Courts and Counsel, 1985; The Burden of Proof, 1987; contributed: Encyclopædia of Soviet Law, 1973 (Leiden); Contemporary Soviet Law, 1974; East-West Business Transactions, 1974; Common Law, Encyclopædia Britannica, 1974; Codification in the Communist World, 1975; Russian Law: Historical Perspectives, 1977; Le

Nuove Frontiere del Diritto, 1979; André Loeber Festschrift, 1988; Nuovi Moti per la Formazione del Diritto, 1988; International Encyclopedia of Comparative Law, 1989; Macerata Conference Papers, 1989 (Italy); Jean Bodin Soc., vol. 52, 1990, vol. 60, 1993; History of Law—Russia and England, 1990 (Moscow); Il Processo Civile Inglese, ed L. Moccia, 1991; European Current Law, 1992–96; Il Diritto Privato Europeo: problemi e prospettive, 1993; Studi in Memoria di Gino Gorla, 1994; *Rapporteur*, The Child without Family Ties, Congress of Jean Bodin Soc., Strasbourg, 1972; contribs to Jl of Legal History; NY Jl of Internat. and Comparative Law; Review of Socialist Laws. *Recreations:* history, languages. *Address:* 58 Cheriton Square, SW17 8AE.
Died 27 April 2001.

KIRBY, Hon. Sir Richard (Clarence), Kt 1961; AC 1985; Chairman, Advertising Standards Council, 1973–88; *b* 22 Sept. 1904; *s* of Samuel Enoch Kirby and Agnes Mary Kirby, N Queensland; *m* 1st, 1937, Hilda Marie Ryan (*d* 1991); two *d*; 2nd, 1998, Joyce Sidaway. *Educ:* The King's Sch., Parramatta; University of Sydney (LLB). Solicitor, NSW, 1928; called to Bar, 1933; served AIF, 1942–44; Mem. Adult Adv. Educl Council to NSW Govt, 1944–46; Judge, Dist Court, NSW, 1944–47; Mem. Austr. War Crimes Commn, 1945, visiting New Guinea, Morotai, Singapore, taking evidence on war crimes; Australia Rep. on War Crimes, Lord Mountbatten's HQ, Ceylon, 1945; Royal Commissioner on various occasions for Federal, NSW and Tasmanian Govts, 1945–47; Acting Judge Supreme Court of NSW, 1947; Chief Judge, Commonwealth Court of Conciliation and Arbitration, 1956–73. Austr. Rep., UN Security Council's Cttee on Good Offices on Indonesian Question, 1947–48, participating in Security Council Debates, Lake Success, USA; Chm., Stevedoring Industry Commn, 1947–49; (first) Pres., Commonwealth Conciliation and Arbitration Commn, 1956–73; Chm., Nat. Stevedoring Conf., 1976–77. Pres., H. V. Evatt Meml Foundn, 1979–85. Mem. Council, Wollongong Univ., 1979–84. Hon. DLitt Wollongong Univ., 1984. Bintaq Jasa Ultama (Indonesia), 1995. *Recreation:* encouraging good will in industry. *Address:* Unit 60, Bayview Gardens Village, Cabbage Tree Road, Bayview, NSW 2104, Australia. *T:* (2) 99972096. *Club:* Athenæum (Melbourne).   *Died 25 Oct. 2001.*

KIRK, Prof. Geoffrey Stephen, DSC 1945; LittD; FBA 1959; Regius Professor of Greek, University of Cambridge, 1974–82, then Emeritus; Fellow of Trinity College, Cambridge, 1974–82; *b* 3 Dec. 1921; *s* of Frederic Tilzey Kirk, MC, and Enid Hilda (*née* Pentecost); *m* 1st, 1950, Barbara Helen Traill (marr. diss. 1975); one *d*; 2nd, 1975, Kirsten Ricks (*née* Jensen). *Educ:* Rossall Sch.; Clare Coll., Cambridge (BA 1946); LittD Cambridge, 1965; MA Yale 1965. Served War in Royal Navy, 1941–45; commissioned 1942; Temp. Lt, RNVR, 1945. Research Fellow, Trinity Hall, 1946–49; Student, Brit. Sch. at Athens, 1947; Commonwealth Fund Fellow, Harvard Univ., 1949–50; Cambridge University: Fellow, Trinity Hall, 1950–70; Asst Lectr in Classics, 1951; Lectr in Classics, 1952–61; Reader in Greek, 1961–65; Prof. of Classics, Yale Univ., 1965–70; Prof. of Classics, Bristol Univ., 1971–73. Vis. Lectr, Harvard Univ., 1958; Sather Prof. of Classical Literature, Univ. of California, Berkeley, 1968–69; Mellon Prof., Tulane Univ., 1979. Pres., Soc. for Promotion of Hellenic Studies, 1977–80. Corresp. Mem., Acad. of Athens, 1993. *Publications:* Heraclitus, the Cosmic Fragments, 1954; (with J. E. Raven) The Presocratic Philosophers, 1958; The Songs of Homer, 1962 (abbrev., as Homer and the Epic, 1965); Euripides, Bacchae, 1970; Myth, 1970; The Nature of Greek Myths, 1974; Homer and the Oral Tradition, 1977; The Iliad: a commentary, Vol.1, books 1–4, 1985, Vol. 2, books 5–8, 1990; Towards the Aegean Sea, 1997; articles in classical, archæological and philosophical jls. *Recreations:* writing, 18th century architecture. *Address:* 12 Sion Hill, Bath BA1 2UH.   *Died 10 March 2003.*

KIRKE, Rear-Adm. David Walter, CB 1967; CBE 1962 (OBE 1945); *b* 13 March 1915; *s* of late Percy St George Kirke and Alice Gertrude, *d* of Sir James Gibson Craig, 3rd Bt; *m* 1st, 1936, Tessa O'Connor (marr. diss. 1950); one *s*; 2nd, 1956, Marion Margaret Gibb; one *s* one *d*. *Educ:* RN Coll., Dartmouth. China Station, 1933–35; Pilot Training, 1937; served War of 1939–45, Russian Convoys, Fighter Sqdns; loaned to RAN, 1949–50; Chief of Naval Aviation, Indian Navy, New Delhi, 1959–62; Rear-Adm. 1965; Flag Officer, Naval Flying Training, 1965–68. MBIM 1967. *Recreation:* golf. *Address:* Lismore House, Pluckley, Kent TN27 0QZ. *T:* (01233) 840439. *Club:* Army and Navy.   *Died 29 Oct. 2004.*

KIRKPATRICK, John Lister, CBE 1981; chartered accountant, retired; *b* 27 June 1927; *s* of late Dr Henry Joseph Rodway Kirkpatrick and Dr Nora Kirkpatrick (*née* Lister); *m* 1st; one *s* one *d*; 2nd, Helen Lindsay (*née* Heap) (marr. diss. 1976);3rd, 1977, Gay Elmslie (*née* Goudielock) (*d* 1995); 4th, 1996, Mary-Alex (*née* Daly). *Educ:* Inverness Royal Acad. Served RNVR, 1944–47. Thomson McLintock & Co., subseq. KMG Thomson McLintock, then Peat Marwick McLintock, later KPMG: apprentice; 1948; qual. CA 1952; Partner, 1958; Joint Senior Partner, Glasgow and Edinburgh, 1974–80; Co-Chm., UK Policy Council, 1974–83; Sen. Partner, Scotland, 1980–87; UK Dep. Chm., 1983–87; Consultant, 1987–90; McLintock Main Lafrenz (MML), subseq. Klynveld Main Goerdeler (KMG): Partner, 1974–87; Mem. Bd of Mgt, and Chm., Eastern Hemisphere Exec. Cttee, 1974–79; Mem., Central Mgt Cttee, and Chm., Region 1 (Europe, Africa, ME, India, Pakistan), 1979–85; Chm., ME, 1985–87. Institute of Chartered Accountants of Scotland: Vice Pres., 1975–77; Pres., 1977–78; Member: Examg Bd, Parly and Law Cttee (Chm.), Acctg and Auditing Standards Cttee (Chm.), and F and GP Cttee (Chm.), 1964–75; Council, 1970–75. Mem. (rep. GB and Ireland), 1978–85, Chm., 1985–87, Internat. Acctg Standards Cttee; Lay Mem., Scottish Solicitors' Discipline Tribunal, 1981–96. Member: BoT Accountants' Adv. Cttee, 1967–72; Exam. Supervisory Bd, Arab Soc. of Certified Accountants, 1988–96 (Hon. FASCA 1997); Rev. Body on Doctors' and Dentists' Remuneration, 1983–89; Panel for Financial Services Tribunal, 1988–95; Audits Jt Cttee, Securities Assoc., 1990–95. Member: Royal Glasgow Inst. of Fine Arts; Merchants House of Glasgow; RSPB; Saints and Sinners Club of Scotland. Trustee, Highland Fund Foundn, 1983–90. FRSA 1989. Addresses and TV presentations to nat. and internat. audiences. *Publications:* various prof. papers and articles. *Recreations:* fishing, gardening, painting (watercolour), protection of precious environment of rural and island Scotland. *Address:* 1 Letham Drive, Newlands, Glasgow G43 2SL. *T:* (0141) 633 1407; The Bungalow, Daliburgh, Isle of South Uist HS8 5SS. *T:* (01878) 700652. *Club:* New (Edinburgh).
Died 21 Dec. 2002.

KITCHEN, Stanley, FCA; Partner, Foster & Stephens, later Touche Ross & Co., chartered accountants, Birmingham, 1948–81; *b* 23 Aug. 1913; *s* of late Percy Inman Kitchen, OBE and Elizabeth Kitchen; *m* 1941, Jean Craig (*d* 1998); two *d*. *Educ:* Rugby Sch. ACA 1937, FCA 1953. Army, 1939–46: Major, RASC. Sec., British Rollmakers Corp. Ltd, Wolverhampton, 1946–48. Chm., STEP Management Services Ltd, 1978–85; Dir, Cobalt (UK) Ltd, 1986–92. Birmingham and West Midlands Society of Chartered Accountants: Mem. Cttee, 1951–81; Sec., 1953–55; Pres., 1957–58; Institute of Chartered Accountants in England and Wales: Mem. Council, 1966–81; Vice-Pres., 1974–75; Dep. Pres., 1975–76; Pres., 1976–77. Liveryman, Chartered Accountants' Co., 1977– (Mem. Court, 1979–85). *Publications:* Learning to Live with Taxes on Capital Gains, 1967; Important Aspects of Professional Partnerships, 1974. *Recreations:* gardening, golf. *Address:* 49 Dovehouse Court, Grange Road, Warwick Road, Solihull B91 1EW. *T:* (0121) 705 6153. *Club:* Lansdowne.   *Died 22 July 2001.*

KLEEMAN, Harry, CBE 1984; Chairman: Kleeman Plastics group of companies, 1968–94; Kleeman Management Ltd, since 1990; *b* 2 March 1928; *s* of Max Kleeman and Lottie Bernstein; *m* 1955, Avril Lees; two *s* two *d*. *Educ:* Westminster Sch.; Trinity Coll., Cambridge. FIMMM (FPRI 1980). Director, O. & M. Kleemann Ltd, 1951–65. President, British Plastics Fedn, 1979–80; Chairman: Polymer Engineering Directorate, SERC, 1980–84; Plastics Processing EDC, NEDO, 1980–85; Small Firms Cttee, OFTEL, 1985–88; Council, Plastics & Rubber Inst., 1985–87; Adv. Bd, London Sch. of Polymer Technology, 1988–94; Member: CBI Smaller Firms Council, 1982–91 (Vice-Chm., 1987–88, Chm., 1988–90); CBI Council, 1984–94. Chairman: Central British Fund for World Jewish Relief, 1991–96 (Treasurer, 1969–91); Hampstead and Highgate Conservative Party Club, 1991–95. Member: Zoological Soc., 1950–; Royal Society of Arts, 1978–; Worshipful Co. of Horners, 1954– (Master, 1992). *Recreations:* horse riding, amateur radio, tennis, sculpture. *Address:* 41 Frognal, NW3 6YD. *T:* (020) 7794 3366; *e-mail:* harry@kleeman.net.
Died 15 April 2004.

KLESTIL, Thomas; President of Austria, 1992–2004; *b* 4 Nov. 1932; *m;* two *s* one *d;* *m* 1999, Margot Loeffler. *Educ:* Economic Univ., Vienna. Mem., Austrian Delegn to OECD, Paris, 1959–62; with Austrian Embassy, Washington, 1962–66; Sec. to Chancellor, 1966–69; Consul-Gen., Los Angeles, 1969–74; Rep. of Austria to UN, 1978–82; Ambassador to Washington, 1982–87; Sec.-Gen. for Foreign Affairs, 1987–92. *Address:* c/o Präsidentschaftskanzlei, Hofburg, 1014 Vienna, Austria.
Died 6 July 2004.

KLEVAN, Hon. Sir Rodney (Conrad), Kt 1998; **Hon. Mr Justice Klevan;** a Judge of the High Court, Queen's Bench Division, since 1998; *b* 23 May 1940; *s* of late Sidney Leopold Klevan and Florence Klevan (*née* Eaton); *m* 1968, Susan Rebecca (*née* Lighthill) (*d* 1991); two *s* one *d*. *Educ:* Temple Primary School; Manchester Central Grammar School; Birmingham Univ. (LLB Hons 1962). Pres., Birmingham Univ. Guild of Undergraduates, 1962–63. Called to the Bar, Gray's Inn, 1966, Bencher, 1992; QC 1984; Deputy Circuit Judge, 1977; a Recorder, 1980–98; Leader, Northern Circuit, 1992–95. *Recreations:* theatre, art, following the fortunes of Lancashire CCC. *Address:* Royal Courts of Justice, Strand, WC2A 2LL.
Died 26 Dec. 2001.

KLIBANSKY, Raymond, CC 2000; GOQ 1999; PhD; FRSC; FRHistS; Frothingham Professor of Logic and Metaphysics, McGill University, Montreal, 1946–75, then Emeritus Professor; Fellow of Wolfson College, Oxford, 1981–95 (Hon. Fellow, 1995); *b* Paris, 15 Oct. 1905; *s* of late Hermann Klibansky; *m* Ethel Groffier. *Educ:* Paris; Odenwald Sch.; Univs of Kiel, Hamburg, Heidelberg. PhD 1928; MA Oxon by decree, 1936. Asst, Heidelberg Acad., 1927–33; Lecturer in Philosophy: Heidelberg Univ., 1931–33; King's Coll., London, 1934–36; Oriel Coll., Oxford, 1936–48; Forwood Lectr in Philosophy of Religion, Univ. of Liverpool, 1938–39. Political Warfare Exec., FO, 1941–46. Dir of Studies, Warburg Inst., Univ. of London, 1947–48. Vis. Prof. of History of Philosophy, Université de Montréal, 1947–68; Mahlon Powell Prof., Indiana Univ., 1950; Cardinal Mercier Prof. of Philosophy, Univ. of Louvain, 1956; Visiting Professor of Philosophy: Univ. of Rome, 1961; Univ. of Genoa, 1964; Univ. of Tokyo, 1971; Prof. Emeritus, Heidelberg Univ., 1975–, Hon. Senator, 1986–. President: Canadian Soc. for History and Philosophy of Sci., 1959–72 (Pres. Emeritus, 1972–); Inst. Internat. de Philosophie, Paris, 1966–69 (Hon. Pres., 1969–); Société Internat. pour l'étude de la Philos. Médiévale, Louvain, 1968–72 (Hon. Pres., 1972–); Centro Studi di Civiltà del Medioevo e del Rinascimento, Parma 1990–. Fellow: Accademia Nazionale dei Lincei, Rome; Acad. of Athens; Académie Internationale d'Histoire des Sciences, Paris; Iranian Acad. of Philosophy, Teheran; Acad. dei Dafnici e degli Zelanti; Acireale;

Corresponding Fellow: Mediaeval Acad. of America; Heidelberg Acad. of Scis; Deutsche Akad. für Sprache und Dichtung, Darmstadt; Braunschweigische Wissenschaftliche Gesellschaft. Hon. Member: Allgemeine Gesellsch. für Philosophie in Deutschland; Assoc. des Scientifiques de Roumanie, Bucarest; Foreign Hon. Mem., Amer. Acad. of Arts and Scis. Hon. Fellow: Oriel Coll., Oxford; Warburg Inst., Univ. of London; Accad. Ligure delle Scienze, Genoa; Canadian Mediterranean Inst., Athens, Rome, Cairo. Guggenheim Foundation Fellow, 1954 and 1965; Vis. Fellow, Wolfson Coll., Oxford, 1976–78. Dir, Canadian Academic Centre in Italy, Rome, 1980. Mem. Exec. Council, Union Académique Internationale, 1978–80. Comité Directeur, Fedn Internat. des Socs de Philosophie, 1958–83. DPhil *hc:* Bologna; Marburg; Ottawa; Reconnaissance de Mérite Scientifique, Québec à Montréal, 1991. Gauss Medal, Brunswick, 1990; Lessing Prize, Hamburg, 1994. Grand Cross, Order of Merit (Germany), 1994; Medal, City of Paris, 1999. Gen. Editor, Corpus Platonicum Medii Aevi, (Plato Latinus and Plato Arabus), Union Académique Internat., 1937–; Joint Editor and contributor to: Magistri Eckardi Opera Latina, 1933–36; Philosophy and History, 1936; Mediaeval and Renaissance Studies, 1941–68; Editor: Philosophical Texts, 1951–62; Philosophy and World Community, 1957–95; Philosophy in the Mid-Century, 1958–59; Contemporary Philosophy, 1968–71; Dir, Bibliographie de la Philosophie, 45 vols, 1954–99. *Publications:* Ein Proklos-Fund und seine Bedeutung, 1929; Heidelberg Acad. edn of Opera Nicolai de Cusa, 5 vols, 1929–82; The Continuity of the Platonic Tradition, 1939, enlarged 4th edn, incl. Plato's Parmenides in the Middle Ages and the Renaissance, 1982; (with E. Panofsky and F. Saxl) Saturn and Melancholy, 1964 (enlarged French, German and Spanish edns, 1989–92); (with F. Regen) Überlieferungsgeschichte der philosophischen Werke des Apuleius, 1993; (ed and contrib.) La Philosophie en Europe, 1993; Le Philosophe et la Mémoire du siècle, 1998; articles in Jahresberichte d. Heidelberger Akademie, Proceedings of British Acad., Enciclopedia Italiana, and elsewhere. *Address:* Wolfson College, Oxford OX2 6UD; Leacock Building, McGill University, Montreal, QC H3A 2T7, Canada.
Died 5 Aug. 2005.

KNAGGS, Kenneth James, CMG 1971; OBE 1959; formerly overseas civil servant; *b* 3 July 1920; *e s* of late James Henry Knaggs and Elsie Knaggs (*née* Walton); *m* 1945, Barbara, *d* of late Ernest James Page; two *s*. *Educ:* St Paul's Sch., London. Served War, 1939–46. Northern Rhodesia Civil Service, 1946; Sec. to Govt, Seychelles, 1955 (Actg Governor, 1957–58); Northern Rhodesia: Asst Sec., 1960; Under Sec., 1961; Permanent Sec., Min. of Finance and subseq. the same in Zambia, 1964; retd 1970. European Rep. and Manager, Zambia Airways, 1970–72; Consultant, Commonwealth Develt Corp., 1974–87. *Recreations:* walking, gardening, cooking. *Address:* High House Farm, Earl Soham, near Framlingham, Suffolk IP13 7SN. *T:* (01728) 685416.
Died 18 Aug. 2001.

KNAPP, Edward Ronald, CBE 1979; Managing Director, Timken Europe, 1973–85, retired; *b* 10 May 1919; *s* of Percy Charles and Elsie Maria Knapp; *m* 1942, Vera Mary Stephenson; two *s* two *d*. *Educ:* Cardiff High Sch.; St Catharine's Coll., Cambridge (MA 1940); Harvard Business Sch. (AMP 1954). Served RNVR, Special Branch, Lt-Comdr, 1940–46: HMS Aurora, 1941–44; US Naval Research, Anacostia, 1944–46. Joined British Timken, 1946, Man. Dir, 1969; Dir, Timken Co., USA, 1976. Technical and Management Educnl Governor, Nene Coll., 1953–80. Pres., Northampton RFC, 1986–88. *Recreations:* gardening, golf; played Rugby for Wales, 1940, Captain of Cambridge Univ. 1940 and Northampton RFC, 1948. *Address:* The Elms, 1 Millway, Duston, Northampton NN5 6ER. *T:* (01604) 584737. *Clubs:* East India, Devonshire, Sports and Public Schools; Northants County Golf; Hawks (Cambridge).
Died 21 Dec. 2005.

KNAPP, James; General Secretary, National Union of Rail, Maritime and Transport Workers, since 1990 (National Union of Railwaymen, 1983–90); *b* 29 Sept. 1940; *s* of James and Jean Knapp; *m* 1965, Sylvia Florence Yeomans; one *d*; *m* 2001, Eva Leigh. *Educ:* Hurlford Primary Sch.; Kilmarnock Academy. British Rail employee (signalman), 1955–72; Hurlford NUR Branch Secretary, 1961–65; Sec., Amalgamated Kilmarnock and Hurlford NUR Br., 1965–72; Glasgow and W Scotland NUR Dist Council Sec., 1970–72; full time Divisional Officer, NUR, 1972–81; Headquarters Officer, NUR, 1981–82. Member: TUC Gen. Council, 1983–; ITF Exec. Bd, 1983–. Dir, Trade Union Unit Trust, 1984–; Pres., Unity Trust Bank, 1989– (Dir, 1984–). Mem. Bd, Transport for London, 2000–. *Recreations:* walking, soccer, countryside. *Address:* (office) Unity House, 205 Euston Road, NW1 2BL. *Died 13 Aug. 2001.*

KNAPP-FISHER, Rt Rev. Edward George; Hon. Assistant Bishop, diocese of Chichester, since 1987; *b* 8 Jan. 1915; *s* of late Rev. George Edwin and Agatha Knapp-Fisher; *m* 1965, Joan, *d* of late R. V. Bradley. *Educ:* King's School, Worcester; Trinity Coll., Oxford (MA). Assistant Curate of Brighouse, Yorks, 1939; Chaplain, RNVR, 1942; Chaplain of Cuddesdon Coll., 1946; Chaplain of St John's Coll., Cambridge, 1949; Vicar of Cuddesdon and Principal of Cuddesdon Theological Coll., 1952–60; Bishop of Pretoria, 1960–75; Canon and Archdeacon of Westminster, 1975–87; Sub-Dean, 1982–87; Asst Bishop, Dio. Southwark 1975–87, Dio. London 1976–87; Custos, St Mary's Hosp., Chichester, 1987–2001. Member: Anglican Roman-Catholic Preparatory Commn, 1967–68; Anglican-Roman Catholic Internat. Commn, 1969–81. *Publications:* The Churchman's Heritage, 1952; Belief and Prayer, 1964; To be or not to be, 1968; Where the Truth is Found, 1975; (ed jtly and contrib.) Towards Unity in Truth, 1981; Eucharist, Many-Sided Mystery, 1988. *Recreations:* walking, theatre, gardening. *Address:* 2 Vicars' Close, Canon Lane, Chichester, West Sussex PO19 1PT. *T:* (01243) 789219. *Died 7 Feb. 2003.*

KNELLER, Sir Alister (Arthur), Kt 1996; Chief Justice of Gibraltar, 1986–95; *b* 11 Nov. 1927; *s* of Arthur Kneller, OBE and Hester (*née* Farr). *Educ:* King's Sch., Canterbury; Corpus Christi Coll., Cambridge (MA 1954; LLM 1985). Kenya: Resident Magistrate, 1955; Sen. State Counsel, 1962; Registrar of the High Court, 1965; Puisne Judge, 1969, Judge of the Court of Appeal, 1982. Hon. Bencher, Gray's Inn, 1995. *Recreations:* music, reading. *Club:* Oxford and Cambridge. *Died 7 Nov. 2005.*

KNIGHT, Sir Arthur (William), Kt 1975; Chairman: National Enterprise Board, 1979–80; Courtaulds Ltd, 1975–79; *b* 29 March 1917; *s* of Arthur Frederick Knight and Emily Scott; *m* 1st, 1945, Beatrice Joan Osborne (*née* Oppenheim) (*d* 1968); one *s* three *d*; 2nd, 1972, Sheila Elsie Whiteman. *Educ:* Tottenham County Sch.; London Sch. of Economics (evening student) (BCom; Hon. Fellow 1984). J. Sainsbury, Blackfriars, 1933–38; LSE, Dept of Business Admin (Leverhulme Studentship), 1938–39; Courtaulds, 1939. Served War, Army, 1940–46. Courtaulds, 1946–79: apptd Dir, 1958; Finance Dir, 1961. Non-exec. Director: Richard Thomas & Baldwin, 1966–67; Pye Holdings, 1972–75; Rolls-Royce (1971), 1973–78; Dunlop Holdings, 1981–84. Member: Council, Manchester Business Sch., 1964–71; Economic Cttee, CBI, 1965–72; Cttee for Arts and Social Studies, CNAA, 1965–71; Commn of Enquiry into siting of Third London Airport, 1968–70; Council of Industry for Management Educn, 1970–73; Court of Governors, London Sch. of Economics, 1971–94; Finance Cttee, RIIA, 1971–75; Council, RIIA, 1975–85; Cairncross (Channel Tunnel) Cttee, 1974–75; NIESR Exec. Cttee, 1976–96; BOTB, 1978–79; The Queen's Award Adv. Cttee, 1981–86; Cttee on Fraud Trials, 1984–85. *Publications:* Private Enterprise and Public Intervention: the Courtauld experience, 1974; various papers. *Recreations:* walking, music, reading. *Address:* Charlton End, Charlton, West Sussex PO18 0HX. *Club:* Reform. *Died 5 April 2003.*

KNIGHT, Dr Geoffrey Wilfred; Regional Medical Officer, North West Thames Regional Health Authority, 1973–76; *b* 10 Jan. 1920; *s* of Wilfred Knight and Ida Knight; *m* 1944, Christina Marion Collins Scott; one *s* one *d*. *Educ:* Leeds Univ. Med. Sch. MB, ChB, MD, DPH (Chadwick Gold Medal). County Med. Officer of Health, Herts, 1962–73. Formerly: Governor, Nat. Inst. of Social Work; Member: Personal Social Services Council; Central Midwives Bd; Exec. Cttee, Child Health Bureau; Adv. Panel, Soc. for Health Educn; formerly Mem., Govt Techn. and Sci. Cttee on Disposal of Toxic Wastes. *Recreations:* painting, golf. *Address:* 114 20655 88th Avenue, Langley, BC V1M 2M5, Canada. *Died 21 April 2003.*

KNILL, Sir John (Lawrence), Kt 1994; PhD, DSc; FREng, FICE; freelance engineering geologist; Director, SAUL Trustee Co., since 1996 (Chairman, 1997–2002); Professor of Engineering Geology, Imperial College of Science, Technology and Medicine, University of London, 1973–93, then Emeritus, and Senior Research Fellow, since 1993; *b* 22 Nov. 1934; *s* of late William Cuthbert Knill and Mary (*née* Dempsey); *m* 1957, Diane Constance Judge; one *s* one *d*. *Educ:* Whitgift Sch.; Imperial Coll. of Science and Technol. (BSc, ARCS 1955; PhD, DIC 1957; DSc 1981). FIGeol 1985; FICE 1981; FHKIE 1982; FREng (FEng 1991). Geologist, Sir Alexander Gibb & Partners, 1957; Imperial College, London: Asst Lectr, 1957; Lectr, 1959; Reader in Engrg Geology, 1965; Dean of Royal Sch. of Mines, 1980–83; Head of Dept of Geology, 1979–88; Chm., Centre for Remote Sensing, 1984–88; Chm. and Chief Exec., NERC, 1988–93. Member: Council, Nat. Stone Centre, 1984–91; Nature Conservancy Council, 1985–91; Radioactive Waste Management Adv. Cttee, 1985–95 (Chm., 1987–95); Univs Cttee for Non-Teaching Staffs, 1987–88; Resources Bd, BNSC, 1988–93; ABRC, 1988–93; Jt Nature Conservation Cttee, 1991–96; Council, Royal Acad. of Engrg, 1992–95. President: Instn of Geologists, 1981–84; Geologists' Assoc., 1982–84 (Hon. Mem., 1990); Section C, BAAS, 1988–89. Chm., UK Coordinating Cttee for UN Decade for Natural Disaster Reduction, 1992–95. Vis. Prof. in Engrg Hydrogeology, Royal Holloway, Univ. of London, 1996–. Lectures: Manuel Rocha, Lisbon, 1991; F. H. Moore, Sheffield, 1991; Wilson Campbell, Newcastle, 1992; Royal Acad. of Engrg, Southampton, 1992; first Hans Cloos, Durban, 2002. Corresp. Mem., Société Geologique de Belgique, 1976. Hon. FCGI 1988. Hon. DSc: Kingston, 1992; Exeter, 1995; Hon. DTech: Nottingham Trent, 1996; East London, 1999. Whitaker Medal, IWEM, 1969; Aberconway Medal, Instn of Geologists, 1989; William Smith Medal, Geol. Soc., 1995; Hans Cloos Medal, Internat. Assoc. for Engrg Geology and the Envmt, 2002. *Publications:* Industrial Geology, 1978; Geological and Landscape Conservation, 1994; articles on geology of Scotland and engrg geology. *Recreation:* viticulture. *Address:* Highwood Farm, Long Lane, Shaw-cum-Donnington, Newbury, Berks RG14 2TB. *Clubs:* Athenæum, Chaps. *Died 31 Dec. 2002.*

KNOTT, Air Vice-Marshal Ronald George, CB 1967; DSO 1944; DFC 1943; AFC 1955 and Bar, 1958; *b* 19 Dec. 1917; *s* of George and Edith Rose Knott; *m* 1941, Hermione Violet (*née* Phayre); three *s* one *d*. *Educ:* Borden Grammar Sch., Sittingbourne, Kent. No 20 Sqdn RAF, 1938–40; No 5 Flight IAFVR, 1940–41; HQ Coast Defence Wing, Bombay, 1942; No 179 Sqdn, 1943–44; No 524 Sqdn, 1944–45; RAF, Gatow (Ops), 1949–50; OC, RAF Eindhoven, 1950–51; HQ 2nd TAF, 1951–52; RAF Staff Coll., 1952; Flying Trng Comd, 1953–55; Chief Flying Instructor, Central Flying Sch., 1956–58; Air Plans, Air Min., 1959; OC, RAF Gutersloh, 1959–61; ACOS Plans, 2 ATAF, 1962–63; Defence Res. Policy Staff, MoD, 1963; DOR2 (RAF), MoD, 1963–67; SASO,

HQ NEAF Cyprus, 1967–70; AOA, HQ Air Support Comd, RAF, 1970–72, retired. *Recreations:* gardening, wine growing. *Address:* 20 Windmill Close, Bridge, Canterbury, Kent CT4 5LY. *Died 29 Nov. 2002.*

KNOX, Col Sir Bryce (Muir), KCVO 1990; MC 1944 and Bar, 1944; TD 1947; Lord-Lieutenant of Ayrshire and Arran (formerly County of Ayr), 1974–91 (Vice-Lieutenant, 1970–74); Vice-Chairman, Lindustries Ltd, 1979 (Director, 1953–79); *b* 4 April 1916; *s* of late James Knox, Kilbirnie; *m* 1948, Patricia Mary Dunsmuir (*d* 1989); one *s* one *d*. *Educ:* Stowe; Trinity Coll., Cambridge. Served with Ayrshire (ECO) Yeomanry, 1939–45, N Africa and Italy; CO, 1953–56; Hon. Col, 1969–71; Hon. Col, The Ayrshire Yeomanry Sqdn, Queen's Own Yeomanry, T&AVR, 1971–77; Pres., Lowlands T&AVR, 1978–83. Member, Queen's Body Guard for Scotland, Royal Company of Archers. Pres., RHAS, 1990–91. CStJ. *Publication:* The History of the Eglinton Hunt, 1984. *Recreation:* country sports. *Address:* Martnaham Lodge, by Ayr KA6 6ES. *T:* (01292) 560204.
Died 22 Nov. 2003.

KNOX, Prof. Henry Macdonald; Professor of Education, The Queen's University of Belfast, 1951–82, then Emeritus Professor; *b* 26 Nov. 1916; *e s* of Rev. R. M. Knox, Edinburgh, and J. E. Church; *m* 1945, Marian (decd), *yr d* of N. Starkie, Todmorden; one *s* one *d*. *Educ:* George Watson's Coll., Edinburgh; University of Edinburgh. MA 1938; MEd 1940; PhD 1949. Served as Captain, Intelligence Corps, commanding a wireless intelligence section, Arakan sector of Burma, and as instructor, War Office special wireless training wing, 1940–46. Lecturer in Education, University Coll. of Hull, 1946; Lecturer in Education, University of St Andrews, 1949; former Dean of Faculty of Education, and acting Dir, Inst. of Educn, 1968–69, QUB. Assessor in Educn, Univ. of Strathclyde, 1984–89; sometime Examiner in Educn, Universities of Durham, Leeds, Sheffield, Aberdeen, Glasgow, Strathclyde, Wales and Ireland (National); occasional Examiner, Universities of Edinburgh, Belfast, Dublin and Bristol. Chm., N Ireland Council for Educn Research, 1979–82; Member: Advisory Council on Educn for N Ireland, 1955–58; 1961–64; Senior Certificate Examination Cttee for N Ireland, 1962–65; Adv. Bd for Postgraduate Studentships in Arts Subjects, Ministry of Educn for N Ireland, 1962–74; Adv. Cttee on Supply and Training of Teachers for NI, 1976–82; NI Council for Educnl Develt, 1980–82. Mem. Governing Body: Stranmillis Coll. of Educn, Belfast, 1968–82 (Vice-Chm., 1975–82); St Joseph's Coll. of Educn, Belfast, 1968–82. *Publications:* Two Hundred and Fifty Years of Scottish Education, 1696–1946, 1953; John Dury's Reformed School, 1958; Introduction to Educational Method, 1961; Schools in Europe (ed W. Schultze): Northern Ireland, 1969; (contrib.) Chambers Scottish Biographical Dictionary, 1992; numerous articles in educational journals. *Address:* 9 Elliot Gardens, Colinton, Edinburgh EH14 1EH. *T:* (0131) 441 6283.
Died 19 July 2004.

KNOX, John; Under-Secretary, Department of Trade and Industry, retired, 1974; Head of Research Contractors Division, 1972–74; *b* 11 March 1913; *s* of William Knox and May Ferguson; *m* 1942, Mary Blackwood Johnston, *d* of late Rt Hon. Thomas Johnston, CH; one *s* one *d*. *Educ:* Lenzie Acad.; Glasgow Univ. (Kitchener's Schol.; MA). Business management trng, 1935–39; joined RAE, 1939; Op. Research with RAF, 1939–45; Asst Chief Scientific Adviser, Min. of Works, 1945–50; Dep. Dir and Dir, Intelligence Div., DSIR, 1950–58; Dep. Dir (Industry), DSIR, 1958–64; Min. of Technology, later DTI: Asst Controller, 1964–65; CSO, Head of External Research and Materials Div., 1965–68; Head of Materials Div., 1968–71; Head of Res. Div., 1971–73. *Publications:* occasional articles on mgt of research, develt and industrial innovation. *Recreation:* golf. *Address:* 6 Mariners Court,

Victoria Road, Aldeburgh, Suffolk IP15 5EH. *T:* (01728) 453657. *Died 12 April 2003.*

KNOX, Hon. Sir William Edward, Kt 1979; FCIT, FAIM; Leader of Parliamentary Liberal Party, Queensland, 1983–88; *b* 14 Dec. 1927; *s* of E. Knox, Turramurra; *m* 1956, Doris Ross; two *s* two *d*. *Educ:* Melbourne High School. State Pres., Qld Young Liberals, 1953–56; Vice-Pres., Qld Div., Liberal Party, 1956–57, Mem. Exec., 1953–58, 1962–65; Sec., Parly Lib. Party, 1960–65. MLA (L) Nundah, Qld, 1957–89; Minister for Transport, Qld, 1965–72; Minister for Justice and Attorney-Gen., Qld, 1971–76; Dep. Premier and Treasurer of Qld, 1976–78; Leader, State Parly Liberal Party, 1976–78 and 1983–88; Minister for Health, Qld, 1978–80; Minister for Employment and Labour Relations, Qld, 1980–83. Chm., Qld Road Safety Council and Mem., Aust. Transport Adv. Council, 1965–72. Mem., Nat. Exec. Aust. Jnr Chamber of Commerce, 1961–62; Senator Jnr Chamber Internat., 1962–. State Pres., Father and Son Movement, 1965; Pres., Assoc. of Independent Schs, Qld, 1991–97. Chm., St John Council for Qld, 1983–95. KStJ 1995. *Address:* 1621 Sandgate Road, Nundah, Queensland 4012, Australia.
Died 22 Sept. 2001.

KNUTTON, Maj.-Gen. Harry, CB 1975; MSc; CEng, FIEE; Director-General, City and Guilds of London Institute, 1976–85; *b* Rawmarsh, Yorks, 26 April 1921; *m* 1958, Pamela Brackley, E Sheen, London; three *s* one *d*. *Educ:* Wath-upon-Dearne Grammar Sch.; RMCS. Commnd RA, 1943; served with 15th Scottish and 1st Airborne Divs, NW Europe, 1944–45; India, 1945–47; Instructor in Gunnery, 1946–49; Project Officer, Min. of Supply, 1949–51; served Middle East, 1953–55; Directing Staff, RMCS, 1955–58; jssc 1958; various staff appts, MoD, 1958–60, 1962–64, 1966–67; Comdr Missile Regt, BAOR, 1964–66; Comdr Air Defence Bde, 1967–69; Fellow, Loughborough Univ. of Technology, 1969–70; Dir-Gen. Weapons (Army), 1970–73; Dir, Royal Ordnance Factories and Dep. Master-Gen. of Ordnance, 1973–75. Col Comdt, RA, 1977–82. Teacher, Whitgift Foundn, 1975–76. Member: Associated Examining Bd, 1976–85; Dep. Chm., Standing Conf. on Schools' Science and Technology, 1983–90. Governor, Imperial Coll., London, 1976–91. FCollP 1983. FCGI 1985. Liveryman, Engineers' Co. *Address:* 85 Hayes Lane, Kenley, Surrey CR8 5JR. *Died 24 Nov. 2001.*

KOHT, Paul; Ambassador of Norway to Denmark, 1975–82; *b* 7 Dec. 1913; *s* of Dr Halvdan Koht and Karen Elisabeth (*née* Grude); *m* 1938, Grete Sverdrup; two *s* one *d*. *Educ:* University of Oslo (Law degree, 1937). Entered Norwegian Foreign Service, 1938; held posts in: Bucharest, 1938–39; London, 1940–41; Tokyo, 1941–42; New York, 1942–46; Lisbon, 1950–51; Mem. Norwegian Delegn to OEEC and NATO, Paris, and Perm. Rep. to Coun. of Europe, 1951–53; Dir Gen., Dept for Econ. Affairs, Min. of For. Affairs, Oslo, 1953–56; Chargé d'Affaires, Copenhagen, 1956–58; Ambassador to: USA, 1958–63; Fed. Republic of Germany, 1963–68; Court of St James's, 1968–75. Comdr, Order of St Olav; Grand Cross, Order of Dannebrog; Grand Cross, Order of Merit (Federal Republic of Germany). *Address:* Lille Frogner Allé 4b, 0263 Oslo, Norway. *Died 26 March 2002.*

KOSSOFF, David; actor, author, illustrator; *b* 24 Nov. 1919; *s* of Louis and Anne Kossoff, both Russian; *m* 1947, Margaret, (Jennie), Jenkins (*d* 1995); one *s* (and one *s* decd). *Educ:* elementary sch.; Northern Polytechnic. Commercial Artist, 1937; Draughtsman, 1937–38; Furniture Designer, 1938–39; Technical Illustrator, 1939–45. Began acting, 1943; working as actor and illustrator, 1945–52, as actor and designer, 1952–. BBC Repertory Company, 1945–51. Took over part of Colonel Alexander Ikonenko in The Love of Four Colonels, Wyndham's, 1952; Sam Tager in The Shrike, Prince's, 1953; Morry in The Bespoke Overcoat, and Tobit in Tobias and the Angel, Arts, 1953; Prof. Lodegger in No Sign of the Dove, Savoy, 1953; Nathan in The

Boychik, Embassy, 1954 (and again Morry in The Bespoke Overcoat); Mendele in The World of Sholom Aleichem, Embassy, 1955, and Johannesburg, 1957; one-man show, One Eyebrow Up, The Arts, 1957; Man on Trial, Lyric, 1959; Stars in Your Eyes, Palladium, 1960; The Tenth Man, Comedy, 1961; Come Blow Your Horn, Prince of Wales, 1962; one-man show, Kossoff at the Prince Charles, 1963, later called A Funny Kind of Evening (many countries); Enter Solly Gold, Mermaid, 1970; Cinderella, Palladium, 1971; Bunny, Criterion, 1972; own Bible storytelling programmes on radio and TV, as writer and teller, 1964–66; solo performance (stage), 'As According to Kossoff', 1970–. Has appeared in many films. Won British Acad. Award, 1956. Elected MSIA 1958. FRSA 1969. Hon. DLitt, Hatfield Poly., 1990. *Play:* Big Night for Shylock, 1968. *Publications:* Bible Stories retold by David Kossoff, 1968; The Book of Witnesses, 1971; The Three Donkeys, 1972; The Voices of Masada, 1973; The Little Book of Sylvanus, 1975; You Have a Minute, Lord?, 1977; A Small Town is a World, 1979; Sweet Nutcracker, 1985; The Old & The New, 2002. *Recreations:* conversation, working with the hands. *Address:* 45 Roe Green Close, Hatfield, Herts AL10 9PD.

Died 23 March 2005.

KRAFT, Rt Rev. Richard Austin; Bishop of Pretoria, 1982–98; *b* 3 June 1936; *s* of Arthur Austin Kraft and Mary Roberta Hudson Kraft; *m* 1958, Phyllis Marie Schaffer; three *s* one *d. Educ:* Ripon Coll., Ripon, Wisconsin, USA (BA); General Theol Seminary, New York (MDiv; Hon. DD 1983). Deacon then priest, 1961; Asst priest, St Alphege's, Scottsville, dio. Natal, 1961–63; Asst priest and Rector, St Chad's Mission, Klip River, 1963–67; Dir of Christian Education, Diocese of Zululand, 1968–76; Rector, All Saints Parish, Melmoth, 1974–76; Dir of Education Dept, Church of Province of S Africa, 1977–79; Dean and Rector, St Alban's Cathedral, Diocese of Pretoria, 1979–82. Canon, Dio. of Zululand, 1971; Canon Emeritus, 1977. *Recreation:* woodwork. *Address:* 12 Maroelana, Maroelana, Pretoria 0081, S Africa. *T:* (12) 4608934, *Fax:* (12) 3229411; *e-mail:* rkraft@cpsa.org.za.

Died 17 Jan. 2001.

KRISH, Tanya, (Mrs Felix Krish); see Moiseiwitsch, T.

KROLL, Natasha, RDI 1966; FCSD; freelance television and film designer; *b* Moscow, 20 May 1914; *d* of Dr (phil.) Hermann Kroll and Sophie (*née* Rabinovich). *Educ:* Berlin. Teacher of window display, Reimann Sch. of Art, London, 1936–40; Display Manager: Messrs Rowntrees, Scarborough and York, 1940–42; Simpson Piccadilly Ltd, 1942–55; Sen. Designer, BBC TV, 1955–66: programmes include: Monitor, Panorama, science programmes, Lower Depths, Death of Danton, The Duel, Ring Round the Moon, La Traviata, Day by the Sea, The Sponge Room and many others; freelance designer, 1966–; TV designs include: The Seagull, 1966; Family Reunion, 1966; Eugene Onegin, 1967; The Soldier's Tale, 1968; La Vida Breve, 1968; Mary Stuart, 1968; Doll's House, 1969; Three Sisters, Cherry Orchard, Rasputin, Wild Duck, 1971; Summer and Smoke, Hedda Gabler, 1972; The Common, 1973; Lady from the Sea, 1974; Love's Labour's Lost, 1975; Very Like a Whale, 1980; production–designer of: The Music Lovers, 1970; The Hireling, 1973 (FTA Film award for best Art Direction); Summer Rag-time, 1976; Absolution, 1978. *Publication:* Window Display, 1954. *Recreations:* painting, family, entertaining. *Address:* 5 Ruvigny Gardens, SW15 1JR. *T:* (020) 8788 1556.

Died 2 April 2004.

KUIPERS, John Melles; *b* 7 July 1918; *s* of late Joh Kuipers and Anna (*née* Knoester); *m* 1947, Joan Lilian Morgan-

Edwards; one *s* three *d. Educ:* Royal Masonic Sch., Bushey. Served RA, 1939–46 (Lt-Col). Ford Motor Co. Ltd, 1947–51; Treasurer, Canadian Chemical Co. Ltd, Montreal, 1951–55; Gp Manager, Halewood, and Dir, Stamping and Assembly Gp, Ford Motor Co. Ltd, 1955–67; EMI Ltd, 1967–80: Chief Exec. Electronic and Industrial Ops, 1969–72; Chm. and Chief Exec., EMI (Australia) Ltd, 1974–77; Man. Dir and Vice-Chm., 1977–79; Dir, Thames TV Ltd, 1977–81; Chairman: Huntleigh Gp PLC, 1980–83; ATT Ltd, 1984–91. Dir, Gowrings, 1980–89. *Address:* 2 Bell Lane, Henley-on-Thames, Oxon RG9 2HP. *T:* (01491) 574760.

Died 23 June 2004.

KURIA, Most Rev. Manasses; Executive Chairman, Jehovah Jireh Christian Homes for Street Children and Families, since 1995; Archbishop of Kenya and Bishop of Nairobi, 1980–94; *b* 22 July 1929; *s* of John Njoroge Kuria; *m* 1947, Mary Kuria (*d* 2002); two *s* four *d. Educ:* locally. Teaching, 1944–53; Deacon, 1955; ordained Priest, 1957; Archdeacon of Eldoret, 1965–70; Asst Bishop of Nakuru, 1970–75; Bishop of Nakuru, 1976–79. *Publication:* Uwakili Katika Kristo (Stewardship of Christ), 1969. *Address:* Jehovah Jireh Christian Homes, PO Box 20050, Nairobi, Kenya.

Died 19 Sept. 2005.

KYPRIANOU, Spyros; Grand Cross of the Order of George I of Greece, 1962; Grand Cross, Order of the Saviour, Greece, 1983; President of the Republic of Cyprus, 1977–88; President: Democratic Party of Cyprus, since 1976; House of Representatives, since 1996; *b* Limassol, 1932; *s* of Achilleas and Maria Kyprianou; *m* Mimi Kyprianou; two *s. Educ:* Greek Gymnasium, Limassol; City of London Coll. Called to the Bar, Gray's Inn, 1954 (Hon. Bencher, 1985); Dip. Comparative Law. Founded Cypriot Students' Union in England (first Pres. 1952–54). Sec. of Archbp Makarios, in London, 1952; Sec. of Cyprus Ethnarchy in London, 1954; left Britain for Greece, 1956, to work for world projection of Cyprus case; later in 1956, rep. Cyprus Ethnarchy, New York, until 1957; resumed London post until signing of Zürich and London Agreements, returning to Cyprus with the Archbp in 1959. On declaration of Independence, 16 Aug. 1960, following brief appt as Minister of Justice, became Foreign Minister, accompanying the Pres. on visits to countries world-wide, 1961–71; rep. Cyprus at UN Security Council and Gen. Assembly sessions, notably during debates on the Cyprus question; signed Agreement in Moscow for Soviet Military Aid to Cyprus, 1964; had several consultations with Greek Govt on Cyprus matter. Mem., Cttee of Ministers of Council of Europe, at meetings in Strasburg and Paris (Pres. Cttee, April–Dec. 1967). Resigned post of Foreign Minister, 1972, after dispute with military régime in Athens. Practised law, withdrawing from politics until the coup and Turkish invasion of Cyprus, 1974; travelled between Athens, London and New York, where led Cyprus delegn during debate on Cyprus in Gen. Assembly of UN, 1974; participated in talks between Greek Govt and Pres. Makarios, 1974; an *ad hoc* member of Cyprus delegn at Security meeting in New York, 1975. Announced estabt of Democratic Party in Cyprus, 1976, becoming Pres. of House of Reps on the party's victory in parly elections. On death of Archbp Makarios, Aug. 1977, became Actg Pres. of Republic, until elected Pres. in same month; re-elected Pres., unopposed, in Feb. 1978 for a full five-year term; re-elected for further five-year term, 1983. Holds numerous foreign decorations. *Recreations:* literature, music, sport. *Address:* Antistaseos 1, Engomi, Nicosia, Cyprus.

Died 12 March 2002.

L

LABOVITCH, Neville, LVO 1993; MBE 1977; *b* Leeds, 20 Feb. 1927; *s* of late Mark and Anne Labovitch; *m* 1958, Sonia Deborah Barney (marr. diss. 1986); two *d. Educ:* Brasenose College, Oxford (MA). Treasurer, Oxford Union, 1945. Dir, 1954–82, Man. Dir, 1966–82, Darley Mills. Chairman: Brenta Construction, 1987–91 (Dir, 1985–91); Brenta Cogifar-Impresit, 1990–91; Brenta AB, 1993–; CP Carpets, Kidderminster, 1991–93. Chairman: Trafalgar Square Assoc., 1974–76; Knightsbridge Assoc., 1978–98 (Hon. Pres., 1998); Cleaner London Campaign, 1978–; Piccadilly Tourist Trust, 1978–82; Great Children's Party for IYC, 1979; London Environmental Campaign, 1983; Westminster Quatercentenary Cttee, 1984; Prince of Wales Royal Parks Tree Appeal, 1987–; Mem., Royal Parks Ministerial Adv. Bd, 1994–99; Mem., London Celebrations Cttee for Queen's Silver Jubilee, and Chm., Silver Jubilee Exhibn, Hyde Park, 1977; Pres., Jubilee Walkway Trust, 2001– (Vice-Chm., 1978–95; Chm., 1995–2001); Chairman: Organizing Cttee, Queen's 60th Birthday Celebrations, 1986; Queen's Anniv. Cttee, Hampton Court Palace 1952–1992, 1992. Mem., Vis. Cttee, RCA, 1983–90. Director: Nat. Children's Charities Fund, 1979–; Spitalfields Market Opera Ltd, 1994–2000. Trustee, Albert Memorial Trust, 1994–. FRSA. Cavaliere Ufficiale, Order of Merit (Italy), 1991. *Recreations:* reading and ruminating. *Club:* Brooks's.
Died 13 April 2002.

LADAS, Diana Margaret; Head Mistress, Heathfield School, 1965–72; *b* 8 Feb. 1913; *er d* of late Bertram Hambro and Margaret Constance Neville (*née* Lubbock, later Mrs Charles Boyle); *m* 1945, Alexis Christopher Ladas, MBE (marr. diss. 1955); one *s. Educ:* Downe House Sch.; Girton Coll., Cambridge. Before the war, Sec. in Geneva, Malta and London; during War of 1939–45, worked as temp. Asst Principal in Min. of economic Warfare, Board of Trade and Political Warfare Executive in Cairo; transferred to UNRRA, worked in Athens, Washington and London; on the staff of British Information Services, in New York, 1948–50; began teaching at Westminster Tutors, 1955; joined staff of Heathfield Sch., 1958; Dep. Head of Moira House Sch., 1959, Head Mistress, 1960; Vice-Principal of Queen's Gate Sch., 1962–65. Since retirement, occupied with voluntary social work and local politics. *Recreations:* gardening, travelling. *Address:* 154 Peckham Rye, SE22 9QH. *Died 8 Oct. 2001.*

LAFITTE, Prof. François; Professor of Social Policy and Administration, University of Birmingham, 1959–80, then Emeritus; *b* 3 Aug. 1913; *s* of John Armistead Collier and Françoise Lafitte and adopted *s* of late Havelock Ellis; *m* 1938, Eileen (*née* Saville) (*d* 1996); (one *s* decd). *Educ:* Collège Municipal, Maubeuge; George Green's Sch., Poplar; St Olave's Grammar Sch., Southwark; Worcester Coll., Oxford. Research and translating for Miners' Internat. Fed., 1936–37; on research staff, and subseq. Dep. Sec., PEP, 1938–43; on editorial staff of The Times, as special writer on social questions, 1943–59; Chm. of PEP research groups on health services, 1943–46, on housing policy, 1948–51. Dean of Faculty of Commerce and Social Science, Birmingham, Univ., 1965–68. Member: Home Office Advisory Council on the Treatment of Offenders, 1961–64; Adv. Cttees Social Science Research Council, 1966–69; Redditch New Town Corp., 1964–75; Chm., British Pregnancy Adv. Service, 1968–88. *Publications:* The Internment of Aliens, 1940, repr. 1988; Britain's Way to Social Security, 1945; Family Planning in the Sixties, 1964; (part author) Socially Deprived Families in Britain, 1970; many PEP Planning monographs; many papers on abortion and related issues;

contribs to British Jl of Delinquency, Eugenics Review, Chambers's Encyclopædia, etc. *Address:* 77 Oakfield Road, Birmingham B29 7HL. *T:* (0121) 472 2709. *Club:* University Staff (Birmingham). *Died 21 Nov. 2002.*

LAING, Alastair Stuart, CBE 1980; MVO 1959; *b* 17 June 1920; *s* of Captain Arthur Henry Laing and Clare May Laing (*née* Ashworth); *m* 1946 Audrey Stella Hobbs, MCSP, *d* of Dr Frederick Hobbs and Gladys Marion Hobbs (*née* George); one *s* decd. *Educ:* Sedbergh School. Served Indian Army, 10th Gurkha Rifles, 1940–46, Captain; seconded to Civil Administration, Bengal, 1944–46. Commonwealth War Graves Commission, 1947–83 (Dep. Dir Gen., 1975–83). Chm., Vale of Aylesbury Hunt, 1981–87. *Publications:* various articles. *Recreations:* gardening, foxhunting, racing, history. *Address:* Wagtails, Lower Wood End, Marlow, Bucks SL7 2HN. *T:* (01628) 484481. *Died 1 July 2004.*

LAING, (William James) Scott; special assignments for United Nations and other international agencies, 1977–98; *b* 14 April 1914; *er s* of late William Irvine Laing and Jessie C. M. Laing (*née* Scott); *m* 1952, Isabelle Mary Durrant-Fox (*d* 1990); one *s. Educ:* George Watson's Coll.; Edinburgh Univ. Appointed to Dept of Overseas Trade, 1937; Asst to Commercial Counsellor, British Embassy, Buenos Aires, 1938; Second Sec. (Commercial), Buenos Aires, 1944; First Sec. (Commercial), Helsinki, 1947; Consul, New York, 1950; Consul-Gen. (Commercial), New York, 1954; Counsellor (Commercial), Brussels and Luxembourg, 1955; Consultant to UN Secretariat, Financial Policies and Institutions Section, 1958, African Training Programme, 1960; Editor, UN Jl, 1964; Chief, Publications Sales Section, UN Secretariat, 1969–76; consultant to motor industry pubns, EIU, 1977–92. *Publications:* The US Market for Motor Vehicle Parts and Accessories, 1977; Concentration and Diversification of the Self-Propelled Heavy Machinery Industries in USA, 1979; (jtly) Financial Assessment of the US Automotive Industry, 1982; (jtly) Foreign Outsourcing by US Auto Manufacturers, 1983. *Address:* 1016 Chantilly Road, Bel–Air, CA 90077, USA. *Club:* Caledonian.
Died 19 June 2003.

LAISTER, Peter; company director; *b* 24 Jan. 1929; *s* of late Horace Laister and Mrs I. L. Bates; *m* 1st, 1951, Barbara Cooke; one *s* one *d*; 2nd, 1958, Eileen Alice Goodchild (*née* Town); one *d. Educ:* King Edward's Sch., Birmingham; Manchester Univ., Coll. of Technology (BSc Tech 1949; FUMIST 1985). FInstPet 1958; FIChemE 1983; CEng; CIMgt. RAF, 1949–51. Esso Petroleum Co. Ltd, 1951–66: Process Engr to UK Refining Co-ordinator, 1960; Gen. Manager, Marketing Ops, 1962–66; British Oxygen Co. Ltd (BOC Intl Ltd), 1966–75 (Gp Man Dir, 1969–75); Chm., BOC Financial Corp. (USA), 1974–75; Gp Man. Dir, Ellerman Lines Ltd, 1976–79; Chairman: Tollemache and Cobbold Breweries, 1977–79; London & Hull Insce Co., 1976–79; Oceonics plc, 1986–88; Group Man. Dir, Thorn Electrical Industries, later THORN EMI, 1979–84, Chm., 1984–85. Director: (non exec.) Inchcape plc, 1982–93; (non exec.) Fluor Daniel, 1985–90; Mirror Hldgs Ltd, 1985–90; Tower Maritime Gp Ltd, 1986–88; (non exec.) A&P Appledore, 1986–87; British Cable Services, 1987–89; Clyde Cable Vision, 1987–89; Metromode Ltd, 1987–90; Pergamon GED Internat. Ltd, 1987–90; Nimbus Records Ltd, 1987 (Chm., 1988–94); Pergamon Media plc, 1987–90; Tower Hotels (Management), 1987–89; VIP Marine and Aviation Ltd, 1987–90; Laister Dickson Ltd, 1988–94; Chairman: Nimbus Manufacturing (UK) Ltd, 1985–94; Nimbus Communications Internat. Ltd,

1985–93; Park Hotels plc, 1985–91; SelecTV plc, 1987–94; MTV Europe, 1988–91; Tower Gp (formerly Finance, Land & General Hldgs), 1988–90; Maxwell Satellite Communications, 1988–91; Maxwell Communication Corp., 1991–92 (Dir, 1985–92). Industrial Society: Council Mem., 1971–86; Mem., Industrial Develt Adv. Bd, 1981–83; Mem., BIM Exec. Bd, 1983–88. Gov., BUPA, 1982–93; Chm., CICI, 1988–94. Vice-Pres., Research into Ageing, 1982–85. Mem. Council, UCL, 1978–88. *Recreations:* private flying, boating and angling, gardening, photography.
Died 14 April 2001.

LANCASTER, Patricia Margaret; Headmistress, Wycombe Abbey School, 1974–88; a Church Commissioner, 1989–98; *b* 22 Feb. 1929; *d* of Vice-Adm. Sir John Lancaster, KBE, CB. *Educ:* Univs of London (BA) and Southampton (Cert. Educn). English Mistress, St Mary's Sch., Calne, 1951–58; Housemistress, St Swithun's Sch., Winchester, 1958–62; Headmistress, St Michael's, Burton Park, Petworth, 1962–73. Pres., Girls' Schools' Assoc., 1979–80. Governor: Berkhamsted Sch., 1989–97; Marlborough Coll., 1989–96; Repton Sch., 1989–95; St Mary's Sch., Calne, 1989–97; St Swithun's Sch., Winchester, 1989–96. *Recreations:* theatre, art galleries, gardening. *Address:* 8 Vectis Road, Alverstoke, near Gosport, Hants PO12 2QF.
Died 27 March 2004.

LANCHBERY, John Arthur, OBE 1990; FRAM; conductor; *b* London, 15 May 1923; *s* of William Lanchbery and Violet (*née* Mewett); *m* 1951, Elaine Fifield (marr. diss. 1960; she *d* 1999); one *d. Educ:* Alleyn's Sch., Dulwich; Royal Academy of Music. Henry Smart Composition Scholarship, 1942. Served, RAC, 1943–45. Royal Academy of Music, 1945–47 (ARAM 1953); Musical Dir, Metropolitan Ballet, 1948–50; Sadler's Wells Theatre Ballet, 1951–57; Royal Ballet, 1957–72 (Principal Conductor, 1959–72); Musical Director: Australian Ballet, 1972–77; American Ballet Theatre, 1978–80. Bolshoi Theatre Medal, Moscow, 1961; Queen Elizabeth II Coronation Award, Royal Acad. of Dancing, 1989; Carina Ari Medal, Stockholm, 1989. *Film scores* include: The Turning Point, 1977; Nijinsky, 1980; Evil Under the Sun, 1983; The Birth of a Nation, 1993; The Iron Horse, 1994; Orphans of the Storm, 2001. *Arrangements and compositions* of ballets include: Pleasuredrome, 1949; Eve of St Agnes (BBC commission), 1950; House of Birds, 1955; La Fille Mal Gardée, 1960; The Dream, 1964; Don Quixote, 1966; Giselle, 1968; La Sylphide, 1970; Tales of Beatrix Potter, 1971; Tales of Hoffman, 1972; Merry Widow, 1975; Month in the Country, 1976; Mayerling, 1978; Rosalinda, 1978; Papillon, 1979; La Bayadère, 1980; Peer Gynt, 1980; The Devil to Pay, 1982; The Sentimental Bloke, 1985; Le Chat Botté, 1985; Midsummer Night's Dream, 1985; Hunchback of Notre Dame, 1988; Figaro, 1992; Madame Butterfly, 1995; The Highwaymen, 1996; Dracula, 1997; The Snow Maiden, 1998; Cleopatra, and Toad, 2000. *Recreations:* walking, reading. *Address:* 71 Park Street, St Kilda West, Vic 3182, Australia. *T:* (3) 95370520, *Fax:* (3) 95370521.
Died 27 Feb. 2003.

LANDEN, Dinsdale (James); actor; *b* 4 Sept. 1932; *s* of Edward James Landen and Winifred Alice Landen; *m* 1959, Jennifer Daniel. *Educ:* King's Sch., Rochester; Hove County Grammar Sch. *Stage:* Dead Secret, Piccadilly, 1957; Auntie Mame, Adelphi; Provok'd Wife, Vaudeville; Philanthropist, May Fair, 1970; London Assurance, New, 1972; Alphabetical Order, May Fair, 1975; Bodies, Ambassadors, 1980; Taking Steps, Lyric, 1980; Loot, Lyric, 1984; Sufficient Carbohydrate, Albery, 1984; Wife Begins at Forty, Ambassadors, 1985; Selling the Sizzle, Hampstead, 1986; Dangerous Obsession, Apollo, then Fortune, 1987; Thark, Lyric, Hammersmith, 1989; Bookends, Apollo, 1990; Twelfth Night, Playhouse, 1991; Chatsky, Almeida, 1993; School for Scandal, 1995; Racing Demon, 1998, Chichester Fest. *National Theatre:* Plunder; The Philanderer; On the Razzle, 1981; Uncle Vanya, 1982. *Films:* The Valiant; Every Home Should Have One;

Digby the Biggest Dog in the World; Mosquito Squadron; Morons from Outer Space; The Steal; *television:* Great Expectations; Mickey Dunne; The Spies; Glittering Prizes; Devenish; Two Sundays; Fathers and Families; Pig in the Middle; Radio Pictures; Absent Friends; Events in a Museum; What the Butler Saw; Some Other Spring; Fighting Against Slavery; Arms and the Man; The Buccaneers; The Wingless Bird. *Recreations:* walking, golf. *Address:* 48 Ashlone Road, SW15 1LR. *Club:* Stage Golfing Society.
Died 29 Dec. 2003.

LANDRETH, Rev. Canon Derek, TD 1963; Vicar of Icklesham, Diocese of Chichester, 1983–89 (Priest-in-charge, 1982–83), also Priest-in-charge of Fairlight, 1984–86; Chaplain to the Queen, 1980–90; Rural Dean of Rye, 1984–89; *b* 7 June 1920; *s* of Rev. Norman Landreth and Muriel Landreth; *m* 1st, 1943, Myra Joan Brown; one *s* three *d*; 2nd, 1986, Dss Mavis Isabella White. *Educ:* Kingswood School, Bath; King's College, Cambridge (MA); Bishops' College, Cheshunt. Commnd, RA, 1942–46 (service India and Burma); CF (TA), 1951–67, (TAVR) 1967–70. Ordained deacon, 1948, priest, 1949; Asst Curate, St George, Camberwell, 1948–53; Vicar, St Mark, Battersea Rise, 1953–59; Deputy Chaplain, HM Prison, Wandsworth, 1954–59; Vicar of Richmond, Surrey, and Chaplain, Star and Garter Home for Disabled Soldiers, Sailors and Airmen, 1959–70; Rector of Sanderstead, Surrey, 1970–77; Hon. Chaplain to Bishop of Southwark, 1962–80; Hon. Canon of Southwark Cathedral, 1968–77; Canon Residentiary and Librarian, Southwark Cathedral, 1977–82, then Canon Emeritus. Proctor in Convocation, 1980–83. Indep. Mem., Richmond Borough Council, 1961–65. *Recreations:* gardening, fishing. *Address:* Gossamer Cottage, Slindon, near Arundel, W Sussex BN18 0QT. *T:* (01243) 814224.
Died 25 Jan. 2003.

LANE, Baron *cr* 1979 (Life Peer), of St Ippollitts; **Geoffrey Dawson Lane,** Kt 1966; AFC 1943; PC 1974; Lord Chief Justice of England, 1980–92; *b* 17 July 1918; *s* of late Percy Albert Lane, Lincoln, and Mary (*née* Dawson); *m* 1944, Jan, *d* of Donald Macdonald; one *s. Educ:* Shrewsbury; Trinity Coll., Cambridge (Hon. Fellow 1981). Served War, RAF, 1939–45; Sqdn-Leader, 1942. Called to the Bar, Gray's Inn, 1946, Bencher 1966; QC 1962. Dep. Chm., Beds. QS, 1960–66; Recorder of Bedford, 1963–66; a Judge of the High Court of Justice, Queen's Bench Div., 1966–74; a Lord Justice of Appeal, 1974–79; a Lord of Appeal in Ordinary, 1979–80. Mem., Parole Board, 1970–72 (Vice-Chm., 1972). Hon. Bencher, Inner Temple, 1980. Hon. LLD Cambridge, 1984. *Address:* Royal Courts of Justice, Strand, WC2A 2LL.
Died 22 Aug. 2005.

LANE, Rev. David John; Principal, College of the Resurrection, Mirfield, 1990–97; *b* 12 June 1935; *s* of late Rex Clayphen Fox Lane and Constance Mary Lane. *Educ:* Hurstpierpoint Coll. (Scholar); Magdalen Coll., Oxford (BA Theol 1958; Oriental Studies 1960; Pusey and Ellerton Schol., 1959; Hall Houghton Syriac Prize, 1961; MA 1962; BD 1989). Nat. Service, Royal Signals, 1953–55. Coll. of the Resurrection, Mirfield, 1960–61; Codrington Coll., Barbados, 1961–62. Ordained deacon and priest, Barbados, 1962; Lectr, 1961, Sen. Tutor, 1963, Codrington Coll., Barbados; Curate, St Peter's, Wolvercote, 1965–66; Associate Chaplain, and Kennicott Hebrew Fellow, 1966–68, Lectr in Theol., 1968–71, Pembroke Coll., Oxford; Lectr and Tutor, St Stephen's House, Oxford, 1968–71; Asst Prof., Near Eastern Studies, 1971, Associate Prof., 1974–83, Univ. of Toronto; Sen. Fellowship, Trinity Coll., Toronto, 1977–82; College of the Resurrection: Lectr and Tutor, 1983; Dir of Studies, 1984; Vice-Principal, 1987–90. Hon. Lectr, Dept of Theology and Religious Studies, Univ. of Leeds, 1983–2001; Seeri Guest Prof., Mahatma Gandhi Univ., Kerala, S India, 1999–. *Publications:* The Old Testament in Syriac: Part II, fasc. 5 ((ed) Ecclesiastes; (ed with J. A. Emerton) Wisdom of Solomon and Song of Songs), 1979,

Part I, fasc. 2 ((ed) Leviticus), 1991; The Peshitta of Leviticus, 1994; Shubhalmaran's Book of Gifts, 2005; articles in learned jls. *Recreations:* gardening, reading, photography. *Club:* Royal Over-Seas League.
Died 9 Jan. 2005.

LANE, Hon. Dame Miriam; *see* Rothschild, Hon. Dame M. L.

LANG, Lt-Gen. Sir Derek (Boileau), KCB 1967 (CB 1964); DSO 1944; MC 1941; DL; General Officer Commanding-in-Chief, Scottish Command, 1966–69; Governor of Edinburgh Castle, 1966–69; *b* 7 Oct. 1913; *s* of Lt-Col C. F. G. Lang and Mrs Lumsden Lang (*née* M. J. L. Forbes); *m* 1st, 1942, Morna Massy Dawson (*d* 1953); one *s* one *d*; 2nd, 1953, Anita Lewis S. Shields (marr. diss. 1969; she *d* 1970); 3rd, 1969, Mrs Elizabeth Harker Balfour (*d* 1982); 4th, 1983, Mrs Maartje McQueen. *Educ:* Wellington Coll.; RMC Sandhurst. Commnd, The Queen's Own Cameron Highlanders, 1933; Adjutant, TA, 1938; active service in France, E and N Africa, 1940–42; Chief Instructor, Sch. of Infantry, 1943–44; Comdr, 5th Camerons, NW Europe, 1944–45; Comdt, Sch. of Infantry, BAOR, 1945–46; Directing Staff, Staff Coll., Camberley, 1947–48; Staff, Australia, 1949–51; GSO1, War Office, 1951–53; Chief Instructor, Sch. of Infantry, 1953–55; AAG, War Office, 1955–57; NDC, 1957–58; Comd Infty Bde (153–TA), 1958–60; Chief of Staff, Scottish Comd, 1960; Gen. Officer Commanding, 51st Highland Div. and District, Perth, 1962–64; Dir of Army Training, 1964–66. Sec., Univ. of Stirling, 1970–73. Hon. Col, 153 (Highland) Regt, RCT (Volunteers), T&AVR, 1970–76; Pres., Army Cadet Force Assoc. (Scotland), 1975–85. Chm., Scottish Veterans Residences, 1975–91. Associate Consultant, PA Management Consultants Ltd, 1975–84. DL Edinburgh, 1978. OStJ. *Publication:* Return to St Valéry, 1974. *Recreations:* golf, fishing, shooting. *Address:* Templeland, Kirknewton, Midlothian EH27 8DJ. *T:* (01506) 883211. *Clubs:* New (Edinburgh); Senior Golfers' Society; Hon. Co. of Edinburgh Golfers (Muirfield). *Died 7 April 2001.*

LANG, Robert; actor, theatre director; *b* 24 Sept. 1934; *s* of Richard Lionel Lang and Lily Violet Lang (*née* Ballard); *m* 1971, Ann Forrest Bell; one *s* one *d*. *Educ:* St Simon's Church Sch., Bristol; Fairfield Grammar Sch., Bristol; Bristol Old Vic Th. Sch. Scientific asst, Meteorological Office, 1952–54. With Bristol Old Vic Co., 1956–58; Nottingham Rep. Co., 1958–61; RSC, 1962; Chichester Fest. Th., 1962 and 1963; joined National Theatre Co., 1963 (Founder Mem.): rôles include: Yefim in Uncle Vanya, 1963; Roderigo in Othello (filmed, 1968), Martín Ruíz in The Royal Hunt of the Sun, Richard Greatham in Hay Fever, 1964; Brazen in The Recruiting Officer, Scandal in Love for Love, Rev. Hale in The Crucible, 1965; toured, Moscow and Berlin, 1965; Kurt in The Dance of Death, 1967 (filmed, 1969); toured Canada, 1967; Corvino in Volpone, 1968; Ash in The National Health, Mirabell in The Way of the World, 1969; Shylock in Merchant of Venice, 1970; toured as Sir Toby Belch in New Shakespeare Co.'s Twelfth Night, 1972; Artistic Dir, Cambridge Theatre Co., 1975–76: directed The Importance of Being Earnest, 1975, The Birthday Party, Home, and The Rivals, 1976; Masquerade, Young Vic, 1982; Larry's Stable, Old Vic, 1991; Midsummer Night's Dream, Regent's Park, Shakespeare in Love, Dallas, 1994; Voyage Round My Father, Oxford Playhouse, and tour, Midsummer Night's Dream, Regent's Park and Cyprus, 1995; Mind Millie for Me, Haymarket, 1996; The Cherry Orchard, RSC tour, 1997; Merry Wives of Windsor, Regent's Park, 1999; The Circle, Oxford Th. Co. tour, 2001; *films* include: Catch Us If You Can, 1965; Walk With Love and Death, 1969; Savage Messiah, 1972; Night Watch, The Mackintosh Man, 1973; Shout at the Devil, 1976; First Great Train Robbery, 1978; Sweet Scent of Death, 1984; Hawks, 1987; Four Weddings and a Funeral, 1994; Rasputin, 1996; Wilde, 1997; *television* includes: An Age of Kings (Shakespeare history plays), 1959; That Was

The Week That Was, 1963; 1990, 1977; For Maddy With Love, 1980; Lady Windermere's Fan, Pinter's The Birthday Party, Antigone, 1986; Vanity Fair, 1988; Parnell and the Englishwoman, Old Boy Network, 1991; Under the Hammer, 1993; Jasper Carrot Trial, A Dance to the Music of Time, 1997; Our Mutual Friend, 1998; Forsyte Saga, 2002. *Recreations:* photography, fishing, reading, parks and beaches. *Address:* c/o Waring & McKenna, 22 Grafton Street, W1S 4EX. *T:* (020) 7491 2666, *Fax:* (020) 7409 7932; *e-mail:* dj@waringandmckenna.demon.co.uk.
Died 6 Nov. 2004.

LANG, Rear-Adm. (William) Duncan, CB 1981; retired; *b* 1 April 1925; *s* of James Hardie Lang and Elizabeth Foggo Paterson Lang (*née* Storie); *m* 1947, Joyce Rose Weeks; one *s* one *d*. *Educ:* Edinburgh Acad. Entered Royal Navy, 1943; trained as Pilot; served in 800, 816 and 825 Sqdns and as Flying Instr and Test Pilot; comd 802 Sqdn, 1958–59; Commander (Air): RNAS Culdrose, 1962–63; HMS Eagle, 1964–65; Fleet Aviation Officer, Far East Fleet, 1966–68; Captain 1969; comd RNAS Lossiemouth, 1970–72; Dep. Comdt, Jt Warfare Estabt, 1973–74; COS to Flag Officer, Naval Air Comd, 1975–76; Dir, Naval Recruiting, 1976–78; Mil. Dep. to Hd of Defence Sales, 1978–81; Dir, Naval Security, MoD, 1981–86. Naval ADC to the Queen, 1978; Rear-Adm. 1978. *Recreation:* golf (Pres., RN Golf Soc., 1979–85). *Address:* c/o HSBC, 19 High Street, Haslemere, Surrey GU27 2HQ. *Club:* Army and Navy.
Died 30 Dec. 2005.

LANGDON, Jonathan Bertram Robert Louis; His Honour Judge Langdon; a Circuit Judge, since 1991; *b* 1 Nov. 1939; *s* of Captain John Edward Langdon, RN and Nancy Langdon; *m* 1962, Hilary Jean Fox Taylor; twin *s* one *d*. *Educ:* Hurstpierpoint Coll.; RNC Dartmouth. Entered RN, 1958; served HM Ships Bermuda, Lincoln and London, 1960–64; Supply Officer, HMS Daring, 1965–68; legal trng, 1968–70; called to the Bar, Gray's Inn, 1970; Staff Legal Advr to FO Plymouth, 1970–73; RN FE Legal Advr, Hong Kong, 1973–75; Comdr, 1977; Supply Officer, HMS Norfolk, 1977–79; various MoD and staff appts, 1980–86; Captain, 1986; Chief Naval Judge Advocate, 1987–90; Sec. to C-in-C Naval Home Command, 1990–91; retired voluntarily from RN, 1991. Hon. Recorder, City of Canterbury, 2000–. *Recreations:* sailing, gardening, croquet, travel. *Address:* The Law Courts, Chaucer Road, Canterbury, Kent CT1 1ZA.
Died 13 Aug. 2004.

LANGDON, Richard Norman Darbey, FCA; Senior Partner, Spicer and Pegler, 1978–84; *b* 19 June 1919; *s* of Norman Langdon and Dorothy Langdon; *m* 1944, June Dixon; two *s*. *Educ:* Shrewsbury Sch. Officer, RA, 1939–46. Admitted Mem. Inst. of Chartered Accountants in England and Wales, 1947; joined Spicer and Pegler, 1949, Partner 1953, Managing Partner, 1971–82. Chairman: Hammond and Champness Ltd, 1966–89; Aspinall Hldg, 1983–89; Finlay Packaging PLC, 1984–93; First National Finance Corp., 1985–92; Beeson Gregory, 1989–95; Director: Time Products PLC, 1984–93 (Chm., 1984–92); Rockware Group PLC, 1985–91; Chemring Gp PLC, 1985–96 (Dep. Chm., 1985–92). Treasurer, CGLI, 1982–90. Mem. Council, Univ. of Surrey, 1988–90. *Recreation:* gardening. *Address:* Whitedale House, Hambledon, Hants PO7 4RZ. *T:* (023) 9263 2457. *Club:* Old Salopian. *Died 24 Aug. 2004.*

LANGE, Rt Hon. David Russell, ONZ 2003; CH 1990; PC 1984; Prime Minister of New Zealand, 1984–89; *b* 4 Aug. 1942; *s* of late Eric Roy Lange and Phoebe Fysh Lange; *m* 1st, 1968, Naomi Joy Crampton; two *s* one *d*; 2nd, 1992, Margaret Forsyth Pope; one *d*. *Educ:* Univ. of Auckland (LLM Hons). Called to the Bar of NZ and admitted Solicitor, 1966. MP (Lab) Mangere, NZ, 1977–96; Dep. Leader of the Opposition, 1979–83, Leader 1983–84; Minister of Foreign Affairs, 1984–87; Minister in charge of Security Intelligence Service, 1984–89; Minister of Education, 1987–89; Attorney Gen., and Minister of

State, 1989–90. *Publications:* Nuclear-Free—the New Zealand Way, 1990; Broadsides, 1992; Cuttings, 1994. *Address:* PO Box 59–120, Mangere Bridge, New Zealand.
Died 13 Aug. 2005.

LANGHAM, Sir James (Michael), 15th Bt *cr* 1660; TD 1965; *b* 24 May 1932; *s* of Sir John Charles Patrick Langham, 14th Bt, and Rosamond Christabel (MBE 1969) (*d* 1992), *d* of late Arthur Rashleigh; *S* father, 1972; *m* 1959, Marion Audrey Eleanor, *d* of O. H. Barratt, Gararagua Estate, Tanzania; two *s* one *d. Educ:* Rossall School, Fleetwood. Served as Captain, North Irish Horse, 1953–67. *Heir: s* John Stephen Langham [*b* 14 Dec. 1960; *m* 1991, Sarah Jane, *d* of late J. D. Verschoyle-Greene; one *s* two *d*]. *Address:* Claranagh, Tempo, Co. Fermanagh BT94 3FJ. *T:* (028) 6654 1247. *Died 23 Dec. 2002.*

LA NIECE, Rear-Adm. Peter George, CB 1973; CBE 1967; *b* 23 July 1920; *s* of late George David Nelson La Niece and Gwynneth Mary (*née* Morgan); *m* 1948, Evelyn Mary Wrixon Babington (*d* 1982); two *s* one *d. Educ:* Whitgift Sch., Croydon. Entered RN, 1937; served War of 1939–45 in battleships, cruisers and destroyers; Gunnery Specialist 1945; Comdr 1953; Captain 1961; comd HMS Rame Head, 1962; Senior UK Polaris Rep., Washington, 1963–66; comd HMS Triumph, 1966–68; Cdre Clyde in Comd Clyde Submarine Base, 1969–71; Rear-Adm. 1971; Flag Officer Spithead and Port Admiral, Portsmouth, 1971–73, retired. Dir in Exco Gp of Cos, 1976–85. *Address:* 31 Crittles Court, Townlands Road, Wadhurst, E Sussex TN5 6BY. *T:* (01892) 782161. *Club:* Army and Navy. *Died 4 April 2003.*

LAPUN, Sir Paul, Kt 1974; *b* 1923; Lois; two *s* one *d. Educ:* Catholic Mission, Vunapope. Teacher, Catholic Mission, 1947–61. Under-Secretary for Forests, Papua and New Guinea, 1964–67. Founder Mem., for S Bougainville, PNG House of Assembly, 1964; Founder, Pangu Party, 1967 (Leader, 1967–68; Dep. Parly Leader, 1968); Minister: for Mines and Energy, 1972–75; for Health, 1975–77. Hon. Mem., Internat. Mark Twain Soc., USA. *Address:* Bougainville, N Solomons Province, Papua New Guinea. *Died 26 Oct. 2003.*

LARCOM, Sir (Charles) Christopher (Royde), 5th Bt *cr* 1868; *b* 11 Sept. 1926; *s* of Sir Philip Larcom, 4th Bt, and Aileen Monica Royde (*née* Colbeck); *S* father, 1967; *m* 1956, Barbara Elizabeth, *d* of Balfour Bowen; four *d. Educ:* Radley; Clare Coll., Cambridge (Wrangler, 1947; BA 1947; MA 1951). ACA 1954, FCA 1965. Served RN (Lieutenant), 1947–50. Articled to Messrs Spicer and Pegler (Chartered Accountants), 1950–53; joined Grieveson, Grant and Co., 1955, Partner, 1960, retired, 1986. Mem., The Stock Exchange, London, 1959 (Mem. Council, 1970–80). *Recreations:* sailing, music. *Address:* 33 Cromwell Tower, Barbican, EC2Y 8DD.
Died 20 Dec. 2004.

LARGE, Sir Peter, Kt 1993; CBE 1987 (MBE 1974); President, Joint Committee on Mobility for Disabled People (formerly Mobility for the Disabled), since 1997 (Chairman, 1971–97); *b* 16 Oct. 1931; *s* of Ethel May Walters and Rosslyn Victor Large; *m* 1st, 1962, Susy Fisher (*d* 1982); one step *s* two step *d; m* 2nd, 1992, Sheenah McCaffrey. *Educ:* Enfield Grammar Sch.; University Coll. London (BSc Civil Engrg 1953). National Service, HM Submarines, 1953–55 (Sub Lt (E)). Joined Shell International, 1956; West Africa, 1957; Ghana, 1957–60; South East Arabia, 1960–61; Indonesia, 1961–62; paralysed by poliomyelitis, 1962; Civil Service, 1966–91. Chm., Assoc. of Disabled Professionals, 1971–93 (Parly Advr, 1993–); Mem., Disabled Persons Transport Adv. Cttee, 1986–2002; Vice-Chm., Disablement Income Group, 1985–93 (Parly Advr, 1973–93); Chairman: Silver Jubilee Cttee on Improving Access for Disabled People, 1977–79; Cttee on Restrictions against Disabled People, 1979–82; Member: Exec. Cttee, British Council for Rehabilitation of the Disabled, 1966–77; Exec. Cttee, RADAR, 1977–2001 (Vice Chm., 1995–99); Access

Cttee for England, 1984–94; Nat. Adv. Council on Employment of People with Disabilities (formerly Disabled People), 1987–98; Disability Living Allowance Adv. Bd, 1991–99. Pres., East Surrey Dial-a-Ride, 2000–. Governor, Mobility, 1978–; Trustee, Motability 10th Anniversary Trust, 1989–. FRSA 1993. Field-Marshal Lord Harding of Petherton Award, Action Res. and RADAR, 1992. *Recreation:* conversing with Siamese cats. *Address:* 14 Birch Way, Warlingham, Surrey CR6 9DA.
Died 23 Jan. 2005.

LARRY; *see* Parkes, T.

LASDUN, Sir Denys (Louis), CH 1995; Kt 1976; CBE 1965 (MBE 1945); RA 1991; RIBA; architect in private practice, since 1935; with Peter Softley & Associates, since 1986; *b* 8 Sept. 1914; *s* of Norman Lasdun and Julie Abrahams; *m* 1954, Susan Bendit; two *s* one *d. Educ:* Rugby Sch.; Architectural Assoc. Served with Royal Engineers, 1939–45 (MBE). Practised with Wells Coates, Tecton and Drake, 1935–48. Hoffman Wood Professor of Architecture, University of Leeds, 1962–63. Assessor, Competitions for Belgrade Opera Hse, 1971, and new Parly Bldg, London, 1971–72. Principal works: housing and schools for Bethnal Green and Paddington; London HQ, NSW Govt; flats at 26 St James's Place; Royal College of Physicians (RIBA Trustees' Medal, 1992); Fitzwilliam College, and Christ's College extension, Cambridge; new University of East Anglia and work for the Universities of London (SOAS, Inst. of Educn, Law Inst., project for Courtauld Inst.), Leicester and Liverpool; National Theatre and IBM, South Bank; EEC HQ for European Investment Bank, Luxembourg; design for new Hurva Synagogue, Old City, Jerusalem; Cannock Community Hosp.; Genoa Opera House competition; office buildings, Fenchurch Street, EC4 and Milton Gate, EC2. Retrospective Exhibn, RA, 1997. Trustee, BM, 1975–85; Member: CIAM and MARS Gp, 1935–59; Jerusalem Town Planning Cttee, 1970; V&A Adv. Cttee, 1973–83; Slade Cttee, 1976–92; Arts Panel, Arts Council of GB, 1980–84; Académie d'Architecture, Paris, 1984–; Accademia Nazionale di San Luca, Rome, 1984–; Academician, Internat. Acad. of Architecture, Bulgaria, 1986. Hon. Fellow, American Institute of Architects, 1966; Hon. FRCP 1975; Hon. FRIAS 1994; Hon. DipAA 1994. Hon. DA Manchester, 1966; Hon. DLitt: E Anglia, 1974; Sheffield, 1978. RIBA London Architecture Bronze Medallist, 1960 and 1964; Civic Trust Awards: Class I, 1967; Group A, 1969; Special Award, São Paulo Biennale, Brazil, 1969; Concrete Society Award, 1976; Royal Gold Medal for Architecture, RIBA, 1977; RIBA Architectural, Award for London Region, 1978; Wolf Prize in Arts (Architecture), Wolf Foundn, 1992; Centenary Medal, Architects' Jl, 1995; Bulgaria Gold Medal, IAA, 1997. *Publications included:* An Architect's Approach to Architecture, 1965 (RIBA Jl); A Language and a Theme, 1976; Architecture in an Age of Scepticism, 1984. *Relevant publication:* Denys Lasdun: architecture, city, landscape, by William Curtis, 1994. *Address:* 51 Rowan Road, W6 7DT. *T:* (020) 7602 7758. *Died 11 Jan. 2001.*

LASKO, Prof. Peter Erik, CBE 1981; FBA 1978; Professor of the History of Art, Courtauld Institute, University of London, 1974–85; Director, Courtauld Institute, 1974–85; *b* 5 March 1924; *s* of Leo Lasko and Wally Lasko (*née* Seifert); *m* 1948, Gwendoline Joan Norman; three *d. Educ:* Courtauld Institute, Univ. of London (BA Hons 1949). Asst Keeper, British Museum, 1950–65; Prof. of the Visual Arts, Univ. of East Anglia, 1965–73. Member: Cathedrals Adv. Commn, 1981–91; Royal Commn on Historical Monuments (England), 1984–91; Cathedrals Fabric Commn, 1991–96; Trustee: British Mus., 1981–95; Royal Armouries, 1984–91. Hon. DLitt East Anglia, 1997. *Publication:* Ars Sacra 800–1200 (Pelican History of Art), 1972, 2nd edn 1994. *Address:* 1 Hawke Lane, Bloxham, Oxon OX15 4PY.
Died 18 May 2003.

LASKY, Melvin Jonah, MA; Editor, Encounter Magazine, 1958–90; *b* New York City, 15 Jan. 1920; *s* of Samuel Lasky and Esther Lasky (*née* Kantrowitz); *m* 1947, Brigitte Newiger (marr. diss. 1974); one *s* one *d. Educ:* City Coll. of New York (BSS); Univ. of Michigan (MA); Columbia Univ. Literary Editor, The New Leader (NY), 1942–43; US Combat Historian in France and Germany, 1944–45; Capt., US Army, 1946; Foreign Correspondent, 1946–48; Editor and Publisher, Der Monat (Berlin), 1948–58 and 1978–83; Editorial Director, Library Press, NY, 1970–80; Publisher, Alcove Press, London, 1972–82. Regular television broadcaster, Cologne, Zürich and Vienna, 1955–. Fellow, Inst. of Advanced Study, Berlin, 1988–89. Hon. PhD York (Canada), 1990. Univ. of Michigan, Sesquicentennial Award, 1967; Distinguished Alumnus Award, City Univ., NY, 1978. *Publications:* (ed) The Hungarian Revolution, 1957; Reisenotizen und Tagebücher, 1958; Africa for Beginners, 1962; Utopia and Revolution, 1976 (Spanish edn 1982; German edn 1989); On the Barricades, and Off, 1989; Voices in a Revolution, 1991 (also German edn); The Language of Journalism, vol I: newspaper culture, 2000, vol. II: pornography, obscenity and the media, 2004; contributor to: America and Europe, 1951; New Paths in American History, 1965; Sprache und Politik, 1969; Festschrift for Raymond Aron, 1971; Koestler, Orwell, Lasky and Der Monat: a history, 1999; Ein Fenster zur Welt (Monat anthol.), 2000. *Address:* Mommsenstrasse 67, 10629 Berlin, Germany; 37 Godfrey Street, Chelsea, SW3 3SX. *Club:* Garrick.
Died 19 May 2004.

LASLETT, (Thomas) Peter (Ruffell), CBE 1997; FBA 1979; Reader in Politics and the History of Social Structure, Cambridge University, 1966–83; Co-Founder and Director, Cambridge Group for the History of Population and Social Structure, since 1964; Fellow of Trinity College, Cambridge, since 1953; *b* 18 Dec. 1915; *s* of Rev. G. H. R. Laslett and E. E. Laslett (*née* Alden); *m* 1947, Janet Crockett Clark; two *s. Educ:* Watford Grammar Sch.; St John's Coll., Cambridge. Served War, Royal Navy, 1940–45: Lieut RNVR, Japanese Naval Intelligence. Producer, BBC, 3rd Programme Talks, 1946–60; Fellow: St John's Coll., Cambridge, 1948–51; Inst. for Advanced Study, Princeton, 1959. With Michael Young and others developed plans for Open Univ. in the 1960s, and for univs of the Third Age in the 1970s; Mem., govt cttee on foundn of Open Univ., 1965; oversaw instn of first Univ. of the Third Age, 1981. Visiting Professor: Johns Hopkins Univ., 1972; Collège de France, Paris, 1976; Yale Univ., 1977; Nihon Univ., Tokyo, 1992. DUniv: Open, 1980; Keele, 1993; Tulane, 2000. Founder and Chief Ed., series, Philosophy, Politics and Society, 1957 (6th series 1992). *Publications:* Sir Robert Filmer, 1949; Locke's Two Treatises of Government, 1960, 3rd edn 1988; The World We Have Lost, 1965, 3rd edn 1983; (with R. Wall) Household and Family in Past Time, 1972; Family Life and Illicit Love in Earlier Generations, 1977; (with R. M. Smith and others) Bastardy and its Comparative History, 1980; (jtly) Family Forms in Historic Europe, 1983; A Fresh Map of Life, 1989, 2nd edn 1996; (with J. Fishkin) Justice between Age Groups and Generations, 1992; (with D. Kertzer) Ageing in the Past, 1995. *Recreations:* book collecting, gardening. *Address:* Trinity College, Cambridge CB2 1TQ; Cambridge Group, 27 Trumpington Street, Cambridge CB2 1QA. *T:* (01223) 333181. *Died 8 Nov. 2001.*

LATHAM, Cecil Thomas, OBE 1976; Stipendiary Magistrate, Greater Manchester (sitting at Salford), 1976–94; *b* 11 March 1924; *s* of Cecil Frederick James Latham and Elsie Winifred Latham; *m* 1945, Ivy Frances (*née* Fowle); one *s* one *d. Educ:* Rochester Cathedral Choir Sch.; King's Sch., Rochester. Qualified as solicitor. Served War, 1942–45. Asst Clerk, Magistrates' Courts: Chatham, 1939–42; Maidstone, 1945; Leicester, 1948–54; Bromley, 1954–63; Dep. Justices' Clerk, Liverpool, 1963–65; Justices' Clerk, Manchester, 1965–76. Member: Magistrates' Courts Rule Cttee, 1966–94; Royal Commn on Criminal Procedure, 1978–81; Criminal Law Revision Cttee, 1981–94. Hon. MA Manchester, 1984. *Publications:* (ed) Stone's Justices' Manual, 101st-109th edns; How Much?: determining maintenance in magistrates' courts, 1976; Care Proceedings, 1989; (ed) Family Law Reports, 1980–86; specialist editor, Justice of the Peace Reports, 1986–93; founder editor, Family Court Reporter, 1987–99; contrib. Criminal Law Review, Justice of Peace, Family Law. *Recreation:* music. *Address:* 12 Oakside Way, Oakwood, Derby DE21 2UH. *T:* (01332) 544338.
Died 2 April 2005.

LATYMER, 8th Baron *cr* 1431; **Hugo Nevill Money-Coutts;** *b* 1 March 1926; *s* of 7th Baron Latymer and Patience (*d* 1982), *d* of late William Courtenay-Thompson; *S* father, 1987; *m* 1st, 1951, Hon. Penelope Ann Clare (marr. diss. 1965), *yr d* of late T. A. Emmet and Baroness Emmet of Amberley; two *s* one *d*; 2nd 1965, Jinty, *d* of late Peter George Calvert; one *s* two *d. Educ:* Eton. *Heir: s* Hon. Crispin James Alan Nevill Money-Coutts [*b* 8 March 1955; *m* 1st, 1978, Hon. Lucy Rose (marr. diss. 1995), *y d* of Rt Hon. Baron Deedes, KBE, MC, PC; one *s* two *d*; 2nd, 1995, Mrs Shaunagh Heneage]. *Address:* Vivero Hortus, Santa Maria, Mallorca, Spain. *Died 10 Nov. 2003.*

LAUGHLAND, His Honour (Graham Franklyn) Bruce; QC 1977; a Circuit Judge, 1989–96, at the Central Criminal Court; *b* 18 Aug. 1931; 3rd *s* of late Andrew and Constance Laughland; *m* 1st, 1969, Victoria Nicola Christina Jarman (*d* 1994); one *s*; 2nd, 1999, Jacqueline Marie Bakes-Bradbury. *Educ:* King Edward's Sch., Birmingham; Christ Church, Oxford (MA). Stick of Honour, Mons Officer Cadet Sch., 1954; Lieut 8th RTR, 1954–56. Called to Bar, Inner Temple, 1958, Bencher, 1985; Dep. Chm., Bucks QS, 1971; Standing Counsel to the Queen's Proctor, 1968; a Recorder, 1972–89; First Prosecuting Counsel to the Inland Revenue (Midland and Oxford Circuit), 1973–77; actg Judge of the Supreme Court of the Falkland Is, 1985. Mem., Gen. Council of the Bar, 1970; Treas., Midland and Oxford Circuit, 1986–89. Chm., Westminster Assoc. for Youth, 1984–89. Liveryman, Curriers' Co., 1992–. *Address:* 30 Monmouth Road, W2 4UT. *T:* (020) 7229 5045. *Club:* Garrick.
Died 1 May 2002.

LAURIE, Robert Peter, OBE 1994; JP; DL; farmer, 1958–89, retired; Vice Lord-Lieutenant, Essex, 1985–92; *b* 20 Aug. 1925; *s* of late Col Vernon Stewart Laurie, CBE, TD, DL, and Mary, 2nd *d* of Selwyn Robert Pryor; *m* 1952, Oonagh Margaret Faber Wild, 3rd *d* of W. P. Wild, Warcop Hall, Westmorland; three *s* one *d. Educ:* Eton College. Served Coldstream Guards, 1943–47, Hon. Captain. Mem., Stock Exchange, 1953; Partner, Heseltine, Powell & Co., then Heseltine, Moss & Co., 1953–80, Consultant, 1980–86; Dir, British Empire Securites & General Trust Ltd, 1954–95 (Chm., 1973–84). Chm., 1977–86, Pres., 1986–, Essex Assoc. of Boys' Clubs; a Vice-Pres., NABC-CYP (formerly NABC), 1986–; President: Essex Agricl Soc., 1986–87; Essex Shire Horse Assoc., 1987–2001; Essex Home Workers, 1986–2000; Chelmsford and Mid Essex Samaritans, 1986–92. Member: Ct, Essex Univ., 1979–; Council, CGLI, 1984–97. Governor: Brentwood Sch., 1974–95; Alleyn's Sch., 1984–95. Master, Saddlers' Co., 1981–82. Vice-Pres., Coldstream Guards Assoc., 2003– (Pres., Essex Br., 1959–2002); Chm., Essex Co. Cttee, TAVRA, 1987–91; Hon. Col, Essex, ACF, 1994–98. JP 1974, High Sheriff 1978–79, DL 1979, Essex. *Recreations:* foxhunting and field sports, gardening, reading. *Address:* The Old Vicarage, Cornish Hall End, Braintree, Essex CM7 4HF.
Died 15 Aug. 2005.

LAURISTON, His Honour Alexander Clifford; QC 1972; a Circuit Judge, 1976–93; a Deputy Circuit Judge, 1993–2000; Chairman, Registered Homes Appeals Tribunal, 1994–98; *b* 2 Oct. 1927; *s* of Alexander Lauriston and Nellie Lauriston (*née* Ainsworth); *m* 1954, Inga Louise Cameron; two *d. Educ:* Coatham Sch.,

Redcar, Yorks; Trinity Coll., Cambridge (MA). National Service: Army, Green Howards and RAPC, 2nd Lieut, 1948–50. Called to Bar, Inner Temple, 1952. A Recorder of the Crown Court, 1972–76. Mem., Loriners' Co., 1969; Freeman, City of London, 1969. *Recreations:* outdoor activities, painting, music. *Address:* 199 Strand, WC2R 1DR. *Clubs:* Oxford and Cambridge; Berkshire Golf. *Died 27 Jan. 2004.*

LAW, Adm. Sir Horace (Rochfort), GCB 1972 (KCB 1967; CB 1963); OBE 1950; DSC 1941; Chairman, R. & W. Hawthorn Leslie & Co., 1973–81; *b* 23 June 1911; *s* of S. Horace Law, MD, FRCSI, and Sybil Mary (*née* Clay); *m* 1941, Heather Valerie Coryton (*d* 1996); two *s* two *d*. *Educ:* Sherborne Sch. Entered Royal Navy, 1929; gunnery specialist, 1937. Served War of 1939–45 (DSC): AA Cruisers: Cairo, 1939; Coventry, 1940; Cruiser Nigeria, 1942; Comdr 1946; Capt. 1952; comd HMS Centaur, 1958 and Britannia, RN Coll., 1960; Rear-Adm. 1961; Vice-Adm. 1965; Flag Officer Sea Training, 1961–63; Flag Officer, Submarines, 1963–65; Controller of the Navy, 1965–70; C-in-C, Naval Home Comd, and Flag Officer, Portsmouth Area, 1970–72; First and Principal Naval Aide-de-Camp to the Queen, 1970–72. Mem., Security Commn, 1973–82. President: RINA, 1975–77; Officers' Christian Union, 1976–86; Chm., Church Army Bd, 1980–87. Grand Cross, Order of the Crown (Netherlands), 1972. *Recreations:* walking, gardening. *Address:* West Harting, Petersfield, Hants GU31 5NT. *Died 30 Jan. 2005.*

LAW, James; QC (Scot.) 1971; *b* 7 June 1926; *s* of late George Law, MA, and Isabella Rebecca Lamb or Law, MA; *m* 1956, Kathleen Margaret, *d* of late Alexander Gibson; two *s* one *d*. *Educ:* Kilmarnock Academy; Girvan High Sch.; Univ. of Glasgow (MA 1948, LLB 1950). Admitted to Faculty of Advocates, 1951; Advocate-Depute, 1957–64. Temp. Sheriff, 1971–96. Mem., Criminal Injuries Compensation Bd, 1970–96. *Address:* 9/3 Silvermills, Edinburgh EH3 5BF. *T:* (0131) 558 9376. *Died 6 March 2001.*

LAW, Sylvia, OBE 1977; *b* 29 March 1931; *d* of late Reginald Howard Law and Dorothy Margaret Law. *Educ:* Lowther Coll.; Girton Coll., Cambridge (MA); Regent Street Polytechnic (DipTP). MRTPI. Teaching, Benenden Sch., 1952–55; market research, Unilever Ltd, 1955–58; town and country planning and policy studies and research, Kent CC and GLC, 1959–86. Royal Town Planning Institute: Mem. Council, 1965–78; Chm. of Educn Cttee, 1970–73; Vice-Pres., 1972–74; Pres., 1974–75. Mem. Planning Cttee, SSRC, 1977–79. Volunteer Advr, CAB, 1986–98. Member: Cambridge Soc., 1981–; Bury St Edmunds Univ. of Third Age, 1999–. *Publications:* (contrib.) Recreational Economics and Analysis, 1974; (ed) Planning and the Future, 1976; articles in RTPI Jl, Official Architecture and Planning, Planning Outlook, Town Planning Rev., Greater London Intelligence Qly, etc. *Recreations:* music, photography, gardening. *Died 1 April 2004.*

LAW, Dr Vivien Anne, (Lady Shackleton), FBA 1999; Fellow, Trinity College, Cambridge, since 1997; Reader in the History of Linguistic Thought, University of Cambridge, since 1998; *b* 22 March 1954; *d* of John Ernest and Anne Elizabeth Law; *m* 1986, Nicholas John Shackleton (Sir Nicholas Shackleton, FRS). *Educ:* Trafalgar Sch. for Girls, Montreal; McGill Univ. (BA 1974); Girton Coll., Cambridge (PhD 1979). MIL 1979. University of Cambridge: Res. Fellow, Jesus Coll., 1977–80; David Thomson Sen. Res. Fellow, 1980–84, Fellow, 1984–97, Sidney Sussex Coll.; Lectr in Hist. of Linguistics, 1984–98; Co-Founder, Post Soviet States in Transition Res. Prog., Sidney Sussex Coll., 1993–97. Invited Lectr, Hungarian Acad. Scis, 1995; O'Donnell Meml Lectr, Toronto, 1998. Associate Ed., Beiträge zur Geschichte der Sprachwissenschaft, 1991–. Mem. Council, Philological Soc., 1990–95 and 1996–2000; Chm., Cambridge Regl Soc., Inst. Linguists, 1994–2001;

Henry Sweet Society for the History of Linguistic Ideas: Membership Sec., 1987–90; Conf. Sec., 1990–93; Chm., 2000–; Mem. Editl Bd, Studies in Hist. of Linguistics, 1995–. Co-founder and Jt Leader, Humanities Res. Gp and Humanities Section in GB, Sch. of Spiritual Sci., 1997–. Fellow, Soc. Internazionale per lo Studio del Medioevo Latino, 1996– (Corresp. Mem., 1981–96); Comité Internat., Soc. d'Histoire et d'Epistémologie des Sciences du Langage, 1998. *Publications:* The Insular Latin Grammarians, 1982; (ed) History of Linguistic Thought in the Early Middle Ages, 1993; Wisdom, Authority and Grammar in the Seventh Century: decoding Virgilius Maro Grammaticus, 1995; (ed jtly) Dionysius Thrax and the Techné Grammatiké, 1995; (ed jtly) Linguists and Their Diversions, 1996; Grammar and Grammarians in the Early Middle Ages, 1997; (jtly) Nation-Building in the Post-Soviet Borderlands: the politics of national identities, 1998; contrib. articles and book chapters. *Recreations:* orchestral flute and piccolo playing, rollerblading. *Address:* Trinity College, Cambridge CB2 1TQ. *T:* (01223) 338549. *Died 19 Feb. 2002.*

LAWRENCE, Sir David (Roland Walter), 3rd Bt *cr* 1906, of Sloane Gardens, Chelsea; late Captain, Coldstream Guards, 1951; *b* 8 May 1929; *er s* of Sir Roland Lawrence, 2nd Bt, MC, and Susan, 3rd *d* of Sir Charles Addis, KCMG; *S* father, 1950; *m* 1955, Audrey, Duchess of Leeds, *yr d* of Brig. Desmond Young, OBE, MC. *Educ:* Radley; RMC Sandhurst. Heir: *b* Clive Wyndham Lawrence [*b* 6 Oct. 1939; *m* 1966, Sophia Annabel Stuart, *d* of late (Ian) Hervey Stuart Black, TD; three *s*]. *Address:* 28 High Town Road, Maidenhead, Berks SL6 1PB. *Died 9 Sept. 2002.*

LAWRENCE, John, OBE 1974; Director, Africa and Middle East Division, British Council, 1990–93; *b* 22 April 1933; *s* of William and Nellie Lawrence. *Educ:* Queens' College, Cambridge (BA 1956, Cert. Ed. 1957, MA 1961); Indiana University (MA 1959). Teaching posts in USA and UK, 1957–60; British Council headquarters appts, 1961; Regional Representative, Sabah, 1965; Representative, Zambia, 1968, Sudan, 1974, Malaysia, 1976; Dir, South Asia Dept, 1980; Controller, America, Pacific and S Asia Div., 1982–87; Rep., Brazil, 1987–90. *Recreations:* walking and talking, simultaneously or otherwise. *Died 17 May 2003.*

LAWSON, John Alexander Reid, OBE 1979; FRCGP; General Medical Practitioner, 1948–86, retired; Regional Adviser in General Practice, Tayside Region, 1972–82; *b* 30 Aug. 1920; *s* of Thomas Reid Lawson and Helen Scrimgour Lawson; *m* 1944, Pat Kirk; two *s* two *d*. *Educ:* High Sch. of Dundee; Univ. of St Andrews (MB, ChB). RAMC, 1944–47 (Major). Surgical Registrar, Royal Infirmary, Dundee, 1947–48. Royal College of General Practitioners: Mem., 1952; Fellow, 1967; Chm. Council, 1973–76; Pres., 1982–85. Mem. Cttee of Enquiry into Competence to Practice, 1974–76; Chairman: Jt Cttee on Postgraduate Training for General Practice, 1975–78; Armed Service Gen. Practice Approval Bd, 1979–87. *Recreations:* shooting, fishing, golf, gardening. *Address:* The Ridges, 458 Perth Road, Dundee DD2 1NG. *T:* (01382) 566675. *Club:* Royal and Ancient Golf (St Andrews). *Died 23 Oct. 2001.*

LAWSON, Col Sir John Charles Arthur Digby, 3rd Bt *cr* 1900, of Weetwood Grange, West Riding of Yorkshire; DSO 1943; MC 1940; Colonel 11th Hussars, retired; Chairman, Fairbairn Lawson Ltd, Leeds, 1968–79; *b* 24 Oct. 1912; *e s* of Sir Digby Lawson, 2nd Bt, TD, JP, and Mrs Gerald Wallis (*née* Iris Mary Fitzgerald); *S* father, 1959; *m* 1st, 1945, Rose (marr. diss. 1950; she *d* 1972), widow of Pilot Officer William Fiske, RAF, and *er d* of late D. C. Bingham and Lady Rosabelle Brand; 2nd, 1954, Tresilla Ann Elinor (de Pret Roose) (*d* 1985), *d* of late Major E. Buller Leyborne Popham, MC; one *s*. *Educ:* Stowe; RMC, Sandhurst; commissioned 11th Hussars (PAO), 1933; Palestine, 1936–37; Transjordan Frontier Force, 1938; Western Desert, 1940–43 (despatches twice,

MC, DSO); Armoured Adviser to Gen. Patton, N Africa, 1943; Staff Coll., 1943; US Marines Staff Course, 1944; Special Liaison Officer to Gen. Montgomery, NW Europe, 1944; Comd Inns of Court Regt, 1945–47; retired, 1947. Colonel, 11th Hussars (PAO), 1965–69; Col, The Royal Hussars (PWO), 1969–73. Legion of Merit (US), 1943. *Heir: s* Charles John Patrick Lawson [*b* 19 May 1959; *m* 1987, Lady Caroline Lowther, *d* of 7th Earl of Lonsdale; three *s* one *d. Educ:* Harrow; Royal Agricl Coll., Cirencester. With Jackson-Stops & Staff]. *Clubs:* Cavalry and Guards, MCC.

Died 19 Nov. 2001.

LAWSON JOHNSTON, Hon. Hugh de Beauchamp, TD 1951; DL; *b* 7 May 1909; *yr s* of 1st Baron Luke, KBE and Hon. Edith Laura (*d* 1941), *d* of 16th Baron St John of Bletsoe; *m* 1946, Audrey Warren, *d* of late Colonel F. Warren Pearl and Mrs A. L. Pearl; three *d. Educ:* Eton; Chillon Coll.; Corpus Christi, Cambridge (BA 1934, MA 1938). With Bovril Ltd, 1935–71, finally as Chm. Territorial Service with 5th Bn Beds and Herts Regt, 1935–; Captain, 1939, and throughout War. Chairman: Tribune Investment Trust Ltd, 1951–86; Pitman Ltd, 1973–81. Chm. of Cttees, United Soc. for Christian Literature, 1949–82. High Sheriff, 1961–62, DL 1964, Beds. *Recreations:* walking, gardening, photography. *Address:* Woodleys Farm House, Melchbourne, Bedfordshire MK44 1AG. *T:* (01234) 708282.

Died 12 Oct. 2002.

LAWTON, Rt Hon. Sir Frederick (Horace), Kt 1961; PC 1972; a Lord Justice of Appeal, 1972–86; *b* 21 Dec. 1911; *o s* of William John Lawton, OBE; *m* 1937, Doreen (*née* Wilton) (*d* 1979); two *s. Educ:* Battersea Grammar Sch.; Corpus Christi Coll., Cambridge (Hon. Fellow, 1968). Barrister, Inner Temple, 1935; Bencher, 1961. Served with London Irish Rifles, 1939–41; invalided out of Army, 1941, and returned to practice at the Bar. QC 1957; Recorder of City of Cambridge, 1957–61; Judge of the High Court of Justice, Queen's Bench Div., 1961–72; Dep. Chm., Cornwall QS, 1968–71; Presiding Judge, Western Circuit, 1970–72. Member: Bar Council, 1957–61; Departmental Cttee on Proceedings before Examining Justices, 1957–58; Standing Cttee on Criminal Law Revision, 1959–86 (Chm., 1977–86); Inter-departmental Cttee on Court of Criminal Appeal, 1964–65; Chm., Adv. Cttee on Legal Educn, 1976–86. President, British Academy of Forensic Sciences, 1964. *Address:* 1 The Village, Skelton, York YO30 6XX. *T:* (01904) 470441. *Club:* Garrick. *Died 3 Feb. 2001.*

LAWTON, Harold Walter, MA; Docteur de l'Univ.; Officier d'Académie; Emeritus Professor, University of Sheffield, since 1964; *b* Stoke-on-Trent, 27 July 1899; *y s* of late William T. C. and Alice Lawton; *m* 1933, Bessie (*d* 1991), *y d* of T. C. Pate; one *d* (and two *s* decd). *Educ:* Middle Sch., Newcastle under Lyme; Rhyl County Sch.; Univ. of Wales (BA Hons 1921; MA 1923; Fellow, 1923–26); Docteur de l'Univ. de Paris, 1926. Served with Cheshire Regt, 1916–18. University College, Southampton: Lecturer in French, 1926–37; Professor of French, 1937–50; Dean of Faculty of Arts, 1945–49; first Warden of New, later Connaught, Hall, 1930–33; University of Sheffield: Professor of French, 1950–64; Warden of Ranmoor House, 1957–63; Deputy Pro-Vice-Chancellor, 1958–61; Pro-Vice-Chancellor, 1961–64. Transcriber, the Gladstone Diaries, 1933–36. Médaille d'Argent de la Reconnaissance Française, 1946; Officier d'Académie, 1948. Chevalier, Légion d'Honneur (France), 1999. *Publications:* Térence en France au XVIe Siècle: éditions et traductions (Paris), 1926; repr. 1970; Handbook of French Renaissance Dramatic Theory, 1950, repr. 1972; J. du Bellay, Poems, selected with introduction and notes, 1961; Térence en France au XVIe Siècle: imitation et influence, 1972; articles and reviews to British and French periodicals. *Address:* Fir Tree Farmhouse, Main Street, Cottesmore, Rutland LE15 7DJ. *Died 23 Dec. 2005.*

LEACH, David Andrew, OBE 1987; potter, designer, lecturer; *b* 7 May 1911; *e s* of Bernard Leach, CH, CBE, and Edith Muriel, *o d* of Dr William Evans Hoyle; *m* 1938, Mary Elizabeth Facey; three *s. Educ:* Prep. Sch., Bristol; Dauntsey's Sch., Wilts. Served War, DCLI, 1941–45. At age of 19, began to work in his father's pottery at St Ives, Cornwall (tuition from him and associates); Manager and Partner, 1946–55; took Manager's course, N Staffs Technical Coll., Stoke-on-Trent, to 1937; taught pottery at Dartington Hall Progressive Sch., 1933; taught at Penzance Sch. of Art and St Ives, 1945; designed and made David Leach Electric Kiln, 1950; helped to start a pottery in Norway, 1951; in charge of Ceramic Dept, and taught, at Loughborough Coll. of Art, 1953 (later Vis. Lectr); started pottery for Carmelite Friars at Aylesford, 1954; started workshop at Bovey Tracey, 1956; researched into glazes and changed from slipware to stoneware, 1961; latterly made a large percentage of porcelain. Formerly Member: Council, Craftsmen Potters Assoc. of GB (Past Chm.); Grants Cttee, Crafts Adv. Commn; Council, Crafts Council, 1977; Chm., Devon Guild of Craftsmen, 1986–87; Adviser, Dartington Pottery Trng Workshop. Has exhibited in Europe, USA and Far East; first major one-man show, CPA, 1966; Internat. Ceramics Exhibn, 1972, and Craftsmen's Art, 1973, V&A Mus., 1973; major one-man show, NY, 1978; exhibns in Germany (Darmstadt, Munich, Deidesheim, Sandhausen-bei-Heidelberg, and Hanover), Holland (Amsterdam), Belgium (Brussels), USA (San Francisco), Japan (Osaka) and Norway (Oslo); Joint Exhibitions: New Ashgate Gall., Farnham, 1982, 1983, (3 Generations Leach) 1986; Beaux Arts Gall., Bath, 1984; (with John Leach) Peter Dingley Gall., Stratford, 1985; Solus Exhibitions: NY, and lecture tour, USA, 1978; Washington DC, and 2nd lecture tour, USA, 1979; British Crafts Centre, London, 1979; Galerie St Martin, Cologne, 1982; St Paul's Sch., Barnes, 1982; Robert Welch Gall., Chipping Campden, 1982; Frontroom Gall., Dallas, 1983; Chestnut Gall., Bourton-on-the-Water, 1984; Century Gall., Henley-on-Thames, 1984; Castle Mus., Norwich, 1985; Galerie F15, Oslo, 1986; Elaine Potter Gall., San Francisco, 1986; Greenwich House Gall., NY, 1987; New Ashgate Gall., Farnham, 1988; Lecture at Setagaya Mus., Tokyo, 1989; Lecture demonstration tours: in USA, 1985, 1986, 1987 and 1988; in Caracas, Venezuela, 1987, 1991 (with exhibn). Craft of the Potter, BBC, 1976. Gold Medal, Istanbul, 1967. *Publication:* David Leach: a potter's life, with workshop notes (introd. by Bernard Leach), 1977. *Address:* Lowerdown Pottery, Bovey Tracey, Devon TQ13 9LE. *T:* (01626) 833408. *Died 15 Feb. 2005.*

LEADBEATER, Howell; Under/Deputy Secretary, Department of the Environment, 1973–76; *b* 22 Oct. 1919; *s* of late Thomas and Mary Ann Leadbeater; *m* 1946, Mary Elizabeth Roberts; two *s* one *d. Educ:* Pontardawe Secondary Sch.; University College, Swansea. Army Service, 1940–46: Adjt 11th E African Div. Signals. Min. of Works, later MPBW and Dept of the Environment: Asst Principal, 1948; Asst Sec., 1958; Under Sec., 1968. Design Co-ordinator for Caernarfon Castle, Investiture of Prince of Wales, 1969. Mem., Crafts Adv. Cttee, 1978–80. FRSA 1968. *Address:* 1 Parsons Mead, East Molesey, Surrey KT8 9DT. *T:* (020) 8979 6160. *Died 3 March 2001.*

LEADBETTER, David Hulse, CB 1958; Assistant Under-Secretary of State, Department of Education and Science, 1964–68 (Under Secretary, Ministry of Education, 1953–64); *b* 14 Aug. 1908; *s* of late Harold Leadbetter; *m* 1933, Marion (*d* 1995), *d* of late Horatio Ballantyne, FRIC, FCS; two *s* two *d* (one *d* decd.). *Educ:* Whitgift; Merton Coll., Oxford (Classical Postmaster). Entered Board of Education, 1933. *Recreations:* photography, gardening. *Address:* The Old Vicarage, Leigh, Sherborne, Dorset DT9 6HL. *T:* (01935) 874020. *Died 26 Sept. 2003.*

LEASK, Lt-Gen. Sir Henry (Lowther Ewart Clark), KCB 1970 (CB 1967); DSO 1945; OBE 1957 (MBE

1945); GOC Scotland and Governor of Edinburgh Castle, 1969–72, retired; *b* 30 June 1913; *s* of Rev. James Leask, MA; *m* Zoë de Camborne, *d* of Col W. P. Paynter, DSO, RHA; one *s* two *d*. 2nd Lt Royal Scots Fusiliers, 1936. Served War of 1939–45 in Mediterranean and Italy; Staff College Camberley, 1942; GSO 1942; Bde Major Inf. Bde 1943; 2nd in Comd and CO, 8 Bn Argyll and Sutherland Highlanders, 1944–45; Comd 1st Bn London Scottish, 1946–47; RAF Staff College, 1947; Gen. Staff Mil. Ops, WO, 1947–49; Instr Staff Coll., 1949–51; Comd 1st Bn The Parachute Regt, 1952–54; Asst Military Sec. to Sec. of State for War, 1955–57; Comdt, Tactical Wing Sch. of Inf., 1957–58; Comd Infantry Bde, 1958–61; idc 1961; Dep. Mil. Sec. to Sec. of State for War, 1962–64; GOC 52 Lowland Div., 1964–66; Dir of Army Training, MoD (Army), 1966–69. Brig. 1961, Maj.-Gen. 1964, Lt-Gen. 1969. Col of the Royal Highland Fusiliers, 1964–69; Col Comdt, Scottish Div. of Infantry, 1968–72. Chm., Army Benevolent Fund, Scotland, 1972–88. *Recreation:* field sports. *Clubs:* Carlton, Hurlingham.

Died 10 Jan. 2004.

LEATHER, Sir Edwin (Hartley Cameron), KCMG 1974; KCVO 1975; Kt 1962; Governor and C-in-C of Bermuda, 1973–77; writer and broadcaster; *b* 22 May 1919; *s* of Harold H. Leather, MBE, Hamilton, Canada, and Grace C. Leather (*née* Holmes); *m* 1940, Sheila A. A. (CStJ) (*d* 1994), *d* of Major A. H. Greenlees, Hamilton; two *d*. *Educ:* Trinity College Sch., Canada; Royal Military Coll., Kingston, Canada (BMilSc 1994). Commnd RCHA; served War of 1939–45 with Canadian Army, UK and in Europe, 1940–45. Contested (C) South Bristol, 1945; MP (C) N Somerset, 1950–64. Mem., Exec. Cttee, British Commonwealth Producers Organisation, 1960–63; Pres., Inst. of Marketing, 1966–67. Chairman: Bath Festival Soc., 1960–65; Horder Centre for Arthritics, 1962–65; Cons. and Unionist Assocs, 1969–70 (Mem. Nat. Exec. Cttee, 1963–70); Member: Cons. Party Bd of Finance, 1963–67; Bd of Dirs, Yehudi Menuhin Sch., 1967–; Dir, N. M. Rothschild (Bermuda), 1978–91, and other cos. Canadian Legion rep. on Exec. Cttee of Brit. Commonwealth Ex-Servicemen's League, 1954–63. Lay Reader, in Anglican Church, 1950–97. Chm., Bermuda Cttee, United World Colls, 1975–91; Mem. Council, Imp. Soc. of Knights Bachelor, 1969–; Nat. Gov., Shaw Fest., Niagara-on-the-Lake, Ontario, 1990–; Trustee, Menuhin Foundn of Bermuda, 1975–96, then Emeritus; Hon. Patron, Bermuda Fest., 1975–; Hon. Mem. Cttee, Canada Meml Foundn, 1991–. Freemason, 1942– (Past Grand Warden, Grand Lodge of England; Past Grand Registrar, Grand Lodge of Canada in Ontario). Grand Senechal Confrerie des Chevaliers du Tastevin, 1990–95. FRSA 1969. Hon. LLD: Bath, 1975; McMaster, 1999. Hon. Citizen: Kansas City, USA, 1957; S Carolina, 1995. Gold Medal, Nat. Inst. Social Scis, NY, 1977. Medal of Merit, Royal Canadian Legion, 1963. KStJ 1974. *Publications:* The Vienna Elephant, 1977; The Mozart Score, 1978; The Duveen Letter, 1980. *Address:* 23 Inwood Drive, Paget, Bermuda PG05. *Clubs:* Carlton; Hamilton (Ontario); Royal Bermuda Yacht.

Died 5 April 2005.

LEATHER, Ted; *see* Leather, Sir E. H. C.

LECHMERE, Sir Berwick (Hungerford), 6th Bt *cr* 1818, of The Rhydd, Worcestershire; JP; Vice Lord-Lieutenant, Hereford and Worcester, 1977–92; Land Agent; *b* 21 Sept. 1917; *s* of Sir Ronald Berwick Hungerford Lechmere, 5th Bt, and Constance Marguerite (*née* Long) (*d* 1981); S father, 1965; *m* 1954, Norah Garrett Elkington; no *c. Educ:* Charterhouse; Magdalene Coll., Cambridge. High Sheriff of Worcs, 1962; JP 1966, DL 1972, Worcs. FRICS. CStJ. *Heir: cousin* Reginald Anthony Hungerford Lechmere [*b* 24 Dec. 1920; *m* 1956, Anne Jennifer Dind; three *s* one *d*]. *Address:* Church End House, Hanley Castle, Worcester WR8 0BL. *T:* (01684) 592130. *Died 24 June 2001.*

LECOURT, Robert; Commander, Legion of Honour; Croix de Guerre; Rosette de la Résistance; Member, Constitutional Council of the French Republic, 1979–89; *b* 19 Sept. 1908; *s* of Léon Lecourt and Angèle Lépron; *m* 1932, Marguerite Chabrerie; one *d. Educ:* Rouen; Univ. de Caen (DenDroit). Advocate, Court of Appeal: Rouen, 1928; Paris, 1932. Served with French Air Force, 1939–40; Mem., Resistance Movt, 1942–44. Deputy for Paris, 1945–58, and for Hautes Alpes, 1958–61, National Assembly; Pres., Parly Gp, MRP, 1945–48 and 1952–57; Minister of Justice, 1948–49 and 1957–58; Minister of State responsible for co-operation with Africa, 1958–61; Judge, Court of Justice, European Community, 1962, President, 1967–76. Hon. Bencher, Gray's Inn, 1972. DUniv Exeter, 1975. Holds numerous foreign decorations. *Publications:* Nature juridique de l'action en réintégrande, 1931; Code pratique du travail, Responsabilité des architectes et entrepreneurs, etc, 1932–39; Le Juge devant le marché commun, 1970; L'Europe des juges, 1976; Concorde sans concordat 1952–1957, 1978. *Address:* 11 Boulevard Suchet, 75016 Paris, France. *Died 9 Aug. 2004.*

LEDGER, Ronald Joseph; casino proprietor and manager, retired; *b* 7 Nov. 1920; *s* of Arthur and Florence Ledger; brought up by Dr Barnardo's, 1923–37; *m* 1946, Madeleine Odette de Villeneuve; three *s* one *d. Educ:* Skinners' Grammar Sch., Tunbridge Wells; Nottingham Univ. (Dip. in Social Sci. 1949). Toolroom Engineer, 1938–42. Served RAF, 1942–47, fitter, Leading Aircraftsman; served three years in India. Staff Training Officer, Enfield Highway Co-op. Soc., 1949; Business Partner, 1950, Co. Director, 1953, Employment Specialists. Mem. Herts CC, 1952–54. Contested (Lab) Rushcliffe Div. of Nottingham, 1951; MP (Lab and Co-op) Romford, 1955–70. Director: Enfield Electronics (CRT) Ltd, 1958; London Co-operative Soc. Ltd, 1961. Chm., Hairdressing Council, 1966–79. Proprietor, Halland Hotel, IoW, 1969–73; Owner, Holliers Casino, IoW, 1973–83; Proprietor, Kebab Steak House, IoW, 1983–97. *Recreations:* tennis, cricket, golf, snooker. *Address:* Lisbon, Heath Gardens, Lake, Isle of Wight PO36 8PQ. *Club:* Ventnor Golf. *Died 11 Dec. 2004.*

LEE, Sir Arthur (James), KBE 1966 (CBE 1959); MC and Bar (1939–45); Company Director; National President, Returned Services League, Australia, 1960–74 (State President, 1954–60); *b* 30 July 1912; *s* of Arthur James and Kathleen Maud Lee; *m* 1945, Valerie Ann Scanlan; three *s* one *d. Educ:* Collegiate School of St Peter, Adelaide. Chm., War Veterans Home, SA, 1967–91. Trustee, Aust. War Meml, 1960–74. *Recreation:* golf. *Clubs:* Naval and Military, Royal Adelaide Golf (Adelaide).

Died 4 July 2003.

LEE, David John, CBE 1989; FREng; Consultant: G. Maunsell and Partners, Consulting Engineers, since 1994 (Partner, 1966–94; Chairman, 1984–94); Maunsell Structural Plastics Ltd, since 1994; Director of Maunsell Group cos; *b* 28 Aug. 1930; *s* of Douglas and Mildred Lee; *m* 1957, Helga Bass; one *s* one *d. Educ:* Manchester Univ. (BSc Tech 1950); Imperial Coll. of Science and Technol. (DIC 1954). MICE 1957, FICE 1966; MIStructE 1960, FIStructE 1968; FREng (FEng 1980). National Service, RE, 1950–52. Engr, Reinforced Concrete Steel Co. Ltd, 1952–53 and 1954–55; G. Maunsell and Partners, Consulting Engineers: Resident Engr, 1955–59; Sen. Engr, 1960–65; Associate, 1965–66. Vis. Prof., Imperial College, London, 1987–94. OC Engr and Logistic (formerly Transport) Staff Corps, RE (TA), 1977–95 (Col). Pres., IStructE, 1985–86; Mem. Council, Concrete Soc., 1968–71, Vice Pres. 1977–78. Chm., Council, CIRIA, 1989–92; Mem., Overseas Project Bd, DTI, 1989–94; Hon. Mem., Internat. Assoc. for Bridge and Structural Engrg. FCGI. George Stephenson Medal, ICE, 1969; Medal, 1974, and Hon. Pres., Fedn Internationale de la Précontrainte. *Publications:* The Theory and Practice of Bearings and Expansion Joints for Bridges, 1971, 2nd edn as Bridge Bearings and Expansion Joints, 1993; (contrib. chapter on bridges) The Civil Engineer's Reference Book,

3rd edn 1975, 4th edn 1989; (contrib. chapter on bridges) Developments in Pre-stressed Concrete, vol. 2 1978; papers in Proc. ICE and Proc. IStructE. *Recreations:* art, music. *Address:* 26 Paget Gardens, Chislehurst, Kent BR7 5RX. *T:* (020) 8325 0942. *Club:* East India.

Died 5 April 2001.

LEE, Air Chief Marshal Sir David (John Pryer), GBE 1969 (KBE 1965; CBE 1947; OBE 1943); CB 1953; retired, 1971; *b* 4 Sept. 1912; *s* of late John Lee, Byron Crescent, Bedford; *m* 1938, Denise, *d* of late Louis Hartoch; one *s* one *d*. *Educ:* Bedford Sch.; RAF Coll., Cranwell. NWFP, India, 1933–36; Central Flying Sch., Upavon, 1937; RAF Examining Officer, Supt. of Reserve, 1938–39; Bomber Command, Hemswell, 1939–40; RAF Staff Coll. (student), 1942; Deputy Director Plans, Air Ministry, 1943–44; OC 904 Fighter Wing, Batavia, Java, 1945–46; Directing Staff, RAF Staff Coll., 1948–50; Deputy Director Policy, Air Ministry, 1951–53; OC RAF Scampton, Lincs, 1953–55; Secretary, Chiefs of Staff Cttee, Ministry of Defence, 1956–59; AOC, AFME (Aden), 1959–61; Comdt, RAF Staff Coll., 1962–65; Air Member for Personnel, MoD, 1965–68; UK Military Rep. to NATO, 1968–71. Vice-Pres., RAF Benevolent Fund, 1988–; Chm., Governing Trustees, Nuffield Trust for Armed Forces, 1975–96; Dir, Utd Services Trustee, 1971–88; Pres., Corps of Commissionaires, 1984–88. *Publications:* Flight from the Middle East, 1981; Never Stop the Engine When It's Hot, 1983; Eastward: a history of the Royal Air Force in the Far East 1945–1972, 1984; Wings in the Sun, 1989; And We Thought the War was Over, 1990. *Address:* The Garden House, Catherine Close, Shrivenham, Swindon SN6 8ER. *T:* (01793) 784264. *Club:* Royal Air Force. *Died 13 Feb. 2004.*

LEE, Edward, PhD; Director, Admiralty Research Laboratory, Teddington, 1971–74, retired; *b* 2 March 1914; *s* of Thomas and Florence Lee; *m* 1942, Joan Pearson; three *d*. *Educ:* Consett Grammar Sch.; Manchester Univ. (MSc); Pembroke Coll., Cambridge (PhD 1939). Admiralty Research Laboratory, 1939–46; Ministry of Defence, 1946–48; Dept of Physical Research, Admiralty, 1948–51; Admiralty Research Laboratory, 1951–55; Dir of Operational Research, Admty, 1955–58; Dep. Dir, Nat. Physical Laboratory, 1958–60; Director, Stations and Industry Div., DSIR, 1960–65; Dep. Controller (R), Min. of Technology, 1965–70; Head of Res. Services, Dept of Trade and Industry, 1970–71. *Publications:* scientific papers. *Address:* 17 Farington Acres, Vale Road, Weybridge, Surrey KT13 9NH. *T:* (01932) 841114. *Died 31 Dec. 2001.*

LEE, (Edward) Stanley, FRCS; Consulting Surgeon Westminster Hospital; formerly Civilian Consultant in Surgery of Neoplastic Diseases, Queen Alexandra Military Hospital; Surgeon Emeritus, Guildford Radiotherapy Centre; *b* 10 Sept. 1907; *m* 1951, Elizabeth Priestnall (*d* 2001); one *s* two *d*. *Educ:* Westminster Hosp. (MB, BS 1931); MS London, 1936. FRCS 1933. Mem. Court of Examiners, RCS, 1953–59; Member: Grand Council British Empire Cancer Campaign; Internat. Union against Cancer; Assoc. of Head and Neck Oncologists of GB. FRSocMed; Sen. Fellow, Assoc. of Surgeons. Hon. Mem. Royal College of Radiologists. *Publications:* contributions to medical literature, etc. *Address:* Ingram, The Grand, Folkestone, Kent CT20 2LR. *Died 23 Oct. 2001.*

LEE, George Ranson, CVO 1980; CBE 1983; HM Diplomatic Service, retired; *b* 26 Sept. 1925; *s* of late Wilfred Lee and Janet (*née* Ranson); *m* 1955, Anne Christine Black; one *d*. Served Indian Army, 6th Gurkha Rifles, NW Frontier Prov., 1945–47; TA, W Yorks Regt, 1948–53. Employed in Trng Dept, Min. of Food, 1948–53; joined CRO, 1954; Karachi, 1955–58; First Sec., Madras, 1959–63; CRO, 1964; Head of Chancery: Singapore, 1965–69; Santiago, 1969–72; FCO, 1972–74; Dep. UK Perm. Rep. to Council of Europe, Strasbourg, 1974–78; Counsellor, Berne, 1978–83. Council of Europe Medal, *pro merito*, 1978. *Address:* Garthmynd, Trevor Hill,

Church Stretton, Shropshire SY6 6JH. *Club:* Royal Commonwealth Society. *Died 21 Sept. 2002.*

LEE, Rowland Thomas Lovell; a Recorder of the Crown Court, 1979–92; *b* 7 March 1920; *s* of late Ronald Lovell Lee and of Jessie Maude Lee; *m* 1944, Marjorie Betty, *d* of late William Holmes and Clare Johnston Braid Holmes; two *d*. *Educ:* Bedford Modern School. Served Royal Navy, 1939–48; POW, Sept. 1942–March 1943. Bedfordshire Constabulary, 1948–52; Articles with E. A. S. Barnard, Dunstable, 1954; qualified as solicitor, 1957; Principal, Wynter Davies & Lee, Hertford, 1959–89. Chairman: Medical Services Cttee, Hertfordshire Family Practitioners Cttee, 1970–77; N Herts HA (formerly Herts AHA), 1977–84. *Publications:* poetry: Scarecrow Galabieh, 1998; Small Lazarus, 2000; Each Different Beauty, 2001; Your Face at the Window, 2002; Rocking Horse, 2002; Knock on Any Door, 2003; East Wind. *Address:* Culpepers, 5 The Green, Letty Green, Hertford, Herts SG14 2NZ. *T:* (01707) 261445. *Died 10 Oct. 2005.*

LEE, Stanley; see Lee, (Edward) S.

LEECH, His Honour Robert Radcliffe; a Circuit Judge (formerly Judge of County Courts), 1970–86; *b* 5 Dec. 1919; *s* of late Edwin Radcliffe Leech; *m* 1951, Vivienne Ruth, *d* of A. J. Rickerby, Carlisle; two *d*. *Educ:* Monmouth Sch.; Worcester Coll., Oxford (Open Classics Exhibnr 1938). Served War, 1940–44, Border Regt (despatches twice). Called to Bar, Middle Temple, 1949 (Harmsworth Law Scholar); Dep. Chm., Cumberland QS, 1966–71; Hon. Recorder of Carlisle, 1985–86. *Recreations:* sailing, golf. *Address:* Scaur House, Cavendish Terrace, Stanwix, Carlisle, Cumbria CA3 9ND. *Club:* Oriental. *Died 30 April 2004.*

LEES-SPALDING, Rear-Adm. Ian Jaffery, (Tim), CB 1973; RN retired; *b* London, 16 June 1920; *s* of Frank Souter Lees-Spalding and Joan (*née* Bodilly); *m* 1946, June Sandys Lyster Sparkes; two *d*. *Educ:* Blundells Sch.; RNEC. Served War of 1939–45 (King's Commendation for Bravery, 1941; Royal Lifesaving Inst. medal, 1942); served in HMS Sirius, HM Submarines Trespasser, Teredo, Truculent and Andrew, HMS Cleopatra and Tiger; Chief of Staff to C-in-C Naval Home Comd, 1969; CSO (Technical) to C-in-C Fleet, 1971; retd 1974. Administrator, London Internat. Film Sch., 1975–79. Joint Editor: Macmillan and Silk Cut Nautical Almanac, 1981–92; Macmillan and Silk Cut Yachtsman's Handbook, 1984–92. *Recreations:* music, travelling. *Address:* St Olaf's, Wonston, Winchester, Hants SO21 3LP. *T:* (01962) 760249. *Club:* Army and Navy. *Died 20 July 2001.*

LEFEBVRE, Prof. Arthur Henry, FREng; Distinguished Reilly Professor of Combustion Engineering, School of Mechanical Engineering, Purdue University, 1979–93, then Emeritus Professor (Professor and Head of School, 1976–80); *b* 14 March 1923; *s* of Henri and May Lefebvre; *m* 1952, Elizabeth Marcella Betts; two *s* one *d*. *Educ:* Long Eaton Grammar Sch; Nottingham Univ.; Imperial Coll., London (DSc (Eng), DIC, PhD). FREng (FEng 1994); FIMechE, FRAeS. Ericssons Telephones Ltd: Engrg apprentice, 1938–41; Prodn Engr, 1941–47; res. work on combustion and heat transfer in gas turbines, Rolls Royce, Derby, 1952–61; Prof. of Aircraft Propulsion, Coll. of Aeronautics, 1961–71; Prof. and Hd of Sch. of Mechanical Engrg, Cranfield Inst. of Technol., 1971–76. Mem., AGARD Combustion and Propulsion Panel, 1957–61; Mem., AGARD Propulsion and Energetics Panel, 1970–76; Chm., Combustion Cttee, Aeronautical Res. Council, 1970–74. Hon. DSc Cranfield Inst. of Technology, 1989. Gas Turbine Award, ASME, 1982; R. Tom Sawyer Award, ASME, 1984; inaugural AIAA Propellants and Combustion Award, 1990; Marshall Award, Instn for Liquid Atomization and Spray Systems, 1993; Internat. Gas Turbine Inst. Scholar Award, ASME, 1995; Aircraft Engine Technology Award, ASME, 1996; George Westinghouse Gold Medal, ASME, 2002.

Publications: Gas Turbine Combustion, 1983; Selected Papers on Fundamentals of Gas Turbine Combustion, 1988; Atomization and Sprays, 1989; papers on combustion and heat transfer in Proc. Royal Soc., internat. symposium vols on combustion, combustion and flame, combustion science and technology. *Recreations:* music, reading. *Address:* Low Furrow, Pebworth, Stratford-upon-Avon, Warwicks CV37 8XW. *T:* (01789) 721429.
Died 24 Nov. 2003.

LEGG, Keith (Leonard Charles), OBE 1981; PhD, MSc (Eng); CEng, FIMechE, FRAeS, FCIT, FILT; FHKIE; Hon. Professor and Advisor to Xian Jiaotung University, Shanghai Polytechnic University and South China Institute of Technology, China; consultant on aerospace engineering and on higher education; *b* 24 Oct. 1924; *s* of E. H. J. Legg; *m* 1947, Joan (*d* 2001), *d* of H. E. Green; two *s*. *Educ:* London Univ. (external); Cranfield Inst. of Technology. Engineering apprenticeship, 1940–45; Dep. Chief Research and Test Engr, Asst Chief Designer, Chief Project and Structural Engr, Short Bros & Harland Ltd, Belfast, 1942–56; Chief Designer and Prof., Brazilian Aeronautical Centre, São Paulo, 1956–60; Head of Dept, 1960–72, and Prof., 1965–72, Loughborough Univ. of Technology (Sen. Pro Vice-Chancellor, 1967–70); Dir, Lanchester Polytechnic, 1972–75; Dir, Hong Kong Polytechnic, 1975–84. Chm., Internat. Directing Cttee, CERI/OECD Higher Educn Institutional Management, 1973–75; Member: Road Transport Industrial Trng Bd, 1966–75 (former Chm.); Hong Kong Bd of Educn, 1975–84; World Council for Co-operative Educn, 1979–84; Adv. Cttee on Environmental Protection, 1977–84 (Chm., Noise Cttee); Hong Kong Management Assoc. Council, 1982–84; Environmental and Pollution Council of Hong Kong; Indust. Develt Bd, 1982–84. Royal Aeronautical Society: Member: Council, 1967–75; Educn Cttee, 1990–; Grading Cttee, 1991–. Adviser to OECD in Paris; mem. various nat. and professional cttees. Member: Council of City Polytechnic of Hong Kong, 1984; Court, Cranfield Inst. of Technology (later Univ.), 1987– (Hon. Vice-Pres. of Convocation, 1987–); Court, Loughborough Univ., 1993–. JP Hong Kong, 1978–84. Fellow, Hong Kong Management Assoc. Hon. DTech Loughborough, 1982; Hon. LLD: Hong Kong Univ., 1984, Hong Kong Poly., 1992. *Publications:* numerous on aerospace structures and design, transport systems, higher educn, educnl analytical models and on Hong Kong/China. *Recreations:* most sports, classical music, theatre, walking, aid to the handicapped, public lectures on Hong Kong and China. *Address:* 408 Hardaker Court, 317–323 Clifton Drive South, St Anne's-on-Sea, Lancs FY8 1HN. *T:* (01253) 725387.
Died 24 April 2004.

LEIGH, 5th Baron *cr* 1839; **John Piers Leigh**; *b* 11 Sept. 1935; *s* of 4th Baron Leigh, TD and Anne (*d* 1977), *d* of Ellis Hicks Beach; *S* father, 1979; *m* 1st, 1957, Cecilia Poppy (marr. diss. 1974), *y d* of late Robert Cecil Jackson; one *s* one *d* (and one *d* decd); 2nd, 1976, Susan (marr. diss. 1982), *d* of John Cleave, Whitnash, Leamington Spa; one *s*; 3rd, 1982, Mrs Lea Hamilton-Russell (marr. diss. 1998), *o d* of Col Noel Wild. *Educ:* Eton; Oxford and London Universities. *Recreations:* horses, hunting, racing, sport, country pursuits. *Heir: s* Hon. Christopher Dudley Piers Leigh [*b* 20 Oct. 1960; *m* 1990, Sophy-Ann, *d* of Richard Burrows; one *s* one *d*].
Died 16 Sept. 2003.

LEINSTER, 8th Duke of, *cr* 1766; **Gerald FitzGerald;** Baron of Offaly, 1205; Earl of Kildare, 1316; Viscount Leinster (Great Britain), 1747; Marquess of Kildare, 1761; Earl of Offaly, 1761; Baron Kildare, 1870; Premier Duke, Marquess, and Earl, of Ireland; Major late 5th Royal Inniskilling Dragoon Guards; *b* 27 May 1914; *o s* of 7th Duke of Leinster and May (*d* 1935), *d* of late Jesse Etheridge; *S* father, 1976; *m* 1st, 1936, Joane (who obtained a divorce, 1946), *e d* of late Major McMorrough Kavanagh, MC, Borris House, Co. Carlow; two *d*; 2nd, 1946, Anne Eustace Smith; two *s*. *Educ:* Eton; Sandhurst. *Recreations:* fishing, shooting. *Heir: s* Marquess of Kildare, *b*

7 April 1948. *Address:* Kilkea House, Ramsden, Chipping Norton, Oxfordshire OX7 3BA. *Died 3 Dec. 2004.*

LEMON, Sir (Richard) Dawnay, Kt 1970; CBE 1958; QPM 1964; Chief Constable of Kent, 1962–74; *b* 29 May 1912; *o s* of late Lieut-Colonel F. J. Lemon, CBE, DSO, and of Mrs Laura Lemon; *m* 1939, Sylvia Marie Kentish; one *s* one *d* (and one *d* decd). *Educ:* Uppingham Sch.; RMC, Sandhurst. Joined West Yorks Regt, 1932; retired 1934. Metropolitan Police, 1934–37; Leicestershire Constabulary, 1937–39; Chief Constable of East Riding of Yorkshire, 1939–42; Chief Constable of Hampshire and Isle of Wight, 1942–62. *Recreations:* cricket, golf. *Address:* 9 Milchester House, Staveley Road, Eastbourne BN20 7JX. *T:* (01323) 649441. *Clubs:* Royal Yacht Squadron (Cowes (hon.)); Royal St Georges Golf (Sandwich).
Died 5 Aug. 2004.

LENG, Christopher Anthony William, OBE 1987; Vice Lord-Lieutenant, Tweeddale, 1994–97; *b* 5 April 1922; *s* of Douglas Christopher Leng and Marcia Mary Leng (*née* Maxwell Stuart); *m* 1953, Patricia Lillywhite; two *s* two *d*. *Educ:* Downside Sch.; Hertford Coll., Oxford (MA); Royal Agricl Coll. (MRAC). Served War, Royal Armoured Corps, 1940–43; Special Ops Executive, 1943–46. Overseas Develt Corp., 1947–50; farmer, 1952–91. *Recreations:* gardening, fishing, reading. *Address:* Juniper Bank, Walkerburn, Peeblesshire EH43 6DE. *T:* (01896) 870230. *Club:* Special Forces.
Died 13 April 2005.

LENNIE, Douglas; *b* 30 March 1910; *e s* of Magnus S. Lennie; *m* 1941, Rhona Young Ponsonby; two *s*. *Educ:* Berkhamsted Sch.; Guy's Hospital (LDS, RCS 1934) Northwestern University, Chicago (DDS 1938). Served War of 1939–45, Temporary Surg. Lt-Comdr (D) RNVR; formerly Surgeon Dentist to Queen Mary. *Address:* 72 Chiltley Way, Liphook, Hants GU30 7HE.
Died 28 Aug. 2005.

LENNOX, Robert Smith, CBE 1978; JP; Lord Provost of Aberdeen, 1967–70 and 1975–77; *b* 8 June 1909; *m* 1963, Evelyn Margaret; no *c*. *Educ:* St Clement Sch., Aberdeen. JP Aberdeen. Hon. LLD Aberdeen, 1970. *Address:* 7 Gillespie Crescent, Ashgrove, Aberdeen AB2 5AX. *T:* (01224) 483862. *Died 2 July 2001.*

LEONARD, Sir (Hamilton) John, Kt 1981; a Judge of the High Court, Queen's Bench Division, 1981–93; Presiding Judge, Wales and Chester Circuit, 1982–86; *b* 28 April 1926; *s* of late Arthur and Jean Leonard, Poole, Dorset; *m* 1948, Doreen Enid (*d* 1996), *yr d* of late Lt-Col Sidney James Parker, OBE, and May Florence Parker, Sanderstead, Surrey; one *s* one *d*. *Educ:* Dean Close Sch., Cheltenham; Brasenose Coll., Oxford (MA). Coldstream Guards (Captain), 1944–47. Called to Bar, Inner Temple, 1951; Master of the Bench, 1977; practised on South-Eastern Circuit; 2nd Junior Prosecuting Counsel to the Crown at Central Criminal Court, 1964–69; QC 1969; Dep. Chm., Surrey QS, 1969–71; Comr, CCC, 1969–71; a Recorder of the Crown Court, 1972–78; a Circuit Judge, 1978–81; Common Serjeant in the City of London, 1979–81. Member: General Council of the Bar, 1970–74; Senate, 1971–74, Senate of Four Inns and the Bar, 1974–77. Chm., Criminal Bar Assoc., 1975–77. Member: Home Sec.'s Adv. Bd on Restricted Patients, 1973–78; Deptl Cttee to Review Laws on Obscenity, Indecency and Censorship, 1977–79; Judicial Studies Bd, 1979–82. Mem. Council, Hurstpierpoint Coll., 1975–83; Gov., Dean Close Sch., Cheltenham, 1986–2000. Liveryman, Plaisterers' Co.; HM Lieutenant, City of London, 1980–81. *Recreations:* books, music, painting. *Address:* Royal Courts of Justice, WC2A 2LL. *Club:* Garrick.
Died 10 Aug. 2002.

LEONARD, His Honour James Charles Beresford Whyte, MA Oxon; a Circuit Judge (formerly Deputy Chairman of Quarter Sessions, Inner London and Middlesex), 1965–79; Judge of the Mayor's and City of

London Court, 1972–79; *b* 26 Jan. 1905; *s* of Hon. J. W. Leonard, Middle Temple, KC (S Africa); *m* 1939, Barbara Helen (*d* 1989), *d* of late Capt. William Incledon-Webber; two *s* one *d*. *Educ:* Clifton Coll.; Christ Church, Oxford. Called to the Bar, Inner Temple, 1928, Bencher 1961. Served 1940–45, with RAF (Sqdn Ldr). Recorder of Walsall, Staffs, 1951–64; Junior Counsel to Ministry of Agriculture, Fisheries and Food, Forestry Commission and Tithe Redemption Commission, 1959–64; Deputy Chairman of QS: Co. of London, 1964–65; Oxfordshire, 1962–71. Chairman: Disciplinary Cttee, Pharmaceutical Soc. of GB, 1960–64; Adv. Cttee dealing with internment under Civil Authorities (Special Powers) Act (NI) 1962, April–Nov. 1972; Comr under Terrorism (N Ireland) Order 1972, 1972–74; Dep. Chm., Appeal Tribunal, 1974–75. *Address:* Cross Trees, Sutton Courtenay, Oxon OX14 4AD. *T:* (01235) 848230. *Died 20 July 2004.*

LEONARD, Sir John; *see* Leonard, Sir H. J.

LEONARD, Michael William, CVO 1984; FREng, FICE, FCIArb; consultant; Founder Secretary, The Fellowship of Engineering, 1976–83; Founder Clerk to the Worshipful Company of Engineers, 1983–86; *b* 25 Dec. 1916; *e s* of late Frank Leonard and Marguerite Leonard (*née* Holborow); *m* 1945, Rosalinna Cushnir; three *s*. *Educ:* Haberdashers' Aske's Sch.; Pupilage in Mechanical Engineering, Messrs Fraser & Chalmers Ltd, Erith; University College London (BSc(Eng)); Pres., Union Society, 1939). MIMechE. Civil Engineer, Mowlem Group of Companies, to 1968; Dir, later Chief Exec., Soil Mechanics Ltd; Dir, Soil Mechanics-Soletanche Ltd; Chm., Engineering Laboratory Equipment Ltd. Mem., BSI Code of Practice Cttee on Site Investigations; Mem., later Chm., Tip Safety Cttee (post Aberfan); Sec., Council of Engineering Institutions, 1969–82; Chm., BSI Code of Practice Cttee on Foundations; Member: Design Council Engineering Design, later Industrial, Adv. Cttee; DoI Cttee for Industrial Technologies. Parliamentary and Scientific Committee: Hon. Treasurer, 1984; Hon. Sec., 1987; Vice-Pres., 1990–; Mem. Council, 1991. Vice Pres., Fédération Européenne d'Associations Nationales d'Ingénieurs; Sec., Commonwealth Engineers' Council; Mem., Executive Cttee, World Fedn of Engineering Organizations (Vice-Pres., 1987–). Hon. Prof., Dept of Civil and Structural Engrg, Sheffield Univ., 1974. FREng (FEng 1983). *Publications:* papers and articles on foundation and geotechnical engineering, and on professional engineering, for jls and confs. *Recreations:* touring, golf, fishing. *Address:* 2 Mossy Vale, Maidenhead, Berks SL6 7RX. *T:* (01628) 412736. *Club:* Athenæum.
Died 30 May 2001.

LE QUESNE, Sir (Charles) Martin, KCMG 1974 (CMG 1963); HM Diplomatic Service, retired; *b* 10 June 1917; *s* of C. T. Le Quesne, QC; *m* 1948, Deirdre Noel (*née* Fisher); three *s*. *Educ:* Shrewsbury; Exeter Coll., Oxford (Hon. Fellow, 1990). Served in Royal Artillery, 1940–45. Apptd HM Foreign Service, 1946; 2nd Sec. at HM Embassy, Baghdad, 1947–48; 1st Secretary: Foreign Office, 1948–51, HM Political Residency, Bahrain, 1951–54; attended course at NATO Defence Coll., Paris, 1954–55; HM Embassy, Rome, 1955–58; Foreign Office, 1958–60; apptd HM Chargé d'Affaires, Republic of Mali, 1960, subsequently Ambassador there, 1961–64; Foreign Office, 1964–68; Ambassador to Algeria, 1968–71; Dep. Under-Sec. of State, FCO, 1971–74; High Comr in Nigeria, 1974–76. Mem., States of Jersey, 1978–90 (Dep. for St Saviour's parish). Hon. Vice-Pres., Royal African Soc. Mem. Council, Southampton Univ. *Recreations:* gardening, books. *Address:* Beau Désert, St Saviour, Jersey, Channel Islands. *T:* (01534) 22076. *Clubs:* Reform (Chairman 1973–74), MCC; Victoria, United (Jersey); Royal Channel Islands Yacht. *Died 3 April 2004.*

LE QUESNE, Sir Martin; *see* Le Quesne, Sir C. M.

LeROY-LEWIS, David Henry, FCA; Director, Touche, Remnant & Co., 1974–88 (Deputy Chairman, 1981–88);

Chairman, Henry Ansbacher Holdings plc, 1982–88; *b* 14 June 1918; *er s* of late Stuyvesant Henry LeRoy-Lewis and late Bettye LeRoy-Lewis; *m* 1953, Cynthia Madeleine, *er d* of late Comdr John C. Boldero, DSC, RN (Retd); three *d*. *Educ:* Eton. FCA 1947. Chairman: TR North America Trust PLC (formerly Continental Union Trust Ltd) 1974–88 (Dir, 1948–88); R. P. Martin plc, 1981–85; Hill Martin, 1989–93; Director: TR Industrial & General Trust PLC, 1967–88; Akroyd & Smithers Ltd, 1970–81 (Chm., 1976–81); TR Trustees Corp. PLC, 1973–88; TR Energy PLC, 1981–88. Mem., 1961–81, a Dep. Chm., 1973–76, Stock Exchange Council. *Recreation:* fishing. *Address:* Stoke House, Stoke, Andover, Hants SP11 0NP. *T:* (01264) 738548. *Club:* MCC. *Died 26 Aug. 2004.*

LESLIE, (Percy) Theodore; retired British Aerospace engineer; *b* 19 Nov. 1915; *s* of Frank Harvey Leslie (*d* 1965) (*g g s* of Sir John Leslie, 4th Bt, WS), Christ's Hospital, and Amelia Caroline (*d* 1918), *d* of Alexander Russon; heir to the Leslie of Wardis and Findrassie baronetcy (*cr* 1625, dormant 1967). *Educ:* London and privately. FSAScot 1983. Freeman, City of London, 1978. Mem., Clan Leslie Soc. *Recreations:* chess, retirement. *Address:* c/o Ranworth House, 39 Orchard Drive, Chorleywood, Herts WD3 5QN.
Died 28 July 2001.

LESLIE, Theodore; *see* Leslie, P. T.

LEVIN, Bernard; *see* Levin, H. B.

LEVIN, (Henry) Bernard, CBE 1990; journalist and author; *b* 19 Aug. 1928; *s* of late Phillip Levin and Rose (*née* Racklin). *Educ:* Christ's Hospital; LSE, Univ. of London. BSc (Econ.). Has written regularly or irregularly for many newspapers and magazines in Britain and abroad, 1953–, principally The Times, Sunday Times, Observer, Manchester Guardian, Truth, Spectator, Daily Express, Daily Mail, Newsweek, International Herald-Tribune; has written and broadcast for radio and television, 1952–, incl. BBC and most ITV cos. Sir Dorab Tata Trust Lectr, India, 1990. Pres., English Assoc., 1984–85, Vice-Pres., 1985–88. Various awards for journalism. Hon. Fellow, LSE, 1977–. Mem., Order of Polonia Restituta (by Polish Government-in-Exile), 1976. *Publications:* The Pendulum Years, 1971; Taking Sides, 1979; Conducted Tour, 1981; Speaking Up, 1982; Enthusiasms, 1983; The Way We Live Now, 1984; A Shakespeare Mystery (English Assoc. Presidential address), 1985; Hannibal's Footsteps, 1985; In These Times, 1986; To The End Of The Rhine, 1987; All Things Considered, 1988; A Walk Up Fifth Avenue, 1989; Now Read On, 1990; If You Want My Opinion, 1992; A World Elsewhere, 1994; I Should Say So, 1995; Enough Said, 1998. *Address:* The Times, 1 Pennington Street, E98 1TT. *Died 7 Aug. 2004.*

LEVY, Allan Edward; QC 1989; a Recorder, 1993–2001 (an Assistant Recorder, 1990–93); author; *b* 17 Aug. 1942; *s* of Sidney Levy and Mabel (*née* Lewis). *Educ:* Bury Grammar Sch.; Hull Univ. (LLB Hons); Inns of Court Law School. Called to the Bar, Inner Temple, 1969, Bencher, 1993. Member: Family Law Bar Assoc. Cttee, 1987–97; Council, Justice, 1988–; Bar Council Law Reform Cttee, 1989–90; Council, Medico-Legal Soc., 1990–; Bar Council, 1995–97. Speaker at seventh Internat. Congress on Child Abuse, Rio de Janeiro, 1988; Keynote speaker, Australasian child abuse conf., Melbourne, 1995; Chm., Staffordshire Pindown Child Care Inquiry, 1990; Member: Gulbenkian Foundn Commn on children and violence, 1994–95; Howard League Commn of Inquiry into violence in penal instns for young people, 1994–95. Hon. Legal Advr, Nat. Children's Bureau, 1990–. Vis. Prof., Washburn Law Sch., Kansas, 2001; Sen. Vis. Fellow, Law Faculty, Southampton Univ., 2002–; Vis. Lectr, Inst. of Educn, London Univ., 2004–. Sidgwick Meml Lectr, Newnham Coll., Cambridge, 2001. Mem., Exec. Bd, History of Childhood Workshop, Oxford Univ., 2003–. Chm., Intercountry Adoption Lawyers' Assoc., 1991–95; Internat. Bar Assoc. Observer, Hague Conf. on Private

Internat. Law (special commn on intercountry adoption), 1992. Patron: Freedom to Care, 1994–; Children's Legal Centre, 1999; Bar Cttee on Rights of the Child, 1999–. Fellow: Internat. Acad. of Matrimonial Lawyers, 1992; Soc. for Advanced Legal Studies, 1998; FRSocMed 1993. Broadcaster on legal topics. *Publications:* Wardship Proceedings, 1982, 2nd edn 1987; Custody and Access, 1983; (with J. F. Josling) Adoption of Children, 10th edn 1985; (ed and contrib.) Focus on Child Abuse, 1989; (with B. Kahan) The Pindown Experience and the Protection of Children, 1991; (ed and contrib.) Re-Focus on Child Abuse, 1994; contributed to: One Scandal Too Many: the case for comprehensive protection for children in all settings, 1993; Medico-Legal Essentials in Health Care, 1996, 2004; Children Who Kill, 1996; Whistleblowing in the Social Services, 1998; Consent, Rights and Choices in Health Care for Children and Young People, 2000; Legal Concepts of Childhood, 2001; Child Abuse Tort Claims against Public Bodies: a comparative law view, 2004; contrib. legal jls and nat. newspapers. *Recreations:* travel, writing, watching sport. *Address:* 17 Bedford Row, WC1R 4EG. *T:* (020) 7831 7314, *Fax:* (020) 7831 0061. *Club:* Reform.   *Died 26 Sept. 2004.*

LEW, Jonathan Michael; Chief Executive, United Synagogue, 1986–98; *b* 23 Nov. 1937; *s* of Rabbi Maurice Abram Lew and Rachel Lew (*née* Segalov); *m* 1963, Linda Samad; one *s* one *d*. *Educ:* Univ. of Witwatersrand (BCom). ACMA. Finance Director: Dorland Advertising, 1973–79; Dancer Fitzgerald Sample Internat., 1979–83; MWK Advertising, 1984–85. Hon. Officer, United Synagogue, 1984–86. Lay Mem., Marylebone Duty Solicitors' Cttee, 1987–; Gen. Comr for Income Taxes, 1992–; Member: Central London Valuation Tribunal, 1998–; Adv. Gp on Religion in Prisons, 1998–; Ind. Review Panels, London Region, NHS Exec., DoH, 1999–; London Regl Cttee, Duty Solicitors' Scheme, 2000–. *Recreations:* bridge, travel, family. *Address:* 41 Eyre Court, St John's Wood, NW8 9TU.

Died 26 Feb. 2003.

LEWANDO, Sir Jan (Alfred), Kt 1974; CBE 1968; *b* 31 May 1909; *s* of Maurice Lewando and Eugenie Lewando (*née* Goldsmid); *m* 1948, Nora Slavouski; three *d*. *Educ:* Manchester Grammar Sch.; Manchester University. Served War of 1939–45, British Army: British Army Staff, Washington DC and British Min. of Supply Mission, 1941–45 (Lt-Col, 1943). Marks & Spencer Ltd, 1929–70 (Dir 1954–70); Chairman: Carrington Viyella Ltd, 1970–75; Consolidated Textile Mills Ltd, Canada, 1972–75; Penn Consultants Ltd, 1975–99; Pres., Carrington Viyella Inc. (USA), 1971–75; Director: Carrington Tesit (Italy), 1971–75; Heal and Son Holdings, 1975–82 (Dep. Chm., 1977–82); Bunzl PLC (formerly Bunzl Pulp & Paper Ltd), 1976–86; W. A. Baxter & Sons Ltd, 1975–99; Johnston Group Inc. (USA) (formerly Johnston Industries Inc.), 1976–85; Edgars Stores Ltd (South Africa), 1976–82; Royal Worcester Spode Ltd, 1978–79; Bunzl and Biach AG (Austria), 1979–80; Johnston Industries Ltd, 1980–85; Chm., Gelvenor Textiles Ltd, S Africa, 1973–75. Vice Chm., Clothing Export Council, 1966–70; Pres., British Textile Confedn, 1972–73; Vice Pres., Comitextil, Brussels, 1972–73; Member: British Overseas Trade Bd, 1972–77; British Overseas Trade Adv. Council, 1975–77; BNEC, 1969–71; Council, UK-S Africa Trade Assoc., 1973–92; Export Council for Europe, 1965–69; European Steering Cttee, CBI, 1968–71; Grand Council, CBI, 1971–75. Vice Pres., Transport Trust, 1973–88 and 1991– (Pres., 1989–91). Chm., Appeal Cttee, British Inst. of Radiology, 1979–84. CCMI (CBIM 1980; FBIM 1972); FRSA 1973. Companion, Textile Inst., 1972. Order of Legion of Merit (USA), 1946.   *Died 2 July 2004.*

LEWIS, David Henry L.; *see* LeRoy-Lewis.

LEWIS, Prof. Edward B., PhD; Thomas Hunt Morgan Professor of Biology, California Institute of Technology, 1966–88, then Emeritus; *b* 20 May 1918; *s* of Edward B.

Lewis and Laura H. Lewis; *m* 1946, Pamela H. Harrah; two *s* (and one *s* decd). *Educ:* Univ. of Minnesota (BA Biostats 1939); California Inst. of Technol. (PhD Genetics 1942; MS Meteorology 1943). Served USAAF (Capt.), 1942–46. Instructor, CIT, 1946–48; Rockefeller Foundn Fellow, Cambridge Univ., 1947–48; California Institute of Technology: Asst Prof. of Biol., 1948–49; Associate Prof., 1949–56; Prof. of Biol., 1956–66. Guest Prof., Inst. of Genetics, Univ. of Copenhagen, 1975–76. Hon. PhD Umeå, Sweden, 1981; Hon. DSc Minnesota, 1993. Nat. Medal of Sci., USA, 1990; (jtly) Nobel Prize in Physiology or Medicine, 1995. *Publications:* (ed) Genetics and Evolution: selected papers of A. H. Sturtevant, 1961; contrib. chapters in books; contrib. numerous papers and articles in Proc. Nat. Acad. Sci., Genetics, Jl Heredity, Nature, Science, Genes and Develt, and others. *Recreations:* flute, swimming, jogging, marine biology. *Address:* California Institute of Technology, Division of Biology 156–29, Pasadena, CA 91125, USA. *Fax:* (626) 5649685.

Died 21 July 2004.

LEWIS, Prof. Graham Pritchard; Dean, Hunterian Institute (formerly Institute of Basic Medical Sciences), 1982–89, Vandervell Professor of Pharmacology, 1974–89, then Emeritus, Royal College of Surgeons; *b* 5 Aug. 1927; *s* of George Henry and Ruth Lewis; *m* 1973, Averil Priscilla Myrtle; two *s* two *d*. *Educ:* Monkton House School, Cardiff; University College Cardiff (BPharm, PhD). Mem., Scientific Staff, Nat. Inst. for Med. Research, MRC, 1953–63; Dep. Dir, Research, and Dir, Biological Research, Ciba-Geigy Pharmaceuticals, 1964–73. Mem., Horserace Scientific Adv. Cttee, Jockey Club, 1989–97. Hon. Mem., British Pharmacol. Soc., 1994. *Publications:* 5-Hydroxytryptamine, 1958; The Role of Prostaglandins in Inflammation, 1976; Mechanisms of Steroid Action, 1981; Mediators of Inflammation, 1986; numerous contribs to British and overseas sci. jls, esp. Jl Physiol., BJ Pharmacol. *Recreations:* writing unfathomable stories, painting indescribable paintings and cooking excruciating dishes.   *Died 1 Jan. 2001.*

LEWIS, Norman; author; *b* 28 June 1908; *s* of Richard and Louise Lewis; *m* 3rd, Lesley; one *s* two *d*, and two *s* one *d* by previous marriages. *Educ:* Enfield Grammar Sch. Served War of 1939–45, in Intelligence Corps. DU Essex, 1987. *Publications:* Sand and Sea in Arabia, 1938; Samara, 1949; Within the Labyrinth, 1950, new edn 1985; A Dragon Apparent, 1951, new edn 1982; Golden Earth, 1952, repr. 1983; A Single Pilgrim, 1953; The Day of the Fox, 1955, new edn 1985; The Volcanoes Above Us, 1957; The Changing Sky, 1959, repr. 1984; Darkness Visible, 1960; The Tenth Year of the Ship, 1962; The Honoured Society, 1964, rev. edn 1984; A Small War Made to Order, 1966; Every Man's Brother, 1967; Flight from a Dark Equator, 1972; The Sicilian Specialist, 1974, new edn 1985; The German Company, 1979; Cuban Passage, 1982; A Suitable Case for Corruption, 1984; A View of the World, 1986; The March of the Long Shadows, 1987; To Run Across the Sea, 1989; A Goddess in the Stones: travels in India, 1991; An Empire of the East, 1993; The Norman Lewis Omnibus, 1995; The Happy Ant Heap and Other Pieces, 1998; In Sicily, 2000; The Tomb in Seville, 2003; *autobiography:* Naples '44, 1978, repr. 1983; Voices of the Old Sea, 1984, new edn 1996; Jackdaw Cake, 1985, rev. edn as I Came, I Saw, 1994; The Missionaries, 1988; The World, The World, 1996. *Address:* c/o Jonathan Cape, 20 Vauxhall Bridge Road, SW1V 2SA.

Died 22 July 2003.

LEWIS, Rev. Canon Robert Hugh Cecil; Chaplain to the Queen, 1987–95; *b* 23 Feb. 1925; *s* of Herbert Cecil and Olive Frances Lewis; *m* 1948, Joan Dorothy Hickman; one *s* one *d*. *Educ:* Manchester Grammar School; New Coll., Oxford (BA 1950, MA 1950); Westcott House, Cambridge. Ordained deacon, 1952, priest 1953; Curate: St Mary, Crumpsall, 1952–54; New Bury, 1954–56; Incumbent, Bury St Peter, 1956–63; Vicar, Poynton, dio. Chester, 1963–91. RD of Stockport, 1972–85, of

Cheadle, 1985–87; Diocesan Ecumenical Officer, and County Ecumenical Officer for Cheshire, 1987–91; Hon. Canon, Chester Cathedral, 1975–91, Canon Emeritus, 1991–. *Recreations:* gardening, poetry. *Address:* 78 Dean Drive, Wilmslow, Cheshire SK9 2EY. *T:* (01625) 524761.
Died 28 Nov. 2004.

LEWIS, Thomas Loftus Townshend, CBE 1979; FRCS; Consultant Obstetric and Gynæcological Surgeon at Guy's Hospital, Queen Charlotte's Maternity Hospital and Chelsea Hospital for Women, 1948–83; Hon. Consultant in Obstetrics and Gynaecology, to the Army, 1973–83; *b* 27 May 1918; *e s* of late Neville Lewis and his first wife, Theodosia Townshend; *m* 1946, Kathleen Alexandra Ponsonby Moore; five *s. Educ:* Diocesan Coll., Rondebosch, S Africa; St Paul's Sch.; Cambridge Univ.; Guy's Hospital. BA Cantab (Hons in Nat. Sci. Tripos), 1939; MB, BChir Cantab, 1942. FRCS 1946; MRCOG 1948; FRCOG 1961. House appointments Guy's Hospital, 1942–43; Gold Medal and Prize in Obstetrics, Guy's Hospital, 1942. Volunteered to join South African Medical Corps, 1944; seconded to RAMC and served as Capt. in Italy and Greece, 1944–45. Returned to Guy's Hospital; Registrar in Obstetrics and Gynæcology, 1946, Obstetric Surgeon, 1948; Surgeon, Chelsea Hosp. for Women, 1950; Surgeon, Queen Charlotte's Maternity Hosp., 1952. Examiner in Obstetrics and Gynæcology: University of Cambridge, 1950; University of London, 1954; Royal College of Obstetricians and Gynæcologists, 1952; London Soc. of Apothecaries, 1955; University of St Andrews, 1960. Hon. Sec. and Mem. Council, Royal College of Obstetricians and Gynæcologists, 1955–68, 1971, Vice-Pres., 1976–78; Mem. Council Obstetric Section, Royal Society of Med., 1953 (Pres. 1981); co-opted Mem. Council, RCS, 1978–81. Guest Prof. to Brisbane, Australia, Auckland, New Zealand, 1959, Johns Hopkins Hosp., Baltimore, 1966; Litchfield Lectr, University of Oxford, 1968; Sims-Black Prof. to Australia, NZ and Rhodesia, 1970. *Publications:* Progress in Clinical Obstetrics and Gynæcology, 2nd edn 1964; (ed jtly and contrib.) Obstetrics by Ten Teachers, 11th edn 1966 to 16th edn 1995; (jtly) Queen Charlotte's Textbook of Obstetrics, 12th edn 1970; (ed jtly and contrib.) Gynaecology by Ten Teachers, 12th edn 1970 to 16th edn 1995; (contrib.) French's Index of Differential Diagnosis, 10th edn 1973 to 12th edn 1984; contributions to: Lancet, BMJ, Practitioner, Proc. Royal Soc. Med., Encyclopædia Britannica Book of the Year (annual contrib.), etc. *Recreations:* ski-ing, sailing, tennis, golf, croquet, wind-surfing, underwater swimming, photography, viniculture on the Isle of Elba. *Address:* 13 Copse Hill, Wimbledon, SW20 0NB. *T:* (020) 8946 5089. *Clubs:* Old Pauline; Royal Wimbledon Golf; Guy's Hospital Rugby Football (ex-Pres.). *Died 9 April 2004.*

LEWIS-JONES, Captain (Robert) Gwilym, CBE 1969; RN retired; *b* 22 Feb. 1922; *s* of Captain David Lewis Jones and Olwen Lewis Jones (*née* Evans), Corris and Dolgellau; *m* 1946, Ann Mary, *d* of David and Margaret Owen, Dolgellau; two *s. Educ:* Tywyn Grammar Sch.; Gonville and Caius Coll., Cambridge. CEng, MRAeS, FBIM. Fleet Air Arm Observers Course, 1942–43; 842 Sqdn in HM Ships Indefatigable, Furious and Fencer on Murmansk and Atlantic convoys, 1943–45; Long Air Communications Course, 1945–46; Long Air Electronics/Electrical Course, 1946–47; RRE Malvern, 1947–49; Long Ships Electrical Course, 1950; RAE Farnborough, 1950–53; Sen. Aircraft Engr Off., HMS Albion, 1953–56; Dep. Comd Engr Off., Staff of Flag Officer Naval Air Comd, 1956–58; Head of Air Electrical Comd, RN Air Stn Brawdy, 1958–61; Sqdn Weapons Off., HMS Caesar and 8th Destroyer Sqdn, 1961–63; Exec. Off. and 2nd in Comd, HMS Condor, 1963–65; Gen. Man., RN Aircraft Yard, Belfast, 1965–67; Dir of Aircraft Armament, MoD (N), 1967–68; Jt Services Planning and Co-ordinating Off. responsible for Armed Forces participation in Investiture of Prince of Wales, 1967–69; Sen. Officers War Course, RNC Greenwich, 1969–70; Staff of Dir Gen. Ships

(Directorate Naval Ship Production), 1970–72; Dir, Fleet Management Services, 1973–75; Dir, Naval Management and Orgn, 1975–76. ADC to the Queen, 1976. Lt-Comdr 1952; Comdr 1958; Captain 1967. Member: (C) for Carshalton, GLC, 1977–81; Mayor of Dolgellau and Chm., Dolgellau Town Council, 1987–88 (Dep. Mayor, 1986–87). Chm., Merioneth SSAFA, 1984–93; Dep. Chm., 1984–88, Chm., 1988–89, Gwynedd Valuation Panel; President: Gwynedd Valuation and Community Charge Tribunal, 1989–93; Meirionydd CAB, 1992–97 (Chm., 1988–92); Member: Snowdonia Nat. Park Cttee, 1982–88; Prince of Wales' Cttee (Mid Wales Gp), 1988–93; Clwyd Social Security Appeals Tribunal, 1988–94. Deacon, Welsh Presbyterian Church, 1983–. JP SE London, 1979–81. High Sheriff of Gwynedd, 1991–92. *Recreations:* golf, choral music, Welsh culture. *Address:* Mansiriol, Dolgellau, Gwynedd LL40 2YS. *T:* (01341) 422526. *Died 18 Sept. 2001.*

LEWTHWAITE, Sir David (Rainald), 5th Bt *cr* 1927, of Broadgate, Thwaites, co. Cumberland; *b* 26 March 1940; *s* of Brig. Sir Rainald Gilfrid Lewthwaite, 4th Bt, CVO, OBE, MC and Margaret Elizabeth (*née* Edmonds), MBE; *S* father, 2003; *m* 1969, Diana Helena, twin *d* of W. R. Tomkinson, TD; two *d. Educ:* Rugby; Trinity Coll., Cambridge (BA 1960). *Address:* Broadgate, nr Millom, Cumbria LA18 5JY. *Died 28 July 2004 (ext).*

LEWTHWAITE, Brig. Sir Rainald Gilfrid, 4th Bt *cr* 1927, of Broadgate, Thwaites, Co. Cumberland; CVO 1975; OBE 1974; MC 1943; *b* 21 July 1913; 2nd *s* of Sir William Lewthwaite, 2nd Bt of Broadgate, Cumberland, and Beryl Mary Stopford Hickman; *S* brother, 1993; *m* 1936, Margaret Elizabeth Edmonds, MBE 1942 (*d* 1990), 2nd *d* of late Harry Edmonds and Florence Jane Moncrieffe Bolton, High Green, Redding, Conn, USA; one *s* (and one *s* two *d* decd). *Educ:* Rugby Sch.; Trinity Coll., Cambridge. BA (Hons) Law 1934. Joined Scots Guards, 1934. Served War of 1939–45 (MC, despatches twice). Retired as Defence and Military Attaché, British Embassy, Paris, 1968. Dir of Protocol, Hong Kong, 1969–76. French Croix-de-Guerre with Palm, 1945. *Recreation:* country life. *Heir:* *s* David Rainald Lewthwaite [*b* 26 March 1940; *m* 1969, Diana Helena, twin *d* of W. R. Tomkinson, TD; two *d*]. *Address:* Broadgate, Millom, Cumbria LA18 5JY. *T:* (01229) 716295. *Club:* Cavalry and Guards. *Died 15 April 2003.*

LICHFIELD, 5th Earl of, *cr* 1831; **Thomas Patrick John Anson;** Viscount Anson and Baron Soberton, 1806; DL; *b* 25 April 1939; *s* of Viscount Anson (Thomas William Arnold) (*d* 1958) and Princess Anne of Denmark (*née* Anne Fenella Ferelith Bowes-Lyon) (*d* 1980); *S* grandfather, 1960; *m* 1975, Lady Leonora Grosvenor (LVO 1997) (marr. diss. 1986), *d* of 5th Duke of Westminster, TD; one *s* two *d. Educ:* Harrow Sch.; RMA, Sandhurst. Joined Regular Army, Sept. 1957, as Officer Cadet; Grenadier Guards, 1959–62 (Lieut). Photographer (known professionally as Patrick Lichfield). Ambassador, VSO, 1989. FBIPP; FRPS. Freeman, City of London, 1981. DL Stafford 1996. *Publications:* The Most Beautiful Women, 1981; Lichfield on Photography (also video cassettes), 1981; A Royal Album, 1982; Patrick Lichfield's Unipart Calendar Book, 1982; Patrick Lichfield Creating the Unipart Calendar, 1983; Hot Foot to Zabriskie Point, 1985; Lichfield on Travel Photography, 1986; Not the Whole Truth (autobiog.), 1986; (ed) Courvoisier's Book of the Best, 1986, 5th edn 1994; Lichfield in Retrospect, 1988; (ed) Queen Mother: the Lichfield selection, 1990; (ed) Elizabeth R: a photographic celebration of 40 years, 1991. *Recreations:* arboriculture, country pursuits. *Heir:* *s* Viscount Anson, *b* 19 July 1978. *Address:* Lichfield Studios, 133 Oxford Gardens, W10 6NE. *T:* (020) 8969 6161; (seat) Shugborough Hall, Stafford. *T:* (01889) 881454. *Club:* White's. *Died 11 Nov. 2005.*

LICKORISH, Leonard John, CBE 1975; Director-General, British Travel Association, 1970–86; *b* 10 Aug. 1921; *s* of Adrian J. and Josephine Lickorish; *m* 1945,

Eileen Maris Wright (*d* 1983); one *s*. *Educ:* St George's Coll., Weybridge; University Coll., London (BA). Served RAF, 1941–46. British Travel Assoc., 1946–86. Vis. Prof., Univ. of Strathclyde, 1989–96. Chm., European Travel Commn, 1984–86 (Hon. Vice-Chm., 1986); Chm., Exhibition Industry Federation, 1987–89; Vice Chm., European Tourism Action Group, 1997– (Sec., 1986–97). Officer of Crown of Belgium, 1967. *Publications:* The Travel Trade, 1955; The Statistics of Tourism, 1975; Tourism Marketing, 1989; Developing Tourism Destinations, 1991; An Introduction to Tourism, 1997; numerous for nat. and internat. organisations on internat. travel. *Recreations:* gardening, walking, fishing. *Address:* 46 Hillway, Highgate, N6 6EP. *Club:* Royal Over-Seas League.   *Died 19 May 2002.*

LIGHT, (Sidney) David; a Civil Service Commissioner, 1978–79; Member, Civil Service Commission's Panel of Selection Board Chairmen, 1980–89; *b* 9 Dec. 1919; *s* of late William Light; *m* Edna Margaret Honey; one *s*. *Educ:* King Edward VI Sch., Southampton. RAF, 1940–46. HM Customs and Excise, 1938; HM Treasury, 1948–68; Asst Sec., CS Commn, 1969–75; Under Sec., CSD, 1975–78. *Recreations:* bricolage, watching cricket, travel. *Address:* Church House Cottage, Bentley, Hampshire GU10 5HY. *Clubs:* Royal Commonwealth Society; Hampshire Cricket.   *Died 12 Aug. 2001.*

LILFORD, 7th Baron *cr* 1797; **George Vernon Powys;** *b* 8 Jan. 1931; *s* of late Robert Horace Powys (*g g grandson* of 2nd Baron) and of Vera Grace Bryant, Rosebank, Cape, SA; *S* kinsman, 1949; *m* 1st, 1954, Mrs Eve Bird (marr. diss.); 2nd, 1957, Anuta Merritt (marr. diss. 1958); 3rd, 1958, Norma Yvonne Shell (marr. diss. 1961); 4th, 1961, Mrs Muriel Spottiswoode (marr. diss. 1969); two *d*; 5th, 1969, Margaret Penman (marr. diss. 1991); one *s* two *d*. *Educ:* St Aidan's Coll., Grahamstown, SA; Stonyhurst Coll. *Recreations:* golf, cricket. *Heir: s* Hon. Mark Vernon Powys, *b* 16 Nov. 1975. *Address:* Le Grand Câtelet, St John, Jersey, Channel Islands JE3 4FL.
                                         Died 3 Jan 2005.

LILLINGSTON, George David I. I.; *see* Inge-Innes-Lillingston.

LIMERICK, 6th Earl of, *cr* 1803 (Ire.); **Patrick Edmund Pery,** KBE 1983; Hon. AM 2001; DL; MA, CA; Baron Glentworth, 1790 (Ire.); Viscount Limerick, 1800 (Ire.); Baron Foxford, 1815 (UK); Chairman, Pirelli UK, since 1989; Chancellor, London Metropolitan University (formerly London Guildhall University), since 1999; *b* 12 April 1930; *e s* of 5th Earl of Limerick, GBE, CH, KCB, DSO, TD, and Angela Olivia, Dowager Countess of Limerick, GBE, CH (*d* 1981); *S* father, 1967; *m* 1961, Sylvia Rosalind Lush; two *s* one *d*. *Educ:* Eton; New Coll., Oxford. CA 1957. Chairman: Mallinson–Denny Ltd, 1979–81; Polymeters Response Internat., 1988–93; AMP Asset Management plc, 1992–98; De La Rue plc, 1993–97 (Dir, 1983–); Dep. Chm., Henderson plc, 1998–2000; Director: Kleinwort Benson Ltd, 1967–87 (Vice Chm., 1983–85; Dep Chm., 1985–87); Kleinwort Benson Gp, 1982–90; Kleinwort Benson Australian Income Fund Inc., subseq. Dresdner RCM Global Strategic Fund Inc., 1986–2000; Commercial Bank of Australia Ltd (London Adv. Bd), 1969–72; TR Pacific Investment Trust, 1987–92; Brooke Bond Gp, 1981–84. Parly Under-Sec. of State for Trade, DTI, 1972–74; Chairman: BOTB, 1979–83 (Mem., 1975–91); BIEC, subseq. British Invisibles, 1984–91; Pres., Inst. of Export, 1983–95; Vice-Pres., Assoc. of British Chambers of Commerce, 1977– (Pres., 1974–77); Member: Cttee for ME Trade, 1968–79 (Chm., 1975–79); Council, London Chamber of Commerce, 1968–79. Pres., Canning House, 1994–97. Chairman: Employability Forum, 2000–; ChildAction Ltd, 2001–. Chairman: Ct of Govs, London Guildhall Univ. (formerly City of London Poly.), 1984–99; Cttee of Univ. Chairmen, 1995–97; Trustees, City Parochial Foundn, 1992–96 (Trustee, 1971–). Pres., South of England Agricl Soc., 1993. Chairman: Britain-Australia

Soc., 1997–99 (Vice-Pres., 2000–); European-Atlantic Gp, 1999–2001 (Pres., 2001–); Sussex Heritage Trust, 2000–. Master, Guild of World Traders, 1991. President: Anglo-Swiss Soc., 1984–2000; Ski Club of GB, 1974–81; Alpine Ski Club, 1985–87 (Vice-Pres., 1975–77); Vice-Pres., Alpine Club, 1989–91. Hon. Colonel: 71st (Yeomanry) Signal Regt (Volunteers), 1993–98; Inns of Court and City Yeomanry (Volunteers), 1993–. Kt Pres., Soc. of Knights of the Round Table, 1999–. DL W Sussex, 1988. Hon. DBA London Guildhall, 2000; Hon. LLD American Internat. Univ. in London, 2001. *Recreations:* ski-ing, mountaineering. *Heir: s* Viscount Glentworth, *b* 10 Feb. 1963. *Address:* Chiddinglye, West Hoathly, East Grinstead, West Sussex RH19 4QT. *T:* (01342) 810214; 30A Victoria Road, W8 5RG. *T:* (020) 7937 0573. *Club:* Cavalry and Guards.   *Died 8 Jan. 2003.*

LINCOLN, 18th Earl of, *cr* 1572; **Edward Horace Fiennes-Clinton;** *b* 23 Feb. 1913; *s* of Edward Henry Fiennes-Clinton (killed in action, 1916) and Edith Annie (*née* Guest) (*d* 1965); *S* to earldom of 10th Duke of Newcastle, 1988; *m* 1st, 1940, Leila Ruth Millen (*d* 1947); one *d* (one *s* decd); 2nd, 1953, Linda Alice O'Brien. *Educ:* Hale School; Govt Schools; Junior Technical Coll., Perth. In goldmining industry, Kalgoorlie, 1935–53; Public Works Dept (water supply) and farming (mainly wheatbelt), 1956–76. *Publication:* Memoirs of an Embryo Earl (family edn), 1992. *Recreations:* boating, gardening. *Heir: g s* Robert Edward Fiennes-Clinton, *b* 17 June 1972. *Address:* Flat 45, Elanora Villas, 37 Hastie Street, Bunbury, WA 6230, Australia. *T:* (8) 97211223.
                                          Died 7 July 2001.

LINDBERGH, Anne Spencer Morrow; author, United States; *b* 22 June 1906; *d* of Dwight Whitney Morrow and Elizabeth Reeve Morrow (*née* Cutter); *m* 1929, Col Charles Augustus Lindbergh, AFC, DFC (*d* 1974); three *s* one *d* (and one *s* one *d* decd). *Educ:* Miss Chapin's Sch., New York City; Smith Coll., Northampton, Mass (two prizes for literature). Received Cross of Honour of United States Flag Association for her part in survey of air route across Atlantic, 1933; received Hubbard Gold Medal of National Geographical Soc. for work as co-pilot and radio operator in flight of 40,000 miles over five continents, 1934. Hon. MA Smith Coll., Mass, 1935. *Publications:* North to the Orient, 1935; Listen, the Wind, 1938; The Wave of the Future, 1940; The Steep Ascent, 1944; Gift from the Sea, 1955; The Unicorn and other Poems, 1935–55, 1958; Dearly Beloved, 1963; Earth Shine, 1970; Bring Me a Unicorn (autobiog.), 1972; Hour of Gold, Hour of Lead (autobiog.), 1973; Locked Rooms and Open Doors: diaries and letters 1933–35, 1974; The Flower and the Nettle: diaries and letters 1936–39, 1976; War Within and Without: diaries and letters 1939–44, 1980. *Address:* c/o Lindbergh Foundation, Suite 110, 708 South 3rd Street, Minneapolis, MN 55415, USA.
                                          Died 7 Feb. 2001.

LINDSAY, Maj.-Gen. Courtenay Traice David, CB 1963; Director-General of Artillery, War Office, 1961–64, retired; *b* 28 Sept. 1910; *s* of late Courtenay Traice Lindsay and Charlotte Editha (*née* Wetenhall); *m* 1934, Margaret Elizabeth, *d* of late William Pease Theakston, Huntingdon; two *s*. *Educ:* Rugby Sch.; RMA Woolwich. 2nd Lt RA, 1930. Mem., Ordnance Board (Col), 1952; Dir of Munitions, British Staff (Brig.), Washington, 1959; Maj.-Gen. 1961. *Address:* Huggits Farm, Stone-in-Oxney, Tenterden, Kent TN30 7JT. *Club:* Rye Golf.
                                          Died 7 Dec. 2002.

LINDSAY, Donald Dunrod, CBE 1972; *b* 27 Sept. 1910; *s* of Dr Colin Dunrod Lindsay (Pres., BMA 1938), and Mrs Isabel Baynton Lindsay; *m* 1936, Violet Geraldine Fox; one *s* one *d*. *Educ:* Clifton Coll., Bristol; Trinity Coll., Oxford. Asst Master, Manchester Gram. Sch., 1932; Asst Master, Repton Sch., 1935; temp. seconded to Bristol Univ. Dept of Education as lecturer in History, 1938; Senior History Master, Repton Sch., 1938–42; Headmaster: Portsmouth Gram. Sch., 1942–53; Malvern

Coll., 1953–71. Dir, ISIS, 1972–77. Chm., Headmasters' Conference, 1968. Governor, Harrow Sch., 1977–82. *Publications:* A Portrait of Britain Between the Exhibitions, 1952; A Portrait of Britain, 1688–1851, 1954; A Portrait of Britain Before 1066, 1962; Authority and Challenge, Europe 1300–1600, 1975; Europe and the World, 1979; Friends for Life: a portrait of Launcelot Fleming, 1981; Forgotten General, 1986; Sir Edmund Bacon: a Norfolk life, 1988; A Form of Gratitude: the life of Angela Limerick, 1992. *Recreations:* walking, theatre, music. *Address:* 29 Teme Avenue, Malvern, Worcs WR14 2XA.
Died 14 Nov. 2002.

LINDSAY of Dowhill, Sir Ronald Alexander, 2nd Bt *cr* 1962, of Dowhill; 23rd Representer of Baronial House of Dowhill; *b* 6 Dec. 1933; *er s* of Sir Martin Lindsay of Dowhill, 1st Bt, CBE, DSO, and Joyce Lady Lindsay (*d* 1998), *d* of late Major Hon. Robert Lindsay, Royal Scots Greys; *S* father, 1981; *m* 1968, Nicoletta, *yr d* of late Captain Edgar Storich, Royal Italian Navy and late Mrs Storich; three *s* one *d. Educ:* Eton College; Worcester Coll., Oxford (MA). National service in Grenadier Guards (Lieut), 1952–54. Insurance broker, 1958– (chiefly Hogg Robinson, and Minets); gen. manager, UK Br., Ocaso SA, Madrid, 1980–84; Lloyd's Members' Agent, 1984–; Director: AHJ Members Agency, 1984–88; Sturge Hldgs members' agencies, 1989–93. Mem., Standing Council of the Baronetage, 1978– (Chm., 1987–89; a Vice-Pres., 2002–); Trustee, Baronets Charitable Trust, 1986–95 (Chm., 1990–92); Vice-Pres., Anglo-Spanish Soc., 1993– (Vice-Chm., 1985–93). Member of Queen's Body Guard for Scotland (Royal Company of Archers), 1963. FCII 1963. Encomienda, Orden de Isabel la Católica (Spain), 1988. *Heir: s* James Martin Evelyn Lindsay [*b* 11 Oct. 1968; *m* 2000, Annabel, *yr d* of Dr Peter Knight]. *Address:* 104 Edith Road, W14 9AP. *T:* (020) 7603 0278.
Died 6 March 2004.

LINES, (Walter) Moray, CBE 1969; Chairman, Lines Brothers Ltd, 1962–71 (Joint Managing Director, 1962–70); *b* 26 Jan. 1922; *er s* of late Walter Lines; *m* 1955, Fiona Margaret Denton; three *s* one *d. Educ:* Gresham Sch. Joined Board of Lines Bros Ltd, 1946; Chm., British Toy Manufacturers Assoc., 1968–70. *Address:* Stable Cottage, Shirwell, near Barnstaple, N Devon EX31 4JU. *T:* (01271) 850265.
Died 15 Oct. 2002.

LINGARD, Anthony; *see* Lingard, P. A.

LINGARD, (Peter) Anthony, CBE 1977; TD; Director General, St John Ambulance Association, 1978–82; *b* 29 Feb. 1916; *s* of late Herbert Arthur Lingard and Kate Augusta Burdett; *m* 1946, Enid Nora Argile (*d* 2002); two *d. Educ:* Berkhamsted Sch.; London Univ. (BCom). Served RA, 1939–46; Major, 1941 (despatches twice). Co. of London Electric Supply Gp, 1936; Area Manager Lambeth and Camberwell, County Group, 1947; Commercial Officer, S Western Sub-Area, 1948, Chief Commercial Officer, 1959–62, London Electricity Board; Commercial and Development Adviser, Electricity Council, 1962–65; Mem., Electricity Council, 1965–77; Chm., E Midlands Electricity Bd, 1972–77. Member: CEGB, 1972–75; Directing Cttee, Internat. Union of Producers and Distributors of Electrical Energy, 1973–77. County Dir, Suffolk, St John Ambulance, 1982–85. Member until 1977: Ct of Governors, Admin. Staff Coll.; Council, IEE; Council of Industrial Soc.; E Midlands Econ. Planning Council; Mem. Nottingham Univ. Ct, 1975–77. CompIEE 1967. FCMI (FBIM 1973). KStJ. *Recreations:* photography, painting, golf, fly-fishing, reading. *Address:* The Dumble, High Street, Orford, Woodbridge, Suffolk IP12 2NW. *T:* (01394) 450622. *Clubs:* Army and Navy; Orford Sailing (Pres.); Aldeburgh Yacht, Aldeburgh Golf. *Died 15 Feb. 2003.*

LINGS, Dr Martin; Keeper Emeritus of Oriental Manuscripts and Printed Books, British Library; *b* 24 Jan. 1909; *e s* of late George Herbert Lings and Gladys Mary Lings (*née* Greenhalgh), Burnage, Lancs; *m* 1944, Lesley,

3rd *d* of late Edgar Smalley. *Educ:* Clifton Coll.; Magdalen Coll., Oxford (Class. Mods 1930, BA English 1932, MA 1937); Sch. of Oriental and African Studies, Univ. of London (BA Arabic 1954, PhD 1959). Lectr in Anglo-Saxon and Middle English, Univ. of Kaunas, 1935–39; Lectr in English Lit., Univ. of Cairo, 1940–51; Asst Keeper, Dept of Oriental Printed Books and Manuscripts, British Museum, 1955–70, Dep. Keeper, 1970, Keeper, 1971–74; seconded to the British Library, 1973. FRAS. *Publications:* The Book of Certainty, 1952 (trans. Spanish, Turkish and French); (with A. S. Fulton) Second Supplementary Catalogue of Arabic Printed Books in the British Museum, 1959; A Moslem Saint of the Twentieth Century, 1961 (trans. French and Arabic); Ancient Beliefs and Modern Superstitions, 1965 (trans. Turkish, Portuguese, French, German and Greek); Shakespeare in the Light of Sacred Art, 1966; The Elements and Other Poems, 1967; The Heralds and Other Poems, 1970; A Sufi Saint of the Twentieth Century, 1971 (trans. Urdu, Persian, Spanish, Turkish, Arabic, German and French); What is Sufism? (trans. French, Italian, Spanish, German, Portuguese and Bosnian); (with Y. H. Safadi) Third Supplementary Catalogue of Arabic Printed Books in the British Library, 1976; (with Y. H. Safadi) The Qur'ān, Catalogue of an Exhibition at the British Library, 1976; The Quranic Art of Calligraphy and Illumination, 1977 (trans. Persian); Muhammad: his life based on the earliest sources, 1983 (trans. French, Urdu, Tamil, Spanish, Arabic, Dutch, Bosnian, German and Italian); The Secret of Shakespeare, 1984 (trans. Italian, Spanish, Persian, Greek and French); The Eleventh Hour, 1987 (trans. German and French); Collected Poems, 1987; Symbol and Archetype: studies in the meaning of existence, 1990 (trans. French); The Sacred Art of Shakespeare, 1998 (trans. French and Turkish); Mecca from before Genesis until Today, 2004; Sufi Poems, 2004; Splendours of Qur'ān Calligraphy and Illumination, 2005 (trans. Arabic, Italian, Spanish, Persian, Turkish, German and French); A Return to the Spirit: questions and answers, 2005; contrib. Encycl. Britannica, Encycl. Islam, Studies in Comparative Religion, Cambridge History of Arabic Literature, etc. *Recreations:* walking, gardening, music. *Address:* 3 French Street, Westerham, Kent TN16 1PN. *T:* (01959) 562855.
Died 12 May 2005.

LINTON, Alan Henry Spencer, LVO 1969; HM Diplomatic Service, retired; Consul-General, Detroit, USA, 1976–79; *b* Nottingham, 24 July 1919; *s* of Rt Rev. James Henry Linton, DD and Alicia Pears (*née* Aldous); *m* 1959, Kaethe Krebs (*d* 1990); four *d. Educ:* St Lawrence, Ramsgate; Magdalen Coll., Oxford (MA). Served War, RA, 1940–46. HM Overseas Civil Service, Tanganyika, 1947–62; FO, 1963–65; First Sec. (Inf.), Vienna, 1965–69; Head of Chancery, Lusaka, Zambia, 1970–73; First Sec. (Commercial), Kingston, Jamaica, 1973–75; Dep. High Comr, Kingston, 1975–76. *Recreations:* walking, photography. *Address:* 29 The Avenue, Poole BH13 6LH.
Died 3 June 2003.

LION, Jacques Kenneth, OBE 1979; President, The London Metal Exchange Ltd, 1987–91; *b* 18 Dec. 1922; *s* of Felix J. Lion and Ethel (*née* Myers); *m* 1947, Jean Elphinstone (*née* Mackenzie); two *s* one *d. Educ:* St Paul's Sch. Sen. Partner, 1969–86, Chm., 1986–90, Philipp & Lion (Holdings) Ltd. Pres., Non-Ferrous Div., Bureau Internationale de la Récupération, 1970–74; Mem. Council, British Secondary Metals Assoc., 1956–77 (Pres., 1959 and 1964). Dir, 1972, Chm., 1984–91, Metal Market & Exchange Co. Ltd. *Recreations:* music, gardening, golf. *Club:* City of London. *Died 18 Nov. 2002.*

LISLE, 8th Baron *cr* 1758 (Ire.), of Mount North, co. Cork; **Patrick James Lysaght;** *b* 1 May 1931; *s* of Horace James William Lysaght (*d* 1977), *yr b* of 7th Baron Lisle, and Joanna Mary (*née* Nolan; *d* 1985); *S* uncle, 1997; *m* 1957, Mrs Mary Louise Shaw-Stuart (marr. diss.); two *s* one *d. Educ:* Shrewsbury. Late Lieut, Grenadier Guards. *Heir: s* Hon. John Nicholas Geoffrey Lysaght, *b* 20 May 1960.

Address: 30 Springhurst House, Greenham, Newbury, Berks RG14 7UD.   *Died 11 Nov. 2003.*

LISTER, Prof. James, MD, FRCS; Professor of Paediatric Surgery, University of Liverpool, 1974–86, then Emeritus; *b* 1 March 1923; *s* of Thomas and Anna Rebecca Lister; *m* 1946, Greta Redpath; three *d. Educ:* St Paul's Sch., London; Edinburgh Univ. (MB, ChB 1945; MD 1972). FRCS 1975, FRCSE 1950, FRCSGlas 1969. Surg. Lieut, RNVR, 1945–48. Surgical training posts, Edinburgh and Dundee, 1948–58; Halstead Res. Fellow, Colorado Univ., 1959; Sen. Lectr in Paediatric Surgery and Consultant Surgeon, Hosp. for Sick Children, Great Ormond St, and Queen Elizabeth Hosp., Hackney Rd, 1960–63; Consultant Paediatric Surgeon, Sheffield Children's Hosp., 1963–74. Civil Consultant in Paediatric Surgery to RN, 1979–86. Past Examiner: Univs of Glasgow and Sheffield (in paediatric surgery); DCH London; Part I and Part II FRCSE. Mem. Council, RCSE, 1977–91 (Convenor of Examinations Cttee, 1986–90; a Vice-Pres., 1988–91); Mem., St Helens & Knowsley DHA, 1983–86. Chm., European Union of Paediatric Surgical Assocs, 1983–86; Hon. Member: British Assoc. of Paediatric Surgeons (Pres., 1975–76); Paediatric Surgical Assocs of Austria, Brazil, Chile, Germany, Greece, Hungary, Peru, Poland, Scandinavia, Yugoslavia. Hon. Fellow: Amer. Acad. of Paediatrics, 1976; Assoc. of Surgeons of India, 1985. Former Member of Editorial Board: Jl of RCSEd; Jl of Paediatric Surgery; Annals of Tropical Paediatrics; Consultant Ed., Eur. Jl of Pediatric Surgery, 1991–2000. *Publications:* Neonatal Surgery, ed jtly 2nd edn 1978 and 3rd edn, 1990; Complications in Paediatric Surgery, 1986; papers on neonatal surgery and myelomeningocele. *Recreations:* gardening, hill walking. *Address:* 6 Penstones Court, Marlborough Lane, Stanford in the Vale, Farington, SN7 8SW.   *Died 9 May 2004.*

LISTER, Raymond (George), LittD; President, Royal Society of Miniature Painters, Sculptors and Gravers, 1970–80; Chairman, Board of Governors, Federation of British Artists, 1976–80 (Governor, 1972–80); *b* 28 March 1919; *s* of late Horace Lister and Ellen Maud Mary Lister (*née* Arnold); *m* 1947, Pamela Helen, *d* of late Frank Bishop Brutnell; one *s* one *d. Educ:* St John's Coll. Choir Sch., Cambridge; Cambridge and County High Sch. for Boys; MA 1975, LittD 1990, Cantab. Served apprenticeship in family firm (architectural metalworking), 1934–39; specialised war service (engrg), 1939–45; Dir of family firm, 1941–94; Man. Editor, Golden Head Press, 1952–72; Dir, John P. Gray and Son, craft bookbinders, 1978–82. Hon. Senior Mem., University Coll., subseq. Wolfson Coll., Cambridge, 1971–75, Mem. Coll. Council, 1983–85, Emeritus Fellow, 1986 (Fellow, 1975–86); a Syndic, Fitzwilliam Mus., Cambridge, 1981–89. Associate Mem. 1946, Mem. 1948, Royal Soc. of Miniature Painters; Pres., Private Libraries Assoc., 1971–74; Vice-Pres., Architectural Metalwork Assoc., 1970–75, Pres., 1975–77. Liveryman, Blacksmiths' Co., 1957, Mem. Ct of Assistants, 1980, Prime Warden, 1989–90. *Publications:* Decorative Wrought Ironwork in Great Britain, 1957; Decorative Cast Ironwork in Great Britain, 1960; Edward Calvert, 1962; Beulah to Byzantium, 1965; Victorian Narrative Paintings, 1966; William Blake, 1968; Hammer and Hand, 1969; Samuel Palmer and his Etchings, 1969; A Title to Phoebe, 1972; British Romantic Art, 1973; Samuel Palmer: a biography, 1974; (ed) The Letters of Samuel Palmer, 1974; Infernal Methods: a Study of William Blake's art techniques, 1975; Apollo's Bird, 1975; For Love of Leda, 1977; Great Images of British Printmaking, 1978; (jtly) Samuel Palmer: a vision recaptured, 1978; Samuel Palmer in Palmer Country, 1980; George Richmond, 1981; Bergomask, 1982; There was a Star Danced, 1983; Prints and Printmaking, 1984; Samuel Palmer and 'The Ancients', (catalogue of exhibn at Fitzwilliam Mus., Cambridge, also selected by R. Lister) 1984; The Paintings of Samuel Palmer, 1985; The Paintings of William Blake, 1986; Samuel Palmer, his Life and Art, 1987; Catalogue Raisonné of the Works of

Samuel Palmer, 1988; British Romantic Painting, 1989; trans., A. M. St Léon, Stenochoreography, 1992; With My Own Wings (autobiog.), 1994; contrib. Climbers' Club Jl, The Irish Book, Blake Studies, Blake Quarterly, Gazette des Beaux-arts, Connoisseur, Studies in Romanticism, Book Collector and TLS. *Recreations:* mountaineering in the fens, merels. *Address:* 9 Sylvester Road, Cambridge CB3 9AF. *T:* (01223) 324443. *Club:* Sette of Odd Volumes (Pres. 1960, 1982).   *Died 2 Nov. 2001.*

LITCHFIELD, Dame Ruby (Beatrice), DBE 1981 (OBE 1959); Director, Festival City Broadcasters Ltd, 1975–86, retired (first woman appointed); Trustee, Adelaide Festival Centre, 1971–82, retired (first woman to be appointed to this position) (Life Member, 1982); *b* 5 Sept. 1912; *d* of Alfred John Skinner and Eva Hanna (*née* Thomas); *m* 1940, Kenneth Lyle Litchfield (*d* 1976); one *d. Educ:* North Adelaide Primary Sch.; Presbyterian Girls' Coll., Glen Osmond. Bd Mem., Kidney Foundn, 1968–; Chairperson: Carclew Youth Performing Arts Centre, 1972–88 (Life Patron, 1988); Families, Religion, Cultural Cttee, S Aust. Jubilee 150th, 1980–86. First woman Mem., Bd of S Aust. Housing Trust, 1962–70; Life Member: Queen Victoria Maternity Hosp., 1972 (Mem. Bd and Vice-Pres., 1953–72); Adelaide Rep. Th., 1967 (Mem. Bd, 1951–68); Hon. Life Mem., Spastic Paralysis Welfare Assoc. Inc. Mayoress of Prospect, 1954–57; Pres., Sportswomen's Assoc., 1969–74; Mem., Divl Council, Red Cross Soc., SA, 1955–71; Councillor, Royal Dist Bush Nursing Soc., 1957–64; Member: S Aust. Davis Cup Cttee, 1952, 1963, 1968; SA Cttee of Royal Acad. of Dancing, 1961–66; Bd, Telethon Channel 9, 1969–86; Mem. Cttee, Adelaide Festival of Arts, 1960 (Mem. Bd of Govs, 1966–90); Council, Sudden Infant Death Syndrome Res. Foundn, 1979–; Bd, Mary Potter Foundn (Chair, Hospice Appeal Cttee, 1988–; Life Mem., 1992); Mem. Bd, Crippled Children's Assoc., 1976–; First Life Mem., Telethon, 1992; Patron: Adelaide Chamber Orch., 1992–; State Theatre Co. Friends Cttee, 1993–; SA Div., Internat. AIDS Meml Fund, 1993–. Silver Jubilee Medal, 1977; Advance Australia Award, 1985; S Australia Great Award, 1987. *Recreation:* tennis (SA Hardcourt Champion, 1932–35). *Address:* 33 Hallett Road, Burnside, SA 5066, Australia. *Club:* Royal Commonwealth Society (Adelaide).   *Died 14 Aug. 2001.*

LITHIBY, John Grant; Director, Panmure Gordon & Co. Ltd, 1958–99 (Chairman, 1986–95); *b* 1 Dec. 1930; *s* of John Stewart Lithiby and Dorothy (*née* Schwartz); *m* 1961, Sarah Branch; two *s* one *d. Educ:* Eton Coll. Nat. Service, Life Guards, 1950–53. Carl M. Loeb Rhoades, 1953–57; joined Panmure Gordon & Co. Ltd, 1957. *Recreations:* bridge, gardening, tennis. *Address:* Stoke House, Stoke Road, Kingston upon Thames KT2 7NX. *Clubs:* White's, Hurlingham.   *Died 22 Dec. 2002.*

LITTLE, Dr Robert Clement; Head of Chemistry Division, Agricultural Science Service, Ministry of Agriculture, Fisheries and Food, 1979–85; *b* 8 Nov. 1925; *s* of Ernest William Little and Hannah Little; *m* 1950, Margaret Isobel Wilson; two *d. Educ:* Carlisle Grammar Sch.; Manchester Univ. (BScTech); Glasgow Univ. (PhD). W of Scotland Agricultural Coll., 1946–55; Agricultural Develt and Adv. Service (formerly National Agricl Adv. Service), MAFF, 1955–85. *Address:* 9 Ashcroft Close, Harpenden, Herts AL5 1JJ. *T:* (01582) 715613.   *Died 24 April 2004.*

LITTLEJOHN, Alan Morrison; Director, Shipbuilders and Shiprepairers Association (formerly Shiprepairers and Shipbuilders Independent Association), 1977–90; Secretary General, UK Land and Hydrographic Survey Association Limited, 1980–90; retired; *b* 17 Oct. 1925; *s* of Frank Littlejohn and (Ethel) Lucy (*née* Main); *m* 1955, Joy Dorothy Margaret (*née* Till); one *d. Educ:* Dame Allan's Boys' Sch., Newcastle upon Tyne; King's Coll., Durham Univ. (BScAgric); Lincoln Coll. and Agricultural Economics Res. Inst., Oxford Univ. (BLitt, DipAgEcon). Assistant Agricultural Economist: King's Coll., Durham

Univ., 1945–47; Wye Coll., London Univ., 1950–51; Agric. Chemical Div., Shell Internat. Chemical Co., London, 1951–67; Economist, Agric. Engineers Assoc., 1968–73; Dir Gen., Clay Pipe Develt Assoc., 1973–77; Dir, Assoc. of High Pressure Water Jetting Contractors, 1980–87. Chm., Catherine Place Personnel Services Ltd, 1981–89. Member: Chorleywood Parish Council, 1979–91 (Vice-Chm., 1984–85, 1987–88; Chm., 1985–87); (C) Three Rivers Dist Council, 1988–96 (Chm., Resources Cttee, 1990–91; Dep. Leader, 1990–91, Leader, 1991–95, Cons. Gp; Leader, 1992–94, Chm., 1995–96, Council). Hon. Life Vice-President: Chorleywood Cons. Br., 1998; SW Herts Cons. Assoc., 1999. *Recreation:* current affairs. *Address:* 5 The Readings, Chorleywood, Herts WD3 5SY. *T:* (01923) 284420.

Died 17 Dec. 2003.

LITTLEWOOD, Joan (Maud); theatre artist; *b* 6 Oct. 1914; *m* Jimmie Miller (later known as Ewan MacColl) (marr. diss.; he *d* 1989). *Educ:* London. Dir, Theatre of Action, Manchester (street theatre), 1931–37; founder, Theatre Union, Manchester, introducing individual work system, 1937–39; freelance writer, 1939–45 (banned from BBC and ENSA for political opinions); founded Theatre Workshop with Gerry Raffles, 1945; touring in GB, Germany, Norway, Sweden with original works, 1945–53; moved to Theatre Royal, Stratford, London, with classics, 1953; invited to Theatre of the Nations, Paris, 1955, then yearly (Best Production of the Year three times); Centre Culturel, Hammamet, Tunisia, 1965–67; Image India, Calcutta, 1968; creation of Children's Environments, Bubble Cities, learn and play areas around Theatre Royal, Stratford, 1968–75. Left England to work in France, 1975; Seminar Relais Culturel, Aix-en-Provence, 1976. Productions include: The Quare Fellow, 1956; Lysistrata, 1958 (Gold Medal, East Berlin, 1958; Olympic Award, Taormina, 1959); A Taste of Honey, 1958; Fings Ain't Wot They Used T'Be, The Hostage, 1959; Sparrers Can't Sing (film), 1962; Oh What a Lovely War (with Gerry Raffles and the Company), 1963. Mem., French Academy of Writers, 1964. SWET Special Award, 1983; Women of Achievement in the Arts Award, Arts Council of GB, 1993; Lifetime's Achievement Award, Director's Guild, 1995; Vildrosen, Stockholm, 1995. Hon. FRIBA 2002. Dr *hc* Univ. of the Air, 1977; DUniv: Flinders, SA, 1995; Open, 1995. Commandeur, Ordre des Arts et des Lettres (France), 1986. *Publications:* Milady Vine: biography of Philippe de Rothschild, 1984; Joan's Book (autobiog.), 1994. *Address:* c/o Theatre Royal Stratford East, Gerry Raffles Square, Newham, E15 1BN.

Died 20 Sept. 2002.

LIVESAY, Adm. Sir Michael (Howard), KCB 1989; Chief of Naval Personnel, Second Sea Lord and Admiral President, Royal Naval College, Greenwich, 1991–93; *b* 5 April 1936; *s* of William Lindsay Livesay and Margaret Eleanor Chapman Steel; *m* 1959, Sara House; two *d*. *Educ:* Acklam Hall Grammar Sch.; Britannia Royal Naval Coll. Joined RN, 1952; training appts, 1954–57; commnd 1957; qual. Aircraft Direction Specialist, 1959; Direction Officer, HMS Hermes, HMS Aisne, Fighter Direction Sch., and 893 Sqdn, 1959–66; i/c HMS Hubberston, 1966–68, HMS Plymouth, 1970–72; Captain Fishery Protection/Captain Mine Counter Measures, 1975–77; 1st CO HMS Invincible, 1979–82; Dir of Naval Warfare, 1982–84; Flag Officer Sea Training, 1984–85; ACNS, 1986–88; Flag Officer Scotland and NI, 1989–91. Director: Scottish Nuclear, 1993–98; ICM (formerly Inter Exec) Scotland Ltd, 1994–98. Comr, Northern Lighthouse Bd, 1994– (Chm., 1997–2001). President: RBL, Scotland, 1996–2001; Royal Naval Benevolent Soc. for Officers, 2001–. *Recreations:* sailing, fishing, golf. *Address:* c/o The Naval Secretary, Victory Building, HM Naval Base, Portsmouth PO1 3LS. *Clubs:* Army and Navy, Royal Navy of 1765 and 1785; Royal Perth.

Died 6 Oct. 2003.

LIVESEY, Ronald John Dearden; QC 1981; **His Honour Judge Livesey;** a Circuit Judge, since 1992; Senior Judge, Sovereign Base Areas, Cyprus, since 1996 (Deputy Senior Judge, 1983–96); *b* 11 Sept. 1935; *s* of John William and Una Florence Livesey; *m* 1965, Elizabeth Jane Coutts; one *s* one *d*. *Educ:* Malvern Coll.; Lincoln Coll., Oxford (MA). Called to the Bar, Lincoln's Inn, 1962, Bencher, 1989; a Recorder, 1991–92. *Recreation:* golf. *Address:* Preston Crown Court, Openshaw Way, Preston PR1 2LL. *Club:* Union (Southport).

Died 17 Jan. 2002.

LIVINGSTON BOOTH, Dick; *see* Livingston Booth, J. D.

LIVINGSTON BOOTH, (John) Dick, OBE 1976; Chairman, Legislation Monitoring Service for Charities, 1981–91; Patron, International Standing Conference on Philanthropy, since 1987 (President, 1975–87); *b* 7 July 1918; *o s* of late Julian Livingston Booth and Grace Marion (*née* Swainson); *m* 1st, 1941, Joan Ashley Tabrum (*d* 1976), *d* of Ashley Tabrum, OBE, LLM, MA; two *s* one *d*; 2nd, 1979, Audrey Betty Hope Harvey, PhD, AcDipEd (Psych), DipHEd, DipSoc, SRN, FRSH, MIHE, *d* of Sqdn Leader John James Haslett, RAF. *Educ:* Melbourne Church of England Grammar Sch.; Sidney Sussex Coll., Cambridge (MA). Served War, 1940–43: T/Captain RA; RWAFF; Instructor, 121 HAC OCTU RHA. Nigerian Administrative Service, 1943–57; Perm. Sec., Min. of Local Govt, Eastern Nigeria, 1956–57; Dir, Charities Aid Foundn, 1957–81. Member: Exec. Cttee, Nat. Council for Voluntary Organisations, 1974–81; Exec. Cttee, Christian Orgs Research and Adv. Trust, 1975–88; Develt and Stewardship Cttee, Central Bd of Finance, 1977–80. Mem. of Lloyd's, 1979–89. Trustee, Europhil Trust, 1987–90 (Chm., 1986–87). Lay Reader, Church of England, 1955–83. *Publications:* Directory of Grant-Making Trusts, 1968, 7th edn 1981; Trusts and Foundations in Europe, 1971; Report on Foundation Activity, 1977; Charity Statistics (annual), 1978–81; articles and booklets on charity. *Recreations:* home-making, travel, philately. *Address:* Goodwill Cottage, North Street, Mayfield, E Sussex TN20 6AN. *T:* and *Fax:* (01435) 872501. *Clubs:* Garrick, Royal Commonwealth Society.

Died 16 July 2001.

LLEWELLYN, His Honour John Desmond S.; *see* Seys-Llewellyn.

LLEWELLYN, Rt Rev. William Somers; first Suffragan Bishop of Lynn, 1963–72; *b* 16 Aug. 1907; *s* of Owen John and Elizabeth Llewellyn; *m* 1947, Innis Mary, *d* of Major Arthur Dorrien Smith, DSO, Tresco Abbey, Isles of Scilly; three *s*. *Educ:* Eton; Balliol Coll., Oxford. (BA 1929; MA 1937); Wycliffe Hall, Oxford; Dip. in Theology (with dist.) 1934. Deacon, 1935, priest, 1936; Curate of Chiswick, 1935–37; Vicar of Badminton, with Acton Turville, 1937–49; Chaplain to the Forces, 1940–46: served with Royal Gloucestershire Hussars in Egypt and Western Desert, and as Senior Chaplain with 8th Army HQ, Canal Area and East Africa; Vicar of Tetbury with Beverston, 1949–61; Rural Dean of Tetbury, 1955–61; Archdeacon of Lynn, 1961–72; Priest-in-charge of Boxwell with Leighterton, 1973–77; Asst Curate, Tetbury with Beverston, 1977–93; Hon. Asst Bishop, dio. of Gloucester, 1973–94. *Address:* Glebe House, Leighterton, Tetbury, Glos GL8 8UW. *T:* (01666) 890236.

Died 22 July 2001.

LLEWELLYN-JONES, His Honour Ilston Percival; a Circuit Judge, 1978–88; *b* 15 June 1916; *s* of Rev. L. Cyril F. Jones and Gertrude Anne Jones; *m* 1963, Mary Evelyn; one *s* by a previous marriage. *Educ:* prep. schs; St John's Sch., Leatherhead. Admitted Solicitor, Nov. 1938; practised privately until served Sussex Yeomanry RA and 23rd Field Regt RA (commnd), 1939–42; Solicitors Dept, Metropolitan Police, New Scotland Yard, 1942–48; private practice, Torquay, 1948–52; Devon County Prosecuting Solicitor, 1952–56; Clerk to N Devon

Justices, 1956–62; private practice, 1962–77; a Recorder of the Crown Court, 1972–78. *Recreation:* swimming. *Address:* Calle Toni Llido, 3–4° pta. 11, 03730 Javea (Alicante), Spain. *T:* (96) 5795584.

Died 14 Aug. 2002.

LLOYD, Rev. (Albert) Kingsley; President of the Conference of the Methodist Church, 1964; *b* 2 Nov. 1903; *s* of Rev. Albert Lloyd; *m* 1926, Ida Marian (*née* Cartledge) (*d* 1969); one *s* one *d*; 2nd, 1972, Katharine G. (*d* 1999), *d* of late A. G. L. Ives, CVO. *Educ:* Kingswood Sch., Bath; Richmond Coll., Surrey (Univ.of London). Methodist Circuit Minister: London, Bedford, Cambridge, 1926–52; Chm., London N Dist, 1951–53; Sec., Dept of Connexional Funds of the Methodist Church, 1952–69. Formerly: Secretary: Central Finance Bd; Ministers' Retirement Fund; Ministers' Children's Fund; Treas. and Vice–Chm., Methodist Ministers' Housing Soc.; Chm., Finance Cttee, BCC, Christian Aid. Formerly: Visitor and Chm. Govs, Kingswood Sch.; Gov., Trinity Hall, Southport. Wesley Historical Soc. Lectr, 1968. *Address:* 13 High Street, Orwell, Royston, Herts SG8 5QN. *Died 24 Jan. 2004.*

LLOYD, Frederick John, CBE 1977; FIA; Chairman, Road Transport Industry Training Board, 1978–83; *b* 22 Jan. 1913; *m* 1942, Catherine Johnson (*née* Parker); one *s* one *d*. *Educ:* Ackworth Sch., Yorks; Liverpool Univ. (BSc). FIA 1947; FIS 1949; FCIT 1968. War Service, Operational Research, Bomber Comd, 1942–45. Royal Insurance Co., 1933–47; London Passenger Transport Bd, 1947–69: Staff Admin Officer, 1952; Divl Supt (South), 1957; Chief Operating Manager (Central Buses), 1961; Chief Commercial and Planning Officer, 1965–69; Dir Gen., West Midlands Passenger Transport Exec., 1969–78. *Publications:* contribs to actuarial and transport jls. *Recreations:* golf, gardening. *Address:* 8 Cliveden Coppice, Sutton Coldfield, West Midlands B74 2RG. *T:* (0121) 308 5683. *Clubs:* Birmingham Rotary; Whittington Heath Golf (Lichfield, Staffs). *Died 8 Oct. 2003.*

LLOYD, Very Rev. Henry Morgan, DSO 1941; OBE 1959; Dean of Truro and Rector of St Mary, Truro, 1960–81, then Dean Emeritus; *b* 9 June 1911; *y s* of late Rev. David Lloyd, Weston-super-Mare, Somerset; *m* 1962, Rachel Katharine (*d* 1998), *d* of late J. R. Wharton, Haffield, near Ledbury; one *d*. *Educ:* Canford Sch.; Oriel Coll., Oxford (MA); Cuddesdon Theological Coll. Deacon, 1935; priest, 1936; Curate of Hendon Parish Church, Middlesex, 1935–40; served War as Chaplain RNVR, 1940–45; Principal of Old Rectory Coll., Hawarden, 1946–48; Secretary of Central Advisory Council of Training for the Ministry, 1948–50; Dean of Gibraltar, 1950–60. Hon. Citizen of the City of Truro, 1978. *Publication:* Flowers of the Field: an anthology of hope, 1996. *Recreation:* reading. *Club:* Royal Commonwealth Society (Fellow).

Died 16 April 2001.

LLOYD, Rev. Kingsley; *see* Lloyd, Rev. A. K.

LLOYD, Leslie, CBE 1981; FCIT; General Manager, Western Region, British Rail, 1976–82; *b* 10 April 1924; *s* of Henry Lloyd and Lilian Wright; *m* 1953, Marie Snowden; one *s* two *d*. *Educ:* Hawarden Grammar Sch. Served War, RAF, 1943–47. British Rail: Management Trainee, Eastern Reg., 1949–52; Chief Controller, Manchester, 1953–56; Freight Officer, Sheffield, 1956–59; Modernisation Asst, King's Cross, 1959–61; Dist Manager, Marylebone, 1961–63; Movements Supt, Great Northern Line, 1963–64; Ops Officer, Eastern Reg., 1964–67; Manager, Sundries Div., 1967; Movements Manager, Western Reg., 1967–69; Chief Ops Manager, British Rail HQ, 1969–76. *Recreations:* golf, gardening. *Address:* 73 The Fairway, Burnham, Bucks SL1 8DY. *Club:* Burnham Beeches Golf (Burnham). *Died 27 June 2004.*

LLOYD, Peter, CBE 1957; Director, Booth International Holdings Ltd, 1973–79 (Consultant, 1980–83); *b* 26 June

1907; *s* of late Godfrey I. H. Lloyd and Constance L. A. Lloyd; *m* 1st, 1932, Nora K. E. Patten (marr. diss. 1947); one *s* one *d*; 2nd, 1951, Joyce Evelyn Campbell. *Educ:* Gresham's Sch.; Trinity Coll., Cambridge (BA 1928, MA 1941). Industrial Research in Gas Light and Coke Co., London, 1931–41; RAE, 1941–44; Power Jets (Research and Development), 1944–46. Nat. Gas Turbine Estabt, Pyestock, 1946–60, Dep. Dir, 1950; Dir-Gen. Engine R&D, Mins of Aviation and Technology, 1961–69; Head of British Defence Research and Supply Staff, Canberra, 1969–72. Chm., Gas Turbine Collaboration Cttee, 1961–68. CEng, FRAeS, SFInstE. Pres., Cambridge Univ. Mountaineering Club, 1928–29; Chm., Mount Everest Foundn, 1982–84 (Vice Chm., 1980–82). Himalayan expeditions: Nanda Devi, 1936; Everest, 1938; Langtang Himal, 1949; Kulu, 1977. *Publications:* various papers in scientific and technical journals. *Recreations:* mountaineering, fishing, gardening. *Address:* 121 Tourist Road, Toowoomba, Qld 4350, Australia. *Clubs:* Alpine (Vice-Pres., 1961–63, Pres., 1977–80); Himalayan (Hon. Mem., 1992); Queensland (Brisbane).

Died 11 April 2003.

LLOYD OWEN, Maj.-Gen. David Lanyon, CB 1971; DSO 1945; OBE 1954; MC 1942; Chairman, Long Range Desert Group Association, since 1945; *b* 10 Oct. 1917; *s* of late Capt. Reginald Charles Lloyd Owen, OBE, RN; *m* 1947, Ursula Evelyn (MBE 1991), *d* of late Evelyn Hugh Barclay and Hon. Phyllis Patty Barclay (MBE 1942) (*e d* of 1st Baron Somerleyton, GCVO, PC); three *s*. *Educ:* Winchester; RMC Sandhurst. 2nd Lieut, The Queen's Royal Regt, 1938; Comdr, Long Range Desert Group, 1943–45; Military Asst to High Commissioner in Malaya, 1952–53; Comdg 1st Queen's Royal Regt, 1957–59; Comdr 24 Infantry Bde Group, 1962–64; GOC Cyprus District, 1966–68; GOC Near East Land Forces, 1968–69. Pres., Regular Commns Bd, 1969–72, retd. Kt of Cross of Merit, SMO Malta, 1946. *Publications:* The Desert My Dwelling Place, 1957; Providence Their Guide, 1980. *Address:* Violet Bank, Swainsthorpe, Norwich NR14 8PR. *T:* (01508) 470468. *Died 5 April 2001.*

LOADER, Sir Leslie (Thomas), Kt 1987; CBE 1980; retired company chairman; *b* 27 April 1923; *s* of Edward Robert Loader and Ethel May Loader (*née* Tiller); *m* 1st, 1957, Jennifer (marr. diss. 1980); three *d*; 2nd, 1981, Elizabeth. *Educ:* Bitterne Park; Bournemouth Municipal Coll.; LSE (occasional student). Served War of 1939–45; commnd Hampshire Regt (later Royal Hampshire Regt); saw active service in Italy. Mem., Southampton Borough Council, 1947–59 (first to propose sale of council houses to tenants, 1949); contested (C) Southampton, Itchen, 1955; Chairman: Southampton Young Conservatives, 1947; Southampton Itchen Cons. Assoc., 1964–70; Wessex Area Cons. Party, 1972–75; Euro-Cons. Council for Wight and Hants E, 1979–82 (Hon. Treas., 1984–87); Mem. Exec., Nat. Union of Cons. and Unionist Assocs, 1967–76 (Mem., Standing Adv. Cttee on Parly Cands; Hon. Life Vice Pres., Wessex Area, 1990); Pres., Eastleigh Cons. Assoc., 1985–98; Founder Chairman: Southern Parishes Cons. Club, Eastleigh; Cosham Cons. Club, Portsmouth N. Mem., Rotary Club, Bitterne and Woolston, 1959–72; founded Rotary Club of Bitterne and Woolston Housing Assoc., 1962 (Chm., 1962–83; Pres., 1983–98); Pres., Swaythling Housing Soc. Ltd, 1983–92 (Chm., 1976–83); Chm., Wessex Body Scanner Appeal, 1980–83; Member: Southampton Harbour Bd, 1951–56; Southampton and SW Hampshire HA, 1981–86; Trustee, Wessex Med. Sch. Trust, 1983–86. Manager, It makes yer fink Don't it campaign, 2002. Formerly Mem. Ct of Governors, UC Southampton, later Univ. of Southampton. Founder, S Hampshire Aviation Historical Soc., 1980. Freeman, City of London; Liveryman, Painter-Stainers' Co. *Publications:* War Prose Poems of a Young Infantry Officer; All of Life is a Learning Curve, 2003; booklets and articles on housing and political matters. *Recreations:* social history research, encouraging people to read Animal Farm again, warning people about the creeping dictatorship that is almost upon us. *Club:* Carlton.   *Died 24 July 2003.*

LOCKLEY, Ven. Harold; Archdeacon of Loughborough, 1963–86, then Archdeacon Emeritus; *b* 16 July 1916; *s* of Harry and Sarah Elizabeth Lockley; *m* 1947, Ursula Margaret, JP (*d* 1990), *d* of Rev. Dr H. Wedell and Mrs G. Wedell (*née* Bonhoeffer); three *s*. *Educ:* Loughborough Coll. (Hons Dip. Physical Educn); London Univ. (BA Hons 1937; BD Hons 1943; MTh 1949); Westcott House, Cambridge; PhD Nottingham 1955; Emmanuel Coll., Cambridge (MLitt 1990). Served War, RN, 1940–45. Chaplain and Tutor, Loughborough Coll., 1946–51; Vicar of Glen Parva and South Wigston, 1951–58; Canon Chancellor of Leicester Cathedral, 1958–63; Vicar of All Saints, Leicester, 1963–78. Postgrad. res student, Emmanuel Coll., Cambridge, 1986–88. OCF Royal Leics Regt, 1951–58; Chaplain: Leicester Royal Infirmary Maternity Hosp., 1967–74; Leics Yeomanry Assoc., 1968–; Proctor in Convocation of Canterbury, 1960–80. Sen. Examining Chaplain to Bishop of Leicester, 1951–79; part-time Lectr in Divinity, Univ. of Leicester, 1953–86; Mem., Leics Educn Cttee, 1973–85. Chm., Anglican Young People's Assoc., 1966–86. Founder Governor, Leicester Grammar Sch., 1981–. Editor, Leicester Cathedral Quarterly, 1960–63. *Publications:* Leicester Grammar School: the first ten years, 1992; Dietrich Bonhoeffer: his 'Ethics' and its value for today, 1993; numerous reviews and theological articles. *Recreations:* walking, foreign travel. *Address:* 21 Saxon Close, Market Harborough, Leics LE16 7PR. *T:* (01858) 465605. *Club:* Leicestershire (Leicester).   *Died 26 Sept. 2004.*

LOFTHOUSE, Reginald George Alfred, FRICS; Member, Advisory Committee, Centre for Agricultural Strategy, Reading University, 1980–98 (Chairman, 1982–92); Convener, 1978–88, Vice-Chairman, 1988–98, Standing Conference on Countryside Sports; *b* Workington, 30 Dec. 1916; *m* 1939, Ann Bernardine Bannan; two *d* (and one *d* decd). *Educ:* Workington Secondary Sch.; with private land agent, Cockermouth. Chartered Surveyor and Land Agent (Talbot-Ponsonby Prizeman). Asst District Officer, Penrith, 1941–42; District Officer, Carlisle, for Cumberland War Agric. Exec. Cttee, 1942–43; Asst Land Comr, West Riding, 1943–46; Land Commissioner: N and E Ridings, 1946–48; Derbys, Leics, Rutland, Northants, 1948–50; Somerset and Dorset, 1950–52; Regional Land Comr, Hdqtrs, 1952–59, and SE Region, 1959–71; Regional Officer, SE Region, Agric., Develt and Adv. Service, 1971–73; Chief Surveyor, MAFF, 1973–76. Chairman: UK Jt Shelter Res. Cttee, 1958–71; Statutory Cttee on Agricl Valuations, 1973–76. Mem., Farming and Wildlife Adv. Gp, 1966–81. Adviser to: Lord Porchester's Exmoor Study, 1977; Nature Conservancy Council, 1978–82; Council for Environmental Conservation, 1980–81. Vis. Lectr in Rural Estate Management and Forestry, Regent Street Polytechnic, 1954–62. Member: Bd of Governors, Coll. of Estate Management, 1963–85 (Chm., 1972–77; Research Fellow, 1982–85, Hon. Fellow 1985; Chm., Centre for Advanced Land Use Studies, 1972–81); Court and Council, Reading Univ., 1973–; Delegacy for Nat. Inst. for Res. in Dairying, Shinfield, 1974–80; Gen. Council, RICS, 1974–76; RICS Land Agency and Agric. Div. Council, 1974–77. Hon. Life Mem., Cambridge Univ. Land Soc.; Chm. Farm Bldgs Cttee 1973–80, Mem. Engrg and Bldgs Res. Bd 1973–80, ARC Jt Consultative Organisation. Liveryman, Loriners' Co., 1976; Freeman, City of London, 1976. *Publications:* The Berwyn Mountains Area of Wales, 1979; Some Countryside Policy Conflicts, 1997; contrib. professional, techn. and countryside jls. *Clubs:* Athenæum, MCC.

                                              Died 4 Oct. 2003.

LOGAN, Sir Douglas; *see* Logan, Sir R. D.

LOGAN, Sir (Raymond) Douglas, Kt 1983; grazier (sheep and cattle), since 1944; *b* 31 March 1920; *s* of Raymond Hough Logan and Agnes Eleanor Logan; *m*

1944, Florence Pearl McGill (MBE 1975); one *s* one *d* (and one *s* decd). *Educ:* Thornburgh College, Charters Towers. Served RAAF, 1941–44 (Flying Officer, pilot; trained EATS, Australia, 1941–42; served with 66 Sqdn RAF, 1942–44). Member: Qld Govt Beef Cttee of Enquiry, 1975–77; Qld Meat Industry Orgn and Marketing Authority (later Livestock and Meat Authority of Qld), 1978–87; United Graziers Assoc. of Qld; Cattlemen's Union, Qld. *Recreations:* tennis, horse riding, sailing, flying. *Address:* PO Box 200, Dobson Road, Malanda, Qld 4885, Australia.   *Died 20 Sept. 2003.*

LOMBINO, Salvatore Albert; *see* Hunter, E.

LONG, Olivier; ambassador; President, Graduate Institute of Public Administration, Lausanne, 1981–89; *b* 1915; *s* of Dr Edouard Long and Dr Marie Landry; *m* 1946, Francine Roels; one *s* two *d*. *Educ:* Univ. de Paris, Faculté de Droit et Ecole des Sciences Politiques; Univ. de Genève. PhD Law, 1938; Rockefeller Foundn Fellow, 1938–39; PhD Pol. Sc., 1943. Swiss Armed Forces, 1939–43; International Red Cross, 1943–46; Swiss Foreign Affairs Dept, Berne, 1946–49; Washington Embassy, 1949–54; Govt Delegate for Trade Agreements, 1955–66; Head of Swiss Delegn to EFTA, 1960–66; Ambassador to UK and Malta, 1967–68; Dir-Gen., GATT, 1968–80. Prof., Graduate Inst. of Internat. Studies, Geneva, 1962–85. Hon. Mem., Internat. Red Cross Cttee, 1985– (Mem., 1980–85). Trustee, Foundn for Internat. Conciliation, Geneva, 1984–96. *Publications:* Law and its Limitations in the GATT Multilateral Trade System, 1985; Le dossier secret des Accords d'Evian—une mission suisse pour la paix en Algérie, 1988. *Address:* 6 rue Constantin, 1206 Geneva, Switzerland.   *Died 19 March 2003.*

LONGFORD, 7th Earl of, *cr* 1785 (Ire.); **Francis Aungier Pakenham,** KG 1971; PC 1948; Baron Longford (Ire.) 1759; Baron Silchester (UK) 1821; Baron Pakenham (UK) 1945; Baron Pakenham of Cowley (Life Peer), 1999; *b* 5 Dec. 1905; 2nd *s* of 5th Earl of Longford, KP, MVO and Lady Mary Child-Villiers, 2nd *d* of 7th Earl of Jersey; *S* brother, 6th Earl of Longford, 1961; *m* 1931, Elizabeth (CBE 1974), *d* of N. B. Harman, FRCS; four *s* three *d* (and one *d* decd). *Educ:* Eton; New Coll., Oxford (1st Class in Modern Greats, 1927; MA). Tutor, University Tutorial Courses, Stoke-on-Trent, 1929–31; Cons. Party Economic Res. Dept, 1930–32; Christ Church, Oxford: Lecturer in Politics, 1932; Student in Politics, 1934–46, and 1952–64. Contested (Lab) Oxford City, 1938. Enlisted Oxford and Bucks LI (TA), May 1939; resigned commission on account of ill-health, 1940. Personal assistant to Sir William Beveridge, 1941–44; a Lord-in-Waiting to the King, 1945–46; Parliamentary Under-Secretary of State, War Office, 1946–47; Chancellor of the Duchy of Lancaster, 1947–48; Minister of Civil Aviation, 1948–51; First Lord of the Admiralty, May–Oct. 1951; Lord Privy Seal, 1964–65; Secretary of State for the Colonies, 1965–66; Leader of the House of Lords, 1964–68; Lord Privy Seal, 1966–68. Chm., The National Bank Ltd, 1955–63; Dir, Sidgwick and Jackson, 1980–85 (Chm., 1970–80). Chm., Nat. Youth Employment Council, 1968–71; Joint Founder: New Horizon Youth Centre, 1964; New Bridge for Ex-Prisoners, 1956; (also Dir) The Help Charitable Trust, 1986. *Publications:* Peace by Ordeal (The Anglo-Irish Treaty of 1921), 1935, repr. 1972; Born to Believe (autobiog.), 1953; (with Roger Opie) Causes of Crime, 1958; The Idea of Punishment, 1961; Five Lives (autobiog.), 1964; Humility, 1969; (with Thomas P. O'Neill) Eamon De Valera, 1970; The Grain of Wheat (autobiog.), 1974; Abraham Lincoln, 1974; Jesus Christ, 1974; Kennedy, 1976; St Francis of Assisi, 1978; Nixon, 1980; (with Anne McHardy) Ulster, 1981; Pope John Paul II, 1982; Diary of a Year, 1982; Eleven at No. 10: a personal view of Prime Ministers, 1984; One Man's Faith, 1984; The Search for Peace, 1985; The Bishops, 1986; Saints, 1987; A History of the House of Lords, 1989; Suffering and Hope, 1990; Punishment and the Punished, 1991; Prisoner or Patient, 1992; Young Offenders, 1993;

Avowed Intent (autobiog.), 1994; Lord Longford's Prison Diary, ed Peter Stanford, 2000. *Heir: s* Thomas Frank Dermot Pakenham, *b* 14 Aug. 1933. *Address:* Bernhurst, Hurst Green, East Sussex TN19 7QN. *T:* (01580) 860248; 18 Chesil Court, Chelsea Manor Street, SW3 5QP. *T:* (020) 7352 7794.   *Died 3 Aug. 2001.*

LONGFORD, Elizabeth, Countess of; Elizabeth Pakenham, CBE 1974; *b* 30 Aug. 1906; *d* of late N. B. Harman, FRCS, and Katherine (*née* Chamberlain); *m* 1931, Hon. F. A. Pakenham (later 7th Earl of Longford, KG, PC; he *d* 2001); four *s* three *d* (and one *d* decd). *Educ:* Headington Sch., Oxford; Lady Margaret Hall, Oxford (MA). Lectr for WEA and Univ. Extension Lectr, 1929–35. Contested (Lab) Cheltenham, 1935, Oxford, 1950; candidate for King's Norton, Birmingham, 1935–43. Mem., Rent Tribunal, Paddington and St Pancras, 1947–54; Trustee, National Portrait Gall., 1968–78; Member: Adv. Council, V&A Museum, 1969–75; Adv. Bd, British Library, 1976–80; Hon. Life Pres., Women Writers and Journalists, 1979. Hon. DLitt Sussex 1970. *Publications:* (as Elizabeth Pakenham): Points for Parents, 1956; (ed) Catholic Approaches, 1959; Jameson's Raid, 1960, new edn 1982; (as Elizabeth Longford): Victoria RI, 1964 (James Tait Black Memorial Prize for Non-Fiction, 1964); Wellington: years of the sword, 1969 (Yorkshire Post Prize); Wellington: pillar of state, 1972; The Royal House of Windsor, 1974; Churchill, 1974; Byron's Greece, 1975; Life of Byron, 1976; A Pilgrimage of Passion: the life of Wilfrid Scawen Blunt, 1979; (ed) Louisa: Lady in Waiting, 1979; Images of Chelsea, 1980; The Queen Mother, a biography, 1981; Eminent Victorian Women, 1981; Elizabeth R, 1983; The Pebbled Shore (autobiog.), 1986; The Oxford Book of Royal Anecdotes, 1989; Darling Loosy; Letters to Princess Louise 1856–1939, 1991; Wellington (abridged), 1992; Poet's Corner: an anthology, 1992; Royal Throne: the future of the Monarchy, 1993; Queen Victoria, 1999. *Recreation:* audio books. *Address:* Bernhurst, Hurst Green, East Sussex TN19 7QN. *T:* (01580) 860248.
                                                Died 23 Oct. 2002.

LONGUET-HIGGINS, Prof. Hugh Christopher, DPhil (Oxon); FRS 1958; Professor Emeritus, University of Sussex, 1989 (Royal Society Research Professor, 1974–88); *b* 11 April 1923; *e s* of late Rev. H. H. L. Longuet-Higgins. *Educ:* Winchester (schol.); Balliol Coll., Oxford (schol., MA). Research Fellow of Balliol Coll., 1946–48; Lecturer and Reader in Theoretical Chemistry, University of Manchester, 1949–52; Prof. of Theoretical Physics, King's Coll., University of London, 1952–54; FRSE; John Humphrey Plummer Professor of Theoretical Chemistry, University of Cambridge, 1954–67; Royal Soc. Res. Prof., Univ. of Edinburgh, 1968–74; Fellow of Corpus Christi Coll., 1954–67, Life Fellow 1968; Hon. Fellow: Balliol Coll., Oxford, 1969; Wolfson Coll., Cambridge, 1977. A Governor, BBC, 1979–84. Warden, Leckhampton House, 1961–67. Editor of Molecular Physics, 1958–61. For. Mem., Amer. Acad. of Arts and Scis, 1961; Foreign Associate, US National Academy of Sciences, 1968. DUniv York, 1973; DU Essex, 1981; Hon. DSc: Bristol, 1983; Sussex, 1989; Hon. DMus Sheffield, 1995. Harrison Meml Prize, Chemical Soc., 1950; Naylor Prize, London Mathematical Soc., 1981. *Publications:* co-author, The Nature of Mind (Gifford Lectures), 1972; Mental Processes, 1987; papers on theoretical physics, chemistry and biology in scientific journals. *Recreations:* music and arguing. *Address:* Department of Psychology, University of Sussex, Falmer, Brighton BN1 9QH. *T:* (01273) 677659.
                                                Died 27 March 2004.

LONSDALE, Maj.-Gen. Errol Henry Gerrard, CB 1969; MBE 1942; Transport Officer-in-Chief (Army), 1966–69; *b* 26 Feb. 1913; 2nd *s* of Rev. W. H. M. Lonsdale, Arlaw Banks, Barnard Castle; *m* 1944, Muriel Allison, *d* of E. R. Payne, Mugswell, Chipstead; one *s* one *d. Educ:* Westminster Sch.; St Catharine's Coll.,

Cambridge (BA 1934, MA 1948). 2nd Lt, RASC, 1934; Bt Lt-Col 1952; Col 1957; Brig. 1961; Maj.-Gen. 1965. Sudan Defence Force, 1938–43 (despatches); Chief Instr, RASC Officers Trng Centre, 1944–45; AQMG FARELF, 1945–47; CRASC 16 Airborne Div., 1947–48; GSOI, 1948–51; AA & QMG, War Office, 1951–53; Korea, 1953–54; Malaya, 1954–56 (despatches); ACOS, G4 Northern Army Group, 1957–60; DDST, 1st Corps, 1960–62; Comdt RASC Trng Centre, 1962–64; Inspector, RASC, 1964–65; ADC to the Queen, 1964–66; Inspector, RCT, 1965–66; psc; jssc. Col Comdt, RCT, 1969–74. Hon. Colonel: 160 Regt RCT(V), 1967–74; 562 Para Sqdn RCT(V), 1969–78. FCIT (MInstT) 1966. Vice-President: Transport Trust, 1969; Internat. Union for Modern Pentathlon and Biathlon, 1976–80; Pres., Modern Pentathlon Assoc. of Great Britain, 1977–88, Hon. Pres., 1988– (Chm., 1967); Chm., Inst. of Advanced Motorists, 1971–79, Vice-Pres., 1979. *Recreations:* modern pentathlon, photography, driving. *Address:* Windleys, Podgers Lane, Ilton, Ilminster, Somerset TA19 9HE.   *Died 3 April 2003.*

LOTHIAN, 12th Marquess of, *cr* 1701; **Peter Francis Walter Kerr,** KCVO 1983; DL; Lord Newbattle, 1591; Earl of Lothian, 1606; Baron Jedburgh, 1622; Earl of Ancram, Baron Kerr of Nisbet, Baron Long-Newton and Dolphingston, 1633; Viscount of Brien, Baron Kerr of Newbattle, 1701; Baron Ker (UK), 1821; Lord Warden of the Stannaries and Keeper of the Privy Seal of the Duke of Cornwall, 1977–83; *b* 8 Sept. 1922; *s* of late Captain Andrew William Kerr, RN, and Marie Constance Annabel, *d* of Capt. William Walter Raleigh Kerr; *S* cousin, 1940; *m* 1943, Antonella (OBE 1997), *d* of late Maj.-Gen. Sir Foster Newland, KCMG, CB, and Donna Agnese Carr; two *s* four *d. Educ:* Ampleforth; Christ Church, Oxford. Lieut, Scots Guards, 1943. Member, British Delegation: UN Gen. Assembly, 1956–57; European Parliament, 1973; UK Delegate, Council of Europe and WEU, 1959. PPS to Foreign Sec., 1960–63; a Lord in Waiting (Govt Whip, House of Lords), 1962–63, 1972–73; Jt Parly Sec., Min. of Health, April–Oct. 1964; Parly Under-Sec. of State, FCO, 1970–72. Chm., Scottish Council, BRCS, 1976–86. Mem., Queen's Body Guard for Scotland (Royal Company of Archers). Mem., Prince of Wales Council, 1976–83. DL, Roxburgh, 1962. Kt, SMO Malta. *Heir: s* Earl of Ancram, *b* 7 July 1945. *Address:* Ferniehirst Castle, Jedburgh, Roxburghshire TD8 6NX. *T:* (01835) 864021; 177 Cranmer Court, Whiteheads Grove, SW3 3HF. *Clubs:* Boodle's; New (Edinburgh).
                                                Died 11 Oct. 2004.

LOTZ, Prof. Dr Kurt; German business executive; *b* 18 Sept. 1912; *m* Elizabeth Lony; two *s* one *d. Educ:* August-Vilmar-Schule, Homberg. Joined Police Service, 1932; Lieut 1934. Served Luftwaffe (Gen. Staff; Major), 1942–45. Employed by Brown Boveri & Cie, Dortmund, 1946; Head of Business Div., Mannheim, 1954; Dir 1957; Chm. 1958–67; Mem. Board of Directors in parent company, Baden, Switzerland, 1961; Managing Director, 1963–67. Dep. Chm., 1967–68, Chm., 1968–71, Volkswagenwerk AG. Chm., Deutscher Rat für Landespflege, 1984–91 (Mem., 1973; Hon. Mem., 1991); Founder Chm., 1984–97, Hon. Chm., 1997, WWF, World Wildlife Fund, Germany. Mem., Rotary Internat. Mem., Stiftung Univ., Heidelberg; Hon. Senator, Heidelberg Univ., 1963; Hon. Prof., Technische Universität Carolo Wilhelmina, Brunswick, 1970. Dr rer. pol. *hc* Mannheim, 1963. *Publication:* Lebenserfahrungen: Worüber man in Wirtschaft und Politik auch sprechen sollte, 1978.   *Died 9 March 2005.*

LOUDOUN, Countess of (13th in line) *cr* 1633; **Barbara Huddleston Abney-Hastings;** Lady Campbell Baroness of Loudoun, 1601; Lady Tarrinzean and Mauchline, 1638; a *co-heiress* (with her sister, nephew and nieces) to the abeyant English baronies of Botreaux 1368, Stanley 1456, and Hastings 1461; *b* 3 July 1919; assumed by deed poll, 1955, the surname of Abney-Hastings in lieu of that of

Griffiths; *S* mother, 1960; *m* 1st, 1939, Capt. Walter Strickland Lord (marr. diss. 1945); one *s*; 2nd, 1945, Capt. Gilbert Frederick Greenwood (*d* 1951); one *s* one *d*; 3rd, 1954, Peter Griffiths (who assumed by deed poll the surname of Abney-Hastings in lieu of his patronymic, 1958); three *d*. *Heir: s* Lord Mauchline, *b* 22 July 1942. *Address:* Mount Walk, Ashby-de-la-Zouch, Leics LE65 1BG. *T:* (01530) 415844.   *Died 1 Nov. 2002.*

LOVE, Prof. Andrew Henry Garmany, CBE 1995; MD; FRCP, FRCPI, FMedSci; Professor of Medicine, Queen's University of Belfast, 1983–99; Director of Education, Research and Development, Royal Group of Hospitals HSS Trust, since 1996; *b* 28 Sept. 1934; *s* of Andrew and Martha Love; *m* 1963, Margaret Jean Lennox; one *s*. *Educ:* Bangor Endowed Sch., NI; Queen's Univ. of Belfast (BSc Hons 1955; MD 1963). FRCP 1973; FRCPI 1972. Lectr in Physiology, 1960–63 and Lectr in Medicine, 1963–64, QUB; MRC Travelling Fellow, and Hon. Consultant, US Naval Med. Res. Unit-2, Taipei, Taiwan, 1964–65; Queen's University, Belfast: Sen. Lectr in Medicine, 1966–73 (on leave of absence, Res. Fellow, Boston City Hosp., Mass, 1966); Prof. of Gastroenterology, 1973–83; Dean, Faculty of Medicine, 1981–86. Hon. Consultant, SEATO Cholera Labs, Pakistan, 1967–70. Mem., GMC, 1981–87; Chairman: NI Council for Postgrad. Med. and Dental Educn, 1995–99; Review Bd for Overseas Practitioners, 1995–. Pres., Assoc. of Medical Deans of Europe, 1988–91. Censor, RCP, 1996–97. Founder FMedSci 1998. FRSA 1995. *Publications:* articles in learned jls on gen. medicine, intestinal function, trace element metabolism and nutrition. *Recreations:* golf, sailing. *Address:* The Glen Farm, Carrowdore Road, Greyabbey, Co. Down BT22 2LU. *T:* (028) 4278 8414. *Clubs:* East India, Devonshire, Sports and Public Schools; Royal Ulster Yacht (Bangor, Co. Down); Royal County Down Golf (Newcastle).   *Died 3 Jan. 2001.*

LOVELL, Kenneth Ernest Walter; Treasurer to the Greater London Council, 1977–80, retired; *b* 25 Oct. 1919; *s* of Ernest John and Alice Lovell; *m* 1946, Vera Mary Pithouse; one *s* two *d*. *Educ:* Ashford County Grammar School. Mem. CIPFA. Middlesex County Council (Finance Department): Computer Manager, 1961; Asst County Treasurer, 1963; Greater London Council: Asst Treasurer, 1965; Finance Officer, ILEA, 1972. *Recreations:* gardening, cricket, hockey, photography, study of social and economic development of British Isles, study of landscape of British Isles. *Address:* 15 Meadway Close, Staines, Middx TW18 2PR. *T:* (01784) 452806.   *Died 2 Oct. 2002.*

LOVELL-DAVIS, Baron *cr* 1974 (Life Peer), of Highgate, in Greater London; **Peter Lovell Lovell-Davis;** Member: Commonwealth Development Corporation, 1978–84; London Consortium, 1978–88; *b* 8 July 1924; *s* of late William Lovell Davis and Winifred Mary Davis; *m* 1950, Jean Graham; one *s* one *d*. *Educ:* Christ's Coll., Finchley; King Edward VI Sch., Stratford-on-Avon; Jesus Coll., Oxford (BA Hons English, MA). Served War, RAF (Pilot), to Flt-Lt, 1943–47. Oxford, 1947–50. Managing Dir, Central Press Features Ltd, 1952–70; Dir, various newspaper and printing cos. Chairman: Colour Features Ltd; Davis & Harrison Ltd, 1970–73; Features Syndicate, 1971–74; Lee Cooper Licensing Services, 1983–90; Pettifor, Morrow & Associates, 1986–98. Mem., Islington DHA, 1982–85. A Lord in Waiting (Govt Whip), 1974–75; Parly Under-Sec. of State, Dept of Energy, 1975–76. Adviser to various Govt Cttees, Health Educn Council, Labour Party and Govt, on media. Vice-Pres., YHA, 1978–; Trustee, Whittington Hosp. Academic Centre, 1980–. *Recreations:* industrial archaeology, inland waterways, bird-watching, walking, sketching. *Address:* 80 North Road, Highgate, N6 4AA. *T:* (020) 8348 3919.   *Died 6 Jan. 2001.*

LOWE, Prof. Gordon, FRS 1984; CChem, FRSC; Professor of Biological Chemistry, University of Oxford, 1989–2000; Fellow, Lincoln College, Oxford, since 1962

(Tutor, 1962–99); *b* 31 May 1933; *s* of Harry Lowe and Ethel (*née* Ibbetson); *m* 1956, Gwynneth Hunter; two *s*. *Educ:* Imperial Coll. of Science and Technol., Univ. of London (Governors Prize and Edmund White Prize, 1954; Edmund White Prize, 1957; BSc , ARCS 1954; PhD, DIC 1957); MA 1960, DSc 1985, Oxon. CChem, FRSC 1981. University of Oxford: Pressed Steel Res. Fellow, 1957–59; Deptl Demonstrator, 1959–65; Weir Jun. Res. Fellow, University Coll., 1959–61; Lectr, Organic Chemistry, 1965–88; Aldrichian Praelector in Chemistry, 1988–89; Sub-Rector, Lincoln Coll., 1986–89. Irvine Lectr, Univ. of St Andrews, 1984; Upper Rhine Lectr, Univs of Basle, Mulhouse, Strasbourg, Freiburg and Karlsruhe, 1989; Liversidge Lectr, Univ. of Sydney, 1990. Dir and Founder, Pharminox Ltd, 2002. Member: Biochemistry and Biophysics Cttee, SERC, 1979–82; Molecular Enzymology Cttee, Biochemical Soc., 1978–84; Editorial Adv. Panel, Biochemical Jl, 1981–99; Editorial Bd, Bio-organic Chemistry, 1983–2001. FRSA 1986. Charmian Medal, 1983, Stereochemistry Medal, 1992, RSC. *Publications:* reports on the cysteine proteinases, β-Lactam antibiotics, chiral phosphate and sulphate esters, antitumour and antimalarial agents, and combinatorial chemistry; articles in primary chemical and biochemical jls. *Address:* 17 Norman Avenue, Abingdon, Oxon OX14 2HQ. *T:* (01235) 523029.   *Died 6 Aug. 2003.*

LOWE, Dr John; Head, Country Educational Policy Reviews, Education and Training Division, OECD, 1973–87; *b* 3 Aug. 1922; *s* of John Lowe and Ellen (*née* Webb); *m* 1949, Margaret James (*d* 1982); two *s* one *d*. *Educ:* Univ. of Liverpool (BA Hons 1950); Univ. of London (CertEd 1951, PhD 1960). Served War of 1939–45 and Control Commn for Germany, 1945–47 (Captain). Lectr, subseq. Sen. Lectr, Univ. of Liverpool, 1955–63; Dir, Extra-Mural Studies, Univ. of Singapore, 1963–64; Dir, Dept of Adult Educn and Extra-Mural Studies, subsequently Head, Dept of Educnl Studies, Univ. of Edinburgh, 1964–72; Consultant in field, 1964–. Sec./Treas., Internat. Congress of Univ. Adult Educn, 1972–76. Hon. Prof., Warwick Univ., 1990–2000. *Publications:* On Teaching Foreign Languages to Adults (ed jtly), 1965; Adult Education in England and Wales, 1970; (ed) Adult Education and Nation-Building, 1970; (ed) Education and Nation-Building in the Third World, 1971; The Education of Adults: a world perspective, 1975, rev. edn, 1982; (ed) The Clanricarde Letter Book, 1983; Compulsory Schooling in a Changing World, 1983; (jtly) Schools and Quality, 1989; (jtly) Reviews of National Policies for Education: Ireland, 1991; Educational Trends and Prospects in OECD Countries, 1991; The Pursuit of Literacy, 1997; articles in educnl and hist. jls. *Recreations:* reading, music. *Address:* 3 Rue Ribera, 75016 Paris, France. *T:* 45202515.   *Died 7 July 2003.*

LOWREY, Air Comdt Dame Alice, DBE 1960; RRC 1954; Matron-in-Chief, Princess Mary's Royal Air Force Nursing Service, 1959–63, retired; *b* 8 April 1905; *d* of William John Lowrey and Agnes Lowrey (formerly Walters). *Educ:* Yorkshire; Training Sch., Sheffield Royal Hospital. Joined PMRAFNS, 1932; served in Iraq and Aden; Principal Matron: HQ, MEAF and FEAF, 1956–58; HQ, Home Command and Technical Training Command, 1958–59. Air Commandant, 1959. Officer Sister Order of St John, 1959. *Address:* c/o BUPA, Oakwood House Nursing Home, Norwich, Norfolk.   *Died 19 May 2001.*

LOWRY, Sir John Patrick, (Sir Pat), Kt 1985; CBE 1978; President, Institute of Personnel Management, 1987–89; *b* 31 March 1920; *s* of John McArdle Lowry and Edith Mary Lowry; *m* 1952, Sheilagh Mary Davies; one *s* one *d*. *Educ:* Wyggeston Grammar Sch., Leicester; London Sch. of Economics (evening student; BCom); CIPD, CIMgt. Statistical Clerk, Engineering Employers' Fedn, 1938; served Army, 1939–46; various posts in EEF, 1946–70, Dir 1965–70; Dir of Industrial Relations, British Leyland Motor Corp., 1970, Board Dir 1972; Dir of

Personnel, 1975–77, of Personnel and Admin, 1977–78, of Personnel and External Affairs, 1978–81, British Leyland Ltd. Chairman: ACAS, 1981–87; Nat. Jt Council for Engineering Construction Industry, 1987–; Univs Academic Salaries Cttee, 1987–. Hon. Prof., Sch. of Industrial and Business Studies, Warwick Univ., 1983. Member: UK Employers' Delegn, ILO, 1962, 1963, 1967; Court of Inquiry, Barbican and Horseferry Road Building Disputes, 1967; Court of Inquiry, Grunwick Dispute, 1977. Pres., Inst. of Supervisory Management, 1972–74. FRSA 1984. Hon. LLD Leicester, 1984; Hon. Dr Middlesex, 1994. *Recreation:* travel. *Address:* 18 Chapman Square, Wimbledon Parkside, SW19 5QR. *T:* (020) 8946 3893.   *Died 30 May 2001.*

LOWRY, Sir Pat; see Lowry, Sir J. P.

LOWRY, His Honour Richard John; QC 1968; a Circuit Judge, 1977–95; *b* 23 June 1924; *s* of late Geoffrey Charles Lowry, OBE, TD, and Margaret Spencer Lowry; *m* 1963, Her Honour Noreen Margaret Lowry; one *d*. *Educ:* St Edward's Sch.; University College, Oxford (BA 1948, MA 1949). RAF, 1943; qualified as pilot and commnd, 1944; No 228 Group Staff Officer, India, 1945; Flt-Lieut, 1946; University College, Oxford, 1942–43 and 1946–48. Called to the Bar, Inner Temple, 1949; Bencher 1977. Member, General Council of the Bar, 1965–69. Dep. Chm., Herts QS, 1968; a Recorder, 1972–77. Mem., Home Office Adv. Council on Penal System, 1972–78. Freeman, City of London, 1983. *Recreations:* theatre, swimming, fossicking; formerly rowing. *Clubs:* Garrick, Royal Automobile (Steward); Leander (Henley-on-Thames).   *Died 17 Sept. 2001.*

LOYD, His Honour John Anthony Thomas; QC 1981; a Circuit Judge, assigned to Official Referees' business, London, 1990–97; *b* 18 July 1933; *e s* of Leslie William Loyd and Joan Louisa Loyd; *m* 1963, Rosaleen Iona Ward; one *d* (and one *d* decd). *Educ:* Wycliffe Coll.; Gonville and Caius Coll., Cambridge (BA 1956, MA 1959). RAF Regt, 1951–53. Called to the Bar, Gray's Inn, 1958, Bencher, 1994; a Recorder, 1985–90. *Recreation:* viticulture. *Address:* 31 Swan Street, Boxford, Suffolk CO10 5NZ; Segos, 46800 Le Boulvé, France.   *Died 1 May 2002.*

LOYDEN, Edward; *b* 3 May 1923; *s* of Patrick and Mary Loyden; *m* 1944, Rose Ann Boyle (*d* 1986); one *s* two *d* (and one *d* decd). *Educ:* Friary RC Elem. School. Shop boy, margarine factory, 1937; Able-Seaman, MN, 1938–46; Seaman Port Worker, Mersey Docks & Harbour Co., 1946–74. Transport and General Workers' Union: Shop Steward, 1954; Branch Chm. 1959; Mem. District Cttee, Docks and Waterways, 1967; Mem. Nat. Cttee, 1968; Chm., Parly Gp of MPs, 1991–97. Member: Liverpool City Council, 1960 (Dep. Leader, 1983); Liverpool District Council, 1973; Merseyside Met. CC, 1973; Liverpool Met. Dist Council (St Mary's Ward), 1980–83. MP (Lab) Liverpool, Garston, Feb. 1974–1979 and 1983–97. Member: PLP Transport Cttee, 1983–97; For. Affairs Cttee, 1983–97; Health Cttee, 1983–97. President: Liverpool Trades Council, 1967; Merseyside Trades Council, 1974. *Recreations:* full-time political. *Clubs:* Gillmoss Labour, Woolton Labour.
                                                          Died 27 April 2003.

LUCAS OF CHILWORTH, 2nd Baron *cr* 1946, of Chilworth; **Michael William George Lucas;** *b* 26 April 1926; *er s* of 1st Baron and Sonia (*d* 1979), *d* of Marcus Finkelstein, Libau, Latvia; *S* father, 1967; *m* 1st, 1955, Ann-Marie (marr. diss. 1989), *o d* of Ronald Buck, Southampton; two *s* one *d*; 2nd, 1998, Jill Mary MacKean. *Educ:* Peter Symond's Sch., Winchester; Luton Technical Coll. Served with Royal Tank Regt. A Lord in Waiting (Govt Whip), 1983–84; Parly Under-Sec. of State, DTI, 1984–87. Mem., House of Lords Select Cttee on Science and Technol., 1980–83, on European Communities, 1988–94; UK deleg., N Atlantic Assembly, 1981–83, 1988–98. TEng(CEI); FIMI (Mem. Council, 1972–76; Vice Pres., 1993–); FInstTA; LAE. President: League of

Safe Drivers, 1976–80; Inst. of Transport Administration, 1980–83; Vice-Pres., RoSPA, 1980; Mem., Public Policy Cttee, RAC, 1981–83, 1988–98. Governor, Churcher's Coll., Petersfield, 1985–96. Hon. FIHT. *Heir: s* Hon. Simon William Lucas, late Capt. RE [*b* 6 Feb. 1957; *m* 1993, Fiona, *yr d* of Thomas Mackintosh, Vancouver. *Educ:* Churcher's Coll., Petersfield; Leicester Univ. (BSc). Geophysicist, Canada].   *Died 10 Nov. 2001.*

LUCAS, Sir Cyril (Edward), Kt 1976; CMG 1956; FRS 1966; Director of Fisheries Research, Scotland (Department of Agriculture and Fisheries for Scotland) and Director Marine Laboratory Aberdeen, 1948–70; *b* Hull, Yorks, 30 July 1909; *o s* of late Archibald and Edith Lucas, Hull; *m* 1934, Sarah Agnes (*d* 1974), *o d* of late Henry Alfred and Amy Rose; two *s* one *d*. *Educ:* Grammar Sch., Hull; University Coll., Hull; BSc (London) 1931, DSc (London) 1942. Research Biologist, University Coll., Hull, 1931; Head of Dept of Oceanography, University Coll., Hull, 1942. UK Expert or Delegate to various internat. confs on Marine Fisheries and Conservation, 1948–80, and Chm. of research cttees in connexion with these; Chm., Consultative and Liaison Cttees, Internat. Council for Exploration of Sea, 1962–67; Member: Adv. Cttee on Marine Resources Research, FAO, 1964–71 (Chm. 1966–71); Council for Scientific Policy, 1968–70; Nat. Environmental Res. Council, 1970–78. FRSE 1939 (Vice-Pres., 1962–64; Neill Prize, 1960). Hon. DSc Hull, 1975; Hon. LLD Aberdeen, 1977. *Publications:* various scientific, particularly on marine plankton and fisheries research in Bulletins of Marine Ecology (Joint Editor), Jl of Marine Biological Assoc., etc and various international jls. *Address:* 16 Albert Terrace, Aberdeen AB10 1XY. *T:* (01224) 645568.   *Died 12 Jan. 2002.*

LUNS, Dr Joseph Marie Antoine Hubert, Hon. GCMG; Hon. CH 1971; Officer, Order of Orange-Nassau, 1947; Knight Grand Cross, Order of the Netherlands Lion, 1971; Secretary-General of NATO, 1971–84; *b* 28 Aug. 1911; *m* Baroness E. C. van Heemstra (*d* 1990); one *s* one *d*. *Educ:* sec. schs, Amsterdam and Brussels; universities of Leyden, Amsterdam, London and Berlin. Attaché of Legation, 1938; 2nd Sec., 1942; 1st Sec., 1945; Counsellor, 1949. Served in: Min. for For. Affairs, 1938–40; Berne, 1940–41; Lisbon, 1941–43; London, at Netherlands Min. for For. Affairs, 1943–44, and at Netherlands Embassy, 1944–49; Netherlands Delegn to UN, NY, 1942–52; Minister of Foreign Affairs, The Netherlands, 1952–71. MP (Second Chamber, Netherlands), July-Oct. 1956 and March-June 1959. Hon. Fellow, London Sch. of Economics, 1969. Hon. DCL: Harvard, 1970; Oxon, 1972; Exeter, 1974; Dr Humanities, Hope Coll., USA, 1974. Prix Charlemagne, Aachen, 1967; Gustav Stresemann Medal, 1968. Holds numerous foreign orders. *Publications:* The Epic of The Royal Netherlands Navy; articles on Royal Netherlands Navy in Dutch and foreign jls, and articles on international affairs in International Affairs, La Revue Politique, and others. *Recreation:* swimming. *Address:* 117 Avenue Franklin Roosevelt, 1050 Brussels, Belgium. *Clubs:* Reform (Hon. Mem.); Haagsche, De Witte (Netherlands).
                                                          Died 17 July 2002.

LUNT, Maj.-Gen. James Doiran, CBE 1964 (OBE 1958); FRGS; FRHistS; Domestic Bursar, and Fellow, Wadham College, Oxford, 1973–83, then Emeritus Fellow; *b* 13 Nov. 1917; *s* of late Brig. W. T. Lunt, MBE, Camberley, Surrey; *m* 1940, Muriel, *d* of late A. H. Byrt, CBE, Bournemouth; one *s* one *d*. *Educ:* King William's Coll., IOM; RMC, Sandhurst; MA Oxon. 2nd Lieut, Duke of Wellington's Regt, 1937; served with 4th Bn Burma Rifles, 1939–41; Burma Campaign, 1942; transf. to 16/5th Queen's Royal Lancers, 1949; served with Arab Legion, 1952–55; comd 16/5th Queen's Royal Lancers, 1957–59; comd Federal Regular Army, Aden, 1961–64; Dir of Admin. Planning (Army), MoD, 1964–66; Defence Adviser to British High Commissioner, India, 1966–68; Chief of Staff, Contingencies Planning, SHAPE, 1969–70;

Vice-Adjt-Gen., MoD, 1970–72; Col, 16th/5th The Queen's Royal Lancers, 1975–80. Order of Independence (Jordan), 1956; Commander, Order of South Arabia, 1964. *Publications:* Charge to Glory, 1961; Scarlet Lancer, 1964; The Barren Rocks of Aden, 1966; Bokhara Burnes, 1969; From Sepoy to Subedar, 1970; The Duke of Wellington's Regiment, 1971; 16th/5th The Queen's Royal Lancers, 1973; John Burgoyne of Saratoga, 1975; Imperial Sunset, 1981; Glubb Pasha, 1984; A Hell of a Licking: the retreat from Burma 1941–42, 1986; Hussein of Jordan, 1989; The Scarlet Lancers, 1993; Jai Sixth!: story of the 6th Gurkha Rifles, 1994; The Arab Legion, 1999. *Recreations:* fly fishing, writing. *Address:* 2 Garden Court, Sutton Manor, Sutton Scotney, Hants SO21 3JX. *T:* (01962) 761308. *Clubs:* Cavalry and Guards, Flyfishers'.
Died 1 Oct. 2001.

LYALL, Gavin Tudor; author; *b* 9 May 1932; *s* of J. T. and A. A. Lyall; *m* 1958, Katharine E. Whitehorn; two *s*. *Educ:* King Edward VI Sch., Birmingham; Pembroke Coll., Cambridge (BA 1956, MA 1958). RAF, 1951–53 (Pilot Officer, 1952). Journalist with: Picture Post, 1956–57; BBC, 1958–59; Sunday Times, 1959–63. Hon. Consultant, Air Transport Users' Cttee, CAA, 1985–94 (Mem., 1979–85); Mem., Air Travel Trust Cttee, 1986–2000. *Publications:* The Wrong Side of the Sky, 1961; The Most Dangerous Game, 1964; Midnight Plus One, 1965; Shooting Script, 1966; (ed) Freedom's Battle: the RAF in World War II, 1968; Venus with Pistol, 1969; Blame the Dead, 1972; Judas Country, 1975; Operation Warboard, 1976; The Secret Servant, 1980 (televised, 1984); The Conduct of Major Maxim, 1982; The Crocus List, 1985; Uncle Target, 1988; Spy's Honour, 1993; Flight From Honour, 1996; All Honourable Men, 1997; Honourable Intentions, 1999. *Recreations:* cooking, military history, model making. *Address:* 14 Provost Road, NW3 4ST. *T:* (020) 7722 2308. *Clubs:* Royal Air Force, Detection.
Died 18 Jan. 2003.

LYALL, William Chalmers, MBE 1952; HM Diplomatic Service, retired; *b* 6 Aug. 1921; *s* of John Brown Lyall and Margaret Angus Leighton Stevenson Lyall; *m* 1948, Janet Lawson McKechnie; two *s* one *d*. *Educ:* Kelty Public Sch.; Beath Secondary Sch. Min. of Labour, 1940–48; served War, HM Forces, 1941–47; FO, 1948; Hankow, 1948–51; São Paulo, 1952–53; Manila, 1953–55; FO, 1955–57; Caracas, 1957–60; Bahrain, 1960–64; FO, 1964–65; DSAO, 1965–68; FCO, 1968–69; Consul-Gen., Genoa, 1969–73; FCO, 1973; Counsellor (Administration), Bonn, 1974–78. *Recreations:* music, photography.
Died 3 July 2004.

LYLE, Lt-Col (Archibald) Michael, OBE 1994; JP; Vice Lord-Lieutenant, Perth and Kinross, 1984–95; farmer and landowner; *b* 1 May 1919; 3rd *s* of Col Sir Archibald Lyle, 2nd Bt, MC, TD and Dorothy, *e d* of Sir James de Hoghton, 11th Bt; *m* 1942, Hon. Elizabeth Sinclair (*d* 1994), *yr d* of 1st Viscount Thurso, KT, CMG, PC; three *d* (and one *d* decd). *Educ:* Eton College; Trinity College, Oxford (BA, MA). Hon. Attaché, Rome, 1938–39; served 1939–45 with The Black Watch, RHR (wounded Normandy, 1944 and discharged, 1945); Lt-Col, The Scottish Horse RAC (TA), 1953–56. Chm., T&AFA, 1959–64. Mem., Royal Company of Archers, Queen's Body Guard for Scotland. Member: Perth and Kinross CC, 1946–74; Tayside Regional Council, 1974–79. Chm., Perth Coll. of Further Educn, 1978–91. JP Perth, 1950; DL Perthshire, 1961. *Recreations:* fishing, shooting, music. *Address:* Riemore Lodge, Dunkeld, Perthshire PH8 0HP. *T:* (01350) 724205. *Clubs:* Brooks's, MCC; Puffin's (Edinburgh).
Died 3 Jan. 2001.

LYLE, Lt-Col Michael; see Lyle, Lt-Col A.M.

LYMPANY, Dame Moura, DBE 1992 (CBE 1979); FRAM; FRCM; concert pianist; *b* Saltash, Cornwall, 18 Aug. 1916; British (*née* Mary Johnstone); *d* of John and Beatrice Johnstone; *m* 1944, Lt-Col Colin Defries (marr. diss. 1950); *m* 1951, Bennet H. Korn, American television

executive (marr. diss. 1961); one *s* decd. *Educ:* Belgium, Austria, England. FRAM 1948; FRCM 1995. Has made many recordings. First public performance at age of 12, 1929, at Harrogate, playing Mendelssohn G Minor Concerto. Won second prize out of 79 competitors at Ysaye Internat. Pianoforte Competition at Brussels, 1938. Has played in USA, Canada, South America, Australia, New Zealand, India, and all principal European countries. Commander of the Order of the Crown (Belgium), 1980; Medal of Cultural Merit (Portugal), 1989; Chevalier, Ordre des Arts et des Lettres (France), 1992; Order of Prince Henry the Navigator (Portugal), 1996. *Publication:* Moura Lympany: her autobiography, 1991. *Recreations:* gardening, tapestry, reading.
Died 28 March 2005.

LYNCH, Martin Patrick James; Under Secretary, Overseas Development Administration, Foreign and Commonwealth Office, 1975–83, retired; Secretary, UK Inter Professional Group, 1995–99; *b* 4 June 1924; 2nd *s* of late Frederick Lynch, DSM, and late Elizabeth Yeatman; *m* 1959, Anne, *d* of late Major Gerald McGorty, MC, RAMC; two *s* one *d* (and one *s* decd). *Educ:* London Oratory School; BA Hons London. RAF, 1942–49; Exec. Officer, HM Treasury, 1950; Asst Private Sec. to Financial Sec., 1953–54; Private Sec. to Minister Without Portfolio, 1954–55; Principal, 1958; Asst Sec., Min. of Overseas Develt, 1966 and 1971–75; Counsellor, UK Treasury and Supply Delegn, Washington, and UK Alternate Dir, World Bank, 1967–71. Asst Sec. (Admin), 1984–87; Project Manager, 1993–99, Hon. Mem., 1997, Coll. of Optometrists (formerly British Coll of Ophthalmic Opticians); Asst to Gen. Optical Council, 1989–94. Mem. Council, Assoc. for Latin Liturgy, 1973–92 (Chm., 1976–88). *Publications:* (contrib.) A Voice for All Time, 1993; The College of Optometrists: a history 1980–98, 1999. *Address:* Hillside, Combe Hill, Combe St Nicholas, Chard, Somerset TA20 3NW. *T:* (01460) 65029. *Club:* Reform.
Died 15 Dec. 2001.

LYNCH, Patrick, MA; MRIA; Professor of Political Economy (Applied Economics), University College, Dublin, 1975–80, then Emeritus; *b* 5 May 1917; *s* of Daniel and Brigid Lynch, Co. Tipperary and Dublin; *m* 1st, 1965, Mary Crotty (*née* Campbell), MA (*d* 1982); 2nd, 1991, Mary Moloney. *Educ:* University Coll., Dublin. Fellow Commoner, Peterhouse, Cambridge, 1956. Entered Irish Civil Service, 1941; Asst Sec. to Govt; 1950; Univ. Lectr in Econs, UC Dublin, 1952, Associate Prof., 1966–75. Chm., Aer Lingus, 1954–75; Jt Dep. Chm., Allied Irish Banks, 1976–84. Has acted as economic consultant to OECD, Council of Europe, Dept of Finance, Dublin, Gulbenkian Inst., Lisbon. Directed surveys sponsored by Irish Govt with OECD into long-term Irish educnl needs, 1965, and into requirements of Irish economy in respect of scientific res., develt and technology, 1966; estab. Science Policy Res. Centre in Dept of Applied Econs, UC Dublin, 1969. Mem., various Irish Govt Commns and Cttees, 1952–; Member: Club of Rome, 1973; EEC Economic and Monetary Union 1980 Group, 1974; Nat. Science Council, 1968–78; Higher Educn Authority, 1968–72; Nat. Economic and Social Council, 1973–76; European Science Foundn, 1974–77; Chairman: Medico-Social Research Board, 1966–72; Public Service Adv. Council, 1973–77; Exec. Cttee, Econ. and Social Res. Inst., 1983–88; Editl Bd, Economic and Social Review; Mem. Editorial Bd, University Review. Chm., Nat. Library of Ireland Soc., 1969–72; Chm., Irish Anti-Apartheid Movement, 1972; Member: Irish Assoc. for Civil Liberty; Movement for Peace in Ireland. Chm., Inst. of Public Administration, 1973–77. Member: Governing Body UC Dublin, 1963–75; Senate NUI, 1972–77; Treasurer, RIA, 1972–80. Hon. FTCD 1995. DUniv Brunel, 1976; Hon. LLD: Dublin, 1979; NCEA 2000; Hon. DEconSc: NUI, 1985; Limerick, 1994. *Publications:* Planning for Economic Development in Ireland, 1959; (with J. Vaizey) Guinness's Brewery in the Irish Economy, 1960; (jtly) Economics of Educational Costing, 1969; (with Brian Hillery) Ireland in the

International Labour Organisation, 1969; (with B. Chubb) Economic Development Planning, 1969; Whither Science Policy, 1980; (ed with J. Meenan) Essays in Memory of Alexis Fitzgerald, 1987; (contrib.) Essays in memory of Dáithé Ó h-Uaithe, 1994; essays in various symposia, etc; articles in Administration, The Bell, Encycl. Britannica, Econ. History Review, Irish Hist. Studies, Irish Jl of Educn, Statist, Studies, University Review, etc. *Address:* 79 Wellington Road, Dublin 4, Ireland.

Died 16 Oct. 2001.

LYONS, Sir James (Reginald), Kt 1969; Airport Manager, Cardiff Airport, 1955–75; *b* 15 March 1910; *s* of James Lyons and Hilda (*née* Driscoll); *m* 1937, Doreen Mary Fogg; one *s*. *Educ:* Howard Gardens High Sch.; Cardiff Technical Coll. Served War of 1939–45: Royal Tank Regt, 1940–46 (1939–45 Star, Africa Star, Italy Star, Defence Medal, War Medal of 1939–45). Civil Service, 1929–65: Post Office, Min. of Supply, Min. of Aviation. Chm., Park Lodge Property Co., till 1997. Mem., Wales Tourist Bd. Cardiff City Council: Councillor, 1949–58; Alderman, 1958–74; Lord Mayor of Cardiff, 1968–69; Mem., Glamorgan CC, 1965–74. Mem., Norfolk Cttee for investiture of Prince of Wales, 1968–69. Former Mem., BBC Broadcasting Council. Assessor under Race Relations Act, 1976. President: Welsh Games Council, 1985– (Life Vice-Pres., 1975); Cardiff Horticultural Soc., 1962–. Former Trustee, Wales and Border Counties TSB. Chairman of Governors: UC Cardiff, 1955–70; St Illtyd's Coll., 1956–86; Governor, De La Salle Prep. Sch., 1966–86. JP Cardiff, 1966–82. OStJ; KCSG. *Recreations:* Rugby football, swimming, tennis.

Died 22 Sept. 2004.

LYTHALL, Basil Wilfrid, CB 1966; Director, SACLANT Anti-Submarine Warfare Research Centre, La Spezia, Italy, 1978–81; *b* 15 May 1919; *s* of Frank Herbert Lythall and Winifred Mary (*née* Carver); *m* 1942, Mary Olwen Dando (*d* 1998); one *s*. *Educ:* King Edward's Sch., Stourbridge; Christ Church, Oxford (MA). Joined Royal Naval Scientific Service, 1940; Admiralty Signal and Radar Establishment, 1940–53; Admiralty Research Laboratory, 1954–57; Asst Dir of Physical Research, Admty, 1957–58;

a Dep. Chief Scientist, Admty Signal and Radar Estabt (later Admty Surface Weapons Estabt), 1958–60; first Chief Scientist of Admty Underwater Weapons Estabt, Portland, 1960–64; Member of Admiralty Bd of Defence Council and Chief Scientist (Royal Navy), 1964–78; Dep. Controller, R&D Estab., Procurement Exec., 1971–78. Chm., Policy Bd, Centre for Operational Res. and Defence Analysis, CAP Scientific Ltd, 1986–88. Technical Advr, Monopolies and Mergers Commn, 1989, 1990. Trustee, National Maritime Museum, 1974–80. UK Mem., Editorial Bd, Naval Forces, 1986–. *Publications:* occasional articles in learned jls. *Recreations:* gardening, sculpting, genealogy. *Address:* 48 Grove Way, Esher, Surrey KT10 8HL. *T:* (020) 8398 2958.

Died 22 Sept. 2001.

LYTHGO, Wilbur Reginald, OBE 1964; HM Diplomatic Service, retired; *b* 7 June 1920; *yr s* of late Alfred and Marion Lythgo, Monkton, Ayrshire; *m* 1943, Patricia Frances Sylvia Smith; two *s*. *Educ:* Palmer's Sch., Grays, Essex. Joined Home Office, 1937. Served in RASC, 1939–41 and Indian Army, 1941–46. Rejoined Home Office, 1946; British Information Services, New Delhi, 1948–54; UK High Commn, New Delhi, 1956–59; British High Commn, Ottawa, 1962–66; Head of Office Services and Supply Dept, DSAO, 1966–68; Counsellor, British Embassy, and Consul-Gen., Washington DC, 1968–71; Consul-Gen., Cleveland, Ohio, 1971–73. Hon. Kentucky Col, 1971. *Recreations:* reading, gardening. *Address:* 200 Dovercourt Avenue, Ottawa, ON K1Z 7H2, Canada. *T:* (613) 7223242. *Died 17 Jan. 2002.*

LYTLE, Maj.-Gen. Simon William St John, CB 1995; DL; Director, Army Sport Control Board, since 1995; *b* 1 Oct. 1940; *s* of Dr W. D. F., (Bobby), Lytle, and Anne M. E. Lytle; *m* 1966, Pamela Mary O'Ferrall; three *s*. *Educ:* Sherborne; RMA Sandhurst. Commnd RIrF, 1960; transf. AAC, 1969; Staff Coll., Camberley, 1973; CO 1 Regt AAC, 1980–83; MoD, 1984–87; Comd Avn, BAOR, 1987–89; RCDS, 1989; Director: Army Recruiting, 1990–92; AAC, then Army Aviation, 1992–95. DL Hampshire, 1996. *Recreations:* sailing, bridge, tennis. *Clubs:* MCC; Leckford Golf.

Died 17 Oct. 2004.

M

McAVOY, Sir (Francis) Joseph, Kt 1976; CBE 1969; Chairman: Queensland and Australian Canegrowers Councils, 1963–82 (Member, 1952–82); Australian Canegrowers Council, 1952–82; *b* 26 Feb. 1910; *s* of William Henry McAvoy and Hanorah Catherine McAvoy; *m* 1936, Mary Irene Doolan; four *s* (one *d* decd). *Educ:* Nudgee Coll., Brisbane; Sacred Heart Convent, Innisfail, Qld. Member: Goondi Mill Suppliers Cttee, 1947–82; Innisfail Canegrowers Exec., 1949–82; Metric Conversion Bd (Aust.), 1970–78; Aust. Immigration Adv. Council, 1964–72; Exec. Council of Agriculture, 1963–82; Exec., Aust. Farmers Fedn, 1969–77, Nat. Farmers Fedn, 1977–82. Vice-Pres., Internat. Fedn of Agricultural Producers, 1968–74. Paul Harris Fellow, Rotary Internat., USA, 1986. *Recreation:* lawn bowls. *Address:* PO Box 95, Innisfail, Qld 4860, Australia. *Clubs:* Rotary, IDB (Innisfail, Qld).   *Died 6 July 2002.*

McBAIN, Ed; *see* Hunter, Evan.

McBRIDE, Commandant (Sara) Vonla (Adair), CB 1979; Director, City of London Region, Lloyds Bank Ltd, 1980–91; a Chairman, Civil Service Commissioners' Interview Panel, 1985–91; *b* 20 Jan. 1921; *d* of late Andrew Stewart McBride and Agnes McBride. *Educ:* Ballymena Acad., NI; TCD (Moderatorship in Mod. Lit.; BA Hons). Teacher of English and French, Ballymena Acad., 1942–45; Housemistress, Gardenhurst Sch., Burnham-on-Sea, Somerset, 1945–49. Dir, WRNS, 1976–79 (joined 1949); Hon. ADC to the Queen, 1976–79. Vice-President: Ex Services Mental Welfare Soc., 1983–; Officers' Pension Soc., 1989–96; RNLI, 1992–. Freeman, City of London, 1978; Liveryman, Shipwrights' Co., 1983. *Publication:* Never at Sea (autobiog.), 1966. *Recreations:* golf, theatre entertaining, continental travel. *Address:* c/o 10 Shady Bower, Salisbury, Wilts SP1 2RG. *Clubs:* Army and Navy, Naval.   *Died 2 Aug. 2003.*

McBRIDE, Vonla; *see* McBride, S. V. A.

McCALL, Sir (Charles) Patrick (Home), Kt 1971; MBE 1944; TD 1946; solicitor; Clerk of the County Council, 1960–72, Clerk of the Peace, 1960–71, and Clerk of the Lieutenancy, Lancashire, 1960–74; *b* 22 Nov. 1910; *s* of late Charles and Dorothy McCall; *m* 1944, Anne (*d* 1991), *d* of late Samuel Brown, Sedlescombe, Sussex; two *s* one *d*. *Educ:* St Edward's Sch., Oxford. Served 1939–45; Substantive Major TA. Hon. Lt-Col. Mem., Economic and Social Cttee, EEC, 1973–78. *Address:* 211–6085 Uplands Drive, Nanaimo, BC V9V IT8, Canada.
       Died 29 Aug. 2002.

McCALL, Sir Patrick; *see* McCall, Sir C. P. H.

MAC CANA, Prof. Proinsias; Senior Professor, School of Celtic Studies, Dublin Institute for Advanced Studies, 1985–96, then Senior Professor Emeritus; *b* 6 July 1926; *s* of George Mc Cann and Mary Catherine Mallon; *m* 1952, Réiltín (*née* Supple); one *s* one *d*. *Educ:* St Malachy's Coll., Belfast; The Queen's Univ., Belfast (BA, MA, PhD); Ecole des Hautes Etudes, Paris. Asst Lectr, Celtic Dept, QUB, 1951–54; University College Wales, Aberystwyth: Asst Lectr in Early Irish, 1955–57; Lectr, 1957–61; Prof., Sch. of Celtic Studies, Dublin Inst. for Advanced Studies, 1961–63; Prof. of Welsh, 1963–71, Prof. of Early (incl. Medieval) Irish, 1971–85, UC Dublin. Prof. of Celtic Langs and Lits (Fall semester), Harvard Univ., 1987–92. Mem., Irish Placenames Commn, 1975–2003. Co-editor, Ériu (RIA Jl of Irish Studies), 1973–; General editor, Medieval and Modern Welsh Series, Dublin Inst. for Advanced Studies, 1962–; Chairman, Editorial Board: Dictionary of Medieval Latin in Celtic Countries, 1981–; Dictionary of Irish Biography, 1985–. Chm., Governing Bd, Sch. of Celtic Studies, Dublin Inst. for Advanced Studies, 1975–85; Mem., Bd of Mgt, Centre culturel Irlandais, Paris, 2002–. PRIA, 1979–82. Mem., Academia Europaea, 1989. Foreign Hon. Member: Amer. Acad. Arts and Scis, 1989; Royal Gustavus Adolphus Acad., Sweden, 1994. Hon. LittD Dublin, 1985; Hon. DLitt: Ulster, 1991; Wales, 1995. *Publications:* Scéalaíocht na Ríthe (collection of early Irish tales trans. into Modern Irish), 1956; Branwen Daughter of Llŷr: the second branch of the Mabinogi, 1958; Celtic Mythology, 1970; The Mabinogi, 1977; Regnum and Sacerdotium: notes on Irish Tradition (Rhŷs Meml Lecture, British Academy), 1979; The Learned Tales of Medieval Ireland, 1980; (ed jtly) Rencontres de Religions, 1986; (ed jtly) Mélusines continentales et insulaires, 1999; Collège des Irlandais Paris and Irish Studies, 2001. *Address:* 9 Silchester Road, Glenageary, Co. Dublin, Ireland. *T:* (1) 2805062. *Club:* Kildare Street and University (Dublin).
       Died 21 May 2004.

McCANN, Peter Toland McAree, CBE 1977; JP; DL; Lord Provost of the City of Glasgow and Lord-Lieutenant of the City of Glasgow, 1975–77; *b* 2 Aug. 1924; *s* of Peter McCann and Agnes (*née* Waddell); *m* 1958, Maura Eleanor (*née* Ferris); one *s*. *Educ:* St Mungo's Academy; Glasgow Univ. (BL). Solicitor and Notary Public. Pres., Glasgow Univ. Law Soc., 1946; Pres., St Thomas More Soc., 1959. Mem. Glasgow Corp., 1961. Chm., McCann Cttee (Secondary Educn for Physically Handicapped Children), 1971. DL Glasgow, 1978. OStJ 1977. Silver Sword, 1976, Golden Sword, 1977, City of Jeddah; Medal of King Faisal of Saudi Arabia, 1976; two Golden Swords, Royal House of Saudi Arabia, 1978. *Recreations:* music, history, model aeroplane making. *Address:* 31 Queen Mary Avenue, Glasgow G42 8DS.   *Died 24 Jan. 2004.*

McCARTHY, Eugene Joseph; writer, since 1971; *b* 29 March 1916; *s* of Michael J. and Anna Baden McCarthy; *m* 1945, Abigail Quigley McCarthy (*d* 2001); one *s* two *d* (and one *d* decd). *Educ:* St John's Univ., Collegeville (BA); Univ. of Minnesota (MA). Teacher in public schools, 1935–40; Coll. Prof. of Econs and Sociology, and civilian techn. Asst in Mil. Intell. for War Dept, 1940–48; US Representative in Congress of 4th District, Minnesota, 1949–58; US Senator from Minnesota, 1959–70. Independent. Holds hon. degrees. *Publications:* Frontiers in American Democracy, 1960; Dictionary of American Politics, 1962; A Liberal Answer to the Conservative Challenge, 1964; The Limits of Power, 1967; The Year of the People, 1969; Other Things and the Aardvark (poetry), 1970; The Hard Years, 1975; Mr Raccoon and his Friends (children's stories), 1977; (with James Kilpatrick) A Political Bestiary, 1978; Ground Fog and Night (poetry), 1978; America Revisited: 150 years after Tocqueville, 1978; The Ultimate Tyranny: the majority over the majority, 1980; Gene McCarthy's Minnesota, 1982; Complexities and Contraries, 1982; The View from Rappahannock, 1984; Up 'Til Now, 1987; Required Reading, 1988; The View from Rappahannock II, 1989; Colony of the World, 1993; Collected Poetry, 1997; No-Fault Politics, 1997; contribs to Saturday Review, Commonweal, Harper's, New Republic, USA Today. *Address:* 271 Hawlin Road, Woodville, VA 22749, USA.
       Died 10 Dec. 2005.

McCARTHY, Rt Hon. Sir Thaddeus (Pearcey), ONZ 1994; KBE 1974; Kt 1964; PC 1968; Justice of the Court of Appeal of New Zealand, 1963–76, President, 1973–76; Chairman, New Zealand Press Council, 1978–89; *b* 24 Aug. 1907; *s* of Walter McCarthy, Napier, merchant; *m*

1938, Joan Margaret Miller; one *s* two *d* (and one *d* decd). *Educ:* St Bede's Coll., Christchurch, New Zealand; Victoria University Coll., Wellington (LLM (1st Class Hons) 1931). Served War of 1939–45 in MEF with 22 Bn 2 NZEF, later as DJAG, 2 NZEF. Practised as Barrister and Solicitor until 1957 when appointed to Supreme Court. Chairman: Royal Commn on State Services, 1961–62; Winston Churchill Memorial Trust, 1966–76; Royal Commissions: on Salary and Wage Fixing Procedures in the State Services, 1968; on Social Security, 1969; on Horse Racing, Trotting and Dog Racing, 1969; on Salaries and Wages in the State Services, 1972; on Nuclear Power Generation, 1976–78; on Maori Land Courts, 1979–; Chm., Security Review Authority and Comr of Security Appeals, 1977–94. Chm. Adv. Cttee, NZ Computer Centre, 1977–86. Vice-Pres., NZ Sect., Internat. Commn of Jurists. Chm., Queen Elizabeth II Nat. Trust, 1978–84. Fellow, NZ Inst. of Public Admin, 1984. Hon. Bencher, Middle Temple, 1974. Hon. LLD Victoria Univ. of Wellington, 1978. *Recreations:* golf (Captain, Wellington Golf Club, 1952, Pres., 1973–77), sailing. *Address:* Wharenui, 274 Oriental Parade, Wellington, New Zealand. *Club:* Wellington (Wellington, NZ) (Pres., 1976–78; Trustee, 1978–).
Died 11 April 2001.

McCAUGHEY, (John) Davis, AC 1987; Governor of Victoria, Australia, 1986–92; *b* 12 July 1914; *s* of John and Lizzie McCaughey; *m* 1940, Jean Middlemas Henderson; three *s* two *d*. *Educ:* Pembroke Coll., Cambridge (MA; Hon. Fellow, 1988); New Coll., Edinburgh; Presbyterian Coll., Belfast. Ordained in Presbyterian Ch in Ireland, 1942; Study Sec., SCM, 1946–52; Prof. of NT Studies, Ormond Coll., Univ. of Melbourne, 1953–64, Master of the Coll., 1959–79; Dep. Chancellor, Univ. of Melbourne, 1978–79, 1982–85. Pres., Uniting Church in Australia, 1977–79. Hon. FRACP 1988; FAHA 1990. Hon. DD Edinburgh, 1966; Hon. LLD: Melbourne, 1982; QUB, 1987; Monash, 1993; Hon. DLitt La Trobe, 1992; Hon. STD Melbourne Coll. of Divinity, 1992. *Publications:* Christian Obedience in the University, 1958; Diversity and Unity in the New Testament Picture of Christ, 1969; Piecing Together a Shared Vision (Boyer Lectures), 1988; Victoria's Colonial Governors 1839–1900, 1993; Tradition and Dissent, 1997; articles in Colloquium, Aust. Biblical Review, etc. *Recreations:* reading, listening, golf. *Address:* 36 Chapman Street, North Melbourne, Vic 3051, Australia. *Clubs:* Melbourne, Royal Melbourne Golf.
Died 25 March 2005.

McCLELLAN, Col Sir (Herbert) Gerard (Thomas), Kt 1986; CBE 1979 (OBE 1960); TD 1955; company director; *b* 24 Sept. 1913; *s* of late George McClellan and Lilian (*née* Fitzgerald); *m* 1939, Rebecca Ann (Nancy) Desforges (*d* 1982); one *s* three *d*. Served War of 1939–45, Loyal (N Lancs) Regt, RA, London Irish Rifles, in ME and Italy (wounded; despatches). Vernons of Liverpool, 1934–82: formerly: Vice Chm. and Man. Dir, Vernons Trust Corp., Vernons Finance Corp., and Vernons Insurance Brokers; Dir, Vernons Orgn; Man. Dir, Competition Management Services. Chm., Intro-Merseyside Ltd, 1988–94; Director: JS Mortgage Corp., 1986–93; Richmond Storage & Transit Co. (UK) Ltd, 1990–93; Richmond Freight Services Ltd, 1990–93. Commanded 626 HAA (Liverpool Irish) Regt and 470 LAA (3rd West Lancs) Regt, RA TA, 1955–60; County Comdt, W Lancs ACF, 1961–66; Member: W Lancs T&AVRA, 1955–66 (Vice-Chm., 1966–68); NW England and IoM T&AVRA, 1968–70 (Vice-Chm., 1970–75; Chm., 1975–79). Former Mem. (C) for Childwall, Liverpool City Council; Member: Liverpool Cons. Assoc., 1960–95 (Vice-Chm., 1966–75; Chm., 1975–85; Vice-Pres., 1985–95); NW Area Cons. Assoc., 1971–90; Exec. Cttee, Nat. Union of Cons. and Unionist Assocs, 1982–87; Chairman: Wavertree Cons. Assoc., 1962–67 (Pres., 1967–76); Liverpool European Cons. Constituency Council, 1978–84; Merseyside W European Cons. Constit. Council, 1984–85 (Pres., 1985–88);

President: Garston Cons. Assoc., 1979–90; Halewood Cons. Club, 1983–88; Vice-Pres. Woolton Ward Cons. Assoc., 1981–95; Patron, Crosby Cons. Assoc., 1994–2000 (Pres., 1986–89; Chm., 1989–91). Vice-President: Merseyside Co. SSAFA, 1975–; Incorp. Liverpool Sch. of Tropical Medicine, 1987–92. Governor: Archbp Whiteside Secondary Modern Sch. and St Brigid's High Sch., 1961–91; Mabel Fletcher Technical Coll., 1969– (Chm., 1971–86); Sandown Coll., Liverpool, 1989–91. FIAM. DL Lancs, later Merseyside, 1967–97; JP Liverpool, 1968–83; High Sheriff of Merseyside, 1980–81. *Address:* Ince Blundell Hall, Ince Blundell, Merseyside L38 6JL. *T:* (0151) 929 2269, *Fax:* (0151) 929 2188. *Clubs:* Army and Navy; Athenæum (Liverpool).
Died 7 Aug. 2004.

McCLINTOCK, Surg. Rear-Adm. Cyril Lawson Tait, CB 1974; OBE 1964; Medical Officer in Charge, Royal Naval Hospital, Haslar and Command Medical Adviser on staff of Commander-in-Chief Naval Home Command, 1972–75; *b* 2 Aug. 1916; *o surv. s* of late Lawson Tait McClintock, MB, ChB, Loddon, Norfolk; *m* 1966, Freda Margaret, *o d* of late Robert Jones, Caergwle, Denbighshire; two step *s*. *Educ:* St Michael's, Uckfield; Epsom; Guy's Hospital. DLO 1955. MRCS, LRCP 1940; MFCM 1975. Joined RN Medical Service, 1940; served War of 1939–45 in Western Approaches, N Africa, Eritrea, India and Singapore; Korea, 1950–51; ENT Specialist, RN Hosps, Port Edgar, Chatham, Hong Kong, Portland, Haslar, Malta and Russell Eve Building, Hamilton, Bermuda; MO i/c RN Hosp. Bighi, Malta, 1969; David Bruce RN Hosp. Mtarfa, Malta, 1970–71; Comd Med. Adviser to C-in-C Naval Forces Southern Europe, 1969–71. QHS 1971–75. FRSocMed 1948. CStJ 1973. *Recreations:* cricket, tennis, Rugby refereeing, history. *Address:* 5 Ambleside Court, Alverstoke, Hants PO12 2DJ. *Clubs:* Army and Navy, MCC. *Died 20 Aug. 2005.*

McCLINTOCK, David Charles, TD; writer, naturalist and plantsman; *b* 4 July 1913; *o s* of Rev. E. L. L. McClintock, Glendaragh, Crumlin, Co. Antrim, and Margaret McClintock, *d* of John Henry Buxton, Easneye, Ware, Herts; *m* Elizabeth Anne (*d* 1993), *d* of Maj. V. J. Dawson, Miserden, Glos; two *s* two *d*. *Educ:* West Downs Sch., Winchester; Harrow Sch.; Trinity Coll., Cambridge (BA 1934, MA 1940). FCA 1937; FLS 1953. 2nd Lieut, Herts Yeomanry RA TA, 1938; HQ 54 Div., Captain, 1941; Intelligence Trng Centre, 1941–43; Major, 1942; Civil Affairs Trng Centre, 1943–44; Lt-Col, 1944; BAOR, 1944–45. K-H Newsletter, 1938–46; Commercial Manager, Air Contractors Ltd, 1946–47; Chief Accountant and Admin. Officer, Coal Utilisation Council, 1951–73. Member: Wild Flower Soc., 1934– (Chm., 1981–93; Treasurer, 1978–82; Vice-Pres., 1994–97; Pres., 1997–2000); Council, Botanical Soc. of British Isles, 1954–64 (Pres., 1971–73; Hon. Mem., 1994–); Council, Kent Trust for Nature Conservation, 1958–62 (Vice-Pres., 1963–); Council, Ray Soc., 1968–72, 1976–80 (Vice-Pres., 1972–76; Pres., 1980–83; Hon. Vice-Pres., 1983–); Council, Linnean Soc., 1970–78 (Vice-Pres., 1971–74; Editl Sec., 1974–78; Editor, Biological Jl, 1976); Plant Variety Rights Adv. Panel for heathers, 1973–; Royal Horticultural Society: Scientific Cttee, 1978–94 (Vice-Chm., 1983–92; Actg Chm. 66 times), Publications Cttee, 1982–87; Council, Internat. Dendrology Soc., 1979– (Editor, 1979–83; Vice-Pres., 1990–2000); Council, Nat. Trust, 1980–84; Heather Soc., 1963– (Vice-Pres., 1980–89; Pres., 1989–2000); President: Kent Field Club, 1978–80 (Hon. Mem., 1994–); London Natural Hist. Soc., 2000–02. Internat. Registrar for heather cultivars, 1970–95; holder of national collection of Sasa bamboos, 1986–. Broadcast many times, 1962–96. Membre d'Honneur, Soc. Guernesiaise, 1968–. Veitch Meml Medal in gold, RHS, 1981; H. H. Bloomer Award, Linnean Soc., 1993; VMH 1995. *Publications:* Pocket Guide to Wild Flowers (with R. S. R. Fitter), 1956; Supplement to the Pocket Guide to Wild Flowers, 1957; (jtly) Natural History of the Garden of Buckingham

Palace, 1964; Companion to Flowers, 1966; Guide to the Naming of Plants, 1969, 2nd edn 1980; Wild Flowers of Guernsey, 1975, Supplement, 1987; (with J. Bichard) Wild Flowers of the Channel Islands, 1975; Joshua Gosselin of Guernsey, 1976; (with F. Perring and R. E. Randall) Picking Wild Flowers, 1977; (ed) H. J. van de Laar, The Heather Garden, 1978; Guernsey's Earliest Flora, 1982; Heathers of the Lizard, 1998; contribs to 26 other books and over 100 periodicals, incl. more than 2,500 book reviews. *Recreations:* anything to do with wild life and gardening, music, formerly shooting, fishing, tennis etc. *Address:* Bracken Hill, Platt, Sevenoaks, Kent TN15 8JH. *T:* (01732) 884102. *Clubs:* Horticultural, Linnean Dining. *Died 23 Nov. 2001.*

McCLINTOCK, Nicholas Cole, CBE 1979; Secretary-General of the Order of St John, 1968–81 (Deputy Secretary-General, 1963–68); *b* 10 Sept. 1916; *s* of late Col Robert Singleton McClintock, DSO (3rd *s* of Adm. Sir Leopold McClintock), and Mary Howard, *d* of Sir Howard Elphinstone, VC; *m* 1953, Pamela Sylvia, *d* of late Major Rhys Mansel, Smedmore, Dorset; two *s* two *d*. *Educ:* Stowe Sch.; Trinity Coll., Cambridge (MA; Capt., Univ. Fencing Team). Entered Colonial Admin. Service, N Nigeria, 1939 but went immediately on War Service with 18th and 28th Field Regts RA, Dunkirk 1940, India and Burma, 1942–45; commanded 1st Field Battery RA in final Burma campaign. Asst Principal, Appointments Dept, CO, Feb.–Oct. 1946; Asst Dist Officer, N Nigeria, 1946–49; Private Sec. to Governor (Sir John Macpherson), 1949–50; Clerk to Exec. Council and Clerk, Legislature, N Nigeria, 1951–53; Sen. Dist Officer and Actg Resident, Kano Province, 1955–59; Admin. Officer Grade 1 and Resident, Bornu Province, 1960–62. Chm., Aidis Trust, 1988–94. KStJ 1968. *Publication:* Kingdoms in the Sand and Sun, 1992. *Address:* Lower Westport, Wareham, Dorset BH20 4PR. *T:* (01929) 553252.
Died 23 Nov. 2001.

McCLUNE, Rear-Adm. (William) James, CB 1978; *b* Londonderry, 20 Nov. 1921; *s* of James McClune, MBE, Carrickmacross, Co. Monaghan, and Matilda (*née* Burns); *m* 1953, Elizabeth, *yr d* of A. E. D. Prideaux, LDS, Weymouth; one *s* one *d*. *Educ:* Model Sch. and Foyle Coll., Derry; QUB (BSc 1st cl. Hons Elec. Engrg, 1941); RN Staff Coll., Greenwich (1961); Univ. of Birmingham (Ratcliff Prizeman, MSc 1970); RN War Coll. (1971). Bronze Medal, CGLI, 1940; Belfast Assoc. of Engrs' Prize, 1940, 1941. CEng, MIEE. Radar Officer, RNVR, 1941–47; Engrg Dept, GPO, 1947–49; RN, 1949–78; CSO (Engrg) to C-in-C Fleet, 1976–78. A Life Vice-Pres., RNLI. Patron, Monkton Combe Sch. CCMI. *Recreation:* sailing. *Died 4 Dec. 2004.*

McCOLL, Ian, CBE 1983; Chairman, Scottish Express Newspapers Ltd, 1975–82; *b* 22 Feb. 1915; *e s* of late John and Morag McColl, Glasgow and Bunessan, Isle of Mull; *m* 1968, Brenda, *e d* of late Thomas and Mary McKean, Glasgow; one *d*. *Educ:* Hillhead High Sch., Glasgow. Served War, RAF, 1940–46 (despatches, 1945); Air Crew, Coastal Comd 202 Sqdn. Joined Scottish Daily Express as cub reporter, 1933; held various editorial exec. posts; Editor: Scottish Daily Express, 1961–71; Daily Express, 1971–74; Dir, Express Newspapers Ltd, 1971–82. Mem., Press Council, 1975–78; a Vice-Pres., Newspaper Press Fund, 1981–. Contested (L): Dumfriesshire, 1945; Greenock, 1950. Member: Presbytery of Glasgow and Synod of Clydesdale, 1953–71; Gen. Assembly Publications Cttee, until 1971; Gen. Assembly Bd of Communication, 1983–86; Session Clerk, Sandyford-Henderson Meml Church of Scotland, Glasgow, 1953–71. Mem., Newlands South C of S, Glasgow, 1975–. Chm. Media Div., XIII Commonwealth Games, Scotland 1986, 1983–86. Bank of Scotland Scottish Press Life Achievement Award, 1993. *Address:* 12 Newlands Road, Newlands, Glasgow G43 2JB. *Club:* Saints and Sinners of Scotland (Chm., 1981–82). *Died 21 June 2005.*

McCORMACK, Mark Hume; Chairman and Chief Executive Officer, International Management Group, since 1964; *b* 6 Nov. 1930; *s* of late Ned Hume McCormack and Grace Wolfe McCormack; *m* 1st, 1954, Nancy Breckenridge McCormack (marr. diss. 1984); two *s* one *d*; 2nd, 1986, Betsy Nagelsen; one *d*. *Educ:* Princeton Univ.; William and Mary Coll. (BA 1951); Yale Univ. (LLB 1954). Admitted to Ohio Bar, 1957; Associate in Arter, Hadden, Wykoff & Van Duzer, 1957–63, Partner, 1964–; started Internat. Management Gp, 1962. Commentator for televised golf, BBC. *Publications:* The World of Professional Golf, annually, 1967–; Arnie: the evolution of a legend, 1967; What they don't teach you at Harvard Business School, 1984; The Terrible Truth about Lawyers, 1987; Success Secrets, 1989; What They Still Don't Teach You at Harvard Business School, 1989; The 110% Solution, 1991; Hit the Ground Running, 1993; On Negotiating, 1995; McCormack on Communications, 1996; Getting Results for Dummies, 2000; What You'll Never Learn on the Internet, 2000; monthly newsletters Success Secrets. *Recreations:* golf, tennis. *Address:* 1360 E Ninth Street #100, Cleveland, OH 44114-1782, USA. *T:* 216/522–1200. *Clubs:* Royal & Ancient Golf (St Andrews); Wentworth (Virginia Water); Sunningdale Golf (Berkshire, England); Old Prestwick (Prestwick); Royal Dornoch (Dornoch); Turnberry Hotel Golf; Deepdale (NY); Pepper Pike, Country Club of Cleveland (Ohio); Isleworth, Bay Hill (Florida); Ironwood Country (Calif).
Died 16 May 2003.

McCOWAN, Rt Hon. Sir Anthony (James Denys), Kt 1981; PC 1989; a Lord Justice of Appeal, 1989–97; *b* 12 Jan. 1928; *yr s* of John Haines Smith McCowan, MBE, and Marguerite McCowan, Georgetown, British Guiana; *m* 1961, Sue Hazel Anne, *d* of late Reginald Harvey and of Mrs Harvey, Braiseworth Hall, Tannington, Suffolk; two *s* one *d*. *Educ:* Queen's Coll., British Guiana; Epsom Coll.; Brasenose Coll., Oxford (Open Hist. schol.; MA, BCL). Called to Bar, Gray's Inn, 1951 (Atkin Schol.), Bencher, 1980. Dep. Chm., E Sussex QS, 1969–71; a Recorder of the Crown Court, 1972–81; QC 1972; a Judge of the High Court, QBD, 1981–89. Leader, 1978–81, Presiding Judge, 1986–89, SE Circuit; Sen. Presiding Judge, England and Wales, 1991–95. Member: Parole Bd, 1982–84; Crown Court Rule Cttee, 1982–88. Chm., Fedn of Univ. Cons. and Unionist Assocs, 1951; Founder Mem., Bow Gp, 1951 (author of its first pubn, Coloured Peoples in Britain). Pres., Old Epsomian Club, 1997–98; Vice-Pres., Queen's Coll. of Guyana Assoc. (UK), 1995–. *Recreations:* sport, history, travel. *Died 3 July 2003.*

MacCRINDLE, Robert Alexander; QC 1963; commercial lawyer; Partner, Shearman and Sterling; *b* 27 Jan. 1928; *s* of F. R. MacCrindle; *m* 1959, Pauline Dilys, *d* of Mark S. Morgan; one *s* one *d*. *Educ:* Girvan High Sch.; King's Coll., London (LLB 1948); Gonville and Caius Coll., Cambridge (Chancellor's Medal, LLM 1951). Served RAF, 1948–50, Flt-Lt. Called to the Bar, Gray's Inn, 1952 (Bencher, 1969); Junior Counsel to Board of Trade (Export Credits), 1961–63; Mem., Hong Kong Bar, 1967; Avocat, Barreau de Paris, 1991. Mem., Royal Commn on Civil Liability and Compensation for Personal Injury, 1973–78. Hon. Fellow, American Coll. of Trial Lawyers, 1974. *Publication:* McNair's Law of the Air, 1953. *Recreation:* golf. *Address:* Essex Court Chambers, 24 Lincoln's Inn Fields, WC2A 3ED. *T:* (020) 7813 8000; Shearman and Sterling, 114 avenue des Champs Elysées, 75008 Paris, France. *T:* 153897000; 41 avenue Bosquet, 75007 Paris, France. *T:* 147051858. *Club:* University (New York). *Died 15 March 2005.*

McCRUM, Michael William, CBE 1996; MA; Master of Corpus Christi College, Cambridge, 1980–94; Chairman, Cathedrals Fabric Commission for England, 1991–99; *b* 23 May 1924; 3rd *s* of Captain C. R. McCrum, RN and Ivy Hilda Constance (*née* Nicholson); *m* 1952, Christine Mary Kathleen, *d* of Sir Arthur fforde, GBE; three *s* one *d*. *Educ:* Horris Hill, Newbury; Sherborne Sch.; Corpus Christi

Coll., Cambridge (Entrance Schol., Dec. 1942; Part I, Class. Tripos, 1st cl., 1947; Part II, 1st cl. with dist., 1948; Hon. Fellow, 1994). Served War, RN, 1943–45 (Sub-Lt RNVR, Dec. 1943). Asst Master, Rugby School, Sept. 1948–July 1950 (Lower Bench Master, 1949–50); Fellow CCC, Cambridge, 1949, Second Tutor, 1950–51, Tutor, 1951–62; Headmaster, Tonbridge Sch. 1962–70; Head Master of Eton, 1970–80; Vice-Chancellor, Cambridge Univ., 1987–89. Lectures: Lansdowne, Univ. of Victoria, BC, 1985; Clayesmore, Blandford Forum, 1986; Lady Margaret's Preacher, Univ. of Cambridge, 1987. University of Cambridge: Member: Council of the Senate, 1955–58, 1981–89; Gen. Board of Faculties, 1957–62, 1987–89; Financial Bd, 1985–89; Chairman: Faculty Bd of Educn, 1981–86, 1990–93; Bd of Extra-Mural Studies, 1982–86. Chairman: HMC, 1974; Joint Educnl Trust, 1984–87; GBA, 1989–94 (Dep. Chm., 1982–89); Member: Oxford and Cambridge Schs Exam. Bd, 1960–62, 1966–87 (Chm., 1981–87); BBC/IBA Central Religious Affairs Cttee, 1965–69; Governing Body, Schools Council, 1969–76 (also mem., various cttees); ISJC, 1982–94 (Dep. Chm., 1989–92; Chm., 1992–94). Governor: Bradfield Coll., 1956–62; Eastbourne Coll., 1960–62; King's Sch., Canterbury, 1980–94; Sherborne Sch., 1980–94; Oakham Sch., 1981–85; United World Coll. of the Atlantic, 1981–94; Rugby Sch., 1982–94. Pres., Cambridge Soc., 1989–96. Trustee: King George VI and Queen Elizabeth Foundn of St Catharine's, Cumberland Lodge, 1983–2000; Nat. Heritage Meml Fund, 1984–90; Cambridge Foundn, 1989–99; Henry Fund, 1994–95. Hon. Freeman, Skinners' Co., 1980. Hon. DEd Victoria, BC, 1989. Comendador de la Orden de Isabel la Católica (Spain), 1988. *Publications:* Select Documents of the Principates of the Flavian Emperors AD 68–96 (with A. G. Woodhead), 1961; Thomas Arnold, Head Master, 1989; The Man Jesus, 1999; (contrib.) Dictionary of National Biography, 1971–80 and 1981–85. *Address:* 32 Clarendon Street, Cambridge CB1 1JX. *T:* (01223) 353303. *Clubs:* Athenæum, Oxford and Cambridge, East India, Devonshire, Sports and Public Schools; Hawks (Cambridge).   *Died 16 Feb. 2005.*

MacDERMOT, Brian (Charles), CBE 1966; LVO 1961; HM Diplomatic Service, retired; *b* 29 Jan. 1914; *m* 1949, Mary Arden Hunter; seven *s* two *d.* Probationer Vice-Consul, Peking, China, 1936; served at: Hankow, China, 1939–40; Kobe, Japan, 1940–41; Kunming, South China, 1942; Vice-Consul, Shiraz, Persia, 1943; Paris, 1944, promoted Consul, 1945; Foreign Office, 1946; Consul, Beirut, 1948; First Secretary, Belgrade, 1950; First Secretary, Berne, 1951, acted as Charge d'Affaires, 1951, 1952, 1953; transferred to Foreign Office, 1954; transferred to Holy See, 1955, acted as Chargé d'Affaires, 1958, 1959, 1960 and 1961; HM Consul-General, Oporto, 1962–68; Ambassador and Consul-Gen., Paraguay, 1968–72. *Address:* 2 Henry's Yard, Berwick St James, Salisbury SP3 4TS.   *Died 25 April 2003.*

McDERMOTT, Sir Emmet; *see* McDermott, Sir L. E.

McDERMOTT, Sir (Lawrence) Emmet, KBE 1972; Lord Mayor of Sydney, 1969–72; Alderman, Sydney, 1962–77; dental surgeon; *b* 6 Sept. 1911; *s* of O. J. McDermott; *m* 1st, 1939, Arline Beatrice Olga (*d* 1987); one *s* one *d*; 2nd, 1992, Eula Macdonald, *d* of Robert Murray Ross. *Educ:* St Ignatius Coll., Sydney; Univ. of Sydney (MDS); Northwestern Univ., Chicago (DDS). FICD, FRACDS, FACD; FAIM 1983. Hon. Consultant Dental Surgeon: Royal Prince Alfred Hosp., 1942; Eastern Suburbs Hosp., 1945; Pres., Bd of Control, United Dental Hosp., Sydney, 1967–79. Mem., NSW Dental Bd, 1967–79; Pres., Australian Dental Assoc. (NSW Br.), 1960–61; Councillor, Australian Dental Assoc., 1962–66. Mem., Liberal Party State Council, 1969; Councillor, Sydney County Council, 1973–80, Dep. Chm., 1975–77, Chm., 1977–78. Dir, City Mutual Life Assce Soc. Ltd, 1970–83, Dep. Chm., 1976–83; Member: Sydney Cove Redevelopment Authority, 1971–76; Convocation,

Macquarie Univ., 1966–94; Australia-Britain Soc. (NSW Br.), Vice-Pres., 1972–77. *Recreations:* golf, swimming (Sydney Univ. Blue), bowls. *Address:* 61 Fiddens Wharf Road, Killara, NSW 2071, Australia. *T:* (2) 4984382. *Clubs:* Royal Sydney Golf, Tattersall's, Chatswood Bowling, City Bowling (all Sydney).
Died 29 Aug. 2002.

MacDONAGH, Prof. Oliver Ormond Gerard; W. K. Hancock Professor of History, Australian National University, 1973–90, later Emeritus; *b* 23 Aug. 1924; *s* of Michael A. MacDonagh and Loretto (*née* Oliver); *m* 1952, Mary Carmel Hamilton; three *s* four *d. Educ:* Clongowes Wood Coll., Co. Kildare; University Coll. Dublin (MA); King's Inns, Dublin (BL); Univ. of Cambridge (PhD). Fellow, St Catharine's Coll., Cambridge, 1952–64, Vis. Fellow, 1986, Hon. Fellow, 1987; Foundn Prof. of History, Flinders Univ., SA, 1964–68; Prof. of Modern History, UC, Cork, 1968–73. Vis. Prof., Yale Univ., 1970; Overseas Schol., St John's Coll., Cambridge, 1981; Parnell Sen. Res. Fellow, Magdalene Coll., Cambridge, 1993–94; Res. Prof., Australian Catholic Univ., 1994–95. FASSA 1965; FAHA 1977; Corresp. FBA 1984; Hon. MRIA 1993. Hon. LittD: Flinders, 1982; Sydney, 1989; NUI, 1989. *Publications:* A Pattern of Government Growth, 1961, 2nd edn 1993; Ireland: the Union and its Aftermath, 1968, 2nd edn 1977; Early Victorian Government, 1977; The Inspector-General, 1981; States of Mind, 1983, 2nd edn 1985; The Hereditary Bondsman: Daniel O'Connell 1775–1829, 1987; The Emancipist: Daniel O'Connell 1830–1847, 1989; Jane Austen: Real and Imagined Worlds, 1991; The Life of Daniel O'Connell 1775–1847, 1991; The Sharing of the Green: a modern Irish history for Australians, 1996; (with S. R. Dennison) Guinness: 1886–1939, 1998. *Recreations:* watching Rugby, Nineteenth Century novels. *Address:* 9B Crescent Street, Fairlight, NSW 2094, Australia. *T:* (2) 99497824.   *Died 22 May 2002.*

McDONALD, Hon. Lord; Robert Howat McDonald, MC 1944; a Senator of the College of Justice in Scotland, 1973–89; *b* 15 May 1916; *s* of Robert Glassford McDonald, and Roberta May Howat, Paisley, Renfrewshire; *m* 1949, Barbara Mackenzie, *d* of John Mackenzie, Badcaul, Ross-shire; no *c. Educ:* John Neilson Institution, Paisley. MA 1935, LLB 1937, Glasgow. Served with KOSB, 1939–46 (despatches, 1945). Admitted Faculty of Advocates, 1946; QC (Scot.) 1957. Sheriff Principal of Ayr and Bute, 1966–71. Mem., Criminal Injuries Compensation Board, 1964–71; Pres., Industrial Tribunals for Scotland, 1972–73; Chairman: Mental Welfare Commn for Scotland, 1965–83; Gen. Nursing Council for Scotland, 1970–73; Mem., Employment Appeal Tribunal, 1976–86. Chm., Queen's Nursing Inst., Scotland, 1981–93. *Address:* 5 Doune Terrace, Edinburgh EH3 6EA. *Club:* New (Edinburgh).
Died 6 Jan. 2003.

MACDONALD OF GWAENYSGOR, 2nd Baron *cr* 1949, of Gwaenysgor, Flint; **Gordon Ramsay Macdonald;** business consultant; *b* 16 Oct. 1915; *er s* of 1st Baron Macdonald of Gwaenysgor, PC, KCMG; *S* father, 1966; *m* 1941, Leslie Margaret Taylor; three *d. Educ:* Manchester Univ. MA, Economics and Commerce. Served War, 1940–46; Army, Major, Artillery; GSO2 Operations and Intelligence (despatches, Burma). Board of Trade, 1946–53: Principal, 1946–47; UK Trade Comr, Canberra, ACT, 1947–53. With Tube Investments Ltd, and Man. Dir TI (Export) Ltd, 1953–64; Chief Exec., Telecommunications Group, Plessey Co., 1964–67; Chm., Hayek Engrg (UK) Ltd, 1967–76; Chm. and Chief Exec., Ferro Metal and Chemical Comp., and Satra Consultants (UK) Ltd, 1977. *Recreations:* golf, chess. *Heir:* none.   *Died 27 Jan. 2002 (ext).*

McDONALD, Allan Stuart; Headmaster, George Heriot's School, Edinburgh, 1970–83; *b* 20 Aug. 1922; *s* of Allan McDonald and Clementina Peebles (*née* Stuart), both of Edinburgh; *m* 1948, Margaret Wilson, *d* of late James

Adams, Paisley and Stranraer, and of Margaret Wilson (née Ferguson); one s two d. *Educ:* Royal High Sch., Edinburgh; Giffnock and Eastwood Schs, Renfrewshire; Glasgow Univ. (MA Hons 1944; DipEd 1948); Sorbonne. Commnd, Royal Corps of Signals (21st Army Group Signals), 1943–45. Asst Master: Johnstone High Sch., 1948–50; Eastwood Sch., 1950–54; Principal Teacher: Modern Languages, Fortrose Acad., 1954–59; German, George Heriot's Sch., 1959–70; Depute Headmaster, George Heriot's Sch., 1967–70. *Recreations:* formerly Rugby, cricket; subseq. gardening, photography. *Address:* Mearns Edge, Haulkerton Wood, Laurencekirk, Aberdeenshire AB30 1DZ. *Died 10 Dec. 2005.*

MacDONALD, Ian; *see* Mayfield, Hon. Lord.

MacDONALD, Isabel Lillias, (Mrs J. G. MacDonald); *see* Sinclair, I. L.

McDONALD, Robert Howat; *see* McDonald, Hon. Lord.

MACDONALD, Vice-Adm. Sir Roderick (Douglas), KBE 1978 (CBE 1966); Chief of Staff to Commander, Allied Naval Forces Southern Europe, 1976–79, retired; artist, since 1979; *b* Java, 25 Feb. 1921; *s* of Douglas and Marjorie Macdonald; *m* 1st, 1943, Joan Willis (marr. diss. 1980); two *s* (and one *s* decd); 2nd, 1980, Mrs Pamela Bartosik (née Bowman). *Educ:* Fettes. Entered Royal Navy, 1939; served War: Fleet and Convoy ops throughout 1939–45 (Atlantic, Norway, Mediterranean, Eastern Fleet, East Coast and Normandy); commanded HMS Leeds Castle, 1953, also HMS Essington; Sen. Officer, 104th Mine-Sweeping Sqdn and HMS Walkerton, 1957 (despatches, Cyprus); Comdr Sea Trng, 1959; Comd HMS Falmouth, 1961; Comdr, Naval Forces and Jt Force Comdr, Borneo, 1965 (CBE); Comd HMS Galatea; Captain (D): Londonderry Sqdn, 1968; First Frigate Sqdn, Far East, 1969; Captain of the Fleet, 1970; Comd HMS Bristol, 1972; COS to C-in-C, Naval Home Command, 1973–76; ADC to the Queen, 1975. One-man exhibitions: Naples, 1978; Edinburgh, 1980, 1989; London, 1981, 1983, 1985, 1987, 1991. Younger Brother of Trinity House; Vice-Pres. 1976–85, and Fellow, Nautical Inst. Mem., RNSA. Chieftain, Isle of Skye Highland Games; President: Isle of Skye Piping Soc.; Inverness Sea Cadets. Exec. Trustee, Clan Donald Lands Trust. *Publications:* The Figurehead, 1993; articles in Scottish Rev., Naval Rev., and other jls. *Recreation:* gardening. *Address:* Ollach, Braes, Isle of Skye IV51 9LJ. *Clubs:* Caledonian; Royal Scottish Pipers Society (Edinburgh). *Died 19 Jan. 2001.*

MACDONALD, Maj.-Gen. Ronald Clarence, CB 1965; DSO 1944 and Bar, 1945; OBE 1953; Deputy Chief of Staff, Headquarters, Allied Land Forces, Central Europe, 1962–65; *b* 1 Aug. 1911; 2nd *s* of late Col C. R. Macdonald, CMG; *m* 1st, 1939, Jessie Ross Anderson (*d* 1986); one *s* (one *d* decd); 2nd, 1986, Constance Margaret Davies. *Educ:* Rugby; RMC, Sandhurst. Commnd Royal Warwicks Regt, 1931, Comdr 2nd Bn, 1945–46, Comdr 1st Bn, 1953–55; Bn Comdr, France, Germany Campaign, 1944–45; Mil. Asst to CIGS, 1946–49; GSO1, HQ, West Africa Comd, 1950–53; Col Gen. Staff, SHAPE, 1955–56; Comdr 10th Inf. Bde Gp, 1956–59; DDI, War Office, 1959–60; Chief of Staff, HQ Middle East Comd, 1960–62; retired, 1965. Col Royal Warwicks Fusiliers, 1963–68; Dep. Col (Warwicks), The Royal Regt of Fusiliers, 1968–74. *Address:* 6 The Beeches, Shaw, Melksham, Wilts SN12 8EW. *Died 28 July 2005.*

McDONALD, Sir Tom, Kt 1991; OBE 1983; Chairman: Yorkshire and Humberside and East Midlands Industrial Development Board, 1982–91; West Yorkshire Residuary Body, 1986–91; West Midlands Residuary Body, 1990–91; Education Assets Board, 1988–93; *b* 5 Aug. 1923; *s* of Robert and Edna McDonald; *m* 1951, Pamela Anne Glaisby; three *s* one *d. Educ:* Dewsbury Wheelwright Grammar Sch.; Leeds Univ. (BCom Hons). FCA.

Armitage & Norton: Audit Manager, 1953–62; Partner, 1962–86; Chm., 1982–86. Chairman: Old Swan Hotel (Harrogate) Ltd, 1973–82; Yorkshire Chemicals, 1977–83; Yorkshire Enterprise Ltd, 1990–94; Director: Dale Electric International, 1988–93; S. Jerome & Sons (Holdings), 1988–93; Consultant, KPMG Peat Marwick, 1987–93. Dir, Opera North, 1982–95. Pres., W Yorks Soc. of Chartered Accountants, 1986–87. *Recreations:* history, travel, music. *Address:* 15 Sandmoor Green, Alwoodley, Leeds LS17 7SB. *T:* (0113) 266 4232.

Died 16 July 2001.

McDONALD, William, MBE 2000; CA; JP; Chamberlain, 1962–89, and Secretary, 1971–89, Company of Merchants of City of Edinburgh; Bursar, Carnegie Trust for the Universities of Scotland, 1990–2001; *b* 9 Nov. 1929; *yr s* of late Joseph McDonald and Margaret Pringle (née Gibb); *m* 1956, Anne Kidd Laird Donald; one *s* one *d. Educ:* Perth Acad. Served RAF, 1952–54. Sec., South Mills and Grampian Investment, Dundee, 1957–62. Clerk and Treasurer, Incorp. of Guildry in Edinburgh, 1975–89; Jt Secy., Scottish Council of Independent Schs, 1978–89. Chm., Lothian Region Valuation Appeal Cttee, 1995–2000 (Mem., 1990–95). Scout Association: Dep. Chief Comr of Scotland, 1977–79 (Hon. Treas., Scotland, 1989–93); Chm., Finance Cttee, 1993–98; Chm. Audit Cttee, World Scout Bureau, 2001–03; Hon. Treas., Eur. Scout Region, 1995–2000. Chm., Scottish Environmental and Outdoor Centres Assoc. (formerly Scottish Nat. Camps Assoc.), 1986–91. Member: High Constables of Edinburgh (Colinton Ward), 1983–2002; Rotary Club of Edinburgh, 1989–94. *Recreation:* bridge. *Address:* 1/3 Wyvern Park, Edinburgh EH9 2JY. *Club:* New (Edinburgh).

Died 31 March 2005.

McDONNELL, His Honour Denis Lane, OBE 1945; a Circuit Judge (formerly a County Court Judge), 1967–86; *b* 2 March 1914; *o c* of late David McDonnell, LLD and Mary Nora (née Lane), Riversdale, Sundays Well, Cork and Fairy Hill, Monkstown, Co. Cork and *g s* of Denny Lane, poet and Young Irelander; *m* 1940, Florence Nina (Micky), *d* of late Lt-Col Hugh T. Ryan, DSO and Clare Emily (née Conry), Castle View, Ballincollig, Co. Cork; three *d* (and one *s* one *d* decd). *Educ:* Christian Brothers' Coll., Cork; Ampleforth Coll.; Sidney Sussex Coll., Cambridge (MA). Served in RAFVR, Equipment and Admin. and Special Duties Branches, 1940–45 in UK and with No. 84 Gp in NW Europe (Wing Comdr). Called to Bar, Middle Temple, 1936; Bencher, 1965. Practised at Bar, 1938–40 and 1946–67. Hon. Sec., Council of HM Circuit Judges, 1979–83 (Pres., 1985). *Publications:* Kerr on Fraud and Mistake (7th edn, with J. G. Monroe), 1952; titles on carriage in Encyclopædias of Forms and Precedents and Court Forms and Precedents, and in Halsbury's Laws of England. *Recreations:* family life, listening to music, golf, gardening. *Clubs:* Piltdown Golf, Woking Golf. *Died 18 Nov. 2001.*

MacDOUGALL, Sir (George) Donald (Alastair), Kt 1953; CBE 1945 (OBE 1942); FBA 1966; economist; *b* 26 Oct. 1912; *s* of late Daniel Douglas MacDougall, Glasgow, and Beatrice Amy Miller; *m* 1st, 1937, Bridget Christabel Bartrum (marr. diss. 1977); one *s* one *d*; 2nd, 1977, Laura Margaret Hall (née Linfoot) (*d* 1995). *Educ:* Kelvinside Acad., Glasgow; Shrewsbury Sch.; Balliol Coll., Oxford (Hon. Fellow, 1992). George Webb Medley Junior (1934) and Senior (1935) Scholarships in Political Economy; Asst Lecturer (later Lecturer) in Economics, University of Leeds, 1936–39; First Lord of the Admiralty's Statistical Branch, 1939–40; Prime Minister's Statistical Branch, 1940–45 (Chief Asst, 1942–45). Work on Reparations and German Industry, Moscow and Berlin, 1945; Mem. of Heavy Clothing Industry Working Party, 1946; Official Fellow of Wadham Coll., Oxford, 1945–50, Domestic Bursar, 1946–48, Hon. Fellow, 1964–; Econ. Dir, OEEC, Paris, 1948–49; Faculty Fellow, Nuffield Coll., 1947–50, Professorial Fellow, 1950–52, Official Fellow, 1952–64,

First Bursar, 1958–64, Hon. Fellow, 1967–; Nuffield Reader in Internat. Economics, Oxford Univ., 1950–52; Chief Adviser, Prime Minister's Statistical Branch, 1951–53; Visiting Prof., Australian Nat. Univ., 1959; MIT Center for Internat. Studies, New Delhi, 1961; Dir, Investing in Success Equities, Ltd, 1959–62; Economic Dir, NEDO, 1962–64; Mem. Turnover Tax Cttee, 1963–64; Dir-Gen., Dept of Economic Affairs, 1964–68; Head of Govt Economic Service, and Chief Economic Adviser to the Treasury, 1969–73; Chief Economic Advr, CBI, 1973–84. Mem. Council, Royal Econ. Soc., 1950– (Hon. Sec., 1958–70; Vice-Pres., 1970–72, 1974–; Pres., 1972–74); Pres., Soc. for Strategic and Long Range Planning, 1977–85, Vice-Pres., 1968–77; Vice-Pres., Soc. of Business Economists, 1978–; Chm., Exec. Cttee NIESR, 1974–87; Mem., EEC Study Gp on Economic and Monetary Union, 1974–75; Chm., EEC Study Gp on Role of Public Finance in European Integration, 1975–77. Mem., New Europe Adv. Council, 2001–. Hon. LLD Strathclyde, 1968; Hon. LittD Leeds, 1971; Hon. DSc Aston, 1979. *Publications:* (part author) Measures for International Economic Stability, UN, 1951; The World Dollar Problem, 1957; (part author) The Fiscal System of Venezuela, 1959; The Dollar Problem: A Reappraisal, 1960; Studies in Political Economy (2 vols), 1975; Don and Mandarin: memoirs of an economist, 1987; contrib. to various economic and statistical jls. *Address:* Flat K, 19 Warwick Square, SW1V 2AB. *T:* (020) 7821 1998. *Club:* Reform. *Died 22 March 2004.*

McELHERAN, John; Principal Assistant Solicitor (Under Secretary), Ministry of Agriculture, Fisheries and Food, 1983–89; *b* 18 Aug. 1929; *s* of late Joseph Samuel McElheran and Hilda McElheran (*née* Veale); *m* 1956, Jean Patricia Durham; one *s* two *d. Educ:* Archbishop Holgate's Grammar Sch., York; St Edmund Hall, Oxford (MA English, DipEd). Solicitor. Short period of teaching; articled clerk, Thomson & Hetherton, York, 1954; Asst Solicitor, 1959, Partner, 1962, Leathes Prior & Son, Norwich; Sen. Legal Asst, Land Commn, Newcastle upon Tyne, 1967; Sen. Legal Asst, 1971, Asst Solicitor, 1974, Dept of Trade and Industry and successor Depts. ARPS 2002. *Recreation:* photography. *Address:* 12 Bedern, York YO1 7LP. *T:* (01904) 628987. *Club:* Civil Service. *Died 14 Sept. 2005.*

McENTEE, Peter Donovan, CMG 1978; OBE 1963; HM Diplomatic Service, retired; Governor and Commander-in-Chief of Belize, 1976–80; *b* 27 June 1920; *s* of Ewen Brooke McEntee and Caroline Laura Clare (*née* Bayley); *m* 1945, Mary Elisabeth Sherwood; two *d. Educ:* Haileybury Coll., Herts. Served War, HM Forces, 1939–45, KAR (Major). HM Overseas Civil Service, 1946–63: Dist Commissioner; retired as Principal of Kenya Inst. of Administration; First Secretary: Commonwealth Relations Office, 1963; Lagos, 1964–67; Commonwealth Office (later Foreign and Commonwealth Office), 1967–72; Consul-Gen., Karachi, 1972–75. *Recreations:* music, natural history. *Address:* Flat 2, Glebe House, The Street, Ickham, Canterbury, Kent CT3 1QN. *T:* (01227) 722893. *Club:* Royal Over-Seas League (Chm., 1992–95; Vice Pres., 1995). *Died 30 July 2002.*

McFARLANE, Prof. Ian Dalrymple, MBE 1946; FBA 1978; Professor of French Literature, University of Oxford, 1971–83, then Emeritus; Professorial Fellow, Wadham College, Oxford, 1971–83, then Emeritus Fellow; *b* 7 Nov. 1915; *s* of James Blair McFarlane and Valérie Edith Liston Dalrymple; *m* 1939, Marjory Nan Hamilton (*d* 2001); one *s* (one *d* decd). *Educ:* Lycée St-Charles, Marseilles; Tormore Sch., Upper Deal, Kent; Westminster Sch.; St Andrews Univ. (MA 1st class Hons, 1938; Carnegie Research Scholar, 1938–39). Served 1st Bn Black Watch, RHR, 1940–45. Apptd Lectr in French, Cambridge Univ., 1945; Gonville and Caius College: elected Fellow, 1947 (Hon. Fellow, 1990); appointed Senior Tutor, 1956; Prof. of French Language and Literature, St Andrews, 1961–70. Zaharoff Lectr, Oxford,

1984; Hon. Faculty Prof., University Coll., Cardiff, 1984. Hon. Sen. Res. Fellow, Inst. of Romance Studies, Univ. of London, 1990. Member: Scottish Cert. of Educn Examination Board, 1964; Academic Planning Board, Univ. of Stirling, 1964–67; Cttee on Research and Develt in Modern Languages, 1966. Pres., MHRA, 1986. Doctor of Univ. of Paris, 1950; Dr *hc*, Univ. of Tours, 1982; Hon. DLitt St Andrews, 1982. Officier des Palmes Académiques, 1971. *Publications:* critical edn of M. Scève's Délie, 1966; Renaissance France 1470–1589, 1974; Buchanan, 1981; The Entry of Henri II into Paris, 1549, 1982; various, in learned periodicals. *Recreations:* cricket, music. *Address:* Wadham College, Oxford OX1 3PN.
Died 17 Aug. 2002.

McGARRITY, J(ames) Forsyth, CB 1981; HM Senior Chief Inspector of Schools (Scotland), 1973–81; *b* 16 April 1921; *s* of late James McGarrity and Margaret Davidson; *m* 1951, Violet S. G. Philp, MA; one *s* one *d. Educ:* Bathgate Academy; Glasgow Univ. (MA, MEd, BSc). Schoolmaster, 1949–57; HM Inspector of Schools, 1957–68; HM Chief Inspector of Schools, 1968–73. *Recreations:* golf, gardening. *Address:* 30 Oatlands Park, Linlithgow, Scotland EH49 6AS. *T:* (01506) 843258.
Died 22 July 2003.

McGARVIE, Hon. Richard Elgin, AC 1994; Governor of Victoria, 1992–97; *b* 21 May 1926; *s* of Richard Fleming McGarvie and Mabel Catherine McGarvie; *m* 1953, Lesley, *d* of K. G. and G. D. Kerr; two *s* two *d. Educ:* Camperdown High Sch.; Univ. of Melbourne (LLB Hons, BCom). AB, RAustNR, 1944–46. Admitted Victorian Bar, 1952; QC 1963; Judge, Supreme Court of Victoria, 1976–92. Mem., Law Faculty, Melbourne Univ., 1957–88. Chm., Nat. Cttee on Discrimination in Employment and Occupation, 1973–76; Member: Adv. Cttee on Aust. Judicial System, Constitutional Commn, 1985–87; Constitutional Convention on Republic, 1998. Chm., Victorian Bar Council, 1973–75; Treas., Exec. Law Council of Aust., 1974–76; Dep. Chm., then Chm., Aust. Inst. of Judicial Admin, 1980–86 (Mem., 1976–). Mem. Council, Monash Univ., 1980; Chancellor, La Trobe Univ., 1981–92. Hon. LLD Melbourne, 1990; Monash, 1997; DUniv La Trobe, 1995. *Publications:* (jtly) Cases and Materials on Contract, 1962, 4 edns; Democracy: choosing Australia's republic, 1999; papers on law, judiciary, governorship, and head of state/republican issue; author of McGarvie model for head of state in Australia. *Recreations:* reading, sailing, golf. *Address:* 1/62 Grange Road, Sandringham, Vic 3191, Australia. *T:* (3) 95216802. *Clubs:* Royal Automobile, West Brighton (Victoria); Melbourne Cricket. *Died 24 May 2003.*

McGEOWN, Prof. Mary Graham, (Mrs J. M. Freeland), CBE 1985; FRCP, FRCPE, FRCPI; Professorial Fellow, Queen's University of Belfast, since 1988; *b* 19 July 1923; *d* of James Edward McGeown and Sarah Graham Quinn; *m* 1949, Joseph Maxwell Freeland (*d* 1982); three *s. Educ:* Lurgan Coll.; Queen's Univ. of Belfast (MB, BCh, BAO, with Hons, 1946; MD, PhD). House Physician and Surgeon, Royal Victoria Hosp., Belfast, 1947–48; Sen. House Physician, Royal Belfast Hosp. for Sick Children, 1948; Asst Lectr in Pathology, 1948–50, in Biochemistry, 1950–53, QUB; res. grant, MRC, 1953–56; Res. Fellow, Royal Victoria Hosp., 1956–58; Belfast City Hospital: Sen. Hosp. MO, 1958–62; Consultant Nephrologist, 1962–88; Physician in Admin. Charge, Renal Unit, 1968–88. Hon. Reader in Nephrology, QUB, 1972–87. Chm., UK Transplant Management Cttee, 1983–90; Mem., Unrelated Living Transplant Regulatory Authy, 1990–96. Hon. Treas., Renal Assoc., 1986–89 (Pres., 1983–86); Pres., Ulster Med. Soc., 1985–86. Chm., Corrigan Club, 1987. Hon. Member: British Transplantation Soc.; Eur. Dialysis Transplant Assoc.; Eur. Renal Assoc. Lectures: Graves, Royal Acad. of Medicine, Ireland, 1963; Corrigan, 1987, J. Creery Ferguson, 1997, RCPI. Hon. DSc New Univ. of Ulster, 1983; Hon. DMSc QUB, 1991. *Publications:*

Clinical Management of Electrolyte Disorders, 1983; Clinical Management of Renal Transplantation, 1992; numerous papers and chapters in books on calcium metabolism, renal stones, phosphate metabolism, parathyroid function and disease, renal transplantation, kidney diseases. *Recreations:* gardening, antique collecting, genealogy. *Address:* 14 Osborne Gardens, Belfast BT9 6LE. *T:* (028) 9080 2934.   *Died 21 Nov. 2004.*

McGHEE, George Crews; Legion of Merit; businessman; former diplomat; Director: Mobil Oil Co., 1969–82; Procter and Gamble Co., 1969–82; American Security & Trust Co., 1969–82; Trans World Airlines, 1976–82; *b* Waco, Texas, 10 March 1912; *s* of George Summers McGhee and Magnolia (*née* Spruce); *m* 1938, Cecilia Jeanne DeGolyer (decd); one *s* three *d* (and one *s* one *d* decd). *Educ:* Southern Methodist Univ., Dallas; Univ. of Oklahoma (BS 1933); Oxford Univ. (Rhodes Schol.; DPhil 1937); Univ. of London. Served War, US Navy, 1943–45 (Asiatic ribbon with three battle stars). Geologist and geophysicist, 1930–40; oil producer, sole owner, McGhee Production Co., 1940–. Special Asst to Under-Sec of State for Economic Affairs, 1946; Coordinator for Aid to Greece and Turkey, 1947; Asst Sec. of State for Near Eastern, South Asian and African Affairs, 1949; US Ambassador to Turkey, 1951–53; Consultant, Nat. Security Council, 1958; Mem., President's Cttee to Study Mil. Asst Program, 1958; Counselor of Dept of State and Chm., State Dept Policy Planning Council, 1961; Under-Sec. of State for Political Affairs, 1961; Bd, Panama Canal Co., 1962; Actg Sec., Cuban Missile Crisis, Oct. 1963; US Ambassador to the Federal Republic of Germany, 1963–68; Ambassador-at-Large, 1968–69. Chairman: English Speaking Union of US, 1969–74; Business Council for Internat. Understanding, 1969–73; Vice-Chm., Inst. for Study of Diplomacy, 1978–; Member Board: Geo. C. Marshall Res. Foundn, 1972–85; German-American Cultural Fund, 1992–; Amer. Council on Germany, 1969–86; Resources for Future, 1977–82; Asia Foundn, 1974–84; Atlantic Council, 1975–; Atlantic Inst. for Internat. Affairs, 1977–88; Smithsonian Nat. Associates, 1971– (Chm., 1975–76); Population Crisis Cttee, 1969–82; Council of Amer. Ambassadors, 1983–; Amer. Inst. for Contemp. German Studies, 1983–; Nat. Tree Trust, 1992–; President's Circle, Nat. Acad. of Scis, 1989–; Circle, Nat. Gall. of Art, 1991–; Carnegie Council, 1990–; Council for Econ. Develt Sub-cttee on Global Econ. Strategy for US, 1991–. Member: Inst. of Turkish Studies, 1983–86; Sackler Gall. Vis. Cttee, Smithsonian Instn. Trustee: Duke Univ.; Cttee for Economic Develt, 1957–72; Aspen Inst. for Humanistic Studies, 1958–; Salzburg Seminar, 1969–71; Nat. Civil Service League, 1969–71; Folger Library Council, 1983–85. Chm., Saturday Review World, 1974–77. Mem., Amer. Philos. Soc., 1993–. Hon. Fellow, Queen's Coll., Oxford, 1969. Distinguished Service Citation, Univ. of Oklahoma, 1952; Hon. DCL Southern Methodist Univ., 1953; Hon. LLD: Tulane, 1957; Maryland, 1965; Hon. DSc Tampa, 1969. Ouissam Alaouite Cherifien, Govt Morocco, 1950; Hon. Citizen, Ankara, Turkey, 1954; Outstanding Citizen Award, Amer. Friends of Turkey, 1983. *Publications:* Envoy to the Middle World, 1983; (ed) Diplomacy for the Future, 1987; At the Creation of a New Germany, 1989; (ed) National Interest and Global Goals, 1989; The US-Turkish-NATO Middle East Connection, 1990; Dance of the Billions, 1990; International Community: a goal for a New World Order, 1992; Life in Alanya: Turkish delight, 1992; On the Frontline in the Cold War—an Ambassador Reports, 1997; I Did It This Way (autobiog.), 2001; The Ambassador, 2001; Oxford Letters, 2002; contribs to Foreign Affairs, Gewerkschaftliche Rundschau, Werk und Wir, Europa Archiv, Universitas, Ruperto-Carola Weltraumfahrt-Raketentechnik, Europa, Washington Post, New York Times, etc. *Recreations:* hunting, tennis, photography. *Address:* Farmer's Delight, 36276 Mountville Road, Middleburg, VA 20117–3308, USA. *Clubs:* Bohemian (California); Metropolitan, Cosmos

(Washington, DC); Century Association (New York).
                    Died 4 July 2005.

McGILL, Rt Rev. Stephen; Bishop of Paisley, (RC), 1968–88, then Bishop Emeritus; *b* Glasgow, 4 Jan. 1912; *s* of Peter McGill and Charlotte Connolly. *Educ:* St Aloysius', Glasgow; Blairs College, Aberdeen; Coutances, France; Institut Catholique, Paris (STL). Ordained Priest of St Sulpice, 1936. St Mary's College, Blairs, Aberdeen: Spiritual Director, 1940–51; Rector, 1951–60; Bishop of Argyll and the Isles, 1960–68. *Address:* 13 Newark Street, Greenock PA16 7UH.   *Died 9 Nov. 2005.*

McGIRR, Prof. Edward McCombie, CBE 1978; MD; FRCP, FRCPE, FRCPGlas; FFCM; FRSE; Dean, 1974–81, Administrative Dean, 1978–81, and Professor of Administrative Medicine, 1978–81 (then Professor Emeritus), Faculty of Medicine, University of Glasgow; Dean of Faculties, University of Glasgow, 1992–94; Physician, Glasgow Royal Infirmary, 1952–81; Honorary Consultant Physician to the Army in Scotland, 1975–81; *b* 15 June 1916; *yr s* of William and Ann McGirr, Hamilton, Lanarkshire; *m* 1949, Diane Curzon (*d* 1996), *y c* of Alexander Woods, MBE, TD, DL, and Edith E. C. Woods, Birmingham and London; one *s* three *d*. *Educ:* Hamilton Academy; Glasgow Univ. (BSc 1937; MB, ChB (Hons) 1940; MD (Hons) and Bellahouston Medal, 1960). Served RAMC, 1941–46, in UK, India, Burma, Siam, Indo-China; Medical Specialist; demobilized with hon. rank of Major. Glasgow University: various appointments incl. Lectr and Sen. Lectr in Medicine, at Royal Infirmary, Glasgow, 1947–61; Muirhead Prof. of Medicine, 1961–78. Visitor, RCPSG, 1968–70, Pres., 1970–72. Member: Medical Appeals Tribunals, 1961–88; NRPB, 1976–83; Scottish Health Service Planning Council, 1977–84 (Chm., 1978–84); Nat. Med. Consultative Cttee, 1977–81; Med. Sub-Cttee, UGC, 1977–81; GNC for Scotland, 1978–83; Greater Glasgow Health Bd, 1979–85; Nat. Bd for Nursing, Midwifery and Health Visiting for Scotland, 1980–83; Cttee of ten, Tenovus-Scotland, 1981–89; BBC/IBA Scottish Appeals Adv. Cttee, 1982–86; Chairman: Scottish Council for Postgrad. Med. Educn, 1979–85; Scottish Council for Opportunities for Play Experience, 1985–87; Professional Adv. Panel, Prince and Princess of Wales Hospice, 1985–87; Working Party on Play in Scotland, 1986–87; Clyde Estuary Amenity Council, 1986–90. Member: Assoc. of Physicians of Gt Britain and Ireland, 1955– (mem. of editorial panel, Quarterly Journal of Medicine, 1968–76; Mem. Council, 1972–76; Hon. Mem., 1990–); Scottish Soc. of Physicians; Scottish Soc. for Experimental Med. (Treas., 1960–66); Pres., Harveian Soc. of Edin., 1979; Corresp. Member: Amer. Thyroid Assoc.; Medical Research Soc. (mem. of council, 1967–69); Royal Medico-Chirurgical Soc. of Glasgow (Pres., 1965–66). Hon. FACP. Hon. DSc Glasgow, 1994. *Publications:* chiefly in relation to thyroid gland dysfunction, nuclear medicine, medical education, policy planning in the NHS, and 18th century medical history. *Recreations:* family life, curling. *Address:* Anchorage House, Bothwell, by Glasgow G71 8NF. *T:* (01698) 852194. *Club:* Royal Scottish Automobile.
                    Died 12 May 2003.

McGONAGLE, Stephen; Senator, Seanad Éireann, Dublin, 1983–87; *b* 17 Nov. 1914; *m*; five *s* one *d*. *Educ:* Christian Brothers', Derry. Chm., NI Cttee, Irish Congress of Trade Unions, 1959; Vice-Chm., Derry Develt Commn, 1969–71; Pres., Irish Congress of Trade Unions, 1972–73; Mem., NI Economic Council, Indust. Tribunal, Indust. Ct, until 1973; Dist Sec., Irish Transport and General Workers' Union, Dec. 1973; NI Parly Comr For Admin, and Comr for Complaints, 1974–79; Chm., NI Police Complaints Bd, 1977–83. *Recreations:* fishing, boating, reading.   *Died 4 March 2002.*

McGOWAN, 3rd Baron *cr* 1937; **Harry Duncan Cory McGowan;** Managing Director, WestLB Panmure Ltd, since 1999 (Chairman, 1995–99); Partner, Panmure, Gordon & Co., 1971–86; *b* 20 July 1938; *e s* of Harry

Wilson McGowan, 2nd Baron McGowan, and Carmen (*d* 1996), *d* of Sir (James) Herbert Cory, 1st Bt; *S* father, 1966; *m* 1962, Lady Gillian Angela Pepys, *d* of 7th Earl of Cottenham; one *s* two *d*. *Educ:* Eton. Non-executive Director: BNB Resources plc; Halma plc; Wassall plc. Mem., Jockey Club. *Heir: s* Hon. Harry John Charles McGowan [*b* 23 June 1971; *m* 2001, Emma, *d* of Duncan Hattersley Smith]. *Address:* Highway House, Lower Froyle, Alton, Hants GU34 4NB. *T:* (01420) 22104; 12 Stanhope Mews East, SW7 5QU. *T:* (020) 7370 2346. *Clubs:* Boodle's, Cavalry and Guards.

Died 6 May 2003.

McGOWAN, Bruce Henry, MA; FRSA; Headmaster, Haberdashers' Aske's School, Elstree, 1973–87; *b* 27 June 1924; *er s* of late Rt Rev. Henry McGowan, sometime Bishop of Wakefield, and Nora Heath McGowan (*née* Godwin); *m* 1947, Beryl McKenzie (*née* Liggitt); one *s* three *d*. *Educ:* King Edward's Sch., Birmingham; Jesus Coll., Cambridge. War service, Royal Artillery, 1943–46 (India and Burma). Asst Master, King's Sch., Rochester, 1949–53; Senior History Master, Wallasey Gram. Sch., 1953–57; Headmaster: De Aston Sch., Market Rasen, Lincs, 1957–64; Solihull Sch., 1964–73. Page Scholar of the English-Speaking Union, 1961. Member: Church Assembly, 1963–70; Public Schools Commn, 1968–70; Council, Church Schools Co., 1986–92 (Chm., 1987–92); Cttee, GBGSA, 1989–93; GBA, 1992–95; Chairman: Boarding Schools Assoc., 1967–69; Headmasters' Conference, 1985 (Chairman: London Div. 1977; Community Service Cttee, 1976–80; Political and Public Relations Cttee, 1981–84). Comr, Duke of York's Royal Mil. Sch., Dover, 1986–96; Governor: Bristol Grammar Sch., 1983–95; St George's Sch., Harpenden, 1977–81, 1984–97; Greycotes Sch., Oxford, 1987–96; Ellesmere Coll., 1992–94; Adv. Gov., St Benedict's Sch., Ealing, 1989–2001. Church Warden, St Mary's, N Leigh, Oxford, 1993–96. Fellow Woodard Corp., 1990–94. *Recreations:* foreign travel, motor-caravanning, music, the theatre. *Address:* The Bell House, 29 Union Street, Woodstock, Oxon OX20 1JF. *Club:* East India.

Died 24 May 2004.

McGRATH, John Peter; writer and director, theatre, film and television; Director, Freeway Films, since 1983; *b* 1 June 1935; *s* of John Francis McGrath and Margaret McGrath; *m* 1962, Elizabeth Maclennan; two *s* one *d*. *Educ:* Alun Grammar Sch., Mold; St John's Coll., Oxford. Theatre (playwright), 1958–61; BBC Television, 1960–65; film (screenwriting) and theatre (writing and directing), 1965–70; theatre, with regular forays into television and film, as writer and director, 1970–; founded 7:84 Theatre Co., 1971, Artistic Dir, 1971–88; Dir, C4 Television, 1989–94. Judith E. Wilson Vis. Fellow, Cambridge, 1979, 1988; Vis. Prof. in Media Studies, RHBNC, 1996–. Produced or directed over 75 plays in the theatre, and wrote over 40 plays, including: Why the Chicken, 1959; The Tent, 1960; Comrade Jacob, 1968; Soft or a Girl, 1971; Trees in the Wind, 1971; Sergeant Musgrave Dances On (adaptation), 1972; Boom, 1974; Lay Off, 1975; Out of Our Heads, 1976; Trembling Giant, 1977; Bitter Apples, 1979; Nightclass, 1981; Rejoice!, 1982; The Catch, 1982; Women in Power, 1983; Women of the Dunes, 1983; Six Men of Dorset (adaptation), 1984; The Albannach (adaptation), 1984; The Baby and the Bathwater, 1984; All the Fun of the Fair, 1985; There is a Happy Land, 1986; Mairi Mhor, 1987; Border Warfare, 1989; John Brown's Body, 1990; Watching for Dolphins, 1991; The Wicked Old Man, 1992; The Silver Darlings (adaptation), 1994; Reading Rigoberta, 1995; The Four Estaites, 1996; The Last of the MacEachans, 1996; many TV plays performed on BBC and ITV; prod. film Carrington, 1995; co-prod. film Ma Vie En Rose, 1997; screenplays: The Bofors Gun, 1967; Billion Dollar Brain, 1967; The Virgin Soldiers (adaptation), 1968; The Reckoning, 1968; Blood Red Roses, 1986 (dir); The Dressmaker, 1988 (exec. producer); The Long Roads, 1993; wrote libretto for Alexander Goehr's opera, Behold

the Sun; writes songs and poems. Writer's Award, BAFTA, 1994; Lifetime Achievement Award, Writers Guild of GB, 1997. DUniv Stirling, 1992. *Publications: plays:* Events While Guarding the Bofors Gun, 1966; Random Happenings in the Hebrides, 1972; Bakke's Night of Fame, 1973; The Cheviot, The Stag and The Black Black Oil, 1974, 2nd edn 1981; The Game's A Bogey, 1974; Fish in the Sea, 1977; Little Red Hen, 1977; Yobbo Nowt, 1978; Joe's Drum, 1979; Blood Red Roses (filmed for TV, 1986), and Swings and Roundabouts, 1981; Six Pack: six plays for Scotland, 1996; *general:* A Good Night Out, 1981; The Bone Won't Break, 1990. *Address:* c/o Freeway Films, 33A Pembroke Square, W8 6PD.   *Died 22 Jan. 2002.*

MACGREGOR, Sir Edwin (Robert), 7th Bt *cr* 1828; Mayor, District of Sooke, since 1999; Deputy Minister, Ministry of Lands and Parks, Province of British Columbia, Victoria, BC, 1991–92, retired; *b* 4 Dec. 1931; *e s* of Sir Robert McConnell Macgregor, 6th Bt, and of Annie Mary Lane; *S* father, 1963; *m* 1st, 1952, (Margaret Alice) Jean Peake (marr. diss. 1981); one *s* two *d* (and one *s* decd); 2nd, 1982, (Helen) Linda Herriott; two step *d*. *Educ:* Univ. of British Columbia (BASc 1955, MASc 1957, Metallurgical Engrg). Plant Manager, 1965–72, Marketing Manager, Metals, 1972–74, Union Carbide Canada Ltd. Dep. Minister, Min. of Crown Lands, BC, 1989–91. Life Mem., Assoc. of Professional Engrs and Geoscientists, Province of BC. *Publications:* contribs to Trans Amer. Inst. of Mining, Metallurgical and Petroleum Engrg, Jl Amer. Chem. Soc. *Recreations:* reading; participation in several outdoor sports such as golf, swimming, fishing, etc.; music. *Heir: s* Ian Grant Macgregor, *b* 22 Feb. 1959. *Address:* Scarlet Oak, 6136 Kirby Road, Sooke, BC V0S 1N0, Canada.   *Died 28 March 2003.*

MACGREGOR, Rt Rev. Gregor; Bishop of Moray, Ross and Caithness, 1994–98; *b* 17 Nov. 1933; *m* 1956, Elizabeth Jean Harris; one *s* three *d*. *Educ:* St Andrews Univ. (MA 1964; BD 1967). Ordained deacon, 1976, priest, 1977; NSM, Elie and Earlsferry, and Pittenweem, 1977–81; Rector, Glenrothes, 1981–86; Vice-Provost, Cumbrae, 1986; Rector, Dollar, 1987–90; Mission Priest, St Luke, Wester Hailes, 1991–94. *Address:* Flat 11, John Ker Court, 42 Polwarth Gardens, Edinburgh EH11 1LN. *T:* (0131) 229 6938.   *Died 29 June 2003.*

MacGREGOR OF MacGREGOR, Brig. Sir Gregor, 6th Bt *cr* 1795; ADC 1979; 23rd Chief of Clan Gregor; *b* 22 Dec. 1925; *o s* of Capt. Sir Malcolm MacGregor of MacGregor, 5th Bt, CB, CMG, and Hon. Gylla Lady MacGregor of MacGregor, OBE (*d* 1980); *S* father, 1958; *m* 1958, Fanny, *o d* of C. H. A. Butler, Shortgrove, Newport, Essex; two *s*. *Educ:* Eton. Commissioned Scots Guards, 1944; served: War of 1939–45; Palestine, 1947–48; Malaya, 1950–51; Borneo, 1965. Staff Coll. Course, 1960; Brigade Major, 16th Parachute Bde Gp, 1961–63; Joint Services Staff Coll., 1965; commanding 1st Bn Scots Guards, 1966–69; GSO1 (BLO) Fort Benning, USA, 1969–71; Col Recruiting, HQ Scotland, 1971; Lt-Col commanding Scots Guards, 1971–74; Defence and Mil. Attaché, British Embassy, Athens, 1975–78; Comdr, Lowlands, 1978–80. Grand Master Mason of Scotland, 1988–93. Mem. of the Royal Company of Archers (Queen's Body Guard for Scotland), 1949–. *Heir: s* Major Malcolm Gregor Charles MacGregor of MacGregor, Scots Guards [*b* 23 March 1959; *m* 1988, Cecilia, *er d* of Sir Ilay Campbell of Succoth, 7th Bt]. *Address:* Bannatyne, Newtyle, Blairgowrie, Perthshire PH12 8TR. *T:* (01828) 650314. *Club:* New (Edinburgh).

Died 30 March 2003.

McGUIRE, Gerald, OBE 1974; Vice-President, Council for National Parks, 1983–90 and since 1995 (President, 1990–92; Vice-Chairman, 1981–83); *b* 12 July 1918; *s* of John Charles McGuire and Adelaide Maud McGuire (*née* Davies); *m* 1942, Eveline Mary Jenkins; one *s* one *d*. *Educ:* Trinity County Sch., Wood Green. Youth Hostels Association: Reg. Sec., N Yorks, 1944–64; National

Countryside and Educn Officer, 1964–74; Dep. Nat. Sec., 1974–82; Pres., N England Region, 1989–95. President: Ramblers Assoc., 1975–78 (Vice Pres., 1978–; Pres., Lake Dist Area, 1983–86; Pres., E Yorks and Derwent Area, 1987–90); Assoc. of National Park and Countryside Voluntary Wardens, 1978–80; Chm., Countryside Link Gp, 1982–86. Member: N York Moors Nat. Park Cttee, 1953–72, 1985–91; Exec. Cttee, CPRE, 1966–76, 1981–84; Gosling Cttee on Footpaths, 1967–68; Countryside Commn, 1976–79; Commn on Energy and the Environment, 1978–81; Recreation and Conservation Cttee, Yorks Water Authority, 1984–89; Yorks Regional Cttee, Nat. Trust, 1985–93; Jt Adv. Cttee, Howardian Hills Area of Outstanding Natural Beauty, 1992–97. Vice Pres., Open Spaces Soc., 1982–98 (Vice Chm. 1971–76); Vice Chairman: Standing Cttee on Nat. Parks, 1970–76; Council for Environmental Conservation, 1981–82; Trustee, Gatliff Trust, 1983–94. Hon. Mem., Cyclists Touring Club, 1978–. Cert. of Merit, Internat. Youth Hostel Fedn, 1983; Richard Schirrmann (Founder's) Medal, German Youth Hostels Assoc., 1983; Nat. Blood Transfusion Service Award for 100 donations, 1983; CPRE Medal, 1998. *Recreations:* reading, music, walking in the countryside. *Address:* 24 Castle Howard Drive, Malton, North Yorks YO17 7BA. *T:* (01653) 692521.
Died 10 Feb. 2002.

McINDOE, William Ian, CB 1978; Deputy Secretary, Department of the Environment, 1979–86; *b* 11 March 1929; *s* of John McIndoe, Leven, Fife and Agnes Scott; *m* 1st, 1954, Irene Armour Mudie (*d* 1966); one *s* two *d*; 2nd, 1971, Jamesanna Smart (*née* MacGregor) (*d* 2002). *Educ:* Sedbergh; Corpus Christi Coll., Oxford. 2nd Lieut 2 RHA, 1951–53; CRO, 1953–63, served in Canberra and Salisbury, 1956–62, Private Sec. to Sec. of State, 1962–63; Private Sec. to Sec. of Cabinet, later Asst Sec., Cabinet Office, 1963–66; Scottish Office, 1966–76, Under-Sec., 1971; Dep. Sec., Cabinet Office, 1976–79. Dep. Chm., Housing Corp., 1986–90. *Address:* Lochside Cottage, Lochside, Lochwinnoch, Renfrewshire PA12 4JH. *T:* (01505) 844866. *Died 2 April 2005.*

MacINNES, Archibald, CVO 1977; Under Secretary, Property Services Agency, Department of the Environment, 1973–79; retired 1989; *b* 10 April 1919; *s* of Duncan and Catherine MacInnes; *m* 1950, Nancey Elisabeth Blyth (*d* 1976); one *s* two *d*. *Educ:* Kirkcudbright Academy; Royal Technical Coll., Glasgow. FIMechE. Scott's Shipbuilding and Engineering Co., Greenock, 1937–44; Colonial Service, Nigeria, 1945–59; War Office Works Organisation: Gibraltar, 1959–63; Southern Comd, Salisbury, Wilts, 1963–64; MPBW, Bristol, 1964–68; DoE, Germany, 1968–72; Dir, London Region, PSA, DoE, 1972–79; part-time Planning Inspector, DoE, 1980–89. FCMI. Coronation Medal. *Recreations:* golf, shooting, fishing. *Address:* Heymersh Lodge, Lower Road, Bamford, Salisbury, Wilts SP5 4DU. *T:* (01722) 413088.
Died 23 April 2004.

McINTOSH, Prof. Angus, FRSE 1978; FBA 1989; consultant on linguistics problems; hon. consultant, Institute for Historical Dialectology (formerly Gayre Institute for Medieval English and Scottish Dialectology), University of Edinburgh, since 1986; *b* 10 Jan. 1914; *s* of late Kenneth and Mary McIntosh (*née* Thompson), Cleadon, Sunderland, Co. Durham; *m* 1st, 1939, Barbara (*d* 1988), *d* of late Dr William Seaman and Mrs Bainbridge (*née* June Wheeler), New York City; two *s* one *d*; 2nd, 1988, Karina Williamson (*née* Side), *widow* of Colin Williamson, Fellow of Jesus Coll., Oxford; two step *s* one step *d*. *Educ:* Ryhope Grammar Sch., Co. Durham; Oriel Coll., Oxford (BA, 1st Class Hons, English Lang. and Lit., 1934; MA 1938); Merton Coll., Oxford (Harmsworth Schol.); Dip. of Comparative Philology, Univ. of Oxford, 1936; Harvard Univ. (Commonwealth Fund Fellow, 1936–38; AM 1937). Lecturer, Dept of English, University College, Swansea, 1938–46. Served War of 1939–45, beginning as trooper in Tank Corps, finishing as

Major in Intelligence Corps. University Lecturer in Mediæval English, Oxford, 1946–48; Lecturer in English, Christ Church, Oxford, 1946–47; Student of Christ Church, 1947–48; University of Edinburgh: Forbes Prof. of English Language and General Linguistics, 1948–64, later Forbes Prof. of Eng. Lang., 1964–79; Dir, Middle English Dialect Atlas Project, 1979–86; Hon. Sen. Res. Fellow, Dept of English Language, Glasgow Univ., 1993–. Co-Chm., Hon. Adv. Bd, Pergamon Encyclopedia of Lang. and Linguistics, 1988–94. Rockefeller Foundation Fellowship, US, June-Sept. 1949; Leverhulme Emeritus Res. Fellow, 1984–86. Hon. Fellow, Scottish Text Soc., 1989– (Pres., 1977–89). For. Mem., Finnish Acad. of Science and Letters, 1976. Hon. DPhil Poznan Univ., 1972; Hon. DLitt: Durham, 1980; Glasgow, 1994; Edinburgh, 2004. Sir Israel Gollancz Prize, British Acad., 1989. *Publications:* books, articles and reviews on English language and related topics. *Recreations:* gardening, painting, music. *Address:* 12 Strathearn Place, Edinburgh EH9 2AL. *T:* (0131) 447 8405. *Died 25 Oct. 2005.*

McINTOSH, Rev. Canon Hugh; Hon. Canon, St Mary's Cathedral, Glasgow, since 1983; *b* 5 June 1914; *s* of Hugh Burns McIntosh and Mary (*née* Winter); *m* 1951, Ruth Georgina, *er d* of late Rev. William Skinner Wilson and Enid (*née* Sanders); two *s* one *d*. *Educ:* Hatfield Coll., Durham (Exhibr; LTh, 1941; BA (dist.) 1942; MA 1945); Edinburgh Theological Coll. (Luscombe Schol.). Ordained deacon and priest, 1942; Precentor and Senior Chaplain, St Paul's Cathedral, Dundee, 1942–46; Senior Chaplain, St Mary's Cathedral, Edinburgh, 1946–49; Curate, St Salvador's, Edinburgh, 1949–51; Rector, St Adrian's, Gullane, 1951–54; Rector, St John's, Dumfries, 1954–66; Canon of St Mary's Cathedral, Glasgow, and Synod Clerk of Glasgow and Galloway, 1959; Provost of St Mary's Cathedral, Glasgow, 1966–70; Rector, Christ Church, Lanark, 1970–83. *Recreations:* reading, writing, and (a little) arithmetic. *Address:* 2 Ridgepark Drive, Lanark ML11 7PG. *T:* (01555) 663458.
Died 31 March 2002.

McINTOSH, Vice-Admiral Sir Ian (Stewart), KBE 1973 (MBE 1941); CB 1970; DSO 1944; DSC 1942; Management Selection Consultant, 1973–78; *b* 11 Oct. 1919; *s* of late A. J. McIntosh, Melbourne, Australia; *m* 1943, Elizabeth Rosemary Rasmussen (*d* 1995); three *s* (one *d* decd). *Educ:* Geelong Grammar Sch. Entered RN, 1938; comd HM Submarine: H44, 1942; Sceptre, 1943–44; Alderney, 1946–48; Aeneas, 1950–51; Exec. Officer, HMS Ark Royal, 1956–58; comd 2nd Submarine Sqn, 1961–63; comd HMS Victorious, 1966–68; Dir-Gen., Weapons (Naval), 1968–70; Dep. Chief of Defence Staff (Op. Req.), 1971–73, retd 1973. Captain, 1959; Rear-Adm., 1968; Vice-Adm., 1971. Chairman: Sea Cadet Assoc., 1973–83; HMS Cavalier Trust, 1974–88. *Recreations:* friends, reading, music. *Address:* 19 The Crescent, Alverstoke, Hants PO12 2DH. *T:* (023) 9258 0510. *Club:* Royal Over-Seas League.
Died 30 July 2003.

MacINTYRE, Rt Hon. Duncan, CMG 1992; DSO 1945; OBE 1956; ED; PC (NZ) 1980; Deputy Prime Minister of New Zealand, 1981–84; *b* 1915; *s* of A. MacIntyre; *m* Diana, *d* of Percy Hunter; two *s* three *d*. Sheep farming, 1933–39 and 1946–. Served War, NZ Army, 1939–46; Territorial Force, 1949–60 (Brig. 1956); Col Comdt RNZAC, 1976. MP (National Party) Hastings, 1960–72, Bay of Plenty, 1975–78, East Cape, 1978–84; Minister: of Lands, of Forests, and i/c of Valuation Dept, 1966–72; of Maori Affairs and of Island Affairs, 1969–72; for the Environment, 1972; of Agriculture, of Fisheries, and i/c of Rural Banking and Finance Corp., 1975–84; of Maori Affairs, 1975–78. *Address:* Taikura, RD4, Waipukurau, New Zealand.
Died 7 June 2001.

McINTYRE, Very Rev. Prof. John, CVO 1985; DD; DLitt; FRSE; Professor of Divinity, University of Edinburgh, 1956–86, then Emeritus; Dean of the Order of the Thistle, 1974–89; Chaplain to the Queen in Scotland, 1975–86; an Extra Chaplain to the Queen in Scotland, 1974–75 and since 1986; Moderator of the General Assembly of the Church of Scotland, 1982; *b* 20 May 1916; *s* of late John C. McIntyre, Bathgate, Scotland, and Annie McIntyre; *m* 1945, Jessie B., *d* of late William Buick, Coupar-Angus; two *s* one *d*. *Educ*: Bathgate Academy; University of Edinburgh; MA 1938; BD 1941; DLitt 1953. Ordained, 1941; Locum Tenens, Parish of Glenorchy and Inishail, 1941–43; Minister of Parish of Fenwick, Ayrshire, 1943–45; Hunter Baillie Prof. of Theology, St Andrew's Coll., University of Sydney, 1946–56; Principal of St Andrew's Coll., 1950–56 (Hon. Fellow, 1990); Principal Warden, Pollock Halls of Residence, Univ. of Edinburgh, 1960–71; actg Principal and Vice-Chancellor, Edinburgh Univ., 1973–74, 1979; Principal, New Coll., and Dean of Faculty of Divinity, 1968–74. FRSE 1977 (Vice-Pres., 1983–86). DD *hc* Glasgow, 1961; DHL *hc* Coll. of Wooster, Ohio, 1983; Dr *hc* Edinburgh, 1987. *Publications*: St Anselm and His Critics, 1954; The Christian Doctrine of History, 1957; On the Love of God, 1962; The Shape of Christology, 1966, 2nd edn 1998; Faith, Theology and Imagination, 1987; The Shape of Soteriology, 1992; The Shape of Pneumatology, 1997; Theology after the Storm (ed G. D. Badcock), 1997; articles and reviews in various learned jls of Theology. *Address*: 317 Mayfield Court, 27 West Savile Terrace, Edinburgh EH9 3DT. *T*: (0131) 667 1203.   *Died 18 Dec. 2005.*

McIVOR, Rt Hon. Basil; *see* McIvor, Rt Hon. W. B.

McIVOR, Rt Hon. (William) Basil, OBE 1991; PC (NI) 1971; *b* 17 June 1928; 2nd *s* of Rev. Frederick McIvor, Methodist clergyman and Lilly McIvor; *m* 1953, Frances Jill Anderson (CBE 1994); two *s* one *d*. *Educ*: Methodist Coll., Belfast; Queen's Univ., Belfast (LLB 1948). Called to NI Bar, 1950; Jun. Crown Counsel, Co. Down, Sept. 1974, Resident Magistrate, Dec. 1974. MP (UU) Larkfield, NI Parlt, 1969; Minister of Community Relations, NI, 1971–72; Member (UU) for S Belfast, NI Assembly, 1973–75; Minister of Education, NI, 1974. Founder Mem., 1976–, Chm., 1988–, Fold Housing Assoc. Chm., All Children Together (the pioneering movement for integrated educn by consent), 1990–92 (Mem., 1974–). Governor, Campbell Coll., 1975– (Chm., 1983–85); Chm. Bd of Governors, Lagan Coll., Belfast, 1981– (the first integrated RC and Protestant school in NI). *Publication*: Hope Deferred: experiences of an Irish Unionist, 1998. *Recreations*: golf, music, gardening. *Address*: Larkhill, 98 Spa Road, Ballynahinch, Co. Down BT24 8PP. *T*: (028) 9756 3534. *Club*: Royal Over-Seas League.   *Died 5 Nov. 2004.*

MACK, Keith Robert; Director-General, European Organisation for the Safety of Air Navigation (Eurocontrol), 1989–93; *b* 2 March 1933; *s* of late David Stanley Mack and Dorothy Ivy Mack (*née* Bowes); *m* 1960, Eileen Mary Cuttell; two *s* four *d*. *Educ*: Edmonton County School. RAF Pilot, 1951–58; Civilian Air Traffic Control Officer, Scottish and Oceanic Air Traffic Control Centre, 1960–67; RAF Staff College, Bracknell, 1968; NATS HQ, 1969–71; ATC Watch Supervisor, Scottish ATCC, 1972–73; CAA Chief Officer, Cardiff Airport, 1974; NATS HQ, 1975–76; ATC Watch Supervisor, London ATCC, 1977; NATS Dep. Dir of Control (Airspace Policy), 1978–79; Supt, London ATCC, 1980–82; Dep. Controller, NATS, 1983–84; Mem. Bd and Gp Dir, CAA, and Controller, NATS, 1985–88. *Recreations*: music, walking, reading. *Address*: 67 Forest House, Russell-Cotes Road, Bournemouth BH1 3UB.   *Died 11 March 2001.*

McKANE, Prof. William, FRSE 1984; FBA 1980; Professor of Hebrew and Oriental Languages, University of St Andrews, 1968–90, then Emeritus; Principal of St Mary's College, St Andrews, 1982–86; *b* 18 Feb. 1921; *s* of Thomas McKane and Jemima Smith McKane; *m* 1952, Agnes Mathie Howie; three *s* two *d*. *Educ*: Univ. of St Andrews (MA 1949); Univ. of Glasgow (MA 1952, PhD

1956, DLitt 1980). RAF, 1941–45. University of Glasgow: Asst in Hebrew, 1953–56; Lectr in Hebrew, 1956–65; Sen. Lectr, 1965–68; Dean, Faculty of Divinity, St Andrews, 1973–77. Fellow, Nat. Humanities Center, NC, USA, 1987–88. Foreign Sec., Soc. for Old Testament Study, 1981–86 (Pres., 1978); Corresponding Mem., Göttingen Akad. der Wissenschaften. DD (*hc*) Edinburgh, 1984. Burkitt Medal, British Acad., 1985. *Publications*: Prophets and Wise Men, 1965; Proverbs: a new approach, 1970; Studies in the Patriarchal Narratives, 1979; Jeremiah 1–25 (International Critical Commentary series), 1986; Selected Christian Hebraists, 1989; A Late Harvest, 1995; Jeremiah 26–52 (International Critical Commentary Series), 1996; Micah: introduction and commentary, 1998; articles and reviews in British and European learned jls. *Recreations*: St Andrews association football blue (1949), walking. *Address*: 51 Irvine Crescent, St Andrews, Fife KY16 8LG. *T*: (01334) 73797. *Club*: Royal and Ancient Golf (St Andrews).   *Died 4 Sept. 2004.*

MACKAY OF ARDBRECKNISH, Baron *cr* 1991 (Life Peer), of Tayvallich in the District of Argyll and Bute; **John Jackson Mackay;** PC 1996; DL; Lord Chairman of Committees, House of Lords, since 2001; *b* 15 Nov. 1938; *s* of late Jackson Mackay and Jean Mackay; *m* 1961, Sheena Wagner; two *s* one *d*. *Educ*: Glasgow Univ. (BSc, DipEd). Formerly, Head of Maths Dept, Oban High Sch.; Chief Exec., Scottish Cons. Central Office, 1987–90; Chm., Sea Fish Industry Authy, 1990–93. MP (C): Argyll, 1979–83; Argyll and Bute, 1983–87; Parly Under-Sec. of State, Scottish Office, 1982–87; a Lord in Waiting (Govt Whip), 1993–94; Parly Under-Sec. of State, Dept of Transport, 1994; Minister of State, DSS, 1994–97; Dep. Leader of Opposition, H of L, 1998–2000. Member: H of L Select Cttee on EC, 1991–93; H of L Sub-Cttee on Energy, Industry and Transport, 1991–93; H of L Delegated Powers Scrutiny Cttee, 1992–93. Pres., Glasgow Bn, Boys' Brigade, 1993–98. DL Glasgow, 1997. *Recreation*: fishing. *Address*: Innishail, 51 Springkell Drive, Pollokshields, Glasgow G41 4EZ.
                    Died 21 Feb. 2001.

MACKAY, Charles, CB 1986; FIBiol; Chief Agricultural Officer, Department of Agriculture and Fisheries for Scotland, 1975–87; *b* 12 Jan. 1927; *s* of Hugh and Eliza Mackay; *m* 1956, Marie A. K. Mackay (*née* Mitchell); one *s* one *d*. *Educ*: Strathmore Sch., Sutherland; Lairg Higher Grade Sch., Sutherland; Univ. of Aberdeen (BScAgric); Univ. of Kentucky (MSc). Department of Agriculture and Fisheries for Scotland: Temporary Inspector, 1947–48; Asst Inspector, 1948–54; Inspector, 1954–64; Sen. Inspector, 1964–70; Technical Develt Officer, 1970–73; Dep. Chief Agricl Officer, 1973–75. Hon. Order of Kentucky Colonels, 1960. *Recreations*: fishing, golf. *Address*: The Cottage, 3 West Shinness, Lairg, Sutherland IV27 4DW. *T*: (01549) 402114.   *Died 3 Oct. 2004.*

McKAY, Sir John (Andrew), Kt 1972; CBE 1966; QPM 1968; HM Chief Inspector of Constabulary for England and Wales, 1970–72; *b* 28 Nov. 1912; *s* of late Denis McKay, Blantyre, Lanarkshire; *m* 1st, 1947, Gertrude Gillespie Deighan (*d* 1971); two *d*; 2nd, 1976, Mildred Grace Kilday, *d* of late Dr Emil Stern and Grace Mildred Pleasants, San Francisco. *Educ*: Glasgow Univ. (MA 1934). Joined Metropolitan Police, 1935; Metropolitan Police Coll., 1937–38; seconded to Army for service with Military Govt in Italy and Austria, 1943–47 (Lt-Col); Asst Chief Constable, then Dep. Chief Constable, Birmingham, 1953–58; Chief Constable of Manchester, 1959–66; HM Inspector of Constabulary, 1966–70. Freeman of City of London, 1972. Hon. Fellow, Manchester Polytechnic, subseq. Manchester Metropolitan Univ., 1971. Hon. MA Manchester, 1966. OStJ 1963. *Address*: 212 Mocking Bird Circle, Santa Rosa, CA 95409, USA. *T*: (707) 5388285.
                    Died 24 Oct. 2004.

McKEAN, Douglas, CB 1977; Under-Secretary, HM Treasury, 1962–77, retired; *b* 2 April 1917; *s* of late

Alexander McKean, Enfield, Middx; *m* 1st, 1942, Anne (*d* 1994), *d* of late Roger Clayton, Riding Mill, Northumberland; two *s*; 2nd, 1995, Joyce, *widow* of Alan Beslee; one step *d*. *Educ*: Merchant Taylors' Sch.; St John's Coll., Oxford. War Office, 1947; transferred to HM Treasury, 1949; Asst Sec., 1956; Under-Sec., 1962; on loan to Dept of the Environment, 1970–72. Dir, Agric. Mortgage Corp., 1978–87. Dep. Sec., Central Bd of Finance, Church of England, 1978–83. Trustee, Irish Sailors and Soldiers Land Trust, 1980–99; Governor, Whitelands Coll., 1984–89. *Publication*: Money Matters: a guide to the finances of the Church of England, 1987. *Recreation*: mountain walking. *Address*: 66 Graeme Road, Enfield, Middx EN1 3UT. *T*: (020) 8363 5438. *Club*: Oxford and Cambridge. *Died 28 May 2001.*

McKECHNIE, Dame Sheila (Marshall), DBE 2001 (OBE 1995); Director, Consumers' Association, since 1995; *b* Falkirk, 3 May 1948. *Educ*: Falkirk High School; Edinburgh Univ. (MA Politics and History); Warwick Univ. (MA Industrial Relations). Research Asst, Oxford Univ., 1971–72; Asst Gen. Sec., Wall Paper Workers Union Staff Section, 1972–74; WEA Tutor, Manchester, 1974–76; Health and Safety Officer, ASTMS, 1976–85; Dir, Shelter, 1985–94. A Dir, Bank of England, 1998–2003. DUniv Open, 1994; Hon. DSc(SocSci) Edinburgh, 1994. *Address*: Consumers' Association, 2 Marylebone Road, NW1 4DF; *e-mail*: do@which.co.uk. *Died 2 Jan. 2004.*

McKEE, Major Sir Cecil; *see* McKee, Major Sir William Cecil.

McKEE, Major Sir (William) Cecil, Kt 1959; ERD; JP; estate agent; *b* 13 April 1905; *s* of late W. B. McKee and M. G. B. Bulloch; *m* 1932, Florence Ethel Irene Gill; one *d*. *Educ*: Methodist Coll., Belfast; Queen's Univ., Belfast. Alderman, Belfast Corporation, 1934; High Sheriff, Belfast, 1946; Deputy Lord Mayor, 1947, Lord Mayor of Belfast, 1957–59. JP Belfast, 1957. Pres., NI Br., Inst. of Dirs, 1957–59. Served with Royal Artillery in War of 1939–45. KStJ. 1982. Hon. LLD Queen's Univ., Belfast, 1960. *Recreation*: golf. *Address*: 9 Ailsa Road, Holywood, Co. Down BT18 0AS. *Clubs*: Ulster Reform (Belfast); Royal County Down Golf. *Died 4 Jan. 2003.*

McKENNA, David, CBE 1967 (OBE 1946; MBE 1943); FCIT; Member, British Railways Board, 1968–76 (part-time Member, 1976–78); *b* 16 Feb. 1911; *s* of late Rt Hon. Reginald McKenna and Pamela Margaret McKenna (*née* Jekyll); *m* 1934, Lady Cecilia Elizabeth Keppel, *d* of 9th Earl of Albemarle, MC; three *d*. *Educ*: Eton; Trinity Coll., Cambridge (BA 1933, MA 1946). Served War of 1939–45, Transportation Service, RE, Iraq, Turkey, India and Burma (Lt-Col). London Passenger Transport Board, 1934–39, and 1946–55; Asst Gen. Manager, Southern Region of BR, 1955–61; Chief Commercial Officer, HQ, BR, 1962; Gen. Manager, Southern Region of BR, and Chm., Southern Railway Bd, 1963–68; Chm., British Transport Advertising, 1968–81. Mem., Dover Harbour Bd, 1969–80; Dir, Isles of Scilly Steamship Co., 1976–92. Pres., Chartered Inst. of Transport, 1972. Chm. of Govs, Sadler's Wells, 1962–76. Vice-Pres., Royal College of Music; Chm., Bach Choir, 1964–76. FRCM. Commandeur de l'Ordre National du Mérite, 1974. *Publications*: various papers on transport subjects. *Recreations*: music, sailing. *Address*: Rosteague, Portscatho, Truro, Cornwall TR2 5EF. *Clubs*: Brooks's; Royal Cornwall Yacht (Falmouth). *Died 29 Jan. 2003.*

MacKENNA, Robert Ogilvie; University Librarian and Keeper of the Hunterian Books and MSS, Glasgow, 1951–78; *b* 21 March 1913; *s* of late Dr John G. MacKenna and Katherine Ogilvie; *m* 1942, Ray (*d* 2001), *o d* of late Samuel Mullin, Glasgow. *Educ*: Paisley Grammar Sch.; Glasgow Univ. (MA). MCLIP. Served War, as officer, RNVR, 1939–45. Asst Librarian, Glasgow Univ., 1936; Sub-Librarian, Leeds Univ., 1946; Librarian, King's Coll., Newcastle upon Tyne (Univ. of Durham), 1948–51.

Trustee, Nat. Library of Scotland, 1953–79. Pres., Scottish Library Assoc., 1966; Chm., SCONUL, 1967–69. Pres., Scottish Cricket Union, 1968. Editor: The Philosophical Jl, 1976–77; Glasgow Cathedral Lecture Series, 1986–. *Publication*: Glasgow University Athletic Club: the story of the first hundred years, 1981. *Recreations*: watching and talking cricket, reading. *Address*: 40 Kelvin Court, Glasgow G12 0AE. *Club*: College (Glasgow). *Died 22 Nov. 2004.*

MacKENZIE, Prof. David Neil, PhD; FBA 1996; Professor of Iranian Studies, University of Göttingen, 1975–94, Professor Emeritus since 1994; *b* 8 April 1926; *s* of David MacKenzie and Ada MacKenzie (*née* Hopkins); *m* 1951, Gina Schaefer (marr. diss. 1981); three *s* one *d*. *Educ*: Sch. of Oriental and African Studies, Univ. of London (BA 1951; MA 1953; PhD 1958). School of Oriental and African Studies, University of London: Lectr in Kurdish, 1955–61; Lectr in Iranian Langs, 1961–65; Univ. Reader in Iranian Langs, 1965–75. *Publications*: Kurdish Dialect Studies, I & II, 1961–62; Poems from the Divan of Khushâl Khân Khattak, 1965; The Dialect of Awroman (Hawrāmān-i Luhōn), 1966; The 'Sūtra of the Causes and Effects of Actions' in Sogdian, 1970; A Concise Pahlavi Dictionary, 1971, 2nd edn 1986; The Buddhist Sogdian Texts of the British Library, 1976; The Khwarezmian Element in the Qunyat al-munya, 1990; Iranica Diversa, I and II, 1999; contrib. Festschriften; numerous articles in learned jls, esp. Bull. SOAS. *Recreation*: music. *Address*: 5 Column Grounds, Llanfairpwll, Anglesey LL61 5NJ. *T*: (01248) 715270. *Died 13 Oct. 2001.*

MACKEOWN, Fred; *see* Mackeown, T. F. W.

MACKEOWN, Thomas Frederick William; Administrator and Secretary, University College Hospital, London, 1946–63; *b* 3 Jan. 1904; *s* of Rev. William Mackeown, Rushbrooke, Co. Cork; *m* 1936, Lorraine, *d* of Major R. Hayes, Sherburn-in-Elmet, Yorks; one *d*. *Educ*: Felsted; Worcester Coll., Oxford (MA). Qualified as Chartered Accountant, 1927. Hospital Administrator: Liverpool Stanley Hospital, 1934–37; Clayton Hospital, Wakefield, 1937–45; Royal Infirmary, Sunderland, 1945–46; Hill Homes, Highgate (actg), 1966; King Edward VII Memorial Hospital, Bermuda, 1967; Vice-Chm., Management Cttee, Harefield and Northwoods Hosps, 1960–74; undertook Hosp. Domestic Staff Survey under aegis of King Edward's Hosp. Fund for London, 1968. Lay FRSocMed, 1974. *Address*: Mary Feilding Guild, Kekewich House, 1 View Road, Highgate, N6 4DP. *T*: (020) 8348 1952. *Died 29 Aug. 2001.*

McKERN, Leo, (Reginald McKern), AO 1983; actor; *b* 16 March 1920; *s* of Norman Walton McKern and Vera (*née* Martin); *m* 1946, Joan Alice Southa, (Jane Holland); two *d*. *Educ*: Sydney Techn. High Sch. Engrg apprentice, 1935–37; artist, 1937–40; AIF (Corp., Engrs), 1940–42; actor, 1944; arrived England, 1946; CSEU tour, Germany; Arts Council tours, 1947; Old Vic, 1949–52; Shakespeare Meml Theatre, 1952–54; Old Vic last season, 1962–63; New Nottingham Playhouse, 1963–64; *stage*: Toad of Toad Hall, Princes, 1954; Queen of the Rebels, Haymarket, 1955; Cat on a Hot Tin Roof, Aldwych, 1958; Brouhaha, Aldwych, 1958; Rollo, Strand, 1959; A Man for all Seasons, Globe, 1960; The Thwarting of Baron Bolligrew, RSC, Aldwych, 1965; Volpone, Garrick, 1967; The Wolf, Apollo, 1973; The Housekeeper, Apollo, 1982; Number One, Queen's, 1984; Boswell for the Defence, Australia, later Playhouse, 1989, tour 1991; Hobson's Choice, Chichester, tour, then Lyric, 1995; When We Are Married, Chichester, then Savoy, 1996; She Stoops to Conquer, Sydney Opera House, 1999; *films*: The French Lieutenant's Woman, 1983; Ladyhawke, 1984; The Chain, 1985; Travelling North, 1986; On Our Selection, 1996; Molokai, 1998; *television*: Rumpole of the Bailey (series), 1977–; Reilly—Ace of Spies, 1983; King Lear, 1983; Monsignor Quixote; Murder With Mirrors (film), 1985; The Master Builder, 1988; The Last Romantics (film), 1992; A Foreign Field, 1993; Circles of Deceit (film), 1996. *Publication:* Just Resting (biographical memoir), 1983. *Recreations:* sailing, swimming, photography, painting, environment preservation. *Address:* c/o Richard Hatton Ltd, 29 Roehampton Gate, SW15 5JR.   *Died 23 July 2002.*

McKIERNAN, Most Rev. Francis Joseph, DD; Bishop of Kilmore, (RC), 1972–98; *b* 3 Feb. 1926; *s* of Joseph McKiernan and Ellen McTague. *Educ:* Aughawillan National School; St Patrick's Coll., Cavan; University College, Dublin; St Patrick's Coll., Maynooth. BA, BD, HDE. Ordained priest, 1951; St Malachy's Coll., Belfast, 1951–52; St Patrick's Coll., Cavan, 1952–53; University Coll., Dublin, 1953–54; St Patrick's Coll., Cavan, 1954–62; Pres., St Felim's Coll., Ballinamore, Co. Leitrim, 1962–72. Editor of Breifne (Journal of Breifne Historical Society), 1958–72. *Address:* 5 Brookside, Cavan, Ireland. *T:* (49) 4361804.   *Died 23 Dec. 2005.*

McKINLEY, Air Vice-Marshal David Cecil, CB 1966; CBE 1957; DFC 1940; AFC 1944; Bar 1945; RAF; *b* 18 Sept. 1913; *s* of David McKinley, Civil Engineer, and May McKinley (*née* Ward); *m* 1940, Brenda Alice (*née* Ridgway); three *s. Educ:* Bishop Foy Sch., Waterford; Trinity Coll., Dublin. Radio Engineering, Ferranti Ltd, 1935. Entered (regular) Royal Air Force, 1935; served 1935–68: AOC Malta and Dep. C-in-C (Air), Allied Forces, Mediterranean, 1963–65; SASO, Transport Command, 1966, Air Support Command, 1967–68; retired 1968. Freeman, The Guild of Air Pilots and Air Navigators, 1959. FIN 1949. *Recreations:* sailing, fishing, water ski-ing, gardening. *Address:* 4 Courtil Lubin, Alderney, Channel Islands. *T:* (01481) 822497; HSBC, Alderney, CI. *Club:* Royal Air Force.
            Died 23 April 2002.

MACKSEY, Kenneth John, MC 1944; freelance author, since 1968, and publisher, since 1982; *b* 1 July 1923; *s* of Henry George Macksey and Alice Lilian (*née* Nightingall); *m* 1946, Catherine Angela Joan Little; one *s* one *d. Educ:* Goudhurst Sch.; Sandhurst; Army Staff Coll., Camberley. Served War, RAC: trooper, 1941–44; commnd 141st Regt RAC (The Buffs), 1944; Western Europe, 1944–45; Royal Tank Regt, 1946; served: India, 1947; Korea, 1950; Germany, 1957 and 1960–62; Singapore, 1958–60; retd, 1968. Dep. Editor, Purnell's History of the Second World War, and History of the First World War, 1968–70. Consultant to Canadian Armed Forces, 1981–91; Mil. Consultant, Discovery Channel, 1993. Town Councillor, 1972–83. *Publications:* To the Green Fields Beyond, 1965, 2nd edn 1977; The Shadow of Vimy Ridge, 1965; Armoured Crusader: the biography of Major-General Sir Percy Hobart, 1967, repr. 2004; Afrika Korps, 1968, 4th edn 1976; Panzer Division, 1968, 4th edn 1976; Crucible of Power, 1969; Tank, 1970, 3rd edn 1975; Tank Force, 1970; Beda Fomm, 1971; Tank Warfare, 1971; Vimy Ridge, 1972; Guinness Book of Tank Facts and Feats, 1972, 3rd edn 1980; The Guinness History of Land Warfare, 1973, 2nd edn 1976; Battle, 1974, 2nd edn 2001; The Partisans of Europe, 1975; (jtly) The Guinness History of Sea Warfare, 1975; Guderian, Panzer General, 1975, 4th edn 2003; (with Joan Macksey) The Guinness Guide to Feminine Achievements, 1975; (jtly) The Guinness History of Air Warfare, 1976; The Guinness Book of 1952, 1977; The Guinness Book of 1953, 1978; The Guinness Book of 1954, 1978; Kesselring: the making of the Luftwaffe, 1978, 3rd edn 2003; Rommel: battles and campaigns, 1979, 2nd edn 1997; The Tanks, vol. 3, 1979; Invasion: the German invasion of England July 1940, 1980, 3rd edn 1999; The Tank Pioneers, 1981; A History of the Royal Armoured Corps, 1914–1975, 1983; Commando Strike, 1985; First Clash, 1985; Technology in War, 1986; Godwin's Saga, 1987; Military Errors of World War II, 1987, 12th edn 2004; Tank versus Tank, 1988, 2nd edn 1991; For Want of a Nail, 1989; (jtly) The Penguin Encyclopedia of Modern Warfare, 1991, 2nd edn 1993; Penguin Encyclopedia of Weapons and Military

Technology, 1994; (ed) The Hitler Options, 1995; From Triumph to Disaster, 1996, new edn as Why the Germans Lose at War, 1999; Turning Points (memoirs), 1997; Without Enigma, 2000; They Never Looked Back, 2002; The Searchers, 2003, 2nd edn 2004; contributor to DNB; articles and reviews in RUSI Jl, Army Qly, Brit. Army Rev., and The Tank. *Recreations:* watching ladies' hockey, listening to music, living in Beaminster. *Address:* Whatley Mill, Beaminster, Dorset DT8 3EN. *T:* (01308) 862321.   *Died 30 Nov. 2005.*

MACLAGAN, Michael, CVO 1988; FSA; FRHistS; Richmond Herald of Arms, 1980–89; *b* 14 April 1914; *s* of Sir Eric Robert Dalrymple Maclagan, KCVO, CBE, and Helen Elizabeth (*née* Lascelles); *m* 1st, 1939, Brenda Alexander (marr. diss. 1946); one *s;* 2nd, 1949, Jean Elizabeth Brooksbank Garnett (*d* 2003), *d* of late Lt-Col W. B. Garnett, DSO; two *d* (one *s* decd). *Educ:* Winchester Coll.; Christ Church, Oxford (BA 1st Cl. Hons Modern History, MA). FSA 1948; FRHistS 1961; FSG 1970; FHS 1972. Lectr, Christ Church, Oxford, 1937–39; Fellow of Trinity Coll., Oxford, 1939–81, Emeritus Fellow 1981, Sen. Proctor, 1954–55. 2/Lieut TA, 1938; served war, 1939–46: 16/5 Lancers; sc; Major, GSOII War Office. Slains Pursuivant, 1948–70; Portcullis Pursuivant, 1970–80. Vis. Prof., Univ. of S Carolina, 1974; Fellow of Winchester Coll., 1975–89; Sen. Librarian, 1960–70, Trustee, 1970–99, Oxford Union. Councillor, Oxford CBC, 1946–74; Sheriff, 1964–65; Lord Mayor of Oxford, 1970–71. Chm., Oxford Dio. Adv. Cttee, 1961–85. Master of Scriveners' Co., 1988–89. OStJ 1952. *Publications:* (ed) Bede: Ecclesiastical History I and II, 1949; Trinity College, 1955, rev. edn 1963; (jtly) The Colour of Heraldry, 1958; (ed) Richard de Bury: Philobiblon, 1960; 'Clemency' Canning, 1962 (Wheatley Gold Medal); City of Constantinople, 1968; (with J. Louda) Lines of Succession, 1981 (trans. French; 1984; 3rd edn 1992); articles in DNB, VCH, etc. *Recreations:* real tennis, wine, walking, travel. *Address:* 20 Northmoor Road, Oxford OX2 6UR. *T:* (01865) 558536; Trinity College, Oxford OX1 3BH. *Clubs:* Cavalry and Guards, Pratt's; Oxford Union (Oxford).
            Died 13 Aug. 2003.

McLAREN, Prof. Digby Johns, OC 1987; FRS 1979; FRSC 1968; President, Royal Society of Canada, 1987–90; *b* 11 Dec. 1919; *s* of James McLaren and Louie Kinsey; *m* 1942, Phyllis Matkin (*d* 2003); two *s* one *d. Educ:* Sedbergh Sch.; Queens' Coll., Cambridge (BA, MA); Univ. of Michigan (PhD). Served War, RA (Gunner to Captain), ME and Italy, 1940–46. Field Geologist, Geol Survey of Canada, in Alberta and British Columbia Rocky Mountains, District of Mackenzie, Yukon Territory, Arctic Islands, 1948–80; first Dir, Inst. of Sedimentary and Petroleum Geology, Calgary, Alberta, 1967–73; Dir Gen., Geol Survey of Canada, 1973–80; Prof., Dept of Geology, Univ. of Ottawa, 1981–89; Sen. Science Adviser, Dept of Energy, Mines and Resources, Ottawa, 1981–84. Pres., Commn on Stratigraphy, IUGS, 1972–76; Chm. of Bd, Internat. Geol Correlation Prog., UNESCO-IUGS, 1976–80; IUGS Deleg. to People's Republic of China to advise on participation in internat. sci., 1977. President: Paleontol Soc., 1969; Canadian Soc. Petroleum Geologists, 1971; Geol Soc. of America, 1981. Hon. Mem. and Leopold von Buch Medallist, Geol Soc. of Germany, 1982; Corresp. Mem., Geol Soc. of France, 1975; Foreign Associate, Nat. Acad. of Scis, USA, 1979; For. Mem., Amer. Philosophical Soc., 1994. For. Hon. Fellow, European Union of Geoscis, 1983; Hon. FGS 1989. Hon. DSc: Ottawa, 1980; Carleton, 1993; Waterloo, 1996. Gold Medal (for Pure and Applied Science), Professional Inst. of Public Service of Canada, 1979; Edward Coke Medal, Geol Soc. of London, 1985; Logan Medal, Geol Assoc. of Canada, 1987; Hollis D. Hedberg Award in Energy, Inst. for Study of Earth and Man, 1994. *Publications:* (ed) Resources and World Development (proceedings of 2 Dahlem Workshops), 1987; memoirs, bulletins, papers, geological maps, and scientific contribs to jls on regional geology, paleontology, geological time, correlation, extinctions and global change and resource depletion. *Recreations:* ski-ing, swimming, gardening, music.   *Died 8 Dec. 2004.*

McLAUCHLAN, Madeline Margaret Nicholls; Head Mistress, North London Collegiate School, 1965–85; *b* 4 June 1922; *o c* of late Robert and Gertrude McLauchlan, Birmingham. *Educ:* King Edward VI Grammar Sch. for Girls, Camp Hill, Birmingham; Royal Holloway Coll., Univ. of London. Assistant Mistress: Shrewsbury High Sch., GPDST, 1944; Manchester High Sch., 1952; Senior Walter Hines Page Scholar, E-SU, 1955; Head Mistress, Henrietta Barnett Sch., 1958. Chm., Schoolboy and Schoolgirl Exchange Cttee, E-SU (Mem., Educn Cttee, 1966); Member: Exec. Cttee, Assoc. of Head Mistresses, 1966–76 (Chm., 1974–76); Exec. Cttee, UCCA, 1968–85; Direct Grant Cttee, GBGSA, 1972–; Assisted Places Cttee, ISJC, 1980–85. Member Council: Westfield Coll., Univ. of London, 1975–78; The Francis Holland Schools Trust, 1985– (Chm., 1993–99); Vice-Pres., Church Schs Co., 1996– (Mem. Council, 1985–96). Pres., Brecknock DFAS, 2003– (Chm., 1999–2002). Governor: Imperial Coll., 1968–85; Bedford Coll., 1981–85; St Christopher's Sch., NW3, 1985–98; Rougemont Sch., Newport, Gwent, 1988–92; Llanbedr Village Sch., 1989–2003; NYO, 1985–93 (Mem. Council, 1975, Vice-Chm. Council, 1981). Freeman, Goldsmiths' Co., 1986. *Recreations:* music, housekeeping. *Address:* The Coach House, Moor Park, Llanbedr, Crickhowell, Powys NP8 1SS. *Clubs:* English-Speaking Union, University Women's.   *Died 20 Jan. 2004.*

McLAUCHLAN, Thomas Joseph; Stipendiary Magistrate, 1966–82; *b* 15 May 1917; *s* of Alexander and Helen McLauchlan; *m* 1945, Rose Catherine Gray, MA. *Educ:* St Aloysius Coll., Glasgow; Univ. of Glasgow (BL). War service, Merchant Navy and RAF Y Section, Signals Intell., Wireless Officer, 1940–46. Legal Asst to Manager of large industrial insurance co., 1947–49; Clerk to Glasgow Police Courts, 1949–66. JP Scotland.   *Died 17 July 2002.*

MacLEAN, Vice-Adm. Sir Hector Charles Donald, KBE 1962; CB 1960; DSC 1941; JP; DL; *b* 7 Aug. 1908; *s* of late Captain D. C. H. Maclean, DSO, The Royal Scots; *m* 1933, Opre, *d* of late Captain Geoffrey Vyvyan, Royal Welch Fusiliers; one *s* two *d. Educ:* Wellington. Special Entry into Navy, 1926; Captain 1948; idc 1951; Comd HMS Saintes and 3rd Destroyer Sqdn, 1952–53; Dir of Plans, Admiralty, 1953–56; Comd HMS Eagle, 1956–57; Chief of Staff, Home Fleet, 1958–59; Chief of Allied Staff, Mediterranean, 1959–62; Vice-Adm. 1960; retired 1962. JP, 1963, DL, 1977, Norfolk. *Address:* Deepdale Old Rectory, Brancaster Staithe, King's Lynn, Norfolk PE31 8DD. *T:* (01485) 210281.   *Died 19 Feb. 2003.*

McLEAN, Prof. Malcolm, PhD; FREng, FIMMM, FInstP; Professor of Materials, Imperial College, London, since 1990 (Head, Department of Materials, 1990–2000); *b* 19 Dec. 1939; *s* of Andrew Bell McLean and Jane Pattison McLean (*née* Kilmartin); *m* 1967, Malinda Ruth Conner; two *s. Educ:* Ayr Acad.; Univ. of Glasgow (BSc Natural Phil. 1962; PhD 1965). CEng 1991, FREng 2002; FIMMM (FIM 1984); FInstP 2003. Ohio State Univ., 1965–67; NPL, 1969–90 (Grade 6, Sect. Leader in mech. behaviour of materials at high temps). Fellow, Amer. Soc. Metals, 1992. Rosenhain Medallist, Inst. Metals, 1986; Platinum Medal, Inst. of Materials, Mining and Minerals, 2003. *Publications:* Directionally solidified materials for high temperature service, 1983; (Series Editor) Characterisation of high temperature materials, Vols 1–7, 1988–89; articles on materials sci. and engrg in learned jls. *Recreations:* travel, music, politics. *Address:* Department of Materials, Imperial College, London, Exhibition Road, SW7 2AZ; 20 Strawberry Hill Road, Twickenham, Middx TW1 4PT. *T:* (020) 8892 0617.   *Died 28 Dec. 2005.*

McLELLAND, Charles James; Director General, Association of British Travel Agents, 1987; *b* 19 Nov. 1930; *s* of Charles John McLelland and Jessie Steele Barbour; *m* 1961, Philippa Mary Murphy; one *s* three *d. Educ:* Kilmarnock Acad.; Glasgow Acad.; Glasgow Univ. (MA). Commnd Royal Artillery, 1952–54. Sub-Editor, Leader Writer, Glasgow Herald, 1954–58; Scriptwriter, European Productions, BBC, 1958–61; Head of Programmes, Radio Sarawak, 1962–64; Indian Programme Organiser, BBC, 1964–67; Asst Head, Arabic Service, BBC, 1967–71; Head of Arabic Service, 1971–75; Controller, BBC Radio 2, 1976–80 (also Radio 1, 1976–78); Dep. Man. Dir and Dir of Progs, BBC Radio, 1980–86. Chm., EBU Radio Prog. Cttee, 1985–86; Pres., Overseas Broadcasters' Club, 1985–89, Hon. Vice-Pres., 1990–. Mem. Council, 1989–2003, Vice Patron, 2003–, Officers' Assoc. Trustee, Bourke Trust, 1991–92. *Address:* 14 High Street, Tisbury, Wilts SP3 6HG.   *Died 2 Dec. 2004.*

McLEOD, Sir Ian (George), Kt 1984; JP; director of companies; *b* 17 Oct. 1926; *s* of George Gunn McLeod; *m* 1st, 1950, Audrey Davis (*d* 1996); two *d*; 2nd, 1997, Margaret Palmer, OBE, *d* of Rev. Harold Palmer. *Educ:* Kearsney College, Natal; Natal University; ACIS. Played for Rosslyn Park Rugby Team, 1951. Chm., London Transport Passengers Cttee, 1979–83; Board Mem., SE Electricity Board, 1983–89; Dir, Seeboard plc, 1990–94; Chm., IGI Gp plc, 1997–. Chairman: Croydon Central Cons. Assoc., 1973–76; Greater London Area Conservatives, 1981–84; Cons. Policy Gp for London, 1984–87; Nat. Union of Cons. and Unionist Assocs, 1988–90 (Vice-Chm., 1985–87); Mem., Nat. Union Exec. Cttee, Cons. Party, 1974–91; Chm., Brighton Cons. Conf., 1988. Mem., Croydon Borough Council, 1974–78; Dep. Mayor, 1976–77. Governor, Old Palace Girls' Sch., Croydon, 1974–87. JP SE London, 1977. *Recreations:* politics, reading history. *Address:* 23 Albemarle Park, Albemarle Road, Beckenham, Kent BR3 5XG. *T:* (020) 8658 4970. *Clubs:* Carlton, MCC.   *Died 18 Jan. 2001.*

MACLEOD, Nigel Ronald Buchanan; QC 1979; a Recorder of the Crown Court, since 1981; a Deputy High Court Judge, 1992–2001; *b* 7 Feb. 1936; *s* of Donald Macleod, MB, ChB, and Katherine Ann Macleod; *m* 1966, Susan Margaret (*née* Buckley) (*d* 2002); one *s* one *d. Educ:* Wigan Grammar Sch. (school captain); Christ Church, Oxford (MA, BCL). Served RAF, 1954–56. Called to the Bar, Gray's Inn, 1961 (Bencher, 1993), Inner Temple *ad eundem*, 1984. Asst Comr, Boundary Commn for England, 1981–85; a Pres., Mental Health Review Tribunals, 2000. Chm., IOM Commn of Inquiry into Mount Murray concerning irregularities in planning matters, 2002–04. Chm., Planning and Environment Bar Assoc., 1998–2000 (Vice Chm., 1994–98; Hon. Mem., 2002); Mem., Gen. Council of the Bar, 1998–2000. Hon. Mem., Parly Bar Assoc., 2001. Fellow, Soc. for Advanced Legal Studies, 1998. *Publications:* contribs to legal jls. *Recreations:* boats, gardening, travel. *Address:* Russet House, 27 Warwick Road, Upper Boddington, Northants NN11 6DH. *T:* (01327) 264256. *Club:* Garrick.   *Died 1 March 2005.*

McLUSKEY, Very Rev. J(ames) Fraser, MC; DD; Minister at St Columba's Church of Scotland, Pont Street, London, 1960–86; Moderator of the General Assembly of the Church of Scotland, 1983–84; *b* 19 Sept. 1914; *s* of James Fraser McLuskey and Margaret Keltie; *m* 1st, 1939, Irene (*d* 1959), *d* of Pastor Calaminus, Wuppertal; two *s*; 2nd, 1966, Ruth Quartermaine (*née* Hunter), *widow* of Lt-Col Keith Briant. *Educ:* Aberdeen Grammar Sch.; Edinburgh Univ. (MA, BD). Ordained Minister of Church of Scotland, 1938; Chaplain to Univ. of Glasgow, 1939–47; service as Army Chaplain, 1943–46 (1st Special Air Service Regt, 1944–46); Sub Warden, Royal Army Chaplains' Training Centre, 1947–50; Minister at: Broughty Ferry East, 1950–55; New Kilpatrick, Bearsden, 1955–60. *Publications:* Parachute Padre, 1951; The Cloud and the Fire, 1994. *Recreations:* walking, music, reading. *Address:* 54/5 Eildon Terrace, Edinburgh EH3 5LU. *Clubs:* Caledonian, Special Forces; New (Edinburgh). *Died 24 July 2005.*

McMAHON, Andrew, (Andy); *b* 18 March 1920; *s* of Andrew and Margaret McMahon; *m* 1944; one *s* (one *s* decd). *Educ:* District School, Govan. Boilermaker, Govan shipyards, 1936; unemployed, 1971–79. MP (Lab) Glasgow, Govan, 1979–83; first and only boilermaker to enter House of Commons. Member, Glasgow Dist Council, 1973–79. Chm., Scottish Arab Friendship Assoc., 1972–85; Sec. Gen., British-Iraqi Friendship Assoc., 1989 (Pres., 1986–89). *Recreations:* youth work, care and comfort for elderly. *Died 26 April 2005.*

MacMAHON, Gerald John, CB 1962; CMG 1955; Under-Secretary, Board of Trade, 1964–70; *b* 26 Sept. 1909; 2nd *s* of late Jeremiah MacMahon and Kathleen MacMahon (*née* Dodd); unmarried. *Educ:* Clongowes Wood Coll., Co. Kildare, Ireland; Emmanuel Coll., Cambridge (BA). Entered Board of Trade, 1933; Asst Sec., 1942; Imperial Defence Coll., 1949; Senior UK Trade Commissioner in India, 1952–58; Under-Secretary: Board of Trade 1958–62; Admiralty, 1962–64. *Address:* 19 Lower Park, Putney Hill, SW15 6QY. *Club:* Reform. *Died 23 July 2001.*

McMILLAN, Rt Rev. Mgr Donald Neil; Parish Priest, St Nicholas' Church, Winchcombe, 1986–99; *b* 21 May 1925; *s* of Daniel McMillan and Mary Cameron McMillan (*née* Farrell). *Educ:* St Brendan's Coll., Bristol; Prior Park Coll., Bath; Oscott Coll., Sutton Coldfield; Open Univ. (BA (Hons) 1996; MA 1999). Ordained priest, Dio. Clifton, 1948; Curate: Bath, 1948–49; Gloucester, 1949–51; Taunton, 1951; commissioned Army Chaplain, 1951; served: BAOR, 1961–63, 1966–68, 1975–77; Middle East, 1956–59, 1968–70; Far East, 1952–55; Principal RC Chaplain and Vicar Gen. (Army), 1977–81; Parish Priest: St Augustine's Church, Matson Lane, Gloucester, 1981–85; St Teresa's Church, Filton, Bristol, 1985–86. Apptd Prelate of Honour by Pope Paul VI, 1977. *Recreations:* reading, walking. *Address:* Nazareth House, London Road, Charlton Kings, Cheltenham, Glos GL52 6YJ. *T:* (01242) 529029. *Club:* Army and Navy. *Died 16 March 2001.*

MACMILLAN, Matthew, CBE 1983 (OBE 1977); Controller, English Language and Literature Division, British Council, 1978–83; *b* 14 July 1926; *s* of late David Craig Macmillan and Barbara Cruikshank Macmillan (*née* Gow); *m* 1949, Winifred (*née* Sagar); one *s* two *d. Educ:* Robert Gordon's Coll., Aberdeen; Aberdeen Univ. (MA Hons); Manchester Univ. (Teacher's Dip.). Served Royal Air Force, 1944–47. Schoolmaster, Chatham House Grammar Sch., Ramsgate, 1951–57; Sen. Lectr, Univ. of Science and Technology, Kumasi, Ghana, 1958–62; Associate Prof., University Coll. of Cape Coast, Ghana, 1962–64; Prof. of English, Univ. of Khartoum, The Sudan, 1965–70; British Council, London: Director, English-Teaching Information Centre, 1970–72; Dep. Controller, English Teaching Div., 1972–74; Asst Educn Adviser (English Studies), British Council, India, 1974–78; Prof. of English, 1983–89, Principal, 1986–89, University Coll., Univ. of E Asia, Macau; Prof., English Programmes, E Asia Open Inst., Hong Kong, 1989–90. English examiner, Trinity Coll. London, 1992–99. Mem., ESU, 1993–. *Publications:* articles on the teaching of English as a second/foreign language. *Recreations:* travel, antiques. *Address:* Yeoman's Cottage, 49 North Lane, Canterbury, Kent CT2 7EF. *T:* (01227) 766429. *Club:* Royal Commonwealth Society. *Died 27 Aug. 2001.*

MACMILLAN, Very Rev. William Boyd Robertson; Moderator of the General Assembly of the Church of Scotland, 1991–92; an Extra Chaplain to the Queen in Scotland, since 1997 (Chaplain, 1988–97); *b* 3 July 1927; *s* of Robert and Annie Simpson Macmillan; *m* 1962, Mary Adams Bisset Murray. *Educ:* Royal High Sch., Edinburgh;

Univ. of Aberdeen (MA, BD). Served RN, 1946–48. Minister: St Andrew's, Bo'ness, 1955–60; Fyvie, 1960–67; Bearsden, South, 1967–78; Dundee Parish Church (St Mary's), 1978–93; Chaplain, City of Dundee DC, 1978–93. Convener, General Assembly, Church of Scotland: Bd of Practice and Procedure, 1985–88; Business Cttee, 1985–88. Mem. Cttee, Chaplains to HM Forces, 1995–99. Chm. Bd of Dirs, High Sch. of Dundee, 1993–96. Chm., Murray Home, 1994–96; Trustee, Scottish Nat. War Meml, 1994–; Mem., Cttee of Mgt, Royal Soc. for Relief of Indigent Gentlewomen, Scotland, 1994–. Pres., Scottish Church Soc., 1994–97. Freeman of Dundee, 1991. Hon. LLD Dundee, 1990; Hon. DD Aberdeen, 1991. ChStJ 1993 (Prelate, 1993–96). *Recreations:* reading, golf, exploring towns. *Address:* 3/5 Craigend Park, Edinburgh EH16 5XY. *Club:* New (Edinburgh). *Died 16 Oct. 2002.*

MacMURRAY, Her Honour Mary Bell McMillan, (Mrs Ian Mills); QC 1979; a Circuit Judge, 1988–96; *d* of Samuel Bell MacMurray and Constance Mary MacMurray (*née* Goodman); *m* 1971, Ian Donald Mills. *Educ:* Queen Margaret's School, Escrick, York. Called to the Bar, Lincoln's Inn, 1954, Bencher, 1986. Barrister-at-Law, 1954–88; a Recorder of the Crown Court, 1978–88. Coronation Medal, 1953. *Recreation:* golf. *Address:* c/o Courts Administrator, Westgate House, Westgate Road, Newcastle upon Tyne NE1 1RR. *Clubs:* Durham County; Whitburn Golf; Lady Taverners. *Died 20 Oct. 2001.*

MACNAIR, His Honour (Maurice John) Peter; a Circuit Judge, 1972–91; *b* 27 Feb. 1919; *s* of late Brig. J. L. P. Macnair and Hon. Mrs Macnair (*née* Atkin); *m* 1952, Vickie Reynolds, *d* of Hugh Reynolds; one *s* two *d. Educ:* Bembridge Sch.; St Paul's Sch.; St Edmund Hall, Oxford (BA 1947). Served War of 1939–45: Western Desert, Sicily, Italy; wounded 1944; Captain, RA. Called to Bar, Gray's Inn, 1948. Dep. Chm., W Sussex QS, 1968–72. *Recreations:* reading, painting. *Address:* 28 Rawlings Street, SW3 2LS. *Died 17 June 2003.*

McNAIR SCOTT, Thomas Frederick; *see* Scott, T. F. M.

McNICOL, David Williamson, CBE 1966; Australian Diplomatic Service, retired; *b* 20 June 1913; *s* of late Donald McNicol, Adelaide; *m* 1947, Elsa Margaret, *d* of N. J. Hargrave, Adelaide; one *s. Educ:* Carey Grammar Sch., Melbourne; Kings Coll., Adelaide; Adelaide Univ. (BA). RAAF, 1940–45, Pilot, 201 and 230 Sqdns RAF, Atlantic, Madagascar, Italy and Dodecanese. Australian Minister to Cambodia, Laos and Vietnam, 1955–56; idc 1957; Australian Comr to Singapore, 1958–60; Asst Sec., Dept of External Affairs, Australia, 1960–62; Australian High Comr to Pakistan, 1962–65 and to New Zealand, 1965–68; Australian Ambassador to Thailand, 1968–69; Australian High Comr to Canada, 1969–73; Dep. High Comr for Australia in London, 1973–75; Ambassador to S Africa, and High Comr to Botswana, Lesotho and Swaziland, 1975–77. *Recreations:* golf, gardening. *Address:* Unit 7/23, Burkitt Street, Page, ACT 2614, Australia. *Clubs:* Naval and Military (Melbourne); Royal Canberra Golf. *Died 19 Sept. 2001.*

MACQUAKER, Donald Francis, CBE 1991; solicitor, retired; Partner, T. C. Young & Son, Glasgow, 1957–93, Consultant, 1993–96; *b* 21 Sept. 1932; *s* of Thomas Mason Macquaker, MC, MA, BL and Caroline Bertha Floris Macquaker; *m* 1964, Susan Elizabeth, *d* of Mr and Mrs W. A. K. Finlayson, High Coodham, Symington, Ayrshire; one *s* one *d. Educ:* Winchester Coll.; Trinity Coll., Oxford (MA); Univ. of Glasgow (LLB). Admitted Solicitor, 1957. Mem. Bd of Management, Glasgow Royal Maternity Hosp. and associated hosps, 1965–74 (Vice-Chm., 1972–74); Greater Glasgow Health Board: Mem., 1973–87; Chm., 1983–87; Convener, F and GP Cttee, 1974–83; Chm., Common Services Agency for Scottish Health Service, 1987–91. Dir, Lithgows Ltd, 1987–98.

Dir, Prince and Princess of Wales Hospice, Glasgow, 1991–94. Chm., Western Meeting Club, Ayr Racecourse, 1996–2002. *Recreations:* shooting, fishing, gardening. *Address:* Blackbyres, by Ayr KA7 4TS. *T:* (01292) 441088. *Club:* Leander (Henley-on-Thames).

Died 15 Aug. 2004.

MACTAGGART, William Alexander, CBE 1964; Chairman, 1960–70, and Managing Director, 1945–68, Pringle of Scotland Ltd, Knitwear Manufacturers, Hawick; *b* 17 Aug. 1906; *o s* of late William Alexander and Margaret Mactaggart, Woodgate, Hawick; *m* 1932, Marjorie Laing Innes (decd); two *s* one *d. Educ:* Sedbergh Sch., Yorks. Joined Robert Pringle & Son Ltd (later Pringle of Scotland Ltd), 1925; Dir, 1932; Joint Managing Dir, 1933. Served War of 1939–45: Captain, RASC, Holland, Belgium, France, 1942–45. *Address:* Bewlie House, Lilliesleaf, Melrose, Roxburghshire TD6 9ER. *T:* (01835) 870267.

Died 23 May 2002.

McWHIRTER, Norris Dewar, CBE 1980; author, publisher, broadcaster; Director, Guinness Publications Ltd (formerly Guinness Superlatives Ltd), 1954–96 (Managing Director, 1954–76); *b* Winchmore Hill, N London, 12 Aug. 1925; *er (twin) s* of William Allan McWhirter, Managing Director of Associated Newspapers and Northcliffe Newspapers Group, and Margaret Williamson; *m* 1st, 1957, Carole (*d* 1987), *d* of late George H. Eckert; one *s* one *d;* 2nd, 1991, Tessa Mary, *d* of late Joseph Dunsdon Pocock and Dorothy Pocock (*née* von Weichardt). *Educ:* Marlborough; Trinity Coll., Oxford. BA (Internat. Rel. and Econs), MA (Contract Law). Served RN, 1943–46: Sub-Lt RNVR, 2nd Escort Gp, Atlantic; minesweeping Pacific. Dir, McWhirter Twins Ltd, 1950–; Chm., Wm McWhirter & Sons, 1955–86; co-founder, Redwood Press (Chm., 1966–72); Dir, Gieves Group plc, 1972–95. Founder Editor (with late Ross McWhirter till 1975) and compiler, Guinness Book of Records, 1954–86 (1st edn 1955). Adv. Editor, 1986–96; by 2003, in 37 languages; 100 million sales. Athletics Correspondent: Observer, 1951–67; Star, 1951–60; BBC TV Commentator, Olympic Games, 1960–72; What's In the Picture, 1957; The Record Breakers, 1972–94; Guinness Hall of Fame, 1986. Mem., Sports Council, 1970–73. Pres., Freedom Assoc., 2001– (Chm., 1983–2000). Pres., Marlburian Club, 1983–84. Contested (C) Orpington, 1964, 1966. Trustee: Ross McWhirter Foundn (Chm., 1994–); Police Rehabilitation Trust. *Publications:* Get To Your Marks, 1951; (ed) Athletics World, 1952–56; Dunlop Book of Facts, 5 edns, 1964–73; Guinness Book of Answers, 1976, 10th edn 1995; Ross: story of a shared life, 1976; Guinness Book of Essential Facts, 1979 (US); (jtly) Treason at Maastricht, 1994; Time and Space, 1998; Book of Extremes, 1998; Book of Millennium Records, 1999; Book of Historical Records, 2000; (contrib.) Whitaker's Almanack, 1990–. *Recreations:* family tennis, watching athletics (Oxford 100 yds, Scotland 1950–52, GB in Norway 1951) and Rugby football (Saracens and Mddx XV, 1950). *Address:* c/o Lloyds Bank (Law Courts), 222 Strand, WC2R 1BB. *Clubs:* Carlton; Vincent's (Oxford); Achilles.   *Died 19 April 2004.*

MADDEN, Adm. Sir Charles (Edward), 2nd Bt *cr* 1919, of Kells, co. Kilkenny; GCB 1965 (KCB 1961 CB 1955); Vice Lord-Lieutenant of Greater London, 1969–81; *b* 15 June 1906; *s* of Admiral of the Fleet Sir Charles E. Madden, 1st Bt, GCB, OM, and Constance Winifred (*d* 1964), 3rd *d* of Sir Charles Cayzer, 1st Bt; *S* father, 1935; *m* 1942, Olive (*d* 1989), *d* of late G. W. Robins, Caldy, Cheshire; one *d. Educ:* Royal Naval Coll., Osborne. ADC to the Queen, 1955. Served War: Exec. Officer, HMS Warspite, 1940–42 (despatches); Captain, HMS Emperor, 1945 (despatches); Naval Asst to 1st Sea Lord, 1946–47. Captain, 1946; Rear-Admiral, 1955; Vice-Admiral, 1958; Admiral, 1961. Chief of Naval Staff, NZ, 1953–55; Dep. Chief of Naval Personnel, 1955–57; Flag Officer, Malta, 1957–59; Flag Officer, Flotillas, Home Fleet, 1959–60; C-in-C Plymouth, 1960–62; C-in-C Home Fleet and

NATO C-in-C Eastern Atlantic Command, 1963–65; retired, 1965. Chairman, Royal National Mission to Deep Sea Fishermen, 1971–81 (Dep. Chm., 1966–71); Vice-Chairman, Sail Training Assoc., 1968–70. Trustee: National Maritime Museum, 1968– (Chm., 1972–77); Portsmouth Royal Naval Museum, 1973–77. Chm., Standing Council of the Baronetage, 1975–77. Dep. Warden, Christ Church, Victoria Rd, 1970–86. Grand Cross of Prince Henry the Navigator, Portugal, 1960. *Recreation:* painting. *Heir: nephew* Peter John Madden [*b* 10 Sept. 1942; *m* 1993, Mrs Vellie Laput Co; three step *d*]. *Address:* 21 Eldon Road, W8 5PT. *Club:* Arts.

Died 23 April 2001.

MADDOCKS, Sir Kenneth (Phipson), KCMG 1958 (CMG 1956); KCVO 1963; Governor and Commander-in-Chief, Fiji, 1958–63; *b* 8 Feb. 1907; *s* of Arthur P. Maddocks, Haywards Heath, Sussex; *m* 1st, 1951, Elnor Radcliffe, CStJ (*d* 1976), *d* of late Sir (Edward) John Russell, OBE, FRS; no *c;* 2nd, 1980, Patricia Josephine, *d* of Algernon and Irma Hare Duke and *widow* of Sir George Mooring, KCMG. *Educ:* Bromsgrove Sch.; Wadham Coll., Oxford. Colonial Administrative Service, Nigeria, 1929; Northern Region, Nigeria: Civil Secretary, 1955–57; Dep. Governor, 1957–58; Acting Governor, 1956 and 1957. Dir and Secretary, E Africa and Mauritius Assoc., 1964–69. KStJ (Mem. Chapter-Gen., Order of St John, 1969–75). *Recreation:* gardening. *Address:* 11 Lee Road, Aldeburgh, Suffolk IP15 5HG. *T:* (01725) 453443.

Died 28 Aug. 2001.

MAGINNIS, John Edward; JP; *b* 7 March 1919; *s* of late Edward Maginnis and Mary E. Maginnis, Mandeville Hall, Mullahead, Tanderagee; *m* 1944, Dorothy, *d* of late R. J. Rusk, JP, of Cavanaleck, Fivemiletown, Co. Tyrone; one *s* four *d. Educ:* Moyallon Sch., Co. Down; Portadown Technical Coll. Served War of 1939–45, Royal Ulster Constabulary. MP (UU) Armagh, Oct. 1959–Feb. 1974. JP, Co. Armagh, 1956. Group Secretary, North Armagh Group, Ulster Farmers' Union, 1956–59. Hon. LLD, 1990. *Recreations:* football, hunting, shooting. *Address:* Mandeville Hall, 68 Mullahead Road, Tandragee, Craigavon, Co. Armagh, N Ireland BT62 2LB. *T:* (028) 3884 0260.   *Died 7 July 2001.*

MAGUIRE, (Albert) Michael, MC 1945; MM 1943; QC 1967; *b* 30 Dec. 1922; *s* of late Richard Maguire and Ruth Maguire. *Educ:* Hutton Grammar Sch.; Trinity Hall, Cambridge (BA 1948). Served War of 1939–45, North Irish Horse (Captain), in Africa (MM) and Italy (MC). Inns of Court Regt, 1946. War Crimes Investigation Unit, 1946. Called to the Bar, Middle Temple, 1949 (Harmsworth Scholar); Bencher, 1973; Leader, Northern Circuit, 1980–84. Last Recorder of Carlisle (1970–71). *Address:* Goldsmith Building, Temple, EC4Y 7BL; Chestnuts, 89 Lower Bank Road, Fulwood, Preston PR2 4NU. *T:* (01772) 719291.   *Died 12 Dec. 2001.*

MAGUIRE, (Benjamin) Waldo, OBE 1973; *b* 31 May 1920; *s* of Benjamin Maguire and Elizabeth Ann Eldon; *m* 1944, Lilian Joan Martin (*d* 1998); four *s. Educ:* Portadown Coll.; Trinity Coll., Dublin (BA 1st cl. hons Philosophy). Intell. Service, WO and FO, 1942–45; BBC Latin American Service, 1945; BBC Radio News, 1946–55; BBC TV News, 1955; Editor, BBC TV News, 1962–64; Controller, News and Public Affairs, NZ Broadcasting Corp., 1965–66; BBC Controller, NI, 1966–72; Head of Information Programmes, NZ TV2, 1975–76. *Recreations:* gardening, conversation, angling. *Address:* c/o The Sloane Nursing Home, Beckenham, Kent.

Died 23 Nov. 2005.

MAGUIRE, Air Marshal Sir Harold John, KCB 1966 (CB 1958); DSO 1946; OBE 1949; Director, Commercial Union Assurance Co., 1975–82 (Political and Economic Adviser, 1972–79); *b* 12 April 1912; *s* of Michael Maguire, Maynooth, Ireland, and Harriett (*née* Warren), Kilkishen, Co. Clare, Ireland; *m* 1940, Mary Elisabeth Wild (*d* 1991), Dublin; one *s* one *d. Educ:* Wesley Coll., Dublin; Dublin

Univ. Royal Air Force Commn, 1933; service in flying boats, 230 Sqdn, Egypt and Far East, 1935–38; commanded night fighter sqdn, UK, 1939–40 and day fighter sqdn, 1940; OC 266 (Fighter) Wing, Dutch E Indies, 1942; POW, Java, 1942; Staff Coll., 1947; Fighter Command Staff Duties, 1948–50; OC, RAF Odiham, 1950–52; Senior Air Staff Officer, Malta, 1952–55; staff of CAS, Air Ministry, 1955–58; Senior Air Staff Officer, HQ No 11 Group, RAF, 1958–59; AOC No 13 Group, RAF, 1959–61; AOC No 11 Group, Fighter Command, 1961–62; SASO Far East Air Force, 1962–64; ACAS (Intelligence), 1964–65; Dep. Chief of Defence Staff (Intelligence), 1965–68; retired, 1968; Dir-Gen. of Intelligence, MoD, 1968–72. *Club:* Royal Air Force.
Died 1 Feb. 2001.

MAGUIRE, Michael; see Maguire, A. M.

MAGUIRE, Waldo; see Maguire, B. W.

MAHER, Very Rev. William Francis, SJ; Provincial Superior of the English Province of the Society of Jesus, 1976–81; *b* 20 June 1916. *Educ:* St Ignatius' College, Stamford Hill; Heythrop College, Oxon. STL. Entered the Society of Jesus, 1935; ordained priest, 1948; Principal, Heythrop College, 1974–76. *Address:* Our Lady of the Rosary, 40 Margaret Street, Ammanford, Dyfed SA18 2NP. *T:* (01269) 592533. *Died 11 Nov. 2005.*

MAINWARING, Captain Maurice Kildare C.; see Cavenagh-Mainwaring.

MALCOLM, Ellen, RSA 1976 (ARSA 1968); *b* 28 Sept. 1923; *d* of John and Ellen Malcolm; *m* 1962, Gordon Stewart Cameron, RSA (*d* 1994). *Educ:* Aberdeen Acad.; Gray's Sch. of Art, Aberdeen; DA (Aberdeen) 1944. Teacher of Art, Aberdeen Grammar Sch. and Aberdeen Acad., 1945–62. Paintings in public galleries in Southend, Aberdeen, Perth, Milngavie, Edinburgh, and in private collections in Scotland, England, Wales, America, Switzerland, Sweden and Australia. Chalmers-Jervise Prize, 1946; Guthrie Award, Royal Scottish Acad., 1952; David Cargill Award, Royal Glasgow Inst., 1973. *Recreation:* reading. *Address:* c/o Dr I. Malcolm, 4 Deemount Gardens, Aberdeen AB11 7UE.
Died 14 March 2002.

MALCOLM, Prof. John Laurence; Regius Professor of Physiology, University of Aberdeen, 1959–75, retired; *b* 28 Aug. 1913; *s* of late Prof. J. Malcolm, Dunedin, New Zealand; *m* 1st, 1940, Sylvia Bramston (*d* 1958), *d* of late Basil B. Hooper, Auckland, New Zealand; one *s* one *d*; 2nd, 1961, Margaret Irvine S impson (*d* 1967), *d* of late Col J. C. Simpson, Skene, Aberdeenshire. *Publications:* contribs to Proceedings of Royal Society, Journal of Physiology, Journal of Neuro-physiology. *Address:* Heath Cottage, Crathie, Aberdeenshire AB3 5UP.
Died 9 Oct. 2001.

MALDEN, Charles Peter S.; see Scott-Malden.

MALLET, Roger; Chairman, North Western Electricity Board, 1972–76, retired; *b* 7 June 1912; British; *m* 1942, Kathleen Els Walker; two *s* two *d*. *Educ:* Eastbourne Coll.; Trinity Hall, Cambridge (BA Mech. Sci. Tripos). CEng, FIEE. West Cambrian Power Co., S Wales, 1937–40; Buckrose Light & Power Co., Yorks, 1940–45; Shropshire, Worcestershire and Staffordshire Electric Power Co., 1945–47; Midlands Electricity Board, 1948–72. *Recreation:* golf. *Died 21 June 2001.*

MALLETT, Edmund Stansfield; Director of Applications Programmes, European Space Agency, Paris, 1981–85; *b* 21 April 1923; *s* of Cecil Finer Mallett and Elsie Stansfield; *m* 1st, 1953, Nancy Campbell (*d* 1983); three *s*; 2nd, 1985, Jocelyn Maynard Ghent, BA, MA, PhD. *Educ:* Bradford Grammar Sch.; Leeds Univ. (BSc). CEng, MIEE, FBIS. Gramophone Co., 1944; Fairey Aviation Co., 1948; Royal Aircraft Establishment: joined 1950; Head, Data Transmission and Processing Div., 1961; Supt, Central

Unit for Scientific Photography, 1966; Head: Instrumentation Div., 1968; Instruments Br., Min. of Technol., 1969; Instrumentation and Ranges Dept, RAE, 1971; Director Space, DoI, 1976; Under Sec., and Head of Res. and Technol. Requirements and Space Div., DoI, 1978; Dir, Nat. Maritime Inst., 1979. *Publications:* papers and articles on instrumentation and measurement. *Recreations:* music, art, genealogy, solving problems. *Address:* 580 Old Prospect Road, Ottawa, ON K1M 0X7, Canada. *T:* (613) 7487219. *Died 8 Aug. 2004.*

MALONEY, Michael John, MA; Principal, Moreton Hall, 1990–92; *b* 26 July 1932; *s* of John William Maloney and Olive Lois Maloney; *m* 1960, Jancis Ann (*née* Ewing); one *s* one *d*. *Educ:* St Alban's Sch.; Trinity Coll., Oxford (MA). Nat. Service, 2nd Lieut RA, served with RWAFF, 1955–57. May & Baker Ltd, 1957–58; Asst Master, Shrewsbury Sch., 1958–66; Sen. Science Master, Housemaster, Dep. Headmaster, Eastbourne Coll., 1966–72; Headmaster: Welbeck Coll., 1972–85; Kamazu Acad., Malawi, 1986–89. JP Worksop, 1975–86, Shrewsbury, 1991–2002. *Publication:* (with D. E. P. Hughes) Advanced Theoretical Chemistry, 1964. *Recreations:* ornithology, cryptography, very hard crosswords. *Address:* Lower Lane Cottage, Chirbury, Montgomery, Powys SY15 6UD. *T:* (01938) 561303.
Died 24 Oct. 2004.

MANCHESTER, 12th Duke of, *cr* 1719; **Angus Charles Drogo Montagu;** Baron Montagu, Viscount Mandeville, 1620; Earl of Manchester, 1626; *b* 9 Oct. 1938; *yr s* of 10th Duke of Manchester, OBE, and Nell Vere (*d* 1966); *S* brother, 1985; *m* 1st, 1961, Mary Eveleen McClure (marr. diss. 1970); two *s* one *d*; 2nd, 1971, Diane Pauline Plimsaul (marr. diss. 1985); 3rd, 1989, Mrs Ann-Louise Bird, *d* of Dr Alfred Butler Taylor, Cawthorne, S Yorks; 4th, 2000, Biba Hiller (marr. diss.). *Educ:* Gordonstoun. Heir: *s* Viscount Mandeville, *b* 11 Dec. 1962.

Died 25 July 2002.

MANCHESTER, William; Purple Heart (US) 1945; author; Fellow, East College, 1968–86, writer in residence since 1974, and Adjunct Professor of History, 1979–92, then Professor Emeritus, Wesleyan University; Fellow, Pierson College, Yale University, since 1991; *b* 1 April 1922; *s* of William Raymond Manchester and Sallie E. R. (*née* Thompson); *m* 1948, Julia Brown Marshall (*d* 1998); one *s* two *d*. *Educ:* Springfield Classical High School; Univ. of Massachusetts; Dartmouth Coll., NH; Univ. of Missouri. Served US Marine Corps, 1942–45. Reporter, Daily Oklahoman, 1945–46; Reporter, foreign corresp., war corresp., Baltimore Sun, 1947–55; Man. editor, Wesleyan Univ. Publications, 1955–64; Fellow, Center for Advanced Studies, 1959–60, Lectr in English, 1968–69, Wesleyan Univ. Trustee: Friends of Univ. of Massachusetts Library, 1970–76 (Pres., 1970–72); Winston Churchill Travelling Fellowships, 1992–96; Mem., Soc. of Amer. Historians. Guggenheim Fellow, 1959; Hon. Dr of Humane Letters: Univ. of Mass, 1965; Univ. of New Haven, 1979; Hon. LittD: Skidmore Coll., 1987; Univ. of Richmond, 1988; Wesleyan Univ., 2002; Hon. LHD Russell Sage Coll., NY, 1990. Dag Hammarskjold Internat. Prize in Literature, 1967; Overseas Press Club (New York) Award for Best Book of the Year on Foreign Affairs, 1968; Univ. of Missouri Medal, 1969; Connecticut Book Award, 1974; President's Cabinet Award, Detroit Univ., 1981; Frederick S. Troy Medal, 1981; McConaughy Award, 1981; Lincoln Literary Award, 1983; Distinguished Public Service Award, Conn Bar Assoc., 1985; Washington Irving Lit. Award, 1991; Sarah Josepha Hale Award, 1993; Nat. Humanities Medal, USA, 2001. *Publications:* Disturber of the Peace, 1951 (publ. UK as The Sage of Baltimore, 1952); The City of Anger, 1953; Shadow of the Monsoon, 1956; Beard the Lion, 1958; A Rockefeller Family Portrait, 1959; The Long Gainer, 1961; Portrait of a President, 1962; The Death of a President, 1967; The Arms of Krupp, 1968; The Glory and the Dream, 1974; Controversy and other Essays in

Journalism, 1976; American Caesar, 1978; Goodbye, Darkness, 1980; One Brief Shining Moment, 1983; The Last Lion: vol. 1, Visions of Glory, 1983; vol. 2, Alone, 1987 (publ. UK as The Caged Lion, Winston Spencer Churchill 1932–1940, 1988); This is Our Time, 1989; A World Lit Only By Fire, 1992; contrib. to Encyclopedia Britannica and to periodicals. *Recreation:* photography. *Address:* 316 Pine Street, Middletown, CT 06457, USA. *T:* (860) 6853884. *Club:* Century (New York).

Died 1 June 2004.

MANCHESTER, Sir William (Maxwell), KBE 1987 (CBE 1973); FRCS, FRACS, FACS; retired; *b* 31 Oct. 1913; *s* of James Manchester and Martha Browne; *m* 1945, Lois Yardley Cameron (*d* 1990). *Educ:* Waimate Primary Sch.; Timaru Boys' High Sch.; Otago Univ. Med. Sch. (MB ChB 1938). FRCS 1949; FRACS 1957; FACS 1973. NZ Medical Corps: joined as RMO, Feb. 1940; 2nd NZ Exped. Force, May 1940; seconded for training as plastic surgeon, Nov. 1940; served in UK, Egypt and NZ (mostly in plastic surgery) until 1947. Head of plastic surgical services, Auckland Hosp. Bd, 1950–79; Prof. of Plastic and Reconstructive Surgery, Univ. of Auckland, 1977–79; private plastic surgery practice, 1979–89; Mem., Auckland Hosp. Bd, 1980–89. Mem., James IV Assoc. of Surgeons, 1969. *Publications:* chapters in: Operative Surgery, 1956, 3rd edn 1976; Long-term Results in Plastic and Reconstructive Surgery, 1980; The Artistry of Reconstructive Surgery, 1987; Management of Cleft Lip and Palate, ed J. Bardach and H. L. Morris, 1990; contribs to British and US med. jls. *Recreations:* classical music, gardening, cooking. *Address:* Watch Hill, Jeffs Road, RD1, Papatoetoe, Auckland, New Zealand. *T:* (9) 2746702. *Club:* Northern (Auckland).

Died 25 Dec. 2001.

MANDER, Noel Percy, MBE 1979; FSA; Managing Director, N. P. Mander Ltd, since 1946; *b* 19 May 1912; *s* of late Percy Mander and Emily Pike, Hoxne, Suffolk; *m* 1948, Enid Watson; three *s* two *d.* *Educ:* Haberdashers' Aske's Sch., Hatcham. Organ building from 1930, interrupted by war service with RA (Hampshire Bde) in N Africa, Italy and Syria, 1940–46. FSA 1974. Mem., Nat. Council of Christians and Jews (former Chm., N London Council). Former Governor, Sir John Cass Foundn. Liveryman, Musicians' Co.; Past Master, Parish Clerks' Co. of City of London; Mem., Art Workers' Guild. Churchill Life Fellow, Westminster Coll., Fulton, 1982; Hon. DFA Westminster Coll., 1984. Builder of Winston Churchill Meml Organ, Fulton, Missouri, and organs in many parts of world; organ builder to St Paul's Cathedral, London and Canterbury Cathedral, and to HM Sultan of Oman. *Publications:* St Lawrence Jewry, A History of the Organs from the Earliest Times to the Present Day, 1956; St Vedast, Foster Lane, A History of the Organs from Earliest Times to the Present Day, 1961; St Vedast Foster Lane, in the City of London: a history of the 13 United Parishes, 1973; (with C. M. Houghton) St Botolph Aldgate: a history of the organs from the Restoration to the Twentieth Century, 1973. *Recreations:* archaeology, horology, reading. *Address:* The Street, Earl Soham, Woodbridge, Suffolk IP13 7SM. *T:* (01728) 685312; The Lodge, St Peter's Organ Works, St Peter's Close, E2 7AF. *T:* (020) 7739 4746. *Club:* Savage.

Died 18 Sept. 2005.

MANN, (Francis) George, CBE 1983; DSO 1942; MC 1941; Director, 1977–87, and non-executive Deputy Chairman, 1980–86, Extel Group; *b* 6 Sept. 1917; *s* of Francis Thomas, (Frank), Mann and Enid Mann (*née* Tilney); *m* 1949, Margaret Hildegarde Marshall Clark (*d* 1995); three *s* one *d.* *Educ:* Eton; Pembroke Coll., Cambridge (BA). Served War of 1939–45, Scots Guards (DSO, MC). Director: Mann Crossman and Paulin, Watney Mann, Watney Mann and Truman Brewers, 1946–77. Middlesex County Cricket Club: first played, 1937; Captain, 1948–49; Pres., 1983–87; captained England in SA, 1948–49 and against NZ, 1949. Chairman:

TCCB, 1978–83; Cricket Council, 1983. *Address:* West Woodhay, Newbury, Berks RG20 0BP. *T:* (01488) 668243. *Club:* MCC (Pres., 1984–85; Hon. Life Vice-Pres., 1989).

Died 8 Aug. 2001.

MANN, George; *see* Mann, F. G.

MANN, Pauline, (Mrs R. D. Mann); *see* Vogelpoel, P.

MANN, William Neville, MD, FRCP; Consultant Physician Emeritus, Guy's Hospital, 1976; *b* 4 April 1911; *s* of William Frank Mann and Clara, *d* of John Chadwick; *m* 1957, Pamela, *yr d* of late H. E. Chasteney; three *d*; one *s* one *d* (and one *s* decd) from previous marr. *Educ:* Alleyn's Sch.; Guy's Hospital (MB, BS 1935); MD London, 1937. MRCP 1937, FRCP 1947. House Physician, Demonstrator of Pathology and Medical Registrar, Guy's Hospital, 1935–39; served, 1940–45, in RAMC in Middle East and Indian Ocean (Temp. Lt-Col); Physician, Guy's Hosp., 1946–76. Hon. Visiting Physician to Johns Hopkins Hosp., Baltimore, USA. Physician: to HM Household, 1954–64; to HM the Queen, 1964–70; King Edward VII's Hosp. for Officers, 1965–76. Sen. Censor and Sen. Vice-Pres., RCP, 1969–70. Hon. DHL Johns Hopkins, 1986. *Publications:* (jtly) Clinical Examination of Patients, 1950; (jtly) The Medical Works of Hippocrates, 1950; (ed) Conybeare's Text-book of Medicine, 14th edn 1964, 16th edn 1975. *Address:* 90 Alleyn Road, SE21 8AH. *T:* (020) 8670 2451. *Club:* Garrick.

Died 25 June 2001.

MANS, Maj.-Gen. Rowland Spencer Noel, CBE 1971 (OBE 1966, MBE 1956); Director, Military Assistance Office, 1973–76, retired; defence consultant and writer on defence and political affairs; *b* 16 Jan. 1921; *s* of Thomas Frederick Mans and May Seigenberg; *m* 1945, Veeo Ellen Sutton; three *s.* *Educ:* Surbiton Grammar Sch.; RMC, Sandhurst; jssc, psc. Served War, Queen's Royal Regt and King's African Rifles, 1940–45. Regtl and Staff Duty, 1945–59; Instr, Staff Colleges, Camberley and Canada, 1959–63; Comd, 1st Tanganyika Rifles, 1963–64; Staff Duty, Far East and UK, 1964–68; Comd, Aldershot, 1969–72; DDPS (Army), 1972–73. Col, Queen's Regt, 1978–83 (Dep. Col (Surrey), 1973–77). Mem., Hampshire CC, 1984–89. Pres., KAR & EAF Assoc., 1997–. *Publications:* Kenyatta's Middle Road in a Changing Africa, 1977; Canada's Constitutional Crisis, 1978. *Recreations:* writing, reading, gardening. *Address:* Ivy Bank Cottage, Vinegar Hill, Milford-on-Sea, Hants SO41 0RZ. *T:* (01590) 643982. *Clubs:* Army and Navy; Royal Lymington Yacht.

Died 16 Oct. 2002.

MANSFIELD, Sir Philip (Robert Aked), KCMG 1984 (CMG 1973); HM Diplomatic Service, retired; Ambassador to the Netherlands, 1981–84; *b* 9 May 1926; *s* of Philip Theodore Mansfield, CSI, CIE and Helen Rosamond Aked; *m* 1953, Elinor Russell MacHatton; two *s.* *Educ:* Winchester; Pembroke Coll., Cambridge (BA 1949, MA 1987). Grenadier Guards, 1944–47. Sudan Political Service, 1950–55. Entered HM Diplomatic Service, 1955; served in: Addis Ababa, Singapore, Paris, Buenos Aires; Counsellor and Head of Rhodesia Dept, FCO, 1969–72; RCDS, 1973; Counsellor and Head of Chancery, 1974–75, Dep. High Comr, 1976, Nairobi; Asst Under Sec. of State, FCO, 1976–79; Ambassador and Dep. Perm. Representative to UN, 1979–81. Consultant to: Rank Xerox, 1987–95; BPB Industries, 1987–95. *Recreations:* reading, walking. *Address:* Palmers Farm, St Breward, Bodmin, Cornwall PL30 4NT. *T:* (01208) 850378.

Died 14 May 2003.

MANTHORP, Brian Robert, MA; FCollP; Principal, Lawrence College, Murree Hills, 1996–97; *b* 28 July 1934; *s* of Alan Roy Manthorp and Stella Manthorp; *m* 1st, 1955, Jennifer Mary Caradine (marr. diss. 1995); three *s* one *d*; 2nd, 1997, Maureen Walker (*née* Webster). *Educ:* Framlingham Coll.; Pembroke Coll., Oxford (MA Hons English); Westcott House, Cambridge. Instructor Lieut, RN, 1955–58. Ordained priest, Guildford, 1961; resigned holy orders, 1994. Assistant Master, Charterhouse, 1958–65; Head of English: Lawrence Coll., Pakistan, 1965–67; Aitchison Coll., Pakistan, 1968–70; Oakbank Sch., Keighley, 1970–73; Headmaster, Holy Trinity Senior Sch., Halifax, 1973–80; Headmaster, Worcester Coll. for the Blind, 1980–87; Principal: RNIB New Coll., Worcester, 1987–94; Sandal Public Sch., Faisalabad, 1994–96. *Publication:* Fifty Poems for Pakistan, 1971. *Recreations:* sport, sketching. *Address:* 9 Waterman's Reach, Brook Street, Oxford OX1 4LQ. *T:* (01865) 204866; La Petite Botellerais, à Broons 22250, France.

Died 21 April 2001.

MANTON, 3rd Baron *cr* 1922, of Compton Verney; **Joseph Rupert Eric Robert Watson;** DL; landowner and farmer; *b* 22 Jan. 1924; *s* of 2nd Baron Manton and Alethea (*d* 1979), 2nd *d* of late Colonel Philip Langdale, OBE; *S* father, 1968; *m* 1951, Mary Elizabeth, twin *d* of Major T. D. Hallinan, Ashbourne, Glounthaune, Co. Cork; two *s* three *d* (of whom two *s* one *d* are triplets). *Educ:* Eton. Joined Army, 1942; commnd Life Guards, 1943; Captain, 1946; retired, 1947; rejoined 7th (QO) Hussars, 1951–56. Sen. Steward, Jockey Club, 1982–85. DL Humberside, 1980. *Recreations:* hunting, shooting, racing. *Heir:* *s* Major the Hon. Miles Ronald Marcus Watson, Life Guards [*b* 7 May 1958; *m* 1984, Elizabeth, *e* *d* of J. R. Story; two *s*]. *Address:* Houghton Hall, Sancton, York YO4 3RE. *T:* (01430) 873234. *Clubs:* White's, Jockey.   *Died 8 Aug. 2003.*

MANTON, Sir Edwin (Alfred Grenville), Kt 1994; Senior Adviser, American International Group Inc., since 1982; *b* 22 Jan. 1909; *s* of John H. Manton and Emily C. Manton (*née* Denton); *m* 1936, Florence V. Brewer; one *d*. *Educ:* Shaftesbury GS; Coll. of Insurance, NY. AIIA. With B. W. Noble, Paris, 1927–33; American International Underwriters Corp.: Casualty Underwriter, 1933–37; Sec., 1937–38; Vice-Pres., 1938–42; Pres., 1942–69; Chm., 1969–75. Hon. DHL Coll. of Insurance, NY. *Publications:* various papers in insurance press. *Recreations:* walking, art, formerly cricket and hockey. *Address:* American International Group, 70 Pine Street, 59th Floor, New York, NY 10270-0002, USA.

Died 1 Oct. 2005.

MAPLES, Ven. Jeffrey Stanley; Archdeacon of Swindon and Hon. Canon Diocesan, Bristol Cathedral, 1974–82, Archdeacon Emeritus, 1982; *b* 8 Aug. 1916; *o s* of Arthur Stanley and Henrietta Georgina Maples; *m* 1945, Isobel Eileen Mabel Wren; four *s* (and one *s* decd). *Educ:* Downing Coll., Cambridge; Chichester Theological Coll. Deacon 1940, priest 1941; Assistant Curate: St James, Milton, Portsmouth, 1940–46; Watlington, Diocese of Oxford, 1946–48; Vicar of Swinderby, Dio. Lincoln, and Diocesan Youth Chaplain, 1948–50; Vicar of St Michael-on-the-Mount, Lincoln, 1950–56; Canon of Lincoln Cathedral, 1954–56; Director of Religious Education: for Lincoln Dio., 1950–56; for Salisbury Dio., 1956–63; Canon, 1957–60, Canon Residentiary and Chancellor, 1960–67, Canon Emeritus, 1967–, Salisbury Cathedral; Director of the Bible Reading Fellowship, 1963–67; Vicar of St James, Milton, Portsmouth, 1967–74; Rural Dean of Portsmouth, 1968–73; Hon. Canon, Portsmouth Cathedral, 1972–74. Proctor in Convocation for Salisbury Diocese, 1957–70. *Address:* Flat 1, 95 Crane Street, Salisbury, Wilts SP1 2PU. *T:* (01722) 323848.

Died 14 Sept. 2001.

MARA, Rt Hon. Ratu Sir Kamisese Kapaiwai Tuimacilai, GCMG 1983; KBE 1969 (OBE 1961); CF 1996; MSD 1996; PC 1973; Tui Nayau; Tui Lau; President of the Republic of Fiji, 1994–2000; Hereditary High Chief of the Lau Islands; *b* 13 May 1920; *s* of late Ratu Tevita Uluilakeba, Tui Nayau; *m* 1951, Adi Lady Lala Mara (Roko Tui Dreketi); two *s* five *d* (and one *s* decd). *Educ:* Fiji; Sacred Heart Coll., NZ; Otago Univ., NZ; Wadham Coll., Oxford (MA; Hon. Fellow, 1971); London Sch. of Economics (Dip. Econ. & Social Admin.; Hon. Fellow, 1985). Administrative Officer, Colonial

Service, Fiji, Oct. 1950; Fijian MLC, 1953–89, and MEC, 1959–61 (elected MLC and MEC, 1959). Member for Natural Resources and Leader of Govt Business; Alliance Party, 1964–66 (Founder of Party); Chief Minister and Mem., Council of Ministers, Fiji, 1967; Prime Minister, Fiji, 1970–87, Republic of Fiji, 1987–92; Minister for Foreign Affairs and Civil Aviation, 1986–87. Mem. Bd, Internat. Raoul Wallenberg Foundn, 2001–. Hon. Dr of Laws: Univ. of Guam, 1969; Univ. of Papua New Guinea, 1982; Hon. LLD: Univ. of Otago, 1973; New Delhi, 1975; Hon. DPolSc Korea, 1978; Hon. Dr Tokai Univ., 1980; DU Univ. of South Pacific, 1980. Man of the Pacific Award, 1984. KStJ 1975. Grand Cross, Order of Lion, Senegal, 1975; Order of Diplomatic Service Merit, Korea, 1978. *Publication:* The Pacific Way: a memoir, 1997. *Recreations:* athletics, cricket, Rugby football, golf, fishing. *Clubs:* Oxford and Cambridge, Achilles (London); Defence (Suva, Fiji).   *Died 18 April 2004.*

MARDELL, Peggy Joyce, CBE 1982; Regional Nursing Officer, North West Thames Regional Health Authority, 1974–82; *b* 8 July 1927; *d* of Alfred Edward and Edith Mary Mardell. *Educ:* George Spicer Sch., Enfield; Highlands Hosp., London (RFN); E Suffolk Hosp., Ipswich (Medallist, SRN); Queen Charlotte's Hosp. Battersea Coll. of Further Educn (Hons Dip., RNT). Queens Inst. of District Nursing, Guildford, 1951–52 (SCM); Ward Sister, Night Sister, Bethnal Green Hosp., 1953–55; Sister Tutor, Royal Surrey County Hosp., 1957–64; Asst Regional Nursing Officer, NE Metrop. Regional Hosp. Bd, 1964–70; Chief Regional Nursing Officer, NW Metrop. Regional Hosp. Bd, 1970–74. Lectr, British Red Cross, 1958–60; Examr, Gen. Nursing Council, 1962–70; Nurse Mem., Surrey AHA, 1977–82; Member: Royal Coll. of Nursing; Regional Nurse Trng Cttee, 1970–82; Assessor for Nat. Nursing Staff Cttee, 1970–82. *Recreations:* renovating old furniture, gardening, reading. *Address:* 3 Corvill Court, Shelley Road, Worthing, W Sussex BN11 4DF. *T:* (01903) 211876.

Died 2 May 2004.

MARGADALE, 2nd Baron *cr* 1964, of Islay, Co. Argyll; **James Ian Morrison,** TD, DL; director of companies; farmer; *b* 17 July 1930; *e s* of 1st Baron Margadale, TD and Hon. Margaret Esther Lucie Smith (*d* 1980), 2nd *d* of Viscount Hambleden; *S* father, 1996; *m* 1952, Clare Barclay; two *s* one *d*. *Educ:* Eton Coll.; RAC, Cirencester. 2nd Lieut, Life Guards, 1949–50; Major, Royal Wilts Yeo., 1960–68; Hon. Colonel: A (RWY) Sqn Royal Yeomanry RAC TA, and B (RWY) Sqn Royal Wessex Yeomanry, 1982–89; Royal Wessex Yeomanry RAC TA, 1984–89. Mem., Queen's Body Guard for Scotland, 1960–. County Councillor, Wilts, 1955 and 1973–77, County Alderman, 1969; Chm., W Wilts Cons. Assoc., 1967–71, Pres., 1972–84; Chm., Wilts CLA, 1978–81. Chm., Tattersalls Cttee, 1969–80. High Sheriff, 1971, DL, 1977, Wilts. *Recreations:* racing, shooting, hunting. *Heir:* *s* Hon. Alastair John Morrison [*b* 4 April 1958; *m* 1988, Lady Sophia Louise Sydney Murphy (marr. diss. 1999), *yr d* of 11th Duke of Devonshire; one *s* one *d*; *m* 1999, Mrs Amanda Wace, *d* of late Michael Fuller]. *Address:* Fonthill House, Tisbury, Salisbury, Wilts SP3 5SA; Islay Estate Office, Bridgend, Islay, Argyll PA44 7PA. *Clubs:* White's, Jockey.   *Died 6 April 2003.*

MARGASON, Geoffrey, CEng, FICE; Director, Transport and Road Research Laboratory, Crowthorne, 1984–88 (Deputy Director, 1980–84); *b* 19 Sept. 1933; *s* of Henry and Edna Margason; *m* 1958, Bernice Thompson; one *s* two *d*. *Educ:* Humberston Foundation Sch., Cleethorpes; Loughborough Coll. of Advanced Technology (DLCEng). With British Transport Commn and Mouchel Associates, Consulting Engineers, until 1960; Transport and Road Research Laboratory: Researcher in Geotechnics, 1960–69; Research Manager in Construction Planning, Scottish Br. and Transport Planning, 1969–75; Sen. Research Manager in Transport Ops, 1975–78; Head of Research and Science Policy Unit,

Depts of Environment and Transport, 1978–80. *Publications:* papers in jls of various professional instns and to nat. and internat. confs on range of topics in highway transportation; reports of TRRL. *Recreations:* pétanque, golf. *Address:* Franche Cottage, Pankridge Street, Crondall, Farnham, Surrey GU10 5QZ. *T:* (01252) 850399. *Club:* Crondall Pétanque.   *Died 22 Nov. 2004.*

MARJORIBANKS, Sir James Alexander Milne, KCMG 1965 (CMG 1954); Chairman, Scotland in Europe, 1979–90; *b* 29 May 1911; *y s* of Rev. Thomas Marjoribanks of that Ilk, DD, and Mary Ord, *d* of William Logan, Madras CS; *m* 1936, Sonya Patricia (*d* 1981), *d* of David Stanley-Alder, Alderford Grange, Sible Hedingham, Essex, and Sylvia Marie Stanley; one *d*. *Educ:* Merchiston; Edinburgh Academy; Edinburgh Univ. (MA, 1st class hons). Entered Foreign Service, Nov. 1934; HM Embassy, Peking, 1935–38; Consulate-General, Hankow, 1938; Marseilles, 1939–40; Consul, Jacksonville, 1940–42; Vice-Consul, New York, 1942–44; Asst to UK Political Rep., Bucharest, 1944–45; Foreign Office, 1945–49; Dep. to Secretary of State for Foreign Affairs in Austrian Treaty negotiations, 1947–49; Official Secretary, UK High Commn, Canberra, 1950–52; Dep. Head of UK Delegation to High Authority of European Coal and Steel Community, 1952–55; Cabinet Office, 1955–57; HM Minister (Economic), Bonn, 1957–62; Asst Under-Secretary of State, Foreign Office, 1962–65; Ambassador and Head of UK Delegn to European Economic Community, European Atomic Energy Community and ECSC, 1965–71. Director: Scottish Council (Develt and Industry), 1971–81 (Vice-Pres., 1981–83); The Distillers Co. Ltd, 1971–76; Governing Mem., Inveresk Research International, 1978–90. Gen. Council Assessor, Edinburgh Univ. Ct, 1975–79. *Recreation:* hill walking. *Club:* New (Edinburgh).   *Died 29 Jan. 2002.*

MARK, James, MBE 1943; Under-Secretary, Ministry of Overseas Development, 1965–74, retired; *b* 12 June 1914; *s* of late John Mark and Louisa Mary (*née* Hobson); *m* 1941, Mary Trewent Rowland (*d* 1994); three *s* two *d*. *Educ:* William Hulme's Grammar Sch., Manchester; Trinity Coll., Cambridge (MA 1939, PhD 1939); Universities of Munich and Münster. Intelligence Corps, 1940–46. Principal, Control Office for Germany and Austria, 1946–48; HM Treasury, 1948–64: Asst Secretary, 1950; Economic Counsellor, Washington, 1951–53. Jt Editor, Theology, 1976–83. *Publications:* The Question of Christian Stewardship, 1964; articles and reviews on theological and related subjects. *Recreations:* reading, music, theatre. *Address:* Highfield, Mandeville Road, Saffron Walden, Essex CB11 4AQ. *T:* (01799) 521623.
                                    Died 7 Jan. 2001.

MARKING, Sir Henry (Ernest), KCVO 1978; CBE 1969; MC 1944; CRAeS 1953; Deputy Chairman and Managing Director, British Airways, 1972–77; *b* 11 March 1920; *s* of late Isaac and Hilda Jane Marking. *Educ:* Saffron Walden Grammar Sch.; University Coll., London. Served War of 1939–45: 2nd Bn The Sherwood Foresters, 1941–45; North Africa, Italy and Middle East; Adjutant, 1944–45. Middle East Centre of Arab Studies, Jerusalem, 1945–46. Admitted solicitor, 1948. Asst Solicitor, Cripps, Harries, Hall & Co., Tunbridge Wells, 1948–49; Asst Solicitor, 1949, Sec., 1950, Chief Exec., 1964–72, Chm., 1971–72, BEA; Mem. Bd, BOAC, 1971–72; Mem., British Airways Board, 1971–80. Chm., Rothmans UK, 1979–86; Director: Rothmans International, 1979–86; Barclays International, 1977–86. Mem., 1969–77, Chm., 1977–84, British Tourist Authority. Trustee, 1962–95, Chm. Internat. Cttee, 1970–91, Leonard Cheshire Foundn. FIMgt (FBIM 1971); FCIT. *Club:* Reform.
                                    Died 16 May 2002.

MARKOVA, Dame Alicia, (Dame Lilian Alicia Marks), DBE 1963 (CBE 1958); Prima Ballerina Assoluta; Professor of Ballet and Performing Arts, College-Conservatory of Music, University of Cincinnati, since 1970; President, English National (formerly London Festival) Ballet, since 1986; *b* London, 1 Dec. 1910; *d* of Arthur Tristman Marks and Eileen Barry. With Diaghilev's Russian Ballet Co., 1925–29; Rambert Ballet Club, 1931–33; Vic-Wells Ballet Co., 1933–35; Markova-Dolin Ballet Co., 1935–37; Ballet Russe de Monte Carlo, 1938–41; Ballet Theatre, USA, 1941–46. Appeared with Anton Dolin, guest and concert performances, 1948–50. Co-Founder and Prima Ballerina, Festival Ballet, 1950–51; Guest Prima Ballerina: Buenos Aires, 1952; Royal Ballet, 1953 and 1957; Royal Danish Ballet, 1955; Scala, Milan, 1956; Teatro Municipal, Rio de Janeiro, 1956; Festival Ballet, 1958 and 1959; guest appearances at Metropolitan Opera House, New York, 1952, 1953–54, 1955, 1957, 1958; partnered Ram Gopal, Prince's Th., London and Edin. Fest., 1960; Dir, Metropolitan Opera Ballet, 1963–69; produced Les Sylphides for Festival Ballet and Aust. Ballet, 1976, for Royal Ballet School and Northern Ballet Theatre, 1978, for Royal Winnipeg Ballet, Canada, 1979. Guest Professor: Royal Ballet Sch., 1973–; Paris Opera Ballet, 1975; Australian Ballet Sch., 1976; Yorkshire Ballet Seminars, 1975–; Pres., All England Dance Competition, 1983–. Vice-Pres., Royal Acad. of Dancing, 1958–; Governor, Royal Ballet, 1973–; President: Pavlova Meml Mus., 1978; London Ballet Circle, 1981–; Trust of the Arts Educational Schs, 1984–. Concert, television and guest appearances (general), 1952–61. BBC series, Markova's Ballet Call, 1960; Masterclass, BBC2, 1980. Queen Elizabeth II Coronation Award, Royal Acad. of Dancing, 1963; Special Ballet Award, Evening Standard, 1994. Hon. DMus: Leicester, 1966; East Anglia, 1982. *Publications:* Giselle and I, 1960; Markova Remembers, 1986; *relevant publication:* Markova: the legend, by Maurice Leonard, 1995. *Address:* c/o Royal Ballet School, 46 Floral Street, Covent Garden, WC2E 9DA.
                                    Died 2 Dec. 2004.

MARKS, John Emile, CBE 1970; Chairman, Peckerbond Ltd; *b* 1 Dec. 1913; *s* of late Hyam and Miriam Marks; *m* 1947, Cassandra Emily (*née* Brierly); two *s* two *d*; *m* 1975, Averil May Hannah (*née* Davies). *Educ:* Eton College. Served War of 1939–45 (despatches 1944). Emigrated to Canada, 1951; established: John Marks Ltd, importers and distribrs of sporting goods, 1952; Canair Ltd, Windsor, England, 1962; President: Douglas Engrg Co. Ltd, Toronto, 1956; DV Gp Ltd, 1958; returned to England, 1972. President: British Canadian Trade Assoc., 1966–67, 1969–70; Canada UK Chamber of Commerce, 1975–76; Vice-Chm., Westminster Chamber of Commerce. *Recreations:* snooker, bowls. *Address:* Teignmouth, Devon.
                                    Died 25 July 2003.

MARKS, Dame Lilian Alicia; *see* Markova, Dame A.

MARRE, Romola Mary, (Lady Marre), CBE 1979; Vice Chairman, City Parochial Foundation, 1989–93 (Trustee, 1975–89); *b* 25 April 1920; *d* of late Aubrey John Gilling and Romola Marjorie Angier; *m* 1943, Sir Alan Samuel Marre, KCB (*d* 1990); one *s* one *d*. *Educ:* Chelmsford County High Sch. for Girls; Bedford Coll., Univ. of London (BA Hons Philosophy). Asst Principal (Temp.), Min. of Health, 1941–42; Sgt, subseq. Jun. Comdr, ATS Officer Selection Bd, 1942–45. Organiser, West Hampstead Citizen's Advice Bureau, 1962–65; Dep. Gen. Sec., Camden Council of Social Service, 1965–73; Adviser on Community Health Councils to DHSS, 1974–75; Chairman: London Voluntary Service Council (formerly London Council of Social Service), 1974–84; Cttee on the Future of the Legal Profession, 1986–88; Panel of Four Commn of Enquiry into Human Aids to Communication, 1990–92; Camden and Islington (formerly Bloomsbury, Camden and Islington) HA Dist Ethics Cttee, 1993–2000; Mem., Middlesex, later UCL, Hosp. Res. Ethics Cttee, 1990–2000. Member: Milk Marketing Bd, 1973–82; Lord Chancellor's Adv. Cttee on Legal Aid, 1975–80; BBC and IBA Central Appeals Adv. Cttee, 1980–87 (Chm., 1984–87); Council of Management, Charity Projects, 1987–90; Dep. Chm., Royal Jubilee Trusts, 1981–88; Chairman: Volunteer Centre, 1973–78; Adv. Gp on

Hospital Services for children with cancer in North Western Region, Jan.-June 1979; Prince of Wales' Adv. Gp on Disability, 1982–84; Child Mental Health Res. Trust, 1996–; Founder Pres., Barnet Voluntary Service Council, 1979–. *Recreations:* cooking, gardening, painting, talking. *Address:* 27 Edmunds Walk, N2 0HU. *T:* (020) 8883 4420; 8 North Quarter Steading, Kingsbarns, St Andrews, Fife KY16 8NE. *T:* (01334) 880313.
Died 6 March 2005.

MARRIOTT, Sir John (Brook), KCVO 1995 (CVO 1991; LVO 1978); Keeper of the Royal Philatelic Collection, 1969–95; *b* 27 July 1922; *er s* of late John Morley Marriott and Maud Marriott (*née* Brook)q; *m* 1952, Mary Eleanor Norcliffe Thompson; two *s*. *Educ:* Merchant Taylors' Sch., Northwood; St John's Coll., Cambridge (Wrangler Math. Tripos; MA). Army Op. Res. Gp, Min. of Supply, 1943; Foreign Office, Bletchley Park, 1944. Asst Master, Charterhouse, 1945–82, Housemaster 1960–75. Mem., Nat. Postal Mus. Bd, 1989–97; Royal Philatelic Society, London: Hon. Fellow, 1993; Council Mem., 1969; Vice-Pres., 1979–83; Pres., 1983–86; Tilleard Medal, 1968; Tapling Medal, 1976; London Medal, 1987. Corresp. Mem., l'Académie de Philatelie, Paris. Liveryman, Merchant Taylors' Co., 1950. Gov., St Edmund's Sch., Hindhead, 1979–87. Roll of Distinguished Philatelists, Philatelic Congress of GB, 1972; Alfred F. Lichtenstein Award, Collectors Club, NY, 1988; Lindenberg Medal, Berlin 1888 Philatelic Club, 1988. *Publications:* Philatelic History of Trinidad to 1862, 1963; contribs to London Philatelist. *Recreations:* cricket, football, philately.
Died 3 July 2001.

MARSH, Nevill Francis, CBE 1969; Director-General, St John Ambulance, 1972–76; *b* 13 Aug. 1907; *m* 1st, 1935, Betty Hide (decd); one *s* one *d*; 2nd, 1989, Gillian Hodnett. *Educ:* Oundle Sch., Northants; Clare Coll., Cambridge (MA). Traction Motor Design Staff, Metropolitan-Vickers Electrical Co. Ltd, 1930–32; Mid-Lincolnshire Electric Supply Co. Ltd: Dist Engineer, 1932–38; Engineer and Manager, 1938–48; Chief Commercial Officer, E Midlands Electricity Board, 1948–55; Dep.-Chm., N Eastern Electricity Board, 1955–57; Dep.-Chm., E Midlands Electricity Board, 1957–59; Chm., East Midlands Electricity Board, 1959–61; a Dep. Chm., Electricity Council, 1962–71; Chm., British Electrotechnical Cttee, 1970–72. Dir for Gtr London, St John Ambulance Assoc., 1971–72. Also formerly: Dir, Altrincham Electric Supply Ltd, and Public Utilities (Elec.) Ltd, and Supervising Engineer, Campbeltown & Mid-Argyll Elec. Supply Co. Ltd, and Thurso & District Elec. Supply Co. Ltd. FIEE; Pres. of Assoc. of Supervising Electrical Engineers, 1966–68. KStJ 1973. *Publications:* jt contrib. Jl Inst. Electrical Engineers, 1955. *Address:* Stocksfield, 20 Main Road, Dowsby, near Bourne, Lincs PE10 0TL. *Club:* Royal Air Force.
Died 12 March 2004.

MARSHALL, Alexander Badenoch, (Sandy); Chairman, Commercial Union Assurance Co. plc, 1983–90 (Director, 1970–90); *b* 31 Dec. 1924; *m* 1961, Mona Kurina Douglas Kirk, South Africa; two *s* one *d*. *Educ:* Trinity Coll., Glenalmond; Worcester Coll., Oxford (MA). Served War, Sub-Lieut RNVR, 1943–46. P&O Group of Companies: Mackinnon Mackenzie & Co., Calcutta, 1947–59; Gen. Manager, British India Steam Navigation Co., 1959–62; Man. Dir, Trident Tankers Ltd, 1962–68; Dir, 1968–79, Man. Dir, 1972–79, Peninsular and Oriental Steam Navigation Co.; Dir, 1979–95, Vice-Chm., 1983–87, Chm., 1987–93, Maersk Co. Ltd; Chairman: Bestobell Plc, 1979–85; Royal Bank of Canada Hldgs UK Ltd, 1988–95; Vice-Chm., The Boots Co. Plc, 1985–91 (Dir, 1981–91); Director: Royal Bank of Canada, 1985–95; Seascope Shipping Hldgs Plc, 1997–99. Pres., Chamber of Shipping of UK, 1994–95. Co-Chm., British-N American Cttee, 1984–90. *Publication:* Taking the Adventure, 2000. *Recreation:* grandchildren. *Address:* Crest

House, Woldingham, Surrey CR3 7DH. *Clubs:* Oriental; Tollygunge (Calcutta).
Died 12 Jan. 2005.

MARSHALL, Geoffrey, MA, PhD; FBA 1971; Provost, The Queen's College, Oxford, 1993–99 (Fellow and Tutor in Politics, 1957–93; Hon. Fellow, 1999); *b* 22 April 1929; *s* of Leonard William and Kate Marshall; *m* 1957, Patricia Ann Christine Woodcock; two *s*. *Educ:* Arnold Sch., Blackpool, Lancs; Manchester Univ. (MA); MA Oxon; PhD Glasgow. Research Fellow, Nuffield Coll., Oxford,1955–57. Andrew Dixon White Vis. Prof., Cornell Univ., Ithaca, NY, 1985–91. Pres., Study of Parliament Gp, 1994–2000. Mem. Oxford City Council, 1965–74; Sheriff of Oxford, 1970–71. *Publications:* Parliamentary Sovereignty and the Commonwealth, 1957; (with G. C. Moodie) Some Problems of the Constitution, 1959; Police and Government, 1965; Constitutional Theory, 1971; Constitutional Conventions, 1984; Ministerial Responsibility, 1989. *Recreation:* Blackpool FC. *Address:* 33 The Villas, Rutherway, Oxford OX2 6QY. *T:* (01865) 516114.
Died 24 June 2003.

MARSHALL, James; MP (Lab) Leicester South, Oct. 1974–1983, and since 1987; *b* 13 March 1941; *m* 1962, Shirley (marr. diss.), *d* of W. Ellis, Sheffield; one *s* one *d*; *m* 1986, Susan, *d* of G. Carter, Leicester. *Educ:* City Grammar Sch., Sheffield; Leeds Univ. BSc, PhD. Joined Lab Party, 1960. Mem., Leeds City Council, 1965–68; Leicester City Council: Mem., 1971–76; Chm., Finance Cttee, 1972–74; Leader, 1974. Contested (Lab): Harborough, 1970; Leicester South, Feb. 1974, 1983. An Asst Govt Whip, 1977–79. *Address:* House of Commons, SW1A 0AA.
Died 27 May 2004.

MARSHALL, Air Cdre Philippa Frances, CB 1971; OBE 1956; Director of the Women's Royal Air Force, 1969–73; *b* 4 Nov. 1920; *d* of late Horace Plant Marshall, Stoke-on-Trent. *Educ:* St Dominic's High Sch., Stoke-on-Trent. Joined WAAF, 1941; Comd WRAF Admin. Officer, Strike Comd, 1968–69, Air Cdre 1969; ADC, 1969–73. *Recreations:* music, cookery. *Club:* Royal Air Force.
Died 4 Feb. 2005.

MARTIN, Archer John Porter, CBE 1960; FRS 1950; PhD; *b* 1 March 1910; *s* of Dr W. A. P. and Mrs L. K. Martin; *m* 1943, Judith Bagenal; two *s* three *d*. *Educ:* Bedford Sch.; Peterhouse, Cambridge (BA 1932, MA 1936; PhD 1937; Hon. Fellow, 1974). Nutritional Lab., Cambridge, 1933–38; Chemist, Wool Industries Research Assoc., Leeds, 1938–46; Research Dept, Boots Pure Drug Co., Nottingham, 1946–48; staff, Medical Research Council, 1948–52; Head of Phys. Chem. Div., National Inst. of Medical Research, 1952–56; Chemical Consultant, 1956–59; Director, Abbotsbury Laboratories Ltd, 1959–70; Consultant to Wellcome Research Laboratories, 1970–73. Extraordinary Prof., Technological Univ. of Eindhoven, 1965–73; Professorial Fellow, Univ. of Sussex, 1973–78; Robert A. Welch Prof. of Chemistry, Univ. of Houston, Texas, 1974–79; Invited Prof. of Chemistry, Ecole Polytechnique Fédérale de Lausanne, 1980–84. Berzelius Gold Medal, Swedish Medical Soc., 1951; (jointly with R. L. M. Synge) Nobel Prize for Chemistry, 1952; John Scott Award, 1958; John Price Wetherill Medal, 1959; Franklin Institute Medal, 1959; Leverhulme Medal, Royal Society, 1963; Koltoff Medal, Acad. of Pharmaceutical Science, 1969; Callendar Medal, Inst. of Measurement and Control, 1971; Fritz-Pregl Medal, Austrian Soc. of Microchem. and Analytical Chem., 1985. Hon. DSc Leeds, 1968; Hon. LLD Glasgow, 1973.
Died 28 July 2002.

MARTIN, Frank Vernon, MA (Oxon); graphic artist; printmaker; engraver; illustrator; *b* Dulwich, 14 Jan. 1921; *er s* of late Thomas Martin; *m* 1942, Mary Irene Goodwin (*d* 2004); three *d*. *Educ:* Uppingham Sch.; Hertford Coll., Oxford (History Schol.); St Martin's Sch. of Art. Army, 1941–46. Studied wood engraving with Gertrude Hermes and etching with John Buckland Wright. In free-lance professional practice as wood engraver and book

illustrator, 1948–. Teacher of etching and engraving, Camberwell Sch. of Art, 1953–80 (Hd of Dept of Graphic Arts, 1976–80). Printmaker, 1966–; etchings, drypoints, woodcuts in colour. Twenty-five one-man exhibitions in UK, Europe and USA, 1956–; works in various public and private collections in UK and abroad. RE 1955–74; MSIA 1955–71; Mem., Soc. of Wood Engravers; Hon. Academician, Accademia delle Arti del Disegno, Florence, 1962. *Publications:* (also illus.) Newhaven-Dieppe, 1996; Twenty-eight Wood Engravings, 1999; (also illus.) Shadowland, 2002; Drawn from Life, 2004; *relevant publication:* The Wood Engravings of Frank Martin, by Hal Bishop, 1998. *Address:* 55 St Mary's Grove, W4 3LW.
Died 29 July 2005.

MARTIN, Ronald, MBE 1945; *b* 7 Nov. 1919; *o s* of late Albert and Clara Martin; *m* 1943, Bettina, *o d* of late H. E. M. Billing; one *d*. *Educ:* St Olave's Grammar Sch. Asst Traffic Superintendent, GPO, 1939. Served War of 1939–45, Royal Signals, NW Europe. GPO: Asst Princ., 1948; Princ., 1950; Treasury, 1954; Princ. Private Sec. to PMG, 1955; Staff Controller, GPO, London, 1956; Asst Sec., 1957; Dir Establishments and Organisation, GPO, 1966; Dir Telecommunications Personnel, 1967; Dir of Marketing, Telecommunications HQ, 1975–79; Sen. Dir, Customer Services, 1975–79. *Recreations:* music, motoring, horology. *Address:* 23 Birch Close, Send, Woking, Surrey GU23 7BZ.
Died 6 Oct. 2004.

MARTIN, Rosamund Mary H., (Lady Holland-Martin); *see* Holland-Martin.

MARTIN, Victor Cecil, OBE; HM Diplomatic Service, retired; *b* 12 Oct. 1915; *s* of late Cecil Martin and Isabel Katherine Martin (*née* Hickman). *Educ:* Cheltenham Coll.; Jesus Coll., Cambridge (Scholar; Classical Tripos Parts 1 and 2; MA). Served Intelligence Corps, 1940–45; Major 1944, Persia and Iraq Force. Asst Principal, Board of Education, 1939; Principal, Min. of Education, 1946; transferred to CRO, 1948; British High Commn, New Delhi, 1951–54, 1956–60; Asst Sec., CRO, 1962; Head of West Africa Dept, 1961–64; Head of S Asia Dept, 1964–66; Head of Cultural Relations Dept, 1966–68; Dep. High Comr, Madras, 1968–71; Special Adviser to High Comr, British High Commn, New Delhi, 1972–75. *Recreations:* ornithology, music. *Address:* 76 Swan Court, Flood Street, SW3 5UD. *Clubs:* Oxford and Cambridge, Royal Commonwealth Society, Royal Over-Seas League.
Died 6 April 2001.

MARTIN-BATES, James Patrick, MA; JP; FCIS; Director: Atkins Holdings Ltd, 1986–90 (Chairman, 1987–89); W. S. Atkins Ltd, 1986–94; W. S. Atkins Group Ltd, 1970–86; *b* 17 Aug. 1912; *er s* of late R. Martin-Bates, JP, Perth, Scotland; *m* 1939, Clare, *d* of late Prof. James Miller, MD, DSc; one *s* two *d*. *Educ:* Perth Academy; Glenalmond; Worcester Coll., Oxford (BA 1933, MA 1944). Lamson Industries, 1933–36; Dorman Long & Co. Ltd, 1936–38; PE Group, 1938–61: Man. Dir, Production Engineering Ltd, 1953–59; Vice-Chm., PE Holdings, 1959–61; Director: Hutchinson Ltd, 1958–78; Avery's Ltd, 1970–77; Charringtons Industrial Holdings Ltd, 1972–77. Principal, Administrative Staff Coll., Henley-on-Thames, 1961–72. Chm., Management Consultants Association, 1960; Member: Council, British Institute of Management, 1961–66; UK Advisory Council on Education for Management, 1961–66; Council, Glenalmond, 1963–82; Bd of Visitors, HM Borstal, Huntercombe, 1964–67; The Council for Technical Education and Training for Overseas Countries, 1962–73; Council, University Coll., Nairobi, 1965–68; Council, Chartered Institute of Secretaries, 1965–74; EDC for Rubber Industry, 1965–69; Council, Univ. of Buckingham (formerly University Coll. at Buckingham), 1977–87. Governor, Aylesbury Grammar Sch., 1983–89. UN Consultant in Iran, 1972–78. High Sheriff of Buckinghamshire, 1974; Chm., Marlow Bench, 1978–82. FCIS 1961; CCMI (FBIM 1960); Fellow Internat. Acad. of Management, 1964. DUniv Buckingham, 1986.

Burnham Medal, BIM, 1974. *Publications:* The History of the Maurice Lubbock Memorial Fund, 1993; various articles in management jls. *Recreations:* golf, fishing. *Address:* Ivy Cottage, Fingest, near Henley-on-Thames, Oxon RG9 6QD. *T:* (01491) 638202. *Clubs:* Caledonian; Royal and Ancient (St Andrews); Huntercombe Golf.
Died 28 Sept. 2003.

MARTINEAU, Charles Herman; Chairman, Electricity Consultative Council for South of Scotland, 1972–76; *b* 3 Sept. 1908; *s* of Prof. Charles E. Martineau, Birmingham; *m* 1939, Margaret Shirley Dolphin; two *s* one *d*. *Educ:* King Edward's Sch., Birmingham. Jas Williamson & Son Ltd, Lancaster and Nairn-Williamson Ltd, Kirkcaldy: Man. Dir, 1952–66. Part-time Mem., S of Scotland Electricity Bd, 1971–76. Mem., Fife CC, 1967 (Vice-Convener, 1970–73); Mem., Fife Regional Council, 1978–82. *Recreations:* chess, golf. *Address:* Gladsmuir, Hepburn Gardens, St Andrews, Fife. *T:* (01334) 473069. *Club:* Royal & Ancient (St Andrews).
Died 8 March 2003.

MASSEY, Prof. Vincent, PhD; FRS 1977; J. Lawrence Oncley Distinguished University Professor of Biological Chemistry, University of Michigan, since 1995; *b* 28 Nov. 1926; *s* of Walter Massey and Mary Ann Massey; *m* 1950, Margot Eva Ruth Grünewald; one *s* two *d*. *Educ:* Univ. of Sydney (BSc Hons 1947); Univ. of Cambridge (PhD 1952). Scientific Officer, CSIRO, Australia, 1947–50; Ian McMaster Scholar, Cambridge, 1950–53, ICI Fellow, 1953–55; Researcher, Henry Ford Hosp., Detroit, 1955–57; Lectr, then Sen. Lectr, Univ. of Sheffield, 1957–63; Prof. of Biol Chemistry, Univ. of Michigan, 1963–95. Visiting Professor: Univ. of Ill, 1960; Univ. of Konstanz, Germany, 1973–74 (Permanent Guest Prof., 1975–); Inst. of Applied Biochem., Mitake, Japan, 1985; Guest Prof., Yokohama City Univ., Japan, 1988. Mem., NAS, USA, 1995–. Hon. DSc Tokushima Univ. Med. Sch., 1994. *Publications:* (ed jtly) Flavins and Flavoproteins, 1982, Flavins and Flavoproteins 1996, 1997 (proc. of internat. symposia); over 400 articles in scholarly jls and books. *Recreations:* walking, sailing, gardening. *Address:* Department of Biological Chemistry, University of Michigan, Ann Arbor, MI 48109, USA. *T:* (734) 7647196, *Fax:* (734) 7634581; *e-mail:* massey@umich.edu.
Died 26 Aug. 2002.

MASSY-GREENE, Sir (John) Brian, AC 1989; Kt 1972; Chairman, Hazelton Air Lines (formerly Hazelton Air Services Investments) Ltd, 1984–97; *b* Tenterfield, NSW, 20 April 1916; *s* of late Sir Walter Massy-Greene, KCMG, and Lula May Lomax; *m* 1942, Margaret Elizabeth Ritchie Sharp, *d* of late Dr Walter Alexander Ramsay Sharp, OBE; two *s* two *d*. *Educ:* Sydney C of E Grammar Sch.; Geelong Grammar Sch.; Clare Coll., Cambridge (MA). Served War 1939–45: New Guinea, AIF, as Lieut, 1942–45. Joined Metal Manufacturers Ltd, as Staff Cadet, 1939; later transferred to their wholly-owned subsid. Austral Bronze Co. Pty Ltd; Gen. Manager, 1953–62. Managing Dir, 1962–76, and Chm., 1966–77, Consolidated Gold Fields Australia Ltd; Chairman: The Bellambi Coal Co. Ltd, 1964–72; Goldsworthy Mining Ltd, 1965–76; The Mount Lyell Mining & Railway Co. Ltd, 1964–76; Lawrenson Alumasc Holdings Ltd, 1964–73 (Dir, 1962–73); Pacific Dunlop (formerly Dunlop Olympic) Ltd, 1979–86 (Dir, 1968–86; Vice-Chm., 1977–79); Santos Ltd, 1984–88 (Dir, 1984); Commonwealth Banking Corp., 1985–88 (Dep. Chm., 1975–85; Dir, 1968–88); Director: Associated Minerals Consolidated Ltd, 1962–76; Commonwealth Mining Investments (Australia) Ltd, 1962–72 and 1978–85; Consolidated Gold Fields Ltd, London, 1963–76; Dalgety Australia Ltd, 1967–78 (Dep. Chm., 1975–78); Zip Holdings Ltd, 1964–73; Australian European Finance Corp., 1975–89 (Chm., 1987–88); Nat. Mutual Life Assoc. Ltd, 1977–85. Member: Exec. Cttee, Australian Mining Industry Council, 1967–78 (Pres. 1971); Manuf. Industries Adv. Council, 1968–77; NSW Adv. Cttee, CSIRO, 1968–75. Mem., Aust. Inst. Mining

and Metallurgy. FAIM; FIEAust. *Recreations:* farming, fishing, flying. *Address:* c/o Level 9, 1 York Street, Sydney, NSW 2000, Australia. *T:* (2) 92500077. *Club:* Australian.
Died 6 July 2001.

MATHESON, Sir (James Adam) Louis, KBE 1976 (MBE 1944); CMG 1972; FTSE; FREng; Vice-Chancellor, Monash University, Melbourne, 1959–76; Chancellor, Papua New Guinea University of Technology, 1973–75; Chairman, Australian Science and Technology Council, 1975–76; *b* 11 Feb. 1912; *s* of William and Lily Edith Matheson; *m* 1937, Audrey Elizabeth Wood; three *s. Educ:* Bootham Sch., York; Manchester Univ. (MSc 1933); PhD Birmingham 1946. Lectr, Birmingham Univ., 1938–46; Prof. of Civil Engineering, Univ. of Melbourne, Australia, 1946–50; Beyer Prof. of Engineering, Univ. of Manchester, 1951–59. Member: Mission on Technical Educn in W Indies, 1957; Ramsay Cttee on Tertiary Educn in Victoria, 1961–63; CSIRO Adv. Council, 1962–67; Royal Commn into failure of King's Bridge, 1963; Exec., Aust. Council for Educational Research, 1964–69; Interim Council, Univ. of Papua New Guinea, 1965–68; Enquiry into Post-Secondary Educn in Victoria, 1976–78; Chairman: Council, Papua New Guinea Inst. of Technology, 1966–73; Aust. Vice-Chancellors' Cttee, 1967–68; Assoc. of Commonwealth Univs, 1967–69; Newport Power Stn Review Panel, 1977; Schools Commn Buildings Cttee, 1977–81; Victorian Planning and Finance Cttee, Commonwealth Schools Commn, 1979–83; Sorrento Harbour Inquiries, 1984 and 1987; St Kilda Harbour Inquiry, 1986. Trustee, Inst. of Applied Science (later Science Mus. of Victoria), 1963–83 (Pres., 1969–73). Dir, Nauru Phosphate Corp., 1977–79. Hon. FICE (Mem. Council, 1965); Hon. FIEAust (Mem. Council, 1961–81, Vice-Pres., 1970–74, Pres., 1975–76); FTSE (FTS 1976); FREng (FEng 1980). Hon. DSc Hong Kong, 1969; Hon. LLD: Manchester, 1972; Monash, 1975; Melbourne, 1975. Kernot Meml Medal, 1972; Peter Nicol Russell Medal, 1976. *Publications:* Hyperstatic Structures: Vol. 1, 1959, Vol. 2, 1960; Still Learning, 1980; various articles on engineering and education. *Recreations:* music, woodcraft. *Address:* 26/166 West Toorak Road, South Yarra, Victoria 3141, Australia.
Died 27 March 2002.

MATHESON, Maj.-Gen. John Mackenzie, OBE 1950; TD 1969; retired; *b* Gibraltar, 6 Aug. 1912; *s* of late John Matheson and Nina Short, Cape Town; *m* 1942, Agnes (*d* 1995), *d* of Henderson Purves, Dunfermline; one *d. Educ:* George Watson's Coll., Edinburgh; Edinburgh Univ. (Vans Dunlop Schol.). MB, ChB 1936; MD 1945. FRCSEd 1946; FRCS 1962; FRCP 1972 (MRCP 1939). Royal Victoria Hosp. Tuberculosis Trust Research Fellow, 1936–37; Lieut, RAMC (TA), 1936. Served War of 1939–45: Middle East, N Africa and Italy; Regular RAMC Commn, 1944 (despatches). Clinical Tutor, Surgical Professorial Unit, Edinburgh Univ., 1947–48; Med. Liaison Officer to Surgeon-Gen. US Army, Washington, DC, 1948–50; Asst Chief, Section Gen. Surgery, Walter Reed Army Hosp., Washington, DC, 1950–51; Cons. Surgeon: MELF, 1963–64; BAOR, 1967; Far East, 1967–69; Jt Prof. Mil. Surg., RAM Coll. and RCS of Eng., 1964–67; Brig. 1967; Comdt and Dir of Studies, Royal Army Med. Coll., 1969–71; Postgrad. Dean, Faculty of Medicine, Univ. of Edinburgh, 1971–80. QHS 1969–71. Hon. Col, 205 (Scottish) Gen. Hosp., T&AVR, 1978–80. Alexander Medal, 1961; Simpson-Smith Memorial Lectr, 1967; Gordon-Watson Lectr, RCS of Eng., 1967; Mitchiner Meml Lectr, RAM Coll., Millbank, 1988. Senior Fellow, Assoc. of Surgeons of GB and Ireland; British Medical Association: Mem., Armed Forces Cttee, 1983–88; Mem., Bd of Educn and Science, 1985–88; Pres., Lothian Div., 1978–80. President: Scottish Br., Royal Soc. of Tropical Medicine and Hygiene, 1978–80; Military Surgical Soc., 1984–86; Edinburgh Univ. Graduates Assoc., 1987–89 (Vice-Pres., 1985–86); Chm. Council, Edinburgh Royal Infirmary Samaritan

Soc., 1983–. *Publications:* (contrib.) Military Medicine, in Dictionary of Medical Ethics, 1977; papers (on gun-shot wounds, gas-gangrene and sterilisation) to medical jls. *Recreation:* travel. *Address:* c/o Croxton Old Rectory, Croxton, St Neots, Cambs PE19 6SU.
Died 9 Nov. 2003.

MATHESON, Sir Louis; *see* Matheson, Sir J. A. L.

MATHEWS, Terence Francis, CBE 1995; Consultant, Financial Services Authority, since 1999; *b* 1 May 1935; *s* of Frank Mathews and Alice Elizabeth (*née* Lever); *m* 1st, 1958, Anna Dawson (marr. diss. 1973); one *s* one *d*; 2nd, 1976, Barbara Scott. *Educ:* Balham Central Sch. Nat. Service, RAF, 1953–55. HM Treasury, 1952–86; Building Socs Commn, 1986–96, Comr, 1988–96, retd. Mem., Gibraltar Financial Services Commn, 1995–. *Recreation:* amateur theatre. *Address:* Financial Services Authority, 25 The North Colonnade, Canary Wharf, E14 5HS.
Died 28 Nov. 2004.

MATHISON, Peter Yorke; Chief Executive, Benefits Agency, Department of Social Security, 1995–2000; *b* 29 March 1945; *s* of Donald and late Jean Mathison; *m* 1966, Betty McCarthy. *Educ:* Lancashire Poly. (BA Business Studies 1983). FCMA 1981. Rover Group: Financial Controller, 1982–84; Systems Manager, 1984–86; Leyland Trucks; Ops Dir, Engines and Foundry Plants, 1986–88; Gen. Manager, Power Systems Div., Lucas Aerospace, 1989; Man. Dir, Guns and Vehicles Div., Royal Ordnance, 1990–91; Chief Exec., War Pensions Agency, DSS, 1992–95. *Recreations:* theatre, good restaurants, travelling, meeting people. *Died 21 Nov. 2002.*

MATTHEWS, Prof. Geoffrey, PhD; CMath, FIMA; Shell Professor of Mathematics Education, Centre for Science and Mathematics Education, Chelsea College, University of London, 1968–77, then Emeritus; *b* 1 Feb. 1917; *s* of Humphrey and Gladys Matthews; *m* 1st, 1941, Patricia Mary Jackson (marr. diss. 1972); one *s* one *d*; 2nd, 1972, Julia Comber. *Educ:* Marlborough; Jesus Coll., Cambridge (MA); PhD (London). CMath 1991; FIMA 1964. Wiltshire Regt, Intelligence Officer 43rd (Wessex) Div., 1939–45, Captain (dispatches, 1945; US Bronze Star, 1945). Teacher: Haberdashers' Aske's Sch., 1945–50; St Dunstan's Coll., 1950–64, Dep. Head and Head of Mathematics Dept; Organiser, Nuffield Mathematics Teaching Project, 1964–72; Co-director (with Julia Matthews), Schools Council Early Mathematical Experiences project, 1974–79; Co-dir (with Prof. K. W. Keohane) SSRC funded prog. Concepts in Secondary Sch. Maths and Sci., 1974–79. Hon. Res. Associate, Greenwich Univ., 1996. Presenter of BBC TV programmes in series Tuesday Term, Middle School Mathematics, and Children and Mathematics; consultant to BBC series Maths in a Box and You and Me, and to ATV series Towards Mathematics. Consultant to maths teaching projects in Italy, Greece, Portugal, Sri Lanka and Thailand; has lectured extensively abroad. Pres., Mathematical Assoc., 1977–78 (Hon. Mem., 1990); Founder Mem., Commonwealth Assoc. of Sci. and Maths Educators, 1964; Member: Internat. Cttee, 3rd Congress, ICME, 1976; Council, Inst. of Maths and its Applications, 1978–81; Cttee, Soc. of Free Painters and Sculptors, 1978–89. One man shows: Loggia Gall., 1986, 1989; St Martin's-in-the-Fields Gall., 1993, 1996. *Publications:* Calculus, 1964; Matrices I & II, 1964; Mathematics through School, 1972; Mainly on the Bright Side, 1989, 2nd edn 2001; papers in Proc. Kon. Akad. Wetensch. (Amsterdam); numerous articles in Math. Gaz., etc. *Recreations:* painting, travel. *Address:* 50 Sydney Road, Bexleyheath, Kent DA6 8HG. *T:* (020) 8303 4301. *Died 13 Sept. 2002.*

MATTHEWS, George Lloyd; Archivist, Communist Party of Great Britain, 1980–89; *b* 24 Jan. 1917; *s* of James and Ethel Matthews, Sandy, Beds; *m* 1940, Elisabeth Lynette Summers (*d* 2002); no *c. Educ:* Bedford Modern Sch.; Reading Univ. Pres., Reading Univ. Students Union, 1938–39; Vice-Pres., Nat. Union of Students,

1939–40; Vice-Pres., University Labour Fedn, 1938–39. County Chm., Nat. Union of Agricultural Workers, 1945–49; Mem. Exec. Cttee, Communist Party, 1943–79; Asst Gen. Sec., Communist Party, 1949–57; Asst Editor, 1957–59, Editor, 1959–74, Daily Worker, later Morning Star; Head of Press and Publicity Dept, Communist Party of GB, 1974–79. Mem., New Politics Network, 2000–. *Publication:* (ed with F. King) About Turn, 1990. *Recreation:* music. *Address:* 74 Hungerford Road, N7 9LP. *T:* (020) 7607 1527. *Died 29 March 2005.*

MATTHEWS, Sir Peter (Jack), Kt 1981; CVO 1978; OBE 1974; QPM 1970; DL; Chief Constable of Surrey, 1968–82; *b* 25 Dec. 1917; *s* of Thomas Francis Matthews and Agnes Jack; *m* 1944, Margaret, *er d* of Cecil Levett, London; one *s*. *Educ:* Blackridge Public Sch., West Lothian. Joined Metropolitan Police, 1937; Flt-Lt (pilot) RAF, 1942–46; Metropolitan Police, 1946–65: seconded Cyprus, 1955; Chief Supt P Div., 1963–65; Chief Constable: East Suffolk, 1965–67; Suffolk, 1967–68. President: British Section, Internat. Police Assoc., 1964–70 (Internat. Pres. 1966–70); Assoc. of Chief Police Officers of England, Wales and NI, 1976–77 (Chm., Sub-Cttee on Terrorism and Allied Matters, 1976–82; Rep. at Interpol, 1977–80); Chief Constables' Club, 1980–81; Vice-Chm., Home Office Standing Adv. Cttee on Police Dogs, 1982– (Chm., 1978–82; Chm., Training Sub-Cttee, 1972–82); led British Police Study Team to advise Singapore Police, 1982; specialist advr to Parly Select Cttee on Defence, 1984; Mem., MoD Police Review Cttee, 1985. Pres., Woking Br., Aircrew Assoc., 1990–2000. Lecture tour of Canada and USA, 1979; Lecturer: Airline Training Associates Ltd, 1984–91; Internat. Military Services Ltd, 1987–91. Final Reader, HM The Queen's Police Gold Medal Essay Competition, 1983–92. CCMI (CBIM 1978). DL Surrey, 1981. Special Cert. for Extraordinary Service, Office of Special Investigation, USAF, 1968. *Club:* Royal Air Force. *Died 6 Jan. 2003.*

MATTHEWS, Prof. Walter Bryan; Professor of Clinical Neurology, University of Oxford, 1970–87, then Emeritus; Fellow of St Edmund Hall, Oxford, 1970–87, then Emeritus; *b* 7 April 1920; *s* of Very Rev. Dr Walter Robert Matthews, KCVO, CH and Margaret (*née* Bryan); *m* 1943, Margaret Forster; one *s* one *d*. *Educ:* Marlborough Coll.; University Coll., Oxford (MA; DM 1949). FRCP 1963. RAMC, 1943–46. Senior Registrar, Oxford, 1948; Chief Asst, Dept of Neurology, Manchester Royal Infirmary, 1949–52; Senior Registrar, King's College Hosp., 1952–54; Consultant Neurologist, Derbyshire Royal Infirmary, 1954–68; Consultant Neurologist, Manchester Royal Infirmary and Crumpsall Hosp., 1968–70. President: Section of Neurology, RSM, 1981; Assoc. of British Neurologists, 1982; Second Vice-Pres., RCP, 1986–87. Osler Orator, RCP, 1981. Editor-in-Chief, Jl of Neurological Scis, 1977–83. *Publications:* Practical Neurology, 1963, 3rd edn 1975; (with H. G. Miller) Diseases of the Nervous System, 1972, 3rd edn 1979; (ed) Recent Advances in Clinical Neurology I, 1975, II, 1978, IV, 1984; Multiple Sclerosis: the facts, 1978; (ed) McAlpine's Multiple Sclerosis, 1985, 2nd edn 1991; papers in Brain, Quarterly Jl of Medicine, etc. *Recreation:* trying to walk. *Address:* Sandford House, Henley Road, Sandford-on-Thames, Oxford OX4 4YN. *Died 12 July 2001.*

MAXWELL-SCOTT, Dame Jean (Mary Monica), DCVO 1984 (CVO 1969); Lady in Waiting to HRH Princess Alice, Duchess of Gloucester, since 1959; *b* 8 June 1923; *d* of Maj.-Gen. Sir Walter Maxwell-Scott of Abbotsford, 1st Bt, CB, DSO, DL and Mairi MacDougall of Lunga. *Educ:* Couvent des Oiseaux, Westgate-on-Sea. VAD Red Cross Nurse, 1941–46. *Recreations:* gardening, reading, horses. *Address:* Abbotsford, Melrose, Roxburghshire TD6 9BQ. *T:* (01896) 752043. *Club:* New Cavendish. *Died 5 May 2004.*

MAY, John Otto, CBE 1962 (OBE 1949); HM Diplomatic Service, retired; *b* 21 April 1913; *s* of late Otto May, FRCP, MD; *m* 1939, Maureen McNally; one *d*. *Educ:* Sherborne; St John's Coll., Cambridge (BA 1936). Apptd to Dept of Overseas Trade, 1937. Private Sec. to Comptroller-General, 1939; Assistant Commercial Secretary: Copenhagen, 1939; Helsinki, 1940; Ministry of Economic Warfare (Representative in Caracas), 1942–44; First Secretary (Commercial): Rome, 1945, Bucharest, 1948; Foreign Office, 1950–53; First Sec., Helsinki, 1954; acted as Chargé d'Affaires in 1954, 1955, and 1956; Counsellor (Commercial) and Consul-General, Athens, 1957–60; Consul-General: Genoa, 1960–65; Rotterdam, 1965–68; Gothenburg, 1968–72. Coronation Medal, 1953. *Recreations:* travel, photography, walking, philately. *Address:* 6 Millhedge Close, Cobham, Surrey KT11 3BE. *T:* (01932) 864645. *Club:* Oxford and Cambridge. *Died 27 Nov. 2002.*

MAY, His Honour Sir Richard (George), Kt 2004; a Judge of the International Criminal Tribunal for the Former Yugoslavia, 1997–2004; *b* 12 Nov. 1938; *s* of late George William May, MB, and Phyllis May; *m* 1974, Radmila Monica, *er d* of late J. D. A. Barnicot, OBE, and Elizabeth Barnicot; one *s* two *d*. *Educ:* Haileybury; Selwyn Coll., Cambridge (Hon. Fellow, 2002). National Service, 2nd Lieut, DLI, 1958–60. Called to the Bar, Inner Temple, 1965, Bencher, 2001; Midland and Oxford Circuit; a Recorder, 1985–87; a Circuit Judge, 1987–97. Vis. Fellow, US Federal Judicial Center, Washington, 1997. Contested (Lab): Dorset South, 1970; Finchley, 1979. Councillor, Westminster CC, 1971–78 (Leader of the Opposition, 1974–77). *Publications:* (ed jtly) Phipson on Evidence, 12th edn 1976, 13th edn 1982; Criminal Evidence, 1986, 4th edn 1999; (jtly) International Criminal Evidence, 2002; articles on criminal procedure and evidence. *Club:* Savile. *Died 1 July 2004.*

MAYFIELD, Hon. Lord; Ian MacDonald, MC 1945; a Senator of the College of Justice in Scotland, 1981–95; *b* 26 May 1921; *s* of H. J. and J. M. MacDonald; *m* 1946, Elizabeth de Vessey Lawson; one *s* one *d*. *Educ:* Colston's Sch., Bristol; Edinburgh Univ. (MA, LLB). Served War of 1939–45, Royal Tank Regt (Capt.), 1939-46. TA Lothians and Border Horse, later Queen's Own Lowland Yeomanry, 1948–62. Called to Bar, 1952; QC (Scot.) 1964. Mem., Criminal Injuries Compensation Board, 1972–74. Sheriff Principal of Dumfries and Galloway, Feb.-Dec. 1973; Pres., Industrial Tribunals for Scotland, 1973–81; Scottish Chm., Employment Appeal Tribunal, 1986–92. *Recreation:* sport. *Address:* Shiskine, Duncur Road, Muirfield, Gullane, E Lothian, EH31 2EF. *T:* (01620) 842084. *Clubs:* Royal Scottish Automobile (Glasgow); Hon. Company of Edinburgh Golfers. *Died 30 Oct. 2002.*

MAYNARD, Brian Alfred, CBE 1982; Partner, Coopers & Lybrand, Chartered Accountants, 1950–81; *b* 27 Sept. 1917; *s* of late Alfred A. Maynard and Clarissa L. (*née* Shawe); *m* 1946, Rosemary Graham (*d* 2001), *y d* of late Col E. C. Boutflower; two *s*. *Educ:* Leighton Park Sch.; Cambridge Univ. (MA). RNVR Officer, 1939–46, served Middle East and Europe. Member: Oxford Univ. Appts Cttee, 1959–81; Cttee of Duke of Edinburgh's Award Scheme, 1961–67; Council, Industry for Management Educn, 1968–81; Cttee of Enquiry into the Financial Control of Catering in the Services, 1973; Cttee of Enquiry into Problems facing the Nat. Theatre, 1978; Council for the Securities Industry, 1978; Chm., Adv. Cttee on Local Govt Audit, 1979–82. Mem. Council, Inst. of Chartered Accountants in England and Wales, 1968–81 (Pres., 1977–78); Chm., Management Consultants Assoc., 1970; Pres., Inst. of Management Consultants, 1974; Vice-Pres., European Fedn of Management Consultants Assoc., 1972–75; Pres., OECD Mission to USA, on Computers, 1960. *Recreations:* racing, shooting, farming. *Address:* Cowick Farm, Hilmarton, Calne, Wilts SN11 8RZ. *T:* (01249) 760397. *Died 15 Aug. 2001.*

MAYNARD SMITH, Prof. John, FRS 1977; Professor of Biology, University of Sussex, 1965–85, then Emeritus; *b* 6 Jan. 1920; *s* of Sidney Maynard Smith and Isobel Mary (*née* Pitman); *m* 1941; two *s* one *d. Educ:* Eton Coll.; Trinity Coll., Cambridge (BA Engrg, 1941); UCL (BSc Zool., 1951; Fellow, 1979). Aircraft stressman, 1942–47; Lectr in Zool., UCL, 1952–65; first Dean of Biol Sciences, Univ. of Sussex, 1965–72. For. Associate, US Nat. Acad. of Scis, 1982; Mem., Hungarian Acad. of Scis, 1993. Hon. DSc: Kent, 1983; Oxon, 1987; Sussex, 1988; Chicago, 1988; Edinburgh, 1995. Balzan Prize, Fondazione Internazionale Premio E. Balzan, 1991; Craoord Prize, Royal Swedish Acad. of Sci., 1999; Darwin Medal, 1986, Royal Medal, 1997, Copley Medal, 1999, Royal Soc.; Kyoto Prize, Inamori Foundn, 2001. *Publications:* The Theory of Evolution, 1958, 3rd edn 1975; Mathematical Ideas in Biology, 1968; On Evolution, 1972; Models in Ecology, 1974; The Evolution of Sex, 1978; Evolution and the Theory of Games, 1982; The Problems of Biology, 1985; Evolutionary Genetics, 1989; (with E. Szathmáry) The Major Transitions in Evolution, 1995; (with E. Szathmáry) The Origins of Life, 1999. *Recreations:* gardening, talking. *Address:* 5 Mountfield House, Mountfield Road, Lewes, East Sussex BN7 2XA. *T:* (01273) 474659. *Died 19 April 2004.*

MEADE, Patrick John, OBE 1944; consultant in meteorology to various international organisations, 1974–88; Director of Services, and Deputy Director-General, Meteorological Office, 1966–73; *b* 23 Feb. 1913; *s* of late John Meade, Caterham, Surrey; *m* 1937, Winifred Jessie, *d* of Bertram Kent, Fawley, Hants; one *s* one *d* (and one *s* decd). *Educ:* Sir Joseph Williamson's Math. Sch., Rochester; Imperial Coll. of Science and Technology (Royal College of Science) (ARCS, BSc); Lubbock Meml Prize in Maths, London Univ., 1933. Entered Met. Office, 1936; Southampton, 1937; Flt Lt RAFVR, Fr., 1939–40; Sqdn Leader, Sen. Met. Off., GHQ Home Forces, 1940–42; Wing Comdr (Gp Capt. 1944), Chief Met. Off., MAAF, 1943–45; Chief Met. Off., ACSEA, 1945–46; Head of Met. Office Trng Sch., 1948–52; London Airport, 1952–55; Research, 1955–60; idc 1958; Dep. Dir for Outstations Services, 1960–65. Hon. Sec., Royal Meteorological Society, 1956–61, Vice-Pres., 1961–63. *Publications:* papers in jls on aviation meteorology and on meteorological aspects of air pollution, atmospheric radioactivity and hydrology. *Recreations:* music, gardening. *Address:* Luccombe, Coronation Road, South Ascot, Berks SL5 9LP. *T:* (01344) 623206. *Died 7 Jan. 2002.*

MEADOWS, Bernard William; sculptor; Professor of Sculpture, Royal College of Art, 1960–80; *b* Norwich, 19 Feb. 1915; *s* of W. A. F. and E. M. Meadows; *m* 1939, Marjorie Winifred Payne; two *d. Educ:* City of Norwich Sch. Studied at Norwich Sch. of Art, 1934–36; worked as Asst to Henry Moore, 1936–40; studied at Royal College of Art, 1938–40 and 1946–48. Served with RAF, 1941–46. Commissioned by Arts Council to produce a work for Festival of Britain, 1951. Rep. (Brit. Pavilion) in Exhib. of Recent Sculpture, Venice Biennale, 1952; in Exhib., Kassel, Germany, 1959, etc. Exhibited in International Exhibitions of Sculpture (Open Air): Battersea Park, 1951, 1960; Musée Rodin, Paris, 1956; Holland Park, 1957; in 4th International Biennial, São Paulo, Brazil, 1957; also in Exhibns (Open Air) in Belgium and Holland, 1953–. *One man exhibitions:* Gimpel Fils, London, 1957, 1959, 1963, 1965, 1967; Paul Rosenberg, New York, 1959, 1962, 1967; Taranman, London, 1979. *Works in Collections:* Tate Gallery; Victoria and Albert Museum; Arts Council; British Council; Museum of Modern Art, New York; also in public collections in N and S America, Israel, Australia, and in Europe. Mem., Royal Fine Art Commn, 1971–76. Awarded Italian State Scholarship, 1956. *Publication:* 34 etchings and box (for Molloy by Samuel Beckett), 1967. *Address:* 34 Belsize Grove, NW3 4TR. *T:* (020) 7722 0772. *Died 12 Jan. 2005.*

MEAKIN, Wilfred, CB 1982; CEng, FIMechE; defence systems consultant (W. M. Associates); Executive Director, Royal Ordnance plc, 1986; Chairman, Royal Ordnance Inc., 1986; *b* 3 Oct. 1925. *Educ:* engineering apprenticeship in industry. Served War of 1939–45, RN. Technical Asst, ROF, Maltby, 1951; posts in ROF and former Inspectorate of Armaments; Asst Dir, ROF, Blackburn, 1966–72; Dir, ROF, Birtley, 1972–75; Dir, ROF Leeds, during 1975; Dir-Gen., Ordnance Factories (Weapons and Fighting Vehicles), 1975–79; Chief Exec. and Dep. Chm., Bd of ROF, later Royal Ordnance plc, 1979–86. Hon. FCGI. *Died 19 Sept. 2004.*

MEDD, Mary Beaumont, (Mrs D. L. Medd), OBE 1964; retired; *b* 4 Aug. 1907; *d* of Ralph Henry Crowley and Muriel Crowley (*née* Priestman); *m* 1949, David Leslie Medd, OBE, architect. *Educ:* Bedales Sch.; Architectural Assoc. Pre-war work connected with housing and Building Centre, London; Hertfordshire County Council: Educn Dept, 1941–46; Architects' Dept, 1946–49; Develt Gp, Architects and Building Br., Min. of Education, later DES, 1949–72; consultancy work, educnl and architectural, in England and abroad, 1972–93. Hon. DSc Hull, 1993. SADG Medal (France), 1932. *Publications:* contribs to jls and books, educnl and architectural, incl. HMSO building bulletins. *Recreations:* art, music, architecture, travel. *Address:* 5 Pennyfathers Lane, Harmer Green, Welwyn, Herts AL6 0EN. *T:* (01438) 714654. *Died 6 June 2005.*

MEEK, Brian Alexander, OBE 1982; JP; Director, Capital Publicity Ltd, since 1987; *b* 8 Feb. 1939; *s* of Walter Harold Meek and Elsbeth Dearden Meek; *m* 1st, 1962, Glenda (*née* Smith) (marr. diss. 1983); one *s* one *d*; 2nd, 1983, Frances (*née* Horsburgh). *Educ:* Royal High Sch. of Edinburgh; Edinburgh Commercial Coll. Sub-editor, The Scotsman and Edinburgh Evening Dispatch, 1958–63; Features and Leader Writer, Scottish Daily Express, 1963–74; Rugby Football Correspondent, Scottish Daily Express and Sunday Express, 1974–86; Political Columnist, Glasgow Herald, 1986–. Dep. Chm., Livingston Develt Corp., 1986–97. Councillor: Edinburgh Corp., 1969–74; Edinburgh Dist Council, 1974–82 (Chm., Recreation Cttee, 1974–77); Lothian Regional Council, 1974–92 (Leader, Conservative Opposition, 1974–82, 1986–90; Convener and Leader of the Admin, 1982–86); Edinburgh DC, 1992–96; City of Edinburgh Council, 1995– (Chm., Cons. Gp, 1995–). Vice-Pres., Scottish Cons. and Unionist Assoc., 1989–92. Magistrate, Edinburgh, 1971, JP 1974. *Recreations:* golf, theatre, cinema, travel. *Address:* City Chambers, High Street, Edinburgh EH1 1YJ. *T:* (0131) 200 2000. *Died 2 Aug. 2004.*

MEEK, Prof. John Millar, CBE 1975; DEng; FREng, FInstP, FIEE; David Jardine Professor of Electrical Engineering, University of Liverpool, 1946–78; Public Orator, 1973–76, and Pro-Vice-Chancellor, 1974–77, University of Liverpool; *b* Wallasey, 21 Dec. 1912; *s* of Alexander Meek and Edith Montgomery; *m* 1942, Marjorie, *d* of Bernard Ingleby; two *d. Educ:* Monkton Combe Sch.; University of Liverpool. College Apprentice, Metropolitan-Vickers Electrical Co. Ltd, 1934–36; Research Engineer, Metropolitan-Vickers Electrical Co. Ltd, 1936–38, 1940–46. Commonwealth Fund Research Fellow, Physics Dept, University of California, Berkeley, 1938–40. Mem. of Council, IEE, 1945–48, 1960–73 (Vice-Pres. 1964–68, Pres., 1968–69), Faraday Medal, 1975. Mem., IBA (formerly ITA), 1969–74. FREng (FEng 1976). Hon. DSc Salford, 1971. *Publications:* The Mechanism of the Electric Spark (with L. B. Loeb), 1941; Electrical Breakdown of Gases (with J. D. Craggs), 1953, new edn 1978; High Voltage Laboratory Technique (with J. D. Craggs), 1954; papers in various scientific journals concerning research on electrical discharges in gases. *Recreations:* golf, gardening, theatre. *Address:* 4 The Kirklands, West Kirby, Wirral CH48 7HW. *T:* (0151) 625 5850. *Died 26 May 2005.*

MEHEW, Peter; Assistant Under Secretary of State (Civilian Management) (C), Ministry of Defence, 1983–86, retired; *b* 22 Jan. 1931; *er s* of Oliver Mehew and Elsie (*née* Cox); *m* 1st, 1956, Gwyneth Sellors (*d* 1982); one *s* one *d*; 2nd, 1992, Margaret McComish; one step *s. Educ:* Bishop Wordsworth's Sch.; St Catharine's Coll., Cambridge (BA 1954). Asst Principal, Admiralty, 1954, Principal, 1959; Assistant Secretary: CSD, 1970–73; MoD, 1973–80; Dep. Head, UK Delegn to Negotiations on Mutual and Balanced Force Reductions, 1975–77; Asst Under Sec. of State (Sales Admin), MoD, 1981–83. Fellow Commoner, CCC Cambridge, 1980. *Address:* 6 Anderson Road, Salisbury SP1 3DX. *T:* (01722) 326364.
Died 28 June 2002.

MEHROTRA, Prof. Ram Charan, DPhil, PhD, DSc; Vice-Chancellor, University of Allahabad, 1991–93; Professor of Chemistry, University of Rajasthan, Jaipur, 1962–82, then Emeritus; *b* 16 Feb. 1922; *s* of late R. B. Mehrotra; *m* 1944, Suman; one *s* two *d. Educ:* Allahabad Univ. (MSc 1943, DPhil 1948); London Univ. (PhD 1952, DSc 1964). Research Chemist, Vigyan Kala Bhawan, Meerut, 1943–44; Lectr, Allahabad Univ., 1944–54; Reader, Lucknow Univ., 1954–58; Prof., 1958–62, Dean, Faculty of Science, 1959–62, Gorakhpur Univ.; Prof., 1962–74, Dean, Faculty of Science, 1962–65, Chief Rector, 1965–67, Vice-Chancellor, 1968–69 and 1972–73, Rajasthan Univ., Jaipur; Vice-Chancellor, Univ. of Delhi, 1974–79. Mem., UGC, 1982–85. President: Chemistry Section, Indian Sci. Congress, 1967; Indian Chemical Soc., 1976–77; Indian Science Congress, 1978–79; Vice-Pres., Indian Nat. Science Acad., 1977–78; Member: Inorganic Chem. Div., IUPAC, 1977–81; Inorganic Nomenclature Commn, 1981–; Convener, Internat. Symposium, Nanjing, 1987. Fedn of Asian Chem. Socs Lecture, Seoul, 1987. Sir S. S. Bhatnagar award, 1965; Fedn of Indian Chambers of Commerce and Industry award, 1975; Prof. T. R. Seshadri's Birthday Commem. Medal, 1976; P. C. Ray Meml Medal, 1981; Golden Jubilee Medal, Inst. of Science, Bombay, 1983; Popularization of Science Award (by the Prime Minister), 1985; J. C. Ghosh Medal, Indian Chem. Soc., 1986; Achievement Award, Inst. of Oriental Phil., 1987; Platinum Jubilee Distinguished Service Award, Indian Science Congress, 1988; Atma Ram Award, for popularization of science, 1989; Dhar Meml Award, Diamond Jubilee Nat. Acad. of Science, 1991; Chatterjee Award, Indian Science Congress Assoc., 1991. Hon. DSc Meerut, 1976. *Publications:* (contrib.) Sol-Gel Science and Technology, 1989; Organometallic Chemistry, 1991; (contrib.) Chemistry, Spectroscopy and Applications of Sol-Gel Glasses, 1991; (contrib.) Chemistry of Silicon and Tin, 1991; treatises on: Metal Alkoxides and Metal β-Diketonates and Allied Derivatives, 1978; Metal Carboxylates, 1983; numerous research papers in nat. and internat. jls of chemistry; continuous references in the chemistry progress reports of Chem. Soc. London. *Recreation:* photography. *Address:* P4, University Campus, Jaipur 302004, India. *T:* (office) 510306, *T:* (home) 511476.
Died 11 July 2004.

MELLOR, His Honour David John; a Circuit Judge, 1989–2005; *b* 12 Oct. 1940; *s* of John Robert Mellor and Muriel Mary (*née* Field); *m* 1966, Carol Mary Clement, LLB, BA, AKC, Barrister, *o d* of late David Morris Clement, CBE, FCA; two *d. Educ:* Plumtree Sch., S Rhodesia; King's Coll., London (LLB). Called to the Bar, Inner Temple, 1964; a Recorder, 1986–89; Principal Judge in Civil Matters for counties of Cambridge, Norfolk and Suffolk, 1991–98; Resident Judge, Norwich, 1998–2004. Chairman: Essex, Suffolk and Norfolk Area Criminal Justice Liaison Cttee, 1998–2001; Norfolk Area Criminal Justice Strategy Cttee, 2001–03. *Recreations:* reading, gardening, travelling, swimming. *Address:* The Old Hall, Mulbarton, Norwich NR14 8JS; 3 Place de Verdun, 14950 Beaumont-en-Auge, Calvados, France. *Club:* Norfolk (Norwich). *Died 9 Sept. 2005.*

MELVILLE, Sir Leslie Galfreid, KBE 1957 (CBE 1953); Member: Board, Reserve Bank, Australia, 1959–63, and 1965–74; Commonwealth Grants Commission, 1979–82 (Chairman, 1966–74); *b* 26 March 1902; *s* of Richard Ernest Melville and Lilian Evelyn Thatcher; *m* 1925, Mary Maud Scales; two *s. Educ:* Sydney Church of England Grammar Sch.; University of Sydney (BEcon 1925). Public Actuary of South Australia, 1924–28; Prof. of Economics, University of Adelaide, 1929–31; Economic Adviser to Commonwealth Bank of Australia, 1931–49; Asst Gov. (Central Banking) Commonwealth Bank of Australia, 1949–53; Mem. of Commonwealth Bank Bd, 1951–53; Exec. Dir, International Monetary Fund and International Bank for Reconstruction and Development, 1950–53; Vice-Chancellor, ANU, Canberra, 1953–60. Mem. of Cttees on Australian Finances and Unemployment, 1931 and 1932; Financial Adviser to Australian Delegates at Imperial Economic Conference, 1932, and to Australian Delegate at World Economic Conference, 1933; Mem. of Financial and Economic Advisory Cttee, 1939; Chm. of Australian Delegation to United Nations Monetary Conf. at Bretton Woods, 1944; Mem. of Advisory Council of Commonwealth Bank, 1945–51; Chm. UN Sub-Commn on Employment and Economic Stability, 1947–50; Member: Immigration Planning Council, 1956–61; Develt Adv. Service of Internat. Bank, 1963–65; Chairman: Tariff Bd, Australia, 1960–62; Tariff Adv. Cttee of Papua and New Guinea, 1969–71. Hon. LLD: Toronto, 1958; ANU, 1978; Hon. DSc Econ Sydney, 1980. *Address:* Unit 61 The Grange, 67 MacGregor Street, Deakin, Canberra, ACT 2600, Australia. *Club:* Commonwealth.
Died 30 April 2002.

MELVILLE, Sir Ronald (Henry), KCB 1964 (CB 1952); Permanent Secretary, attached Civil Service Department, 1971–72; *b* 9 March 1912; *e s* of Henry Edward Melville; *m* 1940, Enid Dorcas Margaret, *d* of late Harold G. Kenyon, Ware; two *s* one *d. Educ:* Charterhouse; Magdalene Coll., Cambridge (1st Class Classical Tripos, Pts I and II, Charles Oldham Scholarship). Entered Air Ministry, 1934; Private Sec. to Chief of Air Staff, 1936, to Sec. of State, 1940; Asst Under-Sec., 1946; Dep. Under-Sec., 1958; Dep. Under-Sec., War Office, 1960–63; Second Permanent Under-Sec. of State, Ministry of Defence, 1963–66; Permanent Sec., Ministry of Aviation, 1966. Director: Electronic Components Industry Fedn, 1972–81; Westland Aircraft, 1974–83. Chairman: Nat. Rifle Assoc., 1972–84 (Captain, GB Rifle Team, touring USA and Canada, 1976, and for Kolapore match in UK, 1977); Jt Shooting Cttee for GB, 1985–89; President: Council for Cadet Rifle Shooting, 1990–2000; Herts Rifle Assoc., 1963–98; has represented Cambridge Univ., TA and Scotland (40 times) at rifle shooting. Member Council: Herts TAA, 1960–80; Herts Conservation Soc. (formerly Herts Soc.), 1963–98; ACFA, 1972–84. *Publication:* (trans.) Lucretius, *De Rerum Natura,* 1997. *Recreations:* painting, gardening. *Address:* The Old Rose and Crown, Braughing, Ware, Herts SG11 2QA. *Club:* Brooks's.
Died 4 June 2001.

MERCER, Rt Rev. Eric Arthur John; *b* 6 Dec. 1917; *s* of Ambrose John Mercer, Kent; *m* 1951, Rosemary Wilma, *d* of John William Denby, Lincs; one *s* one *d. Educ:* Dover Gram. Sch.; Kelham Theol. Coll. Enlisted Sherwood Foresters, 1940; Capt. and Adjt, 14th Foresters, 1943; served Italy (despatches), 1944; Staff Coll., Haifa, 1944; DAA&QMG, 66 Inf. Bde, Palestine, 1945; GSO2 (SD), HQ, MEF, 1945. Returned Kelham Theol. Coll., 1946–47. Ordained, Chester; Curate, Coppenhall, Crewe, 1947–51; Priest in charge, Heald Green, 1951–53; Rector, St Thomas', Stockport, 1953–59; Chester Diocesan Missioner, 1959–65; Rector, Chester St Bridget, 1959–65; Hon. Canon of Chester Cathedral, 1964; Bishop Suffragan of Birkenhead, 1965–73; Bishop of Exeter, 1973–85. Church Commissioners: Dep. Chm., Pastoral Cttee, 1976–85; Mem., Bd of Governors, 1980–85. Nat. Chm., CEMS, 1974–78. *Publication:* (contrib.) Worship in a

Changing Church, 1965. *Address:* Frickers House, Chilmark, Salisbury SP3 5AJ. *T:* (01722) 761400.
Died 8 Nov. 2003.

MERCHANT, Ismail Noormohamed; film producer, since 1960; Partner, Merchant Ivory Productions, since formation, 1961; *b* 25 Dec. 1936; *s* of Noormohamed Haji Abdul Rehman and Hazra Memon. *Educ:* St Xavier's Coll., Bombay (BA); New York Univ. (MBA). Collaborator with Ruth Prawer Jhabvala and James Ivory on most of the following: *feature films:* The Householder, 1963; Shakespeare Wallah, 1965 (won Best Actress award, Berlin Film Fest., 1965); The Guru, 1969; Bombay Talkie, 1970; Savages, 1972; The Wild Party, 1976; Roseland, 1977; The Europeans, 1979 (official Brit. entry, Cannes Film Fest.); Quartet, 1981; Heat and Dust, 1983 (Brit. entry, Cannes Film Fest.); The Bostonians, 1984 (feature, Cannes Film Fest.); A Room with a View, 1986; Maurice, 1987 (Silver Lions for Best Picture, Best Actor and Best Composer); The Deceivers, 1988; The Perfect Murder, 1988; Slaves of New York, 1989; Mr and Mrs Bridge, 1990; The Ballad of the Sad Cafe, 1991; Howards End, 1992; The Remains of the Day, 1993; (directed) In Custody, 1994; Jefferson in Paris, 1995; Feast of July, 1995; Surviving Picasso, 1996; (directed) The Proprietor, 1996; Gaach, 1997; A Soldier's Daughter Never Cries, 1998; Side Streets, 1998; (directed) Cotton Mary, 1999; The Golden Bowl, 2000; (directed) The Mystic Masseur, 2002; Le Divorce, 2003; *shorts:* The Creation of Woman, 1960 (Academy award nomination); Helen, Queen of the Nautch Girls, 1973; (directed) Mahatma and the Mad Boy, 1974; Sweet Sounds, 1976; *television:* Adventures of a Brown Man in Search of Civilization, 1972 (BBC); Autobiography of a Princess, 1975 (TV special, NY); Hullabaloo over Georgie and Bonnie's Pictures, 1978 (feature, LWT); Jane Austen in Manhattan, 1980 (feature, LWT and Polytel); (directed for Channel 4) The Courtesans of Bombay, 1983; The Curry Connection, 1990 (series, Channel 4); Street Musicians of Bombay, 1995 (Channel 4). *Publications:* Ismail Merchant's Indian Cuisine, 1986; Hullabaloo In Old Jaypoore, 1988; Ismail Merchant's Florence, 1994; Ismail Merchant's Passionate Meals, 1994; Once Upon a Time—The Proprietor, 1996; Ismail Merchant's Paris: filming and feasting in France, 1999; My Passage From India, 2002. *Recreations:* squash, bicycling, cooking. *Address:* 400 East 52nd Street, New York, NY 10022, USA. *T:* (212) 5828049; Garden View, Sutter Street, Bombay, India. *T:* 2020083.
Died 25 May 2005.

MEREDITH, John Michael; barrister-at-law; Magistrate, Deputy District Judge and Coroner, Hong Kong, 1988–94, retired; *b* 23 Oct. 1934; *s* of late John Stanley Meredith and Lily Meredith; *m;* one *s* three *d; m* 1988, Linda (*née* Crossland) (*d* 2000). *Educ:* Crossley and Porter Schs, Halifax, Yorks; Leeds Univ. (LLB Hons 1956). Called to the Bar, Gray's Inn, 1958; Junior, NE Circuit, 1964; a Recorder, 1976–88. Dir, 1955–64, Chm. Dirs, 1964–88, J. T. Meredith (Carboniser) Ltd. *Recreations:* shooting, sailing. *Address:* China Rose, c/o Puerto Galera Yacht Club, Puerto Galera, Mindoro Island, Philippines. *Clubs:* Royal Hong Kong Yacht (Life Mem.); Puerto Galera Yacht.
Died 9 June 2003.

MERLE, Robert Jean Georges; Croix du Combattant, 1945; Officier de l'Instruction publique, 1953; Professor of English Literature, University of Paris X, Nanterre, since 1965; Titular Professor: University of Rennes, Brittany, since 1944 (on leave, 1950–51); University of Toulouse, since 1957; University of Caen-Rouen, since 1960; University of Algiers, since 1963; *b* 29 Aug. 1908; father an officer; *m* 1st; one *d;* 2nd, 1949; three *s* one *d;* 3rd, 1965; one *s. Educ:* Lycée Michelet, Paris; Sorbonne, Paris. Professor, 1944. Mobilised, 1939; Liaison agent with BEF (prisoner, 1940–43). *Publications:* Oscar Wilde, 1948, 3rd edn 1996; Week-end à Zuydcoote, 1949 (awarded Prix Goncourt); La Mort est mon métier, 1953; L'Ile, 1962 (awarded Prix de la Fraternité) (translated, as The Island,

1964); Un Animal doué de raison, 1967 (translated, as The Day of the Dolphin, 1969); Derrière la vitre, 1970; Malevil, 1972 (Campbell Award, USA); Les hommes protégés, 1974 (translated, as The Virility Factor, 1977); Madrapour, 1976; Fortune de France, 1978; En nos vertes années, 1979; Paris ma bonne ville, 1980; Le Prince que voilà, 1982; La violente amour, 1983; La Pique du jour, 1985; Le Jour ne se lève pas pour nous, 1986; L'Idole, 1987 (translated, as The Idol, 1989); Le Propre de l'Homme, 1989; La Volte des Vestugadins, 1991; L'Enfant-roi, 1993; Les Roses de la Vie, 1995; Le Lys et la Pourpre, 1997; La gloire et le périls, 1999; *plays:* Nouveau Sisyphe, 1950; Flamineo (inspired by Webster's White Devil), 1953; Pièces pies et impies, 1995; *historical essays:* Moncada, 1965; Ben Bella, 1965; translations, articles. *Recreation:* swimming. *Address:* La Malmaison, Grosrouvre, 78490 Montfort L'Amaury, France.
Died 27 March 2004.

MERTENS DE WILMARS, Baron Josse (Marie Honoré Charles), Grand Croix de l'Ordre de la Couronne; Chevalier de l'Ordre de Léopold; Judge, 1967–80, and President, 1980–84, Court of Justice of the European Communities; Emeritus Professor, Faculty of Law, Catholic University of Leuven, since 1971; Member of the University Curatorium, 1972–90; *b* 12 June 1912; *s* of (Marie Antoine Joseph) Albert Mertens and Jeanne Eugénie Marie Anne Meert; *m* 1939, Elisabeth Simonne M. Hubertine van Ormelingen; three *s* five *d. Educ:* Abdijschool, Zevenkerke, Bruges; Catholic Univ. of Leuven (Dr in Law, Dr in Pol. and Diplomatic Science). Hon. Assessor, Legislative Dept of Council of State (Conseil d'Etat) (Assessor, 1950–52). Mem., Chambre des Représentants de Belgique (Lower House of Parlt), 1952–62; former Mem., Bar Council. Hon. Mem., Bar of Antwerp. Chief Editor, Revue Internationale Droit Economique, 1989–93. CStJ. Groot kruis van de Orde van Orange Nassau (Neth.); Grand Croix de l'Ordre de la Couronne de Chêne (Lux.); Grosskreuz des Verdienstordens der Bundesrepublik Deutschland. *Publications:* several works on Belgian and European Law. *Address:* 192 Jan Van Rijswijcklaan, 2020 Antwerpen 2, Belgium. *T:* (3) 2380768, *Fax:* (3) 2486504.
Died 1 August 2002.

METCALF, Dame Helen, DBE 1998; Headteacher, Chiswick Community School, 1988–2001; *b* 7 Oct. 1946; *d* of Thomas Pitt and Winifred Pitt (*née* Nicholas); *m* 1968, Prof. David Harry Metcalf; one *s. Educ:* Manchester Univ. (BA); London Sch. of Econs (MSc). Head of 6th Form and history teacher, Islington Green Comprehensive, 1974–82; Dep. Head, Acland Burghley Comprehensive, 1982–88. Mem. (Lab), Islington LBC, 1971–78. FRSA 1996. *Recreations:* gardening, travel, politics, detective stories.
Died 3 Dec. 2003.

METCALFE, Hugh, OBE 1969; FREng, FRAeS; Director, Redcliffe Holdings, since 1996; *b* 26 June 1928; *s* of late Clifford Metcalfe, CBE and Florence Ellen Metcalfe; *m* 1952, Pearl Allison Carter (*d* 1998); three *s; m* 1999, Jennifer Mary Reid. *Educ:* Harrow County Grammar School; Imperial College, Univ. of London. BSc, ARCS. FREng (FEng 1983). RAF, 1946–48; joined Bristol Aeroplane Co., 1951; Divisional Dir, 1974; British Aerospace Dynamics Group: Group Dir, Naval Weapons, 1978; Man. Dir, Bristol Div., 1980; Man. Dir, Hatfield Div., 1981; Chief Exec., 1982; Dir, 1982–88, and Dep. Chief Exec. (Ops), 1986–88, BAe; Dir, SAC Internat., then Ricardo Internat., later Ricardo Gp, 1989–95. Pres., RAeS, 1989–90. Hon. DSc Hatfield Polytechnic, 1988; Hon. DEng Bristol Univ., 1992. RAeS gold medal, 1984. *Recreation:* choral music. *Address:* 46 Frogwell Park, Chippenham SN14 0RB. *Clubs:* Athenæum; Leander; Savage's (Bristol).
Died 21 June 2002.

MEYER, Sir Anthony John Charles, 3rd Bt *cr* 1910; lecturer on European affairs; *b* 27 Oct. 1920; *o s* of Sir Frank Meyer, MP, 2nd Bt, Ayot House, Ayot St Lawrence, Herts; *S* father, 1935; *m* 1941, Barbadee Violet, *o c* of late A. Charles Knight, JP, FSA, and of Mrs Charles

Knight, Herne Place, Sunningdale; one *s* three *d. Educ:* Eton (Capt. of Oppidans); New Coll., Oxford. Served Scots Guards, 1941–45 (wounded). Entered HM Foreign Service, 1946; HM Embassy, Paris, 1951; 1st Sec., 1953; transferred to HM Embassy, Moscow, 1956; London, 1958. MP (C): Eton and Slough, 1964–66; W Flint, 1970–83, Clwyd NW, 1983–92. PPS to Sec. of State for Employment, 1972–74. Chm., Franco-British Parly Relations Cttee, 1979–92; Vice-Chm., Cons. European Affairs Cttee, 1979–89. Vice-Chm., Franco-British Council, 1986–2000; Mem. Bd, British Council of European Movement, 1990–99, then Mem. Mgt Bd, British European Movement, 1999–2001; Chm., Federal Union, 2000–02. Trustee of Shakespeare National Memorial Theatre. Officier, Légion d'Honneur, France, 1983. *Publications:* A European Technological Community, 1966; Stand Up and Be Counted, 1990; A Federal Europe: why not?, 1992. *Recreations:* music, travel, cooking. *Heir: s* Anthony Ashley Frank Meyer [*b* 23 Aug. 1944; *m* 1966, Susan Mathilda (marr. diss. 1980), *d* of John Freestone; one *d*]. *Address:* 9 Cottage Place, Brompton Square, SW3 2BE. *T:* (020) 7589 7416.
Died 24 Dec. 2004.

MEYRICK, Sir David (John Charlton), 4th Bt *cr* 1880; *b* 2 Dec. 1926; *e s* of Colonel Sir Thomas Frederick Meyrick, 3rd Bt, TD, DL, JP, and Ivy Frances (*d* 1947), *d* of Lt-Col F. C. Rushton; *S* father, 1983; *m* 1962, Penelope Anne, *d* of late Comdr John Bertram Aubrey Marsden-Smedley, RN; three *s. Educ:* Eton; Trinity Hall, Cambridge (MA). FRICS. *Heir: s* Timothy Thomas Charlton Meyrick [*b* 5 Nov. 1963. *Educ:* Eton; Bristol Univ.]. *Address:* Bush House, Gumfreston, Tenby, Pembrokeshire SA70 8RA. *Died 6 Feb. 2004.*

MEYSEY-THOMPSON, Sir (Humphrey) Simon, 4th Bt *cr* 1874, of Kirby Hall, Yorkshire; *b* 31 March 1935; *s* of Guy Herbert Meysey-Thompson (*d* 1961), *g s* of 1st Bt, and Miriam Beryl Meysey-Thompson (*d* 1985); *S* kinsman, Sir Algar de Clifford Charles Meysey-Thompson, 1967. *Address:* 10 Church Street, Woodbridge, Suffolk IP12 1DH.
Died 10 Sept. 2002 (ext).

MIALL, (Rowland) Leonard, OBE 1961; research historian; *b* 6 Nov. 1914; *e s* of late Rowland Miall and S. Grace Miall; *m* 1st, 1941, Lorna (*d* 1974), *o d* of late G. John Rackham; three *s* one *d*; 2nd, 1975, Sally Bicknell, *e d* of late Gordon Leith. *Educ:* Bootham Sch., York (Scholar); Freiburg Univ.; St John's Coll., Cambridge (Sizar), MA. Pres. Cambridge Union, 1936; Ed. Cambridge Review, 1936. Lectured in US, 1937; Sec. British-American Associates, 1937–39; joined BBC; inaugurated talks broadcast to Europe, 1939; BBC German Talks and Features Editor, 1940–42. Mem. British Political Warfare Mission to US, 1942–44 (Dir of News, San Francisco, 1943; Head of New York Office, 1944); Personal Asst to Dep. Dir-Gen., Political Warfare Exec., London, 1944; attached to Psychological Warfare Division of SHAEF, Luxembourg, 1945. Rejoined BBC: Special Correspondent, Czechoslovakia, 1945; Actg Diplomatic Corresp., 1945; Chief Corresp. in US, 1945–53; Head of Television Talks, 1954; Asst Controller, Current Affairs and Talks, Television, 1961; Special Asst to Dir of Television, planning start of BBC-2, 1962; Asst Controller, Programme Services, Television, BBC, 1963–66; BBC Rep. in US, 1966–70; Controller, Overseas and Foreign Relations, BBC, 1971–74; Research Historian, BBC, 1975–84. Inaugurated BBC Lunchtime Lectures, 1962; Advisor, Cttee on Broadcasting, New Delhi, 1965; Delegate to Commonwealth Broadcasting Confs, Jamaica, 1970, Kenya, 1972, Malta, 1974. Dir, Visnews Ltd (Dep. Chm., 1984–85); Overseas Dir, BAFTA, 1974–; Mem. Council, RTS, 1984–91. FRTS 1986; FRSA. Cert. of Appreciation, NY City, 1970. *Publications:* Richard Dimbleby, Broadcaster, 1966; Inside the BBC, 1994; contribs to DNB and various jls. *Recreation:* writing. *Address:* Maryfield Cottage, High

Street, Taplow, Maidenhead, Berks SL6 0EX. *T:* (01628) 604195. *Club:* Union (Cambridge).
Died 24 Feb. 2005.

MILES, John Edwin Alfred, CBE 1979 (OBE 1961; MBE 1952); HM Diplomatic Service, retired; *b* 14 Aug. 1919; *s* of late John Miles and Rose Miles (*née* Newlyn); *m* 1952, Barbara Fergus Ferguson; two *s* one *d. Educ:* Hornsey County Sch. Apptd to Dominions Office, 1937. Served War: joined Queen's Royal West Surrey Regt, 1940; commissioned in N Staffordshire Regt, 1941; attached Royal Indian Army Service Corps, 1942 (Maj. 1943); released, Sept. 1946, and returned to Dominions Office. Served in: Wellington, NZ, 1948–51; Calcutta, 1953–56; CRO, 1957–61; Trinidad (on staff of Governor-Gen.), 1961; Jamaica (Adviser to Governor, and later First Sec. in British High Commission), 1961–64; Wellington, NZ, 1964–68; Counsellor, 1968; Accra, Ghana, 1968–71; Dep. High Comr, Madras, India, 1971–75; High Comr to Swaziland, 1975–79. *Address:* Cartref, Ladyegate Road, Dorking, Surrey RH5 4AR. *T:* (01306) 884346.
Died 22 Jan. 2004.

MILES, Peter Charles H.; *see* Hubbard-Miles.

MILL, Robert Duguid Forrest P.; *see* Pring-Mill.

MILLAR, George Reid, DSO 1944; MC; farmer and writer; *b* 19 Sept. 1910; 2nd *s* of Thomas Andrew Millar, architect, and Mary Reid Morton; *m* 1st, Annette Stockwell; 2nd, 1945, Isabel Beatriz (*d* 1990), *d* of Montague Paske-Smith, CMG, CBE; no *c. Educ:* Loretto; St John's, Cambridge. Architect, 1930–32; journalist, with Daily Telegraph and Daily Express, 1934–39; Paris correspondent Daily Express, 1939; served War of 1939–45, The Rifle Bde; escaped from German POW camp to England, then served as agent in France; Chevalier de la Légion d'Honneur; Croix de Guerre avec Palmes. Farmer of 1,000 acres, 1962–90. *Publications:* Maquis, 1945; Horned Pigeon, 1946; My Past was an Evil River, 1946; Isabel and the Sea, 1948; Through the Unicorn Gates, 1950; A White Boat from England, 1951; Siesta, 1952; Orellana, 1954; Oyster River, 1963; Horseman, 1970; The Bruneval Raid, 1974; Road to Resistance, 1979. *Recreation:* sailing. *Address:* Uploders Place, Bridport, Dorset DT6 4PF. *T:* (01308) 485653. *Clubs:* Special Forces, Royal Cruising; Royal Yacht Squadron (Cowes).
Died 15 Jan. 2005.

MILLER, (Alan) Cameron, FCIT; advocate; Tutor at Fettes College, 1974–94; *b* 10 Jan. 1913; *o s* of late Arthur Miller, Edinburgh; *m* 1945, Audrey Main; one *d* (one *s* decd). *Educ:* Fettes Coll.; Edinburgh Univ. (MA 1934; LLB 1936). Advocate, 1938; served War of 1939–45, RN (discus record, athletics meeting, Sicily, 1943). Interim Sheriff-Substitute at Dundee, 1946; Sheriff-Substitute of Inverness, Moray, Nairn, Ross and Cromarty, at Fort William, 1946–52; Legal Adviser (Scotland): British Transport Commn, 1952–62; BR Board, 1962–73. Chm., Inst. of Transport (Scotland), 1971–72. *Recreations:* golf, music. *Address:* 12A Quality Street, North Berwick, Scotland.
Died 19 Oct. 2004.

MILLER, Alastair Cheape, MBE 1948; TD; Prison Governor, retired 1972; *b* 13 March 1912 (twin-brother); *s* of John Charles Miller, Banker, Glasgow, and Jessie Amelia Miller; *m* 1943, Elizabeth S. Hubbard (marr. diss. 1967); one *s* one *d. Educ:* Melville Coll., Edinburgh; Bedford Sch., Bedford. Territorial Army, 1930–51; War Service (Gibraltar and Italy); 5th Beds and Herts Regt, 1st Herts Regt and 4th KOYLI, 1948–51. Barclays Bank Ltd: Junior Clerk to Cashier, 1929–45. Housemaster, Approved Sch., April-Nov. 1946; Prison Service: Asst Governor, Wakefield, 1946–53; Governor: Dover, 1953–59; Winchester, 1959–62; Hindley Borstal, 1962–65; Parkhurst Prison, 1966–70; Pentonville, 1970–72. Associated with St Mungo Community Trust i/c Old Charing Cross Hosp. project for homeless people, 1974–75. Freeman, City of London, 1980. *Publication:*

Inside Outside, 1976. *Recreations:* golf, sailing. *Clubs:* Hampstead Golf; Cowes Corinthian Yacht (Cowes).
Died 16 July 2001.

MILLER, Arthur; playwright; *b* 17 Oct. 1915; *s* of Isadore Miller and Augusta Barnett; *m* 1940, Mary Grace Slattery (marr. diss. 1956); one *s* one *d*; *m* 1956, Marilyn Monroe (marr. diss. 1961; she *d* 1962); *m* 1962, Ingeborg Morath (*d* 2002); one *d*. *Educ:* University of Michigan, USA (AB). Pres. of PEN Club, 1965–69. Cameron Mackintosh Prof. of Contemporary Theatre, Oxford Univ., 1995. *Publications:* Honors at Dawn, 1936; No Villains (They Too Arise), 1937; The Pussycat and the Expert Plumber who was a Man, 1941; William Ireland's Confession, 1941; The Man who had all the Luck, 1944; That They May Win, 1944; Situation Normal (reportage), 1944; Focus (novel), 1945; Grandpa and the Statue, 1945; The Story of Gus, 1947; Jane's Blanket, 1963; I Don't Need You Anymore (collected stories), 1967; (jt author) In Russia, 1969; Fame, and the Reason Why, 1970; The Portable Arthur Miller, 1971; (with Inge Morath) In the Country, 1977; (ed Robert Martin) The Theater Essays of Arthur Miller, 1978; (with Inge Morath) Chinese Encounters, 1979; Salesman in Beijing, 1984; Timebends (autobiog.), 1987; Plain Girl (novel), 1995; *plays:* All My Sons, 1947 (NY Drama Critics Award, 1948); Death of a Salesman (NY Drama Critics Award, Pulitzer Prize), 1949 (filmed 1985); The Crucible, 1953 (filmed 1996); A View from the Bridge, 1955 (filmed 1962); A Memory of Two Mondays, 1955; Collected Plays, 1958; After the Fall, 1963; Incident at Vichy, 1964; The Price, 1968 and 1990; The Creation of the World and Other Business, 1972 (musical version, Up From Paradise, 1974); The American Clock, 1980 (TV version, 1993); Playing for Time (Peabody Award, CBS–TV), 1981; Two Way Mirror, 1985; Danger: Memory!, 1986; Ride Down Mount Morgan, 1990; The Last Yankee, 1992; Broken Glass, 1994; Mr Peter's Connections, 1998; Resurrection Blues, 2002; Finishing the Picture, 2004; *screenplays:* The Misfits, 1960; Everybody Wins, 1990; contrib. stories and essays to Esquire, Colliers, Atlantic Monthly, etc. *Address:* c/o ICM, 40 W 57th Street, New York, NY 10019, USA.
Died 10 Feb. 2005.

MILLER, Sir Bernard; see Miller, Sir O. B.

MILLER, Cameron; see Miller, A. C.

MILLER, Edward, CBE 1988; Director of Education, Strathclyde, 1974–88; *b* 30 March 1930; *s* of Andrew and Elizabeth Miller; *m* 1955, Margaret; two *s*. *Educ:* Eastbank Academy; Glasgow Univ. (MA, MEd). Taught at Wishaw High Sch., 1955–57 and Whitehill Secondary Sch., 1957–59; Depute Dir of Educn, West Lothian, 1959–63; Sen. Asst Dir of Educn, Stirlingshire, 1963–66; Depute, later Sen. Depute Dir of Educn, Glasgow, 1966–74. Hon. MLitt Glasgow Coll., 1985. *Recreations:* reading, walking, gardening.
Died 15 Jan. 2005.

MILLER, John Ireland; Vice-President, Methodist Conference of Great Britain, 1973–74; *b* 20 June 1912; *s* of John William Miller and Emma Miller (*née* Minkley); *m* 1943, Vida Bertha Bracher; one *s* one *d*. *Educ:* Hardye's School, Dorchester; Taunton School, Taunton. Admitted Solicitor and Member of Law Society, 1933. HM Coroner: Poole Borough, 1972–74 (Deputy Coroner, 1939–72); East Dorset, 1974–85. *Address:* Summerdyne, Cleobury Road, Bewdley, Worcs DY12 2QQ. *T:* (01299) 405063.
Died 21 May 2004.

MILLER, Air Vice-Marshal John Joseph, CB 1981; Director of Studies, St George's House, Windsor Castle, 1989–94; *b* 27 April 1928; *s* of Frederick George Miller and Freda Ruth Miller; *m* 1950, Adele Mary Colleypriest; one *s* two *d*. *Educ:* Portsmouth Grammar School. Commissioned RAF, 1947; called to the Bar, Gray's Inn, 1958; CO RAF Support Unit Fontainbleau, 1965; Directing Staff, RAF Staff Coll., 1967; DGPS (RAF) Staff, MoD, 1970; Group Captain Admin., RAF Halton, 1971;

Comd Accountant, HQ Strike Comd, 1973; RCDS 1975; Dir, Personnel Management (Policy and Plans) RAF, MoD, 1976; Asst Chief of Defence Staff (Personnel and Logistics), 1978–81; Head of Administrative Branch, RAF, 1979–83; Dir Gen., Personal Services, RAF, 1982–83. Dir, Inst. of Personnel Management, 1983–89. Pres., Eur. Assoc. for Personnel Management, 1987–89. *Recreations:* walking, swimming, theatre, music, collecting (especially antiquarian books). *Address:* 24 Floral Farm, Canford Magna, Wimborne, Dorset BH21 3AU. *T:* (01202) 883701. *Club:* Royal Air Force.
Died 5 Jan. 2005.

MILLER, Maurice Solomon, MB; *b* 16 Aug. 1920; *s* of David Miller; *m* 1944, Renée, *d* of Joseph Modlin, Glasgow; two *s* two *d*. *Educ:* Shawlands Academy, Glasgow; Glasgow University (MB, ChB 1944). Elected Mem. of Glasgow Corporation, 1950; Bailie of Glasgow, 1954–57; JP Glasgow, 1957. MP (Lab): Glasgow Kelvingrove, 1964–74; E Kilbride, 1974–87. Asst Govt Whip, 1968–69. Visited Russia as mem. of medical delegation, 1955. *Publication:* Window on Russia, 1956. *Recreation:* oil painting.
Died 30 Oct. 2001.

MILLER, Sir (Oswald) Bernard, Kt 1967; *b* 25 March 1904; *s* of late Arthur Miller and Margaret Jane Miller; *m* 1931, Jessica Rose Marie ffoulkes (*d* 1985); three *s*. *Educ:* Sloane Sch.; Jesus Coll., Oxford (Stanhope Prize, 1925; BA 1927; MA 1930; Hon. Fellow, 1968). Joined John Lewis Partnership, 1927; Dir, 1935; Chm., 1955–72. Chm., Retail Distributors Assoc., 1953; Member: Council of Industrial Design, 1957–66; Monopolies Commn, 1961–69; EDC for Distributive Trades, 1964–71. Chm. Southern Region, 1974–80, Mem. Council, 1977–82, RSA. Southampton University: Treasr, 1974–82; Chm. Council, 1982–87; Pro-Chancellor, 1983–90. Hon. LLD Southampton, 1981. *Publication:* Biography of Robert Harley, Earl of Oxford, 1927. *Recreations:* fishing, gardening, opera and theatre. *Address:* 3 Sutton Manor Mews, Sutton Scotney, Hants SO21 3JX. *T:* (01962) 760997.
Died 23 Feb. 2003.

MILLER, Walter George, CPFA; FCCA; Chief Executive, Bristol City Council, 1990–91 (Acting Chief Executive, 1987–90); *b* 2 March 1932; *s* of Bert and Rosina Miller; *m* 1956, Sheila Mary Daw; one *s* two *d*. *Educ:* Howardian High Sch., Cardiff. Clerk, City Treasurer's Dept, Cardiff, 1948–50. Served RA, Hong Kong and Korea, 1950–52. Audit Asst, City Treasurer's Dept, Cardiff, 1952–55; Accountant, Treasurer's Dept: Nairobi, 1955–58; Cardiff, 1958–60; Caerphilly, 1960–63; Ilford, 1963–65; Redbridge, 1965; Bromley, 1965–68; Asst Borough Treasurer, Bromley, 1968–72; Bristol: Asst City Treasurer, 1972–73; Dep. City Treasurer, 1973–80; City Treasurer, 1980–90. *Publications:* Morgan at Gatehaven (novel), 1994; contrib. local government and accountancy press. *Recreations:* writing, gardening, walking. *Address:* 21 Heron Gardens, Portishead, Bristol BS20 7DH. *T:* (01275) 818743.
Died 28 Sept. 2004.

MILLICHIP, Sir Frederick Albert, (Sir Bert), Kt 1991; Member of Council, since 1970, and Life Vice President, since 1990, The Football Association (Chairman, 1981–96); *b* 5 Aug. 1914; *s* of late Hugh Bowater Millichip; *m* 1950, Joan Barbara Brown; one *s* one *d*. *Educ:* Solihull Sch., Warwicks. Qualified as solicitor, 1950; Sen. Partner, Sharpe & Millichip, subseq. Tyndelwood & Millichip, 1959–88, Consultant, 1988–96; Consultant, Edge & Ellison, 1996–. Served War, 1939–45, in England, N Africa, Sicily and Italy; joined S Staffs Regt as private, commnd RA (Captain). Union of European Football Associations: Chairman: Cttee for Five-a-Side Football, 1988–92; Juridical Cttee, 1992–93; Member: Exec. Cttee, 1988–96 (Advr, 1996–); Organising Cttee for European Championship, 1981–96; Referees' Cttee, 1992–97 (Chm., 1994–96); Hon. Mem., UEFA, 1996. Mem., FIFA Organising Cttee for World Cup, 1983–; Chm., FA Disciplinary Cttee, 1978–81. West Bromwich Albion Football Club: Dir, 1964–84; Chm., 1976–83; Pres.,

1984–. Hon. DLitt Loughborough, 1995. Ordre du Mérite, FIFA, 1998. *Recreation:* golf. *Address:* 1 The Woodlands, 1 Fiery Hill, Barnt Green, Birmingham B45 8LB. *T:* (0121) 445 4688. *Club:* Blackwell Golf (Blackwell, Worcs). *Died 18 Dec. 2002.*

MILLIGAN, Rt Hon. Lord; James George Milligan; PC 2000; a Senator of the College of Justice in Scotland, 1988–2001; *b* 10 May 1934; *s* of Rt Hon. Lord Milligan; *m* 1st, 1961, Elizabeth Carnegie Thomson (*d* 1982), *e d* of late Hon. Lord Migdale and Louise (*née* Carnegie; later Mrs Thomson); two *s* three *d*; 2nd, 1985, Elizabeth Cynthia Rae Ashworth, *widow* of Rupert S. H. Ashworth, and *y d* of late P. Rae Shepherd. *Educ:* St Mary's Sch., Melrose; Rugby Sch.; Oxford Univ. (BA); Edinburgh Univ. (LLB). Admitted to Faculty of Advocates, 1959; Standing Junior Counsel to the Scottish Home and Health Dept and Dept of Health and Social Security in Scotland; Advocate-Depute, 1971–78; QC (Scot.) 1972; Chm., Med. Appeal Tribunal (Scotland), 1979–88. Chm., RSSPCC Edinburgh, 1978–92. *Publication:* (contrib. small part of) Armour on Valuation for Rating, 3rd edn, 1961. *Recreations:* gardening, golf. *Died 7 March 2005.*

MILLIGAN, James George; *see* Milligan, Rt Hon. Lord.

MILLIGAN, Terence Alan, (Spike Milligan), Hon. KBE 2000 (Hon. CBE 1992); actor; author; *b* 16 April 1918; *s* of late Captain L. A. Milligan, MSM, RA retd, and Florence Winifred Milligan; *m* 1st, 1952, June Marlowe (marr. diss. 1961); one *s* two *d*; 2nd, 1962, Patricia Margaret Ridgeway (*d* 1978); one *d;* 3rd, 1983, Shelagh Sinclair. *Educ:* Convent of Jesus and Mary, Poona; Brothers de La Salle, Rangoon; SE London Polytechnic, Lewisham. Lifetime Achievement Award, British Comedy Awards, 1994. Appearances (comedy) as Spike Milligan: *stage:* The Bed-Sitting Room; Son of Oblomov; Ben Gunn, in Treasure Island, Mermaid, 1973, 1974; One man shows, 1979, 1980, 1998, 1999; writer, Ubu Roi, 1980; Spike Milligan and Friends, Lyric, 1982; *radio:* Goon Show (inc. special performance, 1972, to mark 50th Anniversary of BBC); Best British Radio Features Script, 1972; The Milligan Papers, 1987; *TV:* Show called Fred, ITV; World of Beachcomber, BBC; Q5, BBC; Oh in Colour, BBC; A Milligan for All Seasons, BBC, 1972–73; Marty Feldman's Comedy Machine, ITV (writing and appearing; awarded Golden Rose and special comedy award, Montreux, 1972); The Melting Pot, BBC, 1975; Q7, BBC series, 1977; Q8, 1978; Q9, 1979; TV Writer of the Year Award, 1956; *films:* The Magic Christian, 1971; The Devils, 1971; The Cherry Picker, 1972; Digby the Biggest Dog in the World, 1972; Alice's Adventures in Wonderland, 1972; The Three Musketeers, 1973; The Great McGonagall, 1975; The Last Remake of Beau Geste, 1977; The Hound of the Baskervilles, 1978; Monty Python's Life of Brian, 1978; History of the World, Part 1, 1980; Yellowbeard, 1983. *Publications:* Dustbin of Milligan, 1961; Silly Verse for Kids, 1963; Puckoon, 1963; The Little Pot Boiler, 1965; A Book of Bits, 1965; Milliganimals, 1968; The Bedside Milligan, 1968; The Bed-Sitting Room (play), 1969; The Bald Twit Lion, 1970; Adolf Hitler, My Part in his Downfall, 1971 (filmed 1973; on record, 1980); Milligan's Ark, 1971; Small Dreams of a Scorpion, 1972; The Goon Show Scripts, 1972; Rommel: Gunner Who?, 1973; (for children) Badjelly the Witch, 1973; (with J. Hobbs) The Great McGonagall Scrapbook, 1975; The Milligan Book of Records, Games, Cartoons and Commercials, 1975; Dip the Puppy, 1975; Transports of Delight, 1975; William McGonagal, the truth at last, 1976; Monty, His Part in my Victory, 1976; Goblins (with Heath Robinson illus), 1978; Mussolini, His Part in my Downfall, 1978; Open Heart University, 1978; Spike Milligan's Q Annual, 1979; Get in the Q Annual, 1980; Unspun Socks from a Chicken's Laundry, 1981; Indefinite Articles and Scunthorpe, 1981; The 101 Best and Only Limericks of Spike Milligan, 1982; (for children) Sir Nobonk and the Terrible, Awful, Dreadful, Naughty, Nasty Dragon (illus. by Carol Barker), 1982; The Goon

Cartoons, 1982; More Goon Cartoons, 1983; There's A Lot Of It About, 1983; The Melting Pot, 1983; Spike Milligan's Further Transports of Delight, 1985; Where have all the Bullets Gone? (autobiog.), 1985; Floored Masterpieces with Worse Verse (illus. by Tracey Boyd), 1985; Goodbye Soldier, 1986; The Looney: an Irish fantasy, 1987; The Mirror Running (poetry), 1987; Startling Verse for all the Family (children's poetry), 1987; The Lost Goon Shows, 1987; Milligan's War, 1988; McGonagall Meets George Gershwin, 1988; It Ends With Magic, 1990; Dear Robert, Dear Spike, 1991; Peacework (autobiog.), 1991; Condensed Animals, 1991; Hidden Words (poetry), 1993; (with A. Clare) Depression and How To Survive It, 1993; The Bible According to Spike Milligan, 1993; Lady Chatterly's Lover According to Spike Milligan, 1994; Wuthering Heights According to Spike Milligan, 1995; Fleas, Knees and Hidden Elephants (poetry), 1995; Spike Milligan: a celebration, 1995; D. H. Lawrence's John Thomas and Lady Jane According to Spike Milligan, 1995; The Adventures of Black Beauty According to Spike Milligan, 1996; Frankenstein According to Spike Milligan, 1997; The Hound of the Baskervilles According to Spike Milligan, 1998; Robin Hood According to Spike Milligan, 1998; A Mad Medley of Milligan, 1999; The Family Album–An Illustrated Biography, 1999; A Children's Treasury of Milligan, 1999; Treasure Island According to Spike Milligan, 2000. *Recreations:* restoration of antiques, oil painting, water colours, gardening, eating, drinking, talking, wine, jazz. *Address:* 9 Orme Court, W2 4RL. *T:* (020) 7727 1544. *Died 27 Feb. 2002.*

MILLING, Peter Francis, MB, BChir, FRCS; formerly: Surgeon, Ear, Nose and Throat Department, University College Hospital; Surgeon in charge, Throat and Ear Department, Brompton Hospital; Consultant Ear, Nose and Throat Surgeon: Epsom District Hospital; Oxted and Limpsfield Cottage Hospital; Visiting Laryngologist Benenden Chest Hospital; *m* Peggy. *Educ:* Trinity Hall, Cambridge (BA Hons 1937; MA, MB BChir 1941). MRCS, LRCP 1940; FRCS 1946. Formerly Chief Assistant, Ear, Nose and Throat Department, St Thomas' Hospital; Chief Clinical Assistant and Registrar, Ear, Nose and Throat Department, Guy's Hosp.; Surgical Registrar, Ear, Nose and Throat Dept, Royal Cancer Hospital. Member British Association of Otolaryngologists. *Publications:* contributions to medical text-books and journals. *Address:* Abbotswood House, Crossag Road, Ballasalla, Isle of Man IM9 3DZ. *T:* (01624) 823072. *Died 31 Jan. 2004.*

MILLNER, Ralph; QC 1965; *b* 25 Jan. 1912; *o s* of Ralph Millner, merchant, Manchester; *m* 1st, 1935, Bruna (marr. diss. 1949), *d* of Arturo Rosa, Este, Italy; one *d* decd; 2nd, 1949, Monica, *d* of Prof. P. W. Robertson, Wellington, NZ; one *s* two *d*. *Educ:* William Hulme's Grammar Sch., Manchester; Clare Coll., Cambridge (MA); Bedford Coll., London (BA, Italian). Called to English Bar, Inner Temple, 1934; Ghana Bar (Gold Coast), 1950; Sierra Leone Bar, 1957; Nigerian Bar and S Cameroons Bar, 1959; Guyana Bar (formerly British Guiana), 1961; also appeared in courts of Aden and Kenya. Lectr in Italian, QUB, 1972–79. Vis. Lectr in Italian, Univ. of Leicester, 1980–92. Member: Soc. for Italian Studies; Haldane Soc. *Address:* 69 Anson Road, N7 0AS.
Died 22 Nov. 2001.

MILLS, Eric Robertson, CBE 1981; Registrar of the Privy Council, 1966–83; *b* 27 July 1918; *s* of late Thomas Piercy Mills, Woking, Surrey; *m* 1950, Shirley Manger; two *d*. *Educ:* Charterhouse; Trinity Coll., Cambridge (BA). Served Royal Artillery, 1939–46; Major 1944. Called to Bar, Inner Temple, 1947; Mem. of Western Circuit. Dep. Judge Advocate, 1955; Chief Clerk, Judicial Cttee of Privy Council, 1963. *Publications:* contribs to legal text books. *Address:* Lamber Green, 10 St Catherines Drive, Guildford, Surrey GU2 4HE. *T:* (01483) 537218.
Died 17 Nov. 2003.

MILLS, Ivor Henry, FRCP; Professor of Medicine in the University of Cambridge, 1963–88, then Emeritus; Fellow, Churchill College, Cambridge, 1963–88; Hon. Consultant to United Cambridge Hospitals, since 1963; *b* 13 June 1921; 3rd *s* of late J. H. W. Mills and Priscilla Mills; *m* 1947, Sydney Elizabeth Puleston (*née* Roberts); one *s* one *d*. *Educ:* Selhurst Grammar Sch., Croydon; Queen Mary Coll., London (BSc 1942; PhD 1946); Trinity Coll., Cambridge (Sen. Schol., 1948; BA 1948; MB, BChir 1951; MD 1956; MA 1963). MRCP 1953, FRCP 1964. Pres. Cambridge Univ. Medical Soc., 1947–48; MRC (Eli Lilly) Trav. Fellow, 1956; Vis. Scientist, Nat. Inst. of Health, 1957; Lectr in Medicine and Chem. Path., St Thomas's Hosp. Medical Sch., 1954; Reader in Medicine, St Thomas's Hosp. Medical Sch., London, 1962. Vis. Prof. in Physiology and Medicine, N Carolina Med. Sch., USA, 1972. Mem., Hunter Working Party on Medical Administrators, 1970–72. Royal College of Physicians: Mem. Council, 1971–74; Pro-Censor, 1974–75, Censor, 1975–76; Croonian Lectr, 1977; Sec., Soc. for Endocrinology, 1963–71; Chm., Scientific Adv. Cttee, Mason Med. Res. Foundation, 1982–88. Hon. FACP. *Publications:* Clinical Aspects of Adrenal Function, 1964; contrib. Lancet, Science Jl of Endocr., Clin. Science, etc. *Recreations:* gardening, letters to The Times. *Address:* 6 Spinney Drive, Great Shelford, Cambridge CB2 5LY. *Died 15 Dec. 2005.*

MILLS, John Faithful Fortescue P.; *see* Platts-Mills.

MILLS, Sir John (Lewis Ernest Watts), Kt 1976; CBE 1960; actor, producer, director; *b* 22 Feb. 1908; *m* 1941, Mary Hayley Bell, playwright; one *s* two *d*. *Educ:* Norwich. 1st appearance, stage, 1929. *Plays:* Cavalcade, London Wall, Words and Music, Five O'clock Girl, Give Me a Ring, Jill Darling, Floodlight, Red Night, We at the Cross Roads, Of Mice and Men, Men in Shadow, Duet for Two Hands, etc.; Old Vic Season, 1938; Top of the Ladder; Figure of Fun, Aldwych; Ross, New York, 1961; Power of Persuasion, Garrick, 1963; Veterans, Royal Court, 1972; At the End of the Day, Savoy, 1973; The Good Companions, Her Majesty's, 1974; Separate Tables, Apollo, 1977; Goodbye, Mr Chips, Chichester Fest., 1982; Little Lies, Wyndham's, 1983; The Petition, NT, (transf. Wyndham's) 1986; Pygmalion, Guildford and NY, 1987; When the Wind Blows (TV play), 1987. *Films:* The Midshipmaid, Britannia of Billingsgate, Brown on Resolution, OHMS, Cottage To Let, The Young Mr Pitt, We Dive at Dawn, In Which We Serve, The Way to the Stars, Great Expectations, So Well Remembered, The October Man, Scott of the Antarctic, The History of Mr Polly, The Rocking Horse Winner, Morning Departure, Mr Denning Drives North, Gentle Gunman, The Long Memory, Hobson's Choice, The Colditz Story, The End of the Affair, Above Us the Waves, Town on Trial, Escapade, Its Great to be Young, The Baby and the Battleship, War and Peace, Around the World in Eighty Days, Dunkirk, Ice Cold in Alex, I Was Monty's Double, Summer of the Seventeenth Doll, Tiger Bay, Swiss Family Robinson, The Singer not the Song, Tunes of Glory, Flame in the Streets, The Valiant, Tiara Tahiti, The Chalk Garden, The Truth about Spring, King Rat, Operation X Bow, Red Waggon, Sky West and Crooked (directed), The Wrong Box, The Family Way, Chuka, Showdown, Oh! What a Lovely War, The Return of the Boomerang, Ryan's Daughter (Best Supporting Actor Award, Oscar Award, 1971), Run Wild, Run Free, Emma Hamilton, Dulcima, Lamb, Young Winston, Oklahoma Crude, Trial by Combat, The Devil's Advocate, Great Expectations, The Big Sleep, Zulu Dawn, The 39 Steps, The Human Factor, Gandhi, Masks of Death, Murder with Mirrors, Who's That Girl?, Frankenstein, the Real Story, Deadly Advice, Hamlet, Bright Young Things. Tribute to Her Majesty (film documentary), 1986. *TV and TV series:* The Zoo Gang, 1974; Quatermass, 1979; Tales of the Unexpected, 1979, 1980, 1981; Young at Heart, 1980, 1981, 1982; The True Story of Spit MacPhee; A Tale of Two Cities; Ending Up; A Woman of Substance;

Harnessing Peacocks, 1993; The Big Freeze; Martin Chuzzlewit, 1994. Member: SFTA (Vice-Pres.); RADA Council, 1965–; Chm., Stars Organization for Spastics, 1975–79. Pres., Mountview Theatre Sch., 1983–. Vice Pres., Gtr London Fund for Blind, 1998–. Patron Life Mem., Variety Club. *Publications:* Up in the Clouds, Gentlemen Please (autobiog.), 1980; Book of Famous Firsts, 1984; Still Memories (autobiog.), 2000. *Recreations:* ski-ing, golf, painting. *Address:* c/o ICM, Oxford House, 76 Oxford Street, W1D 1BS. *Clubs:* Garrick, St James's. *Died 23 April 2005.*

MILLS, John William, OBE 1945; QC 1962; *b* 24 Oct. 1914; *s* of late John William Mills, OBE and Jessie Mills; *m* 1942, Phyllis Mary, *yr d* of late Arthur Gibson Pears; no *c*. *Educ:* Clifton; Corpus Christi Coll., Cambridge (MA). Called to Bar, Middle Temple, 1938; Bencher, 1968; Treas., 1985; retired 1987. Lt-Col, Royal Signals, 1944; Comdr, Royal Signals, 46 Div., 1944; Hon. Lt-Col 1946. Member: Bar Council, 1961–64; Clifton Coll. Council, 1967–80. *Publication:* (editor/author) Wurtzburg, Law Relating to Building Societies, subseq. Wurtzburg and Mills, Building Society Law, 10th edn 1952 to 14th edn 1988, Ed. Emeritus of 15th edn 1989. *Recreations:* sailing, golf. *Address:* Greenleas, Highleigh, Chichester, Sussex PO20 7NP. *T:* (01243) 641396. *Died 27 Dec. 2001.*

MILLS, Mary Bell McMillan, (Mrs Ian Mills); *see* MacMurray, M. B. McM.

MILLS, Air Cdre Stanley Edwin Druce, CB 1968; CBE 1959; Royal Air Force, retired; *b* 13 Nov. 1913; *s* of Edwin J. Mills; *m* 1938, Joan Mary, *d* of Robert Ralph James; one *s* one *d*. *Educ:* Collegiate Sch., Bournemouth; RAF Staff Coll. Entered RAF, 1939; served RAF Middle East and Italy, 1942–45; Station Comdr, RAF Innsworth, 1957–60; Comd Accountant, RAF Germany, 1960–63; Dir of Personnel (Policy) (Air), MoD, 1963–65; Dir of Personal Services (Air), MoD, 1966–68. Bursar, Roedean Sch., 1968–73. FCA. *Recreation:* travel. *Address:* Maryland, Lullington Close, Seaford, E Sussex BN25 4JH. *T:* (01323) 895468. *Club:* Royal Air Force. *Died 19 Jan. 2001.*

MILLSON, John Albert; Assistant Under-Secretary of State, Ministry of Defence, 1972–78; *b* 4 Oct. 1918; *s* of late George Charles Millson and Annie Millson, London; *m* 1953, Megan Laura Woodiss (*d* 1999); one *s* one *d*. *Educ:* St Olave's. Entered Air Min., 1936; Private Sec. to Parly Under-Sec. of State for Air, 1947–50; Principal, Air Min., 1955; Asst Sec., MoD, 1961; Asst Under-Sec. of State, 1972. Chm. of Governors, Homefield Prep. Sch., Sutton, 1975. *Recreations:* walking, listening to music. *Address:* Roseacre, Holly Hill Drive, Banstead, Surrey SM7 2BD. *T:* (01737) 359646. *Died 13 Aug. 2005.*

MILNE, 2nd Baron *cr* 1933, of Salonika and of Rubislaw, Co. Aberdeen; **George Douglass Milne,** TD; *b* 10 Feb. 1909; *s* of 1st Baron Milne, GCB, GCMG, DSO, Field Marshal from 1928, and Claire Marjoribanks, MBE, DGStJ (*d* 1970), *d* of Sir John N. Maitland, 5th Bt; *S* father, 1948; *m* 1940, Cicely, 3rd *d* of late Ronald Leslie; two *s* one *d*. *Educ:* Winchester; New Coll., Oxford. Mem., Inst. of Chartered Accountants of Scotland. Partner, Arthur Young McClelland Moores Co., 1954–73; Dir, London & Northern Group Ltd, 1973–87 (Dep. Chm., 1981). Master of the Grocers' Company, 1961–62; Sen. Court Mem., 1984–90. Served War of 1939–45, Royal Artillery (TA); prisoner of war, 1941; NWEF and MEF (wounded, despatches). *Recreation:* art (has exhibited RA, ROI, RP). *Heir: s* Hon. George Alexander Milne, *b* 1 April 1941. *Address:* 33 Lonsdale Road, Barnes, SW13 9JP. *T:* (020) 8748 6421. *Died 1 Feb. 2005.*

MILNE, (Alexander) Berkeley, OBE 1968; HM Diplomatic Service, retired; *b* 12 Feb. 1924; *s* of George and Mary Milne; *m* 1952, Patricia Mary (*née* Holderness); one *s* two *d*. *Educ:* Keith Grammar and Buckie High Schs, Banffshire, Scotland; Univ. of Aberdeen (MA (Hons Mental Phil.) 1943); University Coll., Oxford (BA (Hons

Persian and Arabic) 1949). Served 3/2nd Punjab Regt, Indian Army, India and Java, 1943–46. Scarborough Schol., Tehran Univ., 1950–51; Lectr in Persian, Edinburgh Univ., 1951–52. Foreign Office, 1952–53; BMEO, Cyprus, 1953–54; Third, later Second Sec., Tehran, 1954–57; FO, 1958–61; Second, later First Sec., Brussels, 1961–64; FO (later FCO), 1964–65; First Secretary: British Residual Mission, Salisbury, Rhodesia, 1966–67; Jedda, Saudi Arabia, 1968–70; FCO, 1971–74; Counsellor, Tehran, 1974–77; GCHQ, 1978–83. Consultant, Oman Govt, 1983–86. *Recreations:* gardening, reading; playing chamber music, preferably second violin in string quartets. *Address:* 6 Merestones Close, Cheltenham, Glos GL50 2ST. *T:* (01242) 242370.

Died 22 Feb. 2003.

MILNE, Berkeley; *see* Milne, A. B.

MILNER OF LEEDS, 2nd Baron *cr* 1951; **Arthur James Michael Milner,** AE 1952; Consultant, Gregory, Rowcliffe & Milners (formerly Milners, Curry & Gaskell), Solicitors, London, since 1988 (Partner, 1953–88); *b* 12 Sept. 1923; *o s* of 1st Baron Milner of Leeds, PC, MC, TD and Lois Tinsdale (*d* 1982), *d* of Thomas Brown, Leeds; *S* father, 1967; *m* 1st, 1951, Sheila Margaret (*d* 2000), *d* of Gerald Hartley, Leeds; one *s* one *d* (and one *d* decd); 2nd, 2002, Helen Cutting Wilmerding, *yr d* of Lucius Wilmerding Jr, Princeton, NJ. *Educ:* Oundle; Trinity Hall, Cambridge (BA 1948, MA 1951). Served: RAFVR, 1942–46, Flt Lt; 609 (W Riding) Sqn, RAuxAF, 1947–52, Flt Lt. Admitted Solicitor, 1951. Opposition Whip, House of Lords, 1971–74; Member: Jt Cttee on Consolidation Bills, 1982–92; Select Cttees on Private Bills, 1990–96; elected Mem., H of L, 1999. Member: Clothworkers' Co.; Pilgrims; Hon. Treas. Soc. of Yorkshiremen in London, 1967–70. *Heir: s* Hon. Richard James Milner [*b* 16 May 1959; *m* 1988, Margaret, *y d* of G. F. Voisin; two *d*]. *Address:* 2 The Inner Court, Old Church Street, SW3 5BY. *Club:* Royal Air Force.   *Died 20 Aug. 2003.*

MILNER, Ralph; *see* Millner, Ralph.

MILOSZ, Czeslaw; poet, author; Professor of Slavic Languages and Literatures, University of California, Berkeley, 1961–78, then Emeritus; *b* Lithuania, 30 June 1911; *s* of Aleksander and Weronika Milosz; naturalised US citizen, 1970. *Educ:* High Sch., Wilno; Univ. of Wilno. MJuris 1934. Programmer, Polish Nat. Radio, 1935–39; Mem., Polish diplomatic service, Washington, Paris, 1945–50. Vis. Lectr, Univ. of Calif, Berkeley, 1960–61. Guggenheim Fellow, 1976. Member: Polish Inst. Letters and Scis in America; Amer. Acad. of Arts and Scis; PEN Club in Exile; Amer. Acad. of Arts and Letters. Hon. LittD Michigan, 1977; Hon. doctorates: Catholic Univ. of Lublin, 1981; Harvard Univ., 1989; Jagiellonian Univ., Krakow, 1989; Rome Univ., 1992. Prix Littéraire Européen, Les Guildes du Livre, Geneva, 1953; Neustadt Internat. Prize for Literature, Univ. of Oklahoma, 1978; citation, Univ. of Calif, Berkeley, 1978; Nobel Prize for Literature, 1980. Order of White Eagle (Poland), 1994; Order of Gedyminas (Lithuania), 1997. *Publications:* Poemat o czasie zastyglym (Poem on Time Frozen), 1933; Trzy zimy (Three Winters), 1936; Ocalenie (Rescue), 1945; Zniewolony umysl (The Captive Mind), 1953; Zdobycie wladzy, 1953, trans. as The Usurpers (in US as Seizure of Power), 1955; Dolina Issy, 1955, trans. as The Issa Valley, 1981; Swiatlo dzienne (Daylight), 1955; Traktat poetycki (Poetic Treatise), 1957; Rodzinna Europa, 1958, trans. as Native Realm, 1968; Postwar Polish Poetry, 1965; Widzenia nad Zatoka San Francisco (Views from San Francisco Bay), 1969; The History of Polish Literature, 1970; Prywatne obowiazki (Private Obligations), 1972; Selected Poems, 1973, rev. edn 1981; Ziemia Ulro (The Land of Ulro), 1977; Emperor of the Earth, 1977; Bells in Winter, 1978; Hymn o perle, 1982; Visions from San Francisco Bay, 1983; The Witness of Poetry, 1983; Separate Notebooks, 1984; The Land of Ulro, 1985; Unattainable Earth, 1986; Collected Poems, 1988; Provinces, 1991; Beginning With My Streets, 1992;

A Year of the Hunter, 1994; Facing the River, 1995; A Book of Luminous Things, 1996; Road-side Dog, 1998. *Address:* Department of Slavic Languages and Literatures, 5416 Dwinelle Hall, University of California, Berkeley, CA 94720, USA.   *Died 14 Aug. 2004.*

MILSTEIN, César, CH 1995; PhD; FRS 1975; Scientific Staff of Medical Research Council, 1963–95; Fellow, Darwin College, University of Cambridge, 1981–95. Hon. Fellow, 2002; Joint Head, Division of Protein and Nucleic Acid Chemistry, 1981–93, Deputy Director, 1988–95, MRC Laboratory of Molecular Biology; *b* 8 Oct. 1927; *s* of Lázaro and Máxima Milstein; *m* 1953, Celia Prilleltensky. *Educ:* Colegio Nacional de Bahia Blanca; Univ. Nacional de Buenos Aires; Fitzwilliam Coll., Cambridge (Hon. Fellow 1982); Licenciado en Ciencias Quimicas 1952; Doctor en Quimica 1957; PhD Cantab 1960. British Council Fellow, 1958–60; Scientific Staff, MRC, Dept of Biochemistry, Cambridge Univ., 1960–61; Staff of Instituto Nacional de Microbiologia, Buenos Aires, 1957–63; Head of Div. de Biologia Molecular, 1961–63; Staff of MRC Laboratory of Molecular Biology, 1963–95: Mem. Governing Bd, 1975–79; Head of Sub-div. of Protein Chemistry, 1969–80; Head Sub-div. of Molecular Immunobiology, 1980. For. Associate, Nat. Acad. of Scis, USA, 1981; Founding Fellow, Third World Acad. of Scis, 1983. Hon. FRCP, 1983; Hon. FRCPath, 1987; Hon. FRSocMed, 1992. Hon. DSc: Cambridge, 1999; Vigo, Spain, 1999; Helsinki, 2000. Biochem. Soc. Ciba Medal, 1978; Rosenstiel Medal, 1979; Avery-Landsteiner Preis, 1979; Rosenberg Prize, 1979; Mattia Award, 1979; Gross Horwitz Prize, 1980; Koch Preis, 1980; Wolf Prize in Med., 1980; Wellcome Foundn Medal, 1980; Gimenez Diaz Medal, 1981; William Bate Hardy Prize, Camb. Philos. Soc., 1981; Sloan Prize, General Motors Cancer Res. Foundn, 1981; Gairdner Award, Gairdner Foundn, 1981; Royal Medal, Royal Soc., 1982; Nobel Prize for Physiology or Medicine (with Prof. N. Jerne and Dr G. Koehler), 1984; Dale Medal, Soc. for Endicronology, 1984; Galen Medal, Apothecaries' Soc., 1985; Walker Prize, RCS, 1986; Copley Medal, Royal Soc., 1989; Nat. Biotechnology Ventures Award, USA, 1990; Konex de Brillante Award, Argentina, 1993; Award for Excellence in Res. in Immunology, Duke Univ., USA, 1996; MRC Millennium Medal, 2000. Silver Jubilee Medal, 1977; Orden de Mayo (Argentina), 1999. *Publications:* original papers and review articles on structure, evolution and genetics of immunoglobulins and phosphoenzimes. *Recreations:* open air activities, cooking. *Address:* Medical Research Council Laboratory of Molecular Biology, Hills Road, Cambridge CB2 2QH. *Club:* Sefe (Cambridge).

Died 24 March 2002.

MINTO, 6th Earl of, *cr* 1813; **Gilbert Edward George Lariston Elliot-Murray-Kynynmound,** OBE 1986 (MBE (mil.) 1955); JP; Bt 1700; Baron Minto, 1797; Viscount Melgund, 1813; late Captain Scots Guards; Vice Lord-Lieutenant, Borders Region (Roxburgh, Ettrick and Lauderdale), 1992–2003; *b* 19 June 1928; *er s* of 5th Earl of Minto and Marion, OBE (*d* 1974), *d* of G. W. Cook, Montreal; *S* father, 1975; *m* 1st, 1952, Lady Caroline Child-Villiers (from whom he obtained a divorce, 1965), *d* of 9th Earl of Jersey; one *s* one *d*; 2nd, 1965, Mary Elizabeth (*b* 29 Dec. 1936; *d* 24 Jan. 1998), *d* of late Peter Ballantine and of Mrs Ballantine, Gladstone, New Jersey, USA; 3rd, 1991, Mrs Caroline Larlham. *Educ:* Eton; RMA, Sandhurst. Served Malaya, 1949–51; ADC to C-in-C FARELF, 1951, to CIGS, 1953–55, to HE Governor and C-in-C Cyprus, 1955; transferred to RARO, 1956. Lieut, Queen's Body Guard for Scotland (Royal Company of Archers). Director, Noel Penny Turbines Ltd, 1971–92. Regional Councillor (Hermitage Div.), Borders Region, 1974–80, 1986–96; Convener, Borders Regional Council, 1990–96; Mem. Exec., COSLA, 1990–96. Dep. Traffic Comr for Scotland, 1975–81; Property Comr for Local Govt, Scotland, 1995–98. Pres., S of Scotland Chamber of Commerce, 1980–82 (Exec. Vice-Pres., 1978–80). Chm., 1973–87, Pres., 1987–, Scottish Council on Alcohol. JP

Roxburghshire, 1961–; DL Borders Region, Roxburgh, Ettrick and Lauderdale, 1983. *Heir: s* Viscount Melgund, *b* 1 Dec. 1953. *Address:* Minto, Hawick, Scotland TD9 8SB. *T:* (01450) 870321. *Died 7 Sept. 2005.*

MISSELBROOK, (Bertram) Desmond, CBE 1972; FRSE 1978; Chairman, Livingston Development Corporation, 1972–78; *b* 28 May 1913; *s* of late C. J. and E. P. Misselbrook; *m* 1949, Anne, *er d* of late F. O. Goodman; two *s. Educ:* Chatham House, Ramsgate; Bristol Univ. Admiralty Psychologist, 1942–45. Lectr in Psychology and Dir, Unit of Applied Psychology, Edinburgh Univ., 1945–49; Senr Res. Fellow in Business Studies, 1970–71, Hon. Fellow, 1971. Personnel Adviser, 1949, Dir. 1955, Dep. Chm. 1963–70, British-American Tobacco Co. Ltd; Chm., Eversed and Vignoles Ltd, 1961–65; Chm., Mardon Packaging International Ltd, 1962–70; Dir, 1963, Dep. Chm. 1966–69, Wiggins Teape Ltd; Director: Charterhouse Gp Ltd, 1969–72; Anderson Mavor Ltd, 1971–74; Dep. Chm., Standard Life Assurance Co., 1977–80 (Dir, 1970–84); Chairman: Anderson Strathclyde Ltd, 1974–77; Seaforth Maritime Ltd, 1977–78. Mem. Council, British Inst. of Management, 1967–72 (a Vice-Chm., 1969); Chairman: Bd of Governors, Oversea Service, 1963–70; Construction Ind. Trng Bd, 1970–73; Council, Scottish Business Sch., 1972–77; Economic Development Cttees for Building and Civil Engineering Industries, 1969–72; Member: Adv. Council on Social Work (Scotland), 1970–74; Economic Consultant, Scottish Office, 1970–72. Hon. DSc Edinburgh, 1977. *Recreations:* fishing, gardening, walking. *Address:* Welton House, Coupar Angus, Blairgowrie, Perthshire PH13 9EY. *T:* (01828) 640577. *Died 5 March 2005.*

MITCHELL, Air Cdre Sir (Arthur) Dennis, KBE 1977; CVO 1961; DFC 1944, and Bar, 1945; AFC 1943; Founder and Managing Director, Aero Systems SA, since 1972; an Extra Equerry to the Queen since 1962; *b* 26 May 1918; 2nd *s* of Col A. Mitchell, DSO, Carrickfergus, Belfast, N Ireland, and Dorothy (*née* Mitchell), Rathmelton, Co. Donegal; *m* 1949, Comtesse Mireille Caroline Cornet de Ways Ruart (*d* 1999); one *s. Educ:* Nautical Coll., Pangbourne; RAF Coll., Cranwell; Army Staff Coll., Camberley; RAF Flying Coll., Manby. Joined RAF, 1936. Served 1938–45, India, Burma, UK and NW Europe; RAF Delegn, Belgium, 1948–49; US Air Force, 1951–53; HQ Allied Air Forces Central Europe, NATO, Fontainebleau, 1953–56; o/c RAF Cottesmore Bomber Comd, 1959–62; Dep. Captain and Captain of the Queen's Flight, 1956–59 and 1962–64; ADC to the Queen, 1958–62. Founder: Brussels Airways; Aero Distributors SA. French Croix de Guerre, 1945. *Recreation:* golf. *Address:* (office) 10 chemin des Chasseurs, 1380 Ohain, Belgium. *T:* (2) 6522222, *Fax:* (2) 6531517; (home) (2) 6531301. *Clubs:* Royal Air Force, Naval and Military. *Died 25 Dec. 2001.*

MITCHELL, Bob; *see* Mitchell, R. C.

MITCHELL, Sir Dennis; *see* Mitchell, Sir A. D.

MITCHELL, Sir (Edgar) William (John), Kt 1990; CBE 1976; FRS 1986; Fellow of Wadham College, Oxford, 1978–92, then Emeritus Fellow; *b* Kingsbridge, S Devon, 25 Sept. 1925; *s* of late Edgar and Caroline Mitchell; *m* 1948; one *s*; *m* 1985, Prof. Margaret Davies (*née* Brown). *Educ:* Univ. of Sheffield (BSc, MSc); Univ. of Bristol (PhD). FInstP. Metropolitan Vickers Research Dept, 1946–48, 1950–51; Univ. of Bristol, 1948–50; University of Reading, 1951–78: Prof. of Physics, 1961–78; Dean, Faculty of Science, 1966–69; Dep. Vice-Chancellor, 1976–78; University of Oxford: Dr Lee's Prof. of Experimental Philosophy, 1978–88; Prof of Physics, 1988–89. Science and Engineering Research Council (formerly Science Research Council): Mem., 1970–74, 1982–85; Chm., 1985–90; Mem., 1965–70, Chm., 1967–70, Physics Cttee; Chm., Neutron Beam Res. Cttee, 1966–74 (devised scheme for extensive University

use of nuclear res. reactors for condensed matter res.); Member: Sci. Planning Gp for Spallation Neutron Source, 1978–85; Sci. Bd (formerly Univ. Sci. and Tech. Bd), 1967–70; Nuclear Physics Bd, 1980–85. Mem., Management Bd, British National Space Centre, 1986–90. Acting Jt Dir, 1973, Mem., 1973–80, Sci. Council of Inst. Laue-Langevin, Grenoble; Member: Comité de Direction, Solid State Physics Lab., Ecole Normale and Univ. of Paris VI, 1975–79; Exec. Cttee, Univ. Council for Non-Academic Staff, 1979–82; UGC Phys. Sci. Cttee, 1982–85; Council, Inst. of Physics, 1982–86; ABRC, 1985–90; Council, Foundn of Sci. and Technol., 1985–90; Innovation Adv. Bd, DTI, 1988–90; Scientific Adv. Cttee for Nat. Gall., 1988–; Chm., SE Reg. Computing Cttee, 1974–76; Vice-Pres., European Sci. Foundn, 1989–92; Member: Council, CERN, 1985–93 (Vice-Pres., 1990; Pres., 1991–93); CODEST, EEC, 1991–94; ESTA, EU, 1994–97. Mem., Academia Europaea, 1989 (Chm., Physics Section, 1994–96). Hon. DSc: Reading, 1987; Kent, 1988; Budapest, 1988; Birmingham, 1990. Glazebrook Medal, Inst. of Physics, 1995. Officer's Cross, Order of Merit (Germany), 1990. *Publications:* numerous papers on solid state physics. *Recreations:* good food, opera, motoring, physics. *Address:* Wadham College, Oxford OX1 3PN. *Died 30 Oct. 2002.*

MITCHELL, James; writer these many years; *b* South Shields, 12 March 1926; *s* of James Mitchell and Wilhelmina Mitchell; *m* 1st (marr. diss. 1965); two *s*; 2nd, 1968, Delia (*d* 1990), *d* of Major and Mrs K. J. McCoy. *Educ:* South Shields Grammar Sch.; St Edmund Hall, Oxford (BA 1948, MA 1950); King's Coll., Newcastle upon Tyne, Univ. of Durham (DipEd 1950). Worked in rep. theatre, 1948, then in shipyard, travel agency and Civil Service; taught for some fifteen years in almost every kind of instn from secondary modern sch. to coll. of art. Free-lance writer: novels; more than a hundred television scripts; several screenplays and a theatre play. *Publications:* Here's a Villain, 1957; A Way Back, 1959; Steady Boys, Steady, 1960; Among Arabian Sands, 1963; The Man Who Sold Death, 1964; Die Rich, Die Happy, 1965; The Money that Money can't Buy, 1967; The Innocent Bystanders, 1969; Ilion like a Mist, 1969; A Magnum for Schneider, 1969; The Winners, 1970; Russian Roulette, 1973; Death and Bright Water, 1974; Smear Job, 1975; When the Boat Comes In, 1976; The Hungry Years, 1976; Upwards and Onwards, 1977; The Evil Ones, 1982; Sometimes You Could Die, 1985; Dead Ernest, 1986; Dying Day, 1988; A Woman To Be Loved, 1990; An Impossible Woman, 1992; Leading Lady, 1993; So Far from Home, 1995; Indian Summer, 1996; Dance For Joy, 1997. *Recreations:* travel, military history, aristology. *Club:* Lansdowne. *Died 15 Sept. 2002.*

MITCHELL, (James Lachlan) Martin, RD 1969; Sheriff of Lothian and Borders (formerly Lothians and Peebles), 1974–95 (as a floating Sheriff, 1974–78, and at Edinburgh, 1978–95); *b* 13 June 1929; *o s* of late Dr L. M. V. Mitchell, OBE, MB, ChB and Harriet Doris Riggall; *m* 1993, Jane Anne, *d* of late Patrick Clement Cox. *Educ:* Cargilfield; Sedbergh; Univ. of Edinburgh (MA 1951, LLB 1953). Admitted Mem. Faculty of Advocates, 1957, in practice, 1957–74; Standing Junior Counsel in Scotland to Admty Bd, 1963–74; Temp. Sheriff, 1971–75 and 1995–98. Hon. Sheriff, Inverness, 1983. Nat. Service, RN, 1954–55; Sub-Lt (S) RNVR 1954; Perm. Reserve, 1956; Comdr RNR 1966, retd 1974. Chm., Lothian Allelon, 1978–2001; Mem. Exec. Cttee, 1978–87, Mem. Main Bd, 1987–88, Scottish Council for Spastics. Gov., Cargilfield Sch., 1966–91. *Recreations:* fishing, photography, listening to music. *Address:* 8 St Colme Street, Edinburgh EH3 6AA. *T:* (0131) 225 3384. *Club:* New (Edinburgh). *Died 26 Nov. 2001.*

MITCHELL, Joseph Rodney; Director General of Defence Accounts, Ministry of Defence, 1973, retired; *b* 11 March 1914; *s* of late Joseph William and Martha

Mitchell, Sheffield; *m* 1936, Marian Richardson; two *s* three *d. Educ:* Sheffield Central Secondary School. FCCA, ACMA, ACIS. Works Recorder and Junior Costs Clerk, United Steel Cos Ltd, Sheffield, 1930–35; Senior Accounts Clerk, Cargo Fleet Iron Co. Ltd, Middlesbrough, 1936–39; Royal Ordnance Factories, 1940–55: Chief Exec. Officer, 1951–55; Min. of Supply/Aviation/ Technology, 1956–71: Dir of Accounts, 1967–71; Dep. Dir Gen. of Defence Accounts, MoD, 1971–72. *Recreation:* hill-walking. *Address:* 154 Earlsbrook Road, Redhill, Surrey RH1 6HZ. *Died 10 March 2004.*

MITCHELL, Martin; see Mitchell, J. L. M.

MITCHELL, Dame Mona (Ann), DCVO 1992 (CVO 1985; LVO 1976); Extra Lady-in-Waiting to HRH Princess Alexandra, the Hon. Lady Ogilvy, since 1968; *b* 20 Feb. 1938; *d* of Maj.-Gen. Francis Neville Mitchell, CB, CBE, DSO and late Ann Christian Mitchell (*née* Livingstone-Learmouth; she *m* 2nd, 1962, Brig. Richard Headlam Keenlyside, CBE, DSO (decd)). *Educ:* North Foreland Lodge. Secretary to: Fulke Walwyn, 1958–62; E. Hardy Amies, 1963–68; Sec., 1968–74, Private Sec., 1974–91, to HRH Princess Alexandra. *Recreations:* gardening, music, the arts in general. *Address:* High House, Harvest Lane, Charlton Horethorne, Sherborne, Dorset DT9 4PH. *T:* (01963) 220441. *Club:* Army and Navy. *Died 17 Dec. 2002.*

MITCHELL, Richard Charles, (Bob); Lecturer in Business Studies, Eastleigh College of Further Education, 1984–93; *b* 22 Aug. 1927; *s* of Charles and Elizabeth Mitchell; *m* 1950, Doreen Lilian Gregory; one *s* one *d. Educ:* Taunton's Sch., Southampton; Godalming Co. Grammar Sch.; Southampton Univ. (BSc(Econ) Hons 1951). Bartley County Secondary School: Sen. Master and Head of Maths and Science Dept, 1957–65; Dep. Headmaster, 1965–66. MP (Lab) Southampton Test, 1966–70; MP (Lab 1971–81, SDP 1981–83) Southampton, Itchen, May 1971–1983. Contested Southampton, Itchen (SDP) 1983, (SDP/Alliance) 1987. Mem., European Parlt, 1975–79. Member: Bureau of European Socialist Gp, 1976–79; Chairman's Panel, House of Commons, 1979–83. Gov., Itchen Sixth Form Coll., 1984–. *Publication:* (jtly) Public Administration: a casebook approach, 1991. *Recreation:* postal chess (rep. Brit. Correspondence Chess Assoc. against other countries). *Address:* 49 Devonshire Road, Polygon, Southampton SO15 2GL. *T:* (023) 8022 1781. *Died 18 Sept. 2003.*

MITCHELL, Sir William; see Mitchell, Sir E. W. J.

MOBBS, Sir (Gerald) Nigel, Kt 1986; Lord-Lieutenant of Buckinghamshire, since 1997; Chairman: Slough Estates plc, 1976–2005; Bovis Homes Group, since 1996; Director, Barclays Bank PLC, 1979–2003; *b* 22 Sept. 1937; *s* of Gerald Aubrey Mobbs and Elizabeth (*née* Lanchester); *m* 1961, Hon. Pamela Jane Marguerite Berry, 2nd *d* of 2nd Viscount Kemsley; one *s* twin *d. Educ:* Marlborough Coll.; Christ Church, Oxford. Joined Slough Estates plc, 1960; Director, 1963; Man. Dir, 1971; Chief Exec., 1976–96. Director: Barclays Bank Trust Co. Ltd, 1973–86 (Chm., 1985–86); Charterhouse Gp, 1974–84 (Chm., 1977–83); Kingfisher plc (formerly Woolworth Holdings), 1982–96 (Dep. Chm., 1990–95; Chm., 1995–96); Cookson Gp plc, 1985–93; Howard de Walden Estates Ltd, 1989–; Chm., Groundwork Foundn, 1990–94. Chairman: Corporate Health (formerly Slough Occupational Health Service), 1976–; Slough Social Fund, 1975–; Property Services Agency Adv. Bd, 1980–86; Aims of Industry, 1985–2002; Adv. Panel on Deregulation, DTI, 1988–94. Pres., Slough & Dist Chamber of Commerce, 1969–72; Vice-Pres., Assoc. of British Chambers of Commerce, 1976–90 (Chm. 1974–76); Pres., British Property Fedn, 1979–81. Mem., Cttee on Corporate Governance, 1996–98. Mem., Commonwealth War Graves Commn, 1988–97; Trustee: Nat. Army Mus., 1994–; Historic Royal Palaces, 2002– (Chm. Trustees, 2003–); Comr, Royal Hosp., Chelsea,

2000–. Chm., Wembley Task Force, 1999–2002. President: Bucks Assoc. of Boys' Clubs, 1984–97; British Council for Offices, 1990–91; South East RFCA, 2004–. Hon. Treas., Cons. Party, 1993–96. Chm., Council, Univ. of Buckingham, 1987–98. CCMI. Master, Spectacle Makers' Co., 1989. High Sheriff, 1982, DL, 1985, Bucks. Hon. Col No 1 (Royal Bucks Yeomanry) Signal Sqn (Special Communications), 2001–. Hon. Fellow, Coll. of Estate Management, 1978; Hon. Mem., RICS, 1990. Hon. DSc City, 1988; DUniv: Buckingham, 1993; Bucks Chilterns UC, 2003; Hon. LLD Reading, 2000. KStJ (Pres. Council, Bucks, 1997–). *Recreations:* riding, ski-ing, golf, travel. *Club:* Brooks's. *Died 21 Oct. 2005.*

MOBERLY, Sir John (Campbell), KBE 1984; CMG 1976; HM Diplomatic Service, retired; Associate Fellow (formerly Consultant), Middle East Programme, Royal Institute of International Affairs, 1986–2003; *b* 27 May 1925; *s* of Sir Walter Moberly, GBE, KCB, DSO; *m* 1959, Patience, *d* of Major Sir Richard George Proby, 1st Bt, MC; two *s* one *d. Educ:* Winchester College; Magdalen College, Oxford. War Service in Royal Navy, 1943–47 (despatches). Entered HM Foreign (later Diplomatic) Service, 1950; Political Officer, Kuwait, 1954–56; Political Agent, Doha, 1959–62; First Secretary, Athens, 1962–66; Counsellor, Washington, 1969–73; Dir, Middle East Centre for Arab Studies, 1973–75; Ambassador, Jordan, 1975–79; Asst Under-Sec. of State, FCO, 1979–82; Ambassador, Iraq, 1982–85. CStJ 1979. *Recreation:* walking. *Address:* 27 The Ridgeway, Caversham, Reading RG4 8NX. *T:* and *Fax:* (0118) 947 9512; The Cedars, Temple Sowerby, Penrith, Cumbria CA10 1RZ. *T:* (01768) 361437. *Clubs:* Royal Automobile; Leander (Henley-on-Thames). *Died 14 Sept. 2004.*

MOBERLY, Maj.-Gen. Richard James, CB 1957; OBE 1944; Director, Communications Electronic Equipment, War Office, 1960–64; *b* 2 July 1906; *o s* of late J. E. Moberly; *m* 1st, 1935, Mary Joyce Shelmerdine (*d* 1964); three *d*; 2nd, 1971, Mrs Vivien Mary Cameron (*d* 1981), *d* of Victor Bayley, CIE, CBE. *Educ:* Haileybury; Royal Military Academy, Woolwich. Commissioned Royal Signals, 1926; India, 1928–35; comd 1st Airborne Div. Signal Regt, 1942–43; CSO 1st Airborne Corps, 1943–45; Comdt Indian Signal Trng Centre, 1946–47; Dep. Comdt, Sch. of Signals, 1949–52; Dep. Dir of Signals, WO, 1952–54; CSO, Northern Army Gp, 1954–57; Signal Officer-in-Chief, WO, 1957–60, retired 1960. Col Comdt, Royal Signals, 1960–66. Comr for Dorset, St John Ambulance, 1968–76. KStJ 1986. *Address:* Galsworthy House, 177 Kingston Hill, Kingston upon Thames, Surrey KT2 7LX. *T:* (020) 8547 2640. *Died 21 Dec. 2001.*

MODIGLIANI, Prof. Franco; Institute Professor Emeritus, Massachusetts Institute of Technology, since 1988 (Professor of Economics and Finance, 1962–70; Institute Professor, 1970–88); *b* Rome, 18 June 1918; *s* of Enrico Modigliani and Olga (*née* Flaschel); *m* 1939, Serena Calabi; two *s. Educ:* Univ. of Rome (DJur 1939) DSocSci New Sch. for Social Research, New York, 1944. Instr in Economics and Statistics, New Jersey Coll. for Women, 1942; Instr, Associate in Economics and Statistics, Bard Coll. of Columbia Univ., 1942–44; Lectr, 1943–44, Asst Prof. of Math. Econ. and Econometrics, 1946–48, New Sch. for Social Research; Res. Associate and Chief Statistician, Inst. of World Affairs, NY, 1945–48; Res. Consultant, Cowles Commn for Res. in Economics, Univ. of Chicago, 1949–54; Associate Prof., 1949, Prof. of Economics, 1950–52, Univ. of Illinois; Prof. of Econ. and Indust. Admin, Carnegie Inst. of Technology, 1952–60; Prof. of Economics, Northwestern Univ., 1960–62. Social Science Research Council: Mem., Bd of Dirs, 1963–68; Mem., Cttee on Econ. Stability and Growth, 1970–; Jt Chm., Adv. Sub-Cttee on MIT-Pennsylvania SSRC Model, 1970–81; Mem., Sub-Cttee on Monetary Res., 1970–77. Academic Consultant, Bd of Governors, Federal Reserve System, 1966–; Sen. Adviser, Brookings Panel on Econ. Activity, 1971–; Consultant, Bank of Italy, Rome;

Mem., Consiglio Italiano per le Scienze Sociali, 1974–; Perm. Mem., Conf. on Income and Wealth, Nat. Bureau of Econ. Res. Mem., Adv. Bd, Jl of Money, Credit and Banking, 1969–. Mem., Nat. Acad. of Scis, 1973–; Fellow, Econometric Soc., 1949; Fellow, 1960–, Council Mem., 1978–80, Amer. Acad. of Arts and Scis. Numerous hon. degrees. Nobel Prize in Economic Science, 1985. Kt Grand Cross, Italy, 1985. *Publications:* National Incomes and International Trade (with Hans Neisser), 1953; (jtly) Planning Production, Inventories and Work Forces, 1960; (with Kalman J. Cohen) The Role of Anticipations and Plans in Economic Behavior and their Use in Economic Analysis and Forecasting, 1961; (with Ezio Tarantelli) Mercato del Lavoro, Distribuzione del Reddito e Consumi Privati, 1975; (ed with Donald Lessard) New Mortgage Designs for Stable Housing in an Inflationary Environment, 1975; The Collected Papers of Franco Modigliani, vols 1, 2, 3, 1980, vols 4, 5, 1989 (trans. Hungarian, 1988); The Debate Over Stabilization Policy, 1986; Il caso Italia, 1986; Reddito, Interesse, Inflazione, 1987; (with Frank Fabozzi) Capital Markets—Institutions and Instruments, 1991; Consumo, Risparmio, Finanza, 1992; (with Frank Fabozzi) Mortgage and Mortgage Backed Securities Markets, 1992; Avventure di un Economista (autobiog.), 1999 (trans. English, 2001); contribs to Corriere Della Sera, periodicals and learned jls. *Address:* Massachusetts Institute of Technology, Sloan School of Management, Cambridge, MA 02139, USA.
Died 25 Sept. 2003.

MODISE, Johannes, (Joe); Minister of Defence, Republic of South Africa, 1994–99; b Doornfontein, 23 May 1999; m Jackie Sedibe; two d; three d from previous m (and two s decd). *Educ:* Fred Clark Meml Sch., Nancefield. Commander, Umkhonto we Sizwe, 1963; worked for underground movement and went into exile, 1963; returned to SA, 1990. African National Congress: Mem., NEC, 1963–; Mem., Nat. Wkg Cttee, 1963–; mem., first gp of ANC negotiators to hold talks with Pretoria govt, March 1990; mem., negotiating team of TEC Sub-Council on Defence until elections, April 1994. Grand Cross (Gold), Order of the Star (South Africa), 2001. *Address:* c/o African National Congress, 51 Plein Street, Johannesburg 2001, South Africa.
Died 26 Nov. 2001.

MOGG, Gen. Sir (Herbert) John, GCB 1972 (KCB 1966; CB 1964); CBE 1960; DSO and Bar, 1944; Deputy Supreme Allied Commander, Europe, 1973–76; b 17 Feb. 1913; s of late Capt. H. B. Mogg, MC and Alice Mary (née Ballard); m 1939, Cecilia Margaret Molesworth; three s. *Educ:* Malvern Coll.; RMC Sandhurst. Coldstream Guards, 1933–35; RMC Sandhurst (Sword of Honour) 1935–37; commissioned Oxfordshire and Buckinghamshire Light Infantry, 1937. Served War of 1939–45 (despatches twice, 1944); comd 9 DLI (NW Europe), 1944–45; Instructor, Staff Coll., 1948–50; Commander 10th Parachute Bn, 1950–52; Chief Instructor, School of Infantry, Warminster, 1952–54; Instructor (GSO1), Imperial Defence Coll., 1954–56; Comdr, Commonwealth Brigade Gp, Malaya, 1958–60; Meritorious Medal (Perak, Malaya); Dir of Combat Development, War Office, 1961–62; Comdt, Royal Military Academy, Sandhurst, 1963–66; Comdr 1st (British) Corps, 1966–68; GOC-in-C Southern Comd, 1968; GOC-in-C Army Strategic Comd, 1968–70; Adjutant-Gen., MoD (Army), 1970–73. ADC Gen. to the Queen, 1971–74. Col Comdt: Army Air Corps, 1963–74; The Royal Green Jackets, 1965–73; Hon. Col, 10th Parachute Bn, TA, 1973–78. Kermit Roosevelt Lectr, 1969. President: Army Cricket Assoc.; Army Saddle Club, 1969; Army Boxing Assoc., 1970; Army Parachute Assoc., 1971; BHS, 1972; Ex Services Mental Welfare Soc.; Army Benevolent Fund, 1980– (Chm., 1976); Normandy Veterans Assoc., 1982–; Chairman: Army Free Fall Parachute Assoc., 1970; Army Football Assoc., 1960–63; Royal Soldiers' Daughters Sch., 1976; Operation Drake for Young Explorers, 1978–; Operation Drake Fellowship,

1980–83; Royal Internat. Horse Show, 1979; Vice-Pres., Operation Raleigh. Pres., Council Services Kinema Corp., 1970. Dir, Lloyds Bank S Midland Regional Bd, 1976. Member Council: Wessex TA&VRA, 1976; British Atlantic Cttee, 1977; Fairbridge Drake Soc., 1987. Comr, Royal Hospital Chelsea, 1976. Governor: Malvern College, 1967; Bradfield College, 1977; Chm. of Governors, Icknield Sch., 1981–. Hon. Liveryman, Fruiterers' Co. DL Oxfordshire, 1979, Vice Lord-Lieut, 1979–89. *Recreations:* cricket, most field sports, helicopter pilot. *Address:* Church Close, Watlington, Oxon OX9 5QR. *Clubs:* Army and Navy, Flyfishers', MCC, Cavalry and Guards, Pitt.
Died 28 Oct. 2001.

MOGG, Sir John; see Mogg, Sir H. J.

MOISEIWITSCH, Tanya, (Mrs Felix Krish), CBE 1976; designer for the theatre; b 3 Dec. 1914; d of late Benno Moiseiwitsch, CBE, and 1st wife, Daisy Kennedy; m 1942, Felix Krish (decd). *Educ:* various private schs; Central School of Arts and Crafts, London; scenic painting student at Old Vic, London. Abbey Theatre, Dublin, 1935–39; Q. Theatre, 1940; 1st West End prod. Golden Cuckoo, Duchess, 1940; Weekly Repertory, Oxford Playhouse, 1941–44. Stage designs include: Bless the Bride, Adelphi, 1947; Peter Grimes, Covent Garden, 1947; Beggar's Opera, English Opera Group, Aldeburgh Festival, 1948; Treasure Hunt, Apollo, 1949; Home at Seven, Wyndham's, 1950; The Holly and the Ivy, Lyric (Hammersmith) and Duchess, 1950; Captain Carvallo, St James's, 1950; Figure of Fun, Aldwych, 1951. Designed for Old Vic Co., 1944–; at Playhouse, Liverpool, 1944–45; at Theatre Royal, Bristol, 1945–46; productions for Old Vic Company include: (at New Theatre) Uncle Vanya, The Critic, Cyrano de Bergerac, 1945–46, The Cherry Orchard, 1948, A Month in the Country, 1949; (at Old Vic) Midsummer Night's Dream, 1951, Timon of Athens, 1952, Henry VIII, 1953, Two Gentlemen of Verona, 1957. Designed for Royal Shakespeare Theatre, Stratford upon Avon: Henry VIII, 1950; The History Cycle (assisted by Alix Stone), 1951; Othello, 1954; Measure for Measure, 1956; Much Ado about Nothing (scenery), 1958; All's Well that Ends Well, 1959; also for 1st, and subsequent seasons, Shakespearean Festival, Stratford, Ont, incl. Cymbeline, 1970; The Imaginary Invalid, 1974 (Australian tour for Elizabethan Theatre Trust); All's Well that Ends Well, 1977; Mary Stuart (costumes), 1982; Tartuffe, 1983; (with Polly Scranton Bohdanetzky) The Government Inspector, Stratford, Ont, 1985; consultant to designer, Œdipus Rex, Stratford, Ont, 1997; for The Matchmaker, Edinburgh Fest., 1954, and NY, 1955; for Cherry Orchard, Piccolo Teatro, Milan, 1955; for Merchant of Venice, Habimah Theatre, Israel, 1959; Tyrone Guthrie Theatre, Minneapolis, USA: 1963: Hamlet, The Miser, Three Sisters; 1964: St Joan, Volpone; 1965: The Way of the World; Cherry Orchard; 1966: As You Like It; Skin of our Teeth (with Carolyn Parker); 1967: The House of Atreus; 1973: (with J. Jensen) The Government Inspector (costumes); Metropolitan Opera, New York: Peter Grimes, 1967; Rigoletto, 1977; La Traviata, 1981; National Theatre: Volpone, 1968; The Misanthrope, 1973; Phaedra Britannica, 1975; The Double Dealer, 1978; Macook's Corner, Ulster Players, Belfast, 1969; Caucasian Chalk Circle, Sheffield Playhouse, 1969; Swift, Abbey Theatre, Dublin, 1969; Uncle Vanya, Minneapolis, 1969; The Barber of Seville, Brighton Festival, 1971; The Misanthrope, St James' Theater, NY, 1975; The Voyage of Edgar Allan Poe (world première), Minnesota Opera Co., USA, 1976; Œdipus the King and Œdipus at Colonus (costumes and masks), Adelaide Fest., 1978; Red Roses for Me, Abbey Theatre, Dublin, 1980; The Clandestine Marriage, Compass Theatre Co. tour and Albery, 1984. Cons. designer, Crucible Theatre, Sheffield, 1971–73. Designed costumes for Granada TV, King Lear, 1983. Assoc. Dir Laureate, Stratford Festival, Canada. Diplôme d'Honneur, Canadian Conference of the Arts; Hon. Fellow, Ontario Coll. of Art, 1979. Hon. DLitt: Birmingham, 1964;

Waterloo, Ont, 1977; Minnesota, 1994; Hon. LLD Toronto, 1988. Hon. OC 2003. *Address:* 17B St Alban's Studios, St Alban's Grove, W8 5BT.

Died 19 Feb. 2003.

MOLLOY, Baron *cr* 1981 (Life Peer), of Ealing in Greater London; **William John Molloy**, TD 1945; FRGS; *b* 26 Oct. 1918; *m* 1st, 1946, Eva Lewis (*d* 1980); one *d*; 2nd, 1980, Doris Paines (marr. diss. 1986), *d* of Joseph Foxton. *Educ:* elementary sch., Swansea; University Coll., Swansea (Political Economy, extra-mural). Served TA, 1938, Field Co., RE, 1939–46. Member: TGWU, 1936–46; Civil Service Union, 1946–52; Co-op and USDAW, 1952; Parliamentary Adviser: COHSE, 1974–; Civil Service Union, 1974–79. Editor, Civil Service Review, 1947–52; Chm., Staff-Side Whitley Council, Germany and Austria Sections, FO, 1948–52, and Staff-Side Lectr, 1946–52. Member: Fulham Borough Council, 1954–62 (Leader, 1959–62); Fulham and Hammersmith Council, 1962–66. MP (Lab) Ealing N, 1964–79; PPS to Minister of Posts and Telecom., 1969–70. Former Vice-Chm., Parly Labour Party Gp for Common Market and European Affairs; Chm., PLP Social Services Gp, 1974; Parly Adviser, London Trades Council Transport Cttee, 1968–79; Mem., House of Commons Estimates Cttee, 1968–70; Chm., British Tunisia Soc., 1987–; Vice-Chm., All Party British/ Tunisian Parly Gp, 1987–. Member: CPA, 1964; IPU, 1964 (Mem. Exec., 1984–); Assemblies, Council of Europe and WEU, 1969–73; Mem., Parly and Scientific Cttee, 1982–; EC Mem., CAABU. MEP, 1976–79. Political Consultant: Confedn of Health Service Employees, 1979–; British Library Assoc., 1984–; Consultant and Adviser to Arab League, 1982–88. Vice-Pres., and a Trustee, Health Visitors Assoc., 1987–. Pres., Metropolitan Area,1984–, and Nat. Vice Pres., 1993–, Royal British Legion. Hon. Life Pres., London Univ. Debating Soc., 1970; Hon. Pres., London Univ. Union, 1983–; Hon. Patron, Stirling Univ. Debating Soc., 1991–; Mem. Court, Reading Univ., 1968–. FRGS 1967 (former Mem. Exec. Council); Fellow, World Assoc. of Arts and Sciences, 1982. Hon. Fellow, UC of Swansea, Wales, 1987; Hon. Associate, BVA, 1988. *Recreations:* music, collecting dictionaries. *Address:* 2a Uneeda Drive, Greenford, Middx UB6 8QB. *T:* (office) (020) 7219 6710; (home) (020) 8578 7736. *Died 26 May 2001.*

MONCREIFF, 5th Baron *cr* 1873; **Harry Robert Wellwood Moncreiff;** Bt (NS) 1626, (UK) 1871; Lt-Col (Hon.) RASC, retired; *b* 4 Feb. 1915; *s* of 4th Baron Moncreiff and Lucy Vida (*née* Lechmere-Anderson); *S* father, 1942; *m* 1952, Enid Marion Watson (*d* 1985), *o d* of Major H. W. Locke, Belmont, Dollar; one *s. Educ:* Fettes Coll., Edinburgh. Served War of 1939–45 (despatches). Retired, 1958. *Recreations:* Rugby football, tennis, shooting. *Heir: s* Hon. Rhoderick Harry Wellwood Moncreiff [*b* 22 March 1954; *m* 1982, Alison Elizabeth Anne, *e d* of late James Duncan Alastair Ross; two *s*]. *Address:* Tulliebole Castle, Fossoway, Kinross-shire KY13 7QN. *T:* (01577) 840236. *Died 22 April 2002.*

MONTEFIORE, Rt Rev. Hugh William, MA, BD; Hon. DD; Hon. Assistant Bishop, Diocese of Southwark, since 1987; *b* 12 May 1920; *s* of late Charles Sebag-Montefiore, OBE, and Muriel Alice Ruth Sebag-Montefiore; *m* 1945, Elisabeth Mary Macdonald Paton (*d* 1999), *d* of late Rev. William Paton, DD, and Mrs Grace Paton; three *d. Educ:* Rugby Sch.; St John's Coll., Oxford (Hon. Fellow, 1981). Served during war, 1940–45; Capt. RA (Royal Bucks Yeo). Deacon 1949, priest 1950. Curate, St George's, Jesmond, Newcastle, 1949–51; Chaplain and Tutor, Westcott House, Cambridge, 1951–53; Vice-Principal, 1953–54; Examining Chaplain: to Bishop of Newcastle, 1953–70; to Bishop of Worcester, 1957–60; to Bishop of Coventry, 1957–70; to Bishop of Blackburn, 1966–70; Fellow and Dean of Gonville and Caius Coll., 1954–63; Lectr in New Testament, Univ. of Cambridge, 1959–63; Vicar of Great Saint Mary's, Cambridge, 1963–70; Canon Theologian of Coventry,

1959–70; Hon. Canon of Ely, 1969–70; Bishop Suffragan of Kingston-upon-Thames, 1970–78; Bishop of Birmingham, 1978–87. Mem., Archbishops' Commn on Christian Doctrine, 1967–76; Chm., General Synod Bd for Social Responsibility, 1983–87. Pres., Heathrow Assoc. for Reduction of Aircraft Noise, 1976–78; Chairman: Indep. Commn on Transport, 1973; Pedestrians Assoc., 1975–78; Transport 2000, 1987–92; Friends of the Earth Trust, 1992–98; Nat. Trust for the Homeless, 1992–96; Natural Justice, 2000–. Hon. Fellow, Gonville and Caius Coll., Cambridge, 2000. Hon. DD: Aberdeen, 1976; Birmingham, 1985. *Publications:* (contrib.) The Historic Episcopate and the Fullness of the Church, 1954; To Help You To Pray, 1957; (contrib.) Soundings, 1962; Josephus and the New Testament, 1962; (with H. E. W. Turner) Thomas and the Evangelists, 1962; Beyond Reasonable Doubt, 1963; (contrib.) God, Sex and War, 1963; Awkward Questions on Christian Love, 1964; A Commentary on the Epistle to the Hebrews, 1964; Truth to Tell, 1966; (ed) We Must Love One Another Or Die, 1966; (contrib.) The Responsible Church, 1966; Remarriage and Mixed Marriage, 1967; (contrib.) Journeys in Belief, 1968; (ed) Sermons From Great St Mary's, 1968; My Confirmation Notebook, 1968; The Question Mark, 1969; Can Man Survive, 1970; (ed) More Sermons From Great St Mary's, 1971; Doom or Deliverance?, 1972; (ed) Changing Directions, 1974; (ed) Man and Nature, 1976; Apocalypse, 1976; (ed) Nuclear Crisis, 1977; (ed) Yes to Women Priests, 1978; Taking our Past into our Future, 1978; Paul the Apostle, 1981; Jesus Across the Centuries, 1983; The Probability of God, 1985; So Near And Yet So Far, 1986; Communicating the Gospel in a Scientific Age, 1988; God, Sex and Love, 1989; Christianity and Politics, 1990; Reclaiming the High Ground, 1990; (ed) The Gospel and Contemporary Culture, 1992; The Womb and The Tomb, 1992; Preaching for Our Planet, 1992; Credible Christianity, 1994; Oh God, What Next?, 1995; Time to Change, 1996; On Being a Jewish Christian, 1998; The Paranormal: a bishop investigates, 2002; Looking Afresh: soundings in creative dissent, 2002; The Miracles of Jesus, 2005; contribs to New Testament and Theological jls. *Address:* White Lodge, 23 Bellevue Road, Wandsworth Common, SW17 7EB. *Clubs:* Beefsteak, Royal Commonwealth Society. *Died 13 May 2005.*

MONTEITH, Rt Rev. George Rae, BA; Assistant Bishop of Auckland, 1965–76; *b* 14 Feb. 1904; *s* of John Hodge Monteith and Ellen (*née* Hall); *m* 1st, 1931, Kathleen Methven Mules; two *s* one *d*; 2nd, 1982, Hilary Llewellyn Etherington. *Educ:* St John's Coll., Auckland; Univ. of NZ (BA 1927). Deacon, 1928; priest, 1929; Curate: St Matthew's, Auckland, 1928–30; Stoke-on-Trent, 1931–33; Vicar of: Dargaville, NZ, 1934–37; Mt Eden, Auckland, NZ, 1937–49; St Mary's Cathedral Parish, Auckland, 1949–69; Dean of Auckland, 1949–69; Vicar-General, 1963–76. *Publications:* Enjoy Europe With Me, 1993; More Travels with Monty and Other Stories, 1996; The Cathedral of the Holy Trinity, Auckland, New Zealand, 1997. *Address:* 10A Mahoe Avenue, Remuera, Auckland 1005, NZ. *T:* (9) 5221188; *e-mail:* hilarymonteith@xtra.co.nz. *Died 12 June 2003.*

MONTGOMERY, (Charles) John, CBE 1977; Director: Lloyds Bank Plc, 1972–84 (a Vice-Chairman, 1978–84); Lloyds Bank International, 1978–84; Yorkshire Bank, 1980–84; *b* 18 Feb. 1917; *s* of late Rev. Charles James Montgomery; *m* 1950, Gwenneth Mary McKendrick; two *d. Educ:* Colwyn Bay Grammar School. Served with RN, 1940–46. Entered Lloyds Bank, 1935; Jt Gen. Manager, 1968; Asst Chief Gen. Manager, 1970; Dep. Chief Gen. Manager, 1973; Chief Gen. Manager, 1973–78. Pres., Inst. of Bankers, 1976–77, Vice Pres., 1977–. Chm., Chief Exec. Officers' Cttee, Cttee of London Clearing Bankers, 1976–78. *Recreations:* walking, photography, travel. *Address:* High Cedar, 6 Cedar Copse, Bickley, Kent BR1 2NY. *T:* (020) 8467 2410. *Clubs:* Naval, Bankers. *Died 29 May 2001.*

MONTGOMERY, Prof. Desmond Alan Dill, CBE 1981 (MBE 1943); MD; FRCP, FRCPI; Chairman, Northern Ireland Council for Postgraduate Medical Education, 1979–87; *b* 6 June 1916; 3rd *s* of late Dr and Mrs J. Howard Montgomery, China and Belfast; *m* 1941, Dr Susan Holland, 2nd *d* of late Mr and Mrs F. J. Holland, Belfast; one *s* one *d. Educ:* Inchmarlo Prep Sch.; Campbell Coll.; QUB (3rd, 4th and final yr scholarships; MB, BCh, BAO 1st Cl. Hons 1940; MD (Gold Medal) 1946). Sinclair Medal in Surgery, Butterworth Prize in Medicine, Prize in Mental Disease, QUB. MRCP 1948, FRCP 1964; FRCPI 1975; FRCOG (*ae*) 1981. Served War, RAMC, 1941–46: Temp. Major India Comd; DADMS GHQ India, 1943–45. House Physician and Surgeon, Royal Victoria Hosp., Belfast, 1940–41, Registrar, 1946; Registrar, Royal Postgrad. Med. Sch. and Hammersmith Hosp., and Nat. Heart Hosp., London, 1946–48; Royal Victoria Hospital, Belfast: Sen. Registrar, 1948–51; Consultant Physician, 1951–79, Hon. Consultant 1980–; Physician i/c Sir George E. Clark Metabolic Unit, 1958–79; Endocrinologist, Royal Maternity Hosp., Belfast, 1958–79; Hon. Reader in Endocrinol., Dept of Medicine, QUB, 1969–75, Hon. Prof., 1975–. Hon. Secretary: Royal Victoria Med. Staff Cttee, 1964–66 (Chm., 1975–77); Ulster Med. Soc., 1954–58 (Pres., 1975–76). Member: NI Council for Health and Personal Social Services, 1974–83 (Chm., Central Med. Adv. Cttee, 1974–83, Mem. 1983–87); NI Med. Manpower Adv. Cttee, 1974–83; Distinction and Meritorious Awards Cttee, 1975–87 (Chm., 1982–87); Faculty of Medicine, QUB, 1969–87 (Chm., Ethical Cttee, 1975–81); Senate, QUB, 1979–96; GMC, 1979–84; Pres., QUB Assoc., 1988–89. Member: BMA; Assoc. of Physicians of GB and NI; Eur. Thyroid Assoc.; Corrigan Club (Chm., 1969); Irish Endocrine Soc. (1st Chm., Founder Mem.); Internat. Soc. for Internal Medicine; formerly Mem., Eur. Soc. for Study of Diabetes; Hon. Mem., British Dietetic Assoc. Lectured in USA, India, Greece, Australia and Nigeria; visited Russia on behalf of British Council, 1975. Pres., Belfast City Mission, 1973–92; Mem., Bd of Trustees, Presbyterian Church in Ireland. DSc (*hc*) NUI, 1980. Jt Editor, Ulster Med. Jl, 1974–84. *Publications:* (contrib.) Whita's Dictionary of Treatment, 1957; (contrib.) Good Health and Diabetes, 1961, 3rd edn 1976; (contrib.) R. Smith, Progress in Clinical Surgery, 1961; (with R. B. Welbourn) Clinical Endocrinology for Surgeons, 1963; (contrib.) Progress in Neurosurgery, 1964; (with R. B. Welbourn) Medical and Surgical Endocrinology, 1975; (contrib.) M. D. Vickers, Medicine for Anaesthetists, 1977; articles in med. jls on endocrinology, diabetes mellitus and related subjects. *Recreations:* travel, photography, music, gardening, philately. *Address:* 59 Church Road, Newtownbreda, Belfast BT8 7AN. *T:* (028) 9064 8326; 15 Carrickmore Road, Ballycastle BT54 6QS. *T:* (028) 2076 2361.   *Died 7 July 2003.*

MONTGOMERY, John; *see* Montgomery, C. J.

MONTMORENCY, Sir Arnold Geoffroy de; *see* de Montmorency.

MOODY, Peter Edward, CBE 1981; Director: Prudential Corporation, 1981–91 (Deputy Chairman, 1984–88); The Laird Group, 1981–92; *b* 26 Aug. 1918; *s* of late Edward Thomas Moody and Gladys (*née* Flint); *m* 1945, Peggy Elizabeth (decd), *d* of Edward Henry Causer and Elizabeth Theodora (*née* Finke); one *s* one *d. Educ:* Christ's Coll., Finchley. FIA. Prudential Assurance Co. Ltd: Dep. Investment Manager, 1960; Jt Sec. and Chief Investment Manager, 1973–80; Jt Sec. and Group Chief Investment Manager, Prudential Corp., 1979–80; Director: Triton Petroleum Ltd, 1971–89; United Dominions Trust, 1972–81; British American and General Trust, 1981–85; Inmos International, 1981–84; 3i Group plc (formerly FFI, then Investors in Industry), 1981–89; Equity Trustee Ltd, 1985–90. Mem., PO Bd, 1981–85. Trustee, Thalidomide Trust, 1984–93. Institute of Actuaries: Hon. Sec., 1968–70; Vice-Pres., 1972–75; Pres., 1978–80; Master,

Worshipful Co. of Actuaries, 1988–89. *Publications:* contrib. Jl of Inst. of Actuaries. *Address:* 46 Brookmans Avenue, Brookmans Park, Herts AL9 7QJ.
                                                    Died 12 May 2004.

MOORE, Alexander Wyndham Hume S.; *see* Stewart-Moore.

MOORE, Brian Baden; Football Commentator/ Presenter: London Weekend Television, 1968–98; The Match, Independent Television, 1988–98; *b* 28 Feb. 1932; *s* of Baden Kimberley Moore and Elsie Norah (*née* Sharpe); *m* 1955, Betty (*née* Cole); two *s. Educ:* Cranbrook Sch., Kent. Sports Sub-Editor, World Sports, 1954–56; journalist: Exchange Telegraph, 1956–58; The Times, 1958–61; Football Commentator/Presenter: BBC Radio, 1961–68; Mid-Week Sports Special, Thames TV, 1978–86; Presenter, Brian Moore Meets (TV documentary series), 1979–84. *Publications:* The Big Matches 1970–1980, 1980; The Final Score (autobiog.), 1999. *Recreations:* being at home, animal care, golf. *Address:* c/o Sommerfield Ltd, 35 Old Queen Street, SW1H 9JD.
                                                    Died 1 Sept. 2001.

MOORE, Air Vice-Marshal Charles Stuart, CB 1962; OBE 1945; *b* London, 27 Feb. 1910; *s* of late E. A. Moore and E. B. Moore (*née* Druce); *m* 1st, 1937, Anne (*d* 1957), *d* of Alfred Rogers; 2nd, 1961, Jean Mary (marr. diss. 1993), *d* of John Cameron Wilson; one *d. Educ:* Sutton Valence Sch.; RAF Coll., Cranwell. Commissioned in General Duties Branch, Dec. 1930; served in Egypt, 1932–34 and 1936–41; Sqdn Ldr 1938; Sudan, 1941–42; Wing Comdr 1940; 11 Group, 1943–44; Gp Capt. 1943; OC, OTU, 1944–45; Gp Capt. Org., HQFC, 1945–46; Staff Coll., Bracknell, 1946–47; Dep. Dir Plans, Air Ministry, London, 1947–49; Student, US National War Coll., Washington, 1949–50; Staff of USAF Air War Coll., Alabama, 1950–53; Air Commodore, 1953; AOC 66 Group, 1953–55; Dir of Intelligence, Air Ministry, London, 1955–58; AOA, NEAF, 1958–62; Actg Air Vice-Marshal, 1960; retired, 1962. Joined HM Foreign Service, Oct. 1962; posted to British Embassy, Tehran, Iran; left HM Diplomatic Service, March 1969. *Recreations:* music, photography and travelling. *Address:* Ferndene, The Avenue, Crowthorne, Berks RG45 6PB. *T:* (01344) 772300. *Club:* Royal Air Force.   *Died 26 May 2005.*

MOORE, Dudley Stuart John, CBE 2001; actor (stage, films, TV and radio); composer (film music and incidental music for plays, etc); *b* 19 April 1935; *s* of late Ada Francis and John Moore; *m* 1st, 1968, Suzy Kendall (marr. diss.); 2nd, 1975, Tuesday Weld (marr. diss.); one *s*; 3rd, 1988, Brogan Lane (marr. diss.); 4th, 1994, Nicole Rothschild (marr. diss.); one *s. Educ:* County High Sch., Dagenham, Essex; Guildhall Sch.; Magdalen Coll., Oxford (BA, BMus). *Stage:* Beyond the Fringe, 1960–62 (London), 1962–64 (Broadway, New York); Behind the Fringe, 1971–72; Good Evening, NY, 1974; Mikado (Los Angeles, UK/LA Fest.), 1988; Vic Lewis, John Dankworth Jazz Bands, 1959–60; composed incidental music, Royal Court Theatre (various plays), 1958–60; Play it again Sam, Woody Allen, Globe Theatre, 1970; Behind the Fridge, Cambridge Theatre, 1972–73; Good Evening, Broadway, New York, 1973–74; tour of USA, 1975. *BBC TV:* own series with Peter Cook: Not only . . . but also, 1964, 1966, 1970; *series:* It's Lulu, not to mention Dudley Moore, 1973; in the sixties, *ITV:* Goodbye again; Royal Command Performance; *series:* Orchestra! (co-presenter with Sir Georg Solti), 1991; Concerto!, 1993. Various TV and radio guest spots with Jazz piano trio. *Films:* The Wrong Box, 1966; 30 is a Dangerous Age Cynthia, 1967; Bedazzled, 1968; Monte Carlo or Bust, The Bed-sitting room, 1969; Alice in Wonderland, 1972; The Hound of the Baskervilles, 1977; Foul Play, "10", 1979; Wholly Moses, 1980; Arthur, 1981; Lovesick, Romantic Comedy, 1982; Unfaithfully Yours, Best Defense, 1983; Mickey & Maude, 1984; Santa Claus—The Movie, 1985; Like Father Like Son, 1987; Arthur 2—On The Rocks, 1988; Crazy People, 1990; Blame it on the Bellboy, 1992. *Film* *music* composed for: Bedazzled, 30 is a dangerous age Cynthia, The Staircase, Inadmissable Evidence, Six Weeks, and various TV films. *Publications:* Dud and Pete: The Dagenham Dialogues, 1971, new edn 1988; Musical Bumps, 1986; The Complete Beyond the Fringe, 1987. *Recreations:* films, theatre, music.

Died 27 March 2002.

MOORE, Sir Harry; *see* Moore, Sir H. R.

MOORE, Sir Henry Roderick, (Sir Harry), Kt 1978; CBE 1971; Chairman, Molins plc, 1978–86; *b* 19 Aug. 1915; *er s* of late Roderick Edward Moore; *m* 1944, Beatrice Margaret, *d* of late Major J. W. Seigne; one *s* one *d. Educ:* Malvern Coll.; Pembroke Coll., Cambridge. Qualified as Mem. of Institute of Chartered Accountants, 1939. Served War of 1939–45: North Africa, Italy, Europe; 2nd Lieut Royal Fusiliers, 1939; Lt-Col 1944. Director: Hill Samuel Group Ltd, 1949–80; Estates House Investment Trust Ltd, 1975–76; Chairman: Associated Engineering Ltd, 1955–75; Staveley Industries, 1970–79; Vice-Chm., Philip Hill Investment Trust plc, 1949–86. Dep. Chm., Adv. Panel on Institutional Finance in New Towns, 1970–81. Chm., Bd of Governors, The London Hospital, 1960–74; Mem. Council, British Heart Foundn, 1961; Chm., North East Thames RHA, 1974–84. Trustee, Countryside Foundn, 1986–97. High Sheriff of Bucks, 1966. *Address:* 15 Chesterfield House, South Audley Street, W1Y 5TB. *T:* (020) 7491 0666. *Clubs:* White's, Pratt's; Leander; Rand (Johannesburg).

Died 7 May 2001.

MOORE, Rt Rev. James Edward; Bishop of Connor, 1995–2001; *b* 1933; *m* 1962, Pamela Mary Fetherston; one *s* one *d. Educ:* Trinity Coll., Dublin (BA 1954; MA 1964). Ordained deacon, 1956, priest, 1957; Assistant Curate: Knock, 1956–60; St Comgall, Bangor, 1960–62; Priest-in-charge, Belvoir, 1962–68; Incumbent: Groomsport, 1968–75; Dundela, 1975–95; Archdeacon of Down, 1989–95. Canon, 1985–89, Treasurer, 1987–89, Down Cathedral. *Address:* 1 Plantation Road, Bangor, Co. Down BT19 6AF. *T:* (028) 9147 7295.

Died 16 March 2005.

MOORE, Dr John Michael; JP; Headmaster, The King's School, Worcester, 1983–98; *b* 12 Dec. 1935; *s* of late Roy Moore, CBE; *m* 1960, Jill Mary Maycock (*d* 1995); one *s*. *Educ:* Rugby Sch.; Clare Coll., Cambridge (John Stewart of Rannoch Scholar, 1956; George Charles Winter Warr Scholar, 1957; 1st Cl. Hons Classical Tripos; MA; PhD 1960). Asst Master: Winchester Coll., 1960–64; Radley Coll., 1964–83; Jun. Fellow, Center for Hellenic Studies, Washington, DC, 1970–71. Hon. Fellow, Inst. for Advanced Res. in the Humanities, Birmingham Univ., 1986. Governor: Cranleigh Sch., 1998–; Woodhouse Grove Sch., 1999–; Cokethorpe Sch., 1999–. FRSA 1994. JP Worcester City, 1986. Silver Jubilee Medal, 1977. *Publications:* The Manuscript Tradition of Polybius, 1965; (ed with P. A. Brunt) Res Gestae Divi Augusti, 1967, repr. with corrections 1973; (with J. J. Evans) Variorum, 1969; Timecharts, 1969; Aristotle and Xenophon on Democracy and Oligarchy, 1975, 2nd edn 1983; articles and reviews in Gnomon, Jl Soc. for Promotion of Hellenic Studies, Classical Qly, Greek, Roman and Byzantine Studies. *Recreations:* painting, gardening, travel. *Address:* Rattenbury House, Church Lane, Ombersley, Droitwich, Worcs WR9 0ER. *Died 4 April 2005.*

MOORE, Jonathan Guy J.; *see* James-Moore.

MOORE, Richard Valentine, GC 1940; CBE 1963; FIMechE; FIEE; Managing Director (Reactor Group), 1961–76, Member, 1971–76, UK Atomic Energy Authority; retired; *b* 14 Feb. 1916; *s* of Randall and Ellen Moore; *m* 1944, Ruby Edith Fair (decd); two *s* (and one *s* decd). *Educ:* Strand Sch., London; London Univ. (BSc (Eng)). County of London Electric Supply Co., 1936–39. RNVR, 1939–46: HMS Effingham, 1939–40; HMS President, 1940–41; HMS Dido, 1942–44; British

Admiralty Delegn, Washington, DC, 1944–46; Lieut-Comdr 1944. AERE Harwell, 1946–53; Dept of Atomic Energy, Risley, 1953; Design and Construction of Calder Hall, 1953–57; Chief Design Engineer, 1955; UKAEA, 1955; Dir of Reactor Design, 1958–61. Faraday Lectr, 1966. Hon. DTech Bradford, 1970. *Publications:* various papers to technical institutions. *Recreations:* golf, gardening. *Address:* Culleen House, Cann Lane, Appleton, Ches WA4 5NQ. *T:* (01925) 261023. *Club:* Naval.

Died 25 April 2003.

MOORE, Thomas William; JP; Chairman (since inception) of Trojan Metals Ltd, Carseview Holdings Ltd, Dundee Timber Market Ltd, Inverlaw Property Co. Ltd, 1974–2002; *b* 9 Aug. 1925; Scottish; *m* 1945, Mary Kathleen Thompson; four *s* two *d. Educ:* Stobswell Secondary Sch.; Leicester Coll. of Art and Technology. MCMI. Contested (Lab), Perth and East Perthshire, 1959. Lord Provost of Dundee, and Lord Lieutenant of County of City of Dundee, 1973–75; Chairman: Tay Road Bridge Jt Cttee, 1973; Tayside Steering Cttee, 1973. FInstD. *Recreations:* golf, reading. *Address:* Cidhmore, 492A Perth Road, Dundee DD2 1LR. *Club:* Royal Automobile.

Died 23 Sept. 2004.

MOORER, Admiral Thomas Hinman; Defense Distinguished Service Medals, 1973 and 1974; Navy DSM 1965, 1967, 1968, 1970; Army DSM 1974; Air Force DSM 1974; Silver Star 1942; Legion of Merit, 1945; DFC 1942; Purple Heart, 1942; Presidential Unit Citation, 1942; Board Member: Blount Inc.; Fairchild Industries; USLICO; CACI; *b* Mount Willing, Alabama, 9 Feb. 1912; *s* of Dr R. R. Moorer and Hulda Hill Hinson, Eufaula, Ala; *m* 1935, Carrie Ellen Foy Moorer; three *s* one *d. Educ:* Cloverdale High Sch., Montgomery, Ala; USN Acad.; Naval Aviation Trg Sch.; Naval War Coll. First ship, 1933; serving at Pearl Harbour in Fleet Air Wing, Dec. 1941; Pacific and East Indies areas, 1942; Mining Observer, C-in-C, US Fleet in UK, 1943; Strategic Bombing Survey in Japan, 1945; Naval Aide to Asst Sec. of Navy (Air), 1956; CO, USS Salisbury Sound, 1957; Special Asst to CNO, 1959; Comdr, Carrier Div. Six, 1960; Dir, Long Range Objectives Group, CNO, 1962; Comdr Seventh Fleet, 1964; C-in-C: US Pacific Fleet, 1965; Atlantic and Atlantic Fleet, and Supreme Allied Commander, Atlantic, 1965–67; Chief of Naval Operations, 1967–70; Chm., Jt Chiefs of Staff, USA, 1970–74, retired US Navy 1974. Captain 1952; Rear-Adm. 1958; Vice-Adm. 1962; Adm. 1964. Enshrined in Nat. Aviation Hall of Fame, 1987; introduced into Naval Aviation Hall of Honor, 1988. Gold Medal, Nat. Football Hall of Fame, 1990. Holds seventeen foreign decorations. Hon. LLD Auburn, 1968; Hon. DH Samford, 1970; Hon. Dr Mil. Science, The Citadel, 1983. *Recreations:* golfing, fishing, hunting. *Clubs:* Brook (New York); International, Army-Navy Town (Washington, DC); US Naval Inst. (Annapolis, Md); Chevy Chase (Chevy Chase, Md). *Died 5 Feb. 2004.*

MOORES, Hon. Frank Duff; formerly Chairman, Executive Committee, Government Consultants International; Chairman and Chief Executive Officer, SSF (Holdings) Inc.; Premier of the Province of Newfoundland, 1972–79; *b* 18 Feb. 1933; *s* of Silas Wilmot Moores and Dorothy Duff Moores; *m* 1st, 1952, Dorothy Elizabeth Pain; one *s* six *d* ; 2nd, 1973, Janis Johnson; one *s*; 3rd, 1982, Beth Champion. *Educ:* United Church Academy, Carbonear; St Andrew's Coll., Aurora, Ont. MP, Canada, for Bonavista-Trinity-Conception, 1968–71; MHA for Humber W, Newfoundland, 1971; Pres., Progressive Conservative Party in Canada, 1969; Leader, Progressive Conservative Party, Newfoundland, 1970–79. Mem., Royal Commn on Economic Prospects of Newfoundland. Director: Council for Canadian Unity; Atlantic Salmon Fedn (Canada). Gov., Olympia Trust. Freemason. Hon. LLD Meml Univ. of Newfoundland, 1975. *Recreations:* tennis, salmon fishing, golf. *Clubs:* Forest and Stream (Montreal); Mid Ocean (Bermuda); Hobe Sound Golf (Florida). *Died 10 July 2005.*

MOOREY, (Peter) Roger (Stuart), DPhil; FBA 1977; FSA; Keeper, Department of Antiquities, Ashmolean Museum, Oxford, 1983–2002; Fellow, Wolfson College, Oxford, 1976–2004, then Emeritus (Senior Research Fellow and Vice-gerent, 2002–04); *b* 30 May 1937; *s* of late Stuart Moorey and Freda (*née* Harris). *Educ:* Mill Hill Sch.; Corpus Christi Coll., Oxford (MA, DPhil). FSA 1967. Nat. Service, 1956–58, Intelligence Corps. Asst Keeper, 1961–73, Sen. Asst Keeper, 1973–82, Ashmolean Museum, Oxford. Editor of Levant, 1968–86. Pres., British Sch. of Archaeology in Jerusalem, 1990–98. *Publications:* Catalogue of the Ancient Persian Bronzes in the Ashmolean Museum, 1971; Ancient Persian Bronzes in the Adam Collection, 1974; Biblical Lands, 1975; Kish Excavations 1923–1933, 1978; Cemeteries of the First Millennium BC at Deve Hüyük, 1980; Excavation in Palestine, 1981; (ed) C. L. Woolley, Ur of the Chaldees, revd edn 1982; (with B. Buchanan) Catalogue of Ancient Near Eastern Seals in the Ashmolean Museum, II, 1984, III, 1988; Materials and Manufacture in Ancient Mesopotamia: the evidence of archaeology and art, 1985; A Century of Biblical Archaeology, 1991; Ancient Mesopotamian Materials and Industries, 1994; Idols of the People: miniature images of clay in the Ancient Near East, 2003; museum booklets and articles in learned jls. *Recreations:* travel, walking. *Address:* 343 Iffley Road, Oxford OX4 4DP. *T:* (01865) 248655.
Died 23 Dec. 2004.

MORAES, Dom; Indian poet, author and columnist; *b* 19 July 1938; *s* of Frank Moraes (Editor of the Indian Express and biographer of Nehru); partner, Judith St John; one *s*; *m* 1970, Leela Naidu (marr. diss.). *Educ:* Jesus Coll., Oxford. Read English, 1956–59. Took up residence in England at age of 16, after world-wide travel and a 2-yr stay in Ceylon. *Publications:* A Beginning (poems), 1957 (Hawthornden Prize, 1958); Gone Away (Travel), 1960; Poems, 1960; John Nobody (poems), 1965; The Brass Serpent (trans. from Hebrew poetry), 1964; Poems 1955–65 (collected poems), 1966; My Son's Father (autobiography), 1968; The People Time Forgot, 1972; The Tempest Within, 1972; A Matter of People, 1974; (ed) Voices for Life (essays), 1975; Mrs Gandhi, 1980; Bombay, 1980; Collected Poems 1957–1987, 1988; Serendip (poems), 1990; Never At Home (autobiog.), 1994; In Cinnamon Shade: new and selected poems, 2001; (ed) The Penguin Book of Indian Journeys, 2001; (with Sarayu Srivatsa) The Long Strider: how Thomas Coryate walked from England to India in the year 1613, 2003.
Died 2 June 2004.

MORGAN, Edwin John; Director, Civil Service Selection Board, 1981–87, retired; *b* 10 Jan. 1927; *s* of Thomas Grosvenor Morgan and Florence (*née* Binmore); *m* 1954, Joyce Beryl, *o d* of Reginald and Gladys Ashurst, Bebington, Wirral; two *s* one *d*. *Educ:* Dauntsey's Sch.; St Edmund Hall, Oxford (Sen. Scholar, BA 1st Cl. Hons 1951). Served Army, Intell. Corps, Palestine and Cyprus, 1944–48. Lecteur d'anglais, Ecole normale supérieure, Paris, 1952; Asst, Dept of French Studies, Glasgow Univ., 1953; Asst Principal, Air Min., 1957, Principal, 1960; MoD, 1965; Registrar, RMCS, 1968; Asst Sec., 1970; CSD, 1971; CS Commn, 1975; Under Sec., 1980; CS Comr, 1980–87. Chm., CS Retirement Fellowship, 1987–92. FIPM 1985. *Recreations:* reading, music, gardening, domesticity. *Address:* Southcote, Petersfield Road, Ropley, Alresford, Hants SO24 0EQ. *T:* (01962) 772321. *Club:* Civil Service. *Died 5 Sept. 2002.*

MORGAN, (Frank) Leslie, CBE 1988 (MBE 1973); Chairman: Morgan Bros (Mid Wales) Ltd, 1959–2000; Development Board for Rural Wales (Mid Wales Development), 1981–89 (Member, 1977–81); *b* 7 Nov. 1926; *s* of Edward Arthur Morgan and Beatrice Morgan; *m* 1962, Victoria Stoker (*née* Jeffery); one *s* two *d*. *Educ:* Llanfair Primary Sch.; Llanfair Grammar Sch.; University College of Wales, Aberystwyth (BA Econ Hons). Post graduate trainee and parts executive in motor industry,

1950–56. Chm. and Pres., Montgomery Conservative Assoc., 1964–81; Mem., Welsh Council, 1970–79; Dep. Chm., Mid Wales New Town Development Corp., 1973–77; Director: Develt Corp. for Wales, 1981–83; Wales Adv. Bd, Abbey National (formerly Abbey National Bldg Soc.), 1982–90; Member: Welsh Development Agency, 1981–89; Wales Tourist Bd, 1982–89; Infrastructure Cttee, BTA, 1982–89; Design Council Welsh Cttee, 1981–85. Pres., Montgomeryshire Agricl Soc., 1986. Pres., Montgomery Cons. Assoc., 1989–92. Chm., Campaign for Montgomeryshire, 1997–98 (Chm. Policy Cttee, 1993–98). *Recreations:* reading, travel, jogging, swimming, cycling. *Address:* Wentworth House, Llangyniew, Welshpool, Powys SY21 9EL. *T:* (01938) 810462.
Died 21 Dec. 2002.

MORGAN, Kenneth Smith; Editor of the Official Report (Hansard), House of Commons, 1979–89; *b* 6 Aug. 1925; *er s* of Edward and Florence Morgan; *m* 1952, Patricia Hunt; one *s* one *d*. *Educ:* Battersea and Dartford Grammar Schools. Commissioned Royal West Kent Regt, 1944; Burma, 1944–46. Weekly newspapers, 1947–51; Derby Evening Telegraph, 1951–52; Reuters Parliamentary Staff, 1952–54; joined Official Report, 1954; Dep. Asst Editor, 1972, Dep. Editor, 1978. Founded Commonwealth Hansard Editors Assoc., 1984. *Publication:* The Falklands Campaign: a digest of parliamentary debates on the Falklands, 1982. *Recreations:* Napoleonic warfare history, model soldiers, cricket, bridge. *Address:* 3 Highfield Road, Bexleyheath, Kent DA6 7HX. *Died 26 March 2005.*

MORGAN, Leslie; see Morgan, F. L.

MORGAN, Rev. Philip; Minister, St Andrew's United Reformed Church, Frognal, London, 1990–95; *b* 22 June 1930; *s* of David Lewis and Pamela Morgan; *m* 1954, Greta Mary Hanson; one *s* one *d*. *Educ:* Overdale Coll.; Selly Oaks Colls; Univ. of Birmingham (BA Hons Theology). Ordained 1952; Ministries: Aberfan, Godreaman, Griffithstown, Merthyr Tydfil and Treharris, 1952–58; Eltham, London, 1958–62; Leicester and South Wigston, 1962–67; General Secretary, Churches of Christ in GB and Ireland, 1967–80; Gen. Sec., BCC, 1980–90. Moderator, URC, 1984–85. Hon. DD Christian Theological Seminary, USA, 1980. *Recreations:* hill walking, Celtic history, steam railways. *Address:* 1 Ellesmere Avenue, Mill Hill, NW7 3EX. *Died 17 Oct. 2005.*

MORGAN, Tom, CBE 1982; DL; Lord Provost of the City of Edinburgh and Lord Lieutenant of the City and County of Edinburgh, 1980–84; *b* 24 Feb. 1914; *s* of Thomas Morgan; *m* 1940, Mary Montgomery (*d* 1991), *d* of Stephen McLauchlan; two *s*. *Educ:* Longside Public Sch., Aberdeenshire; Aberdeen Univ.; W of Scotland Coll. of Agriculture. Unigate Ltd for 36 yrs (Regional Dir for Scotland). Member, Edinburgh Corp., 1954–71 and Edinburgh DC, 1977–84. Chairman: Edinburgh Festival Soc., 1980–84; Edinburgh Mil. Tattoo Policy Cttee, 1980–84. Formerly: Magistrate; City Treasurer; Curator of Patronage, Univ. of Edinburgh; Governor: George Heriot's Trust; Edinburgh and E of Scotland Coll. of Agric.; Dir, Edinburgh Chamber of Commerce and Manufactures; Pres., Edinburgh City Business Club; Gen. Comr of Income Tax; Chm., Edinburgh Abbeyfield Soc. DL Edinburgh, 1984. OStJ. *Recreations:* golf, gardening. *Address:* 400 Lanark Road, Edinburgh EH13 0LX. *T:* (0131) 441 3245. *Died 9 Aug. 2002.*

MORGAN, Prof. Walter Thomas James, CBE 1959; FRS 1949; Director, Lister Institute of Preventive Medicine, London, 1972–75 (Deputy Director, 1952–68); *b* London, 5 Oct. 1900; *s* of Walter and Annie E. Morgan; *m* 1930, Dorothy Irene Price (*d* 1993); one *s* two *d*. *Educ:* Univ. of London (Grocers' Co. Schol., 1925–27; PhD 1927, DSc 1937); DrSc (Tech.) Zürich, 1938. CChem, FRSC (FRIC 1929). Beit Memorial Med. Res. Fellow, 1927–28; First Asst and Biochemist, Lister Institute Serum Dept (Elstree), 1928–37; Rockefeller Research Fellow (Eidgenössische Tech. Hochschule, Zürich), 1937; Reader,

Lister Inst., 1938–51; Prof. of Biochemistry, Univ. of London, 1951–68, then Prof. Emeritus. Hon. Secretary: Biochemical Soc., 1940–45; Biological Council, 1944–47. Chm. Bd of Studies, Biochem., Univ. of London, 1954–57; Member: Scientific Advisory Council, 1956–60; MRC, 1966–70. Mem., Lawes Agricl Trust Cttee, 1964–76. Guest Lecturer, 100th meeting of Gesellschaft Deutscher Naturforscher und Ärzte, Germany, 1959; Royal Society: Croonian Lectr, 1959; Vice-Pres., 1961–64; Royal Medal, 1968. Vis. Prof., Japan Soc. for Promotion of Science, 1979. Hon. Member: Biochem. Soc., 1969; Internat. Soc. Blood Transfusion, 1980; British Soc. Blood Transfusion, 1984; Internat. Endotoxic Soc., 1987. Hon. FRCP 1982; Hon. FMedSci 2000. MD *hc* Basel, 1964; DSc *hc* Michigan, 1969. Conway Evans Prize, RCP, 1964; (jtly) Laridsteiner Memorial Award (USA), 1967; (jtly) Paul Ehrlich and Ludwig Darmstädter Prizes (Germany), 1968; Philip Levine Medal, Amer. Soc. of Clinical Pathologists, 1990. *Publications:* papers on biochemistry, immunology and pathology. *Address:* 57 Woodbury Drive, Sutton, Surrey SM2 5RA. *T:* (020) 8642 2319. *Club:* Athenæum. *Died 10 Feb. 2003.*

MORGAN, Air Vice-Marshal William Gwyn, CB 1968; CBE 1960 (OBE 1945); RAF, retired 1969; *b* 13 Aug. 1914; *s* of T. S. Morgan; *m* 1962, Joan Russell. *Educ:* Pagefield Coll., Swansea. Joined Royal Air Force, 1939; Group Capt., 1958; Command Acct, HQ, FEAF, 1962; Air Commodore, 1965; DPS (2), RAF, 1965–66; AOA Technical Training Comd, 1966–68, Training Comd, 1968–69; Air Vice-Marshal, 1967; jssc; psc. FCCA; ACMA. *Recreation:* fell walking. *Address:* c/o Lloyds TSB, 7 Pall Mall, SW1Y 5NH. *Club:* Royal Air Force. *Died 12 Jan. 2002.*

MORIARTY, Brigid Mary B.; *see* Beattie-Moriarty.

MORISHIMA, Prof. Michio, FBA 1981; Sir John Hicks Professor of Economics, London School of Economics and Political Science, 1984–88 (Professor of Economics, 1970–84); Emeritus Professor, University of London, 1988; *b* 18 July 1923; *s* of Kameji and Tatsuo Morishima; *m* 1953, Yoko; two *s* one *d*. *Educ:* Univ. of Kyoto (BA Econ). Assistant Professor: Kyoto Univ., 1950–51; Osaka Univ., 1951–63; Prof., Osaka Univ., 1963–69. Sen. Vis. Fellow, All Souls Coll., Oxford, 1963–64; Vis. Prof., Stanford Univ., 1964; Temp. Prof. and Keynes Vis. Prof., Essex Univ., 1968–70. *Publications:* Equilibrium, Stability and Growth, 1964; Theory of Economic Growth, 1969; The Working of Econometric Models, 1972; Marx's Economics, 1973; Theory of Demand: real and monetary, 1973; The Economic Theory of Modern Society, 1976; Walras' Economics, 1977; Value, Exploitation and Growth, 1978; Why Has Japan 'Succeeded'?, 1982; The Economics of Industrial Society, 1985; Ricardo's Economics, 1989; Capital and Credit, 1992; Dynamic Economic Theory, 1996; Japan at a Dead Lock, 2000; Collaborative Development in Northeast Asia, 2000. *Address:* Ker, Greenway, Hutton Mount, Brentwood, Essex CM13 2NP. *T:* (01277) 219595. *Died 13 July 2004.*

MORISON, Hon. Lord; Alastair Malcolm Morison; a Senator of the College of Justice, Scotland, 1985–97; *b* 12 Feb. 1931; 2nd *s* of Sir Ronald Peter Morison, QC (Scotland); *m* 1st, 1957, Lindsay Balfour Oatts (marr. diss. 1977); one *s* one *d*; 2nd, 1980, Birgitte Hendil. *Educ:* Cargilfield; Winchester Coll.; Edinburgh Univ. Admitted to Faculty of Advocates, 1956; QC (Scotland) 1968. Chairman: Medical Appeals Tribunal, 1972–85; Performing Right Tribunal, 1984–85. *Recreations:* fishing, music, esp. opera. *Club:* New (Edinburgh). *Died 31 July 2005.*

MORISON, Niall Maclaine; Chief Executive, General Council of the Bar, 1994–2004; *b* 3 May 1944; *s* of Dr Neil Morison and Dorothy Morison; *m* 1969, Alison Linda Hill; three *s* one *d*. *Educ:* Edinburgh Academy. Asst Sec., Bar Council, 1973–74; Senate of the Inns of Court and the

Bar: Asst Sec., 1974–85; Dep. Sec., 1985–86; Dep. Chief Exec., Gen. Council of the Bar, 1987–94. Hon. Sec., Internat. Council of Advocates and Barristers, 2001–04. Governor, Stonegate C of E Primary Sch., 1996–2000. *Recreations:* catching up with things I should have done over the last thirty years, reacquainting myself with my family, enjoying music, reading, gardening, watching Rugby, fishing, ski-ing. *Address:* Bramdean Cottage, Stonegate, Wadhurst, E Sussex TN5 7EP. *T:* (01580) 200142. *Died 25 June 2005.*

MORLEY, John Harwood, FMA; writer and consultant (buildings and interiors); Keeper of Furniture and Interior Design, Victoria and Albert Museum, 1985–89; *b* 5 Dec. 1933; *s* of George Frederick Morley and Doris Simpson Morley; *m* 1960, Jacqueline Morgan; three *d*. *Educ:* Henry Mellish Grammar Sch.; Exeter Coll., Oxford (MA). FMA 1965. Archivist, Ipswich Corp., 1958–59; Art Asst, Herbert Art Gall., Coventry, 1959–61; Keeper of Art, Leicester Museums, 1961–65; Director: Bradford City Museums, 1965–68; Royal Pavilion, Art Gall. and Museums, Brighton, 1968–85; exhibitions, 1969–85, incl. The Jazz Age, and Death, Heaven and the Victorians. Mem. Council, Nat. Trust, 1985–89; Chairman (and Founder Member): Decorative Arts Soc. 1890–1940, 1975– (Pres., 1989–); The Brighton Soc., 1973–75; Sec. (and Founder Mem.), Friends of the Royal Pavilion, 1972–85; Trustee: Edward James Foundn, 1976–82; Geffrye Mus., 1990–95; Patron, Twentieth Century Soc.; Mem. Council, Attingham Summer Sch. Trust, 1983–87. *Publications:* Death, Heaven and the Victorians, 1971; Designs and Drawings: The Making of the Royal Pavilion, 1984; Regency Design 1790–1840: Gardens: Buildings: Interiors: Furniture, 1993; Furniture–the Western Tradition: History; Style; Design, 1999. *Recreations:* music, gardening, reading, museums, houses. *Address:* 11 Vine Place, Brighton, East Sussex BN1 3HE. *Died 3 May 2001.*

MORRIS OF CASTLE MORRIS, Baron *cr* 1990 (Life Peer), of St Dogmaels in the County of Dyfed; **Brian Robert Morris,** DPhil; Principal, St David's University College, Lampeter, 1980–91; *b* 4 Dec. 1930; *o s* of William Robert Morris and Ellen Elizabeth Morris (*née* Shelley); *m* 1955, Sandra Mary James, JP; one *s* one *d*. *Educ:* Cardiff High School; Worcester Coll., Oxford (MA, DPhil). National service with Welch Regt, 1949–51. Fellow of Shakespeare Inst., Univ. of Birmingham, 1956–58; Asst Lectr, 1958–60, Lectr, 1960–65, Univ. of Reading; Lectr, 1965–67, Sen. Lectr, 1967–71, Univ. of York; Prof. of English Literature, Univ. of Sheffield, 1971–80. General Editor: New Mermaid Dramatists, 1964–86; New Arden Shakespeare, 1974–82. Opposition Dep. Chief Whip, H of L, 1992–97; principal opposition spokesman on educn, 1994–97. Member: Council, Yorkshire Arts Assoc., 1973–81 (Chm. Literature Panel, 1973–77); Welsh Arts Council, 1983–86 (Mem. Lit. Cttee, 1978–86); Archbishops' Council on Evangelism, 1971–75; Yr Academi Gymreig, 1979–; British Library Bd, 1980–91; Council, Poetry Soc., 1980–90 (Vice-Pres., 1990–); Council, Nat. Library of Wales, 1981–91; Chairman: Museums and Galls Commn, 1985–90 (Mem., 1975– (formerly Standing Commn on Museums and Galls)); Council, Prince of Wales's Inst. of Architecture, 1993–97. President: Welsh Historic Gdns Trust, 1990–; Brontë Soc., 1996–; Dir, Middleton Botanic Garden, 1994–97; Vice President: Council for Nat. Parks, 1985–; Museums Assoc., 1985–; Arkwright Soc., 1992–; Prayer Book Soc., 1993–. Trustee: Nat. Portrait Gall., 1977– (Vice-Chm., 1993–); Nat. Heritage Meml Fund, 1980–91; Welsh Adv. Cttee, British Council, 1983–91; Anthony Panizzi Foundn, 1987–91; Museum of Empire and Commonwealth, 1991–; Campaign for the Protection of Rural Wales, 1991–. Broadcaster, scriptwriter and presenter of television programmes. Hon. LittD Sheffield, 1991; Hon. LLD Wales, 1992. *Publications:* John Cleveland: a Bibliography of his Poems, 1967; (with Eleanor Withington) The Poems of John Cleveland, 1967;

(ed) New Mermaid Critical Commentaries I–III, 1969–72; Mary Quant's London, 1973; (ed) Ritual Murder, 1980; Harri Webb, 1993; *edited plays:* Ford's The Broken Heart, 1965, and 'Tis Pity She's a Whore, 1968; (with Roma Gill) Tourneur's The Atheist's Tragedy, 1976; Shakespeare's The Taming of the Shrew, 1981; *poetry:* Tide Race, 1976; Stones in the Brook, 1978; Dear Tokens, 1987; The Waters of Comfort, 1998; The Collected Poems, 2001; contribs to journals. *Recreations:* music, mountains, museums. *Address:* The Old Hall, Foolow, Eyam, Hope Valley, Derbyshire S32 5QR. *T:* (01433) 631186. *Club:* Athenæum.   *Died 30 April 2001.*

MORRIS OF KENWOOD, 2nd Baron *cr* 1950, of Kenwood; **Philip Geoffrey Morris;** JP; Company Director, retired 1990; *b* 18 June 1928; *s* of 1st Baron Morris of Kenwood, and Florence (*d* 1982), *d* of Henry Isaacs, Leeds; *S* father, 1954; *m* 1958, Hon. Ruth, *o d* of late Baron Janner and Lady Janner; one *s* three *d. Educ:* Loughborough Coll., Leics. Served RAF, Nov. 1946–Feb. 1949, July 1951–Oct. 1955. JP Inner London, 1967. *Recreations:* tennis, golf, ski-ing. *Heir:* *s* Hon. Jonathan David Morris [*b* 5 Aug. 1968; *m* 1996, Melanie, *d* of Robin Klein]. *Address:* 35 Fitzjohns Avenue, NW3 5JY. *T:* (020) 7431 6332.   *Died 2 Dec. 2004.*

MORRIS, Owen Humphrey, CB 1977; CMG 1967; Deputy Under-Secretary of State, Welsh Office, 1974–81, retired; *b* 15 June 1921; *o c* of late David Humphreys Morris, Ton Pentre, Rhondda, Glam., and Mrs Amy Ann Morris (*née* Jones); *m* 1972, Mair Annetta Evans, *d* of late Capt. Daniel Evans, DSC, Tynllys, Morfa Nefyn. *Educ:* Public Elem. Schs; King's Coll. Sch., Wimbledon (Schol.); Balliol Coll., Oxford (Schol.; MA). Served War of 1939–45: The Welch Regt and King's African Rifles, 1941–45 (Capt.). Colonial Office: Asst Principal, 1946; Principal, 1948; seconded Sierra Leone Administration, 1952–53; Asst Sec., 1955; Dept of Techn. Cooperation, 1962; Min. of Overseas Development, 1964; Min. of Housing and Local Govt, 1966; Welsh Office, 1969; Asst Under-Sec., 1970; Dep. Sec., 1974. Chm., Gwynedd Archaeol Trust, 1984–87. *Address:* Taltreuddyn Fawr, Dyffryn Ardudwy, Gwynedd LL44 2RQ.
                                    Died 20 Dec. 2005.

MORRISH, John Edwin, (Jack); school governor and education consultant; Chairman, Northamptonshire Association of School Governing Bodies, 1994–97 (General Secretary, 1992–94; Research Officer, 1994–95); *b* 23 Sept. 1915; *s* of Henry Edwin Morrish and Ada Minnie (*née* Tapping); *m* 1st, 1937, Norah Lake (marr. diss.); one *d*; 2nd, 1944, Violet Saunders (marr. diss.); one *s* one *d*; 3rd, 1984, Betty Lupton (*née* Wear) (*d* 1990). *Educ:* Fleet Road, Hampstead, Elem. Sch.; University Coll. Sch.; Northampton Polytechnic, London; various work-faces; MA Leicester, 1991. Post Office Techn. Officer, 1932–54; coalminer, 1944–45. Trade Union Official: Civil Service Union, 1954–72 (Asst Gen. Sec.); Soc. of Civil and Public Servants, 1972–76 (Gen. Sec., Customs and Excise Gp). Panel Mem., Industrial Tribunals in London, Reading and Bedford, 1970–84. Administrator, Northants Rural Community Council, 1979. Census Officer, 1980–81, 1990–91. Mem. (Lab), Dep. Leader, and Chm., Educn Cttee, Northants CC, 1981–85; Mem. (Lab), Hounslow BC, 1986–90 (Vice-Chm., Educn Cttee). Vice-Chm., E Midlands Further Educn Council, 1982–85; Member: Adv. Cttee, Supply and Educn of Teachers; Assoc. of County Councils, 1981–85; Burnham Cttee on Teachers' Pay, 1983–85, 1986–87; AMA, 1986–90; co-opted Member: Northants Educn Cttee, 1993–98; Som Schs Review Cttee, 2000–01; Vice-Chairman: Nat. Governors' Council, 1994–98; Som Assoc. of Governing Bodies. Hon. Chm., Northants Child Poverty Action Gp, 1980–84. Hon. Treas., UK Reading Assoc. (World Congress Local Arrangements Cttee), 1985–86. Chm., Nene Coll. Governors, 1981–85. *Publications:* The Future of Forestry, 1971; contrib. trade union and educn jls. *Recreations:* thinking, pursuit of justice, music, talking.

Address: 7 De Combe House, Mount Pleasant, Crewkerne, Somerset TA18 7AH. *T:* (01460) 77203. *Club:* Civil Service.   *Died 7 March 2003.*

MORRISON, Hon. Sir Charles (Andrew), Kt 1988; *b* 25 June 1932; 2nd *s* of 1st Baron Margadale, TD; *m* 1st, 1954, Hon. Sara Long (marr. diss. 1984); one *s* one *d*; 2nd, 1984, Mrs Rosalind Ward (marr. diss. 1999). *Educ:* Eton. Nat. Service in The Life Guards, 1950–52; Royal Wilts Yeo. (TA), 1952–66. County Councillor, Wilts, 1958–65 (Chm., Educn Cttee, 1963–64). MP (C) Devizes, May 1964–1992. Chm., Nat. Cttee for Electoral Reform, 1985–91; Mem. Bd of Dirs, Global Cttee of Parliamentarians on Population and Develt, 1984–91. Chairman: South West Regional Sports Council, 1966–68; Young Volunteer Force Foundn, 1971–74; British Trust for Conservation Volunteers, 1973–78; Game Conservancy, 1987–94; Allerton Res. and Educn Trust, 1994–2001; Population Concern, 1995–2001. Chm., Handicapped Anglers Trust, 2000–. Patron, Wilts Wildlife Trust, 1999–. A Vice-Chm., 1922 Cttee, 1974–83 (Mem. Exec., 1972). Freeman, City of London; Prime Warden, Fishmongers' Co., 1986–87. DL Hereford and Worcester, 1995–2000. Hon. Freeman, Devizes, 1992. *Recreations:* gardening, shooting, fishing. *Address:* Cowpens, Fonthill Bishop, Salisbury, Wilts SP3 5RZ. *Clubs:* Beefsteak, Pratt's.   *Died 9 May 2005.*

MORRISON, Prof. John Lamb Murray, CBE 1957; DSc; FREng, FIMechE; Professor Emeritus of Mechanical Engineering, University of Bristol, 1971 (Professor of Mechanical Engineering, 1946–71); *b* 22 May 1906; *s* of late Latto A. Morrison, Biggar, Lanarkshire; *m* 1936, Olga, *d* of late M. Nierenstein, DSc; two *s. Educ:* Biggar High Sch.; Univ. of Glasgow (DSc 1939). Formerly: Lecturer in Mechanical Engineering; Reader in Mechanical Engineering, Univ. of Bristol. Pres., IMechE, 1970–71. FREng (FEng 1977). Hon. DSc Salford, 1972. *Publications:* An Introduction to the Mechanics of Machines, 1964; various papers on strength of materials and design of machines. *Recreations:* gardening; formerly golf. *Address:* Dreva, Rayleigh Road, Bristol BS9 2AU. *T:* (0117) 968 1193.   *Died 6 Feb. 2001.*

MORRISON, Margaret Jane, OBE 1991; BEM 1972; Co-Chairman, Women's National Commission, 1989–91; *b* 20 March 1924; *d* of William and May Campbell; *m* 1943, Thomas Morrison; one *d. Educ:* Royal Jubilee Juniors, Newcastle; Sandyford Secondary Modern, Newcastle. Civil Service Union: Nat. Exec. Cttee, 1968–78; Vice-Pres., 1978–79; Pres., 1980–87; Dep. Pres., Nat. Union of Civil and Public Servants, 1987–89; Vice-Chm., Northern Regional TUC, 1980 (Chm., Women's Adv. Gp, 1980); Mem., TUC Women's Cttee, 1979–89; Director: Northern Development Co., 1984–89; Entrust, 1984; Mem., European Women's TUC and Steering Cttee, 1982. Mem., Civil Service Appeal Bd, 1991. TUC Gold Badge, Woman Trade Unionist of the Year, 1973. *Publication:* (jtly) Homelessness Amongst Women, report, 1983. *Recreations:* music, reading, swimming, conversation.   *Died 5 March 2001.*

MORRISON, Maj.-Gen. Reginald Joseph Gordon, CB 1969; CBE 1959; MD, FRCP; retired; Physician, The Royal Hospital, Chelsea, 1969–79; Director of Medicine, Ministry of Defence (Army), and Consulting Physician to the Army, 1965–68; *b* 29 March 1909; *s* of R. Morrison; *m* 1947, Norma Jacqueline Nicholson; two *s. Educ:* Dulwich Coll.; St Joseph's Coll., SE19; St Bartholomew's Hosp. House Phys., St Bart's Hosp., 1934; Res. MO, Hove Gen. Hosp. Commnd RAMC, 1936; served as Med. Specialist, RAMC. Adviser in Medicine, EA Command, 1947–50; OC, Med. Div., QA Mil. Hosp., 1950–56; Cons. Phys., Far East, 1956–59; Prof. of Trop. Med., Royal Army Medical College, 1959–65. QHP 1963–68. *Publications:* (with W. H. Hargreaves) The Practice of Tropical Medicine, 1965; chapter in: Exploration Medicine, 1965; Medicine in the Tropics, 1974; various articles in Lancet, BMJ, Proc. RSM, etc.

Recreations: rose growing, golf. *Address:* 1 Hollington Court, High Street, Chislehurst, Kent BR7 5AJ.
Died 23 Dec. 2003.

MORRISON, Dr Stuart Love; Professor of Community Medicine, University of Edinburgh, 1964–75, retired; *b* 25 Nov. 1922; *o s* of late William James Morrison, Ironfounder, Glasgow and Isabella Murdoch, Edinburgh; *m* 1947, Dr Audrey Butler Lornie; one *d. Educ:* Glasgow Acad.; Dundee High Sch.; St Andrews Univ. (MB ChB 1951); London Univ. (DPH 1954). MRCPE 1966, FRCPE 1968; FFCM 1975. Served RAF, 1939–46. Hosp. and gen. practice, 1951–53; Public Health appts, 1954–56; Mem., Scientific Staff, MRC Social Medicine Research Unit, 1956–62; Sen. Lectr in Social Med., Univ. of Edinburgh, 1962–64. Vis. Fellow, Epidemiology and Statistics, Univ. of N Carolina, 1961–62; Professorial Fellow in Community Medicine, 1976–82 and Dir, Centre for Med. Res., 1979–82, Univ. of Sussex; Vis. Prof. of Community Medicine, LSHTM, 1982–84; Prof. of Community Medicine, Univ. of Malta, 1984–86. *Publications:* (jtly) The Image and the Reality, 1978; contribs to med. jls on epidemiology and medical care, and to Book Collector on bibliography. *Recreation:* book collecting. *Address:* 4 Roselands, Sidmouth, Devon EX10 8PB. *Died 30 April 2002.*

MORROGH, Henton, CBE 1969; FRS 1964; FREng; Director, BCIRA (formerly British Cast Iron Research Association), 1959–85; *b* 29 Sept. 1917; *s* of Clifford and Amy Morrogh; *m* 1949, Olive Joyce Ramsay; one *d.* Distinguished for his work on the microstructure and solidification of cast iron and for the development of ductile cast iron. Visiting Prof., Dept of Industrial Engrg and Management, Univ. of Technology, Loughborough, 1967–72. President: Instn of Metallurgists, 1967–68; Inst. of British Foundrymen, 1972–73; Internat. Cttee of Foundry Technical Assocs, 1978. FREng (FEng 1979). Hon. Member: Japanese Foundrymen's Soc., 1984; Inst. of British Foundrymen, 1986. DSc (*hc*) Univ. of Birmingham, 1965. Iron and Steel Inst. Andrew Carnegie Gold Medal, 1946; E. J. Fox Medal Inst. of Brit. Foundrymen, 1951; McFadden Gold Medal, Amer. Foundrymen's Soc., 1952; Robert Hadfield Medal, Iron & Steel Inst., 1956; Gold Medal, Amer. Gray Iron Founders' Soc., 1961; Bessemer Gold Medal, Metals Soc., 1977. *Address:* Cedarwood, Penn Lane, Tanworth-in-Arden, Warwicks B94 5HH. *T:* and *Fax:* (01564) 742414; *e-mail:* hentonmorrogh@btopenworld.com.
Died 20 Sept. 2003.

MORTON, Sir Alastair; *see* Morton, Sir R. A. N.

MORTON, Kenneth Valentine Freeland, CIE 1947; OBE 1971; Secretary, East Anglian Regional Hospital Board, 1947–72, retired; *b* 13 May 1907; *s* of Kenneth John Morton; *m* 1936, Mary Hadwin Hargreaves (*d* 1996); four *s* one *d. Educ:* Edinburgh Acad.; University Coll., Oxford. Joined ICS, 1930; Under-Sec. (Political), Punjab Govt, 1934–36; Dep. Comr, 1936–39; Colonisation Officer, 1939–43; Dep. Sec., Develt Dept, 1943–46; Sec., Electricity and Industries Depts, 1946–47; retired, 1947. *Address:* Temple End House, 27 Temple End, Great Wilbraham, Cambridge CB1 5JF. *T:* (01223) 880691. *Club:* East India, Devonshire, Sports and Public Schools.
Died 17 Jan. 2003.

MORTON, Sir (Robert) Alastair (Newton), Kt 1991; Chairman, Strategic Rail Authority, 1999–2001; *b* 11 Jan. 1938; *s* of late Harry Newton Morton and Elizabeth Martino; *m* 1964, Sara Bridget Stephens; one *s* one *d. Educ:* St John's Coll. and Witwatersrand Univ., Johannesburg (BA); Worcester Coll., Oxford (MA; Hon. Fellow, 1994). Special grad. student, MIT, 1964. Anglo American Corp. of SA (mining finance), London and Central Africa, 1959–63; Internat. Finance Corp., Washington, 1964–67; Industrial Reorganisation Corp., 1967–70; Exec. Dir, 117 Group of investment trusts, then Chm., Draymont Securities, 1970–76; Man. Dir, BNOC, 1976–80; Chief

Exec., 1982–87, Chm., 1987, Guinness Peat Gp; Co-Chm., Eurotunnel, 1987–96 (Gp Chief Exec., 1990–94). Chairman: Kent TEC, 1990–95; Chancellor's Private Finance Panel, 1993–95; CIT, 1992–94. Mem. Council, RIIA, 1990–96. Chm., NYO of GB, 1994–. Hon. LLD: Bath, 1990; Kent, 1992; DUniv Brunel, 1992; Hon. DSc: Warwick, 1994; Cranfield, 1996; Hon. DBA Robert Gordon, 2002. Commandeur de la Légion d'Honneur (France), 1994. *Recreations:* sailing, walking. *Clubs:* University (New York); Itchenor Sailing; Country (Johannesburg). *Died 1 Sept. 2004.*

MORTON-SANER, Robert, CVO 1966; CBE 1962 (OBE 1946 MBE 1941); HM Diplomatic Service, retired; *b* 30 Dec. 1911; *o s* of late Major A. E. Saner; *m* 1943, Katharine Mary Gordon (*d* 1981); two *d. Educ:* Westminster Sch.; Christ Church, Oxford. ICS, 1935; served in United Provinces; Under Sec., Defence Department, Government of India, 1940; Deputy Secretary and Chief Administrative Officer, General Headquarters, New Delhi, 1943–45; served with Resettlement Directorate, 1945–47; retired from Indian Civil Service and entered Foreign (subseq. Diplomatic) Service, 1947; served in Madras, 1947–50; Foreign Office, 1950–52; Budapest, 1953–55; NATO Defence College, 1955; Counsellor and Consul-General, Djakarta, 1955–59; Counsellor, Buenos Aires, 1960–64; Consul-General, Antwerp, 1964–70. Acted as Chargé d'Affaires, 1953, 1954, 1956, 1958, 1959, 1960. Member, Skinners' Company. Commander, Order of Leopold II (Belgium). *Recreations:* gardening, old churches. *Address:* Hethe Cottage, Hethe, Oxon OX6 9EU. *Club:* Anglo-Belgian.
Died 26 Sept. 2001.

MOSAR, Nicolas; barrister; Ambassador from Luxembourg to Italy, 1989–92; *b* Luxembourg, 25 Nov. 1927; *m*; three *c. Educ:* Athénée Grand-Ducal; Faculté de Droit, Paris University. Called to Bar, 1955. Mem. Town Council, Luxembourg, 1959–70, 1975–85. Member of Luxembourg Parliament, 1964–74, 1976–85. Social Christian Party: Sec.-Gen., 1959–72; Chm., 1972–74; Chm., Party Parly Gp, 1979–85. Mem., EEC, 1985–88. *Publications:* political and legal papers. *Address:* (office) 8 rue Notre-Dame, 2240 Luxembourg. *T:* 2280231, *Fax:* 462676. *Died 6 Jan. 2004.*

MOUNT, Air Cdre Christopher John, CBE 1956; DSO 1943; DFC 1940; DL; retired; *b* 14 Dec. 1913; *s* of Capt. F. Mount; *m* 1947, Audrey Mabel Clarke; two *s. Educ:* Eton; Trinity Coll., Oxford. Royal Auxiliary Air Force, 1935; Royal Air Force, 1938. Consultant, Wrights (formerly C. R. Thomas & Son), Solicitors, Maidenhead (Partner, 1970–79). DL Berks, 1984. *Address:* Garden House, Bagshot Road, Sunninghill, Ascot, Berks SL5 9JL. *T:* (01344) 622225. *Died 23 July 2002.*

MOUNTAIN, Sir Denis Mortimer, 3rd Bt *cr* 1922; Chairman and Managing Director: Eagle Star Insurance Co. Ltd, 1974–85; Eagle Star Holdings plc, 1979–85 (Hon. Pres., 1985–93); Chairman, Eagle Star Insurance Co. of America, 1978–85; *b* 2 June 1929; *er s* of Sir Brian Edward Stanley Mountain, 2nd Bt, and Doris Elsie, *e d* of E. C. E. Lamb; *S* father, 1977; *m* 1958, Hélène Fleur Mary Kirwan-Taylor (*d* 2004); two *s* one *d. Educ:* Eton. Lieut, Royal Horse Guards. Chairman: Australian Eagle Insurance Co. Ltd, 1977–85; South African Eagle Insurance Co. Ltd, 1977–85, and other companies both in UK and overseas; Pres., Compagnie de Bruxelles Risques Divers SA d'Assurances (Belgium), 1977–85; Director: Rank Organisation PLC, 1968–94; Grovewood Securities Ltd, 1969–85 (Dep. Chm.); Philip Hill Investment Trust plc, 1967–86; Bank of Nova Scotia (Toronto), 1978–2000; BAT Industries plc, 1984–85; Allied London Properties, 1986–99, and other UK and overseas companies. *Recreations:* fishing, shooting. *Heir: s* Edward Brian Stanford Mountain [*b* 19 March 1961; *m* 1987, Charlotte Sarah Jesson, *d* of His Honour Henry Pownall, QC; two *s* one *d*]. *Died 24 Oct. 2005.*

MOUNTFORT, Guy Reginald, OBE 1970; Director, Ogilvy & Mather International Inc., New York, 1964–66; Managing Director, Ogilvy and Mather Ltd, London, 1964–66; *b* 4 Dec. 1905; *s* of late Arnold George Mountfort, artist, and Alice Edith (*née* Hughes); *m* 1931, Joan Hartley (*née* Pink); two *d*. *Educ*: grammar sch. General Motors Corporation (France), 1928–38. War service, 1939–46: 12 Regt HAC and British Army Staff (Washington), Lt-Col; service in N Africa, Italy, Burma, Pacific, Germany. Procter & Gamble Inc., USA, 1946–47; Mather & Crowther Ltd, subseq. Ogilvy and Mather, 1947, Dir, 1949–66. Vice-Chm., Dollar Exports Bd Advertising Cttee, 1948–49. Hon. Sec., Brit. Ornithologists' Union, 1952–62, Pres. 1970–75 (Union Medal, 1967); Leader of scientific expedns to: Coto Doñana, 1952, 1955, 1956; Bulgaria, 1960; Hungary, 1961; Jordan, 1963, 1965; Pakistan, 1966, 1967. Vice Pres., World Wildlife Fund, 1978– (Gold Medal, 1978). Scientific FZS (Stamford Raffles Award, 1969). Medal of Société d'Acclimatation, 1936. Commander, Order of the Golden Ark, Netherlands, 1980. *Publications*: A Field Guide to the Birds of Europe (jtly), 1954, 5th edn, Birds of Britain and Europe, 1994; The Hawfinch, 1957; Portrait of a Wilderness, 1958; Portrait of a River, 1962; Portrait of a Desert, 1965; The Vanishing Jungle, 1969; Tigers, 1973; So Small a World, 1974; Back from the Brink, 1977; Saving the Tiger, 1981; Wild India, 1985; Rare Birds of the World, 1988; Memories of Three Lives, 1991; contribs to ornithol and other scientific jls; television and radio broadcasts on ornithology and exploration. *Recreations*: ornithology, gardening, photography, travel. *Address*: Queensmount, 18 Queens Park West Drive, Bournemouth, Dorset BH8 9DA.

Died 23 April 2003.

MOUNTGARRET, 17th Viscount *cr* 1550 (Ireland); **Richard Henry Piers Butler;** Baron (UK), 1911; *b* 8 Nov. 1936; *s* of 16th Viscount Mountgarret; *S* father, 1966; *senior known heir* to Earldoms of Ormonde and Ossory and Chief Butler of Ireland; *m* 1st, 1960, Gillian Margaret (marr. diss. 1970), *o d* of Cyril Francis Stuart Buckley, London, SW3; two *s* one *d*; 2nd, 1970, Mrs Jennifer Susan Melville Fattorini (marr. diss. 1983), *yr d* of Captain D. M. Wills, Barley Wood, Wrington, near Bristol; 3rd 1983, Mrs Angela Ruth Waddington, *e d* of Major T. G. Porter, The Croft, Church Fenton, Tadcaster. *Educ*: Eton; RMA, Sandhurst. Commissioned, Irish Guards, 1957; retd rank Capt., 1964. Pres., Yorks CCC, 1984–90. *Recreations*: shooting, stalking, cricket, golf. *Heir*: *s* Hon Piers James Richard Butler [*b* 15 April 1961; *m* 1995, Laura Brown Gary (marr. diss. 2000), *d* of Albert Dickens Williams, Jr; two *d*]. *Address*: Stainley House, South Stainley, Harrogate, Yorks HG3 3LX. *T*: (01423) 770087. *Clubs*: White's, Pratt's.

Died 7 Feb. 2004.

MOWAT, Ian Robert Mackenzie, FCLIP; FRSE; Librarian, University of Edinburgh, since 1997; *b* 20 April 1946; *s* of Robert John Bain Mowat and Violet Mowat (*née* Mackenzie); *m* 1968, Margaret Louise Jackson; one *s* one *d*. *Educ*: Univ. of Aberdeen (MA); Univ. of Sheffield (MA); Univ. of St Andrews (BPhil). FCLIP (FLA 1991). Assistant Librarian: St Andrews Univ., 1970–72; Heriot-Watt Univ., 1972–75; Asst Keeper, Nat. Liby of Scotland, 1975–78; Sub-Librarian, Glasgow Univ., 1978–86; Librarian: Hull Univ., 1986–91; and Keeper, Pybus Collection, Newcastle Univ., 1992–97. FRSE 1998. *Publications*: Easter Ross 1750–1850, 1981; Bibliography of Scotland 1976–77, 1978, 1977–78, 1979; (ed jtly) Networking and the Future of Libraries 2, 1995; (ed with M. Sliwinska) Library Management: East-West relations, 1995; contrib. numerous reports, articles, papers and reviews on librarianship, history and architectural history. *Recreations*: hill-walking, swimming, music, architectural history. *Address*: Main Library, George Square, Edinburgh EH8 9LJ. *T*: (0131) 650 3378. *Died 6 Sept. 2002.*

MOWAT, John Stuart; QC (Scot.) 1988; Sheriff Principal of South Strathclyde, Dumfries and Galloway, 1988–93; *b* 30 Jan. 1923; *s* of George Mowat and Annie Barlow; *m* 1956, Anne Cameron Renfrew; two *s* two *d*. *Educ*: Glasgow High Sch.; Belmont House; Merchiston Castle Sch.; Glasgow Univ. (MA, LLB). Served RAF Transport Comd, 1941–46; Flt-Lt 1944. Journalist, 1947–52; Advocate, 1952; Sheriff-Substitute, then Sheriff, of Fife and Kinross at Dunfermline, 1960–72; Sheriff: of Fife and Kinross at Cupar and Kinross, 1972–74; of Lanark and Glasgow, subseq. Glasgow and Strathkelvin, 1974–88. Chm., Sheriff Court Rules Council, 1989–92. Contested (L) Caithness and Sutherland, 1955; Office-bearer, Scottish Liberal Party, 1954–58. Life Trustee: Carnegie Dunfermline Trust, 1967–73; Carnegie UK Trust, 1971–73. *Recreations*: golf, curling, watching football. *Address*: Old Mill of Camserney, Camserney, Aberfeldy, Perthshire PH15 2JF. *T*: (01887) 829572.

Died 31 Oct. 2001.

MOWBRAY, Sir John, Kt 1983; Chairman, Wellington Diocesan Board of Trustees (Anglican), 1970–95, then Past Chairman; *b* 23 Sept. 1916; *s* of Harry Logan Campbell Mowbray and Therese Josephine Mowbray; *m* 1946, Audrey Burt Steel; was *s* one *d*. *Educ*: King's Coll., Auckland; Auckland University Coll. BCom, Dip. in Banking, Univ. of NZ; FCA NZ 1973. Served War, 2nd NZ Div. Field Artillery, ME, 1940–46 (Lieut). Joined staff of The National Bank of New Zealand, 1934; Gen. Man.'s Asst, 1957; Asst Gen. Man., 1961; Gen. Man. and Chief Exec., 1966–76. Chairman: Develt Finance Corp. of NZ, 1976–85; GEC New Zealand Ltd, 1976–86; Motor Hlldgs Ltd, 1980–84; DIC Ltd, 1982–86. Chairman: NZ Bankers' Assoc., 1966, 1972 and 1975; Higher Salaries Cttee in the State Services, 1972–78; Bd of Trustees, NZ Inst. of Econ. Res., 1978–; Asean NZ Business Council, 1984–88; NZ Technol. Advancement Trust, 1984–; Japan/NZ Business Council, 1974–78; NZ Cttee, Pacific Basin Econ. Council, 1972–74. Life Member: NZ Admin. Staff Coll. (formerly Chm.); Arthritis and Rheumatism Foundn of NZ; Barnados NZ. Distinguished Fellow, NZ Inst. of Dirs, 1999. FNZIM 1974; Hon. Fellow, NZ Inst. of Bankers, 1975; FRSA 1970. A Lay Canon Emeritus, Wellington Cathedral. *Recreations*: golf, bridge, gardening. *Address*: 167 Karori Road, Karori, Wellington 5, New Zealand. *T*: 766334. *Clubs*: Wellington (Wellington); Northern (Auckland); Wellington Golf.

Died 1 Nov. 2001.

MOWLAM, Rt Hon. Marjorie; PC 1997; PhD; broadcaster and writer; *b* 18 Sept. 1949; *d* of late Frank William Mowlam and Bettina Mary Mowlam; *m* 1995, Jon Norton. *Educ*: Coundon Court Comprehensive Sch., Coventry; Durham Univ. (BA Social Anthrop. 1971); Iowa Univ. (MA; PhD 1978). Lecturer: Florida State Univ., 1977–78; Newcastle upon Tyne Univ., 1979–83; Administrator, Northern Coll., Barnsley, 1984–87. MP (Lab) Redcar, 1987–2001. Opposition front bench spokesman on NI, 1988–89 and 1994–97, on city and corporate affairs, 1989–92, on Citizen's Charter and women, 1992–93, on nat. heritage, 1993–94; Mem., Shadow Cabinet, 1992–97; Sec. of State for NI, 1997–99; Minister for the Cabinet Office and Chancellor of the Duchy of Lancaster, 1999–2001. Has held various Labour Party offices at constituency and dist levels; Mem., NEC, 1995–2001. Mem., Internat. Crisis Gp, 2001–. Talks countrywide on her career and current topics. *Publications*: (ed jtly) Debate on Disarmament, 1982; Momentum (autobiog.), 2002; (contrib.) Over Our Dead Bodies, ed D. Thompson, 1983. *Recreations*: travelling, swimming, jigsaws. *Died 19 Aug. 2005.*

MOWLL, Christopher Martyn; Clerk to The Clothworkers' Company of the City of London and Secretary to The Clothworkers' Foundation, 1978–92; *b* 14 Aug. 1932; *s* of late Christopher Kilvinton Mowll and Doris Ellen (*née* Hutchinson); *m* 1958, Margaret Frances (*née* Laird); four *s*. *Educ*: Epsom Coll.; Gonville and Caius

Coll., Cambridge (MA). Admitted Solicitor, 1956. Member: Council, National Library for the Blind, 1964–79; Council, Metropolitan Society for the Blind, 1964–2004 (Chm., 1979–2000); Exec. Council, RNIB, 1982–2002; Britain-Australia Bicentennial Cttee, 1984–88; Exec. Cttee, Assoc. of Charitable Foundns, 1989–92; Council, Shaftesbury Soc., 1993–98. Mem. Court, Univ. of Leeds, 1979–92, 1995–2001. Hon. LLD Leeds, 1992. *Address:* 15 West Hill, Sanderstead, South Croydon, Surrey CR2 0SB. *T:* (020) 8657 1207.
Died 18 April 2005.

MOYNIHAN, Daniel Patrick; University Professor, Maxwell School of Citizenship and Public Affairs, Syracuse University, since 2001; Senior Policy Scholar, Woodrow Wilson International Center for Scholars, since 2001; *b* Tulsa, Oklahoma, 16 March 1927; *s* of John Henry and Margaret Ann Phipps Moynihan; *m* 1955, Elizabeth Therese Brennan; two *s* one *d*. *Educ:* City Coll., NY; Tufts Univ.; Fletcher Sch. of Law and Diplomacy. MA, PhD. Gunnery Officer, US Navy, 1944–47. Dir of Public Relations, Internat. Rescue Cttee, 1954; successively Asst to Sec., Asst Sec., Acting Sec., to Governor of NY State, 1955–58; Mem., NY Tenure Commn, 1959–60; Dir, NY State Govt Res. Project, Syracuse Univ., 1959–61; Special Asst to Sec. of Labor, 1961–62; Exec. Asst to Sec., 1962–63, Asst Sec. of Labor, 1963–65; Dir, Jt Center Urban Studies, MIT and Harvard Univ., 1966–69; Harvard: Prof. of Educn and Urban Politics, 1966–73; Senior Mem., 1966–77; Prof. of Govt, 1972–77; Asst to Pres. of USA for Urban Affairs, 1969–70; Counsellor to Pres. (with Cabinet rank), 1969–70; Consultant to Pres., 1971–73; US Ambassador to India, 1973–75; US Permanent Rep. to the UN and Mem. of Cabinet, 1975–76; Senator from New York State, 1977–2001; Ranking Minority Mem., Senate Finance Cttee; Mem., Senate Cttees, Rules, Envmt and Public Works, (jt) Taxation and Library. Chm., Commn on Protecting and Reducing Govt Secrecy, 1995–97. Member: US delegn 26th Gen. Assembly, UN, 1971; President's Sci. Adv. Cttee, 1971–73. Mem., Usage Panel, Amer. Heritage Coll. Dictionary, 1968–. Member: Amer. Philosophical Soc.; AAAS (formerly Vice-Pres.); Nat. Acad. Public Admin; Fellow, Amer. Acad. Arts and Scis. Hon. Fellow, LSE, 1970. Holds numerous hon. degrees. Meritorius Service Award, US Dept of Labor, 1965; Internat. League for Human Rights Award, 1975; John LaFarge Award for Interracial Justice, 1980; Hubert Humphrey Award, Amer. Pol. Sci. Assoc., 1983; Medallion, State Univ. of NY at Albany, 1984; Henry Medal, Smithsonian Instn, 1985; Seal Medallion, CIA, 1986; Meml Sloan-Kettering Cancer Center Medal, 1986; Britannica Award, 1986; AIA Award, 1992; Laetare Medal, Notre Dame Univ., 1992; Thomas Jefferson Medal, Amer. Philosophical Soc., 1993; US Presidential Medal of Freedom, 2000. *Publications:* (jtly) Beyond the Melting Pot, 1963; (ed) The Defenses of Freedom, 1966; (ed) On Understanding Poverty, 1969; Maximum Feasible Misunderstanding, 1969; (ed) Toward a National Urban Policy, 1970; (ed jtly) On Equality of Educational Opportunity, 1972; The Politics of a Guaranteed Income, 1973; Coping: on the practice of government, 1974; (ed jtly) Ethnicity: theory and experience, 1975; A Dangerous Place, 1979; Counting Our Blessings, 1980; Loyalties, 1984; Family and Nation, 1986; Came the Revolution, 1988; On the Law of Nations, 1990; Pandaemonium: ethnicity in international politics, 1993; Miles to Go: a personal history of social policy, 1996; Secrecy: the American experience, 1998. *Address:* Woodrow Wilson International Center for Scholars, One Woodrow Wilson Plaza, 1300 Pennsylvania Avenue NW, Washington, DC 20004-3027, USA. *Clubs:* Century, Harvard (NYC); Federal City (Washington).
Died 26 March 2003.

MOYOLA, Baron *cr* 1971 (Life Peer), of Castledawson; **James Dawson Chichester-Clark;** PC (NI) 1966; DL; *b* 12 Feb. 1923; *s* of late Capt. J. L. C. Chichester-Clark, DSO and bar, DL, MP, and Mrs C. E. Brackenbury; *m*

1959, Moyra Maud Haughton (*née* Morris); two *d*, and one step *s*. *Educ:* Eton. Entered Army, 1942; 2nd Lieut Irish Guards, Dec. 1942; wounded, Italy, 1944; ADC to Governor-General of Canada (Field-Marshal Earl Alexander of Tunis), 1947–49; attended Staff Coll., Camberley, 1956; retired as Major, 1960. MP (U), S Derry, NI Parlt, 1960–72; Asst Whip, March 1963; Chief Whip, 1963–67; Leader of the House, 1966–67; Min. of Agriculture, 1967–69; Prime Minister, 1969–71. County Derry: DL 1954; Vice Lieutenant, 1975–93. *Recreations:* shooting, fishing, ski-ing. *Address:* Moyola Park, Castledawson, Co. Derry, N Ireland BT45 8ED.
Died 17 May 2002.

MUIR, (Isabella) Helen (Mary), CBE 1981; MA, DPhil, DSc; FRS 1977; Director, Kennedy Institute of Rheumatology, London, 1977–90 (Head of Division of Biochemistry, 1966–86); *b* 20 Aug. 1920; *d* of late G. B. F. Muir, ICS, and Gwladys Muir (*née* Stack). *Educ:* Downe House, Newbury; Somerville Coll., Oxford (MA 1944, DPhil 1947, DSc 1973; Hon. Fellow, 1978). Research Fellow, Dunn's Sch. of Pathology, Oxford, 1947–48; Scientific Staff, Nat. Inst. for Med. Research, 1948–54; Empire Rheumatism Council Fellow, St Mary's Hosp., London, 1954–58; Pearl Research Fellow, St Mary's Hosp., 1959–66; Visiting Professor: Queen Elizabeth Coll., Univ. of London, 1981–85; Newcastle Univ.; Manchester Univ., 1997–. Hon. Prof., Charing Cross and Westminster Med. Sch., 1979–. Scientific Mem. Council, Med. Research Council (first woman to serve), Oct. 1973–Sept. 1977. Mem., Connective Tissue Res. Adv. Bd, 1971–85; Governor, Strangeways Res. Lab., 1980–90; Trustee, Wellcome Trust, 1982–90. Heberden Orator, London, 1976; Bunim Lectr, US Arthritis Assoc., New Orleans, 1978. Member, Editorial Board: Biochemical Jl, 1964–69; Annals of the Rheumatic Diseases, 1971–77; Connective Tissue Res., 1971–85; Jl of Orthopaedic Res., 1983–. For. Mem., Royal Swedish Acad. of Scis, 1989; Honorary Member: Amer. Soc. of Biological Chemists, 1982; European Soc. of Arthrology, 1988. Hon. DSc: Edinburgh, 1982; Strathclyde, 1983; Brunel, 1990. Feldberg Foundn Award, 1977; Neil Hamilton Fairley Medal, RCP, 1981; Ciba Medal, Biochem. Soc., 1981; Steindler Award, Orthop. Soc., USA, 1982; Ciba Internat. Award, 1993. *Publications:* many scientific papers, mainly on biochem. of connective tissues in reln to arthritis and inherited diseases in Biochem. Jl, Biochim. et Biophys. Acta, Nature, etc; contribs to several specialist books. *Recreations:* gardening, music, horses, natural history and science in general. *Address:* Langlands House, Hornby, Bedale, N Yorks DL8 1NG. *T:* (01677) 450307; School of Biological Sciences, University of Manchester, Stopford Building, Oxford Road, Manchester M13 9PT. *T:* (0161) 275 5074.
Died 28 Nov. 2005.

MULLETT, Aidan Anthony, (Tony), CBE 1993; QPM 1982; Director-General, National Criminal Intelligence Service, 1992–93; *b* 24 May 1933; *s* of Bartholomew Joseph and Mary Kate Mullett; *m* 1957, Monica Elizabeth Coney; one *s* one *d*. *Educ:* Moat Boys' Sch., Leicester. Served Royal Air Force, 1950–56; joined Leicester City Police, 1957; Leicestershire and Rutland Constabulary, 1966, Chief Superintendent, 1973; Asst Chief Constable, W Mercia Constabulary, 1975–82; Dep. Chief Constable, Dyfed Powys Police, 1982–85; Chief Constable, W Mercia Constabulary, 1985–91. Chm., Crime Cttee, ACPO, 1990–91 (Hon. Sec., 1989). *Recreations:* golf, swimming.
Died 3 Sept. 2004.

MULLETT, Tony; *see* Mullett, A. A.

MULLIGAN, Andrew Armstrong; President: Mulligan Communications Inc., since 1983; European Satellite Radio Ltd; EuroMedia Group, since 1989; *b* 4 Feb. 1936; *s* of Col Hugh Waddell Mulligan, CMG, MD, DSc and Rita Aimee Armstrong; *m* 1964, Pia Ursula Schioler; two *s* two *d*. *Educ:* Magdalene Coll., Cambridge (Geog. and Anthropol. Tripos (Hons)). Personal Asst to Man. Dir, De La Rue Co., London, 1958–60; special assignment to

Australia and NZ for Irish Export Bd, 1961–62; Foreign Correspondent: Daily Telegraph and London Observer in Paris, 1962–68; Independent Television News at Ten, 1968; Producer and reporter, BBC's Panorama, 1969–73; Head of General Reports Div., EEC, Brussels, 1973–74; Dir of Press and Information, Delegn of Commn of European Communities to the US, 1975–83. Dir, American Ireland Fund (formerly Ireland Fund of the US), 1976. Publisher, Europe magazine, 1975–82. Rugby Blue (three times), Cambridge Univ., 1955–57. Played Rugby for London Irish (Capt., 1958–59); internat. début, Ireland *v* France, 1956; 22 caps for Ireland, 1956–61 (three times Captain, 1960); toured Australia and NZ with British Lions, 1959. *Publications:* Ouvert l'Après Midi, 1963; The All Blacks, 1964. *Recreations:* Rugby, tennis, ski-ing, sailing, landscape painting. *Address:* 1855 Shepherd Street, Washington, DC 20011, USA. *Clubs:* Annabel's; Hawks (Cambridge); Kildare Street and University (Dublin); Anglo-American Press Association (Paris); National Press (Washington, DC).   *Died 24 Feb. 2001.*

MUMFORD, William Frederick, CB 1989; Deputy Under-Secretary of State for Research Establishments, Ministry of Defence, 1989, retired; Chairman's Panel, Civil Service Selection Board, 1989–95; government departments recruitment consultant; *b* 23 Jan. 1930; *s* of late Frederick Charles Mumford and Hester Leonora Mumford; *m* 1958, Elizabeth Marion, *d* of Nowell Hall; three *s* one *d. Educ:* St Albans Sch.; Lincoln Coll., Oxford (MA PPE). Nat. Service commission, RA and Herts Yeomanry (TA), 1949–53. Appointed to Home Civil Service, 1953; Asst Principal, 1953–58, Principal, 1958–60, Air Ministry; First Sec., UK Delegn to NATO, Paris, 1960–65; Principal, 1965–67, Asst Sec., 1967–73, Defence Secretariat, MoD; Dep. Head of UK Delegn to MBFR Exploratory Talks, Vienna, 1973; Principal Private Sec. to Secretaries of State for Defence: Rt Hon. Lord Carrington, 1973–74, Rt Hon. Ian Gilmour, MP and Rt Hon. Roy Mason, MP, 1974–75; Under-Sec., Machinery of Govt Div., CSD, 1975–76; Asst Sec.-Gen. for Defence Planning and Policy, NATO, Brussels, 1976–80; Assistant Under-Secretary of State: (Material-Naval), MoD, 1980–84; (Estabts and Res.), MoD, 1984–90. Advr to Coopers & Lybrand, management consultants, 1991–95. *Recreations:* antique book collecting, music, swimming.
Died 8 Feb. 2002.

MUNFORD, William Arthur, MBE 1946; PhD; FCLIP; Librarian Emeritus, National Library for the Blind; *b* 27 April 1911; *s* of late Ernest Charles Munford and Florence Margaret Munford; *m* 1934, Hazel Despard Wilmer; two *s* one *d. Educ:* Hornsey County Sch.; LSE (BScEcon, PhD). Asst, Hornsey Public Libraries, 1927–31; Chief Asst, Ilford Public Libraries, 1931–34; Borough Librarian, Dover, 1934–45 (Food Exec. Officer, 1939–45); City Librarian, Cambridge, 1945–53; Dir-Gen., Nat. Library for the Blind, 1954–82. Hon. Sec., Library Assoc., 1952–55, Hon. Fellow 1977. Trustee Emeritus, Ulverscroft Foundn. *Publications:* Books for Basic Stock, 1939; Penny Rate: aspects of British public library history, 1951; William Ewart, MP, 1960; Edward Edwards, 1963; (with W. G. Fry) Louis Stanley Jast, 1966; James Duff Brown, 1968; A History of the Library Association 1877–1977, 1976; (with S. Godbolt) The Incomparable Mac (biog. of Sir J. Y. W. MacAlister), 1983; Who was Who in British Librarianship 1800–1985, 1987; contribs to librarianship jls, 1933–. *Recreations:* reading, rough gardening, wood sawing, cycling, serendipity. *Address:* 11 Manor Court, Pinehurst, Grange Road, Cambridge CB3 9BE. *T:* (01223) 362962. *Club:* National Liberal.   *Died 23 Dec. 2002.*

MUNRO, Sir Kenneth (Arnold William), 16th Bt *cr* 1634, of Foulis-Obsdale, Ross-shire; *b* 26 June 1910; *s* of Arnold Harry Munro (*d* 1968), *g s* of Sir Charles Munro, 9th Bt, and Hilda Marion Smith (*d* 1961); *S* cousin, 1996, but his name does not appear on the Official Roll of the Baronetage; *m* 1935, Olive Freda, *d* of Francis Broome;

one *s* one *d. Heir: s* Ian Kenneth Munro, *b* 5 April 1940.
Died 3 April 2004.

MURPHY, James Joseph, (Jim); Director of Social Services, Manchester City Council, 1995–2000; *b* 11 July 1952; *s* of George Joseph Murphy and Christina Frances Murphy; *m* 1983, Dorothy Anne Lewis; one *s* one *d. Educ:* St Bede's Coll., Manchester; Liverpool Univ. (BA Hons 1973; CQSW 1976); Manchester Univ. (MA Econ 1983). Social Worker, Gateshead, 1974–75; Social Worker and Team Leader, Liverpool, 1976–86; Manchester City Council: Team Leader, Social Services Dept, 1986–88; Policy Officer, Chief Exec's Dept, 1988–90; Asst Dir of Recreation, 1991–92; Purchasing Manager, 1992–93, Asst Dir, 1993–95, Social Services Dept; Sen. Manager, Quality Control, Wigan, 1990–91. Trustee and Hon. Treas., Russian European Trust for Welfare Reform, 1997–2000. *Recreations:* reading, travel, family activities.
Died Nov. 2002.

MURRAY OF EPPING FOREST, Baron *cr* 1985 (Life Peer), of Telford in the County of Shropshire; **Lionel Murray,** OBE 1966; PC 1976; General Secretary of the Trades Union Congress, 1973–84; *b* 2 Aug. 1922; *m* 1945, Heather Woolf; two *s* two *d. Educ:* Wellington (Salop) Grammar Sch.; QMC, London, 1940–41; NCLC; New Coll., Oxford, 1945–47 (Hon. Fellow, 1975). War Service, KSLI. Economic Dept, TUC, 1947, Head of Dept, 1954–69; Asst Gen. Sec., TUC, 1969–73. Mem., NEDC, 1973–84; Vice-President: ICFTU, 1973; European Trade Union Confedn, 1974. President: Friends of Epping Forest; Friends of Ironbridge Gorge Museum; Vice-President: Nat. Children's Home; Hearing and Speech Trust; Ironbridge Mus. Trust; Wesley's Chapel; Nat. Youth Theatre. Trustee, ADAPT. Patron: St Clare Hospice; Shropshire Soc.; Vice-Patron, Winged Fellowship. Fellow, QMW, 1988; Hon. Fellow, Sheffield City Polytechnic, 1979. Hon. DSc: Aston, 1977; Salford, 1978; Hon. LLD: St Andrews, 1979; Leeds, 1985. *Address:* 29 The Crescent, Loughton, Essex IG10 4PY. *T:* (020) 8508 4425.   *Died 20 May 2004.*

MURRAY, Dame (Alice) Rosemary, DBE 1977; MA, DPhil; JP; DL; President, New Hall, Cambridge, 1964–81 (Tutor in Charge, 1954–64); Vice-Chancellor, Cambridge University, 1975–77; *b* 28 July 1913; *d* of late Adm. A. J. L. Murray and Ellen Maxwell Spooner. *Educ:* Downe House, Newbury; Lady Margaret Hall, Oxford (Hon. Fellow, 1968). MA (Oxon and Cantab); BSc, DPhil (Oxon). Lecturer in chemistry: Royal Holloway Coll., 1938–41; Sheffield Univ., 1941–42. Served War of 1939–45, Experimental Officer, Admiralty Signals Establishment, 1941; WRNS, 1942–46, Chief Officer. Lectr in Chemistry, Girton Coll., Cambridge, 1946–54, Fellow, 1949, Tutor, 1951, Hon. Fellow, 1976; Demonstrator in Chemistry, Univ. of Cambridge, 1947–52. Dir, Midland Bank Ltd, 1978–84; Independent Dir, The Observer, 1981–93. Member: Lockwood Cttee on Higher Educn in NI, 1963–65; Wages Councils, 1968–93; Council, GPDST, 1969–93; Armed Forces Pay Review Body, 1971–81; Pres., Nat. Assoc. of Adult Educn, 1977–80, Vice-Pres., 1980–83. Governor and Chm., Keswick Coll. of Education, 1953–83; Mem. Delegacy, Goldsmiths' Coll., London Univ., 1986–89; Visitor, Homerton Coll., Cambridge, 1990–. Mem. Council, Toynbee Hall, 1983–89. Liveryman, Goldsmiths' Co., 1978–. JP City of Cambridge, 1953–83; DL Cambs, 1982. Hon. Fellow: LMH, Oxford, 1970; Girton Coll., Cambridge, 1975; New Hall, Cambridge, 1981; Robinson Coll., Cambridge, 1985. Hon. DSc: New Univ. of Ulster, 1972; Leeds, 1975; Pennsylvania, 1975; Wellesley Coll., 1976; Hon. DCL Oxon, 1976; Hon. DL Univ. Southern California, 1976; Hon. LLD: Sheffield, 1977; Cantab, 1988. *Recreations:* gardening, book binding and restoring. *Address:* 3 Oxford Road, Old Marston, Oxford OX3 0PQ.   *Died 7 Oct. 2004.*

MURRAY, Sir Antony; *see* Murray, Sir J. A. J.

MURRAY, George Sargent; Forestry Commissioner, 1981–84; *b* 2 Oct. 1924; *s* of James and Helen Murray; *m* 1951, Anita Garden Fraser; two *s*. *Educ*: Buckie High School. Inland Revenue, 1941–43; Royal Navy, 1943–46; Inland Revenue, 1946–49; Dept of Agriculture and Fisheries for Scotland, 1949–67; Scottish Development Dept, 1967–71; Scottish Economic Planning Dept, Scottish Office, 1971–76; Dept of Agriculture and Fisheries for Scotland, 1976–81. *Recreation:* golf. *T*: (0131) 449 2538.   *Died 22 March 2004.*

MURRAY, Rev. Gordon, CB 1994; PhD; Methodist Minister, Edinburgh and Forth Circuit, since 1999; Training and Development Officer, Scotland District, Methodist Church, since 1999; *b* 25 Aug. 1935; *s* of late James Murray, Aberdeen, and Annie Hardie (*née* Center); *m* 1964, Janet Yerrington; two *s* one *d*. *Educ*: Kirkcaldy High Sch.; Edinburgh Univ. (BSc (Hons), PhD). Research Fellow: Atomic Energy of Canada, 1960–62; UKAEA, Harwell, 1962–65; Lectr, Univ. of Manchester, 1965–69; Principal, Scottish Home and Health Dept, 1970–77; Assistant Secretary: Scottish Educn Dept, 1977–79; Central Services, Scottish Office, 1979–86; Dir, Scottish Courts Admin, 1986–95. Ordained, 1992; Methodist Minister, Poole and Swanage Circuit, 1995–99. *Recreations:* reading, hill walking, gardening. *Address:* 12 Liggars Place, Dunfermline, Fife KY12 7XZ. *T*: (01383) 624065.   *Died 4 Sept. 2002.*

MURRAY, Sir (John) Antony (Jerningham), Kt 1987; CBE 1980; Hon. Adviser to Government of Barbados in United Kingdom, since 1961; *b* 21 Jan. 1921; *s* of Captain John Challenger Murray and Cecilia Annette Murray (*née* Jerningham); *m* 1943, Hon. Winifred Mary, *e d* of 2nd Baron Hardinge of Penshurst, PC, GCB, GCVO, MC; one *s*. *Educ*: Eton College; New College, Oxford (2 terms). Grenadier Guards, 1940–46 (Major). Dir,

Christmas Island Phosphate Co. Ltd, 1947–51; Mem. Exec. Cttee, West India Cttee, 1957– (Chm., 1963–65; Vice-Pres., 1966–). *Recreation:* fishing. *Address:* Woodmancote Manor Cottage, Cirencester, Glos GL7 7ED. *T*: (01285) 831226. *Clubs:* Boodle's, MCC.
                                    Died 20 March 2002.

MURRAY, Nigel Ormiston Gauvain; Master of the Supreme Court, Queen's Bench Division, since 1991; a Recorder, since 1994; *b* 22 Jan. 1944; *s* of late Dr Ronald Ormiston Murray, MBE and Dr Catherine Joan Suzette Gauvain, FFCM; *m* 1970, Shirley Arbuthnot; one *s* one *d*. *Educ*: Stowe. Called to the Bar, Inner Temple, 1965; Mem. of Bar, Republic of Ireland and Sierra Leone; in practice, Western Circuit, specialising in Privy Council Appeals and Commonwealth Law, 1966–84 and 1987–90; Judge of High Court of Botswana, 1984–87; Asst Recorder, 1982–94. An Editor, Supreme Court Practice, 1991–99. *Recreation:* golf. *Address:* Royal Courts of Justice, Strand, WC2A 2LL. *T*: (020) 7936 6000, *Fax:* (020) 7936 7165. *Clubs:* Garrick; Berkshire Golf, Rye Golf.
                                    Died 9 Jan. 2002.

MURRAY, Dame Rosemary; *see* Murray, Dame A. R.

MURTAGH, Miss Marion; Managing Director: Stats (MR) Ltd, 1985–87 (Chairman, 1970–85); CSB Data Processing Ltd, 1985–87 (Chairman, 1970–85). *Educ*: Waverley Grammar Sch., Birmingham. Qualified as: Certified Accountant, 1947; Chartered Secretary, 1948. Proprietor, The Calculating Bureau, 1938–51, Joint Owner, 1951–61. Mem., and Pres., West Midlands Bridge Club. Pres., Dorridge Village Hall Assoc. *Recreation:* bridge. *Address:* 42 Dovehouse Court, Warwick Grange, Solihull, West Midlands B91 1EW. *T*: (0121) 704 0873.
                                    Died 8 Nov. 2001.

N

NAIR, C(hengara) V(eetil) Devan; President of Singapore, 1981–85; *b* Malacca, Malaysia, 5 Aug. 1923; *s* of Karunakaran Illath Vayalakkara and Devaki Chengara Veetil Nair; *m* 1953, Avadai Dhanam Lakshimi (*d* 2005); three *s* one *d*. *Educ:* Victoria Sch., Singapore. Teacher, St Andrew's Sch., 1949–51; Gen. Sec., Singapore Teachers' Union, 1949–51; Convenor, and Mem. Central Exec. Cttee, People's Action Party, 1954–56; Political Sec., Min. of Education, 1959–60; Chm., Singapore Adult Educn Bd, 1961–64; National Trades Union Congress: Sec. Gen., 1962–65, 1969–79; Dir, Res. Unit, 1969–81; Pres., 1979–81; Pres., Asian Regl Orgn, ICFTU, 1976–81. MP Malaysia, 1964–69, Singapore, 1979–81; first Sec. Gen., Democratic Action Party, Malaysia, 1964–69. Member: Nat. Wages Council, 1972–81; Housing and Develt Bd, 1975–81; Presidential Council for Minority Rights, 1979–81; Chm., Singapore Labour Foundn, 1977–81. Mem. Council, Nat. Univ. of Singapore, 1980–81. Life Member: Singapore Cancer Soc.; Ramakrishna Mission; Sri Aurobindo Soc. Hon. DLitt Nat. Univ. of Singapore, 1976. *Publications:* (ed) Who Lives if Malaysia Dies?, 1969; (ed) Singapore: Socialism that Works, 1976; (ed) Tomorrow: the peril and the promise, 1976; (ed) Asian Labour and the Dynamics of Change, 1977; (ed) Not by Wages Alone, 1982. *Address:* 176 Buckingham Drive, Hamilton, Ont L9C 2G7, Canada.

Died 7 Dec. 2005.

NALL, Sir Michael (Joseph), 2nd Bt *cr* 1954, of Hoveringham, co. Nottingham; Vice Lord-Lieutenant of Nottinghamshire, 1989–91; *b* 6 Oct. 1921; *er s* of Col Sir Joseph Nall, 1st Bt and Edith Elizabeth, *y d* of John Liell Francklin, JP and Hon. Alice Maude (*e d* of 3rd Viscount St Vincent); *S* father, 1958; *m* 1951, Angela Loveday Hanbury, *e d* of Air Chief Marshal Sir Alec Coryton, KCB, KBE, MVO, DFC; two *s*. *Educ:* Wellington College, Berks. Joined Royal Navy, 1939; served War of 1939–45 (at sea); psc(mil.) 1949; Lt-Comdr, 1950–61, retired. General Manager, Guide Dogs for the Blind Association, 1961–64. Appeal Comr, Inland Revenue, 1981–96. Pres., Nottingham Chamber of Commerce and Industry, 1972–74. DL Notts, 1970; High Sheriff, Notts, 1971. Chairman: Notts Scout Assoc., 1968–88 (Silver Acorn, 1979; Silver Wolf, 1989); Papplewick Pumping Station Trust, 1974–2000. *Recreations:* field sports, flying. *Heir: s* Edward William Joseph Nall, *b* 24 Nov. 1952. *Address:* Hoveringham Hall, Nottingham NG14 7JR.

Died 8 Sept. 2001.

NAPPER, John Pelham; painter; *b* London, 17 Sept. 1916; *e s* of late John Mortimer Napper and Dorothy Charlotte (*née* Hill); *m* 1st, 1935, Hedvig Sophie Armour (marr. diss.; she *d* 1996); 2nd, 1945, Pauline Davidson. *Educ:* Frensham Heights, Surrey and privately; Dundee Sch. of Art; Royal Acad. Schs of Art. Served War of 1939–45: commnd RA, 1941; Ceylon, 1942, War Artist to Ceylon Comd, 1943–44; seconded to RNVR, 1944, E Africa, 1944; demobilised, 1945. Taught life painting at St Martin's Sch. of Art, London, 1949–57. Lived in France, 1957–70. One-man exhibitions: Leicester Galleries, London, 1949, 1961, 1962; Adams Gallery, London, 1957, 1959; La Maison de la Pensée Française, Paris, 1960; Galerie Lahumière, Paris, 1963; Galleries Hervé and Lahumière, Paris, 1965; Larcada Gallery, New York, 1968, 1970, 1972, 1975, 1977; Browse and Darby Gall., 1978, 1980; Ludlow Fest., 1985, 1994; Thos Agnew and Sons, 1986; Albemarle Gall., 1988, 1990, 1991; Gillian Jason Gall., London, 1993; Silk Top Hat Gall., Ludlow, 1998 (retrospective), 1999, 2000; retrospective exhibitions: Walker Art Gall., Liverpool, 1959; Oldham Art Gall., 1984; Machynlleth Art Centre, 1993, 2000; Colnaghi &

Co., London, 1996; Harley Gall., Welbeck, 1996; Burford House, Herefordshire, 1996; Sotheby's, 1998. Paintings acquired by: BM; Contemp. Art Soc.; Courtauld Inst.; Fitzwilliam Mus.; Walker Art Gall., Liverpool; Musée d'Art Moderne, Paris; Musée Municipale, Dieppe; Nat. Gall., Kenya; Columbus Gall. of Fine Arts, Ohio, and other public and pvte collections. Vis. Prof. of Fine Arts, Southern Illinois Univ., USA, 1968–69. Médaille d'argent, Salon des Artistes françaises, Paris, 1947; prize, International Exhibition of Fine Arts, Moscow, 1957; International Assoc. of Art Critics Prize, 1961. *Publication:* The Rose and the Flame, 1994. *Address:* Steadvallets Farmhouse, Bromfield, Ludlow, Shropshire SY8 2LB.

Died 17 March 2001.

NARASIMHAN, Chakravarthi Vijayaraghava, MBE 1946; Senior Fellow, UN Institute for Training and Research, 1978–93; *b* 21 May 1915; *s* of Chakravarthi V. and Janaki Vijayaraghavachari; *m* 1938, Janaki, *d* of Dr M. T. Chari; two *d*. *Educ:* University of Madras (BA); Oxford (MA). Indian Civil Service, 1936; Dep. Sec., Development Dept, Government of Madras, 1945–48; Min. of Agriculture, Govt of India, 1950–53; Joint Sec., Economic Affairs Dept, Ministry of Finance, 1953–56; Executive Sec., UN Economic Commission for Asia and Far East, 1956–59; Under-Sec. for Special Political Affairs, UN, 1959–62; Chef de Cabinet of the Sec.-Gen., UN, 1961–73; Under-Sec., 1962–67, Under-Sec.-Gen. 1967–69, for Gen. Assembly Affairs, UN; Dep. Administrator, UN Devlt Prog., 1969–72; Under-Sec.-Gen. for Inter-Agency Affairs and Co-ordination, UN, 1973–78; Organizing Exec. Sec., Cotton Devlt Internat., UN Devlt Programme, 1979–81. Hon. Doctor of Laws, Williams Coll. Williamstown, Mass, 1960; Hon. Dr of Humane Letters, Colgate Univ., 1966. *Publications:* The Mahabharata (selected verses), 1965; The United Nations: an inside view, 1988; History of United Nations University, 1994; UN at 50: recollections, 1996. *Recreations:* Sanskrit literature, South Indian classical music, tennis. *Address:* 5527 Uppingham Street, Chevy Chase, MD 20815, USA. *T:* (301) 6578571.

Died 2 Nov. 2003.

NARAYAN, Rasipuram Krishnaswamy, (R. K. Narayan); author; *b* Madras, 10 Oct. 1906; *m* 1934 (wife *d* 1939); (one *d* decd). *Educ:* Maharaja's College, Mysore, India. Padma Bushan award for distinguished services to literature. Hon. LittD Leeds, 1967. *Publications: novels:* Swami and Friends, 1935; The Bachelor of Arts, 1937; The Dark Room, 1939; The English Teacher, 1945; Mr Sampath, 1947; The Financial Expert, 1952; Waiting for the Mahatma, 1955; The Guide, 1958; The Man-Eater of Malgudi, 1961; Gods, Demons and Others, 1964; The Sweet Vendor, 1967; The Painter of Signs, 1977; A Tiger for Malgudi, 1983; (ed) The Ramayana, 1973; (ed) The Mahabharata, 1978; Talkative Man, 1986; The World of Nagaraj, 1990; The Grandmother's Tale, 1993; *autobiography:* My Days, 1975; *short stories:* An Astrologer's Day; The Lawley Road; A Horse and Two Goats, 1970; Malgudi Days, 1982; Under the Banyan Tree and Other Stories, 1985, etc; *essays:* Next Sunday, 1955 (India); My Dateless Diary, 1960 (India). *Address:* c/o Sheil Land Associates, 43 Doughty Street, WC1N 2LF; Yadavagiri, Mysore 2, India.

Died 13 May 2001.

NARAYANAN, Kocheril Raman; President of India, 1997–2002 (Vice-President, 1992–97); *b* 27 Oct. 1920; *s* of late Raman Vaidyan Narayanan; *m* 1951, Usha Ma Tint Tint; two *d*. *Educ:* Travancore Univ. (MA); LSE (BSc 1948; Hon. Fellow, 1972). Lectr, Univ. of Travancore, 1942; journalist, 1944–45; entered Foreign Service, 1949;

served Rangoon, Tokyo, London and Min. of External Affairs, 1949–60; Actg High Comr, Australia, 1961–62; Consul-Gen., Hanoi, 1962–63; Dir, China Div., 1963–67; Ambassador to Thailand, 1967–69; Jt Sec. for Policy Planning, 1969–70; Prof., Jawaharlal Nehru Univ., 1970–72; Ambassador to Turkey, 1973–75; Addtl Sec. for Policy Planning Div., 1975–76; Sec. (East), 1976; Ambassador to China, 1976–78; Mem., Indian Delegn to UN Gen. Assembly, 1979; Ambassador to USA, 1980–84; elected MP for Ottapalam, Kerala, Lok Sabha, 1984; Minister of State for: Planning, 1984–85; External Affairs, 1985–86; Atomic Energy, Space, Electronics and Ocean Develt, 1986–87; Sci. and Technol., 1986–89. Hon. Fellow, Centre for Develt Studies, Trivandrum. *Publications:* (jtly) India and America: essays in understanding; Images and Insights; (jtly) Nonalignment in Contemporary International Relations; contribs on internat. relns, Indian politics, and literature. *Address:* c/o Rashtrapati Bhavan, New Delhi 110004, India.

Died 9 Nov. 2005.

NEALON, Dr Catherina Theresa, (Rina), CBE 1979; JP; Chairman, Lothian Health Board, 1973–81; *b* 8 Aug. 1915; *d* of John and Margaret O'Reilly, Glasgow; *m* 1940, James Patrick Nealon (*d* 1989); one *s*. *Educ*: Convent of Mercy, Garnethill, Glasgow. Mem., Edinburgh Town Council for Pilton Ward, 1949–74; served as Magistrate Visiting Prisons, 1954–57; Licensing Court, 1954–57; Judge of Police, 1957–62; Chm., Health Cttee, 1972–73. Member: Educn Cttee, Civil Defence Commn, 1949–73; Royal Infirmary and Associated Hosp's Bd of Management, 1952–56; NHS Exec. Council for City of Edinburgh, 1953–74 (Vice-Chm., May 1966–74); Exec. Cttee of Scottish Assoc. of Exec. Councils, 1967–74 (Vice-Pres., 1971, Pres., 1972); SE Regional Hosp. Bd, Scotland, 1966–74 (Chm., 1969–74); Med. Educn Cttee, 1969–74 (Chm., 1972–74); Livingston New Town Jt Health Service Adv. Cttee, 1969–73; Scottish Health Service Planning Council, 1974–81; Common Services Agency, Management Cttee, and Convenor, Estabt and Accommodation Sub-Cttee, Scottish Health Service, 1974–77; Univ. Liaison Cttee, 1974– (Chm., 1978–81); Edinburgh and SE District Cttee, Scottish Gas Consultative Council, 1967–74 (Chm., 1970–74; Mem. Council, 1969–74); Clean Air Council for Scotland, 1966–75; Nat. Soc. for Clean Air, Scottish Div., 1963– (Vice-Pres., 1970–72, Pres., 1972–74); A&C Whitley Council, 1973–81 (Vice-Chm., 1975–81); Nat. Negotiating Cttee; Ambulance Officers' Negotiating Cttee (Management Side Chm., 1979–81); Gen. Whitley Council (Mem., Gen. Purposes Cttee and Jt Negotiating Cttee, 1980–81); Nat. Appeals Panel; SE Dist Cttee, Gas Consumers' Council, 1981–87; Chm., Scottish Hosp. Supplies Steering Cttee, 1972–74. Former Member: Edin. and Lothian Probation Cttee; Animal Disease Res. Assoc.; Edin. Coll. of Art; Royal Blind Asylum and Sch.; Scottish Accident Prevention Council; Marriage Guidance Council; Nat. Assoc. for Maternal and Child Welfare; Nat. Council on recruitment of Nurses and Midwives; Scottish Assoc. for Mental Health; Assoc. of Sea and Airport Authorities; Edin. and Lothians Tourist Assoc.; Youth Employment Cttee; Extra-Mural Cttee, Edin. Univ., 1960–65; Mem. Bd of Governors: Napier Coll. of Science and Technology, 1964–73 (Vice-Chm., 1971–73); Telford Coll. for Further Education, 1969–72; Moray House Coll. of Educn; Wellington Farm Approved Sch.; Dr Guthrie's Girls' Sch. JP Edinburgh, 1957; Mem. Justices Cttee, 1975; Justice on District Court, 1975–83; Mem. Extra-Parliamentary Panel, 1976–86; Mem., Crossroads Cttee, 1987–98. Attended 25th Anniv. Meeting, President's Cttee on Employment of Handicapped, Washington, 1972. Travelled to many countries with Internat. Hosp. Fedn study tours. Member, Church of Scotland. Dr *hc* Edinburgh, 1977. *Recreation:* reading. *Address:* 34 Learmonth Crescent, Edinburgh EH4 1DE. *T:* (0131) 332 6191. *Died 23 July 2004.*

NEEDHAM, Prof. Roger Michael, CBE 2001; FRS 1985; FREng; Managing Director, Microsoft Research Ltd, since 1997; Professor of Computer Systems, 1981–98, then Emeritus, and Fellow of Wolfson College, since 1967, University of Cambridge; *b* 9 Feb. 1935; *s* of Leonard William Needham and Phyllis Mary Needham; *m* 1958, Karen Ida Boalth Spärck-Jones. *Educ:* Cambridge Univ. (BA 1956, PhD 1961). FBCS; FREng (FEng 1993). Cambridge University: Sen. Asst in Research, Computer Lab., 1963–64; Asst Dir of Research, 1964–73; Reader in Computer Systems, 1973–81; Hd of Computer Lab., 1980–95; Pro-Vice-Chancellor, 1996–98. Member: UGC, 1985–89; DASC, 1999–. Member: Chesterton RDC, 1971–74; South Cambs DC, 1974–86. Fellow, Assoc. for Computing Machinery, USA, 1994; MAE 1998. Hon. DSc: Kent, 1983; Birmingham, 1995; Twente, 1996; Anglia Poly. Univ., 1998; East Anglia, 1999; Sheffield, 2000; Loughborough, 2001; DUniv N London, 1999. Faraday Medal, IEE, 1998. *Publications:* (with M. V. Wilkes) The Cambridge CAP Computer and its Operating System, 1979; (with A. J. Herbert) The Cambridge Distributed Computing System, 1982; contribs to publications on computer operating systems, communications, security and protection. *Recreation:* sailing. *Address:* Microsoft Research Ltd, 7 JJ Thomson Avenue, Cambridge CB3 0FB. *T:* (01223) 479700, *Fax:* (01223) 479999. *Clubs:* Naval; Royal Harwich Yacht.

Died 28 Feb. 2003.

NEHRU, Braj Kumar, Padma Vibhushan, 1999; Chairman: Indian Advisory Board, Grindlays Bank, 1988–94; Hindustan Oil Exploration Co. Ltd, 1987–94; Director, East India Hotels Ltd, since 1988; *b* Allahabad, 4 Sept. 1909; *s* of Brijlal and Rameshwari Nehru; *m* 1935, Magdalena Friedmann; three *s*. *Educ:* Allahabad Univ. (BSc); LSE (BSc Econ; Fellow); Balliol Coll., Oxford. Called to the Bar, Inner Temple. Joined ICS, 1934; Asst Comr, 1934–39; Under-Sec., Dept of Education, Health and Lands, 1939; Mem., Indian Legislative Assembly, 1939; Officer on special duty, Reserve Bank of India, and Under-Sec., Finance Dept, 1940–44; Jt Sec., 1946; Exec. Dir, IBRD (World Bank), and Minister, Indian Embassy, Washington, 1949–54 and 1958–62; Advr to Sudan Govt, 1955; Sec., Dept of Econ. Affairs, 1957–58; Comr-Gen. for Econ. Affairs, Min. of Finance, and Ambassador-at-Large, 1958–61; Ambassador to USA, 1961–68; Governor: Assam and Nagaland, 1968–73; Meghalaya, Manipur and Tripura, 1972–73; High Comr in London, 1973–77; Governor: Jammu and Kashmir, 1981–84; Gujarat, 1984–86. Representative of India: Reparations Conf., 1945; Commonwealth Finance Ministers Confs, UN Gen. Assembly, 1949–52 and 1960; FAO Confs, 1949–50; Sterling Balance Confs, 1946–49; Bandung Conf., 1955. Deputed to enquire into Australian Fed. Finance, 1946; Member: UN Adv. Cttee on Admin and Budgetry Questions, 1951–53; UN Investments Cttee, 1962–91 (Chm., 1977–91; Mem. Emeritus, 1991); Vice-Chm., Vienna Inst. for Develt, 1962–90; Mem. Internat. Adv. Council, Vienna Inst. for Develt & Co-operation, 1990–. Mem., Governing Body, Dyal Singh Coll., 1988– (Chm., 1988–97); Trustee: Indira Gandhi Meml Trust, 1986–; Dyal Singh Coll. Trust, 1988– (Pres., 1988–98); Dyal Singh Library Trust, 1988– (Pres., 1988–2000); Tribune Trust, 1988– (Pres., 1996–2000); World Meml Fund for Disaster Relief, 1989–; Soc. for Preservation of Kasauli and its environs, 1991– (Pres., 1991). Hon. LLD Mo Valley Coll.; Hon. LittD Jacksonville; Hon. DLitt Punjab. *Publications:* Australian Federal Finance, 1947; Speaking of India, 1966; Thoughts on the Present Discontents, 1986; Nice Guys Finish Second, 1997. *Recreations:* reading, writing. *Address:* Fair View, Kasauli 173204, India. *T:* (01792) 72189, *Fax:* (01792) 72929. *Clubs:* Gymkhana, India International Centre (Delhi).

Died 31 Oct. 2001.

NEIL, Thomas, CMG 1962; TD 1951; Director, Thomson Foundation, 1963–79; *b* 23 Dec. 1913; *s* of late W. R. Neil; *m* 1939, Phyllis Selina Gertrude Sargeant; one *d*.

Educ: King's Coll., Univ. of Durham (BSc, NDA). Served War of 1939–45 with Devonshire Regiment (TA), in UK, E Africa, Middle East (Lt Col). Lectr in Agriculture, Devon County Council, 1936–39; Chief Technical Officer, 1946. Colonial Service: District Officer, Kenya, 1947; Asst Chief Sec., 1957; Permanent Sec., 1957; Ministry of State, Kenya, 1959–63. Directed Africanisation of CS. Director, Kenya Famine Relief, 1961–63. Lay Mem., Immigration Appeal Tribunal, 1971–84. *Recreation:* country life. *Address:* 5 Cakeham Way, West Wittering, Chichester, W Sussex PO20 8EQ.

Died 7 May 2002.

NEILL, Major Rt Hon. Sir Ivan, Kt 1973; PC (NI) 1950; *b* Belfast, 1 July 1906; *m* 1928, Margaret Helena Allen. *Educ:* Ravenscroft Nat. Sch., Belfast; Shaftesbury House Tutorial Coll., Belfast; Queen's Univ., Belfast (BSc Econ). FRGS. Served War of 1939–45: RE in UK and FE, 1939–46; Major. MP Ballynafeigh Div. of Belfast, Parlt of NI, 1949–73; Government of Northern Ireland: Minister: of Labour and National Insurance, 1950–62; of Home Affairs, Aug.-Oct. 1952; of Education, 1962–64; of Finance, 1964–65; Leader, House of Commons, Oct. 1964; resigned from Govt, April 1965; Minister of Develt, Dec. 1968–March 1969; Speaker, House of Commons, 1969–73. Represented NI at Internat. Labour Confs, 1950–61. Councillor and Alderman in Belfast Corp., 1946–50 (specialised in educn, housing and youth welfare). DL Belfast, 1966–86. *Publications:* Travel Experiences, 1991; A Story in Verse, 1995; Church and State, 1995. *Address:* Cranagh Cottage, Warren Road, Donaghadee, Co. Down, Northern Ireland BT21 0PQ.

Died 4 Nov. 2001.

NEILL, Very Rev. Ivan Delacherois, CB 1963; OBE 1958; Provost of Sheffield and Vicar of the Cathedral Church of St Peter and St Paul, 1966–74, then Emeritus; Chaplain to the Queen, 1962–66; *b* 10 July 1912; *s* of Rev. Robert Richard Neill and Bessie Montrose (*née* Purdon); *m* 1938, Enid Eyre Godson (*née* Bartholomew) (*d* 1995); one *s* one *d*. *Educ:* St Dunstan's College; Jesus College, Cambridge (MA); London College of Divinity. Deacon 1936, priest 1937; Curate: St Mary, West Kensington, 1936–38; Christ Church, Crouch End, 1938–39; CF 4th Cl., Chatham; served BEF and UK with 3rd Div., Orkneys, Sandhurst, 1941–43; Sen. Chaplain, N Aldershot, 1943; 43rd (Wessex) Div., 1943–45 (despatches); DACG, 1st British Corps, 1945–46; Sen. Chaplain, Guards Depot, Caterham, 1947–50; DACG, N Canal, Egypt, 1950–53; Catterick, 1953; Warden, Royal Army Chaplains Dept Trng Centre, 1954–57; Sen. Chaplain, SHAPE 1957–58; Asst Chaplain-Gen., Middle East Land Forces, 1958–60; QHC 1960; Chaplain General to HM Forces, 1960–66. Chairman of Governors, Monkton Combe Sch., Bath, 1969–81; Pres. of Foundn, St Paul's and St Mary's C of E Coll. of Educn, Cheltenham, 1978–88. Knight Officer, Order of Orange Nassau (with Swords) (Netherlands), 1946. *Publication:* Far from Tipperary (memoirs), 2000. *Address:* York House, 194 High Street, Uckfield, E Sussex TN22 1RD. *T:* (01825) 766184. *Club:* National. *Died 18 June 2001.*

NELSON, Air Marshal Sir Richard; *see* Nelson, Air Marshal Sir S. R. C.

NELSON, St Elmo Dudley, CMG 1964; Permanent Secretary, Military Governor's Office, Kano, 1968–76; Acting Secretary to Military Government, and Head of Kano State Civil Service, 1970, 1973 and 1975; *b* 18 March 1919; *s* of late Dudley Nelson and Dorothy Maida (*née* Browne), Highton, Victoria, Australia; *m* 1958, Lynette Margaret, *o d* of late Phillip Anthony Browne, Yarram and Frankston, Victoria, Australia. *Educ:* privately; Geelong School; Oxford University; Sorbonne. Served War of 1939–45 (despatches): 2/7 Australian Infantry Bn (Major); campaigns N Africa, Greece, Crete, New Guinea; Instructor Staff Coll., Cabalah, 1944. Joined HM Colonial Administrative Service, 1947; Nigeria: Cadet, 1947; Administrative Officer (Class II), 1957; Resident, Plateau Province, 1961; Resident and Provincial Sec., Kabba Province, 1962; Provincial Sec., Kano Province, 1963–67, Sokoto, 1967–68. Chm., Cttee which divided assets of Northern Region between the six Northern States, 1967. Election supervisor, Rhodesian independence elecns, 1980. Gen. Tax Comr, S Wilts, 1980. *Recreations:* fishing, polo, squash. *Address:* Home Farm House, Teffont Evias, Salisbury, Wilts SP3 5RG. *Club:* MCC.

Died 18 July 2001.

NELSON, Air Marshal Sir (Sidney) Richard (Carlyle), KCB 1963 (CB 1962); OBE 1949; Director-General, Royal Air Force Medical Services, 1962–67; Director of Research and Medical Services, Aspro-Nicholas Ltd, 1967–72; *b* Ponoka, Alberta, Canada, 14 Nov. 1907; *s* of M. O. Nelson, BA; *m* 1939, Christina Elizabeth Powell; two *s*. *Educ:* Univ. of Alberta (MD). Commissioned RAF, 1935; served: England 1935–36; Egypt and Western Desert, 1936–42; Fighter Command, 1943; UK Delegation (Canada), 1943–44; British Jt Services Mission (Washington), 1945–48; RAF Staff Coll., 1949; Air Ministry, 1949–52; Comd RAF Hosp., Nocton Hall, 1953–55; SMO British Forces, Arabian Peninsula, 1956–57; PMO Technical Training Comd, 1957–59; Bomber Comd, 1959–62; QHP 1961–67. *Recreations:* fishing, golf. *Address:* Caffyn's Copse, Shappen Hill Lane, Burley, Hants BH24 4EP. *T:* (01425) 403308. *Club:* Royal Air Force. *Died 5 Nov. 2001.*

NEPEAN, Lt-Col Sir Evan Yorke, 6th Bt *cr* 1802 of Bothenhampton, Dorsetshire; late Royal Signals; *b* 23 Nov. 1909; *s* of Sir Charles Evan Molyneux Yorke Nepean, 5th Bt, and Mary Winifred, *o d* of Rev. William John Swayne, formerly Vicar of Heytesbury, Wilts, and Custos of St John's Hospital, Heytesbury; *S* father, 1953; *m* 1940, (Georgiana) Cicely, *o d* of late Major Noel Edward Grey Willoughby, Middlesex Regiment, of Chancel End House, Heytesbury, Wilts; three *d*. *Educ:* Winchester; Downing College, Cambridge (BA 1931; MA 1946). CEng; MIEE. North West Frontier of India (Mohmand), 1935. Served War of 1939–45: GSO3, War Office, 1939–40; with Royal Signals (Lt-Col 1943), UK, and Middle East, Major 1946; on Staff Southern Command, 1947; GSO1 Royal Signals, Ministry of Defence, 1950–53; Lt-Col 1952; GHQ FARELF, Singapore, 1953–55; Cmdg 11 Air Formation Signal Regt, BAOR, 1955–56, retired. Civil Servant, 1957–59; CSO's branch at HQ Southern Command (Retired Officers' Staff appt), 1959–73. Mem., Salisbury Diocesan Guild of Ringers. *Recreations:* bell-ringing, amateur radio. *Heir:* none. *Address:* Elm View, 31 High Street, West Lavington, Devizes, Wilts SN10 4HQ.

Died 11 March 2002 (ext).

NESTOR, Rt Rev. Donald Patrick; Hon. Assistant Bishop, Diocese of Durham, since 2001; *b* 6 Oct. 1938; *s* of Edwin Roy Nestor and Elsie Myrtle Nestor. *Educ:* Heath Grammar Sch., Halifax, Yorks; Exeter Coll., Oxford (MA); Queen's Coll., Birmingham and Univ. of Birmingham (DipTh); MA Lancaster 2001. Ordained deacon, 1965, priest, 1966; Curate: Woodkirk, dio. Wakefield, 1965–68; Forton, dio. Portsmouth, 1968–72; Asst Chaplain, Univ. of Botswana, Lesotho and Swaziland, Roma, 1972–74, Chaplain of Univ. (from 1975 called Nat. Univ. of Lesotho), 1974–79; Warden of Diocesan Seminary, Roma, 1974–79; Suffragan Bishop, Diocese of Lesotho, 1979–92; Priest-in-Charge, Bretherton, 1992–2000; Asst Bp, Dio. of Blackburn, 1992–2000; Diocesan Ecumenical Officer, Blackburn, 1998–2000. Mem., SSM, 2001–. *Recreations:* singing, travel. *Address:* St Antony's Priory, 74 Claypath, Durham DH1 1QT. *T:* (0191) 384 3747. *Died 10 Jan. 2003.*

NEUMANN, Prof. Bernhard Hermann, AC 1994; FRS 1959; FAA 1964; Hon. Fellow, CSIRO Division of Mathematical and Information Sciences (formerly Mathematics and Statistics), since 2000 (Hon. Research Fellow, 1978–99); *b* Berlin-Charlottenburg, 15 Oct. 1909; *s* of late Richard Neumann and Else (*née* Aronstein); *m* 1st,

1938, Hanna Neumann (*née* von Caemmerer) (*d* 1971), DPhil, DSc, FAA, formerly Prof. and Head of Dept of Pure Mathematics, Sch. of Gen. Studies, ANU; three *s* two *d*; 2nd, 1973, Dorothea Neumann (*née* Zeim), MA, PhD. *Educ:* Herderschule, Berlin; Univs of Freiburg, Berlin, Cambridge. Dr phil Berlin, 1932; PhD Cambridge 1935; DSc Manchester 1954. FACE 1970. Asst Lectr, University Coll, Cardiff, 1937–40. Army Service, 1940–45. Lectr, University Coll., Hull, 1946–48; Lectr, Senior Lectr, Reader, Univ. of Manchester, 1948–61; Prof. and Hd of Dept of Maths, Inst. of Advanced Studies, ANU, Canberra, 1962–74, Emeritus Prof., 1975–; Sen. Res. Fellow, CSIRO Div. of Maths and Stats, 1975–77. Visiting Lecturer: Australian Univs, 1959; Univ. of Cambridge, 1970; Monash Univ., 1980; Visiting Professor: Tata Inst. of Fundamental Research, Bombay, 1959; New York Univ., 1961–62; Univ. of Wisconsin, 1966–67; Vanderbilt Univ., 1969–70; G. A. Miller Vis. Prof., Univ. of Illinois at Urbana-Champaign, 1975; Univ. of Manitoba, 1979; Vis. Fellow, Fitzwilliam Coll., Cambridge, 1970; SERC Visiting Fellow: Univ. of Glasgow, 1985; Univ. of Wales Coll. of Cardiff, 1991; Deutscher Akademischer Austauschs-Dienst Visitor, Univ. of Bielefeld, 1987; Matthew Flinders Lectr, Aust. Acad. Sci., 1984. Wiskundig Genootschap te Amsterdam Prize, 1949; Adams Prize, Univ. of Cambridge, 1952–53. Mem., Aust. Subcommn, Internat. Commn Math. Instruct., 1967–75 (Chm.), and 1979–83; Mem.-at-large, Internat. Commn Math. Instruct., 1975–82, Mem. Exec. Cttee, 1979–82; Mem., Programme Adv. Cttee, Congress Math. Educn, Karlsruhe, 1976, Berkeley, Calif., 1980, Adelaide, Australia, 1984. Member Council: London Math. Society, 1954–61 (Vice-Pres., 1957–59); Aust. Math. Society, 1963–79 (Vice-Pres., 1963–64, 1966–68, 1971–73, Pres., 1964–66; Hon. Mem. 1981–; Fellow, 1994); Aust. Acad. of Science, 1968–71 (a Vice-Pres., 1969–71). Mem. Aust. Nat. Cttee for Mathematics, 1963–75 (Chm., 1966–75); (Foundation) Pres., Aust. Assoc. Math. Teachers, 1966–68, Vice-Pres., 1968–69, Hon. Mem., 1975–; (Foundn) Pres., Canberra Math. Assoc., 1963–65, Vice-Pres., 1965–66, Hon. Mem., 1975–; Hon. Mem., NZ Math. Soc., 1975–; Member: Acad. Adv. Council, RAN Coll., 1978–87; Sci. and Industry Forum, 1989–93. Chairman: Internat. Math. Olympiad Site Cttee, 1981–83; Aust. Math. Olympiad Cttee, 1980–86. Hon. DSc: Univ. of Newcastle, NSW, 1974; Monash Univ., 1982; Univ. of WA, 1995; Univ. of Hull, 1995; ANU, 2001; Hon. DMath Univ. of Waterloo, 1986; Hon. Dr rer. nat. Humboldt Univ., 1992. Non-res. Fellow (Tutor), Bruce Hall, ANU, 1963–; Hon. Fellow: Inst. of Advanced Studies, Math. Scis Inst. (formerly Sch. of Mathematical Scis), ANU, 1975–; Inst. of Combinatories and its Applications, 1990–. Pres., Amateur Sinfonia of Canberra Inc., 1978–80, Vice-Pres., 1980–81, 1983–84, Hon. Mem., 1984–85; Vice-Pres., Friends of the Canberra Sch. of Music, 1983– (Hon. Life Mem., 2001); Pres., Woden Valley Chess Club, 1994–95. Hon. Editor, Proc. London Math. Soc., 1959–61; Assoc. Editor, Pacific Jl Math., 1964–92; (Foundation) Editor, Bulletin of Aust. Math. Soc., 1969–79, Hon. Editor, 1979–; Member Editorial Board: Communications in Algebra, 1973–84; Houston Jl Math., 1974–; Mem., Adv. Bd, Zentralblatt Didaktik Math. 1970–84; Editorial Advr, SE Asian Math. Bull. 1987–; Founder Editor and Publisher, IMU Canberra Circular, 1972–99; Hon. Editor, Algebra Colloquium, Beijing, 1994–; Mem. and Regional Chm., IMU Exchange Commn, 1975–78. *Publications:* Appendix to German and Hungarian translations of A. G. Kuroš: Teoriya Grupp, 1953, 1955: Topics in the Theory of Infinite Groups, Bombay, 1961; Special Topics in Algebra, Vol. I: Universal Algebra, Vol. II: Order Techniques, New York, 1962; Selected Works of B. H. Neumann and Hanna Neumann, 6 vols, 1988; papers, mainly on theory of groups, in various mathematical journals. *Recreations:* chess, cycling, music, camping. *Address:* 20 Talbot Street, Forrest, ACT 2603, Australia. *T:* (2) 62733447, *Fax:* (2)

61255549; *e-mail:* bernhard.neumann@maths.anu.edu.au.
Died 21 Oct. 2002.

NEVILL, Maj.-Gen. Cosmo Alexander Richard, CB 1958; CBE 1954 (OBE 1944); DSO 1944; War Office, 1958–60; Colonel, Royal Fusiliers, 1959–63, retired; *b* 14 July 1907; *s* of late Maj. Cosmo Charles Richard Nevill, DSO, OBE, Eccleston, Leamington Spa; *m* 1934, Grania, *d* of late Maj. G. V. Goodliffe, MC, Birdstown, co. Donegal; one *s* one *d. Educ:* Harrow; Royal Military College. Commissioned as Second Lieutenant, Royal Fusiliers, 1927; served War of 1939–45 (DSO, OBE): on staff, India; commanded 2nd battalion Devonshire Regiment, Normandy; Lieutenant-Colonel, 1944. A General Staff Officer, Military Staff Committee, UN, New York, 1946–48; Chief Instr, Sch. of Infantry, 1948–50; commanded 1st battalion Royal Fusiliers, 1950–51; a Brigade Commander, 1951–54; Commandant School of Infantry, 1954–56; Major-General 1957; GOC 2nd Infantry Division, 1956–58. CC West Suffolk, 1962–67. Lay Canon, St Edmundsbury Cathedral, 1979–85. Freeman, City of London, 1962. *Address:* Holt, Edwardstone, Sudbury, Suffolk CO10 5PJ. *T:* (01787) 210428. *Clubs:* Army and Navy; I Zingari.
Died 19 Sept. 2002.

NEVILLE, Sir Roger (Albert Gartside), Kt 1994; VRD 1965; FCA; Group Chief Executive, Sun Alliance Group, 1987–94 (Director, 1979–96); *b* 23 Dec. 1931; *s* of Geoffrey Graham Gartside Neville and Veronica Lily Neville; *m* 1957, Brenda Mary Parke Hamilton; one *s* three *d.* Royal Navy, 1950–52; joined Sun Alliance Insurance, 1962; General Manager, 1977; Dep. Chief General Manager, 1984. Chm., Eyretel Ltd, 1995–2001; Dir, Equitas Holdings Ltd, 1996–99. Chairman: Policyholders Protection Bd, 1991–94; Pool RE, 1993–96. *Recreations:* sailing, fly fishing, cabinet making. *Address:* Possingworth Manor, Blackboys, near Uckfield, East Sussex TN22 5HE. *Clubs:* Royal Automobile, Royal Ocean Racing. *Died 18 Oct. 2005.*

NEWMAN, Karl Max, CB 1979; Second Counsel to the Chairman of Committees and Legal Adviser to the European Communities Committee, House of Lords, 1982–87; *b* 26 March 1919; *s* of Karl Neumann, DrJur, and Licie Neumann; *m* 1952, Annette, *d* of late Ronald Cross Sheen; one *s* one *d. Educ:* Ottershaw Coll., Surrey; Christ Church, Oxford (MA). Bacon Scholar of Gray's Inn, 1939. Served War in Army, 1940–42. Called to the Bar, Gray's Inn, 1946, Bencher 1987; joined Lord Chancellor's Office, 1949; Asst Solicitor, 1962; Under-Sec., 1972–82; part-time Legal Adviser to European Unit of Cabinet Office, 1972–82; Head of Delegn negotiating UK accession to EEC Convention on Jurisdiction and Judgments, 1972–78. Member: UK delegns to Internat. Diplomatic Confs on Nuclear Liability, 1962–63; expert Cttees of Council of Europe, 1961–68; 10th and 11th Session of Hague Conf. on Private Internat. Law, 1964–68; EEC expert cttees, 1972–82. Hon. Life Mem., British Inst. of Internat. and Comparative Law, 2000 (Hon. Fellow, 1991–99). *Publications:* Das Englisch-Amerikanische Beweisrecht, 1949 (Heidelberg); contribs to legal publications on EEC law, internat. jurisdiction and recognition of judgments. *Recreations:* philately, looking at paintings. *Address:* 17 Marryat Road, Wimbledon, SW19 5BB. *T:* (020) 8946 3430. *Club:* Oxford and Cambridge.
Died 12 Jan. 2001.

NEWMAN, Col Sir Stuart (Richard), Kt 1993; CBE 1984; TD 1952; *b* 13 June 1919; *e s* of late Capt. Thomas Pacey Newman, MC, DCM, and Dorothy, *y d* of Richard Booth Beverley. Served War of 1939–45, Queen's Royal Regt, in Western Desert and in India; service in TA with London Rifle Bde (Col, 56th London Inf. Bde, 1962). Joined Cons. party, 1949; agent for various constituencies in London, N and E Midlands, then posts at Central Office. *Address:* 47 Gilkes Crescent, Dulwich Village, SE21 7BP. *Died 1 Sept. 2002.*

NEWSOME, David Hay, MA; LittD Cantab 1976; FRSL 1981; Master of Wellington College, 1980–89; *b* 15 June 1929; *s* of Captain C. T. Newsome, OBE; *m* 1955, Joan Florence (*d* 1999), *d* of Lt-Col L. H. Trist, DSO, MC; four *d. Educ:* Rossall Sch., Fleetwood; Emmanuel Coll., Cambridge (Schol.; First Cl. in Hist. Tripos Parts I and II, 1952, 1953). Asst Master, Wellington Coll., 1954–59 (Head of History Dept, 1956–59); Fellow of Emmanuel Coll., Cambridge, 1959–70; Asst Lectr in Ecclesiastical History, Univ. of Cambridge, 1961–66; Univ. Lectr, 1966–70; Sen. Tutor, Emmanuel Coll., Cambridge, 1965–70; Headmaster of Christ's Hospital, 1970–79. Lectures: Gore Memorial, Westminster Abbey, 1965; Bishop Westcott Memorial, Cambridge, 1968; Birkbeck, Univ. of Cambridge, 1972. Council of: Ardingly Coll., 1965–69; Eastbourne Coll., 1966–70; Epsom Coll., 1966–70. FRHistS, 1970. *Publications:* A History of Wellington College, 1859–1959, 1959; Godliness and Good Learning, Four Studies in a Victorian Ideal, 1961; The Parting of Friends, a study of the Wilberforces and Henry Manning, 1966; Bishop Westcott and the Platonic Tradition, 1969; Two Classes of Men: Platonism and English Romantic Thought, 1974; On the Edge of Paradise: A. C. Benson the Diarist, 1980 (Whitbread Book of the Year Award); (ed) Edwardian Excursions, 1981; The Convert Cardinals: Newman and Manning, 1993; The Victorian World Picture, 1997; articles in Jl of Theological Studies, Jl of Ecclesiastical History, Theology, History Today, Historical Jl, Recusant History. *Recreations:* music, fell-walking. *Address:* The Retreat, Thornthwaite, Keswick, Cumbria CA12 5SA. *T:* (017687) 78372. *Club:* East India.   *Died 28 April 2004.*

NEWTON-CLARE, Herbert Mitchell, (Bill), CBE 1976; MC 1943; Executive Chairman, Albemarle Group PLC, 1986–98; *b* 5 May 1922; *s* of Herbert John and Eileen Marguerite Newton-Clare; *m*; three *d*; *m* 1992, Harriet Mary Sheila (*née* Nye) (*d* 2003). *Educ:* Cheltenham Coll. TA, Middlesex Regt, 1938; served War of 1939–45: mobilised, 1939; commnd, Wiltshire Regt, 1941; wounded, Normandy, 1944; demobilised, 1945 (Major). Joined Bowyers (Wiltshire) Ltd, as trainee, 1945; Factory Manager, 1955, Gen. Manager, 1957, Man. Dir, 1960, Chm., 1966; following take-over by Unigate of Scot Bowyers (formerly Bowyers (Wiltshire) Ltd), became Director of Unigate, 1973, Vice-Chm., 1974–76; Dir, FMC Ltd, and ancillary cos, 1976–77. Chm., Meat Manufrs Assoc., 1970–82; Member: Exec. and Council, Food Manufrs Fedn, 1970–82; Food and Drink Industries Fedn, 1970–82; Exec. Centre de Liaison des Industries Transformatrice de Viandes de la Commune Européenne, 1970–82. *Recreations:* golf, tennis, swimming, fishing. *Address:* Fallowfield, Hightown Hill, Ringwood, Hants BH24 3HE. *T:* (01425) 476011. *Club:* Sunningdale Golf.   *Died 27 April 2004.*

NIBLETT, Prof. (William) Roy, CBE 1970; MLitt; Professor of Higher Education, University of London, 1967–73, then Professor Emeritus; *b* 25 July 1906; *m* 1938, Sheila Margaret (*d* 1997), OBE 1975, *d* of A. C. Taylor, Peterborough; one *s* one *d. Educ:* Cotham Sch., Bristol; University of Bristol (BA 1st cl. hons English; DipEd 1st cl.; John Stewart Schol.); St Edmund Hall, Oxford. Sen. English Master, Doncaster GS, 1930–34; Lectr in Educn, King's Coll., Newcastle, 1934–45 (Registrar, Durham Univ., 1940–44); Prof. of Educn, University Coll., Hull, 1945–47; Prof. of Education, and Dir, Inst. of Education, Univ. of Leeds, 1947–59; Dean, Univ. of London Inst. of Education, 1960–68. Hibbert Lectr, 1965; Fulbright Schol. (Harvard) and Kellogg International Fellow, 1954; sometime Visiting Professor, Universities of California, Otago and Japanese Govt Vis. Prof., Univs of Japan; Nuffield Fellow, Univ. of Melbourne, 1960. Mem., UGC, 1949–59; Chairman: UGC Sub-Cttee on Halls of Residence, 1956 (Report 1957); Educn Dept, BCC, 1965–71; Cttee on Future of Ministry of URC, 1973–75; President: European Assoc. for Res. in Higher Educn, 1972; Higher Educn Foundn, 1984–97 (Chm. Trustees,

1980–81). Vice-President: World Univ. Service (UK), 1963–90; Soc. for Res. in Higher Educn, 1978–. Member: Nat. Advisory Coun. on Trng and Supply of Teachers, 1950–61; Council on Army Educn, 1961–70; Council, Royal Holloway College, 1963–76; Council, Cheltenham Ladies' College, 1967–79; Trustee, Westhill Coll., Birmingham, 1979–91. Chm., Editl Bd, Studies in Higher Education, 1975–82. FSRHE 1992. Hon. Fellow, Sarum Coll., 2003. Hon. DEd UWE, 2003. *Publications:* Education and the Modern Mind, 1954; Christian Education in a Secular Society, 1960; (ed) The Expanding University, 1962; (ed) Moral Education in a Changing Society, 1963; (ed) Higher Education: Demand and Response, 1969; (ed with R. F. Butts) World Year Book of Education, 1972–73; Universities Between Two Worlds, 1974; (with D. Humphreys and J. Fairhurst) The University Connection, 1975; (ed) The Sciences, The Humanities and the Technological Threat, 1975; (contrib.) International Encyclopedia of Higher Education, 1977; (contrib.) The Study of Education, 1980; (contrib.) Validation in Higher Education, 1983; (contrib.) Academic Community: discourse or discord?, 1994; (contrib.) Christian Thinking and Social Order, 1999; Life, Education, Discovery, 2001. *Recreations:* theology, music. *Address:* Moreton Hill Farm, Stonehouse, Glos GL10 3BZ. *T:* (01453) 826000.   *Died 6 May 2005.*

NICHOLAS, Barry; *see* Nicholas, J. K. B. M.

NICHOLAS, (John Keiran) Barry (Moylan), FBA 1990; Principal of Brasenose College, Oxford, 1978–89 (Fellow, 1947–78; Hon. Fellow, 1989); *b* 6 July 1919; *s* of Archibald John Nicholas and Rose (*née* Moylan); *m* 1st, 1948, Hildegart (*d* 1995), *d* of Prof. Hans Cloos, Bonn: one *s* one *d*; 2nd, 1998, Rosalind, *widow* of Prof. Alan Williams, FRS. *Educ:* Downside; Brasenose Coll., Oxford (Schol.; 1st cl. Class Mods, 1939 and Jurisprudence, 1946). Royal Signals, 1939–45: Middle East, 1941–45; Major, 1943. Called to Bar, Inner Temple, 1950, Hon. Bencher, 1984. University of Oxford: Tutor, 1947–71 and Vice-Principal, 1960–63, Brasenose Coll.; All Souls Reader in Roman Law, 1949–71; Prof. of Comparative Law, 1971–78; Mem., Hebdomadal Council, 1975–83. Visiting Professor: Tulane Univ., 1960; Univ. of Rome, 1964, 1993; Fordham Univ., 1968, 1985; Georgetown Univ., 1990; Univ. of Florida, 1997. UK Deleg. to UN Conf. on Internat. Sales Law, 1980. Mem., Louisiana State Law Inst., 1960. Dr *hc* Paris V, 1987. *Publications:* Introduction to Roman Law, 1962; (trans. Spanish, 1987, Chinese, 2000); Jolowicz's Historical Introduction to Roman Law, 3rd edn 1972; French Law of Contract, 1982, 2nd edn 1992. *Address:* 18A Charlbury Road, Oxford OX2 6UU. *T:* (01865) 558512.   *Died 3 March 2002.*

NICHOLSON, (Edward) Max, CB 1948; CVO 1971; Chairman, Land Use Consultants, 1966–89; *b* 12 July 1904; *m* 1st, 1932, Eleanor Mary Crawford (marr. diss., 1964); two *s*; 2nd, Marie Antoinette Mauerhofer (*d* 2002); one *s. Educ:* Sedbergh; Hertford Coll., Oxford (Hon. Fellow, 1993). Head of Allocation of Tonnage Div., Ministry of War Transport, 1942–45; Sec., Office of The Lord President of the Council, 1945–52. Mem., Adv. Council on Scientific Policy, 1948–64; Dir-Gen., Nature Conservancy, 1952–66; Convener, Conservation Section, Internat. Biological Prog., 1963–74; Sec., Duke of Edinburgh's Study Conference on the Countryside in 1970, 1963; Albright Lecturer, Univ. of California, 1964; a Dir and Managing Editor, Environmental Data Services Ltd, 1978–80. President: RSPB, 1980–85; Trust for Urban Ecology (formerly Ecological Parks Trust), 1987–88 (Chm., 1977–87); New Renaissance Gp, 1998–2000 (Chm., 1996–98); Vice-President: RSA, 1978–82; Wildfowl and Wetlands Trust; WWF, UK; Trustee, Earthwatch Europe, 1985–93; Member: Council, Internat. Inst. of Environment and Develt, 1972–88; Internat. Council, WWF, 1983–86. Chairman: Environmental Cttee, London Celebrations for the Queen's Silver Jubilee, 1976–77; London Looks Forward

Conf., 1977; UK Standing Cttee for World Conservation Strategy Prog., 1981–83. Hon. Member: IUCN; British Ecol Soc.; WWF; RTPI. Hon. Fellow: American Ornithologists' Union; RIBA; RGS 2001; IBiol 2002. Hon. LLD Aberdeen, 1964; Hon. Dr, RCA, 1970; Hon. DL Birmingham, 1983. John C. Phillips Medallist, Internat. Union for Conservation of Nature and Natural Resources, 1963; Europa Preis für Landespflege, 1972; Stamford Raffles Award, Zool Soc., 1999. Comdr, Order of Golden Ark, Netherlands, 1973. *Publications:* Birds in England, 1926; How Birds Live, 1927; Birds and Men, 1951; Britain's Nature Reserves, 1958; The System, 1967; The Environmental Revolution, 1970 (Premio Europeo Cortina-Ulisse, 1971); The Big Change, 1973; The New Environmental Age, 1987; (ed jtly) The Birds of the Western Palearctic, Vol. I, 1977, Vol. II, 1980, Vol. III, 1983, Vol. IV, 1985, Vol. V, 1988, Vol. VI, 1992, Vol. VII, 1993, Vol. VIII and Vol. IX, 1994, and other books, scientific papers and articles. *Address:* 13 Upper Cheyne Row, SW3 5JW. *Club:* Athenæum.

Died 26 April 2003.

NICHOLSON, Max; see Nicholson, E. M.

NICHOLSON, Robert; publisher, designer, artist; *b* Sydney, Australia, 8 April 1920; *m* 1951, Kate Poulter, ARCA (marr. diss. 1976); one *s* one *d*; *m* 1989. *Educ:* Troy Town Elementary Sch., Rochester; Rochester Tech. Sch.; Medway Sch. of Art. Served 1939–45, RAMC. Responsible with brother, Roger Nicholson, for major design projects during post-war design boom, 1945–55, including Festival of Britain Exhibition in Edinburgh, 1951 and Design Centre, London, 1956. Writer and publisher of guide books including: Nicholson's London Guide; Street Finder; Guide to Great Britain, guides to the Thames, the canals, etc. Benjamin Franklin medal, 1960. Continued to paint and exhibit occasionally.

Died 19 Oct. 2004.

NICOL, Prof. Donald MacGillivray, FBA 1981; FKC 1980; Koraës Professor of Modern Greek and Byzantine History, Language and Literature, University of London, King's College, 1970–88, then Emeritus; Vice Principal, King's College, 1980–81 (Assistant Principal, 1977–80); *b* 4 Feb. 1923; *s* of late Rev. George Manson Nicol and Mary Patterson (*née* MacGillivray); *m* 1950, Joan Mary Campbell, *d* of Sir Walter Campbell, KCIE; three *s*. *Educ:* King Edward VII Sch., Sheffield; St Paul's Sch., London; Pembroke Coll., Cambridge (MA, PhD). Friends' Ambulance Unit, 1942–46; Scholar at British Sch. of Archæology, Athens, 1949–50; Lectr in Classics, University Coll., Dublin, 1952–64; Vis. Fellow, Dumbarton Oaks, Washington, DC, 1964–65; Vis. Prof. of Byzantine History, Indiana Univ., 1965–66; Sen. Lectr and Reader in Byzantine History, Univ. of Edinburgh, 1966–70. Dir, Gennadius Library, Athens, 1989–92. Birkbeck Lectr, Cambridge, 1976–77. Pres., Ecclesiastical Hist. Soc., 1975–76. MRIA 1960; FRHistS 1971. Hon. Citizen of Arta, Greece, 1990. Editor, Byzantine and Modern Greek Studies, 1973–83. *Publications:* The Despotate of Epiros, 1957; Meteora, the Rock Monasteries of Thessaly, 1963, rev. edn, 1975; The Byzantine Family of Kantakouzenos (Cantacuzenus) ca 1100–1460: a genealogical and prosopographical study, 1968; The Last Centuries of Byzantium, 1261–1453, 1972, 2nd edn 1993; Byzantium: Its Ecclesiastical History and Relations with the Western World, 1972; Church and Society in the Last Centuries of Byzantium, 1979; The End of the Byzantine Empire, 1979; The Despotate of Epiros 1267–1479: a contribution to the history of Greece in the middle ages, 1984; Studies in Late Byzantine History and Prosopography, 1986; Byzantium and Venice: a study in diplomatic and cultural relations, 1988; Joannes Gennadios—The Man: a biographical sketch, 1990; A Biographical Dictionary of the Byzantine Empire, 1991; The Immortal Emperor: the life and legend of Constantine Palaiologos, last Emperor of the Romans, 1992; The Byzantine Lady: ten portraits 1250–1500, 1994; The

Reluctant Emperor: a biography of John Cantacuzene, Byzantine emperor and monk, *c* 1295–1383, 1996; (ed and trans.) Theodore Spandounes, On the Origin of the Ottoman Emperors, 1997; articles in Byzantine, classical and historical jls. *Recreation:* bookbinding. *Address:* 4 Westberry Court, Pinehurst, Grange Road, Cambridge CB3 9BG. *T:* (01223) 360955. *Died 25 Sept. 2003.*

NICOL, Dr Joseph Arthur Colin, FRS 1967; Professor of Zoology, University of Texas Institute of Marine Science, 1967–80, then Professor Emeritus; *b* 5 Dec. 1915; *s* of George Nicol and Noele Petrie; *m* 1941, Helen Wilhelmina Cameron; one *d*. *Educ:* Universities of McGill, Western Ontario and Oxford. BSc (hons Zool.) 1938, McGill; MA 1940, Western Ontario; DPhil 1947, DSc 1961, Oxford. Canadian Army, RCCS, 1941–45. Asst Professor in Zoology, University of British Columbia, 1947–49; Experimental Zoologist, Marine Biological Assoc., UK, 1949 (research on marine animals, comparative physiology, luminescence, vision, at Plymouth Laboratory, 1949–66). Guggenheim Fellow, Scripps Inst. Oceanography, 1953–54. Vis. Prof., Univ. of Texas, 1966–67. *Publications:* Biology of Marine Animals, 1960; Eyes of Fishes, 1989; papers on comparative physiology and anatomy in Jl Marine Biol. Assoc. UK, Proc. Royal Soc, Jl Exp. Biol., Biol. Review, etc. *Recreation:* English literature. *Address:* Ribby, Lerryn, Lostwithiel, Cornwall PL22 0PG; *e-mail:* head@ calstock.cornwall.sch.uk. *Died 20 Dec. 2004.*

NICOLSON, Nigel, OBE 2000 (MBE 1945); FSA; FRSL; author; Director of Weidenfeld and Nicolson Ltd, 1948–92; *b* 19 Jan. 1917; 2nd *s* of late Hon. Sir Harold Nicolson, KCVO, CMG and Hon. V. Sackville-West, CH; *heir-pres.* to 4th Baron Carnock; *m* 1953, Philippa Janet (marr. diss. 1970; she *d* 1987), *d* of Sir Gervais Tennyson d'Eyncourt, 2nd Bt; one *s* two *d*. *Educ:* Eton Coll.; Balliol Coll., Oxford. Capt. Grenadier Guards. Served War of 1939–45 in Tunisian and Italian Campaigns (MBE). Contested (C) NW Leicester, 1950, and Falmouth and Camborne, 1951; MP (C) Bournemouth East and Christchurch, Feb. 1952–Sept. 1959. Chm. Exec. Cttee, UNA, 1961–66. Columnist: The Spectator, 1992–95; Sunday Telegraph, 1995–2002. *Publications:* The Grenadier Guards, 1939–45, 1949 (official history); People and Parliament, 1958; Lord of the Isles, 1960; Great Houses of Britain, 1965, revd edn 1978; (editor) Harold Nicolson: Diaries and Letters, 3 vols, 1966–68, new edn 2004; Great Houses, 1968; Alex (FM Alexander of Tunis), 1973; Portrait of a Marriage, 1973; (ed) Letters of Virginia Woolf, 1975–80 (6 vols); The Himalayas, 1975; Mary Curzon, 1977 (Whitbread Award); Napoleon: 1812, 1985; (with Adam Nicolson) Two Roads to Dodge City, 1986; Kent, 1988; The World of Jane Austen, 1991; Vita and Harold: the letters of Vita Sackville-West and Harold Nicolson 1910–1962, 1992; Long Life (autobiog.), 1997; Virginia Woolf, 2000; Fanny Burney, 2002; The Queen and Us, 2003. *Recreation:* archæology. *Address:* Sissinghurst Castle, Cranbrook, Kent TN17 2AB. *T:* (01580) 714239. *Club:* Beefsteak. *Died 23 Sept. 2004.*

NIGHTINGALE, Sir John (Cyprian), Kt 1975; CBE 1970; BEM 1941; QPM 1965; DL; Chief Constable, Essex, 1962–69 and 1974–78, retired (Essex and Southend-on-Sea Joint Constabulary, 1969–74); *b* 16 Sept. 1913; *s* of Herbert Paul Nightingale, Sydenham, London; *m* 1947, Patricia Mary, *d* of Norman Maclaren, Glasgow University. *Educ:* Cardinal Vaughan Sch., Kensington; University Coll., London. Joined Metropolitan Police, 1935; Asst Chief Constable, Essex, 1958. Chm., Police Council, 1976–78; Mem., Parole Bd, 1978–82. Served with RNVR, 1943–45. DL Essex 1975. *Publications:* various police pubns. *Address:* The Hoppet Barn, Chapel Lane, Little Baddow, Essex CM3 4BD.

Died 1 Oct. 2002.

NIKLASSON, Birgit, (Fru Bertil Niklasson); see Nilsson, B.

NIKLAUS, Prof. Robert, PhD; Officier de l'Ordre National du Mérite, 1972; Professor of French, 1952–75, then Emeritus, also Head of Department of French and Spanish, 1958–64, French and Italian, 1964–75, University of Exeter (formerly University College of the South West); *b* 18 July 1910; *s* of late Jean Rodolphe and Elizabeth Niklaus; *m* 1st, 1935, Thelma (*née* Jones) (*d* 1970); two *s* one *d*; 2nd, 1973, Kathleen (*née* Folta). *Educ:* Lycée Français de Londres; University Coll. London (PhD); Univ. of Lille (LèsL). Sen. Tutor, Toynbee Hall, London, 1931–32; Asst and Asst Lecturer at University Coll. London, 1932–38; Asst Lecturer, Lecturer, Univ. of Manchester, 1938–52. Dean of the Faculty of Arts, Exeter, 1959–62; Dep. Vice-Chancellor, 1965–67. Visiting Professor: Univ. of Calif, Berkeley, 1963–64; Case Western Reserve Univ., Ohio, 1971; Univ. of British Columbia, 1975–76; Univ. of Natal, Pietermaritzburg, 1978; Rhodes Univ., S Africa, 1990. Hd of Dept of Langs, Univ. of Nigeria, Nsukka, 1977–78. Pres., Assoc. of Univ. Teachers, 1954–55, Mem. Executive Cttee, 1948–62; Pres., Internat. Assoc. of Univ. Profs and Lecturers, 1960–64 (Vice-Pres., 1958–60, 1964–66); Member: Cttee of Modern Humanities Research Association, 1956–71; Cttee, Soc. for French Studies, 1965–72 (Vice-Pres., 1967–68 and 1970–71; Pres. 1968–69); Pres., British Soc. for XVIIIth Century Studies, 1970–72; Treasurer, Internat. Soc. for Eighteenth-century Studies, 1969–79; Member: Post-graduate Awards Cttee of Min. of Education, 1956–61; Management Cttee, British Inst., Paris, 1965–67. Mem., Acad. of Verbano, 1996– (Academical Grand Officier, 2000). Gen. Editor, Textes Français Classiques et Modernes, Hodder & Stoughton. DrUniv *hc* Rennes, 1963; Hon. DLitt Exon, 1981. *Publications:* Jean Moréas, Poète Lyrique, 1936; The Nineteenth Century (Post-Romantic) and After, in The Year's Work in Modern Language Studies, vols VII-XIII, 1937–52; Diderot and Drama, 1942; Beaumarchais, Le Barbier de Séville, 1968; A Literary History of France, the Eighteenth Century, 1970; Beaumarchais, Le Mariage de Figaro, 1983; critical editions of: J.-J. Rousseau, Les Rêveries du Promeneur Solitaire, 1942; Denis Diderot, Pensées Philosophiques, 1950; Denis Diderot, Lettre sur les Aveugles, 1951; Marivaux, Arlequin poli par l'Amour, 1959 (in collab. with Thelma Niklaus); Sedaine, La Gageure imprévue, 1970; (contrib.) Diderot: Œuvres Complètes, vol. II, 1975, vol. IV, 1979; Complete Works of Voltaire: vol. I, Eriphyle, 1998; articles in Encyclopaediæ and learned journals; textbooks for schools and universities. *Recreations:* the theatre, the cinema. *Address:* 17 Elm Grove Road, Topsham, Exeter, Devon EX3 0EQ. *T:* (01392) 873627. *Died 16 Jan. 2001.*

NILSSON, Birgit, (Fru Bertil Niklasson); Swedish operatic soprano; *b* Karup, Kristianstadslaen, 17 May 1918; *d* of Nils Svensson; *m* 1948, Bertil Niklasson. *Educ:* Stockholm Royal Academy of Music. Debut as singer, 1946; with Stockholm Opera, 1947–51. Has sung at Glyndebourne, 1951; Bayreuth, 1953, 1954, 1957–70; Munich, 1954; Hollywood Bowl, Buenos Aires, Florence, 1956; La Scala, Milan, 1958; Covent Garden, 1957, 1960, 1962, 1963, 1973 and 1977; Edinburgh, 1959; Metropolitan, New York, 1959; Moscow, 1964; also in most leading opera houses and festivals of the world. Particularly well-known for her Wagnerian rôles. Austrian Kammersängerin, 1968; Bavarian Kammersängerin, 1970. Hon. Professor: Swedish Govt, 1998; Royal Music Sch., Stockholm, 2000. Hon. RAM, 1970; Hon. Mem., Vienna Philharmonic Orch., 1999. Hon. Dr: Andover Univ., Mass, 1970; Manhattan Sch. of Music, NY, 1982; East Lansing Univ. of Fine Arts, Mich, 1982; Sibelius Acad., Helsinki, 1997. Swedish Royal Acad. of Music's Medal for Promotion of Art of Music, 1968; Swedish Golden Medal (cl. 18 *illis quorum*) (only lady to be so honoured). Comdr of the Vasa Order (1st cl.), Sweden, 1974. Comdr des Arts et des Lettres, France, 1991. *Publication:* Mina Minnesbilder (autobiog.), 1977, (trans.) My Memoirs in Pictures, 1981. *Address:* Box 527, 10130 Stockholm, Sweden. *Died 25 Dec. 2005.*

NISBET, Prof. Stanley Donald; Professor of Education, University of Glasgow, 1951–78; *b* 26 July 1912; *s* of Dr J. L. and Isabella Nisbet; *m* 1942, Helen Alison Smith; one *s* one *d*. *Educ:* Dunfermline High Sch.; Edinburgh Univ. (MA 1st cl. Hons (Classics) 1934; Dip. in Educn 1935; BEd (with dist. in Educn and Psychol.) 1940). Taught in Moray House Demonstration Sch., Edinburgh, 1935–39. Served War in RAF, 1940–46; research officer at Air Ministry, 1944–46. Lecturer in Education, Univ. of Manchester, Feb.-Sept. 1946; Prof. of Education, Queen's Univ. of Belfast, 1946–51. FRSE 1955; FEIS 1976. *Publications:* Purpose in the Curriculum, 1957; (with B. L. Napier) Promise and Progress, 1970; articles in psychological and educational journals. *Recreations:* walking, sailing, Esperanto. *Address:* 6 Victoria Park Corner, Glasgow G14 9NZ. *Died 25 Feb. 2004.*

NOAKES, Philip Reuben, OBE 1962; HM Diplomatic Service, retired; *b* 12 Aug. 1915; *y s* of late Charles William and Elizabeth Farey Noakes; *m* 1940, Moragh Jean Dickson; two *s*. *Educ:* Wyggeston Grammar Sch.; Wycliffe Coll.; Queens' Coll., Cambridge (Open Schol.; Mod. Langs Tripos Part I, Hist. Tripos Part II; BA 1937; MA 1945; Pres., Cambridge Union Soc., 1937). Served War, 1940–46; Capt.-Adjt 2nd Fife and Forfar Yeomanry, RAC (despatches). Public Relations Officer, Royal Over-Seas League, 1947–48; Sen. Information Officer, Colonial Office, 1948; Prin. Information Officer, CO, 1953; Information Adviser to Governor of Malta, 1960–61; Chief Information Officer, CO, 1963–66; Commonwealth Office, 1967; Counsellor (Information), Ottawa, 1967–72; Consul-Gen., Seattle, 1973–75. *Recreations:* bird-watching, protection of country living and wildlife. *Died 11 Dec. 2003.*

NOBLE, David; WS; JP; Sheriff of North Strathclyde at Oban and Fort William, 1983–95; *b* 11 Feb. 1923; *s* of late Donald Noble, Solicitor, Inverness, and Helen Kirk Lynn Melville or Noble; *m* 1947, Marjorie Scott Smith or Noble; two *s* one *d*. *Educ:* Inverness Royal Academy; Edinburgh Univ. (MA, LLB *summa cum laude*). Royal Air Force Bomber Command, 1942–46. Partner in Miller Thomson & Robertson, WS, Edinburgh, 1953–82. Chm., Central and Southern, Cons. & Unionist Assoc. of Scotland, until 1983. JP Midlothian, 1970. *Address:* Woodhouselee, North Connel, Argyll PA37 1QZ. *T:* (01631) 710678. *Died 31 May 2005.*

NOBLE, Sir Fraser; *see* Noble, Sir T. A. F.

NOBLE, Sir (Thomas Alexander) Fraser, Kt 1971; MBE 1947; Principal and Vice-Chancellor, University of Aberdeen, 1976–81, then Principal Emeritus; *b* 29 April 1918; *s* of late Simon Noble, Grantown-on-Spey and Jeanie Graham, Largs, Ayrshire; *m* 1945, Barbara A. M. Sinclair, Nairn; one *s* one *d*. *Educ:* Nairn Acad.; Univ. of Aberdeen. After military service with Black Watch (RHR), entered Indian Civil Service, 1940: served in NW Frontier Province, 1941–47, successively as Asst Comr, Hazara; Asst Polit. Agent, N Waziristan; Controller of Rationing, Peshawar; Under-Sec., Food Dept and Develt Dept; Sec., Home Dept; Joint Dep. Comr, Peshawar; Civil Aide to Referendum Comr. Lectr in Political Economy, Univ. of Aberdeen, 1948–57; Sec. and Treas., Carnegie Trust for Univs of Scotland, 1957–62; Vice-Chancellor, Leicester Univ., 1962–76. Mem. and Vice-Chm., Bd of Management, Aberdeen Mental Hosp. Group, 1953–57. Sec., Scottish Economic Soc., 1954–58, Vice-Pres., 1962–. Chm., Scottish Standing Conf. of Voluntary Youth Organisations, 1958–62; Vice-Chm., Standing Consultative Council on Youth Service in Scotland, 1959–62. Mem., Departmental Cttee on Probation Service, 1959–62; Chairman: Probation Advisory and Training Board, 1962–65; Television Research Cttee, 1963–69; Advisory Council on Probation and After-Care, 1965–70; Univs Council for Adult Educn, 1965–69; Min. of Defence Cttee for Univ. Assistance to Adult Educn in HM Forces, 1965–70; Advisory Board, Overseas Students' Special Fund, 1967–71, Fees Awards

Scheme, 1968–75; Cttee of Vice-Chancellors and Principals of Univs of UK, 1970–72; British Council Cttee on Exchanges between UK and USSR, 1973–78; Scottish Council for Community Educn, 1979–80. Member: Academic Advisory Cttee, Univs of St Andrews and Dundee, 1964–66; E Midlands Economic Planning Council, 1965–68; Council, Assoc. Commonwealth Univs, 1970–79; Exec. Cttee, Inter-Univ. Council for Higher Educn Overseas, 1972–79; Exec. Cttee, British Council, 1973–79; British Council Cttee for Commonwealth Univ. Interchange, 1973–79; US-UK Educnl Commn, 1973–76. Hon. LLD: Aberdeen, 1968; Leicester, 1976; Glasgow, 1981; Washington Coll., Maryland, 1981. *Publications:* Something in India (autobiog.), 1997; articles in economic jls and on educn. *Recreation:* golf. *Address:* Hedgerley, Victoria Street, Nairn IV12 4HH. *Club:* Nairn Golf.   *Died 21 Aug. 2003.*

NOLAN, Brig. Eileen Joan, CB 1976; Director, Women's Royal Army Corps, 1973–77; *b* 19 June 1920; *d* of late James John and Ethel Mary Nolan. *Educ:* King's Norton Grammar Sch. for Girls. Joined ATS, Nov. 1942; commissioned, 1945. Lt-Col, 1967; Col, 1970; Brig., 1973. Hon. ADC to the Queen, 1975–77; Chm., NATO Senior Women Officers' Cttee, 1975–77; Dep. Controller Comdt, WRAC, 1977–84. *Address:* c/o Barclays Bank, High Street, Crowthorne, Berkshire RG45 7AR.
    Died 29 Dec. 2005.

NORELL, Dr Jack; *see* Norell, Dr Jacob C.

NORELL, Dr Jacob Solomon, (Jack), FRCGP; principal in general practice, 1956–90; *b* 3 March 1927; *s* of Henry (formerly Habib) Norell and Malka Norell; *m* 1948, Brenda Honeywell (marr. diss. 1973); three *s*. *Educ:* South Devon Technical Coll.; Guy's Hosp. Med. Sch. (MB BS 1953). MRCS, LRCP 1953; LMSSA 1952; MRCGP 1972, FRCGP 1982. Exec. Officer, Jt Cttee on Postgrad. Educn for Gen. Practice, 1976–81. Dean of Studies, 1974–81, Mem. Council, 1984–90, RCGP; Pres., Section of Gen. Practice, RSM, 1989–90. Pres., Balint Soc., 1984–87; Internat. Balint Fedn, 1989–93; ambassadorial rôle in Eastern Europe, 1994–. William Pickles Lectr, RCGP, 1984. Editor, The Practitioner, 1982–83. *Publications:* (co-ed) Six Minutes for the Patient, 1973; Entering General Practice, 1981; papers and chapters on general practice topics: the Balint philosophy, consultation, practice orgn, postgrad. educn, women doctors, measuring quality of med. care, professional self-regulation, doctor-patient relationship. *Recreations:* rural walks, driving open-topped cars, spotting unclad emperors. *Address:* 50 Nottingham Terrace, York Gate, Regent's Park, NW1 4QD. *T:* (020) 7486 2979.
    Died 11 Dec. 2001.

NORFOLK, 17th Duke of, *cr* 1483; **Miles Francis Stapleton Fitzalan-Howard,** KG 1983; GCVO 1986; CB 1966; CBE 1960; MC 1944; DL; Royal Victorian Chain, 2000; Earl of Arundel, 1139; Baron Beaumont, 1309; Baron Maltravers, 1330, Earl of Surrey, 1483; Baron FitzAlan, Clun, and Oswaldestre, 1627; Earl of Norfolk, 1644; Baron Howard of Glossop, 1869; Earl Marshal and Hereditary Marshal and Chief Butler of England; Premier Duke and Earl; *b* 21 July 1915; *s* of 3rd Baron Howard of Glossop, MBE, and Baroness Beaumont (11th in line), OBE; *S* to barony of mother, 1971, and of father, 1972, and to dukedom of cousin, 1975; *m* 1949, Anne Mary Teresa, CBE, *e d* of late Wing Commander Gerald Joseph Constable Maxwell, MC, DFC, AFC; two *s* three *d*. *Educ:* Ampleforth Coll.; Christ Church, Oxford (MA; Hon. Student, 1983). 2nd Lieut, Grenadier Guards, 1937. Served War of 1939–45, France, North Africa, Sicily, Italy (despatches, MC), NW Europe. Appointed Head of British Military Mission to Russian Forces in Germany, 1957; Commanded 70 Bde KAR, 1961–63; GOC 1 Div., 1963–65 (Maj.-Gen.); Dir, Management and Support Intelligence, 1965–66, Service Intelligence, 1966–67, MoD; retd 1967. Chm., Arundel Castle Trustees, Ltd, 1976–. Pres., Building Socs Assoc., 1982–86. Prime

Warden, Fishmongers' Co., 1985–86. Hon. Fellow, St Edmund's House, Cambridge, 1983; Hon. Bencher, Inner Temple, 1984. DL West Sussex, 1977. Knight, SMO Malta; Kt Grand Cross, Order of Pius IX. *Heir: s* Earl of Arundel and Surrey, *b* 2 Dec. 1956. *Address:* Arundel Castle, Sussex BN18 9AB. *T:* (01903) 882173; Carlton Towers, Goole, North Humberside DN14 9LZ. *T:* (01405) 860243; Bacres House, Hambleden, Henley-on-Thames, Oxfordshire RG9 6RY. *T:* (01491) 571350. *Club:* Pratt's.   *Died 24 June 2002.*

NORMAN, Desmond; *see* Norman, N. D.

NORMAN, (Nigel) Desmond, CBE 1970; CEng; FRAeS; Chairman and Managing Director, AeroNorTec Ltd, since 1988; *b* 13 Aug. 1929; 2nd *s* of Sir Nigel Norman, 2nd Bt (*d* 1943), CBE, and Patricia Moyra (*d* 1987) (who *m* 2nd, 1944, Sir Robert Perkins); *m* 1st, Anne Fogg-Elliott; two *s*; 2nd, 1965, Mrs Boel Elizabeth Holmsen; two *s* two *d*. *Educ:* Eton; De Havilland Aeronautical Technical Sch. (1946–49). RAF GD Pilot, thereafter 601 Sqdn, RAuxAF Fighter Sqdn, until disbandment, 1948–57. Export Asst at SBAC, 1951–53; Founder of Britten-Norman Ltd with F. R. J. Britten, 1954. *Recreations:* aviation, sailing, shooting. *Address:* Flat 4, 73 Duke Street, W1M 5DH; Le Palland, 87400 St Leonard de Noblat, France. *Clubs:* Royal Air Force, Royal Yacht Squadron.   *Died 13 Nov. 2002.*

NORRIS, Air Chief Marshal Sir Christopher Neil F.; *see* Foxley-Norris.

NORRIS, Sir Eric (George), KCMG 1969 (CMG 1963); HM Diplomatic Service, retired; Director: Inchcape & Co., 1977–88 (Deputy Chairman, 1981–86); London Sumatra Plantations Ltd, 1978–88; Gray Mackenzie Ltd, 1978–88; *b* 14 March 1918; *s* of late H. F. Norris, Bengeo, Hertford; *m* 1941, Pamela Crane; three *d*. *Educ:* Hertford Grammar Sch.; St Catharine's Coll., Cambridge. Served Royal Corps of Signals, 1940–46 (Major). Entered Dominions Office, 1946. Served in British Embassy, Dublin, 1948–50; UK High Commission in Pakistan, 1952–55; UK High Commission in Delhi, 1956–57; Dep. High Commissioner for the UK, Bombay, 1957–60; IDC 1961; British Dep. High Comr, Calcutta, 1962–65; Commonwealth Office, 1966–68; High Comr, Kenya, 1968–72; Dep. Under Sec. of State, FCO, 1972–73; High Comr, Malaysia, 1974–77. Chm., Royal Commonwealth Soc., 1980–84. PMN (Malaysia), 1974. *Address:* Tilings, 55 Goring Road, Steyning, W Sussex BN44 3GF. *T:* (01903) 879064. *Club:* Royal Commonwealth Society.
    Died 15 March 2005.

NORTHCOTE, Prof. Donald Henry, FRS 1968; Fellow of Sidney Sussex College, Cambridge, since 1992 (Master, 1976–92); Professor of Plant Biochemistry, University of Cambridge, 1972–89 (Reader, 1965–72), Emeritus Professor, 1989; *b* 27 Dec. 1921; *m* Eva Marjorie Mayo; two *d*. *Educ:* Sir George Monoux Grammar Sch., London; London Univ.; Cambridge Univ. (ScD 1964). Fellow, St John's College, Cambridge, 1960–76. Hon. Fellow, Downing Coll., Cambridge, 1976. *Publications:* 300 pubns in scientific jls on plant cell differentiation. *Recreations:* sitting and chatting; strolling about. *Address:* Sidney Sussex College, Cambridge CB2 3HU. *T:* (01223) 338821; *e-mail:* dhn21@cam.ac.uk; (home) 100 North Street, Burwell, Cambs CB5 0BB. *T:* (01638) 743924. *Club:* Oxford and Cambridge.   *Died 7 Jan. 2004.*

NORTHCOTT, Prof. Douglas Geoffrey, MA, PhD, Cambridge; FRS 1961; Town Trust Professor of Mathematics, University of Sheffield, 1952–82, then Emeritus; *b* London, 31 Dec. 1916; *m* 1949, Rose Hilda Austin (*d* 1992), Twickenham, Middlesex; two *d*. *Educ:* Christ's Hospital; St John's Coll., Cambridge; Princeton Univ., USA. *Publications:* Ideal Theory, 1953; An Introduction to Homological Algebra, 1960; Lessons on Rings, Modules and Multiplicities, 1968; A First Course of Homological Algebra, 1973; Finite Free Resolutions,

1976; Affine Sets and Affine Groups, 1980; Multilinear Algebra, 1984. *Address:* 25 Parkhead Road, Sheffield S11 9RA. *Died 8 April 2005.*

NORTON, Captain Gerard Ross, VC 1944; MM; 1/4th Hampshire Regiment; *b* S Africa, 7 Sept. 1915; *m* 1942, Lilia Morris, East London, S Africa; three *d. Educ:* Selborne Coll., East London, S Africa. Bank clerk. *Recreations:* Rugger-provincial, tennis, cricket. *Address:* Annandale Farm, Box 112, Banket, Zimbabwe.
Died 29 Oct. 2004.

NORTON, Marjorie; *see* Mowlam, M.

NUGENT, Sir Peter Walter James, 5th Bt *cr* 1831; *b* 26 Jan. 1920; *s* of Sir Walter Richard Nugent, 4th Bt and of Aileen Gladys, *y d* of late Middleton Moore O'Malley, JP, Ross, Westport, Co. Mayo; *S* father, 1955; *m* 1947, Anne Judith, *o d* of Major Robert Smyth, Gaybrook, Mullingar, Co. Westmeath; two *s* two *d. Educ:* Downside. Served War of 1939–45: 2nd Lieut, Hampshire Regt, 1941; Major, 1945. *Heir: s* Walter Richard Middleton Nugent [*b* 15 Nov. 1947; *m* 1985, Okabe Kayoko]. *Address:* Bay Bush, Straffan, Co. Kildare, Eire.
Died 12 Dec. 2002.

NUTMAN, Dr Phillip Sadler, FRS 1968; Head of Department of Soil Microbiology, Rothamsted Experimental Station, Harpenden, 1957–79; *b* 10 Oct. 1914; *s* of John William Nutman and Elizabeth Hester Nutman (*née* Hughes); *m* 1940, Mary Meta Stanbury; two *s* one *d. Educ:* Teignmouth Grammar Sch.; Imperial Coll., London Univ. Research Asst, Rothamsted Experimental Station, 1940; Senior Research Fellow, Canberra, Australia, 1953–56; Rothamsted, 1956–79; Hannaford Res. Fellow, Waite Inst., Adelaide, 1980. Huxley Medal, 1959. *Publications:* research papers in plant physiological, genetical and microbiological journals. *Recreations:* music, woodworking. *Address:* Melbury, Hensleigh Drive, St Leonards, Exeter EX2 4NZ. *T:* (01392) 276877.
Died 4 May 2004.

NUTTGENS, Patrick John, CBE 1983; Director, Leeds Polytechnic, 1969–86; *b* 2 March 1930; 2nd *s* of late Joseph Edward Nuttgens, stained glass artist, and Kathleen Mary Nuttgens (*née* Clarke); *m* 1954, Bridget Ann Badenoch; five *s* three *d*, and one adopted *s. Educ:* Ratcliffe Coll., Leicester; Univ. of Edinburgh; Edinburgh Coll. of Art. MA, PhD, DA (Edin.). ARIBA. Lectr, Dept of Architecture, Univ. of Edinburgh, 1956–61; Dir, Inst. of Advanced Architectural Studies, Univ. of York, 1962–68; Prof. of Architecture, Univ. of York, 1968–69; Hoffman Wood Prof. of Architecture, Univ. of Leeds, 1968–70. Member: Royal Commn on Ancient and Historical Monuments of Scotland, 1967–76; Ancient Monuments Bd, 1975–78; Royal Fine Art Commn, 1983–90; Yorks

Sculpture Park, 1964–65; Chairman: BBC North Region Adv. Council, 1970–75; BBC Continuing Educn Adv. Council, 1977–82; CNAA Cttee for Art and Design, 1981–84; Cttee, Employment of People with Disabilities (Leeds/York), 1992–94; Educn Cttee, Nat. Mus. of Film and Photography, 1963–73; Trustee, Leonard Cheshire Foundn, 1993–2000 (Chm. Bldg Rev. Team, 1993–98). Chm. Bd, York Theatre Royal, 1990–96. President: York Georgian Soc.; York Univ. of Third Age. Trustee, Selby Abbey, 1997–. Hon. Prof., York Univ., 1986–. Hon. Fellow, Leeds Polytechnic. DUniv: York, 1986; Open, 1986; Leeds Metropolitan, 1998; Hon. DLitt: Sheffield, 1987; Heriot-Watt, 1990. Television includes: In Search of the City (series on Leeds), 1973; York: a journey, 1975; A Full Life and an Honest Place (on arts and crafts movement), 1975; Edwin Lutyens: last architect of the age of humanism, 1981; Five Meditations for Holy Week, 1985; The Flight from Utopia (series), 1985; The Home Front (series), 1989; radio: (contributor) A Word in Edgeways, Round Britain Quiz. *Publications:* Reginald Fairlie, a Scottish Architect, 1959; York, City Building Series, 1971; The Landscape of Ideas, 1972; (contrib.) Spirit of the Age, 1975; York: the continuing city, 1976, 2nd edn 2000; Leeds, Old and New, 1976; Leeds, 1979; Yorkshire section, Shell Guide to English Villages, 1980; Pocket Guide to Architecture, 1980; (Gen. Editor) World's Great Architecture, 1980; (contrib.) Study Service, 1982; The Story of Architecture, 1983, 2nd edn 1997; What should we teach and How should we teach it?, 1988; Understanding Modern Architecture, 1988; The Home Front, 1989; The Art of Learning, 2000; (ed) The History of York, 2002; regular contributor to jls on architecture, planning, education and environmental studies. *Recreations:* drawing, painting, broadcasting. *Address:* Roselea Cottage, Terrington, York YO60 6PP.
Died 15 March 2004.

NYE, Ven. Nathaniel Kemp; Archdeacon Emeritus, diocese of Canterbury, 1982; *b* 4 Nov. 1914; *s* of Charles Frederick and Evelyn Nye; *m* 1941, Rosa Jackson; two *s* one *d. Educ:* Merchant Taylors' Sch.; KCL (AKC 1935); Cuddesdon Coll., Oxford. Ordained deacon, 1937, priest, 1938; Curate, St Peter's, St Helier Estate, dio. Southwark, 1937–40; Chaplain RAF, 1940–46 (POW 1941–43; escaped from Italy at liberation); Rector, Holy Trinity, Clapham, 1946–54; Vicar, St Peter's, St Helier Estate, 1954–60; Vicar, All Saints, Maidstone (Parish Church), and Rural Dean, 1960–66; Tait Missioner, Canterbury Diocese, 1966–72; Archdeacon of Maidstone, 1972–79. Hon. Canon of Canterbury, 1960, Canon Emeritus, 1979. *Recreations:* woodcraft, sailing, travel, family life! *Address:* Appledore, Ashley, Box, Wilts SN13 8AQ. *T:* (01225) 743933.
Died 9 Jan. 2003.

O

OAKES, Rt Hon. Gordon James; PC 1979; *b* 22 June 1931; *o s* of late James Oakes and Florence (*née* Hewitt), Widnes, Lancs; *m* 1952, Esther O'Neill (*d* 1998), *e d* of late Councillor Joseph O'Neill; three *s. Educ:* Wade Deacon Gram. Sch., Widnes; Univ. of Liverpool. BA (Hon.) English, 1952. Admitted Solicitor, 1956. Entered Widnes Borough Council, 1952 (Mayor, 1964–65). Chm. Widnes Constituency Labour Party, 1953–58; contested (Lab): Bebington, 1959; Moss Side (Manchester) by-election, 1961; MP (Lab): Bolton West, 1964–70; Widnes, Sept. 1971–1983; Halton, 1983–97. PPS, Home Office, 1966–67, DES, 1967–70; Front Bench Opposition spokesman on local govt and the environment, 1970–74; Parly Under-Secretary of State: DoE, 1974–76; Dept of Energy, 1976; Minister of State, DES, 1976–79; Front Bench Opposition spokesman on Environment, 1979–83. British Deleg., NATO Parliamentarians, 1967–70; Member: Select Cttee on Race Relations, 1969–70; Executive, NW Region of Labour Party, 1971–73; Exec. Cttee, CPA, 1979–97; Chairman: All-Party Energy Efficiency Gp, 1980–97; All-Party Chem. Industry Gp, 1990–97 (Vice-Chm., 1982–90); Jt Chm., All-Party Gp for the Licensing Trade, 1986–97. Vice-President: Rural District Councils Assoc., 1972–74; County Councils Assoc., 1982–97; Environmental Officers' Assoc. (formerly Inst. of Public Health Inspectors), 1973–97; Building Societies Assoc., 1984–89; Jt Chm., Nat. Waste Management Adv. Council, 1974–76. Gov., Commonwealth Inst., 1992–97. Hon. Alderman and Hon. Freeman, Borough of Halton. *Publications:* The Management of Higher Education in the Maintained Sector, 1978; various articles. *Recreations:* conversation, caravanning, maps. *Address:* Upton Bridle Path, Widnes, Cheshire WA8 9HB. *Died 15 Aug. 2005.*

OAKSHOTT, Hon. Sir Anthony (Hendrie), 2nd Bt *cr* 1959; *b* 10 Oct. 1929; *s* of Baron Oakshott, MBE (Life Peer), and Joan (*d* 1986), *d* of Marsden Withington; *S* to baronetcy of father, 1975; *m* 1965, Mrs Valerie de Pret-Roose (marr. diss. 1981; she *d* 1988), *d* of Jack Vlasto. *Educ:* Rugby. *Heir: b* Hon. Michael Arthur John Oakshott [*b* 12 April 1932; *m* 1st, 1957, Christina Rose Methuen (*d* 1985), *d* of late Thomas Banks; three *s*; 2nd, 1988, Mrs (Helen) Clare Jones, *d* of late Edward Ravell]. *Club:* White's. *Died 11 Dec. 2002.*

OATES, Prof. (Edward Ernest) David (Michael), FSA; FBA 1974; Professor of Western Asiatic Archaeology, University of London, 1969–82; *b* 25 Feb. 1927; *s* of Thomas Oates and Dora B. Strike; *m* 1956, Joan Louise Lines; one *s* two *d. Educ:* Callington County Sch.; Oundle Sch.; Trinity Coll., Cambridge (BA, MA). Fellow of Trinity Coll., Cambridge, 1951–65; British School of Archaeology in Iraq: Dir, 1965–69; Chm., 1988–96; Vice Pres., 1997–2000; Pres., 2000–; Gertrude Bell Meml Medal, 1997. Director, British Archaeological Expedition to Tell Brak, Syria, 1976–. FSA 1954. *Publications:* (contrib.) The Great Palace of the Byzantine Emperors, ed D. Talbot Rice, 1958; (contrib.) The Dark Ages, ed D. Talbot Rice, 1965; Studies in the Ancient History of N Iraq, 1968; (with J. Oates): The Rise of Civilisation, 1976; Excavations at Tell Brak, Vol. 1: the Mitanni and Old Babylonian periods, 1998, Vol. 2: Nagar in the 3rd Millennium, 2001; Nimrud, Ancient Kalhu: an Assyrian Imperial City, 2001; (with C. Postgate and J. Oates) The Excavations at Tell al Rimah: the pottery, 1998; papers of the British School at Rome, Iraq, etc. *Recreations:* history, carpentry. *Address:* 86 High Street, Barton, Cambridge CB3 7BG. *T:* (01223) 262273. *Died 22 March 2004.*

OBOLENSKY, Sir Dimitri, Kt 1984; PhD, DLitt; FBA 1974; FSA; FRHistS; Emeritus Professor, University of Oxford, since 1985 (Professor of Russian and Balkan History, 1961–85, and Student of Christ Church, 1950–85, Emeritus Student, since 1985); *b* Petrograd, 1 April 1918; *s* of late Prince Dimitri Obolensky and late Countess Mary Shuvalov; *m* 1947, Elisabeth Lopukhin (marr. diss. 1989). *Educ:* Lycée Pasteur, Paris; Trinity Coll., Cambridge (BA 1st Class Modern and Medieval Langs Tripos Parts I and II; Amy Mary Preston Read and Allen Schol.; MA 1944; PhD 1943; Hon. Fellow 1991); MA 1948, DLitt, Oxon. Univeristy of Cambridge: Fellow, 1942–48, Lectr, 1945, Trinity Coll.; Faculty Asst Lecturer, 1944; Lecturer in Slavonic Studies, 1946; Reader in Russian and Balkan Medieval History, Univ. of Oxford, 1949–61. Sen. Associate Mem., St Antony's Coll., Oxford, 1993–. Vis. Schol., Dumbarton Oaks Center for Byzantine Studies, Harvard Univ., 1952, 1964, 1977, Vis. Fellow, 1981–82; Visiting Professor: of Russian History, Yale Univ., 1957; of European Hist., Univ. of California, Berkeley, 1973; Davis Prof. in Slavic Studies, Wellesley Coll., Mass, 1982; Vis. Mellon Prof., Inst. for Advanced Study, Princeton, 1985–86; Birkbeck Lecturer in Ecclesiastical History, Trinity Coll., Cambridge, 1961; Raleigh Lectr, British Acad., 1981. Vice-Pres., British Acad., 1983–85. Gen. Sec. Thirteenth Internat. Congress of Byzantine Studies, Oxford, 1966; British Co-Chairman: Anglo-Bulgarian Conf. of Historians, 1973; Anglo-Romanian Conf. of Historians, 1975; Chm., British Nat. Cttee, Association Internationale d'Etudes du Sud-Est Européen, 1985–93. Corresp. Mem., Acad. of Athens; Foreign Member: Serbian Acad. of Scis and Arts, 1988; Amer. Philosophical Soc., 1990; Russian Acad. of Scis, 1994. Hon. Dr Univ: Paris, Sorbonne, 1980; Sofia, 1989; Hon. DLitt Birmingham, 1988. *Publications:* The Bogomils, A Study in Balkan Neo-Manichaeism, 1948; (ed) The Penguin Book of Russian Verse, 1962; (jointly) The Christian Centuries, vol. 2: The Middle Ages, 1969; Byzantium and the Slavs, 1971; The Byzantine Commonwealth, 1971; (ed jtly) Companion to Russian Studies, 3 vols, 1976–80; The Byzantine Inheritance of Eastern Europe, 1982; Six Byzantine Portraits, 1988. *Address:* 29 Belsyre Court, Woodstock Road, Oxford OX2 6HU. *T:* (01865) 556496. *Club:* Athenæum. *Died 23 Dec. 2001.*

OBOTE, Dr (Apollo) Milton; President of Uganda and Minister of Foreign Affairs, 1980–85; former Leader, Uganda People's Congress Party; *b* 28 Dec. 1924; *m*; three *s* one *d.* Migrated to Kenya and worked as labourer, clerk and salesman, 1950–55; Founder Mem., Kenya Africa Union. Mem., Uganda Nat. Congress, 1952–60; Mem., Uganda Legislative Council, 1957–71; Founder and Mem., Uganda People's Congress, 1960–71; Leader of the Opposition, 1961–62; Prime Minister, 1962–66; Minister of Defence and Foreign Affairs, 1963–65; President of Uganda, 1966–71 (deposed by military coup); in exile in Tanzania, 1971–80; returned to Uganda, 1980. *Died 10 Oct. 2005.*

O'BRIEN, Rt Rev. Kevin; *see* O'Brien, Rt Rev. T. K.

O'BRIEN, Rt Rev. (Thomas) Kevin; Auxiliary Bishop of Middlesbrough, (RC), and Titular Bishop of Ard Carna, 1981–98; *b* Cork City, Republic of Ireland, 18 Feb. 1923; *s* of Jack and Mary O'Brien. *Educ:* Christian Brothers Coll., Cork. Ordained, All Hallows College, Dublin, 1948; Curate at Batley, Yorks, 1948–51, and St Anne's Cathedral, Leeds, 1951–56; Catholic Missionary Society, 1956–71, Superior 1960–71; Vicar General, Diocese of Leeds, 1971–81; Parish Priest: St Patrick's, Huddersfield,

1971–79; St Francis, Bradford, 1979–81. Chm., Home Mission Cttee of Bishops' Conference, 1983–; Mem., Co-ordinating Gp for Evangelisation, Churches Together in England, 1986–. Hon. DD Hull, 1998. *Address:* Mount St Joseph's, Shire Oak Road, Headingley, Leeds LS6 2DE.
Died 27 Dec. 2004.

O'CONNELL, John Eugene Anthony, FRCS; Consulting Neurological Surgeon, St Bartholomew's Hospital; *b* 16 Sept. 1906; *s* of Thomas Henry and Catherine Mary O'Connell (*née* O'Sullivan); *m* Marjorie Hutchinson Cook, MBE (*d* 1986). *Educ:* Clongowes Wood and Wimbledon Colleges; St Bartholomew's Hospital; MS London, 1943. Held posts of House Surgeon, Senior Demonstrator of Anatomy, and Surgical Chief Assistant, St Bartholomew's Hospital, 1931–39; studied at Universities of Michigan and Chicago on Rockefeller Foundation Travelling Fellowship, 1935–36; Surgeon in charge of an EMS Neurosurgical Unit, 1941–46; Surgeon i/c Dept of Neurol Surgery, St Bartholomew's Hosp., 1946–71. Hunterian Professor, Royal College of Surgeons, 1943 and 1950. Emeritus Mem., Soc. of Brit. Neurol Surgeons (ex-Pres.); FRSocMed (ex-Vice-Pres.); Hon. Member: Neurosurgical Soc. Australasia; Deutsche Gesellschaft für Neurochirurgie; Corresp. Mem., Amer. Assoc. Neurol Surgeons. *Publications:* papers in neurological, surgical and other journals and books. *Recreations:* fly-fishing, bird watching. *Address:* Sutton Manor Nursing Home, Sutton Scotney, Winchester, Hants SO21 3JX.
Died 27 April 2001.

O'CONNOR, Surgeon Rear-Adm. Anthony, LVO 1967; Director, Red Cross Blood Transfusion Service, Western Australia, 1981–84 (Deputy Director, 1975–81); *b* 8 Nov. 1917; *s* of Armel John O'Connor and Lucy Violet O'Connor (*née* Bullock-Webster); *m* 1946, Catherine Jane (*née* Hayes); three *d. Educ:* KCL; Westminster Hosp. Med. Sch. MRCS, LRCP, MB, BS. FFARCS, MFCM. Qualified Medical Practitioner, 1941; joined Royal Navy (RNVR), 1942; Permanent Commn, 1945; Dep. Medical Director General (Naval), 1969; MO i/c, Inst. of Naval Med. and Dean of Naval Med., 1972–75. QHP 1970–75. *Recreations:* gardening, photography. *Address:* c/o Lloyds TSB, Ludlow, Shropshire SY8 1NQ. *Died 3 May 2004.*

O'CONNOR, Air Vice-Marshal Patrick Joseph, CB 1976; OBE 1943; MD; FRCPE, FRCPsych; Civil Consultant in Neuropsychiatry, Royal Air Force, 1978–98; Consultant in Neurology and Psychiatry to Civil Aviation Authority and to British Airways, 1978–98; *b* 21 Aug. 1914; *s* of Charles O'Connor, farmer, Straffan, Co. Kildare, Eire; *m* 1946, Elsie, *o d* of David Craven, Leeds, Yorks; one *s* two *d* (and one *d* decd). *Educ:* Roscrea Coll.; UC, Dublin, NUI (MB, BCh 1938; DPM 1953; MD 1950). MRCPE 1950, FRCPE 1960; MRCP 1960; FRCPsych 1970. Joined RAF, 1940; Air Cdre 1966; Air Vice-Marshal 1971; Consultant Adviser in Neurology and Psychiatry to RAF, 1964–78; Senior Consultant to RAF at Central Medical Establishment, 1975–78, retired; Hon. Consultant, RAF, 1978–98. QHP 1967–78. Member: Med. Council to Migraine Trust; Med. Council on Alcoholism; EEG Soc.; Assoc. of British Neurologists; Internat. Acad. of Aviation and Space Med., 1977; Internat. League against Epilepsy; Flying Personnel Res. Cttee. Fellow, Aerospace Med. Assoc.; FRSocMed. *Publications:* contrib. Journal Neurology, Psychiatry and Neurosurgery, British Journal Psychiatry, BMJ. *Recreations:* gardening, shooting. *Address:* St Benedicts, Bacombe Lane, Wendover, Bucks HP22 6EQ. *T:* (01296) 623329. *Club:* Royal Air Force. *Died 5 March 2001.*

O'CONNOR, Rt Hon. Sir Patrick McCarthy, Kt 1966; PC 1980; a Lord Justice of Appeal, 1980–89; *b* 28 Dec. 1914; *s* of late William Patrick O'Connor; *m* 1938, Mary Garland (*d* 1984), *d* of William Martin Griffin, KC, Vancouver, BC; two *s* two *d. Educ:* Downside; Merton Coll., Oxford (Hon. Fellow 1987). Called to the Bar,

Inner Temple, 1940; Bencher, 1966. Junior Counsel to the Post Office, 1954–60; Dep. Chairman, IoW QS, 1957–71; QC 1960; Recorder: of King's Lynn, 1959–61; of Southend, 1961–66; a Judge of the High Ct of Justice, QBD, 1966–80. Vice-Chm., Parole Bd, 1974–75. A Governor of Guy's Hospital, 1956–60. *Recreation:* golf. *Address:* 210 Rivermead Court, Ranelagh Gardens, SW6 3SG. *T:* (020) 7731 3563. *Club:* Hurlingham.
Died 3 May 2001.

ODLING, Thomas George, CB 1974; *b* 18 Sept. 1911; *yr s* of late Major W. A. Odling, Paxford, Glos and late Mary Bennett Odling (*née* Case); *m* 1st, Camilla Haldane Paterson (marr. diss.); two *s*; 2nd, Hilary Katharine, *d* of late W. J. Palgrave-Ker, Lilliput, Dorset. *Educ:* Temple Grove; Rugby Sch.; New Coll., Oxford (MA). House of Commons: Asst Clerk, 1935; Clerk of Private Bills, Examr of Petitions for Private Bills and Taxing Officer, 1961–73; Clerk of Select Cttee on Parly Comr for Admin, 1969–73; Clerk of Committees, 1974–76, retired 1976. Temp. attached to Consultative Assembly of Council of Europe during 1949 and later sessions. *Recreations:* music, gardening. *Address:* Paxford, Campden, Glos GL55 6XQ. *Clubs:* Athenæum, MCC. *Died 12 Jan. 2002.*

O'FLYNN, Rt Hon. Francis Duncan, (Frank); PC 1987; QC 1968; Chairman, Community Trust, Trust Bank, Wellington, 1988–94 (Director, Trust Bank, 1988–91); *b* 24 Oct. 1918; *s* of Hon. Francis E. O'Flynn, MLC; *m* 1942, Sylvia Elizabeth Hefford; one *s* three *d. Educ:* Christchurch Boys' High School; Victoria University of Wellington (BA, LLM). Flight Lieut, RNZAF, 1942–46; Flying Instructor, NZ and 6 Flying Boat Sqdn, Pacific. Barrister and Solicitor, 1948; in practice on own account, 1954–78. MP (Lab): Kapiti, 1972–75; Island Bay, 1978–87. Minister of State and of Defence, and Dep. Minister of Foreign Affairs, NZ, 1984–87. Member: Otaki Borough Council, 1968–71; Wellington City Council, 1977–83. Mem. Council, Wellington District Law Soc., 1970–74. *Recreation:* reading. *Address:* 11 Rosetta Road, Raumati South, Wellington, New Zealand. *T:* (4) 9021669.
Died 17 Oct. 2003.

OGDEN, Sir (Edward) Michael, Kt 1989; QC 1968; barrister, 1950–97; a Recorder (formerly Recorder of Hastings), 1971–97; a Deputy High Court Judge, 1977–96; *b* 9 April 1926; *er s* of late Edward Cannon Ogden and Daisy (*née* Pank); *m* 1951, Joan Kathleen (*d* 2002), *er d* of late Pius Charles Brodrick and Kathleen (*née* Moran); two *s* two *d. Educ:* Downside Sch.; Jesus Coll., Cambridge (MA). FCIArb 1990; Fellow, Singapore Inst. of Arbitrators, 1996. Served in RAC (Royal Glos Hussars and 16th/5th Lancers), 1944–47 (Capt.); Inns of Court Regt (TA) 1950–56. Called to the Bar, Lincoln's Inn, 1950 (Bencher, 1977; Treasurer, 1998); Dep. Recorder, Southend-on-Sea, 1964–71; Dep. Official Referee, 1996–97. Leader, SE Circuit, 1975–78. Member: Bar Council, 1960–64, 1966–70, 1971–78 (responsible for fee negotiations, 1968–72, Treas., 1972–74, Chm., Internat. Relns Cttee, 1974–75); Senate of the Inns of Court, 1966–70, 1972–78. Member: Council of Union Internationale des Avocats, 1962–83; Council of Legal Educn, 1969–74; Council, Internat. Bar Assoc., 1983–87. Chairman: Criminal Injuries Compensation Bd, 1975–89 (Mem., 1968–89); Wkg Party publishing Actuarial Tables for Personal Injury and Fatal Accident Cases (4th edn 2000; Ogden Tables enacted Civil Evidence Act 1995); Disciplinary Appeal Cttee, ICAEW, 1993–98; Mem., Lord Chancellor's Adv. on Legal Education, 1972–74. Dir, Internat. Assoc. of Crime Victim Compensation Bds, 1978–89 (Co-Chm. 1983–87). The Independent Assessor for Home Sec. of compensation for miscarriages of justice, 1978–89, and for Minister of Defence, 1986–89. Pres., Sea Fish Licence Tribunal, 1993–94. Proponent, Criminal Procedure (Right of Reply) Act, 1964. Mem. Bd, Internat. and Comparative Corp. Law Jl, 1998–. Hon. Fellow, Soc. of Advanced Legal Studies, 1998; Hon. FIA

1999; Hon. Mem., Litigation Section, Amer. Bar Assoc., 1979. *Publication:* Variety is the Spice of Legal Life (memoirs), 2002. *Address:* 1 Paper Buildings, Temple, EC4Y 7ET. *T:* (020) 7797 8100, *Fax:* (020) 7797 8101.
Died 31 Jan. 2003.

OGILVY, Rt Hon. Sir Angus (James Bruce), KCVO 1989; PC 1997; *b* 14 Sept. 1928; *s* of 12th (*de facto* 9th) Earl of Airlie, KT, GCVO, MC and Lady Alexandra Marie Bridget Coke, *d* of 3rd Earl of Leicester, GCVO, CMG; *m* 1963, HRH Princess Alexandra of Kent, Lady of the Order of the Garter, GCVO; one *s* one *d*. *Educ:* Eton Coll.; Trinity Coll., Oxford (MA). Scots Guards, 1946–48; Mem., HM Body Guard for Scotland (The Royal Company of Archers). Chm. Adv. Council, PYBT, 1986–99; Chm. Adv. Council and Trustee, Prince's Trust, 1999–. President: Imperial Cancer Res. Fund, 1964–94; Youth Clubs UK (formerly NAYC), 1969–89 (Chm. 1964–69); Carr-Gomm Soc., 1983–; Vice-President: Friends of the Elderly & Gentlefolk's Help, 1969– (Treas., 1952–63; Chm., 1963–69); Gtr London Fund for the Blind, 1999–; Head and Neck Cancer Res. Trust, 2003–. Patron: Arthritis Care (formerly British Rheumatism and Arthritis Soc.), 1978–2003 (Chm. 1963–69; Pres., 1969–78); Scottish Wildlife Trust, 1974–90 (Pres., 1969–74); Friends of UK Youth (formerly Youth Clubs UK), 1993–; Vice-Patron, NCH Action for Children (formerly Nat. Children's Homes), 1986–2002. Mem., Governing Council, Society for Promoting Christian Knowledge, 1984–94. Dir, various public cos. Trustee: Leeds Castle Foundn, 1975–; King George's Jubilee Trust, 1995–2001; Queen's Jubilee Trust, 1995–2001. *Recreations:* architecture, reading, music. *Address:* Thatched House Lodge, Richmond Park, Surrey TW10 5HP. *T:* (020) 8546 8833. *Club:* White's. *Died 26 Dec. 2004.*

OGMORE, 2nd Baron *cr* 1950, of Bridgend; **Gwilym Rees Rees-Williams;** *b* 5 May 1931; *er s* of 1st Baron Ogmore, PC, TD, and Constance (*d* 1998), *er d* of W. R. Wills; *S* father, 1976; *m* 1967, Gillian Mavis, *d* of late M. K. Slack; two *d*. *Educ:* Mill Hill School; St Luke's Coll., Exeter. *Heir:* *b* Hon. Morgan Rees-Williams [*b* 19 Dec. 1937; *m* 1st, 1964, Patricia (marr. diss. 1970), *o d* of C. Paris Jones; 2nd, 1972, Roberta (marr. diss. 1976), *d* of Captain Alec Cunningham-Reid, DFC; 3rd, 1990, Beata, *o d* of late Z. Solski; two *s*]. *Address:* 12 Lavant Road, Summersdale, Chichester, West Sussex PO19 5RQ.
Died 9 Nov. 2004.

O'HAGAN, Desmond, CMG 1957; *b* 4 March 1909; *s* of Captain Claud O'Hagan, Nyeri, Kenya and Eva O'Hagan (*née* Napier Magill); *m* 1942, Pamela, *d* of Major A. H. Symes-Thompson, DSO, Kiambu, Kenya; one *s* two *d*. *Educ:* Wellington Coll.; Clare Coll., Cambridge. Entered Colonial Administrative Service, Kenya, 1931. Called to Bar, Inner Temple, 1935. Private Secretary to British Resident, Zanzibar, 1937; served with E African Forces in N Province, Kenya, 1940–42; Native Courts Adviser, 1948–51; Provincial Commissioner, Coast Province, Kenya, 1952–59; Chairman, Transport Licensing Authority, Tanganyika, 1959–63. *Recreations:* bridge, golf. *Address:* Kianjibbi, Box 68, Kiambu, Kenya. *Clubs:* East India, Devonshire, Sports and Public Schools; Muthaiga, Nairobi (life mem.). *Died 12 Dec. 2001.*

O'HIGGINS, Hon. Thomas Francis; SC (Ireland) 1954; a Judge of the European Court of Justice, 1985–92; *b* 23 July 1916; *e s* of Dr Thomas F. O'Higgins and Agnes McCarthy; *m* 1948, Thérèse Keane; five *s* two *d*. *Educ:* St Mary's Coll., Rathmines; Clongowes Wood Coll.; University Coll., Dublin (BA); King's Inns, Dublin (BL). Called to Irish Bar, 1938; Bencher of King's Inns, 1967; Judge of High Court, 1973; Chief Justice of Ireland, 1974–85. Elected to Dail Eireann, 1948; Minister for Health, 1954; contested Presidency, 1966 and 1973. *Publication:* Double Life (memoirs), 1996. *Recreations:* fishing, golf. *Address:* Glenville Cottage, 75 Monkstown Road, Monkstown, Co. Dublin. *T:* (1) 2809119. *Clubs:*

Stephen's Green (Dublin); Royal Irish Yacht.
Died 25 Feb. 2003.

O'KEEFFE, (Peter) Laurence, CMG 1983; CVO 1974; HM Diplomatic Service, retired; *b* 9 July 1931; *s* of Richard O'Keeffe and Alice (*née* Chase); *m* 1954, Suzanne Marie Jousse; three *d*. *Educ:* St Francis Xavier's Coll., Liverpool; University Coll., Oxford (schol.). HM Customs and Excise, 1953–62; 2nd, later 1st Sec. (Economic), Bangkok, 1962–65; FO, 1965–68; 1st Sec. and Head of Chancery, Athens, 1968–72; Commercial Counsellor, Jakarta, 1972–75; Head of Hong Kong and Indian Ocean Dept, FCO, 1975–76; Dir-Gen., British Information Services, and Dep. Consul Gen. (Information), New York, 1976–78; Counsellor, Nicosia, 1978–81; Research Associate, Inst. for the Study of Diplomacy, Georgetown Univ., Washington, DC, 1981–82; Ambassador to Senegal, 1982–85, and concurrently (non-resident) to Guinea, Guinea-Bissau, Mali, Mauritania and Cape Verde, 1982–85; Diplomatic Service Chm., CSSB, 1985–86; Head, British Delegn to CSCE Rev. Conf., Vienna, 1986–88; Ambassador to Czechoslovakia, 1988–91. *Publications:* (as Laurence Halley): Simultaneous Equations (novel), 1975; Ancient Affections, 1985; Abiding City (novel), 1986. *Recreations:* gardening, church recording, lecturing. *Address:* Wylye Cottage, Great Wishford, Salisbury, Wilts SP2 0PD. *Died 2 May 2003.*

O'KELLY, Surgeon Rear-Adm. Francis Joseph, OBE 1965; Royal Navy, retired 1980; Occupational Health Consultant, Medical and Health Department, Government of Hong Kong, 1980–86; *b* 24 Dec. 1921; *s* of Francis John O'Kelly and Elizabeth Mary O'Kelly (*née* Rogan); *m* 1954, Winifred Mary Teresa Henry; one *s* three *d*. *Educ:* St Patrick's Coll., Cavan; University Coll., Dublin. MB, BCh 1945; FFCM, FFOM (RCPI), MFOM (RCPE); Hon. FACOM; DPH, DIH. Hosp. appts in Dublin, 1946–48; joined RN 1948; served with RM Commandos, Middle and Far East, 1948–52; HM Ships Unicorn, St Bride's Bay and Centaur, RNB Chatham and RN Air Station, Brawdy, 1952–63; Naval MOH appts, Far East Fleet, Scotland and NI Comd, Portsmouth and Chatham Comd, 1963–72; Dep. Dir, Health and Research, 1972–74; MO i/c RN Hosp. Gibraltar, 1974–77; Surgeon Rear-Adm. (Ships and Establishments), 1977–78; Surg. Rear-Adm. (Naval Hosps), 1978–80; QHP 1977–80. Adviser in Preventive and Industrial Medicine to Med. Dir Gen. (Naval), 1972–77, in Community Medicine, 1977–80. *Publications:* articles in med jls. *Recreations:* reading and travel. *Address:* Large Barn, North Bersted Street, Bognor Regis, W Sussex PO22 9AH. *Died 11 Nov. 2005.*

OKEOVER, Sir Peter Ralph Leopold W.; *see* Walker-Okeover.

OKOTH, Rt Rev. Yona; Archbishop of Uganda and Bishop of Kampala, 1984–94; *b* 15 April 1927; *s* of Nasanairi Owora and Tezira Akech; *m* Jessica Naome Okoth (*d* 2001); four *s* five *d*. Bishop's clerk, 1947; Ordination Class, 1953–54 (certificate); deacon 1954, priest 1955; Parish Priest, Nagongera, 1956–60; St Augustine's Coll., Canterbury, 1963 (Diploma); Diocesan Treasurer, Mbale Diocese, 1961–65; Provincial Sec., Kampala, 1965–66; studies, Wycliffe Coll., Toronto Univ., 1966–68 (Dip. and LTh); Provincial Sec., Kampala, 1968–72; Diocesan Bishop of Bukedi, 1972–83. Hon. DD Wycliffe Coll., Toronto, 1978. *Recreation:* interest in farming. *Address:* c/o PO Box 255, Tororo, Uganda.
Died 24 Nov. 2001.

OLANG', Most Rev. Festo Habakkuk; *b* 11 Nov. 1914; *m* 1937, Eseri D. Olang' (*d* 1997); two *s* eight *d* (and two *s* decd). *Educ:* Alliance High School. Teacher, 1936–43; ordained 1945; consecrated Assistant Bishop of Mombasa in Namirembe Cathedral, by Archbishop of Canterbury, 1955; Bishop of Maseno, 1961; Bishop of Nairobi, 1970; Archbishop of Kenya, 1970–79. Hon. DD Univ. of the

South Sewanee, USA. *Address:* PO Box 1, Maseno, Kenya. *Died 3 Feb. 2004.*

OLAYAN, Suliman Saleh, Hon. KBE 1987; Founder and Chairman, The Olayan Group, since 1947; *b* 5 Nov. 1918; *s* of Saleh Olayan and Haya Al Ghanim; *m* 1974, Mary Perdikis; one *s* three *d. Educ:* Bahrain. Founding Chairman: Arab Commercial Enterprises, 1950–84; Nat. Gas Co., 1951–54; Saudi British Bank, 1978–89; Saudi Spanish Bank, 1979–84; Director: Al Khobar Power Co., 1950–54; Riyad Bank, 1963–78; Saudi Arabian Airlines, 1965–81; Mobil Corp., 1980–83; CS First Boston, 1988–95. Member: Internat. Council of Morgan Guaranty Trust Co., 1979–90; Internat. Adv. Bd, Amer. Internat. Gp, 1982–99; Adv. Bd, Energy Internat. NV, 1983–92. Chairman: Riyadh Chamber of Commerce and Industry, 1981–89; Council of Saudi Chambers of Commerce and Industry, 1984–87. Member: Internat. Industrial Conf., 1961–97; Gp of Thirty, 1984–87; Bd, Inst. for Internat. Econs, 1987–; Internat. Council, INSEAD, 1991–97. Mem., Rockefeller Univ. Council, 1974–87 (Alumnus Mem., 1987–). Founding Vice Chm., Handicapped Children's Assoc., Riyadh, 1983–88. Medal of Honour, Madrid Chamber of Commerce and Industry, 1985. Great Cross, Order of Merit (Spain), 1984; Comdr First Class, Royal Order of Polar Star (Sweden), 1988. *Publications:* contribs to Washington Qly, Fortune, Wall Street Jl, Financial Times. *Address:* PO Box 8772, Riyadh, Saudi Arabia. *Clubs:* Equestrian (Riyadh); Knickerbocker, New York Athletic (New York); Pacific–Union, Bohemian (San Francisco). *Died 4 July 2002.*

OLDENBOURG-IDALIE, Zoë; Chevalier, Légion d'Honneur, 1980; Officier du Mérite des Arts et des Lettres, 1978; writer (as Zoë Oldenbourg); *b* 31 March 1916; *d* of Sergius Oldenbourg, writer and historicist, and of Ada (*née* Starynkevitch); *m* 1948, Heinric Idalie; one *s* one *d. Educ:* Lycée Molière, Paris; Sorbonne, Paris. Prix Fémina, 1953. *Publications:* Argile et cendres, 1946 (The World is Not Enough, 1949); La Pierre angulaire, 1953 (The Cornerstone, 1954); Réveillés de la Vie, 1956 (The Awakened, trans. E. Hyams, 1957); Les Irréductibles, 1958 (The Chains of Love, 1959); Bûcher de Montségur, 1959 (Massacre at Montségur, 1962); Les Brûlés, 1961 (Destiny of Fire, trans. P. Green, 1961); Les Cités charnelles, 1961 (Cities of the Flesh, 1963); Les Croisades: un essai historique, 1963 (The Crusades, trans. Anne Carter, 1966); Catherine de Russie, 1965 (Catherine the Great, 1965); Saint Bernard, 1969; La Joie des pauvres, 1970 (The Heirs of the Kingdom, trans. Anne Carter, 1972); L'Epopée des cathédrales, 1973; Que vous a donc fait Israël?, 1974; Visages d'un autoportrait (autobiog.), 1977; La Joie-Souffrance, 1980; Le Procès du Rêve, 1982; Que nous est Hécube?, 1984; Les Amours égarées, 1987; Déguisements, 1989; Aliénor, 1992. *Recreation:* painting. *Address:* 4 rue de Montmorency, 92100 Boulogne, France. *Died 8 Nov. 2002.*

OLIPHANT, Air Vice-Marshal David Nigel Kington B.; *see* Blair-Oliphant.

OLIVER, John Laurence; journalist; *b* 14 Sept. 1910; *s* of late Harold and Teresa Oliver; *m* 1946, Renée Mary Webb; two *s. Educ:* Haberdashers' Aske's Hampstead School. Publicity Manager, The Book Society, 1934; Art Editor, The Bystander, 1935–39. War of 1939–45: served in the Field Security Corps; commissioned 1941, The Suffolk Regt (transferred The Cambridgeshire Regt). Joined staff of The Sphere, 1946; Art Editor, 1947; Assistant Editor, 1956; Editor, 1960–64; Editor, The Tatler, 1961–65. *Publications:* Saint John's Wood Church (with Rev. Peter Bradshaw), 1955; Malcolm Morley at the Everyman, 1977; occasional short stories and articles. *Recreations:* reading, theatre going, watching cricket. *Address:* Smokehouse Farm, Sandy Lane, Sternfield, Saxmundham IP17 1RT. *T:* (01728) 603160. *Clubs:* Garrick, MCC. *Died 16 June 2004.*

OLIVER, Michael Edgar; writer and broadcaster; *b* 20 July 1937; *s* of Alan Oliver and Marguerite (*née* Moore). *Educ:* St Clement Danes GS; Isleworth Poly.; London Sch. of Printing. Work in librarianship, publishing and business, 1953–73; Presenter: BBC Radio London, 1970–75; BBC Radio: Kaleidoscope, 1974–87; Music Weekly, 1975–90; Soundings, 1990–92; contributor, CD (formerly Record) Review, 1973–. Reviewer, Gramophone, 1973–; contributor: Classic CD, 1990–; Classic FM mag., 1996–; Internat. Record Review, 2000–. *Publications:* Igor Stravinsky, 1995; Benjamin Britten, 1996; Settling the Score, 1999. *Recreation:* travel. *Address:* 129 Crouch Hill, N8 9QH; via Castello 34, 06066 Oro, Piegaro, Italy. *Died 1 Dec. 2002.*

OLIVER, Peter Richard, CMG 1965; HM Diplomatic Service, retired; Ambassador to Uruguay, 1972–77; *b* 3 June 1917; *yr s* of William Henry Oliver and Muriel Daisie Elisabeth Oliver (*née* Widdicombe); *m* 1940, Freda Evelyn Gwyther (*d* 2002); two *s* two *d. Educ:* Felsted Sch.; Hanover; Berlin; Trinity Hall, Cambridge. Indian Civil Service, 1939–47; served in Punjab and Bahawalpur State. Transferred to HM Foreign (subsequently Diplomatic) Service, 1947; served in Karachi, 1947–49; Foreign Office, 1949–52; The Hague, 1952–56; Havana, 1956–59; Foreign Office, 1959–61; Djakarta, 1961–64; Bonn, 1965–69; Dep. High Comr, Lahore, 1969–72. *Recreations:* publisher-hunting, Bumbloclasm. *Address:* Room 1, Annethy Lowen, Sarah's Lane, Padstow, Cornwall PL28 8EL. *T:* (01841) 532558. *Clubs:* Royal Commonwealth Society; Hawks (Cambridge); Union (Cambridge). *Died 16 Dec. 2003.*

OLYOTT, Ven. Leonard Eric; Archdeacon of Taunton and Prebendary of Milverton, 1977–92, Archdeacon Emeritus, 1992; *b* 11 Jan. 1926; *s* of Thomas Olyott and Maude Ann Olyott (*née* Purser); *m* 1951, Yvonne Winifred Kate Keele; two *s* one *d. Educ:* Colchester Royal Grammar School; London Univ. (BA 1950); Westcott House, Cambridge. Served RNVR, 1944–47; commissioned, 1945. Asst Curate, St George, Camberwell, 1952–55; Priest-in-Charge, St Michael and All Angels, Birchwood, Hatfield, Herts, 1955–60; Vicar of Chipperfield, Herts, 1960–68; Vicar of Crewkerne, 1968–71; Rector of Crewkerne with Wayford, 1971–77; Rural Dean of Crewkerne, 1972–77; Prebendary of Timberscombe, 1976. Hospital Chaplains Adviser to Bishop of Bath and Wells, 1983–92. *Recreations:* sailing, gardening, music, genealogy. *Address:* 5 Greendale, Ilminster, Somerset TA19 0EB. *Died 6 April 2005.*

OMAN, Julia Trevelyan, (Lady Strong), CBE 1986; RDI 1977; designer; Director, Oman Productions Ltd; *b* 11 July 1930; *d* of late Charles Chichele Oman and Joan Trevelyan; *m* 1971, Sir Roy Colin Strong. *Educ:* Royal College of Art, London (Royal Scholar, 1953; Silver Medal, 1955). Designer: BBC Television, 1955–67. Designer: *theatre:* Brief Lives, London and NY, 1967; Country Dance, London and Edinburgh, 1967; 40 Years On, 1968; The Merchant of Venice, NT, 1970; Othello, RSC, 1971; Getting On, Queen's, 1971; The Importance of Being Earnest, Vienna, 1976; Hay Fever and The Wild Duck, Lyric, Hammersmith, 1980; The Shoemakers' Holiday, NT, 1981; Mr and Mrs Nobody, Garrick, 1986; A Man for All Seasons, Chichester and Savoy, 1987; The Best of Friends, Apollo, 1988; Beatrix, Chichester, 1996; *opera:* Mefistofele, WNO, 1957; Eugene Onegin, Covent Garden, 1971; Un Ballo in Maschera, Hamburgische Staatsoper, 1973; La Bohème, Covent Garden, 1974, 1995; Die Fledermaus, Covent Garden, 1977; Die Csardasfürstin, Kassel, 1982; Otello, Stockholm, 1983; Arabella, Glyndebourne, 1984, 1985, 1989, 1996; The Consul, Connecticut Grand Opera, USA, 1985; *ballet:* Enigma Variations, Royal Ballet, 1968, Birmingham Royal Ballet, 1994; A Month in the Country, Royal Ballet, 1976, Nat. Ballet of Canada, 1995; Sospiri, 1980; Swan Lake, Boston, 1981; The Nutcracker, Royal Ballet, 1984; *films:* Alice in Wonderland (BBC TV), 1966

(Designer of the Year Award, 1967); (Art Dir (England)) The Charge of the Light Brigade, 1967; (Art Dir) Laughter in the Dark, 1968; (prodn designer) Julius Caesar, 1969; The Straw Dogs, 1971; *television:* Hay Fever, 1979; Separate Tables, 1982; *exhibitions:* Samuel Pepys, Nat. Portrait Gall., 1971; Mme Tussaud's hist. tableaux, 1979; The Bear's Quest for Ragged Staff, Warwick Castle, 1981. Mem., DES Vis. Cttee for RCA, 1981–85. DesRCA (1st cl.), 1955; FCSD. Hon. DLitt Bristol, 1987. Award for Cable Excellence, for best art direction, NCTA, 1983. *Publications:* Street Children (photographs by Julia Trevelyan Oman; text by B. S. Johnson), 1964; (with Roy Strong) Elizabeth R, 1971; (with Roy Strong) Mary Queen of Scots, 1972; introd. The Merchant of Venice, Folio Soc. edn, 1975; (with Roy Strong) The English Year, 1982; (with Roy Strong) A Celebration of Gardens, 1991; (with Roy Strong) A Country Life, 1994; (with Roy Strong) On Happiness, 1998; (with Roy Strong) Garden Party, 2000; contrib. Architectural Review (photographs), Vogue (text and photographs), Country Life (text and drawings). *Address:* c/o Oman Productions Ltd, The Laskett, Much Birch, Hereford HR2 8HZ.
Died 10 Oct. 2003.

ONG Teng Cheong; Chairman, Ong & Ong Architects, since 1999; President of Singapore, 1993–99; *b* 22 Jan. 1936; *m* 1963, Ling Siew May (*d* 1999); two *s. Educ:* Chinese High Sch.; Univ. of Adelaide (BArch 1961); Univ. of Liverpool (MCD 1967). Architect, Adelaide and Singapore, 1962–65; town planner in Singapore CS, 1967–71; architect and town planner in private sector, 1971–75. MP: for Kim Keat, 1972–88; Toa Payoh Gp, 1988–93; Sen. Minister of State for Communications, 1975–78; Minister for Communications, 1978–83; Actg Minister for Culture, 1978–80; Minister for Labour, 1980–83; Minister Without Portfolio, 1983–85; 2nd Dep. Prime Minister, 1985–90; Dep. Prime Minister, 1990–93. Chm., People's Action Party Central Exec. Cttee, 1981–93. Sec.-Gen., NTUC, 1983–93. *Address:* Ong & Ong Architects, 510 Thomson Road, 11-00 SLF Building, Singapore 298135.
Died 8 Feb. 2002.

ONSLOW OF WOKING, Baron *cr* 1997 (Life Peer), of Woking in the co. of Surrey; **Cranley Gordon Douglas Onslow,** KCMG 1993; PC 1988; *b* 8 June 1926; *s* of late F. R. D. Onslow and Mrs M. Onslow, Effingham House, Bexhill; *m* 1955, Lady June Hay, *yr d* of 13th Earl of Kinnoull; one *s* three *d. Educ:* Harrow; Oriel Coll., Oxford; Geneva Univ. Served in RAC, Lieut 7th Queen's Own Hussars, 1944–48, and 3rd/4th Co. of London Yeo. (Sharpshooters) (TA) as Captain, 1948–52. Joined HM Foreign Service, 1951; Third Sec. Rangoon, 1953–55; Consul at Maymyo, N Burma, 1955–56; resigned, 1960. Served on Dartford RDC, 1960–62, and Kent CC, 1961–64. MP (C) Woking, 1964–97. Parly Under-Sec. of State, Aerospace and Shipping, DTI, 1972–74; an Opposition spokesman on health and social security, 1974–75, on defence, 1975–76; Minister of State, FCO, 1982–83. Chairman: Select Cttee on Defence, 1981–82; Cons. Aviation Cttee, 1970–72, 1979–82; Mem., Select Cttee on Trade and Industry, 1992–97. Mem. Exec., 1922 Cttee, 1968–72, 1981–82, 1983–92, Chm., 1984–92. Mem., UK delegn to Council of Europe and WEU, 1977–81. Dir, Argyll Group PLC, 1983–93. Chm., Nautical Museums Trust, 1983–. Vice Pres., Nat. Rifle Assoc.; Council Mem., Salmon & Trout Assoc.; Vice Chm., Anglers' Conservation Assoc. MRAeS. Liveryman, Fishmongers' Co., 1991–. *Publication:* (ed) Asian Economic Development, 1965. *Recreations:* fishing, shooting, watching cricket. *Address:* House of Lords, SW1A 1PW. *Clubs:* Travellers, English-Speaking Union.
Died 13 March 2001.

OPPENHEIM, Sir Duncan (Morris), Kt 1960; Adviser to British-American Tobacco Co. Ltd, 1972–74 (Chairman 1953–66, President, 1966–72); Chairman, Tobacco Securities Trust Co. Ltd, 1969–74; Deputy Chairman, Commonwealth Development Finance Co.,

1968–74; *b* 6 Aug. 1904; *s* of Watkin Oppenheim, BA, TD, and Helen, 3rd *d* of Duncan McKechnie, JP; *m* 1st, 1932, Joyce Mary (*d* 1933), *d* of Stanley Mitcheson; no *c;* 2nd, 1936, Susan May (*d* 1964), *e d* of Brig.-Gen. E. B. Macnaghten, CMG, DSO; one *s* one *d. Educ:* Repton Sch. Admitted Solicitor of the Supreme Court, 1929; Asst Solicitor, Messrs Linklaters & Paines, London, 1929–34; joined British-American Tobacco Ltd group as a Solicitor, 1934; Director: British-American Tobacco Co. Ltd, 1943; Lloyds Bank Ltd, 1956–75; Equity and Law Life Assurance Society, 1966–80. Chairman: Council, Royal College of Art, 1956–72; Council of Industrial Design, 1960–72 (Mem. 1959); British Nat. Cttee of Internat. Chamber of Commerce, 1963–74; Overseas Investment Cttee CBI, 1964–74; RIIA (Chatham House), 1966–71; Member: Adv. Council, V&A Mus., 1967–79 (Chm. V&A Associates, 1976–81); Crafts Council (formerly Crafts Adv. Cttee), 1972–83 (acting Chm., 1977; Dep. Chm., 1978); Trustee and Mem., Council, 1973–94, Chm. of Council, 1990–, St John's, Smith Square. Governing Body of Repton School, 1959–79; Chm. Court of Governors, Admin. Staff Coll., 1963–71. Pt-time Civil Defence, City of Westminster, 1938–45; pictures painted of air-raid incidents in Westminster in archives of Imperial War Mus. Exhibitor: London Gp, 1954; RA Summer Exhibns, 1957, 1962–1982; one-man shows: Upper Grosvenor Galls, 1971; Spinks, 1980, 1983; New Grafton Gall., 1985, 1988, 1992. Hon. Dr and Senior Fellow, Royal College of Art; Hon. FCSD (Hon. FSIAD 1972). Bicentenary Medal, RSA, 1969. *Recreations:* painting, sailing. *Address:* 43 Edwardes Square, Kensington, W8 6HH. *T:* (020) 7603 7431. *Clubs:* Athenæum; Royal Yacht Squadron.
Died 5 Jan. 2003.

ORAM, Rt Rev. Kenneth Cyril; Assistant Bishop, Diocese of Lichfield, 1987–97; *b* 3 March 1919; *s* of Alfred Charles Oram and Sophie Oram; *m* 1943, Kathleen Mary Malcolm; three *s* one *d. Educ:* Selhurst Grammar Sch., Croydon; King's Coll., London (BA Hons English; AKC 1st cl.); Lincoln Theol Coll. Deacon 1942, priest 1943; Assistant Curate: St Dunstan's, Cranbrook, 1942–45; St Mildred's, Croydon, 1945–46; Upington with Prieska, S Africa, 1946–48; Rector of Prieska and Dir of Prieska Mission District, 1949–51; Rector of Mafeking, 1952–59; Dir of Educn, dio. Kimberley and Kuruman, 1953–62; Archdeacon of Bechuanaland, 1953–59; Dean and Archdeacon: of Kimberley, 1960–64; of Grahamstown, 1964–74; Bishop of Grahamstown, 1974–87. *Address:* Flat 1, Ramsay Hall, Byron Road, Worthing, West Sussex BN11 3HN. *T:* (01903) 204119.
Died 7 Jan. 2001.

ORANMORE and BROWNE, 4th Baron *cr* 1836 (Ireland); **Dominick Geoffrey Edward Browne;** Baron Mereworth of Mereworth Castle (UK) 1926; *b* 21 Oct. 1901; *e s* of 3rd Baron Oranmore and Browne and Lady Olwen Verena Ponsonby (*d* 1927), *e d* of 8th Earl of Bessborough; *S* father, 1927; *m* 1st, 1925, Mildred Helen (who obtained a divorce, 1936; she *d* 1980), *e d* of Hon. Thomas Egerton; two *s* one *d* (and two *d* decd); 2nd, 1936, Oonagh (marr. diss. 1950; she *d* 1995), *d* of late Hon. Ernest Guinness; one *s* (and two *s* decd); 3rd, 1951, Sally Gray, 5b Mount Street, London, W. *Educ:* Eton; Christ Church, Oxford. *Heir: s* Hon. Dominick Geoffrey Thomas Browne [*b* 1 July 1929; *m* 1957, Sara Margaret (marr. diss. 1974), *d* of late Dr Herbert Wright, 59 Merrion Square, Dublin, and Mrs C. A. West, Cross-in-Hand, Sussex]. *Address:* 52 Eaton Place, SW1X 8AL.
Died 7 Aug. 2002.

ORME, Baron *cr* 1997 (Life Peer), of Salford in the co. of Greater Manchester; **Stanley Orme;** PC 1974; *b* 5 April 1923; *s* of Sherwood Orme, Sale, Cheshire; *m* 1951, Irene Mary, *d* of Vernon Fletcher Harris, Worsley, Lancashire. *Educ:* elementary and technical schools; National Council of Labour Colleges and Workers' Educational Association classes. Warrant Officer, Air-Bomber Navigator, Royal Air Force Bomber Command, 1942–47. Joined the Labour party, 1944; Member of Sale Borough Council,

1958–65; contested (Lab) Stockport South, 1959. MP (Lab) Salford West, 1964–83, Salford East, 1983–97. Minister of State: NI Office, 1974–76; DHSS, 1976; Minister of State for Social Security, 1976–77, Minister for Social Security, and Mem. Cabinet, 1977–79; Opposition Spokesman on Health and Social Services, June 1979–Dec. 1980, on Industry, 1980–83, on Energy, 1983–87; Chm., PLP, 1987–92. Member: AEU; District Committee, Manchester; shop steward. Hon. DSc Salford, 1985. *Address:* House of Lords, SW1A 0PW.

Died 28 April 2005.

O'ROURKE, Sarah Louise E.; *see* Evans O'Rourke.

ORR EWING, Major Sir Ronald Archibald, 5th Bt *cr* 1886, of Ballikinrain, Stirlingshire, Lennoxbank, co. Dunbarton; Major (retired) Scots Guards; *b* 14 May 1912; *e s* of Sir Norman Orr Ewing, 4th Bt, CB, DSO, and Lady Orr Ewing (*née* Robarts), Tile House, Buckingham; *S* father, 1960; *m* 1938, Marion Hester (*d* 1997), *yr d* of late Colonel Sir Donald Walter Cameron of Lochiel, KT, CMG, and of Lady Hermione Cameron of Lochiel, *d* of 5th Duke of Montrose, KT; two *s* two *d*. *Educ:* Eton; RMC, Sandhurst. Scots Guards, 1932–53, Major. Served War of 1939–45, Middle East (POW 1942). JP 1956, DL 1963, Perthshire. Grand Master Mason of Scotland, 1965–69. *Recreation:* forestry. *Heir: s* Archibald Donald Orr Ewing [*b* 20 Dec. 1938; *m* 1st, 1965, Venetia Elizabeth (marr. diss. 1972), *y d* of Major and Mrs Richard Turner, Co. Dublin; 2nd, 1972, Nicola Jean-Anne, *d* of Reginald Baron Black, Fovant, near Salisbury; one *s*]. *Address:* Cardross, Port of Menteith, Kippen, Stirling FK8 3JY. *T:* (01877) 385220. *Club:* New (Edinburgh).

Died 14 Sept. 2002.

OSBORNE, Anthony David, CB 1995; Chief Executive, Government Property Lawyers, 1993–95; *b* 21 March 1935; *s* of Frederick Charles Osborne and Eva Mary Osborne (*née* Tutt); *m* 1958, Ethelwyn Grieve; two *s* one *d*. *Educ:* Brighton College. Articled: Aldrich and Crowther, Brighton; Ashurst, Morris, Crisp & Co., London; admitted Solicitor, 1958; private practice, London, 1958–65; joined Treasury Solicitor's Dept, 1965; Asst Treasury Solicitor, 1975; Solicitor to Health and Safety Commn and Health and Safety Exec., 1985–90; Principal Asst Treasury Solicitor, 1990; Head of Property Div., Taunton, 1990–93. *Recreations:* music, theatre, travel, photography. *Died 28 April 2004.*

OSIFELO, Sir Frederick (Aubarua), Kt 1977; MBE 1972; Speaker of Legislative Assembly, Solomon Islands, 1974–78; Chairman: Public Service Commission, 1975–78; Police and Prison Service Commission, 1977–78; Member, Judicial and Legal Service Commission, 1977–78; *b* 15 Oct. 1928; *s* of late Paul Iromea and Joy Ngangale Iromea; *m* 1949, Margaret Tanai; three *s* three *d*. *Educ:* Torquay Technical Coll., England (Dip. Public Admin). Office cleaner, 1945; clerk, 1950; 1st Cl. Magistrate, 1967; Admin. Officer, Cl. B, 1967, Cl. A, 1972; District Comr, Eastern Solomons, 1972; Sen. Sec., 1973; Comr of Lands, 1974. Chairman: Cttee of Prerogative of Mercy, 1979; ad hoc cttee on Solomon Islands Honours and Awards, 1979. Pres., Amateur Sports Assoc., 1975–. Lay Canon, 1977. *Publication:* Kanaka Boy (autobiog.), 1985. *Address:* PO Box 548, Honiara, Solomon Islands. *T:* (office) 21529, (home) 22018. *Died 26 March 2001.*

OSOLA, (Victor) John, (Väinö Juhani), CBE 1980; FREng, FIMechE; Chairman, John Osola & Associates Ltd, 1983–98; *b* 24 Jan. 1926; *s* of Väinö Kaarlo Osola and Violet Agenoria (*née* Jones); *m* 1948, Brenda Lilian Davison; two *s* one *d*. *Educ:* Hymers Coll., Hull; Sunderland Technical Coll., Univ. of Durham (BSc). FIMechE 1966; FREng (FEng 1979); Life Fellow ASME. Technical Commn, RE, 1945–48. Gas Turbine Res. Engr, C. A. Parsons & Co. Ltd, 1951–52; Sen. Proj. Design Engr, Procter & Gamble Ltd, 1952–57; Chief Engr, Lankro Chemicals Ltd, 1957–65; Technical

Director: Fibreglass Ltd, 1965–72; Triplex Safety Glass Co. Ltd, 1972–79; Chm., Fibreglass Pilkington Ltd, Bombay, 1967–72; Director: Triplex Ireland Ltd, 1976–79; Triclover Safety Glass Co. Ltd, 1976–79; (non-exec.) Kongsberg Systems Technology Ltd, 1983–85; Cranfield Precision Engrg Ltd, 1990–95; Mem., Pilkington Brothers European Safety Glass Bd, 1977–79; Group Chief Exec., Redman Heenan Internat. plc, 1979–82, non-exec. Dir, 1982–84. Pres., IMechE, 1982–83; Ind. Mem., Mech. Engrg and Machine Tool Requirements Bd, Dept of Industry, 1974–77, Chm. 1977–79; Chm., NEDO Adv. Manufacturing Systems Cttee, 1983–86; Member: Parly and Scientific Cttee, 1983–89; (Founder), Parly Gp for Engrg Develt, 1985–89; Court of Cranfield Inst. of Technol., 1979–85; Policy Bd, Cranfield Product Engrg Centre, 1980–85; Chm., Engrg Doctorate Prog., Cranfield Univ., 1994–98. Sec., Fellowship of Engrg, 1983–89; Chm., Royal Acad. of Engrg MacRobert Award Trust, 1994–98; Trustee and Dir, 1996–2001, Chm., 1998–2001, Smallpeice Trust. Foreign Mem., Finnish Nat. Acad. of Technology, 1989. Associate, St George's House, Windsor, 1980–; Governor, Malvern Coll., 1981–. Freeman, City of London, 1984; Liveryman, Worshipful Co. of Engineers, 1984–. FRSA 1976. Hon. Fellow, Humberside Coll. of Higher Educn, 1986. MacRobert Award, 1978. *Publications:* papers in specialised engrg jls. *Recreations:* offshore sailing (BoT yachtmaster), music. *Address:* Whiddon End, Yarhampton Cross, near Stourport-on-Severn, Worcs DY13 0UY. *T:* (01299) 896293. *Clubs:* Army and Navy; Royal Dee Yacht (Cheshire); Royal Irish Yacht (Dublin); North West Venturers Yacht (Beaumaris). *Died 11 April 2003.*

O'SULLIVAN, Rt Rev. Mgr James, CBE 1973 (MBE 1963); Officiating Chaplain (RC), Defence Medical Services Training Centre (formerly RAMC Depot and Training Centre), since 1973; *b* 2 Aug. 1917; *s* of Richard O'Sullivan and Ellen (*née* Ahern). *Educ:* St Finnbarr's Coll., Cork; All Hallows Coll., Dublin. Ordained, 1941; joined Royal Army Chaplain's Dept, 1942; 49 Infantry Div., Normandy, 1944; Senior RC Chaplain, Malaya, 1952–54 (despatches 1953); Chaplain Irish Guards, 1954–56; Senior RC Chaplain, Berlin, 1956–59; Staff Chaplain (RC), War Office, 1959–64; Senior RC Chaplain, BAOR, 1965–69; Principal RC Chaplain (Army), 1969–73. *Recreation:* golf. *Address:* Osgil, Vicarage Lane, Ropley, Alresford, Hants SO24 0DU. *Died 7 March 2001.*

OTUNGA, HE Cardinal Maurice Michael; Archbishop of Nairobi, (RC), 1971–97, then Emeritus; *b* Jan. 1923. Priest, 1950; Titular Bishop of Tacape, 1957; Bishop of Kisii, 1960; Titular Archbishop of Bomarzo, 1969; Cardinal 1973; Military Ordinary for Kenya, 1981–97, now Emeritus. *Address:* c/o Archbishop's House, PO Box 14231, Nairobi, Kenya. *Died 6 Sept. 2003.*

OUSBY, Dr Ian Vaughan Kenneth; writer and broadcaster; *b* 26 June 1947; *s* of Arthur Valentine Ousby and Betty Lettice Grace (*née* Green); *m* 1st 1969, Heather Dubrow (marr. diss. 1979); 2nd, 1984, Mary Dustan Turner (marr. diss. 1993); 3rd, 1998, Anna Saunders. *Educ:* Bishop's Stortford Coll.; Magdalene Coll., Cambridge (BA 1965); Harvard Univ. (PhD 1973). Temp. Lectr in English, Univ. of Durham, 1974–75; University of Maryland: Asst Prof. of English, 1975–79; Associate Prof., 1979–82. John Simon Guggenheim Meml Foundn Fellow, 1980–81. *Publications:* Bloodhounds of Heaven: the detective in English fiction from Godwin to Doyle, 1976; The Blue Guide to Literary Britain and Ireland, 1985, 2nd edn 1990; (jtly) The Correspondence of John Ruskin and Charles Eliot Norton, 1987; The Cambridge Guide to Literature in English, 1988, 2nd edn 1993, concise edn 1996; The Blue Guide to England, 10th edn 1989, 11th edn 1995; The Englishman's England: taste, travel and the rise of tourism, 1990; James Plumptre's Britain: the journals of a tourist in the 1790s, 1992; The Blue Guide to Burgundy, 1992; Occupation: the ordeal of France 1940–1944, 1997 (Edith McLeod Literary Prize,

Stern Silver PEN Award, 1998); The Crime and Mystery Book, 1997; The Cambridge Guide to Fiction in English, 1998; *posthumous publication*: The Road to Verdun: France, nationalism and the First World War, 2002. *Recreations*: looking at pictures and buildings, listening to music. *Address*: c/o Andrew Lownie Literary Agency, 17 Sutherland Street, SW1V 4JU. *T*: (020) 7828 1274.
Died 6 Aug. 2001.

OVERALL, Sir John (Wallace), Kt 1968; CBE 1962; MC 1941 and Bar 1942; architect, town planner and company director; *b* 15 July 1913; *s* of late W. Overall, Sydney; *m* 1943, Margaret J. (*d* 1988), *d* of C. W. Goodman; four *s*. *Educ*: Sydney Tech. College. AIF, 1940–45: CO, 1 Aust. Para. Bn (Lt-Col). Chief Architect, S Australian Housing Trust, 1946–48; private practice, Architect and Town Planner, 1949–52; Dir of Architecture, Commonwealth Dept of Works, 1952–57; Comr, Nat. Capital Develt Commn, 1958–72; Chm., Nat. Capital Planning Cttee, 1958–72; Comr, Cities Commn (Chm., Adv. Cttee), 1972–73; Principal, John Overall and Partners, 1973–81. Director: Lend Lease Corp. Ltd, 1973–83; General Property Trust, 1975–83; Alliance Holdings Ltd, 1975–83 (Chm., 1980–83); CSR Ltd, 1973–85. Mem., Parliament House Construction Authority (Commonwealth Govt of Australia), 1979–85; Chm. Assessors, Parlt House Design Competition, 1979–80. Chm. of Olympic Fine Arts Architecture and Sculpture Exhibn, Melb., 1956. Life Fellow, RAIA and API; Hon. Fellow, AIA, 1984; Pres., Austr. Inst. of Urban Studies, 1970–71. Past Pres., Canberra Legacy Club. Sydney Luker Meml Medal, 1970; Sir James Barrett Medal, 1970; Gold Medal, RAIA, 1982. *Publications*: Observations on Redevelopment Western Side of Sydney Cove, 1967; Canberra: yesterday, today and tomorrow, 1995; sundry papers to professional jls. *Recreations*: golf, tennis. *Address*: Unit 1, Kingston Tower, 9 Jardine Street, Kingston, ACT 2604, Australia. *Club*: Commonwealth (Canberra).   *Died 2 Sept. 2001.*

OWEN, Maj.-Gen. David Lanyon Ll.; *see* Lloyd Owen.

OWEN, Rt Rev. Edwin, MA; Bishop of Limerick and Killaloe, 1976–81; *b* 3 Nov. 1910; *s* of late William Rowland Owen; *m* 1940, Margaret Mary Williams, BA; one *s* one *d*. *Educ*: Royal School, Armagh; Trinity College, Dublin (MA). Deacon 1934, priest 1935, Dublin; Curate of Glenageary, 1934–36; Christ Church, Leeson Park, Dublin, 1936–38; Minor Canon of St Patrick's Cathedral, Dublin, 1935–36; Chancellor's Vicar, 1936–38; Succentor, 1938–42; Incumbent of Birr with Eglish, 1942–57; Canon, Killaloe Cathedral, 1954–57; Rector of Killaloe and Dean of Killaloe Cathedral, 1957–72; Diocesan Secretary of Killaloe and Kilfenora, 1957–72; Bishop of Killaloe, Kilfenora, Clonfert and Kilmacduagh, 1972–76, when diocese amalgamated with Limerick, Ardfert and Aghadoe, and Emly. *Recreation*: classical music. *Address*: 4 Cypress, Hazeldene, Anglesea Road, Dublin 4, Ireland.   *Died 2 April 2005.*

OWEN, Dr Gareth, CBE 1988; MRIA; CBiol, FIBiol; Principal, University College of Wales, Aberystwyth, 1979–89; Vice-Chancellor, University of Wales, 1985–87; *b* 4 Oct. 1922; *s* of J. R. and B. M. Owen; *m* 1953, Beti Jones; one *s* two *d*. *Educ*: Pontypridd Boys' Grammar Sch.; University Coll., Cardiff (BSc 1950; Fellow, 1982); DSc Glasgow, 1959. FIBiol 1964. Served War, RAF Pilot, 1942–47. Lectr in Zoology, Univ. of Glasgow, 1950–64; Prof. of Zool., 1964–79, and Pro-Vice-Chancellor, 1974–79, Queen's Univ. of Belfast. Welsh Supernumerary, Jesus Coll., Oxford, 1981–82 and 1986–87. Mem., Nature Conservancy Council, 1984–91 (Chm., Adv. Cttee for Wales, 1985–91). Pres., Welsh Centre of Internat. Affairs, 1989–93. Mem., RSPB Adv. Cttee for Wales, 1991–97. MRIA 1976. Hon. Fellow: UCW, Cardiff, 1982; AFRC Inst. for Grassland and Envmtl Res., 1991. Hon. Mem. of the Gorsedd, 1983. Hon. DSc QUB, 1982; Hon. LLD Wales, 1989. *Publications*: contrib. Trans Royal Soc., Proc. Malacol. Soc. London, Jl Mar. Biol. Soc., and Qly Jl Micro. Sci.

Recreation: photography. *Address*: 6A St Margaret's Place, Whitchurch, Cardiff CF14 7AD. *T*: (029) 2069 2199.
Died 4 May 2002.

OWEN, Sir Hugh (Bernard Pilkington), 5th Bt *cr* 1813; Orielton, Pembrokeshire; *b* 28 March 1915; *s* of Sir John Arthur Owen, 4th Bt and Lucy Fletcher (*d* 1985), *e d* of F. W. Pilkington; *S* father, 1973. *Educ*: Chillon Coll., Switzerland. *Heir*: none. *Address*: 63 Dudsbury Road, Ferndown, Dorset BH22 8RD.
Died 22 Feb. 2002 (ext).

OWEN, Philip Loscombe Wintringham, TD 1950; QC 1963; *b* 10 Jan. 1920; *er s* of late Rt Hon. Sir Wintringham Stable, MC, and Lucie Haden (*née* Freeman); assumed surname of Owen in lieu of Stable by deed poll, 1942; *m* 1949, Elizabeth Jane, *d* of late Lewis Trelawny Widdicombe, Effingham, Surrey; three *s* two *d*. *Educ*: Winchester; Christ Church, Oxford (MA). Served War of 1939–45, Royal Welch Fusiliers: W Africa, India, Ceylon, Burma, 1939–47; Major TARO. Called to the Bar, Middle Temple, 1949; Bencher, 1969; Mem., Gen. Council of the Bar of England and Wales, 1971–77. A Deputy Chairman of Quarter Sessions: Montgomeryshire, 1959–71; Cheshire, 1961–71; Recorder of Merthyr Tydfil, 1971; a Recorder of the Crown Court, 1972–82; Leader, Wales and Chester Circuit, 1975–77. Chm., Adv. Bd constituted under Misuse of Drugs Act, 1974. Legal Assessor to: Gen. Med. Council, 1970; Gen. Dental Council, 1970; RICS, 1970. Contested (C) Montgomeryshire, 1945. JP Montgomeryshire, 1959; JP Cheshire, 1961. Vice-Pres., Montgomeryshire Cons. and Unionist Assoc.; Pres., Montgomeryshire Soc., 1974–75. Dir, Swansea City AFC Ltd, 1976–87. Trustee, and Mem. Cttee of Mgt, Young Musicians Symphony Orch., 1988–. Received into Roman Catholic Church, 1943. *Recreations*: shooting, fishing, forestry, music, Association football. *Address*: Plas Llwyn Owen, Llanbrynmair, Powys SY19 7BE. *T*: (01650) 521542. *Clubs*: Carlton, Pratt's; Cardiff and County (Cardiff); Welshpool and District Conservative; Bristol Channel Yacht (Mumbles).
Died 3 April 2001.

OWEN, Robert Penrhyn; Director and Secretary, The Water Companies' Association, 1974–83, retired; *b* 17 Dec. 1918; *s* of late Captain Richard Owen; *m* 1949, Suzanne (decd), *d* of late L. H. West; one *s* one *d*. *Educ*: Friar's School. War service in Royal Welch Fusiliers, 1939–46, in Madagascar, India, The Arakan and North and Central Burma. Admitted Solicitor, 1947. Asst Solicitor: Berks CC, 1948–50; Leics CC, 1950–54; Chief Asst Solicitor, Lancs CC, 1954–60; 2nd Dep. Clerk and 2nd Dep. Clerk of the Peace, Lancs CC, 1960–63; Gen. Manager, Telford Develt Corp. (New Town), 1963–69; Sec., Chief Exec. Officer and Solicitor, Thames Conservancy, 1969–74. *Recreations*: all sport, gardening, reading. *Address*: Pilgrims Wood, Three Gables Lane, Streatley, Reading RG8 9LJ. *T*: (01491) 874294. *Clubs*: MCC; Phyllis Court (Henley-on-Thames).
Died 8 Dec. 2003.

OWENS, Bernard Charles; Director, British Jewellery and Giftware Federation, 1987–96 (Vice-President, 1990–91; President, 1991–92; Deputy President, 1992–93); *b* 20 March 1928; *s* of late Charles A. Owens and Sheila (*née* O'Higgins); *m* 1954, Barbara Madeline Murphy; two *s* four *d*. *Educ*: Solihull Sch.; LSE. Commnd 2nd Lieut, RASC, 1947; transf. RARO, 1949 (Lieut). Chm. and Man. Dir, Bernard Owens and Partners, 1962; Managing Director: Stanley Bros, 1962–67; Coronet Industrial Securities, 1965–67; Chairman: Unochrome Industries, 1964–79; Silverthorne Group, 1972–79; Director: Hobbs Savill & Bradford, 1957–62; Trinidad Sugar Estates, 1965–67; Cornish Brewery, 1987–93; Local Dir, Alexander Stenhouse UK (formerly Reed Stenhouse UK), 1980–87. Mem. of Lloyd's, 1978–. Mem., Monopolies and Mergers Commn, 1981–93. Chm., Metal Finishing Assoc., 1982–85 (Vice-Chm., 1981–82; Dep. Chm., 1985–88); Treas. and Trustee, British Jewellery

Giftware and Leathergoods Benevolent Soc., 1992–96; Member: Cttee, Nat. Clayware Fedn, 1962–67; Council, Zoological Society, 1987–90. Mem., Solihull Council, 1953–63 (Chm., Finance Cttee, 1957–63); contested (C) Birmingham, Small Heath, 1959 and March 1961. Freeman, City of London, 1981; Liveryman: Gardeners' Co., 1982; Basketmakers' Co., 1994; Mem., HAC, 1984–. Life Governor, RNLI, 1984. FRSA 1972. Mem., SMO Malta, 1979. *Clubs:* MCC, City Livery Yacht (Cdre, 1995–97).   *Died 12 Dec. 2002.*

OXBURY, Harold Frederick, CMG 1961; Deputy Director-General, British Council, 1962–66 (Assistant Director-General, 1959); *b* 11 Nov. 1903; *s* of Fredric Thomas Oxbury; *m* 1st, 1928, Violet Bennets (*d* 1954); one *s* one *d*; 2nd, 1954, Helen Shipley (*d* 1975), *d* of Amos Perry, FLS, VMH. *Educ:* Norwich Sch.; Trinity Coll., Cambridge (Senior Scholar). Entered Indian Civil Service, 1928; Chief Collector of Customs, Burma, 1940; in charge of civilian evacuation from N Burma, 1942; Government of Burma Representative, Burma Office, 1942–44; Dep. Controller Finance (Colonel), Military Administration, Burma, 1945; Finance Secretary, Government of Burma, 1946; British Council: Director, Colonies Dept, 1947; Controller Finance, 1956. *Publications:* Great Britons: twentieth century lives, 1985; contrib. number of articles to Dictionary of National Biography, and compiled epitomes for 1961–1985 in Concise edn, 3 vols, 1992. *Recreations:* writing, painting. *Address:* 122B Woodstock Road, Oxford OX2 7NF.   *Died 31 Oct. 2005.*

OXFUIRD, 13th Viscount of, *cr* 1651; **George Hubbard Makgill,** CBE 1997; Bt 1627; Lord Macgill of Cousland, 1651; *b* 7 Jan. 1934; *s* of Richard James Robert Haldane Makgill, RNZAF (*d* 1948) (*yr s* of 11th Bt) and Elizabeth Lyman (*d* 1981), *d* of Gorham Hubbard, Boston, USA; *S* uncle, 1986; *m* 1st, 1967, Alison Campbell (marr. diss. 1977), *er d* of late Neils Max Jensen, Randers, Denmark; three *s* (inc. twin *s*); 2nd, 1980, Venetia Cunitia Mary, *o d* of Major Charles Anthony Steward, Crondall, Farnham, Surrey; one *s*. *Educ:* St Peter's School, Cambridge, NZ; Wanganui Collegiate School. Commissioned RAF, 1955–58. Overseas Exec., Lansing Bagnall Ltd, 1964–92. A Deputy Speaker, House of Lords, 1990–; Vice-Chm., Assoc. of Cons. Peers, 1993–; Member: Jt Cttee on Statutory Instruments, 1991–97; Hybrid Bills Cttee, 1995–, Offices Cttee, 1995–97, H of L; elected Mem., H of L, 1999. *Recreations:* fishing, gardening, shooting. *Heir: s* Master of Oxfuird, *b* 14 Oct. 1969. *Address:* House of Lords, SW1A 0PW. *Club:* Caledonian.
                                        Died 3 Jan. 2003.

OXLADE, Zena Elsie, CBE 1984; SRN, RNT; Regional Nursing Officer, East Anglian Regional Health Authority,

1981–87, retired; *b* 26 April 1929; *d* of James and Beatrice May Oxlade. *Educ:* Latymer Grammar Sch., N9. SRN 1950; RNT (London Univ.). Ward Sister, 1952; Theatre Sister 1953; Night Sister, 1954; Sister Tutor, 1956; Principal Tutor, 1963; Principal Nursing Officer, 1969; Chief Nursing Officer, 1973; District Nursing Officer, 1974; Area Nursing Officer, Suffolk AHA, 1978–81. Chm., GNC, 1977–83 (Mem., 1975–83; Chm., GNC Trust, 1983–); Mem., UK Council for Nurses, Midwives and Health Visitors, 1983–89. DUniv Surrey, 1993. *Publication:* Ear, Nose and Throat Nursing, 1972. *Recreations:* motoring, reading, handicrafts. *Address:* 5 Morgan Court, Claydon, Suffolk IP6 0AN. *T:* (01473) 831895.   *Died 16 March 2002.*

OXLEE, Colin Hamilton; formerly consultant; Technical Director, Military Division, Defence Research Agency, 1991–92; *s* of Leonard William and Margaret Hamilton Oxlee; *m* 1960, Robyn Rosemary Gardner; one *s* one *d*. *Educ:* St Lawrence College, Ramsgate; Univ. of Nottingham (BSc Hons 1959; MSc 1961). MIM 1960; CEng 1977. Technical apprentice, Appleby-Frodingham Steel Co., 1954–56; Materials Res. Scientist, RARDE, 1961–71; PSO to Chief Scientist (Army), 1971–74; Supt Materials Res., 1974–77, Supt Ammunition, 1977–81, RARDE; Dep. Dir, Scientific and Technical Intell., 1981–84, Dir, Heavy Weapons Projects, 1984–89, MoD; Dep. Dir (Armaments), RARDE, 1989–91. *Publications:* Low Alloy Steels, 1968; Proc. of Iron and Steel Institute Council of Scientific and Industrial Research, India, 1966, and of Iron and Steel Institute of Japan, 1970; official reports. *Recreations:* tennis, jazz, guitar, photography/video, churches, cathedrals, castles and historic houses, travel. *Address:* 9 Springhead, Tunbridge Wells, Kent TN2 3NY.   *Died 27 July 2001.*

OXLEY, Humphrey Leslie Malcolm, CMG 1966; OBE 1956; HM Diplomatic Service, retired; *b* 9 Oct. 1909; *s* of W. H. F. Oxley, MRCS, LRCP, FRCOG, and Lily Malcolm; *m* 1945, Frances Olga, *d* of George Bowden, San Jose, Costa Rica; twin *s*. *Educ:* Epsom Coll. Admitted Solicitor, 1933; Junior Legal Asst, India Office, 1933; Comr for Oaths, 1934; Asst Solicitor, 1944; CRO, 1947; Asst Legal Adviser, 1961; Legal Counsellor, Commonwealth Office, 1965–67; HM Diplomatic Service, 1967; Dep. Legal Adviser, FCO, 1967–69. Legal Consultant to HM Comr, Magistrate, various legal appts, Anguilla, 1971–72. *Recreation:* gardening. *Address:* Sandpipers, Crooked Lane, Birdham, Chichester, West Sussex PO20 7ET. *Club:* Civil Service.
                                        Died 28 Feb. 2003.

OXLEY, James Keith R.; *see* Rice-Oxley.

P

PACKER, Kerry Francis Bullmore, AC 1983; Chairman, Consolidated Press Holdings Ltd, since 1974; *b* 17 Dec. 1937; *s* of late Sir Douglas Frank Hewson Packer, KBE, and Lady (Gretel Joyce) Packer (*née* Bullmore); *m* 1963, Roslyn Redman Weedon; one *s* one *d*. *Educ:* Cranbrook Sch., Sydney, NSW; Geelong C of E Grammar Sch., Vic. Largest shareholder in Publishing and Broadcasting Ltd (publisher of magazines; major TV broadcaster). *Recreations:* golf, tennis, cricket, polo. *Address:* 54 Park Street, Sydney, NSW 2000, Australia. *T:* (2) 92828000. *Clubs:* Athenæum (Melbourne); Royal Sydney Golf, Australian Golf, Elanora Country, Tattersall's (NSW). *Died 26 Dec. 2005.*

PAGE, family name of **Baron Whaddon**.

PAGE, Maj.-Gen. Charles Edward, CB 1974; MBE 1944; DL; Director of Combat Development (Army), 1971–74, retired; *b* 23 Aug. 1920; *s* of late Sir (Charles) Max Page, KBE, CB, DSO, FRCS and Lady (Helen) Page; *m* 1948, Elizabeth Marion, *d* of late Sir William Smith Crawford, KBE; two *s* one *d*. *Educ:* Marlborough Coll.; Trinity Coll., Cambridge; BSc (Eng) London 1949. CEng, FIEE 1968. Commissioned 2nd Lieut Royal Signals from TA, 1941; regimental appts Guards Armd Divisional Signals, 1941–45; CO 19 Indian Div. Signals, 1945–46; psc 1951; GSO2 Staff Coll., 1955–58; GSO1 Combat Develt Directorate, WO, 1960–63; CO 1st Div. Signal Regt, 1963–65; CCR Signals 1 (BR) Corps, 1966–68; Sec., NATO Mil. Cttee, Brussels, 1968–70. Col Comdt, Royal Corps of Signals, 1974–80. Chm. Adv. Council, Women's Transport Service (FANY), 1994–97 (Hon. Col, 1976–93). DL W Sussex, 1986. *Recreations:* shooting, golf, fishing. *Address:* 104 Rivermead Court, Ranelagh Gardens, SW6 3SB. *Club:* Royal and Ancient (St Andrews). *Died 31 Jan. 2001.*

PAGE, Cyril Leslie, OBE 1965; Controller, Personnel, Television, BBC Television Service, 1971–76, retired; *b* 20 Oct. 1916; *s* of Cyril Herbert Page and Rosamund Clara Page; *m* 1939, Barbara Mary Rowland; one *s* one *d*. *Educ:* Sherborne Sch. Royal Air Force, 1936–46 (Wing Comdr). British Broadcasting Corporation, 1946–: Asst. Appts Dept, 1947; Asst Admin. Officer, Overseas Services, 1949; Asst Head of TV Admin., 1951; Establt Officer, TV, 1958; Head of TV Establt Dept, 1961; Asst Controller, TV Admin., 1964. Consultant, Osborne Management Ltd, 1998– (Dir, 1984–98; Chm., 1984–92). Mem. Council, Royal Postgrad. Med. Sch., 1975–89. *Recreations:* reading, gardening. *Address:* 95 Fountain Gardens, Windsor, Berks SL4 3SU. *Died 22 Dec. 2003.*

PAGE, Sir Frederick (William), Kt 1979; CBE 1961; FRS 1978; FREng; Hon. FRAeS; Member of the Board, British Aerospace PLC, 1977–83; Chairman and Chief Executive, Aircraft Group of British Aerospace PLC, 1977–82; retired 1983; *b* 20 Feb. 1917; *s* of Richard Page and Ellen Potter; *m* 1940, Kathleen Edith de Courcy (*d* 1993); three *s* one *d*. *Educ:* Rutlish Sch., Merton; St Catharine's Coll., Cambridge (MA). Hawker Aircraft Co., 1938; English Electric, 1945; Chief Engr, 1950, and Dir and Chief Exec. (Aircraft), English Electric Aviation, 1959; Managing Dir, Mil. Aircraft Div. of BAC, 1965–72, Chm., 1967; apptd Managing Dir (Aircraft), BAC, and Chm., Commercial Aircraft Div., 1972. Jt Chm. of SEPECAT, the Anglo-French co. formed for management of Jaguar programme, 1966–73; apptd to Bd of Panavia Aircraft GmbH, 1969, Chm. 1977; apptd Chm. BAC Ltd (a co. of Brit. Aerospace), 1977. Mem. Council, Soc. of Brit. Aerospace Cos Ltd; apptd to Bd of BAC (Operating) Ltd, 1963; Dir, BAC (USA) Inc., 1975–77. FRAeS, 1951–80, Hon. FRAeS, 1980 (Gold Medal, 1974); FREng (FEng 1977). Hon. Fellow, UMIST, 1970. Hon. DSc Cranfield, 1979. British Gold Medal for Aeronautics, 1962. *Recreation:* gardening. *Address:* 28 Farm Lane, Mudeford, Christchurch, Dorset BH23 4AH. *T:* (01425) 280024. *Died 29 May 2005.*

PAGE, John Brangwyn; Chairman, Agricultural Mortgage Corporation, 1982–85; Director: Standard Chartered Bank, 1982–89; Nationwide Building Society, 1982–92; *b* 23 Aug. 1923; *s* of late Sidney John Page, CB, MC; *m* 1948, Gloria Vail; one *s* one *d*. *Educ:* Highgate Sch. (Foundation Schol.); King's Coll., Cambridge (BA). RAF, 1942–46; Cambridge, 1946–48; Bank of England, 1948; seconded to IMF, 1953; Chief Cashier, 1970–80; Exec. Dir, 1980–82. FCIB; CCMI; FRSA. *Recreations:* gardening, music, travel. *Died 2 Feb. 2005.*

PAIGE, Prof. Edward George Sydney, PhD; FRS 1983; Professor of Electrical Engineering, and Fellow of St John's College, University of Oxford, 1977–97, then Emeritus Professor of Engineering Science and Emeritus Fellow; *b* 18 July 1930; *s* of Sydney and Maude Paige; *m* 1953, Helen Gill; two *s* two *d*. *Educ:* Reading University (BSc, PhD). FInstP. Junior Research Fellow to DCSO, Royal Radar Establishment, Malvern, 1955–77. *Address:* c/o Department of Engineering Science, University of Oxford, Parks Road, Oxford OX1 3PJ. *T:* (01865) 273110. *Died 20 Feb. 2004.*

PAIN, Lt-Gen. Sir (Horace) Rollo (Squarey), KCB 1975 (CB 1974); MC 1945; late 4th/7th Royal Dragoon Guards; Head of British Defence Staff, Washington, 1975–78, retired; *b* 11 May 1921; *s* of late Horace Davy Pain, Levenside, Haverthwaite, Ulverston, and Audrey Pain (*née* Hampson); *m* 1950, Denys Sophia (*née* Chaine-Nickson); one *s* two *d*. Commissioned into Reconnaissance Corps during War of 1939–45: served NW Europe (MC). After War, served for two years in E Africa and Brit. Somaliland before joining 4th/7th Royal Dragoon Gds in Palestine, 1947; attended Staff Coll., Camberley, 1951; subseq. served in Mil. Ops Directorate, in War Office; served with his Regt in BAOR, 1955–56; Mem. Directing Staff, Staff Coll., Camberley, 1957; GSO1, Brit. Army Staff, Washington, DC, 1960; commanded his Regt in BAOR, 1962; commanded one of the three divs, Staff Coll., Camberley, 1964; commanded 5 Inf. Bde in Borneo, 1965; IDC, 1968; ADC to the Queen, 1969; BGS, HQ, BAOR, 1969–70; GOC 2nd Div., 1970–72; Dir of Army Training, MoD, 1972–75; Col Comdt, Mil. Provost Staff Corps, 1974–83; Col 4th/7th Royal Dragoon Guards, 1979–83. *Address:* Eddlethorpe Hall, Malton, North Yorkshire YO17 9QS. *T:* (01653) 658218. *Club:* Cavalry and Guards. *Died 14 April 2005.*

PAIN, Hon. Sir Peter (Richard), Kt 1975; a Judge of the High Court of Justice, Queen's Bench Division, 1975–88; *b* 6 Sept. 1913; *s* of Arthur Richard Pain and Elizabeth Irene Pain (*née* Benn); *m* 1941, Barbara Florence Maude Riggs; two *s*. *Educ:* Westminster; Christ Church, Oxford. Called to the Bar, Lincoln's Inn, 1936, Bencher 1972; QC 1965. Chairman: Race Relations Board Conciliation Cttee for Greater London, 1968–71; South Metropolitan Conciliation Cttee, 1971–73; Mem., Parole Bd, 1978–80. Pres., Holiday Fellowship, 1977–83. *Publications:* Manual of Fire Service Law, 1951; The Law Relating to the Motor Trade (with K. C. Johnson-Davies), 1955. *Recreations:* forestry, cricket, mountain walking. *Address:* Loen, St Catherine's Road, Frimley, Surrey GU16 7NJ. *T:* (01252) 835639. *Died 15 Jan. 2003.*

PAIN, Sir Rollo; *see* Pain, Sir H. R. S.

PAINTAL, Prof. Autar Singh, Padma Vibhushan 1986; MD, PhD, DSc; FRS 1981; FRSE; Director-General, Indian Council for Medical Research, New Delhi, 1986–91; *b* 24 Sept. 1925; *s* of Dr Man Singh and Rajwans Kaur; *m* 1st; one *s* two *d*; 2nd, 1988, Ashima Anand. *Educ:* SSBS Khalsa High Sch., Lahore; Forman Christian Coll., Lahore; Lucknow Univ. (MB, BS, MD); Edinburgh Univ. (PhD, DSc). Lectr in Physiol., King George's Med. Coll., Lucknow Univ., 1949; Rockefeller Fellow, 1950; Lectr in Physiol., Edinburgh Univ., 1951; Control Officer, Technical Develt Estabt Labs, Min. of Defence, Kanpur, 1952–54; Prof. of Physiology, All-India Inst. of Med. Sciences, New Delhi, 1958–64; Prof. of Physiology and Dir, Vallabhbhai Patel Chest Inst., Delhi Univ., 1964–90 (Asst Dir, 1954–56); Dean, Faculty of Med. Sciences, Delhi Univ., 1966–77. Associate Prof., Albert Einstein Coll. of Medicine, New York, 1956; Vis. Associate Prof. of Physiol., Univ. of Utah, 1957; Commonwealth Vis. Prof., St Bartholomew's Hosp. Med. Sch., London, 1966. FRSE 1966; Fellow: Indian Acad. of Med. Sciences, 1966; Indian National Science Acad., 1971 (Vice Pres., 1981–83; Pres., 1987–88); President: Nat. Coll. of Chest Physicians, 1981–86; Indian Sci. Congress, 1984–85; Member: Physiol Soc., UK, 1953 (Hon. Mem., 1988); Ergonomics Res. Soc., UK, 1954; Foreign Mem., USSR Acad. of Scis, 1988; Hon. Mem., Amer. Physiol. Soc., 1990. B. C. Roy Orator, New Delhi, 1973; Sharpey-Schafer Lectr, Univ. of Edin., 1981; Dr Zakir Husain Meml Lectr, Jawaharlal Nehru Univ., 1984. Hon. FRCP, 1987. Hon. DSc: Benares Hindu Univ., 1982; Delhi Univ., 1984; Aligarh Muslim Univ., 1986; N Bengal Univ., 1990; Guru Nanak Dev Univ., 1996; Lucknow Univ., 1996; Punjabi Univ., Patiala, 1997. Basanti Devi Amir Chand Prize, 1967; Silver Jubilee Res. Award, 1978; Barclay Medal, Asiatic Soc., 1982; R. D. Birla Award, 1982; Nehru Sci. Award, 1983; Maharishi Dayanand Centenary Gold Medal, 1983; Acharya J. C. Bose Medal, Bose Inst., 1985; C. V. Raman Medal, Indian Nat. Sci. Acad., 1994; Ashutosh Mukherjee Medal, Indian Science Congress Assoc., 1994; J. L. Nehru Birth Centenary Award, Indian Sci. Congress Assoc., 2001; Om Prakash Bhasin Award for Science and Technol., 2002. *Publications:* (ed) Morphology and Mechanisms of Chemoreceptors, 1976; (ed) Respiratory Adaptations, Capillary Exchange and Reflex Mechanisms, 1977; Respiratory Control Mechanisms and Sensations, 1998; papers in Jl of Physiol. and in other physiol jls. *Recreations:* swimming, rowing, bird watching. *Address:* DST Centre for Visceral Mechanisms, Vallabhbhai Patel Chest Institute, Delhi University, PO Box 2101, Delhi 110007, India. *T:* (11) 27667749, (11) 27667856. *Club:* Roshanara (Delhi). *Died 21 Dec. 2004.*

PAINTER, George Duncan, OBE 1974; biographer and incunabulist; Assistant Keeper in charge of fifteenth-century printed books, British Museum, 1954–74; *b* Birmingham, 5 June 1914; *s* of George Charles Painter and Minnie Rosendale (*née* Taylor); *m* 1942, Isabel Joan, *d* of Samuel Morley Britton, Bristol; two *d*. *Educ:* King Edward's Sch., Birmingham; Trinity Coll., Cambridge (Schol.; Bell Exhibnr; John Stewart of Rannoch Schol.; Porson Schol.; Waddington Schol.; 1st cl. hons Class. Tripos pts I and II; Craven Student; 2nd Chancellor's Class. Medallist, 1936; MA 1945). Asst Lectr in Latin, Univ. of Liverpool, 1937; joined staff of Dept of Printed Books, BM, 1938. FRSL 1965. Hon. DLitt Edinburgh, 1979. *Publications:* André Gide, A Critical Biography, 1951, rev. edn 1968; The Road to Sinodun, Poems, 1951; André Gide, Marshlands and Prometheus Misbound (trans.), 1953; Marcel Proust, Letters to his Mother (trans.), 1956; Marcel Proust, A Biography, vol. 1, 1959, vol. 2, 1965 (Duff Cooper Memorial Prize), rev. and enl. edn in 1 vol., 1989, new edn 1996; The Vinland Map and the Tartar Relation (with R. A. Skelton and T. E. Marston), 1965, rev. edn 1996; André Maurois, The Chelsea Way (trans.), 1966; William Caxton, a Quincentenary Biography, 1976; Chateaubriand, A Biography, vol. 1, The Longed-for Tempests, 1977 (James Tait Black Meml Prize); Studies in Fifteenth-Century Printing, 1984;

articles on fifteenth-century printing in The Library, Book Collector, Gutenberg-Jahrbuch. *Recreations:* family life, gardening, music. *Address:* 10 Mansfield Road, Hove, East Sussex BN3 5NN. *T:* (01273) 416008.
Died 8 Dec. 2005.

PAKENHAM, Elizabeth; *see* Longford, Elizabeth, Countess of.

PALLOT, Arthur Keith, CB 1981; CMG 1966; Secretary and Director-General, Commonwealth War Graves Commission, 1975–82 (Director of Finance and Establishments, 1956–75); *b* 25 Sept. 1918; *s* of Harold Pallot, La Tourelle, Jersey; *m* 1945, Marjorie, *d* of J. T. Smith, Rugby; two *d*. *Educ:* Newton College. Royal Navy, 1936; retired as Lt-Comdr, 1947. Commonwealth War Graves Commission, 1947. Awarded the Queen's Commendation for brave conduct, 1958.
Died 13 July 2004.

PALMER, Charles Stuart William, OBE 1973; Vice-President, British Olympic Association, since 1988 (Vice-Chairman, 1977–83; Chairman, 1983–88); President, British Judo Association, since 1977 (Chairman, 1962–85); *b* London, 15 April 1930; *s* of Charles Edward Palmer and Emma Byrne. *Educ:* Drayton Manor County Sch. Represented GB in internat. judo comps, 1949–59; studied judo in Japan, 1951–55; obtained 1st Dan 1948, 4th Dan 1955, 8th Dan 1980, 9th Dan 1989, 10th Dan 1997; Mem. 1957, Capt. 1958, 1959, European Judo Champs winning team. Pres., Internat. Judo Fedn, 1965–79 (Hon. Life Pres., 1979–); Vice-Pres., British Schs Judo Assoc., 1967–; Chm., British Univs Judo Assoc., 1968–75. Sec.-Gen., Gen. Assoc of Internat. Sports Fedns, 1975–84; Member: IOC Tripartite Commn, 1974–81; Sports Council, 1983–94; Exec. Council, Assoc. of European Nat. Olympic Cttees, 1985–89 (Pres., Scientific and Medical Commn, 1988–89); Exec. Cttee, CCPR, 1975– (Chm., Games and Sports Div., 1980–97; Chm., cttee studying amateurism and eligibility in sport (Palmer Report published, 1988)); Programme Commn, IOC, 1989–. Governor, Sports Aid Foundn, 1979–. Mem., Lloyd's, 1988–. Mem. Council, Royal Albert Hall, 1987–. Manning Award, Sports Writers' Assoc., 1976. Olympic Order (silver), 1980; Gold Medal, European Judo Union, 1982. Key of City of Taipei, 1974, Key of City of Seoul, 1981; Diploma and Bronze Medal, City of Bordeaux, 1970; Distinguished Service Gold Medal (China), 1974; Merito Deportivo Gold Medal (Spain), 1976. *Publications:* technical papers and articles on judo and sports politics. *Recreations:* judo, ski-ing, sport generally, flying light aircraft, orchestral music, opera, languages. *Address:* 4 Hollywood Road, SW10 9HY. *T:* (020) 7352 6238. *Clubs:* Budokwai, Kandahar, Ski of Great Britain.
Died 17 Aug. 2001.

PALMER, Rev. Canon Derek George; Chaplain to the Queen, 1990–98; Team Rector of Dronfield with Holmesfield, 1987–95; *b* 24 Jan. 1928; *s* of late George Palmer, MBE and Edna Palmer; *m* 1952, June Cecilie Goddard; two *s* two *d*. *Educ:* Clifton Coll.; Selwyn Coll., Cambridge (MA); Wells Theological Coll. Deacon 1952, priest 1953; Priest in Charge, Good Shepherd, Bristol, 1954–58; first Vicar of Hartcliffe, 1958–68; Vicar of Christ Church, Swindon, 1968–77; Archdeacon of Rochester and Canon Residentiary of Rochester Cathedral, 1977–83; Home Secretary, Bd for Mission and Unity, 1983–87. Mem., General Synod, 1971–81. Hon. Canon: Rochester Cathedral, 1983–87; Derby Cathedral, 1992–. Chm., Christian Enquiry Agency, 1988–99; Ecumenical Officer, Bucks, 1995–. *Publications:* All Things New, 1963; Quest, 1971; Strangers No Longer, 1990. *Recreation:* canals. *Address:* 124 Bath Road, Banbury, Oxon OX16 0TR. *Died 20 March 2002.*

PALMER, Sir John (Chance), Kt 1979; solicitor; Consultant, Bevan Ashford; Vice Lord-Lieutenant of Devon, 1991–95; *b* 21 March 1920; *s* of Ernest Clephan Palmer and Claudine Pattie Sapey; *m* 1945, Mary

Winifred, d of Arthur Sidney Ellyatt, OBE, and Winifred Mary Ellyatt (née East); four s. Educ: St Paul's Sch.; St Edmund Hall, Oxford (MA). Served War, RNVR, Atlantic and Mediterranean, 1939–46. Admitted a Solicitor, 1948; elected Council of Law Society, 1963, Pres., 1978–79; Member: Criminal Injuries Compensation Board, 1981–92; SW Region Mental Health Tribunal, 1983–92. President: Devon and Exeter Law Soc., 1972; S Western Law Socs, 1973; Gov., Coll. of Law, 1965–83; Chm., Govs of Blundells Sch., 1980–91. Chairman: Exmoor Calvert Trust, 1991–94; Trustees, London Sailing Project, 1982–92. Chm., Internat. Technol Univ., 1988–95; Mem. Council, Exeter Univ., 1983–96. Hon. Member: Amer. Bar Assoc., 1978; Canadian Bar Assoc., 1979; Florida Defence Lawyers Assoc., 1981. Hon. Sec., Soc. for Protection of Animals in N Africa, 1989–98. Freeman, City of London, 2000. Hon. Citizen, Texas, 1980. DL Devon, 1984. Hon. LLD Exeter, 1980. Recreations: gardening, woodland, boats. Address: Lower Withleigh Farmhouse, Tiverton, Devon EX16 8JJ. T: (01884) 252959. Clubs: Athenæum, Royal Over-Seas League, Naval; Western (Glasgow); Royal Yacht Squadron. *Died 13 July 2003.*

PALMER, Sidney John, CB 1972; OBE 1953; Head of Royal Corps of Naval Constructors, 1968–73; b 28 Nov. 1913; s of Sidney Palmer; m 1941, Mavis Beatrice Blennerhassett Hallett; four s. Educ: RNC Greenwich. WhSch 1937. Admty Experiment Works, Haslar, 1938; Portsmouth Dockyard, 1942; Chief Constructor, Sydney, 1945; Constructor Comdr, Hong Kong, 1946; Chief Constructor Aircraft Carriers, 1948; Prof. of Naval Architecture, RNC Greenwich, 1952; Asst Dir Dreadnought Project, 1959; Dep. Dir Polaris Programme, 1963; Dir Naval Ship Production, 1966; Dep. Dir General Ships, 1968–73. Hon. Research Fellow, UCL, 1968. Mem. Council, RINA, 1960; Mem., Cttee of Management, RNLI, 1974–78; Liveryman, Shipwrights' Co., 1968. Address: 89 Bloomfield Avenue, Bath BA2 3AE. T: (01225) 312592. *Died 14 April 2001.*

PALMER, Maj.-Gen. Tony Brian, CB 1984; CEng, FIMechE; conducted a study on maintenance philosophy and organisation in the Army, 1986; retired 1986; b 5 Nov. 1930; s of Sidney Bernard Palmer and Ann (née Watkins); m 1953, Hazel Doris Robinson; two s. Educ: Wolverton Technical College; Luton College of Technology; General Motors Inst. of Technology, USA. General Motors UK, 1948–51 and 1953–54; commissioned REME 1954; RMCS, 1960–62; Tank Gunnery Trials, Infantry Workshop, staff duties MoD, JSSC, Ops and Plans MoD, 1962–70; Head, DG FVE Secretariat, 1970–72; Comdr REME, 3 Div., 1972–74; Head, Tech. Intell. (Army), 1974–76; Dir, Elect. and Mech. Engineering (Organisation and Training), 1977–79; Comdt, REME Training Centre, 1979–83; Dir-Gen. of Elect. and Mech. Engrg, MoD (Army), 1983–85. Col Comdt, REME, 1986–91. Vice-Pres., S Region, British Sports Assoc. for Disabled, 1980–96; Chairman: Somerset Br., Army Benevolent Fund, 1988–; Dorset Cttee for Employment of Disabled People, 1989–91; Somerset Cttee for Employment of People with Disabilities, 1991–94. Mem., Parish Council, Stoke St Gregory, 1995– (Chm., 1999–2001); Gov., Stoke St Gregory Primary Sch., 1997–2001. MIMgt. Recreations: history, gardening. Address: Little Deer Leaps, Windmill, Stoke St Gregory, Taunton, Somerset TA3 6EL. *Died 21 April 2002.*

PANNETT, Juliet Kathleen, MBE 1993; FRSA; portrait artist; b Hove, 15 July 1911; 2nd d of Charles Somers and May (née Brice); m 1938, Major M. R. D. Pannett (d 1980), late the Devonshire Regt; one s one d. Educ: Wistons Sch., Brighton; Brighton College of Art. Special Artist to Illustrated London News, 1957–64. Exhibitions: Royal Festival Hall, 1957, 1958; Qantas Gallery, 1959; New York, 1960; Cleveland, Ohio, 1960; Cooling Gallery, London, 1961; Coventry Cathedral Festival, 1962; Gloucester Three Choirs Festival, 1962; Brighton

Corporation Gallery, Rottingdean, 1967; Arun Art Centre, 1967, 1969, 1972; Fine Art Gall., London, 1969; Mignon Gall., Bath, 1970; Brotherton Gall., London, 1980; Pacific and Fringe Clubs, Hong Kong, 1986; Wigmore Hall, 1989, 1991; RNCM, 1989; Stamford Arts Centre, 1995. Exhibitor: Royal Academy; Royal Society of Portrait Painters; Royal Inst. of Painters in Watercolours, etc. Official Artist on several Qantas and Air Canada inaugural flights. Freeman: City of London, 1960; Painter Stainers' Company, 1960 (Gold Medal, 1995). Work in permanent collections: 22 portraits in National Portrait Gall.; 3 portraits in Scottish Nat. Portrait Gall.; Bodleian Library; Ashmolean Mus.; Oxford and Cambridge colls; RCM; Painter Stainers' Hall, London; Edinburgh Univ.; D Day painting for Devon and Dorset Regt, 1963; Commemorative Stained Glass Window (St Alban), Garrison Church, Munster, 1967; painting of Duke of Kent presenting new colours to Devon and Dorset Regt, 1982; Portraits, many for official bodies, include: HM The Queen (twice); HRH Princess Alexandra, 1984; HRH Prince Andrew, HRH Prince Edward, for HM The Queen, 1974; HRH Princess Marina, Duchess of Kent, 1968; Field Marshal Viscount Alanbrooke; Louis Armstrong; Dame Peggy Ashcroft; Earl Attlee; W. H. Auden; Prof. A. J. Ayer; Gp Capt. Sir Douglas Bader; David Ben-Gurion; Sir Adrian Boult; Sir Benjamin Britten; Lord Callaghan; Pablo Casals; Lord David Cecil; Gp Capt. Leonard Cheshire; Sir Winston Churchill; Jean Cocteau; Sir Colin Davis; Walter de la Mare; Victoria de los Angeles; Lord Denning; Sir Alec Douglas-Home; Jacqueline du Pré; Duke Ellington; Gracie Fields; Sir Ranulph Fiennes; Lord Grimond; Lord Hailsham; Michael Heseltine; Cardinal Basil Hume; Augustus John; Colonel 'H' Jones, VC; Otto Klemperer; C. S. Lewis; Sophia Loren; Humphrey Lyttelton; Sir Neville Marriner; Golda Meir; Yehudi Menuhin; Naomi Mitchison; Field Marshal Lord Montgomery; Patrick Moore; Lord Mountbatten of Burma; Dame Marie Rambert; Ginger Rogers; Sir Malcolm Sargent; Sir Harry Secombe; Igor Stravinsky; A. J. P. Taylor; Lady Thatcher; Sir Wilfred Thesiger; Sir Michael Tippett; Sir Laurens van der Post; Sir William Walton; Sir Ralph Vaughan Williams; Sir Harold Wilson, and many other members of the political, legal, military, academic, musical, artistic and literary professions. Has broadcast on art subjects on TV in UK and USA. Publications: cover portraits for books by Sir Thomas Beecham, Charles Causley, Henry Cecil, Canon John Collins, Mary Drewery, Louis Golding, Gerald Pawle and Cyril Scott; drawings reproduced in The Times, Daily Telegraph, Birmingham Mail, Radio Times, The Lancet, Leisure Painter, The Artist, Law Guardian, Guardian Gazette, etc. Recreation: water colour painting, esp. landscapes and old buildings. Address: Pound House, Roundstone Lane, Angmering Village, Sussex BN16 4AL. T: (01903) 784446. *Died 22 Aug. 2005.*

PANTON, Air Cdre Alastair Dyson, CB 1969; OBE 1950; DFC 1939; Provost Marshal and Director of RAF Security, 1968–71; b 2 Nov. 1916; third s of William Dickson Panton, Aberdeen, and Mary Ethel Langley, Bedford; m 1939, Eileen Isabel Lumley, Bedford; three s (and one s decd). Educ: Bedford School; RAF Coll., Cranwell. Pilot Officer, No 53 Sqdn RAF, 1937; POW 1940–45; OC, Nos 58 and 540 Sqdns, 1946–47; Air Staff, Hong Kong, 1948–50; Wing Comdr Flying, RAF Coningsby, 1951–53; Staff Coll., 1953–54; Air Ministry, 1954–57; Station Comdr, RAF Cranwell, 1957–60, RAF Bircham Newton, 1961–62, RAF Tern Hill, 1963–64; HQ Far East Air Force, 1965–67. Recreations: sleeping, reading. Address: Bridge House, Bankwell Road, Giggleswick, Settle, N Yorks BD24 0AN. *Died 29 Dec. 2002.*

PANTRIDGE, Prof. (James) Frank, CBE 1978; MC 1942; b 3 Oct. 1916. Educ: Queen's Univ., Belfast (MD). FRCP 1957; FACC 1967. Research Fellow, Univ. of Mich., 1948–49; Dir, Regional Medical Cardiology Centre, NI, 1977–82; Hon. Prof. of Cardiol., QUB.

Canadian Heart Foundn Orator; St Cyres Orator, National Heart Hosp., London. Chm., British Cardiac Soc., 1978. Developer of the Portable Defibrillator, and initiator (with J. S. Geddes) of pre-hospital coronary care. Hon. FRCPI. DUniv Open, 1981; Hon. DSc NUU, 1981; Hon. DMedSc QUB. *Publications:* The Acute Coronary Attack, 1975; An Unquiet Life (autobiog), 1989, 4th edn 1995. *Recreation:* fishing. *Address:* Hillsborough, Co. Down, N Ireland BT26 6EH. *T:* (028) 9268 9976.

Died 26 Dec. 2004.

PAOLOZZI, Sir Eduardo (Luigi), Kt 1989; CBE 1968; RA 1979 (ARA 1972); sculptor; HM Sculptor in Ordinary for Scotland, since 1986; Hon. Professor, Royal College of Art, 2000 (Tutor in Ceramics, 1968–89; Visiting Professor, 1989); *b* 7 March 1924; *s* of Rudolpho Antonio Paolozzi and Carmella (*née* Rossi), both Italian; *m* 1951, Freda Elliott (marr. diss. 1988); three *d*. *Educ:* Edinburgh School of Art; Slade Sch. Worked in Paris, 1947–50; Instructor, Central School of Arts and Crafts, London, 1950–55; Lecturer, St Martin's School of Art, 1955–56; Prof. of Ceramics at Fachhochschule, Cologne, 1977–81; Prof. of Sculpture, Akad. der Bildenden Künste, Munich, 1981–91. Trustee, Nat. Portrait Gall., 1988–2000. Fellow: UCL, 1986; Edinburgh Coll. of Art, 2003. Hon. Dr RCA, 1979; Hon. RSA; Hon. DLitt: Glasgow, 1980; Heriot-Watt, 1987; London, 1987; St Andrews, 1994; Cambridge, 1995; Birmingham, 1996. British Critics Prize, 1953; David E. Bright Foundn Award, 1960; Watson F. Blaire Prize, 1961; Purchase Prize, Internat. Sculpture Exhibn at Solomon R. Guggenheim Mus., 1967; First Prize for Sculpture, Carnegie Internat. Exhibn, 1967; Sculpture Prize, European Patent Office, Munich, 1978; First Prize, Rhinegarten Cologne comp., 1981; Grand Prix d'Honneur, Print Biennale at Ljubljana, Yugoslavia, 1983. *One-man exhibitions include:* first in London, Mayor Gallery, 1947; first in New York, Betty Parsons Gallery, 1960, also 1962; Tate Gallery, 1971, 1996; V&A Mus., 1973, 1977 (print retrospective); Nationalgal., W Berlin, 1975; Fruit Market Gall., Edinburgh, 1976; Kassel, Germany, 1978; Glasgow League of Artists, 1979; Edinburgh Univ., 1979; Cologne, Germany, 1979; Museum for Künste und Gewerbe, Hamburg, 1982; Aedes Gall., Berlin, 1983; Architectural Assoc., London; Royal Scottish Acad., 1984; Stadische Galerie im Lenbachhaus, Munich; Mus. Ludwig, Cologne; De Beyerd Mus., Breda, Holland; Contemporary Art Centre, Lyon, France; Ivan Dougherty Gall., Sydney, Aust., 1985; Cork, Ireland, 1985; Mus. of Mankind, 1986; RA, 1986; Serpentine Gall., 1987; Nat. Portrait Gall., 1988; Talbot Rice Art Gall., Edinburgh, 1989; Goethe Inst., London, 1991; Fitzwilliam Mus., Cambridge, 1992, 1996; Yorks Sculpture Park, 1994; Jason and Rhodes, London, 1996; Hayward Gall., 1996; Paolozzi Gall. and Studio, Dean Gall., Nat. Galls of Scotland, 1999; retrospective, Dean Gall., Edinburgh, 2004. Invited artist, 6th Internat. Drawing Biennale, Cleveland (UK), 1983. Designed: glass mosaics for Tottenham Ct Road Underground Station, London; film sets for Percy Adlon's Herschel and the Music of the Stars, 1984–85. Work in permanent collections: Tate Gallery; Contemporary Art Society; Museum of Modern Art, New York; Kowloon Park, Hong Kong, etc. Work exhibited in: British Pavilion, Venice Biennale, 1952; Documenta 2, Kassel, 1959; New Images of Man, New York, 1959; British Pavilion, 30th Venice Biennale; Open Air Sculpture, Battersea Park, London; British Sculpture in the Sixties, Tate Gallery. Corresponding Mem., Bayerische Akad. der Schöner Künste, 1990. Hon. Member: AA, 1980; RGI, 1993; Hon. RIAS, 1991. Eduardo Paolozzi Art Sch. inaugurated at Ipswich Sch., 1987. Goethe Medal, 1991. Cavalieri Ufficiale, Ordine al Merito (Italy), 1991. *Relevant publication:* Eduardo Paolozzi: writings and interviews, by Robin Spencer, 2000. *Recreation:* music. *Clubs:* Athenæum, Chelsea Arts. *Died 22 April 2005.*

PARK, Hon. Sir Hugh (Eames), Kt 1965; Judge of the High Court of Justice, Queen's Bench Division, 1973–85

(Family Division, 1965–73); retired; *b* 24 April 1910; *er s* of late William Robert and Helen Beatrice Park; *m* 1938, Beryl Josephine, *d* of late Joseph and Margery Coombe; three *d*. *Educ:* Blundell's; Sidney Sussex Coll., Cambridge (Hon. Fellow, 1968). Served War, 1940–45; Sqdn Leader, 1945. Called to the Bar, Middle Temple, 1936, Bencher, 1965; Member Western Circuit; QC 1960; Recorder: of Penzance, 1959–60; of Exeter, 1960–64; of Southampton, 1964–65; Commn of Assize, North East Circuit, 1963; Judge of the Courts of Appeal, Channel Islands, 1964–65; Chairman, County of Devon Quarter Sessions, 1964–71; Deputy Chairman, Cornwall County Quarter Sessions, 1959–71; Presiding Judge, Western Circuit, 1970–75. Member, Court of Exeter Univ., 1961; Member, Board of Governors, Blundell's Sch., 1961–81. Hon. LLD Exeter, 1984. *Recreation:* fishing. *Died 24 Jan. 2001.*

PARKE, Prof. Dennis Vernon William, PhD, DSc; CChem, FRSC, FIBiol, FRCPath; (first) Professor and Head of Department of Biochemistry, University of Surrey, 1967–87; University Professor of Biochemistry, 1986–90, then Emeritus; *b* London, 15 Nov. 1922; *e s* of William Parke and Florence Parke; *m* 1943, Doreen Joan Dunn; two *s* one *d*. *Educ:* West Ham Municipal Secondary Sch. (Gurney Scholar); Chelsea and University Colls, Univ. of London (MBBS 1943; BSc Special (1st cl. hons Chemistry) 1948); BS (Stanford) 1945; St Mary's Hosp. Med. Sch., London (PhD, DSc). War Service, RA RAMC, 1942–47. Head, Dept of Microbiol Chem., Glaxo Labs Ltd, 1948–49; St Mary's Hospital Medical School, University of London: Res. Asst to Prof. R. T. Williams, FRS, 1949–52; Lectr in Biochem., 1952–58, Sen. Lectr, 1958–62; Reader in Biochem., 1962–67; Dean, Faculty of Biol and Chem. Sciences, Univ. of Surrey, 1971–75. Visiting Professor: Univ. of Calif, Davis, 1978; Edmonton, Canada, 1984. Sometime Examnr, Univs of Dublin (Trinity), Edinburgh, Glasgow, Liverpool, London, Newcastle upon Tyne, Reading, Strathclyde, Wales, Auckland, Ibadan, Nairobi, Singapore, Sydney and Wellington. Sigma Xi Lectr, Univ. of Calif (Davis), 1978. Member: Cttee on Safety of Drugs, 1968–70; Cttee on Safety of Medicines, 1970–83; Cttee on Med. Aspects of Chemicals in Food and Environment, DHSS, 1972–86; Food Additives and Contaminants Cttee, MAFF, 1972–80; WHO Expert Panel on Food Additives, 1975–88; WHO Sci. Gp on Toxicity Evaluation of Chemicals, 1975; WHO Cons. in Indust. Toxicol., 1974, 1979, 1981, 1983; Sci. Dir, NATO Workshop on Ecotoxicology, July-Aug. 1977; Consultant to Environmental Protection Agency, Washington, 1985. Dir, Food and Veterinary Labs Ltd, 1988–92. Mem., Internat. Acad. of Environmental Safety. Editor, Xenobiotica, 1970–93. Hon. FRCP 1998; Hon. Member: Polish Soc. of Toxicology, 1984; Biochemical Soc., 1991; Soc. of Toxicology, USA, 1996; Hon. Fellow, Polish Soc. of Occupational Medicine, 1984. MD *hc* Lødz, 1995. Nobel Laureate, Medicine, 1989; Scheele Lectr and Medal, Uppsala, 1989. *Publications:* The Biochemistry of Foreign Compounds, 1968; (ed) Enzyme Induction, 1975; Drug Metabolism from Microbe to Man, 1977; Mucus in Health and Disease, 1977; Immunotoxicology, 1983; The Future of Predictive Safety Evaluation, 1987; Food, Nutrition and Chemical Toxicity, 1993; chapters in books and res. papers in biochem., pharm., toxicol. and med. jls. *Recreations:* landscape gardening, music. *Address:* Trevelen, 11 Poyle Road, Guildford, Surrey GU1 3SL. *T:* (01483) 573667. *Died 23 Nov. 2002.*

PARKER, Charles George Archibald; DL; Vice Lord-Lieutenant for Oxfordshire, 1996–99; *b* 30 Jan. 1924; *s* of late Capt. Charles Edward Parker, MC, and Hilda Margaret, *o d* of Sir John Starkey, 1st Bt, DL; *m* 1958, Shirley, *d* of late Col Frank Follett Holt, TD, and of Yvonne (*née* duMont); one *d*. *Educ:* Eton; New Coll., Oxford (MA). Served War, 1942–46, Rifle Bde (Capt.), NW Europe. Times Publishing Co., 1949–56; Charringtons, 1956–61; BMA Pubns, 1961–76; Chm., R. Hazell & Co., 1976–. Pres., ALPSP, 1978–99. Chm.,

Tower Hill Improvement Trust, 1987–. Chm., Anglo-US Cttee, RAF Upper Heyford, 1991–94. FRGS 1958 (Mem. Council, 1966–69); FRSA 1969. Liveryman, Co. of Stationers, 1964. JP: W Central Div., London, 1978–89; Oxford City, 1990–94; High Sheriff 1989–90, DL 1992, Oxon. KStJ 1996 (Chm., St John Council, Oxon, 1989–95; Chapter-Gen., 1994–99). *Address:* The White House, Nuffield, Oxon RG9 5SR. *T:* (01491) 641289; 19 Lennox Gardens, SW1X 0DB. *T:* (020) 7589 2645. *Clubs:* Beefsteak, Garrick, White's, Pilgrims.
Died 18 July 2004.

PARKER, Comdr (John) Michael (Avison), CVO 1957 (MVO 1953); AM 1995; RN (retired); *b* 23 June 1920; *s* of late Capt. C. A. Parker, CBE, RAN, Melbourne; *m* 1st, 1943, Eileen Margaret Anne Allan (marr. diss. 1958); one *s* one *d*; 2nd, 1962, Carol (marr. diss.; she *d* 1977); one *d* (one *s* decd); 3rd, 1976, Mrs Jean Lavinia Grice Ramsay. *Educ:* Xavier College, Melbourne, Australia. Royal Navy, 1938–47. Equerry-in-Waiting to Princess Elizabeth and the Duke of Edinburgh, 1947–52; Private Sec. to Duke of Edinburgh, 1947–57. Dir, Brain Behavioural Res. Cttee, La Trobe Univ., 1984–. Chm., Australian Dredging and Gen. Services Co., 1987–; Director: Spoerry, Australia, 1975– (Rep., Spoerry, port and town planners, France, 1980–); Spacelift Australia, 1999–. Member: Aust.-Britain Soc. (Vice-Pres.); Navy League; RSL; Australian Ballet Trust; Victorian Harbour Corp.; Chairman: Royal Navy Assoc.; Trustees, Melbourne Maritime Trust; Trustee: World Wildlife Australia; The World Ship Trust (UK). Chm., Plain English Foundn, Aust.; Dir, Day Cttee, Melbourne Foundn, 1996–. *Recreations:* painting, tennis, golf, sailing. *Address:* Santosa, 33 Albany Road, Toorak, Vic 3142, Australia. *Clubs:* Melbourne; Sandringham Yacht (Melbourne); Robe Golf (SA).
Died 29 Dec. 2001.

PARKER, Margaret Annette McCrie Johnston, (Margaret Johnston); actress; *b* 10 Aug. 1914; *d* of James and Emily Dalrymple Johnston; *m* 1946, Albert E. W. Parker (*d* 1974). *Educ:* North Sydney and Neutral Bay High School; Sydney University, Australia. Student, RADA; studied with Dr Stefan Hock; in repertory and acted as understudies. *Plays:* Murder without Crime, 1943; Fifth Column, 1944; Last of Summer, 1944; Time of Your Life, 1946; Shouting Dies, 1946; Barretts of Wimpole Street, 1947; Always Afternoon, 1949; Summer and Smoke, 1950; Second Threshold, 1951; The Dark is Light Enough, 1954; Sugar in the Morning, 1959; The Ring of Truth, 1959; Masterpiece, 1961. Stratford Memorial Theatre, 1956 season: Othello, The Merchant of Venice, Measure for Measure; Chichester Festival Theatre, 1966 Season: Lady Macbeth. *Films* include: Rake's Progress, 1945; Man About the House, 1946; Portrait of Clare, 1949; Magic Box, 1951; Knave of Hearts, 1953; Touch and Go, 1955; Night of the Eagle, 1962; Nose on her Face; Life at the Top, 1965; Psychopath, 1966; Sebastian, 1968. Television plays.
Died 29 June 2002.

PARKER, Comdr Michael; *see* Parker, Comdr J. M. A.

PARKER, His Honour Michael Clynes; QC 1973; a Circuit Judge, 1978–94; *b* 2 Nov. 1924; *s* of late Herbert Parker and Elsie Vera Parker (*née* Kirk) (sometime Pres., NUT); *m* 1950, Molly Leila Franklin; one *s* two *d*. *Educ:* City of London Sch.; Pembroke Coll., Cambridge (BA 1948, LLB 1949). Sec., Cambridge Union, 1943. Flt-Sgt/Air Gunner, RAF, 1943–47. Called to Bar, Gray's Inn, 1949; practised in London and SE Circuit; a Recorder of the Crown Court, 1972–78. Contested (Lab) S Kensington, 1951. *Recreations:* theatre, watching cricket. *Address:* 22 Priory Avenue, W4 1TY. *Clubs:* Oxford and Cambridge, MCC.
Died 27 April 2003.

PARKER, Sir Peter, KBE 1993; Kt 1978; LVO 1957; Chairman, Mitsubishi Electric Europe BV, since 1996; *b* 30 Aug. 1924; *s* of late Tom and Dorothy S. Parker; *m* 1951, Gillian Rowe-Dutton, *d* of late Sir Ernest Rowe-Dutton, KCMG, CB, and of Lady Rowe-Dutton; three *s*

one *d*. *Educ:* Bedford Sch.; London Univ.; Lincoln Coll., Oxford (Hon. Fellow, 1980). Major, Intelligence Corps, 1943–47. Commonwealth Fund Fellowship to Cornell and Harvard, 1950–51. Phillips Electrical, 1951–53; Head of Overseas Dept, Industrial Soc. 1953–54; Sec., Duke of Edinburgh's Study Conf. on Human Problems of Industry, 1954–56 (Vice-Chm., UK Trustees, Commonwealth Study Confs, 1986–); joined Booker McConnell Ltd, 1956; Dir, Booker Bros McConnell & Co. Ltd, 1960–70; Chairman: Bookers Engineering & Industrial Holdings Ltd, 1966–70; Associated British Maltsters Ltd, 1971–73; Curtis Brown Ltd, 1971–76; Victoria Deep Water Terminal Ltd, 1971–76; Dawnay Day Group, 1971–76; British Railways Bd, 1976–83; Mitsubishi Electric UK Ltd, 1984–96; Whitehead Mann Ap plc, 1984–2000; Horace, Holman Gp Ltd, 1988–93; Evered, subseq. Bardon Gp, 1989–94; Apricot Computers, 1990–99; Arcadian Internat., 1990–98; Accuread, 1996–; Vice-Chm., H. Clarkson & Co. (Hldgs), 1984–93 (Dir, 1976–93; Chm., 1975–76); Director: Rockware Gp, 1976–92 (Chm., 1971–76, and 1983–92); Group 4 Securitas (UK), 1984–2000. Chairman: Clothing EDC, 1971–78; DETR (formerly DoE) Adv. Cttee on Packaging, 1996–; Nat. Steering Gp, DTI Nat. Langs for Export Campaign, 1993–. Member: British Tourist Authy Bd, 1969–75; British Airways Bd, 1971–81; Royal Nat. Theatre Bd, 1986–91; Political and Econ. Planning Exec. (Vice-Chm., 1969–70); Hon. Treasurer, 1973–78); Council, BIM (Chm., 1984–86); Engineering Industries Council, 1975–76; NEDC, 1980–83. Dir, UK-Japan 21st Century Gp, 1986–; Chm., Japan Fest. 1991. Contested (Lab) Bedford, 1951. Founder Mem., Council of Foundn for Management Educn; Chairman: Westfield College, 1969–76 (Hon. Fellow, 1979); Ct of Governors, LSE, 1988–98; Dep. Chm., Ct of London Univ., 1970–. Mem. Council, Oxford Mus. of Modern Art, 1984–; Trustee, British Architecture Library Trust, 1984; Chm., Young Vic, 1993–96; Pres., Industry Council for Packaging and Envmt, 1990–99. Dimbleby Lecture, BBC TV, 1984. Hon. Patron, Langs NTO. Hon. Fellow: SIAD; SOAS, 1991; London Business Sch., 1991; LSE,1999. Hon. LLD: London, 1981; Manchester Polytechnic, 1981; Bath, 1983; Birmingham, 1991; Hull, 1996; Westminster, 1996; Hon. DBA Robert Gordon, 1997. Communicator of the Year Award, British Assoc. of Indust. Editors, 1981; Bicentenary Medal, RSA, 1990. CStJ 1983. Grand Cordon of Order of Sacred Treasure (Japan), 1991. *Publication:* For Starters (autobiog.), 1989. *Recreations:* Rugby (played for Bedford and E Mids); swimming, browsing. *Address:* 20–23 Lincoln's Inn Fields, WC2A 3ED. *T:* (020) 7936 8233.
Died 28 April 2002.

PARKER, Vice-Adm. Sir (Wilfred) John, KBE 1969 (OBE 1953); CB 1965; DSC 1943; *b* 12 Oct. 1915; *s* of Henry Edmond Parker and Ida Mary (*née* Cole); *m* 1943, Marjorie Stuart Jones (*d* 1999), Halifax, NS, Canada; one *d* (one *d* decd). *Educ:* RN College, Dartmouth. Joined Royal Navy, 1929; War Service in N Atlantic, N Russia, Mediterranean, Pacific, Korea (OBE); sunk in HMS Edinburgh and HMS Trinidad; mined in HMS Sheffield; torpedoed in HMS Newfoundland; DSC (Capture of Sicily); twice mentioned in despatches (HMS Edinburgh on N Russian convoys, and destruction of an Italian convoy, HMS Aurora 1942); Imperial Defence College, 1957; Commodore West Indies, 1958–60; Captain RNC Dartmouth, 1961–63; an Asst Chief of Defence Staff, Min. of Defence, 1963–66; Flag Officer, Medway, and Adm. Supt HM Dockyard, Chatham, 1966–69, retd 1969. Pres., RN Communication Chief Petty Officers Assoc., 1969–94. *Recreation:* 7 grandchildren (3 Mayo, 3 Panton, 1 Polak).
Died 10 May 2005.

PARKES, Terence, (Larry); freelance cartoonist, since 1957; *b* 19 Nov. 1927; *s* of Walter Thomas Parkes and Alice Parkes (*née* Hirons); *m* 1952, Jean Pauline Woodward; one *s* one *d*. *Educ:* Handsworth Grammar Sch., Birmingham; Birmingham Coll. of Art (Art Teacher's Dip.). Regular contributor to Punch, 1954–92;

contrib. Private Eye, 1962–94; illustrations in Observer and Daily and Sunday Telegraph; worked for Joan Littlewood's Theatre Workshop, 1973–74; contrib. HMSO and FO pubns. Fellow, Univ. of W Midlands (formerly Birmingham Poly.), 1991. *Publications:* Man in Apron, 1959; Man in Office, 1961; Man at Work, 1962; Man at Large, 1964; Man and Dog, 1965 (US); Man in Garden, 1966; Man and Wife, 1966 (US); Large Economy Man, 1967 (US); Private Eye Cartoon Library, 1974; Art Collection, 1982; Best of Larry, 1985; Larry on Art, 1986; Larry's Great Western, 1987; Garden Lot, 1988; DIY Man, 1989; Larry on Larry (autobiog.), 1994. *Recreations:* ceramic sculpture, black Labrador dog walking. *Address:* 20 West Street, Stratford-upon-Avon, Warwickshire CV37 6DW. *T:* (01789) 293547; Flat 4, 4 Payton Street, Stratford-upon-Avon, Warwickshire CV37 6VA. *T:* (01789) 292900. *Died 25 June 2003.*

PARKINSON, Sir Nicholas (Fancourt), Kt 1980; consultant; *b* 5 Dec. 1925; *s* of late Rev. C. T. Parkinson, MA Oxon, and Dorothy Fancourt (*née* Mitchell); *m* 1952, Roslyn Sheena Campbell; two *d. Educ:* King's Sch., Parramatta, NSW; Univ. of Sydney (BA). Entered Aust. Foreign Service, 1951; Third Sec., Cairo, 1953–56; First Sec., Hong Kong, 1958–61; Counsellor, Moscow, Wellington, Kuala Lumpur, 1963–67; Chm. Jt Intell. Cttee, Dept of Defence, Canberra, 1967–70; High Comr, Singapore, 1970–74; Dep. Sec., Dept of For. Affairs, Canberra, 1974–76; Ambassador to the US, 1976–77 and 1979–82; Sec., Dept of For. Affairs, Canberra, 1977–79. Dir, Sears World Trade (Australia), 1983–86. Mem., ABC Adv. Council, 1991–93. *Recreation:* bridge. *Address:* 62 Collings Street, Pearce, ACT 2607, Australia. *T:* (2) 62861004. *Club:* Commonwealth (Canberra). *Died 12 Sept. 2001.*

PARRINDER, Prof. (Edward) Geoffrey (Simons); Professor of Comparative Study of Religions, University of London, at King's College, 1970–77, Professor Emeritus, 1977; *b* 30 April 1910; *s* of William Patrick and Florence Mary Parrinder; *m* 1936, Esther Mary Burt; two *s* one *d. Educ:* private sch.; Richmond Coll., London Univ.; Faculté libre de théologie protestante, Montpellier. MA, PhD, DD London. Minister of Methodist Church, Dahomey and Ivory Coast, 1933; ordained 1936; Principal, Séminaire Protestant, Dahomey, 1936–40, 1945–46; Methodist Church: Redruth, 1940; Dahomey, 1943; Guernsey, 1946; Lectr in Religious Studies, 1949, Sen. Lectr, 1950–58, UC Ibadan; Reader in Comparative Study of Religions, Univ. of London, 1958–70; Dean, Faculty of Theology, KCL, 1972–74. Hon. Sec., Internat. Assoc. for History of Religions, British Br., 1960–72, Pres., 1972–77; President: London Soc. for Study of Religion, 1980–82; London Soc. of Jews and Christians, 1981–90 (Hon. Life Pres., 1990). Lectures: Charles Strong (Australian Church), 1964; Wilde, in Natural and Comparative Religion, Oxford Univ., 1966–69; Teape, Delhi, Madras, 1973. Vis. Prof., Internat. Christian Univ., Tokyo, 1977–78; Vis. Lectr, Surrey Univ., 1978–83. FKC 1972; Hon. DLitt Lancaster, 1975. *Publications:* West African Religion, 1949; Bible and Polygamy, 1950; West African Psychology, 1951; Religion in an African City, 1953; African Traditional Religion, 1954; Story of Ketu, 1956; Introduction to Asian Religions, 1957; Witchcraft, 1958; (ed) African Ideas of God, 1961; Worship in the World's Religions, 1961; Comparative Religion, 1962; Upanishads, Gītā and Bible, 1962; What World Religions Teach, 1963; The Christian Debate, 1964; The World's Living Religions, 1965; A Book of World Religions, 1965; Jesus in the Qur'ān, 1965; African Mythology, 1967; Religion in Africa, 1969, repr. as Africa's Three Religions, 1976; Avatar and Incarnation, 1970; Dictionary of Non-Christian Religions, 1971; (ed) Man and his Gods, 1971, repr. as Illustrated History of the World's Religions, 1983; The Indestructible Soul, 1973; Themes for Living, 1973; The Bhagavad Gita, a Verse Translation, 1974; Something after Death?, 1974; The Wisdom of the Forest, 1975; Mysticism in the World's Religions, 1976; The Wisdom

of the Early Buddhists, 1977; Sex in the World's Religions, 1980; Storia Universale delle Religioni, 1984; Encountering World Religions, 1987; A Dictionary of Religious and Spiritual Quotations, 1989; The Sayings of the Buddha, 1991; Son of Joseph, 1992; A Concise Encyclopedia of Christianity, 1998; The Wisdom of Jesus, 2000; In the Belly of the Snake, 2000; articles and reviews in jls of theology, African and Asian religions and Annual Register, 1958–. *Recreations:* travel, gardening, literature. *Address:* 31 Charterhouse Road, Orpington, Kent BR6 9EJ. *T:* (01689) 823887. *Died 16 June 2005.*

PARRY, Baron *cr* 1975 (Life Peer), of Neyland, Dyfed; **Gordon Samuel David Parry;** DL; President, Milford Docks Company, since 1991 (Chairman, 1984–91); *b* 30 Nov. 1925; *s* of Thomas Lewis Parry and Anne Parry (*née* Evans); *m* 1948, Glenys Parry (*née* Incledon); one *d. Educ:* Neyland Board Sch.; Pembroke County Intermediate Sch.; Trinity Coll., Carmarthen; Univ. of Liverpool (Dipl. Advanced Educn). Teacher: Coronation Sch., Pembroke Dock, 1945–46; Llanstadwell Voluntary Primary Sch., Neyland, 1946–47; Barn St Voluntary Sch., Haverfordwest, 1947; County Primary Sch., Neyland, 1947–52; Librarian, Housemaster, County Sec. Sch., Haverfordwest, 1952–62 and 1963–68; Inst. of Educn, Univ. of Liverpool, 1962–63; Warden, Pembs Teachers' Centre, 1969–78. Former member: Welsh Develt Agency; Gen. Adv. Council, IBA; Welsh Arts Council; Schs Council Cttee for Wales; Member: Fac. of Educn, Univ. Coll. of Wales Aberystwyth; Council, Open Univ. (Chm., Adv. Cttee on Studies in Educn, 1978–83); British Tourist Authority, 1978–84; President: Pembs Br., Multiple Sclerosis Soc.; Pembs Spastics Soc.; Spastics Soc., Wales; Commonwealth Games Appeal Cttee for Wales, 1979; Keep Wales Tidy Cttee, 1979– (Chm., 1979–86); BICSc, 1981–91; Tidy Britain (formerly Keep Britain Tidy) Gp, 1991–96 (Chm., 1986–91); Chairman: Wales Tourist Bd, 1978–84; British Cleaning Council, 1983–87; Keep Britain Beautiful Campaign, 1986–96; Clean World Internat., 1991–96; British Travel Educn Trust; Vice President: Nat. Chamber of Trade, 1980; Internat. Year of Disabled People in Wales, 1979; Nat. Soc. for Mentally Handicapped Children, S Wales Region; Soc. of Handicapped Drivers in Wales; Welsh Nat. Council of YMCAs. Chairman: Taylorplan Services, 1987–96; Pembs Radio Co., 1987; non-exec. Bd Mem., Marriott Services UK Ltd, 1996–. Contested (Lab) Monmouth 1959, Pembroke 1970, and Feb. and Oct. 1974. Writer, broadcaster, and TV panel Chm. President: Neyland Ladies' Choir, 1991–; Côr Meibion De Cymru (S Wales Male Voice Choir), 1998–; Vice Pres., London Welsh Choir, 1987. Burgess, Guild of Freemen of Haverfordwest. FRSA; Fellow: Tourism Soc., 1979; HCIMA, 1980; BICSc, 1981; James Cook Univ., N Qld, Aust, 1989. DL Dyfed, 1993. Hon. Fellow: Trinity Coll., Carmarthen, 1990; Polytechnic of Wales, 1991; Pembrokeshire Coll., 1998. Hon. Fellow, Inst. of Wastes Management. Hon. DEd Wales, 1992. *Publication:* Trinity '43–'45: a legacy for life (autobiog.), 1996. *Recreations:* travel; watching Welsh Rugby XV win the Grand Slam; reading. *Address:* Willowmead, 52 Port Lion, Llangwm, Haverfordwest, Pembrokeshire, Dyfed SA62 4JT. *T:* (01646) 600667. *Died 1 Sept. 2004.*

PARRY, John Alderson, CBE 1985; BBC National Governor for Wales, 1986–91; *b* 3 Jan. 1934; *s* of Albert Parry and Mary Parry (*née* Alderson); *m* 1st, 1959, Joan Rathbone (marr. diss. 1992); one *s* one *d*; 2nd, 1998, Ruth Tomkins-Russell (*d* 2001). *Educ:* Leighton Park, Reading; Christ's College, Cambridge (MA, Vet MB). MRCVS; FRAgS 1986. Veterinary practice, Brecon, 1958–96. Mem., Agricl Adv. Council, 1969–73; Chairman: Hill Farming Res. Orgn, 1981–87 (Mem., 1971–85); Welsh Agricl Adv. Cttee, BBC, 1978–85; Welsh Office Hydatid Control Steering Cttee, 1981–96; Member: Sec. of State for Wales' Agricl Adv. Cttee, 1978–94; AFRC, 1982–92 (Chm., Animals Res. Cttee, 1983–87); Develt Bd for Rural Wales, 1985–88; Council, Royal Welsh Agricl Soc.,

1986–; Dir, Animal Disease Res. Assoc., 1987–92. President: BVA, 1976–77; RCVS, 1986–87. Chm., Governing Body, Inst. of Grassland and Animal Prodn, AFRC, 1987–94; Gov., McCauley Land Use Res. Inst., 1987–94. Freeman, City of London, 1978; Liveryman, Co. of Farriers, 1978–. *Recreations:* field sports. *Address:* Trefin, Cradoc Road, Brecon, Powys LD3 9PF. *T:* (01874) 622649. *Clubs:* Oxford and Cambridge, Farmers'; Hawks (Cambridge); Cardiff & County (Cardiff).

Died 21 Sept. 2004.

PARSONS, Air Comdt Dame Pauline, (formerly **Air Comdt Dame Pauline Giles**), DBE 1967; RRC; Matron-in-Chief, Princess Mary's Royal Air Force Nursing Service, 1966–70, retired; *b* 17 Sept. 1912; *m* 1987, Daniel G. Parsons, OBE. *Educ:* Sheffield. Joined PMRAFNS, Nov. 1937; later appointments included Principal Matron for Royal Air Force Command in Britain and Western Europe; became Matron-in-Chief, PMRAFNS, Sept. 1966. *Address:* 3 School View, Wraxall, N Somerset BS48 1HG. *Died 2 Oct. 2005.*

PARTRIDGE, Frances Catherine, CBE 2000; FRSL; writer and literary journalist; *b* 15 March 1900; *d* of William Cecil Marshall, architect, and Margaret Anna Marshall (*née* Lloyd); *m* 1933, Major Reginald Sherring Partridge, (Ralph Partridge), MC and Bar, Croix de Guerre (*d* 1960); one *s* (Lytton Burgo Partridge, *d* 1963). *Educ:* Bedales Sch.; Newnham Coll., Cambridge (BA). Antiquarian bookseller, 1922–28; translator of numerous books from French and Spanish, to 1965. Hon. DLit London, 2000. *Publications:* (ed with husband) The Greville Memoirs (diaries), 8 vols, 1938; A Pacifist's War: diaries 1939–45, 1978; Memories (memoir), 1981; Julia, 1983; Everything to Lose: diaries 1945–60, 1986; Friends in Focus (photographs), 1987; Hanging On: diaries 1960–63, 1990; The Pasque Flower, 1990; Other People: diaries 1963–66, 1993; Good Company: diaries 1967–70, 1994; Life Regained: diaries 1970–72, 1998; Ups and Downs: diaries 1972–75, 2001. *Recreations:* music, reading, botany. *Address:* c/o Rogers, Coleridge & White, 20 Powis Mews, W11 1JN. *T:* (020) 7221 3717; 15 West Halkin Street, SW1X 8JL. *Club:* International PEN.

Died 5 Feb. 2004.

PASLEY, Sir (John) Malcolm (Sabine), 5th Bt *cr* 1794; FBA 1991; Emeritus Fellow, Magdalen College, Oxford; *b* 5 April 1926; *s* of Sir Rodney Marshall Sabine Pasley, 4th Bt, and Aldyth Werge Hamber (*d* 1983); *S* father, 1982; *m* 1965, Virginia Killigrew Wait; two *s*. *Educ:* Sherborne Sch.; Trinity Coll., Oxford (MA). War service, Royal Navy, 1944–46. Laming Travelling Fellow, Queen's Coll., Oxford, 1949–50; Lectr in German, Brasenose and Magdalen Colls, 1950–58; Fellow and Tutor, 1958–86, Vice-Pres., 1979–80, Magdalen Coll. Mem., Deutsche Akademie für Sprache und Dichtung, 1983–. Hon. DPhil Giessen, 1986. Austrian Ehrenkreuz für Wissenschaft und Kunst, 1st cl., 1987. *Publications:* (co-author) Kafka-Symposion, 1965; (ed) Germany: A Companion to German Studies, 1972, 2nd edn 1982; (trans.) Kafka Shorter Works, vol. 1, 1973; (ed) Nietzsche: Imagery and Thought, 1978; (ed) Franz Kafka, Das Schloss, 1982; (ed) Max Brod, Franz Kafka, Reiseaufzeichnungen, 1987; Briefwechsel, 1989; (ed) Franz Kafka, Der Process, 1990; (trans.) Franz Kafka, The Transformation and other stories, 1992; (ed) Franz Kafka, Nachgelassene Schriften und Fragmente I, 1993; Die Schrift ist unveränderlich: Essays zu Kafka, 1995. *Heir: s* Robert Killigrew Sabine Pasley, *b* 23 Oct. 1965. *Address:* 25 Lathbury Road, Oxford OX2 7AT. *Died 4 March 2004.*

PASTERFIELD, Rt Rev. Philip John; an Assistant Bishop, Diocese of Exeter, 1984–90; *b* Canada, 14 Jan. 1920; *s* of Bertie James Pasterfield and Lilian Bishop Pasterfield (*née* Flinn); *m* 1948, Eleanor Maureen (*d* 1999), *d* of William John Symons; three *s* one *d*. *Educ:* Denstone Coll., Staffs; Trinity Hall, Cambridge (MA); Cuddesdon Coll., Oxford. Army Service, 1940–46; commnd in Somerset Light Infantry. Deacon 1951, priest 1952. Curate

of Streatham, 1951–54; Vicar of West Lavington, Sussex, and Chaplain, King Edward VII Hosp., Midhurst, 1954–60; Rector of Woolbeding, 1955–60; Vicar of Oxton, Birkenhead, 1960–68; Rural Dean of Birkenhead, 1966–68; Canon Residentiary and Sub Dean of St Albans, 1968–74; Rural Dean of St Albans, 1972–74; Bishop Suffragan of Crediton, 1974–84. *Recreations:* ornithology, music, hymn writing, poetry. *Died 29 Jan. 2001.*

PATEL, Indraprasad Gordhanbhai, Hon. KBE 1990; PhD; Director, London School of Economics and Political Science, 1984–90 (Hon. Fellow, 1990); *b* 11 Nov. 1924; *s* of F. Patel Gordhanbhai Tulsibhai and M. Patel Kashiben Jivabhai; *m* 1958, Alaknanda Dasgupta; one *d*. *Educ:* Bombay Univ. (BA Hons); King's Coll., Cambridge (BA, PhD; Hon. Fellow, 1986). Prof. of Economics and Principal, Baroda Coll., Maharaja Sayajirao Univ. of Baroda, 1949; Economist, later Asst Chief, IMF, 1950–54; Dep. Economic Adviser, Min. of Finance, India, 1954–58; Alternate Exec. Dir for India, IMF, 1958–61; Chief Economic Adviser, Min. of Finance and Planning Commn, 1962–64, 1965–67; Special Sec. and Sec., Dept of Economic Affairs, 1967–72; Dep. Administrator, UN Develt Programme, 1972–77; Governor, Reserve Bank of India, 1977–82; Dir, Indian Inst. of Management, Ahmedabad, 1982–84. Chm., Bd of Dirs, Hindustan Oil Exploration Co. Ltd, 1999–; Member: Bd of Dirs, State Bank of India, 1995–; Prime Minister's Econ. Adv. Council, 1998–. Vis. Prof., Delhi Univ., 1964. Hon. Prof., Jawaharlal Nehru Univ., New Delhi, 2000–. Chm., Indian Council for Res. in Internat. Economic Relations, 1997–. Hon. DLitt: Sardar Patel Univ.; Maharaja Sayajirao Univ. of Baroda, 1993; Hon. DCL Univ. of Mauritius, 1990; Hon. DPhil Roorkee, 1997; Hon. Dr Banaras Hindu Univ., 2004. Padma Vibhushan, 1991. *Publications:* Essays in Economic Policy and Economic Growth, 1986; Economic Reform and Global Change, 1998; Glimpses of Indian Economic Policy, 2002; An Encounter with Higher Education: my years at LSE, 2003; articles in IMF staff papers etc. on inflation, monetary policy, internat. trade. *Recreations:* music, reading, watching cricket. *Address:* 12 Amee Co-operative Housing Society, Diwali Pura, Old Padra Road, Vadodara 390013, India.

Died 17 July 2005.

PATEMAN, Jack Edward, CBE 1970; FREng; Chairman, Kent County Engineering Society, 1989–96; *b* 29 Nov. 1921; *s* of William Edward Pateman and Lucy Varley (*née* Jetten); *m* 1949, Cicely Hope Turner; one *s* one *d*. *Educ:* Gt Yarmouth Grammar Sch. Served War of 1939–45, RAF, 1940–46. Research Engineer: Belling & Lee, 1946–48; Elliott Bros (London) Ltd, 1948–51; formed Aviation Div. of EBL at Borehamwood, 1951–62; Dep. Chm. and Jt Man. Dir, Elliott Flight Automation Ltd, 1962–71; Man. Dir, 1971–86, Dep. Chm., 1986–87, GEC Avionics; Director: Canadian Marconi Co., 1971–87; GEC Computers Ltd, 1971–89 (Chm., 1978–82); Elliott Brothers (London) Ltd, 1979–89; Marconi Electronic Devices, 1980–87; GEC Avionics Projects Ltd, 1980–89; GEC Information Systems, 1982–86; GEC Avionics Projects (UK) Ltd, 1984–89; General Electric Co. Plc, 1986–88. GEC-Marconi Ltd, 1987–89. FREng (FEng 1981). British Gold Medal, RAeS, 1981. *Recreation:* sailing. *Address:* Spindles, Ivy Hatch, Sevenoaks, Kent TN15 0PG. *T:* (01732) 810364.

Died 28 Aug. 2004.

PATERSON, Dame Betty (Fraser Ross), DBE 1981 (CBE 1973); DL; Chairman: NW Thames Regional Health Authority, 1973–84; National Staff Advisory Committee for England and Wales (Nurses and Midwives), 1975–84; *b* 14 March 1916; *d* of Robert Ross Russell and Elsie Marian Russell (*née* Fraser); *m* 1940, Ian Douglas Paterson; one *s* one *d*. *Educ:* Harrogate Coll.; Western Infirmary, Glasgow. Mem. Chartered Soc. of Physiotherapy (MCSP). County Comr, Herts Girl Guides, 1950–57. Member: Herts CC, 1952–74 (Alderman 1959–74; Chm., 1969–73); NE Metropolitan Regional

Hosp. Bd, 1960–74; Governing Body, Royal Hosp. of St Bartholomew, 1960–74; Commn for the New Towns, England and Wales, 1961–75 (Dep. Chm., 1971–75); Governing Body, Bishop's Stortford Coll., 1967–81; Central Health Services Council, 1969–74; Gen. Council, King Edward's Hosp. Fund for London, 1975–84 (Management Cttee, 1975–80); Chm. Trustees, NHS Pensioners' Trust, 1991–96; Pres., Herts Assoc. of Local Councils, 1980–90; Vice-Pres., Herts Magistrates' Assoc., 1987–. JP Herts, 1950–86 (Chm. Bishop's Stortford Bench, 1978–86); DL Herts, 1980. *Recreations:* family, current affairs, music, talking books. *Address:* Sunrise, Chestnut House, Frognal Avenue, Sidcup, Kent DA14 6LF. *T:* (020) 8302 6200.   *Died 15 March 2005.*

PATERSON, Very Rev. John Thomas Farquhar; Dean of Christ Church, Dublin, 1989–2004; *b* Portadown, Co. Armagh, 21 Dec. 1938; *s* of Henry Paterson and Margreta Elizabeth Paterson (*née* Bell); *m* 2001, Patricia Bray (*née* Daniel); two step *s*. *Educ:* Portadown College; Trinity College, Dublin (BA, MA, BD). Curate-Assistant: Drumglass (Dungannon), 1963; St Bartholomew, Dublin, 1966; Priest-in-charge, St Mark, Dublin and Asst Chaplain, TCD, 1968; Vicar, St Bartholomew with Christ Church, Leeson Park, Dublin, 1972; Dean and Rector of Kildare, 1978. Lectr in Pastoral Liturgy, Church of Ireland Theol Coll., 1984–91. Hon. Sec., Gen. Synod, Church of Ireland, 1985–91. *Publications:* jointly: A Parish Education Handbook, 1987; Mary in the Church, 1990; All Sorts and Conditions: a history of the laity in the Church of Ireland, 2002; articles in Irish theological jls (Search, The Furrow, Doctrine and Life). *Recreations:* travel, reading, music. *Address:* 22 Corr Castle, Howth, Dublin 13, Ireland. *T:* and *Fax:* (1) 8395773; *e-mail:* paterson@iol.ie. *Club:* Kildare Street and University (Dublin).
                    Died 9 Sept. 2005.

PATEY, Very Rev. Edward Henry; Dean of Liverpool, 1964–82, then Dean Emeritus; *b* 12 Aug. 1915; *s* of Walter Patey, MD, and Dorothy Patey; *m* 1942, Margaret Ruth Olivia Abbott, OBE; one *s* three *d*. *Educ:* Marlborough College; Hertford College, Oxford (MA 1941); Westcott House, Cambridge. Ordained deacon, 1939, priest, 1940; Assistant Curate: St Mary-at-the-Walls, Colchester, 1939–42; Bishopwearmouth Parish Church, Sunderland, 1942–50; Youth Chaplain to the Bishop of Durham, 1946–50; Vicar of Oldland, with Longwell Green, Bristol, 1950–52; Secretary, Youth Dept, 1952–55, Asst Gen. Secretary, 1955–58, British Council of Churches; Canon Residentiary, Coventry Cathedral, 1958–64. Hon. LLD Liverpool, 1980. *Publications:* Religion in the Club, 1956; Boys and Girls Growing Up, 1957; Worship in the Club, 1961; A Doctor's Life of Jesus, 1962; Young People Now, 1964; Enquire Within, 1966; Look out for the Church, 1969; Burning Questions, 1971; Don't Just Sit There, 1974; Christian Lifestyle, 1975; All in Good Faith, 1978; Open the Doors, 1978; Open the Book, 1981; I Give You This Ring, 1982; My Liverpool Life, 1983; Becoming An Anglican, 1985; Preaching on Special Occasions, 1985; Questions For Today, 1986; For the Common Good, 1989; Faith in a Risk-Taking God, 1991. *Recreations:* reading, listening to music, walking.
                    Died 5 Sept. 2005.

PATRICK, Margaret Kathleen, OBE 1976; District/ Superintendent Physiotherapist, Central Birmingham Health Authority (Teaching) (formerly United Birmingham Hospitals Hospital Management Committee), 1951–88, retired; *b* 5 June 1923; *d* of late Roy and Rose Patrick. *Educ:* Godolphin and Latymer Sch., London; Guy's Hosp. Sch. of Physiotherapy. BA, Open Univ., 1980. MCSP (Hon. FCSP). Chm. Physio. Adv. Cttee, and Mem. Health Care Planning for Elderly, Birmingham AHA (T). Member: Exec., Whitley Council PTA, 1960–75 (Chm., PTA Cttee C, 1960–75); Tunbridge Cttee on Rehab. Services, 1971–72; Hosp. Adv. Service on Geriatrics, 1972; DHSS Working Party on Stat. Data in Physio., 1969–76; Council, Chartered Soc. of Physio., 1953–75 (Exec. Mem., 1960–75; Vice Chm., 1971–75); Birmingham AHA (Teaching), 1979–82; Vice-Chm., Bromsgrove and Redditch HA, 1982–90. Chm., 1964–75, Pres., 1971–72, Assoc. of Supt Chartered Physiotherapists. *Publications:* Ultrasound Therapy: a textbook for physiotherapists, 1965; (contrib.) Physiotherapy in some Surgical Conditions, ed Joan Cash, 1977, 2nd edn 1979; contrib. Physiotherapy, and articles on ultrasound therapy, geriatric care, and paediatrics. *Recreation:* gardening.   *Died 10 April 2003.*

PATTERSON, John Allan, CB 1989; Panel Chairman, Recruitment and Assessment Services, since 1992; *b* 10 Oct. 1931; *s* of William Gilchrist Patterson and May (*née* Eggie); *m* 1956, Anne Marie Lasson; one *s* one *d* (and one *d* decd). *Educ:* Epsom Coll.; Clare Coll., Cambridge (Major Scholar in Classics, Stewart of Rannoch Scholar; BA 1954); Open Univ. (Dip. German, 2000). HM Diplomatic Service, 1954–65: served in Bangkok, 1957–61 and in Rome, 1961–64 (Private Sec. to the Ambassador); HM Treasury, 1965–81 (on loan to Cabinet Office, 1974–78); Dep. Dir of Savings, 1981–86, Dir of Savings and Head, 1986–91, Dept for Nat. Savings. Chm., Money Management Council, 1991–94; Mem., SW Surrey CHC, 1997–2000. Lay Mem., Guildford Primary Care Gp, 1999–2000. FRSA 1989. *Recreations:* gardening, walking, languages, church. *Address:* 5 Nelson Gardens, Guildford GU1 2NZ. *T:* (01483) 564369.
                    Died 14 April 2002.

PATTERSON, Rev. Canon William James, CBE 1991; Dean of Ely, 1984–90; Vicar of Abbotsley, Everton and Waresley, 1990–93; *b* 25 Sept. 1930; *s* of William Moscrop and Alice Patterson; *m* 1955, Elisabeth Roederer; one *s* two *d*. *Educ:* Haileybury; Balliol College, Oxford (MA). Asst Curate of St John Baptist, Newcastle upon Tyne, 1955–58; Priest-in-Charge, Rio Claro with Mayaro, Dio. Trinidad, 1958–65; Rector of Esher, 1965–72; RD of Emly, 1968–72; Rector of Little Downham, 1972–80; Priest-in-Charge of Coveney, 1978–80; Archdeacon of Wisbech, 1979–84; Vicar of Wisbech St Mary, 1980–84. Hon. Canon, Ely Cathedral, 1990–. *Recreation:* cycling. *Address:* 1 Watledge Close, Tewkesbury, Glos GL20 5RJ.
                    Died 6 April 2002.

PAUL, Air Cdre Gerard John Christopher, CB 1956; DFC 1944; *b* 31 Oct. 1907; *s* of E. W. Paul, FRCS; *m* 1st, 1937, Rosemary (*d* 1975), *d* of Rear-Adm. H. G. E. Lane, CB; two *s* one *d*; 2nd, 1987, Mollie Denise Samuels, *d* of Joseph Samuels, MM. *Educ:* Cheltenham Coll.; St John's Coll., Cambridge (BA 1929, MA 1966). Entered RAF, 1929; Fleet Air Arm, 1931–36; served War of 1939–45 in England and NW Europe; Commandant, Central Flying School, 1954–56; retired, 1958. Sec.-Gen., Air League, 1958–71. Life Vice-Pres., RAF Gliding and Soaring Assoc.; Pres., Popular Flying Assoc., 1969–78. Croix de Guerre avec Palme (Belgium), 1944; Military Cross (Czechoslovakia), 1945. *Recreations:* dogs, garden. *Address:* Wearne House, Old Alresford, Hants SO24 9DH. *Club:* Royal Air Force.   *Died 11 Jan. 2003.*

PAUL, Dame Janet (Elaine), DNZM 1997; painter and writer; *b* 9 Nov. 1919; *d* of Alfred Harry Wilkinson and Eleanor Sinton; *m* 1945, David Blackwood Paul (*d* 1965); four *d* (one *s* decd). *Educ:* Wanganui Girls' Coll.; Victoria Univ. of Wellington (BA Hons 1943). Teacher, 1937–40; Locomotive plan tracer, Railways Dept, Wellington, 1941; Researcher, Historical Br., Dept of Internal Affairs, 1942–45; publishing under imprints: Paul's Book Arcade, Blackwood and Janet Paul, 1945–68; Square and Circle, 1970–73; Art Librarian, Alexander Turnbull Liby, Wellington, 1971–80; occasional lectures in art history, Victoria Univ. of Wellington, and painting, Maroota, NSW, 1985–91. Hon. DLitt Victoria Univ. of Wellington, 1992. *Exhibitions* include: Auckland City Art Gall., 1957, 1958–59, 1962, 1963; Qantas Gall., London, 1964; Victoria Univ. of Wellington Liby, 1971; Arteder '82, Bilbao, Spain, 1982; Wellington City Art Gall., 1983; Loft Gall., Wellington, 1992; Akaroa Art Gall., 1993;

Landmarks in NZ Publishing, Nat. Liby Gall., Wellington, 1995; *solo exhibitions:* Galerie Legard, Wellington, 1981, 1983, 1985; Brooker Gall., Wellington, 1987, 1988, 1990; *work represented in collections:* Auckland City Art Gall.; Waikato Art Mus.; Nat. Art Gall., Wellington; Alexander Turnbull Liby; Victoria Univ. of Wellington; Foreign Affairs Dept; Hocken Liby, Univ. of Otago. *Publications:* (contrib.) Women in New Zealand Society, 1981; (ed jtly) A Musician's Journal, 1986; (contrib.) Beyond Expectations, 1986; Mrs Hobson's Album 1840–1845, 1989; biographies in exhibn catalogues; contribs to Landfall, Turnbull Liby Record, Art NZ, NZ Nature Heritage, Bulletin of NZ Art History. *Recreations:* gardening, drawing, grandchildren. *Address:* 24 Ascot Street, Wellington, New Zealand. *T:* (4) 4722928.
Died 28 July 2004.

PAUL, Sir John (Warburton), GCMG 1965 (KCMG 1962); OBE 1959; MC 1940; Lieutenant Governor, Isle of Man, 1974–80; *b* 29 March 1916; 2nd *s* of Walter George Paul and Phoebe (*née* Bull), Weymouth; *m* 1946, Kathleen Audrey, CStJ 1962, *d* of Dr A. D. Weeden, Weymouth; three *d. Educ:* Weymouth Coll., Dorset; Selwyn Coll., Cambridge (MA; Hon. Fellow, 1982). Secretary, Maddermarket Theatre, Norwich, 1936. Commissioned Royal Tank Regt (Suppl. Res.), 1937; regular commission, RTR, 1938; BEF 1940 (despatches, prisoner-of-war); ADC and Private Secretary to Governor of Sierra Leone, 1945 (seconded). Called to the Bar, Inner Temple, 1947. Colonial Administrative Service, Sierra Leone, 1947; District Commissioner, 1952; Permanent Secretary, 1956; Provincial Commissioner, 1959; Secretary to the Cabinet, 1960; Governor and C-in-C, The Gambia, 1962–65; Governor-General of The Gambia, 1965–66; Governor and C-in-C: British Honduras, 1966–72; The Bahamas, 1972–73; Governor-General, The Bahamas, July-Oct. 1973. Dir, Overseas Relns, St John Ambulance, 1981–89. Member Board, West African Airways Corporation, 1954–56. Chm., St Christopher Motorists' Security Assoc., and associated cos, 1980–93. A Patron, Pain Relief Foundn, 1980–97. Mem., Bd of Governors, Pangbourne Coll., 1981–86. KStJ 1962 (Member: Chapter-Gen., 1981–91; St John Council, Hants, 1990–96). *Recreation:* painting. *Address:* Newlands House, Newlands Road, Corsham, Wilts SN13 0BS. *Clubs:* MCC; Hawks (Cambridge).
Died 31 March 2004.

PAUL, Noël Strange, CBE 1978; Director, Press Council, 1976–79 (Assistant Secretary, 1964, Secretary, 1968–76), retired; *b* 1914; *y s* of late S. Evan Paul, SSC, and Susan, *d* of Dr Henry Habgood; *m* 1950, Mary (*d* 1998), *yr d* of Philip J. Bone, FRSA, MRST, Luton. *Educ:* Kingston Grammar School. Journalist, Press Assoc., 1932; served War of 1939–45, Iran and Italy, Major seconded RAF (despatches). Home Counties Newspapers, 1949; Liverpool Daily Post, 1958. Mem., Steering Cttee on the Mass Media, Council of Europe, 1976–82; Governor, English-Speaking Union, 1980–82. *Publications:* Self-regulation of the Press, 1982; Principles for the Press, 1985. *Recreations:* sailing, photography. *Address:* The Lodge, St Catherine's, Strachur, Argyllshire PA25 8AZ.
Died 5 Dec. 2002.

PAXTON, Peter James, FCIS; FCCA; FCIB; Chief Executive Officer, Cambridge and District Co-operative Society Ltd, 1972–86; *b* 27 April 1923; *m* 1st, 1947, Betty Jane Madden (marr. diss. 1980); one *s* one *d*; 2nd, 1985, Sylvia June Stock. *Educ:* Lawrence Sherriff Sch., Rugby. Served RAF, 1941–46. Accountant, Rugby Co-operative Society Ltd, 1949–55; Chief Accountant, Cambridge and District Co-operative Society Ltd, 1955; Chairman: CWS, 1980–86; Co-operative Bank, 1980–86; First Co-op. Finance, 1980–86; Co-op. City Investments, 1983–86; Dep. Chm., Co-op. Insce Soc., 1983–86. *Address:* Westwood House, Westwood, Broadclyst, Exeter, Devon EX5 3DH. *T:* (01404) 822821. *Died 6 Nov. 2001.*

PAYNE, Arthur Stanley, OBE 1977; HM Diplomatic Service, retired; Director, then Chief Executive, Southern Africa Association, 1988–92; *b* 17 Nov. 1930; *s* of late Arthur and Lilian Gertrude Payne; *m* 1964, Heather Elizabeth Cavaghan; one *d. Educ:* Chatham Tech. Sch.; Gillingham Grammar Sch.; Nat. Defence Coll. HM Forces, 1949–50. Joined BoT, 1949; Raw Materials Dept, Washington, 1951–52; Min. of Materials, London, 1953–55; British Trade Commns, New Delhi, Bombay, Port of Spain, and Georgetown (First Sec.), 1956–67; joined HM Diplomatic Service, 1965; First Sec. (Inf.), Auckland, 1967–70; FCO, 1971–74; Dacca, 1974–76; Bonn, 1976–78; FCO, 1978–79; Dep. High Comr and Head of Chancery, Gabarone, 1980–83; Dep. Hd of Mission, Counsellor and Hd of Commercial Dept, Manila, 1983–87. Hon. Consultant, Southern Africa Business Assoc., 1995–2001. *Recreations:* bridge, music, computing, cooking. *Address:* Hoders Gate, Woodhurst Park, Oxted, Surrey RH8 9HA. *Died 22 June 2001.*

PAYNE, Ian; barrister; *b* 15 July 1926; *s* of late Douglas Harold Payne and of Gertrude (*née* Buchanan); *m* 1st, 1951, Babette (marr. diss. 1975), *d* of late Comte Clarence de Chalus; four *s* two *d*; 2nd, 1977, Colette Eugénie, *d* of late Marinus Jacobus van der Eb, Rotterdam. *Educ:* Wellington Coll. Commnd 60th Rifles, 1944–48. Called to the Bar, Lincoln's Inn, 1953, Hong Kong, 1981; Dep. Recorder of Derby, 1969–72; a Recorder, 1972–81. *Clubs:* Hong Kong; Refreshers Cricket.
Died 3 July 2005.

PAYNE, (Trevor) Ian; *see* Payne, I.

PAYNE-BUTLER, George William; County Treasurer, Surrey County Council, 1973–79 (Assistant, 1962; Deputy, 1970); *b* 7 Oct. 1919; *s* of late George and Letitia Rachel Payne; *m* 1947, Joyce Louise Cockburn; one *s* two *d. Educ:* Woking Sch. for Boys. Joined Surrey CC, 1937. Served War, RAF, 1940–45. Chartered Municipal Treasurer, 1950 (CIPFA). *Recreations:* gardening, handicraft work in wood, reading. *Address:* Janston, Hillier Road, Guildford, Surrey GU1 2JQ. *T:* (01483) 565337.
Died 22 May 2002.

PAYTON, Stanley Walden, CMG 1965; Chief of Overseas Department, Bank of England, 1975–80, retired; *b* 29 May 1921; *s* of late Archibald Walden Payton and Ethel May Payton (*née* Kirtland); *m* 1941, Joan (*née* Starmer); one *s* one *d. Educ:* Monoux School. Fleet Air Arm, 1940–46; Entered Bank of England, 1946; UK Alternate on Managing Board of European Payments Union, Paris, 1957–59; First Governor of Bank of Jamaica, 1960–64.
Died 8 Aug. 2004.

PEACE, David Brian, MBE 1977; FSA; glass engraver; town planner, 1947–82; *b* 13 March 1915; *y s* of Herbert W. F. Peace, Sheffield, and Mabel Peace (*née* Hammond); *m* 1939, Jean Margaret, ARCA (*d* 1989), *d* of Rev. McEwan and Margaret Lawson, Mill Hill; two *d. Educ:* Mill Hill; Univ. of Sheffield. ARIBA, FRTPI. RAF Airfield Construction Service, 1942–46, Sqdn Leader. Glass engraver, 1935–; presentation glass, 1952–; 11 one-man shows, retrospective exhibn, Ruskin Gall., Sheffield, 1990; work in 16 public collections, including: V&A (4); Kettle's Yard, Cambridge (7); Nat. Glass Mus., Stourbridge (2); Keatley Trust (10); Fitzwilliam Mus. (2); Turner Glass Mus., Sheffield (5); Corning Mus., USA; windows, screens and doors, 1956–, in churches and colleges, incl. St Nicholas Liverpool, St Albans Cathedral, Manchester Cathedral, St Botolph Aldgate, St Nicholas Whitehaven, Royal Acad. of Music, Waltham Abbey, Gray's Inn Chapel, Great St Mary's, Cambridge, Chapel Royal, Brighton, St Anthony-in-Meneage; meml inscriptions to G. M. Hopkins and John Betjeman, Westminster Abbey, 1996; with Sally Scott: Westminster Abbey, Norwich Cathedral, Lancaster and Sheffield Univs, Lincoln Coll., Oxford, and St John's Coll., Cambridge, Burwell Church, Cambs, Christ the Cornerstone, Milton Keynes, St Michael and All Angels, Northampton, St

Andrew, Headington, St Alban, Romford, Ealing Green Chapel, St Augustine, Wisbech, St Mary's, Newick, All Saints, Holbeach, Bollington Arts Centre, Cheshire, St Lalluwy, Menheniot, St James, Hanslope, St George, Methwold (RAF Meml). Master, Art Workers Guild, 1973; Guild of Glass Engravers: first Chm., 1975; Pres., 1980–86; Liveryman, Glaziers' Co., 1977. Town Planner: Staffs CC, 1948–61; Cambs CC, Dep. County Planning Officer, 1961–75, then head of envtl planning, 1975–80 (MBE); DoE appeals inspectorate, 1980–82. Member: Council for Visual Education, 1960–80; Council, RTPI, 1961–62, 1972–73; Council for British Archæology, 1965–85. President: Surveyors Club, 1984; ASCHB, 1994; Vice Pres., Betjeman Soc., 1996; Member: Ely DAC for Care of Churches, 1966–98; Council, Artists Gen. Benevolent Inst., 1994–96. Hon. DSc (Tech.) Sheffield Univ., 1991. *Publications:* Glass Engraving: lettering and design, 1985; The Engraved Glass of David Peace: the architecture of lettering, 1990; Eric Gill, the Inscriptions: a descriptive catalogue, 1994; originator of A Guide to Historic Buildings Law, 1965 (The Cambridgeshire Guide); Historic Buildings: maps and guides to the Peak District and N Wales. *Recreations:* townscape, heraldry.
Died 15 Feb. 2003.

PEAKE, Air Cdre (retired) Dame Felicity (Hyde), (Lady Peake), DBE 1949 (MBE 1941); AE; *b* 1 May 1913; *d* of late Colonel Humphrey Watts, OBE, TD, and Mrs Simon Orde; *m* 1st, 1935, John Charles Mackenzie Hanbury (killed on active service, 1939); no *c*; 2nd, 1952, Sir Harald Peake, AE (*d* 1978); one *s*. *Educ:* St Winifreds, Eastbourne; Les Grands Huguenots, Vaucresson, Seine et Oise, France. Joined ATS Co. of the RAF, April 1939; commnd in WAAF, Aug. 1939; served at home and in the Middle East; Director: Women's Auxiliary Air Force, 1946–49; Women's Royal Air Force, from its inception, 1949, until her retirement, 1950; Hon. ADC to King George VI, 1949–50. Mem., Adv. Cttee, Recruitment for the Forces, 1958. Trustee: Imperial War Museum, 1963–85 (Chm., 1986–88, Pres., 1988–92, Friends of Imperial War Museum); St Clement Danes church, 1989–. Governor, London House, 1958–76, 1978–92; Member Council: RAF Benevolent Fund, 1946–96 (a Vice-Pres., 1978–); Union Jack Club, 1950–78. Patron, WAAF Assoc., 1997–. *Publication:* Pure Chance (memoirs), 1993.
Died 2 Nov. 2002.

PEARCE, Sir Austin (William), Kt 1980; CBE 1974; PhD; FREng; Chairman, Oxford Instruments Group, 1987–91; *b* 1 Sept. 1921; *s* of William Thomas and Florence Annie Pearce; *m* 1st, 1947, Maglona Winifred Twinn (*d* 1975); three *d*; 2nd, 1979, Dr F. Patricia Grice (*née* Forsythe) (*d* 1993). *Educ:* Devonport High Sch. for Boys; Univ. of Birmingham (BSc (Hons) 1943; PhD 1945; Cadman Medallist). Joined Agwi Petroleum Corp., 1945 (later Esso Petroleum Co., Ltd): Asst Refinery Manager, 1954–56; Gen. Manager Refining, 1956–62; Dir, 1963; Man. Dir, 1968–71; Chm., 1972–80; Chm., British Aerospace, 1980–87; Director: Esso Europe Inc., 1972–80; Esso Africa Inc., 1972–80; Pres., Esso Holding Co. UK Inc., 1971–80; Chairman: Esso Pension Trust Ltd, 1972–80; Irish Refining Co. Ltd, 1965–71; Director: Williams & Glyn's Bank, 1974–85 (a Dep. Chm., 1980–83; Chm., 1983–85); Royal Bank of Scotland Gp (formerly Nat. & Commercial Banking Gp), 1978–92 (a Vice-Chm., 1985–92); Pearl Assurance PLC, 1985–91; Jaguar PLC, 1986–93; Smiths Ind. PLC, 1987–92; Home Group Ltd, 1998–2001. Part-time Mem., NRDC, 1973–76; Member: Adv. Council for Energy Conservation, 1974–79; Energy Commn, 1977–79; British Aerospace, 1977–87 (Mem., Organising Cttee, 1976); Standing Commn on Energy and the Environment, 1978–81; Takeover Panel, 1987–92. Chm., UK Petroleum Industry Adv. Cttee, 1977–80; Pres., UK Petroleum Industry Assoc. Ltd, 1979–80; CBI: Chm., Industrial Policy Cttee, 1982–85; Chm., Industrial Steering Policy Gp, 1985–86. President: Inst. of Petroleum, 1968–70; The Pipeline Industries Guild,

1973–75; Oil Industries Club, 1975–77; Pres., SBAC, 1982–83. Mem., Bd of Governors, English-Speaking Union, 1974–80; Chm., Bd of Trustees, Science Museum, 1986–95. Treas., RSA, 1988–93. Chairman: Warden Housing Assoc., 1994–2001; Martlets Hospice Ltd, 1994–98; Sussex Victim Support, 1999–2000. Mem. Council, Surrey Univ., 1981–93 (Pro-Chancellor, 1986–93; Pro Chancellor Emeritus, 1994–). FREng (FEng 1978). Hon. DSc: Southampton, 1978; Exeter, 1985; Salford, 1987; Cranfield, 1987; Hon. DEng Birmingham, 1986; DUniv Surrey, 1993. *Recreations:* bowls, woodwork. *Address:* Treeps House, 2 High Street, Hurstpierpoint, Hassocks, W Sussex BN6 9TY.
Died 21 March 2004.

PEARCE, Prof. David William, OBE 2000; Professor of Environmental Economics, University College London, 1983, then Emeritus; *b* 11 Oct. 1941; *s* of William Henry and Gladys Muriel Pearce; *m* 1966, Susan Mary Reynolds; two *s*. *Educ:* Lincoln Coll., Oxford (BA, MA); Univ. of East Anglia (DSc). Lectr in Econs, Lancaster Univ., 1964–67; Sen. Lectr in Econs, Southampton Univ., 1967–74; Dir, Public Sector Econs Res. Centre, 1974–77; Prof. of Political Economy, Univ. of Aberdeen, 1977–83; Dir, 1991–96, Associate Dir, 1996–2000, Centre for Social and Econ. Res. on the Global Envmt, UCL and UEA. Global 500 Award for services to world envmt, UN, 1989. *Publications:* books include: (jtly) Blueprint for a Green Economy, 1989, rev. edn 1999; (jtly) The Economics of Natural Resources and the Environment, 1990; (jtly) Blueprint 2: Greening the World Economy, 1991; (jtly) World Without End: economics, environment and sustainable development, 1993; Economic Values and the Natural World, 1993; (jtly) Environmental Economics: an elementary introduction, 1993; Blueprint 3: Measuring Sustainable Development, 1993; (jtly) Project and Policy Appraisal: integrating economics and environment, 1994; (jtly) The Causes of Tropical Deforestation, 1994; Blueprint 4: Sustaining the Earth—Capturing Global Value, 1995; (jtly) Blueprint 5: The Social Costs of Road Transport, 1996; (ed jtly) Acid Rain: counting the cost, 1997; (jtly) Measuring Sustainable Development: macroeconomics and the environment, 1997; Economics and the Environment: essays in ecological economics and sustainable development, 1999; (jtly) Blueprint for a Sustainable Economy, 2000; numerous papers in refereed jls. *Recreations:* tending seven acres of wild land, drinking wine, birdwatching. *Address:* Department of Economics, University College London, Gower Street, WC1E 6BT.
Died 8 Sept. 2005.

PEARCE, Maj.-Gen. Leslie Arthur, CB 1973; CBE 1971 (OBE 1964; MBE 1956); Chief of General Staff, NZ Army, 1971–73, retd; *b* 22 Jan. 1918; British parents; *m* 1944, Fay Mattocks, Auckland, NZ; two *s* one *d*. *Educ:* in New Zealand. Joined Army, 1937; served War of 1939–45, Greece, Western Desert, Italy; Staff Coll., Camberley, 1948; Directing Staff, Australia Staff Coll., 1958–59; Commandant, Army Schools, NZ, 1960; Comdg Officer, 1 NZ Regt, in NZ and Malaysia, 1961–64; Dep. QMG, NZ Army, 1964–65; Dir of Staff Duties, NZ Army, 1966; IDC, 1967; QMG, 1968–69; Dep. Chief of Defence Staff, 1970. Chm., Vocational Training Council, 1975–81. Co. director: Dep. Chm., NZ Council for Educnl Res., 1983–85 (Mem., 1977–85). *Recreations:* golf, fishing, gardening; Provincial and Services Rugby representative, in youth. *Address:* Apt 218 Park Lane Village, 106 Becroft Drive, Forrest Hill, Auckland, New Zealand.
Died 21 Dec. 2002.

PEARSE, Prof. Anthony Guy Everson, MD; FRCP, FRCPath; Professor of Histochemistry, University of London, Royal Postgraduate Medical School, 1965–81, then Emeritus; *b* 9 Aug. 1916; *o s* of Captain R. G. Pearse, DSO, MC, Modbury, Devon, and Constance Evelyn Steels, Pocklington, Yorks; *m* 1947, Elizabeth Himmelhoch, MB, BS (Sydney), DCP (London); one *s* three *d*. *Educ:* Sherborne Sch.; Trinity Coll., Cambridge

(BA 1937, MB BChir 1941, MD 1950); DCP (London). Kitchener Scholar. Posts, St Bart's Hospital, 1940–41; Surg.-Lt, RNVR, 1941–45 (21st and 24th Destroyer Flotillas). Registrar, Edgware Gen. Hosp., 1946; Asst Lectr in Pathol., PG Med. School, London, 1947–51, Lectr, 1951–57; Cons. Pathol., Hammersmith Hosp., 1951; Fulbright Fellow and Visiting Prof. of Path., Univ. of Alabama, 1953–54; Guest Instructor in Histochemistry: Kansas Univ., 1957, 1958; Vanderbilt Univ., 1967; Reader in Histochemistry, London Univ., 1957–65; Middleton Goldsmith Lectr, NY Path. Soc., 1976; Feulgen Lectr, Deutsch Ges. Histochem., 1983, Hon. Mem., 1986. Member: Path. Soc. (GB), 1949 (Hon. Mem., 1990); Biochem. Soc. (GB), 1957; European Gastro Club, 1969; Hon. Mem. or Mem., various foreign socs incl. Deutsche Akademie der Naturforscher Leopoldina, 1973 and Amer. Assoc. Endocrine Surgeons, 1981; Corresp. Mem., Deutsche Gesellschaft für Endokrinologie, 1978; Hon. Fellow, Royal Microscop. Soc., 1964 (Vice-Pres., 1970–72; Pres., 1972–74). Hon. Mem., Mark Twain Soc., 1977. Hon. MD: Basel, 1960; Krakow, 1978. Raymond Horton-Smith Prize, Univ. of Cambridge, 1950; John Hunter Medal and Triennial Prize, RCS, 1976–78; Ernest Jung Foundn Prize and Medal for Medicine, 1979; Fred W. Stewart Medal and Prize, Sloan-Kettering Cancer Center, NY, 1979; Jan Swammerdam Medal, Soc. for Advancement of Nat. Scis, Amsterdam, 1988; Schleiden Medal, Deutsche Akademie der Naturforscher Leopoldina, 1989. Member Editorial Board: Histochemie, 1958–73; Jl Histochem. Cytochem., 1959–68; Enzymol. biol. clin., 1961–67; Jl of Royal Microscopical Soc., 1967–69; Histochemical Jl, 1968–; Brain Research, 1968–76; Cardiovascular Research, 1968–75; Virchow's Archiv 'B', 1968–91; Jl Microscopy, 1969–81; Jl of Neuro-visceral Relations, 1969–73; Jl of Molecular and Cellular Cardiology, 1970–79; Scand. Jl Gastroenterol., 1971–81; Jl Neural Transmission, 1973–76; Jl of Pathology, 1973–83; Progress in Histochem. Cytochem., 1973–; Histochemistry, 1974–91; Mikroscopie, 1977–88; Basic and Applied Histochem., 1979–90; Acta Histochem., 1980–; Europ. Jl of Basic and Applied Histochem., 1991–92; European Jl of Hystochem., 1993–; Editor, Medical Biology, 1974–84. *Publications:* Histochemistry Theoretical and Applied, 1953, 2nd edn, 1960; 3rd edn, vol. I, 1968, vol. II, 1972; 4th edn vol. I, 1980, vol. II, 1984, vol. III (ed with P. J. Stoward), 1991; numerous papers on theoretical and applied histochemistry, esp. endocrinology (The Neuroendocrine System). *Recreations:* horticulture (plant hybridization, Liliaceae, Asclepiadaceae), ship modelling, foreign touring. *Address:* Church Cottage, Church Lane, Cheriton Bishop, Exeter EX6 6HY. *T:* (01647) 24231. *Club:* Naval.
Died 24 May 2003.

PEASE, Dr (Rendel) Sebastian, FRS 1977; Programme Director for Fusion, UKAEA, 1981–87; *b* 1922; *s* of Michael Stewart Pease and Helen Bowen (*née* Wedgwood); *m* 1st, 1952, Susan Spickernell (*d* 1996); two *s* three *d*; 2nd, 1998, Jean Frances White (*d* 2000); 3rd, 2004, Eleanor Mary Barnes. *Educ:* Bedales Sch.; Trinity Coll., Cambridge (MA, ScD). Scientific Officer, Min. of Aircraft Prodn at ORS Unit, HQ, RAF Bomber Comd, 1942–46; research at AERE, Harwell, 1947–61; Div. Head, Culham Lab. for Plasma Physics and Nuclear Fusion, UKAEA, 1961–67; Vis. Scientist, Princeton Univ., 1964–65; Asst Dir, UKAEA Research Gp, 1967; Dir, Culham Lab., UKAEA, 1968–81. Gordon Godfrey Vis. Prof. of Theoretical Physics, Univ. NSW, 1984, 1988 and 1991; Visitor, Blackett Lab., Imperial Coll., London, 1992–97. Chairman: Adam Hilger Ltd, 1976–77; Plasma Physics Commn, Internat. Union of Pure and Applied Physics, 1975–78; Internat. Fusion Res. Council, Internat. Atomic Energy Agency, 1976–83; British Pugwash Gp, 1988–2002 (Mem., Pugwash Council, 1992–2002). Member: Council, Royal Soc., 1985–87 (a Vice-Pres., 1986–87); Fabian Soc., 1942–; Inst. of Physics (Vice-Pres., 1973–77; Pres., 1978–80); Amer. Inst. of Physics, 1961–; IEE, 1979–; Eur. Atlantic Gp, 1996–. Mem., West Ilsley

Parish Council, 1987–2000 (Chm., 1997–2000). Hon. MINucE 1984. Hon. Fellow, European Nuclear Soc., 1990. DUniv Surrey, 1973; Hon. DSc: Aston, 1981; City Univ., 1987. *Publications:* articles in physics jls, and Pugwash Confs on Science and World Affairs. *Recreation:* music. *Address:* The Poplars, West Ilsley, Newbury, Berks RG20 7AW.
Died 17 Oct. 2004.

PEASE, Sebastian; *see* Pease, R. S.

PEAT, Watson; *see* Peat, W. W. W.

PEAT, (William Wood) Watson, CBE 1972; JP; FRAgS; farmer; broadcaster; Scottish Governor of the BBC, 1984–89; Chairman, Broadcasting Council for Scotland, 1984–89; *b* 14 Dec. 1922; *o s* of William Peat and Margaret Hillhouse; *m* 1955, Jean Frew Paton McHarrie; two *s* one *d*. *Educ:* Denny Public School. Served with Royal Signals, Europe and India, 1941–46; Lieut 1944. Member: Nat. Council, Scottish Assoc. of Young Farmers' Clubs, 1949 (Chm., 1953–54; Vice-Pres., 1975; Pres., 1979); Stirling CC, 1959–74 (Vice-Convenor, 1967–70); Council, NFU Scotland, 1959–78 (Pres., 1966–67); Scottish River Purification Adv. Cttee, 1960–79; Bd of Management, Royal Scottish Nat. Hosp., 1962–72; Council, Hannah Research Inst., 1963–82; Council, Scottish Agricultural Organisation Soc. Ltd, 1963 (Pres., 1974–77); Bd of Management, British Farm Produce Council, 1964–87 (Vice-Chm., 1980–87); Agric. Marketing Develt Exec. Cttee, 1966–67; Central Council for Agric. and Horticultural Co-operation, 1967–83; British Agricl Council, 1974–84; Food from Britain Co-operative Development Board, 1983–89. Chairman: BBC Scottish Agric. Adv. Cttee, 1971–75; Scottish Adv. Cttee, Assoc. of Agriculture, 1974–79 (Vice Pres., 1979–); Council, Scottish Agricl Colls, 1984–90; Gov., West of Scotland Agricl Coll., 1964–90 (Vice Chm., 1975; Chm., 1983–88); Mem. Bd of Mgt, Oatridge Agricl Coll., 1967–75. Director: Agri-Finance (Scotland) Ltd, 1968–79; Fedn of Agricultural Co-operatives (UK) Ltd, 1974–77; FMC PLC, 1974–83. Gen. Comr of Income Tax, 1962. FRAgS 1987. JP Stirlingshire, 1963. OStJ 1990. *Recreations:* amateur radio, flying. *Address:* Carbro, 61 Stirling Road, Larbert, Stirlingshire FK5 4SG. *T:* (01324) 562420. *Clubs:* Farmers', BBC.
Died 1 May 2001.

PECK, (Eldred) Gregory; film actor, US, since 1943; *b* 5 April 1916; *s* of Gregory P. Peck and Bernice Ayres; *m* 1st, 1942, Greta Konen Rice (marr. diss. 1954); two *s* (and one *s* decd); 2nd, 1955, Veronique Passani; one *s* one *d*. *Educ:* Calif Public Schools; Univ. of Calif (BA). Broadway stage, 1941–43. *Films:* Days of Glory, 1943; Keys of the Kingdom, Valley of Decision, 1944; Spellbound, 1945; Duel in the Sun, The Yearling, 1946; The Macomber Affair, Gentlemen's Agreement, 1947; The Paradine Case, 1948; Yellow Sky, The Great Sinner, Twelve O'Clock High, 1949; The Gun Fighter, 1950; Only the Valiant, Captain Horatio Hornblower, David and Bathsheba, 1951; The World in his Arms, 1952; The Snows of Kilimanjaro, 1952; Roman Holiday, 1953; The Million Pound Note, 1953; Night People, 1954; The Purple Plain, 1954; The Man in the Grey Flannel Suit, 1956; Moby Dick, 1956; Designing Woman, 1957; The Bravados, 1958; The Big Country (co-producer), 1958; Pork Chop Hill, On the Beach, 1959; Guns of Navarone, 1960; Cape Fear, 1961; To Kill a Mocking Bird, 1962 (Academy Award for best performance); Captain Newman, MD, 1963; Behold a Pale Horse, 1964; Mirage, Arabesque, 1965; Mackenna's Gold, 1967; The Chairman, The Stalking Moon, 1968; Marooned, 1970; I Walk the Line, Shoot Out, 1971; The Trial of the Catonsville Nine, 1972; Billy Two-Hats, 1974; The Boys From Brazil, 1978; The Sea Wolves, 1980; Amazing Grace and Chuck, 1987; Old Gringo, 1989; Other People's Money, Cape Fear, 1991; *television:* includes:The Blue and the Gray, 1982; The Scarlet and the Black, 1983; (also producer) The Portrait, 1993; Moby Dick, 1998; *produced:* The Dove, 1974; The Omen, 1976; MacArthur, 1977. Nat. Chm., Amer. Cancer Soc., 1966. Mem., Nat. Council on Arts, 1965–67, 1968–; Pres.,

Acad. Motion Picture Arts and Sciences, 1967–70; Chm., Board of Trustees, Amer. Film Inst., 1967–69. Medal of Freedom Award, 1969; Jean Hersholt Humanitarian Award, Acad. of Motion Picture Arts and Sciences, 1968; Nat. Medal of the Arts, 1998. *Recreations:* riding, swimming, bicycling, gardening. *Address:* c/o CAA, 9830 Wilshire Boulevard, Beverly Hills, CA 90212–1825, USA. *Club:* Players (New York). *Died 12 June 2003.*

PEDDER, Air Marshal Sir Ian (Maurice), KCB 1982; OBE 1963; DFC 1949; international aviation consultant, since 1992; *b* 2 May 1926; *s* of Maurice and Elsie Pedder; *m* 1949, Jean Mary (*née* Kellett); one *s* two *d*. *Educ:* Royal Grammar Sch., High Wycombe; Queen's Coll., Oxford. Service in Nos 28, 60, 81, 213 Sqdns, CFS, and with Burma Air Force, 1946–59; Staff Coll., Andover, and MoD, 1959–62; Far East, 1962–64; Staff appts, 1965–70; RCDS, 1971; Comdg RAF Chivenor, 1972–74; Nat. Air Traffic Services, 1974–84, Dep. Controller, 1977–81, Controller and Mem. CAA, 1981–84. Dep. Chm., 1986–89, Chm., 1989–90, Dan-Air Services; Dir, Davies & Newman plc, 1989–92. *Publications:* contribs to Service and aviation jls, UK, US and EU. *Recreations:* study of Victorian times, photography, riding (a bicycle). *Address:* The Chestnuts, Cheddar, Somerset. *Club:* Victory Services. *Died 4 Dec. 2002.*

PEEK, Sir William Grenville, 5th Bt *cr* 1874, of Rousden, Devon; *b* 15 Dec. 1919; *s* of Captain Roger Grenville Peek, 9th Lancers (*d* 1921) and Hon. Joan Penelope Sclater-Booth (*d* 1976), *d* of 2nd Baron Basing; *S* cousin, 1996; *m* 1950, Lucy Jane, *d* of Maj. Edward Dorrien-Smith, DSO; one *s* three *d*. *Educ:* Eton. Served War 1939–45 (despatches). Captain late 9th Lancers. *Heir:* *s* Richard Grenville Peek, *b* 3 Feb. 1955. *Died 14 Sept. 2004.*

PEEL, Sir John; see Peel, Sir W. J.

PEEL, John; see Ravenscroft, J. R. P.

PEEL, Sir John (Harold), KCVO 1960; MA, BM, BCh; FRCP 1971; FRCS 1933; FRCOG 1944; Surgeon-Gynæcologist to the Queen, 1961–73; Consulting Obstetric and Gynæcological Surgeon, King's College Hospital, since 1969; Emeritus Consulting Gynæcologist, Princess Beatrice Hospital, since 1965; *b* 10 Dec. 1904; *s* of Rev. J. E. Peel; *m* 1st, 1936, Muriel Elaine Pellow; one *d*; 2nd, 1947, Freda Margaret Mellish (*d* 1993); 3rd, 1995, Sally Barton. *Educ:* Manchester Grammar Sch.; Queen's Coll., Oxford (MA, BM, BCh 1932; Hon. Fellow, 2002); King's College Hospital Med. Sch., qualified 1930. MRCS, LRCP. Obstetric and Gynæcological Surgeon: King's Coll. Hosp., 1936–69; Princess Beatrice Hosp., 1937–65; Queen Victoria Hosp., East Grinstead, 1941–69; Surgeon EMS, 1939–45. Director of Clinical Studies, King's College Hospital Medical School, 1948–67. Mem., Economic and Social Cttee, EEC, 1973–78. Litchfield Lecturer, Oxford University, 1961 and 1969; Sir Kadar Nath Das Lecturer, Bengal O and G Soc., 1962; Sir A. Mudaliar Lecturer, Madras Univ., 1962; Vis. Prof., Cape Town Univ., 1963; Travelling Prof., S African Council, RCOG, 1968. Past Examiner, Universities of Oxford, Cambridge, London, Liverpool, Bristol, Glasgow, Newcastle, Nat. Univ. of Ireland, Birmingham, Dundee, Sheffield, Conjoint Board, RCOG and CMB. Nuffield visitor to Colonies, 1950 and 1953. President, RCOG, 1966–69 (Hon. Treasurer, 1959–66, Councillor, 1955–); President: Internat. Fedn of Obstetrics and Gynæcology, 1970–73; Chelsea Clinical Society, 1960; BMA 1970 (Chm., Bd of Science and Educn, 1972–76); Family Planning Assoc., 1971–74; Chm., DHSS Cttees of Enquiry: Domiciliary Midwifery and Bed Needs, 1971; The Use of Fetus and Fetal Material for Research, 1972. FKC 1980; Hon. Fellow: American Association of Obstetricians and Gynæcologists, 1962 (Joseph Price Oration, 1961); Edinburgh Obstetrical Soc., 1971; RSM, 1973; Hon. Member: Canadian Assoc. of O and G, 1955; Italian Assoc. O and G, 1960; Hon. Treas., GMC,

1972–75; Hon. FRCS (Canada), 1967; Hon. FCOG (SA), 1968; Hon. MMSA 1970; Hon. FACS 1970; Hon. FACOG 1971; Hon. Fellow, American Gynæcological Soc., 1974. Hon. DSc Birmingham, 1972; Hon. DM Southampton, 1974; Hon. DCh Newcastle, 1980. *Publications:* Textbook of Gynæcology, 1943; Lives of the Fellows of Royal College of Obstetricians and Gynaecologists 1929–69, 1976; Biography of William Blair-Bell, 1986; numerous contributions to Medical Journals. *Recreations:* fishing, gardening. *Address:* 11 Harnwood Road, Harnham, Salisbury SP2 8DD. *T:* (01722) 334892. *Died 31 Dec. 2005.*

PEEL, Sir (William) John, Kt 1973; *b* 16 June 1912; *s* of late Sir William Peel, KCMG, KBE, and Violet Mary Drake, *er d* of W. D. Laing; *m* 1936, Rosemary Mia Minka, *er d* of Robert Readhead; one *s* three *d*. *Educ:* Wellington College; Queens' College, Cambridge. Colonial Administrative Service, 1933–51; on active service, 1941–45; British Resident, Brunei, 1946–48; Res. Comr, Gilbert and Ellice Is Colony, 1949–51. Personal Asst to Man. Dirs of Rugby Portland Cement Co. Ltd, 1952–54. Contested (C) Meriden Division of Warwickshire, 1955; MP (C) Leicester SE, 1957–Feb. 1974; Parliamentary Private Secretary: to Economic Secretary to the Treasury, 1958–59; to Minister of State, Board of Trade, 1959–60; Asst Govt Whip (unpaid), 1960–61; a Lord Comr of the Treasury, Nov. 1961–Oct. 1964. Parly Delegate to: Assemblies of Council of Europe, 1961–74; WEU 1961–74 (Vice-Pres., 1967, Pres. 1972, Chm., Defence and Armaments Cttee, 1970–72, WEU); N Atlantic Assembly, 1959–74 (Leader, 1970–74; Pres., N Atlantic Assembly, Nov. 1972); Mem., British Delegn to European Parlt, Strasbourg, 1973–74; Hon. Dir, Cons. Party Internat. Office, 1975–76. Member Council: Victoria League for Commonwealth Friendship, 1974–83 (Dep. Chm., 1976–81; Chm., 1982–83; Dep. Pres. and Mem., Chairman's Adv. Cttee, 1983–); British Atlantic Cttee; Mem. Central Council, Royal Over-Seas League, 1980–86; Chairman: Hospitality and Branches Cttee of Victoria League, 1974–78, Hospitality Cttee, 1978–81; Overseas Students Adv. Cttee, 1980–81; Jt Standing Cttee of Victoria League and Royal Commonwealth Soc., 1975–83; Westminster for Europe Branch, European Movement, 1974–77. Mem. Ct of Assistants, Framework Knitters' Co. (Master, 1983). Dato Seri Laila Jasa Brunei 1969; Dato Setia Negara Brunei 1971. *Recreations:* varied. *Address:* 51 Cambridge Street, SW1V 4PR. *T:* (020) 7834 8762. *Clubs:* Carlton, Hurlingham; Hawks (Cambridge). *Died 8 May 2004.*

PEIRSON, Margaret Ellen, CB 1996; Under Secretary, Department of Social Security, since 1990; *b* 28 Nov. 1942; *e d* of late David Edward Herbert Peirson, CBE and of Norah Ellen Peirson (*née* Corney). *Educ:* North London Collegiate Sch.; Somerville Coll., Oxford (MA Maths); Yale Univ. HM Treasury, 1965–90; secondment to Bank of England, 1982–84; Under Sec., 1986. *Recreations:* choral singing, theatre. *Address:* Department of Social Security, The Adelphi, 1–11 John Adam Street, WC2N 6HT. *Died 5 May 2001.*

PEMBROKE, 17th Earl of, *cr* 1551, **AND MONTGOMERY**, 14th Earl of, *cr* 1605; **Henry George Charles Alexander Herbert;** Baron Herbert of Cardiff, 1551; Baron Herbert of Shurland, 1605; Baron Herbert of Lea (UK), 1861; DL; Hereditary Grand Visitor of Jesus College, Oxford; *b* 19 May 1939; *s* of 16th Earl of Pembroke and Montgomery, CVO, and Mary Countess of Pembroke, CVO (*d* 1995); *S* father, 1969; *m* 1st, 1966, Claire Rose (marr. diss. 1981), *o d* of Douglas Pelly, Swaynes Hall, Widdington, Essex; one *s* three *d*; 2nd, 1988, Miranda Juliet, *d* of Comdr John Oram, Bulbridge House, Wilton; three *d*. *Educ:* Eton Coll.; Oxford Univ. Royal Horse Guards, 1958–60 (National Service); Oxford University, 1960–63. DL Wilts 1995. *Recreations:* photography, gardening, horse racing. *Heir:* *s* Lord Herbert, *b* 18 May 1978. *Address:* Wilton House,

Salisbury, Wilts SP2 0BJ. *T:* (01722) 746700.
Died 7 Oct. 2003.

PENLINGTON, Ross Grange, CBE 1995 (OBE (mil.) 1980); AE 1972 (Clasp 1979); a Judge of the Court of Appeal of Hong Kong, 1988–95; *b* 3 March 1931; *s* of Cedric Grange Penlington and Elsie May Penlington; *m* 1956, Valerie Ann Wacher; two *d. Educ:* Christ Coll., NZ; Univ. of Canterbury, NZ (LLB 1954). Barrister and Solicitor, Christchurch, NZ, 1954–59; Legal Officer, Magistrate and Attorney Gen., Western Samoa, 1959–64; Hong Kong: Crown Counsel, 1965–75; Dir of Public Prosecutions, 1976–77; District Court Judge, 1977–80; High Court Judge, 1980–88. Commnd Hong Kong RAuxAF, 1964; Pilot's Brevet, 1965; CO (Wing Comdr), 1975–83; Hon. Air Cdre, 1983–93. *Recreations:* flying, golf, tennis, fishing, racing. *Address:* 80 Ngamotu Road, Taupo, New Zealand. *Clubs:* Royal Air Force; Hong Kong; Taupo (Taupo); Northern (Auckland).
Died 12 May 2001.

PENNANT, His Honour David Edward Thornton; a Circuit Judge (formerly County Court Judge), 1961–84; *b* 2 Aug. 1912; *s* of David Falconer Pennant, DL, JP, Barrister-at-law, late of Nantlys, St Asaph, N Wales, and Lilla Agnes Pennant; *m* 1938, Alice Catherine Stainer (*d* 2001); three *s* one *d. Educ:* Charterhouse; Trinity Coll., Cambridge. Called to the Bar, Inner Temple, 1935. Served, 1939–45, with Royal Signals (TA); OC, Signals Officers' Training Sch., Mhow, India, 1944–45. Chm., Radnorshire QS, 1962–64; Deputy Chairman: Brecknockshire QS, 1956–64; Flintshire QS, 1962–71; Dorset QS, 1971. Joint Chairman, Medical Appeals Tribunal for Wales, 1957–61; Mem., County Court Rule Cttee, 1970–78. Chancellor, Dio. Monmouth, 1949–77. Governing, and Representative Bodies, Church in Wales, 1946–83. *Recreation:* gardening. *Address:* 12 Ettrick Road, Branksome Park, Poole, Dorset BH13 6LG. *T:* (01202) 765614.
Died 7 Oct. 2001.

PENNEY, Reginald John; Assistant Under-Secretary of State, Ministry of Defence, 1964–73, retired; *b* 22 May 1919; *s* of Herbert Penney and Charlotte Penney (*née* Affleck); *m* 1941, Eileen Gardiner; one *s* two *d. Educ:* Westminster School. War Service, Royal West Kent Regt, 1939–46. Civil Servant, Air Ministry, until 1964, including service with Far East Air Force, Singapore, 1960–63. Chm., Sherborne Soc., CPRE, 1976. *Recreation:* golf. *Address:* Rumbow Cottage, Acreman Street, Sherborne, Dorset DT9 3NX.
Died 19 June 2001.

PENNING-ROWSELL, Edmund Lionel; wine writer; Wine Correspondent: Country Life, 1954–87; Financial Times, 1964; *b* 16 March 1913; *s* of Edmund Penning-Rowsell and Marguerite Marie-Louise Penning-Rowsell (*née* Egan); *m* 1937, Margaret Wintringham; one *s* two *d. Educ:* Marlborough College. Journalist, Morning Post, 1930–35; Book Publisher, Frederick Muller Ltd, 1935–50; Sales Manager, B. T. Batsford, 1952–57; Dir, book publisher, Edward Hulton & Co./Studio-Vista, 1957–63; Manager, World Book Fair, Earl's Court, 1964. Mem. Cttee of Management, Internat. Exhibition Co-op. Wine Soc., 1959–87 (Chm., 1964–87); Chm., Internat. Co-operative Wine Soc., 1964–87; Founder Mem., William Morris Soc., 1953–54 (Vice-Pres.). Chevalier: Ordre du Mérite Agricole (France), 1971; Ordre du Mérite National (France), 1981. *Publications:* Red, White and Rosé, 1967; The Wines of Bordeaux, 1969, 6th edn 1989; (ed, trans. and updated) Higounet *et al*, Château Latour: the history of a great vineyard 1331–1992, 1993. *Recreation:* drinking wine, particularly claret. *Address:* Yew Trees House, Wootton, Woodstock, Oxford OX20 1EG. *T:* (01993) 811281. *Club:* Travellers.
Died 4 March 2002.

PENRHYN, 6th Baron *cr* 1866; **Malcolm Frank Douglas-Pennant,** DSO 1945; MBE 1943; *b* 11 July 1908; 2nd *s* of 5th Baron Penrhyn and Alice Nellie (*d* 1965), *o d* of Sir William Charles Cooper, 3rd Bt; *S* father, 1967; *m* 1954, Elisabeth Rosemary (*d* 2002), *d* of late Brig. Sir Percy Laurie, KCVO, CBE, DSO, JP; two *d. Educ:* Eton; RMC, Sandhurst. Colonel (retd), KRRC. *Heir: nephew* Simon Douglas-Pennant [*b* 28 June 1938; *m* 1963, Josephine Maxwell, *yr d* of Robert Upcott; two *s* two *d*]. *Address:* Edgedell, Chilland Lane, Martyr Worthy, Hants SO21 1EB. *T:* (01962) 779540. *Club:* Flyfishers'.
Died 8 Nov. 2003.

PEPPER, Kenneth Bruce, CB 1965; Commissioner of HM Customs and Excise, 1957–73; *b* 11 March 1913; *s* of late E. E. Pepper; *m* 1945, Irene Evelyn Watts; two *s. Educ:* County High Sch., Ilford; LSE. Joined HM Customs and Excise, 1932; Asst Sec., 1949; Comr, 1957. Lieutenant, Intelligence Corps, 1944. *Address:* Fairfield, Cae Mair, Beaumaris, Gwynedd LL58 8YN.
Died 1 Dec. 2002.

PERCEVAL, Robert Westby, TD 1968; Clerk Assistant, House of Lords, 1964–74; retired; *b* 28 Aug. 1914; *m* 1948, Hon. J. I. L. Littleton, *er d* of 5th Baron Hatherton; two *s* two *d. Educ:* Ampleforth; Balliol College, Oxford. Joined Parliament Office, House of Lords, 1938. Royal Artillery, 1939–44; General Staff, War Office, 1944–45. *Address:* Pillaton Old Hall, Penkridge, Staffs ST19 5RZ. *Clubs:* Beefsteak, Turf.
Died 19 Jan. 2005.

PERCIVAL-PRESCOTT, Westby William, FIIC; practising conservator and painter; *b* 22 Jan. 1923; *s* of William Percival-Prescott and Edith Percival; *m* 1948, Silvia Haswell Miller; one *s. Educ:* Edinburgh Coll. of Art (DA Hons). FIIC 1957. Andrew Grant Scholar, National Gall., 1945; restoration of Rubens Whitehall ceiling, 1947–51; Restorer i/c House of Lords frescos, 1953; worked in National Gall. Conservation Dept, 1954–56; directed restoration of Painted Hall, Greenwich, 1957–60; National Maritime Museum: estabd Picture Conservation Dept, 1961; Keeper and Head of Picture Dept, 1977–83; organised first internat. conf. on Comparative Lining Techniques, 1973 (Ottawa, 1974); produced and designed historical exhibitions: Idea and Illusion, 1960; Four Steps to Longitude, 1963; The Siege of Malta, 1970; Captain Cook and Mr Hodges, 1979; The Art of the Van de Veldes, 1982. Vis. Sen. Lectr, Dept of Fine Art, Univ. of Leeds, 1980; Leverhulme Trust Res. Award, 1996–97. Internat. Council of Museums: Co-ordinator, Conservation Cttee, 1975–84; Mem., Directory Bd, Conservation Cttee, 1981–84. *Publications:* The Coronation Chair, 1957; The Lining Cycle, 1974, Swedish edn 1975; Handbook of Lining Terms, 1974; Thornhill at Greenwich, 1978; Micro X-Ray Techniques, 1978; Techniques of Suction Lining, 1981; The Art of the Van de Veldes, 1982; technical papers. *Recreations:* listening to music, travel. *Address:* 34 Compayne Gardens, NW6 3DP. *T:* (020) 7624 4577.
Died 22 Jan. 2005.

PEREIRA, Sir (Herbert) Charles, Kt 1977; DSc; FRS 1969; Consultant, tropical agriculture research; *b* 12 May 1913; *s* of H. J. Pereira and Maud Edith (*née* Machin), both of London; *m* 1941, Irene Beatrice, *d* of David and May Sloan, Belfast; three *s* one *d. Educ:* Prince Albert Coll., Saskatchewan; St Albans Sch.; London Univ. Attached Rothamsted Expl Stn for PhD (London) 1941. Royal Engineers, 1941–46 (despatches). Colonial Agric. Service, Coffee Research Stn, Kenya, 1946–52; Colonial Research Service, established Physics Div. at East African Agriculture and Forestry Research Org., Kenya, 1952–61; DSc London 1961; Dir, ARC of Rhodesia and Nyasaland, 1961–63; Dir, ARC of Central Africa (Rhodesia, Zambia and Malawi), 1963–67; Dir, East Malling Research Station, 1969–72; Chief Scientist (Dep. Sec.), MAFF, 1972–77. Member: Natural Environment Res. Council, 1971–77; ARC, 1973–77; ABRC, 1973–77; Chm., Sci. Panel, Commonwealth Develt Corp., 1978–91; Pres., Tropical Agric. Assoc., 1990–2002. Mem. Bd of Trustees, Royal Botanic Gdns, Kew, 1983–86; Trustee, Marie Stopes Internat., 1991–2002. FInstBiol; FRASE 1977. Hon. DSc Cranfield, 1977. Haile Selassie Prize for Research in Africa, 1966. *Publications:* Hydrological Effects of Land Use Changes in East Africa, 1962; Land Use and Water Resources, 1973; Policy and Practice in the

Management of Tropical Watersheds, 1989; Simama (biog.), 2000; papers in research jls. *Recreations:* swimming, sailing. *Address:* Peartrees, Nestor Court, Teston, Maidstone, Kent ME18 5AD. *T:* (01622) 813333.

Died 19 Dec. 2004.

PERRIN, John Henry; Under Secretary, Ministry of Agriculture, Fisheries and Food, 1968–76; *b* 14 Jan. 1916; *s* of Walter William Perrin, Faringdon and Sonning, Berks, and Amelia (*née* Honey), Oxford; *m* 1940, Doris Winifred Barrington-Brider; two *s. Educ:* Minchenden Sch.; London Univ. HM Customs and Excise, 1936–40; Lieut RNVR, Royal Navy, 1940–46; HM Customs and Excise, 1946–48; Ministry of Agriculture and Fisheries, then Ministry of Agriculture, Fisheries and Food, 1948–76: Principal Private Sec. to Minister (Lord Amory), 1955–57; Regional Controller, Eastern Region, 1957–68. Dir-Gen., British Agricl Export Council, 1976–77. Inspector, Public Inquiries, Depts of the Environment and Transport, 1978–84. *Clubs:* Naval, Civil Service, Royal Yachting; RNVR Yacht; Cambridge University Cricket.

Died 18 Jan. 2001.

PERRING, Franklyn Hugh, OBE 1988; writer, lecturer, botanist, and traveller; *b* 1 Aug. 1927; *s* of Frank Arthur and Avelyn Millicent Perring; *m* 1st, 1951, Yvonne Frances Maud Matthews (marr. diss. 1972); one *s*; 2nd, 1972, Margaret Dorothy Barrow; one *d. Educ:* Earls Colne Grammar Sch.; Queens' Coll., Cambridge (MA, PhD). FLS; FIBiol 1979. Botanical Society of British Isles Distribution Maps Scheme: Hd, 1954–59; Dir, 1959–64; Hd, Biological Records Centre, Monks Wood Experimental Station, 1964–79; Botanical Sec., Linnean Soc. of London, 1973–78; Gen. Sec., RSNC, 1979–87. Chm., Wildlife Travel Ltd, 1988–. Pres., Botanical Soc. of the British Isles, 1993–95. Hon. Fellow, UC, Northampton, 2000. Hon. DSc Leicester, 1989. *Publications:* (jtly) Atlas of the British Flora, 1962; (jtly) A Flora of Cambridgeshire, 1964; Critical Supplement to the Atlas of the British Flora, 1968; (ed) The Flora of a Changing Britain, 1970; (ed jtly) The British Oak, 1974; (jtly) English Names of Wild Flowers, 1974, 2nd edn 1986; (jtly) British Red Data Book of Vascular Plants, 1977, 2nd edn 1983; (ed jtly) Ecological Effects of Pesticides, 1977; RSNC Guide to British Wild Flowers, 1984; (jtly) Ecological Flora of the Shropshire Region, 1985; (ed jtly) Changing Attitudes to Nature Conservation, 1988; (jtly) The Macmillan Guide to British Wildflowers, 1989; (ed jtly) The Nature of Northamptonshire, 1989; (ed jtly) Tomorrow is Too Late, 1990; Britain's Conservation Heritage, 1991; (ed jtly) Insects, Plants and Set-aside, 1995; (jtly) Scottish Plants for Scottish Gardens, 1996; sci. papers in Jl of Ecology, Watsonia, etc. *Recreations:* opera-going, poetry reading, gardening. *Address:* 18 High Street, Chesterton, Cambridge CB4 1NG. *T:* (01223) 367306.

Died 11 Oct. 2003.

PERRY OF WALTON, Baron *cr* 1979 (Life Peer), of Walton, Bucks; **Walter Laing Macdonald Perry,** Kt 1974; OBE 1957; FRS 1985; FRSE 1960; Vice-Chancellor, The Open University, 1969–80, Fellow, since 1981; *b* 16 June 1921; *s* of Fletcher S. Perry and Flora M. Macdonald; *m* 1st, 1946, Anne Elizabeth Grant (marr. diss. 1971); three *s*; 2nd, 1971, Catherine Hilda Crawley; two *s* one *d. Educ:* Ayr Acad.; Dundee High Sch.; Univ. of St Andrews (MB, ChB 1943, MD 1948, DSc 1958). MRCP (Edinburgh), 1963; FRCPE 1967; FRCP 1978; Fellow, UCL, 1981–. Medical Officer: Colonial Medical Service (Nigeria), 1944–46; RAF, 1946–47; Staff mem., MRC, 1947–52; Dir, Dept of Biological Standards, Nat. Inst. for Medical Research, 1952–58; Prof. of Pharmacology, Univ. of Edinburgh, 1958–68, Vice-Principal, 1967–68. Mem., British Pharmacopœia Commn, 1952–68; Sec., British Pharmacol Soc., 1957–61. Chairman: Community Radio Milton Keynes, 1979–82; Living Tapes Ltd, 1980–; Videotel Marine Internat., 1985–98 (Pres., 1998–). Chairman: Research Defence Soc., 1979–82 (Pres., 1993–); Delegacy of Goldsmiths' Coll., 1981–84; Standing

Cttee on Continuing Educn, UGC and Nat. Adv. Body for Public Sector Higher Educn, 1985–89. Dep. Leader, SDP peers in House of Lords, 1981–83, 1988–89. Chancellor, Fairfax Univ., 1990–. Hon. DSc Bradford, 1974; Hon. LLD Dundee, 1975; Hon. DHL: Maryland, 1978; State Univ. of NY, 1982; DUniv: Athabasca, 1979; Stirling, 1980; Open, 1981; Hon. DLitt: Deakin Univ., Australia, 1981; Andhra Pradesh Open Univ., 1987; Hon. DEd Univ. of Victoria, 1992. Wellcome Gold Medal, 1994; Royal Medal, RSE, 2000. *Publications:* Open University, 1976; papers in Jl of Physiology, British Jl of Pharmacology and Chemo-therapy, etc. *Recreations:* making music and playing games. *Address:* The Open University, 10 Drumsheugh Gardens, Edinburgh EH3 7QJ. *Club:* Scottish Arts (Edinburgh).

Died 18 July 2003.

PERRY, (George) Edward, MBE 1999; Managing Director, Hyperion Records Ltd, since 1980; *b* 15 May 1931; *s* of William Walter Perry and Olive Mary Monica Perry (*née* Salt); *m* 1959, Doreen Audrey Davies (marr. diss. 1990); one *s* two *d. Educ:* Derby Central GS. Sales asst, then Buyer, subseq. asst to Manager, EMG Handmade Gramophones Ltd, 1949–56; Asst Sales Manager, Heliodor Record Co. (Deutsche Grammophon Ges.), 1956–57; NSW Distributor, Festival Records (Aust.), 1958–61; Dir, Saga Records, 1961–63 and 1973–77; Partner, Meridian Records, 1977–80. FRSA. Hon. ISM. *Recreations:* astronomy, gardening, lazing about. *Address:* The Coach House, 112 Hervey Road, Blackheath, SE3 8BX. *T:* (020) 8319 1544; *e-mail:* gep@debrett.net.

Died 9 Feb. 2003.

PERTH, 17th Earl of, *cr* 1605; **John David Drummond,** PC 1957; Baron Drummond of Cargill, 1488; Baron Maderty, 1609; Baron Drummond, 1686; Lord Drummond of Gilston, 1685; Lord Drummond of Rickertoun and Castlemaine, 1686; Viscount Strathallan, 1686; Hereditary Thane of Lennox, and Hereditary Steward of Menteith and Strathearn; Representative Peer for Scotland, 1952–63; First Crown Estate Commissioner, 1962–77; Chairman, Ditchley Foundation, 1963–66; *b* 13 May 1907; *o s* of 16th Earl of Perth, PC, GCMG, CB, and Hon. Angela Constable-Maxwell (*d* 1965), *y d* of 11th Baron Herries; *S* father, 1951; *m* 1934, Nancy Seymour (*d* 1996), *d* of Reginald Fincke, New York City; two *s. Educ:* Downside; Trinity Coll., Cambridge (BA 1928). Lieut, Intelligence Corps, 1940; seconded to War Cabinet Offices, 1942–43, Ministry of Production, 1944–45. Partner, Schroder's, 1945–56; Minister of State for Colonial Affairs, 1957–62 (resigned). Chm., Reviewing Cttee on Export of Works of Art, 1972–76. Member: Court of St Andrews Univ., 1967–86; Adv. Council, V&A Museum, 1971–72; Trustee, Nat. Library of Scotland, 1968–95. Hon. FRIBA 1978; Hon. FRIAS 1988; Hon. FSA 1994. Hon. LLD St Andrews, 1986. *Heir: s* Viscount Strathallan, *b* 7 July 1935. *Address:* Stobhall, by Perth PH2 6DR. *Died 25 Nov. 2002.*

PERUTZ, Max Ferdinand, OM 1988; CH 1975; CBE 1963; PhD; FRS 1954; Member, scientific staff, Medical Research Council Laboratory of Molecular Biology, since 1979 (Chairman, 1962–79); *b* 19 May 1914; *s* of Hugo and Adèle Perutz; *m* 1942, Gisela Peiser; one *s* one *d. Educ:* Theresianum, Vienna; Univ. of Vienna; Univ. of Cambridge (PhD 1940). Dir, MRC Unit for Molecular Biology, 1947–62. Reader, Davy Faraday Res. Lab., 1954–68, Fullerian Prof. of Physiology, 1973–79, Royal Instn. Chm., EMBO, 1963–69. Hon. FRSE 1976; Hon. FRCP 1993; Hon. Member American Academy of Arts and Sciences, 1963; Corresp. Member, Austrian Acad. of Sciences, 1963; Mem., Akademie Leopoldina, Halle, 1964; Foreign Member: American Philosophical Society, 1968; Royal Netherlands Acad., 1972; French Acad. of Sciences, 1976; Bavarian Acad. of Sciences, 1983; National Acad. of Sciences, Rome, 1983; Accademia dei Lincei, Rome, 1984; Acad. of Science of DDR, 1985; For. Associate, Nat. Acad. of Sciences, USA, 1970; Mem.,

Pontifical Acad. of Sciences, Rome, 1981. Hon. Fellow: Peterhouse, Cambridge, 1962; Darwin Coll., Cambridge, 1984. Hon. degrees: in philosophy: Vienna, 1965; Salzburg, 1972; Wales, 1995; in science: Edinburgh, 1965; East Anglia, 1967; Cambridge, 1981; York, 1990; Oxford, 1993; Paris, 1993; in medicine, Rome, 1988. Nobel Prize for Chemistry (jointly), 1962; Ehrenzeichen für Wissenschaft und Kunst (Austria), 1966; Royal Medal, 1971, Copley Medal, 1979, Royal Soc.; Actonian Prize, Royal Instn, 1984; Lewis Thomas Prize, Rockefeller Univ., NY, 1997. Pour le Mérite (FRG), 1988. *Publications:* Proteins and Nucleic Acids, Structure and Function, 1962; (jtly) Atlas of Haemoglobin and Myoglobin, 1981; Is Science Necessary?, 1988; Mechanisms of Co-operativity and Allosteric Control in Proteins, 1990; Protein Structures: new approaches to disease and therapy, 1992; Science Is No Quiet Life, 1997; I Wish I'd Made You Angry Earlier, 1998. *Address:* 42 Sedley Taylor Road, Cambridge CB2 2PN; Laboratory of Molecular Biology, Hills Road, Cambridge CB2 2QH.
Died 6 Feb. 2002.

PESTELL, Sir John Richard, KCVO 1969; an Adjudicator, Immigration Appeals, Harmondsworth, 1970–87; *b* 21 Nov. 1916; *s* of late Lt-Comdr Frank Lionel Pestell, RN, and Winifred Alice Pestell; *m* 1951, Betty Pestell (*née* Parish); three *d. Educ:* Portsmouth Northern Secondary Sch. Joined British South Africa Police, Southern Rhodesia, 1939; retired, 1965, with rank of Asst Commissioner. Served, 1944–47, Gen. List, MELF, in Cyrenaica Defence Force. Secretary/Controller to Governor of S Rhodesia, Rt Hon. Sir H. V. Gibbs, 1965–69. *Recreation:* walking. *Address:* Batch Cottage, North Road, Charlton Horethorne, near Sherborne, Som DT9 4NS. *Died 5 July 2005.*

PETERS, Prof. George Henry; Research Professor in Agricultural Economics, International Development Centre, Queen Elizabeth House, University of Oxford, 1986–2001; Fellow, Wolfson College, Oxford, 1980–2001, then Emeritus (Vicegerent, 1991–93); *b* 2 Sept. 1934; *s* of William and Mary Peters; *m* 1959, Judith Mary Griffiths; two *d. Educ:* Mold Grammar Sch., Flintshire; University Coll. of Wales, Aberystwyth (BSc, MSc); King's Coll., Cambridge. National Service, Educn Br., RAF, 1957–59. Inst. for Res. in Agricl Econs, Univ. of Oxford, 1959–67; University of Liverpool: Lectr in Econs, 1967–69; Sen. Lectr, 1969–70; Brunner Prof. of Economic Science, 1970–79; Hd of Dept of Econs and Commerce, 1976–79; Dir, Inst. of Agricl Econs, Univ. of Oxford, 1980–86. Pres., Agricl Econs Soc., 1991–92. Ed., Procs of Internat. Assoc. of Agricl Economists, 1991–. *Publications:* Cost Benefit Analysis and Public Expenditure (IEA Eaton Paper 8), 1966, 3rd edn 1973; Private and Public Finance, 1971, 2nd edn 1975; ESRC/RSS Reviews of UK Statistical Sources, vol. 23, Agriculture, 1988; (ed with B. F. Stanton) Sustainable Agricultural Development: the role of international co-operation, 1992; (ed) Agricultural Economics, 1995; (ed with D. D. Hedley) Agricultural Competitiveness: market forces and policy choice, 1995; (ed jtly) Economics of Agro-Chemicals, 1996; (ed with J. von Braun) Food Security, Diversification and Resource Management: refocusing the rôle of agriculture, 1999; (ed with P. Pingali) Tomorrow's Agriculture: incentives, institutions, infrastructure and innovations, 2001; articles in Jl of Agricl Econs, Oxford Agrarian Studies, etc. *Recreations:* all sport, increasingly as a spectator. *Address:* Gable End Cottage, 33 The Moors, Kidlington, Oxford OX5 2AH. *T:* (01865) 372232.
Died 4 Nov. 2001.

PETERSEN, Hon. Sir Johannes B.; *see* Bjelke-Petersen.

PETERSON, Rt Rev. Leslie Ernest; Bishop of Algoma, 1983–94; *b* 4 Nov. 1928; *s* of late Ernest Victor Peterson and of Dorothy Blanche Peterson (*née* Marsh); *m* 1953, Yvonne Hazel Lawton; two *s* three *d. Educ:* Univ. of Western Ontario (BA 1952); Huron College (LTh 1954; DD (*jd*) 1984); Teachers' Coll., North Bay, Ont., 1970.

Deacon 1954, priest 1955; Incumbent of All Saints', Coniston, Ont., 1954–59; St Peter's Elliot Lake, 1959–63; Rector, Christ Church, North Bay, 1963–78; Teacher, Marshall Park Elem. School, 1970–78; Rector, Trinity Church, Parry Sound, 1978–83; Coadjutor Bishop, June-Sept. 1983. STD (*hc*) Thorneloe, 1992. *Recreations:* gardening, woodworking. *Address:* 615 Santa Monica Road, London, ON N6H 3W2, Canada.
Died 25 July 2002.

PETHICK, Brig. Geoffrey Loveston, CBE 1960; DSO 1944; *b* 25 Nov. 1907; *s* of late Captain E. E. Pethick, RN and May (*née* Brook); *m* 1st, 1939, Nancy Veronica Ferrand (*d* 1980); one *d*; 2nd, 1981, Mrs Paula Usborne (*d* 1996); 3rd, 1997, Mrs Neville Carr Selway. *Educ:* Newton Coll. Commissioned, Royal Artillery, 1927; RHA 1934; served War of 1939–45: Staff Coll., Camberley, 1940; CO, Field Regt, 1942; Far East, 1945; jssc 1946; Dep. Dir, WO, 1948; idc, 1950; Commander: 3 Army Gp, RA, 1951; RA 3 Div. 1953; Army Council Staff, 1957; retired, 1960. Dir, British Paper Makers' Association, 1960–74. *Address:* Little Croft, Fireball Hill, Sunningdale, Berks SL5 9PJ. *T:* (01344) 622018. *Died 15 Feb. 2002.*

PETRIE, Prof. James Colquhoun, CBE 1996; FRCP, FRCPE, FRCPI, FFPM, FMedSci; FRSE; Professor of Clinical Pharmacology, since 1985, and Head, Department of Medicine and Therapeutics, since 1994, University of Aberdeen; *b* 18 Sept. 1941; *s* of late Dr James B. Petrie and Dr Cairine R. Petrie; *m* 1964, Dr Xanthe Forbes; two *s* two *d. Educ:* Robert Gordon's Coll., Aberdeen; Aberdeen Univ. (MB ChB). FRCP 1980; FRCPE 1983; FFPM 1989; FRCPI 1996. University of Aberdeen: Sen. Lectr, 1971–81; Reader, 1981–85. Hon. Consultant Physician, Aberdeen Royal Hosps, 1971–. Chm., Lecht Ski Co., Strathdon, 1977–. Pres., RCPE, 1997–2001 (Assessor, 1992–98); Chm., Scottish Royal Colls Intercollegiate Guidelines Network, 1993–. Founder FMedSci 1998; FRSE 2000. *Publications:* (ed jtly) Clinical Effects of Interaction between Drugs, 1975 (trans. Japanese); (ed jtly) The Problem Orientated Medical Record: its use in hospitals, general practice and medical education, 1979 (trans. Italian); (ed) Clinically Important Adverse Drug Reactions, vol. 1, 1980, vol. 2, 1984, vol. 3, 1985; (jtly) Diagnostic Picture Tests in Clinical Medicine, 4 vols, 1984 (trans. Japanese, Greek and French); (ed jtly) Textbook of Medical Treatment, 15th edn 1987; (jtly) Essential Clinical Signs, 1990; (jtly) Illustrated Signs in Clinical Medicine, 1997. *Recreations:* ski-ing, golf. *Address:* 126 Desswood Place, Aberdeen AB15 4DQ. *Club:* Royal Aberdeen Golf. *Died 31 Aug. 2001.*

PFLEGER, Martin Charles; Deputy Auditor General, National Audit Office, 2000–03; *b* 5 May 1948; *m*; two *s* one *d*; *m* 1995, Amanda Jane Dolphin. National Audit Office: Dir, IT Audit, 1986; Dir, Corporate Policy and Finance, 1988; Asst Auditor Gen., 1993. Vis. Prof., Nottingham Trent Univ., 2001–. CIPFA; MInstD 1991. *Publications:* articles on IT and business management in the public sector. *Recreations:* golf, hill walking, bridge.
Died 16 July 2004.

PHELPS, Maj.-Gen. Leonard Thomas Herbert, CB 1973; OBE 1963; *b* 9 Sept. 1917; *s* of Abijah and Jane Phelps; *m* 1st, 1945, Jean Irene Dixon (*d* 1996); one *s* one *d*; 2nd, 2000, Sybil Anne, *widow* of Lt-Col G. L. Ritchie, RAMC. Served War, Hong Kong, 1940–41; India/Burma, 1941–47. Student, Staff Coll., Quetta, 1946; SO2, WO, 1948–51; DAQMG, HQ Land Forces Hong Kong, 1951–53; Second in Command, 4th Trng Bn, RAOC, 1955–57; War Office: DAAG, 1957–59; ADOS, 1961–63; AA & QMG Singapore Mil. Forces, 1963; Chief of Staff and Dep Comdr, 4th Malaysian Inf. Bde, 1964; ADOS, WO, 1965–67; Chief Inspector, Land Service Ammunition, 1967–70; Comdr, Base Organisation, RAOC, 1970; Dir, Ordnance Services, MoD (Army), 1971–73; retired 1973; Col Comdt, RAOC, 1976–78. Man. Dir, The Warrior Gp, 1975–78; Director: Leon Davis & Co., 1975–82; Debenhams Business Systems Ltd,

1982–84. CCMI (CBIM 1980; FBIM 1973). Parchment Award for life saving, Royal Humane Soc., 1936. *Publication:* A History of the Royal Army Ordnance Corps 1945–1982, 1991. *Died 6 Dec. 2003.*

PHILIPS, Prof. Sir Cyril (Henry), Kt 1974; Professor of Oriental History, University of London, 1946–80; Director, School of Oriental and African Studies, London, 1957–76; Vice-Chancellor, University of London, 1972–76 (Deputy Vice-Chancellor, 1969–70); *b* Worcester, 27 Dec. 1912; *s* of William Henry Philips; *m* 1st, 1939, Dorcas (*d* 1974), *d* of John Rose, Wallasey; one *d* (one *s* decd); 2nd, 1975, Joan Rosemary, *d* of William George Marshall. *Educ:* Rock Ferry High School; Univs of Liverpool (MA) and London (PhD). Bishop Chavasse Prizeman; Gladstone Memorial Fellow. Frewen Lord Prizeman (Royal Empire Soc.), 1935; Alexander Prizeman (Royal Hist. Soc.), 1938; Sir Percy Sykes Meml Medal (RSAA), 1976; Asst Lectr, Sch. of Oriental Studies, 1936. Served in Suffolk Infantry, Army Education Corps, 1940–43; Col Commandant, Army School of Education, 1945. Chief Instructor, Dept of Training, HM Treasury, 1945–46. Colonial Office Mission on Community Development, Africa, 1947. Lectures: Montague Burton, Univ. of Leeds, 1966; Creighton, Univ. of London, 1972; James Smart, on Police, 1979; Home Office Bicentenary, 1982; Police, Univ. of Bristol, 1982; Dawtry Meml, Univ. of Leeds, 1983. Chairman: UGC Cttee on Oriental, African and Slavonic Studies, 1965–70; UGC Cttee on Latin American Studies, 1966–70; India Cttee of Inter-University Council and British Council, 1972–; Royal Commn on Criminal Procedure, 1978–80; Police Complaints Bd, 1980–85; Council on Tribunals, 1986–89; Inst. of Archaeology, 1979–85, Inst. of Latin American Studies, 1978–87 (Univ. of London); Member: Social Development Cttee, Colonial Office, 1947–55; Colonial Office Research Council, 1955–57; University Grants Cttee, 1960–69; Commonwealth Education Commn, 1961–70; Postgraduate Awards Cttee (Min. of Education), 1962–64; Modern Languages Cttee (Min. of Education), 1964–67; Inter-Univ. Council, 1967–77; Court, London Univ., 1970–76; Governor: Chinese Univ. of Hong Kong, 1965–75; Mill Hill Sch., 1980–91 (Chm., 1982); Governor and Trustee, Richmond Coll., 1979–84. Pres., Royal Asiatic Soc., 1979–82, 1985–88. Hon. Fellow, Asiatic Soc., Bengal, 1995. Hon. DLitt: Warwick, 1967; Bristol, 1983; Sri Lanka, 1986; Hon. LLD Hong Kong, 1971. India Tagore Medal, 1968; Bombay Freedom Medal, 1977. *Publications:* The East India Company, 1940 (2nd edn 1961); India, 1949; Handbook of Oriental History, 1951 (2nd edn 1962); Correspondence of David Scott, 1951; Historians of India, Pakistan and Ceylon, 1961; The Evolution of India and Pakistan, 1962; Politics and Society in India, 1963; Fort William-India House Correspondence, 1964; History of the School of Oriental and African Studies, 1917–67, 1967; The Partition of India, 1970; The Correspondence of Lord William Bentinck, Governor General of India 1828–35, 1977; Beyond the Ivory Tower, 1995. *Address:* School of Oriental and African Studies, Malet Street, WC1E 7HP. *T:* (020) 7637 2388. *Club:* Athenæum. *Died 29 Dec. 2005.*

PHILIPSON, (John) Trevor (Graham); QC 1989; *b* 3 March 1948; *s* of William Arnold Philipson and Rosalind Philipson; *m* 1974, Victoria Caroline Haskard (marr. diss. 1983). *Educ:* Royal Grammar Sch., Newcastle upon Tyne; Wadham Coll., Oxford (BA Jurisprudence 1970; BCL 1st cl. 1971). Called to the Bar, Middle Temple, 1972, Sen. Harmsworth Schol.; Bencher, 1997. Dir, Bar Mutual Insurance Fund Ltd. Mem. Develt Bd, LAMDA. *Recreations:* walking, gardening, travel. *Address:* Fountain Court, Temple, EC4Y 9DH. *T:* (020) 7583 3335; 17 Gilston Road, SW10 9SJ. *Clubs:* Savile, Royal Automobile. *Died 17 April 2001.*

PHILIPSON, Trevor; *see* Philipson, J. T. G.

PHILIPSON-STOW, Sir Christopher, 5th Bt *cr* 1907; DFC 1944; retired; *b* 13 Sept. 1920; *s* of Henry Matthew Philipson-Stow (*d* 1953) (3rd *s* of 1st Bt) and Elizabeth Willes (*d* 1979), *d* of Sir Thomas Willes Chitty, 1st Bt; *S* cousin, 1982; *m* 1952, Elizabeth Nairn (*d* 1999), *d* of late James Dixon Trees and *widow* of Major F. G. McLaren, 48th Highlanders of Canada; two *s*. *Educ:* Winchester. *Heir: er s* Robert Matthew Philipson-Stow, *b* 29 Aug. 1953. *Address:* 26 Cambridge Street, Penetanguishene, ON L9M 1E6, Canada. *Died 18 Aug. 2005.*

PHILLIMORE, John Gore, CMG 1946; a Managing Director of Baring Brothers & Co. Ltd, 1949–72; *b* 16 April 1908; 2nd *s* of late Adm. Sir Richard Phillimore, GCB, KCMG, MVO and Lady (Violet) Phillimore, Shedfield, Hants; *m* 1951, Jill, *d* of late Captain Mason Scott, Royal Navy retd, Buckland Manor, Broadway, Worcs, and of Mrs Irene Florence, 2nd *d* of 1st Baron Mottistone, CB, CMG, DSO, TD, PC; two *s* two *d*. *Educ:* Winchester College; Christ Church, Oxford. Partner of Roberts, Meynell & Co., Buenos Aires, 1936–48; Representative of HM Treasury and Bank of England in South America, 1940–45. Prime Warden, Fishmongers' Co., 1974–75. High Sheriff of Kent, 1975; DL Kent, 1979–84. Condor de los Andes (Bolivia), 1979; Commander, Orden de Mayo (Argentina), 1961. *Address:* Brooklyn House, Kingsclere, near Newbury, Berks RG20 5QY. *T:* (01635) 298321. *Club:* White's. *Died 22 Sept. 2001.*

PHILLIPS, Edward Thomas John, (Jack), CBE 1985; Controller, English Language and Literature Division, British Council, 1985–89; Consultant, British Executive Service Overseas, 1990–2000; *b* 5 Feb. 1930; *s* of late Edward Emery Kent Phillips and of Margaret Elsie Phillips; *m* 1952, Sheila May (*née* Abbott); two *s* two *d*. *Educ:* Exmouth Grammar Sch., University Coll. London; Inst. of Education, London; School of Oriental and African Studies London; BA Hons, PGCE, and Dip. in linguistics, London Univ. RAF, 1948–49. HMOCS, Educn Officer, Nigeria, 1953–62; British Council: Head, Cultural and Educn Unit, Overseas Students' Dept, 1962–65; English Lang. Officer, Enugu, Nigeria, 1966–67; Sen. Lectr, Coll. of Educn, Lagos Univ., Nigeria, 1967–70; English Lang. Teaching Advr, Min. of Educn, Cyprus, 1970–72; Chief Inspector, English Teaching Div., London, 1972–75; Rep., Bangladesh, Dacca, 1975–77; Dir, Personnel Dept and Dep. Controller Personnel Staff Recruitment Div., 1977–80; Rep, Malaysia, 1980–85. Dir, Project Mala (India), 1992–. Member: British-Malaysia Soc.; Britain-Nigeria Assoc. *Publications:* (ed jtly) Organised English, Books I and II, 1973; contribs to English Language Teaching Jl. *Recreations:* music, theatre, tennis, golf, swimming. *Address:* 1 Bredune, off Church Road, Kenley, Surrey CR8 5DU. *T:* (020) 8660 1929. *Died 12 Oct. 2005.*

PHILLIPS, Sir Henry (Ellis Isidore), Kt 1964; CMG 1960; MBE 1946; Founder Member, 1970, and Hon. Vice-Chairman, since 1996, SIFIDA Investment Co. (SA); director of other companies; *b* 30 Aug. 1914; *s* of late Harry J. Phillips, MBE; *m* 1st, 1941, Vivien Hyamson (marr. diss., 1965); two *s* one *d*; 2nd, 1966, Philippa Cohen. *Educ:* Haberdashers' Sch., Hampstead; University College London (BA 1936; MA 1939; Fellow 1991). FRHistS 1965. Inst. of Historical Research, 1936–39. Commissioned in Beds and Herts Regt, 1939; served War of 1939–45, with 5th Bn, becoming Adjutant; POW, Singapore, 1942. Joined Colonial Administrative Service and appointed to Nyasaland, 1946 (until retirement in 1965); Development Secretary, 1952; seconded to Federal Treasury of Rhodesia and Nyasaland, 1953–57, Dep. Sec., 1956; Financial Sec., Nyasaland Govt, 1957–64, and Minister of Finance, 1961–64. Man. Dir, Standard Bank Finance and Development Corp., 1966–72. Dir, Nat. Bank of Malaŵi, 1983–88; Chm., Ashley Industrial Trust plc, 1986–88. Mem., Civil Aviation Authority, 1975–80; Hon. Consultant, Air Transport Users Council, 1980–.

Hon. Pres., Stonham Housing Assoc., 1995– (Founder Mem.; Hon. Treas., 1984; Vice Chm., 1984–92); Hon. Treasurer: Stonham Meml Trust, 1977– (Vice-Chm., then Chm., 1995–99); SOS Sahel Internat. (UK), 1987–. Mem. Finance Cttee, UCL, 1985–98; Hon. Vice-Pres., Friends of University Coll., 1992–. *Publication:* From Obscurity to Bright Dawn: how Nyasaland became Malawi—an insider's account, 1998. *Address:* 34 Ross Court, Putney Hill, SW15 3NZ. *T:* (020) 8789 1404. *Club:* MCC.
Died 21 Dec. 2004.

PHILLIPS, Sir Horace (Hyman), KCMG 1973 (CMG 1963); HM Diplomatic Service, retired; *b* 31 May 1917; *s* of Samuel Phillips and Polly Yaffie; *m* 1944, Idina Doreen Morgan; one *s* one *d*. *Educ:* Hillhead High Sch., Glasgow. Joined Board of Inland Revenue, 1935. Served War of 1939–45, Dorsetshire and 1st Punjab Regts, 1940–47. Transf. to FO, Oct. 1947; Acting Vice-Consul, Shiraz, Nov. 1947; Vice-Consul, Bushire, 1948; Consul, Shiraz, 1949; 1st Secretary, Kabul, Oct. 1949; Foreign Office, 1951; 1st Secretary, and Consul, Jedda, 1953; Counsellor, 1956; seconded to Colonial Office, Dec. 1956, as Protectorate Secretary, Aden, until Aug. 1960; Counsellor, British Embassy, Tehran, Oct. 1960; Deputy Political Resident in the Persian Gulf, at Bahrain, 1964–66; Ambassador to Indonesia, 1966–68; High Comr in Tanzania, 1968–72; Ambassador to Turkey, 1973–77. Resident Rep., Taylor Woodrow Internat. Ltd: Iran, 1978–79; Hong Kong, 1979–84; Bahrain, 1984–85; China (at Peking), 1985–87. Lecturer in International Relations: Bilkent Univ., Ankara, 1988–92, 1996–97; Erciyes Univ., Kayseri, Turkey, 1993–94. Vice-Pres., Anglo-Turkish Soc., London, 1985–. Hon. LLD Glasgow, 1977. Order of the Taj (Iran), 1961. *Publications:* Envoy Extraordinary, 1995; İhsan Doğramacı, a remarkable Turk, 1997; articles of topical political and diplomatic interest in Asian Wall Street Jl, 1980–86. *Recreations:* languages, long-distance car driving. *Address:* 34a Sheridan Road, Merton Park, SW19 3HP. *T:* (020) 8542 3836. *Club:* Travellers.
Died 19 March 2004.

PHILLIPS, Hugh, DL; FRCS; Emeritus Consultant Trauma and Orthopaedic Surgeon, Norfolk and Norwich University Hospital NHS Trust; President, Royal College of Surgeons of England, since 2004; *b* 19 March 1940; *s* of Morgan William and Elizabeth Phillips; *m* 1966, Patricia Ann Cates Kennard; three *d*. *Educ:* Roan Sch. for Boys, Greenwich; St Bartholomew's Hosp. Med. Coll., Univ. of London (BSc Hons, MB). FRCS 1970. Consultant Trauma and Orthopaedic Surgeon, Norfolk and Norwich Hosp., 1975. Chm., Specialist Adv. Cttee in Trauma and Orthopaedics, Royal Colls of Surgs, 1995–97. President: Orthopaedic Section, RSocMed., 1992; British Orthopaedic Assoc., 1999–2000. Royal College of Surgeons of England: Mem. Council, 1995–2004; Chm., Trauma Cttee, 1996–; Dir, Professional Standards, 2002–04; Vice-Pres., 2003–04; Founder, first Sec. and Pres., British Hip Soc., 1999–. DL Norfolk, 1996. *Publications:* contrib. papers on hip and knee disease. *Recreations:* family, avoidance of all clubs. *Address:* Ashwellthorpe Grange, Norwich, Norfolk NR16 1ET. *T:* (01508) 489713, *Fax:* (01508) 489644; *e-mail:* hphillip78@aol.com. *Died 24 June 2005.*

PHILLIPS, Jack; see Phillips, E. T. J.

PHILLIPS, John, RIBA; architect in private practice, since 1955; *b* 25 Nov. 1926; *s* of John Tudor Phillips and Bessie Maud Phillips; *m* 1955, Eileen Margaret Fryer. *Educ:* Christ's Coll., Finchley; Northern Polytechnic, Holloway. ARIBA 1954. Studied under Romilly B. Craze, Architect, 1948–52. Surveyor to the Fabric: Truro Cathedral, 1961 (Consultant Architect, 1979–); Westminster Cathedral, 1976–97; RIBA 1979–96; Consultant Architect to Brisbane Cathedral, 1988–. Pres., Ecclesiastical Architects' and Surveyors' Assoc., 1982. KSS 1997. *Recreations:* looking at churches, choral singing. *Address:* 8 Friary Way, North Finchley, N12 9PH. *T:* (020) 8445 3414.
Died 24 Dec. 2004.

PHILLIPS, Prof. Neville Crompton, CMG 1973; Vice-Chancellor and Rector, University of Canterbury, Christchurch, New Zealand 1966–77, retired; *b* 7 March 1916; 2nd *s* of Samuel and Clara Phillips, Christchurch, NZ; *m* 1940, Pauline Beatrice, 3rd *d* of Selby and Dorothy Palmer, Te Aratipi, Havelock North, NZ; one *s* two *d*. *Educ:* Dannevirke High Sch.; Palmerston North Boys' High Sch.; Canterbury University College (BA NZ, 1936, MA NZ, 1938); Merton Coll., Oxford. NZ University Post-Grad. Schol. in Arts, Arnold Atkinson Prizeman, 1938; read PPE at Oxford, 1938–39. Served War, RA (Gunner, subseq. Major), 1939–46; service in Tunisia and Italy (despatches). Journalist, Sun and Press, Christchurch, NZ, 1932–38. Lecturer in History and Political Science, Canterbury University College, 1946–47, Senior Lecturer, 1948; Prof. of History and Political Science, Canterbury UC, then Univ. of Canterbury, 1949–62; Prof. of History, Univ. of Canterbury, 1962–66; Emeritus Prof., 1966; presented with Festschrift, 1984. Chm., Canterbury Centennial Provincial Historical Cttee, 1948–66; 1st Pres., Canterbury Historical Assoc., 1953; Editorial Adviser, NZ War Histories, 1957–67; US Dept of State Leader Grantee, 1966; Member: Council, Canterbury Manufacturers' Assoc., 1967–77; Christchurch Teachers' Coll. Council, 1968–76; NZ Vice-Chancellors' Cttee, 1966–77 (Chm., 1973–74); Council, Assoc. of Commonwealth Univs, 1973–74; NZ Council Educational Research, 1973–77. Chm. Mgt Cttee, Canterbury Archaeol Trust, Kent, 1980–83. Hon. LittD Cantuar, 1977. Silver Jubilee Medal, 1977. Settled in Canterbury, Kent, 1978. *Publications:* Italy, vol. 1 (The Sangro to Cassino), 1957 (New Zealand War Histories); Yorkshire and English National Politics, 1783–84, 1961; The Role of the University in Professional Education, 1970; (ed) A History of the University of Canterbury, 1873–1973, 1973; articles, mainly on eighteenth-century English politics, in English and NZ jls. *Recreations:* walking, watching cricket, things Italian. *Address:* Tyle House, Hackington Road, Tyler Hill, Canterbury, Kent CT2 9NF. *T:* (01227) 471708.
Died 29 June 2001.

PHIPPS, Rt Rev. Simon Wilton, MC 1945; Assistant Bishop, Dioceses of Chichester and Southwark, since 1986; *b* 6 July 1921; *s* of late Captain William Duncan Phipps, CVO, RN, and Pamela May Ross; *m* 1973, Mary (*d* 2000), *d* of Sir (Charles) Eric Palmer and *widow* of Rev. Dr James Welch. *Educ:* Eton; Trinity Coll., Cambridge (BA (Hist.) 1948; MA 1953; Pres., Footlights Club, 1949); Westcott House, Cambridge. Joined Coldstream Guards, 1940; commnd, 1941; Capt., 1944; ADC to GOC-in-C Northern Comd India, 1945; Mil. Asst to Adjt Gen. to the Forces, War Office, 1946; Major, 1946. Ordained deacon, 1950, priest, 1951; Asst Curate, Huddersfield Parish Church, 1950; Chaplain, Trinity Coll., Cambridge, 1953; Industrial Chaplain, Coventry Dio., 1958; Hon. Canon, Coventry Cath., 1965; Bishop Suffragan of Horsham, 1968–74; Bishop of Lincoln, 1974–86. Chm. Council, William Temple Foundation, 1985–89; Pres., Assoc. of Pastoral Care and Counselling, 1985–94; Mem., Home Sec.'s Cttee of Inquiry into Liquor Licensing Laws, 1971–72; formerly Mem. Council, Industrial Soc. *Publication:* God on Monday, 1966. *Recreations:* gardening, painting, cooking. *Address:* Sarsens, Shipley, W Sussex RH13 8PX. *T:* (01403) 741354. *Club:* Army and Navy.
Died 29 Jan. 2001.

PICKARD, Prof. Huia Masters, FDSRCS; Professor of Conservative Dentistry, University of London, 1963–74, then Emeritus; *b* 25 March 1909; *o s* of late Ernest Pickard and Sophie Elizabeth Robins; *m* 1945, Daphne Evelyn (*d* 1995), *d* of Hugh F. Marriott; two *d*. *Educ:* Latymer Sch.; Royal Dental Hosp. of London Sch. of Dental Surgery; Charing Cross Hosp. MRCS, LRCP, FDSRCS. Private dental practice, pre-1940; EMS, East Grinstead, 1939. Served War, in RAMC, 8th Army (despatches), 1940–45. Dental practice and teaching, 1945; Dir, Dept of Conservative Dentistry, Royal Dental Hosp., and Consultant, 1955; Reader, London Univ., 1957–63; Dir,

Dept of Restorative Dentistry, Royal Dental Hosp., 1965–74. Mem. Bd of Governors, St George's Hosp., 1969; First Pres., British Soc. for Restorative Dentistry, 1969; Pres., Odontological Section, Royal Soc. Med., 1971. Examr for Univs of London, Newcastle, Glasgow, Birmingham, Wales; also RCS. Governor, Latymer Sch., Edmonton, 1968–84 (Chm., 1980–83). Tomes Medal, BDA, 1983. *Publications:* Manual of Operative Dentistry, 1961, 8th edn 1996; contribs: Dental Record, Brit. Dental Jl, Internat. Dental Jl. *Address:* 12 Heathfield Close, Midhurst, W Sussex GU29 9PS. *T:* (01730) 812869.
Died 17 July 2002.

PICKERING, Sir Edward (Davies), Kt 1977; Executive Vice-Chairman, Times Newspapers Ltd, since 1982; Chairman, The Times Supplements Ltd, since 1989; *b* 4 May 1912; 3rd *s* of George and Louie Pickering; *m* 1st, 1936, Margaret Soutter (marr. diss., 1947); one *d*; 2nd, 1955, Rosemary Whitton; two *s* one *d*. *Educ:* Middlesbrough High Sch. Chief Sub-Editor Daily Mail, 1939. Served Royal Artillery 1940–44; Staff of Supreme Headquarters Allied Expeditionary Force, 1944–45. Managing Editor: Daily Mail, 1947–49; Daily Express, 1951–57; Editor, Daily Express, 1957–62; Dir, Beaverbrook Newspapers, 1956–64; Editorial Dir, 1964–68, Chm., 1968–70, The Daily Mirror Newspapers Ltd; Chairman: International Publishing Corporation Newspaper Div., 1968–70; IPC Magazines, 1970–74; Mirror Group Newspapers, 1975–77; Director: Scottish Daily Record and Sunday Mail Ltd, 1966–69; IPC, 1966–75; Times Newspapers Holdings Ltd, 1981–; William Collins Sons & Co. Ltd, 1981–89; Harper Collins Publishers Ltd, 1989–. Member: Press Council, 1964–69, 1970–82 (Vice-Chm., 1976–82); Press Complaints Commn, 1991–94 (Consultant, 1994–). Treasurer, Fédération Internationale de la Presse Periodique, 1971–75; Chm. Council, CPU, 1977–86. Chm., William Tyndale Quincentenary Appeal, 1991–94; Patron, William Tyndale Soc., 1999–. Hon. Freeman, Stationers' and Newspaper Makers' Co., 1985. Master, Guild of St Bride, 1981–97. Astor Award for distinguished service to Commonwealth Press, 1986. Hon. DLitt City, 1986. *Club:* Garrick. *Died 8 Aug. 2003.*

PICKFORD, Prof. (Lillian) Mary, DSc; FRS 1966; Professor, Department of Physiology, University of Edinburgh, 1966–72 (Reader in Physiology, 1952–66); retired 1972, then Emeritus Professor; *b* 14 Aug. 1902; *d* of Herbert Arthur Pickford and Lillian Alice Minnie Wintle. *Educ:* Wycombe Abbey Sch.; Bedford and University Colls, Univ. of London (BSc 1st cl., Gen. 1924; BSc 2nd cl., Physiology Special 1925; MSc Physiology 1926; DSc 1951). MRCS, LRCP 1933; FRCPE 1977. House Physician and Casualty Officer, Stafford Gen. Infirmary, 1935; Jun. Beit Memorial Research Fellow, 1936–39; Lectr, Dept of Physiology, Univ. of Edinburgh, 1939; Special Prof. of Endocrinology, Nottingham Univ., 1973–83. Fellow, UCL, 1968. FRSE 1954. Hon. DSc Heriot-Watt, 1991. *Publications:* The Central Role of Hormones, 1969; papers in Jl Physiology, British Jl Pharmacology, Jl Endocrinology. *Recreations:* walking, travel, painting. *Address:* Winton House, Nether Wallop, Stockbridge, Hants SO20 8HE. *Died 14 Aug. 2002.*

PICKFORD, Prof. Mary; *see* Pickford, Prof. L. M.

PIERCY, Hon. Joanna Elizabeth; *see* Turner, Hon. J. E.

PIERS, Rear-Adm. Desmond William, DSC 1943; CM 1982; CD; RCN, retd; Agent General of Nova Scotia in the United Kingdom and Europe, 1977–79; *b* 12 June 1913; *s* of William Harrington Piers and Florence Maud Piers (*née* O'Donnell), MD; *m* 1941, Janet, *d* of Dr and Mrs Murray Macneill, Halifax, NS; one step *d*. *Educ:* Halifax County Acad.; RMC of Canada; RN Staff Coll.; Nat. Defence Coll. of Canada. Joined RCN as cadet, 1932; CO, HMC Destroyer Restigouche, and Sen. Officer, Fourth Canadian Escort Gp on N Atlantic convoy routes, 1941–43 (DSC); CO, HMC Destroyer Algonquin with

Brit. Home Fleet, Scapa Flow, and participated in invasion of Normandy and convoys to N Russia, 1944–45, Comdr 1945; Exec. Officer, HMC Aircraft Carrier Magnificent (Comdr), 1947–48; Dir, Naval Plans and Ops, Naval Headquarters, Ottawa (Captain), 1949–50; Asst COS (Personnel and Admin.) to SACLANT, 1952–53; CO, HMC Cruiser Quebec, 1955–56; Sen. Canadian Offr Afloat (Atlantic), 1956–57; Comdt, RMC Canada, and Hon. ADC to the Governor General (Cdre), 1957–60; Asst Chief of Naval Staff (Plans), Naval HQ, 1960–62; Chm., Can. Def. Liaison Staff, Washington DC, and Can. Rep. on NATO Mil. Cttee (Rear-Adm.), 1962–66; retd 1967. Chm., NS Div. Can. Corps of Commissionaires, 1988–91. Hon. Life Mem., Nat. Trust for Scotland, 1984. Hon. DScMil, RMC of Canada, 1978. Freeman of City of London, 1978; KCLJ 1989. *Recreations:* golf, tennis, figure skating, photography. *Address:* The Quarter Deck, Chester, NS B0J 1J0, Canada. *T:* (902) 2754462. *Clubs:* Halifax (Halifax); Halifax Golf and Country, Chester Golf, Chester Tennis, Chester Curling (Nova Scotia).
Died 1 Nov. 2005.

PIKE, Baroness *cr* 1974 (Life Peer), of Melton, Leics; **Irene Mervyn Parnicott Pike,** DBE 1981; Chairman, Broadcasting Complaints Commission, 1981–85; *b* 16 Sept. 1918; *d* of I. S. Pike, company director, Okehampton, Devonshire. *Educ:* Hunmanby Hall; Reading Univ. (BA Hons (Econs and Psychol.) 1941. Served WAAF, 1941–46. Mem., WRCC, 1955–57. Contested (C): Pontefract, 1951; Leek, Staffordshire, 1955. MP (C) Melton, Leics, Dec. 1956–Feb. 1974; Assistant Postmaster-General, 1959–63; Joint Parliamentary Under-Secretary of State, Home Office, 1963–64. Mem., Robens Cttee on Safety and Health of People at their Place of Work, 1970–72. Director: Watts, Blake, Bearne & Co. Ltd; Dunderdale Investments. Chairman: IBA Gen. Adv. Council, 1974–79; WRVS, 1974–81. *Recreations:* gardening, walking. *Address:* Queen's House, Kelso, Roxburgh TD5 7NS.
Died 11 Jan. 2004.

PILKINGTON, Dr Roger Windle; author; *b* 17 Jan. 1915; 3rd *s* of Richard Austin Pilkington and Hon. Hope (*née* Cozens-Hardy); *m* 1st, 1937, Theodora Miriam Jaboor (marr. diss 1973); one *d* (one *s* decd); 2nd, 1973, Fru Ingrid Geijer (*d* 2002), Stockholm. *Educ:* Rugby; Freiburg, Germany; Magdalene Coll., Cambridge (BA 1937, PhD 1941). Research, genetics, 1937. Chairman: London Missionary Soc., 1962; Trustees, Homerton Coll., Cambridge, 1962; Govs, Hall Sch., 1962. Jt author, Sex and Morality Report, Brit. Council of Churches, 1966. Vice-Pres., River Thames Soc., 1967; Master, Glass Sellers' Co., 1967. *Publications:* Males and Females, 1948; Stringer's Folly, Biology, Man and God, Sons and Daughters, 1951; How Your Life Began, 1953; Revelation Through Science, 1954; Jan's Treasure, In the Beginning, 1955; Thames Waters, The Facts of Life, 1956; Small Boat Through Belgium, The Chesterfield Gold, The Great South Sea, The Ways of the Sea, 1957; The Missing Panel, 1958; Small Boat Through Holland, Robert Boyle: father of chemistry, How Boats Go Uphill, 1959; Small Boat to the Skagerrak, World Without End, The Dahlia's Cargo, Don John's Ducats, 1960; Small Boat to Sweden, Small Boat to Alsace, The Ways of the Air, Who's Who and Why, 1961; Small Boat to Bavaria, Nepomuk of the River, Boats Overland, How Boats are Navigated, 1962; The River, (with Noel Streatfeild) Confirmation and After, Facts of Life for Parents, Small Boat to Germany, The Eisenbart Mystery, 1963; Heavens Alive, Small Boat Through France, 1964; Small Boat in Southern France, Glass, 1965; Small Boat on the Thames, The Boy from Stink Alley, 1966; Small Boat on the Meuse, Small Boat to Luxembourg, 1967; Small Boat on the Moselle, 1968; Small Boat to Elsinore, 1968; Small Boat in Northern Germany, 1969; Small Boat on the Lower Rhine, 1970; Small Boat on the Upper Rhine, 1971; Waterways in Europe, 1972; The Ormering Tide, 1974; The Face in the River, 1976; Geijer in England, 1983; Small Boat Down the Years, 1987; Small Boat in the Midi, 1989; I Sailed on the Mayflower, 1990; One Foot in France, 1992; View from the Shore, 1995; History and Legends of the European Waterways, 1998; The Day of the Sheriffs, 2000; contribs to Guardian, Daily Telegraph, Times, Family Doctor, Yachting World, etc. *Recreations:* inland waterways, walking. *Address:* Les Cactus, 34310 Montouliers, France.   *Died 5 May 2003.*

PIMLOTT, Prof. Benjamin John, FBA 1996; Warden, Goldsmiths College, University of London, since 1998; *b* 4 July 1945; *s* of late John Alfred Ralph Pimlott, CB, and Ellen Dench Howes Pimlott; *m* 1977, Jean Ann Seaton; three *s*. *Educ:* Rokeby Sch.; Wimbledon; Marlborough Coll., Wilts; Worcester Coll., Oxford (Open Schol.; MA, BPhil); PhD Newcastle. FRHistS 1993. Lectr, Newcastle Univ., 1970–79; Res. Associate, LSE, 1979–81; Lectr 1981–86, Reader 1986–87, Prof. of Politics and Contemp. Hist., 1987–98, Fellow, 1999, Birkbeck Coll., London Univ. British Acad. Thank Offering to Britain Fellow, 1972–73; Nuffield Foundn Res. Fellow, 1977–78. Mem., Lord Plant Commn on Electoral Systems, 1991–93; Chm., ESRC Whitehall Prog. Commng Panel, 1993–94, Steering Cttee, 1994–99. Contested (Lab): Arundel, Feb. 1974; Cleveland and Whitby, Oct. 1974, and 1979. Mem. Exec., Fabian Soc., 1987– (Chm., 1993–94). Political columnist: Today, 1986–87; The Times, 1987–88; New Statesman (political editor), 1987–88; Sunday Times, 1988–89. Editor, Samizdat, 1988–90. Mem., Governing Body, SOAS, 2002–. FRSA 1996. Hon. Fellow, St Cross Coll., Oxford, 2001. *Publications:* Labour and the Left in the 1930s, 1977, 2nd edn 1986; (ed with Chris Cook) Trade Unions in British Politics, 1982, 2nd edn 1991; (ed) Fabian Essays in Socialist Thought, 1984; Hugh Dalton (Whitbread Biography Prize), 1985, 3rd edn 1995; (ed) The Second World War Diary of Hugh Dalton 1940–45, 1986; (ed) The Political Diary of Hugh Dalton 1918–40, 1945–60, 1987; (ed with Jean Seaton) The Media in British Politics, 1987; (ed with T. Wright and T. Flower) The Alternative, 1990; (ed with S. MacGregor) Tackling the Inner Cities, 1990; Harold Wilson, 1992, 2nd edn 1993; Frustrate Their Knavish Tricks, 1994; The Queen, 1996, 2nd edn 2001; (with Nirmala Rao) Governing London, 2002; articles in learned jls and articles and reviews in Guardian, Independent, Independent on Sunday, Observer, TLS, etc. *Address:* Goldsmiths College, New Cross, SE14 6NW. *T:* (020) 7919 7901.
Died 10 April 2004.

PINCHIN, Malcolm Cyril, CVO 1998; County Education Officer, Surrey, 1982–93; *b* 4 May 1933; *s* of Cyril Pinchin and Catherine Pinchin; *m* 1957, Diana Elizabeth Dawson; three *s*. *Educ:* Cheltenham Grammar Sch.; Univ. of Bristol (BSc). Education Officer, HMOCS, Malawi, 1958–67; Asst Educn Officer, Northampton, 1967–70; Asst Dir of Educn, 1970–74, Asst Dep. Dir of Educn, 1974–76, Leicestershire; Dep. Chief Educn Officer, Devon, 1976–82. Mem., Dio. of Westminster Educn Bd, 1993–97; RC Diocesan rep., Plymouth Educn Cttee, 1997–. Mem. Council, Outward Bound Trust, 1995–97; Trustee: Duke of Edinburgh Award, 1989–97; Children's Trust, Tadworth, 1993–97. FRSA 1986. *Recreations:* gardening, fly fishing, bee keeping, opera. *Address:* Maple Tree House, East Terrace, Budleigh Salterton, Devon EX9 6PG.   *Died 3 June 2002.*

PIRIE, Group Captain Sir Gordon (Hamish Martin), Kt 1984; CVO 1987; CBE 1946; JP; DL; Deputy High Bailiff of Westminster, 1978–87; Member, Westminster City Council, 1949–82 (Mayor, 1959–60; Leader of Council, 1961–69; Alderman, 1963–78; Lord Mayor, 1974–75); Director, Parker Gallery; *b* 10 Feb. 1918; *s* of Harold Victor Campbell Pirie and Irene Gordon Hogarth; *m* 1st, 1943, Margaret Joan Bomford (*d* 1972); no *c*; 2nd, 1982, Joanna, *widow* of John C. Hugill. *Educ:* Eton (King's scholar); RAF Coll., Cranwell. Permanent Commn, RAF, 1938; served War of 1939–45: Dir of Ops, RNZAF, Atlantic and Pacific (despatches, CBE); retired as Group

Captain, 1946. Comr No 1 (POW) Dist SJAB, 1960–69; Comdr St John Ambulance, London, 1969–75; Chm., St John Council for London, 1975–85. Vice-Pres., Services Sound and Vision Corp., 1990– (Chm., 1979–90). Gov., Westminster Sch., 1962–94 (Hon. Fellow, 1995); Mem., Bd of Green Cloth Verge of Palaces, 1962–87; Vice-Pres., Engineering Industries Assoc., 1966–69; Mem., Council of Royal Albert Hall, 1965–92 (a Vice-Pres., 1985–92); Trustee: RAF Museum, 1965–98; Dolphin Square Trust Ltd, 1971–97; Vice-Chm., London Boroughs Assoc., 1968–71; Pres., Conf. of Local and Regional Authorities of Europe, 1978–80 (Vice-Pres., 1974–75, 1977–78, 1980–82); a Vice-Pres., British Sect., IULA/CEM, 1980–88; Mem. Solicitors' Disciplinary Tribunal, 1975–93. Contested (LNat&U) Dundee West, 1955. DL, JP Co. of London, 1962; Mem., Inner London Adv. Cttee on appointment of Magistrates, 1969–87; Chm., S Westminster PSD, 1974–77. Liveryman, Girdlers' Co. (Master, 1996–97). FRSA. KStJ 1969. Pro Merito Medal, Council of Europe, 1982. Comdr, Legion of Honour, 1960; Comdr, Cross of Merit, SMO Malta, 1971; JSM Malaysia, 1974. *Recreations:* motoring, bird-watching. *Address:* Cottage Row, Tarrant Gunville, Blandford, Dorset DT11 8JJ. *T:* (01258) 830212. *Club:* Royal Air Force.   *Died 23 July 2003.*

PITCHER, Prof. Wallace Spencer, PhD, DSc, DIC; George Herdman Professor of Geology, 1962–81, then Emeritus, and Leverhulme Emeritus Research Fellow, 1981–83, University of Liverpool; *b* 3 March 1919; *s* of Harry George and Irene Bertha Pitcher; *m* 1947, Stella Ann (*née* Scutt); two *s* two *d*. *Educ:* Acton Tech. Coll., Chelsea Coll. Asst Analytical Chemist, Geo. T. Holloway & Co., 1937–39. Served War, RAMC, 1939–44. Chelsea Coll., 1944–47; Imperial College: Demonstrator, 1947–48; Asst Lectr, 1948–50; Lectr, 1950–55; Reader in Geology, King's Coll., London, 1955–62. Geological Society London: Hon. Sec., 1970–73; Foreign Sec., 1974–75; Pres., 1976–77; Pres., Section C, British Assoc., 1979. FGS; FIMMM. Hon. MRIA 1977; Hon. FRSE 1993. Hon. Member: GA, 1972; Geol Soc. America, 1982; Geol Soc. Peru, 2001. Hon. ScD Dublin, 1983; Hon. DSc Paris-Sud, 1993. Lyell Fund, 1956, Bigsby Medal, 1963, Murchison Medal, 1979, Geol Soc. of London; Liverpool Geol Soc. Silver Medal, 1969; Aberconway Medal, Instn of Geologists, 1983; Univ. Helsinki Medal, 1986. *Publications:* ed (with G. W. Flinn) Controls of Metamorphism, 1965; (with A. R. Berger) Geology of Donegal: a study of granite emplacement and unroofing, 1972; (with E. J. Cobbing) Geology of Western Cordillera of Northern Peru, 1981; (jtly) Magmatism at a Plate Edge: the Peruvian Andes, 1985; Nature and Origin of Granite, 1993, 2nd edn 1997; (with D. H. W. Hutton) A Masterclass Guide to the Donegal Granites, 2003; many papers on late Precambrian stratigraphy, tillites, Caledonian and Andean granites, structure of the Andes. *Address:* 8 Fletcher Close, Upton, Wirral, Merseyside CH49 5PH. *T:* (0151) 677 6896.   *Died 4 Sept. 2004.*

PITT, Desmond Gordon; Commissioner of HM Customs and Excise, 1979–83; *b* 27 Dec. 1922; *s* of Archibald and Amy Pitt; *m* 1946, Barbara Irene; one *s* two *d*. *Educ:* Bournemouth Sch. FCCA, ACIS, AIB. Officer, HM Customs and Excise, 1947; Inspector, 1958; Asst Sec., 1973; Under Sec., 1979. *Recreations:* history, exploring Wessex. *Address:* 4 Ken Road, Southbourne, Bournemouth, Dorset BH6 3ET.
Died 22 Dec. 2003.

PITT, Rt Rev. Mgr George Edward, CBE 1965; *b* 10 Oct. 1916; *s* of Francis Pitt and Anna Christina Oviedo. *Educ:* St Brendan's Coll., Bristol; Ven. English College, Rome. Priest, 1939; worked in Diocese of Clifton, 1940–43; joined Royal Navy as Chaplain, 1943; Principal Roman Catholic Chaplain, RN, 1963–69; Parish Priest, St Joseph's, Wroughton, Wilts, 1969–86. Nominated a Domestic Prelate, 1963. *Recreation:* music. *Address:* St

Teresa's Nursing Home, Corston BA2 9AG.
Died 9 July 2002.

PITT, Sir Harry (Raymond), Kt 1978; PhD; FRS 1957;
Vice-Chancellor, Reading University, 1964–79; *b* 3 June
1914; *s* of H. Pitt; *m* 1940, Clemency Catherine (*d* 2004),
d of H. C. E. Jacoby, MIEE; four *s. Educ:* King Edward's
Sch., Stourbridge; Peterhouse, Cambridge (BA; PhD
1939). Bye-Fellow, Peterhouse, Cambridge, 1936–39;
Choate Memorial Fellow, Harvard Univ., 1937–38; Univ.
of Aberdeen, 1939–42. Air Min. and Min. of Aircraft
Production, 1942–45. Prof. of Mathematics, Queen's
Univ., Belfast, 1945–50; Deputy Vice-Chancellor, Univ.
of Nottingham, 1959–62; Prof. of Pure Mathematics,
Univ. of Nottingham, 1950–64. Visiting Prof., Yale
Univ., 1962–63. Chm., Universities Central Council on
Admissions, 1975–78. Pres., IMA, 1984–85. Hon. LLD:
Aberdeen 1970; Nottingham 1970; Hon. DSc: Reading,
1978; Belfast, 1981. *Publications:* Tauberian Theorems,
1957; Measure, Integration and Probability, 1963;
Measure and Integration for Use, 1986; mathematical
papers in scientific journals. *Address:* St Mary's Nursing
Home, Brailsford, Derby DE5 3BA.
Died 8 Oct. 2005.

PLATT, Norman, OBE 1985; opera director and writer;
Artistic Director, Kent Opera, 1969–89 and 1991–96; *b* 29
Aug. 1920; *s* of Edward Turner Platt and Emily Jane Platt;
m 1st, 1942, Diana Franklin Clay; one *s* one *d*; 2nd, 1963,
Johanna Sigrid Bishop; one *s* two *d. Educ:* Bury Grammar
Sch.; King's Coll., Cambridge (BA). Principal: Sadler's
Wells Opera, 1946–48; English Opera Group, 1948;
Mem. Deller Consort, and freelance singer, actor, teacher
and producer in Britain and Western Europe; founded
Kent Opera, 1969; co-founded Canterbury Theatre and
Festival Trust, 1983; re-founded Kent Opera, 1991. His
many prodns for Kent Opera include: The Return of
Ulysses; Agrippina; The Seraglio; Dido and Aeneas; Peter
Grimes. Hon. DCL Kent, 1981; Hon. DMus Greenwich,
1996. *Publications:* Making Music, 2001; translations of
numerous songs and operas, incl. L'Incoronazione di
Poppea, Don Giovanni and Fidelio; articles on musical
subjects. *Recreations:* listening to music, being read to by
my wife. *Address:* Pembles Cross Farmhouse, Egerton,
Ashford, Kent TN27 9BN. *T:* (01233) 756237.
Died 4 Jan. 2004.

PLATTS-MILLS, John Faithful Fortescue; QC 1964;
Barrister; *b* 4 Oct. 1906; *s* of John F. W. Mills and Dr Daisy
Platts-Mills, Karori, Wellington, NZ; *m* 1936, Janet
Katherine Cree (*d* 1992); six *s. Educ:* Nelson College, NZ;
Victoria University, NZ (LLB 1st Cl. 1927, LLM 1st Cl.
1928); Balliol College, Oxford (Rhodes Scholar; BA 1st
Cl. 1930, BCL 1931, MA 1948). MP (Lab) Finsbury,
1945–48, (Lab Ind) 1948–50. Pilot Officer, RAF, 1941;
"Bevin Boy", 1944; collier, 1945. Bencher, Inner Temple,
1970. President: Haldane Soc.; Soc. for Cultural Relations
with the USSR; Vice-Pres., Internat. Assoc. of
Democratic Lawyers. Common Councilman, City of
London, 1995–. *Address:* Cloisters, Temple, EC4Y 7AA.
T: (020) 7827 4000. *Clubs:* Athenæum; Vincent's
(Oxford); Leander (Henley-on-Thames).
Died 26 Oct. 2001.

PLOWDEN, Baron *cr* 1959 (Life Peer), of Plowden, co.
Salop; **Edwin Noel Plowden,** GBE 1987 (KBE 1946);
KCB 1951; *b* 6 Jan. 1907; 4th *s* of late Roger H. Plowden;
m 1933, Bridget Horatia Richmond (Lady Plowden, DBE)
(*d* 2000); two *s* one *d* (and one *d* decd). *Educ:* Switzerland;
Pembroke College, Cambridge (Hon. Fellow, 1958).
Temporary Civil Servant, Ministry of Economic Warfare,
1939–40; Ministry of Aircraft Production, 1940–46; Chief
Executive, and Member of Aircraft Supply Council,
1945–46; Vice-Chairman, Temporary Council Cttee of
NATO, 1951–52; Cabinet Office, 1947; HM Treasury,
1947–53, as Chief Planning Officer and Chairman of
Economic Planning Board; Adviser on Atomic Energy
Organization, 1953–54; Chairman, Atomic Energy
Authority, 1954–59. Visiting Fellow, Nuffield College,

Oxford, 1956–64; Chairman, Committee of Enquiry:
Treasury Control of Public Expenditure, 1959–61;
Organisation of Representational Services Overseas,
1963–64; Aircraft Industry, 1964–65; Structure of
Electricity Supply Industry in England and Wales,
1974–75; into CBI's aims and organisation, 1974–75; Dep.
Chm., Cttee of Inquiry on Police, 1977–79; Chm., Police
Complaints Bd, 1976–81; Independent Chm., Police
Negotiating Bd, 1979–82; Chm., Top Salaries Review
Body, 1981–89 (Mem., 1977–81). Pres., TI Gp (formerly
Tube Investments Ltd), 1976–90 (Chm., 1963–76);
Director: Commercial Union Assurance Co. Ltd,
1946–78; National Westminster Bank Ltd, 1960–77;
Chm., Equity Capital for Industry Ltd, 1976–82; Mem.,
Internat. Adv. Bd, Southeast Bank NA, 1982–86. Chm.,
CBI Companies Cttee, 1976–80; Vice-Chm., CBI Pres.'s
Cttee, 1977–80. Pres., London Graduate Sch. of Business
Studies, 1976–90 (Chm. 1964–76); Chm., Standing Adv.
Cttee on Pay of Higher Civil Service, 1968–70; Member:
Civil Service Coll. Adv. Council, 1970–76; Engineering
Industries Council, 1976; Ford European Adv. Council,
1976–83. Hon. Fellow, London Business Sch., 1988. Hon.
DSc: Pennsylvania State Univ., 1958; Univ. of Aston,
1972; Hon. DLitt Loughborough, 1976. *Publication:* An
Industrialist in the Treasury: the post war years (autobiog.),
1989. *Address:* Martels Manor, Dunmow, Essex CM6
1NB. *T:* (01371) 872141.   *Died 15 Feb. 2001.*

PLOWMAN, Hon. Sir John (Robin), Kt 1979; CBE
1970 (OBE 1949); Member of the Legislative Council,
later Senator, Bermuda, 1966–82; Government Leader in
the Senate, 1968–82; Minister of Government and
Commercial Services, Bermuda, 1980–82; *b* Bermuda, 18
Sept. 1908; *s* of Owen and Elizabeth Plowman; *m* 1936,
Marjorie Hardwick (*d* 1990); two *s. Educ:* Bermuda and
England. Member, Ealing Borough Council, 1931–35;
returned to Bermuda, 1935; Bermuda Volunteer
Engineers, 1939–42; Dep. Dir, Dir and later Chm.,
Bermuda Supplies Commission, 1942–47; Man. Director,
Holmes, Williams & Purvey Ltd, 1947–78, Chairman of
Board, 1961–97. Chm. or Mem. of various govt commns
and bds, including Training and Employment, Ports
Facilities, Transport Control and Civil Service; Minister:
of Organisation, 1968–77; of Marine and Air Services,
1977–80. Attached to UK negotiating team for Bermuda
II Civil Aviation agreement, 1977. Chm. Bd of
Governors, Warwick Academy, 1946–73; Life Vice-Pres.
Bermuda Olympic Assoc. and Bermuda Football Assoc.
Recreations: golf, sports administration. *Address:* Chiswick,
Paget, Bermuda. *Club:* Royal Hamilton Dinghy and Mid-
Ocean (Bermuda).   *Died 20 June 2002.*

PLUMB, J. H.; *see* Plumb, Sir John (Harold).

PLUMB, Sir John (Harold), Kt 1982; FBA 1968;
historian; Fellow, since 1946, Master, 1978–82, Christ's
College, Cambridge; Professor of Modern English
History, University of Cambridge, 1966–74, then
Emeritus; *b* 20 Aug. 1911; 3rd *s* of late James Plumb,
Leicester. *Educ:* Alderman Newton's Sch., Leicester;
University Coll., Leicester; BA 1st Cl. Hons Hist. London
1933; Christ's Coll., Cambridge (PhD 1936; LittD 1957).
Ehrman Research Fellow, King's Coll., Cambridge,
1939–46; FO, 1940–45; University of Cambridge:
Steward, 1948–50, Tutor, 1950–59, Vice-Master,
1964–68, Christ's Coll.; Lectr in History, 1946–62;
Reader in Modern English History, 1962–65; Chm. of
History Faculty, 1966–68. Vis. Prof., Columbia Univ.,
1960; Distinguished Vis. Prof., NYC Univ., 1971–72,
1976; Cecil and Ida Green Honors Chair, Texas Christian
Univ., 1974; Dist. Vis. Prof., Washington Univ., 1977;
Lectures: Ford's, Oxford Univ., 1965–66; Saposnekov,
City College, NY, 1968; Guy Stanton Ford, Univ. of
Minnesota, 1969; Stenton, Reading, 1972; George Rogers
Clark, Soc. of the Cincinnati, 1977. Trustee: National
Portrait Gallery, 1961–82; Fitzwilliam Museum, 1985–92
(Syndic, 1960–77); Member: Wine Standards Bd,
1973–75; Council, British Acad., 1977–80; Chm., Centre

of E Anglian Studies, 1979–82. FRHistS; FSA; FRSL 1969. Chm., British Inst. of America, 1982–90; Hon. For. Mem., Amer. Acad. for Arts and Sciences, 1970; Hon. Member: Soc. of Amer. Historians, 1976; Amer. Historical Assoc., 1981. Hon. DLitt: Leicester, 1968; East Anglia, 1973; Bowdoin Coll., 1974; S California, 1978; Westminster Coll., 1983; Washington Univ., St Louis, 1983; Bard Coll., NY, 1988. Editor, History of Human Society, 1959–; Sen. Editor to American Heritage Co. Historical Adviser, Penguin Books, 1960–92; Editor, Pelican Social History of Britain, 1982–. *Publications:* (as J. H. Plumb) England in the Eighteenth Century, 1950; (with C. Howard) West African Explorers, 1952; Chatham, 1953; (ed) Studies in Social History, 1955; Sir Robert Walpole, Vol. I, 1956, Vol. II, 1960, both vols repr. 1972; The First Four Georges, 1956; The Renaissance, 1961; Men and Places, 1962; Crisis in the Humanities, 1964; The Growth of Political Stability in England, 1675–1725, 1967; Death of the Past, 1969; In the Light of History, 1972; The Commercialisation of Leisure, 1974; Royal Heritage, 1977; New Light on the Tyrant, George III, 1978; Georgian Delights, 1980; Royal Heritage: The Reign of Elizabeth II, 1980; (with Neil McKendrick and John Brewer) The Birth of a Consumer Society, 1982; Collected Essays: Vol. I, The Making of a Historian, 1988; Vol. II, The American Experience, 1989; *contrib. to:* Man versus Society in Eighteenth Century Britain, 1968; Churchill Revised, 1969 (Churchill, the historian); *festschrift:* Historical Perspectives: Essays in Honour of J. H. Plumb, 1974. *Address:* Christ's College, Cambridge CB2 3BU. *T:* (01223) 334900. *Club:* Brooks's.
Died 21 Oct. 2001.

PLUMMER, Maj.-Gen. Leo Heathcote, CBE 1974; retired 1979; *b* 11 June 1923; *s* of Lt-Col Edmund Waller Plummer and Mary Dorothy Brookesmith; *m* 1955, Judyth Ann Dolby; three *d. Educ:* Canford Sch.; Queens' Coll., Cambridge. Commnd RA, 1943; War Service, N Africa, Sicily, Italy, 1943–45 (mentioned in despatches, 1945); Adjt, TA, 1947–49; Staff Coll., Camberley, 1952, Directing Staff, 1961–63; Comdt, Sudan Staff Coll., 1963–65; CO, 20 Heavy Regt, 1965–67; Col, Gen. Staff, MoD, 1967; Brig., 1967; Comdr, 1st Artillery Bde, 1967–70; Dep. Dir Manning (Army), 1971–74; Asst Chief of Staff Ops, HQ Northern Army Gp, 1974–76; Maj.-Gen., 1976; Chief, Jt Service Liaison Orgn, Bonn, 1976–78. ADC to HM The Queen, 1974–76; Col Comdt, RA, 1981–86. Chm., Civil Service Commn Selection Bd, 1983–91. Hon. Sec., Old Meeting House Trust, Helmsley, 1993–97; Pres., 78 Div., Battleaxe Club, 1996–2002. *Recreation:* gardening. *Address:* Vivers Lodge, Old Road, Kirkbymoorside, York YO62 6LT.
Died 26 Dec. 2005.

POLAND, Richard Domville, CB 1973; *b* 22 Oct. 1914; *er s* of late Major R. A. Poland, RMLI, and Mrs F. O. Bayly-Jones; *m* 1948, Rosalind Frances, *y d* of late Surgeon-Captain H. C. Devas; one *d* (one *s* decd). *Educ:* RN Coll., Dartmouth. Traffic Trainee, Imperial Airways, 1932; Traffic Clerk, British Continental Airways and North Eastern Airways, 1934–39. Ops Officer, Air Ministry, Civil Aviation Dept, 1939; Civil Aviation Dept Rep., W Africa, 1942–44; Private Secretary to Minister of Civil Aviation, 1944–48; Principal, 1946; Asst Secretary, 1953; Shipping Attaché, British Embassy, Washington, DC, 1957–60; Under-Secretary: Min. of Transport, 1964–70; DoE, 1970–74. Sec., Internat. Maritime Industry Forum, 1976–78. Chm., Kent Branch, CPRE, 1980. *Address:* 63 Alexandra Road, Kew, Surrey TW9 2BT. *T:* (020) 8948 5039.
Died 25 June 2004.

POLLARD, George Neil; Master of Costs Office (formerly Taxing Master) of the Supreme Court, 1994–2003, Deputy Costs Judge, since 2003; *b* 25 Nov. 1935; *s* of late Rev. George Pollard and Elizabeth Beatrice Pollard (*née* Briggs). *Educ:* Queen's Coll., Taunton; Law Society Sch. of Law. Admitted Solicitor, 1958; Solicitor, E. W. Nickerson & Son, 1958–59, J. Clayton & Co.,

1959–61; Partner, Duthie Hart & Duthie, 1962–94. President: W Essex Law Soc., 1984–85; London Criminal Court Solicitors' Assoc., 1988–89; Mem. Cttee, No 1 Legal Aid Area, 1978–94. Lt Bailiff, Royal Ct Guernsey, 2003–. *Recreations:* reading, sailing, music.
Died 22 April 2005.

POLLEN, Sir John Michael Hungerford, 7th Bt *cr* 1795 of Redenham, Hampshire; *b* 6 April 1919; *s* of late Lieut-Commander John Francis Hungerford Pollen, RN; *S* kinsman, Sir John Lancelot Hungerford Pollen, 6th Bt, 1959; *m* 1st, 1941, Angela Mary Oriana Russi (marr. diss. 1956); one *s* one *d*; 2nd, 1957, Mrs Diana Jubb (*d* 1995). *Educ:* Downside; Merton Coll., Oxford. Served War of 1939–45 (despatches). *Heir: s* Richard John Hungerford Pollen [*b* 3 Nov. 1946; *m* 1971, Christianne, *d* of Sir Godfrey Agnew, KCVO, CB; four *s* three *d*]. *Address:* Manor House, Rodbourne, Malmesbury, Wiltshire SN16 0EX.
Died 13 Feb. 2003.

POLWARTH, 10th Lord *cr* 1690 (Scot.); **Henry Alexander Hepburne-Scott,** TD; Vice-Lord-Lieutenant, Borders Region (Roxburgh, Ettrick and Lauderdale), 1975–91; Member, Royal Company of Archers; a Scots Representative Peer, 1945–63; Chartered Accountant; *b* 17 Nov. 1916; *s* of late Hon. Walter Thomas Hepburne-Scott (*d* 1942); *S* grandfather, 1944; *m* 1st, 1943, Caroline Margaret (marr. diss. 1969; she *d* 1982), 2nd *d* of late Captain R. A. Hay, Marlefield, Roxburghshire, and Helmsley, Yorks; one *s* three *d*; 2nd, 1969, Jean, *d* of late Adm. Sir Angus Cunninghame Graham of Gartmore, KBE, CB, and formerly wife of C. E. Jauncey, QC (later Rt Hon. Lord Jauncey); two step *s* one step *d. Educ:* Eton Coll.; King's Coll., Cambridge. Served War of 1939–45, Captain, Lothians and Border Yeomanry. Former Partner, firm of Chiene and Tait, CA, Edinburgh; Governor, Bank of Scotland, 1966–72, Director, 1950–72 and 1974–87; Chm., General Accident, Fire & Life Assurance Corp., 1968–72; Director: ICI Ltd, 1969–72, 1974–81; Halliburton Co., 1974–87; Canadian Pacific Ltd, 1975–86; Sun Life Assurance Co. of Canada, 1975–84. Minister of State, Scottish Office, 1972–74. Chm., later Pres., Scottish Council (Develt and Industry), 1955–72. Member: Franco-British Council, 1981–90; H of L Select Cttee on Trade, 1984–85. Chairman: Scottish Nat. Orchestra Soc., 1975–79; Scottish Forestry Trust, 1987–90. Murrayfield Hosp., 1982–90. Chancellor, Aberdeen Univ., 1966–86. Hon. LLD: St Andrews; Aberdeen; Hon. DLitt Heriot-Watt; DUniv Stirling. FRSE; FRSA; Hon. FRIAS. DL Roxburgh, 1962. *Heir: s* Master of Polwarth, *b* 30 Nov. 1947. *Address:* Wellfield Parva, Hawkchurch, Axminster, Devon EX13 5UT. *T:* (01297) 678735. *Club:* New (Edinburgh).
Died 4 Jan. 2005.

POMEROY, Anthony Michael John, FCIT; Director of Education Training and Membership, Chartered Institute of Transport, 1989–95; *b* 11 Oct. 1930; *s* of Jack Pomeroy and Margaret (*née* Tyler); *m* 1957, Joan Olive Beard (*d* 1993); one *s* one *d. Educ:* Univ. of Nottingham (BA Hist. 1954). FCIT 1967. Traffic Manager, Grey Green Coaches, 1954–57; Claims Manager, N. Francis & Co., 1957–59; Distribn Controller then Trng Exec., Advance Linen Services, 1959–63; Dir of Transport, Louis Reece (Kent) Ltd, 1963–85; freelance lectr in transport studies and transport consultant, 1985–89. Dir, Transport Tutorial Assoc., 1985–89. Chm., Somerset and Dorset Family History Soc., 1998–2001. FRSA 1991. *Publications:* contrib. various distance learning courses in transport hist., operations and policy. *Recreations:* family genealogy, music and theatre, transport, local history. *Address:* The Keep, 3 Stokehouse Street, Poundbury, Dorchester DT1 3GP. *T:* (01305) 257570, *Fax:* (01305) 257912; *e-mail:* tpomerology@aol.com.
Died 21 Aug. 2002.

POOLE, Christopher William Oldfield; Racing Correspondent: BBC World Service, 1968–98; London Evening Standard, 1971–98; *b* 30 Sept. 1937; *yr s* of William Percival Poole and Ellen Elizabeth Poole (*née*

Oldfield); *m* 1959, Diana Faith Bennett; one *s* one *d*. *Educ:* Downs Sch. Bexhill-on-Sea Observer, 1957–59; Sussex Express, 1959–62; Manchester Evening News, 1962–66; Sheffield Telegraph, 1966–68; Daily Telegraph, 1968–71. Vice-Pres., Horserace Writers' Assoc., 1994–97 (Hon. Life Mem., 1998); Member: Press Cttee, Racecourse Assoc., 1976–98; Bd, Independent Betting Arbitration Service, 1999–. Clive Graham Award, 1979. *Publications:* (ed) William Hill Annuals, 1978–82; Classic Treble, 1982; (ed) Playfair Racing Annuals, 1983–88; A Lifetime in Racing, 1984; Guinness Book of Flat Racing, 1990; contrib. to overseas racing jls in France, Italy, USA. *Recreations:* cricket, opera, cooking (and eating), travel. *Address:* Flat 1, Glyne Hall, De La Warr Parade, Bexhill-on-Sea, E Sussex TN40 1LY. *T:* (01424) 214225. *Clubs:* Carbine; Cricketers', Sussex CC. *Died 18 June 2005.*

POPE, Geoffrey George, CB 1986; PhD; FREng, FRAeS; aerospace technology consultant; *b* 17 April 1934; *s* of Sir George Reginald Pope and of Susie (*née* Hendy); *m* 1st, 1961, Rosemary Frances Harnden (*d* 1989); two *s*; 2nd, 1991, Helen Vernon Brewis. *Educ:* Epsom Coll.; Imperial Coll., London. MSc (Eng) 1959, DIC 1959, PhD 1963. FRAeS 1970; FCGI 1982; FREng (FEng 1988). Junior Technical Asst, Hawker Aircraft Ltd, 1952–53; Student, Imperial Coll., 1953–58; Royal Aircraft Establishment: Structures Dept, 1958–73 (Head, Research Div., 1969–73); Aerodynamics Dept, 1973–77 (Head, 1974–77); Gp Head, Aerodynamics, Structures and Materials Depts, 1978–79; Dep. Dir (Weapons), 1979–81; Asst Chief Scientific Advr (Projects), MoD, 1981–82; Dep. Controller and Adviser (Res. and Technol.), MoD, 1982–84; Dir, RAE, 1984–89; Dep. Chief Scientific Advr, MoD, 1989–94. Pres., RAeS, 1993–94. Mem. Council, 1995–, Pro Chancellor and Chair of Council, 1999–, Univ. of Exeter. Mem. Associé Etranger, Acad. Nat. de l'Air et de l'Espace, 1994. FRSA 1994. US Sec. of Defense Medal for Outstanding Public Service, 1994. *Publications:* papers on aeronautical technology in various technical jls. *Recreations:* music, photography, walking. *Address:* 3 Silver Street, Thorverton, Exeter EX5 5LT. *T:* (01392) 860159. *Died 25 Oct. 2004.*

POPE, Air Vice-Marshal John Clifford, CB 1963; CBE 1959; CEng, FIMechE; FRAeS; Senior Technical Staff Officer, Transport Command, 1963–66; *b* 27 April 1911; *s* of George Newcombe-Pope; *m* 1950, Christine Agnes (*d* 1982), *d* of Alfred Hames, Chichester; one *s* two *d*. *Educ:* Tiverton Boys' Middle Sch.; RAF Technical Training Sch., Halton (aircraft apprentice); RAF Coll., Cranwell (cadet; Sir Charles Wakefield Schol.). Graduated as pilot and commnd, 1932; served: No 3 Sqdn, 1933, Nos 27 and 39, on NW Frontier, 1933–36; War of 1939–45: Comd RAF Station, Cleave, 1940–42; Egypt and Palestine, 1943–46; Asst Dir Research and Develt, Min. of Supply, 1947–50; Dir of Engineering, RNZAF, 1951–53; Comd RAF Station, Stoke Heath, 1954–57; Sen. Tech. Staff Officer, No 3 Gp Bomber Comd, 1957–59 and Flying Trng Comd, 1960–61; AOC and Comdt, RAF Technical College, 1961–63. Life Vice-Pres., RAF Boxing Assoc. *Recreations:* scale model steam engineering, clock making. *Address:* Dilston, 47 Oxford Road, Stone, near Aylesbury, Bucks HP17 8PD. *T:* (01296) 748467. *Club:* Royal Air Force. *Died 26 June 2003.*

POPE, Very Rev. Robert William, OBE 1971; Dean of Gibraltar, 1977–82; *b* 20 May 1916; *s* of late Rev. Jonas George Pope and Marjorie Mary Pope (*née* Coates); *m* 1940, Elizabeth Beatrice Matilda (*née* Bressey); two *s* one *d*. *Educ:* English College, Temuco, Chile; Harvey Grammar Sch., Folkestone; Maidstone Grammar Sch.; St Augustine's Coll., Canterbury; Durham Univ. (LTh). Deacon 1939, priest, 1940, Rochester; Curate: Holy Trinity, Gravesend, 1939–41; St Nicholas, Guildford, 1942–43; Priest in charge, Peaslake, 1943–44; Chaplain, Royal Navy, 1944–71; Vicar of Whitchurch with Tufton and Litchfield, Dio. Winchester, 1971–77. Member of Sion College. Minister Provincial of European Province,

1985–91, and Minister Gen., 1987–90, Third Order of Soc. of St Francis. *Address:* c/o P. J. Pope, 20 Ryder Street, Cardiff CF11 9BT. *Died 15 Sept. 2002.*

POPHAM, Maj.-Gen. Christopher John, CB 1982; Director, British Atlantic Committee, 1982–92; *b* 2 April 1927; *s* of late Gordon F. B. Popham and Dorothy A. L. Popham (*née* Yull); *m* 1950, Heather Margaret, *y d* of late Lt-Col and Mrs H. R. W. Dawson; two *s*. *Educ:* Merchant Taylors' School. Commnd Royal Engineers, 1946; served with King George V's Own Bengal Sappers and Miners, RIE and Royal Pakistan Engineers, 1946–48; UK and Germany, 1948–57; Staff Coll., 1958; Cyprus, 1959–62; OC 4 Field Sqdn, 1963–65; JSSC 1965; Mil. Asst to QMG, 1966–68; CO 36 Engineer Regt, 1968–70; CRE 4 Div., 1971–73; Comd 12 Engineer Bde, 1973–75; BGS Intelligence and Security, HQ BAOR and ACOS G-2 HQ Northern Army Group, 1976–79; Asst Chief of Staff (Intell.), SHAPE, 1979–82. Col Comdt, RE, 1982–87. FCMI. *Recreations:* music, photography, railways. *Address:* c/o Barclays Bank, High Street, Andover, Hants SP10 1LN. *Died 25 July 2005.*

POPLE, Sir John (Anthony), KBE 2003; FRS 1961; Trustees' Professor of Chemistry, Northwestern University, Evanston, Illinois, since 1993; *b* 31 Oct. 1925; *e s* of Herbert Keith Pople and Mary Frances Jones, Burnham-on-Sea, Som.; *m* 1952, Joy Cynthia Bowers; three *s* one *d*. *Educ:* Bristol Grammar School; Cambridge Univ. (MA, PhD). Cambridge University: Mayhew Prize, 1948, Smith Prize, 1950; Fellow, Trinity Coll., 1951–58; Lectr in Maths, 1954–58; Superintendent of Basic Physics Division, National Physical Laboratory, 1958–64; Prof. of Chem. Physics, subseq. John Christian Warner Univ. Prof. of Natural Scis, Carnegie-Mellon Univ., Pittsburgh, 1964–93; Adjunct Prof. of Chemistry, Northwestern Univ., 1986–93. Ford Visiting Professor, Carnegie Inst. of Technology, Pittsburgh, 1961–62. Fellow: Amer. Physical Soc., 1970; Amer. Acad. of Arts and Scis, 1971; AAAS 1980. For. Associate, Nat. Acad. of Sci., 1977. Marlow Medal, Faraday Soc., 1958; ACS Pauling Award, 1977; Awards from American Chemical Society: Langmuir, 1970; Harrison Howe, 1971; Gilbert Newton Lewis, 1973; Pittsburgh, 1975; Computers in Chemistry, 1991. Sen. US Scientist Award, Alexander von Humboldt Foundn, 1981; G. Willard Wheland Award, Univ. of Chicago, 1981; Evans Award, Ohio State Univ., 1982; Oesper Award, Univ. of Cincinnati, 1984; Davy Medal, Royal Soc., 1988; Wolf Prize in Chemistry, Israel, 1991; (jtly) Nobel Prize for Chemistry, 1998. *Publications:* High Resolution nuclear magnetic resonance, 1959; Approximate Molecular Orbital Theory, 1970; Ab initio Molecular Orbital Theory, 1986; scientific papers on molecular physics and theoretical chemistry. *Recreations:* music, travel. *Address:* Northwestern University, 2145 Sheridan Road, Evanston, IL 60208–3113, USA; 5850 N Nina, Chicago, IL 60631, USA.

Died 15 March 2004.

POPPLEWELL, (Catharine) Margaret, (Lady Popplewell); JP; DL; Member, Independent Television Commission, 1991–95; *b* 30 July 1929; *d* of Alfred John Storey and Gladys Mabel Storey; *m* 1954, Sir Oliver Bury Popplewell; four *s* (and one *s* decd). *Educ:* Malvern Girls' College; Newnham College, Cambridge (MA Hons); Hughes Hall, Cambridge (PGCE). Mem., Bd of Visitors, Aylesbury Prison, 1974–79; Chm., Bucks County Probation Cttee, 1981–91; Mem., Bucks County Council, 1977–85 (Chm., Educn Cttee, 1981–85). Mem., IBA, 1987–90. Chm., Oxford Dio. Council for the Deaf, 1987–91; Trustee, Bucks Historic Churches Trust, 1985–. Chm., Thames Valley Partnership, 1993–99. Member Council: Open Univ., 1985–95; Buckingham Univ., 1996–99; Chm. Governors, Amersham and Wycombe Coll., 1981–95; School Governor: Godstowe; Winchester House; Ashfold; Sir William Borlase's Grammar. Buckinghamshire: JP, 1968; High Sheriff, 1992–93; DL,

1993. DUniv Open, 1997. *Recreations:* sailing, theatre.
Died 20 April 2001.

POPPLEWELL, Margaret, (Lady Popplewell); *see* Popplewell, C. M.

PORTEOUS, Christopher, MA; Headmaster of Eltham College, 1959–83; *b* 2 April 1921; *e s* of late Rev. Gilbert Porteous; *m* 1944, Amy Clunis, *d* of Theodore J. Biggs; one *s* three *d. Educ:* Nottingham High Sch. (Foundation Scholar); Emmanuel Coll., Cambridge (Senior Scholar; First Classes, with distinction, in Classical Tripos). Master of Classical Sixth, Mill Hill Sch., 1947–55; Asst Director, HM Civil Service Commission, 1955–59. Mem., Admiralty Interview Bd, 1975–94. *Publication:* Eltham College, Past and Present, 1992. *Recreations:* grandchildren, growing unusual trees, travel. *Address:* Little Thatch, Edwardstone, Sudbury, Suffolk CO10 5PR.
Died 28 Oct. 2003.

PORTEOUS, Rev. Prof. Norman Walker; Professor Emeritus, University of Edinburgh, since 1968; *b* Haddington, 9 Sept. 1898; *yr s* of late John Dow Porteous, MA, formerly Rector of Knox Memorial Inst., Haddington, and Agnes Paton Walker; *m* 1929, May Hadwen (*d* 1981), *y d* of late John Cook Robertson, Kirkcaldy; three *s* three *d. Educ:* Knox Meml Inst., Haddington; Univ. of Edinburgh (MA 1st cl. hons Classics, BD); Trinity Coll., Oxford (MA 1st cl. Lit. Hum.); Univs of Berlin, Tübingen and Münster; New Coll., Edinburgh. 1st Bursar at Edinburgh Univ., 1916; C. B. Black Scholar in New Testament Greek, 1920; John Edward Baxter Scholar in Classics, 1923; Ferguson Scholar in Classics, 1923; Senior Cunningham Fellow at New College and Kerr Travelling Scholar, 1927. Served War of 1914–18: in army, 1917–19, commissioned 2nd Lieut, March 1918; served overseas with 13th Royal Scots. Ordained to Ministry of United Free Church of Scotland, 1929; Minister of Crossgates Church, Church of Scotland, 1929–31; Regius Prof., Hebrew and Oriental Languages, Univ. of St Andrews, 1931–35; University of Edinburgh: Prof. of Old Testament Language, Literature and Theology, 1935–37; Prof. of Hebrew and Semitic Languages, 1937–68; Principal of New Coll., and Dean of Faculty of Divinity, 1964–68. Lectures: Stone, Princeton Theological Seminary, 1953; Montague Burton, Leeds, 1974. Pres., Soc. for Old Testament Study, 1954. Hon. DD St Andrews, 1944. *Publications:* Das Alte Testament Deutsch 23: Das Danielbuch, 1962, 4th edn 1985 (English edition, 1965, 2nd, 1979); Living the Mystery: collected essays, 1967; Old Testament and History, 5 lectures in Annual of Swedish Theological Inst., vol. VIII, 1970–71; contributions to: Theologische Aufsätze Karl Barth zum 50 Geburtstag, 1936; Record and Revelation, 1938; The Old Testament and Modern Study, 1951; Peake's Commentary on the Bible, 1962. *Address:* 3 Hermitage Gardens, Edinburgh EH10 6DL. *T:* (0131) 447 4632.
Died 3 Sept. 2003.

PORTER OF LUDDENHAM, Baron *cr* 1990 (Life Peer), of Luddenham in the County of Kent; **George Porter,** OM 1989; Kt 1972; PhD, ScD; FRS 1960; Professor, since 1987, and Chairman of the Centre for Photomolecular Sciences, since 1990, Imperial College of Science, Technology and Medicine, London; Emeritus Professor, Royal Institution, 1988; *b* 6 Dec. 1920; *e s* of late John Smith Porter and Alice Ann Porter, Stainforth; *m* 1949, Stella Jean Brooke; two *s. Educ:* Thorne Grammar Sch.; Leeds Univ. (Ackroyd Schol.; BSc); Emmanuel Coll., Cambridge (MA; PhD 1949; ScD 1960; Hon. Fellow 1967). Served RNVR, Radar Officer, in Western Approaches and Mediterranean, 1941–45. University of Cambridge: Demonstrator in Physical Chemistry, 1949–52; Fellow of Emmanuel Coll., 1952–54; Asst Director of Research in Physical Chemistry, 1952–54; Asst Director of British Rayon Research Assoc., 1954–55; Prof. of Physical Chemistry, 1955–63, Firth Prof. of Chemistry, 1963–66, Univ. of Sheffield; Resident Prof. and Dir, Royal Institution of Great Britain, 1966–85,

Hon. Mem., 1988–. Fairchild Scholar, CIT, 1974; Hitchcock Prof., Univ. of Calif at Berkeley, 1978; Gresham Prof. of Astronomy, Gresham Coll., 1990–94. Lectures: Bakerian, 1977, Humphry Davy, 1985, Royal Soc.; Romanes, Oxford, 1978; Robertson Meml, Nat. Acad. of Scis, USA, 1978; Dimbleby, 1988; many other named lectures. Member: ARC, 1964–66; Adv. Scientific Cttee, Nat. Gall., 1966–68; BBC Sci. Consultative Gp, 1967–75; Open Univ. Council, 1969–75; Science Mus. Adv. Council, 1970–73; Council and Science Bd, SRC, 1976–80; ACOST, 1987–91. Chancellor, Leicester Univ., 1986–95. Trustee, BM, 1972–74. President: Chemical Soc., 1970–72 (Pres. Faraday Div., 1973–74); Comité Internat. de photobiologie, 1968–72; Nat. Assoc. for Gifted Children, 1975–80; R&D Soc., 1977–82; Assoc. for Science Educn, 1985; BAAS, 1985–86; Royal Soc., 1985–90; Internat. Youth Sci. Fortnight, 1987–89; Nat. Energy Foundn, 1990–2000. Counsellor, Inst. for Molecular Sci., Okasaki, Japan, 1980–83. Master, Salters' Co., 1993–94 (Hon. Liveryman, 1981–). Mem., Academia Europaea, 1987; Foreign Associate: Nat. Acad. of Scis; Amer. Acad. of Arts and Scis; Amer. Philos. Soc.; Pontifical Acad.; Japan Acad.; Accad. dei Lincei; Indian Nat. Science Acad.; Indian Acad. of Scis; acads of Madrid, Lisbon, Göttingen, Leopoldina, Hungary and NY; Foreign Mem., USSR Acad. of Sciences, 1988; Hon. Foreign Mem., Korean Acad. of Sci. and Technol., 1995; Hon. Mem., Acad. of Creative Endeavours, Moscow, 1995. Hon. Professor: Univ. of Kent; Beijing Tech. Univ.; Chinese Acad. of Scis. Hon. Fellow: QMC; Imperial Coll., London; Hon. FKC; Hon. FRSE 1983; Hon. FRSC 1991. Hon. doctorates: Utah, Sheffield, East Anglia, Durham, Leeds, Leicester, Heriot-Watt, City, Manchester, St Andrews, London, Kent, Oxon, Hull, Instituto Quimica de Sarria, Barcelona, Pennsylvania, Coimbra, Lille, Open, Surrey, Bristol, Notre Dame, Reading, Loughborough, Brunel, Bologna, Rio de Janeiro, Philippines, Córdoba, Liverpool, Cambridge (LLD), Central Lancashire, Mangalore, Buckingham, Bath. Royal Society of Chemistry: Corday-Morgan Medal, 1955; Tilden Medal, 1958; Liversidge Medal, 1970; Faraday Medal, 1980; Longstaff Medal, 1981; (jtly) Nobel Prize for Chemistry, 1967; Silvanus Thompson Medal, 1969; Royal Society: Davy Medal, 1971; Rumford Medal, 1978; Michael Faraday Award, 1991; Copley Medal, 1992; Kalinga Prize, UNESCO, 1977; first Porter Medal for photochemistry, Eur., Japanese and Inter-Amer. Photochemical Socs, 1988. *Publications:* Chemistry for the Modern World, 1962; Chemistry in Microtime, 1996; scientific papers in Proc. Royal Society, Trans. Faraday Society, etc. TV Series: Laws of Disorder, 1965–66; Young Scientist of the Year, 1966–81; Time Machines, 1969–70; Controversy, 1971–75; Natural History of a Sunbeam, 1976–77. *Recreation:* sailing. *Address:* Departments of Chemistry and Biochemistry, Imperial College, SW7 2AY. *Died 31 Aug. 2002.*

PORTER, Air Marshal Sir Kenneth; *see* Porter, Air Marshal Sir M. K. D.

PORTER, Sir Leslie, Kt 1983; President, Tesco PLC, 1985–90 (Chairman, 1973–85; Deputy Chairman and Managing Director, 1972–73); *b* 10 July 1920; *s* of late Henry Alfred and Jane Porter; *m* 1949, Shirley Cohen (later Dame Shirley Porter, DBE); one *s* one *d. Educ:* Holloway County Sch. Joined family textile business (J. Porter & Co), 1938. Served War: Techn. Quartermaster Sergt, 1st Bn The Rangers, KRRC, in Egypt, Greece, Crete, Libya, Tunisia, Algeria, Italy, 1939–46. Re-joined J. Porter & Co, 1946; became Managing Dir, 1955. Joined Tesco Stores (Holdings) Ltd: Dir, 1959; Asst Managing Dir, 1964; Dep. Chm., 1970. Member of Lloyd's, 1964–. Pres., Inst. of Grocery Distribution, 1977–80. Vice-Pres., NPFA; Chm., Sports Aid Foundn, 1985–88 (Hon. Vice Pres., 1988–). Internat. Vice-Pres., Mus. of the Diaspora, 1984–. Hon. Chm., Bd of Governors, 1989–, Chancellor, 1993–, Tel Aviv Univ.; Hon. PhD (Business Management), Tel Aviv Univ., 1973. OStJ 1992.

Recreations: golf, yachting. *Clubs:* City Livery; Dyrham Park Country (Barnet, Herts). *Died 20 March 2005.*

PORTER, Air Marshal Sir (Melvin) Kenneth (Drowley), KCB 1967 (CB 1959); CBE 1945 (OBE 1942); Air Officer Commanding-in-Chief, Maintenance Command, 1966–70 and Head of RAF Engineer Branch, 1968–70, retired; *b* 19 Nov. 1912; *s* of late Flt Lieut Edward Ernest Porter, MBE, DCM and Helen Porter; *m* 1940, Elena (*d* 1993), *d* of F. W. Sinclair; two *s* one *d*. *Educ:* No 1 Sch. of Technical Training, Halton; RAF Coll., Cranwell. FIEE. Commnd, 1932; Army Co-operation Sqdn, Fleet Air Arm, 1933–36, as PO and FO; specialised on Signals, 1936–37, Flt-Lieut; Sqdn Leader, 1939; served War of 1939–45 (despatches thrice, OBE, CBE, Legion of Merit, USA): Chief Signals Officer, Balloon Command, 1939, Actg Wing Commander; DCSO and CSO, HQ No 11 Group, 1940–42; Temp. Wing Comdr, 1941; CSO HQ No 83 Gp, Temp Gp Captain, 1943; CSO, HQ 2nd TAF, 1943–45; Actg Air Commodore, 1944–45; CSO, HQ Bomber Command, 1945; Air Min. Tech. Plans, 1946–47, Gp Captain, 1946; Member Directing Staff, RAF Staff Coll., Andover, 1947–49; Senior Tech. Staff Officer, HQ No. 205 Group, 1950–52; Comdg Nos 1 and 2 Air Signallers Schools, 1952–54; CSO HQ 2nd ATAF, 1954–55; CSO, HQ Fighter Command, Actg Air Commodore, 1955–58, Air Cdr, 1958; Student Imperial Defence Coll., 1959; Commandant of No 4 School of Technical Training, RAF St Athan, Glamorgan, and Air Officer Wales, 1960–61; Actg Air Vice-Marshal, 1961; Air Vice-Marshal, 1962; Director-General: Ground Training, 1961–63; of Signals (Air), Ministry of Defence, 1964–66; Actg Air Marshal, 1966; Air Marshal, 1967. Dir of Tech. Educn Projects, UC Cardiff, 1970–74. CEng 1966; FRAeS; CCMI. *Recreations:* reading, writing. *Address:* c/o Lloyds TSB, 163 Whiteladies Road, Clifton, Bristol BS8 2RW.
Died 28 March 2003.

PORTER, Rt Rev. Robert George, OBE 1952; Bishop of The Murray, 1970–89; *b* 7 Jan. 1924; *s* of Herbert James and Eileen Kathleen Porter; *m* 1954, Elizabeth Mary Williams; two *d*. *Educ:* Canterbury Boys' High School; St John's Theological Coll., Morpeth, NSW; Moore College, Sydney (ThL Hons). Served with AIF, 1942–44. Deacon 1947, priest 1948; Assistant Curate, Christ Church Cathedral, Ballarat, Victoria, 1947–49; Assistant Curate, St Paul's, Burwood, Sydney, 1949–50; Priest in charge of Isivita and Agenehambo, Diocese of New Guinea, 1950–57; Archdeacon of Ballarat, 1957–70; Assistant Bishop of Ballarat, 1967–70. KSJ 1992. *Recreations:* gardening, reading. *Died 12 July 2001.*

PORTER, Prof. Roy Sydney, PhD; FBA 1994; Professor in the Social History of Medicine, Wellcome Institute for the History of Medicine, since 1993; *b* 31 Dec. 1946; *m* 1st, 1970, Susan Limb (marr. diss.); 2nd, 1983, J. Rainfray (marr. diss.); 3rd, 1987, Dorothy Watkins (marr. diss.); 4th, Hannah Augstein (marr. diss.); partner, Natsu Hattori. *Educ:* Christ's Coll., Cambridge (BA 1968; PhD 1974). Cambridge University: Res. Fellow, Christ's Coll.,1970–72; Fellow and Dir of Studies in History, 1972–79, Dean, 1977–79, Churchill Coll.; Asst Lectr, 1974–77, Lectr, 1977–79, in European Hist.; Sen. Lectr, 1979–91, Reader, 1991–93, Wellcome Inst. Vis. Prof., UCLA, 1988–89; Visiting Fellow: Princeton Univ., 1989; Stanford Univ., 1989. FMedSci 2001. *Publications:* The Making of Geology, 1977; William Hobbs's The Earth Generated and Anatomized, 1981; English Society in the Eighteenth Century, 1982, 2nd edn 1990; (jtly) Documents of the Early Industrial Revolution, 1983; The Earth Sciences: an annotated bibliography, 1983; Mind Forg'd Manacles: madness and psychiatry in England from Restoration to Regency, 1987; Disease, Medicine and Society in England 1550–1860, 1987; A Social History of Madness, 1987; Edward Gibbon: making history, 1988; (jtly) In Sickness and in Health: the British Experience 1650–1850, 1988; Health for Sale: quackery in England

1650–1850, 1989, repr. 2000 as Quacks: fakers and charlatans in English medicine; (jtly) Patient's Progress: doctors and doctoring in eighteenth century England, 1989; (jtly) Exoticism in the Enlightenment, 1990; Doctor of Society: Thomas Beddoes and the sick trade in late Enlightenment England, 1991; (jtly) Consumption and Culture in the Seventeenth and Eighteenth Centuries: a bibliography, 1991; (jtly) Hysteria Beyond Freud, 1993; London: a social history, 1994; (jtly) The Facts of Life: the creation of sexual knowledge in Britain 1650–1950, 1995; (ed) The Cambridge Illustrated History of Medicine, 1996; The Greatest Benefit to Mankind: a medical history, 1997; (jtly) Gout: the patrician malady, 1998; Enlightenment: Britain and the creation of the modern world, 2000 (Wolfson Prize for History, 2001); Science in the Eighteenth Century, 2000; Bodies Politic: disease, death and doctors in Britain 1650–1900, 2001; Madmen: a social history of mad-houses, mad-doctors and lunatics, 2001; Blood and Guts: a short history of medicine, 2002; Madness: a brief history, 2002; also edited and contrib. to many other books; *posthumous publication:* Flesh in the Age of Reason, 2004. *Address:* The Wellcome Institute for the History of Medicine, 183 Euston Road, NW1 2BE.
Died 3 March 2002.

POSNETTE, Prof. Adrian Frank, CBE 1976; FRS 1971; VMH 1982; Director, East Malling Research Station, Kent, 1972–79 (Deputy Director, 1969–72, and Head of Plant Pathology Section, 1957–72); *b* 11 Jan. 1914; *e s* of late Frank William Posnette and Edith (*née* Webber), Cheltenham; *m* 1937, Isabelle, *d* of Dr Montgomery La Roche, New York; one *s* two *d*. *Educ:* Cheltenham Grammar Sch.; Christ's Coll., Cambridge. MA, ScD Cantab; PhD London. AICTA Trinidad; FIBiol. Research at Imperial Coll. of Tropical Agriculture, Trinidad, 1936–37; Colonial Agric. Service, Gold Coast, 1937; Head of Botany and Plant Pathology Dept, W African Cacao Research Inst., 1944; research at East Malling Research Stn, 1949–. Vis. Prof. in Plant Sciences, Wye Coll., Univ. of London, 1971–78. *Publications:* Virus Diseases of Apples and Pears, 1963; numerous research papers in Annals of Applied Biology, Jl of Horticultural Science, Nature, Tropical Agriculture. *Recreations:* ornithology, sailing, gardening. *Address:* Gwyn, Sutton Valence, Maidstone, Kent ME17 3AD. *T:* (01622) 843234. *Club:* Hawks (Cambridge).
Died 17 July 2004.

POSWILLO, Prof. David Ernest, CBE 1989; DDS, DSc; FRCPath, FDSRCS, FRACDS, FIBiol; Professor of Oral and Maxillofacial Surgery, United Medical and Dental Schools of Guy's and St Thomas' Hospitals, 1983–92, then Emeritus Professor of Oral and Maxillofacial Surgery, University of London; *b* 1 Jan. 1927; *s* of Ernest and Amelia Poswillo, Gisborne, NZ; *m* 1956, Elizabeth Alison (*d* 2002), *d* of Whitworth and Alice Russell, Nelson, NZ; two *s* two *d*. *Educ:* Gisborne Boys' High, NZ; Univ. of Otago. BDS 1948, DDS 1962, DSc 1975, Westminster Hosp. FDSRCS 1952, FRACDS 1966, FIBiol 1974, FRCPath 1981. OC S District Hosp., RNZDC, 1949–51; Hill End Hosp., St Albans, 1952; Dir of Oral Surgery, Christchurch Hosp., NZ, 1953–68; Prof. of Teratology, RCS, 1969–77; Consultant Oral Surgeon, Queen Victoria Hosp., East Grinstead, 1969–77; Prof. of Oral Path. and Oral Surgery, Univ. of Adelaide, and Sen. Oral and Maxillofacial Surgeon, Royal Adelaide and Childrens' Hosps, 1977–79; Prof. of Oral Surgery, and Mem. Council, Royal Dental Hosp., London, 1977–83. Consultant Adviser to Chief MO, DHSS, 1979–86; Chairman: Wkg Pty on Anaesthesia, Sedation and Resuscitation in Dentistry (Poswillo Report), DoH, 1990; Cttee on Dental and Surgical Materials, DoH, 1993–95; Scientific Cttee on Tobacco and Health, DoH, 1994–98. Mem., Bd of Faculty of Dental Surgery, RCS, 1981–89; Medical Defence Union: Council Mem., 1983–; Chm., Dental Cttee, 1983–88; Mem., Bd of Management, 1992–97. Sec. Gen., Internat. Assoc. of Oral and Maxillofacial Surgeons, 1983–89 (Hon. Fellow, 1992);

President: BAOMS, 1990–91; Section of Odontology, RSM, 1989–90 (Hon. Treas., 1994–). Chm., Facial Surgery Res. Foundn, Saving Faces, 2000–; Trustee, Tobacco Products Research Trust, 1980–95; Human Task Force, WHO, 1976–78. Mem. Council of Govs, UMDS of Guy's and St Thomas' Hosps, 1983–92. Hunterian Trustee, RCS, 1994–. Hunterian Prof., RCS, 1968, 1976; Adjunct Prof. of Maxillofacial Surgery, Case Western Reserve Univ., 1984–93; Regents' Prof., Univ. of California, 1987. Lectures: Arnott Demonstrator, 1972; Erasmus Wilson, 1973; Darwin-Lincoln, Johns Hopkins, 1975; Waldron, Harvard, 1976; Richardson, Harvard, 1981; Tomes, RCS, 1982; President's, BAOMS, 1985; Friel Meml, European Orthodontic Soc., 1987; Sarnat, UCLA, 1989; William Guy, RCSE, 1990; Chalmers Lyons Meml, American Assoc. of Oral and Maxillofacial Surgeons, 1996. Fellow, German Acad. of Nat. Scis (Leopoldina), 1988; Foreign Associate, Inst. of Medicine, Nat. Acad. of Scis, USA, 1989. Hon. FFDRCSI, 1984; Hon. FIMFT, 1985; Hon. FRSocMed 1995. Hon. MD Zürich, 1983. RNZADC Prize, 1948; Tomes Prize, 1966; Down Medal, 1973; Kay-Kilner Prize, 1975; ASOMS Research Award, 1976; Hunter Medal and Triennial Prize, 1976; 2nd Orthog. Surg. Award, Univ. of Texas, 1982; Edison Award, Univ. of Michigan, 1987; Colyer Gold Medal, RCS, 1990; Goldman Medal and Lecture, BPMF, 1992. Por Cristo Medal (Ecuador), 1989. *Publications*: (with C. L. Berry) Teratology, 1975; (with B. Cohen and D. K. Mason) Oral Surgery and Pathology, 1978; (with B. Cohen and D. K. Mason) Oral Medicine and Diagnosis, 1978; (with D. J. Simpson and D. David) The Craniosynostoses, 1982; (with D. Henderson) Atlas of Orthognathic Surgery, 1984; (jtly) Dental, Oral and Maxillofacial Surgery, 1986; (jtly) The Effects of Smoking on the Foetus, Neonate and Child, 1992; Report of the Scientific Cttee on Tobacco and Health, 1998; papers on surgery, pathology and teratology in dental, medical and sci jls. *Recreations*: art, reading, gardening. *Address*: Whitesakes, 5 Oldfield Road, Bickley, Kent BR1 2LE. *T*: (020) 8467 1578. *Died 3 June 2003*.

POTTER, His Honour (Francis) Malcolm; a Circuit Judge, 1978–97; *b* 28 July 1932; *s* of Francis Martin Potter and Zilpah Jane Potter; *m* 1970, Bertha Villamil; one *s* one *d*. *Educ*: Rugby Sch.; Jesus Coll., Oxford. Called to the Bar, Lincoln's Inn, 1956. A Recorder of the Crown Court, 1974–78. *Recreation*: painting. *Address*: 42 Brompton Avenue, Rhos on Sea, Colwyn Bay LL28 4TF. *Club*: Army and Navy. *Died 20 Sept. 2005*.

POTTER, John McEwen, DM; FRCS; Emeritus Fellow, Wadham College, Oxford; Director of Postgraduate Medical Education and Training, University of Oxford, 1972–87; *b* 28 Feb. 1920; *er s* of Alistair Richardson Potter and Mairi Chalmers Potter (*née* Dick); *m* 1943, Kathleen Gerrard; three *s*. *Educ*: Clifton Coll.; Emmanuel Coll., Cambridge (BA, MB BChir 1943; MA 1945); St Bartholomew's Hosp.; MA, BM, BCh 1963, DM 1964, Oxon. FRCS 1951. Active service (Captain, RAMC), Europe, India and Burma, 1944–47. Lectr in Physiol. and Jun. Chief Asst, Surg. Professorial Unit, St Bart's Hosp., 1948–51; Graduate Asst to Nuffield Prof. of Surgery, Oxford, 1951–56; E. G. Fearnsides Scholar, Cambridge, 1954–56; Consultant Neurosurgeon: Manchester Royal Infirmary, 1956–61; Radcliffe Infirm., Oxford, 1961–72; University of Oxford: Clin. Lectr in Neurosurgery, 1962–68; Univ. Lectr, 1968–87; Mem., Gen. Bd of Faculties, 1975–83; Hebdomadal Council, 1983–89; Fellow: Linacre Coll., 1967–69; Wadham Coll., 1969–87 (Professorial Fellow, 1974–87; Sub-Warden, 1978–81; Dean of Degrees, 1984–97). Hon. Cons. Neurosurgeon, Oxford RHA and Oxfordshire HA, 1972–87. Hunterian Prof., RCS, 1955; Vis. Prof., UCLA, 1967; Governor, United Oxford Hosps, 1973. Cairns Lectr, Adelaide, 1974. Examr for Final BM, BCh Oxon; Ext. Examr, Med. Sciences Tripos Pt II, Cambridge Univ. FRSocMed (Pres., Sect. of Neurol., 1975–76); Member: GMC, 1973–89 (Chm., Registration Cttee, 1979–89); Oxfordshire HA,

1982–89; Medical Appeal Tribunal, 1987–92; Soc. of British Neurol Surgeons (formerly Hon. Sec. and Archivist); Vice-Pres., 4th Internat. Congress of Neurol Surgery. Corres. Member: Amer. Assoc. of Neurol Surgeons; Deutsche Gesellschaft für Neurochirurgie; Sociedad Luso-Espanhola de Neurocirurgia; Hon. Mem., Egyptian Soc. of Neurol Surgeons. *Publications*: The Practical Management of Head Injuries, 1961, 4th edn 1984; contrib. to books and jls on subjects relating mostly to neurology and med. educn. *Recreation*: fishing. *Address*: 47 Park Town, Oxford OX2 6SL. *T*: (01865) 557875. *Died 6 Feb. 2002*.

POTTER, Malcolm; *see* Potter, F. M.

POTTER, Ronald Stanley James; Director of Social Services, Surrey County Council, 1970–81; *b* 29 April 1921; *e s* of late Stanley Potter and Gertrude Mary Keable, Chelmsford; *m* 1954, Ann (Louisa Eleanor) Burnett; one *s* one *d*. *Educ*: King Edward VI Grammar Sch., Chelmsford. MISW. Territorial Army, 1939, War Service, 1939–47; commnd RA, 1942; Captain 1946. Area Welfare Officer, Essex CC, 1953–61; Dep. Co. Welfare Officer, Lindsey CC, 1962; County Welfare Officer: Lindsey CC, 1962–64; Herts CC, 1964–70. Dir, Watford Sheltered Workshop Ltd, 1964–70; Mem. Cttee of Enquiry into Voluntary Workers in Social Services, 1966–69; Director: Industrial Advisers to Blind Ltd, 1969–74; Remploy Ltd, 1974–86. Vice Pres., SE Regional Assoc. for Deaf, 1984–88 (Vice-Chm., 1968–76; Chm., 1976–84); Member: Council of Management, RNID, 1968–71, 1976–84; Nat. Jt Council for Workshops for the Blind, 1970–81; Adv. Council, Nat. Corp. for Care of Old People, 1974–77; Local Authorities Adv. Cttee on Conditions of Service of Blind Workers, 1974–81; Exec. Council, RNIB, 1975–81; Nat. Adv. Council on Employment of Disabled People, 1978–81. *Recreations*: walking, swimming, caravanning, bowls. *Died 30 Dec. 2002*.

POTTER, Maj.-Gen. Sir Wilfrid John; *see* Potter, Maj.-Gen. Sir John.

POTTER, Maj.-Gen. Sir (Wilfrid) John, KBE 1968 (CBE 1963; OBE 1951); CB 1966; Chairman, Traffic Commissioners and Licensing Authority, Western Traffic Area, 1973–83; *b* 18 April 1913; *s* of late Major Benjamin Henry Potter, OBE, MC; *m* 1st, 1943, Vivienne Madge (*d* 1973), *d* of late Captain Henry D'Arcy Medlicott Cooke; one *s* one *d*; 2nd, 1974, Mrs D. Ella Purkis (*d* 2001); one step *s* one step *d*. Served War of 1939–45. Major-General, 1962; Colonel Comdt: RAOC, 1965–69; RCT, 1968–73. Director of Supplies and Transport, 1963–65; Transport Officer in Chief (Army), 1965–66; Dir of Movements (Army), MoD, 1966–68; retired. *Address*: Orchard Cottage, The Orchard, Freshford, Bath BA2 7WX. *Died 2 Dec. 2005*.

POULTON, William Dacres Campbell; His Honour Judge Poulton; a Circuit Judge, since 1994; *b* 15 Dec. 1937; *o s* of late Arthur Stanley Poulton and Winifred Evelyn Poulton (*née* Montgomery Campbell); *m* 1970, Carolyn Frances Macken; two *s* one *d*. *Educ*: Dover Coll.; New Coll., Oxford (BA 1961; MA 1964). Tutor and Lectr, New Coll., Oxford, 1962–68. Called to the Bar, Middle Temple, 1965, commenced practice, 1969; Recorder 1992–94. *Publications*: contribs to Law Quarterly Review and Halsbury's Laws of England (Landlord and Tenant). *Recreations*: ski-ing, gardening, walking. *Died 29 Dec. 2002*.

POUNDS, Maj.-Gen. Edgar George Derek, CB 1975; retired; *b* 13 Oct. 1922; *s* of Edgar Henry Pounds, MBE, MSM, and Caroline Beatrice Pounds; *m* 1944, Barbara Winifred May Evans; one *s* one *d*. *Educ*: Reading Sch. Served War of 1939–45: enlisted, RM, 1940 (King's Badge, trng); HMS Kent, 1941–42 (Atlantic); commissioned as Reg. Off., Sept. 1942 (sword for dist., trng); HMS Berwick, 1943–44 (Atlantic and Russia). Co.

Comdr, RM, 1945–51: Far East, Palestine, Malta, UK (Sniping Wing), Korea (US Bronze Star, 1950); Captain 1952; Instr, RM Officers' Trng Wing, UK, 1952–54; Adjt, 45 Commando, RM, 1954–57, Malta, Cyprus (despatches), Suez; RAF Staff Coll., Bracknell, 1958; Staff Captain, Dept of CGRM, London, 1959–60; Major 1960; Amphibious Ops Officer, HMS Bulwark, 1961–62, Kuwait, Aden, E Africa, Borneo; Corps Drafting Off., UK, 1962–64; 40 Commando RM: 2nd in Comd, 1964–65, Borneo, and CO, 1966–67, Borneo and Far East; CO, 43 Commando, RM, 1967–68, UK based; GSO1 Dept CGRM, 1969–70; Col 1970; Naval Staff, MoD, 1970–72; Comdt Commando Trng Centre, RM, 1972–73; Actg Maj.-Gen. 1973; Maj.-Gen., RM, 1974; Commanding Commando Forces, RM, 1973–76, retired. Chief Exec., British Friesian Cattle Soc., 1976–87; Chm., RM Officers' Widows Pension Funds, 1987–92. Agricl Cons. (Europe), 1987. Mem. Council, Devon Co. Agricl Assoc., 1993–. *Publications:* articles on strategy, amphibious warfare, and tactics in professional jls, on cattle breeding and dairying in farming jls, and on computing in computer jls. *Recreations:* computer usages, reading. *Club:* Army and Navy.   *Died 7 Nov. 2002.*

POUNTAIN, Sir Eric (John), Kt 1985; DL; Chairman: James Beattie PLC, 1987–2002 (Deputy Chairman, 1985–87; Director, 1984–2002); Tarmac PLC, 1983–94 (Group Chief Executive, 1979–92); IMI PLC, 1989–2001 (Director, 1988–2001); *b* 5 Aug. 1933; *s* of Horace Pountain and Elsie Pountain; *m* 1960, Joan Patricia Sutton; one *s* one *d. Educ:* Queen Mary Grammar Sch., Walsall. FFB, FIHE, FCIB. Joined F. Maitland Selwyn & Co., auctioneers and estate agents, 1956, joint principal, 1959; founded Midland & General Develts, 1964, acquired by John McLean & Sons Ltd, 1969; Chief Exec., John McLean & Sons, 1969, acquired by Tarmac PLC, 1974; Chief Exec., newly formed Tarmac Housing Div., until 1979. Director: Tarmac PLC, 1977–94; Midland Bank, 1986–92; United Newspapers, 1992–98; Lloyds Chemists plc, 1993–97; John Maunders Gp, 1994–98; Tay Homes plc, 1999–2001. Member: Adv. Council, Prince's Youth Business Trust, 1988–; President's Appeal Cttee, Age Concern, 1991–93; Trustee: Lichfield Cathedral Trust, 1995–; Crimestoppers Trust, 1995–. Pres., Midlands Industrial Council, 1988–; Patron, Staffs Agricl Soc. DL Stafford, 1985. CCMI; FRSA. *Recreations:* golf, shooting, tennis. *Address:* Edial House, Lichfield Road, Burntwood, Staffs WS7 0HZ.   *Died 19 Oct. 2003.*

POWELL, Albert Edward; JP; General President of Society of Graphical and Allied Trades, 1973–82, of SOGAT '82 1982–83; *b* 20 May 1927; *s* of Albert and Mary Powell; *m* 1947, Margaret Neville; one *s* two *d. Educ:* Holy Family Elementary Sch., Morden. FIWSP. London Organiser, SOGAT, 1957, Organising Secretary, 1967. Has served on various Committees and Boards, including: past Chairman, Croydon College of Art, past Governor, London College of Printing. Chairman, Paper & Paper Products Industry Trng Bd, 1975 (Mem. Central Arbitration Cttee, 1976); Member: TUC Printing Industries Cttee, 1971; NEDO Printing Industries Sector Working Party, 1980; Methods-Time Measurement Assoc., 1966. Member: Industrial Tribunal, 1983; Social Security Appeal Tribunal, 1984; Parole Bd, 1986. JP: Wimbledon, 1961–75; Southend-on-Sea, 1975–80; Bexley, 1980. Silver Jubilee Medal, 1977. *Recreations:* gardening, reading (science fiction), music. *Address:* 31 Red House Lane, Bexleyheath, Kent DA6 8JF. *T:* (020) 8304 7480.   *Died 9 July 2004.*

POWELL, Sir Arnold Joseph Philip; *see* Powell, Sir Philip.

POWELL, Geoffrey; *see* Powell, J. G.

POWELL, (John) Geoffrey, CBE 1987; Deputy Chairman, Local Government Boundary Commission for England, 1984–90; *b* 13 Jan. 1928; *s* of H. W. J. and W. A. S. Powell; *m* 1954, Anne (*née* Evans); one *s* three *d. Educ:*

Shrewsbury. FRICS; FSVA; ACIArb. Lieut, Welsh Guards, 1945–48. Chm., Property Adv. Gp, DoE, 1982–86 (Chm., New Towns Sub-Gp, 1982–86); Member: Skelmersdale New Town Corp., 1978–85; Review Cttee of Govt Valuation Services, 1982; British Rail Property Board, 1985–91; NCB Pension Fund Adv. Panel, 1985–90. Sec.-Gen., European Group of Valuers of Fixed Assets, 1982–87; European Rep., Internat. Assets Valuation Standards Cttee, 1984–87. Chm., RICS Cttees, 1960–83, incl. Assets Valuation Standards Cttee, 1981–83. External Examr, Reading Univ., 1986–88; Member: Liverpool Univ. Dept. of Civic Design Adv. Cttee, 1986–90; Adv. Panel, Law Center, USC, 1987–. Mem. Editl Bd, Rent Review and Lease Renewal, 1985–89. *Address:* Whites Farmhouse, Mickleton, near Chipping Campden, Glos GL55 6PU. *T:* (01386) 438146.
           Died 15 March 2005.

POWELL, Sir Philip, CH 1984; Kt 1975; OBE 1957; RA 1977 (ARA 1972); FRIBA; Partner of Powell and Moya, Architects, since 1946, and Powell, Moya and Partners, 1976–91; *b* 15 March 1921; *yr s* of late Canon A. C. Powell and Mary Winnifred (*née* Walker), Epsom and Chichester; *m* 1953, Philippa, *d* of Lt-Col C. C. Eccles, Tunbridge Wells; one *s* one *d. Educ:* Epsom Coll.; AA Sch. of Architecture (Hons Dip.). *Works include:* Churchill Gdns flats, Westminster, 1948–62 (won in open competition; Civic Trust Special Award for most outstanding winner 1960–99); houses and flats at Gospel Oak, St Pancras, 1954, Vauxhall Park, Lambeth, 1972, Covent Garden, 1983; houses at: Chichester, 1950; Toys Hill, 1954; Oxshott, 1954; Baughurst, Hants, 1954; Skylon for Fest. of Britain, 1951 (won in open competition); British Pavilion, Expo 70, Osaka, Japan, 1970; Mayfield Sch., Putney, 1955; Plumstead Manor Sch., Woolwich, 1970; Dining Rooms at Bath Acad. of Art, Corsham, 1970, and Eton Coll., 1974; extensions, Brasenose Coll., Oxford, 1961, and Corpus Christi Coll., Oxford, 1969; picture gall. and undergrad. rooms, Christ Church, Oxford, 1967; Wolfson Coll., Oxford, 1974; Cripps Building, St John's Coll., Cambridge, 1967; Cripps Court, Queens' Coll., Cambridge, 1976; Chichester Fest. Theatre, 1962; Swimming Baths, Putney, 1967; Hosps at Swindon, Slough, High Wycombe, Wythenshawe, Woolwich, Maidstone, Hastings, Ashington, Great Ormond Street, 1959–93; Museum of London, 1976; London and Manchester Assurance HQ, near Exeter, 1978; Sch. for Advanced Urban Studies, Bristol Univ., 1981; NatWest Bank, Shaftesbury Ave, London, 1982; labs etc, and Queen's Building, RHBNC, Egham, 1986–90; Queen Elizabeth II Conf. Centre, Westminster, 1986. Mem. Royal Fine Art Commn, 1969–94; Treas. RA, 1985–95. Trustee, 1978–93, Life Trustee, 1993–2002, Sir John Soane's Museum. Has won numerous medals and awards for architectural work, inc. Royal Gold Medal for Architecture, RIBA, 1974. *Recreations:* travel, listening to music. *Address:* 16 The Little Boltons, SW10 9LP. *T:* (020) 7373 8620.   *Died 5 May 2003.*

POWELL, Sir Raymond, Kt 1996; MP (Lab) Ogmore, since 1979; *b* 19 June 1928; *s* of Albert and Lucy Powell; *m* 1950, Marion Grace Evans; one *s* one *d. Educ:* Pentre Grammar Sch.; National Council of Labour Colls; London School of Economics. British Rail, 1945–50; Shop Manager, 1950–66; Secretary/Agent to Walter Padley, MP, 1967–69, voluntarily, 1969–79; Sen. Administrative Officer, Welsh Water Authority, 1969–79. Welsh Regl Opposition Whip, 1983–95, Opposition Pairing Whip, 1987–95. Member: Select Cttee, Employment, 1979–82; Welsh Select Cttee, 1982–85; Select Cttee, H of C Services, 1983–87; Cttee of Selection, 1983–95; Liaison Select Cttee, 1987–96; Chm., Parly New Building Cttee, 1987–; Chm., All-Party Parly Showman's Guild, 1987–96. Chairman: Labour Party Wales, 1977–78; S Wales Euro-Constituency Labour Party, 1979–. Secretary: Welsh PLP, 1984–90; Welsh Parly Party; Anglo-Bulgarian All Party Gp, 1984–; Treas., Anglo-Romanian All Party Gp, 1984–; Vice-Chm., Parly Agric. Cttee, 1987. *Recreations:*

gardening, sport, music. *Address:* 8 Brynteg Gardens, Bridgend, Mid-Glam CF31 3EW. *T:* (01656) 652159. *Club:* Ogmore Constituency Labour Party Social.

Died 7 Dec. 2001.

POWER, Michael George; Director, Greenwich Hospital, 1982–87; *b* 2 April 1924; *s* of Admiral of the Fleet Sir Arthur Power, GCB, GBE, CVO, and Amy Isabel (*née* Bingham); *m* 1954, Kathleen Maeve (*née* McCaul); one *s* two *d*, and two step *d*. *Educ:* Rugby Sch.; Corpus Christi Coll., Cambridge. Served War, Rifle Bde, 1942–46 (Captain); ME Centre of Arab Studies (Jerusalem), 1946–47; Colonial Admin. Service, 1947–63: District Officer: Kenya, 1948–53; Malaya, 1953–57; Kenya, 1957–63; Home Civil Service, 1963–81: Under-Sec., MoD, 1973–81. Almoner, Christ's Hosp., 1983–88. *Recreations:* carpentry, gardening. *Address:* Hill House, Church Street, Yetminster, Sherborne, Dorset DT9 6LG. *T:* (01935) 873167.

Died 27 March 2001.

POWNALL, His Honour Henry Charles; QC 1979; a Circuit Judge, 1984–99; *b* 25 Feb. 1927; *er s* of late John Cecil Glossop Pownall, CB, and Margaret Nina Pownall (*née* Jesson); *m* 1955, Sarah Bettine, *d* of late Major John Deverell; one *s* one *d* (and one *d* decd). *Educ:* Rugby Sch.; Trinity Coll., Cambridge (BA 1950, MA 1963; LLB 1951). Served War, Royal Navy, 1945–48. Called to Bar, Inner Temple, 1954, Bencher, 1976; joined South-Eastern Circuit, 1954. Junior Prosecuting Counsel to the Crown at the Central Criminal Court, 1964–71; a Sen., subseq. 2nd, Prosecuting Counsel, 1971–79; a Recorder of the Crown Court, 1972–84; Resident Judge, Knightsbridge Crown Court, 1984–88; Permanent Judge, Central Criminal Court, 1997–99 (a Resident Judge, 1988–99); a Judge, Courts of Appeal of Jersey and Guernsey, 1980–86. Mem., Jt Service Review of Honours and Awards, MoD, 1992–2000. Orders and Medals Research Society: Mem. Cttee, 1961–82; Pres., 1971–75, 1977–81; Trustee, 1994–. Freeman, City of London, 1989; Liveryman, Fruiterers' Co., 2001. OStJ 1996. *Publications:* Korean Campaign Medals, 1950–53, 1957; (jtly) Royal Service, Vol. I, 1996, Vols II and III, 2001. *Recreations:* travel, medals and medal ribbons. *Address:* c/o Coutts & Co., 440 Strand, WC2R 0QS. *Clubs:* Pratt's, Hurlingham; Ebury Court.

Died 29 July 2003.

POYNTON, (John) Orde, AO 2000; CMG 1961; MD; Consulting Bibliographer, University of Melbourne, 1962–74; Fellow of Graduate House, University of Melbourne, 1971–84; *b* 9 April 1906; *o s* of Frederick John Poynton, MD, FRCP, and Alice Constance, *d* of Sir John William Powlett Campbell-Orde, 3rd Bt, of Kilmory; *m* 1946, Nina Florence, *d* of late Horace Benson Jackson, QC, Perth, WA; *m* 1965, Lola, *widow* of Group Captain T. S. Horry, DFC, AFC. *Educ:* Marlborough Coll.; Gonville and Caius Coll., Cambridge (BA 1927, MA 1932; BChir 1932; MD 1941); Charing Cross Hospital (Univ. Schol. 1927–30); MD Adelaide 1948. MRCS, LRCP; Horton-Smith prize, University of Cambridge, 1940. Sen. Resident MO, Charing Cross Hosp., 1932–33; Health Officer, Fed. Malay States, 1936–37; Res. Officer Inst. for Med. Research, FMS, 1937–38, Pathologist, 1938–46; Lectr in Pathology, Univ. of Adelaide, 1947–50; Pathologist, Inst. of Med. and Veterinary Science, S Aust., 1948–50, Dir, 1950–61. Dir, Commercial Finance Co., 1960–70. Life Gov., Nat. Gall. of Aust., 1990. Hon. LLD Melbourne, 1977. *Publications:* monographs and papers relating to medicine and bibliography. *Recreation:* bibliognostics. *Address:* The Terraces, 2 Mount Eliza Way, Mount Eliza, Vic 3930, Australia. *T:* (3) 97873660. *Club:* MCC.

Died 13 Feb. 2001.

PRAGNELL, Anthony William, CBE 1982 (OBE 1960); DFC 1944; Deputy Director-General, Independent Broadcasting Authority (formerly Independent Television Authority), 1961–83; Director, Channel Four Television, 1983–88; *b* 15 Feb. 1921; *s* of William Hendley Pragnell and Silvia Pragnell; *m* 1st, 1955, Teresa Mary (*d* 1988), *d* of Leo and Anne Monaghan, Maidstone; one *s* one *d*; 2nd,

1996, Fiona Carter, *d* of James Thomson, CMG, MM, and Ivy Thomson, Edinburgh. *Educ:* Cardinal Vaughan Sch., London. Asst Examiner, Estate Duty Office, 1939. Served RAF, 1942–46. Examiner, Estate Duty Office, 1946. LLB London Univ., 1949. Asst Principal, General Post Office, 1950; Asst Secretary, ITA, 1954; Secretary, ITA, 1955. Vis. Fellow, European Inst. for the Media, Univ. of Manchester, 1983–92, Düsseldorf, 1992–97. Fellow, Royal Television Soc., 1980. Emile Noël European Prize, 1987. *Publications:* Television in Europe: quality and values in a time of change, 1985; (ed) Opening up the Media, 1993. *Recreations:* reading, music. *Address:* 10 Courtwood Drive, Sevenoaks, Kent TN13 2LR. *T:* (01732) 453240. *Club:* Royal Air Force.

Died 17 June 2004.

PREBBLE, John Edward Curtis, OBE 1998; FRSL; writer; *b* 23 June 1915; *o s* of late John William Prebble, Petty Officer, RN, and Florence (*née* Wood); *m* 1st, 1936, Betty (*d* 1993), *d* of late Ernest Golby; two *s* one *d*; 2nd, 1994, Jan, *d* of late Andrew Reid. *Educ:* Sutherland Public Sch., Saskatchewan; Latymer Upper Sch., London. Entered journalism, 1934; in ranks with RA, 1940–45; Sergeant-reporter with No 1 British Army Newspaper Unit (Hamburg), 1945–46; reporter, columnist and feature-writer for British newspapers and magazines, 1946–60; novelist, historian, film-writer (Zulu) and author of many plays and dramatised documentaries for radio and TV. FRSA. Hon. DLitt Glasgow, 1997. *Publications: novels:* Where the Sea Breaks, 1944; The Edge of Darkness, 1948; Age Without Pity, 1950; The Mather Story, 1954; The Brute Streets, 1954; The Buffalo Soldiers, 1959; *short stories:* My Great Aunt Appearing Day, 1958; Spanish Stirrup, 1972; *biography:* (with J. A. Jordan) Mongaso, 1956; *history:* The High Girders, 1956; Culloden, 1961; The Highland Clearances, 1963; Glencoe, 1966; The Darien Disaster, 1968; The Lion in the North, 1971; Mutiny: Highland Regiments in Revolt, 1975; John Prebble's Scotland, 1984; The King's Jaunt: George IV in Edinburgh, 1988; *autobiography:* Landscapes and Memories (McVitie Award), 1993. *Recreation:* serendipity. *Address:* 905 Nelson House, Dolphin Square, SW1V 3PA. *T:* (020) 7798 8253.

Died 30 Jan. 2001.

PRENTICE, Baron *cr* 1992 (Life Peer), of Daventry in the County of Northamptonshire; **Reginald Ernest Prentice,** Kt 1987; PC 1966; company director and public affairs consultant; *b* 16 July 1923; *s* of Ernest George and Elizabeth Prentice; *m* 1948, Joan Godwin; one *d*. *Educ:* Whitgift Sch.; London School of Economics (BSc (Econ)). Temporary Civil Servant, 1940–42; RA, 1942–46; commissioned 1943; served in Italy and Austria, 1944–46. Student at LSE, 1946–49; Member, staff of Transport and General Workers' Union, Asst to Legal Secretary; in charge of Union's Advice and Service Bureau, 1950–57. MP (Lab): E Ham N, May 1957–1974, Newham NE, 1974–Oct. 1977; MP (C): Newham NE, Oct. 1977–1979; Daventry, 1979–87; Minister of State, Department of Education and Science, 1964–66; Minister of Public Building and Works, 1966–67; Opposition Spokesman on Employment, 1972–74; Sec. of State for Educn and Science, 1974–75; Minister for Overseas Develt, 1975–76; Minister of State (Minister for Social Security), DHSS, 1979–81. Exec. Mem. Cttee, Nat. Union of Cons. Assocs, 1988–90. Alderman, GLC, 1970–71. JP County Borough of Croydon, 1961–64. *Publications:* Social Welfare and the Citizen (jtly), 1957; Right Turn, 1978. *Recreations:* walking, golf. *Address:* Wansdyke, Church Lane, Mildenhall, Marlborough, Wilts SN8 2LU.

Died 18 Jan. 2001.

PRENTICE, Hon. Sir William (Thomas), Kt 1977; MBE 1945; Senior Member, Administrative Appeals Tribunal, Australia, 1981–87; *b* 1 June 1919; *s* of Claud Stanley and Pauline Prentice; *m* 1946, Mary Elizabeth, *d* of F. B. Dignam; three *s* one *d*. *Educ:* St Joseph's College, Hunters Hill; Sydney Univ. (BA, LLB). AIF, Middle East and New Guinea, 2–33 Inf. Bn and Staff Captain 25 Aust.

Inf. Bde, Owen Stanleys and Lae Ramu campaigns; Staff Course, Duntroon, 1944; Staff Captain, 7 Aust. Inf. Bde, Bougainville campaign, 1944–45. Resumed law studies, 1946; admitted Bar, NSW, 1947; Judge, Supreme Court, PNG, 1970; Senior Puisne Judge, 1975; Deputy Chief Justice on independence, PNG, 1975; Chief Justice 1978–80. *Recreations:* bush walking, swimming, reading. *Address:* 16 Olympia Road, Naremburn, NSW 2065, Australia. *Clubs:* Tattersall's, Cricketers' (Sydney).
Died 31 Jan. 2004.

PRESCOTT, Peter John; Director, Arts Division, British Council, 1990–93, retired; *b* 6 April 1936; *s* of Wentworth James Prescott and Ellen Marie (*née* Burrows); *m* 1971, Gillian Eileen Lowe. *Educ:* Windsor Grammar School; Pembroke College, Oxford (MA). Joined British Council, 1963; Asst Cultural Attaché, Egypt, 1964–67; London, 1967–70; Sussex Univ., 1970–71; France, 1971–75; London, 1975–79; on secondment to Dept of Education and Science, 1979–81; Australia, 1981–84; Rep., France, and Cultural Counsellor, British Embassy, Paris, 1984–90. *Recreations:* reading, music, painting, theatre, walking, swimming, travel. *Address:* 6/22 Greville Place, NW6 5JG. *T:* (020) 7624 6269. *Died 23 July 2005.*

PRESCOTT, Westby William P.; *see* Percival-Prescott.

PRESTON, Rev. Prof. Ronald Haydn, DD; Professor of Social and Pastoral Theology in the University of Manchester, 1970–80, then Emeritus; *b* 12 March 1913; *o s* of Haydn and Eleanor Jane Preston; *m* 1st, 1948, Edith Mary Lindley (*d* 1994); two *d* (one *s* decd); 2nd, 1997, Mary Elizabeth Smith. *Educ:* London School of Economics, University of London (BSc Econ. 1935); St Catherine's Coll., Oxford (BA 1st Cl. Theol. 1940; MA 1944); MA Manchester 1974; BD, DD Oxon 1983. Industrial Secretary of Student Christian Movement, 1935–38. Curate, St John, Park, Sheffield, 1940–43; Study Secretary, Student Christian Movement, 1943–48; Warden of St Anselm Hall, University of Manchester, 1948–63; Lectr in Christian Ethics, Univ. of Manchester, 1948–70. Examining Chaplain: to Bishop of Manchester, 1948–2000; to Bishop of Sheffield, 1971–80; Canon Theologian of Manchester Cathedral, 1957–71, Sub-Dean 1970–71, Hon. Canon 1971, Canon Emeritus, 1980. Editor, The Student Movement, 1943–48. *Publications:* (jointly) Christians in Society, 1939; (jointly) The Revelation of St John the Divine, 1949; Technology and Social Justice, 1971; (ed) Industrial Conflicts and their Place in Modern Society, 1974; (ed) Perspectives on Strikes, 1975; (ed) Theology and Change, 1975; Religion and the Persistence of Capitalism, 1979; (ed jtly) The Crisis in British Penology, 1980; Explorations in Theology, No 9, 1981; Church and Society in the late Twentieth Century, 1983; The Future of Christian Ethics, 1987; Religion and the Ambiguities of Capitalism, 1991; (jtly) Christian Capitalism or Christian Socialism?, 1994; Confusions in Christian Social Ethics, 1994; The Middle Way: theology, politics and economics in the later thought of R. H. Preston, 2000; contrib. Theology, etc. *Address:* 161 Old Hall Lane, Manchester M14 6HJ. *T:* (0161) 225 3291. *Died 6 Dec. 2001.*

PRESTON, Timothy William; QC 1982; a Recorder of the Crown Court, since 1979; *b* 3 Nov. 1935; *s* of Charles Frank Preston, LDS, RCS and Frances Mary, *o d* of Captain W. Peters, 5th Lancers; *m* 1965, Barbara Mary Haygarth. *Educ:* Haileybury; Jesus Coll., Oxford (BA 1960). 2nd Lt 16/5 Lancers, 1955; Captain, Staffs Yeomanry, retd. Called to the Bar, Inner Temple, 1964; Bencher, 1991. Mem., Criminal Injuries Compensation Bd, 1989–2000. *Recreations:* hunting, golf. *Address:* 2 Temple Gardens, EC4Y 9AY. *T:* (020) 7583 6041. *Club:* Cavalry and Guards. *Died 20 Feb. 2003.*

PRESTT, His Honour Arthur Miller; QC 1970; a Circuit Judge (formerly Judge of County Courts), 1971–90; Hon. Recorder of Manchester and Senior Circuit Judge, Manchester, 1982–90; *b* 23 April 1925; *s* of

Arthur Prestt and Jessie (*née* Miller), Wigan; *m* 1949, Jill Mary, *d* of late Graham Dawbarn, CBE, FRIBA, FRAeS, and of Olive Dawbarn (*née* Topham); one *s* one *d*. *Educ:* Bootham Sch., York; Trinity Hall, Cambridge (BA 1948, MA 1952). Served 13th Bn Parachute Regt, France, Belgium, India, Malaya, Java, 1944–46; Major Legal Staff and War Crimes Prosecutor, 1946–47. Called to Bar, Middle Temple, 1949. Chm., Mental Health Review Tribunal, 1963–70; Dep. Chm., Cumberland QS, 1966–69, Chm., 1970–71. Has held various appts in Scout Assoc. (Silver Acorn, 1970). Pres., SW Lancs Parachute Regt Assoc., 1980–91. JP Cumberland, 1966. 5 years Medal, Ampleforth Lourdes Hospitalite, 1976. *Recreations:* gardening, golf. *Address:* 10 Heigham Grove, Norwich NR2 3DQ. *Club:* Norfolk (Norwich).
Died 26 Oct. 2002.

PRICE, Rear-Adm. Cecil Ernest, CB 1978; AFC 1953; Deputy Assistant Chief of Staff (Operations), SHAPE, 1976–80, retired; *b* 29 Oct. 1921; *s* of Ernest C. Price and Phyllis M. Price; *m* 1946, Megan Morgan; one *s* one *d*. Joined Royal Navy, 1941; Captain 1966; idc 1970; Director: Naval Air Warfare, 1971–72; Naval Operational Requirements, 1972–73. CO RNAS, Culdrose, 1973–75; Rear-Adm. 1976. *Recreations:* golf, fishing, gardening. *Address:* 17 Harefield Road, Croxton, Thetford IP24 1NE.
Died 22 June 2001.

PRICE, Cedric John, RIBA; Sole Principal, Cedric Price Architects, since 1960; *b* 11 Sept. 1934; *s* of Arthur John Price and Doreen Price. *Educ:* St John's Coll., Cambridge (BA 1955; MA 1959); Architectural Assoc., London (Dip. 1959). ARIBA 1959. Major projects include: (jtly) Snowdon Aviary, London Zoo; Interaction Centre, Kentish Town. Hon. DDes East London, 1994. *Publications:* Works, vol. 2, 1984; Cedric Price: opera, ed Samantha Hardingham, 2003. *Address:* (office) 38 Alfred Place, WC1E 7DP. *T:* (020) 7636 5220. *Club:* Hot Stuff (Life Pres.). *Died 10 Aug. 2003.*

PRICE, Maj.-Gen. David; *see* Price, Maj.-Gen. M. D.

PRICE, Leonard Sidney, OBE 1974; HM Diplomatic Service, retired 1981; *b* 19 Oct. 1922; *s* of late William Price and Dorothy Price; *m* 1958, Adrienne Mary (*née* Wilkinson); two *s* one *d*. *Educ:* Central Foundation Sch., EC2. Served War, 1942–45: Inns of Court Regt; D-Day assault to Danish border. Foreign Office, 1939–42 and 1945–48; Chungking, later Vice-Consul, 1948; Mexico City, 1950; Rome, 1953; Vice-Consul, later Second Sec., Katmandu, 1954; FO, 1957; Consul, Split, 1960; Consul and First Sec., Copenhagen, 1963; FO, later FCO, 1967; First Sec. i/c, Kuching, 1970; Suva, 1972; Parly Clerk, FCO, 1975; Counsellor (Admin), Canberra, 1977–81. Dep. Dir, St John Ambulance Assoc., Somerset, 1982–84; Hon. Treas., Council of Order of St John, Somerset, 1983–88. *Recreation:* reading ancient, medieval and military history. *Address:* 5 Staplegrove Manor, Staplegrove, Taunton, Somerset TA2 6EG. *T:* (01823) 337093. *Club:* Civil Service. *Died 20 Jan. 2003.*

PRICE, (Llewelyn) Ralph, CBE 1972; Director, Honeywell, since 1971 (Chairman, 1971–81); *b* 23 Oct. 1912; *s* of late L. D. Price, schoolmaster, and Lena Elizabeth (*née* Dixon); *m* 1939, Vera Patricia Harrison (*d* 2004); one *s* two *d*. *Educ:* Quarry Bank Sch., Liverpool. Chartered Accountant, 1935; Sec. to Honeywell Ltd, 1936; Cost Investigator, Min. of Supply, 1943–46; Dir of Manufacturing (Scotland), Honeywell Ltd, 1947; Financial Dir, Honeywell Europe, 1957; Dir, Computer Div., Honeywell, 1960; Managing Dir, Honeywell Ltd, 1965; Chm., Honeywell UK Adv. Council, 1981–. Chm., ML Hldgs Ltd, 1976–87. Pres., British Industrial, Measuring & Control Apparatus Manufrs Assoc., 1971–76. CCMI. *Recreations:* golf, bridge, music. *Club:* Temple Golf (Maidenhead). *Died 1 July 2004.*

PRICE, Maj.-Gen. (Maurice) David, CB 1970; OBE 1956; *b* 13 Feb. 1915; *s* of Edward Allan Price and Edna

Marion Price (*née* Turner); *m* 1st, 1938, Ella Lacy (*d* 1971), *d* of late H. L. Day; two *s* two *d*; 2nd, 1972, Mrs Olga Marion Oclee (*d* 1989). *Educ*: Marlborough; RMA, Woolwich. 2nd Lt R Signals, 1935; Vice-Quartermaster-Gen., MoD (Army), 1967–70, retired. Col Comdt, Royal Corps of Signals, 1967–74. *Address*: 2 Windsor Court, Kingsbridge, Devon TQ7 1RZ. *T*: (01548) 856503.
Died 17 April 2005.

PRICE, Ralph; *see* Price, L. R.

PRICE, Roy Kenneth, CB 1980; Under-Secretary (Legal), in office of HM Treasury Solicitor, 1972–81; *b* 16 May 1916; *s* of Ernest Price and Margaret Chapman Price (*née* Scott); *m* 1948, Martha (*née* Dannhauser); one *s* one *d*. *Educ*: Eltham Coll. Qualified as Solicitor, 1937. Town Clerk, Borough of Pembroke, and Clerk to Castlemartin Justices, 1939–40. Served War, Army, 1940–46. Officer in Charge, Legal Aid (Welfare), Northern Command, 1946 (Lt-Col). Joined HM Treasury Solicitor, as Legal Asst, 1946; Sen. Legal Asst, 1950; Asst Solicitor, 1962. Mem. Exec. Council, RNIB, 1981–99; Pres., Richmond Assoc., Nat. Trust, 1985–2002; Trustee, Richmond Almshouse Charities, 1987–99; Chm., Portcullis Trust, 1980–90. *Recreations*: theatre, travel, local history. *Address*: 16 Queensberry House, Friars Lane, Richmond, Surrey TW9 1NT. *T*: (020) 8940 6685. *Club*: Law Society.
Died 20 Oct. 2005.

PRICE, (William Frederick) Barry, OBE 1977; HM Diplomatic Service, retired; Consul-General, Amsterdam, 1983–85; *b* 12 Feb. 1925; *s* of William Thomas and Vera Price; *m* 1948, Lorraine Elisabeth Suzanne Hoather; three *s* two *d*. *Educ*: King Edward's High Sch., Birmingham; Worcester Royal Grammar Sch.; St Paul's Training Coll., Cheltenham; Open Univ. (BA Hons 1994). Served War: Armed Forces, 1944–47: commissioned Royal Warwicks, 1945; demobilised, 1947. Primary Sch. Teacher, 1948. Joined Bd of Trade, 1950; Asst Trade Comr: in Delhi, 1954; in Nairobi, 1957; Trade Commissioner, Accra, 1963; transferred to HM Diplomatic Service, 1966; 1st Sec., Sofia, 1967; seconded to East European Trade Council, 1971; Consul-Gen., Rotterdam, 1973–77; Consul, Houston, 1978–81; Counsellor (Commercial and Economic), Bangkok, 1981–82; Kuala Lumpur, 1982. Chm., Anglo-Netherlands Soc., 1989–94. Comdr, Order of Orange-Nassau (Netherlands), 1989. *Recreations*: Dutch literary translation, playing bridge on the Internet. *Address*: 46 Finchley Park, N12 9JL. *T*: (020) 8445 4642. *Club*: Oriental.
Died 29 Oct. 2005.

PRICHARD, Air Cdre Richard Julian Paget, CB 1963; CBE 1958; DFC 1942; AFC 1941; Air Officer Commanding Northern Sector of Fighter Command, 1965–66, retired; *b* 4 Oct. 1915; *o s* of Major W. O. Prichard, 24th Regt; *m* 1995, Rosemary Bennett (widow). *Educ*: Harrow; St Catharine's Coll., Cambridge. Entered RAF, 1937; Air Armament Sch., Eastchurch and Manby, 1937–39; Flying Instructor, South Cerney, 1939–41; No 21 (LB) Squadron, 1942–43; Staff Coll. (psa), 1943; AEAF, 1943–45; Chief Intelligence Officer, Burma and FEAF, 1946–47; Chief Flying Instructor, RAF Coll., Cranwell, 1947–49; Ministry of Defence, 1949–52; Instructor, RAF Staff Coll., 1953–55; Station Comdr, RAF Tengah, Singapore, 1956–58; IDC, 1959; Director Air Plans, Air Ministry, 1960–63; AOC No 13 Scottish Sector, Fighter Command, 1963–64. US Legion of Merit, 1944. *Recreation*: fishing. *Club*: Royal Air Force.
Died 26 April 2001.

PRIESTLEY, Rev. Canon John Christopher; Vicar of Christ Church, Colne, 1975–2002; Chaplain to the Queen, since 1990; *b* 23 May 1939; *s* of Ronald Edmund Priestley and Winifred Mary Priestley (*née* Hughes); *m* 1964, Margaret Ida Machan; one *s* one *d*. *Educ*: William Hulme Grammar Sch.; Trinity Coll., Oxford (MA); Wells Theol Coll.; MMin Sheffield, 1993; MTh Oxon, 1998. Asst Master, St James Sch., Clitheroe, 1961–64; Dep.

Headmaster, Green Sch., Padiham, 1964–70; ordained deacon 1968, priest 1969; Asst Curate: All Saints, Habergham, Burnley, 1968–70; St Leonard's, Padiham, 1970–75. Convenor, Pastoral Auxiliaries, dio. Blackburn, 1987–91; Rural Dean of Pendle, 1991–96; Dir, Post Ordination Trng, dio. Blackburn, 1996–2000; Hon. Canon of Blackburn Cathedral, 2000–. *Publications*: contribs to Church Times, Church of England Newspaper. *Recreation*: music, reading, long-distance walking, ornithology, flying light aircraft (private pilot's licence). *Address*: 11 Chapman Court, Barnoldswick, Lancs BB18 5EE. *T*: (01282) 812308.
Died 13 Dec. 2005.

PRIGOGINE, Vicomte Ilya; Grand-Croix de l'Ordre de Léopold II, Belgium, 1977 (Commandeur, 1961); Professor, Université Libre de Bruxelles, 1951–87, then Emeritus; Director, Instituts Internationaux de Physique et de Chimie, since 1959; Director, Ilya Prigogine Center of Statistical Mechanics, Thermodynamics and Complex Systems, since 1967, Regental Professor, since 1977 and Ashbel Smith Professor, since 1984, University of Texas at Austin; *b* Moscow, 25 Jan. 1917; created Viscount, 1989; *m* 1st; one *s*; 2nd, 1961, Marina Prokopowicz; one *s*. *Educ*: Univ. of Brussels (Lic. Sc. Physiques, 1939; Dr en Sciences Chimiques, 1941). Prof., Dept of Chemistry, Enrico Fermi Inst. for Nuclear Studies, and Inst. for Study of Metals, Univ. of Chicago, 1961–66. Associate Dir of Studies, l'Ecole des Hautes Etudes en Sciences Sociales, France, 1987; RGK Foundn Centennial Fellow, Univ. of Texas, 1989–90; Dist. Visitor, Inst. for Advanced Study, Princeton, 1993. Special Advr, EEC, 1993. Member: Sci. Adv. Bd, Internat. Acad. for Biomedical Drug Res., 1990; Eur. Assembly of Scis and Technols, EC, 1994. Pres., Séminaire Ilya Prigogine, Penser la Science, Univ. Libre de Bruxelles, 1997. Hon. Pres., Université Philosophique Européenne, Paris, 1985; Member: Acad. Royale de Belgique, 1960; Royal Soc. of Sciences, Uppsala, Sweden, 1967; German Acad. Naturforscher Leopoldina, GDR, 1970; Acad. Internat. de Philosophie des Sciences, 1973; Acad. Européenne des Scis, des Arts et des Lettres, Paris, 1980 (Vice-Pres., 1980); Accad. Mediterranea delle Scienze, Catania, 1982; Acad. Internat. de Prospective Sociale, Geneva, 1983; Haut Conseil de la Francophonie, Paris, 1984–88; Max-Planck Foundn, Fed. Republic of Germany, 1984; World Inst. of Sci., 1992; Assoc. Descartes, 1992; Acad. Scientiarium et Artium Europaea, Salzburg, 1993; MAE 1989; Hon. Member: Amer. Acad. of Arts and Scis, 1960; Chem. Soc., Warsaw, 1971; Soc. for Studies on Entropy, Japan, 1983; Biophys. Soc., China, 1986; Royal Soc. of Chemistry, Belgium, 1987. Fellow: Acad. of Scis, NY, 1962; World Acad. of Art and Science, 1986; Centennial Foreign Fellow, Amer. Chem. Soc., 1976; Foreign Fellow: Indian Nat. Sci. Acad., 1979; Acad. das Ciencias de Lisbôa, 1988; Foreign Associate, Nat. Acad. of Scis, USA, 1967; Hon. Fellow, Nat. Acad. of Scis of India, 1992; Foreign Member: Akad. der Wissenschaften der DDR, Berlin, 1980; USSR Acad. of Scis, 1982; Corresponding Member: Acad. of Romania, 1965; Soc. Royale des Sciences, Liège, 1967; Section of Phys. and Math., Akad. der Wissenschaften, Göttingen, 1970; Akad. der Wissenschaften, Vienna, 1971; Rheinish-Westfälische Akad. der Wissenschaften, Düsseldorf, 1980; Archives de Psychologie, Univ. of Geneva, 1982; Accad. Nazionale di Scienze, Lettere e Arti, Modena, 1992. Dr (*hc*): Newcastle upon Tyne, Poitiers, 1966; Chicago, 1969; Bordeaux, 1972; Uppsala, Liège, 1977; Aix-Marseille, 1979; Georgetown, 1980; Rio de Janeiro, Cracow, Stevens Inst. of Technology, Hoboken, 1981; Heriot-Watt, Universidad Nacional de Educación a Distancia, Madrid, 1985; Tours, France, Nanking, Peking, 1986; Buenos Aires, 1989; Facolta di Magistero, Cagliari Univ., Univ. of Siena, 1990; Nice, France, Philippines, Santiago, Tucumán, Argentina, 1991; Moscow Lomonosov, 1993; 'Al.I. Cuza' Iaşi, Romania, San Luis and Palermo Univs, Argentina, Institut Nat. Polytechnique de Lorraine, 1994; Vrije Univ. Brussel,

SUNY, Valladolid, St Petersburg and Kerala Univs, 1995; Salvador Univ., Buenos Aires, Xanthi Univ., Greece, 1996; Univ. Nacional Autónoma, Mexico, Wroclaw Univ. of Technol., 1998. Prizes: Van Laar, Société Chimique de Belgique, 1947; A. Wetrems 1950, and Annual (jtly) 1952, Acad. Royale de Belgique; Francqui, 1955; E. J. Solvay, 1965; Nobel Prize for Chemistry, 1977; Southwest Science Forum, NY Acad. of Science, 1976; Honda, Honda Foundn, Tokyo, 1983; Umberto Biancamano, Pavia, Italy, 1987; (jtly) Gravity Res. Foundn Award, 1988. Gold Medals: Swante Arrhenius, Royal Acad. of Scis, Sweden, 1969; Cothenius, German Acad. Naturforscher Leopoldina, 1975; Rumford, Royal Soc., 1976; Bourke Medal, Chem. Soc., 1972; Medal, Assoc. for the Advancement of Sciences, Paris, 1975; Karcher Medal, Amer. Crystallographic Assoc., 1978; Descartes Medal, Univ. Descartes, Paris, 1979; Médaille d'Or: Ville de Pavie, 1987; Ville d'Ostende, 1987; l'Université de Padoue, 1988; Distinguished Service Medal, Austin, Texas, 1989. Hon. Citizen: Dallas, USA, 1983; Montpellier, France, 1983; Uccle, Belgium, 1984. Commandeur: l'Ordre du Mérite, France, 1977; l'Ordre des Arts et des Lettres, France, 1984; Légion d'Honneur, France, 1989; Order of the Rising Sun, Japan, 1991. *Publications:* (with R. Defay) Traité de Thermodynamique, conformément aux méthodes de Gibbs et de Donder: Vol. I, Thermodynamique Chimique, 1944 (Eng. trans. 1954); Vol. II, Tension Superficielle et Adsorption, 1951 (Eng. trans. 1965); Etude Thermodynamique des Phénomènes Irreversibles, 1947; Introduction to Thermodynamics of Irreversible Processes, 1954 (3rd edn 1967); (with A. Bellemans and V. Mathot) The Molecular Theory of Solutions, 1957; Non Equilibrium Statistical Mechanics, 1962; (with R. Herman) Kinetic Theory of Vehicular Traffic, 1971; (with P. Glansdorff) Thermodynamic Theory of Structure, Stability and Fluctuations, 1971 (also French edn); (with G. Nicolis) Self-Organization in Non Equilibrium Systems, 1977; (with I. Stengers) La Nouvelle Alliance: les métamorphoses de la science, 1979 (Prix du Haut Comité de la langue française, Paris, 1981) (also English, German, Italian, Yugoslavian, Spanish, Rumanian, Swedish, Dutch, Danish, Portuguese, Russian, Japanese, Chinese, Bulgarian, Korean, Polish, Turkish, Greek and Hungarian edns); From Being to Becoming: time and complexity in the physical sciences, 1980 (also French, German, Japanese, Russian, Italian, Chinese, Rumanian and Portuguese edns); (with I. Stengers) Entre le temps et l'éternité, 1988 (also Dutch, Italian, Portuguese and Spanish edns); (with G. Nicolis) Exploring Complexity, 1989 (also German, Chinese, Russian, Italian, French, Spanish and Japanese edns); (with I. Stengers) Das Paradox der Zeit, 1993; Les Lois du Chaos, 1994; La Fin des Certitudes, 1996 (also Spanish, Portuguese, Dutch, English, Italian, Korean, Japanese and Greek edns); (with Dilip Kondepudi) Modern Thermodynamics: from heat engines to dissipative structures, 1998 (also French edn). *Recreations:* art, music. *Address:* avenue Fond'Roy 67, 1180 Bruxelles, Belgium. *T:* (2)3742952. *Died 28 May 2003.*

PRINCE, Prof. Frank Templeton; Professor of English, University of the West Indies, Jamaica, 1975–78; *b* Kimberley, S Africa, 13 Sept. 1912; 2nd *s* of late H. Prince and Margaret Templeton (*née* Hetherington); *m* 1943, Pauline Elizabeth, *d* of late H. F. Bush; two *d*. *Educ:* Christian Brothers' Coll., Kimberley, S Africa; Balliol Coll., Oxford (MA). Visiting Fellow, Graduate Coll., Princeton, NJ, 1935–36. Study Groups Dept, Chatham House, 1937–40. Served Army, Intelligence Corps, 1940–46. Dept of English, 1946–57, Prof. of English, 1957–74, Southampton Univ. Hurst Vis. Prof., Brandeis Univ., 1978–80; Vis. Prof., Washington Univ., St Louis, 1980–81, Sana'a Univ., N Yemen, 1981–83; Visiting Fellow, All Souls Coll., 1968–69. Clark Lectr, Cambridge, 1972–73. Pres., English Assoc., 1985–86. Hon. DLitt Southampton, 1981; DUniv York, 1982. *Publications:* Poems, 1938; Soldiers Bathing (poems), 1954; The Italian

Element in Milton's Verse, 1954; The Doors of Stone (poems), 1963; Memoirs in Oxford (verse), 1970; Drypoints of the Hasidim (verse), 1975; Collected Poems, 1979; Later On (poems), 1983; Walks in Rome (verse), 1987; Collected Poems, 1993. *Recreations:* music, etc. *Address:* 32 Brookvale Road, Southampton SO17 1QR. *T:* (023) 8055 5457. *Died 7 Aug. 2003.*

PRINCE, Maj.-Gen. Hugh Anthony, CBE 1960; retired as Chief, Military Planning Office, SEATO, Bangkok; *b* 11 Aug. 1911; *s* of H. T. Prince, FRCS, LRCP; *m* 1st, 1938, Elizabeth (*d* 1959), *d* of Dr Walter Bapty, Victoria, BC; two *s*; 2nd, 1959, Claude-Andrée, *d* of André Romanet, Château-de-Tholot, Beaujeu, Rhône; one *s*. *Educ:* Eastbourne Coll.; RMC, Sandhurst. Commissioned, 1931; served in 6th Gurkha Rifles until 1947; The King's Regt (Liverpool), 1947. *Recreations:* golf, gardening, antiques. *Address:* 36 Route de la Crau, 13280 Raphèle-les-Arles, France. *T:* 49984693. *Died 6 Nov. 2005.*

PRING-MILL, Robert Duguid Forrest, DLitt; FBA 1988; Fellow of St Catherine's College, Oxford, since 1965; *b* 11 Sept. 1924; *o s* of late Major Richard Pring-Mill, RA and Nellie (*née* Duguid); *m* 1950, Maria Brigitte Heinsheimer; one *s* one *d*. *Educ:* Colegio de Montesión, Palma de Mallorca; New Coll., Oxford (BA 1st cl. Mod. Langs, 1949; DLitt 1986). Enlisted, 1941; commnd The Black Watch, RHR, 1942; temp. Capt., 1945; despatches, 1947. Oxford University: Sen. Demy, Magdalen Coll., 1950–52; Univ. Lectr in Spanish, 1952–88; Lectr, New Coll., 1956–88, Exeter Coll., 1963–81; Tutor, St Catherine's Coll., 1965–88. English Editor: Romanistisches Jahrbuch, 1953–; Estudios Lulianos, 1957–; Commissió Editora Lul·liana, 1960–. Magister, Maioricensis Schola Lullistica, 1957; Corresponding Member: Inst. d'Estudis Catalans, 1966; Reial Acad. de Bones Lletres, Barcelona, 2002. Pres., Asociación Internacional de Nerudistas, 1995–2001. Premi Pompeu Fabra, 1956; Premi Ciutat de Palma, 1979; Premi Catalònia, 1991. Cross of St George (Generalitat de Catalunya), 1990; Commander, Order of Isabel la Católica (Spain), 1990; Officer, Order of Bernardo O'Higgins (Chile), 1992; Presidential Nevada Centennial Medal (Chile), 2004. *Publications:* Chinese Triad Societies, 1946; (ed) Lope de Vega: Five Plays, 1961; El Microcosmos Lul·lià, 1961; Ramón Llull y el Número Primitivo de las Dignidades, 1963; (with N. Tarn) The Heights of Macchu Picchu, 1966; (with Katya Kohn) Neruda Poems, 1969; (ed) Raymundus Lullus, Quattuor Libri Principiorum, 1969; Neruda: A Basic Anthology, 1975; The Scope of Spanish-American Committed Poetry, 1977; (with Donald Walsh) Cardenal: Apocalypse and Other Poems, 1977; Spanish American Committed Poetry: canciones de lucha y esperanza, 1978; (ed jtly) Studies in Honour of P. E. Russell, 1981; (ed jtly) Hacia Calderón, 1982; Cantas-Canto-Cantemos, 1983; Gracias a la vida: the power and poetry of song, 1990; Estudis sobre Ramón Llull, 1991 (Premi Crítica Serra d'Or, 1992); A Poet for all Seasons, 1993; Der Mikrokosmos Ramón Llulls: eine Einführung in das mittelalterliche Weltbild, 2000; Calderón: estructura y ejemplaridad, 2001; articles in learned jls, Encyc. Britannica, etc, on Ramón Llull, Calderón, modern poetry and Spanish-American protest song. *Recreations:* travel and photography in Latin America. *Address:* 11 North Hills, Brill, Bucks HP18 9TH. *T:* (01844) 237481. *Died 6 Oct. 2005.*

PRIOR, Ven. Christopher, CB 1968; Archdeacon of Portsmouth, 1969–77, Archdeacon Emeritus since 1977; *b* 2 July 1912; *s* of late Ven. W. H. Prior; *m* 1945, Althea Stafford (*née* Coode) (*d* 1999); two *d*. *Educ:* King's Coll., Taunton; Keble Coll., Oxford; Cuddesdon Coll. Curate of Hornsea, 1938–41; Chaplain RN from 1941, Chaplain of the Fleet, 1966–69. Served in: HMS Royal Arthur, 1941; HMHS Maine, 1941–43; HMS Scylla, 1943–44; HMS Owl, 1944–46; various ships, 1946–58; Britannia RNC,

Dartmouth, 1958–61; HMS Blake, 1961–62; HM Dockyard, Portsmouth, 1963–66; QHC, 1966–69. *Recreation:* walking. *Address:* c/o Mrs Field, West Cottage, 9 Albert Road, Dorchester DT1 1SG. *T:* (01305) 259565.
Died 14 Sept. 2004.

PROBY, Sir Peter, 2nd Bt *cr* 1952, of Elton Hall. co. Huntingdon; FRICS; Lord-Lieutenant of Cambridgeshire, 1981–85; *b* 4 Dec. 1911; *s* of Sir Richard George Proby, 1st Bt, MC, and Betty Monica (*d* 1967), *d* of A. H. Hallam Murray; *S* father, 1979; *m* 1944, Blanche Harrison, *o d* of Col Henry Harrison Cripps, DSO; one *s* three *d* (and one *s* decd). *Educ:* Eton; Trinity College, Oxford (BA 1934). Served War of 1939–45, Captain, Irish Guards. Bursar of Eton College, 1953–71. *Heir: s* William Henry Proby, MA, FCA [*b* 13 June 1949; *m* 1974, Meredyth Anne Brentnall; four *d*. *Educ:* Eton; Lincoln Coll., Oxford (MA)]. *Address:* Pottle Green, Elton, Peterborough PE8 6SG. *T:* (01832) 280434.
Died 18 April 2002.

PROCKTOR, Patrick, RA 1996; RWS 1981; RE 1991; painter, since 1962; *b* 12 March 1936; 2nd *s* of late Eric Christopher Procktor and Barbara Winifred (*née* Hopkins); *m* 1973, Kirsten Bo (*née* Andersen) (*d* 1984); one *s*. *Educ:* Highgate; Slade Sch. (Diploma). Many one-man exhibns, Redfern Gallery, 1963–; retrospective tour, England and Wales, 1990; Paintings in Hospitals (exhibn of paintings distributed to hosps), 1999; exhibn in favour of St Marylebone Fire Brigade, 1999. Designed windows for AIDS Recreation Centre, St Stephen's Hosp., Fulham, 1988. *Publications:* One Window in Venice, 1974; Coleridge's Rime of the Ancient Mariner (new illustrated edn), 1976; A Chinese Journey (aquatint landscapes), 1980; (illustrated) Sailing through China, by Paul Theroux, 1983; Patrick Procktor Prints 1959–85 (catalogue raisonné), 1985; A Shropshire Lad, by A. E. Housman (new illustrated edn), 1986; Self-Portrait (autobiog.), 1991; *relevant publications:* Patrick Procktor (monograph by Patrick Kinmonth), 1985; Patrick P, by John McEwen, 1997. *Recreation:* Russian ballet. *Address:* c/o Redfern Gallery, 20 Cork Street, W1X 2HL. *Club:* Garrick.
Died 29 Aug. 2003.

PROCTOR, Ven. Jesse Heighton; Archdeacon of Warwick, 1958–74, then Emeritus; Vicar of Sherbourne, Warwick, 1958–69; *b* 26 May 1908; *s* of Thomas and Sophia Proctor, Melton Mowbray; *m* 1938, Helena Mary Wood (*d* 1992), *d* of John Thomas and Jessie Wood, Melton Mowbray; one *s* two *d*. *Educ:* County Grammar Sch. of King Edward VII, Melton Mowbray; Coll. of St Mark and St John, Chelsea, Univ. of London (MA); St Andrew's Theological Training House, Whittlesford. Asst Master, Winterbourne Sch., Croydon, 1929–32; Sen. History Master, Melton Mowbray Grammar Sch., 1932–35; deacon 1935, priest 1936; Chap. and Tutor, St Andrew's, Whittlesford, 1935–38; Curate, St Philip's, Leicester, 1938–39; Vicar, Glen Parva and South Wigston, and Chap., Glen Parva Barracks, Leicester, 1939–46; Precentor of Coventry Cath., 1946–58; Hon. Canon of Coventry, 1947; Chaplain, Gulson Hosp., 1953–58; Sen. Examining Chap. to Bishop of Coventry, 1947–65; Canon Theologian of Coventry, 1954–59. Vice-Pres. CMS. Governor: Univ. of Warwick, 1966–68; City of Coventry Coll. of Educn, 1966–70. Barnabas of Coventry Evening Telegraph, 1955–75. *Publication:* (contrib.) Neville Gorton (SPCK), 1957. *Recreations:* study of theology and history, the countryside. *Address:* Dilkusha, 22 Bank Crescent, Ledbury, Herefordshire HR8 1AA. *T:* (01531) 632241.
Died 21 May 2001.

PROKHOROV, Prof. Alexander Mikhailovich; Hero of Socialist Labour, 1969, 1986; Order of Lenin (five-fold); Physicist; Director, Centre for Natural Science Research, General Physics Institute, Russian Academy of Sciences, Moscow, since 1998; Editor-in-Chief, Bolshaya Rossiyskaya (formerly Bolshaya Sovetskaya) Encyclopedia Publishing House, since 1970; *b* Atherton, Australia, 11 July 1916; *s* of Mikhail Prokhorov; *m* 1941, Galina Alexeyevna (*née* Shelepina); one *s*. *Educ:* Leningrad State University; Lebedev Inst. of Physics. Academy of Sciences of the USSR, later Russian Academy of Sciences (Department of General Physics and Astronomy): Corresp. Mem., 1960–66; Full Mem., 1966–; Mem. Presidial Body, 1970; Academician-Secretary, 1973–87; Dir, 1983–98; Hon. Dir, 1998–, Gen. Physics Inst. Chm., Nat. Commn of Soviet Physicists, 1973–. Professor, Moscow University, 1958–. Hon. Professor: Delhi Univ.; Bucharest Univ., 1971; Cluz Univ., 1977; Praha Politechnical Inst., 1980. Member: European Phys. Soc., 1977; European Acad. of Scis, Art and Literature, 1986; Hon. Member: Amer. Acad. of Arts and Sciences, 1972; Acad. of Sciences of Hungary, 1976; Acad. of Sciences, German Democratic Republic, 1977; Acad. of Scis of Czechoslavakia, 1982; Acad. of Scis Leopoldina, 1984. Joined Communist Party of the Soviet Union, 1950. Awarded Lenin Prize, 1959; Nobel Prize for Physics (jointly with Prof. N. G. Basov and Prof. C. H. Townes), 1964. *Publications:* contributions on non-linear oscillations, radiospectroscopy and quantum radio-physics. *Address:* General Physics Institute, Russian Academy of Sciences, Vavilova Street 38, Moscow 117942, Russia.
Died 8 Jan. 2002.

PROPHET, Prof. Arthur Shelley, CBE 1980; FDSRCS; FFDRCSI; Professor of Dental Surgery, University of London, 1956–83, then Emeritus; *b* 11 Jan. 1918; *s* of Eric Prophet and Mabel Wightman; *m* 1942, Vivienne Mary Bell; two *s*. *Educ:* Sedbergh Sch.; Univ. of Manchester (BDS Hons (Preston Prize and Medal), 1940; Dip. in Bacteriology, 1948; DDS 1950). FDSRCS 1958; FFDRCS Ireland, 1964. RNVR (Dental Br.), 1941–46; Nuffield Dental Fellow, 1946–48; Lectr in Dental Bacteriology, Univ. of Manchester, 1948–54; Lectr in Dental Surgery, QUB, 1954–56; Dir of Dental Studies, 1956–74, Dean of Dental Studies, 1974–77, UCH Dental Sch.; Dean, UCH Medical Sch., 1977–80; Dean, 1980–82, Vice-Dean, 1982–83, Faculty of Clinical Scis, UCL. Lectures: Charles Tomes, RCS, 1977; Wilkinson, Univ. of Manchester, 1978; Elwood, QUB, 1979; Shefford, UCL, 1983. Rep. of University of London on Gen. Dental Council, 1964–84. Elected Mem. Bd, Faculty of Dental Surgery, RCS, 1964–80 (Vice-Dean, 1972–73); Member: Cttee of Management, Inst. of Dental Surgery, 1963–83; Dental Sub-Cttee, UGC, 1968–78; Bd of Governors, UCH, 1957–74; Camden and Islington AHA(T), 1974–82; Bloomsbury HA, 1982–83. WHO Consultant, 1966; Consultant Dental Advr, DHSS, 1977–83. DSc *hc* Malta, 1987. *Publications:* contrib. to medical and dental journals. *Address:* Morton Rough, Morton Green, Welland, Malvern WR13 6LR. *T:* (01684) 311965.
Died 16 Oct. 2002.

PROSSER, Raymond Frederick, CB 1973; MC 1942; *b* 12 Sept. 1919; *s* of Frederick Charles Prosser and Jane Prosser (*née* Lawless); *m* 1949, Fay Newmarch Holmes; two *s* three *d*. *Educ:* Wimbledon Coll.; The Queen's Coll., Oxford (1938–39 and 1946). Served Royal Artillery (Field), 1939–45 (MC, despatches): service in Egypt, Libya, India and Burma; Temp. Major. Asst Principal, Min. of Civil Aviation, 1947; Sec., Air Transport Advisory Council, 1952–57; Private Sec. to Minister of Transport and Civil Aviation, 1959, and to Minister of Aviation, 1959–61; Counsellor (Civil Aviation), HM Embassy, Washington, DC, 1965–68; Under-Sec., Marine Div., BoT, later DTI, 1968–72; Deputy Sec., Regional Industrial Organisation and Policy, DTI, later DoI, 1972–77; Principal Estabt and Finance Officer, Depts of Industry, Trade, and Prices and Consumer Protection, 1977–79, retired. Dir, European Investment Bank, 1973–77. Mem. (part-time), CAA, 1980–85. *Address:* Juniper House, Shalford Common, Shalford, Guildford, Surrey GU4 8DF. *T:* (01483) 566498.
Died 23 Dec. 2004.

PROWSE, Florence Irene, (Mrs W. A. Prowse); see Calvert, F. I.

PRYCE, Maurice Henry Lecorney, FRS 1951; Professor of Physics, University of British Columbia, 1968–78, then Emeritus; *b* 24 Jan. 1913; *e s* of William John Pryce and Hortense Lecorney; *m* 1939, Susanne Margarete Born (marr. diss., 1959); one *s* three *d*; *m* 1961, Freda Mary Kinsey (*d* 1992). *Educ:* Royal Grammar Sch., Guildford; Trinity Coll., Cambridge (BA 1933, MA 1937). Commonwealth Fund Fellow at Princeton, NJ, USA, 1935–37; Fellow of Trinity Coll., Cambridge, and Faculty Asst Lecturer, Univ. of Cambridge, 1937–39; Reader in Theoretical Physics, Univ. of Liverpool, 1939–45. Engaged on Radar research with Admiralty Signal Establishment, 1941–44, and on Atomic Energy Research with Nat. Res. Council of Canada, Montreal, 1944–45. Univ. Lectr in Mathematics and Fellow of Trinity Coll., Cambridge, 1945–46; Wykeham Prof. of Physics, Univ. of Oxford, 1946–54; Henry Overton Wills Prof. of Physics, Univ. of Bristol, 1954–64; Prof. of Physics, USC, 1964–68. Visiting Professor: Princeton Univ., NJ, USA, 1950–51; Duke Univ., NC, USA, 1958; Univ. of Sussex, 1976–77. Mem., Technical Adv. Cttee to Atomic Energy of Canada Ltd on Nuclear Fuel Waste Management Program, 1979–96. *Publications:* various on theoretical physics, in learned jls. *Recreations:* theoretical scientific research, reading, music. *Address:* 4754 West 6th Avenue, Vancouver, BC V6T 1C5, Canada; Physics Department, University of British Columbia, 6224 Agriculture Road, Vancouver, BC V6T 1Z1, Canada. *Club:* Athenæum.
Died 24 July 2003.

PUGH, Lionel Roger Price, CBE 1975; VRD 1953; Executive Member, British Steel Corporation, 1972–77; *b* 9 May 1916; *s* of late Henry George Pugh, Cardiff; *m* 1942, Joyce Norma Nash; one *s* one *d*. *Educ:* Clifton. FCA. Supply Officer, RNVR, 1938–60; war service mainly in Mediterranean, 1939–46; retired as Lt Comdr, RNR, 1960. With Deloitte & Co., 1933–47; joined Guest Keen Baldwins Iron & Steel Co. Ltd, 1947; Dir 1955; Man. Dir 1960; Chm. 1962; Jt Man. Dir, GKN Steel, 1964. Dir, Product Co-ordination, British Steel Corp., 1967; Dep. Commercial Man. Dir, 1969; Man. Dir, Ops and Supplies, 1970; Mem., Corporate Finance and Planning, 1972; Chairman: BSC (UK) Ltd, 1974–77; BSC Chemicals Ltd, 1974–77; Redpath Dorman Long Ltd, 1974–77. Dir, 1973, Dep. Chm., 1977–86, Bridon plc; Dir, Ryan Internat., 1979–85. Pres., Iron and Steel Inst., 1973; Hon. Member: American Iron and Steel Inst. 1973; Metals Soc., 1976; Inst. of Metals, 1985; Inst. of Materials, 1992. Mem., Civil Aviation Council for Wales, 1962–66; part-time Mem., S Wales Electricity Bd, 1963–67. DL S Glamorgan (formerly Glamorgan), 1963–78. Gold Cross of Merit (Poland), 1942. *Address:* Brook Cottage, Bournes Green, Oakridge, Glos GL6 7NL. *T:* (01452) 770554. *Club:* Cirencester Golf. *Died 11 Feb. 2002.*

PUGH, William David, CBE 1965; JP; FIM; CIMgt; retired; Deputy Chairman, English Steel Corporation Ltd, 1965–67 (Managing Director, 1955–65); Director of Personnel, British Steel Corporation (Midland Group), 1967–70; *b* 21 Nov. 1904; *s* of late Sir Arthur and Lady Pugh; *m* 1936, Mary Dorothea Barber; one *d*. *Educ:* Regent Street Polytechnic; Sheffield Univ. Joined Research Dept, Vickers Ltd, Sheffield, 1926, Director, Vickers Ltd, 1962–67; Chairman: The Darlington Forge Ltd, 1957–66; Taylor Bros & Co. Ltd, 1959–66; Director: (and alternate Chairman), Firth Vickers Stainless Steels Ltd, 1948–67; High Speed Steel Alloys Ltd, 1953–68; Industrial Training Council Service, 1960–67; British Iron and Steel Corp. Ltd, 1962–67; Sheffield Boy Scouts Holdings Ltd, 1965–85 (Scout Silver Wolf, 1983); Sheffield Centre for Environmental Research Ltd. Associate of Metallurgy (Sheffield University; Mappin Medallist). Hon. Fellow, Sheffield Hallam Univ. (formerly Sheffield Poly.), 1969. Hon. DMet Sheffield, 1966.

Recreations: gardening, golf, reading, voluntary work, drystone-walling. *Address:* 8 Royal Croft Drive, Baslow, Bakewell, Derbys DE45 1SN. *T:* (01246) 582386.
Died 10 Jan. 2002.

PULLÉE, Ernest Edward, CBE 1967; ARCA, ACSD, FSAE, NEAC; painter; Chief Officer, National Council for Diplomas in Art and Design, 1967–74; retired; *b* 19 Feb. 1907; *s* of Ernest and Caroline Elizabeth Pullée; *m* 1933, Margaret Fisher, ARCA, NEAC; one *s*. *Educ:* St Martin's Sch., Dover; Royal Coll. of Art, London. Principal: Gloucester Coll. of Art, 1934–39; Portsmouth Coll. of Art, 1939–45; Leeds Coll. of Art, 1945–56; Leicester Coll. of Art and Design, 1956–67. Regular exhibitor, RA summer exhibns and at London and provincial galls. Pres., Nat. Soc. for Art Educn, 1945, 1959; Chm., Assoc. of Art Instns, 1959; Mem., Nat. Adv. Coun. for Art Educn, 1959; Mem., Nat. Coun. for Diplomas in Art and Design, 1961. FRSA 1952. Hon. Life Mem., NEAC, 1986. Hon. Fellow: Portsmouth Polytechnic, 1976; Leicester Polytechnic, 1977. Hon. DA (Manchester), 1961. *Publications:* contribs to professional and academic jls. *Recreation:* travel. *Address:* c/o Michael Pullée, 48 Wray Common Road, Reigate, Surrey RH2 0ND. *Club:* Chelsea Arts. *Died 28 July 2002.*

PULLINGER, Sir (Francis) Alan, Kt 1977; CBE 1970; DL; Chairman, Haden Carrier Ltd, 1961–79; *b* 22 May 1913; *s* of William Pullinger; *m* 1st, 1946, Felicity Charmian Gotch Hobson (*d* 1964); one *s* one *d* (and one *s* decd); 2nd, 1966, Jacqueline Louise Anne Durin (*d* 1992). *Educ:* Marlborough Coll.; Balliol Coll., Oxford (MA). Pres., IHVE, 1972–73. Chm., Hertfordshire Scouts, 1976–91. Vice Chm. Council, Benenden Sch., 1980–97. Hon. FCIBSE, 1977. DL Herts, 1982. *Recreations:* mountaineering, sailing, beagling. *Address:* Grange Farm Cottage, Bovingdon Green Lane, Bovingdon, Herts HP3 0LB. *T:* (01442) 831816. *Clubs:* Alpine, Travellers.
Died 18 Feb. 2002.

PURCHAS, Rt Hon. Sir Francis (Brooks), Kt 1974; PC 1982; a Lord Justice of Appeal, 1982–93; *b* 19 June 1919; *s* of late Captain Francis Purchas, 5th Royal Irish Lancers and Millicent Purchas (*née* Brooks); *m* 1942, Patricia Mona Kathleen, *d* of Lt Milburn; two *s*. *Educ:* Summerfields Sch., Oxford; Marlborough Coll.; Trinity Coll., Cambridge (BA 1947, MA 1962). Served RE, 1940–46: North Africa, 1943 (despatches); Hon. Lt-Col retd (Africa Star, Italy Star, 1939–45 Medal; Defence Medal). Allied Mil. Commn, Vienna. Called to Bar, Inner Temple, 1948, QC 1965, Bencher, 1972; practised at Bar, 1948–74. Leader, SE Circuit, 1972–74; Dep. Chm., E Sussex QS, 1966–71; Recorder of Canterbury, 1969–71 (Hon. Recorder of Canterbury, 1972–74); Recorder of the Crown Court, 1972–74; a Judge of the High Court of Justice, Family Div., 1974–82; Presiding Judge, SE Circuit, 1977–82. Comr, Central Criminal Court, 1970–71. Mem., Bar Council, 1966–68, 1969–71, 1972–74. Judicial Mem., City Disputes Panel, 1994–99; Dep. Appeal Comr, PIA, 1994–2001. FCIArb 1995. Liveryman, Broderers' Co., 1962. *Recreations:* shooting, golf, fishing. *Address:* Parkhurst House, near Haslemere, Surrey GU27 3BY. *T:* (01428) 707280. *Clubs:* Boodle's; Hawks (Cambridge); Royal St George's Golf, West Sussex Golf (Pres., 1994–).
Died 9 Sept. 2003.

PUSEY, Nathan Marsh, PhD; President Emeritus, Harvard University; *b* Council Bluffs, Iowa, 4 April 1907; *s* of John Marsh Pusey and Rosa Pusey (*née* Drake); *m* 1936, Anne Woodward; two *s* one *d*. *Educ:* Harvard University, USA (AB 1928, AM 1932, PhD 1937). Assistant, Harvard, 1933–34; Sophomore tutor, Lawrence Coll., 1935–38; Asst Prof., history and literature, Scripps Coll., Claremont, Calif., 1938–40; Wesleyan University: Asst Prof., Classics, 1940–43; Assoc. Prof., 1943–44; President: Lawrence Coll., Appleton, Wisconsin, 1944–53; Harvard Univ., 1953–71; Andrew Mellon Foundn, 1971–75. Pres., United Bd for Christian Higher

Educn in Asia, 1979–83. Holds many hon. degrees from Universities and colleges in USA and other countries. Officier de la Légion d'Honneur, 1958. *Publications:* The Age of the Scholar, 1963; American Higher Education 1945–1970, 1978. *Address:* 200 East 66th Street (A-501), New York, NY 10021, USA.   *Died 14 Nov. 2001.*

PUTTICK, Richard George; Chairman, 1974–85 and Chief Executive, 1978–85, Taylor Woodrow plc, retired; *b* Kingston, Surrey, 16 March 1916; *e s* of late George Frederick Puttick and Dorothea (*née* Bowerman); *m* 1943, Betty Grace Folbigg; two *s. Educ:* St Mark's, Teddington. Joined Taylor Woodrow Construction Ltd, 1940 (the Taylor Woodrow Group's largest contracting subsidiary co.); Dir, 1955; Asst Managing Dir, 1968; Dir, Taylor Woodrow Ltd, 1969; Jt Dep. Chm., 1972. Mem. Council, CBI, 1967–69; Pres., NW Middx Branch, BIM, 1976–85. FCIOB; CIMgt. Liveryman, Worshipful Co. of Joiners and Ceilers. *Recreations:* music, reading, gardening, supporting sports. *Address:* Woodlawn, Hanger Hill, Weybridge, Surrey KT13 9XU. *T:* (01932) 845131.
Died 20 Feb. 2001.

PYKE, David Alan, CBE 1986; MD, FRCP; Registrar, Royal College of Physicians, 1975–92; Physician-in-charge, Diabetic Department, King's College Hospital, London, 1971–86; *b* 16 May 1921; *s* of Geoffrey and Margaret Pyke; *m* 1948, Janet, *d* of Dr J. Gough Stewart; one *s* two *d. Educ:* Leighton Park Sch., Reading; Cambridge Univ. (MD 1956); University Coll. Hosp. Med. Sch., London. FRCP 1964. Junior med. appts in London and Oxford, 1945–59; Service in RAMC, 1946–48; apptd to staff of King's Coll. Hosp., 1959. Hon. Secretary: Assoc. of Physicians of GB and Ire., 1968–73; Royal Soc. of Med., 1972–74. *Publications:* (ed jtly) Clinical Diabetes and its Biochemical Basis, 1968; (ed) Clinics in Endocrinology and Metabolism, Vol. 1, No 3, 1972; (jtly) Diabetes and its Management, 1973, 3rd edn 1978; articles in med. and sci. jls. *Recreations:* golf, opera. *Address:* 17 College Road, SE21 7BG. *T:* (020) 8693 2313.
Died 12 Jan. 2001.

Q

QUÉGUINER, Jean; Légion d'Honneur, 1970; Administrateur Général des Affaires Maritimes, France; maritime consultant, since 1985; *b* 2 June 1921; *s* of Etienne Quéguiner and Anne Trehin; *m* 1952, Marguerite Gaillard; one *s* one *d. Educ:* Lycée Buffon, Collège Stanislas and Faculté de Droit, Paris; Coll. of Administration of Maritime Affairs, St Malo. Docteur en Droit (maritime), Bordeaux. Head of Maritime Dist of Caen, 1953; Dep. Head of Coll. of Admin. of Maritime Affairs, 1955; Head of Safety of Navigation Section, 1963; Vice-Chm. of Maritime Safety Cttee, 1965–68, Dep. Sec.-Gen., 1968–77, IMCO; Chm., Chantiers Navals de l'Esterel, 1981–85. Maritime expert to the Courts, 1986–. Mem. Cttee, Chambre d'Arbitrage de la Rochelle Centre Ouest-Atlantique (formerly de la Rochelle), 1992–. *Publications:* Législation et réglementation maritime, 1955; Le code de la mer, 1965; La croisière cotière, 1967; Le code fluvial à l'usage des plaisanciers, 1970. *Recreation:* sailing.
Died 6 Aug. 2004.

QUILLEY, Denis Clifford, OBE 2002; actor; *b* 26 Dec. 1927; *s* of Clifford Charles Quilley and Ada Winifred (*née* Stanley); *m* 1949, Stella Chapman; one *s* two *d. Educ:* Bancroft's, Woodford, Essex. First appearance, Birmingham Rep. Theatre, 1945; The Lady's not for Burning, Globe, 1949; Old Vic and Young Vic Cos, 1950–51: parts included: Fabian in Twelfth Night (on tour, Italy), Gratiano in Merchant of Venice; Revue, Airs on a Shoe String (exceeded 700 perfs), Royal Court, 1953; first leading rôle in West End as Geoffrey Morris in Wild Thyme, Duke of York's, 1955; subseq. parts incl.: Tom Wilson in Grab Me a Gondola (over 600 perfs), Lyric; Captain Brassbound, and Orlando, Bristol Old Vic; Candide, Saville; Benedick in Much Ado about Nothing, Open Air Th.; Archie Rice in The Entertainer, Nottingham Playhouse; Krogstad in A Doll's House, Brighton; Nat. Theatre, 1971–76: Aufidius (Coriolanus); Macbeth; Bolingbroke (Richard II); Caliban (The Tempest); Lopakin (Cherry Orchard); Jamie (Long Day's Journey into Night); Claudius (Hamlet); Hector (Troilus and Cressida); Bajazeth (Tamburlaine); Privates on Parade, Aldwych, 1977, Piccadilly, 1978 (SWET award, 1977); Morell in Candida, Albery Theatre, 1977; Deathtrap, Garrick, 1978; title rôle in Sweeney Todd, Theatre Royal Drury Lane (SWET award), 1980; Antony, in Antony and Cleopatra, Chichester, 1985; Fatal Attraction, Haymarket, 1985; La Cage aux Folles, Palladium, 1986; Pizarro in Royal Hunt of the Sun, UK tour, 1989; The School for Scandal, NT, 1990; Brachiano in The White Devil, NT, 1991; Venus Observed, She Stoops to Conquer, Chichester, 1992; Sweeney Todd, RNT, 1993; The Merry Wives of Windsor, RNT, A Patriot for Me, RSC, 1995; Prospero in The Tempest, Regent's Park Open Air Th., 1996; Horsham in Waste, Pozzo in Waiting for Godot, Gloucester in King Lear, Old Vic, 1997; Racing Demon, Katherine Howard, Chichester, 1998; National Theatre: Troilus and Cressida, Candide, Money, 1999; Polonius in Hamlet, 2000; Humble Boy, 2001; Anything Goes, 2002; has played in NY, Melbourne and Sydney. *Films:* Life at the Top, 1965; Anne of the Thousand Days, 1969; Murder on the Orient Express, 1974; The Black Windmill, 1974; The Antagonists, 1980; Evil Under the Sun, 1981; Privates on Parade, 1982; King David, 1985; Foreign Body, 1986; The Shell-seekers, 1989; Mr Johnson, 1990; A Dangerous Man, 1991. *TV plays and series* incl.: Merchant of Venice; The Father; Henry IV (Pirandello); Murder in the Cathedral; Time Slip; Contrabandits (Aust.); Clayhanger; The Serpent Son; The Crucible; Gladstone, in No 10; Masada; Anno Domini; Murder of a Moderate Man, 1988; Rich Tea and Sympathy, 1991. *Recreations:* playing the piano, flute and cello, walking. *Address:* c/o Bernard Hunter Associates, 13 Spencer Gardens, SW14 7AH. *Died 5 Oct. 2003.*

QUILLIAM, Hon. Sir (James) Peter, Kt 1988; **Hon. Mr Justice Quilliam;** Judge of the High Court and Court of Appeal, Cook Islands, since 1988; Chief Justice of the Cook Islands, 1995–2000; *b* 23 March 1920; *s* of Ronald Henry Quilliam, CBE and Gwendoline Minnie Quilliam; *m* 1945, Ellison Jean Gill; two *s* one *d. Educ:* Wanganui Collegiate Sch.; Victoria Univ. of Wellington (LLB). Private practice as barrister and solicitor, 1945–69; Crown Prosecutor, New Plymouth, NZ, 1955–69; Judge, High Court of NZ, 1969–88, and Senior Puisne Judge, 1985–88; Judge of the Ct of Appeal, Fiji, 1992–95. NZ Police Complaints Authy, 1989–92. Pres., Taranaki Dist Law Soc., 1965–67. *Recreations:* golf, fishing, gardening, reading. *Address:* 9 Puketiro Avenue, Northland, Wellington 5, New Zealand. *T:* (4) 758166. *Clubs:* Wellington, Wellington Golf (NZ). *Died 2004.*

QUILLIAM, Prof. Juan Pete, (Peter), OBE 1986; DSc; FRCP; Professor of Pharmacology, University of London, at St Bartholomew's Hospital Medical College, 1962–83, then Emeritus; *b* 20 Nov. 1915; *e s* of late Thomas Quilliam, Peel, IoM and Maude (*née* Pavitt); *m* 1st, 1946, Melita Kelly (*d* 1957); one *s* one *d*; 2nd, 1958, Barbara Lucy Marion, *y d* of late Rev. William Kelly, Pelynt, Cornwall. *Educ:* University Coll. Sch.; UCL (exhibnr); UCH Med. Sch. MSc 1938, MB BS 1941; DSc 1969. FRCP 1975. Vice-Pres., London Univ. Athletic Union, 1938; Pres., London Univ. Boat Club, 1939–40 (rowing purple 1938). Sharpey Physiol Schol., UCL, 1939–41; House Phys. and House Surg., UCH, 1941; House Phys., Brompton Hosp. for Diseases of Chest, 1941–42; Asst TB Officer, Chelsea, 1941–42; Exptl Officer, Min. of Supply, 1942–43; served RAFVR Med. Br. (Central Fighter Estabt), 1943–46; Lectr in Pharmacol., KCL, 1945–55; London Univ. Travelling Fellow, 1949–50; Fellow, Johns Hopkins Hosp. Med. Sch., 1949–50; Sen. Lectr and Head of Pharmacol. Dept, 1956, Reader, 1958, St Bartholomew's Hosp. Med. Coll.; formerly Hon. Clinical Asst, St Bartholomew's Hosp. Gresham Prof. of Physic, 1967–68. University of London Convocation: Mem. Standing Cttee, 1966–73; Senator, Medicine, 1968–73; Chm., 1973–90; Mem. Mgt Cttee, 1973–90; Trustee, 1990–99; Chm., Univ. of London Convocation Trust, 1973–90; Mem. Ct and Senate, London Univ., 1973–90. Examiner in Pharmacol. and Clinical Pharmacol. to Univs of London, Edinburgh, Cambridge, Dundee, Liverpool, Manchester, TCD, NUI and Cardiff, also to Fac. of Anaesthetists and Apothecaries Soc. Mem., 1960–88, Dep. Chm., 1975–88, Gen. Optical Council; Gen. Sec., British Pharmacol Soc., 1968–71 (Hon. Mem., 1999); British Medical Association: Mem. Council, 1971–85; Chairman: Med. Academic Staff Cttee, 1978, 1980, 1982; Bd of Sci. and Educn, 1982–85; Fellow, 1981; Vice-Pres., 1988. Member: CMO's Academic Forum, 1980–81; Academic Medicine Gp, RCP, 1982–90; Cttee CH/30, BSI, 1984–90. Member: IBA Advertising Adv. Cttee, 1984–92; Jt BBC/IBA Central Appeals Adv. Cttee, 1987–92. Crouch Harbour Authority: Mem., 1987; Vice-Chm. 1988; Chm., 1989–94; Mem., 1974, Chm., 1987–90; Crouch Area Yachting Fedn; Associate Mem., Burnham Week Regatta Jt Clubs Cttee, 1984–90. Trustee: City Parochial Foundn, 1977–89; Trust for London, 1986–89; Nat. Heart Forum (formerly Nat. Forum for Coronary Heart Disease Prevention), 1989–2003 (Hon. Treas., 1990–94; Hon. Mem.); Founder Trustee, 1984–94, Co-Chm., 1984–99, Help the Hospices Trust; Mem., Grants Council, Charities Aid Foundn, 1990–99. Vice-Pres., Totteridge Residents' Assoc., 1997–2003. Press Editor,

British Jl of Pharmacol., 1957–60. *Publications: jointly:* Medical Effects of Nuclear War, 1983; Boxing, 1984; Young People and Alcohol, 1986; Long Term Environment Effects of Nuclear War, 1986; Alternative Therapy, 1986; The Torture Report, 1986; papers on visual purple, blood/acqueous humour barrier permability, intra-ocular fluid, DFP and synaptic transmission in heart and muscle, action drugs on the iris, the ocular critical flicker fusion frequency, the auditory flutter fusion frequency, the electro-pharmacology of sedatives, general anaesthetics on autonomic ganglia as a model of brain synapses, GABA-like actions on lobster muscle, effects of staphylococcal α-toxin on intestine, the ultrastructural effects on autonomic ganglia in the presence of chemical substances, World Medicine, University "Cuts" 1983. *Recreations:* work, sailing. *Address:* Hornbeams, 34 Totteridge Common, Totteridge, N20 8NE. *Club:* United Hospitals Sailing (Burnham-on-Crouch) (Cdre, 1974–). *Died 11 Sept. 2003.*

QUILLIAM, Hon. Sir Peter; *see* Quilliam, Hon. Sir J. P.

QUILLIAM, Peter; *see* Quilliam, J. P.

QUINN, Prof. David Beers, DLit, PhD; MRIA, FRHistS; Andrew Geddes and John Rankin Professor of Modern History, University of Liverpool, 1957–76; *b* 24 April 1909; *o s* of late David Quinn, Omagh and Belfast, and Albertina Devine, Cork; *m* 1937, Alison Moffat Robertson, MA (*d* 1993), *d* of late John Ireland Robertson, Edinburgh; two *s* one *d*. *Educ:* Clara (Offaly) No 2 National Sch.; Royal Belfast Academical Institution; Queen's Univ., Belfast (University Schol.; BA 1st Cl. Hons Medieval and Modern Hist. 1931; DLit 1958); King's Coll., University of London (PhD 1934). Asst Lecturer, 1934, and Lecturer, 1937, University College, Southampton; Lecturer in History, QUB, 1939–44; seconded to BBC European Service, 1943; Prof. of History, University College, Swansea, 1944–57. Secretary, Ulster Society for Irish Historical Studies, 1939–44; Member: Council of Hakluyt Society, 1950–54, 1957–60 (Vice-Pres., 1960–82, 1987–, Pres., 1982–87); Council of Royal Historical Society, 1951–55, 1956–60 (Vice-Pres., 1964–68, Hon. Vice-Pres., 1983); Fellow: Folger Shakespeare Lib. (Washington, DC), 1957, 1959, 1963–64; John Carter Brown Lib., 1970, 1982; Leverhulme Res. Fellow, 1963; British Council Visiting Scholar, NZ, 1967; Hungary, 1972; Fellow: Huntington Library, 1980; Nat. Inst. for the Humanities, 1983; Fulbright Fortieth Anniversary Dist. Fellow, 1986–87; Harrison Vis. Prof., Coll. of William and Mary, Williamsburg, Va, 1969–70; Visiting Professor: St Mary's Coll., St Mary's City, Md, 1976–78, 1980–82, 1984; Michigan Univ., 1979. Mem., President's Council, Coll. of William and Mary, Va, 1998–. Founding Mem., Bermuda Maritime Mus. Hon. Mem. American Historical Assoc., 1986. Hon. FBA 1984. Hon. DLitt: Newfoundland, 1964; NUU, 1975; NUI, 1981; Hon. DHL: St Mary's Coll., 1978; Coll. of William and Mary, 1995; Hon. LLD Univ. of N Carolina, 1980. Hon. Phi Beta Kappa, 1984. Medallist, John Carter Brown Library, 1996. *Publications:* The Port Books or Petty Customs Accounts of Southampton for the Reign of Edward IV, 2 vols, 1937–38; The Voyages and Colonising Enterprises of Sir Humphrey Gilbert, 2 vols, 1940; Raleigh and the British Empire, 1947; The Roanoke Voyages, 1584–90, 2 vols, 1955; (with Paul Hulton) The American Drawings of John White, 1577–1590, 1964; (with R. A. Skelton) R. Hakluyt's Principall Navigations (1589), 1965; The Elizabethans and the Irish, 1966; Richard Hakluyt, Editor, 1967; North American Discovery, 1971; (with W. P. Cumming and R. A. Skelton) The Discovery of North America, 1972; (with N. M. Cheshire) The New Found Land of Stephen Parmenius, 1972; (with A. M. Quinn) Virginia Voyages from Hakluyt, 1973; England and the Discovery of America 1481–1620, 1974; The Hakluyt Handbook, 2 vols, 1974; (with W. P. Cumming, S. E. Hillier and G. Williams) The Exploration of North America, 1630–1776, 1974; The Last Voyage of Thomas Cavendish, 1975; North America from First Discovery to Early Settlements, 1977; (with A. M. Quinn and S. Hillier) New American World, 5 vols, 1979; Early Maryland and a Wider World, 1982; (with A. M. Quinn) The First Settlers, 1982; (with A. N. Ryan) England's Sea Empire, 1550–1642, 1983; Set Fair for Roanoke, 1985; (ed) John Derricke, The Image of Ireland, 1986; contrib. to A New History of Ireland, vol. 2, ed A. Cosgrove, 1987; Raleigh and Quinn: the explorer and his Boswell, ed H. G. Jones, 1988; Explorers and Colonies: America 1500–1625, 1990; Ireland and America 1500–1640, 1991; Thomas Harriot and the Problem of America, 1992; (ed with A. M. Quinn) Richard Hakluyt, Discourse of Western Planting, 1994; Sir Francis Drake as seen by his contemporaries, 1996; European Approaches to North America 1450–1640, 1998; contribs on Irish history and the discovery and settlement of N America in historical journals. *Address:* 9 Knowsley Road, Cressington Park, Liverpool L19 0PF. *T:* (0151) 427 2041.
Died 19 March 2002.

QUINNEN, Peter John; Chairman, Frew Macmaster, 1990–99; *b* 4 April 1945; *s* of John Norman Quinnen and Elisabeth Clark; *m* 1972, Pammy Urquhart (*d* 2003); two *s*. *Educ:* St Benedict's School, Ealing; Christ Church, Oxford (MA Jurisp). FCA. Peat, Marwick, Mitchell & Co., 1966–72; James Capel & Co., 1972–90, Dir, 1982, Chm., and Chief Exec., 1986–90. *Recreations:* golf, cricket, reading, music. *Clubs:* St George's Hill Golf, Rye Golf.
Died 4 Oct. 2004.

R

RACE, Ruth Ann; *see* Sanger, R. A.

RADFORD, Joseph; Public Trustee, 1978–80; *b* 7 April 1918; *s* of Thomas Radford and Elizabeth Ann Radford (*née* Sanders); *m* 1976, Rosemary Ellen Murphy. *Educ:* Herbert Strutt, Belper; Nottingham Univ. First Cl. Hons, Law Soc. Intermediate, 1937; Dist., Law Soc. Final, 1940. Admitted solicitor, 1940. Served War, 1940–47, RA; 41st (5th North Staffordshire) RA; 1st Maritime Regt, RA; Staff, MELF (Major). Joined Public Trustee Office, 1949; Chief Admin. Officer, 1973–75; Asst Public Trustee, 1975–78. Mem., Law Soc., 1945– (Hon. Auditor, 1963–65). Freeman, City of London, 1983. Silver Jubilee Medal, 1977. *Address:* 80 Cunningham Park, Harrow, Middx HA1 4QJ.   *Died 30 Dec. 2003.*

RADFORD, Robert Edwin, CB 1979; Assistant Director General, St John Ambulance Association, 1981–84; Deputy Secretary and Principal Finance Officer, Department of Health and Social Security, 1977–81; *b* 1 April 1921; *s* of late Richard James Radford and May Eleanor Radford (*née* Briant); *m* 1945, Eleanor Margaret, *d* of late John Idwal Jones; one *s* one *d*. *Educ:* Royal Grammar Sch., Guildford. Bd of Educn, 1938. Served War, Lieut, RNVR, 1940–46. Colonial Office: Asst Principal, 1947; Private Sec. to Permanent Under-Sec. of State for the Colonies, 1950–51; Principal, 1951; First Sec., UK Commn, Singapore, 1961–63; Asst Sec., Dept of Techn. Co-op., 1963; transferred to ODM, 1964; Counsellor, British Embassy, Washington, and UK Alternate Exec. Dir, IBRD, 1965–67; Under Secretary: FCO (ODA), 1973; DHSS, 1974–76. Mem., SW Surrey HA, 1982–89. *Recreations:* walking, reading. *Address:* 10 Edgeborough Court, Upper Edgeborough Road, Guildford, Surrey GU1 2BL. *T:* (01483) 561822.
Died 17 May 2003.

RADLEY-SMITH, Eric John, FRCS; Surgeon Emeritus: Royal Free Hospital, London; Brentford Hospital; Epsom Hospital; Neurosurgeon, Royal National Throat, Nose and Ear Hospital; *b* 31 March 1910, *né* Eric John Smith; *m* 1937, Eileen Radley (*d* 1987); three *d* (one *s* decd). *Educ:* Paston; King's College, London; King's College Hosp. MB, BS (Hons, Dist. in Medicine, Surgery, Forensic Medicine and Hygiene), 1933; MS London, 1936. LRCP 1933; FRCS 1935 (MRCS 1933). Served War 1939–45, Wing Comdr i/c Surgical Div., RAFVR. Formerly: Surgical Registrar, King's Coll. Hosp.; House Surgeon, National Hosp. for Nervous Diseases, Queen Square. Examnr in Surgery, Univs of London and West Indies. Mem. Court, RCS. Mem. Assoc. of British Neurosurgeons; Fellow, Assoc. of Surgeons of GB. *Publications:* papers in medical jls. *Recreations:* football and farming.   *Died 19 Jan. 2003.*

RAE SMITH, David Douglas, CBE 1976; MC 1946; FCA; Senior Partner, Deloitte Haskins & Sells, Chartered Accountants, 1973–82 (Partner, 1954); *b* 15 Nov. 1919; *s* of Sir Alan Rae Smith, KBE, and Lady (Mabel Grace) Rae Smith; *m* 1947, Margaret Alison Watson, *d* of James Watson; three *s* one *d*. *Educ:* Radley Coll.; Christ Church, Oxford (MA). FCA 1959. Served War, RA, 1939–46; ME, N Africa, Italy and NW Europe; Captain; MC and mentioned in despatches. Chartered accountant, 1950. Director: Thomas Tilling Ltd, 1982–83; Sandoz Products Ltd, 1983–92; Dep. Chm., Bankers Trustee Co., 1984–91. Hon. Treasurer, RIIA, 1961–81. Member: Licensed Dealers Tribunal, 1974–88; Council, Radley Coll. 1966–92 (Chm., 1976–92). *Recreations:* horse racing, golf. *Address:* Oakdale, Crockham Hill, Edenbridge, Kent TN8 6RL. *T:* (01732) 866220.   *Died 28 Dec. 2002.*

RAEBURN, Maj.-Gen. Sir Digby; *see* Raeburn, Maj.-Gen. Sir W. D. M.

RAEBURN, Maj.-Gen. Sir (William) Digby (Manifold), KCVO 1979; CB 1966; DSO 1945; MBE 1941; Major and Resident Governor, HM Tower of London, and Keeper of the Jewel House, 1971–79; *b* 6 Aug. 1915; *s* of late Sir Ernest Manifold Raeburn, KBE, and Lady Raeburn; *m* 1960, Adeline Margaret (*née* Pryor). *Educ:* Winchester; Magdalene College, Cambridge (MA). Commnd into Scots Guards, 1936; despatches, 1942; comd 2nd Bn Scots Guards, 1953; Lieut-Col Comdg Scots Guards, 1958; Comdr, 1st Guards Bde Group, 1959; Comdr, 51st Infty Bde Group, 1960; Director of Combat Development (Army), 1963–65; Chief of Staff to C-in-C, Allied Forces, N Europe, 1965–68; Chief Instructor (Army), Imperial Defence College, 1968–70. Freeman of City of London, 1972. *Recreation:* shooting. *Address:* 25 St Ann's Terrace, NW8 6PH. *Clubs:* Pratt's, Cavalry and Guards; Royal Yacht Squadron.   *Died 8 Dec. 2001.*

RAGG, Rt Rev. Theodore David Butler, DD; Bishop of Huron, 1974–84; *b* 23 Nov. 1919; *s* of late Rt Rev. Harry Richard Ragg, sometime Bishop of Calgary and Winifred Mary Ragg (*née* Groves); *m* 1945, Dorothy Mary Lee; one *s* two *d*. *Educ:* Univ. of Manitoba; Trinity Coll., Univ. of Toronto (BA, LTh); General Synod (BD). Ordained deacon, 1949, priest, 1950; Asst Curate, St Michael and All Angels, Toronto, 1949; Rector: Nokomis, 1951; Wolseley, 1953; St Clement's, N Vancouver, 1955; St Luke's, Victoria, 1957; Bishop Cronyn Meml, London, 1962; St George's, Owen Sound, 1967; Examining Chaplain to Bishop of Huron, 1964–67; Archdeacon of Saugeen, 1967; elected Suffragan Bishop of Huron, 1973. Hon. DD: Huron Coll., London, Ont., 1975; Trinity Coll., Toronto, Ont., 1975. *Recreations:* woodworking, golf. *Address:* 2314 Oak Bay Avenue, Victoria, BC V8R 1G6, Canada.   *Died 1 July 2002.*

RAILTON, Dame Ruth, (Dame Ruth King), DBE 1966 (OBE 1954); Founder and Musical Director of the National Youth Orchestra and National Junior Music School, 1947–65; *b* 14 Dec. 1915; *d* of Rev. David Railton, MC; *m* 1962, Cecil Harmsworth King (*d* 1987). *Educ:* St Mary's School, Wantage; Royal Academy of Music, London (FRAM 1956). Director of Music or Choral work for many schools and societies, 1937–49; Adjudicator, Fedn of Music Festivals, 1946–74; Pres., Ulster Coll. of Music, 1960–; Governor, Royal Ballet School, 1966–74. Founder and Pres., Irish Children's Theatre, 1978–83; Vice-Pres., Cork Internat. Fest., 1960–85; Chm., Nat. Children's Orchestra, 1989–94; Mem., Bd of Dirs, Nat. Concert Hall, Dublin, 1981–86. Hon. Professor: Chopin Conservatoire, Warsaw, 1960; Conservatoire of Azores, 1972. Hon. RMCM 1959; Hon. FRCM 1965; Hon. FTCL 1969. Hon. LLD Aberdeen Univ., 1960. Harriet Cohen Medal for Bach, 1935. *Publication:* Daring to Excel (autobiog.), 1992. *Recreations:* interested in everything. *Address:* 45 Elizabeth Court, Milmans Street, Chelsea, SW10 0DA. *T:* (020) 7351 0089.
Died 23 Feb. 2001.

RAINE, Kathleen Jessie, (Mrs K. J. Madge), CBE 2000; FRSL; poet; *b* 14 June 1908; *o d* of late George Raine, schoolmaster, and Jessie Raine; *m* 1st, 1929, Hugh Sykes Davies (marr. diss.; he *d* 1984); 2nd, 1938, Charles Madge (marr. diss.; he *d* 1996); one *s* one *d*. *Educ:* Girton Coll., Cambridge. Editor, Temenos, a bi-annual Review devoted to the Arts of the Imagination, 1982–93 (Jt Ed., 1981–82) (10th issue 1989); Founder, Temenos Acad., 1990. Hon. DLitt: Leicester, 1974; Durham, 1979; Caen, 1987. Queen's Gold Medal for Poetry, 1992; Kahlil

Gibran Internat. Award, 2001. Comdr, Ordre des Arts et des Lettres (France), 2000 (Officier, 1995). *Publications:* Stone and Flower, 1943; Living in Time, 1946; The Pythoness, 1949; The Year One, 1952; Collected Poems, 1956; The Hollow Hill (poems), 1965; Defending Ancient Springs (criticism), 1967, 1985; Blake and Tradition (Andrew Mellon Lectures, Washington, 1962), Princeton 1968, London 1969 (abridged version, Blake and Antiquity, Princeton 1978, London 1979, trans. Japanese, 1988); (with George Mills Harper) Selected Writings of Thomas Taylor the Platonist, Princeton and London, 1969; William Blake, 1970; The Lost Country (verse), 1971 (W. H. Smith & Son Award, 1972); On a Deserted Shore (verse), 1973; Yeats, the Tarot and The Golden Dawn (criticism), 1973; Faces of Day and Night, 1973; Farewell Happy Fields (autobiog.), 1973 (French trans. as Adieu prairies heureuses, 1978; Prix du meilleur livre étranger); Death in Life and Life in Death (criticism), 1974; The Land Unknown (autobiog.), 1975 (French trans. as Le royaume inconnu, 1978); The Oval Portrait (verse), 1977; The Lion's Mouth (autobiog.), 1977 (French trans. as La Gueul du Lion, 1987); David Jones and the Actually Loved and Known (criticism), 1978; From Blake to a Vision (criticism), 1979; The Oracle in the Heart (verse), 1979; Blake and the New Age (criticism), 1979; Collected Poems, 1981; The Human Face of God, 1982; The Inner Journey of the Poet and other papers (criticism), 1982; L'Imagination Créatrice de William Blake; Yeats the Initiate, 1986; The Presence (verse), 1988; Selected Poems, 1988; Visages du Jour et de la Nuit, 1989; India Seen Afar, 1990; Golgonooza, City of the Imagination, 1991; Living with Mystery (verse), 1992; Le Monde Vivant de l'Imagination, 1998; W. B. Yeats and the Learning of the Imagination, 1999 (French trans. as W. B. Yeats ou le Pouvoir de l'Imagination, 2002); Collected Poems, 2000; Defining the Time, 2002; French trans. of verse: Isis errante, 1978; Sur un rivage désert, 1978; Le Premier Jour, 1980; Le Royaume Invisible, 1991; Spanish trans.: En una desierta orilla, 1980; Swedish trans.: Den Osedda Rosen (selected poetry), 1988; contribs to literary jls. *Address:* 47 Paultons Square, SW3 5DT. *Club:* University Women's.   *Died 6 July 2003.*

RAMACHANDRAN,   Prof.   Gopalasamudram Narayana, FRS 1977; Indian National Science Academy Albert Einstein National Professor, 1984–89; retired; specialist in molecular biology, biophysics and mathematical logic; *b* 8 Oct. 1922; *s* of G. R. Narayana Iyer and Lakshmi Ammal; *m* 1945, Rajalakshmi Sankaran (*d* 1998); two *s* one *d*. *Educ:* Maharaja's Coll., Ernakulam, Cochin; Indian Inst. of Science; Univ. of Madras (MA, MSc, DSc); Univ. of Cambridge (PhD). Lectr in Physics, Indian Inst. of Science, 1946–47, Asst Prof., 1949–52; 1851 Exhibn Scholar, Univ. of Cambridge, 1947–49; Prof., Univ. of Madras, 1952–70 (Dean, Faculty of Science, 1964–67); Indian Institute of Science: Prof. of Biophysics, 1970–78; Prof. of Mathematical Philosophy, 1978–81; Hon. Fellow, 1984; Dist. Scientist, Centre for Cellular and Molecular Biology, Hyderabad, 1981–83. Dir, Univ. Grants Commn Centre of Advanced Study in Biophysics, 1962–70; part-time Prof. of Biophysics, Univ. of Chicago, 1967–78. Member: Physical Res. Cttee, 1959–69; Nat. Cttee for Biophysics, 1961–; Bd of Sci. and Ind. Res., India, 1962–65; Council, Internat. Union of Pure and Applied Biophysics, 1969–72; Commn on Macromolecular Biophysics, 1969; Chm., Nat. Cttee for Crystallography, 1963–70; Senior Vis. Prof., Univ. of Michigan, 1965–66; Jawaharlal Nehru Fellow, 1968–70; Fogarty Internat. Schol., NIH, 1977–78. Fellow, Indian Acad. of Sciences, 1950 (Mem. Council, 1953–70; Sec., 1956–58; Vice-Pres., 1962–64); Fellow, Indian Nat. Sci. Acad., 1963; FRSA 1971. Hon. Mem., Amer. Soc. of Molecular Biology, 1965; Hon. Foreign Mem., Amer. Acad. of Arts and Scis; Founder Member: Indian Acad. of Yoga, 1980; Third World Acad., Rome, 1982. Hon. DSc: Roorkee, 1979; Indian Inst. Technology, Madras, 1985; Hyderabad, 1989; Banaras Hindu, 1991. Bhatnagar Meml Prize, 1961; Watumull Prize, 1964; John Arthur Wilson

Award, 1967; Ramanujan Medal, 1971; Maghnad Saha Medal, 1971; J. C. Bose Gold Medal and Prize of Bose Inst., 1975; Fogarty Medal, 1978; Distinguished Alumni Award, Indian Inst. of Sci., 1978; C. V. Raman Award, 1982; Birla Award for Medical Science, 1984. Editor: Current Science, 1950–58; Jl Indian Inst. of Sci., 1973–77; Member Editorial Board: Jl Molecular Biol., 1959–66; Biochimica et Biophysica Acta, 1965–72; Indian Jl Pure and Applied Physics, 1963–80; Internat. Jl Peptide and Protein Res., 1969–82; Indian Jl Biochem. and Biophys., 1970–78; Connective Tissue Research 1972–84; Biopolymers, 1973–86; Jl Biomolecular Structure and Dynamics, 1984–. *Publications:* Crystal Optics, in Handbuch der Physik, vol. 25; Molecular Structure of Collagen, in Internat. Review of Connective Tissue Research, vol. 1; Conformation of Polypeptides and Proteins, in Advances in Protein Chemistry, vol. 23; Conformation Polypeptide Chains, in Annual Reviews in Biochemistry, vol. 39; Fourier Methods in Crystallography, 1970; (ed) Advanced Methods of Crystallography; (ed) Aspects of Protein Structure; (ed) Treatise on Collagen, 2 vols, 1967; (ed) Conformation of Biopolymers, vols 1 and 2, 1967; (ed) Crystallography and Crystal Perfection; (ed) Biochemistry of Collagen. *Recreations:* Indian and Western music; detective fiction. *Address:* 13–1 Navdeep Apartments, Navjyoth Complex, Near A-One School, Subash Chowk, Memnager, Ahmedabad 380052, India.   *Died 7 April 2001.*

RAMM, Rev. Canon (Norwyn) MacDonald; Vicar of St Michael at the North Gate with St Martin and All Saints, Oxford, 1961–88 (Curate, 1957–61); City Rector, Oxford, 1961–89; Chaplain to the Queen, 1985–94; *b* 8 June 1924; *s* of Rev. Ezra Edward and Dorothy Mary Ramm; *m* 1962, Ruth Ellen, *d* of late Robert James Kirton, CBE, FIA; two *s* one *d*. *Educ:* Berkhamsted School; St Peter's Theological College, Jamaica; Lincoln College, Oxford. Jamaica appointments: Curate, St James, Montego Bay, 1951–53, deacon 1951, priest, 1952; Master, Cornwall College; Rector, St Jude's, Stony Hill with Mount James, 1953–57; Master, Wolmers Girls' School; Chaplain to Approved Sch., Stony Hill; Priest in charge, St Martin and All Saints, Oxford, 1961–71; Hon. Canon, Christ Church Cathedral, Oxford, 1985–88, then Emeritus. Chaplain to: HM Prison, Oxford, 1975–88; British Fire Services Assoc., 1980–96. Pres., Isis Dist Scout Assoc., 1984–99 (Chm., 1969–72); Patron, Headington Sch., 1994– (Mem. Council, 1981–84, Chm., 1984–93); Founder and Pres., Samaritans of Oxford, 1963–. Member: Oxford Rotary Club; Oxford Probus Club, 1996–. *Publication:* Graces Old and New from Oxford, 1990, 2nd edn 1995. *Recreations:* ski-ing, gardening, collecting Graces. *Address:* Fairlawn, Church Lane, Harwell, Abingdon, Oxon OX11 0EZ. *T:* (01235) 835454. *Clubs:* Clarendon, Frewen (Oxford).

Died 8 Jan. 2002.

RANK, Sir Benjamin (Keith), Kt 1972; CMG 1955; MS, FRCS; FRACS; FACS; Consulting Plastic Surgeon, Royal Melbourne Hospital, Repatriation Department, Victoria Eye and Ear Hospital; *b* 14 Jan. 1911; *s* of Wreghitt Rank and Bessie Rank (*née* Smith); *m* 1938, Barbara Lyle Facy (*d* 2000); one *s* three *d*. *Educ:* Scotch College, Melbourne; Ormond College, University of Melbourne (MB, BS 1934; MS 1937). MRCS, LRCP 1938; FRCS 1938. Resident Medical Officer, Royal Melbourne Hospital, 1935–36; Resident Surgical Officer, London County Council, 1938–39 (St James' Hospital, Balham); Assistant Plastic Surgeon (EMS) at Hill End (Bart's), 1939–40; AAMC, 1940–45; Officer i/c AIF Plastic Surgery Unit in Egypt, and later at Heidelberg Military Hospital, Victoria, Australia (Lt-Col); Hon. Plastic Surgeon, Royal Melbourne Hosp., 1946–66. Carnegie Fellow, 1947. Member: Dental Board of Victoria 1949–73, Joske Orator 1974; BMA State Council, 1950–60; Chm. Exec. Cttee, RACS (Pres., 1966–68); Chm., Cttee of Management, Victorian Plastic Surgery Unit (Preston Hosp.), 1966–85; Member: Bd of

Management, Royal Melbourne Hosp., 1976–82 (Vice-Pres., 1979–82); Motor Accident Bd, Victoria, 1972–82. Chm., Consult. Council on Casualty Services, Victoria Health Council; Pres., St John's Ambulance Council, Victoria, 1983–88 (Chm. 1978–83). Sir Arthur Sims Commonwealth Travelling Prof., RCS, 1958; Moynihan Lectr, 1972; Vis. Prof., Harvard Med. Sch., 1976. Syme Orator, RACS, 1976; Stawell Orator, 1977. 87th Mem., James IV Assoc. of Surgeons; Pres., British Assoc. of Plastic Surgeons, 1965. Pres., 5th Internat. Congress of Plastic Surgery, Melbourne, 1971. FRACS 1943; Hon. FACST 1952; Hon. FRCS Canada; Hon. FRCSE 1973; Hon. FACS. Hon. DSc Punjabi Univ., 1970; Hon. Member: Société Française de Chirurgie Plastique; Indian Association of Surgeons. KStJ 1988 (CStJ 1982). *Publications:* (jointly) Surgery of Repair as applied to Hand Injuries, 1953; Jerry Moore, 1975; Head and Hands, 1987; The Family Story, 1992; papers in British, American and Australian Surgical Jls. *Recreations:* golf, gardening, painting. *Address:* 12 Jerula Avenue, Mount Eliza, Victoria 3930, Australia. *Clubs:* Melbourne (Melbourne); Peninsula Golf.   *Died 26 Jan. 2002.*

RANKEILLOUR, 4th Baron *cr* 1932, of Buxted; **Peter St Thomas More Henry Hope;** farmer and landowner; *b* 29 May 1935; *s* of 3rd Baron Rankeillour and Mary Sibyl, *d* of late Col Wilfrid Ricardo, DSO; *S* father, 1967; unmarried. *Educ:* Ampleforth. *Recreations:* architecture, grand-scale landscaping; agricultural equipment inventor. *Heir: cousin* Michael Richard Hope [*b* 21 Oct. 1940; *m* 1964, Elizabeth Rosemary, *e d* of Col F. H. Fuller; one *s* two *d*]. *Address:* Achaderry House, Roy Bridge, West Inverness-shire PH31 4AN. *T:* (01397) 712206.
                    Died 12 April 2005.

RANKIN, Lady Jean (Margaret), DCVO 1969 (CVO 1957); Woman of the Bedchamber to Queen Elizabeth The Queen Mother, 1947–81, Extra Woman of the Bedchamber, since 1982; *b* 15 Aug. 1905; *d* of 12th Earl of Stair and Violet Evelyn, *o d* of Col Frederick Henry Harford, Scots Guards; *m* 1931, Niall Rankin (*d* 1965), *s* of Sir Reginald Rankin, 2nd Bt; one *s* (and one *s* decd). Governor: Thomas Coram Foundation; Magdalen Hosp. Trust. *Address:* 97 Elgin Avenue, W9 2DA.
                    Died 3 Oct. 2001.

RANKIN, Prof. Robert Alexander, PhD, ScD; FRSE, FRSAMD; Professor Emeritus, Glasgow University, since 1982 (Professor of Mathematics, 1954–82); *b* 27 Oct. 1915; *s* of late Rev. Prof. Oliver Shaw Rankin, DD, and Olivia Theresa (*née* Shaw); *m* 1942, Mary Ferrier Llewellyn (*d* 1996), *d* of late W. M. Llewellyn and K. F. Llewellyn, JP; one *s* three *d*. *Educ:* Fettes; Clare Coll., Cambridge (Wrangler, 1936; MA, PhD, ScD). Ministry of Supply (work on rockets), 1940–45. Clare College, Cambridge: Fellow, 1939–51; Asst Tutor, 1947–51; Praelector, 1949–51; Faculty Asst Lectr, 1945–48, University Lectr, 1948–51, Cambridge Univ.; Mason Professor of Pure Mathematics, Birmingham University, 1951–54; Glasgow University: Dean, Faculty of Science, 1967–69; Dean of Faculties, 1986–88; Clerk of the Senate, 1971–78. Vis. Prof., Indiana Univ., 1963–64; Vis. Fellow, Clare Hall, Cambridge, 1971; Salmon Lectr, TCD, 1997. Mem., Special Cttee, Advisory Council on Educn in Scotland, 1959–61; Founder Mem., and Chm., Scottish Mathematical Council, 1967–73. Mathematical Sec. and Editor of Proceedings of Cambridge Philosophical Soc., 1947–51; Pres. Edinburgh Mathematical Soc., 1957–58, 1978–79 (Hon. Mem., 1990); Vice-Pres. Royal Soc. of Edinburgh, 1960–63. Chm., Clyde Estuary Amenity Council, 1969–82. Hon. Pres., Glasgow Gaelic Soc., 1957–; Vice-Pres., Scottish Gaelic Texts Soc., 1967–. Keith Prize, RSE, 1961–63; Senior Whitehead Prize, 1987, De Morgan Medal, 1998, London Mathematical Soc. *Publications:* Matematicheskaya Teorija Dvizhenija Neupravljaemykh Raket, 1951; An Introduction to Mathematical Analysis, 1963; The Modular Group and its Subgroups, 1969; Modular Forms and Functions, 1977;

(ed) Modular Forms, 1985; (with B. C. Berndt) Ramanujan: letters and commentary, 1995; papers on the theory of numbers, theory of functions, rocket ballistics and Gaelic subjects in various journals. *Recreations:* hill-walking, Gaelic studies, organ music. *Address:* 98 Kelvin Court, Glasgow G12 0AH. *T:* (0141) 339 2641.
                    Died 27 Jan. 2001.

RANT, James William, CB 1995; QC 1980; **His Honour Judge Rant;** a Circuit Judge, since 1984, at Central Criminal Court, since 1986; Judge Advocate General of the Army and Royal Air Force, since 1991; *b* 16 April 1936; *s* of late Harry George Rant, FZS and Barbara Rant; *m* 1963, Helen Rant (*née* Adnams), BA; one *s* two *d* (and one *s* decd). *Educ:* Stowe Sch.; Selwyn Coll., Cambridge (BA 1958, MA 1962; LLB 1961, LLM 1985). Called to the Bar, Gray's Inn, 1961, Bencher, 1996; pupillage with late James N. Dunlop, 1962–63. Dep. Circuit Judge, 1975–79; Recorder, 1979–84; an occasional judge, Court of Appeal (Criminal Div.), 1997–. FRSA 1996. Freeman: City of London, 1986; Clockmakers' Co., 1989. *Publications:* Courts-Martial Handbook: practice and procedure, 1998; (with J. Blackett) Courts-Martial, Discipline and the Criminal Process in the Armed Services, 2003. *Recreations:* cookery, music. *Address:* 3 Temple Gardens, Middle Temple Lane, EC4Y 9AA.   *Died 25 May 2003.*

RAO, P(amulaparthi) V(enkata) Narasimha; Prime Minister of India, and Leader of the Congress (I) Party, 1991–96; *b* Karimnagar, Andhra Pradesh, 28 June 1921; widower; three *s* five *d*. *Educ:* Osmania Univ., Hyderabad; Bombay Univ.; Nagpur Univ. (BSc, LLB). Career as leader, writer, poet, agriculturalist, advocate and administrator. Member, Andhra Pradesh Legislative Assembly, 1957–77; Minister in Andhra Pradesh Govt, 1962–71; Chief Minister of the State, 1971–73. Chm., Telugu Academy, Andhra Pradesh, 1968–74; Vice-Pres., Dakshin Bharat Hindi Prachar Sabha, Madras, 1972; Gen. Sec., All India Congress Cttee, 1975–76. Elected to Lok Sabha (from Hanamkonda, Andhra Pradesh) 1972, 1977 and 1980, (from Ramtek) 1984, 1991, 1996; Minister: for External Affairs, 1980–84; for Home Affairs, 1984; of Defence, 1985; of Human Resources Develt, 1985–88; of Health and Family Welfare, 1986–88; of External Affairs, 1988–89. Chairman: Public Accounts Cttee, 1978–79; Bharatiya Vidya Bhavan's Andhra Centre. Has lectured on political matters in univs in USA and Federal Republic of Germany, and has visited many countries. *Publications:* many, including Sahasra Phan (Hindi trans.). *Recreations:* music, cinema, theatre. *Address:* Vangara Post, Karimnagar District, Andhra Pradesh, India.   *Died 23 Dec. 2004.*

RATHBONE, John Rankin, (Tim); Chairman, Sponsorship Consulting Ltd, since 1997; *b* 17 March 1933; *s* of J. R. Rathbone, MP (killed in action 1940) and Beatrice Frederika Rathbone (later Lady Wright, MBE); *m* 1st, 1960, Margarita Sanchez y Sanchez (marr. diss. 1981); two *s* one *d*; 2nd, 1982, Mrs Susan Jenkin Stopford Sackville. *Educ:* Eton; Christ Church, Oxford; Harvard Business School. 2nd Lieut KRRC, 1951–53. Robert Benson Lonsdale & Co., Merchant Bankers, 1956–58; Trainee to Vice-Pres., Ogilvy & Mather Inc., NY, 1958–66; Chief Publicity and Public Relations Officer, Conservative Central Office, 1966–68; Director: Charles Barker Group, 1968–87; Ayer Barker Ltd, 1971–87 (Man. Dir 1971–73; Dep. Chm., 1973–79); Charles Barker City, 1981–87; Charles Barker Manchester, 1983–87 (Chm., 1983–86). MP (C) Lewes, Feb. 1974–1997; contested (C) same seat, 1997. PPS to Minister of Health, 1979–82, to Minister for Trade (Consumer Affairs), 1982–83, to Minister for the Arts, 1985. Member, Select Committee: on Sound Broadcasting of H of C, 1983–87; on Nat. Heritage, 1996–97; Founder Member: All Party Parly Drugs Misuse Gp, 1984 (Chm., 1987–97); Parly Engrg Develt Gp, 1987 (Chm., 1992–97); formerly Member, All-Party Groups: Human Rights; Energy; Envmt; Consumers; Vol Orgns; British-Amer.; British-Latin Amer.; British-Cuban; British-Southern Africa (Chm.);

British-Japanese; British-China; British-Jordan; British-Spanish; British-Lebanon (Chm.); British-UAE; British-Iraqi Shias; Sane Planning. Mem., European Movt. Deleg. to Council of Europe and WEU, 1987–96; formerly Mem., Cons. ME Council. Formerly Mem. Council, Nat. Cttee for Electoral Reform. Mem., Steering Gp on Drugs, the Business Agenda, BITC, 1998–99; Dir, Phoenix House, 1999–; Mem., London Drug Policy Forum, 2000–. Vice-Pres., Tree Council, 1992–. Trustee, Mentor Foundn UK, 1999–. Gov., Bancroft's Sch., 1998–; Mem., Council, Arab-British Centre, 2000–02. FRSA 1979 (Mem. Council, 1985–88). *Publications:* It's my problem as well: drugs prevention and education, 1992; pamphlet on nursery schooling. *Recreation:* family. *Address:* 10 Ursula Street, SW11 3DW. *T:* (020) 7738 1078. *Clubs:* Brooks's, Pratt's; Sussex. *Died 12 July 2002.*

RATHBONE, Tim; *see* Rathbone, J. R.

RAVEN, Andrew Owen Earle, OBE 2004; Chairman, Macaulay Land Use Research Institute, since 2001; Forestry Commissioner, since 2000 (Chairman, National Committee for Scotland, since 2003); *b* 22 Jan. 1959; *s* of John Raven and Faith Raven (*née* Hugh Smith); *m* 1987, Amanda Game. *Educ:* Bristol Univ. (BA Arch.); Aberdeen Univ. (Dip. Land Econ.). MRICS (Rural). Cabinet-maker, 1980–83; Land Agent, Smiths Gore, 1985–95; Director: Ardtornish Estate Co. Ltd, and Partner, Ardtornish Farms, Morven, Lochaber, 1988–; Land Mgt, John Muir Trust, 1995–98. Chm., Deer Commn for Scotland, 1999–2004; Vice-Chm., Rural Forum Scotland, 1995–98; Mem., Scottish Consumer Council, 1995–2001. Trustee, Millennium Forest for Scotland, 1996–2002. Judge, Scottish Awards for Quality in Planning, 1997–2001. *Recreations:* arts and crafts, food, walking. *Address:* 25 Dean Street, Edinburgh EH4 1LN. *T:* (0131) 343 3684, *Fax:* (0131) 332 7460. *Died 2 Oct. 2005.*

RAVEN, Simon Arthur Noël, FRSL; author, critic and dramatist since 1957; *b* 28 Dec. 1927; *s* of Arthur Godart Raven and Esther Kate Raven (*née* Christmas); *m* 1951, Susan Mandeville Kilner (marr. diss.); one *s*. *Educ:* Charterhouse; King's Coll., Cambridge (MA). Research, 1951–52; regular commn, King's Shropshire Light Inf., 1953–57 (Capt.): served in Kenya; resigned, 1957. Member, Horatian Society. FRSL 1993. *Plays and dramatisations for broadcasting:* BBC TV: Royal Foundation, 1961; The Scapegoat, 1964; Sir Jocelyn, 1965; Huxley's Point Counter-Point, 1968; Trollope's The Way We Live Now, 1969; The Pallisers, a serial in 26 episodes based on the six Palliser novels of Anthony Trollope, 1974; Iris Murdoch's An Unofficial Rose, 1975; Sexton Blake, 1978; ABC TV: The Gaming Book, 1965; Thames TV: Edward and Mrs Simpson, a serial based on Edward VIII by Frances Donaldson, 1978; Love in a Cold Climate, a dramatisation of Nancy Mitford's Pursuit of Love and Love in a Cold Climate, 1980; Central TV: Julian Symons's The Blackheath Poisonings, 1993; BBC Radio: Triad, a trilogy loosely based on Thucydides' History of the Peloponnesian War, 1965–68. *Publications: novels:* The Feathers of Death, 1959; Brother Cain, 1959; Doctors Wear Scarlet, 1960; Close of Play, 1962; The Roses of Picardie, 1980; An Inch of Fortune, 1980; September Castle, 1983; The Alms for Oblivion sequence: The Rich Pay Late, 1964; Friends in Low Places, 1965; The Sabre Squadron, 1966; Fielding Gray, 1967; The Judas Boy, 1968; Places Where They Sing, 1970; Sound the Retreat, 1971; Come like Shadows, 1972; Bring Forth the Body, 1974; The Survivors, 1976; The First-born of Egypt sequence: Morning Star, 1984; The Face of the Waters, 1985; Before the Cock Crow, 1986; New Seed for Old, 1988; Blood of My Bone, 1989; In the Image of God, 1990; The Troubadour, 1992; The Islands of Sorrow, 1994; *short stories:* The Fortunes of Fingel, 1976; Remember Your Grammar, 1997; *memoirs:* Shadows on the Grass, 1982; The Old School, 1986; The Old Gang, 1988; Bird of Ill Omen, 1989; Is There Anybody There? Said the Traveller: memories of a private nuisance, 1991;

general: The English Gentleman, 1961; Boys Will be Boys, 1963; Royal Foundation and Other Plays, 1965; contribs to Observer, Spectator, Punch, etc. *Recreations:* cricket, travel, reading, the turf. *Address:* c/o Curtis Brown Ltd, Haymarket House, 28–29 Haymarket, SW1Y 4SP. *Clubs:* MCC; Butterflies Cricket, Trogs' Cricket.

Died 12 May 2001.

RAVENSCROFT, John Robert Parker, (John Peel), OBE 1998; broadcaster/journalist, since 1961; *b* 30 Aug. 1939; *s* of Robert Leslie and Joan Mary Ravenscroft; *m* 1st, Shirley; 2nd, 1974, Sheila Mary Gilhooly; two *s* two *d*. *Educ:* Woodlands Sch., Deganwy, N Wales; Shrewsbury. National Service, Royal Artillery (B2 Radar Operator), 1957–59. Mill operative, Rochdale, 1959–60; office boy, Dallas, Texas, 1960–65; part-time disc-jockey, 1961–; computer programmer, 1965; Pirate Radio, London, 1967; BBC Radio 1, 1967–; Home Truths, BBC Radio 4, 1998–. Hon. MA East Anglia, 1989; Hon. DMus Anglia Polytechnic Univ., 1996; Hon. DLitt Portsmouth, 2001; Hon. Dr: Sheffield Hallam, 1999; Liverpool, 2000; DUniv Open, 2001. Hon. Fellow, Liverpool John Moores Univ., 2001. *Posthumous publication:* (with Sheila Ravenscroft) Margrave of the Marshes, 2005. *Recreations:* looking after first grandchild Archie, checking myself for symptoms of terminal diseases, staring out of the window. *Address:* c/o BBC Radio 1, W1A 4DJ. *T:* (020) 7580 4468.

Died 25 Oct. 2004.

RAVENSWORTH, 8th Baron *cr* 1821; **Arthur Waller Liddell;** Bt 1642; JP; *b* 25 July 1924; *s* of late Hon. Cyril Arthur Liddell (2nd *s* of 5th Baron) and Dorothy L., *d* of William Brown, Slinfold, Sussex; *S* cousin, 1950; *m* 1950, Wendy, *d* of J. S. Bell, Cookham, Berks; one *s* one *d*. *Educ:* Harrow. Radio Engineer, BBC, 1944–50. JP Northumberland, 1959. *Heir: s* Hon. Thomas Arthur Hamish Liddell [*b* 27 Oct. 1954; *m* 1983, Linda, *d* of H. Thompson; one *s* one *d*]. *Address:* Eslington Park, Whittingham, Alnwick, Northumberland NE66 4UR. *T:* (01665) 574239. *Died 28 March 2004.*

RAWLINS, Colin Guy Champion, OBE 1965; DFC 1941; Director of Zoos and Chief Executive, Zoological Society of London, 1966–84; *b* 5 June 1919; *s* of R. S. C. Rawlins and Yvonne Blanche Andrews; *m* 1946, Rosemary Jensen; two *s* one *d*. *Educ:* Prince of Wales Sch., Nairobi; Charterhouse; Queen's Coll., Oxford (MA). Served with RAF, 1939–46: Bomber Comd, NW Europe; POW, 1941–45; Sqdn-Leader. HM Overseas Civil Service, 1946–66: Administrative Officer, Northern Rhodesia (later Zambia); appointments at Headquarters and in field; Provincial Commissioner, Resident Secretary. Mem., Pearce Commn on Rhodesian Opinion, 1972. Past Pres., Internat. Union of Dirs of Zool. Gardens. Chm. of Trustees, Zimbabwe Trust, 1993–2002. FCIS 1967. *Recreations:* aviation, gardening. *Address:* Riverain, Gossmore Lane, Marlow, Bucks SL7 1QF. *T:* (01628) 472796. *Died 23 Oct. 2003.*

RAYNE, family name of **Baron Rayne**.

RAYNE, Baron *cr* 1976 (Life Peer), of Prince's Meadow in Greater London; **Max Rayne,** Kt 1969; Chairman, London Merchant Securities plc, 1960–2000, Life President, since 2000; *b* 8 Feb. 1918; *er s* of Phillip and Deborah Rayne; *m* 1st, 1941, Margaret Marco (marr. diss. 1960); one *s* two *d*; 2nd, 1965, Lady Jane Antonia Frances Vane-Tempest-Stewart, *er d* of 8th Marquess of Londonderry; two *s* two *d*. *Educ:* Central Foundation Sch. and University Coll., London. Served RAF 1940–45. Dir, First Leisure Corp. plc, 1984–99 (Dep. Chm., 1984–92; Chm., 1992–95); Dep. Chm., British Lion Films, 1967–72; Dir, Housing Corp. (1974) Ltd, 1974–78; Dir, other companies. Gov., 1962–74, Special Trustee, 1974–92, St Thomas' Hosp.; Governor: Royal Ballet Sch., 1966–79; Malvern Coll., 1966–; Centre for Environmental Studies, 1967–73; Member: Gen. Council, King Edward VII's Hosp. Fund for London, 1966–96; RADA Council, 1973–; South Bank Bd, 1986–92;

Council, St Thomas's Hospital Medical School, 1965–82; Council of Governors, UMDS of Guy's and St Thomas's Hosps, 1982–89. Vice-Pres., Yehudi Menuhin Sch., 1987– (Gov., 1966–87); Hon. Vice-Pres., Jewish Care, 1966–; Chairman: London Festival Ballet Trust, 1967–75; Nat. Theatre Board, 1971–88; Founder Patron, The Rayne Foundation, 1962–; Founder Mem., Motability, 1979–96 (Life Vice-Pres., 1996). Hon. Fellow: Darwin Coll., Cambridge, 1966; UCL, 1966; LSE 1974; RCPsych, 1977; King's Coll. Hosp. Med. Sch., 1980; UC, Oxford, 1982; King's Coll. London, 1983; Westminster Sch., 1989; RCP, 1992; UMDS, 1992. Hon. LLD London, 1968. Officier, Légion d'Honneur, 1987 (Chevalier 1973). *Address:* 33 Robert Adam Street, W1U 3HR. *T:* (020) 7935 3555.   *Died 10 Oct. 2003.*

RAYNER, Bryan Roy, CB 1987; Deputy Secretary, Department of Health (formerly of Health and Social Security), 1984–91; *b* 29 Jan. 1932; *s* of Harold and Florence Rayner; *m* 1957, Eleanora Whittaker; one *d. Educ:* Stationers' Company's School, N8. Clerical Officer, Customs and Excise, 1948; Asst Private Sec. to Minister of Health, 1960–62; Principal, 1965, Asst Sec., 1970, Under Sec., 1975, DHSS. *Recreation:* listening to music. *Address:* 18 Trevelyan Place, Heath Road, Haywards Heath, W Sussex RH16 3AZ.   *Died 12 Sept. 2003.*

RAYNER, Rabbi John Desmond, CBE 1993; Minister, Liberal Jewish Synagogue, 1957–89, then Rabbi Emeritus; *b* 30 May 1924; *s* of Ferdinand and Charlotte Rahmer; *m* 1955, Jane Priscilla Heilbronn; two *s* one *d. Educ:* Durham Sch.; Emmanuel Coll., Cambridge (MA); Hebrew Union Coll.-Jewish Inst. of Religion, Cincinnati (Hon. DD). Minister, S London Liberal Synagogue, 1953–57; Sen. Minister, Liberal Jewish Synagogue, 1961–89; Leo Baeck College: Lectr in Rabbinic Literature, 1966–2003 (Vice-Pres., 1969–). Hon. Life Pres., Union of Liberal and Progressive Synagogues, 1994; Pres., London Soc. of Jews and Christians, 1990; Chm., Council of Reform and Liberal Rabbis, 1969–71, 1982–84, 1989–92. *Publications:* The Practices of Liberal Judaism, 1958; Towards Mutual Understanding between Jews and Christians, 1960; (ed jtly) Service of the Heart, 1967; Guide to Jewish Marriage, 1975; (ed jtly) Gate of Repentance, 1977; (jtly) Judaism for Today, 1978; (jtly) The Jewish People: their history and their religion, 1987; (ed jtly) Siddur Lev Chadash, 1995; An Understanding of Judaism, 1997; A Jewish Understanding of the World, 1998; Jewish Religious Law, 1998; Principles of Jewish Ethics, 2005; Roadmap to the Messianic Age: sermons and lectures, 2005. *Recreations:* reading, music. *Address:* 37 Walmington Fold, N12 7LD. *T:* (020) 8446 6196.   *Died 19 Sept. 2005.*

REA, James Taylor, CMG 1958; HM Overseas Civil Service, retired; *b* 19 Oct. 1907; *s* of Rev. Martin Rea, Presbyterian Minister, and Mary Rea (*née* Fisher); *m* 1934, Catharine (*d* 1990), *d* of Dr W. H. Bleakney, Whitman College, Walla Walla, Washington, USA; one *s* one *d. Educ:* Royal School, Dungannon; Queen's University, Belfast (BA); St John's College, Cambridge (MA). HM Colonial Administrative Service, later HM Overseas Civil Service, serving throughout in Malaya and Singapore, 1931–58: Principal offices held: Asst Sec., Chinese Affairs, Fedn of Malaya, 1948; Dep. Comr for Labour, Fedn of Malaya, 1949; Dep. Malayan Establishment Officer, 1950; Dep. Pres., 1952–55, Pres., 1955–58, City Council, Singapore, retired. Chairman: Hotel Grants Adv. Cttee, NI, 1963–75; NI Training Exec., 1972–75; Down District Cttee, Eastern Health and Social Services Bd, 1974–78; Mem., NI Housing Trust, 1959–71, Vice Chm., 1970–71. Independent Member: Catering Wages Council, N Ireland, 1965–82; Retail Bespoke Tailoring Wages Council, 1965–82; Laundry Wages Council, 1965–82; Shirtmaking Wages Council, 1965–82. Nominated Member, General Dental Council, under Dentist Act, 1957, 1961–79. Mem. Downpatrick HMC, 1966–73, Chm., 1971–73. *Address:* Craigduff, 29 Downpatrick

Road, Clough, Downpatrick, N Ireland BT30 8NL. *T:* (028) 4481 1258.   *Died 23 Sept. 2001.*

READ, Rt Rev. Allan Alexander; Associate Priest, Merrickville and Burritts Rapids, Ontario, since 1972; Bishop of Ontario, 1981–92; *b* 19 Sept. 1923; *s* of Alex P. Read and Lillice M. Matthews; *m* 1949, (Mary) Beverly Roberts (*d* 2002); two *s* two *d. Educ:* Trinity Coll., Univ. of Toronto (BA, LTh). Incumbent, Mono East and Mono West, 1947–54; Rector, Trinity Church, Barrie, 1954–71; Canon of St James Cathedral, Toronto, 1957; Archdeacon of Simcoe, 1961–72; Bishop Suffragan of Toronto, 1972–81; priest-in-charge: St Patrick's Cathedral, Meath and Kildare, 1992; Dunster, dio. of Bath and Wells, 1993; St Ippolyts, dio. of St Albans, 1994; St Mary, Westerham, dio. of Rochester, 1995; Cathedral of St John the Baptist, dio. of Cashel, Church of Ireland, 1996; All Saints, Goodmayes, Chelmsford, 1997. Chaplain, Simcoe County Gaol, Kingston, Ont, 1954–82. Hon. Asst, St George's Cathedral, Kingston, Ont, 1992–; licensed as a Bishop, dio. of Albany, USA, 1995–. Member: Gen. Synod, Anglican Church of Canada, 1959–89; Provincial Synod of Ontario, 1955–91; Hon. Pres., Rural Workers Fellowship, Episcopal Church, with members from USA and Anglican Church of Canada, 1981–; Hon. Mem., Toronto and Metropolitan Region Conservation Authy, 1977–. Hon. DD: Trinity Coll., Toronto, 1972; Wycliffe Coll., Toronto, 1972; Hon. STD Thornloe Coll., Sudbury, 1982. Citizen of the Year, Barrie, 1966; Honorary Reeve, Black Creek, Toronto, 1980; Govt of Ontario citizenship awards. *Publications:* Shepherds in Green Pastures, 1952; Unto the Hills, 1954. *Recreations:* organ music, reading, Canadian history, 1837 Rebellion Upper Canada. *Address:* 39 Riverside Drive, RR1, Kingston, ON K7L 4V1, Canada.

Died 15 Nov. 2003.

READ, Rev. David Haxton Carswell, DD; Minister of Madison Avenue Presbyterian Church, New York City, USA, 1956–89, then Minister Emeritus; *b* Cupar, Fife, 2 Jan. 1910; *s* of John Alexander Read and Catherine Haxton Carswell; *m* 1936, Dorothy Florence Patricia Gilbert; one *s. Educ:* Daniel Stewart's College, Edinburgh; Edinburgh Univ. (MA (first class Hons in Lit.) 1932); Univs of Montpellier, Strasbourg, Paris, and Marburg; New Coll., Edinburgh (BD (dist. in Dogmatics) 1936). Ordained Minister of the Church of Scotland, 1936; Minister of Coldstream West Church, 1936–39; CF, 1939–45 (despatches; POW, 1940–45, Germany); Minister of Greenbank Parish, Edinburgh, 1939–49; first Chaplain, Univ. of Edinburgh, 1949–55; Chaplain to the Queen in Scotland, 1952–55. Senior Editor, The Living Pulpit, 1991–97, then Editor Emeritus. Guest Lectr and Preacher in USA, Scotland, Canada, Australia. Mem., St Andrew's Soc., NY. Hon. DD: Edinburgh, 1956; Yale, 1959; Lafayette Coll., 1965; Hope Coll., 1969; Knox Coll., Canada, 1979; Hon. LHD: Hobart Coll., 1972; Trinity Univ., 1972; Hon. LittD Coll. of Wooster, 1966; Hon. DHL: Japan Internat. Christian Univ., 1979; Rockford Coll., 1982. *Publications:* The Spirit of Life, 1939; The Church to Come (trans. from German), 1939; Prisoners' Quest, Lectures on Christian doctrine in a POW Camp, 1944; The Communication of The Gospel (Warrack Lectures), 1952; The Christian Faith, 1955 (NY 1956); I am Persuaded, 1961 (NY 1962); Sons of Anak, 1964 (NY); God's Mobile Family, 1966 (NY); Whose God is Dead?, 1966 (Cinn); Holy Common Sense, 1966 (Tenn); The Pattern of Christ, 1967 (NY); The Presence of Christ, 1968 (NJ); Christian Ethics, 1968 (NY 1969); Virginia Woolfe Meets Charlie Brown, 1968 (Mich); Giants Cut Down To Size, 1970; Religion Without Wrappings, 1970; Overheard, 1971; Curious Christians, 1972; Sent from God, 1974; Good News in the Letters of Paul, 1975; Go and make Disciples, 1978; Unfinished Easter, 1978; The Faith is Still There, 1980; Preaching About the Needs of Real People, 1988; *autobiography:* This Grace Given, 1984; Grace Thus Far, 1986; articles and sermons in Atlantic Monthly, Scottish Jl of Theology,

Expository Times, etc. *Recreations:* languages, drama, travel, especially in France. *Address:* 258 Riverside Drive, #9A, New York, NY 10025-6161, USA. *Clubs:* Pilgrims, Century (New York).   *Died 6 Jan 2001.*

REAGAN, Ronald, Hon. GCB 1989; President of the United States of America, 1981–89; *b* Tampico, Ill, 6 Feb. 1911; *m* 1st, 1940, Jane Wyman (marr. diss. 1948); one *s* (one *d* decd); 2nd, 1952, Nancy Davis; one *s* one *d*. *Educ:* public schools in Tampico, Monmouth, Galesburg, and Dixon, Ill; Eureka Coll., Ill (AB). Sports Announcer, WHO, Des Moines, 1932–37; actor, films and television, 1937–66; Host and Program Superviser, Gen. Electric Theater (TV), 1954–62; Host, Death Valley Days (TV), 1962–65. Pres., Screen Actors' Guild, 1947–52, 1959–60; Chm., Motion Picture Industry Council, 1949. Served with USAAF, 1942–45. Governor, State of California, 1967–74; Chairman, State Governors' Assoc., 1969. Republican Candidate for nomination for the Presidency, 1976. Operates horsebreeding and cattle ranch. Hon. Fellow, Keble Coll., Oxford, 1994. Presidential Medal of Freedom, USA, 1992. *Publications:* Where's the Rest of Me? (autobiog.), 1965 (repr. 1981 as My Early Life); Abortion and the Conscience of the Nation, 1984; An American Life (autobiog.), 1990.   *Died 5 June 2004.*

REARDON, Rev. Canon Martin Alan, OBE 1997; General Secretary, Churches Together in England, 1990–97; *b* 3 Oct. 1932; *s* of Ernest William Reardon, CBE and Gertrude Mary; *m* 1964, Ruth Maxim Slade; one *s* one *d*. *Educ:* Cumnor House Sch.; St Edward's Sch., Oxford; Selwyn Coll., Cambridge (MA); Cuddesdon Coll., Oxford; Univ. of Geneva; Univ. of Louvain. Asst Curate, Rugby Parish Church, 1958–61; Sec., Sheffield Council of Churches, 1962–71; Sub-Warden, Lincoln Theol Coll., 1971–78; Sec., Bd for Mission and Unity, Gen. Synod of C of E, 1978–89; Rector, Plumpton with East Chiltington, 1989–90. Hon. Canon, Lincoln Cathedral, 1979–2002, then Emeritus. *Publications:* Christian Unity in Sheffield, 1967; (with Kenneth Greet) Social Questions, 1964; What on Earth is the Church For?, 1985; Christian Initiation, 1991; contribs to One in Christ, Theology, Clergy Review, etc. *Recreations:* walking, sketching. *Address:* The Little School House, 3 Turvey Court, High Street, Turvey, Bedford MK43 8DB.   *Died 3 Jan. 2005.*

RECKITT, Lt-Col Basil Norman, TD 1946; Director, Reckitt and Colman Ltd, retired 1972 (Chairman, 1966–70); *b* 12 Aug. 1905; *s* of Frank Norman Reckitt, Architect, and Beatrice Margaret Hewett; *m* 1st, 1928, Virginia Carre-Smith (*d* 1961); three *d*; 2nd, 1966, Mary Holmes (*née* Peirce), *widow* of Paul Holmes, Malham Tarn, near Settle. *Educ:* Uppingham; King's Coll., Cambridge (MA). Joined Reckitt & Sons Ltd, 1927; Dir, Reckitt & Colman Ltd, 1938. 2nd Lieut, 62nd HAA Regt (TA), 1939; Bde Major, 39th AA Brigade, 1940; CO 141 HAA (M) Regt, 1942; Military Government, Germany, 1944–45. Hull University: Chm. Council, 1971–80; Pro-Chancellor, 1971–93, then Emeritus. Sheriff of Hull, 1970–71. Chm., Friends of Abbot Hall Art Gall. and Museums, Kendal, 1982–87; Vice-Chm., YMCA Nat. Centre, Lakeside, Windermere, 1982–87. Hon. LLD Hull, 1967. *Publications:* History of Reckitt & Sons Ltd, 1951; Charles I and Hull, 1952; The Lindley Affair, 1972; Diary of Military Government in Germany, 1989; The Journeys of William Reckitt, 1989; Diary of Anti-Aircraft Defence, 1990; Brothers at War, 1991; Petronella, 1994; The Death Hole, 1994; Sibella, 1996. *Address:* Haverbrack, Milnthorpe, Cumbria LA7 7AH. *T:* (01539) 563142.   *Died 3 Dec. 2005.*

REDDAWAY, Brian; *see* Reddaway, W. B.

REDDAWAY, Prof. (William) Brian, CBE 1971; FBA 1967; Professor of Political Economy, University of Cambridge, 1969–80, then Emeritus; Fellow of Clare College, Cambridge, since 1938; Economic Consultant to the World Bank, since 1966; *b* 8 Jan. 1913; *s* of late

William Fiddian Reddaway and Kate Waterland Reddaway (*née* Sills); *m* 1938, Barbara Augusta Bennett (*d* 1996); three *s* one *d*. *Educ:* Oundle Sch.; King's Coll., Cambridge (Maj. schol. natural science; 1st cl. Maths tripos, part I, 1st cl. 1st div Economics tripos, part II; Adam Smith Prize; MA). Assistant, Bank of England, 1934–35; Research Fellow in Economics, University of Melbourne, 1936–37; Statistics Division, Board of Trade (final rank Chief Statistician), 1940–47; University Lectr in Economics, 1939–55, Reader in Applied Economics, 1957–65, Dir of Dept of Applied Economics, 1955–69, Univ. of Cambridge. Economic Adviser to OEEC, 1951–52; Visiting Economist, Center for International Studies, New Delhi, 1959–60; Vis. Lectr, Economic Develt Inst. (Washington), 1966–67; Consultant, Harvard Develt Adv. Service (in Ghana), 1967; Vis. Prof., Bangladesh Inst. of Develt Studies, 1974–75. Economic Consultant to CBI, 1972–83. Regional Adviser, Economic Commn for Western Asia, 1979–80; Consultant to World Bank on Nigerian economy, 1983–87. Member: Royal Commn on the Press, 1961–62; NBPI, 1967–71; Chm., Inquiry into Consulting Engineering Firms' Costs and Earnings, 1971–72. Editor, Economic Jl, 1971–76. *Publications:* Russian Financial System, 1935; Economics of a Declining Population, 1939; (with C. F. Carter, Richard Stone) Measurement of Production Movements, 1948; The Development of the Indian Economy, 1962; Effects of UK Direct Investment Overseas, Interim Report, 1967, Final Report, 1968; Effects of the Selective Employment Tax, First Report, 1970, Final Report, 1973; (with G. C. Fiegehen) Companies, Incentives and Senior Managers, 1981; Some Key Issues for the Development of the Economy of Papua New Guinea, 1986; articles in numerous economic journals. *Recreations:* skating, walking. *Address:* 12 Manor Court, Grange Road, Cambridge CB3 9BE. *T:* (01223) 350041.   *Died 23 July 2002.*

REDGRAVE, Rachel, (Lady Redgrave); *see* Kempson, R.

REDGROVE, Peter William, FRSL; poet, analytical psychologist; Resident Author, Falmouth School of Art, 1966–83; *b* 2 Jan. 1932; *s* of late Gordon James Redgrove and Nancy Lena Cestrilli-Bell; *m* Barbara Sherlock; two *s* one *d*; *m* Penelope Shuttle; one *d*. *Educ:* Taunton Sch.; Queens' Coll., Cambridge. Scientific journalist and copywriter, 1954–61; Vis. Poet, Buffalo Univ., NY, 1961–62; Gregory Fellow in Poetry, Leeds Univ., 1962–65; study with John Layard, 1968–69; O'Connor Prof. of Literature, Colgate Univ., NY, 1974–75; Leverhulme Emeritus Fellow, 1985–87; Writer at large, N Cornwall Arts, 1988. FRSL 1982. Hon. DLitt Sheffield, 2001. George Rylands' Verse-speaking Prize, 1954; Fulbright Award, 1961; Poetry Book Society Choices, 1961, 1966, 1979, 1981; Arts Council Awards, 1969, 1970, 1973, 1975, 1977, 1982; Guardian Fiction Prize, 1973; Prudence Farmer Poetry Award, 1977; Cholmondeley Award, 1985; Queen's Gold Medal for Poetry, 1996; Authors' Foundn Grant, 1998. *Publications: poetry:* The Collector, 1960; The Nature of Cold Weather, 1961; At the White Monument, 1963; The Force, 1966; Penguin Modern Poets 11, 1968; Work in Progress, 1969; Dr Faust's Sea-Spiral Spirit, 1972; Three Pieces for Voices, 1972; The Hermaphrodite Album (with Penelope Shuttle), 1973; Sons of My Skin: selected poems, 1975; From Every Chink of the Ark, 1977; Ten Poems, 1977; The Weddings at Nether Powers, 1979; The Apple-Broadcast, 1981; The Working of Water, 1984; The Man Named East, 1985; The Mudlark Poems and Grand Buveur, 1986; In the Hall of the Saurians, 1987; The Moon Disposes, 1987; Poems 1954–1987, 1989; The First Earthquake, 1989; Dressed as for a Tarot Pack, 1990; Under the Reservoir, 1992; The Laborators, 1993; My Father's Trapdoors, 1994; Abyssophone, 1995; Assembling a Ghost, 1996; Orchard End, 1997; What the Black Mirror Saw, 1997; Selected Poems, 1999; From the Virgil Caverns, 2002; *prose fiction:* In the Country of the Skin,

1973; The Terrors of Dr Treviles (with Penelope Shuttle), 1974; The Glass Cottage, 1976; The Sleep of the Great Hypnotist, 1979; The God of Glass, 1979; The Beekeepers, 1980; The Facilitators, 1982; The One Who Set out to Study Fear, 1989; The Cyclopean Mistress, 1993; *plays:* Miss Carstairs Dressed for Blooding (playbook containing several dramatic pieces), 1976; (for radio): In the Country of the Skin, 1973; The Holy Sinner, 1975; Dance the Putrefact, 1975; The God of Glass, 1977 (Imperial Tobacco Award 1978); Martyr of the Hives, 1980 (Giles Cooper Award 1981); Florent and the Tuxedo Millions, 1982 (Prix Italia); The Sin-Doctor, 1983; Dracula in White, 1984; The Scientists of the Strange, 1984; Time for the Cat-Scene, 1985; Trelamia, 1986; Six Tales from Grimm, 1987; Six Views to a Haunt, 1992; An Inspector Named Horse, 1995; (for television): The Sermon, 1963; Jack Be Nimble, 1980; *non-fiction:* The Wise Wound (with Penelope Shuttle), 1978, rev. edn 1986; The Black Goddess and the Sixth Sense, 1987; Alchemy for Women, 1995. *Recreations:* work, photography, judo (1st Kyu Judo: Otani and Brit. Judo Assoc.), yoga. *Address:* c/o David Higham Associates, 5–8 Lower John Street, Golden Square, W1R 4HA.
Died 16 June 2003.

REDMAN, Sydney, CB 1961; *b* 12 Feb. 1914; *s* of John Barritt Redman and Annie Meech; *m* 1939, Barbara Mary Grey; one *s* two *d. Educ:* Manchester Grammar Sch.; Corpus Christi Coll., Oxford. Asst Principal, WO, 1936; Principal Private Sec. to Secretary of State for War, 1942–44; Asst Under-Sec. of State: War Office, 1957–63; Ministry of Defence, 1963–64; Dep. Under-Sec. of State (Navy), MoD, 1964–73. Dir-Gen., Timber Trade Fedn, 1973–82. *Address:* Littlehurst, Birch Avenue, Haywards Heath, West Sussex RH17 7SL. *T:* (01444) 413738.
Died 6 Jan. 2002.

REECE, Sir Gordon; *see* Reece, Sir J. G.

REECE, Sir (James) Gordon, Kt 1986; public affairs consultant, since 1985; *b* 28 Sept. 1929; *m* (marr. diss. 1977); three *s* three *d. Educ:* Ratcliffe Coll.; Downing Coll., Cambridge (Associate Fellow, 1986). Formerly: reporter, Liverpool Daily Post and Echo, then Sunday Express; television producer, ITV, 1960–70; Jt Man. Dir, RM EMI Ltd, 1970–74; Advr to Rt Hon. Margaret Thatcher, 1975–79; Dir of Publicity, Cons. Central Office, 1978–80; a Vice-Pres., Occidental Petroleum Corp., 1980–85. *Recreations:* racing, bridge, books, old movies. *Address:* c/o Wells Fargo Bank, 10850 Wilshire Boulevard, Los Angeles, CA 90025, USA. *Clubs:* Portland, Garrick, Buck's. *Died 22 Sept. 2001.*

REED, Edward John; Clerk to the Clothworkers' Company of the City of London, 1963–78; *b* 2 Sept. 1913; *o c* of late Edward Reed; *m* 1939, Rita Isabel Venus Cheston-Porter; one *s* one *d. Educ:* St Paul's School. Admitted Solicitor, 1938. Territorial Service with HAC; commnd 1940; served BEF and BAOR with 63 (WR) Medium Regt RA; Capt. 1942. Clerk to Governors of Mary Datchelor Girls' Sch., 1963–78. Vice Pres., Metropolitan Soc. for the Blind, 1979– (Chm., 1965–79); Chm., Indigent Blind Visiting Society, 1965–79; Vice-Pres., N London District, St John Ambulance, 1969–81. Cttee, St John Ophthalmic Hosp., Jerusalem, 1964–85. Chm., City Side, Joint Grand Gresham Cttee, 1984. Member: Court of Common Council, City of London, for Tower Ward, 1978–86; Lloyds, 1979–97. Clothworkers' Co.: Liveryman, 1964; Sen. Warden, 1981; Mem., Ct of Assistants, 1982–96, Assistant Emeritus, 1998. Governor: Christ's Hosp., 1981–86; City of London Freemen's Sch., 1982–86. Hon. MA Leeds, 1979. CStJ 1968. Chevalier, Order of Leopold with Palm, and Croix de Guerre with Palm, Belgium, 1944. *Recreations:* sailing, photography. *Address:* 54 Hillcrest Gardens, Hinchley Wood, Esher, Surrey KT10 0BX. *T:* (020) 8398 3904. *Club:* City Livery.
Died 18 June 2001.

REES, Prof. Brinley Roderick, MA Oxon; PhD, Hon. LLD Wales; Principal, Saint David's University College, Lampeter, 1975–80; *b* 27 Dec. 1919; *s* of John David Rees and Mary Ann (*née* Roderick); *m* 1951, Zena Muriel Stella Mayall; two *s. Educ:* Christ Coll., Brecon; Merton Coll., Oxford (Postmaster). 1st Cl., Class Hons Mods and Hon. Mention, Craven and Ireland Schols, 1946. Welch Regt, 1940–45. Asst Classics Master, Christ Coll., Brecon, 1947; Cardiff High Sch., 1947–48; Asst Lectr in Classics, University Coll. of Wales Aberystwyth, 1948–49; Lectr 1949–56; Sen. Lectr in Greek, Univ. of Manchester, 1956–58; UC Cardiff: Prof. of Greek, 1958–70; Dean of Faculty of Arts, 1963–65; Dean of Students, 1967–68; Hon. Lectr, 1980–88; Prof. Emeritus, 1981; Vice-Pres., 1986–88; University of Birmingham: Prof. of Greek, 1970–75; Dean of Faculty of Arts, 1973–75; Hon. Life Mem. of Court, 1983. Welsh Supernumerary Fellow, Jesus Coll., Oxford, 1975–76; Leverhulme Emeritus Fellow, 1984–86. Hon. Secretary, Classical Association, 1963–69, Vice-Pres., 1969–78, 1979–, Pres., 1978–79. Hon. LLD Wales, 1981. *Publications:* The Merton Papyri, Vol. II (with H. I. Bell and J. W. B. Barns); 1959; The Use of Greek, 1961; Papyri from Hermopolis and other Byzantine Documents, 1964; (with M. E. Jervis) Lampas: a new approach to Greek, 1970; Classics: an outline for intending students, 1970; Aristotle's Theory and Milton's Practice, 1972; Strength in What Remains, 1980; Pelagius: a reluctant heretic, 1988; Letters of Pelagius and his Followers, 1991; Pelagius: life and letters, 1998; articles and reviews in various classical and other jls. *Address:* 31 Stephenson Court, Wordsworth Avenue, Cardiff CF24 3FX. *T:* (029) 2047 2058. *Died 21 Oct. 2004.*

REES, Harland, FRCS; Hon. Consultant Urological Surgeon, King's College Hospital; Hon. Consultant Surgeon and Urological Surgeon, Royal Free Hospital; *b* 21 Sept. 1909; *yr s* of Dr David Charles Rees, MRCS, LRCP, and Myrtle May (*née* Dolley); *m* 1950, Helen Marie Tarver (*d* 2001); two *s* (one *d* decd). *Educ:* St Andrew's Coll., Grahamstown, S Africa; University Coll., Oxford (Rhodes Schol.; MA MCh). Charing Cross Hospital. Served RAMC, 1942–46; OC Surgical Div. 53, Indian General Hospital. Adviser in Surgery, Siam (Thailand). Examiner in Surgery, University of Cambridge, 1963–73. Councillor (C), S Beds DC, 1978–95 (Chm., 1986–87). *Publications:* articles and chapters in various books and journals, 1952–63. *Recreations:* walking, cultivation of trees, Rugby football (Oxford *v* Cambridge, 1932–33). *Address:* Kensworth Gorse, Clayhall Road, Kensworth, near Dunstable, Beds LU6 3RF. *T:* (01582) 872411. *Club:* Vincent's (Oxford).
Died 9 July 2002.

REES, Hugh; *see* Rees, J. E. H.

REES, (John Edward) Hugh; chartered surveyor; *b* 8 Jan. 1928; *s* of David Emlyn Rees, Swansea; *m* 1961, Gillian Dian Milo-Jones (decd); two *s*. MP (C) Swansea, West Division, Oct. 1959–64; Assistant Government Whip, 1962–64. UK Rep., Econ. and Soc. Cttee, EEC, 1972–78. Dir, Abbey National plc (formerly Abbey National Building Soc.), 1976–91; Chairman: Cambrian Housing Soc., 1968–; Abbey Housing Association Ltd, 1980–92. Mem., Welsh Develt Agency, 1980–86. Trustee, Ffynone House Sch. Trust, 1973– (Chm. 1977–85). Member Council: Nat. Mus. of Wales, 1968–94; Univ. of Wales Swansea, 1970–. FRICS. *Address:* Sherwood, 35 Caswell Road, Newton, Mumbles, Swansea, W Glamorgan SA3 4SD. *Died 1 Dec. 2003.*

REES, Linford; *see* Rees, W. L. L.

REES, William Hurst; Member of Lands Tribunal, 1973–89; *b* 12 April 1917; *s* of Richard and Florence A. Rees; *m* 1941, Elizabeth Mary Wight; two *s* one *d. Educ:* College of Estate Management, Univ. of London (BSc (Est. Man.)). Served War, RA and RE (SO2), 1940–46; Liaison Officer, Belgian Army Engrs. Head of Valuation Dept, Coll. of Estate Management, 1948–51. Principal in

Private Practice as Chartered Surveyor: City of London, Richard Ellis & Son, 1951–61; East Grinstead, Sx, Turner, Rudge & Turner, 1961–73. Gov., Coll. of Estate Management, 1965–72; Mem. Council, RICS, 1967–70; Chm. Bd of Studies in Estate Management, Univ. of London, 1970–74; Chm., Surveying Bd, CNAA, 1976–77; Hon. Mem., Rating Surveyors Assoc. Pres., BSc (Estate Management) Club, 1961–62; Chm., Exams Bd, RICS (formerly Incorporated Soc. of Valuers and Auctioneers), 1984–. Hon. RICS (Hon. FSVA 1987; FRICS). Hon. DTech Nottingham Trent, 2000. *Publications:* Modern Methods of Valuation, 1943, (jointly) 6th edn 1971; (ed) Valuations: Principles into Practice, 1980, 5th edn 2001. *Recreation:* music, mainly opera. *Address:* Brendon, Carlton Road, South Godstone, Godstone, Surrey RH9 8LD. *T:* and *Fax:* (01342) 892109.
Died 6 Jan. 2004.

REES, (William) Linford (Llewelyn), CBE 1978; FRCP; FRCPsych; Emeritus Professor of Psychiatry, University of London, 1980; Consulting Physician, St Bartholomew's Hospital, since 1981; *b* 24 Oct. 1914; *e s* of late Edward Parry Rees and Mary Rees, Llanelli, Carmarthenshire; *m* 1940, Catherine (*d* 1993), *y d* of late David Thomas, and of Angharad Thomas, Alltwen, Glam; two *s* two *d*. *Educ:* Llanelli Grammar School; University Coll., Cardiff; Welsh Nat. Sch. of Medicine; The Maudsley Hosp.; Univ. of London. BSc 1935; MB, BCh 1938; DPM 1940; MRCP 1942; MD 1943; DSc London 1978. FRCP 1950; FRCPsych 1971 (Pres., 1975–78); Hon. FRCPsych 1978. David Hepburn Medal and Alfred Hughes Medal in Anatomy, 1935; John Maclean Medal and Prize in Obstetrics and Gynaecology, 1937, etc. Specialist, EMS, 1942; Dep. Med. Supt, Mill Hill Emergency Hosp., 1945; Asst Physician and Postgrad. Teacher in Clinical Psychiatry, The Maudsley Hosp., 1946; Dep. Physician Supt, Whitchurch Hosp., 1947; Regional Psychiatrist for Wales and Mon, 1948; Consultant Physician, The Bethlem Royal Hosp. and The Maudsley Hosp., 1954–66; Recognised Clin. Teacher in Mental Diseases, Inst. of Psychiatry, Univ. of London, 1956–78; Lecturer in Psychol Med., St Bartholomew's Med. Coll., 1958–78; Med. Dir, Charter Clinic, London, 1980–89; Chief Psychiatrist and Exec. Med. Dir, Charter Medical, 1984–89; Dir and Med. Advr, Huntercombe Manor Hosp., and Rehabilitation Gp Ltd, 1989– (Pres., 1992–); Consultant, and Chm. Med. Adv. Cttee, Ultramind, 1996. Chm., Armed Services Consultant Adv. Bd in Psych., 1979–90; Consultant Advisor in Psychiatry to RAF; WHO Consultant to Sri Lanka, 1973; Hon. Consultant, Royal Sch. for Deaf Children. Lectures to Univs and Learned Socs in Europe, USA, Asia, Australia and S America. Examiner: Diploma Psychological Medicine, RCP, 1964–69; MRCP, RCP, RCPE and RCPGlas, 1969–; MB and DPM, Univ. of Leeds, 1969–. President: Soc. for Psychosomatic Research, 1957–58; Royal Coll. of Psychiatrists, 1975–78 (Vice-Pres., 1972–75; Chm., E Anglian Region); Section of Psychiatry, RSM, 1971–72 (Vice-Pres., 1968; Hon. Mem., 1982); BMA, 1978–79 (Fellow, 1981); Psychiatric Rehabilitation Assoc., 1995; Welsh Psychiatric Soc., 1996; Chm., Medico-Pharmaceutical Forum, 1982 (Vice-Chm., 1981). Treasurer, World Psychiatric Assoc., 1966– (Hon. Mem., 1982). Member: Clinical Psychiatry Cttee, MRC, 1959; Council, Royal Medico-Psychological Assoc. (Chm., Research and Clinical Section, 1957–63); Soc. for Study of Human Biology; Asthma Research Council; Cttee on Safety of Medicines (also Toxicity and Clinical Trials Sub-Cttee), 1971; Cttee on Review of Medicines (Chm., Psychotropic Drugs Sub-Cttee); Psychological Medicine Group, BMA, 1967. Formerly Chm., Univ. of London Teachers of Psych. Cttee; Member: Bd of Advanced Med. Studies, Univ. of London, 1966–69; Higher Degrees Cttee, Univ. of London; Acad. Council Standing Sub-Cttee in Medicine, Univ. of London; Cttee of Management, Inst. of Psychiatry, Maudsley Hosp., 1968; Council and Exec. Cttee, St Bartholomew's Hosp. Med. Coll., 1972; Jt Policy Cttee, QMC, St Bartholomew's

Hosp. and London Hosp., 1973; Central Health Services Council; Standing Medical Adv. Cttee; Jt Consultants Cttee; Conference of Presidents of Royal Colls; GMC, 1980–84 (Mem., Educn Cttee, Preliminary Health Cttee and Prof. Conduct Cttee). Founder Mem., Internat. Coll. of Neuro-psychopharmacology. Hon. Mem. Learned Socs in USA, Sweden, Venezuela, East Germany, Spain and Greece. FRSocMed; Fellow: Eugenics Soc.; and Vice-Pres., Internat. Coll. of Psychosomatic Medicine, 1973; University Coll., Cardiff, 1980 (Governor, 1984–); Distinguished Fellow, Amer. Psychiatric Assoc., 1968; Hon. Fellow: Amer. Soc. of Physician Analysts; Amer. Coll. Psychiatrists; Biological Psychiatry Assoc., USA; Hong Kong Psychiatric Soc., 1982. Chm. Bd of Trustees, 1981–, Vice-Pres., 1984–, Stress Syndrome Foundn (Chm., Scientific Adv. Council). Governor: The Bethlem Royal Hosp. and The Maudsley Hosp.; Med. Coll. of St Bartholomew's Hosp., 1980–96. President: Extend, 1976; Golden Jubilee Appeal, Welsh Nat. Sch. of Med., 1980. Co-Editor, Jl of Psychosomatic Research. Liveryman: Barber Surgeons; Apothecaries. Hon. LLD Wales, 1981. Bard of Welsh Gorsedd. *Publications:* (with Eysenck and Himmelweit) Dimensions of Personality, 1947; Short Textbook of Psychiatry, 1967; (jtly) Textbook of Psychiatry, 1997; *chapters in:* Modern Treatment in General Practice, 1947; Recent Progress in Psychiatry, 1950; Schizophrenia: Somatic Aspects, 1957; Psychoendocrinology, 1958; Recent Progress in Psychosomatic Research, 1960; Stress and Psychiatric Disorders, 1960. Papers in: Nature, BMJ, Jl of Mental Sci., Jl of Psychosomatic Research, Eugenics Review, etc. Contribs to Med. Annual, 1958–68. *Recreations:* swimming, photography, amusing grandchildren. *Address:* Penbryn, 62 Oakwood Avenue, Purley, Surrey CR8 1AQ. *Club:* Athenæum.
Died 29 July 2004.

REES-JONES, Geoffrey Rippon, MA Oxon; Principal, King William's College, Isle of Man, 1958–79; *b* 8 July 1914; *er s* of W. Rees-Jones, BA, Ipswich; *m* 1950, Unity Margaret McConnell (*d* 1982), *d* of Major P. M. Sanders, Hampstead; one *s* one *d*. *Educ:* Ipswich School (scholar); University College, Oxford (open scholar). Assistant Master, Eastbourne College, 1936–38, Marlborough College, 1938–54 (Housemaster, C2, 1946–54); Headmaster, Bembridge School, 1954–58. Served War mainly in Commandos, 1940–45; Commandant, Commando Mountain Warfare School, 1943; Staff College, Camberley, 1944 (sc); Brigade Major, 4 Commando Bde, 1944–45 (despatches). *Recreations:* sailing, cricket, golf, fives; Oxford Rugby blue, 1933–35, Wales XV, 1934–36. *Address:* Red Lion Cottage, Braaid, Isle of Man IM4 2AJ. *T:* (01624) 851360.
Died 13 Sept. 2004.

REEVES, Marjorie Ethel, CBE 1996; MA (Oxon), PhD (London), DLitt (Oxon); FRHistS; FBA 1974; Vice-Principal, St Anne's College, Oxford, 1951–62, 1964–67; *b* 17 July 1905; *d* of Robert J. W. Reeves and Edith Saffery Whitaker. *Educ:* The High School for Girls, Trowbridge, Wilts; St Hugh's Coll., Oxford; Westfield Coll., London. Asst Mistress, Roan School, Greenwich, 1927–29; Research Fellow, Westfield Coll., London, 1929–31; Lecturer, St Gabriel's Trng Coll., London, 1931–38; Tutor, later Fellow of St Anne's College, 1938–72, Hon. Fellow, 1973. Member: Central Advisory Council, Min. of Educn, 1947–61; Academic Planning Bd, Univ. of Kent; Academic Advisory Cttee, University of Surrey; formerly Member: Educn Council, ITA; British Council of Churches; School Broadcasting Council. Corresp. Fellow, Medieval Acad. of America, 1979. Hon. DLitt: Bath, 1992; London, 1998. Medlicott Medal, Historical Assoc., 1993. Hon. citizenship, Commune of S. Giovanni, Fiore, 1994. *Publications:* Growing Up in a Modern Society, 1946; (ed, with L. Tondelli, B. Hirsch-Reich) Il Libro delle Figure dell'Abate Gioachino da Fiore, 1953; Three Questions in Higher Education (Hazen Foundation, USA), 1955; Moral Education in a Changing Society (ed W. Niblett), 1963; ed, Eighteen Plus: Unity

and Diversity in Higher Education, 1965; The Influence of Prophecy in the later Middle Ages: a study in Joachimism, 1969; Higher Education: demand and response (ed W. R. Niblett), 1969; (with B. Hirsch-Reich) The Figurae of Joachim of Fiore, 1972; Joachim of Fiore and the Prophetic Future, 1976; Sheep Bell and Ploughshare, 1978; Why History, 1980; (with W. Gould) Joachim of Fiore and the Myth of the Eternal Evangel in the Nineteenth Century, 1987; Competence, Delight and the Common Good: reflections on the crisis in higher education, 1988; (with J. Morrison) The Diaries of Jeffery Whitaker, 1989; (ed) Prophetic Rome in the High Renaissance Period, 1992; Pursuing the Muses, 1998; (ed) Christian Thinking and Social Order, 1999; (with Jenyth Worsley) Favourite Hymns: 2000 years of Magnificat, 2000; Then and There Series: The Medieval Town, 1954, The Medieval Village, 1954, Elizabethan Court, 1956, The Medieval Monastery, 1957, The Norman Conquest, 1958, Alfred and the Danes, 1959; The Medieval Castle, 1960, Elizabethan Citizen, 1961; A Medieval King Governs, 1971; Explorers of the Elizabethan Age, 1977; Elizabethan Country House, 1984; The Spanish Armada, 1988; contributions on history in Speculum, Medieval and Renaissance Studies, Traditio, Sophia, Recherches de Théologie, etc, and on education in Times Educational Supplement, New Era, etc. *Recreations:* music, gardening, bird-watching. *Address:* 38 Norham Road, Oxford OX2 6SQ. *T:* (01865) 557039. *Club:* University Women's.
Died 27 Nov. 2003.

REGAN, Hon. Donald Thomas; financier, author; Chief of Staff to the President of the United States, 1985–87; *b* 21 Dec. 1918; *s* of late William F. Regan and Kathleen A. Regan; *m* 1942, Ann Gordon Buchanan; two *s* two *d*. *Educ:* Cambridge Latin Sch.; Harvard Univ. (BA). Served War, US Marine Corps, 1940–46; retd as Lt Col, Marine Corps Reserve. Merrill Lynch, Pierce, Fenner & Smith Inc., 1946–81: Vice Pres., 1959–64; Exec. Vice Pres., 1964–68; Pres., 1968–71; Chm. of Bd, 1971–80; Chm. of Bd, Merrill Lynch & Co., Inc., 1973–81; Sec. of the Treasury, US Treasury Dept, 1981–85. Pres., Regdon Associates, 1987–95. Hon. LLD: Hahnemann Med. Coll. and Hosp., 1968; Tri-State Coll., 1969; Univ. of Penn., 1972; Hon. Dr of Commercial Science, Pace Univ., 1973; Hon DHL Colgate Univ., 1984. Fortune magazine's Hall of Fame for business leadership, 1981. Legion of Honour, 1982. *Publications:* A View from the Street, 1972; For the Record: from Wall Street to Washington, 1988. *Recreations:* golf, reading, painting. *Address:* 266 McLaws Circle, Williamsburg, VA 23185, USA. *Club:* Army-Navy (Washington, DC). *Died 10 June 2003.*

REHNQUIST, William H.; Chief Justice of the United States, since 1986; *b* 1 Oct. 1924; *s* of William Benjamin and Margery Peck Rehnquist; *m* 1953, Natalie Cornell (*d* 1991); one *s* two *d*. *Educ:* Stanford and Harvard Univs. BA, MA 1948, LLB 1952, Stanford; MA Harvard 1949. Law Clerk for Mr Justice Robert H. Jackson, 1952–53; Partner, Phoenix, Ariz: Evans, Kitchell & Jenckes, 1953–55; Ragan & Rehnquist, 1956–57; Cunningham, Carson & Messenger, 1957–60; Powers & Rehnquist, 1960–69; Asst Attorney-Gen., Office of Legal Counsel, Dept of Justice, 1969–72; Associate Justice, Supreme Court, 1972–86. Phi Beta Kappa; Order of the Coif. *Publications:* contrib. US News and World Report, Jl of Amer. Bar Assoc., Arizona Law Review. *Recreations:* swimming, tennis, reading, hiking. *Address:* Supreme Court of the United States, Washington, DC 20543, USA. *Club:* National Lawyers (Washington, DC). *Died 3 Sept. 2005.*

REID, Dougal Gordon, CMG 1983; HM Diplomatic Service, retired; Director of Studies, Royal Institute of Public Administration International, 1985–92; *b* Hong Kong, 31 Dec. 1925; *e s* of late Douglas Reid and Catherine Jean (*née* Lowson), Forfar; *m* 1950, Georgina Elizabeth Johnston; one *s* (and one *s* decd). *Educ:* Sedbergh Sch.; Trinity Hall, Cambridge; LSE. Served in Royal Marines, 1944–46. Cadet, Colonial Admin. Service (later

HMOCS), Sierra Leone, 1949; District Comr 1956; retd as Perm. Sec., Min. of Natural Resources, 1962. Arthur Guinness Son & Co. Ltd, 1962–63. Entered CRO, later FCO, 1963; served in: Accra, 1964–65; CO, 1966; Accra, 1966–68 (concurrently Lomé, 1967–68); Seoul, 1968–71; FCO, 1971–74; Kinshasa (and concurrently at Brazzaville, Bujumbura and Kigali), 1974–77; New Delhi, 1977–78; Singapore, 1979–80; Ambassador to Liberia, 1980–85. Mem., Internat. Cttee, Leonard Cheshire Foundn, 1985–92. *Recreations:* military history, jazz, watching sport. *Clubs:* Royal Commonwealth Society, MCC; London Scottish Football; Sadan Pubin (Seoul).
Died 24 May 2003.

REID, Rev. Prof. John Kelman Sutherland, CBE 1970; TD 1961; Professor of Christian Dogmatics, 1961–70, of Systematic Theology, 1970–76, University of Aberdeen; *b* 31 March 1910; *y s* of late Reverend Dr David Reid, Calcutta and Leith, and Mrs G. T. Reid (*née* Stuart); *m* 1950, Margaret Winifrid Brookes (*d* 1989). *Educ:* George Watson's Boys' College, Edinburgh; Univ. of Edinburgh (MA 1st Cl. Hons Phil. 1933; BD dist. Theol 1938; Cunningham Fellow); Univs of Heidelberg, Marburg, Basel, and Strasbourg. Prof. of Philosophy in Scottish Church Coll., Univ. of Calcutta, 1935–37; ordained into Church of Scotland, 1939; Minister, Parish of Craigmillar Park, Edinburgh, 1939–52; CF, chiefly with Parachute Regt, 1942–46; Prof. of Theology and Head of Department of Theology, University of Leeds, 1952–61. Jt Ed. Scot. Jl Theol. from inception, 1947; Hon. Sec. Jt Cttee on New Translation of the Bible, 1949–82. Hon. DD Edinburgh, 1957. *Publications:* The Authority of Scripture, 1957; Our Life in Christ, 1963; Christian Apologetics, 1969. Translation of: Oscar Cullmann's The Earliest Christian Confessions, 1949; Baptism in the New Testament, 1952; Calvin's Theological Treatises, ed and trans. 1954; Jean Bosc's The Kingly Office of the Lord Jesus Christ, 1959; Calvin's Concerning the Eternal Pre-destination of God, ed and trans., 1961, repr. 1982. *Address:* 8 Abbotsford Court, 18 Colinton Road, Edinburgh EH10 5EH. *Club:* Mortonhall Golf (Edinburgh). *Died 18 March 2002.*

REID, Flight Lt William, VC 1943; agricultural consultant; Agriculture Adviser, The MacRobert Trust, Douneside, Tarland, Aberdeenshire, 1950–59; *b* 21 Dec. 1921; *s* of late William Reid, Baillieston, Glasgow; *m* 1952, Violet Gallagher, 11 Dryburgh Gdns, Glasgow, NW1; one *s* one *d*. *Educ:* Coatbridge Secondary Sch.; Glasgow Univ. (BSc Agric., 1949); West of Scotland Coll. of Agriculture. Student of Metallurgy, Sept. 1940; Post-Graduate World Travelling Scholarship for 6 months, to study Agric. and Installations in India, Australia, NZ, USA and Canada, 1949–50. Joined RAF 1941; trained in Lancaster, Calif, USA. Won VC during a trip to Düsseldorf, 3 Nov. 1943, when member of 61 Squadron; pilot RAFVR, 617 Squadron (prisoner); demobilised, 1946; recalled to RAF for 3 months, Dec. 1951. Joined RAFVR, commissioned Jan. 1949, 103 Reserve Centre, Perth. Nat. Cattle and Sheep Advr, Spillers Ltd, 1959–81. Vice-Chm., VC and GC Assoc., 2000–. Freedom of City of London, 1988. *Recreations:* golf, shooting, fishing, etc. *Address:* Cranford, Ferntower Place, Crieff, Perthshire PH7 3DD. *T:* (01764) 652462. *Club:* Royal Air Force. *Died 28 Nov. 2001.*

REINHARDT, Max; Chairman: Reinhardt Books Ltd (formerly HFL (Publishers) Ltd), since 1947; The Nonesuch Press Ltd, since 1986; *b* 30 Nov. 1915; *s* of Ernest Reinhardt and Frieda Reinhardt (*née* Darr); *m* 1st, 1947, Margaret Leighton, CBE (marr. diss. 1955; she *d* 1976); 2nd, 1957, Joan, *d* of Carlisle and Dorothy MacDonald, NYC; two *d*. *Educ:* English High Sch. for Boys, Istanbul; Ecole des Hautes Etudes Commerciales, Paris; LSE. Acquired HFL (Publishers) Ltd, 1947; founded Max Reinhardt Ltd, 1948, which bought: The Bodley Head Ltd, 1956 (Man. Dir, 1957–81; Chm., 1981–87); Putnam & Co., 1963; Jt Chm., Chatto, Bodley Head and Jonathan Cape Ltd, 1973–87. Mem. Council: Publishers'

Assoc., 1963–69; RADA, 1965–96; The Pilgrims, 1966–. *Recreations:* reading for pleasure, swimming, bridge. *Address:* Flat 2, 43 Onslow Square, SW7 3LR. *T:* (020) 7589 5527. *Club:* Garrick.   *Died 19 Nov. 2002.*

REISZ, Karel; film director; *b* 21 July 1926; *s* of Joseph Reisz and Frederika; *m* 1st, 1953, Julia Coppard (marr. diss. 1963); three *s*; 2nd, 1963, Betsy Blair. *Educ:* Leighton Park Sch., Reading; Emmanuel Coll., Cambridge (BA 1948). Formerly: co-ed with Lindsay Anderson, film magazine, Sequence; worked for BFI; first Programme Dir, National Film Theatre. Co-directed, with Tony Richardson, Momma Don't Allow, 1956; produced: Every Day Except Christmas, 1957; This Sporting Life, 1960; directed: We Are the Lambeth Boys, 1958; Saturday Night and Sunday Morning, 1959; Night Must Fall, 1963; Morgan, a Suitable Case for Treatment, 1965; Isadora, 1967; The Gambler, 1975; Dog Soldiers, 1978; The French Lieutenant's Woman, 1981; Sweet Dreams, 1986; Everybody Wins, 1991; Act Sans Paroles, 2000; *stage plays:* Gardenia, Manhattan Theatre Club, 1991; The Gigli Concert, The Deep Blue Sea, Almeida, 1992; Gate Theatre, Dublin: A Doll's House, 1993; Moonlight, 1994, transf. NY, 1995; Happy Days, transf. NY and Almeida, 1996; A Kind of Alaska, 1997; Long Day's Journey Into Night, 1998; The Yalta Game, 2001. *Publication:* The Technique of Film Editing (also ed), 1953.   *Died 25 Nov. 2002.*

RELPH, Michael Leighton George; film producer, director, designer, writer; *b* 16 Feb. 1915; *s* of late George Relph and Deborah Relph (later Harker); *m* 1st, 1939, Doris Gosden (marr. diss.); one *s*; 2nd, 1950, Maria Barry; one *d*. *Educ:* Bembridge Sch. Stage designer, 1940–50: West-end prodns include: Indoor Fireworks; The Doctor's Dilemma; Up and Doing; Watch on the Rhine; The Man Who Came to Dinner; Frieda; Saloon Bar; Old Acquaintance; Quiet Week-end; Heartbreak House; Relative Values; A Month in the Country; The Last of Summer; Love in Idleness; The White Carnation; The Petrified Forest; The Banbury Nose; They Came to a City. Began film career as apprentice, then Asst Art Dir, Gaumont British Studios; Art Dir, Warner Brothers Studios; Art Dir, Ealing Studios, 1942–45: prodns include: The Bells Go Down; Dead of Night; Champagne Charley; Nicholas Nickleby; Saraband for Dead Lovers (nominated Hollywood Oscar); Associate Producer to Michael Balcon, 1945; subseq. Producer with Basil Dearden as Dir until Dearden's death, 1972: prodns include: The Captive Heart; Kind Hearts and Coronets; The Blue Lamp (Best British Film Award, Brit. Film Acad.); Frieda; Saraband for Dead Lovers; I Believe in You (co-author); The Ship that Died of Shame; The Rainbow Jacket; The Square Ring; The Gentle Gunman; Cage of Gold; Pool of London. Director: Davy, 1957; Rockets Galore, 1958; Producer: Violent Playground; Sapphire (Best British Film Award, Brit. Film Acad.); All Night Long; The Smallest Show on Earth. Founder Dir, Allied Film Makers: produced: League of Gentlemen; Victim; Man in the Moon (co-author); Life for Ruth; The Mind Benders; Woman of Straw; Masquerade (co-author); The Assassination Bureau (also author and designer); The Man Who Haunted Himself (co-author); in charge of production, Boyd's Company, 1978–82: Scum (exec. producer), 1979; An Unsuitable Job for a Woman (co-producer), 1982; Treasure Houses of Britain (TV; exec. producer), 1985; Heavenly Pursuits, 1986; The Torrents of Spring, 1988 (production consultant); screenplays, 1995–96: Seven Against the West; (with Fay Weldon) My Mother's Profession; William Tell: the untold story. Chm., Film Prodn Assoc. of GB, 1971–76; Mem., Cinematograph Films Council, 1971–76; Governor, BFI, 1972–79 (Chm., Prodn Bd, 1972–79). Hon. DLitt De Montfort, 1999. *Recreations:* reading, theatre going, painting. *Address:* c/o The Old Malthouse, Westwood, Bradford-on-Avon, Wilts BA15 2AG. *T:* (01225) 864905.   *Died 30 Sept. 2004.*

RENNIE, James Douglas Milne, CB 1986; Parliamentary Counsel, 1976–92; *b* 2 Nov. 1931; *s* of Douglas Frederick Milne Rennie and Margaret Wilson Fleming Rennie (*née* Keanie); *m* 1962, Patricia Margaret Calhoun Watson; one *s* one *d*. *Educ:* Charterhouse; New Coll., Oxford (Schol.; 1st cl. Hon. Mods 1953; 2nd cl. Lit. Hum. 1955; 2nd cl. Jurisprudence 1957; MA). Called to Bar, Lincoln's Inn, 1958 (Cholmeley Schol.). Asst Lectr, UCW Aberystwyth, 1957; practised at Chancery Bar, 1958–65; Asst Parly Counsel, HM Treasury, 1965; Sen. Asst Parly Counsel, 1972; Dep. Parly Counsel, 1973–75. *Recreations:* opera, travel. *Address:* 8 Wellesley Road, W4 4BL. *T:* (020) 8994 6627.   *Died 3 Dec. 2005.*

RENNIE, John Chalmers; Town Clerk of Aberdeen, 1946–68; retired; *b* 16 April 1907; *s* of late John Chalmers Rennie, Pharmacist, Wishaw; *m* 1937, Georgina Stoddart, *d* of late Henry Bell, Engineer and Ironfounder, Wishaw; one *s*. *Educ:* University of Glasgow (BL). Admitted solicitor, 1929. Town Clerk Depute, Motherwell and Wishaw, 1929–43; Town Clerk Depute, Aberdeen, 1943–46. Dep. Controller, Civil Defence Servs, Motherwell and Wishaw, 1939–43; Secretary: Aberdeen Harbour Bd, 1946–60; NE Fire Area Jt Bd, 1948–68. Mem. Council, Law Soc. of Scotland, 1958–61. Hon. Solicitor (Scotland), NALGO, 1949–64. *Recreation:* surviving. *Address:* 77 Forest Road, Aberdeen AB2 4BJ. *T:* (01224) 638635.   *Died 24 Sept. 2001.*

RENNIE, Sir John Shaw, GCMG 1968 (KCMG 1962; CMG 1958); OBE 1955; Commissioner-General, United Nations Relief and Works Agency for Palestine Refugees, 1971–77 (Deputy Commissioner-General, 1968–71); *b* 12 Jan. 1917; *s* of late John Shaw Rennie, Saskatoon, Canada; *m* 1946, Mary Winifred Macalpine Robertson; one *s*. *Educ:* Hillhead High School; Glasgow University; Balliol College, Oxford. Cadet, Tanganyika, 1940; Asst District Officer, 1942; District Officer, 1949; Deputy Colonial Secretary, Mauritius, 1951; British Resident Comr, New Hebrides, 1955–62; Governor and C-in-C of Mauritius, 1962–March 1968, Governor-General, March-Aug. 1968. Hon. LLD Glasgow, 1972. *Address:* 26 College Cross, N1 1PR. *Club:* Royal Commonwealth Society.   *Died 12 Aug. 2002.*

RENOWDEN, Ven. Glyndwr Rhys, CB 1987; Chaplain in Chief, Royal Air Force, 1983–88; *b* 13 Aug. 1929; *s* of Charles and Mary Elizabeth Renowden; *m* 1956, Mary Kinsey-Jones; one *d*. *Educ:* Llanelli Grammar Sch.; St David's Coll., Lampeter (BA, LTh). Ordained deacon, 1952, priest, 1953; Curate: St Mary's, Tenby, 1952–55; St Mary's, Chepstow, 1955–58; Chaplain, RAF, 1958–88; Asst Chaplain in Chief, 1975–83; Priest i/c, Llanfallteg with Clunderwen and Castell Dwyran, 1989–99. QHC, 1980–88. *Recreations:* Rugby football, bridge. *Address:* Red Cedars, Kenystyle, Penally, near Tenby, Pembrokeshire SA70 7PJ.   *Died 17 Aug. 2002.*

RENSHAW, Sir (Charles) Maurice (Bine), 3rd Bt *cr* 1903, of Coldharbour, Wivelsfield, Sussex; *b* 7 Oct. 1912; *s* of Sir (Charles) Stephen (Bine) Renshaw, 2nd Bt and of Edith Mary, *d* of Rear-Adm. Sir Edward Chichester, 9th Bt, CB, CMG; *S* father, 1976; *m* 1st, 1942, Isabel Bassett (marr. diss. 1947; she *d* 2001), *d* of late Rev. John L. T. Popkin; one *s* one *d* (and one *s* decd); 2nd, Winifred May, *d* of H. F. Gliddon, Ashwater, Devon, and formerly wife of James H. T. Sheldon; three *s* three *d*. *Educ:* Eton. Served as Flying Officer, RAF (invalided). *Heir: s* John David Renshaw [*b* 9 Oct. 1945; *m* 1970, Jennifer (marr. diss. 1988), *d* of Group Captain F. Murray, RAF; one *s* two *d*]. *Address:* Tam-na-Marghaidh, Balquhidder, Perthshire FK19 8PB; Linwood, Instow, N Devon EX39 4HX.   *Died 18 Aug. 2002.*

REVANS, Prof. Reginald William, PhD; MIMinE; Founder, Action Learning Trust, 1977; Professorial Fellow in Action Learning, University of Manchester, since 1986; *b* 14 May 1907; *s* of Thomas William Revans, Principal Ship Surveyor, Board of Trade; *m* 1st, 1932, Annida

Aquist, Gothenburg (marr. diss. 1947); three *d*; 2nd, 1955, Norah Mary Merritt, Chelmsford; one *s*. *Educ:* Battersea Grammar School; University Coll., London (BSc); Emmanuel Coll., Cambridge (PhD 1934). Commonwealth Fund Fellow, Univ. of Michigan, 1930–32; Research Fellow, Emmanuel Coll., Cambridge, 1932–35; Dep. Chief Educn Officer, Essex CC, 1935–45; Dir of Educn, Mining Assoc. of Gt Britain, 1945–47 and NCB, 1947–50; research on management of coalmines, 1950–55; Prof., Industrial Admin., Univ. of Manchester, 1955–65; Res. Fellow, Guy's Hosp. Med. Sch., 1965–68; External Prof., Management Studies, Leeds Univ., 1976–78. Dist. Vis. Scholar, Southern Methodist Univ., USA, 1972. Pres., European Assoc. of Univ. Management Centres, 1962–64. Hon. DSc Bath, 1969. Chevalier, Order of Leopold (Belgium), 1971. *Publications:* Report on Education for Mining Industry, 1945; Education of the Young Worker, 1949; Standards for Morale, 1964; Science and the Manager, 1965; The Theory and Practice of Management, 1965; Developing Effective Managers, 1971; (ed) Hospitals, Communication, Choice and Change, 1972; Workers' Attitudes and Motivation (OECD Report), 1972; Childhood and Maturity, 1973; Action Learning in Hospitals, 1976; The ABC of Action Learning, 1978; Action Learning, 1979; The Origins and Growth of Action Learning, 1982; various in professional magazines upon application of analytical methods to understanding of industrial morale. *Recreations:* British Olympic Team, 1928; holder of Cambridge undergraduate long jump record, 1929–62. *Address:* 21 Tilstock, Whitchurch, Shropshire SY13 3NS.

Died 8 Jan. 2003.

REVELSTOKE, 5th Baron *cr* 1885, of Membland, Devon; **John Baring;** *b* 2 Dec. 1934; *er s* of 4th Baron Revelstoke and Hon. Florence Fermor-Hesketh (*d* 1971), 2nd *d* of 1st Baron Hesketh; *S* father, 1994. *Educ:* Eton. *Heir: b* Hon. James Cecil Baring [*b* 16 Aug. 1938; *m* 1st, 1968, Aneta (marr. diss.), *yr d* of Erskine A. H. Fisher; two *s*; 2nd, 1983, Sarah, *d* of William Edward Stubbs, MBE; one *d*].

Died 5 June 2003.

REYNOLDS, Maj.-Gen. Jack Raymond, CB 1971; OBE 1945; ERD 1948; DL; Director of Movements (Army), Ministry of Defence, 1968–71, retired; *b* 10 June 1916; *s* of Walter Reynolds and Evelyn Marion (*née* Burrows); *m* 1940, Joan Howe Taylor (*d* 1992); one *s* one *d*. *Educ:* Haberdashers' Aske's. Student Apprentice, AEC Ltd, 1934. Commissioned RASC (SR), 1936. Served War of 1939–45, France, Middle East and Italy (despatches). CRASC 7th Armoured Div., 1955–57; GSO 1 War Office, 1958–60; Col GS; UK Delegn to NATO Standing Group, Washington, DC, 1960–62; DDST, Southern Command, 1962–64; Commandant, RASC Training Centre, 1964–65; Imperial Defence College, 1966; Dep. Quarter-Master-General, BAOR, 1967–68. Col Comdt, Royal Corps of Transport, 1972–78. Dir-Gen., BHS, 1971–75; Dir-Gen., 1975–85, Pres., 1985–88, BEF. FCIT. DL Northants, 1984. *Recreation:* fishing. *Address:* Park House, Tyringham, Bucks MK16 9ES.

Died 20 Oct. 2003.

REYNOLDS, William Oliver, OBE 1973 (MBE 1944); General Manager, Eastern Region, British Rail, 1973–76; *b* 2 Nov. 1915; *s* of Edgar Ernest Reynolds and Elizabeth Wilson Biesterfield; *m* 1944, Eleanor Gill; two *s*. *Educ:* Royal Grammar Sch., Newcastle upon Tyne. LNER Traffic apprentice, 1936. Served War, with Royal Engineers, 1940–46: despatches, 1942 and 1944; Lt-Col, 1944. Lt-Col, Engineer and Railway Staff Corps, RE (T&AVR IV), 1971–97. Divisional Manager, London Midland, BR, 1960; Asst Gen. Manager, Scottish Region, 1964; Chief Operating Manager, BR Bd, 1968; Exec. Dir, BR Bd, 1969. Mem., Adv. Council, Science Mus. 1975–84; Chm., Friends of Nat. Railway Mus. 1984–93. FCIT. *Recreations:* fishing, golf, gardening. *Address:* Oak House, Follifoot, Harrogate, N Yorks HG3 1DR. *Club:* Oriental.

Died 13 Jan. 2002.

RHODES, Col Sir Basil (Edward), Kt 1987; CBE 1981 (OBE (mil.) 1945; MBE (mil.) 1944); TD 1946; DL; Partner, Gichard & Co., solicitors, since 1946; *b* Rotherham, 8 Dec. 1915; *s* of late Col Harry Rhodes and of Astri Rhodes (*née* Natvig); *m* 1962, Joëlle, *er d* of Robert Vilgard, Paris; one *s*. *Educ:* St Edward's Sch., Oxford. Served War of 1939–45, Western Desert, Greece, Crete and Burma (wounded; mentioned in despatches). Admitted solicitor, 1946. Director: Carlton Main Brickworks; Wessex Fare; Yorkshire Merchant Securities. Mem. (C) Town Council, Rotherham, 1949–74, Mayor, 1970–71; Chm., 1949–75, Pres., 1975–, Rotherham Cons. Assoc.; Chm., S Yorks Cons. Fedn, 1964–76; Treas., Cons. Central Office Yorks Area, 1983–88. DL 1975, High Sheriff, 1982–83, S Yorks. *Recreations:* fieldsports, ski-ing, gardening. *Address:* Bubnell Hall, Baslow, Bakewell, Derbys DE4 1RL. *T:* (01246) 583266. *Club:* Cavalry and Guards.   *Died 28 Jan. 2003.*

RHODES, Paul; *see* Rhodes, R. P.

RHODES, Sir Peregrine (Alexander), KCMG 1984 (CMG 1976); HM Diplomatic Service, retired; Director-General, British Property Federation, 1986–93; *b* 14 May 1925; *s* of Cyril Edmunds Rhodes and Elizabeth Jocelyn Rhodes; *m* 1st, 1951, Jane Marion Hassell (marr. diss.); two *s* one *d*; 2nd, 1969, Margaret Rosemary Page. *Educ:* Winchester Coll.; New Coll., Oxford (BA Lit. Hum. (1st cl)). Served with Coldstream Guards, 1944–47. Joined FO, 1950; 2nd Sec., Rangoon, 1953–56; Private Sec. to Minister of State, 1956–59; 1st Sec., Vienna, 1959–62; 1st Sec., Helsinki, 1962–65; FCO, 1965–68, Counsellor 1967; Inst. for Study of Internat. Organisation, Sussex Univ., 1968–69; Counsellor, Rome, 1970–73; Chargé d'Affaires, E Berlin, 1973–75; on secondment as Under Sec., Cabinet Office (Chief of Assessments Staff), 1975–78; High Comr, Cyprus, 1979–82; Ambassador, Greece, 1982–85. Chm., Anglo-Hellenic League, 1986–90; Vice-Pres. British Sch., Athens, 1982–2002. FRSA 1988. *Recreations:* photography, reading. *Address:* Pond House, Thorpe Morieux, Bury St Edmunds, Suffolk IP30 0NW. *Club:* Travellers (Chm., 1994–98).

Died 7 March 2005.

RHODES, Philip, FRCS, FRCOG, FRACMA, FFOM; Regional Postgraduate Dean of Medical Studies, and Professor of Postgraduate Medical Education, Southampton University, 1980–87, retired; *b* 2 May 1922; *s* of Sydney Rhodes, Dore, Sheffield; *m* 1946, Mary Elizabeth Worley, Barrowden, Rutland; three *s* two *d*. *Educ:* King Edward VII Sch., Sheffield; Clare Coll., Cambridge (BA 1943, MB BChir 1946); St Thomas's Hospital Medical School. FRCS 1953; MRCOG 1956, FRCOG 1964; FRACMA 1976; FFOM 1990. Major RAMC, 1948–50. Medical appointments held in St Thomas' Hosp., Folkestone, Harrogate, Chelsea Hosp. for Women, Queen Charlotte's Hosp., 1946–58; Consultant Obstetric Physician, St Thomas' Hosp., 1958–63; Prof. of Obstetrics and Gynæcol., St Thomas's Hosp. Med. Sch., Univ. of London, 1964–74, Dean, 1968–74; Dean, Faculty of Medicine, Univ. of Adelaide, 1975–77; Postgrad. Dean and Dir, Regional Postgrad. Inst. for Med. and Dentistry, Newcastle Univ., 1977–80. Member: SW Metropolitan Regional Hosp. Board, 1967–74; SE Thames Reg. Health Authority, 1974; GMC, 1979–89 (Educn Cttee, 1984–89). Mem. Steering Cttee of DHSS on management of NHS, 1971–72. Mem., Adv. Cttee, Nat. Inst. of Medical Hist., Australia, 1976. Chm., Educn Cttee, King Edward's Hosp. Fund for London, 1981–87; Member: UGC Working Party on Continuing Educn, 1983; Council for Postgrad. Med. Educn in England and Wales, 1984–87. Governor: Dulwich Coll., 1966–74; St Thomas' Hosp., 1969–74; Pembroke Sch., Adelaide, 1976–79. FRSA 1989. *Publications:* Fluid Balance in Obstetrics, 1960; Introduction to Gynæcology and Obstetrics, 1967; Reproductive Physiology for Medical Students, 1969; Woman: A Biological Study, 1969; The Value of Medicine, 1976; Dr John Leake's Hospital, 1978;

Letters to a Young Doctor, 1983; An Outline History of Medicine, 1985; Wakerley: a village in Northamptonshire, 1994; A Short History of Clinical Midwifery, 1995; Gynaecology for Everywoman, 1996; Barrowden: a village in Rutland, 1998; Associate Editor, The Oxford Companion to Medicine, 1986; contrib. Encyclopedia Britannica, New DNB; articles in Jl of Obstetrics and Gynæcology of the British Empire, Lancet, Brit. Med. Jl, Med. Jl of Australia. *Recreations:* reading, gardening, photography. *Address:* 1 Wakerley Court, Wakerley, Oakham, Leics LE15 8NZ. *Died 15 July 2002.*

RHODES, Reginald Paul; Chairman, Southern Gas Region, 1975–83; *b* 10 April 1918; *s* of Edwin Rhodes and Dorothy Lena Molyneux; *m* 1940, Margaret Frances Fish; two *s* three *d. Educ:* Merchant Taylors' Sch., Northwood. Joined Gas Light & Coke Co., 1937; North Thames Gas, 1948 (Dep. Chm., 1972). Deputy Chairman: Southampton Industrial Therapy Organisation, 1980–89; Solent Productivity Assoc., 1983–90; Chm., Solent Business Fund, 1983–90; Member: Wessex RHA, 1984–90; Shaw Trust, 1984–90. Mem., Co. of Pikemen, Honourable Artillery Company. FIGasE. *Recreations:* music, gardening. *Address:* 3 The Paddock, Brockenhurst, Hants SO42 7QU. *T:* (01590) 622399.
Died 2 July 2001.

RICE-OXLEY, James Keith, CBE 1981; Chairman, Merchant Navy Training Board, 1981–97; *b* 15 Aug. 1920; *o s* of late Montague Keith Rice-Oxley and Margery Hyacinth Rice-Oxley (*née* Burrell), Kensington; *m* 1949, Barbara, *yr d* of late Frederick Parsons, Gerrards Cross; two *d. Educ:* Marlborough Coll.; Trinity Coll., Oxford. MA(Law). Served War of 1939–45: Wiltshire Regt, Royal West Kents (wounded El Alamein); GSO III, HQ 3 Corps; GSO I, HQ Land Forces, Greece (despatches). Joined Shipping Fedn, 1947, Dir, 1965–75; Dir, Internat. Shipping Fedn, 1970–80; Dir, Gen. Council of British Shipping, 1975–80. Chm., Nat. Sea Training Trust, 1965–80; Mem. Nat. Maritime Bd, 1965–80; Mem., Merchant Navy Welfare Bd, 1965–80; Internat. Shipowners' Chm. and British Shipowners' Rep. on Jt Maritime Commn of ILO, 1970–80; Chm., Shipowners' Gp at Internat. Labour (Maritime) Confs, 1969, 1970, 1975, 1976; a Vice-Pres., IMCO/ILO Maritime Conf., 1978. Chm., Maritime Studies Cttee, BTEC, 1980–87; Mem. Industrial Tribunals (England and Wales), 1981–88; General Comr of Income Tax, 1986–95. Barnardo's: Mem. Council and Exec. Cttee, 1981–95; Vice-Chm. Council, 1988–89 and 1993–94; Chm., Shaftesbury Civic Soc., 1982–85; Mem. Council, King George's Fund for Sailors, 1965–82; UK Mem., Bd of Governors, World Maritime Univ., Malmö, 1982–89. *Recreation:* ceramics. *Address:* Ox House, Bimport, Shaftesbury SP7 8AX. *T:* (01747) 852741. *Died 28 Sept. 2005.*

RICHARDS, Sir Brooks; *see* Richards, Sir F. B.

RICHARDS, David Gordon, CBE 1989; FCA; non-executive Chairman, Walker Greenbank plc, 1990–99 (Director, 1988–99); *b* 25 Aug. 1928; *s* of late Gordon Charles Richards and Vera Amy (*née* Barrow); *m* 1960, Stephanie, *er d* of late E. Gilbert Woodward, Metropolitan Magistrate; one *s* two *d. Educ:* Highgate Sch. FCA 1961. Articled to Harmood Banner & Co., 1945; served, 8th Royal Tank Regt, 1947–49; Partner: Harmood Banner & Co., 1955–74; Deloitte Haskins & Sells, 1974–84. Admitted Associate Mem. ICAEW, 1951 (Council, 1970–87; Vice-Pres., 1977–78; Dep. Pres., 1978–79; Centenary Pres., 1979–80; Mem., Gen. Purposes and Finance Cttee, 1977–83; Chm., Internat. Affairs Cttee, 1980–83); Mem., Cttee of London Soc. of Chartered Accountants, 1966–70, 1981–82 (Chm., 1969–70); Chm., Cons. Cttee of Accountancy Bodies, 1979–80; UK and Ireland rep. on Council, Internat. Fedn of Accountants, 1981–83. Dep. Chm., Monopolies and Mergers Commn, 1983–90; Member: Cttees of Investigation under Agricultural Marketing Act (1958), 1972–88; Council for Securities Industry, 1979–80; Panel on Take Overs and

Mergers, 1979–80; Review Body on Doctors' and Dentists' Remuneration, 1984–90. Chm., Disciplinary Bd, BPsS, 1988–95 (Hon. Life Mem., 1996). Governor: Highgate Sch., 1982–98 (Chm. 1983–98); Associated Bd of Royal Schs of Music, 1987–; Trustee: The Bob Champion Cancer Trust, 1983–94; Royal Acad. of Music Foundn, 1985–2000; Prince's Youth Business Trust, 1986–93; Royal Acad. of Music, 2000–. Pres., Old Cholmeleian Soc., 1988–89. Hon. FRAM 1995. Master, Chartered Accountants' in England and Wales Co., 1986–87. *Publications:* numerous contribs to professional press and lectures on professional topics given internationally. *Recreations:* golf, lawn tennis, sailing, shooting, silviculture, music. *Address:* Eastleach House, Eastleach, Glos GL7 3NW. *T:* (01367) 850416.
Died 9 March 2003.

RICHARDS, Denis George, OBE 1990; author; *b* 10 Sept. 1910; *s* of late George Richards and Frances Amelia Gosland; *m* 1940, Barbara, *d* of J. H. Smethurst, Heaton, Bolton; four *d. Educ:* Owen's Sch.; Trinity Hall, Cambridge (Scholar; BA 1931 (1st Cl. in both Parts of Historical Tripos); MA 1935). Asst Master, Manchester Grammar School, 1931–39; Senior History and English Master, Bradfield Coll., 1939–41; Narrator in Air Ministry Historical Branch, writing confidential studies on various aspects of the air war, 1942–43; Sen. Narrator, 1943–47; Hon. Sqdn Ldr RAFVR, 1943–47; engaged in writing, under Air Min. auspices, an official History of the Royal Air Force in the Second World War, 1947–49; was established in Admin. Civil Service, Principal, Department of Permanent Under Secretary of State for Air, 1949–50; Principal, Morley College, 1950–65; Longman Fellow in Univ. of Sussex, 1965–68. Chm., Women's League of Health and Beauty, 1966–88; Vice-Pres., Purcell Sch. for Young Musicians, 1984–. *Publications:* An Illustrated History of Modern Europe, 1938; Modern Europe (1919–39 section for revised edn of work by Sydney Herbert), 1940; (with J. W. Hunt) An Illustrated History of Modern Britain, 1950; (with late Hilary St G. Saunders) Royal Air Force 1939–45–an officially commissioned history in 3 volumes, 1953–54 (awarded C. P. Robertson Memorial Trophy, 1954); (with J. Evan Cruikshank) The Modern Age, 1955; Britain under the Tudors and Stuarts, 1958; Offspring of the Vic: a history of Morley College, 1958; (with Anthony Quick) Britain 1714–1851, 1961; (with J. A. Bolton) Britain and the Ancient World, 1963; (with Anthony Quick) Britain, 1851–1945, 1967; (with Anthony Quick) Twentieth Century Britain, 1968; (with A. W. Ellis) Medieval Britain, 1973; Portal of Hungerford, 1978; (with Richard Hough) The Battle of Britain: the Jubilee history, 1989; (ed) The Few and the Many, 1990; The Hardest Victory: RAF Bomber Command in the Second World War, 1994; Just to Recall the Flavour: recollections 1910–41, 1999; It Might Have Been Worse: recollections 1941–96, 1999. *Recreations:* music, pictures, residual golf, the lightest tasks in the garden. *Address:* c/o 63 London Road, Tunbridge Wells, Kent TN1 1DT. *Clubs:* Arts, Garrick, Royal Air Force, PEN.
Died 25 Nov. 2004.

RICHARDS, Sir (Francis) Brooks, KCMG 1976 (CMG 1963); DSC and Bar, 1943; HM Diplomatic Service, retired; *b* 18 July 1918; *s* of Francis Bartlett Richards; *m* 1941, Hazel Myfanwy (*d* 2000), *d* of Lt-Col Stanley Price Williams, CIE; one *s* one *d. Educ:* Stowe School; Magdalene College, Cambridge. Served with RN, 1939–44 (Lieut-Comdr RNVR), and in SOE. HM Embassy: Paris, 1944–48; Athens, 1952–54; First Sec. and Head of Chancery, Political Residency, Persian Gulf, 1954–57; Assistant Private Secretary to Foreign Secretary, 1958–59; Counsellor (Information), Paris, 1959–64; Head of Information Policy Dept, 1964, and of Jt Inf. Policy and Guidance Dept, FO/CRO, 1964–65; seconded to Cabinet Office, 1965–69; Minister, Bonn, 1969–71; Ambassador: Saigon, 1972–74; Greece, 1974–78; Dep. Sec., Cabinet Office, 1978–80; NI Office, 1980–81. Chm., CSM Parliamentary Consultants Ltd, 1984–96.

Vice-Pres., Friends of Imperial War Museum, 1991–97 (Chm., 1989–91); Chairman: Paintings in Hosps, 1990–96; Anglo Hellenic League, 1990–93. Chevalier, Légion d'Honneur and Croix de Guerre (France), 1944. *Publication:* Secret Flotillas, 1996 (trans. French 2000). *Recreations:* collecting, gardening, travelling. *Club:* Special Forces.   *Died 13 Sept. 2002.*

RICHARDS, James Alan, OBE 1979; Agent-General for Western Australia in London, 1975–78, retired; *b* 8 Oct. 1913; *s* of James Percival Richards and Alice Pearl Richards (*née* Bullock), Adelaide; *m* 1939, Mabel Joyce, *d* of R. H. Cooper, Riverton, S Austr.; three *s* one *d. Educ:* Unley High Sch.; Coll. of Business Admin, Univ. of Hawaii. Served War of 1939–45, 2nd AIF. Ampol Petroleum Ltd, 1946–75: Sales Man., South Australia, 1952–53; State Man., Western Australia, 1954–75. *Recreation:* bowls.   *Died 25 Nov. 2004.*

RICHARDS, Rt Rev. John; Bishop Suffragan of Ebbsfleet, 1994–98; Episcopal Visitor for the Province of Canterbury, 1994–98; Hon. Assistant Bishop, diocese of Exeter, since 1998; *b* 4 Oct. 1933; *s* of William and Ethel Mary Richards; *m* 1958, Ruth Haynes; two *s* three *d. Educ:* Reading School; Wyggeston Grammar School, Leicester; Sidney Sussex Coll., Cambridge (MA); Ely Theological Coll. Asst Curate, St Thomas, Exeter, 1959–64; Rector of Holsworthy with Hollacombe and Cookbury, 1964–74; RD of Holsworthy, 1970–74; Rector of Heavitree with St Paul's, Exeter, 1974–81; RD of Exeter, 1978–81; Archdeacon of Exeter and Canon Res. of Exeter Cathedral, 1981–94; Assistant Bishop: dios of Lichfield and of Oxford, 1994–98; dio. of Bath and Wells, 1996–98. Chm. of House of Clergy, Exeter Diocesan Synod, 1979–82; Mem. Gen. Synod, 1985–94. Mem., C of E Pensions Bd, 1989–97. A Church Commissioner, 1988–94 (Mem. Bd of Govs, 1993–94). *Recreations:* gardening, fishing, walking. *Address:* Penberth, Stoney Road, Lewdown, Okehampton, Devon EX20 4DQ.   *Died 9 Nov. 2003.*

RICHARDS, Lt-Gen. Sir John (Charles Chisholm), KCB 1980; KCVO 1991; HM Marshal of the Diplomatic Corps, 1982–92; Extra Equerry to the Queen, since 1992; *b* 21 Feb. 1927; *s* of Charles C. Richards and Alice Milner; *m* 1953, Audrey Hidson; two *s* one *d. Educ:* Worksop Coll., Notts. Joined Royal Marines, 1945; 45 Commando, Malaya, 1950–52; Instructor, Officers' Sch., 1953–55; HMS Birmingham, 1955–56; Canadian Army Staff Coll., 1959–61; Adjt and Company Comdr, 43 Commando, 1962–63; Naval staff, 1963–64; Instructor, Staff Coll., Camberley, 1965–67; 45 Commando: 2nd in Comd, Aden, 1967; CO, 1968–69; GSO1 Plymouth Gp, 1969; CO 42 Commando, 1970–72; Chief of Staff, Brit. Def. Staff, Washington DC, UN Deleg., and Mem. Mil. Staff Cttee, 1972–74; Comdr 3rd Commando Bde, 1975–76; Commandant General, Royal Marines, 1977–81. Col Comdt, RM, 1987–88, Representative Col Comdt, 1989–90. Admiral, Texas Navy, 1983. Director: DSC Communications (Europe), 1986–92; Andrew Ltd, 1987–95. CCMI (CBIM 1980). Freeman, City of London, 1982. *Recreations:* golf, swimming, gardening. *Address:* c/o National Westminster Bank, Market Place, Kingston-upon-Thames KT1 1JX. *Club:* Army and Navy.   *Died 5 Oct. 2004.*

RICHARDS, John Deacon, CBE 1978; RSA 1989 (ARSA 1974); PPRIAS; architect, retired; *b* 7 May 1931; *s* of late William John Richards and Ethel Richards; *m* 1958, Margaret Brown, RIBA, ARIAS; one *s* three *d. Educ:* Geelong Grammar Sch., Vic.; Cranleigh Sch.; Assoc. Sch. of Arch., London (Dipl. 1954). RIBA 1955; FRIAS 1968 (PRIAS, 1983–85). RE, 1955–57. Partner, Robert Matthew, Johnson-Marshall and Partners, 1964–86. Buildings include: Stirling Univ., 1965–72; Royal Commonwealth Pool, Edinburgh, 1970. Member: Royal Fine Art Commn for Scotland, 1975–89; Bd, Housing Corp., 1982–89 (Chm., Scottish Cttee, 1982–89); Bd, Scottish Homes, 1988–93 (Dep. Chm., 1989–93).

Housing Assoc. Ombudsman for Scotland, 1994–2000. Mem., Agrément Bd, 1980–83. Trustee, Nat. Galleries of Scotland, 1986–90. DUniv: Stirling, 1976; Napier, 1996. Gold Medallist, RSA, 1972. *Recreation:* country life. *Address:* Lady's Field, Whitekirk, Dunbar, East Lothian EH42 1XS. *T:* (01620) 870206. *Club:* Athenæum.   *Died 29 Oct. 2003.*

RICHARDSON, Baron *cr* 1979 (Life Peer), of Lee in the County of Devon; **John Samuel Richardson,** 1st Bt, *cr* 1963; Kt 1960; LVO 1943; MD, FRCP; President, General Medical Council, 1973–80; Hon. Consulting Physician: St Thomas' Hospital; King Edward VII's Hospital for Officers; Consultant Emeritus to the Army; Consulting Physician: Metropolitan Police, 1957–80; London Transport Board, since 1964; *b* 16 June 1910; *s* of Major John Watson Richardson, solicitor, and Elizabeth Blakeney, *d* of Sir Samuel Roberts, 1st Bt, both of Sheffield; *m* 1933, Sybil Angela Stephanie (*d* 1991), *d* of A. Ronald Trist, Stanmore; two *d. Educ:* Charterhouse; Trinity Coll., Cambridge (Hon. Fellow, 1979); St Thomas' Hosp. (Bristowe Medal; Hadden Prize, 1936; Perkins Fellowship, 1938). MB BChir 1936; MD 1940. FRCP 1948 (MRCP 1937); FRCPE 1975. Major, RAMC (temp.), 1939; Lt-Col, RAMC (temp.), 1942. 1st asst, Med. Professorial Unit, St Thomas' Hosp., 1946; Physician to St Thomas' Hosp., 1947–75. Examiner to Univs of Cambridge, London, Manchester, NUI, RCP London and Edinburgh Conjoint Bd. President: Internat. Soc. of Internal Medicine, 1966–70 (Hon. Pres. 1970); Royal Soc. of Medicine, 1969–71 (Hon. Librarian, 1957–63; Pres., Med. Educn Sect., 1967–68); BMA, 1970–71; 2nd Congress, Assoc. Européene de Médicine Interne d'Ensemble, Bad-Godesberg, 1973 (Hon. Mem. 1974); Assoc. for the Study of Med. Educn, 1978–80 (Vice-Pres., 1974–78, Hon. Mem., 1980); Vice-President: Med. Soc. of London, 1961–63 (Hon. Fellow, 1981); Royal Coll. of Nursing, 1972–; Chairman: Jt Consultants Cttee, 1967–72; Council for Postgrad. Med. Educn in England and Wales, 1972–80; Medico-Pharmaceutical Forum, 1973–76; Armed Forces Med. Adv. Bd, MoD, 1975–80. Mem., Bd of Governors, St Thomas's Hosp., 1953–59, 1964–74. Mem. Ct, Soc. of Apothecaries, 1960–85 (Master, 1971–72). Lectures: Lettsomian, Med. Soc. of London, 1963; Scott Heron, Royal Victoria Hosp., Belfast, 1969; Maudsley, RCPsych, 1971; Wilkinson Meml, Inst. of Dental Surgeons, London Univ., 1976; Harveian Oration, RCP, 1978; Orator, Med. Soc. of London, 1981. Hon. Fellow: Swedish Soc. Med. Scis, 1970; RSocMed 1973; Heberden Soc., 1973; Osler Club of London, 1973; Hon. Mem., Assoc. of Clinical Tutors of GB, 1980; Hon. FRPharms (Hon. FPS 1974); Hon. FRCPI 1975; Hon. FFCM 1977; Hon. FRCPsych 1979; Hon. FRCS 1980; Hon. FRCPSG 1980; Hon. FRCPE 1981; Hon. Fellow: KCL; UMDS. Hon. Bencher, Gray's Inn, 1974. Hon. DSc: NUI, 1975; Hull, 1981; Hon. DCL Newcastle, 1980; Hon. LLD: Nottingham, 1981, Liverpool, 1983. CStJ 1970. Baron de Lancey Law Prize, RSM, 1978; Gold Medal, BMA, 1982; Guthrie Medal, RAMC, 1982. Editor-in-Chief, British Encylopaedia of Medical Practice, 1970–74. *Publications:* The Practice of Medicine, 2nd edn 1960; Connective Tissue Disorders, 1963; Anticoagulant Prophylaxis and Treatment (jointly), 1965. *Heir:* (to baronetcy) none. *Address:* Windcutter, Lee, near Ilfracombe, North Devon EX34 8LW. *T:* (01271) 863198.   *Died 15 Aug. 2004 (Btcy ext).*

RICHARDSON, Hon. James Armstrong; PC (Can.) 1968; President, Jarco Ltd; Chairman, Max Bell Foundation, 1972–97; *b* Winnipeg, Manitoba, 28 March 1922; *s* of late James Armstrong Richardson and Muriel Sprague; *m* 1949, Shirley Anne, *d* of John Rooper, Shamley Green, Surrey, England; two *s* three *d. Educ:* St John's-Ravenscourt, Winnipeg; Queen's Univ., Kingston, Ont. (BA). Pilot with No 10 BR Sqdn, before entering family firm of James Richardson & Sons, Ltd, Winnipeg, Oct. 1945; he was Chm. and Chief Exec. Officer of this company, but resigned to enter public life, 1968. Dir

Emeritus, Canadian Imperial Bank of Commerce; Past Director: Internat. Nickel Co.; Investors' Gp, Hudson's Bay Co.; Canadian Pacific Rly; Canada's America's Cup Challenge 1982–83. MP (L), June 1968 (re-elected Oct. 1972, July 1974); Minister, Canadian Federal Cabinet, July 1968; Minister of Supply and Services, May 1969; Minister of Nat. Defence, 1972–76; resigned from Federal Cabinet over constitutional language issue, Oct. 1976; crossed floor of House to sit as an Independent MP, 27 June 1978. Founding Dir, Canada West Foundn, 1970–97; Hon. Pres., Commonwealth Games Assoc. of Canada, Inc, 1983–97. Former Trustee, Queen's Univ., Kingston; Chm., 1952–65, Hon. Chm., 1965–78, St John's Ravenscourt Sch. *Address:* 407 Bower Boulevard, Winnipeg, MB R3P 0L6, Canada.

Died 17 May 2004.

RICHARDSON, Sir Michael (John de Rougemont), Kt 1990; Chairman, Invesco English & International Trust, since 1961; *b* 9 April 1925; *s* of Arthur Wray Richardson and Audrey de Rougemont; *m* 1949, Octavia Mayhew (*d* 1999); one *s* two *d*. *Educ:* Harrow; Kent Sch., Conn, USA. Captain, Irish Guards, 1943–49. Drayton Gp, 1949–52; Partner: Panmure Gordon & Co., 1952–71; Cazenove & Co., 1971–81; Man. Dir, 1981–90, Vice Chm., 1990–94, N. M. Rothschild & Sons Ltd; Chm., 1990–94, Consultant, 1995–96, Smith New Court plc; Vice-Chairman: J. O. Hambro Magan & Co., 1995–96; NatWest Market Corp. Advy, then Hawkpoint Partners, 1996–99. *Recreations:* fox hunting, sailing. *Clubs:* Cavalry and Guards; Island Sailing, Bembridge Sailing (IoW).

Died 12 May 2003.

RICHARDSON, Prof. Sam Scruton, AO 1980; CBE 1965 (OBE 1960); Commissioner for Law Revision, Northern States of Nigeria, since 1987; Foundation Principal, Canberra College of Advanced Education (subsequently University of Canberra), 1969–84, Emeritus Fellow, 1984–90, Emeritus Professor, since 1990; *b* 31 Dec. 1919; *s* of Samuel and Gladys Richardson; Australian citizen, 1975; *m* 1949, Sylvia May McNeil (*d* 2000); two *s* one *d*. *Educ:* Magnus Sch., Newark-on-Trent; Trinity Coll., Oxford (State Scholar, 1937; BA (PPE) 1940, MA 1946); SOAS, Univ. of London. Called to the Bar, Lincoln's Inn, 1958. Served War, 1940–46: commnd Royal Marines; Commando Bdes, Europe and Far East (despatches); demob., Major, 1946. Dist Comr, Sudan Polit. Service, 1946–54 (served in Kordofan and Darfur, 1946–53; Resident, Dar Masalit, 1953–54); HMOCS, Nigeria, 1954–67: Dist Comr, Bornu Prov., 1954–58; Comr for Local Courts in Attorney Gen.'s Chambers, N Nigeria, 1958–60; Dir, Inst. of Admin, Zaria, 1960–67; Dep. Vice-Chancellor, Ahmadu Bello Univ., Nigeria, 1962–67; Prof. of Public Admin, 1967–68, and Acting Vice-Chancellor, 1968, Univ. of Mauritius; occasional Lectr in Islamic Law, ANU, 1971–82; Vis. Prof., Ahmadu Bello Univ., Nigeria, 1986. Consultant: Aust. Law Reform Commn, 1980–; Museum of Australia, 1985–. Chm., Aust. Conf. of Principals, 1979–80; Pres., Internat. Assoc. of Schs and Insts of Admin, 1982–89; Member: Council, Inst. of Admin, Papua New Guinea, 1970–84; Immigration Adv. Council, 1971–74; Nat. Standing Control Cttee on Drugs of Dependence, 1974–84; Australian Council on Overseas Prof. Qualifications, 1975–; Adv. Council, Aust. Jt Services Staff Coll., 1977–84; Academic Adv. Council, RAN Coll., Jervis Bay, 1978–; Council, ANU, 1981–84; Exec. Cttee, Internat. Inst. of Admin. Scis, 1982–90. Mem., Bd of Management, Aust. Inst. of Sport, 1980–84. Governor, Portsmouth Polytechnic, 1989–92 (Hon. Fellow, 1984). Nat. Pres., Australia Britain Soc., 1980–84; Vice-Pres., Britain Australia Soc., 1984–. Freeman, City of London, 1989–. Hon. Fellow, Univ. of Portsmouth, 1993. Hon. LLD Ahmadu Bello, 1967; Hon. Dr Canberra, 1990. Centenary Medal, Australia, 2003. *Publications:* Notes on the Penal Code of N Nigeria, 1959, 4th edn 1987; (with T. H. Williams) The Criminal Procedure Code of N Nigeria, 1963; (with E. A. Keay) The Native and Customary

Courts of Nigeria, 1965; Parity of Esteem—the Canberra College of Advanced Education 1968–78, 1979; A Saga 1961–1991: the history of International Association of Schools and Institutes of Administration, 1992; Royal Marines and Hong Kong 1840–1997, 1997; No Weariness: the personal memoir of a generalist administrator in public life, 2001; book revs in Canberra Times, 1970–; articles on public admin, customary law and higher educn in learned jls. *Recreations:* travel, reading, community service. *Address:* Wren House, 32 Vicarage Street, Warminster, Wilts BA12 8JF. *T:* (01985) 214862. *Clubs:* Oxford and Cambridge; University House (ANU, Canberra). *Died 23 June 2004.*

RICHLER, Mordecai, OC 2001; FRSL; author; *b* 27 Jan. 1931; *s* of late Moses Isaac Richler and Lily Rosenberg; *m* 1960, Florence Wood; three *s* two *d*. *Educ:* Sir George Williams Univ., Montreal (left without degree). Writer-in-residence, Sir George Williams Univ., 1968–69; Vis. Prof., English Dept, Carleton Univ., Ottawa, 1972–74. Editl Bd, Book-of-the-Month Club, NY. Canada Council Senior Arts Fellowship, 1960; Guggenheim Fellowship, Creative Writing, 1961. FRSL 1998. *Publications: novels:* The Acrobats, 1954; A Choice of Enemies, 1955; Son of a Smaller Hero, 1957; The Apprenticeship of Duddy Kravitz, 1959, repr. 1972 (filmed, Golden Bear Award, Berlin Film Fest., 1974; Writers Guild of America Annual Award, 1974; Academy Award nomination, 1974); The Incomparable Atuk, 1963; Cocksure, 1968 (Governor-General's Award for Literature, 1969); Paris Review Humour Prize, 1969); St Urbain's Horseman, 1971 (Governor-General's Award for Literature, 1972); Joshua Then and Now, 1980 (filmed, 1985); Solomon Gursky Was Here, 1990 (Commonwealth Writers Prize, 1990); Barney's Version, 1997 (Giller Prize, 1997; Leacock Humour Award, 1998); *non-fiction:* Oh Canada! Oh Quebec!, Lament for a Divided Country, 1992; *essays:* Hunting Tigers Under Glass, 1969; Shovelling Trouble, 1973; Home Sweet Home, 1984; Broadsides, 1991; *autobiography:* The Street, 1972; *memoir:* This Year in Jerusalem, 1994; *children's books:* Jacob Two-Two Meets the Hooded Fang, 1975; Jacob Two-Two and the Dinosaur, 1987; Jacob Two-Two's First Spy Case, 1995; *anthology:* (ed) The Best of Modern Humour, 1983; (ed) Writers on World War II, 1991; contrib. Encounter, Commentary, New York Review of Books, etc. *Recreations:* poker, snooker. *Address:* Apt 80C, 1321 Sherbrooke Street W, Montreal, QC H3G 1J4, Canada. *T:* (514) 2882008. *Died 3 July 2001.*

RICHMAN, Stella; television producer; *b* 9 Nov. 1922; *d* of Jacob Richman and Leoni Richman; *m* 1st, 1949, Alec Clunes (marr. diss.; he *d* 1970); 2nd, 1953, Victor Brusa (*d* 1965); one *s* one *d*; 3rd, 1967, Alec Hyams (marr. diss. 1976). *Educ:* Clapton County Secondary Sch. for Girls. Started TV career at ATV, running Script Dept 1960; created and produced Love Story, 1963; joined Rediffusion, 1964; Exec. Head of Series (prod The Informer); Exec. Prod., award-winning Man of Our Times, Half Hour Story and Blackmail; prod first 6 plays, Company of Five, for newly formed London Weekend Television, 1968; Man. Dir, London Weekend Internat., 1969, and Controller of Programmes, London Weekend Television, 1970–71 (first woman to sit on bd of a television co.); in partnership with David Frost formed Stella Richman Productions (first independent TV co.), 1972–78: resp. for Miss Nightingale, Jennie, Clayhanger, Bill Brand, Just William. Chm. and owner, White Elephant Club, 1960–88. FRTS 1982. *Publications:* The White Elephant Cook Books, 1973, 1979. *Recreations:* travel, reading biographies, theatre. *Address:* Garden Flat, 5 Hill Road, NW8 9QE. *Died 24 May 2002.*

RICHMOND, Rear-Adm. Andrew John, CB 1987; Chief Executive (formerly Executive Director), Royal Society for the Prevention of Cruelty to Animals, 1987–91; *b* 5 Nov. 1931; *s* of Albert George Richmond and Emily Margaret (*née* Denbee); *m* 1957, Jane Annette

(née Ley); one s two d. Educ: King's School, Bruton; Nautical College, Pangbourne. Joined RN 1950; staff of C-in-C East Indies, 1953; flying training, 1955; Cyprus 847 Sqdn, 1956; HMS Victorious 824 Sqdn, 1958; staff of FO Arabian Seas, 1960; BRNC Dartmouth, 1963; Sec., FO Carriers and Amphibious Ships, 1968; Supply School, HMS Pembroke, 1970; Fleet Supply Officer, 1974; Asst Dir Naval Manpower, 1976; Sec., C-in-C Naval Home Comd, 1977; Captain, HMS Cochrane, 1979; Dir, Naval Logistic Planning, 1982; ADC 1984; ACDS (Logistics), 1985, and Chief Naval Supply and Secretariat Officer, 1986. Recreations: home, gardening, golf. Address: c/o Royal Bank of Scotland, South Street, Chichester, West Sussex PO19 1DS. Club: Cowdray Park Golf.
Died 22 Sept. 2005.

RICKETTS, Michael Rodney, MA; Headmaster, Sutton Valence School, 1967–80; b 29 Sept. 1923; er s of late Rt Rev. C. M. Ricketts, Bishop of Dunwich, and Dorothy Ricketts; m 1958, Judith Anne Caroline Corry; two s two d. Educ: Sherborne; Trinity Coll., Oxford. Served War of 1939–45: in 8th Army, Africa, Italy, with 60th Rifles, 1942–47. Trinity Coll., Oxford, 1947–50; Asst Master and Housemaster, Bradfield Coll., 1950–67. Dir, ISIS (Eastern England), 1980–93; Nat. ISIS Management Cttee, 1981–93. Member: HMC Cttee, 1976–79 (Chm., HMC/ SHA Services Cttee, 1975–80); British Atlantic Cttee, 1974–93, Council, 1979–93; Chairman: British Atlantic Educn Cttee, 1984–87 (Mem., 1974–93); Atlantic Educn Cttee, 1986–93. Former Governor: Gresham's Sch.; Orwell Park; Vinehall. Fellow, Woodard Corp. Recreations: cricket, shooting, country activities. Address: The Breakers, Atlantic Terrace, New Polzeath, Wadebridge, Cornwall PL27 6UG. Clubs: East India, Devonshire, Sports and Public Schools, Free Foresters, Harlequins, I Zingari, MCC; Vincent's (Oxford).
Died 21 Nov. 2004.

RICKETTS, Sir Robert (Cornwallis Gerald St Leger), 7th Bt cr 1828; retired Solicitor; b 8 Nov. 1917; s of Sir Claude Albert Frederick Ricketts, 6th Bt, and Lilian Helen Gwendoline (d 1955), o d of Arthur M. Hill, late 5th Fusiliers; S father, 1937; m 1945, Anne Theresa Cripps, CBE (d 1998); two s two d. Educ: Haileybury; Magdalene College, Cambridge (2nd Cl. Hons in History and Law, BA 1939, MA 1943). Served War of 1939–45 (Captain, Devon Regiment); Personal Assistant to Chief of Staff, Gibraltar, 1942–45; ADC to Lieutenant-Governor of Jersey, 1945–46. Formerly Partner in Wellington and Clifford. FRSA. Hon. Citizen, Mobile, USA, 1970. Heir: s Robert Tristram Ricketts, b 17 April 1946. Address: Forwood House, Minchinhampton, Stroud, Glos GL6 9AB. T: (01453) 882160.
Died 6 Oct. 2005.

RIDD, John William Gregory; HM Diplomatic Service, retired; International Relations Director (formerly Regional Director), British Executive Service Overseas, since 1994; b 4 June 1931; s of William John and Lilian Gregory Cooke; adoptive s of Philip and Elizabeth Anne Ridd; m 1956, Mary Elizabeth Choat; three s one d. Educ: Lewis' Sch., Pengam; Wallington County Grammar Sch.; St Edmund Hall, Oxford (BA Hons 1954). National Service, 1949–51 (Army). Foreign Office, 1954; Buenos Aires, 1957–61; First Sec., Cairo, 1963–66; Prague, 1968–70, Brasilia, 1974–77; First Sec., later Counsellor, FCO, 1978–91. Recreations: books, distance running, allotment gardening, travel, music, the South Downs.
Died 10 May 2005.

RIDLER, Anne (Barbara), OBE 2001; FRSL; author; b 30 July 1912; o d of late H. C. Bradby, housemaster of Rugby School, and Violet Milford; m 1938, Vivian Hughes Ridler, CBE; two s two d. Educ: Downe House School; King's College, London; and in Florence and Rome. FRSL 1998. Cholmondeley Award for Poetry, 1998. Publications: poems: Poems, 1939; A Dream Observed, 1941; The Nine Bright Shiners, 1943; The Golden Bird, 1951; A Matter of Life and Death, 1959; Selected Poems (New York), 1961; Some Time After,

1972; (contrib.) Ten Oxford Poets, 1978; New and Selected Poems, 1988; Collected Poems, 1994; plays: Cain, 1943; The Shadow Factory, 1946; Henry Bly and other plays, 1950; The Trial of Thomas Cranmer, 1956; Who is my Neighbour?, 1963; The Jesse Tree (libretto), 1972; The King of the Golden River (libretto), 1975; The Lambton Worm (libretto), 1978; Crucifixion Cantata (libretto), 1993; translations: Italian opera libretti: Rosinda, 1973; Orfeo, 1975; Eritrea, 1975; Return of Ulysses, 1978; Orontea, 1979; Agrippina, 1981; Calisto, 1984; Così fan Tutte, 1986; Don Giovanni, 1990; Marriage of Figaro, 1991; Coronation of Poppea, 1992; Gluck's Orfeo, 1996; Magic Flute, 1996; biography: Olive Willis and Downe House, 1967; criticism: (jtly) Profitable Wonders: aspects of Traherne, 1989; A Measure of English Poetry, 1991; Working for T. S. Eliot, 2000; edited: Shakespeare Criticism, 1919–35; A Little Book of Modern Verse, 1941; Best Ghost Stories, 1945; Supplement to Faber Book of Modern Verse, 1951; The Image of the City and other essays by Charles Williams, 1958; Shakespeare Criticism 1935–60, 1963; Poems of James Thomson, 1963; Thomas Traherne, 1966; (with Christopher Bradby) Best Stories of Church and Clergy, 1966; Selected Poems of George Darley, 1979; Poems of William Austin, 1983; A Victorian Family Postbag, 1988. Recreations: music; the theatre; the cinema. Address: 14 Stanley Road, Oxford OX4 1QZ. T: (01865) 247595.
Died 15 Oct. 2001.

RIDLEY, Dame Betty; see Ridley, Dame M. B.

RIDLEY, Sir Harold; see Ridley, Sir N. H. L.

RIDLEY, Jasper Godwin; author; b 25 May 1920; s of Geoffrey Ridley and Ursula (née King), Vera (d 2002), d of Emil Pollak of Prague; two s one d. Educ: Felcourt Sch.; Sorbonne, Paris; Magdalen Coll., Oxford. Certif. of Honour, Bar Finals. Called to Bar, Inner Temple, 1945. St Pancras Borough Council, 1945–49. Pres., Hardwicke Soc., 1954–55. Contested (Lab): Winchester, 1955; Westbury, 1959. Vice-Pres. for life, English Centre of Internat. PEN, 1985; Pres., Tunbridge Wells Writers, 1994–. Mem. Ct of Assts, Carpenters' Co. (Master, 1988–89, 1990–91). Has written many radio scripts on historical subjects. FRSL 1963. Publications: Nicholas Ridley, 1957; The Law of Carriage of Goods, 1957; Thomas Cranmer, 1962; John Knox, 1968; Lord Palmerston, 1970 (James Tait Black Meml Prize, 1970); Mary Tudor, 1973; Garibaldi, 1974; The Roundheads, 1976; Napoleon III and Eugénie, 1979; History of England, 1981; The Statesman and the Fanatic: Thomas Wolsey and Thomas More, 1982; Henry VIII, 1984; Elizabeth I, 1987; The Tudor Age, 1988; The Love Letters of Henry VIII, 1988; Maximillian and Juárez, 1992; Tito, 1994; History of the Carpenters' Company, 1995; Mussolini, 1997; The Freemasons, 1999; Bloody Mary's Martyrs, 2001. Recreations: opera, chess. Address: 6 Oakdale Road, Tunbridge Wells, Kent TN4 8DS. T: (01892) 522460.
Died 1 July 2004.

RIDLEY, Dame (Mildred) Betty, DBE 1975; Third Church Estates Commissioner, 1972–81; a Church Commissioner, 1959–81; b 10 Sept. 1909; d of late Rt Rev. Henry Mosley, sometime Bishop of Southwell; m 1929, Rev. Michael Ridley (d 1953), Rector of Finchley; three s one d. Educ: North London Collegiate School; Cheltenham Ladies' College. Member: General Synod of Church of England, 1970–81, and its Standing Cttee, 1971–81; Central Board of Finance, 1955–79; Mem., Faculty Jurisdiction Commn, 1980–83; Vice-Pres. British Council of Churches, 1954–56. MA (Lambeth) 1958; Hon. DSc (SocSc) Southampton, 1993. Recreation: listening to music. Address: Brendon House, Park Road, Winchester SO23 7BE. T: (01962) 855758. Club: Reform.
Died 1 Aug. 2005.

RIDLEY, Sir (Nicholas) Harold (Lloyd), Kt 2000; MD; FRCS; FRS 1986; Hon. Consultant Surgeon, Moorfields Eye Hospital, 1971 (Surgeon, 1938–71); Hon. Consultant Surgeon, Ophthalmic Department, St Thomas' Hospital,

1971 (Ophthalmic Surgeon, 1946–71); *b* 10 July 1906; *s* of late N. C. Ridley, MB London, FRCS, Royal Navy retired, Leicester; *m* 1941, Elisabeth Jane, *d* of late H. B. Wetherill, CIE; two *s* one *d*. *Educ:* Charterhouse; Pembroke Coll., Cambridge; St Thomas' Hospital, London; MB 1931, MD 1946, Cambridge. FRCS 1932; Hon. FRCOphth (Hon. FCOphth 1989). Temp. Major, RAMC. Originator in 1949 of intraocular implants to cure aphakia. Late Hon. Ophthalmic Surgeon, Royal Buckinghamshire Hospital. Hon. Cons. in Ophthalmology to Min. of Defence (Army), 1964–71. Mem. Advisory Panel, WHO, 1966–71. Life Pres., Internat. Intraocular Implants Club, 1972; late Vice-Pres., Ophthalmological Soc. of UK; Hon. Mem., Oxford Ophthalmological Congress. Hon. Fellow International College of Surgeons, Chicago, 1952; Hon. FRSocMed 1986; Hon. Member: Peruvian Ophthalmic Society, 1957; Ophthalmological Society of Australia, 1963; Irish Ophthalmological Society; Ophthalmological Soc. of UK, 1984; Amer. Intraocular Implants Soc., 1974; European Intra-Ocular Implantlens Council, 1983; Canadian Intraocular Implant Soc. Hon. LHD Med. Univ. of SC, 1989; Hon. DSc City Univ., 1990. Galen Medal, Apothecaries' Soc., 1986; Lord Crook Gold Medal, Spectacle Makers' Co., 1987; Gullstrand Medal, Swedish Med. Soc., 1992; Gonin Medal, Internat. Council of Ophthalmol., 1994. *Publications:* Monograph on Ocular Onchocerciasis; numerous contribs in textbooks and medical journals on intraocular implant surgery and other subjects. *Recreation:* fly-fishing. *Address:* Keeper's Cottage, Stapleford, Salisbury, Wilts SP3 4LT. *T:* (01722) 790209. *Club:* Flyfishers'. *Died 25 May 2001.*

RIDLEY, Rear-Adm. Terence; *see* Ridley, Rear-Adm. W. T. C.

RIDLEY, Rear-Adm. (William) Terence (Colborne), CB 1968; OBE 1954; Admiral Superintendent/Port Admiral, Rosyth, 1966–72; Chairman, Ex-Services Mental Welfare Society, 1973–83; *b* 9 March 1915; *s* of late Capt. W. H. W. Ridley, RN and Vera Constance (*née* Walker); *m* 1st, 1938, Barbara Allen (*d* 1989); one *s*; 2nd, 1993, Joan Elaine Norman. *Educ:* Emsworth House; RNC, Dartmouth (Robert Roxburgh Prize); RNEC, Keyham. HMS Exeter, 1936; HMS Valiant, 1939; HMS Firedrake, 1940 (despatches twice); E-in-C Dept Admty, 1941; HMS Indefatigable, 1944; Admty Fuel Experimental Stn, 1947; Seaslug Project Officer, RAE Farnborough, 1950; HMS Ark Royal, 1956; E-in-C Dept Admty, Dreadnought Project Team, 1958; CO, RNEC, 1962; Staff of C-in-C Portsmouth, 1964. Lt-Comdr 1944; Comdr 1947; Capt. 1957; Rear-Adm. 1966. *Recreations:* gardening, do-it-yourself. *Address:* Flat 18, Fitzroy House, 55–59 Great Pulteney Street, Bath BA2 4DW. *Died 25 Dec. 2001.*

RIDSDALE, Sir Julian (Errington), Kt 1981; CBE 1977; *b* 8 June 1915; *m* 1942, Victoire Evelyn Patricia Bennett (Lady Ridsdale, DBE); one *d*. *Educ:* Tonbridge; Sandhurst. 2nd Lieutenant, Royal Norfolk Regiment, 1935; attached British Embassy, Tokyo, 1938–39; served War of 1939–45: Royal Norfolk Regt, Royal Scots, and Somerset Light Infantry; Asst Mil. Attaché, Japan, 1940; GSO3, Far Eastern Sect., War Office, 1941; GSO2, Joint Staff Mission, Washington, 1944–45; retired from Army with rank of Major, 1946. Contested SW Islington (C), LCC, 1949, N Paddington (C), Gen. Elec., 1951; MP (C) Harwich Div. of Essex, Feb. 1954–1992. PPS to Parly Under-Sec. of State for Colonies, 1957–58; PPS to Minister of State for Foreign Affairs, 1958–60; Parly Under-Sec. of State: for Air and Vice-President of the Air Council, 1962–64; for Defence for the Royal Air Force, Ministry of Defence, April-Oct. 1964. Chairman: British Japanese Parly Group, 1964–92; Parly Gp for Engrg Develt, 1985–92; Vice-Chm., UN Parly Assoc., 1966–82; Mem., Select Cttee of Public Accounts, 1970–74. Leader, Parly Delegns to Japan, 1973, 1975, annually 1977–82, 1988. Member: Trilateral Commn, EEC, USA and Japan,

1973–92; North Atlantic Assembly, 1979–92 (Vice-Pres., Political Cttee, 1983–87); Dep. Chm., Internat. Triangle, USA, Japan and Europe, 1981–85. Chm., Japan Soc., London, 1976–79; British Comr Gen., British Garden Expo 90, Osaka, Japan, 1990; Pres., Ridsdale Charitable Educnl Foundn. Master, Skinners' Co., 1970–71. Hon. Fellow UCL, 1992. Ordre du Commanderie du Bon Temps de Médoc et de Graves, 1996. Order of the Sacred Treasure (Japan), 1967, Grand Cordon, 1990. *Recreations:* tennis, chess, gardening, travelling, sailing. *Address:* 12 The Boltons, SW10 9TD. *T:* (020) 7373 6159.
Died 22 July 2004.

RILEY, Victor; Lord Mayor of Cardiff, 1993–94; *b* 4 Oct. 1916; *s* of William Riley and Constance Evelyn Riley (*née* Cator); *m* 1944, Zoë Marion Elsie Sowden (*d* 1997); four *d*. *Educ:* Hull Grammar Sch. FIHospE 1970. Electrical Apprenticeship, Hull Corp. Engineers Dept, 1932–37; Electrical Engineer: Hull Elect. Dept, 1937–40; HM Ships in Dockyards, NE Coast, 1940–44; Engr in Group of Hosps and subseq. in NHS, 1944–56; Elect. Engr, Crown Agents, Nairobi, 1956–60; Principal Asst Engr, Welsh Health Tech. Services, 1960–81, retired. Councillor, Cardiff City Council, 1976–96. Mem., Whitchurch Royal British Legion, 1967–; Founder Mem., Welsh Chapter, Ordre des Chevaliers Bretvin, 1993–. Hon. FIHEEM. *Recreations:* gardening, Rugby, cricket. *Address:* 12 Coed Arian, Whitchurch, Cardiff CF14 2ND. *T:* (029) 2052 2342. *Club:* Cardiff Athletic. *Died 31 Aug. 2004.*

RING, Prof. James, CBE 1983; Emeritus Professor of Physics, Imperial College of Science, Technology and Medicine, since 1984; *b* 22 Aug. 1927; *s* of James and Florence Ring; *m* 1949, Patricia, *d* of Major H. J. Smith, MBE; two *s*. *Educ:* Univ. of Manchester (BSc, PhD). FInstP, FRAS. Reader in Spectrometry, Univ. of Manchester, 1957; Prof. of Applied Physics, Hull Univ., 1962; Prof. of Physics, 1967, and Associate Hd of Physics Dept, 1979, Imperial Coll. of Sci. and Technol. Director: Queensgate Instruments, 1979–97; Infrared Engrg, 1970–91; IC Optical Systems, 1970–97. Member: IBA, 1974–81; ITC, 1991–94; Inquiry into Cable Expansion and Broadcasting Policy, 1982; Dep. Chm., Cable Authority, 1984–90. *Publications:* numerous papers and articles in learned jls. *Recreations:* stargazing, dinghy sailing. *Address:* 12 Arundel Way, Christchurch, Dorset BH23 5DX. *Died 22 Oct. 2004.*

RIPLEY, Dillon; *see* Ripley, S. D.

RIPLEY, Sir Hugh, 4th Bt *cr* 1880; former Director, John Walker & Sons Ltd, Scotch Whisky Distillers, retired 1981; *b* 26 May 1916; *s* of Sir Henry William Alfred Ripley, 3rd Bt, and Dorothy (*d* 1964), *e d* of late Robert William Daker Harley; *S* father, 1956; *m* 1st, 1946, Dorothy Mary Dunlop Bruce-Jones (marr. diss. 1971); one *s* one *d*; 2nd, 1972, Susan, *d* of W. Parker, Leics; one *d*. *Educ:* Eton. Served in Africa and Italy with 1st Bn KSLI (despatches twice, American Silver Star); retired regular Major. *Publication:* Whisky for Tea, 1991. *Recreations:* golf, fishing, shooting. *Heir: s* William Hugh Ripley, *b* 13 April 1950. *Address:* 20 Abingdon Villas, W8 6BX; The Oak, Bedstone, Bucknell, Salop SY7 0BJ. *Club:* Boodle's. *Died 28 Oct. 2003.*

RIPLEY, (Sidney) Dillon, II, Hon. KBE 1979; PhD; Secretary, Smithsonian Institution, 1964–84, then Secretary Emeritus; *b* 20 Sept. 1913; *s* of Louis Arthur Ripley and Constance Baillie (*née* Rose); *m* 1949, Mary Moncrieffe Livingston (*d* 1996); three *d*. *Educ:* St Paul's Sch., Concord, NH; Yale Univ. (BA 1936); Harvard Univ. (PhD 1943). Staff, Acad. of Natural Sciences, Philadelphia, 1936–39; Volunteer Asst, Amer. Museum of Natural History, New York, 1939–40; Teaching Asst, Harvard Univ., 1941–42; Asst Curator of Birds, Smithsonian Instn, 1942; OSS, 1942–45; Lectr, Curator, Associate Prof. of Zool. and Prof. of Biol., Yale Univ., 1946–64; Dir, Peabody Museum of Nat. Hist., 1959–64. Dir, Riggs Nat. Corp., Washington, 1984. Chm. (US),

ESU, 1984. Pres., 1958–82, Pres. Emeritus, 1982–, ICBP. Benjamin Franklin Fellow, RSA, 1968. Member: Amer. Acad. of Arts and Scis, 1984; Nat. Acad. of Scis, 1968; Hon. Mem., Amer. Inst. of Architects, 1975. Hon. MA Yale, 1961; Hon DHL: Marlboro Coll., 1965; Williams Coll., 1972; Johns Hopkins, 1984; Washington Coll., 1986; Hon. DSc: George Washington, 1966; Catholic, 1968; Maryland, 1970; Cambridge, 1974; Brown, 1975; Trinity Coll., 1977; Hon. LLD: Dickinson Coll., 1967; Hofstra, 1968; Yale, 1975; Gallaudet Coll., 1981; Harvard, 1984; Hon. DE Stevens Inst. of Technol., 1977. Gold Medal: New York Zool Soc., 1966; Royal Zool Soc. of Antwerp, 1970; Thomas Jefferson Award, Amer. Soc. of Interior Designers, 1974; Medal for Distinguished Achievement, Holland Soc. of New York, 1977; F. K. Hutchinson Medal, Garden Club of America, 1979; Medal of Honor, National Soc. of Daughters of Amer. Revolution, 1981; Delacour Medal, ICBP, 1982; Henry Shaw Medal, St Louis Botannical Garden, 1982; Gold Medal, Acad. of Soc. Sci., New York, 1982; Addison Emery Verrill Medal, Peabody Mus., Yale Univ., 1984; Order of James Smithson, Smithsonian Instn, 1984; Olympia Prize, Onassis Foundn, 1984; Medal of Distinction, Barnard Coll., 1985; Cosmos Club Award, Washington, 1988; Bishop Mus. Medal, Hawaii, 1990. President's Medal of Freedom, USA, 1985; Order of the White Elephant (Thailand), 1949; Freedom Medal (Thailand), 1949; Order of the Sacred Treasure, 2nd Cl. (Japan), 1982; Officer: l'Ordre des Arts et des Lettres (France), 1975; Order of Leopold (Belgium), 1981; Légion d'Honneur (France), 1985; Commander: Order of Golden Ark (Netherlands), 1976; Order of Merit (State Council of Polish People's Republic), 1979; Order of Orange-Nassau (Netherlands), 1982; Comdr's Cross, Order of the Dannebrog (Denmark), 1976; Caballero Gran Cruz, Orden del Merito Civil (Spain), 1976; Padma Bhushan (India), 1986. *Publications:* The Trail of the Money Bird, 1942 (Sweden, 1945; UK 1947); Search for the Spiny Babbler, 1952, re-issued as A Naturalist's Adventure in Nepal, 1978; A Paddling of Ducks, 1957 (UK 1959); A Synopsis of the Birds of India and Pakistan, 1961, rev. edn 1982; (ed with Lynette L. Scribner) Ornithological Books in the Yale University Library, 1961; The Land and Wildlife of Tropical Asia, 1964, rev. edn 1971 and 1974; (with H. G. Deignan and R. A. Paynter, Jr) Check-list of Birds of the World, Vol. X (continuation of work of James L. Peters), 1964; The Sacred Grove, 1969; The Paradox of the Human Condition, 1975; Rails of the World, 1977; (with Sálim Ali) A Pictorial Guide to Birds of the Indian Subcontinent, 1983, rev. edn 1988; (with Sálim Ali) Handbook of the Birds of India and Pakistan: Vol. I, 1968, rev. edn 1978; Vol. II, 1969, rev. edn 1979; Vol. III, 1969, rev. edn 1981; Vol. IV, 1970, rev. edn 1984; Vol. V, 1972, rev. edn 1987; Vol. VI, 1971; Vol. VII, 1972; Vol. VIII, 1973; Vol. IX, 1973; Vol. X, 1974. *Recreation:* watching ducks. *Address:* 2324 Massachusetts Avenue, NW, Washington, DC 20008, USA. *T:* (202) 2323131; Box 210, Litchfield, CT 06759, USA. *T:* (860) 5678208. *Clubs:* English-Speaking Union; Alliance Française, Pilgrims of the US, Knickerbocker, Century Association, Yale (New York); Cosmos, Society of Cincinnati, Alibi, Metropolitan (Washington, DC); Himalayan (New Delhi).
Died 12 March 2001.

RITCHIE, Albert Edgar, CC 1975; Canadian Diplomat, retired 1981; *b* 20 Dec. 1916; *m* 1941, Gwendolin Perdue; two *s* two *d*. *Educ:* Mount Allison Univ., New Brunswick (BA 1938). Queen's College, Oxford (Rhodes Scholar, 1940; BA). Officer, Econ. Affairs Dept, UN, and Secretariat of Gen. Agreement on Tariffs and Trade, 1946–48; Counsellor, Office of Canadian High Comr, London, UK, 1948–52; Deputy Under-Secretary of State for External Affairs, Canada, 1964–66; Ambassador to USA, 1966–70; Under-Sec. of State for External Affairs, Canada, 1970–74; Special Advisor to Privy Council Office, Canada, 1974–76; Ambassador to Republic of Ireland, 1976–81. Hon. LLD: Mount Allison, 1966; St Thomas, 1968; Carleton, 1985. *Address:* 1335–1695

Playfair Drive, Ottawa, ON K1H 8J6, Canada. *Club:* Rideau (Ottawa).
Died 24 Jan. 2002.

RITCHIE, Kenneth Gordon, CMG 1968; HM Diplomatic Service, retired; *b* 19 Aug. 1921; *s* of Walter Ritchie, Arbroath; *m* 1951, Esme Stronsa Nash (*d* 1995). *Educ:* Arbroath High Sch.; St Andrews Univ. (MA). Joined FO, 1944; Embassy, Ankara, 1944–47; Foreign Office, 1947–49; Khorramshahr, 1949–50; Tehran, 1950–52; Djakarta, 1952–55; Foreign Office, 1955–57; Peking, 1957–62; Santiago, 1962–64; Elisabethville, 1965–66; Dep. High Comr, Lusaka, 1966–67; High Comr, Guyana, 1967–70; Head of Perm. Under-Sec.'s Dept, FCO, 1970–73; High Comr, Malawi, 1973–77. *Address:* Dalforbie, North Esk Road, Edzell, Angus DD9 7TW.
Died 18 Sept. 2003.

RIVETT-CARNAC, Rev. Canon Sir (Thomas) Nicholas, 8th Bt *cr* 1836; Pastor, Ashburnham Place, Battle, 1993–96; Hon. Canon of Southwark Cathedral, 1980–96, then Canon Emeritus; *b* 3 June 1927; *s* of Vice-Admiral James William Rivett-Carnac, CB, CBE, DSC (2nd *s* of 6th Bt) (*d* 1970), and of Isla Nesta Rivett-Carnac (*d* 1974), *d* of Harry Officer Blackwood; *S* uncle, 1972; *m* 1977, Susan Marigold MacTier Copeland, *d* of late Harold and Adeline Copeland. *Educ:* Marlborough College. Scots Guards, 1945–55. Probation Service, 1957–59. Ordained, 1963; Curate: Holy Trinity, Rotherhithe, 1963–68; Holy Trinity, Brompton, 1968–72; Vicar, St Mark's, Kennington, 1972–89; Rural Dean of Lambeth, 1978–82; Pastor, Kingdom Faith Ministries, Roffey Place, Horsham, 1989–93. *Heir:* *b* Miles James Rivett-Carnac [*b* 7 Feb. 1933; *m* 1958, April Sally Villar; two *s* one *d*]. *Address:* The Haven, Sandhurst Lane, Little Common, Bexhill-on-Sea, East Sussex TN39 4RH.
Died 4 May 2004.

RIZZELLO, Michael Gaspard, OBE 1977; PPRBS; FCSD; sculptor and coin designer; *b* 2 April 1926; *s* of Arthur Rizzello and Maria Rizzello (*née* D'Angelo); *m* 1950, Sheila Semple Maguire (*d* 2002); one *d*. *Educ:* Oratory Central Boys Sch., SW3; Royal College of Art. Military Service, 1944–48; served in India and Far East; commissioned 1945. Major Travelling Scholarship (Sculpture) and Drawing Prize, RCA, 1950. ARCA 1950; ARBS 1955, FRBS 1961, PRBS 1976–86; FCSD (FSIAD 1978). Pres., Soc. of Portrait Sculptors, 1968. Prix de Rome (Sculpture), 1951. Sir Otto Beit Medal for Sculpture, 1961. Sculptor: National Memorial to David Lloyd George, Cardiff; Official Medals for Investiture of the Prince of Wales, 1969, and 25th anniv., 1994; 900th Anniversary of Westminster Abbey, 1965; Churchill Centenary Trust, 1974; Sir Thomas Beecham bust, Royal Opera House, 1979, and Royal Festival Hall, 1986; sculptures at Nat. Postal Mus., 1972, London Docklands, 1988 and 1990 and Plaza, Oxford Street, London, 1997; bronze water feature and fountain, Hemel Hempstead, 1993; meml bronze of Nancy, Lady Astor, H of C, 1996; statues of Edward Jenner, St George's Hosp. Med. Sch., 1996 and Edward Jenner Inst. for Vaccine Res., 1997; bronze of Lord Taylor of Gosforth, Royal Cts of Justice, 1999; bronze heroic statues, Naples, Florida, USA, 2002; bronze portrait roundel of the Queen, St George's Chapel, Windsor, 2003; bronze portrait plaque of Princess Margaret, Royal Opera House, Covent Garden, 2003; designer, Conspicuous Gallantry Cross, 1995. Designer and Sculptor of coinages for over 90 countries, incl. UK £2.00 coin, for 50th Anniversary of UN, 1995. *Recreation:* people. *Address:* Melrose Studio, 7 Melrose Road, SW18 1ND. *T:* (020) 8870 8561. *Club:* Reform.
Died 28 Sept. 2004.

ROB, Prof. Charles Granville, MC 1943; Professor of Surgery, Uniformed Services University of the Health Sciences, Bethesda, Maryland, since 1983; *b* 4 May 1913; *s* of Joseph William Rob, OBE, MD; *m* 1941, Mary Dorothy Elaine Beazley; two *s* two *d*. *Educ:* Oundle School; St John's Coll., Cambridge (BA 1934; MChir 1941); St Thomas's Hospital. FRCS 1939. Lt-Col RAMC. Surgeon, St Thomas' Hospital, 1948; Professor of

Surgery, London University, 1950–60; formerly Surgeon and Director of the Surgical Professorial Unit, St Mary's Hospital; Professor and Chm. Dept of Surgery, Univ. of Rochester, NY, 1960–78; Prof. of Surg., E Carolina Univ., 1978–83. Consultant Vascular Surgeon to the Army. *Publications:* (ed with Rodney Smith) Operative Surgery (8 vols), 1956–57, (14 vols), 1968–69; various surgical. *Recreations:* mountaineering, ski-ing. *Address:* Uniformed Services University of the Health Sciences, Bethesda, MD 20814, USA. *Club:* Alpine.
Died 26 July 2001.

ROBBINS, Prof. Frederick C(hapman), MD; Bronze Star (US Army), 1945; President, Institute of Medicine, National Academy of Sciences, Washington, DC, 1980–85; University Professor, Case Western Reserve University, 1985, Emeritus, since 1986 (Professor of Pediatrics, School of Medicine, 1952–80, Dean, 1966–80, then Emeritus); *b* 25 Aug. 1916; *s* of William J. Robbins and Christine Chapman Robbins; *m* 1948, Alice Havemeyer Northrop; two *d. Educ:* University of Missouri (AB); University of Missouri Medical School (BS); Harvard Medical School (MD). US Army, 1942–46; rank on discharge, Major. Various posts in the Children's Hospital, Boston, 1940–, finishing as Chief Resident in Medicine, 1948; Sen. Fellow in Virus Diseases, Nat. Research Council, 1948–50; Research Fellow in Pediatrics, Harvard Med. Sch., 1948–50; Instr in Ped., 1950–51, Associate in Ped., 1951–52, Harvard Med. Sch.; Dir, Department of Pediatrics, Cleveland Metropolitan Gen. Hosp., 1952–66. Associate, Research Div. of Infectious Diseases, Children's Medical Center, Boston, 1950–52; Research Fellow in Ped., Boston Lying-in Hosp., Boston, Mass, 1950–52; Asst to Children's Medical Service, Mass Gen. Hosp., Boston, 1950–52. Vis. Scientist, Donner Lab., Univ. of California, 1963–64. President: Soc. for Pediatric Research, 1961–62; Amer. Pediatric Soc., 1973–74. Member: Nat. Acad. of Scis, 1972 (Co-Chm., Forum on Human Experimentation, 1974); Amer. Philosophical Soc., 1972; Adv. Cttee, Office of Technol. Assessment for Congress, 1973; Adv. Cttee on Med. Research, Pan American Health Organization, WHO, 1981–. Hon. Dr of Science: John Carroll Univ., 1955; Missouri, 1958; N Carolina, 1979; Tufts, 1983; Med. Coll. of Ohio, 1983; Albert Einstein Coll. of Medicine, 1984; Med. Coll. of Wisconsin, 1984; Hon. Dr of Laws, New Mexico, 1968; Hon. Dr Med. Sci., Med. Coll. of Pa, 1984. First Mead Johnson Award, 1953; (jtly) Nobel Prize in Physiology or Medicine, 1954; Award for Distinguished Achievement (Modern Medicine), 1963; Med. Mutual Honor Award for 1969; Abraham Flexner Award for Distinguished Service to Medical Educn, AAMC, 1987; Camille Cosby World of Children Award, Judge Baker Children's Center, 1988; NASA Public Service Award, 1989; Ohio Sci. and Technology Hall of Fame, 1992. *Publications:* numerous in various jls, primarily on subject of viruses and infectious diseases. *Recreations:* music, tennis, sailing. *Address:* 2626 West Park Boulevard, Shaker Heights, OH 44120, USA; (office) CWRU School of Medicine, 10900 Euclid Avenue, Cleveland, OH 44106–1712, USA. *Died 4 Aug. 2003.*

ROBBINS, (Richard) Michael, CBE 1976; Member, London Transport Executive, 1965–80 (Managing Director, Railways, 1971–78); *b* 7 Sept. 1915; *er s* of late Alfred Gordon Robbins and Josephine, *d* of R. L. Capell, Northampton; *m* 1939, Rose Margaret Elspeth, *er d* of Sir Robert Reid Bannatyne, CB (*d* 1993), Lindfield, Sussex; one *s* two *d. Educ:* Westminster Sch. (King's School.); Christ Church, Oxford (Westminster Schol.; MA); Univ. of Vienna. Joined London Passenger Transport Board, 1939. War service, RE (Transportation), 1939–46: Persia and Iraq, 1941–43; GHQ, MEF, 1943–44; Major, AML (Greece), 1944–45. Rejoined London Transport, 1946; Sec. to Chm., 1947–50; Sec., London Transp. Exec., 1950–55; Sec. and Chief Public Relations Off., 1955–60; Chief Commercial and Pub. Rel. Off., 1960–65. Chm., Transport Adv. Cttee, Transport and Road Res. Lab.,

1977–81. Institute of Transport: Mem. Council, 1957–60 and 1962–64; Chm., Metrop. Sect., 1962–63; Chm., Educn and Trg Cttee, 1969–72; Vice-Pres., 1972–75; Pres., 1975–76. Pres., Omnibus Soc., 1965. Chairman: Middx Victoria County History Council, 1963–76; Middx Local History Council, 1958–65; Internat. Metrop. Rlys Cttee, Internat. Union of Public Transport, 1976–81; Victorian Soc., 1978–81; President: London and Middx Archæol. Soc., 1965–71 (Mem. Council, 1951–56 and 1960–65); Greater London Industrial Archæol. Soc., 1969–; Rly Students Assoc., 1967–68; St Marylebone Soc., 1971–74; Mem., Ancient Monuments Adv. Cttee, English Heritage, 1986–91. Dunhill lectr on industrial design, Australia, 1974. FSA 1957; Pres., Soc. of Antiquaries, 1987–91 (Mem. Council, 1965–67, 1970–71; Treas., 1971–87); Chm., Museum of London, 1979–90 (Governor, 1968–); Vice Chm., Greater Manchester Museum of Science and Industry, 1987–90 (Trustee, 1982–90); Trustee, London Museum, 1970–75. Jt Ed., Jl of Transport History, 1953–65. Hon. DLitt City Univ., 1987. *Publications:* The North London Railway, 1937; 190 in Persia, 1951; The Isle of Wight Railways, 1953; Middlesex, 1953; (ed) Middlesex Parish Churches, 1955; The Railway Age, 1962, rev. edn 1998; (with T. C. Barker) History of London Transport, vol. 1, 1963, vol. 2, 1974; George and Robert Stephenson, 1966, rev. edn 1981; Points and Signals, 1967; A Public Transport Century, 1985; contribs to transport and historical jls. *Recreations:* exploring cities and suburbs; travelling abroad and in branch railway trains; concert-going. *Address:* 18 Fullerton Court, Udney Park Road, Teddington, Middx TW11 9BF. *T:* (020) 8977 6714. *Club:* Athenæum.
Died 21 Dec. 2002.

ROBERTS, His Honour David Ewart; a Circuit Judge, 1982–93; *b* 18 Feb. 1921; *s* of John Hobson Roberts and Dorothy Roberts. *Educ:* Abingdon Sch.; St John's Coll., Cambridge (MA, LLB). Served War, 1941–46; commnd RA (Field); service in Middle East, North Africa, Italy, Yugoslavia and Germany. Called to Bar, Middle Temple, 1948. Asst Recorder, Coventry QS, 1966–71; a Recorder of the Crown Court, 1978–82. *Recreations:* travel, photography. *Address:* 4 Greville Drive, Birmingham B15 2UU. *T:* (0121) 440 3231. *Died 8 July 2002.*

ROBERTS, Rt Rev. Edward James Keymer; Bishop of Ely, 1964–77; *b* 18 April 1908; *s* of Rev. Arthur Henry Roberts; *m* 1st, 1941, Dorothy Frances (*d* 1982), *d* of Canon Edwin David Bowser, Deal; three *s* one *d*; 2nd, 1984, Diana, *widow* of Dr Christopher Grey. *Educ:* Marlborough; Corpus Christi Coll., Cambridge (BA 2nd class Theological Tripos, 1930; MA 1935; Hon. Fellow, 1964); Cuddesdon Theological Coll. Deacon, 1931, priest, 1932; Curate of All Saints, Margaret Street, 1931–35; Vice-Principal, Cuddesdon Coll., 1935–39; Examining Chaplain to Bishop of Portsmouth and Commissary, Johannesburg, 1936–39; Vicar of St Matthew, Southsea, 1940–45; Curate-in-charge of St Bartholomew, Southsea, 1941–45; Examining Chaplain to Bishop of Portsmouth, 1942–56; Proctor in Convocation, Portsmouth, 1944–49; Commissary, Northern Rhodesia, 1946–51; Hon. Canon of Portsmouth, 1947–49; Archdeacon of Isle of Wight, Vicar of Brading, Rector of Yaverland, 1949–52; Archdeacon of Portsmouth, 1952–56; Suffragan Bishop of Malmesbury, 1956–62; Examining Chaplain to Bishop of Bristol, 1959–62; Suffragan Bishop of Kensington, 1962–64. Episcopal Commissary, Portsmouth, 1984–85. Select Preacher, University of Cambridge, 1966, 1978. FRSCM 1977. Hon. DD Cantab, 1965. *Address:* The House on the Marsh, Quay Lane, Brading, IoW PO36 0BD. *T:* (01983) 407434. *Died 29 June 2001.*

ROBERTS, Sir Gordon (James), Kt 1984; CBE 1975; JP; DL; Chairman, Oxford Regional Health Authority, 1978–90; Member, Commission for the New Towns, 1978–94 (Deputy Chairman, 1978–82); *b* 30 Jan. 1921; *s* of Archie and Lily Roberts; *m* 1944, Barbara Leach; one *s* one *d. Educ:* Deanshanger Sch., Northants. Member:

Northants Exec. Council, NHS, 1954–74; St Crispin Hosp. Management Cttee, 1965–74; Oxford Reg. Hosp. Bd, 1968–74; Chairman: Northants AHA, 1973–78; Supervisory Bd, NHS Management Adv. Service, 1982–85; NHS Computer Policy Cttee, 1981–85; RHA Chairmen, 1982–84. Member: E Midlands Econ. Planning Council, 1975–79; Bd, Northampton Develt Corp., 1976–85 (Dep. Chm., 1985). Contested (Lab) S Northants, 1970. Member: Towcester RDC, 1953–56; Northants CC, 1954–77 (Leader, 1973–77). JP Northants, 1952; Chm., Towcester Bench, 1977–83. DL Northants, 1984, High Sheriff, 1989. FRSA 1985. *Publication:* (with Dr O. F. Brown) Passenham—the history of a forest village, 1975. *Recreations:* music, reading, walking, local history. *Address:* 114 Ridgmont, Deanshanger, Milton Keynes, Bucks MK19 6JG. *T:* (01908) 562605.
Died 31 March 2003.

ROBERTS, Dr John Morris, CBE 1996; Warden, Merton College, Oxford, 1984–94; a Governor of the BBC, 1988–93; *b* 14 April 1928; *s* of late Edward Henry Roberts and Dorothy Julia Roberts, Bath, Som.; *m* 1964, Judith Cecilia Mary, *e d* of late Rev. James Armitage and Monica Armitage; one *s* two *d. Educ:* Taunton Sch.; Keble Coll., Oxford (Schol.; Hon. Fellow, 1981). National Service, 1949–50; Prize Fellow, Magdalen Coll., Oxford, 1951–53; Commonwealth Fund Fellow, Princeton and Yale, 1953–54; Merton College, Oxford: Fellow and Tutor, 1953–79 (Hon. Fellow, 1980–84, 1994–); acting Warden, 1969–70, 1977–79; Sen. Proctor, Oxford Univ., 1967–68; Vice-Chancellor and Prof., Southampton Univ., 1979–85. Mem., Inst. for Advanced Study, Princeton, 1960–61; Vis. Prof., Univ. of S Carolina, 1961; Sec. of Harmsworth Trust, 1962–68; Member: Council, European Univ. Inst., 1980–88; US/UK Educn Commn, 1981–88; Gen. Cttee, Royal Literary Fund, 1975–2001; Bd, British Council, 1991–98. Trustee, Nat. Portrait Gall., 1984–98; Rhodes Trustee, 1988–94. Pres. Council, Taunton Sch., 1978–89. Presenter, TV series, The Triumph of the West, 1985. Editor, English Historical Review, 1967–77; General Editor: Purnell's History of the 20th Century, 1967–69; The Short Oxford History of Modern World, 1969–; The New Oxford History of England, 1979–. Hon. DLitt Southampton, 1987. Cavalier, Order of Merit (Italy), 1991. *Publications:* French Revolution Documents, 1966; Europe 1880–1945, 1967, 3rd edn 2001; The Mythology of the Secret Societies, 1972; The Paris Commune from the Right, 1973; Revolution and Improvement: the Western World 1775–1847, 1976; History of the World, 1976, 4th edn 2002; The French Revolution, 1978, 2nd edn 1997; The Triumph of the West, 1985; A History of Europe, 1996; Twentieth Century, 1999; articles and reviews in learned jls. *Recreation:* music. *Address:* c/o Merton College, Oxford OX1 4JD. *Clubs:* Oxford and Cambridge, Groucho, Grillion's.
Died 30 May 2003.

ROBERTS, Percy Charles; Chairman and Chief Executive, Mirror Group Newspapers Ltd, 1977–80; *b* 30 July 1920; *s* of late Herbert Bramwell Roberts and Alice (*née* Lang); *m* 1st 1946, Constance Teresa Violet Butler (marr. diss. 1977); two *s*; 2nd, 1978, Pauline Moore. *Educ:* Brighton Hove and Sussex Grammar Sch. Reporter, Sussex Daily News, 1936–39. Served War of 1939–45, Sussex Yeomanry, in France and ME (Captain). Sub-Editor, Egyptian Mail, Cairo, 1946; Reporter, Mid-East Mail, Palestine, 1947; Sub-Editor: Sussex Daily News, 1948; Liverpool Daily Post, 1949; Editor, Nigerian Citizen, 1949–51; Editorial Adviser, Gen. Manager, Man. Dir, Nigerian Daily Times, 1951–60; Man. Dir, Mirror Gp Newspapers in Caribbean, 1960–62; Gen. Manager, Mirror Newspapers in Manchester, 1962–66; Dir, 1964–80, Man. Dir, 1966–80, Daily Mirror Newspapers Ltd; Vice-Chm., West of England Newspapers Ltd, 1965–69; Man. Dir, IPC Newspapers Ltd, 1968–75; Dir, Scottish Daily Record & Sunday Mail Ltd, 1969–74; Chm., Overseas Newspapers Ltd, 1969–75; Dep. Chm. and Chief Exec., Mirror Gp Newspapers Ltd, 1975–77.

Dir, Reed Publishing Holdings Ltd, 1975–80; Mem., Reed Internat. UK Cttee, 1975–80. Mem., CBI Employment Policy Cttee, 1975–78. Mem. Council, CPU, 1979–83. Pres., Ross Rotary Club, 1992–93; Mem., Ross CAB, 1996–2001. CCMI. *Address:* Magnolia Cottage, Bromsash, Ross-on-Wye, Herefordshire HR9 7PR. *T:* (01989) 750706. *Club:* MCC.
Died 19 Jan. 2003.

ROBERTS, Sir Stephen (James Leake), Kt 1981; Chairman, Milk Marketing Board, 1977–87; *b* 13 April 1915; *s* of Frank Roberts and Annie Leake; *m* 1940, Muriel Hobbins (*d* 2001); two *s* two *d. Educ:* Wellington Grammar Sch. Farmer; founded Wrekin Farmers Ltd, 1960 (Chm., 1960–77); founded Dairy Crest, 1980, Chm., 1980–86. Shropshire delegate to NFU Council, 1962–70; Member: W Midland Region, MMB, 1966–87; Food from Britain Council, 1983–87. *Recreation:* football (latterly a spectator). *Address:* Lydebrook House, Coalmoor Road, Little Wenlock, Telford, Shropshire TF6 5AS. *T:* (01952) 504569. *Club:* Farmers'.
Died 11 June 2002.

ROBERTSON, Hon. Lord; Ian Macdonald Robertson, TD 1946; a Senator of the College of Justice in Scotland, 1966–87; *b* 30 Oct. 1912; *s* of late James Robertson and Margaret Eva Wilson, Broughty Ferry, Angus, and Edinburgh; *m* 1938, Anna Love Glen (*d* 2002), *d* of late Judge James Fulton Glen, Tampa, Florida, USA; one *s* two *d. Educ:* Merchiston Castle School; Balliol College, Oxford (BA (Mod. Greats), 1934); Edinburgh Univ. (LLB 1937; Vans Dunlop Schol. in Law, 1937). Member Faculty of Advocates, 1939; Advocate-Depute, 1949–51; QC (Scot.), 1954; Sheriff of Ayr and Bute, 1961–66; Sheriff of Perth and Angus, 1966. Chairman: Medical Appeals Tribunal, 1957–63; Scottish Jt Council for Teachers' Salaries, 1965–81; Scottish Valuation Adv. Council, 1977–86; Member Court of Session Rules Council; UK Rep., Central Council, Internat. Union of Judges, 1974–87. Formerly, External Examiner in law subjects, Aberdeen, Glasgow, Edinburgh and St Andrews Universities; Member Committee on Conflicts of Jurisdiction affecting Children, 1958; Governor of Merchiston Castle School, 1954, Chm., 1970–96; Assessor on Court of Edinburgh Univ., 1967–81. Chairman: Edinburgh Centre of Rural Economy, 1967–85; Edinburgh Centre for Tropical Veterinary Medicine. Served War of 1939–45, 8th Bn The Royal Scots (The Royal Regt); commd 1939; SO (Capt.), 44th Lowland Brigade (15th Scottish Division), Normandy and NW Europe (despatches). *Publication:* From Normandy to the Baltic, 1945. *Recreation:* golf. *Address:* 13 Moray Place, Edinburgh EH3 6DT. *T:* (0131) 225 6637. *Clubs:* New (Edinburgh); Honourable Company of Edinburgh Golfers (Captain 1970–72).
Died 21 July 2005.

ROBERTSON, Bryan Charles Francis, OBE 1961; author, broadcasting and television, etc; regular contributor to The Spectator; *b* 1 April 1925; *yr s* of A. F. Robertson and Ellen Dorothy Black; unmarried. *Educ:* Battersea Grammar School. Worked and studied in France and Germany, 1947–48; Director: Heffer Gall. Cambridge, 1949–51; Whitechapel Art Gall., London, 1952–68. Member: Arts Council Art Panel, 1958–61, 1980–84; Contemporary Art Soc. Cttee, 1958–73. US Embassy Grant to visit United States, 1956; Lectr on art, Royal Ballet School, 1958; Ford Foundn Grant for research for writing, 1961; British Council Lecture Tour, SE Asia and Australian State Galleries, 1960. Dir, State Univ. of NY Museum, 1970–75. Organized major exhibitions at Whitechapel, 1953–, including Turner, Hepworth, Moore, Stubbs, John Martin, Rowlandson and Gillray, Bellotto, Mondrian, de Stäel, Nolan, Davie, Smith, Malevich, Pollock, Richards, Australian Painting, Rothko, Tobey, Vaughan, Guston, Poliakof, Caro, Medley, etc. *Publications:* Jackson Pollock, a monograph, 1960; Sidney Nolan, a monograph, 1961; (jtly) Private View, 1965; (with H. Tatlock Miller) Loudon Sainthill,

1973; Edward Burra, 1978; contribs (art criticism) to London Magazine, Art News (US), Spectator, Harpers & Queen, Twentieth Century, Listener, Cambridge Review, Museums Jl, etc. *Address:* 73 Barnsbury Street, N1 1EJ. *Club:* Athenæum. *Died 18 Nov. 2002.*

ROBERTSON, Prof. (Charles) Martin, FBA 1967; Lincoln Professor of Classical Archæology and Art, University of Oxford, 1961–78; *b* 11 Sept. 1911; *s* of late Professor Donald Struan Robertson, FBA, FSA, and Petica Coursolles Jones; *m* 1st, 1942, Theodosia Cecil Spring Rice (*d* 1984); four *s* two *d*; 2nd, 1988, Louise Berge (*née* Holstein). *Educ:* Leys School, Cambridge; Trinity College, Cambridge (BA 1934; MA 1947; Hon. Fellow, 1987). Student at British School of Archæology, Athens, 1934–36; Asst Keeper, Dept of Greek and Roman Antiquities, British Museum, 1936–48 (released for service, War of 1939–45, 1940–46); Yates Professor of Classical Art and Archæology in the Univ. of London (Univ. Coll.), 1948–61. Corresp. Mem., German Archæological Inst., 1953; Ordinary Mem., 1953; Chm., Man. Cttee, British School at Athens, 1958–68. Mem., Inst. for Advanced Study, Princeton, 1968–69. Guest Schol., J. Paul Getty Museum, Malibu, 1980 and 1988. Hon. Fellow: Lincoln Coll., Oxford, 1980; UCL, 1980. For. Hon. Mem., Archaeological Inst. of America, 1985. Hon. DLit QUB, 1978. Kenyon Medal, British Acad., 1987. *Publications:* Why Study Greek Art? (Inaugural Lecture), 1949; Greek Painting, 1959; Between Archæology and Art History (Inaugural Lecture), 1963; Crooked Connections (poems), 1970; indexes and editorial work in late Sir John Beazley's Paralipomena, 1971; For Rachel (poems), 1972; A History of Greek Art, 1975; (with Alison Frantz) The Parthenon Frieze, 1975; A Hot Bath at Bedtime (poems), 1977; The Sleeping Beauty's Prince (poem), 1977; (with John Boardman) Corpus Vasorum Antiquorum, Castle Ashby, 1978; A Shorter History of Greek Art, 1981; The Attic Black-figure and Red-figure Pottery, in Karageorghis, Excavations at Kition IV, 1981; Catalogue of Greek, Etruscan and Roman Vases in the Lady Lever Art Gallery, 1987; The Art of Vase-painting in Classical Athens, 1992; articles, notes and reviews since 1935, in British and foreign periodicals. *Address:* 7a Parker Street, Cambridge CB1 1JL. *T:* (01223) 311913. *Died 26 Dec. 2004.*

ROBERTSON, Ian Gordon, FMA; Director, National Army Museum, since 1988; *b* 4 April 1943; *s* of Major Gordon Pentelow Robertson and Florence (*née* Alder); *m* 1968, Barbara Burton; one *d.* *Educ:* Highgate Sch.; Queen's Coll., Oxford (MA). Asst Curator, Chelmsford and Essex Mus., 1965–67; Curator, Passmore Edwards Mus., London, 1967–88. Member: Exec. Council, Area Museums Service for S Eastern England; Exec. Council, ICOM (UK); Ancient Monuments Adv. Cttee, English Heritage, 1984–90. Museums Association: Mem. Council, 1977–88; Hon. Treasurer, 1981–84; Vice Pres., 1984–86; Pres., 1986–88. Founder Pres., London Fedn of Museums and Art Galleries; President: South Midlands Museums Fedn; Soc. for Post-Medieval Archaeology, 1982–85. Member: Bd, Nat. Postal Mus., 1990–98; PO Heritage Bd, 1999–2001; Consignia Heritage Bd, 2001–. Trustee, RA Histl Trust, 1991–; Dir, RA Museums Ltd, 1992–. Served TA, 7th Bn Mddx Regt and 4th/5th Bn Essex Regt. *Publications:* papers on museological and allied topics. *Recreations:* gardening, Essex local history. *Address:* National Army Museum, Royal Hospital Road, Chelsea, SW3 4HT. *T:* (020) 7730 0717. *Died 1 Aug. 2003.*

ROBERTSON, Ian Macdonald; *see* Robertson, Hon. Lord.

ROBERTSON, Maj.-Gen. James Alexander Rowland, CB 1958; CBE 1956 (OBE 1949; MBE 1942); DSO 1944 (Bar 1945); *b* 23 March 1910; *s* of Major James Currie Robertson, CIE, CMG, CBE, IMS, and Catherine Rowland Jones; *m* 1st, 1949, Ann Madeline Tosswill (*d* 1949); 2nd, Joan Wills (*née* Abercromby) (*d* 2003), widow of R. L. J. Wills, CBE, MC. *Educ:* Aysgarth School;

Epsom Coll.; RMC, Sandhurst. Commissioned 2 Lieutenant IA, 1930, attached 1st KOYLI; posted 6th Gurkha Rifles, 1931; Instructor Sch. of Physical Training, 1936–37; Staff Coll., Quetta, July–Dec. 1941; Bde Major 1 (Maymyo) Bde, Jan.–June, 1942; Bde Major, 106 I Inf. Bde, 1942–44; Comdr 1/7 Gurkha Rifles, 1944–45; Comdr 48 Ind. Inf. Bde, 1945–47; GSO 1, Instr Staff Coll., Quetta, June-Nov., 1947; Comdr 1/6th Gurkha Rifles, 1947–48; GSO 1 Gurkha Planning Staff, March-June, 1948; GSO 1 Malaya comd, June–Nov. 1948; BGS 1948–49. GSO 1, War Office, 1950–52; Col GS, 1 Corps, Germany, 1952–54; Comdr 51 Indep. Bde, 1955–57; Commander 17 Gurkha Division Overseas Commonwealth Land Forces, and Maj.-Gen. Brigade of Gurkhas, 1958–61; GOC Land Forces, Middle East Command, 1961–63; Gurkha Liaison Officer, War Office, 1963–64, retd. Personnel Dir, NAAFI, 1964–69. Colonel, 6th Queen Elizabeth's Own Gurkha Rifles, 1961–69; Chm., 1968–80, Pres., 1980–87, Life Vice-Pres., 1987–; Gurkha Brigade Assoc. DL Greater London, 1977–79. *Recreations:* fishing, sculpture. *Died 11 Feb. 2004.*

ROBERTSON, Rev. Canon James Smith, OBE 1984; Canon Emeritus, Zambia, 1965; Secretary, United Society for the Propagation of the Gospel, 1973–83; a Chaplain to the Queen, 1980–87; *b* 4 Sept. 1917; *s* of Stuart Robertson and Elizabeth Mann Smith, Forfar; *m* 1950, Margaret Isabel Mina Mounsey (*d* 2003); one *d.* *Educ:* Glasgow Univ.; Edinburgh Theol Coll.; London Univ. MA Glasgow 1938; PCE London 1953. Curate, St Salvador's, Edinburgh, 1940–45; Mission Priest, UMCA, N Rhodesia, 1945–50; St Mark's Coll., Mapanza, 1950–55; Chalimbana Trng Coll., Lusaka, 1955–65, Principal 1958–65; Head, Educn Dept, Bede Coll., Durham, 1965–68; Sec., Church Colls of Educn, Gen. Synod Bd of Educn, 1968–73; Sec., USPG, 1973–83. British Council of Churches: Chm., Conf. for World Mission, 1977–81; Vice-Pres., 1984–87. Fellow, Selly Oak Colls, Birmingham, 1993. *Publications:* contributed to: Education in South Africa, 1970; The Training of Teachers, 1972; Values and Moral Development in Higher Education, 1974; Grow or Die, 1981; A Dictionary of Religious Education, 1984; Stepping Stones, 1987. *Recreations:* music, electronics, philosophy. *Address:* Flat 8, 26 Medway Street, SW1P 2BD. *T:* (020) 7222 1091.
Died 15 March 2004.

ROBERTSON, Sir John (Fraser), KCMG 1994; CBE 1982; consultant; Chief Ombudsman, New Zealand, 1984–94; *b* 3 Aug. 1925; *s* of Maurice Leigh Robertson and Violet Caroline Robertson (*née* Poultny); *m* 1947, Phyllis Irene Walter; two *s* one *d.* *Educ:* Univ. of Canterbury, NZ; Victoria Univ. of Wellington (DPA). FCA. Public Administration, 1946–82, incl. Sec. of Defence, 1969–79, Sec. for Justice, 1979–82; company dir and management consultant, 1982–84. Harkness Commonwealth Fund Fellow, 1961–62; RCDS 1968. Pres., Internat. Ombudsman Inst., 1992–94. *Publications:* numerous articles on public admin issues. *Recreations:* golf, bowls, bush and beach walking. *Address:* 5 Kabul Street, Khandallah, Wellington 6004, New Zealand. *T:* (4) 4791338. *Died 1 Sept. 2001.*

ROBERTSON, Martin; *see* Robertson, C. M.

ROBERTSON, Prof. Sir Rutherford (Ness), AC 1980; Kt 1972; CMG 1968; DSc, PhD; FRS 1961; FAA; Emeritus Professor, University of Adelaide and Australian National University; *b* 29 Sept. 1913; *o c* of Rev. J. Robertson, MA, and Josephine Robertson; *m* 1937, Mary Helen Bruce Rogerson; one *s.* *Educ:* St Andrew's Coll., NZ; Univ. of Sydney (DSc 1961); St John's Coll., Cambridge (PhD 1939; Hon. Fellow 1973). FAA 1954. Sydney Univ. Science Res. Schol., 1934–35, Linnean Macleay Fellow, 1935–36; Exhibn of 1851 Res. Schol., 1936–39; Res. at Botany Sch., Cambridge, in plant physiology, 1936–39; Asst Lectr, later Lectr, Botany Sch., Univ. of Sydney, 1939–46; Sen. Res. Offr, later Chief Res. Offr, Div. of Food Preservation, CSIRO, 1946–59 (res. in plant physiol. and biochem.); Sydney University: jointly in charge of Plant Physiol. Unit, 1952–59, Hon. Res. Associate, 1954–59; Hon. Vis., Sch. of Biol Scis, 1979–87; Mem. Exec., CSIRO 1959–62; Prof. of Botany, Univ. of Adelaide, 1962–69, then Emeritus; Dir, Res. Sch. of Biol Scis, ANU, 1973–78, then Emeritus Professor (Master, University House, 1969–72); Pro-Chancellor, ANU, 1984–86. Vis Prof., Univ. of Calif, Los Angeles, 1958–59. Kerney Foundn Lectr, Univ. of Calif, Berkeley, 1959; Three Societies Lecture, 1988. Chm., Aust. Res. Grants Cttee, 1965–69; Dep. Chm., Aust. Sci. and Tech. Council, 1977–81. Hon. Sec. Aust. Nat. Res. Council, 1951–55. President: Linnean Soc. of NSW, 1949; Australian Academy of Science, 1970–74 (Sec., Biological Sciences, 1957–58); Aust. and NZ Assoc. for the Advancement of Science, 1964–66; XIII Internat. Botanical Congress, Sydney, 1981. Patron, Aust. Cttee, Cambridge Commonwealth Trust, 1993–97. Corresp. Mem., Amer. Soc. of Plant Physiologists, 1953; For. Associate, US Nat. Acad. of Scis, 1962; Hon. Mem., Royal Soc. of NZ, 1971; Hon. FRSE 1983; For. Mem., Amer. Philosophical Soc., 1971; For. Hon. Mem., Amer. Acad. of Arts and Scis, 1973. Hon. DSc: Tasmania, 1965; Monash, 1970; ANU, 1979; Hon ScD Cambridge, 1969. Clarke Meml Medal, Royal Soc. of NSW, 1955; Farrer Meml Medal, 1963; ANZAAS Medal, 1968; Mueller Medal, 1970; Burnet Medal, 1975. *Publications:* (with G. E. Briggs and A. B. Hope) Electrolytes and Plant Cells, 1961; Protons, Electrons, Phosphorylation and Active Transport, 1968; The Lively Membranes, 1983; various scientific papers on plant physiology and biochemistry. *Recreations:* reading, water colours. *Address:* Unit 12, Linton Retirement Village, Glebe Street, Yass, NSW 2582, Australia. *Club:* Union (Sydney).

Died 5 March 2001.

ROBEY, (Douglas) John (Brett), CMG 1960; HM Diplomatic Service, retired; *b* 7 Aug. 1914; *s* of late E. J. B. and Margaret Robey; *m* 1943, Elizabeth, *d* of late Col David D. Barrett, US Army; two *s* one *d*. *Educ:* Cranleigh School; St John's College, Oxford (BA (History); Editor of The Cherwell); Ecole des Sciences Politiques, Paris. Joined HM Foreign Service, 1937; served in China, USA, Paris, Berlin, Baghdad; Consul-Gen., Chicago, 1966–69; Ambassador and Permanent UK Representative, Council of Europe, Strasbourg, 1969–74. *Publication:* The Innovator, 1945. *Recreations:* reading, writing, the Niebelung Ring. *Address:* Allan Down House, Rotherfield, East Sussex TN6 3RT. *T:* (01892) 852329. *Club:* Cercle Européen de Strasbourg (Hon. Life Pres.).

Died 30 May 2001.

ROBEY, John; *see* Robey, D. J. B.

ROBIN, Dr Gordon de Quetteville; Director, 1958–82, Senior Associate, since 1982, Scott Polar Research Institute, University of Cambridge; Fellow since 1964 and Vice-Master, 1974–78, Darwin College, Cambridge; *b* Melbourne, 17 Jan. 1921; *s* of Reginald James Robin and Emily Mabel Robin; *m* 1953, Jean Margaret Fortt, Bath; two *d*. *Educ:* Wesley Coll., Melbourne; Melbourne Univ. ScD Cantab, MSc Melbourne, PhD Birmingham. FInstP. War service, RANVR: anti-submarine, 1942–44; submarine, RN, 1944–45 (Lieut). Physics Dept, Birmingham Univ.: research student, lectr, ICI Research Fellow, 1945–56; Sen. Fellow, Geophysics Dept, ANU, 1957–58. Meteorologist and Officer i/c Signy Is, South Orkneys, with Falkland Is Dependencies Survey, 1947–48; Physicist and Sen. British Mem. of Norwegian-British-Swedish Antarctic Expedn, 1949–52 (made first effective measurements of Antarctic ice thickness); further researches: in Antarctic in 1959 (ocean wave penetration into pack ice); in Arctic, 1964, 1966, 1973, and Antarctic, 1967, 1969, 1974 (testing and developing airborne radar type sounding technique; discovered largest known sub-ice lake); UK deleg., 1958–84, Sec., 1958–70, Pres., 1970–74, and Hon. Mem., Scientific Cttee on Antarctic Research of ICSU; Mem. Adv. Bd, Geophysical Inst.,

Univ. of Alaska, 1974–81. President: Antarctic Club, 1974; Arctic Club, 1986; Chm., Trans Antarctic Assoc., 1992–97. Hon. DPhil Stockholm, 1978. Kongens Fortjensmedalje, Norway, 1952; Back Grant, RGS, 1953; Bruce Medal, RSE, 1953; Polar Medal, 1956; Patrons Medal, RGS, 1974; Seligman Crystal, Internat. Glaciological Soc., 1986. *Publications:* scientific reports of Norwegian-British-Swedish Antarctic Expedition (Glaciology III, 1958; Upper Winds, 1972); (ed) Annals of the IGY, Vol. 41, Glaciology, 1967; (ed and contrib.) The Climatic Record in Polar Ice Sheets, 1983; papers and articles on polar glaciology in scientific jls, incl. (jtly) paper in Nature, 1996, on freshwater lake beneath ice of central East Antarctica. *Recreations:* Mallorca, walking. *Address:* 10 Melbourne Place, Cambridge CB1 1EQ. *T:* (01223) 358463.

Died 21 Sept. 2004.

ROBIN, Ian (Gibson), FRCS; retired; *b* 22 May 1909; *s* of Dr Arthur Robin, Edinburgh, and Elizabeth Parker; *m* 1st, 1939, Shelagh Marian (*d* 1978), *d* of late Colonel C. M. Croft; one *s* two *d*; 2nd, 1994, Patricia Lawrence. *Educ:* Merchiston Castle School; Clare College, Cambridge. MA, MB, BCh Cantab 1933; LRCP 1933; FRCS 1935. Guy's Hosp.; late House Phys.; Sen. Science Schol., 1930; Treasurer's Gold Medals in Clinical Surgery and Medicine, 1933; Arthur Durham Travelling Schol., 1933; Charles Oldham Prize in Ophthalmology, 1933; Registrar and Chief Clin. Asst, ENT Dept, 1935–36; late Consulting ENT Surgeon: Royal Chest Hosp., 1939–44; Royal Northern Hosp., 1937–74; St Mary's Hosp., Paddington, 1948–74; Princess Louise (Kensington) Hosp. for Children, 1948–69; Paddington Green Children's Hosp., 1969–74; Surgeon EMS, Sector III London Area, 1939–45. Late Vice-Chm., Royal Nat. Institute for the Deaf. Member Hunterian Soc.; Council of Nat. Deaf Children's Soc.; Past Pres., Brit. Assoc. of Otolaryngologists, 1971–72; Past Pres., Laryng. Section, RSM, 1967–68; Vice-Pres., Otolog. Section, RSM, 1967–68, 1969; late Examiner for DLO of RCS of England. Lectures: Yearsley, 1968; Jobson Horne, 1969. Mem., Royal Water-Colour Soc. *Publications:* (jt) Diseases of Ear, Nose and Throat (Synopsis Series), 1957; papers in various med. treatises, jls, etc. *Recreations:* golf, gardening, sketching; formerly athletics and Rugby. *Address:* Merchiston, 4 Lodge Gardens, Oakham, Rutland LE15 6EP. *Clubs:* Hawks (Cambridge); Achilles (Great Britain).

Died 18 April 2005.

ROBINSON, Basil William, FBA 1981; retired; *b* 20 June 1912; *o c* of William Robinson and Rebecca Frances Mabel, *d* of Rev. George Gilbanks; *m* 1st, 1945, Ailsa Mary Stewart (*d* 1954); 2nd, 1958, Oriel Hermione Steel; one *s* one *d*. *Educ:* Winchester (Exhibitioner); Corpus Christi Coll., Oxford (BA 1935; MA, BLitt, 1938). Asst Keeper, Victoria and Albert Museum, 1939; Min. of Home Security, 1939–40. Served as Captain, 2nd Punjab Regt, India, Burma, Malaya, 1943–46. Deputy Keeper, V&A Museum, 1954, Keeper, Dept of Metalwork, 1966–72, Keeper Emeritus, 1972–76. Pres., Royal Asiatic Soc., 1970–73; Vice-Pres., Arms and Armour Soc., 1953; Hon. Pres., Tō-ken Soc. of Great Britain, 1967–93. FSA 1974. *Publications:* A Primer of Japanese Sword-blades, 1955; Persian Miniatures, 1957; Japanese Landscape Prints of the 19th Century, 1957; A Descriptive Catalogue of the Persian Paintings in the Bodleian Library, 1958; Kuniyoshi, 1961; The Arts of the Japanese Sword, 1961, 2nd edn, 1971; Persian Drawings, 1965; part-author, vols 2 and 3, Catalogue of Persian MSS and Miniatures in the Chester Beatty Library, 3 vols, 1958–62; Persian Miniature Painting, 1967; Persian Paintings in the India Office Library, 1976; (ed. and jt author) Islamic painting in the Keir Collection, 1976; Japanese Sword-fittings in the Baur Collection, 1980; Persian Paintings in the John Rylands Library, 1980; Kuniyoshi: the Warrior Prints, 1982 (Uchiyama Meml Prize, Japan Ukiyoe Soc.); Persian Painting and the National Epic (Hertz Lecture, British Acad.), 1983; (jtly) The Aldrich Book of Catches, 1989; Fifteenth Century Persian Painting (Kevorkian Lectures,

NY Univ.), 1991; Collection Jean Pozzi, 1992; Persian Paintings in the Collection of the Royal Asiatic Society, 1998; The Persian Book of Kings, 2002; numerous booklets, articles and reviews on Persian and Japanese art. *Recreations:* catch singing (founder and Chairman, Aldrich Catch Club), cats. *Address:* 41 Redcliffe Gardens, SW10 9JH. *Club:* Hurlingham. *Died 29 Dec. 2005.*

ROBINSON, Ven. David; *see* Robinson, Ven. W. D.

ROBINSON, Dr Derek Charles, FRS 1994; Director, UKAEA Fusion (formerly Research Director, UKAEA Government Division, Fusion), since 1992 (Culham Science Centre Director, since 1998); *b* 27 May 1941; *s* of Alexander Robinson and Grace Kitchen; *m* 1968, Marion Quarmby; one *d. Educ:* Queen Elizabeth Sch., Kirkby Lonsdale; Manchester Univ. (BSc, PhD). FInstP. AERE Harwell, 1965–68; Vis. Scientist, I. V. Kurchatov Inst. of Atomic Energy, Moscow, 1968–69; research at UKAEA Culham Lab., 1970–78; Vis. Scientist, Tokyo, Nagoya and S Australia, 1978–79; Group Leader, 1979–86, Div. Head, 1986–92, Culham Lab. Member: Council, JET, 1996–2001 (Mem. Sci. Council, 1983–); Sci. Adv. Bd, Max Planck Inst. für Plasma Physik, 1988– (Chm., 1997–); Tech. Adv. Cttee, Internat. Thermonuclear Exp. Reactor, 1991–; Conseil Scientifique, CEA, 1994–99; Consultative Cttee for Fusion Prog., 1996–; Chm., European Fusion Physics Cttee, 2000–. Vice Pres., Inst. of Physics, 2001– (Bd Mem., 1999–, Chm., 2001–, Inst. of Physics Publishing). Alfvén Lectr, Swedish Royal Acad. of Scis, 1996. C. V. Boys Prize, 1979, Guthrie Medal and Prize, 1998, Inst. of Physics. *Publications:* contribs to learned jls. *Recreations:* plantsman, photography, hill walking. *Address:* The Thatched Cottage, Church Street, Appleford, Abingdon, Oxon OX14 4PA. *T:* (01235) 848500.
Died 2 Dec. 2002.

ROBINSON, Keith; *see* Robinson, L. K.

ROBINSON, Kenneth Ernest, CBE 1971; MA, FRHistS; *b* 9 March 1914; *o s* of late Ernest and Isabel Robinson, Plumstead, Kent; *m* 1938, Stephanie (*d* 1994), *o d* of late William Wilson, Westminster; one *s* one *d. Educ:* Monoux Grammar School, Walthamstow; Hertford College, Oxford (Scholar, 1st Cl. PPE; 1st Cl. Mod. Hist.; Beit Senior Schol. in Colonial History); London School of Economics. Colonial Office, 1936; Asst Sec. 1946; resigned 1948. Fellow of Nuffield Coll. (Hon. Fellow, 1984) and Reader in Commonwealth Govt, Oxford, 1948–57; Dir, Inst. of Commonwealth Studies and Prof. of Commonwealth Affairs, Univ. of London, 1957–65 (Hon. Life Mem., 1980–); Vice-Chancellor, Univ. of Hong Kong, 1965–72; Hallsworth Res. Fellow, Univ. of Manchester, 1972–74; Dir, Commonwealth Studies Resources Survey, Univ. of London, 1974–76. Leverhulme Res. Fellow, 1952–53; Vis. Lectr, Sch. of Advanced Internat. Studies, Johns Hopkins Univ., 1954; Carnegie Travel Grant, East, Central and S Africa, 1960; Reid Lectr, Acadia Univ., 1963; Vis. Prof., Duke Univ., NC, 1963; Callander Lectr, Aberdeen, 1979. Editor, Jl of Commonwealth Political Studies, 1961–65; Special Commonwealth Award, ODM, 1965. Member: (part-time) Directing Staff, Civil Service Selection Bd, 1951–56; Assessor Panel, 1973–77; Colonial Economic Res. Cttee, 1949–62; Colonial SSRC, 1958–62; Inter-Univ. Council for Higher Educn Overseas, 1973–79; Mem. Council: Overseas Develt Inst. 1960–65; RIIA, 1962–65; Internat. African Inst., 1960–65; African Studies Assoc., UK, 1963–65, 1978–81; ACU, 1967–68; Hong Kong Management Assoc., 1965–72; Chinese Univ. of Hong Kong, 1965–72; Univ. of Cape Coast, 1972–74; Royal Commonwealth Soc., 1974–87 (Vice Pres., 1984–); Royal African Soc., 1983–89 (Pres., 1989–96); Life Mem. Ct, Univ. of Hong Kong, 1972. Governor, LSE, 1959–65. Corresp. Mem., Académie des Sciences d'Outre-Mer, Paris. Hon. LLD Chinese Univ. of Hong Kong, 1969; Hon. DLitt, Univ. of Hong Kong, 1972; DUniv Open, 1978. JP Hong Kong, 1967–72. *Publications:* (with W. J. M. Mackenzie) Five Elections in Africa, 1960; (with A. F.

Madden) Essays in Imperial Government presented to Margery Perham, 1963; The Dilemmas of Trusteeship, 1965; (with W. B. Hamilton & C. D. Goodwin) A Decade of the Commonwealth 1955–64 (USA), 1966. Contrib. to Africa Today (USA), 1955; Africa in the Modern World (USA), 1955; University Cooperation and Asian Development (USA), 1967; L'Europe du XIXe et du XXe Siècle, Vol. 7 (Italy), 1968; Experts in Africa, 1980; Perspectives on Imperialism and Decolonisation, 1984; papers in learned jls; *festschriften:* Imperialism, the State, and the Third World, ed M. Twaddle, 1992; Decolonisation and the International Community, 1993. *Clubs:* Royal Commonwealth Society, Lansdowne; Hong Kong.
Died 18 Jan. 2005.

ROBINSON, (Leonard) Keith, CBE 1981; DL; management consultant, 1985–87; County Chief Executive, Hampshire County Council, 1973–85; Clerk of Lieutenancy, 1973–85; *b* 2 July 1920; *s* of Cuthbert Lawrence Robinson and Hilda Robinson; *m* 1948, Susan May Tomkinson; two *s* two *d. Educ:* Queen Elizabeth's Grammar Sch., Blackburn; Victoria Univ. of Manchester (LLB). Solicitor. Served RAFVR, 1940–46 (Navigator, Sqdn-Ldr). Asst Solicitor, City and County of Bristol, 1948–55; Dep. Town Clerk, Birkenhead Co. Borough Council, 1955–66; Town Clerk, Stoke-on-Trent City Council, 1966–73. Association of County Councils: Mem., Officers Adv. Gp, 1974–83 (Chm., 1977–82); Adviser, Policy Cttee, 1975–82; Adviser, Local Govt Finance Cttee, 1976–85; Chm., Assoc. of County Chief Execs, 1975–77. Member: W Mids Econ. Planning Council, 1967–73; Keele Univ. Council, 1968–73; Central Cttee for Reclamation of Derelict Land, 1971–74; Quality Assce Council, BSI, 1973–77; Job Creation Programme Action Cttee for London and SE, 1976–77; District Manpower Cttee, 1980–83; Adv. Council for Energy Conservation, 1982–84; Local Authorities' Mutual Investment Trust, 1982–83; Hillier Arboretum Management Cttee, 1985–99 (Sec., 1977–85); Southern Arts, 1985–91; Exec. Cttee, Hampshire Develt Assoc., 1985–91; Asst Comr, Local Govt Boundary Commn, 1986–91. Mem. Exec. Cttee, Hampshire Gardens Trust, 1985–; Dir, Salisbury Playhouse, 1979–93; Vice-Chm., Nuffield Theatre Bd, 1985–95; Trustee, New Theatre Royal (Portsmouth) Ltd, 1976–; Pres., Winchester Dramatic Soc., 1984–95. Mem., Barton Stacey PCC, 1997–2001 (Chm., Church Appeal Cttee). DL Hants, 1985. *Publications:* contrib. local govt and legal jls. *Recreations:* fly-fishing, theatre, photography, gardening. *Address:* Bransbury Mill Cottage, Bransbury, Barton Stacey, Winchester, Hants SO21 3QJ. *Club:* MCC.
Died 16 March 2003.

ROBINSON, Prof. Roger James, FRCP, FRCPCH; Professor of Paediatrics, United Medical and Dental Schools of Guy's and St Thomas's Hospitals (formerly Guy's Hospital Medical School), University of London, 1975–90, then Emeritus; *b* 17 May 1932; *s* of Albert Edward and Leonora Sarah Robinson; *m* 1962, Jane Hippisley Packham; two *s* one *d. Educ:* Poole Grammar Sch.; Balliol Coll., Oxford (Brackenbury schol.; MA, DPhil, BM, BCh); PhD (English) Aberdeen, 1998. FRCP 1975; FRCPCH 1996. Lectr of Christ Church, Oxford, 1953; appts at Radcliffe Infirmary, Oxford, National Hosp., Queen Square, and Hammersmith Hosp., 1960–66; Visiting Fellow, Harvard, 1967; Sen. Lectr, Inst. of Child Health, Hammersmith Hosp., 1967; Cons. Paediatrician, Guy's Hosp., 1971. Hon. Fellow, Dept of English, Aberdeen Univ., 1996–2000. Associate Ed., BMJ, 1990–. *Publications:* Brain and Early Behaviour: development in the fetus and infant, 1969; (jtly) Medical Care of Newborn Babies, 1972; papers on paediatrics and child neurology, and on James Beattie, the poet. *Recreations:* literature (especially poetry), theatre, walking. *Address:* 60 Madeley Road, Ealing, W5 2LU.
Died 12 Oct. 2003.

ROBINSON, Victor, CEng, FIChemE; Vice-President, Fédération Européenne d'Associations Nationales d'Ingénieurs, 1992; *b* 31 July 1925; *s* of Arthur Worsley Robinson and Nellie (*née* Halliwell); *m* 1948, Sadie Monica (*née* Grut); one *s* five *d. Educ:* Manchester Grammar Sch.; Cambridge Univ. (MA); Admin. Staff Coll., Henley. CEng, FIChemE 1960. Simon Carves Ltd: R&D Proj. Engrg, 1945; Technical Dir, 1961; Dir, 1964; Man. Dir Overseas Ops and Dir, Sim-Chem Ltd and subsid. cos, 1966; Man. Dir, Turriff Taylor Ltd, 1974–76; Dir, Davy Internat. Projects, 1976–85; Industrial Adviser, Dept of Trade (on secondment from Davy Corp. Ltd), 1978–81. *Recreation:* fell and alpine walking. *Address:* 32 Guilford Avenue, Surbiton, Surrey KT5 5DG.
Died 9 Aug. 2003.

ROBINSON, Ven. (William) David; Archdeacon of Blackburn, 1986–96, then Emeritus; *b* 15 March 1931; *s* of William and Margaret Robinson; *m* 1955, Carol Averil Roma Hamm; one *s* one *d. Educ:* Queen Elizabeth's Grammar School, Blackburn; Durham Univ. (BA 1954, DipTh 1958, MA 1962). Ordained deacon, 1958, priest, 1959; Curate: Standish, 1958–61; Lancaster Priory (i/c St George), 1961–63; Vicar, St James, Blackburn, 1963–73; Diocesan Stewardship Adviser, Blackburn, and Priest-in-charge, St James, Shireshead, 1973–86; Hon. Canon, Blackburn Cathedral, 1975–86; Vicar of Balderstone, 1986–87. *Recreation:* fell walking. *Address:* 21 Westbourne Road, Warton, Carnforth, Lancs LA5 9NP. *T:* (01524) 720591.
Died 12 June 2003.

ROBINSON, Rt Rev. William James; Hon. Assistant, St George's Cathedral, Kingston, Ontario, since 1982; *b* 8 Sept. 1916; *s* of Thomas Albert Robinson and Harriet Mills; *m* 1946, Isobel Morton; one *s* three *d. Educ:* Bishop's Univ., Lennoxville, PQ (BA Theology). Ordained deacon, 1939, priest, 1940; Asst Curate in Trenton, 1939–41; Rector: Tweed and Madoc, 1941–46, Tweed and N Addington, 1946–47; Napanee, 1948–53; St Thomas' Church, Belleville, 1953–55; St John's Church, Ottawa, 1955–62; Church of Ascension, Hamilton, 1962–67; St George's Church, Guelph, 1967–70; Canon of Christ Church Cathedral, Hamilton, 1964–68; Archdeacon of Trafalgar (Niagara Diocese), 1968–70; Bishop of Ottawa, 1970–81, retired. Hon. DCL Bishop's Univ., Lennoxville, 1973. *Recreations:* woodworking, gardening. *Address:* 168 Inverness Crescent, Kingston, ON K7M 6N7, Canada. *T:* (613) 5497599.
Died 9 July 2002.

ROBLIN, Ven. Graham Henry, OBE 1983; Vicar, Bere Regis and Affpuddle with Turnerspuddle, 1993–2001; *b* 18 Aug. 1937; *s* of Ewart and Marjorie Roblin; *m* 1964, Penelope Ann Cumberlege; one *s* one *d. Educ:* Cathedral Sch., Exeter; King's Coll., Taunton; King's Coll., London (AKC). Deacon, 1962; priest, 1963; Curate of St Helier, Southwark, 1962–66; joined Army Chaplaincy Service, 1966; Dep. Asst Chaplain Gen., Hong Kong, 1979–81; Dep. Asst Chaplain Gen., 2nd Armd Div., 1981–83; Warden, RAChD Centre, Bagshot Park, 1983–86; Senior Chaplain: 1st British Corps, 1986–87; BAOR, 1987–89; Dep. Chaplain Gen. to Forces, 1989–93; Archdeacon to the Army, 1990–93, Archdeacon Emeritus, 1994–. QHC 1987–93. Freeman, City of London, 2000. *Recreation:* writing. *Address:* Croft Cottage, High Street, Yetminster, Sherborne, Dorset DT9 6LF. *Died 4 Dec. 2005.*

ROBSON, Brian Ewart, CB 1985; FSA, FRHistS; Deputy Under-Secretary of State (Personnel and Logistics), Ministry of Defence, 1984–86; *b* 25 July 1926; 2nd *s* of late Walter Ewart Robson; *m* 1962, Cynthia Margaret (*d* 1997), *o d* of late William James Scott, Recife, Brazil; two *d. Educ:* Steyning Grammar Sch.; Varndean Sch., Brighton; The Queen's Coll., Oxford (BA Modern History). FRHistS 1995; FSA 1997. Royal Sussex Regt and Kumaon Regt, Indian Army, 1944–47. Air Min., 1950; Asst Private Sec. to Sec. of State for Air, 1953–55; Principal, 1955; Asst Sec., 1965; Imperial Defence Coll., 1970; Mem., UK Delegn to UN Law of the Sea Conf.,

Venezuela, 1974; Ecole Nationale d'Administration, Paris, 1975; Ministry of Defence: Asst Under-Sec. of State (Supply and Orgn), 1976–80, (Operational Requirements), 1980–82; Dep. Under-Sec. of State (Army), 1982–84. Technical Advr, Price Waterhouse, 1986–89. Member: Central Finance Bd of C of E, 1985–95; Chichester Diocesan Finance Bd, 1986–94. Comr, Royal Hosp., 1982–85; Chm., Soc. for Army Historical Res., 1993–98; Member Council: Army Records Soc., 1984–89, 1993–; Nat. Army Museum, 1982–93; Trustee, Imperial War Museum, 1984–86. Chm. Govs, Duke of York's Royal Mil. Sch., 1982–85; Governor: Welbeck Coll., 1982–84; Whitelands Coll., 1988–95; Roehampton Inst., 1991–95; Varndean Coll., 2004–. *Publications:* Swords of the British Army, 1975, 2nd edn 1996; The Road to Kabul: the Second Afghan War 1878–1881, 1986, 2nd edn 2003; Roberts in India: military papers of Lord Roberts, 1993; Fuzzy Wuzzy: the campaigns in the Eastern Sudan 1884–85, 1993; Onward and Upward: a history of Varndean 1884–1975, 1993; Sir Hugh Rose and the Central India Campaign 1858, 2000; Crisis on the Frontier: the third Afghan War and the campaign in Waziristan 1919–1920, 2003; numerous articles on weapons and military history. *Recreations:* military history, cricket, travel. *Address:* 17 Woodlands, Hove, East Sussex BN3 6TJ. *T:* (01273) 505803. *Club:* Oxford Union. *Died 23 June 2005.*

ROCH, Muriel Elizabeth Sutcliffe; Headmistress, School of S Mary and S Anne, Abbots Bromley, Staffs, 1953–77; *b* 7 Sept. 1916; *d* of late Rev. Sydney John Roch, MA Cantab, Pembroke and Manchester. *Educ:* Manchester High Sch.; Bedford Coll., London (BA); Hughes Hall, Cambridge. Teaching appointments at: Devonport High School, 1939–41; Lady Manners, Bakewell, 1941–44; Howells School, Denbigh, 1944–47; Talbot Heath, Bournemouth, 1947–53. *Recreations:* music, travel. *Address:* Northdown Cottage, Lamphey, Pembroke SA71 5PL. *T:* (01646) 672577. *Club:* University Women's.
Died 5 Oct. 2001.

ROCHESTER, Prof. George Dixon, FRS 1958; FInstP; Professor of Physics, University of Durham, 1955–73, then Professor Emeritus; *b* 4 Feb. 1908; *s* of Thomas and Ellen Rochester; *m* 1938, Idaline, *o d* of Rev. J. B. and Mrs Bayliffe; one *s* one *d. Educ:* Wallsend Secondary Sch. and Technical Inst.; Univ. of Durham (Earl Grey Meml Schol.; BSc, MSc, PhD). Earl Grey Fellow, at Stockholm Univ., 1934–35; Commonwealth Fund Fellow at California Univ., 1935–37; Manchester University: Asst Lectr, 1937–46; Lectr, 1946–49; Sen. Lectr, 1949–53; Reader, 1953–55; Second Pro-Vice-Chancellor, Univ. of Durham, 1967–69, Pro-Vice-Chancellor, 1969–70. Scientific Adviser in Civil Defence for NW Region, 1952–55. Member: Council CNAA, 1964–74; Council, British Assoc. for Advancement of Science, 1971–72; Council, Royal Soc., 1972–74; Chm., NE Branch, Inst. of Physics, 1972–74. (Jt) C. V. Boys Prizeman of the Physical Society of London, 1956; Symons Memorial Lecturer of the Royal Meteorological Soc., 1962. Hon. Fellow, Newcastle upon Tyne Polytechnic, 1977. Hon. DSc: Newcastle upon Tyne, 1973; CNAA, 1975. Methodist. *Publications:* (with J. G. Wilson) Cloud Chamber Photographs of the Cosmic Radiation, 1952; scientific papers on spectroscopy, cosmic rays, history of the strange particles, and Durham astronomy. *Recreations:* outdoor activities, history of physics and astronomy. *Address:* 18 Dryburn Road, Durham DH1 5AJ. *T:* (0191) 3864796.
Died 26 Dec. 2001.

ROCKEFELLER, James Stillman; President and Director, Indian Spring Land Co.; Vice-President and Director, Indian Rock Corp.; *b* New York, 8 June 1902; *s* of William Goodsell Rockefeller and Elsie (*née* Stillman); *m* 1925, Nancy Carnegie (*d* 1994); two *s* two *d. Educ:* Yale University (BA). With Brown Bros & Co., NYC, 1924–30; joined National City Bank of New York (later First Nat. City Bank, then Citibank, NA), 1930; Asst

Cashier, 1931; Asst Vice-Pres. 1933; Vice-Pres., 1940–48; Sen. Vice-Pres., 1948–52; Exec. Vice-Pres., 1952; Pres. and Director, 1952–59; Chairman, 1959–67; former director of several Fortune 500 cos. Rep. Greenwich (Conn.) Town Meeting, 1933–42. Served as Lieutenant-Colonel in US Army, 1942–46. Member Board of Overseers, Memorial Hospital for Cancer and Allied Diseases, NY; Trustee of Estate of William Rockefeller; Trustee American Museum of National History. Olympic Gold Medal for rowing, 1924. *Address:* One Indian Spring Road, Greenwich, CT 06831–4430, USA. *Clubs:* Down Town Assoc., Union League, University (New York); Metropolitan (Washington, DC); Field, Round Hill (Greenwich, Conn). *Died 10 Aug. 2004.*

ROCKEFELLER, Laurance Spelman, Hon. CBE 1971; philanthropist; Director, Rockefeller Center Inc., 1936–78 (Chairman, 1953–56, 1958–66); *b* New York, 26 May 1910; *s* of John Davison Rockefeller, Jr, FRS and Abby Greene Aldrich; *m* 1934, Mary French; one *s* three *d. Educ:* Lincoln School of Teachers College; Princeton University (BA). War service, Lt-Comdr, USNR, 1942–45. Chm. Emeritus and Trustee, Jackson Hole Preserve Inc., 1997– (Pres., 1940–87; Chm. and Trustee, 1987–96); Chairman: Citizens' Adv. Council on Environmental Quality, 1969–73 (Mem., 1973–79); Meml Sloan-Kettering Cancer Center, 1960–82 (Hon. Chm., 1982–); NY Zool Soc., 1970–75 (Hon. Chm., 1975–); Woodstock Resort Corp.; Woodstock Foundn, 1968–97 (Chm. Emeritus, 1997–); Dir, Eastern Air Lines, 1938–60, 1977–81, Adv. Dir, 1981–87; Mem. Bd of Dirs, Readers' Digest Assoc., 1973–93; Pres., Palisades Interstate Park Commn, 1970–77 (Comr Emeritus, 1978–); Adv. Trustee, Rockefeller Bros Fund, 1982–85 (Founding Trustee; Chm., 1958–80; Vice-Chm., 1980–82); Charter Trustee, Princeton Univ.; Trustee: Alfred P. Sloan Foundn, 1950–82; Greenacre Foundn; Sleepy Hollow Restorations, 1975–87 (Chm., 1981–85); Hist. Hudson Valley, 1987– (Chm. Emeritus, 1997–); Hon. Trustee, Nat. Geog. Soc.; Life Mem., Mass Inst. of Technology; Dir, Community Blood Council of Gtr NY; Mem., Nat. Cancer Adv. Bd, 1972–79; Chairman: Outdoor Recreation Resources Review Commn, 1958–65; Hudson River Valley Commn, 1956–66; 1965 White House Conf. on Nat. Beauty; Delegate UN Conf. on Human Environment, 1972. Mem., Amer. Conservation Assoc. (Pres., 1958–80; Chm., 1980–85; Hon. Chm., 1985–); Hon. Dir, Nat. Wildflower Center, 1988–. Holds numerous awards, medals and hon. degrees. Comdr, Royal Order of the Lion, Belgium, 1950; US Medal of Freedom, 1969; Congressional Gold Medal, 1990. *Address:* Room 5600, 30 Rockefeller Plaza, New York, NY 10112, USA. *Clubs:* Boone and Crockett, River, Princeton, Lotos, University, Brook, Cosmos, Knickerbocker, Capitol Hill (New York City); Sleepy Hollow (Tarrytown). *Died 11 July 2004.*

RODGER, Rt Rev. Patrick Campbell; an Assistant Bishop, Diocese of Edinburgh, 1986–2000; *b* 28 Nov. 1920; *s* of Patrick Wylie and Edith Ann Rodger; *m* 1952, Margaret Menzies Menzies, MBE (*d* 1989); one *s* (and one *s* decd). *Educ:* Cargilfield; Rugby; Christ Church, Oxford (Hon. Student, 1990); Westcott House, Cambridge. Deacon, 1949; priest, 1950; Asst Curate, St John's Church, Edinburgh, 1949–51, and Chaplain to Anglican Students in Edinburgh, 1951–54; Study Secretary, SCM of GB and Ireland, 1955–58; Rector, St Fillan's, Kilmacolm, with St Mary's Bridge of Weir, 1958–61; Exec. Sec. for Faith and Order, World Council of Churches, 1961–66; Vice-Provost, 1966–67, Provost, 1967–70, St Mary's Cathedral, Edinburgh; Bishop of Manchester, 1970–78; Bishop of Oxford, 1978–86; Mem., House of Lords, 1974–86. Chm., Churches' Unity Commn, 1974–78; Pres., Conf. of European Churches, 1974–86. *Publications:* (ed) The Fourth World Conference on Faith and Order, Montreal, 1964; Songs in a Strange Land, 1989. *Recreations:* music and walking. *Address:* 12 Warrender Park Terrace,

Edinburgh EH9 1EG. *T:* (0131) 229 5075. *Club:* New (Edinburgh). *Died 8 July 2002.*

RODGERS, Prof. Harold William, OBE 1943; FRCS; Professor of Surgery, Queen's University of Belfast, 1947–73, Professor Emeritus, 1973; *b* 1 Dec. 1907; *s* of Major R. T. Rodgers; *m* 1938, Margaret Boycott (*d* 1998); one *s* three *d. Educ:* King's College School; St Bartholomew's Hospital. FRCS 1933. St Bartholomew's Hospital: House Surgeon, Demonstrator in Anatomy, Chief Asst, Casualty Surgeon, Senior Asst Surgeon. Served War of 1939–45, RAMC, North Africa, Italy, France; Hon. Lt-Col. Prof. of Surgery and Head of Div. of Hosp. Care, Univ. of Ife, Nigeria, 1974–77, retd. Nuffield Medical Visitor to African Territories; WHO Vis. Prof. to India; Vice-Pres. Intervarsity Fellowship. FRSocMed 1932 (Past Pres., Section of Surgery); Past President: British Society of Gastro-enterology; Christian Medical Fellowship; British Surgical Research Soc.; Past Chairman, Ct of Examiners of RCS. District Surgeon, St John's Ambulance Brigade. Past Pres., YMCA (Belfast); Pres., Hibernian CMS. Mem., RIIA, 1947–. Mem., Birmingham Med. Inst., 1995; Hon. Fellow, Polish Soc. of Surgeons, 1972. Hon. MD QUB, 1981. OStJ 1968. *Publications:* Gastroscopy, 1937; general articles in surgical and medical journals. *Recreations:* painting, travel, poetry. *Address:* 1 Hartley Place, Vicarage Road, Edgbaston, Birmingham B15 3HS. *Died 24 June 2001.*

ROE, Air Chief Marshal Sir Rex (David), GCB 1981 (KCB 1977; CB 1974); AFC; retired 1981; *b* 1925; *m* 1948, Helen Sophie (*née* Nairn) (*d* 1981); one *s* one *d* (and one *d* decd). *Educ:* City of London Sch.; London University. Joined RAF 1943; trained in Canada; served with Metropolitan Fighter Sector, No 11 Group, 203 Sqn, 1950–51; Sch. of Maritime Reconnaissance, 1951–53; Central Flying School and Flying Training Units, 1953–55; commanded RNZAF Central Flying School, 1956–58; RAF Staff Coll., 1959; commanded No 204 Sqn, 1960–62; Coll. of Air Warfare, 1962–64; SASO No 18 (Maritime) Gp, 1964–67; Stn Comdr RAF Syerston, 1967–69; Dir of Flying Trng, 1969–71; RCDS, 1971; Dep. Controller Aircraft (C), MoD (Procurement Executive), 1972–74; SASO HQ NEAF, 1974–76; AOC-in-C Training Comd, 1976–77; AOC-in-C, Support Comd, 1977–78; Air Mem. for Supply and Organisation, 1978–81. *Recreations:* reading, Rugby football. *Address:* c/o Lloyds TSB, 7 Pall Mall, SW1Y 5NA. *Club:* Royal Air Force. *Died 3 Nov. 2002.*

ROFFEY, (Harry) Norman, CMG 1971; Assistant Secretary, Department of Health and Social Security, 1954–72, retired; *b* 2 March 1911; *s* of Henry Roffey and Ella Leggatt; *m* 1964, Florence Dickie; no *c. Educ:* Brighton Grammar Sch.; St Catharine's Coll., Cambridge (BA Hons, MA); Inst. of Education, London Univ. (Teacher's Dip.). Teaching (languages), 1935–40; Air Ministry and Foreign Office, 1940–45 (left as Wing Comdr); Min. of Health (Principal), 1946–54; Dept of Health and Social Security, 1954–72 (as Asst Sec. i/c Internat. Affairs, on the Health side). *Recreations:* travel, music, etc. *Address:* 2 Sunnyside Place, Wimbledon, SW19 4SJ. *T:* (020) 8946 4991. *Died 27 Feb. 2001.*

ROFFEY, Norman; *see* Roffey, H. N.

ROGERS, Rt Rev. Alan Francis Bright, MA; Hon. Assistant Bishop, diocese in Europe, since 1996; *b* 12 Sept. 1907; *s* of Thomas and Alice Rogers, London, W9; *m* 1st, 1932, Millicent Boarder (*d* 1984); one *s* (and one *s* decd); 2nd, 1985, Barbara Gower. *Educ:* Westminster City Sch.; King's Coll., London; Leeds Univ.; Bishop's Coll., Cheshunt (Kitchener Schol., 1926–30). Curate of St Stephen's, Shepherds Bush, 1930–32; Holy Trinity, Twickenham, 1932–34; Civil Chaplain, Mauritius, 1934–49; Archdeacon of Mauritius, 1946–49; Commissary to Bishop of Mauritius, 1949–59; Vicar of Twickenham, 1949–54; Proctor in Convocation, 1951–59; Vicar of Hampstead, 1954–59; Rural Dean of Hampstead,

1955–59; Bishop of Mauritius, 1959–66; Suffragan Bishop of Fulham, 1966–70; Suffragan Bishop of Edmonton, 1970–75; Priest-in-Charge: Wappenham, 1977–80; Abthorpe with Slapton, 1977–83; Hon. Asst Curate, St Mary's, Twickenham, 1985–2000. An Hon. Assistant Bishop: of Peterborough, 1975–84; Dio. of London (Kensington Area), 1985–91. Chm., Archbishops' Bd of Examiners, USPG, 1972–83. MA Lambeth 1959. *Publications:* Threads of Friendship (autobiog.), 1989; Walking with God as a Friend, 1990. *Recreations:* crosswords, theatre-going, listening to tapes, especially poetry. *Address:* 20 River Way, Twickenham, Middx TW2 5JP. *T:* (020) 8894 2031. *Club:* Royal Over-Seas League.   *Died 16 Oct. 2003.*

ROGERS, Prof. C(laude) Ambrose, FRS 1959; Astor Professor of Mathematics, University College, London, 1958–86, then Emeritus; *b* 1 Nov. 1920; *s* of late Sir Leonard Rogers, KCSI, CIE, FRS; *m* 1952, Mrs J. M. Gordon, *widow* of W. G. Gordon, and *d* of F. W. G. North; two *d. Educ:* Berkhamsted School; University Coll., London; Birkbeck Coll., London. BSc, PhD, DSc (London, 1941, 1949, 1952). Experimental officer, Ministry of Supply, 1940–45; lecturer and reader, University College, London, 1946–54; Prof. of Pure Mathematics, Univ. of Birmingham, 1954–58. Mem. Council, Royal Soc., 1966–68 and 1983–84; Pres., London Mathematical Soc., 1970–72; Chm., Jt Mathematical Council, 1982–84. *Publications:* Packing and Covering, 1964; Hausdorff Measures, 1970, rev. edn 1998; articles in various mathematical journals. *Recreation:* string figures. *Address:* Department of Mathematics, University College, WC1E 6BT; 8 Grey Close, NW11 6QG. *T:* (020) 8455 8027.   *Died 5 Dec. 2005.*

ROGERS, Eric William Evan, DSc(Eng); FRAeS; scientific and engineering recruitment consultant, 1985–2003; Deputy Director (A), Royal Aircraft Establishment, Farnborough, Hants, 1978–85; *b* 12 April 1925; *o s* of late W. P. Rogers, Southgate, N London; *m* 1950, Dorothy Joyce Loveless (*d* 2000); two *s* one *d. Educ:* Southgate County Grammar Sch.; Imperial Coll., London. FCGI, DIC. Aerodynamics Div., NPL, 1945–70 (Head of Hypersonic Research, 1961); Aerodynamics Dept, RAE, 1970 (Head, 1972). *Publications:* various papers on aerodynamics and on industrial aerodynamics, in ARC (R and M series), RAeS jls and elsewhere. *Recreations:* music, history. *Address:* 64 Thetford Road, New Malden, Surrey KT3 5DT. *T:* (020) 8942 7452.   *Died 11 June 2004.*

ROGERS, Sir Frank (Jarvis), Kt 1988; Director, Telegraph Group Ltd (formerly Daily Telegraph, then The Telegraph, plc), 1985–2001 (Deputy Chairman, 1986–95); Director, EMAP plc (formerly East Midland Allied Press), 1971–91 (Chairman, 1973–90); *b* 24 Feb. 1920; *s* of Percy Rogers and Elsie Mary (*née* Jarvis); *m* 1st, 1949, Esma Holland (*d* 1998); two *d*; 2nd, 2001, Sheena Phillips. *Educ:* Wolstanton Grammar School. Journalist, 1937–49; Military Service, 1940–46; Gen. Man., Nigerian Daily Times, 1949–52; Manager, Argus, Melbourne, 1952–55; Man. Dir, Overseas Newspapers, 1958–60; Dir, Daily Mirror, 1960–65; Man. Dir, IPC, 1965–70. Chairman: Nat. Newspaper Steering Gp, 1970–72; Newspaper Publishers Assoc. Ltd, 1990–97 (Vice-Chm., 1968–69); Dir, 1971–73); European Publishers Council, 1991–; Reuters Founders Share Co., 1998–99. Adviser on Corporate Affairs, The Plessey Co. Ltd, 1973–81. Mem., British Exec. Cttee, Internat. Press Inst., 1988– (Chm., 1978–88). Mem. Council and Chm., Exec. Cttee, Industrial Soc., 1976–79; Chm. Council, Industry and Parliament Trust, 1979–81; Mem. Council, Advertising Standards Authority, 1985–90. *Recreations:* motoring, golf. *Address:* Greensleeves, Loudwater Drive, Rickmansworth, Herts WD3 4HJ.   *Died 19 July 2005.*

ROGERS, His Honour John Willis; QC 1975; a Circuit Judge, 1991–99; a Deputy Circuit Judge, 1999–2001; *b* 7 Nov. 1929; *s* of late Reginald John Rogers and Joan Daisy Alexandra Rogers (*née* Willis); *m* 1952, Sheila Elizabeth Cann; one *s* one *d. Educ:* Sevenoaks Sch.; Fitzwilliam House, Cambridge (MA). Called to Bar, Lincoln's Inn, 1955 (Cholmeley Schol.); Bencher, 1984. 1st Prosecuting Counsel to Inland Revenue, SE Circuit, 1969–75; a Recorder, 1974–91. Hon. Recorder, City of Canterbury, 1985–2000. Chm., Adv. Cttee on Conscientious Objectors, 1991–99. Hon. Freeman, City of Canterbury, 2001. *Recreations:* cricket, gardening, change ringing, flying. *Address:* c/o 3 Serjeants' Inn, Temple, EC4Y 1BQ. *Clubs:* Garrick, MCC, Band of Brothers.

Died 12 May 2004.

ROGERS, Maurice Arthur Thorold; Secretary, Royal Institution, 1968–73; Joint Head, Head Office Research and Development Department, ICI, 1962–72; *b* 8 June 1911; *s* of A. G. L. Rogers; *g s* of Prof. J. E. Thorold Rogers; *m* 1947, Margaret Joan (*née* Craven) one *s* two *d. Educ:* Dragon Sch.; Westminster Sch.; University Coll., London. 1st Class hons BSc (Chem.) UCL 1932, PhD (Chem.) 1934. Chemist, ICI Dyestuffs Div., 1934–45; Head of Academic Relations Dept, 1946–58; Head of Head Office Research Dept, ICI, 1958–62. *Publications:* numerous papers in: Jl of Chem. Soc.; Nature; etc. *Recreations:* climbing, gardening, china restoration, conservation of countryside. *Address:* The Skippet, Mount Skippet, Ramsden, Oxon OX7 3AP. *T:* (01993) 868253; *e-mail:* Rogersmat@btopenworld.com.

Died 15 Jan. 2004.

ROGERS, Rev. Percival Hallewell, MBE 1945; Headmaster, Portora Royal School, Enniskillen, 1954–73; *b* 13 Sept. 1912; *s* of Percy Charles Rogers; *m* 1940, Annie Mary Stuart, 2nd *d* of Lt-Col James Morwood; two *s* one *d. Educ:* Brentwood School; St Edmund Hall, Oxford (BA Class II, Hons English, 1935; Diploma in Education, 1936; MA 1946). Two terms of teaching, Westminster School; Master in charge of English, Haileybury, 1936; served War, 1940–45 (despatches twice, MBE): RA, Major; DAAQMG; Bishops' College, Cheshunt, 1946; ordained deacon 1946, priest 1947; Asst Chaplain and English Master, Haileybury, 1947; Chaplain and English Master, 1949; student, Internat. Acad. for Continuous Educn, Sherborne, 1973–74; Chaplain, Gresham's Sch., Holt, 1974–75; Dean, Internat. Acad. for Continuous Educn, 1975–76; Asst Priest, Trinity Episcopal Church, New Orleans, 1976–80; Dir of Ordinands, Warden of Lay Readers, Dio. of Clogher, 1982–84; Priest-in-Charge, Sandford-on-Thames, 1985–86. Life Mem., Oxford Union, 1935. *Publications:* (ed and contrib.) A Guide to Divinity Teaching (SPCK), 1962; The Needs of the Whole Man, Systematics, 1971. *Address:* Ridgemede House, Rareridge Lane, Bishop's Waltham, Southampton SO3 1DX. *T:* (01489) 896224, ext. 206. *Club:* East India, Devonshire, Sports and Public Schools.

Died 24 April 2001.

ROGERS, William Pierce; Partner, law firm of Clifford Chance Rogers & Wells (formerly Rogers & Wells), since 1973 (of Royall, Koegel, Rogers and Wells, 1961–69); *b* 23 June 1913; *s* of Harrison A. and Myra Beswick Rogers; *m* 1937, Adele Langston; three *s* one *d. Educ:* Canton High School, Canton, New York; Colgate University; Cornell Law School. Law firm of Cadwalader, Wickersham and Taft, NY City, 1937; an Asst District Attorney in NY County, 1938; US Navy, 1942–46; Dist Attorney's Office in New York, 1946; Chief Counsel, Senate Investigating Cttee, 1947; Counsel, Senate Permanent Investigating Cttee, 1949; law firm of Dwight, Royall, Harris, Koegel and Caskey, offices in New York and Washington, 1950; Dep. Attorney-General, 1953; Attorney-General of the US, 1957–61; Secretary of State, USA, 1969–73. US Representative: to 20th Session of UN General Assembly, 1965; on UN Ad Hoc Cttee on SW Africa, 1967; Mem., President's Commn on Law Enforcement and Administration of Justice, 1965–67. Several hon. degrees in Law, from Univs and Colls in the USA, 1956–60. Mem. Bar Assocs in the USA. *Recreations:* golf, tennis, swimming. *Address:* Clifford Chance Rogers & Wells, 10th Floor, 607

14th Street NW, Washington, DC 20005, USA. *Clubs:* Metropolitan (Washington); Burning Tree (Bethesda); Racquet and Tennis, The Sky (NYC); Chevy Chase (Chevy Chase). *Died 2 Jan. 2001.*

ROLF, Percy Henry; a Recorder of the Crown Court, 1978–87; Consultant, Robinson Jarvis & Rolf, Solicitors, Isle of Wight, since 1986 (Partner 1948; Senior Partner, 1964); *b* 25 Dec. 1915; *s* of Percy Algernon Rolf and Lydia Kate (*née* Arnold); *m* 1939, Cecilia Florence Cooper; one *s* one *d*. *Educ:* Sandown Grammar Sch.; London Univ. (LLB). Solicitor. Served War, RAF, 1940–46: Wing Comdr; Sen. Air Traffic Control Officer, Transport Comd, 1945–46. Member: Eastbourne Br., Hour of Revival Assoc., 1959–92 (Chm., 1987–90); Holly Soc. of America Inc., 1986–. *Publications:* The Budding of the Fig Tree, 1992; The Seed of Abraham, 1993. *Recreations:* golf, gardening. *Address:* Ashlake Water, Fishbourne, Isle of Wight PO33 4EY. *T:* (01983) 882513. *Club:* Shanklin–Sandown Golf (Hon. Pres., 1990–94).
Died 5 July 2001.

ROLFE, Hume B.; *see* Boggis-Rolfe.

ROLL OF IPSDEN, Baron *cr* 1977 (Life Peer), of Ipsden in the County of Oxfordshire; **Eric Roll,** KCMG 1962 (CMG 1949); CB 1956; Director of the Bank of England, 1968–77; Joint Chairman, S. G. Warburg & Co. Ltd, 1983–87 (Chairman, 1974–83; Deputy Chairman, 1967–74); President, S. G. Warburg Group Plc, 1987–95; Senior Adviser, UBS Ltd (formerly SBC Warburg, then Warburg Dillon Read, then UBS Warburg), since 1995; *b* 1 Dec. 1907; *yr s* of Mathias and Fany Roll; *m* 1934, Winifred (*d* 1998), *o d* of Elliott and Sophia Taylor; two *d*. *Educ:* on the Continent; Univ. of Birmingham (BCom 1928; PhD 1930; Gladstone Memorial Prize, 1928; Univ. Research Scholarship, 1929). Prof. of Economics and Commerce, Univ. Coll. of Hull, 1935–46 (leave of absence 1939–46). Special Rockefeller Foundation Fellow, USA, 1939–41. Member, later Dep. Head, British Food Mission to N America, 1941–46; UK Dep. Member and UK Exec. Officer, Combined Food Board, Washington, until 1946; Asst Sec., Ministry of Food, 1946–47; Under-Secretary, HM Treasury (Central Economic Planning Staff), 1948; Minister, UK Delegation to OEEC, 1949. Deputy Head, United Kingdom Delegation to North Atlantic Treaty Organization, Paris, 1952; Under Secretary Ministry of Agriculture, Fisheries and Food, 1953–57; Executive Dir, International Sugar Council, 1957–59; Chm., United Nations Sugar Conf., 1958; Deputy Secretary, Ministry of Agriculture, Fisheries and Food, 1959–61; Deputy Leader, UK Delegation for negotiations with the European Economic Community, 1961–63; Economic Minister and Head of UK Treasury Delegation, Washington, 1963–64, also Exec. Dir for the UK International Monetary Fund and International Bank for Reconstruction and Development; Permanent Under-Sec. of State, Dept of Economic Affairs, 1964–66. Independent Mem., NEDC, 1971–80. Chm., Bilderberg Meetings, 1986–89. Director: Times Newspapers Ltd, 1967–80; Times Newspapers Holdings Ltd, 1980–83; also other Directorships; President: Mercury Securities Ltd, 1985–87 (Chm., 1974–84); Mercury Internat. Gp, 1985–87. Chancellor, Univ. of Southampton, 1974–84. Hon. DSc Hull, 1967; Hon. DSocSci Birmingham, 1967; Hon. LLD Southampton, 1974. Grosses Goldene Ehrenzeichen mit Stern (Austria), 1979; Comdr 1st Cl., Order of the Dannebrog (Denmark), 1981; Officier, Légion d'Honneur, 1984; Grand Cordon, Order of the Sacred Treasure (Japan), 1993; Grand Cross, Order of Merit (Italy), 2000. *Publications:* An Early Experiment in Industrial Organization, 1930; Spotlight on Germany, 1933; About Money, 1934; Elements of Economic Theory, 1935; Organized Labour (collaborated), 1938; The British Commonwealth at War (collaborated), 1943; A History of Economic Thought, 1954, 5th edn 1992; The Combined Food Board, 1957; The World After Keynes, 1968; The Uses and Abuses of Economics, 1978;

(ed) The Mixed Economy, 1982; Crowded Hours (autobiog.), 1985; Where Did We Go Wrong?, 1995; Where Are We Going?, 2000; articles in Economic Jl, Economica, American Economic Review, etc. *Recreations:* reading, music. *Address:* D2 Albany, Piccadilly, W1J 0AP. *Club:* Brooks's. *Died 30 March 2005.*

ROMER, Mark Lemon Robert; a Metropolitan Stipendiary Magistrate, 1972–96; *b* 12 July 1927; *s* of late Rt Hon. Sir Charles Romer, OBE, PC, and 2nd wife, Hon. Lady (Frances) Romer; *m* 1st, 1953, Philippa Maynard Tomson (marr. diss. 1991); one *s* two *d*; 2nd, 1991, Mary Eileen Hunt (*née* Hernaman). *Educ:* Bryanston; Trinity Hall, Cambridge (MA, LLM). Called to Bar, Lincoln's Inn, 1952; practised privately until 1958 when joined Govt Legal Service. *Recreations:* bird-watching, reading, music. *Address:* Gillings Hill, Arkesden Road, Clavering, Essex CB11 4QU. *T:* (01799) 550792.
Died 22 July 2001.

ROMNEY, 7th Earl of, *cr* 1801; **Michael Henry Marsham;** Bt 1663; Baron of Romney, 1716; Viscount Marsham, 1801; *b* 22 Nov. 1910; *s* of Lt-Col the Hon. Reginald Hastings Marsham, OBE (*d* 1922) (2nd *s* of 4th Earl) and Dora Hermione (*d* 1923), *d* of late Charles North; *S* cousin, 1975; *m* 1939, Frances Aileen (*d* 1995), *o d* of late Lt-Col James Russell Landale, IA. *Educ:* Sherborne. Served War of 1939–45, Major RA. Pres., Marine Soc., 1990–. *Heir: cousin* Julian Charles Marsham [*b* 28 March 1948; *m* 1975, Catriona Ann, *d* of Lt-Col Sir Robert Christie Stewart, KCVO, CBE, TD; two *s* one *d*]. *Address:* Wensum Farm, West Rudham, King's Lynn, Norfolk PE31 8SZ. *T:* (01485) 528249.
Died 5 June 2004.

ROONEY, Maureen Gowran, CBE 2003 (OBE 1996); National Women's Officer, Amalgamated Engineering & Electrical Union, since 1990; Co-Chair, Women's National Commission, 1993–95; *b* Blantyre, Lanarks, 27 April 1947; *d* of James Cunningham and Mary Conroy Cunningham; *m* 1966, Philip Rooney; one *s* three *d*. *Educ:* Elmwood Convent, Bothwell. Hairdresser, 1963–66; machine operator, Hoover plc, 1974–90. Mem., Gen. Council, 1990–, Exec. Council, 1999–, TUC; Mem., Labour Party NEC's Women's Cttee, 1989–. Vice-Pres., Nat. Childminders' Assoc., 1994–96; Bd of Mgt, Adult Literacy and Basic Skills Unit, 1992–95. *Recreations:* music, reading, cinema, theatre, knitting, walking. *Address:* 84 Goodhart Way, West Wickham, Bromley, Kent BR4 0EY. *Club:* Blantyre Miners Welfare.
Died 2 May 2003.

ROPER, Patrick Dacre T.; *see* Trevor-Roper.

ROPNER, Sir Robert Douglas, 4th Bt *cr* 1904; *b* 1 Dec. 1921; *o s* of Sir (E. H. O.) Robert Ropner, 3rd Bt; *S* father, 1962; *m* 1943, Patricia Kathleen, *d* of W. E. Scofield, W Malling, Kent; one *s* one *d*. *Educ:* Harrow. Formerly Captain, RA. *Heir: s* Robert Clinton Ropner, FCA [*b* 6 Feb. 1949; *m* 1978, Diana Felicia Abbott; one *s* one *d* (twins)]. *Address:* Rose Cottage, Swaffham Prior, Cambridge CB5 0LD. *Died 12 Jan. 2004.*

ROSE, Barry, MBE 1981; editor and publisher; Chairman, Barry Rose Law Publishers Ltd, since 1970; *b* 17 July 1923; *s* of late William George Rose and Beatrice Mary (*née* Castle); *m* 1963, Dorothy Jean Colthrup, *d* of Lt-Col W.R. Bowden; one *d*. Chm., own group of companies, 1970–97. Editor: Justice of the Peace and Local Government Review, 1944–72; Justice of the Peace, 1972–74; Local Government Review, 1972–76; law and local govt oriented periodicals. Member: Chichester RDC, 1951–61; West Sussex CC, 1952–73 (Leader, Cons. Group, 1967–72; Alderman, 1972); Pagham Parish Council, 1952–62; Bognor Regis UDC, 1964–68; Hon. Editor, Rural District Review, 1959–63; Mem., RDCA, 1960–63, CCA 1968–72; Chm., SE Area Cons. Local Govt Adv. Cttee, 1969–73; Pres., Assoc. of Councillors, 1975–86 (Treasurer, 1960–69; Chm., Exec. Cttee,

1969–75); posts in Cons. Party, 1945–74, incl. Constituency Chm., Chichester, 1961–69; Pres., Chichester Div., Young Conservatives, 1959–69. Contested (Alternative C) Old Bexley and Sidcup, 1992. Publisher, Centre for Policy Studies, 1974–76. Sometime publisher: Parly All-Party Penal Affairs Gp; Magistrates' Assoc.; NACRO; Council for Science and Society. Liveryman, Stationers' Co., 1974. FRSA 1960; FRSocMed 1998. Hon. Life Mem., Justices' Clerks' Soc., 1985. *Publications:* Change of Fortune (play), 1950; Funny Business (play), 1951; England Looks at Maud, 1970; A Councillor's Work, 1971; History of the Poll Tax, 1993; (as Peter Barton) Encounter by Moonlight (novel), 2001; Anecdotage, 2002. *Recreations:* entertaining and being entertained. *Address:* Courtney Lodge, Sylvan Way, Bognor Regis, West Sussex PO21 2RS. *T:* (01243) 829902. *Clubs:* Athenæum, Garrick, MCC, Oxford and Cambridge. *Died 19 July 2005.*

ROSEHILL, Lord; Alexander Robert MacRae Carnegie; *b* 16 Nov. 1980; *s* and *heir* of 14th Earl of Northesk. *Died 31 Aug. 2001.*

ROSENTHAL, Jack Morris, CBE 1994; writer; *b* 8 Sept. 1931; *s* of Samuel and Leah Rosenthal; *m* 1973, Maureen Lipman, CBE; one *s* one *d*. *Educ:* Colne Grammar School; Sheffield Univ. (BA Eng. Lit. and Lang). *Television:* writer of over 250 productions, incl. That Was the Week That Was, 1963; 129 episodes of Coronation Street, 1961–69; The Evacuees, 1975; Bar Mitzvah Boy, 1976; Ready When You Are, Mr McGill, 1976; Spend Spend Spend, 1977; The Knowledge, 1979; P'tang Yang Kipperbang, 1982; Mrs Capper's Birthday, 1985; London's Burning, 1986; Fools on the Hill, 1986; Day to Remember, 1986; And a Nightingale Sang, 1989; Bag Lady, 1989; Sleeping Sickness, 1991; 'Bye, 'Bye, Baby, 1992; Wide-Eyed and Legless, 1993; Moving Story, 1994; Eskimo Day, 1996; Cold Enough for Snow, 1997; Lucky Jim (adaptation), 2003; *stage:* five plays, incl. Smash!, 1981; *films:* seven feature films including: Lucky Star, 1980; Yentl, 1983 (co-written with Barbra Streisand); The Chain, 1985; Captain Jack, 1999. Hon. MA Salford, 1994; Hon. LittD: Manchester, 1995; Sheffield, 1998. BAFTA Writer's Award, 1976; RTS Writer's Award, 1976; RTS Hall of Fame, 1993. *Publications:* (contrib.) The Television Dramatist, 1973; (anthology) First Love, 1984; numerous TV plays. *Recreations:* work, frying fish, polishing almost anything tarnished, playing the violin in enforced privacy, checking Manchester United's score, minute by minute, on teletext. *Address:* c/o Casarotto Ramsay Ltd, National House, 60–66 Wardour Street, W1V 3HP. *T:* (020) 7287 4450. *Club:* Dramatists'. *Died 29 May 2004.*

ROSS, Alan John, CBE 1982; author, publisher and journalist; Editor of London Magazine, since 1961; Managing Director, London Magazine Editions (Publishers), since 1965; *b* Calcutta, 6 May 1922; *o s* of John Brackenridge Ross, CBE and Clare, *d* of Captain Patrick Fitzpatrick, Indian Army; *m* 1949, Jennifer (marr. diss. 1985), *d* of Sir Geoffrey Fry, 1st and last Bt, KCB, CVO; one *s*; *m* 2000, Jane Rye. *Educ:* Haileybury; St John's College, Oxford (Hon. Fellow). RN, 1942–47: general service, Arctic and North Seas, 1942–44; Asst Staff Officer, Intelligence, 16th Destroyer Flotilla, 1944; on staff of Flag Officer, Western Germany, 1945, and Interpreter to British Naval Commander-in-Chief, Germany, 1946; British Council, 1947–50; on staff of The Observer 1950–71. Toured Australia as correspondent, with MCC, 1954–55, 1962–63; toured South Africa, 1956–57, 1964–65; toured West Indies, 1960, 1968. Atlantic Award for Literature (Rockefeller Foundation), 1946. FRSL 1971. *Publications:* The Derelict Day, 1947; Time Was Away, 1948, repr. 1989; The Forties, 1950; The Gulf of Pleasure, 1951; The Bandit on the Billiard Table, 1954 (revised edition South to Sardinia, 1960), repr. 1989; Something of the Sea, 1954; Australia 55, 1956, repr. 1985; (ed) Abroad, 1957; Cape Summer and the Australians in England, 1957, repr. 1986; To Whom It

May Concern, 1958; The Onion Man, 1959; Through the Caribbean, 1960; (ed) The Cricketer's Companion, 1960; Danger on Glass Island, 1960; African Negatives, 1962; Australia 63, 1963; West Indies at Lord's, 1963, 2nd edn 1986; (ed) London Magazine Stories Nos 1–11, 1964–80; North from Sicily, 1965; Poems 1942–67, 1968; Tropical Ice, 1972; The Taj Express, 1973; (ed) Living in London, 1974; Open Sea, 1975; (ed) Selected Poems of Lawrence Durrell, 1977; Death Valley and Other Poems, 1980; (ed) The Turf, 1982; Colours of War, 1983; Ranji, 1983; (ed) Living out of London, 1984; Blindfold Games (autobiog.), 1986; (ed) London Magazine 1961–85, 1986; The Emissary, 1986; Coastwise Lights (autobiog.), 1988; After Pusan, 1995; Winter Sea, 1998; Green Fading into Blue, 1999; Reflections on Blue Water, 2000; several trans and introductions; contrib. to various jls in England and America. *Recreations:* travel, sport (played cricket and squash for Oxford University and Royal Navy), racing. *Address:* 4 Elm Park Lane, SW3 6DB. *Clubs:* MCC; Vincent's (Oxford). *Died 14 Feb. 2001.*

ROSS, Sir (James) Keith, 2nd Bt *cr* 1960; RD 1967; FRCS; FRCSE; Consultant Emeritus, Southampton and Southwest Hampshire Health Authority, 1990; *b* 9 May 1927; *s* of Sir James Paterson Ross, 1st Bt, KCVO, FRCS, and Marjorie Burton Townsend (*d* 1978); *S* father, 1980; *m* 1956, Jacqueline Annella Clarke; one *s* three *d*. *Educ:* St Paul's School; Middlesex Hosp. MB BS 1950; MS 1965. FRCS 1956; FRCSE 1989. House Surgeon, Registrar, Sen. Registrar, Middlesex Hosp., 1950–67. Surgn Lieut, RNVR, 1952–54; Surg. Lt Comdr, RNR, retd 1972. Heller Fellowship, San Francisco, 1959; Registrar, Brompton Hosp., 1958, 1960; Consultant Thoracic Surgeon, Harefield and Central Middx Hosps, 1964–67; Consultant Surgeon, Nat. Heart Hosp., 1967–72; Consultant Cardiac Surgeon: Wessex Region, 1972–90; King Edward VII Hosp., Midhurst, 1978–92. Hunterian Prof., 1961, Mem. Council, 1986–94, RCS; Pres., Soc. of Cardiothoracic Surgeons, 1988. Hallet Prize, RCS, 1952; Bruce Medal, RCSE, 1989. *Publications:* on cardiac surgery in appropriate medical jls. *Recreations:* fly fishing, golf, painting. *Heir: s* Andrew Charles Paterson Ross, *b* 18 June 1966. *Address:* Moonhills Gate, Exbury Road, Beaulieu, Hants SO42 7YS. *T:* (01590) 612104. *Clubs:* Arts, MCC; Royal Southampton Yacht. *Died 18 Feb. 2003.*

ROSS, Robert, MA, FLS; Keeper of Botany, British Museum (Natural History), 1966–77; *b* 14 Aug. 1912; *e s* of Robert Ross, Pinner, Middx; *m* 1939, Margaret Helen Steadman; one *s* three *d*. *Educ:* St Paul's Sch.; St John's Coll., Cambridge. Asst Keeper, British Museum (Natural History), 1936; Principal Scientific Officer, 1950; Deputy Keeper, 1962. Royal Microscopical Society: Hon. Librarian, 1947–51; Hon. Editor, 1953–71; Vice-Pres., 1959–60. Administrator of Finances, Internat. Assoc. of Plant Taxonomy, 1964–69; Sec., Gen. Cttee for Plant Nomenclature, 1964–69, Chm., 1969–81. President: British Phycological Soc., 1969–71; Quekett Microscopical Club, 1974–76; Pres., Internat. Soc. for Diatom Res., 1994–96 (Vice-Pres., 1992–94). *Publications:* various papers in scientific jls on botanical subjects. *Recreations:* morris dancing (Bagman, Morris Ring, 1946–50), country dancing, gardening. *Address:* The Garden House, Evesbatch, Bishop's Frome, Worcester WR6 5BD. *T:* (01531) 640366. *Died 24 May 2005.*

ROSSER, Sir Melvyn (Wynne), Kt 1974; DL; FCA; Partner, Deloitte, Haskins & Sells, 1961–85; Chairman, HTV Group, 1986–91; *b* 11 Nov. 1926; *s* of late David John and of Anita Rosser; *m* 1957, Margaret; one *s* two *d*. *Educ:* Glanmor Sch., Swansea; Bishop Gore Grammar Sch., Swansea. Chartered Accountant, qual. 1949; joined staff Deloitte Plender Griffiths & Co. (later Deloitte, Haskins & Sells), Swansea, 1950; practised in Swansea, 1961–68, in Cardiff, 1968–80, in London, 1980–85, retired. Director: Develt Corp. for Wales, 1965–80; Land Commn, 1965–68; Nat. Bus Co., 1969–72; Wales and Marches Telecom. Bd, 1970–80; Welsh Regional

Council, CBI, 1970–80; (non-exec.) BSC, 1972–80; (non-exec.) NCB, later British Coal, 1983–89; W Midlands and Wales Regl Bd, Nat. Westminster Bank, 1986–89. Chm., Manpower Services Cttee, Wales, 1976–88; Member: Welsh Econ. Council, 1965–68; Welsh Council, 1968–80 (Chm., 1971–80); Royal Commn on Standards of Conduct in Public Life, 1974; Prime Minister's Adv. Cttee on Outside Business Appts, 1976–83; Nat. Trng Task Force, 1989–91 (Chm., Trng Enterprise and Educn Adv. Gp for Wales, 1989–92). Pres., UCW, Aberystwyth, 1986–98 (Vice-Pres., 1977–86); Mem. Court, Univ. of Wales, 1987–98. Mem. Gorsedd of Bards, Royal Nat. Eisteddfod of Wales. DL West Glamorgan, 1986. Hon. Fellow: Univ. of Glamorgan, 1988; Trinity Coll., Carmarthen, 1997; Univ. of Wales, Aberystwyth, 1998. Hon. LLD Wales, 1987. *Recreations:* music, gardening. *Address:* Corlan, 53 Birchgrove Road, Swansea SA7 9JR. *T:* (01792) 812286. *Club:* Cardiff and County (Cardiff). *Died 4 Feb. 2001.*

ROSTOW, Prof. Eugene Victor; Sterling Professor of Law, Yale University, 1964–84, then Emeritus; *b* 25 Aug. 1913; *s* of Victor A. and Lillian H. Rostow; *m* 1933, Edna B. Greenberg; two *s* one *d*. *Educ:* Yale Coll.; King's Coll., Cambridge (LLD 1962); Yale Law Sch. Practised law, New York, 1937–38; Yale Law Faculty, 1938–: Prof. of Law, 1944–84; Dean of Law Sch., 1955–65. Dist. Vis. Res. Prof. of Law and Diplomacy, Nat. Defense Univ., Washington, 1984–90, 1992–. Assistant: to Asst Sec. of State Acheson, 1942–44; to Exec. Sec., Econ. Commn for Europe, UN, Geneva, 1949–50; Under-Sec. of State for Political Affairs, 1966–69. Dir, Arms Control and Disarmament Agency, 1981–83. Pres., Atlantic Treaty Assoc., 1973–76. Pitt Prof., Cambridge, 1959–60; Eastman Prof., Oxford, 1970–71; Dist. Fellow, US Inst. of Peace, 1990–92. Dir, American Jewish Cttee, 1972–74; Chm. Exec. Cttee, Cttee on the Present Danger (Washington), 1976–81, 1987–92. Hon. LLD Boston, 1976. Dist. Civilian Service Medal, US Army, 1990. Chevalier, Legion of Honour (France), 1960; Grand Cross, Order of the Crown (Belgium), 1969. *Publications:* A National Policy for the Oil Industry, 1948; Planning for Freedom, 1959; The Sovereign Prerogative, 1962; Law, Power and the Pursuit of Peace, 1968; (ed) Is Law Dead?, 1971; Peace in the Balance, 1972; The Ideal in Law, 1978; Toward Managed Peace, 1993; A Breakfast for Bonaparte, 1994; contribs to legal and economic jls. *Address:* Peru, Vermont 05152, USA. *T:* (802) 8246627; 1315 4th Street SW, Washington, DC 20024, USA. *Clubs:* Century (New York); Elizabethan (New Haven); Cosmos (Washington). *Died 25 Nov. 2002.*

ROSTOW, Walt Whitman; Professor of Political Economy, University of Texas at Austin, Texas, 1969–77, then Professor Emeritus; *b* 7 Oct. 1916; 2nd *s* of Victor and Lillian Rostow; *m* 1947, Elspeth, *o d* of Milton J. and Harriet Vaughan Davies; one *s* one *d*. *Educ:* Yale (BA 1936; PhD 1940); Oxford (Rhodes Scholar). Social Science Research Council Fellow, 1939–40; Instructor, Columbia Univ., 1940–41; Office Strategic Services, 1941–45 (Army of the United States, 1943–45, Major; Legion of Merit; Hon. OBE); Asst Chief, Div. German-Austrian Economic Affairs, Dept of State, 1945–46; Harmsworth Prof. American History, Oxford, 1946–47; Special Asst to Exec. Sec., Economic Commn for Europe, 1947–49; Pitt Prof. of American History, Cambridge, 1949–50; Prof. of Economic History, MIT, 1950–61; Dep. Special Asst to the President (USA) for National Security Affairs, Jan. 1961–Dec. 1961; Counselor and Chm., Policy Planning Council, Dept of State, 1961–66; US Mem., Inter-Amer. Cttee on Alliance for Progress, 1964–66; Special Asst to the President, The White House, 1966–69. Chm. and Chief Exec. Officer, Austin Project, 1992–2000. Member: Royal Economic Soc., England; Amer. Acad. of Arts and Scis, 1957; Amer. Philos. Soc.; Massachusetts Historical Soc. Hon. LLD: Carnegie Inst. of Tech., Pittsburgh, 1962; Miami, 1965; Notre Dame, 1966; Middlebury Coll., 1967; Jacksonville, 1974. Presidential

Medal of Freedom, with distinction, 1969. *Publications:* The American Diplomatic Revolution, 1947; Essays on the British Economy of the Nineteenth Century, 1948; The Process of Economic Growth, 1952; (with A. D. Gayer and A. J. Schwartz) The Growth and Fluctuation of the British Economy, 1790–1850, 1953, new edn 1975; (with A. Levin and others) The Dynamics of Soviet Society, 1953; (with others) The Prospects for Communist China, 1954; (with R. W. Hatch) An American Policy in Asia, 1955; (with M. F. Millikan) A Proposal: key to an effective foreign policy, 1957; The Stages of Economic Growth, 1960, 3rd edn 1990; The United States in the World Arena, 1960; (ed) The Economics of Take-off into Sustained Growth, 1963; View from the Seventh Floor, 1964; A Design for Asian Development, 1965; Politics and the Stages of Growth, 1971; The Diffusion of Power, 1972; How It All Began: origins of the modern economy, 1975; The World Economy: history and prospect, 1978; Getting from Here to There, 1978; Why the Poor Get Richer and the Rich Slow Down, 1980; Pre-Invasion Bombing Strategy: General Eisenhower's decision of March 25th 1944, 1981; The Division of Europe after World War II: 1946, 1981; British Trade Fluctuations 1868–1896: a chronicle and a commentary, 1981; Europe after Stalin: Eisenhower's three decisions of March 11th 1953, 1982; Open Skies: Eisenhower's proposal of July 21st 1955, 1982; The Barbaric Counter-Revolution, 1983; Eisenhower, Kennedy and Foreign Aid, 1985; The United States and the Regional Organization of Asia and the Pacific 1965–85, 1985; Rich Countries and Poor Countries: reflections from the past, lessons for the future, 1987; Essays on a Half Century: ideas, policies and action, 1988; History, Policy and Theory: essays in interaction, 1989; Theorists of Economic Growth from David Hume to the Present, with a Perspective on the Next Century, 1990; The Great Population Spike and After: reflections on the 21st century, 1998; various articles contributed to: The Economist, Economic Jl, Economic History Review, Jl of Econ. History, American Econ. Review, etc. *Address:* 1 Wild Wind Point, Austin, TX 78746, USA. *Clubs:* Elizabethan (New Haven, Conn, USA); Cosmos (Washington, DC). *Died 13 Feb. 2003.*

ROTBLAT, Sir Joseph, KCMG 1998; CBE 1965; PhD, DSc; FRS 1995; FInstP; Professor of Physics in the University of London, at St Bartholomew's Hospital Medical College, 1950–76, then Emeritus; Physicist to St Bartholomew's Hospital, 1950–76; President, Pugwash Conferences on Science and World Affairs 1988–97, then Emeritus; *b* 4 Nov. 1908; *e s* of late Z. Rotblat, Warsaw. *Educ:* University of Warsaw, Poland (MA, DSc); PhD Liverpool; DSc London. Research Fellow of Radiological Laboratory of Scientific Society of Warsaw, 1933–39; Asst Director of Atomic Physics Institute of Free Univ. of Poland, 1937–39; Oliver Lodge Fellow of Univ. of Liverpool, 1939–40; work on atomic energy at Liverpool Univ. and Los Alamos, New Mexico, 1939–44; Lecturer and afterwards Senior Lecturer in Dept of Physics, Liverpool Univ., 1940–49; Director of Research in nuclear physics at Liverpool Univ., 1945–49. Treasurer, St Bartholomew's Hosp. Med. Coll., 1974–76; Vice-Dean, Faculty of Sci., London Univ., 1974–76. Member: Adv. Cttee on Med. Res., WHO, 1972–75; WHO Management Gp, 1984–90; Canberra Commn, 1995–96. Ed., Physics in Medicine and Biol., 1960–72. Sec.-Gen., Pugwash Confs on Science and World Affairs, 1957–73; Chm., British Pugwash, 1978–88. President: Hosp. Physicists' Assoc, 1969–70; British Inst. of Radiology, 1971–72 (Hon. Mem., 1990); Internat. Youth Sci. Forum, 1972–74. Mem. Governing Body of Stockholm Internat. Peace Res. Inst., 1966–71; Gov., St Bartholomew's Hosp., 1977–. Vis. Prof. of Internat. Relations, Univ. of Edinburgh, 1975–76; Bertrand Russell Peace Lects, McMaster Univ., 1998; Dag Hammarskjöld Lectr, Uppsala Univ., 2001; Roscoe, Liverpool John Moores Univ., 2002. Member, Polish Academy of Sciences, 1966; Hon. Foreign Member: Amer. Acad. of Arts and Sciences, 1972; Ukraine Acad. of Scis, 1994; For. Mem., Czechoslovak

Acad. of Scis, 1988. Hon. Freeman, London Bor. of Camden, 1996; Hon. Citizen, Seoul, 2001. Hon. FRSE 1998; Hon. FRCR 1998; Hon. FMedSci 2000; Hon. FInstP 2001. Hon. Fellow: UMIST, 1985; QMW, 1996; Liverpool John Moores Univ., 2002. Hon. DSc: Bradford, 1973; Liverpool, 1989; City, 1996; Slovak Acad. of Sciences, 1996; Acadia, 1998; Richmond, 1998; (Medicine) London, 2001; New Brunswick, 2001; Dr hc Moscow, 1988. Bertrand Russell Soc. Award, 1983; Gold Medal, Czechoslovak Acad. of Sciences, 1988; Albert Einstein Peace Prize, 1992; Nobel Peace Prize, 1995; Copernicus Medal, Polish Acad. of Sciences, 1996; Jamnalal Bajaj Peace Award, Jamnalal Bajaj Foundn, Bombay, 1999; Toda Peace Prize, Toda Inst., Hawaii, 2000; Linus Pauling Award, Linus Pauling Foundn, 2002. Commander, Order of Merit (Polish People's Republic), 1987; Order of Cyril and Methodius (1st Cl.) (Bulgaria), 1988; Kt Commander's Cross, OM (Germany), 1989; Kt Comdr's Cross and Star, Order of Polonia Restituta (Poland), 1998. *Publications:* Progress in Nuclear Physics, 1950; (with Chadwick) Radio-activity and Radioactive Substances, 1953; Atomic Energy, a Survey, 1954; Atoms and the Universe, 1956; Science and World Affairs, 1962; Aspects of Medical Physics, 1966; Pugwash, the First Ten Years, 1967; Scientists in the Quest for Peace, 1972; Nuclear Reactors: to breed or not to breed, 1977; Nuclear Energy and Nuclear Weapon Proliferation, 1979; Nuclear Radiation in Warfare, 1981; Scientists, The Arms Race and Disarmament, 1982; The Arms Race at a Time of Decision, 1984; Nuclear Strategy and World Security, 1985; World Peace and the Developing Countries, 1986; Strategic Defence and the Future of the Arms Race, 1987; Coexistence, Co-operation and Common Security, 1988; Verification of Arms Reductions, 1989; Nuclear Proliferation: technical and economic aspects, 1990; Global Problems and Common Security, 1990; Towards a Secure World in the 21st Century, 1991; Striving for Peace, Security and Development in the World, 1992; A Nuclear-Weapon-Free World: Desirable? Feasible?, 1993; A World at the Crossroads: new conflicts, new solutions, 1994; Towards a War-free World, 1995; World Citizenship: allegiance to humanity, 1996; Nuclear Weapons: the road to zero, 1998; Eliminating the Causes of War, 2001; (with Robert Hinde) War No More, 2003; papers on nuclear physics and radiation biology in Proceedings of Royal Society, Radiation Research, Nature, etc. *Recreations:* recorded music, travel. *Address:* 8 Asmara Road, West Hampstead, NW2 3ST. *T:* (020) 7435 1471. *Club:* Athenæum. *Died 31 Aug. 2005.*

ROTHERHAM, Leonard, CBE 1970; DSc; FRS 1963; FREng, FIEE, SFInstE, FIM, FInstP; Hon. Professor, Bath University, since 1985 (Vice-Chancellor, 1969–76); *b* 31 Aug. 1913; *s* of Bernard Rotherham; *m* 1937, Nora Mary Thompson (*d* 1991); one *s* two *d*. *Educ:* Strutt School, Belper; University College London (Fellow, 1959). Physicist, Brown Firth Research Laboratories, 1935–46; Head of Metallurgy Dept, RAE Farnborough, 1946–50; Dir, R&D, UKAEA, Industrial Group, Risley, 1950–58; Mem. for Research, Central Electricity Generating Bd, 1958–69; Head of Research, Electricity Supply Industry and Electricity Council, 1965–69. Chm., Adv. Cttee for Scientific and Technical Information, 1970–74. Member: Defence Scientific Adv. Council, 1967–77 (Chm., 1974–77); Central Adv. Council for Science and Technology, 1968–70; Adv. Council for Energy Conservation, 1974–79; Adv. Council for Applied R&D, 1976–81. Governor, Imperial Coll., 1977–89. Hon. LLD Bristol, 1972; Hon. DSc Bath, 1976. FIC 1987; Hon. Fellow, Inst. of Welding, 1965; Hon. Life Mem., American Society of Mechanical Engineers, 1963. President: Instn of Metallurgists, 1964; Inst. of Metals, 1965; Member of Council, Royal Society, 1965–66. FREng (Founder Fellow, Fellowship of Engineering, 1976; Mem. Exec. Council, 1978–80). *Publications:* Creep of Metals, 1951; Research and Innovation, 1984; various scientific and technical papers; also lectures: Hatfield Memorial, 1961; Coal Science, 1961; Calvin Rice (of

Amer. Soc. of Mech. Engrs), 1963; 2nd Metallurgical Engineering, Inst. of Metals, 1963. *Address:* c/o Jane Lind, Silver Birches, Sparrows Green, Wadhurst, East Sussex, TN5 6DX. *Club:* Athenæum. *Died 23 March 2001.*

ROTHES, 21st Earl of, *cr* before 1457; **Ian Lionel Malcolm Leslie;** Lord Leslie 1445; Baron Ballenbreich 1457; *b* 10 May 1932; *o s* of 20th Earl of Rothes and Beryl (*d* 1994), *o d* of J. Lionel Dugdale; *S* father, 1975; *m* 1955, Marigold, *o d* of Sir David M. Evans Bevan, 1st Bt; two *s*. *Educ:* Eton. Sub-Lt RNVR, 1953. *Heir:* *s* Lord Leslie, *b* 4 June 1958. *Address:* Tanglewood, West Tytherley, Salisbury, Wilts SP5 1LX. *Died 15 April 2005.*

ROTHSCHILD, Hon. Dame Miriam (Louisa), (Hon. Dame Miriam Lane), DBE 2000 (CBE 1982); FRS 1985; *b* 5 Aug. 1908; *e d* of Hon. N. C. Rothschild, 2nd *s* of 1st Baron Rothschild and Rozsika de Wertheimstein; *m* 1943, Capt. George Lane, MC (marriage dissolved, 1957); one *s* three *d* (and one *s* one *d* decd). *Educ:* home. Member: Zoological and Entomological Research Coun.; Marine Biological Assoc.; Royal Entomological Soc.; Systematics Assoc.; Soc. for Promotion of Nature Reserves, etc.; Ed., Novitates Zoologica, 1938–41; Mem., Publications Cttee, Zoological Soc.; Foreign Office, 1940–42; Trustee, British Museum of Natural History, 1967–75. Mem., Amer. Acad. of Arts and Scis. Vis. Prof. in Biology, Royal Free Hosp. Romanes Lectr, Oxford, 1985. Hon. Fellow, St Hugh's Coll., Oxford. Hon. DSc: Oxford, 1968; Gothenburg, 1983; Hull, 1984; Northwestern (Chicago), 1986; Leicester, 1987; Open Univ., 1989; Essex, 1998; Cambridge, 1999. Floral Medal, Lynn Soc., 1968; Wigglesworth Gold Medal, Royal Entomol Soc., 1982; Silver Medal, Internat. Soc. of Chemical Ecology, 1989; VMH 1991; Bloomer Award, Linnean Soc.; Mendel Award, Czech Sci. Acad., 1993. Defence Medal (1940–45). *Publications:* Catalogue Rothschild Collection of Fleas (British Museum): vol. I 1953, vol. II 1956, vol. III 1962, vol. IV 1966, vol. V 1971, vol. VI 1983; (with Theresa Clay) Fleas, Flukes and Cuckoos, 1952; (with Clive Farrell) The Butterfly Gardener, 1983; Dear Lord Rothschild (biog.), 1983; (with Prof. Schlein and Prof. Ito) Atlas of Insect Tissue, 1985; Animals & Man, 1986; Butterfly Cooing Like a Dove, 1991; The Rothschilds Gardens, 1996; Rothschild's Reserves, 1997; 300 contribs to scientific jls. *Recreations:* natural history, conservation. *Address:* Ashton Wold, Peterborough PE8 5LZ. *Clubs:* Queen's, Entomological. *Died 20 Jan. 2005.*

ROTHSTEIN, Saul; Solicitor to the Post Office, 1976–81; *b* 4 July 1920; *s* of late Simon Rothstein and late Zelda Rothstein; *m* 1949, Judith Noemi (*née* Katz); two *d*. *Educ:* Church Institute Sch., Bolton; Manchester Univ (LLB). Admitted solicitor, 1947. War service, RAF, 1941–46 (Flt-Lt). Entered Solicitor's Dept, General Post Office, 1949, Asst Solicitor, 1963; Director, Advisory Dept, Solicitor's Office, Post Office, 1972–76. *Recreations:* chamber music, walking, travel. *Address:* 9 Templars Crescent, Finchley, N3 3QR. *T:* (020) 8346 3701. *Died 9 Feb. 2005.*

ROWE, Richard Brian; District Judge (formerly Registrar) of the High Court (Family Division), 1979–98; *b* 28 April 1933; *s* of Charles Albert Rowe and Mabel Florence Rowe; *m* 1959, Shirley Ann Symons; two *d*. *Educ:* Greenford County Grammar Sch.; King's Coll., London Univ. (LLB Hons). National Service, RAF, 1952–54. High Court (Probate, Divorce and Admiralty Div.), 1954–66; Land Commn, 1966–69; Lord Chancellor's Office, 1969–75; Sec., High Court (Family Div.), 1975–79. Mem., Booth Cttee on Matrimonial Causes Procedure, 1982–85. Chm., AFA, 1995–2001 (Life Vice-Pres., 1991). *Publications:* (ed) Rayden on Divorce, 10th edn, 1967; (ed) Tristram and Coote's Probate Practice, 25th edn, 1978, to 28th edn, 1995. *Recreations:* most sports. *Address:* c/o Principal Registry of the Family Division, First Avenue House, 42–49 High Holborn, WC1V 6NP. *Died 3 March 2002.*

ROWLANDS, (John) Martin, CBE 1980; Secretary for Civil Service, Hong Kong Government, 1978–85; *b* 20 July 1925; *s* of late John Walter Rowlands and Mary Ace Maitland (*née* Roberts); *m* 1956, Christiane Germaine Madeleine Lacheny (*d* 2003); two *d. Educ:* Charterhouse; Selwyn Coll., Cambridge (MA). Military service, 1943–47 (Captain, 3rd Royal Indian Artillery Field Regt, HQ XV Indian Corps, HQ ALFSEA). HMOCS, Hong Kong Admin. Service, 1952–85: Dep. Dir of Urban Services, 1966–68; Principal Asst Colonial Sec., 1968–71; Dep. Sec. for Home Affairs, 1971–74; Dir of Immigration, 1974–78; Mem., Hong Kong Legislative Council, 1978–84. *Recreations:* railways, bird-watching. *Address:* Flat 3, 15 Collingham Road, SW5 0NU. *Clubs:* Hong Kong, Hong Kong Jockey (Hong Kong). *Died 19 Aug. 2004.*

ROWLANDS, Martin; *see* Rowlands, J. M.

ROWLANDS, Martyn Omar, PPCSD, FIMMM; Chairman, Martyn Rowlands Design Consultants Ltd, 1960–88; retired; *b* 27 July 1923; *s* of Edward and Mildred Rowlands; *m* 1st, 1951, Ann Patricia (*d* 1974); two *s* one *d*; 2nd, 1978, Mary Winifred (marr. diss. 1986). *Educ:* Eltham Coll.; Central Sch. of Art and Design. FCSD (FSIAD 1960); FIMMM (FPRI 1973). Served War, RAF, 1940–45: India and Burma. Central Sch. of Art and Design, 1946–49; Head of Indust. Design, Ekco Plastics, 1954–59; started own design consultancy, 1959. Pres., SIAD, 1975–76. Hon. Fellow, Arts Inst. at Bournemouth, 2002. *Recreation:* photography. *Died 15 Sept. 2004.*

ROWLEY, Peter, MC 1944; Vice President, Leonard Cheshire Foundation, since 1993 (Chairman, 1982–90); Chairman, Cheshire Homes European Regional Council, 1990–94; *b* 12 July 1918; *s* of late Roland and Catherine Isabel Rowley; *m* 1940, Ethnea Louis Florence Mary Howard Kyan; four *d. Educ:* Wembley County Sch.; University Coll., Oxford (MA). Served War of 1939–45: Queen's Westminster Rifles, 1938–39; 14th Bn Sherwood Foresters, 1940–46; Adjt, Middle East, N Africa; Company Comdr, Italy; Bde Major 13 Bde, 1944–45; GSOII 8 Corps, 1945–46. Admitted Solicitor, Titmuss Sainer & Webb, 1950; Sen. Partner, 1981–83, retd. Member, Law Society Land Law Cttee, 1970–87. Liveryman, Distillers Co., 1975. *Address:* Underlea, 34 Radnor Cliff, Folkestone, Kent CT20 2JL. *T:* (01303) 248689. *Club:* Royal Automobile. *Died 17 June 2002.*

ROWNTREE CLIFFORD, Rev. Paul; *see* Clifford.

ROWSELL, Edmund Lionel P.; *see* Penning-Rowsell.

ROXBURGH, Vice-Adm. Sir John (Charles Young), KCB 1972 (CB 1969); CBE 1967; DSO 1943; DSC 1942 (Bar, 1945); *b* 29 June 1919; *s* of Sir (Thomas) James (Young) Roxburgh, CIE and Mona Heymerdinguer; *m* 1942, Philippa, 3rd *d* of late Major C. M. Hewlett, MC; one *s* one *d. Educ:* RNC, Dartmouth. Naval Cadet, 1933; Midshipman, 1937; Sub-Lt 1939; Lt 1941; Lt-Comdr 1949; Comdr 1952; Capt. 1958; Rear-Adm. 1967; Vice-Adm. 1970. Served in various ships, 1937–39; joined Submarine Br., 1940; served in ops off Norway, in Bay of Biscay and Mediterranean, 1940–42; comd HM Submarines H43, United and Tapir, 1942–45 in ops in Mediterranean and off Norway; HMS Vanguard, 1948–50; comd HM Submarine Turpin, 1951–53; HMS Triumph, 1955; HMS Ark Royal, 1955–56; comd HMS Contest, 1956–58; Brit. Jt Services Mission, Wash., 1958–60; comd 3rd Submarine Sqdn and HMS Adamant, 1960–61; idc 1962; Dep. Dir of Defence Plans (Navy), MoD, 1963–65; comd HMS Eagle, 1965–67; Flag Officer: Sea Training, 1967–69; Plymouth, 1969; Submarines, and NATO Comdr Submarines, E Atlantic, 1969–72, retired 1972. Chm., Grovebell Group Ltd, 1972–75. Mem. Management Cttee, The Freedom Assoc., 1978–85. Pres., Royal Naval Benevolent Trust, 1978–84. Mem., Friends of Hong Kong Cttee, 1986–95 (Chm., 1987–95). Co. Councillor, Surrey, 1977–81. *Recreations:* golf, sailing, walking, music. *Address:* Oakdene, Wood Road, Hindhead, Surrey GU26 6PT. *T:* (01428) 605600. *Clubs:*

Army and Navy; Liphook Golf, Woking Golf. *Died 13 April 2004.*

ROY, Andrew Donald; economist; *b* 28 June 1920; *er s* of late Donald Whatley Roy, FRCS, FRCOG, and Beatrice Anne Roy (*née* Barstow); *m* 1947, Katherine Juliet Grove-White (*d* 2001); one *s* two *d. Educ:* Malvern Coll.; Sidney Sussex Coll., Cambridge (Maths Trip. Pt I 1939 and Econ. Trip. Pt II 1948, Class I hons). Served War of 1939–45: RA, in UK, India and Burma (8 Medium Regt; Adjt, 1942–44). Cambridge University: Asst Lectr, 1949–51; Lectr, 1951–64; Jun. Proctor, 1956–57; Sidney Sussex College: Fellow, 1951–64; Tutor, 1953–56; Sen. Tutor, 1956–62; Financial Bursar, 1959–61; HM Treasury: Economic Consultant, 1962; Sen. Economic Adviser, 1964; Under-Sec. (Economics), 1969–72; Under-Sec., DTI, 1972–74, MoD, 1974–76; Chief Economic Adviser, DHSS, 1976–80. Consultant, NIESR, 1981–83. Governor, Malvern Coll., 1960–. *Publications:* British Economic Statistics (with C. F. Carter), 1954; articles in economic and statistical jls. *Address:* 15 Rusholme Road, Putney, SW15 3JX. *T:* (020) 8789 3180. *Club:* Oxford and Cambridge. *Died 11 March 2003.*

ROY, Prof. Arthur Douglas, FRCS, FRCSE, FRCSGlas, FRCSI; FACS; Chief of Surgical Services, Ministry of Health, Sultanate of Oman, 1985–88, and Professor of Surgery, Sultan Qaboos University, 1986–88, retired; Professor Emeritus, Queen's University of Belfast, 1985; *b* 10 April 1925; *s* of Arthur Roy and Edith Mary (*née* Brown); *m* 1st, 1954, Monica Cecilia Mary Bowley; three *d*; 2nd, 1973, Patricia Irene McColl. *Educ:* Paisley Grammar Sch.; Univ. of Glasgow (MB, ChB, Commendation). RAMC, 1948–50; Surgical Registrar posts in Glasgow and Inverness, 1950–54; Sen. Surgical Registrar, Aylesbury and Oxford, 1954–57; Cons. Surgeon and Hon. Lectr, Western Infirmary, Glasgow, 1957–68; Foundn Prof. of Surgery, Univ. of Nairobi, 1968–72; Prof. of Surgery, QUB, 1973–85. Non-exec. Dir, Exeter Dist Community NHS Trust, 1991–. Mem. Council, RCSE, 1979–85; Pres., Devon and Exeter Med. Soc., 1994–95 (Vice-Pres., 1993–94). *Publications:* Lecture Notes in Surgery: tropical supplement, 1975; various papers on gastro-enterology, endocrine surgery, tropical medicine, etc. *Recreations:* sailing, gliding, gardening. *Address:* Garden House, Old Feniton Village, near Honiton, Devon EX14 0BE. *T:* (01404) 850055. *Club:* Devon and Somerset Gliding. *Died 21 July 2003.*

ROY, Ian; Assistant Under-Secretary of State, Home Office, 1963–72; *b* 2 Aug. 1912; *o s* of late John Roy and Annie Froude Marshall; *m* 1939, Betty Louise Blissett (*d* 1999); one *s* two *d. Educ:* Manchester Grammar School; Peterhouse, Cambridge. Assistant Inspector of Taxes, 1935; Assistant Principal, Home Office, 1936; Private Secretary to Permanent Under-Secretary of State, 1938; to Parliamentary Under-Secretary of State, 1939–40; Asst Secretary, 1947. *Address:* Flat 47, Cholmeley Lodge, Cholmeley Park, Highgate, N6 5EN. *T:* (020) 8340 3143. *Died 17 Feb. 2001.*

ROYLE, family name of **Baron Fanshawe of Richmond.**

RUBENS, Bernice Ruth, FRSL; writer and director of documentary films, since 1957; *b* 26 July 1928; *m* 1947, Rudi Nassauer (marr. diss.; he *d* 1997); two *d. Educ:* University of Wales, Cardiff (BA, Hons English; Fellow 1982; Hon. DLitt 1991). Followed teaching profession, 1950–55. FRSL 1999. American Blue Ribbon award for documentary film, Stress, 1968. *Publications:* Set on Edge, 1960; Madame Sousatzka, 1962 (filmed, 1989); Mate in Three, 1965; The Elected Member, 1969 (Booker Prize, 1970); Sunday Best, 1971; Go Tell the Lemming, 1973; I Sent a Letter to my Love, 1975 (filmed, 1981); The Ponsonby Post, 1977; A Five Year Sentence, 1978; Spring Sonata, 1979; Birds of Passage, 1981; Brothers, 1983; Mr Wakefield's Crusade, 1985 (televised, 1992); Our Father, 1987; Kingdom Come, 1990; A Solitary Grief, 1991; Mother Russia, 1992; Autobiopsy, 1993; Yesterday in the Back Lane, 1995; The Waiting Game, 1997; I, Dreyfus,

1999; Milwaukee, 2001; Nine Lives, 2002; The Sergeants' Tale, 2003. *Recreation:* plays piano and 'cello. *Address:* 213A Goldhurst Terrace, NW6 3ER. *T:* (020) 7625 4845.
Died 13 Oct. 2004.

RUBINSTEIN, Michael Bernard; Senior Partner, 1969–86, Consultant, 1986–94, Rubinstein Callingham Polden & Gale (formerly Rubinstein, Nash & Co., then Rubinstein Callingham), Solicitors; *b* 6 Nov. 1920; *s* of late H. F. Rubinstein and Lina (*née* Lowy); *m* 1955, Joy Douthwaite; two *s* two *d*. *Educ:* St Paul's Sch. Admitted solicitor, 1948. Served War, RE (TA), 1939, and RA; Captain 1945. Mem., Lord Chancellor's Cttee on Defamation, 1971–74. A Vice Pres., SPNM, 1994– (Trustee, 1967–96; Chm., 1986–94). *Publications:* (ed and contrib.) Wicked, Wicked Libels, 1972; Rembrandt and Angels (monograph), 1982; (with Rowland Parker) The Cart-Ruts on Malta and Gozo (monograph), 1984, repr. with The People of the Temples of Malta and Gozo (monograph with Rowland Parker) as Malta's Ancient Temples and Ruts, 1988; Music to my Ear, 1985; Nasrudin on his toes and other feats, 1999; contrib. legal and other jls. *Recreations:* faxing loose-ball letters to Editors when inspired, experiencing right hemisphere mentation, ruminating, regularly reading poems with friends, composing haikus, otherwise practising to get along without practising, reacting to events and people from what I mistakenly perceive as the real world. *Address:* 1 Walkern Road, Benington, Herts SG2 7LN. *T:* (01438) 869539. *Club:* Garrick.   *Died 12 Jan. 2001.*

RUBINSTEIN, Prof. Nicolai, FBA 1971; FRHistS; Professor of History, Westfield College, London University, 1965–78, then Emeritus; *b* 13 July 1911; *s* of Bernhard and Irene Rubinstein; *m* 1954, Ruth Kidder Olitsky. *Educ:* Univs of Berlin and Florence (LittD). Lectr, UC Southampton, 1942–45; Lectr, 1945–62, Reader, 1962–65, Westfield Coll., Univ. of London. Corresp. Mem., Accad. Toscana La Colombaria, 1976; Hon. Fellow: Warburg Inst., 1985; Westfield Coll., 1986. Hon. Diploma di perfezionamento, Scuola Normale Superiore, Pisa, 1991. Serena Medal, British Acad., 1974; Premio Internazionale Galileo Galilei, 1985; Fiorino d'oro, Florence, 1990; Premio della Cultura della Presidenza del Consiglio, 1993. Hon. Citizen, Florence, 1991. *Publications:* The Government of Florence under the Medici 1434–94, 1966, 2nd edn 1997; (ed) Florentine Studies: politics and society in Renaissance Florence, 1968; Gen. Editor, Letters of Lorenzo de'Medici and ed vol. 3, 1977, and vol. 4, 1981; The Palazzo Vecchio 1298–1532, 1995; articles in Jl of Warburg and Courtauld Insts, Italian Studies, Archivio Storico Italiano, Rinascimento, etc. *Address:* 16 Gardnor Mansions, Church Row, NW3 6UR. *T:* (020) 7435 6995.
Died 19 Aug. 2002.

RUCK, Peter Frederick C.; *see* Carter-Ruck.

RUE, Dame (Elsie) Rosemary, DBE 1989 (CBE 1977); Regional General Manager, 1984–88, and Regional Medical Officer, 1973–88, Oxford Regional Health Authority; *b* 14 June 1928; *d* of Harry and Daisy Laurence; *m* 1950, Roger Rue (marr. diss.); two *s*. *Educ:* Sydenham High Sch.; Univ. of London; Oxford Univ. Med. School. (MB, BS 1951). DCH 1962; MRCP 1972, FRCP 1977; FFPH (FFCM 1972); MRCPsych 1975, FRCPsych 1980, Hon. FRCPsych 1990; FRCGP *ad eundem* 1982; FRCS 1994. Gen. Practitioner, 1952–58; Public Health Service, 1958–65; Hospital Service, 1965–73; SAMO, Oxford RHB, 1971. President: Faculty of Community Medicine, 1986–89; BMA, 1990–91; Past-Pres., Medical Women's Fedn. Hon. Fellow, Green Coll., Oxford, 1985. Hon. MA Oxford, 1988. *Publications:* papers on gen. practice, women in medicine, ward design, community hosps, health services, individuals requiring security. *Address:* 2 Stanton St John, Oxford OX33 1ET.
Died 24 Dec. 2004.

RUMBOLD, Sir Jack (Seddon), Kt 1984; QC (Zanzibar) 1963; President of the Industrial Tribunals, England and Wales, 1979–84, retired; *b* 5 March 1920; *s* of William Alexander Rumbold and Jean Lindsay Rumbold (*née* Mackay), Christchurch, NZ; *m* 1st, 1949, Helen Suzanne (marr. diss. 1969), *d* of Col J. B. Davis, Wanganui, NZ; two *d*; 2nd, 1970, Veronica Ellie Hurt (*née* Whigham). *Educ:* St Andrew's Coll., NZ; Canterbury Univ., NZ (LLB 1940); Brasenose Coll., Oxford (Rhodes Schol.; BCL 1948). Served Royal Navy, Lieut RNZNVR, 1941–45 (despatches). Called to Bar, Inner Temple, 1948; Crown Counsel, Kenya, 1957, Sen. Crown Counsel, 1959; Attorney General, Zanzibar, 1963; Legal Adviser, Kenya Govt, 1964–66; Academic Director, British Campus of Stanford Univ., USA, 1966–72. Chairman of Industrial Tribunals (part-time), 1968; (full-time) 1972; Regional Chairman (London South), 1977. FRSA 1985. *Recreations:* books, music; formerly cricket (Oxford Blue). *Address:* 5 Church Row, Moore Park Road, SW6 2JW; Le Mas du Vallon, Le Brulat du Castellet, Var 83330, France. *Clubs:* Garrick, MCC.   *Died 9 Dec. 2001.*

RUSH, Most Rev. Francis Roberts, DD; RC Archbishop of Brisbane, 1973–91, then Archbishop Emeritus; *b* 11 Sept. 1916; *s* of T. J. Rush. *Educ:* Christian Brothers' Coll., Townsville; Mt Carmel, Charters Towers; St Columba's Coll., Springwood; Coll. de Propaganda Fide, Rome. Ordained priest, 1939; Assistant Priest, Townsville, Mundingburra and Ingham; Parish Priest, Abergowrie and Ingham; Bishop of Rockhampton, 1960–73. *Address:* Verona Villa, 169 Seventeen Mile Rocks Road, Oxley, Brisbane, Qld 4075, Australia.
Died 21 July 2001.

RUSSELL, 5th Earl *cr* 1861; **Conrad Sebastian Robert Russell,** FBA 1991; Viscount Amberley 1861; Professor of British History, King's College London, 1990–2002; *b* 15 April 1937; *s* of 3rd Earl Russell, OM, FRS and Patricia Helen, *d* of H. E. Spence; *S* half brother, 1987; *m* 1962, Elizabeth Franklyn Sanders (*d* 2003); two *s*. *Educ:* Merton College, Oxford (BA 1958, MA 1962; Sir Henry Savile Fellow, 1994); MA Yale 1979. FRHistS 1971. Lectr in History, 1960–74, Reader, 1974–79, Bedford Coll., London Univ.; Prof. of History, Yale Univ., 1979–84; Astor Prof. of British History, UCL, 1984–90. Ford Lectr, Univ. of Oxford, 1987–88; Trevelyan Lectr, Univ. of Cambridge, 1995. Took Liberal Democrat whip, H of L; elected Mem., H of L, 1999. *Publications:* The Crisis of Parliaments: English History 1509–1660, 1971; (ed) The Origins of the English Civil War, 1973; Parliaments and English Politics 1621–1629, 1979; The Causes of the English Civil War, 1990; Unrevolutionary England 1603–1642, 1990; The Fall of the British Monarchies 1637–1642, 1991; Academic Freedom, 1993; An Intelligent Person's Guide to Liberalism, 1999; articles in jls. *Recreations:* swimming, cricket. *Heir:* *s* Viscount Amberley, *b* 12 Sept. 1968. *Address:* House of Lords, Westminster, SW1A 0PW.   *Died 14 Oct. 2004.*

RUSSELL, Rev. Arthur Colin, CMG 1957; ED; *b* 2 Nov. 1906; *e s* of late Arthur W. Russell, OBE, WS; *m* 1939, Elma (*d* 1967), *d* of late Douglas Strachan, Hon. RSA; three *d*. *Educ:* Harrow; Brasenose Coll., Oxford (Heberden Schol.; MA). Called to the Bar, Inner Temple, 1939. Cadet, Gold Coast (later Ghana), 1929; Asst Dist Comr, 1930; Dist Comr, 1940; Judicial Adviser, 1947; Senior, 1951; Regional Officer, 1952; Permanent Sec., Min. of Educn and Social Welfare, 1953; Governor's Sec., 1954; Chief Regional Officer, Ashanti, 1955–57, retd. Trained for the Ministry, 1957–59; ordained (Church of Scotland), 1959; Parish Minister, Aberlemno, 1959–76, retd. Dist Councillor, Angus Dist, 1977–84. *Publications:* Stained Glass Windows of Douglas Strachan, 1972, 3rd edn 2002; Gold Coast to Ghana, 1996. *Address:* Balgavies Lodge, by Forfar, Angus DD8 2TH. *T:* (01307) 818571.
Died 5 Sept. 2003.

RUSSELL, Barbara Winifred, MA; Headmistress, Berkhamsted School for Girls, 1950–71; *b* 5 Jan. 1910; *er d* of Lionel Wilfred and Elizabeth Martin Russell. *Educ:* St Oran's School, Edinburgh; Edinburgh University (MA);

Oxford University, Dept of Education. History Mistress, Brighton and Hove High School, 1932–38; Senior History Mistress, Roedean School, 1938–49. *Recreations:* reading, gardening. *Club:* East India, Devonshire, Sports and Public Schools. *Died 29 April 2002.*

RUSSELL, Sir David Sturrock W.; *see* West-Russell.

RUSSELL, Sir Mark; *see* Russell, Sir R. M.

RUSSELL, Hon. Sir Patrick; *see* Russell, Hon. Sir T. P.

RUSSELL, Sir (Robert) Mark, KCMG 1985 (CMG 1977); HM Diplomatic Service, retired; *b* 3 Sept. 1929; *s* of Sir Robert E. Russell, CSI, CIE; *m* 1954, Virginia Mary Rogers; two *s* two *d. Educ:* Trinity Coll., Glenalmond; Exeter Coll., Oxford (Hon. Mods cl. 2, Lit. Hum. cl. 1; MA). Royal Artillery, 1952–54; FO, 1954–56; 3rd, later 2nd Sec., HM Legation, Budapest, 1956–58; 2nd Sec., Berne, 1958–61; FO, 1961–65; 1st Sec., 1962; 1st Sec. and Head of Chancery, Kabul, 1965–67; 1st Sec., DSAO, 1967–69; Counsellor, 1969; Dep. Head of Personnel (Ops) Dept, FCO, 1969–70; Commercial Counsellor, Bucharest, 1970–73; Counsellor, Washington, 1974–78, and Head of Chancery, 1977–78; Asst Under Sec. of State, FCO and Dep. Chief Clerk and Chief Inspector, HM Diplomatic Service, 1978–82; Ambassador to Turkey, 1983–86; Dep. Under-Sec. of State (Chief Clerk), FCO, 1986–89. Chairman: Margaret Blackwood Housing Assoc., 1990–98; Scottish Trust for the Physically Disabled, 1990–98; Centre for Maritime and Industrial Safety Technol. Ltd, 1992–2003. *Recreations:* reading, music. *Address:* 20 Meadow Place, Edinburgh EH9 1JR. *Died 11 July 2005.*

RUSSELL, Rt Hon. Sir (Thomas) Patrick, Kt 1980; PC 1987; a Lord Justice of Appeal, 1987–96; *b* 30 July 1926; *s* of late Sidney Arthur Russell and Elsie Russell; *m* 1951, Doreen (Janie) Ireland; two *d. Educ:* Urmston Grammar Sch.; Manchester Univ. (LLB). Served in Intelligence Corps and RASC, 1945–48. Called to Bar, Middle Temple, 1949, Bencher, 1978. Prosecuting Counsel to the Post Office (Northern Circuit), 1961–70; Asst Recorder of Bolton, 1963–70; Recorder of Barrow-in-Furness, 1970–71; QC 1971; a Recorder of the Crown Court, 1972–80; a Judge of the High Court of Justice, QBD, 1980–86. Leader, 1978–80, Presiding Judge, 1983–87, Northern Circuit. A Justice of the Court of Appeal, Gibraltar, 1998–99. Member: Senate, Inns of Court and Bar, 1978–80; Lord Justice James Cttee on Distribution of Criminal Business, 1973–76. Pres., Manchester and Dist Medico-Legal Soc., 1978–79 (Patron, 1987); Vice-Pres., Lancs CCC, 1980–98 and 2001– (Pres., 1999–2001). Hon. LLD Manchester, 1988. *Recreation:* cricket. *Address:* Oakfield, 65 Crofts Bank Road, Urmston, Manchester M41 0UB. *Died 28 Oct. 2002.*

RUSSELL-DAVIS, John Darelan, FRICS; chartered surveyor, retired; *b* 23 Dec. 1912; *s* of Edward David Darelan Davis, FRCS, and Alice Mildred (*née* Russell); *m* 1st, 1938, Barbarina Elizabeth Graham Arnould (*d* 1985); one *s* one *d*; 2nd, 1986, Gaynor, *widow* of Lt-Col A. V. Brooke-Webb, RA. *Educ:* Stowe Sch.; Germany; Coll. of Estate Management, London. FRICS 1934. Served War, HAC, 1939; commnd RA, 1940; Captain 1942; mentioned in despatches, 1945. Partner, C. P. Whiteley & Son, Chartered Surveyors, 1938; Sen. Partner, Whiteley, Ferris & Puckridge, and Kemsley, Whiteley & Ferris, City of London, 1948–72. Mem., Lands Tribunal, 1972–77. Royal Institution of Chartered Surveyors: formerly Mem. Council (twice); Chm., City branch, 1959; Hon. Treasurer, Benevolent Fund. Mem., East Grinstead UDC, 1957–60 (Vice-Chm., 1960). Formerly: Mem. Council, Wycombe Abbey Sch.; Trustee, Cordwainer and Bread Street Foundn; Mem. Court, Turners' Co. (Renter-Warden, 1975). *Recreation:* Somerset and Dorset countryside. *Died 4 July 2005.*

RUTHERFORD, (Herman) Graham, CBE 1966; QPM 1957; DL; Chief Constable of Surrey, 1956–68; *b* 3 April 1908; *m* 1940, Dorothy Weaver (*d* 1987); two *s* one *d* (and

one *s* decd). *Educ:* Grammar School, Consett, Co. Durham. Metropolitan Police, 1929–45. Called to the Bar, Gray's Inn, 1941. Served Army, Allied Military Government, 1943–45, Lt-Col. Chief Constable: Oxfordshire, 1945–54; Lincolnshire, 1954–56. DL Surrey, 1968. *Address:* Hankley Farm, Elstead, Surrey GU8 6LJ. *T:* (01252) 702200. *Died 29 July 2003.*

RUTTER, Sir Frank (William Eden), KBE 1986 (CBE 1981); general medical practitioner; *b* 5 June 1918; *s* of Edgar and Nellie Rutter; *m* 1947, Mary Elizabeth Milton; six *d. Educ:* Welsh National Sch. of Medicine, Cardiff; Westminster Hosp. Med. Sch., London. MRCGP, FRCGP, MRCS, LRCP; DipObst. Served War of 1939–45, RAMC (Airborne Forces), 1942–46; OC 195 (Parachute) Field Ambulance, 1946. Chm., Health Cttee, Cardiff RDC, 1960–62; Member: Auckland Hosp. Bd, 1971–88 (Chm., 1974–88); Auckland Area Health Bd, 1988–89; Pres., Hosp. Bds Assoc., NZ, 1977–81 and 1983–85. Chairman, National Advisory Committee: Cancer Treatment Services, 1978–89; Organ Imaging Services, 1982–89; Life-Mem., NZ National Multiple Sclerosis Soc. Patron, South Island Airedale Terrier Club, 1989–93. CStJ 1989. Silver Jubilee Medal, 1977. *Recreation:* watching development of fourteen grandchildren. *Address:* 266 Meola Road, Point Chevalier, Auckland, New Zealand. *T:* (9) 8542544.

Died 28 Oct. 2002.

RYAN, John; Senior Lecturer in Management Studies, Napier University; *b* 30 April 1940; *m* 1964, Eunice Ann Edmonds; two *s. Educ:* Lanark Grammar School; Glasgow University (MA, MBA). Member, National Association of Labour Student Organisations, 1958–62; formerly Youth Organiser, Lanark City Labour Party; Member, Executive Committee, North Paddington Labour Party, 1964–66. Contested (Lab) Buckinghamshire South, 1964; MP (Lab) Uxbridge, 1966–70. Member, Fabian Society, 1961; Dir, Tribune Publications Ltd, 1969. Mem., Inst. of Marketing; Associate Member: Market Res. Soc.; Inst. of Mgt. *Recreations:* golf, walking. *Address:* Napier Business School, 219 Colinton Road, Edinburgh EH14 1DJ. *T:* (0131) 455 5004, *Fax:* (0131) 455 5046. *Died 26 March 2002.*

RYAN, Most Rev. Laurence, DD; Bishop of Kildare and Leighlin, (RC), 1987–2002, then Bishop Emeritus; *b* 13 May 1931; *s* of Michael Ryan and Brigid Foley. *Educ:* St Patrick's Coll., Maynooth (BA, DD). Lectr in Theology, St Patrick's Coll., Carlow, 1958–80, Pres. 1974–80; Parish Priest of Naas, Co. Kildare, 1980–85; Vicar General of Kildare and Leighlin, 1975–87; Coadjutor Bishop of Kildare and Leighlin, 1984–87. Sec., 1966–71, Chm., 1974–76, Irish Theological Assoc.; Pres., Nat. Conf. of Priests of Ireland, 1976–82. *Publications:* contribs to Irish Theological Qly, The Furrow, Irish Ecclesiastical Record, Christus Rex. *Recreation:* walking. *Address:* Teach Moling, Oak Park, Carlow, Ireland. *T:* (59) 9136835.

Died 13 Oct. 2003.

RYDER OF EATON HASTINGS, Baron *cr* 1975 (Life Peer), of Eaton Hastings, Oxfordshire; **Sydney Thomas Franklin, (Don), Ryder,** Kt 1972; Chairman, National Enterprise Board, 1975–77; *b* 16 Sept. 1916; *s* of John Ryder; *m* 1950, Eileen Dodds (*d* 1999); one *s* one *d. Educ:* Ealing County GS. Ed., Stock Exchange Gazette, 1950–60; Jt Man. Dir, 1960–61, Sole Man. Dir, 1961–63, Kelly Iliffe Holdings, and Associated Iliffe Press Ltd; Dir, Internat. Publishing Corp., 1963–70; Man. Dir, Reed Paper Gp, 1963–68; Chm. and Chief Executive, Reed International Ltd, 1968–75; Dir, MEPC Ltd, 1972–75. Industrial Advr to the govt, 1974. Member: British Gas Corp., 1973–78; Reserve Pension Bd, 1973; NEDC, 1976–77. Member: Council and Bd of Fellows, BIM, 1970; Court and Council, Cranfield Inst. of Technology, 1970–74; Council, UK S Africa Trade Assoc., 1974; Nat. Materials Handling Centre (Pres., 1970–77); Council, Industrial Soc., 1971. Vice-Pres., RoSPA, 1973. *Recreations:* sailing, chess. *Address:* House of Lords, SW1A 0PW. *Died 12 May 2003.*

S

SACHS, Hon. Sir Michael (Alexander Geddes), Kt 1993; **Hon. Mr Justice Sachs;** a Judge of the High Court of Justice, Queen's Bench Division, since 1993; *b* 8 April 1932; *s* of Dr Joseph Sachs, MB, ChB, DPH, and Mrs Ruby Mary Sachs (*née* Ross); *m* 1957, Patricia Mary (*née* Conroy); two *s* two *d* (and one *s* decd). *Educ:* Sedbergh; Manchester Univ. (LLB 1954). Admitted solicitor, 1957. Partner in Slater, Heelis & Co., Solicitors, Manchester, 1962–84. A Recorder, 1980–84; a Circuit Judge, 1984–93. Pres., Manchester Law Soc., 1978–79; Chm., Greater Manchester Legal Services Cttee, 1977–81; Member: No 7 (NW) Area, Legal Aid Cttee, 1966–80 (Chm., 1975–76); Council, Law Soc., 1979–84 (Chm., Standing Cttee on Criminal Law, 1982–84); Court, Univ. of Manchester, 1977–84. Hon. Bencher, Middle Temple, 1993; Hon. Mem., Law Soc., 1993. Hon. LLD Manchester, 1994. KSS 1980. *Address:* Royal Courts of Justice, WC2A 2LL. *Died 25 Sept. 2003.*

SACKVILLE, 6th Baron *cr* 1876; **Lionel Bertrand Sackville-West;** *b* 30 May 1913; *s* of late Hon. Bertrand George Sackville-West, *y b* of 4th Baron and Eva Adela Mabel Inigo (*d* 1936), *d* of late Maj.-Gen. Inigo Richmond Jones, CB, CVO; *S* cousin, 1965; *m* 1st, 1953, Jacobine Napier (*d* 1971), *widow* of Captain John Hichens, RA, and *d* of J. R. Menzies-Wilson; five *d*; 2nd, 1974, Arlie, Lady de Guingand (marr. diss. 1983; she *d* 1991); 3rd, 1983, Jean, *widow* of Sir Edward Imbert-Terry, 3rd Bt. *Educ:* Winchester; Magdalen Coll., Oxford. Formerly Capt. Coldstream Gds; served War, 1939–42 (POW). Member of Lloyd's, 1949. *Heir: nephew* Robert Bertrand Sackville-West [*b* 10 July 1958; *m* 1st, 1985, Catherine Dorothea Bennett (marr. diss. 1992); 2nd, 1994, Margot Jane MacAndrew; one *s* two *d*]. *Address:* Knole, Sevenoaks, Kent TN15 0RP. *Died 27 March 2004.*

SADIE, Stanley (John), CBE 1982; writer on music; Music Critic for The Times, 1964–81, thereafter freelance; Editor: The Musical Times, 1967–87; The New Grove Dictionary of Music and Musicians, 1970–2000; Master Musicians series, since 1976; *b* 30 Oct. 1930; *s* of David Sadie and Deborah (*née* Simons); *m* 1st, 1953, Adèle Bloom (*d* 1978); two *s* one *d*; 2nd, 1978, Julie Anne Vertrees; one *s* one *d*. *Educ:* St Paul's Sch.; Gonville and Caius Coll., Cambridge Univ. (MA, PhD, MusB; Hon. Fellow, 2001). Prof., Trinity Coll. of Music, London, 1957–65. President: Royal Musical Assoc., 1989–94 (Vice-Pres., 1985–89; Mem., 1957–); Internat. Musicological Soc., 1992–97 (Mem., 1955–; Directorium, 1987–92); Member: Critics' Circle, 1963–; American Musicological Soc., 1970– (Foreign Corresp. Mem., 1994). Chairman: Handel House Trust, 1994–96 (Pres., 1996–); English Bach Fest. Trust, 2001–03; Music & Letters Trust, 2004–. Writer and broadcaster on musical subjects, *circa* 1955–; Music Consultant, Man and Music, Granada TV, 1984–89; editor of many edns of 18th-century music, 1955–; Series Editor, Man and Music, 8 vols, 1989–93. Hon. RAM 1981; Hon. FRCM 1994. Hon. DLitt Leicester, 1981. *Publications:* Handel, 1962; Mozart, 1966; Beethoven, 1967; Handel, 1968; (with Arthur Jacobs) Pan Book of Opera/The Opera Guide, 1964, new edns 1969, 1984; Handel Concertos, 1973; (ed) The New Grove Dictionary of Music and Musicians, 1980, rev. edn 2001; Mozart (The New Grove Biographies), 1982; (ed) New Grove Dictionary of Musical Instruments, 1984; (with Alison Latham) The Cambridge Music Guide, 1985, rev. edn 1993 (trans. German, French, Swedish and Chinese); Mozart Symphonies, 1986; (ed with H. Wiley Hitchcock) The New Grove Dictionary of American Music, 1986; (ed) The Grove Concise Dictionary of Music, 1988, rev. edn 1994; (ed) History of Opera, 1989; (ed with H. M. Brown) Performance Practice, 1989; (ed with D. W. Krummel) Music Printing and Publishing, 1989; (ed) The New Grove Dictionary of Opera, 1992; (ed) Wolfgang Amadè Mozart: essays on his life and works, 1996; (ed) New Grove Book of Operas, 1996; contrib. The Musical Times, Gramophone, Opera, Music and Letters, Musical Quarterly, Proc. Roy. Musical Assoc. *Recreations:* watching cricket, drinking (mainly wine and coffee), bridge, travel, reading. *Address:* The Manor, Cossington, Bridgwater, Somerset TA7 8JR. *T:* (01278) 723655, *Fax:* (01278) 723656; *e-mail:* s.sadie@ukgateway.net.
Died 21 March 2005.

SAGAN, Françoise; pen-name of Françoise Quoirez; authoress; *b* France, 21 June 1935; *y c* of Paul Quoirez; *m* 1958, Guy Schoeller (marr. diss. 1960); *m* 1962, Robert James Westhoff (marr. diss.); one *s*. *Educ:* convent and private school. Published first novel at age of 18. Wrote some songs and collaborated in scheme for ballet Le Rendez-vous Manqué, produced Paris and London, 1958. *Publications:* Bonjour Tristesse, 1954; Un Certain Sourire, 1956 (filmed, 1958); Dans un mois, dans un an, 1957 (Those Without Shadows, 1958); Aimez-vous Brahms ..., 1959 (1960); Château en Suède (play), 1960; Les Violons, parfois ... (play), 1961; La Robe Mauve de Valentine (play), 1963; Bonheur, impair et passe (play), 1964; Toxique ... (trans. 1965); La Chamade, 1965 (trans. 1966) (filmed, 1970); Le Cheval Evanoui (play), 1966; L'Echarde, 1966; Le Garde du cœur, 1968 (The Heart-Keeper, 1968); Un peu de soleil dans l'eau froide, 1969 (Sunlight and Cold Water, 1971); Un piano dans l'herbe (play), 1970; Des bleus à l'âme, 1972 (Scars on the Soul, 1974); Zaphorie (play), 1973; Lost Profile, 1976; Silken Eyes (short stories), 1977; The Unmade Bed, 1978; Le Chien Couchant, 1980; La femme fardée, 1981 (The Painted Lady, 1982); The Still Storm, 1984; Incidental Music (short stories), 1985; Avec mon meilleur souvenir (With Fondest Regards), 1986; Un sang d'aquarelle, 1987; Dear Sarah Bernhardt, 1989; (with W. Denker) The Eiffel Tower, 1989; La Laisse, 1989 (The Leash); Les Faux-fuyants, 1991 (The Evasion, 1993); Répliques, 1992; Oeuvres (collected works), 1993; ----- et toute ma sympathie (essays), 1993; Un Chagrin de Passage, 1994; Le Miroir égaré, 1996; Dernière l'épaule ..., 1998. *Address:* c/o Editions Julliard, 24 avenue Marceau, 75008 Paris, France. *Died 24 Sept. 2004.*

SAGE, Prof. Lorna; journalist and critic; Professor of English Literature, University of East Anglia, since 1994 (Dean of the School of English and American Studies, 1985–88, and 1993–96); *b* 13 Jan. 1943; *d* of Eric and Valma Stockton; *m* 1st, 1959, Victor Sage (marr. diss. 1974); one *d*; 2nd, 1979, Rupert Hodson. *Educ:* Univ. of Durham (BA 1st Cl. Hons 1964); Univ. of Birmingham (MA 1966). Asst Lectr in English Literature, Univ. of East Anglia, 1965, Lectr 1968, Sen. Lectr, 1975. Florence B. Tucker Vis. Prof., Wellesley Coll., Mass, USA, 1981. *Publications:* (ed) Peacock, Satirical Novels, 1976; Doris Lessing, 1983; Women in the House of Fiction, 1992; (ed) Flesh and the Mirror, 1994; Angela Carter, 1994; (ed) The Cambridge Guide to Women's Writing in English, 1999; Bad Blood, 2000 (Whitbread Biography Prize, 2001); reviews in Observer, TLS, London Review of Books, Vogue, New York Times, etc; *posthumous publications:* Moments of Truth: twelve twentieth-century women writers, 2001; Good as Her Word: selected journalism, 2003. *Address:* School of English and American Studies, University of East Anglia, Norwich NR4 7TJ. *T:* (01603) 456161. *Died 11 Jan. 2001.*

SAID, Prof. Edward W(adie), PhD; University Professor, English and Comparative Literature, Columbia University, since 1992; *b* 1 Nov. 1935; *m* 1st, 1962, Maire Jaanus (marr. diss. 1967); 2nd, 1970, Mariam Cortas; one *s* one *d. Educ:* Princeton Univ. (AB 1957); Harvard Univ. (AM 1960; PhD 1964). Columbia University: Instructor in English, 1963–65; Asst Prof., 1965–67, Associate Prof., 1968–70, Prof., 1970–77, Parr Prof., 1977–88, of English and Comparative Literature; Old Dominion Foundn Prof. in Humanities, 1989–91. Reith Lectr, 1993. *Publications:* Joseph Conrad and the Fiction of Autobiography, 1966; Beginnings: intention and method, 1975; Orientalism, 1978; The Question of Palestine, 1979; (ed) Literature and Society, 1980; Covering Islam, 1981; The World, the Text and the Critic, 1983; After the Last Sky, 1986; (ed jtly) Blaming the Victims, 1988; Musical Elaborations, 1991; Culture and Imperialism, 1993; The Politics of Dispossession, 1994; Representations of the Intellectual, 1994; Peace and Its Discontents: Gaza to Jericho 1993–1995, 1995; Out of Place: a memoir, 1999; The End of the Peace Process: Oslo and after, 2000; Reflections on Exile and Other Essays, 2000; Power, Politics and Culture: interviews with Edward W. Said, 2001; (with D. Barenboim) Parallels and Paradoxes: explorations in music and society, 2003. *Address:* 602 Philosophy Hall, Department of English, Columbia University, New York, NY 10027, USA.   *Died 24 Sept. 2003.*

SAINSBURY, Edward Hardwicke, TD 1945; consultant; Partner, Dawson, Hart & Co., Uckfield, 1961–92 (ceased to practice, 1993), retired; District Notary Public, Uckfield, since 1965; *b* 17 Sept. 1912; *e s* of Henry Morgan Sainsbury, and *g s* of James C. Hardwicke, a pioneer of technical and other educn in S Wales; *m* 1946, Ann, 2nd *d* of late Kenneth Ellis, Tunbridge Wells; one *s* one *d. Educ:* Cardiff High Sch.; Univ. of S Wales and Monmouth. Solicitor in private practice, 1935–93; commnd (TA) 1936; Prosecuting Solicitor, Cardiff, 1938, Sen. Pros. Solicitor, 1939. Served War of 1939–45: Adjutant, 77th HAA Regt, 1940; comd 240 HAA Battery Gibraltar, 1944; demobilised Nov. 1945. Hong Kong: Asst Crown Solicitor, 1946; comr for revision of the laws of Hong Kong, 1947; magistrate, 1948; registrar, High Court, 1949; sen. magistrate, Kowloon, 1951; Barrister, Inner Temple, 1951; Land Officer and sen. crown counsel, Hong Kong, 1952; legal draftsman, Nigeria, 1953; Principal Legal Draftsman, Fed. of Nigeria, 1958; Judge, High Court of Lagos, 1960–63, and of Southern Cameroons, 1961–63; Speaker, House of Assembly, 1958–63, Chm., Public Service Commn, 1961–63, Southern Cameroons. Pres., Commonwealth Parly Assoc., Southern Cameroons, 1959–63. *Publication:* (jtly) Revised Laws of Hong Kong, 1948. *Recreations:* squash (a memory), golf. *Address:* 35 Allington Road, Newick, Lewes, East Sussex BN8 4NB. *T:* (01825) 723682.   *Died 24 Sept. 2003.*

ST CLAIR, Malcolm Archibald James; *b* 16 Feb. 1927; *o s* of late Maj.-Gen. George James Paul St Clair, CB, CBE, DSO and Charlotte Theresa Orme Little; *m* 1955, Mary-Jean Rosalie Alice, *o d* of Wing-Comdr Caryl Liddell Hargreaves, Broadwood House, Sunningdale; two *s* one *d. Educ:* Eton. Served with Royal Scots Greys, 1944–48. Formerly Hon. Sec. to Sir Winston Churchill. Contested (C) Bristol South-East, 1959; MP (C) Bristol South-East, 1961–63. Lt Col Comdg, Royal Gloucestershire Hussars (TA), 1967–69. High Sheriff Glos, 1972. *Address:* Long Newnton Priory, Tetbury, Glos GL8 8RR. *Club:* White's.   *Died 1 Feb. 2004.*

ST JOHN-BROOKS, Dr Caroline; Editor, Times Educational Supplement, 1997–2000; *b* 24 March 1947; *d* of Maj. Julian Gordon de Renzy St John-Brooks and Diana Wintersladen; *m* 1972, Roger Hampson; one *s* one *d. Educ:* Royal Sch., Bath; Thornbury Grammar Sch., Glos; Trinity Coll., Dublin (BA Hons); Univ. of Ulster (MA); Univ. of Bristol (PhD 1981). Lecturer: Portrush Hotel and Catering Coll., 1971–73; Bristol Poly.,

1976–79; Educn Corresp., New Society, 1979–87; Educn Ed., Sunday Times, 1987–91; Asst Editor, TES, 1991–94; Administrator, Centre for Educnl Research and Innovation, OECD, Paris, 1994–97. *Publications:* Schools Under Scrutiny, 1995; Mapping the Future: young people and career guidance, 1996; Parents as Partners in Schooling, 1997. *Address:* 1 Grove Hall, West Grove, Greenwich, SE10 8QT. *T:* (020) 8469 0703.
      Died 8 Sept. 2003.

SALINGER, Pierre (Emil George); politician, journalist; independent public relations counselor, since 1996; International Consultant, ABC News, American Broadcasting Company, since 1993; *b* San Francisco, 14 June 1925; *s* of Herbert and Jehanne Salinger; *m* 1st; one *s* (and one *s* one *d* decd); 2nd, 1957, Nancy Brook Joy (marr. diss. 1965); 3rd, 1965, Nicole Gillmann (marr. diss. 1988), Paris, France; one *s*; 4th, 1989, Nicole Beauvillain. *Educ:* Lowell High School, San Francisco; State Coll., San Francisco; Univ. of San Francisco. Served War, 1942–45, with US Navy. With San Francisco Chronicle, 1942–55; Guest Lectr, Mills Coll., Calif, 1950–55; Press Officer, Democratic Presidential Campaign (Calif), 1952; West Coast Editor, Contributing Editor, Collier's Magazine, 1955–56; Investigator, Senate Labor Rackets Cttee, 1957–59; Press Sec. to President Kennedy (when Senator), 1959–61, and to President of the United States, 1961–64; appointed to serve as a US Senator, 4 Aug. 1964–2 Jan. 1965; Roving Editor, L'Express, Paris, 1973–78; ABC News: Correspondent, Paris, 1978–79; Paris Bureau Chief, 1979–87; Chief Foreign Corresp., 1983–93; Sen. Ed., Europe, 1988–93. Vice Chm., Burson Marsteller, 1993–96; Vice Pres., Continental Airlines, Continental Air Services, 1965–68. Trustee, Robert F. Kennedy Meml Foundn; Hon. Chm., Bd of Trustees, American Coll. in Paris. Mem., Legion of Honour, 1978; US Navy and Marine Corps Medal, 1946. *Publications:* articles on county jail conditions in California, 1953; A Tribute to John F. Kennedy, Encyclopedia Britannica, 1964; With Kennedy, 1966; A Tribute to Robert F. Kennedy, 1968; For the Eyes of the President Only, 1971; Je suis un Americain, 1975; La France et le Nouveau Monde, 1976; America Held Hostage—the secret negotiations, 1981; (with Leonard Gross) The Dossier, 1984; (with Robert Cameron) Above Paris, 1985; (with Leonard Gross) Mortal Games, 1988; (with Eric Laurent) La Guerre du Golfe: le dossier secret, 1990; P.S.: a memoir, 1995; John F. Kennedy, Commander in Chief, 1997.
      Died 16 Oct. 2004.

SALISBURY, 6th Marquess of, *cr* 1789; **Robert Edward Peter Gascoyne-Cecil;** DL; Baron Cecil, 1603; Viscount Cranborne, 1604; Earl of Salisbury, 1605; Captain Grenadier Guards; High Steward of Hertford since 1972; *b* 24 Oct. 1916; *s* of 5th Marquess of Salisbury, KG, PC, FRS, and Elizabeth Vere (*d* 1982), *e d* of late Lord Richard Cavendish, PC, CB, CMG; *S* father, 1972; *m* 1945, Marjorie Olein (Mollie), *d* of late Captain Hon. Valentine Wyndham-Quin, RN; four *s* one *d* (and two *s* decd). MP (C) Bournemouth West, 1950–54. Pres., Monday Club, 1974–81. DL Dorset, 1974. *Heir: s* Viscount Cranborne, *b* 30 Sept. 1946. *Address:* Hatfield House, Hatfield, Herts AL9 5NF.
      Died 11 July 2003.

SALMON, Brian Lawson, CBE 1972; Chairman, J. Lyons & Co. Ltd, 1972–77 (Director, 1961–77, Joint Managing Director, 1967–69, Deputy Chairman, 1969–71); *b* 30 June 1917; *s* of Julius Salmon; *m* 1946, Annette Wilson Mackay; two *s* one *d. Educ:* Grenham Hse; Malvern Coll. Chm., Cttee on Sen. Nursing Staff Structure, 1963–66. Vice-Chm., Bd of Governors, Westminster Hosp. Gp, 1963–74; Chairman: Camden and Islington AHA, 1974–77; Supply Bd Working Gp, DHSS, 1977–78. *Recreations:* theatre, ballet, food and wine. *Address:* 34 Kingston House North, Princes Gate, SW7 1LN.
      Died 28 May 2001.

SALT, George, FRS 1956; ScD; Fellow of King's College, Cambridge, since 1933; Reader in Animal Ecology, University of Cambridge, 1965–71, then Emeritus; *b* Loughborough, 12 Dec. 1903; *s* of late Walter Salt and Mary Cecilia (*née* Hulme); *m* 1939, Joyce Laing (*d* 2002), Newnham Coll. and Stockton-on-Tees; two *s. Educ:* Crescent Heights Collegiate Inst., Calgary; Univ. of Alberta (BSc); Harvard Univ. (SM, SD); Univ. of Cambridge (PhD 1933, ScD 1941). Nat. Res. Fellow, Harvard Univ., 1927–28; Entomologist, Imperial Inst. Entom., 1929–31; Royal Soc. Moseley Res. Student, 1932–33; Univ. Lectr in Zoology, Cambridge, 1937–65; Lectr in Natural Scis, 1937, Lay Dean, 1939–45, Tutor for Advanced Students, 1945–51, King's Coll., Cambridge. Vis. Prof., Univ. of Calif, Berkeley, 1966. Biological expedns in NW Canada and Rocky Mts, Cuba, Republic of Colombia, E Africa, Pakistan. Murchison Grant, RGS, 1951. *Publications:* The Cellular Defence Reactions of Insects, 1970; papers in scientific jls on insect parasitism and ecology. *Recreations:* mountaineering, gardening, calligraphy and palaeography. *Address:* King's College, Cambridge CB2 1ST.   *Died 17 Feb. 2003.*

SALTER, Harry Charles, CMG 1983; DFC 1945; Director, Financing of Community Budget, European Economic Community, 1973–82, retired; *b* 29 July 1918; *er s* of late Harry Arnold Salter and Irene Beatrice Salter; *m* 1st, 1946, Anne Hooper (marr. diss. 1980); one *d*; 2nd, 1983, Mrs Janet Watford (marr. diss. 1999); one step *d. Educ:* St Albans Sch. Entered Ministry of Health, 1936. Served War, Royal Artillery, 1939–46 (despatches, DFC). Asst Sec., Min. of Health, 1963; Under-Sec., DHSS, 1971–73. *Recreations:* living, bridge, chess, reading. *Address:* 27 Streatley Lodge, Pegasus Grange, White House Road, Oxford OX1 4QF. *T:* (01865) 201856.
Died 17 Aug. 2003.

SAMPSON, Anthony (Terrell Seward); writer and journalist; *b* 3 Aug. 1926; *s* of Michael Sampson and Phyllis, *d* of Sir Albert Seward, FRS; *m* 1965, Sally, *d* of Dr P. G. Bentlif, Jersey, and of Mrs G. Denison-Smith, Islip, Oxon; one *s* one *d. Educ:* Westminster School; Christ Church, Oxford. Served with Royal Navy, 1944–47; Sub-Lieut, RNVR, 1946. Editor of Drum Magazine, Johannesburg, 1951–55; Editorial staff of The Observer, 1955–66; Associate Prof., Univ. of Vincennes, Paris, 1968–70; Chief American Corresp., The Observer, 1973–74. Contributing Editor, Newsweek, 1977–; Editorial Conslt, The Brandt Commn, 1978–79; Editor, The Sampson Letter, 1984–86. Presenter and narrator: The Midas Touch (BBC2), 1990; The Two-Edged Sword (BBC2), 1991. Chm., Soc. of Authors, 1992–94. Trustee, Scott Trust (Guardian/Observer), 1993–96; Mem., Internat. Adv. Bd, Independent Newspapers (S Africa), 1995–. *Publications:* Drum, a Venture into the New Africa, 1956; The Treason Cage, 1958; Commonsense about Africa, 1960; (with S. Pienaar) South Africa: two views of Separate Development, 1960; Anatomy of Britain, 1962; Anatomy of Britain Today, 1965; Macmillan: a study in ambiguity, 1967; The New Europeans, 1968; The New Anatomy of Britain, 1971; The Sovereign State: the secret history of ITT, 1973; The Seven Sisters, 1975 (Prix International de la Presse, Nice, 1976); The Arms Bazaar, 1977; The Money Lenders, 1981; The Changing Anatomy of Britain, 1982; Empires of the Sky, 1984; (with Sally Sampson) The Oxford Book of Ages, 1985; Black and Gold: tycoons, revolutionaries and apartheid, 1987; The Midas Touch, 1989; The Essential Anatomy of Britain, 1992; Company Man, 1995; The Scholar Gypsy: the quest for a family secret, 1997; Mandela: the authorised biography, 1999; Who Runs This Place?, 2004. *Recreations:* vertical gardening, opera. *Address:* 10 Hereford Mansions, Hereford Road, W2 5BA. *T:* (020) 7727 4188, *Fax:* (020) 7221 5738; Quarry Garden, Wardour, Tisbury, Wilts SP3 6HR. *T:* (01747) 870407. *Clubs:* Beefsteak, Groucho, Academy, Grillions.   *Died 18 Dec. 2004.*

SANDELSON, Neville Devonshire; Barrister-at-Law; public affairs and business consultant; Deputy Chairman, Westminster and Overseas Trade Services Ltd, since 1985; Co-Founder, 1988, President, since 1990, The Radical Society (Co-Chairman, 1988–90); Executive Director, Profundis Ltd, since 1989; *b* Leeds, 27 Nov. 1923; *s* of late David I. Sandelson, OBE, and Dora Sandelson, (*née* Lightman); *m* 1959, Nana Karlinski, Neuilly sur Seine, France; one *s* two *d. Educ:* Westminster School; Trinity College, Cambridge (MA). Called to Bar, Inner Temple, 1946; for some years director of local newspaper and book publishing cos and producer of TV documentary programmes until resuming practice at Bar, 1964. Dep. Circuit Judge and Asst Recorder, 1977–85. Mem. London County Council, 1952–58. Travelled extensively in USA, Middle East, Asia and Europe. Contested (Lab): Ashford (Kent) 1950, 1951 and 1955; Beckenham (by-election) 1957; Rushcliffe 1959; Heston & Isleworth 1966; SW Leicester (by-election) 1967; Chichester 1970; (SDP) Hayes and Harlington, 1983. MP (Lab 1971–81, SDP 1981–83) Hayes and Harlington, June 1971–83; Founder Mem., SDP, 1981, resigned 1987. Parly spokesman on NI, 1981–82, and on the arts, 1982–83; Vice-Chm., All-Party Productivity Gp; Sec., All-Party Theatre Gp; Jt Sec., British-Greek Parly Gp; Sec., British Gibraltar Parly Gp; Vice-Chm., Afghanistan Parly Support Cttee. Promoted, as a Private Mem's Bill, the Matrimonial Proceedings (Polygamous Marriages) Act, 1972. Member: Council, Nat. Cttee for Electoral Reform, 1977–88 (resigned); Nat. Council of European Movement, 1985–; Exec. Cttee, Wider Share Ownership Council, 1979–92; founder Mem., Manifesto Gp, 1975–80 (Hon. Treas.). Mem. Ct, Brunel Univ., 1975–81. *Address:* 71 Valiant House, Vicarage Crescent, SW11 3LX. *T:* and *Fax:* (020) 7223 5211; Villecelle, 34240 Lamalou-les-Bains, France. *T:* and *Fax:* 467952502. *Club:* Reform.   *Died 12 Jan. 2002.*

SANDERS, John Derek, OBE 1994; Director of Music, Cheltenham Ladies' College, 1968–97; Organist and Master of the Choristers, Gloucester Cathedral, 1967–94, Organist Emeritus, 1997; *b* 26 Nov. 1933; *s* of Alderman J. T. Sanders, JP, CA and Mrs E. M. Sanders (*née* Trivett); *m* 1967, Janet Ann Dawson; one *s* one *d. Educ:* Felsted Sch., Essex; Royal Coll. of Music; Gonville and Caius Coll., Cambridge. MusB 1956; MA 1958. ARCM 1952; FRCO 1953. Dir of Music, King's Sch., Gloucester, and Asst Organist, Gloucester Cathedral, 1958–63; Organist and Master of the Choristers, Chester Cathedral, 1964–67. Conductor: Gloucestershire Symphony Orchestra, 1967–94; Gloucester Choral Soc., 1967–94. Conductor of Three Choirs Festival, triennially, 1968–94. Pres., Cathedral Organists' Assoc., 1990–92; Mem. Council, RCO, 1979–94, and 1996–2000. Liveryman, Co. of Musicians, 1987. Freeman, City of London, 1986. DMus Lambeth, 1990. Hon. FRSCM 1991. *Publications:* Festival Te Deum, 1962; Soliloquy for Organ, 1977; Toccata for Organ, 1979; Te Deum Laudamus, 1985; Jubilate Deo, 1986; Two Prayers, 1988; A Canticle of Joy, 1991; The Reproaches, 1993; St Mark Passion, 1993. *Recreations:* gastronomy, travelling. *Address:* Ridge Cottage, Upton Bishop, Ross-on-Wye, Herefordshire HR9 7UD. *T:* (01989) 780482.   *Died 23 Dec. 2003.*

SANDERSON, George Rutherford, CBE 1978; British Council Representative, Spain, and Cultural Attaché, British Embassy, Madrid, 1976–79; *b* 23 Nov. 1919; *er s* of late George Sanderson and Edith Mary Sanderson, Blyth, Northumberland; *m* 1947, Jean Cecilia, *d* of late James C. McDougall, Chesterfield, Derbyshire; two *s. Educ:* Blyth Grammar Sch.; Univ. of London (BA 1st Cl. Hons French and Italian). War Service, 1940–46: RA, Malta and Egypt (Major). British Council, 1949–79: Actg Dir, Anglo Argentine Cultural Inst., La Plata, Argentina, 1949; Dir, Tucuman, Argentina, 1950–52; Asst Rep., Santiago, Chile, 1952–58; Dep. Area Officer, Oxford, 1958–62; Reg. Dir, and Dir Anglo Argentine Cultural Assoc., Rosario, Argentina, 1962–66; Asst Rep., Buenos Aires, 1966–69; Reg. Dir, and Dir Anglo Brazilian Cultural Soc.,

São Paulo, Brazil, 1969–72; Dir, Drama and Music Dept, and Dep. Controller, Arts Div., 1973; Educnl Attaché, British Embassy, Washington, 1973–76. Administering Officer, The Kennedy Scholarships and Knox Fellowships, ACU, 1979–82. *Recreations:* art, reading. *Address:* Leafield House, Holton, Oxford OX33 1PZ. *T:* (01865) 872526. *Club:* Athenæum. *Died 24 March 2002.*

SANDFORD, Prof. Cedric Thomas; Professor of Political Economy, University of Bath, 1965–87, then Professor Emeritus; Director of Bath University Centre for Fiscal Studies, 1974–86; *b* 21 Nov. 1924; *s* of Thomas Sandford and Louisa (*née* Hodge); *m* 1945, Evelyn Belch (*d* 1982); one *s* one *d*; *m* 1984, Christina Privett; one *d*. *Educ:* Manchester Univ. (BAEcon 1948, MAEcon 1949); London Univ. (BA History (external) 1955). Undergraduate, Manchester Univ., 1942–43 and 1946–48; RAF, 1943–46 (Pilot). Graduate Research Schol., Univ. of Manchester, 1948–49; Lectr, Burnley Municipal Coll., 1949–60; Sen. Lectr, subseq. Head of General and Social Studies Dept, Bristol Coll. of Science and Technology, 1960–65; Head of Sch. of Humanities and Social Sciences, Univ. of Bath, 1965–68, 1971–74, 1977–79. Visiting Prof., Univ. of Delaware, USA, 1969; Visiting Fellow: ANU, 1981, 1985; Univ. of Melbourne, 1990; Univ. of Newcastle, NSW, 1994. Mem., Meade Cttee on Reform of Direct Tax System, 1975–78; Consultant: Fiscal Div., OECD, 1976–79, 1985–87; Irish Commn on Taxation, 1982–85; World Bank, 1986; UN 1986; IMF 1989, 1992; Nat. Audit Office, 1992–94; UK Inland Revenue, 1995–97. Partner, Fiscal Publications, 1989–. *Publications:* Taxing Inheritance and Capital Gains (Hobart Paper 32, IEA), 1965, 2nd edn 1967; Economics of Public Finance, 1969, 4th edn 1992; Realistic Tax Reform, 1971; Taxing Personal Wealth, 1971; (sen. editor and jt author) Case Studies in Economics (3 vols), 1971, 2nd edn 1977; National Economic Planning, 1972, 2nd edn 1976; Hidden Costs of Taxation, 1973; (jtly) An Accessions Tax, 1973; (jtly) An Annual Wealth Tax, 1975; Social Economics, 1977; (jtly) Grants or Loans?, 1980; (jtly) The Costs and Benefits of VAT, 1981; The Economic Framework, 1982; (jtly) Tax Policy-Making in the United Kingdom, 1983; (jtly) The Irish Wealth Tax: a study in economics and politics, 1985; Taxing Wealth in New Zealand, 1987; (jtly) Administrative and Compliance Costs of Taxation, 1989; (jtly) The Compliance Costs of Business Taxes in New Zealand, 1992; Successful Tax Reform: lessons from an analysis of tax reform in six countries, 1993; (jtly) Key Issues in Tax Reform, 1993; (jtly) More Key Issues in Tax Reform, 1995; (jtly) Tax Compliance Costs: measurement and policy, 1995; (jtly) Further Key Issues in Tax Reform, 1998; Why Tax Systems Differ: a comparative study of the political economy of taxation, 2000; numerous articles in wide range of learned jls. *Recreations:* fishing, gardening, busking. *Address:* Old Coach House, Fersfield, Perrymead, Bath BA2 5AR. *T:* (01225) 832683. *Died 5 March 2004.*

SANDFORD, Jeremy; writer, journalist, musician; *b* 5 Dec.; *s* of late Christopher Sandford, owner/director of the Golden Cockerel Press, and Lettice Sandford, wood engraver, chalk worker; *m* 1st, 1956, Nell Dunn (marr. diss. 1986); three *s*; 2nd, 1988, Philippa Finnis. *Educ:* Eton; Oxford. Executive Mem., Gypsy Council. Formerly editor, Romano Drom (Gypsy newspaper); author/ researcher of many plays and documentaries for radio, stage and television. Screen Writers' Guild of Gt Britain Award, 1967, 1971; Prix Italia prize for TV drama, 1968; Critics Award for TV drama, 1971. *Publications:* Synthetic Fun, 1967; Cathy Come Home, 1967; Whelks and Chromium, 1968; Edna the Inebriate Woman, 1971; Down and Out in Britain, 1971; In Search of the Magic Mushrooms, 1972; Gypsies, 1973; Tomorrow's People, 1974; Prostitutes, 1975; Smiling David, 1975; Virgin of the Clearways, 1977; Figures and Landscapes, 1991; Hey Days in Hay, 1992; Castle by the Sea, 1998; Spirit of the Gypsies, 1999; Rokkering to the Gorjios, 1999; contribs to

Guardian, Sunday Times, etc. *Recreations:* painting, traditional and Romany Gypsy music (accordion and Irish whistle), travel, mountain exploration, riding, wandering, windsurfing, wondering, festivals, holistic educational camps, sacred circle dance. *Address:* Hatfield Court, Hatfield, Leominster, Herefordshire HR6 0SD. *Died 12 May 2003.*

SANDFORD, Kenneth Leslie, CMG 1974; retired barrister; *b* 14 Aug. 1915; *s* of Albert Edgar Sandford and Barbara Ivy (*née* Hill); *m* 1946, Airini Ethel Scott Sergel (decd); one *s* one *d* (and one *d* decd). *Educ:* King's Coll., Auckland, NZ; Auckland University Coll. (LLB 1938). Served War: 34 Bn (NZ), rank of Captain, 1940–45. Barrister and Solicitor, 1939–72; Crown Solicitor (Hamilton), 1950–72; Chm., Accident Compensation Commn (NZ), 1972–80. *Publications:* Dead Reckoning, 1955; Dead Secret, 1957; Mark of the Lion, 1962. *Recreation:* cricket (Pres. NZ Cricket Council, 1971–73). *Died 13 Oct. 2005.*

SANDHURST, 5th Baron *cr* 1871; **(John Edward) Terence Mansfield,** DFC 1944; *b* 4 Sept. 1920; *er s* of 4th Baron Sandhurst, OBE, and Morley Victoria (*née* Upcher; *d* 1961); *S* father, 1964; *m* 1947, Janet Mary, *er d* of late John Edward Lloyd, NY, USA; one *s* one *d*. *Educ:* Harrow. Served RAFVR, 1939–46: Bomber Command (as Navigator and Bombing Leader): 149 Sqdn, 1941; 419 (RCAF) Sqdn, 1942; 12 Sqdn, 1943–45. Metropolitan Special Constabulary 'C' Div., 1946–55, Sergeant, 1949–52; long service medal, 1955. Hon. ADC to Lieutenant-Governor of Jersey, 1969–74. *Recreation:* golf. *Heir: s* Hon. Guy Rhys John Mansfield, *b* 31 May 1943. *Educ:* Harrow; Oriel Coll., Oxford (MA). Called to Bar, Middle Temple, 1972]. *Address:* La Volière, Les Ruisseaux, St Brelade, Jersey JE3 8DD. *Clubs:* Royal Air Force, MCC; United (Jersey). *Died 2 June 2002.*

SANER, Robert M.; *see* Morton-Saner.

SANGER, Dr Ruth Ann, (Mrs R. R. Race), FRS 1972; Director, Medical Research Council Blood Group Unit, 1973–83 (Member of Scientific Staff, 1946–83); *b* 6 June 1918; *yr d* of late Rev. Hubert Sanger and Katharine M. R. Sanger (*née* Cameron), Urunga, NSW; *m* 1956, Robert Russell Race, CBE, FRS (*d* 1984); no *c*. *Educ:* Abbotsleigh, Sydney; Sydney Univ. (BSc 1939); London Univ. (PhD 1948). Scientific Staff of Red Cross Blood Transfusion Service, Sydney, 1940–46. Hon. Member: Sociedad de Hematologia del Instituto Mexicano del Seguro Social; Deutsche Gesellschaft für Bluttransfusion; Toronto Antibody Club; Norwegian Soc. of Immunohaematology; Internat. Soc. of Blood Transfusion; Genetical Soc. Hon. MD Helsinki, 1990. Landsteiner Meml Award, USA, 1957; Philip Levine Award, USA, 1970; Gairdner Foundn Award, Canada, 1972; Oliver Meml Award for Blood Transfusion, British Red Cross, 1973. *Publications:* (with R. R. Race) Blood Groups in Man, 1950, 6th edn, 1975; many papers in genetical and med. jls. *Address:* 22 Vicarage Road, East Sheen, SW14 8RU. *T:* (020) 8876 1508. *Died 4 June 2001.*

SANGSTER, Robert Edmund; *b* 23 May 1936; *o c* of late Mr Vernon Sangster and of Mrs Sangster. *Educ:* Repton Coll. Chairman: Vernons Orgn, 1980–88; Sangster Gp, 1988–. Owner of: The Minstrel (won Derby, 1977); Alleged (won Prix de l'Arc de Triomphe, 1977, 1978); Jaazeiro (won Irish Derby, 1978); Detroit (won Prix de l'Arc de Triomphe, 1980); Beldale Ball (won Melbourne Cup, 1980); Kings Lake (won Irish 2,000 Guineas, 1981); Our Paddy Boy (won Australian Jockey Club Cup, 1981); Golden Fleece (won Derby, 1982); Assert (won Irish Sweeps Derby, and French Derby, 1982); Lomond (won 2,000 Guineas, 1983); Caerleon (won French Derby, 1983); El Gran Señor (won 2,000 Guineas, Irish Sweeps Derby, 1984); Sadler's Wells (won Irish 2,000 Guineas, 1984); Gildoran (won Ascot Gold Cup, 1984, 1985, Goodwood Cup, 1984); Law Society (won Irish Derby,

1985); Committed (won Prix de l'Abbaye de Longchamp; Champion European Sprinter); Royal Heroine (Champion Grass Mare, USA, 1984); Marooned (won Sydney Cup, 1986); Prince of Birds (won Irish 2,000 Guineas, 1988); Rodrigo de Triano (won 2,000 Guineas and Irish 2,000 Guineas, 1992); Las Meninas (won 1,000 Guineas, 1994); Turtle Island (won Irish 2,000 Guineas, 1994); Riverina Charm (Champion, Australia, 1989); Kostroma (Champion, USA, 1991, 1992); Royal Heroine (Champion, USA, 1984); Revoque (Champion European Two Year Old, 1996). Leading winning race-horse owner, 1977, 1978, 1982, 1983 and 1984 seasons; owner of 741 Stakes winners, 1977–. *Recreation:* golf. *Address:* Manton House, Manton House Estate, Marlborough, Wilts SN8 1PN. *Club:* Jockey. *Died 7 April 2004.*

SARELL, Captain Richard Iwan Alexander, DSO 1939; RN retd; *b* 22 Feb. 1909; *s* of late Philip Charles Sarell; *m* 1961, Mrs Ann Morgan (*née* Keenlyside). *Educ:* Royal Naval Coll., Dartmouth. Entered RNC Dartmouth, 1922; Comdr 1943; Capt. 1948; specialised in Gunnery, 1934; DSO for action against enemy submarines while in command of HMS Broke, 1939; despatches, 1943. Naval Attaché, Moscow and Helsinki, 1949–51; student Imperial Defence Coll., 1952; Defence Research Policy Staff, 1954; retd 1957. *Recreation:* fishing. *Address:* 43 Rivermead Court, Ranelagh Gardens, SW6 3RX. *Died 31 Oct. 2001.*

SARELL, Sir Roderick (Francis Gisbert), KCMG 1968 (CMG 1958); KCVO 1971; HM Diplomatic Service, retired; *b* 23 Jan. 1913; *y s* of late Philip Charles Sarell, HM Consular Service and Ethel Ida Rebecca, *d* of late John Dewar Campbell; *m* 1946, Pamela Muriel (*d* 1994), *d* of late Vivian Francis Crowther-Smith; three *s*. *Educ:* Ashdown House, Sussex; Radley; Magdalen College, Oxford. HM Consular Service, 1936; Vice-Consul, Persia, 1937; Italian East Africa, 1939; Iraq, 1940; 2nd Secretary, Addis Ababa, 1942; 1st Secretary, HM Foreign Service, 1946; Rome, Bucharest, 1946; Foreign Office, 1949; Acting Counsellor, 1952; Counsellor and Consul-General, Rangoon, 1953; Consul-General, Algiers, 1956–59; Head of Southern Dept, Foreign Office, 1959–61, General Dept, 1961–63; Ambassador: to Libya, 1964–69; to Turkey, 1969–73. Coronation Medal, 1953. *Recreations:* swimming, building, walking. *Address:* The Litten, Hampstead Norreys, Thatcham, Berks RG18 0TD. *T:* (01635) 201274. *Clubs:* Oriental, Royal Over-Seas League; Leander. *Died 15 Aug. 2001.*

SARGINSON, Edward William; retired from Civil Service, 1976; with Confederation of British Industry until 1982; *b* 22 May 1919; *s* of Frederick William and Edith Sarginson; *m* 1944, Olive Pescod; one *s* one *d*. *Educ:* Barrow-in-Furness Grammar School. Entered Civil Service, War Office, 1936; served Infantry, 1939–46; Principal, Min. of Supply, 1955; Asst Sec., Min. of Aviation, 1965; Asst Under Sec. of State, MoD (PE), 1972–76. Voluntary work: with Childline, 1987–89; with Victim Support, 1990–91. *Recreations:* gardening, bowls. *Address:* 41 Kendall Avenue South, Sanderstead, Surrey CR2 0QR. *T:* (020) 8660 4476. *Died 16 Feb. 2004.*

SAUGMAN, Per Gotfred, Hon. OBE 1990; Knight of the Order of Dannebrog; Chairman, Blackwell Scientific Publications Ltd, Oxford, 1972–92 (Managing Director, 1954–87); *b* 26 June 1925; *s* of Emanuel A. G. Saugman and Esther (*née* Lehmann); *m* 1950, Patricia (*née* Fulford) (*d* 2005); two *s* one *d* (and one *s* decd). *Educ:* Gentofte Grammar Sch.; Commercial Coll., Copenhagen. Bookselling and publishing training in Denmark, Switzerland and England, 1941–49; Sales Manager, Blackwell Scientific Publications Ltd, 1952; Director, University Bookshops (Oxford) Ltd, 1963–92; Mem. Board, B. H. Blackwell Ltd, 1964–92; Chairman: William George's Sons Ltd, Bristol, 1965–92; Oxford Illustrators Ltd, 1968–98; Blackwell North America, Inc., 1975–92; Ejnar Munksgaard Publishers Ltd, Copenhagen, 1967–92; Kooyker Boekhandel Leiden, 1973–92; Athenaeum

Bookshop, Copenhagen, 1992; Oxford Shutter Co. Ltd, 1994–98. Member Council: International Publishers' Assoc., 1976–79; Publishers' Assoc. of GB and Ireland, 1977–82; President, Internat. Group of Scientific, Technical and Medical Publishers, 1977–79. Chairman: Oxford Round Table, 1953–55; Sunningwell Sch. of Art, 1972–. Trustee, City of Oxford Orch., 1996–. Hon. Mem., British Ecological Soc., 1960–; Governor: Oxford Polytechnic, 1972–85; Dragon Sch., Oxford, 1975–2000; Headington Sch., Oxford, 1988–2003. Fellow, St Cross Coll., Oxford, 1978; Hon. MA Oxford, 1978; Hon. Fellow, Green Coll., Oxford, 1981. Chevalier, Order of Icelandic Falcon, 1984. *Publications:* From the First Fifty Years, 1989, 2nd edn 1992; The Way I Think it Was (autobiog.), 1992; Ejnar Munksgaard: a biography, 1992, 2nd edn 1997; The Way it Was (autobiog.), 1994. *Recreations:* reading, art—English watercolours, golf. *Address:* Hollen House, Buckland, Faringdon, Oxon SN7 8QN. *T:* (01367) 870570, *Fax:* (01367) 870590. *Clubs:* Athenæum, Royal Automobile; Frilford Golf (Oxford). *Died 25 Nov. 2005.*

SAUNDERS, Dame Cicely (Mary Strode), OM 1989; DBE 1980 (OBE 1967); FRCP, FRCS; President, St Christopher's Hospice, since 2000 (Medical Director, 1967–85; Chairman, 1985–2000); *b* 22 June 1918; *d* of Gordon Saunders and Mary Christian Knight; *m* 1980, Prof. Marian Bohusz-Szyszko (*d* 1995), *s* of Antoni Bohusz-Szyszko, Wilno, Poland. *Educ:* Roedean Sch.; St Anne's Coll., Oxford (BA (war degree) 1945, MA 1960; Hon. Fellow, 1986); Nightingale Sch. of Nursing (SRN 1944); St Thomas's Hosp. Med. Sch. (MB, BS, 1957). FRCP 1974 (MRCP 1968); FRCN 1981; FRCS 1986. Founded St Christopher's Hospice, 1967 (St Christopher's became a Registered Charity in 1961 and was opened as a Hospice in 1967). Mem., MRC, 1976–79; Dep. Chm., Attendance Allowance Bd, 1979–85. Hon. Consultant, St Thomas' Hosp., 1985. AIMSW 1947. Freedom of London Boroughs: Bromley, 1987; Lewisham, 2000. Hon. FRCPsych 1988; Hon. FRSocMed 1995; Hon. Fellow: Sheffield City Polytechnic, 1983; Newnham Coll., Cambridge, 1986; Guy's and St Thomas' Med. Schs (UMDS), 1993; Liverpool John Moores, 1998; Middlesex Univ., 2000. Hon. DSc: Yale, 1969; London, 1983; Glasgow, 1990; Durham, 1995; McGill, 1997; Dr of Medicine, Lambeth, 1977; Hon. MD Belfast, 1984; DUniv: Open, 1978; Middlesex, 2000; Hon. LLD: Columbia, NY, 1979; Leicester, 1983; South Bank, 2003; Bath, 2005; DHL Jewish Theological Seminary of America, 1982; DU Essex, 1983; Hon. DCL: Canterbury, 1984; Cambridge, 1986; Oxford, 1986; Hon. Dr Med. TCD, 1988; Hon. MD Wales at Aberystwyth, 2002. Gold Medal, Soc. of Apothecaries of London, 1979; Gold Medal, BMA, 1987; Templeton Foundation Prize, 1981; Conrad N. Hilton Humanitarian Prize, 2001. DSG 1996. *Publications:* Care of the Dying, 1960, 2nd edn 1977; (ed) The Management of Terminal Disease, 1978, 3rd edn 1993; (ed jtly) Hospice: the living idea, 1981; Living with Dying, 1983, 2nd edn 1989; (ed) St Christopher's in Celebration, 1988; Beyond the Horizon, 1990; (ed) Hospice and Palliative Care, 1990; Watch With Me, 2003; various papers on terminal care. *Recreations:* theology, ethics, classical music. *Address:* St Christopher's Hospice, 51–59 Lawrie Park Road, Sydenham, SE26 6DZ. *T:* (020) 8768 4500. *Died 14 July 2005.*

SAUNDERS, James; playwright; *b* Islington, 8 Jan. 1925; *s* of Walter Percival Saunders and Dorcas Geraldine (*née* Warren); *m* 1951, Audrey Cross; one *s* two *d*. *Educ:* Wembley County Sch.; Southampton Univ. *Plays:* Moonshine, 1955; Alas, Poor Fred, The Ark, 1959; Committal, Barnstable, Return to a City, 1960; A Slight Accident, 1961; Double Double, 1962; Next Time I'll Sing to You (Evening Standard Drama Award), The Pedagogue, Who Was Hilary Maconochie?, 1963; A Scent of Flowers, Neighbours, 1964; Triangle, Opus, 1965; A Man's Best Friend, The Borage Pigeon Affair, 1969; After Liverpool, 1970; Games, Savoury Meringue, 1971; Hans

Kohlhaas, 1972; Bye Bye Blues, 1973; The Island, 1975; Bodies, 1977; Birdsong, 1979; Fall, 1981; Emperor Waltz, 1983; Scandella, 1985; Menocchio, 1985 (BBC Radio Play Award, 1986); Making it Better, 1992; Retreat, 1995; Lancelot, 2000; *stage adaptations:* The Italian Girl, 1968; The Travails of Sancho Panza, 1969; A Journey to London, 1973; Player Piano, 1978; Random Moments in a May Garden, 1980; The Girl in Melanie Klein, 1980; *television:* Watch Me I'm a Bird, 1964; Bloomers, 1979 (series); television adaptations of works by D. H. Lawrence, Henry James, H. E. Bates and R. F. Delderfield; *screenplays:* Sailor's Return; The Captain's Doll. Arts Council of GB Drama Bursary, 1960; Writers' Guild TV Adaptation Award, 1966; Arts Council Major Bursary, 1984. *Address:* c/o Casarotto Ramsay Ltd, 60–66 Wardour Street, W1V 3HP.   *Died 29 Jan. 2004.*

SAUNDERS, Sir John (Anthony Holt), Kt 1972; CBE 1970; DSO 1945; MC 1944; Chairman, Hongkong and Shanghai Banking Corporation, 1962–72; *b* 29 July 1917; *s* of late E. B. Saunders; *m* 1942, Enid Mary Durant Cassidy (*d* 1996); two *d. Educ:* Bromsgrove Sch. War Service, 1940–45; OCTU Sandhurst (Belt of Honour); N Africa, Sicily and Italy. Lived in Hong Kong 1950–72; MEC Hong Kong Govt, 1966–72. Chm. of Stewards, Royal Hong Kong Jockey Club, 1967–72.
Died 4 July 2002.

SAUNDERS, Sir Peter, Kt 1982; Chairman and Managing Director, Peter Saunders Group Ltd; Director: West End Theatre Managers Ltd; Theatre Investment Fund Ltd; Theatre Investment Finance Ltd; *b* 23 Nov. 1911; *s* of Ernest and Aletta Saunders; *m* 1st, 1959, Ann Stewart (*d* 1976); no *c*; 2nd, 1979, Catherine Baylis (*née* Imperiali dei Principi di Francavilla) (Katie Boyle); no *c. Educ:* Oundle Sch.; Lausanne. Film cameraman, film director, journalist and press agent; served War of 1939–45 (Captain); started in theatrical production, 1947; has presented over 100 plays incl. The Mousetrap, which ran from 1952 (became world's longest ever run, Dec. 1971; he produced it from 1952 until 1994 when he gave up active theatrical production); other West End productions include: Fly Away Peter; The Perfect Woman; Breach of Marriage; My Mother Said; The Hollow; Witness for the Prosecution; The Manor of Northstead; Spider's Web; The Water Gipsies; The Bride and the Bachelor; Subway in the Sky; Verdict; The Trial of Mary Dugan; The Unexpected Guest; A Day in the Life Of; And Suddenly it's Spring; Go Back For Murder; You Prove It; Fit To Print; Rule of Three; Alfie; The Reluctant Peer; Hostile Witness; Every Other Evening; Return Ticket; Arsenic and Old Lace; Justice Is A Woman; As You Like It; Oh Clarence!; On A Foggy Day; The Jockey Club Stakes; Move Over Mrs Markham; Lover; Cockie; Double Edge; A Murder is Announced; The Family Reunion; Cards On The Table; in 1971 acquired Volcano Productions Ltd, whose productions include: No Sex Please, We're British; The Mating Game; Lloyd George Knew My Father; At The End Of The Day; Touch Of Spring; Betzi; operated repertory at Royal Artillery Theatre, Woolwich, 1951, and at Prince of Wales Theatre, Cardiff, 1956; in 1958, took over a long lease of Ambassadors Theatre; bought Duchess Theatre, 1961, and sold it in 1968; held a long lease of St Martin's Theatre, 1968–94; bought Vaudeville Theatre, 1969, and sold it in 1983; bought Duke of York's Theatre, 1976 and sold it in 1979 to Capital Radio on condition that it remained a live theatre in perpetuity; has produced more than 1500 programmes for Radio Luxembourg; an original Dir, Yorkshire Television; Mem. consortium awarded London Gen. Radio Station by IBA, which became Capital Radio, 1973. Life Pres., Theatre Investment Fund, 1995; Vice-President: Actors' Benevolent Fund, 1972–; Royal General Theatrical Fund Assoc., 1985–; Mem. Bd, SOLT (formerly Mem. Exec. Council, SWET), 1954– (Pres. 1961–62 and 1967–69); Vice Pres., 1988–93; Hon. Vice Pres., 1999); Mem. Council, Theatrical Management Assoc., 1958–64. President: Stage Golfing Soc., 1963; Stage Cricket Club,

1956–65. Life Mem., Dogs Home Battersea Assoc., 1988. Governor, Christ's Hosp. Silver Heart award, Variety Club of GB, 1955. *Publications:* The Mousetrap Man (autobiog.), 1972; Scales of Justice (play), 1978. *Recreations:* cricket, chess, bridge, photography, music of George Gershwin, telephoning, collecting wills. *Address:* Monkswell, Canons Close, The Bishops Avenue, N2 0BH. *Club:* MCC.   *Died 6 Feb. 2003.*

SAUVAGNARGUES, Jean Victor, Commandeur, Légion d'honneur, et l'Ordre National du Mérite; Croix de Guerre avec palme (1939–45); Hon. GCMG 1976; French Ambassador; *b* Paris, 2 April 1915; *s* of Edmond Sauvagnargues and Alice Caplan; *m* 1948, Lise Marie L'Evesque; one *s* one *d* (and one *s* one *d* decd). *Educ:* Ecole normale supérieure; agrégé (in German); Dip., Ecole libre des sciences politiques. Attaché, Embassy, Bucharest, 1941. Served War with Free French Forces, 1943 (Army, June 1944–May 1945). Cabinet of: the High Commn, Beirut, 1943; M Massigli, 1944; Gen. de Gaulle, 1945–46; Specialist on German questions, Quai d'Orsay, 1947–55; Cabinet of M Pinay, 1955. In negotiations about the Saar, Jan.-June 1956; Ambassador to Ethiopia, 1956–60; Director, African and Middle-Eastern Affairs, Min. of Foreign Affairs, 1960–62; Ambassador to: Tunisia, 1962–70; FRG, 1970–74; Minister for Foreign Affairs, France, 1974–76; Ambassadeur de France, 1976; Ambassador to UK, 1977–81. *Address:* 14 avenue Pierre 1er de Serbie, 75116 Paris, France.
Died 6 Aug. 2002.

SAVAGE, Sir Ernest (Walter), Kt 1979; FCA; company director, retired; *b* 24 Aug. 1912; *s* of Walter Edwin Savage and Constance Mary Sutton; *m* 1938, Dorothy Winifred Nicholls; one *s* one *d. Educ:* Brisbane Grammar School; Scots Coll., Warwick, Qld. In public practice as chartered accountant, 1940–76; retd as Sen. Partner of Coopers & Lybrand, Queensland. Chairman, Bank of Queensland, 1960–84; Director of several other public companies, retired. Institute of Chartered Accountants in Australia: Mem. Queensland State Council, 1951–74 (Chm. three years); Nat. Council, 1961–73; Aust. Pres., 1968–70; elected Life Member, 1978. Hon. Consul for Norway at Brisbane, 1950–76. Chairman: Queensland Govt Cttee of Review of Business Regulations, 1985–86; Public Sector Review Cttee, 1987. Member: Bd of Governors, Cromwell UC, 1950–77 (Chm. 1958–67); Faculty of Commerce and Economics, Univ. of Queensland, 1960–67; Bd of Advanced Education, 1978–82 (Finance Cttee, 1974–83); Salvation Army Adv. Bd, 1981–92. Trustee, Leukaemia Foundn, 1983–; Chm., Geriatric Medical Foundn, 1986–94. Knight 1st class, Order of St Olav (Norway), 1966. *Recreation:* brick and concrete work. *Address:* Forest Place, R42/356 Blunder Road, Durack, Qld 4077, Australia. *T:* (7) 33722669. *Clubs:* Queensland, Brisbane (Brisbane).   *Died 16 July 2003.*

SAVORY, Hubert Newman, DPhil; FSA; Keeper of Archæology, National Museum of Wales, Cardiff, 1956–76; *b* 7 Aug. 1911; *s* of William Charles Newman Savory and Alice Amelia (*née* Minns); *m* 1949, Priscilla Valerie Thirkell; four *s* two *d. Educ:* Magdalen College Sch., Oxford; St Edmund Hall, Oxford Univ. (BA 1934 (Lit. Hum. 1st Cl.); DPhil 1937). Randall MacIver Student in Iberian Archæology, 1936–38. Assistant, 1938, Asst Keeper, 1939, Dept of Archæology, National Museum of Wales. Chm., Royal Commn on Ancient Monuments (Wales), 1979–83 (Mem., 1970–83); Mem., Ancient Monuments Board for Wales, 1957–84. Pres., Cambrian Archæological Assoc., 1975–76; Chm., Glamorgan Gwent Archæological Trust, 1975–84. Conducted excavations of various Welsh megaliths, round barrows, hill-forts, etc. Served War of 1939–45, in Army, 1940–45. *Publications:* Spain and Portugal: the Prehistory of the Iberian Peninsula, 1968; Guide Catalogues of the Early Iron Age Collections, 1976, and the Bronze Age Collections, 1980, National Museum of Wales; (ed) Glamorgan County History, vol. II, 1984; contrib. to: Celtic Art in Ancient

Europe, 1976; Hillforts, 1976; Settlement and Society in Wales, 1989; Proc. of Prehistoric Soc.; Archæologia Cambrensis, etc. *Recreations:* walking, gardening, genealogy. *Address:* 31 Lady Mary Road, Cardiff CF2 5NT. *T:* (029) 2075 3106. *Died 21 Feb. 2001.*

SAXON, David Stephen, PhD; President Emeritus, University of California; Hon. Chairman of the Corporation, Massachusetts Institute of Technology, 1990–95 (Chairman, 1983–90); *b* 8 Feb. 1920; *s* of Ivan Saxon and Rebecca Moss; *m* 1940, Shirley Goodman; six *d*. *Educ:* Massachusetts Institute of Technology (BS 1941; PhD 1944). Massachusetts Institute of Technology: Res. physicist, Radiation Lab., 1943–46; Philips Labs, 1946–47. Univ. of California at Los Angeles: Mem. of Faculty, 1947–75; Prof. of Physics, 1958–75; Chm. of Dept, 1963–66; Dean of Physical Sciences, 1966–68; Vice-Chancellor, 1968–75; Provost, Univ. of California, 1974–75, Pres., 1975–83. Guggenheim Fellow, 1956–57 and 1961–62; Fulbright grant, 1961–62. Vis. Prof., Univ. of Paris, Orsay, France, 1961–62; Vis. scientist, Centre d'Etudes Nucléaires, France, 1968–69; Vis. Research Fellow, Merton Coll., Oxford, 1981; consultant to research organisations, 1948–. Special research into theoretical physics: nuclear physics, quantum mechanics, electromagnetic theory and scattering theory. Dir, Eastman Kodak Co., 1983–90. Fellow: Amer. Acad. of Arts and Scis; Amer. Phys. Soc.; Member: Amer. Phil Soc.; Amer. Assoc. Physics Teachers; Amer. Inst. Physics; Amer. Assoc. for the Advancement of Science; Technical Adv. Council for Ford Motor Co., 1979–; Corp. of MIT, 1977–; Dir, Houghton Mifflin Co., 1984–90. Recipient of several honorary degrees. Member: Phi Beta Kappa; Sigma Pi Sigma; Sigma Xi. Royal Order of the Northern Star (Nordstjärnan), 1979. *Publications:* Elementary Quantum Mechanics, 1968; The Nuclear Independent Particle Model (with A. E. S. Green and T. Sawada), 1968; Discontinuities in Wave Guides (with Julian Schwinger), 1968; Physics for the Liberal Arts Student (with William B. Fretter), 1971. *Address:* University of California, Los Angeles, Department of Physics, Knudsen Hall Room 3145J, 405 Hilgard Avenue, Los Angeles, CA 90095–1547, USA. *Died 8 Dec. 2005.*

SAYERS, Ross Edward; Chairman, Macquarie European Infrastructure Fund Advisory Panel, since 2004; non-executive Director: Intertek Group plc, since 2002; Network Rail, since 2002; Turbo Genset Inc., since 2005; *b* 1 Sept. 1941; *s* of Stanley and Grace Sayers; *m* 1964, Glenda Seath; two *s*. *Educ:* Auckland GS; Auckland Univ. (Dip. Business and Industrial Admin); Harvard Univ. (AMP). FCA (NZ) 1962. Man. Dir, Holeproof NZ Ltd, 1958–75; Partner, McElroy Speakman & Co., 1976–77; Gen. Manager, Ops, Feltex NZ, 1977–83; Man. Dir, NZ Breweries, 1983–86; Chairman and Chief Executive: NZ Railways Corp., 1986–88; State Rail Authy of NSW, 1988–92; Man. Dir and CEO, China Light and Power Co. (HK), subseq. CLP Hldgs, 1993–2000; Chairman: Innogy Hldgs, 2000–02; Wales & West Utilities Ltd, 2004–; A-Train AB, 2004–; non-exec. Chm., Associated British Ports Hldgs, 2002–04. NZ Commemoration Medal, 1990. *Recreations:* walking, photography. *Address:* (office) Level 30, CityPoint, 1 Ropemaker Street, EC2Y 9HD. *T:* (020) 7065 2201. *Clubs:* Athenæum, Royal Automobile. *Died 25 Nov. 2005.*

SAYNOR, John, CMG 1992; JP; Secretary and Director-General, Commonwealth War Graves Commission, 1989–92; *b* 28 Sept. 1930; *s* of Charles Herbert Saynor and Emily Saynor (*née* Mundie); *m* 1954, Jennifer Ann Nelson; two *s*. *Educ:* Doncaster Grammar Sch. Commnd RASC, 1949–51. Post Office, 1951–69; Dept for National Savings, 1969–74; Commonwealth War Graves Commn, 1974–92. Mem. Bd, High Wycombe YMCA, 1992–2002 (Chm., 1992–98; Vice-Chm., 1998–2000); Mem. Cttee, Flackwell Heath Age Concern, 1998–. JP Berks, 1983. *Recreations:* gardening, golf, bridge, travel, painting. *Address:* 12 The Meadows, Flackwell Heath, High

Wycombe, Bucks HP10 9LX. *T:* (01628) 523459.
Died 16 Aug. 2002.

SCAIFE, Geoffrey Richard, CB 1999; Chief Executive, Avon, Gloucestershire and Wiltshire Strategic Health Authority, since 2003; *b* 12 Jan. 1949; *m* 1971, Janet Elizabeth Woodward; two *s* two *d*. *Educ:* Workington GS. DHSS, 1968–71, 1975–83; seconded to Prime Minister's Private Office, 1971–74; Mersey RHA, 1983–93, Chief Exec., 1989–93; Chief Exec., Mgt Exec. for NHS in Scotland, Scottish Office, then Scottish Exec., DoH, 1993–2000; Chief Exec., Birmingham HA, then Birmingham and The Black Country Strategic HA, 2000–02. Mem. Bd, Nat. Develt Team for People with Learning Disabilities, 1992–95. *Address:* Avon, Gloucestershire and Wiltshire Strategic Health Authority, Jenner House, Langley Park Estate, Chippenham, Wilts SN15 1GG. *Died 20 April 2004.*

SCALES, Prof. John Tracey, OBE 1986; FRCS, LRCP; CIMechE; Hon. Director, 1988–93 and Director, Pressure Sore Prevention, 1994–97, RAFT Institute of Plastic Surgery (formerly Department of Research in Plastic Surgery), Regional Plastic and Oral Surgery Centre, Mount Vernon Hospital; Professor of Biomedical Engineering, Institute of Orthopaedics, University of London, 1974–87, then Emeritus; *b* 2 July 1920; *s* of late W. L. Scales and E. M. Scales (*née* Tracey); *m* 1945, Cecilia May (*d* 1992), *d* of late A. W. Sparrow; two *d*. *Educ:* Haberdashers' Aske's Sch., Hampstead; King's Coll., London; Charing Cross Hosp. Med. Sch. MRCS, LRCP 1944; FRCS 1969. CIMechE 1966. Captain RAMC, 1945–47. Casualty Officer and Resident Anaesthetist, Charing Cross Hosp., 1944; Royal National Orthopaedic Hosp., Stanmore: House Surgeon, 1944–45 and 1947–49; MO i/c Plastics Res. Unit, 1949–50; Hon. Registrar, 1950–52; Hon. Sen Registrar, 1952–57; Lectr i/c Plastics Res. Unit, Inst. of Orth., Stanmore, 1951–52; Sen. Lectr i/c Plastics Res. Unit (re-named Dept. of Biomechanics and Surg. Materials, 1956; re-named Dept of Biomed. Engrg, 1968), Inst. of Orth., Univ. of London, 1952–68; Consultant in Orthopaedic Prosthetics, 1958–68, in Biomedical Engrg, 1968–87, Royal Nat. Orthopaedic Hosp., Stanmore and London (Hon. Consultant); Reader in Biomed. Engrg, Dept of Biomed. Engrg, Inst. of Orth., Univ. of London, 1968–74; Consultant in Biomed. Engrg, Mt Vernon Hosp., Northwood, 1969–85; Consultant, Royal Orthopaedic Hosp., Birmingham, 1978–87. Vis. Prof., Biomed. Centre, Cranfield Univ., 1997–98. Chairman: BSI Cttee on Orthopaedic Joint-replacements, 1981–91; ISO Cttee on Bone and Joint Replacements; Member: IMechE Engrg in Medicine Gp, 1966–91 (Founder Mem.); Adv. Panel on Med. Engrg, National Fund for Res. into Crippling Diseases (Chm., 1981–85); Biol Engrg Soc., 1960– (Founder Mem.); Hon. Member: Eur. Soc. of Biomechanics, 1976– (Former Pres., Founder Mem.); British Assoc. of Plastic Surgeons, 1993–. Ext. Examiner, Univ. of Surrey, 1969–84, and other univs. Freeman, City of London, 1995. FRSocMed 1950; Companion Fellow, British Orth. Assoc., 1959 (Sen. Companion Fellow, 1994); FBES 1994; FIPEM 1995. Thomas Henry Green Prize in Surgery, Charing Cross Hosp. Med. Sch., 1943; Robert Danis Prize, Internat. Soc. of Surgery, Brussels, 1969; James Berrie Prize, RCS, 1973; Clemson Univ. Award, USA, 1974; S. G. Brown Award, Royal Soc., 1974; A. A. Griffith Silver Medal, Materials Science Club, 1980; Jackson Burrows Medal, Royal Nat. Orthopaedic Hosp., Stanmore, 1985; Don Julius Groen Prize, IMechE, 1988. Kentucky Colonel, 1986. Member Editorial Board: Engineering in Medicine; Clinical Materials, 1986–; Wounds, 1989–. Research includes development of: polymeric orthopaedic splints and appliances, 1945–81; bone and joint prostheses and joint replacements, using metals and polymers, 1949–87; British cuirass respirator, 1950–53; Airstrip, 1954–59; air support systems for prevention of pressure sores, 1960–82. *Publications: chapters in:* Modern Trends in Surgical Materials, ed Gillis, 1958; Aspects of Medical Physics, ed

Rotblat, 1966; Surgical Dressings and Wound Healing, ed Harkiss, 1971; (and ed jtly) Bed Sore Biomechanics, 1976; Surgical Dressings in the Hospital Environment, ed Turner and Brain, 1976; Treatment of Burns, ed Donati, Burke and Bertelli, 1976; Scientific Foundations of Orthopaedics and Traumatology, ed Owen, Goodfellow and Bullough, 1980; also jt author of chapters in med. books; contrib. Proc. RSM, Proc. IMechE, Proc. Physiol Soc., BMJ, Jl of Bone and Jt Surg., Lancet, Nature, and other med. and scientific jls; contrib. conf. and symposia reports. *Recreations:* walking dogs, Goss china. *Address:* Fairbanks, Riverview Road, Pangbourne, Berks RG8 7AU. *T:* (0118) 9843568, *Fax:* (0118) 9844945.

Died 30 Jan. 2004.

SCANLON, Baron *cr* 1979 (Life Peer), of Davyhulme in the County of Greater Manchester; **Hugh Parr Scanlon;** President, Amalgamated Union of Engineering Workers, 1968–78; Member, British Gas Corporation, 1976–82; *b* 26 Oct. 1913; *m* 1943, Nora; two *d. Educ:* Stretford Elem. Sch.; NCLC. Apprentice, Instrument Maker, Shop Steward-Convener, AEI, Trafford Park; Divisional Organiser, AEU, Manchester, 1947–63; Member: Exec. Council, AEU, London, 1963–67; TUC Gen. Council, 1968–78; TUC Econ. Cttee, 1968–78. Member: NEDC, 1971–; Metrication Bd, 1973–78; NEB, 1977–79; Govt Cttee of Inquiry into Teaching of Maths in Primary and Secondary Schs in England and Wales, 1978–; Chm., Engineering Industry Training Bd, 1975–82. Vice-Pres., Internat. Metalworkers' Fedn, 1969–78; Pres., European Metal Workers' Fedn, 1974–78. Hon. DCL Kent, 1988. *Recreations:* golf, swimming, gardening. *Address:* 23 Seven Stones Drive, Broadstairs, Kent CT10 1TW. *Club:* Eltham Warren Golf. *Died 27 Jan. 2004.*

SCARBROUGH, 12th Earl of, *cr* 1690; **Richard Aldred Lumley;** Viscount Lumley (Ire.), 1628; Baron Lumley, 1681; Viscount Lumley, 1690; Lord-Lieutenant of South Yorkshire, since 1996 (Vice Lord-Lieutenant, 1990–96); *b* 5 Dec. 1932; *o s* of 11th Earl of Scarbrough, KG, GCSI, GCIE, GCVO, PC, and Katharine Isobel, Dowager Countess of Scarbrough, DCVO, K-i-H (*d* 1979), *d* of late R. F. McEwen; *S* father, 1969; *m* 1970, Lady Elizabeth Ramsay (LVO 2002; Lady of the Bedchamber to Queen Elizabeth the Queen Mother, 1994–2002), *d* of 16th Earl of Dalhousie, KT, GCVO, GBE, MC; two *s* one *d. Educ:* Eton; Magdalen College, Oxford. 2nd Lt 11th Hussars, 1951–52; formerly Lt Queen's Own Yorkshire Dragoons. ADC to Governor and C-in-C, Cyprus, 1956. Hon. Col, 1st Bn The Yorkshire Volunteers, 1975–88. President: Northern Area, Royal British Legion, 1984–93; York Georgian Soc., 1985–92; Northern Assoc. of Building Socs (formerly Yorkshire and North Western Assoc. of Building Socs), 1985–95. Mem., Royal Commn on Historical MSS, 1994–2003. Trustee, Leeds Castle Foundn, 1983–. Hon. RIBA, Yorks Region. Hon. LLD Sheffield, 2001. DL S Yorks, 1974. *Heir: s* Viscount Lumley, *b* 18 May 1973. *Address:* Sandbeck Park, Maltby, Rotherham, S Yorks S66 8PF. *T:* (01302) 742210. *Clubs:* White's; Jockey (Newmarket). *Died 23 March 2004.*

SCARLETT, His Honour **James Harvey Anglin;** a Circuit Judge, 1974–89; *b* 27 Jan. 1924; *s* of Lt-Col James Alexander Scarlett, DSO, RA, and Muriel Scarlett, *d* of Walter Blease; unmarried. *Educ:* Shrewsbury Sch.; Christ Church, Oxford (MA). Served War, Royal Artillery (Lieut), 1943–47. Called to the Bar, Inner Temple, 1950; a Recorder of the Crown Court, 1972–74. Malayan Civil Service, 1955–58. *Recreation:* gardening. *Address:* Chilmington Green, Great Chart, near Ashford, Kent TN23 3DP. *Clubs:* Athenæum; Athenæum (Liverpool). *Died 25 June 2005.*

SCARMAN, Baron *cr* 1977 (Life Peer), of Quatt in the county of Salop; **Leslie George Scarman,** Kt 1961; OBE 1944; PC 1973; a Lord of Appeal in Ordinary, 1977–86; *b* 29 July 1911; *s* of late George Charles and Ida Irene Scarman; *m* 1947, Ruth Clement Wright; one *s. Educ:* Radley College (Classical Schol., 1925); Brasenose

College, Oxford (Open Classical Scholar, 1930; Hon. Mods 1st cl., 1932; Lit. Hum. 1st cl., 1934; Hon. Fellow, 1966). Served RAFVR, 1940–45. Harmsworth Law Scholar, Middle Temple, 1936, Barrister, 1936; QC 1957; a Judge of the High Court of Justice, Probate, Divorce, and Admiralty Div., later Family Div., 1961–73; a Lord Justice of Appeal, 1973–77. Chairman: Law Commn, 1965–73; Council of Legal Educn, 1973–76; President: Constitutional Reform Centre, 1984–; Citizen Action Compensation Campaign, 1988–. Chm., Univ. of London Court, 1970–86 (Dep. Chm., 1966–70); Chancellor, Univ. of Warwick, 1977–89. Vice-Chm., Statute Law Cttee, 1967–72. Pres., Senate of Inns of Court and Bar, 1976–79. Mem. Arts Council, 1968–70, 1972–73; Vice-Chm., ENO, 1976–81. Pres., RIPA, 1981–89. Hon. Fellow: Imperial Coll., Univ. of London, 1975; UCL, 1985; LSE, 1985; Leeds, 1987; Brunel, 1988. Hon. LLD: Exeter, 1965; Glasgow, 1969; London, 1971; Keele, 1972; Freiburg, 1973; Warwick, 1974; Bristol, 1976; Manchester, 1977; Kent, 1981; Wales, 1985; QUB, 1990; Dundee, 1990; Hon. DCL: City, 1980; Oxon, 1982. Chm., Malcolm Clubs, RAF. Order of Battle Merit (Russia), 1945. *Publications:* Pattern of Law Reform, 1967; English Law—The New Dimension, 1975. *Recreations:* gardening, walking. *Address:* House of Lords, SW1A 0PW. *Club:* Royal Air Force. *Died 8 Dec. 2004.*

SCATCHARD, Vice-Adm. **John Percival,** CB 1963; DSC 1941, first Bar, 1944, second Bar, 1945; *b* 5 Sept. 1910; *s* of Dr James P. Scatchard, MB, BS, Tadcaster, Yorks; *m* 1943, Edith Margaret Niven (*d* 1988); one *d. Educ:* Aysgarth School, Yorkshire; RNC Dartmouth. Joined RN, 1924; served War of 1939–45, in HMS Kashmir-Garth and Termagent; Captain (D) Portsmouth, 1951–52; Captain 5th Destroyer Squadron, 1957–58; Director Naval Equipment, Admiralty, 1959–60; Commandant, Joint Services Staff College, Latimer, Bucks, 1960–62; Flag Officer, Second-in-Command, Far East Fleet, 1962–64; retd list, 1964. *Recreation:* gardening. *Address:* Reachfar, 46 Newtown Road, Warsash, near Southampton, Hants SO31 9FZ. *Died 22 June 2001.*

SCHAFFTER, **Ernest Merill James;** Secretary, Royal Aeronautical Society, 1973–82 (Deputy Secretary, 1970–73); Director, Engineering Sciences Data Unit Ltd, 1975–82; *b* 1922; *er s* of late Dr Charles Merill Schaffter and of Bertha Grace Brownrigg, of the CMS in Isfahan, Iran; *m* 1951, Barbara Joy, *o c* of Alfred Bennett Wallis and Hilda Frances Hammond; three *d. Educ:* Trent Coll., Nottinghamshire; King's Coll., Cambridge. BA 1950, MA 1955. Served War: RAF, as Pilot with Coastal and Transport Command, Flt Lt, 1941–46. De Havilland Aircraft Co., Hatfield, as Aerodynamicist and Engr, 1950–54; Marshall's Flying Sch., Cambridge, as Engr, 1954–60; Marshall of Cambridge (Eng) Ltd, as Personal Asst to Chief Designer and later as Design Office Manager, 1960–70. Freeman, GAPAN, 1978. FRAeS, AFAIAA, AFCASI, FCMI. *Address:* 43 Speldhurst Road, W4 1BX. *T:* (020) 8723 1728, *Fax:* (020) 8995 0708. *Died 15 April 2004.*

SCHAPERA, Prof. **Isaac,** FBA 1958; FRSSAf 1934; Emeritus Professor, University of London (London School of Economics), 1969; *b* Garies, South Africa, 23 June 1905; 3rd *s* of late Herman and Rose Schapera. *Educ:* S African Coll. Sch., Cape Town; Univ. of Cape Town (MA 1925);Univ. of London (PhD 1929, DSc 1939). Prof. of Social Anthropology, Univ. of Cape Town, 1935–50; Prof. of Anthropology, LSE, 1950–69 (Hon. Fellow, 1974). Visiting Professor: Univ. of Chicago, 1948; Univ. of Toronto, 1953. Many anthropological field expeditions to Bechuanaland Protectorate, 1929–50. Chm., Assoc. of Social Anthropologists of the British Commonwealth, 1954–57; Pres., RAI, 1961–63. Hon. DLitt: Cape Town, 1975; Botswana, 1985; Hon. LLD Witwatersrand, 1979. *Publications:* The Khoisan Peoples of South Africa, 1930; A Handbook of Tswana Law and Custom, 1938; Married Life in an African Tribe, 1940; Native Land Tenure in the

Bechuanaland Protectorate, 1943; Migrant Labour and Tribal Life, 1948; The Ethnic Composition of Tswana Tribes, 1952; The Tswana, 1953; Government and Politics in Tribal Societies, 1956; Praise Poems of Tswana Chiefs, 1965; Tribal Innovators, 1970; Rainmaking Rites of Tswana Tribes, 1971; Kinship Terminology in Jane Austen's Novels, 1977; editor: Western Civilization and the Natives of South Africa, 1934; The Bantu-speaking Tribes of South Africa, 1937; David Livingstone's Journals and Letters 1841–1856 (6 vols), 1959–63; David Livingstone: South African papers 1849–1853, 1974; contrib. to many learned jls. *Address:* 157 White House, Albany Street, NW1 3UP. *Died 26 June 2003.*

SCHLESINGER, John Richard, CBE 1970; film director; *b* 16 Feb. 1926; *s* of late Bernard Schlesinger, OBE, MD, FRCP and Winifred Henrietta (*née* Regensburg). *Educ:* Uppingham; Balliol Coll., Oxford (BA; Hon. Fellow 1981). Associate Dir, NT, 1973–88. Mem., Theatre Dirs' Guild of GB, 1983–. Directed: *films:* for Monitor and Tonight (BBC TV), 1958–60; Terminus, for British Transport Films, 1960 (Golden Lion Award, Venice Film Fest., 1961); A Kind of Loving, 1961 (Golden Bear Award, Berlin Film Festival, 1962); Billy Liar, 1962–63; Darling, 1964–65 (NY Critics Award); Far from the Madding Crowd, 1966–67; Midnight Cowboy, 1968–69 (Acad. Award for Best Dir; Soc. of TV and Film Acad. Award for Best Dir; Dir's Guild of America Award); Sunday, Bloody Sunday, 1971 (Soc. of TV and Film Acad. Award for Best Dir; David di Donatello Award); contrib. Visions of Eight, 1973; Day of the Locust, 1975; Marathon Man, 1976; Yanks, 1978 (New Evening Standard Award, 1980); Honky Tonk Freeway, 1980; The Falcon and the Snowman, 1984; The Believers, 1987; Madame Sousatzka, 1988 (screenplay with Ruth Prawer Jhabvala); Pacific Heights, 1991; The Innocent, 1994; Eye for an Eye, 1995; The Next Best Thing, 2000; *television:* Separate Tables, 1982; An Englishman Abroad, 1983 (BAFTA Award, Broadcasting Press Guild Award, Barcelona Film Fest. Award and Nat. Bd of Review Award, 1984); A Question of Attribution, 1991 (BAFTA Award); Cold Comfort Farm, 1995 (film, 1996); Sweeney Todd, 1997; *plays:* No, Why, 1964, Timon of Athens, and Days in the Trees, 1964–66, for RSC; I and Albert, Piccadilly, 1972; Heartbreak House, 1975, Julius Caesar, 1977, and True West, 1981, for NT; *opera:* Les Contes d'Hoffmann, 1980 (SWET Award, 1981), and Der Rosenkavalier, 1984, for Covent Garden; Un Ballo in Maschera, for Salzburg Fest., 1989; Peter Grimes, for La Scala, Milan and LA Opera, 2000. Fellow, BAFTA, 1995. David di Donatello Special Award, 1980; Shakespeare Prize, FVS Foundn of Hamburg, 1981; Outstanding Achievement in Directing, Hollywood Film Fest., 1999. *Recreations:* gardening, travel, music, antiques. *Address:* c/o Duncan Heath, ICM, Oxford House, 76 Oxford Street, W1D 1BS. *Died 25 July 2003.*

SCOBLE, (Arthur William) John; Chairman, Economic Planning Board, South West Region (Bristol), 1965–71, retired; *b* Plymouth, 11 Jan. 1910; *er s* of Arthur and Mabel Scoble; *m* 1935, Constance Aveline (*d* 1995), *d* of Samuel Robbins; three *d. Educ:* Sexey's Sch., Bruton, Som. Entered Civil Service, 1930; HM Customs and Excise, 1930–40; Min. of Supply, 1940–44; Min. of Nat. Insce, 1945–50; jssc 1950; Min. of Works, 1951–59; UN, Buenos Aires, 1960–61; Min. of Works, 1962–64; Dept of Economic Affairs, 1965–70; Dept of the Environment, 1970–71, 1972–73. Chm., Agricl Housing Adv. Cttee, 1977–81. Dir, Bath Preservation Trust, 1973–74. Regional Advisor, Employment Fellowship, 1975–79. Clerk to Bathampton Council, 1980–86. *Address:* 4 Somerset Road, Southsea, Hants PO5 2NL. *T:* (023) 9275 0508. *Died 10 Jan. 2001.*

SCOBLE, John; *see* Scoble, A. W. J.

SCORER, Philip Segar; Consultant solicitor, Burton & Co., Lincoln, since 1991 (Partner, 1952–91); *b* 11 March 1916; *s* of late Eric W. Scorer and Maud Scorer (*née* Segar);

m 1950, Monica Smith; one *s* three *d. Educ:* Repton. Admitted Solicitor, 1938; LCC Legal Dept, 1938–40. Served War, Army (Royal Signals: War Office, SHAEF and BAS, Paris), 1940–46. Solicitors' Dept, New Scotland Yard, 1947–51; Clerk of the Peace, City of Lincoln, 1952–71; Under-Sheriff of Lincolnshire, 1954–96, of Humberside, 1974–96; Asst Under-Sheriff of Lincolnshire, 1996–; a Recorder, 1976–83. Pres., Under Sheriffs Assoc., 1978–84. Hon. Solicitor, Lincoln and Dist CAB, 1966–2000. *Address:* (office) Stonebow, Lincoln LN2 1DA. *T:* (01522) 523215. *Club:* National Liberal. *Died 18 May 2003.*

SCOTT, Sir (Charles) Peter, KBE 1978 (OBE 1948); CMG 1964; HM Diplomatic Service, retired; *b* 30 Dec. 1917; *er s* of late Rev. John Joseph Scott and Dorothea Scott (*née* Senior); *m* 1954, Rachael, *yr d* of C. W. Lloyd Jones, CIE; one *s* two *d. Educ:* Weymouth Coll.; Pembroke Coll., Cambridge. Indian Civil Service: Probationer, 1939; appointed to Madras Presidency, 1940; Asst Private Sec. to Viceroy, 1946–47. Entered HM Diplomatic Service, 1947; Second Sec., Tokyo, 1948; First Sec., 1949; Foreign Office, 1950; Private Sec. to Gen. Lord Ismay at NATO, Paris, 1952; First Secretary: Vienna, 1954; British Information Services, NY, 1956; Counsellor and Consul-General, Washington, 1959; idc, 1962; Head of UK Mission to European Office of UN, Geneva, 1963; Minister, Rome, 1966–69; Temp. Vis. Fellow at Centre for Contemporary European Studies, Univ. of Sussex, 1969–70; Asst Under-Sec. of State, FCO, 1970–75; Ambassador to Norway, 1975–77. Private Sec., 1978–79, Treasurer, 1979–81, to HRH Prince Michael of Kent. *Recreations:* walking, and such as offer. *Address:* 284 Kew Road, Kew, Richmond, Surrey TW9 3DU. *T:* (020) 8948 4262. *Clubs:* Oxford and Cambridge; Hawks (Cambridge). *Died 16 Jan. 2002.*

SCOTT, Edward John Rankin, CMG 2002; Chairman, John Swire & Sons Ltd, since 1998; *b* 3 Jan. 1939; *s* of late Lt-Col C. R. Scott, KRRC and Elizabeth Meade, *d* of 5th Earl of Clanwilliam; *m* 1997, Angela Brice; one *d. Educ:* Eton; McGill Univ. (BA Hons). Joined Swire Group, 1960: Swire Hong Kong, 1964–65; Swire Japan, 1965–67; Man. Dir, 1971–76, Chm., 1976–97, John Swire & Sons Pty Ltd; Dir, Swire Pacific, 1993–. Director: Brick & Pipe Industries, 1975–81 (Chm., 1981–88); Cathay Pacific Airways, 1976–; Steamships Trading Co., 1979–96 (Chm., 1997–); United States Cold Storage, 1981–85 (Chm., 1985–2001); James Finlay Ltd, 1991–. Chairman: Internat. Assoc. of Refrigerated Warehousemen, Washington, 1988 (Dir, 1985–89); Australia and NZ Trade Adv. Cttee, 1997–. *Recreations:* fishing, farming. *Address:* Swire House, 59 Buckingham Gate, SW1E 6AJ. *T:* (020) 7834 7717. *Clubs:* White's, MCC; Melbourne; Union, Australian Jockey (Sydney). *Died 29 Jan. 2002.*

SCOTT, Most Rev. Edward Walter, CC 1978; Archbishop, and Primate of All Canada, 1971–86; *b* Edmonton, Alberta, 30 April 1919; *s* of Tom Walter Scott and Kathleen Frances Ford; *m* 1942, Isabel Florence Brannan (*d* 2000); one *s* three *d. Educ:* Univ. of British Columbia; Anglican Theological Coll. of BC. Vicar of St Peter's, Seal Cove, 1943–45; SCM Secretary, Univ. of Manitoba, 1945–59; Staff of St John's Coll., Winnipeg, 1947–48; Rector: St John the Baptist, Fort Garry, 1949–55; St Jude's, Winnipeg, 1955–60; Dir, Diocesan Council for Social Service, Diocese of Rupert's Land, and Priest Dir of Indian Work, 1960–64; Associate Sec., Council for Social Service, Anglican Church of Canada, 1964–66; Bishop of Kootenay, 1966–71. Moderator of Executive and Central Cttees, WCC, 1975–83; Pres., Canadian Council of Churches, 1985. Mem. Commonwealth Eminent Persons Gp on South Africa, Dec. 1985–June 1986. DD Lambeth, 1986; Hon. DD: Anglican Theol Coll., BC, 1966; Trinity Coll., Toronto, 1971; Wycliffe Coll., Toronto, 1971; Huron Coll., Ont., 1973; United Theol Coll., Montreal, 1971; Renison Coll., Waterloo; Coll. of Emmanuel & St Chad, Saskatoon,

1979; Univ. of Victoria Coll., Toronto, 1986; Queen's Univ., Kingston, 1987; Hon. DCL St John's Coll., Winnipeg, 1971; Hon. STD: Dio. Theol Coll., Montreal, 1973; Thorneloe Coll., Ont., 1974; Hon. LLD York, 1987. Human Relations Award, Canadian CCJ, 1987. *Recreation:* carpentry. *Address:* 1177 Yonge Street, Unit 208, Toronto, ON M4T 2Y4, Canada.

Died 21 June 2004.

SCOTT, Sir Ian Dixon, KCMG 1962 (CMG 1959); KCVO 1965; CIE 1947; Ambassador to Norway, 1965–68; *b* Inverness, 6 March 1909; *s* of Thomas Henderson Scott, OBE, MICE, and Mary Agnes Dixon, Selkirk; *m* 1937, Hon. Anna Drusilla Lindsay, *d* of 1st Baron Lindsay of Birker, CBE, LLD; one *s* four *d*. *Educ:* Queen's Royal College, Trinidad; Balliol College, Oxford (MA); London School of Economics. Entered Indian Civil Service, 1932; Indian Political Service, 1935; Assistant Director of Intelligence, Peshawar, 1941; Principal, Islamia College, Peshawar, 1943; Deputy Private Secretary to the Viceroy of India, 1945–47; Dep. Dir of Personnel, John Lewis & Co. Ltd, 1948–50; appointed to Foreign Service, 1950; First Secretary, Foreign Office, 1950–51; British Legation, Helsinki, 1952; British Embassy, Beirut, 1954; Counsellor, 1956; Chargé d'Affaires, 1956, 1957, 1958; idc 1959; Consul-General, then Ambassador to the Congo, 1960–61; Ambassador to Sudan, 1961–65. Chm., Clarksons Holidays Ltd, 1972–73 (Dir, 1969–73). Chm., Suffolk AHA, 1973–77; Member: Council, Dr Barnardo's, 1970–84 (Chm., 1972–78; elected Vice-Pres., 1984–); Bd of Governors, Felixstowe Coll., 1971–84 (Chm., 1972–78); Chm., Indian Civil Service (retd) Assoc., 1977–97 (Hon. Life Pres., 1997). *Publications:* Tumbled House, 1969; A British Tale of Indian and Foreign Service: the memoirs of Sir Ian Scott, 1999. *Recreation:* sailing. *Address:* Leiston Old Abbey Residential Home, Leiston, Suffolk IP16 4RF. *Died 3 March 2002.*

SCOTT, Sir Michael, KCVO 1979 (MVO 1961); CMG 1977; HM Diplomatic Service, retired; *b* 19 May 1923; *yr s* of late John Scott and Kathleen Scott; *m* 1st, 1944, Vivienne Sylvia Vincent-Barwood (marr. diss.); three *s*; 2nd, 1971, Jennifer Slawikowski (*née* Cameron Smith), *widow* of Dr George J. M. Slawikowski. *Educ:* Dame Allan's School; Durham Univ. War Service: Durham Light Infantry, 1941; 1st Gurkha Rifles, 1943–47. Joined Colonial Office, 1949; CRO, 1957; First Secretary, Karachi, 1958–59; Deputy High Commissioner, Peshawar, 1959–62; Counsellor and Director, British Information Services in India, New Delhi, 1963–65; Head of E and Central Africa Dept, FCO, 1965–68; Dep. High Comr, British High Commn, Nicosia, 1968–72; RCDS, 1973; Ambassador to Nepal, 1974–77; High Comr in Malaŵi, 1977–79; High Comr in Bangladesh, 1980–81. Sec.-Gen., Royal Commonwealth Soc., 1983–88. Dir, Tiger Mountain Gp (Nepal and India), 1984–93. Mem., Governing Council, ODI, 1983–93; Trustee, Internat. Agricl Trng Programme, 1988–2001. Dep. Chm., Drive for Youth Programme, 1987–93. *Address:* 87A Cornwall Gardens, SW7 4AY. *T:* (020) 7589 6794. *Club:* Oriental. *Died 9 June 2004.*

SCOTT, Rt Hon. Sir Nicholas (Paul), KBE 1995 (MBE 1964); PC 1989; JP; *b* 5 Aug. 1933; *e s* of late Percival John Scott; *m* 1st, 1964, Elizabeth Robinson (marr. diss. 1976); one *d*, and one adopted *s* (one adopted *d* decd); 2nd, 1979, Hon. Mrs Cecilia Anne Tapsell, *d* of 9th Baron Hawke; one *s* one *d*. *Educ:* Clapham College. Mem., Holborn BC, 1956–59 and 1962–65; contested (C) SW Islington, 1959 and 1964. MP (C): Paddington S, 1966–Feb. 1974; Chelsea, Oct. 1974–1997. PPS to: Chancellor of the Exchequer, Rt Hon. Iain Macleod, 1970; Home Sec., Rt Hon. Robert Carr, 1972–74; Parly Under-Sec. of State, Dept of Employment, 1974; Opposition spokesman on housing, 1974–75; Parly Under Sec. of State, 1981–86; Minister of State, 1986–87, Northern Ireland Office; Minister of State, DHSS, then DSS, 1987–94. Mem., 1922 Exec. Cttee, 1978–81; Dir, London Office, European

Cons. Gp in European Parlt, 1974. Nat. Chm., Young Conservatives, 1963 (Vice-Pres., 1988–89); Chm., Conservative Parly Employment Cttee, 1979–81 (Vice-Chm., 1967–72); formerly Nat. Pres., Tory Reform Gp. Chairman: Westminster Community Relations Council, 1967–72; Paddington Churches Housing Assoc., 1970–76; British Atlantic Gp Younger Politicians, 1970–73; Dep. Chm., British Caribbean Assoc.; Mem. Council, Community Service Volunteers; Governor, British Inst. of Human Rights; Dep. Chm., Youthaid, 1977–79. Mem., Cttee, MCC, 1972–75. Churchwarden, St Margaret's, Westminster, 1971–73. Man. Dir, E. Allom & Co., 1968–70; Chm., Creative Consultants Ltd, 1969–79; Director: A. S. Kerswill Ltd, 1970–81; Eastbourne Printers Ltd, 1970–81; Juniper Studios Ltd, 1970–81; Midhurst White Holdings Ltd, 1977–78; Bonusbond Hldgs Ltd, 1980–81; Bonusplan Ltd, 1977–81; Cleveland Offshore Fund Inc., 1970–81; Throgmorton Securities Ltd, 1970–74; Ede & Townsend, 1977–80; Learplan Ltd, 1978–81; Consultant: Campbell-Johnson Ltd, 1970–76; Roulston & Co. Inc., 1970–78; Lombard North Central Ltd, 1971–74; Clevebourne Investments Ltd, 1974–76; Claremont Textiles Ltd, 1974–76; Procter & Gamble Ltd, 1974–78; Hill & Knowlton (UK) Ltd, 1981; Bank of Ireland, 1994–97; Clarke Smith Industries, 1994–96; Tara Television, 1997–; VSO, 1974–76; Council, Bank Staff Assocs, 1968–77. Freeman, City of London, 1979; Liveryman, GAPAN, 1988. JP London, 1961. *Recreations:* cricket, tennis, golf, flying. *Clubs:* Pratt's, Garrick, Chelsea Arts, MCC, Hurlingham, Queen's; St Enodoc.

Died 6 Jan. 2005.

SCOTT, Norman Bruce St Clair, CMG 1994; Director: Diplomatic Studies Programmes, Graduate Institute of International Studies, Geneva, since 1999 (Visiting Professor, 1963–98); ECPD Regional Institute for Development Studies, Skopje, Macedonia, since 2000; *b* 13 April 1933; *s* of John Reid Scott and Isobel Carmichael-Brown; *m* 1955, Mirjana Matejovic; one *s* one *d*. *Educ:* Glasgow Univ. (MA 1954); Univ. of Belgrade; Univ. of Geneva; Coatbridge Acad. UN Economic Commission for Europe: Sen. Economist, Res. Div., 1966–73; Dir, Technol. Div., 1974–83; Dir, Trade Div., 1983–93; Sen. Dir, UN Secretariat, retd 1993. Consultant, IMF, 1994–. Pres., Centre for Res. on Internat. Instns, Geneva, 1986–. *Publications:* numerous essays on comparative economic systems and policies in collective works; contrib. economic and technical jls. *Recreations:* angling, antique map collecting. *Address:* 2 avenue De Warens, 1203 Geneva, Switzerland. *T:* (22) 3448664; Glower, Birsay, Orkney KW17 2ND. *Clubs:* Athenæum, Oriental.

Died 10 March 2004.

SCOTT, Sir Peter; *see* Scott, Sir C. P.

SCOTT, Col Robert Edmond Gabriel, MBE 1959; MC 1953; Director General, Engineering Industries Association, 1981–82; *b* 3 Aug. 1920; *s* of Edmond James and Lilian Kate Scott; *m* 1942, Anna Maria Larkin; two *s*. *Educ:* Roan, Greenwich. Commissioned into Durham Light Inf., 1942; regimental service with this regt in Western Desert, Italy, Korea and Rhine Army, 1942–52; Staff duties, MoD and Eastern Comd, 1952–56; service with W African Frontier Force, 1956–60; comd inf. batt., Home Service, 1960–66; seconded to Diplomatic Service, as Defence Adviser, Lagos, 1966–70; Dep. Comd, W. Midland Dist, 1970–72; retired, 1972. Engineering Industries Association: Export Sec. and Dep. Dir, 1973–77; Dir, 1977–81. *Recreations:* rough shooting, country pursuits, philately. *Address:* Zaria, 22 Crail Close, Wokingham, Berks RG11 2PZ. *T:* (0118) 977 6595.

Died 4 Jan. 2002.

SCOTT, Prof. Thomas Frederick McNair, MD; MRCS, FRCP; Associate Director of Ambulatory Pediatrics, 1983–85, retired, then Emeritus Professor of Paediatrics, Hahnemann University; Senior Physician, The Children's Hospital of Philadelphia, 1940–69, then Physician Emeritus; *b* 18 June 1901; *e s* of Robert

Frederick McNair Scott, MB, ChB (Edin.), and Alice Nystrom; *m* 1936, Mary Dwight Baker, PhD (Radcliffe), *o d* of late Clarence Dwight Baker, Wisconsin, USA; one *s* one *d*. *Educ*: Cheltenham College; Caius College, Cambridge (Scholar; Natural Science Tripos Pt I Class I, Part II (Physiology) Class II; MA; MD 1938); St George's Hospital (Jun. Univ. Entrance Schol.; Brackenbury Prize in Medicine, 1926); qualified conjoint board, 1927. MRCP 1928, FRCP 1953. Casualty Officer, House Surgeon, House Physn, Resident Obst. Asst, Medical Registrar, at St George's Hospital, 1927–29; House Physician Queens Hospital for Children, 1930; Research Fellow of Medicine, Harvard University, Mass, USA, 1930–31; Instructor in Pædiatrics Johns Hopkins University, Baltimore, Md, USA, 1931–34; Assistant Resident Physician at Hospital of Rockefeller Institute for Medical Research, New York, USA, working on Virus diseases, 1934–36; Assistant Physician i/c of Children's Out-patients, Lecturer in Children's Diseases, at St George's Hospital, SW1, Assistant Physician at Queens Hospital for Children, E2, 1936–38; Prof. of Pediatrics, Temple Univ. Med. Sch., Philadelphia, 1938–40; Research Prof. of Pediatrics, Univ. of Pennsylvania, 1940–66, Prof. of Paediatrics, 1966–69, then Emeritus; Prof. of Paediatrics, 1974, Co-ordinator of Ambulatory Care Teaching, 1974–75, and Co-Dir, Ambulatory Paediatrics, 1975–83, Hahnemann Med. Coll. and Hosp. Dist. Service Award, The Children's Hosp. of Philadelphia, 1977; Corp. medal, Hahnemann Med. Coll., 1978; Alumni Award, Children's Hosp. Alumni Orgn, 1989. Elected Faculty Mem., Medical Students' Honor Soc. (AOA), 1981. *Publications*: papers on cytology and blood diseases, lead poisoning in children, virus diseases of the central nervous system, herpes simplex infections, common exanthemata, history of measles and herpes. *Address*: 2 Franklin Town Boulevard 1605, Philadelphia, PA 19103, USA. *Died 25 Nov. 2001.*

SCOTT, Dame Thora; *see* Hird, Dame T.

SCOTT-BARRETT, Lt-Gen. Sir David (William), KBE 1976 (MBE 1956); MC 1945; GOC Scotland and Governor of Edinburgh Castle, 1976–79; Chairman, Army Cadet Force Association, 1982–96; *b* 16 Dec. 1922; 2nd *s* of late Brig. Rev. H. Scott-Barrett, CB, CBE; *m* 1st, 1948, Marie Elise (*d* 1985), *d* of late Norman Morris; three *s*; 2nd, 1992, Judith, *widow* of Major John Waring. *Educ*: Westminster School. Commnd Scots Guards, 1942; served NW Europe, 3rd Armd Bn Scots Guards; GSO3 Gds Div., 1948; Co. Comdr 2nd Bn Malaya, 1951; GSO2, 1st Div., 1955; DS Camberley, 1961; Comdt Gds Depot, 1963; GSO1, 4th Div. BAOR, 1965; comd 6 Inf. Bde BAOR, 1967; idc 1970; GOC Eastern District, 1971–73; GOC Berlin, 1973–75. Col Comdt, Scottish Div., 1976–79; Hon. Col, 205 (Scottish) Gen. Hosp., RAMC, TAVR, 1981–88. *Club*: Cavalry and Guards.

Died 1 Jan. 2004.

SCOTT-ELLIOT, Aydua Helen, CVO 1970 (MVO 1958); FSA; retired 1970; *b* 11 Dec. 1909; *d* of late Lewis Alexander Scott-Elliot and Princess Eydua Odescalchi. *Educ*: St Paul's Girls' School and abroad. Temp. Asst Civilian Officer, Admty, 1941–46; Keeper of Prints and Drawings, Royal Library, Windsor Castle, 1946–69. *Publications*: articles in Burlington Magazine, Apollo, Papers of the Bibliographical Soc. of America, etc. *Club*: University Women's. *Died 9 July 2003.*

SCOTT-MALDEN, (Charles) Peter, CB 1966; retired civil servant; *b* 29 June 1918; *e s* of late Gilbert Scott Scott-Malden and Phyllis Dorothy Scott-Malden (*née* Wilkinson); *m* 1941, Jean Honor Chamberlain Silver, *yr d* of late Lt-Col J. P. Silver, CBE, DSO, RAMC; two *s* two *d*. *Educ*: Winchester Coll. (Schol.); King's College, Cambridge (major Scholar). Entered Ministry of Transport, 1939. War of 1939–45; RAMC 1940–41; Glider Pilot Regiment, 1942–45. Ministry of Transport, later Department of the Environment: Asst Sec., 1949; Under-Sec., 1959; Dep. Sec., 1968, retired, 1976.

Member: Transport Tribunal, 1978–88; Management Cttee, Hanover Housing Assoc., 1978–93; Nat. Exec. Cttee, Abbeyfield Soc., 1983–90. *Recreations*: music, watching golf. *Address*: 18A Tower Road, Tadworth, Surrey KT20 5QY. *T*: (01737) 215644.

Died 27 Nov. 2001.

SCOTT-MALDEN, Peter; *see* Scott-Malden, C. P.

SCOTT-SMITH, Catharine Mary, MA; Principal of Beechlawn Tutorial College, Oxford, 1966–71, retired; *b* 4 April 1912; *d* of Edward Montagu Scott-Smith and Catharine Lorance (*née* Garland). *Educ*: Wycombe Abbey School, Bucks; Girton College, Cambridge (MA). Classics Mistress: St Katharine's School, Wantage, 1933–37; Godolphin School, Salisbury 1937–41; Classics Mistress and house-mistress, Headington School, Oxford, 1941–47, Second Mistress, 1946–47; Classics Mistress and house-mistress, Wycombe Abbey School, Bucks, 1947–55, Second Mistress, 1951–54; Headmistress of Westonbirt School, Tetbury, Gloucestershire, 1955–64. Member Council: Berkhamsted School for Girls; Berkhamsted School; Mem. Exec. Cttee, GBGSA, 1975–78. Pres., Wycombe Abbey School Seniors, 1974–79. *Club*: University Women's.

Died 28 Jan. 2004.

SCOWEN, Sir Eric (Frank), Kt 1973; MD, DSc; FRCP, FRCS, FRCPE, FRCPath, FRPharmS, FRCGP; Director, Medical Professorial Unit, 1955–75, Physician, 1946–75, St Bartholomew's Hospital; Professor of Medicine, University of London, 1961–75; *b* 22 April 1910; *s* of late Frank Edward Scowen and Eleanor Betsy (*née* Barnes) (*d* 1969). *Educ*: City of London School; St Bartholomew's Hospital Medical College; MD 1935, DSc 1962, London; MA KCL 1988. FRCP 1941; FRCS 1960; FRCPE 1965; FRCPath 1965; FRPharmS 1984; FRCGP 1989. St Bartholomew's Hospital: House Physician, 1931–33, Second Assistant, 1933, to Medical Professorial Unit; Baly Research Fell. in Clin. Med., 1933; First Asst to Med. Professorial Unit, 1935; Asst Dir of Med. Prof. Unit, and Asst Physician, 1937–55; Rockefeller Research Fell. to Columbia Univ., New York, 1937; Reader in Medicine, Univ. of London, 1938–61. Chairman: Council, Imperial Cancer Research Fund, 1967–82 (Vice-Pres., 1982); British Pharmacopœia Commission, 1963–69; Cttee on Safety of Medicines (formerly Cttee on Safety of Drugs), 1969–80 (Mem.), 1963); Cttee on the Review of Medicines, 1975–78; Poisons Bd (Home Office), 1976–83. Chm. Council, Sch. of Pharmacy, Univ. of London, 1979–88 (Hon. Fellow, 1986). FKC 2000. FRSA 2000. Hon. LLD Nottingham, 1979. *Publications*: various in medical and scientific journals. *Address*: Flat 77, 6/9 Charterhouse Square, EC1M 6EX. *T*: (020) 7251 3212. *Club*: Athenæum. *Died 23 Nov. 2001.*

SCRIMSHAW, Frank Herbert; *b* 25 Dec. 1917; *s* of late John Leonard Scrimshaw and Jessie Scrimshaw (*née* Sewell), Lincoln; *m* 1950, Joan Olive, *d* of Leslie Stephen Paskall, Felixstowe; one *s*. *Educ*: The City Sch., Lincoln; University Coll., Nottingham; BSc London. Joined Scientific Civil Service, 1939; various posts at RAE, Farnborough, and Blind Landing Experimental Unit, RAF Martlesham Heath, 1939–58; Dir of Scientific Research (Electronics), Min. of Aviation, 1959–61; RRE, Malvern: Head of Guided Weapons Group, 1961–65; Head of Mil. and Civil Systems Dept, 1965–67; Dir Gen., Electronics R&D, Min. of Technology, later MoD, 1967–72; Dep. Dir, RAE, Farnborough, 1972–78, retired. *Address*: 53 Feoffees Road, Somersham, near Huntingdon, Cambs PE28 3JQ. *T*: (01487) 840143. *Died 23 Feb. 2005.*

SCRIVEN, Wilton Maxwell, AO 1983; Member, Council on the Ageing (Chairman, Seniors Week Committee); *b* 10 Dec. 1924; *m* 1948, Marjorie Reta Shaw; two *s* two *d*. *Educ*: Univ. of Adelaide (BSc). FIEAust. Flying Officer RAAF; served with RAF Sqdn 622 Mildenhall, 1943–45. Engr, PMG's Dept, 1946–64; Regional Dir, Dept of Trade, 1965–66; Chm., Australian

Industrial Research and Develt Grants Bd, 1967–68; Dir of Industrial Develt, S Australian Govt, 1969–76; Agent General for S Australia in London, 1977–80; Director General: S Aust. Dept of Premier and Cabinet, 1980–83; Dept of Lands, SA, 1983–84. Mem. Bd, Investigator Sci. and Technol. Centre, 1992–. *Recreations:* tennis, golf, flute. *Address:* 7 Knightsbridge Road, Leabrook, SA 5068, Australia. *Clubs:* Royal Over-Seas League; Kensington Gardens Tennis (Australia). *Died 20 April 2002.*

SCRIVENER, Ronald Stratford, CMG 1965; HM Diplomatic Service, retired; *b* 29 Dec. 1919; *s* of Sir Patrick Scrivener, KCMG and Margaret, 2nd *d* of Walter Dorling; *m* 1st, 1947, Elizabeth Drake-Brockman (marr. diss. 1952); 2nd, 1962, Mary Alice Olga Sofia Jane Hohler, *d* of late Squadron-Leader Robert Charlton Lane; two step *s* two step *d. Educ:* Westminster School; St Catharine's College, Cambridge. Served with Royal Air Force Volunteer Reserve, 1940–45. Appointed HM Diplomatic Service, 1945; served in Berlin, Buenos Aires, Vienna, Caracas, Berne, Bangkok; Ambassador to: Panama, 1969–70; Czechoslovakia, 1971–74; Asst Under-Sec. of State, FCO, 1974–76. Mem. Council, Franco-British Soc., 1978–97. Freeman of City of London, 1984; Liveryman, Scriveners' Co., 1984–. *Publications:* Economic Handbook to the Soviet Union, 1986; Market Survey of Spain, 1987. *Recreations:* travel, fishing. *Address:* 38 Lysia Street, SW6 6NG. *T:* (020) 7385 3013. *Club:* White's.
Died 14 Jan. 2001.

SEABROOKE, George Alfred; retired consultant in education and training; Director, The Polytechnic, Wolverhampton, 1977–85; *b* 8 Dec. 1923; *s* of late John Arthur Seabrooke and Elsie Seabrooke; *m* 1945, Evelyn Sargent (*d* 2003); two *s. Educ:* Keighley Boys' Grammar Sch.; Bradford Technical Coll.; Stoke-on-Trent Tech. Coll.; King's Coll., London Univ. FBIM 1978. National Service, 1946–48. Post Office Engrg Dept, 1940–50; Estate Duty Office, Comrs of Inland Revenue, 1950–56; SW London Coll. of Commerce, 1956–60; Trent Polytechnic, Nottingham (and precursor Colls), 1960–73; Dep. Dir, NE London Polytechnic, 1974–77. *Publications:* Air Law, 1964; contrib. learned jls. *Recreations:* music, cricket, rugby. *Address:* 6 John Trundle Court, Barbican, EC2Y 8DJ. *Died 2 April 2004.*

SEAGER, Major Ronald Frank, RA, retired; Executive Director, RSPCA, 1971–78 (Secretary, 1966–71); Advisory Director, International Society for Protection of Animals; *b* 27 May 1918; *s* of Frank Seager and Lilias K. (*née* Parr); *m* 1941, Josephine, *d* of Rev. R. M. Chadwick; one *s* one *d. Educ:* St Albans School. Royal Artillery (HAC), 1939; commnd, 1941; Italy, 1944–45; seconded Royal Pakistan Artillery, 1949–50; served Korean War, 1953–54; Perm. Pres. Courts Martial, Eastern Command, 1960–63. Joined RSPCA, 1963. *Recreations:* golf, gardening. *Address:* 4 Thornbank Court, Long Street, Sherborne, Dorset DT9 3BS. *T:* (01935) 816223.
Died 2 Oct. 2001.

SEBRIGHT, Sir Peter Giles Vivian, 15th Bt *cr* 1626, of Besford, Worcs; *b* 2 Aug. 1953; *s* of Sir Hugo Giles Edmund Sebright, 14th Bt and of Deirdre Ann, *d* of late Major Vivian Lionel Slingsby Bethell; *S* father, 1985; *m* 1st, 1977, Regina Maria (marr. diss.), *d* of Francis Steven Clarebrough, Melbourne; one *s*; 2nd, 1987, Madeleine; one *s* one *d*. Heir: *s* Rufus Hugo Giles Sebright, *b* 31 July 1978. *Died 25 Oct. 2003.*

SECCOMBE, Hugh Digorie, CBE 1976; Chairman, Seccombe Marshall & Campion Ltd, 1962–77; *b* 3 June 1917; *s* of Lawrence Henry Seccombe, CBE and Norah (*née* Wood); *m* 1947, Eirene Rosemary Banister, *d* of Richard and Eirene Whittow, and *widow* of Lieut P. C. McC. Banister, DSC, RN; one *s* one *d. Educ:* Stowe; Sidney Sussex Coll., Cambridge (BA 1938, MA 1942). RNVR, 1939–50, retd, Lt-Comdr. Joined Seccombe Marshall & Campion, 1938; Dir, 1947. Chm., YWCA Central Club, 1971–86. Fellow, Inst. of Bankers, 1964.

Recreations: gardening, fishing. *Address:* Brook End, Gosden Common, Bramley, Guildford, Surrey GU5 0AE. *T:* (01483) 893296. *Died 11 June 2001.*

SECOMBE, Sir Harry (Donald), Kt 1981; CBE 1963; actor, comedian and singer; *b* 8 Sept. 1921; *s* of Frederick Ernest Secombe; *m* 1948, Myra Joan Atherton, Swansea; two *s* two *d. Educ:* Dynevor School, Swansea. Served with Royal Artillery, 1939–46. Windmill Theatre, 1947–48; General Variety, 1948–. Appearances included: London Palladium, 1956, 1958, 1959, 1961, 1966; Royal Command Perfs, 1951, 1955, 1957, 1958, 1963, 1966, 1969, 1975, 1978, 1987; (musical) Pickwick, Saville, 1963, Chichester Fest., Sadler's Wells, and nat. tour, 1993; (musical) The Four Musketeers, Drury Lane, 1967; The Plumber's Progress, Prince of Wales, 1975. Radio: Goon Show, 1949–60, and special performance of Goon Show for 50th Anniversary of BBC, 1972. Television: BBC, ITV, CBS (New York), Yorkshire TV, 1950–; Presenter, Highway, Tyne Tees TV, 1983–93; Sunday Morning with Secombe, STV, 1994; Songs of Praise, BBC TV, 1995–. *Films:* Davy, for Ealing Films, 1957; Jetstorm, 1959; Bed-Sitting Room, 1968; Mr Bumble in Oliver!, 1968; Bjornsen in Song of Norway, 1969; Rhubarb, 1969; Doctor in Trouble, 1970; The Magnificent Seven Deadly Sins, 1971; Sunstruck, 1972. Many recordings, 1953–. FRSA 1971. Hon. DMus Wales, 1986. *Publications:* Twice Brightly, 1974; Goon for Lunch, 1975; Katy and the Nurgla, 1978; Welsh Fargo, 1981; Goon Abroad, 1982; The Harry Secombe Diet Book, 1983; Harry Secombe's Highway, 1984; The Highway Companion, 1987; Arias and Raspberries (autobiog.), 1989; The Nurgla's Magic Tear, 1990. *Recreations:* film photography, literature, travel, golf, cricket. *Address:* Willinghurst House, Shamley Green, Guildford, Surrey GU5 0SU. *Clubs:* Savage, Royal Automobile, Lord's Taverners, Variety Club of Great Britain, St James's (Founder Mem.).
Died 11 April 2001.

SEDDON, Richard Harding, PhD; RWS 1976 (ARWS 1972); ARCA; artist and writer; President, Royal Watercolour Society, 1995–96; *b* 1 May 1915; *s* of Cyril Harding Seddon; *m* 1946, Audrey Madeline Wareham. *Educ:* King Edward VII School; RCA; Univ. of Reading (PhD 1946). Served with RAOC Field Park, France, 1940 (King's Badge); facilities by War Office Order to make war drawings in Maginot Line, 1940. Demonstrator in Fine Art, Univ. of Reading, 1944; Extra-Mural Staff Tutor in Fine Art, Univ. of Birmingham, 1947; Dir, Sheffield City Art Galls, 1948–63; Curator, Ruskin Collection, 1948–63; Dir of Art History and Liberal Studies, Sch. of Design and Furniture, Buckinghamshire Coll. of Higher Educn, 1963–80. Hon. Adv. Panel, Hereford Art Galls, 1948; Arts Council Selection Bd (Art Students Exhib.), 1947; Pres. Ludlow Art Soc., 1947–67. Mem., Oxford Bureau for Artists in War-time, 1940; Chm. Selection Cttee, Nottingham Artists Exhibition, 1953; Guest Speaker Educational Centres Assoc. Annual Conference, 1951; West Riding Artists Exhibition Selection Cttee, 1956; Northern Young Artists Exhibition Selection Cttee, 1958. Hon. Member: Sheffield Soc. of Artists; Oxford Folk Art Soc.; Sheffield Photographic Soc. Member Sheffield Univ. Court; Sheffield Diocesan Adv. Cttee, 1948. Exhibitor at: RA; NEAC; RI; RBA; Internat. Artists; Architectural Assoc.; RIBA; Nat. Gall. (War Artists), 1943; Leicester Galls; Redfern Galls. Official acquisitions: V&A Mus., 1939; Pilgrim Trust, 1942; Imperial War Mus. (War Artists), 1943, 1956 (ten paintings); Graves Gall., Sheffield, 1943 and 1956; Atkinson Gall., Southport, 1953; Reading Art Gall., 1956; Leeds Educn Cttee Collection, 1956. Extra Mural and Univ. Extension lectr on art to Univs of Oxford, Birmingham, London and Sheffield, 1948–; initiated Sheffield Conf. on Nation's Art Treasures, 1958; FMA, 1951–74; Mem., Yorkshire Fed. Museums and Art Galls, 1948 (Cttee, 1952 and 1957, Pres., 1954–55, Vice-Pres., 1955–56); Sec., Yorks Museums Regional Fact Finding Cttee, 1959; NACF Rep. for Yorks, 1954–63; Judge for

Wakefield Art Galls Open Art Competition, 1984. Hon. Adviser to Co. of Cutlers in Hallamshire, 1950–64; Dep. Chm., Sheffield Design Council for Gold, Silver and Jewelry Trades, 1960; Member: BBC '51 Soc., 1960; Govg Council, Design and Res. Centre, 1960; Art Adv. Cttee Yorks Area Scheme for Museums and Art Galls, 1963; Art Critic: Birmingham Post, 1963–71; Yorkshire Post, 1974–92; Jl Fedn of British Artists, 1975–83; Mem. Recognised Panel of London Univ. Extension Lectrs, 1964; Mem. Council and Hon. Treasurer, 1976, Trustee, 1983–86, RWS; Hon. Artist Mem., RI, 1996; Hon. Treas., Artists' League of GB, 1984–86. Hon. Mem., Mark Twain Soc., USA, 1976. *Publications:* The Technical Methods of Paul Nash (Memorial Vol.), 1949; The Artist's Vision, 1949; The Academic Technique of Oil Painting, 1960; A Hand Uplifted (war memoirs), 1962; Art Collecting for Amateurs, 1964; (ed) Dictionary of Art Terms, 1981; The Artist's Studio Book, 1983; articles on fine art for Jl of Aesthetics (USA), Burlington Magazine, Apollo, The Studio, The Connoisseur, Arch. Review, The Artist, The Antique Collector and daily press; lectures on art in England and abroad; criticisms; book reviews; broadcasts. *Recreation:* gardening. *Address:* 6 Arlesey Close, Putney, SW15 2EX. *T:* (020) 8788 5899.

Died 17 Aug. 2003.

SEFTON OF GARSTON, Baron *cr* 1978 (Life Peer), of Garston in the County of Merseyside; **William Henry Sefton;** Chairman, North West Economic Planning Council, 1975–89; Vice-Chairman and Board Member, Warrington and Runcorn Development Corporation, 1981–85 (Chairman, 1974–81, Board Member, 1964–81, Runcorn Development Corporation); *b* 5 Aug. 1915; *s* of George and Emma Sefton; *m* 1st, 1940, Phyllis Kerr (*d* 1991); 2nd, 2000, Mrs Evelyn Pimblett. *Educ:* Duncombe Road Sch., Liverpool. Joined Liverpool CC, 1953, Leader 1964; Chm. and Leader, Merseyside CC, 1974–77, Opposition Leader, 1977–79. Joined Runcorn Develt Corp., 1964, Dep. Chm. 1967. Member: New Towns Commn, 1978–85; SSRC, 1978. *Recreations:* gardening, woodwork. *Address:* House of Lords, SW1A 0PW.

Died 9 Sept. 2001.

SEGAL, Ben; *see* Segal, J. B.

SEGAL, Prof. Judah Benzion, (Ben), MC 1942; FBA 1968; Professor of Semitic Languages in the University of London, School of Oriental and African Studies, 1961–79, then Emeritus; *b* 21 June 1912; *s* of Prof. Moses H. Segal and Hannah Leah Segal; *m* 1946, Leah (*née* Seidemann); two *d. Educ:* Magdalen College School, Oxford; St Catharine's College, Cambridge. Jarrett Schol., 1932; John Stewart of Rannoch Schol., in Hebrew, 1933; 1st Cl. Oriental Langs Tripos, 1935; Tyrwhitt Schol. and Mason Prizeman, 1936. BA (Cambridge), 1935, MA 1938; DPhil (Oxford) 1939. Colours, Cambridge Univ. Boxing Club, 1935, 1936. Mansel Research Exhibitioner, St John's Coll., Oxford, 1936–39; James Mew Schol., 1937. Deputy Assistant Director, Public Security, Sudan Government, 1939–41; served War of 1939–45, GHQ, MEF, 1942–44, Captain; Education Officer, British Military Administration, Tripolitania, 1945–46. Head of Dept of Near and Middle East, Sch. of Oriental and African Studies, 1961–68 (Hon. Fellow 1983); Visiting Lectr, Ain Shams Univ., Cairo, 1979; Res. Fellow, Hebrew Univ., Jerusalem, 1980; Leverhulme Emeritus Fellowship, S India, 1981. Principal, Leo Baeck Coll., 1982–85, Pres., 1985–. Mem., Council of Christians and Jews; President: North Western Reform Synagogue; British Assoc. for Jewish Studies, 1980; Vice-Pres., Reform Synagogues of GB, 1985–91. Freedom, City of Urfa, Turkey, 1973. *Publications:* The Diacritical Point and the Accents in Syriac, 1953; The Hebrew Passover, 1963; Edessa, 1970; Aramaic Texts From North Saqqara, 1983; A History of the Jews of Cochin, 1993; Aramaic and Mandaic Incantation Bowls in the British Museum, 2000; Whisper Awhile, 2000; articles in learned periodicals. *Recreations:* reminiscing, meditation. *Address:* 17 Hillersdon Avenue,

Edgware, Middx HA8 7SG. *T:* (020) 8958 4993.

Died 23 Oct. 2003.

SEIFERT, Richard; *see* Seifert, Robin.

SEIFERT, Robin (also known as **Richard**), FRIBA; Principal R. Seifert and Partners, Architects, since 1934; *b* 25 Nov. 1910; *s* of William Seifert; *m* 1939, Josephine Jeanette Harding; two *s* one *d. Educ:* Central Foundation Sch., City of London; University College, London (DipArch; Fellow, 1971). Commenced architectural practice, 1934. Corps of Royal Engineers, 1940–44; Indian Army, 1944–46; Hon. Lt-Col, 1946; Certif. for Meritorious Services Home Forces, 1943. Returned to private practice, 1948. Designed: ICI Laboratories, Dyestuffs Div., Blackley, Manchester; The Times Newspapers building, Printing House Square; Centre Point, St Giles Circus; Drapers Gardens, Nat. West. Bank Tower, City; The Royal Garden Hotel, Kensington; Tolworth Towers, Surbiton; Guiness Mahon Bank, Gracechurch Street; HQ of ICT, Putney; Kellogg House, Baker Street; Dunlop House, King Street, St James's; BSC Res. Labs, Middlesbrough; Britannia Hotel; Park Tower Hotel; London Heathrow Hotel; Sobell Sports Centre; ATV Centre, Birmingham; Central Television Complex, Nottingham; International Press Centre; Metropolitan Police HQ, Putney; Wembley Conference Centre; Princess Grace Hospital, Marylebone Road; Princess Margaret Hospital, Windsor; Churchill Hospital, Harrow; BUPA Hospital, Bushey; The Pirate Castle, Camden; British Rail HQ Offices, Euston Station. RIBA Architectural Exhibition (depicting 50 years of practice), Heinz Gall., 1984. Member: MoT Road Safety Council, 1969 (later disbanded); Home Office Cttee of Management, Housing Assoc. for Discharged Offenders; (part-time) British Waterways Bd, 1971–74; Council, RIBA, 1971–74. FRSA 1976. Liveryman, Glaziers' Co. City of London. JP Barnet, 1969. *Recreations:* chess, violin. *Address:* Eleventrees, Milespit Hill, Mill Hill, NW7 2RS. *T:* (020) 8959 3397. *Clubs:* Army and Navy, City Livery, Arts.

Died 26 Oct. 2001.

SEIGNORET, Sir Clarence (Henry Augustus), GCB 1985; OBE 1966; Award of Honour, Dominica, 1993; President of the Commonwealth of Dominica, 1983–93; *b* 25 Feb. 1919; *s* of Clarence Augustus Seignoret and Violet Elizabeth (*née* Riviere); *m* 1950, Judith Laronde; two *s. Educ:* Dominica Grammar Sch.; Balliol Coll., Oxford. Civil Servant, 1936–77: Principal Asst Sec., Min. of Social Services, 1956–58; Principal Sec., Min. of Trade and Prodn, 1960–67; Sec. to Cabinet, Hd of Civil Service, 1967–77; Administrator's Dep., Governor's Dep., Actg Pres. on six occasions, 1966–83. Exec. Sec., Dominica Assoc. of Industry and Commerce, 1980–83. Pres., Internat. Develt and Management Ltd, 1994–. Mem., Girl Guide Council of Dominica. Patron: Community Hostels Inc.; Nat. Develt Foundn of Dominica; Dominica Special Olympics. Kt Comdr Grand Cross of Grace, Order of Imperial Russian Order of St John of Jerusalem Ecumenical (Kt of Malta), 1992. Collar of Order of the Liberator (Simon Bolivar), Venezuela, 1987. *Recreations:* agriculture, horticulture. *Address:* 24 Cork Street, Roseau, Commonwealth of Dominica, West Indies. *T:* (office) 4498777; (home) 4482108. *Clubs:* Lions Club of Dominica (Hon. Mem.), Rotary Club of Dominica (Hon. Mem.).

Died 5 May 2002.

SELBY, 5th Viscount *cr* 1905, of the City of Carlisle; **Edward Thomas William Gully;** *b* 21 Sept. 1967; *o s* of 4th Viscount Selby and of Mary Theresa Dorothy Gully (*née* Powell); *S* father, 1997; *m* 1992, Charlotte Cathrine Brege (marr. diss. 1995); one *s; m* 2000, Sally Ann Payne. *Educ:* Harrow; Sorbonne, Paris; Lund Univ., Sweden. *Recreations:* travel, chess, squash, sailing. *Heir:* *s* Hon. Christopher Rolf Thomas Gully, *b* 18 Oct. 1993. *Address:* 5 Ardmore Road, Aros, Salen, Isle of Mull, PA72 6JJ. *T:* (01852) 500221.

Died 23 Jan. 2001.

SELDON, Arthur, CBE 1983; economist and writer; a Founder President, Institute of Economic Affairs, since 1990; Founder Editor, Economic Affairs, 1980; *b* 29 May 1916; *m* (Audrey) Marjorie, *d* of Wilfred Willett and Eileen Willett (*née* Stenhouse); three *s*. *Educ:* Dempsey St Elementary Sch., Stepney; Raine's Foundation Sch. (State Scholar); LSE (BCom 1937 (1st cl. hons); Hon. Fellow 2001). Army service in Africa and Italy, 1942–45. Editor, Store, 1946–49; Tutor, Univ. of London Commerce Degree Bureau, 1946–56; economist in industry, 1949–1959; Staff Examr, LSE, 1956–66; Editorial Dir, Inst. of Economic Affairs, 1957–88; Chm., Liberal Party Cttee on the Aged, 1948–49; Mem., BMA Cttee on Health Financing, 1968–70; Adviser, Australian Cabinet Cttee on Welfare, 1968; Vice-Pres., Mont Pèlerin Soc., Switzerland, 1980–86 (first Hon. Fellow, 1996); Founder Trustee, Social Affairs Unit, 1980. Hon. DSocSc Univ. Francisco Marroquin, Guatemala, 1998; Hon. DSc Buckingham, 1999. *Publications:* Pensions in a Free Society, 1957; (jtly) Advertising in a Free Society, 1959; Pensions for Prosperity, 1960; (jtly) Everyman's Dictionary of Economics, 1965, 2nd edn 1976; After the NHS, 1968; The Great Pensions Swindle, 1970; Charge, 1977; (jtly) Over-ruled on Welfare 1963–78, 1979; Corrigible Capitalism, Incorrigible Socialism, 1980; Wither the Welfare State, 1981; Socialism Explained, 1983 (US edn as Socialism: the grand delusion, 1986); (ed) The New Right Enlightenment, 1985; The Riddle of the Voucher, 1986; (jtly) Welfare Without the State, 1987; Capitalism, 1990 (Fisher Prize, 1991); The State is Rolling Back, 1994; (contrib.) Democracy and Public Choice: essays in honour of Gordon Tullock, ed C. K. Rowley, 1987; The Dilemma of Democracy, 1998; The Retreat of the State: nurturing the soul of society, 1998; (jtly) Government: whose obedient servant?, 2000; The Making of the I.E.A., 2002; (jtly) Government Failure; a primer in public choice, 2002; (jtly) The Collected Works of Arthur Seldon, 7 vols, 2004–05. *Recreations:* writing, cricket, opera, parties for non-conformists. *Address:* The Thatched Cottage, Godden Green, Sevenoaks, Kent TN15 0HR. *T:* (01732) 761499.   *Died 11 Oct. 2005.*

SELIGMAN, Madron; *see* Seligman, R. M.

SELIGMAN, (Richard) Madron, CBE 1994; *b* 10 Nov. 1918; 4th *s* of late Dr Richard Seligman, FCGI, FIM, and Hilda Mary (*née* MacDowell); *m* 1947, Nancy-Joan, *d* of Julian Marks; three *s* one *d*. *Educ:* Rokeby Sch., Wimbledon; Harrow Sch.; Balliol Coll., Oxford (BA (Hons) PPE; MA). Oxford Univ. ski team, 1938–39; President, Oxford Union, 1940. Served war, 6th Armoured Divisional Signals, N Africa and Italy, 1941–46, Major 1945. Chm., Incinerator Company, Eaton Socon, 1960–88. MEP (C) Sussex W, 1979–94. Vice Pres., European Energy Foundn, 1982–94. Hon. Treas., Cons. Animal Welfare Gp, 1996–. Chm. UK Br., Confédn Européenne des Anciens Combattants, 1989–. *Recreations:* tennis, ski-ing, gardening, piano, sailing. *Address:* Mile Ash, Tower Hill, Horsham, West Sussex RH13 7AG. *T:* (01403) 240075. *Clubs:* Royal Thames Yacht, Royal Institute of International Affairs, MCC.

Died 9 July 2002.

SELL, Anthony Lawrence, CBE 1999; Chief Executive, British Tourist Authority, 1993–98; *b* 19 April 1943; *s* of late Richard Geoffrey Sell and Zena Warren Sell (*née* Goddard); *m* 1975, Susan Constance; two *s* one *d*. *Educ:* Berkhamsted; Christ's Coll., Cambridge (Open Schol.; BA 1964, MA 1968); Univ. of Wisconsin (Fulbright Schol.); London Business Sch. (MSc). ICI Organics Div., 1965–67; Booz Allen & Hamilton Internat., 1969–73; Internat. Investment Corp. for Yugoslavia, 1973–74; Foseco Internat. Exports, 1974–78; Man. Dir, Kemwell, 1978–82; Commercial Dir, Metalchem Internat., 1982–86; Exec. Dir, Boosey & Hawkes plc, 1986–89; Pres.-Dir-Gen., Buffet Crampon SA, 1986–88; Man. Dir, Continental Europe, Thomas Cook Gp, 1989–93 (Pres., Chm., Mem., Thomas Cook subsids, France, Switzerland, Netherlands,

Italy, Sweden, Czechoslovakia). Mem., London Tourist Bd, 1993–98. Chm., Soc. of Ticket Agents and Retailers, 1997. Gov., Warwick Sch., 1983–85. FRSA. *Recreations:* rowing, music, the clarinet. *T:* (020) 8748 9272. *Club:* Mortlake Boat.   *Died 30 May 2002.*

SENSI, His Eminence Cardinal Giuseppe Maria; *b* 27 May 1907. Ordained, 1929; Sec. of Apostolic Nunciature in Roumania, 1934–38; Secretary and Auditor of Apostolic Nunciature in Switzerland, 1938–46; Councillor of Apostolic Nunciature in Belgium, 1946–47; Chargé d'Affaires of the Holy See in Prague, 1948–49; Councillor in the Secretariat of State of His Holiness, 1949–53; Permanent Observer of the Holy See at UNESCO in Paris, 1953–55; apptd Nuncio Apostolic to Costa Rica, May 1955, and consecrated Titular Archbishop of Sardi, July 1955; Apostolic Delegate to Jerusalem, 1957; Apostolic Nuncio to Ireland, 1962–67; Apostolic Nuncio to Portugal, 1967–76; Cardinal, 1976. Hon. Mem., Accademia Cosentina, 1976. Chevalier, Grand Cross SMO Malta, 1959; Grand Cross: Santi Maurizio e Lazzaro, 1975; Ordre Militaire du Christ (Portugal), 1976; Ordre Equestre du St Sepolcre de Gerusalemme, 1978. *Address:* Piazza S Calisto 16, 00153 Rome, Italy. *T:* (6) 6987265/6987388/5897827.

Died 26 July 2001.

SEROTA, Baroness *cr* 1967 (Life Peer), of Hampstead in Greater London; **Beatrice Serota,** DBE 1992; JP; a Deputy Speaker, House of Lords, since 1985; *b* 15 Oct. 1919; *d* of Alexander Katz; *m* 1942, Stanley Serota, BSc (Eng), FICE; one *s* one *d*. *Educ:* John Howard School; London School of Economics (BSc (Econ); Hon. Fellow, 1976). Member: Hampstead Borough Council, 1945–49; LCC for Brixton, 1954–65 (Chm., Children's Cttee, 1958–65); GLC for Lambeth, 1964–67 (Chief Whip). Baroness in Waiting, 1968–69; Minister of State (Health), DHSS, 1969–70; Prin. Dep. Chm. of Cttees, and Chm., European Communities Select Cttee, H of L, 1986–92; Mem., Public Service Select Cttee, H of L, 1996–98. Founder Chm., Commn for Local Admin, 1974–82; Member: Adv. Council in Child Care, and Central Training Council in Child Care, 1958–68; Adv. Council on Treatment of Offenders, 1960–64; Longford Cttee on "Crime—A Challenge to us all", 1964; Royal Commn on Penal System, 1964–66; Latey Cttee on Age of Majority, 1965–67; Adv. Council on Penal System, 1966–68, 1974–79 (Chm., 1976–79); Seebohm Cttee on Organization of Local Authority Personal Social Services, 1966–68; Community Relations Commn, 1970–76; BBC Complaints Commn, 1975–77; Governor, BBC, 1977–82. JP Inner London (West Central Division). Peerage conferred for services to children. Hon. DLitt Loughborough, 1983. *Recreations:* needlepoint, gardening, collecting shells. *Address:* The Coach House, 15 Lyndhurst Terrace, NW3 5QA.   *Died 21 Oct. 2002.*

SEYMOUR, Dr Francis, FFPHM; Director of Clinical and Scientific Services (formerly Regional Medical Officer), North West Thames Regional Health Authority, 1982–89; *b* 29 June 1928; *s* of Francis Reginald and Drusilla Seymour; *m* 1953, Ivy Esther; two *d*. *Educ:* Wallasey Grammar School; Liverpool University (MB ChB 1951); DPH 1955; FFPHM (MFCM 1972; FFCM 1979). Dep. MOH, N Bucks, 1955–58; MOH, Mid Bucks Districts, 1958–62; Div. MO, Runcorn and Mid Cheshire, 1962–70; Dep. County MO, Herts, 1970–74; Area MO, Herts AHA, 1974–82. FRSA. *Recreations:* walking, music, theatre. *Address:* The Fennings, Back Ends, Chipping Campden, Glos GL55 6AU. *T:* (01386) 840483.

Died 16 March 2001.

SEYS-LLEWELLYN, His Honour John Desmond; a Circuit Judge (formerly a County Court Judge), 1971–85; *b* 3 May 1912; *s* of Charles Ernest Llewellyn, FAI and Hannah Margretta Llewellyn, of Cardiff; *m* 1st, 1939, Elaine (*d* 1984), *d* of H. Leonard Porcher, solicitor, and Mrs Hilda Porcher, JP, of Pontypridd; three *s*; 2nd, 1986, Mrs Joan Banfield James (*d* 2001), *d* of R. H. Cumming,

JP, of Plymouth. *Educ:* Cardiff High School; Jesus Coll., Oxford (Exhibnr, MA). Joined Inner Temple, 1936. War Service, RTR, 1940–46 (Captain). Called to the Bar, Inner Temple, in absentia OAS, 1945; Profumo Prizeman, 1947; practised on Wales and Chester Circuit, 1947–71; Local Insurance Appeal Tribunal, 1958–71; Dep. Chm., Cheshire QS, 1968–71; joined Gray's Inn, *ad eundem*, same day as youngest son, 1967. Contested Chester Constituency (L), 1955 and 1956. *Recreations:* languages, travel, archaeology, art galleries, music, swimming, English Setter. *Address:* Little Chetwyn, Green Pastures, Gresford, Clwyd LL12 8RT. *T:* (01978) 856818. *Club:* Athenæum (Liverpool).   *Died 4 April 2003.*

SHACKLETON, Prof. Robert Millner, PhD; FRS 1971; Hon. Senior Research Fellow, Open University, since 1977; Professor of Geology, University of Leeds, 1962–75, then Emeritus; Director, Research Institute of African Geology, University of Leeds, 1966–75; *b* 30 Dec. 1909; *s* of John M. Shackleton and Agnes Mitford Shackleton; *m* 1st, 1934, Gwen Isabel Harland (marr. diss.); one *s* two *d*; 2nd, 1949, Judith Wyndham Jeffreys (marr. diss. 1978); one *s* one *d*; 3rd, 1984, Gwendolen Margaret, (Peigi), Wallace. *Educ:* Sidcot School; University of Liverpool (BSc (Hons) 1931, PhD 1934). Beit Fellow, Imperial College, 1932–34; Chief Geologist to Whitehall Explorations Ltd in Fiji, 1935–36; on teaching staff, Imperial College, 1936–40 and 1945–48; Geologist, Mining and Geological Dept, Kenya, 1940–45; Herdman Professor of Geology, University of Liverpool, 1948–62. Royal Society Leverhulme Vis. Prof., Haile Sellassie I Univ., 1970–71; Trevelyan Coll. Fellow, Durham Univ., 1984–85. Vice-Pres., Geol Soc. of London, 1966. Hon. FGS. Murchison Medal, 1970. *Publications:* Mining and Geological Dept of Kenya Reports 10, 11, 12; papers in geological journals, etc. *Address:* The Croft Barn, Church Street, East Hendred, Oxon OX12 8LA. *T:* (01235) 834802.   *Died 3 May 2001.*

SHACKLETON, Vivien Anne, (Lady Shackleton); *see* Law, V. A.

SHACKLETON BAILEY, David Roy; *see* Bailey.

SHAFTESBURY, 10th Earl of, *cr* 1672; **Anthony Ashley-Cooper;** Bt 1622; Baron Ashley, 1661; Baron Cooper of Paulet, 1672; *b* 22 May 1938; *o s* of Major Lord Ashley (*d* 1947; *e s* of 9th Earl of Shaftesbury, KP, PC, GCVO, CBE) and Françoise Soulier; *S* grandfather, 1961; *m* 1st, 1966, Bianca Maria Le Vien (marr. diss. 1976), *o d* of late Gino de Paolis; 2nd, 1976, Christina Eva (marr. diss. 2000), *o d* of Ambassador Nils Montan; two *s*; 3rd, 2002, Jamila Ben M'Barek. *Educ:* Eton; Christchurch, Oxford. Chm., London Philharmonic Orchestra Council, 1966–80. Dir, PKL Gp, 1989–96. Vice-Pres., British Butterfly Conservation Soc., 1992–; Pres., Hawk and Owl Trust, 1996–2000. Hon. Pres., Shaftesbury Soc., 1961–97. (Jtly) Nat. Duke of Cornwall's Award for Forestry and Conservation, Royal Forestry Soc., 1992. Hon. Citizen, South Carolina, USA, 1967. Patron of seven livings. *Recreations:* mountains, music, ecology. *Heir:* *s* Lord Ashley, *b* 24 June 1977. *Clubs:* Turf, MCC.
                Died 2004.

SHAFTESBURY, 11th Earl of, *cr* 1672; **Anthony Nils Christian Ashley-Cooper;** Bt 1622; Baron Ashley, 1661; Baron Cooper, 1672; *b* 24 June 1977; *s* of 10th Earl of Shaftesbury and Christina Eva, *o d* of Ambassador Nils Montan; *S* father, 2004. *Educ:* Marlborough Coll.; Studio Art Centers Internat.; Univ. of Bristol (BSc 1999). CA 2003. PricewaterhouseCoopers, audit and business adv. services, 2000–05; Ernst & Young, transaction adv. services, 2005–. *Heir:* *b* Hon. Nicholas Edmund Anthony Ashley-Cooper, *b* 3 June 1979. *Address:* St Giles, Wimborne, Dorset BH21 5NH.   *Died 15 May 2005.*

SHAPCOTT, Sidney Edward, CEng, FIEE, FInstP; Director-General, Airborne Weapons and Electronic Systems, Ministry of Defence, 1976–80; *b* 20 June 1920; *s*

of late Percy Thomas and Beatrice Shapcott; *m* 1943, Betty Jean Richens (*d* 1999); two *s* one *d*. *Educ:* Hele's School, Exeter; King's College, London (BSc). Joined Air Defence Experimental Establishment, 1941; various appointments in Min. of Supply and Min. of Aviation, 1941–62; DCSO, 1963; Dir of Projects, ESRO, 1963–65; Min. of Defence, Navy Dept, 1965–75; CSO, 1968; Dep. Dir, Admiralty Surface Weapons Establishment, 1968–72; Dir, Underwater Weapon Projects, Admiralty Underwater Weapons Establishment, Portland, 1972–75. Defence Engrng Consultant, 1981–85. *Address:* 23 Upper Churston Rise, Seaton, Devon EX12 2HD. *T:* (01297) 21545.
                Died 20 Dec. 2001.

SHARKEY, Colum John, CMG 1984; MBE 1973; HM Diplomatic Service, retired; *b* 9 June 1931; *s* of late Andrew Sharkey and Sarah Josephine Sharkey (*née* Whelan); *m* 1962, Olivia Anne (*née* Brassil); two *s* one *d*. *Educ:* St Malachy's Coll., Belfast. CRO, 1954; served in New Delhi, 1955, Calcutta, 1956–58; Second Secretary: Dacca, 1959–61; Melbourne, 1962–66; Montevideo, 1967–68 (joined HM Diplomatic Service, 1968); First Sec. and Consul, Asuncion, 1969; First Sec., Montevideo, 1971; seconded to Dept of Trade, 1972–74; Consul, Vancouver, 1974–78; Consul-Gen., Bilbao, 1978–81; Ambassador to Honduras, 1981–84 and non-resident Ambassador to El Salvador, 1982–84; Head of British Interests Section, Buenos Aires, 1984–87; Ambassador to Bolivia, 1987–89, to Uruguay, 1989–91; retd, then re-engaged as Personnel Assessor, FCO, 1991–93. *Recreations:* travel, golf.   *Died 24 April 2003.*

SHARP, His Honour Alastair George, MBE 1945; ERD 1996; QC 1961; DL; a Circuit Judge (formerly Judge of County Courts), 1962–84; Liaison Judge, Durham County Magistrates Courts, 1972–84; *b* 25 May 1911; *s* of late Alexander Sharp, Advocate in Aberdeen, and of late Mrs Isabella Sharp, OBE; *m* 1940, Daphne Sybil (*d* 2000), *d* of late Maj. Harold Smithers, RGA, and late Mrs Connor; one *s* two *d*. *Educ:* Aberdeen Grammar School; Fettes; Clare College, Cambridge (Archdeacon Johnson Exhibitionr in Classics; BA 1933, 1st Class Hons Classical Tripos Part II, Aegrotat Part I). Boxed Cambridge Univ., 1931–32; Cambridge Union Debating Team in America, 1933. Commissioned, The Gordon Highlanders, Feb. 1939; served War of 1939–45: Staff Coll., 1943; 2nd Bn The London Scottish, 1943; Gen. Staff, War Office, 1944–45, Temp. Major. On staff of Bonar Law College, Ashridge, 1934–35; Barrister, Middle Temple, 1935; Harmsworth Law Scholar; North Eastern Circuit, 1936. Dep. Chm. of Agricultural Land Tribunal, Northern Area, 1958–62; Asst Recorder of Huddersfield, 1958–60; Recorder of Rotherham, 1960–62; Dep. Chm., N Riding Yorks QS, 1959–65; Dep. Chm., 1965–70, Chm., 1970–71, Durham QS. Chm., Washington New Town Licensed Premises Cttee, 1966–78; Jt Pres., Council of Circuit Judges, 1979. Governor, Sherburn Hosp. Charity, 1972–81. Mem. Board, Faculty of Law, Durham Univ., 1976–84. DL Co. Durham, 1973. *Recreations:* gardening, music, hill walking. *Address:* High Point, Western Hill, Durham DH1 4RG; The Old Kennels, Tomintoul, Banffshire AB37 9EN. *Club:* Durham County.
                Died 26 Oct. 2001.

SHARP, Derek Joseph; British Council Representative, Italy, 1981–85, retired; *b* 12 June 1925; *s* of Joseph Frank Sharp and Sylvia May (*née* Allen); *m* 1957, Hilda Francesca Cernigoj; two *s*. *Educ:* Preston Grammar School; Queen's Coll., Oxford (MA, DipEd). Lectr, British Inst., Milan, 1956–58; British Council, 1958–85: served Indonesia, Bristol, Bangkok, Addis Ababa, Pretoria and London, 1958–77; Controller, Africa and Middle East Div., 1977–81. Mem., British Cttee for Preservation of Venice (Venice in Peril Fund), 1989–2000. *Address:* 3 Hartley Close, Bickley, Kent BR1 2TP.
                Died 14 March 2001.

SHARP, Hon. Mitchell William, CC 1999 (OC 1983); PC (Can.) 1963; Personal adviser to the Prime Minister of

Canada, since 1993; *b* 11 May 1911; *s* of Thomas Sharp and Elizabeth (*née* Little); *m* 1st, 1938, Daisy Boyd (decd); one *s*; 2nd, 1976, Jeannette Dugal (decd); 3rd, 2000, Jeanne d'Arc Labrecque. *Educ:* University of Manitoba; London School of Economics. Statistician, Sanford Evans Statistical Service, 1926–36; Economist, James Richardson & Sons Ltd, 1937–42; Officer, Canadian Dept of Finance, Ottawa, 1942–51; Director Economic Policy Division, 1947–51; Associate Deputy Minister, Canadian Dept Trade and Commerce, 1951–57; Dep. Minister, 1957–58; Minister, 1963–65; elected to Canadian House of Commons, 1963; Minister of Finance, 1965–68; Sec. of State for External Affairs, 1968–74; Pres., Privy Council, 1974–76; Govt Leader in House of Commons, 1974–76; resigned from Parliament, 1978. Comr, Northern Pipeline Agency, 1978–88; Policy Associate, Strategico Inc., Ottawa, 1988–93. Vice-Pres., Brazilian Traction, Light & Power Co., Toronto, 1958–62. Hon. Dip., Royal Conservatory of Music, 1998; Hon. LLD: Univ. of Manitoba, 1965; Univ. of Western Ontario, 1977; Carleton Univ., 1994; McMaster Univ., 1995; Hon. DrSocSci Ottawa, 1970. *Recreations:* music, walking. *Address:* 2–140 Rideau Terrace, Ottawa, ON K1M 0Z2, Canada. *T:* (613) 7451117. *Died 19 March 2004.*

SHARP, Sir Richard (Lyall), KCVO 1982; CB 1977; Ceremonial Officer, Management and Personnel Office (formerly Civil Service Department), 1977–82; *b* 27 March 1915; *s* of late Alexander Sharp, Advocate, Aberdeen, and late Mrs Isabella Sharp, OBE; *m* 1950, Jean Helen, *er d* of late Sir James Crombie, KCB, KBE, CMG; two *s* two *d* (and one *d* decd). *Educ:* Fettes Coll.; Aberdeen Univ. (MA 1st Cl. Hons Classics 1937); Clare Coll., Cambridge (BA 1st Cl. Classical Tripos Pt II 1939). Served Royal Northumberland Fusiliers, 1939–46 (POW, Singapore and Siam, 1942–45). Principal, HM Treasury, 1946; Private Sec. to Chancellor of Exchequer, 1948–50 and to Minister of State for Economic Affairs, 1950; UK Treasury and Supply Delegn, Washington, 1952–56; Asst Sec., 1954; IDC, 1961; Under-Secretary: Nat. Bd for Prices and Incomes, 1966–68; HM Treasury, 1968–77. *Recreations:* playing the viola, viticulture, gardening. *Address:* Home Farm House, Briston, Melton Constable, Norfolk NR24 2HN. *T:* (01263) 860445.
Died 25 July 2002.

SHARP, William Johnstone, CB 1983; Controller and Chief Executive, Her Majesty's Stationery Office and Queen's Printer of Acts of Parliament, 1981–86; *b* 30 May 1926; *s* of Frederick Matthew and Gladys Evelyn Sharp; *m* 1952, Joan Alice Clark, MBE, *d* of Arnold and Violet Clark. *Educ:* Queen Elizabeth Grammar Sch., Hexham; Emmanuel Coll., Cambridge (MA). Army Service, Reconnaissance Corps, Durham LI and Staff, 1944–48. Entered Min. of Transport, 1949; Private Sec. to Perm. Sec., 1951–53; Principal, Min. of Civil Aviation, 1953; Asst Sec., Min. of Transport, 1962; Under-Sec., DoE, 1970; Controller of Supplies, PSA, 1976–80. FRSA 1984. Hon. Life Member: Nat. State Printing Assoc. (USA), 1987; Internat. Govt Printers Assoc., 1988. *Recreation:* the Turf. *Address:* 43 Friars Quay, Norwich NR3 1ES. *T:* (01603) 624258. *Died 16 Jan. 2002.*

SHARPE, Brian Sidney; Consultant, financial and marketing presentation, since 1985; *b* 12 Feb. 1927; *s* of S. H. Sharpe and Norah Sharpe; *m* 1967, Susan Lillywhite; two *s. Educ:* Haberdashers' Aske's Sch., Hampstead; Guildhall Sch. of Music and Drama. Royal Fusiliers (att. Forces Broadcasting Service), 1945–48; BBC: Announcer, Midland Region, 1955; Television Presentation, 1956; Producer, African Service, External Services, 1957; Senior Producer: Overseas Talks and Features, 1965; The Financial World Tonight, Radio 4, 1974; Money Programme, Sept-Dec. 1979; on secondment as Exec. Dir, City Communications Centre, 1976–79; Director: Charles Barker Lyons, 1980–85; Charles Barker City, 1983–85. Town Councillor (Lib Dem), 1986–2000, Town Mayor, 1991–92, Godalming; Bor. Councillor (Lib Dem),

Waverley, 1987–99. *Publications:* How Money Works (with A. Wilson), 1975; several articles on corporate and other forms of communication. *Recreations:* reading, music. *Address:* 26 Hallam Road, Godalming, Surrey GU7 3HW. *T:* (01483) 421551. *Died 16 Feb. 2005.*

SHARPLES, Air Vice-Marshal Christopher John, FFOM; Director General, RAF Medical Services, 1997–2002; *b* 9 April 1942; *s* of Arthur Victor Sharples and Alma Alice Sharples; *m* 1965, Barbara Anne Edwards; one *s* one *d. Educ:* Ashville Coll.; King's Coll., London; St George's Hosp. Med. Sch.; LSHTM (MSc 1981). DAvMed 1972. MRCS, LRCP 1966; MFOM 1980, FFOM 1991. Cadet, RAF Med., 1963; MO, RAF, 1967–2002; Consultant in Occupational Medicine, and RAF Consultant Advr, 1984–97. QHP 1995–2002. Vice-Pres., Peterborough RFC. FRAeS 1999; FRSocMed 1994. Cade Medal, RCS, 1979. CStJ 1999. Silver Jubilee Medal, 1977; Golden Jubilee Medal, 2002. *Publications:* papers in preventive, occupational and aviation medicine. *Recreations:* golf, music. *Address:* One Black Swan Spinney, Wansford, Peterborough, Cambs PE8 6LE. *T:* (01780) 782246. *Club:* Royal Air Force. *Died 7 Jan. 2004.*

SHAUGHNESSY, 3rd Baron *cr* 1916, of Montreal; **William Graham Shaughnessy**, CD 1955; Director: Arbor Memorial Services Inc., Toronto, since 1972; Eurogas Corporation, Calgary, since 1995; *b* 28 March 1922; *s* of 2nd Baron Shaughnessy and Marion (*d* 1936), *d* of late R. K. Graham, Montreal; *S* father, 1938; *m* 1944, Mary Whitley (*d* 1999), *o d* of late John Whitley, Copthorne House, Letchworth; one *s* two *d* (and one *s* decd). *Educ:* Bishop's Coll. Sch. and Bishop's Univ., Lennoxville, Canada (BA 1941); Columbia Univ., NY (MSc 1947). Served War of 1939–45, NW Europe (despatches); Major, Canadian Grenadier Guards, retd. Dir, Canada-UK Chamber of Commerce, 1981–. Member: Jt Cttee on Statutory Instruments, H of L, 1984–99; Delegated Powers Scrutiny Cttee, H of L, 1992–96. Trustee: The Last Post Fund Inc., Canada; Canada Meml Foundn (UK). *Heir: s* Hon. Michael James Shaughnessy, *b* 12 Nov. 1946. *Address:* 27 Melton Court, Old Brompton Road, South Kensington, SW7 3JQ. *Clubs:* Cavalry and Guards; University (Montreal). *Died 22 May 2003.*

SHAVE, Kenneth George, CEng, FIMechE; Member, London Transport Executive, 1967–73, retired; *b* 25 June 1908; *s* of George Shave and Frances Larkin; *m* 1935, Doris May Stone; one *s* one *d. Educ:* St Paul's School. Apprenticed London General Omnibus Company, 1925; Rolling Stock Engineer, East Surrey Traction Company, 1930; London Transport: Asst Divisional Engineer, 1935; Divisional Engineer, 1948; Rolling Stock Engineer, 1956; Chief Mechanical Engineer, 1965. CStJ 1971 (OStJ 1963). *Recreations:* golf, bridge, gardening. *Address:* 19 Hillcrest Lane, Scaynes Hill, Haywards Heath, West Sussex RH17 7PH. *Died 5 July 2003.*

SHAW, (Francis) Michael; Managing Director, 1985–93, Executive Vice Chairman, 1993–94, Britannia Building Society; *b* 12 Aug. 1936; *s* of Joseph Stanley Shaw and Irene Shaw (*née* Weldrake); *m* 1960, Margaret Elinor Russum; two *d. Educ:* Rotherham Grammar Sch. Qualified as chartered accountant, 1957. National Service, RAF, 1958–60; Peat Marwick Mitchell & Co., Sheffield, 1960–61; Company Sec. and Accountant, John Speed & Co., 1961–67; Chief Accountant, Eastern Counties Building Soc., 1967–74; Britannia Building Society: Chief Accountant, 1974–77; Gen. Manager, 1977–83; Chief Gen. Manager, 1983–85. Chm., BSA, 1992–93; Pres., N Staffs Chamber of Commerce, 1993–95. *Recreations:* golf, foreign travel, photography. *Club:* Leek Golf. *Died 18 April 2002.*

SHAW, John Michael, MC 1940; QC 1967; Barrister-at-Law; Regional Chairman of Industrial Tribunals, 1972–84; *b* 14 Nov. 1914; *yr s* of late M. J. Shaw (killed in action, 1916); *m* 1940, Margaret L. (*d* 1997), *yr d* of Robert

T. D. Stoneham, CBE; two s two d. *Educ:* Rugby; Worcester Coll., Oxford. Called to the Bar, Gray's Inn, 1937. Served War of 1939–45 (Major): commissioned Royal Fusiliers, 1940. *Recreation:* gardening.
Died 21 Dec. 2001.

SHAW, Max S.; *see* Stuart-Shaw.

SHAW, Michael; *see* Shaw, F. M.

SHAW, Sir Robert, 7th Bt *cr* 1821; professional engineer, Alberta, retired; *b* Nairobi, Kenya, 31 Jan. 1925; *s* of Sir Robert de Vere Shaw, 6th Bt, MC, and Joan (*d* 1967), *d* of Thomas Cross; *S* father, 1969; *m* 1954, Jocelyn, *d* of late Andrew McGuffie, Swaziland; two *d. Educ:* Harrow; Univ. of Oklahoma (BS Civil Engrg 1962); Univ. of Missouri (MS Civil Engrg 1964). Served RN, 1943–47 (Lt RN, retd). Mem., Assoc., of Prof. Engrs, Geologists and Geophysicists of Alberta. *Recreation:* sailing. *Heir: n* Charles de Vere Shaw [*b* 1 March 1957; *m* 1985, Sonia, *e d* of Thomas Geoffrey Eden; one *s* one *d*]. *Address:* 234 40th Avenue SW, Calgary, AB T2S 0X3, Canada.
Died 18 Dec. 2002.

SHAW-STEWART, Sir Houston (Mark), 11th Bt *cr* 1667; MC 1950; TD; DL; Vice Lord-Lieutenant, Strathclyde Region (Eastwood, Renfrew and Inverclyde Districts), 1980–95; *b* 24 April 1931; *s* of Sir Guy Shaw-Stewart, 9th Bt, MC, and Diana (*d* 1931), *d* of late George Bulteel; *S* brother, 1980; *m* 1982, Lucinda Victoria, *yr d* of Alexander Fletcher, Old Vicarage, Wighill, near Tadcaster; one *s. Educ:* Eton. Joined Coldstream Guards, 1949; served as 2/Lt Royal Ulster Rifles, Korea, 1950 (MC); joined Ayrshire Yeomanry, 1952; retired, 1969; Hon. Col A (Ayrshire Yeomanry) Sqdn, Queen's Own Yeomanry RAC, TA, 1984–87. Member of the Royal Company of Archers, Queen's Body Guard for Scotland. Joint Master, Lanark and Renfrewshire Foxhounds, 1974–79. DL Renfrewshire, 1970. *Recreations:* hunting, shooting and racing. *Heir: s* Ludovic Houston Shaw Stewart, *b* 12 Nov. 1986. *Address:* Ardgowan, Inverkip, Renfrewshire PA16 0DW. *T:* (01475) 521226. *Clubs:* White's, Turf, Pratt's.
Died 21 Feb. 2004.

SHAWCROSS, Baron *cr* 1959 (Life Peer), of Friston; **Hartley William Shawcross,** GBE 1974; Kt 1945; QC 1939; PC 1946; Special Adviser, Morgan Guaranty Trust of New York, 1965–94 (Chairman, International Advisory Council, 1967–74); Director: Hawker Siddeley Group, 1968–82; The Observer, 1981–93; *b* 4 Feb. 1902; *s* of John Shawcross, MA, and Hilda Shawcross; *m* 1st, 1924, Rosita Alberta Shyvers (*d* 1943); 2nd, 1944, Joan Winifred Mather (*d* 1974); two *s* one *d*; 3rd, 1997, Mrs Monique Huiskamp. *Educ:* Dulwich Coll.; abroad. Certificate of Honour for 1st place in Bar Final; called to the Bar, Gray's Inn, 1925, Bencher, 1939; practised on Northern Circuit. Sen. Law Lectr, Liverpool Univ., 1927–34. Chm., Enemy Aliens Tribunal, 1939–40; left practice at Bar for War Service, 1940; Chief Prosecutor for UK before Internat. Military Tribunal at Nuremberg. Asst Chm. of E Sussex QS, 1941; Recorder of Salford, 1941–45; Dep. Regional Comr, South-Eastern Region, 1941; Regional Comr, North-Western Region, 1942–45; Recorder of Kingston-upon-Thames, 1946–61; retired from practice at Bar, 1958. MP (Lab) St Helens, 1945–58; Attorney-General, 1945–51; Pres., BoT, April-Oct. 1951. A Principal Deleg. for UK to Assemblies of UN, 1945–49; a UK Mem., Permanent Court of Arbitration at The Hague, 1950–67. Independent Chm., Kent District Coal Mining Board, 1940–45; Chairman: Catering Wages Commn, 1943–45; Bar Council, 1952–57; Royal Commn on the Press, 1961–62; MRC, 1961–65; Internat. Law Section of British Inst. of Internat. and Comparative Law; Justice (British Br. of Internat. Commn of Jurists), 1956–72; Panel on Take-overs and Mergers, 1969–80; Press Council, 1974–78; ICC Commn on Unethical Practices, 1976. President: Rainer Foundn (formerly London Police Court Mission), 1951–71; British Hotels and Restaurants Assoc., 1959–71. Member: Home Secretary's Adv. Council on

Treatment of Offenders, 1944–45; Council, Internat. Law Assoc., 1958–74; Exec. Cttee, Internat. Commn of Jurists, 1959. Hon. Member: Bar Council; Amer. and NY Bar Assoc.; Fellow, Amer. Bar Foundn. Director: Shell Transport and Trading Co., 1961–72; EMI Ltd, 1965–81; Rank-Hovis-McDougall Ltd, 1965–79; Caffyns Motors Ltd, 1965–93; Morgan et Cie Internat. SA, 1966–77; Morgan et Cie SA, 1967–90; Times Newspapers Ltd, 1967–74; Upjohn & Co Ltd, 1967–76 (Chm.); Birmingham Small Arms Co. Ltd, 1968–73 (Chm., 1971–73); European Enterprises Development Co. SA 1970–78 (Chm., 1973–78); Chairman: Dominion Lincoln Assurance Co. Ltd, 1969–76; Thames Television Ltd, 1969–74; London and Continental Bankers, 1974–80. Chm. Bd of Governors, Dulwich Coll.; Member: Court, London Univ., 1958–74; Council and Exec. Cttee, Sussex Univ., 1959– (Pro-Chancellor, 1960–65; Chancellor, 1965–85); Council, Eastbourne Coll., 1965–70. Hon. FRCS 1981; Hon. FRCOG 1978. Hon. degrees from Univs of Bristol, Columbia, Hull, Lehigh, Liverpool, London, Loughborough, Massachusetts, Michigan. JP Sussex, 1941–68. Chm., Soc. of Sussex Downsmen, 1962–75. Knight Grand Cross, Imperial Iranian Order of Homayoon, 1st Cl., 1974. *Publication:* Life Sentence: the memoirs of Hartley Shawcross, 1995. *Recreation:* sailing. *Address:* Cowbeech Farm, Cowbeech, East Sussex BN27 4JF. *Clubs:* Pratt's, Garrick; Travellers (Paris); Royal Cornwall Yacht (Falmouth); Royal Yacht Squadron (Cowes); New York Yacht (US). *Died 10 July 2003.*

SHEARER, Rt Hon. Hugh Lawson, OJ 1990; PC 1969; President, Bustamante Industrial Trade Union, Jamaica, since 1977; *b* 18 May 1923; *m* 1998, Dr Denise Eldemire. *Educ:* St Simon's Coll., Jamaica. Journalist on weekly newspaper, Jamaica Worker, 1941–44, subseq. Editor. Apptd Asst Gen. Sec., Bustamante Industrial TU, 1947, Island Supervisor, 1953–67, Vice-Pres., 1960–79 (on leave of absence, 1967–72). Mem. Kingston and St Andrew Corp. Council, 1947; MHR for West Kingston, 1955–59; MLC, later Senator, 1962–67; Leader of Govt Business in Senate, 1962–67; MP S Clarendon, 1967–76, SE Clarendon, 1976–93; Prime Minister of Jamaica, 1967–72; Minister of Defence and of External Affairs, 1967–72; Leader of the Opposition, 1972–74; Dep. Prime Minister, and Minister of For. Affairs and For. Trade, 1980–89; Leader, Jamaica Labour Party, 1967–74. Chm., Jt Trade Unions Res. Develt Centre, 1992; Pres., Jamaica Confedn of Trade Unions, 1994. Patron, Nat. Council of Senior Citizens, 1997–. Hon. Dr of Laws: Howard Univ., Washington, 1968; Univ. of WI, Jamaica, 1994. *Address:* Bustamante Industrial Trade Union, 98–100 Duke Street, Kingston, Jamaica. *Died 5 July 2004.*

SHEARER, Very Rev. John, (Jack), OBE 1994; Dean of Belfast, since 1985; *b* 30 Dec. 1926; *s* of William and Isabelle Shearer; *m* 1956, Morag Williamson; one *s* one *d. Educ:* Trinity College, Dublin (BA (Respondent) 1948; MA, BD 1953). Ordained deacon, 1950, priest, 1951; Rector of Ballynahinch, Co. Down, 1958; Rector of Seagoe, Co. Armagh, 1961. *Publication:* Stewardship Step by Step, 1961. *Recreation:* computing. *Address:* The Deanery, 5 Deramore Drive, Belfast BT9 5JQ. *T:* (028) 9066 0980. *Died 12 Jan. 2001.*

SHEARMAN, Prof. John Kinder Gowran, PhD; FBA 1976; Adams University Professor, Harvard University, 1994–2002, then Emeritus; *b* 24 June 1931; *s* of late Brig. C. E. G. Shearman; *m* 1957, Jane Dalrymple Smith (*d* 1983); one *s* three *d*; 2nd, 1983, Deirdre Roskill (marr. diss.); 3rd, 1998, Kathryn Brush. *Educ:* St Edmund's, Hindhead; Felsted; Courtauld Inst., London Univ. (BA, PhD 1957). Lectr, Courtauld Inst., 1957–67; Research Fellow, Inst. for Advanced Study, Princeton, 1964; Reader, 1967–74, Prof. of the History of Art, 1974–79 (Dep. Dir, 1974–78), Courtauld Inst.; Prof., Dept of Art and Archaeology, Princeton Univ., 1979–87 (Chm., 1979–85); Prof. of Fine Arts, Harvard Univ., 1987–94 (Chm. of Dept, 1990–93). Member: Accademia del

Disegno, Florence, 1979; Amer. Acad. of Arts and Scis, 1993; Accademia di S Luca, Rome, 1995; Accademia Raffaello, Urbino, 2001. Serena Medal, British Acad., 1979. *Publications:* Andrea del Sarto, 1965; Mannerism, 1967, 8th edn 1990; Raphael's Cartoons, 1972; Catalogue of the Early Italian Paintings in the Collection of HM the Queen, 1983; Funzione e Illusione, 1983; Only Connect …, 1992; Raphael in Early Modern Sources, 2003; contribs to British, French, German, American jls. *Recreations:* sailing, music. *Address:* 3 Clement Circle, Cambridge, MA 02138, USA. *Club:* Bembridge Sailing.
Died 11 Aug. 2003.

SHEEHY, Terence Joseph; Editor, Catholic Herald, 1983–88; *b* 12 May 1918; 2nd *s* of Michael Sheehy and Mary (*née* O'Sullivan); *m* 1955, Margaret Patricia Barry, *y d* of Dr T. St John Barry; one *s* three *d*. *Educ:* by Jesuits in London and Dublin. Editorial staff, Irish Catholic, Dublin, 1942–46; publisher and Editor, Irish Cinema Quarterly, Editor, Irish Hotelier, and Editor, Irish Licensing World, 1946–50; Gen. Manager and Dir, Ron Harris (Ireland), film distributors, 1950–52; Bord Fáilte Éireann (Irish Tourist Board): Asst Gen. Manager, N America, 1952–56; Gen. Manager (Britain), and Dir of Publicity, 1956–82; Editor, Irish Observer, 1982. Chairman: Friends of the Manor Hosp., Epsom, 1995–; Queen Elizabeth Hosp., Banstead, 1995–. Allied Irish Banks' Irish Post Community Award, 1977. Knight Cross, Order of Polonia Restituta (Poland), 1989. *Publications:* Ireland in Colour, 1975; Ireland, 1978; Ireland and Her People, 1980; Journey through Ireland, 1986; An Irish Moment, 1989. *Recreations:* reading, writing, conversation. *Address:* Ballinona, 7 Tower Road, Tadworth, Surrey KT20 5QY. *T:* (01737) 814241.   *Died 30 Aug. 2001.*

SHEEN, Sir Barry (Cross), Kt 1978; a Judge of the High Court of Justice, Queen's Bench Division (Admiralty Court), 1978–93; *b* 31 Aug. 1918; 2nd *s* of late Ronald Sheen, FCA; *m* 1st, 1946, Diane (*d* 1986), *d* of late C. L. Donne, MD; three *s*; 2nd, 1988, Helen Ursula, *widow* of Philip Spink; two step *d*. *Educ:* Haileybury; Hill School (USA); Trinity Hall, Cambridge (MA). Served in RNVR, 1939–46; Commanding Officer, HMS Kilkenzie (corvette), 1943–45. Called to Bar, Middle Temple, 1947, Master of the Bench, 1971, Reader, 1990; Member Bar Council, 1959–63; QC 1966. Junior Counsel to Admiralty, 1961–66; a Recorder of the Crown Court, 1972–78. On Panel of Wreck Comrs (Eng.) under Merchant Shipping Acts, 1966–78; Mem., Panel of Lloyd's Arbitrators in Salvage Cases, 1966–78, Appeal Arbitrator, 1977–78. Presided over Inquiry into Zeebrugge ferry disaster, 1987; Vice-Pres., British Maritime Law Assoc., 1979–93. Life Governor, Haileybury (Pres., Haileybury Soc., 1982); Hon. Mem., Assoc. of Average Adjusters, 1979– (Chm., 1986). Liveryman, Shipwrights' Co. Younger Brother, Trinity House, 1993–. Hon. FNI 1993. *Recreations:* bowls, travel, carpentry. *Address:* 107 Rivermead Court, Ranelagh Gardens, SW6 3SB. *T:* (020) 7731 7275. *Clubs:* Hurlingham, Pilgrims; Royal Wimbledon Golf.   *Died 25 Oct. 2005.*

SHELDON, Sir Gervase; see Sheldon, Sir J. G. K.

SHELDON, Sir (John) Gervase (Kensington), Kt 1978; a Judge of the High Court, Family Division, 1978–88; an Additional Judge of the High Court, 1988–93; *b* 4 Oct. 1913; *s* of John Henry Sheldon, MD, DPH, and Eleanor Gladys Sheldon, MB, BS; *m* 1st, 1940, Patricia Mary Mardon; one *s*; 2nd, 1960, Janet Marguerite Seager; two *s* one *d*. *Educ:* Winchester Coll.; Trinity Coll., Cambridge (MA; 1st Cl. Hons Law). Barrister-at-Law, called Lincoln's Inn, 1939 (Cert. of Honour, Cholmeley Schol.), Bencher, 1978. Served RA (TA), 1939–45 (despatches twice): Egypt, N Africa, Italy; Major, RA, 1943. A Circuit Judge (formerly a County Court Judge), 1968–78; Presiding Judge, Western Circuit, 1980–84. *Recreation:* family and home. *Address:* Little Hopton, 7 Beech Avenue, Lower Bourne, Farnham, Surrey GU10 3JZ. *T:* (01252) 792035.
Died 15 May 2004.

SHELFORD, Cornelius William; DL; Chairman, Pestalozzi Children's Village Trust, 1983–85; *b* 6 July 1908; *s* of William Heard Shelford and Maud Ethel Shelford, Horncastle, Sharpthorne, Sussex, and Singapore; *m* 1934, Helen Beatrice Hilda Schuster; one *s* two *d*. *Educ:* private tutor and Trinity College, Cambridge. Chartered Accountant, 1934; Partner, Rowley Pemberton & Co., 1940–60; Chm., Mills & Allen Ltd, 1964–69; Chm., London County Freehold & Leasehold Properties Ltd, 1964–70. East Sussex CC, 1952 (CA, 1957; Chm., 1964–67; Chm., Finance Cttee, 1970–74); High Sheriff of Sussex, 1954; DL Sussex, 1968. Governor and Mem. Management Cttee, Chailey Heritage Craft Schs and Hosp., for 30 years (Jt Founder, League of Friends); Pestalozzi Children's Village Trust: Mem. Council, 1974–89; Vice-Chm., 1975–83. *Recreations:* travelling, walking, gardening. *Address:* Heasmans, Chailey Green, near Lewes, E Sussex BN8 4DA. *T:* (01825) 722530. *Club:* Carlton.   *Died 16 Jan. 2001.*

SHELTON, Sir William (Jeremy Masefield), Kt 1989; *b* 30 Oct. 1929; *s* of late Lt-Col R. C. M. Shelton, MBE, St Saviour's, Guernsey, and Mrs R. E. P. Shelton (*née* Coode), London Place, Oxford; *m* 1960, Anne Patricia, *o d* of John Arthur Warder, CBE; one *s* and one adopted *d*. *Educ:* Radley Coll.; Tabor Acad., Marion, Mass; Worcester Coll., Oxford (MA); Univ. of Texas, Austin. Colman, Prentis & Varley Ltd, 1952–55; Corpa, Caracas, Venezuela, 1955–60; Managing Director: CPV (Colombiana) Ltd, Bogota, 1960–64; CPV (International) Ltd, 1967–74 (Dir, 1964); Grosvenor Advertising Ltd, 1969–74 (Dir, 1964); Chairman: Fletcher, Shelton, Delaney & Reynolds Ltd, 1974–81; GGK London Ltd, 1984–86; Dir, Access to Justice Ltd, 1995–97. Member for Wandsworth, GLC, 1967–70; Chief Whip, ILEA, 1968–70. MP (C) Clapham, 1970–74, Streatham, 1974–92; contested (C) Streatham, 1992. PPS to Minister of Posts and Telecommunications, 1972–74; PPS to Rt Hon. Margaret Thatcher, MP, 1975; Parly Under-Sec. of State, DES, 1981–83. Mem., Council of Europe and WEU, 1987–92. *Recreations:* golf, reading, painting. *Address:* Upton Downs House, near Burford, Oxon OX18 4LY. *T:* (01993) 823537. *Club:* Carlton.
Died 2 Jan. 2003.

SHENFIELD, Dame Barbara (Estelle), DBE 1986; Chairman, Women's Royal Voluntary Service, 1981–88 (Vice Chairman, 1976–81); *b* 9 March 1919; *d* of George and Jane Farrow, Bearwood, Staffs; *m* 1st, 1941, Flt-Lt Gwilym Ivor Lewis, RAF (killed in action 1941); one *s*; 2nd, 1951, Arthur A. Shenfield (*d* 1990); one *s*. *Educ:* Langley High Sch., Worcs; Univ. of Birmingham (Hons Social and Political Science). Lectr in Soc. Studies, Univ. of Birmingham, 1945–56; Lectr, Dept of Econs and Soc. Studies, Bedford Coll., London Univ., 1959–65; Academic Dir, UC at Buckingham, 1972–73. Visiting Professor: Michigan State Univ., 1960; Temple Univ., Philadelphia, 1974; Distinguished Vis. Prof., Rockford Coll., Ill, 1969–71, 1974. Consultant, US Dept of Labor, 1964; Dir, PEP Study of Co. Bds' Soc. Responsibilities, 1965–68. Member: UK Govt Cttee on Local Taxation, 1965–66; UK Govt Cttee on Abuse of Welfare Services, 1971–73; Govt Review Team on Social Security, 1984–85. Chairman: Nat Exec., Nat. Old People's Welfare Council (later Age Concern), 1971–73; Friends of the Imperial War Mus., 1991–2002; Pornography and Violence Res. Trust, 1996–2002. Trustee, Social Affairs Unit, 1990–2003. DUniv Buckingham, 1987. *Publications:* Social Policies for Old Age, 1957; The Social Responsibilities of Company Boards, 1971; The Organisation of a Voluntary Service, 1972; Myths of Social Policy, 1975; monographs and articles on gerontological and other social subjects. *Recreations:* gardening, music. *Address:* 22 Lower Sloane Street, SW1W 8BJ. *T:* (020) 7730 5810.   *Died 17 June 2004.*

SHEPHEARD, Sir Peter (Faulkner), Kt 1980; CBE 1972; PPRIBA, MRTPI, PPILA; architect, town planner and landscape architect in private practice, since 1948 (with Bridgwater & Shepheard, later Shepheard, Epstein & Hunter, until 1989, then solo); Professor of Architecture and Environmental Design, Graduate School of Fine Arts, University of Pennsylvania, since 1971; *b* 11 Nov. 1913; *s* of Thomas Faulkner Shepheard, FRIBA, Liverpool; *m* 1943, Mary Bailey; one *s* one *d*. *Educ*: Birkenhead Sch.; Liverpool Sch. of Architecture (BArch 1st Cl. Hons 1936; Grad. Schol. in Civic Design, 1936–37). Asst to Derek Bridgwater, 1937–40; Min. of Supply, Royal Ordnance Factories, 1940–43; Min. of Town and Country Planning: technical officer, first on Greater London Plan (Sir Patrick Abercrombie's staff), later on research and master plan for Stevenage New Town, 1943–47. Dep. Chief Architect and Planner, Stevenage Develt Corp., 1947–48. Vis. Prof., Landscape Architecture, 1959 and 1962–71, and Dean of Fine Arts, 1971–79, Univ. of Pennsylvania. Member: Nat. Parks Commn, 1966–68; Countryside Commn, 1968–71; Royal Fine Art Commn, 1968–71. Artistic Advr, Commonwealth War Graves Commn, 1977–. Works include: housing and schools for GLC and other authorities; Landscape of part of Festival of Britain South Bank Exhibition, London, 1951; Master plan and buildings for University of Lancaster; work for the Universities of Keele, Liverpool, Oxford, and Ghana, and for Winchester College; gardens in England and USA. President: RIBA, 1969–71; Architectural Association, 1954–55; Inst. of Landscape Architects, 1965–66. Master, Art Workers' Guild, 1984. RIBA Distinction in Town Planning, 1956. Hon. FRAIC; Hon. FAIA. *Publications:* Modern Gardens, 1953; Gardens, 1969; various articles, lectures and broadcasts on architecture and landscape; drawings and illustrations of architecture and other things; illustr. A Book of Ducks, and Woodland Birds (King Penguins). *Recreations:* music and poetry; drawing, gardening and the study of natural history. *Address:* 21 Well Road, NW3 1LH. *T:* (020) 7435 3019. *Club:* Athenæum.

Died 11 April 2002.

SHEPHERD, 2nd Baron *cr* 1946, of Spalding, co. Lincoln; **Malcolm Newton Shepherd;** PC 1965; Baron Shepherd of Spalding (Life Peer), 1999; Chairman, Chequepoint International, since 1989; *b* 27 Sept. 1918; *s* of 1st Baron Shepherd, PC, and Ada Newton (*d* 1975); *S* father, 1954; *m* 1941, Allison Wilson Redmond (*d* 1998); two *s*. *Educ:* Lower Sch. of John Lyon; Friends' Sch., Saffron Walden. War of 1939–45: commissioned RASC, 1941; served in Desert, N Africa, Sicily, Italy. Deputy Opposition Chief Whip, House of Lords, 1960; Deputy Speaker, House of Lords, subseq. Opposition Chief Whip, 1964; Captain of the Hon. Corps of Gentlemen-at-Arms and Government Chief Whip, House of Lords, 1964–67; Minister of State, FCO, 1967–70; Deputy Leader of the House of Lords, 1968–70; Opposition Dep. Leader, House of Lords, 1970–74; Lord Privy Seal and Leader, House of Lords, 1974–76, resigned. Mem., PLP Exec., 1964. Dep. Chm., Sterling Gp of Cos, 1976–86. First Chm., CS Pay Res. Unit Bd, 1978–81; Chairman: MRC, 1978–82; Packaging Council, 1978–82; Nat. Bus Co., 1979–84; President: Centre Européen de l'Enterprise Publique, 1985–; Inst. of Road Transport Engrs, 1987–. *Recreation:* golf. *Heir: s* Hon. Graeme George Shepherd [*b* 6 Jan. 1949; *m* 1971, Eleanor; one *s*]. *Address:* 29 Kennington Palace Court, Sancroft Street, SE11 5UL. *T:* (020) 7582 6772.

Died 5 April 2001.

SHEPHERD, William Stanley; Managing Director, Civic Investments Ltd; *b* 12 March 1910; *s* of W. D. Shepherd; *m* 1942, Betty, *d* of late T. F. Howard, MP for Islington S, 1931–35; two *s*. Served War of 1939–45, Army. A man. dir of businesses which he estabd; MP (C): Bucklow Div. of Cheshire, 1945–50; Cheadle Div. of Cheshire, 1950–66. Mem., Select Cttee on Estimates; Jt Hon. Sec., Cons. Parly Cttee in Trade and Industry, 1945–51. Joined SDP, 1982. Hon. Mem., Valuers Instn. FREconS. *Address:* 33 Queens Grove, St John's Wood, NW8 6HJ. *T:* (020) 7722 7526. *Club:* Savile.

Died 11 Oct. 2002.

SHEPPARD OF LIVERPOOL, Baron *cr* 1998 (Life Peer), of West Kirby in the co. of Merseyside; **Rt Rev. David Stuart Sheppard;** Bishop of Liverpool, 1975–97; *b* 6 March 1929; *s* of late Stuart Morton Winter Sheppard, Solicitor, and Barbara Sheppard; one *d*. *Educ:* Sherborne; Trinity Hall, Cambridge (MA; Hon. Fellow, 1983); Ridley Hall Theological Coll. Asst Curate, St Mary's, Islington, 1955–57; Warden, Mayflower Family Centre, Canning Town, E16, 1957–69; Bishop Suffragan of Woolwich, 1969–75. Chairman: Evangelical Urban Training Project, 1968–75; Peckham Settlement, 1969–75; Martin Luther King Foundn, 1970–75; Urban Ministry Project, 1970–75; Area Bd for Merseyside, MSC, 1978–85; Central Religious Adv. Cttee for BBC and IBA, 1989–93; Gen. Synod Bd for Social Responsibility, 1991–96; Churches' Enquiry into Unemployment and the Future of Work, 1995–97; Vice-Chm., Archbishop of Canterbury's Commn on Urban Priority Areas, 1983–85. Nat. Pres., Family Service Units, 1987–97. Chm. (alternating with Archbp of Liverpool), Liverpool Inst. of Higher Educn, later Liverpool Hope UC, 1982–97. Cricket: Cambridge Univ., 1950–52 (Captain 1952); Sussex, 1947–62 (Captain 1953; Pres., Sussex CCC, 2001–02); England (played 22 times), 1950–63 (Captain 1954). Freedom, City of Liverpool, 1995. Hon. LLD Liverpool, 1981; Hon. DTech Liverpool Polytechnic, 1987; Hon. DD: Cambridge, 1991; Exeter, 1998; Birmingham, 1999; Wales, 2000; DUniv Open, 1999. *Publications:* Parson's Pitch, 1964; Built as a City, 1974; Bias to the Poor, 1983; The Other Britain (Richard Dimbleby Lecture), 1984; Steps Along Hope Street: my life in cricket, the church and the inner city, 2002; with Most Rev. D. Worlock: Better Together, 1988; With Christ in the Wilderness, 1990; With Hope in Our Hearts, 1994. *Recreations:* family, reading, music, gardening, following cricket, singing in choir. *Address:* Ambledown, 11 Melloncroft Drive, West Kirby, Merseyside CH48 2JA.

Died 5 March 2005.

SHERIDAN, Peter; QC 1977; *b* 29 May 1927; *s* of Hugo and Marie Sheridan. *Educ:* eight schools; Lincoln Coll., Oxford (BA Hons 1950). Called to the Bar, Middle Temple, 1955, Bencher, 1988. *Recreations:* motor cars, archery. *Address:* 11 Stone Buildings, Lincoln's Inn, WC2A 3TG. *T:* (020) 7831 6381; 17 Brompton Square, SW3 2AD. *T:* (020) 7584 7250; Pile Oak Lodge, Donhead St Andrew, Wilts SP7 9EU. *T:* (01747) 828484.

Died 31 July 2003.

SHERLOCK, Prof. Dame Sheila (Patricia Violet), DBE 1978; MD; FRCP, FRCPE; FRS 2001; Professor of Medicine, University of London, at the Royal Free Hospital School of Medicine, since 1959; *b* 31 March 1918; *d* of late Samuel Philip Sherlock and Violet Mary Catherine Beckett; *m* 1951, David Geraint James, FRCP; two *d*. *Educ:* Folkestone County Sch.; Edinburgh Univ. Ettles Scholar, 1941; Beit Memorial Research Fellow, 1942–47; Rockefeller Fellow, Yale University, USA, 1948. Physician and Lecturer in Medicine, Postgraduate Medical School of London, 1948–59. RCP Lectures: Bradshaw, 1961; Rolleston, 1968; Lumleian, 1978; Harveian, 1985. RCP: Councillor, 1964–68; Censor, 1970–72; Senior Censor and Vice-Pres., 1976–77. Mem. Senate, Univ. of London, 1976–81. Hon. Member: Gastro-enterological Societies of America, 1963, Australasia, 1965, Mexico, 1968, Czechoslovakia, 1968, Yugoslavia, 1981, Sweden, 1983; Assoc. of Amer. Physicians, 1973; Assoc. of Alimentary Surgeons, 1973; Alpha Omega Alpha Assoc., 1992. Hon. FACP; Hon. FRCPC; Hon. FRACP 1984; Hon. FRCPI; Hon. FRCPS 1986; Hon. FRCS 1989. Hon. DSc: City Univ. of NY, 1977; Yale Univ., USA, 1983; Edinburgh, 1985; London, 1989; Cambridge, 1995. Hon. MD: Lisbon, 1981; Oslo, 1981; Leuven, 1984; Barcelona, 1991; Mainz, 1991; TCD, 1992; Valladolid, 1994; Wisconsin, 1995; Santiago de Chile, 1995; Padua, 1996; Toronto, 1996; Oviedo, 1998; Hon. LLD Aberdeen, 1982. William Cullen Prize, 1962 (shared); Jimenez-Diaz Prize, 1980;

Thannhauser Prize, 1980; Fothergill Gold Medal, Med. Soc. of London, 1983; Gold Medal, BMA, 1985. *Publications:* Diseases of the Liver and Biliary System, 1955, 11th edn 2001; papers on liver structure and function in various medical journals, since 1943. *Recreations:* cricket, travel. *Address:* 41 York Terrace East, NW1 4PT. *T:* (020) 7486 4560, (020) 7431 4589. *Died 30 Dec. 2001.*

SHERMAN, Sir Louis, (Sir Lou Sherman), Kt 1975; OBE 1967; JP; Chairman, Housing Corporation, 1977–80; Deputy Chairman, Harlow Development Corporation; *b* 23 May 1914; *m* Sally (CBE 1987); one *s* decd. Taxi driver, 1935–75. Initiated Lea Valley Regional Park Authority. Mem. and Leader, Hackney BC, 1953–61; Mayor of Hackney, 1961. Chm., London Boroughs Assoc., 1971–78. JP Inner London Area. *Recreations:* politics, reading, talking.
Died 16 Nov. 2001.

SHETH, Pranlal, CBE 1994; Director: One World International (formerly One World Online) Ltd, since 1995; Victim Support Ltd, since 1995; Member, Independent Television Commission, 1991–95; *b* 20 Dec. 1924; *s* of Purashotam Virji Sheth and Sakarben Sheth; *m* 1951, Indumati Druva; one *s* one *d*. Called to the Bar, Lincoln's Inn, 1962. Journalist, Kenya, 1943–52; Chm., Nyanza Farmers' Cooperative Soc., 1954–60; Mem., Central Agriculture Bd, Kenya, 1963–66; Chm., Asian Hosp. Authority, 1964–66; Mem., Economic Planning and Devel Council, Kenya, 1964–66. Group Sec., 1971, Legal Advr and Dir, 1985–88, Abbey Life Gp of Cos; Chm. Adv. Bd, Abbey Ethical Unit Trust, 1988–96; Legal Dir, Hartford Europe Gp of Cos, 1977–86; Director: Abbey Life Assurance Co. Ltd, 1977–89; Ambassador Life Assce Co. Ltd, 1980–88; Abbey Life Assurance (Ireland), 1981–85; Reed Exec. plc, 1990–93; Chairman: Sense Internat. Ltd, 1998–; Channel East TV, 1999–2001; Go Education plc, 2000–. Gp Sec., ITT cos in UK, 1983–86. Chairman: ABI Associates Ltd (formerly Asian Business Initiatives), 1997–; Unity Radio, 1997–; Advr, Supervisory Bd, One World Europe BV, Maastricht, 1998–2000. Dir, Shelter, 1987–91; Mem. Bd, Notting Hill Housing Trust, 1997–. Director: Round House Arts Centre, 1986–90; Pan-Centre for Inter-Cultural Arts, 1998–; Member: BBC Consultative Gp on Commerce, Industry and Finance, 1986–89; BBC Asian Progs Adv. Cttee, 1986–89; IBA, 1990. Founder, and Chief Editor, Gujarat Samachar Weekly, 1972–73; Mem., N Metropolitan Conciliation Cttee, Race Relations Bd, 1973–77; a Dep. Chm., CRE, 1977–80; Vice Pres., UKIAS, 1986–93. Trustee: Project Fullemploy (Charitable Trust), 1977–89; Assoc. of Asian Women, 1979–; Find Your Feet, 1980–2000; Runnymede Trust, 1987–1998; Urban Trust, 1987–2000; Windsor Fellowship, 1988–2002; Womankind Worldwide Trust, 1989–96; One World Broadcasting Trust, 1991–; Gujarati Literary Acad., 1992–; Immigrants Aid Trust, 1988–; Uniting Britain Trust, 1997–; Nat. Primary Trust, 1998–; Mem. Oxfam Council, 1993–94, Assembly, 1994– (Mem. Shops and Premises Cttee, 1988–93). Vice-Patron, UK Assoc., Internat. Year of the Child, 1978–80; Patron: Internat. Centre for Child Studies; CRE Race in Media Awards, 1992–2001; Ruth Hayman Trust, 2001–. Chm., One World Internat. Foundn, 1999–. Hon. Legal Advr and Mem. Exec. Cttee, Nat. Assoc. of Victim Support Schemes, 1988–95 (Mem. Adv. Bd, 1995–). FInstD 1977; FIMgt (FBIM 1980); FRSA 1999. Mem., Bd of Dirs, Univ. (formerly Poly.) of N London, 1979–2000. Mem. Editorial Adv. Panel, Equal Opportunities Review, 1984. *Address:* 70 Howberry Road, Edgware, Middx HA8 6SY; *e-mail:* pransheth@aol.com. *Clubs:* Royal Over-Seas League, Royal Commonwealth Society.
Died 30 June 2003.

SHIELDS, Prof. Carol Ann, CC 2002 (OC 1998); writer; Professor, University of Manitoba, 1980–2000, then Emerita; Chancellor, University of Winnipeg, 1996–2000, then Emerita; *b* 2 June 1935; *d* of Robert Warner and Inez Warner (*née* Sellgren); *m* 1957, Donald Shields; one *s* four *d*. *Educ:* Hanover Coll. (BA 1957); Univ. of Ottawa (MA 1975). Lecturer: Univ. of Ottawa, 1977–88; Univ. of BC, 1978–79. Mem., Royal Soc. of Canada, 1997. Hon. degrees from: Ottawa, 1995; Winnipeg, 1996; Hanover Coll., Queen's, Univ. of BC, 1997; Concordia, Toronto, Western Ont, 1998; Carleton, Wilfrid Laurier, 2000; Victoria, Calgary, Lakehead, 2001; Manitoba, Malaspina Univ. Coll., 2003. Guggenheim Fellow, 1999. Marian Engel Award, Toronto, 1990. *Publications:* Small Ceremonies, 1976 (Canadian Authors' Award, 1976); The Box Garden, 1977; Happenstance, 1980; A Fairly Conventional Woman, 1982; Various Miracles, 1985; Swann, 1987 (Arthur Ellis Award, 1987); The Orange Fish, 1989; (with Blanche Howard) A Celibate Season, 1991, (play) 2000; The Republic of Love, 1992; The Stone Diaries, 1993 (Gov. Gen's Award, 1993; Nat. Book Critics Circle Award, Lire Prize, France, Pulitzer Prize, 1995); Coming to Canada: Poems, 1993; Departures and Arrivals (play), 1993; Thirteen Hands (play), 1993; (with Catherine Shields) Fashion, Power, Guilt and the Charity of Families (play), 1995; Larry's Party, 1997 (Orange Prize, UK, 1998); (with David Williamson) Anniversary (play), 1998; Dressing up for the Carnival, 2000; Jane Austen, 2001 (Charles Taylor Prize, 2002); Unless, 2002 (BC Book Award, 2003). *Recreations:* theatre, France, literary theory. *Address:* 990 Terrace Avenue, Victoria, BC V8S 3V3, Canada. *Club:* PEN International.
Died 16 July 2003.

SHIELDS, (Leslie) Stuart; QC 1970; a Recorder of the Crown Court, 1972–91; *b* 15 May 1919; *m* 1st, 1941, Maureen Margaret McKinstry (*d* 1989); two *s* two *d* (and one *s* decd); 2nd, 1990, Barbara Diana Lloyd. *Educ:* St Paul's School; Corpus Christi College, Oxford. Paid Local Sergeant, Oxford and Buckinghamshire Light Infantry, 1945–47. Called to the Bar, Middle Temple, 1948, Bencher, 1977. Member: Criminal Injuries Compensation Bd, 1981–92; Independent Review Body for Coal Industry, 1985–90. *Recreations:* music, travel. *Address:* Devereux Chambers, Devereux Court, Temple, WC2R 3JJ. *Died 22 March 2005.*

SHIELDS, Sir Neil (Stanley), Kt 1964; MC 1946; management consultant and company director; Chairman, Commission for the New Towns, 1982–95 (Chairman designate, 1981–82); *b* 7 Sept. 1919; *o s* of late Archie Shields and Mrs Hannah Shields; *m* 1970, Gloria Dawn Wilson. Member of Honourable Artillery Company 1939–. Served in Royal Artillery, 1939–46; commnd 1940; Major 1943. Chairman: Anglo Continental Investment & Finance Co., 1965–74; Standard Catalogue Co., 1976–84; Holcombe Hldgs, 1978–84; Trianco Redfyre, 1979–84; Director: Chesham Amalgamations & Investments, 1964–84; Continental Bankers Agents, 1965–74; Central and Sheerwood, 1969–84; Newton Chambers & Co., 1972–84; Paxall Engineering, 1976–79. London Transport (formerly London Regional Transport): Mem. Bd, 1986–93; Chm., 1988–89, Dep. Chm., 1989–93; Chm., Property Bd, 1986–95. Prospective candidate (C) North St Pancras 1947 and contested by-election 1949. Chairman: Camden Conservative Cttee, 1965–67; Hampstead Conservative Assoc., 1954–65 (Vice-Chm., 1951–54); Hon. Treas. 1965–67; National Union of Conservative and Unionist Assocs: Chm. of London Area, 1961–63 (Vice-Chm., 1959–61); Mem. of National Executive, 1955–59, 1961–67, 1968–69; Hampstead Borough Council: Mem. 1947–65; Deputy Leader, 1952–61; Chm. of Works Cttee, 1951–55; Chm. of Finance Cttee, 1955–59. Mem. Council, Aims of Industry, 1976–2001. Chm., WNCCC/ Cancer Aware Devel Task Force, 1996–98; Vice-Pres., Women's Nationwide Cancer Control Campaign, 1998–2002. Governor, Bedford Coll., London Univ., 1983–85. Freeman, City of London, 1993; Mem., Ct of Assts, Guild of Freemen, 1998–. Hon. RICS (Hon. MRICS 1993). *Recreations:* reading, music, wining and dining. *Address:* 12 London House, Avenue Road, NW8 7PX. *Clubs:* Carlton, HAC.					*Died 12 Sept. 2002.*

SHIELDS, Stuart; *see* Shields, L. S.

SHILLINGTON, Sir Graham; *see* Shillington, Sir R. E. G.

SHILLINGTON, Sir (Robert Edward) Graham, Kt 1972; CBE 1970 (OBE 1959; MBE 1951); DL; Chief Constable, Royal Ulster Constabulary, 1970–73; *b* 2 April 1911; *s* of Major D. Graham Shillington, DL, MP, and Mrs Louisa Shillington (*née* Collen); *m* 1935, Mary E. R. Bulloch (*d* 1977), Holywood, Co. Down; two *s* one *d*. *Educ:* Sedbergh Sch., Yorks; Clare Coll., Cambridge. Royal Ulster Constabulary: Officer Cadet, 1933; 3rd Class District Inspector, 1934; 2nd Class District Inspector, 1936; 1st Class District Inspector, 1944; County Inspector, 1953; Commissioner, Belfast, 1961; Deputy Inspector General (Deputy Chief Constable), 1969–70. Chm., Belfast Voluntary Welfare Soc., 1976–81. DL Co. Down, 1975. King's Coronation Medal, 1937; Queen's Coronation Medal, 1953; Police Long Service and Good Conduct Medal, 1955; RUC Service Medal, 1985. *Recreations:* golf, gardening. *Address:* Ardeevin, 184 Bangor Road, Holywood, Co. Down BT18 0BY. *T:* (028) 9042 3471. *Clubs:* Royal Over-Seas League; Royal Belfast Golf.					*Died 14 Aug. 2001.*

SHOENBERG, Prof. David, MBE 1944; FRS 1953; Professor of Physics, Cambridge University and Head of Low Temperature Physics Group, Cavendish Laboratory, 1973–78, then Emeritus; Life Fellow of Gonville and Caius College; *b* 4 Jan. 1911; *s* of Isaac and Esther Shoenberg; *m* 1940, Catherine Félicitée Fischmann (*d* 2003); one *s* two *d*. *Educ:* Latymer Upper School, W6; Trinity College, Cambridge (Scholar; Hon. Fellow 2002); PhD 1935. Exhibition of 1851 Senior Student, 1936–39; Research in low temperature physics, 1932–, in charge of Royal Soc. Mond Laboratory, 1947–73; Univ. Lectr in Physics, 1944–52; Univ. Reader in Physics, 1952–73; UNESCO Adviser on Low Temperature Physics, NPL of India, 1953–54. Mellon Prof., Univ. of Pittsburgh, 1962; Gauss Prof., Univ. of Göttingen, 1964; Visiting Professor: Univ. of Maryland, 1968; Univ. of Toronto, 1974; Univ. of Waterloo, 1977; Lectures: Guthrie, 1961; Rutherford Meml, India and Sri Lanka, 1980; Krishnan Meml, New Delhi, 1988. Hon. Foreign Mem., Amer. Acad. of Arts and Sciences, 1982. Dr (*hc*) Univ. of Lausanne, 1973. Fritz London Award for Low Temperature Physics, 1964; Hughes Medal, Royal Soc., 1995. *Publications:* Superconductivity, 1938, revised edn, 1952; Magnetism, 1949; Magnetic Oscillations in Metals, 1984; (ed jtly) Kapitza in Cambridge and Moscow, 1990; scientific papers on low temperature physics and magnetism. *Address:* 2 Long Road, Cambridge CB2 2PS; Cavendish Laboratory, Madingley Road, Cambridge CB3 0HE. *T:* (01223) 337389.					*Died 10 March 2004.*

SHORE OF STEPNEY, Baron *cr* 1997 (Life Peer), of Stepney in the London Borough of Tower Hamlets; **Peter David Shore;** PC 1967; *b* 20 May 1924; *s* of Capt. R. N. Shore; *m* 1948, Elizabeth Catherine Wrong (CB 1980); one *s* two *d* (and one *s* decd). *Educ:* Quarry Bank Grammar Sch., Liverpool; King's Coll., Cambridge. Flying Officer, RAF, 1943–46. Political economist. Joined Labour Party, 1948; Head of Research Dept, Labour Party, 1959–64. Member of Fabian Society. Contested (Lab) St Ives, Cornwall, 1950, Halifax, 1959. MP (Lab) Stepney, 1964–74, Stepney and Poplar, 1974–83, Bethnal Green and Stepney, 1983–97. PPS to the Prime Minister, 1965–66; Jt Parly Sec., Min. of Technology, 1966–67; Dept of Economic Affairs, 1967; Sec. of State for Economic Affairs, 1967–69; Minister without Portfolio, 1969–70; Dep. Leader of House of Commons, 1969–70; Opposition Spokesman on Europe, 1971–74; Sec. of State for Trade, 1974–76; Sec. of State for the Environment, 1976–79; Opposition Spokesman: on Foreign Affairs, 1979–80; on Treasury and Economic Affairs, 1980–83; on

Trade and Industry, 1983–84; Shadow Leader of the House of Commons, 1984–87. Member: Select Cttee on Foreign Affairs, 1987–97; Cttee on Standards in Public Life, 1994–. *Publications:* Entitled to Know, 1966; Leading the Left, 1993; Separate Ways: Britain and Europe, 2000. *Recreations:* swimming, reading, opera. *Address:* House of Lords, SW1A 0PW; 23 Dryburgh Road, SW15 1BN.					*Died 24 Sept. 2001.*

SHORT, Prof. David Somerset, MD, FRCP, FRCPE; Clinical Professor in Medicine, University of Aberdeen, 1983, then Emeritus; Hon. Consultant Physician, Aberdeen Royal Infirmary, since 1983 (Consultant Physician, 1960–83); *b* 6 Aug. 1918; *s* of Latimer James Short, MD, DPH, Bristol, and Mabel Annie Wood, SRN, Nottingham; *m* 1948, Joan Anne McLay, BSc, MB, ChB, Cardiff; one *s* four *d*. *Educ:* Bristol Grammar Sch.; Clare Coll., Cambridge (MD 1948); Bristol Royal Hospitals; PhD London 1957. FRCP 1964; FRCPE 1966. Served with RAMC, 1944–47; Registrar, Southmead Hosp., Bristol, 1947–49; Sen. Registrar, National Heart Hosp. and London Hosp., 1950–54; Lecturer in Medicine, Middlesex Hosp., 1955–59. Physician to the Queen in Scotland, 1977–83. *Publications:* Medicine as a Vocation, 1978, 2nd edn 1987; The Medical Consultation, 1995; Real Success, 1998; contribs to medical journals, mainly on cardiovascular and pulmonary diseases. *Recreations:* touring, music. *Address:* 48 Victoria Street, Aberdeen, Scotland AB10 1PN. *T:* (01224) 645853.					*Died 4 May 2005.*

SHORT, Sir Noel (Edward Vivian), Kt 1977; MBE 1951; MC 1945; Speaker's Secretary, House of Commons, 1970–82; *b* 19 Jan. 1916; *s* of late Vivian A. Short, CIE, Indian Police, and Annie W. Short; *m* 1st, 1949, Diana Hester Morison (*d* 1951); one *s*; 2nd, 1957, Karin Margarete Anders; one *s* one *d*. *Educ:* Radley College; RMA Sandhurst. Commissioned Indian Army, 1936; joined 6th Gurkha Rifles, 1937; active service: NW Frontier of India, 1937, 1940–41; Assam and Burma, 1942, 1944–45; New Guinea, 1943–44; Malaysia, 1950–51, 1952–53, 1956–57; Staff College, 1946–47; jssc, 1953; Comdr, 63 Gurkha Bde, Malaysia, 1960–61; Comdr, 51 Infty Bde, Tidworth, 1962–63. Principal, Home Office, 1964–70. Col, 6th Queen Elizabeth's Own Gurkha Rifles, 1978–83.					*Died 12 June 2001.*

SHORT, Mrs Renee; politician; *b* 26 April 1919; *m* 1940, Dr Andrew Short (*d* 1999); two *d*. *Educ:* Nottingham Co. Grammar Sch.; Manchester Univ. Freelance journalist. Member: Herts CC, 1952–67; Watford RDC, 1952–64; West Herts Group Hosp. Management Cttee; former Chm. Shrodell's Hosp., Watford. Governor: Watford Coll. of Technology; Watford Grammar Sch. Contested (Lab) St Albans, 1955, Watford, 1959. MP (Lab) Wolverhampton NE, 1964–87; TGWU sponsored Member of Parliament. Member: Delegn to Council of Europe, 1964–68; Estimates Cttee, 1964–69; Expenditure Cttee, 1970–79 (Chm., Social Services and Employment Sub-Cttee); Chairman: Select Cttee for Social Services, 1979–87; Parly and Scientific Cttee, 1982–85 (Vice-Pres., 1986; Life Mem.); Associate Mem., Parly IT Cttee, 1987–. Vice-Chm., Parly East-West Trade Gp, 1968–87; Chairman: British-GDR Parly Gp, 1972–87; British-Soviet Parly Gp 1984–87 (Sec., 1972–84); Pres., British-Romanian Friendship Assoc. Mem., Nat. Exec. Cttee of Labour Party, 1970–81, 1983–88. Member: MRC, 1988–93; Research in Patients Cttee, RCP, 1988–91; IVF Cttee, BMA, 1988–91; AIDS Study Gp, Inst. of Medical Ethics, 1989–91; Special Hosps Services Authority, 1991–. National President: Nursery Schools Assoc., 1970–80; Campaign for Nursery Educn, 1970–83; Pres., Action for the Newborn, 1988–; Vice-President: Women's Nat. Cancer Control Campaign; Health Visitors' Assoc. Patron, Rescare, 1990–. Mem., Roundhouse Theatre Council; Chm., Theatres' Advisory Council, 1974–80. Hon. Fellow, Wolverhampton Polytechnic, 1987; Hon. FRCPsych 1988; Hon. MRCP 1989. *Publication:* The

Care of Long Term Prisoners, 1979.

Died 18 Jan. 2003.

SHORT, Roger Guy, MVO 1971; HM Diplomatic Service; HM Consul General, and Director of Trade and Investment Promotion, Istanbul, since 2001; *b* 9 Dec. 1944; *s* of Harold Short and Alice Ames Short (*née* Fox); *m* 1971, Sally Victoria Taylor; one *s* two *d*. *Educ*: Malvern; University Coll., Oxford (schol.; BA Lit.Hum.; MA). Served FCO and Ankara, 1967–78; Consul (Commercial), Rio de Janeiro, 1978–80; Head of Chancery, Ankara, 1981–84; Counsellor and Dep. Head of Permanent Under-Sec. of State's Dept, FCO, 1984–86; Head of Chancery and Consul-Gen., Oslo, 1986–90; Head of Personnel Services Dept, FCO, 1990–94; Ambassador to Bulgaria, 1994–98; COS, Office of High Rep., Sarajevo, 1999–2000. *Recreations:* music, classical studies, languages, wine. *Address:* c/o Foreign and Commonwealth Office, SW1A 2AH. *Died 20 Nov. 2003.*

SHRAPNEL, Norman; Parliamentary Correspondent of the Guardian, 1958–75; *b* 5 Oct. 1912; *yr s* of Arthur Edward Scrope Shrapnel and Rosa Brosy; *m* 1940, Mary Lilian Myfanwy Edwards; two *s*. *Educ:* King's School, Grantham. Various weekly, evening and morning newspapers from 1930; Manchester Guardian (later the Guardian) from 1947, as reporter, theatre critic and reviewer; contributor to various journals. Political Writer of the Year Award (the Political Companion), 1969. *Publications:* A View of the Thames, 1977; The Performers: politics as theatre, 1978; The Seventies, 1980. *Recreations:* walking, music. *Address:* Laburnum Cottage, Far Oakridge, Stroud, Glos GL6 7PB. *Died 1 Feb. 2004.*

SHRUBSOLE, Alison Cheveley, CBE 1982; Principal, Homerton College, Cambridge, 1971–85; Fellow of Hughes Hall, Cambridge, 1974; *b* 7 April 1925; *d* of Rev. Stanley and Mrs Margaret Shrubsole; *m* 1983, George Huntly Hilton Brown (*d* 2002). *Educ:* Milton Mount Coll.; Royal Holloway Coll., London Univ. (BA Hons); Inst. of Educn (Postgraduate Cert. in Educn); MA Cantab 1975. FCP. Teaching in schools in South London, 1946–50; Lectr and Sen. Lectr, Stockwell Coll., 1950–57; Principal: Machakos Training Coll., Kenya, 1957–62; Philippa Fawcett Coll., London SW16, 1963–71. DUniv Open, 1985. *Recreations:* music, architecture, travel, gardening, cooking. *Address:* 4 Chancellor House, Mount Ephraim, Tunbridge Wells, Kent TN4 8BT; Cortijo Abulagar, Rubite, Granada, Spain.

Died 4 Oct. 2002.

SHULL, Prof. Clifford Glenwood, PhD; Professor of Physics, Massachusetts Institute of Technology, 1955–86, then Emeritus; *b* 23 Sept 1915; *s* of David H. and Daisy B. Shull; *m* 1941, Martha-Nuel Summer; three *s*. *Educ:* Carnegie Inst. of Technology (BS 1937); New York Univ. (PhD 1941). Research Physicist: The Texas Co., 1941–46; Oak Ridge Nat. Lab., 1946–55. Hon. ScD New York, 1997. Buckley Prize, Amer. Phys. Soc., 1956; Humboldt Sen. US Scientist Award, 1980; Aminoff Prize, Royal Swedish Acad. of Scis, 1993; (jtly) Nobel Prize for Physics, 1994. *Publications:* numerous scientific articles.

Died 31 March 2001.

SHULMAN, Milton; writer, journalist, critic; *b* Toronto, 1 Sept. 1913; *s* of Samuel Shulman, merchant, and Ethel Shulman; *m* 1956, Drusilla Beyfus, writer, editor and broadcaster; one *s* two *d*. *Educ:* Univ. of Toronto (BA); Osgoode Hall, Toronto. Barrister, Toronto, 1937–40. Armoured Corps and Intelligence, Canadian Army, 1940–46 (despatches, Normandy, 1945); Major. Film critic, Evening Standard and Sunday Express, 1948–58; book critic, Sunday Express, 1957–58; theatre critic, Evening Standard, 1953–91; TV critic, Evening Standard, 1964–73; columnist, social and political affairs, Daily Express, 1973–75; film critic, Vogue Magazine, 1975–87; columnist, art affairs, Evening Standard, 1991–96. Executive producer and producer, Granada TV, 1958–62; Asst Controller of Programmes, Rediffusion TV,

1962–64. Mem., Adv. Council, British Theatre Museum, 1981–83. Mem. Panel of Judges, Evening Standard Drama Awards, 1955–. Regular panel mem., Stop the Week, BBC Radio 4. IPC Award, Critic of the Year, 1966. *Publications:* Defeat in the West, 1948; How To Be a Celebrity, 1950; The Victors, 1963; The Ravenous Eye, 1973; The Least Worst Television in the World, 1973; Marilyn, Hitler and Me (memoirs), 1998; Voltaire, Goldberg and Others, 1999; It Takes All Sorts, 2001; *children's books:* Preep, 1964; Preep in Paris, 1967; Preep and The Queen, 1970; *novel:* Kill Three, 1967; *novel and film story:* (with Herbert Kretzmer) Every Home Should Have One, 1970. *Recreations:* modern art, history, tennis. *Address:* 51 Eaton Square, SW1W 9BE. *T:* (020) 7235 7162. *Clubs:* Garrick, Chelsea Arts, Hurlingham.

Died 21 May 2004.

SIAGURU, Sir Anthony (Michael), KBE 1990; Chairman, Port Moresby Stock Exchange, since 1998; *b* 4 Nov. 1946; *s* of Khaisir Petrus Siaguru and Kandambi Maria Krakemoine; *m* 1972, Wilhelmina Isikini; three *s*. *Educ:* Marist Brothers' Sch., Wewak and Ashgrove; Univ. of Papua New Guinea (Law); Harvard Univ. (Public Admin). Entered Foreign Service as Cadet Diplomat, 1972; Permanent Sec., Foreign Affairs and Trade, 1975–80; MP, 1982; Minister for: Public Service, 1982–84; Youth and Develt, 1985; Dep. Sec.-Gen. (Pol) of the Commonwealth, 1990–95. Partner, Blake Dawson Waldron, 1988–90 and 1996–97; Chm., South Pacific Games Foundn, 1989–90. Columnist, PNG Post Courier, 1988–90 and 1996–. Fulbright Scholar, 1980. FRSA 1992. *Publications:* In-House in Papua New Guinea, 2001; *contributions to:* Ethics in Government, 1983; The United States' Dilemma, 1983; The Red Orchestra, 1987; Ethics of Public Decision Making, 1987. *Recreations:* gardening, tennis, fishing. *Address:* PO Box 5917, Boroko, NCD, Papua New Guinea. *Clubs:* Reform; Aviat, Badili, Papua (Port Moresby). *Died 16 April 2004.*

SIBERRY, John William Morgan; Under-Secretary, Welsh Office, 1963–73, retired; Secretary to Local Government Staff Commission for Wales, and NHS Staff Commission for Wales, 1973–75; *b* 26 Feb. 1913; *s* of late John William and Martha (*née* Morgan) Siberry; *m* 1949, Florence Jane Davies (*d* 1995); one *s* one *d*. *Educ:* Porth County School, Rhondda; Univ. Coll. Cardiff. Entered Civil Service as Asst Principal, Unemployment Assistance Board (later Nat. Assistance Board), 1935; Principal, 1941; Asst Sec., 1947; transferred to Min. of Housing and Local Govt as Under-Sec., 1963; Welsh Secretary, Welsh Office and Office for Wales of the Ministry of Housing and Local Government, 1963–64. Chm., Working Party on Fourth Television Service in Wales, 1975. *Address:* Northgates, 59 Pwllmelin Road, Llandaff, Cardiff CF5 2NG. *T:* (029) 2056 4666. *Died 8 Feb. 2002.*

SIDDALL, Sir Norman, Kt 1983; CBE 1975; DL; FREng; Member of the National Coal Board, 1971–83, Deputy Chairman 1973–82, Chairman 1982–83; *b* 4 May 1918; *s* of late Frederick and Mabel Siddall; *m* 1943, Pauline, *d* of late John Alexander and Edith Arthur; two *s* one *d*. *Educ:* King Edward VII School, Sheffield; Sheffield Univ. (BEng). National Coal Board: Production Manager, 1951–56, General Manager, 1956–57, No 5 Area, East Midlands Div.; General Manager, No 1 Area, East Midlands Div., 1957–66; Chief Mining Engineer, 1966–67; Dir Gen. of Production, 1967–71. Former Mem., Midland Cos Institn of Engrs (Silver Medal, 1951; Past Pres.). Chartered Engineer; FIMinE; CIMgt. DL Notts, 1987. Hon. DSc Nottingham, 1982. National Association of Colliery Managers: Silver Medal, 1955; Bronze Medal, 1960; Coal Science Lecture Medal, 1972; CGLI Insignia Award in Technology (*hc*), 1978; Instn Medal, IME, 1982; Krupinski Medal, 1982. *Publications:* articles in professional journals. *Address:* Brentwood, High Oakham Road, Mansfield, Notts NG18 5AJ.

Died 9 Jan. 2002.

SIDEBOTTOM, Edward John; a Chief Inspector, Department of Education and Science, 1973–80 (Divisional Inspector, 1969–73); *b* 1918; *s* of late Ernest Sidebottom, Wylam, Northumberland; *m* 1949, Brenda Millicent, *d* of late Alec H. Sadler, Wandsworth. *Educ:* Queen Elizabeth Grammar School, Hexham; Hatfield College, Durham (BSc). Entered Iraq Government education service, 1939; lecturer, Leavesden Green Emergency Training College, 1946; County Youth Organiser for Hampshire, 1947; HM Inspector of Schools, 1949–80. Sec. to Albemarle Cttee on the Youth Service in England and Wales, 1958–59; seconded as first Principal, Nat. Coll. for the Training of Youth Leaders, 1960–64. Chm., Jt Working Gp on Training for Staff Working with Mentally Handicapped People, 1981–83. *Address:* 3 Queen's Court, Marlborough Road, West Cliff, Bournemouth, Dorset BH4 8DB.
Died 9 April 2001.

SIDEY, Air Marshal Sir Ernest (Shaw), KBE 1972; CB 1965; MD; FFCM, DPH; Director-General, Chest, Heart and Stroke Association, 1974–85; *b* 2 Jan. 1913; *s* of Thomas Sidey, Alyth, Perthshire; *m* 1946, Doreen Florence, *y d* of late Cecil Ronald Lurring, Dalkey, Ireland; one *d* (and one *d* decd). *Educ:* Morgan Acad., Dundee; St Andrews Univ. (ChB, MD). Commissioned in RAF, 1937. Served in Burma Campaign during War of 1939–45. Recent appts include: Chief, Med. Adv. Staff, Allied Air Forces Central Europe, 1957–59; PMO: Flying Trg Comd, 1961–63; Middle East Comd, 1963–65; Transport Command, 1965–66; DDGMS, RAF, 1966–68. PMO, Strike Command, 1968–70; Dir-Gen., RAF Med. Services, 1971–74; QHS 1966–74. Governor, Royal Star and Garter Home, 1974–86. *Recreations:* racing, golf, bridge. *Address:* Callums, Tugwood Common, Cookham Dean, Berks SL6 9TU. *T:* (01628) 483006. *Club:* Royal Air Force. *Died 18 Sept. 2002.*

SIDMOUTH, 7th Viscount *cr* 1805; **John Tonge Anthony Pellew Addington;** *b* 3 Oct. 1914; *s* of 6th Viscount Sidmouth and of Gladys Mary Dever (*d* 1983), *d* of late Thomas Francis Hughes; *S* father, 1976; *m* 1st, 1940, Barbara Mary (*d* 1989), *d* of Bernard Rochford, OBE; one *s* five *d* (and one *s* decd); 2nd, 1993, Mrs Thérèse Pollen. *Educ:* Downside School (Scholar); Brasenose Coll., Oxford (Scholar). Colonial Service, E Africa, 1938–54. Mem. Council and Chm. Glasshouse Cttee, Nat. Farmers Union, 1962–69; Member: Agricultural Research Council, 1964–74; Central Council for Agricultural Co-operation, 1970–73. Mem., Select Cttee on European Communities, 1984–87. Pres., Nat. Council on Inland Transport, 1978–84. Trustee, John Innes Foundation, 1974–89. Chm. of Governing Body, Glasshouse Crops Research Inst., 1981–84. Knight of Malta, 1962. *Recreation:* gardening. *Heir: s* Hon. Jeremy Francis Addington [*b* 29 July 1947; *m* 1st, 1970, Grete Henningsen; one *s* one *d*; 2nd, 1986, Una Coogan; one *s* two *d*]. *Address:* 12 Brock Street, Bath, Avon BA1 2LW. *T:* (01225) 301946. *Died 30 Jan. 2005.*

SIEFF OF BRIMPTON, Baron *cr* 1980 (Life Peer), of Brimpton in the Royal County of Berkshire; **Marcus Joseph Sieff,** Kt 1971; OBE 1944; Chairman, First International Bank of Israel Financial Trust Ltd, 1983–94; *b* 2 July 1913; *yr s* of Baron Sieff and Rebecca Doro, *d* of Michael Marks; *m* 1st, 1937, Rosalie Fromson (marr. diss. 1947); one *s*; 2nd, 1951, Elsa Florence Gosen (marr. diss. 1953); 3rd, 1956, Brenda Mary Beith (marr. diss. 1962); one *d*; 4th, 1963, Mrs (Pauline) Lily Moretzki (*née* Spatz) (*d* 1997); one *d*. *Educ:* Manchester Grammar School; St Paul's; Corpus Christi College, Cambridge (MA; Hon. Fellow, 1975). Served War 1939–45, Royal Artillery. Joined Marks and Spencer Ltd, 1935; Dir, 1954; Asst Man. Dir, 1963; Vice-Chm., 1965; Jt Man. Dir, 1967–83; Dep. Chm., 1971; Chm., 1972–84; Pres., 1984–85; Hon. Pres., 1985–. Non-exec. Chm., The Independent, 1986–93; non-exec. Director: Wickes PLC, 1986–93; Sock Shop Internat. plc, 1987–89. Mem., BNEC, 1965–71 (Chm.,

Export Cttee for Israel, 1965–68). Hon. President: Anglo-Israel Chamber of Commerce, 1975–; Joint Israel Appeal, 1984–. Chancellor, Weizmann Inst. of Sci. Vice Pres., Policy Studies Institute (formerly PEP) Exec., 1975–. Trustee, Nat. Portrait Gallery, 1986–93. Hon. FRCS 1984. Hon. LLD: St Andrews, 1983; Leicester, 1988; Hon. Dr Babson Coll., Mass, 1984; Hon. DLitt Reading; DUniv Stirling, 1986; Hon. DPhil: Tel Aviv, 1991; Hebrew, 1992. Hambro Award, Businessman of the Year, 1977; Aims National Free Enterprise Award, 1978; B'nai B'rith Internat. gold medallion for humanitarianism, 1982; Retailer of the Year Award, National Retail Merchants' Assoc., USA, 1982; BIM Gold Medal, 1983. *Publications:* Don't Ask the Price (autobiog.), 1987; Marcus Sieff on Management, 1990. *Died 23 Feb. 2001.*

SIEPMANN, Mary Aline, (Mary Wesley), CBE 1995; FRSL; writer; *b* 24 June 1912; *d* of Col Harold Mynors Farmar, CMG, DSO and Violet Hyacinth (*née* Dalby); *m* 1st, 1937, 2nd Baron Swinfen (marr. diss. 1945); two *s*; 2nd, 1952, Eric Siepmann (*d* 1970); one *s*. *Educ:* at home (governesses); LSE (Hon. Fellow 1994). FRSL 1997. DUniv Open, 1993; Hon. DLitt Exeter, 1993. *Publications:* Speaking Terms (for children), 1968; The Sixth Seal (for children), 1968; Haphazard House (for children), 1983; Jumping the Queue, 1983; The Camomile Lawn, 1984; Harnessing Peacocks, 1985; The Vacillations of Poppy Carew, 1986; Not That Sort of Girl, 1987; Second Fiddle, 1988; A Sensible Life, 1990; A Dubious Legacy, 1993; An Imaginative Experience, 1994; Part of the Furniture, 1997; (with Kim Sayer) Part of the Scenery, 2001. *Recreation:* reading. *Address:* c/o Transworld Publishers, 61–63 Uxbridge Road, W5 5SA. *Died 30 Dec. 2002.*

SILKIN, 2nd Baron, *cr* 1950, of Dulwich [disclaimed his peerage for life, 1972]; *see under* Silkin, Arthur.

SILKIN, Arthur; Lecturer in Public Administration, Civil Service College, Sunningdale, 1971–76, on secondment from Department of Employment; retired 1976; *b* 20 Oct. 1916; *e s* of 1st Baron Silkin, PC, CH; *S* father, 1972, as 2nd Baron Silkin, but disclaimed his peerage for life; *m* 1969, Audrey Bennett. *Educ:* Dulwich College; Peterhouse, Cambridge (BA 1938); Dip. in Govt Admin, 1959; Dip. in Hist. of Art, 1990, Dip. in Eng. Lit., 2000, London Univ. Served 1940–45, Royal Air Force (A and SD Branch), Pilot Officer, 1941, subsequently Flying Officer. Entered Ministry of Labour and National Service, 1939; 2nd Secretary, British Embassy, Paris; First Secretary: High Commissioner's Office, Calcutta, 1960–61; British Embassy, Dakar, May 1962–Mar. 1964; British Embassy, Kinshasa, 1964–66. *Publications:* contrib. to Public Administration, Political Qly. *Heir:* to disclaimed title: *nephew* Christopher Lewis Silkin, *b* 12 Sept. 1947. *Address:* Cuzco, 33 Woodnook Road, SW16 6TZ. *T:* (020) 8677 8733. *Died 25 Nov. 2001.*

SILSOE, 2nd Baron *cr* 1963; **David Malcolm Trustram Eve;** Bt 1943; QC 1972; Barrister, Inner Temple, 1955–2002; *b* 2 May 1930; *er* twin *s* of 1st Baron Silsoe, GBE, MC, TD, QC, and Marguerite (*d* 1945), *d* of late Sir Augustus Meredith Nanton, Winnipeg; *S* father, 1976; *m* 1963, Bridget Min, *d* of Sir Rupert Hart-Davis; one *s* one *d*. *Educ:* Winchester; Christ Church, Oxford (MA); Columbia Univ., New York. 2nd Lt, Royal Welch Fusiliers, 1949–50; Lieut, Queen Victoria's Rifles (TA), 1950–53. Bar Auditor, Inner Temple, 1965–70; Bencher, 1970. *Recreations:* music, singing. *Heir: s* Hon. Simon Rupert Trustram Eve, *b* 17 April 1966. *Address:* Neals Farm, Wyfold, Reading, Berks RG4 9JB. *Died 31 Dec. 2005.*

SILVER, Prof. Peter Hele S.; *see* Spencer-Silver.

SIMCOX, Richard Alfred, CBE 1975 (MBE 1956); Hon. Member of the British Council; *b* 29 March 1915; *s* of Alfred William and Alice Simcox; *m* 1951, Patricia Elisabeth Gutteridge; one *s* two *d*. *Educ:* Gonville and Caius Coll., Cambridge (BA Class. Tripos). Served with N

Staffs Regt, 1939–43; British Council from 1943: Rep. in Jordan, 1957–60, in Libya, 1960, in Jordan (again), 1960; Cultural Attaché, British Embassy, Cairo, 1968–71; British Council Representative, Iran, 1971–75. Governor, Gabbitas-Thring Educnl Trust. *Recreations:* gardening, philately. *Address:* 105 Edburton Avenue, Brighton, E Sussex BN1 6EQ. *T:* (01273) 561748.

Died 1 May 2002.

SIMKINS, (Charles) Anthony (Goodall), CB 1968; CBE 1963; *b* 2 March 1912; *s* of Charles Wyckens Simkins; *m* 1938, Sylvia, *d* of Thomas Hartley, Silchester, Hants; two *s* one *d. Educ:* Marlborough; New Coll., Oxford (1st Class Hons Mod. Hist.). Barrister, Lincoln's Inn, 1936; served 1939–45 as Captain, Rifle Bde (POW); attached War Office (later MoD), 1945–71; idc, 1958. *Publication:* (with Sir Harry Hinsley) British Intelligence in the Second World War: vol. IV, security and counter-intelligence, 1990. *Address:* The Cottage, 94 Broad Street, near Guildford, Surrey GU3 3BE. *T:* (01483) 572456. *Clubs:* Naval and Military, MCC; Woking Golf.

Died 29 Dec. 2003.

SIMON OF WYTHENSHAWE, 2nd Baron *cr* 1947, of Didsbury; **Roger Simon;** *b* 16 Oct. 1913; *S* father, 1960 (but did not use the title and wished to be known as Roger Simon); *m* 1951 (Anthea) Daphne May; one *s* one *d. Educ:* Gresham's School; Gonville and Caius Coll., Cambridge (BA 1935, MA 1939). *Heir: s* Hon. Matthew Simon, *b* 10 April 1955. *Address:* Oakhill, Chester Avenue, Richmond, Surrey TW10 6NP. *Died 14 Oct. 2002.*

SIMON, Prof. Brian; Emeritus Professor of Education, University of Leicester; *b* 26 March 1915; *yr s* of 1st Baron Simon of Wythenshawe and Shena D. Potter; *m* 1941, Joan Home Peel; one *s* (and one *s* decd). *Educ:* Gresham's Sch., Holt; Schloss Schule, Salem; Trinity Coll., Cambridge (MA); Inst. of Educn, Univ. of London. Pres., Nat. Union of Students, 1939–40. Royal Corps of Signals, GHQ Liaison Regt (Phantom), 1940–45; teaching Manchester and Salford schs, 1945–50; Univ. of Leicester: Lectr in Educn, 1950–64; Reader, 1964–66; Professor, 1966–80; Dir, Sch. of Educn, 1968–70, 1974–77. Chairman: History of Educn Soc., 1976–79; Internat. Standing Conf. for Hist. of Educn, 1979–82; President: British Educn Res. Assoc., 1977–78; Council for Educational Advance, 1991–. Mem., Nat. Acad. of Educn, USA, 1992–. Editor, Forum (for discussion of new trends in educn), 1958–90; Jt Editor, Students Library of Education, 1966–77. Dr *hc* Cath. Univ. of Leuven, 1980; DUniv Open, 1981; Hon. DEd UWE, 1997; Hon. DLitt: Warwick, 1998; Leicester, 2000; Hon. LLD Manchester, 1999. *Publications:* A Student's View of the Universities, 1943; Intelligence Testing and the Comprehensive School, 1953; The Common Secondary School, 1955; (ed) New Trends in English Education, 1957; (ed) Psychology in the Soviet Union, 1957; Studies in the History of Education 1780–1870, 1960; (ed, with Joan Simon) Educational Psychology in the USSR, 1963; (ed) The Challenge of Marxism, 1963; (ed) Non-streaming in the Junior School, 1964; Education and the Labour Movement 1870–1920, 1965; (ed) Education in Leicestershire 1540–1940, 1968; (with D. Rubinstein) The Evolution of the Comprehensive School 1926–66, 1969 (revised edn 1973); (with Caroline Benn) Half-Way There: Report on the British Comprehensive School Reform, 1970 (revised edn 1972); Intelligence, Psychology and Education, 1971 (revised edn 1978); (ed) The Radical Tradition in Education in Britain, 1972; The Politics of Educational Reform 1920–1940, 1974; (ed with Ian Bradley) The Victorian Public School, 1975; (with Maurice Galton) Inside the Primary Classroom, 1980; Progress and Performance in the Primary Classroom, 1980; (ed with William Taylor) Education in the Eighties, the central issues, 1981; (ed with John Willcocks) Research and Practice in the Primary Classroom, 1981; Does Education Matter?, 1985; (ed with Detlef Müller and Fritz Ringer) The Rise of the Modern Educational

System, 1987; Bending the Rules: the Baker "reform" of education, 1988; (ed) The Search for Enlightenment: the working class and adult education in the twentieth century, 1989; Education and the Social Order 1940–1990, 1991; What Future for Education?, 1992; (ed with Clyde Chitty) Education Answers Back, 1993; (with Clyde Chitty) SOS Save Our Schools, 1993; The State and Educational Change: essays in the history of education and pedagogy, 1994; In Search of a Grandfather: Henry Simon of Manchester 1835–1899, 1997; A Life in Education (autobiog.), 1998; The Monument at Murg, 1998; Henry Simon's Children, 1999. *Address:* 11 Pendene Road, Leicester LE2 3DQ. *T:* (0116) 270 5176.

Died 17 Jan. 2002.

SIMON, Claude (Henri Eugène); French writer and vine grower; *b* Madagascar, 10 Oct. 1913; *s* of Antoine Simon and Suzanne (*née* Denamiel); *m* 1st, 1951, Yvonne Ducuing; 2nd, 1978, Réa Karavas. *Educ:* Collège Stanislas, Paris. Jury Mem., Prix Médicis, 1968–70. Nobel Prize for Literature, 1985. *Publications:* Le tricheur, 1945; La corde raide, 1947; Gulliver, 1952; Le sacre du printemps, 1954; Le vent, 1957; L'herbe, 1958 (trans. The Grass, 1961); La route des Flandres (Prix de l'Express), 1960 (trans. The Flanders Road, 1962); Le palace, 1962 (trans. 1964); Histoire (Prix Médicis), 1967 (trans. 1969); La bataille de Pharsale, 1969 (trans. The Battle of Pharsalus, 1971); Orion aveugle, 1970; Les corps conducteurs, 1971 (trans. Conducting Bodies, 1975); Triptyque, 1973 (trans. 1977); Leçon de choses, 1975; Les Géorgiques, 1981 (trans. 1985); L'Acacia, 1989; Photographies, 1992; Le Jardin des Plantes, 1997; Le Tramway, 2001; articles in journals. *Address:* c/o Editions de Minuit, 7 rue Bernard-Palissy, 75006 Paris, France. *Died 6 July 2005.*

SIMON, Prof. Herbert Alexander, PhD; Richard King Mellon University Professor of Computer Science and Psychology, Carnegie-Mellon University, since 1967; *b* 15 June 1916; *s* of Arthur Simon and Edna Merkel Simon; *m* 1937, Dorothea Pye; one *s* two *d. Educ:* University of Chicago (BA, PhD). Staff member, Internat. City Managers' Assoc., 1936–39; Study Director, Bureau of Public Admin, Univ. of California (Berkeley), 1939–42; Asst Prof., 1942–45, Associate Prof., 1945–47, Prof., 1947–49, Illinois Inst. of Technology (Head, Dept of Pol and Social Sci., 1946–49); Professor of Administration, Carnegie-Mellon Univ., 1949–67 (Associate Dean, Graduate Sch. of Industrial Admin, 1957–73). Mem., Nat. Acad. of Scis, 1967 (Mem. Council, 1978–81, 1983–86). Hon. degrees: DSc: Case Inst. of Technol., 1963; Yale, 1963; Marquette, 1981; Columbia, 1983; Gustavus Adolphus, 1985; Duquesne, 1988; Illinois Inst. of Technol., 1988; Michigan Inst. of Technol., 1988; Carnegie Mellon, 1990; LLD: Chicago, 1964; McGill, 1970; Michigan, 1978; Pittsburgh, 1979; Paul-Valéry, 1984; Harvard, 1990; FilDr Lund, 1968; DrEconSci Erasmus (Rotterdam), 1973; DrPolitSci Pavia, 1988; DPsych Rome, 1993. Hon. Professor: Tianjin Univ., 1980; Beijing Univ., 1986; Hon. Res. Fellow, Inst. of Psych., and For. Mem., Chinese Acad. of Sciences, 1985. Nobel Prize in Economics, 1978; Dist. Sci. Contrib. Award, Amer. Psych. Assoc., 1969; Turing Award, Assoc. for Computing Machinery, 1975; James Madison Award, Amer. Political Science Assoc., 1984; National Medal of Science, 1986; John Von Neumann Theory Prize, Operations Res. Soc. of Amer. and Inst. of Management Sci., 1988; Gold Medal Award in Psychol Sci., Amer. Psychol. Foundn, 1988; Lifetime Contribn to Psychology, Amer. Psychol. Assoc., 1993; Award for Res. Excellence, Internat. Jt Conf. on Artificial Intelligence, 1995. *Publications:* Administrative Behavior, 1947, 4th edn 1997; Models of Man, 1957; (with J. G. March) Organizations, 1958, 2nd edn 1993; The New Science of Management Decision, 1960, rev. edn 1977; The Sciences of the Artificial, 1969, 3rd edn 1996; (with A. Newell) Human Problem Solving, 1972; Models of Discovery, 1977; (with Y. Ijiri) Skew Distributions and the Sizes of Business Firms, 1977; Models of Thought, vol. 1, 1979, vol. 2,

1989; Models of Bounded Rationality vols 1 and 2, 1982, vol. 3, 1997; Reason in Human Affairs, 1983; (with K. A. Ericsson) Protocol Analysis, 1984, 2nd edn 1993; (with P. Langley *et al*) Scientific Discovery, 1987; Models of my Life, 1991; other books, and articles in sci. jls. *Recreations:* walking, piano, painting. *Address:* Department of Psychology, Carnegie-Mellon University, Pittsburgh, PA 15213–3890, USA. *T:* (412) 2682787. *Club:* University (Pittsburgh).   *Died 9 Feb. 2001.*

SIMON, Roger; *see* Simon of Wythenshawe, Baron.

SIMONS, (Alfred) Murray, CMG 1983; HM Diplomatic Service, retired; Head of UK Delegation to Negotiations on Mutual Reduction of Armed Forces and Armaments and Associated Measures in Central Europe, at Vienna, 1982–85, with personal rank of Ambassador; *b* 9 Aug. 1927; *s* of late Louis Simons and of Fay Simons; *m* 1975, Patricia Jill, *d* of late David and May Barclay, Westbury on Trym, Bristol; two *s. Educ:* City of London Sch.; Magdalen Coll., Oxford (MA). FO, 1951; 3rd Sec., Moscow, 1952–55; FO, 1955–56; Columbia Univ., 1956; 2nd Sec., Bogota, 1957; 1st Sec., Office of Comr-Gen. for SE Asia, Singapore, 1958–61; FO, 1961–64; 1st Sec., British High Commn, New Delhi, 1964–68; FCO, 1968–71; Counsellor, 1969; British Embassy, Washington, 1971–75; Head of SE Asia Dept, FCO, 1975–79; Consul General, Montreal, 1980–82. Pres., John Carpenter Club, 1992–93. Freeman, City of London, 1990. *Recreations:* tennis, theatre. *Address:* 128 Longland Drive, Totteridge, N20 8HL. *T:* (020) 8446 3163.   *Died 15 Dec. 2003.*

SIMPSON, Sir Alfred (Henry), Kt 1985; Chief Justice of Kenya, 1982–85; *b* 29 Oct. 1914; *s* of John Robertson Simpson, Dundee; *m* 1st, 1941, Hilda Corson Rodgers (*d* 1999); one *d*; 2nd, 2000, Anne Murtagh. *Educ:* Grove Academy; St Andrews University; Edinburgh University. MA St Andrews 1935; LLB Edinburgh 1938. Solicitor. Served in RASC, 1940–46, Middle East and Italy; Military Mission to the Italian Army and Allied Commission, Austria. Legal Officer, BMA, Cyrenaica, 1946–48. Member of the Faculty of Advocates, 1952. Crown Counsel, Singapore, 1948–56; Legal Draftsman, Gold Coast, 1956; Solicitor-General, Ghana, 1957, then Puisne Judge, Supreme Court, 1957–61; Puisne Judge, Combined Judiciary of Sarawak, North Borneo and Brunei, 1962; Senior Puisne Judge, Fedn of Malaysia High Court in Borneo, 1964; Reader, Faculty of Law, ANU, Canberra, 1965; Barrister-at-Law, NSW, 1967; Puisne Judge, High Court of Kenya, 1967–82. *Publications:* (with others) The Laws of Singapore, revised edn, 1955; Memoirs Legal and Otherwise, 1996. *Recreation:* golf. *Address:* 23 Downes Place, Hughes, ACT 2605, Australia. *Clubs:* Royal Commonwealth Society, Royal Over-Seas League; Royal Canberra Golf.   *Died 8 Sept. 2003.*

SIMPSON, Alfred Moxon, AC 1978; CMG 1959; Chairman, SA Telecasters Ltd, 1964–92 (Director, 1962–92); *b* 17 Nov. 1910; *s* of late A. A. Simpson, CMG, CBE; *m* 1938, Elizabeth Robson Cleland; one *s. Educ:* St Peter's College; University of Adelaide (BSc). Associate (Commerce) of Univ. of Adelaide, 1940. Dir, Simpson Holdings Ltd, 1939–83 (Chm., 1954–81). Pres. Adelaide Chamber of Commerce, 1950–52; Sen. Vice-Pres. Associated Chambers of Commerce of Aust., 1953–55; President: SA Chamber of Manufrs, 1956–58; Associated Chambers of Manufrs of Aust., 1957–58. Director: Bank of Adelaide, 1952–79; Elder Smith Goldsbrough Mort Ltd, 1954–81; Adelaide Steamship Co. Ltd, 1960–83; QBE Insurance Group Ltd, 1975–83 (Local Dir, 1935). Mem. Hulme Cttee on Rates of Depreciation, 1956; Report on employment security of overseas officers in Papua-New Guinea, 1972, adopted by govt, 1973. Mem. Council, Flinders Univ., 1965–76. *Recreations:* carpentry, lawnmowing. *Address:* 31 Heatherbank Terrace, Stonyfell, SA 5066, Australia. *T:* (8) 311285. *Clubs:* Adelaide, Naval, Military and Airforce, Mt Lofty Ski (Adelaide).
                Died 11 Nov. 2001.

SIMPSON, Commander Cortlandt James Woore, CBE 1956; DSC 1945; retired 1961; *b* 2 Sept. 1911; *s* of late Rear-Admiral C. H. Simpson, CBE, and Edith Octavia (*née* Busby); *m* 1st, 1932, Lettice Mary Johnstone; 2nd, 1955, Ann Margaret Cubitt (*née* Tooth); 3rd, 1972, Joan Mary Watson; one *d*; 4th, Vanessa Ann Stainton (*née* Heald). *Educ:* St Ronans, Worthing; RN College, Dartmouth; London Univ. (BSc Hons Engineering). Joined RN (Dartmouth), 1925; Lieut, 1934. Served War of 1939–45 in Home and Mediterranean Fleets; Commander (L), 1948. Summer expeditions to Greenland, 1950, 1951; Leader of British North Greenland Expedition, 1952–54. Polar Medal, 1954; Royal Geographical Society, Founder's Medal, 1955. *Publication:* North Ice, 1957. *Recreations:* mountaineering, sailing, walking. *Address:* Sanctuary Gate, Iddesleigh, Winkleigh, Devon EX19 8SN. *Club:* Alpine.   *Died 9 May 2002.*

SIMPSON, Ffreebairn Liddon, CMG 1967; Secretary to the Cabinet, Mauritius, 1967–76; *b* 11 July 1916; *s* of late James Liddon Simpson and Dorothy (*née* Blyth); *m* 1947, Dorina Laura Magda, MBE (*née* Ilieva) (*d* 1991); one *s. Educ:* Westminster School; Trinity College, Cambridge (Exhibnr, 1938; BA Hons Mod. Lang.). HM Diplomatic/ Foreign Service, 1939–48; HM Treasury, 1948–50; Administrative Officer, Gold Coast, 1950–55; Dep. Colonial Sec., Mauritius, 1955; Perm. Sec., Min. of Works and Internal Communications, 1961; Premier's Office, 1966, Mauritius; Gen. Manager, Central Water Authy, Mauritius, 1976–78. *Recreations:* reading, theatre, family history research. *Club:* Oxford and Cambridge.
                Died 25 Jan. 2001.

SIMPSON, Gordon Russell, DSO 1944 and Bar 1945; LVO 1979; TD; stockbroker; Partner, Bell, Cowan & Co. (later Brewin Dolphin Bell Lawrie Ltd), 1938–82; *b* 2 Jan. 1917; 2nd *s* of A. Russell Simpson, WS; *m* 1943, Marion Elizabeth King (*d* 1976); two *s. Educ:* Rugby School. Served with 2nd Lothians and Border Horse, 1939–46 (comd 1944–46); Col TA, 1950–52. Chm., Edinburgh Stock Exchange, 1961–63; Chm., Scottish Stock Exchange, 1965–66; Pres., Council of Associated Stock Exchanges, 1971–73; Dep. Chm., Stock Exchange, 1973–78. Chm., General Accident Fire & Life Assurance Corporation Ltd, 1979–87 (Dir, 1967–87). Captain, Queen's Body Guard for Scotland (Royal Company of Archers); non-active list, 2003. Mem. Court, Stirling Univ., 1980–88; Comr, Queen Victoria Sch., 1982–92. DL Stirling and Falkirk Dists (Central Region), 1981–92. *Recreations:* music, archery. *Address:* Arntomie, Port of Menteith, by Stirling FK8 3RD. *Club:* New (Edinburgh).
                Died 30 March 2005.

SIMPSON, Sir William (James), Kt 1984; Chairman, Health and Safety Commission, 1974–83; *b* Falkirk, 20 May 1920; *s* of William Simpson and Margaret Nimmo; *m* 1942, Catherine McEwan Nicol; one *s. Educ:* Victoria Sch. and Falkirk Techn Sch., Falkirk. Served War of 1939–45, Argyll and Sutherland Highlanders (Sgt). Apprenticed to moulding trade, 1935; returned to foundry, 1946. Mem., Nat. Exec. Council, Amalgamated Union of Foundry Workers, 1955–67; Gen. Sec., AUEW (Foundry Section), 1967–75. Chm., Labour Party, 1972–73. Member: Race Relations Bd; Ct of Inquiry into Flixborough explosion, 1974; Chm., Adv. Cttee on Asbestos, 1976–79. *Publication:* Labour: the Unions and the Party, 1973.
                Died Nov. 2001.

SINCLAIR, 17th Lord *cr* 1449 (Scotland); Charles Murray Kennedy St Clair, CVO 1990 (LVO 1953); Major, late Coldstream Guards; Extra Equerry to Queen Elizabeth the Queen Mother, 1953–2002; Lord-Lieutenant, Dumfries and Galloway Region (District of Stewartry), 1982–89 (Vice-Lord-Lieutenant, 1977–82); Member Queen's Body Guard for Scotland (Royal Company of Archers); *b* 21 June 1914; *o s* of 16th Lord Sinclair, MVO, and Violet (*d* 1953), *d* of Col J. Murray Kennedy, MVO; *S* father, 1957; *m* 1968, Anne Lettice, *yr d* of Sir Richard Cotterell, 5th Bt, CBE; one *s* two *d. Educ:* Eton; Magdalene Coll.,

Cambridge. Served War of 1939–45, Palestine, 1939 (wounded, despatches). Retired as Major Coldstream Guards, 1947. Portcullis Pursuivant of Arms, 1949–57; York Herald, 1957–68, retired. A Representative Peer for Scotland, 1959–63. DL Kirkcudbrightshire, 1969. *Heir: s* Master of Sinclair, *b* 9 Dec. 1968. *Address:* Knocknalling, St John's Town of Dalry, Castle Douglas, Kirkcudbrightshire, Scotland DG7 3ST. *T:* (01644) 430221.   *Died 1 April 2004.*

SINCLAIR, Alexander Riddell; HM Diplomatic Service, retired; *b* 28 Aug. 1917; *s* of Henry W. Sinclair and Mary Turner; *m* 1948, Alice Evelyn Nottingham; three *d. Educ:* Greenock High School. DipCAM. Inland Revenue, 1935–37; Admty, 1938–47 (Comdr RNVR, 1945–46); 2nd Sec., HM Embassy, Moscow, 1947–48; Vice-Consul: Detroit, 1949; Mosul, 1950; FO, 1952; 1st Secretary, HM Embassy: Saigon, 1953–56; Amman, 1957–58; FO, 1959; 1st Sec. (Cultural), Budapest, 1962; FO, 1964; 1st Secretary (Information): Beirut, 1967–70; Rome, 1970–71; Consul-Gen., Genoa, 1972–76; FCO Library, 1977–85. Pres., St Andrews Probus Club, 1997–98. Silver Jubilee Medal, 1977. *Publications:* literary articles in learned jls. *Recreations:* reading, book browsing, walking. *Address:* 2 Ruthven Place, St Andrews, Fife KY16 8SJ. *Club:* Civil Service.   *Died 23 Jan. 2004.*

SINCLAIR, Sir George (Evelyn), Kt 1960; CMG 1956; OBE 1950; *b* Cornwall, 6 Nov. 1912; 2nd *s* of late F. Sinclair, Chynance, St Buryan, Cornwall; *m* 1st, 1941, Katharine Jane Burdekin (*d* 1971); one *s* three *d*; 2nd, 1972, Mary Violet, *widow* of George Lester Sawday, Saxmundham, Suffolk. *Educ:* Abingdon School; Pembroke College, Oxford (MA; Hon. Fellow, 1986). Entered Colonial Administrative Service, 1936; appointed to Gold Coast Administration; Asst District Comr, 1937. Military service, 1940–43. District Commissioner, Gold Coast, 1943; seconded to Colonial Office, 1943–45; Sec. to Commn on Higher Education in West Africa, 1943–45; returned to Gold Coast, 1945; Senior Assistant Colonial Secretary, 1947; Principal Assistant Secretary, 1950; Regional Officer, Trans-Volta Togoland Region, 1952; Deputy Governor, Cyprus, 1955–60; retired, 1961. MP (C) Dorking, Surrey, Oct. 1964–1979. Member, Parly Select Committees on: Procedure, 1965–66; Race Relations, 1969–70; Overseas Aid, 1969–70; Race Relations and Immigration, 1970–74; Members Interests, 1975; Abortion Act (Amendment) Bill; Joint Secretary: Cons. Parly Commonwealth Affairs Cttee, 1966–68; Cons. Parly Educn Cttee, 1974–79, Vice-Chm., 1974; Member: Intermediate Technology Develt Gp (Vice-Pres., 1966–79; Dir, 1979–82); Nat. Exec. Cttee, UNA (UK Branch), 1968–70; Council, Overseas Services Resettlement Bureau; Council of PDSA, 1964–70; Council, Christian Aid, 1975; Steering Cttee, UN/ FPA World Conf. of Parliamentarians on population and develt, 1978–79; Vice-Chm., Family Planning Assoc., 1979–81; Consultant: UN Fund for Population Affairs, 1979–82; IPPF, 1979–83; special advr to Global Cttee on Population and Develt, 1982–88. Trustee: Runnymede Trust, 1969–75; Human Rights Trust, 1971–74; Physically Handicapped and Able Bodied (Foundn Trustee), 1973–81; Wyndham Place Trust. Mem., Wimbledon Borough Council, 1962–65. Member, Board of Governors: Abingdon Sch., 1970–87 (Chm., 1971–79); Felixstowe Coll., 1980–87; Campion Sch., Athens, 1983–94; Chm., Assoc. of Governing Bodies of Independent Schools, 1979–84 (Mem., 1973–); Member: Direct Grant Jt Cttee, 1974–80; Indep. Schools Jt Council, 1979–84 (Chm. 1980–83, Dep. Chm., 1984); Council, Oxford Soc., 1982–93. Chm. Planning Office, 1988 Internat. Conf. of Spiritual and Parly Leaders on Human Survival, 1986–88. *Recreations:* golf, fishing. *Address:* Rookery Orchard, Kelsale-cum-Carlton, Saxmundham, Suffolk IP17 2NN; South Minack, Porthcurno, Cornwall TR19 6JU. *Clubs:* Athenæum, Royal Commonwealth Society; Aldeburgh Golf.   *Died 21 Sept. 2005.*

SINCLAIR, Isabel Lillias, (Mrs J. G. MacDonald); QC (Scotland) 1964; Sheriff of Lothian and Borders (formerly Roxburgh, Berwick, and Selkirk), 1968–79, then Honorary Sheriff; Honorary Sheriff of Bute; *b* 9 April 1911; *d* of William Sinclair, Glasgow, and Isabella (*née* Thomson), Glasgow; *m* 1938, J. Gordon MacDonald (decd), BL, Solicitor, Glasgow. *Educ:* Shawlands Academy; Glasgow Univ. (MA 1932; BL 1946). Worked as a newspaper-woman from 1932. Admitted to Faculty of Advocates, Edinburgh, 1949. Sheriff-Substitute of Lanarkshire at Airdrie, 1966–68. *Address:* 30 Ravelston Garden, Edinburgh EH4 3LE. *Clubs:* Caledonian, Royal Over-Seas League (Edinburgh).   *Died 16 Oct. 2005.*

SINCLAIR, Air Vice-Marshal Sir Laurence (Frank), GC 1941; KCB 1957 (CB 1946); CBE 1943; DSO 1940 (and Bar, 1943); Controller, National Air Traffic Control Services, Ministry of Aviation and Ministry of Defence, 1962–66; *b* 13 June 1908; *m* 1941, Valerie (*d* 1990), *d* of Lt-Col Joseph Dalton White; one *s* one *d. Educ:* Imperial Service Coll.; RAF Coll. Cranwell. Comd No 110 Sqdn in 1940; Comd RAF Watton, 1941; Comd Tactical Light Bomber Force in North Africa and Italy, 1943–44; ADC to King George VI, 1943–44; subsequently Sen. Air Staff Officer, Balkan Air Force; Imperial Defence Coll., 1947; commanded No 2 Light Bomber Group (Germany), 1948–49; Assistant Commandant RAF Staff College, 1949–50; Commandant: Royal Air Force College Cranwell, 1950–52; School of Land/Air Warfare, 1952–53; Asst Chief of the Air Staff (Operations), 1953–55; Comdr British Forces, Arabian Peninsula, 1955–57; Comdt, JSSC, 1958–60; retd from RAF; Controller of Ground Services, Min. of Aviation, 1960–61. Legion of Merit (USA), 1943; Legion of Honour (France), 1944; Partisan Star (Yugoslavia). *Address:* The Old Prebendal House, Shipton-under-Wychwood, Oxford OX7 6BQ.   *Died 14 May 2002.*

SINDELL, Marion Harwood; Chief Executive, Equal Opportunities Commission, 1979–85; *b* 23 June 1925; *d* of Arthur Barrett Sindell and Ethel Maude Sindell. *Educ:* Lincoln Girls' High Sch.; St Hilda's Coll., Oxford (MA). Solicitor. Deputy Town Clerk: Workington, 1959–64; Nuneaton, 1964–66; Town Clerk, Goole, 1966–74; Chief Exec., Boothferry Bor. Council, 1974–79.
Died 28 Aug. 2002.

SINGER, Harry Bruce, OBE 1995; TD 1955; DL; FCA; Senior Partner, Singer & Partners, Chartered Accountants, 1968–87; *b* 21 June 1921; *er s* of Geoffrey and Agnes Singer; *m* 1945, Betty Alison Brittan (*d* 1993); one *s. Educ:* Cathedral Sch., Hereford. FCA 1960 (Mem., 1953). Served War: commnd 99th (London Welsh) HAA Regt, RA, 1941; served in UK and NW Europe; Instr, Sch. of AA Artillery, 1945; joined 281 (Glam Yeomanry) Field Regt, RA (TA), 1947; in comd, 1959–62. Pres., S Wales Soc. of Chartered Accountants, 1970–71; Inst. of Chartered Accountants in England and Wales: Mem. Council, 1973–85; Vice Pres., 1979–80; Dep. Pres., 1980–81; Pres., 1981–82. Hon. Treasurer, SSAFA 1990–96; Trustee, Yeomanry Benevolent Fund, 1995–2001. Liveryman, Worshipful Co. of Chartered Accountants, 1978–89; Freeman, City of London, 1978. Vice Chm. Wales, TA&VRA, 1984–87. DL Mid Glamorgan, 1985. *Recreations:* golf, foreign travel, Rugby football (originally as player). *Address:* 29 Nottage Mead, Porthcawl, CF36 3SA. *Clubs:* Cardiff and County, Cardiff Golf (Cardiff).   *Died 12 Oct. 2005.*

SINGLETON, Norman, CB 1966; retired civil servant; *b* 21 March 1913; *s* of Charles and Alice Singleton, Bolton, Lancs; *m* 1936, Cicely Margaret Lucas (*d* 2000), Claverdon, Warwick; one *s* two *d. Educ:* Bolton School; Emmanuel College, Cambridge. Min. of Labour, 1935; Under-Secretary: Civil Service Pay Research Unit, 1956–60; Min. of Labour, then Dept of Employment and Productivity, 1960–69; Sec., 1969–72, Dep. Chm., 1973–74, Commn on Industrial Relns; Dep. Chm., Central Arbitration Cttee, 1976–85; Arbitrator and

Mediator, ACAS, 1976–87. *Publication:* Industrial Relations Procedures, 1976. *Address:* 43 Church Lane, Lower Bemerton, Salisbury SP2 9NR.
Died 11 Jan. 2005.

SINOPOLI, Giuseppe; Italian conductor and composer; *b* Venice, 2 Nov. 1946; *s* of Giovanni and Maria Sinopoli; *m* 1979, Silvia Cappellini; two *s*. *Educ:* Benedetto Marcello Conservatoire, Venice; Univ. of Padua Med. Sch. (Doctor's degree in medicine as surgeon and psychiatrist); studied conducting with Swarowsky, Vienna, 1972. Founded Bruno Maderna Ensemble, Venice, 1975; début: Macbeth, Berlin Opera, 1979; Attila, Vienna State Opera, 1980; Manon Lescaut, Covent Garden, 1983; with NY Philharmonic Orchestra, 1983; Tosca, Metropolitan, NY, 1985; Tannhäuser, Bayreuther Festspiele, 1985; Elektra, La Scala, 1994. Musical Director: Philharmonia Orch., London, 1987–94 (Prin. Conductor, 1983–87); Fest. Taormina Arte, 1990–; Chief Conductor, Dresden Staatskapelle, 1992–97; conducted Boston Symphony, Chicago Symphony, Berliner Philharmoniker, Wiener Philharmoniker, Israel Philharmonic, Filarmonica della Scala, etc. *Compositions* included: Numquid et unum; Klavierkonzert; Kammerkonzert; Tombeau d'Amour No 1, 2, 3 for Orch.; Souvenir à la Mémoire; Requiem Hashirim; Lou Salome (opera). *Recreations:* reading, studying archaeology (at University of Rome), collecting antique objects. *Address:* c/o Hannelore Tschöpe, Künstlersekretariat, Zehetmeierstrasse 10, 80939 Munich, Germany. *T:* (89) 32464953, *Fax:* (89) 32450156.
Died 20 April 2001.

SISSON, Charles Hubert, CH 1993; writer; *b* 22 April 1914; *s* of late Richard Percy Sisson and Ellen Minnie Sisson (*née* Worlock); *m* 1937, Nora Gilbertson (*d* 2003); two *d*. *Educ:* Univ. of Bristol, and in France and Germany. Entered Min. of Labour as Asst Principal, 1936; HM Forces, in the ranks, mainly in India, 1942–45; Simon Sen. Res. Fellow, 1956–57; Dir of Establishments (Under Sec.), Min. of Labour, 1962–68; Dir of Occupational Safety and Health (Under Sec.), Dept of Employment, 1972. FRSL 1975. Hon. DLitt Bristol, 1980. Jt Editor, PN Review, 1976–84. *Publications:* An Asiatic Romance, 1953; The Spirit of British Administration, 1959; Christopher Homm, 1965; Art and Action, 1965; Essays, 1967; English Poetry 1900–1950, 1971, rev. edn 1981; The Case of Walter Bagehot, 1972; (ed) The English Sermon, Vol. II 1650–1750, 1976; David Hume, 1976; (ed) Selected Poems of Jonathan Swift, 1977; The Avoidance of Literature, 1978; (ed) Autobiographical and Other Papers of Philip Mairet, 1981; Anglican Essays, 1983; (ed) Selected Poems of Christina Rossetti, 1984; On the Look-out (autobiog.), 1989; In Two Minds, 1990; (ed) Jeremy Taylor: selected writings, 1990; English Perspectives, 1992; Is There a Church of England?, 1993; (ed) Edgar Allan Poe: poems and essays on poetry, 1995; *poetry:* The London Zoo, 1961; Numbers, 1965; The Discarnation, 1967; Metamorphoses, 1968; In the Trojan Ditch, 1974; The Corridor, 1975; Anchises, 1976; Exactions, 1980; Selected Poems, 1981; Collected Poems, 1984, rev. edn 1998; God Bless Karl Marx!, 1987; Antidotes, 1991; What and Who, 1994; Poems: selected, 1995; Collected Poems, 1998; *translations:* Versions and Perversions of Heine, 1955; Catullus, 1966; The Poetic Art: a translation of the Ars Poetica of Horace, 1975; The Poem on Nature, 1976; Some Tales of La Fontaine, 1979; The Divine Comedy, 1980; The Song of Roland, 1983; Les Regrets of Joachim du Bellay, 1983; The Aeneid of Virgil, 1986; Britannicus, Phaedra, Athaliah, of Racine, 1987; Collected Translations, 1996. *Address:* Moorfield Cottage, The Hill, Langport, Somerset TA10 9PU. *T:* (01458) 250845.
Died 5 Sept. 2003.

SKEAT, Theodore Cressy; Keeper of Manuscripts and Egerton Librarian, British Museum, 1961–72; *b* 15 Feb. 1907; *s* of Walter William Skeat, MA; *m* 1942, Olive Martin (*d* 1992); one *s*. *Educ:* Whitgift School, Croydon; Christ's Coll., Cambridge (BA 1929). Student at British School of Archaeology, Athens, 1929–31; Asst Keeper, Dept of Manuscripts, British Museum, 1931; Dep. Keeper, 1948. FBA, 1963–80. *Publications:* (with H. I. Bell) Fragments of an Unknown Gospel, 1935; (with H. J. M. Milne) Scribes and Correctors of the Codex Sinaiticus, 1938; The Reigns of the Ptolemies, 1954; Papyri from Panopolis, 1964; Catalogue of Greek Papyri in the British Museum, vol. VII, 1974; (with C. H. Roberts) The Birth of the Codex, 1983; The Reign of Augustus in Egypt, 1993; The Codex Sinaiticus, the Codex Vaticanus and Constantine, 1999; articles in papyrological jls. *Address:* 12 Berkeley Court, 31/33 Gordon Road, W5 2AE. *T:* (020) 8998 9174.
Died 25 June 2003.

SKEATES, Basil George; Director, Ashdown Gallery, 1985–94; Under Secretary, Department of the Environment, 1980–85; *b* 19 May 1929; *s* of George William Skeates and Florence Rachel Skeates; *m* 1957, Irene Margaret (*née* Hughes); four *s*. *Educ:* Hampton Grammar Sch. RIBA 1955. Mil. Service with RE, W Africa, 1947–49. Architect with LCC schs and special works, 1949–61; Principal Architect: NE Metrop. Reg. Hosp. Bd, 1961–64; MPBW, 1964–71; Superintending Architect, CSD, 1971–73; Asst Dir, Architectural Services, PSA, 1973–75; Dir of Works, PO Services, 1975–80; Dir of Def. Services II, DoE, 1980–85. *Publications:* articles in prof. and technical jls. *Recreation:* designing and making things.
Died 21 Nov. 2001.

SKEET, Sir Trevor (Herbert Harry), Kt 1986; barrister, writer and consultant; *b* 28 Jan. 1918; British; *m* 1st, 1958, Elizabeth Margaret Gilling (*d* 1973); two *s*; 2nd, 1985, Mrs Valerie Anita Edwina Benson. *Educ:* King's College, Auckland; University of New Zealand, Auckland (LLB). Served War of 1939–45, with NZ Engineers (sergeant); 2nd Lieut, NZ Anti-Aircraft (Heavy); Sub-Lieutenant, NZ Roy. Naval Volunteer Reserve; demobilised, 1945. Formerly Barrister and Solicitor of Supreme Court of New Zealand; Barrister, Inner Temple, 1947. Has considerable experience in public speaking. Formerly associated with Commonwealth and Empire Industries Assoc.; Mem. Council, Royal Commonwealth Soc., 1952–55, and 1956–69. Contested (C): Stoke Newington and Hackney, North, Gen. Election, 1951; Llanelly Div. of Carmarthenshire, Gen. Election, 1955; MP (C): Willesden East, 1959–64; Bedford, 1970–83; Bedfordshire North, 1983–97. Mem., Select Cttee on Science and Technol., 1993–97; Vice-Chairman: Cons. Party Power Cttee, 1959–64; Energy Cttee, 1974–77; Chairman: Oil Sub-Cttee, 1959–64; Cons. Party Trade Cttee, 1971–74; Cons. Party Middle East Cttee (Foreign and Commonwealth Affairs), 1973–78; Secretary: All-Party Cttee on Airships, 1971–78; All-Party Gp on Minerals, 1971–97 (Co-Chm., 1979–97); Vice-Pres., Steering Cttee, Parly and Scientific Cttee, 1988–91 (Mem., 1982–97; Sec., 1983–85; Chm., 1985–88); Vice-Chm., British-Japanese and British-Brazilian Gps; Sec., British-Nigerian Gp. Mem., Econ. Cttee, Machine Tool Trades Association for several years; Member Technical Legislation Cttee, CBI. *Publications:* contrib. to numerous journals including New Commonwealth and Mining World, on oil, atomic energy, metals, commodities, finance, and Imperial and Commonwealth development. *Address:* The Gables, Milton Ernest, Bedfordshire MK44 1RS. *T:* (01234) 822307. *Clubs:* Army and Navy, Royal Commonwealth Society.
Died 14 Aug. 2004.

SKELTON, Rt Rev. Kenneth John Fraser, CBE 1972; an Assistant Bishop, Dioceses of Sheffield and Derby; *b* 16 May 1918; *s* of Henry Edmund and Kate Elizabeth Skelton; *m* 1945, Phyllis Barbara (*d* 2002), *y d* of James Emerton; two *s* one *d*. *Educ:* Dulwich Coll.; Corpus Christi Coll., Cambridge (1st Cl. Classics Tripos, Pt 1, 1939; 1st Cl. Theol. Tripos, Pt 1, 1940; BA 1940, MA 1944); Wells Theol Coll. Ordained deacon, 1941, priest, 1942; Curate: Normanton-by-Derby, 1941–43; Bakewell, 1943–45; Bolsover, 1945–46; Tutor, Wells Theol Coll., and Priest-Vicar, Wells Cathedral, 1946–50; Vicar of

Howe Bridge, Atherton, 1950–55; Rector, Walton-on-the-Hill, Liverpool, 1955–62; Exam. Chap. to Bp of Liverpool, 1957–62; Bishop of Matabeleland, 1962–70; Asst Bishop, dio. Durham, Rural Dean of Wearmouth and Rector of Bishopwearmouth, 1970–75; Bishop of Lichfield, 1975–84. Select Preacher, Cambridge Univ., 1971, 1973. *Publications:* Bishop in Smith's Rhodesia, 1985; The Overseas Bishoprics' Fund 1941–1991, 1991. *Recreation:* music. *Address:* 65 Crescent Road, Sheffield S7 1HN. *T:* (0114) 255 1260.   *Died 30 July 2003.*

SKEMPTON, Sir Alec (Westley), Kt 2000; DSc; FRS 1961; FREng, FICE; Professor of Civil Engineering in the University of London (Imperial College), 1957–81, then Emeritus; Senior Research Fellow, Imperial College, since 1981; *b* 4 June 1914; *o c* of late A. W. Skempton, Northampton, and Beatrice Edridge Payne; *m* 1940, Mary (*d* 1993), *d* of E. R. Wood, Brighouse, Yorks; two *d. Educ:* Northampton Grammar School; Imperial College, University of London (Goldsmiths' Bursar); DSc London 1949. Building Research Station, 1936–46; University Reader in Soil Mechanics, Imperial College, 1947–54; Professor of Soil Mechanics, Imperial College, 1955–57. Chm., Jt Cttee on Soils, Min. of Supply and Road Research Bd, 1954–59; Mem., Cathedrals Advisory Cttee, 1964–70; Mem., NERC, 1973–76. President: Internat. Soc. Soil Mechanics and Foundn Engrg, 1957–61; Newcomen Soc., 1977–79; Smeatonian Soc., 1981; Vice-Pres., ICE, 1974–76 (Mem. Council, 1949–54). Hitchcock Foundn Prof., Univ. of Calif, Berkeley, 1978; Lectures: Copenhagen, Paris, Harvard, Univ. of Illinois, Oslo, Stockholm, Madrid, Florence, Sydney, Quebec, Mexico City, Tokyo, Berkeley; Special Lectr, Architectural Assoc., 1948–57; Vis. Lectr Cambridge Univ. School of Architecture, 1962–66. Consultant to Binnie & Partners, John Mowlem & Co., etc. For. Associate, Nat. Acad. of Engineering, USA, 1976. Hon. MRIA 1990. Hon. DSc: Durham, 1968; Aston, 1980; Chalmers, 1982. Ewing Medal, 1968; Lyell Medal, 1972; Dickinson Medal, 1974; Karl Terzaghi Award, 1981; IStructE Gold Medal, 1981; ICE Gold Medal, 2000. Silver Jubilee Medal, 1977. *Publications:* Early Printed Reports in the Institution of Civil Engineers, 1977; (with C. Hadfield) William Jessop, Engineer, 1979; John Smeaton, FRS, 1981; Selected Papers on Soil Mechanics, 1984; British Civil Engineering Literature (1640–1840), 1987; Civil Engineers and Engineering in Britain 1600–1830, 1996; numerous contribs on soil mechanics, engineering geology and history of construction. *Address:* Imperial College, SW7 2AZ. *T:* (020) 7589 5111; 16 The Boltons, SW10 9SU. *T:* (020) 7370 3457. *Clubs:* Athenæum, Hurlingham.
                                       Died 9 Aug. 2001.

SKERMAN, Ronald Sidney, CBE 1974; Deputy Chairman, Prudential Corporation plc, 1985–87 (Director, 1980–87; Group Chief Actuary, 1979); *b* 1 June 1914; *s* of S. H. Skerman; *m* 1939, Gladys Mary Fosdike (*d* 1998); no *c. Educ:* Hertford Grammar School. BA Open Univ. 1989. FIA. Actuarial Trainee with Prudential Assurance Co., 1932; Chief Actuary, 1968–79. Pres., Inst. Actuaries, 1970–72; Chm., Life Offices Assoc., 1973–74; Chm., British Insurers European Cttee, 1972–82; Mem., Royal Commn on Civil Liability, 1973–78. Gold Medal, Inst. of Actuaries, 1980. *Publications:* contrib. Jl Inst. Actuaries. *Recreations:* walking, travel, music. *Address:* 1 Rookes, Little Walden Road, Saffron Walden, Essex CB10 2EP. *T:* (01799) 513158.   *Died 19 April 2002.*

SKYRME, Sir Thomas; *see* Skyrme, Sir W. T. C.

SKYRME, Sir (William) Thomas (Charles), KCVO 1974; CB 1966; CBE 1953; TD 1949; JP, DL; Chairman, Broadcasting Complaints Commission, 1985–87 (Member, 1981–87); Secretary of Commissions, 1948–77; Vice-President, Magistrates' Association of England and Wales, since 1981 (Member of Council, since 1974; Deputy Chairman, 1977–79; Chairman, 1979–81); *b* 20 March 1913; *s* of Charles G. Skyrme, Hereford, and of Katherine (*née* Smith), Maryland, USA; *m* 1st, 1938, Hon.

Barbara Suzanne Lyle (marr. diss. 1953; she *d* 1994), *yr d* of 1st Baron Lyle of Westbourne; one *s* two *d*; 2nd, 1957, Mary (*d* 1999), *d* of Dr R. C. Leaning. *Educ:* Rugby School; New College, Oxford (MA); Universities of Dresden and Paris. Called to the Bar, Inner Temple, 1935, Bencher 1988. Practised in London and on Western Circuit. Served War of 1939–45 in Royal Artillery in Middle East, North Africa and Italy (wounded twice); Lt-Col; Founder and first CO, G Locating Battery, HAC, 1947. Secretary to the Lord Chancellor, 1944. Governor and Member of Committee of Management of Queen Mary's Hosp., London, 1938–48. Mem., Magistrates' Courts Rule Cttee, 1950–66; Chm., Interdepartmental Working Party on Legal Proceedings against Justices and Clerks, 1960; Mem., Interdepartmental Cttee on Magistrates Courts in London, 1961; Life Vice-Pres., Commonwealth Magistrates' and Judges' Assoc. (formerly Commonwealth Magistrates' Assoc.), 1979 (Founder, and first Pres., 1970–79); Chm., Commonwealth Magistrates' Confs, London, 1970, Bermuda, 1972, Nairobi, 1973, Kuala Lumpur, 1975, Tonga, 1976, Jamaica, 1977, Oxford, 1979; Vice-Chm., Adv. Cttee on Training of Magistrates, 1974–80. Hon. Life Mem., Justices' Clerks' Soc., 1979–. A General Comr of Income Tax, 1977–88; Mem., Top Salaries Review Body, 1981–90; Chm., Judicial Salaries Cttee, 1983–90. Chm., Batsford Foundn, 1983–96. Pres., City of London RAOC Assoc., 1987–. FRGS. Freeman of City of London, 1970; HM Lieut for City of London, 1977–. DL Glos 1983; JP: Oxon 1948; London 1952; Glos 1976. *Publications:* The Changing Image of the Magistracy, 1979; History of the Justices of the Peace, 1990; contribs to legal jls. *Recreations:* ski-ing, travel, rifle shooting (captained Oxford University, 1934). *Address:* Amesbury Abbey, Amesbury, Wilts SP4 7EX; Casa Larissa, Klosters, Switzerland. *Clubs:* Army and Navy; Hurlingham.   *Died 24 Jan. 2002.*

SLACK, His Honour George Granville; a Circuit Judge (formerly a County Court Judge), 1966–81; *b* 11 July 1906; *s* of George Edwin and Amy Beatrice Slack; *m* 1st, 1935, Ella Kathleen (*d* 1957), *d* of Henry Alexander Eason; one *d*; 2nd, 1958, Vera Gertrude, *d* of Reginald Ackland Spencer; one *s* one *d. Educ:* Accrington Grammar School; London University. BA (Hons History) 1926; LLB 1929; LLM 1932. Called to Bar, Gray's Inn, 1929. Served RAFVR, 1943–46. Judge of Croydon County Court, 1969–75, of Willesden County Court, 1976–81. Contested (L): Twickenham, 1945; Dewsbury, 1950; Chairman: London Liberal Party, 1947–48, 1950–53; Liberal Party Organisation, 1956–57. Sec., Acton Baptist Church, 1954–77. Chm., West Gp Housing Soc. Ltd (West Haven), 1961–94. *Publications:* Slack on War Damage, 1941; Liabilities (War Time Adjustment) Act, 1941; Liability for National Service, 1942. *Address:* 10 Baronsmede, Ealing, W5 4LT. *T:* (020) 8567 8164. *Club:* National Liberal.   *Died 30 Nov. 2003.*

SLATER, Duncan, CMG 1982; HM Diplomatic Service, retired; Chairman, GEC Marconi (Projects) Ltd, since 1995; *b* 15 July 1934; *m* 1972, Candida Coralie Anne Wheatley; one *s* two *d*. Joined FO, 1958; Asst Polit. Agent, Abu Dhabi, 1962–66; First Secretary: Islamabad, 1966; New Delhi, 1966–68; Head of Chancery, Aden, 1968–69; FO, 1969; Special Asst to Sir William Luce, 1970–71; First Sec., UK Representation to EEC, Brussels, 1973–75; UK Resident Rep. to IAEA and UK Perm. Rep. to UNIDO, Vienna, 1975–78; on staff of Government House, Salisbury, Dec. 1979–April 1980; Counsellor and Head of Chancery, Lagos, 1978–81; Ambassador to Oman, 1981–86; Asst Under Sec. of State, FCO, 1986–92; High Comr, Kuala Lumpur, 1992–94. Part-time Lectr, SOAS, Univ. of London. Chm., Res. Inst. for Study of Conflict and Terrorism, 1994–. Vice Pres., British Malaysian Soc. *Recreations:* walking, sailing, skiing, studying Islamic art. *Address:* 15 Marlborough Street, SW3 3PS.
                                       Died 28 June 2002.

SLATER, John Fell, CMG 1972; Assistant Secretary, HM Treasury, 1968–82; *b* 3 July 1924; *s* of J. Alan Slater, FRIBA, and Friede R. Slater (*née* Flight); *m* 1951, Susan Baron (*d* 1996); two *s* two *d* (and one *d* decd). *Educ:* Abinger Hill Preparatory Sch.; Leighton Park Sch.; New Coll., Oxford (BA). *Recreations:* gardening, photography. *Address:* 20 Upham Park Road, W4 1PG. *T:* (020) 8995 8299.   *Died 14 Oct. 2001.*

SLATER, Richard Mercer Keene, CMG 1962; HM Diplomatic Service, retired; *b* 27 May 1915; *s* of late Samuel Henry Slater, CMG, CIE and Muriel Agnes, *d* of Rev. H. B. Streatfeild; *m* 1939, Barbara Janet Murdoch (*d* 1999); four *s.* *Educ:* Eton; Magdalene Coll., Cambridge. Indian Civil Service (Punjab Commission), 1939–47; joined HM Diplomatic Service, 1947; served in Karachi (on secondment to Commonwealth Relations Office), Lima, Moscow, Rangoon and Foreign Office; Ambassador to Cuba, 1966–70; High Comr in Uganda and Ambassador to Rwanda, 1970–72; Asst Under-Sec. of State, FCO, 1973. Adviser to Commercial Union Assurance Co., 1973–81. Chm., Hampshire Br., CPRE, 1974–85. *Address:* 5 High Street, Odiham, Hook, Hants RG29 1LE.   *Died 8 Oct. 2001.*

SLAUGHTER, Frank Gill, MC; MD, FACS; novelist (self-employed); physician and surgeon, retired; *b* Washington, USA, 25 Feb. 1908; *s* of Stephen Lucius Slaughter and Sallie Nicholson Gill; *m* 1933, Jane Mundy; two *s.* *Educ:* Duke Univ. (AB); Johns Hopkins (MD). Served War, 1942–46 (MC): Major to Lt-Col, US Army Med. Corps. Intern, asst resident, and resident surgeon, Jefferson Hosp., Roanoke, Va, 1930–34; practice, specializing in surgery, Jacksonville, Fla, 1934–42; retired, 1946; Lectr, W. Colston Leigh, Inc., NY City, 1947–49. Res. Diplomate, Amer. Bd of Surgery. Mem., Sons of Amer. Revolution. Presbyterian (Elder). Hon. DHL Jacksonville Univ., 1978. *Publications:* That None Should Die, 1941; Spencer Brade, MD, 1942; Air Surgeon, 1943; Battle Surgeon, 1944; A Touch of Glory, 1945; In a Dark Garden, 1946; The New Science of Surgery, 1946; The Golden Isle, 1947; Sangaree, 1948; Medicine for Moderns, 1948; Divine Mistress, 1949; The Stubborn Heart, 1950; Immortal Magyar, 1950; Fort Everglades, 1951; The Road to Bithynia, 1951; East Side General, 1952; The Galilieans, 1953; Storm Haven, 1953; The Song of Ruth, 1954; Apalachee Gold, 1954; The Healer, 1955; Flight from Natchez, 1955; The Scarlet Cord, 1956; The Warrior, 1956; Sword and Scalpel, 1957; The Mapmaker, 1957; Daybreak, 1958; The Thorn of Arimathea, 1958; The Crown and the Cross, 1959; Lorena, 1959; The Land and the Promise, 1960; Pilgrims in Paradise, 1960; Epidemic, 1961; The Curse of Jezebel, 1961; David: Warrior and King, 1962; Tomorrow's Miracle, 1962; Devil's Harvest, 1963; Upon This Rock, 1963; A Savage Place, 1964; The Purple Quest, 1965; Constantine: The Miracle of the Flaming Cross, 1965; Surgeon, USA, 1966; God's Warrior, 1967; Doctor's Wives, 1967; The Sins of Herod, 1968; Surgeon's Choice, 1969; Countdown, 1970; Code Five, 1971; Convention, MD, 1972; Life blood, 1974; Stonewall Brigade, 1975; Plague Ship, 1977; Devil's Gamble, 1978; The Passionate Rebel, 1979; Gospel Fever, 1980; Doctor's Daughters, 1981; Doctors At Risk, 1983; No Greater Love, 1985; Transplant, 1987. *Recreations:* boating, hiking, reading. *Address:* 5051 Yacht Club Road, Jacksonville, FL 32210, USA. *T:* (904) 3897677. *Club:* Timuquana Country (Jacksonville, Fla).
                                            Died 17 May 2001.

SLOMAN, Peter; retired; Education Officer, Association of Metropolitan Authorities, 1974–79; *b* 5 Oct. 1919; *s* of H. N. P. and Mary Sloman (*née* Trinder); *m* 1950, (Margaret) Barbara Pilkington-Rogers; one *s* one *d.* *Educ:* Winchester Coll.; New Coll., Oxford (BA, MA 1945). War Service (RA), 1939–46; TA, 1951–61. Home Civil Service, 1946–74: Under-Sec., 1968; Min. (later Dept) of Educn; HM Treasury; Ministries of Defence, Land and Natural Resources, Housing and Local Govt; IDC 1960.

Principal Admin. Officer: Newham, 1980–83; Surrey, 1985; Principal Administrator, ACC, 1983–88. *Address:* 11 Lowther Road, SW13 9NX. *T:* (020) 8748 2196.
                                            Died 14 Aug. 2003.

SMALL, Dr Ramsay George; Chief Administrative Medical Officer, Tayside Health Board, 1986–89; *b* 5 Feb. 1930; *s* of Robert Small and Ann Ramsay; *m* 1951, Aileen Masterton; four *s.* *Educ:* Harris Academy, Dundee; Univ. of St Andrews (MB ChB). FFCM; FRCPE; DPH. Asst Medical Officer of Health, Ayr CC, 1958–61; Sen. Asst/ PMO, City of Dundee, 1961–74; Community Medicine Specialist, Tayside Health Bd, 1974–86. Convener, Scottish Affairs Cttee, Faculty of Community Medicine, 1983–86. Pres., Baptist Union of Scotland, 1972–73. OStJ. *Recreations:* music, mediaeval ecclesiastical buildings, shipping. *Address:* 46 Monifieth Road, Broughty Ferry, Dundee DD5 2RX. *T:* (01382) 778408.
                                            Died 7 March 2003.

SMALLEY, Prof. Richard Errett, PhD; Gene and Norman Hackerman Professor of Chemistry, since 1982, Professor, Department of Physics, since 1990, and University Professor, since 2002, Rice University; *b* 6 June 1943; *s* of Frank Dudley Smalley and Virginia Smalley (*née* Rhoads); *m* 1st, 1968, Judith Grace Sampieri (marr. diss. 1979); one *s;* 2nd, 1980, Mary Lynn Chapieski (marr. diss. 1994); 3rd, 1997, JoNell Marie Chauvin (marr. diss. 1998); one *s;* 4th, Deborah Lynn Sheffield. *Educ:* Univ. of Michigan (BS Chemistry 1965); Princeton Univ. (MA Chemistry 1971; PhD Chemistry 1973). Associate, James Franck Inst., Chicago, 1973–76; Asst Prof., subseq. Prof., Rice Univ., 1976–82; Chm., Rice Quantum Inst., 1986–96; Dir, Rice Center for Nanoscale Science and Technology, 1996–2002. Franklin Medal, Franklin Inst., 1996; (jtly) Nobel Prize for Chemistry, 1996. *Publications:* articles in learned jls. *Address:* Department of Chemistry, Rice University, Mail Stop 100, PO Box 1892, Houston, TX 77251–1892, USA.   *Died 28 Oct. 2005.*

SMALLWOOD, Anne Hunter, CMG 1976; Commissioner, Board of Inland Revenue, 1973–81; *b* 20 June 1922; *d* of Martin Wilkinson McNicol and Elizabeth Straiton Harper; *m* 1972, Peter Basil Smallwood (*d* 1977). *Educ:* High Sch. for Girls, Glasgow; Glasgow Univ. Entered Inland Revenue, 1943; Min. of Land and Natural Resources, 1964–66; Min. of Housing and Local Govt, 1966; Under-Sec., Inland Revenue, 1971–73. *Address:* 83 Lyncombe Hill, Bath BA2 4PJ.   *Died 7 July 2002.*

SMART, (Alexander Basil) Peter, CMG 1990; HM Diplomatic Service, retired; *b* 19 Feb. 1932; *s* of late Henry Prescott Smart and Mary Gertrude Todd; *m* 1955, Joan Mary Cumming; three *s* (incl. twin *s*). *Educ:* Ryhope Grammar Sch., Co. Durham. Commnd RAEC, 1951; Supervising Officer, Educn, Gibraltar Comd, 1951–52; entered HM Foreign (later Diplomatic) Service, 1953; Vice Consul, Duala, 1955; Polit. Office, ME Forces, Cyprus, 1956; 2nd Sec. (Information), Seoul, 1959; News Dept, FO, 1964; Head of Chancery, Rangoon, 1968; FCO, 1971; Head of Communications Technical Services Dept, 1975; Counsellor, 1977–82, and Dep. High Comr, 1981–82, Canberra; Counsellor and Head of Chancery, Prague, 1983–86; High Comr, Seychelles, 1986–89; Ambassador to Fiji, and High Comr (non-resident) to Republic of Nauru and to Tuvalu, 1989–92. FRSA. *Recreations:* wild nature, the arts: looking and listening. *Address:* 715 Willoughby House, Barbican, EC2Y 8BN.
                                            Died 9 Feb. 2002.

SMART, Prof. Sir George (Algernon), Kt 1978; MD, FRCP; Director, British Postgraduate Medical Federation, 1971–78, retired; *b* 16 Dec. 1913; *er s* of A. Smart, Alnwick, Northumberland; *m* 1939, Monica Helen Carrick; two *s.* *Educ:* Uppingham; Durham Univ. (BSc 1935, MB BS 1937, MD 1939). MRCP 1940, FRCP 1952. Commonwealth Fund Fellow, 1948–49. Lectr in Med., Univ. of Bristol, 1946–50; Reader in Medicine, Univ. of Durham, 1950–56; Prof. of Medicine, Univ. of

Durham, 1956–68, Univ. of Newcastle upon Tyne, 1968–71 (Post-graduate Sub-Dean, 1962–68, Dean of Medicine, 1968–71). Censor, 1965–67, Senior Censor and Senior Vice-Pres., 1972–73, RCP. Chairman: Review Bd for Overseas Qualified Practitioners, GMC, 1979–82; Cttee of Management, and Med. and Survival Cttee, RNLI, 1979–83. Life Vice Pres., RNLI, 1988. Hon. Fellow, Coll. of Physicians and Surgeons, Pakistan, 1976. *Publications:* contrib. to Price's Textbook of Medicine, and Progress in Clinical Medicine (Daley and Miller); (ed) Metabolic Disturbances in Clinical Medicine, 1958; (co-author) Fundamentals of Clinical Endocrinology, 1969, 2nd edn 1974. *Recreation:* photography. *Address:* Taffrail, Crede Lane, Old Bosham, Chichester, Sussex PO18 8NX.
Died 2 Nov. 2003.

SMART, Ninian; *see* Smart, R. N.

SMART, Peter; *see* Smart, A. B. P.

SMART, Prof. (Roderick) Ninian; J. F. Rowny Professor of Religious Studies, University of California, Santa Barbara, 1988–98 (Professor, 1976–98), then Emeritus; Professor Emeritus, University of Lancaster, since 1989 (Professor of Religious Studies, 1967–82; Hon. Professor, 1982–89); *b* 6 May 1927; *s* of late Prof. W. M. Smart, FRSE, and Isabel (*née* Carswell); *m* 1954, Libushka Clementina Baruffaldi; one *s* two *d* (and one *s* decd). *Educ:* Glasgow Academy; The Queen's College, Oxford (Mods (shortened), Class II, 1949; Lit. Hum. Class I, 1951; BPhil 1954; Hon. Fellow, 1999). Army service with Intelligence Corps, 1945–48, 2nd Lt, Captain, 1947; overseas service in Ceylon. Asst Lecturer in Philosophy, University Coll. of Wales, Aberystwyth, 1952–55, Lecturer, 1955; Vis. Lecturer in Philosophy, Yale Univ., 1955–56; Lecturer in History and Philosophy of Religion, Univ. of London, King's College, 1956–61; H. G. Wood Professor of Theology, University of Birmingham, 1961–66. Pro-Vice-Chancellor, Univ. of Lancaster, 1969–72. Lectures: Banaras Hindu Univ., Summer, 1960; Teape, Univ. of Delhi, 1964; Gifford, Univ. of Edinburgh, 1979–80; Visiting Professor: Univ. of Wisconsin, 1965; Princeton and Otago, 1971; Queensland, 1980 and 1985; Univ. of Cape Town, 1982; Harvard, 1983; Hong Kong, 1989. President: Inst. of Religion and Theology, 1980–85 (first Gen. Sec., 1973–77); British Assoc. History of Religions, 1981–85; Amer. Soc. for Study of Religion, 1984–87; Amer. Acad. of Religion, 2000. Mem., Finnish Acad. of Scis and Letters, 2000–. Hon. LHD Loyola, 1968; Hon. DLitt: Glasgow, 1984; Kelaniya, Sri Lanka, 1991; Lancaster, 1995; Middlesex, 1996; DUniv Stirling, 1986. *Publications:* Reasons and Faiths, 1958; A Dialogue of Religions, 1960; Historical Selections in the Philosophy of Religion, 1962; Philosophers and Religious Truth, 1964; Doctrine and Argument in Indian Philosophy, 1964, 2nd edn 1991; The Teacher and Christian Belief, 1966; The Yogi and the Devotee, 1968; Secular Education and the Logic of Religion, 1968; The Religious Experience of Mankind, 1969, 4th edn as The Religious Experience, 1991; Philosophy of Religion, 1970; The Concept of Worship, 1972; The Phenomenon of Religion, 1973; The Science of Religion and the Sociology of Knowledge, 1973; Mao, 1974; A Companion to the Long Search, 1977; The Phenomenon of Christianity, 1979; Beyond Ideology, 1982; (with R. Hecht) Sacred Texts of the World, 1982; Worldviews, 1983; (with Swami Purnananda) Prophet of a New Hindu Age, 1985; Concept and Empathy, 1986; Religion and the Western Mind, 1986; World Religions, 1989; (with S. Konstantine) A Christian Systematic Theology in World Context, 1991; Buddhism and Christianity: rivals and allies, 1993; The Religions of the West, 1993; Asian Religions, 1993; Religion and Nationalism, 1994; Choosing a Faith, 1995; Dimensions of the Sacred, 1996; Lights of Asia: The Buddha and Christ, 1996; Reflections in the Mirror of Religion, 1997; World Philosophies, 1999; (ed) Atlas of the World's Religions, 1999; contrib. to Mind, Philosophy, Philosophical Quarterly, Review of

Metaphysics, Religion, Religious Studies. *Recreations:* cricket, tennis, poetry, painting. *Address:* Department of Religious Studies, University of Lancaster, Bailrigg, Lancaster LA1 4YG; Department of Religious Studies, University of California at Santa Barbara, CA 93106, USA. *Club:* Athenæum.
Died 29 Jan. 2001.

SMEDLEY, Sir Harold, KCMG 1978 (CMG 1965); MBE 1946; HM Diplomatic Service, retired; *b* 19 June 1920; *s* of late Dr R. D. Smedley, MA, MD, DPH, Worthing; *m* 1950, Beryl Mary Harley Brown, Wellington, New Zealand; two *s* two *d*. *Educ:* Aldenham School; Pembroke College, Cambridge. Served War of 1939–45, Royal Marines. Entered Dominions Office (later Commonwealth Relations Office), 1946; Private Secretary to Permanent Under-Secretary of State, 1947–48; British High Commissioner's Office: Wellington, NZ, 1948–50; Salisbury, Southern Rhodesia, 1951–53; Principal Private Sec. to Sec. of State for Commonwealth Relations, 1954–57; Counsellor, British High Comr's Office: Calcutta, 1957; New Delhi, 1958–60; British High Comr in Ghana, 1964–67; Ambassador to Laos, 1967–70; Asst Under-Sec. of State, FCO, 1970–72; Sec. Gen., Commn on Rhodesian opinion, 1971–72; High Comr in Sri Lanka, and Ambassador to Republic of Maldives, 1972–75; High Comr in NZ and concurrently Governor of Pitcairn Island, 1976–80; High Comr in Western Samoa (non-resident), 1977–80. Chm., London Bd, Bank of NZ, 1983–89. Vice Chm., Victoria League, 1981–90. Pres., Hakluyt Soc., 1987–92. Mem., W Sussex CC, 1989–93. Pres., W Sussex Assoc. for the Blind, 1991–97. *Address:* 11A Beehive Lane, Ferring, Sussex BN12 5NN.
Died 16 Feb. 2004.

SMETHURST, (John) Michael, CBE 1996; Deputy Chief Executive, British Library, London, 1995–96; *b* 25 April 1934; *s* of Albert Smethurst and Nelly Smethurst (*née* Kitchin); *m* 1960, Mary Clayworth; one *s* one *d*. *Educ:* William Hulme's Grammar School, Manchester; Manchester Univ. (BA). MCLIP. Librarian: Bede Coll., Durham Univ., 1964–66; Inst. of Educn, Newcastle upon Tyne, 1966–69; Dep. Librarian, Univ. of Glasgow, 1969–72; Univ. Librarian, Univ. of Aberdeen, 1972–86; British Library: Dir-Gen., Humanities and Social Sciences, 1986–91; Dir-Gen., London Services, 1991–95; Mem. Bd, 1986–96; Mem., Lending Div. Adv. Cttee, 1976–80; Mem., Adv. Council, 1982–86 (Chm., Bibliog. Services Adv. Cttee, 1983–86). Hon. Res. Fellow, UCL, 1987–. Trustee, Nat. Library of Scotland, 1976–86; Chairman: Library and Inf. Services Cttee (Scotland), 1982–86; SCONUL, 1984–86, 1989–90 (Vice-Chm., 1983–84, 1988; Mem. Council, 1977–80, 1983–92); Brotherton Liby Cttee, Leeds Univ., 1986–98; Consortium of Eur. Res. Libraries, 1992–2000; Member: British Council Libraries Adv. Cttee, 1983–92; Bd, Res. Libraries Gp, USA, 1992–96; UNESCO Commn for Rehabilitation of Russian State Liby, Moscow, 1993–98; Expert Panel, Museums, Libraries, Archives Heritage Lottery Fund, 1996–2002; UNESCO Consultative Cttee, Qarawiyyin Library Project, Morocco, 1998–99. President: Scottish Liby Assoc., 1983; Friends of Aberdeen Univ. Liby, 1986–2001; LIBER, 1989–95. Trustee, Lambeth Palace Liby, 1998–. Hon. LittD Sheffield, 1996. *Publications:* papers and articles in professional jls. *Recreations:* music, art, travel, gardening. *Address:* Romney, 72 Grove Road, Tring, Herts HP23 5PB. *Club:* Athenæum.
Died 18 Oct. 2004.

SMETTEM, Colin William; Chairman, North Eastern Region, British Gas Corporation, 1973–76; *b* 1 June 1916; *s* of William Home Smettem and Agnes Grace; *m* 1945, Sylvia Elisabeth (*née* Alcock); two *s* two *d*. Solicitor (Hons) 1938. Asst Solicitor, Scarborough Corp., 1938. Served War, RA, 1939–45: UK, India, Assam; started 14th Army Trng Sch., 1943; GII (Major) at Tactical Trng Centre, India Command, 1944. Asst Town Clerk, Wallasey, 1948; North Western Gas Board: Solicitor, 1950; Commercial

Manager, 1961; Mem. Bd, 1965–68; Dep. Chm., Eastern Gas Bd, 1968. Mem., Law Soc. Mem., Rutland DC, 1983–91. CompIGasE 1966. *Address:* The Rookery, Tinwell, Rutland, via Stamford, Lincs PE9 3UJ. *T:* (01780) 753168. *Died 8 Jan. 2003.*

SMIETON, Dame Mary Guillan, DBE 1949; Permanent Secretary, Ministry of Education, 1959–63, retired; *b* 5 Dec. 1902; *d* of John Guillan Smieton, late librarian and bursar Westminster Coll., Cambridge, and of Maria Judith Toop. *Educ:* Perse Sch., Cambridge; Wimbledon High Sch.; Bedford Coll., London (1 year; Hon. Fellow, 1971); Lady Margaret Hall, Oxford (MA; Hon. Fellow, 1959). Asst Keeper, Public Record Office, 1925–28; Min. of Labour and Nat. Service, 1928–46; on loan to Home Office as Gen. Sec., Women's Voluntary Services, 1938–40, and to UN as Dir of Personnel, 1946–48; Under-Sec., 1946–55, Dep. Sec., 1955–59, Min. of Labour and Nat. Service. UK rep., Unesco Exec. Bd, 1962–68. Trustee, British Museum, 1963–73; Member: Advisory Council on Public Records, 1965–73; Standing Commn on Museums and Galls, 1970–73. Vice Pres., Museums Assoc., 1974–77. Chm., Bedford Coll. Council, 1964–70. *Address:* 14 St George's Road, St Margaret's on Thames, Middlesex TW1 1QR. *T:* (020) 8892 9279. *Club:* Oxford and Cambridge. *Died 23 Jan. 2005.*

SMITH; *see* Abel Smith.

SMITH, Prof. Adam Neil, MD, DSc; FRCSE, FRCPE; retired consultant surgeon; *b* 27 June 1926; *s* of William Blackwood Smith and Janet Elder Robertson; *m* 1953, Sibyl Mary Veitch Johnstone; one *s* three *d. Educ:* Lanark Grammar Sch.; Univ. of Glasgow (MB ChB 1948; MD Hons 1959); DSc Edinburgh, 1995. FRCSE 1956; FRCPE 1988; FRSE 1982; FIBiol 1991. Hall Fellow, Univ. of Glasgow, 1949–50; Faulds Fellow, 1950–51; MRC Clinical Research Fellow, 1951–54; Lectr in Surgery, Univ. of Glasgow, 1954–58; St Mark's Hosp., 1958; Sen. Lectr, 1959–63, Reader in Surgery, 1963–91, Univ. of Edinburgh. James IV and Commonwealth Travelling Fellow, 1963. Royal College of Surgeons of Edinburgh: Wade Prof. of Surgical Studies, 1986–97; Vice-Pres., 1991–94; Medal, 1997. Mem. Council, Assoc. of Coloproctology, 1991–94; President: Pelvic Floor Soc., 1989–92; Scottish Soc. of Coloproctology, 1991–94; Mem., James IV Surgical Assoc. Formerly Ext. Examr, Glasgow, Dundee, Newcastle, overseas. Chm., Clinical Sci. Adv. Body, 1984–94, and Trustee, 1994–2001, Melville Trust for Cancer Research. *Publications:* Scientific Foundations of Gastroenterology, 1980; (contrib.) Nutrition in the Prevention of Disease, 1989; (contrib.) Clinical Measurements in Coloproctology, 1991; (contrib.) The Large Intestine, 1991; (contrib.) Coloproctology and the Pelvic Floor, 1992; (contrib.) Colorectal Physiology: Faecal Incontinence, 1994; papers in surgical, gastroenterological and cancer jls. *Recreations:* golf, gardening (Mem. Council, Royal Caledonian Horticultural Soc.), art. *Address:* 2 Ravelston House Park, Edinburgh EH4 3LU. *T:* (0131) 332 4077. *Club:* Scottish Arts (Edinburgh). *Died 12 June 2004.*

SMITH, Alan; mining engineer; *b* 19 Jan. 1930; *s* of John Smith and Alice (*née* Williams); *m* 1958, Adele Marguerite (*née* Buckle) (marr. diss. 1986); two *s* two *d. Educ:* Rossall; St Catherine's Soc., Oxford. BSc Leeds 1957. MIMinE 1958. NCB, 1957–64; Principal Sci. Officer, Min. of Power, 1964; Sci. Counsellor, HM Embassy, Paris, 1965–70; Cabinet Secretariat, 1970–71; DTI, 1971–73; Dept of Industry, 1973–74; Sci. and Technol. Counsellor, HM Embassy, Washington, 1975–77; Head of Sci. and Technol. Div., OECD, 1977–80; DTI Research Gp, 1980–84. Exec. Sec., Newcomen Soc., 1988–92. De Laune Lectr, Apothecaries' Soc., 1980. *Publications:* learned articles on steam engines. *Recreation:* engineering history. *Address:* 63 Abbey House, Abbey Road, NW8 9BX. *Died 4 Oct. 2002.*

SMITH, Sir Alex; *see* Smith, Sir Alexander M.

SMITH, Sir Alexander Mair, (Sir Alex), Kt 1975; director of various companies; *b* 15 Oct. 1922; *s* of late John S. and Anne M. Smith; *m* 1st, 1944, Muriel (*née* Harris) (*d* 1950); one *d*; 2nd, 1956, Doris Neil (*née* Patrick) (*d* 1980); one *d* (and one *d* decd); 3rd, 1984, Jennifer Lewis (*née* Pearce); two step *s. Educ:* Univ. of Aberdeen (MA Maths and Nat. Phil., PhD). FInstP. Physicist, UKAEA, 1952–56; Head of Advanced Research, Rolls Royce Ltd, 1956–67; Dir and Chief Scientist, Rolls Royce & Associates Ltd, 1967–69; Dir, Manchester Polytechnic, 1969–81. Chairman: Cttee of Dirs of Polytechnics, 1974–76; Schools Council, 1975–78; Member: UGC, 1974–76; BBC Gen. Adv. Council, 1978–81; Council, RSA, 1979–84; Vice-Pres., CGLI, 1981–91; Patron, Educnl Inst. of Design, Craft and Technology, 1977–83. Hon. Fellow: Sheffield Poly., 1977; Poly. of Wales, 1983. *Publications:* Lock Up the Swings on Sundays (memoirs), 1998; papers in learned jls. *Recreation:* music. *Address:* Flat 2, 6 Hall Road, Wilmslow, Cheshire SK9 5BW. *T:* (01625) 522011. *Died 28 Feb. 2003.*

SMITH, Anthony Patrick, CBE 1998; Chief Executive, English National Board for Nursing, Midwifery and Health Visiting, 1990–2002; *b* 7 Aug. 1939; *s* of Edward Smith and Gladys Smith (*née* Green); *m* 1965, Barbara Marie Johnson; one *d. Educ:* Latymer Sch.; Open Univ. (BA Hons); Polytechnic of Central London (MA). RGN, RMN, RNT (Florence Nightingale Scholar, 1971). Asst Dir, Nurse Education, St Bartholomew's Hosp., 1969–75; Dir, Nurse Education, Southampton, 1975–81. Fellow, Florence Nightingale Foundn, 1996. Hon. DSc Southampton, 1998. *Recreations:* countryside pursuits, Staffordshire portrait figures. *Address:* 2 Rosewarne Court, Hyde Street, Winchester SO23 7HL.
Died 8 June 2004.

SMITH, Antony Francis, CMG 2002; HM Diplomatic Service, retired; High Commissioner to Jamaica, 1999–2002; *b* 6 May 1942; *s* of Robert Smith and Barbara (*née* Cunningham); *m* 1963, Marion Frances Hickman; two *d. Educ:* De La Salle Coll., Manchester. Joined FO, 1960; Cambodia, 1963–64; Vice Consul, Luanda, Angola, 1964–68; Warsaw, 1968–70; Persian lang. studies, SOAS, 1970–71; Tehran, 1971–74; FCO, 1975; First Sec., Accra, 1976–78; UK Delegn, OECD, Paris, 1979–83; Lisbon, 1983–85; Counsellor, FCO, 1985–90; Consul Gen. and Counsellor, Washington, 1990–94; Dep. Hd of Mission, Lisbon, 1994–99. Official, Order of Infante Dom Henriques (Portugal), 1985. *Recreation:* ski-ing. *Address:* 136 Elm Park Mansions, Park Walk, SW10 0AS. *Club:* Gremio Literario (Lisbon). *Died 17 Feb. 2003.*

SMITH, Ven. Arthur Cyril, VRD 1955; Archdeacon of Lincoln, 1960–76, then Archdeacon Emeritus; Rector of Algarkirk, 1960–76, then Canon Emeritus; *b* 26 Jan. 1909; *s* of late Arthur Smith and Margaret Ryde, Manchester; *m* 1940, Patricia Marion Greenwood, *d* of late Lt-Col Ranolf Nelson Greenwood, MC, and Beatrice Marion, *d* of late Rev. Llewellyn L. Montford Bebb, DD; two *s* two *d. Educ:* St John's College, Winnipeg, Canada; Sheffield University (MA); Westcott House, Cambridge. Deacon 1934, priest 1935; Curate of: Keighley, 1934–36; Bishop's Hatfield, 1936–40; Chaplain RNVR, 1940; HMS Hawkins, 1940–41; 13th Destroyer Flotilla Gibraltar, 1941–43; HMS Eaglet, 1943–44; Senior Chaplain, Liverpool 1945–46; Rector, South Ormsby Group of Parishes, 1946–60; Rural Dean, Hill North, 1955; Canon and Prebendary of Centum Solidorum, 1960. Member: Standing Cttee, House of Clergy, Church Assembly, 1966–70; General Synod, 1970–76; Inspections Cttee, Adv. Council for Churches Ministry, 1967. Church Comr, 1968. Dir, Ecclesiastical Insurance Office Ltd, 1962–72. *Publications:* The South Ormsby Experiment, 1960; Deaneries: Dead or Alive, 1963; (contrib.) Mission and Communication, 1963; (contrib.) The Caring Church, 1964; Team and Group Ministry, 1965; contrib. Theology. *Address:* 28 London Court, London Road,

Headington, Oxford OX3 7SL. *T:* (01865) 744788. *Club:* Army and Navy. *Died 3 April 2001.*

SMITH, Maj.-Gen. Sir Brian W.; *see* Wyldbore-Smith.

SMITH, Catharine Mary S.; *see* Scott-Smith.

SMITH, Charles Stephen; Member, Commission for Racial Equality, since 2004; Chairman, Gypsy Council, since 1990; *b* 20 June 1956; *s* of Charles Reginald Smith and Peggy Smith; *m*; one *s*. *Educ:* King John's, Thundersley. UK Rep. to the UN for the Romani people, 1992–. Mem., Lay Adv. Panel, Centrex, 2005–. Castle Point Borough Council: Mem. (Lab), 1995–2003; Dep. Mayor, 2001–02, Mayor, 2002–03. *Publications:* Gavvered All Around (collection of Gypsy poems), 1987; The Spirit of the Flame, 1990; Not All Wagons and Lanes, 1995. *Recreations:* antiques, music, gardening, nature, walking my dogs. *Address:* c/o The Gypsy Council, 8 Hall Road, Aveley, Essex RM15 4HD. *T:* and *Fax:* (01708) 868986; *e-mail:* enquiries@thegypsycouncil.org.
Died 8 Nov. 2005.

SMITH, Colin; Secretary-General, International Association Against Painful Experiments on Animals, since 1969; *b* 4 July 1941; *s* of Henry E. Smith and A. E. Smith. *Educ:* Upton House Sch., London. Asst Sec., National Anti-Vivisection Soc., 1962–71, Gen. Sec., 1971–81, Internat. Exec. Dir, 1981–86; Dir, American Fund for Alternatives to Animal Res., 1977–92. Mem., Hon. Nederlandse Laureat van de Arbeid, 1981. Editor, Animals' Defender and Anti-Vivisection News, 1967–72, 1982–86. *Publications:* Progress without Pain, 1973; Animal Experiments: steps towards reform, 1975; Moral and Social Aspects of Vivisection, 1981; (with Robert Sharpe) International Charter for Health and Humane Research, 1989; numerous contribs to med. and scientific jls on the anti-vivisection case. *Recreations:* music, theatre, travel. *Address:* 29 College Place, St Albans, Herts AL3 4PU. *Died 26 Sept. 2001.*

SMITH, Rev. Canon David Cree S.; *see* Stewart-Smith.

SMITH, David Douglas R.; *see* Rae Smith.

SMITH, David Dury H.; *see* Hindley-Smith.

SMITH, Sir Douglas (Boucher), KCB 1992 (CB 1982); Chairman, Advisory, Conciliation and Arbitration Service, 1987–93; *b* 9 June 1932; *m* 1956, Mary Barbara Tarran. *Educ:* Leeds Modern Sch.; Leeds Univ. Entered Ministry of Labour, 1953; successively: Private Sec. to Minister of Labour, 1967–68; to First Sec. of State and Sec. of State for Employment and Productivity, 1968–70; to Sec. of State for Employment, 1970–71; Chief Conciliation Officer, 1971–74, Under Secretary: Dept of Employment, 1974–77; Cabinet Office, 1977–79; Dep. Sec., Dept of Employment, 1979–87. *Address:* 17 Dundas Close, Bracknell, Berkshire RG12 7BX. *T:* (01344) 454573. *Club:* Athenæum. *Died 8 Dec. 2001.*

SMITH, Eric John R.; *see* Radley-Smith.

SMITH, Maj.-Gen. Sir (Francis) Brian W.; *see* Wyldbore-Smith.

SMITH, Sir Gilbert; *see* Smith, Sir T. G.

SMITH, Sir Graham (William), Kt 1999; CBE 1990; HM Chief Inspector of Probation, 1992–2001; *b* 15 Aug. 1939; *s* of William George Smith and Edith May Smith; *m* 1958, Jeanne Lilian Ann Goodyear; two *s* one *d*. *Educ:* Univ. of Durham; Univ. of Newcastle upon Tyne (CQSW 1965). Durham: Probation Officer, 1965–69; Sen. Probation Officer, 1969–73; Inner London Probation Service: Asst Chief Probation Officer, 1973–79; Dep. Chief Probation Officer, 1979–80; Chief Probation Officer, 1980–92. Lectr and Examr for Home Office Probation Course, 1972–78; Vis. Prof., UN Asia and FE Inst., Tokyo, 1982. Member: Home Sec.'s Adv. Bd on Restricted Patients, 1986–92; Lord Chancellor's Adv.

Cttee on Legal Educn and Conduct, 1991–97. Chairman: Assoc. of Chief Probation Officers, 1988–89; Penological Cttee, 1995–, Community Sanctions Cttee, 1997–2000, Council of Europe; Mem. Council, Centre for Crime and Justice Studies, KCL, 2001–. Gov., Nat. Inst. of Social Work, 1992–97. Trustee, Lucy Faithfull Foundn, Birmingham, 2000–. Freeman, City of London, 1974. Margaret Mead Award, Internat. Assoc. of Residential and Community Alternatives, LA, 1990. *Recreations:* sport, gardening, theatre, grandchildren. *Address:* The Cottage, Swanley Village Road, Swanley Village, Kent BR8 7NG. *T:* (01322) 665427. *Died 11 Aug. 2002.*

SMITH, Ivor Otterbein, CMG 1963; OBE 1952; Chairman of Public Service and Police Service Commissions and Member of Judicial Service Commission, British Guiana, 1961–66, retired; *b* Georgetown, British Guiana, 13 Dec. 1907; *s* of late Bryce Otterbein Smith and Florette Maud Smith (*née* Chapman); *m* 1936, Leila Muriel Fowler; one *s* two *d*. *Educ:* Queen's Coll., British Guiana; Pitman's Commercial Coll., London. Joined Brit. Guiana CS, as Clerical Asst, Treas., 1925; Sec., Comrs of Currency, 1933; Asst Dist. Comr, 1941; Private Sec. to Gov., 1943; Dist Comr, 1945; Comr, Cayman Is, 1946–52; Dep. Comr of Local Govt, Brit. Guiana, 1953; Governor's Sec., and Clerk Exec. Coun., 1956; Dep. Chief Sec., 1960; acted as Chief Sec. on several occasions and was Officer Administering the Govt, Sept.-Oct. 1960. Served with S Caribbean Force, 1941–43; Major, Staff Officer, Brit. Guiana Garrison. Hon. Col, British Guiana Volunteer Force, 1962–66. Chm., Nat. Sports Council, 1962–66. *Recreations:* reading; interested in sports of all kinds; rep. Brit. Guiana at Association and Rugby football, cricket, hockey. *Address:* #109–867 KLO Road, Kelowna, BC V1Y 9G5, Canada. *Died 2003.*

SMITH, Sir John (Cyril), Kt 1993; CBE 1983; QC 1979; FBA 1973; Professor of Law in the University of Nottingham 1958–87, then Emeritus, and Head of Department of Law 1956–74, and 1977–86; *b* 15 Jan. 1922; 2nd *s* of Bernard and Madeline Smith; *m* 1957, Shirley Ann Walters (*d* 2000); two *s* one *d*. *Educ:* St Mary's Grammar Sch., Darlington; Downing Coll., Cambridge (BA 1949, LLB 1950, MA 1954, LLD 1975; Hon. Fellow, 1977). Served Royal Artillery, 1942–47 (Captain). Called to the Bar, Lincoln's Inn, 1950; Hon. Bencher, 1977. Nottingham University: Asst Lectr in Law, 1950–52; Lectr, 1952–56; Reader, 1956–57; Pro-Vice-Chancellor, 1973–77; Hon. Pres. of Convocation, 1978–87. Arthur Goodhart Vis. Prof. in Legal Science, Cambridge, 1989–90. Commonwealth Fund Fellow, Harvard Law Sch., 1952–53. Member: Criminal Law Revision Cttee, 1977– (co-opted, 1960–66 (theft reference) and 1970–77); Policy Adv. Cttee, 1975–85. Pres., Soc. of Public Teachers of Law, 1979–80. Hon. LLD: Sheffield, 1984; Nottingham, 1989; Villanova, 1993; De Montfort, 1995. *Publications:* (with J. A. C. Thomas) A Casebook on Contract, 1957, 11th edn 2000; (with Brian Hogan) Criminal Law, 1965, 10th edn 2002; Law of Theft, 1968, 8th edn 1997; Criminal Law, Cases and Materials, 1975, 8th edn 2002; (with I. H. Dennis and E. J. Griew) Codification of the Criminal Law, 1985; Justification and Excuse in the Criminal Law (Hamlyn Lectures), 1989; Contract, 1989, 4th edn 2002; Criminal Evidence, 1995. *Recreations:* walking, gardening. *Address:* 445 Derby Road, Lenton, Nottingham NG7 2EB. *T:* (0115) 978 2323. *Died 14 Feb. 2003.*

SMITH, John Derek, MA, PhD; FRS 1976; Member of Scientific Staff, Medical Research Council, Laboratory of Molecular Biology, Cambridge, 1962–88; *b* 8 Dec. 1924; *s* of Richard Ernest Smith and Winifred Strickland Smith (*née* Davis); *m* 1955, Ruth Irwin Aney (marr. diss. 1968). *Educ:* King James's Grammar Sch., Knaresborough; Clare Coll., Cambridge. Mem., Scientific Staff, Agricl Research Council Virus Research Unit, Cambridge, 1945–59; Research Fellow, Clare Coll., 1949–52; with Institut Pasteur, Paris, 1952–53; Rockefeller Foundn Fellow,

Univ. of California, Berkeley, 1955–57; California Institute of Technology: Sen. Research Fellow, 1959–62; Sherman Fairchild Scholar, 1974–75. *Publications:* numerous papers in scientific jls on biochemistry and molecular biology. *Recreation:* travel. *Address:* 12 Stansgate Avenue, Cambridge CB2 2QZ. *T:* (01223) 247841.
Died 22 Nov. 2003.

SMITH, John Herbert, CBE 1977; FCA, CPFA, CIGasE; Deputy Chairman and Chief Executive, British Gas Corporation, 1976–83; *b* 30 April 1918; *s* of Thomas Arthur Smith and Pattie Lord; *m* 1945, Phyllis Mary Baxter (*d* 2000); two *s* three *d*. *Educ:* Salt High Sch., Shipley, Yorks. Articled Clerk, Bradford and Ilkley, 1934–39. Served War, RAMC, 1940–46. Dep. Clerk and Chief Financial Officer, Littleborough, Lancs, 1946–49; West Midlands Gas Bd, 1949–61 (various posts, finishing as Asst Chief Accountant); Chief Accountant, Southern Gas Bd, 1961–65; East Midlands Gas Board: Dir of Finance and Admin, 1965–68; Mem. (full-time), 1968 (Dep. Chm., 1968–72); Member for Finance: Gas Council, June-Dec. 1972; British Gas Corp., 1973–76. Chm., Nationalised Industries Finance Panel, 1978–83. Chairman: Moracrest Investments, 1977–85; United Property Unit Trust (formerly Industrial and Commercial Property Unit Trust), 1986–89 (Mem., 1983–89, Chm., 1986–89, Management Cttee); Member, Management Committee: Pension Funds Property Unit Trust, 1975–89 (Dep. Chm., 1984–89); Lazard American Exempt Fund, 1976–91; British American Property Unit Trust, 1982–93. Member: Council, Inst. of Chartered Accountants, 1977–81; Trilateral Commn, 1976–85. FRSA 1985. *Recreations:* music, piano playing, walking. *Address:* 105 Albany, Manor Road, East Cliff, Bournemouth, Dorset BH1 3EJ. *T:* (01202) 298157.
Died 31 Aug. 2003.

SMITH, John M.; *see* Maynard Smith.

SMITH, (John) Stephen; HM Diplomatic Service; Head of South Asian Department, Foreign and Commonwealth Office, since 2002; *b* 28 March 1957; *s* of Roy and Ruth Smith; *m* 1984, Wanda Won Min Kim. *Educ:* Clare Coll., Cambridge (MA). Joined FCO, 1978: Third, later Second Sec. (Commercial), Seoul, 1980–85; Second Sec., FCO, 1985–87; Second, later First Sec. (Chancery), UK Mission to UN, NY, 1987–90; First Secretary: FCO, 1990–94; (Political/Internal), Bonn, 1994–98; Dep. Head of Mission, Brussels, 1999–2002. *Recreations:* ski-ing, sailing, retriever training, opera. *Address:* c/o Foreign and Commonwealth Office, King Charles Street, SW1A 2AH.
Died 29 Jan. 2005.

SMITH, Kenneth Graeme Stewart, CMG 1958; JP; Civil Secretary, The Gambia, West Africa, 1959–62, retired; *b* 26 July 1918; 3rd *s* of late Prof. Herbert Arthur Smith, DCL and Mora Stewart, 2nd *d* of Dugald Stewart Macphee, Helensburgh; unmarried. *Educ:* Bradfield; Magdalen College, Oxford. Cadet, Colonial Administrative Service, Tanganyika, 1940; appointments in Colonial Service, Zanzibar, Seychelles, Aden, The Gambia, 1945–62. JP Dorset, 1967. *Address:* The Old House, Newland, Sherborne, Dorset DT9 3AQ. *T:* (01935) 812754.
Died 14 April 2001.

SMITH, Lawrence Joseph, OBE 1976; Assistant General Secretary, Transport and General Workers Union, 1985–88; *m*; two *d*. Served in HM Forces, 1941–47; joined London Transport, 1947; District Officer, TGWU, 1961, London District Secretary, 1965, National Officer, 1966, National Secretary, Passenger Services Group, 1971, Exec. Officer, 1979–85. Part-time Mem., London Transport Bd, 1983. Mem., TUC Gen. Council, 1979–88. *Recreations:* gardening, football. *Address:* c/o TGWU, 16 Palace Street, SW1E 5JD.
Died 29 July 2005.

SMITH, Leslie Charles, OBE 1968; Founder Director, Eastway Zinc Alloy Co. Ltd, 1965–82; *b* 6 March 1918; *s* of Edward A. Smith and Elizabeth Smith; *m* 1948, Nancy Jackson-Moore (*d* 1969); two *s* one *d*. *Educ:* Enfield

Central School. Export Buyer, 1938–40; Lieut, RNVR, 1940–46. Founder Dir, Lesney Products, 1947, Jt Man. Dir 1947–73, Man. Dir 1973–80; Chief Exec. Officer, 1980–81, Vice-Chm., 1981–82. FInstM; FCMI (FBIM 1976); FInstD 1979. Master, Marketors' Co., 1986. *Recreations:* ski-ing, sailing, golf. *Address:* White Timbers, 9a Broad Walk, N21 3DA. *T:* (020) 8886 1656. *Clubs:* Naval, Royal Thames Yacht; Royal Motor Yacht, Parkstone Yacht, Poole Harbour Yacht; Parkstone Golf, Hadley Wood Golf.
Died 26 May 2005.

SMITH, Maurice George, OBE 1988; retired; Under-Secretary, Ministry of Overseas Development, 1968–76; *b* 4 Sept. 1915; *s* of Alfred Graham and Laura Maria Smith; *m* 1940, Eva Margaret Vanstone ; two *s*. *Educ:* Sir Walter St John's School, Battersea. Examiner, Estate Duty Office, 1939. Flt Lieut RAF, 1942–46. Asst Principal, Min. of Civil Aviation, 1947; Principal, 1948; transferred to Colonial Office, 1950; seconded Commonwealth Office, 1954–55; Asst Secretary, Colonial Office, 1959; transferred to Dept of Technical Co-operation, 1961; Min. of Overseas Development, 1964; Under-Sec. and Principal Finance Officer, ODM, 1968. Chairman, Knights' Assoc. of Christian Youth Clubs, Lambeth, 1970–2000, Pres. Emeritus, 2000. *Recreations:* voluntary work in youth service, travel.
Died 16 Dec. 2005.

SMITH, Michael K.; *see* Kinchin Smith.

SMITH, Peter Alexander Charles, OBE 1981; Chairman: Securicor Group plc, 1974–95; Security Services plc, 1974–95; *b* 18 Aug. 1920; *s* of Alexander Alfred Smith and Gwendoline Mary (*née* Beer); *m* 1st, 1945, Marjorie May Humphrey (*d* 1988); one *s*; 2nd, 1994, Jeanette Reeve. *Educ:* St Paul's Sch., London. Served RA, 1941–46: Captain; Adjt, 17th Medium Regt. Admitted solicitor, 1948; Partner, Hextall, Erskine & Co., 1953–79. Chairman: British Security Industry Assoc. Ltd, 1977–81; Metal Closures Gp plc, 1983–87 (Dir, 1972, Dep. Chm., 1981). Mem. Council, Royal Warrant Holders Assoc., 1976–, Vice-Pres., 1981–82, Pres., 1982–83. Vice-Pres., Forest Philharmonic Symphony Orch., 1991–. CCMI; FRSA. *Recreations:* golf, music, photography. *Address:* c/o Sutton Park House, 15 Carshalton Road, Sutton, Surrey SM1 4LE. *Clubs:* British Racing Drivers (Hon. Life Mem.); Chigwell Golf (Chm., 1990–97).
Died 20 Nov. 2002.

SMITH, Sir Raymond (Horace), KBE 1967 (CBE 1960); Consultant to Rolls-Royce, 1949–96; Chairman, Hawker Siddeley, 1960–75, and other British companies in Venezuela; *b* 1917; *s* of Horace P. Smith and Mabelle (*née* Osborne-Couzens); *m* 1943, Dorothy, *d* of Robert Cheney Hart. *Educ:* Salesian College, London; Barcelona University. Served War of 1939–45, with British Security Co-ordination, NY, and with Intelligence Corps, in France, India, Burma, Malaya, Indonesia. Civil Attaché British Embassy, Caracas, 1941; Negotiator, sale of British owned railway cos to Venezuelan Govt and other S American govts, 1946–50; Rep., London Reinsurers in Venezuela, 1954–60; Consultant: Cammell Laird; Mirrlees; British Aerospace, 1952–82; Provincial Insurance Co. Ltd, 1960–75; Director: Daily Journal, 1953–95; Anglo-Venezuelan Cultural Inst., 1946–80; British Venezuelan Chamber of Commerce, 1956–86 (Hon. Pres., 1987); Pres. British Commonwealth Assoc. of Venezuela, 1955–57. Companion of Royal Aeronautical Society. Knight Grand Cross, St Lazarus of Jerusalem; Venezuelan Air Force Cross. *Recreations:* tennis, water ski-ing, winter sports (Cresta Run and ski-ing). *Address:* Quinta San Antonio, Calle El Samancito, Avenida El Saman, Caracas Country Club, Caracas 1062, Venezuela; Carlton Lodge, 37 Lowndes Street, SW1X 9JB. *Clubs:* White's, Naval and Military; Caracas Country, Jockey (Caracas); St Moritz Tobogganing (Switzerland).
Died 4 May 2002.

SMITH, Prof. R(ichard) Selby, OBE 1981; MA (Oxon), MA (Harvard); Professor of Education and Head of

Department of Education, University of Tasmania, 1973–79, then Professor Emeritus; *b* 13 June 1914; *s* of Selby Smith, Hall Place, Barming, Maidstone, Kent, and Annie Rachel Smith (*née* Rawlins); *m* 1940, Rachel Hebe Philippa Pease, Rounton, Northallerton, Yorks; two *s*. *Educ:* Rugby Sch.; Magdalen Coll., Oxford; Harvard Univ. Asst Master, Milton Acad., Milton, Mass, USA, 1938–39; House Tutor and Sixth Form Master, Sedbergh Sch., 1939–40; War of 1939–45: Royal Navy, 1940–46; final rank of Lt-Comdr, RNVR. Administrative Asst, Kent Education Cttee, 1946–48; Asst Education Officer, Kent, 1948–50; Dep. Chief Education Officer, Warwickshire, 1950–53; Principal, Scotch Coll., Melbourne, 1953–64; Foundation Prof. of Educn, Monash Univ., 1964, Dean of Faculty of Educn, 1965–71; Principal, Tasmanian Coll. of Advanced Education, 1971–73. Chairman: Victorian Univs and Schools Examinations Bd, 1967–71; State Planning and Finance Cttee, Australian Schools Commn, 1974–77, 1980–83; Vice-Pres., Australian Council for Educnl Research, 1976–79. Hon. LLD Monash, 1989. *Publications:* Towards an Australian Philosophy of Education, 1965; (ed jtly) Fundamental Issues in Australian Education, 1971; The Education Policy Process in Tasmania, 1980; Australian Independent Schools: yesterday, today and tomorrow, 1983. *Recreations:* fishing, ornithology. *Address:* Apt 234, Derwent Waters Residential Club, Cadbury Road, Claremont, Tas 7011, Australia.   *Died 22 Oct. 2005.*

SMITH, Sir Roland, Kt 1991; a Director, Bank of England, 1991–96; Professor Emeritus of Management Science, University of Manchester, since 1988; *b* 1 Oct. 1928; *s* of late Joshua Smith and of Mrs Hannah Smith; *m* 1954, Joan (*née* Shaw); no *c*. *Educ:* Univs of Birmingham and Manchester. BA, MSc, PhD (Econ). Flying Officer, RAF, 1953. Lectr in Econs, Univ. of Liverpool, 1960; Dir, Univ. of Liverpool Business Sch., 1963; Prof. of Marketing, 1966–88, Hon. Vis. Prof., 1988–, and Chancellor, 1996–2002, UMIST. Non-Exec. Chm., Senior Engineering Ltd, 1973–92; Chairman: Temple Bar Investment Trust Ltd, 1980–99; House of Fraser, 1981–86; Readicut International, 1984–96; Hepworth plc, 1986–97; British Aerospace, 1987–91; P & P plc, 1988–97; Manchester United Plc, 1991–2002; Dir-Consultant to a number of public companies. *Recreation:* walking.
Died 20 Nov. 2003.

SMITH, Ronald Alfred D.; *see* Dingwall-Smith.

SMITH, Sidney William; retired; Regional Administrator, East Anglian Regional Health Authority, 1975–83; *b* 17 May 1920; *s* of late Sidney John and Harriet May Smith; *m* 1943, Doreen Kelly; one *s* one *d*. *Educ:* Wirral Grammar Sch., Cheshire. ACIS. Served RAF, 1940–46. Asst Sec., Bury Infirmary, 1939–48; Dep. Group Sec.: Mansfield HMC, 1948–61; Wolverhampton HMC, 1961–63; Group Sec., Wakefield HMC, 1963–73; Area Administrator, Wakefield AHA, 1973–75. Member: Management Side, Ancillary Staff, Whitley Council, 1969–83 (Chm., 1982–83); Cttee, Assoc. of Chief Administrators of Health Authorities, 1974–84 (Chm., 1974–76); Health Services Panel, ICSA, 1978–84, 1986–95 (Chm., 1978–83); Council, Soc. of Family Practitioner Cttees, 1989–90; Vice Chm., Cambs FPC, 1985–90; Chm., Pharmaceutical Services Panel, Cambs FHSA, then Cambridge and Huntingdon HA, 1991–99. Dir, Sketchley Hosp. Services Ltd, 1983–84. Freeman, City of London, 1985. *Recreations:* gardening, Rugby Union football. *Address:* 77 Gough Way, Cambridge CB3 9LN. *T:* (01223) 362307.   *Died 10 May 2005.*

SMITH, Sir (Thomas) Gilbert, 4th Bt *cr* 1897; area manager; *b* 2 July 1937; *er s* of Sir Thomas Turner Smith, 3rd Bt, and Agnes, *o d* of Bernard Page, Wellington, New Zealand; *S* father, 1961; *m* 1962, Patricia Christine Cooper; two *s* one *d*. *Educ:* Huntley Sch.; Nelson Coll. *Recreation:* ski-ing. *Heir: s* Andrew Thomas Smith, *b* 17 Oct. 1965.   *Died 13 Feb. 2003.*

SMITH, William McGregor, OBE 1970; HM Inspector of Constabulary for Scotland, 1970–75, retired; *b* 14 April 1910; *s* of John Smith, Milngavie and Agnes Smith (*née* Haldane); *m* 1939, Alice Mary Ewen, Montrose; one *s* one *d*. *Educ:* Bearsden Academy; Glasgow University (MA 1930). Joined City of Glasgow Police, 1933; Deputy Commandant, Scottish Police College, 1951; Chief Constable of Aberdeen, 1963. *Recreations:* golf, bridge. *Address:* Sherwood, 2 Cherry Tree Park, Balerno, Midlothian EH14 5AQ. *Clubs:* Luffness New Golf, Baberton Golf.   *Died 16 Feb. 2001.*

SMITHSON, Peter Denham; architect in private practice since 1950; *b* 18 Sept. 1923; *s* of William Blenkiron Smithson and Elizabeth Smithson; *m* 1949, Alison Margaret (*née* Gill) (*d* 1993); one *s* two *d*. *Educ:* The Grammar School, Stockton-on-Tees; King's Coll., Univ. of Durham. Served War of 1939–45, Queen Victoria's Own Madras Sappers and Miners, India and Burma, 1942–45. Asst in Schools Div., LCC, 1949–50; subseq. in private practice with wife. Banister Fletcher Prof. of Architecture, UCL, 1976–77; Vis. Prof. of Architecture: Bath Univ., 1978–90; Univ. of Delft, 1982–83; Univ. of Munich, 1984–85; Univ. of Barcelona, 1985–86. *Buildings:* Hunstanton School, 1950–54; The Economist Building, St James's, 1959–64, Porch 1983; Robin Hood Gardens, Tower Hamlets, 1963–72; Garden Bldg, St Hilda's Coll., Oxford, 1968–70; Ramp at Ansty, Wilts, 1987; for Bath University: Second Arts Bldg, 1978–81; Amenity Bldg, 1979–80, 1984; Arts Barn, 1980–90; Architecture and Building Engrg, 1982–88; Porch, Ansty Plum, Wilts, 1992; Porches at Tecta, Lauenförde, 1992–99; Hexenbesenraum, 1991–96, Hexenhaus Pier, and Tea-Haus, 1997, Lantern Pavilion, 2001, Bad Karlshafen; *furniture:* for Tecta, Germany (with A. Smithson), 1982–; Exhibitions for Tecta, Köln and Berlin, 1993, 1998, 1999, 2000, 2001. *Publications:* (all with A. Smithson) Uppercase 3, 1960; The Heroic Period of Modern Architecture, 1965, rev. edn 1981; Urban Structuring Studies of Alison and Peter Smithson, 1967; Team 10 Primer, 1968; The Euston Arch, 1968; Ordinariness and Light, 1970; Without Rhetoric, 1973; Bath: walks within the walls, 1980; The Shift, 1982; AS in DS, 1983; The 1930s, 1985; Upper Lawn, 1986; Italian Thoughts, 1993 (trans. Italian, 1996); Changing the Art of Inhabitation, 1994; Italian Thoughts Followed Further, 2001; The Charged Void, 2002; theoretical work on town structuring in ILAUD Year Book, Spazio e Società and other periodicals; *relevant publications:* synopsis of professional life in Arch. Assoc.'s Arena, Feb. 1966; selective bibliography in The Shift, 1982; A.+P. Smithson, 1991; Alison & Peter Smithson, 1997. *Address:* Cato Lodge, 24 Gilston Road, SW10 9SR. *T:* (020) 7373 7423.
Died 3 March 2003.

SMYTHE, Clifford Anthony, (Tony); consultant; Director, Medical Action for Global Security (formerly Medical Campaign against Nuclear Weapons), 1989–92; *b* 2 Aug. 1938; *s* of Clifford John and Florence May Smythe; *m*; four *d*. *Educ:* University College School. Conscientious Objector, 1958; General Secretary, War Resisters' International, 1959–64; Treasurer, 1982–86; Council Member, Internat. Confederation for Disarmament and Peace, 1963–71; Gen. Sec., Nat. Council for Civil Liberties, 1966–72; Field Dir, American Civil Liberties Union, 1973; Dir, Mind (Nat. Assoc. for Mental Health), 1973–81. Board Member: Volunteer Centre, 1977–81; Retired Execs Clearing Hse (REACH), 1978–90; Member: Nat. Adv. Council on Employment of Disabled People, 1975–81; Nat. Develt Council for Mentally Handicapped People, 1981; (co-opted), Mddx Area Probation Cttee, 1984–90. Chairman: Campaign for Homeless Single People, 1982–84; National Peace Council, 1982–86; Nat. Assoc. of Voluntary Hostels, 1990–92; Director: Assoc. of Community Health Councils for England and Wales, 1983–86; SHAC, 1986–88. *Publications:* Conscription: a World Survey, 1968; (with D.

Madgwick) The Invasion of Privacy, 1974.
Died 27 March 2004.

SMYTHE, Tony; *see* Smythe, C. A.

SNELL, Philip D.; Member (Lab), Tyne and Wear County Council, 1974–86, Chairman, General Services Committee, 1981–86; *b* 14 Oct. 1915; *s* of Alfred William Snell and Jane Herdman; *m* 1939, Selina Waite; two *d*. *Educ:* Causey Road Council Sch., Gateshead. Miner, Marley Hill Colliery, Gateshead, 1929–57; Industrial Relations Advr, NCB, 1957–61; Education and Welfare Officer: Durham CC, 1961–73; Gateshead MDC, 1973. Chm., Tyne and Wear CC, 1980–81. Trustee, Whickham Glebe Sports Club. *Recreation:* enjoying Northern Federation Brewery Beer. *Address:* 16 Sunhill, Sunniside, Newcastle upon Tyne NE16 5PF. *T:* (0191) 488 7006. *Club:* Sunniside Social (Gateshead).
Died 17 Oct. 2002.

SOAKIMORI, Sir Frederick Pa'Nukuanga, KBE 1996 (OBE 1982); CPM 1976; Commissioner, Royal Solomon Islands Police Force, 1982–96, retired; livestock farmer, since 1996; *b* 7 Jan. 1939; *s* of Alick Rakeitino and Lily Makonavai, Tikopia Is; *m* 1965, Ethel Maesiufia, Malaita Is; six *s* two *d*. *Educ:* Anglican Sen. Primary Sch., Pawa. Joined Solomon Is Police Force, 1960: driver, 1960–64; detective constable, 1964–67; officer i/c station, 1967–70; Chief Instructor, Police Acad., 1970–75; Dist Police Comdr, 1975–79; Dep. Police Comr, 1979–82. OStJ 1984. *Recreations:* walking, swimming, jogging, canoeing, reading, table tennis. *Address:* Mbumbura Ridge, Honiara, PO Box 595, Solomon Islands. *T:* 23838/26789.
Died 10 Feb. 2003.

SOLOMON, His Honour (Alan) Peter; a Circuit Judge, 1973–86; *b* 6 July 1923; *s* of late Jacob Ovid Solomon, Manchester; *m* 1st, 1954, Deirdre Anne Punter (marr. diss. 1969); one *d*; 2nd, 1973, Gloria Sophia Turower (marr. diss. 1979); one *d*; 3rd, 1981, Susan Jennifer Hunter. *Educ:* Mill Hill Sch.; Lincoln College, Oxford (MA). Served War, 1942–46, Fleet Air Arm, Petty Officer Airman. Called to the Bar, Inner Temple, 1949; practised South-Eastern circuit. *Publications: poetry:* The Lunatic, Balance, in Keats Prize Poems: an anthology of poetry, 1973. *Recreations:* the turf, travel, poetry, burgundy.
Died 17 Sept. 2001.

SOLOMON, Peter; *see* Solomon, A. P.

SOMERS, Rt Hon. Sir Edward (Jonathan), Kt 1989; PC 1981; Judge of the Court of Appeal, New Zealand, 1981–90; *b* 9 Sept. 1928; *s* of Ewart Somers and Muriel Ann Crossley; *m* 1953, Mollie Louise Morison; one *s* two *d*. *Educ:* Christ's Coll., Christchurch; Canterbury University Coll., Christchurch, NZ (BA, LLB). Practised as barrister and solicitor, 1952–71; practised as barrister, 1971; QC (NZ) 1973; Judge of Supreme Court of New Zealand, 1974. LLD *hc* Univ. of Canterbury, 1992. *Recreation:* gardening. *Address:* Waverley, Kaiapoi, RD2, New Zealand. *T:* (3) 3277094. *Club:* Christchurch (New Zealand).
Died 3 June 2002.

SOMERSET JONES, Eric; QC 1978; a Recorder of the Crown Court, 1975–98; *b* 21 Nov. 1925; *s* of late Daniel and Florence Somerset Jones; *m* 1966, Brenda Marion, *yr d* of late Hedley Shimmin and Doris (*née* Beacroft) two *d*. *Educ:* Birkenhead Inst.; Lincoln Coll., Oxford (MA). Served RAF, 1944–47. Called to the Bar, Middle Temple, 1952, Bencher, 1988; Mem., Northern Circuit. Member: Lord Chancellor's County Courts Rule Cttee, 1975–78; Gen. Council of the Bar, 1990–94. *Address:* (home) Southmead, Mill Lane, Willaston, Wirral, Cheshire CH64 1RL. *T:* (0151) 327 5138, *Fax:* (0151) 327 8895; 12 Marryat Square, SW6 6UA. *T:* (020) 7381 5360. *Club:* Royal Chester Rowing (Chester).
Died 11 Nov. 2002.

SOMERVILLE, David, CB 1971; Under-Secretary, Department of Health and Social Security, 1968–77; *b* 27 Feb. 1917; *e s* of late Rev. David Somerville and Euphemia Somerville; *m* 1950, Patricia Amy Johnston; two *s* two *d*. *Educ:* George Watson's Coll.; Fettes Coll.; Edinburgh Univ.; Christ Church, Oxford. Served Army, 1940–45, Major, RA. Entered Civil Service as Asst Principal, Min. of Health, 1946; Under-Sec., Min. of Health, 1963–67. *Recreations:* gardening, University of the Third Age. *Address:* 5 Glebe Road, Dorking, Surrey RH4 3DS. *T:* (01306) 885102. *Club:* Boat of Garten Golf.
Died 19 Nov. 2002.

SOMERVILLE, John Arthur Fownes, CB 1977; CBE 1964; DL; an Under-Secretary, Government Communications Headquarters, 1969–78; *b* 5 Dec. 1917; *s* of late Admiral of the Fleet Sir James Fownes Somerville, GCB, GBE, DSO; *m* 1945, Julia Elizabeth Payne; one *s* two *d*. *Educ:* RNC Dartmouth. Lieut-Comdr 1945; retd 1950. Govt Communications Headquarters, 1950–78. DL Somerset, 1985. *Recreation:* walking. *Address:* The Old Rectory, Dinder, Wells, Som BA5 3PL. *T:* (01749) 674900.
Died 16 Nov. 2005.

SOMERVILLE, Walter Patrick, CBE 1979; MD, FRCP; Hon. Physician: to Department of Cardiology, Middlesex Hospital, since 1979 (Physician, 1954–79); to Cardiac Surgical Unit, Harefield Hospital, 1952–78; Lecturer in Cardiology, Middlesex Hospital Medical School, 1954–79; Consultant in Cardiology: to Royal Hospital Chelsea, 1963–79; to the Army, 1963–79, Hon. Consultant, 1980–85, Emeritus Consultant, 1985; Hon. Civil Consultant in Cardiology: to Royal Air Force, since 1963; to Association of Naval Officers, since 1960; to King Edward VII Convalescent Home for Officers, Osborne, since 1970; *b* 2 Oct. 1913; *s* of late Patrick and Catherine Somerville, Dublin; *m* 1957, Jane Platnauer (Prof. Jane Somerville, MD, FRCP); three *s* one *d*. *Educ:* Belvedere Coll., Dublin; University College, Dublin. House appts, Mater Hosp., Dublin, 1937; out-patients Assistant, Brompton Hosp. and Chelsea Chest Clinic, 1938–39. Served in War 1939–45; attached: Canadian Dept of Defense, 1942; US Army, 1943; Lt-Col RAMC 1944. Fellow in Med., Mass General Hosp., Boston, 1946; Registrar, British Postgraduate Med. School, Hammersmith, 1947; studied in Paris, Stockholm and Univ. of Michigan, 1948; Fellow in Medicine, Peter Bent Brigham Hosp. Boston and Harvard Med. Sch., 1949; Med. Registrar, Nat. Heart Hosp. and Inst. of Cardiology, 1951; Sen. Med. Registrar, Middlesex Hosp., 1951–54. Vis. Prof., Cleveland Clinic, Cleveland, Ohio, 1960. Lectures: Carey Coombs, Bristol Univ., 1977; St Cyres, Nat. Heart Hosp., 1978; William Stokes, Irish Cardiac Soc., Belfast, 1983. Editor, British Heart Jl, 1973–80; Editorial Board: American Heart Jl, 1975; Revista Portuguesa de cardiologia, 1982. Mem., Med. Adv. Gp, Brewers' Soc., 1988–92. Pres., British Cardiac Soc., 1976–80; former Pres., British Acad. of Forensic Sciences; Mem., Assoc. of Physicians of Great Britain and Ireland and other socs; Corr. Member: Colombian Soc. of Cardiology; Chilean Soc. of Cardiology; Fellow, Amer. Coll. of Cardiology. Trustee, British Assoc. of Performing Arts Medicine, 1986–. Purkynje Medal, Czechoslovakian Cardiac Soc., 1981. Officer, Legion of Merit, USA, 1945. *Publications:* (ed) Paul Wood's Diseases of the Heart and Circulation, 3rd edn, 1968; various articles on cardiovascular subjects in British, continental European and American jls. *Address:* 30 York House, Upper Montagu Street, W1H 1FR. *T:* (020) 7262 2144.
Died 20 July 2005.

SONTAG, Susan; writer; *b* 16 Jan. 1933; *m* Philip Rieff (marr. diss.); one *s*. *Educ:* Univ. of Chicago (BA 1952); Harvard Univ. (MA 1955). MacArthur Foundn Fellow, 1990–95. Member: American Acad.-Inst. of Arts and Letters, 1979; Amer. Acad. of Arts and Scis, 1993; Pres., PEN Amer. Center, 1987–89. Jerusalem Prize, Jerusalem Book Fair, 2001; (jtly) Prince of Asturias Award for Literature, Spain, 2003. Commandeur de l'Ordre des Arts et des Lettres (France), 1999. *Films:* Duet for Cannibals,

1969; Brother Carl, 1971; Promised Lands, 1974; Unguided Tour, 1983. *Publications: novels:* The Benefactor, 1963; Death Kit, 1967; The Volcano Lover, 1992; In America, 2000 (Nat. Book Award for Fiction, 2000); *stories:* I, etcetera, 1978; The Way We Live Now, 1991; *essays:* Against Interpretation, 1966; Styles of Radical Will, 1969; On Photography, 1977; Illness as Metaphor, 1978; Under the Sign of Saturn, 1980; AIDS and its Metaphors, 1989; Where the Stress Falls, 2001; Regarding the Pain of Others, 2003; *filmscripts:* Duet for Cannibals, 1970; Brother Carl, 1974; *play:* Alice in Bed, 1993. *Address:* c/o The Wylie Agency, 250 West 57th Street, Suite 2114, New York, NY 10107, USA. *Died 28 Dec. 2004.*

SORINJ, Dr Lujo T.; *see* Tončić-Sorinj.

SOUROZH, Metropolitan of; *see* Anthony, Archbishop.

SOUTH, Sir Arthur, Kt 1974; JP; Partner, Norwich Fur Company, since 1947; *b* 29 Oct. 1914; *s* of Arthur and Violet South, Norwich; *m* 1st, 1937, May Adamson (marr. diss. 1976); two *s*; 2nd, 1976, Mary June (*d* 1982), *widow* of Robert Edward Carter, JP, DL. *Educ:* City of Norwich Sch. Served RAF and MAP, 1941–46. Mem., Norwich, Lowestoft, Gt Yarmouth Hosp. Management Cttee, 1948–74 (Vice-Chm., 1954–66, Chm., 1966–74); Chairman: Norfolk Area Health Authority, 1974–78; E Anglian RHA, 1978–87; Mem., E Anglia Regional Hosp. Bd, 1969–74. Member: Assoc. of Educn Cttees, 1963–74; Assoc. of Municipal Corporations, 1965–74; E Anglia Econ. Planning Council, 1966–80; E Anglia Rent Assessment Panel, 1967–74; E Anglia Adv. Cttee to BBC, 1970–74; Univ. of E Anglia Council, 1964–80 (Life Mem., Court, 1964); Chairman: E Anglia Roads to Prosperity, 1987–; Norfolk Energy Forum, 1988–. Norwich: City Councillor, 1935–41 and 1946–61; Alderman, 1961–74; Sheriff, 1953–54; Lord Mayor, 1956–57, Dep. Lord Mayor, 1959–60; JP 1949; Dep. Leader, Norwich City Council, 1959–60; Chm., Labour Party Gp and Leader Norwich City Council, 1960–78. Norwich City Football Club: Vice-Pres., 1957–66; Dir, 1966–73; Chm., 1973–85; Mem., FA Council, 1981–86; Football League: Mem., Management Cttee, 1981–85; Life Vice-Pres., 1985. Hon. DCL East Anglia, 1989. *Recreations:* football, bowls, cricket. *Address:* 23 Hall Lane, Drayton, Norfolk NR8 6DR. *T:* (01603) 868907. *Clubs:* MCC; Mitre Bowls, Norfolk Cricket, Norwich City Football. *Died 28 Jan. 2003.*

SOUTHERN, Michael William; Adviser to HE the Minister of Health, Kingdom of Saudi Arabia, 1978, retired; Regional Administrator, South West Thames Regional Health Authority, 1973–77; *b* 22 June 1918; *s* of William Southern and Ida Frances Southern; *m* 1945, Nancy Russell Golsworthy; two *d* (and one *d* decd). *Educ:* Tiffin Boys' Sch., Kingston-upon-Thames; London Univ. (DPA); Open Univ. (BA Humanities). Surrey CC Public Health Dept, 1934–39 and 1945–48; served with RAMC (NCO), 1939–45: Technician in No 1 Malaria Field Lab., 1940–41; POW Germany, 1941–44; Planning Officer and later Sec. of SW Metropolitan Regional Hosp. Bd, 1948–73. Royal British Legion: Chairman: Surrey Council, 1985–88 (Life Vice Pres., 1989); Richard Sharples Court, Sutton, 1988–93; Duke of Connaught Meml Br., 1993–97 (Pres., 1998). *Recreations:* music, travel, philately. *Address:* 5 Beach Crescent, Littlehampton, West Sussex BN17 5NT. *T:* (01903) 734713.

Died 21 Sept. 2001.

SOUTHERN, Sir Richard (William), Kt 1974; FBA 1960; FRSL; President of St John's College, Oxford, 1969–81, Honorary Fellow, 1981; *b* 8 Feb. 1912; 2nd *s* of Matthew Henry Southern, Newcastle upon Tyne; *m* 1944, Sheila (*née* Cobley), *widow* of Sqdn Ldr C. Crichton-Miller; two *s*. *Educ:* Royal Grammar Sch., Newcastle upon Tyne; Balliol College, Oxford (Domus Exhibnr; 1st Class Hons Modern History, 1932). Junior Research Fellow, Exeter College, Oxford, 1933–37 (Hon. Fellow, 1991); studied in Paris, 1933–34 and Munich, 1935; Fellow and

Tutor, Balliol Coll., Oxford, 1937–61 (Hon. Fellow, 1966); Junior Proctor, Oxford Univ., 1948–49; Chichele Prof. of Modern History, Oxford, 1961–69. President: Royal Historical Soc., 1968–72; Selden Soc., 1973–76. Lectures: Birkbeck, in Ecclesiastical History, Trinity Coll., Cambridge, 1959–60; Raleigh, British Academy, 1962; David Murray, Glasgow Univ., 1963; Gifford, Glasgow Univ., 1970–72; G. M. Trevelyan, Cambridge Univ., 1980–81. FRSL 1973. Corresponding Fellow: Medieval Academy of America, 1965; Monumenta Germaniae Historica, 1982; For. Hon. Mem., Amer. Acad. of Arts and Scis, 1972. Hon. Fellow, Sidney Sussex Coll., Cambridge, 1971. Hon. DLitt: Glasgow, 1964; Durham, 1969; Cantab, 1971; Bristol, 1974; Newcastle, 1977; Warwick, 1978; St Anselm's Coll., 1981; Columbia, 1982; Univ. of the South, 1985; Hon. LLD Harvard, 1977. Balzan Prize, Fondazione Internazionale Balzan, Milan, 1987. Served Oxford and Bucks LI, 1940; 2nd Lieut Durham LI 1941; 155th Regt RAC, 1942; Captain 1943; Major 1944; Political Intelligence Dept, Foreign Office, 1943–45. *Publications:* The Making of the Middle Ages, 1953 (numerous foreign translations); Western Views of Islam in the Middle Ages, 1962; (ed) Eadmer's Vita Anselmi, 1963; St Anselm and his Biographer, 1963; (ed with F. S. Schmitt) Memorials of St Anselm, 1969; Medieval Humanism and other studies, 1970 (RSL award 1970); Western Society and the Church in the Middle Ages, 1970; Robert Grosseteste, 1986, 2nd edn 1992; St Anselm: a portrait in a landscape, 1990; Scholastic Humanism and the Unification of Europe, vol. 1, 1995, vol. 2, 1999; articles in English Historical Review, Medieval and Renaissance Studies, etc. *Address:* 40 St John Street, Oxford OX1 2LH. *Died 6 Feb. 2001.*

SOUTHWARD, Sir Leonard (Bingley), (Sir Len), Kt 1986; OBE 1978; Founder (with Lady Southward) of Southward Museum Trust Inc., Paraparaumu, New Zealand, 1972; *b* 20 Sept. 1905; *s* of Philip Edmund Southward and Elizabeth Sarah Southward; *m* 1st, 1931, Eileen Rose (marr. diss. 1954), *d* of Charles Mitchell; two *s*; 2nd, 1954, Vera Thelma Bellamore. *Educ:* Te Aro Sch., Wellington, NZ. Started motorcycle repair business, 1926; changed to car repairs, 1935; started prodn engrg and manufacture of steel tubing, 1939; Governing Dir, Southward Engrg Co. Ltd, 1957–. The Southward Museum, which was opened to the public in 1979, contained one of the largest and most varied privately owned collection of veteran and vintage cars in the Southern Hemisphere. *Recreations:* veteran and vintage cars, rallies, etc; formerly speed boat racing, Australasia (first man in region to travel at over 100 mph on water). *Address:* 203 State Highway 1, Paraparaumu, New Zealand. *T:* (4) 2984627. *Died 19 Feb. 2004.*

SOUTHWOOD, Prof. Sir (Thomas) Richard (Edmund), Kt 1984; DL; FMedSci; FRS 1977; Professor of Zoology, University of Oxford and Fellow of Merton College, Oxford, 1979–98, then Emeritus Professor and Emeritus Fellow (Linacre Professor of Zoology, 1979–93); Vice-Chancellor, 1989–93, Pro Vice-Chancellor, 1987–89 and 1993–98, University of Oxford; Director, Glaxo Wellcome (formerly Glaxo Holdings) plc, 1992–99; *b* 20 June 1931; *s* of late Edmund W. Southwood and A. Mary, *d* of Archdeacon T. R. Regg; *m* 1955, Alison Langley, *d* of late A. L. Harden, Harpenden, Herts; two *s*. *Educ:* Gravesend Grammar Sch.; Imperial Coll., London (BSc, ARCS 1952; PhD 1955; DSc 1963); MA Oxon 1979; DSc Oxon 1987. FIBiol 1968. ARC Research Schol., Rothamsted Experimental Station, 1952–55; Res. Asst and Lecturer, Zoology Dept, Imperial Coll., London, 1955–64; Vis. Prof., Dept of Entomology, University of California, Berkeley, 1964–65; Reader in Insect Ecology, University of London, 1964–67; Prof. of Zoology and Applied Entomology, London Univ., Head of Dept of Zoology and Applied Entomol., and Dir of Field Station, Imperial Coll., 1967–79; Dean, Royal Coll. of Science, 1971–72; Chm., Division of Life Sciences, Imperial Coll., 1974–77. A. D. White Prof.-at-Large, Cornell Univ.,

1985–91. Member: ARC Adv. Cttee on Plants and Soils, 1970–72; ARC Res. Grants Bd, 1972–78; JCO Arable and Forage Crops Bd, 1972–79; NERC Terrestrial Life Sciences (formerly Nature Conservancy) Grants Cttee, 1971–76 (Chm., 1972–76); Council, St George's House, Windsor, 1974–80; Adv. Bd Research Councils, 1977–80; Trop. Medicine Panel, Wellcome Trust, 1977–79; Chairman: Royal Commn on Envmtl Pollution, 1981–86 (Mem., 1974–86); Management Cttee, Royal Soc., Royal Swedish Acad. and Norwegian Acad. Surface Water Acidification Prog., 1984–90; NRPB, 1985–94 (Mem., 1980–94); Dept of Health and MAFF Working Party on Bovine Spongiform Encephalopathy, 1988–89; UGC Working Party on Biology in Univs, 1988–89; Inter-Agency Cttee on Global Envmtl Change, 1997–2000; UK Round Table on Sustainable Develt, 1995–99. Vice-Pres., Royal Soc., 1982–84; President: British Ecological Soc., 1976–78 (Hon. Treas., 1960–64 and 1967–68; Hon. Mem., 1988); Royal Entomological Soc., 1983–85 (Vice-Pres., 1963–64; Hon. Fellow, 1999); Hon. Vice-President: Inst. of Envmtl Health, 1984–2001; Game Conservancy, 1986–. Governor, Glasshouse Crops Research Inst., 1969–81; Trustee: British Museum (Natural History), 1974–83 (Chm., 1980–83); East Malling Trust, 1984–99; Rhodes Trust, 1986–2002 (Chm., 1999–2002); Lawes Trust, 1987–2005 (Chm., 1991–2005); Rank Prize Funds Trust, 1993–2005; Delegate, OUP, 1980–94; Mem., Hebdomadal Council, 1981–94. Lectures: Spencer, Univ. of British Columbia, 1978; Bawden, British Crop Protection Conf., 1979; Le Conte, Georgia, 1989; F. E. Williams, RCP, 1990; Crookshank, RCR, 1993; Croonian, Royal Soc., 1995. Founder FMedSci 1998; Member: Academia Europaea, 1989; Pontifical Acad. of Scis, 1992; Foreign Member: Amer. Acad. of Arts and Sciences, 1981; Norwegian Acad. of Sci. and Letters, 1987; US Nat. Acad. of Science, 1988; Royal Netherlands Acad., 1996; Hungarian Acad. of Scis, 1998; Hon. Mem., Ecol Soc. of America, 1986. Fellow, Eton Coll., 1993–2001; Hon. Fellow: Imperial Coll., 1984; Kellogg Coll., Oxford, 2000; Mansfield Coll., Oxford, 2000; Harris Manchester Coll., Oxford, 2004; Entomological Soc. of Amer., 1986. Hon. FRCP 1991; Hon. FRCR 1995. Hon. DSc: Griffith, 1983; McGill, 1988; Warwick, 1989; Liverpool, 1992; Durham, 1994; Sussex, 1994; Victoria, 1994; Hon. LLD: London, 1991; Oxford Brookes, 1993; Bristol, 1994; Fil. Doc. *hc* Lund, 1986; Hon. ScD E Anglia, 1987. Scientific Medal, Zool. Soc., London, 1969; Linnean Medal, Linnean Soc. of London, 1988. DL Oxfordshire, 1993. Cavaliere Ufficiale, Order of Merit, Republic of Italy, 1991; Ordem de Merito (cl. II), Republic of Portugal, 1993. *Publications:* (with D. Leston) Land and Water Bugs of the British Isles, 1959; Life of the Wayside and Woodland, 1963; Ecological Methods, 1966, 3rd edn 2000; (jtly) Insects on Plants, 1984; (ed with B. J. Juniper) Insects and the Plant Surface, 1986; (ed with R. R. Jones) Radiation and Health: the biological effects of low-level exposure to ionizing radiation, 1987; (ed jtly) The Treatment and Handling of Wastes, 1992; The Story of Life, 2003; many papers in entomological and ecological jls. *Recreations:* natural history, reading, gardening, conversation. *Address:* Merton College, Oxford OX1 4JD. *Clubs:* Athenæum, Oxford and Cambridge.
Died 26 Oct. 2005.

SOUTHWOOD, William Frederick Walter, MD; FRCS; Consultant Surgeon, Bath Health District, 1966–90; *b* 8 June 1925; *s* of late Stuart W. Southwood, MC, and of Mildred M. Southwood, and *g s* of W. E. W. Southwood; *m* 1965, Margaret Carleton Holderness, *d* of late Sir Ernest Holderness, Bt, CBE, and Lady Holderness; two *s*. *Educ:* Charterhouse; Trinity Coll., Cambridge (MA 1951, MChir 1956, MD 1964); Guy's Hosp. FRCS 1954. Captain, RAMC, 1949–51. Surg. Registrar, West London Hosp. and St Mark's Hosp. for Diseases of the Rectum, 1954–60; Sen. Surg. Registrar, Royal Infirmary, Bristol, 1960–66. Hunterian Prof., RCS, 1961. Vis. Prof. of Surgery, Univ. of Cape Town, 1987. Chm., Professional and Linguistic Assessment Bd, 1984–87 (Mem., 1976–87;

Vice-Chm., 1983–84). Mem., Court of Assts, Worshipful Soc. of Apothecaries of London, 1975– (Chm., Exams Cttee, 1981–85; Jun. Warden, 1984–85; Sen. Warden, 1985–86; Master, 1986–87; Hon. Treas., 1989–99; Hon. Freeman, 2000). Mem. Cttee, Non-Univ. Medical Licencing Bodies, 1979–90. Examr in Anatomy and Surgery to GNC, 1957–72. *Publications:* articles in surgical jls. *Recreations:* fishing, snooker. *Address:* 1 Aldwick Avenue, Bognor Regis, W Sussex PO21 3AQ. *T:* (01243) 823073. *Club:* East India. *Died 27 April 2002.*

SOUZAY, Gérard, Chevalier, Légion d'Honneur; Chevalier de l'Ordre des Arts et des Lettres; French baritone; *b* 8 Dec. 1921; *né* Gérard Marcel Tisserand. *Educ:* Paris Conservatoire Musique. World Première, Stravinsky's Canticum Sacrum, Venice Festival, 1956; Bach B Minor Mass at Salzburg Festival; Pelléas et Mélisande, Rome Opera, Opera Comique, 1962, Scala, Milan, 1973; Don Giovanni, Paris Opera, 1963; second tour of Australia and New Zealand, 1964. Also tours in US, South America, Japan, Africa, Europe. Annual Lieder recitals, Salzburg Festival. Has made recordings; Grand Prix du Disque, for Ravel Recital, etc. *Recreations:* tennis, painting. *Died 17 Aug. 2004.*

SOWRY, Dr Clive; *see* Sowry, Dr G. S. C.

SOWRY, Dr (George Stephen) Clive, FRCP, FRCPEd; FFOM; Physician, Edgware General Hospital, 1953–82; *b* 26 Dec. 1917; *s* of Dr George H. Sowry and Mrs Stella Sowry; *m* 1943, Jeanne (*née* Adams); one *s* one *d*. *Educ:* Bilton Grange, near Rugby; Epsom Coll., Surrey; St Mary's Hosp. Med. Sch., London (MB, BS 1940; MD 1947). FRCP 1963 (MRCP 1946); FRCPEd 1986; FFOM 1987. Served War, RNVR, 1941–45 (Surg. Lieut). Med. appts, St Mary's Hosp., Brompton Hosp. and Hammersmith Hosp., until 1953; med. admin, Edgware Gen. Hosp., 1957–73. Royal College of Physicians: Pro Censor, 1975; Censor, 1976; Sen. Censor and Vice-Pres., 1978–79. Mem. Qualification Cttee, 1981–86, Examnr, 1981–86, Board Mem., 1987–92, Faculty of Occupational Medicine. Med. Sec., MRCP (UK) Pt 2 Exam. Bd, 1983–87; Member: Jt Academic Cttee, Conjoint Bd, 1983–89 (Chm., 1985–87); Med. Adv. Cttee, HSE, 1983–87. Silver Jubilee Medal, 1977. *Publication:* (jtly) article on aetiology of essential hypertension in Clin. Science. *Recreations:* sailing, singing. *Address:* 53 Aldenham Avenue, Radlett, Herts WD7 8JA. *T:* (01923) 856046. *Died 4 Sept. 2001.*

SPAFFORD, George Christopher Howsin; Chancellor, Manchester Diocese, 1976–96; a Recorder of the Crown Court, 1975–88; *b* 1 Sept. 1921; *s* of Christopher Howsin Spafford and Clara Margaret Spafford; *m* 1959, Iola Margaret, 3rd *d* of Bertrand Leslie Hallward; one *s* one *d*. *Educ:* Rugby; Brasenose Coll., Oxford (MA, BCL Hons); Univ. of Wales Coll. of Cardiff (LLM 1994). Served RA, 1939–46 (Captain). Called to Bar, Middle Temple, 1948. Mem., Legal Adv. Commn of Gen. Synod, 1981–96. Treasurer, Friends of the Manchester City Art Gall., 1986–92; Hon. Legal Advr, RCA, 2001– (Hon. Treas., 1995–2001); former Treasurer: Parish and People; Red Rose Guild of Designer Craftsmen. RCA 1989 (ARCamA 1986). Hon. LLM Manchester, 1992. *Recreation:* painting pictures. *Address:* 57 Hawthorn Lane, Wilmslow, Cheshire SK9 5DQ. *Died 9 Oct. 2003.*

SPALDING, Rear-Adm. Ian Jaffery L.; *see* Lees-Spalding.

SPARROW, (Albert) Charles; QC 1966; DL; barrister; *b* Kasauli, India, 16 Sept. 1925; *e s* of Captain Charles Thomas Sparrow, sometime Essex Regt, and Antonia Sparrow; *m* 1949, Edith Rosalie Taylor (*d* 1985); two *s* one *d*. *Educ:* Royal Grammar Sch., Colchester; LLB London Univ., 1951. Served Civil Defence, 1939–43; joined Army, 1943; posted as cadet to India, commnd into Royal Signals and served in Far East, 1944–47; OC, GHQ Signals, Simla, 1947. Admitted to Gray's Inn, 1947

(Holker Sen. Schol., Atkin Schol., Lee Prizeman and Richards Prizeman); called to the Bar, Gray's Inn, 1950 (Bencher, 1976; Master of Pictures and Silver, 1985–2001; Treas., 1994; Barnard's Inn Reader, 1996; Staple Inn Reader, 1998); admitted to Lincoln's Inn, 1967; in practice in Chancery and before Parliament, 1950–99. Member: General Council of the Bar, 1969–73; Senate of the Four Inns of Court, 1970–73; Incorp. Council of Law Reporting, 1977–83. Hon. Legal Adviser to Council for British Archæology (concerned notably with legal protection of antiquities and reform of treasure trove; draftsman of Abinger Bill), 1966– (Hon. Vice-Pres., 2002–). Chairman: ind. Panel of Inquiry for affairs of RSPCA, 1973–74; ind. Cttee of Inquiry for Girl Guides Rally at Crystal Palace, 1985. FSA 1972; Pres., Essex Archaeological Soc., 1975–78. Chm., Stock Branch, British Legion, 1970–75 (Pres., 1999–). Mem., Court, Univ. of Essex, 1985–. Advr to assocs of customary freemen, 1972–; Hon. Counsellor to Freemen of England, 1978–; Freeman, City of London; Hon. Life Mem., Gild of Freemen of City of York; Mem., Freemen of England and Wales; Burgess Freeman, Altrincham. DL Essex, 1985. KStJ 1993 (OStJ 1982; CStJ 1987); Mem. St John Council for Essex, 1977–; Comr for Essex, St John Ambulance Bde, 1983–90; Comdr, St John for Essex, 1989–93. *Recreation:* Romano-British archæology. *Address:* Serle Court Chambers, 6 New Square, Lincoln's Inn, WC2A 3QS. *T:* (020) 7242 6105; Croyde Lodge, Stock, Essex CM4 9QB. *Clubs:* Arts; Essex. *Died 17 May 2005.*

SPARROW, Charles; see Sparrow, A. C.

SPEDDING, Sir David (Rolland), KCMG 1996; CVO 1984; OBE 1980; HM Diplomatic Service, retired; Chief, Secret Intelligence Service, 1994–99; *b* 7 March 1943; *s* of Lt Col Carlisle Montagu Rodney Spedding and Gwynfydd Joan Llewellyn; *m* 1970, Gillian Leslie Kinnear; two *s*. *Educ:* Sherborne School; Hertford College, Oxford (MA; Hon. Fellow, 2000). Third Sec., FO, 1967; Middle East Centre for Arabic Studies, 1968; Second Sec., Beirut, 1970; Santiago, 1972; First Sec., FCO, 1974; Abu Dhabi, 1978; FCO, 1981–83; Counsellor, Amman, 1983–86; Counsellor, FCO, 1987–94. *Recreations:* golf, reading. *Address:* PO Box 317, EC1P 1HD.
Died 13 June 2001.

SPENCE, Captain (Frederick) Michael (Alexander) T.; see Torrens-Spence.

SPENCER, Herbert, RDI 1965; DrRCA; Professor of Graphic Arts, Royal College of Art, 1978–85; *b* 22 June 1924; *m* 1954, Marianne Möls, Dordrecht (*d* 2001); one *d*. DrRCA 1970. FCSD (FSIA 1947). Joined London Typographical Designers, 1946; consultant and designer: W. H. Smith Ltd (formerly W. H. Smith & Son Ltd), 1973–96; Tate Gall., 1981–89; British Rail, 1984–86. Mem., PO Stamp Adv. Cttee, 1968–93; external advr to Design Cttee, British Telecom, 1981–83. Editor: Typographica, 1949–67; Penrose Annual, 1964–73. Sen. Res. Fellow, RCA, 1966–78, Hon. Fellow, 1985. Dir, Lund Humphries Publishers Ltd, 1970–88. Internat. Pres., AGI, 1971–74; Master, Faculty of Royal Designers for Industry, 1979–81; Vice-Pres., RSA, 1979–81. Governor, Bath Acad. of Art, Corsham, 1982–83. One-man exhibitions of paintings: Bleddfa Trust, 1986; Gallery 202, London, 1988–89 and 1990; Eva Jekel Gall., London, 1992; exhibition of photographs, Zelda Cheatle Gall., London, 1991; photographs in perm. collection of V&A Museum. *Publications:* Design in Business Printing, 1952; London's Canal, 1961, 2nd edn 1976; Traces of Man, 1967; The Visible Word, 1968, 2nd edn 1969; Pioneers of Modern Typography, 1969, 2nd edn 1982, German edn 1970, Dutch edn 1983, Spanish edn 1995; (with Colin Forbes) New Alphabets A-Z, 1973, French edn 1974; (with Mafalda Spencer) The Book of Numbers, 1975; The Liberated Page, 1987, 2nd edn 1990; Without Words: photographs by Herbert Spencer, 1999. *Address:* 75 Deodar Road, Putney, SW15 2NU. *T:* and *Fax:* (020) 8874 6352. *Club:* Chelsea Arts. *Died 11 March 2002.*

SPENCER, Mrs Joanna Miriam, CB 1971; CBE 1961; CompIGasE; *b* 26 July 1910; *d* of late Rev. R. S. Franks; *m* 1954, Frank Woolley Sim Spencer (*d* 1975). *Educ:* Redland High School for Girls, Bristol; Girton College, Cambridge (MA). Asst, Lancs County Library, 1934–35; Asst Librarian: Hull Univ. Coll., 1936–37; Regent Street Polytechnic, 1938; Librarian, Selly Oak Colls, 1938–42. Temp. Civil Servant, Min. of Aircraft Production, 1942–45. Principal, Min. of Supply, 1946; Assistant Secretary, Min. of Supply, 1949–55, Board of Trade, 1955–56, Min. of Power, 1957–64; Under-Secretary: Min. of Power, 1964–69; Min. of Technology, 1969–70; DTI, 1970–72. *Address:* Galsworthy House, 177 Kingston Hill, Kingston on Thames, Surrey KT2 7LX.
Died 13 April 2004.

SPENCER, John Loraine, TD; Headmaster, Berkhamsted School, 1972–83; Assistant Director, GAP Activity Projects Ltd, 1985–94; *b* 19 Jan. 1923; *s* of late Arthur Loraine Spencer, OBE, and Emily Maude Spencer, OBE, Woodford Green; *m* 1954, Brenda Elizabeth (*née* Loft); two *s* one *d*. *Educ:* Bancroft's Sch.; Gonville and Caius Coll., Cambridge (MA). 1st cl. hons Class. Tripos Pts I and II. War Service in Essex Regt, 1942–45 (Captain, despatches). Asst Master, Housemaster and Sixth Form Classics Master, Haileybury Coll., 1947–61; Headmaster, Lancaster Royal Grammar Sch., 1961–72. Mem. Chairman's Panel, Civil Service Selection Bds, 1985–90. Pres., Soc. of Schoolmasters, 1985–97. Mem. Council, Lancaster Univ., 1968–72. *Address:* Crofts Close, 7 Aston Road, Haddenham, Bucks HP17 8AF. *T:* (01844) 291235.
Died 31 Dec. 2003.

SPENCER-SILVER, Prof. Peter Hele; S. A. Courtauld Professor of Anatomy in the University of London, at the Middlesex Hospital Medical School, 1974–82, then Emeritus; *b* 29 Oct. 1922; 2nd *s* of late Lt-Col J. H. Spencer Silver; *m* 1948, Patricia Anne, *e d* of late Col J. A. F. Cuffe, CMG, DSO, Wyke Mark, Winchester; two *s* one *d*. *Educ:* Harrow School; Middlesex Hosp. Med. School, Univ. of London (MB, BS 1945); PhD London 1952. MRCS, LRCP. Res., Middlesex Hosp., 1945–46. RAF, 1946–48. Demonstrator in Anatomy, Middlesex Hosp. Med. Sch., 1948–57; Mem. 2nd Internat. Team in Embryology, Hübrecht Laboratory, Utrecht, Netherlands Govt Fellowship, 1956; Reader in Anatomy, Univ. of London, 1957; US Nat. Inst. of Health Post-doctoral Travelling Fellowship, 1961; Carnegie Inst. of Washington, Dept of Embryology, Baltimore, 1961–62; Prof. of Embryology, Mddx Hosp. Medical Sch., 1964–74, Sub-Dean, 1976–81. WHO Vis. Prof., 1976, 1979, 1981; Chm., Dept of Anatomy, King Saud Univ. (Abha Br.), Saudi Arabia, 1984–86. *Publications:* An Introduction to Human Anatomy, 1981; contribs to Jl Embryology and Experimental Morphology, Jl Physiol., Jl Anat., Lancet, etc. *Recreations:* music, George Myers. *Address:* c/o Barclays Bank, Jewry Street, Winchester, Hants SO23 8RG. *Died 27 Dec. 2005.*

SPENCER SMITH, Prof. David, PhD, DPhil; Hope Professor of Zoology/Entomology, University of Oxford, 1980–95; Senior Research Fellow, Jesus College, Oxford, 1995–99, then Emeritus (Fellow, 1980–95); *b* 10 April 1934; *s* of Rev. Harry Chadwick Smith and Mary Edith (*née* Lupton); *m* 1st, 1964, Una Scully; one *d*; 2nd, 1974, Sylvia Hyder. *Educ:* Kingswood Sch.; Cambridge Univ. (BA, MA, PhD); DPhil Oxon 1980. Research Fellow: Rockefeller Univ., NY, 1958–61; St Catharine's Coll., Cambridge, 1961–63 (Res. Fellow); Asst Prof., Univ. of Virginia, 1963–66; Associate Prof. of Medicine and Biology, Univ. of Miami, Fla, 1966–70; Prof. of Medicine, Pharmacology and Biology, Univ. of Miami, 1970–80; engaged in res. on distbn and ecology of butterflies at high altitude in Karakoram, Hunza and Sino-Pakistan border reg., 1994–. Courtesy Prof. of Biol., Fla Internat. Univ., 1995–. Trustee, BM (Natural Hist.), 1984–88. Editor, Tissue & Cell, 1969–94. *Publications:* Insect Cells: their structure and function, 1968; Muscle: a monograph, 1972;

The Butterflies of the West Indies and South Florida, 1994; contrib. Standard Catalog of World Coins, annually, 1983–95; papers and chapters in books and jls. *Recreations:* the coinage of China, early coinage of the Indian subcontinent. *Address:* Jesus College, Oxford OX1 3DW.
Died 22 Oct. 2005.

SPENS, 3rd Baron *cr* 1959, of Blairsanquhar, Fife; **Patrick Michael Rex Spens,** FCA; *b* 22 July 1942; *s* of 2nd Baron Spens and Joan Elizabeth (*d* 1994), *d* of late Reginald Goodall; *S* father, 1984; *m* 1966, Barbara Janet Lindsay, *d* of Rear-Adm. Ralph Lindsay Fisher, CB, DSO, OBE, DSC; one *s* one *d*; one *s* by Mary Elizabeth Hunter Blair (she *d* 2000). *Educ:* Rugby; Corpus Christi Coll., Cambridge (MA). FCA 1967. Director of Morgan Grenfell & Co. Ltd, 1972–82; Man. Dir, Henry Ansbacher & Co. Ltd, 1983–87. Proprietor, Patrick Spens & Co., Chartered Accountants, 1993–. Chm., Patrick Spens & Co. Ltd. *Heir: s* Hon. Patrick Nathaniel George Spens [*b* 14 Oct 1968; *m* 1998, Hon. Philippa Patricia Lennox-Boyd, *yr d* of 2nd Viscount Boyd of Merton; one *s*]. *Address:* Gould, Frittenden, Kent TN17 2DT.
Died 5 Jan. 2001.

SPENS, Colin Hope, CB 1962; FICE, FCIWEM; Chief Engineer, Ministry of Housing and Local Government, 1960–67; *b* 22 May 1906; *er s* of late Archibald Hope Spens, Lathallan, Fife and Hilda Constance Hooper; *m* 1941, Josephine (decd), *d* of late Septimus Simond; two *s* one *d*. *Educ:* Lancing Coll.; Imperial Coll. of Science and Technology. Consulting engrg experience, 1928–39. Served War of 1939–45: Royal Signals, 1939–41; PA to Dir of Works, Min. of Works, 1941–44; Engrg Inspectorate, Min. of Health, 1944–51, Min. of Housing and Local Govt, 1951–60. Sen. Consultant, Rofe, Kennard and Lapworth, 1967–76; Dep. Chm., Sutton District Water Co., 1971–83. Pres., IWES, 1974–75. Hon. FInstPHE. *Address:* Residential Care Home, 20 Saffrons Road, Eastbourne BN21 1DU. *T:* (01323) 638742.
Died 11 March 2003.

SPICER, Clive Colquhoun; retired; Honorary Research Fellow, Exeter University, 1979–91; Director, Medical Research Council Computer Unit, 1967–79; *b* 5 Nov. 1917; *s* of John Bishop Spicer and Marion Isobel Spicer; *m* 1st, 1941, Faith Haughton James, MB (marr. diss. 1979); one *s* two *d*; 2nd, 1979, Anne Nolan. *Educ:* Charterhouse Sch.; Guy's Hospital. Operational research on war casualties, 1941–46; Hon. Sqdn Leader, RAF; Staff, Imperial Cancer Research Fund, 1946–49; Dept of Biometry, University Coll., London, 1946–47; Public Health Laboratory Service, 1949–59; WHO Fellow, Univ. of Wisconsin, 1952–53; Vis. Scientist, US Nat. Insts of Health, 1959–60; Statistician, Imperial Cancer Research Fund, 1960–62; Chief Medical Statistician, General Register Office, 1962–66. Main interest has been in application of mathematical methods to medical problems. *Publications:* papers in scientific journals on epidemiology and medical statistics. *Recreations:* sailing, reading. *Address:* Churchtown, Michaelstow, St Tudy, Bodmin PL30 3PD.
Died 30 March 2004.

SPIEGL, Fritz; musician, writer, broadcaster; *b* 27 Jan. 1926; *s* of Rudolf Spiegl and Josefine Spiegl (*née* Geiringer); *m* 1st, 1952, (Katharine) Bridget Fry (marr. diss. 1970); three *d*; 2nd, 1976, Ingrid Frances Romnes. *Educ:* Magdalen College Sch.; Royal Academy of Music (ARAM; FRAM 1986). Designer/typographer, Colman Prentis & Varley, 1941–46; Principal Flautist, Royal Liverpool Philharmonic, 1948–63 (Hon. Life Mem., 1988); sometime flautist: RPO; CBSO; Hallé; BBC NSO; Founder/Conductor, Liverpool Music Group, Liverpool Wind Ensemble, 1949–; Dir, The Spieglers, 1975–. Founder, Scouse Press, 1965. Columnist: Liverpool Daily Post, 1970–; Classical Music, 1979–81; Classic CD, 1990–92; Wordplay/Usage and Abusage columns, Daily Telegraph, 1989–97; contributor to: Guardian; Oldie; Independent; BBC Music Magazine, 1994–. Broadcaster in various capacities for BBC: Start the Week, 1972–80;

Up to the Hour, 1977–78; Words, 1978; A–Z of Musical Curios, 1978–79; Fritz on Friday, 1978–80; Mainly for Pleasure, 1982–92; Wives of the Great Composers, 1985–86; Loves of the Great Composers, 1986–87; Inflight music programmes, Swissair, Cathay Pacific, 1988–98; Lectr, Swan Hellenic and Noble Caledonia cruises. *Quondam* question-setter, University Challenge. Mem., Local Radio Adv. Council, 1997–2000. Pres., Merseyside Music Teachers' Assoc., 1991–. *Publications:* various edns of music; What the Papers Didn't Mean to Say, 1964; Lern Yerself Scouse, 1965; The Black-on-White Misprint Show, 1966; ABZ of Scouse, 1967; The Growth of a City, 1967; Liverpool Ballads, 1967; The Liverpool Manchester Railway, 1970; Slavers and Privateers, 1970; A Small Book of Grave Humour, 1971; Dead Funny, 1982; Keep Taking the Tabloids, 1983; Music Through the Looking-Glass, 1984; The Joy of Words, 1986; Fritz Spiegl's In-words & Out-words, 1987; Mediaspeak/Mediawrite, 1989; Scally Scouse, 1989; Sing the Titanic, 1993; Sick Notes: a hypochondriacs' dictionary, 1995; Lives, Wives and Loves of the Composers, 1995; Robson Book of Musical Blunders, 1996; A Game of Two Halves, Brian: the language of soccer, 1996; Scouse International, 2001; MuSick Notes: a medical songbook, 2001; contrib. Grove's Dictionary of Music, New Grove Dictionary of Opera. *Recreations:* printing, cooking, inventing and several deadly sins. *Address:* 4 Windermere Terrace, Liverpool L8 3SB. *T:* (0151) 727 2727, *Fax:* (0151) 727 7272; *e-mail:* fritz@scousepress.demon.co.uk. *Clubs:* Garrick; Athenæum (Liverpool). *Died 23 March 2003.*

SPOTSWOOD, Marshal of the Royal Air Force Sir Denis (Frank), GCB 1971 (KCB 1966; CB 1961); CBE 1946; DSO 1943; DFC 1942; *b* 26 Sept. 1916; *s* of late F. H. Spotswood and M. C. Spotswood; *m* 1942, Ann (*née* Child); one *s*. Commissioned in RAF, 1936; UK Service in Squadrons, 1937–41; No 209 Squadron, 1939–41. Served War of 1939–45 (despatches twice, DSO). Chief Instructor, Operation Training Unit, 1941–42; Officer Commanding No 500 (County of Kent) Squadron, RAuxAF, 1942–43; Director of Plans, HQ Supreme Allied Commander, South-East Asia, 1944–46; Directing Staff, RAF Staff Coll., 1946–48; Officer Commanding RAF (Fighter) Stations, Horsham St Faith and Coltishall, 1948–50; Directing Staff, Imperial Defence Coll., 1950–52; Exchange Duties, HQUSAF in USA, 1952–54; Officer Commanding RAF (Fighter) Station, Linton-on-Ouse, 1954–56; Deputy Director of Plans, Air Ministry, 1956–58; AOC and Commandant, RAF Coll., Cranwell, 1958–61; Assistant Chief of Staff (Air Defence), SHAPE, 1961–63; AOC No 3 Group, RAF Bomber Command, 1964–65; C-in-C RAF Germany, 1965–68; Commander, 2nd Allied Tactical Air Force, 1966–68; AOC-in-C, RAF Strike Command, 1968–71; Comdr, UK Air Defence Region, 1968–71; Chief of the Air Staff, 1971–74. Group Captain, 1954; Air Commodore, 1958; Air Vice-Marshal, 1961; Air Marshal, 1965; Air Chief Marshal, 1968; Marshal of the RAF, 1974. ADC to the Queen, 1957–61, Air ADC to the Queen, 1970–74. Vice-Chm. and Dir, Rolls Royce Ltd, 1974–80; Chm., Turbo Union Ltd, 1975–80; Director: RR/Turbomeca Ltd; Dowty Gp, 1980–87; Smiths Industries ADS, 1980–91 (Chm., 1980–82). Pres., SBAC, 1978–79. Chm. of Governors, Royal Star and Garter Home, 1981–85 (Gov., 1974–80); Vice-Patron, RAF Museum (Chm. of Trustees, 1974–80). FRAeS 1975. Officer of the Legion of Merit (USA). *Recreations:* golf, sailing, bridge. *Address:* Coombe Cottage, Hambleden, Henley-on-Thames, Oxon RG9 6SD. *Clubs:* Royal Air Force; Phyllis Court (Henley); Huntercombe Golf. *Died 11 Nov. 2001.*

SPURRIER, Peter Brotherton; design consultant; Design Director, Maritime Insignia Ltd, since 1995; *b* 9 Aug. 1942; *s* of Eric Jack Spurrier, MBE and late Frances Mary (*née* Brotherton); *m* 1973, Hon. Elizabeth Jane Maude, *d* of Baron Maude of Stratford-upon-Avon, TD, PC; two *s* one *d*. *Educ:* Chetham's Hosp. Sch., Manchester;

Manchester Coll. of Art and Design (NDD 1965). MSIAD 1980. Designer for Wade Heath Pottery, Burslem, 1965–66; Asst Design Officer, DoE, 1966–71 (on design team for Investiture of HRH Prince of Wales, 1969); Dir, Dromas Design Ltd, 1971–79; Principal Designer, Idiom Design Ltd, 1979–81; Portcullis Pursuivant of Arms, 1981–93; York Herald of Arms, 1993. Packaging co-ordn and planning advr, human fungal foodstuffs div., The French Garden Ltd, 1995–; Dep. Sen. Asst wall-furniture presentation consultant, Wall Game Ltd, 1996–; heraldic adviser, Burke's Peerage, 1996–. Hon. Asst Curator, Heralds' Mus. at Tower of London, 1981–83. Mem. Council, Heraldry Soc., 1981–90; Chm., Soc. of Heraldic Arts, 1991–. FRSA. Freeman, City of London, 1980; Freeman and Liveryman, Painter Stainers' Co., 1985. OStJ 1990. *Publication:* The Heraldic Art Source Book, 1997. *Recreations:* painting, music, fishing. *Address:* 6 Wroughton Road, SW11 6BG; 23 School Hill, Storrington, W Sussex RH20 4NA. *Died 13 Jan. 2005.*

SQUIRE, Raglan, FRIBA, MSIA; Consultant, Raglan Squire & Partners, Architects, Engineers and Town Planners, since 1981 (Senior Partner, 1948–81); *b* 30 Jan. 1912; *e s* of Sir John (Collings) Squire; *m* 1st, 1938, Rachel (*d* 1968), *d* of James Atkey, Oxshott, Surrey; two *s*; 2nd, 1968, Bridget Lawless (*d* 1997); 3rd, 1997, Mrs Mabel Elizabeth Stone, (Mrs M. E. Stone-Squire). *Educ:* Blundell's; St John's Coll., Cambridge. Started private practice in London, 1935. War service with Royal Engineers, 1942–45. Founded firm of Raglan Squire & Partners, 1948; principal projects: housing, educational and industrial work, 1935–41; pre-fabricated bldgs and industrial design, 1945–48; Eaton Sq. Conversion Scheme, 1945–56; Rangoon Univ. Engineering Coll., 1953–56; Associated Architect, Transport Pavilion, Festival of Britain Exhib., 1951; Town Planning Scheme for Mosul, Iraq, 1955; Bagdad airport report, 1955; factories at Weybridge, Huddersfield, etc; office buildings London, Eastbourne, Bournemouth, etc; gen. practice at home and over-seas incl. major hotels at Teheran, Tunis, Nicosia, Malta and Singapore, Gibraltar, Caribbean and Middle East, 1955–81, retired from active practice. Sec. RIBA Reconstruction Cttee, 1941–42; Council of Architectural Assoc., 1951–52; Guest Editor Architects' Journal, 1947. *Publications:* Portrait of an Architect (autobiog.), 1985; articles in technical press on organisation of Building Industry, Architectural Education, etc. *Recreations:* gardening, chess, ocean racing and designing small yachts. *Address:* c/o Raglan Squire & Partners, The Ivories, Northampton Street, N1 2HY. *T:* (020) 7359 8373; 10 Rochester Gardens, Hove BN3 3AW. *Clubs:* Royal Thames Yacht, Royal Ocean Racing; Royal Southern Yacht. *Died 18 May 2004.*

STABB, His Honour Sir William (Walter), Kt 1981; QC 1968; FCIArb; a Circuit Judge (formerly Official Referee, Supreme Court of Judicature), 1969–78; Senior Official Referee, 1978–85; *b* 6 Oct. 1913; 2nd *s* of late Sir Newton Stabb, OBE and Lady E. M. Stabb; *m* 1940, Dorothy Margaret Leckie (*d* 1999); four *d*. *Educ:* Rugby; University Coll., Oxford. Called to the Bar, 1936; Master of the Bench, Inner Temple, 1964, Treasurer, 1985. Served with RAF, 1940–46, attaining rank of Sqdn Ldr. Junior Counsel to Ministry of Labour, 1960; Prosecuting Counsel to BoT, 1962–68. Dep. Chm. 1961–69, Chm. 1969–71, Bedfordshire QS. *Recreations:* fishing, golf. *Died 19 Dec. 2003.*

STACEY, Air Vice-Marshal John Nichol, CBE 1971; DSO 1945; DFC 1942; *b* 14 Sept. 1920; *s* of Captain Herbert Chambers Stacey and Mrs May Stacey; *m* 1950, Veronica, *d* of late Sinclair Sutherland Rudd-Clarke; two *d*. *Educ:* Whitgift Middle Sch., Croydon. Merchant Marine Apprentice, 1937–38; joined RAF, 1938; flying throughout War of 1939–45 (despatches thrice); comd No 160 Sqdn, 1944–45; Asst Air Attaché, Washington, 1947–48; psc 1949; on staff at Staff Coll., 1958–60; Chief of Air Staff, Royal Malayan Air Force, 1960–63 (JMN);

comd RAF Laarbruch, Germany, 1963–66; AOC, Air Cadets, 1968–71; Dir, Orgn and Admin. Planning (RAF), MoD, 1971–74; AOA, Support Comd, 1974–75, retired. Dir, Stonham Housing Assoc., 1976–81; Member: Tunbridge Wells HA, 1981–86; RAFA Housing Assoc., 1982–86; High Weald Housing Assoc., 1990– (Chm., 1992–96; Pres., 1998–). President: Royal British Legion Gondhurst Br., 1991–; Headcorn Br., RAFA; Trustee: Housing Assoc. Charitable Trust, 1978–86; Bedgebury Sch., 1983– (Vice Pres., 1999–). *Recreations:* sailing, golf. *Address:* Riseden Cottage, Riseden, Goudhurst, Cranbrook, Kent TN17 1HJ. *T:* (01580) 211239. *Clubs:* Royal Air Force; Dale Hill Golf. *Died 25 Dec. 2003.*

STACEY, Prof. Margaret; Professor of Sociology, University of Warwick, 1974–89, Emerita Professor, 1989; *b* 27 March 1922; *d* of Conrad Eugene Petrie and Grace Priscilla Boyce; *m* 1945, Frank Arthur Stacey (*d* 1977); three *s* two *d*. *Educ:* City of London Sch. for Girls; London Sch. of Econs (BScEcon, 1st Cl. Hons Sociology). Labour Officer, Royal Ordnance Factory, 1943–44; Tutor, Oxford Univ., 1944–51; University Coll. of Swansea: Res. Officer and Fellow, 1961–63; Lectr in Sociol., 1963–70; Sen. Lectr in Sociol., 1970–74; Dir, Medical Sociol. Res. Centre, 1972–74. Lucille Petry Loene Vis. Prof. Univ. of Calif., San Francisco, 1988. British Sociological Association: Mem. Exec. Cttee, 1965–70, 1975–79; Hon. Gen. Sec., 1968–70; Chairperson, 1977–79; Pres., 1981–83; Mem. Women's Caucus, 1974–. Pres., Section N, BAAS, 1990. Scientific Advr to DHSS; Temp. Advr to Reg. Dir, WHO EURO. Pres., Assoc. for Welfare of Children in Hosp. (Wales), 1974–; Member: Assoc. for Welfare of Children in Hosp., 1960–; Welsh Hosp. Bd, 1970–74; Davies Cttee on Hosp. Complaints Procedure, 1971–73; GMC, 1976–84; Sociol. Cttee, SSRC, 1969–71; Health and Health Policy Cttee, SSRC, 1976–77. FRSocMed. Hon. Fellow, UC of Swansea, 1987. Hon. LLD Keele, 1998. *Publications:* Tradition and Change: a study of Banbury, 1960, paperback 1970; (ed) Comparability in Social Research, 1969; (ed and jt author) Hospitals, Children and their Families: a study of the welfare of children in hospital, 1970; Methods of Social Research, 1970; (jtly) Power, Persistence and Change: a second study of Banbury, 1975; (ed) The Sociology of the NHS, 1976; (ed jtly and contrib.) Beyond Separation: further studies of children in hospital, 1979; (jtly) Women, Power and Politics, 1981 (Fawcett Book Prize, 1982); (ed jtly) Concepts of Health, Illness and Disease: a comparative perspective, 1986; Sociology of Health and Healing: a textbook, 1988; Regulating British Medicine: the General Medical Council, 1992; (ed) Changing Human Reproduction: social science perspectives, 1992; contrib. to Feminist Rev., Sociol Rev., Sociol., Brit. Jl of Sociol., Sociol Science and Med., Jl of Med. Ethics, and Sociol. of Health and Illness. *Recreations:* walking, gardening. *Address:* 47 Newbold Terrace East, Leamington Spa, Warwicks CV32 4EZ. *T:* (01926) 312094. *Died 10 Feb. 2004.*

STAFFORD, John, OBE 1977; HM Diplomatic Service, retired; *b* 15 June 1920; *s* of late Frank and Gertrude Stafford, Sheffield; *m* 1949, Mary Jocelyn Goodwin, *d* of late Capt. J. G. Budge, RN. *Educ:* High Storrs Grammar Sch. Exchequer and Audit Dept, 1939. RAF, W/O Pilot, 1940. Board of Trade, 1946; Assistant Trade Commissioner, Delhi, Karachi, Bulawayo, 1946–56; Trade Commissioner, Karachi, Lahore, Bombay, Madras, Lahore, 1956–65; Dep. High Comr, Lahore, 1965–69; Consul, Houston, Texas, 1969–71; First Sec. (Commercial), New Delhi, 1974–77; Consul Gen., Brisbane, 1978–80. *Recreations:* cricket, tennis, theatre, music. *Address:* Leacroft, 268 Brooklands Road, Weybridge, Surrey KT13 0QX. *Clubs:* East India, Devonshire, Sports and Public Schools; Royal Bombay Yacht; Punjab (Lahore). *Died 16 Feb. 2001.*

STAGG, Prof. Geoffrey Leonard, MBE 1945; Professor Emeritus, Department of Spanish and Portuguese,

University of Toronto; *b* 10 May 1913; *s* of Henry Percy Stagg and Maude Emily Bradbury; *m* 1948, Amy Southwell (decd), Wellesley Hills, Mass, USA; two *s* one *d*. *Educ*: King Edward's School, Birmingham (Scholar); Trinity Hall, Cambridge (Scholar; BA 1st cl. Hons Modern and Medieval Languages Tripos, 1934; MA 1946); Harvard Univ. (Joseph Hodges Choate Meml Fellow, 1934–36; AM 1935). Modern Languages Master, King Edward's School, Birmingham, 1938–40, 1946–47; served in Intelligence Corps, 1940–46, Allied Commn for Austria, 1945–46; Lecturer in Spanish and Italian, Nottingham Univ., 1947–53, and Head of Dept of Spanish, 1954–56; Prof., 1956–78, Chm., 1956–66, 1969–78, Dept of Italian and Hispanic Studies, Toronto Univ. Fellow, New Coll., Univ. of Toronto, 1962–; Senior Fellow, Massey Coll., Univ. of Toronto, 1965–70; Canada Council Senior Fellowship, 1967–68. Vice-Pres., Assoc. of Teachers of Spanish and Portuguese of GB and Ireland, 1948–; Pres., Canadian Assoc. of Hispanists, 1964–66, 1972–74; Vice-Pres., Internat. Assoc. of Hispanists, 1977–83; Chm., Local Organising Cttee, Sixth Congress of Internat. Assoc. of Hispanists, Toronto, 1977. *Publications*: articles in learned jls on Spanish and Italian literature, Romance Prosody and European folklore; *festschrift*: Ingeniosa Invención: essays on Golden Age Spanish literature, ed E. M. Anderson and A. R. Williamsen, 1999. *Address*: 30 Old Bridle Path, Toronto, ON M4T 1A7, Canada. *Died 10 Nov. 2004.*

STAINFORTH, Maj.-Gen. Charles Herbert, CB 1969; OBE 1955; Head of UK Future Command Structure, Ministry of Defence, 1969–72; *b* 12 Dec. 1914; *s* of Lt-Col Herbert Graham Stainforth, CMG, 4th Cavalry, IA, and Georgina Helen, *d* of Maj.-Gen. H. Pipon, CB; *m* 1942, Elizabeth (*d* 1997), *d* of late John Tait Easdale; one *s* one *d*. *Educ*: Wellington Coll.; RMC, Sandhurst. Commnd into 2nd Royal Lancers, IA; transferred British Army, 1947; Chief of Staff, Southern Comd, 1965–66; GOC Aldershot District and SE Dist, 1966–69. Col Comdt, RCT, 1970–72. Chm. Combined Cadet Forces, 1970–72. Consultant to Nat. Tourist Bds, 1973–75. Editor, Army Quarterly and Defence Journal, 1974–84. *Address*: Beeches, Paice Lane, Medstead, Alton, Hants GU34 5PT. *Died 22 March 2001.*

STAINTON, Keith Monin; *b* 8 Nov. 1921; *m* 1946, Vanessa Ann Heald (marr. diss. 1978); three *s* three *d*; *m* 1980, Frances Easton. *Educ*: Kendal Sch.; Manchester Univ. (BA (Com.) dist. in Economics). Insurance clerk, 1936–39. Served War of 1939–45: Lieut, RNVR, Submarines and with French Resistance, 1940–46. Manchester Univ., 1946–49; Leader Writer, Financial Times, 1949–52; Industrial Consultant, 1952–57; joined Burton, Son & Sanders, Ltd, 1957, Man. Dir 1961–69, Chm. 1962–69; Chm. Scotia Investments Ltd, 1969–72. MP (C) Sudbury and Woodbridge, Dec. 1963–1983; Mem., House of Commons Select Cttees on Expenditure and Science and Technology. Mem. Council of Europe and WEU, 1979–83. Légion d'Honneur, Croix de Guerre avec Palmes, Ordre de l'Armée, 1943. *Address*: Little Bealings House, near Woodbridge, Suffolk IP13 6LX. *T*: (01473) 624205. *Died 3 Nov. 2001.*

STAKIS, Sir Reo (Argyros), Kt 1988; Founder, and Chairman, 1947–91, President, 1966–99, Stakis plc; *b* 13 March 1913; *né* Argyros Anastasis; *s* of Anastasis and Katerina Stakis; *m* 1946, Annitsa Petropoulos; two *s* four *d*. *Educ*: American Acad., Larnaca. Stakis plc included hotels and casinos, and formerly also restaurants, public houses and nursing homes. Hon. Comr for Cyprus at Glasgow, 1968–. Hon. LLD Strathclyde, 1986; Hon. DA Napier, 1991. *Recreations*: shooting, fishing. *Address*: Grant House, Dunblane, Perthshire FK15 0HG.

Died 28 Aug. 2001.

STAMM, Temple Theodore, FRCS; Orthopædic Surgeon Emeritus, Guy's Hospital; *b* 22 Dec. 1905; *s* of Dr Louis Edward Stamm, Streatham, and Louisa Ethel (*née* Perry), Caterham, Surrey; *m* 1945, Pamela (*d* 1998), *d* of

Charles Russell, Chislehurst, Kent. *Educ*: Rose Hill Sch., Surrey; Haileybury Coll.; Guy's Hospital Medical School (MB, BS London 1930). MRCS, LRCP 1928, FRCS 1934. Orthopædic Surgeon, Bromley Hospital, 1941–66; formerly: Asst Orthopædic Surgeon and Orthopædic Registrar, Royal Nat. Orthopædic Hospital; Asst Orthopædic Surgeon, Orthopædic Registrar, Asst Anæsthetist and Demonstrator of Anatomy, Guy's Hospital. Major RAMC. Mem., BMA. FRSocMed; Fellow, British Orthopaedic Assoc. *Publications*: Foot Troubles, 1957; Guide to Orthopædics, 1958; Surgery of the Foot, British Surgical Practice, Vol. 4; contributions to Blackburn and Lawrie's Textbook of Surgery, 1958; articles in: Lancet, Guy's Hospital Reports, Journal of Bone and Joint Surgery, Medical Press, etc. *Recreations*: farming, sailing, music. *Address*: Little Badgers, 6 The Spinney, Itchenor, W Sussex PO20 7DF.

Died 18 Oct. 2001.

STAMPER, John Trevor, MA; FREng, Hon. FRAeS; Corporate Technical Director, British Aerospace, 1977–85, retired; *b* 12 Oct. 1926; *s* of late Col Horace John Stamper and Clara Jane (*née* Collin); *m* 1950, Cynthia Joan Parsons; two *s* one *d*. *Educ*: Loughborough Grammar Sch.; Jesus Coll., Cambridge (MA 1951). FRAeS 1965 (Hon. FRAeS 1984); CEng 1966; FREng (FEng 1977). Blackburn Aircraft Ltd: Post-grad. apprenticeship, 1947; Dep. Head of Aerodynamics, 1955; Head of Structures, 1956; Flight Test Manager, 1960; Chief Designer (Buccaneer), 1961; Dir and Chief Designer, 1963; Hawker Siddeley Aviation Ltd (following merger): Exec. Dir Design (Military), 1966; Exec. Dir and Dep. Chief Engr (Civil), 1968; Tech. Dir, 1968–77. Member: Council, RAeS, 1971–77, 1978–88 (Pres., 1981–82); Tech. Bd, SBAC, 1966–85 (Chm., 1972–74); Council, SBAC, 1981–84; Council, Aircraft Res. Assoc., 1966–85 (Chm., 1976–78); Aeronautical Res. Council, 1971–74; Air Warfare Adv. Bd, Defence Scientific Adv. Council, 1973–84; Noise Adv. Council, 1975–78; Comité Technique et Industriel, Assoc. Européenne des Constructeurs de Matériel Aerospatial, 1971–81 (Chm., 1974–81); Airworthiness Requirements Bd, CAA, 1976–78, 1987–88. CCMI (CBIM 1983). Hon. DSc Loughborough, 1986. Hodgeson Prize, RAeS, 1975 and 1986; British Gold Medal for Aeronautics, RAeS, 1976. *Publications*: (contrib.) The Future of Aeronautics, 1970; Air Power in the Next Generation, 1979; papers in Jl RAeS. *Recreations*: sailing, photography. *Address*: 7 Sycamore Close, The Mount, Fetcham, Surrey KT22 9EX. *T*: (01372) 370336. *Died 15 Nov. 2003.*

STANBRIDGE, Air Vice-Marshal Sir Brian (Gerald Tivy), KCVO 1979 (MVO 1958); CBE 1974; AFC 1952; Director-General, Air Transport Users' Committee, 1979–85; *b* 6 July 1924; *s* of late Gerald Edward and Violet Georgina Stanbridge; *m* 1st, 1949, Kathleen Diana Hayes (marr. diss. 1983); two *d*; 2nd, 1984, Jennifer Anne Jenkins. *Educ*: Thurlestone Coll., Dartmouth. Served War: RAFVR, 1942; commnd, 1944; No 31 Sqdn (SE Asia), 1944–46; No 47 Sqdn, 1947–49; 2FTS/CFS, 1950–52; British Services Mission to Burma, 1952–54; The Queen's Flight (personal pilot and flying instructor to Duke of Edinburgh), 1954–58; Naval Staff Coll., 1958; PSO to AOC-in-C Coastal Comd, 1958–59; W/Cdr, Flying, RAF St Mawgan, 1960–62; jssc, 1962; RAFDS, Army Staff Coll., Camberley, 1962–63; Gp Captain on staff of NATO Standing Gp, Washington, DC, 1963–66; RAF Dir, Jt Anti-Submarine Sch., Londonderry, and Sen. RAF Officer, NI, 1966–68; Gp Captain Ops, HQ Coastal Comd, 1968–70; IDC, 1970; Air Cdre, 1970; Sec., Chiefs of Staff Cttee, MoD, 1971–73; Dep. Comdt, RAF Staff Coll., Bracknell, 1973–75; ADC to the Queen, 1973–75; Air Vice-Marshal, 1975; Defence Services Sec. to the Queen, 1975–79; retired 1979. Pres., No 31 Sqdn Assoc., 1992–2002. *Address*: 20 Durrant Way, Sway, Lymington, Hants SO41 6DQ. *Club*: Royal Air Force.

Died 12 Feb. 2003.

STANBROOK, Ivor Robert; b 13 Jan. 1924; y s of Arthur William and Lilian Stanbrook; m 1946, Joan (née Clement) (d 2000); two s. Educ: state schools; Univs of London (BSc (Econ) 1948), Oxford and East Anglia (PhD 1995). Served RAF, 1942–46. Colonial Administrative Service, Nigeria, 1950–60: Asst Sec., Council of Ministers, Lagos, 1956; Dist Officer, N Region, 1957–60. Called to the Bar, Inner Temple, 1960; practising barrister, 1960–90. Contested (C) East Ham, South, 1966. MP (C) Orpington, 1970–92. Chairman: All Party gps on Nigeria, 1979–92, Zambia, 1985–92, Southern Africa, 1987–92; Cons. parly cttees on constitutional affairs, 1985–92, on Northern Ireland, 1989–92; Mem., Select Cttee on Home Affairs, 1983–91. Founded Britain-Nigeria Assoc., 1961. Publications: Extradition—the Law and Practice, 1979, 2nd edn 1999; British Nationality—the New Law, 1981; A Year in Politics, 1988; How to be an MP, 1993. Recreations: music, books. Club: Royal Commonwealth Society.

Died 18 Feb. 2004.

STANDARD, Prof. Sir Kenneth (Livingstone), Kt 1982; CD 1976; MD, MPH; FFPH; Professor, 1968, and Head of Department of Social and Preventive Medicine, 1966–89, University of the West Indies at Mona; Emeritus Professor, University of the West Indies; b 8 Dec. 1920; m 1955, Evelyn Francis; one d. Educ: UC of West Indies (MB BS); Univ. of Pittsburgh (MPH); Univ. of London (MD). FFPH (FFCM 1972). Schoolmaster, Lynch's Secondary Sch., Barbados, 1940–48 (Headmaster, 1948); Med. House Officer, UCH of WI, 1956; MO, Nutrition Res., Jamaica, 1957–58; MOH, Barbados, 1958–61; MO, MRC Epidemiol. Res. Unit, Jamaica, 1961–66; Lectr, 1961–65, Sen. Lectr, 1965–68, Dept of Social and Preventive Medicine, Univ. of WI, Jamaica. Adjunct Prof. of Public Health, Grad. Sch. Public Health, Univ. of Pittsburgh, 1972–75; Stubenord Vis. Prof., Cornell Univ. Med. Coll., USA, 1975–. Thomas Parran Lecture, Grad. Sch. of Public Health, Univ. of Pittsburgh, 1984. Member: WHO Adv. Cttee on Med. Res., 1969–72; WHO Expert Adv. Panel on Public Health Admin, 1969–. Foundn Pres., Caribbean Public Health Assoc., 1988–92. Fellow, Caribbean Coll. of Family Physicians, 1988. Fellowship, 1980, Medal, 1981, Jacques Parisot Foundn, WHO; Abraham Horwitz Award, Pan American Health and Educn Foundn, 1988; Health for All Medal, WHO, 1988; Medical Alumni Pioneer Award, Univ. of WI, 1988. Publications: (ed jtly) Manual for Community Health Workers, 1974, rev. edn 1983; Epidemiology and Community Health in Warm Climate Countries, 1976; Alternatives in the Delivery of Health Services, 1976; Four Decades of Advances in Health in the Commonwealth Caribbean, 1979. Recreations: reading, poetry, gardening. Address: Department of Social and Preventive Medicine, University of the West Indies, Mona, Kingston 7, Jamaica. T: 9272476. Club: Royal Commonwealth Society.   Died 2 Aug. 2004.

STANFIELD, Rt Hon. Robert Lorne; PC (Canada) 1967; QC; Chairman, Institute for Research on Public Policy, 1981–86; b Truro, NS, 11 April 1914; s of late Frank Stanfield, sometime MLA and Lieutenant-Governor of NS, and Sarah (née Thomas); m 1st, 1940, N. Joyce (d 1954), d of C. W. Frazee, Vancouver; one s three d; 2nd, 1957, Mary Margaret (d 1977), d of late Hon. W. L. Hall, Judge of Supreme Court and formerly Attorney-Gen. of NS; 3rd, 1978, Anne Margaret Austin, d of Dr D. Nelson, Henderson, Toronto. Educ: Colchester County Academy, Truro; Ashbury Coll., Ottawa; Dalhousie Univ.; Harvard Law Sch. Southam Cup, Ashbury Coll.; BA Political Science and Economics 1936, Governor-General's Gold Medal, Dalhousie Univ.; LLB Harvard, 1939. War of 1939–45: attached Halifax Office of Wartime Prices and Trade Bd as Regional Rentals Officer, later as Enforcement Counsel. Admitted Bar of NS, 1940. Practised law, McInnes and Stanfield, Halifax, 1945–56; KC 1950. President, Nova Scotia Progressive Cons. Assoc., 1947–48; Leader, Nova Scotia Progressive Cons. Party, 1948–67; elected to Legislature of NS, 1949, Mem.

for Colchester Co.; re-elected Mem., 1953, 1960, 1963, 1967; Premier and Minister of Education, NS, 1956; resigned as Premier of NS, 1967; MP (Progressive C): Colchester-Hants, NS, 1967–68; Halifax, NS, 1968–79; Leader, Progressive Cons. Party of Canada, and of Opposition in House of Commons, 1967–74. Ambassador at Large and special representative of Govt of Canada in Middle East, 1979–80. Dir, Canada Life. Chm., Commonwealth Foundn. Hon. LLD: University of New Brunswick, 1958; St Dunstan's Univ., PEI, 1964; McGill Univ., PQ, 1967; St Mary's Univ., NS, 1969; Dalhousie, 1982; Université Sainte-Anne, NS, Acadia Univ., NS, and Univ. of Toronto, 1987; Mount Allison Univ., 1990. Anglican. Address: 136 Acacia Avenue, Rockcliffe Park, Ottawa, ON K1M 0R1, Canada.

Died 16 Dec. 2003.

STANLEY, Peter Ian, CBE 2001; PhD; consultant on food, agriculture and environment; Chief Executive, Central Science Laboratory Agency, 1992–2001; b 25 June 1946; m Judy; two s one d. Educ: University College London (PhD 1972). MAF, subseq. MAFF, 1970–2001. Address: Century House, Settrington, N Yorks YO17 8NP.   Died 28 Oct. 2003.

STANYER, Maj.-Gen. John Turner, CBE 1971 (OBE 1967); b 28 July 1920; s of late Charles T. Stanyer and late Mrs R. H. Stanyer; m 1942, Mary Patricia Pattie; three s four d. Educ: Latymer Upper Sch., Hammersmith. Served War, 2/Lieut The Middlesex Regt, 1941; Lieut to Captain, The Middlesex Regt, 1941–47: Iceland, France, Germany, Palestine. Captain, Royal Army Ordnance Corps, 1947; Student, Staff Coll., Camberley, 1951; AA&QMG, UN Force in Cyprus, 1966; Dir of Ordnance Services, BAOR, 1968–71; Commandant, Central Ordnance Depot, Bicester, 1971–73; Comdr, Base Orgn, RAOC, 1973–75, retired. Col Comdt, RAOC, 1977–82. Dir Gen., Supply Co-ordination, MoD, 1975–80. Mem., Oxford City Council, 1983–87. Recreation: sailing. Address: 1 Dukes Road, Lindfield, W Sussex RH16 2JH.

Died 14 May 2005.

STAPLES, Rev. Canon Edward Eric, CBE 1977 (OBE 1973); Chaplain to the Queen, 1973–80; Chaplain to the Anglican congregations in Helsinki and throughout Finland, in Moscow, Leningrad and elsewhere in the Soviet Union, and in Outer Mongolia, 1964–80; Hon. Chaplain, British Embassy: Helsinki, 1967–80, Moscow, 1968–80, Ulan Bator, 1970–81; b 15 Nov. 1910; yr s of Christopher Walter Staples and Esther Jane Staples; m 1962, Kate Ethel Thusberg (née Rönngren); two step d. Educ: Chichester Theol Coll. (earlier opportunities so misused that it is unwise to name the establishments concerned!); MA, PhD. Niger Company, 1932. Served with RNVR, 1939–46. Ordained deacon, 1948, priest, 1949; Curate, Holy Trinity, Wallington, 1948–51; Domestic Chaplain to Bp of Portsmouth, 1951–55; Vicar of Shedfield, 1955–64. Hon. Canon, Gibraltar Cathedral, 1974–. Hon. Lectr in Eng. Hist., Univ. of Helsinki, 1972–80. Assistant of Court of Russia Company, 1977–89, Consul, 1978–88. Life Mem., Finnish-British Soc.; Mem., Anglo-Mongolian Soc. Medal of Univ. of Helsinki, 1980. Kt, Order of the Lion (Finland), 1976; Order of St Vladimir (Russian Orthodox Church), 1977. Recreations: climbing, cricket, fishing, gardening (no longer actively), historical research. Address: The Old Farmhouse, Ramsbury, Marlborough, Wilts SN8 2PG. T: (01672) 521118. Clubs: MCC; Helsinki Cricket (Founder Mem.); Moscow Cricket (Founder Mem.); Ulan Bator Golf (Hon. Life Mem.).   Died 2 Sept. 2002.

STASSEN, Harold Edward; lawyer, executive, politician, educator, United States; Chairman, International Law Committee of Philadelphia Bar Association, 1973; b W St Paul, Minn, 13 April 1907; s of William Andrew Stassen and Elsie Emma Mueller; m 1929, Esther G. Glewwe, artist (d 2000); one s one d. Educ: Univ. of Minnesota Coll. (BA 1927; LLB 1929); Law School. Admitted to Minnesota Bar, 1929; practised South St Paul; County Attorney,

Dakota County, 1930–38; thrice elected Governor of Minnesota, 1939–43; resigned for service with Navy; Lt Comdr, USN; Comdr on staff of Admiral Halsey in Pacific, 1943–45; Asst Chief of Staff, 1944; Capt., USNR; released to inactive duty, 1945. One of US delegates to San Francisco Conference, drafting and signing UN Charter, 1945. Pres., Minnesota Young Republicans; Delegate to Republican Convention, 1936; Temporary Chairman and Keynoter of Republican National Convention and floor manager for Wendell Wilkie, 1940; twice elected National Chairman National Governors' Conference, and of Council of State Governments, 1940–41. Candidate for Republican nomination for President of US, 1948. Director, Foreign Operations Admin, 1953–55; Special Assistant to the President for Disarmament, 1955–58; Dep. US Rep. on Disarmament Commn, UN, 1955–58; Mem., Nat. Security Council, 1953–58; Partner in law firm Stassen, Kephart, Sarkis and Scullin, later Stassen, Kostos and Mason, 1958–91. Chm., Constitutional Law Cttee, Amer. Bar. Assoc., 1950–51. President, International Council of Religious Education, 1942, 1950; Vice-Pres. and a Founder, Nat. Council of Churches, 1951–52; President, Div. of Christian Educn, Nat. Council of Churches, 1953. Pres., Univ. of Pennsylvania, 1948–53; Chief Consultant, Middle East Technical Univ., Ankara, 1958. Mem., Horatio Alger Assoc., 1981. Delivered Godkind Lectures on Human Rights, Harvard Univ., 1946. Chm., World Law Day, Geneva, 1968. Several hon. degrees. Stassen Center for World Peace, Univ. of Minnesota, 1993. Adlai Stevenson World Peace Award, 1989. Bronze Star, 1944; Legion of Merit, Six Battle Stars (Western Pacific campaign), 1945. Baptist. Mason. *Publications:* Where I Stand, 1947; Man was meant to be Free, 1951; (jtly) Eisenhower: turning the world toward peace, 1991; United Nations: a working paper for restructuring in its 50th year 1995, 1993. *Address:* 310 Salem Church Road, Sunfish Lake, MN 55118, USA.
Died 4 March 2001.

STATHAM, Sir Norman, KCMG 1977 (CMG 1967); CVO 1968; HM Diplomatic Service, retired; *b* Stretford, Lancs, 15 Aug. 1922; *s* of Frederick William and Maud Statham; *m* 1948, Hedwig Gerlich; one *s* one *d* (and one *s* decd). *Educ:* Seymour Park Council School, Stretford; Manchester Grammar School; Gonville and Caius College, Cambridge (MA). Intelligence Corps, 1943–47; Manchester Oil Refinery Ltd and Petrochemicals Ltd, 1948–50; Foreign Service, 1951: Foreign Office, 1951; Consul (Commercial), New York, 1954; First Secretary (Commercial), Bonn, 1958; Administrative Staff College, Henley, 1963; Foreign Office, 1964; Counsellor, Head of European Economic Integration Dept, 1965–68, 1970–71; Consul-General, São Paulo, 1968–70; Minister (Economic), Bonn, 1971; Asst Under Sec. of State, FCO, 1975; Dep. Under Sec. of State, FCO, 1975; Ambassador to Brazil, 1977–79. FCO Special Rep. for British-German Co-operation, 1984–86. Vice-Pres., British Chamber of Commerce in Germany, 1981–85; Pres., Council of British Chambers of Commerce in Continental Europe, 1982–84. *Recreations:* reading, birdwatching, calligraphy. *Address:* 11 Underhill Park Road, Reigate, Surrey RH2 9LU.
Died 10 Nov. 2001.

STEAD, Robert, CBE 1965; Controller, BBC North Region, 1958–69, retired; *b* 10 Aug. 1909; *s* of Charles Fearnley Stead and Mary Ellen Taylor; *m* 1932, Constance Ann Sharpley (*d* 1989); two *s. Educ:* Morley Grammar Sch. In journalism, 1926–40; served in RNVR, 1940–45; Talks Producer, BBC North Region, 1946–48; Head of North Regional Programmes, 1948–53; BBC Australian Representative, 1953–57. *Recreations:* golf, gardening, theatre. *Address:* Bushmead Court, 58/60 Bushmead Avenue, Bedford MK40 3QW.
Died 3 April 2001.

STEARN, Dr William Thomas, CBE 1997; botanical consultant; retired as Senior Principal Scientific Officer, Department of Botany, British Museum (Natural History), 1976; Editor, Annales Musei Goulandris, 1976–99; *b* 16

April 1911; *e s* of late Thomas Stearn, Cambridge; *m* 1940, Eldwyth Ruth Alford, *d* of late Roger R. Alford, Tavistock; one *s* two *d. Educ:* Cambridge High Sch. for Boys. Part-time research at Botany Sch., Cambridge; apprentice antiquarian bookseller, Bowes & Bowes, Cambridge, 1929–32; Librarian, Royal Horticultural Soc., 1933–41, 1946–52; served RAF, in Britain, India and Burma, 1941–46; Botanist, British Museum (Natural History), 1952–76. Hon. Sec., Internat. Cttee for Nomenclature of Cultivated Plants, 1950–53. Former Council Member: Botanical Soc. of British Isles (Vice-Pres., 1973–77); British Soc. for History of Science (Vice-Pres., 1969–72); British Soc. for History of Medicine; Field Studies Council; Garden History Soc. (Founder Mem., 1965; Pres., 1977–82); Ray Soc. (Vice-Pres., 1964–67, 1970–73; Pres., 1974–77); Richmond Scientific Soc. (Pres., 1969–71); Soc. for Bibliography of Natural History (Founder Mem., 1936; Hon. Mem., 1976); Systematics Assoc.; Mem., Old Cantabrigian Soc. (Pres., 1984–85). Sandars Reader in Bibliography, Cambridge, 1965; Vis. Prof., Dept of Botany and Agricl Botany, 1977–83, Hon. Res. Fellow, 1983, Univ. of Reading. Masters Meml Lectr, 1964; Wilkins Lectr, Royal Soc., 1985. Botanical collections made in Europe, Jamaica, USA, Australia. Royal Horticultural Society: Hon. Fellow, 1946; Vice-Pres., 1986–; Veitch Meml Medal, 1964; Victoria Medal of Honour, 1965; Linnean Society: FLS 1934; Hon. Botanical Curator, 1959–85; former Mem. Council; Vice-Pres., 1961–62; Pres., 1979–82; Gold Medal, 1976. CBiol 1992, FIBiol 1967 (MIBiol 1965). Hon. Member: Royal Soc. of Scis of Uppsala, 1967; Svenska Linnésällskapet, 1971; Botanical Soc. of Amer., 1982; For. Mem., Royal Swedish Acad. of Scis, 1983; Corresp. Mem., Amer. Soc. of Plant Taxonomists, 1980. Freeman, Gardeners' Co., 1982. Hon. Fellow, Sidney Sussex Coll., Cambridge, 1968. DSc *hc* Leiden, 1960; Hon. ScD Cantab, 1967; FilDr *hc* Uppsala, 1972. Boerhaave Commem. Medal, Leiden, 1969; Linnaeus Medal, Royal Swedish Acad. of Sciences, 1972; Hutchinson Medal, Chicago Horticultural Soc., 1985; Founders Medal, Soc. for the Hist. of Natural Hist., 1986; Engler Medal in Gold, Internat. Assoc. Plant Taxonomy, 1993; Asa Gray Award, American Soc. of Plant Taxonomists, 2000. Comdr, Order of the Star of the North (Sweden), 1980. *Publications:* (with W. Blunt) The Art of Botanical Illustration, 1950, new edn as sole author, 1994; (with H. B. D. Woodcock) Lilies of the World, 1950; (with E. Blatter and W. S. Millard) Some Beautiful Indian Trees, 1955; Introduction to the *Species Plantarum* of Carl Linnaeus, 1957; Early Leyden Botany, 1961; Botanical Latin, 1966, 4th edn 1992 (trans. Chinese, 1981); Three Prefaces on Linnaeus and Robert Brown, 1967; Humboldt, Bonpland, Kunth and Tropical American Botany, 1968; (with C. N. Goulimis and N. Goulandris) Wild Flowers of Greece, 1968; (with A. W. Smith) Gardener's Dictionary of Plant Names, 1972; (with W. Blunt) Captain Cook's Florilegium, 1973; (with M. Page) Culinary Herbs, 1974, 3rd edn 1992; (with W. Blunt) Australian Flower Paintings of Ferdinand Bauer, 1976; The Wondrous Transformation of Caterpillars: M. S. Merian (biog.), 1978; (with H. Hara and L. H. J. Williams) Enumeration of Flowering Plants of Nepal, vol. 1, 1978; The Natural History Museum at South Kensington, 1981; (with E. Rücker) Merian in Surinam, 1982; Plant Portraits from the *Flora Danica*, 1983; (with E. Roberts and C. Opsomer) Livre des Simples Médicines, English trans. and commentaries, 1984; (with P. H. Davis) Peonies of Greece, 1984; (with M. Rix) Redouté's Fairest Flowers, 1987; (with C. Brickell and M. Grierson) An English Florilegium, 1987; (with A. T. Gage) A Bicentenary History of the Linnean Society of London, 1988; (with A. W. Roach) Hooker's Fairest Fruits, 1989; Flower Artists of Kew, 1990; Stearn's Dictionary of Plant Names for Gardeners, 1992; (with J. Stewart) The Orchid Paintings of Franz Bauer, 1993; (with J. Riddell) By Underground to Kew, 1994; (ed English text and contrib.): Siebold's Florilegium of Japanese Plants, 1995;

WHO WAS WHO 2001–2005

C. P. Thunberg's Drawings of Japanese Plants, 1995; (ed) John Lindley Bicentenary Celebration Volume, 1999; numerous bibliographical, biographical, botanical and horticultural contribs to learned jls (listed in Biological Jl of Linnean Soc. vol. 8, 1976, Botanical Jl of Linnean Soc., vol. 109, 1992), RHS Dictionary of Gardening, Chambers's Encyclopaedia, Dictionary of Scientific Biography, Flora Europaea, European Garden Flora, Flora of Australia, Mountain Flora of Greece, etc. *Recreations:* gardening, talking. *Address:* 17 High Park Road, Kew Gardens, Richmond, Surrey TW9 4BL.

Died 8 May 2001.

STEEL, Very Rev. David; Minister of St Michael's, Linlithgow, 1959–76, then Minister Emeritus; Moderator of the General Assembly of the Church of Scotland, 1974–75; *b* 5 Oct. 1910; *s* of John S. G. Steel and Jane Scott, Hamilton; *m* 1937, Sheila Martin, Aberdeen; three *s* two *d*. *Educ:* Peterhead Academy; Robert Gordon's Coll., Aberdeen; Aberdeen Univ. (MA 1932, BD 1935). Minister of Church of Scotland: Denbeath, Fife, 1936–41; Bridgend, Dumbarton, 1941–46; Home Organisation Foreign Mission Sec., 1946–49; Minister of Parish of E Africa and of St Andrew's, Nairobi, 1949–57; Associate Minister, St Cuthbert's, Edinburgh, 1957–59. Vis. Prof., Columbia Theol Seminary, Atlanta, 1979–85. Chm. of Governors, Callendar Park Coll. of Educn, 1974–79; Vice-Pres., Boys' Brigade, 1974–79. Hon. Vice-President: Nat. Bible Soc. of Scotland; W Lothian History and Amenity Soc.; Boys' Brigade. Hon. DD Aberdeen 1964; Hon. LLD Dundee, 1977. *Publications:* History of St Michael's, Linlithgow, 1961; Preaching Through the Year, 1980, 2nd edn 1998; contrib. theol and church jls. *Recreation:* trout fishing. *Address:* 39 Newbattle Terrace, Edinburgh EH10 4SF. *T:* (0131) 447 2180. *Club:* Aberdeen University Senior Common Room.

Died 11 Nov. 2002.

STEEL, Sir David (Edward Charles), Kt 1977; DSO 1940; MC 1945; TD; Chairman, The Wellcome Trust, 1982–89; *b* 29 Nov. 1916; *s* of late Gerald Arthur Steel, CB; *m* 1956, Ann Wynne (*d* 1997), *d* of Maj.-Gen. C. B. Price, CB, DSO, DCM, VD, CD; one *s* two *d*. *Educ:* Rugby School; University Coll., Oxford (BA; Hon. Fellow, 1981). Inns of Court Regt, 1938; Commissioned 9 QR Lancers, 1940; served 1940–45 France, Middle East, North Africa, Italy (DSO, MC, despatches thrice). Admitted a Solicitor, June 1948; Linklaters and Paines, 1948–50; Legal Dept of The British Petroleum Co. Ltd, 1950–56; Pres. BP (N Amer.) Ltd, 1959–61; Man. Dir, Kuwait Oil Co. Ltd, 1962–65; Man. Dir, 1965–75, a Dep. Chm., 1972–75 and Chm., 1975–81, BP. A Dir, Bank of England, 1978–85; Dir, Kleinwort Benson Gp (formerly Kleinwort, Benson, Lonsdale), 1985–92. Pres., London Chamber of Commerce and Industry, 1982–85. Trustee, The Economist, 1979–95; Chairman: Lenta Educn Trust, 1986–90; London Educn Business Partnership, 1986–89; Governors, Rugby Sch., 1984–88. Hon. Freeman, Tallow Chandlers' Co., 1980. Hon. DCL City Univ., 1983. Order of Taj III, Iran, 1974; Comdr, Order of Leopold, Belgium, 1980. *Recreations:* gardening, golf. *Clubs:* Cavalry and Guards, MCC, Hurlingham; Royal and Ancient (St Andrews). *Died 9 Aug. 2004.*

STEELE, Prof. Alan John; Professor of French, University of Edinburgh, 1972–80, retired; *b* Bellshill, Lanarks, 11 April 1916; *s* of John Steele, MA, BD, and Anne (*née* Lawson); *m* 1947, Claire Alice Louise Belet; one *d* (one *s* decd). *Educ:* Royal Grammar School, Newcastle upon Tyne; Blyth Secondary School, Northumberland; Universities of Edinburgh, Grenoble and Paris. MA 1st Cl. Hons in French Language and Literature, Vans Dunlop Schol., Univ. of Edinburgh, 1938. Served War of 1939–45, at sea with 4th Maritime AA Regt, RA, 1941–42; commissioned, 1942, with 64th LAA Regt RA in Algeria, Italy and Greece. Lecturer in French, University of Edinburgh, 1946, Prof. of French Literature, 1961–72. Chairman: Scottish Central Cttee for Modern Languages, 1972–81; Assoc. of Univ. Profs of French, 1974–75; Consultative Cttee, Institut Français d'Ecosse, 1981–88; Vice-Pres., Franco-Scottish Soc., 1961–92. Mem., Church of Scotland Panel on Doctrine, 1978–86. Editor, Modern Language Review (French Section), 1971–79. Chevalier, Légion d'Honneur, 1973; Commandeur, Palmes Académiques, 1988. *Publications:* (with R. A. Leigh) Contemporary French Translation Passages, 1956; Three Centuries of French Verse, 1956, new edn 1961; contrib. to collective volumes, Cahiers de l'Assoc. Internat. des Etudes françaises, Modern Language Review. *Recreation:* music. *Address:* 17 Polwarth Grove, Edinburgh EH11 1LY. *T:* (0131) 337 5092.

Died 6 March 2004.

STEELE, Prof. Anthony, PhD; FCA; Professor of Accounting, University of Warwick, since 1985; *b* 25 April 1951; *s* of late Charles and Brenda Steele; *m* 1977, Judith; one *s* three *d*. *Educ:* Fitzwilliam Coll., Cambridge (BA 1974); Univ. of Lancaster (MA 1979); Univ. of Warwick (PhD 2002). FCA 1977. Programmer, Tube Investments, 1970–71; Chartered Accountant, Price Waterhouse, 1974–77; Lectr in Accounting, Lancaster Univ., 1979–85. Vis. Prof., Univ. of Leuven, 1992–93. Director: Warwick Univ. Training Ltd, 1995–; Warwick Univ. Services Ltd, 1995–. Mem., Competition (formerly Monopolies and Mergers) Commn, 1997–. *Publications:* The Implementation of Current Cost Accounting, 1984; Audit Risk and Audit Evidence, 1992 (trans. Japanese 1997); articles on accounting and finance in learned jls. *Recreations:* theatre, circus. *Address:* Warwick Business School, University of Warwick, Coventry CV4 7AL. *T:* (024) 7652 3523. *Died 21 April 2003.*

STELL, Prof. Philip Michael, MBE 2004; FRCS, FRCSE; Professor of Oto-rhino-laryngology, University of Liverpool, 1979–92, then Emeritus; Research Associate, Centre for Medieval Studies, York, since 1996; *b* 14 Aug. 1934; *s* of Frank Law Stell and Ada Stell; *m* 1959, Shirley Kathleen Mills; four *s* one *d*. *Educ:* Archbishop Holgate's Grammar Sch., York; Edinburgh Univ. (MB, ChB 1958). York Univ. (MA with distinction, 1995). ChM Liverpool, 1976. FRCS 1966; FRCSE 1962. Jun. hosp. appts, Edinburgh and Liverpool, 1958–63; Fellow, Washington Univ., St Louis, USA, 1964–65; Sen. Lectr, Univ. of Liverpool, 1965–78. Hunterian Prof., RCS, 1976. President: Otorhinolaryngological Res. Soc., 1983–86; Assoc. of Head and Neck Oncologists of GB, 1986–89; Liverpool Med. Inst., 1986–87 and 1987–88; Sect. of Laryngology, RSM, 1990–91. Mem., Deutsche Akademie der Naturforscher Leopoldina, 1990. Hon. Life Member: Netherlands ENT Soc., 1992; N of England ENT Soc., 1993. FSH 2003. Yearsley Gold Medal, 1980; Harrison Prize, RSM, 1982; Semon Medal, Univ. of London, 1986; George Davey Meml Prize, Univ. of London, 1987; Centenary Medal, Dudley Road Hosp., Birmingham, 1987; Gold Medal, Irish ENT Soc., 1988; Leegaard Medal, Norwegian ENT Soc., Gold Medal, Marie Curie Inst., Warsaw, Swedish Med. Assoc. Medal, Jobson Horne Prize, BMA, 1989; Gold Medal, German ENT Soc., 1991. *Publications:* approx. 20 books and over 300 articles in learned jls on surgery for cancer of head and neck; 5 books and 5 articles in learned jls on mediaeval history. *Recreation:* history. *Address:* 69 The Village, Haxby, York YO32 2JE. *T:* (01904) 761469. *Died 23 May 2004.*

STEPHEN, Derek Ronald James, CB 1975; Deputy Under-Secretary of State, Ministry of Defence, 1973–82; *b* 22 June 1922; *s* of late Ronald James Stephen; *m* 1948, Gwendolen Margaret, *d* of late William James Heasman, CBE; two *s* one *d* (and one *s* decd). *Educ:* Bec Sch.; Christ's Coll., Cambridge (1st cl. Hons Classics). Served War, 1941–45; 11th Hussars and HQ 7th Armoured Div., N Africa, Italy, NW Europe; Captain. Entered Admin. Class, Home Civil Service: Asst Principal, War Office, 1946; Asst Private Sec. to Sec. of State for War, 1949–50; Principal, 1951; Private Sec. to Sec. of Cabinet, 1958–60; Asst Sec., WO (later MoD), 1960; IDC 1966; HM

Treasury, 1968; Civil Service Dept (on its formation), 1968; Under-Sec., 1969–71; Asst Under-Sec. of State, MoD, 1972–73; Dep. Under-Sec. of State (Navy), MoD, and Mem. Admiralty Bd, 1973–78; Dep. Under-Sec. of State (Army), MoD, and Mem., Army Bd, 1978–82; Asst Sec., Royal Hosp., Chelsea, 1982–88. Army Benevolent Fund: Member: Grants Cttee, 1984–99; Finance Cttee, 1988–99; Mem. Council, Royal Cambridge Home for Soldiers' Widows, 1987–2000. Trustee, Tank Museum, 1982–97. Gov., Royal Sch., Hampstead, 1984–99. *Recreations:* choral singing, listening to music, opera, golf. *Club:* Naval and Military. *Died 2 July 2002.*

STEPHEN, Harbourne Mackay, CBE 1985; DSO 1941; DFC and bar 1940; AE 1943; Director, Telegraph plc (formerly Daily Telegraph), 1963–96 (non-executive, 1986–96); *b* 18 April 1916; *s* of Thomas Milne Stephen, JP, and Kathleen Vincent Park; *m* 1947, Sybil Erica Palmer; two *d. Educ:* Shrewsbury. Staff of Allied Newspapers, London, 1931; Evening Standard, 1936–39; returned to Beaverbrook Newspapers, 1945; Scottish Daily Express, Scottish Sunday Express, and Evening Citizen in Glasgow, 1945–55; General Manager, Sunday Express, 1958; General Manager, Sunday Graphic, 1960, and thereafter General Manager, Thomson Papers, London; Man. Dir, Daily Telegraph and Sunday Telegraph, 1963–86. Dir, Internat. Newspaper Colour Assoc., Darmstadt, 1964–69. Council Member: RSPB, 1972–73; Scientific Exploration Soc., 1992–; Trustee, Raleigh International, 1987–97. RAFVR, 1937; served RAF, 1939–45 (destroyed numerous enemy aircraft): 605 and 74 Sqdns, 1939–40; at MAP, 1941, then comd 234 Sqdn; Far East, 1942–45; Wing Comdr (Flying) Dum Dum; RAF, Bengal; comd 166 Fighter Wing; then to Fighter Ops, 224 Gp Arakan; Ops "A" Air Comd SEA, 1945; OC 602 City of Glasgow (F) Sqdn RAuxAF, 1950–52. *Recreations:* normal, occasionally. *Address:* Donnington Fields, Newbury, Berks RG14 3BA. *T:* (01635) 40105, *Fax:* (01635) 551311. *Clubs:* Naval and Military, Royal Air Force. *Died 20 Aug. 2001.*

STEPHEN, John Low, FRCSE, FRCS; Surgeon, St Mary's Hospital, W2, 1958–77; Senior Surgeon, St Mary's Hospital, W9, 1968–77, retired; *b* 13 May 1912; 2nd *s* of late Dr J. H. Stephen, Aberdeen; *m* 1938, Mary Milne, MA, BSc; one *s* one *d. Educ:* Aberdeen Grammar School; Aberdeen Univ. (MA 1931, MB 1935, ChM 1945); Edinburgh Univ. FRCSEd 1937; FRCS (*ad eundem*), 1968. Various university and hospital appointments in Scotland and England. Associate Teacher in Surgery, St Mary's Hosp. Med. School, 1950–77. FRSocMed. *Publications:* chapters in Operative Surgery (Smith and Rob); various articles on abdominal surgery in Brit. Jl of Surgery. *Recreations:* golf, motoring.
Died 17 May 2001.

STEPHEN, His Honour Lessel Bruce; a Circuit Judge, 1972–89; *b* 15 Feb. 1920; *s* of L. P. Stephen, FRCS(E); *m* 1949, Brenda (*née* Tinkler). *Educ:* Marlborough; Sydney Sussex Coll., Cambridge (BA). Called to the Bar, Inner Temple, 1948; subsequently practised NE Circuit; Recorder, 1972. *Recreations:* golf, wine. *Address:* 2 Harcourt Buildings, Temple, EC4Y 9DB. *T:* (020) 7353 2548. *Died 18 June 2004.*

STEPHENS, William Henry, CB 1961; DSc; CEng; FRAeS; non-Executive Director, General Technology Systems Ltd, 1987–89 (Senior Executive Director, 1973–87); *b* Kilkenny, Ireland, 18 March 1913; *s* of William Henry Stephens, MBE, and Helena Read Stephens (*née* Cantley); *m* 1938, Elizabeth Margaret Brown, BSc (decd); one *s* (one *d* decd). *Educ:* Methodist College, Belfast; Queen's University, Belfast (MSc 1935); DSc. Air Ministry, Royal Aircraft Establishment (aerodynamic research), 1935–38; War Office, Woolwich (rocket research), 1938–39; Ministry of Aircraft Prod., London (air defence research), 1939–44; Asst Scientific Attaché and Asst Director, UK Scientific Mission, British Commonwealth Scientific Office, Washington, USA,

1944–47; Min. of Supply, RAE, Head of Guided Weapons Dept and later Dep. Director, 1947–58; Dir-Gen. Ballistic Missiles, Ministry of Aviation, 1959–62; Technical Dir, European Space Launcher Develt Organisation, Paris, 1962–69; Minister, Defence R&D, British Embassy, Washington, 1969–72; Special Advr (Internat. Affairs), Controllerate of Res., MoD, 1972–73. Mem., Internat. Acad. of Astronautics; Fellow, British Interplanetary Soc. *Publications:* contrib. to Jl Royal Aeronautical Soc., Proc. Brit. Assoc., Proc. Internat. Congress of Aeronautical Sciences. *Recreations:* travel, music, art, theatre. *Address:* Rosebrook House, Oriel Hill, Camberley, Surrey GU15 2JW. *Club:* Athenæum.
Died 12 Aug. 2001.

STEPHENSON, Lt-Col John Robin, CBE 1994 (OBE (mil.) 1976); Secretary: Marylebone Cricket Club, 1987–93; International Cricket Council (formerly International Cricket Conference), 1987–93; *b* 25 Feb. 1931; *s* of John Stewart Stephenson and Edith Gerda Greenwell Stephenson; *m* 1962, Karen Margrethe Koppang; one *s* two *d. Educ:* Christ's Hosp.; RMA Sandhurst. Commnd Royal Sussex Regt, 1951; served Egypt, Korea, Gibraltar, Libya, Germany, N Ireland; Instructor, Mons Officer Cadet Sch., 1958–60; Infantry Rep., Sch. of Signals, 1968–70; SOWC, 1972–73; Comdg Officer, 5 (V) Queen's Regt, 1973–75; Dep. Pres., Regular Commissions Bd, 1976; Staff Officer, Cs-in-C Cttee, 1977–79. Asst Sec. (Cricket), MCC, 1979–86; managed MCC tours, Bangladesh, 1979–80, 2000, E Africa, 1980–81, Canada, 1985, Kenya, 1993. President: Forty Club, 1994–96; Stragglers of Asia CC, 1994–. Governor: St Bede's Sch., Eastbourne, 1989–94; Claysmore Sch., Dorset, 1989–2000; Chm. Governors, Leaden Hall Sch., Salisbury, 1995–. Order of Orange-Nassau, 1972. *Recreations:* Rugby football (RMA Sandhurst (Capt.), Richmond, Army, Sussex), cricket (RMA Sandhurst, Army), golf, boating, gardening. *Address:* Plum Tree Cottage, Barford St Martin, Salisbury, Wilts SP3 4BL. *T:* (01722) 743443. *Clubs:* East India, Farmers', MCC (Mem. Cttee, 2000–); IZ, Free Foresters, Stragglers of Asia. *Died 2 June 2003.*

STERN, Isaac; violinist; *b* Kreminiecz, Russia, 21 July 1920; *s* of Solomon and Clara Stern; *m* 1st, 1948, Nora Kaye (*d* 1987); 2nd, 1951, Vera Lindenblit; three *c*; 3rd, 1996, Linda Reynolds. Studied San Francisco Conservatory, 1930–37. First public concert as guest artist, San Francisco Symphony Orchestra, 1934; played with Los Angeles Philharmonic Orchestra and in concerts in Pacific Coast cities; New York début, 1937; thereafter played in concerts throughout USA, in Europe, Israel, Australia, South America, Japan, China, India, The Philippines, Soviet Union and Iceland; played with major American and European orchestras; took part in Prades Festivals, 1950–52; Edinburgh and other major festivals in Europe and US. Films: Mao to Mozart: Isaac Stern in China (Best Full-length Documentary Acad. Award, 1981); Isaac Stern – a life, 1992; Isaac Stern – life's virtuoso, 2000; (TV prodn) Carnegie Hall – The Grand Reopening, 1987 (Emmy Award). Chm. Emeritus, America-Israel Cultural Foundn, NY. President, Carnegie Hall, NY, 1960–; Artistic Dir, Jerusalem Music Center. Hon. degrees from Columbia, Johns Hopkins, Dalhousie, Brown and Oxford Univs, and San Francisco Conservatory of Music. Over 150 recordings for which many Grammy Awards received. Albert Schweitzer Music Award, 1975; Kennedy Center Honors, 1984; Nat. Medal of Honor, 1991; US Presidential Medal of Freedom, 1992; Polar Music Prize, Sweden, 2000. Commandeur, Légion d'Honneur (France), 1989; Order of the Rising Sun (Japan), 1998. *Publication:* My First 79 Years (memoirs), 2000. *Address:* c/o ICM Artists Ltd, 40 West 57th Street, New York, NY 10019, USA. *Died 22 Sept. 2001.*

STERNE, Laurence Henry Gordon; Deputy Director, National Engineering Laboratory, East Kilbride, 1968–76; *b* 2 July 1916; *o s* of late Henry Herbert Sterne and Hilda

Davey Sterne; *m* 1944, Katharine Clover; two *d. Educ:* Culford Sch.; Jesus Coll., Oxford (Hon. Schol.; MA). Royal Aircraft Establishment, 1940; Chief Supt at Bedford, 1955; Dir, von Karman Inst., Rhode Saint Genèse, Belgium, 1958; Research Policy Staff, MoD, 1962; Dir, Royal Naval Aircraft and Helicopters, 1964. Vis. Prof., Strathclyde Univ., 1971–76. *Publications:* (ed jtly) early vols of Progress in Aeronautical Sciences; reports and memoranda of Aeronautical Research Council. *Address:* 10 Trinity Street, Bungay, Suffolk NR35 1EH.
Died 30 May 2001.

STEVEN, Stewart; Chairman, National Campaign for the Arts, since 1996; *b* 30 Sept. 1935; *s* of Rudolph and Trude Steven; *m* 1965, Inka Sobieniewska; one *s. Educ:* Mayfield Coll., Sussex. Political Reporter, Central Press Features, 1961–63; Political Correspondent, Western Daily Press, 1963–64; Daily Express: Political Reporter, 1964–65; Diplomatic Correspondent, 1965–67; Foreign Editor, 1967–72; Daily Mail: Asst Editor, 1972–74; Associate Editor, 1974–82; Editor: The Mail on Sunday, 1982–92 (Columnist, 1996–); Evening Standard, 1992–95; Chairman: Liberty Publishing & Media Ltd, 1996–98; Punch, 1996–98. Chm., Equity Theatre Commn, 1995–97; Member: Thames Adv. Gp, 1995–98; Better English Campaign, 1995–98; Dir, London Film Commn, 1996–2000. *Publications:* Operation Splinter-Factor, 1974; The Spymasters of Israel, 1976; The Poles, 1982. *Recreation:* the arts. *Address:* 20 Woodstock Road, W4 1UE. *Clubs:* Garrick, Groucho. *Died 19 Jan. 2004.*

STEVENS, Clifford David, CB 1997; Civil Service Commissioner, since 1997; *b* 11 June 1941; *s* of late Robert Stevens and of Ivy (*née* White); *m* 1964, Mary Olive (*née* Bradford); one *s* two *d. Educ:* Stationers' Company's Sch., London. FO, 1959–63; BoT, 1963–64; DEA, 1964–70 (Private Sec. to successive Ministers, 1967–70); CSD, 1970–76; Cabinet Office, 1976–78; CSD, 1978–81; Management and Personnel Office, 1981–86; Welsh Office, 1986–97: Dir, Industry Dept, 1987–94; Principal Establishment Officer, 1994–97. *Recreations:* gardening, bowls, golf. *Address:* c/o Office of the Civil Service Commissioners, 35 Great Smith Street, SW1P 3BQ. *T:* (020) 7276 2615.
Died 29 Oct. 2001.

STEVENS, Prof. Denis William, CBE 1984; President and Artistic Director, Accademia Monteverdiana, since 1961; *b* 2 March 1922; *s* of William J. Stevens and Edith Driver; *m* 1st, 1949, Sheila Elizabeth Holloway; two *s* one *d*; 2nd, 1975, Leocadia Elzbieta Kwasny. *Educ:* Royal Grammar Sch., High Wycombe; Jesus College, Oxford. Served War of 1939–45, RAF Intelligence, India and Burma, 1942–46. Producer, BBC Music Div., 1949–54; Assoc. Founder and Conductor, Ambrosian Singers, 1952; Vis. Professor of Musicology, Cornell Univ., 1955, Columbia Univ., 1956; Secretary, Plainsong and Mediaeval Music Soc., 1958–63; Editor, Grove's Dictionary of Music and Musicians, 1959–63. Professor, Royal Acad. of Music, 1960. Vis. Prof. Univ. of California (Berkeley), 1962; Dist. Vis. Prof., Pennsylvania State Univ., 1962–63; Prof. of Musicology, Columbia Univ., 1964–76; Vis. Prof. Univ. of California (Santa Barbara), 1974–75; Brechemin Dist. Vis. Prof., Univ. of Washington, Seattle, 1976; Visiting Professor: Univ. of Michigan, Ann Arbor, 1977; San Diego State Univ., 1978; Goldsmiths Coll., London Univ., 1995–; Acad. Musicale de Villecroze, 1996. Lectures on music, especially British, and contrib. musicolog. confs, in England, France, Germany, Italy, USA and Russia; Organizer and Leader, Rockefeller Congress on Music, Bellagio, 1974; concerts, conducting own and ancillary ensembles at internat. festivals in GB (incl. 5 proms, the first introducing Monteverdi 1967), Europe and USA; TV and radio programmes in Europe and N America; first broadcast perfs of unknown works by Dufay, Dunstable and Telemann, of Charpentier's Medée and Monteverdi's Orfeo; cons. for films. FSA; Mem., Co. of Musicians.

Hon. RAM, 1960. Hon.D, Humane Letters, Fairfield Univ., Connecticut, 1967. *Publications:* The Mulliner Book, 1952; Thomas Tomkins, 1957, rev. edn 1966; A History of Song, 1960, rev. edn, 1971; Tudor Church Music, 1966; A Treasury of English Church Music (I), 1965; (ed) First and Second Penguin Book of English Madrigals, 1967, 1971; Early Tudor Organ Music (II), 1969; Music in Honour of St Thomas of Canterbury, 1970; Monteverdi: sacred, secular and occasional music, 1978; Musicology: a practical guide, 1980; The Letters of Monteverdi, 1980, 2nd edn 1995; Renaissance Dialogues, 1981; The Worcester Fragments, 1981; Musicology in Practice, 1987; Early Music, 1997; Monteverdi: songs & madrigals, 1999; Monteverdi in Venice, 2001; many edns of early music, including: Monteverdi Vespers, 1961, 2nd edn 1994, and Orfeo; Cavalli's Pompeo Magno, 2002; choral works by Gabrieli, Gesualdo, Lassus, Machaut, Tallis, Tomkins; contrib. Encyclopaedia Britannica, Amer. Acad. Encyclopaedia, Grove's Dictionary, Die Musik in Geschichte und Gegenwart, Enciclopedia della Musica; reviews and articles in English and foreign journals; also many stereo recordings with Ambrosian Singers and Accademia Monteverdiana, ranging from plainsong to Beethoven. *Recreations:* travel, photography. *Address:* The Quadrangle, Morden College, SE3 0PW. *Club:* Garrick.
Died 1 April 2004.

STEVENS, Prof. John Edgar, CBE 1980; PhD; FBA 1975; President of Magdalene College, Cambridge, 1983–88, Fellow, 1950–88, then Emeritus; Professor of Medieval and Renaissance English, University of Cambridge, 1978–88, then Emeritus; *b* 8 Oct. 1921; *s* of William Charles James and Fanny Stevens; *m* 1946, Charlotte Ethel Mary (*née* Somner); two *s* two *d. Educ:* Christ's Hospital, Horsham; Magdalene College, Cambridge (Schol.; MA, PhD). Served Royal Navy; Temp. Lieut RNVR. Cambridge University: Bye-Fellow 1948, Research Fellow 1950, Fellow 1953 and Tutor 1958–74, Magdalene Coll.; Univ. Lectr in English, 1954–74; Reader in English and Musical History, 1974–78. Vis. Dist. Prof. of Medieval Studies, Univ. of California, Berkeley, 1989. Chm., Plainsong and Medieval Music Soc., 1988–95. Hon. MusD Exeter, 1989. *Publications:* Medieval Carols (Musica Britannica vol. 4), 1952, 2nd edn 1958; Music and Poetry in the Early Tudor Court, 1961; Music at the Court of Henry VIII (Musica Britannica vol. 18), 1962, 2nd edn 1969; (with Richard Axton) Medieval French Plays, 1971; Medieval Romance, 1973; Early Tudor Songs & Carols (Musica Britannica vol. 36), 1975; Words and Music in the Middle Ages, 1986. *Recreation:* viol-playing. *Address:* 4 & 5 Bell's Court, Castle Street, Cambridge CB3 0AH. *Died 14 Feb. 2002.*

STEVENS, Kenneth Henry, CBE 1983; DL; Chief Executive Commissioner, The Scout Association, 1970–87; *b* 8 Oct. 1922; *s* of late Horace J. Stevens, CBE, sometime Senior Principal Inspector of Taxes, and late Nora Stevens (*née* Kauntze); *m* 1947, Yvonne Grace Ruth (*née* Mitchell) (decd); one *s* one *d. Educ:* Brighton Coll.; Brighton Technical Coll. South Coast Civil Defence, 1941–44. Alliance Assurance Co., 1944–47; Asst Dir of Adult Leader Training, Internat. Scout Training Centre, Gilwell Park, Chingford, 1947–56; Organising Comr, World Scout Jamboree, Indaba and Rover Moot, Sutton Coldfield, 1956–58; Dep. Dir of Adult Leader Training, Internat. Scout Training Centre, 1958–61; Asst Chief Exec. Comr, The Scout Assoc., 1961–63; Dep. Chief Exec. Comr, 1963–70. DL Surrey, 1989. *Publication:* Ceremonies of The Scout Movement, 1958. *Recreations:* motoring, gardening. *Address:* Drovers, Crampshaw Lane, Ashtead, Surrey KT21 2UF. *T:* (01372) 277841. *Club:* MCC. *Died 18 Nov. 2005.*

STEVENSON, Derek Paul, CBE 1972; Secretary, British Medical Association, 1958–76 (Assistant Secretary, 1946–48; Deputy Secretary, 1948–58); *b* 11 July 1911; *s* of late Frederick Stevenson and Maud Coucher; *m* 1941, Pamela Mary, *d* of late Col C. N. Jervelund, OBE; two *s* one *d. Educ:* Epsom College; Guy's Hospital. MRCS, LRCP 1935. Lieut RAMC, 1935 (Montefiore Prize, Royal Army Med. Coll., 1935); Capt. RAMC, 1936; Maj. 1942; Lt-Col 1943; service in China and Malaya; Asst Director-General, Army Medical Service, War Office, 1942–46; Sec., Army Medical Advisory Bd 1943–46; War Office rep. on Central Med., War Cttee, 1943–46. Sec. Jt Consultants Cttee, 1958–76; Mem., Health Services Bd, and Scottish Cttee, 1977–80. Vice-Pres. British Medical Students Assoc.; Hon. Sec./Treas., British Commonwealth Med. Conf.; Delegate, Gen. Assembly World Medical Association: Sydney, 1968, Paris, 1969, Oslo, 1970, Ottawa, 1971, Amsterdam, 1972, Munich, 1973, Stockholm, 1974 (Mem. Council, 1967; Chm. Council, 1969, 1970–71). Medical Sec. to Nat. Ophthalmic Treatment Board Assoc.; Mem. Council of London Hospital Service Plan; Member, Committee of Management: Medical Insurance Agency; Medical and Dental Retirement Adv. Service; Vice Pres., Private Patients Plan, 1984–. Hon. Sec. and Treas., British Commonwealth Medical Assoc., 1964; Sec. Gen., Permanent Cttee of Doctors, EEC, 1973–76; Member: Chichester HA; West Sussex Gen. Practitioners' Cttee; Hon. Sec., British Life Assurance Trust. Liaison Officer, MoD, 1964. Adviser: Sterling Winthrop; Mediscope Jl; Mem. Adv. Bd, Allied Investments; Dir, Tavistock Computer Services; Gen. Comr, Inland Revenue. Mem. Bd of Governors, Epsom College; Governor, Midhurst Grammar Sch.; Pres., Old Epsomian Club, 1974–75. Mem., Chichester Dio. Bd; Lay Chm., Rural Deanery. Mem., West Sussex CC, 1980–85. Fellow, Royal Commonwealth Soc., 1968; Fellow, BMA, 1976 (Gold Medal, 1976). Hon. FRCGP 1992. Hon. LLD Manchester, 1964. *Publications:* contrib. Irish Medical Jl; BMA Lecture delivered to Irish Medical Assoc.; contrib. Canadian Med. Assoc. Jl, and address at Centennial meeting, Montreal; NHS Reorganisation (in RSH Jl), address to RSH Congress 1973; regular contribs to Medical Interface. *Recreations:* golf, sailing, gardening. *Address:* 19 Marchwood Gate, Chichester, West Sussex PO19 4HA. *T:* (01243) 774237. *Clubs:* Athenæum, Royal Commonwealth Society.   *Died 4 March 2001.*

STEVENSON, Robert Bryce; General President, National Union of Footwear Leather and Allied Trades, 1980–90, retired; *b* 26 June 1926; *s* of Daniel Liddle Stevenson and Christina Stevenson; *m* 1947, Margaret Eugenia; two *d. Educ:* Caldercruix Advanced Sch., Airdrie, Lanarks. Full-time Officer NUFLAT, Street, Som. Branch, 1961–80. Member, 1980–: Internat. Textile, Garment and Leather Workers Fedn Exec. Council and Cttee (Brussels); Jt Cttee, Footwear Industry in Europe (Brussels); Footwear Econ. Develt Cttee, 1980–88; TUC Textile, Clothing and Footwear Industries Cttee; Council, Shoe and Allied Trades Res. Assoc.; Boot and Shoe Repairing Wages Council for GB; Bd of Management, Boot Trade Benevolent Soc.; Mem., Footwear Leather and Fur Skin Industry Trng Bd, 1980–82; Mem., TUC Gen. Council, 1984–90. JP Wells and Glastonbury 1970 (on Supplementary List, Northants, 1981). *Recreations:* listening to and playing music, all sports.
          Died 2 July 2003.

STEWART, Sir Alan, KBE 1981 (CBE 1972); Vice-Chancellor of Massey University, 1964–83; *b* 8 Dec. 1917; *s* of Kenneth and Vera Mary Stewart; *m* 1950, Joan Cecily Sisam; one *s* three *d. Educ:* Massey Agricultural College; University College, Oxford. Lieut, RNZNVR, on loan to RN, 1940–45; CO Minesweeper; served Western Approaches and Bay of Bengal. Sen. Lectr, Massey Agric. Coll., 1950–54; Chief Consulting Officer, Milk Marketing Board, England and Wales, 1954–58; Principal, Massey Agric. Coll., 1959–63. Hon. DSc Massey, 1984. *Address:* PO Box 3, Whakatane, New Zealand. *T:* (7) 3086619.
          Died 1 Sept. 2004.

STEWART, Prof. Sir Frederick (Henry), Kt 1974; FRS 1964; PhD; FRSE; FGS; Regius Professor of Geology,

1956–82, then Emeritus, Dean of Science Faculty, 1966–68, and Member, University Court, 1969–70, Edinburgh University; *b* 16 Jan. 1916; *o s* of Frederick Robert Stewart and Hester Alexander, Aberdeen; *m* 1945, Mary Florence Elinor Rainbow (novelist, as Mary Stewart); no *c. Educ:* Fettes Coll.; Univ. of Aberdeen (BSc); Emmanuel Coll., Cambridge (PhD). Mineralogist in Research Dept of ICI Ltd (Billingham Div.), 1941–43; Lectr in Geology, Durham Colls in the Univ. of Durham, 1943–56. Vice-Pres., Geological Soc. of London, 1965–66; Member: Council for Scientific Policy, 1967–71; Adv. Council for Applied R&D, 1976–79; Chairman: NERC, 1971–73 (Mem., Geol. Geophysics Cttee, 1967–70); Adv. Bd for Res. Councils, 1973–79 (Mem., 1972–73); Mem. Council, Royal Soc., 1969–70; Trustee, BM (Nat. Hist.), 1983–87; Mem. Council, Scottish Marine Biol Assoc., 1983–89. Lyell Fund Award, 1951, J. B. Tyrrell Fund, 1952, Geological Soc. of London; Mineralogical Soc. of America Award, 1952; Lyell Medal, Geological Soc. of London, 1970; Clough Medal, Edinburgh Geol. Soc., 1971; Sorby Medal, Yorks Geol. Soc., 1975. Hon. DSc: Aberdeen, 1975; Leicester, 1977; Heriot-Watt, 1978; Durham, 1983; Glasgow, 1988. *Publications:* The British Caledonides (ed with M. R. W. Johnson), 1963; Marine Evaporites, 1963; papers in Mineralogical Magazine, Jl of Geol. Soc. of London, etc., dealing with igneous and metamorphic petrology and salt deposits. *Recreation:* fishing. *Address:* House of Letterawe, Lochawe, Dalmally, Argyll PA33 1AH. *T:* (01838) 200329. *Club:* New (Edinburgh).
          Died 9 Dec. 2001.

STEWART, Prof. Harold Charles, CBE 1975; DL; FRCP; FRSE; Head of Pharmacology Department, St Mary's Hospital Medical School, 1950–74; Professor of Pharmacology in the University of London 1965–74, then Emeritus Professor (Reader, 1949–64); Consultant in Pharmacology to: St Mary's Hospital, 1946; Ministry of Defence (Army), since 1961; *b* 23 Nov. 1906; *s* of Bernard Halley Stewart, MA, MD, FRSE, FKC, Pres. of Sir Halley Stewart Trust, and Mabel Florence Wyatt; *m* 1st, 1929, Dorothy Irene Lowen (*d* 1969); one *s* one *d*; 2nd, 1970, Audrey Patricia Nicolle. *Educ:* Mill Hill Sch.; University Coll. London; Jesus Coll., Cambridge (BA 1928, MA 1934; MB, BCh 1931, MD 1935); University Coll. Hosp (PhD 1941). MRCP 1949. Gen. practice, Barnet, Herts, 1932–36; Sub-Dean, St Mary's Hospital Med. Sch., 1950–52. Gresham Prof. in Physic, City Univ., 1968–70. Sometime Examr, Univs of London, Cambridge, Birmingham, Bristol and Wales, RCS, Soc. of Apothecaries. Research work, mainly on fat absorption and transport in the human subject, and on problems of pain and analgesia. Cons. in Pharmacology to Army; Med. Adviser and Mem. Commonwealth Council, Brit. Commonwealth Ex-Services League; Pres., Sir Halley Stewart Trust for Research, 1986– (Chm., 1979–86); Mem. Asthma Research Council; Dir-Gen., St John Ambulance Assoc., 1976–78 (Dep Dir-Gen., 1973–76); Dist Surg. for London, SJAB, 1950–64); Mem. Chapter-Gen., Order of St John (KStJ); Mem. Council, Stewart Soc. (Hon. Vice Pres., 1988); Chm., Buttle Trust for Children, 1979–; Vice-Chairman: Med. Council of Alcoholism, 1986–87 (later Patron); St Christopher's Hospice for terminal cases, 1963–87 (Vice Pres., 1987); Sen. Vice-Pres. and British Rep., Assoc. Internat. de Sauvetage et de Premiers Secours en Cas d'Accidents, 1974–. Member: Physiology Soc.; British Pharmacol. Soc. Liveryman, Soc. of Apothecaries of London; Freeman, City of London. FRCA (FFARCS 1969). FRSE 1974. RAMC, T, 1935; Mem. LDV, later Major and Med. Adviser, HG; comd and reformed Med. Unit, Univ. of London STC as Major RAMC, 1942–46. DL Greater London, 1967–82. Defence Medal; Gen. Serv. Medal, 1939–46; Coronation Medal, 1953; Guthrie Meml Medal, 1974. *Publications:* Drugs in Anæsthetic Practice (with F. G. Wood-Smith), 1962; (with W. H. Hughes) Concise Antibiotic Treatment, 2nd edn 1973; contribs to jls. *Recreations:* voluntary service; sport (lacrosse: Cambridge

Half-Blue 1928; lawn tennis); genealogy and heraldry. *Address:* 41 The Glen, Green Lane, Northwood, Mddx HA6 2UR. *T:* (01923) 824893. *Club:* Athenæum.
Died 7 Dec. 2001.

STEWART, Sir Houston Mark S.; *see* Shaw-Stewart.

STEWART, Kenneth Hope, PhD; Director of Research, Meteorological Office, 1976–82; *b* 29 March 1922; *s* of Harry Sinclair Stewart and Nora Hassan Parry; *m* 1950, Hilary Guest (*d* 1993); four *s* four *d. Educ:* Trinity Coll., Cambridge (MA, PhD). Entered Meteorol Office, 1949; Dep. Dir, Physical Res., 1974. *Publications:* Ferromagnetic Domains, 1951; contrib. physical and meteorol jls. *Address:* 19 Harston Road, Newton, Cambridge CB2 5PA.
Died 3 Jan. 2004.

STEWART, Very Rev. Maurice Evan; Dean of St Patrick's Cathedral, Dublin, 1991–99; *b* 8 Jan. 1929; *s* of Robert Carlisle and Annie Stewart; *m* 1965, Wendy Margaret McConnell; two *d. Educ:* Royal Belfast Academical Instn; Trinity Coll., Dublin (MA 1953; BD 1967); Queen's Univ., Belfast (PhD 1975). Ordained: deacon, 1952; priest, 1953; Curate, St James, Belfast, 1952–55; Chaplain, Bishop's Coll., Cheshunt, 1955–58; Head of TCD Mission in Belfast, 1958–61; Rector of Newcastle, Co. Down, 1961–69; Lectr, C of I Theol Coll., 1969–91; Lectr in Divinity, TCD, 1973–91; St Patrick's Cathedral, Dublin: Chancellor, 1980–89; Precentor, 1989–91. *Recreations:* Anglican theology, Swiftiana. *Address:* 12 Mounthaven, New Road, Greystones, Co. Wicklow, Ireland. *Club:* Kildare Street and University (Dublin). *Died 18 Oct. 2004.*

STEWART, Dame Muriel (Acadia), DBE 1968; Headmistress, Northumberland LEA, 1940–70; *b* 22 Oct. 1905; *d* of late James Edmund Stewart. *Educ:* Gateshead Grammar Sch.; Durham Univ. (BA Hons 1926; MA 1929). Teacher: Newcastle upon Tyne, 1927–29; Northumberland, 1929–70 (a headteacher of Secondary Schools, 1940–69); Headmistress, Shiremoor Middle School, 1969–70. Nat. Pres., Nat. Union of Teachers, 1964–65; Chm., Schools Council, 1969–72. Vice-Chm., Bullock Cttee, 1972–74. Pres., Lib Dem Nat. Educn Assoc., 1991. Hon. MEd Newcastle upon Tyne, 1965. *Recreation:* music. *Died 7 Oct. 2001.*

STEWART, Dr Robert William, OC 1979; FRS 1970; FRSC 1967; Adjunct Professor, School of Earth and Ocean Sciences, University of Victoria, since 1989; Hon. Professor of Physics and Oceanography, University of British Columbia, since 1971; Hon. Professor of Science, University of Alberta, since 1985; *b* 21 Aug. 1923; *m* 1st, 1948, V. Brande (marr. diss. 1972); two *s* one *d*; 2nd, 1973, Anne-Marie Robert; one *s. Educ:* Queen's Univ., Ontario (BSc 1945, MSc 1947); PhD Cantab 1952. Canadian Defence Research Bd, 1950–61; Prof. of Physics and Oceanography, Univ. of British Columbia, 1961–70; Dir, Marine Scis Br., Pacific Reg., Environment Canada, 1970–74; Dir-Gen., Ocean and Aquatic Scis, Pacific Reg., Fisheries and Marine Service, Dept of Fisheries and Oceans, Canada, 1974–79; Dep. Minister, Ministry of Univs, Science and Communications, BC, Canada, 1979–84; Pres., Alberta Res. Council, 1984–87; Dir, Centre for Earth and Ocean Res., Univ. of Victoria, 1987–89. Vis. Professor: Dalhousie Univ., 1960–61; Harvard Univ., 1964; Pennsylvania State Univ., 1964; Commonwealth Vis. Prof., Cambridge Univ., 1967–68. Vice-Chm., 1968–72, Chm., 1972–76, Jt Organizing Cttee, Global Atmospheric Res. Program; Pres., Internat. Assoc. of Physical Scis of Ocean, 1975–79; Mem., Cttee on Climatic Changes and the Ocean, 1980–92 (Chm., 1983–87); Vice Chm., Sci. Cttee for Internat. Geosphere-Biosphere Prog., 1991–94. *Publications:* numerous, on turbulence, oceanography and meteorology. *Address:* School of Earth and Ocean Studies, University of Victoria, PO Box 1700, Victoria, BC V8W 2Y2, Canada.
Died 19 Jan. 2005.

STEWART, Dr William, CB 1977; DSc; aerospace consultant, 1983–94; *b* Hamilton, 29 Aug. 1921; *m* 1955, Helen Cairney; two *d. Educ:* St John's Grammar Sch.; Hamilton Acad.; Glasgow Univ. (BSc Hons (engrg); DSc 1958). RAE, Farnborough, 1942–53; British Jt Services Mission, Washington, 1953–56; Dep. Head of Naval Air Dept, RAE, Bedford, 1956–63; IDC, 1964; Asst Dir, Project Time and Cost Analysis, 1965–66; Dir, Anglo-French Combat Trainer Aircraft Projects, 1966–70; Dir-Gen., Multi-Role Combat Aircraft, 1970–73; Dep. Controller, Aircraft A, 1973–78, Aircraft, 1978–81, MoD (PE). Silver Medal, RAeS, 1981. *Address:* 25 Brickhill Drive, Bedford MK41 7QA. *Died 8 Nov. 2002.*

STEWART COX, Maj.-Gen. Arthur George Ernest, DFC 1952; General Officer Commanding Wales, 1978–80; *b* 11 April 1925; *s* of Lt-Col Arthur Stewart Cox and Mrs Dorothea Stewart Cox, *d* of Maj.-Gen. Sir Edward May; *m* 1953, Mary Pamela, *d* of Hon. George Lyttelton; two *s* one *d* (and one *s* decd). *Educ:* Marlborough Coll.; Aberdeen Univ. Commissioned RA, 1944; parachutist, RA regts, 1945–50; army pilot, Far East and Korea, 1950–52; ADC to Comdt, RMA Sandhurst, 1954–56; Staff Coll., 1956; SO 99 Gurkha Inf. Bde, 1957–58; SO MoD, Malaya, 1963–65; CO 29 Commando Light Regt, RA, 1965–68; SO Sch. of Artillery, 1968–69; Comdr RA 4th Div., 1969–72; RCDS, 1973; Dep. Dir of Manning (Army), MoD, 1974–76. Col Comdt, RA, 1980–90; Hon. Colonel: 3rd Bn RWF, TAVR, 1980–85; 289 Commando Battery, RA, TAVR, 1983–91. *Recreations:* shooting, fishing, lepidoptery, gardening. *Address:* Long Mead, Brixton Deverill, Warminster, Wilts BA12 7EJ. *T:* (01985) 840877. *Died 9 Nov. 2003.*

STEWART-MOORE, Alexander Wyndham Hume; DL; Chairman, Gallaher Ltd, 1975–79 (Managing Director, 1966–75); Director, American Brands Inc., 1975–79; *b* 14 Feb. 1915; 2nd *s* of late James Stewart-Moore, DL, Ballydivity, Dervock, Co. Antrim, and of Katherine Marion (*née* Jackson); *m* 1948, Magdalene Clare (*d* 1999), *y d* of Sir David Richard Llewellyn, 1st Bt, LLD, JP; three *s* one *d. Educ:* Shrewsbury. Joined Gallaher Ltd, Nov. 1934. Served War, RA, Middle East and Italy, 1939–46. DL Co. Antrim, 1982. *Recreations:* farming, fishing, gardening. *Address:* Moyarget Farm, 98 Moyarget Road, Ballycastle, Co. Antrim, NI BT54 6HL. *T:* (028) 2076 2287. *Died 22 Jan. 2003.*

STEWART-SMITH, Rev. Canon David Cree; Archdeacon of Rochester and Canon Residentiary of Rochester Cathedral, 1969–76; Hon. Canon of Rochester, 1968–69, 1976–78, then Canon Emeritus; *b* 22 May 1913; 3rd *s* of late Thomas Stewart Stewart-Smith, JP, Heathlands, Kinver, Staffs, and Mabel (*née* McDougall); *m* 1943, Kathleen Georgiana Maule Ffinch, *d* of Rev. K. M. Ffinch, Ifield, Kent. *Educ:* Marlborough; King's Coll., Cambridge; Cuddesdon Theol College. BA 1939, MA 1943. Vicar-Choral and Sacrist, York Minster, 1944–49; Vicar of Shadwell, Leeds, 1949–52; Warden, Brasted Place Coll., 1952–63; Dean of St George's Cath., Jerusalem, and Administrator of St George's Coll., 1964–67; Commissary for Archbishop in Jerusalem, 1968–76; Archdeacon of Bromley, 1968–69. Director of Ordinands, dio. Rochester, 1968–74; Mem., C of E Pensions Bd, 1970–84; a Church Commissioner, 1973–78; Home Sec., Jerusalem and Middle East Church Assoc., 1976–78. Fellow of Woodard Corporation: Northern Div., 1949–52; Southern Div., 1959–64. *Recreations:* architecture, music, travel. *Address:* 16 Capel Court, Prestbury, near Cheltenham GL52 3EL. *T:* (01242) 510972. *Died 1 May 2001.*

STEWART-SMITH, (Dudley) Geoffrey; *b* 28 Dec. 1933; *s* of Dudley Cautley Stewart-Smith; *m* 1956, Kay Mary (marr. diss. 1990); three *s. Educ:* Winchester; RMA Sandhurst. Regular Officer, The Black Watch, 1952–60. Dir, Foreign Affairs Res. Inst., 1976–86. Director: Foreign Affairs Circle; Freedom Communications Internat. News

Agency; Editor, East-West Digest; Dir, Foreign Affairs Publishing Co.; Financial Times, 1968. MP (C) Derbyshire, Belper, 1970–Feb 1974. Liveryman, Grocers' Co., 1962. *Publications:* The Defeat of Communism, 1964; No Vision Here: Non-Military Warfare in Britain, 1966; (ed) Brandt and the Destruction of NATO, 1973; The Struggle for Freedom, 1980. *Recreations:* study of religious and esp. inter-faith matters, gardening.

Died 3 March 2004.

STIRLING, Rear-Adm. Michael Grote; Agent-General for British Columbia in the United Kingdom and Europe, 1968–75; *b* 29 June 1915; *s* of late Hon. Grote Stirling and Mabel Katherine (*née* Brigstocke), Kelowna, BC; *m* 1942, Sheelagh Kathleen Russell; two *s* one *d. Educ:* Shawnigan Lake School, BC; RNC Greenwich. Cadet, RCN, 1933; HMS Frobisher for training till 1934, then as Midshipman and Sub-Lt in RN, returning Canada Jan. 1938; Ships of RCN until 1941; specialized in Signals at HM Signal School, Portsmouth, then Home Fleet; Dep. Dir, Signal Div., Naval Service HQ, Ottawa, 1942–43; SSO to C-in-C, Canadian North-West Atlantic, 1943–44; comd destroyers, 1944–46; Dir Naval Communications, rank of Comdr, 1949–51; promoted Captain and staff of Supreme Allied Commander Atlantic, Norfolk, Va, 1953–55; comd HMCS Cornwallis, 1955–57; 2nd Cdn Escort Sqdn, 1957–58; Naval Member of Directing Staff, Nat. Defence Coll., as Cdre, 1958–61; Sen. Canadian Officer Afloat, 1961–62; Chief of Naval Personnel, 1962–64; Rear-Adm. 1962; Maritime Comdr, Pacific, 1964–66. Dir, Univ. of Victoria Foundn, 1967–68. *Recreations:* golf, ski-ing. *Address:* 302–1280 Newport Avenue, Victoria, BC V8S 5E7, Canada. *Club:* Victoria Golf (Vic, BC).

Died 24 July 2002.

STOCK, His Honour Raymond; QC 1964; DL; a Circuit Judge (formerly Judge of County Courts), 1971–88; *b* 1 Oct. 1913; *s* of late A. E. and M. E. Stock; *m* 1969, E. Dorothy Thorpe, JP. *Educ:* West Monmouth School; Balliol College, Oxford. Barrister-at-law, Gray's Inn, 1936, Bencher, 1969. Royal Artillery, 1939–45. Recorder: Penzance, 1962–64; Exeter, 1964–66; Southampton, 1966–71; Dep. Chm., Dorset QS, 1964–71. DL Hants, 1991. *Address:* Brambridge House, Bishopstoke, Hants SO50 6HL. *Club:* Athenæum.

Died 17 May 2001.

STOCKDALE, Sir (Arthur) Noel, Kt 1986; DFM 1942; Life President, Walmart-ASDA (formerly ASDA), 1986 (Chairman, 1969–86); *b* 25 Dec. 1920; *s* of Arthur and Florence Stockdale; *m* 1944, Betty Monica Shaw; two *s. Educ:* Woodhouse Grove School; Reading University. Joined Hindells Dairy Farmers, 1939; RAF, 1940–46; rejoined Hindells Dairy Farmers, 1946, subseq. Associated Dairies & Farm Stores (Leeds) Ltd, 1949, Associated Dairies Group PLC, 1977. Hon. LLD Leeds, 1986. *Recreations:* fishing, garden. *Address:* 20 The Old Mill, Scott Lane, Wetherby, Yorks LS22 6NB. *T:* (01937) 582970.

Died 2 Feb. 2004.

STOCKDALE, Sir Noel; see Stockdale, Sir A. N.

STOCKER, Prof. Bruce Arnold Dunbar, FRS 1966; MD; Professor of Microbiology and Immunology in Stanford University, 1966–87, then Emeritus Active; *b* 26 May 1917. *Educ:* King's College, London; Westminster Hosp. Med. Sch.; MB, BS, 1940; MD 1947. MRCS, LRCP, 1940. Guinness Prof. of Microbiology, Univ. of London, and Dir of Guinness-Lister Microbiological Research Unit, Lister Inst. of Preventive Med., until Dec. 1965. *Publications:* articles in scientific jls. *Address:* Department of Microbiology and Immunology, Stanford University School of Medicine, Stanford, CA 94305–5124, USA. *T:* (650) 7232673, *Fax:* (650) 7256757; *e-mail:* bstocker@stanford.edu.

Died 30 Aug. 2004.

STODART OF LEASTON, Baron *cr* 1981 (Life Peer), of Humbie in the District of East Lothian; **James Anthony**

Stodart; PC 1974; *b* 6 June 1916; *yr s* of late Col Thomas Stodart, CIE, IMS, and of Mary Alice Coullie; *m* 1940, Hazel Jean Usher (*d* 1995). *Educ:* Wellington. Farming at Kingston, North Berwick, 1934–58, and at Leaston, Humbie, East Lothian, 1959–2001. Contested: (L) Berwick and East Lothian, 1950; (C) Midlothian and Peebles, 1951; Midlothian, 1955; MP (C) Edinburgh West, 1959–Oct. 1974; Jt Under-Sec. of State, Scottish Office, Sept. 1963–Oct. 1964; an Opposition spokesman on Agriculture and on Scottish Affairs, 1966–69; Parly Sec., MAFF, 1970–72; Minister of State, MAFF, 1972–74. Vice-Chm., Conservative Agric. Cttee, H of C, 1962–63, 1964–65, 1966–70; led Parly Delegns to Canada, 1974, 1983. Dir, FMC, 1980–82; Chm., Agricultural Credit Corp. Ltd, 1975–87. Chairman: Cttee of Inquiry into Local Govt in Scotland, 1980; Manpower Review of Vet. Profession in UK, 1984–85. Pres., E Lothian Boy Scouts' Assoc., 1960–63. Hon. Pres., Edinburgh Univ. Agricl Soc., 1952. *Publications:* (jtly) Land of Abundance, a study of Scottish Agriculture in the 20th Century, 1962; contrib. on farming topics to agricultural jls and newspapers. *Recreations:* music, collecting and looking at vintage films, preserving a sense of humour. *Address:* Lorimers, North Berwick, East Lothian EH39 4NG. *T:* (01620) 892457. *Clubs:* Cavalry and Guards; New (Edinburgh); Hon. Company of Edinburgh Golfers. *Died 31 May 2003.*

STOKES, David Mayhew Allen; QC 1989; **His Honour Judge Stokes;** a Permanent Judge, Central Criminal Court, since 1999; *b* 12 Feb. 1944; *s* of late Henry Pauntley Allen Stokes and Marjorie Joan Stokes; *m* 1970, Ruth Elizabeth, *d* of late Charles Tunstall Evans, CMG, Haywards Heath; one *s* one *d. Educ:* Radley College; Inst. de Touraine (Tours); Churchill College, Cambridge (MA History/Law). Admitted Student, Gray's Inn, 1964; Holt Scholar, 1966; called to the Bar, 1968, Bencher, 1998; a Recorder, 1985–99. Dep. Chancellor, dio. of Norwich, 2001–. Mem., Gen. Council of the Bar, 1989–91, Additional Mem., 1992–98, Chm., Professional Conduct Cttee, 1997–98 (Vice-Chm., 1994–96); Chm., SE Circuit Liaison Cttee, 1991–99. Vis. Instructor/Team Leader, Nat. Inst. Trial Advocacy Workshop, Osgoode Hall Law Sch., York Univ., Toronto, 1986–. Trustee/Dir, London Suzuki Gp, 1988–94. Chairman: Cambridge Bar Mess, 1991–99; E Anglian Bar Mess, 1999. *Recreations:* amateur dramatics, madrigals. *Address:* c/o Central Criminal Court, Old Bailey, EC4M 7EH. *Club:* Norfolk (Norwich).

Died 29 Sept. 2004.

STOKES, Sir John (Heydon Romaine), Kt 1988; *b* 23 July 1917; *o surv. s* of late Victor Romaine Stokes, Hitchin; *m* 1st, 1939, Barbara Esmée (*d* 1988), *y d* of late R. E. Yorke, Wellingborough; one *s* two *d*; 2nd, 1989, Elsie Frances (*d* 1990), *widow* of John Plowman; 3rd, 1991, Ruth (marr. diss. 1996), *widow* of Sir Timothy Bligh, KBE, DSO, DSC; 4th, 1996, Frances Jean Stirling, *widow* of Lt Comdr Donald Packham, RN. *Educ:* Temple Grove; Haileybury Coll.; Queen's Coll., Oxford (BA 1938, MA 1946). Hon. Agent and Treas., Oxford Univ. Conservative Assoc., 1937; President: Monarchist Soc., 1937; Mermaid Club, 1937. Asst Master, Prep. Sch., 1938–39. Served War, 1939–46: Dakar Expedn, 1940; wounded in N Africa, 1943; Mil. Asst to HM Minister Beirut and Damascus, 1944–46; Major, Royal Fusiliers. Personnel Officer, ICI, 1946–51; Personnel Manager, British Celanese, 1951–59; Dep. Personnel Manager, Courtaulds, 1957–59; Dir, Clive & Stokes, Personnel Consultants, 1959–80. Contested (C): Gloucester, 1964; Hitchin, 1966; MP (C) Oldbury and Halesowen, 1970–74, Halesowen and Stourbridge, 1974–92. Mem., Select Cttee on Parly Commn for Admin (Ombudsman), 1979–83. Leader, Parly delegations: to Portugal, 1980; to Falkland Is, 1985; to Malta, 1988; to Trinidad and Tobago, 1991. Mem., Delegn to Council of Europe and WEU, 1983–92; Leader, Delegn from Council of Europe to observe elections in Albania, March 1992. Pres., W Midlands Cons. Clubs, 1971–84. Mem., Gen. Synod of C of E, 1985–90. Chm., Gen. Purposes Cttee, Primrose

League, 1971–85; Vice-Pres., Royal Stuart Soc.; Member: Oxford Soc., 1946–; Prayer Book Soc., 1970–; Trustee, Battlefields Trust, 1998–. Evelyn Wrench Speaker, ESU (USA), 1992. *Publications:* articles on political and historical subjects. *Recreations:* gardening, travel, English history, church affairs, writing to The Times. *Address:* 4 The Bradburys, Stratton Audley, near Bicester, Oxon OX6 9BW. *T:* (01869) 277875. *Died 27 June 2003.*

STOLTENBERG, Gerhard, DrPhil; Member of the Bundestag, 1957–71 and 1982–98; Minister of Defence, Federal Republic of Germany, 1989–92; *b* 29 Sept. 1928; *m* 1958, Margot Rann; one *s* one *d*. *Educ:* Bad Oldesloe; Kiel Univ. (DrPhil 1954). Military service, 1944–45; local govt, 1945–46; Asst Lectr, 1954–60, Lectr, 1960–65, Kiel Univ. Mem., CDU, 1947–: Dep. Chm., 1955–71, Chm., 1971–82, Schleswig-Holstein CDU; Nat. Dep. Chm., 1969–. Nat. Chm., Young Union, 1955–61. Schleswig-Holstein Parliament: Mem., 1954–57, 1971–82; Prime Minister, 1971–82. Bundestag: Minister of Scientific Research, 1965–69; Dep. Chm., CDU/CSU, 1969–71; Minister of Finance, 1982–89. *Publications:* The German Reichstag 1871–1873, 1954; Political Currents in Rural Schleswig-Holstein 1919–1933, 1960; State and Science, 1969; Schleswig-Holstein: present and future, 1978. *Died 23 Nov. 2001.*

STONEY, Brigadier Ralph Francis Ewart, CBE 1952 (OBE 1943); Director-General, The Royal Society for the Prevention of Accidents, 1959–68; *b* 28 June 1903; *o s* of late Col R. D. S. Stoney, The Downs, Delgany, Co. Wicklow and Mrs E. M. M. Stoney; *m* 1st, 1939, Kathleen Nina (*née* Kirkland) (*d* 1973); one *d*; 2nd, 1979, Bridget Mary St John Browne. *Educ:* Royal Naval Colls, Osborne and Dartmouth; RMA, Woolwich. Commnd RE, 1923; Staff Coll., Camberley, 1937–38. Served War of 1939–45 as GSO, 1939–43 (OBE) and as CRE, 82 Div., 1943–46, in Burma (despatches twice). CRE 5th Div. and 2nd Div., 1947–48; Col GS (Intelligence), War Office, 1949–51; Brig. GS (Intelligence), Middle East, 1952–54, retired. *Address:* Kinsale, Hook Heath Avenue, Woking, Surrey GU22 0HN. *Died 19 Jan. 2003.*

STORAR, John Robert Allan Montague, CA; Chairman, Mitchell Cotts PLC, 1985–87 (Director, 1973–87; Deputy Chairman, 1978); *b* 6 Nov. 1925; *s* of James and Leonore Storar; *m* 1952, Catherine Swanson Henderson; two *s* one *d*. *Educ:* Dollar Academy. Dir, 1960–74, Dep. Chief Exec., 1972–74, Drayton Corporation Ltd; Dir 1974–85, Dep. Chm. 1974–81, Man. Dir 1981–82, Samuel Montagu & Co. Ltd; Dir, Consolidated Gold Fields PLC, 1969–89. Chm., Assoc. of Investment Trust Cos, 1979–81. *Recreation:* fly fishing. *Address:* 2 Oxford House, Wimbledon, SW19 5NE. *Club:* Caledonian. *Died 1 March 2003.*

STOREY, Graham, OBE 1997; LittD; Emeritus Reader in English, and Emeritus Fellow of Trinity Hall, Cambridge University, since 1988 (Hon. Fellow, Trinity Hall, 1995); *b* 8 Nov. 1920; *o surv. s* of late Stanley Runton Storey, LDS RCS and Winifred Storey (*née* Graham). *Educ:* St Edward's Sch., Oxford; Trinity Hall, Cambridge (MA 1944); LittD Cantab 1997. Served War, RA, 1941–45; Lieut 1942; mentioned in despatches. Called to the Bar, Middle Temple, 1950, but did not practise. Cambridge University: Fellow, 1949–88, Sen. Tutor, 1958–68, Vice-Master, 1970–74, Trinity Hall; Univ. Lectr in English, 1965–81; Reader, 1981–88; Chm., Faculty Bd of English, 1972–74. Vis. Fellow, All Souls Coll., Oxford, 1968. Leverhulme Emeritus Res. Fellowship, 1988. Warton Lectr, British Acad., 1984; Lecture tours for British Council overseas. Syndic, CUP, 1983. Vice-Pres., G. M. Hopkins Soc., 1971; Pres., Dickens Soc. of America, 1983–84. Governor: St Edward's, Oxford, 1959–69; Eastbourne Coll., 1965–69. Jt Gen. Editor, Letters of Dickens, Pilgrim edn, 1965–; General Editor: Cambridge Renaissance and Restoration Dramatists, 1975–89; Cambridge English Prose Texts, 1980–. *Publications:* Reuters' Century, 1951; Journals and Papers of G. M.

Hopkins, 1959 (completed edn on death of Humphry House); (ed) A. P. Rossiter, Angel with Horns, 1961; (ed) Selected Verse and Prose of G. M. Hopkins, 1966; (ed jtly) Letters of Charles Dickens, vol. I, 1965, vol. II, 1969, vol. III, 1974, vol. V, 1981, vol. VI, 1988, vol. VII, 1993, vol. VIII, 1995, vol. IX, 1997, vol. X, 1998; A Preface to Hopkins, 1981; (ed with Howard Erskine-Hill) Revolutionary Prose of the English Civil War, 1983; Bleak House (critical study), 1987; David Copperfield (critical study), 1991; contributions to: New Cambridge Bibliography, 1967; Writers and their Work, 1982; Dickens and Other Victorians, 1988; periodicals. *Recreations:* theatre, gardening, travel. *Address:* Trinity Hall, Cambridge CB2 1TJ. *T:* (01223) 332500; Crown House, Caxton, Cambs CB3 8PQ. *T:* (01954) 719316. *Died 6 Nov. 2005.*

STOREY, Maude, CBE 1987; President, Royal College of Nursing, 1986–90; *b* 24 March 1930; *d* of late Henry Storey and of Sarah Farrimond Storey. *Educ:* Wigan and District Mining and Techn. Coll.; St Mary's Hosp., Manchester; Lancaster Royal Infirmary; Paddington Gen. Hosp.; Royal Coll. of Nursing, Edinburgh; Queen Elizabeth Coll., London. SRN 1952; SCM 1953; RCI (Edin.) 1962; RNT 1965. Domiciliary Midwife, Wigan County Borough, 1953–56; Midwifery Sister, St Mary's Hosp., Manchester, 1956–57; Charge Nurse, Intensive Therapy, Mayo Clinic, USA, 1957–59; Theatre Sister, Clinical Instructor, 1959–63, subseq. Nurse Tutor, 1965–68, Royal Albert Edward Infirmary, Wigan; Lectr in Community Nursing, Manchester Univ., 1968–71; Asst, subseq. Principal Regional Nursing Officer, Liverpool Regional Hosp. Bd, 1971–73; Regional Nursing Officer, Mersey RHA, 1973–77; Registrar, GNC for England and Wales, 1977–81; Registrar and Chief Exec., UKCC, 1981–87. Member: Wigan and Leigh HA, 1974–77; Standing Nursing and Midwifery Adv. Cttee, 1977–90; West Berks HA, 1982–93; non-exec. Dir, Berks HA, 1993–96; Chm., W Berks Res. Ethics Cttee, 1992–96. Mem. Council, 1988–2000, Mem. Court, 2001–, Reading Univ. FRCN 1996. Hon. Fellow, Univ. of Central Lancashire, 1998. CStJ 1987. *Recreations:* travel, theatre. *Address:* 14 Conifer Drive, Long Lane, Tilehurst, Berks RG31 6YU. *T:* (0118) 941 2082. *Died 29 March 2003.*

STORR, (Charles) Anthony, FRCP, FRCPsych; FRSL; writer and psychiatrist; Clinical Lecturer in Psychiatry, Faculty of Medicine, University of Oxford, 1974–84; Fellow, Green College, Oxford, 1979–84, then Emeritus; Hon. Consulting Psychiatrist, Oxford Health Authority, since 1986; *b* 18 May 1920; *y s* of Vernon Faithfull Storr, Subdean of Westminster and Katherine Cecilia Storr; *m* 1st, 1942, Catherine Cole (marr. diss.; she *m* 2nd, Baron Balogh, and *d* 2001); three *d*; 2nd, 1970, Catherine Barton (*née* Peters). *Educ:* Winchester Coll.; Christ's Coll., Cambridge (MB, BChir 1944); Westminster Hosp. Medical School. FRCPsych 1971; FRCP 1975. Postgrad. trng in psychiatry, Maudsley Hosp., 1947–50; held various positions as psychiatrist in different hospitals; Consultant Psychotherapist, Oxford AHA, 1974–84. Member: Parole Bd, 1976–77; Cttee on Obscenity and Film Censorship, 1977–79. Hon. FRCPsych 1993. *Publications:* The Integrity of the Personality, 1960; Sexual Deviation, 1964; Human Aggression, 1968; Human Destructiveness, 1972; The Dynamics of Creation, 1972; Jung, 1973; The Art of Psychotherapy, 1979; (ed) Jung: selected writings, 1983, new edn, as The Essential Jung, 1998; Solitude, 1988; Freud, 1989; Churchill's Black Dog and Other Phenomena of the Human Mind, 1989; Music and the Mind, 1992; Feet of Clay, 1996; contrib. several books and jls. *Recreations:* music, broadcasting, journalism. *Address:* 45 Chalfont Road, Oxford OX2 6TJ. *T:* (01865) 553348. *Club:* Savile. *Died 17 March 2001.*

STOTT, (Charlotte) Mary, OBE 1975; journalist, retired; *b* 18 July 1907; *d* of Robert Guy Waddington and Amalie Waddington (*née* Bates); *m* 1937, Kenneth Stott (*d* 1967);

one d. *Educ:* Wyggeston Grammar Sch., Leicester. Leicester Mail, 1925–31; Bolton Evening News, 1931–33; Co-operative Press, Manchester, editing women's and children's publications, 1933–45; News sub-editor, Manchester Evening News, 1945–50; Women's Editor, The Guardian, 1957–72. Last Pres., Women's Press Club, 1970; Chm., Fawcett Soc., 1980–82; Pres., Nat. Assoc. of Widows, 1993–95. Hon. Fellow, Manchester Polytechnic, 1972. Hon. MA: Open, 1991; Leicester, 1995; Hon. DLitt De Montfort, 1996. *Publications:* Forgetting's No Excuse, 1973, rev. edn 1989; Organization Woman, 1978; Ageing for Beginners, 1981; Before I Go …, 1985; Women Talking, 1987. *Recreations:* committees, music (especially choir singing), painting (water colours), gardening. *Address:* 4/11 Morden Road, Blackheath, SE3 0AA. *T:* (020) 8852 2901.   *Died 16 Sept. 2002.*

STOTT, Mary; *see* Stott, C. M.

STOUT, Samuel Coredon; HM Diplomatic Service, retired; *b* 17 Feb. 1913; *m* 1st, Mary Finn (*d* 1965); two *s* one *d*; 2nd, 1966, Jill Emery. Ministry of National Insurance, 1937–40; Admiralty, 1940–46; Board of Trade, 1946–65 (Trade Commissioner, Singapore, Bombay and Melbourne); Counsellor (Commercial), Canberra, 1966–68; Dep. High Comr and Minister (Commercial), Karachi, 1968–70; Consul-Gen., St Louis, USA, 1970–72. *Address:* Dominies, 25 Stanhope Avenue, Woodhall Spa, Lincs LN10 6SP. *T:* (01526) 352240.

Died 21 Jan. 2001.

STOUT, William Ferguson, CB 1964; Security Adviser to Government of Northern Ireland, 1971–72, retired; *b* Holywood, Co. Down, 22 Feb. 1907; *s* of late Robert and Amelia Stout; *m* 1938, Muriel Kilner; one *s* one *d*. *Educ:* Sullivan Upper Sch., Holywood; Queen's Univ., Belfast. Ministry of Home Affairs: Principal, 1943; Asst Sec., 1954; Senior Asst Sec., 1959; Permanent Sec., 1961–64; Permanent Secretary: Min. of Health and Local Govt, 1964; Min. of Development, 1965–71. *Recreation:* golf. *Died 18 March 2005.*

STOW, Sir Christopher P.; *see* Philipson-Stow.

STRACHAN, Douglas Frederick; Vice-Chairman, Cheltenham & Gloucester plc, 1995–2002 (Director, 1995–2002); *b* 26 July 1933; *s* of Hon. Lord Strachan and Lady (Irene Louise) Strachan (*née* Warren); *m* 1st, 1956, Mary Scott Hardie (*d* 1976); four *s* one *d*; 2nd, 1980, Jane, *widow* of Lt-Col I. D. Corden-Lloyd, OBE, MC; three step *s*. *Educ:* Rugby Sch.; Corpus Christi Coll., Oxford (MA). Brewer, Arthur Guinness Son & Co. (Dublin) Ltd, 1956–67; Man. Dir, Cantrell & Cochrane Gp Ltd, Dublin, 1967–72; Dir, Showerings, Vine Products & Whiteways Ltd, 1972–77; Man. Dir, Allied Breweries Ltd, 1977–85; Dir, Allied-Lyons Plc, 1976–85; Dir (Chief Executive), PRO NED, 1985–89; Dir, Cheltenham & Gloucester BS, 1991–95 (Vice-Chm., 1994–95).Chm., Somerset FHSA, 1989–93; Mem., South Western RHA, 1990–93. *Recreations:* gardening, music, golf. *Address:* North Hill Farm, West Camel, Yeovil, Somerset BA22 7RF. *T:* (01935) 850404.   *Died 13 May 2004.*

STRACHAN, Walter, CBE 1967; CEng, FRAeS; consulting engineer, since 1971; *b* 14 Oct. 1910; *s* of William John Strachan, Rothes, Morayshire, and Eva Hitchins, Bristol; *m* 1937, Elizabeth Dora Bradshaw, Aldershot; two *s*. *Educ:* Newfoundland Road Sch., Bristol; Merchant Venturers Technical Coll., Bristol. Bristol Aeroplane Co.: Apprentice, 1925; Aircraft Ground Engr, 1932; RAE, Farnborough, 1934; Inspector: Bristol Aeroplane Co., 1937. BAC Service Engr, RAF Martlesham Heath, 1938; BAC: Asst Service Manager, 1940; Asst Works Manager, 1942; Manager, Banwell, building Beaufort and Tempest aircraft, 1943; Gen.-Manager, Banwell and Weston Factories, manufg Aluminium Houses, 1945; Gen. Manager, Banwell and Weston Factories, building helicopters and aircraft components, 1951; Managing Dir, Bristol Aerojet,

Banwell, Rocket Motor Develt and Prod., 1958. Liveryman, Coachmakers' & Coach Harness Makers' Co., 1961. *Recreations:* golf, music, ornithology. *Address:* 18 Clarence Road East, Weston-super-Mare, Somerset BS23 4BW. *T:* (01934) 623878. *Clubs:* Naval and Military; Royal Automobile.   *Died 1 Aug. 2004.*

STRAITON, Edward Cornock, OBE 1998; Senior Partner, Veterinary Hospital, Penkridge, Staffs, since 1957; *b* 27 March 1917; *s* of George Ramsay Straiton and May Purcell Straiton (*née* Cornock); *m* 1st, Lorraine (decd); (one *s* decd); 2nd, 1982, Penelope Stanier; one *s* one *d*. *Educ:* Glasgow Univ. MRCVS 1940. Veterinary surgeon, 1940–; BBC vet. and sound broadcaster, 1961–; started as BBC TV vet., 1964; agricl journalist, 1970–. *Publications:* TV Vet series, 1960s: Cattle Diseases; Calving the Cow and Care of the Calf; Pig Book; Sheep Book; Horse Book; Dog Book; Cat Book; Exotic Creatures; *autobiographical:* Animals are my Life; A Vet in Charge; A Vet at Large; Positively Vetted; A Vet on the Set. *Recreation:* sport. *Address:* Darlaston Hall, Darlaston Park, Stone, Staffs ST15 0ND. *T:* (01785) 712235; *e-mail:* tvveted@aol.com.
Died 30 Oct. 2004.

STRANGE, Baroness (16th in line), *cr* 1628; **Jean Cherry Drummond;** *b* 17 Dec. 1928; *e c* of 15th Baron Strange (*d* 1982) and Violet Margaret Florence (*d* 1975), *d* of Sir Robert William Buchanan-Jardine, 2nd Bt; *S* (after termination of abeyance), 1986; *m* 1952, Captain Humphrey ap Evans, MC, who assumed name of Drummond of Megginch by decree of Lord Lyon, 1965; three *s* three *d*. *Educ:* St Andrews Univ. (MA 1951); Cambridge Univ. Pres., War Widows' Assoc. of GB, 1990–. Elected Mem., H of L, 1999. FSAScot 1989. Hon. FIMarEST (Hon. FIMarE 1996). *Publications:* Love from Belinda, 1960; Lalage in Love, 1962; Creatures Great and Small, 1968; Love is For Ever, 1988; The Remarkable Life of Victoria Drummond, Marine Engineer, 1994. *Heir:* *s* Hon. Adam Humphrey Drummond, Major Grenadier Guards [*b* 20 April 1953; *m* 1988, Mary Emma Dewar; one *s* one *d*]. *Address:* Megginch Castle, Errol, Perthshire PH2 7SW. *T:* (01821) 642222; Tresco, 160 Kennington Road, SE11 6QR. *T:* (020) 7735 3681.
Died 11 March 2005.

STRATTON, Air Vice-Marshal William Hector, CB 1970; CBE 1963; DFC 1939 and Bar 1944; Chief of the Air Staff, RNZAF, 1969–71, retired 1971; *b* 22 July 1916; *s* of V. J. Stratton; *m* 1954, Dorothy M., *d* of J. D. Whyte; one *s* two *d*. *Educ:* Hawera Tech. High School, and privately. RAF, 1937–44: No 1 Sqn, France, 1939–40; CO Advanced Trng Sqn, Rhodesia, 1940–43; CO 134 Sqn, ME and India, 1943–44; transf. RNZAF, 1944: appointments include: CO, Ohakea, 1954–57; Hd, NZ Defence Liaison Staff, Aust., 1957–60; Dir of Ops, subseq. Dir of Postings and Personal Services, 1960–61; ACAS, 1961–63; Hd, NZ Liaison Staff, London, 1963–67; Air Member for Personnel, 1967–69. *Address:* 41 Goldsworthy Road, Claremont, Perth, WA 6010, Australia.
Died 27 Dec. 2005.

STRETTON, Eric Hugh Alexander, CB 1972; Deputy Chief Executive in Property Services Agency, Department of the Environment, 1972–76, Deputy Chairman, 1973–76; *b* 22 June 1916; *y s* of Major S. G. Stretton, Wigston, Leicester; *m* 1946, Sheila Woodroffe Anderson, MB, BS (*d* 1997), *d* of Dr A. W. Anderson, Cardiff (formerly of Ogmore Vale); one *s* one *d*. *Educ:* Wyggeston Sch; Pembroke Coll., Oxford. BA 1939, MA 1942. Leics Regt and 2/4 PWO Gurkha Rifles (Major), 1939–46. Asst Sec., Birmingham Univ. Appointments Board, 1946. Entered Ministry of Works, 1947; Prin. Private Sec. to Minister of Works, 1952–54; Asst Sec., 1954; Under-Secretary: MPBW, 1962–70; DoE, 1970–72; Dep. Sec., 1972. Chm., Structure Plan Examns in Public, Salop, 1979, Lincs, 1980, Central and N Lancs, 1981. *Publication:* Dacre Castle, 1994.   *Died 1 Aug. 2004.*

STRETTON, Ross; Director, Royal Ballet, 2001–02; *b* 6 June 1952; *m* Valmai Roberts; two *s* one *d*. Trained at Australian Ballet Sch., Melbourne. Dancer: Australian Ballet, 1972–79 (Prin. Artist); Joffrey Ballet; American Ballet Theatre, NY, 1981–91; Asst Artistic Dir, American Ballet Theatre, 1993–97; Dir, Australian Ballet, 1997–2001. *Died 16 June 2005.*

STRINGER, Pamela Mary; Headmistress, Clifton High School for Girls, 1965–85; *b* 30 Aug. 1928; *e d* of late E. Allen Stringer. *Educ:* Worcester Grammar Sch. for Girls; St Hugh's Coll., Oxford (MA (Hons Lit Hum)). Asst Classics Mistress, Sherborne Sch. for Girls, 1950–59; Head of Classics Dept, Pate's Grammar Sch. for Girls, Cheltenham, 1959–64 (Dep. Head, 1963–64). Member: Exec. Cttee, Assoc. of Headmistresses, 1975–; Exec. Cttee, Girls Schools Assoc., 1975– (Pres., 1978–79; Chm., Educn Cttee, 1981–84); Council, Secondary Heads Assoc., 1978–79 (Pres. Area 7, 1978–79). *Recreations:* travel in Tuscany and Umbria, reading, arctophily, cooking. *Address:* 36 Henleaze Gardens, Bristol BS9 4HJ. *Died 26 Sept. 2005.*

STRONG, John Clifford, CBE 1980; HM Diplomatic Service, retired; Governor, Turks and Caicos Islands, 1978–82; *b* 14 Jan. 1922; *m* 1942, Janet Browning (*d* 1992); three *d*. *Educ:* Beckenham Grammar Sch.; London Sch. of Economics and Political Science. LLB 1953. Served RN, 1942–46; HMOCS Tanzania, 1946–63; CRO, 1963; First Sec., Nairobi, 1964–68; FCO, 1968–73; Counsellor and Head of Chancery, Dar es Salaam, 1973–78. *Address:* Sunrise Assisted Living, Frognal House, Frognal Avenue, Sidcup, Kent DA14 6LF. *Died 24 Sept. 2003.*

STRONG, Julia Trevelyan; see Oman, J. T.

STROUD, Sir (Charles) Eric, Kt 1989; FRCP; Professor of Child Health, King's College School of Medicine and Dentistry (formerly King's College Hospital Medical School), and Director, Department of Child Health, 1968–88; Paediatric Consultant to RAF, 1976–2005; *b* 15 May 1924; *s* of Frank Edmund and Lavinia May Stroud; *m* 1950, June, *d* of Harold Neep; one *s* two *d*. *Educ:* Cardiff High Sch. for Boys; Welsh National Sch. of Medicine (BSc 1945, MB, BCh 1948). MRCP 1955, DCH 1955, FRCP 1968 (London). Sqdn Ldr, RAF, 1950–52. Med. Qual., 1948; Paediatric Registrar, Welsh Nat. Sch. of Med.; Sen. Registrar, Great Ormond Street Children's Hosp., 1957–61; Paediatrician, Uganda Govt, 1958–60; Asst to Dir, Dept of Child Health, Guy's Hosp., 1961–62; Cons. Paediatrician, King's Coll. Hosp., 1962–68. Med. Advr, Eastern Hemisphere, Variety Clubs Internat., 1985–2005; Hon. Med. Dir, Children Nationwide Med. Res. Fund. FKC 1989. *Publications:* chapters in Textbook of Obstetrics, 1958; Childhealth in the Tropics, 1961; various articles in med. jls, mainly on sickle cell anaemia, nutrition and health of ethnic minorities. *Recreations:* bad golf, good fishing, cheap antiques, planning for retirement. *Address:* 84 Copse Hill, Wimbledon, SW20 0EF. *T:* (020) 8947 1336. *Died 29 Dec. 2005.*

STROUD, Sir Eric; see Stroud, Sir C. E.

STRUTT, Sir Nigel (Edward), Kt 1972; TD; DL; formerly Managing Director: Lord Rayleigh's Farms; Strutt & Parker (Farms); *b* 18 Jan. 1916; *yr s* of late Edward Jolliffe Strutt and Amélie, *d* of Frederic Devas. *Educ:* Winchester; Wye Agricultural College (Fellow, 1970). Essex Yeomanry (Major), 1937–56. Member: Eastern Electricity Bd, 1964–76; Agricultural Advisory Council, 1963– (Chm. 1969–73; Chm., Adv. Council for Agriculture and Horticulture, 1973–80); NEDC for Agriculture, 1967–82. President: Country Landowners' Association, 1967–69; British Friesian Cattle Soc., 1974–75; Royal Agricultural Soc. of England, 1982–83. Master, Farmers' Co., 1976–77. DL Essex 1954; High Sheriff of Essex, 1966. Hon. FRASE, 1971. Hon. DSc Cranfield, 1979; DU Essex, 1981; Hon. DPhil Anglia

Polytech. Univ., 1993. Massey Ferguson Award, 1976. Von Thünen Gold Medal, Kiel Univ., 1974. *Recreations:* shooting, travelling. *Address:* Sparrows, Terling, Essex CM3 2QY. *T:* (01245) 233213. *Clubs:* Brooks's, Farmers'. *Died 28 Jan. 2004.*

STUART-SHAW, Max, CBE 1963; Executive Director, Olympic Airways, 1969–71; *b* 20 Dec. 1912; *e s* of Herman and Anne Louise Stuart-Shaw; *m* 1st, 1957, Ella Dorothy (*d* 1966); 2nd, 1967, Janna Job, *d* of C. W. Howard. *Educ:* Belmont School, Sussex; St Paul's, London. Imperial Airways/BOAC, 1931–46; Aer Lingus Irish Airlines, Traffic Manager, Commercial Manager, Asst Gen. Manager, 1947–57; Chief Exec. and Gen. Manager Central African Airways, Salisbury, Rhodesia, 1958–65; Man. Dir, BUA, 1966–67; Vice-Chairman, British United Airways, 1967–68. *Recreation:* air transport. *Died 23 Aug. 2005.*

STUART-WHITE, Sir Christopher (Stuart), Kt 1993; a Judge of the High Court of Justice, Family Division, 1993–99; *b* 18 Dec. 1933; *s* of Reginald Stuart-White and Catherine Mary Wigmore Stuart-White (*née* Higginson); *m* 1957, Pamela (*née* Grant); one *s* two *d*. *Educ:* Winchester; Trinity Coll., Oxford (BA). Called to Bar, Inner Temple, 1957, Bencher 1993. Barrister on the Midland and Oxford Circuit, 1957–78; a Recorder of the Crown Court, 1974–78; a Circuit Judge, 1978–93; Liaison Judge, Family Div., Midland and Oxford Circuit, 1994–98. Chairman: Magisterial Cttee, Judicial Studies Bd, 1985–90; County Court Rule Cttee, 1988–92. Contributing Editor: County Court Practice, 1991–99; Civil Court Practice, 1999–2000. *Recreation:* discussing ailments with other elderly gentlemen. *Died 7 July 2005.*

STUDD, Sir Peter Malden, GBE 1971; KCVO 1979; Kt 1969; DL; *b* 15 Sept. 1916; *s* of late Brig. Malden Augustus Studd, DSO, MC and Netta Cramsie; *m* 1943, Angela Mary Hamilton (*née* Garnier) (*d* 1995); two *s*. *Educ:* Harrow; Clare Coll., Cambridge (BA 1939, MA 1968). Captain of cricket, Harrow and Cambridge Univ. Served War of 1939–45, RA, ME and European campaigns. De La Rue Co., 1939–81; Dir, Lloyds & Scottish plc, 1973–84. Alderman, Cripplegate Ward, City of London, 1959–76; Sheriff, 1967–68; Lord Mayor of London, 1970–71; Hon. DSc City Univ., 1971. Chm., Florence Nightingale Hosp., 1967–71. Chm., King George's Jubilee Trust, 1972; Dep. Chm., Queen's Silver Jubilee Trust, 1976–80; Vice-Pres., Britain-Australia Bicentennial Cttee '88, 1985–; Pres., British Chiropractic Advancement Assoc., 1987–90; Vice-President: The Arts Educational Schools, 1984–; Seven Springs Centre, 1998–2002; Trustee, Royal Jubilee Trusts, 1980–95. Patron, London Bridge Mus. and Educnl Trust, 2001–. Former Governor: Regent Street Poly.; Lady Eleanor Holles Sch.; Pangbourne Coll.; Harrow Sch. Liveryman, Merchant Taylors' Co., 1959 (Asst, 1959–, Master, 1973–74); Hon. Liveryman, Fruiterers' and Plaisterers' Cos. DL Wilts, 1983. KStJ 1968 (Pres., Co. of Surrey, 1967–76). *Recreations:* fishing, photographing, saving St Paul's, 'lighting up the Thames'. *Address:* c/o Messrs C. Hoare & Co., 37 Fleet Street, EC4P 4DQ. *Clubs:* MCC, I Zingari; Hawks (Cambridge); Houghton (Stockbridge). *Died 22 June 2003.*

STURDY, Henry William, OBE 1975 (MBE 1968); HM Diplomatic Service, retired; Deputy Consul General and Counsellor Commercial, Chicago, 1976–78; *b* 17 Feb. 1919; *s* of late Henry William Dawson Sturdy and Jemima Aixill; *m* 1945, Anne Jamieson, (Nan), Marr; one *s* one *d*. *Educ:* Woolwich Polytechnic (Mechanical Engineering). Served War in Middle East, 1939–45; Allied Control Commission, Germany, 1946. Executive Branch of Civil Service and Board of Trade, 1951; tour in Trade Commission Service, 1953; appointments: Pakistan, Bangladesh, Sri Lanka, Canada. First Secretary, Diplomatic Service, 1965; Counsellor, Korea, 1976. Defence Medal; 1939–45 Medal; General Service Medal, 1939, with

Palestine Clasp, 1945. *Recreations:* bridge, reading, argument, international cuisine. *Address:* 12A Homewood Court, Badgers Walk, Chorleywood, Herts WD3 5GB.
Died 29 Dec. 2001.

SUGDEN, Sir Arthur, Kt 1978; Chief Executive Officer, Co-operative Wholesale Society Ltd, 1974–80; Chairman: Co-operative Bank Ltd, 1974–80; Co-operative Commercial Bank Ltd, 1974–80; *b* 12 Sept. 1918; *s* of late Arthur and Elizabeth Ann Sugden; *m* 1946, Agnes Grayston; two *s. Educ:* Thomas Street, Manchester. Certified Accountant, Chartered Secretary. FIB 1975. Served War of 1939–45, RA; CPO 6th Super Heavy Battery; Adjt 12th Medium Regt; Staff Captain 16th Army Group. CWS Ltd: Accountancy Asst, 1946; Office Manager, 1950; Factory Manager, 1954; Group Manager, Edible Oils and Fats Factories, 1964; Controller, Food Div., 1967; Dep. Chief Exec. Officer, 1971. Chairman, 1974–80: FC Finance Ltd; CWS (Longburn) Ltd; CWS (New Zealand) Holdings Ltd; CWS Marketing Ltd; CWS (India) Ltd; Ocean Beach Freezing Co. Ltd; Shaw's Smokers' Products Ltd; formerly Director: Co-operative City Investments Ltd; Co-operative Pension Funds Unit Trust Managers' Ltd; Associated Co-operative Creameries Ltd; CWS Svineslagterier A/S Denmark; CWS (Overseas) Ltd; Tukuyu Tea Estates Ltd; Spillers French Holdings Ltd; J. W. French (Milling & Baking Holdings) Ltd; North Eastern Co-operative Soc. Ltd; Manchester Ship Canal Ltd, 1978–87; Manchester Chamber of Commerce. Formerly Vice-President: Inst. of Bankers; Inst. of Grocery Distribution Ltd. Member: Central Cttee, Internat. Co-operative Alliance; Management Bds, Euro-Coop and Inter-Coop (Pres., 1979–80). Pres., Co-operative Congress, 1978. CCMI; FIGD. *Recreations:* music, reading, walking. *Address:* 56 Old Wool Lane, Cheadle Hulme, Cheadle, Cheshire SK8 5JA.
Died 7 June 2003.

SUMMERFIELD, Prof. Arthur, BSc Tech; BSc; CPsychol, FBPsS, FInstD; Chairman, LearnIT Ltd, 1991–2001; Professor of Psychology, University of London, 1961–88, then Emeritus, and Head of the Department of Psychology at Birkbeck College, 1961–88; *b* 31 March 1923; *s* of late Arthur and Dora Gertrude Summerfield; *m* 1st, 1946, Aline Whalley; one *s* one *d*; 2nd, 1974, Angela Barbara, MA Cantab, PhD London, CPsychol, FBPsS, *d* of late George Frederick and Estelle Steer. *Educ:* Manchester Grammar Sch.; Manchester Univ.; University Coll. London (1st cl. hons Psychology). Served War of 1939–45, Electrical Officer, RNVR, 1943–46: Naval Air Stations, 1943–46; Dept of Sen. Psychologist to the Admiralty, 1946. Lectr in Psychology, University Coll. London, 1949–61, Hon. Research Associate, 1961–70, Hon. Research Fellow, 1970–; first Dean, Fac. of Econs, Birkbeck Coll., 1971–72, Governor, 1982–86; Hon. Lectr in Psychology, Westminster Med. Sch., 1974–76. Member: Univ. of London Acad. Adv. Bd in Medicine, 1974–88; Acad. Council Standing Sub-Cttee on Science and Engrg, 1974–77. Hon. Life Mem., British Psychological Soc., 1993 (Mem. Council, 1953–65, 1967–75, 1977–84; Hon. Gen. Sec., 1954–59; Dep. Pres., 1959–62; Pres., 1963–64; Vice-Pres., 1964–65; first Chm., Scientific Affairs Bd, 1974–75); Member: Cttee on Internat. Relations in Psychology, Amer. Psychological Assoc., 1977–79; Bd of Dirs, European Co-ordination Centre for Res. and Documentation in Social Scis (Vienna Centre), 1977–81; ICSU Study Gp on biol, med. and physical effects of large scale use of nuclear weapons, 1983–87; Pres., IUPS, 1976–80 (Mem., Exec. Cttee, 1963–84, Assembly, 1957–84; Vice-Pres., 1972–76); Pres., Section J (Psychology), BAAS, 1976–77; Pres., Internat. Soc. Sci. Council, 1977–81 (Mem. Prog. Cttee, 1973–83; Mem. Exec. Cttee, 1977–83); Chm., DES Working Party on Psychologists in Educn Services, 1965–68 (Summerfield report). Member: DSIR Human Sciences Res. Grants Cttee, 1962–65; SSRC, 1979–81; Psychology Cttee, SSRC, 1979–81. Vis. Prof., Univ. of California (at Dept of Psychobiology, Irvine Campus), 1968. Governor,

Enfield Coll. of Technology, 1968–72. Dir, British Jl of Educnl Psychology Ltd, 1976–93; Asst Editor, Brit. Jl Psychology (Statistical Section), 1950–54; Editor, British Jl of Psychology, 1964–67; Scientific Editor, British Med. Bulletin issues on Experimental Psychology, 1964, Cognitive Psychology, 1971, (with D. M. Warburton) Psychobiology, 1981. *Publications:* (trans. and ed jtly) Animals and Men, 1951; articles on perception, memory, statistical methods and psycho-pharmacology in scientific periodicals. *Address:* Rose Bank, Sutton-under-Whitestonecliffe, Thirsk, N Yorks YO7 2PR. *T:* (01845) 597395, *Fax:* (01845) 597005. *Club:* Athenæum.
Died 10 Sept. 2005.

SUMMERS, Henry Forbes, CB 1961; Under-Secretary, Department of the Environment (formerly Ministry of Housing and Local Government), 1955–71; *b* 18 Aug. 1911; *s* of late Rev. H. H. Summers, Harrogate, Yorks; *m* 1937, Rosemary (*d* 2003), *d* of late Robert L. Roberts, CBE; two *s* one *d. Educ:* Fettes Coll., Edinburgh; Trinity College, Oxford. Joined Min. of Health, 1935; was Private Sec. to Rt Hon. Aneurin Bevan, Minister of Health, during passage of Nat. Health Bill, 1945. *Publications:* Smoke After Flame, 1944; Hinterland, 1947; Poems in Pamphlet, 1952; Tomorrow is my Love, 1978; The Burning Book, 1982; Brevities, 1991. *Address:* 29A West End, Sherborne St John, Basingstoke, Hants RG24 9LE. *T:* (01256) 889450.
Died 22 Dec. 2005.

SUMSION, John Walbridge, OBE 1991; Senior Fellow, Department of Information Science (formerly Information and Library Studies), Loughborough University, since 1996; *b* 16 Aug. 1928; *s* of late Dr Herbert Sumsion, CBE; *m* 1st, 1961, Annette Dorothea Wilson (marr. diss. 1979); two *s* two *d*; 2nd, 1979, Hazel Mary Jones (*née* English). *Educ:* St George's Choir Sch., Windsor Castle; St Thomas' Choir Sch., NYC; Rendcomb Coll., Cirencester; Clare Coll., Cambridge (BA (Hons) History 1952); Yale Univ., USA (MA Economics); Cornell Univ., USA (Teaching Fellow). Somervell Brothers (K Shoemakers) Ltd: Graduate trainee, 1954; Production Manager (Women's Shoes), 1959; Dir, 1962–81; Registrar, Public Lending Right, 1981–91; Dir, Library and Inf. Statistics Unit, Loughborough Univ., 1991–96. Dir, TeleOrdering Ltd, 1992–94. Mem., Library and Inf. Services Council (England), 1992–95; Chm., Stats Section, IFLA, 1995–99. Ed., Library & Information Res. News, 1997–2001. Hon. FCLIP (Hon. FLA 1990). *Publications:* Setting Up Public Lending Right, 1984; PLR in Practice, 1988, 2nd edn 1991; Practical Performance Indicators, 1992; (with L. England) Perspectives of Public Library Use, 1995; (jtly) Library Economics in Europe: millennium study, 2000; (jtly) Economic Value of Public Libraries, 2001; various statistical reports. *Recreation:* music (flute, singing). *Address:* The Granary, 29 Main Street, Rotherby, Melton Mowbray, Leics LE14 2LP. *T:* (01664) 434485.
Died 21 Feb. 2003.

SURR, Jeremy Bernard, CB 1993; consultant; Director Operations (South and East), Training Enterprise and Education Directorate, Department of Employment, 1990–92; *b* 23 Jan. 1938; *s* of Thomas Bernard Surr, ISO, and Mabel Edith Moore; *m* 1965, Gillian Mary Lapage. *Educ:* Rutlish Sch., Wimbledon; Bury Grammar Sch., Lancs. National Service, RCS, 1956–58. Min. of Labour, 1959–65; computer systems analyst, 1965–70; Asst Private Sec. to Sec. of State for Employment, 1971–74; Principal, Employment Protection, Incomes Policy and Res. and Planning, 1974–78; on secondment to Australian Dept of Employment and Industrial Relations, 1978–80; joined MSC as Head of Sheltered Employment and Employment Rehabilitation Br., 1980; Head of Special Measures Br., 1982–85; Dir of Special Measures, 1985–86; Chief Exec., Employment and Enterprise Gp, 1986–87; Dir of Adult Programmes, 1987–89, Dir, Operations and Trng and Enterprise Councils Develt, 1989–90, Training Agency (formerly MSC, later Training Commn). Dir, Energy Action Grants Agency, 1993–2000. Trustee, Drive for

Youth, 1993–2001. FRSA 1993. *Recreations:* golf, walking, gardening, DIY. *Address:* 48 Oak Hill Road, Nether Edge, Sheffield S7 1SH. *T:* (0114) 255 7554. *Club:* Abbeydale Golf (Sheffield). *Died 25 Sept. 2005.*

SUTCH, Peter Dennis Antony, CBE 1995; GBS 2000; FRAeS; Director, John Swire & Sons Ltd, since 1999; Chairman: Aviation Partners Worldwide plc, since 2000; Magtibay Holdings BV, since 2001; *b* 8 April 1945; *s* of Ronald Antony Sutch and Kathleen (*née* Roden); *m* 1st, 1968, Rosemary Aisling Langan (marr. diss. 1996); three *s* one *d*; 2nd, 1996, Gillian Stevens (marr. diss. 2001). *Educ:* Downside Sch., Stratton-on-Fosse; Exeter Coll., Oxford Univ. (MA Hist.). Joined John Swire & Sons Ltd, Hong Kong, 1966: Shipping Division: Hong Kong, 1966–67; Japan, 1967–69; Cathay Pacific Airways: Manager, W Japan, 1970–72; Passenger Sales Manager, Hong Kong, 1972–76; Gen. Manager, Japan, 1976–81; Dep. Dir and Gen. Manager, Hong Kong, 1981–83; Dep. Man. Dir, 1983–84; Man. Dir, 1984–88; Dep. Chm. and Man. Dir, 1988; Dep. Chm., John Swire & Sons (HK) Ltd and Swire Pacific Ltd, 1988–92; Chairman: Hong Kong Aircraft Engrg Co. Ltd, 1987–95; Swire Gp, Hong Kong, 1992–99; Director: Cathay Pacific Airways Ltd, 1983–2001 (Chm., 1992–99); Swire Pacific Ltd, 1984–2001 (Chm., 1992–99); John Swire & Sons (HK) Ltd, 1984–2000 (Chm., 1992–99); GlobalInflight Services Ltd, 2000–; iVenture Investment Mgt (BVI) Ltd, 2000–; National Jet Italia SpA, 2001–. Board Member: Hongkong & Shanghai Banking Corp., 1992–99; Lee Gardens Internat. Hldgs, 1992–96; Community Chest of Hong Kong, 1992–99; Council Mem., Univ. of Hong Kong, 1992–99; Member: Aviation Adv. Bd; Gen. Cttee, Hong Kong Gen. Chamber of Commerce, 1992–99 (Chm., 1998–99); Hong Kong Trade Develt Council, 1992–99; CIT in Hong Kong, 1992–99; Hong Kong Chief Exec's Commn on Strategic Develt, 1998–99; Mem., Barristers Disciplinary Tribunal Panel, Hong Kong, 1993–99. Mem. Adv. Bd., Hong Kong Red Cross, 1996–99. *Recreations:* golf, travel, boating. *Address:* (office) 132 Ebury Street, SW1W 9QQ; (home) 2/33 Cranley Gardens, SW7 3BD. *Clubs:* Royal Automobile; Naunton Downs Golf; Hong Kong, Hong Kong Jockey, Hong Kong Golf, Shek O Country (Hong Kong). *Died 6 March 2002.*

SUTHERLAND, James, CBE 1974; Partner, McClure Naismith, Solicitors, Glasgow and Edinburgh, 1951–87, Consultant, 1987–90; *b* 15 Feb. 1920; *s* of James Sutherland, JP and Agnes Walker; *m* 1st, 1948, Elizabeth Kelly Barr; one *s* (and one *s* decd); 2nd, 1984, Grace Williamson Dawson, BL. *Educ:* Queens Park Secondary Sch., Glasgow; Glasgow Univ. (MA 1940, LLB 1948). Served Royal Signals, 1940–46. Examr in Scots Law, 1951–55 and Mercantile Law and Industrial Law, 1968–69, Glasgow Univ.; Chm., Glasgow South Nat. Insce Tribunal, 1964–66; Member: Council, Law Soc. of Scotland, 1959–77 (Vice-Pres. 1969–70; Pres. 1972–74); Council, Internat. Bar Assoc., 1972– (Chm., Gen. Practice Section, 1978–80; Sec.-Gen., 1980–84; Pres., 1984–86; Hon. Mem., 1988); GDC, 1975–89; Scottish Dental Estimates Bd, 1982–87; Mem. Bd of Mgt, Glasgow Maternity and Women's Hosps, 1964–74 (Chm., 1966–74); Vice-Chm., Glasgow Eastern Health Council, 1975–77; Sec., Local Dental Cttee, City of Glasgow, 1955–65. Deacon, Incorporation of Barbers, Glasgow, 1962–63; Dean, Royal Faculty of Procurators in Glasgow, 1977–80. Hon. Mem., American Bar Assoc., 1986–. Mem. Court, Univ. of Strathclyde, 1977–92. Hon. LLD Glasgow, 1985. *Recreation:* golf. *Address:* Greenacres, 20/1 Easter Belmont Road, Edinburgh EH12 6EX. *T:* (0131) 337 1888. *Clubs:* Western (Glasgow); Royal and Ancient. *Died 21 Sept. 2001.*

SUTHERLAND, Sir Maurice, Kt 1976; Member, Cleveland County Council, 1973–93 (Leader, 1973–77 and 1981–85; Leader of Opposition, 1977–81); *b* 12 July 1915; *s* of Thomas Daniel and Ada Sutherland; *m* 1st, 1941, Beatrice (*née* Skinner); one *s*; 2nd, 1960, Jane Ellen

(*née* Bell); one step *d*; 3rd, Ellen Margaret (*née* Guy). *Educ:* Stockton Secondary Sch. War service with Green Howards and RCS, N Africa and NW Europe. Solicitor, 1937–. Mem. Stockton Borough Council, 1957–67 (Hon. Alderman, 2000); Chm., Teesside Steering Cttee, 1966–67; Leader of Labour Party, Teesside County Borough Council, 1967–74; Mayor of Teesside, 1972–73. Chm., Northern Econ. Planning Council, 1977–79. Hon. LLM Teesside, 1994. *Recreations:* cricket, walking, chess, politics. *Address:* 8 Manor Close, Low Worsall, Yarm, Cleveland TS15 9QE. *T:* (01642) 782799.
Died 11 March 2001.

SUTTON, Colin Bertie John, QPM 1985; policing consultant, UK and overseas; Director, Police Scientific Development Branch, Home Office, 1991–93; *b* 6 Dec. 1938; *s* of Bertie Sidney Russell Sutton and Phyllis May; *m* 1960, Anne Margaret Davis. *Educ:* King Edward VI Grammar School, Stratford-upon-Avon; University College London (LLB 1970). Police Constable, 1957, Sergeant, 1964, Inspector, 1966, Warwicks County Police; Chief Inspector, 1970, Supt, 1972, Chief Supt, 1974, Warwicks and Coventry Constabulary; Chief Supt, W Midlands Police, 1974–77; Asst Chief Constable, Leics Constabulary, 1977; Metropolitan Police: Dep. Asst Comr, 1983–84; Asst Comr, 1984–88; Dir, Police Requirements Support Unit, Home Office, 1988–91. Columnist, Police Guardian. Freeman, City of London, 1988; Liveryman, Fletchers' Co., 1989. SBStJ 1990. *Recreations:* golf, angling, squash, music, art, literature.
Died 24 March 2004.

SUTTON, Shaun Alfred Graham, OBE 1979; television producer and writer; script consultant, Richard Price Television Associates; Head of Drama Group, BBC Television, 1969–81; *b* 14 Oct. 1919; *s* of Eric Graham Sutton and Beryl Astley-Marsden; *m* 1948, Barbara Leslie; one *s* three *d*. *Educ:* Latymer Upper Sch.; Embassy Sch. of Acting, London. Actor and Stage Manager, Q, Embassy, Aldwych, Adelphi, Arts, Criterion Theatres, 1938–40. Royal Navy, 1940–46, Lieut RNVR. Stage Dir, Embassy and provincial theatres, 1946–48; Producer, Embassy, Buxton, Croydon Theatres, 1948–50; toured S Africa as Producer, 1950; Producer, Embassy, Ipswich, Buxton, 1951–52; entered BBC TV Service, 1952; produced and wrote many children's TV plays and serials; directed many series incl. Z Cars, Softly Softly, Sherlock Holmes, Kipling, etc; Head of BBC Drama Serials Dept, 1966–69; dramatised Rogue Herries and Judith Paris for BBC Radio, 1971; Producer: BBC TV Shakespeare series, 1982–84; Theatre Night series, BBC 2, including Season's Greetings, Make and Break, The Devil's Disciple, What the Butler Saw, Absent Friends, The Master Builder, Strife, The Miser, The Rivals, Journey's End, When We are Married, Once in a Lifetime, Benefactors, The Contractor, The Winslow Boy, Relatively Speaking, Merlin, Re-Joyce, The Spirit of R101, Spy in the Cab. Writer of pantomime for Perth Th., 2002. FRTS. *Publications:* A Christmas Carol (stage adaptation), 1949; Queen's Champion (children's novel), 1961; The Largest Theatre in the World, 1982. *Recreations:* gardening, walking. *Address:* The Cottage, Brewery Road, Trunch, Norfolk NR28 0PX. *Died 14 May 2004.*

SVETLANOV, Yevgeny Fyodorovich; Principal Conductor, Russia (formerly USSR) State Symphony Orchestra, 1965–2000; Chief Conductor, Residentie Orkest, The Hague, since 1992; composer; *b* 6 Sept. 1928; *m* 1st, Nina Moznaim; 2nd, Larissa Avdeyeva; 3rd, 1980, Nina Nikolayeva. *Educ:* Moscow Conservatoire. Conductor, 1955–63, Chief Conductor, 1963–65, Bolshoi Theatre. Prin. Guest Conductor, LSO, 1979–. *Compositions* include: Concerto, 1951; Siberian Fantasy, 1953; Rhapsody, 1954; Symphony, 1957; sonatas, sonatinas. *Address:* Apt 41, Stanislavsky Str. 14, 103009 Moscow, Russia; Residentie Orkest, Spuiplein 150, 2511 DG Den Haag, Netherlands. *Died 3 May 2002.*

SVOBODA, Prof. Josef, RDI 1989; stage designer, 1947–73, head designer, 1951–73, National Theatre, Prague; Professor at Academy of Applied Arts, since 1968; *b* Čáslav, 10 May 1920; *m* 1948, Libuše Hrubešová; one *d. Educ:* Sch. of Fine and Applied Arts, Prague. EXPO 58, Brussels: success with Laterna Magica; EXPO 67, Montreal: polyvision, polydiaekran. Artistic Dir, Laterna Magika, indep. theatre (formerly experimental studio, Nat. Theatre, Prague), 1973–. Stage designs for numerous theatres including: Metropolitan Opera, New York; Covent Garden; Geneva; Bayreuth; Frankfurt; Hamburg; Stuttgart; Berlin; Zurich; Vienna; Barcelona; Milan; Montreal; Banff. Hon. RA 1969. Hon. DFA: Denison, Ohio, 1978; Western Michigan, 1984. Internat. Theatre Award, Amer. Theater Assoc., 1976; Internat. Prize for scenery and costumes, Teatro de l'Europa, 1984. Laureate of State Prize, 1954; Merited Artist of CSSR, 1966; National Artist of CSSR, 1968; Chevalier, Ordre des Arts et des Lettres (France), 1976; Légion d'honneur (France), 1993. *Publications:* relevant monographs: Josef Svoboda (by Theatre Inst.) 1967 (Prague); Josef Svoboda (by Denis Bablet) 1970 (France); The Scenography of J. Svoboda (by Jarka Burian) 1971, 1974 (USA); Teatr Josefa Svobody (by V. Berjozkin) 1973 (USSR); Josef Svoboda: the secret of the theatrical space, Czech edn 1992, Italian edn 1997. *Recreations:* theatre, photography, creative arts, music, literature. *Address:* Filmařská 535/17, 15200 Prague 5, Czech Republic; Laterna Magika, Liliová 9, 11000 Prague 1, Czech Republic. *Died 8 April 2002.*

SWAIN, Henry Thornhill, CBE 1971; RIBA; County Architect, Nottinghamshire County Council, 1964–88, retired; *b* 14 Feb. 1924; *s* of Thornhill Madge Swain and Bessie Marion Swain; *m* 1950, Annie Harthorn (marr. diss.); two *d; m* 1976, Judy Torrington (marr. diss.); one *d. Educ:* Bryanston Sch.; Architectural Assoc. (Hons Dipl.). Served with RN, 1943–46. Herts County Architect's Dept, 1949; worked in primary school group; Notts CC, 1955; Group Leader i/c initial develt of CLASP construction; Dep. County Architect, 1958–64. Vice-Pres., RIBA, 1966–67. *Publications:* many articles in architectural jls. *Recreation:* sailing. *Address:* 50 Loughborough Road, West Bridgford, Nottingham NG2 7JJ. *T:* (0115) 981 8059. *Died 7 Jan. 2002.*

SWANSEA, 4th Baron *cr* 1893; **John Hussey Hamilton Vivian,** Bt 1882; DL; *b* 1 Jan. 1925; *s* of 3rd Baron Swansea, DSO, MVO, TD and Hon. Winifred Hamilton (*d* 1944), 4th *d* of 1st Baron Holm Patrick; *S* father, 1934; *m* 1st, 1956, Miriam Antoinette (marr. diss. 1973; she *d* 1975), 2nd *d* of A. W. F. Caccia-Birch, MC, of Guernsey Lodge, Marton, NZ; one *s* two *d;* 2nd, 1982, Mrs Lucy Temple-Richards (*née* Gough). *Educ:* Eton; Trinity Coll., Cambridge. DL Powys (formerly Brecknock), 1962. CStJ 1994. *Recreations:* shooting, fishing, rifle shooting. *Heir: s* Hon. Richard Anthony Hussey Vivian [*b* 24 Jan. 1957; *m* 1996, Anna Clementine, *d* of M. Austin]. *Address:* 4/89 St George's Square, Pimlico, SW1V 3QW.
Died 24 June 2005.

SWANWICK, Sir Graham Russell, Kt 1966; MBE 1944; Judge of the High Court of Justice, Queen's Bench Division, 1966–80; Presiding Judge, Midland and Oxford Circuit, 1975–78; *b* 24 August 1906; *s* of Eric Drayton Swanwick and Margery Eleanor (*née* Norton), Whittington House, Chesterfield; *m* 1st, 1933, Helen Barbara Reid (marr. diss., 1945; she *d* 1970); one *s* (and one *s* decd); 2nd, 1952, Audrey Celia Parkinson (*d* 1987). *Educ:* Winchester Coll.; University Coll., Oxford (BA). Called to the Bar, Inner Temple, 1930, Bencher, 1962; QC 1956. Wing Comdr RAFVR, 1940–45 (MBE, despatches). Recorder: City of Lincoln, 1957–59; City of Leicester, 1959–66; Judge of Appeal, Channel Islands, 1964–66. Leader, Midland Circuit, 1961–65; Chm., 1963–66, Dep. Chm., 1966–71, Derbys QS. *Recreation:* country pursuits. *Address:* The Rectory House Nursing Home, West Street, Sompting, West Sussex BN15 0DA.

T: (01903) 761863. *Club:* Royal Air Force.
Died 23 June 2003.

SWEET, Prof. Peter Alan, PhD; FRAS; Regius Professor of Astronomy in the University of Glasgow, 1959–82; retired; *b* 15 May 1921; *s* of David Frank Sweet; *m* 1947, Myrtle Vera Parnell (*d* 2002); two *s. Educ:* Kingsbury County Grammar School, London; Sidney Sussex College, Cambridge (Open Maj. Schol. in Maths, 1940–42, Wrangler, 1942, BA 1943, MA 1946); PhD Cantab 1949. FRAS 1949. Junior Scientific Officer, Min. of Aircraft Prod., 1942–45; BA Scholar, Sidney Sussex Coll., Cambridge, 1945–47 (Mayhew Prizeman, 1946); Lectr in Astronomy, Univ. of Glasgow, 1947–52; Lectr in Astronomy and Asst Dir of the Observatory, Univ. of London, 1952–59; Dean, Faculty of Science, Univ. of Glasgow, 1973–75. Visiting Asst Prof. of Astronomy, Univ. of California, Berkeley, 1957–58; Vis. Sen. Res. Fellow, NASA Inst. for Space Studies, NY, 1965–66. *Publications:* papers on stellar evolution, cosmic magnetism, and solar flares in Monthly Notices of Royal Astronomical Soc., etc. *Recreations:* music, gardening. *Address:* 17 Westbourne Crescent, Glasgow G61 4HB. *T:* (0141) 942 4425. *Died 16 Jan. 2005.*

SWINDEN, (Thomas) Alan, CBE 1971; Executive Chairman, Institute of Manpower Studies, 1978–86; *b* 27 Aug. 1915; *s* of Thomas and Ethel Swinden; *m* 1941, Brenda Elise Roe; one *d. Educ:* Rydal Sch.; Sheffield Univ. (BEng). With Rolls-Royce, 1937–55; seconded to AFV Div., Min. of Supply, 1941–45; with Engrg Employers Fedn, 1955–65, Dir, 1964–65; Dir, Engrg Industry Trng Bd, 1965–70; Confederation of British Industry: Dep. Dir Gen. (Industrial Relations), 1970–74; Chief Advr, Social Affairs, 1974–78; Consultant, 1978–81; Chm., 1974–85, Dir, 1980–84, Kingston Regl Mgt Centre. Chm., Derby No 1 HMC, 1953–55. Council Member: British Employers Confedn, 1955–65; ACAS, 1974–84; Inst. for Employment Studies (formerly of Manpower Studies), 1976–96; British Assoc. for Commercial and Industrial Educn, 1982–94; Mem., BBC Consultative Gp on Industrial and Business Affairs, 1977–83. Governor, Box Hill Sch., 1995–99. *Address:* 85 College Road, Epsom, Surrey KT17 4HH. *T:* (01372) 720848. *Club:* Royal Automobile. *Died 27 Sept. 2004.*

SWINSON, Sir John (Henry Alan), Kt 1984; OBE 1974; Commercial Director (Ireland), Forte (formerly Trusthouse Forte) plc, 1965–96; *b* 12 July 1922; *s* of Edward Alexander Stanley Swinson and Mary Margaret McLeod; *m* 1944, Margaret Sturgeon Gallagher; two *s. Educ:* Royal Belfast Academical Institution. Founded J. H. A. Swinson and Co. Ltd, 1946; Man. Dir (also of associated cos), until 1959; merged with Lockhart Gp, 1959, which merged with Trust Houses (later Trusthouse Forte plc), 1965. Chairman: Catering Industry Training Board, 1966–75; NI Training Executive, 1975–83; Livestock Marketing Commn (NI), 1970–85; NI Tourist Bd, 1979–88 (Mem., 1970–88); Member: Council, NIHCA, 1961– (Past Pres.); Catering Wages Council, 1965–82; NI Economic Council, 1977–81; Industrial Forum for NI, 1980–83. *Recreation:* sailing. *Address:* 22A Ailsa Road, Cultra, Co. Down BT18 0AS.
Died 2 Aug. 2001.

SWORD, John Howe; Director, Oral History Project, University of Toronto, 1981–90; a Vice-President, Associated Medical Services Inc., 1984–92; *b* Saskatoon, Saskatchewan, 22 Jan. 1915; *m* 1947, Constance A. Offen; one *s* one *d. Educ:* public and high schs, Winnipeg; Univ. of Manitoba (BA); Univ. of Toronto (MA). Served War, RCAF, Aircrew navigation trg and instr in Western Canada; Armed Services Div., Wartime Inf. Bd, Ottawa, 1945. Taught for six years, before War, in Roland, Teulon and Winnipeg, Manitoba. Secretary, Manitoba Royal Commn on Adult Educn, 1945–46. Univ. of Toronto: Asst Sec. and Sec., Sch. of Grad. Studies, 1947–60; Exec. Asst to the President, 1960–65; Vice-Provost, 1965–67; Actg Pres., 1967–68; Exec. Vice-Pres. (Academic), and

Provost, 1968–71; Actg Pres., 1971–72; Vice-Pres., Institutional Relations and Planning, 1972–74; Special Asst to the President, Institutional Relations, 1974–80, retired; Acting Dir, Sch. of Continuing Studies, 1980–81 and 1983–84. Chm., Art Cttee, 1980–83, Finance Cttee, 1983–88, Mem. Bd of Stewards, 1988–94, Hart House, Univ. of Toronto. Chm., Certificate Review Adv. Cttee, Ministry of Educn, 1984–94. Member: Bd, Addiction Res. Foundn of Ont, 1981–88; Council, Royal Canadian Inst., Toronto, 1981–93. Dir, Toronto Dist Heating Corp., 1983–87. Chm., Toronto Round Table, 1991–93; Mem. Management Bd, Geneva Park YMCA, 1972–85; Trustee: Toronto Sch. of Theology, 1978–83; Wychwood Pk Heritage Conservation Dist, 1986–90. Mem., United Church. Hon. LLD: Univ. of Manitoba, 1970; Univ. of Toronto, 1988. Silver Jubilee Medal, 1977. *Recreations:* lawn bowling, swimming, bridge, tennis, Scrabble. *Address:* #716–602 Melita Crescent, Toronto, ON M6G 3Z5, Canada. *T:* (416) 530 7799. *Clubs:* Faculty (Univ. of Toronto), Arts and Letters, Queen's, Wells Hill Lawn Bowling (Toronto).   *Died 4 July 2001.*

SYKES, Edwin Leonard, CMG 1966; *b* 1 May 1914; *m* 1st, 1946, Margaret Elizabeth McCulloch (*d* 1973); 2nd, 1976, Dorothy Soderberg (*d* 1996). *Educ:* Leys School, Cambridge (Schol.); Trinity Coll., Cambridge (Senior Schol.). Entered Dominions Office, 1937; Asst Private Sec. to Secretary of State, 1939. Served War, 1939–45 (despatches). Served in British High Commissions, Canada, 1945–47, India, 1952–54; idc 1955; Dep. UK High Comr in Fedn of Rhodesia and Nyasaland, 1956–59; Asst Under-Sec. of State, CRO, 1964–65; Dep. UK High Comr in Pakistan, 1965–66; Sec., Office of the Parly Comr for Administration, 1967–74. *Address:* 22 Garth House Nursing Home, Tower Hill Road, Dorking, Surrey RH4 2AY.   *Died 22 May 2005.*

SYKES, Sir John (Charles Anthony le Gallais), 3rd Bt *cr* 1921, of Kingsknowes, Galashiels, co. Selkirk; *b* 19 April 1928; *er s* of Stanley Edgar Sykes (*d* 1963) (2nd *s* of 1st Bt) and Florence Anaise le Gallais (*d* 1955); *S* uncle, 1974; *m* 1954, Aitha Isobel (marr. diss. 1970), *yr d* of Lionel Dean, New Mill, Yorks. *Educ:* Churchers College. Export merchant, retired. Mem., British Epicure Soc. *Recreations:* wine, food, travel. *Heir: nephew* David Michael Sykes [*b* 10 June 1954; *m* 1st, 1974, Susan Elizabeth (marr. diss. 1987), 3rd *d* of G. W. Hall; one *s*; 2nd, 1987, Margaret Lynne, *o d* of J. McGreavy; one *d*].   *Died 12 May 2001.*

SYLVESTER, (Anthony) David (Bernard), CBE 1983; writer on art, etc; exhibitions curator; *b* 21 Sept. 1924; *s* of Philip Silvester and Sybil Rosen; *m* 1950, Pamela Briddon (marr. diss.); three *d*; one *d* with Shena Mackay. *Educ:* University Coll. Sch. Arts Council of Great Britain: Mem., 1980–82; Mem., Art Panel, 1962–70, 1972–77, Chm., 1980–82. Member: Commn d'Acquisitions, Musée Nat. d'Art Moderne, Paris, 1984–96; South Bank Bd, 1998–; Trustee: Tate Gall., 1967–69; Henry Moore Foundn, 1996–. Visiting Lecturer: Slade Sch. of Fine Art, 1953–57; RCA, 1960–70; Swarthmore Coll., Pa, 1967–68. Sen. Fellow, RCA, 1991. Hon. FRA 1986. Golden Lion, Venice Biennale, for art criticism, 1993. Commandeur de l'Ordre des Arts et des Lettres (France), 1995 (Officier, 1985). *Exhibitions:* (curator or co-curator): Henry Moore, Tate, 1951; Stanley Spencer drawings, London, 1954; Alberto Giacometti, Arts Council, 1955; Chaim Soutine, Tate, 1963; Giacometti, Tate, 1965; Moore, Tate, 1968; René Magritte, Tate, 1969; Robert Morris, Tate, 1971; Henri Laurens, Hayward, 1971; Joan Miró bronzes, Hayward, 1972; Islamic carpets, Hayward, 1972; Willem de Kooning, Serpentine, 1977; Dada and Surrealism Reviewed, Hayward, 1978; Moore, Serpentine, 1978; Magritte, Palais des Beaux-Arts, Brussels, and Musée National d'Art Moderne, Paris, 1978–79; Giacometti, Serpentine, 1981; The Eastern Carpet in the Western World, Hayward, 1983; André Masson drawings, London, 1987; Late Picasso, Paris and London, 1988; Magritte, London, NY, Houston and Chicago, 1992–93; Francis

Bacon, Venice, 1993; de Kooning, Washington, NY and London, 1994–95; Leon Kossoff, Venice, 1995; William Turnbull, London, 1995; Bacon, Paris and Munich, 1996–97; Hayward, 1998; Ken Adam, London, 1999; Francis Bacon, Dublin, 2000, etc; *films and TV:* Ten Modern Artists (writer/presenter of series), 1964; Giacometti (writer/producer), 1967; Matisse and His Model (writer), 1968; Magritte: The False Mirror (dir), 1970, etc; *radio:* interviews, talks and discussions for BBC, 1948–. Hawthornden Prize for Art Criticism, 2000. *Publications:* Henry Moore, 1968; Magritte, 1969; Interviews with Francis Bacon, 1975, enlarged edns 1980 and 1987; René Magritte, 1992; (ed and co-author) René Magritte Catalogue Raisonné, 5 vols, 1992–97; Looking at Giacometti, 1994; About Modern Art, 1996, enlarged edn 1997; Looking Back at Francis Bacon, 2000; exhibn catalogues; articles, incl. some on films or sport, 1942–. *Fax:* (020) 7229 4078.   *Died 19 June 2001.*

SYLVESTER-EVANS, Alun, CB 1975; Deputy Chief Executive, Property Services Agency, Department of the Environment, 1973–78, retired; Member, Chairman's Panel of Assessors, Civil Service Selection Boards, 1980–88; *b* 21 April 1918; *o c* of Daniel Elias Evans and Esther Evans, Rhymney, Mon.; *m* 1945, Joan Maureen (*d* 1998), *o c* of A. J. Sylvester, CBE; two *s*. *Educ:* Lewis' School, Pengam; Univ. of Wales, Aberystwyth. Armed services, 1940–46. Asst Research Officer, Min. of Town and Country Planning, 1946–47; Asst Principal, 1947–48; Principal Private Sec. to Minister of Housing and Local Govt, 1954–57; Asst Sec., 1957–66, Under-Sec., 1966–73, Min. of Housing and Local Govt, later DoE. *Recreation:* golf. *Address:* Rudloe Cottage, Rudloe, Corsham, Wilts SN13 0PG. *T:* (01225) 810375. *Club:* Royal Commonwealth Society.   *Died 16 Aug. 2003.*

SYMONS, Prof. Martyn Christian Raymond, FRS 1985; Visiting Research Professor: De Montfort University, since 1993; Nottingham Trent University, since 1995; London University, since 1995; Essex University, since 1997; Greenwich University, since 1997; *b* 12 Nov. 1925; *s* of Marjorie LeBrasseur and Stephen White Symons; *m* 1950, Joy Lendon (decd); one *s* one *d*. *Educ:* Battersea Polytechnic (BSc, PhD, DSc London). CChem, FRSC. Army, 1945–48. Lecturer: Battersea Polytechnic, 1948–53; Southampton Univ., 1953–60; Leicester University: Prof. of Physical Chem., 1960–88; Res. Prof. of Chem., CRC Sen. Fellow, and Dir, CRC Electron Spin Resonance Res. Gp, 1988–93. Royal Soc. of Chemistry: Vice Pres., Faraday Div., 1985–87; Bruker Lectr (first), 1986; R. A. Robinson Lectr, 1987. FRSA. *Publications:* (with P. W. Atkins) The Structure of Inorganic Radicals, 1967; Chemical and Biochemical Aspects of Electron Spin Resonance Spectroscopy, 1978; (jtly) Techniques in Free Radical Research, 1992; (with J. Gutteridge) Free Radicals and Iron: chemistry, biology and medicine, 1998; over 1000 scientific articles mainly in chem. jls. *Recreations:* watercolour landscape painting, piano playing. *Address:* 33 Castle Road, Hadleigh, Essex SS7 2AU.   *Died 28 Jan. 2002.*

SYMS, John Grenville St George, OBE 1981; QC 1962; Barrister-at-Law; a Recorder of the Crown Court, 1972–80; *b* 6 Jan. 1913; *s* of late Harold St George Syms and Margaret (*née* Wordley); *m* 1st, 1951, Yvonne Yolande Rigby (marr. diss. 1971); one *s*; 2nd, 1971, Anne Jacqueline, *d* of Brig. J. B. P. Willis-Fleming, CBE, TD. *Educ:* Harrow; Magdalen College, Oxford (BA). Called to the Bar, 1936. Dep. Chm., Huntingdon and Peterborough QS, 1965–71. Chm., SE Agricultural Land Tribunal, 1972–83. Served in RAFVR, 1940–45 (despatches); Wing Commander, 1944. *Recreation:* fishing. *Address:* Wesley House, New Park Road, Cranleigh, Surrey GU6 7HL. *T:* (01483) 276017.   *Died 14 Dec. 2005.*

SYNGE, Henry Millington; Chairman, Union International Co. Ltd, 1969–88 (Director, 1955–88); Consultant, Tilney (Stockbrokers); *b* 3 April 1921; *s* of Richard Millington Synge, MC, Liverpool and Eileen

Hall; *m* 1947, Joyce Helen (*d* 2000), *d* of Alexander Ross Topping and Mrs Topping (*née* Stileman); two *s* one *d*. *Educ:* Shrewsbury School. Mercantile Marine: Radio Officer, 1941; Purser, Bibby Line, 1943; demobilised, 1946. Partner, Sing White & Co. (Stockbrokers), 1947. Manager, Liverpool Trustee Savings Bank, 1957, Chm. 1968–69; Regional Bd Mem., Trustee Savings Bank, England and Wales, 1970–85. *Recreations:* private flying, fishing, amateur radio. *Address:* 5 Wilmore Street, Much Wenlock, Shropshire TF13 6HR.

Died 24 April 2001.

SYNNOT, Adm. Sir Anthony (Monckton), KBE 1979 (CBE 1972); AO 1976; Hon. JMN 1965; Hon. PSM 1982; *b* 5 Jan. 1922; *s* of Monckton Synnot; *m* 1st, 1959, (Mary) Virginia (*d* 1965), *d* of late Dr W. K. Davenport; two *d*; 2nd, 1968, E. Anne, *d* of late E. Waldron Manifold, MC. *Educ:* Geelong Grammar School. Joined RAN, 1939; served War of 1939–45 in HMAS Canberra, Stuart, Quiberon; HMS Barham, Punjabi; CO HMAS Warramunga, 1956–57, HMAS Vampire, 1961–62; OC Royal Malaysian Navy, 1962–65; CO HMAS Sydney, 1966, HMAS Melbourne, 1967; IDC 1968; Chief of Naval Personnel, 1970; Dep. Chief of Naval Staff, 1971–72; Commanding HM Australian Fleet, 1973; Director Joint Staff, 1974–76; Chief of Naval Staff, 1976–79; Chief of Defence Force Staff, 1979–82, retired. Chm., Australian War Meml Council, 1982–85. *Address:* Ballymoyer, Barton Highway, Yass, NSW 2582, Australia. *Club:* Melbourne (Melbourne).   *Died 4 July 2001.*

SZASZY, Dame Miraka Petricevich, (Dame Mira), DBE 1990 (CBE 1976); QSM 1975; JP; *b* 7 Aug. 1921; *d* of Lovré (Lawrence) Cvitanov Petricevich and Mákeretá Raharuhi; *m* 1956, Albert Szaszy (decd); two *s*. *Educ:* Te Hapua Primary Sch.; Queen Victoria Maori Girls' Sch., Auckland; Auckland Girls' Grammar Sch.; Auckland Teachers' Training Coll. (BCert 1942); Auckland Univ.

(BA 1945); Univ. of Hawaii (Dip. Soc. Sci. 1949). Teacher, 1946, 1968–70; social welfare work, 1946–48, Employment Officer, 1951–52, Maori Affairs Dept; Exec. Sec., Maori Women's Welfare League, 1952–57; Lecturer: Teachers' Training Coll., 1972 and 1974–79; Ardmore Trng Coll., 1973; Dir, Community Dept, Ngatapuwae Sec. Sch., 1980–84; returned to tribal home in north of NZ, 1984; helped re-establish Iwi tribal roots of Ngati Kuri through Waananga (study of history, genealogy and lore), 1989. Member: Wellington UN Club; SE Asian and Pacific Women's Assoc.; Board of Trustees, Queen Victoria and St Stephen's Schs; Anglican Church and Soc. Commn, 1970; Bishopric of Aotearoa, 1988–; NZ Anglican Synod, 1989–; NZ Race Relations Council, 1969–70; Bd, NZ Broadcasting Council (Mem., Northern NZ Broadcasting Council, 1969–70; Dep. Chm., Radio NZ); NZ Council, Protection Citizens Rights (Vice-Pres.); Social Welfare Commn, 1988–90; Maori Educn Foundn Trust Board; Maori Fisheries Commn, 1990–; Shellfish Recovery Trust, 1993–; Women's Adv. Cttee on estabt of Ministry of Women's Affairs; Maori Women's Gp which estabd Te Ohu Whakatupu (Maori Women's Secretariat) within Women's Ministry; Maori Women's Develt Trust Fund, 1988–; Muriwhenua Runanga, 1986; Muriwhenua Incorporation, 1991–; Te Orangikaupapa Trust, 1987–; Ngati Kuri Trust Bd, 1993–; Telethon Family Trust Cttee, 1982–85; Managing Trustee, Waiora Papakainga Trust, 1989–; Chm., Waiora Marae Trustees, 1988–; Maori Women's Welfare League: Rep., 1962–70; 1st Vice-Pres., 1971; Pres., 1974–77; Mem., 1st Delegn to Govt on Equal Pay for Women; Delegate: Maori Congress, 1990; Taitokerau Forum, 1990. Pres., Three Combined Tribes, 1988. LLD *hc* Victoria Univ. of Wellington, 1993. Silver Jubilee Medal, 1977. *Recreations:* tennis, basketball (rep. Auckland Univ., rep. North Island), reading, gardening. *Address:* Ngataki, RD4, Kaitaia, New Zealand. *T:* (9) 4098558.   *Died 29 Dec. 2001.*

T

TABOR, Prof. David, PhD, ScD; FRS 1963; Professor of Physics in the University of Cambridge, 1973–81, then Emeritus; Head of Physics and Chemistry of Solids, Cavendish Laboratory, 1969–81; Fellow of Gonville and Caius College, Cambridge, since 1957; *b* 23 Oct. 1913; *s* of Charles Tabor and Rebecca Weinstein; *m* 1943, Hannalene Stillschweig; two *s. Educ:* Regent St Polytechnic; Universities of London and Cambridge. BSc London 1934; PhD Cambridge 1939; ScD Cambridge 1956. Reader in Physics, Cambridge Univ., 1964–73. Vis. Prof., Imperial Coll., London, 1981. For. Associate, US NAE, 1995. Hon. DSc Bath, 1985. Inaugural Gold Medal of Tribology, Instn of Engrs, 1972; Guthrie Medal, Inst. Physics, 1975. *Publications:* The Hardness of Metals, 1951; Gases, Liquids and Solids, 1969, 3rd edn 1991; (with F. P. Bowden) Friction and Lubrication of Solids, Part I, 1950, rev. edn 1954, repr. 1986; Part II, 1964; contributions to learned jls on friction, adhesion, lubrication and hardness. *Recreation:* Judaica. *Address:* Cavendish Laboratory, Madingley Road, Cambridge CB3 0HE; Gonville and Caius College, Cambridge CB2 1TA.

Died 26 Nov. 2005.

TABOR, Maj.-Gen. David John St Maur, CB 1977; MC 1944; late Royal Horse Guards; GOC Eastern District, 1974–77, retired; *b* 5 Oct. 1922; *y s* of late Harry Tabor, Hitchin, Herts; *m* 1st, 1955, Hon. Pamela Roxane (*d* 1987), 2nd *d* of 2nd Baron Glendyne; two *s*; 2nd, 1989, Marguerite, *widow* of Col Peter Arkwright. *Educ:* Eton; RMA, Sandhurst. Served War: 2nd Lieut, RHG, 1942; NW Europe, 1944–45 (wounded, 1944); Major, 1946. Lt-Col Comdg RHG, 1960; Lt-Col Comdg Household Cavalry, and Silver Stick in Waiting, 1964; Col, 1964; Brig., 1966; Comdr Berlin Inf. Bde, 1966; Comdr, British Army Staff and Mil. Attaché, Washington, 1968; RCDS, 1971; Maj.-Gen., 1972; Defence Attaché, Paris, 1972–74. *Recreations:* shooting, fishing, gardening. *Address:* Lower Farm, Compton Abdale, Cheltenham, Glos GL54 4DS. *T:* (01242) 890234. *Clubs:* Turf, Royal Automobile, MCC.

Died 18 May 2004.

TACON, Air Cdre (Ernest) William, CBE 1958; DSO 1944; LVO 1950; DFC 1940 (Bar 1944); AFC 1942 (Bar 1953); *b* 6 Dec. 1917; *s* of Ernest Richard Tacon, Hastings, New Zealand; *m* 1st, 1949, Clare Keating (*d* 1956), *d* of late Michael Keating, Greymouth, NZ; one *s* two *d*; 2nd, 1960, Bernardine, *d* of Cecil Leamy, Wellington, NZ; three *s. Educ:* St Patrick's Coll., Silverstream, NZ. Joined RNZAF, 1938; served with RAF, 1939–46; transferred to RAF, 1946; CO, King's Flight, Benson, 1946–49; served: Canal Zone, 1951–53; Cyprus, 1956–58; Persian Gulf, 1961–63; Commandant, Central Fighter Establishment, 1963–65; Air Cdre, Tactics, HQ Fighter Comd, 1966–67; AOC Military Air Traffic Ops, 1968–71, retired. MCMI. *Address:* 69 McLeans Road, Bucklands Beach, Auckland, NZ. *T:* (9) 5344757.

Died 9 Sept. 2003.

TAGG, Alan; freelance designer/theatre designer; *b* 13 April 1928; *s* of Thomas Bertram Tagg and Edith Annie Hufton. *Educ:* Mansfield Coll. of Art; Old Vic Theatre Sch. Worked as asst to Cecil Beaton, Oliver Messel, etc; first play, Charles Morgan's The River Line, 1952; worked for H. M. Tennent Ltd; Founder Mem., English Stage Co., 1956: designed: first prodn of Look Back in Anger, 1956; The Entertainer (with Laurence Olivier), 1957, also 15 other prodns at Royal Court Theatre; 4 prodns for RSC, including Graham Greene's The Return of A. J. Raffles, 1975; 12 prodns at Chichester Festival Theatre, including: Dear Antoine (with Edith Evans), 1971; Waters of the Moon (with Ingrid Bergman), 1977; 9 plays by Alan Ayckbourn; 10 prodns for NT; 93 West End prodns,

including: Billy Liar, 1959; How the Other Half Loves, 1970; The Constant Wife, 1973; Alphabetical Order, 1975; Donkeys Years, 1976; The Kingfisher, 1977; Candida, 1977; The Millionairess, 1978; Peter Shaffer's Lettice and Lovage (with Maggie Smith), 1987; 11 prodns on Broadway, including Peter Shaffer's Black Comedy, 1967, Lettice and Lovage, 1990 (US tour 1992); Look Back in Anger, Moscow Arts Theatre, 1957; Sleuth, Berlin, 1991; directors worked with include Lindsay Anderson, Michael Blakemore, John Dexter, John Gielgud, Tony Richardson and Michael Rudman; exhibitions designed include: Shakespeare, Stratford-upon-Avon, 1964; Hector Berlioz, 1969; 25 Years of Covent Garden, V&A Museum, 1971; Byron, 1974. *Address:* 19 Parsons Green, SW6 4UL. *T:* (020) 7731 2787. *Club:* Chelsea Arts.

Died 5 Nov. 2002.

TAIT, Adm. Sir (Allan) Gordon, KCB 1977; DSC 1943; Chief of Naval Personnel and Second Sea Lord, 1977–79; Chairman, Lion Nathan Ltd (incorporating NZ Breweries Ltd, Lion Breweries Ltd and Lion Corporation), 1984–97; *b* 30 Oct. 1921; *s* of Allan G. Tait and Ann Gordon, Timaru, NZ; *m* 1952, Philippa, *d* of Sir Bryan Todd; two *s* two *d. Educ:* Timaru Boys' High Sch.; RNC Dartmouth. War Service, Atlantic and N Russia Convoys, 1939–42; Submarines, Mediterranean and Far East, 1942–45 (despatches); commanded HM Submarines: Teredo, 1947; Solent, 1948; ADC to Governor-General of New Zealand (Lt-Gen. Lord Freyberg, VC), 1949–51; commanded HM Submarines: Ambush, 1951; Aurochs, 1951–53; Tally Ho, 1955; Sanguine, 1955–56; Asst Naval Adviser, UK High Commn, Canada, 1957–59; Dep. Dir Ops, Admiralty, 1963–65; commanded HM Ships: Caprice, 1960–62; Ajax, 1965–67; Maidstone, 1967–68; commanded: 2nd Destroyer Squadron (Far East), 1965–66; 3rd Submarine Sqdn, 1967–69; Chief of Staff, Submarine Comd, 1969–70; commanded, Britannia RNC, 1970–72; Rear-Adm., 1972; Naval Secretary, MoD, 1972–74; Vice-Adm., 1974; Flag Officer, Plymouth, Port Admiral, Devonport, NATO Comdr, Central Sub Area, Eastern Atlantic, 1975–77; Adm., 1978. Naval ADC to the Queen, 1972. Director: NZ Bd, Westpac Banking Corp., 1981–93; Todd Bros Ltd, 1981–87; Todd Corp., 1987–97 (Dep. Chm.); Todd Petroleum Mining, 1994–97 (Dep. Chm.); Owens Gp Ltd, 1984–93; AGC (NZ) Ltd, 1987–93. Pres., and Chm. of Trustees, NZ Sports Foundn, 1981–86; Chairman: NZ Family Trust, 1983–; NZ Internat. Yachting Trust, 1989–94; Trustee, NZ Nat. Maritime Mus., 1990–97; Mem., Spirit of Adventure Trust Board, 1982–91. *Address:* 22 Orakei Road, Auckland 5, New Zealand. *Clubs:* White's; Royal Yacht Squadron; Northern (Auckland).

Died 29 May 2005.

TAIT, Sylvia Agnes Sophia, (Mrs James F. Tait), FRS 1959; Honorary Research Associate and Co-Director, Biophysical Endocrinology Unit, Physics Department, Middlesex Hospital Medical School, 1982; biochemist; distinguished for her work on the hormones controlling the distribution of salts in the body; *b* 8 Jan. 1917; *m* 1956, James Francis Tait, PhD, FRS. Research Asst, Courtauld Inst. of Biochemistry, Middlesex Hosp. Med. Sch., 1944–55; External Scientific Staff, MRC, Middlesex Hosp. Med. Sch., 1955–58; Sen. Scientist, Worcester Foundn for Experimental Biology, USA, 1958–70; Res. Associate and Co-Dir, Biophysical Endocrinology Unit, Dept of Physics as Applied to Medicine, Middlesex Hosp. Med. School, 1970–82. (With Prof. J. F. Tait) R. Douglas Wright Lecture and Medallion, Univ. of Melbourne, 1989. Hon. DSc Hull, 1979. Tadeus Reichstein Award, Internat. Endocrine Society, 1976; Gregory Pincus Meml

Medal, 1977; CIBA Award, American Heart Assoc. for Hypertension Research, 1977; Sir Henry Dale Medal of Soc. for Endocrinology, 1979. *Address:* Moorlands, Main Road, East Boldre, Brockenhurst, Hants SO42 7WT. *T:* (01590) 626312.   *Died 28 Feb. 2003.*

TALBOT, Sir Hilary Gwynne, Kt 1968; a Judge of the High Court of Justice, Queen's Bench Division, 1968–83; Judge of the Employment Appeals Tribunal, 1978–81; *b* 22 Jan. 1912; *s* of late Rev. Prebendary A. T. S. Talbot, RD, and Mrs Talbot; *m* 1963, Jean Whitworth (JP Wilts), *o d* of late Mr and Mrs Kenneth Fisher. *Educ:* Haileybury Coll.; Worcester Coll., Oxford. MA Oxon. Served War of 1939–45; Captain, RA. Called to Bar, Middle Temple, 1935, Bencher, 1968. Dep. Chm., Northants QS, 1948–62; Chm., Derbyshire QS, 1958–63; Dep. Chm. Hants QS, 1964–71; Judge of County Courts, 1962–68; a Presiding Judge, Wales and Chester Circuit, 1970–74. Mem., Parole Bd, 1980–82. Dep. Chm., Boundary Commn for Wales, 1980–83. Formerly Dep. Chm., Agricultural Land Tribunals; formerly Mem., County Court, Divorce Court and Supreme Court Rules Cttees. *Recreations:* fishing, bird-watching. *Address:* Old Chapel House, Little Ashley, Bradford-on-Avon, Wilts BA15 2PN.   *Died 24 May 2004.*

TANGE, Sir Arthur (Harold), AC 1977; Kt 1959; CBE 1955 (OBE 1953); retired civil servant; *b* 18 Aug. 1914; 2nd *s* of late Charles L. Tange, solicitor, Gosford, New South Wales; *m* 1940, Marjorie Florence, 2nd *d* of late Prof. Edward O. G. Shann; one *s* one *d*. *Educ:* Gosford High School; Western Australia University (BA 1st Cl. Hons Economics). Joined Bank of NSW, 1931; Economist, Bank of NSW, 1938; Economic Research in Commonwealth Depts, Canberra, 1942–46; entered Australian Diplomatic Service, 1946; First Secretary, Australian Mission to United Nations, 1946–48; Counsellor, United Nations Division, Canberra, 1948–50; Assistant Secretary, Department of External Affairs, Canberra, 1950–53; Minister at Australian Embassy, Washington, 1953–54; Secretary of Dept of External Affairs, Canberra, 1954–65; High Comr in India and Ambassador to Nepal, 1965–70; Sec., Dept of Defence, 1970–79. Represented Australia at many international diplomatic, economic, trade and defence conferences, 1944–79. *Publications:* (jtly) Australia Foots the Bill, 1942; various articles and collected lectures on defence and public administration. *Recreation:* stream fishing. *Address:* 32 La Perouse Street, Griffith, ACT 2603, Australia. *T:* (6) 2958879. *Club:* Commonwealth (Canberra).
                              Died 10 May 2001.

TANNER, Dr John Benedict Ian, CBE 1979; Founding Director: Royal Air Force Museum, 1963–88; Battle of Britain Museum, 1978–88; Cosford Aero-Space Museum, 1978–88; Bomber Command Museum, 1982–88; Hon. Archivist, since 1980, and Senior Research Fellow, 1982–97, then Supernumary Fellow, Pembroke College, Oxford; *b* London, 2 Jan. 1927; *o s* of R. A. and I. D. M. Tanner; *m* 1st, 1953, April Rothery (marr. diss. 1972, and subseq. by RC Tribunal); one *d*; 2nd, 1991, Dr Andrea Isobel Duncan, FSA. *Educ:* City of London Library Sch.; Universities of London, Nottingham (MA, PhD) and Oxford (MA). Reading Public Library, 1950; Archivist-Librarian, Kensington Library, 1950–51; Leighton House Art Gall. and Museum, 1951–53; Curator, Librarian and Tutor, RAF Coll., 1953–63; Hon. Sec., Old Cranwellian Assoc., 1956–64; Extra-mural Lectr in History of Art, Univ. of Nottingham, 1959–63. Walmsley Lectr, City Univ., 1980. Vis. Fellow, Wolfson Coll., Cambridge, 1983; Prof., The Polish Univ., 1987–94, then Emeritus. Chm., Internat. Air Museum Cttee; Vice-President: Guild of Aviation Artists; Croydon Airport Museum Soc.; Trustee, Manchester Air and Space Museum; Mem. Founding Cttee, All England Lawn Tennis Museum; Mem. Br. Cttee, Caen Memorial Musée pour la Paix; President: Anglo-American Ecumenical Assoc.; USAF European Meml Foundn. Life Vice-Pres., Friends of RAF Mus. FCLIP, FMA, FRHistS, FRAeS, FSA. Freeman, City of London, 1966; Liveryman: Worshipful Co. of Gold and Silver Wyre Drawers, 1966; Scriveners' Co., 1978. Freeman, Guild of Air Pilots and Air Navigators, 1979. Hon. Mem. Collegio Araldico of Rome, 1963. Hon. DLitt City, 1982; Hon. LLD The Polish Univ., 1989; Hon. DCL Assumption Coll., Worcester, Mass, 1993. Tissandier Award, Fedn Aeronautique Internat., 1977. KStJ 1978 (OStJ 1964); St John Service Medal, 1985); KCSG 1977; KCSG, with Star, 1985; Cross of Merit, Order of Malta, 1978. Grand Comdr, OM Holy Sepulchre (Vatican); Order of Polonia Restituta (Poland), 1985; Nile Gold Medal (Egypt), 1987. *Publications:* (ed) List of Cranwell Graduates, 2nd edn, 1963; (jtly) Encyclopedic Dictionary of Heraldry, 1968; How to trace your Ancestors, 1971; Man in Flight (limited edn), 1973; The Royal Air Force Museum: one hundred years of aviation history, 1973; (with W. E. May and W. Y. Carman) Badges and Insignia of the British Armed Services, 1974; Charles I, 1974; Who's Famous in Your Family: a Reader's Digest guide to genealogy, 1975, 2nd edn 1979; Wings of the Eagle (exhibition catalogue), 1976; (ed) They Fell in the Battle, 1980 (limited edn, to commemorate 40th anniv. of Battle of Britain); Sir William Rothenstein: an RAF Museum exhibition catalogue, 1985; RAF Museum — a combined guide, 1987; Editor, RAF Museum Air Publication series, 10 vols; General Editor: Museums and Libraries (Internat. Series); Studies in Air History; reviews and articles in professional and other jls. *Recreations:* cricket, opera, reading. *Address:* Flat One, 57 Drayton Gardens, SW10 9RU. *Clubs:* Athenæum, Reform, MCC.
                              Died 18 May 2004.

TATHAM, Francis Hugh Currer, (Tom); Editor of Whitaker's Almanack, 1950–81; *b* 29 May 1916; *s* of late Harold Lewis Tatham, Gravesend, Kent, and late Frances Eva (*née* Crook); *m* 1945, Nancy Margaret, *d* of John Robins, Newton Abbot; two *s*. *Educ:* Charterhouse; Christ Church, Oxford. Missioner, Shrewsbury School Mission, Liverpool, 1939–42; Sub-Warden, Mary Ward Settlement, 1942–45; Army Cadet Force, 1943–45; Editor, Church of England Newspaper, 1945–47. Vice-Pres., Harrow RFC. *Recreations:* watching cricket, travel in England. *Address:* 27 Montacute Road, Lewes, East Sussex BN7 1EN. *T:* (01273) 473585. *Club:* MCC.
                              Died 21 April 2002.

TATHAM, Tom; *see* Tatham, F. H. C.

TAUBE, Prof. Henry, PhD; Professor, Department of Chemistry, Stanford University, 1962–86, then Emeritus; *b* 30 Nov. 1915; *s* of Samuel and Albertina (Tiledetski) Taube; *m* 1952, Mary Alice Wesche; two *s* oned (and one *d* decd). *Educ:* Univ. of Saskatchewan (BS 1935, MS 1937); Univ. of California, Berkeley (PhD 1940). Instructor, Univ. of California, Berkeley, 1940–41; Instructor and Asst Prof., Cornell Univ., 1941–46; Asst Prof., Associate Prof., Prof., Univ. of Chicago, 1946–61; Chm., Dept of Chemistry, Univ. of Chicago, 1956–59; Chm., Dept of Chemistry, Stanford Univ., 1972–74 and 1978–79. Foreign Mem., Royal Soc., 1988; Hon. Member: Canadian Soc. for Chemistry, 1986; Hungarian Acad. of Scis, 1988; Corresponding Member: Brazilian Acad. of Scis, 1991; Australian Acad. of Sci., 1991; Foreign Associate, Engrg Acad. of Japan, 1991. Hon. FRSC 1989; Hon. Fellow, Indian Chem. Soc., 1989; Hon. FRS(Can) 1997. Hon. LLD Saskatchewan, 1973; Hon. PhD Hebrew Univ. of Jerusalem, 1979; Hon. DSc: Chicago, 1983; Polytechnic Inst., NY, 1984; State Univ. of NY, 1985; Guelph Univ., 1987; Seton Hall Univ., 1988; Lajos Kossuth Univ., Debrecen, Hungary, 1988. Guggenheim Fellow, 1949, 1955. ACS Award for Nuclear Applications in Chemistry, 1955; ACS Award for Distinguished Service in the Advancement of Inorganic Chemistry, 1967; Willard Gibbs Medal, Chicago Section, ACS, 1971; Nat. Medal of Science, Washington DC, 1977; T. W. Richards Medal of the Northwestern Section, ACS, 1980; ACS

Award in Inorganic Chemistry of the Monsanto Co., 1981; Nat. Acad. of Sciences Award in Chemical Sciences, 1983; Robert A. Welch Foundn Award in Chemistry, 1983; Nobel Prize for Chemistry, 1983; Priestley Medal, ACS, 1985; Dist. Achievement Award, Internat. Precious Metals Inst., 1986. *Publications:* numerous papers in scientific jls on the reactivity of coordination compounds. *Recreations:* gardening, collecting classical vocal records. *Address:* 441 Gerona Road, Stanford, CA 94305, USA. *T:* (415) 3282759. *Died 16 Nov. 2005.*

TAUSKY, Vilem, CBE 1981; FGSM 1968; conductor; Director of Opera, Guildhall School of Music, 1966–87; *b* 20 July 1910; *s* of Emil Tausky, MD, Prerov, Czechoslovakia, and Josefine Ascher, opera singer; *m* 1948, Margaret Helen Powell (*d* 1982). *Educ:* Univ. of Brno; Janáček Conservatoire, Brno; Meisterschule, Prague. Military Service in France and England, 1939–45. National Opera House, Brno, Czechoslovakia, 1929–39; Musical Director, Carl Rosa Opera, 1945–49; Artistic Dir, Phoenix Opera Co., 1967. BBC Conductor, 1950. Guest Conductor: Royal Opera House, Covent Garden, 1951; Sadler's Wells Opera, 1953. Freeman, City of London, 1979. Ambassador, City of Coventry, 2003. Jan Masaryk Gratias Agit Prize, 2000; Gold Medal, Acad. of Performing Arts, Prague Univ., 2000. Czechoslovak Military Cross, 1944; Czechoslovak Order of Merit, 1945. *Publications:* Coventry: a meditation for string quartet, 1940; Czechoslovak Christmas Carols, 1942; Coventry: a meditation for orchestra, 1956; Oboe Concerto, 1957; Concertino for harmonica and orchestra, 1963; Divertimento for strings, 1966; Soho: Scherzo for orchestra, 1966; Concert Overture for Brass Band, 1969; Cakes and Ale: Overture for Brass Band, 1971; Ballad for Cello and Piano; From Our Village: orchestral suite, 1972; Sonata for Cello and Piano, 1976; Suite for Violin and Piano, 1979; String Quartet, 1981; (book) Vilem Tausky Tells his Story, 1979; Leoš Janáček, Leaves from his Life, 1982; contribs to: Tension in the Performance of Music, 1979; The Spectator, 1979. *Recreation:* country life. *Address:* Ivor Newton House, 10–12 Edward Road, Sundridge Park, Bromley, Kent BR1 3NQ. *T:* (020) 8466 5112. *Died 16 March 2004.*

TAVENAS, Prof. François Aimé; Founding Rector, Université du Luxembourg, since 2003; Rector, and Professor, Department of Civil Engineering, Laval University, 1997–2002; *b* 12 Sept. 1942; *s* of Adrien Tavenas and Marie-Thérèse Bazin; *m* 1963, Gundula Schlichting; one *s* two *d*. *Educ:* Inst. Nat. des Scis Appliquées, Lyons, France (Diplôme Ingénieur 1963); Univ. of Grenoble (doctorate in soil mech. 1965). Laval University: Lectr, Dept of Civil Engrg, 1968–70; Asst Prof., 1970–73; Associate Prof., 1973–78; Prof., 1978–89; Dean, Faculty of Sci. and Engrg, 1985–89; McGill University: Prof., Dept of Civil Engrg and Applied Mechanics, 1989–97; Vice-Principal, Planning and Computing, 1989–90; Planning and Resources, 1990–97; actg Vice Principal, Macdonald Campus, 1995–97. President: Canadian Geotechnical Soc., 1990–92 (Robert F. Legget Award, 1995); Assoc. Canadienne-Française pour l'Avancement des Sciences, 1997–98; Réseau Interordinateurs Scientifique Québecois, 1998–2001; Chm., Standing Adv. Cttee on Univ. Res., Assoc. of Univs and Colls of Canada, 1998–; Mem. Council, Natural Scis and Engrg Res. Council, Ottawa, 1989–95. Fellow, Canadian Acad. of Engrg, 1998. Keefer Gold Medal, 1980, Julian C. Smith Medal, 2001, Engrg Inst. of Canada; Telford Premium, ICE, 1986, 1989. Chevalier, Légion d'honneur (France), 2000. *Publications:* Remblais sur argiles molles, 1985; papers in jls, conf. proceedings and other pubns. *Recreations:* tennis, sailing, travelling. *Address:* c/o Rector's Office, Université Laval, Québec, QC G1K 7P4, Canada. *T:* (418) 6562272. *Died 13 Feb. 2004.*

TAYLOR OF GRYFE, Baron *cr* 1968 (Life Peer), of Bridge of Weir, Renfrewshire; **Thomas Johnston Taylor;** DL; FRSE 1977; Chairman, Morgan Grenfell

(Scotland) Ltd, 1973–85; *b* 27 April 1912; *s* of John Sharp Taylor, Glasgow; *m* 1943, Isobel Wands; two *d*. *Educ:* Bellahouston Acad., Glasgow. Member: British Railways Bd, 1968–80 (Chm., Scottish Railways Board, 1971–80); Board of Scottish Television Ltd, 1968–82; Forestry Commn, 1963–76 (Chm., 1970–76). President, Scottish CWS, 1965–70; Mem., Scottish Economic Council, 1971–74. Director: Whiteaway Laidlaw & Co. Ltd, 1971–89; Friends' Provident Life Office, 1972–82; Scottish Metropolitan Property Co. Ltd, 1972–88; BR Property Bd, 1972–82; Mem., Internat. Adv. Council, Morgan Grenfell. Chm., Economic Forestry Group, 1976–81. Chm., All-Party Parly Forestry Gp, 1995–. Trustee, Dulverton Trust, 1980–; Chm., Scottish Action on Dementia, 1989–95. DL Renfrewshire, 1970. Hon. LLD Strathclyde, 1974. Comdr's Cross, OM (Germany), 1992. *Recreations:* theatre, golf, walking. *Address:* 33 Seagate, Kingsbarns, Fife KY16 8SR. *T:* (01334) 880430. *Clubs:* Caledonian; Royal and Ancient (St Andrews). *Died 13 July 2001.*

TAYLOR, Lt-Gen. Sir Allan (Macnab), KBE 1972; MC 1944; Deputy Commander-in-Chief, United Kingdom Land Forces, 1973–76, retired; *b* 26 March 1919; *s* of Alexander Lawrence Taylor and Winifred Ethel (*née* Nisbet); *m* 1945, Madeleine Turpin (marr. diss. 1963); two *d*. *Educ:* Fyling Hall School, Robin Hood's Bay. Joined TA, 1938; Troop Leader, 10th Royal Tank Regt, 1940; Squadron Leader, 7th Royal Tank Regt, 1942; 6th Royal Tank Regt, 1946; Staff College, 1948; GSO 2, 56 London Armoured Div., 1949; Bde Major 20 Armoured Bde, 1952; Instructor, Staff College, 1954; Squadron Leader, 1st R Tank Regt, 1957; Second in Comd 5th RTR, 1959; Comdg Officer: 5th RTR, 1960 and 3rd, 1961; AA&QMG, 1st Div., 1962; Commandant, RAC Gunnery School, 1963; Comd Berlin Brigade, 1964; Imperial Defence College, 1967; Comdr, 1st Div., 1968; Commandant, Staff College, Camberley, 1969–72; GOC South East District, April–Dec. 1972. Chm., Cttee on Regular Officer Training, 1972. Col Comdt, RTR, 1973–77. *Recreation:* golf. *Address:* 4 Mill Close, Middle Assendon, Henley-on-Thames, Oxon RG9 6BA. *T:* (01491) 575167. *Died 13 June 2004.*

TAYLOR, Andrew James, CBE 1965; Chairman, British Manufacturing and Research Co., Grantham, Lincs, 1968–73; *b* 1902; *s* of late Alfred George Ralph Meston Taylor, Broughty Ferry, Dundee; *m* 1925, Mary Ann Symmers (*d* 1996), *d* of George Cowie, Aberdeen; one *d* (and three *s* decd). *Educ:* Robert Gordon's Coll., Aberdeen. Dir of Manufacture and Exec. Dir, 1962–65, Deputy Managing Director, 1965–67, Ford Motor Co. Ltd. *Recreations:* photography, fishing. *Address:* 2 Drummond Road, Blairgowrie, Perthshire PH10 6PD. *T:* (01250) 873358. *Club:* Royal Automobile. *Died 17 March 2001.*

TAYLOR, Arnold Joseph, CBE 1971; DLitt, MA; FBA 1972; FSA; Hon. Vice-President, Society of Antiquaries, since 1978 (Vice-President, 1963–64; Secretary, 1964–70; Director, 1970–75; President, 1975–78); *b* 24 July 1911; *y s* of late John George Taylor, Headmaster of Sir Walter St John's School, Battersea; *m* 1940, Patricia Katharine, *d* of late S. A. Guilbride, Victoria, BC; one *s* one *d*. *Educ:* Merchant Taylors' School; St John's College, Oxford (MA). Asst master, Chard School, Somerset, 1934; Asst Inspector of Ancient Monuments, HM Office of Works, 1935. Served War of 1939–45, Intelligence Officer, RAF, 1942–46. Inspector of Ancient Monuments for Wales, Min. of Works, 1946–54, Asst Chief Inspector, 1954–61; Chief Inspector of Ancient Monuments and Historic Buildings, MPBW, later DoE, 1961–72. Commissioner: Royal Commissions on Ancient and Historical Monuments (Wales and Monmouthshire), 1956–83; Historical Monuments (England), 1963–78; Mem., Ancient Monuments Board: for England, 1973–82; for Scotland, 1974–79; for Wales, 1974–82. Member: Cathedrals Advisory Cttee, 1964–80; Adv. Bd for

Redundant Churches, 1973–82 (Chm., 1975–77); Westminster Abbey Architectural Adv. Panel, 1979–92; Vice-President: English Place-Name Soc., 1986–; British Archaeol Assoc., 1993; Hon. Vice-President: Flintshire Hist. Soc., 1953; Royal Archaeol Inst., 1979– (Vice-Pres., 1968–72); Surrey Archaeol Soc., 1979; President: Oxford Univ. Archaeol Soc., 1932; Cambrian Archaeol Assoc., 1969; London and Middx Archaeol Soc., 1971–74; Soc. for Medieval Archaeology, 1972–75; Friends of Lydiard Tregoze, 1983–86; Sir Walter St John's Old Boys' Assoc., 1969–70 (Hon. Life Patron, 1992); Old Merchant Taylors' Soc., 1985–86. Mem., Sir Walter St John's Schools Trust, 1970. Reckitt Lectr, British Acad., 1977. Hon. Corres. Mem., Société Jersiaise, 1983. Hon. Pres., Colloque Internat. du Château Gaillard, 1992. Hon. DLitt Wales, 1970; Docteur hc Caen, 1980. Reginald Taylor Prize, British Archaeol Assoc., 1949; G. T. Clark Prize, Cambrian Archaeol Assoc., 1956; Gold Medal, Soc. of Antiquaries, 1988. Médaille d'Honneur de la Ville de Saint-Georges d'Espéranche, 1988. Silver Jubilee Medal, 1977. *Publications:* Records of the Barony and Honour of the Rape of Lewes, 1940; official guides to various historical monuments in care Ministry of Works (later DoE), 1939–80; chapter on Military Architecture, in vol. Medieval England, 1958; (part author) History of the King's Works, 1963; Four Great Castles, 1983; Studies in Castles and Castle-Building, 1986; contribs on medieval architectural history in Eng. Hist. Rev., Antiquaries Jl, Archaeologia Cambrensis, etc. *Recreations:* reading and using records, resisting iconoclasts. *Address:* Rose Cottage, Lincoln's Hill, Chiddingfold, Surrey GU8 4UN. *T:* (01428) 682069.   *Died 24 Oct. 2002.*

TAYLOR, Dr Daniel Brumhall Cochrane; JP; Vice-Chancellor, Victoria University of Wellington, New Zealand, 1968–82; Referee of the Small Claims Tribunal, Wellington, 1985–88; *b* 13 May 1921; *s* of Daniel Brumhall Taylor, Coleraine, NI and Anna Martha Taylor (*née* Rice); *m* 1955, Elizabeth Page, Christchurch, NZ; one *s* one *d*. *Educ:* Coleraine Academical Instn, NI; Queen's Univ., Belfast. BSc (Mech. Engrg) 1942, BSc (Elec. Engrg) 1943, MSc 1946, PhD 1948, QUB; MA Cantab 1956. FIMechE 1968. Lecturer in Engineering: Liverpool Univ., 1948–50; Nottingham Univ., 1950–53; ICI Fellow, Cambridge Univ., 1953–56; Lectr in Mechanical Sciences, Cambridge Univ., 1956–68; Fellow of Peterhouse, 1958–68, Fellow Emeritus, 1968; Tutor of Peterhouse, 1958–65, Senior Tutor, 1965–68. Member: NZ/USA Educnl Foundn, 1970–82; Council, Assoc. of Commonwealth Univs, 1974–77 (Chm., 1975–76); Chm., NZ Vice-Chancellors' Cttee, 1975–77. JP New Zealand, 1985. Hon. LLD Victoria Univ. of Wellington, 1983. *Publications:* numerous engrg and metallurgical papers. *Address:* 361 Fergusson Drive, Heretaunga, New Zealand. *T:* (4) 5280720. *Club:* Leander (Henley-on-Thames).   *Died 28 Dec. 2003.*

TAYLOR, David John; writer and editor; *b* 17 March 1947; *s* of John Whitfield Taylor and Alice Elaine Oldacre; *m* 1972, Ann Robinson; two *d* (and one *s* one *d* decd). *Educ:* High Sch., Newcastle-under-Lyme; Magdalene Coll., Cambridge (MA (English)). Reporter, Staffordshire Evening Sentinel, 1966; Editor, Varsity, 1969; BBC TV, Late Night Line-Up, 1969; Asst Editor, 1970–78, Dep. Editor, 1978–87, Editor, 1988, Punch; Editor: Business Life, 1988–93; Business Standards (BSI), 1996–. Columnist, Daily Telegraph. *Recreations:* bell-ringing, golf, personal computers. *Address:* Premier Magazines, Haymarket House, 1 Oxendon Street, SW1Y 4EE.
Died 13 Nov. 2001.

TAYLOR, Frank Henry; Principal, Frank H. Taylor & Co., City of London, Chartered Accountants; *b* 10 Oct. 1907; 2nd *s* of George Henry Taylor, Cambridgeshire; *m* 1936, Margaret Dora Mackay (*d* 1944), Invernesshire; one *d*; *m* 1948, Mabel Hills (*d* 1974), Hertfordshire; two *s*; *m* 1978, Glenys Mary Edwards, MBE, Bethesda, N Wales. *Educ:* Rutlish School, Merton, Surrey. FCIS 1929; FCA

1930. Commenced in practice as Chartered Accountant, 1930; Ministry of Food Finance Director of Tea, Coffee, Cocoa and Yeast, 1942; Min. of War Transport Finance Rep. overseas, 1944; visited over 40 countries on financial and political missions. Lt-Colonel comdg 1st Caernarvonshire Bn Home Guard, 1943. Contested (C) Newcastle under Lyme, 1955, Chorley, 1959; MP (C) Manchester, Moss Side, Nov. 1961–Feb. 1974. Governor of Rutlish School, 1951–89. Liveryman, City of London; Master, Bakers' Co., 1981–82; Mem. Ct, Worshipful Co. of World Traders (formerly Co. of World Traders), 1982–. Mem., GAPAN. *Publication:* Called to Account (autobiog.), 1993. *Recreations:* numerous including Rugby (for Surrey County), sculling (Thames Championship), punting (several Thames championships), golf (Captain RAC 1962). *Address:* 4 Barrie House, Lancaster Gate, W2 3QJ. *T:* (020) 7262 5684. *Clubs:* City Livery, Royal Automobile, Dinosaurs.   *Died 1 Oct. 2003.*

TAYLOR, Geoffrey H.; *see* Handley-Taylor.

TAYLOR, Geoffrey William, FCIB; Chairman, Private and Commercial Finance Group (formerly The Asset Management Corporation) PLC, 1995–2001; *b* 4 Feb. 1927; *s* of late Joseph William and Doris Taylor; *m* 1951, Joyce (*née* Walker); three *s* one *d*. *Educ:* Heckmondwike Grammar School; Univ. of London (BComm). Joined Midland Bank Ltd, 1943; Gen. Man. and Man. Dir, Midland Bank Finance Corp. Ltd, 1967–76; Asst Chief General Manager, 1974–80, Dep. Group Chief Exec., 1980–82, Group Chief Exec., 1982–86, Dir, 1982–87, Vice-Chm., 1986–87, Midland Bank Plc; Chm., Daiwa Europe Bank, 1987–94. Dir, Y. J. Lovell (Hldgs), 1987–96; Chairman: Fosters Trading Co. (formerly Foster Brother Menswear), 1992–98; Atkins Hldgs, 1994–2000. Mem., Internat. Adv. Council, Wells Fargo & Co., 1987–95. Mem., Banking Law Review, (Jack), Cttee, 1987–90. *Recreations:* golf, reading, music. *Club:* Burhill Golf.   *Died 18 Nov. 2004.*

TAYLOR, Hermon, MD; FRCS; formerly Consulting Surgeon: London Hospital, E1; King George Hospital, Ilford; *b* 11 May 1905; *s* of Enoch Oliver Taylor and L. M. Taylor (*née* Harrison); *m* 1st, 1932, Méarie Amélie Pearson (*d* 1981); three *s* two *d*; 2nd, 1983, Mrs Noreen Cooke. *Educ:* Latymer School, Edmonton; St John's Coll., Cambridge (Scholar; BA 1926; MB, BChir 1930; MA 1931; MChir 1932; MD (Raymond Horton-Smith Prize, 1934)); St Bartholomew's Hospital (Entrance Scholar). MRCS, LRCP 1929; FRCS 1930. Luther Holden Res. Scholar in Surg., St Bartholomew's Hosp., 1932; BMA Res. Scholar, 1937–38, and Surgical First Asst, London Hosp. Formerly: House Surgeon, Demonstr of Pathology, St Bart's Hosp.; Resident Surgical Officer: Hertford Co. Hosp.; Lincoln Co. Hosp.; Surgical Registrar, Prince of Wales' Hosp., Tottenham. Moynihan Fellow, Assoc. of Surgeons of GB and Ireland; Hunterian Professor, RCS. Founder Mem. and former Sec., Treas. and Pres., British Society of Gastro-enterology; Hon. Member, Amer. Gastro-enterological Assoc. Hon. Fellow, London Hosp. Med. Coll., 1988. Hermon Taylor Endoscopy Unit, St Bart's and Royal London Hosp., opened 1999. *Publications:* Carcinoma of the Stomach, in Modern Trends in Gastro-Enterology, 1952; contrib. to BMJ, Lancet, etc, 1942–. *Address:* Coppice Field, Bosham Hoe, Chichester, West Sussex PO18 8ET. *T:* (01243) 573385.
Died 10 Jan. 2001.

TAYLOR, Dame Jean (Elizabeth); *see* Dowling, Dame J. E.

TAYLOR, Sir John Lang, (Sir Jock Taylor), KCMG 1979 (CMG 1974); HM Diplomatic Service, retired; *b* 3 Aug. 1924; *y s* of Sir John William Taylor, KBE, CMG; *m* 1952, Molly, *o d* of James Rushworth; five *s* three *d*. *Educ:* Prague; Vienna; Imperial Services Coll., Windsor; Baltimore Polytechnic Inst., Md; Cornell Univ.; Trinity Coll., Cambridge (BA 1949, MA 1954). Served RAFVR, 1944–47 (Flt-Lt 1946). Joined HM Foreign (later

Diplomatic) Service, 1949; served in: FO, 1949–50 and 1957–60; Saigon, 1950–52; Hanoi, 1951; Beirut, 1952–55; Prague, 1955–57; Montevideo, 1960–64; Bonn, 1964–69; Minister (Commercial), Buenos Aires, 1969–71; RCDS, 1972; Head of Industry, Science and Energy Dept, FCO, 1972–73; Asst Under-Sec. of State, FCO, 1973–74; Under-Sec., Dept of Energy, 1974–75; Ambassador to: Venezuela, 1975–79; the Netherlands, 1979–81; FRG, 1981–84. Non-executive Chairman: Klöckner INA Ltd, 1984–92; Siemens Ltd, 1985–91; non-exec. Dir, Schering Ltd, 1985–91. Chm., Latin Amer. Trade Adv. Gp, BOTB, 1986–89. Hon. Vice Pres., Hispanic and Luso-Brazilian Councils (Canning House), 1989 (Vice-Chm., 1987; Chm., 1987–89); Trustee, Anglo-German Foundn for the Study of Industrial Soc., 1988. *Address:* 44 Danemere Street, Putney, SW15 1LT. *Died 30 Sept. 2002.*

TAYLOR, Rt Rev. John Vernon; Bishop of Winchester, 1975–85; *b* 11 Sept. 1914; *s* of late Rt Rev. J. R. S. Taylor and Margaret Irene Taylor (*née* Garrett); *m* 1940, Margaret Wright; one *s* two *d. Educ:* St Lawrence Coll., Ramsgate; Trinity Coll., Cambridge (Hon. Fellow, 1987); St Catherine's Soc., Oxford; Wycliffe Hall, Oxford; Institute of Education, London. Deacon 1956, priest 1957; Curate, All Souls, Langham Place, W1, 1938–40; Curate in Charge, St Andrew's Church, St Helens, Lancs, 1940–43; Warden, Bishop Tucker College, Mukono, Uganda, 1945–54; Research Worker, Internat. Missionary Council, 1955–59; Africa Sec., CMS, 1959–63; Gen. Sec., CMS, 1963–74. Chm., Doctrine Commn of C of E, 1978–85. Examng Chap. to Bishop of Truro, 1974–75. Hon. Canon of Namirembe Cathedral, 1963–74. Hon. Fellow: New Coll., Oxford, 1985; Magdalen Coll., Oxford, 1986; Selly Oak Colls, Birmingham, 1987. Hon. DD Wycliffe Coll., Toronto, 1964; Hon. DLitt CNAA, 1991. *Publications:* Man in the Midst, 1955; Christianity and Politics in Africa, 1957; The Growth of the Church in Buganda, 1958; African Passion, 1958; Christians of the Copperbelt, 1961; The Primal Vision, 1963; For All the World, 1966; Change of Address, 1968; The Go-Between God, 1972; Enough is Enough, 1975; Weep not for Me, 1986; A Matter of Life and Death, 1986; Kingdom Come, 1989; A Christmas Sequence and Other Poems, 1989; The Christlike God, 1992; *posthumous publications:* The Easter God, 2003; The Incarnate God, 2004. *Recreations:* theatre, music. *Address:* 65 Aston Street, Oxford OX4 1EW. *T:* (01865) 248502. *Died 30 Jan. 2001.*

TEBALDI, Renata; Italian soprano; *b* Pesaro, Italy, 1 Feb. 1922; *o c* of Teobaldo and Giuseppina (Barbieri) Tebaldi. *Educ:* Arrigo Boito Conservatory, Parma; Gioacchino Rossini Conservatory, Pesaro; subsequently a pupil of Carmen Melis and later of Giuseppe Pais. Made professional début as Elena in Mefistofele, Rovigo, 1944; first sang at La Scala, Milan, at post-war reopening concert (conductor Toscanini), 1946; sang at Covent Garden and in opera houses of Naples, Rome, Venice, Pompeii, Turin, Cesana, Modena, Bologna and Florence; toured England, France, Spain and South America; American début in title rôle Aïda, San Francisco, 1950; Metropolitan Opera House Season, New York, 1955, and regularly until retirement from public perf., 1976; subseq. teaching. Recordings of complete operas include: Otello; Adriana Lecouvreur; Il Trittico; Don Carlo; La Gioconda; Un Ballo in Maschera; Madame Butterfly; Mefistofele; La Fanciulla Del West; La Forza Del Destino; Andrea Chenier; Manon Lescaut; La Tosca; Il Trovatore; Aida, La Bohème. *Address:* 1 Piazzetta della Guastalla, 20122 Milan, Italy. *T:* (02) 5512273. *Died 19 Dec. 2004.*

TEDFORD, Prof. David John, OBE 1997; ScD; CEng; FIEE; CPhys; FInstP; Professor of Electrical Engineering, University of Strathclyde, 1972–97, then Emeritus; Fellow, University of Strathclyde, 1999; *b* 12 July 1931; *s* of Thomas Tedford and Eliza Jane (*née* Yates); *m* 1956, Mary White Gardner; three *s* one *d. Educ:* Coatbridge High Sch.; Royal Tech. Coll., Glasgow (ARCST 1952; Pres., Sports Union, 1953–55; BSc 1952, PhD 1955,

Glasgow Univ.). CEng, FIEE 1970; CPhys, FInstP 1970. Res. Engr, Ferranti Ltd, Edinburgh, 1955–57; Strathclyde University (formerly Royal College of Science and Technology): Lectr, 1957–64; Sen. Lectr, 1964–69; Reader, 1969–72; Dep. Principal, 1982–84; Vice-Principal, 1984–88; Dep. Principal (Internat. Affairs), 1988–91; Special Advr to Principal, 1991–92. Scientific Advr to Scottish Office Industry Dept, 1992–94; Chief Scientific Advr to Sec. of State for Scotland, 1994–97. Non-exec. Dir, Startech Partners Ltd, 1997–; Dir, Scottish Academic Consultants, 1996–. Chm., Technol. Educn Adv. Gp, Scottish Consultative Council on Curriculum, 1996–2001. Member: Scottish Univ. Council on Entrance, 1982–94 (Chm., 1989–94); Brit. Nat. Cttee and Exec. Cttee, CIGRE 1985–96; Standing Conf. on Univ. Entrance, 1989–93; Scottish Exam. Bd, 1986–93; Mgt Bd, SCOTVEC, 1993–97; Scottish Science Trust, 1997– (Chm., Scientific Adv. Cttee, 2001–); Steering Gp, Skills Strategy for Electronics Industry, Scotland, 1996–2001; Dundee Science Trust, 1998–; Business Services Steering Gp, Glasgow Sci. Centre, 1998–2002; Planning Cttee and Council, Hong Kong Univ. of Sci. and Technol., 1987–91; Mgt Bd, Bell Coll. of Technol., Hamilton, 1990– (Chm. College Council, 1990–93; Fellow, 2002); Chm. Court, Univ. of Abertay Dundee, 1997–2002 (Fellow 2003). Member: Council, RSE, 1989–95 (Vice-Pres., 1992–95); Educn Cttee and Internat. Relns Cttee, Royal Soc., 1991–93; Council, IEE, 1992–95; SMIEE, 1982. FRSE 1978; FRSA 1983. FUniv Strathclyde, 1999. Hon. ScD Lodz, 1988; Hon. DTech Abertay Dundee, 1995; Hon. DSc Robert Gordon, 1997; DUniv Strathclyde, 1997. Achievement Medal, IEE, 1997; Distinguished Mem., CIGRE, 1998. Civil Defence Medal, 1982. Commander's Cross, Order of Merit (Poland), 2001. *Publications:* numerous in scientific and engrg jls. *Recreations:* hill-walking, music, amateur astronomy, current affairs. *Address:* 76 Woodlands Drive, Coatbridge, Lanarkshire ML5 1LB. *T:* and *Fax:* (01236) 422016; *e-mail:* david.tedford@blueyonder.co.uk. *Died 11 Nov. 2004.*

TELLER, Prof. Edward; Senior Research Fellow, Hoover Institution, since 1975; University Professor, University of California, Berkeley, 1971–75, then Emeritus (Professor of Physics, 1960–71); Chairman, Department of Applied Science, University of California, 1963–66; Associate Director, Lawrence Radiation Laboratory, University of California, 1954–75, then Emeritus; *b* Budapest, Hungary, 15 Jan. 1908; *s* of a lawyer; became US citizen, 1941; *m* 1934, Augusta Harkanyi (*d* 2000); one *s* one *d. Educ:* Karlsruhe Technical Inst., Germany; Univ. of Munich; Leipzig (PhD). Research Associate: Leipzig, 1929–31; Göttingen, 1931–33; Rockefeller Fellow, Copenhagen, 1934; Lectr, Univ. of London, 1934–35; Professor of Physics: George Washington Univ., Washington, DC, 1935–41; Columbia Univ., 1941–42; Physicist, Manhattan, Engineer District, 1942–46, Univ. of Chicago, 1942–43; Los Alamos Scientific Laboratory, 1943–46; Prof. of Physics, Univ. of Chicago, 1946–52; Asst Dir, Los Alamos (on leave, Chicago), 1949–52; Consultant, Livermore Br., Univ. of Calif, Radiation Laboratory, 1952–53; Prof. of Physics, Univ. of Calif, 1953–60; Dir, Livermore Br., Lawrence Livermore Lab., Univ. of Calif, 1958–60, then Dir Emeritus. Mem. Nat. Acad. of Sciences, etc. Held several hon. degrees, 1954–. Awards, 1957–, incl. Enrico Fermi Award, 1962; Harvey Prize, Israel, 1975; Gold Medal, Amer. Coll. of Nuclear Med., 1980; Man of the Year, Achievement Rewards for College Scientists, 1980; Nat. Medal of Science, 1983. *Publications:* The Structure of Matter, 1949; Our Nuclear Future, 1958; The Legacy of Hiroshima, 1962; The Reluctant Revolutionary, 1964; The Constructive Uses of Nuclear Explosives, 1968; Great Men of Physics, 1969; Nuclear Energy in a Developing World, 1977; Energy from Heaven and Earth, 1979; Pursuit of Simplicity, 1980; Better a Shield than a Sword, 1987; Conversations on the Dark Secrets of Physics, 1991. *Address:* Stanford, CA 94305, USA. *Died 10 Sept. 2003.*

TEMPLE, Ven. George Frederick; Archdeacon of Bodmin, 1981–89, then Archdeacon Emeritus; *b* 16 March 1933; *s* of George Frederick and Lilian Rose Temple; *m* 1961, Jacqueline Rose Urwin; one *s* one *d*. *Educ:* St Paul's, Jersey; Wells Theol Coll. Ordained deacon, 1968, priest 1969, Guildford; Curate: St Nicholas, Gt Bookham, 1968–70; St Mary the Virgin, Penzance, 1970–72; Vicar: St Just in Penwith with Sancreed, 1972–74; St Gluvias, Penryn, 1974–81; Saltash, 1982–85. Mem., Gen. Synod of C of E, 1981–85; Chm., House of Clergy, Truro Diocesan Synod, 1982–85; Diocesan Dir of Ordinands, 1985–87. Hon. Canon of Truro, 1981–89. *Recreations:* poetry, history, walking. *Address:* 3 Sycamore Close, Bodmin, Cornwall PL31 1QB. *Died 8 Jan. 2003.*

TENNANT, Harry; Commissioner of Customs and Excise, 1975–78; *b* 10 Dec. 1917; *s* of late Robert and Mary Tennant; *m* 1944, Bernice Baker; one *s*. *Educ:* Oldham High School. Appointed Officer of Customs and Excise, 1938; Inspector, 1960; Principal Inspector, 1970; Asst Sec., 1971; Dep. Chief Inspector, 1973; Mem., CS Appeal Bd, 1980–87. *Publications:* Back to the Bible, 1962, repr. 1984; Moses My Servant, 1966, repr. 1990; The Man David, 1968, repr. 1996; The Christadelphians: what they believe and preach, 1986; Steps to True Marriage, 1999. *Recreations:* walking, travel. *Address:* Strathtay, Alexandra Road, Watford, Herts WD17 4QY. *T:* (01923) 222079. *Died 31 May 2004.*

TERRAINE, John Alfred, FRHistS; author; *b* 15 Jan. 1921; *s* of Charles William Terraine and Eveline Holmes; *m* 1945, Joyce Eileen Waite; one *d*. *Educ:* Stamford Sch.; Keble Coll., Oxford (Hon. Fellow, 1986). Joined BBC, 1944; Pacific and S African Programme Organiser, 1953–63; resigned from BBC, 1964. Associate producer and chief scriptwriter of The Great War, BBC TV, 1963–64; part-scriptwriter The Lost Peace, BBC TV, 1965; scriptwriter, The Life and Times of Lord Mountbatten, Rediffusion/Thames TV, 1966–68; scriptwriter, The Mighty Continent, BBC TV, 1974–75. Founder Pres., Western Front Assoc., 1980–97, Patron, 1997–. Mem. Council, RUSI, 1976–84. FRHistS 1987. Chesney Gold Medal, RUSI, 1982. C. P. Robertson Meml Trophy, Air Public Relations Assoc., 1985. *Publications:* Mons: The Retreat to Victory, 1960; Douglas Haig: The Educated Soldier, 1963; The Western Front, 1964; General Jack's Diary, 1964; The Great War: An Illustrated History, 1965 (NY), unillustrated reprint, The First World War, 1983; The Life and Times of Lord Mountbatten, 1968; Impacts of War 1914 and 1918, 1970; The Mighty Continent, 1974; Trafalgar, 1976; The Road to Passchendaele, 1977; To Win a War: 1918 The Year of Victory, 1978; The Smoke and the Fire, 1980; White Heat: The New Warfare 1914–1918, 1982; The Right of the Line: the Royal Air Force in the European War 1939–45, 1985 (Yorkshire Post Book of the Year Award, 1985); Business in Great Waters: the U-Boat Wars 1916–1945, 1989. *Recreation:* convivial and congenial conversation. *Address:* 77 Sirdar Road, W11 4EQ. *T:* (020) 7229 8152. *Died 28 Dec. 2003.*

TERRELL, Colonel Stephen, OBE 1952; TD; QC 1965; DL; *b* June 1916; *m* 1951, Diana Marion, *d* of Maj.-Gen. J. R. Hartwell, CB, DSO; two *s*, and one step *s* one step *d*. *Educ:* Trinity Coll., Glenalmond; University Coll. London. Called to the Bar, Gray's Inn, 1946; Bencher, Gray's Inn, 1970. South Eastern Circuit. Pres., Liberal Party, 1972. Contested (L) Eastbourne, 1964, 1966, 1970 and Feb. 1974. DL Middlesex, then Gtr London, 1961. *Died 16 Aug. 2004.*

TERRINGTON, 5th Baron *cr* 1918, of Huddersfield, co. York; **Christopher Montague Woodhouse,** DSO 1943; OBE 1944; *b* 11 May 1917; 2nd *s* of 3rd Baron Terrington, KBE and 1st wife, Valerie (*d* 1958), 2nd *d* of G. A. Phillips, Edenbridge, Kent; *S* brother, 1998; *m* 1945, Lady (Cynthia Mary Millicent) Davina (*d* 1995), *d* of 2nd Earl of Lytton, KG, GCSI, GCIE, PC, and *widow* of 5th Earl of Erne; two *s* one *d*. *Educ:* Winchester; New Coll.,

Oxford (Craven and Hertford Schols, Gaisford Prizeman; First Cl. Hon. Mods 1937; First Class Lit. Hum. 1939; MA 1947; Hon. Fellow, 1982). Lord Justice Holker Schol., Gray's Inn, 1939. Enlisted RA, 1939, commissioned 1940; Col 1943, in command of Allied Military Mission to Greek Guerillas in German-occupied Greece (despatches twice, DSO, OBE, Officer of Legion of Merit (USA), Commander of Order of the Phoenix, with Swords (Greece)). Served in HM Embassy, Athens, 1945, Tehran, 1951; Secretary-General, Allied Mission for Observing Greek Elections, 1946; worked in industry 1946–48; Asst Secretary, Nuffield Foundation, 1948–50; Foreign Office, 1952; Director-General, RIIA, and Dir of Studies, 1955–59; Dir, Educn and Training, CBI, 1966–70. MP (C) Oxford, 1959–66 and 1970–Sept. 1974; Parliamentary Secretary, Ministry of Aviation, 1961–62; Joint Under-Secretary of State, Home Office, 1962–64. President, Classical Assoc., 1968; Chm. Council, RSL, 1977–86. Fellow of Trinity Hall, Cambridge, 1950; Visiting Fellow, Nuffield Coll., Oxford, 1956; Vis. Prof., King's Coll., London, 1978. FRSL 1951. Special Mem., Acad. of Athens, 1980. *Publications:* Apple of Discord, 1948; One Omen, 1950; Dostoievsky, 1951; The Greek War of Independence, 1952; Britain and the Middle East, 1959; British Foreign Policy since the Second World War, 1961; (with J. G. Lockhart) Rhodes, 1963; The New Concert of Nations, 1964; The Battle of Navarino, 1965; Post-War Britain, 1966; The Story of Modern Greece, 1968, retitled Modern Greece, 5th edn 1991; The Philhellenes, 1969; Capodistria: the founder of Greek independence, 1973; The Struggle for Greece (1941–1949), 1976; Something Ventured, 1982; Karamanlis: the restorer of Greek democracy, 1982; The Rise and Fall of the Greek Colonels, 1985; Gemistos Plethon: the last of the Hellenes, 1986; Rhigas Velestinlis, 1995; numerous articles, translations, broadcasts. *Heir:* *s* Hon. Christopher Richard James Woodhouse [*b* 20 Sept. 1946; *m* 1975, Hon. Anna Margaret Philipps, *er d* of 3rd Baron Milford; one *s* one *d*]. *Address:* 59 Pegasus Grange, Whitehouse Road, Oxford OX1 4QQ. *T:* (01865) 724642. *Died 13 Feb. 2001.*

TESH, Robert Mathieson, CMG 1968; HM Diplomatic Service, retired; Ambassador to Ethiopia, 1979–82; *b* 15 Sept. 1922; *s* of late E. Tesh, Hurst Green, Surrey; *m* 1950, Jean Bowker; two *s* one *d*. *Educ:* Queen Elizabeth's, Wakefield; Queen's College, Oxford (MA). Oxford, 1940–42 and 1945–47; Rifle Brigade, 1942–45; HM Foreign Service, 1947: New Delhi, 1948–50; FO, 1950–53 and 1957–60; Delegation to NATO, Paris, 1953–55; Beirut, 1955–57; Bangkok, 1960–64; Dep. High Comr, Ghana, 1965–66; Lusaka, 1966; Consul-General British Interests Section, Canadian Embassy, Cairo, 1966–67; Counsellor, British Embassy, Cairo, 1968; IDC, 1969; Head of Defence Dept, FCO, 1970–72; Ambassador to: Bahrain, 1972–75; the Democratic Republic of Vietnam, 1976; the Socialist Republic of Vietnam, 1976–78; FCO, 1978–79. *Recreations:* music, theatre. *Address:* 2 Belvedere House, 115 High Street, Esher, Surrey KT10 9LG. *T:* (01372) 464192. *Club:* Travellers. *Died 15 March 2002.*

TETT, Sir Hugh (Charles), Kt 1966; Chairman, Esso Petroleum Co. Ltd, 1959–67; *b* Exeter, Devon, 28 Oct. 1906; *e s* of late James Charles Tett and Florence Tett (*née* Lihou); *m* 1st, 1931, Katie Sargent (*d* 1948); one *d*; 2nd, 1949, Joyce Lilian (*née* Mansell) (*d* 1979); one *d*; 3rd, 1980, Barbara Mary (*née* Mackenzie). *Educ:* Hele's School, Exeter; University College of SW of England, Exeter; Royal College of Science (Kitchener's Scholar; ARCS); BSc, DIC. Joined Esso Petroleum Co. Ltd, 1928; Managing Director, Esso Research Ltd, 1947–49; Director, Esso Petroleum Co. Ltd, 1951. Technical Advisory Committee, Petroleum Board, 1940–45; Lieut-Colonel, Combined Intelligence Objectives Sub-Cttee, 1944–45. Chairman of Council, Institute of Petroleum, 1947–48; Member: Council for Scientific and Industrial Research, 1961–64; Advisory Council, Ministry of Technology, 1964–67. Chairman, Economic

Development Cttee for Motor Manufacturing Industry, 1967–69. Pro-Chancellor, Univ. of Southampton, 1967–79. Fellow, Imperial Coll. of Science and Technology, 1964. Hon. DSc: Southampton, 1965; Exeter, 1970. *Address:* Primrose Cottage, Bosham, Chichester, West Sussex PO18 8HZ. *T:* (01243) 572705, *Fax:* (01243) 572765. *Died 2 Jan. 2001.*

THATCHER, Sir Denis, 1st Bt *cr* 1991, of Scotney in the County of Kent; MBE (mil.) 1944; TD 1946; company director; *b* 10 May 1915; *m* 1st, 1942, Margaret Doris (marr. diss. 1946), *o d* of Leonard Kempson; 2nd, 1951, Margaret Hilda Roberts (later Baroness Thatcher, LG, OM, PC, FRS); one *s* one *d* (twins). *Educ:* Mill Hill Sch. Major, RA, 1938–46. Man. Dir, Atlas Preservative Co., 1949; Director: Castrol, 1963; Burmah Oil Trading Ltd, 1969–; non-exec. Dir, various cos, 1975–. *Recreation:* golf. *Heir: s* Hon. Mark Thatcher [*b* 15 Aug. 1953; *m* 1987, Diane Bergdorf, Dallas, Texas; one *s* one *d*]. *Address:* 73 Chester Square, SW1W 9DU. *Clubs:* Carlton, East India, Buck's, Pratt's. *Died 26 June 2003.*

THAW, John Edward, CBE 1993; actor; *b* 3 Jan. 1942; *s* of John Edward Thaw and Dorothy (*née* Abblott); *m* 1st, Sally Alexander (marr. diss.); one *d*; 2nd, 1973, Sheila Hancock, OBE; one *d* and one step *d*. *Educ:* Ducie Technical High Sch., Manchester; RADA (Vanbrugh Award; Liverpool Playhouse Award). *Theatre* appearances include: A Shred of Evidence, Liverpool Playhouse, 1960; The Fire Raisers, Royal Court, 1961; Women Beware Women, Arts, 1962; Semi-Detached, Saville, 1962; So What About Love?, Criterion, 1969; Random Happenings in the Hebrides, Edinburgh Fest., 1970; The Lady from the Sea, Greenwich, 1971; Collaborators, Duchess, 1973; Absurd Person Singular (tour), 1976; Night and Day, Phoenix, 1978; Sergeant Musgrave's Dance, NT, 1982; Twelfth Night, The Time of Your Life, Henry VIII, RSC, 1983; Pygmalion, Shaftesbury, 1984; All My Sons, Royal Exchange, Manchester, 1988; The Absence of War, Royal NT, 1993 (televised, 1995); *television* appearances include: Redcap, 1965–66; Thick As Thieves, 1973; The Sweeney, 1974–78; Sir Francis Drake, 1981; Mitch, 1983; The Life and Death of King John, 1984; Home to Roost, 1985–89; Inspector Morse, 1986–2000; Stanley and the Women, 1991; A Year in Provence, 1993; Kavanagh QC, 1994–99; Plastic Man, 1999; The Waiting Time, 1999; Monsignor Renard, 2000; The Glass, 2001; Buried Treasure, 2001; films include: The Bofors Gun, 1968; The Sweeney, 1976; The Sweeney II, 1977; The Grass is Singing, 1982; Cry Freedom, 1987; Charlie, 1992. Fellow, BAFTA, 2001. *Address:* c/o John Redway Associates, Nederlander House, 7 Great Russell Street, WC1B 3NH. *Died 21 Feb. 2002.*

THELWELL, Norman; freelance artist-cartoonist since 1957; *b* Birkenhead, 3 May 1923; *s* of Christopher Thelwell and Emily (*née* Vick); *m* 1949, Rhona Evelyn Ladbury; one *s* one *d*. *Educ:* Rock Ferry High Sch., Birkenhead; Liverpool Coll. of Art. Nat. Diploma of Art; ATD. Teacher of Art, Wolverhampton Coll. of Art, 1950–57. Regular contributor to Punch, 1952–; cartoonist for: News Chronicle, 1956–60; Sunday Dispatch, 1960–61; Sunday Express, 1962–. Drawings for general publications, advertising, book jackets, illustrations, etc. *Publications:* Angels on Horseback, 1957; Thelwell Country, 1959; A Place of Your Own, 1960; Thelwell in Orbit, 1961; A Leg at Each Corner, 1962; The Penguin Thelwell, 1963; Top Dog, 1964; Thelwell's Riding Academy, 1965; Drawing Ponies, 1966; Up the Garden Path, 1967; Thelwell's Compleat Tangler, 1967; Thelwell's Book of Leisure, 1968; This Desirable Plot, 1970; The Effluent Society, 1971; Penelope, 1972; Three Sheets in the Wind, 1973; Belt Up, 1974; Thelwell Goes West, 1975; Thelwell's Brat Race, 1977; A Plank Bridge by a Pool, 1978; Thelwell's Gymkhana, 1979; Thelwell Annual, 1980; A Millstone Round My Neck, 1981; Thelwell Annual, 1981; Pony Cavalcade, 1981; How to

Draw Ponies, 1982; Some Damn Fool's Signed the Rubens Again, 1982; Thelwell's Magnificat, 1983; Thelwell's Sporting Prints, 1984; Wrestling with a Pencil: the life of a freelance artist, 1986; Play It As It Lies: Thelwell's golfing manual, 1987; Penelope Rides Again, 1988; The Cat's Pyjamas, 1992. *Recreations:* trout and salmon angling, painting. *Address:* Herons Mead, Timsbury, Romsey, Hants SO51 0NE. *T:* (01794) 368238. *Died 7 Feb. 2004.*

THESIGER, Roderic Miles Doughty; Director, P. & D. Colnaghi and Co. Ltd, 1955–71; *b* 8 Nov. 1915; *y s* of late Hon. Wilfred Thesiger, DSO, and Kathleen Mary, CBE (*née* Vigors; later Mrs Reginald Astley); *m* 1st, 1940, Mary Rose (marr. diss. 1946; she *d* 1962), *d* of Hon. Guy Charteris; 2nd, 1946, Ursula, *d* of A. W. Whitworth, Woollas Hall, Pershore; one *s* one *d*. *Educ:* Eton; Christ Church, Oxford; Courtauld Institute. Served War of 1939–45, Welsh Guards, 1939–41; 1st Parachute Bde, 1941–44 (twice wounded, POW). Assistant, Tate Gallery, 1945–46; afterwards worked with Messrs Sotheby and privately until 1954. *Recreation:* visiting Italy and France. *Address:* The Paddocks, Lucton, Leominster, Herefordshire HR6 9PG. *T:* (01568) 780327. *Died 5 March 2005.*

THESIGER, Sir Wilfred (Patrick), KBE 1995 (CBE 1968); DSO 1941; *b* 3 June 1910; *e s* of late Hon. Wilfred Thesiger, DSO, and Mrs Reginald Astley, CBE; *heir-presumptive* to Barony of Chelmsford. *Educ:* Eton; Magdalen Coll., Oxford (MA; Hon. Fellow, 1982). Rep. Oxford at boxing, 1930–33; Captain Oxford Boxing Team, 1933. Hon. Attaché, Duke of Gloucester's Mission to Abyssinia, for Haile Selassie's coronation, 1930; explored Danakil country of Abyssinia and the Aussa Sultanate, 1933–34 (awarded Back Grant by RGS, 1935); Sudan Political Service, Darfur-Upper Nile, 1935–40; served: ME 1941 (DSO); in Ethiopian, Syrian and Western Desert campaigns with SDF and SAS regt, rank of Major; explored in Southern Arabia, 1945–49; twice crossed the Empty Quarter. Hon. Vice-Pres., RSAA, 1990–. FRSL 1966; Hon. FBA 1982. Hon. DLitt: Leicester, 1967; Bath, 1992. Founder's Medal, RGS, 1948; Lawrence of Arabia Medal, RCAS, 1955; Livingstone Medal, RSGS, 1962; W. H. Heinemann Award (for 1964), RSL, 1965; Burton Memorial Medal, Roy. Asiatic Soc., 1966. 3rd Class Star of Ethiopia, 1930; Order of Independence (UAE), 2000. *Publications:* Arabian Sands, 1959; The Marsh Arabs, 1964; Desert, Marsh and Mountain: the world of a nomad, 1979; The Life of my Choice (autobiog.), 1987; Visions of a Nomad, 1987; My Kenya Days, 1994; The Danakil Diary: journeys through Abyssinia 1930–34, 1996; Among the Mountains: travels in Asia, 1998; Crossing the Sands, 1999; A Vanished World, 2001. *Recreations:* travelling, photography. *Address:* Woodcote Grove House, Meadow Hill, Coulsdon, Surrey CR5 2XL. *T:* (020) 8668 5309. *Clubs:* Travellers' (Special Mem.), Beefsteak (Hon. Life Mem.). *Died 24 Aug. 2003.*

THIMONT, Bernard Maurice, CB 1979; Secretary, Churches' Main Committee, 1981–90; *b* 1 July 1920; *s* of Georges André Thimont; *m* 1949, Joy Rowe; one *s* one *d*. *Educ:* St Ignatius Coll., London. Served War of 1939–45, in Army (Major), 1939–48. Foreign Office, 1948–50; HM Treasury, 1950–65; IDC, 1966; Cabinet Office, 1967; HM Treasury, 1967–68; Civil Service Dept, 1968–77; Controller, HM Stationery Office and Queen's Printer of Acts of Parlt, 1977–80. MA Lambeth, 1990. *Recreations:* music, building. *Address:* Trusham, Kingsnorth Close, Bridport, Dorset DT6 4BZ. *T:* (01308) 425426. *Died 5 Dec. 2005.*

THISTLETHWAITE, Prof. Frank, CBE 1979; founding Vice-Chancellor, 1961–80, and Emeritus Professor, University of East Anglia; *b* 24 July 1915; *s* of late Lee and Florence Nightingale Thistlethwaite; *m* 1940, Jane (*d* 1992), *d* of H. Lindley Hosford, Lyme, Connecticut, USA; one *s* three *d* (and one *s* decd). *Educ:* Bootham School; St John's Coll., Cambridge (Exhibnr and Schol.; BA 1938,

MA 1941; Hon. Fellow 1974). FRHistS. Ed., The Cambridge Review, 1937. Commonwealth Fund Fellow, Univ. of Minnesota, 1938–40; British Press Service, NY, 1940–41. Served RAF, 1941–45; seconded to Office of War Cabinet (Joint-Amer. Secretariat), 1942–45. Cambridge University: Fellow, St John's Coll., 1945–61 (at various times, Tutor, Praelector, Steward); Lectr in Faculty of Economics and Politics, 1949–61. Vis. Prof. of Amer. Civilization, Univ. of Pennsylvania, 1956; Vis. Fellow, Henry E. Huntington Library, Calif, 1973; Leverhulme Emeritus Fellow, 1981; Hill Vis. Prof., Univ. of Minnesota, 1986. Chairman: British Assoc. for Amer. Studies, 1955–59; Cttee of Management, Inst. of US Studies, Univ. of London, 1966–80; IUPC (formerly IUC), 1977–81 (Mem., 1962–81); Member: Inst. for Advanced Study, Princeton, 1954; Academic Adv. Cttee, Open Univ., 1969–74; Provisional Council, Univ. of Zambia, 1965–69; Univ. of Malaŵi, 1971–75; Univ. of Mauritius, 1974–84; Marshall Aid Commemoration Commn, 1964–80; US-UK Educnl (Fulbright) Commn, 1964–79; European Adv. Council, Salzburg Seminar in Amer. Studies, 1969–74; Bd, British Council, 1971–82; British Cttee of Award, Harkness Fellowships, 1974–80; Adviser to Nat. Council of Higher Educn, Ceylon, 1967. Governor, Sedbergh Sch., 1958–73. Pres., Friends of Cambridge Univ. Library, 1983–95. Hon. Prof. of History, Univ. of Mauritius, 1981. Hon. FRIBA 1985. Hon. LHD Colorado, 1972; Hon. DCL East Anglia, 1980; Hon. DSc Minnesota, 1994. Publications: The Great Experiment: an introduction to the history of the American people, 1955 (trans. 14 languages); The Anglo-American Connection in the Early Nineteenth Century, 1958; Dorset Pilgrims: the story of West Country pilgrims who went to New England in the 17th century, 1989; Migration from Europe Overseas in the Nineteenth and Twentieth Centuries, in, A Century of European Migrations 1830–1930, 1991; A Lancashire Family Inheritance, 1996; Our War 1938–1945, 1997; Cambridge Years 1945–1961, 1999; Origins, 2000; A Reminiscence of Undergraduate Life; contributed to: New Cambridge Modern History and other historical works and jls; New Universities in the Modern World (ed M. G. Ross). Recreation: music. Address: 15 Park Parade, Cambridge CB5 8AL. Club: Athenæum. Died 17 Feb. 2003.

THOMAS, Rt Rev. Eryl Stephen; Hon. Assistant Bishop of Swansea and Brecon, since 1988; b 20 Oct. 1910; s of Edward Stephen and Margaret Susannah Thomas; m 1939, Jean Mary Alice Wilson; three s one d. Educ: Rossall Sch.; St John's Coll., Oxford (BA 2nd Class Hons Theology, 1932; MA 1935); Wells Theological Coll. Ordained deacon, 1933, priest, 1934; Curate of Colwyn Bay, 1933–38, of Hawarden, 1938–43; Vicar of Risca, Mon, 1943–48; Warden of St Michael's Theological Coll., Llandaff, 1948–54; Dean of Llandaff, 1954–68; Bishop of Monmouth, 1968–71, of Llandaff, 1971–75. Chm., Church in Wales Liturgical Commn for revision of Prayer Book, 1954–68. Chaplain and Sub-Prelate, Order of St John of Jerusalem, 1969. Address: 17 Orchard Close, Gilwern, Abergavenny NP7 0EN. T: (01873) 831050. Died 6 Dec. 2001.

THOMAS, Sir (Godfrey) Michael (David), 11th Bt cr 1694; Member of Stock Exchange, London, 1959–88; b 10 Oct. 1925; o s of Rt Hon. Sir Godfrey Thomas, PC, GCVO, KCB, CSI, 10th Bt, and Diana (d 1985) , d of late Ven. B. G. Hoskyns; S father, 1968; m 1956, Margaret Greta Cleland, yr d of John Cleland, Stormont Court, Godden Green, Kent; one s two d (of whom one s one d are twins). Educ: Harrow. The Rifle Brigade, 1944–56. Heir: s David John Godfrey Thomas, b 11 June 1961. Address: 81 Rivermead Court, Ranelagh Gardens, SW6 3SA. T: (020) 7736 6896. Clubs: MCC, Hurlingham. Died 10 Jan. 2003.

THOMAS, Graham Stuart, OBE 1975; VMH 1968; Gardens Consultant to National Trust, since 1974; b 3 April 1909; s of W. R. Thomas and L. Thomas. Educ: horticultural and botanical training, Cambridge Univ. Botanic Garden, 1926–29. Six Hills Nursery, Stevenage, 1930; Foreman, later Manager, T. Hilling & Co., Chobham, 1931–55; Manager, Sunningdale Nurseries, Windlesham, 1956, Associate Dir, 1968–71; Gardens Adviser, Nat. Trust, 1955–74. Vice-President: RHS; Garden History Soc.; British Hosta and Hemerocallis Soc.; Vice-Patron, Royal Nat. Rose Soc. (Dean Hole Medal, 1976); Hon. Mem., Irish Garden Plant Soc. Veitch Meml Medal, RHS, 1966; Nat. Trust Founders' Award, 1996; Lifetime Achievement Award, Garden Writers' Guild, 1996. Publications: The Old Shrub Roses, 1955, 5th edn 1978; Colour in the Winter Garden, 1957, 3rd edn 1984; Shrub Roses of Today, 1962, rev. edn 1980; Climbing Roses Old and New, 1965, new edn 1983; Plants for Ground Cover, 1970, rev. edn 1989; Perennial Garden Plants, 1976, rev. and enlarged edn 1990; Gardens of the National Trust, 1979; Three Gardens, 1983; Trees in the Landscape, 1983; The Art of Planting, 1984; A Garden of Roses, 1987; The Complete Flower Paintings and Drawings of Graham Stuart Thomas, 1987; The Rock Garden and its Plants, 1989; An English Rose Garden, 1991; Ornamental Shrubs, Climbers and Bamboos, 1992; The Graham Stuart Thomas Rose Book, 1994; Cuttings from my Garden Notebooks, 1997; Treasured Perennials, 1999; Thoughts from a Garden Seat, 2000; The Garden Through the Year, 2002. Recreations: horticulture, music, painting and drawing plants. Address: 21 Kettlewell Close, Horsell, Woking, Surrey GU21 4HY.
Died 16 April 2003.

THOMAS, Sir (John) Maldwyn, Kt 1984; President, Welsh Liberal Party, 1985–86; b 17 June 1918; s of Daniel and Gwladys Thomas; m 1975, Maureen Elizabeth (Dame Maureen Thomas, DBE 1999). Educ: Porth Rhondda Grammar Sch. FCIS. Called to Bar, Gray's Inn, 1953; Solicitor, 1965; readmitted to Gray's Inn, 1987. Lewis & Tylor Ltd, Cardiff, 1940–56; Signode Ltd, Swansea, 1956–59; Commercial Agreements Manager, UKAEA, 1959–63; Rank Xerox Ltd: Sec., 1964–70; Man. Dir, 1970–72; Chm., 1972–79; Dir, Xerox Corp., USA, 1974–79; non-executive Director: Internat. Military Services, 1978–84; Thos Cook Inc. (USA), 1978–84; Westland PLC, 1985–94; non-exec. Dep. Chm., John Brown plc, 1984–86. Chm., European Govt Business Relations Council, 1978–79. Contested (L) Aberavon, 1950. Pres., London Welsh Assoc. and Trust. Trustee, London Welsh Sch. Address: 9 Chester Terrace, Regent's Park, NW1 4ND. Clubs: Reform, National Liberal.
Died 31 July 2002.

THOMAS, Sir Maldwyn; see Thomas, Sir J. M.

THOMAS, Sir Michael, 11th Bt; see Thomas, Sir G. M. D.

THOMAS, Ralph Philip, MC 1942; film director; b Hull, Yorks, 10 Aug. 1915; m 1944, Joy Spanjer; one s one d. Educ: Tellisford School, Clifton. Entered film industry, 1932, and worked in all production depts, particularly editing, until 1939; served War of 1939–45, as Regimental Officer 9th Lancers until 1944; thereafter Instructor Royal Military College; returned to Film Industry, in Rank Organisation Trailer Dept, 1946; joined Gainsborough Pictures, 1948, and directed Once Upon a Dream, Traveller's Joy. Films directed at Pinewood Studios: The Clouded Yellow, Appointment with Venus, The Venetian Bird, A Day to Remember, Doctor in the House, Mad About Men, Above Us The Waves, Doctor at Sea, The Iron Petticoat, Checkpoint, Doctor at Large, Campbell's Kingdom, A Tale of Two Cities, The Wind Cannot Read, The 39 Steps, Upstairs and Downstairs, Conspiracy of Hearts, Doctor in Love, No My Darling Daughter, No Love for Johnnie, The Wild and the Willing, Doctor in Distress, Hot enough for June, The High Bright Sun, Doctor in Clover, Deadlier than the Male, Nobody Runs Forever, Some Girls Do, Doctor in Trouble, Quest, Percy, It's a 2 foot 6 inch Above the Ground World, Percy's Progress, A Nightingale Sang in Berkeley Square, Doctors' Daughters, Pop Pirates. Address: Kirrin House, Blyton

Close, Beaconsfield, Bucks HP9 2LX. *T:* (01494) 671865.
Died 17 March 2001.

THOMAS, Dr Reginald; Austrian Ambassador, retired; Lecturer on protocol, etiquette and diplomatic correspondence, Diplomatic Academy, Vienna, and in other foreign institutions, 1994–2001; *b* 28 Feb. 1928; *s* of Dr Leopold Thomas and Irma Thomas (*née* von Smekal); *m* 1960, Ingrid Renate Leitner; three *s* one *d. Educ:* Univ. of Vienna (Dr jur 1950). Entered Austrian Foreign Service, 1951; Austrian Legation, Bern, 1952–56; Dep. Legal Adviser on Internat. Law, Min. of Foreign Affairs, Vienna, 1956–59; Austrian Embassy, Tokyo, 1959–62; Head of Office of Sec. Gen. for Foreign Affairs, Vienna, 1962–68; Ambassador: to Pakistan and concurrently accredited to Union of Burma, 1968–71; to Japan and concurrently accredited to Republic of Korea, 1971–75; Head of Dept of Administration, Min. of Foreign Affairs, Vienna, 1975–82; concurrently Dep. Sec. Gen. for Foreign Affairs, Vienna, 1978–82; Ambassador to UK, 1982–87; Inspector Gen. in Min. of Foreign Affairs, Vienna, 1988–93. Mem., Austrian Assoc. for Foreign Policy and Internat. Relations, Vienna. Knight Comdr's Cross (Austria), 1993; Foreign orders include: Grand Cross: Order of the Rising Sun (Japan); Order of Diplomatic Service (Korea); Independence Order (Jordan); Order of F. de Miranda (Venezuela); Hilal-i-Qaid-i-Azam (Pakistan). *Recreation:* sports. *Address:* Schwarzenbergstrasse 8, 1010 Wien, Austria. *Club:* Queen's (Life Mem.).
Died 1 Aug. 2001.

THOMAS, Sir Robert (Evan), Kt 1967; JP, DL; Leader, Greater Manchester Metropolitan County Council, 1973–77; Deputy Chairman, Manchester Ship Canal, 1971–74; *b* 8 Oct. 1901; *s* of Jesse and Anne Thomas; *m* 1924, Edna Isherwood (*d* 1992); one *s* one *d. Educ:* St Peter's, Leigh, Lancs. Miner, 1914; served Army, 1919–21; Bus Driver, 1924–37; Trade Union Official, 1937–66; Member, Manchester City Council, 1944–74; Lord Mayor of Manchester, 1962–63. Chairman: Assoc. of Municipal Corps, 1973–74; Assoc. of Metropolitan Authorities, 1974–77; British Sector, Internat. Union of Local Authorities, 1974–77. JP Manchester, 1948; DL: County Palatine of Lancaster, 1967–73, County Palatine of Greater Manchester, 1974. Hon. MA Manchester, 1974. *Publication:* Sir Bob (autobiog.), 1984. *Recreations:* gardening, golf. *Address:* Gorton Parks, 121 Taylor Street, Gorton, Manchester M18 8DF. *Died 17 April 2004.*

THOMAS, Roydon Urquhart; QC 1985; a Recorder, 1986–2002; *b* 17 May 1936; *s* of Rowland Daniel Thomas and Jean Milne Thomas; *m* 1984, Caroline (marr. diss.); one *s* one *d* (and one *s* decd). *Educ:* Fettes College; Sidney Sussex Coll., Cambridge (BA 1959). Called to the Bar, Middle Temple, 1960, Bencher, 1993; practised on South Eastern Circuit. *Publication:* (Asst Ed.) Tolstoy on Divorce, 1964. *Recreations:* golf, fishing, erratic ski-ing. *Address:* 1 Essex Court, Temple, EC4Y 9AR. *T:* (020) 7583 2000. *Clubs:* Hurlingham; High Post Golf.
Died 24 Feb. 2003.

THOMAS, Sir William James Cooper, 2nd Bt *cr* 1919; TD; JP; DL; Captain RA; *b* 7 May 1919; *er s* of Sir William James Thomas, 1st Bt, and Maud Mary Cooper, Bexhill-on-Sea; *S* father, 1945; *m* 1947, Freida Dunbar (*d* 1990), *yr d* of late F. A. Whyte; two *s* one *d. Educ:* Harrow; Downing Coll., Cambridge. Barrister, Inner Temple, 1948. Member TA, 1938. Served War of 1939–45. Monmouthshire: JP 1958; DL 1973; High Sheriff, 1973. *Heir: s* William Michael Thomas, *b* 5 Dec. 1948. *Address:* Green Gates, 2 Hernes Road, Oxford OX2 7PT.
Died 9 Oct. 2005.

THOMPSON, Charles Allister; HM Diplomatic Service, retired; *b* 21 July 1922; *yr s* of late Herbert Ivie and Margaret (*née* Browne-Webber) Thompson, Managua, Nicaragua; *m* 1950, Jean Margaret, *er d* of late Alexander Bruce Dickson; one *s* two *d* (and one *s* decd). *Educ:* Haileybury; Hertford Coll., Oxford (MA, BLitt). War

Service, 1942–46, 1st King's Dragoon Guards. Joined Foreign Service (later Diplomatic Service), 1947, and served in FO until 1949; 3rd Sec., Prague, 1949–50; 2nd Sec. (Commercial), Mexico City, 1950–53; FO 1953–56; 1st Sec., Karachi, 1956–59; Head of Chancery, Luxembourg, 1959–62; FO, 1962–65; Counsellor, 1965; Dep. Consul-Gen., New York, 1965–67; Dep. High Comr, Port of Spain, 1967–70; HM Consul-Gen., Philadelphia, 1970–74; Vis. Fellow, Centre for Internat. Studies, LSE, 1974–75; Head of Training Dept, FCO, and Dir, Diplomatic Service Language Centre, 1975–76. Founding Chm., HELP Jávea, 1978. *Recreations:* gardening, golf, gerontology. *Address:* Calle San Joaquín 9–4° 25, Jávea 03730, Alicante, Spain. *T:* (96) 5792283.
Died 22 Aug. 2002.

THOMPSON, Sir Donald, Kt 1992; *b* 13 Nov. 1931; *s* of Geoffrey and Rachel Thompson; *m* 1957, Patricia Ann Hopkins; two *s. Educ:* Hipperholme Grammar Sch. Nat. Service, 1950–52. Farmer/butcher, 1952–74; formerly Dir, Halifax Farmers' Trading Assoc.; Man. Dir, Armadillo Plastics (Glass Fibre Manufacturers), 1974–79. Member: WR CC, 1967–74; W Yorks CC, 1974–75; Calderdale Dist Council, 1975–79. Contested (C): Batley and Morley, 1970; Sowerby, Feb. and Oct. 1974. MP (C) Sowerby, 1979–83, Calder Valley, 1983–97; contested (C) Calder Valley, 1997. An Asst Govt Whip, then a Lord Comr of HM Treasury, 1981–86; Parly Sec., MAFF, 1986–89. A Govt Whip, Council of Europe and WEU, 1990–94. Chm., Cons. Candidates' Assoc., 1972–74. Chm. Appeal Fund, Animal Health Trust, 1989–2004. Dir-Gen., Friends of War Memls, 1997–. *Recreations:* Rugby football, poor golf, conversation. *Address:* Moravian House, Lightcliffe, Halifax HX3 8AL. *Clubs:* Beefsteak, Pratt's, St Stephen's; Brodleians (Hipperholme); Octave (Elland).
Died 14 March 2005.

THOMPSON, Godfrey; *see* Thompson, W. G.

THOMPSON, Sir (Humphrey) Simon M.; *see* Meysey-Thompson.

THOMPSON, Rt Rev. James Lawton; Assistant Bishop, diocese of Exeter, since 2002; Bishop of Bath and Wells, 1991–2001; *b* 11 Aug. 1936; *s* of Bernard Isaac and Marjorie May Thompson; *m* 1965, Sally Patricia Stallworthy; one *s* one *d. Educ:* Dean Close School, Cheltenham; Emmanuel Coll., Cambridge (BA 1964, MA 1971; Hon. Fellow, 1992). FCA 1959. 2nd Lt, 3rd Royal Tank Regt, 1959–61. Ordained deacon, 1966, priest, 1967; Curate, East Ham, 1966–68; Chaplain, Cuddesdon Coll., Oxford, 1968–71; Rector of Thamesmead and Ecumenical Team Leader, 1971–78; Suffragan, then Area, Bishop of Stepney, 1978–91. Mem., House of Bishops, Gen. Synod of C of E, 1988–2001. Chairman: Cttee for Relations with People of Other Faiths, BCC, 1983–89; Urban Studies Centre, then Urban Learning Foundn, 1985–91; Interfaith Network (UK), 1987–92; London Churches Broadcasting Gp, 1987–91; Church at Work, London, 1989–91; Social Policy Cttee, 1990–95, Social, Economic and Industrial Affairs Cttee, 1996–97, Bd for Social Responsibility; Children's Soc., 1997–2001; Jt Pres., English Churches Housing Trust, 1995–2000. Pres., Royal Bath and West Soc., 1997–98. Visitor, Wadham Coll., Oxford, 1992. Entered House of Lords, 1997. Hon. Fellow, QMC, 1986. Hon. DLitt: E London Poly., 1989; Bath, 1998; Hon. DD Exeter, 1995. (Jtly) Sir Sigmund Sternberg Award for Christian-Jewish Relations, 1987. *Publications:* Halfway: reflections in midlife, 1986; (contrib.) Trevor Huddleston, ed D. D. Honoré, 1989; The Lord's Song, 1990; Stepney Calling, 1991; Why God?, 1996; Good Morning, 2003. *Recreations:* riding, painting, a horse, sport, Exmoor.
Died 19 Sept. 2003.

THOMPSON, John Alan, CMG 1974; HM Diplomatic Service, retired; *b* 21 June 1926; *m* 1956, Maureen Sayers. *Educ:* Bromsgrove Sch.; Brasenose Coll., Oxford. Control Commission for Germany, 1952; Vice-Consul, Hanoi,

1954; Second Sec., Saigon, 1956; Warsaw, 1959; Foreign Office, 1961; First Sec. (Commercial), Havana, 1964; First Sec., FO (later FCO), 1966–75; Counsellor, 1973. *Recreations:* music, mountains. *Address:* Sun House, Hall Street, Long Melford, Suffolk CO10 9HZ. *T:* (01787) 378252. *Died 5 Feb. 2001.*

THOMPSON, (John) Peter (Stuart); Director, Solicitors' Complaints Bureau, 1986–90; *b* 6 July 1925; *s* of Frederick Charles Victor Thompson and Hilda Mary (*née* Hampton); *m* 1956, Valerie Merriel (*née* Harman). *Educ:* Burton Grammar Sch.; Royal Naval Coll., Dartmouth; Royal Naval Engineering Coll., Devonport; Univ. of Birmingham (LLB 1955). Admitted Solicitor, 1966. Served Royal Navy, 1943–47. Arts Council Drama Dept and associated theatres: Actor/Stage Dir, 1947–52. Asst Company Sec., Saunders-Roe Ltd, Aircraft Manufrs, 1955–61; articled clerk, Helder Roberts & Co., Solicitors, London, 1961–66, Partner 1966–70; Law Soc. Professional Purposes Dept, 1971–86. *Recreations:* gardening, marine technology, 18th Century music, flora and fauna of tropical islands. *Address:* Parkhurst Lodge, Abinger Common, Dorking, Surrey RH5 6LL. *T:* (01306) 730522. *Died 3 Feb. 2002.*

THOMPSON, Norman Sinclair, CBE 1980; *b* 7 July 1920; *s* of Norman Whitfield Thompson and Jane Thompson (*née* Robinson); *m* 1945, Peggy Sivil; two *s* (one *d* decd). *Educ:* Middlesbrough High Sch. Qual. Chartered Accountant, 1947 (FCA); Cost and Management Accountant (ACMA), 1949. Served War, Merchant Seaman, 1940–45. Asst Sec., Paton's and Baldwin's Ltd, 1947; Commercial Manager, Cowan's Sheldon & Co. Ltd, 1955; Group Secretary, Richardson's Westgarth & Co. Ltd, 1957; Financial Dir, David Brown & Sons (Huddersfield) Ltd, 1961; Gen. Manager, Malta Drydocks, Swan Hunter Group Ltd, 1963; apptd Swan Hunter Bd, 1964; Overseas Dir, 1967; Dep. Managing Dir, 1969; The Cunard Steam-Ship Co. Ltd: Man. Dir, Cargo Shipping, 1970; Man. Dir, 1971–74; Chairman: Mass Transit Railway Corp., Hong Kong, 1975–86; Poole Harbour Comrs, 1984–86; Dep. Chm., New Hong Kong Tunnel Co., 1986–92; Director: Hong Kong and Shanghai Banking Corp., 1978–86; British Shipbuilders, 1983–86; Portland Port Ltd, 1995–96. Chm., Burton Bradstock Parish Council, 1999–2002. *Recreations:* dogs, music. *Address:* The Old Coach House, Burton Bradstock, Bridport, Dorset DT6 4QG. *Clubs:* Oriental; Hong Kong, Royal Hong Kong Yacht, Hong Kong Jockey. *Died 19 April 2005.*

THOMPSON, Peter; *see* Thompson, J. P. S.

THOMPSON, (William) Godfrey; library planning consultant, 1983; *b* 28 June 1921; *s* of late A. and E. M. Thompson, Coventry; *m* 1946, Doreen Mary Cattell; one *s*. *Educ:* King Henry VIII Sch., Coventry; MA Loughborough, 1977. FSA. Served with Royal Signals and Indian Signal Corps, 1941–46. Entered Library Service, Coventry, 1937; Dep. Borough Librarian, Chatham, 1946; Deputy City Librarian: Kingston-upon-Hull, 1952; Manchester, 1958; City Librarian, Leeds, 1963; Guildhall Librarian, Dir of Libraries and Art Galls, City of London, 1966–83; Cultural Consultant, UAE, Abu Dhabi, 1983–86. Organiser, City Treasures exhibns in Brussels, 1967, Vienna, 1968, San Francisco, 1970–71, etc. Hon. Librarian to Clockmakers' Co., Gardeners' Co., Charles Lamb Soc.; Pres., Assoc. of Asst Librarians, 1962. Member: Council, Library Assoc., 1968–81 (Hon. Treasurer, 1974–77; Pres., 1978); Council, Aslib, 1968–71; Liby Adv. Bd, British Council, 1974–83; Adv. Panel to Sec. of State on allocation of books received under Capital Transfer Tax; Adv. Panel to Sec. of State on Export of Works of Art. Mem. Exec. Cttee, Friends of the Nat. Libraries; Founding Hon. Sec. Internat. Assoc. Metropolitan Libraries, 1968–70. Governor, St Bride Foundn. Mem. Adv. Bd, New Library World; Libraries Specialist, Architects' Jl, 1968–74; consultant on libraries to more than 20 overseas governments and nat. bodies, including the planning of twelve nat. libraries; Advr, Botswana Nat. Liby project, 1994, 1996. FRSA. *Publications:* London's Statues, 1971; Planning and Design of Library Buildings, 1972, 3rd edn 1989; edited: London for Everyman, 1969; Encyclopædia of London, 1969. *Recreation:* reading — at last. *Address:* Southdown, Down Lane, Compton, Surrey GU3 1DN. *Died 11 Dec. 2002.*

THOMPSON HANCOCK, P(ercy) E(llis); *see* Hancock.

THOMSON, Robert John Stewart, CMG 1969; MBE 1955; Ministry of Defence, 1969–81; *b* 5 May 1922; *s* of late John Stewart Thomson, FRIBA, and Nellie Thomson (*née* Morris). *Educ:* Bromsgrove Sch.; Worcester Coll., Oxford. Service with Sudan Defence Force, 1943–45. Sudan Political Service, 1943–54 (District Commissioner, 1950–54). Attached Ministry of Defence, 1955–56; First Sec., British High Commission, Accra, 1956–60, 1962–64, Counsellor, 1966–69. *Recreations:* gardening, singing. *Address:* Ardgowan, 119 Lenthay Road, Sherborne, Dorset DT9 6AQ. *Died 19 June 2002.*

THOMSON, Rosemary Edith Robertson, CBE 1997 (OBE 1992); JP; DL; Vice-President, Magistrates' Association, since 1996 (Chairman of Council, 1993–96); *b* 3 Oct. 1934; *d* of James Heggie and Cecilia (*née* Walker); *m* 1958, Peter Thomson; one *s* one *d*. *Educ:* Watford Grammar Sch. for Girls; Girton Coll., Cambridge (MA); McGill Univ., Montreal. Open University: Tutor-counsellor, 1974–96; counsellor to students in Broadmoor Hosp., 1974–84. Feltham Young Offenders' Institution: Mem., 1980–86; Chm., Bd of Visitors, 1984–86. Mem., Berks Probation Cttee, 1987–96. Magistrates' Association: Mem. Council, 1975–96; Chm., Trng Cttee, 1981–87; Chm., Berks Br., 1987–92; Dep. Chm., Council, 1987–93. Member: Lord Chancellor's Adv. Cttee on Trng of Magistrates, 1981–84; Judicial Studies Bd, 1985–88; Criminal Justice Consultative Council, 1992–99; Magistrates' Courts Consultative Council, 1992–96; Berkshire and Oxfordshire Magistrates' Courts Cttee, 1997–99; Council, Commonwealth Magistrates and Judges Assoc., 1991–95 (Mem., Trng Cttee, 1987–95); Criminal Injuries Compensation Appeal Panel, 1996–; Lord Chancellor's Adv. Cttee on Legal Educn and Conduct, 1997–99; Home Office Correctional Bd, subseq. Strategy Bd for Correctional Services, 1999–; Vice Chm., Thames Valley Magistrates' Courts Cttee, 1999–. Non-executive Director: Prison Service, 1997–; Nat. Probation Service, 2000–; Expert Consultee, Criminal Justice Rev., 1999–2001. JP Maidenhead, 1971; DL Berks, 2000. Hon. Dr Central England, 1995. *Publications:* numerous articles on magisterial matters mostly in The Magistrate. *Recreations:* sedentary and literary pursuits, looking at pictures, family life. *Address:* Little Lodge, Lower Cookham Road, Maidenhead, Berks SL6 8JT. *T:* (01628) 626816. *Died 23 Oct. 2001.*

THORLEY, Charles Graham; *b* 4 Jan. 1914; *s* of Charles Lord Thorley; *m* 1958, Peggy Percival Ellis (*née* Boor); one step *s* one step *d*. *Educ:* Manchester Grammar Sch.; King's Coll., Cambridge (Mod. Lang. Scholar). Served War of 1939–45, Eritrea and Cyrenaica (Lt-Col). Entered Civil Service as Economist, Bd of Trade, 1936; attached to British Embassy, China, 1936–38; Mem. British Economic Mission to Belgian Congo, 1940–41; HM Treasury, 1940–57; served on UK financial delegns and missions in Japan, US, Egypt, France, Switzerland, W Germany, etc; Min. of Power, 1957; Under-Secretary and Head of Coal Div., 1965–69; Acct-Gen. and Dir of Finance, 1969. Chm., NATO Petroleum Planning Cttee, 1962–65; Under-Sec., Min. of Technology and DTI, 1969–74. Specialist Advr, House of Lords, 1975–79. *Address:* 4 Penstones Court, Marlborough Lane, Stanford in the Vale, Faringdon, Oxon SN7 8SW. *T:* (01367) 718085. *Died 13 Nov. 2004.*

THORNE, Sir Peter (Francis), KCVO 1981; CBE 1966; ERD; Serjeant at Arms, House of Commons, 1976–82; *b*

6 Aug. 1914; *y s* of late Gen. Sir Andrew Thorne, KCB, CMG, DSO; *m* 1959, Lady Anne Pery, MA, DPhil (Senior Res. Fellow, Imperial College, London), *d* of 5th Earl of Limerick, GBE, CH, KCB, DSO, TD; one *s* two *d* (and one *d* decd). *Educ:* Eton; Trinity Coll., Oxford. Served War of 1939–45: with 3rd Bn Grenadier Guards (wounded), 1939–41; HQ 2nd Div., 1941–42; Staff College, Quetta, 1942; on staff of India Command and HQ, SACSEA, 1943–45; demobilised with rank of Hon. Lieut-Col, 1946. With Imperial Chemical Industries Ltd, 1946–48. Assistant Serjeant at Arms, House of Commons, 1948–57, Dep. Serjeant at Arms, 1957–76. *Publications:* The Royal Mace in the House of Commons, 1990; various HMSO pamphlets and articles in parly and historical pubns. *Address:* Chiddinglye Farmhouse, West Hoathly, East Grinstead, West Sussex RH19 4QS. *T:* (01342) 810338. *Clubs:* Cavalry and Guards; Royal Yacht Squadron. *Died 16 March 2004.*

THORNE, Robin Horton John, CMG 1966; OBE 1963; HM Overseas Service, retired; *b* 13 July 1917; *s* of late Sir John Anderson Thorne; *m* 1946, Joan Helen Wadman (*d* 2000); one *s*. *Educ:* Dragon Sch., Oxford; Rugby (open scholar); Exeter College, Oxford (open scholar; MA). War Service, Devonshire Regiment and King's African Rifles, 1939–46. Colonial Administrative Service (later HM Overseas Civil Service), 1946–67; Tanganyika Administration, 1946–58; Aden, 1958–67; Asst Chief Sec. (Colony), MLC and Mem. of Governor's Exec. Coun., 1959–63; Ministerial Sec. to Chief Minister, 1963–65; Assistant High Commissioner, 1966–67. With Vice-Chancellors' Cttee, 1967–77; part-time admin. work, Univ. of Sussex, 1978–81. Trustee of Aden Port Trust, 1959–66; Chm., Staines Trust, 1979–85; Mem., Management Cttee, Sussex Housing Assoc. for the Aged, 1983–87. *Recreations:* various. *Address:* Care Village, Winsley Road, Limpley Stoke, Bath BA2 7FF. *T:* (01255) 722447. *Club:* Royal Commonwealth Society. *Died 11 May 2004.*

THRING, Rear-Adm. George Arthur, CB 1958; DSO 1940 and Bar 1952; DL; *b* 13 Sept. 1903; *s* of Sir Arthur Thring, KCB; *m* 1929, Betty Mary (*d* 1983), *er d* of Colonel Stewart William Ward Blacker, DSO; two *s* two *d*. *Educ:* Royal Naval Colleges, Osborne and Dartmouth. Commander, 1941; Captain, 1946; Rear-Admiral, 1956; retired, 1958. Commanded: HMS Deptford, 1940–41; 42nd and 20th Escort Groups, Atlantic, 1943–45; HMS Ceylon, 1951–52; Flag Officer, Malayan Area, 1956–58. Officer, Legion of Merit (USA), 1945. DL Somerset, 1968. *Recreations:* golf, fishing. *Address:* Alford House, Castle Cary, Somerset BA7 7PN. *T:* (01963) 240329. *Died 15 Dec. 2001.*

THYSSEN BORNEMISZA de KASZON, Baron Hans Heinrich; industrialist and art collector; *b* The Hague, 13 April 1921; Swiss citizen; *s* of Baron Dr Heinrich Thyssen-Bornemisza and Baroness Margit Bornemisza de Kaszon; *m* 1st, 1946, Theresa zur Lippe (marr. diss.); one *s*; 2nd, 1954, Nina Dyer (marr. diss.); 3rd, 1956, Fiona Campbell-Walter (marr. diss. 1964); one *s* one *d*; 4th, 1964, Denise Shorto (marr. diss.); one *s*; 5th, 1985, Carmen Cervera; one adopted *s*. *Educ:* Realgymnasium, The Hague; Fribourg Univ. Chm., and Hon. Pres. Supervisory Bd, TBG Holdings NV (formerly Thyssen-Bornemisza Gp NV). Hon. Chairman: Fundación Colección Thyssen-Bornemisza, Madrid; Thyssen-Bornemisza Foundation, Lugano; Foundation Friends of Mauritshuis, The Hague. Emeritus Mem., Trustees' Council, Nat. Gallery of Art, Washington; Mem., Sotheby's Holdings Adv. Bd. Corresp. Mem., Acad. of Fine Arts, San Fernando, Madrid. Art collection housed and exhibited in Museum Thyssen-Bornemisza, Madrid and partially in Villa Favorita, Castagnola-Lugano. Johann Wolfgang von Goethe Gold Medal, Hamburg, 1992; Royal Museum Medal, Netherlands, 1993. OStJ. Gran Cruz, Orden Carlos III (Spain), 1988; Order of the Banner (Hungary), 1990; Grande Ufficiale, Order of Merit of the Republic (Italy), 1991; Commander, Order of Orange Nassau (Netherlands), 1995; Middle Cross of Merit (Hungary), 1996. *Address:* Villa Favorita, 6976 Castagnola, Lugano, Switzerland. *Clubs:* Corviglia (St Moritz); Eagle Ski (Gstaad); Knickerbocker (NY). *Died 27 April 2002.*

TIBBITS, Captain Sir David (Stanley), Kt 1976; DSC 1942; FNI; RN retired; Deputy Master and Chairman of Board, Trinity House, 1972–76; *b* 11 April 1911; *s* of late Hubert Tibbits, MB, BCh, Warwick, and Edith Lucy Tibbits (*née* Harman); *m* 1938, Mary Florence Butterfield, Hamilton, Bermuda; two *d*. *Educ:* Wells House, Malvern Wells; RNC, Dartmouth. RN Cadet 1925; navigation specialist, 1934; served War, 1939–45, HM Ships York, Devonshire and Anson; Comdr 1946; Captain 1953; Dir, Radio Equipment Dept, Admty, 1953–56; comd, HM Ships Manxman, Dryad and Hermes, 1956–61, retd. Trinity House: Elder Brother, 1961; Warden, 1969. Hon. Sec., King George's Fund for Sailors, 1974–80; Lay Vice-Pres., Missions to Seamen, subseq. Mission to Seafarers, 1972–. Engaged in various voluntary activities in Bermuda including: Mem., Marine Board and Port Authy, 1978–92; Chm., Pilotage Commn, 1978–92; Pres., Sea Cadet and Sail Trng Assoc., 1978–87; Chm. and Pres., Bermuda Soc. for Blind, 1982– (Mem. Cttee, 1977–). Mem. Court, Shipwrights' Co., 1976–. Trustee, Nat. Maritime Mus., 1974–77. Gov., Pangbourne Coll., 1973–78. Founder Mem., 1972, Fellow 1979–, Nautical Inst. CStJ 1993 (Mem. Council for Bermuda, 1978–). *Recreations:* sailing, colour photography, classical music. *Address:* Harting Hill, PO Box HM 1419, Hamilton, Bermuda HM FX; c/o Trinity House, Tower Hill, EC3N 4DH. *Clubs:* Army and Navy, Hurlingham; Royal Bermuda Yacht (Bermuda). *Died 17 May 2003.*

TICEHURST, Maj.-Gen. (Arthur) Christopher; Medical Officer, Army Medical Directorate (Medico-Legal), 1994–95; *b* 22 April 1933; *s* of late Arthur William Ticehurst and Edith Violet Ticehurst (*née* Adams); *m* 1959, Valerie Jean Hughes; four *s*. *Educ:* Chichester High Sch.; King's Coll. London; Westminster Hosp. (MB BS 1955). MFCM 1977; FFPHM 1990. House appointments, Westminster Hosp., 1955–56; National Service, RAMC, 1958–60; Regular Commn, 1961; Medical Officer: Kent, Cyprus, 1958–61; Singapore, Brunei, Thailand, 1962–65; CO, 11 Field Dressing Station, BAOR, 1965–67; Instructor, RAMC Trng Centre, 1967–68; Army Staff Coll., 1968–69; MoD, 1970–72; CO, 4 Armoured Field Ambulance, 1972–74; ndc, 1974–75; Army Med. Directorate, MoD, 1976–80; Chief Instructor, RAMC Trng Centre, 1980–83; Comdr, Med. HQ, NE Dist, 1983–84; Dep. Comdr, Med. HQ, BAOR, 1984–87; Asst Surgeon Gen., MoD, 1987–90; Comdr Med., HQ UKLF, 1990–93. QHS 1991–93. FIMgt (FBIM 1992). OStJ 1972. *Publications:* (ed jtly) Royal Army Medical Corps 1898–1998: reflections of one hundred years of service, 1997; articles on use of medical services in disaster relief to professional jls. *Recreations:* tennis, military history, maps, water colours. *Address:* c/o Lloyds TSB, 19 Obelisk Street, Camberley, Surrey GU15 3SE. *Died 31 July 2002.*

TICEHURST, Maj.-Gen. Christopher; see Ticehurst, Maj.-Gen. A. C.

TIDBURY, Sir Charles (Henderson), Kt 1989; DL; Chairman, Whitbread PLC, 1978–84; Deputy Chairman, Inspec PLC, 1994–98; *b* 26 Jan. 1926; *s* of late Brig. O. H. Tidbury, MC, and Beryl (*née* Pearce); *m* 1950, Anne, *d* of late Brig. H. E. Russell, DSO, and Lady O'Connor; two *s* three *d*. *Educ:* Eton Coll. Served KRRC, 1944–52: Palestine, 1946–48 (despatches); Queen's Westminsters TA, 1952–60. Joined Whitbread & Co. Ltd, 1952; a Man. Dir, 1959; Chief Exec., 1971; Dep. Chm., 1977; Dir, 1984–88. Chm., Brickwoods Brewery Ltd, 1966–71. Director: Whitbread Investment Co. PLC, 1975–93; Barclays Bank PLC, 1978–91; Mercantile Gp plc, 1985–91; Nabisco Gp Ltd, 1985–88; Vaux Gp plc,

1985–91; ICL (Europe, formerly UK), 1985–93; Pearl Assurance PLC, 1985–94; Gales Brewery, Horndean, 1989–96. Dir, Centre for Policy Studies, 1988–93. Pres., Inst. of Brewing, 1976–78; Chm., 1982–84, Vice-Pres., 1985–, Brewers' Soc.; President: Shire Horse Soc., 1985–87; British Inst. of Innkeeping, 1985–92 (Vice-Pres., 1992–); Brewing Res. Foundn Internat. (formerly Brewing Res. Foundn), 1993– (Chm., 1985–93). Chairman: Mary Rose Development Trust, 1980–86; William and Mary Tercentenary Trust, 1986–93; Hampshire Enterprise Partnership (formerly Business Liaison Exec. Bd), 1993–; Mem., Portsmouth and SE Hants Health Commn, 1992–96; Trustee, Nat. Maritime Museum, 1984–96. Governor: Nat. Heart and Chest Hosps, 1988–90; Portsmouth Univ. (formerly Polytechnic), 1988–96; Chm. Govs, Portsmouth High Sch., 1992–96. Master, Brewers' Co., 1988–89. DL Hampshire, 1989. Hon. LLD Portsmouth, 1997. *Recreations:* my family, messing about in boats, rough shooting, the countryside. *Address:* Crocker Hill Farm, Forest Lane, Wickham, Hants PO17 5DW. *Clubs:* Royal Yacht Squadron, Bembridge Sailing.

Died 3 July 2003.

TILLEY, John Vincent; Head, Parliamentary Office, Co-operative Group, 2000–02; *b* 13 June 1941; *m* 1st, Tracey (marr.diss.); one *d*; 2nd, Kathryn Riley; one *d*. *Educ:* Trinity Hall, Cambridge (BA 1963). Mem., Wandsworth Borough Council, 1971–78. MP (Lab) Lambeth Central, Apr. 1978–83. Contested (Lab): Kensington Div. of Kensington and Chelsea, Feb. and Oct. 1974; Southwark and Bermondsey, 1983. Chief Economic Advisor, London Borough of Hackney, 1983–88; Parly Sec., Co-operative Union, 1988–99. *Publication:* Churchill's Favourite Socialist: a life of A. V. Alexander, 1995. *Address:* 35 Point Hill, SE10 8QW. *Died 18 Dec. 2005.*

TILLOTSON, Prof. Kathleen Mary, CBE 1991 (OBE 1983); FRSL; FBA 1965; Hildred Carlile Professor of English in the University of London, at Bedford College, 1958–71, then Emeritus; *b* 3 April 1906; *e d* of late Eric A. Constable, BLitt (Durham), journalist, and Catherine H. Constable, Berwick-on-Tweed and Birmingham; *m* 1933, Geoffrey Tillotson, FBA (*d* 1969); two adopted *s*. *Educ:* Ackworth School; Mount School, York; Somerville College, Oxford (Exhibitioner and Shaw Lefevre Scholar; Charles Oldham Shakespeare Scholarship, 1926; BA 1927; BLitt 1929; Hon. Fellow, 1965). Temporary tutor, Somerville College, 1928–29; teaching at Somerville and St Hilda's Colleges, 1929–39; part-time Assistant, later Junior Lecturer, 1929, Lecturer, 1939, Fellow, 1971, Bedford College, London; Reader in the University of London at Bedford College, 1947–58. General Editor, Clarendon Dickens, 1957–; nine novels published by 1994. Vice-President: Dickens Fellowship; Brontë Soc.; Trustee: Wordsworth Trust; Bosanquet Trust. Lectures: Warton, British Academy, 1956; James Bryce Memorial, Somerville College, Oxford, 1963; Annual Brontë, 1966, 1986; Dickens Meml, 1970; Annual Tennyson, 1974; Robert Spence Watson, 1978. Hon. DLitt Belfast, 1972; Hon. DLitt: Oxon, 1982; London, 1982. Rose Mary Crawshay prize, British Academy, 1943, 1988. *Publications:* (with J. W. Hebel and B. H. Newdigate) Works of Michael Drayton, vol. V, 1941; Novels of the Eighteen-Forties, 1954; Matthew Arnold and Carlyle (Warton Lecture), 1957; (with John Butt) Dickens at Work, 1957; Introductions to Trollope's Barsetshire novels, 1958–75; The Tale and the Teller (inaug. lect.), 1959; (with G. Tillotson) Mid-Victorian Studies, 1965; Letters of Charles Dickens (General Editor, 1978–95): vol. 1, 1965 (Mem., Editl Cttee); vol. 2, 1969 (Associate Editor); vol. 3, 1974 (Associate Editor); vol. 4, 1977; vol. 5, 1981; vol. 6, 1988 (Joint Editor); vol. 7, 1993 (Joint Editor); vol. 8, 1995; vol. 9, 1997 (Consultant Editor); vol. 10, 1998 (Consultant Editor); James Kinsley (memoir, British Acad.), 1989; *edited:* (with G. Tillotson) Vanity Fair, 1963; Oliver Twist, 1966; (with A. Trodd) The Woman in White, 1969; Oliver Twist (World's Classics), 1982; contributions to

periodicals. *Address:* c/o Henry Tillotson, 43 Evershot Road, N4 3DG. *Club:* University Women's.

Died 3 June 2001.

TILNEY, Charles Edward, CMG 1956; Minister for Finance and Economics, Tanganyika, 1957–60; *b* 13 April 1909; *yr s* of late Lt-Col Norman Eccles Tilney, CBE, DSO, and Cicely Sara Tilney (*née* Alston); *m* 1952, Rosalind Hull (*d* 1993), *e d* of late Lt-Col Edward Cuthbert de Renzy-Martin, CMG, DSO, MC, and Winifred Grace Alicia de Renzy-Martin; two *s*. *Educ:* Rugby School; Oriel College, Oxford. Ceylon Civil Service, 1932; Tanganyika: Asst Chief Secretary (Finance), 1948; Dep. Financial Secretary, 1948; Secretary for Finance, 1950; Member for Finance and Economics, 1953; retd from E Africa, 1960. *Address:* 8 Butts Close, Biddestone, Chippenham, Wilts SN14 7DZ. *T:* (01249) 714770. *Died 28 Feb. 2002.*

TIMBERLAKE, Herman Leslie Patterson, (Tim); Director, Abbey National Building Society, 1972–84 (Chief General Manager, 1971–79; Deputy Chairman, 1976–79); *b* 3 Feb. 1914; *s* of William Walter and Mabel Timberlake; *m* 1940, Betty (*née* Curtis); two *s*. *Educ:* Watford Grammar Sch. FCIS; FCIB. Served War of 1939–45. Joined Abbey Road Building Soc., 1930 (became Abbey Nat. Building Soc., 1944); Asst Branch Manager, Watford, 1936; Branch Manager appts, 1946–59; Manager: Branches Admin Dept, 1959; Investments Admin Dept, 1964; Branches and Agencies, 1966; Jt Gen. Manager, 1968. Mem. Council, Building Societies Assoc., 1975–79; Pres., Building Societies Institute, 1977–78. *Address:* 1 Rochester Drive, Pinner, Middx HA5 1DA. *T:* (020) 8866 1554.

Died 31 May 2003.

TIMPSON, John Harry Robert, OBE 1987; writer and broadcaster; *b* 2 July 1928; *s* of late John Hubert Victor Timpson and Caroline (*née* Willson); *m* 1951, (Muriel) Patricia Whale; one *s* (and one *s* decd). *Educ:* Merchant Taylors' Sch. National Service, RASC, 1946–49. Reporter: Wembley News, 1945–46 and 1949–51; Eastern Daily Press, 1951–59; BBC News Staff, 1959–87; BBC Dep. Court Correspondent, 1962–67 (reporting Australian, Ethiopian and other Royal tours); Presenter: Newsroom, BBC2, 1968–70; Tonight, BBC1, 1976–78; Today, BBC Radio 4, 1970–76, 1978–86; Chm., Any Questions, BBC Radio 4, 1984–87, Presenter, Timpson's Country Churches, ITV, 1995–98. Hon. MA UEA, 1991. Sony Gold Award for outstanding services to radio, 1986. *Publications:* Today and Yesterday (autobiog.), 1976; The Lighter Side of Today, 1983; The Early Morning Book, 1986; Timpson's England—A Look beyond the Obvious, 1987; Paper Trail (novel), 1989; Timpson's Towns, 1989; Timpson's Travels in East Anglia, 1990; Sound Track (novel), 1991; Timpson's English Eccentrics, 1991; Little Trains of Britain, 1992; Timpson's English Villages, 1992; Timpson's Other England, 1993; Timpson's Timepaths, 1994; Timpson's English Country Inns, 1995; Timpson's Book of Days, 1996; Timpson's Adaptables, 1997; Timpson's Country Churches, 1998; Timpson's Leylines, 2000; Timpson's Norfolk Notebook, 2001; Timpson on the Verge, 2002. *Recreation:* enjoying Norfolk. *Address:* Kennel House, The Green, Weasenham St Peter, King's Lynn, Norfolk PE32 2TD. *Died 19 Nov. 2005.*

TIPPETTS, Rutherford Berriman; Under-Secretary, Export Services Division, Department of Trade and Industry, 1970–73; *b* 8 Feb. 1913; *s* of late Percy William Berriman Tippetts and Katherine Brown Rutherford; *m* 1948, Audrey Helen Wilson Cameron; one *s* one *d*. *Educ:* Rugby; Trinity Coll., Oxford (MA). Asst Principal, BoT, 1936; Principal Private Sec. to Ministers of Supply and Presidents of BoT, 1941–45; idc 1954; Chief Exec., Dollar Exports Council, 1959–61; served in Commercial Relations and Exports, Industry and Tourism Divs of BoT. Mem., Council, CGLI. Master, Armourers' and Brasiers' Co., 1975–76. *Address:* 74 Ebury Mews East, SW1W

9QA. *T:* (020) 7730 6464. *Club:* Carlton.
Died 6 Sept. 2003.

TITMAN, Sir John (Edward Powis), KCVO 1991
(CVO 1982; LVO 1966; MVO 1957); JP; DL; Secretary
of the Lord Chamberlain's Office, 1978–91; Serjeant-at-
Arms to the Queen, 1982–91; *b* 23 May 1926; *s* of late Sir
George Titman, CBE, MVO, sometime Secretary, Lord
Chamberlain's Office, and Lady Titman; *m* 1953, Annabel
Clare (*née* Naylor); two *s. Educ:* City of London School.
Entered Lord Chamberlain's Office, 1947; State
Invitations Asst, 1956; Asst Sec., 1976; retired 1991.
Master, Wax Chandlers' Co., 1984. JP, 1971, DL, 1991,
Surrey. *Address:* Friars Garth, The Parade, Epsom, Surrey
KT18 5DH. *T:* (01372) 722302. *Clubs:* Royal
Automobile, MCC. *Died 11 Jan. 2003.*

TOBIN, Prof. James, PhD; Sterling Professor of
Economics, Yale University, 1957–88, then Emeritus; *b* 5
March 1918; *s* of Louis Michael and Margaret Edgerton
Tobin; *m* 1946, Elizabeth Fay Ringo; three *s* one *d. Educ:*
Harvard Univ. (AB 1939 (*summa cum laude*); MA 1940;
PhD 1947). Economist, Office of Price Admin, and
Civilian Supply and War Production Bd, Washington,
1941–42; line officer, destroyer, USN, 1942–46. Teaching
Fellow in Econs, 1946–47, Jun. Fellow, Soc. of Fellows,
1947–50, Harvard Univ.; Yale University: Associate Prof.
of Econs, 1950–55; Prof. of Econs, 1955–57; Mem.,
1955–, Dir, 1955–61, Cowles Foundn for Res. in Econs;
Chm., Dept of Econs, 1968–69, 1974–78. Vis. Prof.,
Univ. of Nairobi, 1972–73; Ford Vis. Res. Prof. of Econs,
Univ. of Calif, Berkeley, 1983; P. K. Seidman Vis. Dist.
Prof. of Internat. Studies, Rhodes Coll., 1992. Mem.,
Pres.'s Council of Econ. Advrs, 1961–62. Corresp. FBA
1984. LLD *hc:* Syracuse Univ., 1967; Univ. of Illinois,
1969; Dartmouth Coll., 1970; Swarthmore Coll., 1980;
New Sch. for Social Res., and New York Univ., 1982;
Univ. of Hartford, 1984; Colgate Univ., 1984; Western
Maryland Coll., 1984; Univ. of New Haven, 1986;
Harvard, 1995; Univ. of Wisconsin-Madison, 1996;
DEcon *hc* New Univ. of Lisbon, 1980; Hon. DHL: Bates
Coll., 1982; Hofstra Univ., 1983; Gustavus Adolphus
Coll., 1986; Sacred Heart Univ., 1990; Bard Coll., 1995;
Beloit Coll., 1996; Quinnipiac Univ., 2001; DSocSc *hc*
Helsinki, 1986; DEcon and Bus *hc* Athens, 1992. Foreign
Associate, Acad. of Sciences, Portugal, 1980. Nobel Prize
in Economics, 1981; Centennial Medal, Harvard Univ.
Graduate Sch., 1989. Grand Cordon, Order of the Sacred
Treasure (Japan), 1988. *Publications:* (jtly) The American
Business Creed, 1956; National Economic Policy, 1966;
Essays in Economics: vol. 1, Macroeconomics, 1971; vol.
2, Consumption and Econometrics, 1975; vol. 3, Theory
and Policy, 1982; vol. 4, National and International, 1996;
The New Economics One Decade Older, 1974; Asset
Accumulation and Economic Activity, Reflections on
Contemporary Macroeconomic Theory, 1980; Policies
for Prosperity, 1987; Two Revolutions in Economic
Theory, 1988; Full Employment and Growth, 1996;
Money Credit and Capital, 1997; contribs to professional
jls. *Recreations:* tennis, ski-ing, sailing, canoeing, fishing,
chess. *Address:* Cowles Foundation for Research in
Economics, Yale University, Box 208281, New Haven,
CT 06520–8281, USA. *T:* (203) 4323720. *Clubs:* Yale
(New York); Mory's Association, The Club (New
Haven). *Died 11 March 2002.*

TODD, Hon. Sir Garfield; *see* Todd, Hon. Sir R. S. G.

TODD, John Rawling, CVO 1972; OBE 1985; Secretary
for Housing, Hong Kong Government, 1986–88; *b* 15
Feb. 1929; *s* of William Rawling Todd and Isabella May
Todd; *m* 1960, Ingrid von Rothermann; one *s* one *d. Educ:*
Durham Univ. (BSc). Nat. Service, RA, 1952. Joined
HMOCS; Admin. Officer, Gambia, 1955; New Hebrides,
1962; Administrator, British Indian Ocean Territory,
1966; Dep. Governor, Seychelles, 1970; seconded to
FCO, 1974; Hong Kong: Dep. Sec., 1976; Dir of Lands,
1982. Sen. British Rep., Sino-British Land Commn,
1984–88; Chm., Special Cttee on Compensation and

Betterment, Hong Kong, 1991. *Recreations:* reading,
gardening, walking, croquet. *Address:* Longridge,
Crudwell, Malmesbury, Wilts SN16 9ER. *Club:* Royal
Commonwealth Society. *Died 18 July 2002.*

TODD, Mary Williamson Spottiswoode, MA;
Headmistress of Harrogate College, 1952–73; *b* 11 June
1909; *d* of John and Mary Todd, Oxford. *Educ:* Oxford
High School; Lady Margaret Hall, Oxford (MA Hons
Oxon; Final Hon. Sch.: Mathematics, 1932, Nat. Science,
1933); London Diploma in Theology, 1941. Various
teaching posts: St Felix School, Southwold, 1933–37;
Clifton High School, Bristol, 1937–39; Westonbirt
School, Glos, 1939–46; Headmistress of Durham,
1946–52. Lay Reader, 1975–. *Address:* Hampden House,
Duchy Road, Harrogate, North Yorks HG1 2HE. *T:*
(01423) 566411. *Died 6 April 2005.*

TODD, Hon. Sir (Reginald Stephen) Garfield, Kt
1986; Prime Minister of South Rhodesia, 1953–58;
Member, Senate, Parliament of Zimbabwe, 1980–85; *b* 13
July 1908; *s* of late Thomas and Edith C. Todd; *m* 1932,
Jean Grace Wilson (*d* 2001); three *d. Educ:* Otago Univ.;
Glen Leith Theol Coll., NZ; Univ. of Witwatersrand.
Superintendent, Dadaya Mission, 1934–53, Chm.
Governing Bd,1963–85. MP for Shabani, 1946–58. First
Vice-Pres., World Convention of Churches of Christ,
1955–60; awarded Citation for Christian Leadership in
Politics and Race Relations; former Member Executive:
United Coll. of Educn, Bulawayo; Rhodesian Christian
Council. Arrested by Smith regime in 1965 and confined
to Hokonui Ranch for one year; arrested by Smith regime
in 1972 and imprisoned, then detained, Jan. 1972–June
1976. Received medal acknowledging efforts for peace
and justice in Rhodesia, from Pope Paul, 1973. Holds hon.
doctorates, NZ and USA. Knighted for services to NZ and
Africa. *Address:* Box FM 693, Famona, Bulawayo,
Zimbabwe. *Club:* Bulawayo. *Died 13 Oct. 2002.*

TODD, Ronald; General Secretary, Transport and General
Workers' Union, 1985–92; *b* 11 March 1927; *s* of late
George Thomas Todd and of Emily Todd; *m* 1945,
Josephine Tarrant; one *s* two *d. Educ:* St Patrick's Sch.,
Walthamstow, E17. Served with Royal Marine
Commandos; spent considerable time in China. Joined
TGWU: worked at Ford Motor Co., 1954–62, latterly
Dep. Convener; full-time officer of TGWU, 1962;
Regional Officer, 1969; Reg. Sec., 1976; Nat. Organiser,
1978. Mem., TUC Gen. Council, 1984–92; Chm., TUC
Internat. Cttee, 1985–92. Chm. (TU side), Ford Nat. Jt
Council, 1978–85; Jt Sec., Nat. Jt Council for Stable Staff
(Workpeople's side), 1978–85. Member: NEDC,
1985–92; MSC, 1986–88; former Mem., Employment
Appeal Tribunal. Member: Unity Trust, 1986– (Pres.,
1986–89); Council for Charitable Support, 1988–; Bd,
Royal Marines Assoc. Vice-Pres., Retired Members
Assoc., TGWU; Hon. Vice-President: CND; BDA.
Patron, Margaret Centre Macmillan Appeal. *Recreations:*
collecting Victorian music covers, archaeology. *Address:* 65
Surrey Road, Dagenham, Essex RM10 8ET.
Died 30 April 2005.

TOKATY, Prof. Grigori Alexandrovich; aerospace
adviser; Professor Emeritus, City University; *b* North
Caucasus, Russia, 13 Oct. 1910; Ossetian by mother
tongue; *m* 1936, Aza Bayeva (*d* 2003); one *d. Educ:*
Leningrad Rabfak, 1929–30; Rykov Rabfak of Moscow
Higher Technical Coll. MVTU, 1930–32; Zhukovsky Air
Force Academy of Aeronautics, Moscow, 1932–37. DEng,
PhD, DAeSc. CEng, CanTechSc. Lt Col, Air Force.
Zhukovsky Academy: Aeronautical Research Engineer,
1937–38; Head of Aeronautics Laboratory, 1938–41; Dep.
Head of Res. Dept, 1941; Lectr in Aerodynamics and
Aircraft Design, 1941–45; Acting Prof. of Aviation,
Moscow Engrg Inst, 1939–45; Rocket research and
development, 1944–45; Rocket scientist, Berlin, 1945–47.
Varied work for HM Govt, London, 1948–52; Imperial
Coll., and Coll. of Aeronautics, Cranfield, 1953–56; work
on theoretical rocket dynamics and orbital flight mechanics

associated with Apollo programme, 1956–68; Reader in Aeronautics and Astronautics, Northampton Coll. of Advanced Technology, 1960–61; Head, 1961–75, and Prof., 1967–75, Dept of Aeronautics and Space Technology, Northampton Coll. of Advanced Technology and City Univ. Chief Scientific Adviser, WTI, 1976–78. Visiting Professor: Univs of the US, Jordan, Nigeria, Iran, Turkey, Holland. FRAeS, FAIAA, FIMA. *Publications:* numerous, including seven books: Rocketdynamics, 1961; The History of Rocket Technology (jt), 1964; A History and Philosophy of Fluid Mechanics, 1971; Cosmonautics-Astronautics, 1976; Higher Education, 1982; Scientific Technological Education for the shape of things to come, 1988; Theoretic Principles of Spaceship Design, 1989; articles and booklets (alone or jointly) in the fields of fluid mechanics, gasdynamics, rocketdynamics, theory and philosophy of educn, and non-scientific subjects. *Recreations:* writing, broadcasting, travelling. *Address:* Centre for Aeronautics, City University, Northampton Square, EC1V 0HB. *Club:* National Liberal.

Died 23 Nov. 2003.

TOLOLO, Sir Alkan, KBE 1985 (CBE); Chairman, National Agricultural Research Institute, Papua New Guinea; High Commissioner for Papua New Guinea in Malaysia, 1986; *m* Nerrie Tololo, MBE; two *s* two *d.* Teaching, 1957–61; supervisory teacher, 1963–65; Superintendent of Schools, 1967–69; Mem., Public Service Board, 1969–70; First Comr, PNG Teaching Service, 1971–73; Dir of Education, 1973–79; Chm., Public Services Commn, 1979–80; Consul-General Sydney, 1981; High Comr in Australia, 1983–86. Chairman: PNG Federation of Savings and Loan Soc.; East New Britain Savings and Loan Soc. Dep. Chm., Res. and Conservation Foundn, PNG. Former Mem. or Chm. of numerous Boards and Cttees on education, culture and employment, PNG. Hon. LLD 1982, Hon. DTech 1982, Univ. of Papua New Guinea. *Address:* PO Box 3014, Boroko NCD, Papua New Guinea.

Died 26 Aug. 2003.

TOMLINSON, Prof. John Race Godfrey, CBE 1983; Professor of Education, 1985–97 and Director, 1985–96, Institute of Education, University of Warwick, then Professor Emeritus; Chair, National Forum for Learners with Learning Difficulties and Disabilities, Learning and Skills Council, 2001–04; *b* 24 April 1932; *s* of John Angell Tomlinson and Beatrice Elizabeth Race Godfrey; *m* 1954, Audrey Mavis Barrett; two *s* two *d. Educ:* Stretford Grammar Sch.; Manchester Univ. (MA); London Inst. of Historical Research. Flt Lt, RAF, 1955–58. Teaching, 1958–60; Admin. Asst, Salop LEA, 1960–63; Asst Educn Officer, Lancs LEA, 1963–67; Dep. Dir of Educn, Cheshire LEA, 1967–72; Dir of Educn, Cheshire CC, 1972–84. Chairman: Schools Council, 1978–81; NICEC, 1985–89; Arts in Education Project, SCDC, 1985–90; Academic Sec., UCET, 1997–2000. Member: Court Cttee on Child Health Services, 1973–76; Gulbenkian enquiries into Drama, Music and Dance, 1974–78; Founder Chm., Further Educn Curriculum Review and Develt Unit, 1976; Member: Special Programmes Bd, MSC, 1977–82; Delegacy for Continuing Educn, Open Univ., 1978–81; Study Commn on the Family, 1978–83; Adv. Cttee on Supply and Trng of Teachers, 1979–82; Council, Foundn for Educn Business Partnerships, 1990–91; Educn Advr, RNCM, 1972–85. Chm., Exec. Cttee and Trustees, 1982–95, Patron, 1995–, Nat. Schs Curriculum Award; Chairman: MSC TVEI Quality and Standards Gp, 1986–88; Enquiry into Freedom of Information, ILEA, 1986–87; Gen. Teaching Council initiative, 1991–2000; FEFC Enquiry, Disability and Learning Difficulties, 1993–96; Gulbenkian Enquiry into Personal and Social Education, 1998–2000; Teacher Training for the Arts, 2002–03; Dep. Chm., Gen. Teaching Council for England, 2000–01. Royal Society of Arts: Vice-Pres., 1986; Chm., Exams Bd, 1986–89; Chm. Council, 1989–91 (Mem. Council, 1982–99); FRSA

1976. Pres., Soc. of Educn Officers, 1982; Trustee: Community Service Volunteers, 1981–89; Edward Boyle Trust, 1988–98; Chm., Comino Foundn, 2001– (Trustee, 1989–2001). Governor: Chetham's Sch., Manchester, 1984–92; Menuhin Sch., 1987–89. Hon. Prof., Dept of Educn, Keele Univ., 1981–84; Distinguished Vis. Academic, QUB, 1996. Lectures: Wilfred Fish Meml, GDC, 1978; Charles Gittens Meml, Univ. of Wales, 1980; Lockyer, RCP, 1980; Schools Council, BAAS, 1981; Standing Conf. on Schools' Science and Technology Annual, 1987; Barry and Tye Meml, Manchester Univ., 1987; Internat. Schs Distinguished, Internat. Schs Assoc. Conf., Hamburg, 1994. FCMI (MBIM 1976); FCP 1980. Hon. RNCM 1980. Freeman, City of London, 1989; Liveryman, Goldsmiths' Co., 1991– (Mem., Educn Cttee, 1982–89, 1994–99). DUniv: Open, 1999; Surrey, 1999; Hon. EdD UWE, 1999; Hon. DLitt Hull, 2002. *Publications:* Additional Grenville Papers 1763–65, 1962; (ed) The Changing Government of Education, 1986; Teacher Appraisal: a nationwide approach, 1989; The Control of Education, 1993; School Co-operation: new forms of governance, 1994; articles in various jls. *Recreations:* family and garden, music and walking, a relentless search for good bitter. *Address:* The Barn House, 76 Birmingham Road, Allesley, Coventry CV5 9GX. *Clubs:* Athenæum, Army and Navy.

Died 6 Aug. 2005.

TONČIĆ-SORINJ, Dr Lujo; Secretary-General, Council of Europe, 1969–74; *b* Vienna, 12 April 1915; *s* of Dušan Tončić-Sorinj (formerly Consul-Gen. in service of Imperial Ministry for Foreign Affairs), and Mabel (*née* Plason de la Woesthyne); *m* 1956, Renate Trenker; one *s* four *d. Educ:* Secondary sch. (Gymnasium), Salzburg. Studied law and philosophy at Univs of Vienna and Agram (Zagreb), 1934–41, also medicine and philosophy (LLD Vienna); political science, Institut d'Etudes Politiques, Paris. Head of Polit. Dept of Austrian Research Inst. for Economics and Politics in Salzburg and Editor of Berichte und Informationen (political periodical published by Austrian Research Inst. for Economics and Politics), 1946–49. MP for Land Salzburg, 1949–66; Chairman: Legal Cttee of Austrian Parl., 1953–56; For. Affairs Cttee, 1956–59; in charge of For. Affairs questions, Austrian People's Party, 1959–66. Austrian Parly Observer to Consultative Assembly of Council of Europe, 1953–56; Austrian Mem., Consultative Assembly, 1956–66; Vice-Pres., Council of Europe; Vice-Pres., Political Commn, 1961–62; Minister for Foreign Affairs, Austria, 1966–68. Permanent Rep. of Austrian People's Party to Christian-Democratic Gp, European Parlt, 1980–95; Permanent Rep. of Croatian Democratic Union to European Union of Christian Democrats, 1991–. Chm., Austrian Assoc. of UN, 1978–92; Pres., Union Internationale de la Propriété Immobilière, 1987–99. Grand Cross of several orders including Order of St Michael and St George, Great Britain (Hon. GCMG). *Publications:* Erfüllte Träume (autobiog.), 1982; Am Abgrund vorbei, 1992; Usamljena borba Hrvatske, 1998 (trans. German); Meine Reiseabenteuer, 2003; over 350 articles and essays on politics, economics, internat. law and history. *Recreations:* swimming, diving, history, geography. *Address:* Schloss Fürberg, Pausingerstrasse 11, 5020 Salzburg, Austria. *T:* (662) 642886.

Died 20 May 2005.

TONGE, Brian Lawrence, PhD; Director, Oxford Polytechnic, 1981–85; *b* 19 April 1933; *s* of Lawrence and Louisa Tonge; *m* 1955, Anne Billcliff; one *d. Educ:* Bury High Sch.; London Univ. (BSc 1st Cl. Chemistry); Manchester Univ. (PhD). FRIC 1964. Scientific Officer, Hirst Research Centre, GEC Ltd, 1956–59; Chemist, MRC Carcinogenic Substances Res. Unit, Exeter Univ., 1959; Lectr in Chemistry, Plymouth Coll. of Technol., 1960–63; Res. Manager, Pure Chemicals Ltd, 1963–65; Principal Lectr in Chemistry, West Ham Coll. of Technol., 1965–67; Head, Dept of Applied Science and Dean, Faculty of Science, Wolverhampton Poly., 1967–71; Dep. Dir, Oxford Poly., 1971–81. Mem.,

Wolfson Coll., Oxford, 1975–85. *Publications:* numerous contribs to learned jls and articles in scientific and educnl press. *Recreations:* gardening, reading, music. *Address:* 46 Hillcrest, Ellesmere, Shropshire SY12 0LJ.
Died 4 Dec. 2002.

TOOK, Barry; freelance writer and broadcaster; *b* 19 June 1928; *s* of Charles William Took and Kate Louie Rose Took (*née* Cox); *m* 1st, 1950, Dorothy Bird (marr. diss.); two *s* one *d*; 2nd, 1964, Lynden Leonard; one *d*. *Educ:* Stationers' Co. Sch. First broadcast (radio), 1951; *West End Revues:* performer: For Amusement Only, 1956–58; For Adults Only, 1958–59; *Scriptwriter:* radio series: Beyond Our Ken, 1959–60; Round the Horne, 1965–68; television series: Bootsie and Snudge, 1960–64; Marty, 1968–69; On the Move, 1974–79; writer and presenter, Points of View (TV series), 1979–86; Chair, The News Quiz (radio series), 1979–96. *Publications:* The Max Miller Blue Book, 1975; Laughter in the Air, 1976; Tooks Eye View (essays), 1983; Comedy Greats, 1989; A Point of View (autobiog.), 1990; Star Turns, 1992; Round the Horne: the complete and utter history, 1998; (with Mat Coward) The Best of Round the Horne, 2000. *Recreations:* golf, gossip. *Address:* c/o Jules Bennett, PO Box 25, Moreton in Marsh, Glos GL56 9YJ.
Died 31 March 2002.

TOOMEY, Ralph; Under-Secretary, Department of Education and Science, 1969–78; *b* 26 Dec. 1918; *s* of late James and Theresa Toomey; *m* 1951, Patricia Tizard; two *d*. *Educ:* Cyfarthfa Grammar Sch., Merthyr Tydfil; University Coll., London; Univ. of Caen. Served British and Indian Army, 1940–46. Teacher, Enfield Grammar Sch., 1947; Lecturer, Univ. of London, at Sch. of Oriental and African Studies, 1948. Min. of Education, 1948–60 and 1963–78 (seconded to Govt of Mauritius, 1960–63, Principal Asst Sec. in Colonial Secretary's Office and Min. of Local Govt and Co-operative Develt). A UK Rep., High Council, European Univ. Inst., Florence, 1974–78. DUniv Open, 1979. *Address:* 1 Bullfinch Close, Riverhead, Sevenoaks, Kent TN13 2BB. *T:* (01732) 452553. *Club:* Knole Park Golf (Sevenoaks).
Died 10 May 2004.

TORRANCE, Rev. Prof. James Bruce; Professor of Systematic Theology, King's College, University of Aberdeen, and Christ's College, Aberdeen, 1977–89 (Dean of the Faculty of Divinity, 1978–81), then Professor Emeritus; *b* 3 Feb. 1923; *s* of late Rev. Thomas Torrance and Annie Elizabeth Sharp; *m* 1955, Mary Heather Aitken, medical practitioner; one *s* two *d*. *Educ:* Royal High School, Edinburgh; Edinburgh Univ. (MA Hons Philosophy, 1st Cl.); New Coll., Edinburgh (BD Systematic Theol., Distinction); Univs of Marburg, Basle and Oxford. Licensed Minister of Church of Scotland, 1950; parish of Invergowrie, Dundee, 1954; Lectr in Divinity and Dogmatics in History of Christian Thought, New Coll., Univ. of Edinburgh, 1961; Sen. Lectr in Christian Dogmatics, New Coll., 1972. Visiting Professor: of New Testament, Union Theol. Seminary, Richmond, Va, 1960; of Theology, Columbia Theol. Seminary, Decatur, Ga., 1965, and Vancouver Sch. of Theology, BC, 1974–75, 1988; Regent Coll., Vancouver, 1984, 1988, 1993, 1994, 1995, 1997; Fuller Theol Seminary, Pasadena, 1982, 1984, 1987, 1989, 1991, 1994, 1995; S Africa, 1980, 1984, 1986, 1990; univs and theol schs in Perth, Brisbane, Melbourne, Adelaide and Sydney, 1990, 1993, 1996; in New Zealand, 1987, 1988, 1989; in Fiji, W Samoa, 1993, 1996. Warfield Lects, Princeton Theol Seminary, 2001. *Publications:* (trans. jtly) Oscar Cullmann's Early Christian Worship, 1953; John Duns Scotus in a Nutshell, 1992; Worship, Community and the Triune God of Greece, 1996; contribs: Essays in Christology for Karl Barth (Karl Barth's Festschrift), 1956; Where Faith and Science Meet, 1954; Calvinus Ecclesiae Doctor, 1978; Incarnation (on Nicene-Constantinopolitan Creed, 381 AD), 1981; The Westminster Confession in the Church Today, 1982; Calvinus Reformator, 1982; Calvinus Sacrae Scripturae

Professor, 1994; A Passion for Christ, 1999; articles to Biblical and Biographical Dictionaries, Scottish Jl of Theology, Interpretation, Church Service Society Annual, and other symposia; *festschrift:* Christ in Our Place (ed T. Hart and D. Thimell), 1991. *Recreations:* beekeeping, fishing, gardening, swimming. *Address:* 3 Greenbank Crescent, Edinburgh EH10 5TE. *T:* (0131) 447 3230.
Died 15 Nov. 2003.

TORRENS-SPENCE, Captain (Frederick) Michael (Alexander), DSO 1941; DSC 1941; AFC 1944; Royal Navy retired; Lord Lieutenant of County Armagh, 1981–89; *b* 10 March 1914; *s* of Lt-Col Herbert Frederick Torrens-Spence and Eileen Torrens-Spence; *m* 1944, Rachel Nora Clarke; three *s* one *d*. *Educ:* RNC, Dartmouth. Commnd Sub Lieut, 1934; specialised as pilot, 1936; Battle of Taranto, 1940; commanded 815 Naval Air Sqdn, 1941; Battle of Matapan, 1941; Chief Instructor, Empire Test Pilots Sch., 1947–48; Dep. Dir, Air Warfare Div., Naval Staff, 1952–54; commanded HMS Delight, 1955–56, HMS Albion, 1959–61; ADC to the Queen, 1961. Comdr 1946, Captain 1952. Co. Comdt, Ulster Special Constabulary, 1961–70; commanded 2nd (Co. Armagh) Bn, Ulster Defence Regt, 1970–71. High Sheriff, Co. Armagh, 1979. DFC, Greece, 1941. *Address:* Drumcullen House, Ballydugan, Downpatrick, Co. Down BT30 8HZ. *Club:* MCC. *Died 2 Nov. 2001.*

TORRENS-SPENCE, Captain Michael; *see* Torrens-Spence, F. M. A.

TOWNSEND, Mrs Lena Moncrieff, CBE 1974; Member, Race Relations Board, 1967–72; *b* 3 Nov. 1911; twin *d* of late Captain R. G. Westropp, Cairo, Egypt; *m* (twice); two *s* one *d*. *Educ:* Downe House, Newbury; Somerville Coll., Oxford; Heidelberg Univ., Germany. During War of 1939–45 was an Organiser in WVS and in Women's Land Army, and then taught at Downe House. Mem. for Hampstead, LCC, 1955–65; Alderman, London Borough of Camden, 1964–67; Mem. for Camden, GLC, 1967–70; Alderman, GLC, 1970–77, and Dep. Chm., 1976–77; Inner London Education Authority: Dep. Leader, later Leader, 1967–70; Leader of the Opposition, 1970–71; Chm., Management Panel, Burnham Cttee, 1967–70; Mem., Women's European Cttee, 1972–75. Pres., Anglo-Egyptian Assoc., 1961–87 (when wound-up); Executive Member: British Section, European Union of Women, 1970–81; National Council, European Movement (British Council), 1970–86 (Mem., Speaker's Panel); Cons. Gp for Europe, 1967–88 (Founder Mem.); British Section, Internat. Union of Local Authorities and Council of European Municipalities, 1975–97 (rep. on Jt Twinning Cttee, 1975–83); London Europe Soc., 1977– (a Vice-Pres. 1999–); Arkwright Arts Trust, 1971–84 (Chm., 1971–73). Mem., House Cttee, New End Hosp., then Hampstead Cttee, Royal Free Hosp., 1953–65. Mem. Exec. Cttee, Contemporary Dance Trust, 1968–75. Chm., Students' Accommodation Cttee, Univ. of London, 1977–86 (and Mem., Intercollegiate Halls Management Cttee); Member: Council, Westfield Coll., London Univ., 1965–89; Cons Nat. Adv. Cttee on Education, 1976–82; Governor: Barrett Street Coll., later London Coll. of Fashion, 1958–86 (Chm., 1967–86); Old Vic Trust, 1976–88; Hampstead Parochial Primary Sch., 1979–93. Hon. Vice Pres., Local Govt Gp for Europe, 1998. Patron, Lewis Carroll Soc. Hon. Fellow, QMW (Hon. Fellow, Westfield Coll., 1983). *Recreations:* once foreign languages, travel, the arts, gardening, knitting, sewing; latterly entertaining grandchildren and enjoying the surrounding garden. *Address:* Highgate Nursing Home, 12 Hornsey Lane, Highgate N6 5LX. *T:* (020) 7281 3511. *Died 17 Nov. 2004.*

TRAIN, David, MC 1945; PhD; FCGI, FRPharmS, FRSC; FREng, FIChemE; Partner, 1961–82, Senior Partner, 1980–82, Senior Consultant, 1982–88, Cremer and Warner, Consulting Engineers and Scientists; *b* 27 Feb. 1919; *s* of Charles and Elsie Louisa Train; *m* 1943, Jeanne Catherine, *d* of late William R. and M. M.

Edmunds; two *s*. *Educ:* Lady Hawkins' Grammar Sch., Kington; School of Pharmacy, Univ. of London; Northampton Coll. of Advanced Technology; Imperial Coll., Univ. of London. Fairchild Schol. 1940, MPS 1941, Hewlett Exhibn 1941; BPharm 1942, PhC 1942; BScChemEng 1949, PhD 1956, DIC 1956. ARIC 1949; FRSH 1972; FCGI 1982 (ACGI 1949); FREng (FEng 1983). Apprenticed to F. T. Roper and Daughter, Kington, 1935–38. War service: St John's Hosp. Reserve, 1939; RAMC (non-med.), NW Europe, 1942–45; 212 Fd Amb. 53rd Welsh (Lieut). Lectr in Pharmaceutical Engrg Science, 1949–59, Reader, 1959–61, Fellow, 1991–, Sch. of Pharmacy, London; Vis. Prof., Univ. of Wisconsin, 1959. Examiner: for Pharm. Soc. of Gt Brit., 1949–56; IChemE, 1956–66; Mem. Bd of Studies in Chem. Engrg, Univ. of London, 1958–94. Jt Hon. Secretary: Brit. Pharm. Conf., 1958–64; IChemE, 1972–77; Member: Adv. Cttee on Oil Pollution of the Sea, 1973–84; Parly Gp for Engrg Develt, 1987–; Air Pollution Control Assoc., USA, 1971–84; Fédn Internat. Pharmaceutique, 1970–82. Gov., Bromley Coll. of Further Educn, 1987–95. Liveryman: Worshipful Soc. of Apothecaries, 1975–; Worshipful Co. of Engineers, 1983–. *Publications:* various, on compression of powders, protection of the environment, acidic emissions, hazards in medicaments, preventative toxicology. *Recreations:* gardening, travelling. *Address:* 3 Grayland Close, Bromley, BR1 2PA. *T:* (020) 8464 4701. *Died 18 Dec. 2005.*

TRAPP, Prof. Joseph Burney, CBE 1990; FSA; FBA 1980; Professor of the History of the Classical Tradition and Director, Warburg Institute, University of London, 1976–90, Hon. Fellow since 1990; *b* 16 July 1925; *s* of H. M. B. and Frances M. Trapp; *m* 1953, Elayne M. Falla; two *s*. *Educ:* Dannevirke High Sch. and Victoria University Coll., Wellington, NZ (MA). FSA 1978. Alexander Turnbull Library, Wellington, 1946–50; Jun. Lectr, Victoria University Coll., 1950–51; Asst Lectr, Reading Univ., 1951–53; Warburg Institute: Asst Librarian, 1953–66; Librarian, 1966–76. Visiting Professor: Univ. of Toronto, 1969; Univ. of Melbourne, 1980; Iowa State Univ., Princeton Univ., 1984; Univ. of Warwick, 1992–99; Univ. of Rome (La Sapienza), 2005. J. H. Gray Lectr, Univ. of Cambridge, 1990; Panizzi Lectr, British Liby, 1990; J. P. R. Lyell Reader in Bibliography, Oxford Univ., 1994. Chm., Panizzi Lectures Selection Cttee, 1996–2000 (Mem., 1986–91). Member: Advisory Council: V&A Museum, 1977–83; British Library, 1980–87; Exec. Cttee, British Sch. at Rome, 1983–87, Council, 1984–95; Foreign Sec., British Academy, 1988–95 (Vice-Pres., 1983–85). Chm. and Trustee, Lambeth Palace Liby, 1987–98. Foreign Mem., Royal Swedish Acad. of Letters, History and Antiquities, 1995. *Publications:* (ed) The Apology of Sir Thomas More, 1979; Essays in the Renaissance and the Classical Tradition, 1990; Erasmus, Colet and More ... (Panizzi Lectures), 1991; (ed with L. Hellinga) Cambridge History of the Book in Britain 1400–1557, 1999; Studies of Petrarch and his Influence, 2003; articles in learned jls. *Address:* c/o Warburg Institute, Woburn Square, WC1H 0AB. *Died 13 July 2005.*

TRASLER, Prof. Gordon Blair; JP; PhD; FBPsS; first Professor of Psychology, University of Southampton, 1964–94, then Emeritus; Leverhulme Emeritus Fellow, since 1995; *b* 7 March 1929; *s* of Frank Ferrier Trasler and Marian (*née* Blair); *m* 1953, Kathleen Patricia Fegan. *Educ:* Isleworth Grammar Sch.; Bryanston Sch.; University Coll., Exeter (MA); London Univ. (BSc, PhD). FBPsS 1963; CPsychol. Tutorial Asst, UC, Exeter, 1952–53; Psychologist, HM Prisons, Wandsworth and Winchester, 1955–57; Lectr, Southampton Univ., 1957–64. Visiting Lecturer: LSE, 1962–63; Inst. of Criminology, Cambridge Univ., 1968–; Vis. Prof., Univ. of Alberta at Edmonton, 1977. Mem., Winchester Health Authority, 1981–89. Vice-Pres., Inst. for Study and Treatment of Delinquency, 1987– (Chm., 1981–87); Chm., Div. of Criminolog. and Legal Psychol., BPsS, 1980–83. Chief Scientist's Advr,

DHSS, 1977–80 and 1983–; Member: Adv. Council on Penal System, 1968–74; Wootton Cttee on Non-custodial penalties, 1968–70; Younger Cttee on Young Adult Offenders, 1970–74; Lord Chancellor's Adv. Cttee for Southampton, 1988–96. Editor-in-chief, British Jl of Criminology, 1980–85. JP Hants, 1978. Sellin-Glueck Award (for outstanding scholarly contribs to criminology), Amer. Soc. of Criminology, 1990. *Publications:* In Place of Parents, 1960; The Explanation of Criminality, 1962; The Shaping of Social Behaviour, 1967; (jtly) The Formative Years, 1968; (with D. P. Farrington) Behaviour Modification with Offenders, 1980; many papers in jls and chapters on psychology and criminology. *Recreations:* reading, photography, writing. *Address:* Fox Croft, Old Kennels Lane, Oliver's Battery, Winchester SO22 4JT. *T:* (01962) 852345. *Died 26 March 2002.*

TREASURE, Prof. John Albert Penberthy, PhD; *b* 20 June 1924; *s* of Harold Paul Treasure and Constance Frances Treasure; *m* 1954, Valerie Ellen Bell; three *s*. *Educ:* Cardiff High Sch.; University Coll., Cardiff (BA 1946); Univ. of Cambridge (PhD 1956). Joined British Market Research Bureau Ltd, 1952, Man. Dir 1957; Marketing Dir, J. Walter Thompson Co. Ltd, 1960, Chm. 1967; Dir, J. Walter Thompson Co. USA, 1967, Vice Chm. 1974; Vice-Chm., Saatchi & Saatchi Advertising Ltd (formerly Saatchi & Saatchi Compton Ltd), 1983–89. Chm., Taylor Nelson AGB plc, 1992–97; Director: Rowntree Mackintosh plc, 1976–88; Assi Packaging (UK) Ltd (formerly AFIH Ltd), 1984–94; Household Mortgage Corp. plc, 1986–94. Dean and Prof. of Marketing, City Univ. Business Sch., 1978–82. President: Inst. of Practitioners in Advertising, 1975–77; Market Res. Soc., 1975–78; Nat. Advertising Benevolent Soc., 1977–78; Chm., History of Advertising Trust, 1985–90. Master, Marketors' Co., 2000. *Publications:* articles on marketing, market research and economics in Financial Times, Times, New Soc., Econ. Jl, Commentary, and Advertising Qly. *Recreations:* golf, tennis. *Address:* 20 Queensberry House, Friars Lane, Richmond, Surrey TW9 1NT. *Clubs:* Caledonian, Queen's, Hurlingham; Royal Mid-Surrey Golf (Richmond); Royal and Ancient Golf (St Andrews). *Died 9 Feb. 2004.*

TREGARTHEN JENKIN, Ian Evers; see Jenkin.

TREHANE, Sir Richard; see Trehane, Sir W. R.

TREHANE, Sir (Walter) Richard, Kt 1967; Chairman of the Milk Marketing Board, 1958–77; *b* 14 July 1913; *s* of James Trehane and Muriel Yeoman Cowl; *m* 1948, Elizabeth Mitchell (*d* 1999); two *s*, and one step *s*. *Educ:* Monkton Combe School, Somerset; University of Reading (BSc (Agric)). On staff of School of Agriculture, Cambridge, 1933–36; Manager of Hampreston Manor Farm, Dorset, 1936–79. Member: Dorset War Agric. Exec. Cttee, later Dorset Agricl Cttee, 1942–52 (Dep. Chm., 1947–52); MMB, 1947–77 (Vice-Chm., 1952–58; Chm., 1958–77); Mem. (later Vice-Chm.) Avon and Stour Catchment Bd, subseq. Avon & Dorset Rivers Bd, 1944–53; Mem. Dorset County Council and Chm. Secondary Education Cttee, 1946–49; Chm. Dorset National Farmers' Union, 1947–48; Member, Nat. Milk Publicity Council, 1954–77 (1st Pres. 1954–56); Chm. English Country Cheese Council, 1955–77; Pres. British Farm Produce Council, 1963–78 (Chm. 1960–63). Chm. Govg Body, Grassland Research Institute, Hurley, Berks, 1959–78 (Hon. Fellow, 1981); Chm. and Pres. European Cttee on Milk/Butterfat Recording, 1957–60; Director of British Semen Exports Ltd, 1960–77; Vice-President: World Assoc. Animal Production, 1965–68; President: European Assoc. Animal Prodn, 1961–67 (Hon. Pres., 1967–95); British Soc. Animal Prodn, 1954, 1961; British Friesian Cattle Soc., 1969–70; Royal Assoc. British Dairy Farmers, 1968, 1977; Internat. Dairy Fedn, 1968–72, Hon. Pres., 1972–76. Chm., UK Dairy Assoc., 1963–69. Chm., Alfa-Laval Co. Ltd, 1982–84 (Dir, 1977–84); Director: Southern Television, 1969–81; The Rank Organisation Ltd, 1970–84; Beaumont UK, 1980–83. Trustee, UK

Farming Scholarship Trust, 1970. Governor: Monkton Combe School, 1957–83; British Nutrition Foundn, 1975–77. FRAgSs 1970. Hon. DSc Reading, 1976. Justus-von-Liebig Prize, Kiel Univ., 1968; Gold Medal, Soc. of Dairy Technology, 1969; Massey-Fergusson Award, 1971. Comdr du Mérite Agricole, 1964. *Address:* Hampreston Manor Farm, Wimborne, Dorset BH21 7LX. *Club:* Farmers'.   *Died 28 Nov. 2001.*

TRENAMAN, Nancy Kathleen, (Mrs M. S. Trenaman); Principal of St Anne's College, Oxford, 1966–84 (Hon. Fellow, 1984); *b* 25 Aug. 1919; *d* of Frederick Broughton Fisher and Edith Fisher; *m* 1967, Mervyn S. Trenaman. *Educ:* Bradford Girls' Grammar School; Somerville College, Oxford (Hon. Fellow, 1977). Board of Trade, 1941–51; Assistant Secretary, Ministry of Materials, 1951–54; Counsellor, British Embassy, Washington, 1951–53; Board of Trade, 1954–66, Under-Sec. 1962–66. Mem., Commn on the Constitution, 1969–73. Chm., Exec. Cttee, LEPRA, 1992–95. *Address:* Flat 2, Fairlawn Flats, Fairlawn, Oxford OX2 8AP. *Club:* Oxford and Cambridge.   *Died 17 March 2002.*

TREVELYAN OMAN, Julia; see Oman.

TREVOR, Brig. Kenneth Rowland Swetenham, CBE 1964 (OBE 1952); DSO 1945; Inspector of Boys' Training (Army), 1964–66, retired; *b* 15 April 1914; 2nd *s* of late Mr and Mrs E. S. R. Trevor, formerly of The Acres, Upton Heath, Chester; *m* 1st, 1941, Margaret Baynham (*d* 1988), *er d* of late Rev. J. H. Baynham, ACG; two *s*; 2nd, 1989, Jeanne Alexander (*née* Holmes Henderson). *Educ:* Oriel House, St Asaph; Rossall; RMC, Camberley. Joined 22nd (Cheshire) Regt, 1934; served in India and with RWAFF in Nigeria. War of 1939–45 (despatches and DSO), No. 1 Commando, N Africa and Burma, 1941–45 (as CO, 1943–45). Staff Coll., Camberley, 1945–46; Bde Major, 29 Infantry Brigade Gp, 1949–51; served Korea, 1950–51 (despatches, OBE); GSO1 and Chief Instructor, RMA Sandhurst, 1954–56; comd 1st Bn Cheshire Regt, 1956–58; Malaya, 1957–58 (despatches); Dep. Comdr, 50 Infantry Brigade Gp/Central Area, Cyprus, 1959; Brigade Col Mercian Brigade, 1960–61; Comdr, 2 Infantry Brigade Gp and Devon/Cornwall Sub District, 1961–64; Comdr, British Guiana Garrison, 1963. With Runcorn Develt Corp., 1966–78. Vice-Pres., Commando Assoc., 1964– (Pres., 1965–66, 1985–86, 1989–90). Pres., Norton Priory Museum Trust, Runcorn, 1994–2000. *Address:* Barrelwell Hill, Chester CH3 5BR. *Club:* Army and Navy.   *Died 10 Feb. 2003.*

TREVOR COX, Major Horace Brimson; *b* 14 June 1908; *o s* of late C. Horace Cox, Roche Old Court, Winterslow, Wilts and formerly of Whitby Hall, nr Chester; *m* 1957, Gwenda Mary, *d* of Alfred Ellis, Woodford, Essex; one *d. Educ:* Eton (played football for Eton Field and Wall game, 1926 and 1927, boxed for Eton, 1925, 1926, 1927); Germany and USA. Major late Welsh Guards (SR); served in France with BEF, 1939–40, and on General Staff, 1940–44; Major AA Comd. HQ, 1944–46, RARO, 1946–61. Studied commercial and political conditions in Germany, 1927–29, in America and Canada, 1929–30, and in Near East (Egypt and Palestine), 1934; contested (C) NE Derbyshire, 1935, Stalybridge and Hyde, 1937; MP (C) County of Chester, Stalybridge and Hyde, 1937–45; Parliamentary Private Secretary to: Rt Hon. Sir Ronald Cross when Under-Secretary Board of Trade, 1938–39, and when Minister of Economic Warfare, 1939–40; Minister of Health Rt Hon. H. U. Willink, 1945. Hon. Treas., Russian Relief Assoc., 1945–47. Contested (C) Stalybridge and Hyde, 1945, Birkenhead, 1950; Parly Candidate (C) for Romford and Brentwood, Essex, 1953–55; contested (Ind) Salisbury by-election, 1965; later joined Labour Party; contested (Lab) RDC, Wilts, 1970; Wilts CC, 1973. Member of Exec. County Committee, British Legion, Wilts, 1946–62; Chairman: Salisbury and S Wilts Branch, English-Speaking Union, 1957–63; Salisbury Road Safety Cttee 1985 (Mem., 1977–85); Mem. Exec. Cttee, CLA, for Wilts,

Hants, IoW and Berks. RBL Wilts Co. Award, for 50 yrs service, 2000. Farmer and landowner. Lord of Manor of East Winterslow. *Address:* Roche Old Court, Winterslow, Wilts SP5 1BG. *Club:* Brooks's.   *Died 30 Oct. 2005.*

TREVOR-ROPER, family name of **Baron Dacre of Glanton**.

TREVOR-ROPER, Patrick Dacre, MA, MD, BChir Cantab; FRCS, DOMS England; Hon. FCOphth; FZS; FRGS; Consultant Ophthalmic Surgeon: Westminster Hospital, 1947–82; Moorfields Eye Hospital, 1961–81; King Edward VII Hospital for Officers, 1964–86; Teacher of Ophthalmology, University of London, 1953–82; *b* 1916; *yr s* of Dr B. W. E. Trevor-Roper, Alnwick, Northumberland; unmarried. *Educ:* Charterhouse (senior classical schol.); Clare Coll., Cambridge (exhibitioner); Westminster Hospital Medical Sch. (scholar). Served as Captain, NZ Medical Corps, 1943–46, in Central Mediterranean Forces. Held resident appointments, Westminster Hospital and Moorfields Eye Hospital. Vice-Pres., Ophthalmol Soc. of UK; Founder Mem., Internat. Acad. of Ophthalmology, 1976; FRSocMed (Pres., Ophthalmol Sect., June 1978–80). Formerly: Examnr for Diploma of Ophthalmology, RCS; Mem., Ophth. Group Cttee, BMA; Mem., London Med. Cttee. Hon. Member: Brazilian Society of Ophthalmology, 1958; Ophthalmological Soc. of NZ, 1975; Hon. dipl., Peruvian and Columbian Societies of Otolaryngology and Ophthalmology, 1958; President, etc., of various clubs in connection with sports, music and drama, both hospital and county. Freeman, City of London; Liveryman, Soc. of Spectaclemakers. Doyne medal, 1980; (first) de Lancey medal, RSocMed; Lettsomian Medal, Med. Soc. of London, 1994. Editor, Trans Ophthalmol Soc., UK, 1949–88; Member Editorial Board: Modern Medicine, 1975–; Annals of Ophth., 1972–86; The Broadway, 1946–83. *Publications:* (ed) Music at Court (Four 18th century studies by A. Yorke-Long), 1954; Ophthalmology, a Textbook for Diploma Students, 1955, new edn 1962; Lecture-notes in Ophthalmology, 1960, 7th edn 1986 (trans. French, Spanish, Portuguese, Polish, Malay); (ed) International Ophthalmology Clinics VIII, 1962; The World Through Blunted Sight: an inquiry into the effects of disordered vision on character and art, 1971, 3rd edn 1990; The Eye and Its Disorders, 1973, new edn 1984; (ed) Recent Advances in Ophthalmology, 1975; (ed) The Bowman Lectures, 1980; (ed) Procs 6th Congress of European Ophth. Soc., 1980; Ophthalmology (pocket consultant series), 1981, 2nd edn 1985; miscellaneous articles in medical and other journals. *Recreations:* music, travel. *Address:* Flat 3, Fitzrovia Apartments, 365 Euston Road, NW1 3AR. *T:* (020) 7387 9670; Long Crichel House, near Wimborne, Dorset BH21 5JU. *Clubs:* Athenæum, Beefsteak.   *Died 22 April 2004.*

TREWBY, Vice-Adm. Sir Allan; see Trewby, Vice-Adm. Sir G. F. A.

TREWBY, Vice-Adm. Sir (George Francis) Allan, KCB 1974; FREng; Chief of Fleet Support and Member of Board of Admiralty, 1971–74, retired; *b* Simonstown, S Africa, 8 July 1917; *s* of late Vice-Adm. George Trewby, CMG, DSO, and Dorothea Trewby (*née* Allan); *m* 1942, Sandra Coleridge Stedham; two *s. Educ:* RNC, Dartmouth; RNEC, Keyham; RNC, Greenwich. Naval Cadet, Dartmouth, 1931 (King's Dirk, 1934); served in HMS: Frobisher, Barham, Nelson, Duke of York, Dido, Cadiz, Albion; Comdg Officer, HMS Sultan, 1963–64; IDC, 1965; Captain of Naval Base, Portland, 1966–68; Asst Controller (Polaris), MoD, 1968–71. Commander, 1950; Captain, 1959; Rear-Adm., 1968; Vice-Adm., 1971. Naval ADC to the Queen, 1968. FIMechE; FIMarE; FREng (FEng 1978); CIMgt. Akroyd Stuart Award of InstMarE for 1954–55. *Publications:* papers on naval marine engineering, in UK, USA, Sweden and Italy. *Address:* Gainsborough Apartment, 25 Thamesfield, 3 Wargrave Road, Henley-on-Thames RG9 2LX. *T:*

(01491) 577260. *Clubs:* Naval, MCC, Ebury Court; Phyllis Court (Henley). *Died 23 July 2001.*

TRIBE, Rear-Admiral Raymond Haydn, CB 1964; MBE 1944; DL; *b* 9 April 1908; *s* of Thomas and Gillian Ada Tribe; *m* 1938, Alice Mary (*née* Golby); no *c*. Served War of 1939–45 (MBE, despatches twice). Commander, 1947; Captain, 1955; Rear-Admiral, 1962. Inspector-General, Fleet Maintenance, and Chief Staff Officer (Technical) to C-in-C Home Fleet, 1962–65; retired from Royal Navy, Sept. 1965. CC Berks, 1970–77. DL Berks, 1975. Distinguished Battle Service Medal of Soviet Union, 1943. *Recreations:* gardening, painting.
Died 29 July 2005.

TRICKEY, Edward Lorden, FRCS; Dean, Institute of Orthopaedics, London University, 1981–87, retired; Consultant Orthopaedic Surgeon, Royal National Orthopaedic Hospital, London, and Edgware General Hospital, 1960–85, retired; *b* 22 July 1920; *s* of E. G. W. Trickey and M. C. Trickey; *m* 1944, Ivy Doreen Harold; two *s* one *d*. *Educ:* Dulwich College; King's College, London Univ. (MB BS). Consultant Orthopaedic Surgeon, Ashton under Lyne, 1957–60. *Publications:* various articles on orthopaedic trauma and knee joint surgery. *Recreations:* cricket, bridge. *Address:* 43 Beverley Gardens, Stanmore, Mddx HA7 2AP. *T:* (020) 8863 6964. *Clubs:* MCC, Middlesex CC. *Died 17 April 2002.*

TRIER, Peter Eugene, CBE 1980; FREng, FIEE; FInstP, FIMA; Pro-Chancellor, Brunel University, 1980–99; Director of Research and Development, Philips Electronics UK, 1969–81, retired; *b* Darmstadt, 12 Sept. 1919; *s* of Ernst and Nellie Trier; *m* 1st, 1946, Margaret Nora Holloway (*d* 1998); three *s*; 2nd, 2000, Teresa Watson (*née* Keogh). *Educ:* Mill Hill Sch.; Trinity Hall, Cambridge (Wrangler 1941; MA); MSc Open 1997. Royal Naval Scientific Service, 1941–50; Mullard Research Labs, 1950–69, Dir, 1953–69. Dir, Mullard Ltd and other Philips subsidiaries, 1957–85; Main Bd Dir, Philips Electronics, 1969–85. Specialist Advr, House of Lords Select Cttee on Sci and Technol., 1982–84; Member: Electronics Res. Council, MoD, 1963–80 (Chm., 1976–80); Defence Scientific Adv. Council, 1975–85 (Chm., 1981–85); ACARD sub-group on Annual Review of Govt-funded R&D, 1984–86 (Chm., 1985–86). FREng (FEng 1978; Hon. Sec. for Electrical Engrg, 1985–87; Chm., Membership Cttee, 1987–90); Vice-Pres., IEE, 1974–77 (Faraday Lectr, 1968–69); President: Electronic Engrg Assoc., 1980–81; IMA, 1982–83. Member: Mgt Cttee, Royal Instn, 1978–81; Adv. Bd, RCDS, 1980–90. Brunel University: Mem. Council, 1969–99 (Chm., 1973–78); Chm., Supervisory Bd, Brunel Inst. of Bio-Engineering, 1983–97; Chairman: Engrg Adv. Cttee, UWIST, 1983–86; Technol. Faculty Adv. Bd, Polytechnic South West, subseq. Plymouth Univ., 1989–93; External Examr in Maths: Polytechnic of Central London, 1983–86; Coventry Polytechnic, 1986–92. Mem., Mgt Cttee, The Wine Soc., 1977–92. Liveryman, Co. of Scientific Instrument Makers, 1968–. Hon. DTech Brunel, 1975. Glazebrook Medal and Prize, Inst. of Physics, 1984. *Publications:* Strategic Implications of Micro-electronics, 1982; Mathematics and Information, 1983; papers in scientific and technical jls. *Recreations:* travel, mathematics, Trier family history, railway history. *Address:* 14 Mill View Gardens, Croydon, CR0 5HW. *T:* (020) 8655 0835. *Clubs:* Royal Commonwealth Society, Old Millhillians. *Died 21 March 2005.*

TRISTAM, Brother; *see* Holland, Brother T. K.

TROTMAN, Baron *cr* 1999 (Life Peer), of Osmotherley in the county of North Yorkshire; **Alexander James Trotman,** Kt 1996; Chairman, Imperial Chemical Industries, 2002–03 (Director, 1997–2003); *b* 22 July 1933; *m* 1963, Valerie Anne Edgar; two *s* two *d*. *Educ:* Boroughmuir Sch., Edinburgh; Michigan State Univ. (MBA). Various positions, Ford of Britain, 1955–67; Dir, Car Product Planning, Ford Europe, 1967–69; positions in

Car Product Planning and Sales Planning Depts, Ford US, 1969–75; Chief Car Planning Manager, Ford Motor Co., 1975–79; Vice Pres., European Truck Ops, 1979–83; President: Ford Asia-Pacific, 1983–84; Ford of Europe, 1984–88; Exec. Vice Pres., North American Automotive Ops, 1989–93; Pres., Ford Automotive Gp, 1993; Chm. and CEO, Ford Motor Co., 1993–98. Member, Board of Directors: IBM Corp., 1995–; NY Stock Exchange, 1996–2002. Pres., Hakluyt Foundn, 2002–. *Address:* c/o House of Lords, SW1A 0PW. *Club:* Royal Air Force.
Died 26 April 2005.

TROUP, His Honour Alistair Mewburn; a Circuit Judge, 1980–95; *b* 23 Nov. 1927; *y s* of late William Annandale Troup, MC, MD, and Margaret Loïs Troup (*née* Mewburn); *m* 1st, 1952, S. B. Wylde (marr. diss. 1963); three *d*; 2nd, 1963, C. F. Hancock (marr. diss. 1968); one *s*; 3rd, 1969, (Marjorie) Cynthia (*née* Hutchinson). *Educ:* Merchant Taylors' School; New College, Oxford (BA). Served Army, 1946–48. Called to the Bar, Lincoln's Inn, 1952; Crown Counsel, Tanganyika, 1955–62; Sen. Crown Counsel, 1962–64; returned to practice at English Bar, 1964; Dep. Circuit Judge, 1975–77; a Recorder, 1977–80. Member Panel of Counsel: for Courts Martial Appeals Court, 1970–80; for Comrs of Customs and Excise at VAT Tribunals, 1973–80; Inspector for Dept of Trade, Hartley-Baird Ltd Inquiry, 1974–76. *Recreations:* golf, gardening. *Address:* The Rough, Firle Road, East Blatchington, Seaford, East Sussex BN25 2JD. *Club:* Seaford Golf.
Died 10 May 2001.

TROWBRIDGE, George William Job, CBE 1969; CEng; Chairman, AMT (Birmingham) Ltd, 1981–90; *b* 21 July 1911; *s* of George Clarke Trowbridge and Thirza Lampier Trowbridge (*née* Dingle); *m* 1938, Doris Isobel Morrison (*d* 1967); one *s*. *Educ:* Southall Technical Coll. Works Manager, Gays (Hampton) Ltd, 1938–45; Works Dir, Kingston Instrument Co. Ltd, 1945–52; Wickman Ltd, Coventry, 1952–79: London Area Manager, 1952–57; General Sales Manager, 1957–62; General Sales Dir, 1962–64; Dep. Man. Dir, 1966–79; Man. Dir, Machine Tool Sales Ltd, 1964–79; Director: John Brown & Co. Ltd, 1969–79; Machine Tools (India) Ltd, Calcutta, 1976–79; Drury Wickman Ltd, Johannesburg, 1976–79; Wickman (Australia) Ltd, Melbourne, 1976–79; Chairman: Wickman Machine Tools Inc., USA; Wickman Machine Tools SA, France. President: Machine Tool Trades Assoc., 1975–77; Comité Européen de Coopération des Industries de la Machine-Outil, 1975–77; Mem., Economic Develt Cttee for Machine Tools, 1968–79. MIProdE. *Publications:* A Handbook for Marketing Machinery, 1970; A Financial Study of British Machine Tool Companies, 1974. *Recreations:* walking, fishing. *Address:* 6 Moultrie Road, Rugby CV21 3BD. *T:* (01788) 560946. *Club:* Institute of Directors.
Died 8 March 2001.

TROWBRIDGE, Martin Edward O'Keeffe, CBE 1987; FCGI; public affairs, environmental, regulatory and EC consultant; Chairman, since 1973, and Chief Executive, since 1987, Martin Trowbridge Ltd; *b* 9 May 1925; *s* of late Edward Stanley Trowbridge and Ida Trowbridge (*née* O'Keeffe); *m* 1946, Valerie Ann Glazebrook; one *s*. *Educ:* RCS, Imperial Coll. of Science and Technology, London Univ. (BSc Eng (Chem. Eng); ACGI 1946); Amer. Management Assoc. Coll., NYC (Dip. Bus. Studies). Technical Officer, ICI (Billingham Div.) Ltd, 1946–48; Div. Manager, HWP/Fluor, 1948–53; Technical Dir, 1953–57, Man. Dir, 1957–59, Sharples Co.; Internat. Man. Dir, Sharples Corp., 1959–63; Group Managing Director: Pennwalt Internat. Corp., 1963–72; Pegler-Hattersley Ltd, 1972–73; Dir Gen., Chemical Industries Assoc., 1973–87. Member: Process Plant Working Party, NEDO, 1970–77; Chemicals EDC, NEDO, 1973–87; Process Plant EDC, NEDO, 1977–80; CBI Council; CBI Heads of Sector Group; CBI Europe Cttee; Eur. Chem. Ind. PR Council, Brussels; CEFIC R&D Cttee, Brussels;

Anglo-German Gp for Chem. Ind.; Anglo-French Gp for Chem. Ind.; ESRC Govt Industry Relns Cttee, 1973–87; Adv. Cttee, Eur. Business Inst., 1984–90; Bd, NRPB, 1987–91; IMRO Ltd, 1988–95. Chm., NEDO Task-Group on Tech., Research and Develt; Pres., Conseil d'Administration/CEFIC, Brussels, 1984–87 (Mem., 1973–87). Chm., Professional Develt Cttee, IChemE; Mem. Council, IChemE, 1987–89. Trustee, Chemical Ind. Museum, 1985–89. Hinchley Medal, IChemE, 1946; Internat. Medal, SCI, 1987. *Publications:* Purification of Oils for Marine Service, 1960; Scaling Up Centrifugal Separation Equipment, 1962; Collected Poems, 1963; Centrifugation, 1966; Exhibiting for Profit, 1969; Market Research and Forecasting, 1969; The Financial Performance of Process and Plant Companies, 1970; Poems for the Second Half, 1975; The Particular World of Directors General, 1987. *Recreations:* having fun, painting, shooting, mineralogy, print making, kitsch, wooden containers. *Died 24 Dec. 2002.*

TROWBRIDGE, Rear-Adm. Sir Richard (John), KCVO 1975; Governor of Western Australia, 1980–83; *b* 21 Jan. 1920; *s* of A. G. Trowbridge, Andover, Hants; *m* 1955, Anne Mildred Perceval; two *s*. *Educ:* Andover Grammar Sch.; Royal Navy. Joined RN as Boy Seaman, 1935. Served War of 1939–45, commnd as Sub Lieut, Dec. 1940 (despatches Aug. 1945). Comdr, 1953; comd Destroyer Carysfort, 1956–58; Exec. Officer, HMS Bermuda, 1958–59, and HMS Excellent, 1959–60; Captain, 1960; comd Fishery Protection Sqdn, 1962–64; completed course IDC, 1966; comd HMS Hampshire, 1967–69; Rear-Adm., 1970; Flag Officer Royal Yachts, 1970–75. An Extra Equerry to the Queen, 1970–. Younger Brother of Trinity Hse, 1972. KStJ 1980. *Recreations:* fishing, sailing, golf; most outdoor pursuits. *Address:* Old Idsworth Garden, Finchdean, Waterlooville PO8 0BA. *T:* (01705) 412714. *Club:* Army and Navy. *Died 4 May 2003.*

TRUBSHAW, Brian; *see* Trubshaw, E. B.

TRUBSHAW, (Ernest) Brian, CBE 1970 (OBE 1964); MVO 1948; FRAeS; aviation consultant; *b* 29 Jan. 1924; *s* of late Major H. E. Trubshaw, DL, and Lumly Victoria (*née* Carter); *m* 1972, Mrs Yvonne Edmondson, *d* of late J. A. Clapham, Harrogate, Yorks, *widow* of Richard Edmondson. *Educ:* Winchester College. Royal Air Force, 1942–50: Bomber Command, 1944; Transport Command, 1945–46; The King's Flight, 1946–48; Empire Flying School, 1949; RAF Flying Coll., 1949–50. Joined Vickers-Armstrongs (Aircraft) Ltd as Experimental Test Pilot, 1950; Dep. Chief Test Pilot, 1953; Chief Test Pilot, 1960; Dir of Flight Test, 1966–80; Divl Dir and Gen. Man. (Filton), Civil Aircraft Div., BAe plc, 1980–86. Mem. Bd (part-time), CAA, 1986–93. Warden, Guild of Air Pilots, 1958–61; Fellow, Society Experimental Test Pilots, USA. Hon. DTech Loughborough, 1986. Derry and Richards Memorial Medal, 1961 and 1964; Richard Hansford Burroughs Memorial Medal, 1964; R. P. Alston Memorial Medal, 1964; Segrave Trophy, 1970; Air League Founders' Medal, 1971; Iven C. Kinchloe Award, USA, 1971; Harmon Aviation Trophy, 1971; Bluebird Trophy, 1973; French Aeronautical Medal, 1976. *Recreation:* gardening. *Address:* The Walled Garden, Cherington, near Tetbury, Glos GL8 8SN. *T:* (01285) 841423, *Fax:* (01285) 841484. *Clubs:* Royal Air Force, MCC. *Died 24 March 2001.*

TRUSCOTT, Sir George (James Irving), 3rd Bt *cr* 1909; *b* 24 Oct. 1929; *s* of Sir Eric Homewood Stanham Truscott, 2nd Bt, and Lady (Mary Dorcas) Truscott (*née* Irving) (*d* 1948); *S* father, 1973; *m* 1962, Yvonne Dora (*née* Nicholson); one *s* one *d*. *Educ:* Sherborne School. *Heir: s* Ralph Eric Nicholson Truscott, *b* 21 Feb. 1966. *Address:* BM QUILL, London WC1N 3XX. *Died 26 March 2001.*

TRYON-WILSON, Brig. Charles Edward, CBE 1945 (MBE 1943); DSO 1944; Vice Lord-Lieutenant of Cumbria, 1980–83; *b* 20 Sept. 1909; 2nd *s* of late Charles Robert Tryon; *m* 1st, 1937, Cicely Joan (*d* 1969), *y d* of Captain Henry Whitworth; one *d* (and one *d* decd); 2nd, 1975, Rosemary Lucas. *Educ:* Shawnigan Lake School, BC; Trinity Coll., Glenalmond. Served 60th Rifles, 1927–30, Royal Fusiliers, 1930–36 and 1938–46 (N Africa, Italy, Austria; despatches twice). DL Westmorland (later Cumbria), 1971–85. *Recreations:* shooting, fishing. *Address:* Dallam Tower, Milnthorpe, Cumbria LA7 7AG. *T:* (015395) 63368. *Clubs:* Army and Navy, Lansdowne, Flyfishers'. *Died 18 April 2001.*

TUCK, Prof. John Philip; Professor of Education, University of Newcastle upon Tyne (formerly King's College, University of Durham) 1948–76, then Emeritus; *b* 16 April 1911; *s* of late William John and Annie Tuck, Uplyme, Lyme Regis; *m* 1936, Jane Adelaide (*d* 2001), *d* of late George William Wall and Maria Ellen Wall, Ulceby, N Lincs; two *s* (and one *s* decd). *Educ:* Strand School; Jesus College, Cambridge (BA Hons English and History, Class I, 1933; Certificate in Education, 1934; MA 1937); Christ's Coll., Cambridge (Adelaide Stoll Bachelor Research Scholar, 1935). English Master: Gateshead Grammar School, 1936; Manchester Central High School, 1938; Wilson's Grammar School, 1939 and 1946; Lecturer in Education, King's College, Newcastle upon Tyne, 1946–48. Served War of 1939–45, East Surrey Regt, and Army Education Corps, N Africa, Sicily, Italy, Austria. Mem. Council, GPDST, 1976–84. FRSA 1970. Hon. Fellow, Coll. of Speech Therapists, 1966. *Address:* 7 Chesterford House, Southacre Drive, Chaucer Road, Cambridge CB2 2TZ. *T:* (01223) 324655.
Died 7 Dec. 2001.

TUKE, Sir Anthony (Favill), Kt 1979; Chairman, Barclays Bank Ltd, 1973–81; *b* 22 Aug. 1920; *s* of late Anthony William Tuke and Agnes Edna, *d* of Henry George Gannaway; *m* 1946, Emilia Mila; one *s* one *d*. *Educ:* Winchester; Magdalene Coll., Cambridge. Scots Guards, 1940–46. Barclays Bank Ltd, 1946–90 (Dir, 1965–90); Vice-Chm, 1972–73); Dir, Barclays Bank UK, 1971–81; Barclays Bank International: Dir, 1966–85; Vice-Chm., 1968–72; Chm., 1972–79. Chm., Savoy Hotel, 1984–94 (Dir, 1982–94); Dep. Chm., Royal Insurance, 1985–92 (Dir, 1978–92); Director: Merchants Trust, 1969–94; RTZ Corp., 1980–91 (Chm., 1981–85); Whitbread Investment Company PLC, 1984–93. Vice-President: Inst. of Bankers, 1973–81; British Bankers' Assoc., 1977–81; Chm., Cttee of London Clearing Bankers, 1976–78 (Dep. Chm., 1974–76); Pres., Internat. Monetary Conference, 1977–78. Mem., Trilateral Commn, 1973–91. Chm., 1980 British Olympic Appeal; Pres., MCC, 1982–83. Mem., Stevenage Develt Corp., 1959–64. Governor, Motability, 1978–85. Mem. Council, Warwick Univ., 1966–73; Treas., English-Speaking Union, 1969–73. *Recreation:* gardening. *Address:* Freelands, Wherwell, near Andover, Hants SP11 7JS. *Club:* MCC.
Died 6 March 2001.

TUMIM, Sir Stephen, Kt 1996; HM Chief Inspector of Prisons for England and Wales, 1987–95; *b* 15 Aug. 1930; *yr s* of late Joseph Tumim, CBE (late Clerk of Assize, Oxford Circuit) and Renée Tumim; *m* 1962, Winifred Borthwick (CBE 2003); three *d*. *Educ:* St Edward's Sch., Oxford; Worcester Coll., Oxford (Scholar; Hon. Fellow, 1994). Called to Bar, Middle Temple, 1955, Bencher, 1990. A Recorder of the Crown Court, 1977–78; a Circuit Judge, 1978–96; a Judge of Willesden County Court, 1980–87. Principal, St Edmund Hall, Oxford, 1996–98. Chm., Nat. Deaf Children's Soc., 1974–79. Chairman: Friends of Tate Gall., 1983–90; British Art Market Standing Cttee, 1990–95; Koestler Award Trust, 1993–; Pres., Royal Lit. Fund, 1990–. Pres., Unlock, 1997–. Gov., Dr Johnson's House Trust, 2002–. Fellow, Royal Philanthropic Soc., 1994. Hon. FRCPsych 1993; Hon. Fellow: LSE, 1993; UEA, 1994; Oxford Brookes Univ, 1995; Hon. Sen. Fellow, Cayman Is Law Sch., 1994. High Steward, Wallingford, 1995–2001. DUniv:

Stirling, 1993; Open, 1997; UCE, 1997; Hon. LLD: Leicester, UWE, 1994; Birmingham, Essex, Southampton, 1995; Keele, Exeter, 1996; N London, 2001. *Publications:* Great Legal Disasters, 1983; Great Legal Fiascos, 1985; Crime and Punishment, 1997; occasional reviews. *Recreations:* books and pictures. *Clubs:* Garrick, Beefsteak.
Died 8 Dec. 2003.

TURECK, Rosalyn; concert artist; conductor, writer, teacher; *b* Chicago, 14 Dec. 1914; *d* of Samuel Tureck and Monya (*née* Lipson); *m* 1st, 1961, James Hainds (marr. diss.); 2nd, 1964, George Wallingford Downs (*d* 1964). *Educ:* Juilliard Sch. of Music, NY. Piano studies with Sophia Brilliant-Liven, Jan Chiapusso and Olga Samaroff; harpsichord with Gavin Williamson. Member Faculty: Philadelphia Conservatory of Music, 1935–42; Mannes Sch., NYC, 1940–44; Juilliard Sch. of Music, 1943–53; Columbia Univ., NY, 1953–55; Professor of Music: Univ. of California, San Diego, 1966–72; Univ. of Maryland, 1981–85; Yale Univ., 1991–93. Vis. Prof., Washington Univ., 1963–64; Visiting Fellow: St Hilda's Coll., Oxford, 1974 (Hon. Life Fellow, 1974); Wolfson Coll., Oxford, 1975; Lectures: educnl instns in USA, S America, Canada, Israel, Russia and Europe; Royal Instn of GB, and Boston Univ., 1993; Smithsonian Instn, 1994; Regents' Lectr, Univ. of Calif, 1995; Oxford Univ. (and master classes), 1995. Has appeared as soloist and conductor of leading orchestras in US, Europe and Israel, and toured US, Canada, S Africa, S America; début solo recital, Chicago, 1924; NY début, Carnegie Hall, 1936; European début, Copenhagen, 1947, since when toured extensively in Europe, and played at festivals in Edinburgh, Venice, Holland, Wexford, Schaffhausen, Bath, Brussels World Fair, Glyndebourne, Barcelona, Puerto Rico, St Petersburg, etc, and in major Amer. festivals including Mostly Mozart Festival, NY, Caramoor, Detroit, etc; extensive tours: India, Australia and Far East, 1971; S America, 1986–; Spain, 1986–; Rome and Florence, 1996–; Europe and US, 1998–99. Founder: Composers of Today, 1949–53; also Director: Tureck Bach Players, London, 1957 (conductor, 1960–72), NY, 1981–86; Internat. Bach Soc., Inst. for Bach Studies, 1968–93; Tureck Bach Inst. Inc., 1981; Tureck Bach Res. Foundn, Oxford, 1994. Hon. Member, GSMD, London, 1961; Member: Royal Musical Assoc., London; Inc. Soc. of Musicians, London; Amer. Musicol Soc; Amer. Br., New Bach Soc. Editor, Tureck/Bach Urtext series, 1979–. Numerous recordings, 1945–. Hon. Dr of Music, Colby Coll., USA, 1964; Hon. DMus: Roosevelt Univ., 1968; Wilson Coll., 1968; Oxford, 1977; Music and Arts Inst. of San Francisco, 1987. Numerous awards, USA, UK, Germany and S America. Officer's Cross, Order of Merit, Fed. Republic of Germany, 1979. *Television films:* Fantasy and Fugue: Rosalyn Tureck plays Bach, 1972; Rosalyn Tureck plays on Harpsichord and Organ, 1977; Joy of Bach, 1978; Bach and Tureck at Ephesus, 1985; Tureck on Television, 1999; also many appearances, US. *Publications:* An Introduction to the Performance of Bach, 1960; Authenticity, 1994; (contrib.) Music and Mathematics, 1995; edited: Bach: Sarabande, C minor, 1950; (transcribed) Paganini: Moto Perpetuo, 1950; (Urtext and performance edns) Bach: Italian Concerto, 1983, 2nd edn 1991; J. S. Bach, Lute Suite in E minor, set for classical guitar, 1984, Lute Suite in C minor, 1985; Interaction: the journal of the Tureck Bach Research Foundation, Vol. I, 1997, Vol. II, 1998, Vol. III, 1999; many articles. *Address:* Hotel El Paraiso, Ctra Cádiz, Km 167-Apdo 134, 29680 Estepona-Marbella, Spain. *Club:* Century (NY).
Died 17 July 2003.

TURNBULL, Ven. David Charles; Archdeacon of Carlisle, and Canon Residentiary, Carlisle Cathedral, since 1993; *b* 16 March 1944; *m* Elaine; one *s* one *d. Educ:* Leeds Univ. (BA 1965); Chichester Theol Coll.; Sheffield Univ. (MEd 1992). Ordained deacon, 1969, priest, 1970; Curate of Jarrow, 1969–74; Vicar, Carlinghow, 1974–83; Vicar of Penistone, 1983–86, and Priest in charge of Thurlstone, 1985–86, Team Rector of Penistone and Thurlstone,

1986–93; RD of Barnsley, 1988–93. Mem., Gen. Synod of C of E, 1996–. Hon. Canon, Wakefield, 1993. *Address:* 2 The Abbey, Carlisle CA3 8TZ. *T:* (01228) 23026.
Died 5 May 2001.

TURNER, Dudley Russell Flower, CB 1977; Secretary, Advisory, Conciliation and Arbitration Service, 1974–77; *b* 15 Nov. 1916; *s* of Gerald Flower Turner and Dorothy May Turner (*née* Gillard), Penang; *m* 1941, Sheila Isobel Stewart; one *s* one *d. Educ:* Whitgift Sch.; London Univ. (BA Hons). Served RA (Captain), 1940–46. Entered Ministry of Labour, 1935; HM Treasury, 1953–56; Principal Private Sec. to Minister of Labour, 1956–59; Assistant Secretary: Cabinet Office, 1959–62; Ministry of Labour, 1962–64, 1966; Under-Sec., Ministry of Labour, 1967; Asst Under-Sec. of State, Dept of Employment and Productivity, 1968–70; Under-Sec., Trng Div., 1970–72, Manpower Gen. Div., 1972–73, Dept of Employment; Sec., Commn on Industrial Relations, 1973–74. Imperial Defence Coll., 1965. Pres., East Surrey Decorative and Fine Arts Soc., 1986– (Chm., 1980–86). *Recreations:* music, gardening. *Address:* 9 Witherby Close, Croydon, Surrey CR0 5SU. *Club:* Civil Service.
Died 11 July 2003.

TURNER, Janet; *see* Kear, J.

TURNER, Hon. Joanna Elizabeth, (Hon. Mrs Turner), MA; Classics Teacher, Ellesmere College, Salop, 1975–80; *b* 10 Jan. 1923; 2nd *d* of 1st Baron Piercy, CBE, and Mary Louisa, *d* of Hon. Thomas Pelham; *m* 1968, James Francis Turner (*d* 1983), *er s* of late Rev. P. R. Turner. *Educ:* St Paul's Girls' Sch.; Somerville Coll., Oxford (Sen. Classics Schol.). Assistant Classics Mistress: Downe House, Newbury, 1944–46; Gordonstoun Sch., 1947–48; Badminton Sch., Bristol, 1948–65; Headmistress, Badminton Sch., Bristol, 1966–69. JP Inner London (Juvenile Courts), 1970–75. *Publications:* B. M. Sanderson and Badminton School 1947–1966, 1988; Quarries and Craftsmen of the Windrush Valley, 1988. *Address:* Gable Cottage, 55 Witney Street, Burford, Oxon OX18 4RX. *T:* (01993) 822368.
Died 10 Feb. 2001.

TURNER, His Honour John Turnage; a Circuit Judge, 1976–98; Resident Judge at Ipswich, 1984–98; *b* 12 Nov. 1929; *s* of Wilfrid Edward and May Martha Turner; *m* 1956, Gillian Mary Rayner; two *d. Educ:* Earls Colne Grammar School. Called to the Bar, Inner Temple, 1952. *Recreations:* music appreciation, travelling, watching cricket, philately. *Club:* MCC. *Died 17 March 2004.*

TURPIN, Kenneth Charlton; Provost of Oriel College, Oxford, 1957–80, and Hon. Fellow since 1980; Vice-Chancellor, Oxford University, 1966–69 (Pro-Vice Chancellor, 1964–66, 1969–79); Member, Hebdomadal Council, 1959–77; *b* 13 Jan. 1915; *e s* of late Henry John Turpin, Ludlow. *Educ:* Manchester Grammar Sch.; Oriel College, Oxford. HM Treasury, 1940–43; Asst Private Sec. to C. R. Attlee, Lord President of the Council and Dep. Prime Minister, 1943–45; 2nd Asst Registrar, University Registry, Oxford, 1945–47; Sec. of Faculties, Univ. of Oxford, 1947–57; Professorial Fellow, Oriel Coll., 1948. A Church Commissioner, 1984–89. Hon. Fellow, Trinity Coll., Dublin, 1968. *Recreations:* gardening, walking. *Address:* 13 Apsley Road, Oxford OX2 7QX. *Clubs:* Athenæum; Vincent's (Oxford).
Died 14 Sept. 2005.

TURTON, Victor Ernest; Managing Director: V. E. Turton (Tools) Ltd; V. E. Turton (Wholesalers) Ltd; *b* 29 June 1924; *s* of H. E. Turton; *m* 1951, Jean Edith Murray; two *d. Educ:* Paget Secondary Modern Sch.; Aston Techn. Coll.; Birmingham Central Techn. Coll. Birmingham City Councillor (Lab) Duddeston Ward, 1945–63; Saltley Ward, 1970–71; Alderman, Birmingham, 1963–70 and 1971–74, Hon. Alderman, 1974–; Lord Mayor of Birmingham, 1971–72, Dep. Lord Mayor, 1972–73; West Midlands County Council: Mem., 1974–77, 1981–86; Vice-Chm., 1983–84, Chm., 1984–85; Chm., Airport

Cttee, 1974–77; Member: Airport and Fire Bde Cttee; Transportation Cttee. Chm., Birmingham Airport, 1959–66; Dir, Birmingham Exec. Airways, 1983–89. Chairman: Smallholdings and Agric. Cttee, 1954–58; West Midlands Regional Adv. Cttee for Civil Aviation, 1966–72; Jt Airports Cttee of Local Authorities, 1975–77. Vice Pres., Heart of England Tourist Bd, 1977– (Chm., 1975–77). Chm., Hall Green Div. Labour Party, 1957–59. Former Governor, Coll. of Technology (later Univ. of Aston in Birmingham). *Recreations:* football, cricket, table tennis, philately. *Address:* 121 Maypole Lane, King's Heath, Birmingham B14 4PF. *Club:* Rotary (Birmingham). *Died 3 Oct. 2002.*

TUTIN, Dame Dorothy, (Dame Dorothy Barton-Chapple), DBE 2000 (CBE 1967); actress (stage and films); *b* 8 April 1931; *d* of late John Tutin, DSc, and Adie Evelyn Tutin; *m* 1963, Derek Barton-Chapple (stage name Derek Waring); one *s* one *d. Educ:* St Catherine's, Bramley, Surrey; RADA. Began career, 1950; Stratford Festival, 1958, 1960. *Parts included:* Rose, in The Living Room; Katherine, in Henry V; Sally Bowles, in I am a Camera; St Joan, in The Lark; Catherine, in The Gates of Summer; Hedwig, in The Wild Duck; Viola, in Twelfth Night; Juliet, in Romeo and Juliet; Ophelia, in Hamlet; during Shakespeare Memorial Theatre tour of Russia, 1958, played parts of Ophelia, Viola and Juliet; Dolly, in Once More, With Feeling, New, 1959; Portia, Viola, Cressida, Stratford, 1960; Sister Jeanne, in The Devils, Aldwych, 1961, 1962; Juliet, Desdemona, Stratford, 1961; Varya, in The Cherry Orchard, Stratford, and Aldwych, 1961; Cressida, Prioress, in The Devils, Edinburgh, 1962; Polly Peachum, in The Beggar's Opera, Aldwych, 1963; The Hollow Crown, New York, 1963; Queen Victoria, in Portrait of a Queen, Vaudeville, 1965, NY, 1968; Rosalind, As You Like It, Stratford, 1967, Los Angeles, 1968; Play on Love, St Martin's, 1970; Old Times, Aldwych, 1971; Peter Pan, Coliseum, 1971, 1972; What Every Woman Knows, 1973, Albery, 1974; Natalya Petrovna, in A Month in the Country, Chichester, 1974, Albery, 1975; Cleopatra, in Antony and Cleopatra, Edinburgh, 1977; Madame Ranevsky, The Cherry Orchard, Lady Macbeth, in Macbeth, Lady Plyant, in The Double Dealer (SWET Award, 1978), Nat. Theatre, 1978; Undiscovered Country, Nat. Theatre, 1979; Reflections, Theatre Royal, Haymarket, 1980; The Provok'd Wife, Nat. Theatre, 1980; Hester, in The Deep Blue Sea, Greenwich, 1981; After the Lions, Royal Exchange, Manchester, 1982; Ballerina, Churchill Theatre, Bromley, 1984; A Kind of Alaska, Duchess, 1985; The Chalk Garden, Chichester, 1986; Are you sitting comfortably, Watford, 1986; Brighton Beach Memoirs, Aldwych, 1987; Thursday's Ladies, Apollo, 1987; Harlequinade and The Browning Version (double-bill), Royalty, 1988; A Little Night Music, Chichester Fest., transf. Piccadilly, 1989; Henry VIII, Chichester, 1991; Getting Married, Chichester, 1993; After October, Chichester, 1997; Gin Game, Savoy, 1999. *Films:* Cecily, in The Importance of Being Earnest, 1951; Polly Peachum, in The Beggar's Opera, 1954; Lucie Manette, in A Tale of Two Cities, 1956; Henrietta Maria in Cromwell; Sophie Breska in Savage Messiah (Variety Club of GB Film Actress Award, 1972); The Shooting Party; Great Moments in Aviation, 1992; The Great Kandinsky, 1993; Alive and Kicking, 1997; Maybe Next Year, 1998. Appeared on television. *Recreations:* music; Isle of Arran. *Address:* c/o Michael Whitehall, 10 Lower Common South, SW15 1BP.
Died 6 Aug. 2001.

TUTTE, Prof. William Thomas, OC 2001; FRS 1987; FRSC 1958; Professor of Mathematics, University of Waterloo, Ontario, 1962–85, Professor Emeritus, 1985; *b* 14 May 1917; *s* of William John Tutte and Annie Tutte

(*née* Newell); *m* 1949, Dorothea Geraldine Mitchell (*d* 1994). *Educ:* Cambridge and County High Sch.; Trinity Coll., Cambridge (BA, MA, PhD). Fellow of Trinity Coll., Cambridge, 1942–49; Lectr to Associate Prof., Univ. of Toronto, 1948–62. *Publications:* Connectivity in Graphs, 1966; Introduction to the Theory of Matroids, 1971; Graph Theory, 1984; Graph Theory as I have known it, 1998; papers in mathematical jls. *Address:* Apt 804, 25 Westmount Road North, Waterloo, ON N2L 5G7, Canada. *Died 2 May 2002.*

TWEEDDALE, 13th Marquis of, *cr* 1694; **Edward Douglas John Hay;** Lord Hay of Yester, 1488; Earl of Tweeddale, 1646; Viscount Walden, Earl of Gifford, 1694; Baron Tweeddale (UK), 1881; Hereditary Chamberlain of Dunfermline; *b* 6 Aug. 1947; *s* of 12th Marquis of Tweeddale, GC, and of Sonia Mary, *d* of 1st Viscount Ingleby; *S* father, 1979. *Educ:* Milton Abbey, Blandford, Dorset; Trinity Coll., Oxford (BA Hons PPE). *Heir:* yr twin *b* Lord Charles David Montagu Hay, *b* 6 Aug. 1947.
Died 1 Feb. 2005.

TWIGG, Patrick Alan; QC 1986; FCIArb; a Recorder, since 1987; *b* 19 May 1943; *s* of late Alan Oswald Twigg and of Gwendoline Mary Twigg; *m* 1974, Gabrielle Madeline Bay Green; one *s* one *d. Educ:* Repton Sch., Derbyshire; Universities of: The Sorbonne, Paris; Perugia, Italy; Bristol (LLB); Virginia, USA (LLM). FCIArb 1998. Called to the Bar, Inner Temple, 1967; Mem., Western Circuit. Arbitrator (Internat. Panel), Singapore Internat. Arbitration Centre; Mediator, Singapore Acad. of Law, 1997. Dir, Canterbury Festival, 1991–. Pres., Bishopsbourne Cricket Club, 1989–. *Recreations:* family, landscape and other gardening, restoring country house, music (particularly church, piano and chamber music), musical composition, amateur dramatics (Mem. Old Stagers 1969–), travel, tennis. *Address:* 2 Temple Gardens, Temple, EC4Y 9AY. *T:* (020) 7583 6041, *Fax:* (020) 7583 2094. *Club:* Delta Theta Phi Fraternity (Charlottesville, Virginia). *Died 14 May 2001.*

TYRRELL, Dr David Arthur John, CBE 1980; FRCP, FRCPath; FRS 1970; Director, MRC Common Cold Unit, 1982–90, retired; *s* of late Sidney Charles Tyrrell and Agnes Kate (*née* Blewett); *m* 1950, Betty Moyra Wylie; two *d* (one *s* decd). *Educ:* Sheffield University (MB, ChB Hons; MD Hons). FRCP 1965. Junior hosp. appts, Sheffield, 1948–51; Asst, Rockefeller Inst., New York, 1951–54; Virus Research Lab., Sheffield, 1954–57; MRC Common Cold Unit, Salisbury, 1957–90; Dep. Dir of Clin. Res. Centre, Northwick Park, Harrow, and Head of Div. of Communicable Diseases, 1970–84. Chairman: (first), Adv. Cttee on Dangerous Pathogens, 1981–91; Consultative Cttee on Res. into Spongiform Encephalopathies, 1989–90; Spongiform Encephalopathy Adv. Cttee, 1990–95; Biol Sub-Cttee, Cttee on Safety of Medicines, 1989–92; Task Force on Chronic Fatigue Syndrome/Myalgic Encephalomyelitis/Post Viral Fatigue Syndrome, 1993–99. Managing Trustee, Nuffield Foundn, 1977–92. Sir Arthur Sims Commonwealth Travelling Prof., 1985. Hon. DSc Sheffield, 1979; Hon. DM Southampton, 1990. Stewart Prize, BMA, 1977; Ambuj Nath Bose Prize, 1983, Conway Evans Prize, 1986, RCP. *Publications:* Common Colds and Related Diseases, 1965; Interferon and its Clinical Potential, 1976; (jtly) Microbial Diseases, 1979; The Abolition of Infection: hope or illusion?, 1982; numerous papers on infectious diseases and viruses. *Recreations:* music-making, gardening, walking; various Christian organizations. *Address:* Ash Lodge, Dean Lane, Whiteparish, Salisbury, Wilts SP5 2RN. *T:* and *Fax:* (01794) 884352.
Died 2 May 2005.

U

UNDERHILL, Herbert Stuart; President, Victoria (BC) Press, 1978–79; Publisher, Victoria Times, 1971–78, retired; *b* 20 May 1914; *s* of Canon H. J. Underhill and Helena (*née* Ross); *m* 1937, Emma Gwendolyn MacGregor; one *s* one *d. Educ:* University Sch., Victoria, BC. Correspondent and Editor, The Canadian Press, Vancouver, BC, Toronto, New York and London, 1936–50; Reuters North American Editor, 1950; Asst General Manager, Reuters, 1958; Managing Editor, 1965–68; Dep. Gen. Manager, with special responsibility for North and South America and Caribbean, 1963–70. Director: Canadian Daily Newspaper Publishers' Assoc., 1972–76; The Canadian Press, 1972–78. *Publication:* The Iron Church, 1984. *Recreations:* travel, reading. *Address:* 308 Beach Drive, Victoria, BC V8S 2M2, Canada.
Died 28 Feb. 2003.

UNWIN, Rev. Canon Christopher Philip, TD 1963; Archdeacon of Northumberland, 1963–82; *b* 27 Sept. 1917; *e s* of Rev. Philip Henry and Decima Unwin. *Educ:* Repton Sch.; Magdalene Coll., Cambridge (MA); Queen's Theological Coll., Birmingham. Ordained deacon, 1940, priest, 1941; Assistant Curate of: Benwell, 1940–43; Sugley, 1944–47; Vicar of: Horton, Northumberland, 1947–55; Benwell, 1955–63. *Recreations:* reading, walking. *Address:* 60 Sandringham Avenue, Benton, Newcastle upon Tyne NE12 8JX. *T:* (0191) 270 0418. *Died 21 Dec. 2004.*

UPJOHN, Maj.-Gen. Gordon Farleigh, CB 1966; CBE 1959 (OBE 1955); *b* 9 May 1912; *e s* of late Dudley Francis Upjohn; *m* 1946, Rita Joan, *d* of late Major Clarence Walters; three *d. Educ:* Felsted School; RMC Sandhurst. 2nd Lieut, The Duke of Wellington's Regt; RWAFF, 1937; Adjt 3rd Bn The Nigeria Regt, 1940; Staff Coll., 1941; GSO2 Ops GHQ Middle East, 1941; Bde Maj. 3 West African Inf. Bde, 1942 (despatches); Lt-Col Comd 6 Bn The Nigeria Regt, 1944 (despatches); DAA&QMG Southern Comd, India, 1946; GSO2 Mil. Ops Directorate WO, 1948; Lt-Col Chief Instructor RMA Sandhurst, 1951; Lt-Col Comd West African Inf. Bn, 1954; Bde Comdr 2 Inf. Bde Malaya, 1957 (despatches; Meritorious Medal (Perak Malaya)); Provost Marshal WO, 1960; GOC Yorkshire District, 1962–65. Automobile Assoc., 1965–76. *Recreations:* golf, cricket, field sports. *Address:* c/o Lloyds TSB, Grayshott, Hindhead, Surrey GU26 6LG.
Died 19 March 2001.

URIE, Wing Comdr Dunlop; *see* Urie, Wing Comdr J. D.

URIE, Wing Comdr (John) Dunlop; AE 1942, bar 1945; *b* 12 Oct. 1915; *s* of late John Urie, OBE, Glasgow; *m* 1939, Mary Taylor, *d* of Peter Bonnar, Dunfermline; one *s* two *d. Educ:* Sedbergh; Glasgow Univ. Served War of 1939–45: with RAuxAF, in Fighter Command and Middle East Command; Wing Comdr, 1942. DL Co. of Glasgow, 1963. OStJ. *Address:* Tottington, RMB 5194, St Arnaud, Vic 3478, Australia. *Club:* Royal Northern and Clyde Yacht. *Died 20 July 2001.*

USHER, Sir Leonard (Gray), KBE 1986 (CBE 1971); CF 1997; JP; Secretary, Fiji Press Council, 1985–94; Chairman, Suva Stock Exchange, 1978–92; *b* 29 May 1907; *s* of Robert Usher and Mary Elizabeth (*née* Johnston); *m* 1st, 1940, Mary Gertrude Lockie (marr. diss. 1962; she *d* 1997); one *s* one *d;* 2nd, 1962, Jane Hammond Derné (*d* 1984). *Educ:* Auckland Grammar Sch., NZ; Auckland Training Coll. (Trained Teachers Cert. B); Auckland Univ. (BA). Headmaster, Levuka Public Sch., Provincial Schs, Queen Victoria Sch., 1930–43; Fiji Govt PRO, 1943–56; Exec. Dir, Fiji Times and Herald Ltd, 1957–73; Editor, Fiji Times, 1958–73; Org. Dir, Pacific Is News Assoc., 1974–85 (Councillor and Life Mem., 1985–). Chm., Fiji Develt Bank, 1978–82; Dep. Chm., Nat. Bank of Fiji, 1974–83. Mem., Suva CC, 1962–71, 1975–77; Mayor of Suva, 1966–70, 1975–76. Chm., Fiji Coll. of Honour, 1995–97. *Publications:* Satellite Over The Pacific, 1975; 50 Years in Fiji, 1978; (jtly) Suva—a history and guide, 1978; Levuka School Century, 1979; (jtly) This is Radio Fiji, 1979; The Lodge of Fiji 1882–1982, 1982; (ed) Pacific News Media, 1986; Mainly About Fiji, 1987; 60 Years in Fiji, 1988; Letters From Fiji 1987–1990, 1992; More Letters from Fiji 1990–1994, 1994. *Recreations:* reading, computer programmes, conversation. *Address:* 24 Des Voeux Road, Suva, Fiji. *T:* 302025, *Fax:* 303025; PO Box 13250, Suva, Fiji. *Clubs:* Defence, Fiji, United, Ex-Servicemen's (Fiji); Royal Automobile (Sydney).
Died 26 Aug. 2003.

USTINOV, Sir Peter (Alexander), Kt 1990; CBE 1975; FRSA, FRSL; actor, dramatist, film director; Chancellor, Durham University, since 1992; Rector of the University of Dundee, 1971–73; Goodwill Ambassador for UNICEF, 1969; *b* London, 16 April 1921; *s* of late Iona Ustinov and Nadia Benois, painter; *m* 1st, 1940, Isolde Denham (marr. diss. 1950); one *d;* 2nd, 1954, Suzanne Cloutier (marr. diss. 1971); one *s* two *d;* 3rd, 1972, Hélène du Lau d'Allemans. *Educ:* Westminster School. Served in Army, Royal Sussex Regt and RAOC, 1942–46. Author of plays: House of Regrets, 1940 (prod Arts Theatre 1942); Blow Your Own Trumpet, 1941 (prod Playhouse [Old Vic] 1943); Beyond, 1942 (prod Arts Theatre, 1943); The Banbury Nose, 1943 (prod Wyndham's, 1944); The Tragedy of Good Intentions, 1944 (prod Old Vic, Liverpool, 1945); The Indifferent Shepherd (prod Criterion, 1948); Frenzy (adapted from Swedish of Ingmar Bergman, prod and acted in St Martin's, 1948); The Man in the Raincoat (Edinburgh Festival, 1949); The Love of Four Colonels (and acted in, Wyndham's, 1951); The Moment of Truth (Adelphi, 1951); High Balcony, 1952 (written 1946); No Sign of the Dove (Savoy, 1953); The Empty Chair (Bristol Old Vic, 1956); Romanoff and Juliet (Piccadilly, 1956, film, 1961; musical, R loves J, Chichester, 1973); Photo Finish (prod and acted in it, Saville, 1962); The Life in My Hands, 1963; The Unknown Soldier and his Wife, 1967 (prod and acted in it, Chichester, 1968, New London, 1973); Halfway up the Tree (Queen's), 1967; compiled, prod and acted in The Marriage, Edinburgh, 1982; wrote and acted in Beethoven's Tenth (Vaudeville, 1983, 1987–88); An Evening with Peter Ustinov, (Haymarket), 1990, 1991, 1994. Co-Author of film: The Way Ahead, 1943–44. Author and Director of films: School for Secrets, 1946; Vice-Versa, 1947. Author, director, producer and main actor in film Private Angelo, 1946; acted in films: One of Our Aircraft is Missing, 1941; The Way Ahead, 1944; Odette, Quo Vadis, Hotel Sahara, 1950; Beau Brummell, The Egyptian, We're No Angels, 1954; Lola Montez, 1955; The Spies, 1955; I Girovaghi, 1956; An Angel Flew Over Brooklyn, 1957; Spartacus, 1960 (Academy Award, Best Supporting Actor, 1961); The Sundowners, 1961; Romanoff and Juliet, 1961; Topkapi (Academy Award, Best Supporting Actor), 1964; John Goldfarb, Please Come Home, 1964; Blackbeard's Ghost, 1967; The Comedians, 1968; Hot Millions, 1968; Viva Max, 1969; Big Truck and Poor Clare, 1971; One of our Dinosaurs is Missing, 1974; Logan's Run, 1975; Treasure of Matecumbe, 1977; Un Taxi Mauve, 1977; The Last Remake of Beau Geste, 1977; Death on the Nile, 1978 (Best Film Actor, Variety Club of GB); Ashanti, The Thief of Baghdad, 1979; Charlie Chan and the Curse of the Dragon Queen, 1981; Evil under the Sun, 1981; Appointment with Death, 1988; The French Revolution,

1989; Lorenzo's Oil, 1992; The Phoenix and the Magic Carpet, 1994; Stiff Upper Lips, 1998; director, producer and actor in film Billy Budd, 1961; director and actor in films: Hammersmith is Out, 1971; Memed My Hawk, 1984. Directed operas at: Covent Garden, 1962; Hamburg Opera, 1968, 1985, 1987; Paris Opera, 1973; Edinburgh Fest., 1973, 1981; Deutsche Oper, Berlin, 1978; Piccola Scala, Milan, 1981, 1982; Dresden Opera, 1993; Bolshoi, 1997. Master's Course (opera direction), Salzburg, 1986. Acted in: revues: Swinging the Gate, 1940, Diversion, 1941; plays: Crime and Punishment, New Theatre, 1946; Love in Albania, St James's, 1949; King Lear, Stratford, Ont, 1979; Beethoven's Tenth, Berlin, 1987; directed Lady L, 1965; *television:* Omnibus: the life of Samuel Johnson (Emmy Award), 1957–58; Barefoot in Athens (Emmy Award), 1966; Storm in Summer (Emmy Award), 1970; The Mighty Continent (series), 1974; Einstein's Universe (series), 1979; 13 at Dinner, 1985; Dead Man's Folly, 1985; World Challenge (series), 1985; Peter Ustinov's Russia (series), 1987; Peter Ustinov in China, 1987 (ACE Award, 1988); Around the World in 80 Days, 1988–89; Secret Identity of Jack the Ripper, 1989; Ustinov aboard the Orient Express, 1992; Ustinov Meets Pavarotti, 1993; Inside the Vatican, 1994; The Old Curiosity Shop, 1995; Haydn Gala, 1995; Sir Peter Ustinov in Thailand, Sir Peter Ustinov in Hong Kong, 1995; Paths of Gods, 1995; Planet Ustinov, 1998; Alice in Wonderland, 2000; Victoria and Albert, 2001. Member: British Film Academy; Acad. of Fine Arts, Paris, 1988. Pres., World Federalist Movt, 1992–; Mem., British USA Bicentennial Liaison Cttee, 1973–. Hon. doctorates include: Hon. DMus Cleveland Inst. of Music, 1967; Hon. DHL Georgetown Univ., 1988; Hon. LLD Ottawa, 1991; Hon. DLitt Durham, 1992; Hon. Dr St Michael's Coll., Toronto, 1995; Dr *hc* Free Flemish Univ., Brussels, 1995. Benjamin Franklin Medal, Royal Society of Arts, 1957; UNICEF award, 1978, 1995; Gold Medal, City of Athens, 1990; Medal of the Greek Red Cross, 1990; Medal of Honour, Charles Univ., Prague, 1991; Grammy Award; Britannia Award, LA Br., BAFTA, 1992; Critics' Circle Award, 1993; German Cultural Award, 1994; German Bambi, 1994; Internat. Child Survival Award, UNICEF, 1995; Rudolph Valentino Award for Lifetime Achievement in Motion Pictures, 1995; Norman Cousins Global Governance Award, World Federalist Movt, 1995. Order of the Smile (for dedication to idea of internat. assistance to children), Warsaw, 1974; Commandeur des Arts et des Lettres (France), 1985; Order of El Istiglal (Jordan); Order of Yugoslav Flag (Yugoslavia); Ordem Nacional do Cruzerio do Sul (Brazil), 1994. *Publications:* House of Regrets, 1943; Beyond, 1944; The Banbury Nose, 1945; Plays About People, 1950; The Love of Four Colonels, 1951; The Moment of Truth, 1953; Romanoff and Juliet (Stage and Film); Add a Dash of Pity (short stories), 1959; Ustinov's Diplomats (a book of photographs), 1960; The Loser (novel), 1961; The Frontiers of the Sea, 1966; Krumnagel, 1971; Dear Me (autobiog.), 1977; Overheard (play), 1981; My Russia, 1983; Ustinov in Russia, 1987; The Disinformer, 1989; The Old Man and Mr Smith, 1990; Ustinov at Large (compilation of articles in The European), 1991; Still at Large (compilation of articles in The European), 1993 and

1995; Quotable Ustinov, 1995; Monsieur René, 1998; contributor short stories to Atlantic Monthly. *Recreations:* lawn tennis, squash, collecting old masters' drawings, music. *Address:* The Ustinov Foundation Office, Höhenberg Strasse 20, 82340 Feldafing, Germany. *Clubs:* Garrick, Savage, Royal Automobile, Arts Theatre, Queen's.   *Died 28 March 2004.*

UVAROV, Dame Olga (Nikolaevna), DBE 1983 (CBE 1978); FRCVS; Vice-President, Universities Federation for Animal Welfare, 1986–92; *d* of Nikolas and Elena Uvarov. *Educ:* Royal Vet. Coll. (Bronze Medals for Physiol. and Histol.). MRCVS 1934; FRCVS 1973. Asst in gen. mixed practice, 1934–43; own small animal practice, 1944–53; licence to practice and work at greyhound stadium, 1945–68; clinical res., pharmaceutical industry, 1953–70; Head of Vet. Adv. Dept, Glaxo Laboratories, 1967–70; BVA Technical Inf. Service, 1970–76; Advr on Tech. Inf., BVA, 1976–78; Mem. MAFF Cttees under Medicines Act (1968), 1971–78. Royal College of Veterinary Surgeons: Mem. Council, 1968–88; Chm. Parly Cttee, 1971–74; Jun. Vice-Pres., 1975; Pres., 1976–77; Sen. Vice-Pres., 1977–78; President: Soc. Women Vet. Surgeons, 1947–49 (Sec., 1946); Central Vet. Soc., 1951–52; Assoc. Vet. Teachers and Res. Workers, 1967–68 (Pres. S Reg., 1967–68); Section of Comparative Medicine, RSocMed, 1967–68 (Sec., 1965–67; Sec. for Internat. Affairs, 1971–78, 1983–92); Lab. Animal Science Assoc., 1984–86 (Vice-Pres., 1983–84); Vice-Pres., Inst. of Animal Technicians, 1983–; Member Council: BVA, 1944–67; RSocMed, 1968–70 (Hon. Fellow, 1982); Res. Defence Soc., 1968–82 (Hon. Sec., 1978–82; Vice-Pres., 1982–); Member: Medicines Commn, 1978–82; Vet. Res. Club, 1967–; British Small Animal Vet. Assoc.; British Codex Sub-Cttee, Pharmaceutical Soc., 1970–71. FRVC 1979; Hon. FIBiol 1983. Hon. DSc Guelph, 1976. Victory Gold Medal, Central Vet. Soc., 1965. *Publications:* contribs to: The Veterinary Annual; International Encyclopaedia of Veterinary Medicine, 1966; also papers in many learned jls. *Recreations:* work, travel, literature, flowers. *Address:* Silverlands, 36 Wellington Road, Hatch End, Middx HA5 4NW. *Club:* Royal Society of Medicine.
                                             Died 29 Aug. 2001.

UZIELL-HAMILTON, Her Honour Adrianne Pauline; a Circuit Judge, 1990–2002; *b* 14 May 1932; *e d* of late Dr Marcus and Ella Grantham; *m* 1952, Mario Reginald Uziell-Hamilton (*d* 1988); one *s* one *d. Educ:* Maria Gray's Academy for Girls and privately. Called to the Bar, Middle Temple, 1965; *ad eundem* Mem., Inner Temple, 1976; Head of Chambers, 1976–90; a Recorder, 1985–90. Vice-Chm., Ethics Cttee, Nat. Hosp., 1993–95 (Mem., 1991–95); Member: Legal Aid Panel, 1969–90; Parole Bd, 1994–96; General Council of the Bar, 1970–74 (Exec. Cttee, 1973–74). Pres., Mental Health Review Tribunals, 1988. Gov., North London Univ. (formerly Polytechnic of N London), 1986–2000. FRSA. *Publications:* articles on marriage contracts. *Recreations:* collecting ballet and theatre costume design, cooking for friends, conversation.   *Died 13 April 2005.*

V

VALLIS, Rear-Adm. Michael Anthony, CB 1986; FREng, CEng; *b* 30 June 1929; *s* of R. W. H. Vallis and S. J. Dewsnup; *m* 1959, Pauline Dorothy Abbott, Wymondham, Leics; three *s* one *d*. *Educ:* RN College, Dartmouth; RN Engineering College, Plymouth; RN College, Greenwich. MIMechE; FREng 1987. RN Service, 1943–86; Dir Gen., Surface Ships, 1983–84, Marine Engrg, 1984–86, MoD. Hon. FIMarEST. *Recreations:* fishing, gardening, walking, food and wine, theatre. *Address:* 4A St Stephen's Close, Bath, BA1 5PP. *Club:* Royal Over-Seas League. *Died 24 Oct. 2003.*

VALOIS, Dame Ninette de; *see* de Valois.

VANCE, Cyrus Roberts, Hon. KBE 1994; Secretary of State, USA, 1977–80; barrister-at-law; *b* Clarksburg, W Va, 27 March 1917; *m* 1947, Grace Elsie Sloane; one *s* four *d*. *Educ:* Kent Sch.; Yale Univ. (BA 1939); Yale Univ. Law Sch. (LLB 1942). Served War, USNR, to Lieut (s.g.), 1942–46. Asst to Pres., The Mead Corp., 1946–47; admitted to New York Bar, 1947; Associate and Partner of Simpson Thacher & Bartlett, New York, 1947–60, Partner, 1956–60, 1967–77 and 1980–98. Special Counsel, Preparedness Investigation Sub-cttee of Senate Armed Services Cttee, 1957–60; Consulting Counsel, Special Cttee on Space and Astronautics, US Senate, 1958; Gen. Counsel, Dept of Defense, 1961–62; Sec. of the Army, 1962–64; Dep. Sec. of Defense, 1964–67; Special Rep. of the President: in Civil Disturbances in Detroit, July-Aug. 1967 and in Washington, DC, April 1968; in Cyprus, Nov.-Dec. 1967; in Korea, Feb. 1968; one of two US Negotiators, Paris Peace Conf. on Vietnam, May 1968–Feb. 1969; Personal Envoy of UN Secretary-General: in Yugoslavia crisis, 1991–93; to Nagorno-Karabakh, 1992; to South Africa, 1992; Mem., Commn to Investigate Alleged Police Corruption in NYC, 1970–72. Mem., Bd of Govs, Federal Reserve Bank of NY (Chm., 1989–91). Pres., Assoc. of Bar of City of New York, 1974–76. Mem. Bd of Trustees: Rockefeller Foundn, 1970–77, 1980–82 (Chm., 1975–77); Yale Univ., 1968–78, 1980–87; Amer. Ditchley Foundn, 1980– (Chm., 1981–); Mayo Foundn, 1980–90. Hon. degrees: Marshall, 1963; Trinity Coll., 1966; Yale, 1968; West Virginia, Bowling Green, 1969; Salem Coll., 1970; Brandeis, 1971; Amherst, W Virginia Wesleyan, 1974; Harvard, Colgate, Gen. Theol Seminary, Williams Coll., 1981. Medal of Freedom (US), 1969. *Publications:* The Choice is Ours, 1983; Hard Choices, 1983. *Address:* Simpson Thacher & Bartlett, 425 Lexington Avenue, New York, NY 10017–3954, USA. *T:* (212) 4557190.
Died 12 Jan. 2002.

van der LOON, Prof. Piet; Professor of Chinese, University of Oxford, and Fellow of University College, Oxford, 1972–87, then Emeritus Professor and Emeritus Fellow; *b* 7 April 1920; *m* 1947, Minnie C. Snellen; two *d*. *Educ:* Univ. of Leiden (Litt. Drs); MA Cantab 1949. University of Cambridge: Asst Lectr, 1948; Lectr, 1949–72. *Publications:* Taoist Books in the Libraries of the Sung Period, 1984; The Classical Theatre and Art Song of South Fukien, 1992; articles in Asia Major, T'oung Pao, Jl Asiatique. *Recreations:* travel, gardening. *Address:* Midhurst, Old Boars Hill, Oxford OX1 5JQ. *T:* (01865) 739318.
Died 22 May 2002.

VANDORE, Peter Kerr; QC (Scot.) 1982; *b* 7 June 1943; *s* of James Vandore and Janet Kerr Fife; *m* 1970, Hilary Ann Davies; two *d*. *Educ:* Berwickshire High Sch., Duns; Edinburgh Univ. (MA Hons Hist.; LLB). Called to the Scottish Bar, 1968; Standing Counsel to Sec. of State for Scotland, for private legislation procedure, 1975–86.

Mem., Legal Aid Central Cttee, 1972–85. *Publications:* contribs to Juridical Rev. *Died 2 Nov. 2005.*

VANE, Sir John (Robert), Kt 1984; FRS 1974; Hon. President, William Harvey Research Institute, since 1997 (Director, 1986–90; Director-General, 1990–97); Professor of Pharmacology and of Medicine, New York Medical College, since 1986; *b* 29 March 1927; *s* of Maurice Vane and Frances Florence Vane (*née* Fisher); *m* 1948, Elizabeth Daphne Page; two *d*. *Educ:* Birmingham Univ. (BSc Chemistry, 1946); St Catherine's Coll., Oxford (BSc Pharmacology, 1949; DPhil 1953; DSc 1970; Hon. Fellow, 1983). Stothert Research Fellow of Royal Soc., 1951–53; Asst Prof. of Pharmacology, Yale Univ., 1953–55; Sen. Lectr in Pharmacology, Inst. of Basic Medical Sciences, RCS, 1955–61; Reader in Pharmacology, RCS, Univ. of London, 1961–65; Prof. of Experimental Pharmacology, RCS, Univ. of London, 1966–73; Gp Res. and Develt Dir, Wellcome Foundn, 1973–85. Visiting Professor: King's Coll., London, 1976; Charing Cross Hosp. Med. Sch., 1979; Harvard Univ., 1979; St Marianna Univ., Japan, 1993. British Pharmacological Soc.: Meetings Sec., 1967–70; Gen. Sec., 1970–73; For. Sec., 1979–85; Hon. Mem., 1985; a Vice Pres., Royal Soc., 1985–87. Founder FMedSci 1998. Mem., Royal Acad. of Medicine, Belgium, 1978 (Hon. Foreign Mem., 1983). Foreign Member: Royal Netherlands Acad. of Arts and Scis, 1979; Polish Acad. of Scis, 1980; For. Associate, US Nat. Acad. of Scis, 1983; For. Hon. Mem., Amer. Acad. of Arts and Scis, 1982; Hon. Member: Polish Pharmacological Soc., 1973; Japanese Pharm. Soc., 1990; Alpha Omega Alpha Honor Med. Soc., USA, 1990; Polish Acad. of Medicine, 1995; Hon. FACP 1978; Hon. FRCP 1983; Hon. FRCPath 1990; Hon. FRCS 1995; Hon. FFPM 1996; Hon. Fellow: Swedish Soc. of Medical Scis, 1982; Royal Acad. of Medicine, Spain, 1996; QMW, 1996. Hon. DM: Krakow, 1977; Vienna, 1993; Hon. Dr René Descartes Univ., Paris, 1978; Hon. DSc: Mount Sinai Med. Sch., NY, 1980; Aberdeen, 1983; NY Med. Coll., 1984; Birmingham, 1984; Camerino, 1984; Catholic Univ., Louvain, 1986; London, 1995; DUniv Surrey, 1984; Dr *hc* Buenos Aires, 1986; Hon. DPharm Milan, 1993; Hon. Dr Med. Surg. Florence, 1991. (Jtly) Albert Lasker Basic Med. Res. Award, 1977; Baly Medal, RCP, 1977; (jtly) Peter Debye Prize, Univ. of Maastricht, 1980; Feldberg Foundn Prize, 1980; Ciba Geigy Drew Award, Drew Univ., 1980; Dale Medal, Soc. for Endocrinol., 1981; Nobel Prize for Physiology or Medicine (jtly), 1982; Galen Medal, Apothecaries' Soc., 1983; Biol Council Medal, 1983; Louis Pasteur Foundn Prize, Calif, 1984; Royal Medal, Royal Soc., 1989; Special Award, Tsukuba City, Japan, 1990; Meml Prize, Fernandez-Cruz Foundn, 1991; Golden Medal Medicus Magnus, Polish Acad. of Medicine, 1995. Freeman: Scranton, USA, 1988; Taipei, Taiwan, 1989; New Orleans, USA, 1995. *Publications:* (ed jtly) Adrenergic Mechanisms, 1960; (ed jtly) Prostaglandin Synthetase Inhibitors, 1974; (ed jtly) Metabolic Functions of the Lung, Vol. 4, 1977; (ed jtly) Handbook of Experimental Pharmacology, 1978; (ed jtly) Prostacyclin, 1979; (ed jtly) Interactions between Platelets and Vessel Walls, 1981; (ed jtly) Endothelin, Vol. I, 1989, Vol. II, 1991, Vol. III, 1993, Vol. IV, 1995; (ed jtly) Aspirin and Other Salicylates, 1992; (ed jtly) Prostacyclin: new perspectives in basic research and novel therapeutic indications, 1992; (ed jtly) Therapeutic Applications of Prostaglandins, 1993; (ed jtly) The Endothelial Cell in Health and Disease, 1995; (ed jtly) Improved Non-steroid Anti-inflammatory Drugs, 1995; (ed jtly) New Targets in Inflammation: inhibitors of Cox-2 or adhesion molecules,

1996; (ed jtly) Eicosanoids, Aspirin and Asthma, 1998; (ed jtly) Selective Cox-2 Inhibitors: pharmacology, clinical effects and therapeutic potential, 1998; numerous papers in learned jls. *Recreations:* photography, travel, underwater swimming. *Address:* John Vane Science Centre, St Bartholomew's and The Royal London School of Medicine and Dentistry, Charterhouse Square, EC1M 6BQ. *Clubs:* Athenæum, Garrick.

Died 19 Nov. 2004.

VARNAM, Ivor; Deputy Director, Royal Armament Research and Development Establishment, 1974–82, retired; *b* 12 Aug. 1922; *s* of Walter Varnam and Gertrude Susan Varnam (*née* Vincent); *m* 1942, Doris May Thomas; two *s*. *Educ:* Alleyn's Coll., Dulwich; University Coll., Cardiff (BSc Wales 1941); Birkbeck Coll., London Univ. (BSc (Hons) 1952). Served War, RAF, 1940–46 (commnd 1944). Joined Tannoy Products, 1946; Atomic Energy Research Estabt, 1947; Siemens Bros., 1948; Royal Armament Research and Development Estabt, 1953–60 and 1962–82 (Defence Research Staff, Washington, USA, 1960–62), as: Supt Mil. ADP Br., 1964; Supt GW Br., 1967; Prin. Supt Systems Div., 1969; Head, Applied Physics Dept, 1972. *Publications:* official reports. *Recreations:* gardening, photography, bridge, music.

Died 9 May 2005.

VASCONCELLOS, Josefina Alys Hermes de, MBE 1985; sculptor; Founder, The Harriet Trust, Beached Trawler adapted for Nature-observation Base for Young Disabled; *b* 26 Oct. 1904; *d* of late H. H. de Vasconcellos, Brazilian Consul-General in England, and Freda Coleman; *m* 1930, Delmar Banner (*d* 1983), painter; one adopted *s* (and one adopted *s* decd). *Educ:* sculpture: London, Paris, Florence; Royal Academy Schools. Former FRBS. Exhibited RA, Leicester Galls; High Altar and Statue, Varengeville, Normandy, 1925; Bronze St Hubert, Nat. Gall. of Brazil, 1926; Music in Trees, in stone, Southampton Gall., 1933; Ducks, in marble, Glasgow Art Gall., 1946; exhibn with husband, of 46 sculptures in 20 materials at RWS Gall., 1947; Episcopal Crook, in perspex, for Bristol Cathedral, 1948; Refugees, in stone, Sheffield Art Gall., 1949; Last Chimera, Canongate Kirk, Edinburgh; 8ft Christ (in Portland Stone), Nat. War Meml to Battle of Britain, Aldershot, 1950; two works, Festival of Britain, Lambeth Palace, 1951; sculpture exhibn, with husband, RWS Galls, 1955; War Memorial, St Bees School, 1955; two figures, St Bees Priory, 1955; life-size Mary and Child and design group of 11 sculptures by 11 collaborators, for Nativity, St Paul's Cathedral, Christmas 1955; Mary and Child bought for St Paul's, 1956; life-size Resurrection for St Mary, Westfield, Workington, 1956–57; Madonna and Child, St James's, Piccadilly (subseq. in Burrswood, Dorothy Kerin Trust), 1957; Rising Christ in St Bartholomew the Great, Smithfield; Winter, carving in Perspex, Oldham Gallery, 1958; Nativity (for ruins of Coventry Cathedral), 1958; Flight into Egypt, for St Martin-in-the-Fields, 1958 (subseq. in Cartmel Priory); War Memorial, Reredos of carved oak, Rossall School Chapel, 1959; Nativity Set, life-size figures, St Martin-in-the-Fields, annually in Trafalgar Sq.; Winged Victory Crucifix, Clewer Church, 1964, and Canongate Kirk, Edinburgh; life-size Holy Family, Liverpool Cathedral and Gloucester Cathedral, 1965; life-size Virgin and Child, Blackburn Cathedral, 1974; Reunion, Bradford Univ., 1977, rededicated as Reconciliation when cast taken for two bronzes, 1995 (for Coventry Cathedral and Hiroshima Peace Park Hall, bronze casts also for grounds of Stormont, NI, and for site on remains of Berlin Wall, 1999); Return of the Carpenter, group of 10 life-size children, Samlesbury Hall, 1978; life-size Holy Family, for St Martin-in-the-Fields, 1983, 1992; life-size Holy Family, in cold cast stone, Norwich Cathedral, 1985; Revelation XXI, 'and God shall wipe the tears from their eyes', life-size two figure group, in plaster, for Lake Artists Exhibn, Grasmere, 1986; life-size Virgin and Child, Ambleside Parish Church, 1988; Reredos, Wordsworth Chapel,

1988; life-size Mary and Babe, Carlisle Cathedral, 1989; Sea Legend, in bronze, Hutton in the Forest, 1990; Childline to God, life-size figures of Christ, angels and 4 children, the Fratery, Carlisle Cathedral, 1990; life-size Holy Family, Manchester Cathedral, 1992 (exhibited Lake Artists Exhibn); Father Forgive, Rydal Hall, 1993, later at Brougham Hall; St Michael, life-size bronze, Cartmel Priory, 1995; The Weight of our Sins, St Martin-in-the-Fields, 1999–2000; Escape to Light, 2001, later at Haverigg; Young Martyr, Virgin and Infant and The True Vine, Cartmel Priory, 2003; The First Christian Stone Circle, Mungrisdale; Silver Medal of the Winged Cross, 2004; The Adoration of the Holy Innocents, Childrise, St Bees Priory; one man exhibn, A Christmas Exhibition of Sculpture, Painting and Poems, Manchester Cath., 1991–92; sculptures at Dallas, Tulsa, Chicago, USA; Portraits: bronze of Lord Denning, 1969; Bishop Fleming; Rev. Austen Williams; Mario Borelli; and Rev. Dr M. S. Israel. Documentary film Out of Nature (on her work), 1949; BBC programme, Viewpoint TV, 1968; film, Moments of Truth, Border TV, 1993. President: Guild of Lakeland Craftsmen, 1971–73; Cumbria Sculptors, 1999–; Brother, Art Workers Guild. Mem., Inst. of Patentees and Inventors; Hon. Member, Glider Pilots Regimental Assoc. Founder, Childrise, 2000. Hon. DLitt Bradford, 1977. Jean Masson Davidson Medal, Soc. of Portrait Sculptors, 2000. *Publications:* Woodcut illustrations for The Cup (Poems by F. Johnson), 1938; (contrib.) They Became Christians (ed Dewi Morgan), 1966; She was Loved: memories of Beatrix Potter, 2003 (2 awards for Book of the Year, Cumbria Tourist Bd, 2004); *relevant publications:* Sculptor: Josefina de Vasconcellos, by Linda Clifford, 2000; Josefina de Vasconcellos: her life and art, by Dr Margaret Lewis, 2002. *Address:* Top Floor Studio, 15 Rowan Court, Rothay Road, Ambleside, Cumbria LA22 0EE.

Died 20 July 2005.

VASEY, Rt Rev. Mgr Kevin, OBE 1990; QHC 1999; Principal Roman Catholic Chaplain and Vicar General (Army), Ministry of Defence, since 1997; *b* 8 April 1949; *s* of late Frederick Vasey and of Edna Mary Vasey (*née* Stoddart). *Educ:* St Mary's Primary Sch., Hartlepool; St Mary's Coll., Middlesbrough; Ushaw College. Ordained priest, 1973; Curate, St Mary's Cathedral, Newcastle upon Tyne and Dio. Tribunal Asst, 1973–76; Royal Army Chaplains' Department: TA commn, 1976–79; Regular Army commn, 1979; Dortmund Garrison, 1979–81; 3 Inf. Bde, 1981; 8 Inf. Bde, 1981–82; 12 Armd Bde, 1982–84; Dhekelia Garrison, 1984–85; RMA, Sandhurst, 1985–88; Sen. RC Chaplain, HQ NI, 1988–90; 1 (Br) Corps, 1990–93; HQ ARRC, 1993–94; HQ BAOR, 1994–95; HQ UK Support Comd (Germany), 1995; 4th Div., 1995–97. *Recreations:* performing arts, travel. *Address:* Ministry of Defence Chaplains (A), Trenchard Lines, Upavon, Pewsey, Wilts SN9 6BE. *T:* (01980) 615803. *Club:* Army and Navy.

Died 4 March 2002.

VAUGHAN, Rt Rev. Benjamin Noel Young; Bishop of Swansea and Brecon, 1976–87, Hon. Assistant Bishop, since 1988; *b* 25 Dec. 1917; *s* of late Alderman and Mrs J. O. Vaughan, Newport, Pembs; *m* 1st, 1945, Nesta Lewis (*d* 1980); 2nd, 1987, Magdalene Reynolds. *Educ:* St David's Coll., Lampeter (BA 1940; Hon. Fellow, 1990); St Edmund Hall, Oxford (BA 1942, MA 1946); Westcott House, Cambridge. Ordained deacon, 1943, priest, 1944; Curate of: Llannon, 1943–45; St David's, Carmarthen, 1945–48; Tutor, Codrington Coll., Barbados, 1948–52; Lecturer in Theology, St David's Coll., Lampeter, and Public Preacher, Diocese of St David's, 1952–55; Rector, Holy Trinity Cathedral, Port of Spain, and Dean of Trinidad, 1955–61; Bishop Suffragan of Mandeville, 1961–67; Bishop of British Honduras, 1967–71; Assistant Bishop and Dean of Bangor, 1971–76. Examining Chaplain to Bishop of Barbados, 1951–52, to Bishop of Trinidad, 1955–61; Commissary for Barbados, 1952–55. Formerly Chairman: Nat. Council for Educn in British Honduras; Govt Junior Secondary Sch.; Provincial

Commn on Theol Educn in WI; Provincial Cttee on Reunion of Churches, Christian Social Council of British Honduras; Ecumenical Commn of British Honduras; Agric. Commn of Churches of British Honduras; Pres., Belize Church Assoc., 1974–98. Chairman: Provincial Cttee on Missions, Church in Wales; Church and Society Dept, Council of Churches for Wales; Adv. Cttee on Church and Society, Church in Wales, 1977; Judge of Provincial Court, Church in Wales. Pres., Council of Churches for Wales, 1980–82. Member: Council, St David's Univ. Coll., Lampeter, 1976–89 (Sub-Visitor, 1987–); Council and Ct, Swansea Univ. Coll., 1976–89; Ct, Univ. of Wales, 1986–89. Chm. of Govs, Christ Coll., Brecon, 1976–87. Sub-Prelate, OStJ, 1977; Order of Druids, Gorsedd y Beirdd. *Publications:* Structures for Renewal, 1967; Wealth, Peace and Godliness, 1968; The Expectation of the Poor, 1972. *Address:* 4 Caswell Drive, Caswell, Swansea, West Glamorgan SA3 4RJ. *T:* (01792) 360646.   *Died 5 Aug. 2003.*

VAUGHAN, Sir Gerard (Folliott), Kt 1984; FRCP; Consultant, Guy's Hospital, 1958–79, then Emeritus; *b* Xinavane, Portuguese E Africa, 11 June 1923; *s* of late Leonard Vaughan, DSO, DFC, and Joan Vaughan (*née* Folliott); *m* 1955, Joyce Thurle (*née* Laver); one *s* one *d*. *Educ:* privately in E Africa; London Univ.; Guy's Hosp. MB, BS 1947; Academic DPM London 1952. MRCP 1949, FRCP 1966; FRCPsych 1972. Alderman: LCC, 1955–61; LCC Streatham, 1961–64; GLC Lambeth, 1966–70; Alderman, GLC, 1970–72; Chm., Strategic Planning Cttee GLC, 1968–71; Mem., SE Economic Planning Council, 1968–71. Contested (C) Poplar, 1955. MP (C) Reading, 1970–74, Reading South, 1974–83, Reading East, 1983–97. Minister for Health, DHSS, 1979–82; Minister of State (Consumer Affairs), Dept of Trade, 1982–83. Member: Select Cttee on Educn, 1983–93; Select Cttee on Sci. and Technol., 1993–97. Chm., Parly and Scientific Cttee, 1991–94. Parly Mem., MRC, 1973–76. Governor, UCL, 1959–68. Liveryman, Barbers' Co. (Master, 1992–93). Hon. FASI (FFAS 1978); Hon. FRCS 1993. *Publications:* various professional and gen. literary pubns. *Recreations:* painting, fishing. *Clubs:* Carlton, White's.   *Died 29 July 2003.*

VAUGHAN-JACKSON, Oliver James, VRD 1951; FRCS; Consulting Orthopaedic Surgeon to London Hospital, since 1971; *b* 6 July 1907; *e s* of Surgeon Captain P. Vaughan-Jackson, RN, Carramore, Ballina, County Mayo; *m* 1939, Joan Madeline (*d* 1996), *er d* of E. A. Bowring, CBE, St Johns, Newfoundland; two *s*. *Educ:* Berkhamsted School; Balliol Coll., Oxford; The London Hospital. Kitchener Scholar; BA, BM, BCh Oxon, 1932. MRCS, LRCP, 1932; FRCS 1936. Surgical Registrar, The London Hosp. Surgeon Lieut-Comdr RNVR, Retd, Surgical specialist, Roy. Naval Hosp., Sydney, Australia. Sen. Registrar (Orthopædic), The London Hosp.; Orthopaedic Surgeon to: The London Hosp., 1946–71; St Bartholomew's Hosp., Rochester, 1947–70; Medway Hosp., 1970–71; Claybury Mental Hosp., 1946–64; Halliwick Cripples Sch., 1946–71; Cons. In Orthopaedics to Royal Navy, 1956–71; Vis. Prof. of Orthopaedics, Memorial Univ. of Newfoundland, 1971–73; Senior Consultant in Orthopaedics at St John's Gen. Hosp., St Clare Mercy Hosp. and Janeway Child Health Centre, St John's, Newfoundland, 1971–73. Sen. Fellow, British Orthopædic Assoc.; Fellow: RSM (Pres., Section of Orthopædics, 1968–69); Med. Soc. London; Mem., Soc. Internat. de Chirurgie Orthopédique et de Traumatologie; Hon. Mem., British Soc. for Surgery of the Hand. Trustee, Meml Univ. of Newfoundland's Harlow Campus Trust, 1988–91. Former Mem., Editorial Board of Jl of Bone and Joint Surgery. Hon. DSc Memorial Univ. of Newfoundland, 1973. *Publications:* Sections on: Arthrodesis (Maingot's Techniques in British Surgery), 1950; Arthrodesis of the Hip, and Osteotomy of the Upper End of Femur (Operative Surgery, ed Rob and Smith), 1958; Surgery of the Hand; Orthopædic Surgery in Spastic

conditions; Peripheral Nerve Injuries (Textbook of British Surgery, ed Sir Henry Souttar and Prof. J. C. Goligher), 1959; The Rheumatoid Hand; Carpal Tunnel Compression of the Median Nerve (Clinical Surgery, ed Rob and Smith), 1966; Surgery in Arthritis of the Hand, in Textbook of Rheumatic Diseases, 1968; The Rheumatoid Hand, in Operative Surgery, 2nd edn, 1971; contribs to Jl of Bone and Joint Surgery, etc. *Recreations:* gardening, photography. *Address:* 25 Barton Farm, Cerne Abbas, Dorchester, Dorset DT2 7LF.

Died 7 Nov. 2003.

VAUX OF HARROWDEN, 10th Baron *cr* 1523; **John Hugh Philip Gilbey;** *b* 4 Aug. 1915; 2nd *s* of William Gordon Gilbey (*d* 1965) and Grace Mary Eleanor, 8th Baroness Vaux of Harrowden (*d* 1958); *S* brother, 1977; *m* 1939, Maureen Pamela (*d* 1999), *e d* of Hugh Gilbey; three *s* one *d*. *Educ:* Ampleforth College; Christ Church, Oxford (BA 1937). Formerly Major, Duke of Wellington's Regt; served War of 1939–45. *Heir: s* Hon. Anthony William Gilbey [*b* 25 May 1940; *m* 1964, Beverley Anne, *o d* of Charles Alexander Walton; two *s* two *d*]. *Address:* Cholmondeley Cottage, 2 Cholmondeley Walk, Richmond, Surrey TW9 1NS.   *Died 31 Aug. 2002.*

VENABLES, Richard William Ogilvie; Member of Council and Board, Direct Mail Services Standards Board, 1983–95; *b* 23 Feb. 1928; *s* of late Canon and Mrs E. M. Venables; *m* 1952, Ann Richards; three *s* two *d*. *Educ:* Marlborough Coll.; Christ Church, Oxford (BA, MA). Joined Mather and Crowther Ltd, as trainee, 1952; Account Group Director, 1965; Board Member, 1966; Mem. Executive Cttee, 1972; Managing Director, 1974; joined Board of Ogilvy and Mather International, 1975; Chm., Ogilvy Benson and Mather Ltd, 1978–81; retired early, 1981, to pursue new career in the making of violins, violas, lutes, harpsichords. Chm., Apple and Pear Develt Council, 1980–83. *Recreations:* fly fishing, hill walking, cabinet making, golf. *Address:* First Field, Combe Hay, Bath BA2 8RD. *T:* (01225) 833694.

Died 4 April 2005.

VERCO, Sir Walter (John George), KCVO 1981 (CVO 1970; MVO 1952); Secretary of the Order of the Garter, 1974–88; Secretary to the Earl Marshal, 1961–96; Surrey Herald of Arms Extraordinary, since 1980; *b* 18 Jan. 1907; *s* of John Walter Verco, RN (killed in action, 1940); *m* 1929, Ada Rose (*d* 1989), *d* of late Bertram Leonard Bennett, Lymington, Hants; one *s* one *d*. Served War, 1940–45, with RAFVR, Flight Lt. Secretary to Garter King of Arms, 1949–60; Rouge Croix Pursuivant of Arms, 1954–60; Chester Herald, 1960–71; Norroy and Ulster King of Arms, 1971–80. Hon. Genealogist to Royal Victorian Order, 1968–88; Inspector, RAF Badges, 1970–96, RAAF Badges, 1971–96; Adviser on Naval Heraldry, 1970–96. OStJ 1954. *Address:* College of Arms, Queen Victoria Street, EC4V 4BT; Pettswood, Five Acres, Funtington, West Sussex PO18 9LX.

Died 10 March 2001.

VEREKER, Peter William Medlicott; HM Diplomatic Service, retired; Ambassador and UK Permanent Representative to OECD, Paris, 1995–99; *b* 13 Oct. 1939; *s* of late Comdr Charles William Medlicott Vereker and Marjorie Hughes Whatley; *m* 1967, Susan Elizabeth, *d* of Maj.-Gen. A. J. Dyball, CBE, MC; three *s*. *Educ:* Elstree Sch.; Marlborough Coll.; Trinity Coll., Cambridge (MA); Harvard Univ. (Henry Fellow, 1962). CU Air Sqdn (RAFVR), 1958–61. Assistant d'Anglais, Paris, 1963; joined FO, 1963; Bangkok, 1964; Chiang Mai, 1967; FCO, 1968; Canberra, 1971; Head of Chancery, Athens, 1975; Asst Head, W European Dept, FCO, 1978; RCDS, 1982; Counsellor and Consul-Gen., Bangkok, 1983; Dep. Perm. Rep., UK Mission at Geneva, 1987; Head, Arms Control and Disarmament Dept, FCO, 1991; Sen. Civilian Dir, RCDS, 1994; Chm., Directing Staff, RCDS, 1995. *Recreations:* writing, tennis, golf, ski-ing, sailing.

Address: c/o National Westminster Bank, 208 Piccadilly, W1A 2DG. *Died 12 Sept. 2001.*

VEREY, Rosemary Isabel Baird, OBE 1996; garden designer; author, and broadcaster; *b* 21 Dec. 1918; *d* of late Lt Col Prescott Sandilands, DSO and Gladys Baird Sandilands (*née* Murton); *m* 1939, David Cecil Wynter Verey (*d* 1984); two *s* two *d. Educ:* Eversley Sch.; Folkestone; University Coll. London. Creator (with David Verey), Barnsley House Garden, Glos, 1950 (Christie's/ HHA Garden of the Year Award, 1988); lectr on gardening subjects in USA, Australia, England, Ireland. Member: Royal Horticultural Soc., 1960; Gardening History Soc., 1966. Hon. DHL South Carolina, 1994. Lifetime Achievement Award, Garden Writers Guild, 1995; VMH 1999. *Publications:* The Englishwoman's Garden, 1980; The Scented Garden, 1981; The Englishman's Garden, 1982; The American Woman's Garden, 1983; Classic Garden Design, 1984; The New Englishwoman's Garden, 1987; The Garden in Winter, 1988; The Flower Arranger's Garden, 1989; The American Man's Garden, 1990; Good Planting, 1990; The Garden Gate, 1991; A Countrywoman's Notes, 1991; A Gardener's Book of Days, 1992; Rosemary Verey's Garden Plans, 1993; Secret Garden, 1994; Rosemary Verey's Making of a Garden, 1995; The English Country Garden, 1996. *Recreation:* travelling. *Address:* The Close, Barnsley, Cirencester, Glos GL7 5EE. *T:* (01285) 740281. *Died 31 May 2001.*

VERMEULE, Prof. Emily Dickinson Townsend, FSA, Zemurray-Stone-Radcliffe Professor, Harvard University, 1970–94, then Emerita; Fellow for Research, Museum of Fine Arts, Boston, 1963, then Emerita; *b* 11 Aug. 1928; *d* of Clinton Blake Townsend and Eleanor Mary Meneely; *m* 1957, Cornelius Clarkson Vermeule III; one *s* one *d. Educ:* The Brearley Sch.; Bryn Mawr Coll. (BA, PhD); Radcliffe Coll. (MA). FSA 1975. Instructor in Greek: Bryn Mawr Coll., 1956–57; Wellesley Coll., 1957–58; Asst Prof. of Classics, 1958–61, Associate Prof. of Classics, 1961–64, Boston Univ.; Prof. of Greek and Fine Arts, Wellesley Coll., 1965–70. James Loeb Vis. Prof. of Classical Philology, Harvard Univ., 1969; Sather Prof. of Classical Literature, Univ. of California, Berkeley, 1975; Geddes-Harrower Prof. of Greek Art and Archaeology, Univ. of Aberdeen, 1980–81; Bernhard Vis. Prof., Williams Coll., 1986. Corresp. Member: German Archaeological Inst., 1964; British Academy, 1982. Member: Archaeological Inst. of America, 1950; Soc. for Preservation of Hellenic Studies, 1954; Amer. Philosophical Soc., 1971; Amer. Acad. of Arts and Scis, 1970; Bd of Scholars, Library of Congress, 1982–87; Smithsonian Council, 1983–90. National Endowment for the Humanities Jefferson Lectr, 1981. Hon. degrees: DLitt: Douglass Coll., Rutgers, 1968; Smith Coll., 1971; Wheaton Coll., 1973; Tufts, 1980; Pittsburgh, 1983; Bates Coll., 1983; DFA, Massachusetts at Amherst, 1970; LLD: Regis Coll., 1970; LHD: Trinity Coll., Hartford, Conn, 1974; Emmanuel Coll., Boston, 1980; Princeton, 1989; Bard Coll., 1994; Harvard, 1997. Gold Medal, Radcliffe Coll., 1968; Charles Goodwin Award of Merit, American Philological Assoc., 1980. *Publications:* Euripides' Electra, 1959; Greece in the Bronze Age, 1964, 7th edn 1980; The Trojan War in Greek Art, 1964; Götterkult, Archaeologia Homerica V, 1974; The Mound of Darkness, 1974; The Art of the Shaft Graves, 1975; Death in Early Greek Art and Poetry, 1979; (with V. Karageorghis) Mycenaean Pictorial Vase-Painting, 1982; (jtly) Toumba tou Skourou, A Bronze Age Potters' Quarter on Morphou Bay in Cyprus, 1990; contribs to Jl of Hellenic Studies, American Jl of Archaeology, Jahrbuch des d.Arch. Insts, Classical Philology, etc. *Recreations:* dogs, gardening. *Address:* 47 Coolidge Hill Road, Cambridge, MA 02138, USA. *T:* (617) 8641879. *Died 6 Feb. 2001.*

VERNEY, Sir Ralph (Bruce), 5th Bt *cr* 1818, of Claydon House, Buckinghamshire; KBE 1974; JP; landowner; Vice-Lord-Lieutenant (formerly Vice-Lieutenant) of Buckinghamshire, 1965–84; *b* 18 Jan. 1915; *e s* of Sir Harry Calvert Williams Verney, 4th Bt, DSO, and Lady Rachel Bruce (*d* 1964), *d* of 9th Earl of Elgin; *S* father, 1974; *m* 1948, Mary Vestey; one *s* three *d. Educ:* Canford; Balliol Coll., Oxford. 2nd Lieut Bucks Yeomanry, 1940; Major, Berks Yeomanry, 1945 and Bucks Yeomanry, 1946. Pres., Country Landowners' Assoc., 1961–63; Vice-President for Great Britain, Confédération Européenne de l'Agriculture, 1965–71, Counsellor, 1971; Chairman, Forestry Commn Cttee for England, 1967–80; Member: Forestry Commn, 1968–80; Milton Keynes New Town Corporation, 1967–74; BBC Adv. Cttee on Agriculture, 1970–78; Royal Commn on Environmental Pollution, 1973–79; Chm., Nature Conservancy Council, 1980–83 (Mem., 1966–71); Chm., Sec. of State for the Environment's Adv. Cttee on Aggregates for Construction Industry, 1972–77. Trustee: Radcliffe Trust; Chequers Trust; Sch. of Water Sciences, Cranfield, 1982–87. Member, Council: Buckingham Univ., 1983–87; Royal Soc. of Arts, 1983–87 (FRSA 1972). Buckinghamshire County Council: Member, 1951; Chairman, Finance Cttee, 1957; Planning Cttee, 1967; CA 1961. JP Bucks, 1954; High Sheriff of Buckinghamshire, 1957–58; DL Bucks, 1960; High Steward of Buckingham, 1966. Prime Warden, Worshipful Co. of Dyers, 1969–70. Hon. Fellow: RIBA, 1977; Green Coll., Oxford, 1980. DUniv Buckingham, 1991. Chevalier de Tastevin, Clos Vougeot, 1978. *Recreations:* trees, wine. *Heir: s* Edmund Ralph Verney [*b* 28 June 1950; *m* 1982, Daphne Fausset-Farquhar; one *s* one *d*]. *Address:* Ballams, Middle Claydon, Buckingham MK18 2ET. *T:* (01296) 730297; Plas Rhôscolyn, Holyhead LL65 2NZ. *T:* (01407) 860288. *Club:* Cavalry and Guards. *Died 17 Aug. 2001.*

VESTEY, Sir Derek; *see* Vestey, Sir J. D.

VESTEY, Sir (John) Derek, 2nd Bt *cr* 1921; *b* 4 June 1914; *s* of John Joseph Vestey (*d* 1932) and Dorothy Mary (*d* 1918), *d* of John Henry Beaver, Gawthorpe Hall, Bingley, Yorkshire; *g s* of Sir Edmund Vestey, 1st Bt; *S* grandfather, 1953; *m* 1938, Phyllis Irene, *o d* of H. Brewer, Banstead, Surrey; one *s* one *d. Educ:* Leys Sch., Cambridge. Served War of 1939–45: Flt-Lieut, RAFVR, 1940–45. *Heir: s* Paul Edmund Vestey [*b* 15 Feb. 1944; *m* 1971, Victoria Anne Scudamore, *d* of John Salter, Tiverton, Devon; three *d. Educ:* Radley]. *Address:* Park Penthouse, 355 Kings Road, Chelsea, SW3 5ES. *T:* (020) 7352 5940. *Clubs:* Royal Over-Seas League, MCC. *Died 29 June 2005.*

VIAL, Sir Kenneth Harold, Kt 1978; CBE 1969; chartered accountant; *b* 11 Aug. 1912; *s* of G. O. Vial, Melbourne; *m* 1937, Adele, *d* of R. G. R. Ball; one *s* two *d. Educ:* Scotch Coll., Melbourne. Served RAAF, 1941–46 (Flight Lieut). Partner, Arthur Andersen & Co. (formerly Fuller King & Co.), 1946–69; Chairman: Yarra Falls Ltd, 1969–74; Rocke Tompsitt & Co. Ltd, 1975–79; Director: Michaelis Bayley Ltd, 1969–81 (Chm., 1975–81); Mono Pumps (Aust.) Pty Ltd, 1969–81; F. H. Faulding & Co. Ltd, 1978–84; Hortico Ltd, 1981–84 (Chm., 1981–84). Member: Aust. Nat. Airlines Commn, 1956–79 (Chm., 1975–79); Aviation Industry Adv. Council, 1978–79; Council, Aust. Services Canteens Organisation, 1959–76 (Chm., Bd of Management, 1971–76); Council, La Trobe Univ., 1966–74 (Dep. Chancellor, 1970–72); Melbourne Underground Rail Loop Authority, 1971–81. *Address:* White Haven, 15 Murray Street, Newcomb, Vic 3219, Australia. *Club:* Naval and Military (Melbourne). *Died 29 Jan. 2001.*

VIEIRA DE MELLO, Dr Sergio; United Nations High Commissioner for Human Rights, since 2002; United Nations Special Representative to Iraq, 2003; *b* 15 March 1948; *s* of Arnaldo and Gilda Vieira De Mello; two *s. Educ:* Univ. of Paris I (Panthéon-Sorbonne) (Licence et Maîtrise d'Enseignement en Philosophie; Dr d'État ès Lettres et Sciences Humaines 1985). United Nations High Commission for Refugees: Field Officer, Special Op. in E

Pakistan/Bangladesh, 1971–72; Programme Officer: S Sudan Op., 1972–73; and Asst Rep. (N), Special Op. in Cyprus, 1974–75; Dep. Rep. and Rep. *ai*, Mozambique, 1975–77; Regl Rep. for Northern Latin America, Peru, 1978–80; Sen. Pol Advr, UN Interim Force in Lebanon, 1981–83; Dep. Chief of Personnel, Geneva, 1983–85; Chef de Cabinet to High Comr for Refugees, 1986–87; Director: for Asia and Oceania, 1988–90; for Ext. Relns, 1990–92; Special Envoy to Cambodia, 1992–93; Pol Dir, Bosnia, and Hd, Civil Affairs, UN Protection Force, Former Yugoslavia, 1993–94; Dir, Policy and Ops, 1995; Asst High Comr for Refugees, 1996–97; Under-Sec.-Gen. for Humanitarian Affairs and Emergency Relief Co-ordinator, UN, 1998–99; Special Representative of UN Secretary-General: Kosovo, June–July 1999; and Transitional Administrator, E Timor, 1999–2002. *Recreations:* jogging, travel, reading, music. *Address:* United Nations High Commission for Human Rights, Palais Wilson, 1211 Geneva 10, Switzerland. *T:* (22) 9179239, *Fax:* (22) 9179012; *e-mail:* de_mello.ohchr@unoy.ch.
Died 19 Aug. 2003.

VINCENT, Prof. John Joseph, CText, FTI; Professor of Textile Technology, University of Manchester Institute of Science and Technology, 1957–74, then Emeritus; *b* 29 June 1907; 2nd *s* of J. H. Vincent, MA, DSc; *m* 1935, M. Monica Watson, MSc, PhD (*d* 1992), Sheffield; one *s* one *d. Educ:* County Grammar Sch., Harrow; University Coll., London (MSc); MSc Tech Manchester. Mathematics Dept, University Coll., London, 1927–29; Shirley Inst., Manchester, 1929–42 and 1945–57; Ministry of Aircraft Production, 1942–45. Hon. Life Mem., Textile Institute, 1976 (Mem. Council, 1959–74; Vice-Pres., 1971–74); Pres., British Assoc. of Managers of Textile Works, 1963–64; Mem., Cotton and Allied Textiles Industry Training Bd, 1966–74. Textile Inst. Medal, 1968; Leverhulme Emeritus Fellowship, 1976. *Publications:* Shuttleless Looms, 1980; papers on textile technology. *Recreations:* gardening, reading, listening to music. *Address:* The White House, Perranarworthal, Truro, Cornwall TR3 7QE. *T:* (01872) 863504. *Died 24 April 2001.*

VINE, Col (Roland) Stephen, FRCPath, FZS; Chief Inspector, Cruelty to Animals Act (1876), Home Office, 1962–75; *b* 26 Dec. 1910; *s* of late Joseph Soutter Vine and of Josephine Vine (*née* Moylan); *m* 1935, Flora Betty, *d* of Charles Strutton Brookes, MBE, Dovercourt; three *d. Educ:* Southend-on-Sea High Sch.; Guy's Hosp. BSc; MRCS, LRCP. FRCPath; FZS(Scientific). Royal Army Medical Corps, 1934–60 (incl. War of 1939–45); Home Office, 1960–75. Mem. Council, Res. Defence Soc., 1977–85. *Publications:* chapter in: Biomedical Technology in Hospital Diagnosis, 1972; Animals in Scientific Research, 1983; articles in RAMC Jl. *Recreations:* gardening, bowling. *Address:* Shola, Fielden Road, Crowborough, Sussex TN6 1TR. *T:* (01892) 661381. *Club:* Civil Service. *Died 4 Feb. 2003.*

VINE, Stephen; *see* Vine, R. S.

VINES, Eric Victor, CMG 1984; OBE 1971; HM Diplomatic Service, retired; *b* 28 May 1929; *s* of late Henry E. Vines; *m* 1953, Ellen-Grethe Ella Küppers; one *s. Educ:* St Dunstan's Coll., London; St Catharine's Coll., Cambridge (MA). Army service, 1947–49. Joined Commonwealth Relations Office, 1952; Colombo, 1954–55; 1st Sec., Singapore, 1958–61; Canberra, 1961–65; Diplomatic Service Administration Office, 1965–68; 1st Sec., Information, Mexico City, 1968–70; Counsellor, Exec. Sec.-Gen., SEATO Conf., London, 1971; Head, Cultural Exchange Dept, FCO, 1971–74; Counsellor (Commercial), Tel Aviv, 1974–77, Stockholm, 1977–80; Consul-Gen., Barcelona, 1980–83; Ambassador: to Mozambique, 1984–85; to Uruguay, 1986–89; Staff Assessor, FCO, 1991–94. Chm., British–Uruguayan Soc., 1995–; Vice-Chm., Britain–Mozambique Soc., 1999–2000. Trustee: Centre for S African Studies, York Univ., 1989–94; Gemini

Ethiopian Trust, 1990–99. *Recreations:* opera, archaeology. *Address:* 80 Farquhar Road, SE19 1LT. *Club:* Royal Commonwealth Society. *Died 17 Nov. 2001.*

VINEY, Elliott (Merriam), DSO 1945; MBE 1946; TD; DL; FSA; Director: British Printing Corporation Ltd, 1964–75; Hazell, Watson & Viney Ltd, 1947–78; *b* 21 Aug. 1913; *s* of late Col Oscar Viney, TD, DL, and Edith Merriam; *m* 1950, Rosamund Ann Pelly; two *d. Educ:* Oundle; University Coll., Oxford. Bucks Bn, Oxford and Bucks Light Infantry (TA), 1932–46. Governor and Trustee, Museum of London, 1972–88. Pres., British Fedn of Master Printers, 1972–73. Master, Grocers' Company, 1970–71. County Dir, Bucks St John Amb. Assoc., 1953–55; Trustee, Bucks Historic Churches Trust, 1957; Pres., Bucks Archaeol. Soc., 1979–98 (Hon. Sec., 1954–79); Pres., CPRE (Bucks), 1990–93 (Chm., 1976–90); Chm., Bucks Record Soc., 1986–99. JP Bucks DL 1952, High Sheriff, 1964, Buckinghamshire. Editor: Oxford Mountaineering, 1935; Climbers' Club Jl, 1936–39; (jt) Records of Bucks, 1947–74. *Publications:* The Sheriffs of Buckinghamshire, 1965; (jtly) Old Aylesbury, 1976. *Recreations:* conservation, music. *Address:* Cross Farmhouse, Quainton, Aylesbury, Bucks HP22 4AR. *Clubs:* Alpine; County Hall (Aylesbury). *Died 9 Aug. 2002.*

VINTER, (Frederick Robert) Peter, CB 1965; *b* 27 March 1914; *e s* of P. J. Vinter (Headmaster, Archbishop Holgate's Grammar Sch., York, 1915–37) and Harriet Mary (*née* Cammack); *m* 1938, Margaret (*d* 1998), *d* of S. I. Rake, Pembroke; two *s. Educ:* Haileybury Coll.; King's Coll., Cambridge (MA). Min. of Economic Warfare, 1939; Cabinet Office, 1943; HM Treasury, 1945–69, Third Sec., 1965–69; Dep. Sec., Min. of Technology and DTI, 1969–73. Overseas Adviser to CEGB, 1973–79; Dir (non-Exec.), Vickers Ltd, 1974–80. Nuffield Travelling Fellowship (in India), 1950–51. *Died 8 March 2002.*

VINTER, Peter; *see* Vinter, F. R. P.

VIVIAN, 6th Baron *cr* 1841; **Nicholas Crespigny Laurence Vivian;** Bt 1828; *b* 11 Dec. 1935; *s* of 5th Baron Vivian and Victoria (*d* 1985), *er d* of late Captain H. G. L. Oliphant, DSO, MVO; *S* father, 1991; *m* 1st, 1960, Catherine Joyce (marr. diss. 1972), *y d* of late James Kenneth Hope, CBE; one *s* one *d*; 2nd, 1972, Carol, *e d* of F. Alan Martineau, MBE; two *d. Educ:* Eton; Madrid Univ. CO 16th/5th The Queen's Royal Lancers, 1976–79; Col, MoD, 1980–84; Dep. Comdr Land Forces and Chief of Staff, Cyprus, 1984–87; Brig., 1987; Comdr, British Communication Zone (Antwerp), 1987–90. Conservative; Chm., H of L Defence Gp, 1999–2001; Mem., Statutory Instruments Cttee, 1997–; elected Mem., H of L, 1999; Cons. defence spokesman, 2001–; an Opposition Whip, 2001–. Member: IPU; CPA; Dep. Chm., Assoc. of Cons. Peers, 1998–. Comr, Royal Hosp. Chelsea, 1994–2000; Special Trustee, Chelsea and Westminster Hosp., 1996–. Hon. Col, 306 Field Hosp. RAMC(V), 1995–2001. *Recreation:* travel. *Heir: s* Hon. Charles Crespigny Hussey Vivian, *b* 20 Dec. 1966. *Address:* House of Lords, SW1A 0PW. *Clubs:* White's, Cavalry and Guards. *Died 28 Feb. 2004.*

VOGELPOEL, Pauline, (Mrs R. D. Mann), MBE 1962; Vice-President, Contemporary Art Society, since 1984; *d* of late Pieter Vogelpoel and Yvonne Vogelpoel, Mozambique; *m* 1975, Richard David Mann, *s* of F. A. Mann, CBE, FBA. *Educ:* Herschel School, Cape Town; Univ. of Cape Town (BA). Joined Contemporary Art Soc., 1954, as Organising Sec.; Dir, 1976–82. Zurich Ed., Harpers & Queen Magazine, 1982–86. Member: Adv. Council, V&A Mus., 1977–82; Internat. Council, Tate Gall., 1997–. *Publications:* occasional journalism. *Recreations:* cooking, music, junkshops, pugs. *Address:* Hebelstrasse 15, 4056 Basle, Switzerland.
Died 22 Dec. 2002.

VOGT, Dr Marthe Louise, Dr med Berlin, Dr phil Berlin; PhD Cantab; FRS 1952; *b* 8 Sept. 1903; *d* of Oskar Vogt and Cécile Vogt (*née* Mugnier). *Educ:* Auguste Viktoria-Schule, Berlin; University of Berlin. Research Assistant, Department of Pharmacology, Berlin Univ., 1930; Research Assistant and head of chemical division, Kaiser Wilhelm Institut für Hirnforschung, Berlin, 1931–35; Rockefeller Travelling Fellow, 1935–36; Research Worker, Dept of Pharmacology, Cambridge Univ., 1935–40; Alfred Yarrow Research Fellow of Girton Coll., 1937–40; Member Staff of College of Pharmaceutical Society, London, 1941–46; Lecturer, later Reader, in Pharmacology, University of Edinburgh, 1947–60; Head of Pharmacology Unit, Agricultural Research Council Institute of Animal Physiology, 1960–68. Vis. Associate Prof. in Pharmacology, Columbia Univ., New York, 1949; Vis. Prof., Sydney 1965, Montreal 1968. Life Fellow, Girton Coll., Cambridge, 1970. For. Hon. Mem., Amer. Acad. of Arts and Scis, 1977. Hon. Fellow RSM 1980. Corresp. Mem., Deutsche Physiologische Gesellschaft, 1976; Hon. Member: Physiological Soc., 1974; British Pharmacological Soc., 1971; Hungarian Acad. of Scis, 1981; British Assoc. for Psychopharmacol., 1983. Hon. DSc: Edinburgh, 1974; Cambridge, 1983. Royal Medal, Royal Soc., 1981. *Publications:* papers in neurological, physiological and pharmacological journals. *Address:* Chateau La Jolla Terrace, 7544 La Jolla Boulevard, La Jolla, CA 92037, USA.				*Died 9 Sept. 2003.*

W

WADDELL, Sir James (Henderson), Kt 1974; CB 1960; Deputy Chairman, Police Complaints Board, 1977–81; *b* 5 Oct. 1914; *s* of D. M. Waddell and J. C. Fleming; *m* 1940, Dorothy Abbie Wright (decd); one *s* one *d*. *Educ:* George Heriot's Sch.; Edinburgh Univ. Assistance Board, 1936; Ministry of Information, 1940; Reconnaissance Corps, 1942; Ministry of Housing and Local Government, 1946; Under-Secretary, 1955; Under-Secretary, Cabinet Office, 1961–63; Dep.-Secretary, Min. of Housing and Local Government, 1963–66; Dep. Under-Sec., Home Office, 1966–75. *Address:* Long Meadow, East Lavant, Chichester, W Sussex PO18 0AH. *T:* (01243) 527129.
Died 3 Jan. 2004.

WADE, Prof. Sir (Henry) William (Rawson), Kt 1985; QC 1968; MA; LLD (Cantab); DCL (Oxon); FBA 1969; Master of Gonville and Caius College, Cambridge, 1976–88; Barrister-at-Law; *b* 16 Jan. 1918; *s* of late Colonel H. O. Wade and E. L. Rawson-Ackroyd; *m* 1st, 1943, Marie (*d* 1980), *d* of late G. E. Osland-Hill; two *s*; 2nd, 1982, Marjorie (*d* 2001), *d* of late Surgeon-Capt. H. Hope-Gill, RN, and *widow* of B. C. Browne. *Educ:* Shrewsbury Sch. (Governor, 1977–85); Gonville and Caius Coll., Cambridge. Henry Fellow, Harvard Univ., 1939; temp. officer, Treasury, 1940–46. Called to the Bar, Lincoln's Inn, 1946; Hon. Bencher, 1964. Fellow of Trinity Coll., Cambridge, 1946–61, Hon. Fellow, 1991; University Lecturer, 1947; Reader, 1959; Prof. of English Law, Oxford Univ., 1961–76; Fellow, St John's College, Oxford, 1961–76, Hon. Fellow, 1976; Rouse Ball Prof. of English Law, Cambridge Univ., 1978–82. Lectr, Council of Legal Education, 1957; British Council Lectr in Scandinavia, 1958, and Turkey, 1959; Cooley Lectr, Michigan Univ., 1961; Vithalbai Patel Lectr, New Delhi, 1971; Chettyar Lectr, Madras, 1974; Chitaley Lectr, New Delhi, 1982; Cassel Lectr, Stockholm, 1987; Nambyar Lectr, India, 1992. Vice-Pres., British Acad., 1981–83. Member: Council on Tribunals, 1958–71; Relationships Commn, Uganda, 1961; Royal Commn on Tribunals of Inquiry, 1966. Hon. LittD Cantab, 1999. *Publications:* The Law of Real Property, 1957 (with Rt Hon. Sir Robert Megarry), 6th edn 2000; Administrative Law, 1961, 8th edn (with Dr C. F. Forsyth) 2000; Towards Administrative Justice, 1963; (with Prof. B. Schwartz) Legal Control of Government, 1972; Constitutional Fundamentals (Hamlyn Lectures), 1980, rev. edn 1989; articles in legal journals; broadcast talks. *Recreations:* climbing, gardening. *Address:* 1A Ludlow Lane, Fulbourn, Cambridge CB1 5BL. *T:* (01223) 881745; Gonville and Caius College, Cambridge CB2 1TA. *T:* (01223) 332400, *Fax:* (01223) 332456. *Club:* Alpine. *Died 12 March 2004.*

WADE, Joseph Frederick; General Secretary, National Graphical Association, 1976–84; Visiting Professor, University of Strathclyde, 1985–88; *b* 18 Dec. 1919; *s* of James and Ellen Wade; *m* Joan Ann; two *s*. *Educ:* elementary sch., Blackburn, Lancs. Trained as compositor, The Blackburn Times, 1934–40; served UK and overseas, East Lancs Regt and RAOC, 1940–46; newspaper compositor, 1946–56. Full-time Trade Union official, Typographical Assoc., 1956; Nat. Officer, NGA, 1964; Asst Gen. Sec., NGA, 1968; Gen. Sec., NGA, 1976, NGA '82 (after amalgamation) 1982. Member: Exec. Cttee, Printing and Kindred Trades Fedn, 1971–74; Exec. Cttee, Internat. Graphical Fedn, 1976–85 (Vice-Pres.); TUC Printing Industries Cttee, 1976–84; TUC Gen. Council, 1983–84; Printing and Publishing Industry Training Bd, 1977–82; Printing Industries EDC, 1979–84. Mem., Blackburn County Borough Council, 1952–56. *Recreations:* walking, Scrabble, gardening. *Address:* 10 Spring Vale, Swarthmoor, Ulverston, Cumbria LA12 0XA. *Died 5 Oct. 2004.*

WADE, Air Chief Marshal Sir Ruthven (Lowry), KCB 1974 (CB 1970); DFC 1944; Chief of Personnel and Logistics, Ministry of Defence, 1976–78, retired 1978; Director, Acatos and Hutcheson, since 1979; *b* 15 July 1920. *Educ:* Cheltenham Coll.; RAF Coll., Cranwell. RAF, 1939; served War of 1939–45, UK and Mediterranean (DFC); psa, 1953; HQ 2nd Tactical Air Force, Germany; RAF Flying Coll.; Gp Captain 1960; Staff Officer, Air HQ, Malta; Comdr, Bomber Comd station, RAF Gaydon, 1962–65; Air Cdre, 1964; idc 1965; Air Exec. to Deputy for Nuclear Affairs, SHAPE, 1967–68; AOC No 1 (Bomber) Gp, Strike Comd, 1968–71; Air Vice-Marshal, 1968; Dep. Comdr, RAF Germany, 1971–72; ACAS (Ops), 1973; Vice Chief of Air Staff, 1973–76; Air Marshal, 1974; Air Chief Marshal, 1976. *Address:* White Gables, Westlington, Dinton, Aylesbury, Bucks HP17 8UR. *T:* (01296) 748884.
Died 24 Sept. 2001.

WADE, Sir William; *see* Wade, Sir H. W. R.

WAIDE, (Edward) Bevan, OBE 1988; Partner, Coopers & Lybrand, 1988–93; Chairman, Oxford Policy Management Ltd, since 1996; *b* 14 Sept. 1936; *s* of William Leathley Waide and Louisa Winifred Waide (*née* Evershed); *m* 1st, 1961, Pu-Chin (marr. diss. 1993); one *s* one *d*; 2nd, 1995, Urmila Kumari, Kathiwada. *Educ:* Farnham Grammar Sch.; Emmanuel Coll., Cambridge (BA 1959, MA 1978); Univ. of Calif, Berkeley (MA). Teaching Asst, Univ. of Calif, 1959–61; Sen. Economist, Asia, World Bank, 1962–69; Chief Advr, Min. of Economic Affairs and Devlt Planning, Govt of Tanzania, 1969–73; Dir, N Region Strategy Team, DoE, 1973–76; World Bank: Chief Economist, S Asia, 1976–79; Director: Devlt Policy, 1979–82; Country Policy Dept, 1982–84; New Delhi Office, 1984–88. Chief Advr, Privatisation, Tanzanian Govt, 1993–97; Advisor, Privatisation: Indonesian Govt, 1979–99; Bangladeshi Govt, 1999–; Indian Govt, 2001–. Mem., Commonwealth Devlt Corp., 1990–93. *Publications:* (jtly) India: an industrialising economy in transition, 1989; World Devlt Reports, World Bank; Government of Indonesia: privatisation masterplan, 1998; articles on devlt and regional planning issues; country reports. *Recreations:* tennis, car restoration. *Address:* Laburnum Cottage, The Butts, Napton-on-the-Hill, Southam, Warwicks CV47 8NW. *T:* (01926) 817024; *e-mail:* bevan@waide.net. *Clubs:* Reform; Vintage Sports Car. *Died 13 March 2003.*

WAINWRIGHT, Richard Scurrah; MP (L) Colne Valley, 1966–70 and Feb. 1974–1987, retired; *b* 11 April 1918; *o s* of late Henry Scurrah and Emily Wainwright; *m* 1948, Joyce Mary Hollis; one *s* two *d* (and one *s* decd). *Educ:* Shrewsbury Sch.; Clare Coll., Cambridge (Open Schol.; BA Hons (History), 1939). Friends Ambulance Unit, NW Europe, 1939–46. Partner, Peat Marwick Mitchell & Co., Chartered Accountants, retired. Pres., Leeds/Bradford Soc. of Chartered Accountants, 1965–66. Chairman: Liberal Party Research Dept, 1968–70; Liberal Party, 1970–72; Mem., Select Cttee on Treasury, 1979–87; Liberal spokesman on the economy, 1979–85, on employment, 1985–87. Dep. Chm., Wider Share Ownership Council, 1968–92. Pres., Yorks Fedn of Lib Dems, 1989–97. *Recreations:* gardening, swimming. *Address:* 8 Dunstarn Lane, Leeds LS16 8EL. *T:* (0113) 267 3938. *Died 16 Jan. 2003.*

WAKELING, Rt Rev. John Denis, MC 1945; Bishop of Southwell, 1970–85; *b* 12 Dec. 1918; *s* of Rev. John Lucas

Wakeling and Mary Louise (*née* Glover); *m* 1941, Josephine Margaret (*d* 2004), *d* of Dr Benjamin Charles Broomhall and Marion (*née* Aldwinckle); two *s* (and one *s* decd). *Educ:* Dean Close Sch., Cheltenham; St Catharine's Coll., Cambridge (MA 1944); Ridley Hall, Cambridge. Commnd Officer in Royal Marines, 1939–45 (Actg Maj.). Ordained deacon, 1947, priest, 1948; Asst Curate, Barwell, Leics, 1947; Chaplain of Clare Coll., Cambridge, and Chaplain to the Cambridge Pastorate, 1950–52; Vicar of Emmanuel, Plymouth, 1952–59; Prebendary of Exeter Cathedral, 1957, Prebendary Emeritus, 1959; Vicar of Barking, Essex, 1959–65; Archdeacon of West Ham, 1965–70. Entered House of Lords, June 1974. Chairman: Archbishops' Council on Evangelism, 1976–79; Lee Abbey Council, 1976–84. Hon. DD Nottingham, 1985. *Recreations:* formerly cricket and hockey (Cambridge Univ. Hockey Club, 1938, 1939, 1945, 1946, English Trials Caps, 1939, 1946–49). *Club:* Hawks (Cambridge).
Died 10 Oct. 2004.

WAKERLEY, Hon. Sir Richard (MacLennon), Kt 2003; **Hon. Mr Justice Wakerley;** a Judge of the High Court of Justice, Queen's Bench Division, since 2003; *b* 7 June 1942; *s* of late Charles William Wakerley and Gladys MacLennon Wakerley; *m* 1966, Marian Heather Dawson; two *s* two *d*. *Educ:* De Aston Sch., Market Rasen; Emmanuel Coll., Cambridge (MA). Called to the Bar, Gray's Inn, 1965, Bencher, 1991. Practised on Midland and Oxford Circuit, 1965–2001 (Dep. Leader, 1989–92, Leader, 1992–96); QC 1983; a Recorder, 1982–2001, Hon. Recorder of Birmingham, 2001–03; a Sen. Circuit Judge, 2001–03. *Recreations:* theatre, bridge, gardening. *Address:* Royal Courts of Justice, Strand, WC2A 2LL.
Died 24 July 2005.

WAKLEY, His Honour Bertram Joseph, MBE 1945; a Circuit Judge, 1973–92; *b* 7 July 1917; *s* of Major Bertram Joseph Wakley and Hon. Mrs Dorothy Wakley (*née* Hamilton); *m* 1953, Alice Margaret Lorimer (*d* 2000). *Educ:* Wellington Coll.; Christ Church, Oxford (BA 1939, MA 1943). Commnd S Lancs Regt, 1940; Captain 1941; Major 1943; served N Africa, Italy, Greece (despatches). Called to Bar, Gray's Inn, 1948. A Recorder of the Crown Court, 1972–73. Reader, Diocese of Southwark, 1977–96. *Publications:* History of the Wimbledon Cricket Club, 1954; Bradman the Great, 1959; Classic Centuries, 1964. *Recreations:* cricket, golf. *Address:* 4 The Watergardens, Warren Road, Kingston Hill, Surrey KT2 7LF. *T:* (020) 8546 7587. *Clubs:* Carlton, MCC, Roehampton.
Died 11 Sept. 2001.

WALDEN, Herbert Richard Charles, CBE 1986; part-time Member, Building Societies Commission, 1986–94; *b* 6 Oct. 1926; *s* of Reginald George Walden and Matilda Ethel Walden; *m* 1950, Margaret Walker (*d* 1995); two *d*. *Educ:* Westgate Sch., Warwick. FCIS; FCIB. War service, 1944–47, Royal Warwickshire Regt and Royal Leicestershire Regt, UK and Gold Coast (Captain). Asst Sec., Warwick Building Soc., 1955, Gen. Manager 1962; Gen. Manager, Rugby and Warwick Building Soc. (on merger), 1967; Gen. Manager, Heart of England Building Soc. (on merger), 1974, Dir and Gen. Manager, 1974–86. Mem. Bd, Housing Corp., 1985–88. Chm., Midland Assoc. of Building Socs, 1972–73, Vice-Pres., 1986; Vice President: CBSI, 1988–93; Building Societies Assoc., 1994– (Mem. Council, 1974–86, Dep. Chm. 1981–83, Chm., 1983–85). Mem., Warwick BC, 1955–63; Chm., S Warwickshire HMC, 1964–72; Mem., Warwick Schs Foundn, 1962–90 (Chm., 1986–90); Trustee, various Warwick charities; Founder Pres., Rotary Club of Warwick, 1965; Vice Pres., Warwickshire Scout Assoc., 1969– (Hon. Treas., 1958–68). Mem., Finance Cttee, Northgate Methodist Church, Warwick, 1965–2002. Chm., Warwicks Adv. Cttee, Tax Comrs, 1983–96 (Mem., 1969–96). *Recreation:* watching cricket. *Address:* Fieldgate House, 24 Hill Wootton Road, Leek Wootton, Warwick CV35 7QL. *T:* (01926) 854291. *Club:* Naval and Military.
Died 29 Oct. 2002.

WALDER, Ruth Christabel, (Mrs Wesierska), OBE 1956; National General Secretary, YWCA of Great Britain, 1949–67; *b* 15 Jan. 1906; *d* of Rev. Ernest Walder; *m* 1955, Maj.-Gen. George Wesierski (*d* 1967), formerly Judge Advocate General of the Polish Forces. *Educ:* Cheltenham Ladies' College. General Organiser, National Federation of Women's Institutes, 1934–40; Admiralty, 1940–41; Relief Department, Foreign Office, 1942–44; Secretary: Food Cttee of Council for Europe, UNRRA, 1944–47; UN Appeal for Children (in the UK), 1948. Lectr for the European Community, 1970–. Defence Medal, 1946. Polish Gold Cross of Merit, 1969. *Publication:* (as Ruth Walder Wesierska) They built a Jolly Good Mess (memoirs, in Europe 1939–45), 1987. *Address:* Westhope, Langton Herring, Weymouth, Dorset DT3 4HZ. *T:* (01305) 871233. *Clubs:* Naval and Military; Royal Dorset Yacht.
Died 14 Jan. 2002.

WALKER OF DONCASTER, Baron *cr* 1997 (Life Peer), of Audenshaw in the co. of Greater Manchester; **Harold Walker,** Kt 1992; PC 1979; DL; *b* 12 July 1927; *s* of Harold and Phyllis Walker; *m* 1st, 1956, Barbara Hague (*d* 1981); one *d*; 2nd, 1984, Mary Griffin. *Educ:* Manchester College of Technology. Served RN, 1946–48. MP (Lab) Doncaster, 1964–83, Doncaster Central, 1983–97. An Assistant Government Whip, 1967–68; Jt Parly Under-Sec. of State, Dept of Employment and Productivity, 1968–70; Opposition Front-Bench spokesman on Industrial Relations, 1970–74, on Employment, 1979–83; Parly Under-Sec. of State, Dept of Employment, 1974–76; Minister of State, Dept of Employment, 1976–79; Chm. of Ways and Means and Dep. Speaker, H of C, 1983–92. Chm., All Party Gardening and Horticulture Gp, 1997–. DL S Yorks, 1997. Freeman, Borough of Doncaster, 1999. Lifetime Achievement Award, Inst. of Occupational Safety and Health, 1999. *Recreations:* reading, gardening. *Address:* House of Lords, SW1A 0PW. *Clubs:* Westminster, Clay Lane, Doncaster Trades, RN, Catholic (all Doncaster); Wimbledon Village.
Died 11 Nov. 2003.

WALKER, Rev. Sir Alan (Edgar), Kt 1981; OBE 1955; Principal, Pacific College for Evangelism, 1989–95, Principal Emeritus, Alan Walker College of Evangelism, since 1995; *b* 4 June 1911; *s* of Rev. Alfred Edgar Walker, former Pres., NSW Methodist Conf., and Violet Louisa Walker; *m* 1938, Winifred Garrard Walker (*née* Channon); three *s* one *d*. *Educ:* Leigh Theol Coll., Sydney; Univ. of Sydney (BA, MA); Bethany Biblical Seminary, Chicago (Hon. DD 1954). Ordained, Sydney, 1934; Associate Dir, NSW Methodist Youth Dept, 1936–38; England and Europe, 1938–39; Minister, Cessnock, NSW, 1939–44; Supt, Waverley Methodist Mission, 1944–54; Dir, Australian Mission to the Nation, 1953–55; led Mission to America, 1956–57; Visiting Professor: of Evangelism, Boston Sch. of Theol., 1957; of Evangelism and Preaching, Claremont Sch. of Theol., USA, 1973; Supt, Central Methodist Mission, Sydney, 1958–78; Dir, World Evangelism, World Methodist Council, 1978–87. Deleg. to First Assembly of WCC, Amsterdam, 1948; Adviser to: Aust. Delegn at UN, 1949; Third Ass. of WCC, New Delhi, 1962; Fourth Ass., WCC, Uppsala, 1968; Missions to: Fiji, S Africa, S America, Singapore and Malaysia, Sri Lanka, 1962–75; Founder, Sydney Life Line Tel. Counselling Centre, 1963 (Pres., Life Line Internat., 1966–87); Sec., NSW Methodist Conf., 1970, Pres., 1971; lectures, various times, USA. Inst. de la Vie award, Paris, for services to humanity, 1978; (with Lady Walker) World Methodist Peace Award, 1986; Australian Nat. Living Treasure, 1998. Order of Jerusalem, 1999. *Publications: include:* There is Always God, 1938; Everybody's Calvary, 1943; Coal Town, 1944; Heritage Without End, 1953; The Whole Gospel for the Whole World, 1957; The Many Sided Cross of Jesus, 1962; How Jesus Helped People, 1964; A Ringing Call to Mission, 1966; The Life Line Story, 1967 (USA, As Close as the Telephone); Breakthrough, 1969; God, the Disturber, 1973 (USA); Jesus, the Liberator, 1973 (USA); The New Evangelism, 1974 (USA); Love in Action, 1977; Life Grows with

Christ, 1981; Life Ends in Christ, 1983; Standing Up To Preach, 1983; Your Life Can Be Changed, 1985; Life in the Holy Spirit, 1986; Try God, 1990; Herald of Hope, 1994; The Contrast Society of Jesus, 1997; *relevant publications*: Reach for the World: the Alan Walker story, by Harold Henderson, 1981; Conscience of the Nation, by Don Wright, 1997. *Recreations:* swimming, tennis. *Address:* Wesley Gardens, 2B Morgan Road, Belrose, NSW 2085, Australia. *Died 29 Jan. 2003.*

WALKER, Alexander; Film Critic, London Evening Standard, since 1960; *b* Portadown, NI, 22 March 1930; *s* of Alfred and Ethel Walker. *Educ:* Portadown Grammar Sch.; QUB (BA); Collège d'Europe, Bruges; Univ. of Michigan, Ann Arbor. Lectr in political philosophy and comparative govt, Univ. of Michigan, 1952–54; features ed., Birmingham Gazette, 1954–56; leader writer and film critic, Birmingham Post, 1956–59; columnist, Vogue magazine, 1974–86. Frequent broadcaster on the arts on radio and television; author: TV series, Moviemen; BBC Radio series, Film Star; author and co-producer of TV progs on History of Hollywood, Garbo and Chaplin. Member: British Screen Adv. Council (formerly Wilson Interim Action Cttee on the Film Industry), 1977–92; Bd of Govs, BFI, 1989–95. Critic of the Year, in annual British Press awards, 1970, 1974, 1998, commended, 1985; Award of Golden Eagle, Philippines, for services to internat. cinema, 1982. Chevalier de l'Ordre des Arts et des Lettres, 1981. *Publications:* The Celluloid Sacrifice: aspects of sex in the movies, 1966; Stardom: the Hollywood phenomenon, 1970; Stanley Kubrick Directs, 1971; Hollywood, England: the British film industry in the sixties, 1974; Rudolph Valentino, 1976; Double Takes: notes and afterthoughts on the movies 1956–1976, 1977; Superstars, 1978; The Shattered Silents: how the talkies came to stay, 1978; Garbo, 1980; Peter Sellers: the authorized biography, 1981; Joan Crawford, 1983; Dietrich, 1984; (ed) No Bells on Sunday: journals of Rachel Roberts, 1984; National Heroes: British cinema industry in the seventies and eighties, 1985; Bette Davis, 1986; trans., Benayoun, Woody Allen: beyond words, 1986; Vivien: the life of Vivien Leigh, 1987; It's Only a Movie, Ingrid: encounters on and off screen, 1988; Elizabeth: the life of Elizabeth Taylor, 1990; (jtly) Zinnemann: an autobiography, 1992; Fatal Charm: the life of Rex Harrison, 1992; Audrey: her real story, 1994; (contrib.) Screen Violence, 1996; Projections 8, 1998; Stanley Kubrick, Director, 1999; contrib. to many British and foreign pubns. *Recreations:* ski-ing, persecuting smokers. *Address:* 1 Marlborough, 38–40 Maida Vale, W9 1RW. *T:* (020) 7289 0985. *Died 15 July 2003.*

WALKER, Prof. Arthur Geoffrey, FRS 1955; Professor of Pure Mathematics, Liverpool University, 1952–74, then Emeritus; *b* 17 July 1909; 2nd *s* of late A. J. Walker, Watford, Herts; *m* 1939, Phyllis Ashcroft, *d* of late Sterry B. Freeman, CBE. *Educ:* Watford Grammar Sch.; Balliol Coll., Oxford (MA); PhD, DSc Edinburgh. FRSE. Lectr at Imperial Coll. of Science and Technology, 1935–36; at Liverpool Univ., 1936–47; Prof. of Mathematics in the Univ. of Sheffield, 1947–52. Mem. of Council, Royal Soc., 1962–63. Pres., London Mathematical Soc., 1963–65. Junior Berwick Prize of London Mathematical Soc., 1947; Keith Medal of Royal Society of Edinburgh, 1950. *Publication:* (with H. S. Ruse and T. J. Willmore) Harmonic Spaces, 1962. *Address:* Beechcroft, Roundabout Lane, West Chiltington, Pulborough, W Sussex RH20 2RL. *T:* (01798) 812412. *Died 31 March 2001.*

WALKER, Sir (Baldwin) Patrick, 4th Bt *cr* 1856; *b* 10 Sept. 1924; *s* of late Comdr Baldwin Charles Walker, *o s* of Sir Francis Walker, 3rd Bt and Mary, *d* of F. P. Barnett of Whalton, Northumberland; *S* grandfather, 1928; *m* 1948, Joy Yvonne (marr. diss. 1954); *m* 1954, Sandra Stewart; *m* 1966, Rosemary Ann, *d* of late Henry Hollingdrake; one *s* one *d*; *m* 1980, Vanessa Hilton. *Educ:* Gordonstoun. Served Royal Navy, Fleet Air Arm, 1943–58. Lieut, RN, retired. *Heir: s* Christopher Robert

Baldwin Walker, *b* 25 Oct. 1969. *Address:* 5 Voortrekker Road, Blanco 6531, South Africa. *Died 6 June 2005.*

WALKER, Sir (Charles) Michael, GCMG 1976 (KCMG 1963; CMG 1960); HM Diplomatic Service, retired; Chairman, Commonwealth Scholarship Commission in the UK, 1977–87; *b* 22 Nov. 1916; *s* of late Col C. W. G. Walker, CMG, DSO; *m* 1945, Enid Dorothy, *d* of late W. A. McAdam, CMG; one *s* one *d*. *Educ:* Charterhouse; New Coll., Oxford. Clerk of House of Lords, June 1939. Enlisted in Army, Oct. 1939, and served in RA until 1946 when released with rank of Lt-Col. Dominions Office, 1947; First Sec., British Embassy, Washington, 1949–51; Office of United Kingdom High Comr in Calcutta and New Delhi, 1952–55; Establishment Officer, Commonwealth Relations Office, 1955–58. Imperial Defence Coll., 1958; Asst Under-Sec. of State and Dir of Establishment and Organisation, CRO, 1959–62; High Commissioner: Ceylon, 1962–65 (concurrently Ambassador to Maldive Islands, July–Nov. 1965); Malaysia, 1966–71; Sec., ODA, FCO, 1971–73; High Comr, India, 1974–76. Chm., Festival of India Trust, 1980–83. Hon. DCL City, 1980. *Recreations:* fishing, gardening, golf. *Address:* Herongate House, West Chiltington Common, Pulborough, Sussex RH20 2NL. *T:* (01798) 813473. *Club:* Sloane. *Died 16 Dec. 2001.*

WALKER, Dr George Patrick Leonard, FRS 1975; G. A. Macdonald Professor of Volcanology, University of Hawaii, 1981–96, Professor Emeritus since 1999; *b* 2 March 1926; *s* of Leonard Richard Thomas Walker and Evelyn Frances Walker; *m* 1958, Hazel Rosemary (*née* Smith); one *s* one *d*. *Educ:* Wallace High Sch., Lisburn, NI; Queen's Univ., Belfast (BSc, MSc); Univ. of Leeds (PhD 1956); Univ. of London (DSc 1982). Research, Univ. of Leeds, 1948–51; Asst Lectr and Lectr, Imperial Coll., 1951–64; Reader in Geology, Imperial Coll., 1964–79; Captain J. Cook Res. Fellow, Royal Soc. of NZ, 1978–80. Visiting Professor: Bristol Univ.; Cheltenham & Gloucester Coll. of Higher Educn. Fellow: Geol Soc. of America, 1987; Amer. Geophysical Union, 1988. Awarded moiety of Lyell Fund of Geological Soc. of London, 1963, Lyell Medal, 1982; Wollaston Medal, 1995. Hon. Member: Vísindafjelag Íslendinga, (Iceland), 1968; Royal Soc. of NZ, 1987. Hon. DSc Iceland, 1988. McKay Hammer Award, Geol Soc. of NZ, 1982. Icelandic Order of the Falcon, Knight's Class, 1980. *Publications:* scientific papers on mineralogy, the geology of Iceland, and volcanology. *Recreation:* visiting volcanoes. *Address:* Department of Earth Sciences, Wills Memorial Building, Queen's Road, Bristol University, Bristol BS8 1RJ. *Died 17 Jan. 2005.*

WALKER, Sir Gervas (George), Kt 1979; JP; DL; Chairman and Leader, Avon County Council, 1973–81; *b* 12 Sept. 1920; *yr s* of late Harry James Walker and Susanna Mary Walker; *m* 1944, Jessie Eileen (*née* Maxwell); two *s*. *Educ:* Monmouth Sch. Bristol City Council: Councillor, 1956–74; Alderman, 1970–74; Leader of Council, 1966–72; Leader of Opposition Party, 1972–74; Chm., Planning and Transportation Cttee, 1960–63 and 1966–72; Chm., Bristol Avon River Authority, 1963–66. Member: SW Regional Economic Planning Council, 1972–79; Local Authorities' Conditions of Service Adv. Bd, 1974–81; Severn Barrage Cttee, 1978–81; British Rail (Western) Bd, 1979–85. Chm., Assoc. of County Councils, 1979–81 (Vice-Chm., 1978–79). Chairman, Bristol Conservative Assoc., 1975–79. JP Bristol, 1969; DL Avon, 1982. *Recreation:* fly-fishing. *Address:* Bulverton Well Farm, Sidmouth, Devon EX10 9DW. *T:* (01395) 516902. *Died 19 Aug. 2001.*

WALKER, Major Sir Hugh (Ronald), 4th Bt *cr* 1906; *b* 13 Dec. 1925; *s* of Major Sir Cecil Edward Walker, 3rd Bt, DSO, MC, and Violet (*née* McMaster); *S* father, 1964; *m* 1971, Norna, *er d* of Lt-Cdr R. D. Baird, RNR; two *s*. *Educ:* Wellington Coll., Berks. Joined Royal Artillery, 1943; commissioned Sept. 1945; 2 iC, RA Range,

Benbecula, Outer Hebrides, 1964–66; Commanding No 1 Army Information Team, in Aden and Hong Kong, 1966–68; Larkhill, 1969–73, retired. Mem., Assoc. of Supervisory and Executive Engineers. *Recreation:* horses. *Heir: s* Robert Cecil Walker, *b* 26 Sept. 1974. *Address:* Ballinamona, Hospital, Kilmallock, Co. Limerick, Ireland.
Died 10 Jan. 2004.

WALKER, Sir James Heron, 5th Bt *cr* 1868; *b* 7 April 1914; *s* of Major Sir Robert Walker, 4th Bt and Synolda, *y d* of late James Thursby-Pelham; *S* father, 1930; *m* 1st, 1939, Angela Margaret, *o d* of Victor Alexandre Beaufort; one *s* (one *d* decd); 2nd, 1972, Sharrone, *er d* of David Read; one *s*. *Educ:* Eton Coll.; Magdalene Coll., Cambridge. *Recreations:* long haired Dachshunds, music. *Heir: s* Victor Stewart Heron Walker [*b* 8 Oct. 1942; *m* 1st, 1969, Caroline Louise (marr. diss. 1982), *d* of late Lt-Col F. E. B. Wignall; two *s* one *d*; 2nd, 1982, Svea, *o d* of late Captain Ernst Hugo Gothard Knutson Borg and of Mary Hilary Borg]. *Address:* Oakhill, Port Soderick, Isle of Man.
Died 9 Jan. 2003.

WALKER, John Malcolm; Principal Assistant Director of Public Prosecutions (Grade 3), 1985–86, retired; *b* 25 Feb. 1930; *s* of James and Mary Walker; *m* 1955, Barbara Anne Fawcett (*d* 1989); two *d*. *Educ:* St Edward's Sch., Oxford; Leeds Univ. (LLB). Served Royal Artillery, 1948–50. Called to the Bar, Gray's Inn, 1955; joined Director of Public Prosecutions as Temp. Legal Asst, 1956; Legal Asst, 1958; Sen. Legal Asst, 1964; Asst Solicitor, 1974; Asst Director, 1977. *Recreations:* music, painting. *Address:* 10 Second Cross Road, Twickenham, Middx TW2 5RF.
Died 26 March 2001.

WALKER, Sir Michael; *see* Walker, Sir C. M.

WALKER, Sir Patrick; *see* Walker, Sir B. P.

WALKER, Robert; HM Diplomatic Service, retired; *b* 1 May 1924; *s* of Young and Gladys Walker, Luddendenfoot, Yorks; *m* 1949, Rita Thomas; one *s* one *d*. *Educ:* Sowerby Bridge Grammar Sch.; Peterhouse, Cambridge, 1942–43 and 1946–48 (BA Hons History, 1948; MA 1963). Commissioned RNVR 1944; served in minesweepers in home waters. Joined CRO, 1948; served Peshawar and Karachi, 1949–51; New Delhi, 1955–59; Sen. First Sec., Accra, 1962–64; Dep. British High Comr, in Ghana, 1964–65; FCO, 1965–68. IDC, 1969; Commercial Counsellor, Ankara, 1970–71; Dep. High Comr, Nairobi, 1971–72. Dep. Registrar, Hull Univ., 1972–79. Mem., Craven DC, 1984–98 (Chm., 1991–92 and 1996–97). Contested (L): Haltemprice, Feb. and Oct. 1974, 1979; Humberside, European election, 1979; South Ribble, 1983. Mem., Liberal Party Council, 1976–87; Chm., Yorkshire Liberal Fedn, 1977–81. Mem. Council, Lancaster Univ., 1986–94. Founder Mem. and first Chm., Ribblesdale Trust, 1987–94. Mem. Cttee, Yorkshire Dales Nat. Park, 1992–98. Chm., Camberwell After Sch. Project, 2001–02. *Recreations:* croquet, travel. *Address:* 13 Acacia Grove, West Dulwich, SE21 8ER. *T:* (020) 8670 7029.
Died 9 Dec. 2004.

WALKER, Sheila Mosley, (Mrs Owen Walker), CBE 1981; JP; Chief Commissioner, Girl Guides Association, 1975–80; *b* 11 Dec. 1917; *yr d* of late Charles Eric Mosley Mayne, Indian Cavalry, and Evelyn Mary, *d* of Sir Thomas Skewes-Cox, MP; *m* 1st, 1940, Major Bruce Dawson, MC, Royal Berkshire Regt (killed, Arnhem, 1944); one *s* one *d*; 2nd, 1955, Henry William Owen, *s* of late Sir Henry Walker, CBE; one step *s* one step *d*. *Educ:* St Mary's Hall, Brighton; St James' Secretarial Coll., London. Midlands Regional Chief Comr, 1970–75, Vice-Pres., 1988–2003, Girl Guides Assoc. Vice-Chm., CPRE, 1988–95. JP Nottingham City, 1970. *Recreations:* children, animals, all country and nature conservation. *Address:* Dingley Hall, near Market Harborough, Leics LE16 8PJ. *T:* (01858) 535388. *Club:* New Cavendish (Chm. Bd 1983–93).
Died 6 Dec. 2005.

WALKER, Gen. Sir Walter (Colyear), KCB 1968 (CB 1964); CBE 1959 (OBE 1949); DSO 1946 and Bars, 1953 and 1965; Commander-in-Chief, Allied Forces Northern Europe, 1969–72, retired; *b* 11 Nov. 1912; *s* of late Arthur Colyear Walker; *m* 1938, Beryl (*d* 1990), *d* of late E. N. W. Johnston; two *s* one *d*. *Educ:* Blundell's; RMC, Sandhurst. Waziristan, 1939–41 (despatches twice); Burma, 1942, 1944–46 (despatches, DSO); Malaya, 1949–59 (despatches twice, OBE, Bar to DSO, CBE); Bt Lt Col, 1952; Atomic Trials, Maralinga, SA, 1956; Dir of Operations, Borneo, 1962–65 (CB, Bar to DSO); Deputy Chief of Staff, HQ AFCENT, 1965; Acting Chief of Staff, 1966–67; GOC-in-C, Northern Command, 1967–69. psc† 1942; jssc 1950; idc 1960. Col, 7th Duke of Edinburgh's Own Gurkha Rifles, 1964–75. Dato Seri Setia, Order of Paduka Stia Negara (Brunei), 1964; Hon. Panglima Mangku Negara (Malaysia), 1965. *Publications:* The Bear at the Back Door, 1978; The Next Domino, 1980; Fighting On (autobiog.), 1997. *Recreations:* normal. *Address:* Haydon Farmhouse, Sherborne, Dorset DT9 5JB.
Died 12 Aug. 2001.

WALKER-OKEOVER, Sir Peter (Ralph Leopold), 4th Bt *cr* 1886; DL; *b* 22 July 1947; *s* of Colonel Sir Ian Peter Andrew Monro Walker-Okeover, 3rd Bt, DSO, TD, and of Dorothy Elizabeth, *yr d* of Captain Josceline Heber-Percy; *S* father, 1982; *m* 1st, 1972, Catherine Mary Maule (marr. diss. 1991), *d* of Colonel George Maule Ramsay; two *s* one *d*; 2nd, 1993, Patricia Margaret Sevier, *er d* of Laurance Sanderson. *Educ:* Eton; RMA Sandhurst. Captain, Blues and Royals, retired. DL Staffs, 1992. *Heir: s* Andrew Peter Monro Walker-Okeover, *b* 22 May 1978. *Address:* Okeover Hall, Ashbourne, Derbyshire DE6 2DE; House of Glenmuick, Ballater, Aberdeenshire.
Died 6 Nov. 2003.

WALL, Prof. Patrick David, DM; FRCP; FRS 1989; Professor of Anatomy and Director, Cerebral Functions Research Group, University College London, 1967–90, then Professor Emeritus, based at Physiology Department, St Thomas' Hospital; *b* 5 April 1925; *s* of T. Wall, MC, and R. Wall (*née* Cresswell); *m* 1st, 1950, Betty Tucker (marr. diss.); 2nd, 1976, Vera Ronnen, enamellist (marr. diss.), *d* of Ernst Bischitz; 3rd, 1999, Mary. *Educ:* St Paul's; Christ Church, Oxford (MA 1947; BM, BCh 1948; DM 1960). Instructor, Yale School of Medicine, 1948–50; Asst Prof., Univ. of Chicago, 1950–53; Instructor, Harvard Univ., 1953–55; Assoc. Prof., 1957–60, Professor 1960–67, MIT. Vis. Prof., Hebrew Univ., Jerusalem, 1973–. Founding Chm., Brain Research Assoc. Founder FMedSci 1998. Hon. FRCA 1992. Hon. MD: Sienna, 1987; Debrecen, 1994. Bonica Award, Internat. Assoc. Study of Pain, 1987; Sherrington Medal, RSM, 1988; Wakeman Award, Duke Univ., 1988; Research on Pain Award, Bristol-Myers, 1988. First Editor in Chief, Pain. *Publications:* Trio, The Revolting Intellectuals' Organizations (novel), 1966 (US 1965); (with R. Melzack) The Challenge of Pain, 1982, 2nd edn 1989; The Textbook of Pain, 1983, 4th edn 1999; Pain: the science of suffering, 1999; many papers on anat. and physiol. of nervous system. *Recreation:* kibbitzing. *Address:* Flat 1, Lake House, South Hill Park, NW3 2SH.
Died 8 Aug. 2001.

WALL, Prof. William Douglas, PhD, DLit; CPsychol, FBPsS; Professor of Educational Psychology, Institute of Education, University of London, 1973–78, then Professor Emeritus; *b* 22 Aug. 1913; *s* of late John Henry Wall and Ann McCulloch Wall, Wallington, Surrey; *m* 1st, 1936, Doris Margaret (*née* Satchel) (marr. diss. 1960); two *s* one *d*; 2nd, 1960, Ursula Maria (*née* Gallusser); one *s*. *Educ:* Univ. Coll. London, 1931–34 (BA Hons); Univ. Coll. London/Univ. of Birmingham, 1944–48 (PhD (Psychol.)); DLit (London) 1979. FBPsS 1978, CPsychol 1994. Mem., Social Psych. Sect., Child and Educnl Psych. Sect., BPsS. Univ. of Birmingham Educn Dept, 1945–53; Reader, 1948–53; Head, Educn and Child Develt Unit, UNESCO, Paris, 1951–56; Dir, Nat. Foundn for Educnl Res. in England and Wales, 1956–68; Dean, Inst. of

Educn, Univ. of London, 1968–73; Scientific Advr, Bernard van Leer Foundn, 1978–82. Visiting Professor: Univ. of Michigan, 1957; Univ. of Jerusalem, 1962; Univ. of Tel Aviv, 1967. Chm., Internat. Project Evaluation of Educnl Attainment, 1958–62; Mem., Police Trng Council, 1970–78; Co-Dir, 1958–75, and Chm., Nat. Child Develt Study, 1958–78; Mem. Council, Internat. Children's Centre, Paris, 1970–78. *Publications:* (many trans. various langs): Adolescent Child, 1948 (2nd edn, 1952); Education and Mental Health, 1955; Psychological Services for Schools, 1956; Child of our Times, 1959; Failure in School, 1962; Adolescents in School and Society, 1968; Longitudinal Studies and the Social Sciences, 1970; Constructive Education for Children, 1975; Constructive Education for Adolescents, 1977; Constructive Education for Handicapped, 1979; contrib: British Jl Educnl Psych.; British Jl Psych., Educnl Res. (Editor, 1958–68), Educnl Rev., Enfance, Human Develt, Internat. Rev. Educn. *Recreations:* painting (one-man exhibitions: Windsor, 1986, 1988; London, 1987; Open Studio, Visual Images Gp, 1993), church architecture, gardening. *Address:* La Geneste, Rose Hill, Burnham, Bucks SL1 8LW. *Died 7 Oct. 2003.*

WALLACE OF COSLANY, Baron *cr* 1974 (Life Peer), of Coslany in the City of Norwich; **George Douglas Wallace;** *b* 18 April 1906; *e s* of late George Wallace, Cheltenham Spa, Gloucestershire; *m* 1932, Vera Randall, Guildford, Surrey; one *s* one *d. Educ:* Central School, Cheltenham Spa. Mem. of Management Cttee, in early years, of YMCA at East Bristol and Guildford; Mem. Chislehurst-Sidcup UDC, 1937–46; has been Divisional Sec. and also Chm., Chislehurst Labour Party; also Chm. of Parks and Cemeteries Cttee of UDC, Schools Manager and Member of Chislehurst, Sidcup and Orpington Divisional Education Executive; Mem., Cray Valley and Sevenoaks Hosp. Management Cttee; Chm., House Cttee, Queen Mary's Hosp.; Vice-Chm., Greenwich and Bexley AHA, 1974–77. Joined Royal Air Force, reaching rank of Sergeant. Served in No 11 Group Fighter Command, 1941–45. MP (Lab) Chislehurst Div. of Kent, 1945–50; Junior Govt Whip, 1947–50; MP (Lab) Norwich North, Oct. 1964–Feb. 1974; PPS: to Lord President of the Council, Nov. 1964–65; to Sec. of State for Commonwealth Affairs, 1965; to Minister of State, Min. of Housing and Local Govt, 1967–68; Mem. Speaker's Panel of Chairmen, 1970–74; a Lord in Waiting (Govt Whip), 1977–79; opposition spokesman and Whip, H of L, 1979–84. Delegate to Council of Europe and WEU, 1975–77. Member: Commonwealth Parly Assoc.; Commonwealth War Graves Commn, 1970–86; Kent CC, 1952–57. *Recreations:* interested in Youth Movements and social welfare schemes. *Address:* 44 Shuttle Close, Sidcup, Kent DA15 8EP. *T:* (020) 8300 3634.
Died 11 Nov. 2003.

WALLACE, Ian Alexander; JP; Headmaster, Canford School, 1961–76; *b* 5 Oct. 1917; *s* of late Very Rev. A. R. Wallace and Winifred, *d* of late Rev. H. C. Sturges; *m* 1947, Janet Glossop; two *s* two *d. Educ:* Clifton; Corpus Christi College, Cambridge (Open Scholar; Classical Tripos, Part I, 1st Cl.; Theological Tripos Part I, 2nd Cl. Div. One). Served War of 1939–45, Mountain Artillery, NW Frontier, India, 1941; School of Artillery, India, 1942–43; Arakan, 1944; Mandalay, 1945 (despatches). Rossall School: Assistant Master, 1946; Housemaster, 1951–61. SW Regional Sec., Independent Schools Careers Organisation, 1976–84; Project Manager for India, GAP Activity Projects, 1984–89; Wilts Regional Dir, HOST, 1992–95. Governor: Portsmouth Grammar Sch., 1977–89; King's Sch., Bruton, 1977–92. JP Poole Borough, 1966. *Address:* Steeple Close, Hindon, Salisbury, Wilts SP3 6DJ. *Died 14 June 2002.*

WALLACE, Walter Wilkinson, CVO 1977; CBE 1973 (OBE 1964); DSC 1944; Foreign and Commonwealth Office, 1980–99; *b* 23 Sept. 1923; *s* of late Walter Wallace and Helen Wallace (*née* Douglas); *m* 1955, Susan Blanche,

d of Brig. F. W. B. Parry, CBE; one *s* one *d. Educ:* George Heriot's, Edinburgh. Served War, Royal Marines, 1942–46 (Captain). Joined Colonial Service, 1946; Asst Dist Comr, Sierra Leone, 1948; Dist Comr, 1954; seconded to Colonial Office, 1955–57; Sen. Dist Comr, 1961; Provincial Comr, 1961; Develt Sec., 1962–64; Estabt Sec., Bahamas, 1964–67; Sec. to Cabinet, Bermuda, 1968–73; HM Commissioner, Anguilla, 1973; Governor, British Virgin Islands, 1974–78. Constitutional Comr, St Helena, 1987, Cayman Islands, 1991, Turks and Caicos Is, 1992, British Virgin Islands, 1993, Falkland Islands, 1995. *Recreation:* golf. *Address:* Becketts, Itchenor, Sussex PO20 7DE. *T:* (01243) 512438. *Died 14 Oct. 2005.*

WALLEN, Ella Kathleen, MA; Headmistress, St Mary's School, Wantage, 1977–80; *b* 15 Feb. 1914. *Educ:* Camden Sch. for Girls; St Hugh's Coll., Oxford (MA). History Mistress, Queen Victoria High Sch., Stockton-on-Tees, 1937–41; Sen. History Mistress, High Sch. for Girls, Gloucester, 1942–59; Headmistress: Queen Victoria High Sch., Stockton-on Tees, 1959–65; Bedford High Sch., 1965–76. *Address:* 10 Dove House Close, Upper Wolvercote, Oxford OX2 8BG. *Died 22 June 2003.*

WALLEY, Sir John, KBE 1965; CB 1950; Deputy Secretary, Ministry of Pensions and National Insurance, later Ministry of Social Security, 1958–66, retired; *b* Barnstaple, Devon, 3 April 1906; *e s* of late R. M. Walley; *m* 1934, Elisabeth Mary (*d* 2002), *e d* of late R. H. Pinhorn, OBE; two *s* two *d. Educ:* Hereford High Sch.; Hereford Cathedral Sch.; Merton Coll., Oxford (Postmaster, 1924–28; Hons Maths and Dip., Pol. and Econ. Sci.). Ministry of Labour: Asst Principal, 1929; Sec., Cabinet Cttee on Unemployment, 1932; Principal, 1934; Asst Sec., Min. of Nat. Service, 1941; promoted Under-Sec. to take charge of legislation and other preparations for Beveridge Nat. Insce Scheme, in new Min. of Nat. Insurance, 1945; Chm., Dental Benefit Council, 1945–48. Chm., Hampstead Centre, National Trust, 1969–79, Pres., 1980–90. *Publications:* Social Security-Another British Failure?, 1972; contribs: to The Future of the Social Services, ed Robson and Crick, 1970; on Children's Allowances, in Family Poverty, ed David Bull, 1971; vol. in British Oral Archive of Political and Administrative History, 1980; articles in jls and the press on social security matters. *Died 1 Nov. 2002.*

WALLINGTON, Jeremy Francis; publisher and television producer; Managing Director, Headwater Cross-Media (formerly Headwater Communications), since 1996 (Publishing Director, 1994–96); Founder and Managing Director, The Magazine Channel Ltd, since 1998; *b* 7 July 1935; *s* of Ernest Francis Wallington and Nell (*née* Howe); *m* 1955, Margaret Ivy Willment; three *s* one *d. Educ:* Royal Grammar Sch., High Wycombe, Bucks. Reporter on several Fleet Street newspapers, 1956–62; Managing Editor, Topic Magazine, 1962; Co-Founder of Insight, Sunday Times, 1963; Assistant Editor: Sunday Times, 1963–65; Daily Mail, 1965–67; Editor, Investigations Bureau, World in Action, Granada Television, 1967–68; Jt Editor, then Editor, World in Action, 1968–72; Head of Documentaries, Granada Television, 1972–77 (prod Burgess, Philby and Maclean, 1977); Dir of Progs, Southern TV, 1977–81; Chief Exec., Limehouse Prodns, 1982–86. Dir, Wallington, Irving, Jackson Ltd, 1990–. *Publication:* (jtly) Scandal '63, 1963. *Recreations:* choral singing, France. *Address:* 28 Merrick Square, SE1 4JB. *T:* (020) 7403 0570.
Died 14 Aug. 2001.

WALLIS-JONES, His Honour Ewan Perrins; a Circuit Judge (formerly County Court Judge), 1964–84; *b* 22 June 1913; *s* of late William James Wallis-Jones, MBE, and Ethel Perrins Wallis-Jones; *m* 1940, Veronica Mary (*née* Fowler); one *s* two *d. Educ:* Mill Hill Sch.; University Coll. of Wales, Aberystwyth (LLB Hons 1934); Balliol Coll., Oxford (BA 1936, MA 1941). Qualified Solicitor, 1935; called to the Bar, Gray's Inn, 1938. Chm., Carmarthenshire QS, 1966–71 (Dep. Chm., 1965–66); Jt

Pres., Council of Circuit Judges, 1982. ARPS. *Recreations:* music, reading and photography. *Address:* 25 Cotham Grove, Bristol BS6 6AN. *T:* (0117) 924 8908. *Club:* Royal Photographic Society. *Died 29 Jan. 2003.*

WALLROCK, John; Chairman, Conocean International Consultants Group, Hong Kong, 1984–92; *b* 14 Nov. 1922; *s* of Samuel and Marie Kate Wallrock; *m* 1967, Audrey Louise Ariow; one *s* two *d*. *Educ:* Bradfield Coll., Berks. Cadet, Merchant Navy, 1939; Lieut RNR, 1943; Master Mariner, 1949; J. H. Minet & Co. Ltd, 1950, Dir, 1955–79, Chm., 1972–79; Chairman: Minet Holdings, 1972–82; St Katherine Insurance Co. Ltd, London, 1972–82; Dir, Tugu Insce Co. Ltd, Hong Kong, 1976–84. Underwriting Mem. of Lloyd's, 1951–86. Mem., Council of Management, White Ensign Assoc. Ltd, 1974–83. Liveryman, Master Mariners' Co., 1954–; Freeman, City of London, 1965. FCIB, MNI. *Recreations:* yachting, shooting. *Address:* 14 Lowndes Square, SW1X 9HB; Kits Croft, Up Green, Eversley, Hants RG27 0PE. *Clubs:* East India, Naval; Royal London Yacht, Royal Southern Yacht. *Died 9 Dec. 2004.*

WALLS, Prof. John, FRCP; Professor of Nephrology, University of Leicester, since 1990; Clinical Director, Renal Directorate, Leicester General Hospital NHS Trust, since 1989; *b* 25 Dec. 1939; *s* of Mark Stanley Walls and Doris Walls; *m* 1966, Adele L. Raine; two *s*. *Educ:* Bingley Grammar Sch.; Univ. of Leeds Sch. of Medicine (MB ChB 1963). FRCP 1979. Jun. hosp. posts, Leeds, York and Newcastle upon Tyne, 1964–70; Asst Prof., Washington Univ., St Louis, Mo, 1971–73; Consultant Nephrologist, Leicester General Hosp., 1974– (Clin. Tutor, 1976–82); Clin. Sub Dean, Univ. of Leicester, 1986–93; Postgrad. Dean, Univ. of Leicester and S Trent, 1993–2000. President: Renal Assoc., 1995–98; Internat. Soc. Nut. Metabol. in Renal Disease, 2000–. Censor, RCP, 1997–99. Founder FMedSci 1998. Foundn Trustee, Leicester Grammar Sch., 1980–. Internat. Medal of Distinction, Nat. Kidney Foundn, USA, 1998. *Publications:* numerous contribs on nephrology in peer reviewed jls. *Recreations:* marathon running, squash, trout fishing. *Address:* 26 Morland Avenue, Stoneygate, Leicester LE2 2PE. *T:* (0116) 270 7602. *Club:* Royal Society of Medicine. *Died 1 March 2001.*

WALLWORTH, Cyril; Assistant Under-Secretary of State, Ministry of Defence, 1964–76; Gwilym Gibbon Fellow, Nuffield College, Oxford, 1975–76; *b* 6 June 1916; *s* of Albert A. Wallworth and Eva (*née* Taylor; unmarried. *Educ:* Oldham High Sch.; Manchester Univ. (BA (Hons) History, 1937). Asst Principal, Admiralty, 1939; Asst Private Secretary to First Lord, 1941–45, Principal, 1943; Asst Secretary, 1951; IDC 1960; Under-Secretary, 1964. Liveryman: Basketmakers' Co., 1990; Upholders' Co., 1991. *Recreations:* music, wine, cooking, photography. *Address:* 5 Leinster Mews, W2 3EY. *Clubs:* Hurlingham, Lansdowne, United Wards, City Livery. *Died 26 Sept. 2002.*

WALSH, Sir John (Patrick), KBE 1960; Professor of Dentistry and Dean and Director, University of Otago Dental School, 1946–72; *b* 5 July 1911; *s* of John Patrick Walsh and Lillian Jane (*née* Burbidge), Vic, Australia; *m* 1934, Enid Morris; one *s* three *d*. *Educ:* Ormond Coll.; Melbourne Univ. (BDSc 1st Cl. Hons; MB, BS 1943; DDSc 1950); LDS Victoria, 1936; MDS NUI, 1952. FDSRCS 1950; FDSRCS Edinburgh, 1951; FRSNZ 1961; FACD 1962. Hosp. and teaching appointments in Melbourne till 1946. MO, RAAF, 1945–46. Consultant, WHO Dental Health Seminars: Wellington, 1954; Adelaide, 1959. Speaker: 11th and 12th Internat. Dental Congresses, London and Rome; Centennial Congress of Amer. Dental Assoc., New York, 1959; 12th, 14th and 15th Australian Dental Congresses. Chairman: Dental Council of NZ, 1956–72; Mental Health Assoc. of Otago, 1960. Dominion Pres., UNA, 1960–64. Member: MRC of NZ, 1950–72 (Chm. Dental Cttee, 1947–60); Scientific Commn; Fedn Dentaire Internat., 1954–61; Council,

Univ. of Otago, 1958–63; Nat. Commn for UNESCO, 1961–69; Educn Commn, 1961–; Expert Panel on Dental Health, WHO, 1962; Nat. Council, Duke of Edinburgh's Award, 1963–68. CC, Dunedin, 1968–73. Pres., Dunedin Rotary Club, 1960, Governor Dist 298, 1966–67. Paul Harris Fellow, 1981. Hon. Mem., American Dental Assoc., 1969–; Hon. FACDS 1967. List of Honour, FDI, 1969–. Holds hon. degrees, incl. Hon. DSc Otago, 1975. *Publications:* A Manual of Stomatology, 1957; Living with Uncertainty, 1968; Psychiatry and Dentistry, 1976; numerous articles in scientific literature. *Recreation:* retirement. *Address:* Elizabeth Knox Home, 10 Ranfurly Road, Epsom, Auckland 3, New Zealand. *T:* (9) 5207102. *Died 22 Aug. 2003.*

WALSH, Lt-Col Noel Perrings; Under Secretary, and Director of Home Regional Services, Department of the Environment, 1976–79; *b* 25 Dec. 1919; *s* of late John and Nancy Walsh; *m* 1st, 1945, Olive Mary (*d* 1987), *y d* of late Thomas Walsh, Waterford; three *s* one *d*; 2nd, 1988, Mary Ruth, *d* of late Rev. R. D. M. Hughes. *Educ:* Purbrook Park Grammar Sch.; Open Univ.; Birmingham Univ. (MSocSc). Served Army, 1939–66; India, 1941–44; Arakan Campaign, 1944–45; DAQMG, 52 (L) Div., 1951–53; GSO2 RA, HQ BAOR, 1955–57; GSO1 PR, MoD Army, 1964–66; retired Lt-Col, RA, 1966. Entered Home Civil Service as Principal, MPBW, 1966; Regional Director: Far East, 1969–70; Midland Region, 1970–75. Vice-Chm., Midland Study Centre for Building Team, 1982–90; Regional Chm., W Midlands Council, CIOB, 1988–90. Vice-Pres., W Midlands Central SSAFA, 1995– (Chm., 1991–95); Chm., RBL Birmingham Poppy Appeal, 1996–2001; Chm., Lord Mayor's Birmingham Ex-Service Appeals Cttee, 2001–. FCIOB 1972; FCMI (FBIM 1978); FRSA 1987. *Recreations:* gardening, economic history, gauge O railway modelling. *Address:* 25 Oakfield Road, Selly Park, Birmingham B29 7HH. *T:* (0121) 472 2031. *Club:* Naval and Military. *Died 9 May 2005.*

WALTER, Kenneth Burwood, CVO 1978; Full-time Member, British Airports Authority, 1975–77; *b* 16 Oct. 1918; *s* of late Leonard James Walter and Jessie Florence Walter; *m* 1940, Elsie Marjorie Collett (*d* 1997); two *s*. *Educ:* St Dunstan's Coll., SE6. Dept of Civil Aviation, Air Ministry, 1936. Served War, Royal Artillery (Anti Aircraft and Field), home and Far East, 1940–46. Ministries of: Civil Aviation; Transport and Civil Aviation; Aviation, 1946–66; British Airports Authority: Dep. Dir Planning, 1966; Dir Planning, 1972; Airport Dir, Heathrow, 1973–77. MCIT, MILT, ARAeS. *Publications:* various papers on airports. *Recreations:* music, swimming, fishing, gardening. *Address:* 7 Willersley Avenue, Orpington, Kent BR6 9RT. *Died 20 June 2005.*

WALTERS, Geraint Gwynn, CBE 1958; Director for Wales, Ministry of Public Building and Works and Department of the Environment, 1966–72, retired; *b* Welsh Colony, Patagonia, 6 June 1910; *s* of Rev. D. D. Walters; *m* 1st, 1942, Doreena Owen (*d* 1959); 2nd, 1968, Sarah Ann Ruth Price; no *c*. *Educ:* various schools in Argentina and Wales; University Coll., Bangor (BA). Gladstone Prizeman, Foyle Prizeman. Schoolmaster, 1933–35; political organizer on staff of Rt Hon. David Lloyd George, 1935–40; Min. of Information, 1940–45; Dep. Regional Dir of Inf., Bristol and Plymouth, 1942–45; Principal, Min. of Works HQ, 1945–48; Dir for Wales, Min. of Works, 1948–63; Dir, Far East Region, Min. of Public Building and Works, 1963–66. Govt Housing Comr for Merthyr Tydfil, 1972–72; Member: Welsh Bd for Industry, 1948–62; Housing Production Bd for Wales; Cttee of Inquiry on Welsh Television, 1963. Chm., Royal Inst. of Public Admin (S Wales Br.), 1960–61; Hon. Mem. of Gorsedd, 1961; Pres., St David's Soc. of Singapore, 1965; Leader of Welsh Overseas, at Nat. Eisteddfod of Wales, 1965; Chm., Argentine Welsh Soc., 1976–78, Pres., 1979–82. Chm., Civil Service Sports Council for Wales, 1970–72. Mem. Council, Univ. of Wales Inst. of

Science and Technology, 1970–87 (Vice-Chm., 1980–83); Mem. Court, Univ. of Wales, 1982–88; Life Mem. Court, Univ. of Wales Coll. of Cardiff, 1989–. *Recreations:* reading Talking Books, radio, travel. *Address:* 1 The Mount, Cardiff Road, Llandaff, Cardiff CF5 2AR. *T:* (029) 2056 8739. *Clubs:* Civil Service; Cardiff and County (Cardiff). *Died 6 June 2003.*

WALTERS, Max; *see* Walters, S. M.

WALTERS, S(tuart) Max, ScD; VMH; Director, University Botanic Garden, Cambridge, 1973–83, retired; *b* 23 May 1920; *s* of Bernard Walters and Ivy Dane; *m* 1948, Lorna Mary Strutt; two *s* one *d*. *Educ:* Penistone Grammar Sch.; St John's Coll., Cambridge (1st cl. hons Pt I Nat. Scis Tripos 1940 and Pt II Botany 1946; PhD 1949). Research Fellow, St John's Coll., 1947–50; Curator of Herbarium, Botany Sch., Cambridge, 1948–73; Lectr in Botany 1962–73; Fellow of King's Coll., Cambridge, 1964–84. VMH 1984; Linnean Medal for Botany, 1995. *Publications:* (with J. S. L. Gilmour) Wild Flowers, 1954; (with J. Raven) Mountain Flowers, 1956; (ed, with F. H. Perring) Atlas of the British Flora, 1962; (with F. H. Perring, P. D. Sell and H. L. K. Whitehouse) A Flora of Cambridgeshire, 1964; (with D. Briggs) Plant Variation and Evolution, 1969, 3rd edn 1997; The Shaping of Cambridge Botany, 1981; Wild and Garden Plants, 1993; (with E. A. Stow) Darwin's Mentor: John Stevens Henslow 1796–1861, 2001. *Address:* 1 Symonds Lane, Grantchester, Cambridge CB3 9NU. *T:* (01223) 841295. *Died 11 Dec. 2005.*

WARD, Donald Albert; Secretary General, International Union of Credit and Investment Insurers (Berne Union), 1974–86; *b* 30 March 1920; *s* of Albert and Rosie Ward; *m* 1948, Maureen Molloy; five *s*. *Educ:* Brewery Road Elementary Sch.; Southend-on-Sea High Sch.; Queen's Coll., Oxford (BA Hons Maths; MA). Served War, Indian Army (RIASC), 10th Indian Div., Middle East and Italy, 1940–45 (despatches). Min. of Food, 1946–53; Export Credits Guarantee Dept, 1953–74 (Under-Sec., 1971–74). *Address:* 54 Highlands Road, Leatherhead, Surrey KT22 8NJ. *Died 12 Oct. 2001.*

WARD, Ven. Edwin James Greenfield, LVO 1963; Archdeacon of Sherborne, 1968–84; Archdeacon Emeritus and Canon Emeritus of Salisbury Cathedral, since 1985; Extra Chaplain to the Queen, since 1989 (Chaplain, 1955–89); *b* 26 Oct. 1919; *er s* of Canon F. G. Ward, MC, lately of Canberra, Australia; *m* 1946, Grizell Evelyn Buxton (*d* 1985); one *s* two *d*. *Educ:* St John's, Leatherhead; Christ's Coll., Cambridge (MA). Served King's Dragoon Guards, 1940; Reserve, 1946. Ordained 1948; Vicar of North Elmham, Norfolk, 1950–55; Chaplain, Royal Chapel, Windsor Great Park, 1955–67; Rector of West Stafford, 1967–84. Mem. of Council, Marlborough Coll., 1969–88; Visitor, Milton Abbey School, 1991–94 (Mem., Bd of Govs, 1983–91). *Recreation:* fishing. *Address:* 14 Arle Close, Alresford, Hants SO24 9BG. *T:* (01962) 735501. *Died 22 Nov. 2005.*

WARD, Frank Dixon; *see* Dixon Ward.

WARD, Michael Phelps, CBE 1983; FRCS; FRGS; Emeritus Consultant Surgeon: City and East London Area Health Authority (Teaching) (Consultant Surgeon, 1964–93); St Andrew's Hospital, Bow (Consultant Surgeon, 1964–93); Newham Hospital (Consultant Surgeon, 1983–93); Lecturer in Clinical Surgery, London Hospital Medical College, 1975–93; *b* 26 March 1925; *s* of late Wilfrid Arthur Ward, CMG, MC and Norah Anne Phelps; *m* 1957, Felicity Jane Ewbank; one *s*. *Educ:* Marlborough Coll., Wilts; Peterhouse, Cambridge (Ironmongers' Co. Exhibn; BA Hons 1945, MA 1961; MB BChir 1949, MD 1968; London Hosp. Med. Coll. FRCS 1955. Ho. Surg., Surgical Registrar, Sen. Surgical Registrar, London Hosp.; Asst Resident, Royal Victoria Hosp., Montreal, Canada; Consultant Surg., Poplar Hosp., E14, 1964–75; Hunterian Prof., RCS, 1954. Served

RAMC, Captain, 1950–52. Fellow, Assoc. of Surgs of Gt Britain. Master, Soc. of Apothecaries, 1993–94 (Mem., Court of Assts, 1986). Mount Everest Reconnaissance Expedn, 1951; Mount Everest Expedn, 1953 (1st Ascent); Scientific Expedn to Everest Region, 1960–61 (Leader, 1st Winter Ascents of Amadablam and other peaks); Scientific Expedns to Bhutan Himal, 1964 and 1965; scientific and mountaineering expedn to Pamirs West Kun Lun, China, 1980–81; Royal Soc./Chinese Acad. of Sciences Tibet Geotraverse, 1985–86. FRSocMed; FRGS 1964. Dickson Asia Lectr, RGS, 1966, 1985; Monkton Copeman Lectr, Soc. of Apothecaries, 1994. Cuthbert Peek Award, RGS, 1973; Founder's (Royal) Medal, RGS, 1982; Cullum Medal, Amer. Geog. Soc., 1954. Chm., Mount Everest Foundn, 1978–80. *Publications:* Mountaineers' Companion, 1966; In this Short Span, 1972; Mountain Medicine, 1975; (jtly) High Altitude Medicine and Physiology, 1989, 3rd edn 2000; Everest: a thousand years of exploration, 2003; many scientific and medical papers on the effects of great altitude, exposure to cold, and on exercise; also on exploratory journeys to Nepal, Bhutan, Chinese Central Asia and Tibet. *Recreations:* mountaineering, ski-ing. *Clubs:* Alpine (Vice-Pres., 1968–69; Hon. Mem., 1993); Cambridge Alpine (Pres., 1986–95). *Died 7 Oct. 2005.*

WARD, Maj.-Gen. Sir Philip (John Newling), KCVO 1976; CBE 1972 (OBE 1969); Lord-Lieutenant of West Sussex, 1994–99 (Vice Lord-Lieutenant, 1990–94); *b* 10 July 1924; *s* of George William Newling Ward and Mary Florence Ward; *m* 1948, Pamela Ann Glennie; two *s* two *d*. *Educ:* privately; Monkton Combe Sch. Commnd Welsh Guards, 1943; Adjt, RMA Sandhurst, 1960–62; Bde Major, Household Bde, 1962–65; Comdg 1st Bn Welsh Guards, 1965–67; Comdr Land Forces, Gulf, 1969–71; GOC London Dist and Maj.-Gen. comdg Household Div., 1973–76; Comdt, RMA, 1976–79. Communar of Chichester Cathedral, 1980–83. Dir, Public Affairs, Internat. Distillers and Vintners (UK), 1980–87; Chm., Peter Hamilton Security Consultants, 1986–90; Director: W & A Gilbey (formerly Gilbey Vintners), 1983–89; Morgan Furze, 1983–89; Justerini & Brooks, 1987–89; Southern Reg., Lloyds Bank, 1983–90. Pres., S of England Agricl Soc., 1994–95 (Vice Patron and Life Gov., 1996); Chairman: Queen Alexandra Hosp. Home, 1979–98; Royal Soldiers Daughters School, 1980–83; Governor and Comdt, Church Lads and Church Girls Bde, 1980–86. Patron, Chichester Cathedral Trust, 1995. Freeman, City of London, 1976. DL, 1981, High Sheriff, 1985–86, W Sussex. KStJ 1994. *Recreation:* gardening. *Address:* 15 Tarrant Wharf, Arundel, W Sussex BN18 9NY. *Clubs:* Cavalry and Guards (Chm., 1987–90), Buck's. *Died 6 Jan. 2003.*

WARD, Prof. Richard Hugh, PhD; Professor of Biological Anthropology and Fellow of Linacre College, Oxford University, since 1996. *Educ:* Univ. of Auckland, NZ (BA, BSc, MA); PhD Michigan. Lectr, Auckland Univ., until 1974; Asst Prof. of Anthropology and Res. Affiliate in Child Develt, 1974–78, Associate Prof. in Epidemiology and Biostats, 1978–80, Univ. of Washington; Associate Prof. of Med. Genetics, Univ. of British Columbia, 1980–96. Mem., N Amer. Human Genome Diversity Cttee, 1993–96. *Publications:* contrib. to learned jls. *Address:* Linacre College, Oxford OX1 3JA. *Died 14 Feb. 2003.*

WARD, His Honour Roy Livingstone; QC 1972; a Circuit Judge, 1979–94; *b* 31 Aug. 1925; *m* 1972, Barbara Anne (*née* Brockbank) (marr. diss); one *s* one *d*. *Educ:* Taunton Sch.; Pembroke Coll., Cambridge (BA Hons 1949). Served RAF, 1943–47 (commnd 1945). Called to the Bar, Middle Temple, 1950. A Recorder of the Crown Court, 1972–79. *Address:* Tethers End, Shelsley Drive, Colwall, Worcs WR13 6PS. *Club:* Oxford and Cambridge. *Died 24 June 2003.*

WARD-BOOTH, Maj.-Gen. Anthony; *see* Ward-Booth, Maj.-Gen. J. A.

WARD-BOOTH, Maj.-Gen. (John) Antony, OBE 1971; DL; Consultant, Francis Graves and Partners, 1989–95; *b* 18 July 1927; *s* of Rev. J. Ward-Booth and Mrs E. M. Ward-Booth; *m* 1952, Margaret Joan, *d* of Rev. A. W. Hooper, MC, MA and G. Hooper; one *s* two *d* (and one *s* decd). *Educ:* Worksop College, Notts. Joined Army, 1945; commnd into Worcestershire Regt in India, 1946; served India and Middle East, 1946–48; regular commn Bedfordshire and Hertfordshire Regt, 1948; served BAOR, Far East, Nigeria and Congo, 1950–63, trans. to Parachute Regt, 1963; commanded 3rd Bn, Parachute Regt, 1967–69; Hong Kong, 1969–70; Comdr, 16 Parachute Bde, 1970–73; Nat. Defence Coll., Canada, 1973–74; DAG, HQ BAOR, 1974–75; Dir, Army Air Corps, 1976–79; GOC Western District, 1979–82. Dep. Col, Royal Anglian Regt, 1982–87. Sec., Eastern Wessex TAVRA, 1982–89. Hon. Vice-Pres., Army Rugby Union, 1982. Governor: Enham Village Centre, 1982–97; Clayesmore Sch., Dorset, 1985–2000 (Chm., 1989–94). DL Hants, 1988. *Recreations:* sailing, golf, cricket. *Address:* 19 St Peter's Close, Goodworth Clatford, Andover, Hants SP11 7SF. *Club:* MCC. *Died 25 Aug. 2002.*

WARD-JACKSON, Mrs (Audrey) Muriel; a Director (concerned mainly with Finance), John Lewis Partnership, 1955–74; *b* 30 Oct. 1914; *d* of late William James Jenkins and Alice Jenkins (*née* Glyde); *m* 1946, George Ralph Norman Ward-Jackson (*d* 1982); no *c. Educ:* Queenswood, Hatfield, Herts; Lady Margaret Hall, Oxford (MA). Home Civil Service (Ministries of Works, Town and Country Planning, Housing and Local Government, and Central Econ. Planning Staff, HM Treasury): Asst Principal, 1937; Principal, 1942; Asst Sec., 1946–55. John Lewis Partnership Ltd: Dir, 1957–74; Dir, John Lewis Properties Ltd, 1969–74; Chm., John Lewis Partnership Pensions Trust, 1964–74. On Civil Service Arbitration Tribunal, 1959–64; Chm., Consumers Cttees (Agric. Marketing), 1971–75; Member: Nat. Savings Review Cttee, 1971–73; Royal Commn on Standards of Conduct in Public Life, 1974–76. A Governor, BFI, 1962–65; Mem. Council, Bedford Coll., London Univ., 1967–72. *Recreation:* swimming. *Address:* 91 The Cloisters, Pegasus Grange, White House Road, Oxford OX1 4QQ. *T:* (01865) 725486. *Died 11 Feb. 2003.*

WARDINGTON, 2nd Baron *cr* 1936, of Alnmouth in the County of Northumberland; **Christopher Henry Beaumont Pease;** *b* 22 Jan. 1924; *s* of 1st Baron Wardington and Hon. Dorothy Charlotte (*d* 1983), *er d* of 1st Baron Forster; *S* father, 1950; *m* 1964, Margaret Audrey Dunfee, *d* of John and Eva White; one *s* two *d* (adopted). *Educ:* Eton. Served War of 1939–45, in Scots Guards, 1942–47, Captain. Partner in Stockbroking firm of Hoare Govett Ltd, 1947–86. Alderman of Broad Street Ward, City of London, 1960–63. Mem., Council of Foreign Bondholders, 1967–81. Comr, Public Works Loan Bd, 1969–73. Trustee, Royal Jubilee Trusts, 1967–90; Chm., Athlone Trust, 1983–2001. Pres., Friends of the British Library, 1999– (Chm., 1988–94). *Recreations:* cricket, golf, book collecting. *Heir: b* Hon. William Simon Pease [*b* 15 Oct. 1925; *m* 1962, Hon. Elizabeth Jane Ormsby-Gore (*d* 2004), *d* of 4th Baron Harlech, KG, PC, GCMG]. *Address:* Wardington Manor, Banbury, Oxon OX17 1SW. *T:* (01295) 750202; 29 Moore Street, SW3 2QW. *T:* (020) 7584 5245. *Clubs:* Royal Automobile, Garrick, Roxburghe; All England Lawn Tennis. *Died 6 July 2005.*

WARMINGTON, Sir David (Marshall), 5th Bt *cr* 1908, of Pembridge Square, Royal Borough of Kensington; Policy Adviser: Exeter Friendly Society, since 2002; Sanitas, Spain, since 2002; *b* 14 Feb. 1944; *s* of Sir Marshall Warmington, 3rd Bt and his 2nd wife, Eileen Mary Warmington (*d* 1969); *S* half-brother, *m* 1st, 1966, Susan Mary Chapman (marr. diss. 1980); two *s*; 2nd, 1981, Eileen Victoria Johnston. *Educ:* Charterhouse; Madrid Univ., Spain. Director: Malawi Finance Co., 1975–77; Balfour Wiliamson Inc., NY, 1980–83; British Chamber

of Commerce, Mexico, 1981–83; American British Cowdray Hosp., Mexico, 1982–83; Elders Finance Group Ltd, London, 1985–87; Man. Dir, Marbella Times, 1988–90; Man. Dir, Internat. Product Design Inc., 1991–99. *Recreations:* golf, tennis, horse racing. *Heir: s* Rupert Marshall Warmington, *b* 17 June 1969. *Address:* 139 Highlands Heath, Putney, SW15 3TZ. *T:* (home) (020) 8780 5740; Apartado de Correos 163, Finca Montanchez, Alhaurin El Grande, 29120 Málaga, Spain. *Clubs:* Army and Navy, MCC; Wimbledon Park Golf; El Prat (Barcelona); La Peña Madridista (Madrid). *Died 13 Sept. 2005.*

WARNER, Sir Edward (Redston), KCMG 1965 (CMG 1955); OBE 1948; HM Diplomatic Service, retired; *b* 23 March 1911; *s* of late Sir George Redston Warner, KCVO, CMG, and Margery Catherine (*née* Nicol); *m* 1943, Grizel Margaret Clerk Rattray; three *s* one *d. Educ:* Oundle; King's College, Cambridge. Entered Foreign Office and Diplomatic Service, 1935; UK Delegation to OEEC, Paris, 1956–59; Minister at HM Embassy, Tokyo, 1959–62; Ambassador to Cameroon, 1963–66; UK Rep., Econ. and Social Council of UN, 1966–67; Ambassador to Tunisia, 1968–70. *Address:* The Old Royal Oak, High Street, Blockley, Glos GL56 9EX. *Club:* Oxford and Cambridge. *Died 8 Feb. 2002.*

WARNER, Sir Jean-Pierre (Frank Eugene), Kt 1981; Judge of the High Court of Justice, Chancery Division, 1981–94; a Judge of the Restrictive Practices Court, 1982–94; *b* 24 Sept. 1924; *s* of late Frank Cloudesley ffolliot Warner and of Louise Marie Blanche Warner (*née* Gouet); *m* 1950, Sylvia Frances, *d* of Sir Ernest Goodale, CBE, MC; two *d. Educ:* Sainte Croix de Neuilly; Ecole des Roches; Harrow; Trinity Coll., Cambridge (MA). Served in Rifle Bde, 1943–47, Actg Major, GSO2 (Ops) GHQ Far East. Called to Bar, Lincoln's Inn, 1950 (Cassel Schol.; Bencher 1966, Treasurer 1985). Junior Counsel: to Registrar of Restrictive Trading Agreements, 1961–64; to Treasury (Chancery), 1964–72; QC 1972; Advocate-Gen., Ct of Justice of European Communities, 1973–81. Mem. Gen. Council of Bar, 1969–72. Councillor: Royal Borough of Kensington, 1959–65 (Chm., Gen. Purposes Cttee, 1963–65); Royal Borough of Kensington and Chelsea, 1964–68. Dir, Warner & Sons Ltd and subsids, 1952–70. Pres., UK Assoc. for European Law, 1983–89 (Vice-Pres., 1975–83). Hon. Mem., Soc. of Legal Scholars (formerly Soc. of Public Teachers of Law), 1982. Hon. LLD: Exeter, 1983; Leicester, 1984; Edinburgh, 1987. Liveryman, Co. of Weavers, 1957. Chevalier du Tastevin, 1952, Commandeur 1960; Mem., Confrérie St Etienne d'Alsace, 1981. Grand Cross, Order of Merit, Luxembourg, 1998. *Recreation:* sitting in the sun with a cool drink. *Address:* 32 Abingdon Villas, W8 6BX. *T:* (020) 7937 7023. *Died 1 Feb. 2005.*

WARREN, Stanley Anthony Treleaven, CB 1984; CEng, FRINA, FIMechE; RCNC; Director General Submarines, Ministry of Defence (Procurement Executive), 1979–85, retired; *b* 26 Sept. 1925; *s* of Stanley Howard Warren and Mabel Harriett (*née* Ham); *m* 1950, Sheila Glo May (*née* Rowe); two *s* one *d. Educ:* King's Coll., Univ. of London (BSc 1st Cl. Hons Engrg); RNC, Greenwich (1st Cl. Naval Architecture). FRINA 1967; FIMechE 1970. Sub-Lieut, RN, 1945–47; Constructor Lieut, RCNC, 1947–51; Royal Yacht Britannia design, 1951–54; frigate modernisations, 1954–57; Constructor, HM Dockyard, Malta, 1957–60; Admiralty Constructor Overseer, John Brown and Yarrow, 1960–64; Polaris Submarine design, 1964–67; Chief Constructor and Principal Naval Overseer, Birkenhead, 1967–72; Asst Dir and Invincible Class Proj. Manager, 1972–76; Dep. Dir of Submarines (Polaris), MoD (PE), 1976–79. *Publications:* contribs to learned societies. *Recreations:* golf, travel, gardening. *Died 28 Sept. 2005.*

WARRENDER, Hon. Robin Hugh; Senior Consultant, Aon Insurance Services Ltd (formerly Bain Hogg Ltd), since 1999 (non-executive Director, 1994–99); *b* 24 Dec.

1927; 3rd *s* of 1st Baron Bruntisfield, MC; *m* 1951, Gillian, *d* of Leonard Rossiter; one *s* two *d*. *Educ:* Eton; Trinity Coll., Oxford. Underwriting Member of Lloyd's, 1953; Tudor & Co. (Insurance) Ltd, 1958–62; Managing Director, Fenchurch Insurance Holdings Ltd, 1963–69; Dep. Chm., A. W. Bain & Sons Ltd, 1970; Chairman: Bain Dawes PLC and other group companies, 1973–85; London Wall Hldgs Ltd, 1986–94. Director: Comindus S. A. (France), 1980–82; Worms & Co., 1981–83; Varity Corporation, 1982–96; Varity Holdings Ltd, 1982–91; Heritable Group Holdings Ltd, 1983–94; Société Centrale Préservatrice Foncière Assurances, 1986–89; Gp Athena, 1989–93; Aquilo plc, 2002–. Mem. Council and Cttee of Lloyd's, 1983–86. Mem. Council, Bath Univ., 1979–82. *Recreations:* shooting, gardening, bridge. *Address:* Chadshunt, Coln St Aldwyn, Glos GLY 5AW. *Club:* White's.   *Died 6 April 2004.*

WATERFIELD, John Percival; public servant; *b* Dublin, 5 Oct. 1921; *er s* of late Sir Percival Waterfield, KBE, CB; *m* 1st, 1950, Margaret Lee Thomas (*d* 1990); two *s* one *d*; 2nd, 1991, Tilla Hevesi Vahanian (*d* 1999). *Educ:* Dragon Sch.; Charterhouse (schol.); Christ Church, Oxford (schol.). Served War of 1939–45: 1st Bn, KRRC (60th Rifles), Western Desert, Tunisia, Italy and Austria (despatches). Entered HM Foreign (subseq. Diplomatic) Service, 1946; Third Sec., Moscow, 1947; Second Sec., Tokyo, 1950; FO, 1952; First Sec., Santiago, Chile, 1954; HM Consul (Commercial), NY, 1957; FO, 1960; Ambassador to Mali Republic, 1964–65, concurrently to Guinea, 1965; duties connected with NATO, 1966; Counsellor and Head of Chancery, New Delhi, 1966–68; Head of Western Organizations Dept, FCO, 1969; Man. Dir, BEAMA, 1971; Principal Estabs and Finance Officer, NI Office, 1973–79; on secondment to Internat. Military Services Ltd, 1979–80; retired from public service, 1980; company dir and consultant, 1980–84. *Address:* 5 North Street, Somerton, Somerset TA11 7NY. *T:* (01458) 272389.   *Died 21 Dec. 2002.*

WATKINS, Thomas Frederick; Director, Chemical Defence Establishment, Porton, 1972–74; *b* 19 Feb. 1914; *s* of late Edward and late Louisa Watkins; *m* 1939, Jeannie Blodwen Roberts (*d* 2000); two *d*. *Educ:* Cowbridge Grammar Sch.; Univ. of Wales, Cardiff (BSc Hons 1935; MSc 1936). FRIC 1947. Joined Scientific Staff of War Dept, 1936; seconded to Govt of India, 1939–44; seconded to Dept of Nat. Defence, Canada, 1947–49; Head of Research Section, CDRE, Sutton Oak and Min. of Supply CDE, Nancekuke, 1949–56; Supt Chemistry Research Div., CDE, Porton, 1956; Asst Dir Chemical Research, CDE, Porton, 1963; Dep. Dir, CDE, Porton, 1966. *Address:* 17 Lodge Road, Writtle, Chelmsford CM1 3HY. *T:* (01245) 420294.   *Died 10 March 2005.*

WATKINS, Dr Winifred May, FMedSci; FRS 1969; Visiting Professor and Senior Research Fellow, Imperial College School of Medicine (formerly Royal Postgraduate Medical School), University of London, 1990–2001; Head of Division of Immunochemical Genetics, Clinical Research Centre, Medical Research Council, 1976–89; *b* 6 Aug. 1924; *d* of Albert E. and Annie B. Watkins. *Educ:* Godolphin and Latymer Sch., London; Univ. of London. PhD 1950; DSc 1963. FRCPath 1983. Research Asst in Biochemistry, St Bartholomew's Hosp. Med. Sch., 1948–50; Beit Memorial Research Fellow, 1952–55; Mem. of Staff of Lister Inst. of Preventive Medicine, 1955–75; Wellcome Travelling Research Fellow, Univ. of California, 1960–61; Reader in Biochemistry, 1965; Prof. of Biochemistry, Univ. of London, 1968–75; William Julius Mickle Fellow, London Univ., 1971. Mem. Council, Royal Soc., 1984–86. Hon. Member: Internat. Soc. of Blood Transfusion, 1982; British Blood Transfusion Soc., 1996; Japanese Biochemical Soc., 1990; British Biochem. Soc., 2000; Foreign Member: Polish Acad. of Sciences, 1988; Royal Swedish Acad. of Scis, 1998. Governor: Dulwich Coll., 1987–95; Alleyn's Sch., Dulwich, 1995–97. Founder FMedSci 1998. Hon. FRCP

1990. Hon. DSc Utrecht, 1990. Landsteiner Memorial Award (jtly), 1967; Paul Ehrlich-Ludwig Darmstädter Prize (jtly), 1969; Kenneth Goldsmith Award, British Blood Transfusion Soc., 1986; Royal Medal, Royal Soc., 1988; Franz Oehlecker Medal, German Soc. of Transfusion Medicine and Immunohaematology, 1989; (jtly) Philip Levine Award, Amer. Soc. of Clin. Pathologists, 1990. *Publications:* various papers in biochemical and immunological jls. *Address:* Flat 37 Duneevan, 76 Oatlands Drive, Weybridge, Surrey KT13 9HZ. *T:* (01932) 234830; *e-mail:* w.watkins@ imperial.ac.uk.   *Died 3 Oct. 2003.*

WATKINSON, John Taylor; solicitor; Director, Interconnect Communications Ltd, since 1986; *b* 25 Jan. 1941; *s* of William Forshaw Watkinson; *m* 1969, Jane Elizabeth Miller; two *s* two *d*. *Educ:* Bristol Grammar Sch.; Worcester Coll., Oxford. Schoolmaster, Rugby Sch., Warwicks, 1964–71. Called to the Bar, Middle Temple, 1971; practised, Midland Circuit, 1972–74, South East Circuit, 1978–79; Solicitor of the Supreme Ct, 1986–; Principal, Watkinson & Co., 1989–95. MP (Lab) Gloucestershire West, Oct. 1974–1979; PPS to Sec. of State, Home Office, 1975–79; Member: Public Accounts Cttee, 1976–79; Expenditure Cttee, 1978–79; Speakers' Conf. on Northern Ireland, 1979; Hon. Sec., Anglo-Swiss Parly Gp, 1977–79; Mem. and Rapporteur, Council of Europe and WEU, 1976–79; Rapporteur, first Europ. Declaration on the Police. Contested: (Lab) Warwick and Leamington, 1970; (SDP) Glos West, 1983, 1987. Financial Reporter, BBC TV, 1979–82. Dir, Wyedean Review Ltd, 1987–. Advr to Polish, Macedonian, Bulgarian, Latvian, Austrian, Moroccan, Mauritian, Norwegian, Bosnian, Belarusian, Czech Republic, Slovakian, Ukrainian, Cypriot, Romanian, Jordanian, Lebanon, and Irish Govts on telecommunications, postal and broadcasting laws and regulatory regimes, 1992–93. Visitor, Onley Borstal, Warwicks, 1970–71. Mem., NUJ. Amateur Rugby Fives Champion (Singles 3 times, Doubles 4 times), 1964–70. *Publications:* (jtly) UK Telecommunications Approval Manual, 1987; Telecommunications Approval Report, 1987; European Telecommunications Manual, 1990; The Company Director's Guide, 2001. *Recreations:* rackets, Real tennis, cricket, golf. *Address:* Clanna Lodge, Alvington, Lydney, Glos GL15 6AJ.   *Died 21 Sept. 2004.*

WATSON, Prof. Alan Albert; JP; FRCPath; Regius Professor of Forensic Medicine, University of Glasgow, 1985–92, then Emeritus; *b* 20 Feb. 1929; *s* of Wilfrid Roy Watson and Gladys Cusden or Watson; *m* 1955, Jeannette Anne Pitts or Watson; three *s*. *Educ:* Reading Sch.; St Mary's Hosp. Med. Sch., Univ. of London (MB BS); MA Cantab; BD Glasgow. FRCPGlas; DMJ; DTM&H (Antwerp). Director, Ntondo Hosp., Zaire, 1958; Lectr in Pathology, Glasgow Univ., 1964; Asst Pathologist, Cambridge Univ., 1969, Fellow, Queens' Coll., Cambridge, 1970; Sen. Lectr, Forensic Medicine, Glasgow, 1971. District Court Judge, 1982; JP Glasgow, 1982–93, Kilmarnock and Loudoun Dist, 1993–. Fellow, Royal Belgian Acad. of Medicine, 1983. *Publications:* Legal Aspects of Dental Practice, 1975; Forensic Medicine, 1989; Lecture Notes on Forensic Medicine, 1989; contribs to Jls of Forensic Medicine, and Pathology. *Address:* 76 Arrol Drive, Ayr KA7 4AW. *T:* (01292) 266365.   *Died 17 Nov. 2001.*

WATSON, Anthony Heriot, CBE 1965; Director of Statistics, Ministry of Transport, later Department of the Environment, 1965–73; *b* 13 April 1912; *s* of William Watson and Dora Isabel Watson (*née* Fisher); *m* 1946, Hilary Margaret Fyfe. *Educ:* St Paul's Sch.; Christ Church, Oxford; University Coll., London. Statistical Officer, British Cotton Industry Research Assoc., 1936. Min. of Supply, 1940: Statistician; Asst Dir of Statistics; Min. of Aircraft Production, 1942; Statistician, Dept of Civil Aviation, Air Ministry, 1945; Chief Statistician: Min. of Civil Aviation, 1951; Min. of Transport and Civil

Aviation, 1954; Min. of Aviation, 1959; Min. of Transport, 1964. *Publications:* (ed with D. L. Munby and contrib.) Inland Transport Statistics: Great Britain 1900–1970, vol. 1, 1978; (contrib.) Reviews of UK Statistical Sources, vol. VII. *Recreation:* music, especially singing. *Address:* 66 Murrayfield Avenue, Edinburgh EH12 6AY. *T:* (0131) 337 8121.

Died 23 Dec. 2002.

WATSON, Arthur Christopher, CMG 1977; HM Diplomatic Service, retired; Governor of Montserrat, West Indies, 1985–87; *b* 2 Jan. 1927; *s* of late Dr A. J. Watson and Dr Mary Watson, Kunming, China, and Chinnor; *m* 1956, Mary Cecil Candler (*née* Earl); one *d*, and one step *s* one step *d*. *Educ:* Norwich Sch.; St Catharine's Coll., Cambridge. Naval Service, 1945–48 (commissioned RNVR, 1946). Colonial Administrative Service, Uganda, 1951; District Commissioner, 1959; Principal Asst Sec., 1960; Principal, Commonwealth Relations Office, 1963; HM Diplomatic Service, 1965; Karachi, 1964–67; Lahore, 1967; FCO, 1967–71; HM Comr in Anguilla, 1971–74; Governor, Turks and Caicos Islands, 1975–78; High Comr in Brunei, 1978–83; FCO, 1983–84. *Address:* Old School House, Newport Road, Whitwell, Isle of Wight PO38 2QW. *Club:* Royal Commonwealth Society. *Died 7 May 2001.*

WATSON, Prof. Newton Frank, RIBA; Haden/Pilkington Professor of Environmental Design and Engineering, and Head, Bartlett School of Architecture and Planning, University College London, 1985–88, then Emeritus Professor; Dean of the Faculty of Environmental Studies, 1986–88; *b* 29 July 1923; *s* of Frank Watson and Amy Watson (*née* Cole); *m* 1944, Bridget Williams; two *d*. *Educ:* Holywell Grammar Sch.; King's Coll., Univ. of Durham (BArch). Wartime service, RWF (Lieut). Asst architect in practice, 1951–55; Res. Fellow, Nuffield Foundn Div. for Architectural Studies, 1955–57; Lectr in Arch., Poly. of N London, 1957–60; Lectr/Sen. Lectr in Arch., UCL, 1960–69; Bartlett Prof. of Architecture, UCL, 1969–85. Vis. Prof., Dept. of Arch., Univ. of California at Berkeley, 1965–66; Vis. Scholar, Sch. of Design, N Carolina State Univ., 1989. Awards (jtly) by Illuminating Soc. of Amer. for lighting design of London Stock Exchange, 1974, and Tate Gall., 1980. *Publications:* (jtly) in Design for Research, 1986; contribs to professional jls on lighting design (CIBSE medal (jtly) 1982, for contrib. Preferred Lighting Levels for Viewing Works of Art). *Recreations:* etching, France. *Address:* 1b Oval Road, NW1 7EA. *T:* (020) 7485 4796. *Club:* Athenæum.

Died 24 May 2002.

WATSON, Roy William, CBE 1983; Director General, National Farmers' Union, 1979–85, retired; *b* 7 Feb. 1926; *s* of William and Eleanor Maud Watson; *m* 1st, 1947, Margaret Peasey; two *s*; 2nd, 1977, Phyllis Frances Brotherwood (*née* Farrer). *Educ:* Alleyn's Sch., Dulwich. Intelligence Corps, 1945–48. National Farmers' Union, 1948–85: Asst Dir General, 1973–78; Dep. Dir General, 1978. Mem., UK Employer Delegn to ILO, 1961–76; formerly Mem., ILO Permanent Agric. Cttee and Cttee on Rural Develt; Employer Deleg. to World Employment Conf., 1976. *Recreations:* music, military history, golf, gardening. *Address:* Galilee, 44 Greenway, Frinton-on-Sea, Essex CO13 9AL. *T:* (01255) 679651.

Died 22 Dec. 2003.

WATT; *see* Gibson-Watt.

WATT, Emeritus Prof. William Smith, FBA 1989; Regius Professor of Humanity in the University of Aberdeen, 1952–79, Vice-Principal, 1969–72; *b* 20 June 1913; *s* of John Watt and Agnes Smith; *m* 1944, Dorothea, *e d* of R. J. Codrington Smith; one *s*. *Educ:* Univ. of Glasgow (1st cl. Hons, Classics, 1933; Ferguson Schol., 1934); Balliol Coll., Oxford (Snell Exhibnr and Hon. Schol.; Craven Schol., 1934; 1st cl. Classical Mods, 1935; Hertford and Ireland Schol., 1935; 1st cl. Lit. Hum., 1937; MA 1940). Lecturer in Greek and Greek History, Univ. of

Glasgow, 1937–38; Fellow and Tutor in Classics, Balliol Coll., Oxford, 1938–52. Civilian Officer, Admiralty (Naval Intelligence Div.), 1941–45. Convener, Scottish Univs Council on Entrance, 1973–77. Governor, Aberdeen Coll. of Educn, 1958–75 (Chm. of Governors 1971–75). Pres., Classical Assoc. of Scotland, 1983–88. *Publications:* (ed) Ciceronis Epistulae ad Quintum fratrem, etc, 1958, 1965; (ed) Ciceronis Epistularum ad Atticum Libri I-VIII, 1965; (ed) Ciceronis Epistulae ad familiares, 1982; (ed with P. J. Ford) George Buchanan's Miscellaneorum Liber, 1982; (ed) Vellei Paterculi Historiae, 1988; many articles in classical periodicals. *Address:* 38 Woodburn Gardens, Aberdeen AB15 8JA. *T:* (01224) 314369. *Died 23 Dec. 2002.*

WATTS, Lt-Gen. Sir John Peter Barry Condliffe, KBE 1988 (CBE 1979; OBE 1972); CB 1985; MC 1960; Chief of Defence Staff, Sultan of Oman's Armed Forces, 1984–87; *b* 27 Aug. 1930; *m* 1st, Mary Flynn (marr. diss. 1986); four *s* three *d*; 2nd, 1986, Diana Walker. *Educ:* Westminster Sch.; Phillips Acad., Andover, USA; RMA Sandhurst. Commissioned, RUR, 1951 (Royal Irish Rangers, 1968); served Hong Kong, Malaya (despatches), Cyprus, Oman (MC), BAOR, Borneo and South Arabia; 48 Gurkha Inf. Bde, 1967–69; CO 22 SAS Regt, 1970–72; Directing Staff, Staff Coll., 1972–74; MoD, 1974; Comdr. SAS Gp, 1975–78; Comdr, Sultan of Oman's Land Forces, 1979–84. *Died 10 Dec. 2003.*

WATTS, Thomas Rowland, (Tom), CBE 1978; Chartered Accountant; *b* 1 Jan. 1917; *s* of late Thomas William Watts and Daisy Maud Watts (*née* Bultitude); *m* 1955, Hester Zoë Armitstead; one *s* two *d*. *Educ:* Gresham's Sch., Holt. Served War, TA, 1939–41, Royal Marines (Captain), 1941–46. Articled to Price Waterhouse & Co., 1934–39, Partner, 1963–82. Dir, Jarrold & Sons Ltd, Norwich, 1982–87. Chm., Accounting Standards Cttee (UK and Ireland), 1978–82; Mem. Council, Inst. of Chartered Accountants in England and Wales, 1974–82; Mem. City EEC Cttee, 1974–82; Adviser to Dept of Trade on EEC company law, 1974–83; Vice-Pres. d'honneur, Groupe d'Etudes des experts comptables de la CEE, 1979–88 (Vice-Pres., 1975–79); Chm., EEC Liaison Cttee of UK Accountancy Bodies, 1986–88; Chm., Dental Rates Study Gp, 1982–85. A Gen. Comr of Income Tax, 1986–92. Hon. Vis. Prof., City of London Polytech., 1983–86. Liveryman, Chartered Accountants' Co., 1977–. Chartered Accountants Founding Socs' Centenary Award, 1982. *Publications:* editor, various professional books; papers in professional jls. *Address:* 13 Fitzwalter Road, Colchester, Essex CO3 3SY. *T:* (01206) 573520.

Died 14 Sept. 2005.

WATTS, His Honour Victor Brian; a Circuit Judge, 1980–99; *b* 7 Jan. 1927; *o s* of Percy William King Watts and Doris Millicent Watts; *m* 1965, Patricia Eileen (*née* Steer); one *s* one *d*. *Educ:* Colfe's Grammar Sch.; University Coll., Oxford (BCL 1949; MA 1952). Called to the Bar, Middle Temple, 1950; subseq. Western Circuit; a Recorder of the Crown Court, 1972–80. Flying Officer, Royal Air Force, 1950–52. Churchwarden, St Peter's Church, Hammersmith, 1984–90. *Publications:* Landlord and Tenant Act, 1954; Leading Cases on the Law of Contract, 1955; occasional articles of a legal nature. *Recreations:* the arts, travel, tennis, riding. *Address:* 28 Abinger Road, W4 1EL. *T:* (020) 8994 4435. *Club:* Hurlingham. *Died 9 Nov. 2001.*

WAUGH, Auberon Alexander; Editor, The Literary Review, since 1986; Columnist: The Daily Telegraph, since 1990; The Sunday Telegraph, since 1996; *b* 17 Nov. 1939; *e s* of late Evelyn Waugh, writer, and Laura Waugh, Combe Florey House, Somerset; *m* 1961, Teresa, *o d* of 6th Earl of Onslow, KBE, MC, and *sister* of 7th Earl of Onslow; two *s* two *d*. *Educ:* Downside (schol. in Classics); Christ Church, Oxford (exhibn in English, read PPE). Commissioned Royal Horse Guards, 1957; served Cyprus; retd with wounds, 1958. Editorial staff, Daily Telegraph, 1960–63; weekly columnist, Catholic Herald, 1963–64;

special writer, Mirror group, 1964–67; Political Correspondent: Spectator, 1967–70; Private Eye, 1970–86; weekly columnist: The Times, 1970–71; New Statesman, 1973–76; Sunday Telegraph, 1981–90; columnist, Spectator, 1976–96; Chief Fiction Reviewer: Spectator, 1970–73; Evening Standard, 1973–80; Daily Mail, 1981–86; Chief Book Reviewer, The Independent, 1986–89; monthly contributor, Books and Bookmen, 1973–80. Contested (Dog Lovers' Party) Devon North, 1979. Pres., British Croatian Soc., 1973–92. Nat. Press 'Critic of the Year' commendations, 1976, 1978; 'What the Papers Say' Columnist of the Year, Granada TV, 1979, 1988. *Publications: novels:* The Foxglove Saga, 1960; Path of Dalliance, 1963; Who are the Violets Now?, 1966; Consider the Lilies, 1968; A Bed of Flowers, 1971; *non-fiction:* (with S. Cronje) Biafra: Britain's Shame, 1969; Four Crowded Years: the Diaries of Auberon Waugh, 1976; The Last Word: an Eyewitness Account of the Thorpe Trial, 1980; Auberon Waugh's Yearbook, 1981; The Diaries of Auberon Waugh: a turbulent decade 1976–85, 1985; Waugh on Wine, 1986; Will This Do? the first fifty years of Auberon Waugh (autobiog.), 1991; Way of the World, 1994, vol. 2, The Forgotten Years (illus. W. Rushton), 1997; *essays:* Country Topics, 1974; In The Lion's Den, 1978; Another Voice, 1986; *anthology:* (ed) The Literary Review Anthology of Real Poetry, 1991. *Recreation:* gossip. *Address:* Combe Florey House, near Taunton, Somerset TA4 3JD; 7 Phoenix Lodge Mansions, Brook Green, W6 7BG. *Clubs:* Beefsteak, Academy.
Died 16 Jan. 2001.

WEATHERLEY, Prof. Paul Egerton, FRS 1973; Regius Professor of Botany in the University of Aberdeen, 1959–81, then Emeritus; *b* 6 May 1917; *o s* of late Leonard Roger Weatherley and Ethel Maude (*née* Collin), Leicester; *m* 1942, Margaret Logan, *o d* of late John Pirie, JP, Castle of Auchry, Aberdeenshire; one *s* three *d. Educ:* Wyggeston School; Keble College, Oxford (Open Schol.; Final Sch. of Nat. Sci. (Hons Botany) 1939). Keble Research Schol., 1939–40, elected to Colonial Agric. Schol., 1940. Trained in RE, then Colonial Office cadet at Imperial Coll. of Tropical Agric., Trinidad, 1940–42; Govt Botanist in Dept of Agriculture, Uganda Protectorate, 1942–47; Asst Lectr, Univ. of Manchester, 1947–49; Lecturer in Botany, 1949–59 (Sen. Lectr 1956), Univ. of Nottingham. *Publications:* papers in (mainly) botanical journals. *Recreations:* music, sketching. *Address:* Greystones, Torphins, Aberdeenshire AB31 4HP.
Died 8 Aug. 2001.

WEAVER, Sir Tobias Rushton, (Sir Toby), Kt 1973; CB 1962; Deputy Secretary, Department of Education and Science, 1962–72; *b* 19 July 1911; *s* of late Sir Lawrence Weaver, KBE, and Lady (Kathleen) Weaver (*née* Purcell); *m* 1941, Marjorie, *d* of Rt Hon. Sir Charles Trevelyan, 3rd Bt, PC; one *s* three *d. Educ:* Clifton College; Corpus Christi College, Cambridge. Bank clerk, Toronto, 1932; teaching at Barking, 1935, Eton, 1936; Assistant Director of Education: Wilts CC, 1936, Essex CC, 1939; Admiralty, 1941–42; War Office, 1942–45; Dept of Education and Science, 1946–73 (Under-Secretary, 1956). Visiting Professor of Education: Univ. of Southampton, 1973; Univ. of London Inst. of Educn, 1974; Open Univ., 1976–78. FIC 1986; Hon. Fellow: Manchester Poly., 1970; Huddersfield Poly., 1972; Hatfield Poly., 1973; NE London Poly., 1985. Hon. LLD CNAA, 1972. *Address:* 14 Marston Close, NW6 4EU. *T:* (020) 7624 4263.
Died 10 June 2001.

WEBB, Maysie Florence, CBE 1979; Deputy Director, British Museum, 1971–83 (Assistant Director 1968–71); *b* 1 May 1923; *d* of Charles and Florence Webb. *Educ:* Kingsbury County School; Northern Polytechnic (BSc). Southwark Public Libraries, 1940–45; A. C. Cossor Ltd, 1945–50; British Non-Ferrous Metals Research Assoc., 1950–52; Mullard Equipment Ltd, 1952–55; Morgan Crucible Co. Ltd, 1955–60; Head, Patent Office Library, 1960–66; Keeper, National Reference Library of Science

and Invention, 1966–68. General Comr in England and Wales, 1976–2002. Trustee of the Royal Armouries, 1984–90. *Recreations:* family and friends, thinking.
Died 11 Dec. 2005.

WEBB, William Grierson; freelance conductor and teacher; Musical Director, South Coast Opera, since 1998; *b* 16 Oct. 1947; *s* of Horace James Harry Webb and Marjorie Cairns (*née* Grierson); *m* 1984, Elizabeth Jean Shannon; two *s. Educ:* Rugby School; Merton Coll., Oxford (MA); Salzburg Mozarteum (Dip.). Hon. FLCM. Conductor, Trier Opera House, Germany, 1973–76; Asst General Administrator, Scottish Nat. Orchestra, 1976–78; Founder Administrator, Nat. Youth Orchestra of Scotland, 1978–87; Dep. Dir, 1987–90, Artistic Dir, 1991–96, London Coll. of Music; Associate Artistic Dir, The Rehearsal Orch., 1994–98. Musical Dir, Aberdeen Internat. Youth Festival, 1989–91. Dir, Chase Lodge Music, 1997–. Chm., Mendelssohn and Boise Scholarship Foundns, 1992–94. *Publications:* (trans.) Tyrol through the Ages, 1973; The Music of John McLeod, 1979. *Address:* Chase Lodge, Herbert Road, Bournemouth BH4 8HD.
Died 10 Feb. 2004.

WEBSTER, Alen Gregg, CMG 1999; Assistant Director-General, Director, Development and Training Services and Member, Board of Management, British Council, since 1995; *b* 25 April 1946; *s* of Ian Webster and Helen Elizabeth Webster (*née* Barrs); *m* 1983, Carmel Kennedy; one *s* one *d. Educ:* George Heriot's Sch., Edinburgh. CA. Whinney Murray Ernst & Ernst, London and Germany, 1969–72; Walt Disney Productions, Europe, 1972–74; Chief Accountant, Pergamon Press, 1974–75; British Council, 1975–: posts in Finance Div., 1975–78; Asst Dir, India, 1978–81; Finance Div., 1981–83; Asst Dir, Spain, 1983–86; Dir, Audit, 1986–87; Chief Acct, 1987–89; Director: Singapore, 1989–92; Indonesia, 1992–95. *Address:* British Council, 58 Whitworth Street, Manchester M1 6BB. *T:* (0161) 957 7801.
Died 22 July 2001.

WEBSTER, David (Jay); Chairman, Trans-Atlantic Dialogue on Broadcasting and the Information Society, since 1988; consultant to international companies and institutions; *b* 11 Jan. 1931; *s* of Alec Webster and Clare Webster; *m* 1st, 1955, Lucy Law (marr. diss.), Princeton, NJ; two *s;* 2nd, 1981, Elizabeth Drew, author, Washington, DC. *Educ:* Taunton Sch.; Ruskin Coll., Oxford. British Broadcasting Corporation: Sub-Editor, External Services News Dept, 1953–59; Producer, Panorama, 1959–64; Exec. Producer, Enquiry, and Encounter, BBC 2, 1964–66; Dep. Editor, Panorama, 1966, Editor, 1967–69; Exec. Editor, Current Affairs Group, 1969, Asst Head, 1970; BBC Rep. in USA, 1971–76; Controller, Information Services, 1976–77; Dir, Public Affairs, 1977–80; Dir, US, BBC, 1981–85. Mem., Bd of Management, BBC, 1977–85. Resident Associate, Carnegie Endowment, 1985–87; Sen. Fellow, Annenberg Washington Program on Communications Policy Studies, 1987–92. Pres., RadioSar Internat., 1991–97. Special Adviser, Communications Studies and Planning Internat., 1987–88; Chm., Internat. Disaster Communications Project, 1987–91. Mem., Twentieth Century Fund Task Force on the Flow of the News, 1978. Member: Adv. Council, Ditchley Foundn of US, 1981–; Nat. Adv. Cttee for the William Benton Fellowship Prog., Univ. of Chicago, 1983–89. Fellow, Internat. Council, Nat. Acad. of Television Arts and Scis, USA, 1980– (Chm., Internat. Council, 1974 and 1975). *Address:* 3000 Woodland Drive, Washington, DC 20008, USA. *T:* (202) 2986373, *Fax:* (202) 2986374; *e-mail:* Dwebsweb@aol.com. *Club:* Century Association (NY). *Died 6 Aug. 2003.*

WEBSTER, His Honour Ian Stevenson; a Circuit Judge, 1981–95; *b* 20 March 1925; *s* of late Harvey Webster and Annabella Stevenson Webster (*née* McBain); *m* 1951, Margaret (*née* Sharples); two *s. Educ:* Rochdale Grammar Sch.; Manchester Univ. Sub Lieut (A), RNVR, 1944. Called to the Bar, Middle Temple, 1948; Assistant

Recorder: of Oldham, 1970; of Salford, 1971; a Recorder of the Crown Court, 1972–76, 1981; Chm., Industrial Tribunals for Manchester, 1976–81; Liaison Judge: for Burnley, Reedley and Accrington Benches, 1981–86; for Rochdale, Middleton and Heywood Benches, 1987–95; Resident Judge, Burnley, 1985–95. Hon. Recorder, Burnley, 1991–95. *Club:* Rochdale Golf.

Died 9 March 2002.

WEDGWOOD, John Alleyne, CBE 1984; FCIS; Chairman, Southern Electricity Board, 1977–84; *b* 26 Jan. 1920; *s* of Rev. Charles Henry Wedgwood and Myrtle Winifred Perry; *m* 1st, 1942, Freda Mary Lambert (*d* 1963); one *s*; 2nd, 1974, Lilian Nora Forey (*d* 1992); 3rd, 1992, Jeanette May England. *Educ:* Monkton Combe Sch.; Queens' Coll., Cambridge (MA Hons Hist. Tripos). FCIS, CompIEE. Served War, Lincs Regt and Durham LI, 1940–46 (Actg Major). Asst Principal, Min. of Fuel and Power, 1946–48; Admin. Officer, British Electricity Authority, 1948–55; Dep. Sec., London Electricity Bd, 1955–58; Dep. Sec., Electricity Council, 1958–65, Sec., 1965–74; Dep. Chm., S Eastern Elec. Bd, 1974–77. President: Inst. of Chartered Secs and Administrators, 1976; Electric Vehicle Assoc., 1983–86; Chm. Bd of Management, Electrical and Electronics Industries Benevolent Assoc., 1977–83. Member: Worshipful Co. of Scriveners, 1973–; SE Econ. Planning Council, 1975–79. Founder Master, Worshipful Co. of Chartered Secs and Administrators, 1978. Freeman, City of London, 1973. *Recreations:* gardening, music, railways, ornithology. *Address:* Apartment 24, Swallowfield Park, Swallowfield, Reading, Berks RG7 1GT. *T:* (0118) 988 3799. *Club:* Phyllis Court (Henley). *Died 15 Feb. 2004.*

WEEDON, Prof. Basil Charles Leicester, CBE 1974; DSc; PhD; FRS 1971; FRSC; Vice-Chancellor, Nottingham University, 1976–88; *b* 18 July 1923; *s* of late Charles William Weedon; *m* 1959, Barbara Mary Dawe; one *s* one *d*. *Educ:* Wandsworth Sch.; Imperial Coll. of Science and Technology (ARCS; DIC). Research Chemist, ICI Ltd (Dyestuffs Div.), 1943–47; Lecturer in Organic Chemistry, Imperial Coll., 1947–55, Reader, 1955–60; Prof. of Organic Chemistry, QMC, 1960–76, Fellow, 1984; Hon. Prof., Nottingham Univ., 1988–. Chm., Food Additives and Contaminants Cttee, 1968–83; Mem., EEC Scientific Cttee for Food, 1974–81; Scientific Editor, Pure and Applied Chemistry, 1960–75. Member: UGC, 1974–76; Council, National Stone Centre, 1985–93 (Chm. Council, 1985–91). Chm., E Midlands Reg., Electricity Consumers' Cttee, 1990–94. Tilden Lecturer, Chemical Society, 1966. Hon. DTech Brunel Univ., 1975; Hon. LLD Nottingham, 1988. Meldola Medal, Roy. Inst. of Chemistry, 1952. *Publications:* A Guide to Qualitative Organic Chemical Analysis (with Sir Patrick Linstead), 1956; scientific papers, mainly in Jl Chem. Soc. *Address:* Sheepwash Grange, Heighington Road, Canwick, Lincoln LN4 2RJ. *T:* (01522) 522488. *Died 10 Oct. 2003.*

WEEKES, Philip Gordon, CBE 1993 (OBE 1977); CEng, FIMinE; Chairman: S. V. Waste Services Ltd, since 1992; Goitre Tower Anthracite Ltd, 1994–99; *b* 12 June 1920; *s* of Albert Edwin and Gwladys Magdaline Weekes; *m* 1944, Branwen Mair Jones; two *s* two *d*. *Educ:* Tredegar County Sch.; University Coll., Cardiff (BSc Hons; Fellow, 1982). Jun. official, Tredegar Iron & Coal Co., 1939. Served War, RAF, 1942–44. Manager: Wyllie Colliery, Tredegar (Southern) Colliery Co., 1946; Oakdale Colliery, 1948; seconded to Colonial Office, 1950; Colliery Agent, S Wales, 1951; HQ Work Study Engr, 1952; Gp Manager, Area Prod. Manager, in various areas in S Wales, 1954; Dir of Studies, NCB Staff Coll., 1964; Dep. Dir (Mining), S Midlands Area, 1967; Chief Mining Engr, Nat. HQ, 1970; Dir-Gen. of Mining, Nat. HQ, 1971; Area Dir, S Wales Coalfield, 1973–85; part-time Mem., NCB, 1977–84. Chm., 1992 Garden Fest. Wales Ltd, 1987–94. Member: Prince of Wales' Cttee, 1978–89; IBA Wales Adv. Cttee, 1983–90. Gov., United World Coll. of the Atlantic,

1981–95. *Address:* Hillbrow, Llantwit Major, South Glamorgan CF61 1RE. *Club:* Cardiff and County.

Died 26 June 2003.

WEIGHELL, Sidney; General Secretary, National Union of Railwaymen, 1975–83; Member, Trades Union General Council, 1975–83; *b* 31 March 1922; *s* of John Thomas and Rose Lena Weighell; *m* 1st, 1949, Margaret Alison Hunter (killed, 1956); one *s* (one *d* killed, 1956); 2nd, 1959, Joan Sheila Willetts. *Educ:* Church of England Sch., Northallerton, Yorks. Joined LNER, Motive Power Dept, 1938. Elected to: NUR Exec., 1953; full-time NUR Official, 1954; Asst Gen. Sec., 1965. Labour Party Agent, 1947–52; Mem., Labour Party Exec., 1972–75. Non-exec. Dir, BAA plc (formerly BAA), 1987–88 (pt-time Bd Mem., 1983–87); Mem., Programme Consultative Panel, Tyne Tees TV Ltd, 1984–87. Pres., Great Yorks Rly Preservation Soc., 1986–; Mem., Ditchley Foundn, 1983–89 (Gov., 1983–92). *Publications:* On the Rails, 1983; A Hundred Years of Railway Weighells (autobiog.), 1984. *Recreations:* trout fishing, swimming, gardening; professional footballer, Sunderland FC, 1945–47. *Address:* Blenheim, 2 Moor Park Close, Beckwithshaw, near Harrogate, North Yorkshire HG3 1TR. *Died 13 Feb. 2002.*

WEINSTOCK, Baron *cr* 1980 (Life Peer), of Bowden in the County of Wiltshire; **Arnold Weinstock,** Kt 1970; FSS; Managing Director, General Electric Co. plc, 1963–96, then Chairman Emeritus; *b* 29 July 1924; *s* of Simon and Golda Weinstock; *m* 1949, Netta, *d* of Sir Michael Sobell; one *d* (one *s* decd). *Educ:* LSE, Univ. of London (BSc Econ (Stats); Hon. Fellow 1985). Junior administrative officer, Admiralty, 1944–47; engaged in finance and property development, group of private companies, 1947–54; Radio & Allied Industries Ltd (later Radio & Allied Holdings Ltd), 1954–63 (Managing Director); General Electric Co. Ltd, Director 1961. Dir, Rolls-Royce (1971) Ltd, 1971–73. Vice Pres., Friends of the Ravenna Fest., 1993–94; Trustee: British Museum, 1985–96; Royal Philharmonic Soc., Foundn Fund, 1984–92. Mem., Jockey Club. Hon. FRCR 1975. Hon. Fellow, Peterhouse, Cambridge, 1982. Hon. Bencher, Gray's Inn, 1982. Hon. DSc: Salford, 1975; Aston, 1976; Bath, 1978; Reading, 1978; Ulster, 1987; Hon. LLD: Leeds, 1978; Wales, 1985; Keele, 1997; Hon. DTech Loughborough, 1981; DUniv Anglia Poly., 1994; Hon. DEconSc London, 1997. Commendatore, Ordine al Merito (Italy), 1991; Officier, Légion d'Honneur (France), 1992. *Recreations:* racing, music. *Address:* 7 Grosvenor Square, W1X 9LA.

Died 23 July 2002.

WEIR, Richard Stanton; Director-General, Institutional Fund Managers' Association, 1989–95; *b* 5 Jan. 1933; *o s* of Brig. R. A. Weir, OBE and Dr M. L. Cowan; *m* 1961, Helen Eugenie Guthrie; one *d*. *Educ:* Repton Sch., Derbys; Christ Church, Oxford (MA). Called to the Bar, Inner Temple, 1957. Commnd 3rd Carabiniers (Prince of Wales' Dragoon Guards), 1952. Head of Legal Dept, Soc. of Motor Mfrs and Traders Ltd, 1958–61; Exec., British Motor Corp. Ltd, 1961–64; Dep. Co. Sec., Rank Organisation Ltd, 1964–67; Head of Admin, Rank Leisure Services, 1967–69; Sec., CWS Ltd, 1969–74; Dir, 1975–81, Dir-Gen., 1987–89; Retail Consortium; Sec. Gen. (Chief Exec.), BSA, 1981–86; Dir, British Retailers' Assoc., 1987–89. Mem., Consumer Protection Adv. Cttee set up under Fair Trading Act, 1973, 1973–76. Pres., Old Reptonians Soc., 1998. *Recreations:* reading, walking, shooting. *Address:* PO Box 275, Salt Rock 4391, Republic of South Africa. *Club:* Oxford and Cambridge.

Died 7 March 2004.

WEISSKOPF, Prof. Victor Frederick; Professor of Physics, Massachusetts Institute of Technology, 1946–73, then Emeritus (Chairman, Department of Physics, 1967–73); *b* 19 Sept. 1908; *m* 1st, 1934, Ellen Margrete Tvede (*d* 1989); one *s* one *d*; 2nd, 1991, Duscha Schmid. *Educ:* Univ. of Göttingen, Germany (PhD 1931). Research Associate: Berlin Univ., 1932; Eidgenossiche

Technische Hochschule (Swiss Federal Institute of Technology), Zürich, 1933–35; Inst. for Theoretical Physics, Copenhagen, 1936; Asst Professor of Physics, Univ. of Rochester, NY, USA, 1937–43; Dep. Division Leader, Manhattan Project, Los Alamos, USA, 1943–45; Director-Gen., CERN, Geneva, 1961–65 (on leave of absence from MIT). Chm., High Energy Physics Adv. Panel, AEC, 1967–75. Mem., Nat. Acad. of Sciences, Washington, 1954; Pres., Amer. Acad. of Arts and Sciences, 1976–79; Corresp. Member: French Acad. of Sciences, 1957; Scottish Acad. of Scis, 1959; Royal Danish Scientific Soc., 1961; Bavarian Acad. of Scis, 1962; Austrian Acad. of Scis, 1963; Spanish Acad. of Scis, 1964; Soviet Acad. of Scis, 1976; Pontifical Acad. of Scis, 1976. Hon. Fellow: Weizmann Inst., Rehovot, Israel, 1962; Inst. of Physics, France, 1980. Hon. PhD: Manchester, 1961; Uppsala, 1964; Yale, 1964; Chicago, 1967; Hon. DSc: Montreal, 1959; Sussex, 1961; Lyon, 1962; Basle, 1962; Bonn, 1963; Genève, 1964; Oxford, 1965; Vienna, 1965; Paris, 1966; Copenhagen, 1966; Torino, 1968; Yale, 1968; Upsala, 1969; Harvard, 1984; Graz, 1985. Cherwell-Simon Memorial Lecturer, Oxford, 1963–64. Planck Medal, 1956; Gamov Award, 1969; Prix Mondial Del Duca, 1972; Killian Award, 1973; Smoluchovski Medal, Polish Physical Soc., 1979; Nat. Medal of Science, 1979; Wolf Prize (Israel), 1981; Enrico Fermi Award, 1989; Nat. Acad. Public Welfare Medal, 1991; Compton Award, 1992. Légion d'Honneur (France), 1959; Pour le Mérite Order, Germany, 1978; Grosse Goldene Ehrenzeichen (Austria), 2000. *Publications:* Theoretical Nuclear Physics, 1952; Knowledge and Wonder, 1962; Physics in the XX Century, 1972; Concepts of Particle Physics, 1984; The Privilege of Being a Physicist, 1989; The Joy of Insight, 1991; papers on theoretical physics in various journals. *Address:* 20 Bartlett Terrace, Newton, MA 02459, USA.
Died 21 April 2002.

WEIZMAN, Maj.-Gen. Ezer; President of Israel, 1993–2000; *b* Tel Aviv, 15 June 1924; *s* of Yechiel Weizman and Yehudit Weizman; *m* 1950, Reuma Schwartz; one *d* (one *s* decd). Joined RAF, 1942; fighter pilot, 1944; served ME and FE; co-founder, Israeli Air Force, 1947; fighter pilot, War of Independence, 1948–49; Comdr, first Israeli fighter sqdn, 1949; RAF Staff Coll., 1952; Air Base Comdr, 1953–57; Maj.-Gen. and Comdr, Israeli Air Force, 1958–66; Dep. COS, Israel Defence Forces, 1966–69; retd, 1969. Israeli Government: Mem., Knesset, 1977–92; Minister: of Transport, 1969–70; of Defence, 1977–80; for Arab Affairs, 1984–88; of Sci. and Technol., 1988–90. *Publications:* On Eagles' Wings, 1974; The Battle for Peace, 1981. *Address:* Beit Amot Mishpat, 8 Shaul Hamelech Boulevard, Tel Aviv 64733, Israel.
Died 24 April 2005.

WELBOURN, Prof. Richard Burkewood, MD, FRCS; Professor of Surgical Endocrinology, Royal Postgraduate Medical School, University of London, 1979–82, then Emeritus Professor; *b* 1 May 1919; *γ s* of late Burkewood Welbourn, MEng, MIEE, and Edith Welbourn, Rainhill, Lancs; *m* 1944, Rachel Mary Haighton, BDS, Nantwich, Cheshire; one *s* four *d*. *Educ:* Rugby School; Emmanuel College, Cambridge (MB, BChir 1942; MA, MD 1953); Liverpool University. FRCS 1948. War of 1939–45: RAMC. Senior Registrar, Liverpool Royal Infirmary, 1948; Research Asst, Dept of Surgery, Liverpool Univ., 1949. Fellow in Surgical Research, Mayo Foundation, Rochester, Minn, 1951. Professor of Surgical Science, Queen's University of Belfast, 1958–63; Surgeon, Royal Victoria Hospital, Belfast, 1951–63 and Belfast City Hosp., 1962–63; Prof. of Surgery, Univ. of London and Dir, Dept of Surgery, RPMS and Hammersmith Hosp., 1963–79; Hon. Consultant Surgeon, Hammersmith Hosp., 1979–82. Consultant Adviser in Surgery to Dept of Health and Social Security, 1971–79; Consultant (Vis. Schol., res. in hist. of Endocrine Surgery), Dept of Surgery, UCLA, 1983–89. Member: Council, MRC, 1971–75; Council, Royal Postgraduate Med. Sch., 1963–82. Hunterian Professor, RCS, 1958 (James Berry Prize, 1970); Harvey

Lectr, Yale Univ., 1995. Member: Society of Sigma XI; British Medical Association; Internat. Assoc. of Endocrine Surgeons, 1979– (Peter Heimann Lectr, 1989; Distinguished Service Award, 1991); Internat. Soc. of Surgery, 1979–; British Soc. of Gastro-enterology and Assoc. of Surgeons; 58th Member King James IV Surgical Association Inc.; Fellow, West African Coll. of Surgeons; FRSocMed (former Mem. Council, Section of Endocrinology, former Vice-Pres., Section of Surgery); Hon. Fellow Amer. Surgical Assoc.; Hon. Mem., Soc. for Surgery of the Alimentary Tract; formerly: Pres., Surgical Res. Soc. (Hon. Mem.); British Assoc. of Endocrine Surgeons (Hon. Mem.); Chm., Assoc. of Profs of Surgery; Mem., Jt Cttee for Higher Surgical Training; formerly Examr in Surgery, Univs of Manchester, Glasgow, Oxford, Sheffield, Edinburgh, QUB, and Liverpool; formerly Examr in Applied Physiology, RCS. Chm., Editorial Cttee, Journal of Medical Ethics, 1974–81; former Member: Editorial Cttee, Gut; Exec. Cttee, British Jl of Surgery. Formerly: Pres., Internat. Surgical Gp; Chm. Governing Body, Inst. of Medical Ethics; Pres., Prout Club. Hon. Mem., Royal Coll. of Surgeons of Univs of Denmark, 1978; Hon. FACS 1984. Hon. MD Karolinska Inst., Stockholm, 1974; Hon. DSc QUB, 1985. Biennial Medal and Prize, Internat. Soc. of Surgery, 1995. *Publications:* (with D. A. D. Montgomery) Clinical Endocrinology for Surgeons, 1963, rev. edn, Medical and Surgical Endocrinology, 1975; (with A. S. Duncan and G. R. Dunstan) Dictionary of Medical Ethics, 1977, 2nd edn 1980, American edn 1981; The History of Endocrine Surgery, 1990; chapters in books and papers, mainly on gastro-intestinal and endocrine surgery and physiology, and history of endocrinology in med. and surg. jls. *Recreations:* reading, writing without deadlines, gardening, music. *Address:* 2 The Beeches, Tilehurst, Reading RG31 6RQ. *T:* (0118) 942 9258.
Died 3 Aug. 2005.

WELLBY, Rear-Adm. Roger Stanley, CB 1958; DSO 1940; DL; Head of UK Services Liaison Staff in Australia and Senior Naval Adviser to UK High Commissioner, 1956–59; *b* 28 April 1906; *o s* of Dr Stanley Wellby and Marian Schwann; *m* 1936, Elaine, *d* of late Sir Clifford Heathcote-Smith; three *s*. *Educ:* RNC, Dartmouth. Qualified as Torpedo Officer, 1931; Commander, 1939; Special Service in France, 1940 (DSO, Croix de Guerre); Captain, 1947; Imperial Defence College; Rear-Adm. 1956. Dep. Comr-in-Chief, St John Ambulance Brigade, 1963–71; Comr, St John Ambulance Brigade, Bucks, 1971–75. DL Bucks 1972. KStJ 1966. *Recreation:* hockey, for Navy. *Address:* 2 Kingsmere Road, Wimbledon, SW19 6PX. *T:* (020) 8788 6722.
Died 25 Oct. 2003.

WELLINGS, David Gordon; Group Chief Executive, Cadbury Schweppes plc, 1993–96; *b* 13 Dec. 1940; *s* of Gordon Henry and Muriel Wellings; *m* 1962, Jennifer Christine Simpson; one *s* one *d*. *Educ:* Manchester Grammar Sch.; Oriel Coll., Oxford (MA Mod. Langs). Joined Cadbury Bros Ltd, 1962; Marketing Dir, Associated Fisheries & Food, 1970–73; Man. Dir, Northray Foods Ltd, 1973–78; Dir, Fish Ops, Ross Foods Ltd, 1978–82; Chm. and Chief Exec., Golden Wonder/HP Foods, 1982–86; Managing Director: Cadbury Ltd, 1986–89; Gp Confectionery, Cadbury Schweppes plc, 1989–93. *Recreations:* ornithology, golf. *Club:* Oxford and Cambridge.
Died 25 April 2004.

WELLINGS, Victor Gordon; QC 1973; President of the Lands Tribunal, 1989–92 (Member, 1973–88); Deputy Judge of the High Court, 1975–92; *b* 19 July 1919; *e s* of late Gordon Arthur Wellings, solicitor, and Alice Adelaide Wellings (later Poole); *m* 1948, Helen Margaret Jill Lovell; three *s*. *Educ:* Reading Sch.; Exeter Coll., Oxford (MA). Called to the Bar, Gray's Inn, 1949; practised, 1949–73. War service, 1940–46; Captain Indian Army, 17th Dogra Regt; Intell. Corps, India; Captain, TARO, 1949–. Hon. RICS (Hon. ARICS 1993). *Publications:* (ed) Woodfall, The Law of Landlord and Tenant, 28th edn 1978 (ed jtly 26th and 27th edns, 1963 and 1968), and other works on

same subject. *Recreations:* golf, fishing. *Address:* Cherry Tree Cottage, Whitchurch Hill, Pangbourne, Berks RG8 7PT. *T:* (0118) 984 2918. *Club:* Oxford and Cambridge.
Died 19 June 2001.

WELLINGTON, Peter Scott, CBE 1981; DSC; PhD; ARCS; FLS; FIBiol; FRAgS; Director, National Institute of Agricultural Botany, 1970–81; *b* 20 March 1919; *er s* of late Robert Wellington, MBE, MC; *m* 1947, Kathleen Joyce, *widow* of E. H. Coombe; one *s* one *d. Educ:* Kelly Coll.; Imperial Coll. of Science (BSc 1946). Observer, Fleet Air Arm, 1940–45 (Lt-Comdr (A) RNVR). Research Asst 1948–52, Chief Officer 1953–61, Official Seed Testing Stn for England and Wales; Asst Dir 1961–68, Dep. Dir 1968–69, Nat. Inst. of Agricultural Botany. Vice-Pres., Internat. Seed Testing Assoc., 1953–56 (Chm. Germination Cttee, 1956–70); Chief Officer, UK Variety Classification Unit, 1965–70; Chm., Technical Working Group, Internat. Convention for Protection of Plant Varieties, 1966–68; Mem., Governing Body, Nat. Seed Develt Orgn Ltd, 1982–87. *Publications:* (with V. Silvey) Crop and Seed Improvement: a history of the National Institute of Agricultural Botany 1919–1996, 1997; papers on germination of cereals and weeds, seed-testing and seed legislation. *Recreations:* gardening, walking, reading. *Address:* Colescus, Gorran Haven, St Austell, Cornwall PL26 6JJ. *T:* (01726) 842065.
Died 22 March 2003.

WELLS, Dr Alan Arthur, OBE 1982; FRS 1977; FREng; Director-General, The Welding Institute, 1977–88; *b* 1 May 1924; *s* of Arthur John Wells and Lydia Wells; *m* 1950, Rosemary Edith Alice Mitchell; four *s* one *d. Educ:* City of London Sch.; Univ. of Nottingham (BScEng); Clare Coll., Cambridge (PhD). FREng (FEng 1978); MIMechE (Hon. FIMechE 1999); Hon. FWeldI. British Welding Res. Association: Asst Dir, 1956; Dep. Dir (Scientific), 1963; Queen's University of Belfast: Prof. of Struct. Science, 1964; Head of Civil Engrg Dept, 1970–77; Dean, Faculty of Applied Science and Technol., 1973–76; Professorial Fellow, 1990. Hon. Dr, Faculty of Engrg, Univ. of Ghent, 1972; Hon. DSc Glasgow, 1982; Hon. DScEng QUB, 1986. *Publications:* Brittle Fracture of Welded Plate (jtly), 1967; res. papers on welding technol. and fracture mechanics. *Recreation:* handyman about the house and garden. *Address:* Grove House, Mepal, Ely, Cambs CB6 2AR. *T:* (01353) 778620. *Club:* Athenæum.
Died 28 Nov. 2005.

WELSBY, Rev. Canon Paul Antony; Canon Residentiary and Vice-Dean of Rochester Cathedral, 1966–88, Canon Emeritus, 1988; Permission to Officiate, Diocese of Rochester, since 1988; Chaplain to the Queen, 1980–90; *b* 18 Aug. 1920; *m* 1948, Cynthia Mary Hosmer; one *d. Educ:* Alcester Grammar Sch.; University Coll., Durham (MA); Lincoln Theological Coll.; Univ. of Sheffield (PhD). Ordained deacon, 1944, priest, 1945; Curate at Boxley, Kent, 1944–47; Curate, St Mary-le-Tower, Ipswich, 1947–52; Rector of Copdock with Washbrook, 1952–66; Rural Dean of Samford, 1964–66. Director of Post-Ordination Training for Dio. of Rochester, 1966–88; Examining Chaplain to Bp of Rochester, 1966–88, Personal Chaplain 1988–90. Member, Church Assembly, 1964–70; General Synod, 1970–80; Chm., House of Clergy at Gen. Synod and Prolocutor of Convocation of Canterbury, 1974–80. *Publications:* A Modern Catechism, 1956; Lancelot Andrewes, 1958; How the Church of England Works, 1960, new edn, 1985; The Unwanted Archbishop, 1962; The Bond of Church and State, 1962; Sermons and Society, 1970; (contrib.) Oxford Dictionary of the Christian Church, 2nd edn, 1974, 3rd edn 1997; A History of the Church of England 1945–80, 1984; (contrib.) Faith and Fabric: a history of Rochester Cathedral 604–1994, 1996; contrib. Theology. *Recreations:* reading detective fiction and biographies, visiting National Trust properties. *Address:* 20 Knights Ridge, Pembury, Kent TN2 4HP. *T:* (01892) 823053. *Died 1 March 2002.*

WELTY, Eudora; writer; *b* 13 April 1909. *Educ:* Jefferson Davis Grammar Sch.; Univ. of Wisconsin (grad 1929); Columbia Univ. (postgrad. advertising course). Gold Medal for the Novel, Amer. Acad. and Inst. of Arts and Letters, 1972; National Medal for Literature, 1980; Presidential Medal of Freedom, 1980. *Publications:* A Curtain of Green, 1943; The Robber Bridegroom, 1944; The Wide Net, 1945; Delta Wedding, 1947; Golden Apples, 1950; The Ponder Heart, 1954; The Bride of Innisfallen, 1955; The Shoe Bird, 1964; Losing Battles, 1970; One Time, One Place (photographs), 1971; The Optimist's Daughter, 1972 (Pulitzer Prize, 1973); The Eye of the Story, 1979; The Collected Stories of Eudora Welty, 1980; One Writer's Beginnings, 1984; Eudora Welty Photographs, 1989; A Writer's Eye: collected book reviews, 1994; Monuments to Interruption: collected book reviews, 1994; Complete Novels, and, Stories, Essays and Memoir (Library of America series), 1999. *Address:* 1119 Pinehurst Street, Jackson, MS 39202–1812, USA.
Died 23 July 2001.

WENTWORTH, Maurice Frank Gerard, CMG 1957; OBE 1946; *b* 5 Nov. 1908; *s* of F. B. Wentworth, Finchley, N3; *m* 1962, Belinda Margaret, *d* of late B. S. Tatham and Mrs Tatham, Mickleham, Surrey; one *s* one *d. Educ:* Haileybury; University Coll., London (BA). Military Service, 1939–46, Lieutenant-Colonel. Gold Coast: Inspector of Schools, 1930; Sen. Education Officer, 1945; Principal, Teacher Training Coll., Tamale, 1946; Administrative Officer Class I, 1951; Permanent Secretary, 1953; Establishment Secretary, 1954–57 (Ghana Civil Service); Chairman: Public Service Commission: Sierra Leone, 1958–61; E African High Commn, 1961–64; Appointments Officer, ODM, 1964–73. *Address:* Castania, Burton Street, Marnhull, Sturminster Newton, Dorset DT10 1JJ. *Died 15 Dec. 2005.*

WESIERSKA, Ruth Christabel, (Mrs George Wesierska); *see* Walder, R. C.

WESLEY, Mary; *see* Siepmann, M. A.

WEST, Rt Hon. Henry William; PC (N Ire) 1960; Leader, Ulster Unionist Party, 1974–79; *b* 27 March 1917; *s* of late W. H. West, JP; *m* 1956, Maureen Elizabeth Hall; four *s* three *d. Educ:* Enniskillen Model School; Portora Royal School. Farmer. MP for Enniskillen, NI Parlt, 1954–72; Mem. (U), Fermanagh and S Tyrone, NI Assembly, 1973–75; Parly Sec. to Minister of Agriculture, 1958; Minister of Agriculture, 1960–67, and 1971–72; MP (UUUC) Fermanagh and South Tyrone, Feb.–Sept. 1974; Mem. (UUUC), for Fermanagh and South Tyrone, NI Constitutional Convention, 1975–76. N Ireland representative on British Wool Marketing Board, 1950–58; President, Ulster Farmers' Union, 1955–56. High Sheriff, Co. Fermanagh, 1954. *Address:* Rossmere, Rossahilly, Enniskillen, Northern Ireland BT94 2FP. *T:* (028) 6632 3060. *Died 5 Feb. 2004.*

WEST, Peter; BBC television commentator/anchorman, 1950–86; commentaries for radio, 1947–85; Chairman, West Nally Group (sports marketing), 1971–83; *b* 12 Aug. 1920; *s* of Harold William and Dorcas Anne West; *m* 1946, Pauline Mary Pike; two *s* one *d. Educ:* Cranbrook Sch.; RMC, Sandhurst. Served War of 1939–45, Duke of Wellington's Regt. TV/radio commentaries every year: on Test matches, 1952–86; on Wimbledon, 1955–82; on Rugby Union, 1950–85; Olympics, 1948–60–64–68–72–76. Rugby Football Correspondent of The Times, 1971–82. TV shows: chairman of: Why?, 1953; Guess my Story, 1953–54–55; introduced: At Home, 1955; First Hand and It's Up to You, 1956–57; Box Office, 1957; Come Dancing, 1957–72 (incl.); Be Your Own Boss and Wish You Were Here, 1958; Get Ahead, 1958–62; Good Companions, 1958–62; First Years at Work (Schs TV), 1958–69 (incl.); Miss World, 1961–66 (incl.); Facing West (HTV, Bristol), 1986–88. Children's TV: introduced: Question Marks, 1957; Ask Your Dad, 1958; What's New?, 1962–63–64. Radio: introduced:

What Shall We Call It?, 1955; Sound Idea, 1958; Morning Call, 1960–61; Treble Chance, 1962; Sporting Chance, 1964; Games People Play, 1985. Pres., Cheltenham Cricket Soc., 1984–. Ed., Playfair Cricket Annual, 1948–53. *Publications:* The Fight for the Ashes, 1953; The Fight for the Ashes, 1956; Flannelled Fool and Muddied Oaf (autobiog.), 1986; Clean Sweep, 1987; Denis Compton—Cricketing Genius, 1989. *Recreations:* gardening, rubber bridge. *Address:* 55 Priory Close, Combe Down, Bath BA2 5AW. *Died 2 Sept. 2003.*

WEST-RUSSELL, His Honour Sir David (Sturrock), Kt 1986; President of Industrial Tribunals for England and Wales, 1984–91; *b* 17 July 1921; *o s* of late Sir Alexander West-Russell and Agnes West-Russell (*née* Sturrock); *m* Christine (*née* Tyler); one *s* two *d*. *Educ:* Rugby; Pembroke Coll., Cambridge. Served war: Buffs, 1940; commissioned Queen's Own Cameron Highlanders, 1941; Parachute Regt, 1942–46; N Africa, Italy, France, Greece, Norway and Palestine (despatches, Major). Management Trainee, Guest Keen and Nettlefold, 1948–50; Harmsworth Law Scholar, 1952; called to Bar, Middle Temple, 1953, Bencher, 1986; SE Circuit; Dep. Chm., Inner London Quarter Sessions, 1966–72; Circuit Judge, 1972; Sen. Circuit Judge, Inner London Crown Court, 1979–82, Southwark Crown Court, 1983–84. Mem., Departmental Cttee on Legal Aid in Criminal Proceedings, 1964–65. Comr (NI Emergency Provisions Act), 1974–80; Chairman: Lord Chancellor's Adv. Cttee on Appts of Magistrates for Inner London, 1976–87; Home Sec's Adv. Bd on Restricted Patients, 1985–91; Inner London Probation Cttee, 1988–89 (Mem., 1979–89); Member: Lord Chancellor's Adv. Cttee on the Trng of Magistrates, 1980–85; Judicial Studies Bd, 1980–84, 1987–90; Parole Bd, 1980–82; Parole Review Cttee, 1987–88; Criminal Injuries Compensation Bd, 1991–95. Pres., Inner London Magistrates' Assoc., 1979–85; Jt Pres., Council of HM Circuit Judges, 1985. *Club:* Garrick.

Died 2 July 2004.

WESTBROOK, Eric Ernest, CB 1981; painter and writer; *b* 29 Sept. 1915; *s* of Ernest James and Helen Westbrook; *m* 1st, 1942, Ingrid Nyström (marr. diss. 1962; decd); one *d*; 2nd, 1964, Dawn Sime (*d* 2001). *Educ:* Alleyn's Sch., Dulwich; various schools of art. Lecturer for Arts Council of Gt Britain, 1943; Director, Wakefield City Art Gallery, Yorks, 1946; Chief Exhibitions Officer, British Council, 1949; Director: Auckland City Art Gallery, NZ, 1952–55; National Gallery of Victoria, Melbourne, Aust., 1956–73; Director (Permanent Head), Ministry for the Arts, Victoria, 1973–80, retired. Hon. LLD Monash, 1974. Chevalier de l'Ordre des Arts et Lettres (France), 1972; Palmes Académiques, 1989. *Publications:* Birth of a Gallery, 1968; various articles and reviews in arts and museum pubns. *Recreations:* music, gardening. *Address:* Houghton Park, Odgers Road, Castlemaine, Vic 3450, Australia. *T:* (3) 54724171.

Died 5 Nov. 2005.

WESTBURY, 5th Baron *cr* 1861; **David Alan Bethell,** CBE 1994; MC 1942; DL; *b* 16 July 1922; *s* of Captain The Hon. Richard Bethell, *o c* of 3rd Baron Westbury (*d* 1929); *S* brother, 1961; *m* 1947, Ursula Mary Rose James, CBE; two *s* one *d*. *Educ:* Harrow. 2nd Lieut 1940, Capt. 1944, Scots Guards. Equerry to the Duke of Gloucester, 1946–49. DL N Yorks, formerly NR Yorks, 1973. GCStJ 1988 (KStJ 1977). *Heir: s* Hon. Richard Nicholas Bethell, MBE 1979 [*b* 29 May 1950; *m* 1st, 1975, Caroline Mary (marr. diss. 1991), *d* of Richard Palmer; one *s* two *d*; 2nd, 1993, Charlotte Sarah-Jane, *d* of Jack Gore. *Educ:* Harrow; RMA Sandhurst. Major Scots Guards, retired]. *Address:* Grange Cottage, Thirlby, Thirsk, N Yorks YO7 2DT. *T:* (01845) 597161. *Died 12 Oct. 2001.*

WESTERMAN, Sir Alan; *see* Westerman, Sir W. A.

WESTERMAN, Sir (Wilfred) Alan, Kt 1963; CBE 1962 (OBE 1957); EdD; Chairman, Australian Industry Development Corporation, 1971–83; *b* NZ, 25 March 1913; *s* of W. J. Westerman, Sydney, NSW; *m* 1969, Margaret, *d* of late B. H. White. *Educ:* Knox Grammar School; Universities of Tasmania, Melbourne and Columbia; MA Econ, EdD. Chairman, Commonwealth Tariff Board, 1958–60; Sec., Dept of Trade and Industry, Canberra, 1960–71. Director: Ampol Ltd; Philips Industries Holdings Ltd; Oak Systems of Australia Pty Limited; Chm., Stevedoring Industry Consultative Council, 1978. *Recreation:* tennis. *Address:* 47 Tasmania Circle, Forrest, ACT 2603, Australia. *Clubs:* Commonwealth (Canberra); Athenæum (Melbourne); Union (Sydney). *Died 20 May 2001.*

WESTLAKE, Peter Alan Grant, CMG 1972; MC 1943; *b* 2 Feb. 1919; *s* of A. R. C. Westlake, CSI, CIE, and late Dorothy Louise (*née* Turner); *m* 1943, Katherine Spackman (*d* 1990); two *s*. *Educ:* Sherborne; Corpus Christi Coll., Oxford; Military College of Science. Served with 1st Regt RHA (Adjt 1942), and on the staff (despatches). HM Foreign Service (later Diplomatic Service), 1946–76: served in Japan and at Foreign Office; Joint Services Staff College, 1954; Israel, 1955; Japan, 1957; Administrative Staff Coll., 1961; Counsellor: Foreign Office, 1961; Washington, 1965; British High Commn, Canberra, 1967–71; Minister, Tokyo, 1971–76. Pres., Asiatic Soc. of Japan, 1972–74. UK Comr-General, Internat. Ocean Expo, Okinawa, 1975. BD Wales 1981, MSc Wales, 1981; Deacon, Church in Wales, 1981, priest 1982. FRAS. Order of the Rising Sun, Japan. *Publications:* The Proud Walkers, 1992; Holy Island, 1992; Equations of motion for the Earth's crust, 1993; The Troy Game, 1995; Atlas for the ascent of Pan, 1998; Winter-Fire-Shed, 2000. *Address:* 53 Church Street, Beaumaris, Anglesey LL58 8AB. *Died 10 Dec. 2003.*

WESTON, Bryan Henry; Chairman: Manweb plc (formerly Merseyside and North Wales Electricity Board), 1985–94; The National Grid Holding, 1991–93; *b* 9 April 1930; *s* of Henry James Weston and Rose Grace Weston; *m* 1956, Heather West; two *s* two *d*. *Educ:* St George Grammar School, Bristol; Bristol, Rutherford and Oxford Technical Colleges. CEng, FIEE; CCMI. South Western Electricity Board: Commercial Manager, 1973–75; Bd Mem., 1975; Exec. Mem., 1975–77; Dep. Chm., Yorkshire Electricity Bd, 1977–85. *Recreations:* caravanning, walking, gardening. *Address:* Fountainhead Cottage, Brassey Green, near Tarporley, Cheshire CW6 9UG. *T:* (01829) 733523. *Died 15 April 2003.*

WESTON, Rt Rev. Frank Valentine; Bishop Suffragan of Knaresborough, since 1997; *b* 16 Sept. 1935; *s* of William Valentine Weston and Gertrude Hamilton Weston; *m* 1963, Penelope Brighid, *d* of Marmaduke Carver Middleton Athorpe, formerly of Dinnington, Yorks and Hilda Bridget (*née* Waterfall); one *s* two *d*. *Educ:* Christ's Hospital; Queen's Coll., Oxford (BA 1960; MA 1964); Lichfield Theol Coll. Ordained deacon, 1961, priest, 1962; Curate, St John the Baptist, Atherton, Lancs, 1961–65; Chaplain, 1965–69, Principal, 1969–76, Coll. of the Ascension, Selly Oak, Birmingham; Vice-Pres., Selly Oak Colls, 1973–76; Principal and Pantonian Prof., Edinburgh Theol Coll., 1976–82; Archdeacon of Oxford, 1982–97; Canon of Christ Church, Oxford, 1982–97, Emeritus Student, 1998. Mem., Court of Assistants, Salters' Co., 1984– (Master, 1992–93). Governor: St Augustine's Upper Sch., Oxford, 1983–97; Christ's Hosp., 1988– (Almoner, 1996–2002); Tudor Hall Sch., 1988–97. Provost, Northern Div., Woodard Corp., 1998–. *Publications:* (contrib.) Quel Missionnaire, 1971; (contrib.) Gestalten der Kirchengeschichte, 1984. *Recreations:* wine, persons and song; exploring the countryside. *Address:* 16 Shaftesbury Avenue, Leeds LS8 1DT. *T:* (0113) 266 4800. *Died 29 April 2003.*

WESTON, Garfield Howard, (Garry); Chairman: Associated British Foods plc, 1967–2000 (Chief Executive, 1969–99); Fortnum and Mason, 1979–2000; Wittington Investments Ltd UK, 1979–2000; British Sugar PLC, 1991–2000; *b* 28 April 1927; *s* of late Willard Garfield

Weston and Reta Lila Howard; *m* 1959, Mary Ruth, *d* of late Major-Gen. Sir Howard Kippenberger; three *s* three *d*. *Educ:* Sir William Borlase School, Marlow; New College, Oxford; Harvard University (Economics). Managing Director: Ryvita Co. Ltd, UK, 1951–54; Weston Biscuit Co., Aust., 1954–67; Vice-Chm., Associated British Foods Ltd, 1960; Chm., George Weston Holdings Ltd, 1978. *Recreations:* gardening, tennis, walking. *Address:* Weston Centre, Bowater House, 68 Knightsbridge, SW1X 7LQ. *T:* (020) 7589 6363.
Died 15 Feb. 2002.

WESTON, Garry; *see* Weston, Garfield H.

WHADDON, Baron *cr* 1978 (Life Peer), of Whaddon in the County of Cambridgeshire; **(John) Derek Page;** Chairman, Daltrade, since 1983; *b* 14 Aug. 1927; *s* of John Page and Clare Page (*née* Maher); *m* 1st, 1948, Catherine Audrey Halls (*d* 1979); one *s* one *d*; 2nd, 1981, Angela Rixson. *Educ:* St Bede's College, Manchester; external BSc (Soc.) London Univ. MP (Lab) King's Lynn, 1964–70; contested (Lab) Norfolk NW, Feb. 1974. Chairman: Skorimpex-Rind, 1985–; Cambridge Chemical Co. Ltd, 1991–2000 (Dir, 1962–2000); Crag Group Ltd, 1996–2001. Mem., Council of Management, CoSIRA, 1975–82; Mem., E Anglia Economic Planning Council, 1975–80. Fellow, Cambridge Philosophical Soc., 2000. Golden Insignia of Order of Merit (Poland), 1989. *Club:* Reform.
Died 16 Aug. 2005.

WHALLEY, Richard Carlton; Chairman, Ewden Associates Ltd, since 1981; *b* Quetta, India, 4 July 1922; *s* of Frederick Seymour Whalley, MC, FCGI, MIMechE, and Gwendolen, *d* of Sir William Collingwood; *m* 1945, Mary Christian Bradley; two *s* twin *d*. *Educ:* Shrewsbury Sch.; 151 OCTU, Aldershot. Served War: Private, Royal Berkshire Regt, 1940; commissioned 2nd Lieut, Royal Corps of Signals, 1942; Captain and Adjt, 2nd Div. Signals, India, Assam, Burma, 1942–45 (despatches). War Office, AG II (O), 1945–48; GHQ Singapore, 1948–51. Vulcan Foundry Ltd: Asst Sec., 1952–58; Commercial Manager, 1958–60; Dep. Gen. Manager, 1960–65; Manager, English Electric Diesel Engine Div., 1965–67; Dir and Gen. Manager, Glacier Metal Co., 1968–70. 1970–78: Dep. Chm. and Managing Dir, Millspaugh Ltd; Chm. and Managing Dir, C. A. Harnden Ltd, Westbury Engrg Ltd, Hargreaves & Jennings Ltd, and T. Rowbottom Ltd; Director: Bertram-Scott Ltd; Sulzer Bros (UK) Ltd; Mem., Bd of British Shipbuilders (with special responsibility for personnel, indust. relations, and trng), 1978–80. Chairman: F. & M. Ducker Ltd, 1981–84; A. Spafford & Co. Ltd, 1981–82; Pennine Plastics Ltd, 1981–82; Eaton and Booth Ltd, 1984–87; (also Chief Exec.) Eaton and Booth Rolling Mills Ltd, 1984–87; John King and Co. Ltd, 1985–87; Director: Estridge & Ropner Ltd, 1981–84; Sheffield Photoco, 1983–84; Dep. Chm., Malacarp Group, 1982–84. Freeman, Co. of Cutlers in Hallamshire, 1986. *Recreations:* rowing, walking. *Address:* Sunnybank Farm, Bolsterstone, Sheffield S36 3ST. *T:* (0114) 288 3116. *Clubs:* National Liberal; London Rowing.
Died 18 June 2004.

WHALLEY, Prof. William Basil; Professor of Chemistry and Head of Department of Pharmaceutical Chemistry, School of Pharmacy, 1961–82, then Emeritus Professor of Chemistry, University of London; *b* 17 Dec. 1916; *s* of William and Catherine Lucy Whalley; *m* 1945, Marie Agnes Alston; four *s* one *d*. *Educ:* St Edward's College, Liverpool; Liverpool University (BSc Hons 1938; PhD 1940; DSc 1952). FRIC 1950. MOS and ICI 1940–45; Lectr, 1946–55, Sen. Lectr, 1955–57, Reader, 1957–61, in Organic Chemistry, Liverpool Univ. *Publications:* contrib. on organic chemistry to several books incl. Heterocyclic Compounds, Vol. 7, edited R. C. Elderfield; many pubns in Jl of Chem. Soc., Jl Amer. Chem. Soc., etc. *Recreations:* music, mountaineering. *Address:* 9 Peaks Hill, Purley, Surrey CR8 3JG. *T:* (020) 8668 2244.
Died 30 May 2002.

WHEATLEY, Rev. Canon Arthur; Priest in Charge of St Columba's, Grantown-on-Spey and St John's, Rothiemurchus, 1983–95; Hon. Assistant Priest, Grantown-on-Spey, since 1996; *b* 4 March 1931; *s* of George and Elizabeth Wheatley; *m* 1959, Sheena Morag Wilde; two *s* two *d*. *Educ:* Alloa Acad.; Coates Hall Theol Coll., Edinburgh. Ordained deacon 1970, priest 1970, dio. Brechin; 1st Curate's title, St Salvador's with St Martin's, Dundee, 1970–71; Curate in Charge, St Ninian's Mission, Dundee, 1971–76; Rector of Holy Trinity, Elgin with St Margaret's Church, Lossiemouth, dio. Moray, Ross and Caithness, 1976–80; Canon of St Andrew's Cathedral, Inverness, 1978–80, Provost, 1980–83; Canon of Inverness Cathedral, 1985–. Episcopalian Chaplain to HM Prison, Porterfield, 1980–; Anglican Chaplain to RAF Unit, Grantown-on-Spey, 1984–95. *Recreations:* fishing, bee keeping. *Address:* The Cot, 15 Broomhill Court, Nethy Bridge, Inverness-shire PH25 3EH. *T:* (01479) 821576.
Died 31 Jan. 2003.

WHEELER, Prof. David John, FRS 1981; Professor of Computer Science, Cambridge University, 1978–94, then Emeritus; Fellow of Darwin College, Cambridge, 1967–94, then Emeritus; *b* 9 Feb. 1927; *s* of Arthur William Wheeler and Agnes Marjorie (*née* Gudgeon); *m* 1957, Joyce Margaret Blackler; one *s* two *d*. *Educ:* Camp Hill Grammar Sch., Birmingham; Hanley High Sch., Stoke on Trent; Trinity Coll., Cambridge. Vis. Asst Prof., Univ. of Illinois, USA, 1951–53; Cambridge University: Research Fellow, Trinity Coll., 1951–57; Asst Dir of Research, 1956–66; Reader in Computer Science, 1966–78. Fellow, Assoc. of Computing Machinery, 1994. *Publication:* The Preparation of Programs for an Electronic Digital Computer, 1951. *Address:* 131 Richmond Road, Cambridge CB4 3PS. *T:* (01223) 351319.
Died 13 Dec. 2004.

WHEELER, Sir John (Hieron), 3rd Bt *cr* 1920; formerly Chairman and Managing Director, Raithby, Lawrence & Co. Ltd, retired 1973; *b* 22 July 1905; 2nd *s* of Sir Arthur Wheeler, 1st Bt; *S* brother, Sir Arthur (Frederick Pullman) Wheeler, 1964; *m* 1929, Gwendolen Alice (*née* Oram); two *s*. *Educ:* Charterhouse. Engaged in Print. Served War of 1939–45, Volunteer Trooper, RTR, 1941–45. After the war, returned to printing. *Recreations:* whittling, dry stone walling. *Heir: s* John Frederick Wheeler [*b* 3 May 1933; *m* 1963, Barbara Mary, *d* of Raymond Flint, Leicester; two *s* one *d*]. *Address:* 39 Morland Avenue, Leicester LE2 2PF.
Died 21 April 2005.

WHENT, Sir Gerald Arthur, Kt 1995; CBE 1989; Deputy Chairman, Vodafone Group PLC, 1997–98 (Chief Executive, 1988–96); *b* 1 March 1927; *m* 1st, 1956, Coris Dorothy Bellman-Thomas (marr. diss); one *s* one *d*; 2nd, 1985, Sarah Louise (*née* Donaldson); two step *s* one step *d*. *Educ:* St Mary's College, Southampton. Dent Allcroft & Co.: Management Trainee, 1952; Asst Div. Manager, 1957; Div. Manager, 1959–62; Plessey Co.: Dept Manager, 1962; Div. Gen. Manager, 1966–69; Dir, Racal Recorders, 1970–72; Man. Dir, Racal Comsec, 1973–76; Man. Dir, Racal-Tacticom, 1977–80; Chm. and Man. Dir, Racal Radio Group, 1980–85; Dir, Racal Electronics plc, 1982–; Chm. and Chief Exec., Racal Telecommunications Group, 1983–88. *Recreations:* golf, ski-ing, horse riding, chess, bridge. *Address:* Raffin Stud, West Soley, Chilton Foliat, Hungerford RG17 0TN.
Died 16 May 2002.

WHETSTONE, Keith; *see* Whetstone, N. K.

WHETSTONE, (Norman) Keith, OBE 1983; VRD; journalist and editorial consultant; *b* 17 June 1930; *yr s* of Albert and Anne Whetstone; *m* 1952, Monica Joan Clayton, Leamington Spa; three *s*. *Educ:* King Henry VIII Sch., Coventry. Served Royal Navy, 1949–50, 1951–52; Lt Comdr (S) RNVR, retired, 1965. Coventry Evening Telegraph, 1950–51; Western Morning News, 1952–55; Birmingham Post, 1955–58; Coventry Evening Telegraph, 1958–63; Editor: Cambridge Evening News,

1964–70; Coventry Evening Telegraph, 1970–80; Editor-in-Chief: Birmingham Evening Mail series, 1980–84; Birmingham Post and Birmingham Evening Mail series, 1984–86; Dir, Birmingham Post & Mail Ltd, 1980–86. Nat. Pres., Guild of British Newspaper Editors, 1976–77. Mem. Press Council, 1980–86. *Recreations:* theatre, Rugby football (Pres., Old Coventrians RFC, 2000–), golf. *Address:* 4 The Green, Meriden, Coventry CV7 7PE. *T:* (01676) 522654; Niaudon, 46220 Prayssac, Lot, France. *T:* 565224661.   *Died 1 Sept. 2002.*

WHIFFEN, David Hardy, DPhil, DSc ; FRS 1966; FRSC; Professor of Physical Chemistry, 1968–85, Head of School of Chemistry, 1978–85, Pro-Vice-Chancellor, 1980–83, University of Newcastle upon Tyne (Dean of Science, 1974–77); *b* 15 Jan. 1922; *s* of late Noël H. and Mary Whiffen; *m* 1949, Jean P. Bell (*d* 1998); four *s*. *Educ:* Oundle School; St John's Coll., Oxford (Schol.; BA 1943, MA 1947; DPhil 1948); DSc Birmingham 1959. Sometime Commonwealth Fund Fellow, Sen. Student of Commn for 1851 Exhibition. Lectr in Chemistry, Univ. of Birmingham, 1949–59; Supt, Molecular Science Div., NPL, 1959–68. Vice-Chm., Newcastle HA, 1983–85 (Mem., Newcastle AHA, 1978–82, Newcastle HA, 1982–85). Pres., Faraday Div., RSC, 1981–83. *Publications:* Spectroscopy, 1966; The Royal Society of Chemistry: the first 150 years, 1991; papers in scientific jls.   *Died 2 Dec. 2002.*

WHIPPLE, Prof. Fred Lawrence; Senior Scientist, Smithsonian Astrophysical Observatory, since 1973; Director, Smithsonian Institution Astrophysical Observatory, 1955–73; Phillips Professor of Astronomy, Harvard University, 1968–77; *b* 5 Nov. 1906; *s* of Harry Lawrence Whipple and Celestia Whipple (*née* MacFarland); *m* 1st, 1928, Dorothy Woods (marr. diss. 1935); one *s*; 2nd, 1946, Babette Frances Samelson; two *d*. *Educ:* Long Beach High School, Calif; UCLA; Univ. of California, Berkeley. Lick Observatory Fellow, 1930–31; Staff Member, Harvard Univ., 1931–; Instructor, 1932–38; Lecturer, 1938–45; Assoc. Prof., 1945–50; Professor, 1950–77; Chm. Dept of Astronomy, 1949–56. US Nat. Cttee of Internat. Geophysical Year: Chm. Techn. Panel on Rocketry, 1955–59; Member: Techn. Panel on Earth Satellite Program, 1955–59; Working Group on Satellite Tracking and Computation, 1955–58; Scientific Advisory Bd to USAF, 1953–62; Cttee on Meteorology, Nat. Acad. of Sciences, Nat. Research Coun., 1958–61; Special Cttees on Space Techn., Nat. Advisory Cttee for Aeronautics, 1958–63 (later NASA), US; Space Sciences Working Group on Orbiting Astronomical Observatories, Nat. Acad. of Sciences (Mem. Nat. Acad. of Sciences, 1959–); Advisory Panel to Cttee on Sci. and Astronautics of US House of Representatives, 1960–73; Amer. Philosophical Soc., Philadelphia; Amer. Acad. of Arts and Sciences, Boston; New York Acad. of Science, NY; several technical societies. Associate, Royal Astronomical Soc., 1970–. Benjamin Franklin Fellow, RSA, 1968–. Editor: Smithsonian Contributions to Astrophysics, 1956–73; Planetary and Space Science, 1958–. Hon. degrees: MA, Harvard Univ., 1945; DSc, Amer. Internat. Coll., 1958; DLitt, North-eastern Univ., 1961; DS: Temple Univ., 1961; Arizona, 1979; LLD, CW Post Coll. of Long Island Univ., 1962. J. Lawrence Smith Medal of Nat. Acad. of Sciences, 1949; Donohue Medals, 1932, 1933, 1937, 1940, 1942 (received two medals that year); Presidential Certificate of Merit, 1948; Exceptional Service Award, US Air Force Scientific Adv. Bd, 1960; Space Flight Award, Amer. Astron. Soc., 1961; President's Award for Distinguished Federal Civilian Service, 1963; Space Pioneers Medallion, 1968; NASA Public Services Award, 1969; Kepler Medal, AAAS, 1971; Nat. Civil Service League's Civil Service Award, 1972; Henry Medal, Smithsonian Instn, 1973; Alumnus of the Year Award, UCLA, 1976; Gold Medal, Royal Astronomical Soc., 1983; Bruce Gold Medal, Astronomical Soc. of Pacific, 1986; UCLA Medal, 1997; other foreign awards. Depicted on postal stamp, Mauritania, 1986 (in recognition of contribn to understanding of comets, and to commemorate Halley's Comet) and on stamp of St Vincent, 1994. *Publications:* Earth, Moon and Planets, 1942, 3rd edn 1968; Orbiting the Sun, 1981; The Mystery of Comets, 1985; many technical papers in various astronomical and geophysical journals and books; popular articles in magazines and in Encyclopædia Britannica. *Recreation:* cultivation of roses. *Address:* Smithsonian Astrophysical Observatory, 60 Garden Street, Cambridge, MA 02138, USA. *T:* (617) 8647383.

Died 30 Aug. 2004.

WHIPPMAN, Michael Lewis, CB 1998; PhD; independent consultant, since 1998; Policy Director, Department of Social Security, 1994–98; *b* 20 Sept. 1938; *s* of Matthew Whippman and Adelina Whippman (*née* Abrahams); *m* 1967, Constance Baskett; two *d*. *Educ:* King Edward VII Sch.; Univ. of the Witwatersrand; Clare Coll., Cambridge (PhD). Res. Fellow 1963–65, Asst Prof. 1965–71, Univ. of Pennsylvania; Sen. Res. Fellow, Univ. of Helsinki, 1971–73; Principal 1973, Asst Sec. 1980, Under Sec. 1988, DHSS; Under Sec., Home and Educn Gp, HM Treasury, 1990–94. Bd Mem., 1998–, Chm., 1999–, Homeless Network. Trustee, Big Brothers and Sisters (UK), 1999–; Trustee, 1999–, Treas., 2001–, Chartered Soc. of Queens' Square. Fellow, Amer. Phys. Soc., 1971. *Publications:* papers in Phys. Rev., Annals of Physics, Il Nuovo Cimento, etc. *Recreation:* opera. *Address:* 33 Dunmore Road, SW20 8TN.   *Died 1 Oct. 2001.*

WHITBY, Charles Harley; QC 1970; a Recorder of the Crown Court, Western Circuit, 1972–98; *b* 2 April 1926; *s* of late Arthur William Whitby and Florence Whitby; *m* 1981, Eileen Scott. *Educ:* St John's, Leatherhead; Peterhouse, Cambridge (Open Schol., 1943; BA (History) 1st cl. 1949, MA 1951). Served RAFVR, 1944–48. Called to the Bar, Middle Temple, 1952, Bencher, 1977, Lent Reader, 1996. Mem., Bar Council, 1969–71, 1972–78. Member: Criminal Injuries Compensation Bd, 1975–2000; Criminal Injuries Compensation Appeals Panel, 2000–02. Chm. Council, St John's Sch., Leatherhead, 1985–97 (Mem., 1977–97). *Publications:* contributed to: Master and Servant in Halsbury's Laws of England, 3rd edn, Vol. 25, 1959; Master and Servant in Atkin's Encyclopaedia of Court Forms, 2nd edn, Vol. 25, 1962. *Recreations:* golf, watching soccer, boating, fishing, swimming, theatre, cinema. *Address:* 12 King's Bench Walk, Temple, EC4Y 7EL. *T:* (020) 7583 0811. *Clubs:* Oxford and Cambridge, Royal Automobile (Steward, 1985–), Garrick; Woking Golf.   *Died 29 Aug. 2003.*

WHITE, Hon. Byron R(aymond); Associate Justice of the Supreme Court of the United States, 1962–93; *b* Fort Collins, Colorado, 8 June 1917; *s* of Alpha White, Wellington, Colorado; *m* 1946, Marion Lloyd Stearns, *d* of Dr Robert L. Stearns; one *s* one *d*. *Educ:* Wellington High Sch.; Univ. of Colorado; Oxford Univ. (Rhodes Scholar); Yale Univ. Law Sch (before and after War). Professional American footballer, 1938–41. Served War of 1939–45: USNR, Naval Intell., Pacific (two Bronze Stars). Law Clerk to Chief Justice of the United States, 1946–47; law practice in Denver, Colorado, 1947–60, with firm of Lewis, Grant, Newton, Davis and Henry (later Lewis, Grant and Davis). Dep. Attorney-Gen., 1961–62. Phi Beta Kappa, Phi Gamma Delta. As a Democrat, he was a prominent supporter of John F. Kennedy in the Presidential campaign of 1960. *Recreations:* fishing, walking. *Address:* c/o US Supreme Court, 1 First Street NE, Washington, DC 20543, USA.

Died 15 April 2002.

WHITE, Sir Christopher Stuart S.; *see* Stuart-White.

WHITE, Maj.-Gen. Gilbert Anthony, MBE 1944; *b* 10 June 1916; *s* of Cecil James Lawrence White and Muriel (*née* Collins); *m* 1939, Margaret Isabel Duncan Wallet; two *d*. *Educ:* Christ's Hosp., Horsham. Member of Lloyd's, 1938. Joined TA Artists Rifles, 1937; TA Commn, E

Surrey Regt, 1939; served BEF, 1940, N Africa, 1943–44, Italy, 1944–45; Staff Coll., 1944; Instructor, Staff Coll., Haifa, 1946; with UK Delegn to UN, 1946–48; served on Lord Mountbatten's personal staff in MoD, 1960–61; idc 1965; BAOR, 1966–69; Chief, Jt Services Liaison Orgn, Bonn, 1969–71; retd 1971. Mem. Council, Guide Dogs for the Blind, 1971–92. *Recreation:* racing.

Died 27 Aug. 2003.

WHITE, Harold Clare, MBE 1967; HM Diplomatic Service, retired; Consul-General, Seattle, 1976–79; *b* 26 Oct. 1919; *s* of Alfred John White and Nora White; *m* 1951, Marie Elizabeth Richardson; two *d. Educ:* Grammar Sch., Warrington. Served War, Royal Signals, 1939–45. GPO, 1937–39 and 1946; FO, 1947; Third Sec., Djakarta, 1951; FO, 1955; Vice-Consul, Piraeus, Kirkuk, San Francisco, and Durban, 1957–64; 1st Secretary: Kinshasa, 1964; Kuala Lumpur, 1968; FCO, 1972; Dep. Consul-Gen., Chicago, 1974. *Recreation:* cricket. *Address:* 31 Stuart Avenue, Eastbourne, East Sussex BN21 1UR. *T:* (01323) 731148. *Club:* Civil Service. *Died 7 Dec. 2003.*

WHITE, James; author and art historian; Professor of History of Painting, Royal Hibernian Academy, 1968; *b* 16 Sept. 1913; *s* of Thomas John White and Florence Coffey; *m* 1941, Agnes Bowe; three *s* two *d. Educ:* Belvedere Coll., Dublin; privately in European museums and collections. Art Critic: Standard, 1940–50; Irish Press, 1950–59; Irish Times, 1959–62; Curator, Municipal Gall. of Modern Art, Dublin, 1960–64; Dir, Nat. Gall. of Ireland, 1964–80. Chm., Irish Arts Council, 1978–84; Hon. Sec., Royal Dublin Soc., 1986–90. Ext. Lectr in History of Art, University Coll., Dublin, 1955–77; Vis. Lectr in Univs and Socs in GB, Italy, USA, Canada. Trustee, Chester Beatty Library of Oriental Art, Dublin. Radio and television contribs: BBC, RTE, and in the USA. Irish Comr to Biennale at Venice and at Paris on various occasions; Organiser of Exhibns in Dublin, London, Paris, etc., incl. Paintings from Irish Collections, 1957. Corresp. Mem., Real Academia de Bellas Artes de San Fernando, 1975. Hon. LLD NUI, 1970. Arnold K. Henry Medal., RCS of Ireland. Chevalier, Légion d'Honneur (France), 1974; Order of Merit, Govt of Italy, 1977; Commander of the Order of Merit (FRG), 1983. *Publications:* Irish Stained Glass (with Michael Wynne), 1963; The National Gallery of Ireland, 1968; Jack B. Yeats, 1971; John Butler Yeats and the Irish Renaissance, 1972; Masterpieces of the National Gallery of Ireland, 1978; Pauline Bewick: painting a life, 1985; Gerard Dillon, a Biography, 1993; monographs on Louis Le Brocquy, George Campbell, Brian Bourke; contributions to: Apollo, Art News, Studio, Connoisseur, Blackfriars, Manchester Guardian, The Furrow, Doctrine and Life, Art Notes, Merian, Werk, Das Munster, Hollandsche Art, La Biennale, La Revue Française, Il Milione, Encyclopaedia of Art, etc. *Recreations:* golf, swimming, gardening, bridge. *Address:* 66 Cedars, Herbert Park Lane, Dublin 4, Ireland. *T:* (1) 6683723. *Club:* Kildare Street and University (Dublin). *Died 2 June 2003.*

WHITE, Lawrence John, CMG 1972; Assistant Secretary, Board of Customs and Excise, 1961–75, retired; *b* 23 Feb. 1915; *s* of Arthur Yirrell White and Helen Christina White; *m* 1936, Ivy Margaret Coates; one *s. Educ:* Banbury Grammar Sch. Joined Customs and Excise, 1933; Commonwealth Relations Office, 1948–50; Customs and Excise, 1951–75. *Recreations:* reading, walking. *Address:* Peach Tree Cottage, Fifield, Oxon OX7 6HL. *T:* (01993) 830806. *Died 9 May 2002.*

WHITE, Sir Lynton (Stuart), Kt 1985; MBE (mil.) 1943; TD 1950; DL; Chairman, Hampshire County Council, 1977–85; *b* 11 Aug. 1916; 2nd *s* of Sir Dymoke White, 2nd Bt, JP, DL; *m* 1945, Phyllis Marie Rochfort Worley (decd), *er d* of Sir Newnham Arthur Worley, KBE; four *s* one *d. Educ:* Harrow; Trinity College, Cambridge (MA 1938). Associate RIBA, 1947–82. TA 1939, as 2nd Lieut RA; served War of 1939–45: UK, 1939–40; Far East, 1940–45 (despatches, 1943, 1944, 1945); Hon. Lieut-Col

RA, TA, 1946; TARO, 1948–71. Member Hampshire CC, 1970; Vice-Chm., 1976. DL Hants 1977.

Died 2 April 2005.

WHITEHEAD, His Honour (Garnet) George (Archie), DFC 1944; a Circuit Judge, 1977–89; *b* 22 July 1916; *s* of late Archibald Payne Whitehead and Margaret Elizabeth Whitehead; *m* 1946, Monica (*née* Watson); two *d. Educ:* Wisbech. Admitted Solicitor, 1949. Served War, 1939–45, RAF, Pilot, Bomber Comd and Transport Comd; demob. as Flt Lt, 1 Jan. 1947. Articled to Edmund W. Roythorne, MBE, Solicitor, Spalding. Formerly Senior Partner, Roythorne & Co., Solicitors, Boston, Lincs (Partner, 1950–77); a Recorder of the Crown Court, 1972–77. Formerly Alderman, Boston Borough Council; Mayor of Boston, 1969–70. Reader, Diocese of Lincoln. *Recreations:* photography, walking. *Address:* 15 Burton Close, Boston, Lincs PE21 9QW. *T:* (01205) 364977.

Died 21 Nov. 2001.

WHITEHEAD, His Honour George; *see* Whitehead, His Honour G. G. A.

WHITEHEAD, Phillip; writer and television producer; Member (Lab) East Midlands Region, European Parliament, since 1999 (Staffordshire East and Derby, 1994–99); *b* 30 May 1937; adopted *s* of late Harold and Frances Whitehead; *m* 1967, Christine, *d* of T. G. Usborne; two *s* one *d. Educ:* Lady Manners' Grammar Sch., Bakewell; Exeter Coll., Oxford. President, Oxford Union, 1961. BBC Producer, 1961–67, and WEA Lecturer, 1961–65; Editor of This Week, Thames TV, 1967–70. Guild of TV Producers Award for Factual Programmes, 1969; BPG Best Documentary Award and Emmy Award for Best Script, for the Kennedys, 1993. Vice-Chm., Young Fabian Group, 1965; Chm., Fabian Soc., 1978–79 (Centenary Dir, 1983–84). Chairman: New Society Ltd, 1986; Statesman and Nation Publications Ltd, 1985–90; Director: Goldcrest Film and Television Hldgs Ltd, 1984–87; Brook Productions, 1986–97; Brook Lapping Prodns, 1997–2003 (Chm., 2002). Member: Annan Cttee on Future of Broadcasting, 1974–77; Council, Consumers' Assoc., 1982– (Chm., 1990–94). Vis. Fellow, Goldsmiths' Coll., Univ. of London, 1985–91; MacTaggart Lectr, Edinburgh Internat. Television Festival, 1987. MP (Lab) Derby N, 1970–83; Front bench spokesman on higher educn, 1980–83 and on the arts, 1982–83; Member: Procedure Cttee, 1977–79; Select Cttee on Home Affairs, 1979–81; PLP Liaison Cttee, 1975–79; Council of Europe Assembly, 1975–80. European Parliament: Chairman: Intergroup on Consumer Affairs, 1994–99; Internal Mkt and Consumer Protection Cttee, 2004–; Member: Temp. Cttee of Enquiry into BSE, 1996–97; Temp. Cttee on Foot and Mouth Disease, 2002; Vice Pres., Delegn to Czech Republic, 1997–; parly rapporteur for Eur. Food Safety Authy, 2001–02. Chm., Eur. PLP, 1999–2004. Contested (Lab) W Derbys, 1966, Derby N, 1983, 1987. Member: NUJ; RMT. Times columnist, 1983–85; Presenter, Credo series, LWT, 1983–84. FRSA 1983. *Publications:* (jtly) Electoral Reform: time for change, 1982; (contrib.) Fabian Essays in Socialist Thought, 1984; The Writing on the Wall, 1985; (jtly) Stalin, a time for judgment, 1990; (jtly) The Windsors, a Dynasty Revealed, 1994; (jtly) Dynasty: the Nehru/Gandhi story, 1997. *Recreations:* walking, cinema, old model railways. *Address:* Mill House, Rowsley, Matlock, Derbys DE4 2EB. *T:* (01629) 732659. *Club:* Derbyshire CC. *Died 31 Dec. 2005.*

WHITEHEAD, Prof. Thomas Patterson, CBE 1985; MCB, FRCPath, FRSC; Professor of Clinical Chemistry, University of Birmingham, 1968–87, then Emeritus Professor; Consultant Biochemist, Queen Elizabeth Medical Centre, 1960–87; *b* 7 May 1923; *m* 1947, Doreen Grace Whitton, JP; two *s* one *d. Educ:* Salford Royal Technical Coll.; Univ. of Birmingham (PhD). Biochemist to S Warwickshire Hospital Gp, 1950–60. Dean, Faculty of Medicine and Dentistry, Birmingham Univ., 1984–87. Dir, Wolfson Research Laboratories, 1972–84. Council

Mem., Med. Research Council, 1972–76; Mem., Health Service Research Bd, 1973–75; Chairman: Div. of Path. Studies, Birmingham, 1974–80; Board of Undergraduate Med. Educn, Birmingham, 1982–84; W Midlands RHA Res. Cttee, 1982–86; DHSS Adv. Cttee on Assessment of Laboratory Standards, 1969–84; W Midlands RHA Scientific Services Cttee, 1984–86; Member: Adv. Bd, CS Occupational Health Service, 1988–96; Med. Adv. Panel on Driving and Alcohol and Substance Abuse, Dept of Transport, 1989–97. Chief Scientific Advr, BUPA Med. Res., London, 1987–91; Consultant to: BUPA Medical Centre, London, 1969–91; BUPA Hosps, London, 1983–91; BUPA Med. R&D, 1991–95; Centro Diagnostico Italiano, Milan, 1972–92; WHO, Geneva, 1974–86; Unilabs Clinical Pathology Services (formerly JS Pathology Services), London, 1983–99. Pres., Assoc. of Clinical Biochemists, 1981–83; Mem. Council, RCPath, 1982–84. Hon. MRCP 1985. Kone Award Lectr, 1983. Wellcome Prize, 1972; Dade Award, Geneva, 1975; Disting. Internat. Services Award, Internat. Fedn of Clinical Chemistry, 1987; Rank Prize for Opto-Electronics, 1991. *Publications:* Quality Control in Clinical Chemistry, 1976; papers in med. and scientific jls. *Recreations:* monitoring air pollution, gardening. *Address:* 70 Northumberland Road, Leamington Spa CV32 6HB. *T:* (01926) 421974. *Club:* Athenæum.

Died 4 Oct. 2005.

WHITEHORN, John Roland Malcolm, CMG 1974; a Deputy Director-General, Confederation of British Industry, 1966–78; *b* 19 May 1924; *s* of late Alan and Edith Whitehorn; *m* 1st, 1951, Josephine (*née* Plummer) (marr. diss. 1973; she *d* 1990); no *c*; 2nd, 1973, Marion FitzGibbon (*née* Gutmann). *Educ:* Rugby Sch. (Exhbnr); Trinity Coll., Cambridge (Exhbnr). Served War, 1943–46, RAFVR (Flying Officer). Joined FBI, 1947; Dep. Overseas Dir, 1960; Overseas Dir, 1963; Overseas Dir, CBI, 1965–68; Dir, Mitchell Cotts plc, 1978–86; Consultant Dir, Lilly Industries, 1978–89. Member: BOTB, 1975–78; Bd, British Council, 1968–82; Gen. Adv. Council, BBC, 1976–82. Chm., Cocking Parish Council, 1991–99. *Address:* Casters Brook, Cocking, near Midhurst, W Sussex GU29 0HJ. *T:* (01730) 813537. *Club:* Reform. *Died 30 May 2003.*

WHITEHOUSE, Mary, CBE 1980; Founder and President Emeritus, National Viewers' and Listeners' Association (Hon. General Secretary, 1965–80; President, 1980–93); freelance journalist, broadcaster; *b* 13 June 1910; *d* of James and Beatrice Hutcheson; *m* 1940, Ernest R. Whitehouse; three *s. Educ:* Chester City Grammar Sch.; Cheshire County Training Coll. Art Specialist: Wednesfield Sch., Wolverhampton, 1932–40; Brewood Grammar Sch., Staffs, 1943; Sen. Mistress, and Sen. Art Mistress, Madeley Sch., Shropshire, 1960–64. Co-founder, "Clean up TV campaign", 1964. *Publications:* Cleaning Up TV, 1966; "Who Does She Think She Is?", 1971; Whatever Happened to Sex?, 1977; A Most Dangerous Woman?, 1982; Mightier than the Sword, 1985; Quite Contrary (autobiog.), 1993. *Recreations:* reading, gardening, walking. *Address:* c/o Abberton Manor, Layer Road, Abberton, Colchester, Essex CO5 7NL. *Died 23 Nov. 2001.*

WHITEHOUSE, Prof. Norman Harold; Professor of Dental Public Health, and Dean, Dental School, University of Wales College of Medicine, 1993–99 (Pro Vice Chancellor, 1997–99); Chief Executive, University Dental Hospital NHS Trust, 1995–99 (Chief Executive, Cardiff Dental Hospital, 1993–94); *b* 22 April 1938; *y s* of late Norman Lester Whitehouse, builder and Maud Whitehouse, Bloxwich, Walsall, Staffs; *m* 1963, Barbara Palmer; one *s* one *d. Educ:* Univ. of Leeds (LDS 1961; BChD 1962); Univ. of Birmingham (DDH 1970); DDPH RCS 1970; FDSRCSE (*ad hominem*) 1995; FDSRCS (by election) 1995. Chief Admin. Dental Officer and Specialist in Community Dental Health, S Glam and E Dyfed HAs, 1974–86; British Dental Association: Sec., 1986–91; Chief

Exec. and Sec., 1991–93; Chief Admin. Dental Officer and Dir, Dental Public Health, Mid Glam HA, 1993–99; Hon. Consultant in Dental Public Health, S and Mid Glam HAs, 1993–99. Mem., BroTaf HA, 2000–03. Chm., Offa's Dyke Assoc., 2002–. Trustee, Borrow Foundn, 2000–. Hon. DDSc Wales, 2003. *Publications:* contrib. articles in jls. *Recreation:* hill-walking. *Address:* White Cottage, Craig Penllyn, Cowbridge, Vale of Glamorgan CF71 7RT. *T:* (01446) 774184; *e-mail:* whitehousenh@ tesco.net. *Died 10 Oct. 2003.*

WHITEHOUSE, Walter Alexander; Professor of Theology, University of Kent, 1965–77; Master of Eliot College, University of Kent, 1965–69, and 1973–75; *b* 27 Feb. 1915; *e s* of Walter and Clara Whitehouse, Shelley, near Huddersfield; *m* 1st, 1946, Beatrice Mary Kent Smith (*d* 1971); 2nd, 1974, Audrey Ethel Lemmon (*d* 2003). *Educ:* Penistone Grammar Sch.; St John's Coll., Cambridge (BA 1936, MA 1940); Mansfield Coll., Oxford. Minister of Elland Congregational Church, 1940–44; Chaplain, Mansfield Coll., Oxford, 1944–47; University of Durham: Reader in Divinity, 1947–65; Principal, St Cuthbert's Soc., 1955–60; Pro-Vice-Chancellor, and Sub-Warden, 1961–64. Minister at High Chapel, Ravenstonedale, 1977–82. Mem. (Lab), Glos CC, 1989–93. Hon. DD Edinburgh, 1960. *Publications:* Christian Faith and the Scientific Attitude, 1952; Order, Goodness, Glory (Riddell Memorial Lectures), 1959; The Authority of Grace, 1981. *Address:* 5 Penlee Manor Drive, Penzance, Cornwall TR18 4HW.

Died 11 April 2003.

WHITFORD, Hon. Sir John (Norman Keates), Kt 1970; Judge of the High Court, Chancery Division, 1970–88; *b* 24 June 1913; *s* of Harry Whitford and Ella Mary Keates; *m* 1946, Rosemary, *d* of John Barcham Green and Emily Paillard; four *d. Educ:* University College School; Munich University; Peterhouse, Cambridge. President, ADC. Called to the Bar: Inner Temple, 1935; Middle Temple, 1946 (Bencher 1970). Served with RAFVR, 1939–44: Wing Comdr, 1942; Chief Radar Officer and Dep. Chief Signals Officer, Air Headquarters Eastern Mediterranean; Advisor on patents and information exchanged for war purposes, HM Embassy, Washington, 1944–45. QC 1965. Member of Bar Council, 1968–70. Chm., Departmental Cttee on Law Relating to Copyright and Designs, 1974–76. *Address:* 140 High Street, West Malling, Kent ME19 6NE.

Died 5 Nov. 2001.

WHITLEY, Oliver John; Managing Director, External Broadcasting, British Broadcasting Corporation, 1969–72, retired; *b* 12 Feb. 1912; *s* of Rt Hon. J. H. Whitley and Marguerite (*née* Marchetti); *m* 1939, Elspeth Catherine (*née* Forrester-Paton); four *s* one *d. Educ:* Clifton Coll.; New Coll., Oxford. Barrister-at-Law, 1935; BBC, 1935–41. Served in RNVR, 1942–46; Coastal Forces and Combined Ops. BBC 1946–72: seconded to Colonial Office, 1946–49; Head of General Overseas Service, 1950–54; Assistant Controller, Overseas Services, 1955–57; Appointments Officer, 1957–60; Controller, Staff Training and Appointments, 1960–64; Chief Assistant to Dir-Gen., 1964–68. Valiant for Truth Award, Order of Christian Unity, 1974. *Recreations:* reading, gardening. *Address:* Greenacre, Ganavan Road, Oban, Argyll PA34 5TU. *T:* (01631) 562555.

Died 22 March 2005.

WHITLOCK, William Charles; *b* 20 June 1918; *s* of late George Whitlock and Sarah Whitlock, Sholing, Southampton; *m* 1943, Jessie Hilda, *d* of George Reardon, Armagh; five *s*, and two adopted *d. Educ:* Itchen Grammar Sch.; Southampton Univ. Army Service, 1939–46. Apptd full-time Trade Union Officer, Area Organiser of Union of Shop, Distributive and Allied Workers, 1946. President: Leicester and District Trades Council, 1955–56; Leicester City Labour Party, 1956–57; North-East Leicester Labour Party, 1955–56, and 1958–59. Member East Midlands Regional Council of Labour Party, 1955–67, Vice-

Chairman 1961–62, Chairman 1962–63. MP (Lab) Nottingham N, Oct. 1959–1983; Opposition Whip, House of Commons, 1962–64; Vice-Chamberlain of the Household, 1964–66; Lord Comr of Treasury, March 1966–July 1966; Comptroller of HM Household, July 1966–March 1967; Dep. Chief Whip and Lord Comr of the Treasury, March–July 1967; Under Sec. of State for Commonwealth Affairs, 1967–68; Parly Under-Sec. of State, FCO, 1968–69. Contested (Lab) Nottingham N, 1983. DPhil *hc* Ukranian Free Univ., 1986.

Died 2 Nov. 2001.

WHITSON, Thomas Jackson, OBE 1985; Commandant, Scottish Police College, 1987–91; *b* 5 Sept. 1930; *s* of Thomas and Susan Whitson; *m* 1953, Patricia Marion Bugden; two *s. Educ:* Knox Acad., Haddington. RN, 1949–56. Lothian and Peebles Police, 1956–75: Police Constable, 1956; Detective Constable, 1959; Detective Sergeant, 1966; Inspector, 1969; Chief Inspector, 1972; Superintendent, 1974; Lothian and Borders Police, 1975–80: Chief Superintendent, 1976; Dep. Chief Constable, Central Scotland Police, 1980–87. *Recreations:* golf, curling, angling. *Address:* Glenelg, Orchard Grove, Polmont, Falkirk FK2 0XE. *Died 26 May 2004.*

WHITTICK, Richard James; Assistant Under-Secretary of State, Home Office, 1967–72; *b* 21 August 1912; *s* of Ernest G. Whittick and Grace M. Shaw; *m* 1938, Elizabeth Mason; two *s. Educ:* George Heriot's Sch.; Edinburgh Univ. British Mus. (Natural History), 1936; Home Office, 1940; Principal Private Sec. to Home Sec., 1952–53; Asst Sec., 1953. *Recreations:* gardening, photography (FRPS 1988). *Address:* Coombe Cottage, Coombe, Sherborne, Dorset DT9 4BX. *T:* (01935) 814488.

Died 3 May 2003.

WHITTINGTON, Thomas Alan, CB 1977; TD 1986; Circuit Administrator, North Eastern Circuit, 1974–81; *b* 15 May 1916; *o s* of late George Whittington, JP and Mary Elizabeth Whittington; *m* 1939, Audrey Elizabeth, *y d* of late Craven Gilpin, Leeds; four *s. Educ:* Uppingham Sch.; Leeds Univ. (LLB). Commnd W Yorks Regt (Leeds Rifles) TA, 1937, serving War of 1939–45 in UK and 14th Army in India (Major). Solicitor of Supreme Court, 1945; Clerk of the Peace, Leeds, 1952–70; Senior Partner, Marklands, Solicitors, Leeds, 1967–70, Consultant, 1981–2001; Under-Sec., Lord Chancellor's Office, 1970; Circuit Administrator, Northern Circuit, 1970–74. *Recreations:* fishing, gardening. *Address:* The Cottage, School Lane, Collingham, Wetherby LS22 5BQ. *T:* (0113) 257 3881. *Died 16 May 2004.*

WHITTOME, Sir Alan; *see* Whittome, Sir L. A.

WHITTOME, Sir (Leslie) Alan, Kt 1991; Special Adviser to Managing Director, International Monetary Fund, 1990–91; *b* 18 Jan. 1926; *s* of Leslie Whittome and Beryl Treherne-Thomas; *m* 1984, Eleanor Duncan Wood Moose, *o d* of James Moose, US Ambassador; two *d* by previous marr. *Educ:* Marlborough Coll.; Pembroke Coll., Cambridge (MA). Capt., RAC, 1944–48. Bank of England, 1951–64, Dep. Chief Cashier; International Monetary Fund: Dir, European Dept, 1964–86; Dir, ETR, 1986–90. *Address:* 23411 Walston Place Drive, Accomac, VA 23301, USA. *T:* (757) 7871472.

Died 21 Jan. 2001.

WHITWORTH, Maj.-Gen. Reginald Henry, CB 1969; CBE 1963; MA; *b* 27 Aug. 1916; 2nd *s* of late Aymer William Whitworth and late Alice (*née* Hervey), Eton College; *m* 1st, 1946, June Rachel (*d* 1994), *o d* of late Sir Bartle Edwards, CVO, MC, and of Daphne, MBE, *d* of late Sir Cyril Kendall Butler, KBE; two *s* one *d* (and one *s* decd); 2nd, 1999, Victoria Mary Rose (*née* Buxton), *widow* of Major David Faulkner, Irish Guards. *Educ:* Eton; Balliol College, Oxford (1st cl. Hons, Modern History, 1938); Laming Travelling Fellow, Queen's Coll., Oxford, 1938–39. 2nd Lt Grenadier Guards, 1940; War Service in N Africa and Italy, 1943–45; GSO2, 78 Division, 1944;

Bde Major, 24 Guards Brigade, 1945–46; comdg 1st Bn Grenadier Guards, 1956–57; Comdr Berlin Infantry Bde, 1961–63; DMS 1, Ministry of Defence, 1964–66; GOC: Yorkshire District, 1966–67; Northumbrian District, 1967–68; Chief of Staff, Southern Command, 1968–70. Bursar and Official Fellow, Exeter College, Oxford, 1970–81. Bronze Star, USA, 1945. *Publications:* Field Marshal Earl Ligonier, 1958; Famous Regiments: the Grenadier Guards, 1974; Gunner at Large, 1988; William Augustus, Duke of Cumberland, 1992. *Recreations:* church crawling, fishing, military history. *Address:* Abbey Farm, Goosey, Faringdon, Oxon SN7 8PA. *T:* (01367) 710252. *Club:* Army and Navy. *Died 22 May 2004.*

WHYTE, Very Rev. James Aitken; Moderator of the General Assembly of the Church of Scotland, 1988–89; Professor of Practical Theology and Christian Ethics, University of St Andrews, 1958–87; *b* 28 Jan. 1920; 2nd *s* of late Andrew Whyte, Leith, and Barbara Janet Pittillo Aitken; *m* 1st, 1942, Elisabeth (*d* 1988), *er d* of Rev. G. S. Mill, MA, BSc, Kalimpong, India; two *s* one *d*; 2nd, 1993, Ishbel Christina Rathie (*née* Macaulay), *widow* of William Rathie, MA. *Educ:* Daniel Stewart's Coll., Edinburgh; University of Edinburgh (Arts and Divinity, MA 1st Cl. Hons Phil., 1942). Ordained, 1945; Chaplain to the Forces, 1945–48; Minister of: Dunollie Road, Oban, 1948–54; Mayfield, Edinburgh, 1954–58; Associate, Hope Park, St Andrews, 1987–96. St Andrews University: Dean, Faculty of Divinity, 1968–72; Principal, St Mary's Coll., 1978–82. Guest Lectr, Inst. for the Study of Worship and Religious Architecture, Birmingham, 1965–66; Lectures: Kerr, Univ. of Glasgow, 1969–72; Croall, Univ. of Edinburgh, 1972–73; Margaret Harris, Univ. of Dundee, 1990. Pres., Soc. for Study of Theol., 1983–84. Hon. LLD Dundee, 1981; Hon. DD St Andrews, 1989; DUniv Stirling, 1994. *Publications:* (ed jtly) Worship Now: Vol. 1, 1972, Vol. 2, 1989; Laughter and Tears, 1993; The Dream and the Grace, 2001; contributor to various dictionaries, composite volumes, journals, etc. *Address:* 13 Hope Street, St Andrews, Fife KY16 9HJ. *Club:* New (Edinburgh). *Died 17 June 2005.*

WICKHAM, Glynne William Gladstone; Professor of Drama, University of Bristol, 1960–82, thenEmeritus, and Senior Research Fellow, since 1995 (Hon. Fellow, 1996); *b* 15 May 1922; *s* of W. G. and Catherine Wickham; *m* 1954, Marjorie Heseltine (*née* Mudford); two *s* one *d*. *Educ:* Winchester College; New College, Oxford (BA, 1947; DPhil, 1951). Entered RAF, 1942; commissioned as Navigator, 1943; discharged as Flt Lt, 1946. President of OUDS, 1946–47. Bristol University: Asst Lectr, Drama Dept, 1948; Sen. Lectr and Head of Dept, 1955; Dean, Faculty of Arts, 1970–72. Worked sporadically as actor, script-writer and critic for BBC, from 1946; attended General Course in Broadcasting, BBC Staff Trg Sch., 1953. Travelled in America on Rockefeller Award, 1953. Visiting Prof., Drama Dept, State Univ. of Iowa, 1960; Ferens Vis. Prof. of Drama, Hull Univ., 1969; Vis. Prof. of Theatre History, Yale Univ., 1970; Killam Res. Prof., Dalhousie Univ., 1976–77; S. W. Brooks Vis. Prof., Univ. of Qld, 1983; Vis. Prof. in British Studies (Drama), Univ. of the South, Sewanee, 1984; Adjunct Prof. (Arts and Letters), Univ. of Notre Dame (London Campus), 1987–96; Hon. Prof., Univ. of Warwick, 1990–95. Lectures: G. F. Reynolds Meml, Univ. of Colorado, 1960; Judith E. Wilson, in Poetry and Drama, Cambridge, 1960–61; Festvortrag, Deutsche Shakespeare Gesellschaft, 1973; Shakespeare, British Acad., 1984; British Council, in Europe, annually 1969–79. Directed: Amer. première, The Birthday Party, for Actors' Workshop, San Francisco, 1960; world première, Wole Soyinka's Brother Jero's Metamorphosis, 1974. Consultant to Finnish National Theatre and Theatre School on establishment of Drama Department in Univ. of Helsinki, 1963. Governor of Bristol Old Vic Trust, 1963–83; Vandyck Theatre, Bristol Univ., renamed Glynne Wickham Studio Theatre, 1983. Consultant to Univ. of E Africa on establishment of a Sch. of Drama in University Coll., Dar-es-Salaam, Tanzania,

1965; Dir, Theatre Seminar, for Summer Univ., Vaasa, Finland, 1965; External Examr to Sch. of Drama in Univ. of Ibadan, Nigeria, 1965–68. Chm., Nat. Drama Conf., Nat. Council of Social Service, 1970–76; Chm., and Chief Exec., Radio West plc (ILR Bristol), 1979–83; Pres., Soc. for Theatre Research, 1976–99; Member: Adv. Cttee, British Theatre Museum, 1974–77; Culture Adv. Panel, UK Nat. Commn to UNESCO, 1984–86. Mem., Edit. Cttee, Shakespeare Survey, 1974–94; Chairman: Adv. Bd, Theatre Research International, 1975–; Gen. Edit. Bd, Theatre in Europe: documents and sources, 1979–. Trustee, St Deiniol's Residential Library, Hawarden, 1985–2000; Dir, Bd of Internat. Shakespeare Globe Centre, 1986–91. Mem., Polish Acad. of Arts and Letters, 1991. Hon. Fellow, St Deiniol's Residential Liby, 2002–. Hon. DLitt: Loughborough, 1984; Univ. of the South, Sewanee, 1984. Sam Wanamaker Award for services to the theatre, 1999. *Publications:* Early English Stages 1300–1660, Vol. I (1300–1576), 1959, 2nd edn 1980; Vol. II (1576–1660, Pt 1), 1962; Vol. II (Pt 2), 1972; Vol. III, 1981; Vols I–III repr. 2002; Vol. IV, 2002; Editor: The Relationship between Universities and Radio, Film and Television, 1954; Drama in a World of Science, 1962; Gen. Introd. to the London Shakespeare, 6 vols (ed J. Munro), 1958; Shakespeare's Dramatic Heritage, 1969; The Medieval Theatre, 1974, 3rd edn 1987; English Moral Interludes, 1975, 2nd edn 1985; A History of the Theatre, 1985, 2nd edn 1992; English Professional Theatre 1530–1660: a documentary history, 2001. *Recreations:* gardening , travel. *Address:* 6 College Road, Clifton, Bristol BS8 3JB. *T:* (0117) 973 4918. *Clubs:* Garrick, National Liberal.   *Died 27 Jan. 2004.*

WIDDOWS, Roland Hewlett, CB 1989; a Deputy Special Commissioner of Income Tax and Chairman (part-time) of Value Added Tax Tribunals, 1990–94; *b* 14 Aug. 1921; *s* of late A. E. Widdows, CB; *m* 1945, Diana Gweneth, *d* of late E. A. Dickson, Malayan Civil Service; two *s* one *d*. *Educ:* Stowe Sch.; Hertford Coll., Oxford (MA). Served in Royal Navy, Coastal Forces, 1941–45. Called to Bar, Middle Temple, 1948; entered Inland Revenue Solicitor's Office, 1951; Asst Solicitor, 1963; on staff of Law Commission, 1965–70; Lord Chancellor's Office, 1970–77; Under Secretary, 1972; Special Comr of Income Tax, 1977–90, Presiding Comr, 1984–90. *Recreations:* sailing, playing the clarinet. *Address:* 1 Chaucer Drive, Milford-on-Sea, Hants SO41 0SS. *T:* (01590) 644661. *Clubs:* Oxford and Cambridge; Royal Lymington Yacht.   *Died 20 Oct. 2004.*

WIDDUP, Malcolm, CB 1979; Under-Secretary, HM Treasury, 1971–80; retired 1981; *b* 9 May 1920; *s* of John and Frances Ellen Widdup; *m* 1947, Margaret Ruth Anderson (*d* 2002); one *s* one *d*. *Educ:* Giggleswick Sch.; Trinity Coll., Oxford (MA). Served War, Army, RA and Staff, 1940–45. Ministry of Food, 1946–53; HM Treasury, 1953–55; Cabinet Office, 1955–57; HM Treasury, 1957–60; Min. of Health, 1960–62; HM Treasury, 1962–66; UK Delegn to OECD, 1966–68; HM Treasury, 1968–80; Sen. Clerk, House of Lords, 1980–81. *Recreations:* gardening, bridge, bowling.
                                                   Died 15 Feb. 2003.

WIGGLESWORTH, Gordon Hardy, RIBA; Consultant, Alan Turner Associates, architects, planning and development consultants, 1988–92 (Director, 1984–88); *b* 27 June 1920; *m* 1952, Cherry Diana Heath; three *d*. *Educ:* Highgate; University Coll., London; Architectural Association. AADipl; RIBA 1948. Served War of 1939–45: Royal Engineers, 1941–46. Architectural Assoc., 1946–48; private practice and Univ. of Hong Kong, 1948–52; private practice: London, 1952–54; Hong Kong, 1954–56; London, 1956–57. Asst Chief Architect, Dept of Education and Science, 1957–67; Dir of Building Develt, MPBW, later DoE, 1967–72; Principal Architect, Educn, GLC (ILEA), 1972–74; Housing Architect, GLC, 1974–80. Vice-Pres., RIBA, 1980–81. FRSA 1983.

Address: 48 Northcote Avenue, W5 3UT. *T:* (020) 7226 7734.   *Died 13 July 2005.*

WIGODER, Baron *cr* 1974 (Life Peer), of Cheetham in the City of Manchester; **Basil Thomas Wigoder;** QC 1966; Vice-President, British United Provident Association, since 1992 (Chairman, 1981–92); *b* 12 Feb. 1921; *s* of late Dr P. I. Wigoder and Mrs R. R. Wigoder, JP, Manchester; *m* 1948, Yoland Levinson; three *s* one *d* (of whom one *s* one *d* are twins). *Educ:* Manchester Grammmar Sch.; Oriel Coll., Oxford (Open Scholar, Mod. Hist.; MA 1946). Served RA, 1942–45. Pres. Oxford Union, 1946. Called to Bar, Gray's Inn, 1946, Master of the Bench, 1972, Vice-Treas., 1988, Treas., 1989. A Recorder of the Crown Court, 1972–84. BoT Inspector, Pinnock Finance (GB) Ltd, 1967. Member: Council of Justice, 1960–; Gen. Council of the Bar, 1970–74; Crown Court Rules Cttee, 1971–77; Council on Tribunals, 1980–86; Home Office Adv. Cttee on Service Candidates, 1984–; Chm., Health Services Bd, 1977–80; a Tribunal Chm., Securities Assoc., 1988–92. Chm., Liberal Party Exec., 1963–65; Chm., Liberal Party Organising Cttee, 1965–66; Liberal Chief Whip, House of Lords, 1977–84 (Dep. Whip, 1976–77). Contested (L): Bournemouth, 1945 and by-election, Oct. 1945; Westbury, 1959 and 1964. Vice-President: Nuffield Hosps, 1981–92; Statute Law Soc., 1984–90; Mem. Court, Nene Coll., 1982–90; Trustee, Oxford Union Soc., 1982–92. *Recreations:* cricket, music. *Address:* House of Lords, SW1A 0PW. *Clubs:* National Liberal, MCC.
                                                   Died 12 Aug. 2004.

WIGRAM, Major Sir (Edward) Robert (Woolmore), 8th Bt *cr* 1805, of Walthamstow, Essex; *b* 19 July 1913; *yr s* of Robert Ainger Wigram and Evelyn Dorothy (*née* Henslowe); *S* brother, 2000; *m* 1944, Viva Ann (*d* 1997), *d* of Douglas Bailey; one *d*. *Educ:* Winchester; Trinity Coll., Cambridge (BA 1934). Attached 2nd Bn S Staffordshire Regt, Bangalore, 1935; Major, 19th King George V Own Lancers, Lahore, 1938. Former master, Westminster Sch. *Heir: cousin* John Woolmore Wigram [*b* 25 May 1957; *m* 1996, Sally Winnington; three *s*]. *Address:* 1 Skipster Hagg, Sinnington, York YO62 6SP.
                                                   Died 11 Oct. 2003.

WILBERFORCE, Baron *cr* 1964 (Life Peer); **Richard Orme Wilberforce,** Kt 1961; CMG 1956; OBE 1944; PC 1964; a Lord of Appeal in Ordinary, 1964–82; Fellow, All Souls College, Oxford, since 1932; *b* 11 Mar. 1907; *s* of late S. Wilberforce; *m* 1947, Yvette, *d* of Roger Lenoan, Judge of Court of Cassation, France; one *s* one *d*. *Educ:* Winchester; New Coll., Oxford. Called to the Bar, 1932; served War, 1939–46 (Hon. Brig.); Under Sec., Control Office Germany and Austria, 1946–47; returned to Bar, 1947; QC 1954; Judge of the High Court of Justice (Chancery Division), 1961–64; Bencher, Middle Temple, 1961. Chm. Exec. Council, Internat. Law Assoc., 1966–88; Mem., Perm. Ct of Arbitration; President: Fédération Internat. du Droit Européen, 1978; Appeal Tribunal, Lloyd's of London, 1983–87. Jt Pres., Anti-Slavery Soc.; Vice-President: (jt) RCM; David Davies Meml Inst. Chancellor, Univ. of Hull, 1978–94; University of Oxford: High Steward, 1967–90; Visitor: Wolfson Coll., 1974–90; Linacre Coll., 1983–90; Hon. Fellow: New Coll., 1965; Wolfson Coll., 1991. Hon. FRCM. Hon. Comp. Royal Aeronautical Society. Hon. Mem., Scottish Faculty of Advocates, 1978. Hon. DCL Oxon, 1968; Hon. LLD: London, 1972; Hull, 1973; Bristol, 1983. Diplôme d'Honneur, Corp. des Vignerons de Champagne. US Bronze Star, 1944; Grand Cross, St Jean de Penafort (Spain), 1970. *Publications:* The Law of Restrictive Trade Practices, 1956; articles and pamphlets on air law and internat. law. *Recreations:* the turf, travel, opera. *Address:* House of Lords, SW1A 0PW. *Club:* Athenæum.   *Died 15 Feb. 2003.*

WILBERFORCE, William John Antony, CMG 1981; HM Diplomatic Service, retired; *b* 3 Jan. 1930; *s* of late Lt-Col W. B. Wilberforce and Cecilia (*née* Dormer); *m* 1953,

Laura Lyon, *d* of late Howard Sykes, Englewood, NJ; one *s* two *d*. *Educ:* Ampleforth; Christ Church, Oxford. Army National Service, 2nd Lieut KOYLI, 1948–49. HM Foreign Service, 1953; served: Oslo, 1955–57; Berlin, 1957–59; Ankara, 1962–64; Abidjan, 1964–67; Asst Head of UN (Econ. and Social) Dept, 1967–70, and of Southern European Dept, 1970–72; Counsellor, 1972–74, and Head of Chancery, 1974–75, Washington; Hd of Defence Dept, FCO, 1975–78; Asst Under-Sec., RCDS, 1979; Leader of UK Delegn to Madrid Conf. on Security and Cooperation in Europe Review Meeting, with rank of Ambassador, 1980–82; High Comr in Cyprus, 1982–88. Hon. DHum Wilberforce, 1973. *Recreations:* the turf, travel, gardening. *Address:* Markington Hall, Harrogate HG3 3PQ. *T:* (01765) 677356. *Club:* Athenæum.

Died 2 Sept. 2001.

WILCOX, Albert Frederick, CBE 1967; QPM 1957; Chief Constable of Hertfordshire, 1947–69, retired; *b* 18 April 1909; *s* of late Albert Clement Wilcox, Ashley Hill, Bristol; *m* 1939, Ethel, *d* of late E. H. W. Wilmott, Manor House, Whitchurch, Bristol; one *s* two *d*. *Educ:* Fairfield Grammar School, Bristol. Joined Bristol City Police, 1929; Hendon Police Coll., 1934; Metropolitan Police, 1934–43. Barrister-at-Law, Gray's Inn, 1941. Served Allied Mil. Govt, Italy and Austria (Lt-Col), 1943–46. Asst Chief Constable of Buckinghamshire, 1946. Cropwood Fellowship, Inst. of Criminology, Cambridge, 1969. Pres. Assoc. of Chief Police Officers, Eng. and Wales, 1966–67; Chm. of Management Cttee, Police Dependents' Trust, 1967–69. Regional Police Commander (designate), 1962–69. Member, Parole Board, 1970–73. Criminological Res. Fellowship, Council of Europe, 1974–76. *Publication:* The Decision to Prosecute, 1972. *Address:* 34 Roundwood Park, Harpenden, Herts AL5 3AF.   *Died 8 Feb. 2002.*

WILD, His Honour David Humphrey; a Circuit Judge, 1972–92; *b* 24 May 1927; *s* of John S. Wild and Edith Lemarchand; *m* 1st, 1950, Joy Josephine, *d* of A. C. Nesbitt, Lincoln's Inn; one *d*; 2nd, 1963, Estelle Grace Prowett, *d* of James Marshall, Aberdeen and Malaya; one *s*. *Educ:* Whitgift Middle Sch., Croydon. Served War of 1939–45, Royal Navy, 1944–48. Called to Bar, Middle Temple, 1951. Practised, London and SE Circuit, 1951–58, Midland Circuit, 1958–72; resident judge, Cambridge Crown Court, 1973–84. Councillor, Oundle and Thrapston RDC, 1968–72. Mem., St Catharine's Coll., Cambridge, 1973. *Publication:* The Law of Hire Purchase, 1960 (2nd edn, 1964). *Clubs:* Naval and Military, Savile, Sette of Odd Volumes.

Died 30 Jan. 2004.

WILDENSTEIN, Daniel Leopold; art historian; President: Fondation Wildenstein, Paris, 1970–90; Wildenstein Institute, Paris, since 1990; Chairman, Wildenstein & Co Inc., New York, 1967–94 (Vice-President, 1943–59, President, 1959–68); Vice-President, Florence Gould Foundation, since 1983; *b* Verrières-le-Buisson, France, 11 Sept. 1917; *s* of Georges Wildenstein; *m* 1939, Martine Kapferer (marr. diss. 1968); two *s*; *m* 1978, Sylvia Roth. *Educ:* Cours Hattemer; Sorbonne (LèsL 1938). Gp Sec., French Pavilion, World's Fair, 1937; went to US, 1940; with Wildenstein & Co. Inc., New York, 1940–; Director: Wildenstein & Co. Inc., London, 1963–; Wildenstein Arte, Buenos Aires, 1963–. Dir, Gazette des Beaux Arts, 1963–; Dir of Activities, Musée Jacquemart-André, Paris, 1956–62; Musée Chaalis, Institut de France, Paris, 1956–62; organiser of art competitions (Hallmark art award). Mem., French Chamber of Commerce in US (Conseiller), 1942–; Founder (1947) and Mem, Amer. Inst. of France (Sec.). Mem., Institut de France (Académie des Beaux-Arts), 1971; Membre du Haut Comité du Musée de Monaco. *Publications:* Claude Monet, vol. 1, 1975, vols 2 and 3, 1979, vol. 4, 1985, vol. 5, 1992; Edouard Manet, vol. 1, 1976, vol. 2, 1977; Gustave Courbet, vol. 1, 1977, vol. 2, 1978. *Recreation:* horse racing (leading owner, 1977). *Address:* Bauernhofstrasse 14, 8853

Lachen, Switzerland; (office) 57 rue La Boétie, 75008 Paris, France. *T:* (1) 45616161. *Clubs:* Brooks's; Turf and Field, Madison Square Garden (New York); Cercle de Deauville, Tir au Pigeon (Paris); Jockey (Buenos Aires).

Died 23 Oct. 2001.

WILES, Rev. Prof. Maurice Frank, FBA 1981; Canon of Christ Church, Oxford, and Regius Professor of Divinity, University of Oxford, 1970–91; *b* 17 Oct. 1923; *s* of late Sir Harold Wiles, KBE, CB and Lady Wiles; *m* 1950, Patricia Margaret (*née* Mowll); two *s* one *d*. *Educ:* Tonbridge School; Christ's College, Cambridge. Ordained deacon, 1950, priest, 1951; Curate, St George's, Stockport, 1950–52; Chaplain, Ridley Hall, Cambridge, 1952–55; Lectr in New Testament Studies, Ibadan, Nigeria, 1955–59; Lectr in Divinity, Univ. of Cambridge, and Dean of Clare College, 1959–67; Prof. of Christian Doctrine, King's Coll., Univ. of London, 1967–70. Bampton Lectr, Univ. of Oxford, 1986. FKC 1972. *Publications:* The Spiritual Gospel, 1960; The Christian Fathers, 1966; The Divine Apostle, 1967; The Making of Christian Doctrine, 1967; The Remaking of Christian Doctrine, 1974; (with M. Santer) Documents in Early Christian Thought, 1975; Working Papers in Doctrine, 1976; What is Theology?, 1976; Explorations in Theology 4, 1979; Faith and the Mystery of God, 1982 (Collins Biennial Religious Book Award, 1983); God's Action in the World, 1986; Christian Theology and Interreligious Dialogue, 1992; A Shared Search, 1994; The Archetypal Heresy, 1996; Reason to Believe, 1999; Scholarship and Faith, 2003. *Address:* Christ Church, Oxford OX1 1DP.

Died 3 June 2005.

WILKINS, Sir Graham John, (Bob), Kt 1980; Chairman, THORN EMI, 1985–89, retired (Chief Executive, 1985–87); President, Beecham Group Ltd, 1984–89 (Chairman and Chief Executive, 1975–84); *b* 22 Jan. 1924; *s* of George William and Anne May Wilkins; *m* 1st, 1945, Daphne Mildred Haynes (*d* 1989); 2nd, 1990, Helen Catherine McGregor. *Educ:* Yeovil Sch.; University Coll., South West of England, Exeter (BSc). Dir and Vice-Pres., Beecham (Canada) Ltd, 1954–59; C. L. Bencard Ltd, and Beecham Research Labs Ltd: Asst Man. Dir, 1959; Man. Dir, 1960; Dir, Beecham Pharmaceutical Div., 1962–64; Beecham Group Ltd: Dir and Chm., Pharmaceutical Div., 1964–72; Man. Dir (Pharmaceuticals), 1972; Exec. Vice-Chm., 1974; Chm., ICC UK, 1985–89 (Vice Chm., 1984–85); Director: Beecham Inc., 1967–86; Hill Samuel Gp Ltd, 1977–87; THORN EMI (formerly Thorn Electrical Industries) Ltd, 1978–89; Rowntree, 1985–88 (Dep. Chm., 1988); Courage Pensions, 1989–; Eastern Electricity, 1989–95. Mem., Doctors' and Dentists' Remuneration Rev. Bd, 1980–90 (Chm., 1986–90). Vice-Chm., Proprietary Assoc. of GB, 1966–68; President: Assoc. of Brit. Pharmaceutical Industry, 1969–71 (Vice-Pres., 1968–69); European Fedn of Pharmaceutical Industries Assoc., 1978–82; Chm., Medico-Pharmaceutical Forum, 1971–73 (Vice-Chm., 1969–70). Mem., BOTB, 1977–80. Pres., Advertising Assoc., 1983–89. Mem. Council, Sch. of Pharmacy, London Univ., 1984–2000 (Chm., 1987–2000). Hon. FRCP 1984. *Publications:* various papers on pharmaceutical industry. *Recreations:* golf, theatre-going. *Address:* Alceda, Walton Lane, Shepperton-on-Thames, Middx TW17 8LQ.   *Died 2 July 2003.*

WILKINS, Maurice Hugh Frederick, CBE 1963; PhD; FRS 1959; Professor of Bio-physics, 1970–81, Emeritus Professor of Biophysics since 1981, and Fellow, since 1973, King's College, University of London; Director, Medical Research Council Cell Biophysics Unit, 1974–80 (Deputy Director, 1955–70, Director, 1970–72, Biophysics Unit; Director Neurobiology Unit, 1972–74); *b* 15 Dec. 1916; *s* of late Edgar Henry Wilkins and of Eveline Constance Jane (*née* Whittaker), both of Dublin; *m* 1959, Patricia Ann Chidgey; two *s* two *d*. *Educ:* King Edward's Sch., Birmingham: St John's College, Cambridge (MA; Hon. Fellow, 1972). Research on luminescence of solids at Physics Department, Birmingham University, with Ministry of Home Security and Aircraft Production, 1938; PhD 1940; Manhattan Project (Ministry of Supply), Univ. of California (research on separation of uranium isotopes by mass spectrograph), 1944; Lectr in Physics, St Andrews Univ., 1945; MRC Biophysics Unit in Physics Department, King's College, London, 1946; Hon. Lecturer in the sub-department of Biophysics, 1958; Prof. of Molecular Biology, King's Coll., 1963–70. President: British Soc. for Social Responsibility in Science, 1969–91; Food and Disarmament Internat., 1984–. Hon. Mem., Amer. Soc. of Biological Chemists, 1964; For. Hon. Mem., Amer. Acad. of Arts and Scis, 1970. Albert Lasker Award, Amer. Public Health Assoc., 1960. Hon. LLD Glasgow, 1972; Hon. ScD: TCD, 1992; Birmingham, 1992; Hon. DSc London, 1998. (Jtly) Nobel Prize for Medicine, for work on structure of DNA, 1962. *Publications:* The Third Man of the Double Helix (autobiog.), 2003; papers in scientific journals on luminescence and topics in bio-physics, *eg* molecular structure of nucleic acids and structure of nerve membranes. *Address:* 30 St John's Park, SE3 7JH. *T:* (020) 8858 1817.   *Died 5 Oct. 2004.*

WILKINSON, Prof. (Elizabeth) Mary, PhD; FBA 1972; Professor of German, University College London, 1960–76, then Emeritus; *b* 17 Sept. 1909; *d* of Frank Wilkinson and Martha E. Gilleard, Keighley, Yorks. *Educ:* Whalley Range High Sch., Manchester; Bedford Coll., London (BA, PhD; Hon. Fellow 1985); DipEd Oxford. Vis. Prof., Univ. of Chicago, 1955; first Virginia C. Gildersleeve Prof., Barnard Coll., Columbia Univ., 1958; Prof.-at-Large of Cornell Univ., 1967. President: English Goethe Soc., 1974–86; Modern Language Assoc., GB, 1964; Hon. Mem., Modern Language Assoc. of America, 1965. Former Governor, Bedford Coll., London. Korresp. Mitglied, Akademie der Wissenschaften zu Göttingen, 1973; Deutsche Akad. für Sprache und Dichtung, 1976. Hon. LLD Smith Coll., Mass., 1966; Hon. DLitt Kent, 1971. Medaille in Gold des Goethe-Instituts, 1965; Preis für Germanistik im Ausland der Deutschen Akad. für Sprache und Dichtung, 1974. German Editor, Notebooks of Samuel Taylor Coleridge, 1950–62 (vols 1 and 2); Editor, publications of the English Goethe Soc., 1951–70. *Publications:* (ed) Thomas Mann's Tonio Kröger, 1943; (ed with L. A. Willoughby) Schiller's Kabale und Liebe, 1944; J. E. Schlegel: A German Pioneer in Aesthetics, 1945, German edn 1973 (Wissenschaftliche Buchges.) (J. G. Robertson Prize); Edward Bullough's Aesthetics, 1957; (with L. A. Willoughby) Goethe: poet and thinker, 1962 (German edn 1974); (with L. A. Willoughby) Schiller: On the Aesthetic Education of Man, 1967 (German edn 1977); Goethe Revisited, 1983; contrib. on Goethe to Encyclopædia Britannica, 1963 and subsq. edns. *Address:* 33 Queen Court, Queen Square, WC1N 3BB.
Died 2 Jan. 2001.

WILKINSON, Geoffrey Crichton, CBE 1986; AFC 1956; Chief Inspector of Accidents (Aircraft), 1981–86; *b* 7 Nov. 1926; *s* of Col W. E. D. Wilkinson and Mrs E. K. Wilkinson; *m* 1958, Virginia Mary Broom; two *d*. *Educ:* Bedford Sch. Graduate, Empire Test Pilots Sch.; FRAeS. Royal Indian Mil. Coll., 1943–44; served RN, 1944–47; aeronautical engrg course, 1948; served RAF, 1949–59 (AFC); Turner and Newall, 1959–61; Mercury Airlines, 1961–65; Accidents Investigation Br., 1965–86. Air Medal, USA, 1953. *Recreations:* sailing, ski-ing, music. *Address:* Buckingham House, 50 Hyde Street, Winchester, Hants SO23 7DY. *T:* (01962) 865823. *Club:* Royal Air Force.   *Died 21 Jan. 2005.*

WILLCOCKS, Alison Ann; Head, Bedales School, 1995–2001; *b* 22 July 1952; *d* of Patrick MacNamara and Sibyl MacNamara; *m* 1st, 1976, Jonathan Willcocks; one *s* one *d*; 2nd, David Strutt. *Educ:* St Francis Coll., Letchworth; New Hall, Cambridge Univ. (MA Hist.); Birmingham Univ. (BMus). Asst Mistress, Portsmouth High Sch., 1976–79; Bedales Sch., 1980–2001: History

teacher, 1980–83; Housemistress, 1983–88; Dep. Head, 1988–94. *Recreations:* writing, music, reading, Christian counselling.   *Died 23 Dec. 2004.*

WILLESEE, Hon. Donald Robert; Member of Senate for Western Australia, 1949–75; *b* 14 April 1916; *m* Gwen; four *s* two *d*. *Educ:* Carnarvon, Western Australia. Special Minister of State, Minister assisting Prime Minister, Minister assisting Minister for Foreign Affairs and Vice-Pres. of Exec. Council, 1972–73; Minister for Foreign Affairs, 1973–75; Leader of Opposition in the Senate, 1966–67; Dep. Leader of Opposition in Senate, 1969–72; Dep. Leader of Govt in Senate, 1972. *Recreation:* swimming. *Address:* 5 Walton Place, Quinns Rock, WA 6030, Australia.   *Died 9 Sept. 2003.*

WILLIAMS OF MOSTYN, Baron *cr* 1992 (Life Peer), of Great Tew in the County of Oxfordshire; **Gareth Wyn Williams;** PC 1999; QC 1978; Lord Privy Seal, Leader of the House of Lords, since 2001; *b* 5 Feb. 1941; *s* of Albert Thomas Williams and Selina Williams; *m* 1st, 1962, Pauline Clarke (marr. diss.); one *s* two *d*; 2nd, 1994, Veena Maya Russell; one *d*. *Educ:* Rhyl Grammar Sch.; Queens' Coll., Cambridge (Open Schol. (History) 1958; Univ. Prize, Jurisprudence 1962; Foundn Schol. 1964; LLB (1st Cl.) 1964; MA 1965). Called to the Bar, Gray's Inn, 1965, Bencher, 1991; a Recorder, 1978–; Leader, Wales and Chester Circuit, 1987–89. Mem., Bar Council, 1986–92 (Chm., 1992). Parly Under-Sec. of State, Home Office, 1997–98; Minister of State, Home Office, 1998–99; Attorney Gen., 1999–2001. Pro-Chancellor, Univ. of Wales, 1994–. Fellow, UCW, Aberystwyth, 1993. *Address:* House of Lords, SW1A 0PW.   *Died 20 Sept. 2003.*

WILLIAMS, Prof. Alan Harold, FBA 2002; Professor in the Centre for Health Economics, University of York, since 1968; *b* 9 June 1927; *s* of Harold George Williams and Gladys May Williams (*née* Clark); *m* 1953, June Frances Porter; two *s* one *d*. *Educ:* King Edward's, Birmingham; Univ. of Birmingham (BCom). Lecturer, Exeter Univ., 1954–63; Sen. Lectr and Reader, Univ. of York, 1964–68. Visiting Lecturer: MIT, 1957–58; Princeton, 1963–64; Director of Economic Studies, HM Treasury Centre for Administrative Studies, 1966–68. Member: Yorkshire Water Authority, 1973–76; DHSS Chief Scientists Research Cttee, 1973–78; Royal Commission on the NHS, 1976–78; various SSRC Cttees and Panels, 1973–; Nat. Water Council, 1980–83. Hon. DPhil Lund, 1977. *Publications:* Public Finance and Budgetary Policy, 1963; (with Robert Anderson) Efficiency in the Social Services, 1975; (with Robert Sugden) Principles of Practical Cost-Benefit Analysis, 1978; Being Reasonable about the Economics of Health, 1997; articles in Economica, Jl of Political Econ., Jl of Public Econs, Nat. Tax Jl, Jl of Health Econ., BMJ and elsewhere; numerous conf. papers on various aspects of public expenditure appraisal, esp. health and health care. *Recreations:* music, walking, teasing.
Died 2 June 2005.

WILLIAMS, Sir Alwyn, Kt 1983; PhD; FRS 1967; FRSE, MRIA, FGS; Principal and Vice-Chancellor , University of Glasgow, 1976–88, Hon. Senior Research Fellow in Geology, since 1988; *b* 8 June 1921; *s* of D. Daniel Williams and E. May (*née* Rogers); *m* 1949, E. Joan Bevan; one *s* one *d*. *Educ:* Aberdare Boys' Grammar Sch.; University College of Wales, Aberystwyth (Hon. Fellow, 1990). PhD Wales. Fellow, Univ. of Wales, 1946–48. Harkness Fund Fellow at US National Museum, Washington, 1948–50; Lecturer in Geology in University of Glasgow, 1950–54; Prof. of Geology, 1954–74, Pro-Vice-Chancellor, 1967–74, Queen's Univ. of Belfast; Lapworth Prof. of Geology, and Head of Dept, Univ. of Birmingham, 1974–76. Co-ordinating Author, Treatise on Invertebrate Paleontology, Geol Soc. of America, 1955–65, 1988–. Pres., Palaeontological Assoc., 1968–70. Trustee, British Museum (Nat. History), 1971–79, Chm. of Trustees, 1974–79. Member: Equip. and Phys. Sci. sub-cttees, UGC, 1974–76; NERC, 1974–76; Adv. Council,

British Library, 1975–77; Scottish Tertiary Educn Adv. Council, 1983–87; Adv. Bd for the Res. Councils, 1985–88; Chairman: Cttee on Nat. Museums and Galls in Scotland, 1979–81; Cttee on Scottish Agricl Colls, 1989; Scottish Hospitals Endowment Res. Trust, 1989–96; Vice-Chm., Cttee of Vice-Chancellors and Principals, 1979–81. Dir, Scottish Daily Record & Sunday Mail Ltd, 1984–90. Pres., Royal Soc. of Edinburgh, 1985–88. Hon. FRSAMD 1988; Hon. Fellow, Geol Soc. of America, 1970–; For. Mem., Polish Academy of Sciences, 1979–; Hon. Associate, BM (Nat. Hist.), 1981–; Hon. FRCPS; Hon. FDS RCPS; Hon. DSc: Wales, 1974; Belfast, 1975; Edinburgh, 1979; Hon. LLD: Strathclyde, 1982; Glasgow, 1988; Hon. DCL Oxford, 1987; DUniv Paisley, 1993. Bigsby Medal, 1961, Murchison Medal, 1973, Geol Soc.; Clough Medal, Edin. Geol. Soc., 1976; T. Neville George Medal, Glasgow Geol. Soc., 1984; Lapworth Medal, Palaeontol Assoc., 2002. *Publications:* contrib. to Trans Royal Socs of London and Edinburgh, Washington Acad. of Scis, Geological Socs of London and America; Jl Geological Soc., Palaeontology, Jl of Paleontology, Nature, Science, Structural Biology, etc. *Address:* Palaeobiology Unit, The University, Glasgow G12 8QQ; 25 Sutherland Avenue, Pollokshields, Glasgow G41 4HG. *T:* (0141) 427 0589. *Died 4 April 2004.*

WILLIAMS, Hon. Atanda F.; *see* Fatayi-Williams.

WILLIAMS, Rev. Austen; *see* Williams, Rev. S. A.

WILLIAMS, Sir Bernard (Arthur Owen), Kt 1999; FBA 1971; Fellow of All Souls College, Oxford, 1951–54 and since 1997; Monroe Deutsch Professor of Philosophy, University of California, Berkeley, since 1988; *b* 21 Sept. 1929; *s* of late O. P. D. Williams, OBE and H. A. Williams; *m* 1955, Shirley Vivienne Teresa Brittain Catlin (later Baroness Williams of Crosby, PC) (marr. diss. 1974); one *d*; *m* 1974, Patricia Law Skinner; two *s*. *Educ:* Chigwell Sch., Essex; Balliol Coll., Oxford (BA 1951, MA 1954; Hon. Fellow 1984). RAF (Gen. Duties Br.), 1951–53; Fellow of New Coll., Oxford, 1954–59; Vis. Lectr, Univ. Coll. of Ghana, 1958–59; Lectr in Philosophy, UCL, 1959–64; Prof. of Philosophy, Bedford Coll., London, 1964–67 (Hon. Fellow 1985); Knightbridge Prof. of Philosophy, Cambridge Univ., 1967–79; Fellow, 1967–79 and 1988–, Provost, 1979–87, King's Coll., Cambridge; White's Prof. of Moral Philosophy, Oxford Univ., and Fellow of CCC, Oxford, 1990–96 (Hon. Fellow, 1996). Visiting Professor: Princeton Univ., USA, 1963; Harvard Univ., 1973; Univ. of California, Berkeley, 1986; Sather Prof. of Classics, Univ. of Calif, Berkeley, 1989; Vis. Fellow, Inst. of Advanced Studies, ANU, 1969; Sen. Vis. Fellow, Princeton, 1978, 1991; Gauss Seminar in Criticism, Princeton, 1992. Member: Public Schools Commn, 1965–70; Royal Commn on Gambling, 1976–78; Commn on Social Justice, 1993–94; Ind. Inquiry into the Misuse of Drugs Act (1971), 1997–2000; Chairman: Cttee on Obscenity and Film Censorship, 1977–79; Fitzwilliam Mus. Syndicate, 1984–87. Dir, English Nat. Opera (formerly Sadler's Wells Opera), 1968–86. Author and presenter, What is Truth? series, Channel 4, 1988. Foreign Hon. Mem., Amer. Acad. of Arts and Sciences, 1983. FRSA 1993. Hon. LittD: Dublin, 1981; Cambridge, 2002; Hon. DLitt: Aberdeen, 1987; Keele, 1995; Yale, 2001; Hon. DHL Chicago, 1999; Hon. LLD Harvard, 2002. *Publications:* (ed with A. C. Montefiore) British Analytical Philosophy, 1966; Morality, 1972; Problems of the Self, 1973; A Critique of Utilitarianism, 1973; Descartes: The Project of Pure Enquiry, 1978; Moral Luck, 1981; (ed with A. K. Sen) Utilitarianism and Beyond, 1982; Ethics and the Limits of Philosophy, 1985; Shame and Necessity, 1993; Making Sense of Humanity, 1995; Plato, 1998; Truth and Truthfulness, 2002; articles in philosophical jls, etc. *Recreation:* music, particularly opera. *Address:* All Souls College, Oxford OX1 4AL. *Died 10 June 2003.*

WILLIAMS, Clifford; Associate Director, Royal Shakespeare Company, 1963–91, Hon. Associate Artist,

since 1991; *b* 30 Dec. 1926; *s* of George Frederick Williams and Florence Maud Williams (*née* Gapper); *m* 1st, 1952, Joanna Douglas (marr. diss. 1959); no *c*; 2nd, 1962, Josiane Eugenie Peset; two *d*. *Educ:* Highbury County Grammar Sch. Acted in London (These Mortals, Larissa, Wolves and Sheep, Great Catherine), and repertory theatres, 1945–48; founded and directed Mime Theatre Company, 1950–53; Dir of Productions: at Marlowe Theatre, Canterbury, 1955–56; at Queen's Theatre, Hornchurch, 1957. Directed at Arts Theatre, London: Yerma, 1957; Radio Rescue, 1958; Dark Halo, Quartet for Five, The Marriage of Mr Mississippi (all in 1959); Moon for the Misbegotten, The Shepherd's Chameleon, Victims of Duty (all in 1960); The Race of Adam, Llandaff Festival, 1961. Joined Royal Shakespeare Company, 1961; directed: Afore Night Come, and The Comedy of Errors, 1962; productions for RSC in Stratford and London: The Tempest, The Representative, The Comedy of Errors (revival), 1963; Richard II, Henry IV Pts I and II (co-dir), Afore Night Come (revival), The Jew of Malta, 1964; The Merchant of Venice, The Jew of Malta (revival), The Comedy of Errors (revival), 1965; The Meteor, Twelfth Night, Henry IV Pts I and II (co-dir, revivals), 1966; Doctor Faustus, 1968; Major Barbara, 1970; The Duchess of Malfi, 1971; The Comedy of Errors (revival), 1972; The Taming of the Shrew, A Lesson in Blood and Roses, 1973; Cymbeline (co-dir), 1974; The Mouth Organ, Too True to be Good, 1975; Wild Oats, 1976, 1979; Man and Superman, 1977; The Tempest, 1978; The Love-Girl and the Innocent, 1981; The Happiest Days of Your Life, 1984; Il Candelaio, 1986; The Beaux' Stratagem, 1988. Other productions include: Savitri, Venus and Adonis, English Opera Gp, London and Aldeburgh, 1956; Our Man Crichton, 1964, and The Flying Dutchman, 1966, in London; The Gardener's Dog, 1965, and The Merry Wives of Windsor, 1967, for the Finnish National Theatre; Volpone at Yale Univ., 1967; Othello, for Bulgarian Nat. Theatre, Soldiers, New York and London, 1968; Dido and Aeneas, Windsor Festival, Famine, English Stage Soc., 1969; As You Like It, 1967, and Back to Methuselah, 1969, both for the Nat. Theatre of GB; The Winter's Tale, 1969, for Yugoslav Nat. Theatre; Sleuth, London, NY and Paris, 1970; Oh! Calcutta!, London and Paris, 1970; Emperor Henry IV, New York, 1973; As You Like It (revival), New York, What Every Woman Knows, London, Emperor Henry IV, London, 1974; Murderer, London, 1975; Mardi-Gras, London, Carte Blanche, London, 1976; Stevie, The Old Country, Rosmerholm, London, 1977; The Passion of Dracula, London, 1978; Richard III, Mexican Nat. Theatre, 1979; Threepenny Opera, 1979, and The Love-Girl and the Innocent, 1980, Aalborg; Born in the Gardens, London, 1980; Overheard, London, To Grandmother's House We Go, NY, The Carmelites, Aalborg, 1981; Othello, Bad Hersfeld, Chapter 17, London, 1982; A Child's Christmas in Wales, 1982, USA, 1983; Richard III, Madrid, Merry Wives of Windsor, USA, Scheherazade, Festival Ballet, 1983; Pack of Lies, London, 1983, NY, 1985; Rise and Fall of the City of Mahagonny, Aalborg, 1984; Aren't We All?, London, 1984, NY, 1985; The Cherry Orchard, Tokyo, 1984; Measure for Measure, Norrköping, St Joan, British tour, 1985; Legends, USA, 1986; Breaking the Code, London, 1986, NY, 1987; Aren't We All?, Australia, 1986; The Importance of Being Earnest, Copenhagen, 1987; A Chorus of Disapproval, British tour, Richard II, London, 1988; Richard III, London, Song at Nightfall, Dorset Music Fest., Wheel of Fire, Mérida Fest., Spain, 1989; Bellman's Opera, Stockholm, 1990; A Slight Hangover, British tour, Painting Churches, Southampton, It's Ralph, London, 1991; Pygmalion, Denmark, Breaking the Code, British tour, Bellman's Opera, London, 1992; A Murder of No Importance, Matters Matrimonial, British tours, 1993; Arsenic and Old Lace, British tour, 1994; Harvey, London, 1995; The Father, NY, 1996, LA, 1998; Separation, Frankfurt, 1997. Also directed plays for the Arena Theatre, Triumph Theatre Co., Theatre Workshop, Guildford, Oxford, Coventry, Windsor,

Toronto, Los Angeles, Washington, Houston, Johannesburg, Edinburgh Festival; Malvern Festival; Dir, Man and Superman (film), 1986. Mem. Welsh Arts Council, 1963–72; Chairman: Welsh Nat. Theatre Co., 1968–72; British Theatre Assoc., 1977–90; Chm., British Children's Theatre Assoc., 1968–71; Governor, Welsh Coll. of Music and Drama, 1981–90. Associate Artist of Yugoslav Nat. Theatre, 1969; FTCL 1960; FRWCMD (FWCMD 1994). *Publications:* (ed) John O'Keeffe, Wild Oats, 1977; (ed) Frederick Lonsdale, Plays 1, 2000, Plays 2, 2004; *plays:* The Disguises of Arlecchino, 1951; The Sleeping Princess, 1953; The Goose Girl, 1954; The Secret Garden, 1955; (with Donald Jonson, after James Joyce) Stephen Dedalus, 1956; Matters Matrimonial, 1993; (after Daphne du Maurier) Rebecca, 1994; The Keys of the Kingdom, 1996; Saints and Sinners, 1997; (after Albert Camus) The Fall, 1997; (after Georges Bernanos) The Carmelites, 1998; (after Rex Warner) The Wild Goose Chase, 1998; (after Benjamin Disraeli) Sybil, or The Two Nations, 2000; (after Susan Ferrier) Marriage, 2001; (after Fyodor Dostoyevsky) A Gentle Spirit, 2003; The Trial of Babeuf, 2004; *translations:* Ionesco, The Duel, Double Act, 1979; Pirandello, As You Desire Me, 1981; Chekhov, The Cherry Orchard, 1981; Musset, A Door Must Be Either Open Or Shut. *Recreations:* motor boating, water-ski-ing. *Address:* 62 Maltings Place, Bagleys Lane, SW6 2BY; 12 chemin Cambarnier Nord, 06650 Opio, France.
Died 20 Aug. 2005.

WILLIAMS, Dafydd Wyn J.; *see* Jones-Williams.

WILLIAMS, Derek Alfred H.; *see* Hutton-Williams.

WILLIAMS, Douglas, CB 1977; CVO 1966; Deputy Secretary, Ministry of Overseas Development (later Overseas Development Administration), 1973–77, retired; *b* 14 May 1917; *s* of late James E. Williams and Elsie Williams; *m* 1948, Marie Jacquot; no *c. Educ:* Wolverhampton Sch.; Exeter Coll., Oxford. Served War, 1939–46 (despatches): Major, RA. Colonial Office, 1947; Principal, 1949; Colonial Attaché, Washington, 1956–60; Asst Sec., Colonial Office, 1961; transferred to ODM (later ODA), 1967, Under-Sec., 1968–73. Member: Bd, Crown Agents, 1978–84; EEC Econ. and Social Cttee, 1978–82; Governing Council, ODI, 1979–85. Trustee, Help the Aged and associated charities, 1984–92 (Chm. of Exec. Cttee, 1985–87, Chm., Overseas Cttee, 1987–88); Mem. Exec. Cttee, David Davies Meml Inst. of Internat. Studies, 1986–. *Publications:* The Specialized Agencies and the United Nations: the system in crisis, 1987; contrib. to United Kingdom—United Nations, 1990; articles on human rights and economic development, British colonial history. *Address:* 14 Gomshall Road, Cheam, Sutton, Surrey SM2 7JZ. *T:* (020) 8393 7306. *Club:* Oxford and Cambridge.
Died 25 June 2002.

WILLIAMS, Frank Denry Clement, CMG 1956; *b* 3 May 1913; *s* of Frank Norris Williams and Joanna Esther Williams; *m* 1941, Traute Kahn; no *c. Educ:* Leighton Park School, Reading; London School of Economics (BSc Econ.). Cadet, Colonial Administrative Service, 1946; Asst Financial Sec., Nigeria, 1952; Financial Secretary: Jamaica, 1954; Federation of Nigeria, 1956; Economic Adviser, Federation of Nigeria, 1957–58; Permanent Secretary, Prime Minister's Dept, Fedn of The W Indies, 1958–62; Financial Sec., The Gambia, 1962–65. *Recreation:* languages. *Address:* 51 The Priory, London Road, Brighton, Sussex BN1 8QT.
Died 23 Nov. 2001.

WILLIAMS, Sir Glanmor, Kt 1995; CBE 1981; FBA 1986; Professor of History, University College of Swansea, 1957–82; Chairman, Ancient Monuments Board (Wales), 1983–95; *b* 5 May 1920; *s* of Daniel and Ceinwen Williams, Dowlais, Glam; *m* 1946, Margaret Fay Davies; one *s* one *d. Educ:* Cyfarthfa Grammar Sch., Merthyr Tydfil; University Coll. of Wales, Aberystwyth (MA 1947); DLitt 1962. University College of Swansea: Asst Lectr in History, 1945; Sen. Lectr, 1952; a Vice-Principal, 1975–78; Hon. Fellow, 1988. Nat. Governor, BBC, for

Wales, 1965–71; Chm., Royal Commn on Ancient and Historical Monuments in Wales, 1986–90 (Mem., 1962–90); Member: Historic Bldgs Council for Wales, 1962–; British Library Bd, 1973–80 (Chm., Adv. Council, 1981–85); Adv. Council on Public Records, 1974–82; Welsh Arts Council, 1978–81; Council, Nat. Museum of Wales, 1983–90; Chm., Welsh Folk-Museum Cttee, 1987–90. Vice-Pres., Univ. of Wales, Aberystwyth, 1986–96, and Hon. Fellow, 1993. Chm., Pantyfedwen Foundations, 1973–79; Pres., Cambrian Arch. Assoc., 1980. Freeman, Bor. of Merthyr Tydfil, 2002. FRHistS 1954 (Vice-Pres., 1979–83); FSA 1978. Hon. LLD Wales, 1998. Medal of Hon. Soc. of Cymmrodorion, 1991. *Publications:* Yr Esgob Richard Davies, 1953; The Welsh Church, 1962; Owen Glendower, 1966; Welsh Reformation Essays, 1967; (ed) Glamorgan County History, vol. II 1984, vol. III 1971, vol. IV 1974, vol. V 1980, vol. VI 1988; Religion, Language and Nationality in Wales, 1979; Grym Tafodau Tân, 1984; Henry Tudor and Wales, 1985; Wales 1415–1642, 1987; (ed) Swansea: an illustrated history, 1990; (ed) The Celts and the Renaissance, 1990; The Welsh and their Religion, 1991; (ed) Social Policy, Crime and Punishment, 1994; Wales and the Reformation, 1997; Cymru a'r Gorffennol, 2000; Glanmor Williams: a life (autobiog.), 2002; contrib. to: History, Welsh History Review, etc. *Recreations:* music, camera. *Address:* 11 Grosvenor Road, Swansea SA2 0SP. *T:* (01792) 204113.
Died 24 Feb. 2005.

WILLIAMS, Sir (Henry) Sydney, Kt 1983; OBE 1978; company director; *b* 10 Jan. 1920; *s* of Edward Stratten Williams and Zilla Williams (*née* McHugh); *m* 1940, Joyce Veronica Meldon; four *s. Educ:* Mt Carmel Coll., Charters Towers, Qld, Aust. Served War, 7th Aust. Div. Cavalry Regt, ME and PNG, 1940–45; 51st Inf. Bn (Far North Qld Regt), 1947–57, Lt-Col Comd 1954–57. Chairman: Air Queensland Ltd (formerly Bush Pilots Airways Ltd), 1960–86; Willtrac Pty Ltd, 1964–; Lizard Island Pty Ltd, 1970–86; Director: Carlton & United Breweries (NQ) Ltd, 1964–90; Placer Pacific Ltd, 1986–90. Member: Queensland Art Gall., 1981–; Cairns Port Authority, 1982–; Life Mem., Cairns RSSAILA; Trustee, WWF, 1981–; Councillor, Enterprise Australia, 1980–; Pres., Far North Queensland Amateur Turf Club, 1959–; past Dep. Chm., Australian Tourist Commn; past Pres., Cairns Legacy Club. Hon. Col, 51st Infantry Bn (Far North Qld Regt), 1987–; Patron, Light Horse Assoc. Ltd, Qld, 1989–93. *Recreations:* fishing, bowls, golf. *Address:* 14 Bellevue Crescent, Edge Hill, Cairns, Qld 4870, Australia. *T:* (7) 40531489. *Clubs:* North Queensland (Townsville); United Services, Brisbane (Brisbane).
Died 11 May 2003.

WILLIAMS, Hubert Glyn, AE 1944; a Recorder of the Crown Court, 1974–77; Senior Partner, Blake, Lapthorn, Rea & Williams, Solicitors, Portsmouth and District, 1973–83; *b* 18 Dec. 1912; *s* of John Christmas Williams and Florence Jane Williams (*née* Jones); *m* 1952, Audrey Elizabeth Righton; one *s* one *d. Educ:* Ruthin. Admitted solicitor, 1934 (2nd cl. Hons). Served War of 1939–45 (Sqdn Ldr; AE): AAF, 1939–41; RAFVR, 1941–45; UK, Egypt, E Africa, Palestine. Pres., Hampshire Inc. Law Soc., 1977–78. *Recreation:* cricket. *Address:* 29 The Avenue, Alverstoke, Gosport, Hants PO12 2JS. *T:* (023) 9258 3058. *Club:* MCC.
Died 28 Sept. 2003.

WILLIAMS, Ven. John Charles; Archdeacon of Worcester, 1975–80, then Archdeacon Emeritus; Residentiary Canon of Worcester Cathedral, 1975–80; *b* 17 July 1912; *s* of William and Edith Williams; *m* 1940, Agnes Mildred Hutchings, MA; one *s* one *d. Educ:* Cowbridge Sch.; St David's University Coll., Lampeter; University College, Oxford; Queen's Coll., Birmingham. Ordained deacon, 1937, priest, 1938; Asst Curate, Christ Church, Summerfield, Birmingham, 1937–39; Asst Curate, Hales Owen, in charge of St Margaret's, Hasbury, 1939–43; Vicar: Cradley Heath, Staffs, 1943–48; Redditch, Worcs, 1948–59; Surrogate, 1951–71; Rural

Dean of Bromsgrove, 1958–59; Rector, Hales Owen, 1959–70; Archdeacon of Dudley, 1968–75; Vicar of Dodderhill, 1970–75. Hon. Canon, Worcester Cathedral, 1965–75; Examng Chaplain to Bishop of Worcester, 1969–80; Dir, Worcester Diocesan Central Services, 1974–75; Director of Ordination Candidates, 1975–79. Substitute Chaplain, HM Prison Long Lartin, Evesham, 1982–87. *Publication:* One Hundred Years, 1847–1947: a history of Cradley Heath Parish, 1947. *Recreations:* history of architecture, sailing. *Address:* The Old Vicarage, Norton with Lenchwick, Evesham, Worcs WR11 4TL. *Clubs:* Oxford University Occasionals, Oxford and Cambridge.
Died 27 Aug. 2002.

WILLIAMS, Prof. John Eryl Hall; Professor of Criminology with Special Reference to Penology, London School of Economics, University of London, 1984–86, then Emeritus; *b* 21 Sept. 1921; *s* of late Edward Hall Williams and Kitty Hall Williams; *m* 1951, Constance Mary Evans. *Educ:* Barry County Sch.; University Coll. of Wales, Aberystwyth (LLB 1942, LLM 1953). Called to the Bar, Middle Temple, 1949. Lectr, Dept of Law, University Coll. of Hull, 1946–50; London School of Economics: Lectr, Law Dept, 1950–59; Reader in Criminology, 1959–84. Vis. Associate Prof., NY Univ. Sch. of Law, 1955–56; Senior Fellow and Vis. Lectr, Yale Law Sch., 1965–66. Mem., Parole Bd, 1970–72, 1976–78. Pres., British Soc. of Criminology, 1970–72; Sec.-Gen., Internat. Soc. for Criminology, 1974–79, Vice-Pres., 1985–94; Mem., Criminological Scientific Council, Council of Europe, 1985–89. Hon. LLD JFK Univ., Calif., 1981. Jt Editor, British Jl of Criminology, 1966–79. *Publications:* The English Penal System in Transition, 1970; Changing Prisons, 1975; (with L. H. Leigh) The Management of the Prosecution Process in Denmark, Sweden and The Netherlands, 1981; Criminology and Criminal Justice, 1982; (ed) The Role of the Prosecutor, 1988; (ed jtly) Punishment, Custody and the Community: reflections and comments on the Green Paper, 1989; A Page of History in Relief, 1993. *Recreations:* landscape painting, foreign travel. *Address:* Law Department, London School of Economics and Political Science, Houghton Street, Aldwych, WC2A 2AE. *T:* (020) 7405 7686.
Died 25 April 2005.

WILLIAMS, Rev. John Herbert, LVO 1989; Chaplain to the Royal Victorian Order and Chaplain of the Queen's Chapel of the Savoy, 1983–89; Chaplain to the Queen, 1988–89; *b* 15 Aug. 1919; *s* of Thomas and Mary Williams; *m* 1948, Joan Elizabeth (*née* Morgan); one *s. Educ:* St David's Coll., Lampeter (BA Hons); Salisbury Theological Coll. Deacon 1943; priest 1944; Curate: Blaenavon (Gwent), 1943–46; Llanishen, Cardiff, 1946–48; Priest in Charge, Rogerstone (Gwent), 1948–51; Asst Chaplain, HM Prison, Manchester, 1951; Chaplain, HM Prison: Holloway, 1952; Birmingham, 1957; Wormwood Scrubs, 1964; South East Regional Chaplain, 1971; Deputy Chaplain General, Home Office Prison Dept, 1974–83; Priest-in-Ordinary to the Queen, 1980–83. *Recreations:* Rugby, classical music/opera, Francophile. *Address:* 75 Monks Drive, W3 0ED. *T:* (020) 8992 5206.
Died 16 Dec. 2003.

WILLIAMS, Michael Leonard; actor; Associate Artist, Royal Shakespeare Company, since 1966; *b* 9 July 1935; *s* of Michael Leonard Williams and Elizabeth (*née* Mulligan); *m* 1971, Judith Olivia Dench (Dame Judi Dench, DBE); one *d. Educ:* St Edward's Coll., Liverpool; RADA (Coronation Scholar). Début, Nottingham Playhouse, 1959; London début, Celebration, Duchess Theatre, 1961; joined RSC, 1963; rôles included: Puck in A Midsummer Night's Dream, Filch in The Beggar's Opera, Eichmann in The Representative, 1963; Oswald in King Lear (also NY), Pinch in The Comedy of Errors, Kokol in Marat/Sade, Lodowick in The Jew of Malta, 1964; Dromio of Syracuse in The Comedy of Errors, Guildenstern in Hamlet, Herald in Marat/Sade (also NY), 1965; Arthur in Tango, 1966; Petruchio in The Taming of the Shrew,

Orlando in As You Like It, 1967; Fool in King Lear, Troilus in Troilus and Cressida, 1968; Charles Courtly in London Assurance, 1970; Bassanio in The Merchant of Venice, Ferdinand in The Duchess of Malfi, title rôle in Henry V, 1971; Mole in Toad of Toad Hall, 1972; Stellio in Content to Whisper, 1973; Private Meek in Too True to be Good, 1975; title rôle in Schweyk in the Second World War, Dromio in The Comedy of Errors (musical version), Autolycus in The Winter's Tale, Fool in King Lear, 1976; title rôle in national tour, Quartermaine's Terms, 1982; Bob in Pack of Lies, Lyric, 1983; George in Two Into One, Shaftesbury, 1984; Charles Pooter in Mr and Mrs Nobody, Garrick, 1986; George in Out of Order, Shaftesbury, 1990; Brief Lives, Duchess, 1998; The Forest, RNT, 1999; *films* included: The Marat/Sade, 1966; Eagle in a Cage, 1969; Dead Cert, 1974; In Search of Alexander the Great, 1980; Enigma, 1981; Educating Rita, 1982; Henry V, 1990; Tea with Mussolini, 1999; *television* included: Elizabeth R, 1971; A Raging Calm, The Hanged Man, 1974; My Son, My Son, 1978; Love in a Cold Climate, 1980; Quest of Eagles, 1980; A Fine Romance, 1980–81, 1982; Blunt, 1986; Double First, 1988; Angel Voices, 1989; Can you hear me thinking?, 1990; September Song, 1992–94; Conjugal Rites, 1993–94; A Dance to the Music of Time, 1997; Leprechauns, 1999. Chm., Catholic Stage Guild, 1977–87; KSG 2000. *Recreations:* family, pottering, gardening. *Address:* c/o Julian Belfrage Associates, 46 Albemarle Street, W1X 4PP. *Club:* Garrick. *Died 11 Jan. 2001.*

WILLIAMS, Noel Ignace B.; *see* Bond-Williams.

WILLIAMS, Peter F.; *see* Firmston-Williams.

WILLIAMS, Prof. Philip James Stradling, PhD; FRAS, FInstP; Professor of Physics, University of Wales, Aberystwyth (formerly University College of Wales, Aberystwyth), since 1991; Member (Plaid Cymru) South East Wales, National Assembly for Wales, 1999–2003; *b* 11 Jan. 1939; *s* of Glyndwr and Morfydd Williams; *m* 1962, Ann Green; one *s* one *d. Educ:* Lewis Sch., Pengam; Clare Coll., Cambridge (BA 1960, MA 1964; PhD 1964). FRAS 1984; FInstP 1992. Fellow, Clare Coll., Cambridge, 1964–67; Lectr, then Sen. Lectr, 1967–86, Reader, 1986–91, UCW, Aberystwyth. Pres., ASE Cymru, 2002–03. Plaid Cymru spokesperson for Econ. Develt, 1999–2003. Plaid Cymru: Nat. Chm., 1970–76; Co-ordinator, Campaign for Self-Govt, 1996–. Welsh Politician of the Year, Channel 4, 2000. *Publications:* (with D. Wigley) An Economic Plan for Wales, 1970; A Voice from the Valleys, 1981; The Welsh Budget, 1998; contrib. numerous papers to internat. refereed jls on radio astronomy, space and atmospheric physics. *Recreations:* jazz (alto sax), dancing, hill-walking, history, poetry. *Address:* Rhydyfrian, Aberystwyth, Ceredigion SY23 4LU. *T:* (01970) 612857. *Club:* Bryn Amlwg Sports and Social (Aberystwyth). *Died 10 June 2003.*

WILLIAMS, Sir Robert (Evan Owen), Kt 1976; MD, FRCP, FRCPath; FFPHM; Director, Public Health Laboratory Service, 1973–81; Chairman, Advisory Committee on Genetic Manipulation, Health and Safety Executive, 1984–86 (Chairman, Genetic Manipulation Advisory Group, 1981–84); *b* 30 June 1916; *s* of Gwynne Evan Owen Williams and Cicely Mary (*née* Innes); *m* 1944, Margaret (*née* Lumsden) (*d* 1990); one *s* two *d. Educ:* Sherborne Sch., Dorset; UCL(Fellow 1968); UCH. Assistant Pathologist, EMS, 1941–42; Pathologist, MRC Unit, Birmingham Accident Hospital, 1942–46; on staff Public Health Laboratory Service, 1946–60 (Dir, Streptococcus, Staphylococcus and Air Hygiene Lab., 1949–60); Prof. of Bacteriology, Univ. of London, at St Mary's Hosp. Med. Sch., 1960–73, Dean 1967–73. Mem. MRC, 1969–73. Pres., RCPath, 1975–78. Hon. FRCPA, 1977. Hon. MD Uppsala, 1972; Hon. DSc Bath, 1977; Dr *hc* Lisbon, 1992. *Publications:* (jtly) Hospital Infection, 1966; Microbiology for the Public Health, 1985; numerous pubns in jls on bacteriol and epidemiol subjects. *Recreation:* horticulture. *Address:* Little Platt, Plush,

Dorchester, Dorset DT2 7RQ. *T:* (01300) 348320. *Club:* Athenæum. *Died 24 May 2003.*

WILLIAMS, Rev. (Sidney) Austen, CVO 1980; Vicar of St Martin-in-the-Fields, 1956–84; Chaplain to the Queen's Household, 1961–82, Extra Chaplain since 1982; a Prebendary of St Paul's Cathedral, since 1973; *b* 23 Feb. 1912; *s* of Sidney Herbert and Dorothy Williams; *m* 1945, Daphne Joan McWilliam; one *s* one *d. Educ:* Bromsgrove School; St Catharine's College, Cambridge (MA); Westcott House, Cambridge. Ordained deacon, 1937, priest, 1938; Curate of St Paul, Harringay, 1937–40. Chaplain, Toc H, France and Germany, 1940–48 (POW, 1940–44). Curate of: All Hallows, Barking by the Tower, 1945–46; St Martin-in-the-Fields, 1946–51; Vicar of St Albans, Westbury Park, Clifton, Bristol, 1951–56. Freeman of the City of London, 1977. *Recreations:* photography, ornithology. *Address:* 37 Tulsemere Road, SE27 9EH. *T:* (020) 8670 7945. *Died 9 Dec. 2001.*

WILLIAMS, Sir Sydney; *see* Williams, Sir Henry S.

WILLIAMS, Prof. Thomas Eifion Hopkins, CBE 1980; CEng; Research Professor of Civil Engineering, University of Southampton, 1983–93, then Emeritus Professor (Professor of Civil Engineering, 1967–83); *b* 14 June 1923; *s* of David Garfield Williams and Annie Mary Williams (*née* Hopkins), Cwmtwrch, Brecon; *m* 1947, Elizabeth Lois Davies; one *s* two *d. Educ:* Ystradgynlais Grammar Sch.; Univ. of Wales (BSc, MSc); Univ. of Durham (PhD). FICE, FIHT, FCIT. Research Stressman, Sir W. G. Armstrong-Whitworth Aircraft, 1945; Asst Engr, Trunk Roads, Glam CC, 1946; Asst Lectr in Civil Engrg, UC Swansea, 1947; Lectr in Civil Engrg, King's Coll., Univ. of Durham, 1948; Resident Site Engr, R. T. James & Partners, 1952; Sen. Lectr, Reader and Prof. of Civil and Transport Engrg, King's Coll., Univ. of Durham (subseq. Univ. of Newcastle upon Tyne), 1958–67. Post-doctoral Visitor, Univ. of California at Berkeley, 1955; Vis. Prof., Civil Engrg, Northwestern Univ., 1957. Chairman: Civil Engrg EDC, 1976–78; Standing Adv. Cttee on Trunk Rd Assessment, Dept of Transport, 1980–87 (Mem., Adv. Cttee, 1977–80); Member: EDC Civil Engrg, 1967–76; Transport Cttee, SRC; Roads Engrg Bd, ICE; British Nat. Cttee, PIARC; Council and Transp. Engrg Bd, Inst. Highway Engrs (Pres. 1979–80); Public Policy Cttee, RAC, 1981–97. Visitor, TRRL, 1982–88 (Mem., Adv. Cttee on Traffic and Safety, 1977–80); Special Advisor, H of L Select Cttee on European Transport, 1989. Mem. Council, Church Schools Co., 1982–90. *Publications:* (ed) Urban Survival and Traffic, 1961; Capacity, in Traffic Engineering Practice, 1963; Prediction of Traffic in Industrial Areas, 1966; Autostrade: Strategia, di sviluppo industriale e la vitalita delle nostre citta, 1965; Inter-City VTOL: Potential Traffic and Sites, 1969; Mobility and the Environment, 1971; (ed) Transportation and Environment: policies, plans and practice, 1973; Integrated Transport: developments and trends, 1976; Air, Rail and Road Inter-City Transport Systems, 1976; Land Use, Highways and Traffic, 1977; Motor Vehicles in a Changing World, 1978; Traffic Engineering 1960–81, 1981; Transport Policy: facts; frameworks; econometrics, 1983; Assessment of Urban Roads, 1986; contribs to Proc. ICE, Highway Engrs, IMunE, Road International, Traffic Engrg and Control, Segnalazioni Stradali, OTA/PIARC Confs. *Recreation:* music. *Address:* Willowdale, Woodlea Way, Ampfield, Romsey, Hants SO51 9DA. *T:* (023) 8025 3342. *Club:* Royal Automobile.

Died 17 June 2001.

WILLIAMS, Prof. William David, DPhil; Professor of German, Liverpool University, 1954–80; *b* 10 March 1917; *s* of William Williams and Winifred Ethel Williams (*née* Anstey); *m* 1946, Mary Hope Davis; one *s* one *d. Educ:* Merchant Taylors' School; St John's Coll., Oxford (MA, DPhil). Served War of 1939–45, with Sudan Defence Force, Middle East, and as Liaison Officer with Polish Army in Italy; Asst Lecturer in German, Leeds Univ.,

1946; Lecturer in German, Oxford Univ., 1948–54; Pro-Vice-Chancellor, Liverpool Univ., 1965–68. *Publications:* Nietzsche and the French, 1952; The Stories of C. F. Meyer, 1962; reviews, etc, in Modern Language Review, and Erasmus. *Recreation:* gardening. *Address:* Strangers Corner, 5 Summerfield Rise, Goring-on-Thames, near Reading, Berks RG8 0DS. *T:* (01491) 872603.

Died 21 April 2005.

WILLIAMS, Col William Trevor, FCIS; Director General, Engineering Industries Association, 1981–95; *b* 16 Oct. 1925; *s* of Francis Harold and Ellen Mabel Williams, Newton Manorbier; *m* 1951, Elizabeth, *d* of late Brig. Arthur Goldie; two *s* two *d. Educ:* Darwin Coll., Univ. of Kent (MA). MCIT. Commissioned in Infantry, 1945; regimental service, India and Malaya, to 1949; seconded to Guyanese Govt, 1964, 1965; Commander, Maritime Air Regt, Far East, 1967–69; Project Office, National Defence Coll., 1970–71; Adviser, Ethiopian Govt, 1971–72; Col Q BAOR, 1973–76 (Chm., Berlin Budget Cttee); Head of Secretariat, MoD, 1976–77; Director, SATRA, 1979–80. FCMI. *Publications:* military. *Recreations:* golf, photography. *Address:* 15 Mill Lane, Lower Harbledown, Canterbury CT2 8NE. *T:* (01227) 768170. *Died 7 July 2004.*

WILLIAMSON, David Stewart, OBE 1999; QC (Scot.) 2002; WS; FCIArb; Solicitor Advocate, since 1993; Senior Litigation Partner, Brodies Solicitors, Edinburgh, since 1976; *b* 6 May 1949; *s* of Kenneth and Annie Williamson; *m* 1988, Dorothy, (Dee), Smyth. *Educ:* Royal High Sch., Edinburgh; Edinburgh Univ. (LLB). FCIArb 1994. Admitted solicitor, 1971; Partner, Simpson & Marwick Solicitors, Edinburgh, 1974–76. Pt-time Chm., Employment Tribunals, 1990–; Temp. Sheriff, 1996–99; Pt-time Sheriff, 2000–. Member: Criminal Injuries Compensation Bd, 1996–2001; Criminal Injuries Compensation Appeals Panel, 2001–. *Publication:* (contrib.) Sport and the Law in Scotland, 2000. *Recreations:* cricket, hill-walking, golf. *Address:* 48 Garscube Terrace. Edinburgh EH12 6BN. *T:* (0131) 337 8971; *e-mail:* williamsonws@msn.com. *Club:* MCC.

Died 27 Jan. 2004.

WILLIAMSON, Dame (Elsie) Marjorie, DBE 1973; PhD; Principal, Royal Holloway College, University of London, 1962–73; *b* 30 July 1913; *d* of late Leonard Claude Williamson and Hannah Elizabeth Cary. *Educ:* Wakefield Girls' High School; Royal Holloway College, London (MSc, PhD). Demonstrator in Physics, Royal Holloway College, University of London, 1936–39; Lecturer in Physics: University College of Wales, Aberystwyth, 1939–45; Bedford Coll., Univ. of London, 1945–55; Principal, St Mary's Coll., Univ. of Durham, 1955–62; Deputy Vice-Chancellor, Univ. of London, 1970–71, 1971–72. Fellow, Bedford Coll., Univ. of London, 1975. A Manager, The Royal Instn, 1967–70, 1971–74. Mem., Commonwealth Scholarship Commn, 1975–83. *Recreations:* music, gardening. *Address:* Priory Barn, Lower Raydon, Ipswich, Suffolk IP7 5QT. *T:* (01473) 824033. *Died 12 Aug. 2002.*

WILLIAMSON, Malcolm Benjamin Graham Christopher, CBE 1976; composer, pianist, organist; Master of the Queen's Music, since 1975; *b* 21 Nov. 1931; *s* of Rev. George Williamson, Sydney, Australia, and Bessie (*née* Wrigley); *m* 1960, Dolores Irene Daniel (marr. diss. 1978); one *s* two *d. Educ:* Barker Coll., Hornsby, NSW; Sydney Conservatorium. Asst Organist, Farm Street, London, 1955–58; Organist, St Peter's, Limehouse, 1958–60; Lectr in Music, Central Sch. of Speech and Drama, 1961–62; Composer-in-Residence: Westminster Choir Coll., Princeton, NJ, 1970–71 (Hon. Fellow, 1971); Florida State Univ., 1975; Creative Arts Fellow, ANU, 1974–81; Ramaciotti Medical Research Fellow, Univ. of NSW, 1982–83; Vis. Prof. of Music, Strathclyde Univ., 1983–86. Mem. Exec. Cttee, Composers' Guild of GB, 1964. President: Beauchamp Sinfonietta, 1972–; Birmingham Chamber Music Soc., 1975–; Univ. of

London Choir, 1976–; Purbeck Festival of Music, 1976–; RPO, 1977–82; Sing for Pleasure, 1977–; British Soc. for Music Therapy, 1977–; Stevenage Music Soc., 1987–; Ditchling Choral Soc., 1989–; Finchley Children's Music Gp, 1991–; Vice President: Elgar Foundn; St Michael's Singers; Nat. Music Council of GB; NYO of GB; patron of orchestras, choirs, trusts, etc. Hon. DMus: Westminster Choir Coll., Princeton, NJ, 1970; Melbourne, 1982; Sydney, 1982; DUniv Open, 1983. Hon. AO 1987. *Compositions include: grand operas:* Our Man in Havana (also orchestral suite); The Violins of Saint-Jacques; Lucky Peter's Journey; *chamber operas:* English Eccentrics (also choral suite); The Happy Prince; Julius Caesar Jones; Dunstan and the Devil; The Growing Castle; The Red Sea; The Death of Cuchulain; The Musicians of Bremen; *operatic sequence:* The Brilliant and the Dark; *choral operas or cassations:* The Moonrakers; Knights in Shining Armour; The Snow Wolf; Genesis; The Stone Wall; The Winter Star; The Glitter Gang; The Terrain of the Kings; The Valley and the Hill; The Devil's Bridge; *ballets:* Sun into Darkness; Spectrum; Heritage; *orchestral:* seven symphonies; Santiago de Espada (overture); Sinfonia concertante (also ballet); The Display (concert suite; also ballet); Sinfonietta (also ballet); Concerto Grosso; Symphonic Variations; Serenade and Aubade; Epitaphs for Edith Sitwell (also organ arrangement); The Bridge that Van Gogh Painted; Perisynthion (also ballet); The House of Windsor (orchestral suite); Fiesta; Ochre; Fanfarade; Ode for Queen Elizabeth; In Thanksgiving—Sir Bernard Heinze; Cortège for a Warrior; Lento for Strings; Bicentennial Anthem; *concerti:* three piano concerti (ballet, Have Steps Will Travel, to Piano Concerto No 3); Concerto for Two Pianos and Strings; Organ Concerto; Violin Concerto; Lament in Memory of Lord Mountbatten of Burma (violin and strings); Au Tombeau du Martyr Juif Inconnu (harp and strings); *solo voice and orchestra:* Six English Lyrics (also arrangement for solo voice and piano); Hammarskjold Portrait; Les Olympiques; Tribute to a Hero; Next Year in Jerusalem; White Dawns (also arrangement for solo voice and piano); *solo voice and piano:* A Vision of Beasts and Gods; Celebration of Divine Love; Three Shakespeare Songs; A Christmas Carol; From a Child's Garden; The Fly; The Mower to the Glow-worm; The White Island or Place of the Blessed; Day that I Have Loved; Two Vocalises; *chorus and orchestra:* The Icy Mirror; Ode to Music; Jubilee Hymn; Mass of Christ the King (to celebrate the Queen's Silver Jubilee); Little Mass of Saint Bernadette; Now is the Singing Day; A Pilgrim Liturgy; Songs for a Royal Baby; The True Endeavour; The Dawn is at Hand; The Cradle of the Hope of Peace; *choral:* Two Motets; Adoremus; Dawn Carol; Ascendit Deus; Tu es Petrus; Agnus Dei; Dignus est Agnus; Procession of Psalms; Easter Carol; Jesu, Lover of My Soul; Symphony for Voices; Harvest Thanksgiving; Let Them Give Thanks; Wrestling Jacob; The Morning of the Day of Days; An Australian Carol; Epiphany Carol; Mass of Saint Andrew; A Young Girl; Sweet and Low; A Canon for Stravinsky; Sonnet; Cantate Domino—Psalm 98; In Place of Belief; Te Deum; Love, the Sentinel; Canticle of Fire; The World at the Manger; This Christmas Night; Kerygma; Mass of Saint Margaret of Scotland; Three Choric Hymns; Now is the Singing Day; Galilee; Easter in St Mary's Church; *unison voices:* Planctus; 12 New Hymn Tunes; 6 Christmas Songs for the Young; Mass of Saint Andrew; 6 Evening Hymns; A Psalm of Praise; Hallo Everybody; 5 Carols of King David; 6 Wesley Songs for the Young; Communion Hallelujahs; 16 Hymns and Processionals; Love Chorales (8 hymns); Dove Chorales (8 hymns); Above Chorales (8 hymns); Mass of Saint James; 20 Psalms of the Elements; Mass of the People of God; Our Church Lives; *chamber music:* Nonet; Variations for Violoncello and Piano; Concerto for Wind Quartet and Two Pianos; Serenade for Flute, Piano and String Trio; Pas de Quatre for Piano and Woodwind Quartet (also ballet as BigfellaTootsquoodgeandNora); Piano and String Quintet; Partita for Viola on Themes of Walton; Pietà; Piano Trio; The Feast of Eurydice; Champion Family

Album; Channukkah Sketches for Flute and Guitar; *brass ensembles:* Canberra Fanfare; Adelaide Fanfare; Konstanz Fanfare; Richmond Fanfare; Fontainebleau Fanfare; Ceremony for Oodgeroo; Fanfares and Chorales; Bratsvo-Brotherhood; Music for a Quiet Day; Concertino for Charles; *piano solos:* 2 piano sonatas; Five Preludes for Piano; Ritual of Admiration; Himna Titu; Sonata for Two Pianos; Springtime on the River Moskva (piano duet); 7 books of travel diaries; 2 books of peace pieces; *organ:* Fons Amoris; Résurgence du Feu; Symphony for Organ; Vision of Christ Phœnix; Elegy—JFK; Little Carols of the Saints; Mass of a Medieval Saint; Organ Fantasies on This is my Father's World and O Paradise!; The Lion of Suffolk; Mass of the People of God; *musicals:* No Bed for Bacon; Trilby; also arrangements, film scores, music for television and radio. *Recreation:* literature. *Address:* c/o Campion Press, Sandon, Buntingford, Herts SG9 0QW.

Died 2 March 2003.

WILLIAMSON, Dame Marjorie; *see* Williamson, Dame E. M.

WILLIS, Vice-Adm. Sir (Guido) James, KBE 1981; AO 1976; Chief of Naval Staff, Australia, 1979–82, retired; *b* 18 Oct. 1923; *s* of late Dr Jack Rupert Law Willis and Théa Willis; *m* 1st, 1949; one *s* two *d*; 2nd, 1976, Marjorie J. Campbell-Smith, *d* of W. E. R. Rogers, Adelaide, SA. *Educ:* Wesley Coll., Melbourne; Royal Australian Naval Coll. IDC, 1967; Dir Gen. Ops and Plans, 1968–71; CO HMAS Melbourne, 1971–72; DDL Project Dir, 1972–73; Chief of Naval Personnel, 1973–75; Chief of Naval Material, 1975–76; Asst Chief of Defence Force Staff, 1976–78; Flag Officer Commanding HMA Fleet, 1978–79. Commander 1956, Captain 1962, Rear-Adm. 1973, Vice-Adm. 1979. *Address:* 20 Wilsden Street, Walkerville, SA 5081, Australia.   *Died 15 June 2003.*

WILLIS, Sir James; *see* Willis, Sir G. J.

WILLIS, Joseph Robert McKenzie, CB 1952; CMG 1946; Deputy Chairman, Board of Inland Revenue, 1957–71; *b* 18 March 1909; 2nd *s* of Charles Frederick Willis and Lucy Alice McKenzie; *m* 1945, Elizabeth Browning, *er d* of James Ewing; one *s* one *d*. *Educ:* Eton; Christ Church, Oxford. Entered Inland Revenue Dept, 1932; Under Secretary, Central Economic Planning Staff, Treasury, 1948–49; Commissioner of Inland Revenue, 1949; Student of Imperial Defence Coll., 1948. Professorial Res. Fellow and Vis. Prof., Bath Univ., 1972–79. Specialist advr to Select Cttee on Wealth Tax, 1975. *Publications:* (with C. T. Sandford and D. J. Ironside) An Accessions Tax, 1973; An Annual Wealth Tax, 1975; (with P. J. W. Hardwick) Tax Expenditures in the United Kingdom, 1978. *Address:* Bunbury, Lower Shiplake, Henley-on-Thames, Oxon RG9 3PD. *T:* (0118) 940 2726.   *Died 14 Feb. 2001.*

WILLISON, Sir John (Alexander), Kt 1970; OBE 1964; QPM 1968; DL; Chief Constable, West Mercia Constabulary, 1967–74; *b* 3 Jan. 1914; *s* of John Willison Gow Willison and Mabel Willison, Dalry, Ayrshire; *m* 1947, Jess Morris Bruce (*d* 1996). *Educ:* Sedbergh School. Joined City of London Police, 1933; served with RNVR, 1943–46; Chief Constable: Berwick, Roxburgh and Selkirk, 1952–58; Worcestershire Constabulary, 1958–67. DL Worcs 1968. KStJ 1973. *Address:* Ravenhills Green, Lulsley, near Worcester WR6 5QW.

Died 20 Oct. 2002.

WILLMAN, George, FIA; Chief Executive, United Synagogue, since 1999; *b* 5 July 1940; *s* of Rabbi Dr Alfred Willman and Gabrielle Willman; *m* 1973, Agnes Weiss; two *s* one *d*. *Educ:* W Hartlepool Grammar Sch.; Oriel Coll., Oxford (MA). FIA 1967. Confederation Life Insurance Company: Chief Actuary for UK, 1972–85; Dir of Mktg, 1985–86; Vice-Pres., Individual Insce, 1986–92; Sen. Vice Pres. and Gen. Manager, 1992–94; Asst Gen. Manager, 1994–96, Consultant, 1996–99, Sun Life Insce Co. of Canada. *Publication:* Penguin Guide to Insurance,

1973. *Recreations:* reading, theatre, family. *Address:* United Synagogue, Adler House, 735 High Road, N12 0US. *T:* (020) 8343 8989. *Died 13 April 2001.*

WILLMER, Prof. (Edward) Nevill, ScD; FRS 1960; Emeritus Professor of Histology, University of Cambridge, since 1969; Fellow of Clare College, Cambridge, since 1936; *b* 15 Aug. 1902; 5th *s* of Arthur W. Willmer, Birkenhead; *m* 1939, Henrietta Noreen, (Penny) (*d* 1999), 2nd *d* of H. Napier Rowlatt; two *s* two *d*. *Educ:* Birkenhead Sch.; Corpus Christi Coll., Oxford (BA 1924, MA 1965; Hon. Fellow, 1983); MSc Manchester, 1927; ScD Cambridge, 1944. Demonstrator and Assistant Lecturer in Physiology, Manchester, 1924–29; Lecturer in Histology, Cambridge, 1930–48, Reader, 1948–65, Prof., 1966–69. Editor, Biological Reviews, 1969–80. *Publications:* Tissue Culture, 1934; Retinal Structure and Colour Vision, 1946; Cytology and Evolution, 1960, 2nd edn 1970; (ed) Cells and Tissues in Culture, vols 1 and 2, 1965, vol. 3, 1966; Old Grantchester, 1976; The River Cam, 1979; Waen and the Willmers, 1988; What the Poet Saw, 1994; The Sallow Bush, 1999; contrib. physiological and biological journals. *Recreations:* painting, gardening. *Address:* Yew Garth, Grantchester, Cambridge CB3 9ND. *T:* (01223) 840360. *Died 8 April 2001.*

WILLMER, Nevill; *see* Willmer, E. N.

WILSON, Alexander, CBE 1986; FLA; Director General, British Library Reference Division, 1980–86; *b* 12 Feb. 1921; *s* of late William Wilson and Amelia Wilson; *m* 1949, Mary Catherin Traynor; two *s*. *Educ:* Bolton County Grammar Sch. FLA 1950, Hon. FLA 1984. Served War, RAF, 1941–46. Librarian at Bolton, Harrogate, Taunton, and Swindon, 1946–52; Dir of Library and Cultural Services, Dudley and later Coventry, 1952–72; Dir, Cheshire Libraries and Museums Service, 1972–79. Member: Library Adv. Council (England), 1971–74; British Library Bd, 1974–86. Pres., LA, 1986. Fellow, Birmingham Polytechnic, 1989. Hon. DLit Sheffield, 1989. *Publications:* contrib. books and periodicals on libraries and other cultural services. *Recreations:* walking, listening to music. *Address:* 1 Brockway West, Tattenhall, Chester CH3 9EZ. *Died 13 Feb. 2002.*

WILSON, Lt.-Gen. Sir (Alexander) James, KBE 1974 (CBE 1966; MBE 1948); MC 1945; DL; Chief Executive, Tobacco Advisory Council, 1983–85 (Chairman, 1977–83); *b* 13 April 1921; *s* of Maj.-Gen. Bevil Thomson Wilson, CB, DSO, and of Florence Erica, *d* of Sir John Starkey, 1st Bt; *m* 1958, Hon. Jean Margaret Paul, 2nd *d* of 2nd Baron Rankeillour; two *s*. *Educ:* Winchester Coll.; New Coll., Oxford (BA Law, MA). Served War of 1939–45, North Africa and Italy, Rifle Bde (despatches); Adjt, IMA Dehra Dun, 1945–47; PS to C-in-C Pakistan, 1948–49; Co. Comdr, 1st Bn Rifle Bde, BAOR 1949 and 1951–52, Kenya 1954–55 (despatches); psc 1950; Bde Major 11th Armd Div., BAOR, 1952–54; Instr, Staff Coll. Camberley, 1955–58; 2nd in comd 3rd Green Jackets, BAOR, 1959–60; GSO1 Sandhurst, 1960–62; CO 1st Bn XX Lancs Fus, 1962–64; Chief of Staff, UN Force in Cyprus, 1964–66 (Actg Force Comdr, 1965–66); Comdr, 147 Inf. Bde TA, 1966–67; Dir of Army Recruiting, MoD, 1967–70; GOC NW District, 1970–72; Vice Adjutant General, MoD, 1972–74; GOC SE District, 1974–77. Dep. Col (Lancashire), RRF, 1973–77, Col, 1977–82; Hon. Col, Oxford Univ. OTC, 1978–82. Col Commandant: Queen's Division, 1974–77; RAEC, 1975–79; Royal Green Jackets, 1977–81. Director: Standard Commercial Corp., 1983–92; Standard Wool, 1987–92; Mem., Marketing Council, 1990–92, and Adv. Consultant, 1992–94, Drake Beam Morin (UK); adviser in politics and economics, Standard Commercial Corp., 1992–2000. Chm., Council, RUSI, 1973–75. Member: Sports Council, 1973–82; Council, CBI, 1977–85; Pres., Army Cricket Assoc., 1973–76; Vice-Pres., Army Football Assoc., 1973–76, Chm., 1976–77, Pres., 1977–82; Hon. Vice-Pres., FA, 1976–82; Pres., British Assoc. for Physical Trng, 1998–2000. Chm., Crown and Manor Club,

Hoxton, 1977–95 (Pres., 1995–2002); Vice Pres., NABC Clubs for Young People, 1990– (Vice Chm., 1977–90); President: Notts Clubs for Young People, 1986–98; Broadway Lodge (formerly Broadway Foundn), 1989–99. Association Football Correspondent, Sunday Times, 1957–90; Review Editor, Army Quarterly, 1985–2000. DL Notts, 1993. *Publications:* Unusual Undertakings: a military memoir, 2002; articles and book reviews on mil. subjects. *Recreations:* cricket, Association football. *Address:* 151 Rivermead Court, SW6 3SF. *T:* (020) 7736 7228. *Clubs:* Travellers, MCC; Notts CC.
Died 17 Dec. 2004.

WILSON, Bryan Ronald, PhD, DLitt; FBA 1994; Reader in Sociology, University of Oxford, 1962–93; Fellow, 1963–93, and Domestic Bursar, 1989–93, All Souls College, Oxford (Sub-Warden, 1988–90); *b* 25 June 1926. *Educ:* University Coll., Leicester (BSc Econ London); London Sch. of Economics (PhD); MA, DLitt Oxon. Lectr in Sociology, Univ. of Leeds, 1955–62. Commonwealth Fund Fellow (Harkness), 1957–58; Fellow, Amer. Council of Learned Socs, 1966–67; Visiting Professor or Fellow, Universities of: Louvain, 1976, 1982, 1986, 1993; Toronto, 1978; Melbourne (Ormond Coll.), 1981; Queensland, 1986; California, Santa Barbara, 1987. Pres., Conf. Internat. de sociologie religieuse, 1971–75. Sen. Treasurer, Oxford Union Soc., 1983–91. Hon. DLitt Soka Univ., Japan, 1985; Dr *hc* Louvain, 1992. *Publications:* Sects and Society, 1961; Religion in Secular Society, 1966; (ed) Patterns of Sectarianism, 1967; The Youth Culture and the Universities, 1970; (ed) Rationality, 1970; Religious Sects, 1970; Magic and the Millennium, 1973; (ed) Education, Equality and Society, 1975; The Noble Savages, 1975; Contemporary Transformations of Religion, 1976; (ed) The Social Impact of New Religious Movements, 1981; Religion in Sociological Perspective, 1982; (with Daisaku Ikeda) Human Values in a Changing World, 1984; (ed with Brenda Almond) Values: a symposium, 1988; The Social Dimensions of Sectarianism, 1990; (ed) Religion: contemporary issues, 1992; (with K. Dobbelaere) A Time to Chant, 1994; (ed with Jamie Cresswell) New Religious Movements: challenge and response, 1999; (ed with D. Machacek) Global Citizens: the Soka Gakkai Buddhist movement in the world, 2000; contribs to learned jls. *Address:* 12 Victoria Court, London Road, Headington, Oxford OX3 7SP.
Died 9 Oct. 2004.

WILSON, Brig. Charles Edward T.; *see* Tryon-Wilson.

WILSON, Sir Charles Haynes, Kt 1965; MA; Principal and Vice-Chancellor, University of Glasgow, 1961–76; *b* 16 May 1909; 2nd *s* of late George Wilson and Florence Margaret Hannay; *m* 1935, Jessie Gilmour Wilson; one *s* two *d*. *Educ:* Hillhead High School; Glasgow Univ. (MA). Glasgow Univ. Faulds Fellow in Political Philosophy, 1932–34; Lectr in Political Science, LSE, 1934–39; Oxford University: Fellow and Tutor in Modern History, Corpus Christi Coll., 1939–52; Junior Proctor, 1945; Faculty Fellow, Nuffield Coll.; Principal, The University College of Leicester, 1952–57; Vice-Chancellor, Univ. of Leicester, 1957–61. Vis. Prof. in Comparative Govt, Ohio State Univ., 1950. Chairman: Commn on Fourah Bay Coll., Sierra Leone, 1957; Acad. Planning Bd for Univ. of E Anglia, 1960; Member: Acad. Planning Cttee and Council of UC of Sussex, 1958; Acad. Adv. Cttee, Royal Coll. of Science and Technology, Glasgow (later Univ. of Strathclyde), 1962; Acad. Planning Bd, Univ. of Stirling, 1964. Chairman: CVCP, 1964–67; ACU, 1966–67 and 1972–74. Hon. Fellow: Corpus Christi Coll., Oxford, 1963; LSE, 1965. Hon. LLD: Glasgow, 1957; Leicester, 1961; Rhodes Univ., 1964; Queen's Univ., Kingston, Ont, 1967; Ohio State Univ., 1969; Pennsylvania, 1975; Hon. DLitt: Strathclyde, 1966; NUU, 1976; Heriot-Watt, 1977; Hon. DCL East Anglia, 1966. Comdr, St Olav (Norway), 1966; Chevalier, Legion of Honour (France), 1976. *Address:* Whinnymuir, Dalry, Castle Douglas DG7 3TT. *T:* (01644) 430218. *Died 9 Nov. 2002.*

WILSON, Sir Donald; *see* Wilson, Sir R. D.

WILSON, Frank Richard, CMG 1963; OBE 1946; Controller of Administration, Commonwealth Development Corporation, 1976–80; retired HMOCS, 1963; *b* 26 Oct. 1920; *er s* of Sir Leonard Wilson, KCIE and late Muriel Wilson; *m* 1947, Alexandra Dorothy Mary (*née* Haigh); two *s. Educ:* Oundle Sch.; Trinity Hall, Cambridge (1939–40 only). Commnd Indian Army, 1941; retired as Lieut-Col, 1946. Joined Colonial Administrative Service (later HMOCS) in Kenya, 1947; Dist Comr, 1950–56; Private Sec. to the Governor, 1956–59; Provincial Comr, Central Province, 1959–63; Civil Sec., Central Region, 1963. With Commonwealth Develt Corp., 1964–80. *Address:* Chelsea House, Mickleton, Chipping Campden, Glos GL55 6SD.
Died 14 Oct. 2002.

WILSON, Sir Geoffrey Masterman, KCB 1969 (CB 1968); CMG 1962; Chairman, Oxfam, 1977–83; *b* 7 April 1910; 3rd *s* of late Alexander Cowan Wilson and Edith Jane Brayshaw; *m* 1st, 1946, Julie Stafford Trowbridge (marr. diss. 1979); two *s* two *d*; 2nd, 1989, Stephanie Stainsby (*née* Ross). *Educ:* Manchester Grammar School; Oriel College, Oxford. Chairman, Oxford Univ. Labour Club, 1930; Pres., Oxford Union, 1931. Harmsworth Law Scholar, Middle Temple, 1931; called to Bar, Middle Temple, 1934. Served in HM Embassy, Moscow, and Russian Dept of Foreign Office, 1940–45. Cabinet Office, 1947; Treasury, 1948; Director, Colombo Plan Technical Co-operation Bureau, 1951–53; Under-Secretary, Treasury, 1956–58; Deputy Head of UK Treasury Delegn and Alternate Exec. Dir for UK, Internat. Bank, Washington, 1958; Vice-President, International Bank, Washington, 1961–66; Deputy Secretary, ODM, 1966–68, Permanent Secretary, 1968–70; Dep. Sec.-Gen. (Economic), Commonwealth Secretariat, 1971. Chm., Race Relations Bd, 1971–77. Hon. Fellow: Wolfson Coll., Cambridge, 1971; Inst. of Develt Studies, Brighton, 1981; Oriel Coll., Oxford, 1992. *Address:* 1 Rawlinson Road, Oxford OX2 6UE.
Died 11 July 2004.

WILSON, Geoffrey Studholme, CMG 1961; Commissioner of Police, Tanganyika Police Force, 1958–62; *b* 5 June 1913; *s* of late J. E. S. Wilson; *m* 1936, Joy Noel (decd), *d* of Capt. C. St G. Harris-Walker; two *s. Educ:* Radley Coll. Joined Hong Kong Police, 1933; Comr of Police, Sarawak Constabulary, 1953–58. KPM 1950. OStJ 1961. *Recreations:* golf, fishing, sailing. *Address:* British Bank of the Middle East, 29 Hill Street, W1X 7FD. *Club:* Hong Kong (Hong Kong).
Died 21 April 2003.

WILSON, George Pritchard Harvey, CMG 1966; JP; Chairman, Victorian Inland Meat Authority, 1973–77 (Deputy Chairman, 1970–73); *b* 10 March 1918; *s* of late G. L. Wilson; *m* 1945, Fay Hobart Duff; two *s* one *d. Educ:* Geelong Grammar School. Nuffield Scholar (Farming), 1952. Council Member, Monash University, 1961–69; Royal Agricultural Society of Victoria: Councillor, 1950; President, 1964–73; Trustee, 1968–. Member: Victoria Promotion Cttee, 1968–81; Victoria Economic Develt Corp., 1981–82. Chm., Australian Nuffield Farming Scholars Assoc., 1973–89; Hon. Trustee, UK Nuffield Farming Scholarship Trust, 1989–. JP 1957. *Recreation:* fishing. *Address:* Wilson House, Berwick, Vic 3806, Australia. *T:* (3) 97071271. *Clubs:* Melbourne, Royal Automobile of Victoria (Melbourne); Melbourne Cricket.
Died 30 Oct. 2003.

WILSON, Henry Braithwaite; Assistant Under-Secretary of State, Home Office, 1963–71; *b* 6 Aug. 1911; *s* of Charles Braithwaite Wilson and Ellen Blanche Hargrove; *m* 1936, Margaret Bodden; two *s* two *d. Educ:* Leighton Park School; Lincoln College, Oxford. Editorial work for Joseph Rowntree Social Service Trust, 1933–40; Sub-Warden, Toynbee Hall, 1940–41; Home Office: Temp. Administrative Asst, 1941–44; Sec., Departmental Cttee on War Damaged Licensed Premises and Reconstruction, 1942–44; Principal, 1944 (estab. 1946); Asst Sec., 1956.

Address: 14 Lawn Terrace, Silloth, Wigton CA7 4AW.
Died 29 April 2001.

WILSON, Sir James; *see* Wilson, Sir A. J.

WILSON, James Elliott, OBE 1978; JP; Lord-Lieutenant, County Borough of Belfast, 1991–2000; *b* 3 May 1925; *s* of Samuel Robinson Wilson and Clarice Evelyn (*née* Duckham); *m* 1954, Rosemary Clarke; three *d. Educ:* Clifton Coll., Bristol. Served Royal Inniskilling Fusiliers, 1943–48. Ormeau Bakery Ltd, Belfast, 1948–80. Chm., Trustee Savings Bank of NI, 1974–82; Dir, First Trust Bank, NI, 1994–96. Chm., Assoc. Citizens' Advice Bureaux, NI, 1985–88. Member, Board of Management: Somme Hosp., Belfast, 1965–98; NI Fever Hosp., 1968–73; Chm., Glendhu Children's Hostel, Belfast, 1981–85. DL 1982, JP 1991, Belfast. Hon. Col, 40th Ulster Signal Regt (V), 1982–90. CStJ 1993. *Recreations:* golf, gardening, travel. *Address:* White Lodge, The Temple, Boardmills, Lisburn, Co. Antrim BT27 6UQ. *T:* (028) 9263 8413. *Club:* Royal County Down Golf (Newcastle, Co. Down).
Died 24 April 2004.

WILSON, Prof. Peter Northcote, CBE 1987; FRSE; General Secretary, Royal Society of Edinburgh, 1996–2001; *b* 4 April 1928; *s* of Llewellyn W. C. M. Wilson and F. Louise Wilson; *m* 1950, Maud Ethel (*née* Bunn); two *s* one *d. Educ:* Whitgift School; Wye College, Univ. of London (BSc (Agric), MSc, PhD); Univ. of Edinburgh (Dip. Animal Genetics). CBiol, FIBiol; FRSE 1987; FRAgS 2001. Lectr in Agriculture, Makerere Coll., UC of E Africa, 1951–57; Sen. Lectr in Animal Production, Imperial Coll. of Tropical Agriculture, 1957–61; Prof. of Agriculture, Univ. of W Indies, 1961–64; Senior Scientist, Unilever Res. Lab., 1964–68; Agricl Dir, SLF Ltd (Unilever), 1968–71; Chief Agricl Advr, BOCM Silcock Ltd (Unilever), 1971–83; Prof. of Agric. and Rural Economy and Hd of Sch. of Agric., Univ. of Edinburgh, 1984–90; Principal, East of Scotland Coll. of Agric., 1984–90; Scientific Dir, Edinburgh Centre for Rural Res., 1990–97. Vis. Prof. Univ. of Reading, 1975–83. Mem., Medicines Commn, 1976–79. President: Brit. Soc. of Animal Production, 1977 (Vice-Pres., 1976); Edin. Agricl Soc., 1992–93 (Vice-Pres., 1991–92); Scotia Club, 1992–93 (Vice-Pres., 1990–92); Hon. Sec., Inst. of Biol., 1992–96 (Vice-Pres., 1977–79, 1991–92); Mem. Council, Scottish Agricl Colls, 1995– (Sec.-Gen., 1985–86; Mem. Exec. Bd, 1987–90); Vice Convener Business Cttee, Gen. Council, Univ. of Edinburgh, 1997–2000. Chm., Frank Parkinson Agricl Trust, 1980–99; Trustee, Frank Parkinson Yorks Trust, 1992–. DUniv Stirling, 2000. *Publications:* Agriculture in the Tropics, 1965, 3rd edn 1998; Improved Feeding of Cattle and Sheep, 1981; A Tale of Two Trusts, 2000; Purchase Two Kilts, 2001; numerous papers in learned jls. *Recreations:* hill walking, ornithology, photography, foreign travel, philately. *Address:* 8 St Thomas' Road, Edinburgh EH9 2LQ. *T:* (0131) 667 3182. *Club:* Farmers'.
Died 29 Jan. 2004.

WILSON, Quintin Campbell, OBE 1975; HM Inspector of Constabulary for Scotland, 1975–79; *b* 19 Nov. 1913; *s* of William Wilson and Mary (*née* Cowan); *m* 1939, Adelia Campbell Scott; two *s. Educ:* Barr Primary Sch.; Girvan High Sch. Halifax Borough Police, April 1936; Ayrshire Constabulary, Nov. 1936; Chief Supt, Police Research and Planning Branch, Home Office, London, 1965; Dep. Chief Constable, Ayrshire, 1966; Chief Constable, Ayrshire, 1968–75. *Recreation:* golf. *Address:* 15 Portmark Avenue, Alloway, Ayr KA7 4DN. *T:* (01292) 443034.
Died 2001.

WILSON, Sir Robert, Kt 1989; CBE 1978; FRS 1975; Perren Professor of Astronomy, University College London, 1972–94, then Emeritus; *b* 16 April 1927; *s* of Robert Graham Wilson and Anne Wilson; *m* 1st, Eileen Flora Milne (marr. diss.); two *s* one *d*; 2nd, 1986, Fiona (*née* Nicholson). *Educ:* King's Coll., Univ. of Durham (BSc. Physics 1948); Univ. of Edinburgh (PhD

Astrophysics 1952). SSO, Royal Observatory, Edinburgh, 1952–57; Research Fellow, Dominion Astrophysical Observatory, Canada, 1957–58; Leader of Plasma Spectroscopy Gp, CTR Div., Harwell, 1959–61; Head of Spectroscopy Div., Culham Laboratory, 1962–68; Dir, Science Research Council's Astrophysics Research Unit, Culham, 1968–72; Dean, Faculty Sci., 1982–85, Head, Dept of Physics and Astronomy, 1987–93, UCL. Member: SERC, 1985–89; NERC, 1985–88; Chairman: British National Cttee for Space Res., 1983–88; Anglo-Australian Telescope Bd, 1986–89; James Clerk Maxwell Telescope Bd, 1987–91; Council, Royal Instn, 1992–93. Foreign Member: Société Royale des Sciences, Liège; Amer. Philosophical Soc., 1996; Vice-Pres., Internat. Astronomical Union, 1979–85; Trustee, Internat. Acad. of Astronautics, 1985; Mem., COSPAR Bureau, 1986–90. Hon. Fellow, UCL, 1990. Hon. DSc QUB, 1995. (Jtly) Herschel Medal, RAS, 1986; Science Award, Internat. Acad. of Astronautics, 1987; President Reagan's Award for design excellence (on behalf of UK team on the Internat. Ultraviolet Explorer), 1988; Royal Soc./COSPAR Massey Award, 1994. *Publications:* Astronomy Through the Ages, 1998; papers in many jls on: optical astronomy, plasma spectroscopy, solar physics, ultraviolet astronomy. *Address:* Department of Physics and Astronomy, University College London, Gower Street, WC1E 6BT. *T:* (020) 7380 7154.   *Died 2 Sept. 2002.*

WILSON, Sir (Robert) Donald, KBE 1995; Kt 1987; DL; farmer; Chairman, Electricity Consultative Council (North West), 1981–85; *b* 6 June 1922; *s* of John and Kate Wilson; *m* 1946, (Edna) Elizabeth Ellis. *Educ:* Grove Park Sch., Wrexham, Clwyd. Served RAF, 1940–46. Tyre industry, 1946–60; farming, 1954–; Director of various farming and property companies; Board Mem. (part-time), North West Electricity Bd (NORWEB), 1981–87. Chairman: Mersey RHA, 1982–93, 1993–94; West Midlands RHA, 1993; NW RHA, 1994–96. Mem., School Teachers' Review Body, 1991–92. Chairman: Ayrshire Cattle Soc., 1966–67; Cheshire Br., CLA, 1980–82; Nat. Staff Cttee, Admin, Catering and Other Services, 1983–85. Vice-Chm. Governors, Cheshire Coll. of Agric., 1980–84. High Sheriff, 1985–86, DL 1987, Cheshire. FRSA 1986. Hon. Fellow, Liverpool John Moores, 1994. Hon. LLD Liverpool, 1994. *Recreation:* fishing. *Address:* The Oldfields, Pulford, Chester, Cheshire CH4 9EJ. *T:* (01244) 570207. *Clubs:* Farmers'; City (Chester).   *Died 29 July 2001.*

WILSON, Rt Rev. Roger Plumpton, KCVO 1974; Clerk of the Closet to the Queen, 1963–75; Hon. Assistant Bishop, Diocese of Bath and Wells, since 1974; *b* 3 Aug. 1905; *s* of Rev. Canon Clifford Plumpton Wilson, Bristol, and Hester Marion Wansey; *m* 1935, Mabel Joyce Avery (*d* 1995), Leigh Woods, Bristol; two *s* one *d*. *Educ:* Winchester Coll. (Exhibitioner); Keble Coll., Oxford (Classical Schol.; Hons Mods in Classics 1st Class, Lit. Hum. 2nd Class, BA 1928; MA 1932); Westcott House, Cambridge. Classical Master: Shrewsbury Sch., 1928–30, 1932–34; St Andrew's Coll., Grahamstown, S Africa, 1930–32. Deacon, 1935; priest, 1936; Curacies: St Paul's, Prince's Park, Liverpool, 1935–38; St John's, Smith Square, SW1, 1938–39; Vicar of South Shore, Blackpool, 1939–45; Archdeacon of Nottingham and Vicar of Radcliffe on Trent, 1945–49; also Vicar of Shelford (in plurality), 1946–49; Bishop of Wakefield, 1949–58; Bishop of Chichester, 1958–74. Chm., Church of England Schools Council, 1957–71; Mem., Presidium, Conf. of European Churches, 1967–74. DD Lambeth 1949. *Recreations:* Oxford University Authentics Cricket Club, Oxford University Centaurs Football Club, golf. *Clubs:* Athenæum, Royal Commonwealth Society.
          Died 1 March 2002.

WILSON, Hon. Sir Ronald (Darling), AC 1988; KBE 1979; CMG 1978; Justice of the High Court of Australia, 1979–89; President: Uniting Church in Australia, 1988–91; Human Rights and Equal Opportunity Commission, 1990–97; *b* 23 Aug. 1922; *s* of Harold Wilson and Jean Ferguson Wilson (*née* Darling); *m* 1950, Leila Amy Gibson Smith; three *s* two *d*. *Educ:* Geraldton State School; Univ. of Western Australia (LLB Hons; Hon. LLD 1980); Univ. of Pennsylvania (LLM). Assistant Crown Prosecutor, Western Australia, 1954–59; Chief Crown Prosecutor, WA, 1959–61; Crown Counsel, WA, 1961–69; QC 1963; Solicitor General, WA, 1969–79. Moderator, Presbyterian Church in Western Australia, 1965; Moderator, WA Synod, Uniting Church in Australia, 1977–79. Chancellor, Murdoch Univ., 1980–95. Hon. Pres., Australian Council for Overseas Aid, 1997–2001. Hon. DEd Keimyung Univ., Korea, 1989; DUniv Murdoch, 1995; Hon. DLitt Univ. of Technology, Sydney, 1998. *Address:* 6B Atkins Road, Applecross, WA 6153, Australia.   *Died 15 July 2005.*

WILSON, Prof. Thomas, OBE 1945; FBA 1976; FRSE; Adam Smith Professor of Political Economy, University of Glasgow, 1958–82; *b* 23 June 1916; *s* of late John Bright and Margaret G. Wilson, Belfast; *m* 1943, Dorothy Joan Parry (MVO 1945) (*d* 1998); one *s* two *d*. *Educ:* Methodist College and Queen's University, Belfast; London School of Economics (Hon. Fellow, 1979). Mins of Economic Warfare and Aircraft Production, 1940–42; Prime Minister's Statistical Branch, 1942–45; Fellow of University College, Oxford, 1946–58; Faculty Fellow of Nuffield College, Oxford, 1950–58. Nuffield Foundation Visiting Prof., Univ. of Ibadan, 1962; Vis. Fellow, All Souls Coll., Oxford, 1974–75. Editor, Oxford Economic Papers, 1948–58. Vice-Chm., Scottish Council's Cttee of Inquiry into the Scottish Economy, 1960–61; Economic Consultant: to Govt of N Ireland, 1964–65, 1968–70; to Sec. of State for Scotland, 1963–64 and 1970–83; Shipbuilding Industry Cttee, 1965; Assessor, DoE, 1984–85. Dir, Scottish Mutual Assce Soc., 1966–87 (Chm., 1978–81). FRSE 1980; FRSA 1992. DUniv Stirling, 1982. *Publications:* Fluctuations in Income and Employment, 1941; (ed) Ulster under Home Rule, 1955; Inflation, 1960; Planning and Growth, 1964; (ed) Pensions, Inflation and Growth, 1974; (ed with A. S. Skinner) Essays on Adam Smith, 1975; (ed with A. S. Skinner) The Market and the State, 1976; The Political Economy of Inflation (British Acad. Keynes Lecture), 1976; (with D. J. Wilson) The Political Economy of the Welfare State, 1982; Inflation, Unemployment and the Market, 1985; Ulster—Conflict and Consent, 1989; (ed with D. J. Wilson) The State and Social Welfare, 1991; Churchill and the Prof, 1995. *Recreations:* sailing, hill walking. *Address:* 1 Chatford House, The Promenade, Clifton, Bristol BS8 3NG. *T:* (0117) 973 0741. *Club:* Athenæum.   *Died 27 July 2001.*

WILSON, William Moore; Director, Royal Bank of Scotland Group, since 1993; *b* 21 May 1937; *s* of late Thomas Martin Wilson and Mary Wilson (*née* Moore); *m* 1966, Margaret Roan Spalding; one *s* two *d*. *Educ:* Belmont House Prep. Sch., Glasgow; Merchiston Castle Sch., Edinburgh. CA; FCIBS. CA apprenticeship, Deloittes, Glasgow, 1955–60; Peat Marwick Mitchell, 1960–61; Stenhouse Holdings, Glasgow, 1961–73; Reed Stenhouse Companies, Toronto: Dir, 1973–95 (Pres. and CEO, 1979–89); Alexander & Alexander: Chm. and CEO, NY, 1985–88; Chm. and CEO, Europe, 1988–92, Chm., Europe, 1993–97. Dir, Soc. Gen. de Courtages d'Assurances, Paris, 1989–97 (Vice-Chm., 1993–97). Director of numerous organisations, incl. Scottish Rugby Union plc. *Recreations:* yachting, shooting, Rugby. *Address:* Silverton Farmhouse, Braco, by Dunblane, Perthshire FK15 9QZ. *T:* (01786) 880688. *Clubs:* Caledonian; London Scottish Football; Toronto.
          Died 25 Dec. 2003.

WILTSHIRE, Edward Parr, CBE 1965; HM Diplomatic Service, retired; *b* 18 Feb. 1910; 2nd *s* of late Major Percy Wiltshire and Kathleen Olivier Lefroy Parr Wiltshire, Great Yarmouth; *m* 1942, Gladys Mabel Stevens (*d* 1995); one *d*. *Educ:* Cheltenham College; Jesus College,

Cambridge. Entered Foreign Service, 1932. Served in: Beirut, Mosul, Baghdad, Tehran, Basra, New York (one of HM Vice-Consuls, 1944); promoted Consul, 1945; transf. Cairo, 1946 (Actg Consul-Gen., 1947, 1948); transf. Shiraz (having qual. in Arabic, and subseq. in Persian); Consul, Port Said, 1952; 1st Sec. and Consul: Baghdad, 1952, Rio de Janeiro, 1957; promoted Counsellor, 1959; Political Agent, Bahrain, 1959–63; Consul-General, Geneva, 1963–67; Dir, Diplomatic Service Language Centre, London, 1967–68; worked for Council for Nature (Editor, Habitat), 1968–69; Consul, Le Havre, 1969–75. Hon. Associate, BM (Nat. Hist.), 1980. *Publications:* The Lepidoptera of Iraq, 1957; A Revision of the Armadini, 1979. *Recreations:* music, entomology. *Address:* Wychwood, High Road, Cookham, Berks SL6 9JF.
Died 8 July 2004.

WINFIELD, Dr Graham, CBE 1991; Chairman: Booker Tate Ltd, 1993–98; Zinc Corporation PLC, 1997–98; *b* 28 May 1931; *s* of Josiah and Gladys Winfield; *m* 1959, Olive Johnson; three *s* one *d*. *Educ:* Univ. of Liverpool (BSc, PhD Chemistry). Chemist, Min. of Supply, 1956–57; Lectr, Univ. of Liverpool, 1957–58; Chief Chemist, later Develt Manager, Ciba ARL, 1958–62; Develt Manager, MaxMeyer Co., Milan, 1962–63; BOC Group, 1963–89: R&D, marketing, gen. management; Chief Executive: Metals Div. UK, 1969–74; Gases Div. UK, 1974–79; Overseas Gp, 1979–89. Non-exec. Dir., Baker Perkins Group, 1984–87. Mem., ESRC, 1985–90; Chairman: Post Grad. Trng Bd, 1987–90; Retail and Distbn Panel, Technol. Foresight, Cabinet Office, 1994–97. *Publications:* numerous papers in pure and applied chemistry. *Recreations:* golf, bridge, music, reading. *Address:* Tawelfan, Crossing Lane, Claydon, Banbury, Oxon OX17 1EX.
Died 15 Nov. 2002.

WINKS, Prof. Robin W(illiam Evert), PhD; Randolph W. Townsend Professor of History, Yale University, since 1957; *b* 5 Dec. 1930; *s* of Evert McKinley Winks and Jewell Sampson; *m* 1952, Avril Flockton, Wellington, NZ; one *s* one *d*. *Educ:* Univ. of Colorado (BA Hons 1952, MA 1953); Victoria Univ., NZ (Cert. 1952); Johns Hopkins Univ. (PhD 1957). Yale University: Dir, Office of Special Projects and Foundns, 1974–76; Master of Berkeley Coll., 1977–90; Chairman: Council of Masters, 1978–84, 1986–88; Studies in the Envmt, 1993–96; Dept of History, 1996–99. Smith-Mundt Prof., Univ. of Malaya, 1962; Vis. Prof., Univ. of Sydney, 1963; Vis. Fellow, Inst. of Commonwealth Studies, 1966–67; Guggenheim Fellow, 1976–77; Vis. Prof. of Economics, Univ. of Stellenbosch, 1983; Fellow, Amer. Sch. for Research, 1985 and 1991; George Eastman Vis. Prof., 1992–93, Harmsworth Vis. Prof., 1999–2000, Oxford Univ. Cultural Attaché, Amer. Embassy, London, 1969–71; Advisor to Dept of State, 1971–. Chm., Nat. Park Service Adv. Bd, 1981–83; Trustee, Nat. Parks and Conservation Assoc., 1985–. Mem. Council on For. Relations. FRHistS; Fellow, Explorers' Club, 1986. Hon. MA: Yale 1967; Oxon, 1992; Hon. DLitt: Nebraska, 1976; Colorado, 1987; Westminster Coll., 1995. *Publications:* Canada and the United States, 1960, 4th edn 1998; The Cold War, 1964, 2nd edn 1977; Historiography of the British Empire-Commonwealth, 1966, 2nd edn 1994; Malaysia, 1966, 2nd edn 1979; Age of Imperialism, 1969; Pastmasters, 1969; The Historian as Detective, 1969; The Blacks in Canada, 1971, 2nd edn 1997; Slavery, 1972; An American's Guide to Britain, 1977, 3rd edn 1987; Other Voices, Other Views, 1978; The Relevance of Canadian History, 1979, 2nd edn 1988; World Civilization, 1979, 3rd edn 1993; Detective Fiction, 1980; The British Empire, 1981; Modus Operandi, 1982; History of Civilization, 1984, 9th edn 1995; Cloak and Gown, 1987, 2nd edn 1996; Asia in Western Language Fiction, 1990; Frederick Billings: a life, 1991, 2nd edn 1998; Laurance S. Rockefeller: catalyst for conservation, 1997; (ed) The Oxford History of the British Empire, vol. V: historiography, 1999; articles in Amer. Hist. Rev.

Recreations: travel, conservation, detective fiction. *Address:* Box 208324 Yale Station, New Haven, CT 06520, USA. *Clubs:* Athenæum, Royal Commonwealth Society, Special Forces; Yale, Explorers' (NY). *Died 7 April 2003.*

WINNING, His Eminence Cardinal Thomas Joseph, DCL, STL, DD; Archbishop of Glasgow, (RC), since 1974; *b* 3 June 1925. *Educ:* Our Lady's High Sch., Motherwell; St Mary's Coll., Blairs; St Peter's Coll., Bearsden; Scots Coll., Rome. Ordained priest, 1948; formerly parish priest, St Luke, Braidhurst, Motherwell; Auxiliary Bishop of Glasgow, 1971–74; parish priest, Our Holy Redeemer's, Clydebank, 1972–74. Cardinal, 1994. Member: Sacred Congregation for the Doctrine of the Faith, 1978–83; Pontifical Council for Promoting Christian Unity, 1994–; Pontifical Council for the Family, 1994–. Pres., Bishops' Conf. of Scotland, 1985–. Grand Prior, Scottish Lieutenancy of Equestrian Order of Holy Sepulchre of Jerusalem, 1989–. Hon. Prof., Univ. of Glasgow, 1996. FEIS 1986. Hon. DD Glasgow, 1983; DUniv Strathclyde, 1992; Hon. LLD Aberdeen, 1996. *Address:* 40 Newlands Road, Glasgow G43 2JD.
Died 17 June 2001.

WINNINGTON, Sir Francis Salwey William, 6th Bt *cr* 1755; Lieutenant, late Welsh Guards; *b* 24 June 1907; *er s* of late Francis Salwey Winnington, *e s* of 5th Bt and Blanch, *d* of Commander William John Casberd-Boteler, RN; *S* grandfather, 1931; *m* 1944, Anne, *o d* of late Captain Lawrence Drury-Lowe; one *d*. *Educ:* Eton. Served War of 1939–45 (wounded, prisoner). Owns 4700 acres. *Heir: nephew* Anthony Edward Winnington [*b* 13 May 1948; *m* 1978, Karyn Kathryn, *d* of F. H. Kettles; one *s* two *d*]. *Died 26 April 2003.*

WINSKILL, Air Commodore Sir Archibald (Little), KCVO 1980 (CVO 1973); CBE 1960; DFC 1941 and Bar 1943; AE 1944; Extra Equerry to The Queen; *b* 24 Jan. 1917; *s* of late James Winskill; *m* 1947, Christiane Amilie Pauline, *d* of M. Bailleux, Calais, France; one *d* (one *s* decd). *Educ:* Carlisle Grammar Sch. Joined RAFVR, 1937; served War of 1939–45: Fighter Pilot: Battle of Britain; European and North African Theatres; evaded capture in enemy territory, in occupied France, 1941, and in Tunisia, 1943; Post War: graduate, Army Staff Coll., Flying Coll.; Air Adviser to Belgian Govt; Station Cmdr, RAF Turnhouse and Duxford; Gp Capt. Ops Germany; Air Attaché, Paris, 1964–67; Dir of Public Relations, MoD (RAF); Captain of the Queen's Flight, 1968–82. Freedom of City of London, 1978. *Recreations:* golf, bridge. *Address:* 28 Swinnerton House, Phyllis Court Drive, Henley-on-Thames, Oxon RG9 2HU. *T:* (01491) 578069. *Clubs:* Royal Air Force; Phyllis Court (Henley).
Died 9 Aug. 2005.

WINTER, Frederick Thomas, CBE 1963; racehorse trainer, 1964–87, retired; *b* 20 Sept. 1926; *s* of late Frederick Neville Winter and Ann (*née* Flanagan); *m* 1956, Diana Pearson; three *d* (incl. twins). *Educ:* Ewell Castle. Served as Lieut, 6th Bn Para. Regt, 1944–47. Jockey, Flat, 1939–42; National Hunt jockey, 1947–64. *Address:* Montague House, Eastbury, Newbury, Berks RG17 7JN. *T:* (01488) 71438. *Died 5 April 2004.*

WINTER, Prof. Gerald Bernard, FDSRCS; Professor and Head of Department of Children's Dentistry, 1966–94, then Emeritus Professor, Dean and Director of Studies, 1983–93, Institute of Dental Surgery, University of London; *b* 24 Nov. 1928; *s* of Morris Winter and Edith (*née* Malter); *m* 1960, Brigitte Eva Fleischhacker; one *s* one *d*. *Educ:* Coopers' Company's Sch.; London Hosp. Med. Coll. (BDS, MB BS); DCH London. FFDRCSI. Ho. Surg./Ho. Phys., London Hosp. Med. Coll., 1955–59; Lectr in Children's Dentistry, Royal Dental Hosp., London, 1959–62; Cons. Dent. Surg., Eastman Dental Hosp., 1962–94 (Hon. Cons. Dent. Surg., 1994–). Hon. Sec. 1962–65, Pres. 1970–71 and 1993–94, Brit. Paedodontic Soc., subseq. British Soc. for Paediatric

Dentistry; Hon. Gen. Sec., Internat. Assoc. of Dentistry for Children, 1971–79; Founder Chm., Brit. Soc. of Dentistry for the Handicapped, 1976–77; Hon. Dir, Oral and Dental Res. Trust, 1996–. FRSA 1996. *Publications:* A Colour Atlas of Clinical Conditions in Paedodontics (with R. Rapp), 1979; many chapters and sci. papers. *Recreations:* painting, theatre, music, gardening.

Died 22 Dec. 2002.

WINTERBOTTOM, Sir Walter, Kt 1978; CBE 1972 (OBE 1963); Director, The Sports Council, 1965–78; retired; *b* 31 March 1913; *s* of James Winterbottom and Frances Holt; *m* 1942, Ann Richards; two *d* (one *s* decd). *Educ:* Chester Coll. of Educn; Carnegie Coll. of Physical Educn. Schoolmaster, Oldham; Lectr, Carnegie Coll. of Phys. Educn; Wing Comdr, RAF, 1939–45; Dir of Coaching and Manager of England Team, Football Assoc., 1946–62; Gen. Sec., Central Council of Physical Recreation, 1963–72. *Publications:* technical, on association football. *Recreations:* golf, bowls. *Address:* 15 Orchard Gardens, Cranleigh, Surrey GU6 7LG. *T:* (01483) 271593.   *Died 16 Feb. 2002.*

WINTON, Walter; Keeper, Department of Electrical Engineering, Telecommunications and Loan Circulation, Science Museum, 1976–80; *b* 15 May 1917; *m* 1942, Dorothy Rickard; two *s* one *d. Educ:* Glossop Grammar Sch.; Manchester Univ. (BSc and Teacher's Diploma). Chemist, Royal Ordnance Factories, 1940–45. Taught science, Harrow Co. and Greenford, 1945–50; Science Museum: Asst and Dep. Keeper, 1950–67; Keeper: Dept of Loan Circulation, Mining and Marine Technol., 1968–73; Dept of Museum Services, 1973; Dept of Mechanical and Civil Engrg and Loan Circulation, 1973–76. *Publications:* contrib. to jls. *Recreations:* Scottish dancing, sailing, fell-walking. *Address:* Lantern Lodge, Village Road, Denham, Bucks UB9 5BN. *T:* (01895) 832692.   *Died 15 Aug. 2002.*

WITHERS, Roy Joseph, CBE 1983; FREng; Director, Vosper Thornycroft (Holdings), 1985–96 (Chairman, 1985–90); *b* 18 June 1924; *s* of Joseph Withers and Irene Ada Withers (*née* Jones); *m* 1947, Pauline M. G. Johnston; four *s. Educ:* Tiffin School, Kingston upon Thames; Trinity College, Cambridge (1st. cl. Hons Mech. Scis Tripos; BA 1945, MA 1957). ICI, 1948–55; Humphreys & Glasgow, 1955–63; Engrg Dir, then Man. Dir, Power-Gas Corp. (subsid. of Davy Corp.), 1963–71; Chief Exec., Davy Powergas Internat., 1972–73; Man. Dir, 1973–83, Vice-Chm., 1983–91, Davy Corp. Director: A. Monk & Co., 1983–88; Transmark, 1987–95 (Chm., 1991–95). Mem., BOTB, 1983–86; Chm., Overseas Projects Board, 1983–86. FIMechE 1972; FREng (FEng 1983). Hon. FIChemE 1983. *Recreations:* painting, golf, walking. *Address:* Wheelwrights Cottage, Bramshaw, Lyndhurst, Hants SO4 7JB. *T:* (023) 8081 2543. *Clubs:* Carlton; Hampstead Golf, Bramshaw Golf.

Died 24 Aug. 2003.

WOJTYLA, Karol Jozef; *see* John Paul II.

WOLEDGE, Brian, FBA 1989; Emeritus Professor of French Language and Literature, University of London; Fielden Professor of French, University College, London, 1939–71; Hon. Research Fellow, University College London; *b* 16 Aug. 1904; *m* 1933, Christine Mary Craven (*d* 1993); one *s* one *d. Educ:* Leeds Boys' Modern School; University of Leeds (BA 1926; MA 1928); Docteur de l'Université de Paris, 1930. Asst Lecturer in French, University College, Hull, 1930–32; Lecturer in French, University of Aberdeen, 1932–39. Visiting Andrew Mellon Professor of French, University of Pittsburg, 1967. Docteur *hc* de l'Université d'Aix-Marseille, 1970. *Publications:* L'Atre périlleux; études sur les manuscrits, la langue et l'importance littéraire du poème, 1930; L'Atre périlleux, roman de la Table ronde (Les Classiques français du moyen âge 76), 1935; Bibliographie des romans et nouvelles en prose française antérieurs à 1500, 1954, repr.

1975, Supplement 1975; The Penguin Book of French Verse, Vol. 1, To the Fifteenth Century, 1961; Répertoire des premiers textes en prose française, 842–1210 (with H. P. Clive), 1964; La Syntaxe des substantifs chez Chrétien de Troyes, 1979; Commentaire sur Yvain (Le Chevalier au Lion) de Chrétien de Troyes, Vol. 1, 1986, Vol. 2, 1988. *Address:* 28a Dobbins Lane, Wendover, Aylesbury, Bucks HP22 6DH. *T:* (01296) 622188.   *Died 3 June 2002.*

WOLFF, Rosemary Langley; Member, Police Complaints Authority, 1985–92 (Member, Police Complaints Board, 1977–85); *b* 10 July 1926; *er d* of late A. C. V. Clarkson; *m* 1956, Michael Wolff, JP (*d* 1976); two *d. Educ:* Haberdashers' Aske's Sch. Mem., Community Relations Commn, 1973–77. Manager of various primary schs in North Kensington and Tower Hamlets, 1963–; Governor, City College; Chm., Conservative Contact Group, 1973–77; Mem., Managing Cttee, Working Ladies' Guild. Assoc. Mem., Kensington, Chelsea and Westminster FHSA, 1994–96. *Address:* 38 Finstock Road, W10 6LU. *T:* (020) 8964 0690.

Died 19 March 2003.

WOLLHEIM, Prof. Richard Arthur, FBA 1972; Professor of Philosophy, University of California, Berkeley, 1985–2002, then Emeritus; Emeritus Grote Professor in the University of London; *b* 5 May 1923; *s* of Eric Wollheim; *m* 1st, 1950, Anne, *yr d* of Lieutenant-Colonel E. G. H. Powell (marr. diss. 1967); two *s*; 2nd, 1969, Mary Day, *er d* of Robert S. Lanier, NYC; one *d. Educ:* Westminster School; Balliol College, Oxford (MA). Served in the Army, N Europe, 1942–45 (POW during Aug. 1944). University College London: Asst Lectr in Philosophy, 1949; Lectr, 1951; Reader, 1960; Hon. Fellow, 1994; Grote Prof. of Philosophy of Mind and Logic in Univ. of London, 1963–82; Prof. of Philosophy, Columbia Univ., 1982–85; Prof. of Philosophy and the Humanities, Univ. of Calif., Davis, 1989–96. Visiting Professor: Columbia Univ., 1959–60, 1970; Visva-Bharati Univ., Santiniketan, India, 1968; Univ. of Minnesota, 1972; Graduate Centre, City Univ. of NY, 1975; Univ. of California, Berkeley, 1981; Harvard Univ., 1982; Sarah Lawrence Coll., 1987; Univ. of Guelph, 1988; Washington Univ., St Louis, 1989; Claremont Coll., 1995–96; Univ. of New Mexico, 1996; Northwestern Univ., 2003, 2004. Lectures: Ernest Jones, British Psychoanalytical Soc., 1969; Power, Univ. of Sydney, 1972; Leslie Stephen, Univ. of Cambridge, 1979; William James, Harvard Univ., 1982; Andrew W. Mellon, Nat. Gall., Washington, 1984; Lewin, Washington Univ., 1989; Tamblyn, Univ. of W Ontario, 1989; Cassirer, Yale Univ., 1991; Hoffmann, Dallas Mus., 1992; David A. Jones, Claremont Coll., 1995–96; Gareth Evans, Univ. of Oxford, 1996; Penrose, Tate Gallery, 1998; Werner Heisenberg, Bavarian Acad., 2001; Lindley, Univ. of Kansas, 2001. President: Aristotelian Soc., 1967–68; British Soc. of Aesthetics, 1993– (Vice-Pres., 1969–93); Pacific Div., Amer. Philos. Assoc., 2002–03. Mem., American Acad. of Arts and Scis, 1986. Hon. Affiliate, British Psychoanalytical Soc., 1982; Hon. Mem., San Francisco Psychoanalytic Inst., 1994. Award for Dist. Services to Psychoanalysis, Internat. Psychoanalytic Soc., 1991. *Publications:* F. H. Bradley, 1959, rev. edn 1969; Socialism and Culture, 1961; On Drawing an Object (Inaugural Lecture), 1965; Art and its Objects, 1968, 2nd edn with suppl. essays, 1980; A Family Romance (fiction), 1969; Freud, 1971; On Art and the Mind (essays and lectures), 1973; The Good Self and the Bad Self (Dawes Hicks lecture), 1976; The Sheep and the Ceremony (Leslie Stephen lecture), 1979; The Thread of Life, 1984; Painting as an Art, 1987; The Mind and its Depths (essays and lectures), 1993; On the Emotions, 1999; edited: F. H. Bradley, Ethical Studies, 1961; Hume on Religion, 1963; F. H. Bradley, Appearance and Reality, 1968; Adrian Stokes, selected writings, 1972; Freud, a collection of critical essays, 1974; J. S. Mill, Three Essays, 1975; (with Jim Hopkins) Philosophical Essays on Freud, 1982; articles in anthologies, philosophical and literary jls. *Address:* 4 Gemini House, 180-182 Bermondsey Street, SE1 3TQ. *Died 4 Nov. 2003.*

WOLRIGE-GORDON, Patrick; *b* 10 Aug. 1935; *s* of late Captain Robert Wolrige-Gordon, MC and Joan Wolrige-Gordon; *m* 1962, Anne, *d* of late Peter D. Howard and Mrs Howard; one *s* two *d. Educ:* Eton; New College, Oxford. MP (C) Aberdeenshire East, Nov. 1958–Feb. 1974. Liveryman Worshipful Company of Wheelwrights, 1966. *Recreations:* reading, golf, music. *Address:* Ythan Lodge, Newburgh, Aberdeenshire AB41 6AD. *Club:* Royal Over-Seas League. *Died 22 May 2002.*

WOLSTENCROFT, Alan, CB 1961; Director, 1974–87, and Chairman, 1979–84, National Counties Building Society; *b* 18 Oct. 1914; *yr s* of late Walter and Bertha Wolstencroft; *m* 1951, Ellen, *d* of late W. Tomlinson. *Educ:* Lancaster Royal Grammar Sch.; Caius Coll., Cambridge (1st Cl. Classical Tripos; BA 1936, MA 1939). Asst Principal, GPO, 1936. Served War of 1939–45, RE (Postal Section), France and Middle East. Principal, 1945, Asst Sec., 1949, GPO; Sec., Independent Television Authority, 1954; General Post Office: Dir of Personnel, 1955; Dir of Postal Services, 1957; Dir of Radio Services, 1960–64; Dep. Dir Gen., 1964–67; Man. Dir Posts, 1967, Posts and GIRO, 1968; Adviser on Special Projects to Chm. of Post Office Corporation, 1969–70; Sec. to Post Office, 1970–73; retired. *Address:* Green Court, 161 Long Lane, Tilehurst, Reading RG31 6YW.
Died Jan. 2002.

WOLSTENHOLME, Sir Gordon (Ethelbert Ward), Kt 1976; OBE (mil.) 1944; MA, MB, BChir; MRCS, FRCP, FIBiol; Founder, 1988, and Life President, 1995–2001, Action in International Medicine (Chairman, 1988–95); *b* Sheffield, 28 May 1913; *o s* of G. Ethelbert Wolstenholme and Clementina Ward; *m* 1st; one *s* two *d*; 2nd, Dushanka; two *d. Educ:* Repton; Corpus Christi Coll., Cambridge (Hon. Fellow, 1998); Middlesex Hosp. Med. Sch. Served with RAMC, 1940–47 (OBE); France, UK, ME and Central Mediterranean; specialist and advr in transfusion and resuscitation; OC Gen. Hosp. in Udine and Trieste; Dir, Ciba Foundn, 1949–78; Harveian Librarian, RCP, 1979–89; Fellow, Green Coll., Oxford, 1986–90. Mem., GMC, 1973–83; Chm., Genetic Manipulation Adv. Gp, 1976–78. Founder Mem. 1954, Treasurer 1955–61, Mem. Exec. Bd 1961–70, UK Cttee for WHO; Organizer and Advr, Haile Selassie I Prize Trust, 1963–74; Advr, La Trinidad Med. Centre, Caracas, 1969–78. Royal Society of Medicine: Hon. Sec. 1964–70; Pres. Library (Sci. Res) Sect., 1968–70; Chm. Working Party on Soc's Future, 1972–73; Pres., 1975–77, 1978; Zoological Society: Scientific Fellow and Vice-Pres.; Member: Finance Cttee, 1962–69; Council, 1962–66, 1967–70, 1976–80; Chm., Nuffield Inst. for Comparative Medicine, 1969–70; Chm. Governors, Inst. for Res. into Mental and Multiple Handicap, 1973–77. Founder Mem. 1950, Hon. Treasurer 1956–69, Renal Assoc. of GB; Chm. Congress Prog. Cttee, 1962–64, Mem. Finance Cttee 1968–72, Internat. Soc. for Endocrinology; Trustee and Mem. Res. Bd, Spastics' Soc., 1963–67; Founder Chm., European Soc. for Clinical Investigation, 1966–67 (Boerhaave Lectr, 1976); Mem. Council 1969–75, Sponsor 1976–, Inst. for Study of Drug Dependence; Dir, Nuffield Foundn Inquiry into Dental Educn, 1978–80; Chairman: Dental Res. Strategy Gp, 1986–89; Oral and Dental Res. Trust, 1989–96. Member: Council, Westfield Coll., London Univ., 1965–73; Planning Bd, University College at Buckingham, 1969. Chm., Anglo-Ethiopian Soc., 1967–70. Emeritus Mem. Ct of Assistants, Soc. of Apothecaries, 1988– (Mem., 1969–88; Master, 1979–80; Chm., Faculty of Hist. and Philosophy of Med. and Pharmacy, 1973–75; Visitor, 1975–78); Chm., Skin Diseases Res. Fund, 1980–85. Vis. Prof., UCSD, 1982, 1983, 1984. Dir, IRL Press Ltd, 1980–88. Trustee, Foulkes Foundn; Trustee, 1978–90, Chm. Acad. Bd,

1978–88, St George's Univ. Sch. of Med., Grenada. Mem. Bd, Dahlem Konferenzen, 1978–90. Vice-Pres., ASLIB, 1979–82. Pres., Brit. Soc. Hist. Medicine, 1983–85. Patron, FRAME, 1977–. Member, Advisory Board: Neem Nagar, India, 1997–99; Imperial Coll. Press, 1997–2000. Hon. Life Governor, Middlesex Hosp., 1938. Fellow UCL, 1991; FRSA 1979. Hon. FACP, 1975; Hon. FDSRCS 1991; Hon. Fellow: Hunterian Soc., 1975 (Orator 1976); Royal Acad. of Med. in Ireland, 1976; European Soc. for Clinical Investigation, 1979; RSocMed, 1982; Faculty of Hist. Med. Pharm., 1982. Hon. Member: Swedish Soc. of Endocrinology, 1955; Soc. of Endocrinology, 1959; Swiss Acad. of Med. Sciences, 1975; Assoc. Med. Argentina, 1977; Internat. Assoc. for Dental Res., 1984; Osler Club, 1986 (Orator, 1986); Foreign Mem., Swedish Med. Soc., 1959; Hon. For. Mem., Amer. Acad. of Arts and Scis, 1981. Hon. LLD Cambridge, 1968; Hon. DTech Brunel, 1981; Hon. MD Grenada, 1982. Linnaeus Medal, Royal Swedish Acad. Sci., 1977; Pasteur Medal, Paris, 1982; Gold Medal: Perugia Univ., 1961; (class 1A) Italian Min. of Educn, 1961. Tito Lik, 1945; Chevalier, Légion d'Honneur, 1959; Star of Ethiopia, 1966. *Publications:* (ed) Ciba Foundation vols, 1950–78; Royal College of Physicians: Portraits, vol. I (ed with David Piper), 1964, vol. II (ed with John Kerslake), 1977; (ed with Valerie Luniewska) Munk's Roll, vol. VI, 1982, vol. VII, 1984, vol. VIII, 1989; (jtly) Portrait of Irish Medicine, 1984. *Recreations:* walking, photography. *Address:* La Villiaze Lodge, Rue de la Villiaze, Forest, Guernsey GY8 0HQ. *T:* (01481) 263034.
Died 29 May 2004.

WONFOR, Andrea Jean, OBE 2003; Director, Liberty Bell Ltd, since 2002; *b* 31 July 1944; *d* of George Duncan and Audrey Joan Player; *m* 1st, 1967, Patrick Masefield (marr. diss. 1988); one *d*; 2nd, 1974, Geoffrey Wonfor; one *d. Educ:* Simon Langton Girls School, Canterbury; New Hall, Cambridge (BA). Graduate trainee, Granada Television, 1966–67; Tyne Tees Television: Researcher, 1969; Director, 1973; Head of Children's and Young People's Programmes, 1976; Dir of Progs, 1983–87; Channel Four Television: Controller, Arts and Entertainment, 1990–93; Dep. Dir of Progs, 1993; Dir of Progs, Granada TV, 1993–94; Jt Man. Dir, Granada TV, then Granada Productions, 1994–99; Creative Dir, Granada Content, 2000–02. Man. Dir, Zenith North, 1988–90. Mem., Bd of Govs, BFI, 1989–94. FRTS 1991 (Chm., 1996–98). *Recreations:* reading, music. *Address:* Fell Pasture, Ingoe, Matfen, Northumberland NE20 0SP. *T:* (01661) 886487. *Died 10 Sept. 2004.*

WOOD, Sir David (Basil) H.; *see* Hill-Wood.

WOOD, Francis Gordon, FIA; Deputy Chief General Manager, Prudential Assurance Co. Ltd, 1982–85; non-executive Director, Prudential Corporation, 1985–90 (Director, 1984); *b* 30 Oct. 1924; *s* of Francis R. and Florence A. Wood; *m* 1950, Margaret Parr; two *d. Educ:* Alleyne's Grammar School, Stone, Staffs. ACII. Prudential Assurance Co. Ltd, 1941–85; Dir, 1981. *Recreation:* golf. *Address:* 6 Matching Lane, Bishop's Stortford, Herts CM23 2PP. *T:* (01279) 315536. *Died 9 Jan. 2004.*

WOOD, Sir Frederick (Ambrose Stuart), Kt 1977; Hon. Life President, Croda International Ltd, since 1987 (Managing Director, 1953–85, Executive Chairman, 1960–85, non-executive Chairman, 1985–86); *b* 30 May 1926; *s* of Alfred Phillip Wood, Goole, Yorkshire, and Patras, Greece, and Charlotte Wood (*née* Barnes), Goole, Yorkshire, and Athens, Greece; *m* 1947, J. R. (Su) King; two *s* one *d. Educ:* Felsted Sch., Essex; Clare Coll., Cambridge. Served War, Sub-Lt (A) Observer, Fleet Air Arm, 1944–47. Trainee Manager, Croda Ltd, 1947–50; Pres., Croda Inc., NY, 1950–53. Chm., Nat. Bus Co., 1972–78. Mem., 1973–78, Chm., 1979–83, NRDC; Chairman: NEB, 1981–83; British Technology Gp, 1981–83. Mem., Nationalised Industries Chms' Gp, 1975–78. Chm. British Sect., Centre Européen d'Entreprise Publique, 1976–78. Hon. LLD Hull, 1983. *Address:* Hearn Wood, The Mount, Headley, Hants GU35 8AG. *T:* (01428) 712134. *Died 9 March 2003.*

WOOD, J(ohn) Laurence; Keeper, Department of Printed Books, British Library, 1966–76, retired; *b* 27 Nov. 1911; *s* of J. A. Wood and Clara Josephine (*née* Ryan); *m* 1947, Rowena Beatrice Ross; one *s* one *d. Educ:* Bishop Auckland; Merton Coll., Oxford (BA); Besançon; Paris. Lecteur, Univ. of Besançon, 1934; Asst Cataloguer, British Museum, 1936; seconded to Foreign Office, 1941; Asst Keeper, 1946; Dep. Keeper, 1959, British Museum. Ed., Factotum, 1978–95. *Publications:* (trans.) The French Prisoner, Garneray, 1957; (trans.) Contours of the Middle Ages, Genicot, 1967. *Recreation:* bookbinding. *Address:* 88 Hampstead Way, NW11 7XY. *T:* (020) 8455 4395. *Died 13 Dec. 2002.*

WOOD, John Peter; freelance gardening journalist and broadcaster; Editor, The Rose, since 1996; *b* 27 March 1925; *s* of Walter Ralph Wood and Henrietta Martin; *m* 1956, Susan Maye White; one *s* one *d. Educ:* Grove Park Grammar Sch.; Seale Hayne Agricultural Coll. (NDH and Dip. in Hort., of College). FIHort 1986. Served War, 1943–46. Horticultural studies, 1946–52; Amateur Gardening: Asst Editor, 1952–66; Dep. Editor, 1966–71; Editor, 1971–86; Cons. Editor, 1986–89. *Publications:* Amateur Gardening Handbook—Bulbs, 1957; Amateur Gardening Picture Book—Greenhouse Management, 1959; (jtly) The Complete Book of Roses, 1993. *Recreations:* gardening, choral singing. *Address:* 1 Charlton House Court, Charlton Marshall, Blandford, Dorset DT11 9NT. *T:* (01258) 454653. *Died 2 Dec. 2001.*

WOOD, Leonard George, CBE 1978; Director of Parent Board, 1965–80, and Group Director, Music, 1966–78, EMI Ltd; *b* 12 June 1910; *s* of Leonard George Wood and Miriam (*née* Barnes); *m* 1936, Christine Florence Reason (*d* 1978). *Educ:* Bishopshalt Sch., Hillingdon, Middx; London Univ. (BCom). Served War, RAF: Sgt, Airfield Controller, 1943; commnd Flying Control Officer, 1944–46. Asst Record Sales Manager, UK, EMI Ltd, 1939, Record Sales Man., 1947; EMI Records Ltd: Gen. Man., 1957; Man. Dir, 1959–66; Chm., 1966–78; EMI Ltd: Gp Divl Dir, 1961; Gp Asst Man. Dir, 1973–77. International Federation of Producers of Phonograms and Videograms: Chm. Council, 1968–73; Pres., 1973–76; Vice Pres. and Mem. Bd, 1967–81, Emeritus Vice-Pres., 1981–82; Mem. Bd, IFPI (Secretariat) Ltd, 1979–81. Chm., Record Merchandisers Ltd, 1975–81; Dep. Chm., Phonographic Performance Ltd, 1967–80; Hon. Pres., Brit. Phonographic Industry, 1980– (Chm., 1973–80); Governor, Brit. Inst. of Recorded Sound, 1974–78; Trustee, British Record Industry Trust, 1989–94. FRSA 1971–85. *Publication:* paper to RSA on growth and develt of recording industry. *Address:* Lark Rise, 39 Howards Thicket, Gerrards Cross, Bucks SL9 7NT. *T:* (01753) 884233. *Died 16 Feb. 2001.*

WOOD, Norman, CBE 1965; Director: Manchester Ship Canal Co., 1954–64; Associated British Foods Ltd, 1964–75, retired; *b* 2 Oct. 1905; *m* 1st, 1933, Ada Entwisle (*d* 1974); two *s* (one *d* decd); 2nd, 1976, Nita Miller (*d* 2001). *Educ:* Bolton Co. Grammar Sch.; Co-operative Coll. Mem. Cttee, Nat. Exec. Co-operative Party, and Central Board of Co-operative Union, 1934; served in Ministry of Information, NW England, 1939; Cttee Mem., Chocolate and Sugar Confectionery War-time Assoc., 1942; elected Dir, CWS, 1942–64, resigned; Mem., British Tourist and Holidays Board (later BTA), 1947–70 (Dep. Chm., 1964–67; sometime Chm., Finance and Exec. Cttee); Trustee, Plunkett Foundation, 1948 (sometime Chm., Exec. Cttee; Vice-Pres. 1972–; Hon. Life Mem., 1994); served on: Cake and Biscuit Alliance, 1948; Wheat Commission, 1950; Mem. Nat. Cttee, Domestic Coal Consumers Council, 1950; Coronation Accommodation Cttee, 1952. Member: British and Irish Millers, 1950–64; White Fish Authority, 1959–63; Food

Res. Adv. Cttee, 1961–65; DTI Japan Trade Adv. Cttee, 1971–; Exec. Mem., British Food Export Council, 1970–75. Chairman: Food and Drink Cttee, British Week, Toronto, 1967, Tokyo, 1969; Chm., ten Food and Drink Missions to Hong Kong and Japan, 1968–76; Dir, Fedn of Agricl Co-ops (UK) Ltd, 1975–; Mem., Lab Party Study Gp on Export Services and Organisation, 1974; Founder Mem., SDP, 1981; Chm., SDP Surrey Forum, 1988–92 (the last expression of the SDP); rejoined Lab. Pty. *Recreations:* walking, music. *Address:* 17 Wallace Fields, Epsom, Surrey KT17 3AX. *T:* (020) 8393 9052. *Club:* Oriental. *Died 1 Feb. 2002.*

WOOD, Peter Edric, OBE 1994; Chairman (part-time), West Yorkshire (formerly Huddersfield), Health Authority, 1982–96; Member, Audit Commission, 1990–96; *b* 17 July 1929; *s* of Edric Wood and Ruby (*née* Revill); *m* 1952, Barbara Evans; one *s* three *d. Educ:* RAF Coll.; Bradford Univ. (MSc); Open Univ. (BA); Huddersfield Univ. (Post-grad. Dip. Law 1999); DipEE. Served RAF, 1946–61. With ICI, 1961–82; Lectr (part-time), Manchester Univ., 1982–84; Sen. Teaching Fellow (part-time), Leeds Univ., 1984–89. Hon. Prof. of Mgt Scis, Lancaster Univ., 1996–2000. Mem. Council, Huddersfield Univ., 1996–. Trustee: Nat. Children's Centre (Chm., 1993–2000); Safe Anchor Trust, 1996–. Hon. Sec., Huddersfield Mencap Soc. *Recreations:* reading, walking, golf. *Address:* 9 Abbey Close, Hade Edge, Holmfirth, Huddersfield HD7 1RT. *T:* (01484) 686977. *Died 17 Aug. 2002.*

WOOD, Prof. Richard Frederick Marshall, RD 1976; MD; FRCSG, FRCS, FRCSE, FMedSci; Professor of Surgery, University of Sheffield, and Hon. Consultant Surgeon, Sheffield Teaching Hospitals (formerly Northern General Hospital) NHS Trust, since 1994; *b* 6 Jan. 1943; *s* of Sir Henry Peart Wood, CBE; *m* 1968, Christine Crawford Smith Jamieson; two *s. Educ:* Glasgow Acad.; Univ. of Glasgow (MB ChB 1967; MD 1976); MA Oxon 1981. FRCS 1972; FRCSG 1972; FRCSE 2001. Surgeon Lt-Comdr, RNR, 1973–87. Jun. surgical appts at Western Infirmary, Glasgow, 1967–74; Lectr and Sen. Lectr in Surgery, Univ. of Leicester, 1974–81; Hon. Consultant Surgeon, Leics AHA, 1977–81; Clinical Reader in Surgery and Fellow of Green Coll., Oxford Univ., and Hon. Consultant Surgeon, Oxford AHA, 1981–84; Prof. of Surgery, St Bartholomew's Hosp. Med. Coll., Univ. of London, and Hon. Consultant Surgeon, City and Hackney Health Dist, 1984–94. Vis. Fellow, Peter Bent Brigham Hosp., Boston, 1980; Hunterian Prof., RCS, 1985. Mem., Management Cttee, UK Transplant Service, 1980–89. Sec., Surgical Res. Soc., 1987–90; Vice-Pres., Transplantation Soc., 1998–2000 (Sec. and Cllr, 1986–96); Founding Pres., Sect. of Transplantation, RSM, 1993–95. Fellow, Assoc. of Surgeons of GB; Mem., European Surgical Assoc., 1998; Founder FMedSci 1998. Member Editorial Board: Transplantation, 1982–; British Jl of Surgery, 1984–89; Transplant International, 1998. *Publications:* Renal Transplantation: a clinical handbook, 1983; Surgical Aspects of Haemodialysis, 1983; Fundamental Anatomy for Operative General Surgery, 1989; (jtly) Small Bowel Transplantation, 1994; papers and chapters in textbooks on transplantation, and vascular surgery. *Recreations:* music, sailing. *Address:* Clinical Sciences Building, Northern General Hospital, Herries Road, Sheffield S5 7AU. *Died 11 April 2003.*

WOOD, Rt Rev. Roland Arthur; Rector, St James' Cathedral, and Dean of the Diocese of Athabasca, 1993–98; Bishop of Saskatoon, 1981–93; *b* 1 Jan. 1933; *s* of Cyril Arthur Wood and Evelyn Mae Wood (*née* Cave); *m* 1959, Elizabeth Nora (*née* Deacon); one *s* two *d. Educ:* Bishop's Univ., Lennoxville, Quebec (BA 1956, LST 1958). Ordained deacon, May 1958, priest, Dec. 1958; Asst Curate, St Matthew's, Winnipeg, 1958–60; Rector, Christ Church, Selkirk, 1960–64; Asst Priest, St John's Cathedral, Saskatoon, 1964–67; Rector, Holy Trinity

Church, Yorkton, 1967–71; Dean, St John's Cathedral, Saskatoon, 1971–81. Hon. DD Coll. of Emmanuel and St Chad, Saskatoon, 1979. *Recreations:* model railroading, camping, painting, refurbishing old furniture.
Died 17 Sept. 2002.

WOODCOCK, Gordon, FCA, CPFA; County Treasurer of Staffordshire, 1973–83; *m* Eileen M. Woodcock. FCA 1953. Served War, Royal Navy, 1942–46; Lieut RNVR. City Treasurer's Dept: Birmingham, 1937–42 and 1946–54; Stoke-on-Trent, 1954–73; City Treasurer of Stoke-on-Trent, 1971–73. *Died 12 April 2004.*

WOODING, Sir Norman (Samuel), Kt 1992; CBE 1986; PhD; Chairman, BEARR Trust, 1993–2003; *b* 20 April 1927; *s* of Samuel and Nellie Gertrude Wooding; *m* 1949, Dorothy Elizabeth Smith; one *s* two *d*. *Educ:* Lawrence Sheriff Sch., Rugby; Univ. of London (BSc); Univ. of Leeds (PhD); Univ. of Manchester. Joined Courtaulds, 1944; Main Board Dir, 1973; Dep. Chm., 1976–87; retd. Earlys of Witney: Dir, 1971–84; Chm., 1978–83; SAICCOR, S Africa: Dir, 1977–86; Chm., 1983–86. Chairman: Agricl Genetics Co. Ltd, 1988–93; E Europ. Trade Council, 1990–96; British Textile Technol. Gp, 1991–94; EIS Group, 1994–98; non-exec. Dep. Chm., Royal London Mutual Insce Soc. Ltd, 1988–96; non-exec. Dir, British Nuclear Fuels plc, 1987–98. Pres., Comité Internat. de Rayon et Fibres Synthétiques, 1981–85. Pres., Russo-British (formerly Brit. Soviet) Chamber of Commerce, 1988–2003; Chm. Council, SSEES, Univ. of London, 1992–99; Chm., govt Review of Soviet and E European Studies, 1989; Member: Governing Body, Brit. Assoc. for Central and Eastern Europe, 1988–; Adv. Bd, British Know How Fund, 1989–99. Sen. Associate Mem., St Antony's Coll., Oxford, 1987–. CCMI (CBIM 1983); FRSA 1992. *Publications:* papers in scientific journals, E European trade jls, etc. *Recreations:* mountain walking, gardening, fast cars. *Club:* Reform. *Died 27 June 2005.*

WOODROOFE, Sir Ernest (George), Kt 1973; PhD; FInstP, FIChemE; Chairman, Unilever Ltd, 1970–74; *b* 6 Jan. 1912; *s* of late Ernest George Woodroofe and Ada (*née* Dickinson); *m* 1st, 1938, Margaret Downes (*d* 1961); one *d*; 2nd, 1962, Enid Grace Hutchinson Arnold. *Educ:* Cockburn High Sch.; Leeds Univ. (PhD 1935). Staff of Loders & Nucoline Ltd, 1935–44; Staff of British Oil & Cake Mills Ltd, 1944–50; Mem., Oil Mills Executive of Unilever Ltd, 1951–55; Director of British Oil & Cake Mills Ltd, 1951–55; Head of Research Division of Unilever Ltd, 1955–61; Director: United Africa Co. Ltd, 1961–63; Unilever NV, 1956–74; Dir, 1956–74, Vice-Chm., 1961–70, Unilever Ltd; Trustee, Leverhulme Trust, 1962–82 (Chm., 1974–82). Vis. Fellow, Nuffield Coll., Oxford, 1972–80. President, International Society for Fat Research, 1962. Member Cttee of Enquiry into the Organisation of Civil Science, 1962–63; A Vice-Pres., Soc. of Chemical Industry, 1963–66; Member: Tropical Products Inst. Cttee, 1964–69; Council for Nat. Academic Awards, 1964–67; Cttee of Award of the Commonwealth Fund, 1965–70; Royal Commn for the Exhibn of 1851, 1968–84; British Gas Corp., 1973–81. Director: Schroders Ltd, 1974–89; Burton Group Ltd, 1974–83; Guthrie Corp. Ltd, 1974–82. Chairman: Review Body on Doctors' and Dentists' Remuneration, 1975–79; CBI Research Cttee, 1966–69. Governor, London Business Sch., 1970–75 (Dep. Chm., 1973–75). Hon. ACT Liverpool, 1963; Hon. Fellow, University of Manchester Inst. of Science and Technology, 1968; Hon. LLD Leeds, 1968; DUniv Surrey, 1970; Hon. DSc: Cranfield, 1974; Liverpool, 1980. Comdr, Order of Orange Nassau (Netherlands) 1972. *Recreation:* fishing. *Address:* 44 The Street, Puttenham, Surrey GU3 1AR. *T:* (01483) 810977.
Died 31 March 2002.

WOODRUFF, Prof. Sir Michael (Francis Addison), Kt 1969; DSc; FRS 1968; FRCS; Emeritus Professor of Surgery, University of Edinburgh; Surgeon, Edinburgh Royal Infirmary, 1957–76; Director, Nuffield Transplantation Surgery Unit, Edinburgh, 1968–76; *b* 3 April 1911; *s* of late Prof. Harold Addison Woodruff and Margaret Ada (*née* Cooper); *m* 1946, Hazel Gwenyth Ashby; two *s* one *d*. *Educ:* Wesley Coll., Melbourne; Queen's Coll., University of Melbourne (MB, BS 1937, MD 1940, MS 1941). FRCS 1946. Captain, Australian Army Medical Corps, 1940–46. Tutor in Surgery, Univ. of Sheffield, 1946–48; Lecturer in Surgery, Univ. of Aberdeen, 1948–52; Prof. of Surgery, Univ. of Otago, Dunedin, NZ, 1953–56; Prof. of Surgery, Univ. of Edinburgh, 1957–76. Travelling Fellow, WHO, 1949. Hunterian Prof., RCS, 1952. Pres., Transplantation Soc., 1972–74. A Vice-Pres., Royal Soc., 1979. Associé Etranger, Académie de Chirurgie, 1964; Hon. Fellow, American Surgical Assoc., 1965; Korrespondierenden Mitglied, Deutsche Gesellschaft für Chirurgie; Hon. FACS 1975; Hon. FRCPE 1982. Lister Medal, 1969; Gold Medal, Soc. of Apothecaries, 1974. *Publications:* (jtly) Deficiency Diseases in Japanese Prison Camps, 1951; Surgery for Dental Students, 1954; Transplantation of Tissues and Organs, 1960; On Science and Surgery (essays), 1977; The Interaction of Cancer and Host, 1980; Cellular Variation and Adaptation in Cancer, 1990; (contrib.) Encyclopedia of Human Biology, 1991; Nothing Venture Nothing Win (autobiog.), 1997; articles on surgical topics and on experimental tissue transplantation. *Recreations:* music, sailing. *Address:* The Bield, 506 Lanark Road, Juniper Green, Edinburgh EH14 5DH. *Clubs:* Athenæum; New (Edinburgh).
Died 10 March 2001.

WOODRUFF, William Charles, CBE 1985; FRAeS; Controller, National Air Traffic Services, 1977–81; *b* 14 Aug. 1921; *s* of late Thomas and Caroline Woodruff; *m* 1st, 1946, Ethel May Miles (*d* 1981); one *s* one *d*; 2nd, 1987, Olivia Minerva Henson. *Educ:* St George's, Ramsgate. Served RAF, 1941–46: Navigator/Observer, 1409 Flight; POW Germany, 1943–45. Seconded Air Min., 1945, and later Min. of Civil Aviation for Air Traffic Control planning; various air traffic control appts at Hurn, Northolt, Southern Centre, Heston and MTCA Hdqrs, 1946–56; Air Traffic Control Officer i/c Heathrow, 1956–62; Sec. of Patch Long-term Air Traffic Control Planning Group, 1960–61; Dep. Dir, 1962–67, Dir, 1967–69, Civil Air Traffic Ops; National Air Traffic Services: Jt Field Comdr, 1969–74; Dep. Controller, 1974–77. Assessor, Stanstead/Heathrow Airports Public Inquiries, 1981–84; Specialist Advr, H of C Transport Select Cttee on Air Safety, 1988–89. Guild of Air Traffic Control Officers: Clerk, 1952–56; Master, 1956. *Publications:* articles on aviation subjects. *Address:* 21 Atwater Court, Lenham, Kent ME17 2PW. *T:* (01622) 850560. *Died 25 July 2003.*

WOODS, Sir Colin (Philip Joseph), KCVO 1977; CBE 1973; QPM 1980; HM Chief Inspector of Constabulary, 1977–79; Commissioner, Australian Federal Police, 1979–82; *b* London, 20 April 1920; *s* of late Michael Woods, Sub-divisional Inspector, Metropolitan Police; *m* 1941, Gladys Ella May (*née* Howell); one *d*. *Educ:* LCC Primary and Secondary Schs; Finchley Grammar Sch. Served War, in 60th Rifles and RUR, 1939–46. Metropolitan Police: Constable, through ranks, to Dep. Comdr; Commander, Traffic Dept, 1966–67; Head of Management Services, 1968; Comdt, National Police Coll., 1969–70; Asst Comr (Traffic Dept), 1970; Asst Comr (Crime), 1972; Dep. Comr, 1975–77. Chm. Council, BSIA, 1987–92. *Recreations:* walking, gardening, caravanning. *Address:* Doversmead, Littleworth Road, The Sands, Farnham, Surrey GU10 1JW. *T:* (01252) 782514.
Died 27 Jan. 2001.

WOODWARD, Barry; His Honour Judge Woodward; a Circuit Judge, since 1990; Resident Judge, Manchester Minshull Street Crown Court, since 2002; Temporary Additional Judge, Employment Appeal Tribunal, since

2002; *s* of Wilfred and Mary Hannah Woodward; *m* 1963, Patricia Holland; two *d*. *Educ*: Sheffield Univ. (LLM). Called to the Bar, Gray's Inn, 1970. Teaching positions, 1961–70; practice on Northern Circuit, 1970–84; Chm., Industrial Tribunals, Manchester Region, 1984; a Recorder, 1988. *Recreations*: ski-ing, motorcycling, golf, any other sporting activity that time and fitness permits, messing with classic motor cars. *Address*: Minshull Street Crown Court, Manchester M1 3FS. *T*: (0161) 954 7500.
Died 21 Dec. 2005.

WOOF, Robert Samuel, CBE 1998; PhD; Director, Wordsworth Trust, Dove Cottage, Grasmere, since 1989; *b* 20 April 1931; *s* of late William Woof and Annie (*née* Mason); *m* 1958, Pamela Shirley Moore; two *s* two *d*. *Educ*: Lancaster Royal Grammar School; Pembroke College, Oxford (MA); University of Toronto (PhD). Goldsmith Travelling Fellow, 1953–55; Lectr, Univ. of Toronto, 1958–61; University of Newcastle: Lord Adams of Ennerdale Fellow, 1961–62; Lectr, 1962; Reader in Eng. Lit., 1971–92; Leverhulme Fellow, 1983–84. Vice-Chm., Northern Arts Assoc., 1974–81; Hon. Keeper of Collections, Trustees of Dove Cottage, Grasmere, 1974–89, Hon. Sec. and Treasurer, 1978–95. Mem., 1982–88, Rep., 1988–, Arts Council: Vice-Chm., 1982–88, acting Chm, 1985–86, Drama Panel; Chm., Literature Panel, 1984–88 (Vice-Chm., 1983–84). Chairman: Century Theatre, 1991–92; English Touring Theatre, 1993–2000. FRSL 2000. Hon. DLitt: Lancaster, 1994; Newcastle upon Tyne, 2001. Creative Briton Award, Arts & Business, 1999. *Publications*: (ed) T. W. Thompson, Wordsworth's Hawkshead, 1970; The Wordsworth Circle, 1979; (with Peter Bicknell) The Discovery of the Lake District 1750–1810, 1982; (with Peter Bicknell) The Lake District Discovered 1810–50, 1983; Thomas De Quincey: an English opium-eater 1785–1859, 1985; (with David Thomason) Derwentwater, the Vale of Elysium, 1986; The Artist as Evacuee, 1987; (with Jonathan Wordsworth and Michael C. Jaye) William Wordsworth and the Age of English Romanticism, 1987; Matthew Arnold, a Centennial Exhibition, 1988; Byron: a dangerous romantic?, 1989, rev. 2003; Tennyson: a bicentenary tribute, 1992; Shelley: an ineffectual angel?, 1992; (with Stephen Hebron) John Keats 1795–1995, 1995; (with David Brown and Stephen Hebron) Benjamin Robert Haydon: painter and writer, friend of Wordsworth and Keats, 1996; (with Fay Godwin) A Perfect Republic of Shepherds, 1997; (with Stephen Hebron) The Ancient Mariner, 1997; (with Stephen Hebron, Claire Tomalin and Pamela Woof) Hyenas in Petticoats, 1997; (with Stephen Hebron) Towards Tintern Abbey, 1998; (with Stephen Hebron) Romantic Icons, 1999; (with Stephen Hebron and Pamela Woof) English Poetry, 850–1850: the first thousand years, 2000; Wordsworth: the critical heritage, 2001; (with Stephen Hebron and Howard Hanley) Paradise Lost: the poem and its illustrators, 2004. *Recreations*: the arts, the Lake District. *Address*: The Wordsworth Trust, Dove Cottage, Grasmere, Cumbria LA22 9SH. *T*: (015394) 63500/35544.
Died 7 Nov. 2005.

WOOLF, Harry, PhD; Professor-at-Large, Institute for Advanced Study, Princeton, USA, 1987–94, then Emeritus (Director, 1976–87); *b* 12 Aug. 1923; *s* of Abraham Woolf and Anna (*née* Frankman); *m* 1961, Patricia A. Kelsh (marr. diss.); two *s* two *d*. *Educ*: Univ. of Chicago (BS Physics and Maths 1948; MA Physics and History 1949); Cornell Univ. (PhD Hist. of Science 1955). Served US Army, 1943–46. Instructor: Boston Univ., Mass, 1953–55; Brandeis Univ., Waltham, Mass, 1954–55; Asst Prof., Associate Prof., and Prof., Univ. of Washington, Seattle, 1955–61; Johns Hopkins University: Prof., Hist. of Science Dept, 1961–76 (Chm. of Dept, 1961–72); Provost, 1972–76; Mem. Adv. Council, Depts of Philosophy, 1980–84, and of Comparative Lit., 1982–86, Princeton Univ. Pres., Chm. of Bd, Johns Hopkins Program for Internat. Educn in Gynecology and Obstetrics, Inc., 1973–76, Trustee 1976–; Mem. Adv. Bd, Smithsonian Research Awards, 1975–79; Member: Vis. Cttee Student Affairs, MIT, 1973–77; Corp. Vis. Cttee, Dept of Linguistics and Philosophy, MIT, 1977–83; Corp. Vis. Cttee, Dept of Physics, MIT, 1979–85; Vis. Cttee, Res. Center for Language Scis, Indiana Univ., 1977–80; Nat. Adv. Child Health and Human Develt Council, NIH, 1977–80. Trustee: Associated Universities Inc., Brookhaven Nat. Laboratories, Nat. Radio Astronomy Observatory, 1972–82; Hampshire Coll., Amherst, Mass, 1977–81; Merrill Lynch Cluster C Funds, 1982–95; Reed Coll., 1992–97; Dibner Inst. for the Hist. of Science, 1992–98; Trustee-at-Large, Univs Research Assoc. Inc., Washington, DC (Fermi Nat. Accelerator Lab.), 1978–91, Chm. Bd 1979–89. Member: Council on Foreign Relations Inc., 1979–; Adv. Panel, WGBH, NOVA, 1979–; Internat. Research and Exchanges Bd, NY, 1980–94; Scientific Adv. Bd, Wissenschaftskolleg zu Berlin, 1981–87; Board of Directors: Alex. Brown Mutual Funds, Inc., Baltimore, 1981–96; W. Alton Jones Cell Science Center, 1982–86; Westmark Corp., 1987–92; Family Health Internat., 1992–; Advanced Technology Labs, 1992–99; Spacelabs Medical, 1992–98; Pres., Bankers Trust/Alex. Brown Funds Inc., 1997–99. Member: Adv. Council, Nat. Science Foundn, 1984–89; Bd of Trustees, Rockefeller Foundn, 1984–94; Dir-at-large, Amer. Cancer Soc., 1982–86. Member: Académie Internat. d'Histoire des Sciences; Amer. Philos. Soc.; Phi Beta Kappa; Sigma Xi (also Bicentennial Lectr, 1976). Ed., ISIS Internat. Review, 1958–64; Associate Ed., Dictionary of Scientific Biog., 1970–80; Member: Editl Bd, Interdisciplinary Science Revs, 1975–; Editl Adv. Bd, The Writings of Albert Einstein, 1977–. Fellow, Amer. Acad. of Arts and Scis; FAAAS. Hon. DSc: Whitman Coll., 1979; Amer. Univ., Washington, DC, 1982; Hon. LHD: Johns Hopkins Univ., 1983; St Lawrence Univ., 1986. *Publications*: The Transits of Venus: a study in eighteenth-century science, 1959, repr. 1981; (ed) Quantification: essays in the history of measurement in the natural and social sciences, 1961; (ed) Science as a Cultural Force, 1964; (ed and contrib.) Some Strangeness in the Proportion: a centennial symposium to celebrate the achievements of Albert Einstein, 1980; (ed) The Analytic Spirit: essays in the history of science, 1981. *Address*: Institute for Advanced Study, Princeton, NJ 08540, USA. *T*: (609) 7348018.
Died 6 Jan. 2003.

WOOLF, John Moss, CB 1975; Deputy Chairman of the Board of Customs and Excise, and Director-General (Customs and Establishments), 1973–78; *b* 5 June 1918; *o s* of Alfred and Maud Woolf; *m* 1940, Phyllis Ada Mary Johnson (*d* 1990); one *d*. *Educ*: Drayton Manor Sch.; Hon. Soc. of Lincoln's Inn. Called to the Bar, 1948. Served War, 1939–46, Captain, RA. Inland Revenue, 1937; Asst Principal, Min. of Fuel and Power, 1948; HM Customs and Excise, 1950: Principal, 1951; Asst Sec., 1960; Chm., Valuation Cttee, Customs Cooperation Council, Brussels, 1964–65; National Bd for Prices and Incomes, 1965; Under-Sec., 1967; Asst Under-Sec. of State, Dept of Employment and Productivity, 1968–70; HM Customs and Excise: Comr, 1970; Dir of Estabts and Organisation, 1971–73. Advr on Price Problems, Govt of Trinidad & Tobago, 1968. Association of First Division Civil Servants: Mem., Exec. Cttee, 1950–58 and 1961–65; Hon. Sec., 1952–55; Chm., 1955–58 and 1964–65; Mem., Civil Service National Whitley Council (Staff Side), 1953–55. Leader of Review Team to examine responsibilities of Dirs of Nat. Museums and Galleries, 1978–79; Review of Organisation and Procedures of Chancery Div. of High Court, 1979–81. Overseas Adviser to CEGB, 1979–82. Commandeur d'Honneur, Ordre du Bontemps de Médoc et des Graves (France), 1973; Hon. Borgenerális (Hungary), 1974. *Publications*: Report on Control of Prices in Trinidad and Tobago (with M. M. Eccleshall), 1968; Report of the Review Body on the Chancery Division of the High Court (with Lord Oliver of Aylmerton and R. H. H. White), 1981. *Recreation*: reading. *Address*: 20

Bushey Park, High Street, Bushey, Herts WD23 1BJ. *T:* (020) 8950 4918. *Club:* Civil Service.

Died 15 July 2003.

WOOLLEY, His Honour Roy Gilbert; a Circuit Judge, 1976–93; *b* 28 Nov. 1922; *s* of John Woolley and Edith Mary Woolley; *m* 1953, Doreen, *d* of Humphrey and Kathleen Morris; two *s* two *d*. *Educ:* Overton and Marchwiel Primary Schs; Deeside Secondary Sch.; UCL (LLB Hons 1949); BA Hons 2003. Served War, 1939–45, Air Gunner, RAF. Christopher Tancred Student, Lincoln's Inn, 1948; called to the Bar, 1951; Wales and Chester Circuit; Recorder, 1975. Reader: Diocese of Chester, 1955–77; Diocese of Lichfield, 1977–95. Member: Lichfield Diocesan Synod, 1988–; General Synod of C of E, 1990–95; Legal Adv. Commn of C of E, 1991–96. *Recreations:* outdoor pursuits, incl. horse riding, gardening; interested in music, poetry, art and antique furniture. *Address:* Henlle Hall, Gobowen, Oswestry, Salop SY10 7AX. *T:* (01691) 661257.

Died 8 Oct. 2005.

WOOLMAN, (Joseph) Roger, CB 1997; Deputy Secretary, and Legal Adviser and Solicitor to Ministry of Agriculture, Fisheries and Food, Forestry Commission and Intervention Board for Agricultural Produce, 1993–97; *b* 13 Feb. 1937; *s* of late Maurice Wollman and Hilda Wollman; *m* 1st, 1973, Elizabeth Ingham (marr. diss. 1999), *d* of late Eric Ingham; one *s* one *d*; 2nd, 2000, Dr Judith Bronkhurst, art historian. *Educ:* Perse School, Cambridge; Trinity Hall, Cambridge (Exhibnr; MA). Solicitor, 1974. DTI and OFT Legal Departments, 1976–93: Under Sec., DTI, 1985–88 and 1991–93; Legal Dir, OFT, 1988–91. *Died 19 May 2005.*

WOOLRYCH, Prof. Austin Herbert, FBA 1988; Professor of History, University of Lancaster, 1964–85, then Emeritus; *b* 18 May 1918; *s* of Stanley Herbert Cunliffe Woolrych and May Gertrude (*née* Wood); *m* 1941, Muriel Edith Rolfe (*d* 1991); one *s* one *d*. *Educ:* Westminster Sch.; Pembroke Coll., Oxford (BLitt, MA). Served War, RAC, 1939–46: commnd RTR, 1940; Captain 1943. Lectr in History, subseq. Sen. Lectr, Univ. of Leeds, 1949–64; Pro-Vice-Chancellor, Univ. of Lancaster, 1971–75. Vis. Fellow, All Souls Coll., Oxford, 1981–82; Commonwealth Vis. Fellow to univs in Australia and NZ, 1983. Hon. DLitt Lancaster, 1986. *Publications:* Battles of the English Civil War, 1961, rev. edn 2000; Oliver Cromwell, 1964; (introd) Complete Prose Works of John Milton, vol. 7, 1980; Commonwealth to Protectorate, 1982; England without a King, 1983; Soldiers and Statesmen, 1987; Britain in Revolution 1625–1660, 2002; articles and reviews in jls and symposia. *Recreations:* walking, travel, listening to music. *Address:* 9 Hollowrayne, Burton-in-Kendal, Carnforth LA6 1NS. *T:* (01524) 782471.

Died 14 Sept. 2004.

WORDLEY, Ronald William; Chairman, The Buckingham Group (Winslow Press) Ltd, 1987–93; Director, BCS Developments Ltd, since 1989; Managing Director, 1978–87, Chairman, 1985–86, HTV Ltd; *b* 16 June 1928; *s* of William Wordley and Elizabeth Anne Hackett; *m* 1953, Pamela Mary Offord; two *s* one *d* (and one *s* decd). *Educ:* Barnet Grammar Sch.; City of London Coll.; RMA, Sandhurst. Regular Army Officer: 2/Lieut RA, 1948; regtl duty, UK, Far East and Europe; Liaison Officer, RM Commando Bde, 1951, Captain; Air OP Pilot, 1953; Army Light Aircraft Sch., 1955; seconded Army Air Corps Cadre, 1957; resigned commn, 1958. Unilever (United Africa Co.), 1958–59; Anglia Television Ltd: Sales Exec., 1959; Gen. Sales Manager, 1962; Dep. Sales Controller, 1964; joined Harlech Consortium as Sales Controller, 1967; Sales Dir on bd of HTV Ltd, 1971. Director: Instock Ltd; Independent Television Publications Ltd; (also Mem. Council), Independent Television Cos Assoc. Ltd; HTV Gp plc; HTV Equipment Ltd; HTV Property Ltd., 1971–87. Hon. Patron, Royal

Regt of Wales, 1986–91. Mem., Inst. of Marketing; FRSA 1983; FInstD 1986. *Recreations:* music, travel, golf, swimming. *Address:* 1 Deanery Walk, Avon Park Village, Limpley Stoke, Bath BA3 7JQ; TSDY Tirion II, Quay 11, Berth 14, Port de La Rague, Theoule-sur-Mer 06590, France. *Clubs:* Clifton (Bristol); Bristol and Clifton Golf.

Died 1 June 2003.

WORMALD, Brian; *see* Wormald, T. B. H. G.

WORMALD, (Thomas) Brian (Harvey Goodwin); University Lecturer in History, Cambridge, 1948–79; Fellow of Peterhouse, 1938–79; *b* 24 July 1912; *s* of late Rev. C. O. R. Wormald and Mrs A. W. C. Wormald (*née* Brooks); *m* 1946, Rosemary (*d* 2003), *d* of E. J. B. Lloyd; two *s* (and two *s* decd). *Educ:* Harrow; Peterhouse, Cambridge (Scholar; BA 1934 (1st Class Hons Hist. Tripos, Parts I and II); Members Prize (English Essay), 1935; Prince Consort Prize, 1938; MA 1938); Chichester Theol. Coll. Ordained deacon, 1940, priest, 1943; Cambridge University: Strathcona Research Student, St John's College, 1936–38; Chaplain and Catechist, 1940–48, Dean, 1941–44; Tutor, 1952–62, Peterhouse; Junior Proctor, 1951–52. Select Preacher, Cambridge, 1945 and 1954. Received into Roman Catholic Church, 1955. *Publications:* Clarendon: Politics, History and Religion, 1951; Francis Bacon: History, Politics, Science, 1993. *Address:* c/o Peterhouse, Cambridge CB2 1RD. *Club:* Travellers. *Died 22 March 2005.*

WORSFOLD, Reginald Lewis, CBE 1979; Member for Personnel, British Gas Corporation (formerly Gas Council), 1973–80, retired; *b* 18 Dec. 1925; *s* of Charles S. and Doris Worsfold; *m* 1st, 1952, Margot Kempell (marr. diss. 1974); one *s* one *d*; 2nd, 1982, Christine McKeown. *Educ:* Sch. of Technol., Art and Commerce, Oxford; LSE. MIPM. Served War of 1939–45, Lieut 44 Royal Marine Commandos, 1943–46. Organising Comr, Scout Council of Nigeria, 1947–49; Personnel Manager: BEA, 1953–65; W Midlands Gas Bd, 1965–69; Gas Council: Dep. Personnel Dir, 1969–70; Personnel Dir, 1970–72. *Recreations:* sailing, camping, music. *Address:* Beck House, 43 Wychwood Grove, Chandler's Ford, Hants SO53 1FQ. *T:* (023) 8026 9873. *Died 23 Nov. 2002.*

WORSWICK, David; *see* Worswick, G. D. N.

WORSWICK, (George) David (Norman), CBE 1981; FBA 1979; Director, National Institute of Economic and Social Research, 1965–82; *b* 18 Aug. 1916; *s* of Thomas Worswick, OBE, and Eveline (*née* Green); *m* 1940, Sylvia, *d* of A. E. Walsh, MBE; one *s* two *d* (and one *s* decd). *Educ:* St Paul's Sch.; New Coll., Oxford (Scholar; Final Hons (Maths), 1937); Dipl. in Economics and Political Science, 1938. Research staff, Oxford Univ. Institute of Statistics, 1940–60; Fellow and Tutor in Economics, Magdalen Coll., Oxford, 1945–65 (Sen. Tutor, 1955–57; Vice-President, 1963–65; Emeritus Fellow, 1969). Vis. Prof. of Economics, MIT, 1962–63. Mem., SSRC, 1966–70. President: Sect. F, British Assoc., 1971; Royal Econ. Soc., 1982–84. Hon. DSc City, 1975. *Publications:* (ed jtly) The British Economy 1945–50, 1952; (ed jtly) The Free Trade Proposals, 1960; (ed jtly) The British Economy in the 1950s, 1962; (jtly) Profits in the British Economy 1909–1938, 1967; (ed) Uses of Economics, 1972; (ed jtly) The Medium Term, 1974; (ed) The Concept and Measurement of Involuntary Unemployment, 1976; (ed jtly) Keynes and the Modern World, 1983; (ed) Education and Economic Performance, 1985; Unemployment: a problem of policy, 1991; articles in academic jls. *Address:* 25 Beech Croft Road, Oxford OX2 7AY. *T:* (01865) 552486. *Club:* Oxford and Cambridge.

Died 18 May 2001.

WORTH, Irene, Hon. CBE 1975; actress; *b* 23 June 1916. *Educ:* University of California, Los Angeles (BE). Antoinette Perry Award for distinguished achievement in the Theatre, 1965. First appeared as Fenella in Escape Me

Never, New York, 1942; debut on Broadway as Cecily
Harden in The Two Mrs Carrolls, Booth Theatre, 1943.
Studied for six months with Elsie Fogerty, 1944–45.
Subsequently appeared frequently at Mercury, Bolton's,
Q, Embassy, etc. Parts include: Anabelle Jones in Love
Goes to Press, Duchess Theatre, 1946 (after Embassy);
Ilona Szabo in The Play's the Thing, St James's, 1947 (after
tour and Lyric, Hammersmith); Eileen Perry in Edward
my Son, Lyric, 1948; Lady Fortrose in Home is
Tomorrow, Cambridge Theatre, 1948; Olivia Raines in
Champagne for Delilah, New, 1949; Celia Coplestone in
The Cocktail Party, New, 1950 (after Edinburgh Festival,
1949; Henry Miller Theatre, New York, 1950);
Desdemona in Othello, Old Vic, 1951; Helena in
Midsummer Night's Dream, Old Vic, 1952; Catherine de
Vausselles in The Other Heart, Old Vic, 1952; Lady
Macbeth in Macbeth, Desdemona in Othello, Helena in
Midsummer Night's Dream, Catherine de Vausselles in
The Other Heart, Old Vic tour of S Africa, 1952; Portia
in The Merchant of Venice, Old Vic, 1953; Helena in All's
Well That Ends Well and Queen Margaret in Richard III,
First Season Shakespeare Festival Theatre, Stratford, Ont,
Canada, 1953; Frances Farrar in A Day By The Sea,
Haymarket, 1953–54; Alcestis in A Life in the Sun,
Edinburgh Festival, 1955; leading rôles in: The Queen and
the Rebels, Haymarket, 1955; Hotel Paradiso, Winter
Garden, 1956; Mary Stuart, Phœnix Theatre, NY, 1957,
Old Vic, 1958; The Potting Shed, Globe Theatre,
London, 1958; Rosalind in As You Like It, Shakespeare
Festival Theatre, Stratford, Ont, 1959; Albertine Prine in
Toys in the Attic, Hudson Theatre, New York, 1960 (NY
Newspaper Guild Page One Award); Season at Royal
Shakespeare Theatre, Stratford, 1962; Goneril in King
Lear, Aldwych, 1962; Doctor Mathilde von Zahnd in The
Physicists, Aldwych, 1963; Clodia Pulcher in The Ides of
March, Haymarket, 1963; World tour of King Lear for
Royal Shakespeare Company, 1964; Alice in Tiny Alice,
Billy Rose Theatre, New York, 1965 (Tony award 1965),
Aldwych, 1970; Hilde in A Song at Twilight, Anne in
Shadows of the Evening, Anna-Mary in Come into the
Garden Maud (Noël Coward Trilogy), Queen's, 1966
(Evening Standard Award); Hesione Hushabye in
Heartbreak House, Chichester and Lyric, 1967 (Variety
Club of GB Award, 1967); Jocasta in Seneca's Oedipus,
National Theatre, 1968; Hedda in Hedda Gabler,
Stratford, Ont, 1970; worked with internat. Co. for
Theatre Res., Paris and Iran, 1971; Notes on a Love Affair,
Globe, 1972; Madame Arkadina, The Seagull, Chichester,
1973; Hamlet, Ghosts, The Seagull, Greenwich, 1974;
Sweet Bird of Youth, Lake Forest, Washington, NY
(Tony Award, Jefferson Award), 1975; Misalliance, 1976,
Old Times, 1977, After the Season, 1978, Lake Forest, Ill;
The Cherry Orchard, NY, 1977 (Drama Desk Award,
1977); Happy Days, NY, 1979; The Lady from Dubuque,
NY, 1980; L'Olimpiade, Edinburgh Fest., 1982; The
Chalk Garden, NY, 1982; The Physicists, Washington,
1983; The Golden Age, NY, 1984; Coriolanus, Nat.
Theatre, 1984; The Bay at Nice, Nat. Theatre, 1986; You
Never Can Tell, Haymarket, 1987; Volumnia in
Coriolanus, Public Theatre, NY, 1988–89; Lost in
Yonkers, NY (Tony Award), 1991; A Week's Worth,
Almeida, 1996; Irene Worth's Portrait of Edith Wharton;
The Gypsy and the Yellow Canary, 1997; Chère Maître,
Almeida, 1999. Films: Orders to Kill, 1957 (British Film
Academy Award for Best Woman's Performance, 1958);
The Scapegoat, 1958; King Lear (Goneril), 1970; Nicholas
and Alexandra, 1971; Eye Witness, 1980; Deathtrap, 1982;
Fast Forward, 1985; Lost in Yonkers, 1993; A Piece of
Cake, 1997. Television: The Lady from the Sea, BBC,
1953; The Lake, BBC, 1953 (Daily Mail National
Television Award, 1953–54), and has subseq. appeared on
television and acted with CBC Television in NY and
Canada; Coriolanus (BBC Shakespeare series), 1984. Hon.
Dr Arts Tufts Univ., 1980; Hon. DFA Queen's Coll., NY,
1986. Whitbread Anglo-American Award for Outstanding
Actress, 1967; NY Theatre Hall of Fame, 1979; Obie

Award for outstanding achievement in the theatre, 1989.
Recreation: music. Address: c/o ICM, Sam Cohn, 40 West
57th Street, New York, NY 10019, USA.
                                                          Died 9 March 2002.

WORTHINGTON, Edgar Barton, CBE 1967; PhD;
environmental consultant; b 13 Jan. 1905; s of Edgar
Worthington and Amy E. Beale; m 1st, 1930, Stella
Desmond Johnson (d 1978); three d; 2nd, 1980, Harriett
Stockton, Cape Cod. Educ: Rugby; Gonville and Caius
Coll., Cambridge (MA, PhD 1930). Expeditions to
African Lakes, 1927–31; Balfour Student, 1930–33, and
Demonstrator in Zoology, Cambridge Univ., 1933–37;
Scientist for the African Research Survey, 1934–37;
Director of Laboratories and Secretary of Freshwater
Biological Assoc., Windermere, 1937–46; Scientific
Adviser to Middle East Supply Centre, 1943–45;
Development Adviser, Uganda, 1946; Scientific Secretary
to Colonial Research Council, 1946–49, to E Africa High
Commission, 1950–51; Secretary-General to Scientific
Council for Africa South of the Sahara, 1951–55; Deputy
Director-General (Scientific) Nature Conservancy,
1957–65; Scientific Dir, Internat. Biological Programme,
1964–74. Pres., Cttee on Water Res., ICSU, 1973–77.
Mem. of Honour, IUCN, 1978; Mem. (hc), Linnean Soc.,
1991. Gill Meml award, RGS, 1932; Mungo Park Medal,
RSGS, 1938; Avicenne Medal, UNESCO, 1993. Order of
Golden Ark (Netherlands), 1976. Publications: (with Stella
Worthington) Inland Waters of Africa, 1933; Science in
Africa, 1938; Middle East Science, 1946; Development
Plan for Uganda, 1947; (with T. T. Macan) Life in Lakes
and Rivers, 1951, rev. edn 1973; Science in the
Development of Africa, 1958 (trans. French, 1960); (ed)
Man-made Lakes: problems and environmental effects,
1973; Evolution of the IBP, 1975; (ed) Arid Land
Irrigation: problems and environmental effects, 1976; The
Nile, 1978; The Ecological Century, 1983; official reports
and papers in scientific journals. Recreations: nature
conservation, field sports and farming. Address: Colin
Godmans, Furner's Green, Uckfield, East Sussex TN22
3RR. T: (01825) 740322.   Died 14 Dec. 2001.

WRAGG, Prof. Edward Conrad; Professor of Education,
Exeter University, 1978–2003, then Emeritus (Director,
School of Education, 1978–94); b 26 June 1938; s of late
George William and of Maria Wragg; m 1960, Judith (née
King); one s two d. Educ: King Edward VII Grammar Sch.,
Sheffield; Durham Univ. (BA Hons German Cl. 1;
Postgrad. CertEd, Cl. 1); Leicester Univ. (MEd); Exeter
Univ. (PhD). Asst Master, Queen Elizabeth Grammar
Sch., Wakefield, 1960–64; Head of German, Wyggeston
Boys' Sch., Leicester, 1964–66; Lectr in Education, Exeter
Univ., 1966–73; Prof. of Educn, Nottingham Univ.,
1973–78. Pres., British Educnl Research Assoc., 1981–82.
Specialist Adviser, Parliamentary Select Cttee, 1976–77;
Chairman: School Broadcasting Council for UK,
1981–86; Educnl Broadcasting Council for UK, 1986–87;
BBC Regl Adv. Council for South and West, 1989–92,
for South, 1992–96; Member: Educnl Res. Bd, SSRC,
1974–78; Educn Sub-Cttee, UGC, 1981–89; Bd,
Qualifications and Curriculum Authty, 1997–2003; Chm.
of Judges, Nat. Teaching Awards, 2000–. Specialist Advr
in Educn, UFC, 1989–92. Chm., Univ. of the First Age,
2004. Chm., Devon Children's Trust, 2003–. Presenter of
radio and TV series and items on education, including
Chalkface (Granada), Crisis in Education (BBC), The
Education Roadshow (BBC), The Education Programme
(BBC), Pebble Mill at One (BBC), Teaching Today
(BBC). Editor, Research Papers in Education, 1986–. FCP
1988. DUniv: Open, 1989; Strathclyde, 1993; Hon. DCL
Northumbria, 1999; Hon. DLitt London, 2002; Hon.
DEd E London, 2004. Publications: Teaching Teaching,
1974; Teaching Mixed Ability Groups, 1976; Classroom
Interaction, 1976; A Handbook for School Governors,
1980; Class Management and Control, 1981; A Review of
Teacher Education, 1982; Swineshead Revisited, 1982;
Classroom Teaching Skills, 1984; Pearls from Swineshire,

1984; The Domesday Project, 1985; Education: an action guide for parents, 1986; Teacher Appraisal, 1987; The Wragged Edge, 1988; Parents and Schools, 1989; Riches from Wragg, 1990; Mad Curriculum Disease, 1991; Class Management, 1993; Questioning, 1993; Explaining, 1993; Primary Teaching Skills, 1993; The Parents' File, 1993; No, Minister!, 1993; An Introduction to Classroom Observation, 1994; Flying Boot, 1994; Effective Teaching, 1994; A Parent's Guide to the National Curriculum, 1995; The Ted Wragg Guide to Education, 1995; Teacher Appraisal Observed, 1996; (jtly) The Longman Parent's and Students' Guides, 1996; The Last Quango, 1996; Assessment and Learning, 1997; The Cubic Curriculum, 1997; Teach Your Child French, 1997; The Prince of Darkness, 1998; Improving Literacy in the Primary School, 1998; Failing Teachers?, 2000; Explaining in the Primary School, 2001; Questioning in the Primary School, 2001; Class Management in the Primary School, 2001; Assessment and Learning in the Primary School, 2001; Explaining in the Secondary School, 2001; Questioning in the Secondary School, 2001; Class Management in the Secondary School, 2001; Assessment and Learning in the Secondary School, 2001; Education, Education, Education, 2004; Performance Pay for Teachers, 2004; The Routledge Falmer Reader in Teaching and Learning, 2004; The Art and Science of Teaching and Learning, 2005; frequent contributor to Guardian, Times Educnl Supp. (regular columnist), Times Higher Educn Supp., Observer, Independent, Good Housekeeping. *Recreations:* football playing, watching and coaching; cooking, running, writing, music. *Address:* Higher Duryard House, Pennsylvania Road, Exeter EX4 5BQ. *T:* (01392) 491052.   *Died 10 Nov. 2005.*

WRAXALL, 2nd Baron *cr* 1928, of Clyst St George, co. Devon; **George Richard Lawley Gibbs**; DL; landowner, farmer and forester, since 1954; *b* 16 May 1928 (for whom Queen Mary was sponsor); *er s* of 1st Baron Wraxall, PC and Hon. Ursula Mary Lawley, OBE 1945, RRC (*d* 1979), *e d* of 6th Baron Wenlock; *S* father, 1931. *Educ:* Eton; RMA Sandhurst. Coldstream Guards, 1946–53; 2nd Lieut, 1948; Actg Captain, 1953; Captain, RARO, 1954; Lieut North Somerset Yeomanry/44 Royal Tank Regt (TA), 1958; Captain, 1962; Major, 1965; retired 1967. Chairman: N Somerset Conservative Assoc., 1970–74; Avon County Scout Council, 1976–95 (Pres., 1995–); N Somerset Yeo. Regtl Assoc., 1989– (Trustee, 1970–); President: Assoc. of Professional Foresters, 1991–95; Woodspring Cons. Assoc., 1992–97 (Life Vice-Pres., 1984, and Trustee, 1984–2000). Fellow, Woodard Schs (Western Div.), 1979–92; Mem., Exec. Cttee, Woodard Corporation, 1983–92; Chm. Governors, St Katherine's Sch., Avon, 1976–81. Mem. Council, Royal Bath and West Show, 1955–89; Patron, N Somerset Agricl Soc., 1988–. Patron of benefices: Flax Bourton, dio. Bath and Wells; Exwick, and Clyst St George, dio. Exeter. DL Avon, 1974, Somerset, 1996. *Heir:* b Hon. Sir Eustace Hubert Beilby Gibbs [*b* 3 July 1929; *m* 1957, Evelyn Veronica Scott; three *s* two *d*]. *Address:* Tyntesfield, Wraxall, Bristol BS48 1NU. *T:* (01275) 462923. *Clubs:* Royal Automobile, Cavalry and Guards.
                                Died 19 July 2001.

WRAY, Prof. Gordon Richard, FRS 1986; FREng; Eur Ing; Royal Academy of Engineering Professor in Principles of Engineering Design, Engineering Design Institute, Loughborough University of Technology, 1988–93, then Professor Emeritus; *b* 30 Jan. 1928; *s* of Joseph and Letitia Wray (*née* Jones); *m* 1954, Kathleen Senior; one *s* one *d*. *Educ:* Bolton Tech. Coll., Univ. of Manchester (BScTech 1952, MScTech 1957, PhD 1965); DSc Loughborough 1978. FTI 1963; FIMechE 1973; FREng (FEng 1980). Engineering apprentice, Bennis Combustion, Bolton, 1943; Design draughtsman, Dobson & Barlow, Bolton, 1946; Sir Walter Preston Scholar, Univ. of Manchester, 1949; Develt Engineer, Platts (Barton), 1952; Lectr in Mech. Engrg, Bolton Tech. Coll.,

1953–55; Lectr in Textile Engrg, UMIST, 1955–66; Loughborough University of Technology: Reader, 1966–70, Prof., 1970–88, and Hd, 1983–88, Dept of Mech. Engrg; Dir, Engrg Design Inst., 1988–91. Springer Vis. Prof., Univ. of California, Berkeley, 1977; Royal Soc./Royal Acad. of Engrg Vis. Lectr, Australia and NZ, 1992; Lectures: Brunel, BAAS, 1980; Thomas Hawksley Meml, IMechE, 1989; Bill Aldridge Meml, Textile Inst., Auckland, NZ, 1994. Member: DoI Chief Scientist's Requirements Bd, 1974–75; CEI/CSTI Interdisciplinary Bd, 1978–83; SEFI Cttee on Innovation, Brussels, 1980–82; Royal Soc. Working Gp on Agricl Engrg, 1981–82; SERC Applied Mechanics Cttee, 1982–85; Fellowship of Engrg Working Party on DoI Requirements Bds, 1982; SERC Working Party on Engrg Design, 1983; Royal Soc. Sectional Cttee 4 (i), 1986–89; Cttee, Engrg Profs Conf., 1986–88; Royal Soc. Mullard Award Cttee, 1986–92; Royal Soc./SERC Industrial Fellowships Panel, 1986–89; Royal Soc. Technology Activities Cttee, 1989–93; Chm., Engrg Council/Design Council Wkg Party on Attaining Competences in Engrg Design, 1989–91. First recipient of title European Engineer (Eur Ing), Paris, 1987. Mem. Council, IMechE, 1964–67 (Chm., Manip. and Mech. Handling Machinery Gp, 1969–71). Chm., Judging Panel, William Lee Quatercentenary Technology Prize, 1989. FRSA 1974. Hon. FIED 2001 (Hon. MIED 1990). IMechE Prizes: Viscount Weir, 1959; Water Arbitration, 1972; James Clayton, 1975; Warner Medal, Textile Inst., 1976; S. G. Brown Award and Medal, Royal Soc., 1978; Engrg Merit Award, ASME, 1977. Mem., East Leake Summer Wine Club. *Publications:* (contrib.) Textile Engineering Processes, ed Nissan, 1959; Modern Yarn Production from Man-made Fibres, 1960; Modern Developments in Weaving Machinery, 1961; An Introduction to the Study of Spinning, 3rd edn 1962; (contrib.) Contemporary Textile Engineering, ed Happey, 1982; State/Industry Linkages, 1993; (contrib.) Mechatronic Design in Textile Engineering, ed Acar, 1995; numerous papers to learned jls. *Recreations:* fell-walking, photography, steam traction engines, theatre, music, gardening, DIY.
                                Died 17 Aug. 2005.

WRIGHT, Beatrice Frederika, (Lady Wright), MBE 1996; Vice-President, Royal National Institute for the Deaf, since 1978; Co-Founder, Hearing Dogs for Deaf People, 1982 (President, 1983–88; Life Vice President, 2001); *b* New Haven, Conn, 17 June 1910; *d* of Mr and Mrs F. Roland Clough; *m* 1st, 1932, John Rankin Rathbone (Flight Lieut, RAFVR, MP, killed in action, 1940); one *d* (one *s* decd); 2nd, 1942, Paul Hervé Giraud Wright (later Sir Paul Wright, KCMG, OBE); one *d*. *Educ:* Ethel Walker Sch., Simsbury, Conn; Radcliffe Coll., Oxford. MP (U) Bodmin Div. of Cornwall, 1941–45. *Address:* 62 Westminster Gardens, Marsham Street, SW1P 4JG.   *Died 17 March 2003.*

WRIGHT, Sir Denis (Arthur Hepworth), GCMG 1971 (KCMG 1961; CMG 1954); HM Diplomatic Service, retired; *b* 23 March 1911; *s* of late A. E. Wright, Hong Kong, and Margery Hepworth Chapman, York; *m* 1939, Iona Craig, Bolney, Sussex; no *c*. *Educ:* Brentwood School; St Edmund Hall, Oxford (Hon. Fellow 1972). Asst Advertising Manager to Gallaher & Co. (Tobacco Manufacturers), 1935–39. Employed from outbreak of war as Vice-Consul on economic warfare work at HM Consulate at Constantza (Roumania), 1939–41. Vice-Consul-in-charge of HM Consulate at Trebizond (Turkey), 1941–43; Acting-Consul-in-charge of HM Consulate, Mersin (Turkey), 1943–45; First Secretary (Commercial) to HM Embassy, Belgrade, 1946–48; Superintending Trade Consul at Chicago for Middle-Western Region of USA, 1949–51; Head of Economic Relations Department in the Foreign Office, 1951–53; appointed Chargé d'Affaires, Tehran, on resumption of diplomatic relations with Persia, Dec. 1953; Counsellor, HM Embassy, Tehran, 1954–55; Asst Under-Sec., FO,

1955–59; Ambassador to Ethiopia, 1959–62; Asst Under-Sec., FO, 1962; Ambassador to Iran, 1963–71. Dir, Shell Transport & Trading Co., Standard Chartered Bank, and Mitchell Cotts Gp, 1971–81. Governor, Oversea Service, Farnham Castle, 1972–86; Mem. Council, British Inst. of Persian Studies, 1973– (Pres., 1978–87); Pres., Iran Soc., 1989–95 (Chm., 1976–79). Hon. Fellow St Antony's Coll., Oxford, 1976. Sir Percy Sykes Meml Medal, RSAA, 1990. *Publications:* Persia (with James Morris and Roger Wood), 1969; The English Amongst the Persians, 1977; The Persians Amongst the English, 1985; contrib. Encycl. Iranica, Oxford DNB, Jl British Inst. of Persian Studies and other jls. *Address:* Duck Bottom, 15 Flint Street, Haddenham, Aylesbury, Bucks HP17 8AL. *Club:* Travellers. *Died 18 May 2005.*

WRIGHT, Desmond Garforth; QC 1974; *b* 13 July 1923; *s* of late Arthur Victor Wright and Doris Greensill; *m* 1952, Elizabeth Anna Bacon; one *s* one *d*. *Educ:* Giggleswick; Royal Naval Coll., Greenwich; Worcester Coll., Oxford (MA). Served War of 1939–45: RNVR, 1942–46; Staff of Flag Officer Malaya Forward Area, 1946. Called to Bar, Lincoln's Inn, 1950 (Cholmondley Scholar; Bencher, 1981). *Publication:* Wright on Walls, 1954. *Recreations:* cartology, conversation. *Address:* 1 Atkin Building, Gray's Inn, WC1R 5BQ. *T:* (020) 7404 0102.
Died 4 Aug. 2005.

WRIGHT, Sir Edward (Maitland), Kt 1977; DPhil; FRSE; Research Fellow, University of Aberdeen, 1976–83; *b* 13 Feb. 1906; *s* of M. T. Wright, Farnley, Leeds; *m* 1934, Elizabeth Phyllis (*d* 1987), *d* of H. P. Harris, Bryn Mally Hall, N Wales; one *s*. *Educ:* Jesus Coll., Oxford (Schol., 1926–30; Hon. Fellow, 1963); Christ Church, Oxford (Sen. Schol., 1930–33); MA Oxon, DPhil Oxon 1932; Univ. of Göttingen. Master, Chard School, Somerset, 1923–26; Lecturer: King's College, London, 1932–33; Christ Church, Oxford, 1933–35; Flt Lieut, RAFVR, 1941–43; Principal Scientific Officer, Air Ministry, 1943–45; Prof. of Mathematics, 1935–62, Vice-Principal, 1961–62, Principal and Vice-Chancellor, 1962–76, Univ. of Aberdeen. Member: Anderson Cttee on Grants to Students, 1958–60; Hale Cttee on Univ. Teaching Methods, 1961–64; Scottish Universities Entrance Bd, 1948–62 (Chm. 1955–62); Royal Commission on Medical Education, 1965–67. Vice-Pres., RUSI, 1969–72. Hon. Editor: Zentralblatt Math., 1950–; Jl Graph Theory, 1983–. Hon. LLD: St Andrews, 1963; Pennsylvania, 1975; Aberdeen, 1978; Hon. DSc Strathclyde, 1974. Macdougall-Brisbane Prize, RSE, 1952; Sen. Berwick Prize, London Math. Soc., 1978. Gold Medal, Order of Polonia Restituta (Poland), 1978. *Publications:* Introduction to the Theory of Numbers (with Professor G. H. Hardy), 1938, 5th edn 1979; 170 mathematical papers in scientific journals. *Club:* Caledonian. *Died 2 Feb. 2005.*

WRIGHT, Prof. Esmond; Emeritus Professor of American History, University of London, since 1983; Vice-President, Automobile Association, since 1985 (Vice-Chairman and Hon. Treasurer, 1971–85; Chairman, Drive Publications, 1980–85); *b* 5 Nov. 1915; *s* of Esmond Wright and Isabella Gray; *m* 1945, Olive Adamson. *Educ:* Univ. of Durham (Open Entrance Schol.); Univ. of Virginia (Commonwealth Fund Fellow). War Service, 1940–46, demob. as Lt-Col, 1946. Glasgow Univ., 1946–67, Prof. of Modern History, 1957–67. MP (C) Glasgow, Pollok, March 1967–1970; Dir, Inst. of US Studies and Prof. of American History, Univ. of London, 1971–83; Principal, Swinton Cons. Coll., 1972–76. Chm., Border TV, 1981–85 (Vice-Chm., 1976–81). Founder-Mem., British Assoc. for American Studies (Chm., 1965–68). Mem., Marshall Aid Commemoration Commn, 1966–83; Vice-Chm., British Road Fedn, 1981–85. For. Mem., Amer. Philos. Soc., 1990–. FRHistS; FRSA (Franklin Medal, 1988). Hon. LHD Pennsylvania, 1983; Hon. DLitt New Brunswick, 1984.

Publications: A Short History of Our Own Times, 1951; George Washington and the American Revolution, 1957; The World Today, 1961, 4th edn 1978; Fabric of Freedom, 1961, 2nd edn 1978; (ed) Illustrated World History, 1964; Benjamin Franklin and American Independence, 1966; (ed) Causes and Consequences of the American Revolution, 1966; (ed) American Themes, 1967; American Profiles, 1967; (ed) Benjamin Franklin, a profile, 1970; A Time for Courage, 1971; A Tug of Loyalties, 1974; Red, White and True Blue, 1976; (with A. G. Nicolson) Europe Today, 1979; The Great Little Madison (British Academy Lecture), 1981; The Fire of Liberty, 1983; (ed) History of the World: Pre-History to Renaissance, 1985; The Last Five Hundred Years, 1986; Franklin of Philadelphia, 1986; Franklin: his life as he wrote it, 1989; The Sayings of Benjamin Franklin, 1995; The Search for Liberty, 1995; An Empire for Liberty, 1995; The American Dream, 1995; articles in periodicals. *Address:* Radleigh House, Masham, N Yorks HG4 4EF. *Club:* Athenæum. *Died 9 Aug. 2003.*

WRIGHT, Georg Henrik von, Hon. GCVO 1976; Research Professor in the Academy of Finland, 1961–86; *b* Helsingfors, 14 June 1916; *s* of Tor von Wright and Ragni Elisabeth Alfthan; *m* 1941, Maria Elisabeth von Troil, Hon. CVO; one *s* one *d*. *Educ:* Svenska Normallyceum, Helsingfors; Helsingfors Univ. MA. Helsingfors University: Lectr and Acting Prof. of Philosophy, 1943–46; Prof. of Philosophy, 1946–61 (also in Univ. of Cambridge, 1948–51); Prof. at Large, Cornell Univ., 1965–77; Chancellor, Abo Acad., 1968–77. Visiting Professor: Cornell Univ., 1954 and 1958; UCLA, 1963; Univ. Pittsburg, 1966; Univ. Karlsruhe, 1975; Univ. Leipzig, 1994–95; Lectures: Shearman Meml, UCL, 1956; Gifford, Univ. of St Andrews, 1959–60; Tarner, Trinity Coll., Cambridge, 1969; Woodbridge, Columbia Univ., 1972; Nellie Wallace, Univ. of Oxford, 1978; Tanner, Helsingfors Univ., 1984. President: Internat. Union of History and Philosophy of Science, 1963–65; Acad. of Finland, 1968–69; Philos. Soc. of Finland, 1962–73; Inst. Internat. de Philosophie, 1975–78. Fellow: Finnish Soc. of Scis (Pres., 1966–67, Hon. Fellow 1978); New Soc. of Letters, Lund; Royal Swedish Acad. of Scis; Royal Soc. of Letters, Lund; British Acad.; Royal Swedish Acad. of Letters, History and Antiquities; Finnish Acad. of Scis; Royal Danish Acad. of Scis and Letters; Royal Acad. of Arts and Scis, Uppsala; Norwegian Acad. of Science and Letters; Royal Acad. of Science, Trondheim; European Acad. of Arts, Scis and Humanities; World Acad. of Arts and Scis; Serbian Acad. of Scis and Arts; Hon. Foreign Mem., Amer. Acad. of Arts and Scis. Sometime Fellow, Trinity College, Cambridge, Hon. Fellow 1983. Hon. degrees: Helsingfors (doctor of pol. sci.); Liverpool (DLitt); doctor of philosophy: Lund; Bologna; Abo Acad.; Tromsø; Leipzig; Innsbruck; Turku (doctor of philosophy; doctor of law); Saint Olaf Coll., Northfield, Minn. (doctor of humane letters); Tampere (doctor of soc. sci.); Stockholm (doctor of law); Buenos Aires; Salta. Wilhuri Foundn Internat. Prize, 1976; Alexander von Humboldt Foundn Forschungspreis, 1986; Gold Medal, Swedish Acad., 1986; Selma Lagerlöf Foundn Literature Prize, 1993; Tage Danielsson Humanist Prize, Linköping, 1998. *Publications:* The Logical Problem of Induction, 1941, rev. edn 1957; Den logiska Empirismen, 1943; Über Wahrscheinlichkeit, 1945; A Treatise on Induction and Probability, 1951; An Essay in Modal Logic, 1951; Logical Studies, 1957; The Varieties of Goodness, 1963; The Logic of Preference, 1963; Norm and Action, 1963; An Essay in Deontic Logic, 1968; Time, Change, and Contradiction, 1969; Explanation and Understanding, 1971; Causality and Determinism, 1974; Freedom and Determination, 1980; Wittgenstein, 1982; Philosophical Papers I-III, 1983–84; Vetenskapen och förnuftet, 1986; (contrib.) The Philosophy of Georg Henrik von Wright, 1989; The Tree of Knowledge, 1993; Normen, Werte und Handlungen, 1994; Six Essays in Philosophical Logic, 1996; In the Shadow of Descartes, 1998; Mitt Liv (autobiog.), 2001. *Address:* 4 Skepparegatan, Helsingfors, Finland. *Died 16 June 2003.*

WRIGHT, Prof. H(enry) Myles, RIBA; RTPI; Lever Professor of Civic Design, University of Liverpool, 1954–75, then Emeritus Professor; University Planning Consultant, 1957–77; *b* 9 June 1908; *s* of H. T. Wright, Gosforth, Newcastle upon Tyne; *m* 1939, Catharine Noble (*d* 1981), *y d* of Very Rev. H. N. Craig, Dean of Kildare; two *d*. *Educ:* Fettes College, Edinburgh (Foundationer); King's College, Newcastle upon Tyne; St John's College, Cambridge. Assistant in various private offices, 1930–35; Asst Editor, The Architects' Journal, and in private practice, 1935–40; Partner in firm of Sir William Holford, 1948–54; principally engaged on planning proposals for Cambridge and Corby New Town. Member British Caribbean Federal Capital Commn, 1956. *Publications:* The Planner's Notebook, 1948; Cambridge Planning Proposals, 1950, and Corby New Town (with Lord Holford), 1952; Land Use in an Urban Environment (Editor and contributor), 1961; The Dublin Region: Preliminary and Final Reports, 1965 and 1967; Lord Leverhulme's Unknown Venture, 1982; other technical publications. *Recreations:* gardening, reading. *Address:* 9 Pine Hey, Neston, S Wirral, Cheshire CH64 3TJ.
Died 24 Sept. 2005.

WRIGHT, Joseph, OBE 1978; FRPharmS; FCIS; Secretary (Chief Executive), National Pharmaceutical Association (formerly National Pharmaceutical Union), 1961–81; *b* 7 Jan. 1917; *s* of late Thomas Wright and Margaret (*née* Cardwell); *m* 1942, Margaretta May Hart Talbot, BA, MRPharmS; two *s* two *d*. *Educ:* Blackpool Boys' Grammar Sch.; Chelsea Polytechnic (Dip., Chem. and Druggist and PhC examinations). Called to the Bar, Middle Temple, 1952. In retail pharmacy, 1933–47, incl. 4 years apprenticeship in Blackpool, with subseq. experience in London. Served war, RAF, commnd wireless navigator, Coastal Comd. On staff, Pharm. Section, Min. of Health, 1947–48; joined NPU, 1948: Asst Sec., 1949, Dep. Sec., 1955, Sec. and Manager, 1961; Dir, NPA Gp, 1971 (Gp comprises Nat. Pharm. Assoc. Ltd, Chemists' Def. Assoc. Ltd, Pharmacy Mutual Insce Co. Ltd, Pharm. and Gen. Prov. Soc., NPU Ltd (t/a NPA Sces), NPU Holdings Ltd): Director: NPU Holdings Ltd, 1965–81; NPU Ltd, 1971–81; Indep. Chemists Marketing Ltd, 1972–81; NPU Marketing Ltd, 1966–81; Member: Standing Pharm. Adv. Cttee, 1964–82; Poisons Bd, 1963–84; Panel of Fellows of Pharm. Soc., 1965–82; Gen. Practice Sub-Cttee, PSGB, 1963–81; Bd, Nat. Chamber of Trade, 1973–82; Trade & Professional Alliance, 1975–81; Legislation & Taxation Cttee, Nat. Ch. of Trade, 1964–81; Adviser to Pharm. Services Negotiating Cttee, 1977–81. Hon. Life Mem., S African Retail Chem. and Druggists Assoc., 1974. Freeman, City of London; Liveryman, Worshipful Soc. of Apoth. of London, 1978–. Distinguished Service Award, Pharmacy Guild of Aust., 1978; Charter Gold Medal of Pharmaceutical Soc. of GB, 1980. *Recreations:* reading, travel and—intermittently—grandchildren. *Address:* 116 Wynchgate, Winchmore Hill, N21 1QU. *T:* (020) 8886 1645. *Died 6 July 2002.*

WRIGHT, Kenneth Campbell, CMG 1987; OBE 1973; PhD; HM Diplomatic Service, retired; Political Affairs Adviser, Saferworld Foundation, since 1992; with Research Department, The Economist, since 1992; *b* 31 May 1932; *s* of James Edwin Wright and Eva Rebecca Wright (*née* Sayers); *m* 1958, Diana Yolande Binnie; one *s* two *d*. *Educ:* George Heriot's Sch., Edinburgh; Univ. of Edinburgh (MA 1st Cl. Hons Mod Langs, PhD); Univ. of Paris (LèsL). Short-service commission, RAF, 1957–60. Lecturer, Inst. Politique Congolais and Lovanium Univ., Congo (Zaire), 1960–63; Lectr, later Sen. Lectr, Dept of Modern Languages, Univ. of Ghana, 1963–65; entered HM Diplomatic Service, 1965; FO, 1965–68; First Sec., Bonn, 1968–72; FCO, 1972–75; First Sec., later Counsellor, UK Permanent Representation to the European Communities, Brussels, 1975–79; FCO, 1979–82; Counsellor, Paris, 1982–85; Asst Under-Sec. of State, FCO, 1985–89. Dir, BIEC, subseq. BI, 1989–91. *Recreations:* people, places, books. *Address:* Leven House, 2 The Meadway, Heath Lane, SE3 0UP. *T:* (020) 8852 3650. *Clubs:* Athenæum, Special Forces.
Died 18 Nov. 2004.

WRIGHT, Lance Armitage, RIBA; Associate Director, International Committee of Architectural Critics, since 1978; *b* 25 Dec. 1915; *s* of Edmund Lancelot Wright and Elizabeth Helen (*née* Bonser); *m* 1942, Susan Melville Foster; two *s* two *d*. *Educ:* Haileybury; UCL; Architectural Assoc. Sch. Architect in private practice, 1946–73; Registrar, Royal West of England Academy Sch. of Architecture, 1950–53; Technical Ed., The Architects Jl, 1954; Ed., The Architectural Review, 1973–80. Exhibn of drawings, Hot Bath Gall., Bath, 1995. Chevalier, Order of St Gregory the Great, 1971. *Publication:* (with D. A. C. A. Boyne) Architects Working Details, vols 4–15, 1953–69. *Address:* The White House, Summerside, Buckland, near Faringdon, Oxon, OX7 8RA. *Died 31 July 2003.*

WRIGHT, Sir Paul (Hervé Giraud), KCMG 1975 (CMG 1960); OBE 1952; HM Diplomatic Service, retired; Chairman: Irvin Great Britain Ltd, 1979–88; British American Arts Association, 1983–88; Member Council, Forte plc (formerly Trusthouse Forte), 1987–97; *b* 12 May 1915; *o s* of late Richard Hervé Giraud Wright; *m* 1942, Beatrice Frederika Rathbone, MBE (*d* 2003), widow of Flt-Lt J. R. Rathbone, MP; one *d*. *Educ:* Westminster Sch. (Hon. Fellow, 1992). Employed by John Lewis Partnership Ltd, 1933–39. Served HM Forces, War of 1939–45; Major, KRRC; HQ 21 Army Group, 1944–45 (despatches). Contested (L) NE Bethnal Green, 1945. Asst Dir, Public Relations, National Coal Bd, 1946–48; Dir, Public Relations, Festival of Britain, 1948–51. HM Foreign Service: Paris and New York, 1951–54; Foreign Office, 1954–56; The Hague, 1956–57; Head of Information, Policy Dept in FO, 1957–60; Cairo, 1960–61; UK Delegn to N Atlantic Council, 1961–64; Minister (Information), Washington, 1965–68, and Dir-Gen., British Inf. Services, NY, 1964–68; Ambassador to Congo (Kinshasa) and to Republic of Burundi, 1969–71; Ambassador to the Lebanon, 1971–75. Special Rep. of Sec. of State for Foreign and Commonwealth Affairs, 1975–78. Chairman: British Lebanese Assoc., 1987–90; Assoc. of Papal Orders in GB, 1999–. Hon. Sec. Gen., London Celebrations Cttee for Queen's Silver Jubilee, 1977; Vice-Chm., The American Fest., 1985; Pres., Elizabethan Club, 1988–95; Governor, Westminster Cathedral Choir School, 1981–2000 (Chm., 1993–2000); Chm., Westminster Sch. Develt Council, 1994–97. Trustee, Trusthouse Charitable Foundn, 1996–2000; Life Vice-Pres., Hearing Dogs for Deaf People, 2001. Hon. RCM 1990. GCSG 2000 (KCSG 1996). Kt of the Order of the Cedar of Lebanon, 1990. *Publication:* A Brittle Glory (autobiog.), 1986. *Address:* 62 Westminster Gardens, Marsham Street, SW1P 4JG. *Club:* Garrick.
Died 10 June 2005.

WRIGHT, Peter, FRCP, FRCS, FRCOphth; Consultant Ophthalmic Surgeon, Moorfields Eye Hospital, 1973–94, Consulting Ophthalmic Surgeon, 1994; President, Royal College of Ophthalmologists, 1991–94; *b* 7 Sept. 1932; *s* of late William Victor Wright and Ada Amelie (*née* Craze); *m* 1960, Elaine Catherine Donoghue (marr. diss. 1992); two *d* (one *s* decd). *Educ:* St Clement Danes; KCL; KCH (MB BS 1955; AKC 1955). MRCS, LRCP 1955; FRCS 1964; DO 1959; FCOphth 1988 (Hon. FRCOphth 1998); FRCP 1994. Resident appts, KCH and Guy's Hosp., 1955–57; ophthalmic specialist, RAF Med. Br., 1957–59; Lectr in Anatomy and Physiology, Guy's Hosp. Med. Sch., 1959–61; House Surgeon and Sen. Resident, Moorfields Eye Hosp., 1961–65; Lectr in Physiology, Inst. of Ophthalmology, 1965–68; Consultant Ophthalmic Surgeon: KCH, 1966–78; Sydenham Children's Hosp.,

1967–73; Clinical Sub-Dean, Inst. Ophthalmology, 1980–86; Surgical Tutor, Moorfields Eye Hosp., 1981–86; Cons. Advr in Ophthalmology, DoH, 1988–. Cons. Advr, Royal Soc. of Musicians, 1986–. Examiner: DO, 1967–73; Ophthalmic Nursing Bd, 1973–78 (Mem., 1974–87); Mem., Court of Examnrs, RCS, 1977–83. Ophthalmic Section, Royal Society of Medicine: Mem. Council and Vice-Pres., 1968–75; Pres., 1988–90; Ophthalmological Society of UK: Sec., 1968–70; Mem. Council, 1970–74; Vice-Pres., 1985–87; Pres., 1987–88; Southern Ophthalmic Society: Mem. Council, 1970–74; Pres., 1984–85; Sen. Vice-Pres., Coll. of Ophthalmologists, 1988–92; Mem. Council, RCS, 1992–; Trustee and Mem. Council, Assoc. for Eye Res., 1966– (Treas. 1966–82). Lectures: Charnwood, 1977; Doyne (and Medal), 1986; Mauerberger Meml, 1987. Hon. Mem., NZ Ophthalmol Soc.; Mem., French and German Ophthalmol Socs; Internat. Mem., Amer. Acad. Ophthal. Freeman, City of London; Liveryman, Soc. of Apothecaries. *Publications:* chapters in: Clinical Aspects of Immunology, 1981; Clinical Ophthalmology, 1987; Relationships in Dermatology, 1988; contribs on external eye disease and immunology to med. jls. *Recreations:* playing the piano, gardening. *Address:* Southbrook Court, Southbrook Lane, Bovey Tracey, Devon TQ13 9NB.

Died 26 May 2003.

WRIGHT, Rt Rev. Roderick; Bishop (RC) of Argyll and the Isles, 1991–96; *b* 28 June 1940; *m* 1998, Kathleen McPhee. *Educ:* St Mary's Coll., Blairs, Grampian; St Peter's Coll., Cardross, Strathclyde. Ordained 1964; Assistant Priest: St Laurence's, Drumchapel, 1964–66; St Jude's, Barlanark, 1966–69; Procurator, Blairs Coll., Grampian, 1969–74; Assistant Priest: Dunoon, Argyll, 1974–76; Fort William, 1976–80; Parish Priest: Ardkenneth, South Uist, 1980–87; St Anne's Corpach and St John the Evangelist, Caol, 1987–91. Mem., Cttee on local and regl ecumenism of Action of Churches Together in Scotland. *Publication:* Feet of Clay (autobiog.), 1999.

Died 23 May 2005.

WU Shu-Chih, Hon. Alex, CBE 1983 (OBE 1973); JP; company director; Chairman, Fidelity Management Ltd, since 1965; Vice-Chairman, Dai Nippon Printing Co. (HK) Ltd, 1964–2003; *b* 14 Sept. 1920; *s* of Wu Chao-Ming and Yeh Huei-Cheng; *m* 1946; three *s* three *d*. *Educ:* National South West Associated Univ., Kunming, China. Director: Hong Kong Ferry Co. Ltd, 1976–; Hong Kong Aircraft Engineering Co. Ltd, 1983–; Pearson China (formerly Longman Group (Far East) Ltd, subseq. Longman China Ltd), 1984–; Nat. Electronics (Consolidated) Ltd, 1984–; K. Wah Stones (Holdings) Ltd, 1986–; Hung Hing Printing Group Ltd, 1992–; Dransfield Hldgs Ltd, 1993–2000; Paliburg Hldgs Ltd, 1995–; Alpha General (Hldgs) Ltd, 1997–; Consultant: Austdairy Ltd, 1987– (Dir, 1983–87); China Daily, 1988–; Proprietor, Sino-Scottish Trading Co., 1960–2000; Publisher, Sino-American Publishing Co., 1960–. Chairman: Supplementary Med. Professions Council, 1981–89; Printing Industry Trng Bd, 1967–89; Council for the Performing Arts, 1982–89; Council, Hongkong Acad. for Performing, 1982–86; Vice-Chairman: Hong Kong Trade Develt Council, 1974–83; Vocational Trng Council, 1982–89; Nominating Cttee, Stock Exchange of Hong Kong Ltd, 1992– (Chm., 1989–91; Vice-Chm., 1991–92); Member: Hong Kong Heart Foundn Ltd, 1975–; Aviation Adv. Bd, 1980–89; Med. Sub-Cttee, Univ. and Polytechnic Grants Cttee, 1983–89; Hong Kong Indust. Estates Corp., 1984–89; Hong Kong Inst. for Promotion of Chinese Culture, 1985–; Securities and Futures Commn Adv. Cttee, 1993–; Hong Kong Affairs Advrs, 1995–; Selection Cttee for first Govt of HKSAR, 1996–. Mem., Bd of Governors, Hong Kong Philharmonic Soc. Ltd, 1978–. Pres., Hongkong Jun. Chamber of Commerce, 1960; Hon. Life Pres., Hong Kong Printers Assoc., 1983–. MLC Hong Kong, 1975–85. JP Hong Kong, 1973. Fellow, Hong Kong Management Assoc.,

1983; FCMI (FBIM 1979); FInstD 1980; FIP3 (FIOP 1984). Hon. LLD Hong Kong, 1992. *Recreations:* classical music, Western and Peking opera, tennis, soccer, swimming, contract bridge. *Address:* 14/F, Hart House, 12–14 Hart Avenue, Tsimshatsui, Kowloon, Hong Kong. *T:* 23668789. *Clubs:* Hong Kong, Rotary of Hong Kong; Hong Kong Jockey; Hong Kong Golf.

Died 10 Jan. 2005.

WYATT, Gavin Edward, CMG 1965; Director of Projects Department, Europe, Middle East and North Africa Region, World Bank, 1975–76 (Assistant Director, 1973–75); *b* 12 Jan. 1914; *s* of Edward Adolphus Wyatt and Blanche M. Muller; *m* 1950, Mary Mackinnon, *d* of John Macdonald, Oban; one *s* one *d*. *Educ:* Newton Abbot Grammar Sch. CEng, FIEE 1951; FIMechE 1962. Engineer and Manager, East African Power & Lighting Co. Ltd, Tanganyika and Kenya, 1939–57; Chief Exec. Officer and General Manager, Electricity Corp. of Nigeria, 1957–62; Man. Dir, East Africa Power & Lighting Co. Ltd, 1962–64; World Bank, 1965–76. *Recreations:* gardening, viticulture, oenology. *Address:* Holne Bridge Lodge, Ashburton, South Devon TQ13 7NW.

Died 17 July 2001.

WYLDBORE-SMITH, Maj.-Gen. Sir (Francis) Brian, Kt 1980; CB 1965; DSO 1943; OBE 1944; General Officer Commanding, 44th Division (TA) and Home Counties District, 1965–68; Director, Conservative Board of Finance, 1970–92; *b* 10 July 1913; *s* of Rev. W. R. Wyldbore-Smith and Mrs D. Wyldbore-Smith; *m* 1944, Hon. Molly Angela Cayzer (*d* 2001), *d* of 1st Baron Rotherwick; three *d* (and one *s* one *d* decd). *Educ:* Wellington Coll.; RMA, Woolwich. Served Middle East, Italy, France and Germany, 1941–45; Military Asst to CIGS, 1947–49; GSO1, 7 Armoured Div., 1951–53; Comd 15/19 King's Royal Hussars, 1954–56; IDC 1959; BGS Combat Development, 1959–62; Chief of Staff to Commander-in-Chief, Far East Command, 1962–64. Col, 15/19 Hussars, 1970–77. *Recreations:* hunting, shooting. *Address:* Grantham House, Grantham, Lincs NG31 6SS. *T:* (01476) 564705. *Club:* Buck's. *Died 6 Dec. 2005.*

WYLIE, Rt Hon. Lord; Norman Russell Wylie; PC 1970; VRD 1961; a Senator of the College of Justice in Scotland, 1974–90; *b* 26 Oct. 1923; *o s* of late William Galloway Wylie and Mrs Nellie Smart Wylie (*née* Russell), Elderslie, Renfrewshire; *m* 1963, Gillian Mary, *yr d* of late Dr R. E. Verney, Edinburgh; three *s*. *Educ:* Paisley Grammar Sch.; St Edmund Hall, Oxford (BA 1948; Hon. Fellow, 1975); Univ. of Glasgow (LLB 1951); Univ. of Edinburgh. Served in Fleet Air Arm, 1942–46; subseq. RNR; Lt-Comdr, 1954. Admitted to Faculty of Advocates, 1952; QC (Scot.) 1964. Appointed Counsel to Air Ministry in Scotland, 1956; Advocate-Depute, 1959; Solicitor-General for Scotland, April-Oct. 1964. MP (C) Pentlands Div., Edinburgh, Oct. 1964-Feb. 1974; Lord Advocate, 1970–74. Mem., Parole Bd for Scotland, 1991–93. Justice of Appeal, Republic of Botswana, 1994–96. Trustee, Carnegie Trust for Univs of Scotland, 1976–96; Chm., Scottish Nat. Cttee, English-Speaking Union of the Commonwealth, 1978–84. *Address:* 30 Lauder Road, Edinburgh EH9 2JF. *T:* (0131) 667 8377. *Club:* New (Edinburgh). *Died 7 Sept. 2005.*

WYLIE, Rt Hon. Norman Russell; *see* Wylie, Rt Hon. Lord.

WYNFORD, 8th Baron *cr* 1829; **Robert Samuel Best,** MBE 1953; DL; Lt-Col Royal Welch Fusiliers; *b* 5 Jan. 1917; *e s* of 7th Baron Wynford and Evelyn (*d* 1929), *d* of Maj.-Gen. Sir Edward S. May, KCB, CMG; *S* father, 1943; *m* 1941, Anne Daphne Mametz, *d* of Maj.-Gen. J. R. Minshull Ford, CB, DSO, MC; one *s* two *d*. *Educ:* Eton; RMC, Sandhurst. 2nd Lieut, RWF, 1937; served BEF; GHQ Home Forces; North Africa (Croix de Guerre); Egypt; Italy; wounded, 1944; Instructor, Staff College, 1945–46; War Office, 1947–49; OC Depot,

RWF, 1955–57; Instructor Joint Service Staff Coll., 1957–60; RARO 1960. DL Dorset, 1970. *Heir: s* Hon. John Philip Robert Best [*b* 23 Nov. 1950; *m* 1981, Fenella Christian Mary, *o d* of Arthur Reginald Danks; one *s* one *d*]. *Club:* Army and Navy.   *Died 21 Jan. 2002.*

WYNN, Arthur Henry Ashford; Adviser on Standards, Department of Trade and Industry (formerly Ministry of Technology), 1965–71; *b* 22 Jan. 1910; *s* of late Prof. William Henry Wynn, MD, MSc and Florence, *d* of G. B. Ashford; *m* 1938, Margaret Patricia Moxon; three *s* one *d. Educ:* Oundle Sch.; Trinity Coll., Cambridge (Entrance Scholar, Nat. Science and Mathematics; MA). Barrister-at-Law, Lincoln's Inn, 1939. Director of Safety in Mines Research Establishment, Ministry of Fuel and Power, 1948–55; Scientific Member of National Coal Board, 1955–65; Member: Advisory Council on Research and Development, Ministry of Power, 1955–65; Safety in Mines Research Advisory Board, 1950–65; Exec. Cttee, British Standards Institution, 1966–71; Advisory Council on Calibration and Measurement, 1967–71; Chairman: Standing Joint Cttee on Metrication, 1966–69; Adv. Cttee on Legal Units of Measurement, 1969–71. *Publications:* (with Margaret Wynn): The Protection of Maternity and Infancy in Finland, 1974; The Right of Every Child to Health Care in France, 1974; Nutrition Counselling in Canada, 1975; Prevention of Handicap of Perinatal Origin in France, 1976; Prevention of Preterm Birth, 1977; Prevention of Handicap and Health of Women, 1979; Prevention of Handicap of Early Pregnancy Origin, 1981; Lead and Human Reproduction, 1982; The Case for Preconception Care, 1991. *Address:* 9 View Road, N6 4DJ. *T:* (020) 8348 1470.   *Died 23 Sept. 2001.*

X

XENAKIS, Iannis; composer, architect, civil engineer; Professor, Université de Paris I (Panthéon-Sorbonne), 1973–89, then Emeritus; *b* 29 May 1922; *s* of Clearchos Xenakis and Fotini Pavlou; *m* 1953, Françoise Gargouïl; one *d*. *Educ:* Athens Polytechnic Inst.; Ecole Normale de Musique, Paris; Gravesano; Paris Conservatoire; studied with Milhaud, Scherchen, Messiaen; studied engineering, Athens. DèsL Sorbonne, 1976. Fought in Greek Resistance, war of 1939–45, sentenced to death; exile, France, 1947; with Le Corbusier as engineer and architect, 1947–60. Numerous musical compositions through introd. of mass concept of music, stochastic music, symbolic music, through probability calculus and set theory, including instrumental, electro-acoustic and computerized works; designer of pavilions and spectacles. Numerous academic appts, including Associate Prof., Indiana Univ., Bloomington, USA, 1967–72, and Gresham Prof. of Music, 1975. Member: Centre Nat. de la Recherche Scientifique; Acad. des Beaux-Arts, 1983; Akademie der Künste, Berlin and Munich, 1983; For. Mem., Swedish Royal Acad. of Music, 1989; Hon. Member: Amer. Acad. of Arts and Letters, 1975; Scottish Soc. of Composers, 1987. Hon. DMus: Edinburgh, 1989; Glasgow, 1990; Bath, 1996. Maurice Ravel Gold Medal, 1974; Beethoven Prize, FRG, 1977; Kyoto Prize, Inamuri Foundn, 1997; Polar Prize, Stockholm, 1999. Officier: Ordre National du Mérite (France), 1985; Légion d'Honneur (France), 1991 (Chevalier, 1982); Commandeur, Ordre des Arts et des Lettres (France), 1991 (Officier, 1981). *Compositions included: orchestral:* Métastasis, 1954; Pithoprakta, 1956; Stratégie, 1962; Terretektorh, 1966; Nomos Gamma, 1968; Kraanerg (ballet score), 1969; Antikhthon 1971; Erikhthon (pno and orch.), 1974; Noomena, 1974; Jonchaies, 1977; Lichens, 1984; Alax, 1985; Keqrops (pno and orch.), 1986; Horos, 1986; Ata, 1987; Kyania, 1990; Dox-Orkh (violin and orch.), 1991; Roäi, 1991; Krinoïdi, 1991; Troorkh, 1991; Dämmerschein, 1994; Koïranoï, 1994; Ioolkos, 1995; Voile, 1995; Sea-Change, 1997; *vocal and orchestral:* Cendrées, 1973; Anemoessa, 1979; Aïs, 1979; Nekuïa, 1981; Kassandra: Oresteïa II, 1987; *choral:* Oresteïa, 1966; Medea, 1967; Pour la Paix, 1981; *instrumental ensemble:* Atrées, 1960; Eonta, 1963; N'Shima, 1975; Tetras, 1983; Thallein, 1984; Jalons, 1986; Waarg, 1988; Tetora, 1990; Plekto, 1993; Ergma, 1994; Kaï, 1995; Kuïlenn, 1995; Ittidra, 1996; O-Mega, 1997; *solo instrumental:* Nomos Alpha ('cello), 1966; Persephassa (perc.), 1969; Gmeeoorh (organ), 1974; Psappha, 1975; Khoaï (hpchd), 1976; Pléïades (perc.), 1978; Komboï (hpchd and perc.), 1981; Naama (hpchd), 1984; *electro-acoustic:* Bohor, 1962; Hibiki Hana Ma, 1970; Persepolis, 1971; Polytope de Cluny, 1972; La Légende d'Eer, 1977; Voyage Absolu des Unari vers Andromède, 1989; Gendy 3, 1991; S.709, 1994. *Publications:* Musiques Formelles, 1963 (Formalized Music, 1970, rev. and enlarged edn, 1991); Musique Architecture, 1970; Xenakis, les Polytopes, 1975; Arts and Sciences: Alloys, 1979; Kéléütha, 1994. *Address:* 9 rue Chaptal, 75009 Paris, France.　　　　　　*Died 4 Feb. 2001.*

Y

YARNOLD, Rev. Edward John, SJ; DD; Tutor in Theology, Campion Hall, Oxford, since 1964 (Master, 1965–72; Senior Tutor, 1972–74); *b* 14 Jan. 1926; *s* of Edward Cabré Yarnold and Agnes (*née* Deakin). *Educ:* St Michael's Coll., Leeds; Campion Hall, Oxford (MA); Heythrop College (STL). Taught classics at St Francis Xavier's Coll., Liverpool, 1954–57; ordained, 1960; taught classics at St Michael's Coll., Leeds, 1962–64; Lectr (part-time), Heythrop Coll., London, 1978–80; Res. Lectr, Oxford Univ., 1991–. Vis. Prof., Univ. of Notre Dame, 1982–; Murray Vis. Prof. of Catholic Thought, Univ. of Toledo, Ohio, 1995; Francis P. Wade Vis. Prof. in Theology, Marquette Univ., 1997; Vis. Scholar, Seton Hall Univ., NJ, 1999. Sarum Lectr, Univ. of Oxford, 1972–73. Gen. Sec., Ecumenical Soc. of Blessed Virgin Mary, 1994–97 (Associate Gen. Sec., 1975–94); Mem., Anglican-Roman Catholic Internat. Commn, 1970–81 and 1983–91; Pres., Catholic Theol. Assoc. of GB, 1986–88. Order of St Augustine, 1981. *Publications:* The Theology of Original Sin, 1971; The Awe-Inspiring Rites of Initiation, 1972; The Second Gift, 1974; (with H. Chadwick) Truth and Authority, 1977; (ed jtly and contrib.) The Study of Liturgy, 1978; They are in Earnest, 1982; Eight Days with the Lord, 1984; (ed jtly and contrib.) The Study of Spirituality, 1986; In Search of Unity, 1989; Time for God, 1991; (ed jtly and contrib.) Anglicans and Roman Catholics: the search for unity, 1994; (ed jtly and contrib.) Anglican Orders: the documents in the debate, 1997; Cyril of Jerusalem, 2000; (ed jtly and contrib.) Studia Patristica, vols xxxiv–xxxviii, 2001; articles in learned jls. *Recreations:* opera, cricket. *Address:* Campion Hall, Oxford OX1 1QS. *T:* (01865) 286111, *Fax:* (01865) 286148; *e-mail:* edward.yarnold@campion.ox.ac.uk. *Died 23 July 2002.*

YARRANTON, Sir Peter (George), Kt 1992; Chairman: Sports Council, 1989–94; Sports Partner Ltd, 1990–95; *b* 30 Sept. 1924; *s* of late Edward John Yarranton and Norah Ellen (*née* Atkins); *m* 1947, Mary Avena (*née* Flowitt); one *s* one *d*. *Educ:* Willesden Technical Coll. Prelim. ARIBA. Joined RAF, 1942: commnd 1944; Flying Officer, 1945; Flt Lieut, 1949; voluntarily retd, 1957. Shell Mex & BP Ltd: management trainee, 1957–58; Ops Officer, Reading, 1958–61; UK Indust. Relations Officer, 1961–63; i/c Indust. Relations, 1963–66; Manager, Indust. Relations, 1966–69; Regional Ops Manager, SE Region, 1969–75; Manager, Plant and Engrg, Distbn Div., Shell UK Oil, 1975–77; Gen. Manager, Lensbury Club, 1978–92. Founder Dir, London Docklands Arena Ltd, 1984–93; non-exec. Dir, Drug Check UK Ltd, 1995–. Consultant: Jet Heritage, 1994–96; Stuart Canvas Products, 1996–. Governor: Sports Aid Foundn, 1989–; London Marathon Ltd, 1989–94; Trustee, Golden Globe Charity Trust, 1990–93; Vice Pres., Comet Foundn, 1996–98. Fellow, 1979–, and Patron, 1998–, Recreation Managers Assoc.; President: Rugby Football Union, 1991–92 (Public Relations Advr to the Union, 1983–94); Lensbury RFC, 1978–; Wasps FC, 1982–85; Middx County RFU, 1986–88. England Internat. (5 caps), Rugby Union Football: *v* Ireland, New Zealand and Wales, 1954, Scotland and France 1955; played for and captained Barbarians, London, Mddx, Wasps, British Combined Services, and RAF Rugby Clubs; formerly: Mem., London and Mddx Premier Swimming and Water Polo Teams; Captain, RAF Swimming and Water Polo Teams. Patron: Royal Canoe Club Trust, 1993–; Cottesloe Veterans Surf Life Saving Assoc., 1999–; Trustee, Richmond Boat Project, 1992–97; Pres., The Great River Race, 1993–99. Chm., Sport Supports St John Ambulance Cttee, 1999–. Pres., Ready, 1996–. Gov., Queen's Coll., Taunton, 1993–2000. Freeman, City of London, 1977;

Liveryman, Gold and Silver Wyre Drawers' Co., 1977 (Mem., Court of Assts, 1987; Master, 2001). FCMI (FBIM 1980); FIPD (FIPM 1975). Hon. DArts De Montfort, 1993. *Recreations:* all sports, indoor and outdoor, particularly Rugby, soccer, cricket, swimming, water polo and sub-aqua diving. *Address:* Broom Point, Broom Water West, Teddington, Middx TW11 9QH; 2 Sunnydale Villas, Durlston Road, Swanage, Dorset BH19 2HY. *Clubs:* East India, Royal Air Force, MCC.
Died 1 June 2003.

YEO, Kok Cheang, CMG 1956; MD; *b* 1 April 1903; *s* of Yeo Kim Hong; *m* 1933, Florence, *d* of late Sir Robert Ho-tung, KBE; one *s* two *d*. *Educ:* Hong Kong Univ. (MB, BS, 1925, MD 1930); London School of Hygiene and Tropical Medicine (DTM&H 1927); Cambridge Univ. (DPH 1928). Assistant Medical Officer of Health, Hong Kong, 1928; Lecturer and Examiner in public health, Hong Kong Univ., 1936–37; Official JP 1938; Chinese Health Officer, senior grade, 1939–47; Deputy Director of Health Services, and Vice-Chairman of Urban Council, 1947–50; Deputy Director of Medical and Health Services, 1950–52; MLC, Hong Kong, 1951–57; Director of Medical and Health Services, Hong Kong, 1952–58; part-time Professor of Social Medicine, Hong Kong Univ., 1952–58; retd 1958. *Address:* 10 Rowbarns, Battle, East Sussex TN33 0JQ. *Died 24 May 2004.*

YOUDS, His Honour Edward Ernest; a Circuit Judge, Bedford, 1972–85; *b* 21 Nov. 1910; *s* of late Edward Youds. *Educ:* Birkenhead Sch.; Magdalene Coll., Cambridge (BA, LLB (Hons)). Called to Bar, Gray's Inn, 1936. Practised on Northern Circuit as Barrister-at-law. Served 1940–45, France and Germany (despatches, 1945). Dep. Chm., Lancs County Sessions, 1961–66; County Court Judge, 1966–69; Puisne Judge, High Court, Uganda, 1969–72. *Died Aug. 2003.*

YOUNG, Baroness *cr* 1971 (Life Peer), of Farnworth in the County Palatine of Lancaster; **Janet Mary Young**; PC 1981; DL; *b* 23 Oct. 1926; *d* of John Norman Leonard Baker and Phyllis Marguerite Baker (*née* Hancock); *m* 1950, Geoffrey Tyndale Young; three *d*. *Educ:* Dragon School Oxford; Headington School; in America; St Anne's Coll., Oxford (MA PPE; Hon. Fellow, 1978). Baroness in Waiting (Govt Whip), 1972–73; Parly Under-Sec. of State, DoE, 1973–74; Minister of State, DES, 1979–81; Chancellor, Duchy of Lancaster, 1981–82; Leader of House of Lords, 1981–83; Lord Privy Seal, 1982–83; Minister of State, FCO, 1983–87. A Vice-Chm., Cons. Party Organisation, 1975–83; Dep. Chm., 1977–79; Pres., Assoc. of Cons. Peers, 2000– (Chm., 1995–2000). Co-Chm., Women's Nat. Commn, 1979–83. Councillor, Oxford City Council, 1957; Alderman, 1967–72; Leader of Conservative Group, 1967–72. A Vice-Pres., Assoc. of Dist Councils, 1990–; Pres., West India Cttee, 1995– (a Vice-Pres., 1987–95). Director: UK Provident Instn, 1975–79; Nat. Westminster Bank, 1987–96; Marks and Spencer Plc, 1987–97. Mem., BR Adv. Bd, Western Reg., 1977–79. Chairman: ISJC, 1989–92, 1994–97; GBGSA, 1989–94. Patron, Family and Youth Concern, 1997–2000. Chancellor, Univ. of Greenwich, 1993–98. Member: Council of Management, Ditchley Foundn, 1990–; Court, Cranfield Univ. (formerly Inst. of Technology), 1991–; Chm. Council, Headington Sch., Oxford, 1993–2001. DL Oxon, 1989. Hon. FICE. Hon. DCL Mt Holyoke Coll., 1982; DUniv Greenwich, 1998. Max Beloff Award, 2001; Parliamentarian of the Year Award, The Spectator, 2001; Peer of the Year, Channel 4 Political Awards, 2001. *Recreation:* music. *Address:* House of Lords, SW1A 0PW. *Died 6 Sept. 2002.*

YOUNG OF DARTINGTON, Baron *cr* 1978 (Life Peer), of Dartington in the County of Devon; **Michael Young,** PhD; Director, Institute of Community Studies since 1953; Trustee, Dartington Hall, 1942–92; *b* 9 Aug. 1915; father a musician, mother a writer; *m* 1st, 1945, Joan Lawson (*d* 1989); two *s* one *d*; 2nd, 1960, Sasha Moorsom (*d* 1993); one *s* one *d*; 3rd, 1995, Dorit Uhlemann; one *d*. *Educ:* Dartington Hall Sch.; London Univ. (BSc Econ, MA, PhD). Barrister, Gray's Inn. Dir of Political and Economic Planning, 1941–45; Sec., Research Dept, Lab. Party, 1945–51. Chairman: Social Science Research Council, 1965–68; Dartington Amenity Research Trust, 1967–; Internat. Extension Coll., 1970–; Nat. Consumer Council, 1975–77; Mutual Aid Centre, 1977–; Coll. of Health, 1983–90; Health Information Trust, 1987–; Argo Venture, 1984–; Open Coll. of the Arts, 1987–90; Open Sch., 1989–; Language Line, 1989–; Educn Extra, 1990–; Sch. for Social Entrepreneurs, 1997–; Dir, Mauritius Coll. of the Air, 1972; Member: Central Adv. Council for Education, 1963–66; NEDC, 1975–78; Policy Cttee, SDP, 1981–83; President: Consumer's Assoc., 1965– (Chm., 1956–65); National Extension Coll., 1971– (Chm., 1962–71); Adv. Centre for Educn, 1976– (Chm., 1959–76); Birkbeck Coll., London Univ., 1989–92. Chm., Tawney Soc., 1982–84. Fellow, Churchill Coll., Cambridge, 1961–66 (Hon. Fellow, 1995); Vis. Prof. of Extension Educn, Ahmadu Bello Univ., Nigeria, 1974; Regents' Lectr, UCLA, 1985. Hon. FBA 1995. Hon. Fellow: LSE, 1978; Plymouth Polytechnic, 1980; QMC, 1983. Hon. LittD Sheffield, 1965; DUniv Open, 1973; Hon. DLitt: Adelaide, 1974; Keele, 1991; Hon. LLD Exeter, 1982. *Publications:* Family and Kinship in East London (with Peter Willmott), 1957; The Rise of the Meritocracy, 1958; (with Peter Willmott) Family and Class in a London Suburb, 1960; Innovation and Research in Education, 1965; (with Patrick McGeeney) Learning Begins at Home, 1968; (ed) Forecasting and the Social Sciences, 1968; (with Peter Willmott) The Symmetrical Family, 1973; (ed) The Poverty Report, 1974 and 1975; (with Marianne Rigge) Mutual Aid in a Selfish Society, 1979; (with others) Distance Teaching for the Third World, 1980; The Elmhirsts of Dartington—the creation of an Utopian Community, 1982; (with Marianne Rigge) Revolution From Within: co-operatives and co-operation in British industry, 1983; Social Scientist as Innovator, 1984; The Metronomic Society, 1988; (ed with Tom Schuller) The Rhythms of Society, 1988; (with Tom Schuller) Life After Work—the arrival of the ageless society, 1991; Your Head in Mine (poetry), 1994; (with Lesley Cullen) A Good Death, 1996; (with G. Lemos) Communities We Have Lost and Can Regain, 1997. *Recreation:* painting. *Address:* 18 Victoria Park Square, E2 9PF. *Died 14 Jan. 2002.*

YOUNG, Prof. Alec David, OBE 1964; FRS 1973; FREng; Professor and Head of the Department of Aeronautical Engineering, Queen Mary College, London University, 1954–78, then Emeritus; Vice-Principal, Queen Mary College, 1966–78; *b* 15 Aug. 1913; *s* of Isaac Young and Katherine (*née* Freeman); *m* 1st, 1937, Dora Caplan (*d* 1970); two *s* one *d*; 2nd, 1971, Rena Waldmann (*née* Szafer). *Educ:* Caius Coll., Cambridge (Wrangler, Mathematical Tripos, 1935; MA). Research Student in Aeronautics, Cambridge, 1935–36; Mem. of staff, Aerodynamics Dept, Royal Aircraft Estab., 1936–46; College of Aeronautics: Senior Lectr and Dep. Head of Dept of Aerodynamics, 1946–50; Prof. and Head of Dept of Aerodynamics, 1950–54; London University: Dean, Faculty of Engineering, 1962–66; Mem. Senate, 1970–78. Member: Fluid Dynamics Panel, AGARD, 1965–90; various Cttees of Aeronautical Research Council (Chm. of Council, 1968–71). Exec. Sec., Internat. Council of Aeronautical Scis, 1987–90. Chm., Bd of Direction, Von Karman Institute for Fluid Dynamics, 1964–93; Mem., Advisory Bd, RAF Coll., Cranwell, 1966. FRAeS 1951 (Hon. FRAeS 1984; Past Chm., Aerodynamics Data Sheets Cttee; Gold Medal, 1972); FREng (FEng 1976). Fellow: QMC, 1980; AIAA, 1987. Editor, Progress in Aerospace Sciences, 1983–93. Ludwig Prandtl Ring, Deutsche Ges. für Luft-und Raumfahrt, 1976; Von Karman Medal, AGARD, 1979. Commandeur de l'Ordre de Leopold, 1976. *Publications:* (jtly) An Elementary Treatise on the Mechanics of Fluids, 1960, 2nd edn 1970; (jtly) Aircraft Excrescence Drag, 1981; Boundary Layers, 1989; various, of Aeronautical Research Council, Coll. of Aeronautics Reports series, and in Proc. and Reports of AGARD; articles in Aeronautical Quarterly and Jl of Royal Aeronautical Soc., Quarterly Jl of Mechanics and Applied Mathematics, and Aircraft Engineering. *Recreations:* drama, sketching, etching. *Address:* 70 Gilbert Road, Cambridge CB4 3PD. *T:* (01223) 354625.
Died 27 Jan. 2005.

YOUNG, Bertram Alfred, OBE 1980; dramatic critic, 1964–91, and arts editor, 1971–77, The Financial Times; *b* 20 Jan. 1912; *y* (twin) *s* of Bertram William Young and Dora Elizabeth Young (*née* Knight); unmarried. *Educ:* Highgate. Served with Artists Rifles, 1930–35, and Lancs Fusiliers, KAR and Staff, 1939–48; Asst Editor, Punch, 1949–62; Dramatic Critic, Punch, 1962–64. Mem., British Council Drama Adv. Cttee, 1973–83; Pres., Critics' Circle, 1978–80. Hon. Kentucky Col, 1980. *Publications:* Tooth and Claw, 1958; How to Avoid People, 1963; Bechuanaland, 1966; Cabinet Pudding, 1967; Colonists from Space, 1979; The Mirror up to Nature, 1982; The Rattigan Version, 1986; author of about 20 radio plays broadcast 1938–49. *Recreation:* music (consumer only). *Address:* Cheltenham, Glos. *Club:* Garrick.
Died 17 Sept. 2001.

YOUNG, David Wright; teacher; *b* Greenock, Scotland, 12 Oct. 1930; *s* of late William Shaw Young and Susan (*née* Redhead); *m* 1st, 1960, Grace McCowat (*d* 1992); 2nd, Vera Dingwall. *Educ:* Greenock Acad.; Glasgow Univ.; St Paul's Coll., Cheltenham. Head of History Dept; subseq. insurance executive. Joined Labour Party, 1955; contested (Lab): South Worcestershire, 1959; Banbury, 1966; Bath, 1970. MP (Lab) Bolton E, Feb. 1974–1983, Bolton SE, 1983–97. PPS to Sec. of State for Defence, 1977–79. Mem., Select Cttee on Employment, 1982–97. Alderman, Nuneaton BC, 1982; Councillor, Nuneaton DC. Chm., Coventry E Labour Party, 1964–68. Member: TGWU; Co-operative Party. Especially interested in comprehensive educn, defence, pensions, economics. *Recreations:* reading, motoring. *Died 1 Jan. 2003.*

YOUNG, Edward Preston, DSO 1944; DSC 1943; writer and retired book designer; *b* 17 Nov. 1913; *m* 1st, 1945, Diana Lilian Graves (marr. diss.); two *d*; 2nd, 1956, Mary Reoch Cressall (*d* 2001). *Educ:* Highgate Sch. Served War, 1940–45: RNVR; entered submarine service 1940 (despatches, DSC); first RNVR officer to comd operational submarine, 1943 (DSO, Bar to DSC); temp. Commander RNVR, 1945. Man. Dir, Rainbird Publishing Gp Ltd, 1970–73. *Publications:* One of Our Submarines, 1952; Look at Lighthouses, 1961; The Fifth Passenger, 1962; Look at Submarines, 1964. *Address:* 15 Maple Walk, Rustington, W Sussex BN16 3QP.
Died 28 Jan. 2003.

YOUNG, Gavin David, FRSL, FRGS; author and traveller; *b* 24 April 1928; *s* of late-Col Gavin David Young and Daphne, *yr d* of Sir Leolin Forestier-Walker, 1st and last Bt, KBE. *Educ:* Rugby; Trinity Coll., Oxford (MA). FRSL 1987; FRGS 1989. National Service, Lieut, Welsh Guards, 1946–48; served Palestine, 1947–48. Lived with Marsh Arabs of S Iraq, 1952–54; at large in SW Arabia (Hejaz, Tihama and Asir), with Desert Locust Control, 1954–56; foreign corresp. with The Observer, 1959–90, covering wars, etc, in Algeria, Cuba, Nagaland, Congo, Middle East, Kurdistan, Yemen, Bangladesh, Angola, Vietnam, Cambodia; Observer's corresp. in NY, 1962–63, Paris, 1967. *Publications:* Return to the Marshes, 1977; Iraq: land of two rivers, 1979; Slow Boats to China, 1981; Slow Boats Home, 1985; Worlds Apart, 1987; Beyond Lion Rock, 1988; In Search of Conrad, 1991 (jtly, Thomas Cook Travel Book Award, 1992); From Sea to Shining

Sea: a present day journey through America's past, 1995; A Wavering Grace: a Vietnamese family in war and peace, 1997; Eye on the World, 1998; contribs to jls and magazines. *Recreations:* travel in remote places, reading, walking, music, talking late. *Address:* c/o Weil, 49 Earls Court Road, W8 6EE. *T:* and *Fax:* (020) 7937 3538. *Clubs:* Brooks's, Beefsteak, Cavalry and Guards, Pratt's, Shikar; Foreign Correspondents' (Hong Kong).

Died 18 Jan. 2001.

YOUNG, Gerard Francis, CBE 1967; DL; CEng, FIMechE; HM Lord-Lieutenant and Custos Rotulorum for South Yorkshire, 1974–85; *b* 5 May 1910; *s* of Smelter J. Young, MICE, and Edith, *d* of Sir John Aspinall, Pres. ICE and Pres. IMechE; *m* 1937, Diana Graham Murray, MA, BSc, JP, *d* of Charles Graham Murray, MD; one *s* three *d* (and one *s* decd). *Educ:* Ampleforth College. Engrg Apprentice, LNER, Doncaster. Entered family firm, The Tempered Spring Co. Ltd (later Tempered Group Ltd), 1930; Dir, 1936; Man. Dir, 1942; Chm., 1954–78. Dir, 1958, Chm., 1967–80, Sheffield Area Board, Sun Alliance & London Insurance Group; Dir, National Vulcan Engineering Insce Group, 1962–79. Member: Nat. Bd for Prices and Incomes, 1968–71; Top Salaries Review Body, 1971–74; Armed Forces Pay Review Body, 1971–74; Gen. Comr of Income Tax, 1947–74 (Chm., Don Div., 1968–74). Dir, Crucible Theatre Trust Ltd, 1967–75; Sec., Assoc. of Christian Communities in Sheffield, 1940–46; Chm., Radio Hallam Ltd, 1973–79; Trustee: Sheffield Town Trust, 1969–2002 (Town Collector, 1978–81); J. G. Graves Charitable Fund, 1974–2002 (Chm., 1974–85); Freshgate Foundn, 1974–96 (Chm., 1979–86); Mem., Finance Bd, RC Dio. of Hallam, 1981–95. President: Council of St John, South and West Yorks, 1979–85; Yorks Volunteers Council, 1980–81; TAVRA Yorks & Humberside, 1983–85 (Vice-Pres., 1974–82). Univ. of Sheffield: Mem. Council, 1943; Treas., 1947–51; Pro-Chancellor, 1951–67; Chm., 1956–67; Life Mem. of Court, 1983. Mem. Bd of Govs, United Sheffield Hosps, 1948–53 (Chm. of Finance Cttee, 1948–50); Chm., Royal Hosp., 1951–53. Master, Company of Cutlers in Hallamshire, 1961–62. JP Sheffield, 1950–85. (Last) High Sheriff of Hallamshire, 1973–74; DL West Riding of Yorks, 1974. Hon. LLD Sheffield, 1962. KStJ 1976; GCSG 1974. *Address:* 69 Carsick Hill Crescent, Sheffield S10 3LS. *T:* (0114) 230 2834. *Died 6 Jan. 2004.*

YOUNG, Hugo John Smelter; journalist; *b* 13 Oct. 1938; *s* of Gerard Francis Young, CBE and Diana, *d* of Charles Graham Murray, MD; *m* 1st, 1966, Helen Mason (*d* 1989); one *s* three *d*; 2nd, 1990, Lucy Waring. *Educ:* Ampleforth Coll.; Balliol Coll., Oxford (MA Jurisprudence). Yorkshire Post, 1961; Harkness Fellow, 1963; Congressional Fellow, US Congress, 1964; The Sunday Times, 1965–84: Chief Leader Writer, 1966–77; Political Ed., 1973–84; Jt Dep. Ed., 1981–84; Political Columnist, The Guardian, 1984–; Dir, The Tablet, 1985–. Chairman: Scott Trust, 1989–; UK Adv. Cttee, Harkness Fellowships, 1993–95. Hon. DLitt Sheffield, 1993. Columnist of the Year: British Press Awards, 1980, 1983, 1985; Granada TV What the Papers Say Awards, 1985; Gerald Barry Lifetime Achievement Award (posthumous), What the Papers Say Awards, 2003. *Publications:* (jtly) The Zinoviev Letter, 1966; (jtly) Journey to Tranquility, 1969; The Crossman Affair, 1974; (jtly) No, Minister, 1982; (jtly) But, Chancellor, 1984; (jtly) The Thatcher Phenomenon, 1986; One of Us, 1989, rev. edn 1991; This Blessed Plot: Britain and Europe from Churchill to Blair, 1998, rev. edn 1999; Supping with the Devils: political journalism from Thatcher to Blair, 2003. *Address:* c/o The Guardian, 119 Farringdon Road, EC1R 3ER; *e-mail:* hugoyoung@ compuserve.com. *Died 22 Sept. 2003.*

YOUNG, Thomas Nesbitt; HM Diplomatic Service, retired; Director, Regional Centre, Mostar, Bosnia and Herzegovina, Organisation for Security and Co-operation in Europe, since 2003; *b* 24 July 1943; *s* of Sir Frank Young, FRS and Lady (Ruth) Young, DPM; *m* 1971,

Elisabeth Ann Shepherdson (*née* Hick) (MBE 1998); one *s* one *d*. *Educ:* The Leys Sch., Cambridge; Pembroke Coll., Oxford (BA Hons Chem., MA). Teaching, Kigezi Coll., Kabale, Uganda, 1962; joined HM Diplomatic Service, 1966; Ankara, 1969–71; Madrid, 1972–76; Head of Chancery, Ankara, 1979–80; Dep. Dir of Trade Develt, NY, 1981; First Sec., Washington, 1981–84; Asst Head, Nuclear Energy Dept, FCO, 1984–86; Dep. High Comr, Accra, 1987–90; Dir of Trade Promotion, British High Commn, Canberra, 1990–93; Ambassador to Azerbaijan, 1993–97; High Comr to Zambia, 1998–2002. *Recreations:* hill-walking, sailing, Renaissance music, reaching inaccessible places. *Address:* River Cottage, Fittleton, Salisbury, Wilts SP4 9QA. *Died 11 Feb. 2004.*

YOUNG, (William) Hilary, CMG 1957; HM Diplomatic Service, retired; Ambassador to Colombia 1966–70; *b* 14 Jan. 1913; *s* of late Rev. Arthur John Christopher Young and Ethel Margaret (*née* Goodwin); *m* 1st, 1946, Barbara Gordon Richmond, *d* of late Gordon Park Richmond; one *s* one *d*; 2nd, 1986, Virginia, *widow* of Sir Ivo Stourton, CMG, OBE, KPM. *Educ:* Marlborough Coll.; Emmanuel Coll., Cambridge (BA 1934, MA 1938). Entered Consular Service, 1935; served HM Legation, Tehran, 1938–41; FO, 1941–45; 1st Sec., 1945; Berlin (Political Div., Control Commn), 1945–48; HM Legation, Budapest, 1948–50; attached to IDC, 1951; Counsellor: UK High Commn, New Delhi, 1952–54; FO, 1954–57; Minister, Moscow, 1957–60; Sen. Civilian Instructor, IDC, 1960–62; Minister, British Embassy, Pretoria and Cape Town, 1962–65; Fellow, Harvard Univ. Center for Internat. Affairs, 1965–66. *Address:* 2 Sutton Manor Mews, Sutton Scotney, Winchester, Hants SO21 3JX.

Died 13 Aug. 2003.

YOUNGER OF LECKIE, 4th Viscount *cr* 1923, of Alloa, Clackmannanshire; **George Kenneth Hotson Younger;** Baron Younger of Prestwick (Life Peer), 1992; Bt 1911; KT 1995; KCVO 1993; TD 1964; PC 1979; DL; FRSE; Lord High Commissioner, General Assembly, Church of Scotland, 2001 and 2002; *b* 22 Sept. 1931; *e s* of 3rd Viscount Younger of Leckie, OBE and Evelyn Margaret, MBE (*d* 1983), *e d* of Alexander Logan McClure, KC; *S* father, 1997; *m* 1954, Diana Rhona, *er d* of Captain G. S. Tuck, RN, Little London, Chichester, Sussex; three *s* one *d*. *Educ:* Cargilfield Sch., Edinburgh; Winchester Coll. (Fellow, 1992–); New Coll., Oxford (Hon. Fellow, 1997). Commnd in Argyll and Sutherland Highlanders, 1950; served BAOR and Korea, 1951; 7th Bn Argyll and Sutherland Highlanders (TA), 1951–65; Hon. Col, 154 (Lowland) Transport Regt, RCT, 1977–85. Chairman: Siemens Plessey Electronic Systems, 1990–97; Royal Bank of Scotland, 1990–2001 (Dir, 1989–2001; Dep. Chm., 1990); Royal Bank of Scotland Gp, 1991–2001; SPEED plc, 1992–98; Murray Johnstone Trusts, 1993–; Director: George Younger & Son Ltd, 1958–68; J. G. Thomson & Co. Ltd, Leith, 1962–66; Maclachlans Ltd, 1968–70; Tennant Caledonian Breweries Ltd, 1977–79; Scottish Equitable Life Assurance Soc., 1990–94; Prestwick Hldgs (formerly Ayrshire Community Airport Project, then PIK Ltd), 1991–98. Contested (U) North Lanarkshire, 1959; Unionist Candidate for Kinross and West Perthshire, 1963, but stood down in favour of Sir A. Douglas-Home. MP (C) Ayr, 1964–92; Scottish Conservative Whip, 1965–67; Parly Under-Sec. of State for Develt, Scottish Office, 1970–74; Minister of State for Defence, 1974; Secretary of State: for Scotland, 1979–86; for Defence, 1986–89. Chm., Cons. Party in Scotland, 1974–75 (Dep. Chm., 1967–70); Pres., Nat. Union of Cons. and Unionist Assocs, 1987–88. Chancellor, Napier Univ., 1993–; Warden, Winchester Coll., 1997–. President: Royal Highland and Agricl Soc., 1990; Council, TA&VRAs, 1993; RSGS, 1993–99; Chairman: Royal Anniversary Trust, 1990–; Romanian Orphanage Trust, 1990; Festival City (formerly Empire, then Edinburgh Fest.) Theatre Trust, 1991–; Royal Armouries, 1994–; Trustees, The Former Royal Yacht Britannia Trust, 1998–. Brig., Queen's Body Guard for Scotland

(Royal Co. of Archers). DL Stirlingshire, 1968. Hon. LLD Glasgow, 1992; Dr *hc* Edinburgh, 1992; Hon. DLitt Napier, 1992; DUniv Paisley, 1994. *Recreations:* music, tennis, sailing, golf. *Heir: s* Hon. James Edward George Younger [*b* 11 Nov. 1955; *m* 1988, Jennie Veronica, *d* of William Wootton; one *s* two *d*]. *Address:* c/o Chairman's Office, Royal Bank of Scotland, 42 St Andrew Square, Edinburgh EH2 2YE. *T:* (0131) 523 2123. *Clubs:* Caledonian; Highland Brigade.   *Died 26 Jan. 2003.*

YOUNGER, Maj.-Gen. Sir John William, 3rd Bt *cr* 1911, of Auchen Castle, co. Dumfries; CBE 1969 (MBE 1945); Commissioner-in-Chief, St John Ambulance Brigade, 1980–85; *b* 18 Nov. 1920; *s* of Sir William Robert Younger, 2nd Bt, and of Joan Gwendoline Johnstone (later Mrs Dennis Wheatley; she *d* 1982); *S* father, 1973; *m* 1st, 1948, Mrs Stella Jane Dodd (marr. diss. 1952), *d* of Rev. John George Lister; one *s* one *d*; 2nd, 1953, Marcella Granito, Princess Pignatelli Di Belmonte (*d* 1989), *d* of Prof. Avv. R. Scheggi; 3rd, 1991, Anne Henrietta Maria St Paul Seely (*d* 1996), *o d* of Horace George St Paul Butler. *Educ:* Canford Sch.; RMC Sandhurst. Served War 1939–45, Middle East (PoW) (MBE); 2nd Lt, Coldstream Gds, 1939; staff coll., Camberley, 1949; Lt Col 1959; Comd, 1st Bn Coldstream Guards; AQMG, HQ London Dist, 1961–63; Col 1963; AAG, War Office, 1963–65; NDC, New Delhi, 1966; Brig. 1967; Dep. Dir, Army Staff Duties, MoD, 1967–70; Dir of Quartering (A), MoD, 1970–73; Maj.-Gen. 1971; Dir, Management and Support of Intelligence, 1973–76. Chm. or Mem., various Civil Service Commn and Home Office Interview Bds. Dep. Comr, St John Ambulance Bde, London (Prince of Wales's) Dist, 1978. KStJ 1980. *Recreations:* reading, photography, travel. *Heir: s* Julian

William Richard Younger, [*b* 10 Feb. 1950; *m* 1981, Deborah Ann Wood; one *s*]. *Address:* Flat 4, 10 Wilbraham Place, SW1X 9AA. *Club:* Boodle's.
Died 14 May 2002.

YOUNGSON, Prof. Alexander John, CBE 1987; Emeritus Professor, Australian National University, since 1980; *b* 28 Sept. 1918; *s* of Alexander Brown, MA, MB, ChB and Helen Youngson; *m* 1948, Elizabeth Gisborne Naylor; one *s* one *d*. *Educ:* Aberdeen Grammar Sch.; Aberdeen Univ. (MA 1947). Pilot, Fleet Air Arm, 1940–45. Commonwealth Fellow, 1947–48. Lecturer, University of St Andrews, 1948–50; Lecturer, University of Cambridge, 1950–58; Prof. of Political Economy 1963–74, and Vice-Principal, 1971–74, Univ. of Edinburgh; Dir, Res. Sch. of Social Scis, ANU, 1974–80; Prof. of Econs, Univ. of Hong Kong, 1980–82. Chm., Royal Fine Art Commn for Scotland, 1983–90 (Mem., 1972–74). Hon. FRIAS 1984. DLitt Aberdeen, 1952; DUniv York, 1993. *Publications:* The American Economy, 1860–1940, 1951; Possibilities of Economic Progress, 1959; The British Economy, 1920–1957, 1960; The Making of Classical Edinburgh, 1966; Overhead Capital, 1967; After the Forty-Five, 1973; Beyond the Highland Line, 1974; Scientific Revolution in Victorian Medicine, 1979; (ed) China and Hong Kong: the economic nexus, 1983; The Prince and the Pretender, 1985; Urban Development and the Royal Fine Art Commission, 1990; Edinburgh and the Border Country, 1993, enlarged edn as Edinburgh and the Borders, 2001; (contrib.) The Dictionary of Art, 1997; contrib. to various journals devoted to economics and economic history. *Recreation:* gardening. *Address:* 17 The Horseshoe, York YO24 1LY.
Died 6 April 2004.

Z

ZHAO ZIYANG; General Secretary, Central Committee, Chinese Communist Party, 1987–89; *b* Huaxian County, Henan Prov., 1919; *m* Liang Boqi; four *s* one *d*. Joined Chinese Communist Youth League, 1932, Chinese Communist Party, 1938; held various posts, S China Sub-Bureau of Central Cttee, Guangdong Provincial Cttee, and Cttee of Inner Mongolia Autonomous Reg., 1950–74; First Sec. of Provincial Cttee and Chm. of Revolutionary Cttee, Guangdong, 1974, Sichuan, 1975–80; First Political Commissar, Chengdu Mil. Reg., Chinese People's Liberation Army, 1976–80; Vice-Chm., 5th Nat. Cttee, Chinese People's Political Consultative Conf., 1978–80; Vice Premier, State Council, 1980, Premier, 1980–87. Mem., 10th Central Cttee, Chinese Communist Party, 1973; Alternate Mem., 1977, Mem., 1979, Mem. Standing Cttee, 1980, Political Bureau, and Vice Chm., 1981, 11th Central Cttee; Mem., 1982, and Mem. Standing Cttee, 1982, Political Bureau, 12th Central Cttee. *Address:* 6 Fuqiang Alley, Beijing, People's Republic of China. *Died 17 Jan. 2005.*

ZIJLSTRA, Jelle; President, Netherlands Bank, 1967–81; Member, Supervisory Board, Royal Dutch Petroleum, since 1982; *b* 27 Aug. 1918; *s* of Ane Zijlstra and Pietje Postuma; *m* 1946, Hetty Bloksma; two *s* three *d*. *Educ:* Netherlands Sch. of Economics. Asst, Netherlands Sch. of Economics, 1945; Prof., Theoretical Economics, 1948–52, Prof., Public Finance, 1963–66, Free Univ. of Amsterdam; Minister: of Economic Affairs, 1952–58; of Finance, 1959–63; Prime Minister, 1966–67. Mem., Chm. Board, and Pres., BIS, 1967–82; Governor, IMF, 1967–81. *Publications:* Planned Economy, 1947; The Velocity of Money and its Significance for the Value of Money and for Monetary Equilibrium, 1948; Economic Order and Economic Policy, 1952. *Recreations:* sailing, skiing. *Address:* Park Oud Wassenaar, flat 44, 2243 BX Wassenaar, Netherlands. *Died 23 Dec. 2001.*

ZIMAN, Prof. John Michael, FRS 1967; Emeritus Professor of Physics, University of Bristol, 1988; *b* 16 May 1925; *s* of late Solomon Netheim Ziman, ICS, retired, and Nellie Frances Ziman (*née* Gaster); *m* 1st, 1951, Rosemary Milnes Dixon (*d* 2001); one adopted *s* two adopted *d* (and one adopted *s* decd); 2nd, 2002, Joan Henriette Solomon (*née* Diamond). *Educ:* Hamilton High Sch., NZ; Victoria University Coll., Wellington, NZ; Balliol Coll., Oxford. Junior Lectr in Mathematics, Oxford Univ., 1951–53; Pressed Steel Co. Ltd Research Fellow, Oxford Univ., 1953–54; Lectr in Physics, Cambridge Univ., 1954–64; Fellow of King's Coll., Cambridge, 1957–64; Editor of Cambridge Review, 1958–59; Tutor for Advanced Students, King's Coll., Cambridge, 1959–63; University of Bristol: Prof. of Theoretical Physics, 1964–69; Melville Wills Prof. of Physics, 1969–76; Dir, H. H. Wills Physics Lab., 1976–81; Henry Overton Wills Prof. of Physics, 1976–82. Vis. Prof., Dept of Social and Economic Studies, 1982–87, Dept of Humanities, 1982–, Imperial Coll., London. Rutherford Memorial Lectr in India and Pakistan, 1968. Dir, Sci. Policy Support Gp, 1986–91; Chairman: Council for Science and Society, 1976–90; European Assoc. for Study of Science and Technology, 1982–86; Member: Scientific Council, Internat. Centre for Theoretical Physics, Trieste, 1970–79; CNAA, 1982–87. Hon. DSc Victoria Univ. of Wellington, NZ, 1985. Jt Editor, Science Progress, 1965–92. *Publications:* Electrons and Phonons, 1960; Electrons in Metals, 1963; (with Jasper Rose) Camford Observed, 1964; Principles of the Theory of Solids, 1965; Public Knowledge, 1968; Elements of Advanced Quantum Theory, 1969; The Force of Knowledge, 1976; Reliable Knowledge, 1978; Models of Disorder, 1979; Teaching and Learning about Science and Society, 1980; Puzzles, Problems and Enigmas, 1981; An Introduction to Science Studies, 1984; (with Paul Sieghart and John Humphrey) The World of Science and the Rule of Law, 1986; Knowing Everything about Nothing, 1987; Prometheus Bound, 1994; Of One Mind, 1995; Real Science, 2000; numerous articles in scientific jls. *Address:* 27 Little London Green, Oakley, Aylesbury, Bucks HP18 9QL. *T:* and *Fax:* (01844) 237464. *Died 2 Jan. 2005.*

ZOLEVEKE, Sir Gideon (Asatori Pitabose), KBE 1983 (MBE 1968); retired as public servant, 1973 and as politician, 1980; farmer since 1980; *b* 3 Aug. 1922; *s* of Pita Pitabose and Mata Taburana; *m* 1954, Melody Sukuluta'a Watanamae; three *s* three *d* (and one *s* decd). *Educ:* primary schs, Solomon Is; secondary sch. and tertiary educn, Fiji. Dip. in Surgery and Medicine, Fiji Sch. of Medicine, Suva; DCMHE London. Served British Solomon Is Protectorate Defence Force, 1942–45 (Pacific Stars). Govt MO, 1951–62; Sen. Health Educn Officer, 1962–73; Mem., Governing Council, 1973–74 (Chm., Works and Public Utilities); MLA, 1974–78 (Backbencher, 1975–76); Minister of: Works and Public Utilities, 1974–75; Home Affairs, April–July 1975; Educn, July–Nov. 1975; Agriculture and Lands, 1976–78; Health and Med. Services, 1978–80. Mem. and leader, various govt delegns, 1953–. Mem., Solomon Is Public Service Commn, 1981–; Chairman: Solomon Is Electricity Authy Bd of Management, 1983–; Solomon Is Water Authy, 1994–. Dir, Boral Gas (SI), 1983–. Founder and first Pres., Solomon Is Med. Officers Assoc., 1952–69; President: W Pacific Br.,BMA, 1961–70; Choiseul People's Assoc., 1955–71; Civil Servants Assoc., British Solomon Is Protectorate, 1966–67; Solomon Is Br., BRCS, 1974–78 (BRCS award, 1978; Life Mem., 1982); Solomon Is Red Cross, 1978–82; St John's Primary Sch., Rove, Honiara, 1968–76; Honiara Club, 1963–68; Foundn Mem., 1967–, Pres. and Chm., 1980–, Sir Winston Churchill Trust Fund, Solomon Is. *Publications:* A Man from Choiseul (autobiog.), 1980; (contrib.) Lands in the Solomon Islands, 1982; (contrib.) Solomon Island Politics, 1983. *Recreations:* writing, reading. *Address:* Kaiti Hill, PO Box 243, Honiara, Solomon Islands. *T:* 22927.

Died 12 Nov. 2003.